RAND McNALLY

THE NEW COSMOPOLITAN WORLD ATLAS

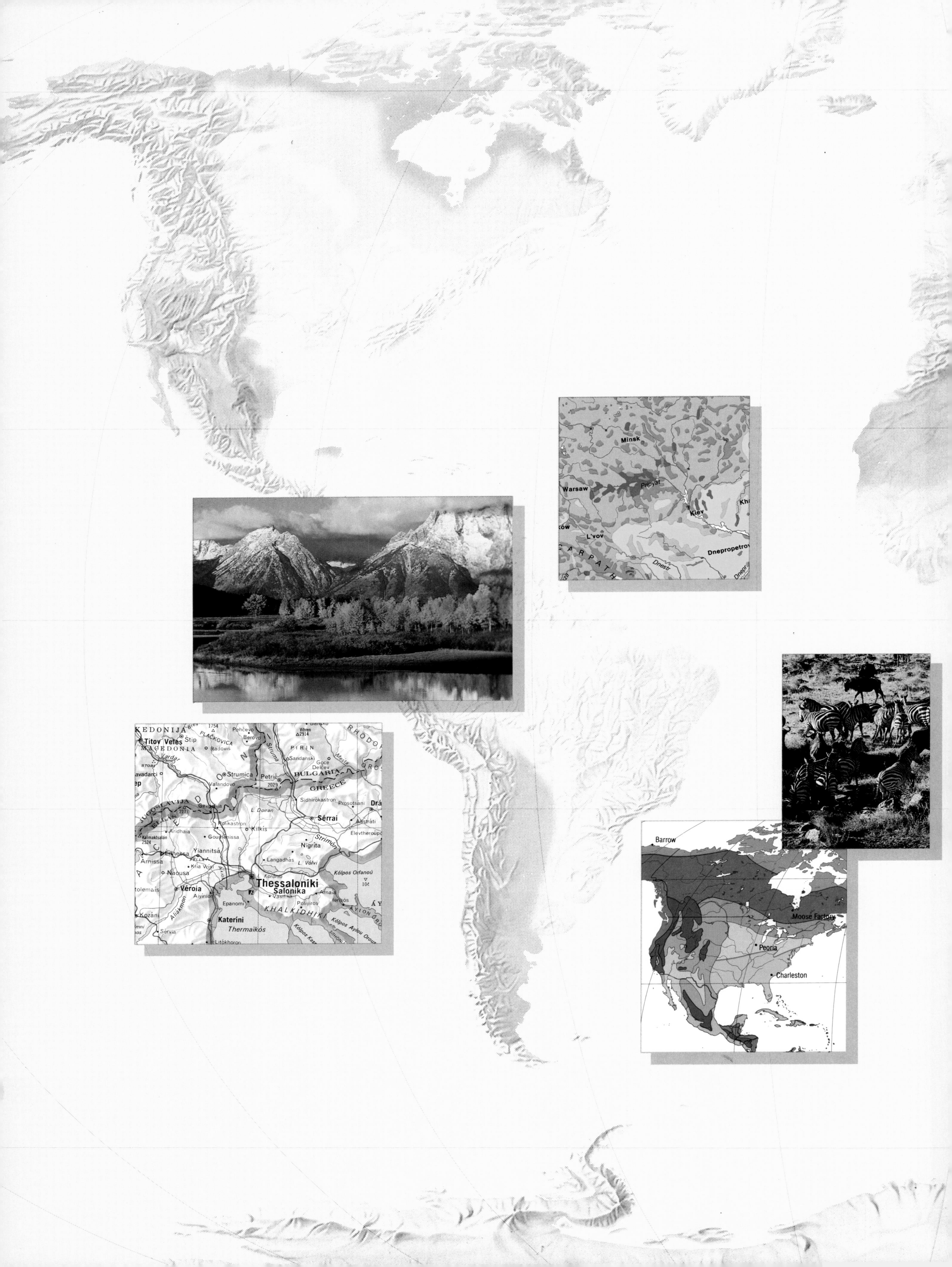

Minsk
Warsaw
Pripyat
Kiev
L'vov
Dnestr
Titov Veles
Stip
MACEDONIA
Radoviš
PIRIN
Sandanski
Goce Delčev
Strumica
Petrič
BULGARIA
GREECE
Gevgelija
Sidhirokastron
Sérrai
L. Doïran
Kilkís
Nigríta
Langadhás
L. Vólvi
Yiannitsá
Náousa
Véroia
Thessaloniki
Salonika
Epanomí
Kateríni
Thermaïkós
KHALKIDHIKI
Kólpos Orfanoú
Barrow
Moose Factory
Peoria
Charleston

THE NEW COSMOPOLITAN WORLD ATLAS

RAND McNALLY
CHICAGO · NEW YORK · SAN FRANCISCO

CONTENTS

THIS FRAGILE EARTH
An Environmental Essay............**I•1 – I•32**
Earth in Balance ....I•2 – I•9
Upsetting the Balance.............I•10 – I•17
Restoring the Balance.............I•18 – I•32

USING THE ATLAS................I•33 – I•35

WORLD TIME ZONES ....I•36

REFERENCE MAPS.......................1 – 160
Map Symbols and Index Map................1
World ....2 – 3
Europe..4 – 5
Northern Europe..............................6 – 7
British Isles ....8 – 9
Central Europe.............................10 – 11
Belgium, Netherlands,
  and Luxembourg 12
Switzerland 13
France and the Alps ....14 – 15
Spain and Portugal.......................16 – 17
Italy ....18 – 19
Southeastern Europe ....20 – 21
Western and
  Central Soviet Union ....22 – 23
Central and
  Eastern Soviet Union................24 – 25
Baltic and Moscow Regions ....26 – 27
Asia ....28 – 29
China, Japan, and Korea ....30 – 31
Northeastern China
  and Korea ....32 – 33
Eastern and
  Southeastern China...................34 – 35
Japan ....36 – 37
Southeastern Asia ....38 – 39
Burma, Thailand,
  and Indochina ....40 – 41
India, Pakistan, and
  Southwestern Asia ....42 – 43
Northern India and Pakistan...........44 – 45
Southern India and Sri Lanka................46
Southern Arabian Peninsula..................47
The Middle East...........................48 – 49
Israel and
  Southern Lebanon ....50 – 51
Africa ....52 – 53
Western North Africa....................54 – 55
Eastern North Africa ....56 – 57
Southern Africa............................58 – 59
Egypt and Sudan ....60 – 61
Northwestern Africa ....62 – 63
West Africa..................................64 – 65
Southern Africa
  and Madagascar ....66 – 67
Australia.....................................68 – 69
Eastern Australia ....70 – 71
New Zealand.......................................72
Antarctica 73

South America ....74 – 75
Northern South America ....76 – 77
Southern South America......................78
Southeastern Brazil 79
Central Argentina and Chile .... 80 – 81
Peru, Bolivia,
  and Western Brazil ....82 – 83
Colombia, Ecuador,
  Venezuela, and Guyana ....84 – 85
North America............................86 – 87
Middle America
  and Caribbean ....88 – 89
Mexico.. 90 – 91
Central America ....92 – 93
Caribbean Region ....94 – 95
Canada ....96 – 97
Alberta 98
British Columbia..................................99
Manitoba...100
New Brunswick, Nova Scotia,
  and Prince Edward Island...............101
Newfoundland 102
Ontario..103
Quebec 104
Saskatchewan....................................105
United States of America.......... 106 – 107
Alabama..108
Alaska 109
Arizona 110
Arkansas.. 111
California 112
Colorado 113
Connecticut.......................................114
Delaware...115
Florida...116
Georgia 117
Hawaii 118
Idaho...119
Illinois 120
Indiana..121
Iowa 122
Kansas...123
Kentucky 124
Louisiana...125
Maine..126
Maryland...127
Massachusetts....................................128
Michigan 129
Minnesota 130
Mississippi...131
Missouri 132
Montana..133
Nebraska 134
Nevada 135
New Hampshire 136
New Jersey 137
New Mexico......................................138
New York 139
North Carolina 140
North Dakota 141

Ohio..142
Oklahoma 143
Oregon 144
Pennsylvania 145
Rhode Island......................................146
South Carolina...................................147
South Dakota.....................................148
Tennessee 149
Texas 150
Utah 151
Vermont...152
Virginia..153
Washington 154
West Virginia 155
Wisconsin..156
Wyoming...157
Pacific and Indian Oceans........ 158 – 159
Atlantic Ocean 160

INDEX TO REFERENCE MAPS...161 – 256

WORLD
GEOGRAPHICAL TABLES.....257 – 259
World Political Information.......257 – 260
General Information..........................261
Principal Mountains 262
World Oceans, Seas, Gulfs,
  Lakes, Rivers, and Islands..............263
World Populations..................264 – 279

UNITED STATES
GEOGRAPHICAL TABLES....280 – 304
United States General Information......280

United States Populations and
Zip Codes.......................281 – 304
Latest 1990 Census Information

The New Cosmopolitan World Atlas

Cartography

Michael W. Dobson, V. Patrick Healy, Timothy J. Carter, Winifred V. Farbman, Susan K. Hudson, Robert K. Argersinger, Ronald F. Peters.

Editorial and Design

Jon M. Leverenz, Elizabeth G. Fagan, Laura C. Schmidt, Vito M. DePinto, Corasue Nicholas, Jerry M. Sullivan (writer).

The New Cosmopolitan World Atlas

Printed in the United States of America.

Library of Congress Cataloging-in-Publication Data

Rand McNally and Company.
  Cosmopolitan world atlas.–Census/environmental ed.
    p. cm.
  Rev. ed. of: Rand McNally cosmopolitan world atlas.
  Includes index.
  ISBN 0-528-83442-8
  1. Atlases. I. Rand McNally and Company.
Rand McNally cosmopolitan world atlas. II. Title.
G1021.R35 1991 <G&M> 91-14589
912—dc20 CIP
MAP

THIS FRAGILE EARTH

THE FRAGILE BIOSPHERE I·2
THE RESTLESS EARTH I·4
THE GREEN MANTLE I·6
THE DOMINANT SPECIES I·8

UPSETTING THE BALANCE

LAND AND AIR I·10
FRESH AND SALT WATER I·12
PLANT AND ANIMAL LIFE I·14
HUMAN LIFE I·16

RESTORING THE BALANCE

EUROPE I·18
ASIA I·20
AFRICA I·22
OCEANIA I·24
POLAR REGIONS I·26
SOUTH AMERICA I·28
NORTH AMERICA I·30

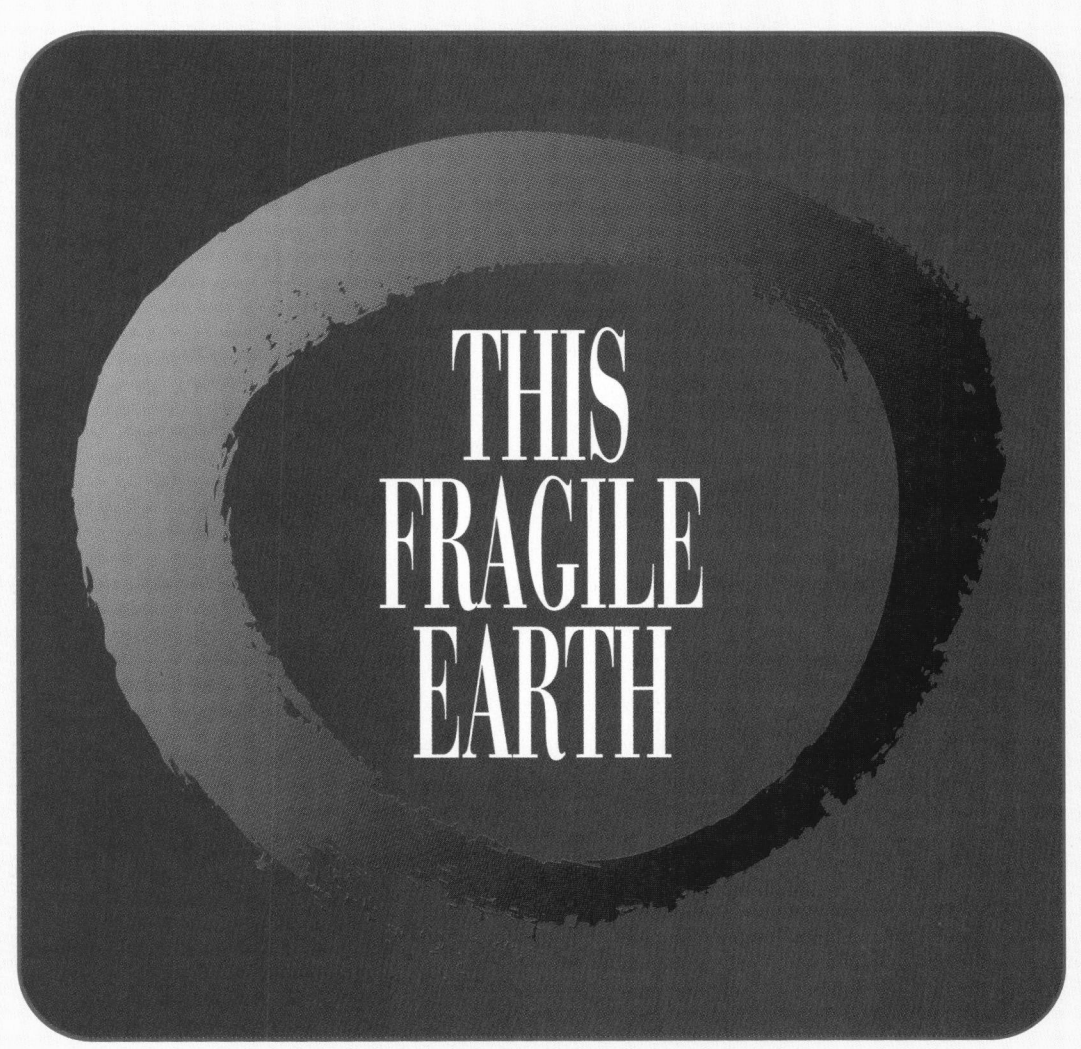

EARTH IN BALANCE
The Fragile Biosphere

The most lasting value of humanity's exploration of space may be the clear picture it has given us of our own home, the earth. It has been said that the environmental movement began when astronauts brought back the first pictures of the earth taken from the moon. Suddenly we realized that the earth of our tradition-bound imaginations—a vast globe filled with remote reaches scarcely touched by humanity—was really just a tiny ball floating in empty space.

Since those first voyages, spaceships from the earth have explored the rest of the solar system. They have brought us pictures of worlds stranger than our most outlandish ideas. And they have shown us that of all the worlds that swing in their orbits around the sun, only the earth has life.

Even here, life is confined to a thin layer that covers the planet like a coat of paint. This is the *biosphere*, the sphere of life.

The continuous movement of energy, minerals, air, and water through the biosphere connects every part of it with every other part. Clouds, for example, carry the water vapor from the oceans to the hearts of the continents. Ocean currents carry the warmth of tropical sunlight to cold northern regions. Winds blow the nutrient-rich dust from the Great Plains to places far from the United States. A seabird in one part of the world sweeps down on a fish and captures some of the energy its prey gained while feeding in the waters of another part of the world.

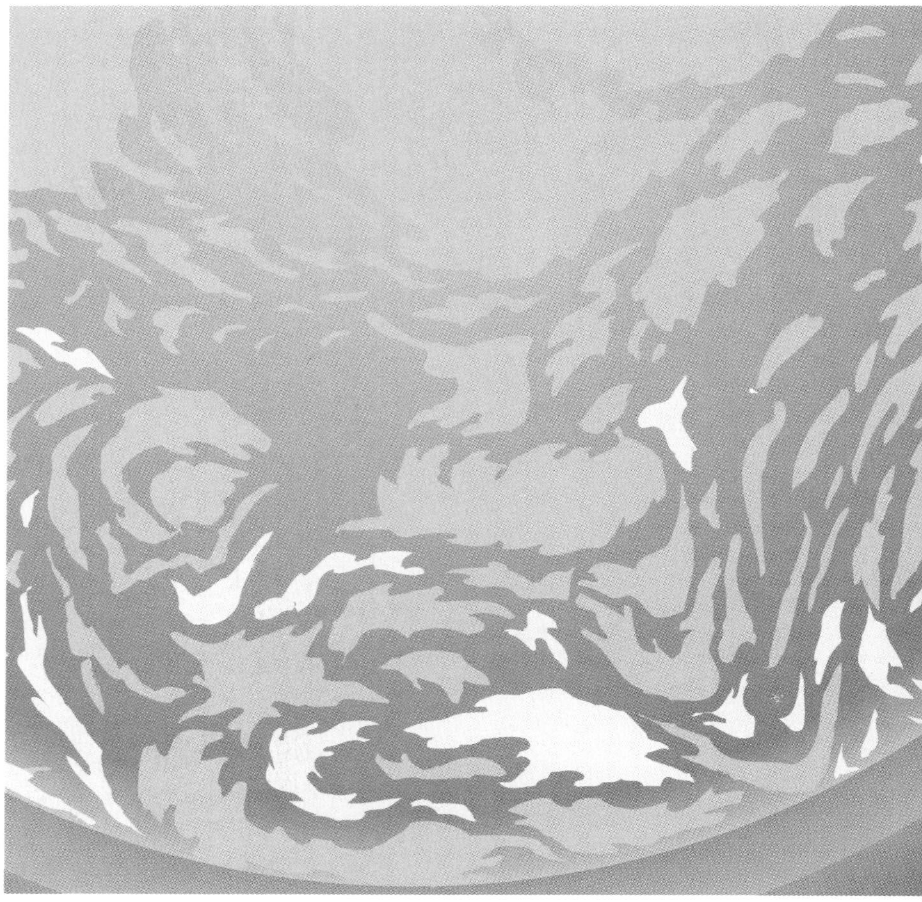

The Miracle of the Biosphere
Life clings to the surface of the earth. The interior of our planet is a fiery caldron, a place of temperatures and pressures beyond endurance for any living thing. Just a few miles above our heads, the airless cold of outer space creates an environment as dead as the surface of the moon. Yet here in the biosphere, life has thrived for billions of years. In all that time, the earth has stayed warm enough to keep everything from freezing, and cool enough to keep the oceans from boiling away. As far as we know, there is no other place like this in the universe.

The variety of life in the biosphere is immense. Each species is unique—and therefore precious. Koalas live in Australia, spending their lives in the eucalyptus trees whose leaves are their only food. Destruction of their habitat has made them a rare species.

The raw materials this complex global system needs—minerals, water, air—come from the earth, but the operation of the system depends on a constant flow of energy from the sun. The movement of currents in the oceans and winds in the atmosphere is created by solar power.

The *hydrologic cycle* that bathes the earth in life-giving rain is another gift of the sun. Solar energy evaporates water from oceans, from lakes and rivers, from the leaves of plants, and from the land itself. This moisture rises, condenses into clouds, and then falls as rain and snow.

The energy that feeds living things also comes from the sun. Green plants have evolved the means to capture a fraction of the sun's radiant energy through the process called *photosynthesis*. *Chlorophyll*, the pigment that makes green plants green, converts light to chemical energy by breaking down molecules of carbon dioxide from the air and water absorbed from the earth and remaking them as molecules of a simple sugar called *glucose*. Modified in countless ways, this sugar both builds the plant and feeds life on earth.

The only waste product of photosynthesis is oxygen. The constant infusion of oxygen into the atmosphere by green plants balances the consumption of this vital element by animals through respiration and maintains the balance of gases in the atmosphere.

Ecologists call green plants *producers* because they produce energy. Animals and plants without chlorophyll are called *consumers*. They depend on the energy produced by green plants. Both plants and animals live in communities where there is intensive interaction and complex interdependence between species. The term *ecosystem* describes a collection of interdependent producers and consumers. Ecosystems are the basic building blocks of the biosphere. All species live in ecosystems.

Water, air, and minerals are endlessly recycled through ecosystems, but the movement of energy is a one-way trip. Plants use much of the energy they capture as fuel for their own physiologies. Herbivorous animals from mice to elephants use much of the energy they consume carrying on their lives. Only a small amount remains to sustain the carnivores who live by consuming the plant-eating animals.

Human beings have become the most successful species in the history of life on earth largely because of our ability to bend natural processes to fit our own needs and wants. A wheat field is a simplified version of a natural ecosystem. It has only one kind of plant rather than hundreds and only one major herbivore: us. With the domestic animals that supply us with meat, milk, eggs, and hides, we take the role of carnivore, harvesting herbivores from our position at the top of the food chain.

Above: The diversity of life on earth is almost beyond comprehension. This lily is one of about 250,000 different kinds of flowering plants. The dragonfly is one of more than a million species of insects.

Right: Energy flows through the biosphere, from the sun to algae in the sea, from algae to small crustaceans, from crustaceans to small fish, from small fish to salmon, and from salmon to brown bear.

Left: The diversity of human beings and their cultures is one of our strengths as a species. It allows us to live in many different places in many different ways. But we must remember that we need to share the biosphere with all living things.

As human populations have grown and spread, we have modified a substantial portion of the earth's land areas to fit our needs. Plowed fields and pasturelands have replaced forests and grasslands. Our once-scattered settlements have grown into huge urban concentrations covering thousands of square miles.

Our intrusions into natural systems have become so massive that they are interfering with the operations of the processes that sustain life on earth. The difficult environmental problems we face arise from this fact. And the search for solutions to these problems is really the search for ways to sustain human life without disrupting the processes that sustain all life.

On pages I•4 through I•9, we will be looking at the processes that sustain the biosphere and some of the ways we humans have remade the earth. Pages I•10 through I•17 will focus on major environmental problems created by our interference with natural processes and look at some attempts to deal with these problems. Pages I•18 through I•32 look at each of the continents, telling of the most severe environmental problems each continent faces and of the work being done to try to solve them.

Food and Water from the Sun

The sun's energy pulls water from the sea and drops it on the mountains, where gravity takes over to return it to the sea. The sun's radiant energy is transformed by plants to chemical energy. The converted energy then feeds grasshoppers and the meadowlarks that eat them. The same energy sustains the zebra and supports the lion that preys on that zebra. This way, the sun's energy circulates through the biosphere.

EARTH IN BALANCE
The Restless Earth

The face of the moon is pocked with ancient craters, records of meteor impacts suffered when the solar system was young. They dominate a surface that has not changed in billions of years.

The ancient history of the earth is much harder to read, because on our planet, the crust is in constant motion; the surface is continuously changing. About two hundred million years ago, when dinosaurs were the dominant land animals, the continents were clustered in a single, enormous land mass geologists call Pangaea (Greek for "all land"). Then North America and Europe, South America and Africa began to split along a widening crack that eventually grew into the Atlantic Ocean. Antarctica drifted south toward the pole and India drifted north. Eventually, India collided with Asia, producing the gigantic uplift called the Himalayas. Fossils in the rocks at the top of Mount Everest, the highest place on earth, reveal that the rock was originally part of the seafloor.

The hard rocks of the earth's crust float on a super-heated layer of soft rock. The crust is broken into six large plates and several smaller ones. Driven by forces deep in the earth, these plates are in constant motion. In the middle of the Atlantic, the Eurasian and American plates are pulling apart. Lava flows up through the widening crack between the plates, creating islands like Iceland.

In California, the Pacific Plate and the American Plate are sliding past each other, and the friction of their passing creates many earthquakes. In the western Pacific, the Pacific Plate is sliding under the Eurasian Plate and raising volcanoes like Japan's Mount Fuji.

The history of the earth is a story of 4.6 billion years of processes like these. It is a story of mountain ranges raised up and eroded away. Of continents and oceans changing shape, size, and location. Of minerals rising from the earth's interior to the surface.

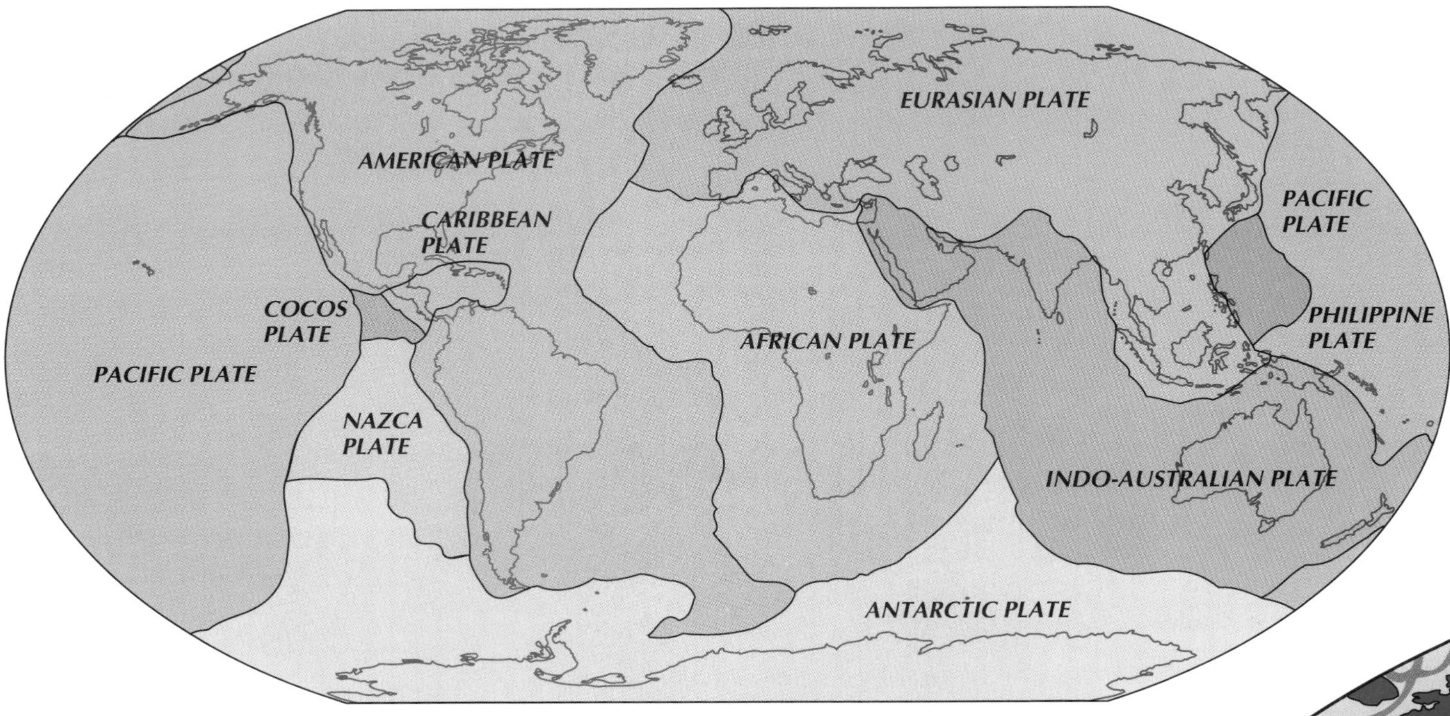

The earth's crust is thinner over midoceanic regions than over the continents. This allows molten magma from the mantle to force its way to the surface and form ridges and new crust. Growth at the midoceanic ridges slowly forces the plates apart. As they spread, their outer edges collide with other plates. One plate is forced beneath the other in a subduction zone, and its crust is melted back into the mantle.

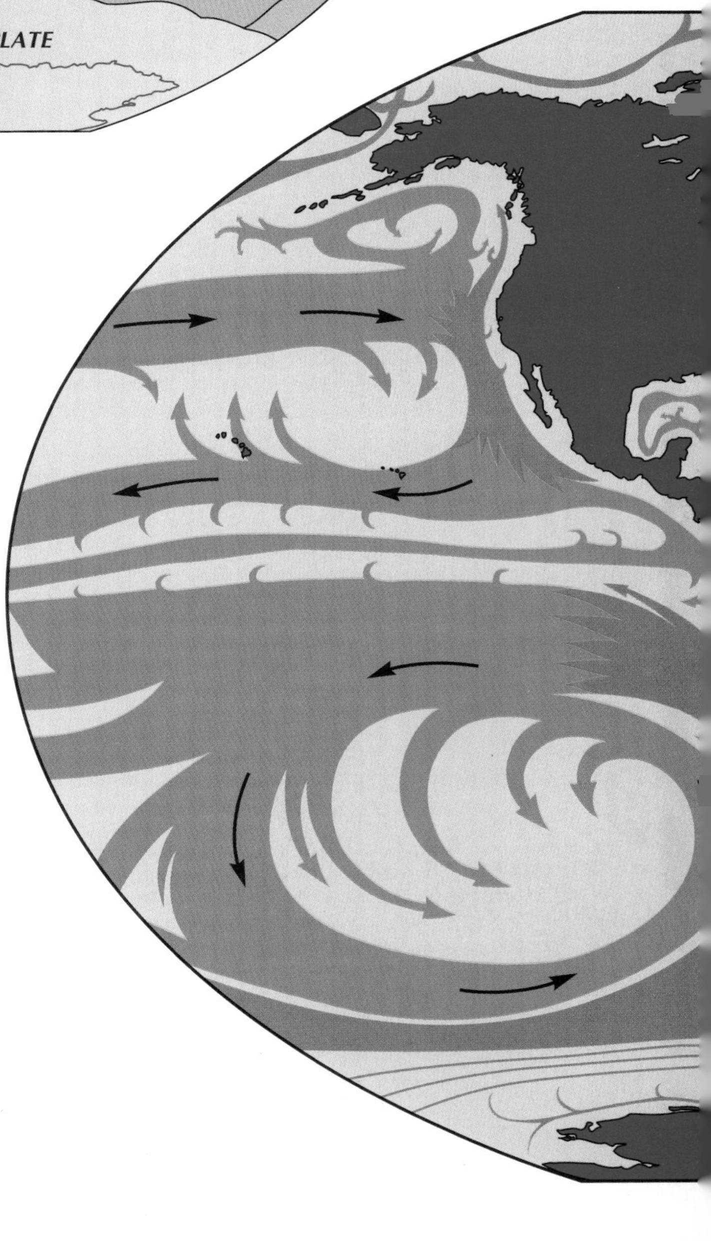

The ocean current called the Gulf Stream carries warm water from the American tropics to the northwest coast of Europe. Westerly winds blow across the warm water and then onto the continent. Because of the Gulf Stream, British farmers can grow wheat at latitudes that, in Canada, grow polar bears.

The waters of the world ocean are in constant motion, too. Water near the surface flows in well-established currents that are like rivers within the ocean. The rotation of the earth on its axis creates a force called *Coriolis force* that bends these currents into giant circles called *gyres*. In the Northern Hemisphere, these gyres flow clockwise. In the Southern Hemisphere, they flow counterclockwise. You can see the same sort of circulation—also caused by Coriolis force—around the drain in your bathtub.

The deep waters flow too. Cold water from the poles flows toward the equator. This cold water is heavy and rich in mineral nutrients. In a few locations, conditions are right for this water to rise to the surface. The minerals make these upwelling zones rich in life. One such zone, off the coast of Peru, provides one-seventh of the world's total catch of ocean fish.

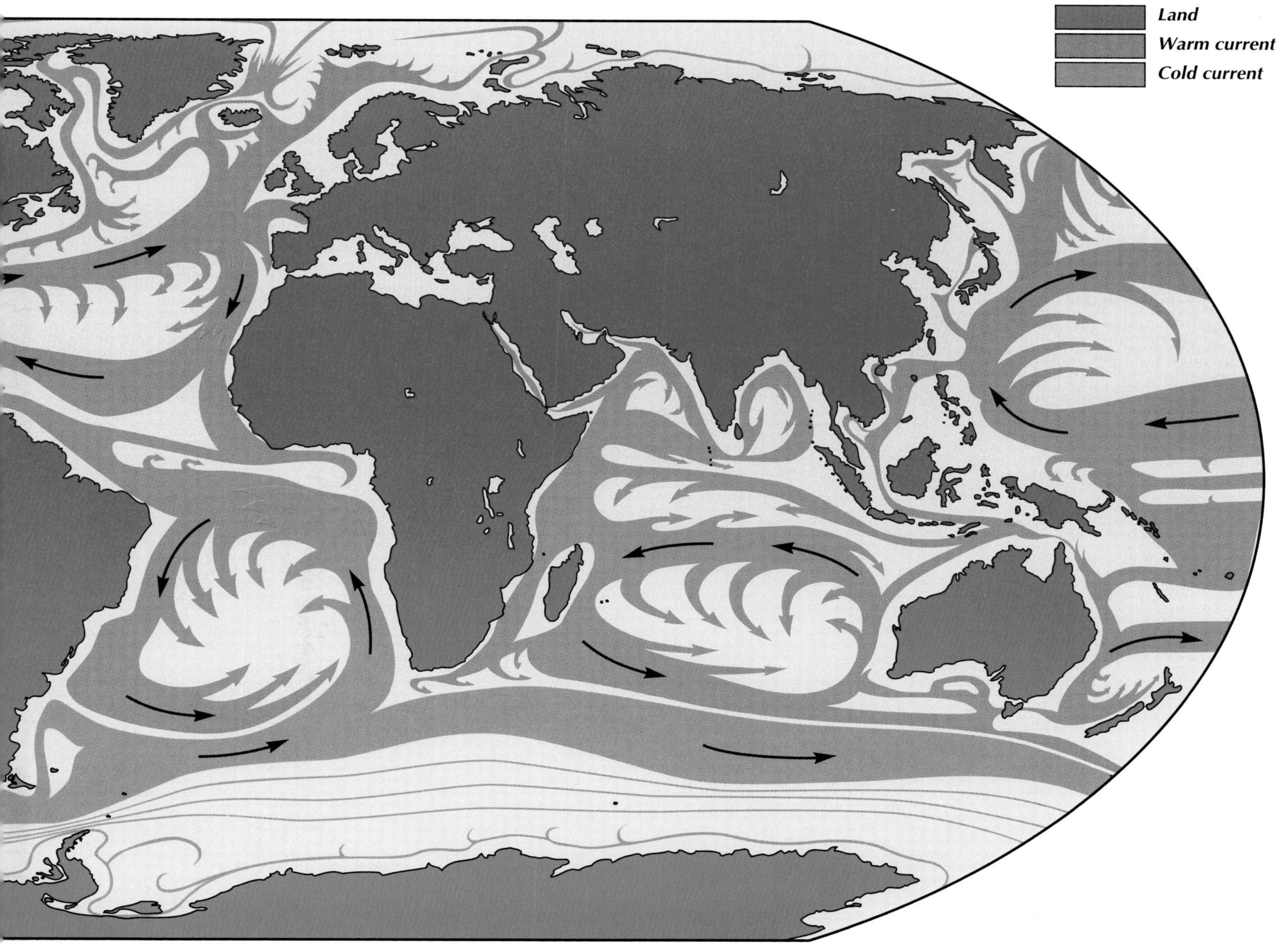

EARTH IN BALANCE
The Green Mantle

One of the maps on these pages shows the pattern of climates around the world. The other shows the distribution of vegetation types that would exist if humans did not intervene. Notice how similar they are. The fit is not exact, but we can see that tundra vegetation grows in polar climates. The evergreen forests of northern Eurasia and North America appear in moist climates with cold winters and cool summers. The steppes of central Asia and the short-grass prairies of North America grow in cool climates with dry summers. The rain forests of South America, Africa, and Asia are found in hot, wet climates near the equator. Climate is the single most important factor in determining where plants can grow. And vegetation is a major factor determining where animals—including human beings—can live.

We use the word *biome* to describe these divisions of the earth's vegetation and the animals that depend on that vegetation. Thus the tropical forest biome includes both the trees and the monkeys that live in them.

Cold winters and warm dry summers in the temperate zone create grasslands like the steppes of central Asia or this prairie in North America's Great Plains.

The earth's atmosphere is an ocean of gases with currents that span the globe. The sun drives these currents, and their continuing patterns shape global climate.

Winds flow down a pressure gradient, from areas of high atmospheric pressure to areas of low pressure. Along the equator air pressure is generally low. Air flows in and, heated by the sun, rises. Rising air cools. Its moisture condenses and falls as rain. Equatorial regions receive a constant heavy flow of energy from the sun, and their climates tend to be warm and wet all year.

Around the tropics—about 23 degrees north and south of the equator—is a belt of continuing high pressure where air sinks and creates a hot, dry climate. Notice the cluster of deserts along the tropics. The Sahara and Kalahari in Africa, the deserts of Australia and Arabia are all at those latitudes.

North and south of the tropics, in the temperate zones, we find changeable climates and enough rainfall to support rich forests and grasslands. Near the poles, high pressure areas again dominate, and rain and snow are scarce. The tundra is a very cold desert.

Between the tropics, the prevailing winds blow from east to west. These are the trade winds that used to carry ships from Europe west across the Atlantic to Central and South America. In the temperate zones, the prevailing winds blow from west to east. When the Spanish sent gold from their American colonies back to Europe, the ships skirted Florida and then turned north to catch the westerlies that would blow them home to Spain.

Prevailing winds have a major impact on climate. Coastal California enjoys mild temperatures year-round because of the winds blowing over the waters of the Pacific Ocean. On the east coast at the same latitudes, westerlies blowing across the continent bring hotter summers and colder winters. In North America, the rain shadow of the Sierra Nevada lies to the east of the range because the prevailing winds are from the west. Deserts cover much of Nevada, Utah, and Arizona.

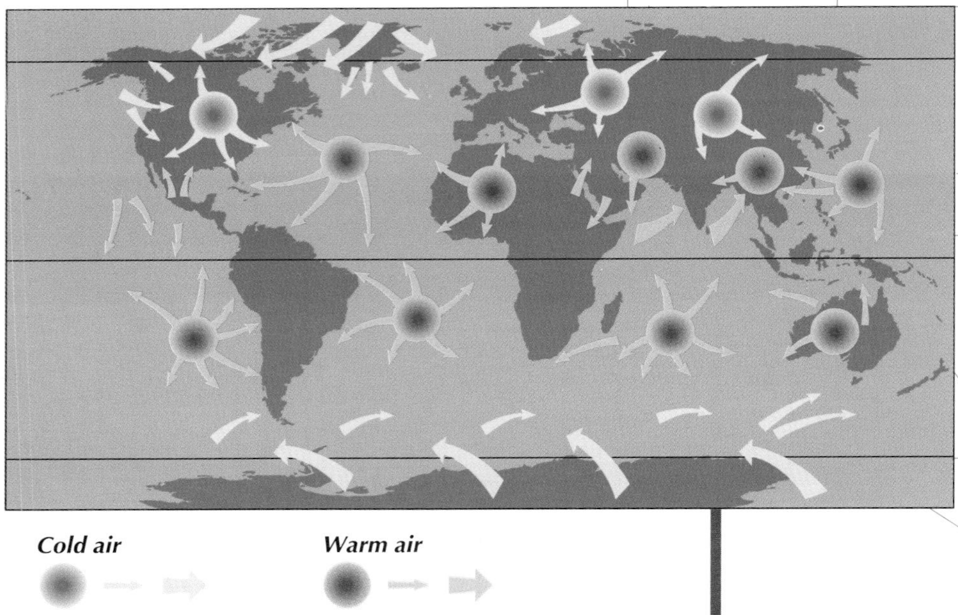

The lush green of this forest in Oregon is the product of a climate with mild winters, cool summers, and precipitation all year.

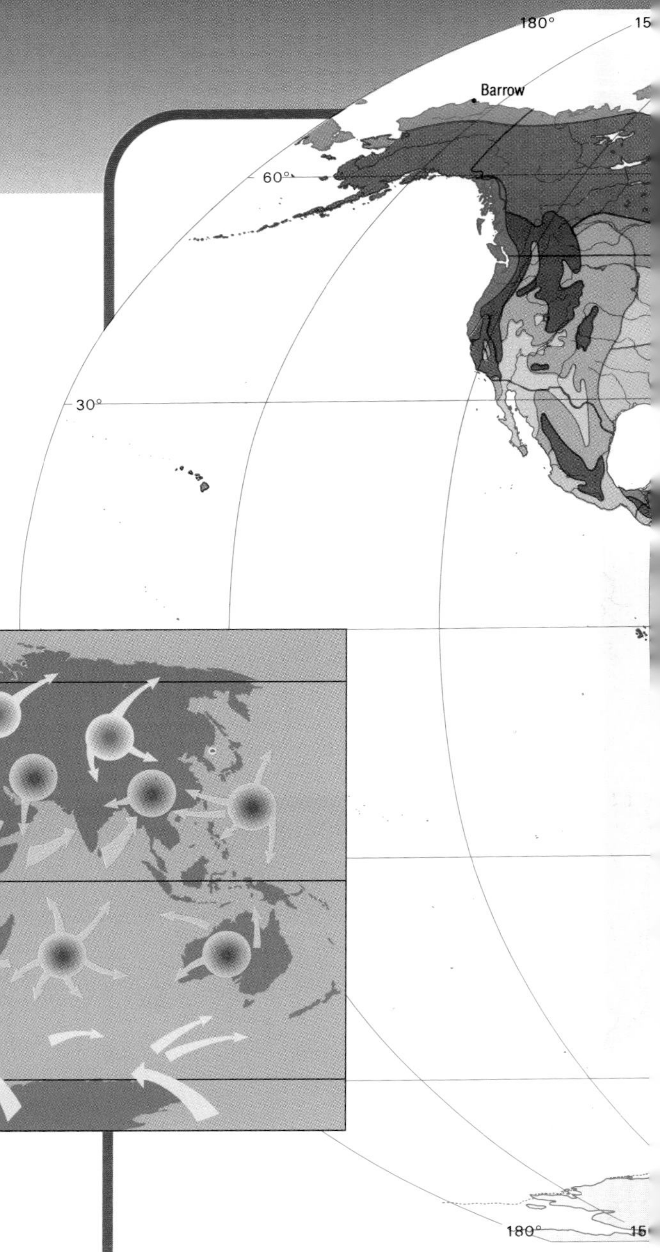

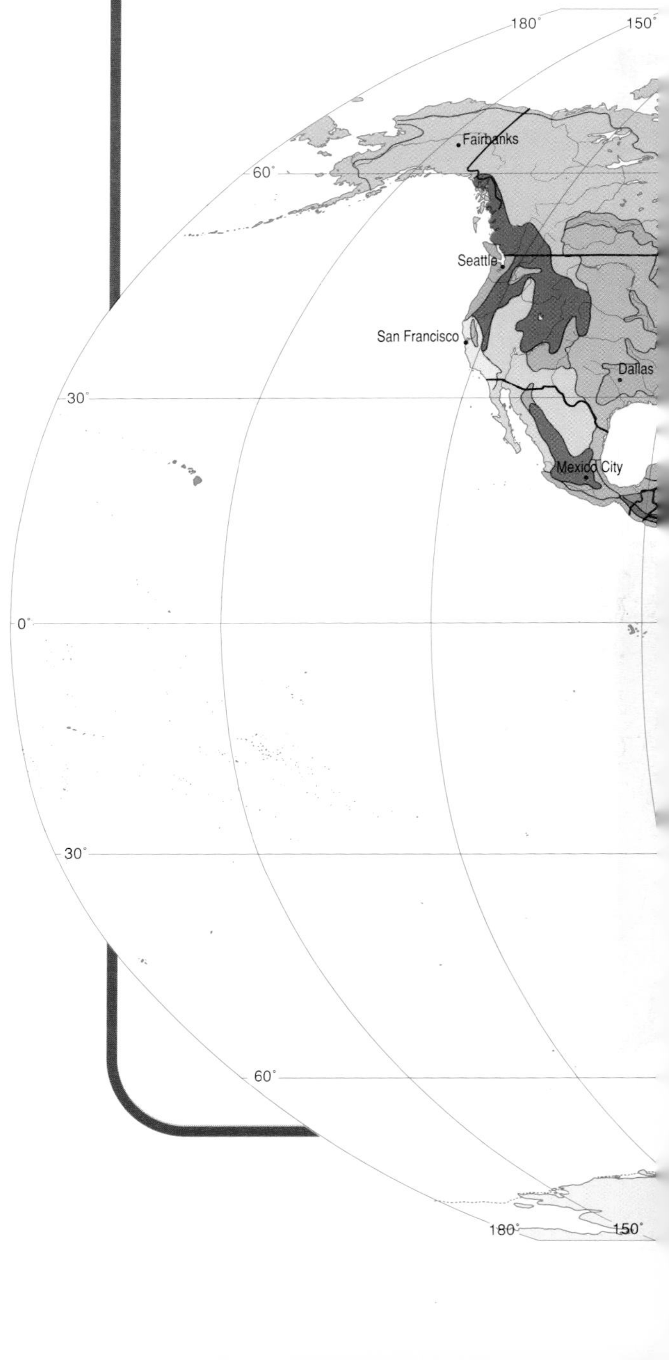

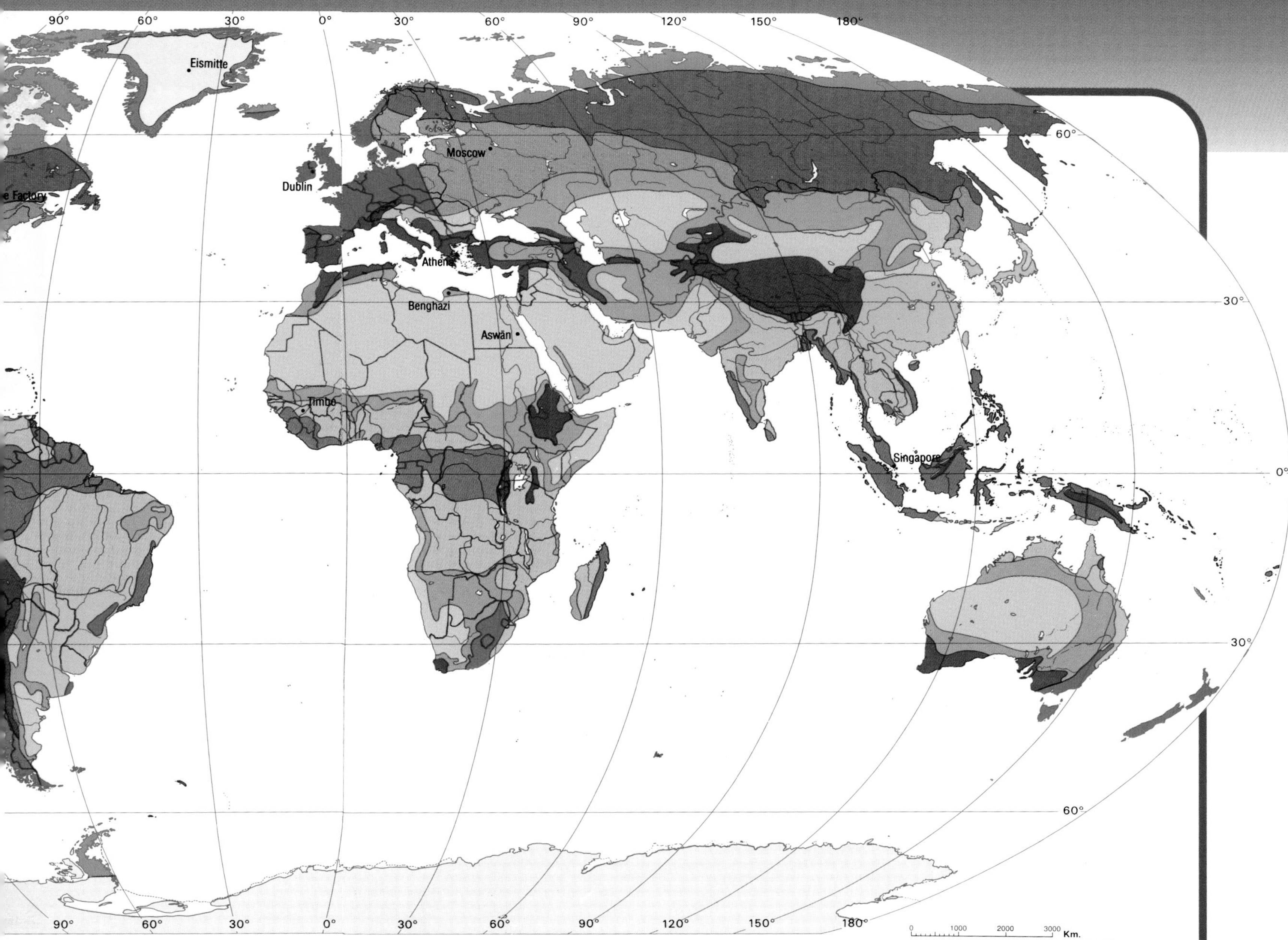

Types of Climate

TROPICAL
- Hot and rainy all year
- Hot, with rainy and dry seasons

DRY
- Desert, with some rain
- Desert

TEMPERATE
(Mild and rainy winter)
- Hot and dry summer
- Warm and humid summer
- Mild and rainy summer

TEMPERATE
(Cold and snowy winter)
- Long, warm, humid summer
- Short, warm, humid summer
- Very short, cool, humid summer

POLAR
- Tundra (very cold and dry)
- Ice cap

HIGHLAND
- Varies with height and latitude

0 1000 2000 3000 Km.
0 1000 2000 3000 Mi.
Equatorial Scale

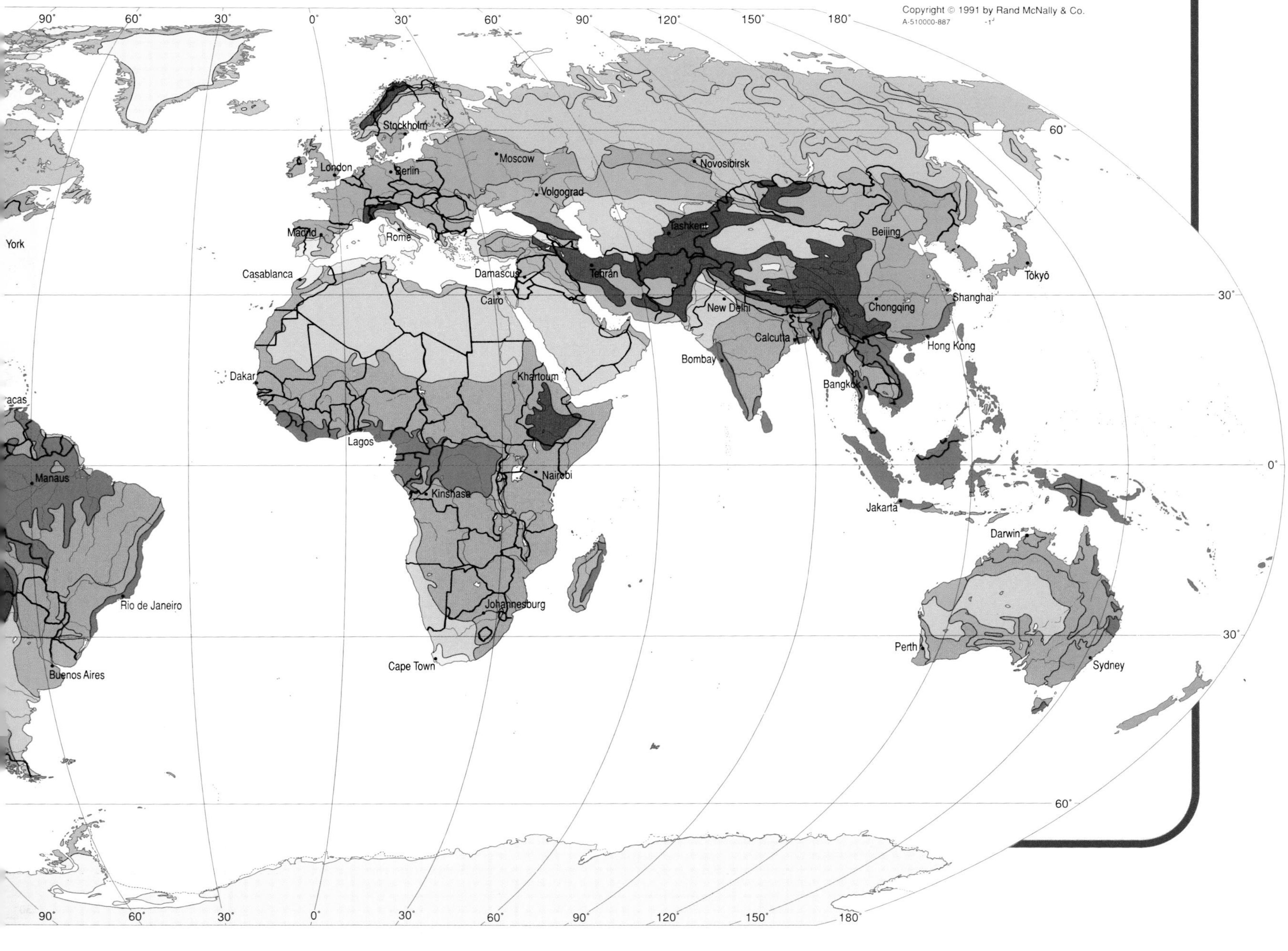

Vegetation Regions

- Tropical and subtropical forests
- Savanna
- Desert
- Mediterranean
- Temperate grassland
- Temperate forest
- Taiga (northern forests)
- Tundra (lichen and moss)
- Mountain
- Polar (high mountain)

EARTH IN BALANCE
The Dominant Species

Farming with tractors, with oxen, or by hand, the world's people have turned more than 2 billion acres of our earth into cropland.

Human beings are unique in the history of life on earth. Today, we say that dinosaurs once dominated the earth. But the species known as dinosaurs were a huge group of animals with many different variations and modes of life. No single species has ever dominated the biosphere the way we do. We are the dominant species in practically every land environment on earth, and our technology has put us at the top of the food chain in the world's oceans as well.

We reached this powerful position by being smart, adaptable, and willing to eat almost anything. Other animals have to wait for the slow processes of evolution to open up new habitats for them. We invent what we need, replacing genetic change with the much faster processes of cultural change. It took only a few thousand years for human beings to colonize the entire Western Hemisphere, from the Arctic environments of northern Alaska to the dense rain forests of the Amazon. The restless intelligence of humanity created the clothing, tools, houses, boats, and other equipment we needed to thrive in almost any environment. We sought out the local varieties of plants and animals suitable for domestication and remade the landscape to fit our needs.

Of all our inventions, none is more important than agriculture. It was discovered independently in several places in the world, and it provided the basis for the development of civilization. Farmers and herdsmen could produce enough food to feed potters, masons, weavers, and eventually, priests, artists, astronomers, and politicians. Modern agriculture has enabled us to feed concentrated human populations, some of which have grown big enough to show up as urban regions on even small-scale maps.

Agriculture also has had a bigger impact on the surface of our planet than any other human activity. Look at the map of world environments on these pages. Millions of square miles of land that were once forests or grasslands are now plowed fields and pastures. Much of North America, Europe, and Asia—especially southern Asia—has been almost completely remade by farmers. Native species of plants and animals have been drastically reduced in numbers—in some cases driven to extinction—by the replacement of their habitats with croplands and pastures.

More than 40 percent of the world's people now live in towns and cities, and estimates are that by the year 2010, more than half of humanity will be urban.

If you compare the maps on these pages with the vegetation and climate maps on the preceding pages, you will discover the unsurprising fact that human populations are concentrated in temperate and tropical regions with moderate to heavy rainfall. These are areas that were covered with forests or grasslands before humans began remaking the landscape. They are, by and large, the areas that are the most habitable, with the most productive farmland. The only completely uninhabited regions of the earth are those lands perpetually covered with ice, the most arid deserts, or mountains too rugged and inhospitable to offer any space for humans to live.

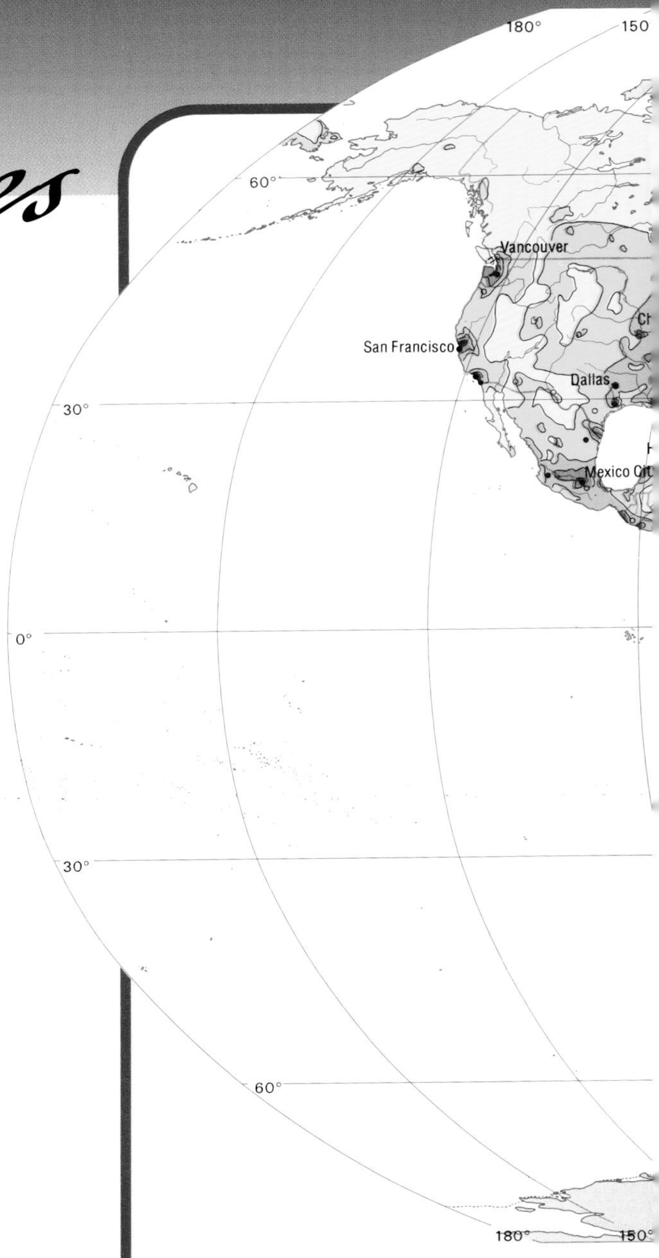

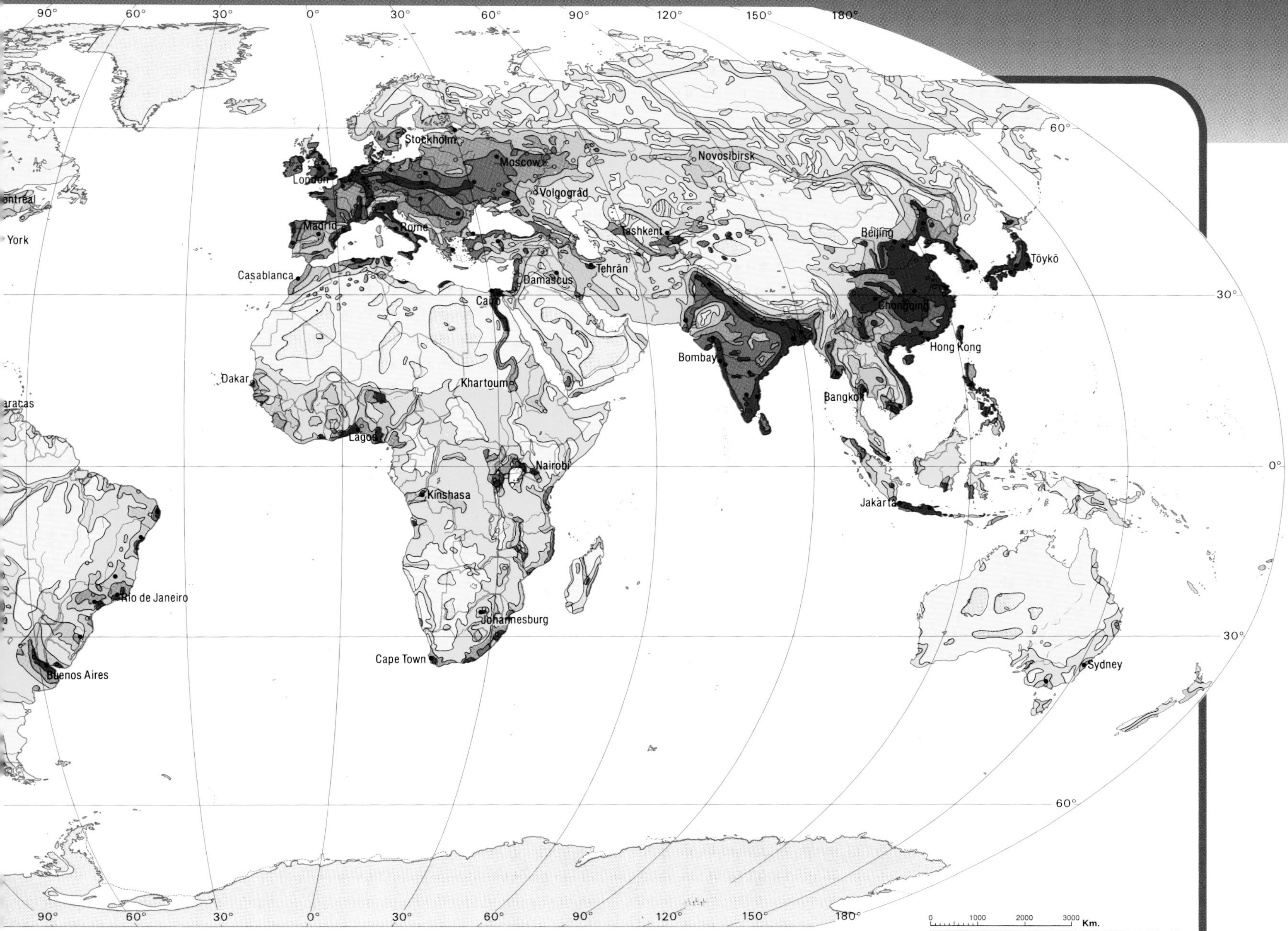

Population Density

Per square mile

- Uninhabited
- Under 2 inhabitants
- 2-25 inhabitants
- 25-60 inhabitants
- 60-125 inhabitants
- 125-250 inhabitants
- Over 250 inhabitants

- • Metropolitan areas over 2,000,000 population
- ◦ Metopolitan areas 1,000,000 to 2,000,000 population

0 1000 2000 3000 Km.
0 1000 2000 3000 Mi.
Equatorial Scale

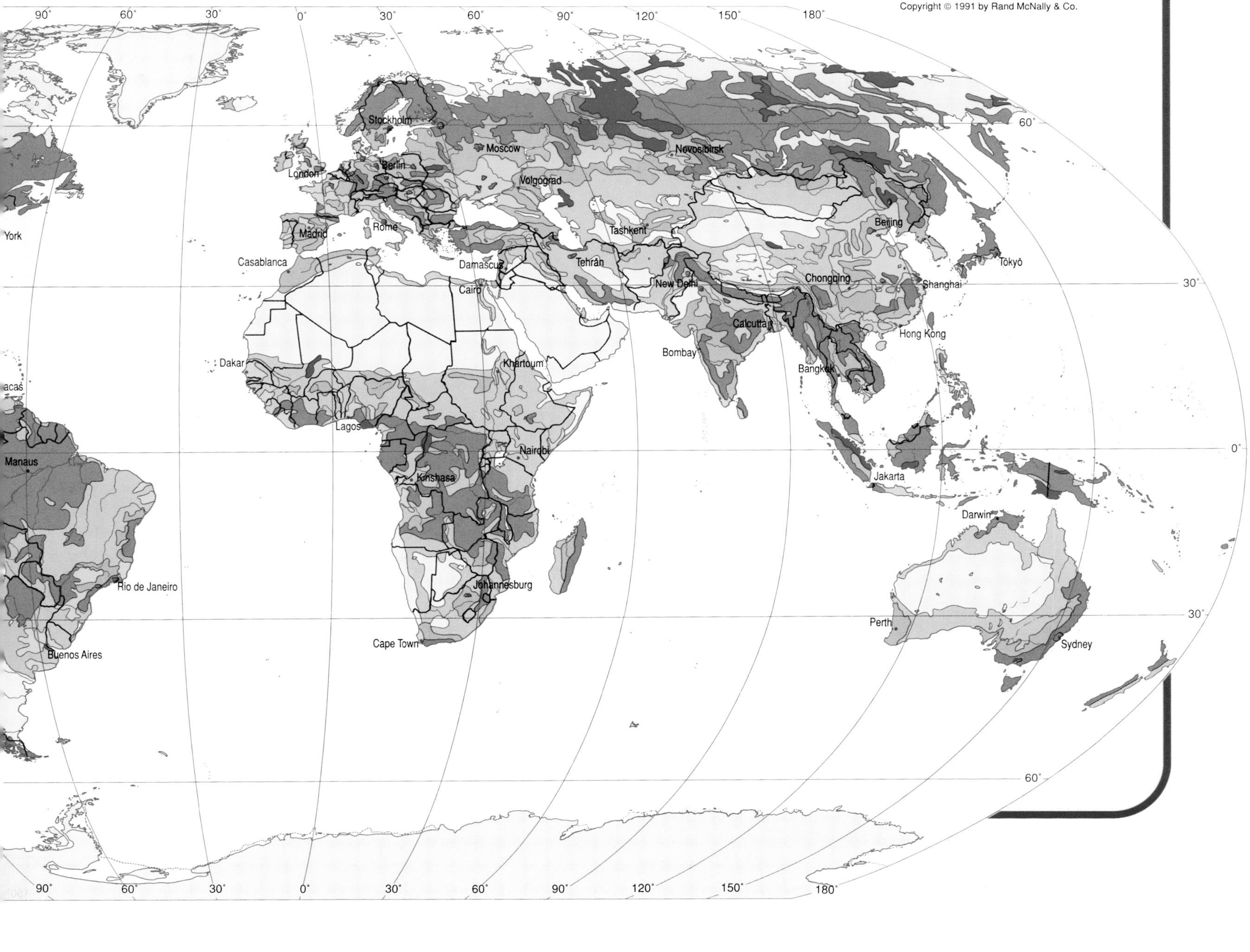

Environments

- Urban
- Cropland
- Cropland and Woodland
- Cropland and Grazing Land
- Grassland, Grazing Land
- Forest, Woodland
- Swamp, Marshland
- Tundra
- Shrub, Sparse Grass and Wasteland (desert)
- Barren Land (polar and high mountain)

UPSETTING THE BALANCE *Land and Air*

The soil is filled with living things. Some of these—insects, spiders, centipedes—are large enough to see. Many others—algae, bacteria, nematodes—are visible only through a microscope. The air is not a living system. It is a mixture of gases. But the proportions of the gases in the mix are maintained by living things. Both earth and air are affected by the actions of human beings. Both are under stress created by our misuse of them.

Most of the organisms that live in the soil get their energy by consuming the remains of plants and animals. Their work releases the nutrients held in the remains, making them available for new growth. All soils are subject to erosion by rain and wind. In a balanced ecosystem, life in the soil compensates for these losses by moving deeper into the subsoil.

Balanced, sustainable systems of agriculture imitate natural systems. Good systems employ crop rotation and fertilizers to replace the nutrients lost in the harvest. They use contour plowing, strip cropping, and other methods to reduce erosion to sustainable levels. With the help of these methods, farmers are also able to keep use of chemical pesticides to a minimum.

Continuing research is developing productive and ecologically sensible ways to grow food. Unfortunately, these methods are not being used on most of the world's cultivated land. Massive erosion reduces fertility, and the heavy use of pesticides releases large amounts of these chemicals into the environment, endangering people and wildlife.

Contour plowing means letting the land dictate the direction of furrows. By plowing across the slope rather than up and down, the farmer creates barriers to erosion that hold both soil and water in place.

Farming Methods Make a Difference

The diagram below shows poor agricultural methods. Spray irrigation loses more water to evaporation and runoff than it supplies to crops. Excessive irrigation also leaves salt deposits in the soil. Crop dusting with aircraft releases large amounts of pesticides into the environment, creating a hazard for wildlife and humans. Plowing up and down slopes rather than across them increases erosion, lowers soil fertility, and muddies streams as well.

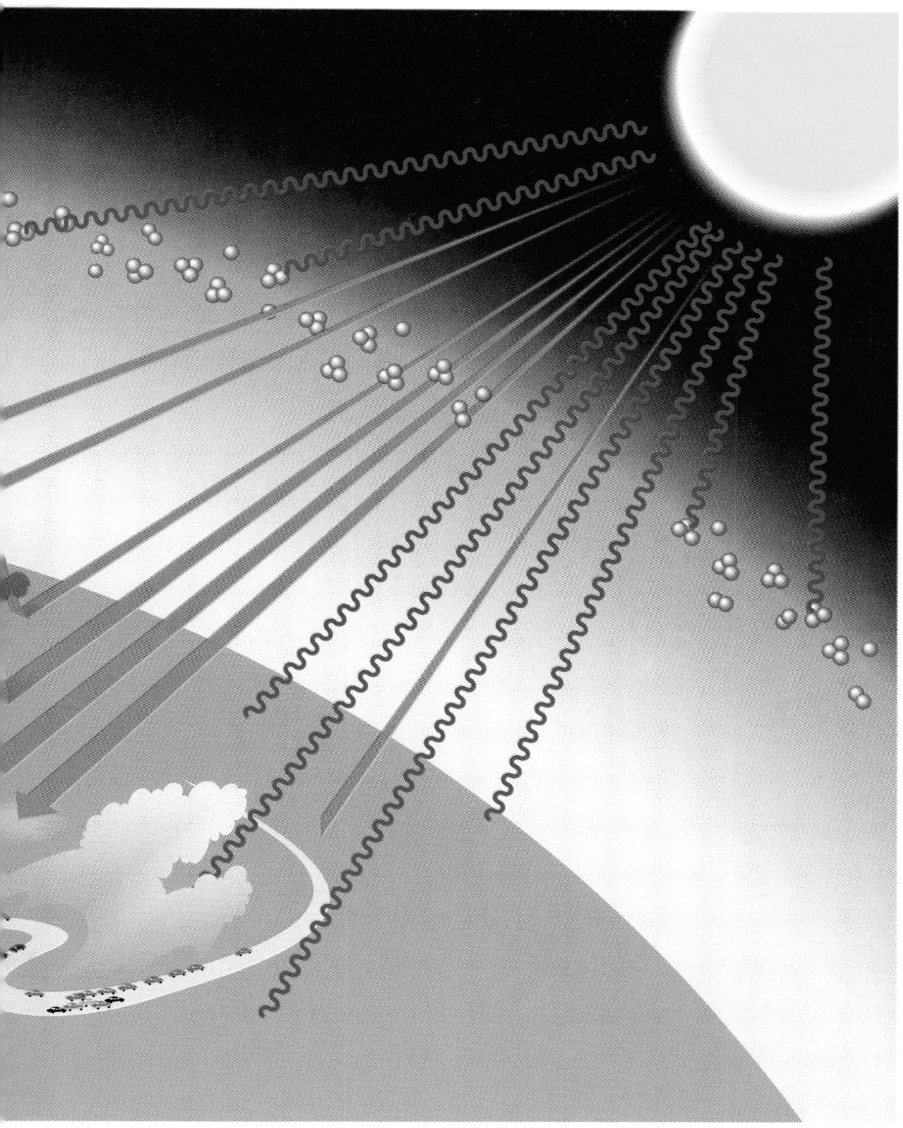

Hazards to the Ozone Layer
Carbon dioxide from the burning of coal and oil and from the massive burning of tropical forests accounts for 56 percent of the greenhouse gases released into the air. Chlorofluorocarbons (CFCs) account for another 23 percent. The chlorine in these compounds—and in other chemicals—is also a major cause of ozone depletion. The amount of carbon dioxide (CO_2) in the air has been rising at an increasing rate since the beginning of the industrial revolution.

These giant wind generators in California produce electricity without burning fossil fuels and without posing the kind of environmental dangers created by nuclear power. Holding off the greenhouse effect will require more use of renewable, non-polluting sources of energy such as these.

Irrigating arid land creates other problems. Most irrigation methods lose to evaporation up to two-thirds of the water they use. The fresh water used for irrigation carries tiny amounts of salt. The salt accumulates in irrigated fields and in time, renders them unfit for agriculture. More efficient methods of irrigation would not only save water, they would also slow salinization and make soil usable longer.

The atmosphere is under two kinds of stresses. One type is readily visible; the other kind is hidden, subtle, and ultimately, far more dangerous. The visible type of stress is the pollution that creates the pall of dirty brown smog that hangs over many of the world's cities. The hidden, subtle, and more dangerous stresses are *ozone depletion* and the *greenhouse effect.*

Most of the world's free oxygen exists in molecules containing two atoms. The chemical formula is O_2. But high above the earth is a layer of the atmosphere where *ozone,* a form of oxygen whose molecules have three atoms (O_3), is common. Ozone has the ability to absorb ultraviolet radiation. The *ozone layer* is a sort of shield that protects the biosphere from a portion of the sun's energy that is very harmful to living things. Without the ozone layer, the ability of the biosphere to support life would be reduced, and humans would suffer a dramatic increase in dangerous skin cancers.

The principal threat to the ozone layer is a group of gases called *chlorofluorocarbons* (CFCs), which are used in refrigerators, air conditioners, and some aerosol sprays. These gases break up ozone molecules, destroying the protective barrier. International agreements signed by the major producers of CFCs now call for the elimination of these gases by the turn of the century.

Chlorofluorocarbons play a role in the greenhouse effect too, but the most important gas in that process is CO_2. Our massive use of fossil fuels—oil and coal—is releasing large amounts of carbon into the atmosphere. The carbon is combined with oxygen to make carbon dioxide, a gas that holds the sun's heat in the atmosphere just as the glass roof of a greenhouse holds heat.

The amount of CO_2 in our atmosphere has been growing, and the rate of growth is increasing. If the earth does get warmer, major agricultural areas—such as the American Midwest—could be struck by severe and continuing droughts. Melting of polar ice caps could raise sea levels enough to flood coastal areas. Significant reductions in our use of fossil fuels will be needed to combat the greenhouse effect.

UPSETTING THE BALANCE
Fresh and Salt Water

The human imagination knows no more potent symbol than water. Our religions, our myths, our stories are filled with symbolic springs, cool flowing streams, gentle rains that revive the earth. Water is life.

Yet in the contemporary world, water is not treated wisely. We dump our wastes in it. We use it heedlessly, as if the world had a limitless supply. Even the vast oceans are being stripped of resources and fouled with wastes. Three-fourths of the fresh water we use is devoted to irrigating crops, yet our irrigation methods are so wasteful that most of it never reaches the plants for which it is intended.

Some farmers are now using an irrigation method called *trickle-drip.* This pumps water through hoses or pipes in the fields, and these pipes and hoses apply very small amounts of water to the soil directly over the plant roots. The method provides a double benefit: it saves water, and it reduces the deposition of salt in the soil.

Household use of water accounts for only a small fraction of our water use worldwide—although it makes up a larger proportion in the industrial countries. Wastewater from households is, however, a very serious problem. In most of the world, sewage is dumped untreated into the nearest river, lake, or harbor.

Industrial wastes are also an enormous strain on our freshwater resources. In many respects, they are worse than sewage, because sewage is a natural product that can be attacked by bacteria and eventually reduced to its constituent elements. Industrial wastes include metals—nickel, cadmium, mercury, lead—and other substances that cannot be rendered harmless by natural processes. Once in the water, they stay there.

The world's oceans seem so large that it is hard to imagine how we could harm them. But much of the open sea is virtually the equivalent of a desert; a shortage of mineral nutrients—phosphorus, nitrogen, potassium, and others—limits the growth of the algae that form the base of the food chain. This in turn limits the numbers of animals farther up the chain.

Most of the life in the world's oceans is in shallow water near the shore. Here sunlight and nutrients flowing from the land combine to make a rich environment that supports thousands of species of living things. Some of the animals of the open sea spend the early parts of their lives in these rich offshore locations.

Mangroves dominate thousands of miles of shoreline in tropical regions. These shrubby

Sewage-treatment plants like this one in Austin, Texas, use natural bacterial processes to remove human wastes from water before it is returned to rivers or lakes.

Dirtying the Fresh Water

We misuse fresh water in two major ways: We waste it, and we poison it. We waste it with dams that impound large lakes in arid regions where evaporation takes much of the water. We use more water for irrigation than for any other purpose, but only 25 percent of the water reaches the roots of crops. Arsenic and other poisons leach from mine tailings into streams and ground water. In many cases, wastewater from factories is returned to streams in a highly polluted state, and rivers are routinely used as dumps for toxic byproducts. Many cities dump raw sewage into the nearest river.

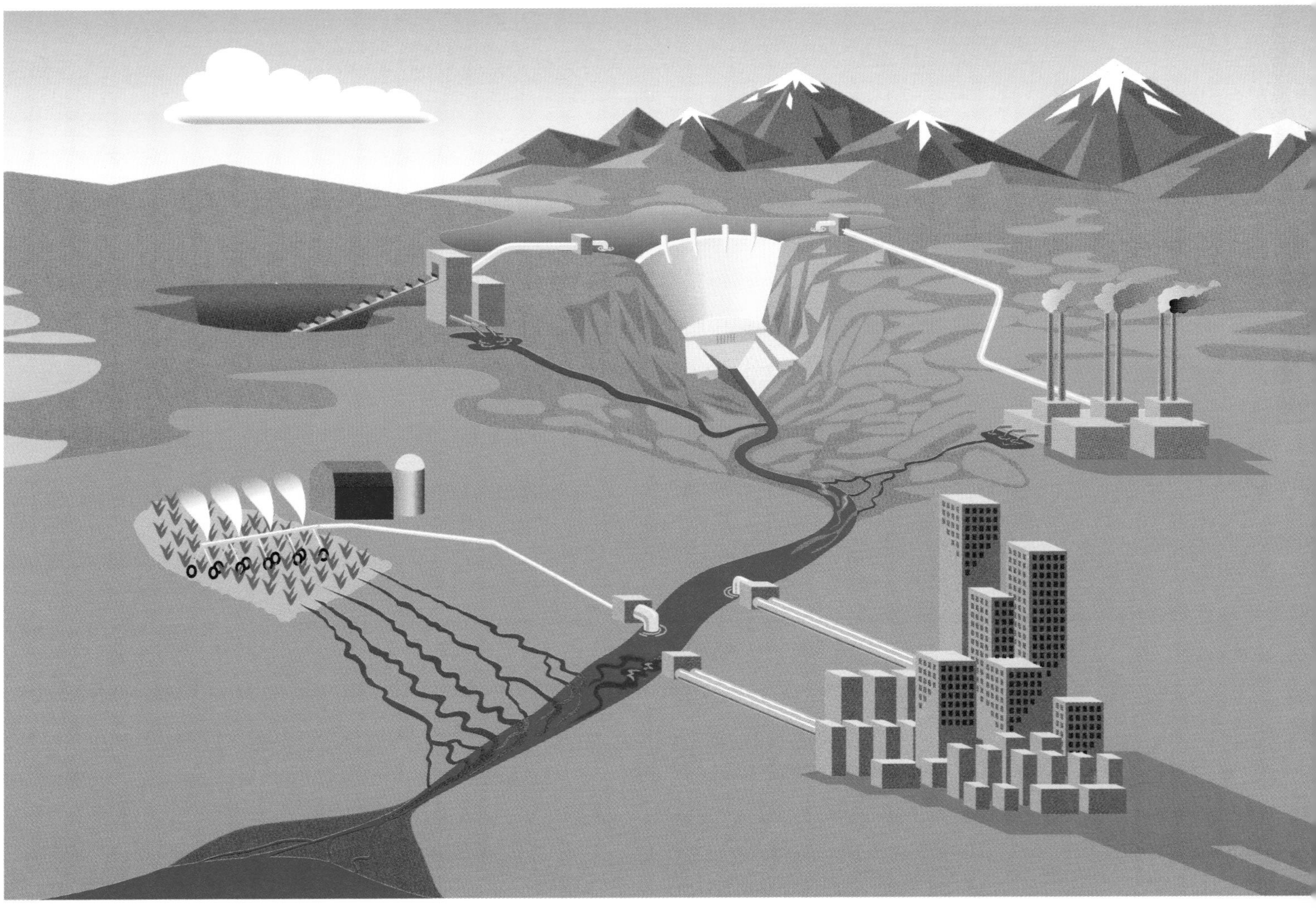

trees provide a shelter from storms for a variety of aquatic life. Offshore, coral reefs create one of the most diverse environments on earth. Along temperate shores, salt marshes teem with life. Estuaries, where fresh and salt water mix, are equally fecund.

The threats to these marine environments come from several sources. Dumping of municipal wastes offshore is a major contributor of pollution. Oil tankers are another source. The big, accidental spills get all the publicity, but ordinary operations such as the cleaning of empty tanks actually account for more oil dumped into the oceans than do the accidental spills. Shoreline development also obliterates hundreds of miles of delicate environments every year.

In both near-shore and open-sea environments, overfishing is a major problem. The annual catch of many important food fish is dropping as the animals become more scarce. Huge floating factories, some of them dragging nets several miles long, capture every living thing in their path: fish, dolphins, sea turtles, even birds.

The plight of whales also calls our attention to our overexploitation of the oceans. Several species have been hunted nearly to extinction. International agreements have reduced hunting, but existing agreements could use strengthening. Saving these marine mammals, and commercially important fish species as well, will require a major diplomatic effort to bring all nations into compliance.

Protecting both fresh and salt waters from waste dumping is equally urgent. A beginning has been made on this problem through international agreements limiting dumping of oil, toxics, and industrial and municipal waste, but more remains to be done.

Perhaps the most important change will have to take place in our minds. We need to remember our ancient images of water as life and stop thinking of it as a convenient place to put our garbage.

Workers scour the beaches of Prince William Sound near Valdez, Alaska, the site of the largest accidental oil spill in United States history. Cleanups are expensive; this one cost $1.3 billion. Looking for better ways to prevent such spills would pay off more in the long run.

Fouling the Salt Water
Most of the life in the oceans is near shore in the shallow waters of the continental shelves. Coral reefs, mangrove swamps, and salt marshes are rich in life and are often nurseries for the young of animals of the open sea. Shoreline development can destroy these habitats, and waste dumping can poison them. Offshore oil drilling and spills from oil tankers pollute the seas. Deliberate spills by oil tankers flushing out tanks actually dump more oil than accidental spills. Overfishing has driven some whales nearly to extinction, and huge trawlers pulling enormous nets catch all the ocean life in their path.

UPSETTING THE BALANCE
Plant and Animal Life

Evolution is a process that happens in ecosystems. A constant interplay of complex forces—relations between competitors, between predators and prey, between mutually dependent species, between living things and nonliving factors such as climate—both sustains the ecosystem and creates the selection pressure that gives rise to new species.

Diversity begets diversity. The presence of large numbers of species promotes ever finer divisions of available resources. In the evergreen forests of Canada and the northern United States, the tiny, bright-colored insect-eating birds called wood warblers demonstrate the process. Four species of the genus Dendroica divide tall trees into distinct zones for feeding and nesting. Magnolia warblers nest and feed within fifteen feet of the ground. Black-throated green warblers concentrate in the area between fifteen and forty feet. Blackburnian warblers nest and feed between forty and fifty-five feet, while Cape May warblers concentrate in the tree tops, above fifty-five feet.

Simplicity also begets simplicity. Remove a species, and the effects of the loss ripple through the ecosystem like the waves that radiate from a pebble thrown into the water. When a plant goes extinct, the specialized insects that fed on that plant go with it. A decline in the numbers and variety of insects in the system affects birds, shrews, toads, lizards, and other insect eaters. A decline in these species harms hawks, herons, snakes, and other predators.

Remove enough species, and the whole system may collapse. We cut tropical forests for farmland and pasture. If the farms and pastures are abandoned, often the forest does not reclaim the land. The forest ecosystem has been so badly damaged it cannot bounce back.

The demands of human beings are putting all of nature under stress. In the entire North Temperate Zone, in Europe, Asia, and North America, only the area centered on Yellowstone Park in Wyoming can still be considered a functioning ecosystem. Elsewhere, the parks and preserves, while they do provide a measure of protection for many species, are too small and too closely pressed by human populations to function naturally.

Now the destruction of natural areas that has already had such a powerful effect on the North Temperate Zone is spreading to the tropics. Tropical forests, the oldest and richest ecosystems on earth, are being turned into farms and pastures at a dizzying rate. One recent estimate suggests that an area twice the size of Austria is cleared every year.

Usually the best thing we can do for nature is leave it alone. This pine forest in Grand Teton National Park was burned a few years before this picture was taken. Left alone, the forest can restore itself with new growth.

Kill the forest, and you also kill the thousands of species of plants and animals that live in the forest. Tropical forests cover only about 7 percent of the earth, but they harbor half of the earth's species of plants and animals. If the destruction continues, we may lose a million different forms of life by the year 2000.

Most of the world's endangered species—both plants and animals—are on the brink of extinction because their habitats have been destroyed. But some species are threatened in other ways. As many as seventy thousand African elephants are ruthlessly slaughtered each year for their ivory. Rhinos are killed for their horns. Leopards and cheetahs provide pelts worth thousands of dollars each. Parrots by the millions are captured in the wild and sold by the pet trade.

The scope of our destruction of nature is so immense that it is hard to know where to start dealing with it. Stopping the trade in endangered species is the easy part. International agreements already exist, notably the Convention on International Trade in Endangered Species of Wild Fauna and Flora (CITES). Over one hundred countries are now signatories to this convention. CITES is successful only when true international cooperation supports it. Enforcement in the developing nations where the animals come from has to be combined with enforcement in the richer nations that provide the markets.

The more profound problem is the destruction of whole biomes, the loss of the ecosystems that support all life—including human life. Our challenge—in the face of growing human populations—is to satisfy our needs without taking up all the space available on this planet. We need to think about both housing patterns and farming practices to search for ways to get the most out of every acre we use.

We also need to draw on the wisdom of the people who have learned to gain a livelihood from tropical lands in nondestructive ways. The Indians of the Amazon, the Dayaks of Borneo, and many other cultures have a profound knowledge of the ecological processes that sustain the natural systems of their homelands. It will take a combination of their knowledge and the insights of science to develop ways to enjoy the bounty of the forest without destroying the source of that bounty.

Stripping Away Plant Life

Our attack on nature proceeds on several fronts. We take the timber we need with massive clearcuts that remove every tree and thereby create soil erosion and stream pollution. We drain and fill wetlands, destroying the specialized habitats of many plants and animals. We scatter pollutants in the air and water, often harming plants and animals thousands of miles away. And, increasingly, as our populations grow, we simply do not leave nature any space.

A busload of tourists watch a leopard at a game preserve in Kenya. The rise of *ecotourism* has helped many Third World nations pay for preserves where wildlife can be protected.

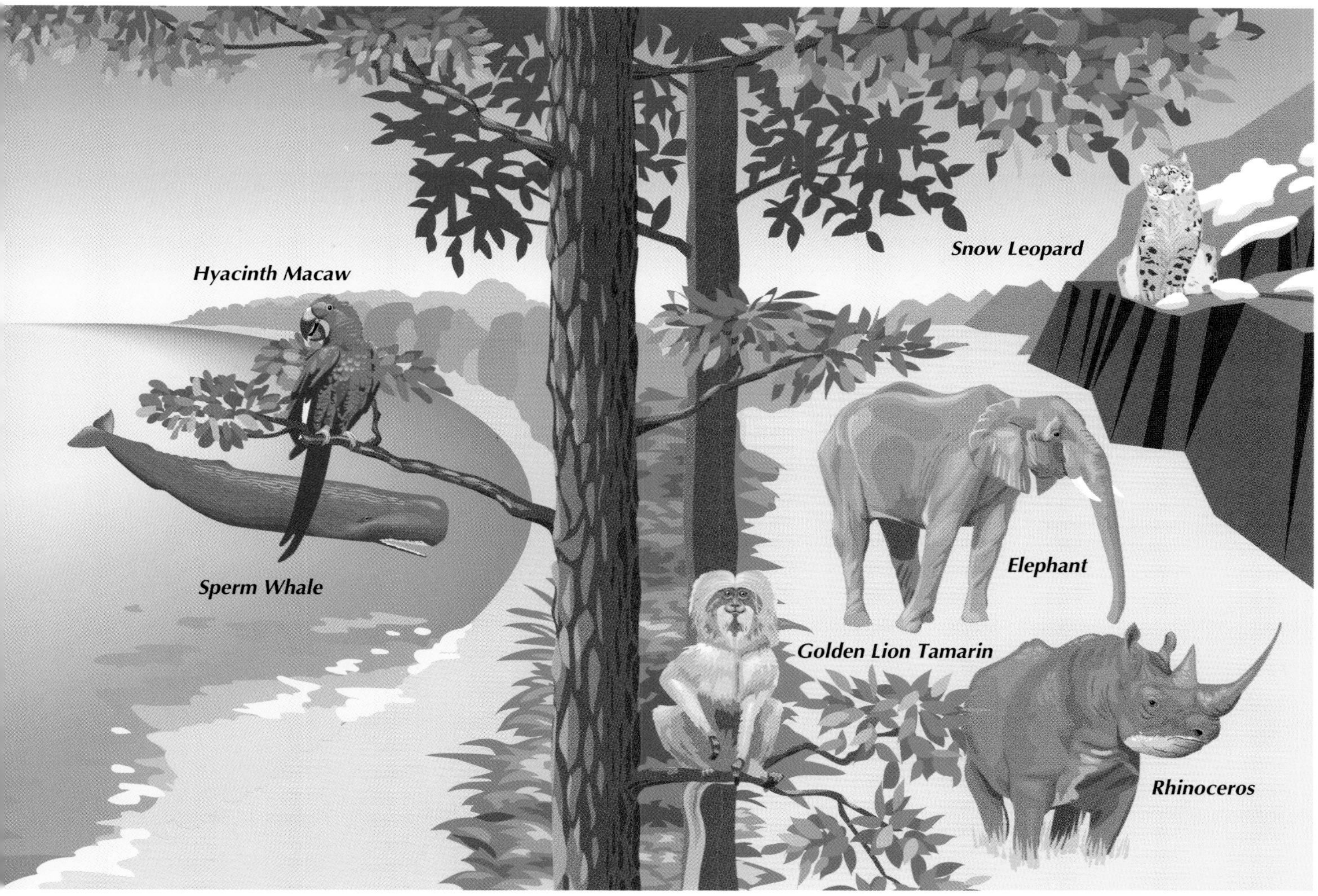

Threatening Animal Life

Most of the damage we have visited upon wildlife has been caused by destruction of natural habitats. But some species are undergoing an even more direct assault. We kill whales for their meat and oil. We kill elephants for their ivory tusks and rhinos for their horns. Snow leopards are victims of vanity as they become coats. Parrots are captured from the wild to be locked in cages. Because the slaughter of these animals does not stem from a larger and tougher-to-solve issue, such as habitat destruction, solutions should be easier to find.

UPSETTING THE BALANCE *Human Life*

Human numbers grew very slowly through most of our history. Births and deaths remained more or less in balance. Our best estimate of world population in A.D. 1 is 150 million. By about 1650, the total was up to 500 million. And then, the explosion began.

By 1850, there were 1.2 billion people in the world. By 1950, that number had doubled to 2.5 billion. By 1990, human numbers had doubled again, to 5.3 billion. It is likely that another three billion will be added to world population by the year 2025.

This explosion is not fueled by an increase in birth rates. People have not been having any more children than they used to have. The critical difference is a major decline in death rates. More food, better sanitation, better housing, and better health care combined to extend the average life span and dramatically lower infant mortality.

But then in Europe, Japan, and North America—the industrialized countries where the benefits of a higher standard of living were spread widely through the population—birth rates began to go down. Instead of having six or eight babies in her lifetime, the average woman had two. Europe, Japan, the United States, and Canada have essentially achieved zero population growth. In some countries—Sweden, Denmark, West Germany, Austria, Hungary—population has actually been declining. Demographers speak of the industrial countries as having completed the demographic transition, of having once again balanced birth rates and death rates.

The situation in the Third World is quite different. There, improved health care has lowered death rates, especially among children, but birth rates have remained high. Growth rates of 2 to 3 percent are common, which means that numbers will double in less than twenty-five years.

The countries with the high growth rates are also the countries least able to cope with the social, economic, and environmental consequences of such growth. Think of a country desperately trying to train enough teachers and build enough schools to educate its children when every year the first grade class grows by 3 percent.

Rates of growth have been slowing down in recent years, however, even in the countries with the fastest population growth. And several countries have initiated successful population control programs that offer hope for the future.

The programs that work emphasize the fact that population control cannot be separated from other factors in the lives of people. The decision to have many children is usually rooted in traditional cultural attitudes, but it is also rational and sensible in terms of the life-style many people lead. Infant mortality has been reduced, but it is still higher in the Third World than in the industrialized countries, so having several children gives a family a better chance of raising some of them to adulthood. Children also begin to contribute economically to their families at an early age. By the time they reach puberty, they are likely to be earning more than the cost of their subsistence. Finally, in the absence of Social Security or extensive private pension plans, children are the only way to ensure a comfortable old age.

Successful population control programs—such as those in Sri Lanka and some of the Indian states—address the problems of poverty as well as teach mothers how to use contraceptive devices. They teach infant and child care and provide immunizations and other health-care assistance so women can feel confident that their babies will live.

The status of women in society also plays a very significant role in the success of family-planning efforts. In cultures where women are subservient to men, where education and the possibility of economic independence are masculine monopolies, it is very difficult to carry out successful population-control programs. In cultures where women have some control over their lives, they generally respond favorably to the opportunity to limit their childbearing.

The long-term question is whether the countries of the Third World will be able to make the demographic transition already accomplished in industrialized countries. Countries that have successfully lowered their birth rates are generally also countries where economic growth has made a difference in the lives of large numbers

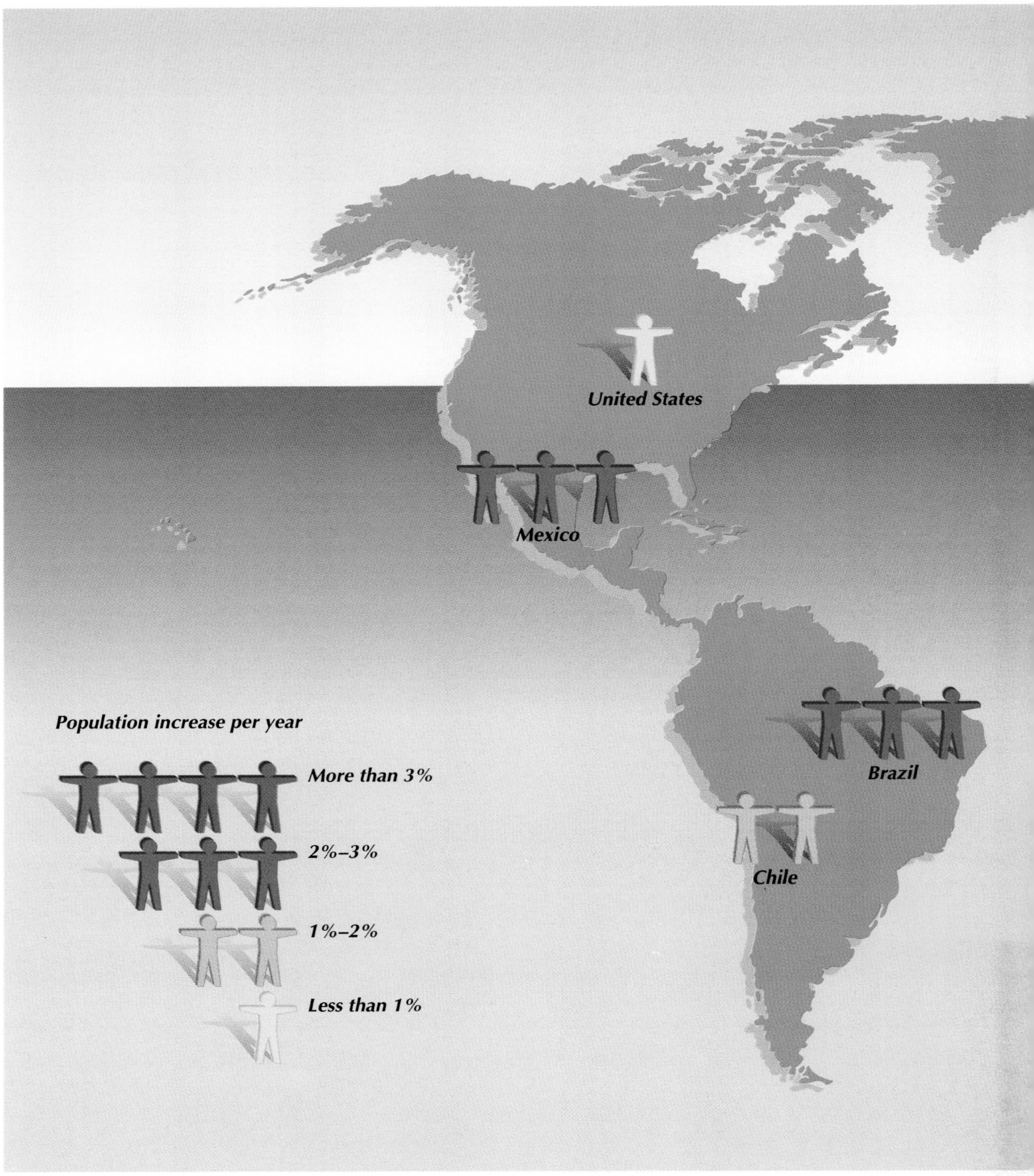

Crowding Human Life
This map shows very clearly the relationship between economic status and population growth. The industrialized countries, with strong economies—France, the Soviet Union, and the United States—show little or no population growth. Chile, a country that is in the middle rank of nations economically, has slightly faster growth. The countries with high growth rates are all among the world's poorer nations. China has managed to cut its growth with the help of an aggressive campaign to limit family size. Countries with high growth rates have young populations who must pass through their child-bearing years before growth will come to a stop.

of people. Continuing development and improvement in the lives of ordinary people must be a major part of population-control efforts.

If population control requires, however, that China's one billion inhabitants and India's 800 million inhabitants consume as much of the earth's resources per person as present-day North Americans or Europeans, then population control is unobtainable. The strain on the biosphere would be so great that the processes that sustain life—including human life—would break down.

That is why our search for sustainable forms of development must be intensified. We need to bend natural processes without breaking them. We need to imitate the actions of nature rather than trying to impose our own vision of how things ought to be done. In agriculture and industry, in the decisions we make about how we want to use the earth, we need to recognize that our grandchildren will someday need to take their living from the same earth that supports us today.

The sprawl of suburban growth around our cities is swallowing up both farmland and natural areas.

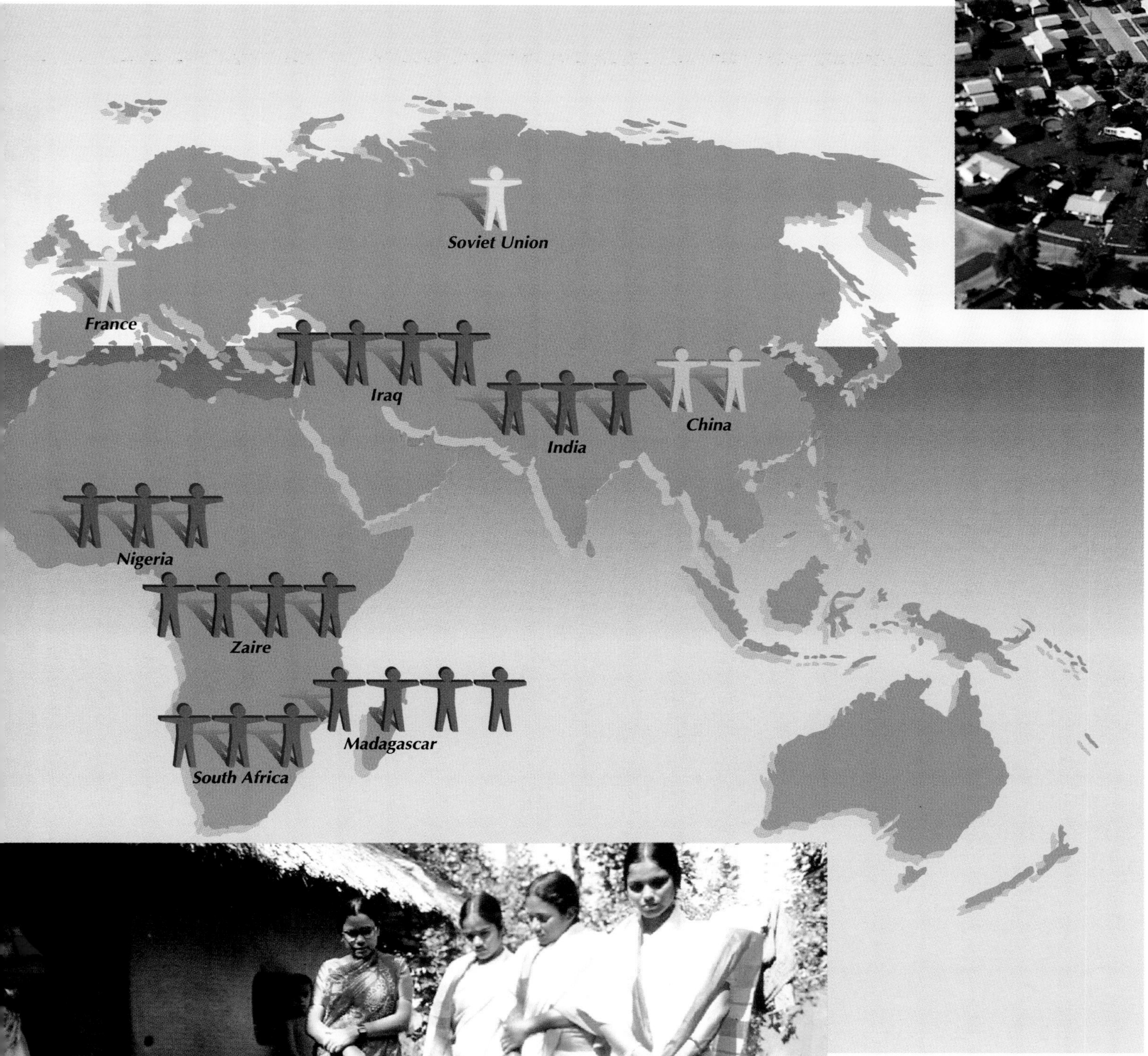

These women in a village in Bangladesh are learning to raise healthy babies as part of a population-control project.

RESTORING THE BALANCE

Europe

A thousand years ago, much of Europe was wilderness. Human populations were small, and ancient forests covered most of the land. And then humans began to expand into these forests, converting woodlands to wheat fields, establishing towns on wilderness rivers. By the end of the Middle Ages, so much forest had been cut that some settlements experienced a shortage of firewood and began mining coal as a substitute fuel. Coal became the fuel that powered the steam engines that powered the Industrial Revolution—perhaps the biggest change in human life since the discovery of agriculture. The power of steam also provided energy for railroads and ships that made travel faster and more reliable.

The Industrial Revolution began in England in the late 18th century, and by 1840, England had become the first nation in which most of the people lived in towns. The rest of Europe followed. Today, nearly three-fourths of all Europeans live in cities; Albania and Yugoslavia are the only European nations in which the majority lives in rural areas. In Great Britain, more than 90 percent of the population is urban. Industry dominates European economies. In Germany and France, almost half the work force is employed in industry.

Rural areas are occupied by farms that tend to be small compared to those in the United States. Less than 2 percent of Great Britain's work force is employed in agriculture. In France, the largest producer and exporter of farm products in western Europe, only 9 percent of the work force is in agriculture.

Centuries of occupation have altered nearly all the natural landscape of the continent. Europe in its natural state survives only in the far north and in a few isolated—mostly mountainous—areas in the east. Even such seemingly wild areas as Germany's Black Forest are actually carefully tended gardens watched over by foresters who literally know every tree.

But those carefully tended woodland gardens are now being threatened by a by-product of the Industrial Revolution called *acid rain*. When we burn coal or oil, the sulphur and nitrogen in these fuels combine with oxygen and escape

Large populations and heavy industry create scenes like this one in Europe. Here a Bulgarian shepherd tends his flock in the shadow of a giant industrial complex.

Almost three-fourths of Europe's people live in cities. Among the most beautiful of these is Nice on France's Mediterranean coast. Unfortunately, the large numbers of people living near that fragile sea are creating pollution problems. The nations of the Mediterranean are now working together on those problems.

into the air as sulphur dioxide and nitrogen oxide. In the atmosphere, chemical changes convert these oxides to sulfuric and nitric acid. Some of these acids fall to earth as dry particles. Most fall with rain and snow.

Rainfall is naturally acidic, but in industrialized regions, concentrations as much as one hundred times more acid than natural rainfall may occur. The effects are profound. Forty-three percent of the conifers in Switzerland's central alpine region are dead or dying. At least four thousand lakes in Sweden are so heavily acidified that no fish survive in them. Every year, Norway experiences some rainfall that is as acidic as lemon juice.

Who Can Stop the Rain?

Controlling the emissions that create acid rain is difficult and expensive, and the fragmentation of Europe into many countries creates additional problems. Who should pay for emission controls—the countries producing the emissions or the countries suffering from them? Until recently, the division of Europe into two blocs compounded the difficulties.

However, major efforts are now underway. The countries belonging to the European Community have agreed to cut sulfur dioxide emissions from power plants by 60 percent by 2003 and nitrogen oxides by 40 percent by 1998. Twenty-one other nations have agreed to somewhat less stringent standards. There is reason to hope that the problem can be resolved.

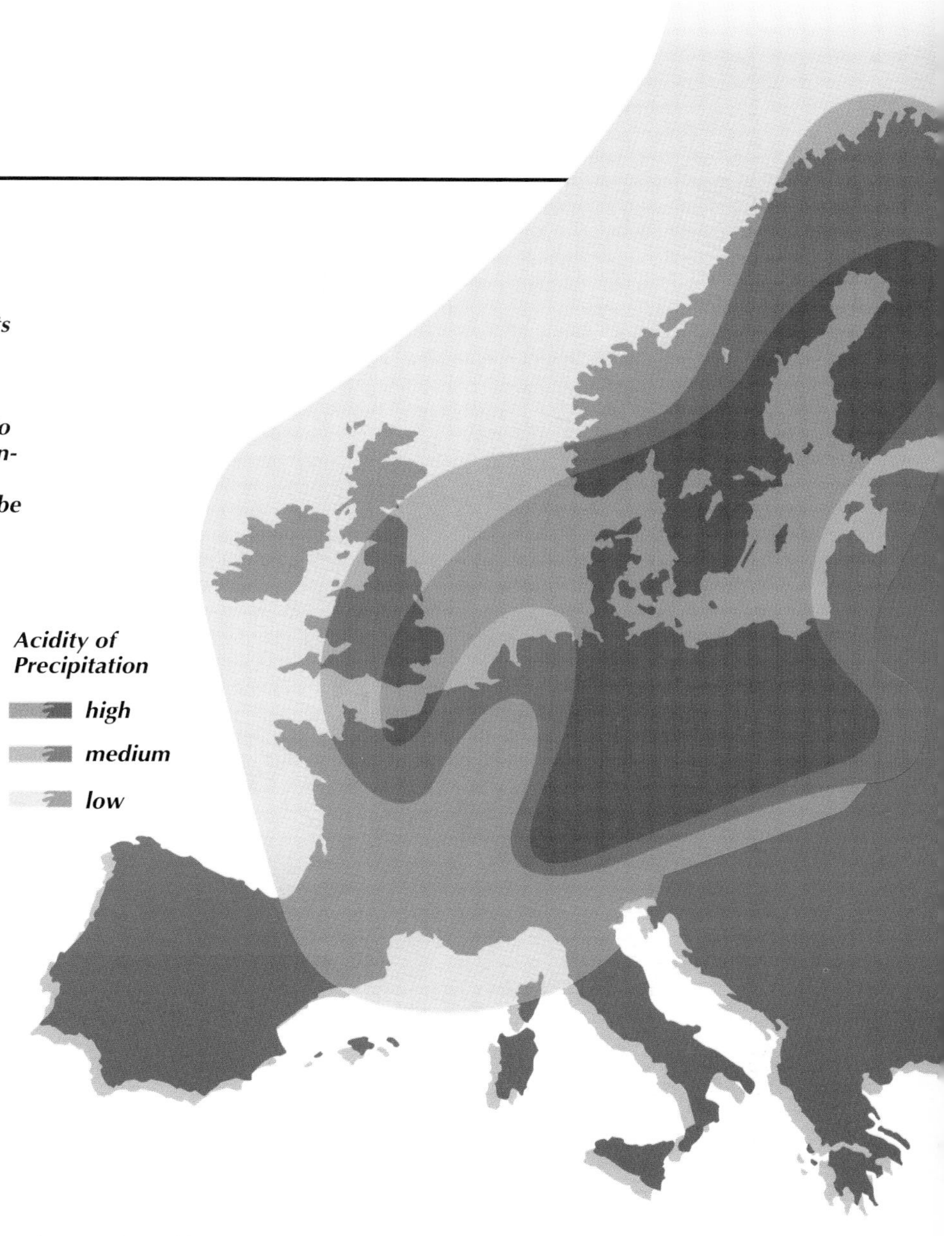

The map shows where acid rain falls in Europe. Regions with acidic bedrock such as Germany and Scandinavia are especially vulnerable. In Germany's Black Forest (left), as many as half the trees are damaged.

RESTORING THE BALANCE
Asia

Asia is a land of superlatives. It is the largest continent in both area and population. It contains the world's highest (Mount Everest) and lowest (the Dead Sea) points. The rain forests at its southern edge are some of the wettest places on earth; the deserts of Arabia are some of the driest. Those same deserts are among the hottest places on earth, and Siberia is one of the coldest.

At the northern edge of the continent, along the shores of the Arctic Ocean, tundra dominates the land. South of that is a broad belt of evergreen forest called *taiga*. Human settlements are widely scattered in these northern regions, and vast expanses of wilderness still exist. However, large development schemes in this region are now having a major impact.

South of the taiga, a narrow belt of grasslands called *steppe* runs east and west across the continent. Some areas here have been converted to wheat fields; others support herds of cattle, horses, sheep, and goats. In the heart of the continent are large, sparsely populated deserts and short-grass steppes.

In eastern China, where deciduous forests were once the dominant vegetation, there exists some of the most intensely used land in the

world. China has a billion mouths to feed, and only about 10 percent of its land is arable, so maximum yields must be produced from every available acre.

Some portions of India are as thickly populated as eastern China, as are some regions in Southeast Asia. Rich tropical forest is the natural vegetation of much of Southeast Asia and the islands of Indonesia. In recent years, however, millions of acres of this forest have been cut—some for timber, some to clear land for agriculture, some to provide firewood.

The cutting of these forests is a major contributor to one of Asia's most serious environmental problems: soil erosion. Asia is losing twenty-five billion tons of topsoil every year. This is twenty-five times the rate of erosion in the United States.

The problem is visible in its starkest form on the slopes of the Himalayas. Stripped of their protective forests, the soils of these slopes slide downhill, carried along by rushing waters. Springs on the mountainsides dry up because so much of the rainwater flows away rather than soaking into the ground. Rivers that once ran clear become choked with silt. The useful life of dams is drastically shortened as silt deposits deepen behind them. Instead of a steady, reliable flow, the rivers oscillate between extremes. Catastrophic floods follow rainy seasons, while beds dry up completely in dry seasons. Major rivers such as the Ganges, the Brahmaputra, the Irriwaddy, the Salween, and the Mekong no longer supply regular amounts of irrigation water.

These hillside terraces in Nepal are an effective way to increase the amount of arable land and a traditional way to control erosion, but they do require heavy, continuing labor to build and maintain.

Nearly twenty million people live in the vast sprawl of Tokyo-Yokohama, Japan. Japan's overall population density is among the highest in the world.

The people of Asia, with help from their governments and from private organizations, are planting millions of trees every year. The trees will protect the soil and provide fuel and wood for the future.

Protecting the Soil

The nations of southern Asia have undertaken major reforestation efforts to fight erosion and the loss of water resources. India alone plants more than three million acres of trees every year. Despite these efforts, India is still losing forest.

The challenge is to provide food, fuel, and land to large and growing populations without destroying the soil that supports human life. Everything from better farming methods to more efficient stoves can contribute to reducing the problem. Thus far, the most successful efforts have been those that involve local people both in the reforestation efforts and in the decisions about how to use their forest resources.

RESTORING THE BALANCE
Africa

Africa inspires myths of Eden. Humanity can trace its beginnings to the ancient savannas of the Rift Valley in East Africa. There, too, is a richness of wildlife unique in the world. In Eurasia and North America, mass extinctions at the end of the Ice Age wiped out many species of large mammals. The antelopes, elephants, zebras, lions, and giraffes of Africa survived that wave of extinctions and are now living reminders of the world that shaped our earliest ancestors.

Deserts dominate much of Africa. In the north, the Sahara, the largest desert on earth, covers 3.5 million square miles. With the Kalahari and the Namib in the south, a full third of the continent is covered by bare sand and sparse scrub.

Along the southern edge of the Sahara, the climate grows gradually more moist. In the region called the Sudan, grasslands and savannas replace the deserts. The people of Africa have long used this land both for pasture and for growing crops such as millet. In recent years, some of this land has been planted in peanuts and other crops grown primarily for export rather than for local consumption.

Farther south, as the climate grows wetter, trees become more common and forests dominate the land. The forest becomes richer and denser near the equator and becomes a region of rain forest in and around the Congo River Basin. South of the basin, drier conditions support more grasslands, deserts, and open woodlands.

Until very recently, most of Africa had been only lightly touched by human activity. The deserts have very small, scattered populations. Large portions of them are totally uninhabited. Even outside the desert areas, population density over most of the continent averages less than ten persons per square mile—about the same density as the states of Nevada and North Dakota. The people of the continent are concentrated in areas whose climate and soils make them particularly attractive for human settlement.

For centuries, the small populations of farmers and herdsmen in Africa's Sudan, or Sahel,

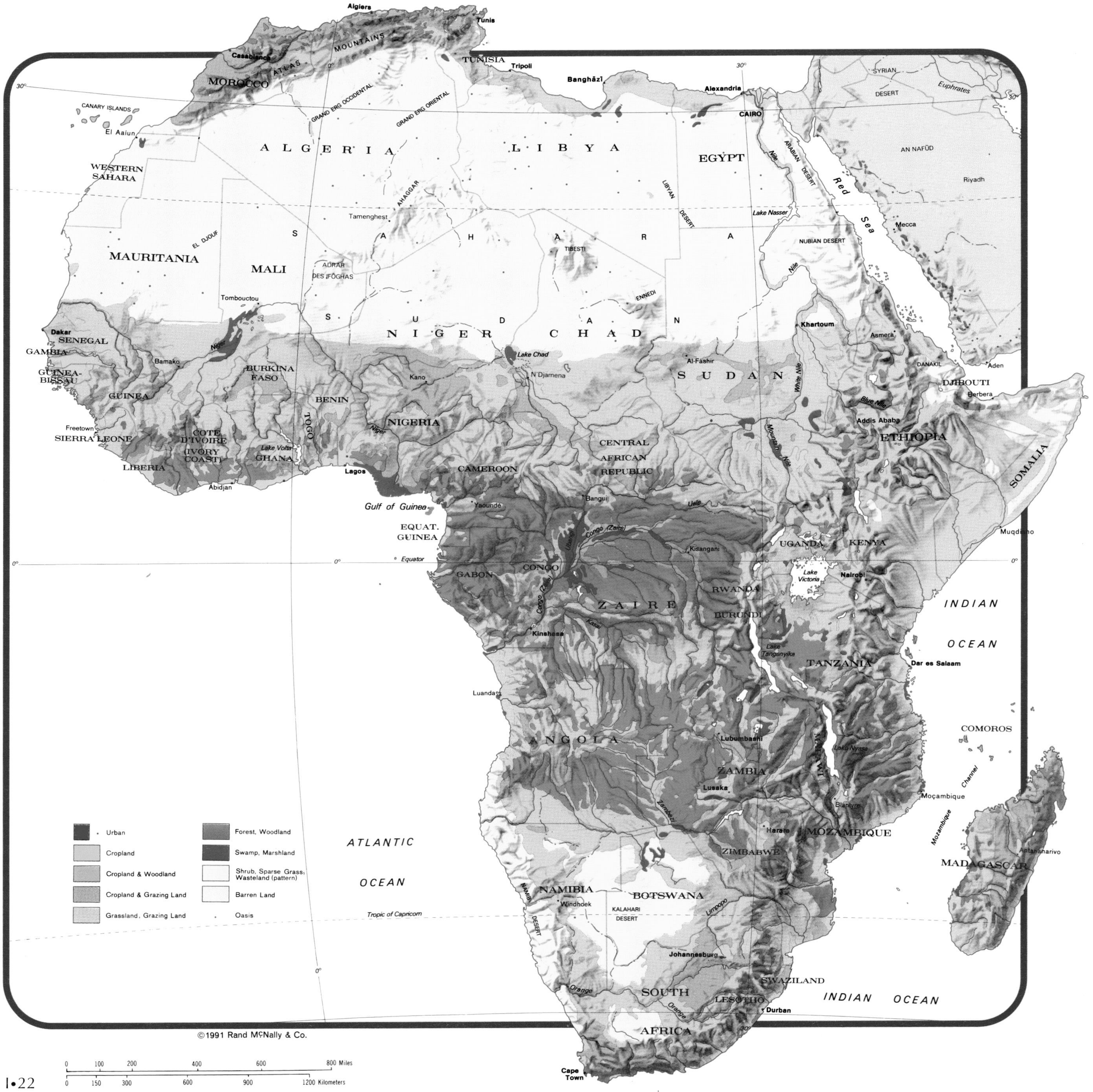

Far left: Africa's cities are growing almost 5 percent a year, but two-thirds of the continent's people still live in rural villages like this one in Zimbabwe.

Left: Africa's herds of large animals are among the living wonders of the world. Preserving them in the face of growing human populations is one of the world's more difficult problems.

made a living from the harsh land. They moved their herds periodically; they rotated crops; they let land lie fallow—sometimes for as long as twenty years—to allow it to regain fertility. In recent years, population growth and the conversion of land to crops grown for export have forced people to abandon the traditional ways. Now, drought and overexploitation have stripped the land of its plant cover and turned more than 160 million acres of land into desert. Stripping land of its vegetation actually makes the climate drier, so deserts feed on themselves. The process is called *desertification*, and people in Africa are suffering as it continues.

Garden or Desert?

Africans, on their own or with the help of international agencies, have found ways to reverse desertification through practices such as agroforestry. Shelter belts of trees protect and enrich the soil, provide a source of fuel, and turn back the advancing desert.

Simple stone fences, built by hand, can impound water from infrequent rains. In Burkina Faso, such structures have increased crop yields by 50 percent. Projects like these must be done on a much larger scale to be truly effective, but their success in small-scale projects shows what can be done.

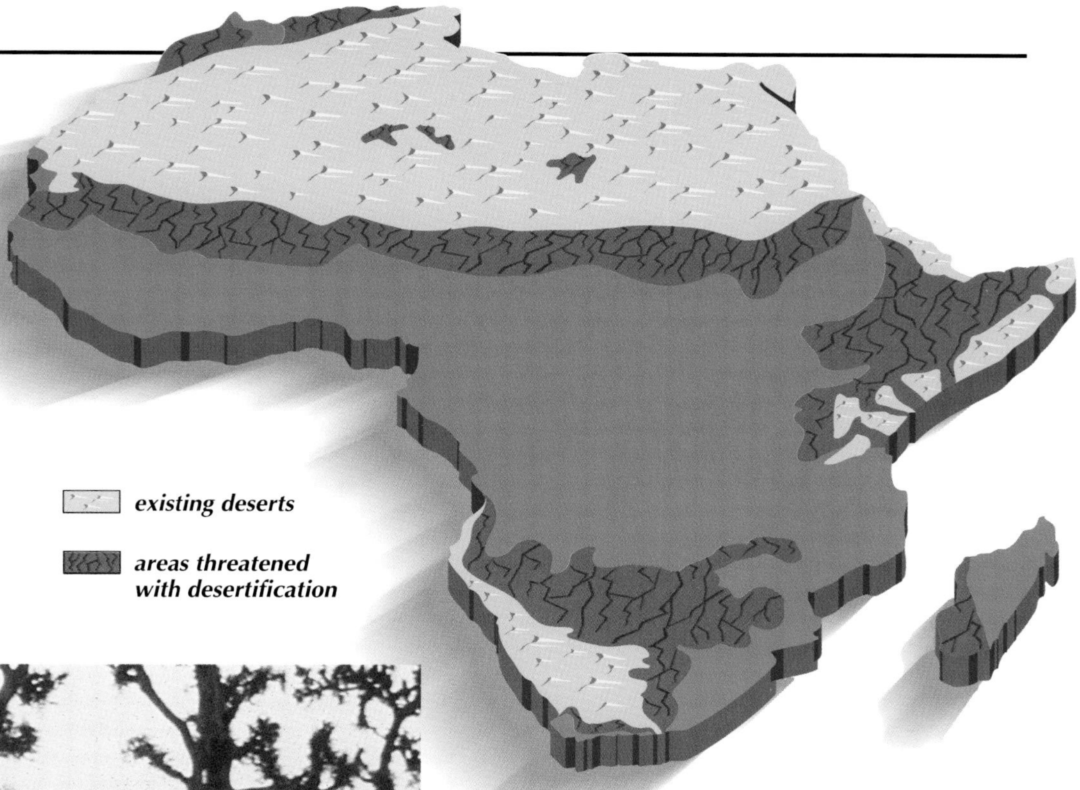

This Senegalese farmer cannot plant a crop because drought has turned his land into a desert. He is working his team of oxen to keep them in practice while waiting and hoping for the rains to come.

RESTORING THE BALANCE
Oceania

Strewn across the South Pacific are thousands of islands, ranging in size from Australia—so big, it is considered a continent—to tiny dots of land in remote waters. These islands—commonly grouped together as Oceania—have been isolated from larger land forms for thousands of years. The isolation of Oceania began to crumble, however, when the Polynesians advanced across the Pacific. It ended only two centuries ago when the British began to settle first Australia, and then New Zealand.

Most of the interior of Australia is very dry. Forests, savannas, and grasslands dominate the northern, eastern, and southern coastal regions. As rainfall decreases inland, short grass and desert scrub replace these richer terrains. Most of Australia's cropland and urban areas are along the coasts. The grasslands of the interior are mainly used as grazing land for over 150 million sheep, a flock that produces 30 percent of the world's wool.

When English settlement began in New Zealand, all of North Island and over half of South Island were forested. Timber and other forest products are still very important to New Zealand's economy. Sheep are there, too; a national flock of sixty-four million animals.

The smaller islands of the Pacific range from coral atolls such as the Gilberts, where the highest point is less than fifteen feet above sea level, to mountainous lands of volcanic origin such as Tahiti.

There is a biological boundary in Indonesia. West of it are Borneo, Java, and Sumatra with their typically Asian plants and animals. East of it are Celebes, New Guinea, and Australia with a unique flora and fauna developed through millions of years of isolation.

English settlers in Oceania found it a world almost unimaginably strange. On Australia's broad grasslands kangaroos replaced the familiar sheep and cattle of home. New Zealand had no mammals at all outside of two species of bats, and its birds included the world's only flightless parrot and the world's only flightless songbird.

The newcomers immediately set about

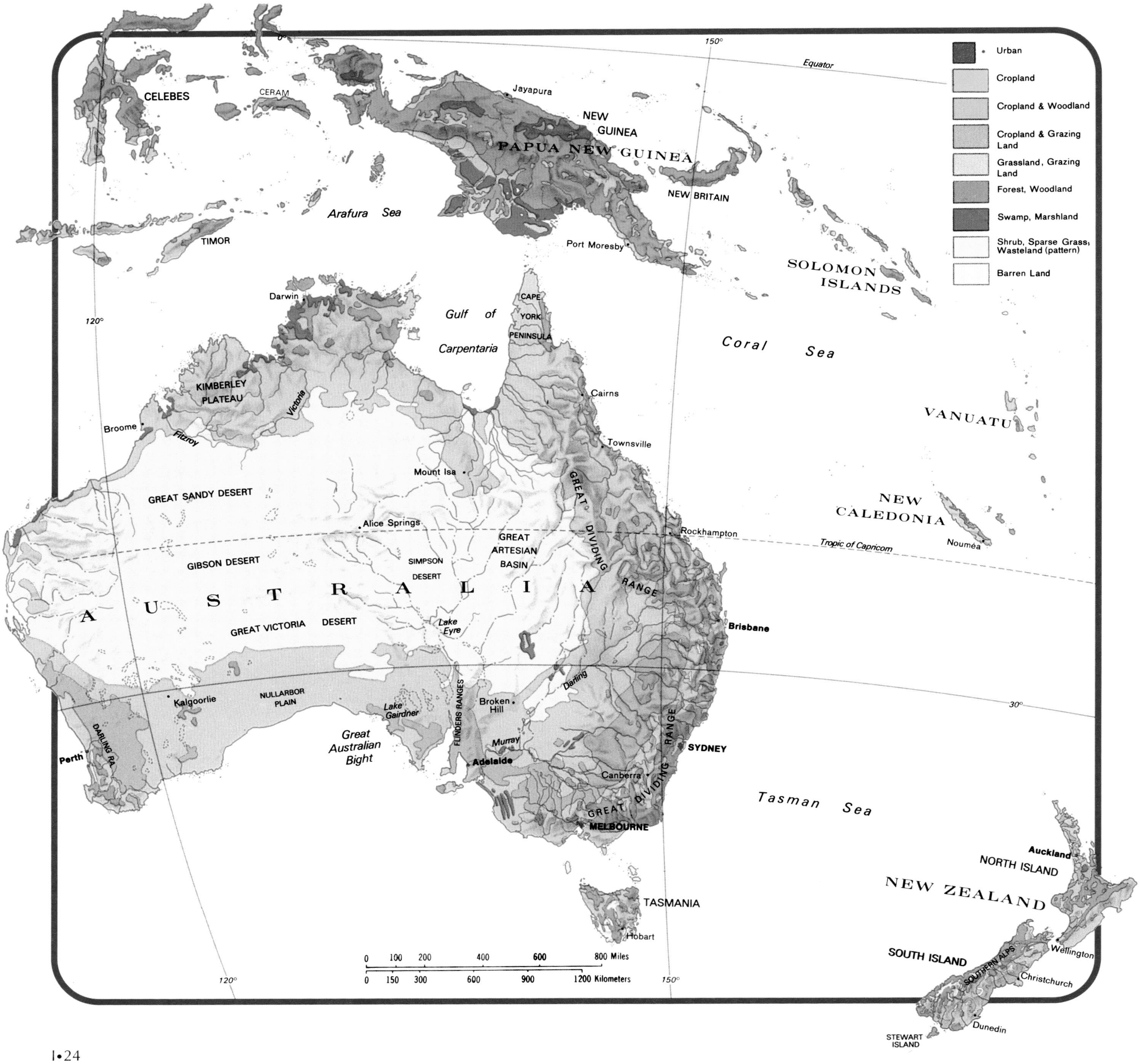

remaking nature in the new lands. They imported rabbits, red deer, Canada geese, and hosts of other birds. When rabbits became pests in New Zealand, weasels and ferrets were brought in to control them.

The imports—whether competitors or predators—had catastrophic effects on the native species. Australia has lost eighteen species of native mammals in the past two hundred years.

Above: The dry interior of Australia supports very sparse vegetation and very few people. Sheep can be grazed on this sort of land in small numbers.

Left: This beach in Sydney attracts large numbers of Australians. Nearly all of the population of the country lives near the coast, more than 20 percent in the city of Sydney alone.

Domestic cats eliminated New Zealand's flightless songbird within a year of its discovery, and its flightless parrot is barely hanging on in the face of predation by weasels and competition for food from both red deer and sheep. Red deer became such pests that New Zealand's government at one time offered to buy ammunition for anyone willing to shoot them.

Island ecosystems tend to have few species. Many have no land predators and a shortage of competitors for scarce resources. This makes them very vulnerable to disturbances from outside. Animals that have never faced competition or predation are likely to go extinct before they can learn to adapt to the introduction of alien species.

Leaving Nature Alone

The governments of Oceania are faced with a huge task of damage control. They have begun with strict controls on imports of exotic animals to prevent a repeat of the mistakes of the past. A variety of programs are under way to protect native species from the exotics already there. In New Zealand, the kakapo, the flightless parrot, is surviving on a preserve where continued trapping keeps out predators and competitors. Transfer to an off-shore island, a measure already protecting kiwis, may provide a long-term answer. Continuing efforts to control exotics involve hunting, trapping, and even the injection of birth control drugs into females.

This is not a lizard. It is a tuatara, the sole survivor of an ancient order of reptiles. It is threatened by exotic species in New Zealand.

The arrows mark some of the exotic species imported into New Zealand since 1840. The native bat and laughing owl are now extinct; fewer than one hundred kakapos survive.

RESTORING THE BALANCE
Polar Regions

The South Pole lies in the middle of a continent, hundreds of miles from the nearest shore. The North Pole is in the middle of the Arctic Ocean. Nearly all of Antarctica is buried under an ice cap up to two miles thick. Greenland has a similar cap, but other Arctic lands are ice-free in the summer months.

Antarctica's largest land animal is a tiny insect. The ice-free lands in the Arctic have a well-developed fauna, with grazing animals like caribou and musk-oxen and carnivores like grizzly bears and wolves.

Antarctica has no people. The closest thing to human habitations on this inhospitable continent are the scientific stations established by various nations in recent years. The Arctic has been peopled for millennia. The Inuit (or Eskimo), various Indian tribes, the Lapps of northern Scandinavia—all have contrived ways to make a sustained living from the harsh lands of the north.

For all these differences, the earth's polar regions have much in common. They are both very cold and very dark for much of the year. Since the sun is the source of the energy that makes ecosystems work, polar ecosystems are characterized by low productivity. Each year, an acre of tundra produces about 1 percent of the plant material produced by an acre of rich, temperate-zone forests. The caribou herds of Alaska and Canada must range over thousands of square miles to find good grazing. North of the Brooks Range on the Alaskan tundra, it takes one hundred square miles to support one grizzly bear.

A lack of precipitation contributes to this low productivity. Arctic lands average less than two inches of rain and snow a year. Amazingly, the ice-free dry valleys of Antarctica have had no precipitation in two million years.

When polar ecosystems are damaged, recovery is a long, slow process. Tracks left by trucks and other vehicles driving across the Alaskan tundra during World War II are still visible half a century later. With little rain to cleanse the atmosphere, air pollution lingers, too.

There are riches in the sea. Essential minerals are abundant. The seas around Antarctica abound in *krill*, a small relative of the shrimp that is the principal food of penguins, albatross-

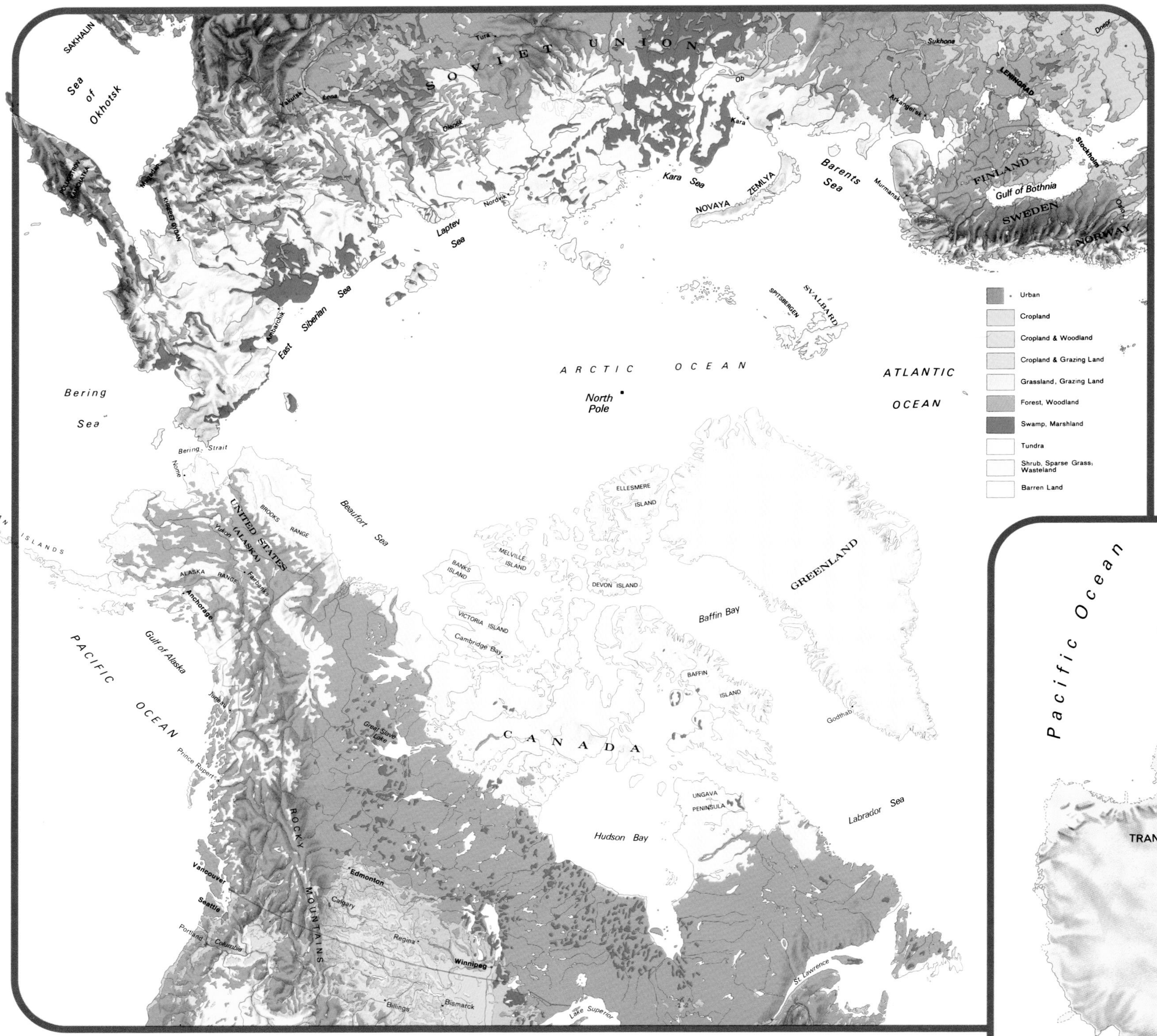

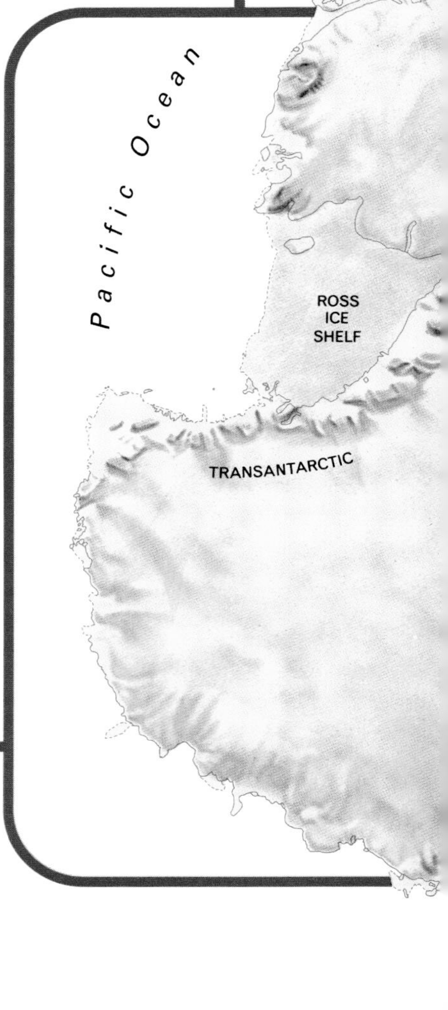

es, seals, and whales. The shallower waters of the Arctic Ocean yield about 10 percent of the world's annual catch of fish. The Inuit have traditionally drawn much of their subsistence from seals, walruses, and other creatures of the sea. This abundance can be deceiving, however. If a disaster such as an oil spill seriously affected the krill, all the animals that feed on this one small creature would be harmed.

Many are calling for intensive development of the polar regions. When we contemplate such development, we must keep in mind the fragility of polar ecosystems.

The Lapps of Scandinavia follow their reindeer herds across the tundra. By drawing food, clothing, and other necessities from the herds, the Lapps sustain their way of life in the Arctic without damaging the ecosystem.

These penguins feed at sea, but they come ashore on Antarctica to nest. They are among the few animals to inhabit the continent at the South Pole.

The Vulnerable Wilderness

***Arctic haze** hangs in the air around Prudhoe Bay, Alaska. It is pollution from the oil fields, and in the cold, dry climate, it is a sort of permanent smog. Conditions are even worse near the Soviet nickel smelters on the Kola Peninsula.*

Protection of the poles requires a major international effort. The eight countries with lands in the Arctic met in 1989 to begin such an effort. Fishing rights, mining, and industry are among the issues these nations will have to deal with. Twenty-nine nations have signed a protection agreement for Antarctica, but the most hopeful sign is that some countries are now backing the idea of making the continent a preserve.

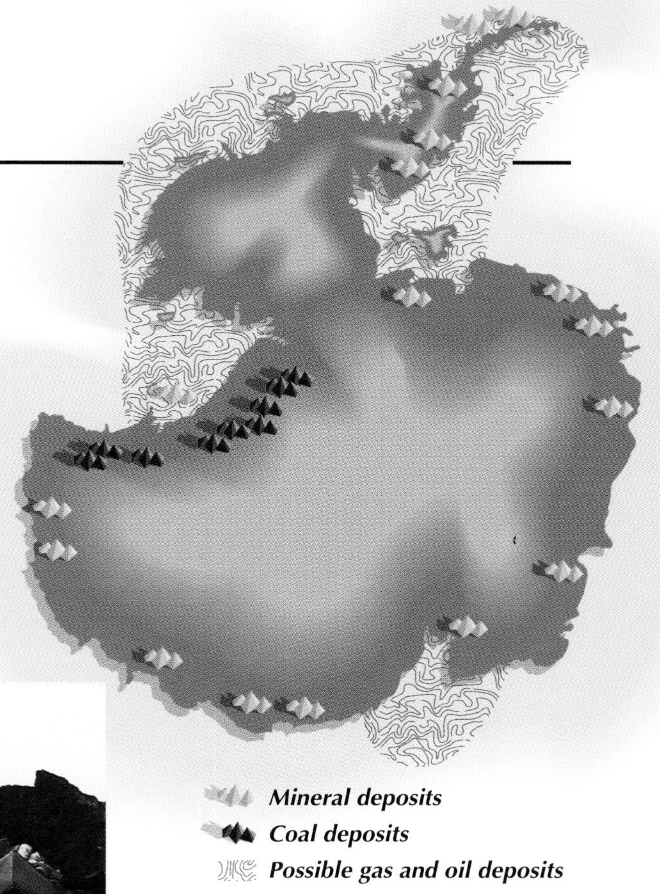

This map shows some of the mineral resources of Antarctica. The presence of these minerals is tempting many nations to consider development of this fragile region. Damage from mining or oil drilling could have catastrophic effects.

Trash left behind at a research station in Antarctica will be preserved indefinitely in the cold, dry climate. The results of any human action at the poles may endure virtually forever.

RESTORING THE BALANCE
South America

Most of South America lies between the tropics. At the northern end of the continent, grasslands called *llanos* dominate the lowlands east of the Andes. South of the llanos is the vast Amazon River Basin, containing the world's largest tropical forest.

South of the Amazon Basin, the forest becomes more open; grasslands again become prominent parts of the landscape. In Argentina, the lush grassland called the *pampa* gives way to drier grass and scrub vegetation in Patagonia to the south.

When Francisco Pizarro entered South America in 1532, he found a high civilization dominating the Andes Mountains, the spine of the continent. Building on the foundation of a thousand years of Andean culture, the Incas had consolidated an empire that extended from present-day Chile to Colombia. When Francisco de Orellana and his followers became the first Europeans to descend the Amazon in 1540, they found the riverbank lined with settlements.

Things have changed since those days. Now, Peru and Bolivia are two of the poorest countries on the continent. The Indian population of the Amazon Basin is dropping, and indigenous culture may soon be extinct. Today, the richest countries in South America have extractive economies. Suriname with its bauxite mines and Venezuela with its oil wells have the highest per capita incomes on the continent.

In the last few hundred years, settlement in South America has mainly been concentrated in a few favored areas such as the Atlantic highlands of Brazil and the pampa of Argentina. Recently, however, the rapid increase in population and the hopes of South American nations for major economic growth have stimulated invasions of the sparsely peopled parts of the continent. Tropical forests are falling at a terrifying rate. South America has already lost a third of its wet tropical forest. In the mountains, too,

Hope shines in the bright greens of these seedlings planted in a forest-restoration project. Careful husbandry is needed to restore the forest after clearing.

The effects of deforestation show plainly in the heavily eroded soil of this cleared rain forest. With nutrients leached away by heavy rains, the soil can no longer support the forest that once grew here.

vast regions of forest have been felled to clear land for the production of coffee, cacao, and coca.

Farms and cattle ranches on the cleared land are seldom successful because tropical forest soils lose their fertility quickly when the tree cover is removed. Despite the conversion of hundreds of thousands of acres from forest to pasture, for example, the Amazon regions of Brazil still have to import much of their beef. Fueled by government subsidies, however, the Amazon land rush continues to destroy the forest and drive thousands of species to extinction.

A coalition of Indians and rubber tappers called the Forest People is now trying to convince the people of Brazil that there is a better way. The Forest People have a knowledge—built up over generations—of how the forest works. Their ways of farming and extraction adapt natural processes to allow a sustained use of the rain forest.

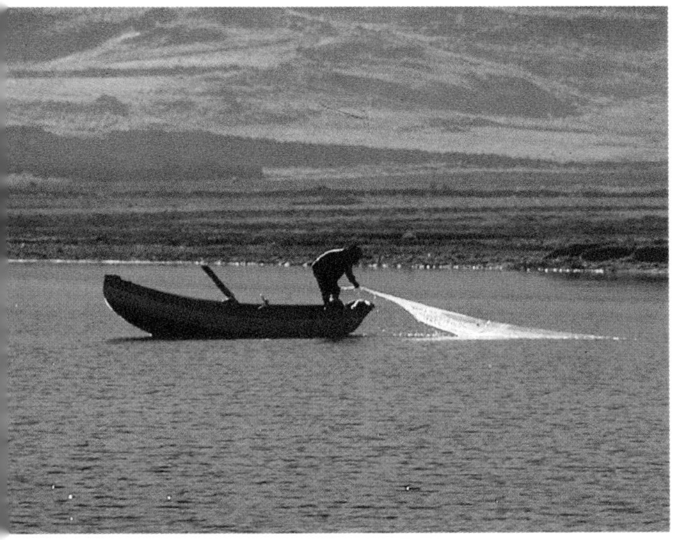

A fisherman spreads his net on Lake Titicaca just as his ancestors did a thousand years ago. The Andean highlands were home to the great Inca civilization.

The skyline of the Andes is rugged and snowcapped even at the equator. The high plains in the foreground are the habitat of such grazing animals as the guanaco.

Preserving the Rain Forest

The assault on the forest includes wasteful logging methods that destroy more trees than they harvest. Bulldozers clear land for farms. Fires set to burn away dead wood spread to uncleared parts of the forest, destroying whole species of plants and animals.

The cleared land is planted in grasses for cattle or plowed for crops. Both have very low rates of success. Only one of the many cattle ranches built with government subsidies in the Brazilian Amazon has ever shown a profit. And when the pastures and fields are abandoned, the forest is often unable to reclaim the land.

RESTORING THE BALANCE
North America

At the turn of the twentieth century, Phoenix, Arizona, was a dusty little town with only 5,000 inhabitants. Today, nearly 2 million people live in the Phoenix metropolitan area. Dallas, Texas, jumped from 42,000 to 2.7 million in the same span of time.

The boomtown is a familiar story in North America. A flood of settlers from every part of the world has spread across the continent in the past two centuries. Sprawling metropolises have sprung up in the wilderness. Whole biomes have been plowed up and turned into cornfields. The face of the continent has been irrevocably changed.

Even the remote tundra at the northern end of North America has been invaded by oil fields and miners. The taiga, the broad belt of evergreen forest that extends from Alaska across Canada and the northern United States to Maine and the maritime provinces, has been hit by logging and by massive industrial projects like Canada's nickel-smelting operations at Sudbury, Ontario.

The hardwood forests of the eastern United States and southern Canada were once so dense that people said a squirrel could travel from the Atlantic Coast to the Mississippi without ever touching ground. Today, the only remaining extensive tracts of this forest are in the more rugged portions of the Appalachian Mountains. Elsewhere, the landscape is dominated by cities and farms, and the forest has been reduced to

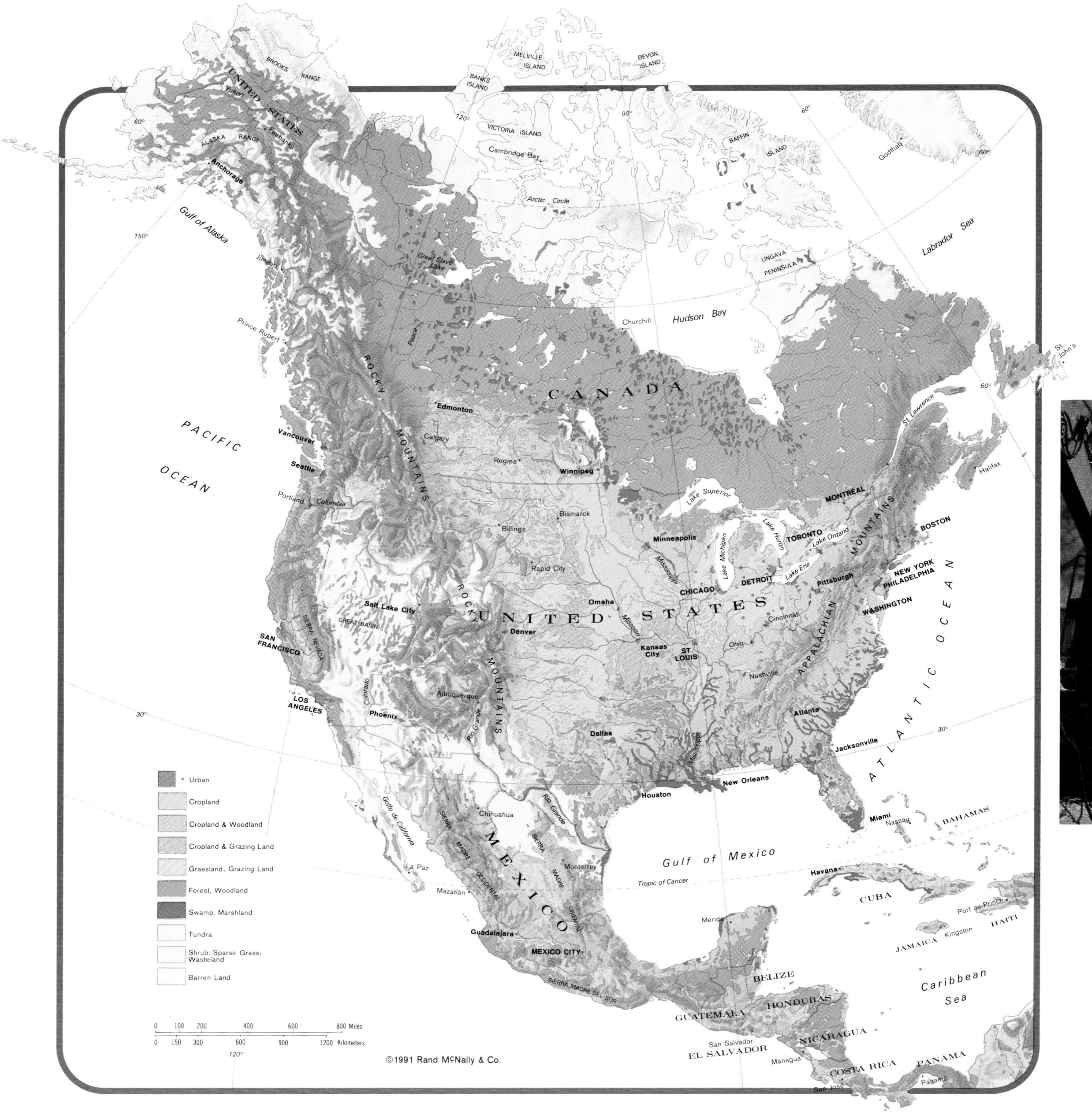

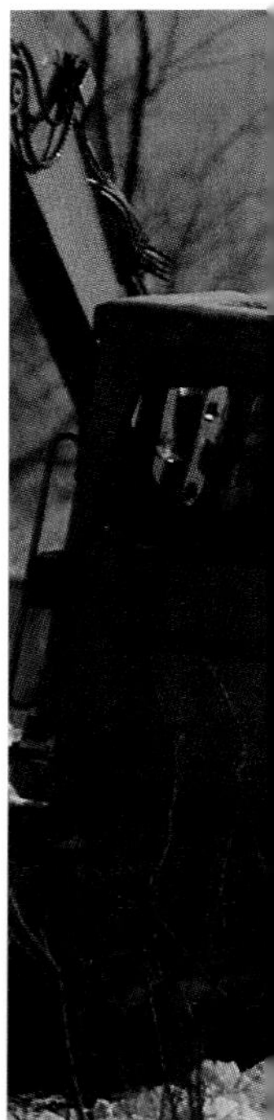

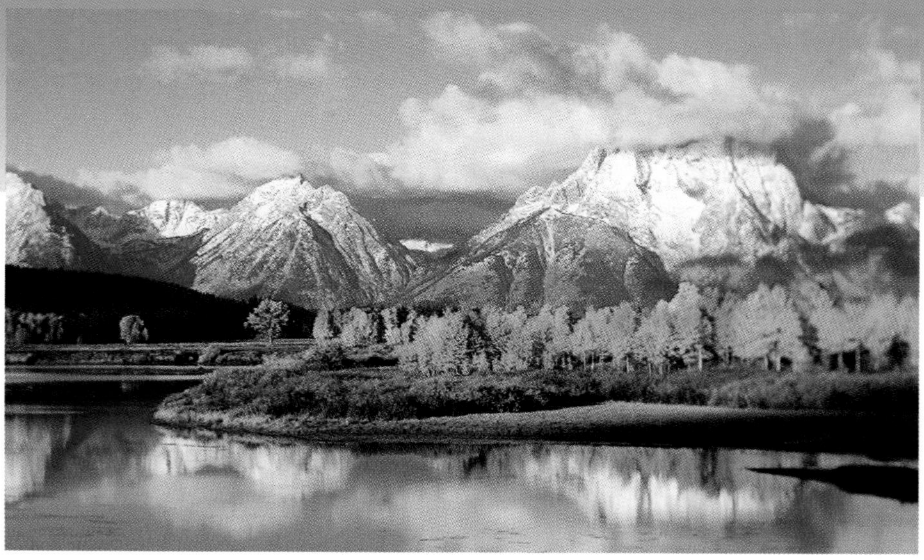

North America's once-vast wilderness is now confined to preserves such as Grand Teton National Park in Wyoming where the peak of Mt. Moran rises over the Snake River.

The huge circles of green in these barley and potato fields in Colorado are created by rotating sprinklers that irrigate the fields. Much of what was once grassland in North America is now cropland such as this.

scattered patches.

The tall-grass prairie that once extended from western Indiana to Nebraska and from Saskatchewan to Texas has almost completely disappeared. The rich soils the prairies built through several millenia of growth are now covered with corn, soybean, and wheat fields. On the short-grass prairies of the high plains, cattle have replaced the native buffalo as the main grazing animal.

In the arid lands of the southwestern United States and northern Mexico, huge dams provide irrigation water for vast fruit and vegetable farms that now spread over hundreds of thousands of acres of what was once desert.

In southern Mexico and Central America, ruins of ancient civilizations recall a time when large human populations had a major effect on the landscape. The forests of these regions have reclaimed lands that once provided corn, beans, and peppers for the Mayans, but in recent years, the forests have begun to fall again. Increasing populations and the development of large-scale farming and ranching for world markets are remaking this region as thoroughly as the settlers of a century ago remade the midwestern United States.

Urbanization and industrialization have also had a powerful effect. Mexico City may be the largest city in the world. Monterrey in northern Mexico joins the manufacturing cities of the United States and Canada as a major world center of industry.

Cleaning Up

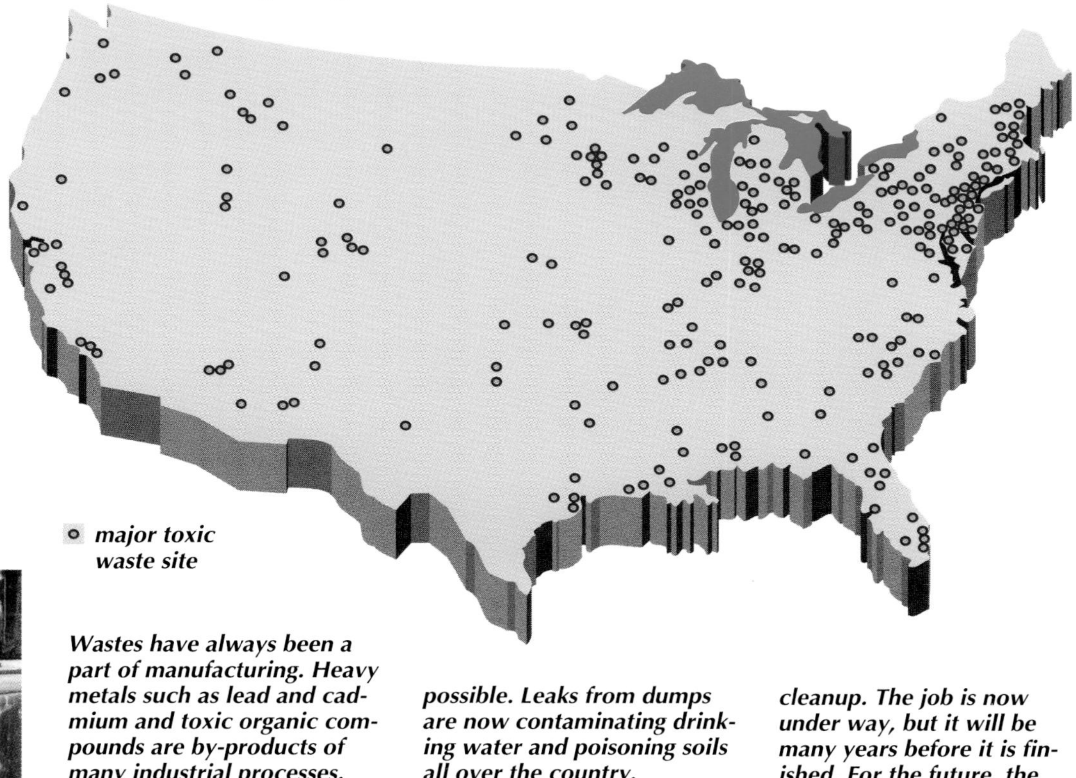

Wastes have always been a part of manufacturing. Heavy metals such as lead and cadmium and toxic organic compounds are by-products of many industrial processes.

During much of the history of industry in America, these toxic chemicals were dumped in the cheapest way possible. Leaks from dumps are now contaminating drinking water and poisoning soils all over the country.

In 1980, the United States Congress voted to tax the chemical industry to create the Superfund to pay for a cleanup. The job is now under way, but it will be many years before it is finished. For the future, the answer lies in redesigning production processes so they will not generate toxics.

Above, left: Cleanup begins on a toxic-waste dump targeted by the Superfund project. Note the protective clothing on the worker in the picture.

Left: Toxics carelessly dumped in leaking drums can contaminate both drinking water and the soil itself.

Almost all the cars on this freeway are carrying one person. In many American households, getting to work and back uses more energy than any other activity. Any serious attempt to cut America's energy use will have to address this problem.

This elementary school was designed to use solar energy for a large part of its heat. New designs in houses and public building can cut energy use as much as two-thirds.

Energy Use or Abuse?

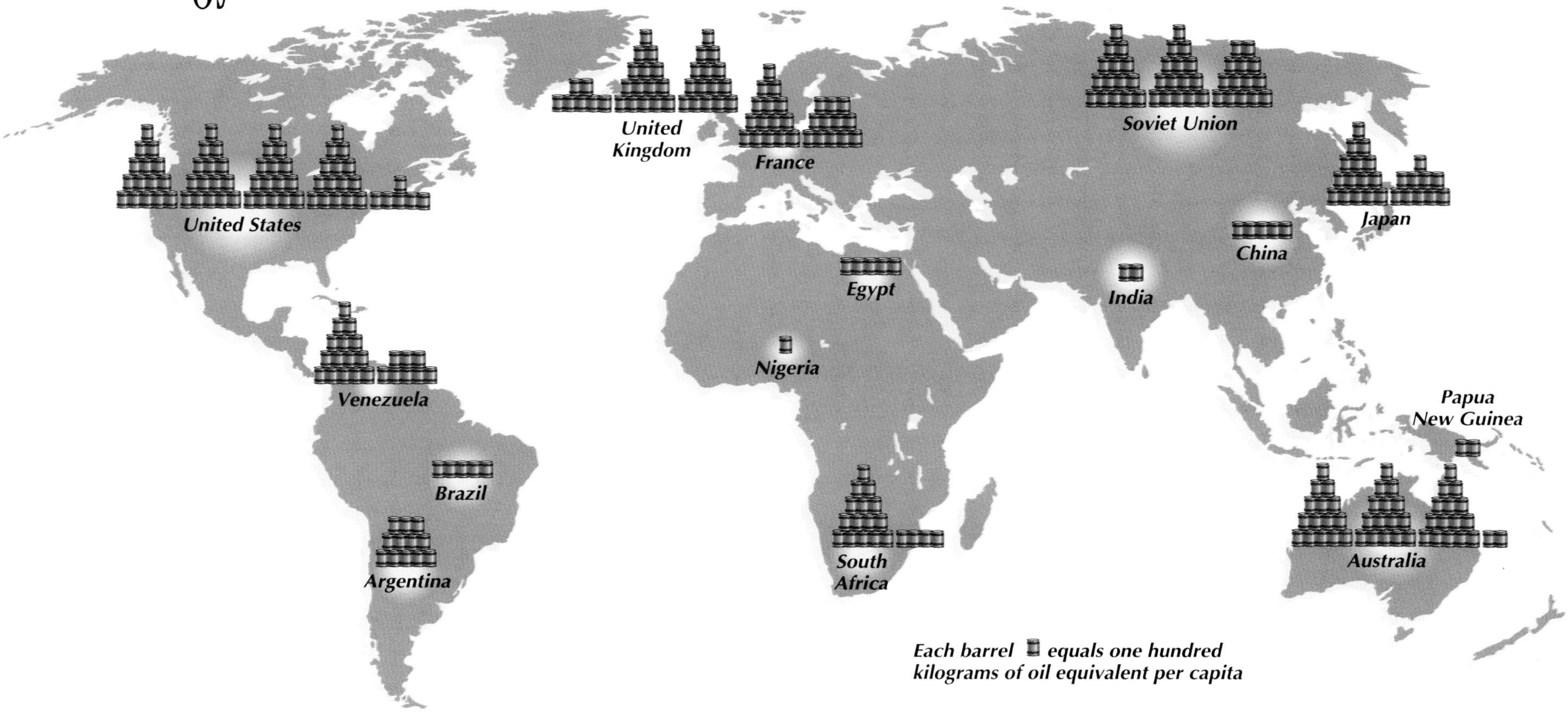

Historically, energy has been cheap in the United States, and Americans have responded to those low prices by using more energy than any other people on earth.

America produces 30 percent of the gases that are thought to be creating the greenhouse effect, and most of that comes from consumption of coal and oil.

We have at least begun to deal with the problem. Since the Arab oil embargo of 1973, the overall economy has been growing four times as fast as energy use.

Household energy use has declined. The United States will need to continue the search for ways to reduce overall energy use and for ways to switch to non-polluting, renewable sources before energy problems can be solved.

Photograph credits

Pages I-2,3 Koalas: John Cancalosi/Tom Stack & Associates. Children: John Isaac/UNICEF. Lily & dragonfly: John Gerlach/Tom Stack & Associates. Brown bear: John Shaw/Tom Stack & Associates. ***I-4,5*** England: David M. Dennis/Tom Stack & Associates. Polar bear: Mark Newman/Tom Stack & Associates. ***I-6,7*** Oregon forest: Milton Rand/Tom Stack & Associates. Prairie: Brian Parker/Tom Stack & Associates. ***I-8,9*** Nepalese woman: CARE photo by Rudolph von Bernuth. Gary, Indiana: AP/Wide World Photos. ***I-10,11*** North Dakota: John Running. Wind generators: Kevin Shafer/Tom Stack & Associates. ***I-12,13*** Treatment plant: Byron Augustin/Tom Stack & Associates. Cleanup: AP/Wide World Photos. ***I-14,15*** Pines: Diana L. Stratton/Tom Stack & Associates. Leopard: Jeff Foott/Tom Stack & Associates. ***I-16,17*** Family planning: CARE photo by Rudolph von Bernuth. Subdivision: Gary Milburn/Tom Stack & Associates. Bulgaria: AP/Wide World Photos. Black Forest: Spencer Swanger/Tom Stack & Associates. Nice, France: David C. London/Tom Stack & Associates. ***I-20,21*** Tokyo: Sheryl S. McNee/Tom Stack & Associates. Planting tree: CARE photo by Rudolph von Bernuth. Nepal: CARE photo by Rudolph von Bernuth. ***I-22,23*** Zebra & wildebeest: Jeff Foott/Tom Stack & Associates. Zimbabwe: Rod Allin/Tom Stack & Associates. Senegal: Clyde McNair/AID. ***I-24,25*** Outback: Greg Vaughn/Tom Stack & Associates. Sydney beach: Greg Vaughn/Tom Stack & Associates. Tuatara: John Cancalosi/Tom Stack & Associates. ***I-26,27*** Penguins: Anna E. Zuckerman/Tom Stack & Associates. Trash: Jack Stein Grove/Tom Stack & Associates. Lapps: Warren & Genny Garst/Tom Stack & Associates. ***I-28,29*** Andes: Gary Milburn/Tom Stack & Associates. Lake Titicaca: Gary Milburn/Tom Stack & Associates. Colombia: Clyde McNair/AID. Seedlings: Chip & Jill Isenhart/Tom Stack & Associates. ***I-30,31*** Mount Moran: Gerald & Buff Corsi/Tom Stack & Associates. Fields: Shattil/Rozinski/Tom Stack & Associates. Leakage: Gary Milburn/Tom Stack & Associates. Cleanup: Gary Milburn/Tom Stack & Associates. ***I-32,33*** Freeway: Jack Swenson/Tom Stack & Associates. School: Stewart M. Green/Tom Stack & Associates.

USING THE ATLAS

MAPS AND ATLASES

Satellite images of the world (figure 1) constantly give us views of the shape and size of the earth. It is hard, therefore, to imagine how difficult it once was to ascertain the look of our planet. Yet from early history we have evidence of humans trying to work out what the world actually looked like.

Twenty-five hundred years ago, on a tiny clay tablet the size of a hand, the Babylonians inscribed the earth as a flat disk (figure 2) with Babylon at the center. The section of the Cantino map of 1502 (figure 3) is an example of a *portolan* chart used by mariners to chart the newly discovered Americas. Handsome and useful maps have been produced by many cultures. The Mexican map drawn in 1583 marks hills with wavy lines and roads with footprints between parallel lines (figure 4). The methods and materials used to create these maps were dependent upon the technology available, and their accuracy suffered considerably. A modern topographic map (figure 5), as well as those in this atlas, shows the detail and accuracy that cartographers are now able to achieve. They benefit from our ever-increasing technology, including satellite imagery and computer assisted cartography.

In 1589 Gerardus Mercator used the word *atlas* to describe a collection of maps. Atlases now bring together not only a variety of maps but an assortment of tables and other reference material as well. They have become a unique and indispensable reference for graphically defining the world and answering the question *where*. Only on a map can the countries, cities, roads, rivers, and lakes covering a vast area be simultaneously viewed in their relative locations. Routes between places can be traced, trips planned, boundaries of neighboring states and countries examined, distances between places measured, the meandering of rivers and streams and the sizes of lakes visualized–and remote places imagined.

FIGURE 1

FIGURE 4

FIGURE 2

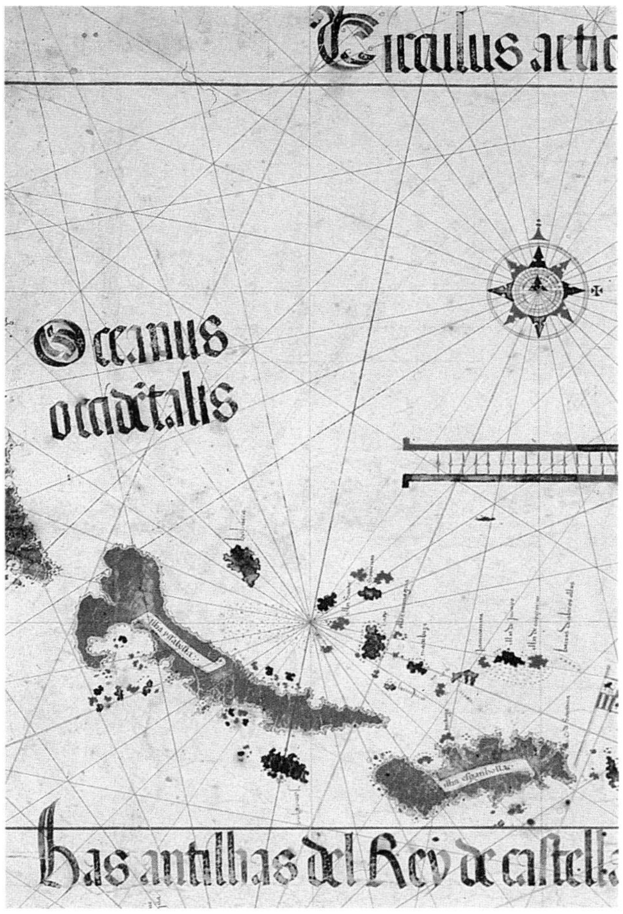

FIGURE 3

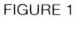

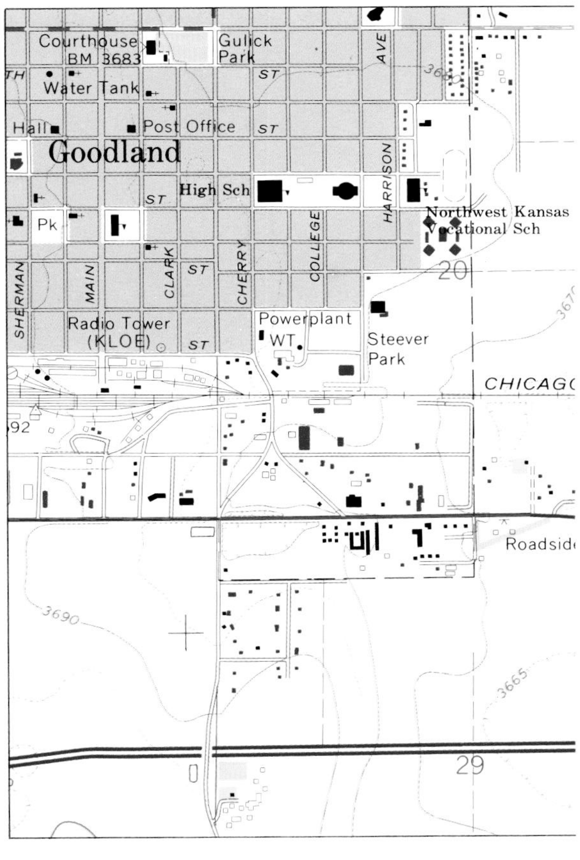

FIGURE 5

SEQUENCE OF THE MAPS

The world is made up of seven major landmasses: the continents of Europe, Asia, Africa, Antarctica, Australia, South America, and North America (figure 6). The maps in this atlas follow this continental sequence. To allow for the inclusion of detail, each continent is broken down into a series of maps, and this grouping is arranged so that as consecutive pages are turned, a continuous successive part of the continent is shown. Larger-scale maps are used for regions of greater detail (having many cities, for example) or for areas of global significance.

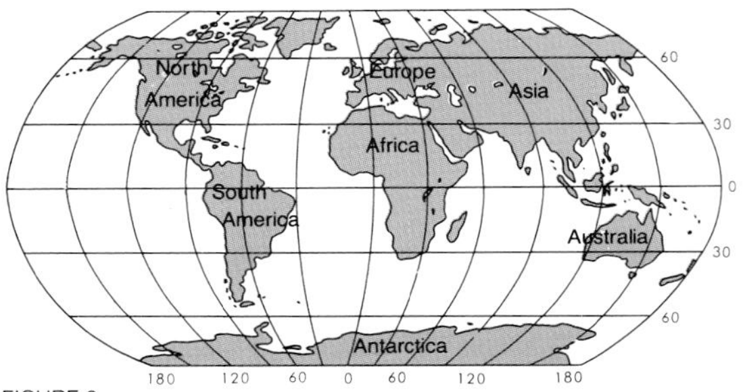

FIGURE 6

GETTING THE INFORMATION

An atlas can be used for many purposes, from planning a trip to finding hot spots in the news and supplementing world knowledge. To realize the potential of an atlas the user must be able to:

1. Find places on the maps
2. Measure distances
3. Determine directions
4. Understand map symbols

FINDING PLACES

One of the most common and important tasks facilitated by an atlas is finding the location of a place in the world. A river's name in a book, a city mentioned in the news, or a vacation spot may prompt your need to know where the place is located. The illustrations and text below explain how to find Yangon (Rangoon), Burma.

1. Look up the place-name in the index at the back of the atlas. Yangon, Burma can be found on the map on page 38, and it can be located on the map by the letter-number key *B2* (figure 7).

Yancey, co., N.C., U.S.	**f10**	140
Yanceyville, N.C., U.S.	**A3**	140
Yanchang, China	**D9**	30
Yancheng, China	**B9**	34
Yandoon, Burma	**F3**	40
Yangjiang, China	**G9**	30
Yangon (Rangoon), Burma	**B2**	38
Yangquan, China	**D9**	30
Yangtze see Chang, stm., China	**E10**	30
Yangzhou, China	**C8**	34
Yanji, China	**C12**	30
Yankton, S.D., U.S.	**E8**	148
Yankton, co., S.D., U.S.	**D8**	148
Yanqi, China	**C4**	30
Yantai (Chefoo), China	**D11**	30
Yantic, stm., Ct., U.S.	**C7**	114
Yapen, Pulau, i., Indon.	**F10**	38
Yaqui, stm., Mex.	**C5**	90
Yaraka, Austl.	**D8**	68

FIGURE 7

2. Turn to the map of Southeastern Asia found on page 38. Note that the letters *A* through *H* and the numbers *1* through *11* appear in the margins of the map.

3. To find Yangon, on the map, place your left index finger on *B* and your right index finger on *2*. Move your left finger across the map and your right finger down the map. Your fingers will meet in the area in which Yangon is located (figure 8).

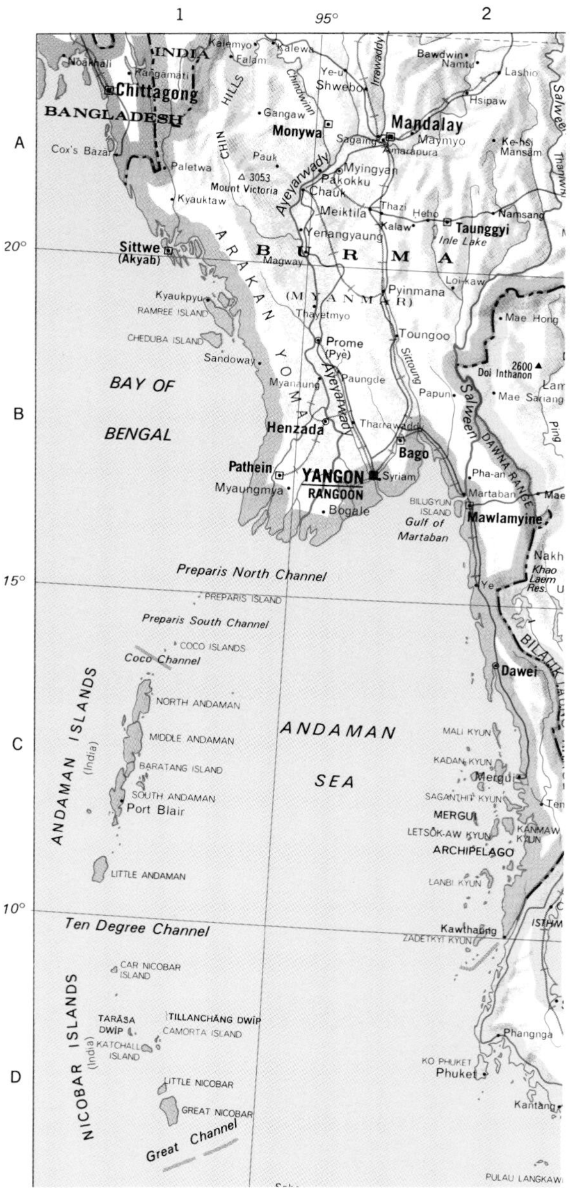

FIGURE 8

MEASURING DISTANCES

In planning trips, determining the distance between two places is essential, and an atlas can help in travel preparation. For instance, to determine the approximate distance between Paris and Rouen, France, follow these three steps:

1. Lay a slip of paper on the map on page 10 so that its edge touches the two cities. Adjust the paper so one corner touches Rouen. Mark the paper directly at the spot where Paris is located (figure 9).

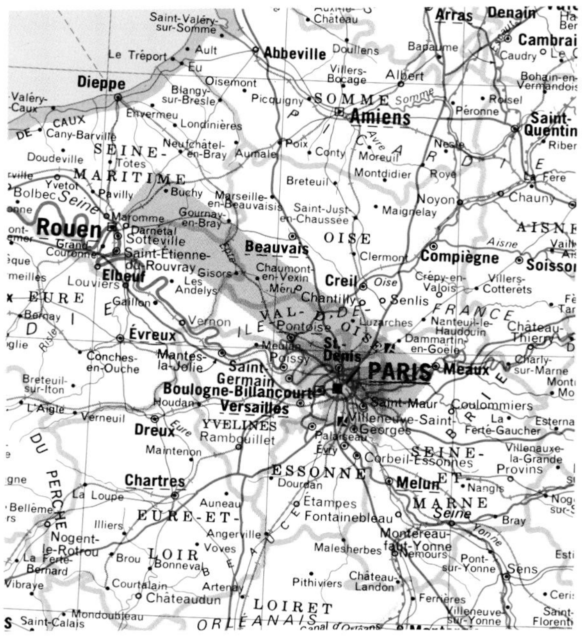

FIGURE 9

2. Place the paper along the scale of miles beneath the map. Position the corner at 0 and line up the edge of the paper along the scale. The pencil mark on the paper indicates Rouen is between 50 and 100 miles from Paris (figure 10).

3. To find the exact distance, move the paper to the left so that the pencil mark is at 100 on the scale. The corner of the paper stands on the fourth 5-mile unit on the scale. This means that the two towns are 50 plus 20, or 70 miles apart (figure 11).

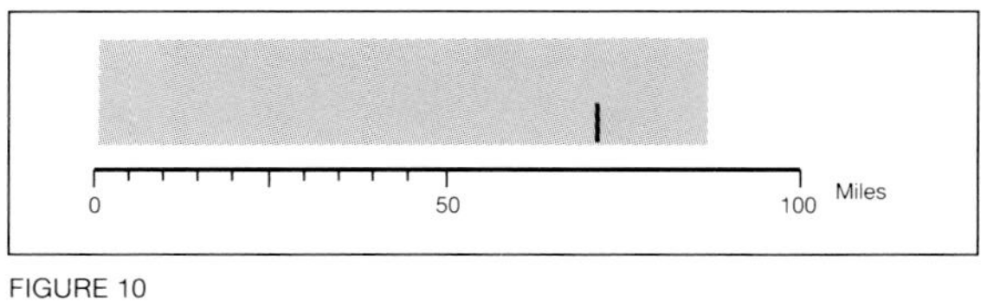

FIGURE 10

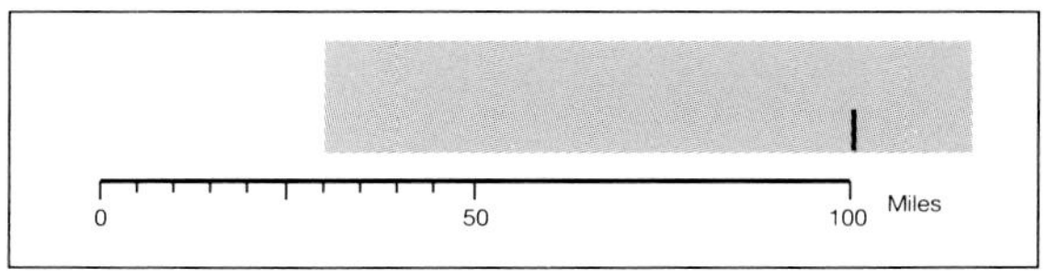

FIGURE 11

DETERMINING DIRECTION

Most of the maps in the atlas are drawn so that when oriented for normal reading, north is at the top of the map, south is at the bottom, west is at the left, and east is at the right. Most maps have a series of lines drawn across them–the lines of *latitude* and *longitude*. Lines of latitude, or *parallels* of latitude, are drawn east and west. Lines of longitude, or *meridians* of longitude, are drawn north and south (figure 12).

Parallels and meridians appear as either curved or straight lines. For example, in the section of the map of Europe (figure 13) the parallels of latitude appear as curved lines. The meridians of longitude are straight lines that come together toward the top of the map. Latitude and longitude lines help locate places on maps. Parallels of latitude are numbered in degrees north and south of the *Equator*. Meridians of longitude are numbered in degrees east and west of a line called the *Prime Meridian*, running through Greenwich, England, near London. Any place on earth can be located by the latitude and longitude lines running through it.

To determine directions or locations on the map, you must use the parallels and meridians. For example, suppose you want to know which is farther north, Bergen, Norway, or Stockholm, Sweden. The map in figure 13 shows that Stockholm is south of the 60° parallel of latitude and Bergen is north of it. Bergen is farther north than Stockholm. By looking at the meridians of longitude, you can determine which city is farther east. Bergen is approximately 5° east of the 0° meridian (Prime Meridian), and Stockholm is almost 20° east of it. Stockholm is farther east than Bergen.

UNDERSTANDING MAP SYMBOLS

In a very real sense, the whole map is a symbol, representing the world or a part of it. It is a reduced representation of the earth; each of the world's features–cities, rivers, etc.–is represented on the map by a symbol. Map symbols may take the form of points, such as dots or squares (often used for cities, capital cities, or points of interest), or lines (roads, railroads, rivers). Symbols may also occupy an area, showing extent of coverage (terrain, forests, deserts). They seldom look like the feature they represent and therefore must be identified and interpreted. For instance, the maps in this atlas define political units by a colored line depicting their boundaries. Neither the colors nor the boundary lines are actually found on the surface of the earth, but because countries and states are such important political components of the world, strong symbols are used to represent them. The Map Symbols page in this atlas identifies the symbols used on the maps.

FIGURE 12

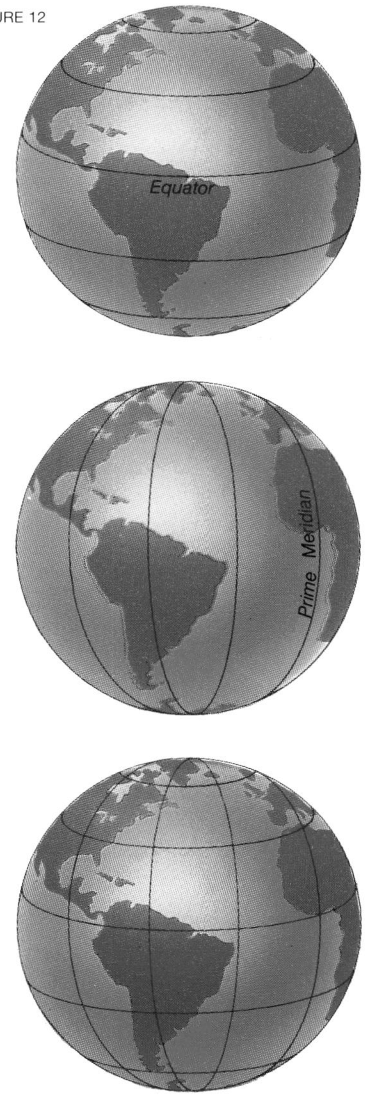

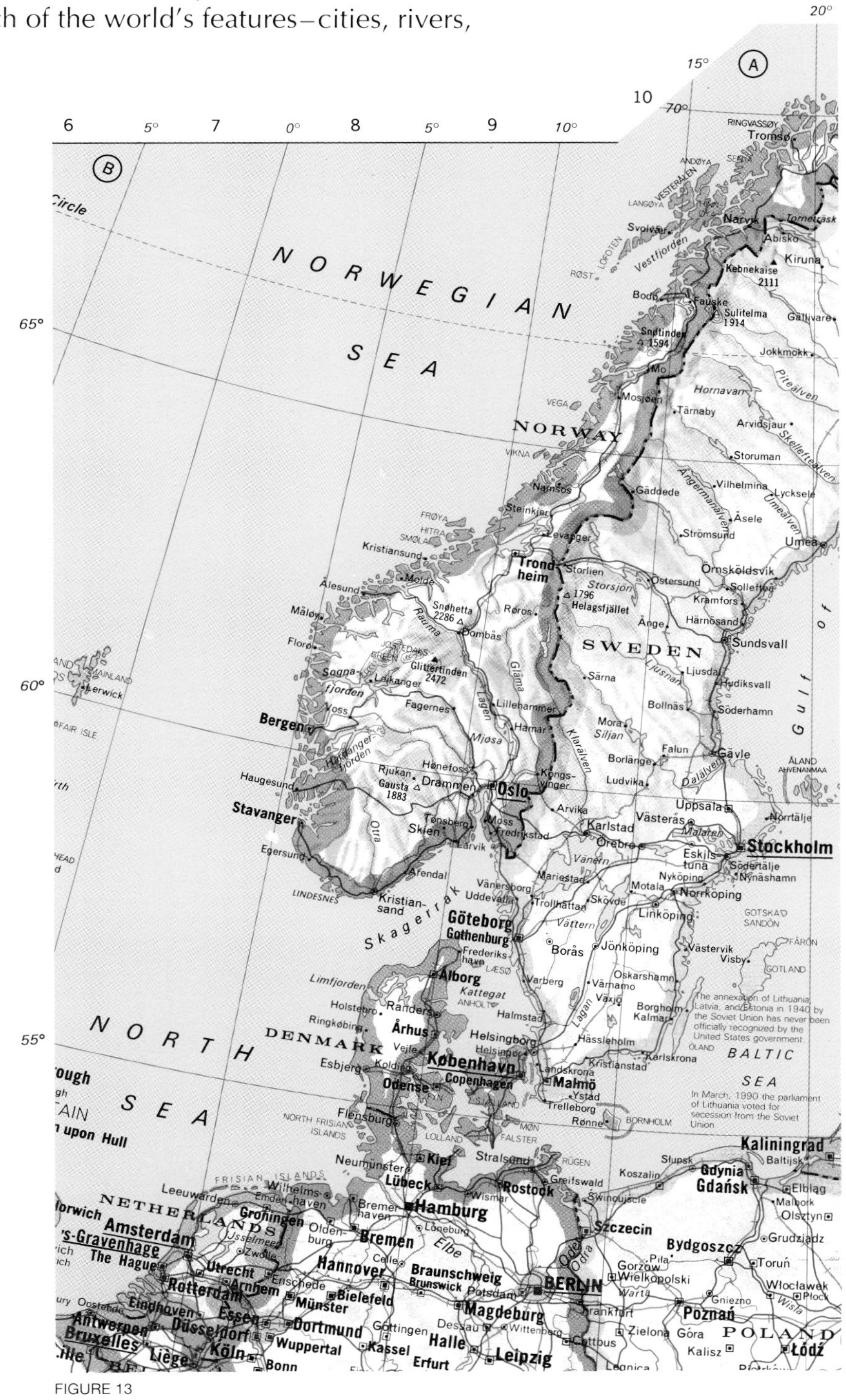

FIGURE 13

World Time Zones

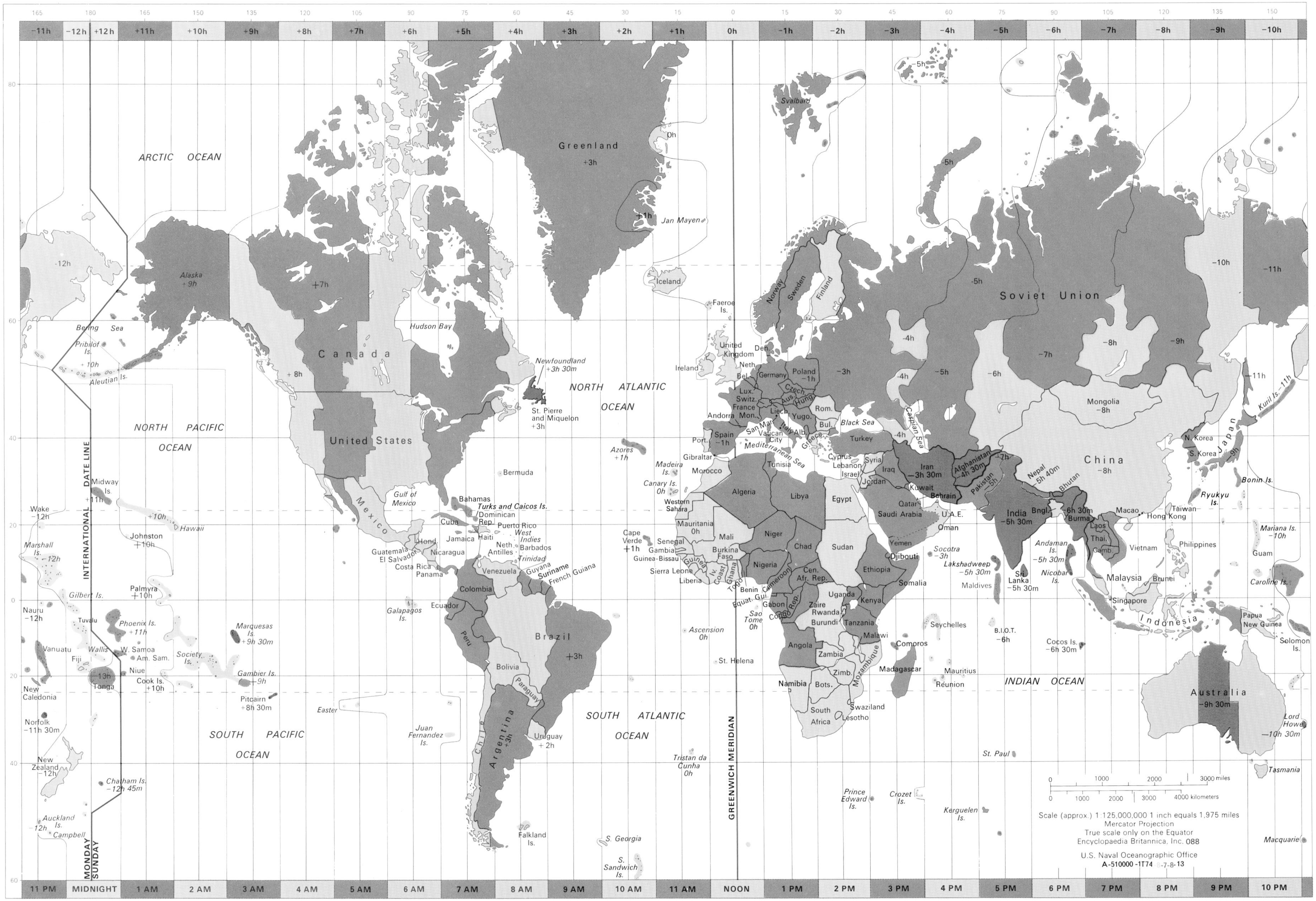

Time Zones

- Standard time zone of even-numbered hours from Greenwich time
- Standard time zone of odd-numbered hours from Greenwich time
- Time varies from the standard time zone by half an hour
- Time varies from the standard time zone by other than half an hour

h m hours, minutes

The standard time zone system, fixed by international agreement and by law in each country, is based on a theoretical division of the globe into 24 zones of 15° longitude each. The mid-meridian of each zone fixes the hour for the entire zone. The zero time zone extends 7½° east and 7½° west of the Greenwich meridian, 0° longitude. Since the earth rotates toward the east, time zones to the west of Greenwich are earlier, to the east, later.
Plus and minus hours at the top of the map are added to or subtracted from local time to find Greenwich time. Local standard time can be determined for any area in the world by adding one hour for each time zone counted in an easterly direction from one's own, or by subtracting one hour for each zone counted in a westerly direction. To separate one day from the next, the 180th meridian has been designated as the international date line. On both sides of the line the time of day is the same, but west of the line it is one day later than it is to the east.
Countries that adhere to the international zone system adopt the zone applicable to their location. Some countries, however, establish time zones based on political boundaries, or adopt the time zone of a neighboring unit. For all or part of the year some countries also advance their time by one hour, thereby utilizing more daylight hours each day.

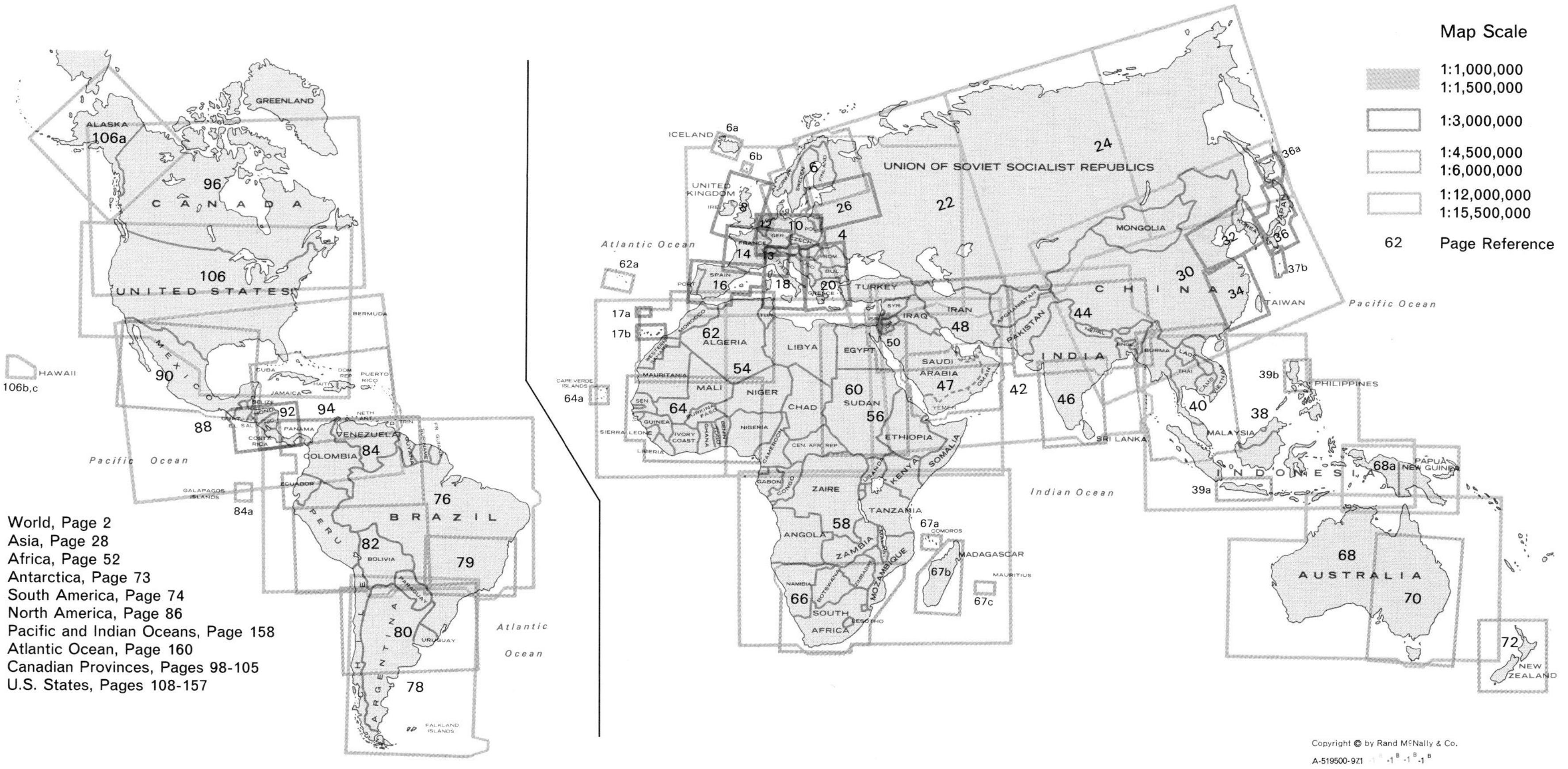

World Maps Symbols

Inhabited Localities

The size of type indicates the relative economic and political importance of the locality

Écommoy | Lisieux | **Rouen**

Trouville | **Orléans** | **PARIS**

Bi'r Safājah ° Oasis

Alternate Names

MOSKVA
MOSCOW

Basel
Bâle

English or second official language names are shown in reduced size lettering

Volgograd
(Stalingrad)

Historical or other alternates in the local language are shown in parentheses

Urban Area (Area of continuous industrial, commercial, and residential development)

Capitals of Political Units

BUDAPEST Independent Nation

Cayenne Dependency (Colony, protectorate, etc.)

Recife State, Province, County, Oblast, etc.

Political Boundaries

International (First-order political unit)

- Demarcated and Undemarcated
- Disputed de jure
- Indefinite or Undefined
- Demarcation Line

Internal

- State, Province, etc. (Second-order political unit)
- *MURCIA* Historical Region (No boundaries indicated)
- GALAPAGOS (Ecuador) Administering Country

Transportation

- Primary Road
- Secondary Road
- Minor Road, Trail
- Railway
- *Canal du Midi* Navigable Canal
- Bridge
- Tunnel
- TO MALMÖ Ferry

Hydrographic Features

- Shoreline
- Undefined or Fluctuating Shoreline
- *Amur* River, Stream
- Intermittent Stream
- Rapids, Falls
- Irrigation or Drainage Canal
- Reef
- *The Everglades* Swamp
- RIMO GLACIER Glacier
- *L. Victoria* Lake, Reservoir
- *Tuz Gölü* Salt Lake
- Intermittent Lake, Reservoir
- Dry Lake Bed
- *(395)* Lake Surface Elevation

Topographic Features

- Matterhorn △ 4478 Elevation Above Sea Level
- 76 ▽ Elevation Below Sea Level
- Mount Cook ▲ 3764 Highest Elevation in Country
- 133 ▼ Lowest Elevation in Country
- Khyber Pass 1067 Mountain Pass

Elevations are given in meters.
The highest and lowest elevations in a continent are underlined

- Sand Area
- Lava
- Salt Flat

State, Province Maps Symbols

- Capital
- County Seat
- Military Installation
- Point of Interest
- Mountain Peak
- International Boundary
- State, Province Boundary
- County Boundary
- Railroad
- Road
- Urban Area

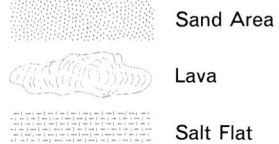

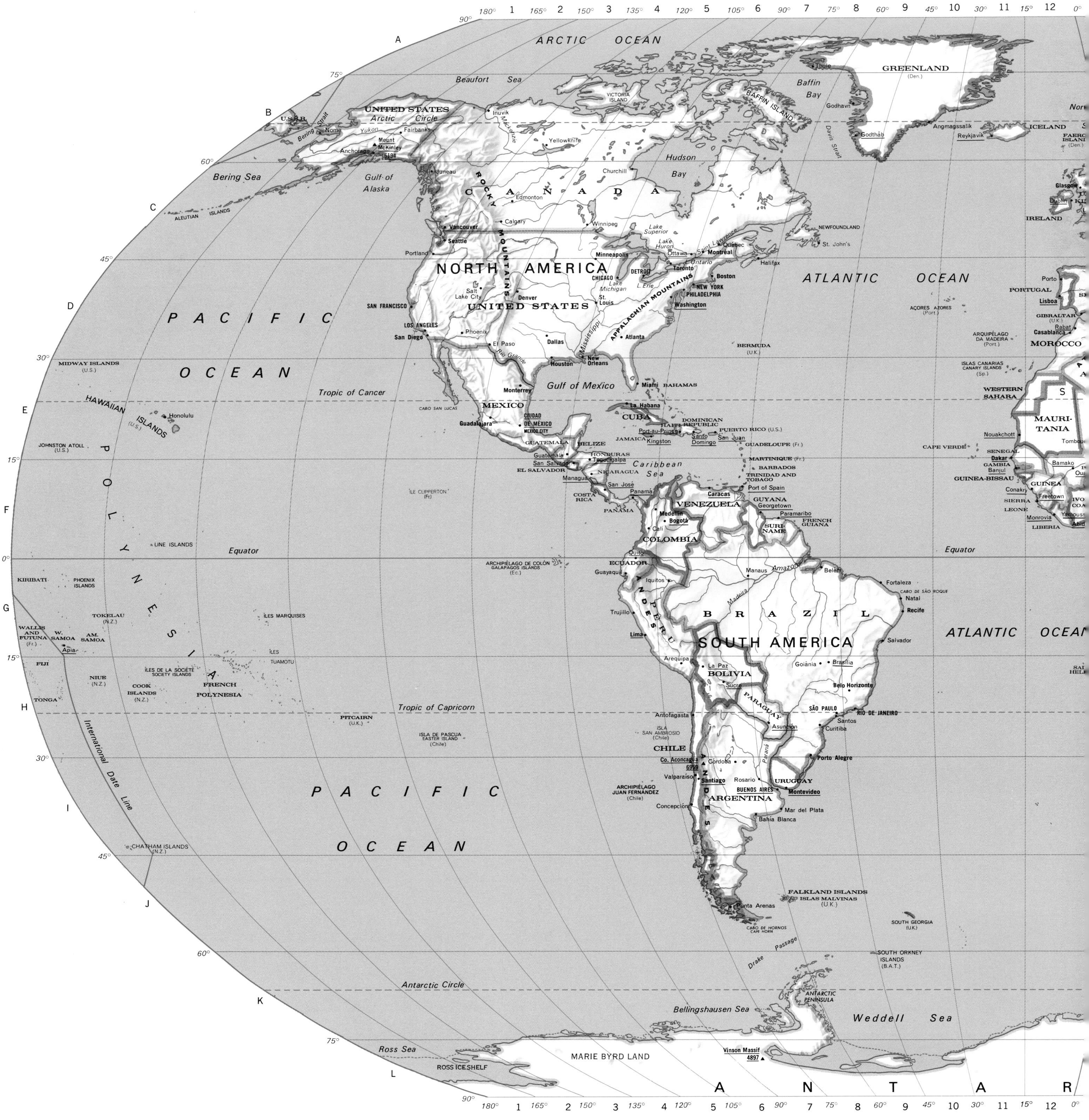
ARCTIC OCEAN
Beaufort Sea
GREENLAND (Den.)
Baffin Bay
BAFFIN ISLAND
VICTORIA ISLAND
Thule
Godhavn
Godthåb
Angmagssalik
Reykjavík
ICELAND
Davis Strait
U.S.S.R.
Bering Strait
UNITED STATES
Arctic Circle
Yukon
Nome
Fairbanks
Mount McKinley 6194
Anchorage
Inuvik
Mackenzie
Yellowknife
Bering Sea
Gulf of Alaska
Juneau
ROCKY MOUNTAINS
C A N A D A
Edmonton
Churchill
Hudson Bay
ALEUTIAN ISLANDS
Calgary
Vancouver
Seattle
Winnipeg
Lake Superior
Lake Huron
NEWFOUNDLAND
St. John's
Québec
Saint Lawrence
Montreal
Ottawa
Toronto
Lake Ontario
Halifax
Portland
Minneapolis
NORTH AMERICA
CHICAGO
DETROIT
Lake Michigan
L. Erie
Boston
NEW YORK
PHILADELPHIA
Washington
APPALACHIAN MOUNTAINS
Salt Lake City
Denver
UNITED STATES
St. Louis
SAN FRANCISCO
LOS ANGELES
San Diego
Phoenix
El Paso
Dallas
Atlanta
Mississippi
Rio Grande
Houston
New Orleans
ATLANTIC OCEAN
AÇORES AZORES (Port.)
BERMUDA (U.K.)
PORTUGAL
Porto
Lisboa
GIBRALTAR (U.K.)
Rabat
Casablanca
MOROCCO
ARQUIPÉLAGO DA MADEIRA (Port.)
ISLAS CANARIAS CANARY ISLANDS (Sp.)
WESTERN SAHARA
MAURITANIA
Nouakchott
Tombouctou
CAPE VERDE
SENEGAL
Dakar
GAMBIA
Banjul
GUINEA-BISSAU
GUINEA
Conakry
SIERRA LEONE
Freetown
Monrovia
LIBERIA
Bamako
IRELAND
Dublin
Glasgow
FAEROE ISLANDS (Den.)
P A C I F I C
O C E A N
MIDWAY ISLANDS (U.S.)
HAWAIIAN ISLANDS (U.S.)
Honolulu
Tropic of Cancer
Gulf of Mexico
Monterrey
Miami
BAHAMAS
MEXICO
CABO SAN LUCAS
CIUDAD DE MÉXICO
MEXICO CITY
Guadalajara
La Habana
CUBA
DOMINICAN REPUBLIC
HAITI
Port-au-Prince
Santo Domingo
PUERTO RICO (U.S.)
San Juan
JAMAICA
Kingston
GUADELOUPE (Fr.)
MARTINIQUE (Fr.)
BARBADOS
TRINIDAD AND TOBAGO
Port of Spain
GUATEMALA
BELIZE
Guatemala
HONDURAS
Tegucigalpa
San Salvador
EL SALVADOR
NICARAGUA
Managua
Caribbean Sea
COSTA RICA
San José
Panamá
PANAMA
JOHNSTON ATOLL (U.S.)
POLYNESIA
ÎLE CLIPPERTON (Fr.)
Caracas
VENEZUELA
GUYANA
Georgetown
SURINAME
Paramaribo
FRENCH GUIANA
Medellín
Bogotá
Cali
COLOMBIA
LINE ISLANDS
Equator
Quito
ECUADOR
Guayaquil
ARCHIPIÉLAGO DE COLÓN GALAPAGOS ISLANDS (Ec.)
Iquitos
Manaus
Amazon
Belém
Fortaleza
CABO DE SÃO ROQUE
Natal
Recife
KIRIBATI
PHOENIX ISLANDS
TOKELAU (N.Z.)
WALLIS AND FUTUNA (Fr.)
W. SAMOA
AM. SAMOA
Apia
ÎLES MARQUISES
Trujillo
PERU
ANDES
Madeira
B R A Z I L
SOUTH AMERICA
Lima
ATLANTIC OCEAN
Salvador
FIJI
NIUE (N.Z.)
COOK ISLANDS (N.Z.)
ÎLES DE LA SOCIÉTÉ SOCIETY ISLANDS
ÎLES TUAMOTU
FRENCH POLYNESIA
Arequipa
La Paz
BOLIVIA
Sucre
Goiânia
Brasília
Belo Horizonte
TONGA
Tropic of Capricorn
PITCAIRN (U.K.)
Antofagasta
PARAGUAY
SÃO PAULO
RIO DE JANEIRO
Santos
Asunción
Curitiba
International Date Line
ISLA DE PASCUA EASTER ISLAND (Chile)
ISLA SAN AMBROSIO (Chile)
CHILE
Co. Aconcagua 6959
Córdoba
Paraná
Porto Alegre
Valparaíso
Santiago
Rosario
URUGUAY
BUENOS AIRES
Montevideo
ARCHIPIÉLAGO JUAN FERNÁNDEZ (Chile)
Concepción
ARGENTINA
Mar del Plata
Bahía Blanca
P A C I F I C
O C E A N
CHATHAM ISLANDS (N.Z.)
FALKLAND ISLANDS ISLAS MALVINAS (U.K.)
Punta Arenas
CABO DE HORNOS CAPE HORN
SOUTH GEORGIA (U.K.)
Drake Passage
SOUTH ORKNEY ISLANDS (B.A.T.)
Antarctic Circle
ANTARCTIC PENINSULA
Bellingshausen Sea
Weddell Sea
Ross Sea
MARIE BYRD LAND
ROSS ICE SHELF
Vinson Massif 4897
A N T A R

One centimeter represents 750 kilometers.
One inch represents approximately 1200 miles.
Robinson Projection
Scale 1:75,000,000

Europe

Copyright © by Rand McNally & Co.
Map prepared by Esselte Map Service AB, Stockholm

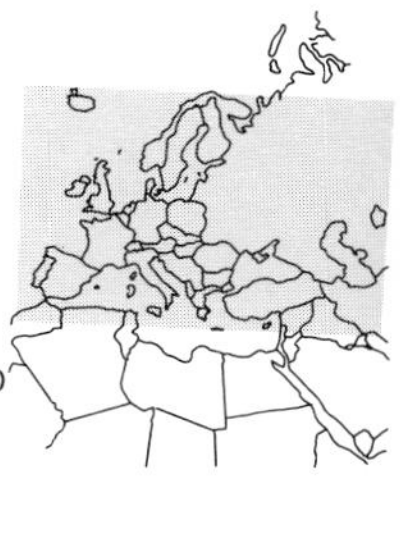

Kilometers 0 200 400 600 Km.

Statute Miles 0 200 400 600 Mi.

Scale 1:12,000,000

One centimeter represents 120 kilometers.

One inch represents approximately 190 miles.

Miller Oblated Stereographic Projection

Northern Europe

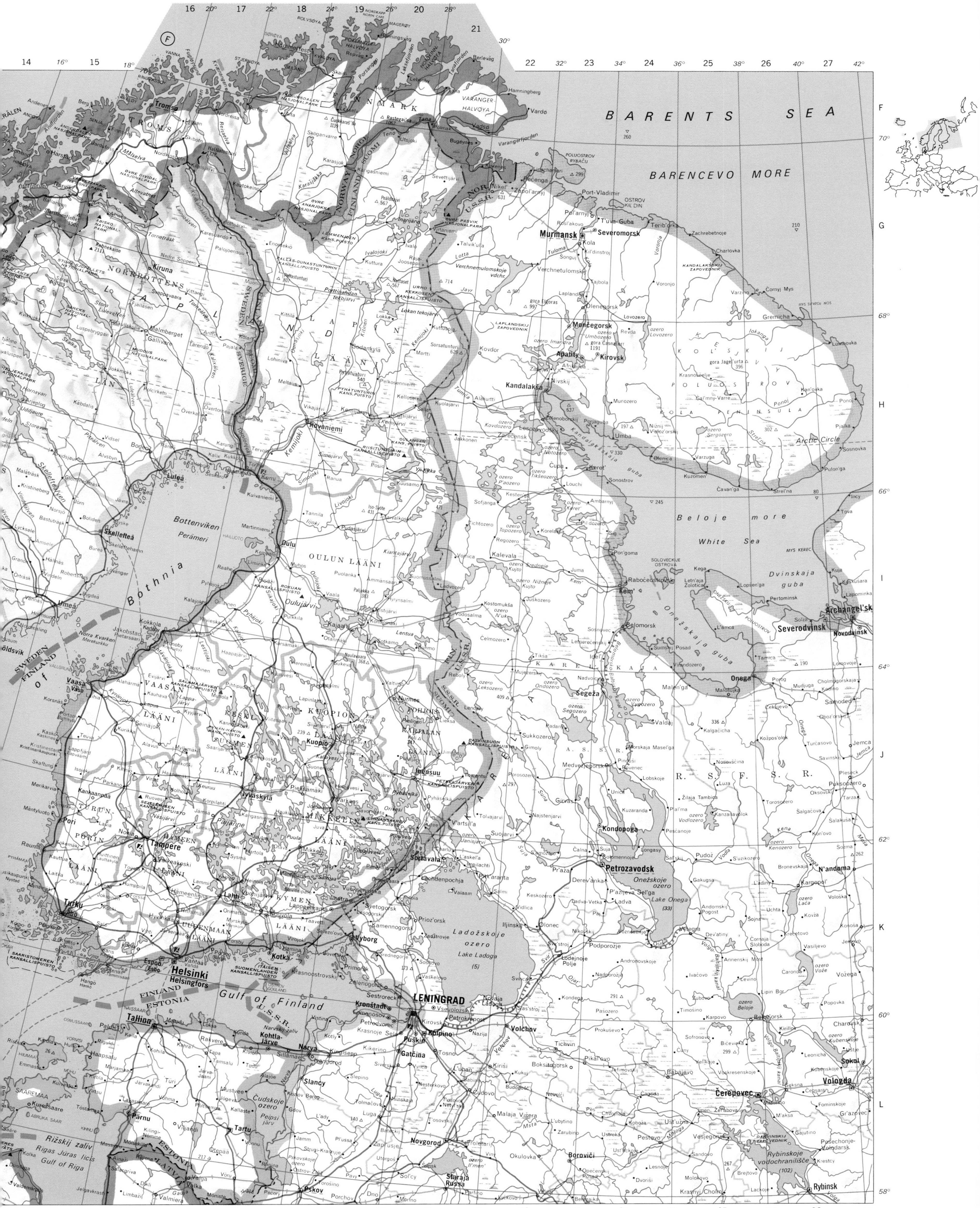

Kilometers 0 100 200 Km.

Statute Miles 0 100 200 Mi.

Scale 1:4,500,000

One centimeter represents 45 kilometers.
One inch represents approximately 71 miles.

Lambert Conformal Conic Projection

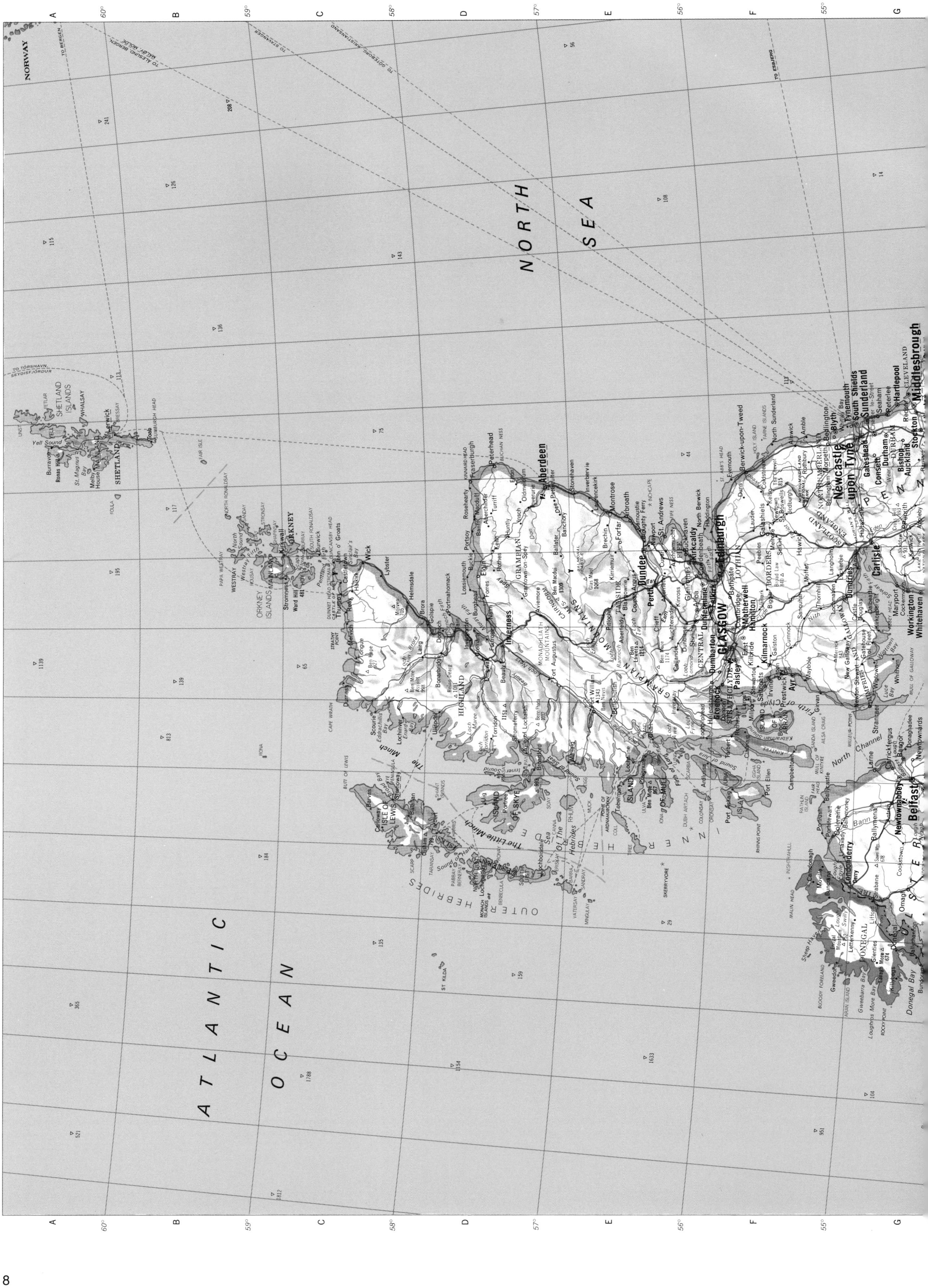
NORTH SEA
ATLANTIC OCEAN
NORWAY
SHETLAND ISLANDS
SHETLAND
Lerwick
FAIR ISLE
ORKNEY
ORKNEY ISLANDS
Kirkwall
Stromness
Thurso
Wick
Inverness
Aberdeen
Peterhead
Fraserburgh
Dundee
Perth
Edinburgh
GLASGOW
Paisley
Kilmarnock
Ayr
Dumfries
Carlisle
Newcastle upon Tyne
Sunderland
Middlesbrough
Belfast
Londonderry
Ballymena
Larne
GRAMPIAN
HIGHLAND
GRAMPIAN MOUNTAINS
CAIRNGORM MOUNTAINS
MONADHLIATH MOUNTAINS
CENTRAL
FIFE
LOTHIAN
BORDERS
STRATHCLYDE
TAYSIDE
ISLE OF LEWIS
ISLE OF SKYE
OUTER HEBRIDES
The Minch
The Little Minch
ST KILDA
ROCKALL
North Channel
Donegal Bay
DONEGAL
ULSTER
SCOTLAND
ENGLAND
NORTHUMBERLAND
DURHAM
CLEVELAND
CUMBRIA

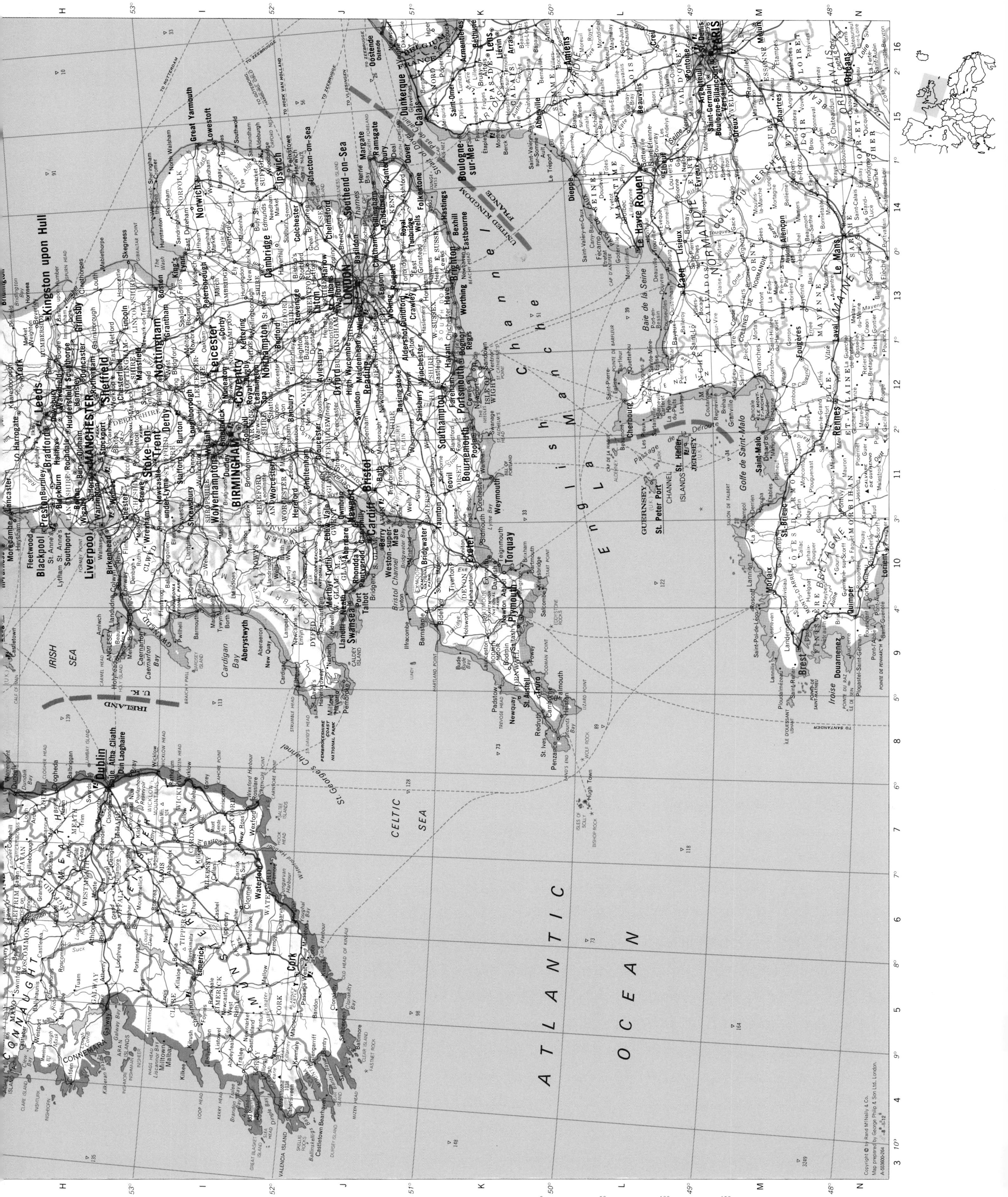

Kilometers 0 50 100 150 Km.

Statute Miles 0 50 100 150 Mi.

Scale 1:3,000,000

One centimeter represents 30 kilometers.

One inch represents approximately 47 miles.

Conic Projection, Two Standard Parallels

Central Europe

Kilometers 0 50 100 150 Km.

Statute Miles 0 50 100 150 Mi.

Scale 1:3,000,000

One centimeter represents 30 kilometers.
One inch represents approximately 47 miles.
Conic Projection, Two Standard Parallels.

BALTIC SEA
Pomeranian Bay
Gulf of Gdansk
Kaliningrad (Königsberg)
Gdańsk (Danzig)
Gdynia
Szczecin (Stettin)
Koszalin (Köslin)
Kołobrzeg
Słupsk (Stolp)
Elbląg (Elbing)
Olsztyn (Allenstein)
Białystok
Grodno
Bydgoszcz
Toruń
Poznań
Gorzów Wielkopolski (Landsberg)
WARSZAWA WARSAW
Łódź
Radom
Lublin
Brest
Wrocław (Breslau)
Częstochowa
Katowice
Kraków
Kielce
Rzeszów
Opole (Oppeln)
Wałbrzych
Legnica (Liegnitz)
Dresden
Berlin
Frankfurt an der Oder
PRAHA PRAGUE
Brno
Ostrava
Olomouc
České Budějovice
Plzeň
WIEN VIENNA
Linz
Graz
Bratislava
Košice
Prešov
Žilina
BUDAPEST
Debrecen
Miskolc
Győr
Szeged
Pécs
Sopron
Oradea
Arad
Subotica
Kikinda
Klagenfurt
Maribor
Varaždin
POLAND
U.S.S.R.
CZECHOSLOVAKIA
AUSTRIA
HUNGARY
ROMANIA
YUGOSLAVIA
CARPATHIAN MOUNTAINS
Danube
Wisła
Odra
Warta
Bug
Tisza
Drava
Balaton
46°
47°
48°
49°
50°
51°
52°
53°
54°
13
14
15
16
17
18
19
20
21
22
23
24
A
B
C
D
E
F
G
H
I
J

Belgium, Netherlands, and Luxembourg

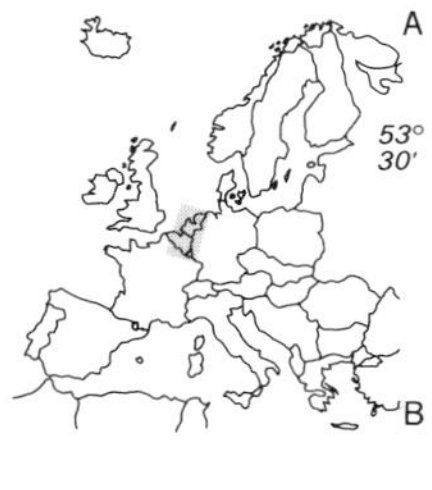

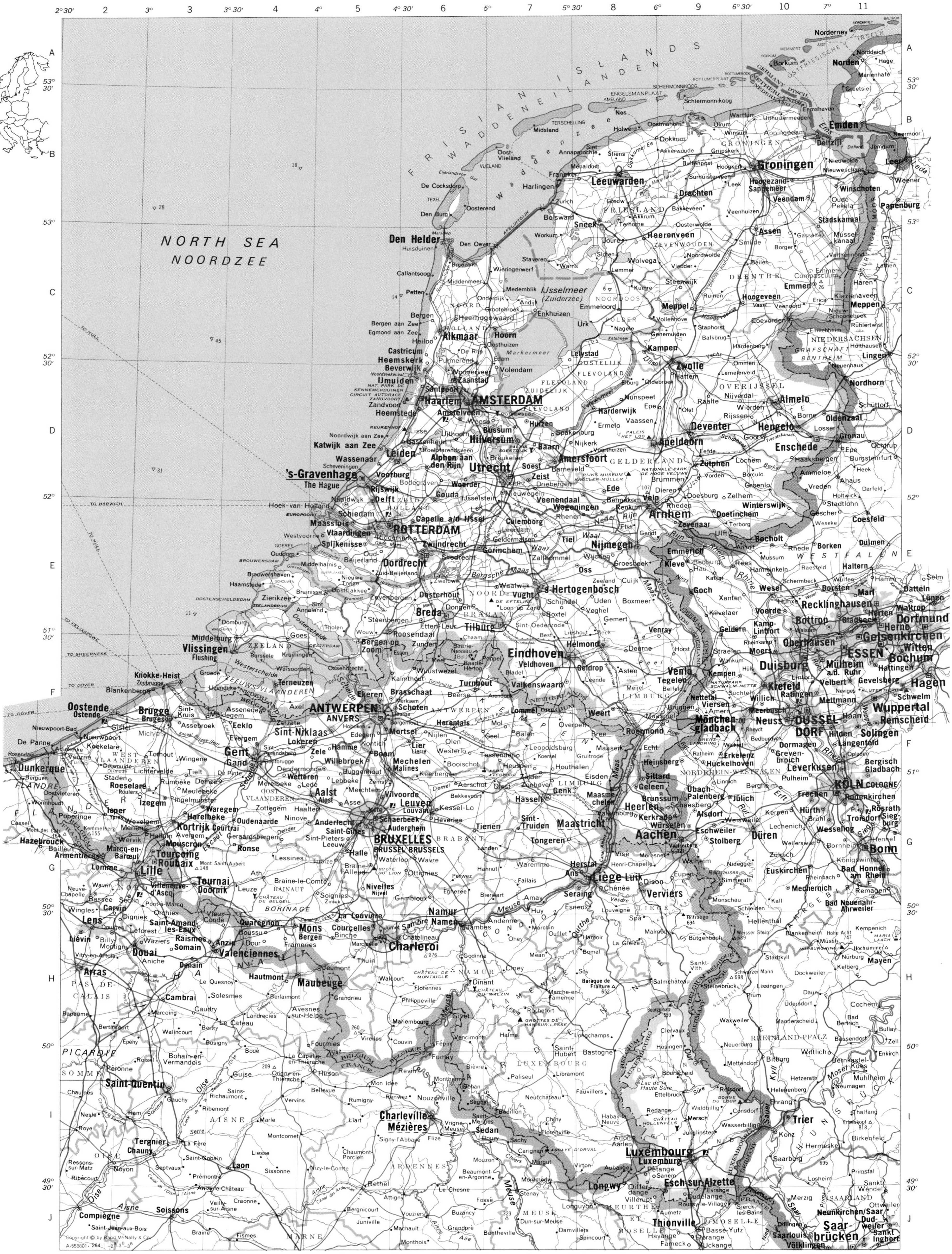

Scale 1:1,500,000

One centimeter represents 15 kilometers.
One inch represents approximately 24 miles.

Lambert Conformal Conic Projection

Kilometers 0 10 20 30 40 50 Km.

Statute Miles 0 10 20 30 40 50 Mi.

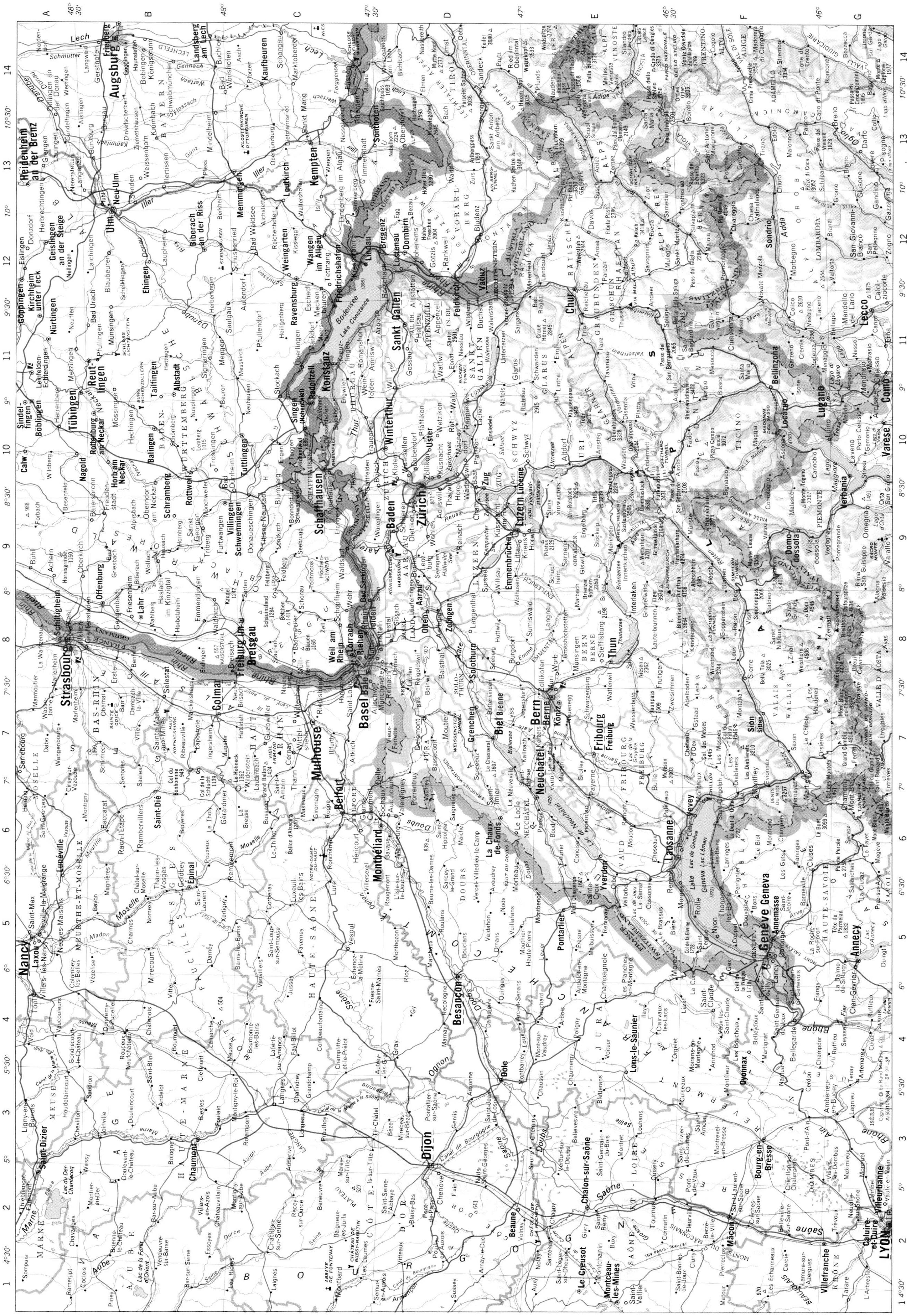

Scale 1:1,500,000

One centimeter represents 15 kilometers.
One inch represents approximately 24 miles.
Lambert Conformal Conic Projection

Kilometers 0 10 20 30 40 50 Km.

Statute Miles 0 10 20 30 40 50 Mi.

English Channel
La Manche
ATLANTIC OCEAN
Bay of Biscay
Golfe de Saint-Malo
Baie de la Seine
Strait of Dover
Pas de Calais
UNITED KINGDOM
FRANCE
GUERNSEY (U.K.)
St. Peter Port
CHANNEL ISLANDS
JERSEY (U.K.)
St. Helier
Southampton
Portsmouth
Bournemouth
Brighton
Plymouth
Torquay
Exeter
Dover
Dunkerque
Calais
Boulogne-sur-Mer
Lille
Roubaix
Amiens
Dieppe
Le Havre
Rouen
Cherbourg
Caen
PARIS
Versailles
Rennes
Brest
Quimper
Lorient
Vannes
Saint-Brieuc
Saint-Malo
Nantes
Saint-Nazaire
Angers
Le Mans
Tours
Orléans
Blois
Bourges
Poitiers
La Rochelle
Rochefort
Limoges
Clermont-Ferrand
Bordeaux
Périgueux
Agen
Toulouse
Montauban
Bayonne
Biarritz
Pau
Tarbes
Carcassonne
Narbonne
Béziers
Perpignan
Montpellier
Sète
Santander
Bilbao
Donostia San Sebastián
Vitoria
Pamplona
Burgos
Logroño
ANDORRA
PYRÉNÉES
BRETAGNE
NORMANDIE
POITOU
LIMOUSIN
AUVERGNE
MASSIF CENTRAL
GASCOGNE
LANGUEDOC
ROUSSILLON

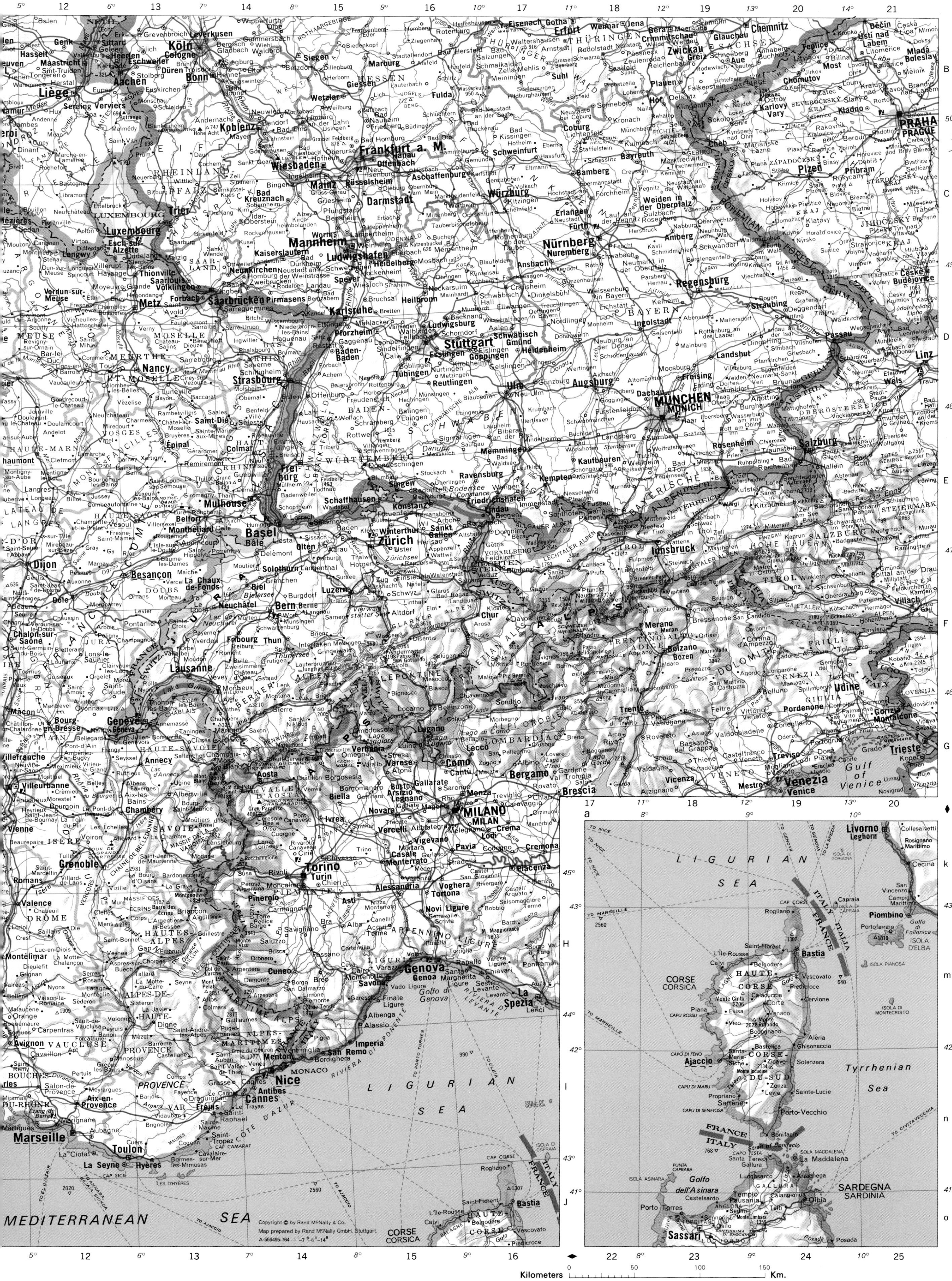

Kilometers 0 50 100 150 Km.

Statute Miles 0 50 100 150 Mi.

Scale 1:3,000,000

One centimeter represents 30 kilometers.

One inch represents approximately 47 miles.

Lambert Conformal Conic Projection

Spain and Portugal

Kilometers 0 50 100 150 Km.

Statute Miles 0 50 100 150 Mi.

Scale 1:3,000,000

One centimeter represents 30 kilometers.

One inch represents approximately 47 miles.

Conic Projection, Two Standard Parallels

ADRIATIC SEA
LIGURIAN SEA
Gulf of Venice
In June 1991, the republics of Croatia (Hrvatska) and Slovenia (Slovenija) declared independence from Yugoslavia.
WIEN VIENNA
BUDAPEST
Bratislava
München Munich
Innsbruck
Salzburg
Linz
Graz
Zürich
Bern Berne
Basel Bâle
Ljubljana
Zagreb
Trieste
Rijeka
Zadar
Split
Sarajevo
Mostar
Dubrovnik
MILANO MILAN
Torino Turin
Genova Genoa
Venezia Venice
Verona
Padova
Trento
Bolzano
Bologna
Firenze Florence
Pisa
Livorno Leghorn
La Spezia
Perugia
Ancona
Pescara
San Marino
Nice
Cannes
MONACO
Bastia
CORSE CORSICA

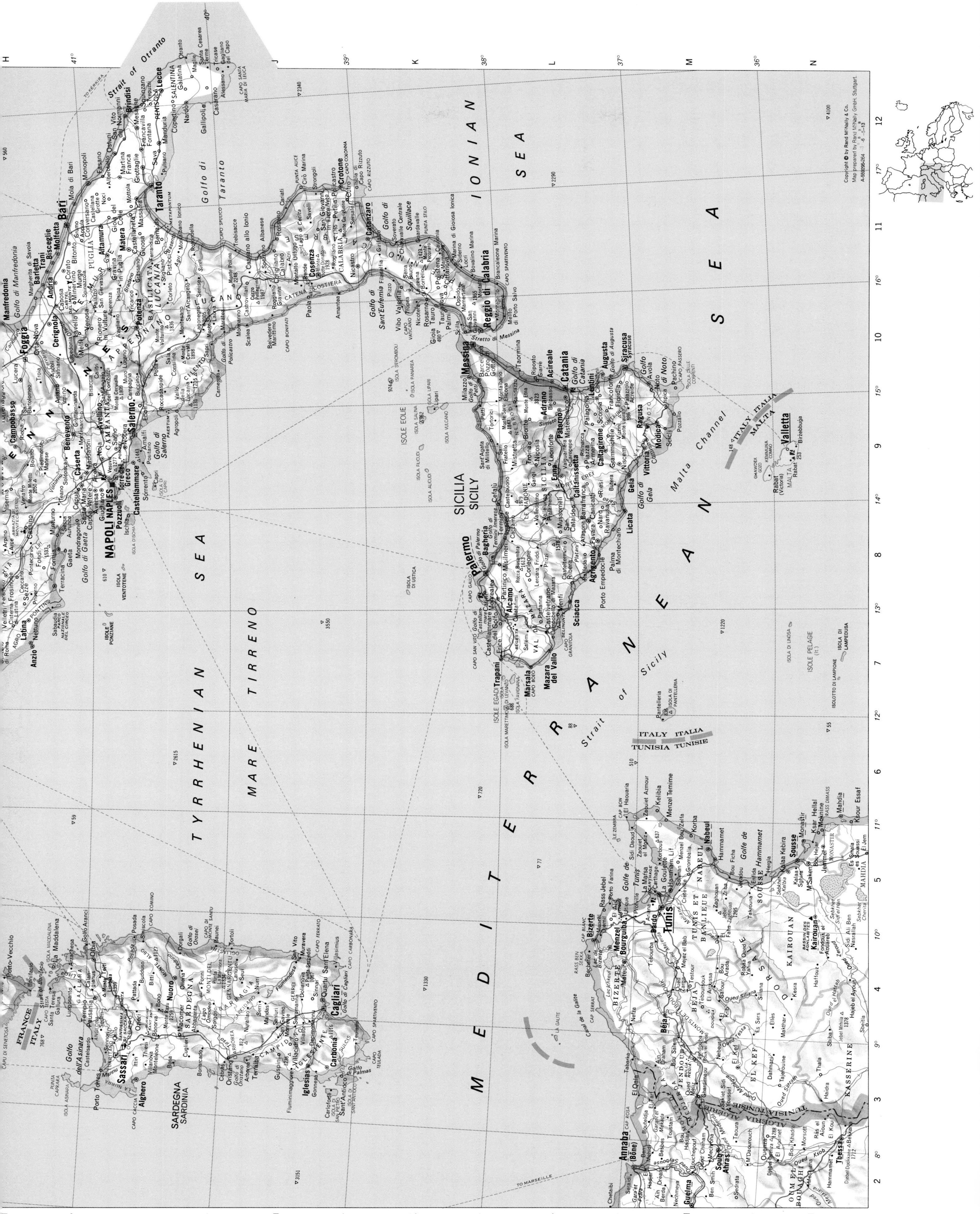

Kilometers 0 50 100 150 Km.

Statute Miles 0 50 100 150 Mi.

Scale 1:3,000,000

One centimeter represents 30 kilometers.

One inch represents approximately 47 miles.

Conic Projection, Two Standard Parallels

BLACK SEA
Mouths of the Danube
CARPATHIAN MOUNTAINS
BUDAPEST
BUCUREŞTI
Beograd
Sofija

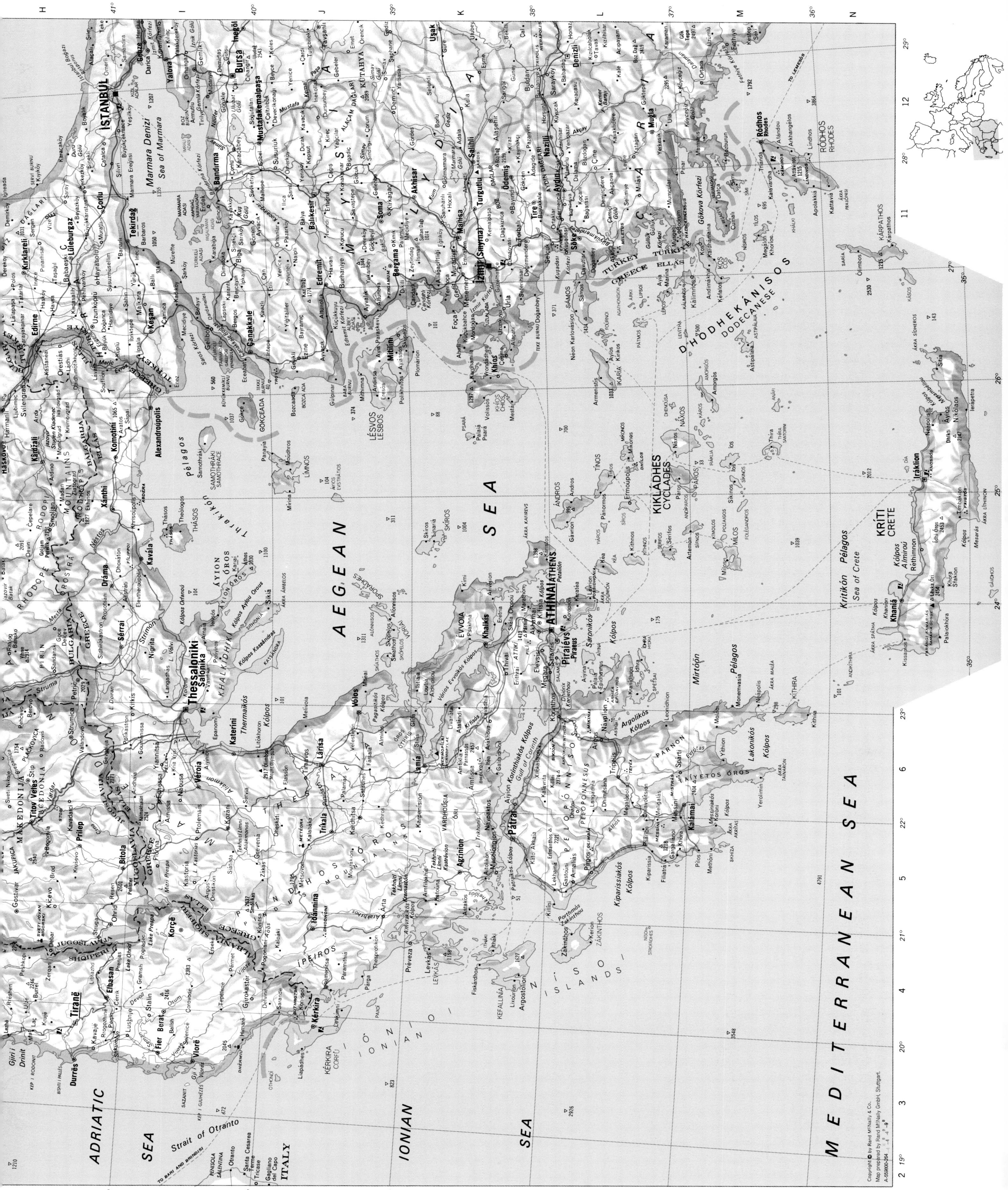

Kilometers 0 50 100 150 Km.

Statute Miles 0 50 100 150 Mi.

Scale 1:3,000,000

One centimeter represents 30 kilometers.

One inch represents approximately 47 miles.

Conic Projection, Two Standard Parallels

Late in 1991 a number of Republics (S.S.R.s) of the Soviet Union declared their intentions to secede.

Kilometers 0 200 400 600 Km.
Statute Miles 0 200 400 600 Mi.

Scale 1:12,000,000
One centimeter represents 120 kilometers.
One inch represents approximately 190 miles.
Lambert Conformal Conic Projection

Central and Eastern Soviet Union

Kilometers 0 200 400 600 Km.
Statute Miles 0 200 400 600 Mi.

Scale 1:12,000,000

One centimeter represents 120 kilometers.
One inch represents approximately 190 miles.
Lambert Conformal Conic Projection

ALASKA
UNITED STATES
Chukchi Sea
Bering Strait
SAINT LAWRENCE ISLAND
NUNIVAK ISLAND
SAINT MATTHEW ISLAND
Bering Sea
OSTROV VRANGEL'A
proliv Longa
VOSTOČNO-SIBIRSKOJE MORE
EAST SIBERIAN SEA
OSTROVA DE-LONGA
OSTROV KOTEL'NYJ
OSTROV BOL'ŠOJ L'ACHOVSKIJ
proliv Sannikova
proliv Dmitrija Lapteva
Janskij zaliv
Arctic Circle
ČUKOTSKIJ POLUOSTROV
Providenija
zaliv Kresta
Anadyrskij zaliv
Anadyr'
Uelen
Pevek
Čaunskaja guba
Ust'-Čaun
Ambarčik
Čerskij
Malyj An'uj
Bol'šoj An'uj
AN'UJSKIJ CHREBET
EKIATAPSKIJ CHREBET
ANADYRSKOJE PLOSKOGORJE
KOL'MSKAJA NIZMENNOST'
Kolyma
Omolon
Indigirka
Alazeja
Chroma
Jana
JUKAGIRSKOJE PLOSKOGORJE
KOR'AKSKOJE NAGORJE
PENŽINSKIJ CHREBET
Penžina
Penžinskaja guba
Gižiginskaja guba
MOMSKIJ CHREBET
CHREBET ČERSKOGO
CHREBET VERCHOJANSKIJ
Verchojansk
Srednekolymsk
Zyr'anka
Ust'-Nera
Oim'akon
Susuman
SUNTAR-CHAJATA
CHREBET SETTE-DABAN
Magadan
Tauiskaja guba
Ochotsk
zaliv Šelichova
Lena
Aldan
Amga
Jakutsk
Pokrovsk
UNION OF SOVIET SOCIALIST REPUBLICS
SIBERIA
ALDANSKOJE NAGORJE
STANOVOJ CHREBET
CHREBET DŽUGDŽUR
Ajan
Udskaja guba
Čumikan
Zeja
Zejskoje vodochranilišče
Skovorodino
Never
Tynda
Uda
Selemdža
Bureja
BUREINSKIJ CHREBET
Amur
Heilong
Svobodnyj
Blagoveščensk
Komsomol'sk-na-Amure
Chabarovsk
Birobidžan
Ussuri
SICHOTE-ALIN'
Vladivostok
Nachodka
Ussurijsk
Ozero Chanka
Arsen'jev
Dal'nerečensk
Lesozavodsk
Nikolajevsk-na-Amure
Sachalinskij zaliv
OSTROV SACHALIN SAKHALIN
Ocha
Aleksandrovsk-Sachalinskij
Poronajsk
zaliv Terpenija
Južno-Sachalinsk
zaliv Aniva
Cholmsk
Tatarskij proliv
Sovetskaja Gavan'
Vanino
La Perouse Strait
SEA OF OKHOTSK
OCHOTSKOJE MORE
POLUOSTROV KAMČATKA KAMCHATKA
SREDINNYJ CHREBET
Petropavlovsk-Kamčatskij
Ust'-Kamčatsk
Kamčatskij zaliv
KOMANDORSKIJE OSTROVA
Kronockij zaliv
Kliučevskaja Sopka 4750
Pervyj Kuril'skij proliv
KURIL'SKIJE OSTROVA
KURIL ISLANDS
proliv Kruzenšterna
proliv Friza
proliv Jekateriny
OSTROV ITURUP
OSTROV KUNAŠIR
OSTROV PARAMUŠIR
OSTROV ŠUMŠU
Habomai, Shikotan, Kunashiri, and Etorofu, occupied by the U.S.S.R. since 1945, are claimed by Japan pending a final peace treaty.
HOKKAIDŌ
Wakkanai
Asahikawa
Sapporo
Otaru
Tomakomai
Muroran
Obihiro
Kushiro
Nemuro
Hakodate
JAPAN
HONSHŪ
Aomori
Hirosaki
Hachinohe
Akita
Morioka
Miyako
Kamaishi
SEA OF JAPAN
PACIFIC OCEAN
CHINA
MANCHURIA
HEILONGJIANG
NEI MONGGOL ZIZHIQU
DA HINGGAN LING
XIAO HINGGAN LING
Harbin
Qiqihar Tsitsihar
Jiamusi
Shuangyashan
Hegang
Yichun
Bei'an
Mudanjiang
Jixi
JILIN
Songhua
Nen

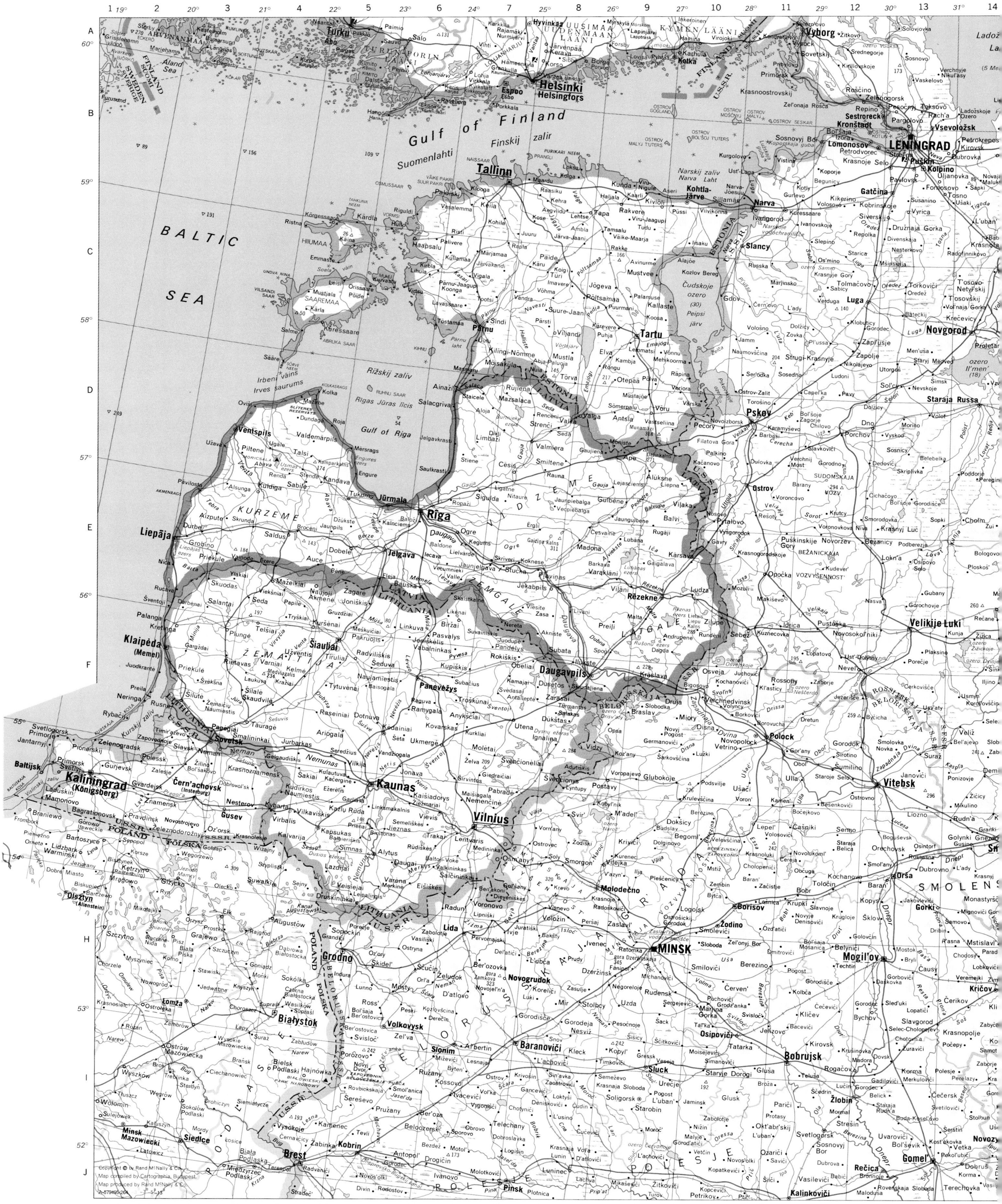
Gulf of Finland
Suomenlahti
Finskij zalir
BALTIC SEA
Rižskij zaliv
Rīgas Jūras līcis
Gulf of Riga
Irbenskij proliv
Åland Sea
Helsinki
Helsingfors
Espoo
Esbo
Turku
Åbo
Hanko
Kotka
Vyborg
LENINGRAD
Kronštadt
Puškin
Pavlovsk
Gatčina
Narva
Kohtla-Järve
Tallinn
Pärnu
Tartu
Pskov
Novgorod
Staraja Russa
Velikije Luki
Vitebsk
Orša
Mogil'ov
Gomel'
Bobrujsk
MINSK
Borisov
Molodečno
Baranoviči
Pinsk
Brest
Grodno
Lida
Vilnius
Kaunas
Šiauliai
Panevėžys
Klaipėda
(Memel)
Liepāja
Ventspils
Jūrmala
Riga
Jelgava
Daugavpils
Rēzekne
Polock
Kaliningrad
(Königsberg)
Sovetsk
Baltijsk
Białystok
Olsztyn
(Allenstein)
Siedlce
SAAREMAA
HIIUMAA
KURZEME
VIDZEME
ZEMGALE
LATGALE
ŽEMAITIJA
POLESJE
ESTONIA
LATVIA
LITHUANIA
BELORUSSKAJA S.S.R.
ROSSIJSKAJA S.S.S.R.
FINLAND
SUOMI
U.S.S.R.
POLAND
POLSKA
SWEDEN
SVERIGE
Čudskoje ozero
(Peipsi järv)
Ozero Il'men'
Copyright © by Rand McNally & Co.
Map compiled by Cartographia, Budapest.
Map produced by Rand McNally & Co.

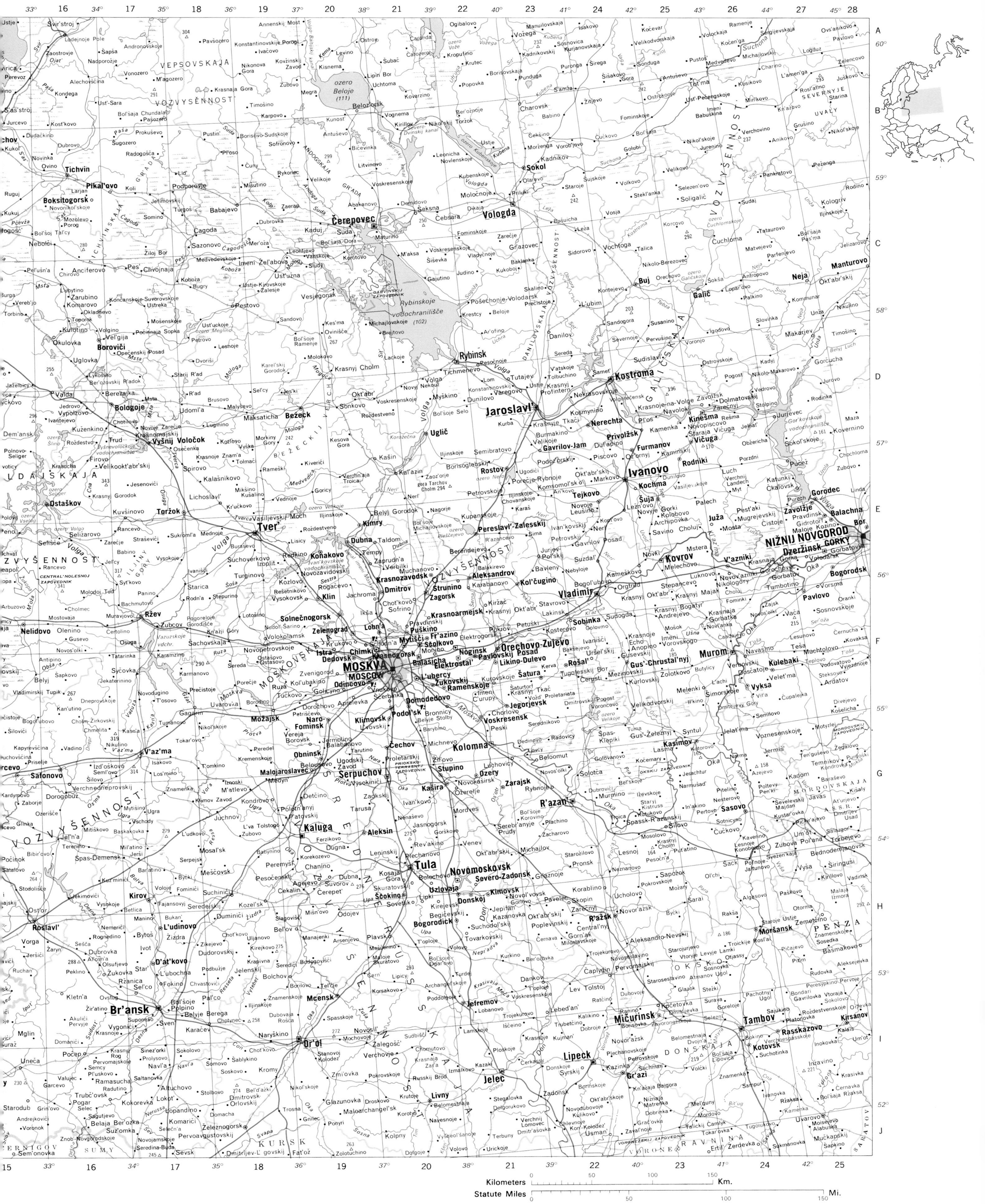

Kilometers 0 50 100 150 Km.

Statute Miles 0 50 100 150 Mi.

Scale 1:3,000,000

One centimeter represents 30 kilometers.

One inch represents approximately 47 miles.

Lambert Conformal Conic Projection

ARCTIC
OCEAN
North Pole
ATLANTIC
OCEAN
GREENLAND
ICELAND
Reykjavik
Greenland Sea
Norwegian Sea
Barents Sea
Kara Sea
Laptevych more
Laptev Sea
Chukchi Sea
Bering Sea
Bering Strait
UNITED STATES
ALEUTIAN BASIN
SVALBARD
ZEML'A FRANCA-IOSIFA
FRANZ JOSEF LAND
SEVERNAJA ZEML'A
NOVOSIBIRSKIE OSTROVA
OSTROV VRANGEL'A
Vostočno-Sibirskoje more
East Siberian Sea
Arctic Circle
North Sea
Baltic Sea
UNITED KINGDOM
IRELAND
Dublin
Belfast
Glasgow
Edinburgh
Liverpool
Manchester
Birmingham
Cardiff
LONDON
NORWAY
SWEDEN
FINLAND
DENMARK
Oslo
Stockholm
Helsinki
København
Copenhagen
Trondheim
Bergen
Göteborg
Malmö
Gulf of Bothnia
Gulf of Finland
NETHERLANDS
BELGIUM
Amsterdam
Bruxelles
GERMANY
BERLIN
Hamburg
Essen
Köln
Bonn
Frankfurt
Stuttgart
München
Leipzig
POLAND
Warszawa
Gdańsk
Kraków
Katowice
CZECHOSLOVAKIA
Praha
AUSTRIA
WIEN
VIENNA
HUNGARY
BUDAPEST
ROMANIA
București
BULGARIA
Sofija
YUGOSLAVIA
Beograd
ALPS
CARPATHIAN MOUNTAINS
Black Sea
Caspian Sea
Aral'skoje more
Aral Sea
EUROPE
UNION OF SOVIET SOCIALIST REPUBLICS
MOSKVA
MOSCOW
LENINGRAD
KIJEV
Minsk
Riga
Vilnius
Tallinn
Smolensk
Char'kov
Odessa
Dnepropetrovsk
Doneck
Rostov-na-Donu
Voronež
Tula
Kursk
Jaroslavl'
Vologda
Archangel'sk
Murmansk
Nižnij Novgorod
Kazan'
Samara
Saratov
VOLGOGRAD
Astrachan'
Penza
Perm'
Kirov
Ufa
SVERDLOVSK
Čel'abinsk
Magnitogorsk
Orenburg
Orsk
Nižnij Tagil
URAL'SKIJE GORY
URAL MOUNTAINS
BOL'ŠOJ KAVKAZ
CAUCASUS
TBILISI
Jerevan
BAKU
ZAPADNO-SIBIRSKAJA RAVNINA
SIBERIA
SREDNESIBIRSKOJE PLOSKOGORJE
CHREBET ČERSKOGO
Omsk
Novosibirsk
Novokuzneck
Tomsk
Kemerovo
Barnaul
Krasnojarsk
Irkutsk
Ulan-Ude
Čita
Jakutsk
Noril'sk
Magadan
Chabarovsk
Vladivostok
Komsomol'sk-na-Amure
Petropavlovsk-Kamčatskij
Celinograd
Karaganda
Semipalatinsk
Ust'-Kamenogorsk
Alma-Ata
Frunze
TAŠKENT
Samarkand
Nukus
PLATO UST'URT
KAZACHSKIJ MELKOSOPOČNIK
ozero Bajkal
Lake Baikal
ozero Balchaš
Lake Balkhash
Sea of Okhotsk
Ochotskoje more
KURIL'SKIJE OSTROVA
KURIL ISLANDS
OSTROV SACHALIN
SAKHALIN
SICHOTE-ALIN
STANOVOJ CHREBET
MONGOLIA
Ulaanbaatar
GOBI
ALTAI
ASIA
TIEN SHAN
PAMIR
HINDU KUSH
KUNLUN SHAN
TARIM PENDI
ALTUN SHAN
QAIDAM PENDI
DA HINGGAN LING
Harbin
Qiqihar
Changchun
Shenyang
MUKDEN
Fushun
Dandong
Dalian
BEIJING
PEKING
TIANJIN
TIENTSIN
Huhehaote
Zhangjiakou
Taiyuan
Jinan
Qingdao
Zhengzhou
XI'AN
Lanzhou
Yinchuan
NANJING
SHANGHAI
WUHAN
Ningbo
Ürümqi
Yining
Kashi
Shache
NORTH KOREA
P'yongyang
SOUTH KOREA
SOUL
PUSAN
Taegu
JAPAN
HOKKAIDO
HONSHU
KYUSHU
Sapporo
Asahikawa
Hakodate
Aomori
Sendai
Niigata
Nagoya
Kyoto
Osaka
Hiroshima
Fukuoka
Kagoshima
Sea of Japan
Yellow Sea
EAST CHINA SEA
TURKEY
ASIA MINOR
ANKARA
ISTANBUL
Izmir
Adana
Samsun
SYRIA
DIMASHQ
DAMASCUS
Halab
LEBANON
Bayrut
ISRAEL
Tel Aviv-Yafo
Yerushalayim
JORDAN
Amman
Dead Sea
IRAQ
BAGHDAD
Al-Basrah
Al-Mawsil
KUWAIT
IRAN
TEHRAN
Tabriz
Esfahan
Mashhad
Hamadan
Rasht
Yazd
AFGHANISTAN
Kabol
Herat
Mediterranean Sea
SAUDI ARABIA

INDIAN OCEAN
ARABIAN SEA
Bay of Bengal
Andaman Sea
Laccadive Sea
SOUTH CHINA SEA
INDIA
SRI LANKA
BANGLADESH
BURMA
THAILAND
LAOS
CAMBODIA
VIETNAM
MALAYSIA
INDONESIA
GREATER SUNDA ISLANDS
SUMATERA
BORNEO
JAWA
PHILIPPINES
AUSTRALIA
MADAGASCAR
SOMALIA
ETHIOPIA
YEMEN
OMAN
ARABIAN PENINSULA
MALDIVES
SEYCHELLES
MAURITIUS
NEW DELHI
DELHI
BOMBAY
CALCUTTA
MADRAS
BANGALORE
Colombo
DHAKA
YANGON (RANGOON)
KRUNG THEP (BANGKOK)
SINGAPORE
JAKARTA
HONG KONG
NINETYEAST RIDGE
CARLSBERG RIDGE
MID-INDIAN RIDGE
SOUTHWEST INDIAN RIDGE
BROKEN RIDGE
WHARTON BASIN
Tropic of Cancer
Tropic of Capricorn
Equator
Scale 1:24,000,000
One centimeter represents 240 kilometers.
One inch represents approximately 380 miles.
Lambert Azimuthal Equal-Area Projection
Kilometers
Statute Miles
Copyright © by Rand McNally & Co.

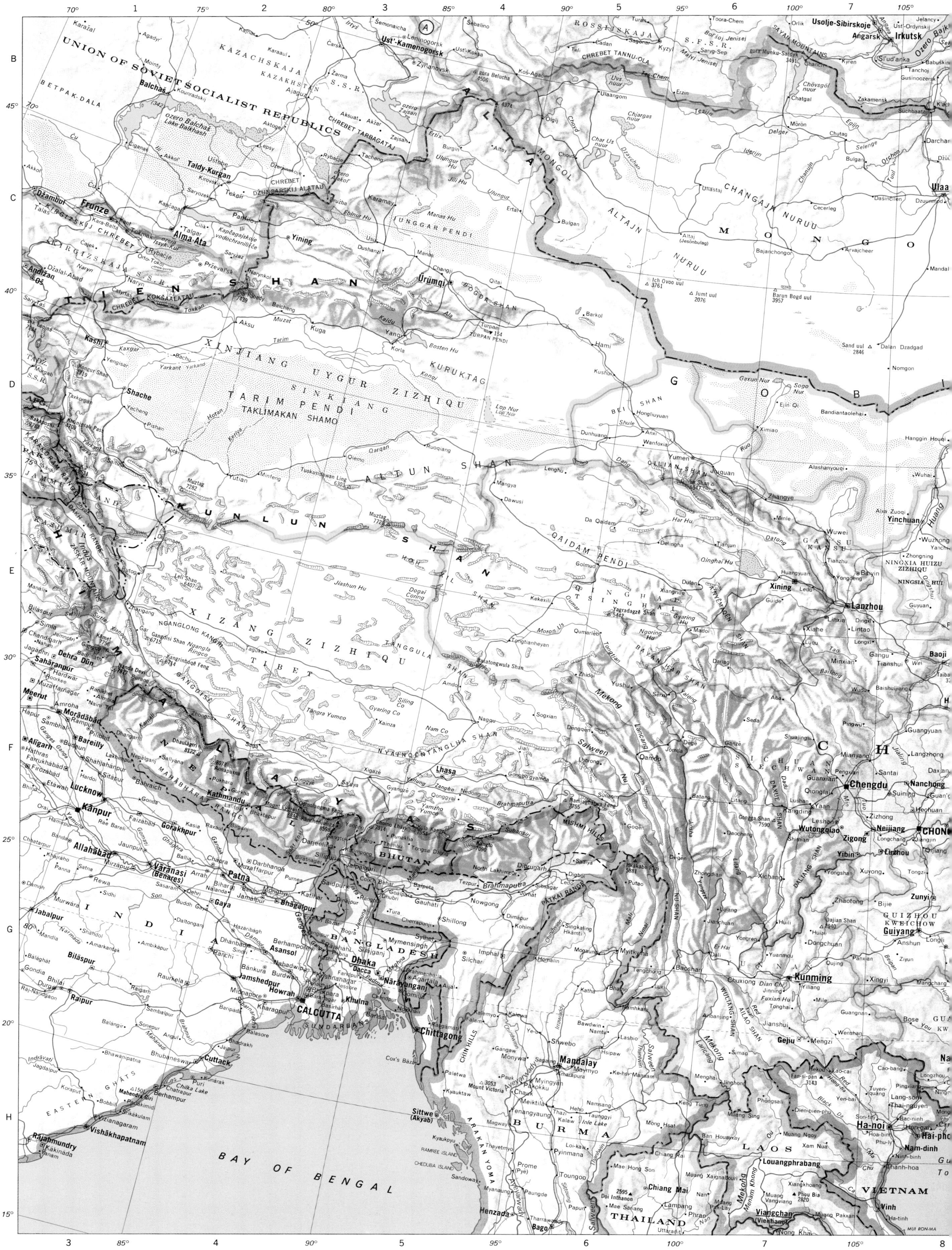
UNION OF SOVIET SOCIALIST REPUBLICS
KAZACHSKAJA S.S.R.
KAZAKHSTAN
ROSSIJSKAJA S.F.S.R.
BETPAK-DALA
Balchaš
ozero Balchaš
Lake Balkhash
Ust'-Kamenogorsk
Irkutsk
Angarsk
Usolje-Sibirskoje
SAYAN MOUNTAINS
CHREBET TANNU-OLA
Uvs nuur
Kyzyl
Ulaangom
ALTAJ
CHREBET TARBAGATAJ
DŽUNGARSKIJ ALATAU
Taldy-Kurgan
Alma-Ata
Frunze
Džambul
KIRGIZSKIJ CHREBET
KIRGIZSKAJA S.S.R.
Andižan
Yining
Ürümqi
BOGDA SHAN
TIEN SHAN
JUNGGAR PENDI
MONGOL ALTAJN NURUU
CHANGAJN NURUU
M O N G O
Bulgan
Barun Bogd uul
Ich Ovoo uul
Jumt uul
Sand uul
Dalan Dzadgad
Kashi
Aksu
Kuga
Korla
TURPAN PENDI
Hami
KURUKTAG
XINJIANG UYGUR ZIZHIQU
SINKIANG
TARIM PENDI
TAKLIMAKAN SHAMO
Shache
Hotan
Lop Nur
BEI SHAN
G O B I
Dunhuang
Yumen
Jiuquan
QILIAN SHAN
Zhangye
ALTUN SHAN
KUNLUN SHAN
QAIDAM PENDI
Golmud
QINGHAI
TSINGHAI
Xining
Lanzhou
Yinchuan
NINGXIA HUIZU ZIZHIQU
GANSU
KANSU
XIZANG ZIZHIQU
TIBET
NGANGLONG KANGRI
TANGGULA SHAN
NYAINQENTANGLHA SHAN
Lhasa
Xigazê
BAYAN HAR SHAN
Mekong
Lancang
Salween
Nu
Yangtze
Qamdo
SICHUAN
SZECHWAN
Chengdu
Chongqing
Baoji
Kunming
GUIZHOU
KWEICHOW
Guiyang
Zunyi
YUNNAN
Kashmir
Jammu
KARAKORAM RANGE
Srinagar
Simla
Dehra Dūn
Meerut
Sahāranpur
Morādābād
Bareilly
Alīgarh
Lucknow
Kānpur
Allahābād
Vārānasi (Benares)
Patna
Gaya
Jabalpur
Bilāspur
Raipur
INDIA
NEPAL
Kathmandu
MAHĀBHĀRAT RANGE
HIMALAYA
Mount Everest
BHUTAN
Darjeeling
BANGLADESH
Dhaka
Dacca
Nārāyanganj
Khulna
Jamshedpur
Howrah
CALCUTTA
SUNDARBANS
Asansol
Bhāgalpur
Cuttack
Bhubaneswar
Vishākhapatnam
Rājahmundry
Kākināda
EASTERN GHATS
Chittagong
Brahmaputra
Gauhati
Shillong
Imphal
MISHMI HILLS
PATKAI RANGE
CHIN HILLS
BURMA
Mandalay
Sittwe (Akyab)
ARAKAN YOMA
Prome
Henzada
Bago
RAMREE ISLAND
CHEDUBA ISLAND
BAY OF BENGAL
THAILAND
Chiang Mai
LAOS
Louangphrabang
Viangchan (Vientiane)
VIETNAM
Ha-noi
Hai-phong
Nam-dinh
Vinh
Gulf of Tonkin

Kilometers 0 200 400 600 Km.
Statute Miles 0 200 400 600 Mi.

Scale 1:12,000,000
One centimeter represents 120 kilometers.
One inch represents approximately 190 miles.
Lambert Conformal Conic Projection

Northeastern China and Korea

Kilometers 0 50 100 150 Km.

Statute Miles 0 50 100 150 Mi.

Scale 1:3,000,000

One centimeter represents 30 kilometers.

One inch represents approximately 47 miles.

Lambert Conformal Conic Projection

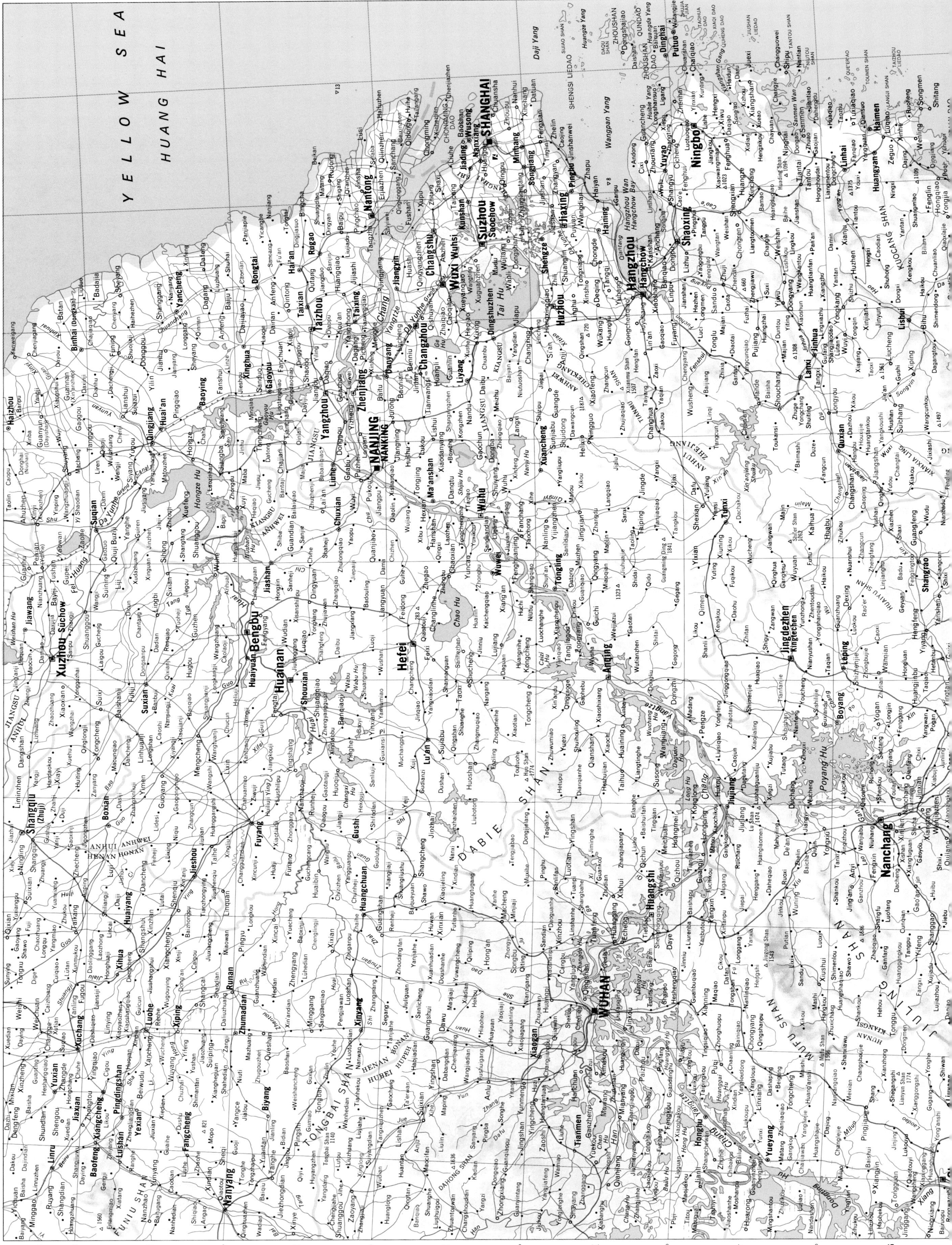
YELLOW SEA
HUANG HAI
SHANGHAI
NANJING
NANKING
WUHAN
Hangzhou
Hangchow
Suzhou
Soochow
Wuxi
Ningbo
Hefei
Nanchang
Bengbu
Huainan
Xuzhou
Suchow
Nantong
Yangzhou
Zhenjiang
Changzhou
Anqing
Wuhu
Jingdezhen
Tai Hu
Chao Hu
Poyang Hu
Hongze Hu
DABIE SHAN
TONGBAI SHAN
FUNIU SHAN
MUFU SHAN
JIANGSU
ANHUI
HENAN
HUBEI
ZHEJIANG
JIANGXI
HUNAN
Chang Jiang
Huai

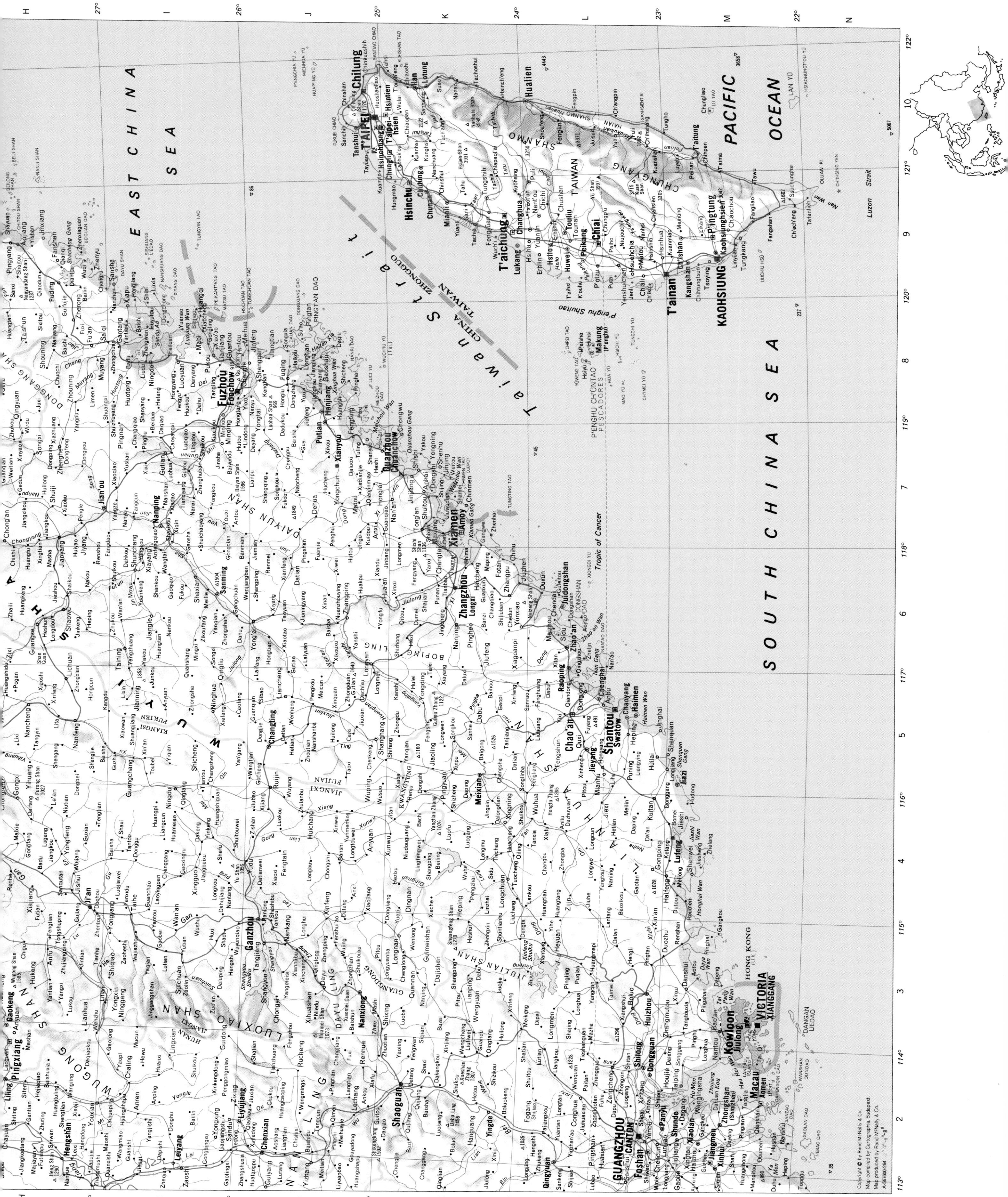

Kilometers 0 50 100 150 Km.

Statute Miles 0 50 100 150 Mi.

Scale 1:3,000,000

One centimeter represents 30 kilometers.

One inch represents approximately 47 miles.

Lambert Conformal Conic Projection

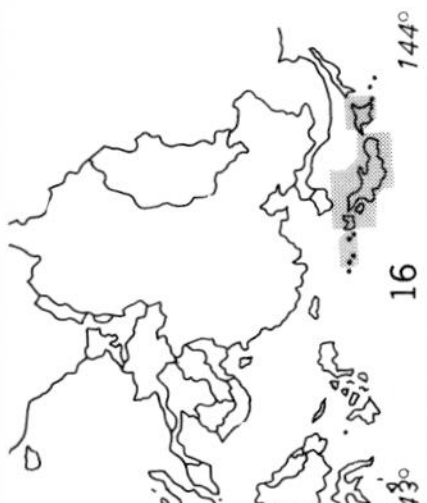

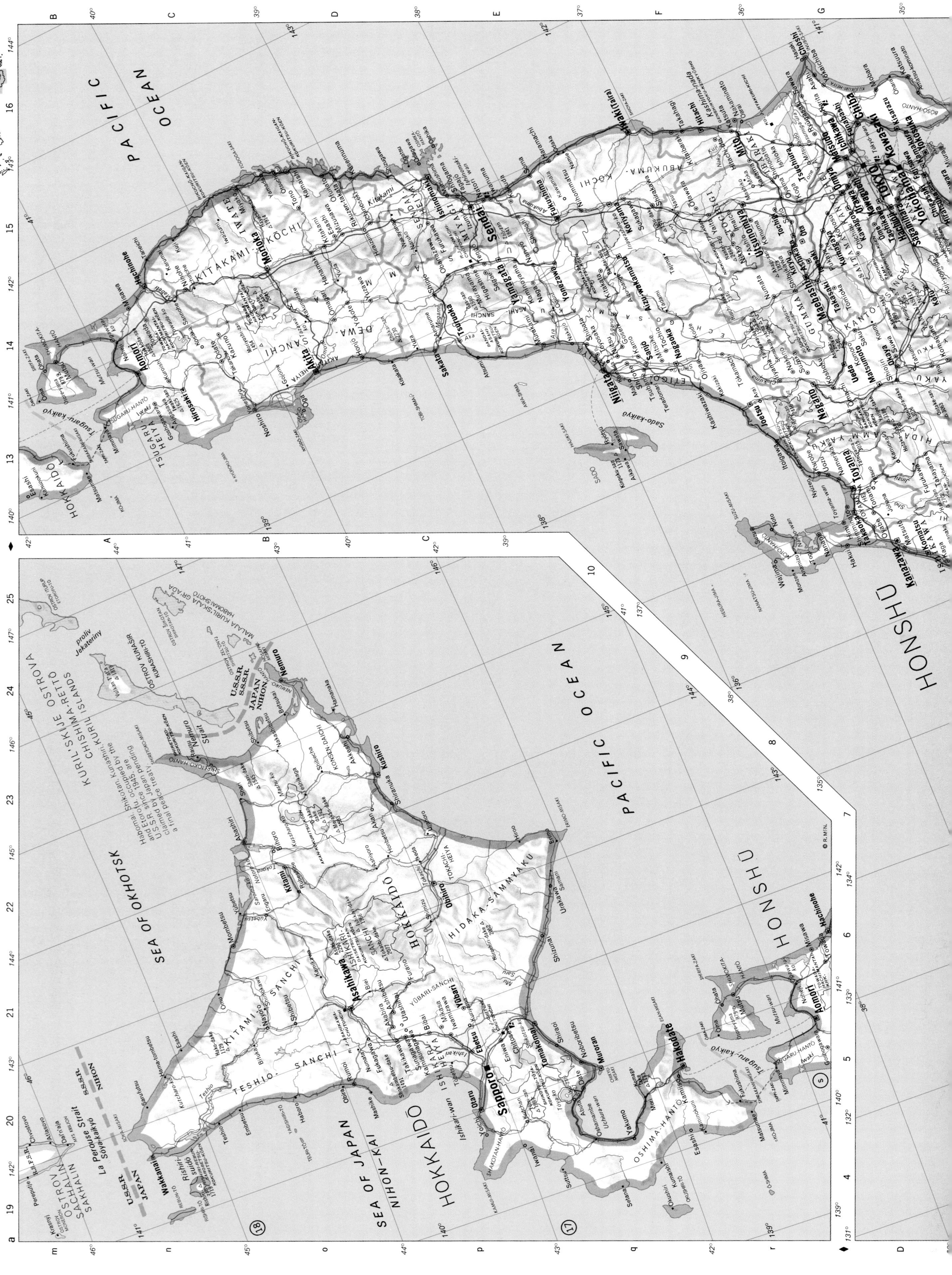

PACIFIC OCEAN
SEA OF OKHOTSK
SEA OF JAPAN
NIHON-KAI
HOKKAIDŌ
HONSHŪ
KURIL'SKIJE OSTROVA
CHISHIMA-RETTŌ
KURIL ISLANDS
La Perouse Strait
Sōya-kaikyō
Tsugaru-kaikyō
Sado-kaikyō
Nemuro Strait
OSTROV SAKHALIN
U.S.S.R.
JAPAN
Sapporo
Asahikawa
Hakodate
Otaru
Muroran
Kushiro
Obihiro
Aomori
Akita
Morioka
Sendai
Niigata
TŌKYŌ
Yokohama
Kawasaki
Chiba

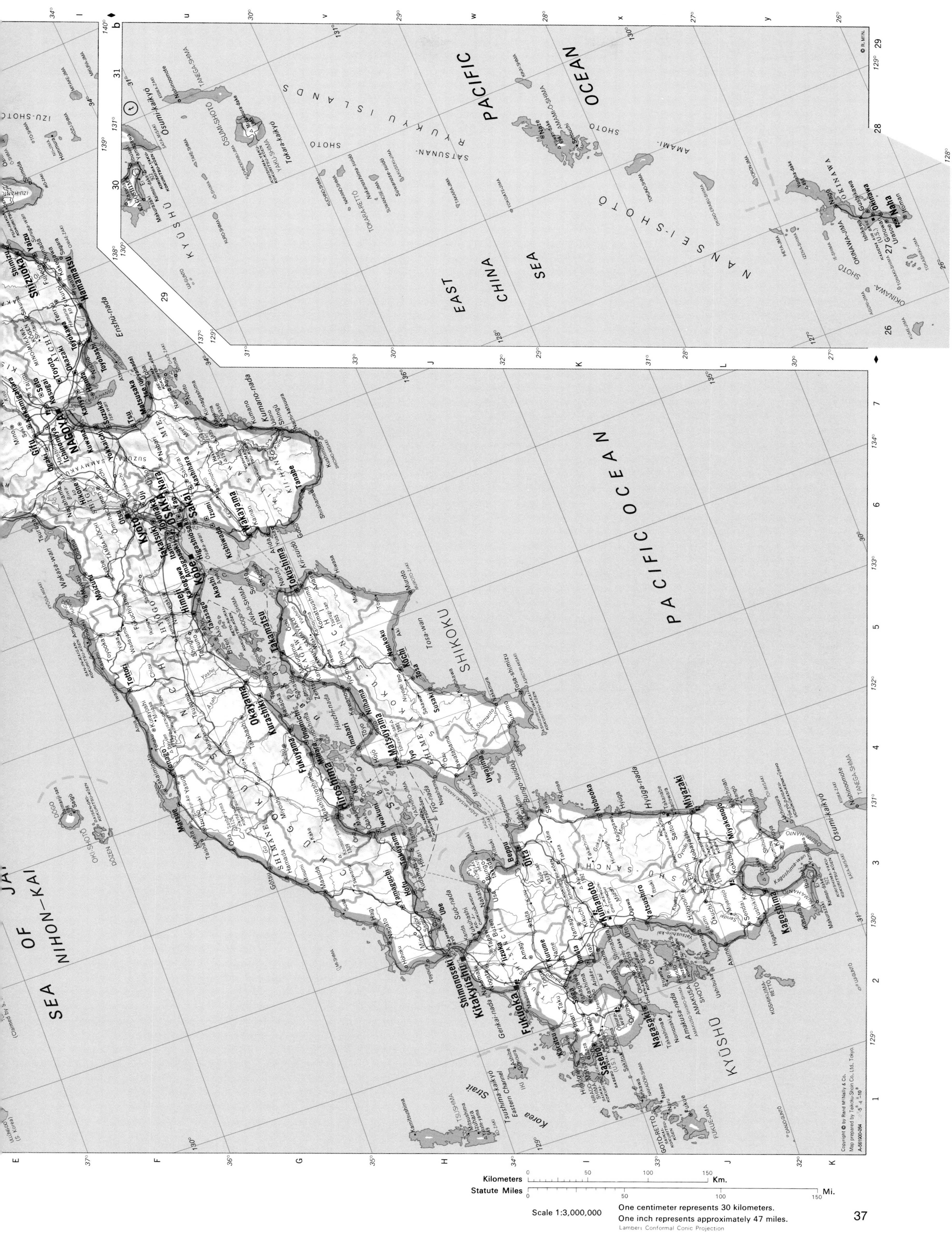

Kilometers 0 50 100 150 Km.

Statute Miles 0 50 100 150 Mi.

Scale 1:3,000,000

One centimeter represents 30 kilometers.

One inch represents approximately 47 miles.

Lambert Conformal Conic Projection

CHINA
YUNNAN
GUANGXI
Nanning
ZHUANGZU
ZIZHIQU
GUANGDONG
GUANGZHOU
CANTON
Shantou
Swatow
Foshan
Dongguan
New Kowloon Xinjiulong
VICTORIA XIANGGANG
HONG KONG
(U.K.)
Aomen Macau
Zhanjiang
Haikou
HAINAN
HAINAN DAO
Gulf of Tonkin
Ha Noi
Hai Phong
Nam Dinh
Thanh Hoa
Vinh
Hue
Da Nang
Qui Nhon
Nha Trang
Phan Thiet
THANH PHO HO CHI MINH
(SAIGON)
VIETNAM
LAOS
Louangphrabang
Viangchan
(Vientiane)
Savannakhet
Pakxe
CAMBODIA
Phnum Penh
Batdambang
Kampong Saom
THAILAND
Chiang Mai
Khon Kaen
Nakhon Ratchasima
KRUNG THEP
BANGKOK
Gulf of Thailand
Songkhla
Hat Yai
BURMA
(MYANMAR)
Mandalay
Monywa
Sittwe
(Akyab)
Taunggyi
Prome
(Pye)
Henzada
Pathein
YANGON
RANGOON
Bago
Mawlamyine
Gulf of Martaban
Dawei
BANGLADESH
Chittagong
INDIA
BAY OF BENGAL
ANDAMAN SEA
ANDAMAN ISLANDS
(India)
Port Blair
Preparis North Channel
Preparis South Channel
Coco Channel
Ten Degree Channel
NICOBAR ISLANDS
(India)
Great Channel
Banda Aceh
Medan
Pematangsiantar
Padang
Pekanbaru
Jambi
Palembang
Bengkulu
Tanjungkarang-Telukbetung
SUMATERA
SUMATRA
Strait of Malacca
MALAYSIA
SEMENANJUNG MALAYSIA
George Town
(Pinang)
Ipoh
Kota Baharu
Kuala Terengganu
Kuantan
Kuala Lumpur
Melaka
Johor Baharu
SINGAPORE
KEPULAUAN RIAU
KEPULAUAN LINGGA
Pangkalpinang
PULAU BANGKA
BELITUNG
SOUTH CHINA SEA
SPRATLY ISLANDS
XISHA QUNDAO
PARACEL ISLANDS
(claimed by China, Taiwan and Vietnam)
KEPULAUAN NATUNA BESAR
BRUNEI
Bandar Seri Begawan
Kota Kinabalu
(Jesselton)
Kuching
Pontianak
BORNEO
KALIMANTAN
Balikpapan
Samarinda
Banjarmasin
Palangkaraya
GREATER SUNDA ISLANDS
INDONESIA
LAUT JAWA
JAVA SEA
JAKARTA
Bogor
BANDUNG
Cirebon
Semarang
Yogyakarta
Surakarta
Madiun
SURABAYA
Malang
Jember
JAWA
JAVA
MADURA
BALI
Denpasar
LOMBOK
Mataram
SUMBAWA
Laut Bali
Bali Sea
INDIAN OCEAN
CHRISTMAS ISLAND
(Austl.)
Equator
KEPULAUAN MENTAWAI

A-569800-264

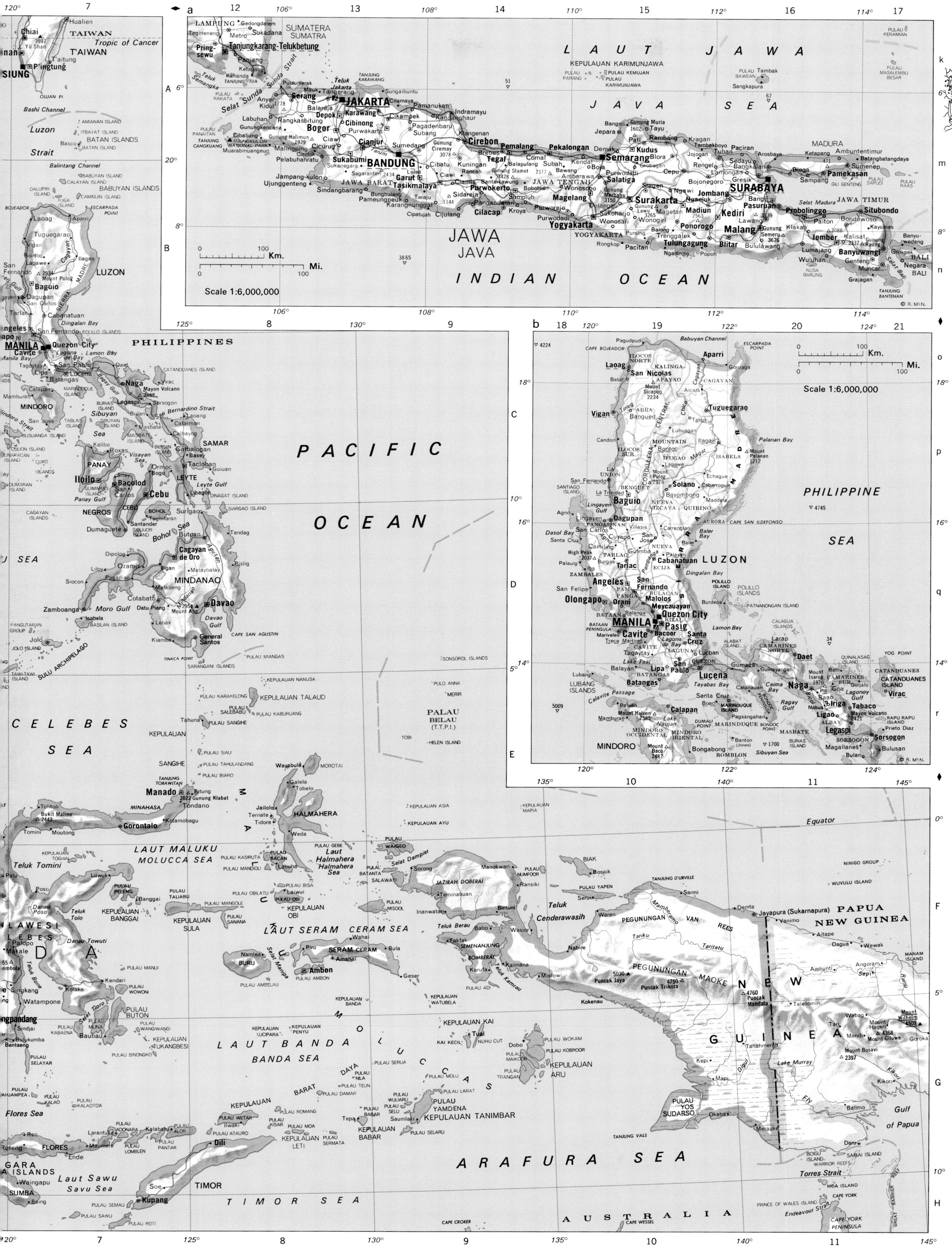

Kilometers 0 200 400 600 Km.

Statute Miles 0 200 400 600 Mi.

Scale 1:12,000,000

One centimeter represents 120 kilometers.
One inch represents approximately 190 miles.
Lambert Conformal Conic Projection

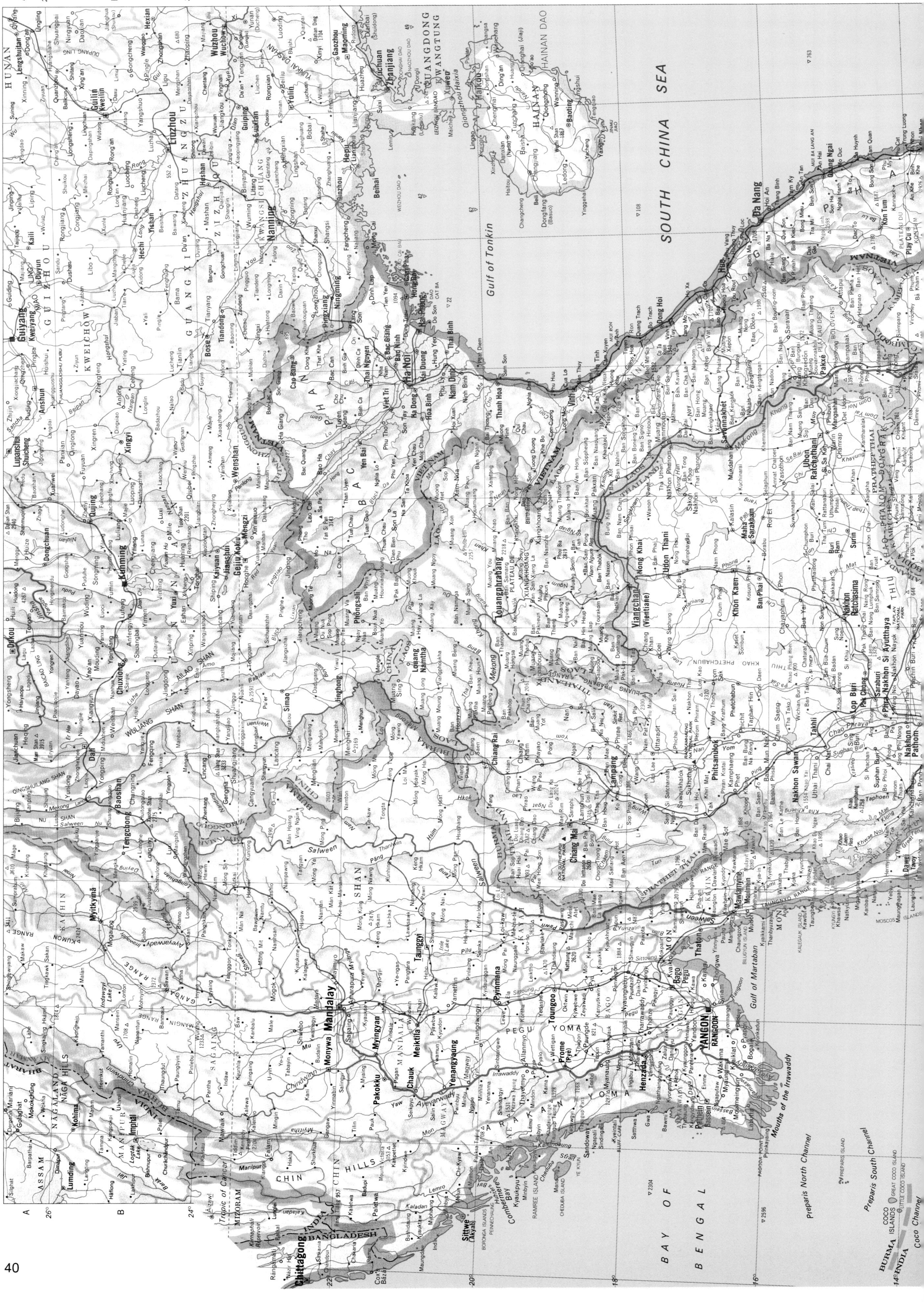
SOUTH CHINA SEA
Gulf of Tonkin
Gulf of Martaban
BAY OF BENGAL
HAINAN
HAINAN DAO
GUANGDONG
KWANGTUNG
GUIZHOU
KWEICHOW
HUNAN
YUNNAN
ASSAM
NAGALAND
MANIPUR
MIZORAM
BANGLADESH
CHIN HILLS
ARAKAN YOMA
PEGU YOMA
SHAN
KACHIN
Mandalay
Monywa
Myitkyina
Chittagong
Sittwe (Akyab)
Bassein
Henzada
Prome (Pye)
Pegu
Toungoo
Taunggyi
Pakokku
Meiktila
Mawlamyine
Moulmein
Thaton
Dawei
Kunming
Guiyang
Kweiyang
Nanning
Liuzhou
Guilin
Zhanjiang
Haikou
Hanoi
Ha Noi
Hai Phong
Nam Dinh
Thanh Hoa
Vinh
Hue
Da Nang
Dong Hoi
Luang Prabang
Viangchan (Vientiane)
Savannakhet
Pakxe
Udon Thani
Khon Kaen
Nakhon Ratchasima
Ubon Ratchathani
Chiang Mai
Chiang Rai
Lampang
Phitsanulok
Nakhon Sawan
Lop Buri
Ayutthaya
Saraburi
Nakhon Pathom
Mekong
Salween
Irrawaddy
Mouths of the Irrawaddy
Tropic of Cancer
Preparis North Channel
Preparis South Channel
Coco Channel
COCO ISLANDS
BURMA
INDIA
RAMREE ISLAND
CHEDUBA ISLAND

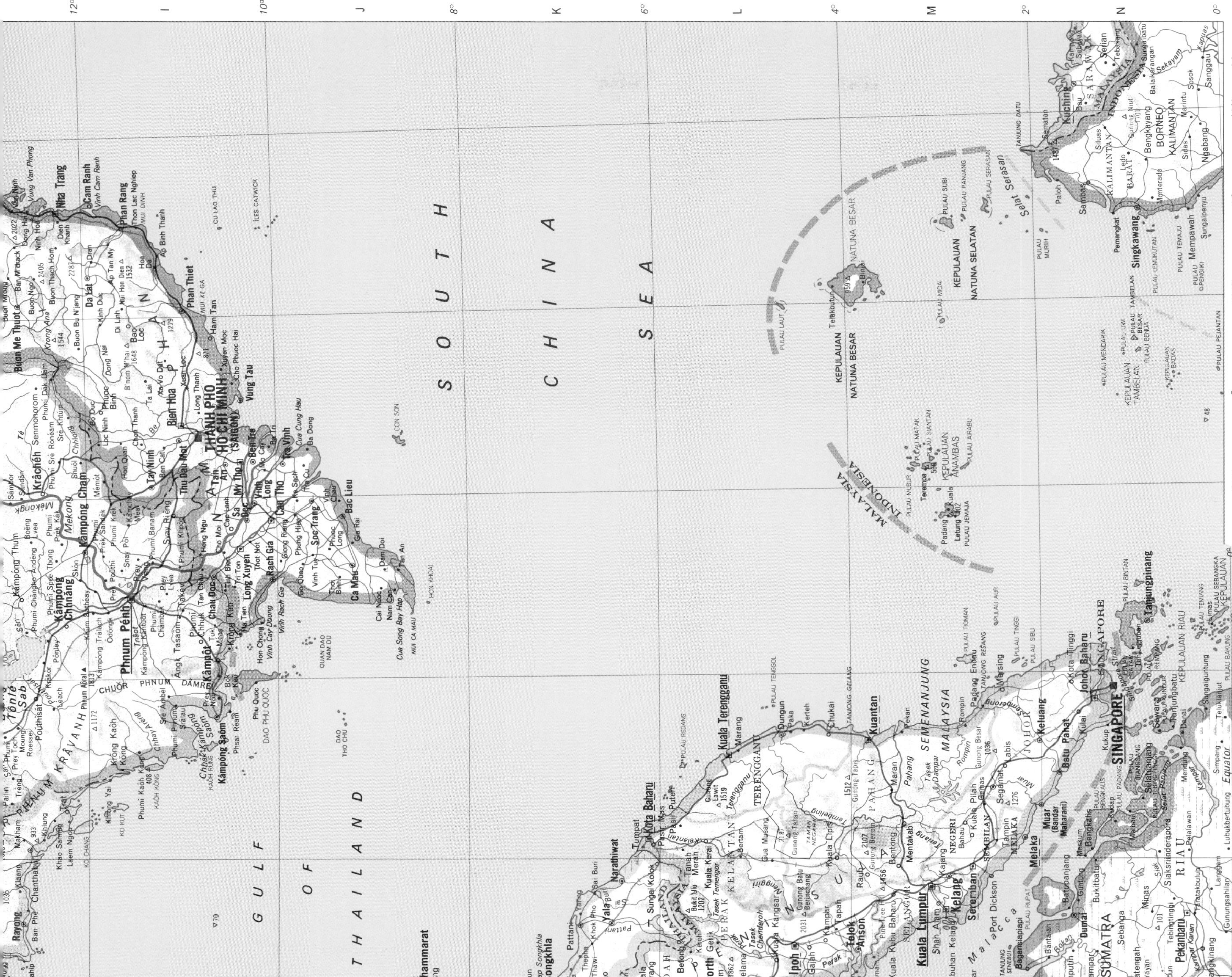

Kilometers 0 100 200 300 Km.
Statute Miles 0 100 200 300 Mi.

Scale 1:6,000,000
One centimeter represents 60 kilometers.
One inch represents approximately 95 miles.
Lambert Conformal Conic Projection

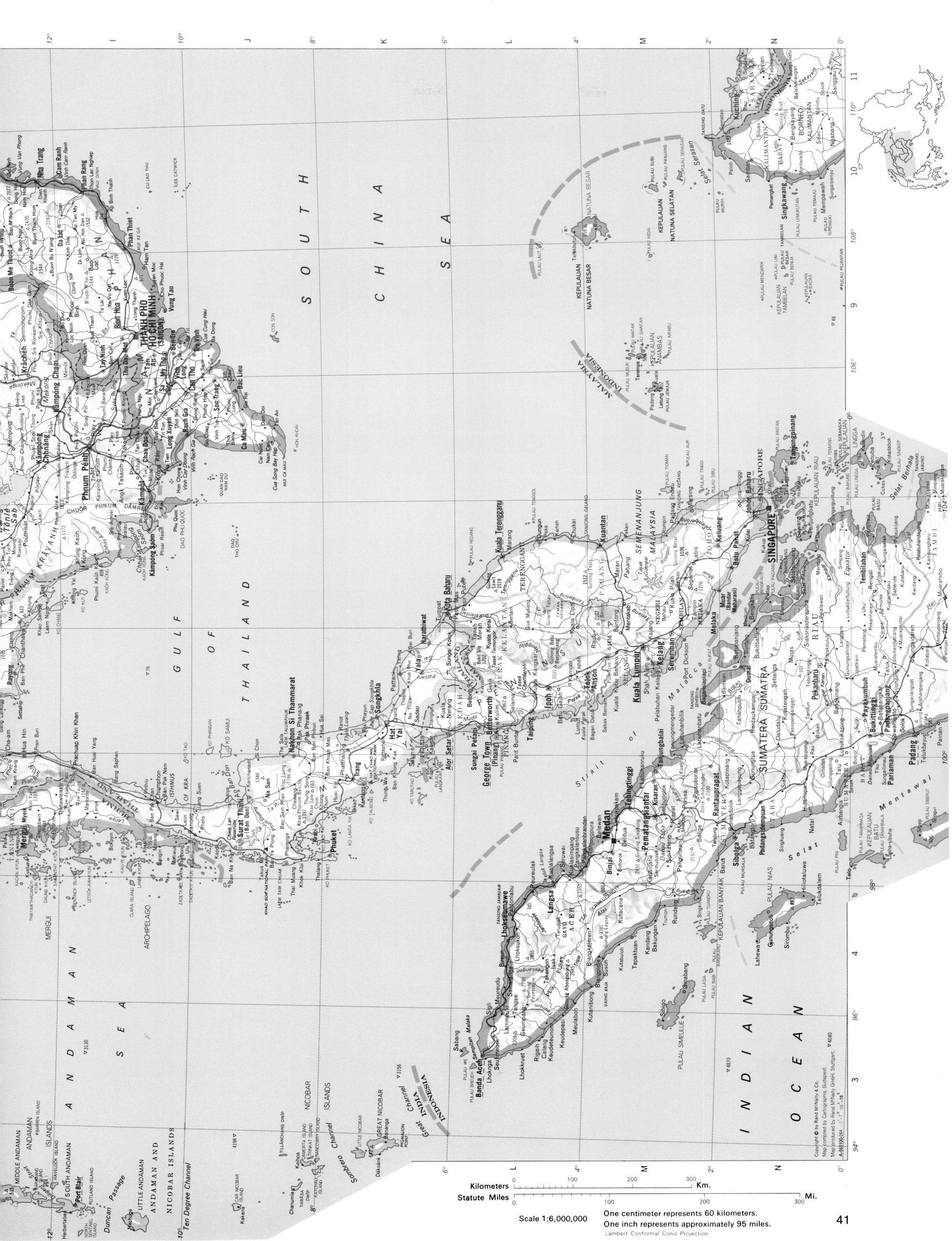

Scale 1:12,000,000
One centimeter represents 120 kilometers.
One inch represents approximately 190 miles.
Lambert Conformal Conic Projection

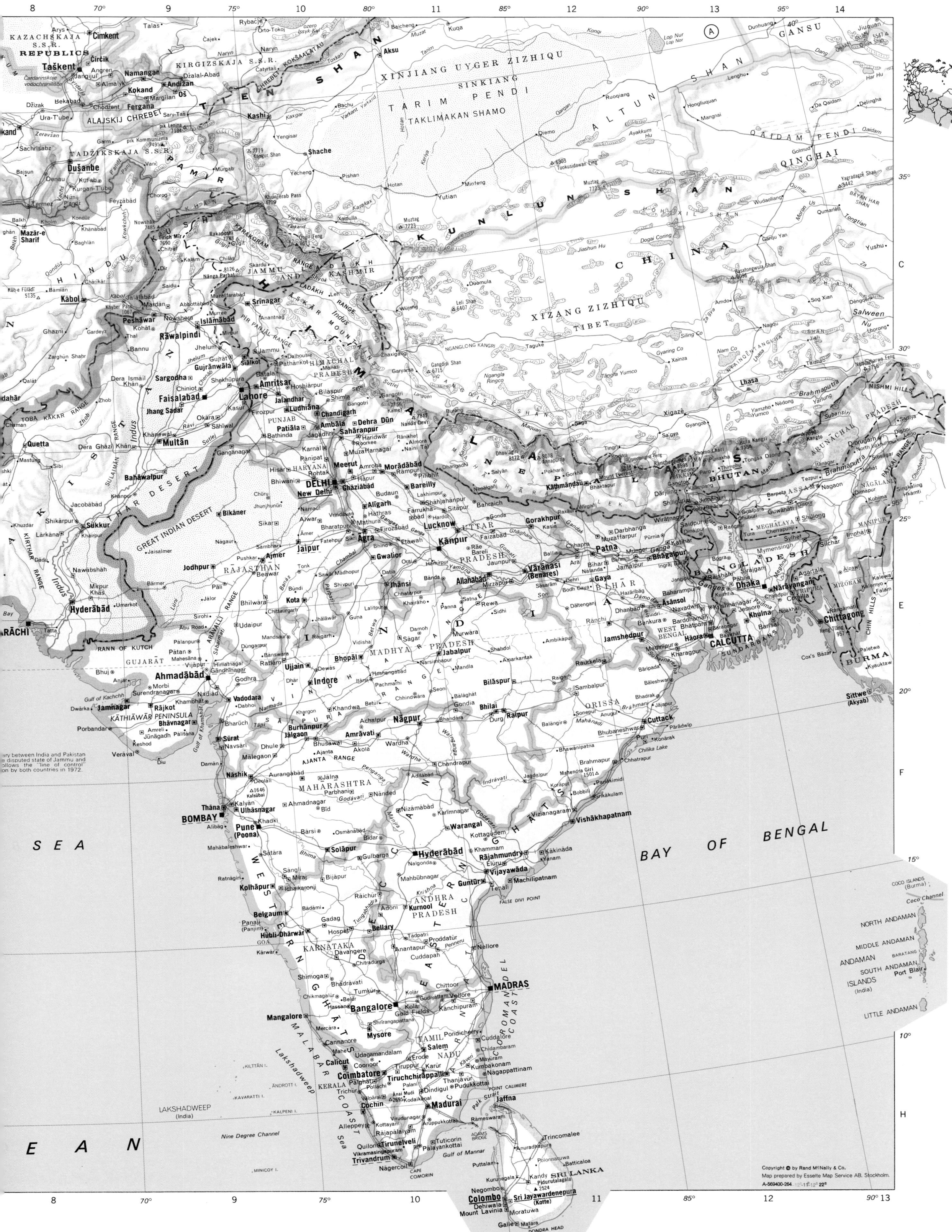
KAZACHSKAJA S.S.R.
REPUBLICS
Taškent
Cimkent
KIRGIZSKAJA S.S.R.
TADŽIKSKAJA S.S.R.
Dušanbe
ALAJSKIJ CHREBET
PAMIR
TIEN SHAN
XINJIANG UYGER ZIZHIQU
SINKIANG
TARIM PENDI
TAKLIMAKAN SHAMO
Kashi
Aksu
Lop Nur
ALTUN SHAN
QAIDAM PENDI
QINGHAI
GANSU
KUNLUN SHAN
HINDU KUSH
KARAKORAM
JAMMU AND KASHMIR
Srinagar
Kābol
Peshāwar
Islāmābād
Rawalpindi
Lahore
Amritsar
Faisalabad
Multān
Quetta
HIMALAYA
XIZANG ZIZHIQU
TIBET
CHINA
Lhasa
NEPAL
Kathmandu
BHUTAN
BANGLADESH
Dhaka
Chittagong
BURMA
Sittwe (Akyab)
PAKISTAN
THAR DESERT
GREAT INDIAN DESERT
Hyderābād
KARĀCHI
RANN OF KUTCH
Ahmadābād
RAJASTHAN
Jaipur
Jodhpur
DELHI
New Delhi
Agra
Kānpur
Lucknow
UTTAR PRADESH
Vārānasi (Benares)
Allahābād
Patna
BIHAR
WEST BENGAL
CALCUTTA
Jamshedpur
MADHYA PRADESH
Bhopāl
Indore
Jabalpur
VINDHYA RANGE
SATPURA RANGE
Nāgpur
Raipur
ORISSA
Cuttack
GUJARAT
KĀTHIĀWĀR PENINSULA
Vadodara
Sūrat
MAHARASHTRA
Nāshik
BOMBAY
Pune (Poona)
Hyderābād
Vishākhapatnam
ANDHRA PRADESH
Vijayawāda
KARNATAKA
Bangalore
MADRAS
Mysore
TAMIL NADU
Madurai
Coimbatore
Cochin
Trivandrum
KERALA
WESTERN GHATS
EASTERN GHATS
DECCAN
MALABAR COAST
COROMANDEL COAST
SEA
BAY OF BENGAL
ANDAMAN ISLANDS (India)
NORTH ANDAMAN
MIDDLE ANDAMAN
SOUTH ANDAMAN
LITTLE ANDAMAN
Port Blair
LAKSHADWEEP (India)
Nine Degree Channel
Gulf of Mannar
Palk Strait
SRI LANKA
Colombo
Sri Jayawardenepura (Kotte)
Jaffna
Trincomalee
CAPE COMORIN
OCEAN
Copyright © by Rand McNally & Co.
Map prepared by Esselte Map Service AB, Stockholm.

A Area occupied by Pakistan and claimed by India.
B Area claimed and occupied by India; status disputed by Pakistan.
C Area occupied by China and claimed by India.
D Area occupied by India and claimed by China.
ARABIAN SEA
Tropic of Cancer
RANN OF KUTCH
GREAT INDIAN DESERT
THAR DESERT
HINDU KUSH
KARAKORAM RANGE
PAMIR
KASHMIR
AFGHANISTAN
PAKISTAN
INDIA
CHINA
Kābol
Peshāwar
Islāmābād
Rāwalpindi
Lahore
Amritsar
Delhi
New Delhi
Quetta
Multān
Hyderābād
Karāchi
Ahmadābād
Jaipur
Agra
Srīnagar
Copyright © by Rand McNally & Co.
Map prepared by George Philip & Son Ltd., London.

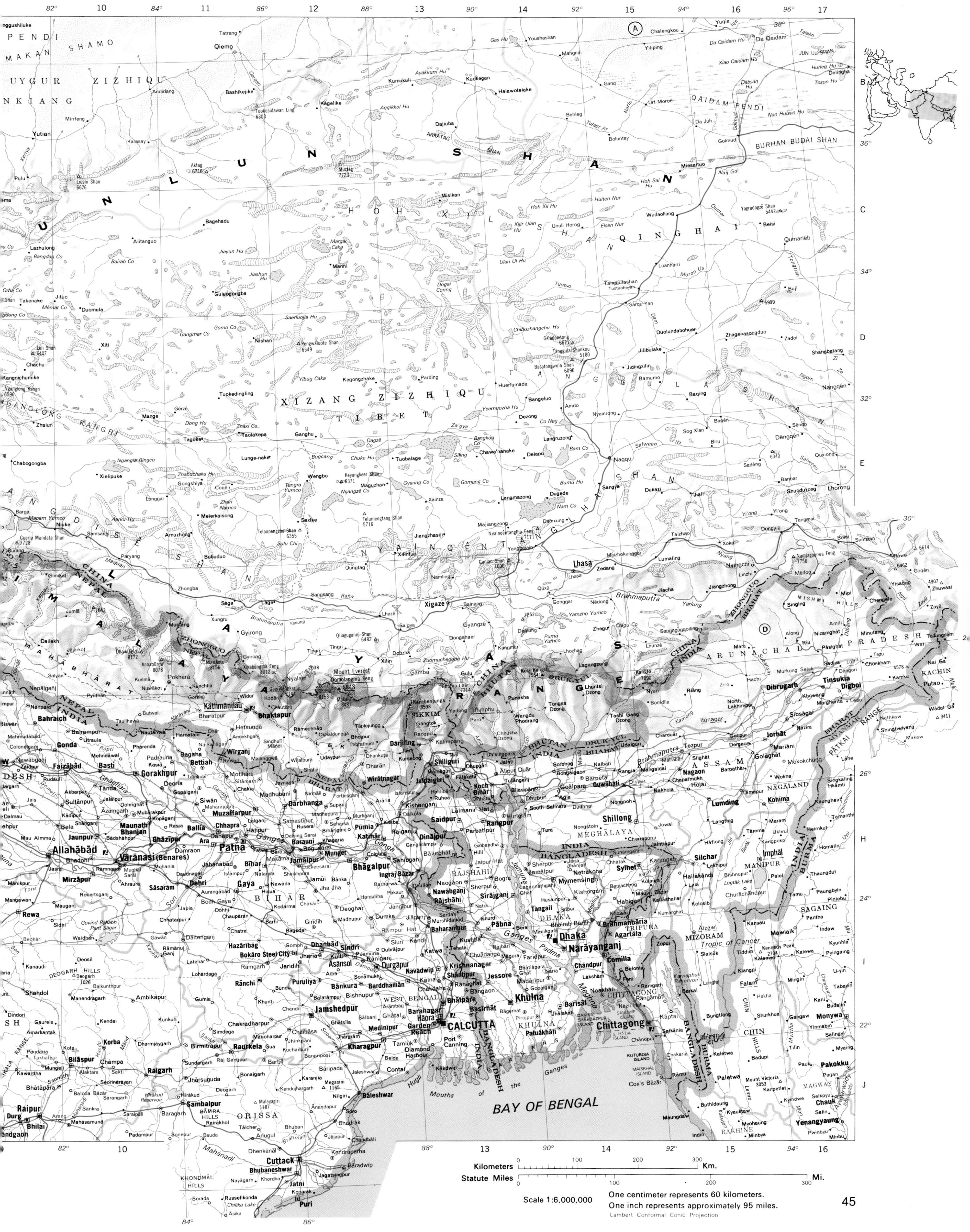

Kilometers 0 100 200 300 Km.
Statute Miles 0 100 200 300 Mi.
Scale 1:6,000,000
One centimeter represents 60 kilometers.
One inch represents approximately 95 miles.
Lambert Conformal Conic Projection

Southern India and Sri Lanka

Kilometers 0 100 200 300 Km.

Statute Miles 0 100 200 300 Mi.

Scale 1:6,000,000

One centimeter represents 60 kilometers.

One inch represents approximately 95 miles.

Lambert Conformal Conic Projection

Southern Arabian Peninsula

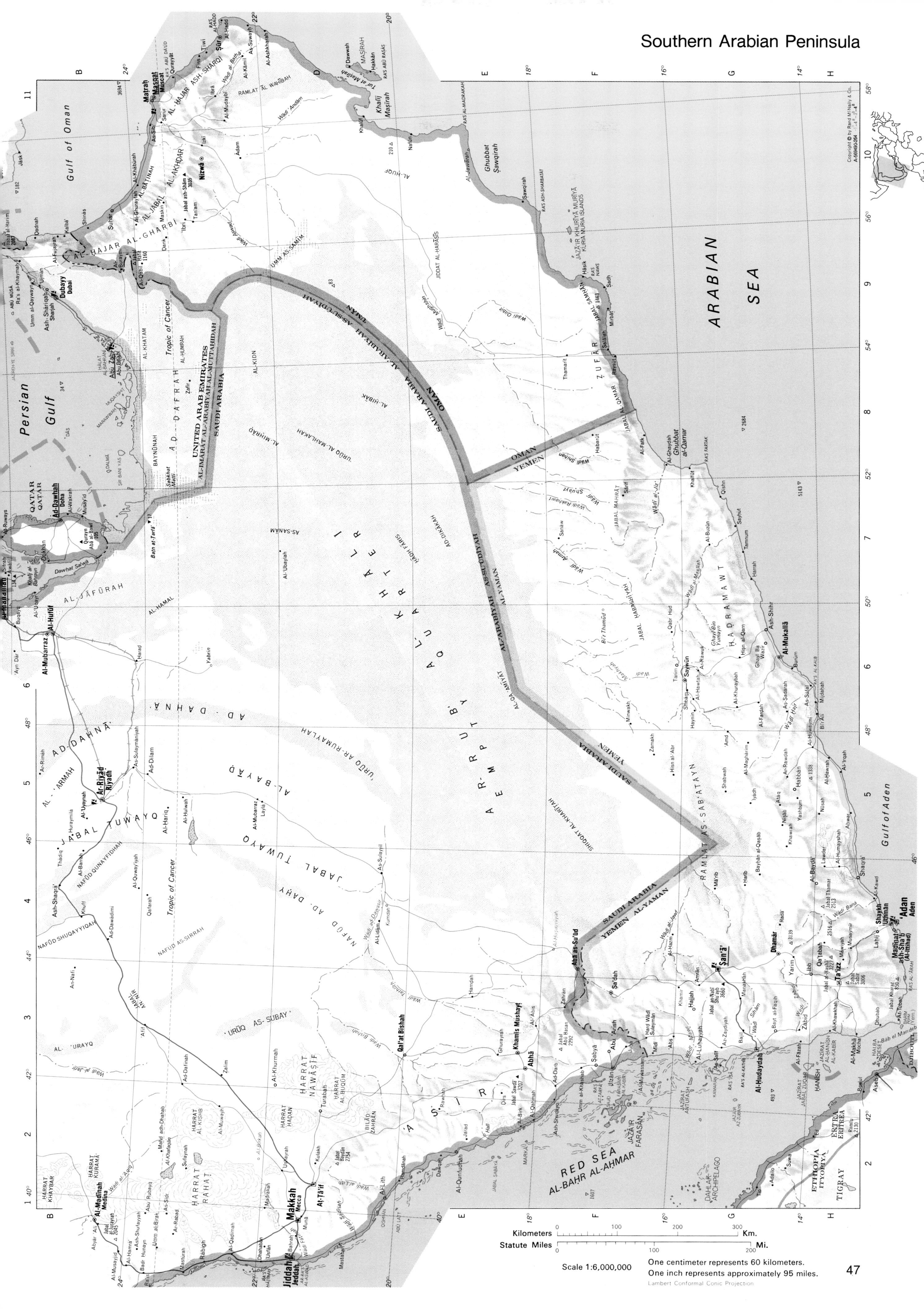

Kilometers 0 100 200 300 Km.
Statute Miles 0 100 200 Mi.

Scale 1:6,000,000

One centimeter represents 60 kilometers.
One inch represents approximately 95 miles.

Lambert Conformal Conic Projection

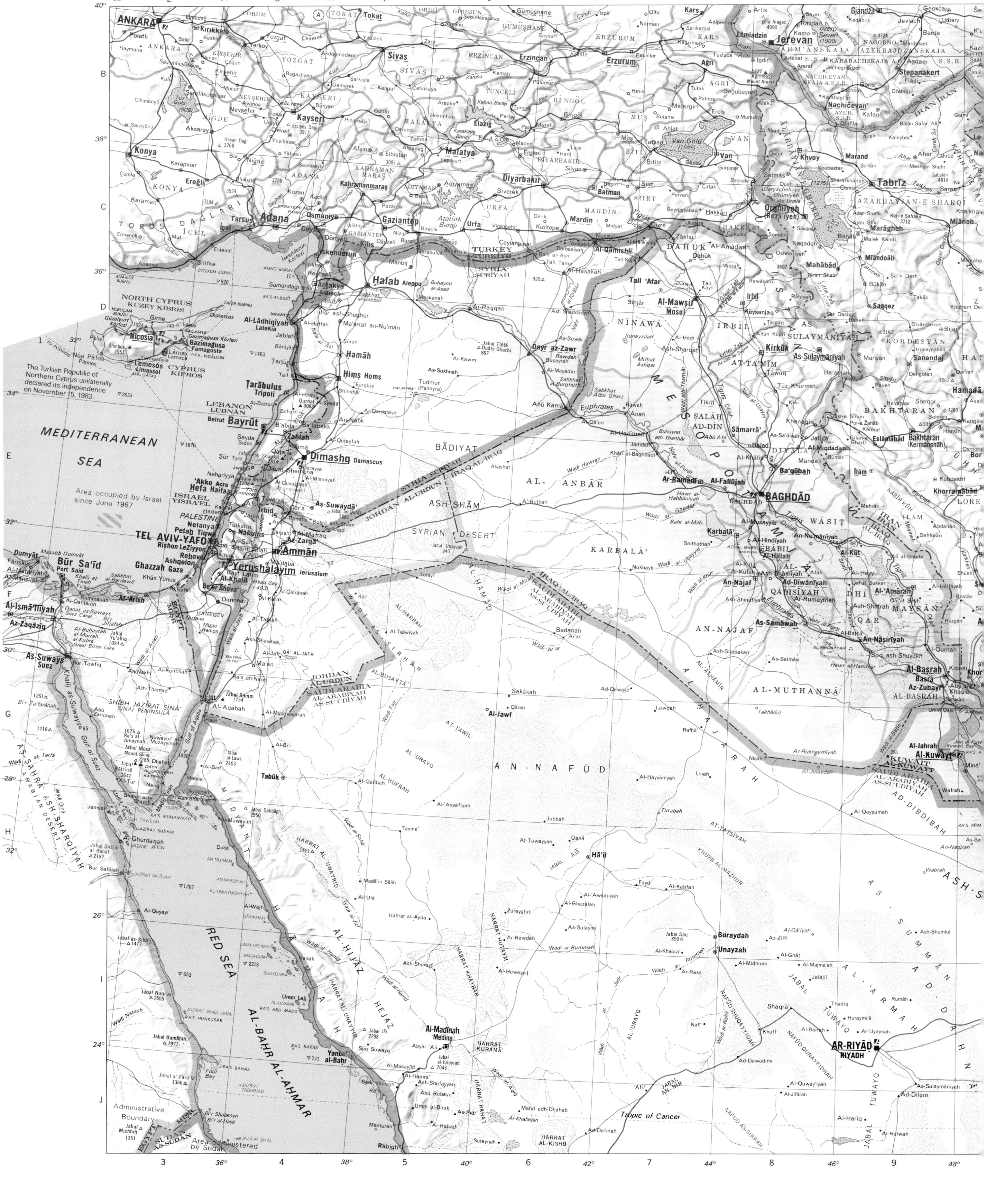
ANKARA
Konya
Adana
Kayseri
Sivas
Erzincan
Erzurum
Malatya
Diyarbakır
Gaziantep
Jerevan
Tabrīz
Halab Aleppo
Hamāh
Ḥimṣ Homs
Dimashq Damascus
Bayrūt
LEBANON
LUBNAN
NORTH CYPRUS
KUZEY KIBRIS
Nicosia
CYPRUS
KIPROS
The Turkish Republic of Northern Cyprus unilaterally declared its independence on November 15, 1983.
MEDITERRANEAN SEA
Area occupied by Israel since June 1967
ISRAEL
YISRA'EL
PALESTINE
TEL AVIV-YAFO
Yerushalayim Jerusalem
'Ammān
Būr Sa'īd Port Said
As-Suways Suez
Al-Mawṣil Mosul
Kirkūk
BAGHDĀD
Al-Baṣrah Basra
Al-Kuwayt
AR-RIYĀḌ RIYADH
Al-Madīnah Medina
Tabūk
Ḥā'il
Buraydah
'Unayzah
RED SEA
AL-BAḤR AL-AḤMAR
AL-ḤIJĀZ
HEJAZ
AN-NAFŪD
SYRIAN DESERT
BĀDIYAT ASH-SHĀM
AL-ANBĀR
Tropic of Cancer
Administrative Boundary
Area administered by Sudan
EGYPT
MIṢR
SUDAN
AS-SŪDĀN

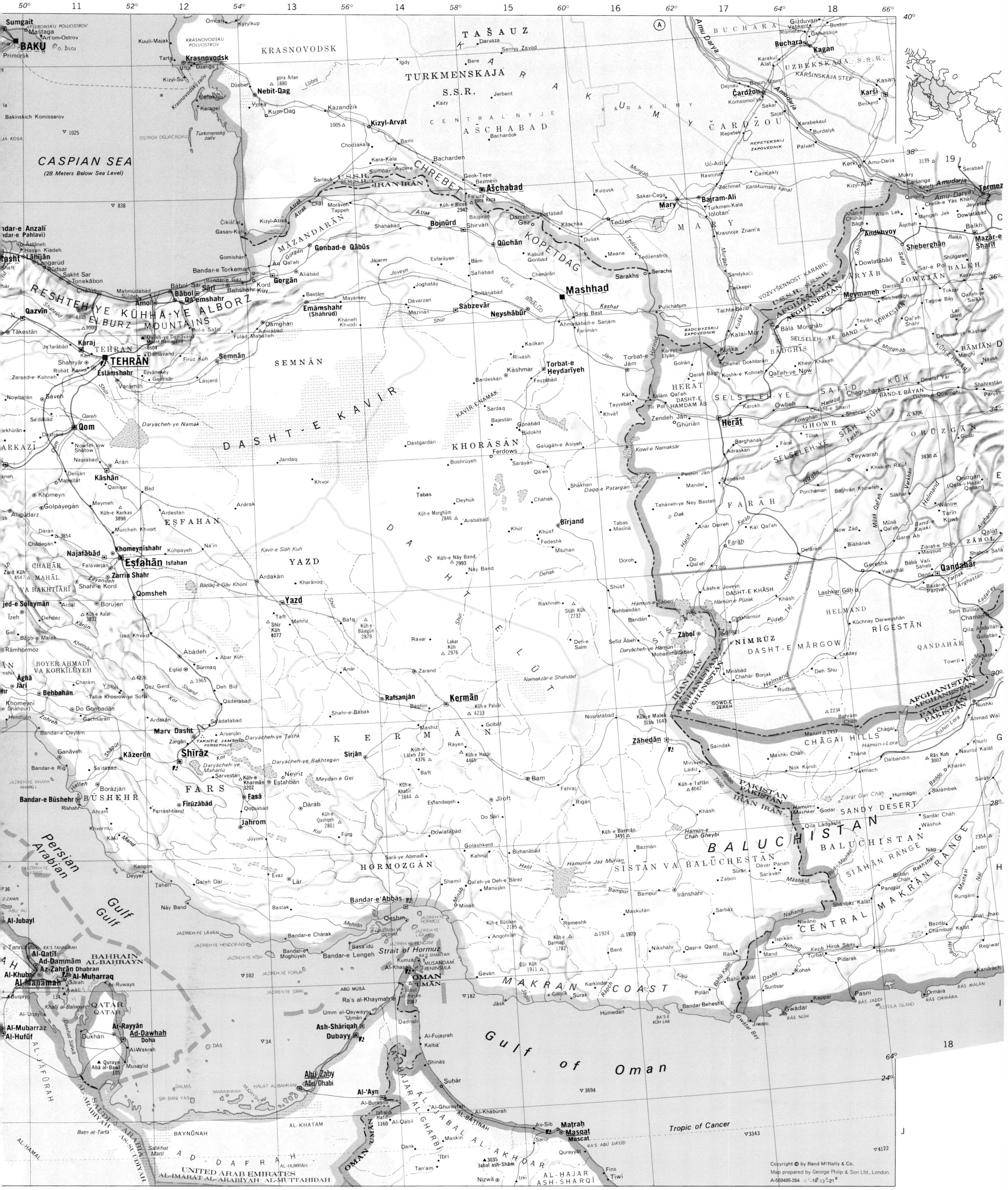

Kilometers 0 100 200 300 Km.
Statute Miles 0 100 200 300 Mi.

Scale 1:6,000,000
One centimeter represents 60 kilometers.
One inch represents approximately 95 miles.
Lambert Conformal Conic Projection

MEDITERRANEAN
SEA
Area occupied by Israel.
A Area occupied by United Nations Disengagement Observer Force since 1974.
B Golan Heights area. Occupied by Israel since 1967. Unilaterally annexed by Israel, 1981.
C West Bank area. Unilaterally annexed by Jordan, 1950. Occupied by Israel since 1967. Status to be determined.
D East Jerusalem portion of West Bank. Unilaterally annexed by Israel, 1980.
E Gaza Strip. Occupied by Israel since 1967. Status to be determined.

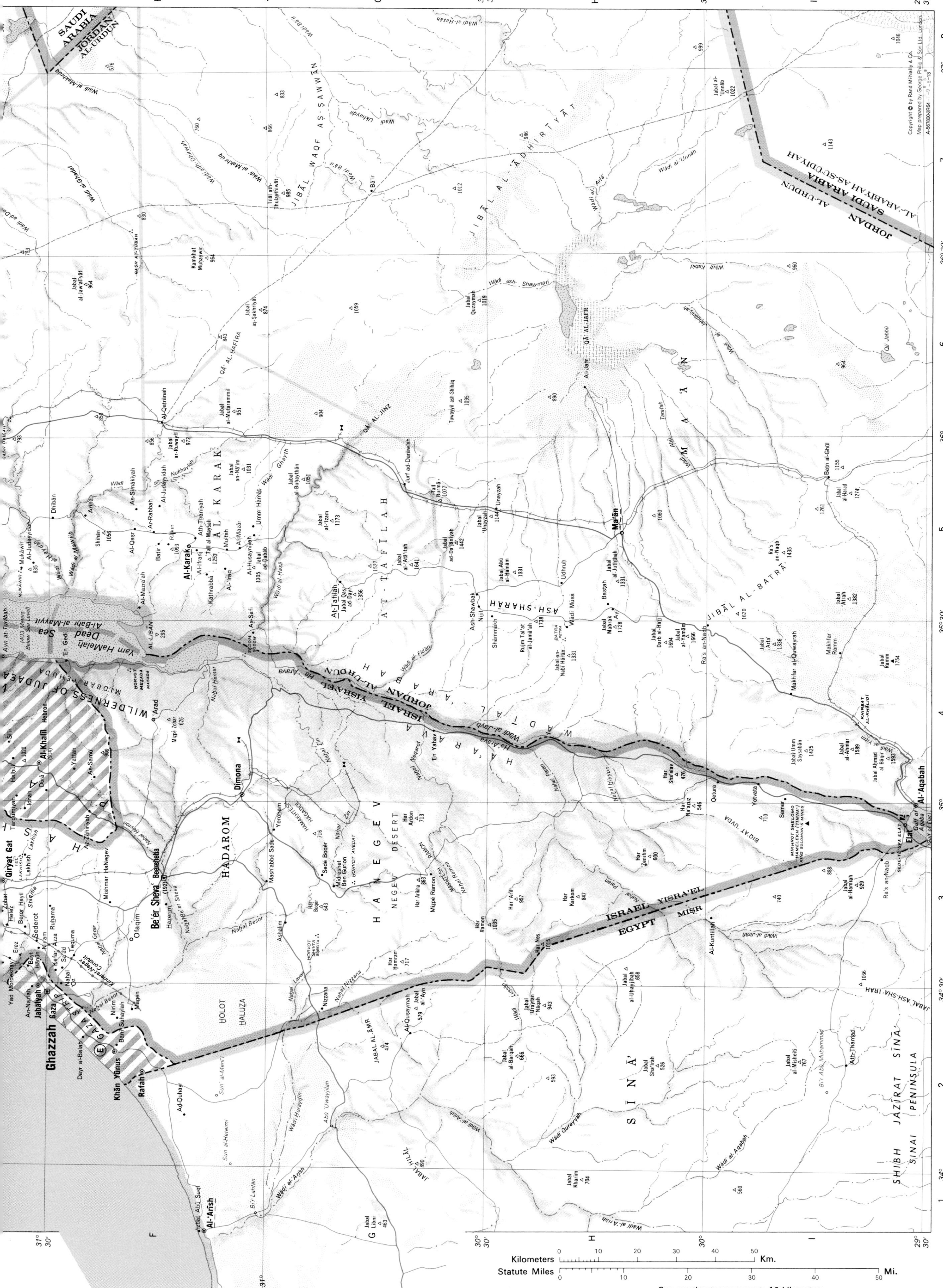

Kilometers 0 10 20 30 40 50 Km.

Statute Miles 0 10 20 30 40 50 Mi.

Scale 1:1,000,000

One centimeter represents 10 kilometers.
One inch represents approximately 16 miles.
Lambert Conformal Conic Projection

ATLANTIC OCEAN
MID-ATLANTIC RIDGE
WEST EUROPEAN BASIN
ROCKALL RISE
ICELAND BASIN
REYKJANES RIDGE
IRMINGER BASIN
LABRADOR BASIN
Labrador Sea
Davis Strait
Denmark Strait
CANADA
GREENLAND (Den.)
ICELAND
Reykjavík
NORWEGIAN BASIN
Norwegian Sea
LOFOTEN BASIN
GREENLAND BASIN
Greenland Sea
SPITSBERGEN SVALBARD (Nor.)
Barents Sea
Kara Sea
NOVAJA ZEML'A
AZORES-GIBRALTAR RIDGE
AZORES
CANARY BASIN
ISLAS CANARIAS CANARY ISLANDS (Sp.)
ARQUIPÉLAGO DA MADEIRA (Port.)
Tropic of Cancer
Arctic Circle
E U R O P E
A S I A
UNION OF SOVIET SOCIALIST REPUBLICS
URAL'SKIJE GORY URAL MOUNTAINS
ZAPADNO-SIBIRSKAJA RAVNINA
NORWAY
SWEDEN
FINLAND
DENMARK
UNITED KINGDOM
IRELAND
FRANCE
SPAIN
PORTUGAL
GERMANY
POLAND
CZECHOSLOVAKIA
AUSTRIA
HUNGARY
ROMANIA
BULGARIA
YUGOSLAVIA
ALBANIA
GREECE
ITALY
SWITZ.
TURKEY
ASIA MINOR
SYRIA
IRAQ
IRAN
SAUDI ARABIA
ARABIAN PENINSULA
JORDAN
ISRAEL
LEBANON
KUWAIT
QATAR
BAHRAIN
UNITED ARAB EMIRATES
OMAN
EGYPT
LIBYA
TUNISIA
ALGERIA
MOROCCO
WESTERN SAHARA
MAURITANIA
SAHARA
Mediterranean Sea
Black Sea
Caspian Sea
Aral'skoje more Aral Sea
Baltic Sea
North Sea
English Channel
Bay of Biscay
Adriatic Sea
Tyrrhenian Sea
Ionian Sea
Aegean Sea
Red Sea
Persian Gulf
Gulf of Oman
London
Paris
Madrid
Lisboa
Roma
Berlin
Warszawa
Praha
Wien
Budapest
Bucuresti
Beograd
Sofija
Tirane
Athinai
Moskva
Leningrad
Kijev
Stockholm
Oslo
København
Helsinki
Dublin
Amsterdam
Bruxelles
İstanbul
Ankara
Baku
Tbilisi
Jerevan
Tehrān
Baghdād
Dimashq
Bayrūt
'Ammān
Al-Qāhirah
Al-Iskandarīyah
Tarābulus
Tunis
El Djazaïr
Rabat
Casablanca
Nouakchott
Ar-Riyāḍ
Al-Kuwayt

INDIAN OCEAN
ATLANTIC OCEAN
AFRICA
Gulf of Aden
Gulf of Guinea
Bight of Benin
Bight of Biafra
Mozambique Channel
Equator
Tropic of Capricorn
SOMALIA
ETHIOPIA
DJIBOUTI
KENYA
UGANDA
RWANDA
BURUNDI
TANZANIA
MALAWI
MOZAMBIQUE
ZAMBIA
ZIMBABWE
BOTSWANA
NAMIBIA
SOUTH AFRICA
LESOTHO
SWAZILAND
TRANSKEI
CISKEI
MADAGASCAR
COMOROS
MAYOTTE (Fr.)
MAURITIUS
REUNION (Fr.)
SEYCHELLES
ANGOLA
ZAIRE
CONGO
GABON
EQUAT. GUI.
CAMEROON
CENTRAL AFRICAN REPUBLIC
NIGERIA
BENIN
TOGO
GHANA
BURKINA FASO
IVORY COAST
LIBERIA
SIERRA LEONE
GUINEA
GUINEA-BISSAU
SAO TOME AND PRINCIPE
SAINT HELENA (U.K.)
CABINDA (Angola)
Adis Abeba
Mogadisho
Nairobi
Kampala
Kigali
Bujumbura
Dar es Salaam
Lilongwe
Maputo
Harare
Lusaka
Gaborone
Windhoek
Pretoria
Maseru
Mbabane
Antananarivo
Luanda
Kinshasa
Brazzaville
Libreville
Yaoundé
Bangui
N'Djamena
Lagos
Porto-Novo
Lomé
Accra
Ouagadougou
Abidjan
Monrovia
Freetown
Conakry
Bissau
Cape Town
Johannesburg
Durban
Kalahari Desert
Namib Desert
Congo Basin
Lake Victoria
Lake Tanganyika
Lake Nyasa
Zambezi
Congo
Orange
Niger
White Nile
Blue Nile
Kilometers
Statute Miles
One centimeter represents 240 kilometers.
One inch represents approximately 380 miles.
Lambert Azimuthal Equal-Area Projection
Scale 1:24,000,000
Copyright © by Rand McNally & Co.
Map prepared by Rand McNally & Co.

Western North Africa

ATLANTIC
OCEAN
ARQUIPÉLAGO DA MADEIRA
MADEIRA ISLANDS
(Portugal)
Funchal
ISLAS CANARIAS
CANARY ISLANDS
(Spain)
Santa Cruz de Tenerife
Las Palmas de Gran Canaria
Arrecife
CAPE VERDE
Mindelo
Praia
Tropic of Cancer
Western Sahara has been occupied by Morocco
WESTERN SAHARA
El Aaiún
Laayone
Tarfaya
Dakhla
La Gouèra
Nouâdhibou
MAURITANIA
Nouakchott
Atâr
Akjoujt
Chinguetti
Tidjikja
Boutilimit
Aleg
Kiffa
Néma
Rosso
Saint-Louis
SENEGAL
Dakar
Thiès
Rufisque
Diourbel
Kaolack
Louga
Banjul
GAMBIA
Ziguinchor
GUINEA-BISSAU
Bissau
ARQUIPÉLAGO DOS BIJAGÓS
GUINEA
Conakry
Kindia
Labé
Kankan
SIERRA LEONE
Freetown
Bo
LIBERIA
Monrovia
Buchanan
Harper
IVORY COAST
Abidjan
Bouaké
Man
Daloa
Gagnoa
San-Pédro
Yamoussoukro
GHANA
Accra
Kumasi
Tamale
Sekondi-Takoradi
Cape Coast
BURKINA FASO
Ouagadougou
Bobo Dioulasso
Ouahigouya
MALI
Bamako
Ségou
Mopti
Tombouctou
Timbuktu
Kayes
Sikasso
Niger
MOROCCO
Rabat
Casablanca
Dar-el-Beida
Mohammedia
Kenitra
Salé
Meknès
Fès
Marrakech
Safi
El-Jadida
Essaouira
Agadir
Sidi Ifni
Tanger
Tangier
Tétouan
Ceuta (Sp.)
Gibraltar (U.K.)
Strait of Gibraltar
Málaga
SPAIN
Oujda
Melilla
Béchar
ATLAS
ANTI-ATLAS
HAMADA DU DRA'A
Tindouf
SAHARA
Taoudenni
Arawane
Equator
Copyright © by Rand McNally & Co.
Map prepared by Esselte Map Service AB, Stockholm.

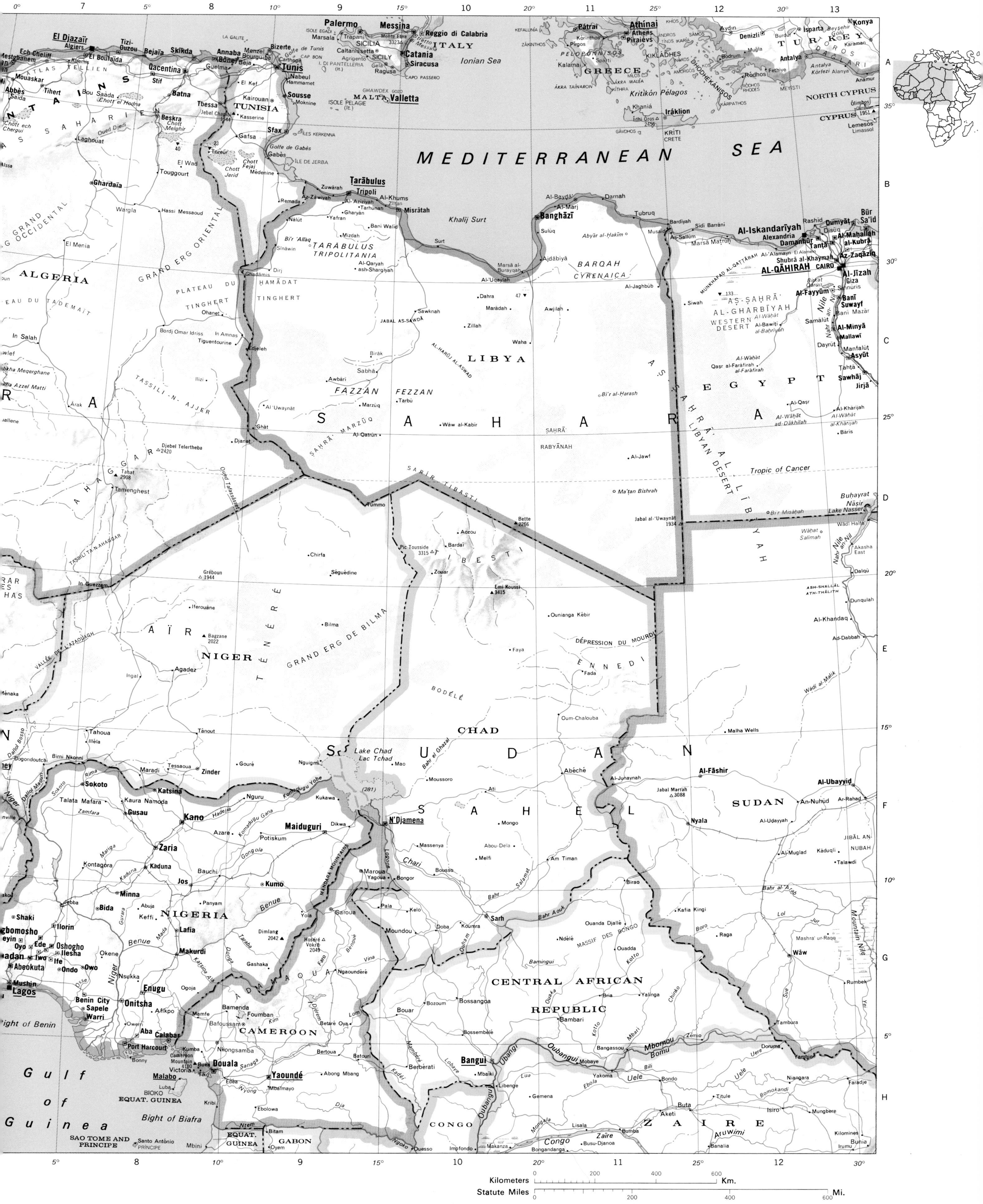

One centimeter represents 120 kilometers.
One inch represents approximately 190 miles.

Eastern North Africa

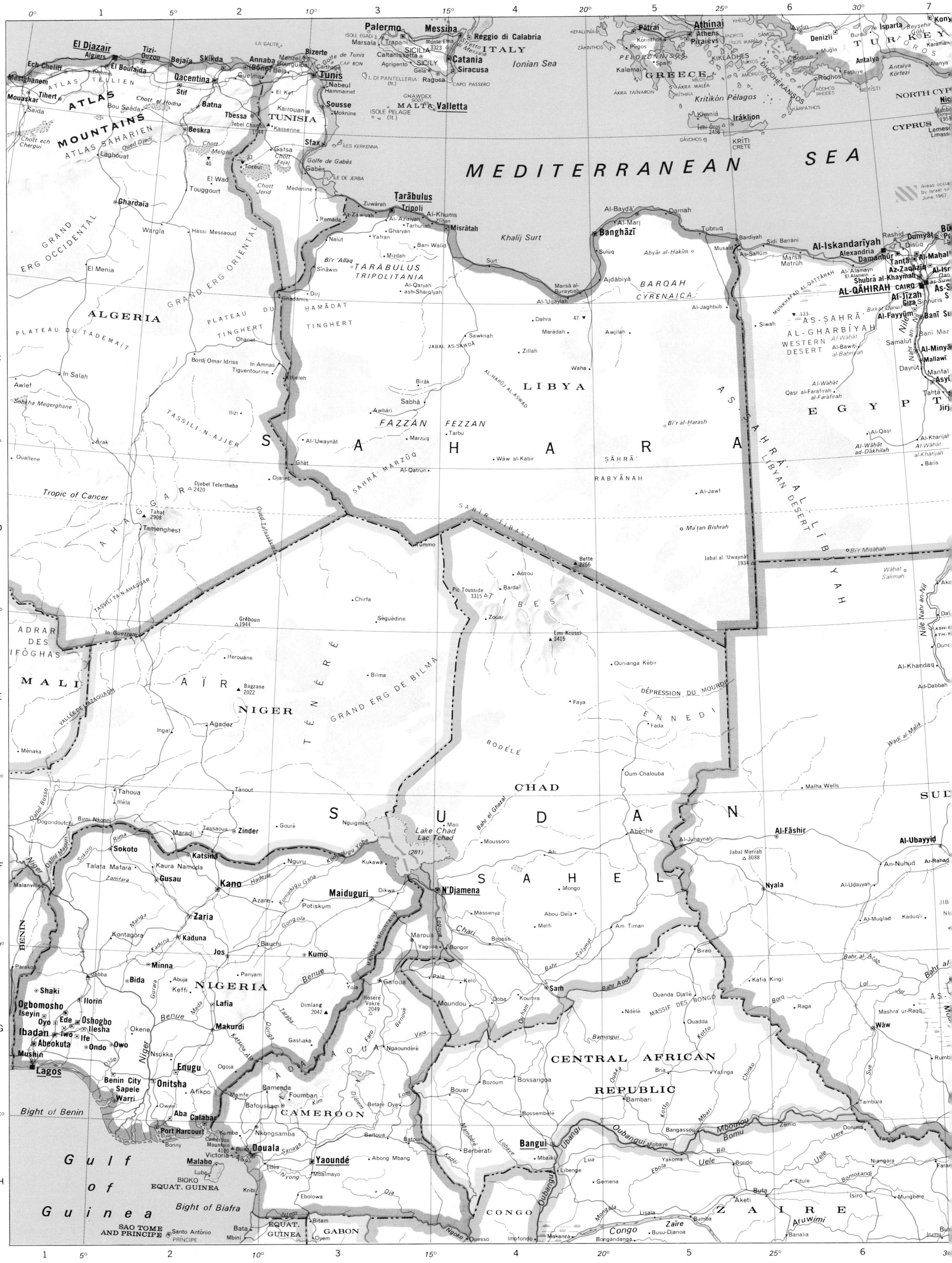

MEDITERRANEAN SEA
Ionian Sea
Khalij Surt
Kritikón Pélagos
Gulf of Guinea
Bight of Benin
Bight of Biafra
Golfe de Gabès
ITALY
SICILIA
GREECE
TURKEY
CYPRUS
TUNISIA
ALGERIA
LIBYA
EGYPT
NIGER
MALI
CHAD
NIGERIA
BENIN
CAMEROON
CENTRAL AFRICAN REPUBLIC
CONGO
GABON
ZAIRE
SUDAN
EQUAT. GUINEA
SAO TOME AND PRINCIPE
SAHARA
SUDAN
SAHEL
ATLAS MOUNTAINS
GRAND ERG OCCIDENTAL
GRAND ERG ORIENTAL
GRAND ERG DE BILMA
TÉNÉRÉ
TIBESTI
AÏR
ENNEDI
BODÉLÉ
AHAGGAR
TASSILI-N-AJJER
ADRAR DES IFÔGHAS
ADAMAOUA
FAZZAN
FEZZAN
TARABULUS
TRIPOLITANIA
BARQAH
CYRENAICA
WESTERN DESERT
LIBYAN DESERT
Tropic of Cancer
El Djazaïr
Algiers
Tunis
Tarābulus
Tripoli
Banghāzī
Al-Iskandarīyah
Alexandria
AL-QĀHIRAH
CAIRO
Valletta
Palermo
Messina
Catania
Athínai
Athens
N'Djamena
Lake Chad
Lac Tchad
Kano
Lagos
Ibadan
Yaoundé
Douala
Bangui
Malabo
Niamey
Agadez
Zinder
Maiduguri
Sokoto
Kaduna
Zaria
Jos
Enugu
Port Harcourt
Sarh
Abéché
Al-Fāshir
Nyala
Sabhā
Ghāt
Misrātah
Sfax
Sousse
Bizerte
Annaba
Qacentina
Tamenghest
Ghardaïa
In Salah
Faya
Bilma
Mao
Moundou
Garoua
Tropic of Cancer
0°
5°
10°
15°
20°
25°
30°
35°
1
2
3
4
5
6
7
B
D
G

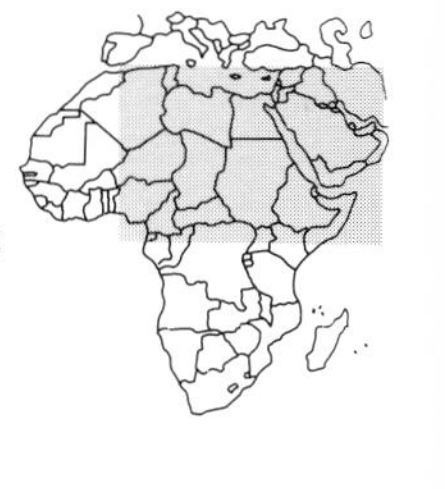

Kilometers 0 200 400 600 Km.

Statute Miles 0 200 400 600 Mi.

Scale 1:12,000,000 One centimeter represents 120 kilometers.
One inch represents approximately 190 miles.
Miller Oblated Stereographic Projection

SAO TOME AND PRINCIPE
São Tomé
Libreville
EQUATORIAL GUINEA
GABON
Port Gentil
ANNOBÓN (Equat. Gui.)
CONGO
Brazzaville
KINSHASA (LÉOPOLDVILLE)
Pointe-Noire
CABINDA (Angola)
Boma
Matadi
Mbandaka (Coquilhatville)
Kisangani (Stanleyville)
Z A I R E
Kananga (Luluabourg)
Mbuji-Mayi (Bakwanga)
Kikwit
Bandundu
Kigali
RWANDA
BURUNDI
Bujumbura
Bukavu
Lake Tanganyika
Kalemie (Albertville)
KATANGA
Kolwezi
Likasi (Jadotville)
Lubumbashi (Elisabethville)
Luanda
A N G O L A
Lobito
Benguela
Huambo (Nova Lisboa)
Malanje
Namibe
Lubango
ATLANTIC
OCEAN
ZAMBIA
Kitwe
Ndola
Chingola
Kabwe (Broken Hill)
Lusaka
Livingstone
Lake Kariba
ZIMBABWE
Bulawayo
Gweru
CAPRIVI ZIPFEL
OVAMBOLAND
Etosha Pan
Tsumeb
N A M I B I A
Windhoek
DAMARALAND
Swakopmund
Walvis Bay (S. Afr.)
Tropic of Capricorn
N A M I B D E S E R T
KAOKO VELD
OKAVANGO DELTA
B O T S W A N A
K A L A H A R I
D E S E R T
Gaborone
GREAT NAMAQUALAND
Keetmanshoop
Lüderitz
Orange
BUSHMAN LAND
BOPHUTHATSWANA
Pretoria
JOHANNESBURG
Kimberley
Bloemfontein
LESOTHO
Maseru
S O U T H
A F R I C A
TRANSKEI
CISKEI
GREAT KARROO
Cape Town
Kaapstad
Port Elizabeth
East London
Pietermaritzburg
CAPE OF GOOD HOPE
CAPE AGULHAS

Kilometers 0 200 400 600 Km.
Statute Miles 0 200 400 600 Mi.

Scale 1:12,000,000
One centimeter represents 120 kilometers.
One inch represents approximately 190 miles.
Miller Oblated Stereographic Projection

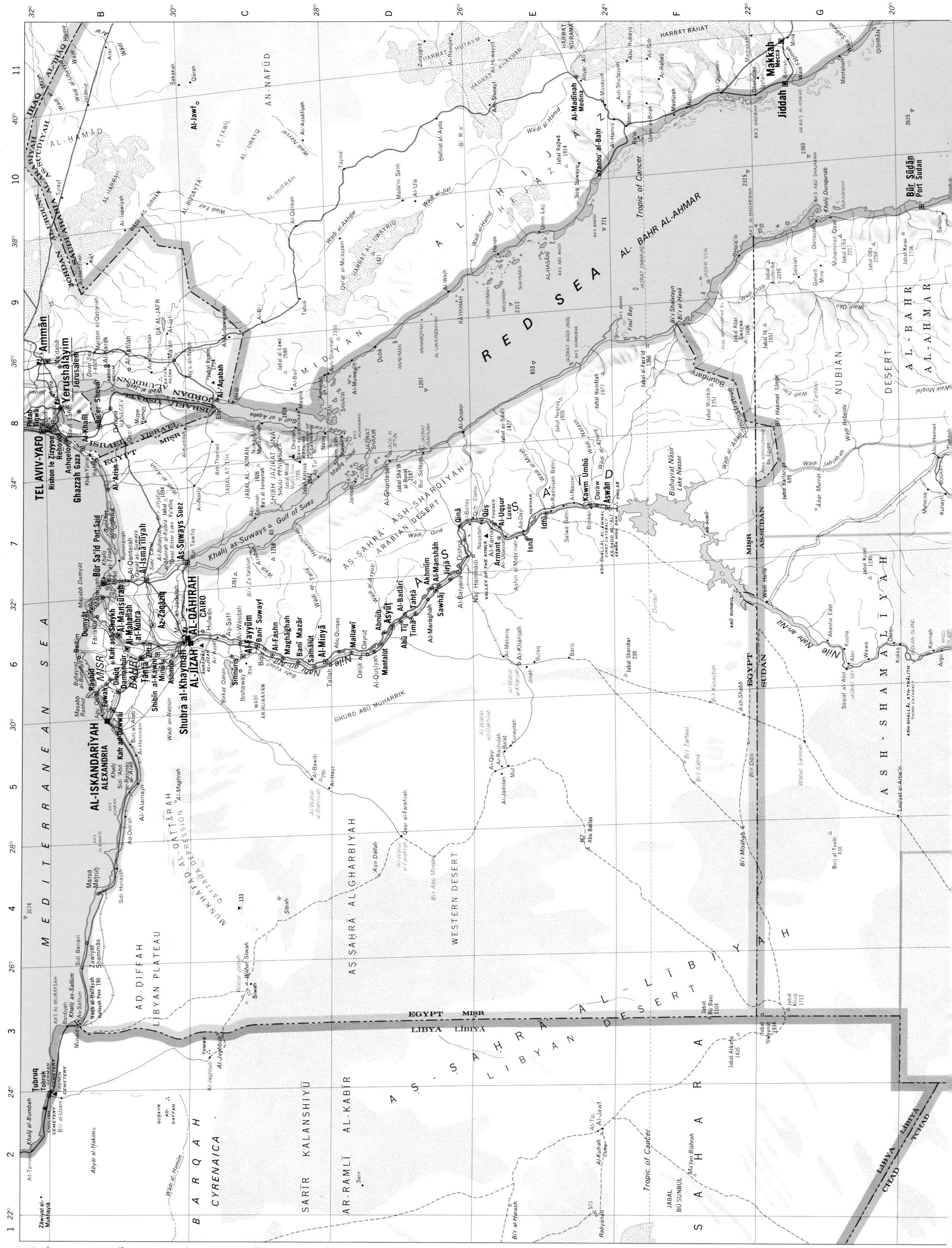
MEDITERRANEAN SEA
RED SEA
AL-BAHR AL-AHMAR
AL-QAHIRAH
CAIRO
AL-ISKANDARĪYAH
ALEXANDRIA
AL-JIZAH
Shubrā al-Khaymah
Būr Sa'īd Port Said
As-Suways Suez
Gulf of Suez
Al-Minyā
Asyūṭ
Aswān
Luxor
Qinā
Lake Nasser
Jiddah
Makkah
Mecca
Būr Sūdān
Port Sudan
Al-Madīnah
Medina
TEL AVIV-YAFO
Yerushalayim
Jerusalem
'Ammān
Tropic of Cancer
WESTERN DESERT
LIBYAN PLATEAU
BARQAH
CYRENAICA
SAHARA
NUBIAN
DESERT
AN-NAFŪD
EGYPT
SUDAN
LIBYA
CHAD

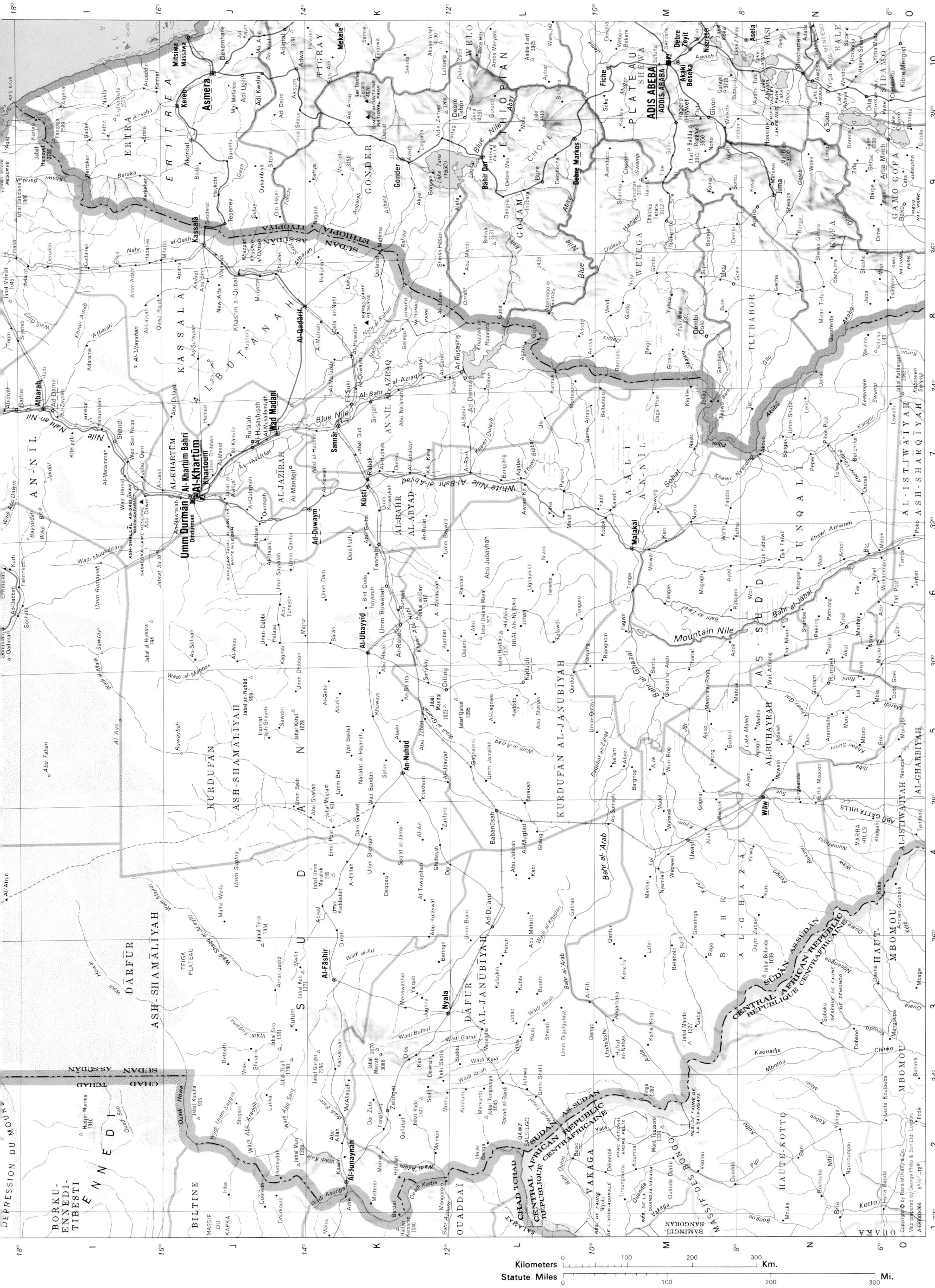

Scale 1:6,000,000

One centimeter represents 60 kilometers.

One inch represents approximately 95 miles.

Lambert Azimuthal Equal-Area Projection

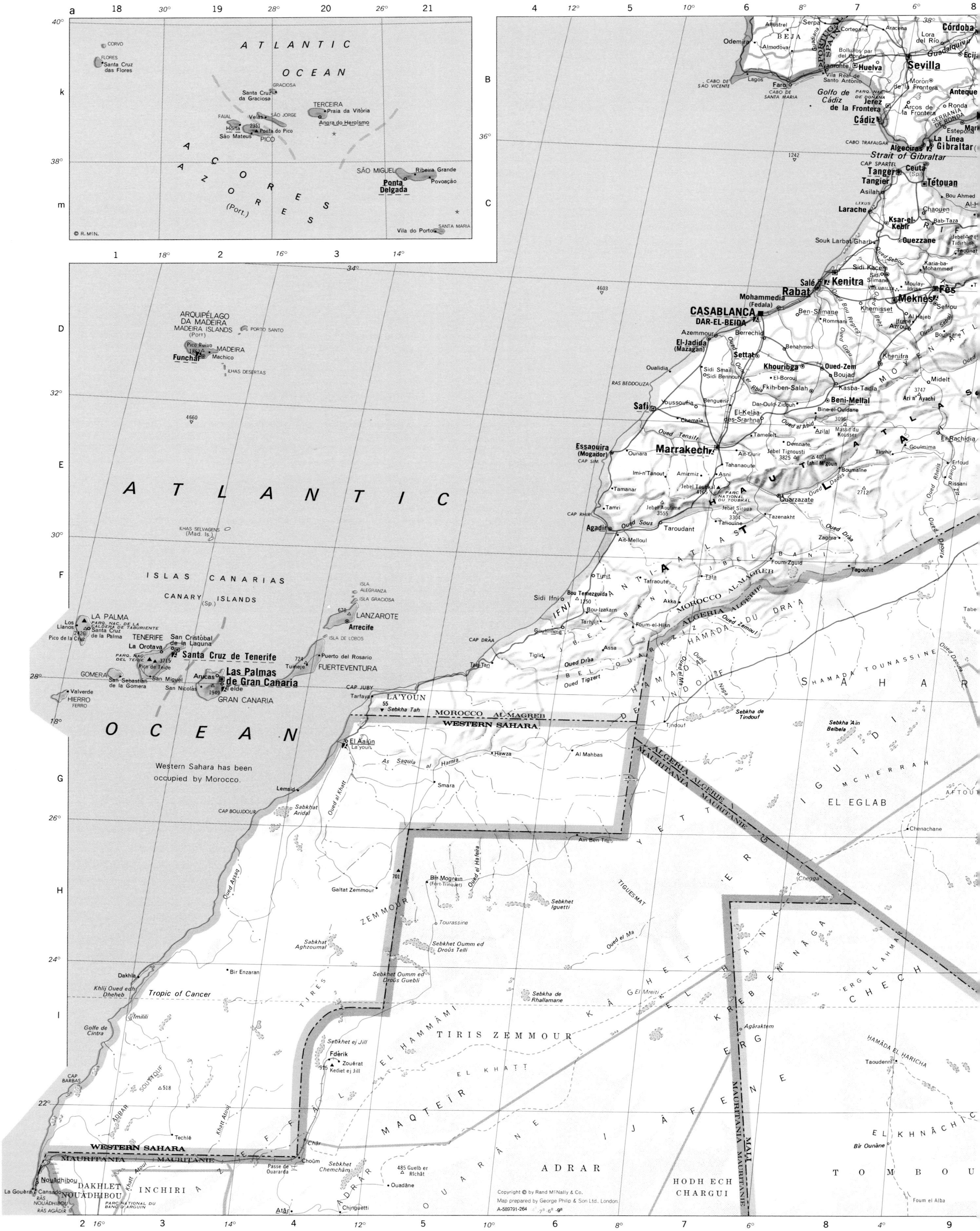

ATLANTIC OCEAN
AÇORES (Port.)
CORVO
FLORES
Santa Cruz das Flores
GRACIOSA
Santa Cruz da Graciosa
TERCEIRA
Praia da Vitória
Angra do Heroísmo
FAIAL
Horta
SÃO JORGE
Velas
PICO
São Mateus
SÃO MIGUEL
Ribeira Grande
Ponta Delgada
Povoação
SANTA MARIA
Vila do Porto
ATLANTIC OCEAN
ARQUIPÉLAGO DA MADEIRA
MADEIRA ISLANDS (Port.)
PORTO SANTO
Pico Ruivo
MADEIRA
Funchal
Machico
ILHAS DESERTAS
ILHAS SELVAGENS (Mad. Is.)
ISLAS CANARIAS
CANARY ISLANDS (Sp.)
LA PALMA
Los Llanos
Santa Cruz de la Palma
TENERIFE
San Cristóbal de la Laguna
La Orotava
Santa Cruz de Tenerife
Pico de Teide
GOMERA
San Sebastián de la Gomera
HIERRO
Valverde
GRAN CANARIA
Las Palmas de Gran Canaria
Arucas
Telde
San Nicolás
San Miguel
LANZAROTE
Arrecife
ISLA DE LOBOS
FUERTEVENTURA
Puerto del Rosario
Tuineje
ISLA ALEGRANZA
ISLA GRACIOSA
Western Sahara has been occupied by Morocco.
Tropic of Cancer
CAP JUBY
Tarfaya
LA'YOUN
El Aaiún
MOROCCO AL-MAGREB
WESTERN SAHARA
MAURITANIA
MAURITANIE
ALGERIA ALGÉRIE
Sebkha Tah
As Saquia al Hamra
Hawza
Al Mahbas
Smara
Lemsid
CAP BOUJDOUR
Sabkhat Aridal
Oued Assag
Galtat Zemmour
Bir Mogrein (Fort-Trinquet)
Oued el Hafeira
ZEMMOUR
Sebkhet Iguetti
Tourassine
Sebkhet Oumm ed Droûs Telli
Sebkhet Oumm ed Droûs Guebli
Sabkhat Aghzoumal
Dakhla
Khlij Oued edh Dheheb
Bir Enzaran
Imlili
Golfe de Cintra
CAP BARBAS
SOUTTOUF
ADRAR
Techlé
WESTERN SAHARA
MAURITANIA
MAURITANIE
Nouâdhibou
La Gouèra
Cansado
RÂS NOUÂDHIBOU
RÂS AGÂDIR
DAKHLET NOUÂDHIBOU
PARC NATIONAL DU BANC D'ARGUIN
INCHIRI
Sebkhet ej Jill
Fdérik
Zouérat
Kediet ej Jill
Choûm
Passe de Ouarâda
Sebkhet Chemchâm
Guelb er Rîchât
Ouadâne
Chinguetti
Atâr
TIRIS ZEMMOUR
EL HAMMÂMI
EL KHATT
MAQTEÏR
OUARÂNE
ADRAR
HODH ECH CHARGUI
IJÂFENE
KHNÂCHICH
TOMBOUCTOU
Bîr Ounâne
Foum el Alba
Taoudenni
HAMÂDA EL HARICHA
Agârâktem
EL MREITI
ERG CHECH
Sebkha de Rhallamane
TIGUESMAT
Oued el Ma
ERG IGUIDI
EL EGLAB
Chenachane
Chegga
YETTI
HAMADA DU DRA'A
HAMADA TOUNASSINE
Tindouf
Sebkha de Tindouf
Sebkha 'Ain Belbela
MCHERRAH
SAHARA
Oued Drâa
JBEL OUARKZIZ
Oued Tigzert
Tiglit
Assa
Foum-el-Hisn
Akka
Tata
Foum-Zguid
Tagounit
Zagora
JBEL BANI
ANTI-ATLAS
IFNI
Sidi Ifni
Tiznit
Bou Tamezguida
Goulimine
Tan-Tan
CAP DRÂA
Tafraoute
Agadir
Aït-Melloul
Taroudant
Oued Sous
Tazenakht
Jebel Siroua
Tamri
CAP RHIR
Tamanar
Essaouira (Mogador)
CAP SIM
Marrakech
Ounara
Chemaïa
Safi
Youssoufia
Oualidia
RAS BEDDOUZA
El-Kelaa-des-Srarhna
Benguerir
Tamelelt
Demnate
Azilal
Jebel Toubkal
PARC NATIONAL DU TOUBKAL
Asni
Amizmiz
Imi-n'Tanout
Tahanaoute
Aït-Ourir
Jebel Tignousti
Irhil M'goun
Ouarzazate
Boumalne
Tinerhir
Goulmima
Er-Rachidia
Erfoud
Rissani
HAUT ATLAS
MOYEN ATLAS
Beni-Mellal
Kasba-Tadla
Boujad
Oued-Zem
Khouribga
Fkih-ben-Salah
Settat
Benahmed
El-Jadida (Mazagan)
Azemmour
Berrechid
CASABLANCA
DAR-EL-BEIDA
Mohammedia (Fedala)
Rabat
Salé
Kenitra
Ben-Slimane
Rommani
Khemisset
Meknès
Fès
Sefrou
Ifrane
Azrou
Khenifra
Midelt
Ari n' Ayachi
Sidi Kacem
Sidi Slimane
Moulay-Idriss
Souk Larbat Gharb
Ouezzane
Ksar-el-Kebir
Larache
Asilah
Tanger
Tangier
Tétouan
Ceuta (Sp.)
Chaouen
Bab-Taza
RIF
CAP SPARTEL
Strait of Gibraltar
Gibraltar
La Línea
Algeciras
Estepona
CABO TRAFALGAR
Cádiz
Jerez de la Frontera
Arcos de la Frontera
Ronda
SERRANÍA DE RONDA
Golfo de Cádiz
Sevilla
Morón de la Frontera
Antequera
Córdoba
Lora del Río
Guadalquivir
Huelva
Bollullos par del Condado
Ayamonte
Vila Real de Santo António
Faro
Lagos
CABO DE SÃO VICENTE
CABO DE SANTA MARIA
PORTUGAL
SPAIN
BEJA
Odemira
Almodôvar
Aljustrel
Serpa
Cortegana
Aracena
Copyright © by Rand McNally & Co.
Map prepared by George Philip & Son Ltd. London.
A-589791-264

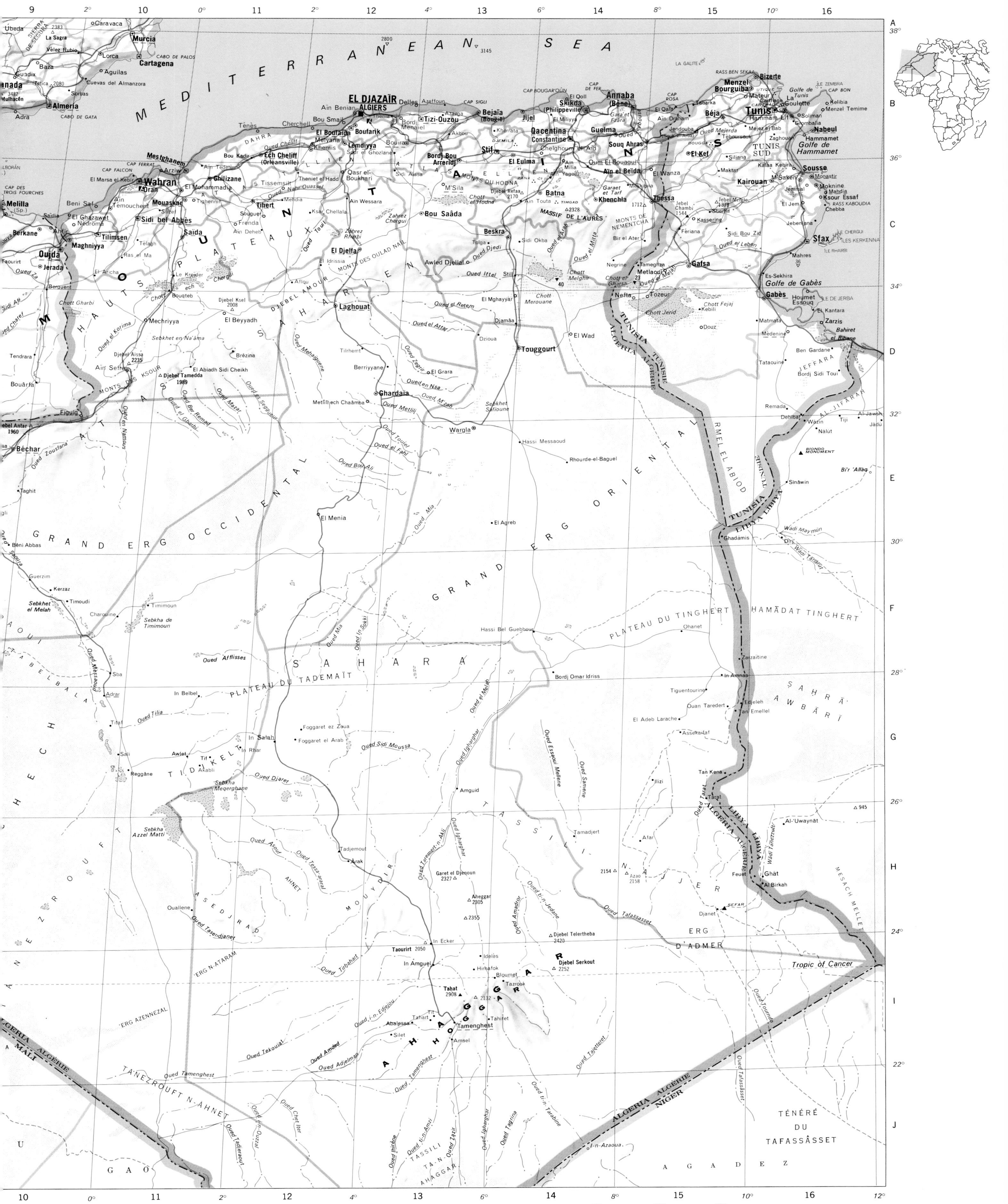

Kilometers 0 100 200 300 Km.

Statute Miles 0 100 200 300 Mi.

Scale 1:6,000,000

One centimeter represents 60 kilometers.

One inch represents approximately 95 miles.

Lambert Azimuthal Equal-Area Projection

ATLANTIC OCEAN
GRAIN COAST
IVORY COAST
Dakar
Banjul (Bathurst)
Bissau
Conakry
Freetown
Monrovia
Bamako
Nouakchott
Abidjan
Saint-Louis
Thiès
Kaolack
Ziguinchor
Kayes
Ségou
Sikasso
Bouaké
Yamoussoukro
Kankan
Bo
Man
San Pédro
Atâr
Tidjikja
Kiffa
Kaédi
Rosso
Nouâmghâr
Oualâta
Néma
Tambacounda
Labé
Kindia
Koidu
Kenema
Buchanan
Harper
Korhogo
Daloa
Gagnoa
DAKHLET NOUADHIBOU
INCHIRI
ADRAR
TAGANT
TRARZA
BRAKNA
GORGOL
GUIDIMAKA
ASSABA
HODH EL GHARBI
HODH ECH CHARGUI
SAINT-LOUIS
LOUGA
THIÈS
DIOURBEL
KAOLACK
FERLO
TAMBACOUNDA
KOLDA
KAYES
KOULIKORO
SÉGOU
SIKASSO
NORTHERN
EASTERN
SOUTHERN
WESTERN AREA
MALI
MAURITANIA MAURITANIE
SENEGAL SÉNÉGAL
GAMBIA
GUINEA-BISSAU GUINÉ-BISSAU
GUINEA GUINÉE
SIERRA LEONE
LIBERIA
IVORY COAST CÔTE D'IVOIRE
FOUTA DJALON
ARQUIPÉLAGO DOS BIJAGÓS
CAPE VERDE CABO VERDE
SANTO ANTÃO
SÃO VICENTE
SÃO NICOLAU
SAL
BOA VISTA
MAIO
SANTIAGO
FOGO
BRAVA
Praia
Mindelo
Copyright © by Rand McNally & Co.
Map prepared by George Philip & Son Ltd., London.

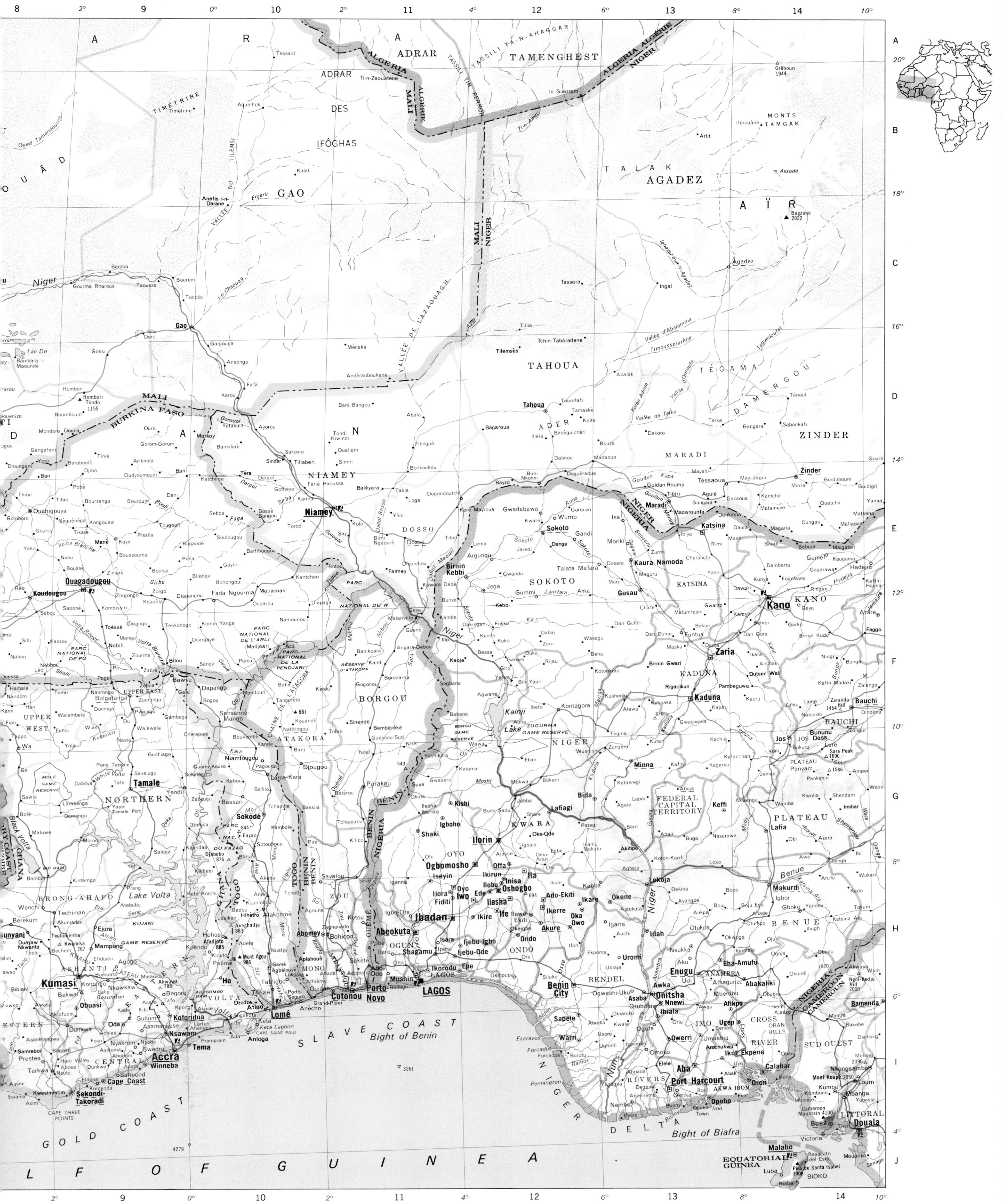

Kilometers 0 100 200 300 Km.

Statute Miles 0 100 200 300 Mi.

Scale 1:6,000,000

One centimeter represents 60 kilometers.

One inch represents approximately 95 miles.

Lambert Azimuthal Equal-Area Projection

Kilometers 0 100 200 300 Km.

Statute Miles 0 100 200 300 Mi.

Scale 1:6,000,000

One centimeter represents 60 kilometers.

One inch represents approximately 95 miles.

Lambert Azimuthal Equal-Area Projection

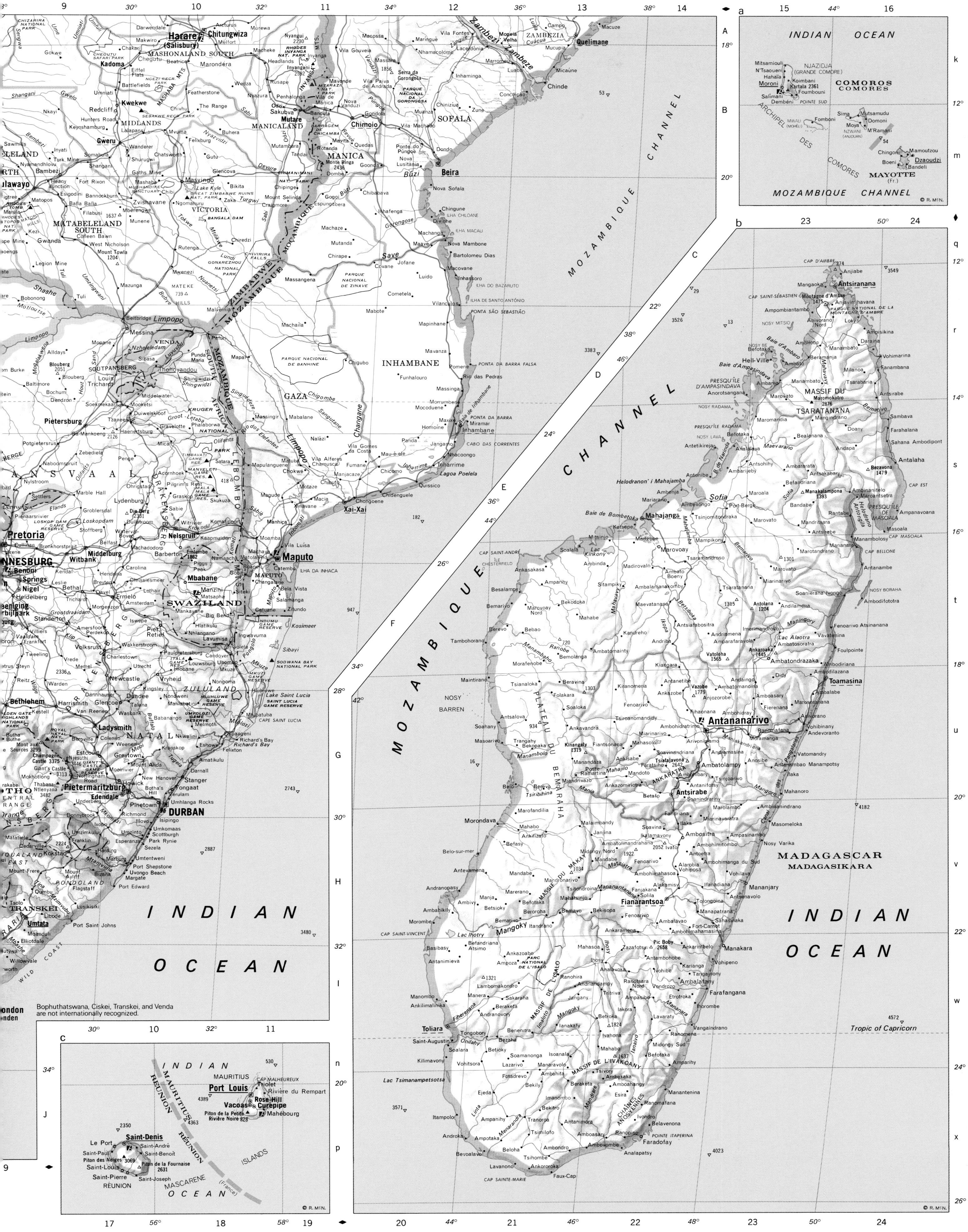

INDIAN OCEAN
MOZAMBIQUE CHANNEL
MADAGASCAR
MADAGASIKARA
Antananarivo
Toamasina
Mahajanga
Antsiranana
Fianarantsoa
Toliara
Antsirabe
Morondava
Manakara
Farafangana
Taolanaro
Tropic of Capricorn
MASSIF DU TSARATANANA
PLATEAU DU BEMARAHA
MASSIF DE L'ISALO
MASSIF DE L'IVAKOANY
CHAÎNE ANOSYENNES
PRESQU'ÎLE DE MASOALA
PRESQU'ÎLE D'AMPASINDAVA
CAP SAINT-ANDRÉ
CAP SAINTE-MARIE
CAP SAINT-VINCENT
CAP D'AMBRE
CAP EST
CAP MASOALA
CAP BELLONE
Sofia
Betsiboka
Mangoky
Onilahy
Lac Alaotra
NOSY BARREN
NOSY BORAHA
INDIAN OCEAN
NJAZIDJA (GRANDE COMORE)
COMOROS
COMORES
Moroni
Fomboni
Mutsamudu
Domoni
Dzaoudzi
MAYOTTE (Fr.)
ARCHIPEL DES COMORES
MOZAMBIQUE CHANNEL
MOZAMBIQUE
ZIMBABWE
SOUTH AFRICA
SWAZILAND
Harare (Salisbury)
Chitungwiza
Kadoma
Kwekwe
Gweru
Masvingo
Mutare
Bulawayo
MASHONALAND SOUTH
MIDLANDS
MANICALAND
VICTORIA
MATABELELAND SOUTH
Quelimane
Beira
Chimoio
Maputo
Xai-Xai
Inhambane
Zambezi
Save
Limpopo
MANICA
SOFALA
ZAMBÉZIA
INHAMBANE
GAZA
MAPUTO
Pretoria
Witbank
Middelburg
Nelspruit
Mbabane
Manzini
Pietersburg
Ladysmith
Pietermaritzburg
DURBAN
Umtata
TRANSKEI
NATAL
ZULULAND
PONDOLAND
WILD COAST
Lake Saint Lucia
INDIAN OCEAN
Bophuthatswana, Ciskei, Transkei, and Venda are not internationally recognized.
INDIAN OCEAN
MAURITIUS
Port Louis
Rose-Hill
Curepipe
Vacoas
Mahébourg
Saint-Denis
Le Port
Saint-Pierre
Saint-Louis
Saint-Paul
Saint-Benoît
Saint-André
Saint-Joseph
RÉUNION
Piton des Neiges 3069
Piton de la Fournaise 2631
MASCARENE ISLANDS
OCEAN
(France)
© R. McN.

PACIFIC OCEAN
Km.
Mi.
Equator
PULAU WAIGEO
Selat Dampier
Sorong
Manokwari
KEPULAUAN SCHOUTEN
BIAK
PULAU NUMFOOR
PULAU YAPEN
TANJUNG D'URVILLE
SALAWATI
PULAU MISOOL
Teluk Berau
Teluk Cenderawasih
Fakfak
SERAM
Bula
Kaimana
Jayapura (Sukarnapura)
NINIGO GROUP
HERMIT ISLANDS
MUSSAU ISLAND
ADMIRALTY ISLANDS
MANUS ISLAND
NEW HANOVER
Kavieng
NEW IRELAND
BISMARCK ARCHIPELAGO
Aitape
Wewak
Sepik
Rabaul
Namatanai
PEGUNUNGAN MAOKE
Puncak Jaya 5030m
Puncak Trikora 4750m
KEPULAUAN BANDA
PULAU ADI
INDONESIA
KEPULAUAN KAI
KAI KECIL
Dobo
PULAU WOKAM
KEPULAUAN ARU
PULAU KOBROOR
NEW GUINEA
Mt. Giluwe 4368m
Mt. Wilhelm 4509m
Madang
KARKAR ISLAND
UMBOI ISLAND
WITU ISLANDS
Talasea
PAPUA NEW GUINEA
Lae
NEW BRITAIN
PULAU YAMDENA
PULAU TRANGAN
KEPULAUAN TANIMBAR
PULAU SELARU
Digul
Strickland
Fly
Huon Gulf
Arafura Sea
TANJUNG VALS
Merauke
Gulf of Papua
Morobe
Popondetta
KIRIWINA ISLANDS
Torres Strait
Port Moresby
OWEN STANLEY RANGE
MOA ISLAND
CAPE YORK
MELVILLE ISLAND
CROKER ISLAND
WESSEL ISLANDS
Gulf of Carpentaria
GREAT BARRIER REEF
Coral Sea
Samarai
D'ENTRECASTEAUX ISLANDS
BATHURST ISLAND
Van Diemen Gulf
Darwin
AUSTRALIA
A-592200-264-1-1-1-2
©1979 R.McN.
Laut Sawu
Savu Sea
TIMOR
Soe
Kupang
PULAU SEMAU
PULAU ROTI
Timor Sea
HIBERNIA REEF
ASHMORE ISLANDS
CARTIER ISLANDS (Austl.)
MELVILLE ISLAND
CAPE CROKER
COBOURG PENINSULA
BATHURST ISLAND
Van Diemen Gulf
Beagle Gulf
Clarence Strait
Darwin
Humpty Doo
ARNHEM
POINT BLAZE
Rum Jungle
Pine Creek
Daly
Katherine
Joseph Bonaparte Gulf
CAPE LONDONDERRY
BROWSE ISLAND
Admiralty Gulf
BONAPARTE ARCHIPELAGO
York Sound
Queens Channel
Wyndham
Kununurra
Ord
Victoria
Lake Argyle
Victoria River Downs
Daly Waters
ADÈLE ISLAND
BEAGLE REEF
Collier Bay
BUCCANEER ARCHIPELAGO
CAPE LEVEQUE
Drysdale
KIMBERLEY PLATEAU
DURACK RANGES
KING LEOPOLD RANGES
Mount Ord 937
King Sound
Derby
Fitzroy Crossing
Halls Creek
Wave Hill
ROWLEY SHOALS
Broome
Fitzroy
CAPE LATOUCHE TREVILLE
La Grange
NORTHERN TERRITORY
TANAMI DESERT
Lake Gregory
EIGHTY MILE BEACH
INDIAN OCEAN
Port Hedland
Goldsworthy
Shay Gap
GREAT SANDY DESERT
De Grey
MONTE BELLO ISLANDS
DAMPIER ARCHIPELAGO
Dampier
Karratha
Roebourne
Marble Bar
Lake White
Lake Wills
Lake Mackay
BARROW ISLAND
Nullagine
Lake Dora
Lake Auld
MUIRON ISLANDS
Onslow
Pannawonica
Fortescue
Wittenoom
HAMERSLEY RANGE
NORTH WEST CAPE
Exmouth
Exmouth Gulf
Mount Brockman 1132
Mount Bruce 1235
Tom Price
Mount Meharry 1251
Paraburdoo
Ashburton
Lake Disappointment
Lake Macdonald
Mount Leisler 897
Mount Liebig 1524
MACDONNELL RANGES
POINT CLOATES
Newman
Savory Cr.
WESTERN AUSTRALIA
GIBSON DESERT
Lake Neale
Lake Amadeus
CAPE CUVIER
Lake Macleod
Lyons
1105
Mount Augustus
906 Mount Essendon
Mount Olga 1069
Ayers Rock 867
Mount Cockburn 1138
Tropic of Capricorn
Geographe Channel
Carnarvon
Gascoyne
ROBINSON RANGE
Peak Hill
Lake Carnegie
Lake Gillen
Mount Aloysius 1085
Mount Woodroffe 1440
BERNIER ISLAND
DORRE ISLAND
Shark Bay
Naturaliste Channel
Wooramel
DIRK HARTOG ISLAND
STEEP POINT
Denham
Murchison
Wiluna
Lake Wells
Meekatharra
Nannine
GREAT VICTORIA DESERT
Cue
Lake Austin
Sandstone
Agnew
Yeo Lake
Kalbarri
Mount Magnet
Mount Redcliffe 562
Laverton
Lake Maurice
Malcolm
Lake Carey
Leonora
Northampton
Yalgoo
Mullewa
Pindar
Lake Ballard
Lake Raeside
Lake Barlee
Lake Minigwal
HOUTMAN ABROLHOS
Geraldton
Mongers Lake
Menzies
Maralinga
Ooldea
Dongara
Three Springs
Lake Moore
Deakin
Forrest
Rawlinna
Haig
NULLARBOR PLAIN
GREEN HEAD
Dalwallinu
Bonnie Rock
Kalgoorlie
Coolgardie
Boulder
Zanthus
Eucla
Moora
Bencubbin
Bullfinch
Lake Lefroy
Southern Cross
Lake Cowan
CAPE ADIEU
SAINT PETER
Eyre
DARLING RANGE
Northam
Merredin
Kellerberrin
Wanneroo
Perth
Fremantle
York
Beverley
Brookton
Hyden
Lake Johnston
Norseman
Lake Dundas
POINT CULVER
Pinjarra
Narrogin
Newdegate
Wagin
Ravensthorpe
Bunbury
Geographe Bay
Collie
Nyabing
Katanning
Gnowangerup
Esperance
CAPE ARID
Great Australian Bight
CAPE NATURALISTE
Busselton
Bridgetown
Manjimup
Bluff Knoll 1096
Hopetoun
Esperance Bay
ARCHIPELAGO OF THE RECHERCHE
HOOD POINT
Augusta
Pemberton
Mount Barker
CAPE LEEUWIN
Albany
Denmark
CAPE VANCOUVER
POINT D'ENTRECASTEAUX
WEST CAPE HOWE
King George Sound
SOUTHERN OCEAN
Copyright © by Rand McNally & Co.
Map prepared by Esselte Map Service AB, Stockholm.
A-590200-264 -8-9-16

Kilometers 0 200 400 600 Km.

Statute Miles 0 200 400 600 Mi.

Scale 1:12,000,000

One centimeter represents 120 kilometers.

One inch represents approximately 190 miles.

Lambert Conformal Conic Projection

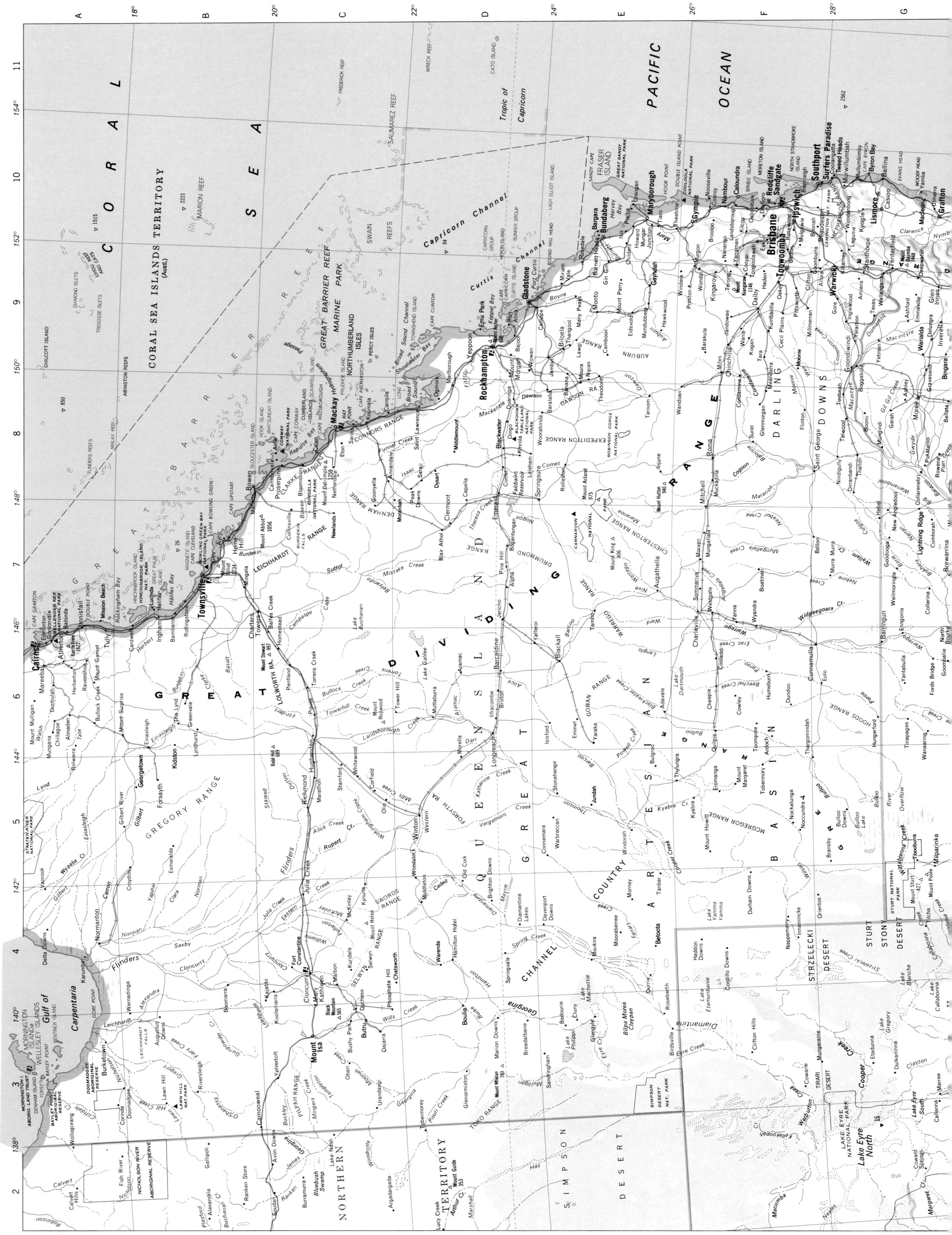
CORAL SEA
PACIFIC OCEAN
CORAL SEA ISLANDS TERRITORY (Austl.)
GREAT BARRIER REEF
GREAT BARRIER REEF MARINE PARK
Capricorn Channel
Tropic of Capricorn
GREAT DIVIDING RANGE
QUEENSLAND
GREAT ARTESIAN BASIN
NORTHERN TERRITORY
SIMPSON DESERT
STURT STONY DESERT
STRZELECKI DESERT
CHANNEL COUNTRY
DARLING DOWNS
Gulf of Carpentaria
Brisbane
Rockhampton
Townsville
Cairns
Mackay
Bundaberg
Maryborough
Gladstone
Toowoomba
Mount Isa
Cloncurry
Longreach
Charleville
Roma
Birdsville
Boulia
Winton
Hughenden
Charters Towers
Bowen
Ipswich
Southport
Surfers Paradise
Lismore
Grafton
Warwick
Gympie
Emerald
Barcaldine
Lake Eyre North
Lake Eyre South

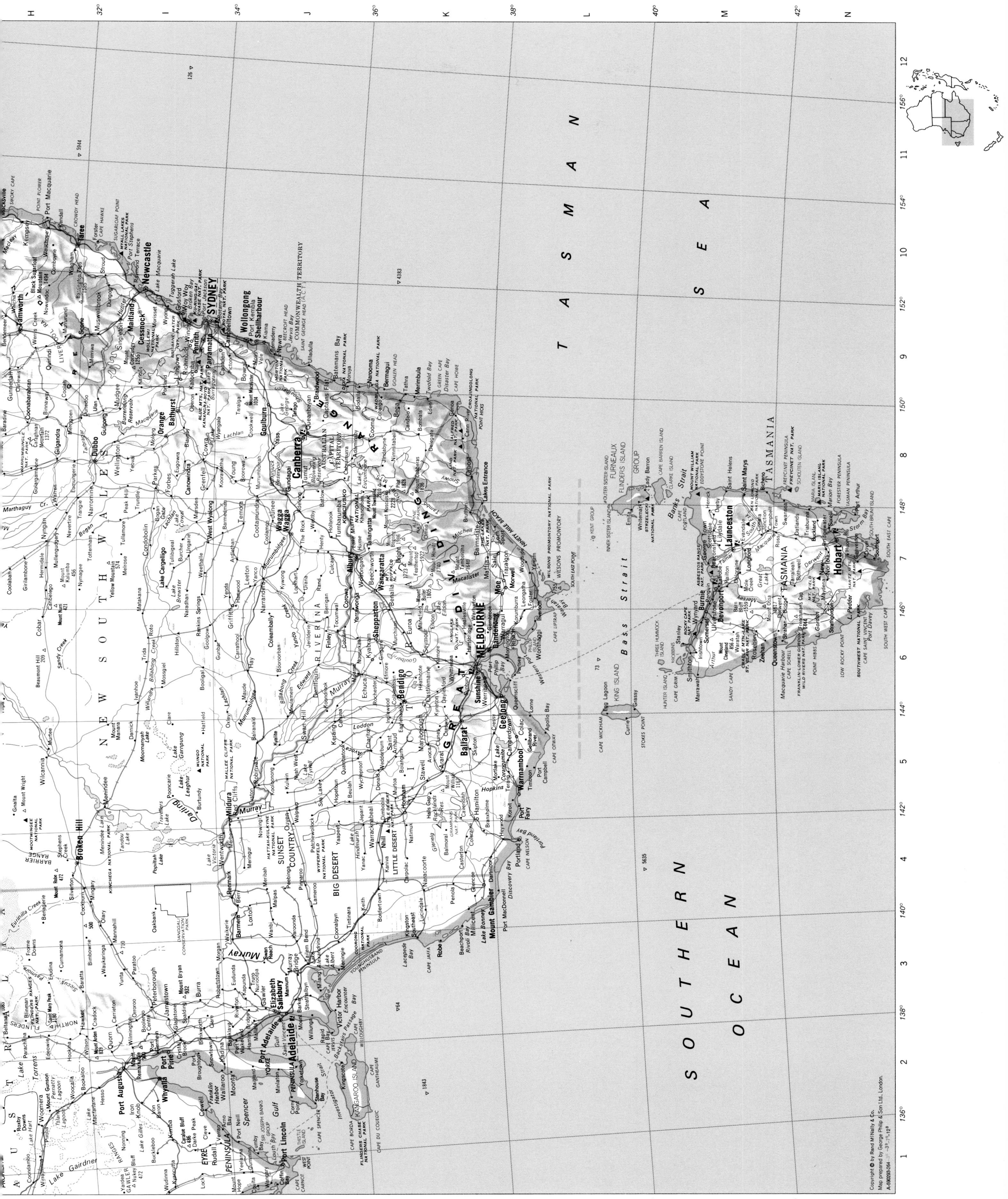

Kilometers 0 100 200 300 Km.

Statute Miles 0 100 200 300 Mi.

Scale 1:6,000,000

One centimeter represents 60 kilometers.
One inch represents approximately 95 miles.
Lambert Conformal Conic Projection

New Zealand

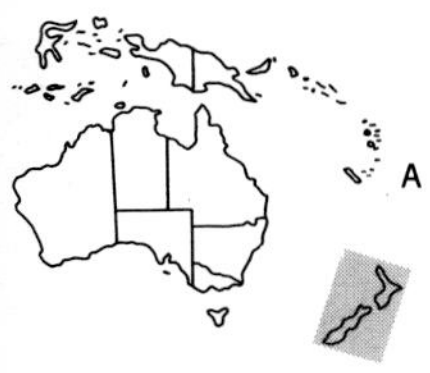

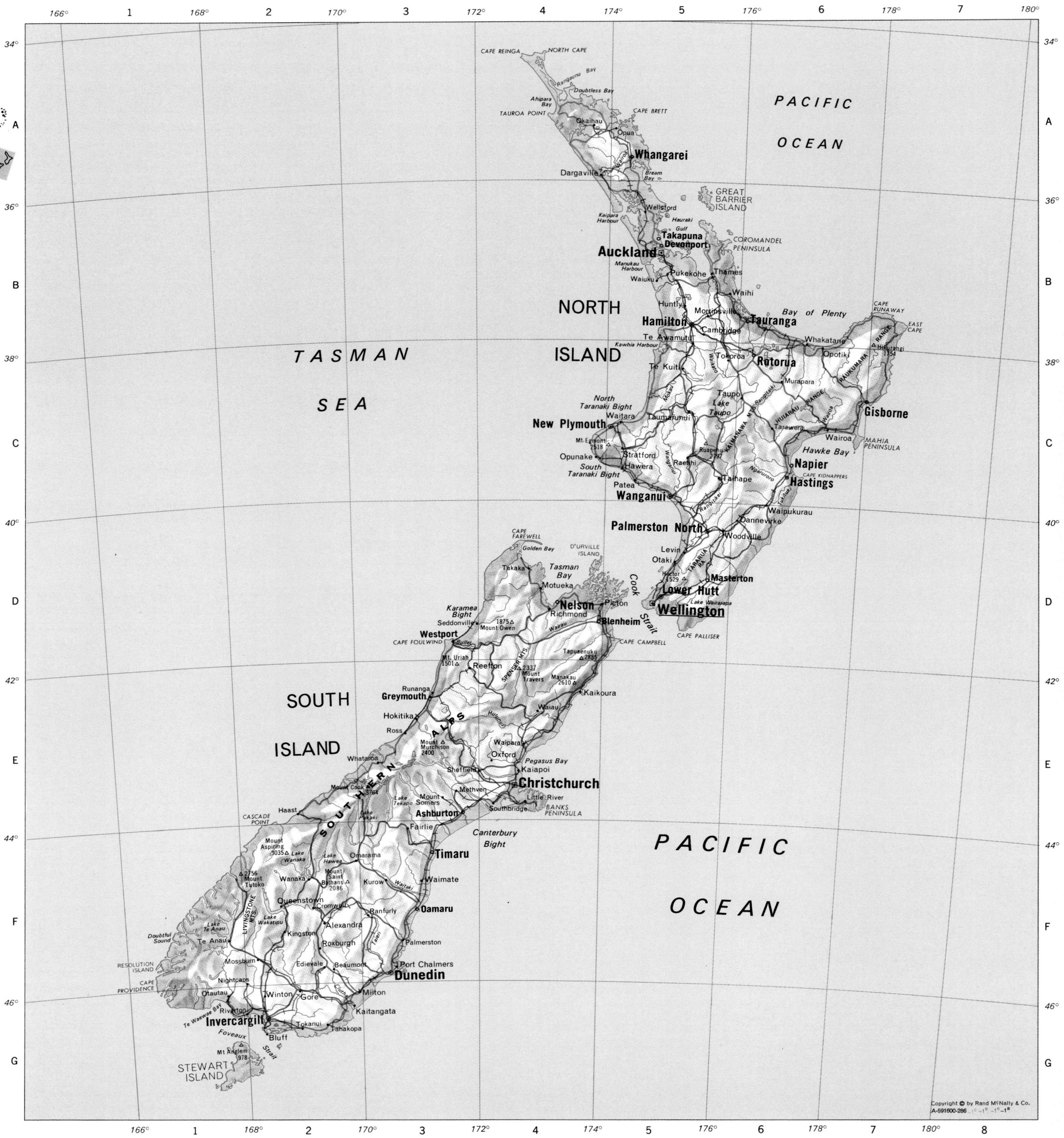

Scale 1:6,000,000

One centimeter represents 60 kilometers.
One inch represents approximately 95 miles.
Lambert Conformal Conic Projection

Kilometers 0 100 200 300 Km.
Statute Miles 0 100 200 300 Mi.

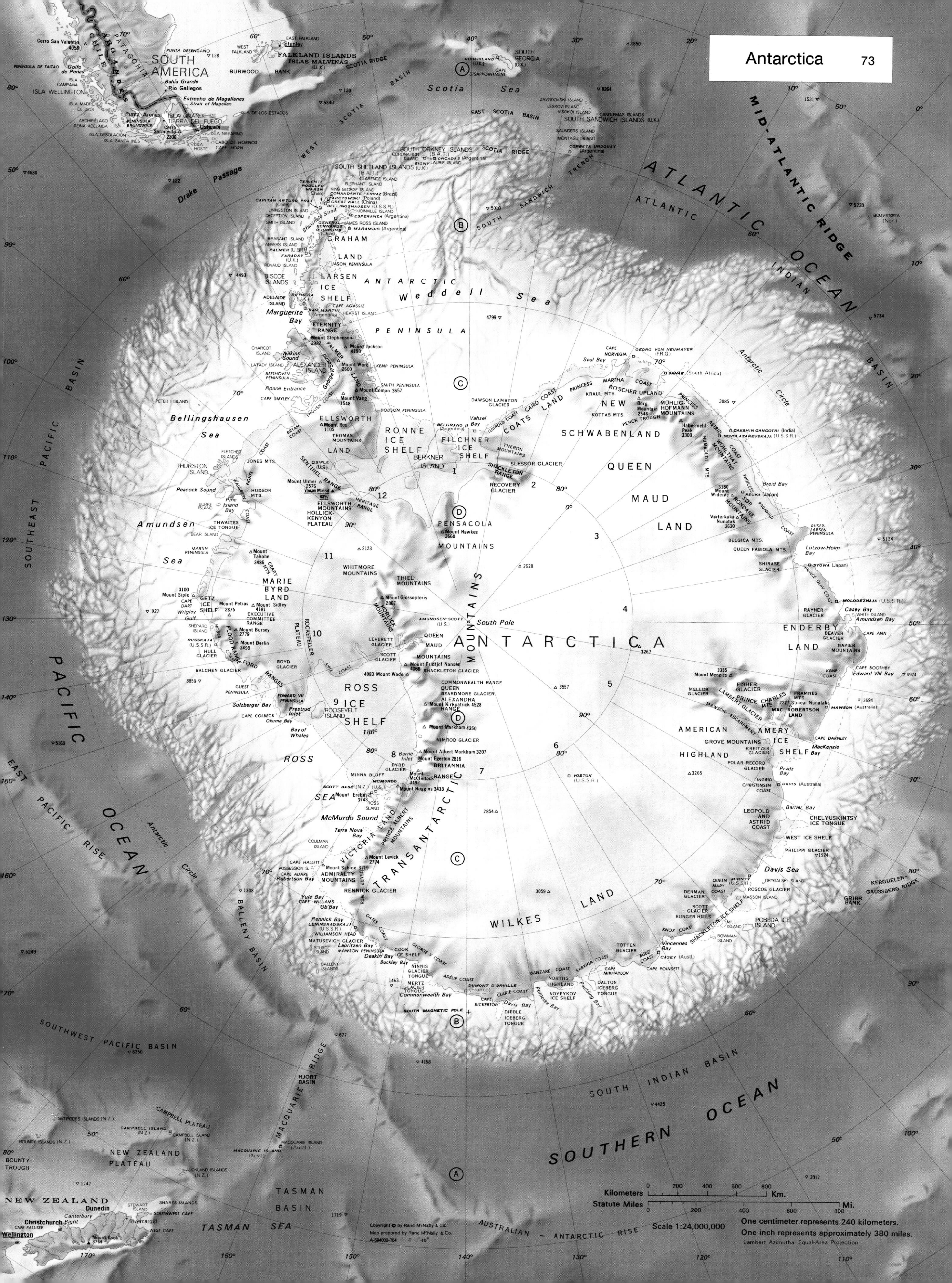
SOUTH AMERICA
PATAGONIA
CHILE
ARGENTINA
FALKLAND ISLANDS
ISLAS MALVINAS
(U.K.)
Stanley
EAST FALKLAND
WEST FALKLAND
BURWOOD BANK
SCOTIA RIDGE
SOUTH GEORGIA
(U.K.)
Scotia Sea
EAST SCOTIA BASIN
SOUTH SANDWICH ISLANDS (U.K.)
SOUTH ORKNEY ISLANDS
SCOTIA RIDGE
SOUTH SHETLAND ISLANDS
Drake Passage
WEST SCOTIA
SOUTH SANDWICH TRENCH
ATLANTIC OCEAN
MID-ATLANTIC RIDGE
ATLANTIC - INDIAN BASIN
Antarctic Circle
GRAHAM LAND
LARSEN ICE SHELF
ANTARCTIC PENINSULA
Weddell Sea
Marguerite Bay
ALEXANDER ISLAND
Bellingshausen Sea
ELLSWORTH LAND
RONNE ICE SHELF
FILCHNER ICE SHELF
BERKNER ISLAND
COATS LAND
NEW SCHWABENLAND
QUEEN MAUD LAND
ENDERBY LAND
AMERY ICE SHELF
AMERICAN HIGHLAND
Davis Sea
WILKES LAND
Amundsen Sea
MARIE BYRD LAND
ROSS ICE SHELF
ROSS SEA
McMurdo Sound
VICTORIA LAND
TRANSANTARCTIC MOUNTAINS
PENSACOLA MOUNTAINS
ANTARCTICA
South Pole
AMUNDSEN-SCOTT (U.S.)
VOSTOK (U.S.S.R.)
Vinson Massif 4897
SOUTH MAGNETIC POLE
PACIFIC OCEAN
SOUTHEAST PACIFIC BASIN
EAST PACIFIC RISE
BALLENY BASIN
SOUTHWEST PACIFIC BASIN
MACQUARIE RIDGE
HJORT BASIN
CAMPBELL PLATEAU
NEW ZEALAND PLATEAU
BOUNTY TROUGH
NEW ZEALAND
Christchurch
Dunedin
Wellington
TASMAN BASIN
TASMAN SEA
AUSTRALIAN - ANTARCTIC RISE
SOUTH INDIAN BASIN
SOUTHERN OCEAN
KERGUELEN-GAUSSBERG RIDGE
Kilometers 0 200 400 600 800 Km.
Statute Miles 0 100 200 300 400 500 Mi.
Scale 1:24,000,000
One centimeter represents 240 kilometers.
One inch represents approximately 380 miles.
Lambert Azimuthal Equal-Area Projection
Copyright © by Rand McNally & Co.
Map prepared by Rand McNally & Co.
A-504000-764

ATLANTIC OCEAN
NORTH AMERICAN BASIN
Sargasso Sea
MID-ATLANTIC RIDGE
CAPE VERDE BASIN
GUIANA BASIN
AZORES PLATEAU
AÇORES (AZORES) (Port.)
Tropic of Cancer
Equator
NORTH AMERICA
UNITED STATES
ROCKY MTS.
GREAT PLAINS
APPALACHIAN MOUNTAINS
GULF OF MEXICO
MEXICO BASIN
MEXICO
SIERRA MADRE ORIENTAL
SIERRA MADRE DEL SUR
CIUDAD DE MÉXICO
BAHAMAS
Straits of Florida
CUBA
La Habana
HAITI
DOMINICAN REPUBLIC
PUERTO RICO
PUERTO RICO TRENCH
JAMAICA
WEST INDIES
GREATER ANTILLES
LESSER ANTILLES
CARIBBEAN SEA
COLOMBIAN BASIN
VENEZUELAN BASIN
GUATEMALA
HONDURAS
EL SALVADOR
NICARAGUA
COSTA RICA
PANAMA
BELIZE
MIDDLE AMERICA TRENCH
GUATEMALA BASIN
COCOS RIDGE
CARNEGIE RIDGE
PANAMA BASIN
COLÓN RIDGE
ARCHIPIÉLAGO DE COLÓN (GALÁPAGOS ISLANDS) (Ec.)
SOUTH AMERICA
COLOMBIA
VENEZUELA
GUYANA
SURINAME
FRENCH GUIANA
ECUADOR
PERU
BRAZIL
BOGOTÁ
CARACAS
LIMA
Quito
Georgetown
Paramaribo
Cayenne
TRINIDAD AND TOBAGO
BARBADOS
GRENADA
SAINT LUCIA
DOMINICA
SAINT VINCENT AND THE GRENADINES
ANTIGUA AND BARBUDA
NETHERLANDS ANTILLES
BERMUDA (U.K.)
PERU-CHILE TRENCH
CHICAGO
NEW YORK
PHILADELPHIA
WASHINGTON
Miami
New Orleans
Houston
Dallas
Denver
Manaus
Belém
Recife
Salvador
Fortaleza

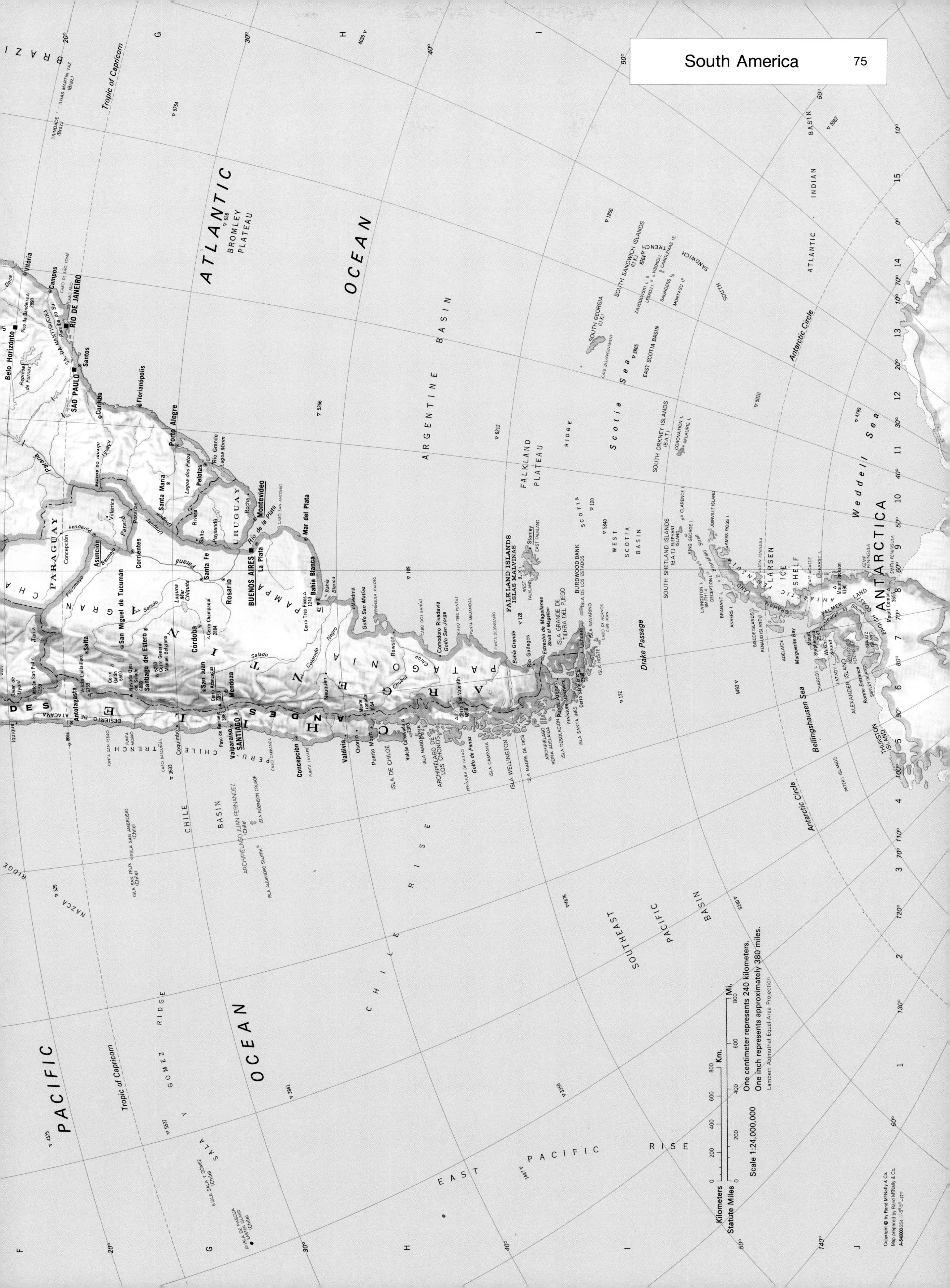
ATLANTIC
OCEAN
PACIFIC
OCEAN
BROMLEY PLATEAU
ARGENTINE BASIN
FALKLAND PLATEAU
Scotia Sea
Weddell Sea
ANTARCTICA
Drake Passage
Bellingshausen Sea
Tropic of Capricorn
Antarctic Circle
SOUTH GEORGIA (U.K.)
SOUTH SANDWICH ISLANDS (U.K.)
SOUTH ORKNEY ISLANDS (B.A.T.)
SOUTH SHETLAND ISLANDS (B.A.T.)
FALKLAND ISLANDS ISLAS MALVINAS (U.K.)
Stanley
BURDWOOD BANK
WEST SCOTIA BASIN
EAST SCOTIA BASIN
SOUTH SANDWICH TRENCH
LARSEN ICE SHELF
ALEXANDER ISLAND
PALMER LAND
THURSTON ISLAND
PETER I ISLAND
CHILE BASIN
CHILE RISE
SOUTHEAST PACIFIC BASIN
EAST PACIFIC RISE
SALA Y GOMEZ RIDGE
NAZCA RIDGE
ISLA DE PASCUA (EASTER ISLAND) (Chile)
ISLA SALA Y GÓMEZ (Chile)
ARCHIPIÉLAGO JUAN FERNÁNDEZ (Chile)
ISLA ROBINSON CRUSOE
ISLA ALEJANDRO SELKIRK
ISLA SAN FÉLIX (Chile)
ISLA SAN AMBROSIO (Chile)
TRINDADE (Braz.)
ILHAS MARTIN VAZ (Braz.)
BRAZIL
PARAGUAY
URUGUAY
PATAGONIA
PAMPAS
GRAN CHACO
Belo Horizonte
Vitória
Campos
RIO DE JANEIRO
SÃO PAULO
Santos
Curitiba
Florianópolis
Porto Alegre
Pelotas
Rio Grande
Montevideo
Asunción
Corrientes
Santa Fe
Rosario
BUENOS AIRES
La Plata
Mar del Plata
Bahía Blanca
Viedma
Rawson
Comodoro Rivadavia
Río Gallegos
Ushuaia
ISLA GRANDE DE TIERRA DEL FUEGO
Estrecho de Magallanes
Punta Arenas
CABO DE HORNOS (CAPE HORN)
Salta
San Miguel de Tucumán
Santiago del Estero
Córdoba
San Juan
Mendoza
Neuquén
Antofagasta
SANTIAGO
Valparaíso
Concepción
Valdivia
Osorno
Puerto Montt
ISLA DE CHILOÉ
ARCHIPIÉLAGO DE LOS CHONOS
Golfo de Penas
ISLA WELLINGTON
Cerro Aconcagua 6959
Scale 1:24,000,000
One centimeter represents 240 kilometers.
One inch represents approximately 380 miles.
Lambert Azimuthal Equal-Area Projection
Kilometers
Statute Miles

Northern South America

Kilometers 0 200 400 600 Km.
Statute Miles 0 200 400 600 Mi.

Scale 1:12,000,000
One centimeter represents 120 kilometers.
One inch represents approximately 190 miles.
Oblique Conic Conformal Projection

ATLANTIC OCEAN
BRAZIL
SURINAME
FRENCH GUIANA
Equator
Tropic of Capricorn
Georgetown
Paramaribo
Cayenne
Belém
São Luís
Fortaleza
Natal
João Pessoa
Recife
Maceió
Aracaju
Salvador
Teresina
Brasília
Goiânia
Anápolis
Belo Horizonte
Vitória
RIO DE JANEIRO
SÃO PAULO
Santos
Campinas
Niterói
Petrópolis
Cuiabá
Corumbá
Campo Grande
Uberlândia
Uberaba
Ribeirão Prêto
Feira de Santana
Vitória da Conquista
Ilhéus
Itabuna
Juazeiro do Norte
Campina Grande
Caruaru
Olinda
Parnaíba
Macapá
Santarém
Amazon
Amazonas
Pará
Xingu
Tocantins
Araguaia
Tapajós
São Francisco
Paraguai
Paraná
ILHA DE MARAJÓ
ILHA DO BANANAL
PLANALTO DO MATO GROSSO
PLANALTO CENTRAL
SERRA DO CACHIMBO
SERRA DOS CARAJÁS
SERRA DO RONCADOR
SERRA DO ESPINHAÇO
TUMUC-HUMAC MTS.
ACARAI MTS.
CABO ORANGE
CABO DE SÃO ROQUE
CABO FRIO
ATOL DAS ROCAS
ILHA FERNANDO DE NORONHA (Brazil)
Juliana Top 1230
7
8
9
10
11
12
55°
50°
45°
40°
35°
10°
5°
0°
15°
20°
A
B
C
D
E
F
G
H

Southern South America

Kilometers 0 200 400 600 Km.

Statute Miles 0 200 400 600 Mi.

Scale 1:12,000,000

One centimeter represents 120 kilometers.
One inch represents approximately 190 miles.

Oblique Conic Conformal Projection

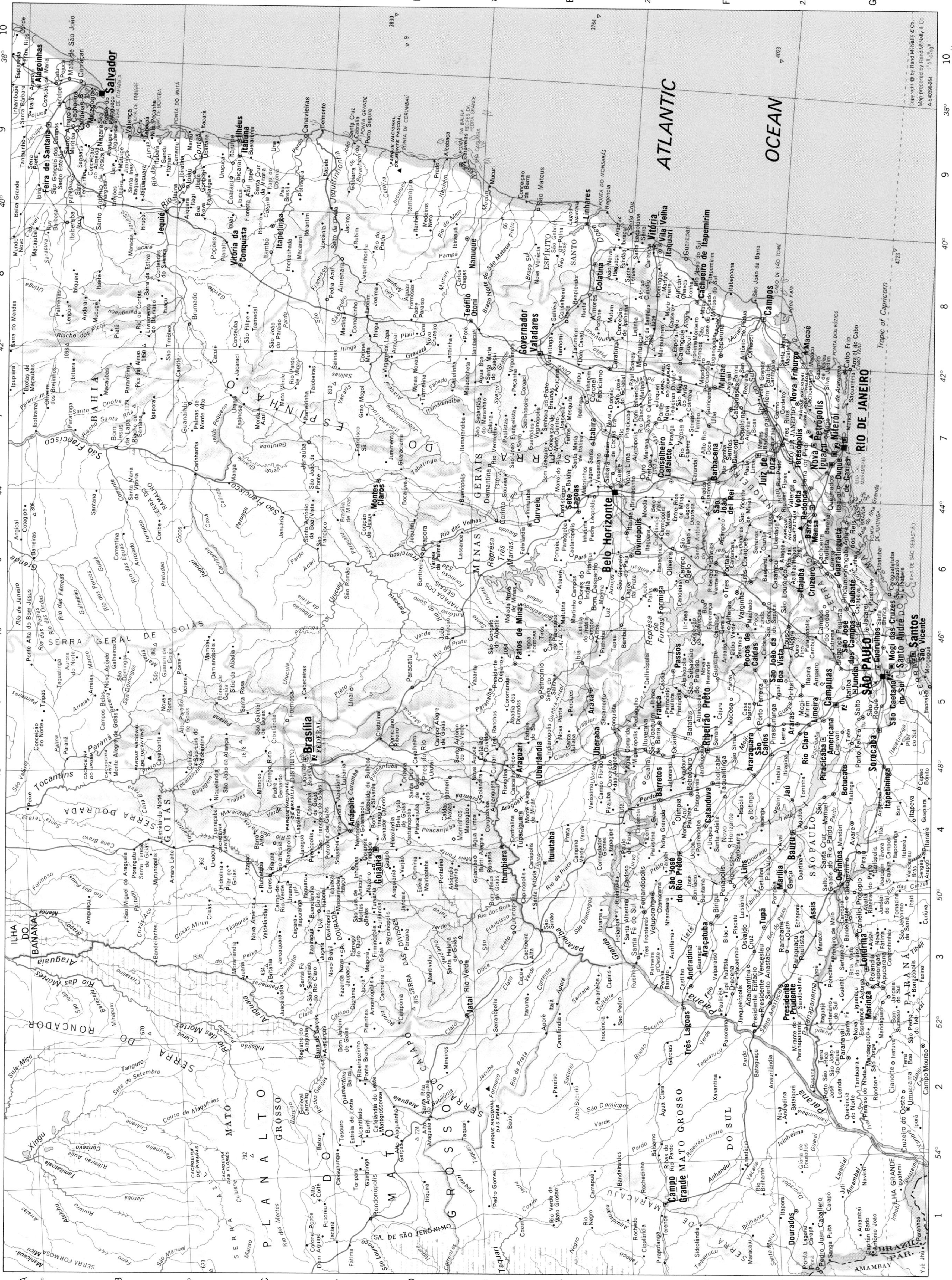

Kilometers 0 100 200 300 Km.
Statute Miles 0 100 200 300 Mi.

Scale 1:6,000,000
One centimeter represents 60 kilometers.
One inch represents approximately 95 miles.
Oblique Conic Conformal Projection

Central Argentina and Chile

Kilometers 0 100 200 300 Km.

Statute Miles 0 100 200 300 Mi.

Scale 1:6,000,000

One centimeter represents 60 kilometers.

One inch represents approximately 95 miles.

Oblique Conic Conformal Projection

Peru, Bolivia, and Western Brazil

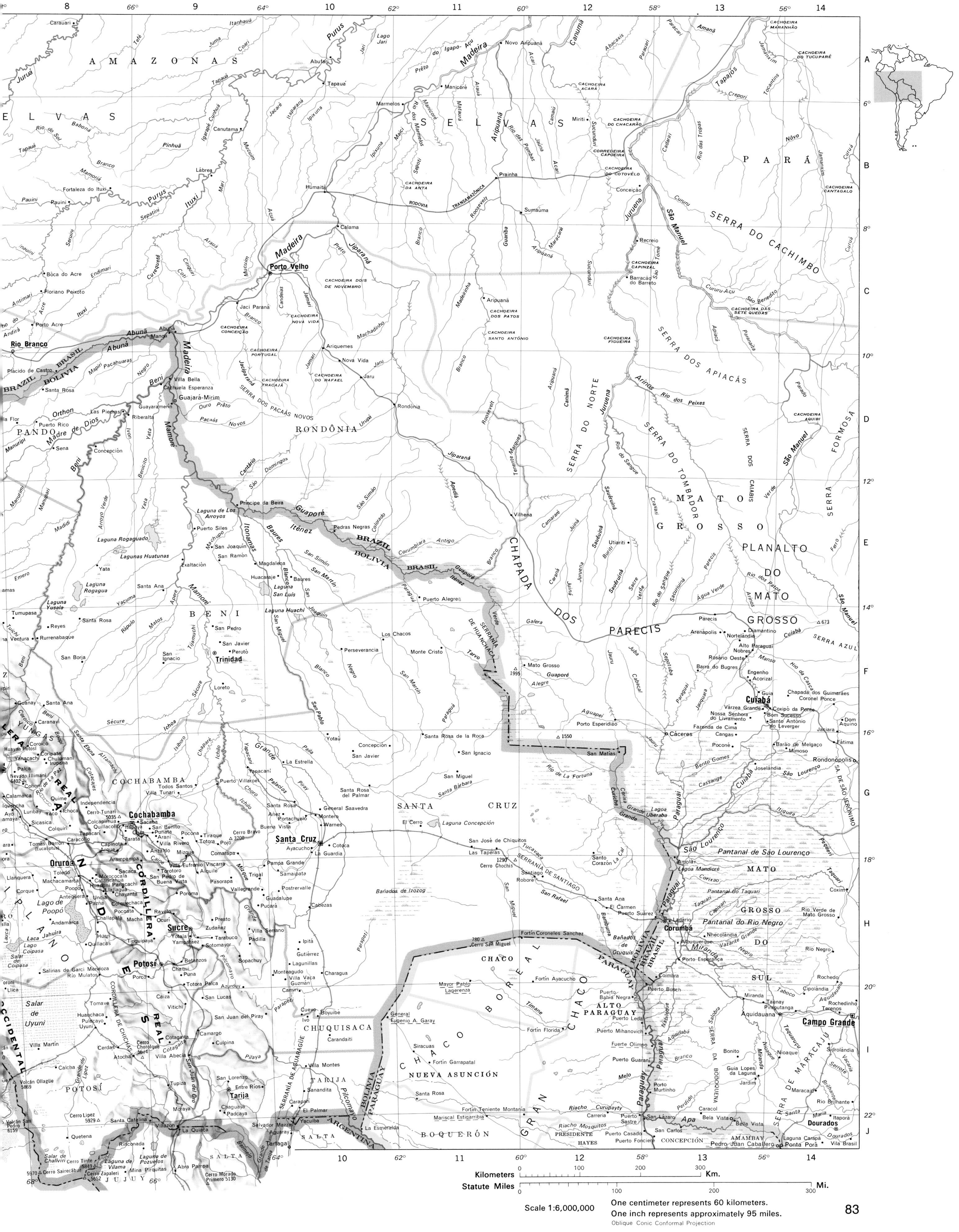

Scale 1:6,000,000
One centimeter represents 60 kilometers.
One inch represents approximately 95 miles.
Oblique Conic Conformal Projection

Colombia, Ecuador, Venezuela, and Guyana

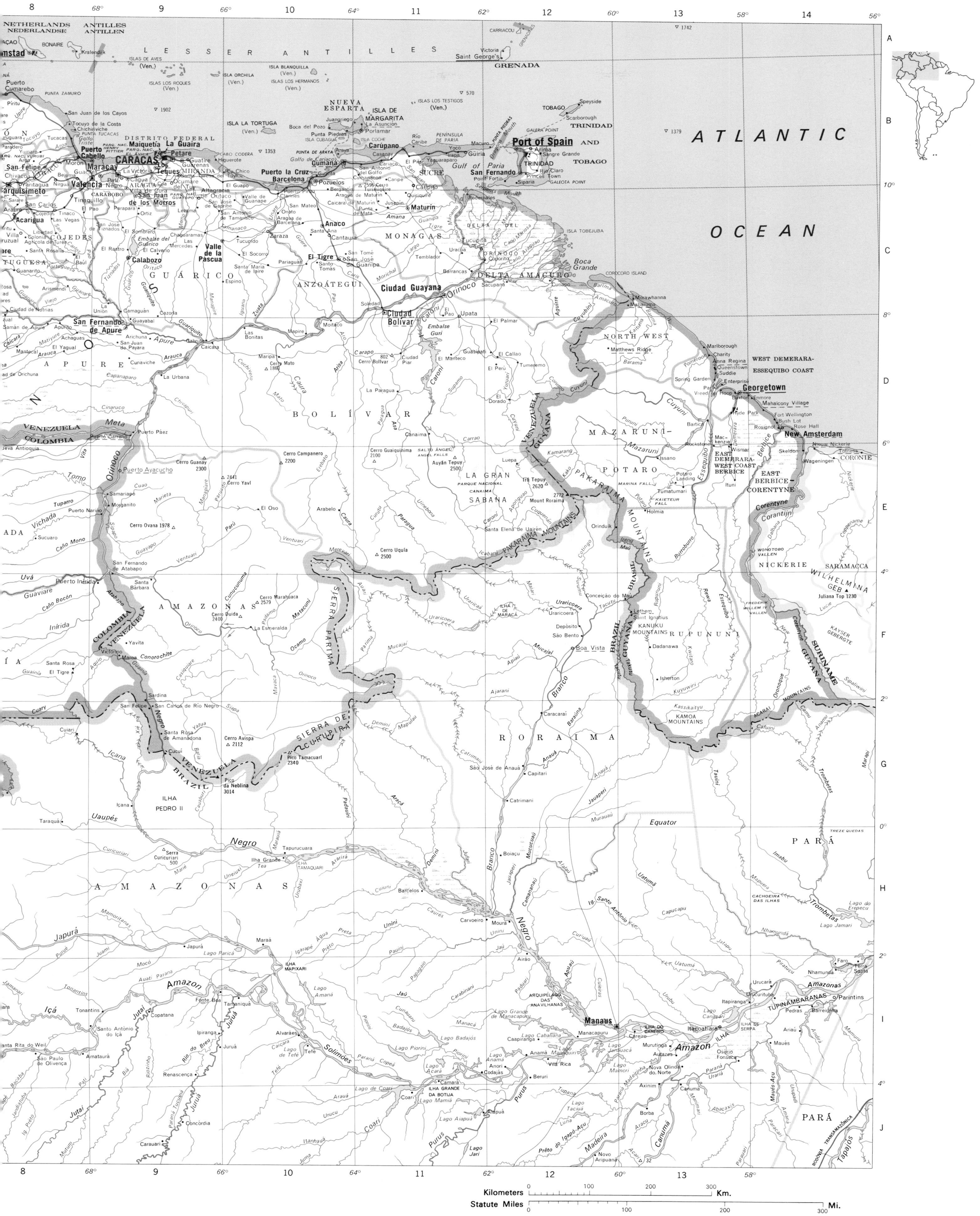

Kilometers 0 100 200 300 Km.
Statute Miles 0 100 200 300 Mi.

Scale 1:6,000,000
One centimeter represents 60 kilometers.
One inch represents approximately 95 miles.
Oblique Conic Conformal Projection

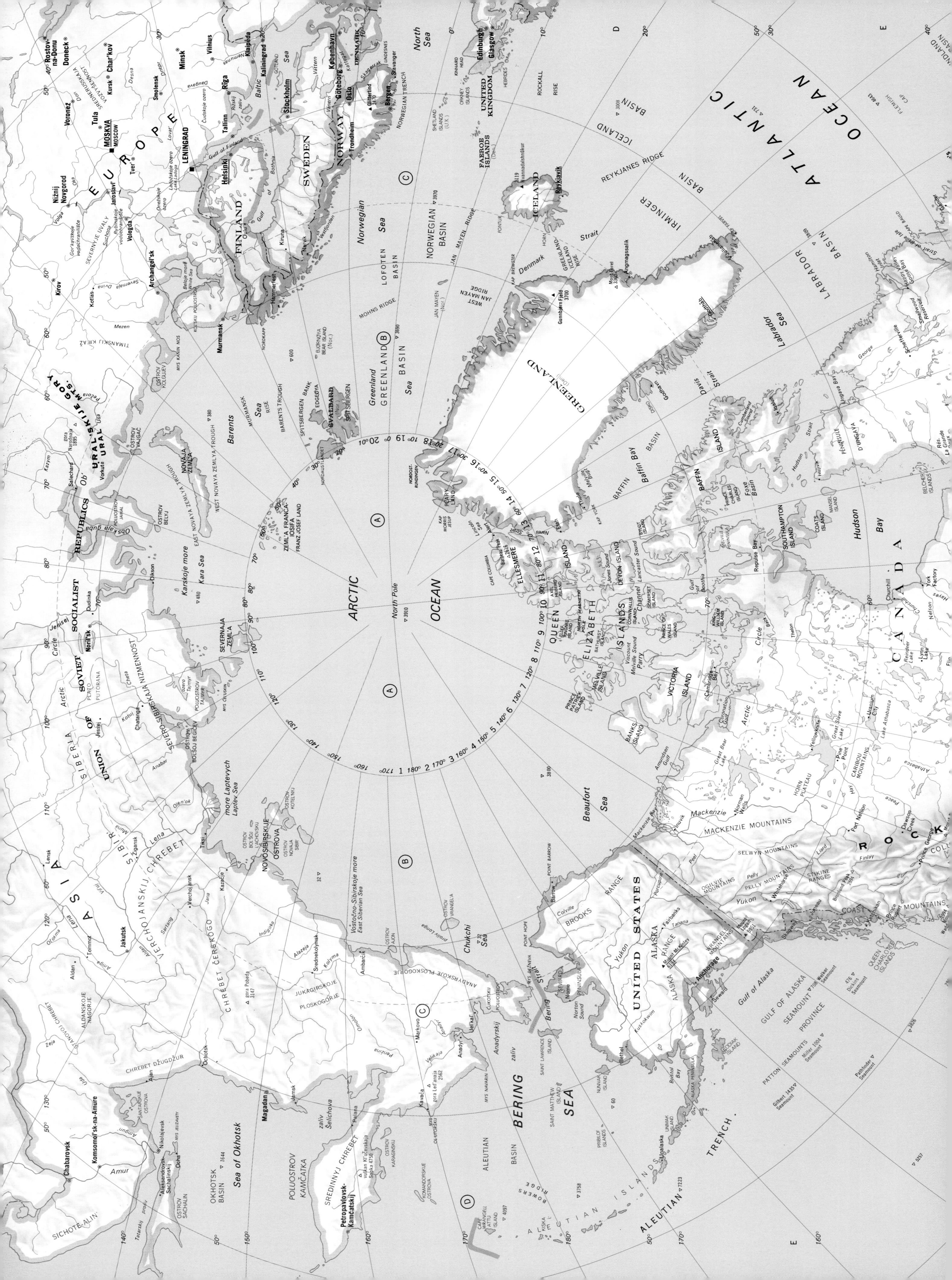

ARCTIC OCEAN
North Pole
ATLANTIC OCEAN
EUROPE
ASIA
SIBERIA
CANADA
UNITED STATES
ALASKA
GREENLAND
ICELAND
BERING SEA
Barents Sea
Kara Sea
Laptev Sea
East Siberian Sea
Chukchi Sea
Beaufort Sea
Baffin Bay
Hudson Bay
Labrador Sea
Norwegian Sea
Greenland Sea
North Sea
Sea of Okhotsk
Gulf of Alaska
UNION OF SOVIET SOCIALIST REPUBLICS
ALEUTIAN ISLANDS
QUEEN ELIZABETH ISLANDS
ELLESMERE ISLAND
BAFFIN ISLAND
VICTORIA ISLAND
SVALBARD
NOVAJA ZEML'A
SEVERNAJA ZEML'A

NORTH AMERICA
ATLANTIC
NORTH
OCEAN
Sargasso Sea
GULF OF MEXICO
CARIBBEAN SEA
UNITED STATES
MEXICO
PACIFIC
OCEAN
SOUTH AMERICA
GREAT PLAINS
ROCKY MOUNTAINS
APPALACHIAN MOUNTAINS
SIERRA MADRE ORIENTAL
SIERRA MADRE OCCIDENTAL
CHIHUAHUAN DESERT
SONORAN DESERT
BAJA CALIFORNIA
Golfo de California
Tropic of Cancer
Equator
COLOMBIA
VENEZUELA
ECUADOR
PERU
BRAZIL
CUBA
BAHAMAS
JAMAICA
HAITI
DOMINICAN REPUBLIC
PUERTO RICO
BELIZE
GUATEMALA
HONDURAS
EL SALVADOR
NICARAGUA
COSTA RICA
PANAMÁ
WASHINGTON
NEW YORK
PHILADELPHIA
BOSTON
CHICAGO
DETROIT
CLEVELAND
ST. LOUIS
LOS ANGELES
SAN FRANCISCO
CIUDAD DE MÉXICO
MEXICO CITY
La Habana
Havana
CARACAS
BOGOTÁ
MONTRÉAL
TORONTO
Ottawa
MURRAY FRACTURE ZONE
CLARION FRACTURE ZONE
CLIPPERTON FRACTURE ZONE
MOLOKAI FRACTURE ZONE
MATHEMATICIANS SEAMOUNTS
EAST PACIFIC RISE
MIDDLE AMERICA TRENCH
COCOS RIDGE
CARNEGIE RIDGE
COLÓN RIDGE
GUATEMALA BASIN
PANAMA BASIN
Kilometers 0 200 400 600 800 Km.
Statute Miles 0 200 400 600 800 Mi.
Scale 1:24,000,000
One centimeter represents 240 kilometers.
One inch represents approximately 380 miles.
Lambert Azimuthal Equal-Area Projection
Copyright © by Rand McNally & Co.
Map prepared by Rand McNally & Co.

UNITED STATES
MEXICO
GULF OF MEXICO
PACIFIC OCEAN
Golfo de California
Tropic of Cancer
SIERRA MADRE OCCIDENTAL
SIERRA MADRE ORIENTAL
SIERRA MADRE DEL SUR
BAJA CALIFORNIA
TEXAS
EDWARDS PLATEAU
LLANO ESTACADO
NEW MEXICO
ARIZONA
OKLAHOMA
ARKANSAS
LOUISIANA
MISSISSIPPI
TENNESSEE
MISSOURI
CALIFORNIA
YUCATAN PENINSULA
GUATEMALA
EL SALVADOR
BELIZE
Bahía de Campeche
Golfo de Tehuantepec
MISSISSIPPI DELTA
ISLAS REVILLAGIGEDO
ISLAS MARÍAS
ÎLE CLIPPERTON (Fr.)
Rio Grande
San Diego
Tijuana
Mexicali
Ensenada
Phoenix
Tucson
Albuquerque
El Paso
Ciudad Juárez
Amarillo
Lubbock
Oklahoma City
Tulsa
Fort Smith
Little Rock
Memphis
Wichita Falls
Fort Worth
Dallas
Abilene
Midland
Odessa
Shreveport
Waco
Jackson
Austin
San Antonio
Houston
Beaumont
Lake Charles
Baton Rouge
New Orleans
Mobile
Galveston
Corpus Christi
Laredo
Nuevo Laredo
Brownsville
Matamoros
Reynosa
Monterrey
Saltillo
Monclova
Piedras Negras
Chihuahua
Hermosillo
Ciudad Obregón
Culiacán
Mazatlán
Durango
Torreón
Gómez Palacio
Zacatecas
Aguascalientes
San Luis Potosí
Ciudad Victoria
Tampico
Tepic
Guadalajara
León
Irapuato
Querétaro
Celaya
Morelia
CIUDAD DE MEXICO
Pachuca
Toluca
Cuernavaca
Puebla
Xalapa
Veracruz
Córdoba
Orizaba
Acapulco
Oaxaca
Coatzacoalcos
Villahermosa
Campeche
Mérida
Tuxtla Gutiérrez
Tapachula
Guatemala
San Salvador
Santa Ana
San Pedro Sula
Tegucigalpa
Belize City
La Paz
Colima
Uruapan del Progreso
Copyright © by Rand McNally & Co.
Map prepared by Esselte Map Service AB, Stockholm.

Kilometers 0 200 400 600 Km.

Statute Miles 0 200 400 600 Mi.

Scale 1:12,000,000

One centimeter represents 120 kilometers.
One inch represents approximately 190 miles.
Oblique Conic Conformal Projection

Kilometers 0 100 200 300 Km.

Statute Miles 0 100 200 300 M

Scale 1:6,000,000

One centimeter represents 60 kilometers.
One inch represents approximately 95 miles.
Lambert Conformal Conic Projection

9
10
11
12
13
14
15
16
100°
98°
96°
94°
92°
90°
88°
32°
30°
28°
26°
24°
22°
20°
18°
16°
A
B
C
D
E
F
GULF
OF
MEXICO
Bahía de Campeche
Tropic of Cancer
TEXAS
LOUISIANA
MISSISSIPPI
ALABAMA
EDWARDS
PLATEAU
UNITED STATES
MEXICO
NUEVO LEÓN
TAMAULIPAS
SAN LUIS POTOSÍ
SIERRA MADRE ORIENTAL
SIERRA MADRE DEL SUR
SIERRA MADRE DE CHIAPAS
YUCATÁN
YUCATAN PENINSULA
PENÍNSULA DE YUCATÁN
QUINTANA ROO
CAMPECHE
TABASCO
CHIAPAS
OAXACA
VERACRUZ
PUEBLA
HIDALGO
QUERÉTARO
GUANAJUATO
MÉXICO
MORELOS
GUERRERO
ISTMO DE TEHUANTEPEC
Golfo de Tehuantepec
GUATEMALA
BELIZE
HONDURAS
Gulf of Honduras
Fort Worth
Dallas
Arlington
Richardson
Garland
Abilene
Shreveport
Longview
Tyler
Jackson
Monroe
Meridian
Waco
Killeen
Temple
San Angelo
Bryan
College Station
Austin
Houston
Baytown
Beaumont
Port Arthur
Lake Charles
Lafayette
Baton Rouge
New Orleans
Houma
Hattiesburg
Gulfport
Biloxi
Mobile
Alexandria
San Antonio
Galveston
Texas City
Victoria
Corpus Christi
Kingsville
Laredo
Nuevo Laredo
Del Rio
Ciudad Acuña
Piedras Negras
Eagle Pass
Nueva Rosita
Monclova
McAllen
Harlingen
Brownsville
Matamoros
Reynosa
Monterrey
San Nicolás de los Garza
Guadalupe
Saltillo
Ciudad Victoria
Ciudad Mante
Ciudad Madero
Tampico
San Luis Potosí
León
Celaya
Querétaro
Pachuca
Morelia
Toluca
CIUDAD DE MÉXICO
MÉXICO CITY
Tlalnepantla
Nezahualcóyotl
Puebla
Cuernavaca
Xalapa
Veracruz
Orizaba
Córdoba
Poza Rica
Tuxpan
Tehuacán
Acapulco
Chilpancingo de los Bravo
Iguala
Oaxaca
Minatitlán
Coatzacoalcos
Villahermosa
Tuxtla Gutiérrez
Ciudad del Carmen
Campeche
Mérida
Progreso
Valladolid
Cancún
Cozumel
Chetumal
Belize City
Belmopan
Tapachula
Guatemala
San Pedro Sula
Puerto Cortés
Juchitán de Zaragoza
Salina Cruz
Laguna Madre
Matagorda Bay
Galveston Bay
Baffin Bay
Lake Pontchartrain
Río Grande
Rio Bravo
Colorado
Brazos
Trinity
Sabine
Red
Mississippi
Pearl
Usumacinta
Grijalva
Balsas
Pecos
Nueces
Frio
Guadalupe
San Antonio
Atchafalaya

PACIFIC
OCEAN
Gulf of Honduras
MEXICO
GUATEMALA
GUATEMALA
BELIZE
GUATEMALA
HONDURAS
EL SALVADOR
CHIAPAS
PETÉN
ALTA VERAPAZ
BAJA VERAPAZ
IZABAL
QUICHÉ
HUEHUETENANGO
SAN MARCOS
TOTONICAPÁN
QUETZALTENANGO
SOLOLÁ
CHIMALTENANGO
SACATEPÉQUEZ
SUCHITEPÉQUEZ
RETALHULEU
ESCUINTLA
SANTA ROSA
JUTIAPA
JALAPA
EL PROGRESO
ZACAPA
CHIQUIMULA
COPÁN
OCOTEPEQUE
SANTA BÁRBARA
CORTÉS
YORO
ATLÁNTIDA
COMAYAGUA
INTIBUCÁ
LEMPIRA
LA PAZ
FRANCISCO MORAZÁN
EL PARAÍSO
VALLE
CHOLUTECA
CHINANDEGA
LEÓN
MANAGUA
CARAZO
TOLEDO
SIERRA MADRE DE CHIAPAS
SIERRA DE LAS MINAS
SIERRA DE LOS CUCHUMATANES
MONTAÑAS DEL MICO
Tapachula
Comitan de Dominguez
Quetzaltenango
Retalhuleu
Mazatenango
Escuintla
Guatemala
Antigua Guatemala
Cobán
Zacapa
Puerto Barrios
Puerto Cortés
San Pedro Sula
El Progreso
Tela
La Ceiba
Santa Ana
Sonsonate
San Salvador
Nueva San Salvador
San Miguel
La Unión
Usulután
Zacatecoluca
Chalatenango
Tegucigalpa
Choluteca
Chinandega
León
Managua
Puerto San Jose
La Libertad
Acajutla
Golfo de Fonseca
Bahía de Jiquilisco
Lago de Atitlán
Lago de Izabal
Lago de Ilopango
Lago de Managua
Islas de la Bahía
Isla de Roatán
Isla de Utila
Copyright © by Rand McNally & Co.
Map prepared by Rand McNally & Co.
A-533600-264

Kilometers 0 50 100 150 Km.

Statute Miles 0 50 100 150 Mi.

Scale 1:3,000,000

One centimeter represents 30 kilometers.

One inch represents approximately 47 miles.

Lambert Conformal Conic Projection

GULF OF MEXICO
Straits of Florida
Canal de Yucatán
UNITED STATES
The FLORIDA
Everglades
Florida Bay
FLORIDA KEYS
Key West
Fort Myers
West Palm Beach
Palm Beach
Lake Worth
Delray Beach
Boca Raton
Pompano Beach
Fort Lauderdale
Hollywood
Hialeah
MIAMI
Miami Beach
Coral Gables
Homestead
Key Largo
Naples
Lake Okeechobee
Belle Glade
Freeport
GRAND BAHAMA
Marsh Harbour
ABACO
Northwest Providence Channel
Northeast Providence Channel
Nassau
NEW PROVIDENCE
ELEUTHERA
ANDROS
Andros Town
GREAT BAHAMA BANK
Tongue of the Ocean
Exuma Sound
EXUMA
CAT ISLAND
LONG ISLAND
Clarence Town
Crooked
RAGGED ISLAND
CAY SAL BANK
Nicholas Channel
Santaren Channel
Old Bahama Channel
LA HABANA
HAVANA
San Antonio de los Baños
Matanzas
Cárdenas
Güines
Pinar del Río
Golfo de Batabanó
Sagua la Grande
Santa Clara
Placetas
Cienfuegos
Trinidad
Sancti Spíritus
Ciego de Ávila
Morón
Florida
Camagüey
Nuevitas
Puerto Padre
Las Tunas
Holguín
Banes
Bayamo
Manzanillo
Palma Soriano
Guantánamo
Santiago de Cuba
SIERRA MAESTRA
Golfo de Guacanayabo
Golfo de Ana María
ARCH. DE LOS JARDINES DE LA REINA
Nueva Gerona
ISLA DE LA JUVENTUD
(ISLA DE PINOS)
CUBA
CAYMAN ISLANDS
(U.K.)
George Town
GRAND CAYMAN
LITTLE CAYMAN
CAYMAN BRAC
GREATER
WEST
Montego Bay
Falmouth
Ocho Rios
Saint Ann's Bay
Port Maria
Port Antonio
Mandeville
May Pen
Spanish Town
Kingston
Blue Mountain Peak
JAMAICA
Portland Bight
Morant Bay
Jamaica Channel
PEDRO CAYS
(Jam.)
MORANT CAYS
(Jam.)
ROSALIND BANK
CARIBBEAN
YUCATÁN
MÉXICO
MEXICO
QUINTANA ROO
Cancún
Isla Mujeres
Puerto Morelos
Playa del Carmen
Cozumel
Tulum
YUCATAN PENINSULA
PENÍNSULA DE YUCATÁN
Bahía Emiliano Zapata
Bahía Venustiano Carranza
BANCO CHINCHORRO
LIGHTHOUSE REEF
(Belize)
GLOVERS REEF (Belize)
Gulf of Honduras
ISLAS DE LA BAHÍA
Roatán
Guanaja
Utila
ISLAS SANTANILLA
(Hond.)
Tela
La Ceiba
Trujillo
Olanchito
Yoro
Catacamas
Juticalpa
Tegucigalpa
Choluteca
LA MOSQUITIA
HONDURAS
NICARAGUA
CORD. ISABELIA
COSTA DE MOSQUITOS
Puerto Cabezas
Waspam
Prinzapolka
Estelí
Matagalpa
León
Chinandega
Managua
Masaya
Granada
Lago de Nicaragua
Bluefields
El Bluff
Rama
Juigalpa
San Carlos
Rivas
Corn Islands
ISLAS DEL MAÍZ
(Nic.)
SAN ANDRÉS Y PROVIDENCIA
(Col.)
San Andrés
ISLA DE PROVIDENCIA
CAYOS DE ALBUQUERQUE
CAYOS DEL ESTE SUDESTE
CAYO DE SERRANA
CAYO DE SERRANILLA
(Col.)
BAJO NUEVO
(Col.)
QUITASUEÑO
CAYOS DE RONCADOR
CAYOS MISKITOS
ARRECIFES DE LA MEDIA LUNA
COSTA RICA
Liberia
Puntarenas
San José
Cartago
Puerto Limón
Alajuela
Heredia
CORD. DE GUANACASTE
CORD. DE TALAMANCA
PANAMÁ
Colón
Panamá
Bocas del Toro
Golfo de los Mosquitos
ISTMO DE PANAMÁ
Golfo de San Blas
SERRANÍA DE SAN BLAS
Barranquilla
Cartagena
Sincelejo
CÓRDOBA
SUCRE
BOLÍVAR
ATLÁNTICO
Golfo de Morrosquillo
Santa Marta
PACIFIC OCEAN
Golfo de Papagayo
Golfo de Nicoya
PENÍNSULA DE NICOYA
CABO BLANCO

ATLANTIC OCEAN
Sargasso Sea
Tropic of Cancer
TURKS AND CAICOS ISLANDS (U.K.)
CAICOS ISLANDS
TURKS ISLANDS
Caicos Passage
Turks Island Passage
Mouchoir Passage
Silver Bank Passage
SILVER BANK
GREAT INAGUA
INDIES
HAITI
HAÏTI
Cap-Haïtien
Port-au-Prince
HISPANIOLA
Santiago
Santo Domingo
San Pedro de Macorís
La Romana
DOMINICAN REPUBLIC
REPÚBLICA DOMINICANA
Canal de la Mona
PUERTO RICO (U.S.)
SAN JUAN
Arecibo
Mayagüez
Ponce
Caguas
Bayamón
CORDILLERA CENTRAL
BRITISH VIRGIN ISLANDS
VIRGIN ISLANDS (U.S.)
Road Town
Charlotte Amalie
SAINT CROIX
Christiansted
Frederiksted
Anegada Passage
ANGUILLA (U.K.)
The Valley
SAINT MARTIN
Philipsburg
LEEWARD ISLANDS
SAINT KITTS AND NEVIS
Basseterre
Charlestown
ANTIGUA AND BARBUDA
Saint John's
MONTSERRAT (U.K.)
Plymouth
Guadeloupe Passage
GUADELOUPE (Fr.)
Pointe-à-Pitre
Basse-Terre
GRANDE-TERRE
DOMINICA
Dominica Passage
Roseau
Martinique Passage
MARTINIQUE (Fr.)
Fort-de-France
Saint Lucia Channel
SAINT LUCIA
Castries
Saint Vincent Passage
SAINT VINCENT AND THE GRENADINES
Kingstown
BARBADOS
Bridgetown
GRENADA
Saint George's
TOBAGO
TRINIDAD AND TOBAGO
Port of Spain
San Fernando
Gulf of Paria
Serpents Mouth
LESSER ANTILLES
WINDWARD ISLANDS
ANTILLES
SEA
TILLES
ISLA DE AVES (Ven.)
ARUBA (Neth.)
Oranjestad
NETHERLANDS ANTILLES
NEDERLANDSE ANTILLEN
CURAÇAO
BONAIRE
Willemstad
Kralendijk
ISLA LA ORCHILA
ISLAS LOS ROQUES (Ven.)
ISLA BLANQUILLA (Ven.)
ISLAS LOS HERMANOS
ISLAS LOS TESTIGOS (Ven.)
ISLA LA TORTUGA (Ven.)
ISLA DE MARGARITA
NUEVA ESPARTA
La Asunción
Porlamar
LA GUAJIRA
PENINSULA DE LA GUAJIRA
Riohacha
Golfo de Venezuela
Maracaibo
Lago de Maracaibo
Cabimas
Ciudad Ojeda
ZULIA
FALCÓN
Coro
Punto Fijo
Puerto Cumarebo
LARA
Barquisimeto
Carora
TRUJILLO
Valera
Guanare
PORTUGUESA
COJEDES
Acarigua
San Carlos
Valencia
Puerto Cabello
Maracay
CARACAS
DISTRITO FEDERAL
Maiquetia
Petare
Los Teques
San Juan de los Morros
Calabozo
GUÁRICO
Valle de la Pascua
MIRANDA
Barcelona
Puerto la Cruz
ANZOÁTEGUI
Anaco
El Tigre
Cumaná
SUCRE
Carúpano
Maturín
MONAGAS
DELTA AMACURO
SERRANIA DE PERIJA
COLOMBIA
VENEZUELA
NORTE DE SANTANDER

Kilometers 0 100 200 300 Km.

Statute Miles 0 100 200 300 Mi.

Scale 1:6,000,000

One centimeter represents 60 kilometers.

One inch represents approximately 95 miles.

Lambert Conformal Conic Projection

Beaufort Sea
Gulf of Alaska
PACIFIC OCEAN
ALASKA RANGE
UNITED STATES
CANADA
ROCKY MOUNTAINS
COAST MOUNTAINS
CASCADE RANGE
SIERRA NEVADA
MACKENZIE MTS.
N O R T H W E S T
BRITISH COLUMBIA
ALBERTA
SASKATCHEWAN
MANITOBA
WASHINGTON
OREGON
IDAHO
MONTANA
WYOMING
NORTH DAKOTA
SOUTH DAKOTA
NEBRASKA
MINNESOTA
NEVADA
UTAH
COLORADO
CALIFORNIA
VICTORIA ISLAND
BANKS ISLAND
Great Bear Lake
Great Slave Lake
Lake Athabasca
Lake Winnipeg
Fairbanks
Anchorage
Vancouver
Victoria
Seattle
Tacoma
Portland
Spokane
Edmonton
Calgary
Saskatoon
Regina
Winnipeg
Great Falls
Billings
Boise
Salt Lake City
Reno
Sacramento
SAN FRANCISCO
Oakland
San Jose
Fresno
Bismarck
Fargo
Minneapolis
Sioux Falls
Rapid City

Kilometers 0 200 400 600 Km.

Statute Miles 0 200 400 600 Mi.

Scale 1:12,000,000

One centimeter represents 120 kilometers.
One inch represents approximately 190 miles.
Lambert Conformal Conic Projection

Alberta

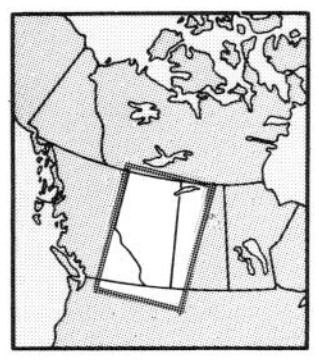

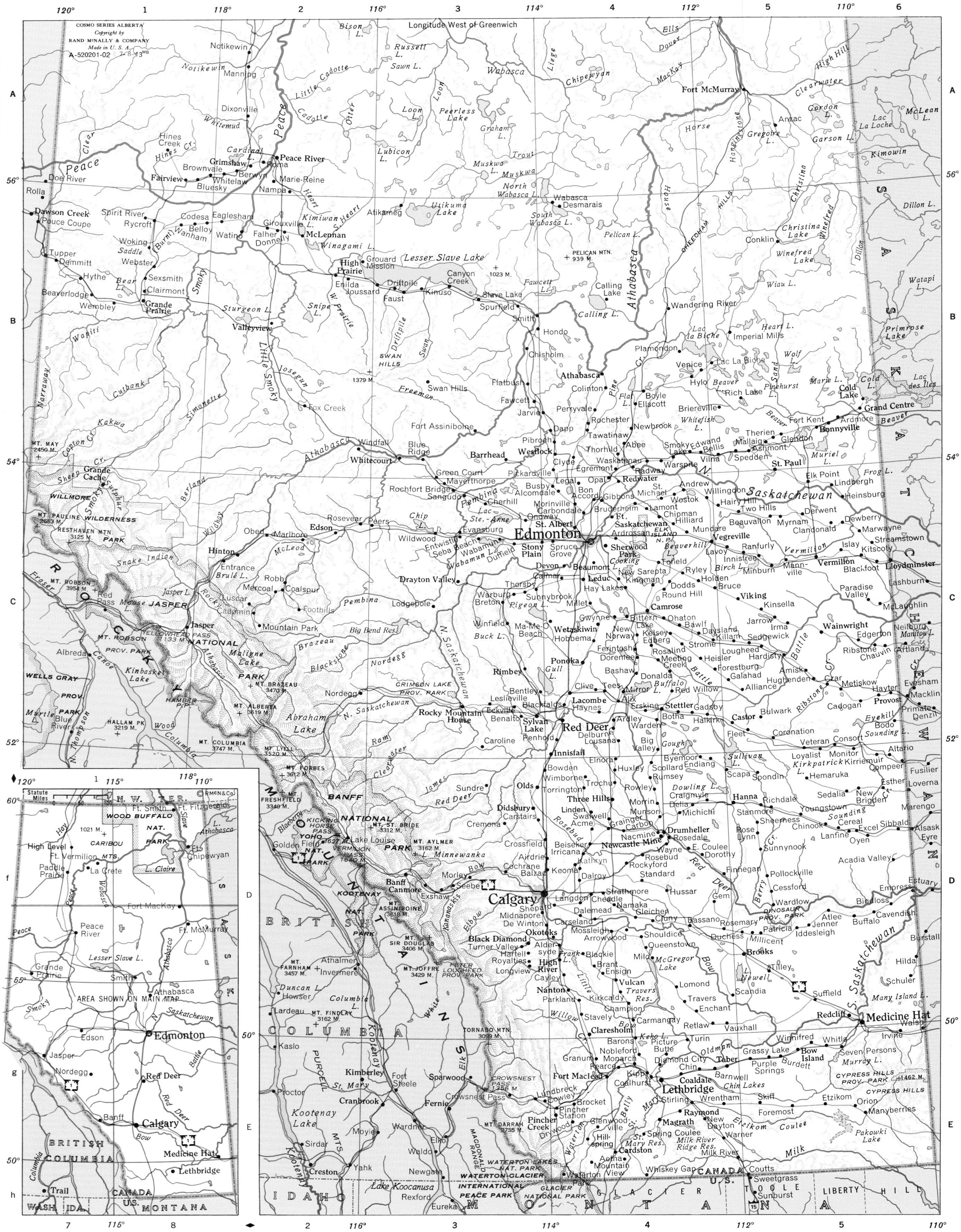

Statute Miles 10 0 10 20 30 40 50 60 70

Kilometers 10 0 10 20 40 60 80 100

Oblique Cylindrical Projection

SCALE 1:3,110,000 1 Inch = 49 Statute Miles

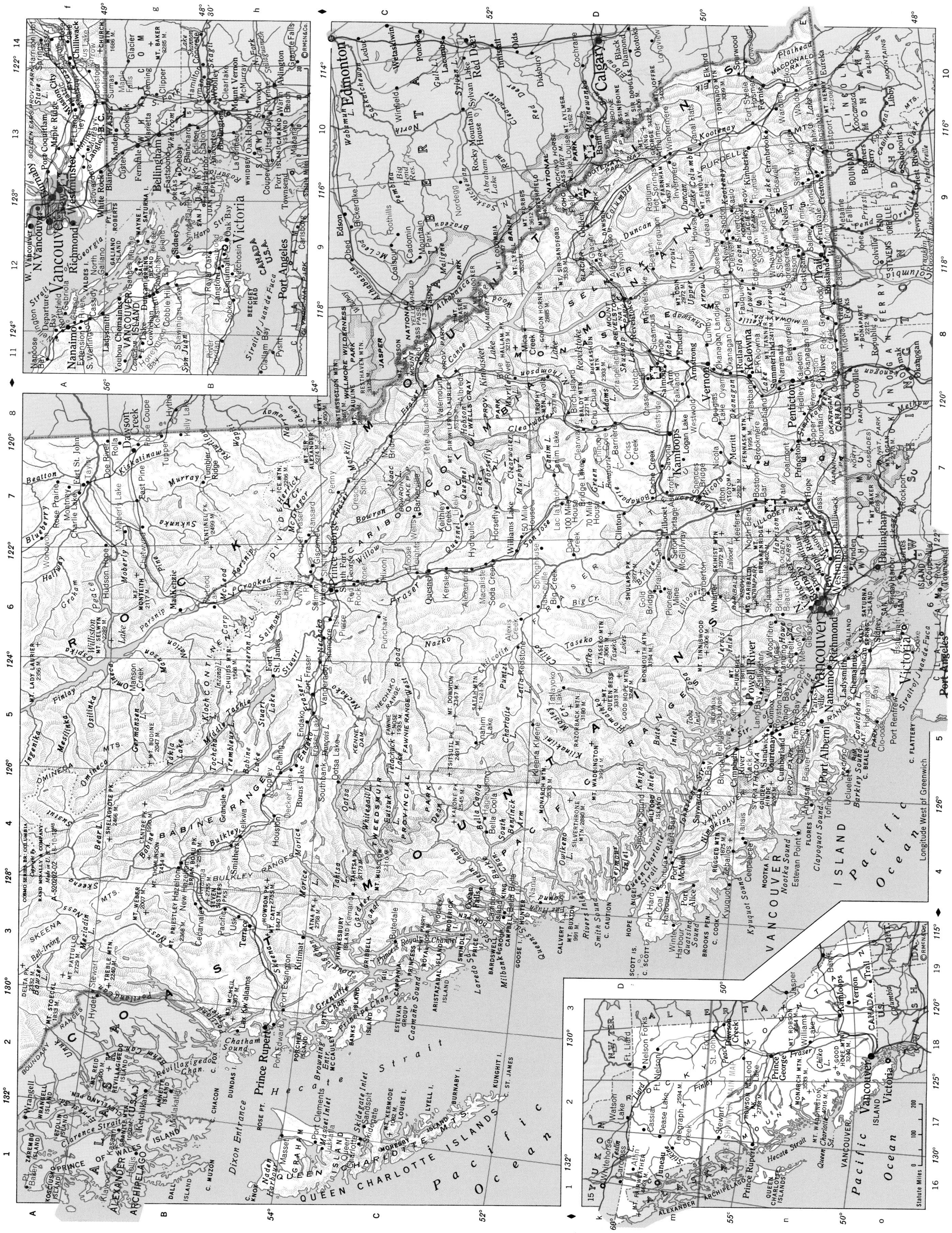

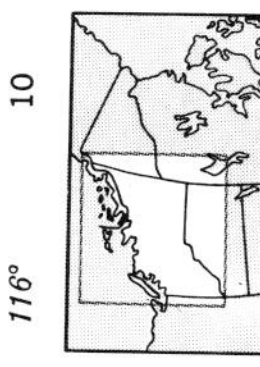

Oblique Cylindrical Projection
SCALE 1:4,255,000 1 Inch = 67 Statute Miles

Statute Miles 10 0 10 20 30 40 50 60 70 80 90 100
Kilometers 10 0 10 20 40 60 80 100 120 140

Manitoba

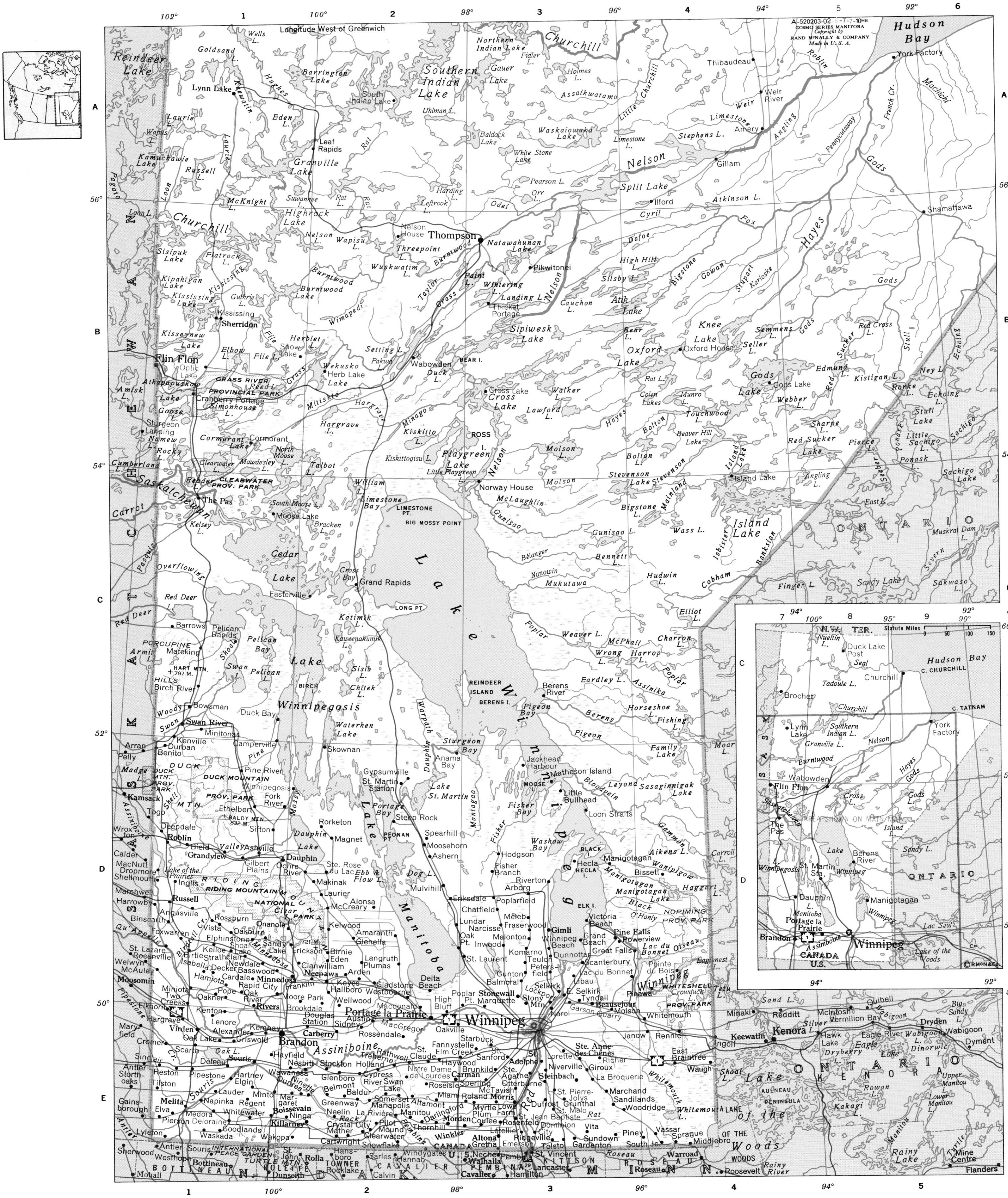

Statute Miles 10 0 10 20 30 40 50 60 70

Kilometers 10 0 10 20 40 60 80 100

Oblique Cylindrical Projection

SCALE 1:3,167,000 1 Inch = 50 Statute Miles

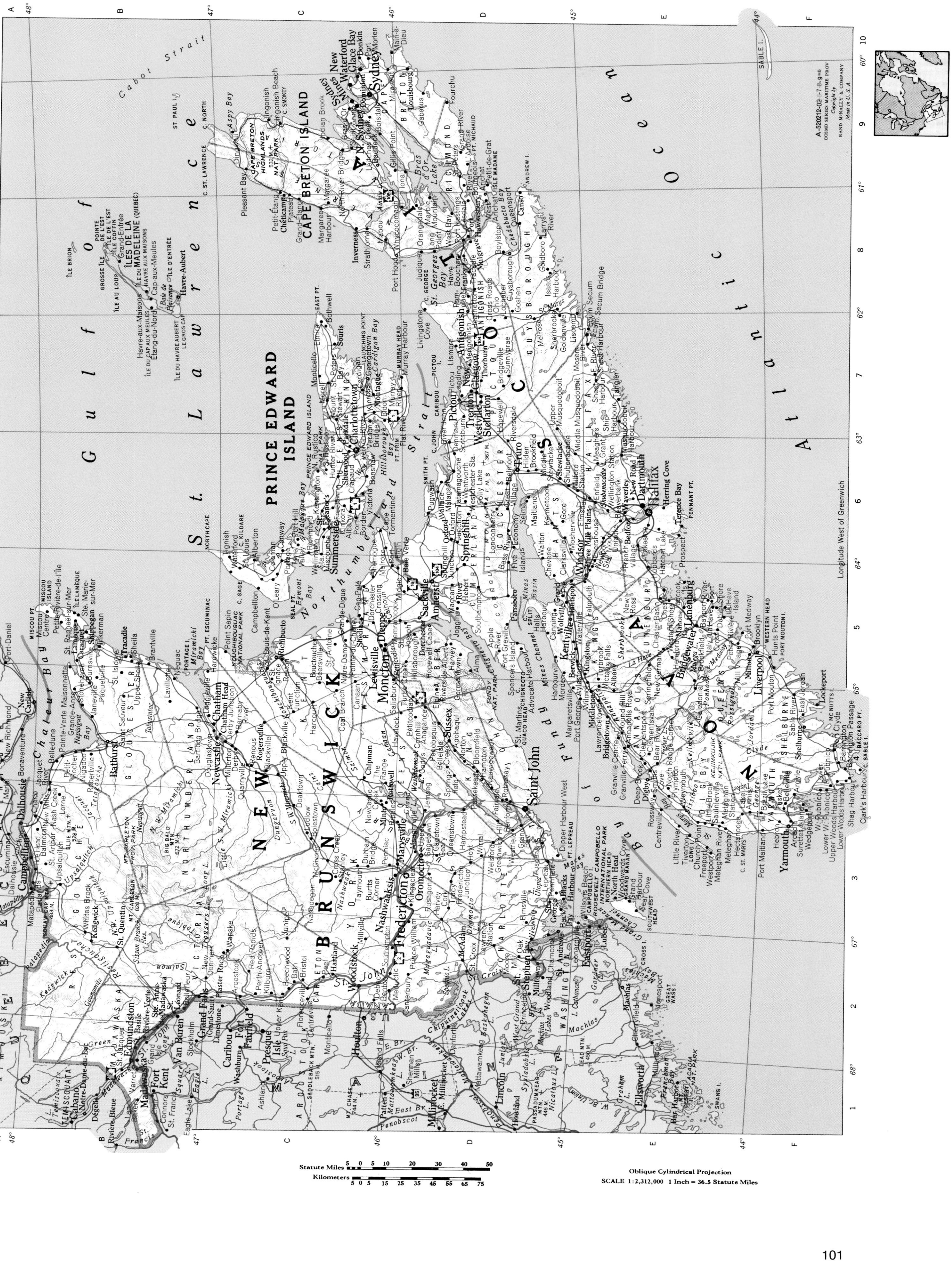

Statute Miles 5 0 5 10 20 30 40 50

Kilometers 5 0 5 15 25 35 45 55 65 75

Oblique Cylindrical Projection

SCALE 1:2,312,000 1 Inch = 36.5 Statute Miles

Newfoundland

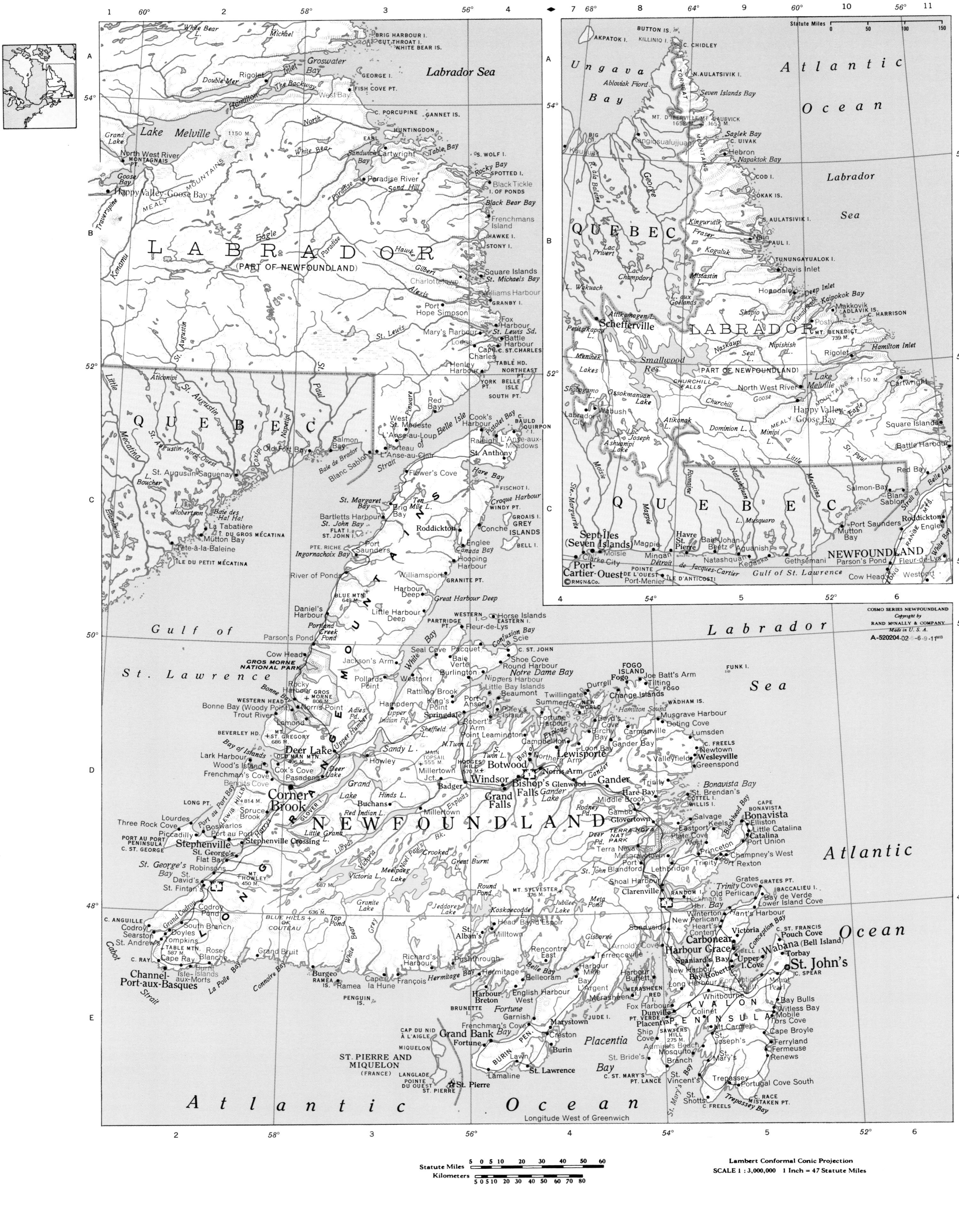

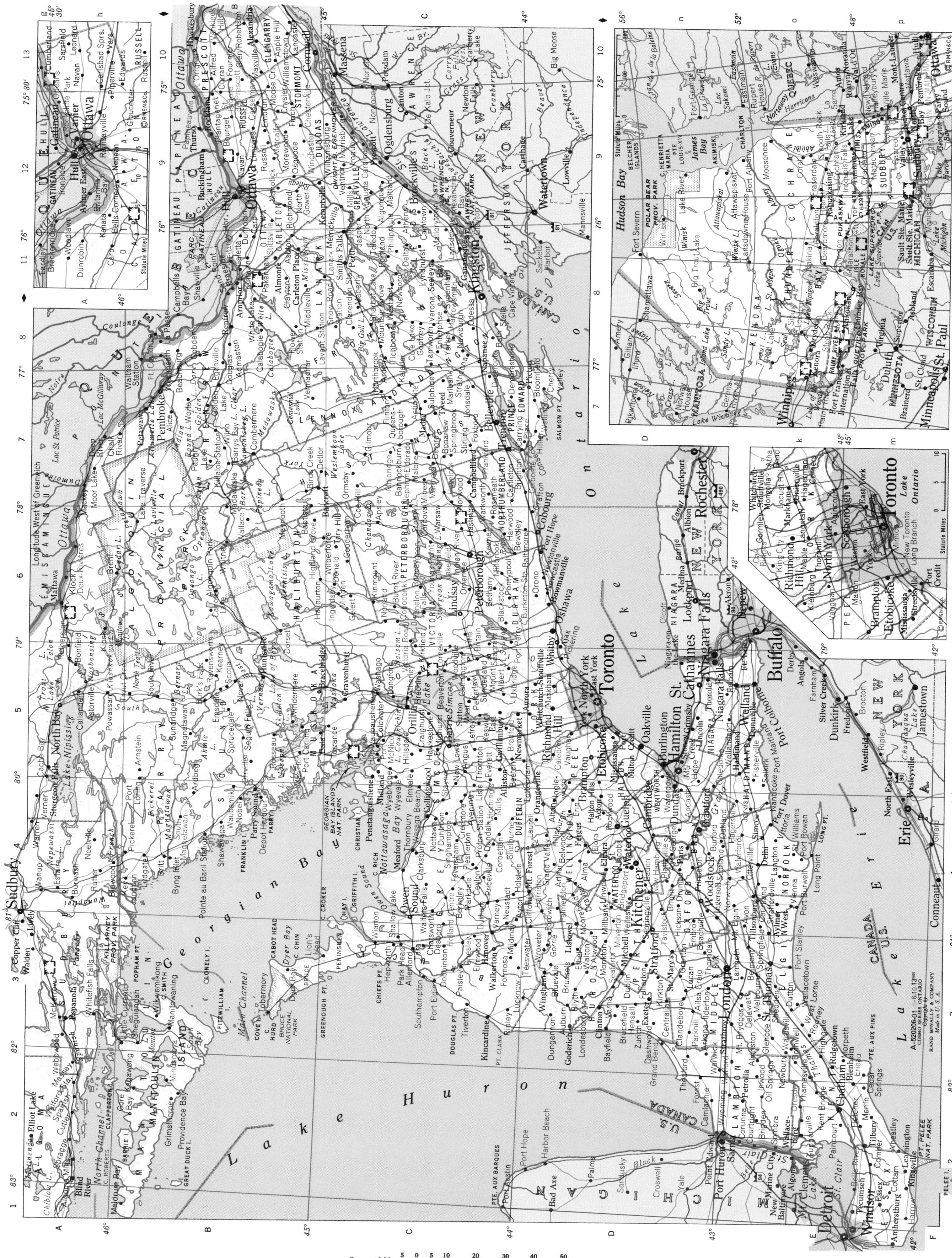

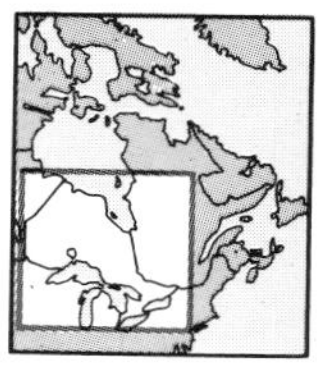

Statute Miles 5 0 5 10 20 30 40 50
Kilometers 5 0 5 15 25 35 45 55 65 75

Oblique Cylindrical Projection
SCALE 1:2,226,000 1 Inch = 35 Statute Miles

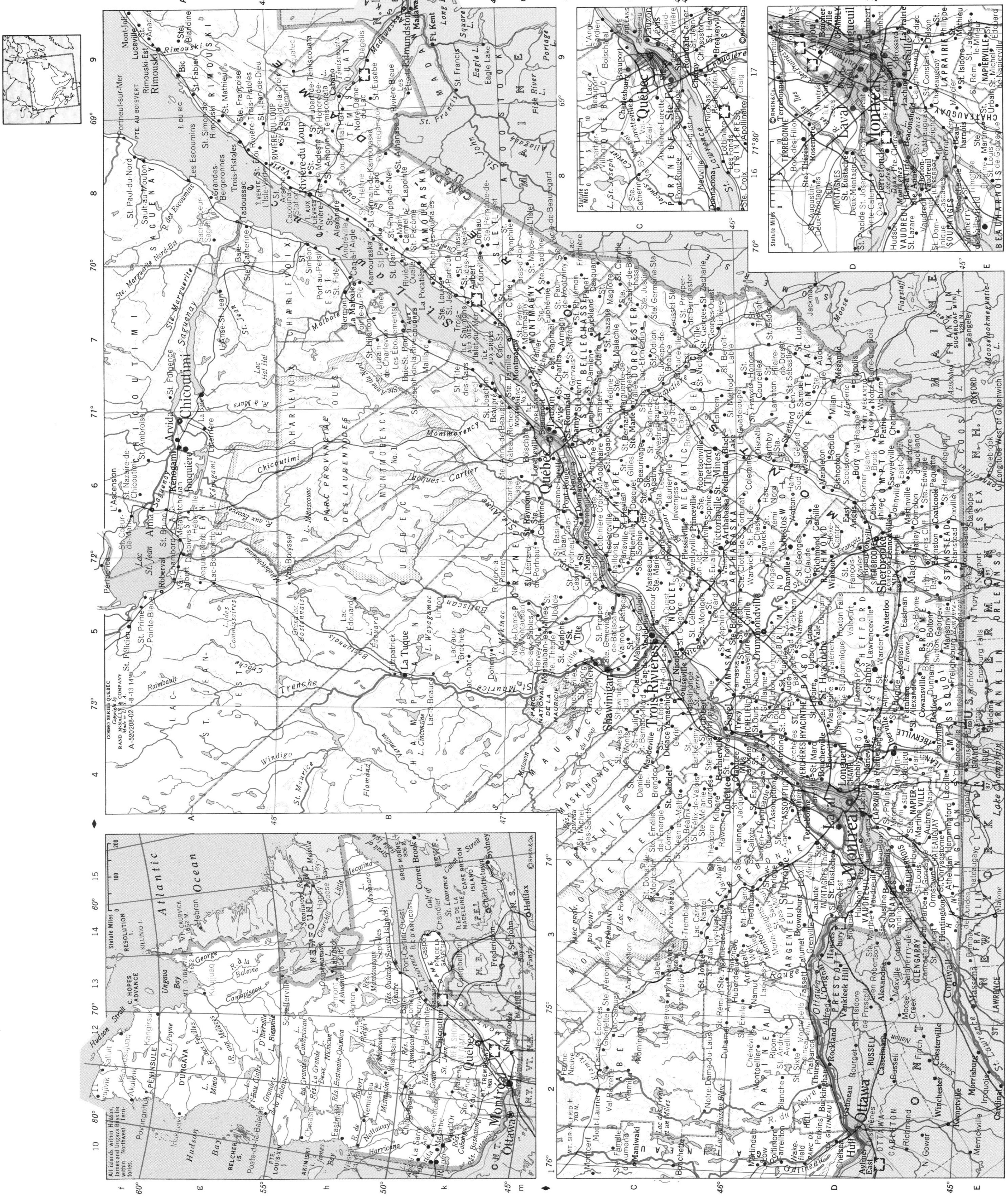

Statute Miles 5 0 5 10 20 30 40

Kilometers 5 0 5 15 25 35 45 55

Oblique Cylindrical Projection
SCALE 1:1,929,000 1 Inch = 30.5 Statute Miles

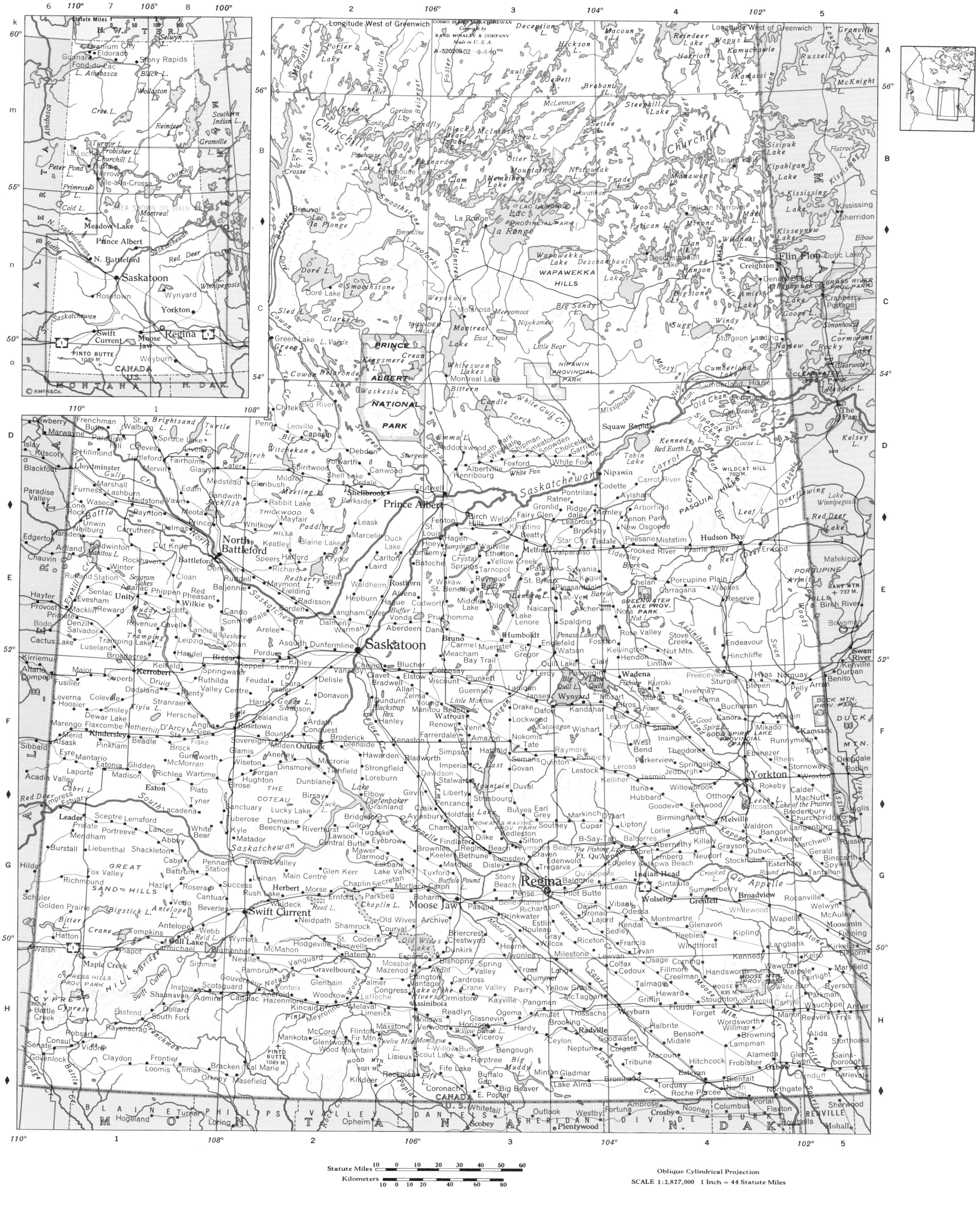
Longitude West of Greenwich
COSMO SERIES SASKATCHEWAN
Copyright by RAND McNALLY & COMPANY
Made in U.S.A.
Saskatoon
Regina
Prince Albert
North Battleford
Moose Jaw
Swift Current
Yorkton
Flin Flon
Lloydminster
Estevan
Weyburn
Melville
Humboldt
Kindersley
Tisdale
Hudson Bay
Nipawin
Creighton
La Ronge
Uranium City
Prince Albert National Park
Lac la Ronge
Lake Diefenbaker
Saskatchewan
South Saskatchewan
North Saskatchewan
Churchill
Qu'Appelle
Assiniboine
Souris
ALBERTA
MANITOBA
MONTANA
N. DAK.
CANADA
U.S.
Statute Miles
Kilometers
Oblique Cylindrical Projection
SCALE 1:2,827,000 1 Inch = 44 Statute Miles

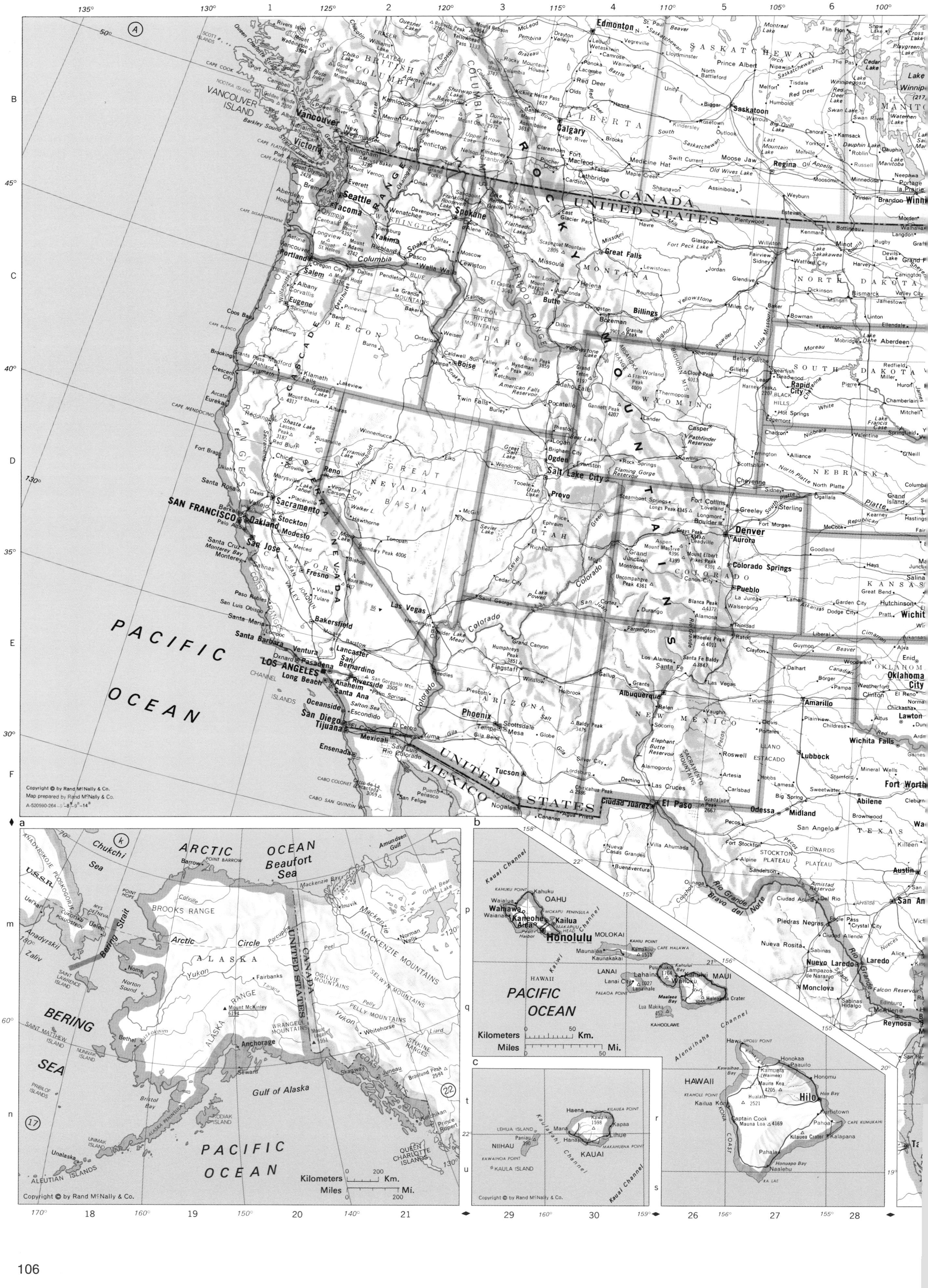
PACIFIC OCEAN
CANADA
UNITED STATES
MEXICO
UNITED STATES
ROCKY MOUNTAINS
BRITISH COLUMBIA
ALBERTA
SASKATCHEWAN
WASHINGTON
OREGON
IDAHO
MONTANA
WYOMING
NORTH DAKOTA
SOUTH DAKOTA
NEBRASKA
KANSAS
CALIFORNIA
NEVADA
UTAH
COLORADO
ARIZONA
NEW MEXICO
TEXAS
OKLAHOMA
GREAT BASIN
SIERRA NEVADA
CASCADE RANGE
COAST RANGES
VANCOUVER ISLAND
Vancouver
Victoria
Seattle
Tacoma
Spokane
Portland
Salem
Eugene
Boise
Calgary
Edmonton
Saskatoon
Regina
Great Falls
Helena
Butte
Billings
Salt Lake City
Ogden
Provo
Reno
Sacramento
SAN FRANCISCO
Oakland
San Jose
Fresno
Bakersfield
Las Vegas
LOS ANGELES
Long Beach
San Diego
Tijuana
Phoenix
Tucson
Albuquerque
Santa Fe
El Paso
Ciudad Juárez
Denver
Colorado Springs
Pueblo
Cheyenne
Amarillo
Lubbock
Oklahoma City
Wichita Falls
Odessa
Midland
San Angelo
Rio Grande
Copyright © by Rand McNally & Co.
Map prepared by Rand McNally & Co.
ARCTIC OCEAN
Beaufort Sea
Chukchi Sea
BROOKS RANGE
ALASKA
Arctic Circle
ALASKA RANGE
Mount McKinley 6194
Fairbanks
Anchorage
Gulf of Alaska
BERING SEA
Bering Strait
PACIFIC OCEAN
Kilometers 0 200 Km.
Miles 0 200 Mi.
Copyright © by Rand McNally & Co.
OAHU
Honolulu
MOLOKAI
LANAI
MAUI
KAHOOLAWE
KAUAI
NIIHAU
HAWAII
Hilo
PACIFIC OCEAN
Kilometers 0 50 Km.
Miles 0 50 Mi.
Copyright © by Rand McNally & Co.

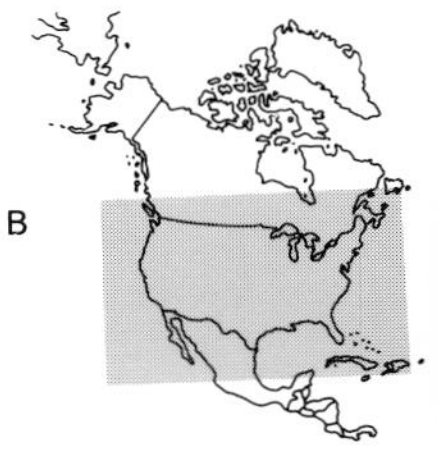

Kilometers 0 200 400 600 Km.

Statute Miles 0 200 400 600 Mi.

Scale 1:12,000,000

One centimeter represents 120 kilometers.
One inch represents approximately 190 miles.
Albers Conical Equal-Area Projection

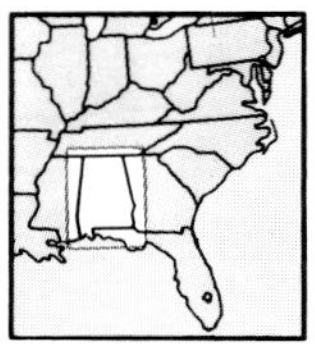

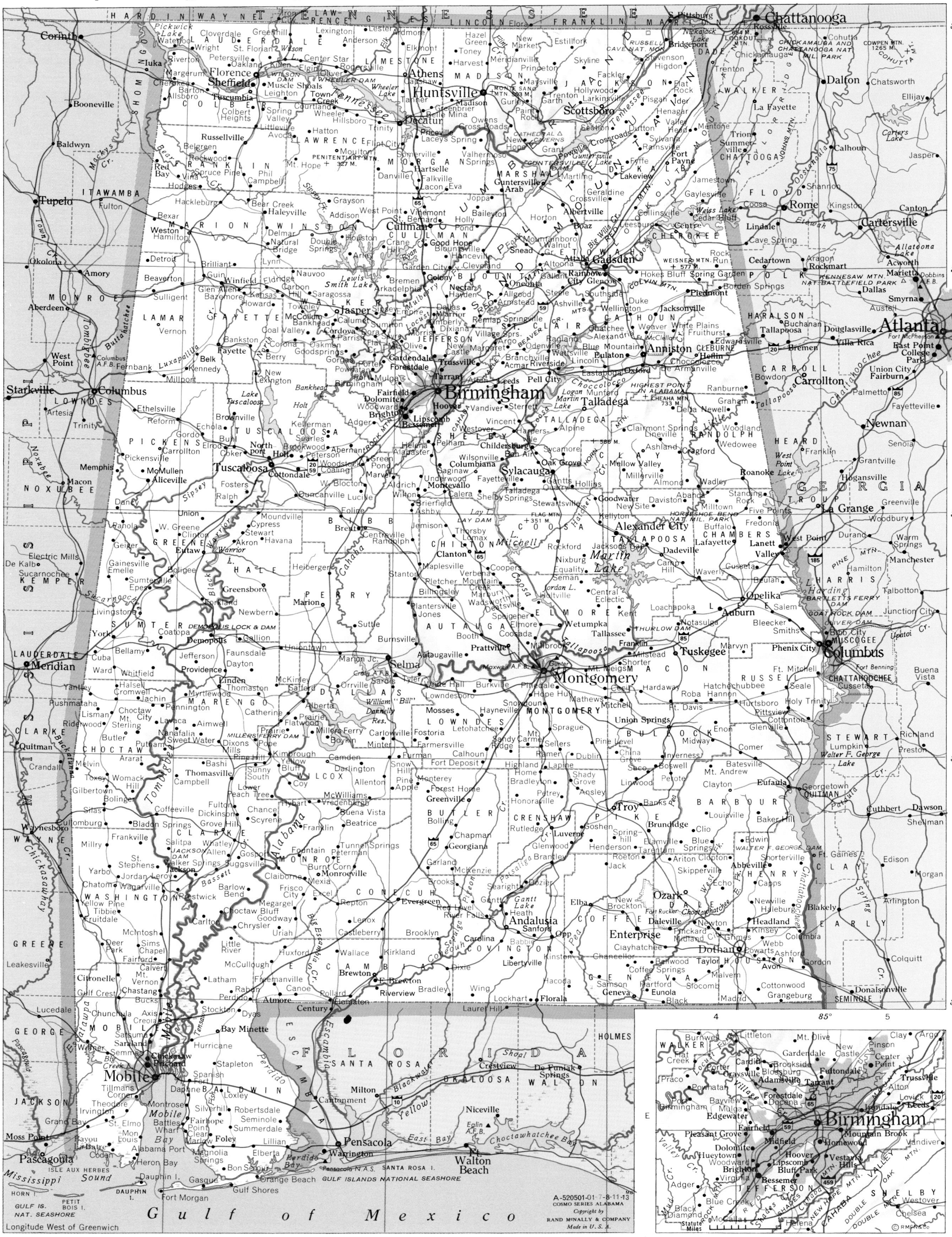

Statute Miles 5 0 5 10 20 30 40

Kilometers 5 0 5 15 25 35 45 55

Lambert Conformal Conic Projection

SCALE 1:1,831,000 1 Inch = 29 Statute Miles

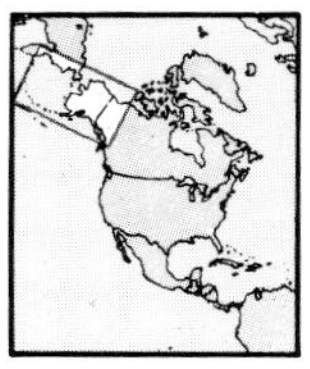

Statute Miles 50 25 0 50 100 150 200 250

Kilometers 50 0 100 200 300

Polyconic Projection

SCALE 1:12,000,000 1 Inch = 189 Statute Miles

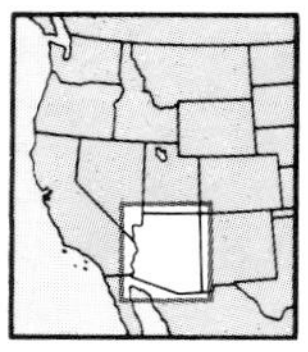

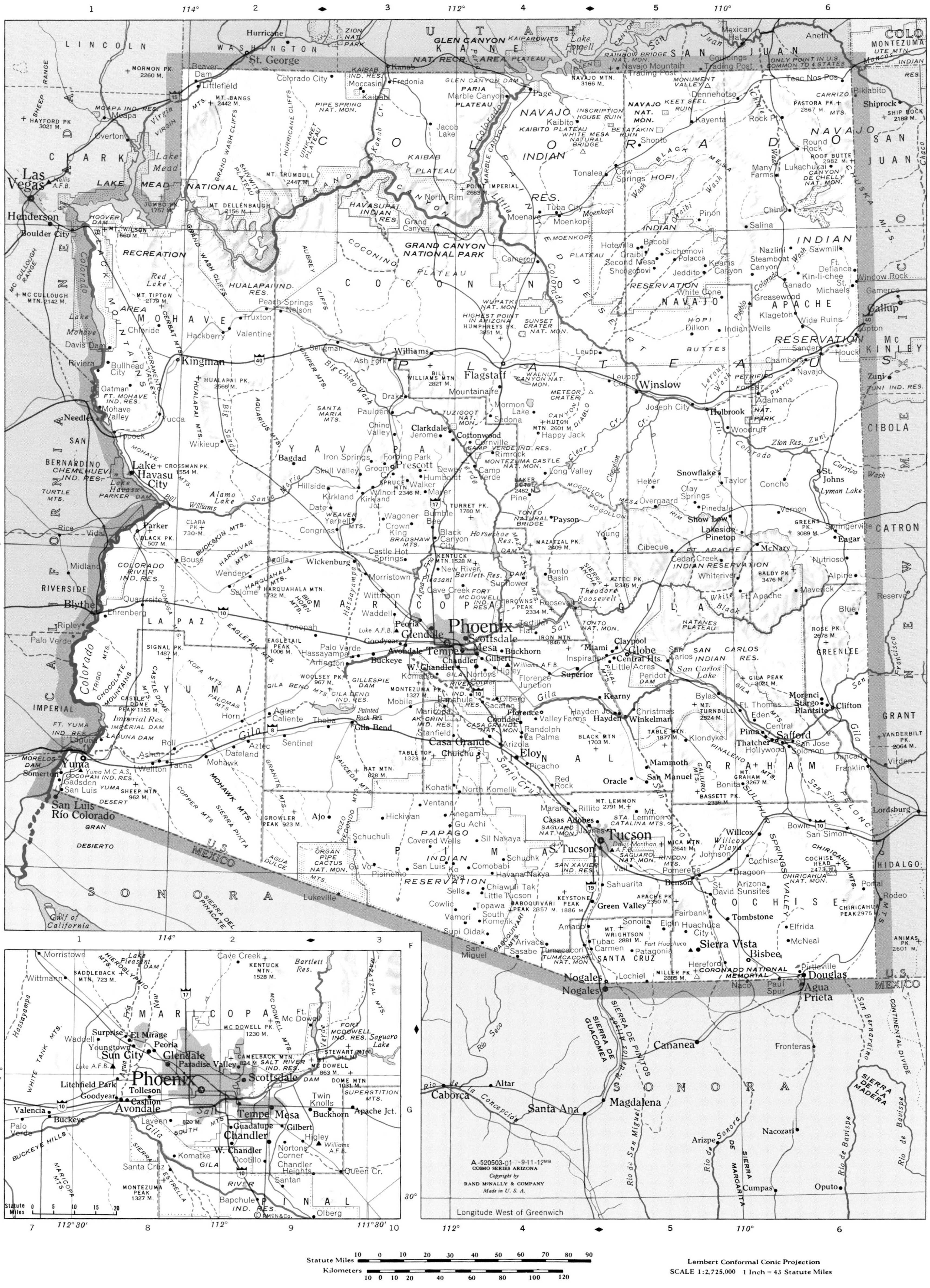
UTAH
COLO
NEVADA
CALIFORNIA
SONORA
U.S.
MEXICO
Las Vegas
Henderson
St. George
Kingman
Flagstaff
Winslow
Holbrook
Prescott
Phoenix
Glendale
Scottsdale
Tempe
Mesa
Chandler
Casa Grande
Tucson
Nogales
Douglas
Bisbee
Sierra Vista
Yuma
Lake Havasu City
Safford
Globe
Gallup
Lordsburg
GRAND CANYON NATIONAL PARK
NAVAJO INDIAN RES.
HOPI INDIAN RESERVATION
FORT APACHE INDIAN RESERVATION
SAN CARLOS INDIAN RES.
PAPAGO INDIAN RESERVATION
MOHAVE
COCONINO
YAVAPAI
MARICOPA
YUMA
LA PAZ
PINAL
PIMA
GRAHAM
COCHISE
SANTA CRUZ
GILA
APACHE
NAVAJO
GREENLEE
Inset: Phoenix area
A-520503-01 -9-11-12MB
COSMO SERIES ARIZONA
Copyright by
RAND McNALLY & COMPANY
Made in U. S. A.
Longitude West of Greenwich
Statute Miles
Kilometers
Lambert Conformal Conic Projection
SCALE 1:2,725,000 1 Inch = 43 Statute Miles

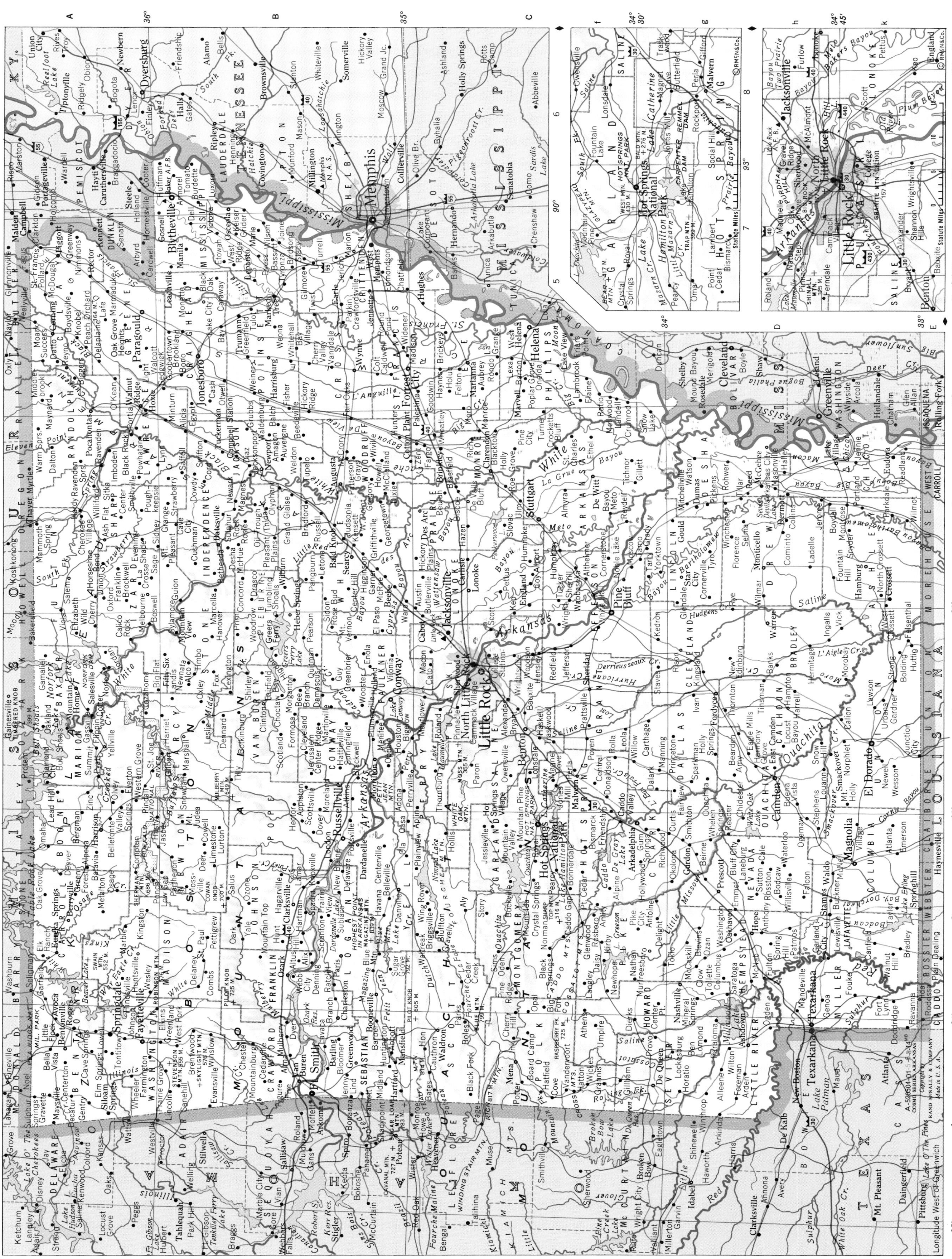

Statute Miles 5 0 5 10 20 30 40

Kilometers 5 0 5 15 25 35 45 55

Lambert Conformal Conic Projection
SCALE 1:1,832,000 1 Inch = 29 Statute Miles

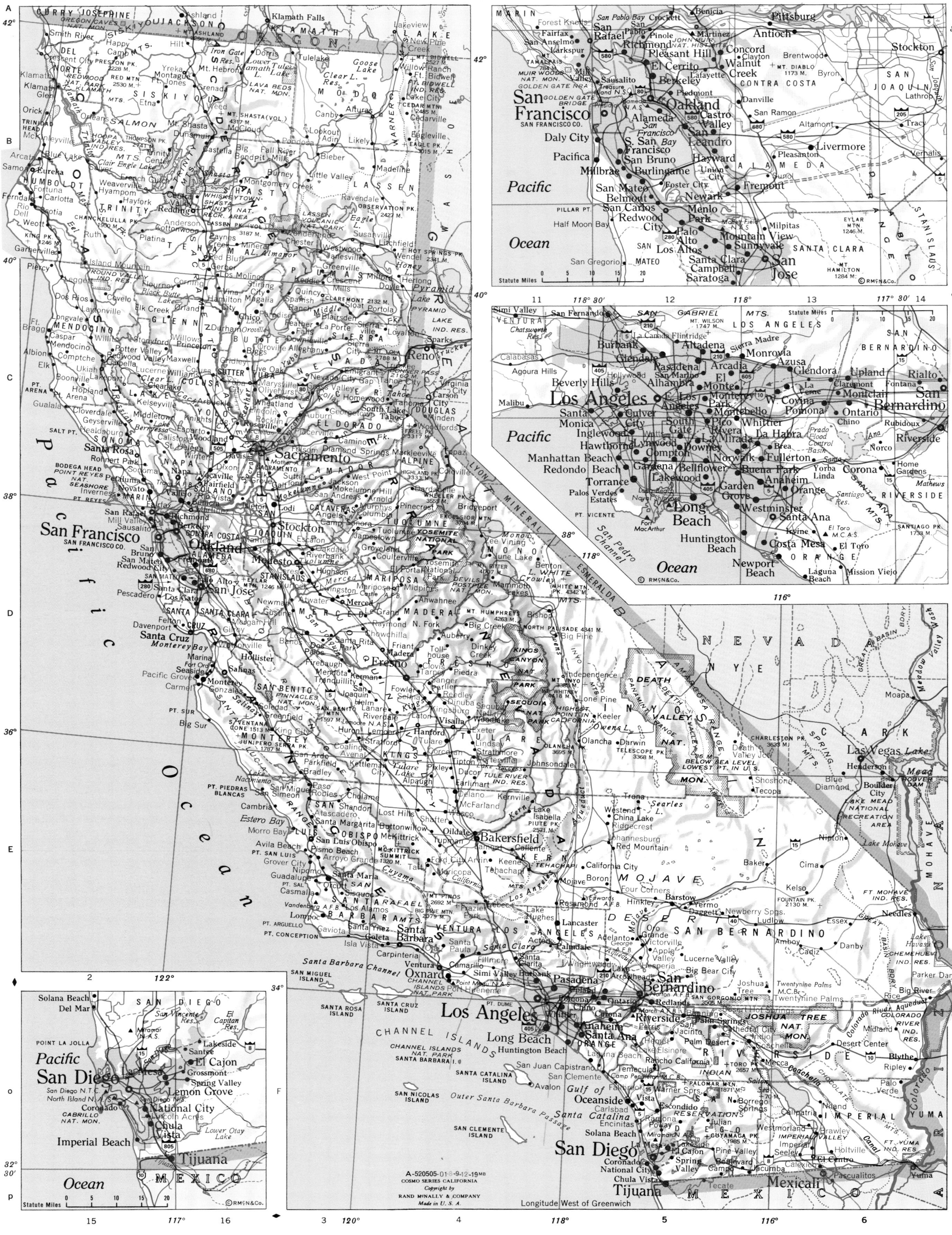

Statute Miles 10 0 10 20 30 40 50 60 70 80 90

Kilometers 10 0 10 20 40 60 80 100 120

Lambert Conformal Conic Projection
SCALE 1:3,733,000 1 Inch = 59 Statute Miles

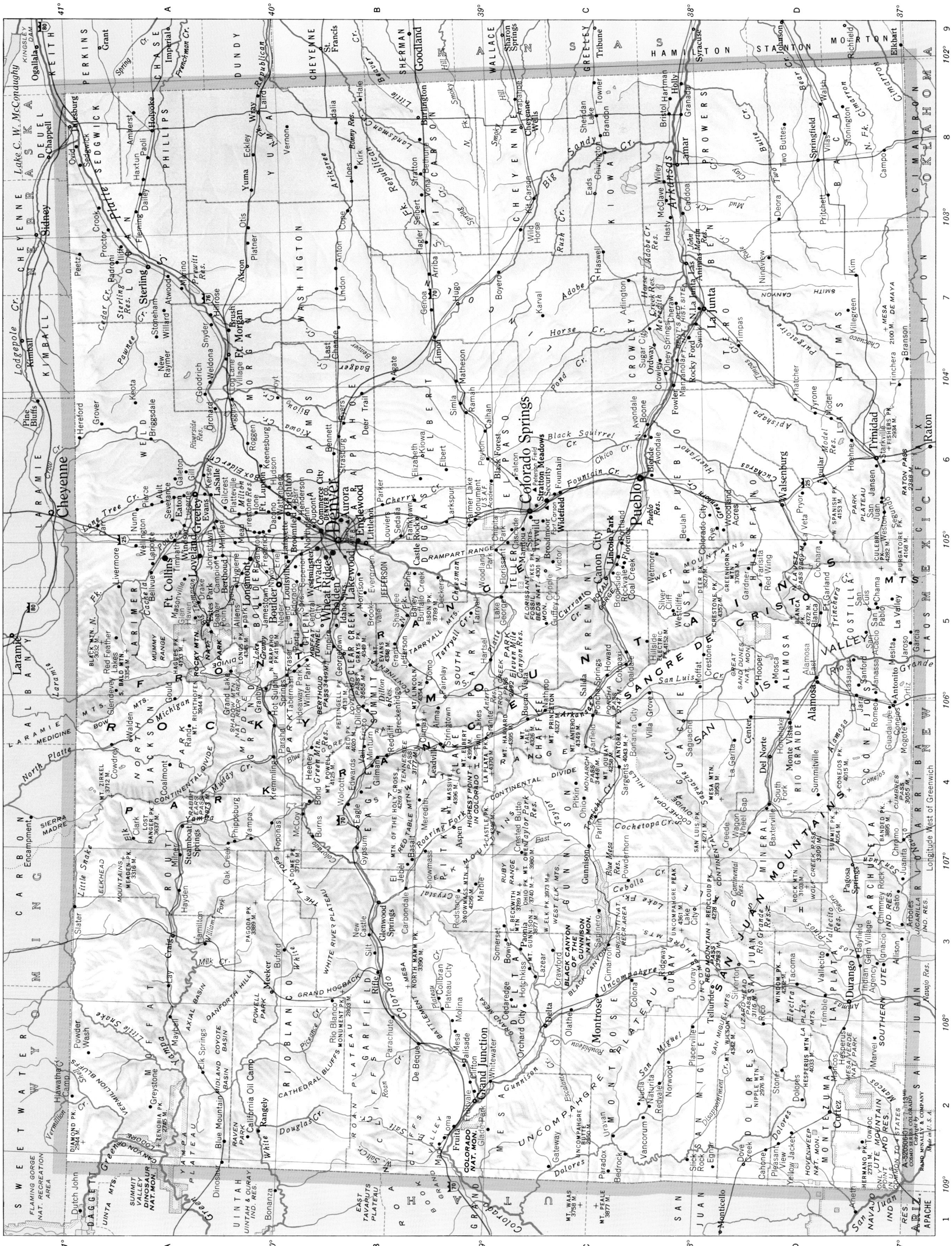

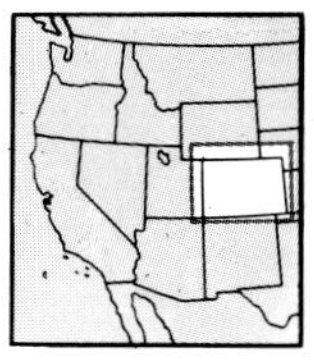

Statute Miles 5 0 5 10 20 30 40 50

Kilometers 5 0 5 15 25 35 45 55 65 75

Lambert Conformal Conic Projection

SCALE 1:2,186,000 1 Inch = 34.5 Statute Miles

Connecticut

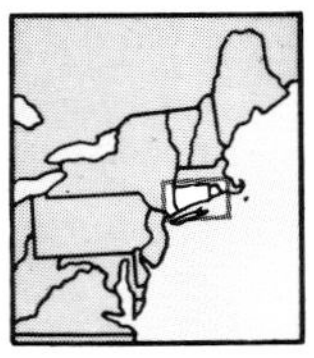

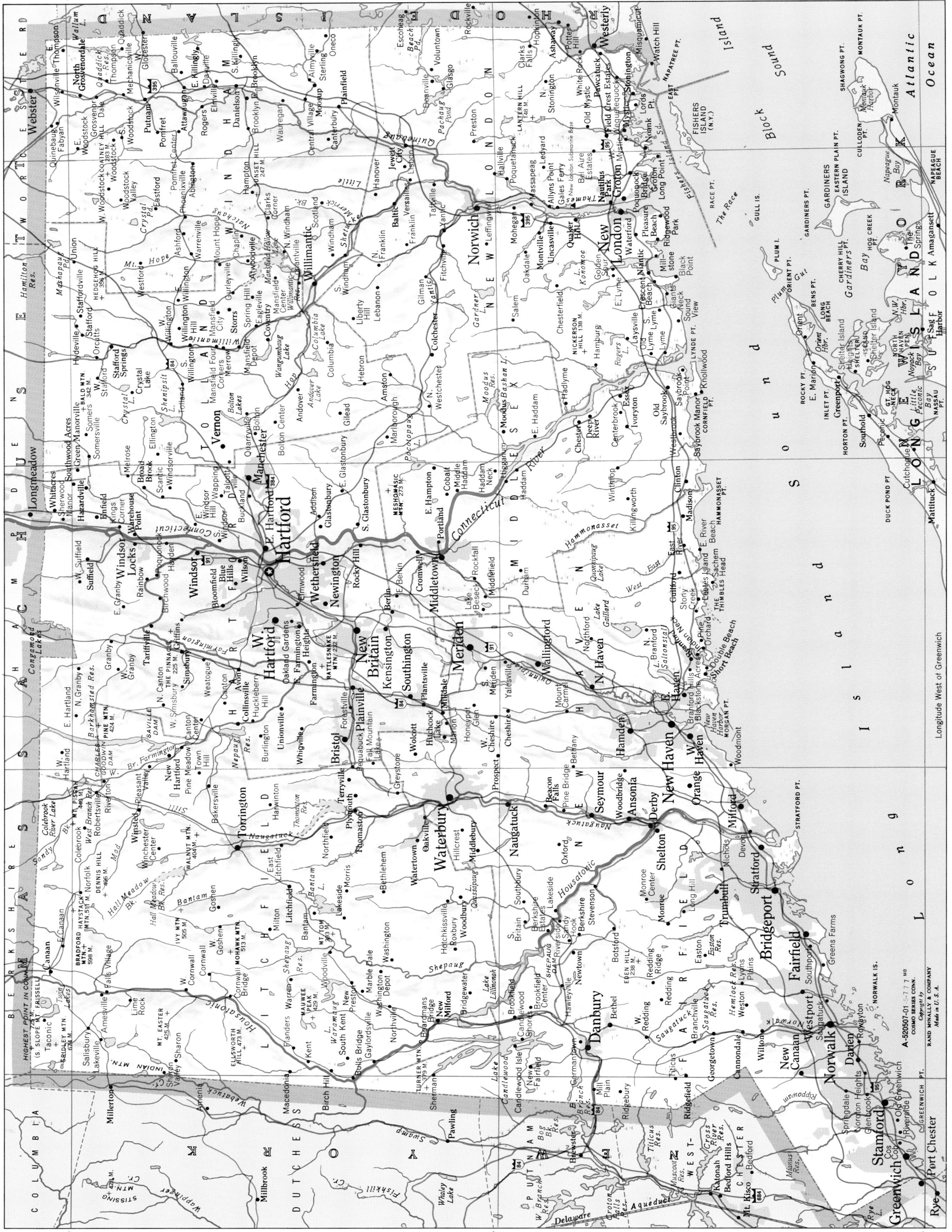

Statute Miles 5 0 5 10 15

Kilometers 5 0 5 10 15 20

Lambert Conformal Conic Projection
SCALE 1:545,000 1 Inch = 8.6 Statute Miles

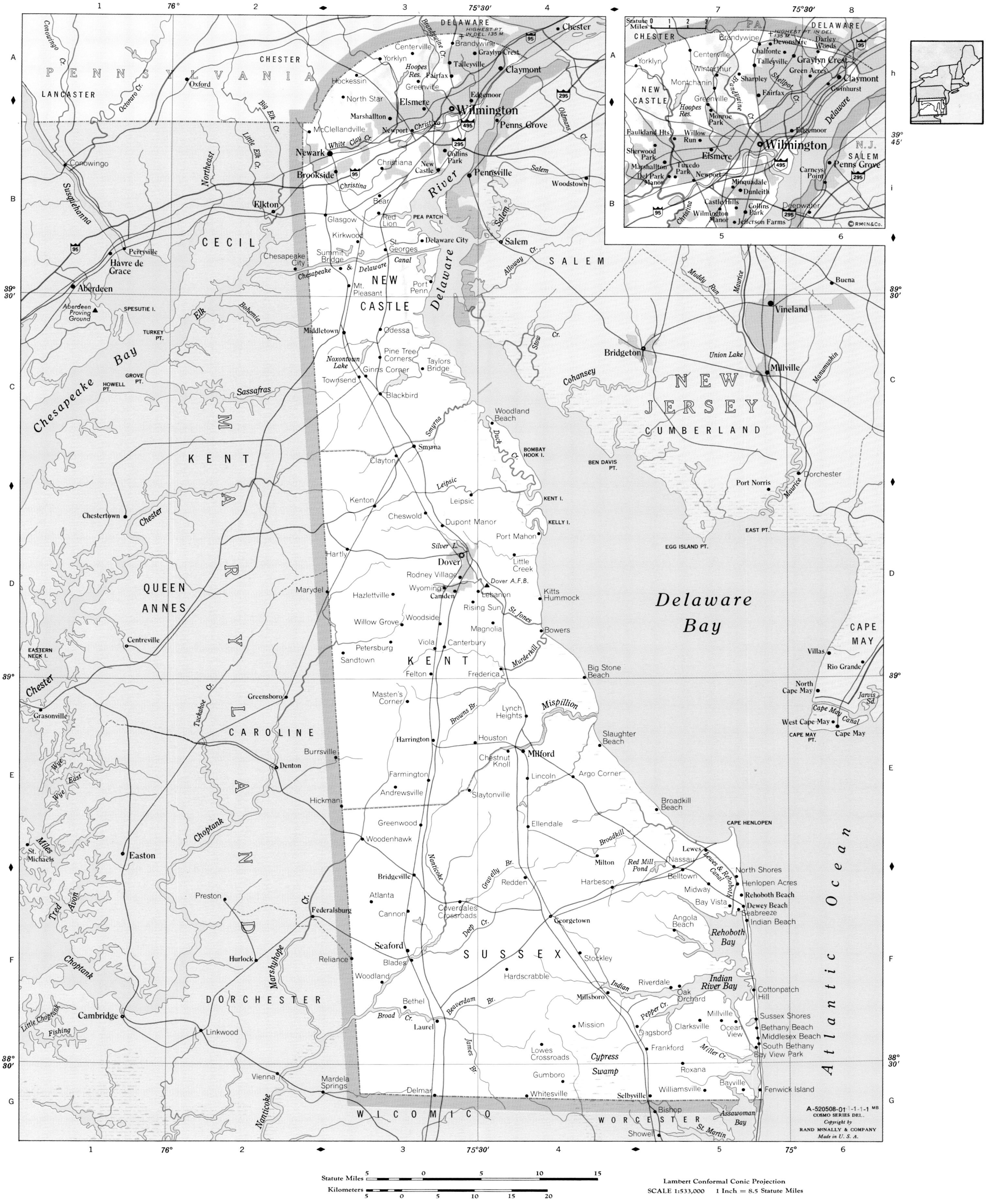
PENNSYLVANIA
LANCASTER
CHESTER
DELAWARE
HIGHEST PT. IN DEL. 135 M.
Conowingo Cr.
Octoraro Cr.
Oxford
Big Elk Cr.
Little Elk Cr.
Northeast
Conowingo
Susquehanna
Elkton
CECIL
Perryville
Havre de Grace
Aberdeen
Aberdeen Proving Ground
SPESUTIE I.
Elk
Bohemia
TURKEY PT.
Chesapeake Bay
GROVE PT.
HOWELL PT.
Sassafras
KENT
Chestertown
Chester
QUEEN ANNES
Centreville
EASTERN NECK I.
Grasonville
Greensboro
Tuckahoe Cr.
CAROLINE
Denton
Wye
Wye East
St. Michaels
Miles
Easton
Choptank
Tred Avon
Preston
Federalsburg
Hurlock
Marshyhope Cr.
DORCHESTER
Cambridge
Little Choptank
Fishing
Linkwood
Vienna
Nanticoke
Mardela Springs
WICOMICO
WORCESTER
MARYLAND
Centerville
Yorklyn
Hockessin
North Star
Brandywine
Brandywine Cr.
Graylyn Crest
Talleyville
Claymont
Chester
Hoopes Res.
Fairfax
Greenville
Elmsere
Edgemoor
Marshallton
Wilmington
Newport
Christina
McClellandville
Newark
White Clay Cr.
Christiana
Collins Park
New Castle
Brookside
Bear
Glasgow
Red Lion
PEA PATCH I.
Kirkwood
St. Georges
Delaware City
Chesapeake City
Summit Bridge
Chesapeake & Delaware Canal
Mt. Pleasant
NEW CASTLE
Port Penn
Middletown
Odessa
Noxontown Lake
Pine Tree Corners
Ginns Corner
Taylors Bridge
Townsend
Blackbird
Smyrna
Clayton
Woodland Beach
Duck Cr.
BOMBAY HOOK I.
Leipsic
Kenton
Cheswold
Dupont Manor
KENT I.
KELLY I.
Port Mahon
Silver L.
Hartly
Dover
Little Creek
Rodney Village
Dover A.F.B.
Marydel
Hazlettville
Wyoming
Camden
Lebanon
Kitts Hummock
Rising Sun
St. Jones
Willow Grove
Woodside
Magnolia
Bowers
Petersburg
Sandtown
Viola
Canterbury
Murderkill
Felton
Frederica
Big Stone Beach
Masten's Corner
Browns Br.
Lynch Heights
Mispillion
Harrington
Houston
Milford
Slaughter Beach
Chestnut Knoll
Burrsville
Farmington
Lincoln
Argo Corner
Andrewsville
Slaytonville
Hickman
Broadkill Beach
Greenwood
Ellendale
CAPE HENLOPEN
Woodenhawk
Broadkill
Lewes
Nassau
Lewes & Rehoboth Canal
Milton
Red Mill Pond
Belltown
North Shores
Bridgeville
Nanticoke
Gravelly Br.
Redden
Harbeson
Henlopen Acres
Rehoboth Beach
Atlanta
Midway
Bay Vista
Dewey Beach
Seabreeze
Cannon
Coverdales Crossroads
Georgetown
Angola Beach
Indian Beach
Deep Cr.
Rehoboth Bay
Seaford
Blades
SUSSEX
Stockley
Reliance
Woodland
Hardscrabble
Indian
Riverdale
Indian River Bay
Millsboro
Oak Orchard
Cottonpatch Hill
Bethel
Beaverdam Br.
Pepper Cr.
Millville
Sussex Shores
Broad Cr.
Laurel
Mission
Clarksville
Ocean View
Bethany Beach
Dagsboro
Middlesex Beach
James Br.
Frankford
South Bethany
Miller Cr.
Bay View Park
Lowes Crossroads
Cypress Swamp
Roxana
Gumboro
Bayville
Fenwick Island
Williamsville
Delmar
Whitesville
Selbyville
Bishop
Assawoman Bay
St. Martin
Showell
Atlantic Ocean
Delaware Bay
Delaware River
Salem
Oldmans Cr.
Penns Grove
Pennsville
Woodstown
Alloway Cr.
SALEM
Muddy Run
Maurice
Buena
Vineland
Stow Cr.
Bridgeton
Union Lake
Millville
Manumuskin
Cohansey
NEW JERSEY
CUMBERLAND
BEN DAVIS PT.
Dorchester
Port Norris
EAST PT.
EGG ISLAND PT.
CAPE MAY
Villas
Rio Grande
North Cape May
Jarvis Sd.
Cape May Canal
West Cape May
Cape May
CAPE MAY PT.
Statute Miles 0 1 2 3
PA
DELAWARE
HIGHEST PT. IN DEL. 135 M.
CHESTER
Yorklyn
Centerville
Winterthur
Montchanin
NEW CASTLE
Greenville
Hoopes Res.
Monroe Park
Chalfonte
Devonshire
Darley Woods
Talleyville
Graylyn Crest
Green Acres
Shellpot Cr.
Sharpley
Fairfax
Claymont
Gwinhurst
Faulkland Hts.
Willow Run
Sherwood Park
Marshallton
Del Park Manor
Tuxedo Park
Newport
Elsmere
Wilmington
Edgemoor
N.J.
SALEM
Penns Grove
Carneys Point
Minquadale
Dunleith
Castle Hills
Wilmington Manor
Collins Park
Jefferson Farms
Deepwater
©RMcN&Co.
39° 45′
39° 30′
39°
38° 30′
76°
75°30′
75°
A-520508-01-1-1-1 MB
COSMO SERIES DEL.
Copyright by
RAND McNALLY & COMPANY
Made in U. S. A.
Statute Miles 5 0 5 10 15
Kilometers 5 0 5 10 15 20
Lambert Conformal Conic Projection
SCALE 1:533,000 1 Inch = 8.5 Statute Miles

Florida

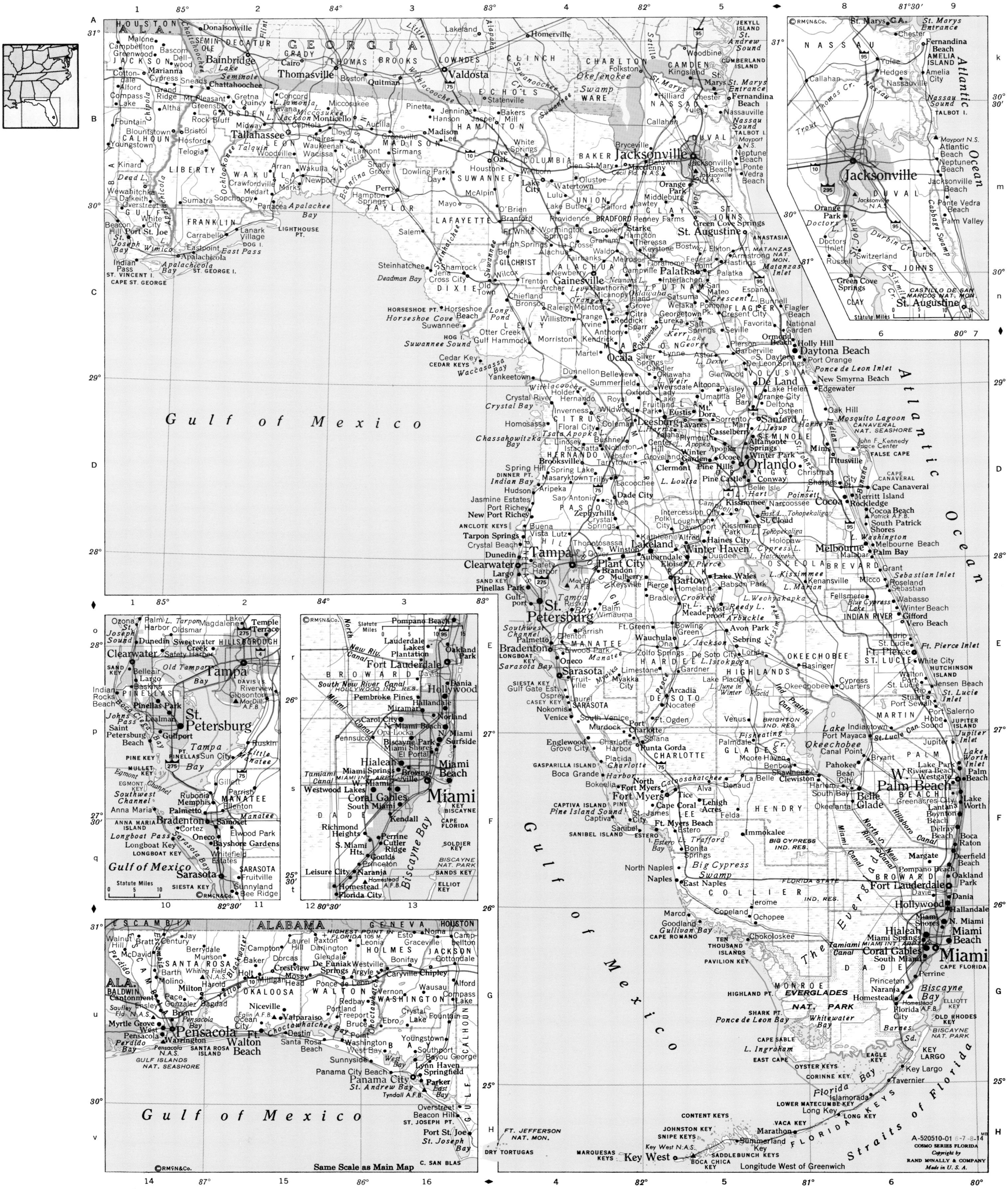
Gulf of Mexico
Atlantic Ocean
Straits of Florida
Florida Bay
Biscayne Bay
G E O R G I A
A L A.
ALABAMA
Jacksonville
Tallahassee
Pensacola
Gainesville
Ocala
Orlando
Daytona Beach
Tampa
St. Petersburg
Clearwater
Lakeland
Sarasota
Fort Myers
W. Palm Beach
Fort Lauderdale
Hollywood
Miami
Key West
St. Augustine
Okeechobee
Lake Okeechobee
Big Cypress Swamp
EVERGLADES NAT. PARK
Valdosta
Thomasville
Bainbridge
Panama City
Same Scale as Main Map
Longitude West of Greenwich
A-520510-01
COSMO SERIES FLORIDA
Copyright by RAND McNALLY & COMPANY
Made in U. S. A.
Statute Miles
Kilometers
Lambert Conformal Conic Projection
SCALE 1:2,425,000 1 Inch = 38 Statute Miles

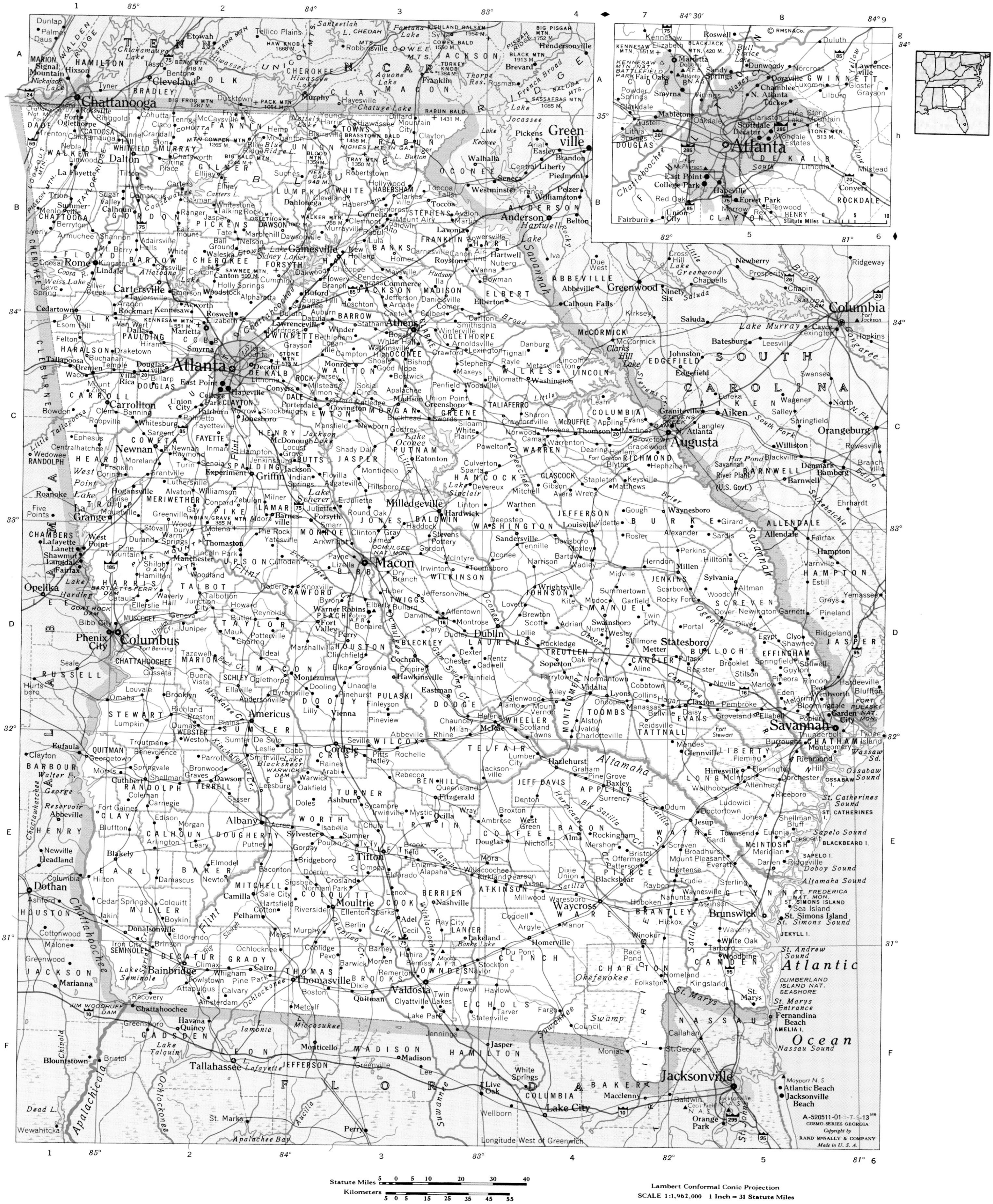
Atlanta
Statute Miles 0 5 10
A-520511-01-5-7-9-13 MB
COSMO SERIES GEORGIA
Copyright by
RAND McNALLY & COMPANY
Made in U. S. A.
Longitude West of Greenwich
Statute Miles 5 0 5 10 20 30 40
Kilometers 5 0 5 15 25 35 45 55
Lambert Conformal Conic Projection
SCALE 1:1,962,000 1 Inch = 31 Statute Miles

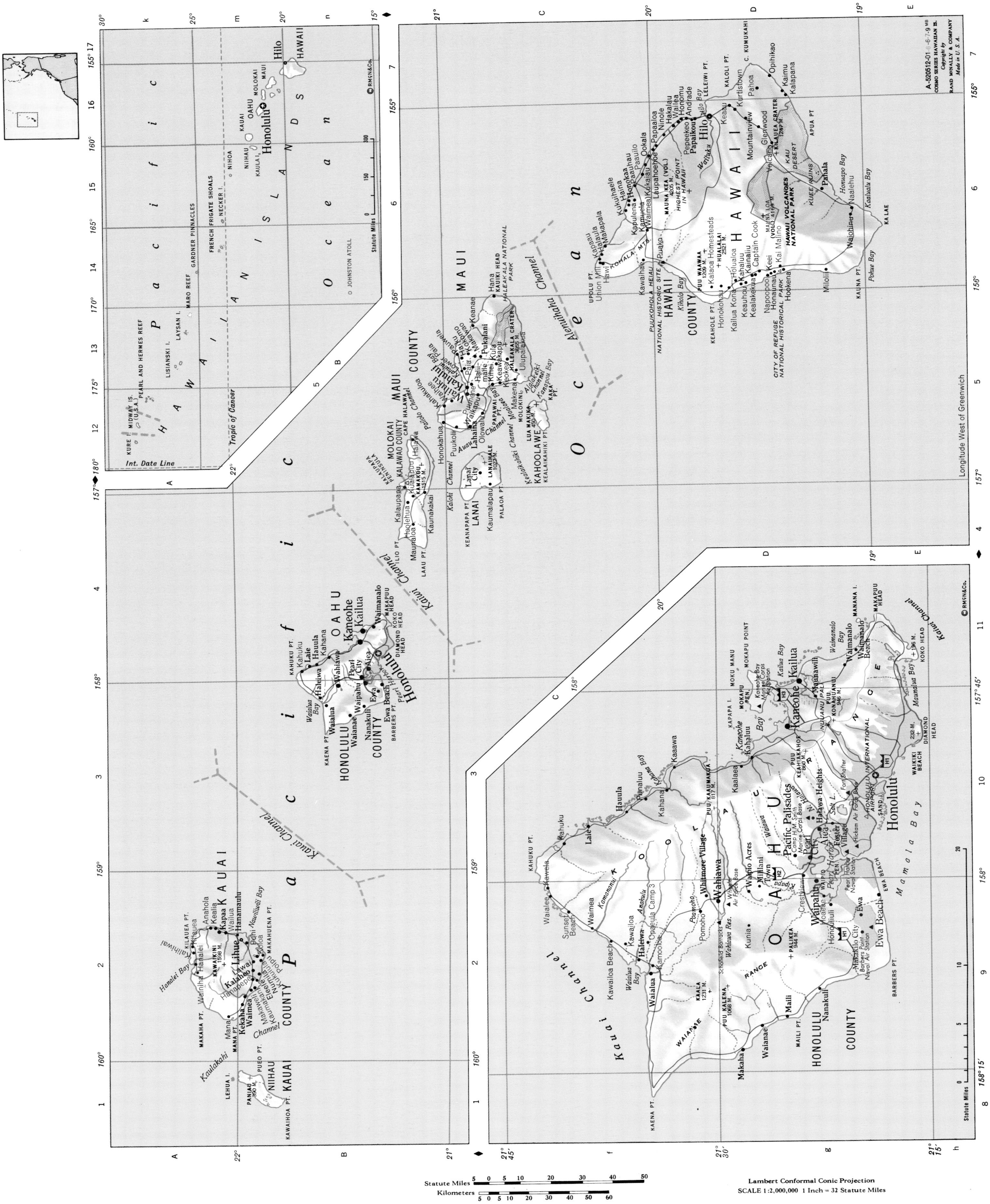
Pacific Ocean
HAWAIIAN ISLANDS
Tropic of Cancer
Int. Date Line
KAUAI
OAHU
MOLOKAI
LANAI
MAUI
KAHOOLAWE
HAWAII
NIIHAU
Honolulu
Hilo
Kauai Channel
Kaiwi Channel
Alenuihaha Channel
HONOLULU COUNTY
KAUAI COUNTY
MAUI COUNTY
HAWAII COUNTY
KALAWAO COUNTY
HAWAII VOLCANOES NATIONAL PARK
HALEAKALA NATIONAL PARK
CITY OF REFUGE NATIONAL HISTORICAL PARK
Longitude West of Greenwich
Statute Miles
Kilometers
Lambert Conformal Conic Projection
SCALE 1:2,000,000 1 Inch = 32 Statute Miles
A-520512-01-6-7-9 MB
COSMO SERIES HAWAIIAN IS.
Copyright by RAND McNALLY & COMPANY
Made in U. S. A.

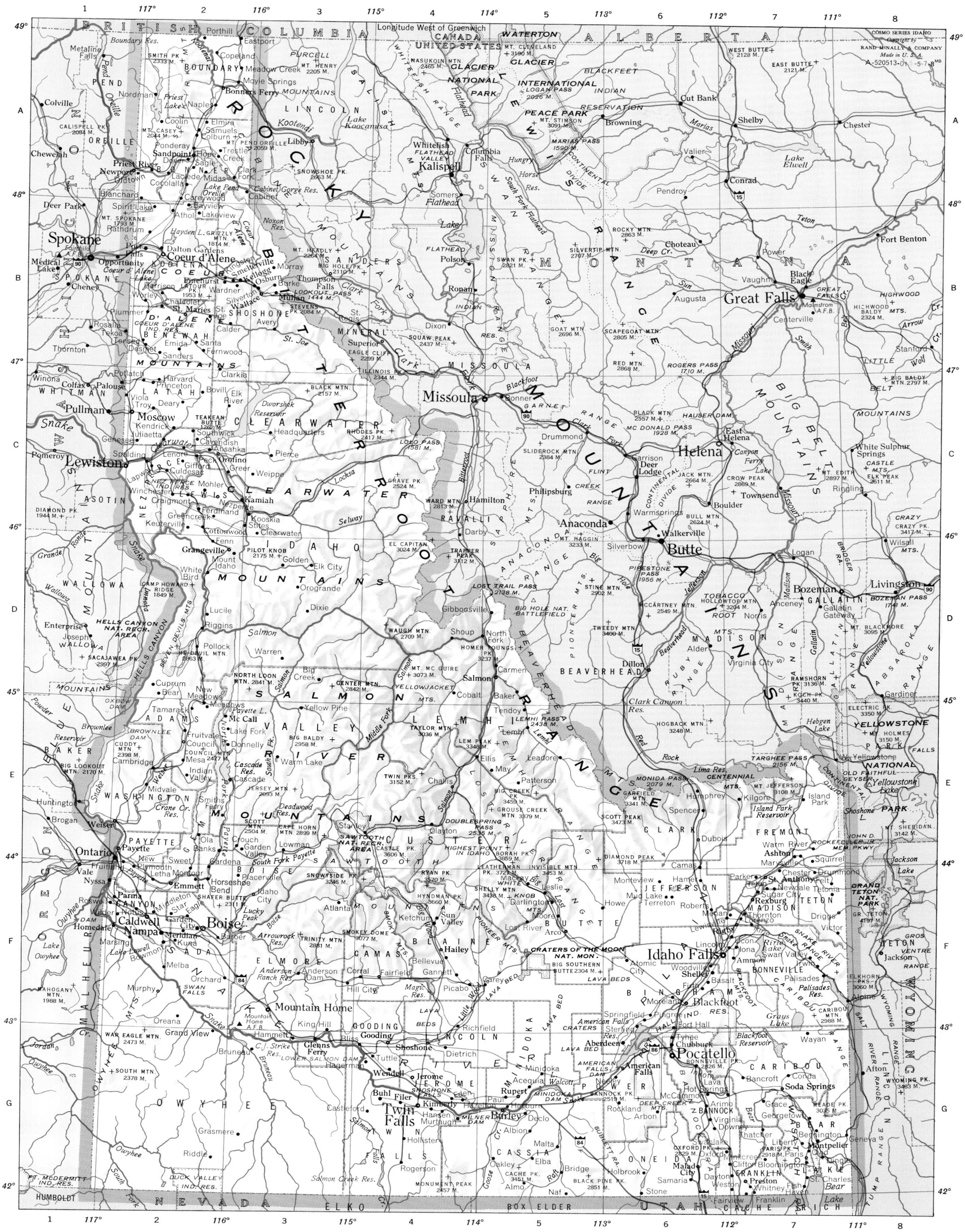

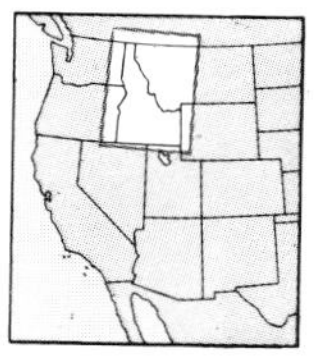

Statute Miles 5 0 5 10 20 30 40 50 60

Kilometers 5 0 5 15 25 35 45 55 65 75

Lambert Conformal Conic Projection

SCALE 1:2,633,000 1 Inch = 41.5 Statute Miles

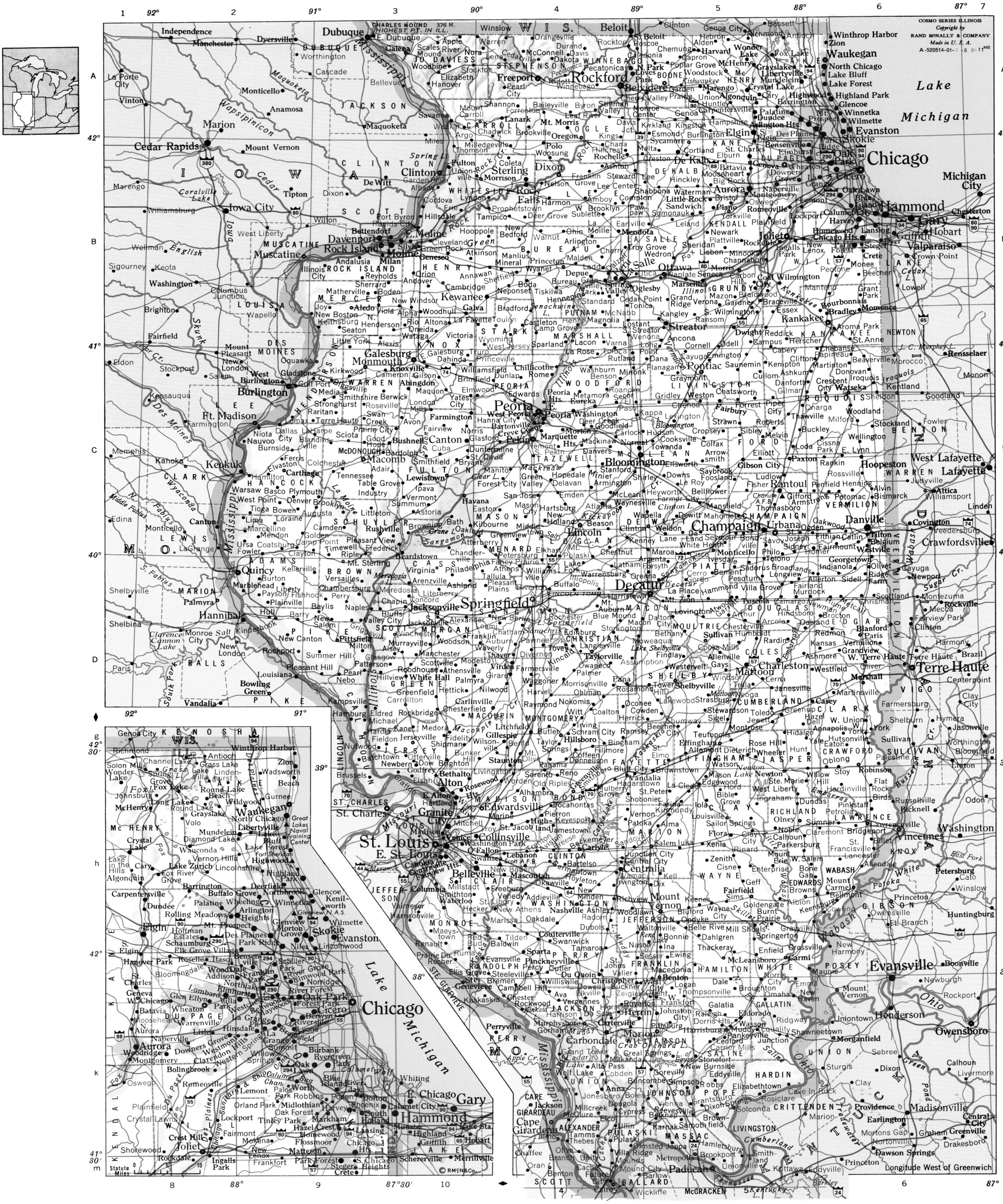
COSMO SERIES ILLINOIS
Copyright by RAND McNALLY & COMPANY
Made in U. S. A.
CHARLES MOUND 376 M. HIGHEST PT. IN ILL.
Lake Michigan
IOWA
MO.
WIS.
Chicago
Peoria
Springfield
Rockford
Decatur
Champaign
Bloomington
St. Louis
Evansville
Terre Haute
Dubuque
Davenport
Rock Island
Moline
Quincy
Galesburg
Joliet
Aurora
Elgin
Waukegan
Kankakee
Danville
Hammond
Gary
Paducah
Cape Girardeau
Belleville
Alton
Mississippi
Illinois
Ohio
Wabash
Longitude West of Greenwich
Statute Miles
Kilometers
Lambert Conformal Conic Projection
SCALE 1:1,997,000 1 Inch = 31.5 Statute Miles

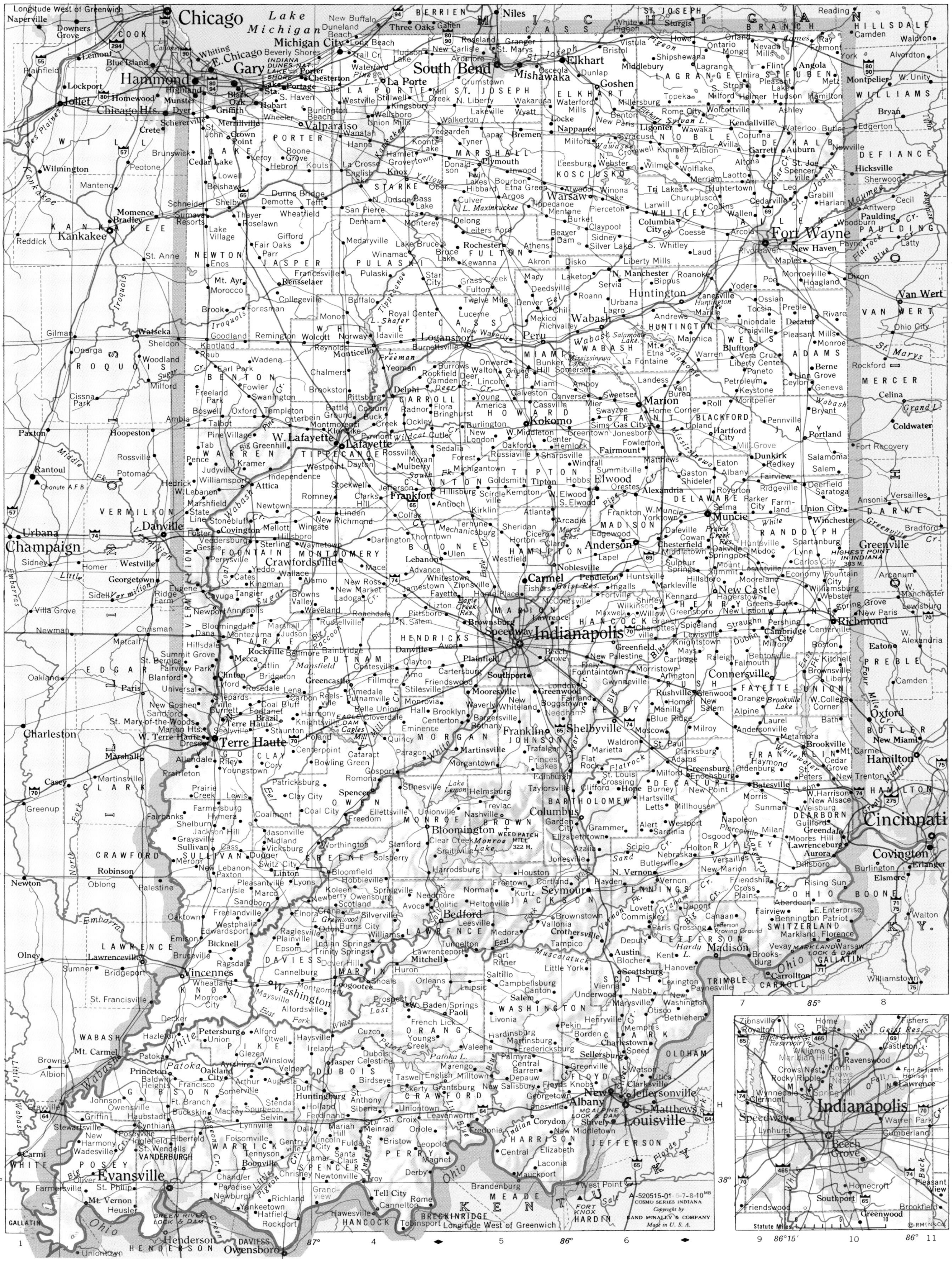

Statute Miles 5 0 5 10 15 20 25 30

Kilometers 5 0 5 15 25 35

Lambert Conformal Conic Projection

SCALE 1:1,465,000 1 Inch=23 Statute Miles

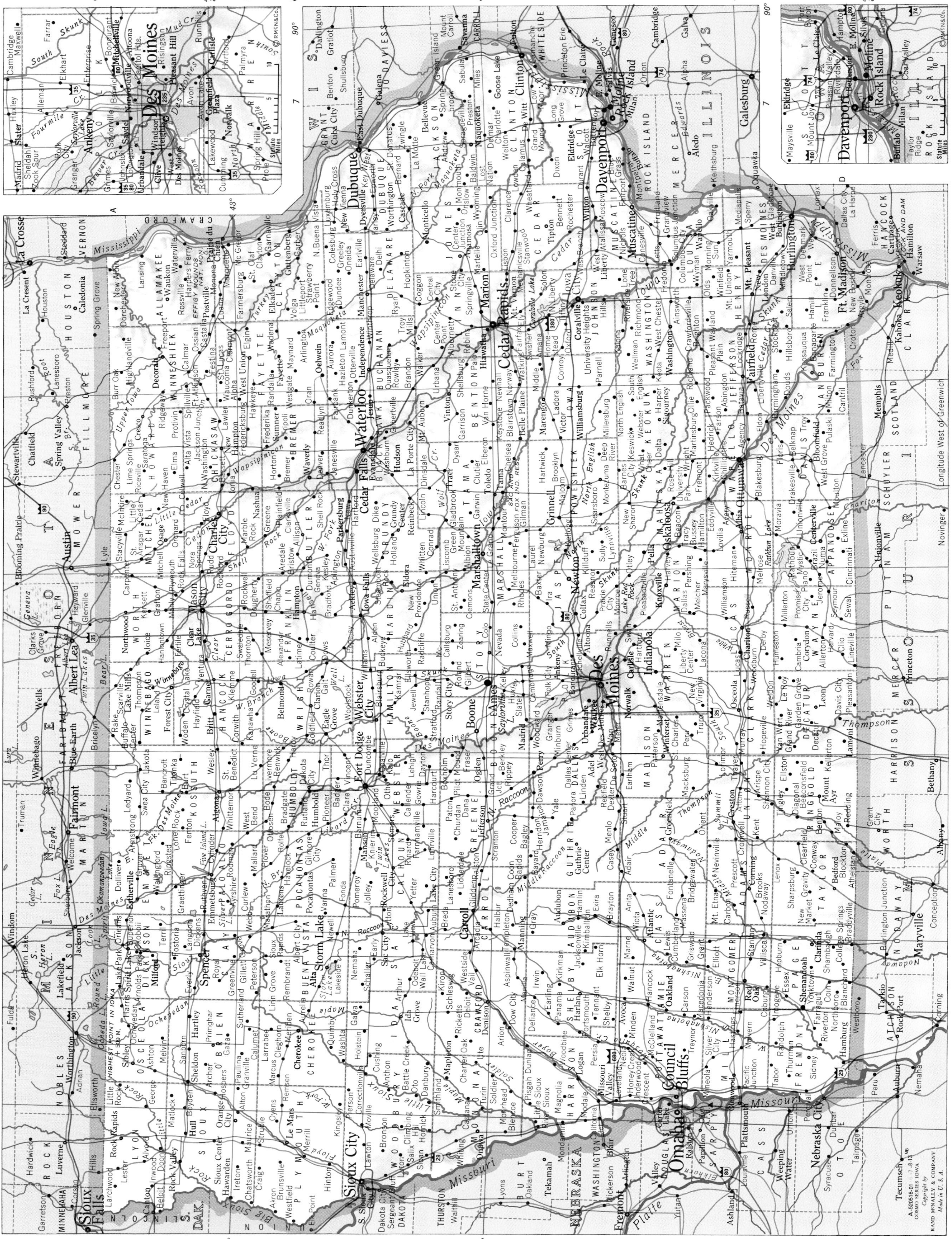

Statute Miles 5 0 5 10 20 30 40
Kilometers 5 0 5 15 25 35 45 55

Lambert Conformal Conic Projection
SCALE 1:1,834,000 1 Inch = 29 Statute Miles

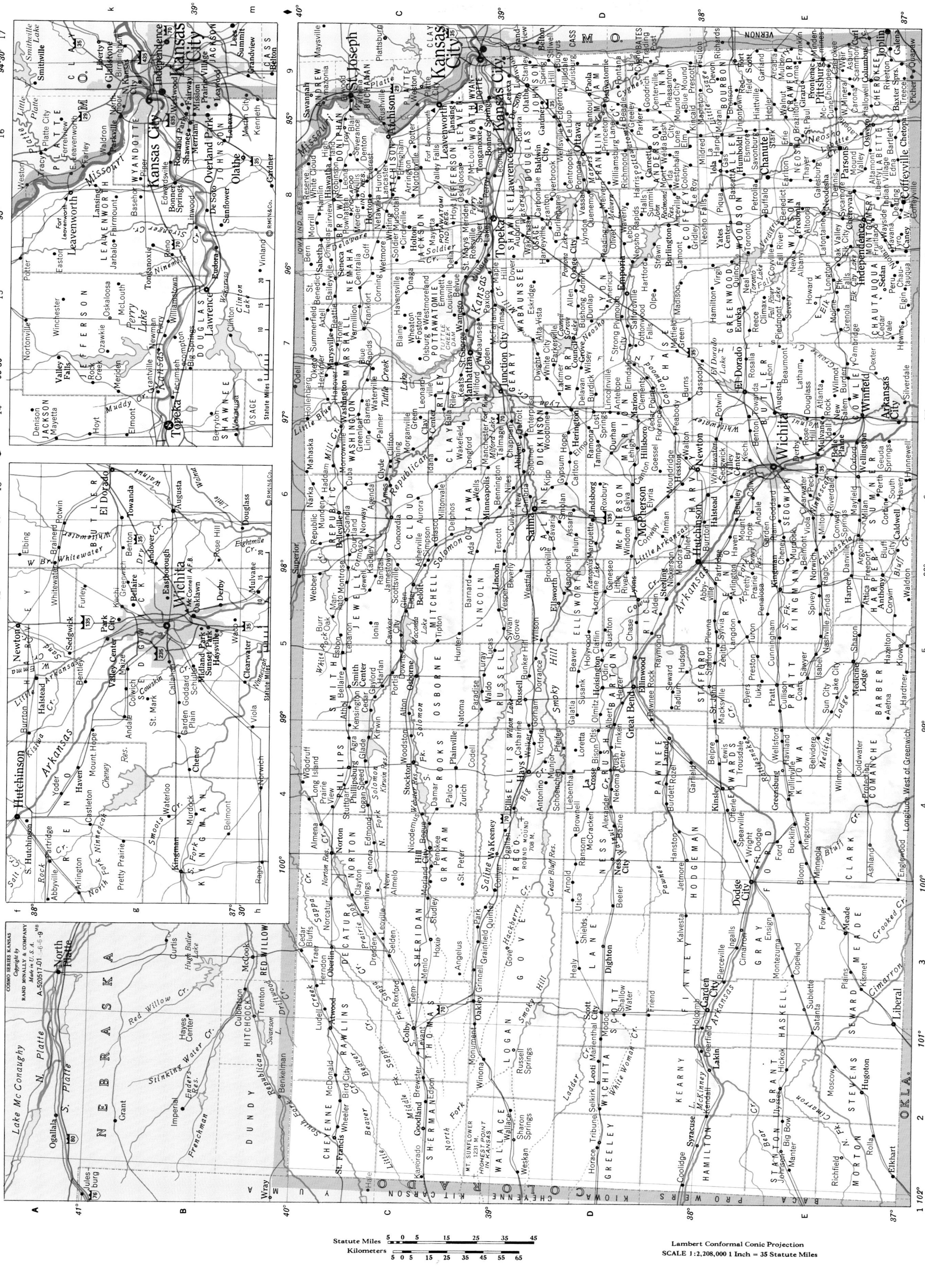

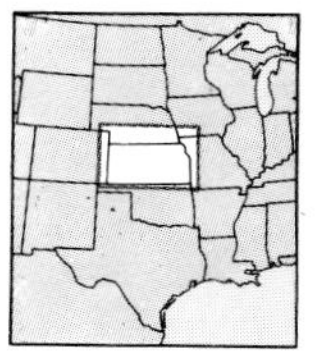

Statute Miles 5 0 5 15 25 35 45

Kilometers 5 0 5 15 25 35 45 55 65

Lambert Conformal Conic Projection

SCALE 1:2,208,000 1 Inch = 35 Statute Miles

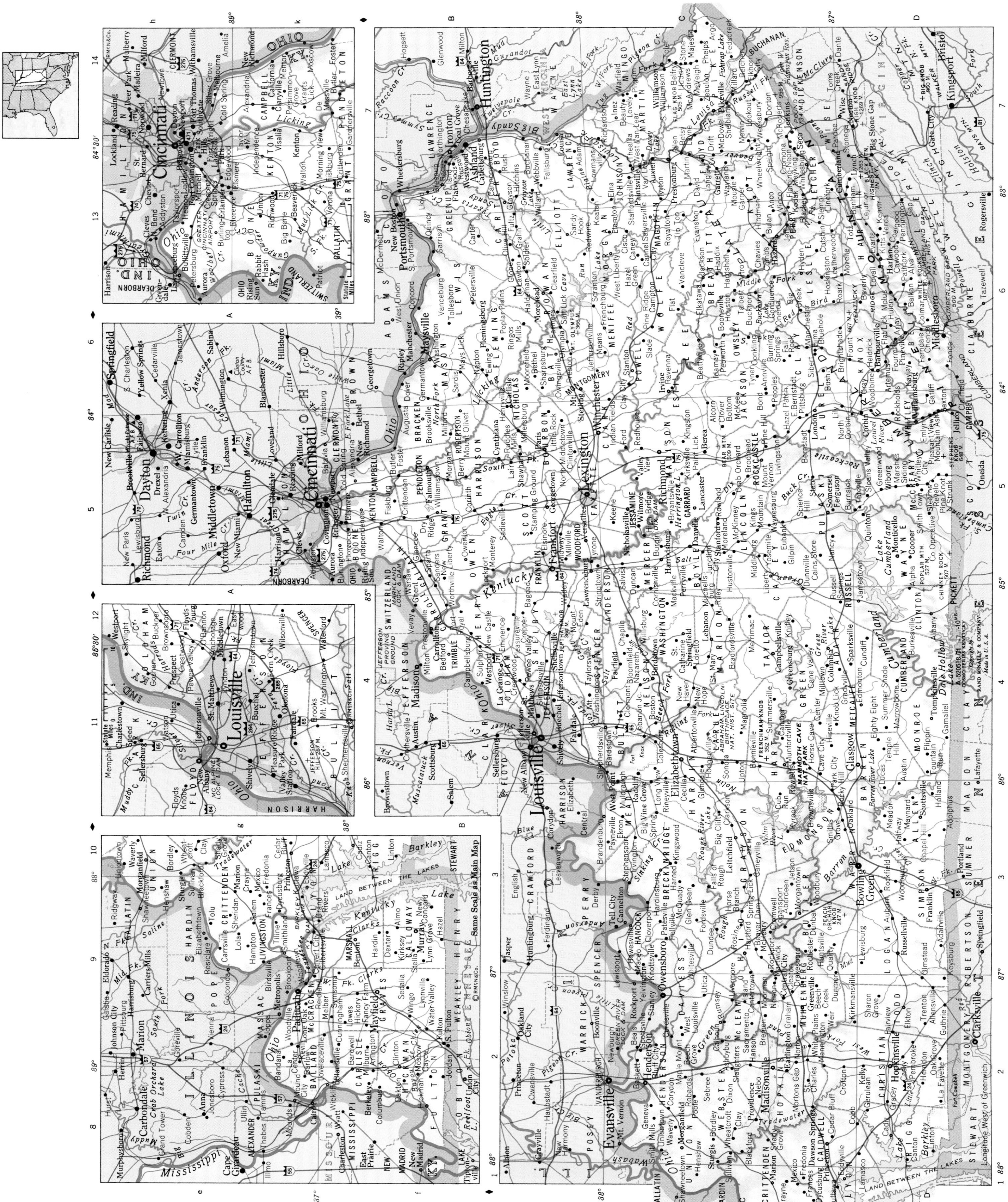
Statute Miles 5 0 5 10 20 30 40
Kilometers 5 0 5 10 20 30 40 50 60
Lambert Conformal Conic Projection
SCALE 1:1,738,000 1 Inch = 27 Statute Miles

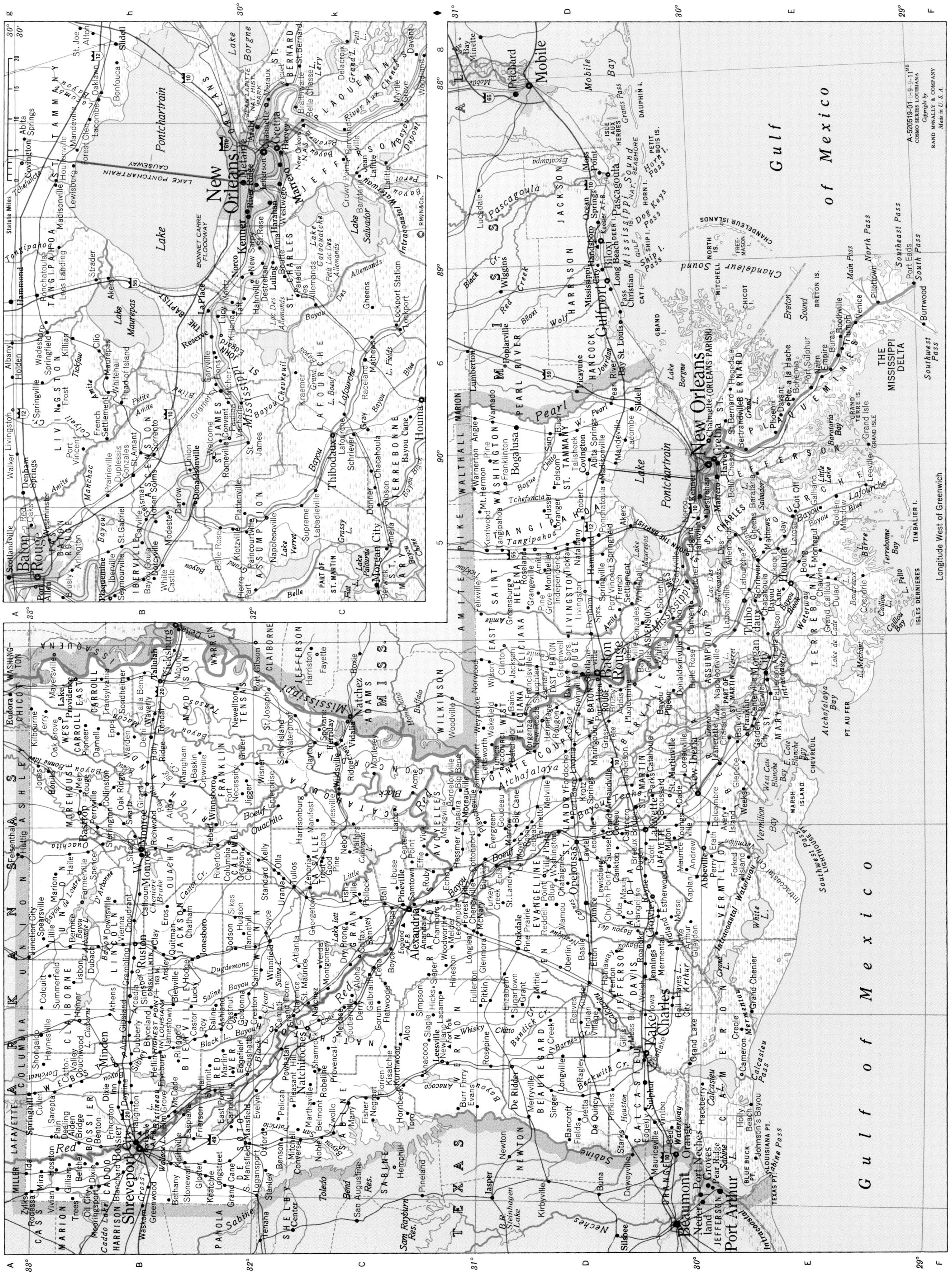

Statute Miles 5 0 5 10 20 30 40

Kilometers 5 0 5 15 25 35 45 55

Lambert Conformal Conic Projection

SCALE 1:2,083,000 1 Inch = 33 Statute Miles

Maine

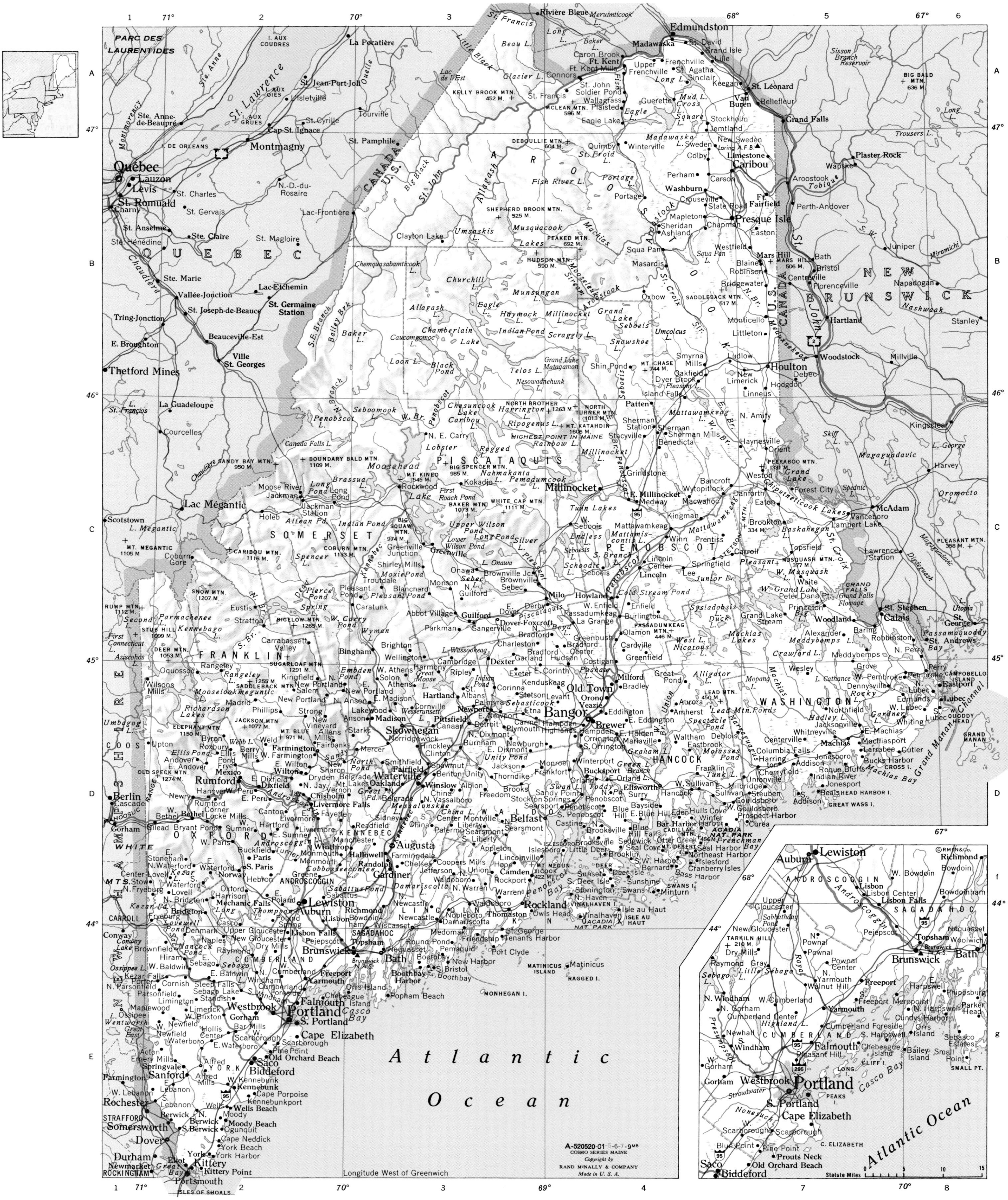

Statute Miles 5 0 5 10 20 30

Kilometers 5 0 5 10 20 30 40

Lambert Conformal Conic Projection

SCALE 1:1,581,000 1 Inch = 25 Statute Miles

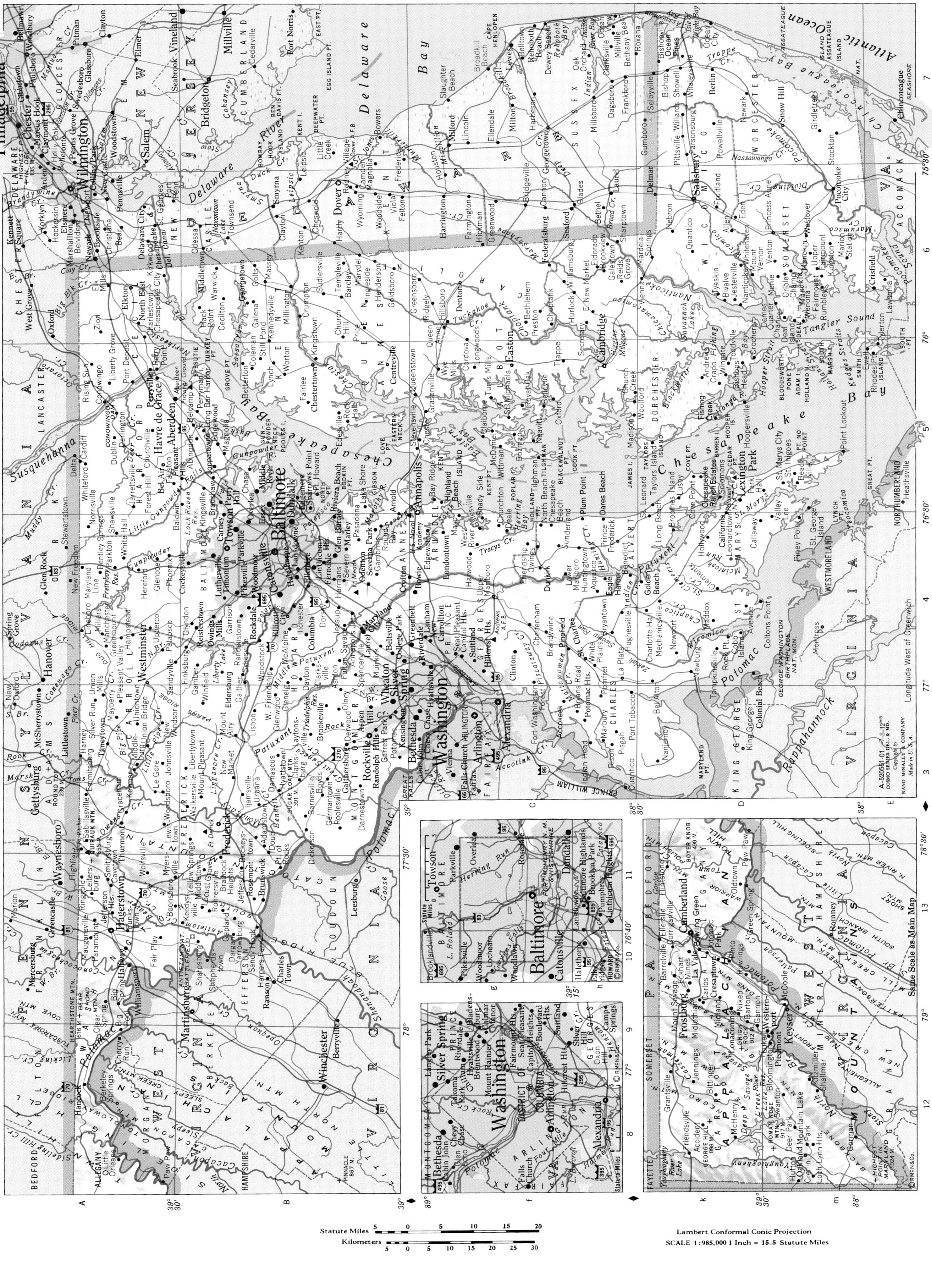

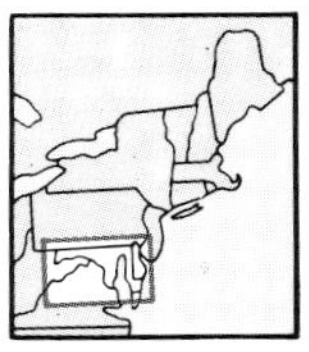

Statute Miles 5 0 5 10 15 20

Kilometers 5 0 5 10 15 20 25 30

Lambert Conformal Conic Projection

SCALE 1:985,000 1 Inch = 15.5 Statute Miles

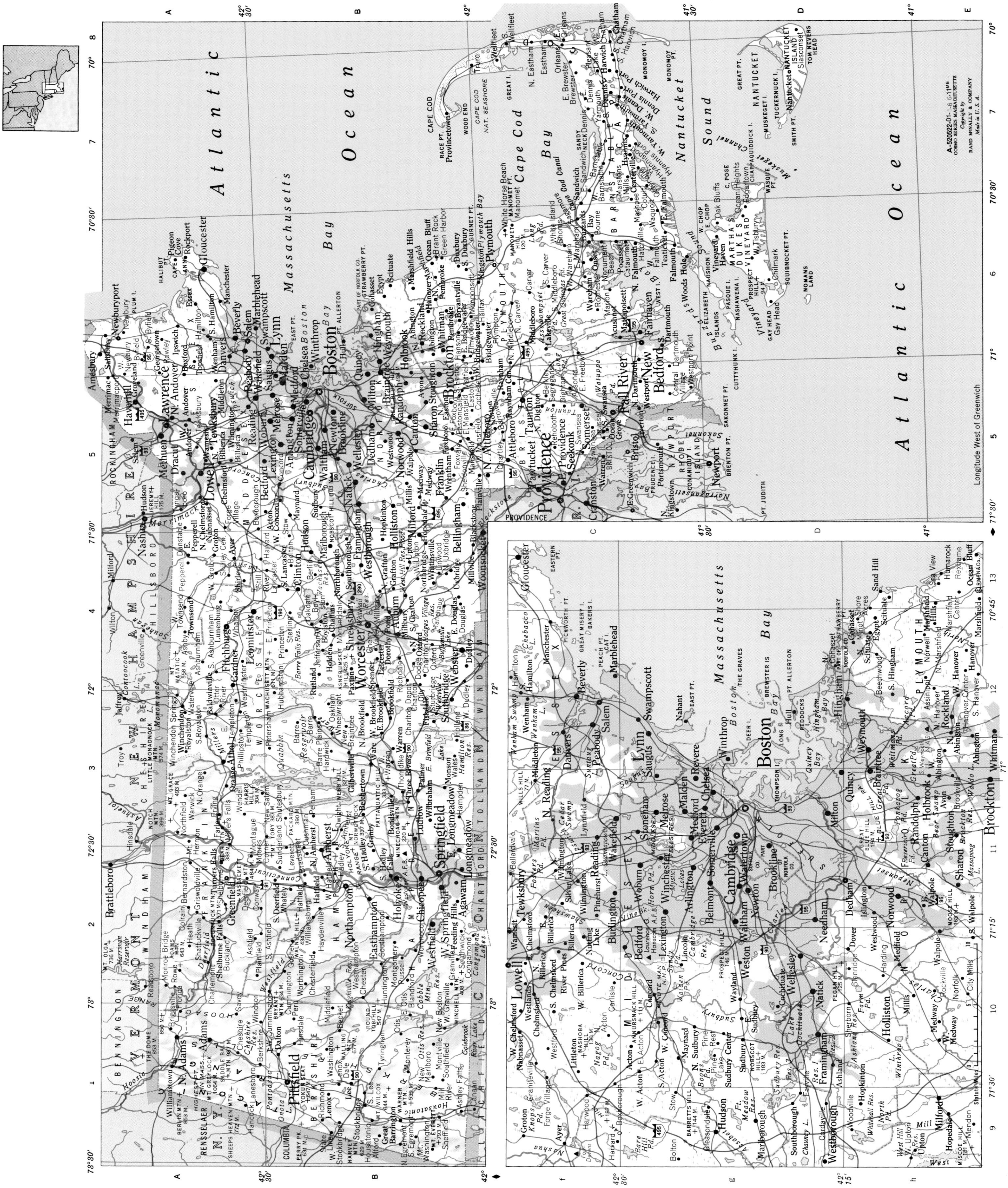

Statute Miles 5 0 5 10 15 20

Kilometers 5 0 5 10 15 20 25

Lambert Conformal Conic Projection

SCALE 1:978,000 1 Inch = 15.5 Statute Miles

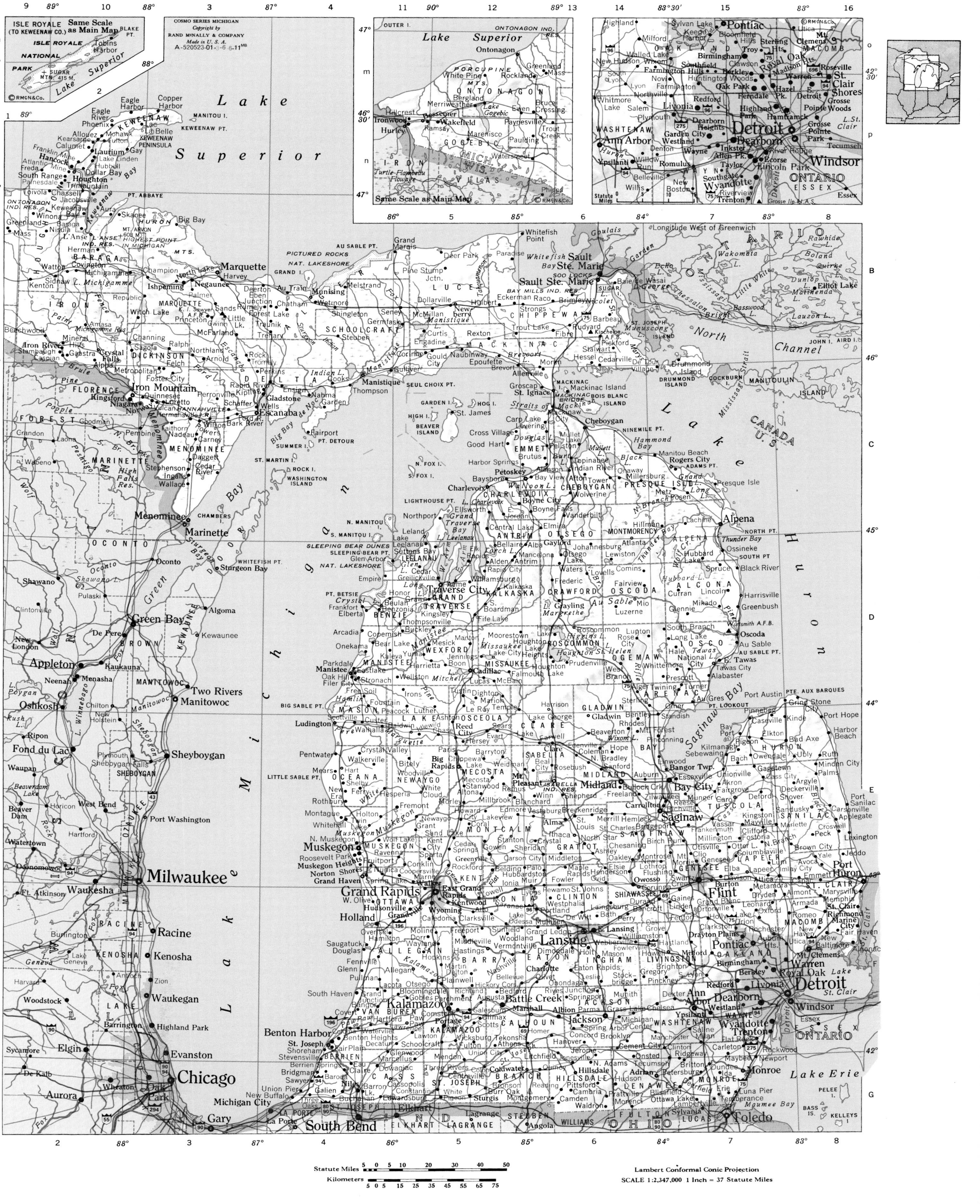
ISLE ROYALE (TO KEWEENAW CO.)
Same Scale as Main Map
ISLE ROYALE NATIONAL PARK
COSMO SERIES MICHIGAN
Copyright by RAND McNALLY & COMPANY
Made in U. S. A.
Same Scale as Main Map
Lake Superior
Lake Michigan
Lake Huron
Lake Erie
North Channel
Green Bay
Saginaw Bay
Straits of Mackinac
ONTARIO
CANADA
U.S.
OHIO
Detroit
Lansing
Grand Rapids
Flint
Kalamazoo
Saginaw
Ann Arbor
Milwaukee
Chicago
Toledo
Marquette
Sault Ste. Marie
Escanaba
Traverse City
Alpena
Muskegon
Battle Creek
Jackson
Pontiac
Windsor
South Bend
Green Bay
Statute Miles
Kilometers
Lambert Conformal Conic Projection
SCALE 1:2,347,000 1 Inch = 37 Statute Miles

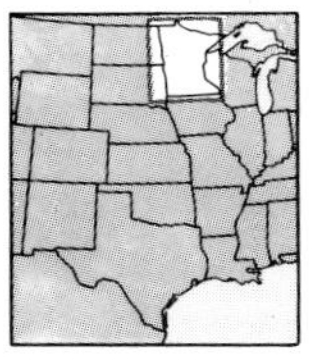

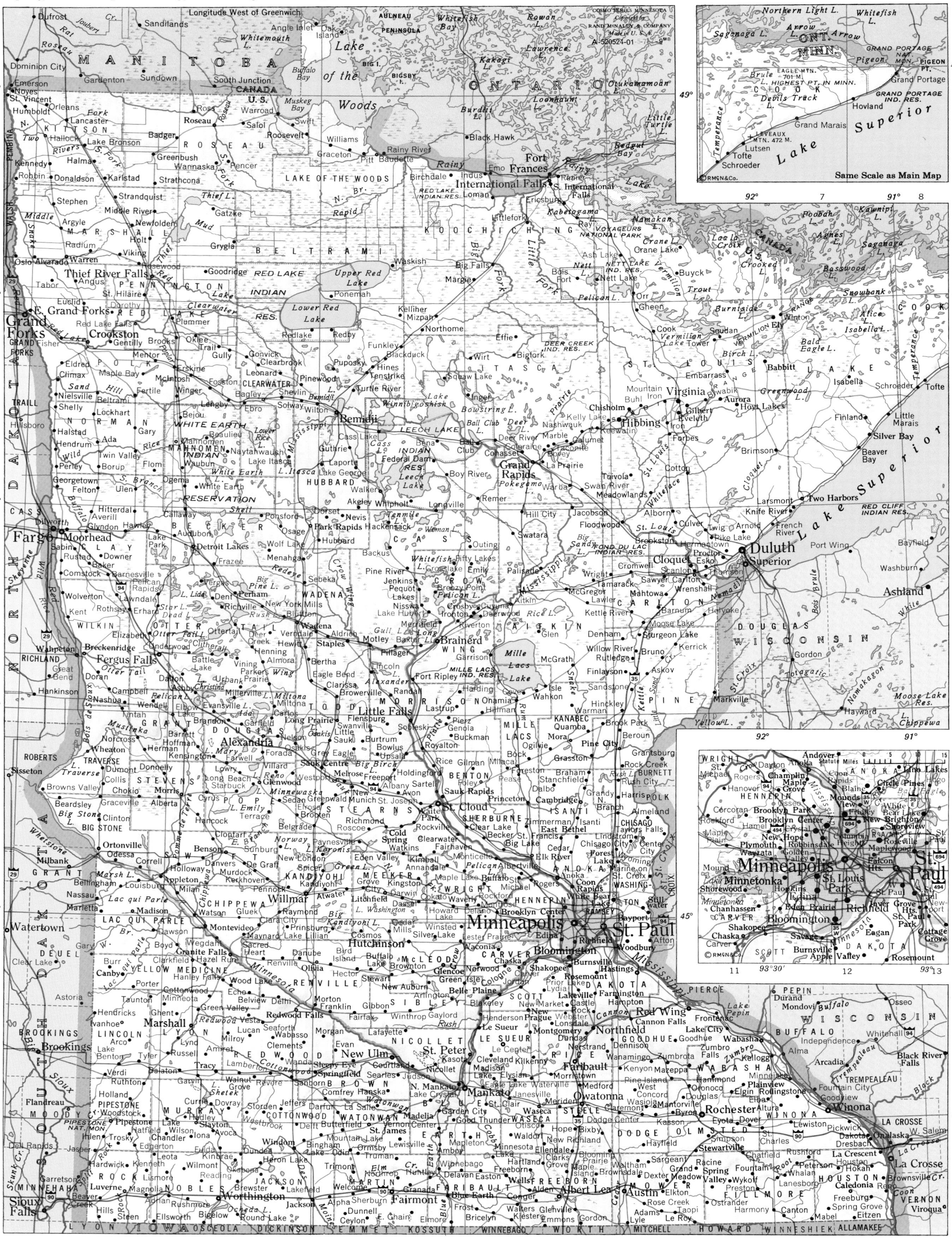

Statute Miles 5 0 5 10 20 30 40 50

Kilometers 5 0 5 15 25 35 45 55 65

Lambert Conformal Conic Projection

SCALE 1:2,179,000 1 Inch = 34 Statute Miles

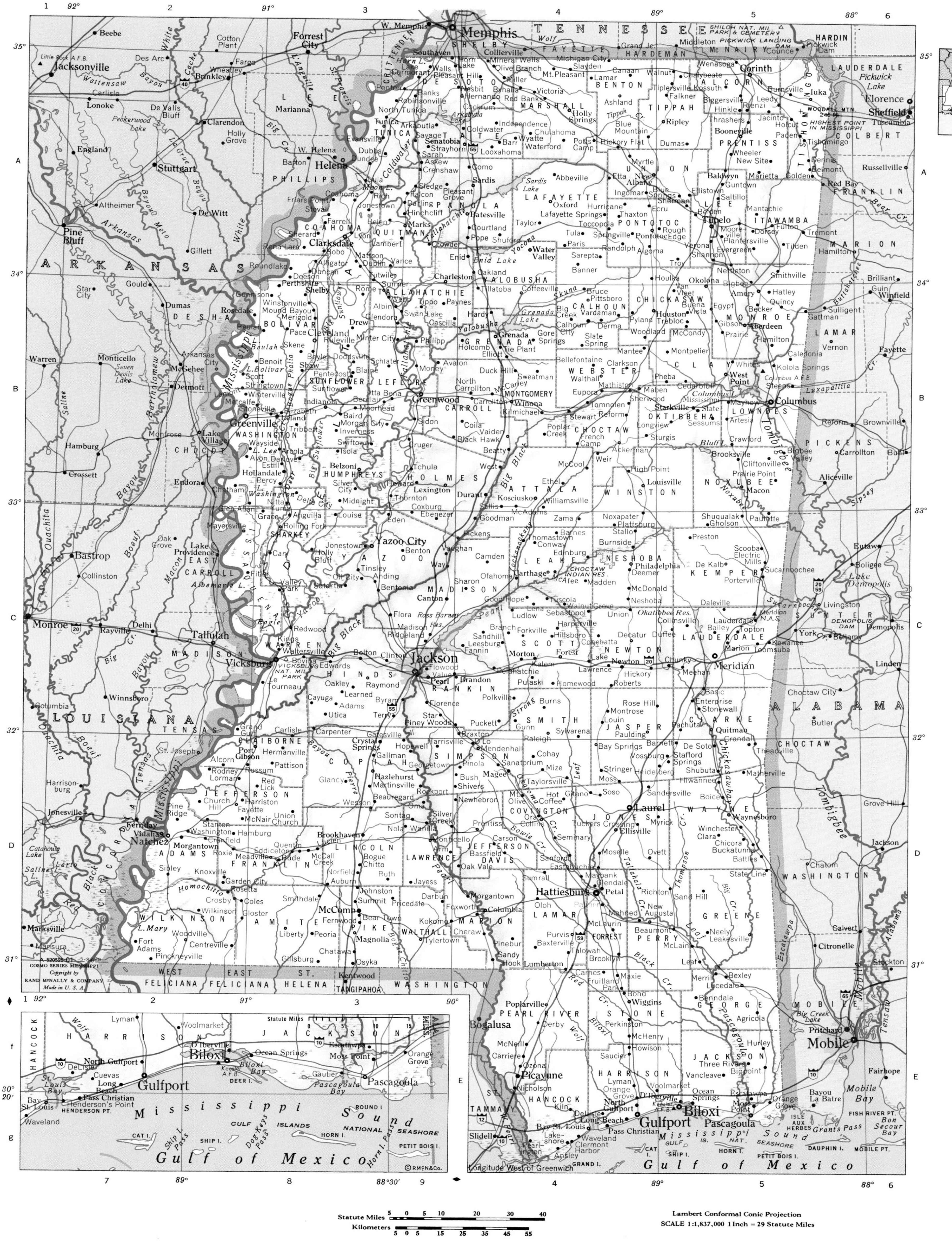
TENNESSEE
ARKANSAS
LOUISIANA
ALABAMA
Memphis
Jackson
Vicksburg
Natchez
Greenville
Greenwood
Clarksdale
Tupelo
Columbus
Meridian
Hattiesburg
Laurel
Gulfport
Biloxi
Pascagoula
Mobile
McComb
Brookhaven
Yazoo City
Corinth
Starkville
Oxford
Grenada
Cleveland
Picayune
Pine Bluff
Monroe
Helena
Tallulah
Bogalusa
Mississippi Sound
Gulf of Mexico
Lambert Conformal Conic Projection
SCALE 1:1,837,000 1 Inch = 29 Statute Miles
Statute Miles
Kilometers
Longitude West of Greenwich
COSMO SERIES MISSISSIPPI
Copyright by RAND McNALLY & COMPANY Made in U. S. A.

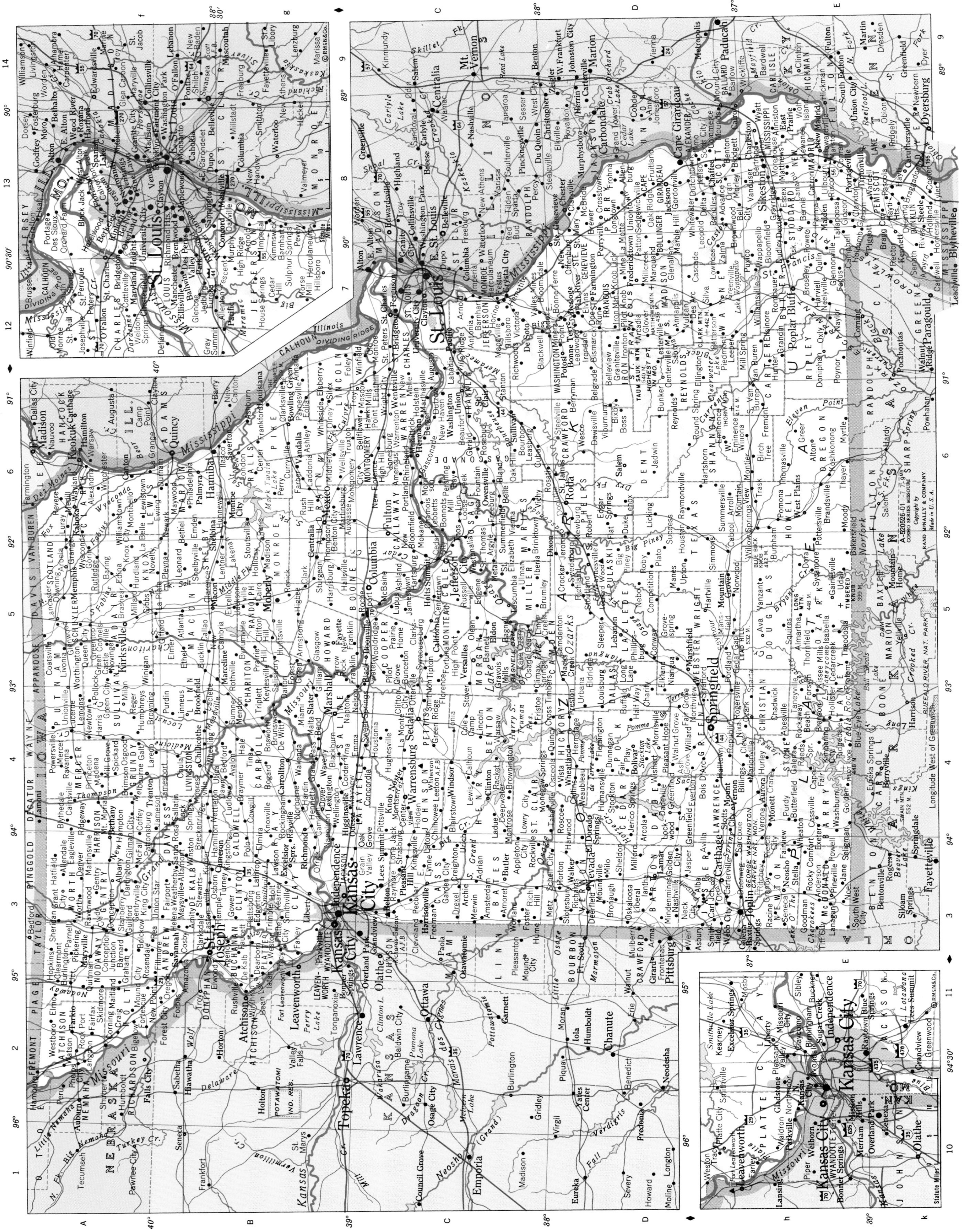

Statute Miles 5 0 5 15 25 35 45
Kilometers 5 0 5 15 25 35 45 55 65

Lambert Conformal Conic Projection
SCALE 1:2,283,000 1 Inch = 36 Statute Miles

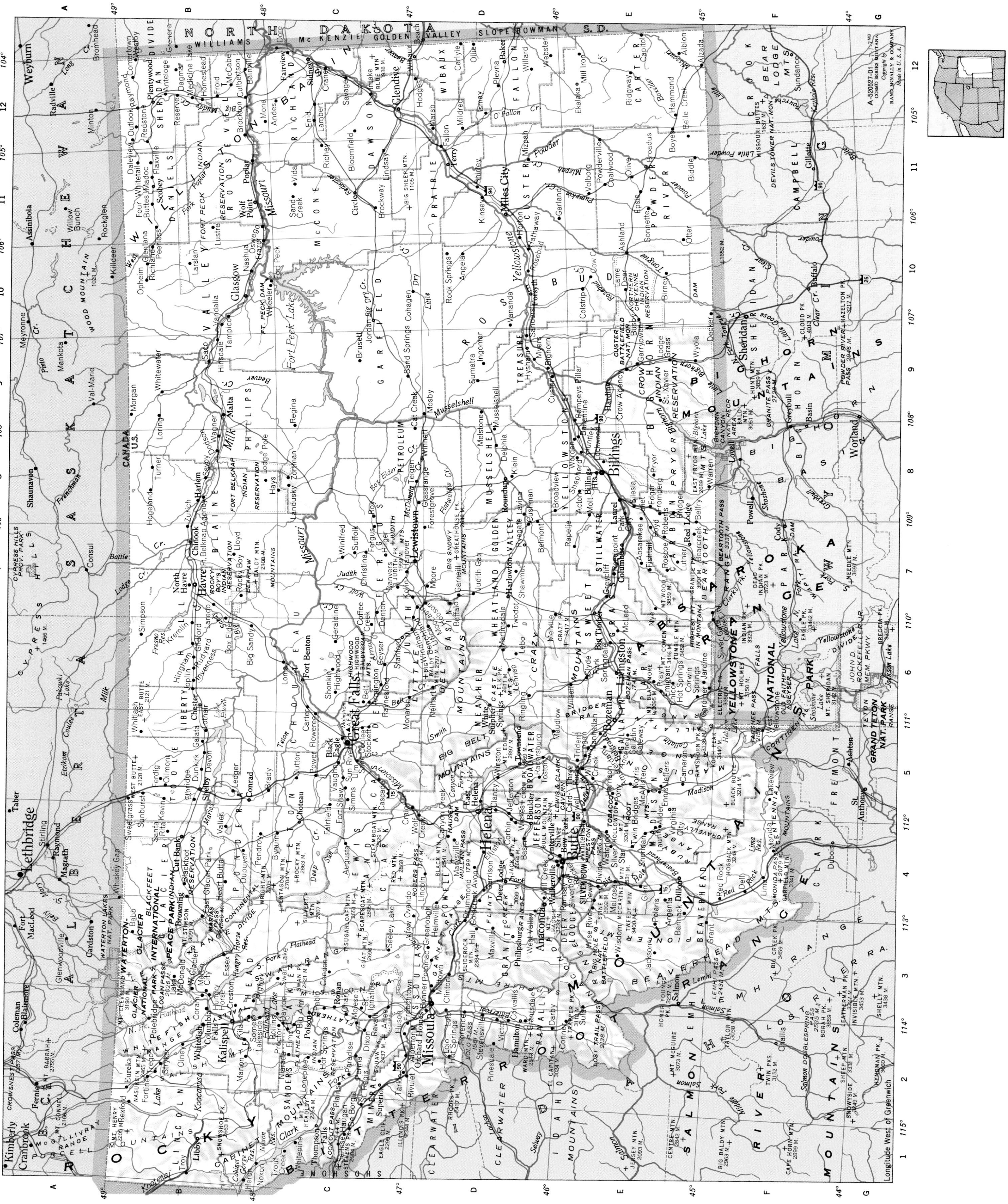

Statute Miles 10 0 10 20 30 40 50 60 70

Kilometers 10 0 10 30 50 70 90

Lambert Conformal Conic Projection

SCALE 1:3,000,000 1 Inch = 47.5 Statute Miles

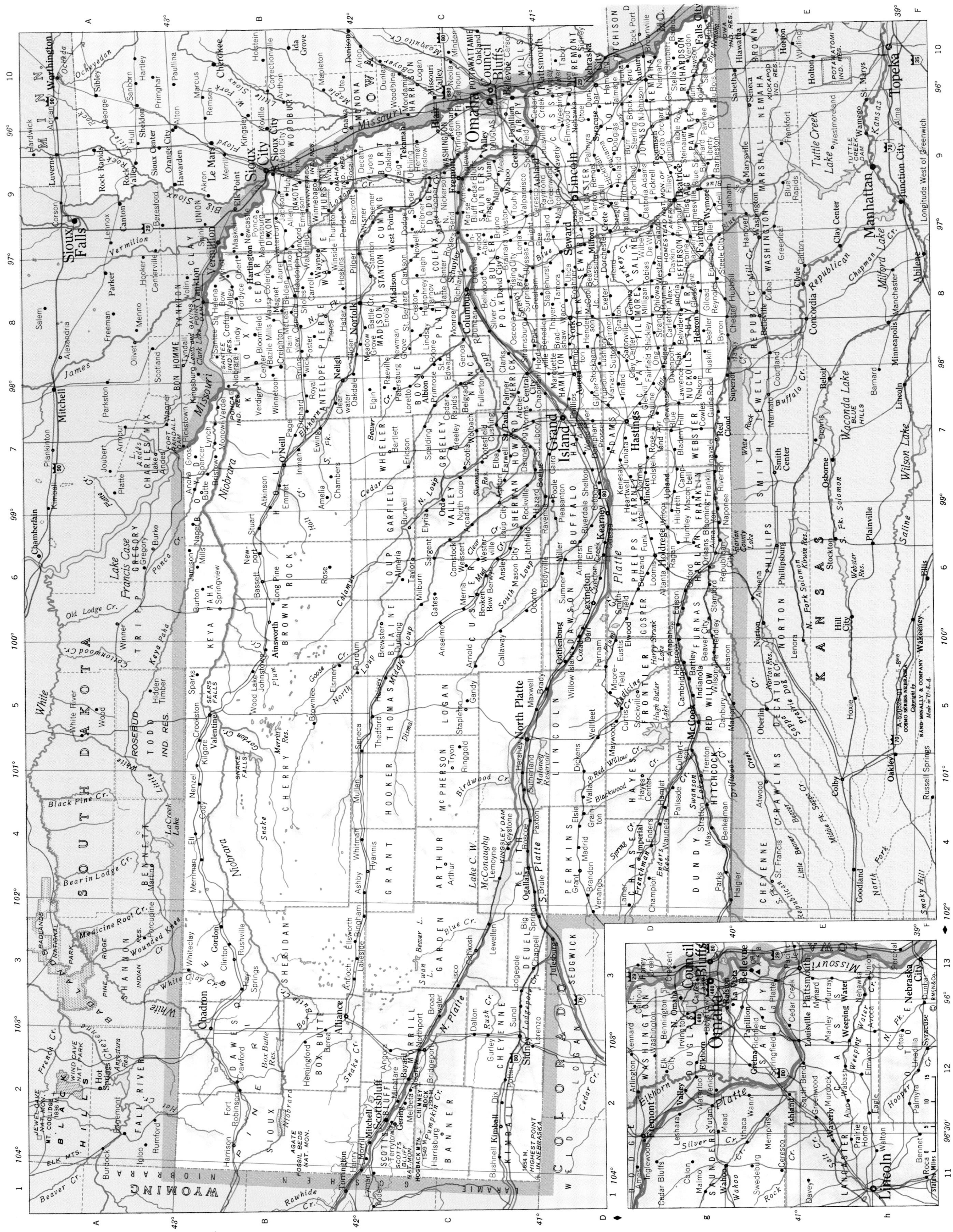

Statute Miles 5 0 5 10 20 30 40 50 60

Kilometers 5 0 5 15 35 55 75 95

Lambert Conformal Conic Projection

SCALE 1:2,460,000 1 Inch = 39 Statute Miles

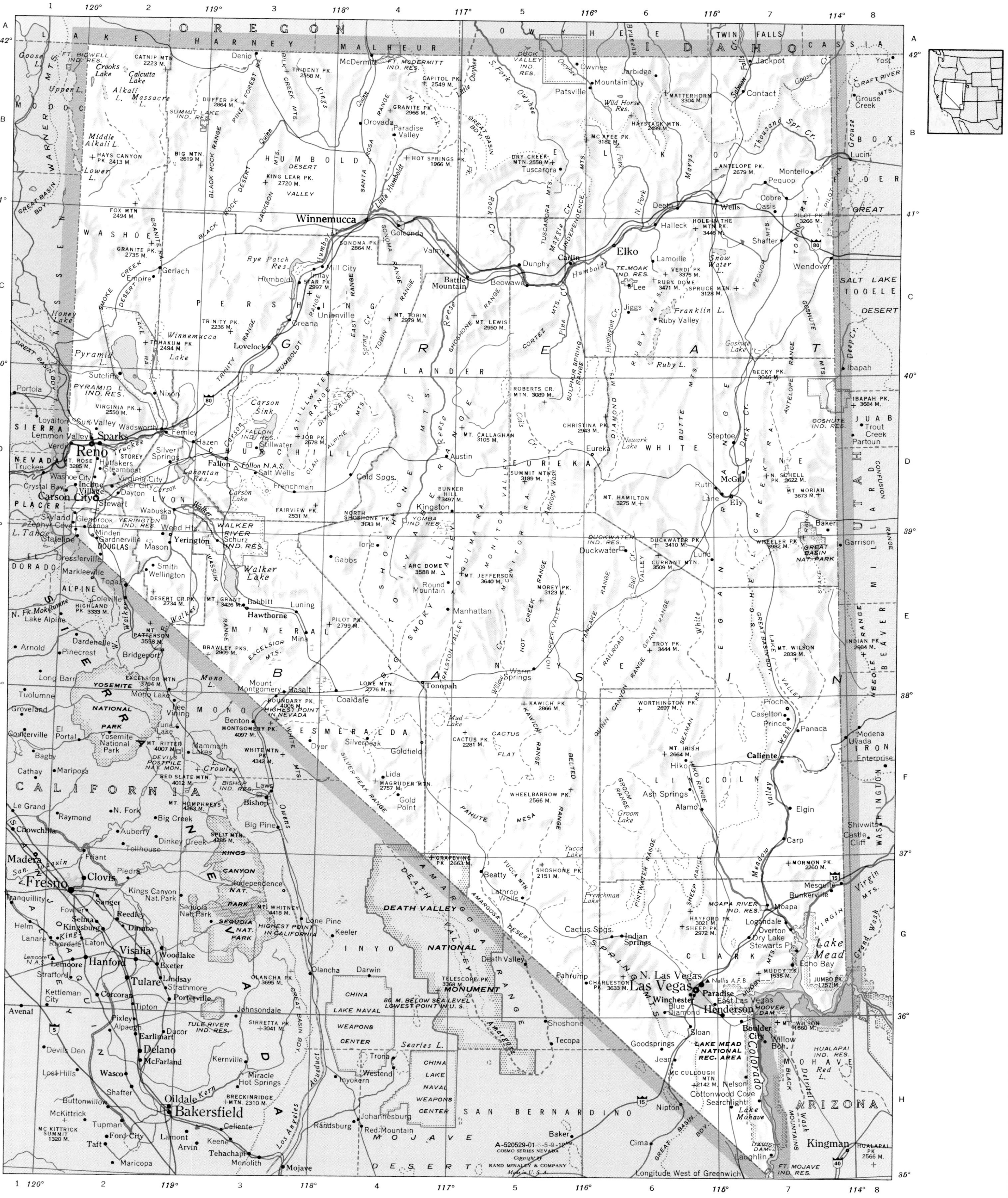

Statute Miles 0 5 10 20 30 40 50 60 70 80

Kilometers 0 5 10 20 40 60 80 100 120

Lambert Conformal Conic Projection

SCALE 1:2,630,000 1 Inch = 41.5 Statute Miles

New Hampshire

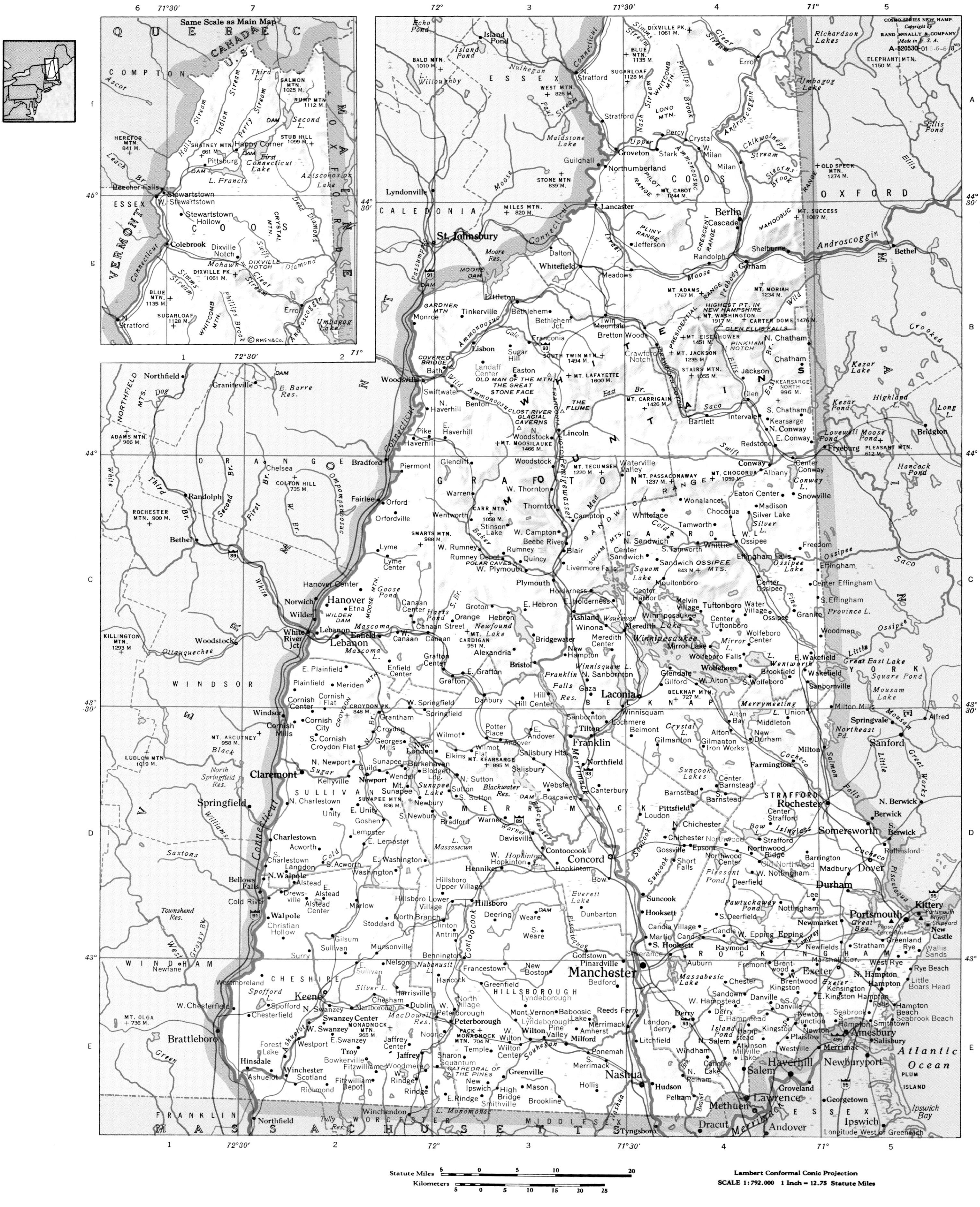

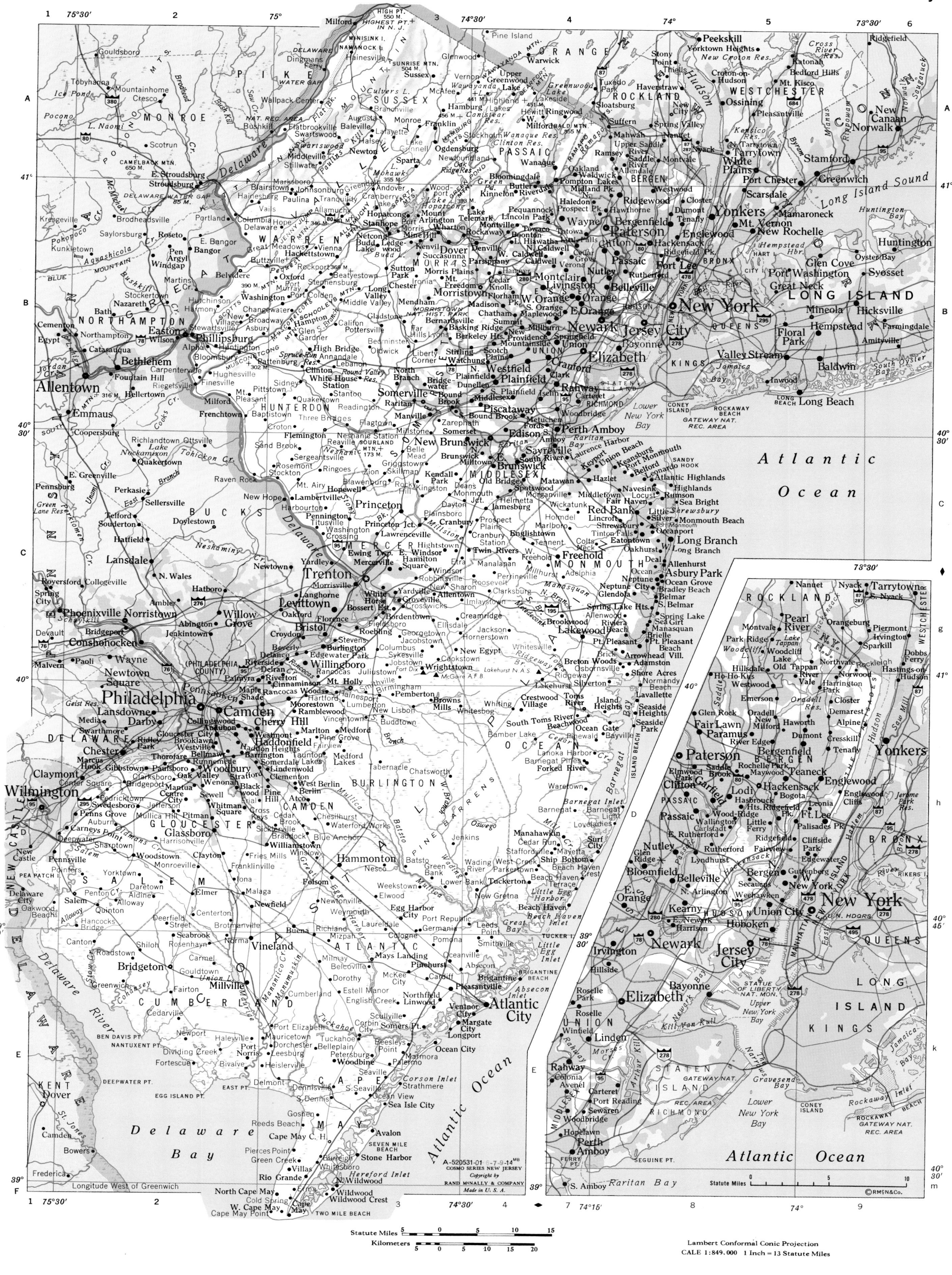

New Jersey
Atlantic Ocean
Delaware Bay
Long Island Sound
New York
Jersey City
Newark
Elizabeth
Paterson
Trenton
Camden
Philadelphia
Atlantic City
Wilmington
Allentown
Bethlehem
New Brunswick
Princeton
Perth Amboy
Asbury Park
Long Branch
Vineland
Millville
Bridgeton
Cape May C. H.
Cape May
SUSSEX
WARREN
MORRIS
PASSAIC
BERGEN
HUNTERDON
SOMERSET
MIDDLESEX
MONMOUTH
MERCER
BURLINGTON
OCEAN
CAMDEN
GLOUCESTER
SALEM
CUMBERLAND
ATLANTIC
CAPE MAY
UNION
LONG ISLAND
STATEN ISLAND
PINE BARRENS
Lambert Conformal Conic Projection
CALE 1:849,000 1 Inch = 13 Statute Miles
Statute Miles
Kilometers
Longitude West of Greenwich
A-520531-01
COSMO SERIES NEW JERSEY
Copyright by RAND McNALLY & COMPANY
Made in U. S. A.
©RM©N&Co.

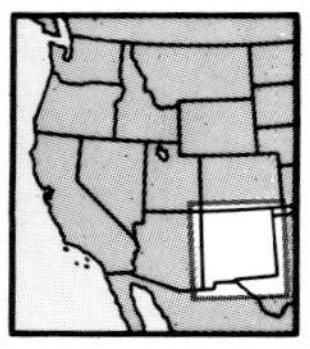

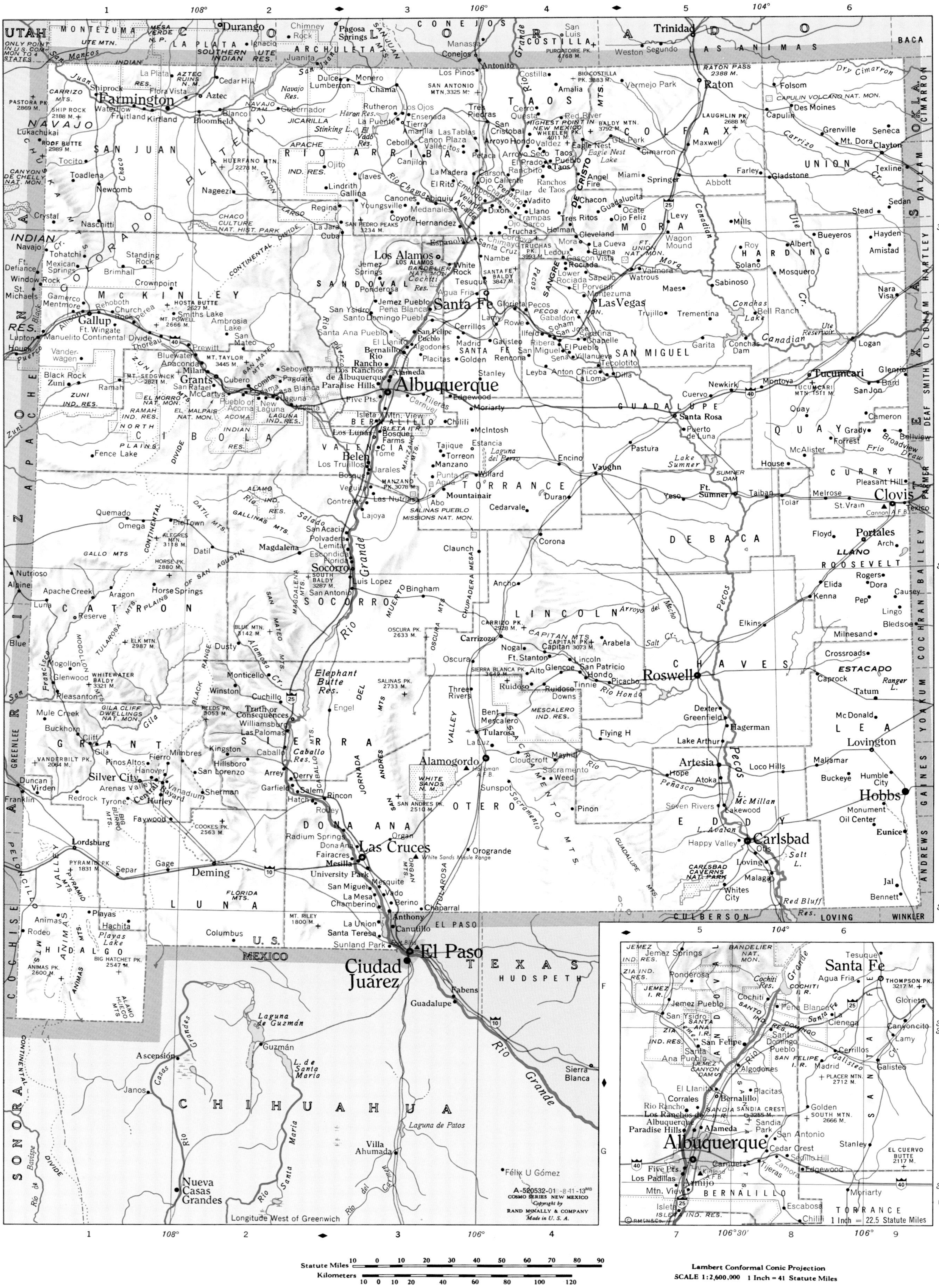
UTAH
COLORADO
ARIZONA
OKLAHOMA
TEXAS
MEXICO
CHIHUAHUA
SONORA
SAN JUAN
RIO ARRIBA
TAOS
COLFAX
UNION
MORA
HARDING
McKINLEY
SANDOVAL
SANTA FE
SAN MIGUEL
GUADALUPE
QUAY
CIBOLA
BERNALILLO
VALENCIA
TORRANCE
DE BACA
CURRY
ROOSEVELT
CATRON
SOCORRO
LINCOLN
CHAVES
SIERRA
OTERO
GRANT
DONA ANA
EDDY
LEA
LUNA
HIDALGO
Farmington
Gallup
Grants
Albuquerque
Santa Fe
Los Alamos
Las Vegas
Raton
Tucumcari
Clovis
Portales
Roswell
Socorro
Alamogordo
Las Cruces
Carlsbad
Hobbs
Artesia
Deming
Lordsburg
Silver City
Truth or Consequences
El Paso
Ciudad Juárez
Rio Grande
Pecos
Canadian
Elephant Butte Res.
Longitude West of Greenwich
A-520532-01 -8-11-13 MB
COSMO SERIES NEW MEXICO
Copyright by
RAND McNALLY & COMPANY
Made in U. S. A.
TORRANCE
1 Inch = 22.5 Statute Miles
Statute Miles
Kilometers
Lambert Conformal Conic Projection
SCALE 1:2,600,000 1 Inch = 41 Statute Miles

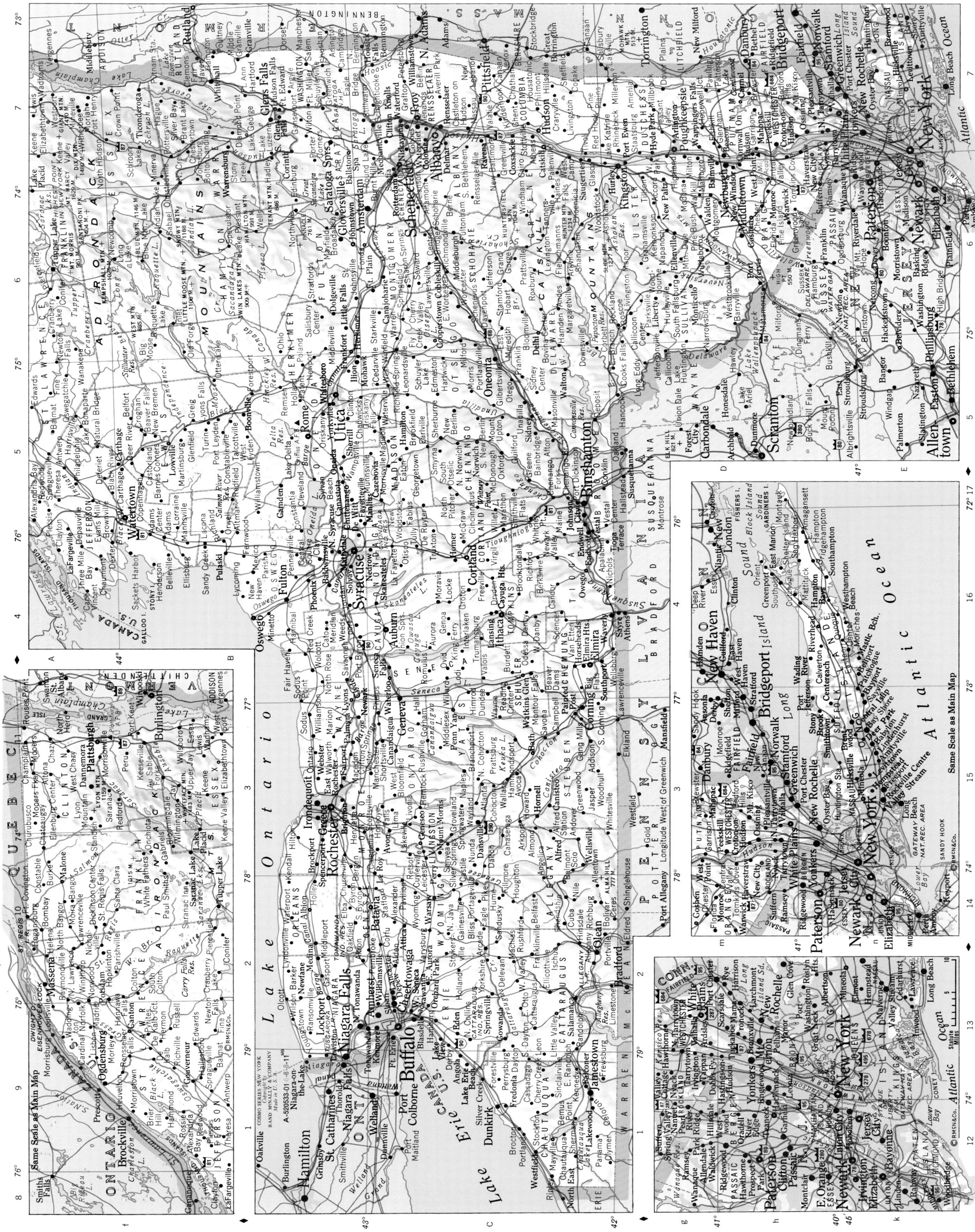

Statute Miles 5 0 5 10 20 30 40

Kilometers 5 0 5 15 25 35 45 55

Lambert Conformal Conic Projection
SCALE 1:1,862,000 1 Inch = 29 Statute Miles

Statute Miles 5 0 5 10 20 30 40

Kilometers 5 0 5 15 25 35 45 55

Lambert Conformal Conic Projection

SCALE 1:1,950,000 1 Inch = 31 Statute Miles

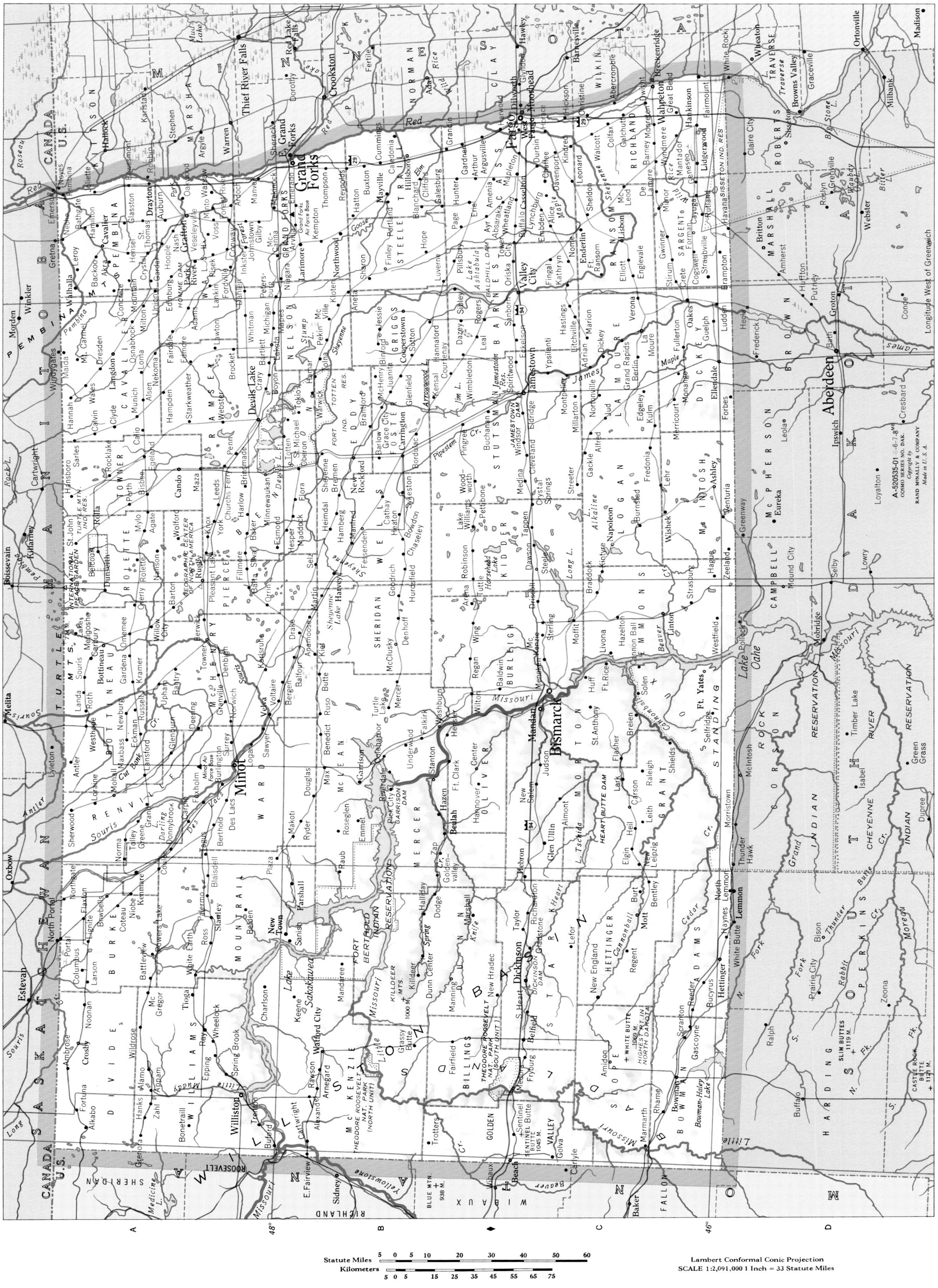

Statute Miles 5 0 5 10 20 30 40 50 60
Kilometers 5 0 5 15 25 35 45 55 65 75

Lambert Conformal Conic Projection
SCALE 1:2,091,000 1 Inch = 33 Statute Miles

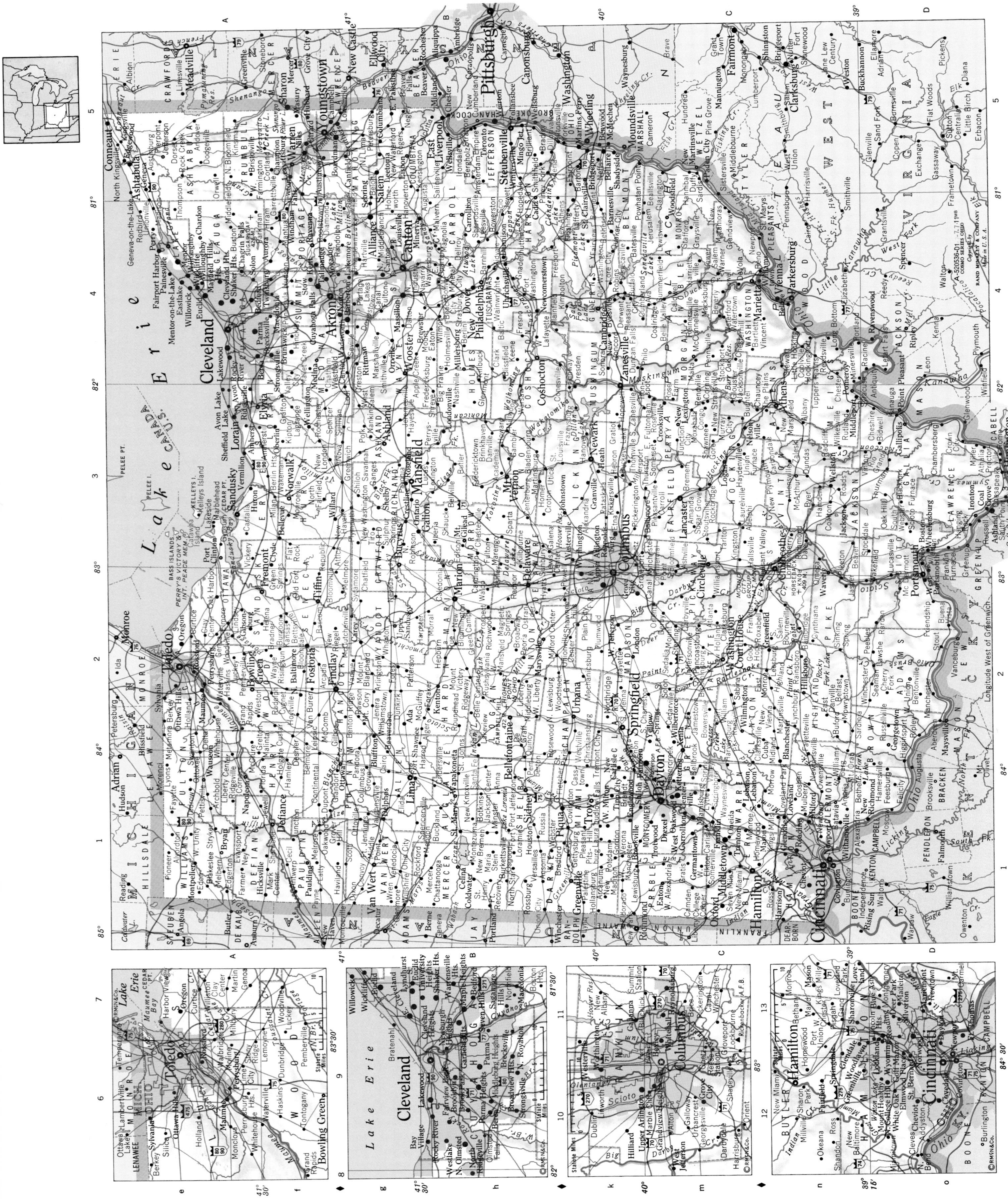

Statute Miles 5 0 5 10 20 30 40
Kilometers 5 0 5 15 25 35 45 55

Lambert Conformal Conic Projection
SCALE 1:1,714,000 1 Inch = 27 Statute Miles

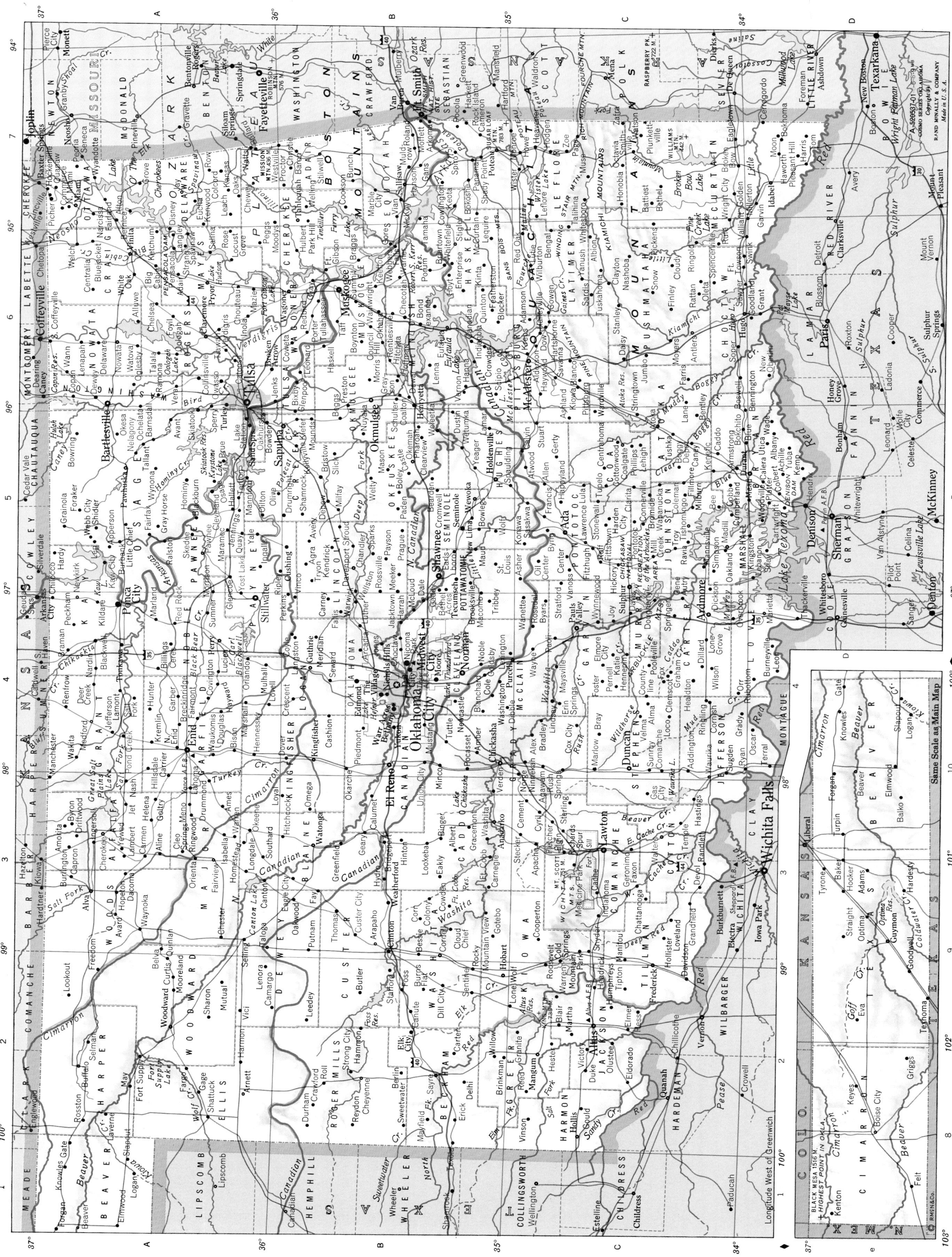

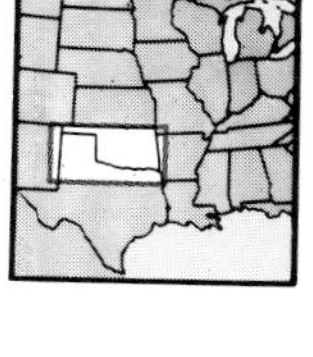

Statute Miles 5 0 5 10 20 30 40

Kilometers 5 0 5 15 25 35 45 55

Lambert Conformal Conic Projection

SCALE 1:1,957,000 1 Inch = 31 Statute Miles

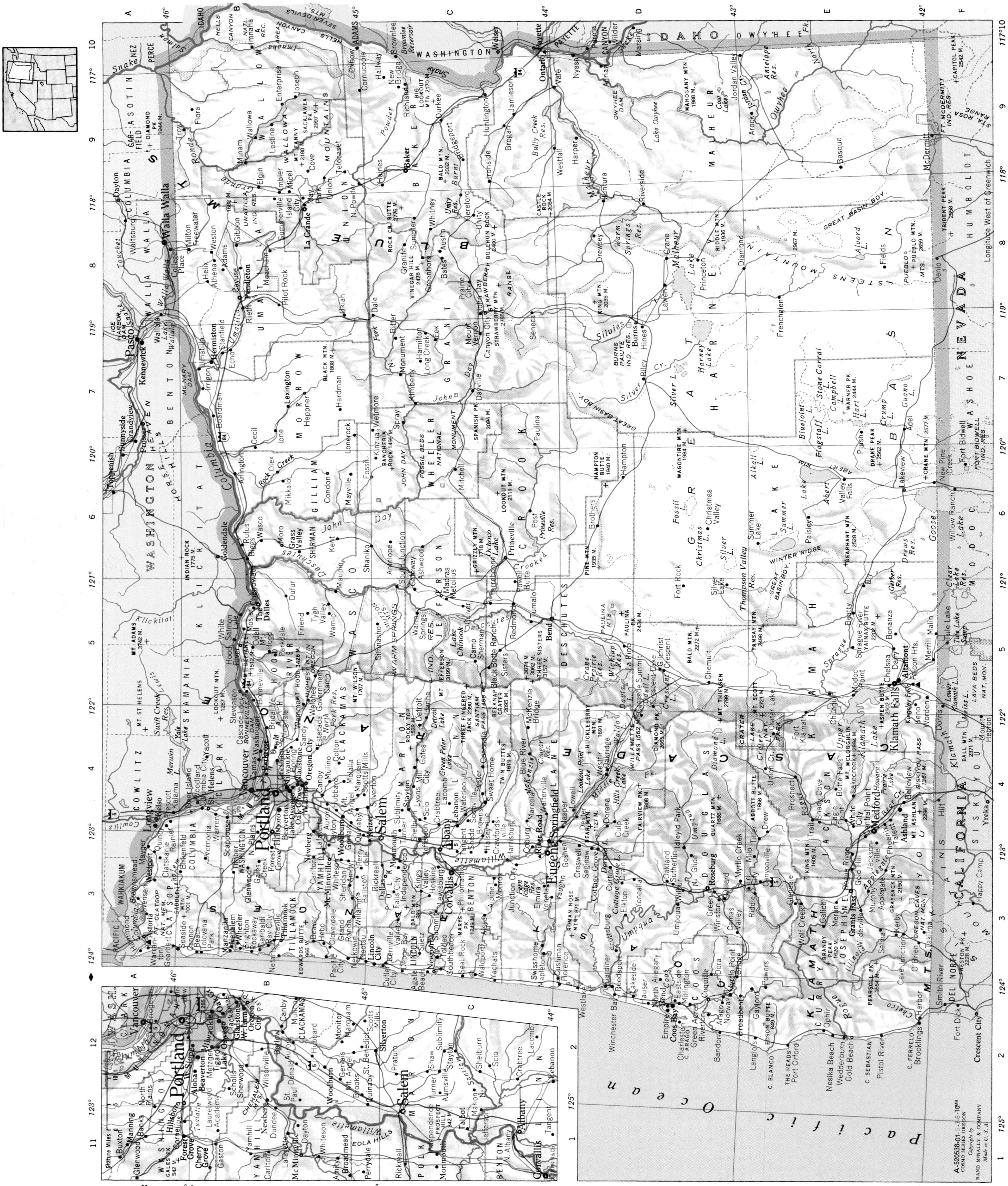

Statute Miles 5 0 5 10 20 30 40 50

Kilometers 5 0 5 15 25 35 45 55 65 75

Lambert Conformal Conic Projection

SCALE 1:2,329,000 1 Inch = 37 Statute Miles

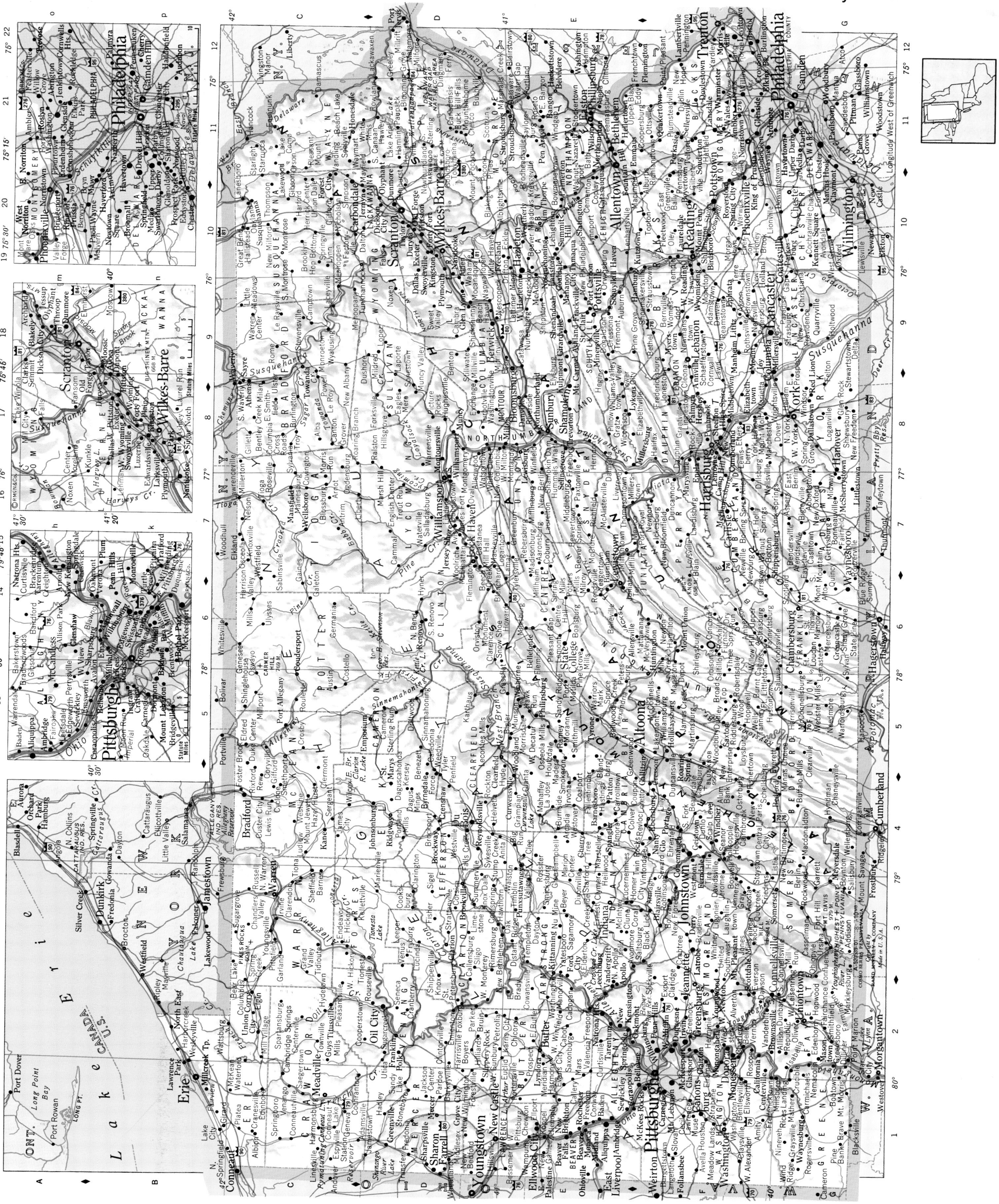

Statute Miles 5 0 5 10 20 30

Kilometers 5 0 5 15 25 35 45

Lambert Conformal Conic Projection

SCALE 1:1,593,000 1 Inch = 25 Statute Miles

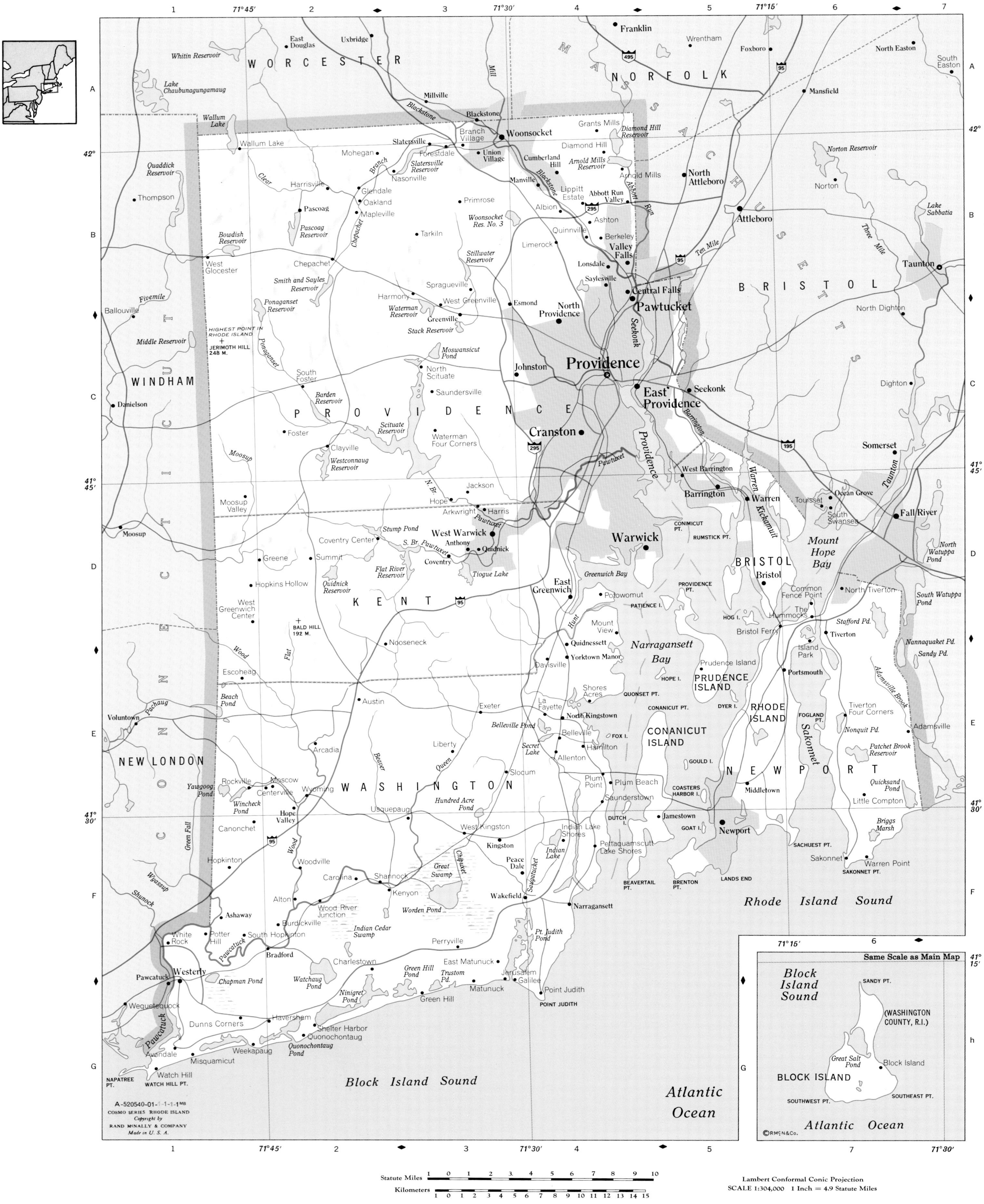

71°45′
71°30′
71°15′
42°
41° 45′
41° 30′
41° 15′
71°30′
WORCESTER
NORFOLK
MASSACHUSETTS
BRISTOL
WINDHAM
CONNECTICUT
NEW LONDON
PROVIDENCE
KENT
WASHINGTON
NEWPORT
BRISTOL
Franklin
Wrentham
Foxboro
North Easton
South Easton
Mansfield
East Douglas
Uxbridge
Whitin Reservoir
Lake Chaubunagungamaug
Millville
Blackstone
Wallum Lake
Woonsocket
Branch Village
Union Village
Slatersville
Forestdale
Slatersville Reservoir
Nasonville
Mohegan
Grants Mills
Diamond Hill Reservoir
Diamond Hill
Cumberland Hill
Arnold Mills Reservoir
Arnold Mills
North Attleboro
Manville
Lippitt Estate
Abbott Run Valley
Albion
Quaddick Reservoir
Thompson
Harrisville
Glendale
Oakland
Mapleville
Pascoag
Pascoag Reservoir
Primrose
Woonsocket Res. No. 3
Tarkiln
Ashton
Quinnville
Berkeley
Valley Falls
Attleboro
Norton Reservoir
Norton
Lake Sabbatia
Bowdish Reservoir
West Glocester
Chepachet
Limerock
Stillwater Reservoir
Lonsdale
Saylesville
Central Falls
Pawtucket
Taunton
Smith and Sayles Reservoir
Ponaganset Reservoir
Harmony
Spragueville
West Greenville
Waterman Reservoir
Greenville
Stack Reservoir
Esmond
North Providence
North Dighton
Ballouville
Middle Reservoir
HIGHEST POINT IN RHODE ISLAND
JERIMOTH HILL 248 M.
Moswansicut Pond
North Scituate
Johnston
Providence
South Foster
Saundersville
Barden Reservoir
East Providence
Seekonk
Dighton
Danielson
Foster
Scituate Reservoir
Waterman Four Corners
Cranston
Clayville
Westconnaug Reservoir
Somerset
West Barrington
Barrington
Warren
Touisset
Ocean Grove
South Swansea
Fall River
Moosup Valley
Jackson
Hope
Arkwright
Harris
Moosup
Stump Pond
Coventry Center
West Warwick
Anthony
Quidnick
Coventry
Tiogue Lake
Warwick
CONIMICUT PT.
RUMSTICK PT.
Mount Hope Bay
North Watuppa Pond
Greene
Summit
Flat River Reservoir
Greenwich Bay
Bristol
Hopkins Hollow
Quidnick Reservoir
East Greenwich
Potowomut
PROVIDENCE PT.
PATIENCE I.
Common Fence Point
North Tiverton
South Watuppa Pond
West Greenwich Center
BALD HILL 192 M.
Mount View
HOG I.
The Hummocks
Stafford Pd.
Bristol Ferry
Tiverton
Nooseneck
Quidnessett
Yorktown Manor
Narragansett Bay
Island Park
Nannaquaket Pd.
Sandy Pd.
Davisville
Prudence Island
Portsmouth
Escoheag
HOPE I.
PRUDENCE ISLAND
Shores Acres
QUONSET PT.
Beach Pond
Austin
La Fayette
CONANICUT PT.
DYER I.
RHODE ISLAND
Tiverton Four Corners
Voluntown
Exeter
North Kingstown
FOGLAND PT.
Belleville Pond
Belleville
FOX I.
CONANICUT ISLAND
Nonquit Pd.
Adamsville
Arcadia
Secret Lake
Hamilton
Liberty
Allenton
Patchet Brook Reservoir
GOULD I.
Slocum
Rockville
Moscow
Centerville
Wyoming
Plum Point
Plum Beach
COASTERS HARBOR I.
Middletown
Quicksand Pond
Yawgoog Pond
Wincheck Pond
Hundred Acre Pond
Saunderstown
Little Compton
Usquepaug
Hope Valley
DUTCH I.
Jamestown
Canonchet
West Kingston
Indian Lake Shores
GOAT I.
Newport
Briggs Marsh
Kingston
Pettaquamscutt Lake Shores
SACHUEST PT.
Hopkinton
Woodville
Peace Dale
Indian Lake
Sakonnet
Warren Point
SAKONNET PT.
Great Swamp
Carolina
Shannock
BEAVERTAIL PT.
BRENTON PT.
LANDS END
Kenyon
Wakefield
Rhode Island Sound
Alton
Wood River Junction
Worden Pond
Narragansett
Ashaway
Burdickville
Indian Cedar Swamp
Pt. Judith Pond
White Rock
Potter Hill
South Hopkinton
Perryville
Bradford
Charlestown
East Matunuck
Pawcatuck
Westerly
Chapman Pond
Watchaug Pond
Green Hill Pond
Trustom Pd.
Jerusalem
Galilee
Point Judith
POINT JUDITH
Ninigret Pond
Matunuck
Green Hill
Wequetequock
Haversham
Shelter Harbor
Dunns Corners
Quonochontaug
Quonochontaug Pond
Weekapaug
Avondale
Misquamicut
Watch Hill
NAPATREE PT.
WATCH HILL PT.
Block Island Sound
Atlantic Ocean
Same Scale as Main Map
Block Island Sound
SANDY PT.
(WASHINGTON COUNTY, R.I.)
Great Salt Pond
Block Island
BLOCK ISLAND
SOUTHWEST PT.
SOUTHEAST PT.
Atlantic Ocean
©RMcN&Co.
A-520540-01-1-1-1-1MB
COSMO SERIES RHODE ISLAND
Copyright by
RAND McNALLY & COMPANY
Made in U. S. A.
Statute Miles
Kilometers
Lambert Conformal Conic Projection
SCALE 1:304,000 1 Inch = 4.9 Statute Miles

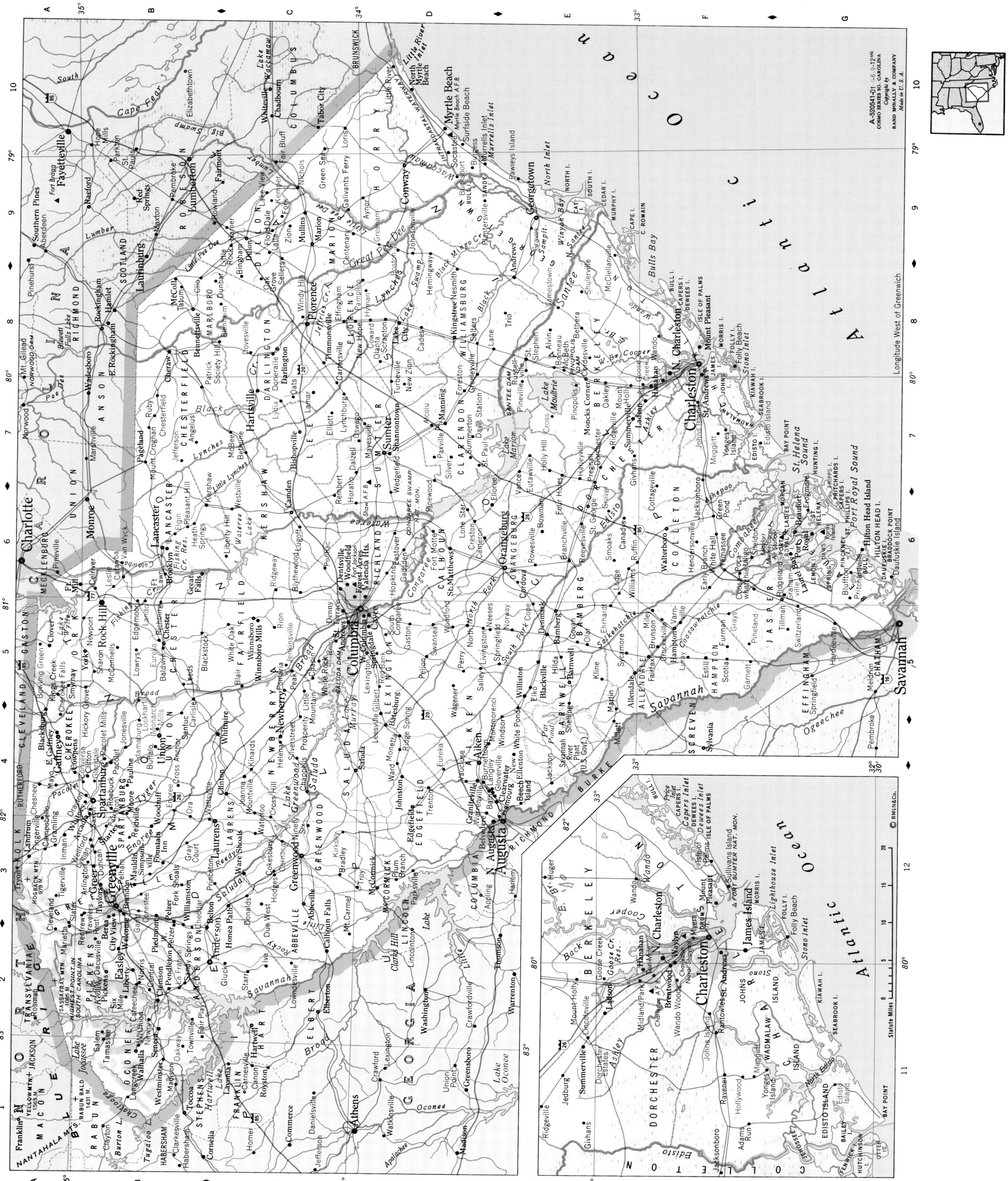

Statute Miles 5 0 5 10 20 30

Kilometers 5 0 5 15 25 35 45

Lambert Conformal Conic Projection

SCALE 1:1,566,000 1 Inch = 25 Statute Miles

South Dakota

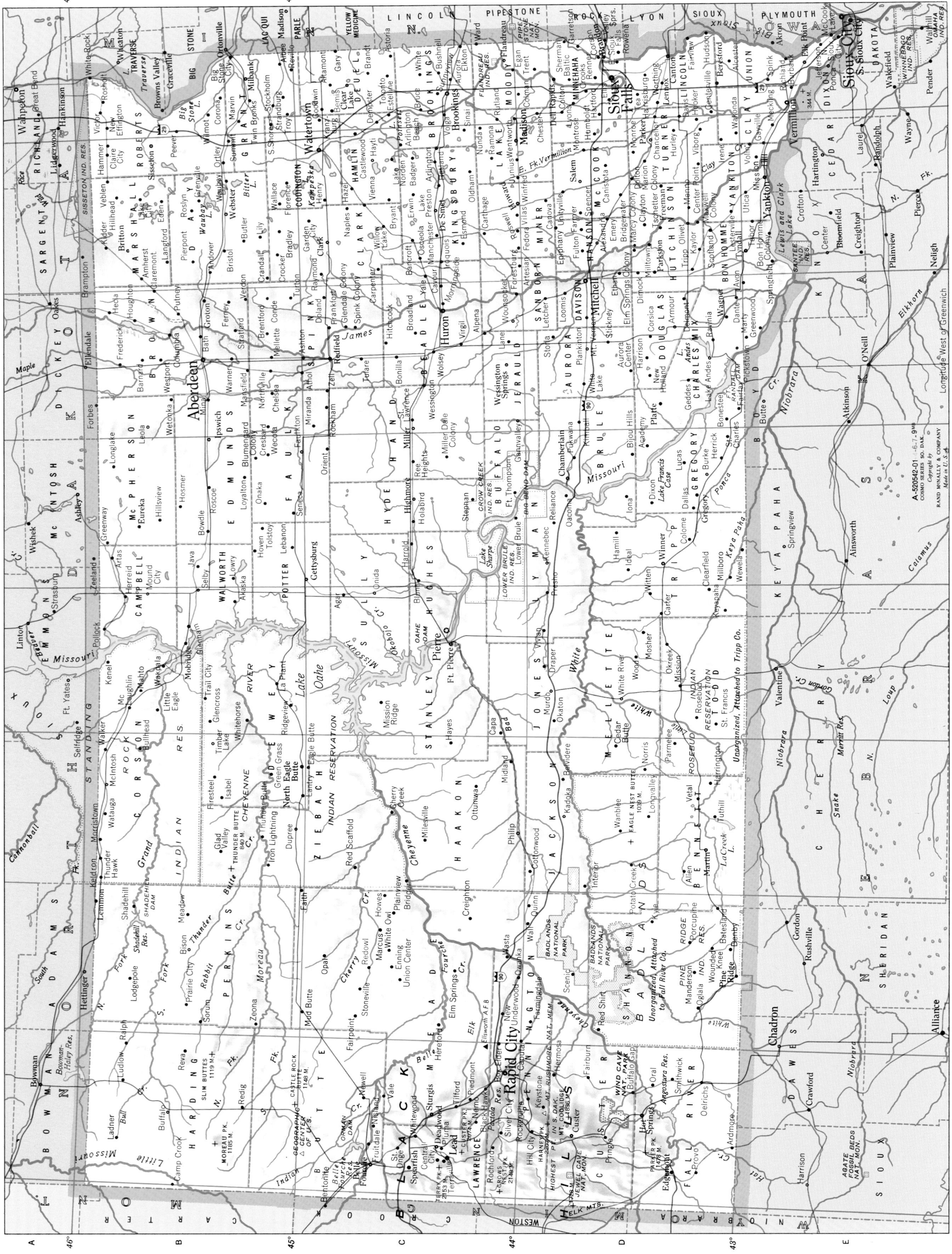

Statute Miles 5 0 5 10 20 30 40 50 60

Kilometers 5 0 5 15 25 35 45 55 65 75

Lambert Conformal Conic Projection

SCALE 1:2,091,000 1 Inch = 33 Statute Miles

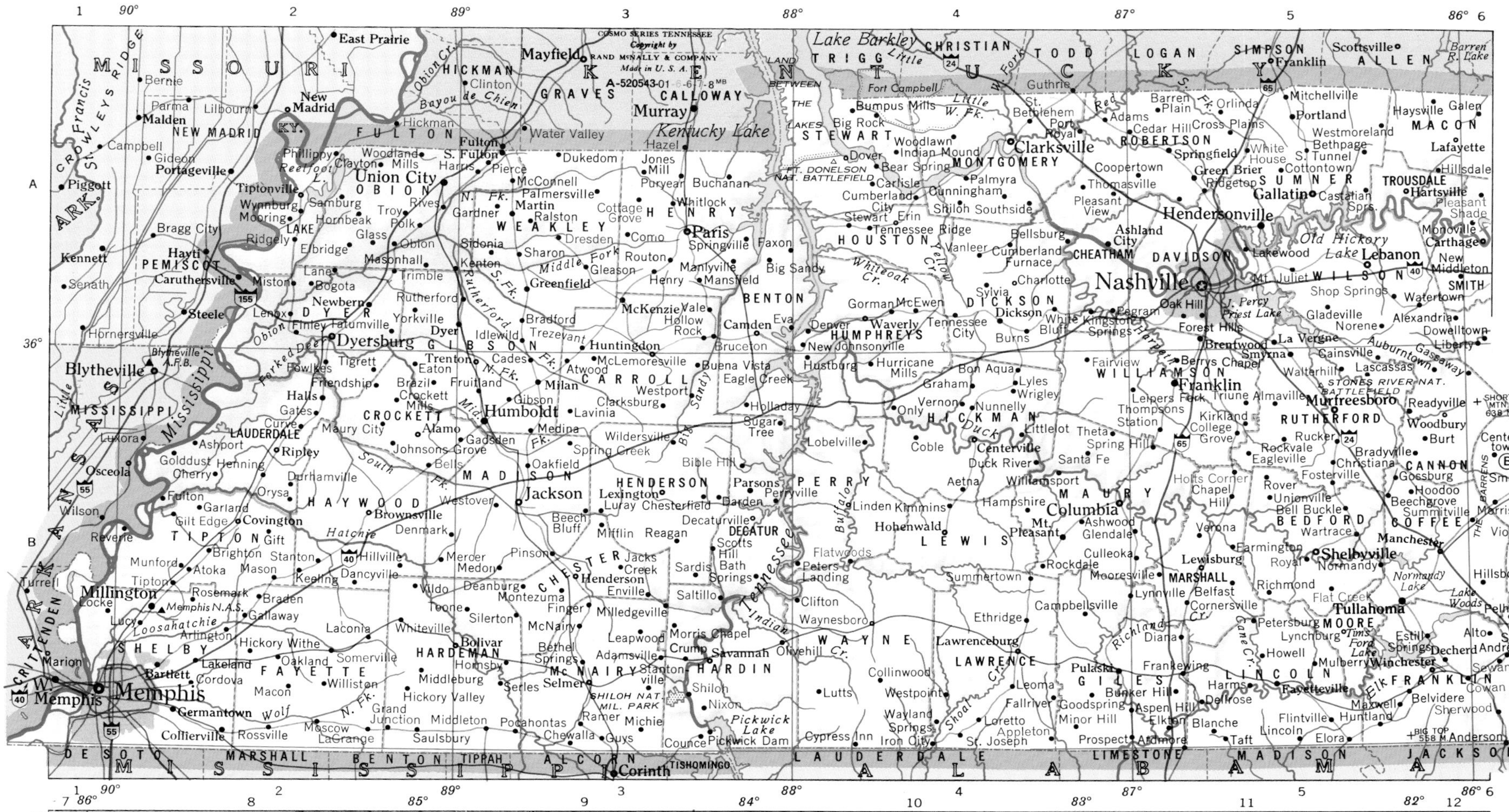

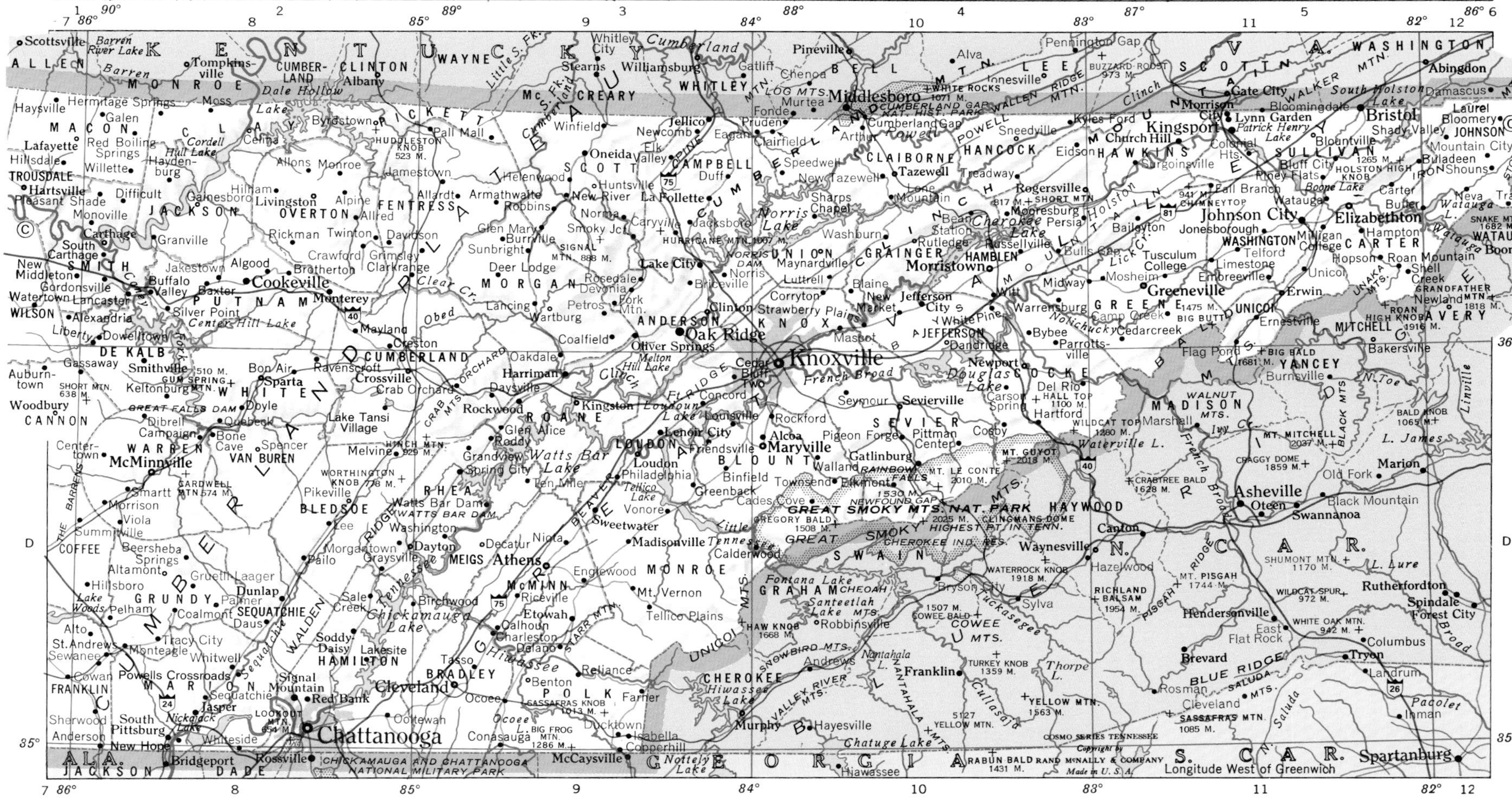

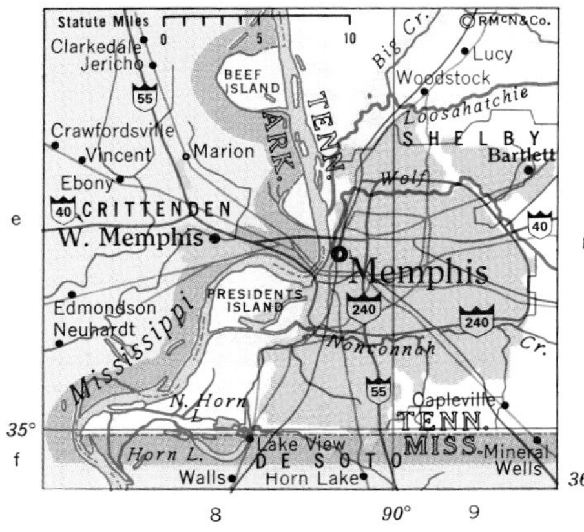

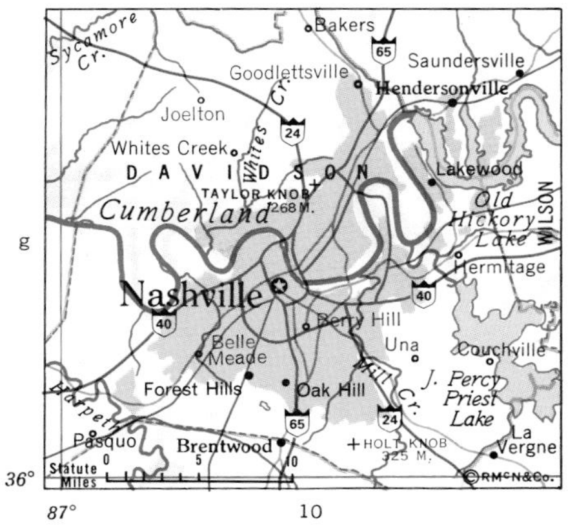

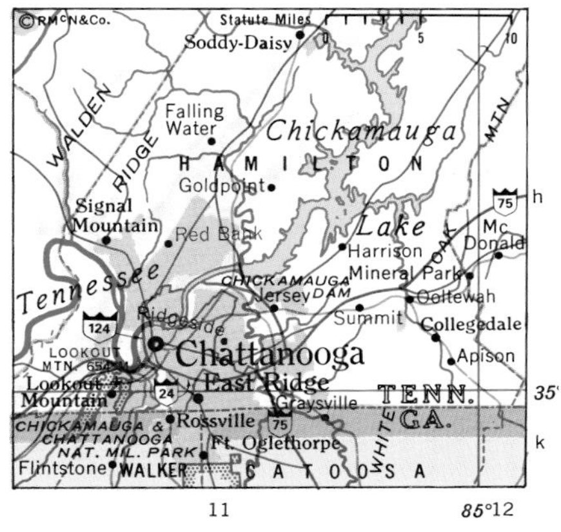

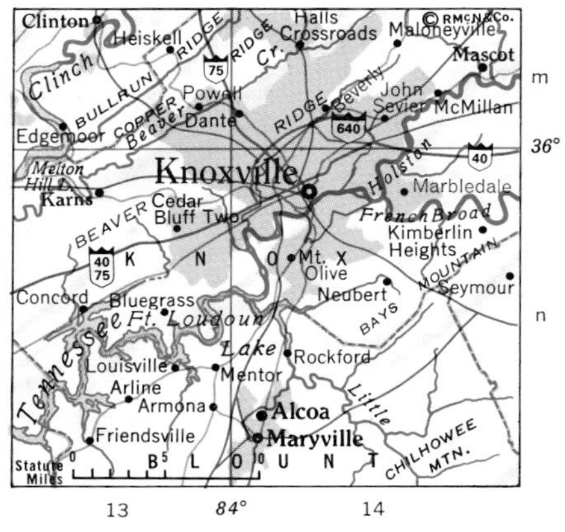

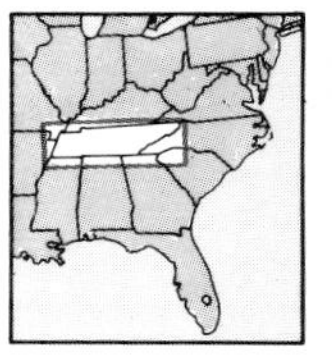

Statute Miles 5 0 5 10 20 30 40

Kilometers 5 0 5 15 25 35 45 55

Lambert Conformal Conic Projection

SCALE 1:1,713,000 1 Inch = 27 Statute Miles

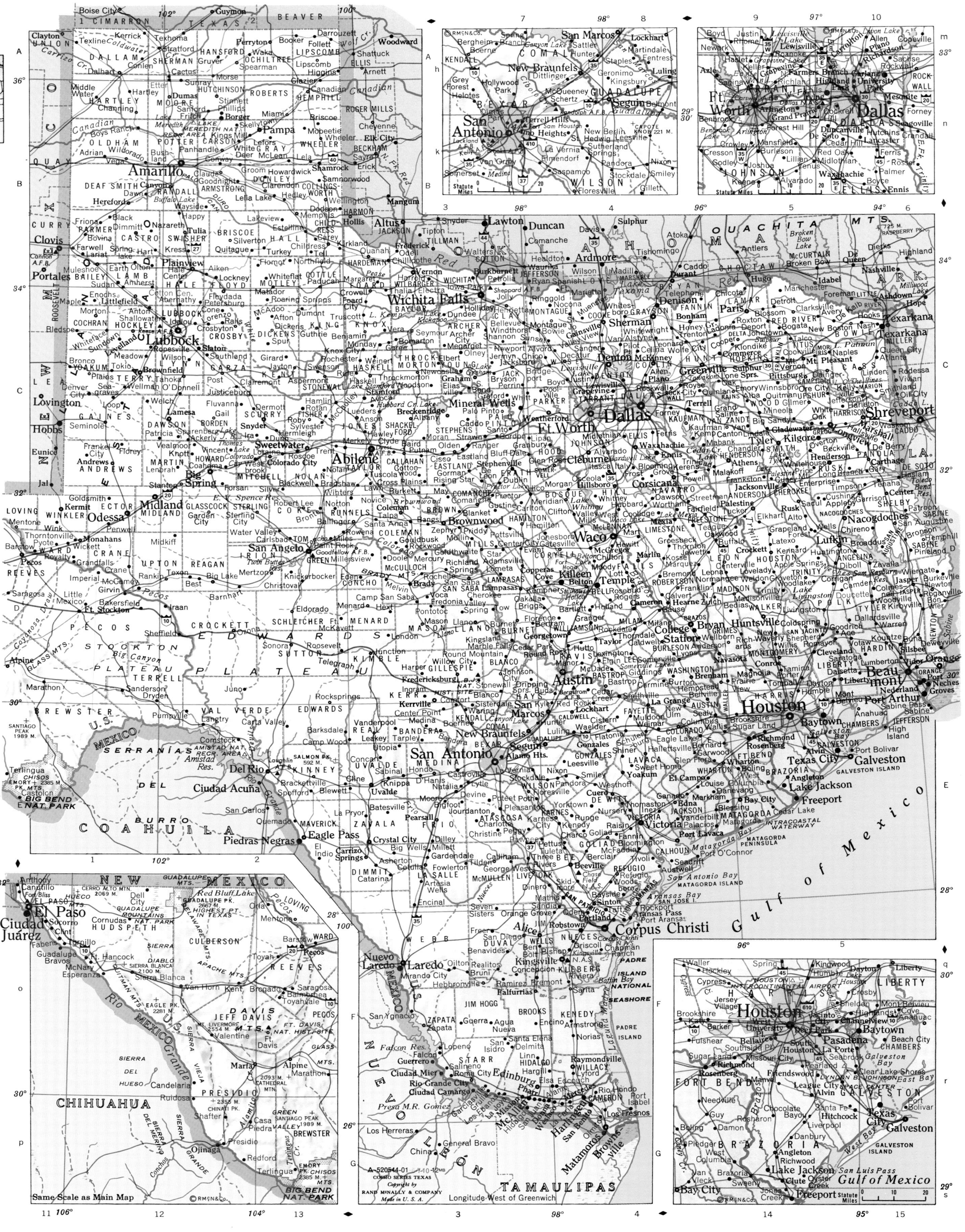
Gulf of Mexico
COAHUILA
CHIHUAHUA
NUEVO LEÓN
TAMAULIPAS
Same Scale as Main Map
Longitude West of Greenwich
A-520544-01
COSMO SERIES TEXAS
Copyright by RAND McNALLY & COMPANY Made in U. S. A.
Statute Miles 10 0 10 20 30 40 50 60 70 80 90 100
Kilometers 10 0 10 20 40 60 80 100 120 140
Lambert Conformal Conic Projection
SCALE 1:4,118,000 1 Inch = 65 Statute Miles
Amarillo
Lubbock
Abilene
Wichita Falls
Dallas
Ft. Worth
Waco
Austin
San Antonio
Houston
Corpus Christi
El Paso
Laredo
Shreveport
Beaumont
Galveston

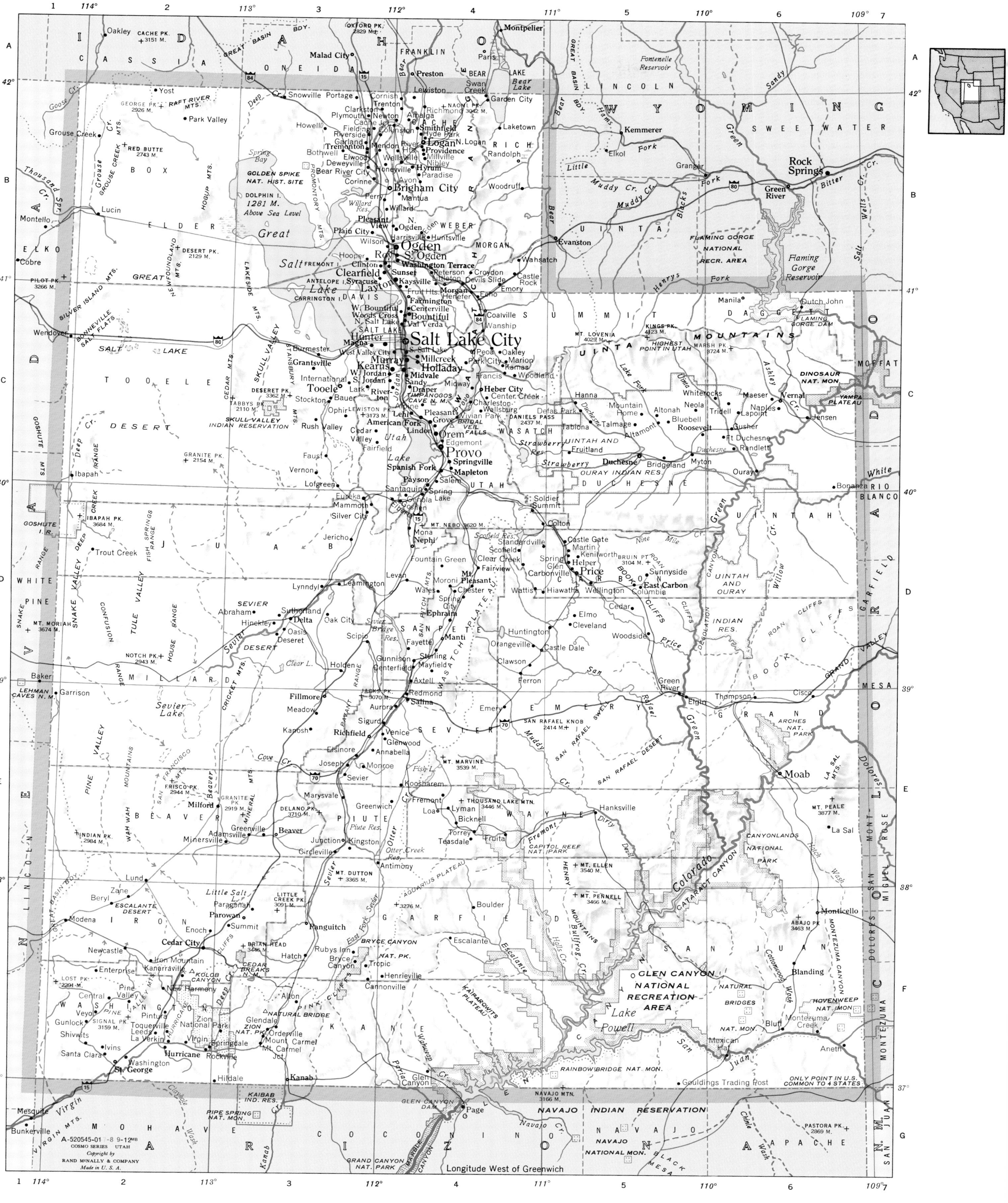

Statute Miles 5 0 5 10 20 30 40 50 60

Kilometers 5 0 5 20 30 40 50 60 70 80

Lambert Conformal Conic Projection

SCALE 1:2,100,000 1 Inch = 33 Statute Miles

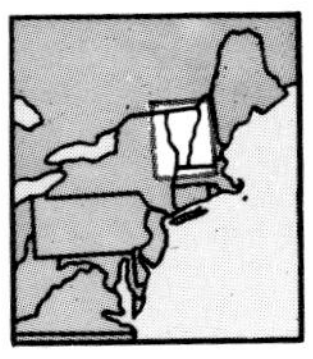

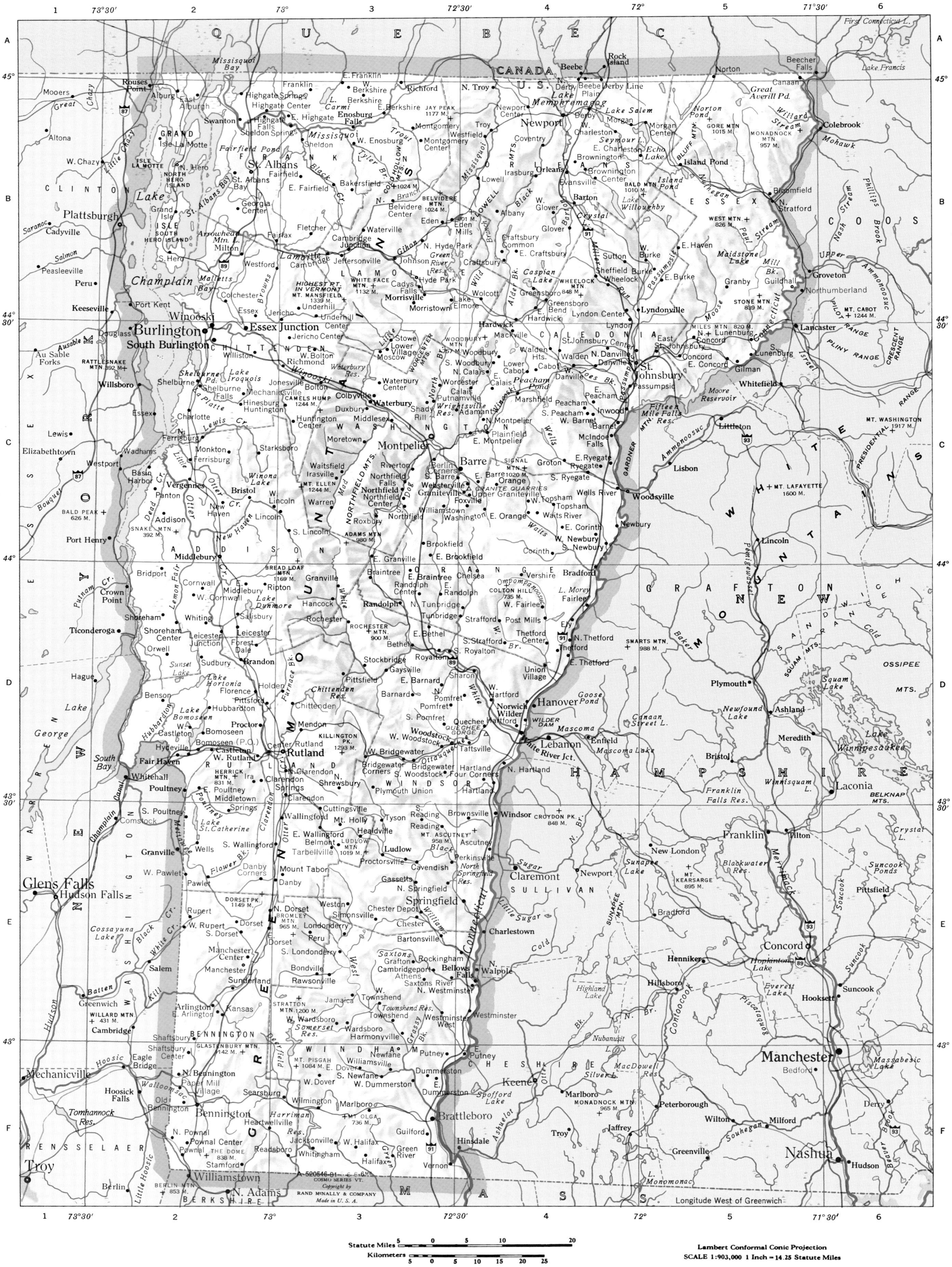
QUEBEC
CANADA
U.S.
CLINTON
ESSEX
COOS
FRANKLIN
GRAND ISLE
LAMOILLE
ORLEANS
CALEDONIA
CHITTENDEN
WASHINGTON
ADDISON
ORANGE
RUTLAND
WINDSOR
WINDHAM
BENNINGTON
GRAFTON
SULLIVAN
CHESHIRE
HAMPSHIRE
MASS.
WASHINGTON
WARREN
RENSSELAER
BERKSHIRE
GREEN MOUNTAINS
WHITE MOUNTAINS
Lake Champlain
Lake Memphremagog
Lake George
Lake Winnipesaukee
Connecticut
Burlington
South Burlington
Winooski
Essex Junction
St. Albans
Swanton
Newport
St. Johnsbury
Montpelier
Barre
Middlebury
Rutland
Brandon
Randolph
White River Jct.
Woodstock
Springfield
Bellows Falls
Brattleboro
Bennington
Manchester
Plattsburgh
Glens Falls
Hudson Falls
Troy
Hanover
Lebanon
Claremont
Keene
Concord
Manchester
Nashua
Laconia
Franklin
HIGHEST PT. IN VERMONT MT. MANSFIELD 1339 M.
CAMELS HUMP 1244 M.
KILLINGTON PK. 1293 M.
MT. WASHINGTON 1917 M.
MT. ASCUTNEY 958 M.
Longitude West of Greenwich
45°
44° 30′
44°
43° 30′
43°
73°30′
73°
72°30′
72°
71°30′
Statute Miles 5 0 5 10 20
Kilometers 5 0 5 10 15 20 25
Lambert Conformal Conic Projection
SCALE 1:903,000 1 Inch = 14.25 Statute Miles
COSMO SERIES VT.
Copyright by RAND McNALLY & COMPANY
Made in U. S. A.

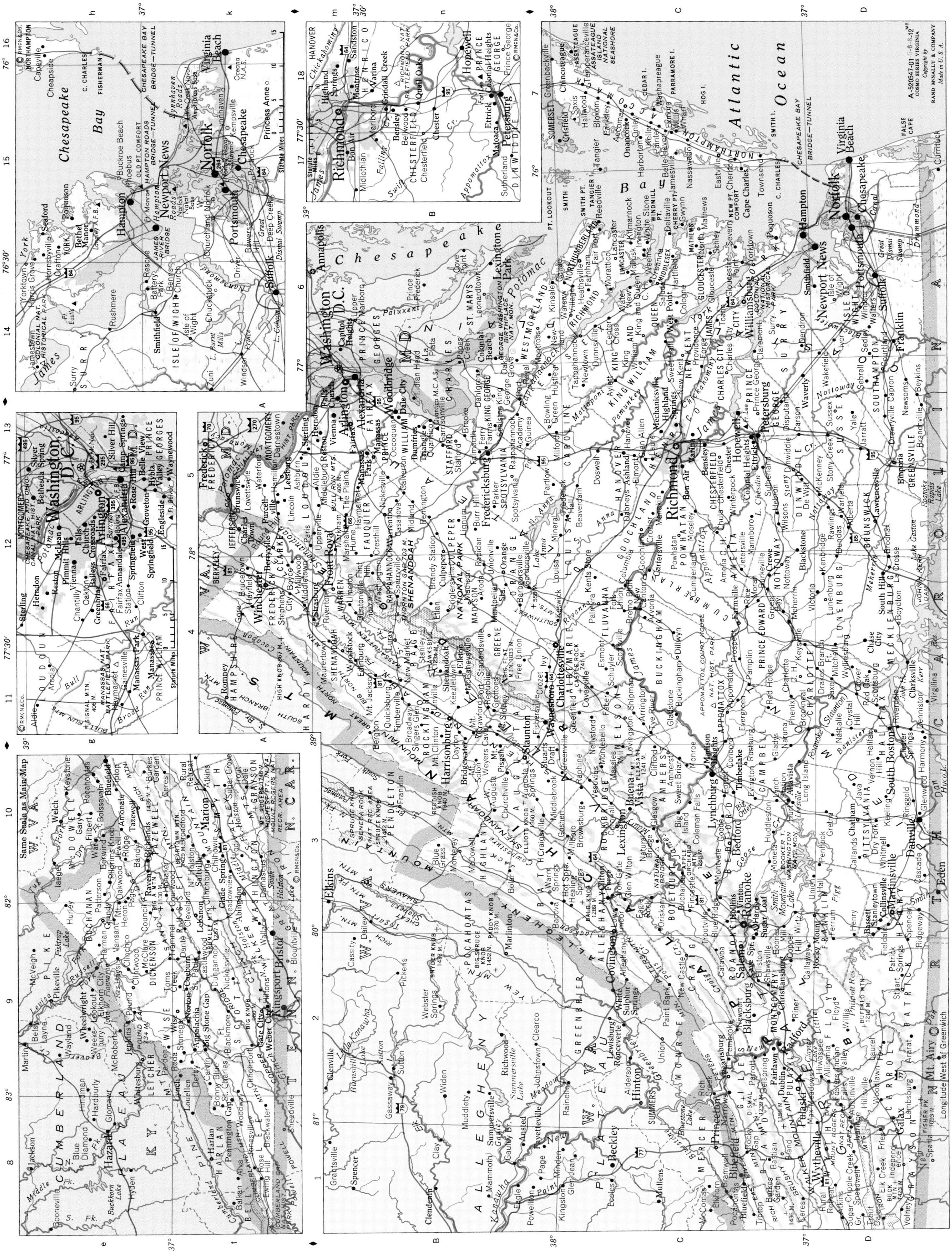

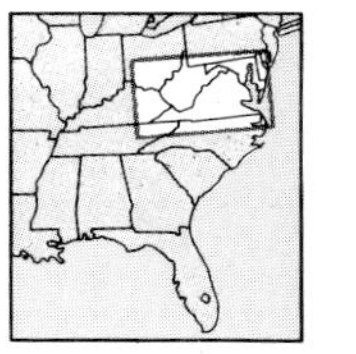

Statute Miles 5 0 5 10 20 30 40
Kilometers 5 0 5 15 25 35 45 55

Lambert Conformal Conic Projection
SCALE 1:1,822,000 1 Inch = 29 Statute Miles

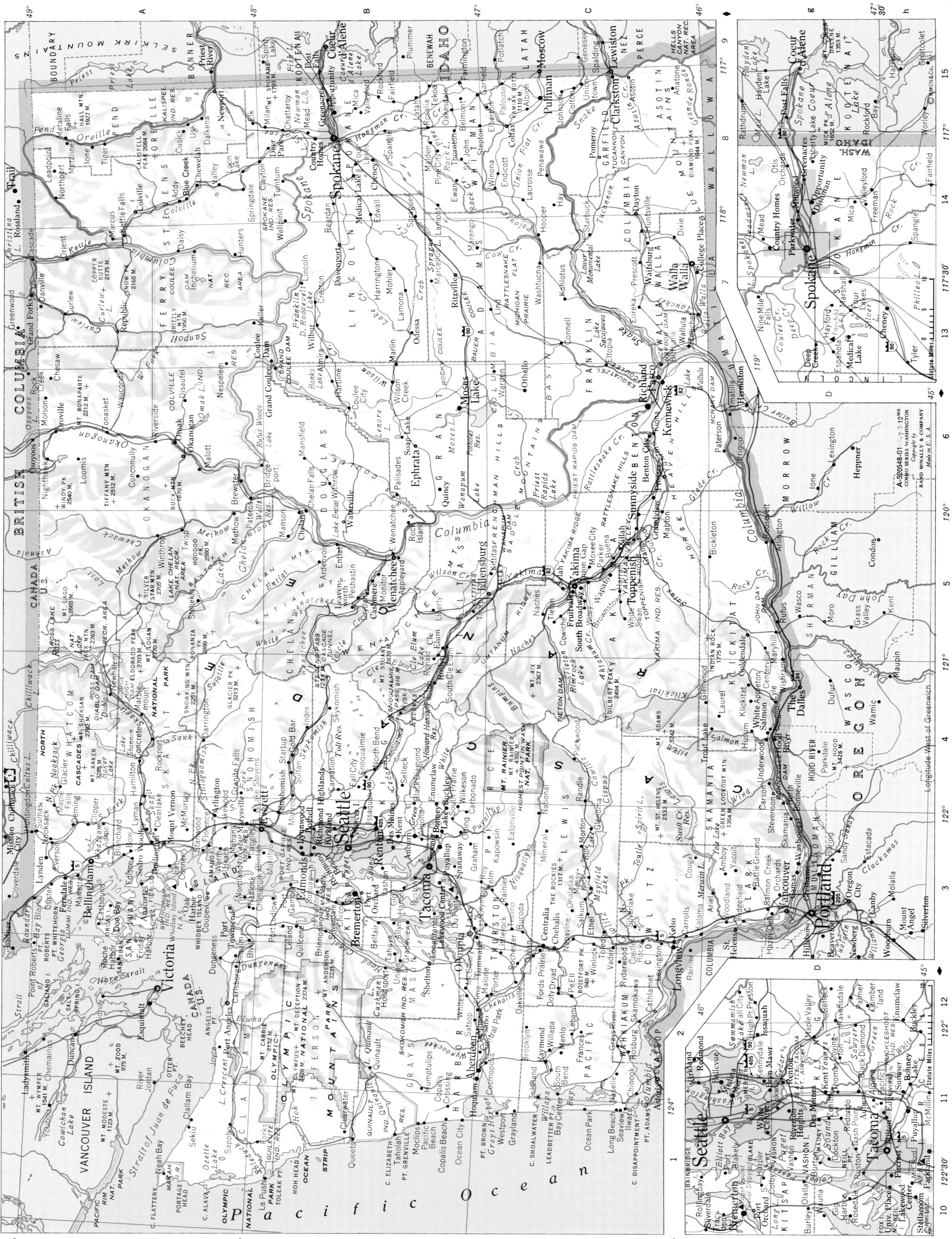

Statute Miles 5 0 5 10 20 30 40 50

Kilometers 5 0 5 15 25 35 45 55 65

Lambert Conformal Conic Projection

SCALE 1:2,068,000 Inch = 33 Statute Miles

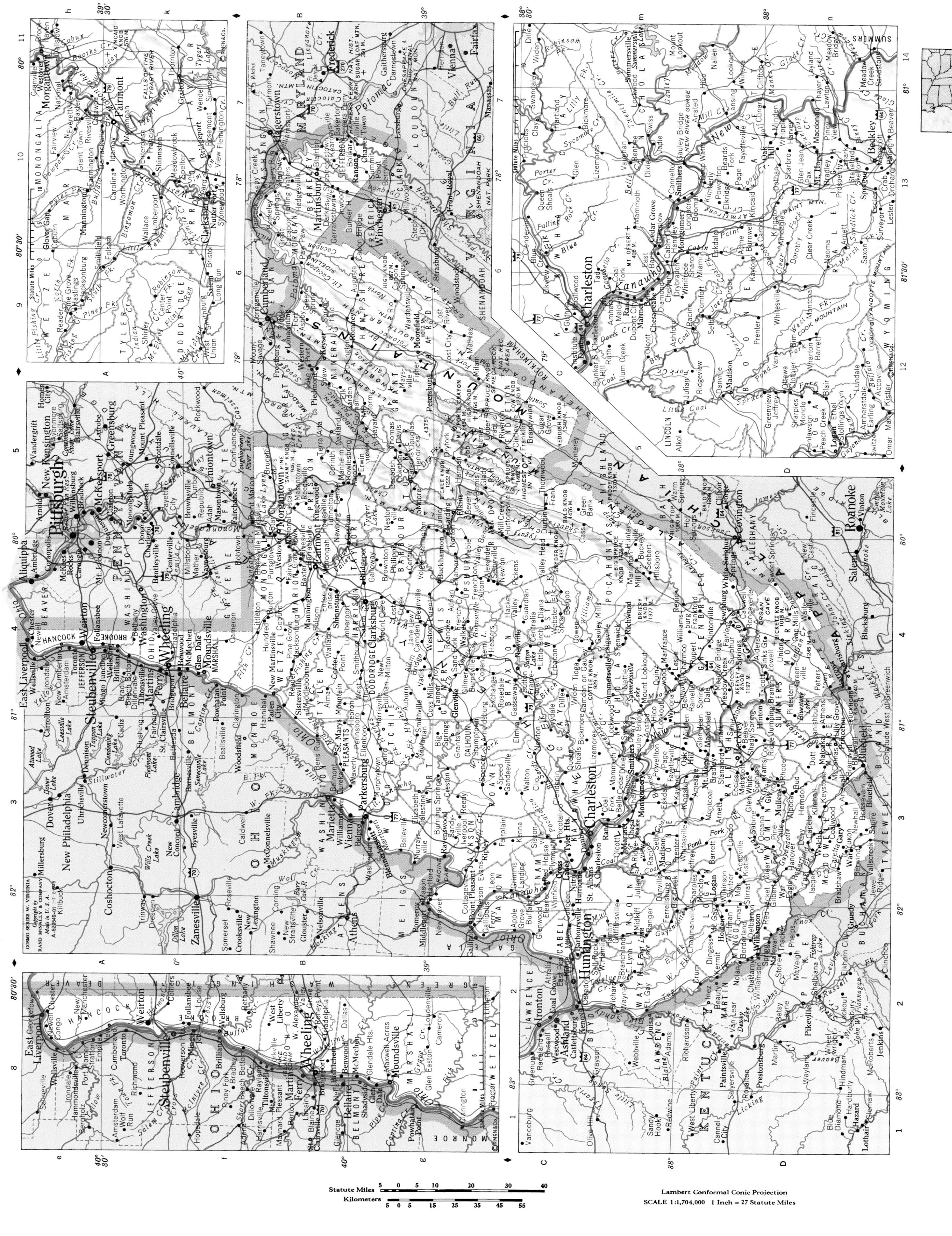

Lambert Conformal Conic Projection
SCALE 1:1,704,000 1 Inch = 27 Statute Miles

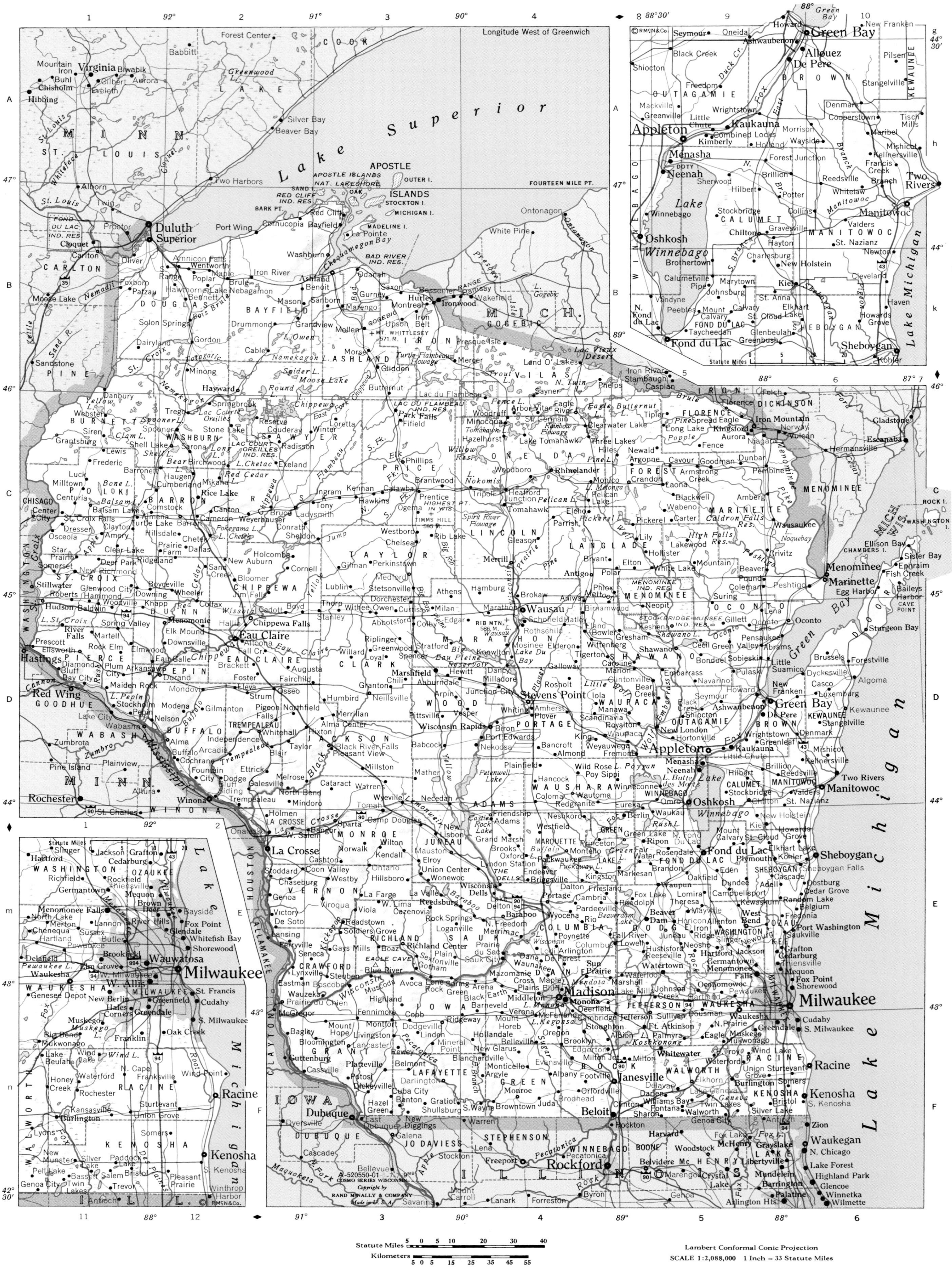
Longitude West of Greenwich
Lake Superior
Lake Michigan
APOSTLE ISLANDS NAT. LAKESHORE
MICH.
MINN.
IOWA
ILL.
Green Bay
Milwaukee
Madison
Duluth
Superior
Eau Claire
La Crosse
Wausau
Stevens Point
Appleton
Oshkosh
Sheboygan
Racine
Kenosha
Janesville
Beloit
Rockford
Dubuque
Manitowoc
Fond du Lac
Lake Winnebago
Statute Miles
Kilometers
Lambert Conformal Conic Projection
SCALE 1:2,088,000 1 Inch = 33 Statute Miles
Copyright by RAND McNALLY & COMPANY
Made in U.S.A.

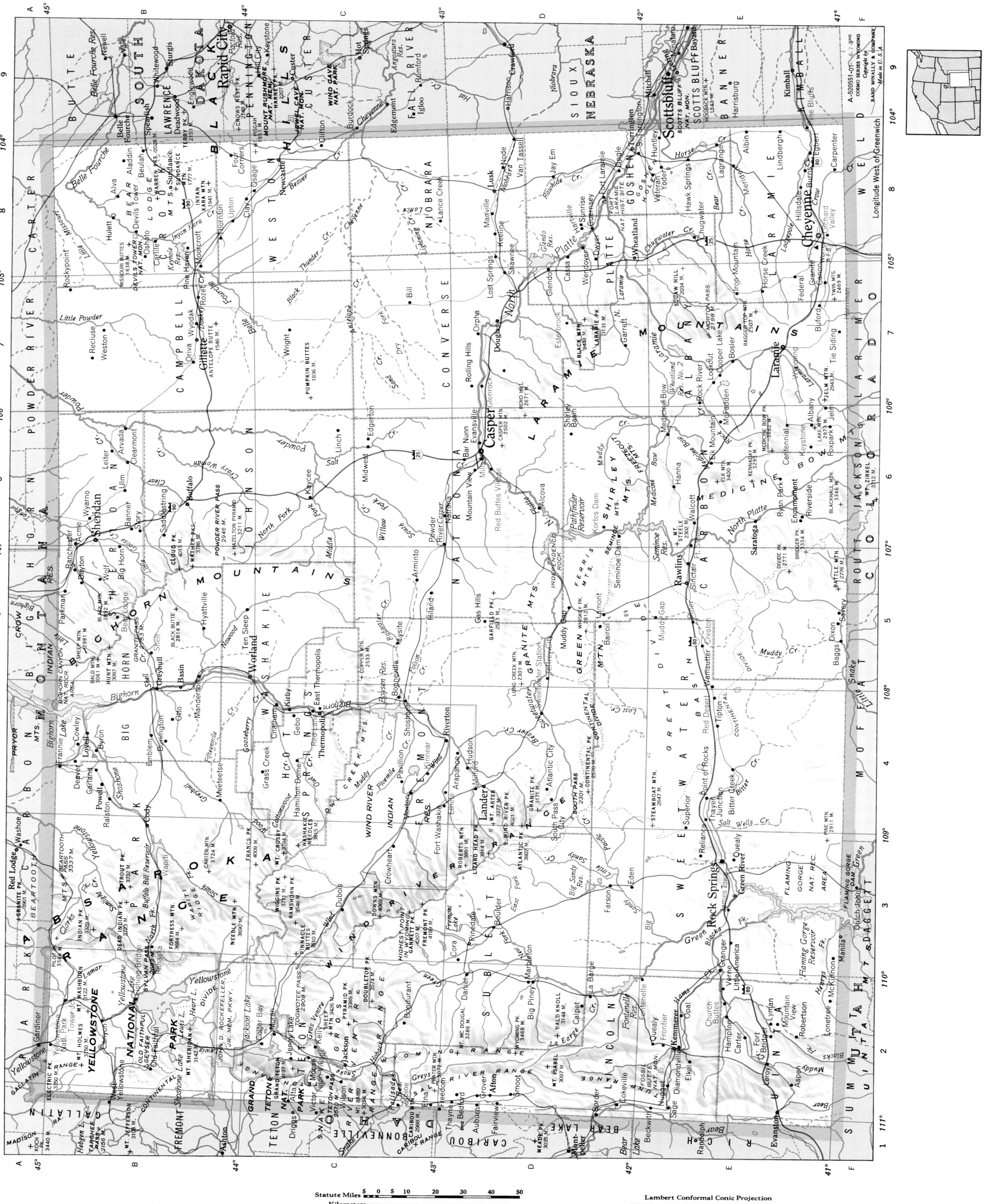

Statute Miles 5 0 5 10 20 30 40 50

Kilometers 5 0 5 15 25 35 45 55 65 75

Lambert Conformal Conic Projection

SCALE 1:2,186,000 1 Inch = 34.5 Statute Miles

GREENLAND
Greenland Sea
Barents Sea
Arctic Circle
ICELAND
Norwegian Sea
NORWAY
SWEDEN
FINLAND
UNITED KINGDOM
IRELAND
North Sea
FRANCE
GERMANY
POLAND
ROMANIA
BULGARIA
YUGO.
HUNGARY
AUSTRIA
TURKEY
ASIA MINOR
Black Sea
Caspian Sea
MEDITERRANEAN SEA
TUNISIA
LIBYA
EGYPT
SAHARA
Tropic of Cancer
SUDAN
ETHIOPIA
SOMALIA
KENYA
UGANDA
TANZANIA
ZAMBIA
ZIMBABWE
MOZAMBIQUE
BOTSWANA
NAMIBIA
SOUTH AFRICA
SWAZILAND
LESOTHO
MADAGASCAR
AFRICA
SAUDI ARABIA
ARABIAN PENINSULA
YEMEN
OMAN
IRAQ
IRAN
SYRIA
JORDAN
ISRAEL
LEBANON
KUWAIT
QATAR
UNITED ARAB EMIRATES
AFGHANISTAN
PAKISTAN
INDIA
NEPAL
BHUTAN
BNGL.
BURMA
THAILAND
CAMB.
VIET-NAM
LAOS
MALAYSIA
BRUNEI
SRI LANKA
MALDIVES
CHINA
MONGOLIA
UNION OF SOVIET SOCIALIST REPUBLICS
SIBERIA
URAL'SKIJE GORY
URAL MOUNTAINS
ZAPADNO-SIBIRSKAJA RAVNINA
SREDNESIBIRSKOJE PLOSKOGORJE
ALTAI
TIEN SHAN
HIMALAYAS
HINDU KUSH
GOBI
KUNLUN SHAN
QING ZANG GAOYUAN
N. KOREA
S. KOREA
JAPAN
Sea of Japan
Yellow Sea
East China Sea
Sea of Okhotsk
TAIWAN
PHILIPPINES
Philippine Sea
South China Sea
SUNDA SHELF
BORNEO KALIMANTAN
SULAWESI CELEBES
GREATER SUNDA ISLANDS
INDONESIA
NEW GUINEA
Arafura Sea
Timor Sea
Gulf of Carpentaria
AUSTRALIA
GREAT SANDY DESERT
GIBSON DESERT
GREAT VICTORIA DESERT
GREAT DIVIDING RANGE
GREAT BARRIER REEF
Great Australian Bight
TASMANIA
ARABIAN SEA
Bay of Bengal
ARABIAN BASIN
SOMALI BASIN
MID-INDIAN BASIN
CARLSBERG RIDGE
CHAGOS-LACCADIVE PLATEAU
NINETY-EAST RIDGE
WHARTON BASIN
INDIAN OCEAN
Tropic of Capricorn
MID-INDIAN RIDGE
SOUTHWEST INDIAN RIDGE
MADAGASCAR BASIN
MASCARENE BASIN
MOZAMBIQUE PLATEAU
Mozambique Channel
NORTH AUSTRALIAN BASIN
PERTH BASIN
BROKEN RIDGE
CROZET BASIN
AGULHAS BASIN
SOUTHERN OCEAN
SOUTHEAST INDIAN RIDGE
SOUTH INDIAN BASIN
SOUTH AUSTRALIAN BASIN
KERGUELEN PLATEAU
ATLANTIC-INDIAN RIDGE
ATLANTIC-INDIAN BASIN
Antarctic Circle
ENDERBY LAND
AMERY ICE SHELF
AMERICAN HIGHLAND
WILKES LAND
ANTARCTICA
PRINCESS MARTHA COAST
PRINCESS RAGNHILD COAST

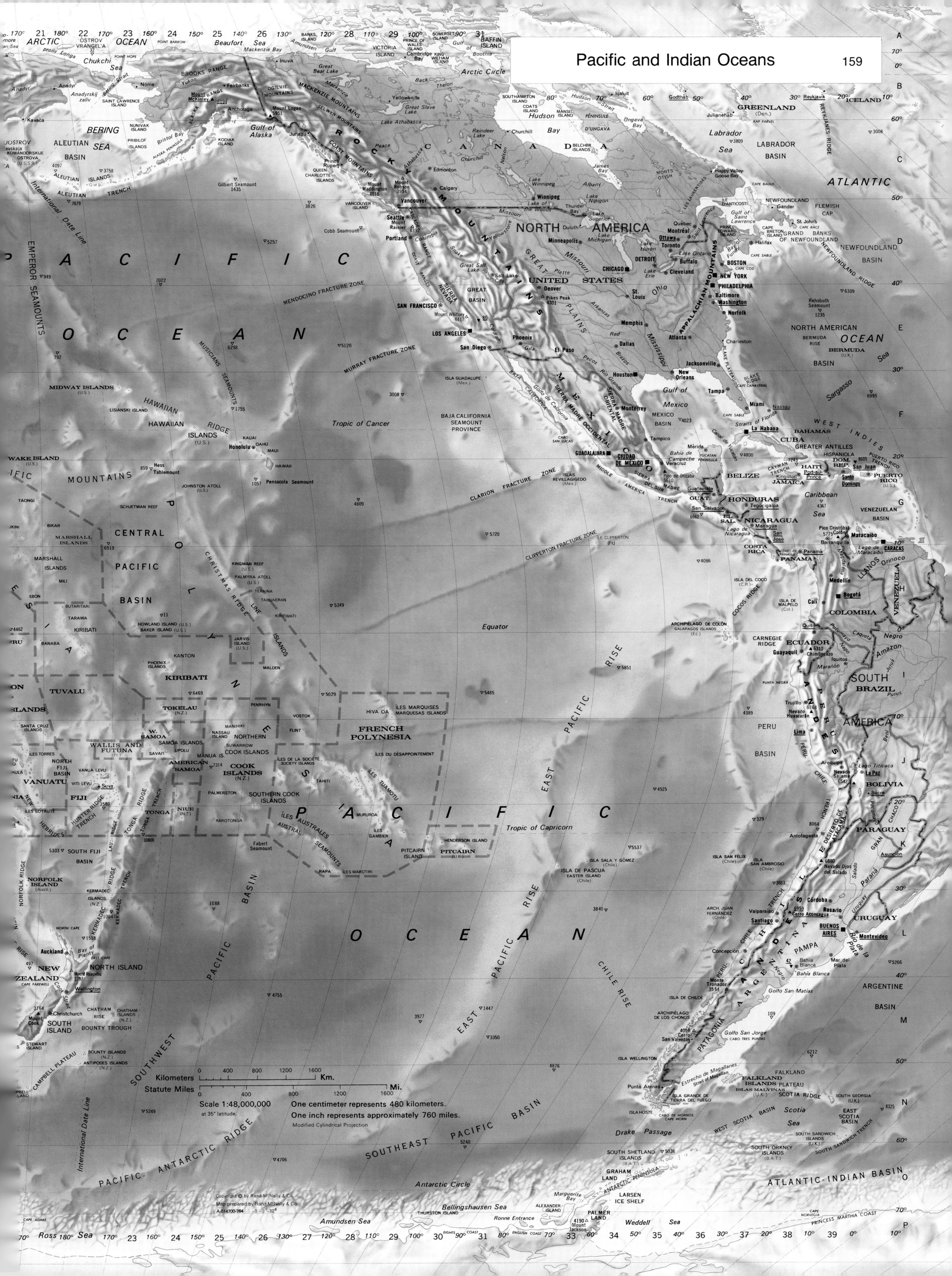
PACIFIC OCEAN
NORTH AMERICA
SOUTH AMERICA
ATLANTIC OCEAN
ARCTIC OCEAN
CANADA
UNITED STATES
MEXICO
ROCKY MOUNTAINS
APPALACHIAN MOUNTAINS
GREAT PLAINS
Gulf of Alaska
BERING SEA
ALEUTIAN BASIN
ALEUTIAN TRENCH
Hudson Bay
Labrador Sea
LABRADOR BASIN
GREENLAND (Den.)
ICELAND
NEWFOUNDLAND BASIN
NORTH AMERICAN BASIN
BERMUDA (U.K.)
Sargasso Sea
Gulf of Mexico
Caribbean Sea
VENEZUELAN BASIN
Tropic of Cancer
Equator
Tropic of Capricorn
Arctic Circle
Antarctic Circle
International Date Line
EMPEROR SEAMOUNTS
MENDOCINO FRACTURE ZONE
MURRAY FRACTURE ZONE
CLARION FRACTURE ZONE
CLIPPERTON FRACTURE ZONE
HAWAIIAN ISLANDS (U.S.)
HAWAIIAN RIDGE
MIDWAY ISLANDS (U.S.)
WAKE ISLAND (U.S.)
MID-PACIFIC MOUNTAINS
CENTRAL PACIFIC BASIN
POLYNESIA
MICRONESIA
KIRIBATI
TUVALU
TOKELAU (N.Z.)
W. SAMOA
AMERICAN SAMOA
WALLIS AND FUTUNA (Fr.)
VANUATU
FIJI
TONGA
NIUE (N.Z.)
COOK ISLANDS (N.Z.)
FRENCH POLYNESIA
PITCAIRN (U.K.)
NEW ZEALAND
NORTH ISLAND
SOUTH ISLAND
SOUTH FIJI BASIN
KERMADEC TRENCH
TONGA TRENCH
EAST PACIFIC RISE
PERU BASIN
PERU-CHILE TRENCH
CHILE RISE
SOUTHWEST PACIFIC BASIN
SOUTHEAST PACIFIC BASIN
PACIFIC-ANTARCTIC RIDGE
ARGENTINE BASIN
SCOTIA SEA
Drake Passage
Bellingshausen Sea
Amundsen Sea
Ross Sea
Weddell Sea
ATLANTIC-INDIAN BASIN
COLOMBIA
VENEZUELA
ECUADOR
PERU
BOLIVIA
BRAZIL
PARAGUAY
URUGUAY
ARGENTINA
CHILE
FALKLAND ISLANDS (ISLAS MALVINAS) (U.K.)
Kilometers 0 400 800 1200 1600 Km.
Statute Miles 0 400 800 1200 1600 Mi.
Scale 1:48,000,000 at 35° latitude.
One centimeter represents 480 kilometers.
One inch represents approximately 760 miles.
Modified Cylindrical Projection
Copyright © by Rand McNally & Co.
Map prepared by Rand McNally & Co.

GREENLAND
Baffin Bay
Arctic Circle
ICELAND
Norwegian Sea
Barents Sea
FAEROE IS.
Labrador Sea
LABRADOR BASIN
NORTH AMERICA
CANADA
Hudson Bay
BAFFIN ISLAND
UNITED STATES
Gulf of Mexico
MEXICO
Caribbean Sea
WEST INDIES
BAHAMAS
CUBA
HAITI
DOM. REP.
PUERTO RICO
JAMAICA
BELIZE
GUAT.
HONDURAS
EL SAL.
NICARAGUA
COSTA RICA
PANAMA
VENEZUELA
COLOMBIA
GUYANA
SURINAME
FRENCH GUIANA
ECUADOR
PERU
BRAZIL
BOLIVIA
PARAGUAY
CHILE
ARGENTINA
URUGUAY
SOUTH AMERICA
PATAGONIA
FALKLAND ISLANDS ISLAS MALVINAS
Drake Passage
Scotia Sea
ATLANTIC OCEAN
NORTH AMERICAN BASIN
BERMUDA RISE
Sargasso Sea
Tropic of Cancer
MID-ATLANTIC RIDGE
CAPE VERDE
CAPE VERDE BASIN
GUIANA BASIN
Equator
BRAZIL BASIN
ANGOLA BASIN
Tropic of Capricorn
ARGENTINE BASIN
CAPE BASIN
AGULHAS BASIN
WEST EUROPEAN BASIN
NEWFOUNDLAND BASIN
PACIFIC OCEAN
INDIAN OCEAN
UNITED KINGDOM
IRELAND
NORWAY
SWEDEN
FINLAND
DENMARK
FRANCE
SPAIN
PORTUGAL
GERMANY
POLAND
ITALY
UNION OF SOVIET SOCIALIST REPUBLICS
EUROPE
Mediterranean Sea
Black Sea
TURKEY
GREECE
MOROCCO
ALGERIA
LIBYA
EGYPT
SAHARA
MAURITANIA
MALI
NIGER
CHAD
SUDAN
ETHIOPIA
SENEGAL
GUINEA
LIBERIA
NIGERIA
CAMEROON
AFRICA
ZAIRE
ANGOLA
ZAMBIA
NAMIBIA
BOTSWANA
SOUTH AFRICA
MOZAMBIQUE
TANZANIA
SAUDI ARABIA
ANTARCTICA
Weddell Sea
Antarctic Circle
Kilometers 0 400 800 1200 1600 Km.
Statute Miles 0 400 800 1200 1600 Mi.
Scale 1:48,000,000
at 35° latitude.
One centimeter represents 480 kilometers.
One inch represents approximately 760 miles.
Modified Cylindrical Projection
Copyright © by Rand McNally & Co.
Map prepared by Rand McNally & Co.
A-513700-764

Index to World Reference Maps

Introduction to the Index

This universal index includes in a single alphabetical list approximately 69,000 names of features that appear on the reference maps. Each name is followed by the name of the country or continent in which it is located, a map-reference key and a page reference.

Names The names of cities appear in the index in regular type. The names of all other features appear in *italics*, followed by descriptive terms (hill, mtn., state) to indicate their nature.

Names that appear in shortened versions on the maps due to space limitations are spelled out in full in the index. The portions of these names omitted from the maps are enclosed in brackets — for example, Acapulco [de Juárez].

Abbreviations of names on the maps have been standardized as much as possible. Names that are abbreviated on the maps are generally spelled out in full in the index.

Country names and names of features that extend beyond the boundaries of one country are followed by the name of the continent in which each is located. Country designations follow the names of all other places in the index. The locations of places in the United States, Canada, and the United Kingdom are further defined by abbreviations that indicate the state, province, or political division in which each is located.

All abbreviations used in the index are defined in the List of Abbreviations below.

Alphabetization Names are alphabetized in the order of the letters of the English alphabet. Spanish *ll* and *ch*, for example, are not treated as distinct letters. Furthermore, diacritical marks are disregarded in alphabetization — German or Scandinavian *ä* or *ö* are treated as *a* or *o*.

The names of physical features may appear inverted, since they are always alphabetized under the proper, not the generic, part of the name, thus: 'Gibraltar, Strait of'. Otherwise every entry, whether consisting of one word or more, is alphabetized as a single continuous entity. 'Lakeland', for example, appears after 'La Crosse' and before 'La Salle'. Names beginning with articles (Le Havre, Den Helder, Al Manşūrah) are not inverted. Names beginning 'St.', 'Ste.' and 'Sainte' are alphabetized as though spelled 'Saint'.

In the case of identical names, towns are listed first, then political divisions, then physical features. Entries that are completely identical are listed alphabetically by country name.

Map-Reference Keys and Page References The map-reference keys and page references are found in the last two columns of each entry.

Each map-reference key consists of a letter and number. The letters appear along the sides of the maps. Lowercase letters indicate reference to inset maps. Numbers appear across the tops and bottoms of the maps.

Map reference keys for point features, such as cities and mountain peaks, indicate the locations of the symbols. For extensive areal features, such as countries or mountain ranges, locations are given for the approximate centers of the features. Those for linear features, such as canals and rivers, are given for the locations of the names.

Names of some important places or features that are omitted from the maps due to space limitations are included in the index. Each of these places is identified by an asterisk (*) preceding the map-reference key.

The page number generally refers to the main map for the country in which the feature is located. Page references to two-page maps always refer to the left-hand page.

List of Abbreviations

Afg.	Afghanistan
Afr.	Africa
Ak., U.S.	Alaska, U.S.
Al., U.S.	Alabama, U.S.
Alb.	Albania
Alg.	Algeria
Alta., Can.	Alberta, Can.
Am. Sam.	American Samoa
anch.	anchorage
And.	Andorra
Ang.	Angola
Ant.	Antarctica
Antig.	Antigua and Barbuda
Ar., U.S.	Arkansas, U.S.
Arg.	Argentina
Aus.	Austria
Austl.	Australia
Az., U.S.	Arizona, U.S.
b.	bay, gulf, inlet, lagoon
Bah.	Bahamas
Bahr.	Bahrain
Barb.	Barbados
B.A.T.	British Antarctic Territory
B.C., Can.	British Columbia, Can.
Bdi.	Burundi
Bel.	Belgium
Ber.	Bermuda
Bhu.	Bhutan
B.I.O.T.	British Indian Ocean Territory
Bngl.	Bangladesh
Bol.	Bolivia
Boph.	Bophuthatswana
Bots.	Botswana
Braz.	Brazil
Bru.	Brunei
Br. Vir. Is.	British Virgin Islands
Bul.	Bulgaria
Burkina	Burkina Faso
c.	cape, point
Ca., U.S.	California, U.S.
Cam.	Cameroon
Camb.	Cambodia
Can.	Canada
Cay. Is.	Cayman Islands
Cen. Afr. Rep.	Central African Republic
Christ. I.	Christmas Island
clf.	cliff, escarpment
co.	county, parish
Co., U.S.	Colorado, U.S.
Col.	Colombia
Com.	Comoros
cont.	continent
C.R.	Costa Rica
crat.	crater
Ct., U.S.	Connecticut, U.S.
ctry.	country
C.V.	Cape Verde
Cyp.	Cyprus
Czech.	Czechoslovakia
D.C., U.S.	District of Columbia, U.S.
De., U.S.	Delaware, U.S.
Den.	Denmark
dep.	dependency, colony
depr.	depression
dept.	department, district
des.	desert
Dji.	Djibouti
Dom.	Dominica
Dom. Rep.	Dominican Republic
Ec.	Ecuador
El Sal.	El Salvador
Eng., U.K.	England, U.K.
Eq. Gui.	Equatorial Guinea
est.	estuary
Eth.	Ethiopia
Eur.	Europe
Faer. Is.	Faeroe Islands
Falk. Is.	Falkland Islands
Fin.	Finland
Fl., U.S.	Florida, U.S.
for.	forest, moor
Fr.	France
Fr. Gu.	French Guiana
Fr. Poly.	French Polynesia
F.S.A.T.	French Southern and Antarctic Territory
Ga., U.S.	Georgia, U.S.
Gam.	Gambia
Ger.	Germany
Gib.	Gibraltar
Grc.	Greece
Gren.	Grenada
Grnld.	Greenland
Guad.	Guadeloupe
Guat.	Guatemala
Gui.	Guinea
Gui.-B.	Guinea-Bissau
Guy.	Guyana
Hi., U.S.	Hawaii, U.S.
hist.	historic site, ruins
hist. reg.	historic region
H.K.	Hong Kong
Hond.	Honduras
Hung.	Hungary
i.	island
Ia., U.S.	Iowa, U.S.
I.C.	Ivory Coast
Ice.	Iceland
ice	ice feature, glacier
Id., U.S.	Idaho, U.S.
Il., U.S.	Illinois, U.S.
In., U.S.	Indiana, U.S.
Indon.	Indonesia
I. of Man	Isle of Man
Ire.	Ireland
is.	islands
Isr.	Israel
Isr. Occ.	Israeli Occupied Territories
Jam.	Jamaica
Jord.	Jordan
Kir.	Kiribati
Ks., U.S.	Kansas, U.S.
Kuw.	Kuwait
Ky., U.S.	Kentucky, U.S.
l.	lake, pond
La., U.S.	Louisiana, U.S.
Leb.	Lebanon
Leso.	Lesotho
Lib.	Liberia
Liech.	Liechtenstein
Lux.	Luxembourg
Ma., U.S.	Massachusetts, U.S.
Madag.	Madagascar
Malay.	Malaysia
Mald.	Maldives
Man., Can.	Manitoba, Can.
Marsh. Is.	Marshall Islands
Mart.	Martinique
Maur.	Mauritania
May.	Mayotte
Md., U.S.	Maryland, U.S.
Me., U.S.	Maine, U.S.
Mex.	Mexico
Mi., U.S.	Michigan, U.S.
Micron.	Federated States of Micronesia
Mid. Is.	Midway Islands
mil.	military installation
Mn., U.S.	Minnesota, U.S.
Mo., U.S.	Missouri, U.S.
Mon.	Monaco
Mong.	Mongolia
Monts.	Montserrat
Mor.	Morocco
Moz.	Mozambique
Mrts.	Mauritius
Ms., U.S.	Mississippi, U.S.
Mt., U.S.	Montana, U.S.
mth.	river mouth or channel
mtn.	mountain
mts.	mountains
Mwi.	Malawi
N.A.	North America
N.B., Can.	New Brunswick, Can.
N.C., U.S.	North Carolina, U.S.
N. Cal.	New Caledonia
N. Cyp.	North Cyprus
N.D., U.S.	North Dakota, U.S.
Ne., U.S.	Nebraska, U.S.
Neth.	Netherlands
Neth. Ant.	Netherlands Antilles
Newf., Can.	Newfoundland, Can.
N.H., U.S.	New Hampshire, U.S.
Nic.	Nicaragua
Nig.	Nigeria
N. Ire., U.K.	Northern Ireland, U.K.
N.J., U.S.	New Jersey, U.S.
N. Kor.	North Korea
N.M., U.S.	New Mexico, U.S.
N. Mar. Is.	Northern Mariana Islands
Nmb.	Namibia
Nor.	Norway
Norf. I.	Norfolk Island
N.S., Can.	Nova Scotia, Can.
Nv., U.S.	Nevada, U.S.
N.W. Ter., Can.	Northwest Territories, Can.
N.Y., U.S.	New York, U.S.
N.Z.	New Zealand
Oc.	Oceania
Oh., U.S.	Ohio, U.S.
Ok., U.S.	Oklahoma, U.S.
Ont., Can.	Ontario, Can.
Or., U.S.	Oregon, U.S.
Pa., U.S.	Pennsylvania, U.S.
Pak.	Pakistan
Pan.	Panama
Pap. N. Gui.	Papua New Guinea
Para.	Paraguay
P.E.I., Can.	Prince Edward Island, Can.
pen.	peninsula
Phil.	Philippines
Pit.	Pitcairn
pl.	plain, flat
plat.	plateau, highland
Pol.	Poland
Port.	Portugal
P.R.	Puerto Rico
prov.	province, region
Que., Can.	Quebec, Can.
reg.	physical region
res.	reservoir
Reu.	Reunion
rf.	reef, shoal
R.I., U.S.	Rhode Island, U.S.
Rom.	Romania
Rw.	Rwanda
S.A.	South America
S. Afr.	South Africa
Sask., Can.	Saskatchewan, Can.
Sau. Ar.	Saudi Arabia
S.C., U.S.	South Carolina, U.S.
sci.	scientific station
Scot., U.K.	Scotland, U.K.
S.D., U.S.	South Dakota, U.S.
Sen.	Senegal
Sey.	Seychelles
Sing.	Singapore
S. Kor.	South Korea
S.L.	Sierra Leone
S. Mar.	San Marino
Sol. Is.	Solomon Islands
Som.	Somalia
Sp. N. Afr.	Spanish North Africa
Sri L.	Sri Lanka
state	state, republic, canton
St. Hel.	St. Helena
St. K./N	St. Kitts and Nevis
St. Luc.	St. Lucia
stm.	stream (river, creek)
S. Tom./P.	Sao Tome and Principe
St. P./M.	St. Pierre and Miquelon
strt.	strait, channel, sound
St. Vin.	St. Vincent and the Grenadines
Sud.	Sudan
Sur.	Suriname
sw.	swamp, marsh
Swaz.	Swaziland
Swe.	Sweden
Switz.	Switzerland
Tai.	Taiwan
Tan.	Tanzania
T./C. Is.	Turks and Caicos Islands
ter.	territory
Thai.	Thailand
Tn., U.S.	Tennessee, U.S.
Tok.	Tokelau
Trin.	Trinidad and Tobago
T.T.P.I.	Trust Territory of the Pacific Islands
Tun.	Tunisia
Tur.	Turkey
Tx., U.S.	Texas, U.S.
U.A.E.	United Arab Emirates
Ug.	Uganda
U.K.	United Kingdom
Ur.	Uruguay
U.S.S.R.	Union of Soviet Socialist Republics
U.S.	United States
Ut., U.S.	Utah, U.S.
Va., U.S,	Virginia, U.S.
val.	valley, watercourse
Vat.	Vatican City
Ven.	Venezuela
Viet.	Vietnam
V.I.U.S.	Virgin Islands (U.S.)
vol.	volcano
Vt., U.S.	Vermont, U.S.
Wa., U.S.	Washington, U.S.
Wal./F.	Wallis and Futuna
Wi., U.S.	Wisconsin, U.S.
W. Sah.	Western Sahara
W. Sam.	Western Samoa
wtfl.	waterfall
W.V., U.S.	West Virginia, U.S.
Wy., U.S.	Wyoming, U.S.
Yugo.	Yugoslavia
Yukon, Can.	Yukon Territory, Can.
Zam.	Zambia
Zimb.	Zimbabwe

Index

A

Name	Map Ref.	Page
Aachen, Ger.	E6	10
Aalen, Ger.	G10	10
Aarau, Switz.	D9	13
Aarburg, Switz.	D8	13
Aare, stm., Switz.	C9	13
Aargau, state, Switz.	D9	13
Aarlen (Arlon), Bel.	I8	12
Aaronsburg, Pa., U.S.	E7	145
Aazanèn, Mor.	J8	16
Aba, China	E7	30
Aba, Nig.	I13	64
Abā as-Su'ūd, Sau. Ar.	F4	47
Abacaxis, stm., Braz.	E7	76
Abacaxis, stm., Braz.	A12	82
Abaco, i., Bah.	A6	94
Abacou, Pointe, c., Haiti	E8	94
Ābādān, Iran	F10	48
Ābādeh, Iran	F12	48
Abadia dos Dourados, Braz.	E5	79
Abadiânia, Braz.	D4	79
Abadla, Alg.	E9	62
Abaeté, Braz.	E6	79
Abaeté, stm., Braz.	E6	79
Abaetetuba, Braz.	D9	76
Abagner Qi, China	C10	30
Abag Qi, China	C9	30
Abaí, Para.	D11	80
Abaj, U.S.S.R.	H12	22
Abaji, Nig.	G13	64
Abajo Peak, mtn., Ut., U.S.	F6	151
Abak, Nig.	I13	64
Abakaliki, Nig.	H14	64
Abakan, U.S.S.R.	G10	24
Abakan, stm., U.S.S.R.	G16	22
Abala, Niger	D11	64
Abalak, Niger	D13	64
Abalessa, Alg.	I13	62
Abancay, Peru	E5	82
Abanda, Al., U.S.	B4	108
Abar Kūh, Iran	F12	48
Abashiri, Japan	C19	36a
Abasolo, Mex.	E7	90
Abasolo, Mex.	E10	90
Abatiá, Braz.	G3	79
Abatimbo el Gumas, Eth.	L8	60
Abau, Pap. N. Gui.	B9	68
Abaya, Lake, l., Eth.	N9	60
Abay see Blue Nile, stm., Afr.	K7	60
Abaza, U.S.S.R.	G16	22
Abbaye, Point, c., Mi., U.S.	B2	129
Abbeville, Fr.	B8	14
Abbeville, Al., U.S.	D4	108
Abbeville, Ga., U.S.	E3	117
Abbeville, La., U.S.	E3	125
Abbeville, Ms., U.S.	A4	131
Abbeville, S.C., U.S.	C3	147
Abbeville, co., S.C., U.S.	C2	147
Abbey, Sask., Can.	G1	105
Abbeyfeale, Ire.	I4	8
Abbiategrasso, Italy	D3	18
Abbot, Mount, mtn., Austl.	C7	70
Abbotsford, Wi., U.S.	D3	156
Abbottābād, Pak.	C5	44
Abbott Butte, mtn., Or., U.S.	E4	144
Abbott Run, stm., U.S.	B4	146
Abbott Run Valley, R.I., U.S.	B4	146
Abbyville, Ks., U.S.	E5	123
'Abd al-Kūrī, i., Yemen	G5	42
'Abd Allāh, Sud.	K2	60
'Abd Allāh, Khawr, strt., Asia	G10	48
Abdulino, U.S.S.R.	G8	22
Abe, Lake, l., Afr.	F9	56
Abéché, Chad	F5	56
Abee, Alta., Can.	B4	98
Abéjar, Spain	D9	16
Abejonal, Cerro, mtn., Nic.	F8	92
Abejorral, Col.	E5	84
Abekr, Sud.	K5	60
Abelek, Sud.	N5	60
Abelti, Eth.	M9	60
Abengourou, I.C.	H8	64
Abenójar, Spain	G7	16
Abeokuta, Nig.	H11	64
Aberavon see Port Talbot, Wales, U.K.	J10	8
Abercorn, Que., Can.	D5	104
Abercrombie, N.D., U.S.	C9	141
Aberdeen, Sask., Can.	E2	105
Aberdeen, S. Afr.	I7	66
Aberdeen, Scot., U.K.	D11	8
Aberdeen, Id., U.S.	G6	119
Aberdeen, Ky., U.S.	C3	124
Aberdeen, Md., U.S.	A5	127
Aberdeen, Ms., U.S.	B5	131
Aberdeen, N.C., U.S.	B3	140
Aberdeen, Oh., U.S.	D2	142
Aberdeen, S.D., U.S.	B7	148
Aberdeen, Wa., U.S.	C2	154
Aberdeen Proving Ground, mil., Md., U.S.	A5	127
Abernant, Al., U.S.	B2	108
Abernathy, Tx., U.S.	C2	150
Abernethy, Sask., Can.	G4	105
Abert, Lake, l., Or., U.S.	E6	144
Abert Rim, clf, Or., U.S.	E6	144
Abetone, Italy	E5	18
Abez', U.S.S.R.	D10	22
Abhā, Sau. Ar.	E3	47
Abhar, Iran	C10	48
Ābhē Bid Hāyk', l., Afr.	G3	42
'Abīdīyah, Sud.	H7	60
Abidjan, I.C.	I7	64
Abie, Ne., U.S.	C9	134
Abilene, Ks., U.S.	D6	123
Abilene, Tx., U.S.	C3	150
Abingdon, Il., U.S.	C3	120
Abingdon, Md., U.S.	B5	127
Abingdon, Va., U.S.	f10	153
Abington, Ct., U.S.	B7	114
Abington, Ma., U.S.	B6	128
Abington Reefs, rf., Austl.	B8	70
Abington [Township], Pa., U.S.	o21	145
Abiquiu, N.M., U.S.	A3	138
Abita Springs, La., U.S.	D5	125
Abitau, stm., Can.	D11	96
Abitibi, stm., Ont., Can.	o19	103
Abitibi, Lake, l., Can.	G17	96
Abiy Adi, Eth.	K10	60
Abiyata, Lake, l., Eth.	N10	60
Ablis, Fr.	D8	14
Abnūb, Egypt	D6	60
Abohar, India	E6	44
Abomey, Benin	H10	64
Abongabong, Gunung, mtn., Indon.	L4	40
Abong Mbang, Cam.	H9	54
Abonnema, Nig.	I13	64
Abony, Hung.	H20	10
Aborigen, pik, mtn., U.S.S.R.	E21	24
Abou-Deïa, Chad	F4	56
Abraham Lake, res., Alta., Can.	C2	98
Abraham Lincoln Birthplace National Historic Site, hist., Ky., U.S.	C4	124
Abraka, Nig.	I13	64
Abrams, Wi., U.S.	D5	156
Abrantes, Port.	F3	16
Abra Pampa, Arg.	B6	80
Abre Campo, Braz.	F7	79
Ábrego, Col.	C6	84
Abreojos, Punta, c., Mex.	D3	90
'Abrī, Sud.	L6	60
Abruzzi, prov., Italy	G8	18
'Abs, Yemen	G3	47
Absaroka Range, mts., U.S.	F7	157
Absarokee, Mt., U.S.	E7	133
Absecon, N.J., U.S.	E4	137
Absecon Inlet, b., N.J., U.S.	E4	137
Abū 'Alī, i., Sau. Ar.	H10	48
Abū al-Khaṣīb, Iraq	F9	48
Abū 'Arīsh, Sau. Ar.	F3	47
Abū Dawm, Sud.	I7	60
Abu Dhabi see Abū Ẓaby, U.A.E.	B9	47
Abufari, Braz.	A10	82
Abū Gelba, Sud.	K6	60
Abū Ḥamad, Sud.	H7	60
Abuja, Nig.	G13	64
Abū Jubayhah, Sud.	L6	60
Abū Kamāl, Syria	D6	48
Abū Madd, Ra's, c., Sau. Ar.	I4	48
Abu Mendi, Eth.	L8	60
Abū Mūsā, i., Asia	I13	48
Abunã, Braz.	C9	82
Abunã (Abunā), stm., S.A.	C8	82
Abū Na'āmah, Sud.	K8	60
Abū Qashsh, Isr. Occ.	E4	50
Abū Qurqāṣ, Egypt	D6	60
Ābu Road, India	H5	44
Abū Rubayq, Sau. Ar.	C1	47
Abū Shajarah, Ra's, c., Sud.	G9	60
Abū Shanab, Sud.	K4	60
Abū Tīj, Egypt	D6	60
Abū Tunaytin, Sud.	J6	60
Abū Zabad, Sud.	K5	60
Abū Ẓaby, U.A.E.	B9	47
Abū Zanīmah, Egypt	C7	60
Abyad, Sud.	K4	60
Abyār 'Alī, Sau. Ar.	B1	47
Acacías, Col.	F6	84
Academia, Oh., U.S.	B3	142
Acadia, co., La., U.S.	D3	125
Acadia National Park, Me., U.S.	D4	126
Acadia Valley, Alta., Can.	D5	98
Acahay, Para.	C10	80
Acajutla, El Sal.	D5	92
Acámbaro, Mex.	G9	90
Acandí, Col.	C4	84
Acaponeta, Mex.	F7	90
Acaponeta, stm., Mex.	F7	90
Acapulco [de Juárez], Mex.	I10	90
Acará, Cachoeira, wtfl, Braz.	A12	82
Acará, Lago, l., Braz.	I11	84
Acarai Mountains, mts., S.A.	G14	84
Acaraú, Braz.	D10	76
Acaray, stm., Para.	C11	80
Acari, Peru	F4	82
Acari, stm., Braz.	C6	79
Acari, stm., Braz.	A12	82
Acarí, stm., Peru	F4	82
Acarigua, Ven.	C8	84
Acatlán de Juárez, Mex.	G8	90
Acatlán de Osorio, Mex.	H10	90
Acay, Nevado de, mtn., Arg.	C5	80
Acayucan, Mex.	I12	90
Accokeek, Md., U.S.	C3	127
Accomac, Va., U.S.	C7	153
Accomack, co., Va., U.S.	C7	153
Accord Pond, l., Ma., U.S.	h12	128
Accoville, W.V., U.S.	D3	155
Accra, Ghana	I9	64
Acebal, Arg.	G8	80
Acebuches, Mex.	C8	90
Aceguá, Braz.	F11	80
Acequia, Id., U.S.	G5	119
Acerra, Italy	I9	18
Acevedo, Arg.	G8	80
Achacachi, Bol.	G7	82
Achaguas, Ven.	D8	84
Achalpur, India	J7	44
Achar, Ur.	G10	80
Acheng, China	B12	30
Achern, Ger.	G8	10
Achí, Col.	C5	84
Achiguate, stm., Guat.	C4	92
Achille, Ok., U.S.	D5	143
Achill Island, i., Ire.	H3	8
Achiras, Arg.	G6	80
Achsu, U.S.S.R.	A10	48
Achtuba, stm., U.S.S.R.	H7	22
Achtubinsk, U.S.S.R.	H7	22
Achtyrka, U.S.S.R.	G4	22
Achuapa, Nic.	D8	92
Ačinsk, U.S.S.R.	F10	24
Acıpayam, Tur.	L13	20
Acireale, Italy	L10	18
Ačisaj, U.S.S.R.	I11	22
Ackerman, Ms., U.S.	B4	131
Ackley, Ia., U.S.	B4	122
Acklins, i., Bah.	C8	94
Acklins, Bight of, Bah.	C7	94
Acmar, Al., U.S.	B3	108
Acme, Alta., Can.	D4	98
Acme, Mi., U.S.	D5	129
Acme, Wa., U.S.	A3	154
Acme, Wy., U.S.	B6	157
Acobamba, Peru	E4	82
Acolla, Peru	D4	82
Acoma Indian Reservation, N.M., U.S.	C2	138
Acomayo, Peru	E6	82
Acomayo, Peru	C3	82
Acomita, N.M., U.S.	B2	138
Aconcagua, Cerro, mtn., Arg.	G3	80
Aconchi, Mex.	C4	90
Açores (Azores), is., Port.	k19	62a
Acoria, Peru	E4	82
Acorizal, Braz.	F13	82
Acornhoek, S. Afr.	E10	66
Acoyapa, Nic.	F9	92
Acoyapa, stm., Nic.	F9	92
Acquapendente, Italy	G6	18
Acqui Terme, Italy	E3	18
Acre, state, Braz.	C6	82
Acre, stm., S.A.	C8	82
Acre see 'Akko, Isr.	C4	50
Acree, Ga., U.S.	E2	117
Acri, Italy	J11	18
Acrotambo, Cerro, mtn., Peru	C3	82
Actinolite, Ont., Can.	C7	103
Acton, Ca., U.S.	E4	112
Acton, Ma., U.S.	B5	128
Acton, Mt., U.S.	E8	133
Acton Vale, Que., Can.	D5	104
Actopan, Mex.	G10	90
Açuã, stm., Braz.	B10	82
Açucena, Braz.	E7	79
Acuña, Arg.	E10	80
Acuracay, Peru	A4	82
Acurauá, stm., Braz.	B6	82
Acushnet, Ma., U.S.	C6	128
Acworth, Ga., U.S.	B2	117
Acworth, N.H., U.S.	D2	136
Ada, Ks., U.S.	C6	123
Ada, La., U.S.	B2	125
Ada, Mn., U.S.	C2	130
Ada, Oh., U.S.	B2	142
Ada, Ok., U.S.	C5	143
Ada, Yugo.	D4	20
Ada, co., Id., U.S.	F2	119
Ada, Mount, mtn., Ak., U.S.	m22	109
Adaba, Eth.	N10	60
Adailo, Eth.	G2	47
Adair, Il., U.S.	C3	120
Adair, Ia., U.S.	C3	122
Adair, Ok., U.S.	A6	143
Adair, co., Ia., U.S.	C3	122
Adair, co., Ky., U.S.	C4	124
Adair, co., Mo., U.S.	A5	132
Adair, co., Ok., U.S.	B7	143
Adair, Bahía, b., Mex.	B3	90
Adairsville, Ga., U.S.	B2	117
Adairville, Ky., U.S.	D3	124
Adak Island, i., Ak., U.S.	E4	109
Adak Naval Station, mil., Ak., U.S.	E4	109
Adala, Tur.	K12	20
Ādam, Oman	C10	47
Adamantina, Braz.	F3	79
Adamaoua, mts., Afr.	G9	54
Adamclisi, Rom.	E11	20
Adam Island, i., Md., U.S.	D5	127
Adami Tulu, Eth.	N10	60
Adamów, Pol.	D22	10
Adams, In., U.S.	F6	121
Adams, Ma., U.S.	A1	128
Adams, Mn., U.S.	G6	130
Adams, Ne., U.S.	D9	134
Adams, N.Y., U.S.	B4	139
Adams, N.D., U.S.	A7	141
Adams, Ok., U.S.	e9	143
Adams, Tn., U.S.	A4	149
Adams, Wi., U.S.	E4	156
Adams, co., Co., U.S.	B6	113
Adams, co., Id., U.S.	E2	119
Adams, co., Il., U.S.	D2	120
Adams, co., In., U.S.	C8	121
Adams, co., Ia., U.S.	C3	122
Adams, co., Ms., U.S.	D2	131
Adams, co., Ne., U.S.	D7	134
Adams, co., N.D., U.S.	C3	141
Adams, co., Oh., U.S.	D2	142
Adams, co., Pa., U.S.	G7	145
Adams, co., Wa., U.S.	B7	154
Adams, co., Wi., U.S.	D4	156
Adams, Mount, mtn., N.H., U.S.	B4	136
Adams, Mount, mtn., Wa., U.S.	C4	154
Adams Bridge, rf., Asia	H5	46
Adams Center, N.Y., U.S.	B5	139
Adams Mountain, mtn., Ma., U.S.	A2	128
Adams Mountain, mtn., Vt., U.S.	C3	152
Adams Peak, mtn., Sri L.	I6	46
Adams Point, c., Mi., U.S.	C7	129
Adams Run, S.C., U.S.	k11	147
Adamstown, Pa., U.S.	F9	145
Adamsville, Al., U.S.	f7	108
Adamsville, R.I., U.S.	E6	146
Adamsville, Tn., U.S.	B3	149
Adamsville Brook, stm., R.I., U.S.	E6	146
'Adan (Aden), Yemen	H4	47
Adana, Tur.	C3	48
Adanero, Spain	E7	16
Adapazarı, Tur.	G14	4
Adarama, Sud.	I8	60
Adare, Cape, c., Ant.	C8	73
Adarot, Sud.	I9	60
Adavale, Austl.	E6	70
Adda, stm., Italy	D4	18
Ad-Dab'ah, Egypt	B5	60
Ad-Dabbah, Sud.	H6	60
Ad-Dafīnah, Sau. Ar.	C2	47
Ad-Dahnā', des., Sau. Ar.	C6	47
Ad-Damazin, Sud.	L8	60
Ad-Dāmir, Sud.	I7	60
Ad-Dammām, Sau. Ar.	A7	47
Ad-Dāmūr, Leb.	A4	50
Ad-Darb, Sau. Ar.	F3	47
Ad-Dawādimī, Sau. Ar.	B4	47
Ad-Dawhah (Doha), Qatar	I11	48
Ad-Dayr, Egypt	E7	60
Addieville, Il., U.S.	E4	120
Ad-Diffah (Libyan Plateau), plat., Afr.	B3	60
Ad-Dilam, Sau. Ar.	C5	47
Addis, La., U.S.	D4	125
Addis Ababa see Adis Abeba, Eth.	G8	56
Addison, Al., U.S.	A2	108
Addison, Ct., U.S.	C5	114
Addison, Il., U.S.	k8	120
Addison, Me., U.S.	D5	126
Addison, N.Y., U.S.	C3	139
Addison, co., Vt., U.S.	C2	152
Ad-Dīwānīyah, Iraq	F8	48
Ad-Du'ayn, Sud.	L4	60
Ad-Duhayr, Egypt	F2	50
Ad-Duwayd, Sau. Ar.	F7	48
Ad-Duwaym, Sud.	J7	60
Addy, Wa., U.S.	A8	154
Addyston, Oh., U.S.	o12	142
Adel, Ga., U.S.	E3	117
Adel, Ia., U.S.	C3	122
Adelaide, Austl.	J3	70
Adelaide, Bah.	B6	94
Adelaide, S. Afr.	I8	66
Adelaide Island, i., Ant.	B12	73
Adelaide Peninsula, pen., N.W. Ter., Can.	C13	96
Adelanto, Ca., U.S.	E5	112
Adèle Island, i., Austl.	C4	68
Adélie Coast, Ant.	B7	73
Adell, Wi., U.S.	E6	156
Aden, Gulf of, b.	F10	56
Adena, Oh., U.S.	B5	142
Aden see 'Adan, Yemen	H4	47
Adéta, Togo	H10	64
Adger, Al., U.S.	B2	108
'Ādhirīyāt, Jibāl al-, hills, Jord.	H7	50
Adi Arkay, Eth.	K9	60
Adi Dairo, Eth.	J10	60
Adieu, Cape, c., Austl.	F6	68
Adige, stm., Italy	D7	18
Adigrat, Eth.	J10	60
Adi Keyih, Eth.	J10	60
Adi Kwala, Eth.	J10	60
Ādilābād, India	C5	46
Adin, Ca., U.S.	B3	112
Adirondack Mountains, mts., N.Y., U.S.	A6	139
Adis Abeba (Addis Ababa), Eth.	M10	60
Adis Zemen, Eth.	K9	60
Adi Ugri, Eth.	J10	60
Adıyaman, Tur.	C5	48
Adjohon, Benin	H11	64
Adjud, Rom.	C11	20
Adjuntas, Presa de las, res., Mex.	F10	90
Adliswil, Switz.	D10	13
Admer, Erg d', des., Alg.	H15	62
Admirals Beach, Newf., Can.	E5	102
Admiralty Bay, b., Ak., U.S.	A9	109
Admiralty Gulf, b., Austl.	B5	68
Admiralty Inlet, b., N.W. Ter., Can.	B15	96
Admiralty Island, i., Ak., U.S.	m22	109
Admiralty Islands, is., Pap. N. Gui.	k16	68a
Admiralty Mountains, mts., Ant.	C8	73
Admire, Ks., U.S.	D7	123
Adobe Acres, N.M., U.S.	B3	138
Adobe Creek, stm., Co., U.S.	C7	113
Adobe Creek Reservoir, res., Co., U.S.	C7	113
Ado-Ekiti, Nig.	H12	64
Adok, Sud.	M6	60
Adolfo López Mateos, Mex.	C6	90
Adolfo López Mateos, Presa, res., Mex.	E6	90
Adolphus, Ky., U.S.	D3	124
Adona, Ar., U.S.	B3	111
Ādoni, India	E4	46
Ado-Odo, Nig.	H11	64
Adour, stm., Fr.	I5	14
Adra, Spain	I8	16
Adra, Spain	B9	62
'Adrā, Syria	A7	50
Adrano, Italy	L9	18
Adrar, Alg.	C6	54
Adrâr, reg., Maur.	J4	62
Adria, Italy	D7	18
Adrian, Ga., U.S.	D4	117
Adrian, Mi., U.S.	G6	129
Adrian, Mn., U.S.	G3	130
Adrian, Mo., U.S.	C3	132
Adrian, W.V., U.S.	C4	155
Adrianople see Edirne, Tur.	H10	20
Adriatic Sea, Eur.	G11	4
Advance, In., U.S.	D4	121
Advance, Mo., U.S.	D8	132
Advocate Harbour, N.S., Can.	D5	101
Adwa, Eth.	J10	60
Adyča, stm., U.S.S.R.	D19	24
Aegean Sea	J8	20
Aetna, Alta., Can.	E4	98
Aetna, Tn., U.S.	B4	149
Afándou, Grc.	M12	20
Afar, Alg.	H15	62
Afars and Issas see Djibouti, ctry., Afr.	F9	56
Afghanistan (Afghānestān), ctry., Asia	C8	42
Afgooye, Som.	H10	56
'Afīf, Sau. Ar.	C3	47
Afikpo, Nig.	I13	64
Aflou, Alg.	C12	62
Afodo, Eth.	L8	60
Afognak Island, i., Ak., U.S.	D9	109
Afonso Cláudio, Braz.	F8	79
Africa	G9	52
Afsluitdijk, Neth.	B7	12
Afton, Ia., U.S.	C3	122
Afton, Mn., U.S.	F6	130
Afton, N.Y., U.S.	C5	139
Afton, Ok., U.S.	A7	143
Afton, Wy., U.S.	D2	157
'Afula, Isr.	C4	50
Afyon, Tur.	H14	4
Agadez, Niger	C13	64
Agadir, Mor.	E6	62
Agadyr', U.S.S.R.	H12	22
Agaie, Nig.	G13	64
Agalak, Sud.	L7	60
Agalega Islands, is., Mrts.	D11	58
Agan, stm., U.S.S.R.	E7	24
Agar, S.D., U.S.	C5	148
Agaro, Eth.	N9	60
Agartala, India	I14	44
Agaru, Sud.	L8	60
Agassiz, Cape, c., Ant.	B12	73
Agate Fossil Beds National Monument, Ne., U.S.	B2	134
Agattu Island, i., Ak., U.S.	E2	109
Agawam, Ma., U.S.	B2	128
Agbaja, Nig.	H13	64
Agboville, I.C.	I7	64
Agdam, U.S.S.R.	B9	48
Agejevo, U.S.S.R.	G19	26
Agen, Fr.	H7	14
Agency, Ia., U.S.	D5	122
Agency, Mo., U.S.	B3	132
Āghā Jārī, Iran	F10	48
Aginskoje, U.S.S.R.	G14	24
Agogo, Sud.	N5	60
Agouna, Benin	H10	64
Agoura Hills, Ca., U.S.	m11	112
Āgra, India	G8	44
Agra, Ks., U.S.	C4	123
Agra, Ok., U.S.	B5	143
Agraciada, Ur.	G9	80
Agrado, Col.	F5	84
Agram see Zagreb, Yugo.	D10	18
Agreda, Spain	D10	16
Ağrı, Tur.	B7	48
Agricola, Ms., U.S.	E5	131
Ağrı Dağı (Mount Ararat), mtn., Tur.	B8	48
Agrigento, Italy	L8	18
Agrinion, Grc.	K5	20
Agrio, stm., Arg.	J3	80
Agryz, U.S.S.R.	F8	22
Agua, Volcán de, vol., Guat.	C4	92
Água Boa, Braz.	D7	79
Agua Caliente, Mex.	F7	90
Agua Caliente, Mex.	D5	90
Agua Caliente Grande, Mex.	D5	90
Aguachica, Col.	C6	84
Água Clara, Braz.	F2	79
Água Comprida, Braz.	F4	79
Aguada de Pasajeros, Cuba	C4	94
Aguadas, Col.	E5	84
Agua de Dios, Col.	E5	84
Aguadilla, P.R.	E11	94
Água Doce, Braz.	D13	80
Aguadulce, Pan.	C2	84
Agua Dulce Mountains, mts., Az., U.S.	E2	110
Agua Fria, N.M., U.S.	B3	138
Agua Fria, stm., Az., U.S.	D3	110
Aguaí, Braz.	G5	79
Agualeguas, Mex.	D10	90
Água Limpa, Braz.	E4	79
Aguán, stm., Hond.	B8	92
Aguanaval, stm., Mex.	E8	90
Aguapeí, stm., Braz.	F12	82
Aguapey, stm., Arg.	E10	80
Água Preta, Igarapé, stm., Braz.	H10	84
Agua Prieta, Mex.	B5	90
Aguaragüe, Serranía de, mts., Bol.	I10	82
Aguaray, Arg.	B7	80
Aguaray-Guazú, stm., Para.	B10	80
Aguaray-Guazú, stm., Para.	C9	80
Aguarico, stm., S.A.	H4	84
Aguaruto, Mex.	E6	90
Aguascalientes, Mex.	G8	90
Águas Formosas, Braz.	D8	79
Água Verde, stm., Braz.	E13	82
Aguayo, Arg.	F6	80
Aguaytía, stm., Peru	C4	82
Agudo, Braz.	E12	80
Agudos, Braz.	G4	79
Águeda, stm., Eur.	E5	16
Aguelhok, Mali	B10	64
Aguié, Niger	E13	64
Aguila, Az., U.S.	D2	110
Aguilar, Spain	H7	16
Aguilar, Co., U.S.	D6	113
Aguilares, Arg.	D6	80
Aguilares, El Sal.	D5	92
Águilas, Spain	H10	16
Aguililla, Mex.	H8	90
Aguirre, stm., Ven.	C12	84
Aguja, Punta, c., Peru	A1	82
Agulhas, Cape, c., S. Afr.	J5	66
Agulhas Negras, Pico das, mtn., Braz.	G6	79
Agustín Codazzi, Col.	B6	84
Ahaggar (Hoggar), mts., Alg.	I13	62
Ahaggar, Tassili ta-n-, plat., Alg.	A12	64
Aha Hills, hills, Afr.	B5	66
Ahar, Iran	B9	48
Ahaus, Ger.	C7	10
Ahfir, Mor.	C9	62
Ahklun Mountains, mts., Ak., U.S.	D7	109
Ahlat, Tur.	B7	48
Ahlen, Ger.	D7	10
Ahmadābād, India	I5	44
Ahmadnagar, India	C3	46
Ahmadpur East, Pak.	F4	44
Ahmad Wāl, Pak.	F1	44
Ahmar Mountains, mts., Eth.	G9	56
Ahnet, Tanezrouft n-, des., Alg.	I11	62
Ahome, Mex.	E5	90
Ahoskie, N.C., U.S.	A6	140
Ahrensburg, Ger.	B10	10
Ahsahka, Id., U.S.	C2	119
Ahtanum Creek, stm., Wa., U.S.	C5	154
Ahu, China	I6	32
Ahuacatlán, Mex.	G7	90
Ahuachapán, El Sal.	D5	92
Ahumada, Mex.	B6	90
Ahuzhen, China	I6	32
Ahvāz, Iran	F10	48
Ahvenanmaa, prov., Fin.	K16	6
Ahwahnee, Ca., U.S.	D4	112
Ahwar, Yemen	H5	47
Aialik, Cape, c., Ak., U.S.	D10	109
Aiapuá, Braz.	J11	84
Aiapuá, Lago, l., Braz.	J11	84
Aiea, Hi., U.S.	B4	118
Aigen im Mühlkreis, Aus.	G13	10
Aigle, Switz.	F6	13
Aiguá, Ur.	H11	80
Aigueperse, Fr.	F10	14
Aigüestortes, Parc National d', Spain	C13	16
Aiguilles, Fr.	H13	14
Aihui, China	A12	30
Aija, Peru	C3	82
Aiken, S.C., U.S.	D4	147
Aiken, co., S.C., U.S.	D4	147
Ailao Shan, mts., China	B6	40
Ailey, Ga., U.S.	D4	117
Ailigandí, Pan.	C3	84
Ailsa Craig, Ont., Can.	D3	103
Aimogasta, Arg.	E5	80
Aimorés, Braz.	E8	79
Ain, dept., Fr.	F12	14
Ainaži, U.S.S.R.	D7	26
Aïn Benian, Alg.	B12	62
Aïn Ben Tili, Maur.	G6	62
Aïn Berda, Alg.	M2	18
Aïn Deheb, Alg.	C11	62
Aïn Draham, Tun.	M3	18
Aïn el Beïda, Alg.	C14	62
Aïn Milia, Alg.	B14	62
Aïn Sefra, Alg.	D10	62
Ainslie Lake, l., N.S., Can.	C8	101
Ainsworth, Ia., U.S.	C6	122
Ainsworth, Ne., U.S.	B6	134
Aïn Tedelès, Alg.	B11	62
Aïn Témouchent, Alg.	C10	62
Aïn Touta, Alg.	C13	62
Aïn Wessara, Alg.	C12	62
Aïn Yagout, Alg.	C14	62
Aiora, Spain	F10	16
Aipe, Col.	F5	84
Aiquara, Braz.	C9	79
Aiquile, Bol.	H9	82
Aïr, mts., Niger	C14	64
Airão, Braz.	H12	84
Airdrie, Alta., Can.	D3	98
Aire, Fr.	I6	14
Air Force Island, i., N.W. Ter., Can.	C18	96
Airline, Ga., U.S.	B3	117
Airolo, Switz.	E10	13
Air Park West, Ne., U.S.	D9	134
Airvault, Fr.	F6	14
Aishihik Lake, l., Yukon, Can.	D5	96
Aisne, dept., Fr.	C10	14
Aisne, stm., Fr.	C10	14
Aïssa, Djebel, mtn., Alg.	D10	62
Aitape, Pap. N. Gui.	F11	38
Aitkin, Mn., U.S.	D5	130
Aitkin, co., Mn., U.S.	D5	130
Aït-Melloul, Mor.	E6	62
Aitolikón, Grc.	K5	20
Ait Youssef ou Ali, Mor.	J8	16
Aiud, Rom.	C7	20
Aiuruoca, Braz.	F6	79
Aix, Mount, mtn., Wa., U.S.	C4	154
Aix-en-Provence, Fr.	I12	14
Aix-la-Chapelle see Aachen, Ger.	E6	10
Aix-les-Bains, Fr.	G12	14
Aíyion, Grc.	K6	20
Āīzawl, India	I15	44
Aizpute, U.S.S.R.	E4	26
Aizu-wakamatsu, Japan	J14	36
Ajaccio, Fr.	M23	15a
Ajaguz, U.S.S.R.	H8	24
Ajajú, stm., Col.	G6	84
Ajan, stm., U.S.S.R.	C10	24
Ajanta, India	B3	46
Ajarani, stm., Braz.	F12	84
Ajasso, Nig.	I14	64
Ajax, Ont., Can.	D6	103
Ajdābiyā, Libya	B5	56
Ajibar, Eth.	L10	60
Ajjer, Tassili-n-, plat., Alg.	H14	62
Ajka, Hung.	H17	10
'Ajlūn, Jord.	D5	50
Ajmer, India	G6	44
Ajo, Az., U.S.	E3	110
Ajok, Sud.	M5	60
Ajon, ostrov, i., U.S.S.R.	D25	24
Ajoya, Mex.	E6	90
Ajtos, Bul.	G11	20
Ajuterique, Hond.	C7	92
Akabli, Alg.	G11	62
Akademii, zaliv, b., U.S.S.R.	G19	24
Akaki Beseka, Eth.	M10	60
Akan, Japan	D19	36a
'Akasha East, Sud.	G6	60
Akashi, Japan	M9	36
Akbou, Alg.	B13	62
Akçadağ, Tur.	B4	48
Akçaova, Tur.	L12	20
Ak-Chin Indian Reservation, Az., U.S.	E3	110
Akdağmadeni, Tur.	B3	48
Akeley, Mn., U.S.	C4	130
Aken, Ger.	D12	10
Akershus, co., Nor.	K12	6
Aketi, Zaire	H5	56
Akharnaí, Grc.	K7	20
Akhdar, Al-Jabal al-, mts., Oman	C10	47
Akhisar, Tur.	K11	20
Akhmīm, Egypt	D6	60
Akiachak, Ak., U.S.	C7	109
Akiak, Ak., U.S.	C7	109
Akimiski Island, i., N.W. Ter., Can.	F16	96
Akita, Japan	H15	36
Akjoujt, Maur.	B2	64
Akkeshi, Japan	D19	36a
'Akko (Acre), Isr.	C4	50
Akkol', U.S.S.R.	I12	22
Aklavik, N.W. Ter., Can.	C5	96
'Aklé 'Aouâna, reg., Afr.	B7	64
Akmeqit, China	E8	26
Akniste, U.S.S.R.	E8	26
Aknoul, Mor.	C9	62
Akobo, Sud.	N7	60
Akobo (Akūbū), stm., Afr.	N8	60
Akola, India	B4	46
Akop, Sud.	M5	60
Akordat, Eth.	E8	56

Name	Map Ref.	Page
Akot, India	B4	46
Akpatok Island, i., N.W. Ter., Can.	D19	96
Akranes, Ice.	B2	6a
Akrítas, Ákra, c., Grc.	M5	20
Akron, Al., U.S.	C2	108
Akron, Co., U.S.	A7	113
Akron, In., U.S.	B5	121
Akron, Ia., U.S.	B1	122
Akron, Mi., U.S.	E7	129
Akron, N.Y., U.S.	B2	139
Akron, Oh., U.S.	A4	142
Akron, Pa., U.S.	F9	145
Aksaray, Tur.	B3	48
Aksarka, U.S.S.R.	D5	24
Akşehir, Tur.	H14	4
Aksu, China	C3	30
Aksuat, U.S.S.R.	H8	24
Aksum, Eth.	J10	60
Aktogaj, U.S.S.R.	H7	24
Akt'ubinsk, U.S.S.R.	G9	22
Akūbū (Akobo), stm., Afr.	G7	56
Akulivik, Que., Can.	f11	104
Akune, Japan	O5	36
Akureyri, Ice.	B4	6a
Akutan, Ak., U.S.	E6	109
Akwanga, Nig.	G14	64
Akwaya, Cam.	H14	64
Akyel, Eth.	K9	60
Akžar, U.S.S.R.	H8	24
Ala, stm., China	C4	30
Alabama, state, U.S.	C3	108
Alabama, stm., Al., U.S.	D2	108
Alabama Port, Al., U.S.	E1	108
Alabaster, Al., U.S.	B3	108
Al-ʻAbbāsīyah, Sud.	K6	60
Āl-ʻĀbis, Sau. Ar.	E3	47
Alacant, Spain	G11	16
Alachua, Fl., U.S.	C4	116
Alachua, co., Fl., U.S.	C4	116
Alacrán, Arrecife, rf., Mex.	F15	90
Alacranes, Presa, res., Cuba	C4	94
Alagir, U.S.S.R.	I6	22
Alagoa, Braz.	G6	79
Alagoa Grande, Braz.	E11	76
Alagoinhas, Braz.	B9	79
Alagón, Spain	D10	16
Al-Aḥmadī, Kuw.	G10	48
Alaior, Spain	F16	16
Al-Ait, Sud.	K4	60
Alajskij chrebet, mts., U.S.S.R.	J12	22
Alajuela, C.R.	G10	92
Alajuela, prov., C.R.	G10	92
Alajuela, Lago, res., Pan.	H15	92
Alakamisy, Madag.	R22	67b
Alakanuk, Ak., U.S.	C7	109
Alakol', ozero, l., U.S.S.R.	H8	24
Alalakeiki Channel, strt., Hi., U.S.	C5	118
Al-ʻAlamayn, Egypt	B5	60
Alalaú, stm., Braz.	H12	84
Al-ʻAmādīyah, Iraq	C7	48
Alamance, co., N.C., U.S.	B3	140
Al-ʻAmārah, Iraq	F9	48
Alameda, Sask., Can.	H4	105
Alameda, Ca., U.S.	h8	112
Alameda, N.M., U.S.	B3	138
Alameda, co., Ca., U.S.	D3	112
Alameda Naval Air Station, mil., Ca., U.S.	h8	112
Alamein see Al-ʻAlamayn, Egypt	B5	60
Alamito Creek, stm., Tx., U.S.	p12	150
Alamo, Ga., U.S.	D4	117
Alamo, Nv., U.S.	F6	135
Alamo, Tn., U.S.	B2	149
Alamo, Tx., U.S.	F3	150
Alamogordo, N.M., U.S.	E4	138
Alamo Heights, Tx., U.S.	E3	150
Alamo Hueco Mountains, mts., N.M., U.S.	F1	138
Alamo Indian Reservation, N.M., U.S.	C2	138
Alamo Lake, res., Az., U.S.	C2	110
Alamor, Ec.	J2	84
Álamos, Mex.	D5	90
Álamos, stm., Mex.	C9	90
Alamosa, Co., U.S.	D5	113
Alamosa, co., Co., U.S.	D5	113
Alamosa, stm., Co., U.S.	D4	113
Alamosa Creek, stm., N.M., U.S.	D2	138
Alamosa East, Co., U.S.	D5	113
Álamos de Márquez, Mex.	C8	90
Åland (Ahvenanmaa), is., Fin.	K16	6
Aland Islands see Åland, is., Fin.	K16	6
Alanje, Pan.	I12	92
Alanson, Mi., U.S.	C6	129
Alanya, Tur.	H14	4
Alaotra, Lac, l., Madag.	P23	67b
Alapaha, Ga., U.S.	E3	117
Alapaha, stm., U.S.	E3	117
Alapajevsk, U.S.S.R.	F10	22
Al-ʻAqabah, Jord.	I4	50
Alarcón, Embalse de, res., Spain	F9	16
Al-ʻArīsh, Egypt	B7	60
Alarobia Vohiposa, Madag.	R22	67b
Alaşehir, Tur.	K12	20
Alashanyouqi, China	C7	30
Alaska, state, U.S.	C9	109
Alaska, Gulf of, b., Ak., U.S.	D10	109
Alaska Peninsula, pen., Ak., U.S.	D8	109
Alaska Range, mts., Ak., U.S.	C9	109
Alassio, Italy	E3	18
Alat, U.S.S.R.	B17	48
Al'at, U.S.S.R.	B10	48
Al-ʻAthāmīn, mts., Asia	F7	48
Alatna, stm., Ak., U.S.	B9	109
Al-ʻAṭrūn, Sud.	H4	60
Alatyr', U.S.S.R.	G7	22
Alausí, Ec.	I3	84
Alava, Cape, c., Wa., U.S.	A1	154
Alawa, Nig.	F13	64
Al-ʻAyn, U.A.E.	I13	48
Al-ʻAyyāṭ, Egypt	C6	60
Alazeja, stm., U.S.S.R.	C22	24
Al-ʻAzīzīyah, Libya	B3	56
Alba, Italy	E3	18
Alba, Mo., U.S.	D3	132
Alba, co., Rom.	C7	20
Albacete, Spain	G10	16
Al-Badārī, Egypt	D6	60
Alba Iulia, Rom.	C7	20
Al-Ballāṣ, Egypt	D7	60
Al-Balyanā, Egypt	D6	60
Alban, Fr.	I9	14
Albania (Shqipëri), ctry., Eur.	G12	4
Albano Laziale, Italy	H7	18
Albany, Austl.	G3	68
Albany, P.E.I., Can.	C6	101
Albany, Ga., U.S.	E2	117
Albany, Il., U.S.	B3	120
Albany, In., U.S.	D7	121
Albany, Ky., U.S.	D4	124
Albany, La., U.S.	g10	125
Albany, Mn., U.S.	E4	130
Albany, Mo., U.S.	A3	132
Albany, N.Y., U.S.	C7	139
Albany, Oh., U.S.	C3	142
Albany, Or., U.S.	C3	144
Albany, Tx., U.S.	C3	150
Albany, Vt., U.S.	B4	152
Albany, Wi., U.S.	F4	156
Albany, Wy., U.S.	E6	157
Albany, co., N.Y., U.S.	C6	139
Albany, co., Wy., U.S.	E7	157
Albany, stm., Ont., Can.	o18	103
Al-Baqʻah, Jord.	D5	50
Albardón, Arg.	F4	80
Al-Barrah, Sau. Ar.	B4	47
Al-Barun, Sud.	L7	60
Al-Baṣrah (Basra), Iraq	F9	48
Al-Batrūn, Leb.	D3	48
Al-Bauga, Sud.	H7	60
Al-Bawīṭī, Egypt	C5	60
Al-Bayḍā', Libya	B5	56
Al-Bayḍā', Yemen	G4	47
Albemarle, N.C., U.S.	B2	140
Albemarle, co., Va., U.S.	C4	153
Albemarle Lake, l., Ms., U.S.	C2	131
Albemarle Sound, strt., N.C., U.S.	A6	140
Albenga, Italy	E3	18
Alberdi, Para.	D9	80
Alberga Creek, stm., Austl.	E6	68
Albert, Fr.	B9	14
Albert, Ks., U.S.	D4	123
Albert, Lake, l., Afr.	A6	58
Alberta, Al., U.S.	C2	108
Alberta, Va., U.S.	D5	153
Alberta, prov., Can.	C4	98
Alberta, Mount, mtn., Alta., Can.	C2	98
Albert City, Ia., U.S.	B3	122
Albert Edward Bay, b., N.W. Ter., Can.	C12	96
Alberti, Arg.	H8	80
Al'bertin, U.S.S.R.	H8	26
Albertinia, S. Afr.	J5	66
Albertkanaal (Canal Albert), Bel.	G8	12
Albert Lea, Mn., U.S.	G5	130
Albert Markham, Mount, mtn., Ant.	D8	73
Albert Nile, stm., Ug.	H7	56
Alberton, P.E.I., Can.	C5	101
Alberton, Mt., U.S.	C2	133
Albertson, N.Y., U.S.	k13	139
Albertville, Sask., Can.	D3	105
Albertville, Fr.	G13	14
Albertville, Al., U.S.	A3	108
Albertville, Mn., U.S.	E5	130
Albi, Fr.	I9	14
Albia, Ia., U.S.	C5	122
Albin, Wy., U.S.	E8	157
Albina, Sur.	B8	76
Albino, Italy	D4	18
Albion, Ca., U.S.	C2	112
Albion, Id., U.S.	G5	119
Albion, Il., U.S.	E5	120
Albion, In., U.S.	B7	121
Albion, Ia., U.S.	B5	122
Albion, Me., U.S.	D3	126
Albion, Mi., U.S.	F6	129
Albion, Ne., U.S.	C7	134
Albion, N.Y., U.S.	B2	139
Albion, Pa., U.S.	C1	145
Albion, R.I., U.S.	B4	146
Albion, Wa., U.S.	C8	154
Al-Biqāʻ (Bekaa Valley), val., Leb.	A6	50
Al-Birk, Sau. Ar.	E2	47
Alborán, Isla de, i., Spain	J8	16
Alborán Sea	I8	16
Ålborg, Den.	M11	6
Alborn, Mn., U.S.	D6	130
Alborz, Reshteh-ye Kūhhā-ye (Elburz Mountains), mts., Iran	C12	48
Albrightsville, Pa., U.S.	D10	145
Ālbū Gharz, Sabkhat, l., Asia	D6	48
Albuñol, Spain	I8	16
Albuquerque, Braz.	H13	82
Albuquerque, N.M., U.S.	B3	138
Albuquerque, Cayos de, is., Col.	H4	94
Al-Buraymī, U.A.E.	B9	47
Alburg, Vt., U.S.	B2	152
Alburnett, Ia., U.S.	B6	122
Alburtis, Pa., U.S.	F10	145
Albury, Austl.	K7	70
Al-Buṭaynah, Syria	C7	50
Alca, Peru	F5	82
Alcalá de Guadaira, Spain	H6	16
Alcalá de Henares, Spain	E8	16
Alcalde, N.M., U.S.	A3	138
Alcamo, Italy	L7	18
Alcanar, Spain	E12	16
Alcañiz, Spain	D11	16
Alcântara, Braz.	D10	76
Alcántara, Spain	F5	16
Alcántara, Embalse de, res., Spain	F5	16
Alcantarilla, Spain	H10	16
Alcantilado, Braz.	D2	79
Alcaudete, Spain	H7	16
Alcázar de San Juan, Spain	F8	16
Alcester, S.D., U.S.	D9	148
Alcira (Gigena), Arg.	G6	80
Alcoa, Tn., U.S.	D10	149
Alcobaça, Braz.	D9	79
Alcobaça, Port.	F3	16
Alcoi, Spain	G11	16
Alcolu, S.C., U.S.	D7	147
Alcomdale, Alta., Can.	C4	98
Alcona, co., Mi., U.S.	D7	129
Alcorn, co., Ms., U.S.	A5	131
Alcorta, Arg.	G8	80
Alcoutim, Port.	H4	16
Alcova, Wy., U.S.	D6	157
Alcovy, stm., Ga., U.S.	C3	117
Alcoy, Nevado, mtn., Peru	D3	82
Alda, Ne., U.S.	D7	134
Aldabra Island, i., Sey.	C9	58
Aldama, Mex.	C7	90
Aldama, Mex.	F10	90
Aldan, U.S.S.R.	F17	24
Aldan, stm., U.S.S.R.	F18	24
Aldanskoje nagorje, plat., U.S.S.R.	F17	24
Aldeburgh, Eng., U.K.	I15	8
Alden, Il., U.S.	A5	120
Alden, Ia., U.S.	B4	122
Alden, Ks., U.S.	D5	123
Alden, Mi., U.S.	D5	129
Alden, Mn., U.S.	G5	130
Alden, N.Y., U.S.	C2	139
Alden, Pa., U.S.	D9	145
Alder, Mt., U.S.	E4	133
Alder Brook, stm., Vt., U.S.	B4	152
Alderney, i., Guernsey	L11	8
Aldershot, Eng., U.K.	J13	8
Alderson, Ok., U.S.	C6	143
Alderson, W.V., U.S.	D4	155
Aldersyde, Alta., Can.	D4	98
Aldora, Ga., U.S.	C2	117
Aldrich, Al., U.S.	B3	108
Aledo, Il., U.S.	B3	120
Alefa, Eth.	L9	60
Aleg, Maur.	C3	64
Alegre, Braz.	F8	79
Alegre, stm., Braz.	F12	82
Alegres Mountain, mtn., N.M., U.S.	C2	138
Alegrete, Braz.	E11	80
Alejandro Roca, Arg.	G7	80
Alejandro Selkirk, Isla, i., Chile	H6	74
Alejo Ledesma, Arg.	G7	80
Alejsk, U.S.S.R.	G8	24
Aleknagik, Ak., U.S.	D8	109
Aleksandrija, U.S.S.R.	H4	22
Aleksandro-Nevskij, U.S.S.R.	H23	26
Aleksandrov, U.S.S.R.	E21	26
Aleksandrov Gaj, U.S.S.R.	G7	22
Aleksandrovskoje, U.S.S.R.	E13	22
Aleksandrovsk-Sachalinskij, U.S.S.R.	G20	24
Aleksejevka, U.S.S.R.	G5	22
Aleksejevka, U.S.S.R.	G12	22
Aleksejevsk, U.S.S.R.	F13	24
Aleksin, U.S.S.R.	G20	26
Aleksinac, Yugo.	F5	20
Alemania, Arg.	C6	80
Alemania, Chile	C4	80
Além Paraíba, Braz.	F7	79
Alençon, Fr.	D7	14
Alenquer, Braz.	D8	76
Alentejo, hist. reg., Port.	G3	16
Alenuihaha Channel, strt., Hi., U.S.	C5	118
Aleppo see Ḥalab, Syria	C4	48
Aléria, Fr.	G4	18
Alert Bay, B.C., Can.	D4	99
Alès, Fr.	H11	14
Alessandria, Italy	E3	18
Ålesund, Nor.	J10	6
Aletschhorn, mtn., Switz.	F9	13
Aleutian Islands, is., Ak., U.S.	E3	109
Aleutian Range, mts., Ak., U.S.	D9	109
Aleutian Trench	D3	86
Alevina, mys, c., U.S.S.R.	F22	24
Alex, Ok., U.S.	C4	143
Alexander, Man., Can.	E1	100
Alexander, Ar., U.S.	C3	111
Alexander, Ga., U.S.	C5	117
Alexander, Il., U.S.	D3	120
Alexander, N.D., U.S.	B2	141
Alexander, co., Il., U.S.	F4	120
Alexander, co., N.C., U.S.	B1	140
Alexander, Lake, l., Mn., U.S.	D4	130
Alexander Archipelago, is., Ak., U.S.	D12	109
Alexander Bay, S. Afr.	G3	66
Alexander City, Al., U.S.	C4	108
Alexander Island, i., Ant.	C12	73
Alexander Mills, N.C., U.S.	B1	140
Alexandra, N.Z.	F2	72
Alexandra, stm., Austl.	B4	70
Alexandra Falls, wtfl, N.W. Ter., Can.	D9	96
Alexandretta, Gulf of see İskenderun Körfezi, b., Tur.	H15	4
Alexandretta see İskenderun, Tur.	C4	48
Alexandria, B.C., Can.	C6	99
Alexandria, Ont., Can.	B10	103
Alexandria, Rom.	F9	20
Alexandria, Al., U.S.	B4	108
Alexandria, In., U.S.	D6	121
Alexandria, Ky., U.S.	B5	124
Alexandria, La., U.S.	C3	125
Alexandria, Mn., U.S.	E3	130
Alexandria, Mo., U.S.	A6	132
Alexandria, Ne., U.S.	D8	134
Alexandria, N.H., U.S.	C3	136
Alexandria, S.D., U.S.	D8	148
Alexandria, Tn., U.S.	A5	149
Alexandria, Va., U.S.	B5	153
Alexandria see Al-Iskandarīyah, Egypt	B5	60
Alexandria Bay, N.Y., U.S.	A5	139
Alexandrina, Lake, l., Austl.	J3	70
Alexandroúpolis, Grc.	I9	20
Alexis, Il., U.S.	B3	120
Alexis Creek, B.C., Can.	C6	99
Alfalfa, co., Ok., U.S.	A3	143
Alfaro, Ec.	I3	84
Alfaro, Spain	C10	16
Al-Fāshir, Sud.	K3	60
Al-Fashn, Egypt	C6	60
Al-Fāw, Iraq	G10	48
Al-Fayyūm, Egypt	C6	60
Alfeld, Ger.	D9	10
Alfenas, Braz.	F6	79
Al-Fifi, Sud.	L3	60
Alfiós, stm., Grc.	L5	20
Alföld, pl., Hung.	H20	10
Alford, Fl., U.S.	B1	116
Alfred, Ont., Can.	B10	103
Alfred, Me., U.S.	E2	126
Alfred, N.Y., U.S.	C3	139
Alfredo Chaves, Braz.	F8	79
Alga, U.S.S.R.	H9	22
Ålgård, Nor.	L9	6
Al-Garef, Sud.	K8	60
Algarrobal, Chile	E3	80
Algarrobo, Arg.	J7	80
Algarrobo, Chile	G3	80
Algarrobo del Águila, Arg.	I5	80
Algarrobo Verde, Arg.	F4	80
Algarve, hist. reg., Port.	H3	16
Algasovo, U.S.S.R.	H24	26
Al-Gebir, Sud.	K5	60
Algeciras, Col.	F5	84
Algeciras, Spain	I6	16
Algemesí, Spain	F11	16
Algena, Eth.	I10	60
Alger, Oh., U.S.	B2	142
Alger, co., Mi., U.S.	B4	129
Algeria (Algérie), ctry., Afr.	C7	54
Al-Ghāṭ, Sau. Ar.	H8	48
Al-Ghawr, val., Asia	D5	50
Al-Ghayḍah, Yemen	F8	47
Al-Ghazālah, Sau. Ar.	H6	48
Alghero, Italy	I3	18
Al-Ghurayfah, Oman	B10	47
Al-Ghurdaqah, Egypt	D7	60
Algiers see El Djazaïr, Alg.	B12	62
Alginet, Spain	F11	16
Algodón, stm., Peru	I6	84
Algodones, N.M., U.S.	B3	138
Algoma, Ms., U.S.	A4	131
Algoma, Wi., U.S.	D6	156
Algona, Ia., U.S.	A3	122
Algona, Wa., U.S.	B3	154
Algonac, Mi., U.S.	F8	129
Algonquin, Ont., Can.	C9	103
Algonquin, Il., U.S.	A5	120
Algonquin Provincial Park, Ont., Can.	B6	103
Algood, Tn., U.S.	C8	149
Algorta, Spain	B8	16
Algorta, Ur.	G10	80
Al-Ḥadīthah, Iraq	D7	48
Al-Ḥadīthah, Sau. Ar.	E8	50
Al-Ḥajarah, reg., Asia	F8	48
Al Hajeb, Mor.	D8	62
Al-Ḥamād, pl., Sau. Ar.	E5	48
Alhama de Murcia, Spain	H10	16
Alhambra, Ca., U.S.	m12	112
Alhambra, Il., U.S.	E4	120
Al-Ḥammām, Egypt	B5	60
Al-Ḥamrā', Sau. Ar.	C1	47
Al-Ḥarīq, Sau. Ar.	C5	47
Al-Harūj al-Aswad, hills, Libya	C4	56
Al-Ḥasakah, Syria	C6	48
Alhaurín el Grande, Spain	I7	16
Al-Hawātah, Sud.	K8	60
Al-Ḥawrah, Yemen	H5	47
Al-Ḥawṭah, Yemen	G6	47
Al-Ḥayy, Iraq	E9	48
Al-Ḥayyānīyah, Sau. Ar.	G7	48
Al-Ḥayz, Egypt	C5	60
Al-Ḥijāz, reg., Sau. Ar.	I5	48
Al-Ḥillah, Iraq	E8	48
Al-Ḥillah, Sud.	K4	60
Al-Hirmil, Leb.	D4	48
Al-Ḥiṣn, Jord.	D5	50
Al-Hoceïma, Mor.	A6	54
Al Hoceïma, Baie d', b., Afr.	J8	16
Alhucemas, Peñón de, i., Sp. N. Afr.	J8	16
Al-Ḥudaydah, Yemen	G3	47
Al-Hufūf, Sau. Ar.	B6	47
Al-Ḥulwah, Sau. Ar.	J9	48
Al-Humayshah, Yemen	H4	47
Al-Ḥuṣayḥiṣah, Sud.	J7	60
Al-Ḥuwaylizah, Isr. Occ.	B5	50
Al-Ḥuwayyiṭ, Sau. Ar.	I6	48
ʻAlīābād, Iran	C13	48
Aliaga, Spain	E11	16
Aliákmon, stm., Grc.	I6	20
Aliákmonos, Tekhnití Límni, res., Grc.	I5	20
ʻAlī al-Gharbī, Iraq	E9	48
Alībāg, India	C2	46
Ali-Bajramly, U.S.S.R.	B10	48
Alibej, ozero, l., U.S.S.R.	D14	20
Alibunar, Yugo.	D4	20
Alice, Ciskei	I8	66
Alice, Tx., U.S.	F3	150
Alicedale, S. Afr.	I8	66
Alice Lake, l., Mn., U.S.	C7	130
Alice Springs, Austl.	D6	68
Alice Town, Bah.	B5	94
Aliceville, Al., U.S.	B1	108
Alicia, Ar., U.S.	B4	111
Alida, Sask., Can.	H5	105
Alīgarh, India	G8	44
Alīgūdarz, Iran	E10	48
Alijos, Islas, is., Mex.	E2	90
Al-Ikhwān, is., Yemen	G5	42
Aline, Ok., U.S.	A3	143
Aliquippa, Pa., U.S.	E1	145
Al-ʻĪrāq, Jord.	F5	50
Al-ʻĪsāwīyah, Sau. Ar.	F4	48
Al-Iskandarīyah (Alexandria), Egypt	B5	60
Al-Ismāʻīlīyah, Egypt	B7	60
Aliwal North, S. Afr.	H8	66
Alix, Alta., Can.	C4	98
Alix, Ar., U.S.	B2	111
Al-Jabalayn, Sud.	K7	60
Al-Jadīdah, Egypt	E5	60
Al-Jafr, Jord.	H6	50
Al-Jaghbūb, Libya	C3	60
Al-Jawf, Libya	E2	60
Al-Jawf, Sau. Ar.	G5	48
Al-Jaylī, Sud.	I7	60
Al-Jazīrah, reg., Sud.	J7	60
Aljezur, Port.	H3	16
Al-Jifārah, Sau. Ar.	J8	48
Al-Jifārah (Jeffara), pl., Afr.	D16	62
Al-Jīzah, Egypt	B6	60
Al-Jubayl, Sau. Ar.	H10	48
Al-Jubayn, Sud.	K8	60
Al-Judayyidah, Jord.	E5	50
Al-Julaydah, well, Asia	G8	48
Al-Junaynah, Sud.	K2	60
Aljustrel, Port.	H3	16
Al-Kafr, Syria	C7	50
Alkali Lake, l., Nv., U.S.	B2	135
Alkali Lake, l., Or., U.S.	E6	144
Alkaline Lake, l., N.D., U.S.	C6	141
Al-Kāmil, Oman	C11	47
Al-Karabah, Sud.	H7	60
Al-Karak, Jord.	F5	50
Al-Karnak, Egypt	E7	60
Al-Kawah, Sud.	K7	60
Al-Khabrā', Sau. Ar.	H7	48
Al-Khābūrah, Oman	C10	47
Al-Khalīl (Hebron), Isr. Occ.	E4	50
Al-Khālis, Iraq	E8	48
Al-Khandaq, Sud.	H6	60
Al-Khārijah, Egypt	E6	60
Al-Kharṭūm (Khartoum), Sud.	J7	60
Al-Kharṭūm Baḥrī, Sud.	J7	60
Al-Khaṣab, Oman	A10	47
Al-Khubar, Sau. Ar.	A7	47
Al-Khums, Libya	B3	56
Al-Khuraybah, Jord.	C5	50
Al-Khuraybah, Yemen	G6	47
Al-Khurmah, Sau. Ar.	D3	47
Al-Kidn, reg., Asia	C9	47
Alkmaar, Neth.	C6	12
Alkol, W.V., U.S.	m12	155
Al-Kuntillah, Egypt	B8	60
Al-Kūt, Iraq	E8	48
Al-Kuwayt, Kuw.	G9	48
Allada, Benin	H11	64
Al-Lādhiqīyah (Latakia), Syria	D3	48
Allagash, stm., Me., U.S.	B3	126
Allagash Lake, l., Me., U.S.	B3	126
Al-Lagowa, Sud.	L5	60
Allahābād, India	H9	44
Allakaket, Ak., U.S.	B9	109
Allamakee, co., Ia., U.S.	A6	122
Allamuchy Mountain, mtn., N.J., U.S.	B3	137
Allan, Sask., Can.	F2	105
Allanche, Fr.	G9	14
Allanmyo, Burma	E3	40
ʻAllāq, Biʼr, well, Libya	E16	62
Allardt, Tn., U.S.	C9	149
Allatoona Lake, res., Ga., U.S.	B2	117
Al-Layyah, Sud.	I8	60
Alldays, S. Afr.	D9	66
Alleene, Ar., U.S.	D1	111
Allegan, Mi., U.S.	F5	129
Allegan, co., Mi., U.S.	F5	129
Allegany, N.Y., U.S.	C2	139
Allegany, co., Md., U.S.	k13	127
Allegany, co., N.Y., U.S.	C2	139
Allegany Indian Reservation, N.Y., U.S.	C2	139
Alleghany, co., N.C., U.S.	A1	140
Alleghany, co., Va., U.S.	C2	153
Allegheny, co., Pa., U.S.	E2	145
Allegheny, stm., U.S.	E2	145
Allegheny Front, mtn., W.V., U.S.	B5	155
Allegheny Mountain, mts., U.S.	B3	153
Allegheny Plateau, plat., U.S.	E1	145
Allegheny Reservoir, res., U.S.	B4	145
Alleman, Ia., U.S.	e8	122
Allemands, Bayou Des, stm., La., U.S.	k11	125
Allemands, Lac Des, l., La., U.S.	E5	125
Allen, Arg.	J5	80
Allen, Ks., U.S.	D7	123
Allen, Ky., U.S.	C7	124
Allen, Md., U.S.	D6	127
Allen, Ne., U.S.	B9	134
Allen, Ok., U.S.	C5	143
Allen, S.D., U.S.	D4	148
Allen, Tx., U.S.	m10	150
Allen, Tx., U.S.	C4	150
Allen, co., In., U.S.	B7	121
Allen, co., Ks., U.S.	E8	123
Allen, co., Ky., U.S.	D3	124
Allen, co., La., U.S.	D3	125
Allen, co., Oh., U.S.	B1	142
Allen, Mount, mtn., Ak., U.S.	C11	109
Allendale, Il., U.S.	E6	120
Allendale, In., U.S.	F3	121
Allendale, N.J., U.S.	A4	137
Allendale, S.C., U.S.	E5	147
Allendale, co., S.C., U.S.	F5	147
Allende, Mex.	C9	90
Allenford, Ont., Can.	C3	103
Allenhurst, Ga., U.S.	E5	117
Allen Park, Mi., U.S.	p15	129
Allens Mills, Me., U.S.	D2	126
Allenspark, Co., U.S.	A5	113
Allenstein see Olsztyn, Pol.	B20	10
Allensville, Ky., U.S.	D2	124
Allenton, Mo., U.S.	f12	132
Allenton, R.I., U.S.	E4	146
Allenton, Wi., U.S.	E5	156
Allentown, Ga., U.S.	D3	117
Allentown, N.J., U.S.	C3	137
Allentown, Pa., U.S.	E11	145
Allentsteig, Aus.	G15	10
Allenwood, N.J., U.S.	C4	137
Alleppey, India	H4	46
Aller, stm., Ger.	C9	10
Allerton, Il., U.S.	D6	120
Allerton, Ia., U.S.	D4	122
Allerton, Point, c., Ma., U.S.	B6	128
Allgäu, reg., Ger.	H10	10
Allgäuer Alpen, mts., Eur.	E17	14
Allgood, Al., U.S.	B3	108
Alliance, Alta., Can.	C5	98
Alliance, Ne., U.S.	B3	134
Alliance, N.C., U.S.	B6	140
Alliance, Oh., U.S.	B4	142
Al-Lidām, Sau. Ar.	D4	47
Allier, dept., Fr.	F9	14
Allier, stm., Fr.	F10	14
Alligator, Ms., U.S.	A3	131
Alligator, stm., N.C., U.S.	B6	140
Alligator Lake, l., Me., U.S.	D4	126
Allison, Ia., U.S.	B5	122
Allison, Pa., U.S.	G2	145
Allison Park, Pa., U.S.	h14	145
Alliston, Ont., Can.	C5	103
Al-Līth, Sau. Ar.	D2	47
Alloa, Scot., U.K.	E10	8
Allons, Tn., U.S.	C8	149
Allora, Austl.	G9	70
Allouez, Wi., U.S.	h9	156
Alloway, N.J., U.S.	D2	137
Alloway Creek, stm., N.J., U.S.	D2	137
Allport, Ar., U.S.	C4	111
Al-Luḥayyah, Yemen	G3	47
Allumette Lake, l., Can.	B7	103
Allyn, Wa., U.S.	B3	154
Alma, N.B., Can.	D5	101
Alma, Ont., Can.	D4	103
Alma, Que., Can.	A6	104
Alma, Ar., U.S.	B1	111
Alma, Co., U.S.	B4	113
Alma, Ga., U.S.	E4	117
Alma, Il., U.S.	E5	120
Alma, Ks., U.S.	C7	123
Alma, Mi., U.S.	E6	129
Alma, Mo., U.S.	B4	132
Alma, Ne., U.S.	D6	134
Alma, Wi., U.S.	D2	156
Alma-Ata, U.S.S.R.	I13	22
Alma Center, Wi., U.S.	D3	156
Almada, Port.	G2	16
Almadén, Spain	G7	16
Al-Madīnah (Medina), Sau. Ar.	B1	47
Al-Mafāzah, Sud.	K8	60
Al-Mafraq, Jord.	D6	50
Almafuerte, Arg.	G6	80
Almagro, Spain	G8	16
Al-Maḥallah al-Kubrā, Egypt	B6	60
Al-Maḥārīq, Egypt	E6	60
Al Mahbas, W. Sah.	G6	62
Alma Hill, hill, N.Y., U.S.	C2	139
Al-Majmaʻah, Sau. Ar.	I8	48
Al-Makhā' (Mocha), Yemen	H3	47
Almalyk, U.S.S.R.	I11	22
Al-Manāmah, Bahr.	H11	48
Almanor, Lake, l., Ca., U.S.	B3	112
Almansa, Spain	G10	16
Al-Manshāh, Egypt	D6	60
Al-Manṣūrah, Egypt	B6	60
Al-Manzilah, Egypt	F1	48
Almanzor, mtn., Spain	E6	16
Al-Marāghah, Egypt	D6	60
Al-Marj, Libya	B5	56
Almas, Pico das, mtn., Braz.	B8	79
Almas, Rio das, stm., Braz.	B9	79
Al-Masīd, Sud.	J7	60
Almassora, Spain	F11	16
Al-Matammah, Sud.	I7	60
Al-Maṭarīyah, Egypt	B7	60
Al-Matnah, Sud.	K8	60
Almaville, Tn., U.S.	B5	149
Al-Mawṣil (Mosul), Iraq	C7	48
Al-Mayādīn, Syria	D6	48
Al-Mazār, Jord.	F5	50
Al-Mazraʻah, Jord.	F5	50
Almeida, Port.	E5	16
Almeirim, Port.	F3	16
Almelo, Neth.	D10	12
Almelund, Mn., U.S.	E6	130
Almena, Ks., U.S.	C4	123
Almena, Wi., U.S.	C1	156
Almenara, Braz.	D8	79
Almendralejo, Spain	G5	16
Almería, Spain	I9	16
Almería, Golfo de, b., Spain	I9	16
Al'metjevsk, U.S.S.R.	G8	22
Al-Midhnab, Sau. Ar.	I8	48
Al-Minyā, Egypt	C6	60
Almira, Wa., U.S.	B7	154
Almirante, Pan.	C1	84
Almirante, Bahía de, b., Pan.	H12	92
Almirante Latorre, Chile	E3	80
Al-Mismīyah, Syria	B6	50
Almo, Id., U.S.	G5	119
Almodôvar, Port.	H3	16
Almolonga, Guat.	C3	92
Almon, Ga., U.S.	C3	117
Almond, Wi., U.S.	D4	156
Almont, Mi., U.S.	F7	129
Almont, N.D., U.S.	C4	141
Almonte, Ont., Can.	B8	103
Almonte, Spain	H5	16
Almora, India	F8	44
Al-Mubarraz, Sau. Ar.	C5	47
Al-Mubarraz, Sau. Ar.	B6	47
Al-Mudawwarah, Jord.	G3	48
Al-Muglad, Sud.	L4	60
Al-Muḥarraq, Bahr.	H11	48
Al-Mukallā, Yemen	G6	47
Almuñécar, Spain	I8	16
Al-Musallamīyah, Sud.	J7	60
Al-Musayfirah, Syria	C6	50
Al-Musayjid, Sau. Ar.	B1	47
Al-Mutayn, Leb.	A5	50
Al-Muwayh, Sau. Ar.	C2	47
Al-Muwayliḥ, Sau. Ar.	H3	48
Almyra, Ar., U.S.	C4	111
Alnwick, Eng., U.K.	F12	8
Aloândia, Braz.	D4	79
Aloha, Or., U.S.	h12	144
Aloja, U.S.S.R.	D7	26
Alonsa, Man., Can.	D2	100
Alor, Pulau, i., Indon.	G7	38
Alor Setar, Malay.	K6	40
Alosno, Spain	H4	16
Alost (Aalst), Bel.	G5	12
Alpachiri, Arg.	I7	80
Alpaugh, Ca., U.S.	E4	112
Alpena, Ar., U.S.	A2	111
Alpena, Mi., U.S.	C7	129
Alpena, S.D., U.S.	C7	148
Alpena, co., Mi., U.S.	D7	129
Alpes-de-Haute-Provence, dept., Fr.	H13	14
Alpes Maritimes, dept., Fr.	I14	14
Alpha, Austl.	D7	70
Alpha, Il., U.S.	B3	120
Alpha, N.J., U.S.	B2	137
Alpharetta, Ga., U.S.	B2	117
Alpine, Al., U.S.	B3	108
Alpine, Az., U.S.	D6	110
Alpine, Ar., U.S.	C2	111
Alpine, N.J., U.S.	h9	137
Alpine, Tn., U.S.	C8	149
Alpine, Tx., U.S.	D1	150
Alpine, Ut., U.S.	C4	151
Alpine, Wy., U.S.	C1	157
Alpine, co., Ca., U.S.	C4	112
Alpine National Park, Austl.	K7	70
Alpinópolis, Braz.	F5	79

Name — Map Ref. — Page

Alpoca, W.V., U.S. D3 155
Alps, mts., Eur. F10 4
Al-Qābil, Oman C9 47
Al-Qaḍārif, Sud. J8 60
Al-Qadīmah, Sau. Ar. C1 47
Al-Qāhirah (Cairo), Egypt B6 60
Al-Qahmah, Sau. Ar. E2 47
Al-Qalībah, Sau. Ar. G4 48
Al-Qāmishlī, Syria C6 48
Al-Qanṭarah, Egypt B7 60
Al-Qaryah ash-Sharqīyah, Libya B3 56
Al-Qaṣr, Egypt E5 60
Al-Qaṣr, Jord. F5 50
Al-Qaṭīf, Sau. Ar. A7 47
Al-Qaṭrānah, Jord. F6 50
Al-Qaṭrūn, Libya D3 56
Al-Qaysūmah, Sau. Ar. G9 48
Al-Qiṣfah, Jord. C5 50
Al-Quds see Yerushalayim, Isr. E4 50
Al-Qunayṭirah, Syria B5 50
Al-Qunfudhah, Sau. Ar. E2 47
Al-Qurnah, Iraq F9 48
Al-Quṣaymah, Egypt G2 50
Al-Quṣayr, Egypt D8 60
Al-Qūṣīyah, Egypt D6 60
Al-Quṭayfah, Syria A7 50
Al-Quṭaynah, Sud. J7 60
Al-Quwayʻīyah, Sau. Ar. B4 47
Al-Quwaysī, Sud. K8 60
Alsace, hist. reg., Fr. D14 14
Alsask, Sask., Can. F1 105
Alsea, Or., U.S. C3 144
Alsen, N.D., U.S. A7 141
Alsey, Il., U.S. D3 120
Alsfeld, Ger. E9 10
Alsina, Arg. G9 80
Alstead, N.H., U.S. D2 136
Alstead, stm., Sask., Can. B2 105
Alstead Center, N.H., U.S. D2 136
Alston, Ga., U.S. D4 117
Alsunga, U.S.S.R. E4 26
Alta, Ia., U.S. B2 122
Alta, Wy., U.S. C1 157
Altadena, Ca., U.S. m12 112
Alta Gracia, Arg. F6 80
Altagracia, Nic. F9 92
Altagracia, Ven. B7 84
Altagracia de Orituco, Ven. C9 84
Altai, mts., Asia H16 22
Altaj (Jesönbulag), Mong. B6 30
Altamachi, stm., Bol. G8 82
Altamaha, stm., Ga., U.S. E4 117
Altamaha Sound, strt., Ga., U.S. E5 117
Altamira, Braz. D8 76
Altamira, Chile C4 80
Altamira, C.R. G10 92
Altamont, Man., Can. E2 100
Altamont, Il., U.S. D5 120
Altamont, Ks., U.S. E8 123
Altamont, Mo., U.S. B3 132
Altamont, N.Y., U.S. C6 139
Altamont, Or., U.S. E5 144
Altamont, Tn., U.S. D8 149
Altamonte Springs, Fl., U.S. D5 116
Altamura, Italy I11 18
Altamura, Isla, i., Mex. E5 90
Altar, Mex. B4 90
Altar, stm., Mex. B4 90
Altar, Desierto de, des., Mex. B3 90
Altar de Los Sacrificios, hist., Guat. I14 90
Altario, Alta., Can. D5 98
Altata, Mex. E6 90
Alta Verapaz, dept., Guat. B4 92
Alta Vista, Ia., U.S. A5 122
Alta Vista, Ks., U.S. D7 123
Altavista, Va., U.S. C3 153
Altay, China B4 30
Altdorf, Switz. E10 13
Altenburg, Ger. E12 10
Altenburg, Mo., U.S. D8 132
Altha, Fl., U.S. B1 116
Altheimer, Ar., U.S. C4 111
Althofen, Aus. I14 10
Altinópolis, Braz. F5 79
Altiplano, plat., S.A. H7 82
Altkirch, Fr. E14 14
Altmark, hist. reg., Ger. C11 10
Altmühl, stm., Ger. F10 10
Alto, Ga., U.S. B3 117
Alto, N.M., U.S. D4 138
Alto, Tx., U.S. D5 150
Alto Araguaia, Braz. D2 79
Alto Cedro, Cuba D7 94
Alto Coité, Braz. C1 79
Alto del Carmen, Chile E3 80
Alto Garças, Braz. D2 79
Alto Madre de Dios, stm., Peru E6 82
Altomünster, Ger. G11 10
Alton, Al., U.S. B3 108
Alton, Il., U.S. E3 120
Alton, Ia., U.S. B2 122
Alton, Ks., U.S. C5 123
Alton, La., U.S. h12 125
Alton, Mo., U.S. E6 132
Alton, N.H., U.S. D4 136
Altona, Man., Can. E3 100
Altona, Il., U.S. B3 120
Altona, In., U.S. B7 121
Alton Bay, N.H., U.S. D4 136
Altoona, Al., U.S. A3 108
Altoona, Fl., U.S. D5 116
Altoona, Ia., U.S. C4 122
Altoona, Ks., U.S. E8 123
Altoona, Pa., U.S. E5 145
Altoona, Wi., U.S. D2 156
Alto Paraguai, Braz. F13 82
Alto Paraguay, dept., Para. I12 82
Alto Paraíso de Goiás, Braz. C5 79
Alto Paraná, dept., Para. C11 80
Alto Parnaíba, Braz. E9 76
Alto Pass, Il., U.S. F4 120
Alto Purús, stm., Peru D6 82
Alto Rio Doce, Braz. F7 79
Alto Río Senguerr, Arg. F2 78
Alto Sucuriú, Braz. E2 79
Altötting, Ger. G12 10
Alto Yurua, stm., Peru C5 82
Altro, Ky., U.S. C6 124
Altstätten, Switz. D12 13
Altuchovo, U.S.S.R. I17 26
Altunoluk, Tur. J10 20
Altun Shan, mts., China D4 30
Altura, Mn., U.S. F7 130
Alturas, Ca., U.S. B3 112
Altus, Ar., U.S. B2 111
Altus, Ok., U.S. C2 143
Altus Air Force Base, mil., Ok., U.S. C2 143
Altus Reservoir, res., Ok., U.S. C2 143
Al-ʻUbaylah, Sau. Ar. D7 47
Al-Ubayyiḍ, Sud. K6 60
Al-ʻUdaysāt, Egypt E7 60
Al-Udayyah, Sud. K5 60
Aluk, Sud. M4 60
Alūksne, U.S.S.R. D10 26
Al-ʻUlā, Sau. Ar. H4 48
Alum Bank, Pa., U.S. F4 145
Alum Creek, W.V., U.S. m12 155
Alum Creek, stm., Oh., U.S. k11 142
Aluminé, Lago, l., Arg. J3 80
Al-ʻUqaylah, Libya B4 56
Al-ʻUqayr, Sau. Ar. B7 47
Al-Uqṣur (Luxor), Egypt E7 60
Al-ʻUwaynāt, Libya C3 56
Al-ʻUyaynah, Sau. Ar. B5 47
Alva, Fl., U.S. F5 116
Alva, Ok., U.S. A3 143
Alva, Wy., U.S. B8 157
Alvarado, Mex. H12 90
Alvarado, Mn., U.S. B2 130
Alvarado, Tx., U.S. C4 150
Alvarães, Braz. I10 84
Álvaro Obregón, Presa, res., Mex. D5 90
Alvdal, Nor. J12 6
Alvear, Arg. E10 80
Alvena, Sask., Can. E2 105
Alvernia, Mount, hill, Bah. B7 94
Alvesta, Swe. M14 6
Alvin, Il., U.S. C6 120
Alvin, Tx., U.S. E5 150
Alvinópolis, Braz. F7 79
Alvinston, Ont., Can. E3 103
Alvito, Port. G4 16
Älvkarleby, Swe. K15 6
Alvo, Ne., U.S. h12 134
Alvord, Ia., U.S. A1 122
Alvord, Tx., U.S. C4 150
Alvord Lake, l., Or., U.S. E8 144
Älvros, Swe. J14 6
Älvsborgs Län, co., Swe. L13 6
Al-Wajh, Sau. Ar. H4 48
Al-Wakrah, Qatar I11 48
Alwar, India G7 44
Al-Wāsiṭah, Egypt C6 60
Al-Wazz, Sud. J6 60
Alxa Zuoqi, China D8 30
Alytus, U.S.S.R. G7 26
Alzamaj, U.S.S.R. F11 24
Alzira (Alcira), Spain F11 16
Ama, La., U.S. k11 125
Amacuro, stm., S.A. C12 84
Amadeus, Lake, l., Austl. D6 68
Amadjuak Lake, l., N.W. Ter., Can. C18 96
Amador, co., Ca., U.S. C3 112
Amagansett, N.Y., U.S. n16 139
Amagasaki, Japan M10 36
Amagi, Japan N5 36
Amagon, Ar., U.S. B4 111
Amagunze, Nig. H13 64
Amahai, Indon. F8 38
Amaichá del Valle, Arg. D6 80
Amajac, stm., Mex. G10 90
Amaka, stm., Nic. C9 92
Amakusa-shotō, is., Japan O5 36
Amakuso-Shimo-shima, i., Japan O5 36
Åmål, Swe. L13 6
Amalfi, Col. D5 84
Amalfi, Italy I9 18
Amalga, Ut., U.S. B4 151
Amalia, N.M., U.S. A4 138
Amaliás, Grc. L5 20
Amambaí, Braz. G1 79
Amambaí, stm., Braz. G1 79
Amambay, dept., Para. B10 80
Amambay, Cordillera de, mts., S.A. B11 80
Amami-Ō-shima, i., Japan S4 37b
Amami-shotō, is., Japan T3 37b
Amana, Ia., U.S. C6 122
Amaná, stm., Braz. J14 84
Amana, stm., Ven. J13 94
Amaná, Lago, l., Braz. I10 84
Amanda, Oh., U.S. C3 142
Amapá, Braz. D9 74
Amapá, Braz. C8 76
Amapala, Hond. D7 92
Amapala, Punta de, c., El Sal. D7 92
Amarante, Braz. E10 76
Amaranth, Man., Can. D2 100
Amarapura, Burma D4 40
ʻAmārat Abū Sinn, Sud. J8 60
Amares, Port. D3 16
Amarete (Charazani), Bol. F7 82
Amargosa, Braz. B9 79
Amargosa, stm., U.S. D5 112
Amargosa Desert, des., U.S. G5 135
Amargosa Range, mts., U.S. G5 135
Amarillo, Tx., U.S. B2 150
ʻAmar Jadīd, Sud. J3 60
Amarkantak, India G3 30
Amarnāth, India C2 46
Amaro Leite, Braz. B4 79
Amasa, Mi., U.S. B2 129
Amasya, Tur. G15 4
Amataurá, Braz. I8 84
Amatignak Island, i., Ak., U.S. E4 109
Amatikulu, S. Afr. G10 66
Amatique, Bahía de, b., N.A. B6 92
Amatitlán, Guat. C4 92
Amatitlán, Lago de, l., Guat. C4 92
Amazon (Solimões) (Amazonas), stm., S.A. D7 76
Amazonas, state, Braz. H10 84
Amazonas, dept., Col. H7 84
Amazonas, dept., Peru A2 82
Amazonas, ter., Ven. F9 84
Amazonia, Mo., U.S. B3 132
Ambakaka, Madag. T22 67b
Ambāla, India E7 44
Ambalanjanakomby, Madag. P22 67b
Ambalavao, Madag. R22 67b
Ambalema, Col. E5 84
Amba Maryam, Eth. L10 60
Ambanja, Madag. N23 67b
Ambar, Peru D3 82
Ambararata, Madag. O23 67b
Ambarčik, U.S.S.R. D24 24
Ambargasta, Salinas de, pl., Arg. E6 80
Ambarnyj, U.S.S.R. I23 6
Ambato, Ec. H3 84
Ambatofinandrahana, Madag. R22 67b
Ambatolampy, Madag. Q22 67b
Ambatondrazaka, Madag. P23 67b
Ambelos, Ákra, c., Grc. J7 20
Ambenja, Madag. O22 67b
Amber, Ok., U.S. B4 143
Amberg, Ger. F11 10
Amberg, Wi., U.S. C6 156
Ambergris Cay, i., Belize H16 90
Ambérieu-en-Bugey, Fr. G12 14
Ambert, Fr. G10 14
Ambevongo, Madag. O22 67b
Ambia, In., U.S. D2 121
Ambikāpur, India I10 44
Ambilobe, Madag. N23 67b
Ambinanindrano, Madag. R23 67b
Ambivy, Madag. R21 67b
Ambler, Ak., U.S. B8 109
Ambler, Pa., U.S. F11 145
Ambo, Peru D3 82
Amboahangy, Madag. T22 67b
Ambodifototra, Madag. P23 67b
Ambodiriana, Madag. P23 67b
Ambohidray, Madag. Q23 67b
Ambohimahamasina, Madag. R22 67b
Amboise, Fr. E7 14
Ambon, Indon. F8 38
Ambondro, Madag. T21 67b
Ambositra, Madag. R22 67b
Ambovombe, Madag. T22 67b
Amboy, Il., U.S. B4 120
Amboy, In., U.S. C6 121
Amboy, Mn., U.S. G4 130
Amboy, Wa., U.S. D3 154
Ambre, Cap d', c., Madag. M23 67b
Ambridge, Pa., U.S. E1 145
Ambrières, Fr. D6 14
Ambriz, Ang. C2 58
Ambrose, Ga., U.S. E3 117
Ambunti, Pap. N. Gui. F11 38
Amchitka Island, i., Ak., U.S. E3 109
Amchitka Pass, strt., Ak., U.S. E4 109
ʻAmd, Yemen G6 47
Amderma, U.S.S.R. D10 22
Amdo, China E5 30
Ameagle, W.V., U.S. D3 155
Ameca, Mex. G7 90
Ameca, stm., Mex. G7 90
Amecameca [de Juárez], Mex. H10 90
Ameghino, Arg. H7 80
Ameland, i., Neth. B8 12
Amelia, Italy G7 18
Amelia, La., U.S. E4 125
Amelia, Oh., U.S. C1 142
Amelia, co., Va., U.S. C4 153
Amelia Court House, Va., U.S. C5 153
Amelia Island, i., Fl., U.S. k9 116
Amenia, N.Y., U.S. D7 139
Amenia, N.D., U.S. B8 141
Āmer, India G6 44
American, stm., Ca., U.S. C3 112
American, South Fork, stm., Ca., U.S. C3 112
Americana, Braz. G5 79
American Falls, Id., U.S. G6 119
American Falls Dam, Id., U.S. G6 119
American Falls Reservoir, res., Id., U.S. F5 119
American Fork, Ut., U.S. C4 151
American Highland, plat., Ant. C5 73
American Samoa, dep., Oc. G1 2
Americus, Ga., U.S. D2 117
Americus, Ks., U.S. D7 123
Amersfoort, Neth. D7 12
Amersfoort, S. Afr. F9 66
Amery, Wi., U.S. C1 156
Amery Ice Shelf, Ant. B5 73
Ames, Ia., U.S. B4 122
Ames, Ok., U.S. A3 143
Amesbury, Ma., U.S. A6 128
Ámfissa, Grc. K6 20
Amga, U.S.S.R. E18 24
Amga, stm., U.S.S.R. E18 24
Amguema, stm., U.S.S.R. D27 24
Amguid, Alg. G13 62
Amgun', stm., U.S.S.R. G19 24
Amherst, N.S., Can. D5 101
Amherst, Ma., U.S. B2 128
Amherst, Ne., U.S. D6 134
Amherst, N.H., U.S. E3 136
Amherst, N.Y., U.S. C2 139
Amherst, Oh., U.S. A3 142
Amherst, S.D., U.S. B8 148
Amherst, Tx., U.S. B1 150
Amherst, Va., U.S. C3 153
Amherst, Wi., U.S. D4 156
Amherst, co., Va., U.S. C3 153
Amherstburg, Ont., Can. E1 103
Amherstdale, W.V., U.S. n12 155
Amiens, Fr. C9 14
Amili, China F16 44
Amīndīvi Islands, is., India G2 46
Aminga, Arg. E5 80
Aminuis, Nmb. D4 66
Amirante Islands, is., Sey. C10 58
Amisk, Alta., Can. C5 98
Amisk Lake, l., Sask., Can. C4 105
Amistad, Parque Internacional de la, C.R. H11 92
Amistad National Recreation Area, Tx., U.S. E2 150
Amite, La., U.S. D5 125
Amite, co., Ms., U.S. D3 131
Amite, stm., La., U.S. D5 125
Amity, Ar., U.S. C2 111
Amity, Or., U.S. B3 144
Amityville, N.Y., U.S. E7 139
Amizmiz, Mor. E6 62
Amlia Island, i., Ak., U.S. E5 109
ʻAmm-Adām, Sud. I9 60
ʻAmmān, Jord. E5 50
Ammarnäs, Swe. I15 6
Ammon, Id., U.S. F7 119
Ammonoosuc, stm., N.H., U.S. B3 136
Amne Machin Shan see A'nyêmaqên Shan, mts., China D6 30
Amnok-kang (Yalu), stm., Asia C13 32
Amo, In., U.S. E4 121
Amo, stm., Asia G13 44
Āmol, Iran C12 48
Amolar, Braz. H13 82
Amonate, Va., U.S. e10 153
Amoret, Mo., U.S. C3 132
Amorgós, i., Grc. M9 20
Amorinópolis, Braz. D3 79
Amory, Ms., U.S. B5 131
Amos, Que., Can. k11 104
Amoy see Xiamen, China K7 34
Ampanihy, Madag. T21 67b
Amparihy, Madag. S22 67b
Amparo, Braz. G5 79
Ampato, Nevado, mtn., Peru F6 82
Amper, Nig. G14 64
Ampiyacu, stm., Peru I6 84
Ampombiantambo, Madag. N23 67b
Amposta, Spain E12 16
Ampotaka, Madag. T21 67b
ʻAmrān, Yemen G3 47
Amrāvati, India J7 44
Amreli, India J4 44
Amritsar, India E6 44
Amroha, India F8 44
Amsel, Alg. I13 62
Åmsele, Swe. I16 6
Amsteg, Switz. E10 13
Amsterdam, Neth. D6 12
Amsterdam, S. Afr. F10 66
Amsterdam, Ga., U.S. F2 117
Amsterdam, Mo., U.S. C3 132
Amsterdam, Mt., U.S. E5 133
Amsterdam, N.Y., U.S. C6 139
Amsterdam, Oh., U.S. B5 142
Amsterdam, Île, i., F.S.A.T. L11 158
Amsterdam-Rijnkanaal, Neth. E7 12
Amstetten, Aus. G14 10
Amston, Ct., U.S. C6 114
Am Timan, Chad F5 56
Amubri, C.R. H12 92
Amu-Darja, U.S.S.R. C18 48
Amu Darya (Amudarja), stm., Asia B2 44
Amukta Pass, strt., Ak., U.S. E5 109
Amundsen Gulf, b., N.W. Ter., Can. B8 96
Amundsen-Scott, sci., Ant. D10 73
Amundsen Sea, Ant. C11 73
Amuntai, Indon. F6 38
Amur (Heilong), stm., Asia B14 30
Amurrio, Spain I3 14
Amuzhong, China E11 44
Amvrakikós Kólpos, b., Grc. K4 20
Amy, Ar., U.S. D3 111
Anabar, stm., U.S.S.R. C14 24
Anaco, Ven. C10 84
Anacoco, La., U.S. C2 125
Anacoco, Bayou, stm., La., U.S. D2 125
Anaconda, Mt., U.S. D4 133
Anaconda, N.M., U.S. B2 138
Anaconda Range, mts., Mt., U.S. E3 133
Anacortes, Wa., U.S. A3 154
Anacostia, stm., U.S. C4 127
Anacostia, Northwest Branch, stm., Md., U.S. B3 127
Anadarko, Ok., U.S. B3 143
Anadyr', U.S.S.R. E27 24
Anadyr', stm., U.S.S.R. E26 24
Anadyrskij zaliv, b., U.S.S.R. E28 24
Anadyrskoje ploskogorje, plat., U.S.S.R. D26 24
Anagance, N.B., Can. D4 101
Anagni, Italy H8 18
ʻĀnah, Iraq D6 48
Anaheim, Ca., U.S. F5 112
Anahim Lake, B.C., Can. C5 99
Anahola, Hi., U.S. A2 118
Anáhuac, Mex. C6 90
Anáhuac, Mex. D9 90
Anahuac, Tx., U.S. E5 150
Anahulu, stm., Hi., U.S. f9 118
Ānai Mudi, mtn., India G4 46
Analalava, Madag. O22 67b
Analapatsy, Madag. T22 67b
Anamã, Braz. I12 84
Anamã, Lago, l., Braz. I12 84
Anama Bay, Man., Can. D2 100
Ana María, Golfo de, b., Cuba D5 94
Anambas, Kepulauan, is., Indon. M9 40
Anamoose, N.D., U.S. B5 141
Anamosa, Ia., U.S. B6 122
Anamu, stm., Braz. G14 84
Anamur, Tur. C2 48
Ānand, India I5 44
Anandale, La., U.S. C3 125
Ananea, Peru F7 82
Ananjev, U.S.S.R. B13 20
Anantapur, India E4 46
Anantnāg (Islāmābād), India D6 44
Anápolis, Braz. D4 79
Anār, Iran F13 48
Anārak, Iran E12 48
Anār Darreh, Afg. E16 48
Anastácio, Braz. F1 79
Anastasia Island, i., Fl., U.S. C5 116
ʻAnātā, Isr. Occ. E4 50
Añatuya, Arg. E7 80
Anauá, stm., Braz. G12 84
Anaurilândia, Braz. G2 79
Anavilhanas, Arquipélago das, is., Braz. I12 84
Anawalt, W.V., U.S. D3 155
Anbanjing, China C6 40
Anbu, China L5 34
Anbyŏn, N. Kor. D15 32
Ancash, dept., Peru C3 82
Ancaster, Ont., Can. D4 103
Ancasti, Arg. E6 80
Ancasti, Sierra de, mts., Arg. E6 80
Ancha, Sierra, mts., Az., U.S. D4 110
Anchang, China E9 34
Anchorage, Ak., U.S. C10 109
Anchorage, Ky., U.S. g11 124
Anchorena, Arg. H6 80
Anchor Point, Ak., U.S. D9 109
Anchor Point, c., Ak., U.S. h15 109
Anci (Langfang), China D4 32
Ancien Goubéré, Cen. Afr. Rep. O4 60
Ancienne-Lorette, Que., Can. C6 104
Anciferovo, U.S.S.R. C17 26
Anclote Keys, is., Fl., U.S. D4 116
Anco, Ky., U.S. C6 124
Ancón, Peru D3 82
Ancona, Italy F8 18
Ancón de Sardinas, Bahía de, b., S.A. G3 84
Ancoraimes, Bol. F7 82
Ancud, Chile E2 78
Ancud, Golfo de, b., Chile E2 78
Anda, China B12 30
Andacollo, Arg. I3 80
Andacollo, Chile F3 80
Andahuaylas, Peru E5 82
Andale, Ks., U.S. E6 123
Andalgalá, Arg. D5 80
Åndalsnes, Nor. J10 6
Andalucía, prov., Spain H7 16
Andalucía, hist. reg., Spain H7 16
Andalusia, Al., U.S. D3 108
Andalusia, Il., U.S. B3 120
Andaman Islands, is., India H2 40
Andaman Sea, Asia I3 40
Andamarca, Bol. H8 82
Andamarca, Peru D4 82
Andamooka, Austl. H2 70
Andapa, Madag. O23 67b
Andaraí, Braz. B8 79
Andaray, Peru F5 82
Andeer, Switz. E11 13
Andelot, Fr. D12 14
Andenes, Nor. G15 6
Andéranboukane, Mali D11 64
Andermatt, Switz. E10 13
Andernach, Ger. E7 10
Anderson, Al., U.S. A2 108
Anderson, Ak., U.S. C10 109
Anderson, Ca., U.S. B2 112
Anderson, In., U.S. D6 121
Anderson, Mo., U.S. E3 132
Anderson, S.C., U.S. B2 147
Anderson, Tn., U.S. D8 149
Anderson, Tx., U.S. D4 150
Anderson, co., Ks., U.S. D8 123
Anderson, co., Ky., U.S. C4 124
Anderson, co., S.C., U.S. B2 147
Anderson, co., Tn., U.S. C9 149
Anderson, co., Tx., U.S. D5 150
Anderson, stm., N.W. Ter., Can. C7 96
Anderson, stm., In., U.S. H4 121
Anderson, Mount, mtn., Wa., U.S. B2 154
Anderson Ranch Reservoir, res., Id., U.S. F3 119
Andersonville, Ga., U.S. D2 117
Andersonville, In., U.S. F7 121
Andes, Col. E5 84
Andes, mts., S.A. G8 74
Andes, Lake, l., S.D., U.S. D7 148
Andevoranto, Madag. Q23 67b
Andhra Pradesh, state, India D5 46
Andikíthira, i., Grc. N7 20
Andimákhia, Grc. M11 20
Andīmeshk, Iran E10 48
Andirá, stm., Braz. I14 84
Andirá, Riozinho do, stm., Braz. C8 82
Andirlang, China B10 44
Ándissa, Grc. J9 20
Andižan, U.S.S.R. I12 22
Andkhvoy, Afg. B1 44
Andoas, Peru I4 84
Andong, S. Kor. G16 32
Andorra, And. C13 16
Andorra, ctry., Eur. G8 4
Andover, Ct., U.S. C6 114
Andover, Il., U.S. B3 120
Andover, Ks., U.S. g12 123
Andover, Me., U.S. D2 126
Andover, Ma., U.S. A5 128
Andover, Mn., U.S. m12 130
Andover, N.H., U.S. D3 136
Andover, N.Y., U.S. C3 139
Andover, Oh., U.S. A5 142
Andover, S.D., U.S. B8 148
Andover Lake, res., Ct., U.S. C6 114
Andøya, i., Nor. G14 6
Andrade, Hi., U.S. D6 118
Andradina, Braz. F3 79
Andranopasy, Madag. R20 67b
Andranovory, Madag. S21 67b
Andreanof Islands, is., Ak., U.S. E4 109
Andreapol', U.S.S.R. E15 26
Andrejevo, U.S.S.R. F24 26
Andréville, Que., Can. B8 104
Andrew, Alta., Can. C4 98
Andrew, Ia., U.S. B7 122
Andrew, co., Mo., U.S. B3 132
Andrew Island, i., N.S., Can. D9 101
Andrews, In., U.S. C6 121
Andrews, N.C., U.S. f9 140
Andrews, S.C., U.S. E8 147
Andrews, Tx., U.S. C1 150
Andrews, co., Tx., U.S. C1 150
Andrews Air Force Base, mil., Md., U.S. C4 127
Andria, Italy H11 18
Andriamena, Madag. P22 67b
Andriandampy, Madag. S21 67b
Andrijevica, Yugo. G3 20
Androka, Madag. T21 67b
Ándros, Grc. L8 20
Ándros, i., Bah. B6 94
Ándros, i., Grc. L8 20
Androscoggin, co., Me., U.S. D2 126
Androscoggin, stm., Me., U.S. D2 126
Androscoggin Lake, l., Me., U.S. D2 126
Andros Town, Bah. B6 94
Ändrott Island, i., India G2 46
Andrychów, Pol. F19 10
Andújar, Spain G7 16
Anécho, Togo H10 64
Anegada, i., Br. Vir. Is. E12 94
Anegada Passage, strt., N.A. E13 94
Añelo, Arg. J4 80
Aneroid, Sask., Can. H2 105
Aneta, N.D., U.S. B8 141
Aneth, Ut., U.S. F6 151
Aneto, Pico de, mtn., Spain C12 16
Áñez, Bol. G10 82
Anfeng, China B9 34
Anfeng, China C9 34
Anfengqiao, China I7 34
Anfu, China H3 34
Angamos, Punta, c., Chile B3 80
Ang'angxi, China B11 30
Angao, China B1 34
Angara, stm., U.S.S.R. F17 22
Angara-Débou, Benin F11 64
Angarbaka, Sud. M3 60
Angarsk, U.S.S.R. G12 24
Angastaco, Arg. C5 80
Angatuba, Braz. G4 79
Ángel, Salto (Angel Falls), wtfl, Ven. E11 84
Ángel de la Guarda, Isla, i., Mex. C3 90
Angeles, Phil. N19 39b
Angeles Point, c., Wa., U.S. A2 154
Angel Falls see Ángel, Salto, wtfl, Ven. E11 84
Angelica, N.Y., U.S. C2 139
Angelina, co., Tx., U.S. D5 150
Angels Camp, Ca., U.S. C3 112
Angereb, stm., Afr. K9 60
Angermünde, Ger. B14 10
Angers, Fr. E6 14
Angerville, Fr. D9 14
Angical, Braz. B6 79
Angicos, Braz. E11 76
Angier, N.C., U.S. B4 140
Angkor Wat, hist., Camb. H7 40
Ângk Tasaôm, Camb. I8 40
Angle Inlet, Mn., U.S. A3 130
Anglesey, i., Wales, U.K. H9 8
Angleton, Tx., U.S. E5 150
Angling Lake, l., Man., Can. C5 100
Angmagssalik, Grnld. C16 86
Angoche, Moz. E7 58
Angoche, Ilha, i., Moz. E7 58
Angol, Chile I2 80
Angola, In., U.S. A8 121
Angola, N.Y., U.S. C1 139
Angola, ctry., Afr. D3 58
Angola Swamp, sw., N.C., U.S. C5 140
Angoon, Ak., U.S. D13 109
Angora see Ankara, Tur. B2 48
Angoram, Pap. N. Gui. F11 38
Angostura, Mex. E5 90
Angostura, Presa de la, res., Mex. I13 90
Angostura Reservoir, res., S.D., U.S. D2 148
Angoulême, Fr. G7 14
Angoumois, hist. reg., Fr. G6 14
Angra dos Reis, Braz. G6 79
Angren, U.S.S.R. I12 22
Angualasto, Arg. F4 80
Anguciana, Cerro, mtn., C.R. I11 92
Anguilla, Ms., U.S. C3 131
Anguilla, dep., N.A. E13 94
Anguilla Cays, is., Bah. C5 94
Anguille, Cape, c., Newf., Can. E2 102
Anguo, China E3 32
Angusville, Man., Can. D1 100
Anhai, China K7 34
Anhanduí, stm., Braz. F1 79
Anhanguera, Braz. E4 79
Anhui (Anhwei), prov., China E10 30
Aniak, Ak., U.S. C8 109
Aniche, Fr. H3 12
Anicuns, Braz. D4 79
Anié, Togo H10 64
Animas, N.M., U.S. F1 138
Animas, stm., U.S. D3 113
Animas, Cerro de las, mtn., Ur. H11 80
Animas Mountains, mts., N.M., U.S. F1 138
Animas Peak, mtn., N.M., U.S. F2 138
Animas Valley, val., N.M., U.S. F1 138
Anina, Rom. D5 20
Anita, Ia., U.S. C3 122
Anita, Pa., U.S. D4 145
Aniva, zaliv, b., U.S.S.R. H20 24
Anivorano, Madag. Q23 67b
Anjangaon, India B4 46
Anjār, India I4 44
ʻAnjar, Leb. A5 50
Anji, China E8 34
Anjiabe, Madag. N23 67b
Anjiang, China C5 32
Anjou, Que., Can. p19 104
Anjou, hist. reg., Fr. E6 14
Anju, N. Kor. D13 32
Ankang, China E8 30
Ankara, Tur. B2 48
Ankaratra, mts., Madag. Q22 67b
Ankarimbelo, Madag. S22 67b
Ankasakasa, Madag. P21 67b
Ankavandra, Madag. Q21 67b
Ankazoabo, Madag. S21 67b
Ankazobe, Madag. Q22 67b
Ankazomiriotra, Madag. Q22 67b
Ankeny, Ia., U.S. C4 122
Ankilimalinika, Madag. S20 67b
Ankisabe, Madag. Q22 67b
Ankleshwar, India B2 46
Ankober, Eth. G8 56
Ankou, China J2 34
An'kovo, U.S.S.R. E22 26

Name	Map Ref.	Page
Ankpa, Nig.	H13	64
Anliu, China	L4	34
Anlu, China	D2	34
Ann, Cape, c., Ant.	B4	73
Ann, Cape, c., Ma., U.S.	A6	128
Anna, Il., U.S.	F4	120
Anna, Oh., U.S.	B1	142
Anna, Lake, res., Va., U.S.	B5	153
Annaba (Bône), Alg.	B14	62
Annabella, Ut., U.S.	E3	151
Annaberg-Buchholz, Ger.	E13	10
An-Nabk, Syria	D4	48
An-Nafī, Sau. Ar.	B3	47
An-Nafūd, des., Sau. Ar.	G6	48
An-Najaf, Iraq	F8	48
An-Nakhl, Egypt	C7	60
Anna Maria, Fl., U.S.	p10	116
Anna Maria Island, i., Fl., U.S.	q10	116
Annamitique, Chaîne, mts., Asia	F9	40
Annandale, Austl.	C8	70
Annandale, Mn., U.S.	E4	130
Annandale, N.J., U.S.	B3	137
Annandale, Va., U.S.	g12	153
Annapolis, In., U.S.	E3	121
Annapolis, Md., U.S.	C5	127
Annapolis, Mo., U.S.	D7	132
Annapolis, stm., N.S., Can.	E4	101
Annapolis Junction, Md., U.S.	B4	127
Annapolis Royal, N.S., Can.	E4	101
Annapūrna, mtn., Nepal	F10	44
Ann Arbor, Mi., U.S.	F7	129
Anna Regina, Guy.	D13	84
An-Nāsirīyah, Iraq	F9	48
An-Nāsirīyah, Syria	A7	50
Annawan, Il., U.S.	B4	120
An-Nawfalāb, Sud.	J7	60
Anne Arundel, co., Md., U.S.	B4	127
Annecy, Fr.	G13	14
Annemasse, Fr.	F13	14
Annenskij Most, U.S.S.R.	A20	26
An Nhon, Viet.	H10	40
Anniston, Al., U.S.	B4	108
Anniston, Mo., U.S.	E8	132
Annobón, i., Eq. Gui.	B1	58
Annonay, Fr.	G11	14
An-Nuhūd, Sud.	K5	60
An-Nu'māniyah, Iraq	E8	48
Annursnack Hill, hill, Ma., U.S.	g10	128
Annville, Ky., U.S.	C6	124
Annville, Pa., U.S.	F8	145
Anoka, Mn., U.S.	E5	130
Anoka, co., Mn., U.S.	E5	130
Anopino, U.S.S.R.	F23	26
Anori, Braz.	I12	84
Anorí, Col.	D5	84
Anping, China	D4	32
Anpu, China	D11	40
Anqing, China	E6	34
Anqiu, China	G7	32
Ansbach, Ger.	F10	10
Anse-d'Hainault, Haiti	E7	94
Anselmo, Ne., U.S.	C6	134
Anserma, Col.	E5	84
Anshan, China	B10	32
Anshun, China	A8	40
Ansina, Ur.	F11	80
Ansley, Ms., U.S.	E4	131
Ansley, Ne., U.S.	C6	134
Anson, Me., U.S.	D3	126
Anson, Tx., U.S.	C3	150
Anson, co., N.C., U.S.	B2	140
Ansŏng, S. Kor.	F15	32
Ansongo, Mali	D10	64
Ansonia, Ct., U.S.	D3	114
Ansonia, Oh., U.S.	B1	142
Ansonville, N.C., U.S.	B2	140
Ansted, W.V., U.S.	C3	155
Anta, Peru	E5	82
Anta, Cachoeira, wtfl, Braz.	B4	79
Anta, Cachoeira da, wtfl, Braz.	B11	82
Antabamba, Peru	F5	82
Antakya (Antioch), Tur.	C4	48
Antalaha, Madag.	O24	67b
Antalovcy, U.S.S.R.	G22	10
Antalya, Tur.	H14	4
Antalya Körfezi, b., Tur.	H14	4
Antambohobe, Madag.	S22	67b
Antanambao Manampotsy, Madag.	Q23	67b
Antananarivo, Madag.	Q22	67b
Antanetibe, Madag.	Q22	67b
Antanifotsy, Madag.	Q22	67b
Antarctica	D5	73
Antarctic Peninsula, pen., Ant.	B12	73
Antas, Rio das, stm., Braz.	E13	80
Antelope, Mt., U.S.	B12	133
Antelope, co., Ne., U.S.	B7	134
Antelope Butte, mtn., Wy., U.S.	B7	157
Antelope Creek, stm., Wy., U.S.	C7	157
Antelope Island, i., Ut., U.S.	B3	151
Antelope Mine, Zimb.	C9	66
Antelope Peak, mtn., Nv., U.S.	B7	135
Antelope Range, mts., Nv., U.S.	D7	135
Antelope Reservoir, res., Or., U.S.	E9	144
Antelope Wash, val., Nv., U.S.	D5	135
Antequera, Bol.	H8	82
Antequera, Para.	C10	80
Antequera, Spain	H7	16
Antero, Mount, mtn., Co., U.S.	C4	113
Antero Reservoir, res., Co., U.S.	C5	113
Antevamena, Madag.	R21	67b
Anthon, Ia., U.S.	B2	122
Anthony, Fl., U.S.	C4	116
Anthony, Ks., U.S.	E5	123
Anthony, N.M., U.S.	F3	138
Anthony, R.I., U.S.	D3	146
Anthony, Tx., U.S.	o11	150
Anthony Creek, stm., W.V., U.S.	D4	155
Anti-Atlas, mts., Mor.	E6	62
Antibes, Fr.	I14	14
Anticosti, Île d', i., Que., Can.	k14	104
Antietam Creek, stm., Md., U.S.	B2	127
Antietam National Battlefield, hist., Md., U.S.	B2	127
Antigo, Wi., U.S.	C4	156
Antigonish, N.S., Can.	D8	101
Antigua, i., Antig.	F14	94
Antigua and Barbuda, ctry., N.A.	F14	94
Antigua Guatemala, Guat.	C4	92
Antiguo Morelos, Mex.	F10	90
Anti-Lebanon see Sharqī, Al-Jabal ash-, mts., Asia	A6	50
Antilla, Arg.	D6	80
Antilla, Cuba	D7	94
Antimari, stm., Braz.	C8	82
Antioch, Ca., U.S.	h9	112
Antioch, Il., U.S.	A5	120
Antioch see Antakya, Tur.	C4	48
Antioquia, Col.	D5	84
Antioquia, dept., Col.	D5	84
Antipodes Islands, is., N.Z.	M21	158
Antisana, vol., Ec.	H3	84
Antlers, Ok., U.S.	C6	143
Antofagasta, Chile	B3	80
Antofagasta, prov., Chile	B4	80
Antofagasta de la Sierra, Arg.	D5	80
Antofalla, Salar de, pl., Arg.	C5	80
Antofalla, Volcán, vol., Arg.	C5	80
Antoine, Ar., U.S.	C2	111
Antón, Pan.	C2	84
Anton, Tx., U.S.	C1	150
Anton Chico, N.M., U.S.	B4	138
Antongila, Helodrano, b., Madag.	O23	67b
Antonia, Mo., U.S.	C7	132
Antonina, Braz.	C14	80
Antonio Amaro, Mex.	E7	90
Antônio João, Braz.	G1	79
Antônio Prado, Braz.	E13	80
Antonito, Co., U.S.	D5	113
Antón Lizardo, Punta, c., Mex.	H12	90
Antopol', U.S.S.R.	I7	26
Antora Peak, mtn., Co., U.S.	C4	113
Antou, China	I7	34
Antrain, Fr.	D5	14
Antrim, N. Ire., U.K.	G7	8
Antrim, N.H., U.S.	D3	136
Antrim, co., Mi., U.S.	C5	129
Antrodoco, Italy	G8	18
Antropovo, U.S.S.R.	C26	26
Antsalova, Madag.	Q21	67b
Antsenavolo, Madag.	R23	67b
Antsiafabositra, Madag.	P22	67b
Antsirabe, Madag.	O23	67b
Antsirabe, Madag.	Q22	67b
Antsiranana, Madag.	N23	67b
Antsla, U.S.S.R.	D9	26
Antsohihy, Madag.	O22	67b
Antuševo, U.S.S.R.	B20	26
Antwerp, Oh., U.S.	A1	142
Antwerp see Antwerpen, Bel.	F5	12
Antwerpen (Anvers), Bel.	F5	12
Antwerpen, prov., Bel.	F6	12
Anugul, India	B8	46
Anuradhapura, Sri L.	H6	46
Anvers (Antwerpen), Bel.	F5	12
Anvers Island, i., Ant.	B12	73
Anxi, China	C6	30
Anxi, China	J7	34
Anxin, China	E3	32
Anyama, I.C.	I7	64
Anyang, China	G2	32
A'nyêmaqên Shan, mts., China	D6	30
Anyi, China	G4	34
Anykščiai, U.S.S.R.	F8	26
Anyuan, China	H2	34
Anzac, Alta., Can.	A5	98
Anzaldo, Bol.	G9	82
Anžero-Sudžensk, U.S.S.R.	F15	22
Anzhen, China	D9	34
Anzhou, China	E3	32
Anzin, Fr.	B10	14
Anzio, Italy	H7	18
Anzoátegui, state, Ven.	C10	84
Anžu, ostrova, is., U.S.S.R.	B20	24
Aoga-shima, i., Japan	E14	30
Aohan Qi (Xinhui), China	A7	32
Aoji, N. Kor.	A18	32
Aojiang, China	H9	34
Aojiao, China	L6	34
Aomori, Japan	G15	36
Aôös (Vijosë), stm., Eur.	J4	20
Aôral, Phnum, mtn., Camb.	H8	40
Aosta, Italy	D2	18
Aotou, China	M3	34
Aouderas, Niger	C14	64
Aouk, Bahr, stm., Afr.	G5	56
Aoukâr, reg., Maur.	B5	64
Aourou, Mali	D4	64
Aozou, Chad	D4	56
Apa, stm., S.A.	B10	80
Apache, Ok., U.S.	C3	143
Apache, co., Az., U.S.	B6	110
Apache Junction, Az., U.S.	m9	110
Apache Peak, mtn., Az., U.S.	F5	110
Apalachee, Ga., U.S.	C3	117
Apalachee Bay, b., Fl., U.S.	B2	116
Apalachicola, Fl., U.S.	C2	116
Apalachicola, stm., Fl., U.S.	B1	116
Apalachicola Bay, b., Fl., U.S.	C2	116
Apalachin, N.Y., U.S.	C4	139
Apanas, Laguna de, res., Nic.	D9	92
Apaporis, stm., S.A.	H7	84
Aparados da Serra, Parque Nacional dos, Braz.	E13	80
Aparri, Phil.	L19	39b
Apartadó, Col.	D4	84
Apaseo El Grande, Mex.	G9	90
Apatin, Yugo.	D2	20
Apatity, U.S.S.R.	D4	22
Apatzingán de la Constitución, Mex.	H8	90
Apaxtla de Castrejón, Mex.	H10	90
Ape, U.S.S.R.	D9	26
Apediá, stm., Braz.	E8	82
Apeldoorn, Neth.	D8	12
Apennines see Appennino, mts., Italy	F7	18
Apex, N.C., U.S.	B4	140
Api, mtn., Nepal	F9	44
Apía, Col.	E5	84
Apia, W. Sam.	G1	2
Apiacá, Braz.	F8	79
Apiacá, stm., Braz.	C13	82
Apiacás, Serra dos, plat., Braz.	D13	82
Apiaí, Braz.	C14	80
Apiaú, stm., Braz.	F12	84
Apisancho, stm., Peru	B3	82
Apishapa, stm., Co., U.S.	D6	113
Apison, Tn., U.S.	h11	149
Apizaco, Mex.	H10	90
Apizolaya, Mex.	E8	90
Aplahoué, Benin	H10	64
Aplao, Peru	G5	82
Aplin, Ar., U.S.	C3	111
Aplington, Ia., U.S.	B5	122
Apo, Mount, mtn., Phil.	D8	38
Apohaqui, N.B., Can.	D4	101
Apolakkiá, Grc.	M11	20
Apolda, Ger.	D11	10
Apolinario Saravia, Arg.	C6	80
Apollo, Pa., U.S.	E2	145
Apolo, Bol.	F7	82
Apón, stm., Ven.	B6	84
Aponguao, stm., Ven.	E12	84
Apopa, El Sal.	D5	92
Apopka, Fl., U.S.	D5	116
Apopka, Lake, l., Fl., U.S.	D5	116
Aporé, Braz.	E2	79
Aporé, stm., Braz.	E3	79
Apostle Islands, is., Wi., U.S.	A3	156
Apostle Islands National Lakeshore, Wi., U.S.	A3	156
Apóstoles, Arg.	D11	80
Apostolovo, U.S.S.R.	H4	22
Appalachia, Va., U.S.	f9	153
Appalachian Mountains, mts., N.A.	C11	106
Appanoose, co., Ia., U.S.	D5	122
Appennino (Apennines), mts., Italy	F7	18
Appenzell, Switz.	D11	13
Appenzell-Ausser Rhoden, state, Switz.	D11	13
Apple, stm., Wi., U.S.	C1	156
Apple Creek, Oh., U.S.	B4	142
Applegate, Or., U.S.	E3	144
Applegate, stm., Or., U.S.	E3	144
Apple Grove, W.V., U.S.	C2	155
Apple Hill, Ont., Can.	B10	103
Apple Orchard Mountain, mtn., Va., U.S.	C3	153
Apple River, N.S., Can.	D5	101
Apple River, Il., U.S.	A3	120
Appleton, Ar., U.S.	B3	111
Appleton, Me., U.S.	E2	130
Appleton, Wi., U.S.	D5	156
Appleton City, Mo., U.S.	C3	132
Apple Valley, Ca., U.S.	E5	112
Apple Valley, Mn., U.S.	n12	130
Applewood, Co., U.S.	B5	113
Appleyard, Wa., U.S.	B5	154
Appling, Ga., U.S.	C4	117
Appling, co., Ga., U.S.	E4	117
Appomattox, Va., U.S.	C4	153
Appomattox, co., Va., U.S.	C4	153
Appomattox, stm., Va., U.S.	C4	153
Appomattox Court House National Historical Park, Va., U.S.	C4	153
Aprelevka, U.S.S.R.	F20	26
Apšeronskij poluostrov, pen., U.S.S.R.	A11	48
Apsley, Ont., Can.	C6	103
Apt, Fr.	I12	14
Apua Point, c., Hi., U.S.	D6	118
Apuaú, stm., Braz.	I12	84
Apucarana, Braz.	G3	79
Apure, state, Ven.	D8	84
Apure, stm., Ven.	D9	84
Apurímac, dept., Peru	E5	82
Apurímac, stm., Peru	E5	82
Apurito, Ven.	D8	84
Aqaba, Gulf of, b.	C8	60
'Aqīq, Sud.	H10	60
Aquarius Mountains, mts., Az., U.S.	C2	110
Aquarius Plateau, plat., Ut., U.S.	E4	151
Aquidabã, stm., Braz.	I13	82
Aquidabán, stm., Para.	B10	80
Aquidauana, Braz.	I14	82
Aquidauana, stm., Braz.	I14	82
Aquila, Mex.	H8	90
Aquila, Switz.	E10	13
Aquiles Serdán, Mex.	C7	90
Aquiles Serdán, Mex.	E11	90
Aquin, Haiti	E8	94
Aquitania, Col.	F9	84
Ara, India	H11	44
Arab, Al., U.S.	A3	108
'Arab, Bahr al-, stm., Sud.	M4	60
Arab, Shatt al-, stm., Asia	G10	48
'Arabah, Wādī al-, val., Jord.	C5	50
'Arabah, Wādī al- (Ha'Arava), val., Asia	G4	50
Arabako, prov., Spain	C9	16
Arabelo, Ven.	E10	84
Arabi, Ga., U.S.	E3	117
Arabi, La., U.S.	k11	125
Arabian Desert see Sharqīyah, As-Sahrā' ash-, des., Egypt	D7	60
Arabian Gulf see Persian Gulf, b., Asia	H11	48
Arabian Peninsula, pen., Asia	G5	28
Arabian Sea	H7	28
Araçá, stm., Braz.	G11	84
Aracaju, Braz.	F11	76
Aracataca, Col.	B5	84
Aracati, Braz.	D11	76
Araçatuba, Braz.	F3	79
Aracena, Spain	H5	16
Aracruz, Braz.	E8	79
Aracu, stm., Braz.	J13	84
Araçuaí, Braz.	D7	79
Araçuaí, stm., Braz.	D7	79
Arad, Rom.	C5	20
Arad, co., Rom.	C5	20
Arada, Hond.	C6	92
Arafura Sea	I17	158
Aragarças, Braz.	C2	79
Arago, Cape, c., Or., U.S.	D2	144
Aragoiânia, Braz.	D4	79
Aragon, Ga., U.S.	B1	117
Aragon, N.M., U.S.	D1	138
Aragón, prov., Spain	D10	16
Aragón, stm., Spain	C10	16
Aragua, state, Ven.	B9	84
Araguacema, Braz.	E9	76
Araguaçu, Braz.	B4	79
Aragua de Barcelona, Ven.	C10	84
Aragua de Maturín, Ven.	C11	84
Araguaia, stm., Braz.	E9	76
Araguaia, Braço Menor, stm., Braz.	B3	79
Araguainha, Braz.	D2	79
Araguao, Caño, mth., Ven.	C12	84
Araguari, Braz.	E4	79
Araguari, stm., Braz.	C8	76
Araguari, stm., Braz.	E4	79
Araguatins, Braz.	E9	76
Ārak, Alg.	H12	62
Arāk, Iran	D10	48
Arakan Yoma, mts., Burma	E3	40
Árakhthos, stm., Grc.	J4	20
Araks (Aras), stm., Asia	B10	48
Aral Sea see Aral'skoje more, U.S.S.R.	H10	22
Aral'sk, U.S.S.R.	H10	22
Aral'skoje more (Aral Sea), U.S.S.R.	H10	22
Aramac, Austl.	D6	70
Aramac, stm., Austl.	D6	70
Aramari, Braz.	B9	79
Arambaza, Col.	I6	84
Aramberri, Mex.	E10	90
Arampampa, Bol.	G8	82
Aramtalla, Sud.	N5	60
Ārān, Iran	D11	48
Aranda de Duero, Spain	D8	16
Arandas, Mex.	G8	90
Aranđelovac, Yugo.	E4	20
Arandis, Nmb.	D2	66
Arani, Bol.	G9	82
Aran Islands, is., Ire.	H4	8
Aranjuez, Spain	E8	16
Aransas, co., Tx., U.S.	E4	150
Aransas Bay, b., Tx., U.S.	E4	150
Aransas Pass, Tx., U.S.	F4	150
Aranyaprathet, Thai.	H7	40
Arao, Japan	O5	36
Araouane, Mali	E6	54
Arapa, Laguna, l., Peru	F6	82
Arapaho, Ok., U.S.	B3	143
Arapahoe, N.C., U.S.	C8	113
Arapahoe, Ne., U.S.	D6	134
Arapahoe, N.C., U.S.	B6	140
Arapahoe, co., Co., U.S.	B6	113
Arapey, Ur.	F10	80
Arapey Chico, stm., Ur.	F10	80
Arapey Grande, stm., Ur.	F10	80
Arapiraca, Braz.	E11	76
Arapkir, Tur.	B5	48
Arapongas, Braz.	G3	79
Arapoti, Braz.	H4	79
Araquari, Braz.	D14	80
'Ar'ar, Sau. Ar.	F6	48
'Ar'ar, Wādī, val., Asia	B11	60
Araranguá, Braz.	E14	80
Araraquara, Braz.	F4	79
Araras, Braz.	G5	79
Ararat, Austl.	K5	70
Ararat, U.S.S.R.	B8	48
Ararat, Mount see Ağrı Dağı, mtn., Tur.	B8	48
Araríra, stm., Braz.	H10	84
Araruama, Lagoa de, b., Braz.	G7	79
Aras (Araks), stm., Asia	B10	48
Aratiba, Braz.	D12	80
Áratos, Grc.	H9	20
Aratuípe, Braz.	B9	79
Arauá, stm., Braz.	C9	82
Arauá, stm., Braz.	A11	82
Arauá, stm., Braz.	J10	84
Arauca, Col.	D7	84
Arauca, dept., Col.	D7	84
Arauca, stm., S.A.	D9	84
Araucária, Braz.	C14	80
Arauco, Chile	I2	80
Arauco, Golfo de, b., Chile	I2	80
Araújos, Braz.	E6	79
Arauquita, Col.	D7	84
Araure, Ven.	C8	84
Arāvalli Range, mts., India	H5	44
Araxá, Braz.	E5	79
Araya, Ven.	B10	84
Araya, Punta de, c., Ven.	B10	84
Arba Minch, Eth.	N9	60
Arboga, Swe.	L14	6
Arbois, Fr.	F12	14
Arboledas, Arg.	I8	80
Arboletes, Col.	C4	84
Arbon, Switz.	C11	13
Arborfield, Sask., Can.	D4	105
Arborg, Man., Can.	D3	100
Arbroath, Scot., U.K.	E11	8
Arbuckle, Ca., U.S.	C2	112
Arbuckle, Lake, l., Fl., U.S.	E5	116
Arbuckle Mountains, mts., Ok., U.S.	C4	143
Arbuckles, Lake of the, res., Ok., U.S.	C5	143
Arbyrd, Mo., U.S.	E7	132
Arc, Bayou des, stm., Ar., U.S.	B4	111
Arcachon, Fr.	H5	14
Arcade, Ca., U.S.	c3	112
Arcade, Ga., U.S.	B3	117
Arcade, N.Y., U.S.	C2	139
Arcadia, N.S., Can.	F3	101
Arcadia, Ca., U.S.	m12	112
Arcadia, Fl., U.S.	E5	116
Arcadia, In., U.S.	D5	121
Arcadia, Ia., U.S.	B2	122
Arcadia, Ks., U.S.	E9	123
Arcadia, La., U.S.	B3	125
Arcadia, Mi., U.S.	D4	129
Arcadia, Mo., U.S.	D7	132
Arcadia, Ne., U.S.	C6	134
Arcadia, Oh., U.S.	A2	142
Arcadia, Ok., U.S.	B4	143
Arcadia, S.C., U.S.	B4	147
Arcadia, Wi., U.S.	D2	156
Arcângelo, Braz.	F6	79
Arcanum, Oh., U.S.	C1	142
Arcas, Cayos, is., Mex.	G14	90
Arcata, Ca., U.S.	B1	112
Arcatao, El Sal.	C6	92
Arc Dome, mtn., Nv., U.S.	E4	135
Arcelia, Mex.	H9	90
Archambault, Lac, l., Que., Can.	C3	104
Archangel'sk, U.S.S.R.	E6	22
Archbald, Pa., U.S.	m18	145
Archbold, Oh., U.S.	A1	142
Archdale, N.C., U.S.	B3	140
Archer, Fl., U.S.	C4	116
Archer, co., Tx., U.S.	C3	150
Archer City, Tx., U.S.	C3	150
Archerwill, Sask., Can.	E4	105
Arches National Park, Ut., U.S.	E6	151
Archidona, Spain	H7	16
Archie, Mo., U.S.	C3	132
Archipovka, U.S.S.R.	E24	26
Archuleta, co., Co., U.S.	D3	113
Arciz, U.S.S.R.	C13	20
Arco, Id., U.S.	F5	119
Arcola, Sask., Can.	H4	105
Arcola, Il., U.S.	D5	120
Arcola, Ms., U.S.	B3	131
Arcola, Va., U.S.	g11	153
Arcos, Braz.	F6	79
Arcos de la Frontera, Spain	I6	16
Arcot, India	F5	46
Arcoverde, Braz.	E11	76
Arctic Bay, N.W. Ter., Can.	B15	96
Arctic Ocean	A1	86
Arctic Red, stm., N.W. Ter., Can.	C6	96
Arctowski, sci., B.A.T.	B1	73
Arcturus, Zimb.	A10	66
Arda, stm., Eur.	H9	20
Ardabīl, Iran	B10	48
Ardahan, Tur.	G16	4
Ardakān, Iran	F12	48
Ardakān, Iran	E12	48
Ardalstangen, Nor.	K10	6
Ardatov, U.S.S.R.	F26	26
Ardèche, dept., Fr.	H11	14
Arden, Man., Can.	D2	100
Arden, Ont., Can.	C8	103
Arden, Ar., U.S.	D1	111
Arden, Mount, mtn., Austl.	I2	70
Ardennes, dept., Fr.	C11	14
Ardennes, reg., Eur.	E5	10
Ardestān, Iran	E12	48
Ardila, stm., Eur.	G4	16
Ardino, Bul.	H9	20
Ardlethan, Austl.	J7	70
Ardmore, Alta., Can.	B5	98
Ardmore, Al., U.S.	A3	108
Ardmore, In., U.S.	A5	121
Ardmore, Ok., U.S.	C4	143
Ardmore, Pa., U.S.	F11	145
Ardmore, Tn., U.S.	B5	149
Ardoch, Austl.	F6	70
Ardrossan, Alta., Can.	C4	98
Ardsley, N.Y., U.S.	g13	139
Åre, Swe.	J13	6
Areado, Braz.	F5	79
Arecibo, P.R.	E11	94
Areguá, Para.	C10	80
Areia, Ribeirão da, stm., Braz.	C6	79
Areia Branca, Braz.	D11	76
Arena, Wi., U.S.	E4	156
Arena, Point, c., Ca., U.S.	C2	112
Arena, Punta, c., Mex.	F5	90
Arenac, co., Mi., U.S.	D7	129
Arena de la Ventana, Punta, c., Mex.	E5	90
Arenal, C.R.	G10	92
Arenal, Laguna de, l., C.R.	G10	92
Arenal, Volcán, vol., C.R.	G10	92
Arenápolis, Braz.	F13	82
Arenas, Cayo, i., Mex.	F14	90
Arenas, Punta, c., Chile	I6	82
Arenas Valley, N.M., U.S.	E1	138
Arendal, Nor.	L11	6
Arendtsville, Pa., U.S.	G7	145
Arenillas, Ec.	I2	84
Arenys de Mar, Spain	D14	16
Arenzville, Il., U.S.	D3	120
Arequipa, Peru	G6	82
Arequipa, dept., Peru	F5	82
Arequito, Arg.	G8	80
Arès, Fr.	H5	14
Arezzo, Italy	F6	18
Argadargada, Austl.	C2	70
Arganda, Spain	E8	16
Arga-Sala, stm., U.S.S.R.	D13	24
Argelès-Gazost, Fr.	I7	14
Argelès-sur-Mer, Fr.	J10	14
Argenta, Italy	E6	18
Argenta, Il., U.S.	D5	120
Argentan, Fr.	D6	14
Argentat, Fr.	G8	14
Argentera, mtn., Italy	E2	18
Argentina, ctry., S.A.	C4	78
Argentino, Lago, l., Arg.	G2	78
Argenton-Château, Fr.	F6	14
Argenton-sur-Creuse, Fr.	F8	14
Argeș, co., Rom.	E8	20
Argeș, stm., Rom.	E9	20
Arghandāb, stm., Afg.	D2	44
Argirita, Braz.	F7	79
Argo, Sud.	H6	60
Argo, Al., U.S.	B3	108
Argo, Ky., U.S.	C7	124
Argo Corner, De., U.S.	E4	115
Argolikós Kólpos, b., Grc.	L6	20
Argonia, Ks., U.S.	E6	123
Argonne, Wi., U.S.	C5	156
Argonne, reg., Fr.	C12	14
Árgos, Grc.	L6	20
Argos, In., U.S.	B5	121
Argostólion, Grc.	K4	20
Arguello, Point, c., Ca., U.S.	E3	112
Argun' (Ergun), stm., Asia	G16	24
Argusville, N.D., U.S.	B9	141
Argyle, N.S., Can.	F4	101
Argyle, Ga., U.S.	E4	117
Argyle, Mn., U.S.	B2	130
Argyle, Mo., U.S.	C5	132
Argyle, N.Y., U.S.	F4	156
Argyle, Wi., U.S.	F4	156
Argyle, Lake, res., Austl.	C5	68
Århus, Den.	M12	6
Ariana, Tun.	M5	18
Ariano Irpino, Italy	H10	18
Ariari, stm., Col.	F6	84
Arias, Arg.	G7	80
Ariaú, Braz.	I14	84
Aribinda, Burkina	D9	64
Arica, Chile	H6	82
Arica, Col.	I7	84
Arichat, N.S., Can.	D8	101
Arichuna, Ven.	D9	84
Arid, Cape, c., Austl.	F4	68
Ariège, dept., Fr.	J8	14
Ariguaní, stm., Col.	C6	84
Arīhā (Jericho), Isr. Occ.	E4	50
Arīhā, Jord.	F5	50
Arikaree, stm., U.S.	B8	113
Arima, Trin.	I14	94
Arimo, Id., U.S.	G6	119
Arinos, stm., Braz.	D12	82
Ario de Rosales, Mex.	H9	90
Ariogala, U.S.S.R.	F6	26
Ariporo, stm., Col.	D7	84
Aripuanã, Braz.	C11	82
Aripuanã, stm., Braz.	B11	82
Ariquemes, Braz.	C10	82
Arisa, stm., Ven.	D10	84
'Arīsh, Wādī al-, val., Egypt	B7	60
Arismendi, Ven.	C8	84
Aristazabal Island, i., B.C., Can.	C3	99
Ariton, Al., U.S.	D4	108
Arivaca, Az., U.S.	F4	110
Arivonimamo, Madag.	Q22	67b
Arizaro, Salar de, pl., Arg.	C5	80
Arizgoiti, Spain	B9	16
Arizona, Arg.	H6	80
Arizona, state, U.S.	C4	110
Arizona Sunsites, Az., U.S.	F6	110
Arizpe, Mex.	B4	90
Arjay, Ky., U.S.	D6	124
Arjeplog, Swe.	H15	6
Arjona, Col.	B5	84
Arkabutla, Ms., U.S.	A3	131
Arkabutla Lake, res., Ms., U.S.	A4	131
Arkadelphia, Ar., U.S.	C2	111
Arkalyk, U.S.S.R.	G11	22
Arkansas, co., Ar., U.S.	C4	111
Arkansas, state, U.S.	C3	111
Arkansas, stm., U.S.	D8	106
Arkansas, Salt Fork, stm., U.S.	A3	143
Arkansas City, Ar., U.S.	D4	111
Arkansas City, Ks., U.S.	E6	123
Arklow, Ire.	I7	8
Arkoma, Ok., U.S.	B7	143
Arkona, Ont., Can.	D3	103
Arkona, Kap, c., Ger.	A13	10
Arktičeskij, mys, c., U.S.S.R.	A11	24
Arktičeskogo Instituta, ostrova, is., U.S.S.R.	B14	24
Arkwright, Ga., U.S.	D3	117
Arlberg pass, Aus.	D13	13
Arlberg-Tunnel, Aus.	D13	13
Arlee, Mt., U.S.	C2	133
Arles, Fr.	I11	14
Arley, Al., U.S.	A2	108
Arli, Burkina	F10	64
Arlington, Az., U.S.	D3	110
Arlington, Ga., U.S.	E2	117
Arlington, Il., U.S.	B4	120
Arlington, In., U.S.	E6	121
Arlington, Ia., U.S.	B6	122
Arlington, Ks., U.S.	E5	123
Arlington, Ky., U.S.	f9	124
Arlington, La., U.S.	h9	125
Arlington, Ma., U.S.	B5	128
Arlington, Mn., U.S.	F4	130
Arlington, Ne., U.S.	C9	134
Arlington, N.Y., U.S.	D7	139
Arlington, N.C., U.S.	A2	140
Arlington, Oh., U.S.	B2	142
Arlington, Or., U.S.	B6	144
Arlington, S.C., U.S.	B3	147
Arlington, S.D., U.S.	C8	148
Arlington, Tn., U.S.	B2	149
Arlington, Tx., U.S.	n9	150
Arlington, Vt., U.S.	E2	152
Arlington, Va., U.S.	B5	153
Arlington, Wa., U.S.	A3	154
Arlington, Wi., U.S.	E4	156
Arlington, co., Va., U.S.	g12	153
Arlington, Lake, res., Tx., U.S.	n9	150
Arlington Heights, Il., U.S.	A5	120
Arlit, Niger	B13	64
Arm, stm., Sask., Can.	F3	105
Arma, Ks., U.S.	E9	123
Armada, Mi., U.S.	F8	129
Armageddon see Tel Megiddo, hist., Isr.	C4	50
Armagh, Que., Can.	C7	104
Armagh, N. Ire., U.K.	G7	8
Armagnac, hist. reg., Fr.	I7	14
Arm'anskaja Sovetskaja Socialističeskaja Respublika, state, U.S.S.R.	I6	22
Armant, Egypt	E7	60
Armavir, U.S.S.R.	H6	22
Armazém, Braz.	E14	80
Armenia, Col.	E5	84
Armenia see Arm'anskaja Sovetskaja Socialističeskaja Respublika, state, U.S.S.R.	I6	22
Armentières, Fr.	B9	14
Armería, Mex.	H8	90
Armero, Col.	E5	84
Armidale, Austl.	H9	70
Armijo, N.M., U.S.	k7	138
Armington, Il., U.S.	C4	120
Armington, Mt., U.S.	C6	133
Armorel, Ar., U.S.	B6	111
Armour, S.D., U.S.	D7	148
Armstrong, Arg.	G8	80
Armstrong, B.C., Can.	D8	99
Armstrong, Il., U.S.	C6	120
Armstrong, Ia., U.S.	A3	122
Armstrong, Mo., U.S.	B5	132
Armstrong, co., Pa., U.S.	E2	145
Armstrong, co., Tx., U.S.	B2	150
Armstrong Creek, stm., W.V., U.S.	m13	155
Armuchee, Ga., U.S.	B1	117
Armaudville, La., U.S.	D4	125
Arnay-le-Duc, Fr.	E11	14
Arnedo, Spain	C9	16

Name	Map Ref.	Page
Arnegard, N.D., U.S.	B2	141
Årnes, Nor.	K12	6
Arnett, Ok., U.S.	A2	143
Arnett, W.V., U.S.	D3	155
Arnhem, Neth.	E8	12
Arnhem, Cape, c., Austl.	B7	68
Arnhem Land, reg., Austl.	B6	68
Árnissa, Grc.	I5	20
Arno, stm., Italy	F5	18
Arno Bay, Austl.	I2	70
Arnold, Ca., U.S.	C3	112
Arnold, Md., U.S.	B5	127
Arnold, Mn., U.S.	D6	130
Arnold, Mo., U.S.	C7	132
Arnold, Ne., U.S.	C5	134
Arnold, Pa., U.S.	h14	145
Arnold Mills, R.I., U.S.	B4	146
Arnold Mills Reservoir, res., R.I., U.S.	B4	146
Arnold's Cove, Newf., Can.	E4	102
Arnolds Park, Ia., U.S.	A2	122
Arnoldstein, Aus.	I13	10
Arnoldsville, Ga., U.S.	C3	117
Arnprior, Ont., Can.	B8	103
Arnsberg, Ger.	D8	10
Arnstadt, Ger.	E10	10
Arnstein, Ont., Can.	B5	103
Aro, stm., Ven.	D10	84
Aroa, Ven.	B8	84
Aroa, stm., Ven.	B8	84
Aroab, Nmb.	F4	66
Aroma, Sud.	J9	60
Aroma Park, Il., U.S.	B6	120
Arona, Italy	D3	18
Aroostook, N.B., Can.	C2	101
Aroostook, co., Me., U.S.	B4	126
Aros, stm., Mex.	C5	90
Arosa, Switz.	E12	13
Arpin, Wi., U.S.	D3	156
Arpoador, Ponta do, c., Braz.	C15	80
Arque, Bol.	G8	82
Ar-Rabad, Sau. Ar.	K8	47
Ar-Radīsīyah Baḥrī, Egypt	E7	60
Arraga, Arg.	E6	80
Ar-Rahad, Sud.	K6	60
Arraial do Cabo, Braz.	G7	79
Arraias, Braz.	B5	79
Arraias, stm., Braz.	A1	79
Arraias, stm., Braz.	B5	79
Ar-Ramādī, Iraq	E7	48
Ar-Ramthā, Jord.	C6	50
Arran, Sask., Can.	F5	105
Arran, Island of, i., Scot., U.K.	F8	8
Ar-Rank, Sud.	L7	60
Ar-Raqqah, Syria	D5	48
Arras, Fr.	B9	14
Ar-Rāshidah, Egypt	E5	60
Ar-Rass, Sau. Ar.	I7	48
Ar-Rawḍah, Sau. Ar.	H6	48
Ar-Rāwuk, Yemen	G6	47
Ar-Rayyān, Qatar	I11	48
Arrecife, Spain	O27	17b
Arrecifes, Arg.	H8	80
Arrey, N.M., U.S.	E2	138
Arriaga, Mex.	I13	90
Arriba, Co., U.S.	B7	113
Ar-Rimāh, Sau. Ar.	B5	47
Arrington, Va., U.S.	C4	153
Ar-Riyāḍ (Riyadh), Sau. Ar.	B5	47
Arroio Grande, Braz.	G12	80
Arrojado, stm., Braz.	B6	79
Arronches, Port.	F4	16
Arrow Creek, stm., Mt., U.S.	C6	133
Arrowhead Mountain Lake, res., Vt., U.S.	B2	152
Arrowrock Reservoir, res., Id., U.S.	F3	119
Arrowsmith, Il., U.S.	C5	120
Arrowsmith, Mount, mtn., Austl.	H4	70
Arrowwood, Alta., Can.	D4	98
Arrowwood Lake, res., N.D., U.S.	B7	141
Arroyito, Arg.	F7	80
Arroyo de la Luz, Spain	F5	16
Arroyo Grande, Ca., U.S.	E3	112
Arroyo Hondo, N.M., U.S.	A4	138
Arroyo Seco, N.M., U.S.	A4	138
Arroyos y Esteros, Para.	C10	80
Ar-Ru'at, Sud.	K7	60
Ar-Rub' al-Khālī (Empty Quarter), des., Asia	D7	47
Ar-Rukhaymīyah, well, Asia	G8	48
Ar-Rumaythah, Iraq	F8	48
Ar-Rummān, Jord.	D5	50
Ar-Ruṣayfah, Jord.	D6	50
Ar-Ruṣayriṣ, Sud.	L8	60
Ar-Ruṭbah, Iraq	E6	48
Ar-Ruways, Qatar	H11	48
Arsenjev, U.S.S.R.	I18	24
Arsenjevo, U.S.S.R.	H19	26
Árta, Grc.	J4	20
Artašat, U.S.S.R.	B8	48
Arteaga, Mex.	H8	90
Artemisa, Cuba	C3	94
Artémou, Maur.	D3	64
Artemus, Ky., U.S.	D6	124
Artenay, Fr.	D8	14
Arter, Mount, mtn., Wy., U.S.	D4	157
Artesia, Ms., U.S.	B5	131
Artesia, N.M., U.S.	E5	138
Artesian, S.D., U.S.	C8	148
Arth, Switz.	D10	13
Arthabaska, Que., Can.	C6	104
Arthur, Ont., Can.	D4	103
Arthur, Il., U.S.	D5	120
Arthur, Ia., U.S.	B2	122
Arthur, Ne., U.S.	C4	134
Arthur, N.D., U.S.	B8	141
Arthur, Tn., U.S.	C10	149
Arthur, co., Ne., U.S.	C4	134
Arthur, Lake, l., La., U.S.	D3	125
Arthur, Lake, res., Pa., U.S.	E1	145
Arthur Kill, stm., N.J., U.S.	k8	137
Arthur's Town, Bah.	B7	94
Artibonite, stm., Haiti	E8	94
Artigas, Ur.	F10	80
Artik, U.S.S.R.	A7	48
Artois, hist. reg., Fr.	B9	14
Art'om, U.S.S.R.	I18	24
Art'om-Ostrov, U.S.S.R.	A11	48
Art'omovsk, U.S.S.R.	G10	24
Art'omovskij, U.S.S.R.	F10	22
Artvin, Tur.	G16	4
Artyk, U.S.S.R.	E21	24
Aru, Kepulauan, is., Indon.	G9	38
Aruaddin, Eth.	I10	60
Aruanã, Braz.	C3	79
Aruba, dep., N.A.	H9	94
Arunāchal Pradesh, state, India	F16	44
Arundel, Que., Can.	D3	104
Aruppukkottai, India	H5	46
Arusha, Tan.	B7	58
Aruwimi, stm., Zaire	H6	56
Arvada, Co., U.S.	B5	113
Arvada, Wy., U.S.	B6	157
Arvajcheer, Mong.	B7	30
Arvi, India	B5	46
Arvidsjaur, Swe.	I16	6
Arvika, Swe.	L13	6
Arvilla, N.D., U.S.	B8	141
Arvin, Ca., U.S.	E4	112
Arvon, Mount, mtn., Mi., U.S.	B2	129
Arvonia, Va., U.S.	C4	153
Árvorezinha, Braz.	E12	80
Arxan, China	H15	24
Arys', U.S.S.R.	I11	22
Arzachena, Italy	H4	18
Arzamas, U.S.S.R.	F6	22
Arziw, Alg.	C10	62
Aš, Czech.	E12	10
Aša, U.S.S.R.	F9	22
Asa, stm., Ven.	D11	84
Asab, Nmb.	E3	66
Asad, Buḥayrat al-, res., Syria	C5	48
Asahikawa, Japan	D17	36a
Asamankese, Ghana	I9	64
Asansol, India	I12	44
Asbest, U.S.S.R.	F10	22
Asbestos, Que., Can.	D6	104
Asbury, Mo., U.S.	D3	132
Asbury Park, N.J., U.S.	C4	137
Ascensión, Mex.	B6	90
Ascension, co., La., U.S.	D5	125
Ascension, i., St. Hel.	I5	52
Aščhabad, U.S.S.R.	J9	22
Aschach an der Donau, Aus.	A9	18
Aschaffenburg, Ger.	F9	10
Aschersleben, Ger.	D11	10
Ascoli Piceno, Italy	G8	18
Ascona, Switz.	F10	13
Ascope, Peru	B2	82
Ascotán, Chile	A4	80
Ascutney, Vt., U.S.	E4	152
Ascutney, Mount, mtn., Vt., U.S.	E4	152
Aseb, Eth.	H3	47
Åseda, Swe.	M14	6
Asela, Eth.	N10	60
Åsele, Swe.	I15	6
Asendabo, Eth.	M9	60
Asenovgrad, Bul.	G8	20
Asfūn al-Maṭā'inah, Egypt	E7	60
Ashaway, R.I., U.S.	F1	146
Ashburn, Ga., U.S.	E3	117
Ashburn, Va., U.S.	A5	153
Ashburnham, Ma., U.S.	A4	128
Ashburton, N.Z.	E3	72
Ashburton, stm., Austl.	D3	68
Ashby, Al., U.S.	B3	108
Ashby, Mn., U.S.	D3	130
Ashby, Ne., U.S.	B4	134
Ashcroft, B.C., Can.	D7	99
Ashdod, Isr.	E3	50
Ashdot Ya'aqov, Isr.	C5	50
Ashdown, Ar., U.S.	D1	111
Ashe, co., N.C., U.S.	A1	140
Asheboro, N.C., U.S.	B3	140
Ashepoo, stm., S.C., U.S.	F6	147
Asher, Ok., U.S.	C5	143
Ashern, Man., Can.	D2	100
Asherton, Tx., U.S.	E3	150
Asheville, N.C., U.S.	f10	140
Ashfield, Ma., U.S.	A2	128
Ash Flat, Ar., U.S.	A4	111
Ashford, Austl.	G9	70
Ashford, Eng., U.K.	J13	8
Ashford, Al., U.S.	D4	108
Ashford, W.V., U.S.	m12	155
Ash Fork, Az., U.S.	B3	110
Ash Grove, Mo., U.S.	D4	132
Ashibetsu, Japan	D17	36a
Ashikaga, Japan	K14	36
Ashkum, Il., U.S.	C6	120
Ashland, Al., U.S.	B4	108
Ashland, Il., U.S.	D3	120
Ashland, Ks., U.S.	E4	123
Ashland, Ky., U.S.	B7	124
Ashland, La., U.S.	B2	125
Ashland, Me., U.S.	B4	126
Ashland, Ma., U.S.	g10	128
Ashland, Ms., U.S.	A4	131
Ashland, Mo., U.S.	C5	132
Ashland, Mt., U.S.	E10	133
Ashland, Ne., U.S.	C9	134
Ashland, N.H., U.S.	C3	136
Ashland, Oh., U.S.	B3	142
Ashland, Or., U.S.	E4	144
Ashland, Pa., U.S.	E9	145
Ashland, Va., U.S.	C5	153
Ashland, Wi., U.S.	B3	156
Ashland, co., Oh., U.S.	B3	142
Ashland, co., Wi., U.S.	B3	156
Ashland, Mount, mtn., Or., U.S.	E4	144
Ashland City, Tn., U.S.	A4	149
Ashland Reservoir, res., Ma., U.S.	h10	128
Ashley, Il., U.S.	E4	120
Ashley, In., U.S.	A7	121
Ashley, Mi., U.S.	E6	129
Ashley, N.D., U.S.	C6	141
Ashley, Oh., U.S.	B3	142
Ashley, Pa., U.S.	n17	145
Ashley, co., Ar., U.S.	D4	111
Ashley, stm., S.C., U.S.	F7	147
Ashley Creek, stm., Ut., U.S.	C6	151
Ashmont, Alta., Can.	B5	98
Ashmore, Il., U.S.	D5	120
Ashmore Islands, is., Austl.	B4	68
Ashmūn, Egypt	B6	60
Ashokan Reservoir, res., N.Y., U.S.	D6	139
Ashport, Tn., U.S.	B2	149
Ashqelon, Isr.	E3	50
Ash-Shajarah, Jord.	C5	50
Ash-Shaqrā', Sau. Ar.	B4	47
Ash-Shāriqah (Sharjah), U.A.E.	B9	47
Ash-Sharmah, Sau. Ar.	G3	48
Ash-Shaṭrah, Iraq	F9	48
Ash-Shawbak, Jord.	G5	50
Ash-Shawmarah, Leb.	B4	50
Ash-Shiḥr, Yemen	G6	47
Ash-Shufayyah, Sau. Ar.	C1	47
Ash-Shumlul, Sau. Ar.	H9	48
Ash-Shuqayq, Sau. Ar.	F3	47
Ash-Shurayf, Sau. Ar.	I5	48
Ash-Shurayk, Sud.	H7	60
Ashtabula, Oh., U.S.	A5	142
Ashtabula, co., Oh., U.S.	A5	142
Ashtabula, Lake, res., N.D., U.S.	B8	141
Ashton, Ont., Can.	B8	103
Ashton, S. Afr.	I5	66
Ashton, Id., U.S.	E7	119
Ashton, Il., U.S.	B4	120
Ashton, Ia., U.S.	A2	122
Ashton, Md., U.S.	B3	127
Ashton, Ne., U.S.	C7	134
Ashton, R.I., U.S.	B4	146
Ashton, S.D., U.S.	C7	148
Ashuanipi Lake, l., Newf., Can.	h8	102
Ashuelot, N.H., U.S.	E2	136
Ashuelot, stm., N.H., U.S.	E2	136
Ashville, Man., Can.	D1	100
Ashville, Al., U.S.	B3	108
Ashville, Oh., U.S.	C3	142
Ashwaubenon, Wi., U.S.	D5	156
Ashwood, Tn., U.S.	B4	149
Asi (Nahr al-'Āṣī), stm., Asia	C3	48
Asia	D11	28
Asia, Kepulauan, is., Indon.	E9	38
Asia Minor, hist. reg., Tur.	H14	4
Asilah, Mor.	C7	62
Asino, U.S.S.R.	F9	24
'Asīr, reg., Sau. Ar.	E2	47
Aşkale, Tur.	B6	48
Askew, Ms., U.S.	A3	131
Askham, S. Afr.	F5	66
Askov, Mn., U.S.	D6	130
Asmār, Afg.	C4	44
Asmera, Eth.	J10	60
Asnebumskit Hill, hill, Ma., U.S.	B4	128
Asola, Italy	D5	18
Asosa, Eth.	F7	56
Asotin, Wa., U.S.	C8	154
Asotin, co., Wa., U.S.	C8	154
Asotin Creek, stm., Wa., U.S.	C8	154
Asp, Spain	G11	16
Aspang Markt, Aus.	H16	10
Aspen, Co., U.S.	B4	113
Aspen Butte, mtn., Or., U.S.	E4	144
Aspen Hill, Md., U.S.	B3	127
Aspermont, Tx., U.S.	C2	150
Aspinwall, Pa., U.S.	k14	145
Aspres-sur-Buëch, Fr.	H12	14
Aspy Bay, b., N.S., Can.	C9	101
Asquith, Sask., Can.	E2	105
As-Sa'ata, Sud.	K5	60
Assabet, stm., Ma., U.S.	g9	128
As-Ṣaff, Egypt	C6	60
As-Saffānīyah, Sau. Ar.	H10	48
As-Ṣāfī, Jord.	F4	50
As-Ṣāfiyah, Sud.	J6	60
Assai, Braz.	G3	79
'Assāl al-Ward, Syria	A6	50
As-Sallūm, Egypt	B3	60
As-Salṭ, Jord.	D5	50
Assam, state, India	G15	44
As-Samāwah, Iraq	F8	48
Assaria, Ks., U.S.	D6	123
Aş-Şarīḥ, Jord.	C5	50
Assateague Island, i., U.S.	D7	127
Assateague Island National Seashore, U.S.	D7	127
Assawoman Bay, b., Md., U.S.	D7	127
Assawompset Pond, l., Ma., U.S.	C6	128
Assekaifaf, Alg.	G15	62
Assenede, Bel.	F4	12
As-Sidr, Sau. Ar.	C1	47
Assiniboia, Sask., Can.	H2	105
Assiniboine, stm., Can.	E2	100
Assiniboine, Mount, mtn., Can.	D3	98
Assinippi, Ma., U.S.	h12	128
Assis, Braz.	G3	79
Assisi, Italy	F7	18
Assomada, C.V.	m17	64a
Assonet, Ma., U.S.	C5	128
As-Sudd, reg., Sud.	N6	60
Aş-Şufayyah, Sud.	J8	60
As-Sulaymānīyah, Iraq	D8	48
As-Sulaymānīyah, Sau. Ar.	B5	47
As-Sulaymī, Sau. Ar.	H6	48
As-Sulayyil, Sau. Ar.	D4	47
As-Sumayh, Sud.	M4	60
Assumption, Il., U.S.	D4	120
Assumption, co., La., U.S.	E4	125
Assumption Island, i., Sey.	C9	58
As-Suwaydā', Syria	C7	50
As-Suways (Suez), Egypt	C7	60
Astaffort, Fr.	H7	14
Āstāneh, Iran	C10	48
Āstāneh, Iran	E10	48
Āstārā, Iran	B10	48
Astara, U.S.S.R.	J7	22
Asti, Italy	E3	18
Astica, Arg.	F5	80
Astillero, Spain	B8	16
Astipálaia, Grc.	M10	20
Astipálaia, i., Grc.	M10	20
Aston Jonction, Que., Can.	C5	104
Astor, Fl., U.S.	C5	116
Astorga, Braz.	G3	79
Astorga, Spain	C5	16
Astoria, Il., U.S.	C3	120
Astoria, Or., U.S.	A3	144
Astoria, S.D., U.S.	C9	148
Astrachan', U.S.S.R.	F17	4
Astrachan-Bazar, U.S.S.R.	B10	48
Asturias, prov., Spain	B5	16
Asuka, sci., Ant.	C3	73
Asunción, Para.	C10	80
Asunción, Bahía, b., Mex.	D2	90
Asunción Mita, Guat.	C5	92
Asunción Nochixtlán, Mex.	I11	90
Asunga, Wādī, val., Afr.	K2	60
Aswān, Egypt	E7	60
Aswān High Dam see 'Āli, As-Sadd al-, Egypt	F7	60
Asyūṭ, Egypt	D6	60
Aszód, Hung.	H19	10
Atabapo, stm., S.A.	F9	84
Atacama, prov., Chile	D3	80
Atacama, Desierto de, des., Chile	G8	74
Atacama, Puna de, plat., S.A.	C5	80
Atacama, Salar de, pl., Chile	B4	80
Ataco, Col.	F5	84
Atacuari, stm., Peru	I7	84
Ataki, U.S.S.R.	A11	20
Atakpamé, Togo	H10	64
Atalándi, Grc.	K7	20
Atalaya, Pan.	I14	92
Atalaya, Peru	D5	82
Atalaya, Cerro, mtn., Peru	E6	82
Atalissa, Ia., U.S.	C6	122
Atami, Japan	L14	36
Atâr, Maur.	A3	64
Atascadero, Ca., U.S.	E3	112
Atascosa, co., Tx., U.S.	E3	150
Atasu, U.S.S.R.	H12	22
Atauro, Pulau, i., Indon.	G8	38
Atbara ('Aṭbarah), stm., Afr.	I8	60
'Aṭbarah, Sud.	I7	60
'Aṭbarah (Atbara), stm., Afr.	E7	56
Atbasar, U.S.S.R.	G11	22
Atchafalaya, stm., La., U.S.	D4	125
Atchafalaya Bay, b., La., U.S.	E4	125
Atchison, Ks., U.S.	C8	123
Atchison, co., Ks., U.S.	C8	123
Atchison, co., Mo., U.S.	A2	132
Atco, N.J., U.S.	D3	137
Atebubu, Ghana	H9	64
Ateca, Spain	D10	16
Atelchu, stm., Braz.	B1	79
Atenguillo, Mex.	G7	90
Ath (Aat), Bel.	G4	12
Athabasca, Alta., Can.	B4	98
Athabasca, stm., Alta., Can.	f8	98
Athabasca, Lake, l., Can.	m7	105
Athārān Hazāri, Pak.	E5	44
Athena, Or., U.S.	B8	144
Athens, Ont., Can.	C9	103
Athens, Al., U.S.	A3	108
Athens, Ar., U.S.	C2	111
Athens, Ga., U.S.	C3	117
Athens, Il., U.S.	D4	120
Athens, In., U.S.	B5	121
Athens, La., U.S.	B2	125
Athens, Me., U.S.	D3	126
Athens, Mi., U.S.	F5	129
Athens, N.Y., U.S.	C7	139
Athens, Oh., U.S.	C3	142
Athens, Pa., U.S.	C8	145
Athens, Tn., U.S.	D9	149
Athens, Tx., U.S.	C5	150
Athens, W.V., U.S.	D3	155
Athens, Wi., U.S.	C3	156
Athens, co., Oh., U.S.	C3	142
Athens see Athínai, Grc.	L7	20
Atherley, Ont., Can.	C5	103
Atherton, Austl.	A6	70
Athiémé, Benin	H10	64
Athínai (Athens), Grc.	L7	20
Athlone, Ire.	H6	8
Athok, Burma	F3	40
Athol, Id., U.S.	B2	119
Athol, Ma., U.S.	A3	128
Athol, S.D., U.S.	C7	148
Áthos, mtn., Grc.	I8	20
Ath-Thamad, Egypt	C8	60
Ati, Chad	F4	56
Atico, Peru	G5	82
Aticonipi, Lac, l., Que., Can.	C2	102
Atik Lake, l., Man., Can.	B4	100
Atikonak Lake, l., Newf., Can.	h8	102
Atiquizaya, El Sal.	D5	92
Atitlán, Lago de, l., Guat.	C3	92
Atitlán, Volcán, vol., Guat.	C3	92
Atka, U.S.S.R.	E22	24
Atka Island, i., Ak., U.S.	E5	109
Atkarsk, U.S.S.R.	G7	22
Atkins, Ar., U.S.	B3	111
Atkins, Va., U.S.	D1	153
Atkinson, Ga., U.S.	E5	117
Atkinson, Il., U.S.	B3	120
Atkinson, Ne., U.S.	B7	134
Atkinson, N.H., U.S.	E4	136
Atkinson, co., Ga., U.S.	E4	117
Atlanta, Ar., U.S.	D2	111
Atlanta, Ga., U.S.	C2	117
Atlanta, Il., U.S.	C4	120
Atlanta, In., U.S.	D5	121
Atlanta, Ks., U.S.	E7	123
Atlanta, Mi., U.S.	C6	129
Atlanta, Mo., U.S.	B5	132
Atlanta, Ne., U.S.	D6	134
Atlanta, Tx., U.S.	C5	150
Atlantic, Ia., U.S.	C2	122
Atlantic, N.C., U.S.	C6	140
Atlantic, co., N.J., U.S.	E3	137
Atlantic Beach, Fl., U.S.	m9	116
Atlantic City, N.J., U.S.	E4	137
Atlantic Highlands, N.J., U.S.	C4	137
Atlantic-Indian Ridge	N5	158
Atlantic Mine, Mi., U.S.	A2	129
Atlántico, dept., Col.	B5	84
Atlantic Ocean	I11	160
Atlantic Peak, mtn., Wy., U.S.	D3	157
Atlántida, Ur.	H11	80
Atlántida, dept., Hond.	B7	92
Atlas Mountains, mts., Afr.	B6	54
Atlas Saharien, mts., Alg.	D11	62
Atlas Tellien, mts., Alg.	C11	62
Atlin, B.C., Can.	m16	99
Atlin Lake, l., Can.	E6	96
'Atlit, Isr.	C3	50
Atmore, Al., U.S.	D2	108
Atna Peak, mtn., B.C., Can.	C3	99
Atocha, Bol.	I8	82
Atoka, Ok., U.S.	C5	143
Atoka, Tn., U.S.	B2	149
Atoka, co., Ok., U.S.	C5	143
Atoka Reservoir, res., Ok., U.S.	C5	143
Atotonilco, Mex.	E8	90
Atoui, Khatt (Khaṭṭ Atoui), val., Afr.	J3	62
Atoyac, stm., Mex.	H10	90
Atoyac de Álvarez, Mex.	I9	90
Atoyaquillo, stm., Mex.	I11	90
Atrak (Atrek), stm., Asia	C12	48
Atrato, stm., Col.	D4	84
Atrek (Atrak), stm., Asia	C12	48
Atri, Italy	G8	18
Aṭ-Ṭafīlah, Jord.	G5	50
Aṭ-Ṭā'if, Sau. Ar.	D2	47
At-Tāj, Libya	E2	60
Attala, co., Ms., U.S.	B4	131
At-Tall, Syria	A6	50
Attalla, Al., U.S.	A3	108
Attapu, Laos	G9	40
Attapulgus, Ga., U.S.	F2	117
Attawapiskat, stm., Ont., Can.	n18	103
Attawaugan, Ct., U.S.	B8	114
Attean Pond, l., Me., U.S.	C2	126
Attica, In., U.S.	D3	121
Attica, Ks., U.S.	E5	123
Attica, Mi., U.S.	E7	129
Attica, N.Y., U.S.	C2	139
Attica, Oh., U.S.	A3	142
Attigny, Fr.	C11	14
Attikí, hist. reg., Grc.	K7	20
Attir, Sud.	N6	60
Attleboro, Ma., U.S.	C5	128
Attock, Pak.	D5	44
Attu Island, i., Ak., U.S.	E2	109
Aṭ-Ṭunayb, Jord.	E5	50
Aṭ-Ṭūr, Egypt	C7	60
Āttūr, India	G5	46
Aṭ-Ṭuwayshah, Sud.	K4	60
Aṭ-Ṭuwayyah, Sau. Ar.	H6	48
Atucatiquini, stm., Braz.	B7	82
Atucha, Arg.	G9	80
Atuel, stm., Arg.	H5	80
Atuel, Bañados del, sw., Arg.	I5	80
Atuntaqui, Ec.	G3	84
Atwater, Sask., Can.	G4	105
Atwater, Ca., U.S.	D3	112
Atwater, Mn., U.S.	E4	130
Atwood, Ont., Can.	D3	103
Atwood, Co., U.S.	A7	113
Atwood, Il., U.S.	D5	120
Atwood, In., U.S.	B6	121
Atwood, Ks., U.S.	C2	123
Atwood, Ok., U.S.	C5	143
Atwood, Tn., U.S.	B3	149
Atwood Lake, res., Oh., U.S.	B4	142
Auari, stm., Braz.	F11	84
Auati Paraná, mth., Braz.	I9	84
Auau Channel, strt., Hi., U.S.	C5	118
Aubagne, Fr.	I12	14
Aube, dept., Fr.	D11	14
Aube, stm., Fr.	D11	14
Auberry, Ca., U.S.	D4	112
Aubigny-sur-Nère, Fr.	E9	14
Aubin, Fr.	H9	14
Aubrey, Ar., U.S.	C5	111
Aubrey Cliffs, clf, Az., U.S.	B2	110
Auburn, Ont., Can.	D3	103
Auburn, Al., U.S.	C4	108
Auburn, Ca., U.S.	C3	112
Auburn, Ga., U.S.	B3	117
Auburn, Il., U.S.	D4	120
Auburn, In., U.S.	B7	121
Auburn, Ia., U.S.	B3	122
Auburn, Ks., U.S.	D8	123
Auburn, Ky., U.S.	D3	124
Auburn, Me., U.S.	D2	126
Auburn, Ma., U.S.	B4	128
Auburn, Mi., U.S.	E6	129
Auburn, Ne., U.S.	D10	134
Auburn, N.H., U.S.	D4	136
Auburn, N.Y., U.S.	C4	139
Auburn, Pa., U.S.	E9	145
Auburn, Wa., U.S.	B3	154
Auburn, Wy., U.S.	D1	157
Auburn, stm., Austl.	E9	70
Auburndale, Fl., U.S.	D5	116
Auburndale, Wi., U.S.	D3	156
Auburn Heights, Mi., U.S.	F7	129
Auburn Range, mts., Austl.	E9	70
Auburntown, Tn., U.S.	B5	149
Aubusson, Fr.	G9	14
Auca Mahuida, Arg.	I4	80
Auca Mahuida, Cerro, mtn., Arg.	I4	80
Aucará, Peru	F4	82
Auce, U.S.S.R.	E5	26
Auch, Fr.	I7	14
Aucilla, stm., Fl., U.S.	B3	116
Auckland, N.Z.	B5	72
Auckland Islands, is., N.Z.	N20	158
Aude, dept., Fr.	I9	14
Aude, stm., Fr.	I10	14
Audierne, Fr.	D2	14
Audincourt, Fr.	E13	14
Audrain, co., Mo., U.S.	B6	132
Audubon, Ia., U.S.	C3	122
Audubon, Mn., U.S.	D3	130
Audubon, N.J., U.S.	D2	137
Audubon, co., Ia., U.S.	C2	122
Aue, Ger.	E12	10
Augathella, Austl.	E7	70
Auglaize, co., Oh., U.S.	B1	142
Auglaize, stm., Oh., U.S.	A1	142
Au Gres, Mi., U.S.	D7	129
Augsburg, Ger.	G10	10
Augusta, Austl.	F3	68
Augusta, Italy	L10	18
Augusta, Ar., U.S.	B4	111
Augusta, Ga., U.S.	C5	117
Augusta, Il., U.S.	C3	120
Augusta, Ks., U.S.	E7	123
Augusta, Ky., U.S.	B6	124
Augusta, Me., U.S.	D3	126
Augusta, Mi., U.S.	F5	129
Augusta, Mo., U.S.	C7	132
Augusta, Mt., U.S.	C4	133
Augusta, Wi., U.S.	D2	156
Augusta, co., Va., U.S.	B3	153
Augusta Springs, Va., U.S.	B3	153
Augustów, Pol.	B22	10
Auiá, Ribeirão, stm., Braz.	B2	79
Aulander, N.C., U.S.	A5	140
Aulnay, Fr.	F6	14
Aulneau Peninsula, pen., Ont., Can.	E4	100
Ault, Fr.	B8	14
Ault, Co., U.S.	A6	113
Aumale, Fr.	C8	14
Aumsville, Or., U.S.	k12	144
Auna, Nig.	F12	64
Auneau, Fr.	D8	14
Auob, stm., Afr.	F5	66
Aurangābād, India	C3	46
Auray, Fr.	E4	14
Aurelia, Ia., U.S.	B2	122
Aurès, Massif de l', mts., Alg.	C14	62
Aurich, Ger.	B7	10
Auriflama, Braz.	F3	79
Aurilândia, Braz.	D3	79
Aurillac, Fr.	H9	14
Auronzo di Cadore, Italy	C7	18
Aurora, Ont., Can.	C5	103
Aurora, Co., U.S.	B6	113
Aurora, Il., U.S.	B5	120
Aurora, In., U.S.	F8	121
Aurora, Ks., U.S.	C6	123
Aurora, Mn., U.S.	C6	130
Aurora, Mo., U.S.	E4	132
Aurora, Ne., U.S.	D7	134
Aurora, N.C., U.S.	B6	140
Aurora, Oh., U.S.	A4	142
Aurora, Or., U.S.	B4	144
Aurora, S.D., U.S.	C9	148
Aurora, Ut., U.S.	E4	151
Aurora, W.V., U.S.	B5	155
Aurora, Wi., U.S.	C5	156
Aurora, co., S.D., U.S.	D7	148
Aurora do Norte, Braz.	B5	79
Aurukun, Austl.	B8	68
Aus, Nmb.	F3	66
Au Sable, Mi., U.S.	D7	129
Au Sable, stm., Mi., U.S.	D6	129
Ausable, stm., N.Y., U.S.	f11	139
Au Sable, North Branch, stm., Mi., U.S.	D6	129
Au Sable Forks, N.Y., U.S.	f11	139
Au Sable Point, c., Mi., U.S.	B4	129
Au Sable Point, c., Mi., U.S.	D7	129
Auschwitz see Oświęcim, Pol.	E19	10
Aust-Agder, co., Nor.	L10	6
Austell, Ga., U.S.	h7	117
Austin, Man., Can.	E2	100
Austin, Ar., U.S.	C4	111
Austin, In., U.S.	G6	121
Austin, Mn., U.S.	G6	130
Austin, Nv., U.S.	D4	135
Austin, Tx., U.S.	D4	150
Austin, co., Tx., U.S.	E4	150
Austinburg, Oh., U.S.	A5	142
Austin Channel, strt., N.W. Ter., Can.	A12	96
Austintown, Oh., U.S.	A5	142
Austinville, Va., U.S.	D2	153
Australes, Îles, is., Fr. Poly.	K24	158
Australia, ctry., Oc.	D7	68
Australian Capital Territory, ter., Austl.	G9	68
Austria (Österreich), ctry., Eur.	F10	4
Autauga, co., Al., U.S.	C3	108
Autaugaville, Al., U.S.	C3	108
Autazes, Braz.	I13	84
Autlán de Navarro, Mex.	H7	90
Au Train, Mi., U.S.	B4	129
Autun, Fr.	F11	14
Auvergne, Ar., U.S.	B4	111
Auvergne, hist. reg., Fr.	G10	14
Auxerre, Fr.	E10	14
Auxier, Ky., U.S.	C7	124
Auxi-le-Château, Fr.	B9	14
Auxonne, Fr.	E12	14
Auxvasse, Mo., U.S.	B6	132
Auyán Tepuy, mtn., Ven.	E11	84
Auzances, Fr.	F9	14
Auzangate, Nevado, mtn., Peru	E6	82
Ava, Il., U.S.	F4	120
Ava, Mo., U.S.	E5	132
Avaí, Braz.	G4	79
Avallon, Fr.	E10	14
Avalon, Ca., U.S.	F4	112
Avalon, Ga., U.S.	B3	117
Avalon, Ms., U.S.	B3	131
Avalon, N.J., U.S.	E3	137
Avalon, Pa., U.S.	h13	145
Avalon, Lake, res., N.M., U.S.	E5	138
Avalon Peninsula, pen., Newf., Can.	E5	102
Ávalos, Mex.	C6	90
Avanos, Tur.	C3	48
Avant, Ok., U.S.	A5	143
Avaré, Braz.	G4	79
Avegbadje, mtn., Afr.	H10	64
Aveiro, Port.	E3	16
Avelgem, Bel.	G3	12
Avella, Pa., U.S.	F1	145
Avellaneda, Arg.	H9	80
Avellaneda, Arg.	F8	80
Avellino, Italy	I9	18
Avenal, Ca., U.S.	E3	112
Avenel, N.J., U.S.	k7	137
Avening, Ont., Can.	C4	103
Avera, Ga., U.S.	C4	117
Averill Park, N.Y., U.S.	C7	139
Aversa, Italy	I9	18
Avery, Id., U.S.	B3	119
Avery, Ia., U.S.	C5	122
Avery, co., N.C., U.S.	e11	140
Avery Island, La., U.S.	E4	125
Aves, Islas de, is., Ven.	A9	84
Aveyron, dept., Fr.	H9	14
Avezzano, Italy	G8	18
Aviemore, Scot., U.K.	D10	8
Avigliano, Italy	I10	18
Avignon, Fr.	I11	14
Ávila, Spain	E7	16
Ávila, prov., Spain	E7	16
Avila Beach, Ca., U.S.	E3	112
Avilés, Spain	B6	16
Avilla, In., U.S.	B7	121
Avis, Pa., U.S.	D7	145
Avispa, Cerro, mtn., Ven.	G10	84
Aviston, Il., U.S.	E4	120
Aviz, Port.	F4	16
Avoca, Ar., U.S.	A1	111
Avoca, In., U.S.	G4	121
Avoca, Ia., U.S.	C2	122
Avoca, Mn., U.S.	G3	130
Avoca, Ne., U.S.	h12	134

Name	Map Ref.	Page

Avoca, N.Y., U.S. C3 139
Avoca, Pa., U.S. m18 145
Avoca, Wi., U.S. E3 156
Avola, B.C., Can. D8 99
Avola, Italy M10 18
Avon, Ont., Can. E4 103
Avon, Al., U.S. D4 108
Avon, Ct., U.S. B4 114
Avon, Il., U.S. C3 120
Avon, In., U.S. E5 121
Avon, Ma., U.S. B5 128
Avon, Mn., U.S. E4 130
Avon, Ms., U.S. B2 131
Avon, Mt., U.S. D4 133
Avon, N.Y., U.S. C3 139
Avon, N.C., U.S. B7 140
Avon, Oh., U.S. A3 142
Avon, S.D., U.S. E7 148
Avon, co., Eng., U.K. J11 8
Avon, stm., Eng., U.K. I12 8
Avondale, Az., U.S. D3 110
Avondale, Co., U.S. C6 113
Avondale, Mo., U.S. h10 132
Avondale, Pa., U.S. G10 145
Avondale Estates, Ga., U.S. h8 117
Avon Downs, Austl. C2 70
Avon Lake, Ia., U.S. e8 122
Avon Lake, Oh., U.S. A3 142
Avonlea, Sask., Can. G3 105
Avonmore, Pa., U.S. E3 145
Avon Park, Fl., U.S. E5 116
Avontuur, S. Afr. I6 66
Avoyelles, co., La., U.S. C3 125
Avranches, Fr. D5 14
A'waj, Nahr al-, stm., Syria B6 50
Awaji-shima, i., Japan M9 36
'Awālī, Bahr. H11 48
Awasa, Eth. N10 60
Awash, Eth. G9 56
Awash, stm., Eth. M10 60
Awaso, Ghana H8 64
Awbārī, Libya C3 56
Awe, Nig. G14 64
Awegyun, Burma H5 40
Awjilah, Libya C5 56
Awled Djellal, Alg. C13 62
Awlef, Alg. G11 62
Aworo Kit, Sud. L7 60
Axel Heiberg Island, i., N.W. Ter., Can. B10 86
Axial Basin, Co., U.S. A2 113
Axim, Ghana I8 64
Axinim, Braz. J13 84
Axiós (Vardar), stm., Eur. I6 20
Axis, Al., U.S. E1 108
Ax-les-Thermes, Fr. J8 14
Axson, Ga., U.S. E4 117
Axtell, Ks., U.S. C7 123
Axtell, Ne., U.S. D6 134
Ayabaca, Peru J3 84
Ayabe, Japan L10 36
Ayacucho, Arg. I9 80
Ayacucho, Bol. G10 82
Ayacucho, Peru E4 82
Ayacucho, dept., Peru E4 82
Ayamonte, Spain H4 16
Ayangba, Nig. H13 64
Ayapel, Col. C5 84
Ayarza, Laguna de, l., Guat. C4 92
Ayaviri, Peru F6 82
Ayaviri, stm., Peru F6 82
Ayden, N.C., U.S. B5 140
Aydın, Tur. L11 20
Ayer, Ma., U.S. A4 128
Ayers Cliff, Que., Can. D5 104
Ayers Rock, mtn., Austl. E6 68
Ayeyarwady (Irrawaddy), stm., Burma F3 40
Ayía Paraskeví, Grc. J10 20
Ayiássos, Grc. J10 20
Áyion Óros, pen., Grc. I8 20
Áyios Kírikos, Grc. L10 20
Áyios Nikólaos, Grc. N9 20
Ayíou Órous, Kólpos, b., Grc. I8 20
Ayl, Jord. H5 50
Aylen Lake, l., Ont., Can. B7 103
Aylesbury, Sask., Can. G3 105
Aylesford, N.S., Can. D5 101
Aylmer, Mount, mtn., Alta., Can. D3 98
Aylmer East, Que., Can. D2 104
Aylmer Lake, l., N.W. Ter., Can. D11 96
Aylmer West, Ont., Can. E4 103
Aylsham, Sask., Can. D4 105
'Ayn Dār, Sau. Ar. B6 47
Aynor, S.C., U.S. D9 147
'Aynūnah, Sau. Ar. G3 48
Ayo, Peru F5 82
Ayo Ayo, Bol. G7 82
Ayod, Sud. M6 60
Ayom, Sud. N5 60
'Ayoûn el 'Atroûs, Maur. C5 64
Ayr, Austl. B7 70
Ayr, Scot., U.K. F9 8
Ayr, Ne., U.S. D7 134
'Aytā al-Fakhkhār, Leb. A5 50
Ayton, Ont., Can. C4 103
Ayu, Kepulauan, is., Indon. E9 38
Ayutla, Mex. G7 90
Ayutla de los Libres, Mex. I10 90
Ayvacık, Tur. J10 20
Ayvalık, Tur. J10 20
Azacualpa, Hond. C8 92
Azacualpa, Hond. B6 92
Azalia, In., U.S. F6 121
Azambuja, Port. F3 16
Āzamgarh, India G10 44
Azángaro, Peru F6 82
Azángaro, stm., Peru F6 82
Azaouagh, Vallée de l', val., Afr. D11 64
Azapa, Quebrada de, stm., Chile H6 82
Azar, val., Afr. C12 64
Azare, Nig. F15 64
Āzar Shahr, Iran C8 48
Azazga, Alg. B13 62
Azeffâl, dunes, Afr. J4 62
Azeffoun, Alg. B13 62
Azemmour, Mor. D6 62
Azerbaijan see Azerbajdžanskaja Sovetskaja Socialističeskaja Respublika, state, U.S.S.R. I7 22
Azerbajdžanskaja Sovetskaja Socialističeskaja Respublika, state, U.S.S.R. I7 22
Azezo, Eth. K9 60
Aziscohos Lake, l., Me., U.S. C1 126
Azle, Tx., U.S. n9 150
Azogues, Ec. I3 84
Azores see Açores, is., Port. k19 62a
Azoum, Bahr (Wādī 'Azūm), val., Afr. K2 60
Azov, U.S.S.R. H5 22
Azov, Sea of see Azovskoje more, U.S.S.R. H5 22
Azovskoje more (Sea of Azov), U.S.S.R. H5 22
Azpeitia, Spain B9 16
Azraq, Al-Baḥr al- see Blue Nile, stm., Afr. K8 60
Azrou, Mor. D8 62
Aztec, N.M., U.S. A2 138
Aztec Peak, mtn., Az., U.S. D5 110
Aztec Ruins National Monument, N.M., U.S. A1 138
Azua, Dom. Rep. E9 94
Azuaga, Spain G6 16
Azuay, prov., Ec. I3 84
Azucena, Arg. I9 80
Azuero, Peninsula de, pen., Pan. D2 84
Azul, Arg. I9 80
Azul, Cerro, mtn., C.R. H9 92
Azul, Cerro, mtn., Hond. C6 92
Azul, Serra, plat., Braz. F14 82
Azur, Côte d', Fr. I14 14
Azurduy, Bol. H9 82
Azusa, Ca., U.S. m13 112
Az-Zabadānī, Syria A6 50
Az-Zahrān (Dhahran), Sau. Ar. A7 47
Az-Zaqāzīq, Egypt B6 60
Az-Zarqā', Jord. D6 50
Az-Zāwiyah, Libya B3 56
Az-Zaydīyah, Yemen G3 47
Azzel Matti, Sebkha, pl., Alg. H11 62
Az-Zilfī, Sau. Ar. H8 48
Az-Zubayr, Iraq F9 48

B

Ba, stm., Viet. H10 40
Baalbek see Ba'Labakk, Leb. D4 48
Baar, Switz. D10 13
Baardheere, Som. H9 56
Baarle-Hertog (Baerle-Duc), Bel. F6 12
Baarle-Nassau, Bel. F6 12
Baba, Ec. H3 84
Babadağ, Tur. L12 20
Babahoyo, Ec. H3 84
Babailiqiao, China C7 34
Babajevo, U.S.S.R. B18 26
Babana, Nig. F11 64
Babanango, S. Afr. G10 66
Babanūsah, Sud. L4 60
Babar, Kepulauan, is., Indon. G8 38
Babar, Pulau, i., Indon. G8 38
Babb Creek, stm., Pa., U.S. C7 145
Babbie, Al., U.S. D3 108
Babbitt, Mn., U.S. C7 130
Babbitt, Nv., U.S. E3 135
Bab el Mandeb see Mandeb, Bab el, strt. H3 47
Babilônia, stm., Braz. D2 79
Babimost, Pol. C15 10
Babina Greda, Yugo. D2 20
Babinda, Austl. A6 70
Babine, stm., B.C., Can. B4 99
Babine Lake, l., B.C., Can. B5 99
Babine Range, mts., B.C., Can. B4 99
Babino, U.S.S.R. B14 26
Babino, U.S.S.R. B23 26
Babo, Indon. F9 38
Bābol, Iran C12 48
Bābol Sar, Iran C12 48
Babonã, stm., Braz. B8 82
Baboosic Lake, N.H., U.S. E3 136
Baboquivari Mountains, mts., Az., U.S. F4 110
Baboquivari Peak, mtn., Az., U.S. F4 110
Babson Park, Fl., U.S. E5 116
Babuškin, U.S.S.R. G13 24
Babuyan Islands, is., Phil. B7 38
Babylon, N.Y., U.S. n15 139
Babynino, U.S.S.R. G18 26
Baca, co., Co., U.S. D8 113
Bacaba, Igarapé, stm., Braz. I8 84
Bacabal, Braz. D10 76
Bacadéhuachi, Mex. C5 90
Bacan, Pulau, i., Indon. F8 38
Bacău, Rom. C10 20
Bacău, co., Rom. C10 20
Bac Can, Viet. C8 40
Baccarat, Fr. D13 14
Baccaro Point, c., N.S., Can. F4 101
Bacerac, Mex. B5 90
Bac Giang, Viet. D9 40
Bachaquero, Ven. C7 84
Bacharden, U.S.S.R. J9 22
Bachi, China K4 34
Bachiniva, Mex. C6 90
Bachmutovo, U.S.S.R. E17 26
Bachu, China D2 30
Bachuma, Eth. N8 60
Back, stm., N.W. Ter., Can. C13 96
Back, stm., S.C., U.S. h12 147
Bačka Palanka, Yugo. D3 20
Bačka Topola, Yugo. D3 20
Back Bay, N.B., Can. D3 101
Backbone Mountain, mtn., U.S. m12 127
Backnang, Ger. G9 10
Backstairs Passage, strt., Austl. J2 70
Bac Lieu, Viet. J8 40
Bac Ninh, Viet. D9 40
Bacoachi, Mex. B5 90
Bacobi, Az., U.S. B5 110
Bacolod, Phil. C7 38
Bacon, co., Ga., U.S. E4 117
Baconton, Ga., U.S. E2 117
Bacoor, Phil. N19 39b
Bács-Kiskun, co., Hung. I19 10
Bácum, Mex. D4 90
Bad, stm., S.D., U.S. C5 148
Bad, stm., Wi., U.S. B3 156
Badagara, India G3 46
Badajia, China B9 34
Badajós, stm., Braz. I11 84
Badajós, Lago, l., Braz. I11 84
Badajoz, Spain G5 16
Badalona, Spain D14 16
Bādāmi, India E3 46
Badanah, Sau. Ar. F6 48
Badaohao, China B9 32
Badaohe, China C10 32
Bad Aussee, Aus. H13 10
Bad Axe, Mi., U.S. E8 129
Bad Brückenau, Ger. E9 10
Baddeck, N.S., Can. C9 101
Bad Doberan, Ger. A11 10
Bad Dürkheim, Ger. F8 10
Bad Dürrenberg, Ger. D12 10
Badeggi, Nig. G13 64
Badéguichéri, Niger D12 64
Bad Ems, Ger. E7 10
Baden, Ont., Can. D4 103
Baden, Eth. I9 60
Baden, Switz. D9 13
Baden, Pa., U.S. E1 145
Baden-Baden, Ger. G8 10
Badenweiler, Ger. H7 10
Baden-Württemberg, state, Ger. G8 10
Badgastein, Aus. H13 10
Badger, Newf., Can. D3 102
Badger, Ia., U.S. B3 122
Badger, Mn., U.S. B2 130
Badger, S.D., U.S. C8 148
Badger Creek, stm., Co., U.S. B7 113
Bad Hall, Aus. G14 10
Bad Harzburg, Ger. D10 10
Bad Hersfeld, Ger. E9 10
Bad Homburg [vor der Höhe], Ger. E8 10
Badin, N.C., U.S. B2 140
Badin Lake, res., N.C., U.S. B2 140
Badiraguato, Mex. E6 90
Bad Kissingen, Ger. E10 10
Bad Kreuznach, Ger. F7 10
Badlands, hills, S.D., U.S. D3 148
Badlands, reg., U.S. C2 141
Badlands National Park, S.D., U.S. D3 148
Bad Langensalza, Ger. D10 10
Bad Lauterberg, Ger. D10 10
Bad Leonfelden, Aus. G14 10
Bad Mergentheim, Ger. F9 10
Bad Muskau, Ger. D14 10
Bad Nauheim, Ger. E8 10
Bad Neustadt an der Saale, Ger. E10 10
Bad Oeynhausen, Ger. C8 10
Bado, Mali F5 64
Bad Oldesloe, Ger. B10 10
Badou, China G5 32
Badou, Togo H10 64
Badoumbé, Mali E4 64
Bad Pyrmont, Ger. D9 10
Bad Ragaz, Switz. D12 13
Bad Reichenhall, Ger. H12 10
Badr Hunayn, Sau. Ar. C1 47
Bad River Indian Reservation, Wi., U.S. B3 156
Bad Salzuflen, Ger. C8 10
Bad Salzungen, Ger. E10 10
Bad Sankt Leonhard im Lavanttal, Aus. I14 10
Bad Schwalbach, Ger. E8 10
Bad Schwartau, Ger. B10 10
Bad Segeberg, Ger. B10 10
Bad Tölz, Ger. H11 10
Badu, China I8 34
Badulla, Sri L. I6 46
Badupi, Burma D2 40
Bad Vöslau, Aus. H16 10
Bad Waldsee, Ger. H9 10
Badwater Creek, stm., Wy., U.S. C5 157
Bad Wildungen, Ger. D9 10
Badiam, Maur. D4 64
Baena, Spain H7 16
Baependi, Braz. F6 79
Baeza, Ec. H4 84
Bafatá, Gui.-B. E2 64
Baffin Bay, b., N.A. B13 86
Baffin Bay, b., Tx., U.S. E4 150
Baffin Island, i., N.W. Ter., Can. C18 96
Bafing, stm., Afr. F4 54
Bafoulabé, Mali E4 64
Bafoussam, Cam. G9 54
Bāfq, Iran F13 48
Bāft, Iran G14 48
Bafwasende, Zaire A5 58
Bagaces, C.R. G9 92
Bagagem, stm., Braz. C4 79
Bāgalkot, India D3 46
Bagansiapiapi, Indon. M6 40
Bağarası, Tur. L11 20
Bagawi, Sud. K8 60
Bagdad, Az., U.S. C2 110
Bagdad, Fl., U.S. u14 116
Bagdad, Ky., U.S. B4 124
Bagdarin, U.S.S.R. G14 24
Bagé, Braz. F11 80
Baggs, Wy., U.S. E5 157
Baghdād, Iraq E8 48
Bagheria, Italy K8 18
Baghlān, Afg. B3 44
Bagley, Ia., U.S. C3 122
Bagley, Mn., U.S. C3 130
Bagley, Wi., U.S. F2 156
Bagnell Dam, Mo., U.S. C5 132
Bagnères-de-Bigorre, Fr. I7 14
Bagnères-de-Luchon, Fr. J7 14
Bagnols-sur-Cèze, Fr. H11 14
Bago (Pegu), Burma F4 40
Bagoé, stm., Afr. F6 64
Bagrationovsk, U.S.S.R. G3 26
Bagua, Peru A2 82
Baguio, Phil. M19 39b
Bagzane, mtn., Niger C14 64
Bahama, N.C., U.S. A4 140
Bahamas, ctry., N.A. D9 88
Bahār, Iran D10 48
Baharampur, India H13 44
Bahāwalnagar, Pak. F5 44
Bahāwalpur, Pak. F4 44
Bahechuan, China C12 32
Bahia, state, Braz. B7 79
Bahía, Islas de la, is., Hond. A8 92
Bahía Azul, Pan. H13 92
Bahía Blanca, Arg. J7 80
Bahía de Caráquez, Ec. H2 84
Bahía Kino, Mex. C4 90
Bahir Dar, Eth. L9 60
Bahrah, Sau. Ar. D1 47
Bahraich, India G9 44
Bahrain (Al-Bahrayn), ctry., Asia D5 42
Bahrayn, Khalīj al-, b., Asia B7 47
Bāhū Kālāt, Iran I16 48
Baï, Mali E8 64
Baia Mare, Rom. B7 20
Baia Sprie, Rom. B7 20
Baicao, China B4 32
Baicheng, China B11 30
Baicheng, China C3 30
Baie-Comeau, Que., Can. k13 104
Baie-d'Urfé, Que., Can. q19 104
Baie-Saint-Paul, Que., Can. B7 104
Baie Verte, N.B., Can. C5 101
Baie Verte, Newf., Can. D3 102
Baigong, China K5 34
Baihebu, China C4 32
Baijian, China D3 32
Baiju, China B9 34
Baikal, Lake see Bajkal, ozero, l., U.S.S.R. G13 24
Bailadores, Ven. C7 84
Baile, China D2 32
Baile Átha Cliath see Dublin, Ire. H7 8
Băile Govora, Rom. D8 20
Bailén, Spain G8 16
Băileşti, Rom. E7 20
Bailey, Co., U.S. B5 113
Bailey, N.C., U.S. B4 140
Bailey, co., Tx., U.S. B1 150
Bailey Brook, stm., Me., U.S. B2 126
Bailey Island, Me., U.S. g8 126
Bailey Island, i., S.C., U.S. k11 147
Baileys Crossroads, Va., U.S. g12 153
Baileys Harbor, Wi., U.S. C6 156
Baileyton, Al., U.S. A3 108
Baileyton, Tn., U.S. C11 149
Baileyville, Il., U.S. A4 120
Baileyville, Ks., U.S. C7 123
Bailin, China H9 34
Bailique, Ilha, i., Braz. C9 76
Bailleul, Fr. B9 14
Bailong, stm., China E7 30
Bailundo, Ang. D3 58
Baimaguan, China C4 32
Baimashi, China F7 34
Baimiaozi, China C8 32
Bainbridge, Ga., U.S. F2 117
Bainbridge, In., U.S. E4 121
Bainbridge, N.Y., U.S. C5 139
Bainbridge, Oh., U.S. C2 142
Bainbridge Island, i., Wa., U.S. e10 154
Bain-de-Bretagne, Fr. E5 14
Bainiqiao, China F3 34
Bains-les-Bains, Fr. D13 14
Bainville, Mt., U.S. B12 133
Baipu, China C9 34
Baiquan, China E11 34
Baird, Tx., U.S. C3 150
Bairdford, Pa., U.S. h14 145
Baird Inlet, b., Ak., U.S. C7 109
Baird Mountains, mts., Ak., U.S. B7 109
Bairin Zuoqi, China C10 30
Bairnsdale, Austl. K7 70
Bairoil, Wy., U.S. D5 157
Bairuopu, China G1 34
Baisha, China E10 40
Baishanji, China B5 34
Baishatan, China G9 32
Baishuifan, China E4 34
Baishuijiang, China E8 30
Baisogala, U.S.S.R. F6 26
Baitazi, China A8 32
Baitu, China D8 34
Baixa Grande, Braz. A8 79
Baixiang, China F2 32
Baiyin, China D7 30
Baizhongpu, China B3 34
Baja, Hung. I18 10
Baja, Punta, c., Mex. C2 90
Baja California, pen., Mex. C3 90
Baja California Norte, state, Mex. C2 90
Baja California Sur, state, Mex. E4 90
Bajada del Agrio, Arg. J3 80
Bajanaul, U.S.S.R. G13 22
Bajanchongor, Mong. B7 30
Bajánsenye, Hung. I16 10
Baja Verapaz, dept., Guat. B4 92
Bajdarackaja guba, b., U.S.S.R. D11 22
Bajestān, Iran D15 48
Bajiazi, China B11 32
Bajimba, Mount, mtn., Austl. G10 70
Bajkal, ozero (Lake Baikal), l., U.S.S.R. G13 24
Bajkal'skoje, U.S.S.R. F13 24
Bajmak, U.S.S.R. G9 22
Bajo Baudó, Col. E4 84
Bajo Boquete, Pan. C1 84
Bajos de Haina, Dom. Rep. E9 94
Bajram-Ali, U.S.S.R. J10 22
Bakebe, Cam. I14 64
Bakel, Sen. D3 64
Baker, Ca., U.S. E5 112
Baker, Fl., U.S. u15 116
Baker, La., U.S. D4 125
Baker, Mt., U.S. D12 133
Baker, Nv., U.S. D7 135
Baker, Or., U.S. C9 144
Baker, co., Fl., U.S. B4 116
Baker, co., Ga., U.S. E2 117
Baker, co., Or., U.S. C9 144
Baker, stm., N.H., U.S. C3 136
Baker, Mount, mtn., Wa., U.S. A4 154
Baker Air Force Base, mil., Ar., U.S. B6 111
Baker Butte, mtn., Az., U.S. C4 110
Baker Hill, Al., U.S. D4 108
Baker Island, i., Oc. H22 158
Baker Island, i., Ak., U.S. n22 109
Baker Lake, N.W. Ter., Can. D13 96
Baker Lake, l., N.W. Ter., Can. D13 96
Baker Lake, l., Me., U.S. B3 126
Baker Lake, res., Wa., U.S. A4 154
Baker Mountain, mtn., Me., U.S. C3 126
Bakers, N.C., U.S. B2 140
Bakers Bayou, stm., Ar., U.S. k11 111
Bakersfield, Ca., U.S. E4 112
Bakersfield, Mo., U.S. E5 132
Bakersfield, Vt., U.S. B3 152
Bakers Island, i., Ma., U.S. f12 128
Bakerstown, Pa., U.S. h14 145
Bakersville, Ct., U.S. B3 114
Bakersville, N.C., U.S. e10 140
Bakerton, W.V., U.S. B7 155
Bākhtarān (Kermānshāh), Iran D9 48
Bakhtegān, Daryācheh-ye, l., Iran G13 48
Bakkagerði, Ice. B7 6a
Baklanka, U.S.S.R. C23 26
Bako, Eth. O9 60
Bakony, mts., Hung. H17 10
Bakoy, stm., Afr. F5 54
Baku, U.S.S.R. I7 22
Bakun, China D9 44
Bala, Ont., Can. B5 103
Bala, Sen. D3 64
Balā, Tur. B2 48
Balabac Strait, strt., Asia D6 38
Ba'labakk, Leb. D4 48
Balabanovo, U.S.S.R. F19 26
Balachna, U.S.S.R. E26 26
Balad, Iraq D8 48
Bālāghāt, India J9 44
Balaguer, Spain D12 16
Balakirevo, U.S.S.R. E21 26
Balaklava, Austl. J3 70
Balakovo, U.S.S.R. G7 22
Balallan, Scot., U.K. C7 8
Bālā Morghāb, Afg. D17 48
Balāngīr, India B7 46
Balao, stm., Ec. I3 84
Balašicha, U.S.S.R. F20 26
Balašov, U.S.S.R. G6 22
Balassagyarmat, Hung. G19 10
Balāţ, Egypt E5 60
Balaton, Mn., U.S. F3 130
Balaton, l., Hung. I17 10
Balayan, Phil. O19 39b
Balbieriškis, U.S.S.R. G6 26
Balbirini, Austl. C7 68
Balboa, Pan. I15 92
Balboa Heights, Pan. C3 84
Balbriggan, Ire. H7 8
Balcanoona, Austl. H3 70
Balcarce, Arg. I9 80
Balcarres, Sask., Can. G4 105
Balchaš, U.S.S.R. H12 22
Balchaš, ozero (Lake Balkhash), l., U.S.S.R. H12 22
Balcones, Arg. D6 80
Balde, Arg. G5 80
Bald Eagle Lake, l., Mn., U.S. m12 130
Bald Eagle Lake, l., Mn., U.S. C7 130
Bald Hill, hill, R.I., U.S. D2 146
Baldhill Dam, N.D., U.S. B7 141
Baldim, Braz. E7 79
Bald Knob, Ar., U.S. B4 111
Bald Knob, mtn., Va., U.S. c3 153
Bald Knob, mtn., W.V., U.S. C5 155
Bald Knoll, mtn., Wy., U.S. D2 157
Bald Mountain, mtn., Ct., U.S. B6 114
Bald Mountain, mtn., N.J., U.S. A4 137
Bald Mountain, mtn., Or., U.S. C9 144
Bald Mountain, mtn., Or., U.S. D5 144
Bald Mountain, mtn., Vt., U.S. B5 152
Bald Mountain, mtn., Wy., U.S. B5 157
Bald Mountains, mts., N.C., U.S. f10 140
Baldone, U.S.S.R. E7 26
Baldur, Man., Can. E2 100
Baldwin, Fl., U.S. B5 116
Baldwin, Ga., U.S. B3 117
Baldwin, Il., U.S. E4 120
Baldwin, La., U.S. E4 125
Baldwin, Mi., U.S. E5 129
Baldwin, Pa., U.S. k14 145
Baldwin, S.C., U.S. B5 147
Baldwin, Wi., U.S. D1 156
Baldwin, co., Al., U.S. E2 108
Baldwin, co., Ga., U.S. C3 117
Baldwin City, Ks., U.S. D8 123
Baldwinsville, N.Y., U.S. B4 139
Baldwinville, Ma., U.S. A3 128
Baldwyn, Ms., U.S. A5 131
Baldy Mountain, mtn., B.C., Can. D7 99
Baldy Mountain, mtn., Man., Can. D1 100
Baldy Mountain, mtn., Mt., U.S. B7 133
Baldy Mountain, mtn., N.M., U.S. A4 138
Baldy Peak, mtn., Az., U.S. D6 110
Balearic Islands see Balears, Illes, is., Spain F15 16
Balears, prov., Spain F15 16
Balears, Illes (Balearic Islands), is., Spain F15 16
Baleia, Ponta da, c., Braz. D9 79
Baleine, Rivière à la, stm., Que., Can. g13 104
Balej, U.S.S.R. G15 24
Baler, Phil. N19 39b
Bāleshwar, India J12 44
Baléyara, Niger E11 64
Balfate, Hond. B8 92
Balfes Creek, Austl. C6 70
Balfour, N.C., U.S. f10 140
Balgonie, Sask., Can. G3 105
Bali, Laut (Bali Sea), Indon. G6 38
Bali, Selat, strt., Indon. G5 38
Balihan, China B6 32
Balıkesir, Tur. J11 20
Balikpapan, Indon. F6 38
Balimo, Pap. N. Gui. G11 38
Balin, China B11 30
Balingen, Ger. G8 10
Balintang Channel, strt., Phil. B7 38
Baliza, Braz. D2 79
Balkan Mountains see Stara Planina, mts., Eur. G8 20
Balkan Peninsula, pen., Eur. D9 52
Balkbrug, Neth. C9 12
Balkh, Afg. B2 44
Balkhash, Lake see Balchaš, ozero, l., U.S.S.R. H12 22
Ball, La., U.S. C3 125
Ballachulish, Scot., U.K. E8 8
Ballangen, Nor. G15 6
Ballantine, Mt., U.S. E8 133
Ballarat, Austl. K5 70
Ballard, co., Ky., U.S. e8 124
Ballardvale, Ma., U.S. f11 128
Ball Club Lake, l., Mn., U.S. C5 130
Ballé, Mali D5 64
Ballenas, Bahía de, b., Mex. D3 90
Balleny Islands, is., Ant. B8 73
Balleroy, Fr. C6 14
Ballesteros, Arg. G7 80
Balleza, Mex. D6 90
Balleza, stm., Mex. D6 90
Ball Ground, Ga., U.S. B2 117
Ballia, India H11 44
Ballina, Austl. G10 70
Ballina, Ire. G4 8
Ballinger, Tx., U.S. D3 150
Ball Mountain Lake, res., Vt., U.S. E3 152
Ballon, Fr. M14 8
Ballouville, Ct., U.S. B8 114
Balls Pyramid, i., Austl. F11 68
Ballston Spa, N.Y., U.S. B7 139
Ballwin, Mo., U.S. f12 132
Bally, Pa., U.S. F10 145
Balm, Fl., U.S. E4 116
Balmaceda, Chile F2 78
Balmoral, Man., Can. D3 100
Balmoral, N.B., Can. B3 101
Balmorhea, Tx., U.S. o13 150
Balmville, N.Y., U.S. D6 139
Balnearia, Arg. F7 80
Balonne, stm., Austl. F8 70
Bālotra, India H5 44
Balovale, Zam. D4 58
Baloži, U.S.S.R. E7 26
Balrāmpur, India G10 44
Balranald, Austl. J5 70
Balsam, N.C., U.S. f9 140
Balsam Lake, Wi., U.S. C1 156
Balsam Lake, l., Ont., Can. C6 103
Balsam Lake, l., Wi., U.S. C1 156
Bálsamo, Braz. F2 79
Balsas, Braz. E9 76
Balsas, stm., Mex. H8 90
Balsas, Rio das, stm., Braz. E9 76
Balsas Sur, Mex. I10 90
Balsthal, Switz. D8 13
Balta, U.S.S.R. H3 22
Balta, N.D., U.S. A5 141
Baltasar Brum, Ur. F10 80
Baltic, Ct., U.S. C7 114
Baltic, Oh., U.S. B4 142
Baltic, S.D., U.S. D9 148
Baltic Sea, Eur. M16 6
Baltijsk, U.S.S.R. G2 26
Baltijskaja kosa, spit, Eur. A19 10
Balţīm, Egypt B6 60
Baltimore, Ont., Can. C6 103
Baltimore, Ire. J4 8
Baltimore, S. Afr. D9 66
Baltimore, Md., U.S. B4 127
Baltimore, Oh., U.S. C3 142
Baltimore, co., Md., U.S. B4 127
Baltimore Highlands, Md., U.S. h11 127
Baluarte, stm., Mex. F7 90
Balvi, U.S.S.R. D10 26
Balya, Tur. J11 20
Balykši, U.S.S.R. H8 22
Balzar, Ec. H3 84
Bam, Iran G15 48
Bama, China B9 40
Bamaga, Austl. B8 68
Bamako, Mali E5 64
Bamba, Mali C9 64
Bambamarca, Peru B2 82
Bambana, stm., Nic. D11 92
Bambara Maoundé, Mali D8 64
Bambari, Cen. Afr. Rep. G5 56
Bambaroo, Austl. B7 70
Bamberg, Ger. F10 10
Bamberg, S.C., U.S. E5 147
Bamberg, co., S.C., U.S. E5 147
Bambesi, Eth. M8 60
Bambezi, Zimb. C9 66
Bambuí, Braz. F6 79
Bamburra, stm., S.A. H12 82
Bam Co, l., China E14 44
Bamenda, Cam. I15 64
Bami, U.S.S.R. B14 48
Bamingui, stm., Cen. Afr. Rep. G4 56
Bampūr, Iran H16 48
Bamumo, China D15 44
Ba Na, Viet. G9 40
Banaba, i., Kir. I20 158
Banalia, Zaire A5 58
Banana, Zaire C2 58
Bananal, Braz. G6 79
Bananal, Ilha do, i., Braz. F8 76
Banana River, b., Fl., U.S. D6 116

Name	Map Ref.	Page

Banarlı, Tur. H11 20
Banās, Ra's, c., Egypt F8 60
Banat, reg., Eur. D4 20
Banbuji, China B5 34
Banco, Punta, c., C.R. I11 92
Bancroft, Ont., Can. B7 103
Bancroft, Id., U.S. G7 119
Bancroft, Ia., U.S. A3 122
Bancroft, Mi., U.S. F6 129
Bancroft, Ne., U.S. B9 134
Bānda, India H9 44
Banda, Kepulauan, is., Indon. F8 38
Banda, Laut (Banda Sea), Indon. G8 38
Banda Aceh, Indon. L3 40
Bānda Dāūd Shāh, Pak. D4 44
Banda del Río Salí, Arg. D6 80
Bandama, stm., I.C. H7 64
Bandama Blanc, stm., I.C. G7 64
Bandama Rouge, stm., I.C. G6 64
Bandana, Ky., U.S. e9 124
Bandar Beheshtī, Iran I16 48
Bandar-e 'Abbās, Iran H14 48
Bandar-e Anzalī (Bandar-e Pahlavī), Iran C10 48
Bandar-e Būshehr, Iran G11 48
Bandar-e Deylam, Iran F11 48
Bandar-e Khomeynī (Bandar-e Shāhpūr), Iran F10 48
Bandar-e Lengeh, Iran H13 48
Bandar-e Māh Shahr, Iran F10 48
Bandar-e Rīg, Iran G11 48
Bandar-e Torkeman, Iran C13 48
Bandar see Machilīpatnam, India D6 46
Bandar Seri Begawan, Bru. E5 38
Banded Peak, mtn., Co., U.S. D4 113
Bandeira, Pico da, mtn., Braz. F8 79
Bandeirantes, Braz. B3 79
Bandeirantes, Braz. E1 79
Bandeirantes, Braz. G3 79
Bandelier National Monument, N.M., U.S. B3 138
Bandera, Arg. E7 80
Bandera, Tx., U.S. E3 150
Bandera, co., Tx., U.S. E3 150
Bandera, Alto, mtn., Dom. Rep. E9 94
Bandera Bajada, Arg. D7 80
Banderas, Bahía de, b., Mex. G7 90
Bandiagara, Mali D8 64
Bandiantaolehai, China C7 30
Bandırma, Tur. I11 20
Bandon, Ire. J5 8
Bandon, Or., U.S. D2 144
Ban Don, Ao, b., Thai. J5 40
Bandula, Moz. B11 66
Bandundu, Zaire B3 58
Bandung, Indon. J13 39a
Bāneh, Iran D8 48
Banes, Cuba D7 94
Banff, Scot., U.K. D11 8
Banff National Park, Alta., Can. D2 98
Banfora, Burkina F7 64
Bangalore, India F4 46
Bangaon, India I13 44
Bangassou, Cen. Afr. Rep. H5 56
Banggai, Indon. F7 38
Banggai, Kepulauan, is., Indon. F7 38
Banghāzī, Libya B5 56
Bangil, Indon. J16 39a
Bangjang, Sud. L7 60
Bangjun, China D5 32
Bangka, Pulau, i., Indon. F4 38
Bangkalan, Indon. J16 39a
Bangkok see Krung Thep, Thai. H6 40
Bangladesh, ctry., Asia E13 42
Bang Mun Nak, Thai. F6 40
Bangolo, I.C. H6 64
Bangor, Sask., Can. G4 105
Bangor, N. Ire., U.K. G8 8
Bangor, Wales, U.K. H9 8
Bangor, Me., U.S. D4 126
Bangor, Mi., U.S. F4 129
Bangor, Pa., U.S. E11 145
Bangor, Wi., U.S. E3 156
Bangor Township, Mi., U.S. E7 129
Bangs, Tx., U.S. D3 150
Bangs, Mount, mtn., Az., U.S. A2 110
Bang Saphan, Thai. I5 40
Bangshi, China C10 32
Bangued, Phil. M19 39b
Bangui, Cen. Afr. Rep. H4 56
Bangweulu, Lake, l., Zam. D5 58
Ban Hin Heup, Laos E7 40
Ban Houayxay, Laos D6 40
Bani, Burkina D9 64
Baní, Dom. Rep. E9 94
Bani, stm., Mali E7 64
Baniachang, Bngl. H14 44
Banikoara, Benin F11 64
Banī Mazār, Egypt C6 60
Banister, stm., Va., U.S. D4 153
Banī Suwayf, Egypt C6 60
Banī Walīd, Libya B3 56
Bāniyās, Syria B5 50
Banja Luka, Yugo. E12 18
Banjarmasin, Indon. F5 38
Banjin, China C9 34
Banjul (Bathurst), Gam. E1 64
Bankas, Mali D8 64
Bankhead Lake, res., Al., U.S. B2 108
Bankilaré, Niger D10 64
Banks, Al., U.S. D4 108
Banks, Or., U.S. g11 144
Banks, co., Ga., U.S. B3 117
Banks Island, i., B.C., Can. C2 99
Banks Island, i., N.W. Ter., Can. B8 96
Banks Lake, res., Ga., U.S. E3 117
Banks Lake, res., Wa., U.S. B6 154
Banks Peninsula, pen., N.Z. E4 72
Banks Strait, strt., Austl. M8 70
Bankston, Al., U.S. B2 108
Bānkura, India I12 44
Ban Mit, Laos E6 40
Bann, stm., N. Ire., U.K. G7 8
Ban Nahin, Laos E8 40
Ban Namnga, Laos D7 40
Banner, co., Ne., U.S. C2 134
Banner Elk, N.C., U.S. A1 140
Ban Ngam, Laos D8 40
Banning, Ca., U.S. F5 112
Banning, Ga., U.S. C2 117
Bannock, co., Id., U.S. G6 119
Bannockburn, Ont., Can. C7 103
Bannock Peak, mtn., Id., U.S. F6 119
Bannock Range, mts., Id., U.S. G6 119
Bannu, Pak. D4 44
Banon, Fr. H12 14
Baños, Ec. H3 84
Baños, Peru D3 82
Ban Pakneun, Laos E6 40
Ban Pong, Thai. H5 40
Banpu, China A8 34
Banqiao, China E9 34
Banqiaoji, China C5 34
Banquan, China H6 32
Banshi, China J4 34
Banská Bystrica, Czech. G19 10
Banská Štiavnica, Czech. G18 10
Ban Songkhon, Laos F8 40
Bānswāra, India I6 44
Bantam, Ct., U.S. C3 114
Bantam, stm., Ct., U.S. B3 114
Bantam Lake, l., Ct., U.S. C3 114
Ban Thanoun, Laos E6 40
Bantry, Ire. J4 8
Ban Xènkhalôk, Laos E6 40
Banyak, Kepulauan, is., Indon. M4 40
Banyoles, Spain C14 16
Banzare Coast, Ant. B7 73
Banzi, China K6 34
Bao'an, China M3 34
Baode, China D9 30
Baoding, China E3 32
Baofeng, China B2 34
Bao Ha, Viet. C8 40
Baohekou, China C6 32
Baoji, China E8 30
Bao Lac, Viet. I9 40
Baonian, China D8 34
Baoquan, China G7 32
Baoshan, China D10 34
Baoshan, China B5 40
Baoting, China H8 30
Baotou, China C8 30
Baoulé, stm., Afr. E5 64
Baowei, China C9 40
Baoxinji, China C4 34
Baoying, China B8 34
Bāpatla, India E6 46
Bapaume, Fr. B9 14
Bapchule, Az., U.S. D4 110
Baptiste, Ont., Can. B6 103
Bāqa el Gharbīya, Isr. D4 50
Baqên, China E16 44
B'aqlīn, Leb. A5 50
Ba'qūbah, Iraq E8 48
Baquedano, Chile B4 80
Bar, Yugo. G3 20
Baraawe, Som. H9 56
Barabinsk, U.S.S.R. F7 24
Barabinskaja step', pl., U.S.S.R. F7 24
Baraboo, Wi., U.S. E4 156
Baraboo, stm., Wi., U.S. E3 156
Baraboulé, Burkina D9 64
Baracaju, stm., Braz. B3 79
Baracaldo, Spain B9 16
Barachit, Eth. J10 60
Baracoa, Cuba D7 94
Baracoa, Hond. B7 92
Baradero, Arg. G9 80
Baradine, Austl. H8 70
Baraga, Mi., U.S. B2 129
Baraga, co., Mi., U.S. B2 129
Baragarh, India B7 46
Bārah, Sud. K6 60
Barahona, Dom. Rep. E9 94
Barak, Tur. C4 48
Baraka, val., Afr. E8 56
Baralaba, Austl. E8 70
Baram, stm., Malay. E5 38
Barama, stm., Guy. D13 84
Baran', U.S.S.R. G13 26
Baranagar, India I13 44
Baranoa, Col. B5 84
Baranof Island, i., Ak., U.S. m22 109
Baranoviči, U.S.S.R. H9 26
Baranya, co., Hung. J18 10
Barão de Cocais, Braz. E7 79
Barão de Melgaço, Braz. G14 82
Baratang Island, i., India H2 40
Barataria, La., U.S. E5 125
Barataria, Bayou, stm., La., U.S. k11 125
Barataria Bay, b., La., U.S. E6 125
Barat Daya, Kepulauan, is., Indon. G8 38
Bar'atino, U.S.S.R. G17 26
Baraúna, stm., Braz. G12 84
Barauni, India H11 44
Baraut, India F7 44
Baraya, Col. F5 84
Barbacena, Braz. F7 79
Barbacoas, Col. G3 84
Barbados, ctry., N.A. H15 94
Barbar, Sud. H7 60
Bárbara, Col. H6 84
Barbareta, Isla, i., Hond. A8 92
Barbas, Cap, c., W. Sah. I2 62
Barbastro, Spain C12 16
Barbate de Franco, Spain I6 16
Barbeau Peak, mtn., N.W. Ter., Can. A12 86
Barber, co., Ks., U.S. E5 123
Barberena, Guat. C4 92
Barbers Point, c., Hi., U.S. B3 118
Barbers Point Naval Air Station, mil., Hi., U.S. g9 118
Barberton, S. Afr. E10 66
Barberton, Oh., U.S. A4 142
Barbezieux, Fr. G6 14
Barbil, India I11 44
Barbosa, Col. D5 84
Barbosa, Col. E6 84
Barbour, co., Al., U.S. D4 108
Barbour, co., W.V., U.S. B4 155
Barboursville, W.V., U.S. C2 155
Barbourville, Ky., U.S. D6 124
Barbuda, i., Antig. F14 94
Barby, Ger. D11 10
Barcaldine, Austl. D6 70
Barcău (Berettyó), stm., Eur. B6 20
Barce see Al-Marj, Libya B5 56
Barcellona Pozzo di Gotto, Italy K10 18
Barcelona, Mex. D8 90
Barcelona, Spain D14 16
Barcelona, Ven. B10 84
Barcelos, Braz. H11 84
Barcin, Pol. C17 10
Barco, N.C., U.S. A7 140
Barcoo, stm., Austl. E5 70
Barcroft, Lake, res., Va., U.S. g12 153
Barcs, Hung. J17 10
Barczewo, Pol. B20 10
Barda, U.S.S.R. A9 48
Barda del Medio, Arg. J4 80
Bardaï, Chad D4 56
Bardai, Sud. K1 60
Bardawīl, Sabkhat al-, sw., Egypt F2 48
Barddhamān, India I12 44
Bardejov, Czech. F21 10
Barden Reservoir, res., R.I., U.S. C2 146
Bardi, Italy E4 18
Bardīyah, Libya B3 60
Bardo, Tun. M5 18
Bardolph, Il., U.S. C3 120
Bardonecchia, Italy D1 18
Bardstown, Ky., U.S. C4 124
Bardu, Nor. G16 6
Bardufoss, Nor. G16 6
Bardwell, Ky., U.S. f9 124
Bardwell Lake, res., Tx., U.S. C4 150
Bare Hill Pond, l., Ma., U.S. g9 128
Bareilly, India F8 44
Barentin, Fr. C7 14
Barents Sea, Eur. B4 28
Barentu, Eth. J9 60
Barfleur, Fr. C5 14
Barge, Eth. N9 60
Bargersville, In., U.S. E5 121
Bargnop, Sud. M5 60
Barguzin, stm., U.S.S.R. G14 24
Bar Harbor, Me., U.S. D4 126
Bari, Italy H11 18
Baria, stm., Ven. G9 84
Barichara, Col. D6 84
Barillas, Guat. B3 92
Barīm (Perim), i., Yemen H3 47
Barima, stm., S.A. C12 84
Barinas, Ven. C7 84
Barinas, state, Ven. C8 84
Baring, Me., U.S. C5 126
Baring, Mo., U.S. A5 132
Baring, Cape, c., N.W. Ter., Can. B9 96
Barinitas, Ven. C7 84
Bāripada, India J12 44
Bariri, Braz. G4 79
Bārīs, Egypt E6 60
Barisāl, Bngl. I14 44
Barisan, Pegunungan, mts., Indon. F3 38
Barito, stm., Indon. F5 38
Barium Springs, N.C., U.S. B2 140
Barjols, Fr. I13 14
Barkal, Bngl. I15 44
Barker Heights, N.C., U.S. f10 140
Barkhamsted Reservoir, res., Ct., U.S. B3 114
Bark Lake, l., Ont., Can. B7 103
Barkley, Lake, res., U.S. f10 124
Barkley Dam, Ky., U.S. e9 124
Barkley Sound, strt., B.C., Can. E5 99
Barkly East, S. Afr. H8 66
Barkly Tableland, plat., Austl. C7 68
Barkly West, S. Afr. G7 66
Barkmere, Que., Can. C3 104
Barkol, China C5 30
Bark Point, c., Wi., U.S. B2 156
Bark River, Mi., U.S. C3 129
Barksdale Air Force Base, mil., La., U.S. B2 125
Bar-le-Duc, Fr. D12 14
Barlee, Lake, l., Austl. E3 68
Barletta, Italy H11 18
Barling, Ar., U.S. B1 111
Barlow, Ky., U.S. e8 124
Bārmer, India H4 44
Bar Mills, Me., U.S. E2 126
Barnaby River, N.B., Can. C4 101
Barnard, Ks., U.S. C5 123
Barnard, Mo., U.S. A3 132
Barnard, Vt., U.S. D3 152
Barnard Castle, Eng., U.K. G15 8
Barnardsville, N.C., U.S. f10 140
Barnaul, U.S.S.R. G14 22
Barn Bluff, mtn., Austl. M6 70
Barnegat, N.J., U.S. D4 137
Barnegat Bay, b., N.J., U.S. D4 137
Barnegat Inlet, b., N.J., U.S. D4 137
Barnes, Ks., U.S. C7 123
Barnes, co., N.D., U.S. B7 141
Barnesboro, Pa., U.S. E4 145
Barnes City, Ia., U.S. C5 122
Barnes Creek, stm., La., U.S. D2 125
Barnes Ice Cap, N.W. Ter., Can. B18 96
Barnes Sound, strt., Fl., U.S. G6 116
Barneston, Ne., U.S. D9 134
Barnesville, Ga., U.S. C2 117
Barnesville, Mn., U.S. D2 130
Barnesville, Oh., U.S. C4 142
Barnet, Vt., U.S. C4 152
Barnett, Mo., U.S. C5 132
Barneveld, Wi., U.S. E4 156
Barney, Ga., U.S. F3 117
Barney, N.D., U.S. C8 141
Barnhart, Mo., U.S. C7 132
Barnsdall, Ok., U.S. A5 143
Barnstable, Ma., U.S. C7 128
Barnstable, co., Ma., U.S. C7 128
Barnstaple, Eng., U.K. J9 8
Barnstead, N.H., U.S. D4 136
Barnum, Mn., U.S. D6 130
Bar Nunn, Wy., U.S. D6 157
Barnwell, Alta., Can. E4 98
Barnwell, S.C., U.S. E5 147
Barnwell, co., S.C., U.S. E5 147
Baro, stm., Afr. G8 56
Baroda, Mi., U.S. G4 129
Barons, Alta., Can. E4 98
Barpeta, India G14 44
Barqa, China E9 44
Barqah (Cyrenaica), hist. reg., Libya C2 60
Barque Canada Reef, rf., Asia D5 38
Barques, Pointe aux, c., Mi., U.S. D8 129
Barquisimeto, Ven. B8 84
Barr, Co., U.S. B6 113
Barra, Braz. F10 76
Barra, Ponta da, c., Moz. D12 66
Barraba, Austl. H9 70
Barracão, Braz. D12 80
Barracão do Barreto, Braz. C12 82
Barrackville, W.V., U.S. B4 155
Barra da Estiva, Braz. B8 79
Barra do Bugres, Braz. F13 82
Barra do Corda, Braz. E9 76
Barra do Cuanza, Ang. C2 58
Barra do Garças, Braz. C2 79
Barra do Mendes, Braz. A7 79
Barra do Piraí, Braz. G7 79
Barra do Ribeiro, Braz. F13 80
Barra Falsa, Ponta da, c., Moz. D12 66
Barrafranca, Italy L9 18
Barra Mansa, Braz. G6 79
Barranca, Peru D3 82
Barranca, Peru A3 82
Barrancabermeja, Col. D6 84
Barrancas, Chile G3 80
Barrancas, Col. B6 84
Barrancas, Ven. C7 84
Barrancas, Ven. C11 84
Barrancas, stm., Arg. I3 80
Barranqueras, Arg. D9 80
Barranquilla, Col. B5 84
Barras, Braz. D10 76
Barre, Ma., U.S. B3 128
Barre, Vt., U.S. C4 152
Barre, Lake, l., La., U.S. E5 125
Barreal, Arg. F4 80
Barre Falls Reservoir, res., Ma., U.S. B4 128
Barreiras, Braz. B6 79
Barreirinha, Braz. I14 84
Barreiro, Port. G2 16
Barreiro, stm., Braz. C2 79
Barreiros, Braz. E11 76
Barren, co., Ky., U.S. D4 124
Barren, stm., Ky., U.S. C3 124
Barren, Nosy, is., Madag. Q20 67b
Barren Island, i., Md., U.S. D5 127
Barren Islands, is., Ak., U.S. h15 109
Barren River Lake, res., Ky., U.S. D3 124
Barretos, Braz. F4 79
Barrett, Mn., U.S. E3 130
Barrett, W.V., U.S. D3 155
Barretts Hill, hill, Ma., U.S. g9 128
Barrhead, Alta., Can. B3 98
Barrie, Ont., Can. C5 103
Barrie Island, i., Ont., Can. B2 103
Barrière, B.C., Can. D7 99
Barrier Range, mts., Austl. H4 70
Barrington, N.S., Can. F4 101
Barrington, Il., U.S. A5 120
Barrington, N.H., U.S. D4 136
Barrington, N.J., U.S. D2 137
Barrington, R.I., U.S. D5 146
Barrington, stm., R.I., U.S. C5 146
Barrington Lake, l., Man., Can. A1 100
Barrington Passage, N.S., Can. F4 101
Barringun, Austl. G6 70
Barrita Vieja, Guat. D4 92
Barro Alto, Braz. C4 79
Barron, Wi., U.S. C2 156
Barron, co., Wi., U.S. C2 156
Barron Lake, Mi., U.S. G4 129
Barros, Arg. J8 80
Barrow, Ak., U.S. A8 109
Barrow, co., Ga., U.S. B3 117
Barrow, Point, c., Ak., U.S. A8 109
Barrow Creek, Austl. D6 68
Barrow-in-Furness, Eng., U.K. G10 8
Barrow Island, i., Austl. D3 68
Barrows, Man., Can. C1 100
Barrow Strait, strt., N.W. Ter., Can. B13 96
Barry, Il., U.S. D2 120
Barry, co., Mi., U.S. F5 129
Barry, co., Mo., U.S. E4 132
Barrys Bay, Ont., Can. B7 103
Barryton, Mi., U.S. E5 129
Bārsi, India C3 46
Barsinghausen, Ger. C9 10
Barstow, Ca., U.S. E5 112
Barstow, Tx., U.S. D1 150
Bar-sur-Aube, Fr. D11 14
Bar-sur-Seine, Fr. D11 14
Bartang, stm., U.S.S.R. A5 44
Bartelso, Il., U.S. E4 120
Barthélemy, Deo, Viet. E8 40
Bartholomew, co., In., U.S. F6 121
Bartholomew, Bayou, stm., U.S. D4 111
Bartibog Bridge, N.B., Can. B4 101
Bartica, Guy. D13 84
Bartle Frere, mtn., Austl. A6 70
Bartlesville, Ok., U.S. A6 143
Bartlett, Ks., U.S. E8 123
Bartlett, Ne., U.S. C7 134
Bartlett, N.H., U.S. B4 136
Bartlett, Tn., U.S. B2 149
Bartlett, Tx., U.S. D4 150
Bartlett Reservoir, res., Az., U.S. D4 110
Bartletts Ferry Dam, U.S. C4 108
Bartletts Harbour, Newf., Can. C3 102
Bartley, Ne., U.S. D5 134
Bartolomé de las Casas, Arg. C9 80
Bartolomeu Dias, Moz. C12 66
Barton, Al., U.S. A2 108
Barton, Ar., U.S. C5 111
Barton, Md., U.S. k12 127
Barton, Oh., U.S. B5 142
Barton, Vt., U.S. B4 152
Barton, co., Ks., U.S. D5 123
Barton, co., Mo., U.S. D3 132
Barton, stm., Vt., U.S. B4 152
Bartonsville, Vt., U.S. E3 152
Barton-upon-Humber, Eng., U.K. H13 8
Bartonville, Il., U.S. C4 120
Bartoszyce, Pol. A20 10
Bartow, Fl., U.S. E5 116
Bartow, Ga., U.S. D4 117
Bartow, co., Ga., U.S. B2 117
Barú, Volcán, vol., Pan. I12 92
Baruun-Urt, Mong. B9 30
Barva, Volcán, vol., C.R. G10 92
Barwāni, India I6 44
Barwick, Ga., U.S. F3 117
Barwon, stm., Austl. G8 70
Barybino, U.S.S.R. F20 26
Baryš, U.S.S.R. G7 22
Basacato del Este, Eq. Gui. J14 64
Basail, Arg. D9 80
Basalt, Co., U.S. B3 113
Basalt, Id., U.S. F6 119
Basankusu, Zaire A3 58
Basarabi, Rom. E12 20
Basatongwula Shan, mtn., China D14 44
Basavilbaso, Arg. G9 80
Basco, Phil. A7 38
Bascom, Oh., U.S. A2 142
Bascuñán, Cabo, c., Chile G7 74
Basehor, Ks., U.S. k16 123
Basel (Bâle), Switz. C8 13
Basey, Phil. C8 38
Bashan Lake, l., Ct., U.S. D6 114
Bashaw, Alta., Can. C4 98
Bashi, Al., U.S. D2 108
Bashi Channel, strt., Asia G11 30
Basile, La., U.S. D3 125
Basilicata, prov., Italy I11 18
Basílio, Braz. F12 80
Basin, Mt., U.S. D4 133
Basin, Wy., U.S. B4 157
Basīrhāt, India I13 44
Baskahegan Lake, l., Me., U.S. C5 126
Baskakovka, U.S.S.R. G17 26
Baskatong, Réservoir, res., Que., Can. k11 104
Baskett, Ky., U.S. C2 124
Baskin, Fl., U.S. p10 116
Basking Ridge, N.J., U.S. B3 137
Bašmakovo, U.S.S.R. H26 26
Basoko, Zaire A4 58
Basque Lands see Euskal Herriko, prov., Spain B9 16
Basra see Al-Başrah, Iraq F9 48
Bas-Rhin, dept., Fr. D14 14
Bassano, Alta., Can. D4 98
Bassano del Grappa, Italy D6 18
Bassari, Togo G10 64
Bassas da India, rf., Reu. F7 58
Bassecourt, Switz. D7 13
Bassein, mth., Burma F3 40
Bassein see Pathein, Burma F3 40
Basse-Terre, Guad. F14 94
Basseterre, St. K./N. F13 94
Basse-Terre, i., Guad. F14 94
Bassett, Ar., U.S. B5 111
Bassett, Ne., U.S. B6 134
Bassett, Va., U.S. D3 153
Bassett, Wi., U.S. n11 156
Bassett Creek, stm., Al., U.S. D2 108
Bassett Peak, mtn., Az., U.S. E5 110
Basse-Yutz, Fr. J9 12
Bassfield, Ms., U.S. D4 131
Bass Harbor, Me., U.S. D4 126
Bassikounou, Maur. D7 64
Bassila, Benin G10 64
Bass Islands, is., Oh., U.S. A3 142
Bass Lake, In., U.S. B4 121
Bass River, N.S., Can. D6 101
Bass Strait, strt., Austl. L6 70
Basswood, Man., Can. D1 100
Basswood Lake, l., Mn., U.S. B7 130
Baştah, Jord. H5 50
Bastak, Iran H13 48
Bastelica, Fr. L24 15a
Basti, India G10 44
Bastia, Fr. J16 14
Bastian, Va., U.S. C1 153
Bastimentos, Pan. H12 92
Bastimentos, Isla, i., Pan. H12 92
Bastogne (Bastenaken), Bel. H8 12
Bastrop, La., U.S. B4 125
Bastrop, Tx., U.S. D4 150
Bastrop, co., Tx., U.S. D4 150
Bastuträsk, Swe. I17 6
Basutoland see Lesotho, ctry., Afr. G5 58
Bata, Eq. Gui. A1 58
Bataan Peninsula, pen., Phil. N19 39b
Batabanó, Golfo de, b., Cuba C3 94
Bataguaçu, Braz. F2 79
Bataiporã, Braz. G2 79
Batajsk, U.S.S.R. H5 22
Batala, India E6 44
Batan, China A9 34
Batang, China E6 30
Batangas, Phil. O19 39b
Batan Islands, is., Phil. A7 38
Bátaszék, Hung. I18 10
Batatais, Braz. F5 79
Batavia, Arg. H6 80
Batavia, Il., U.S. B5 120
Batavia, Ia., U.S. D5 122
Batavia, N.Y., U.S. C2 139
Batavia, Oh., U.S. C1 142
Batchelor Bay, b., N.C., U.S. B6 140
Batchtown, Il., U.S. D3 120
Bătdâmbâng, Camb. H7 40
Bateckij, U.S.S.R. C13 26
Batemans Bay, Austl. J9 70
Bates, Ar., U.S. C1 111
Bates, co., Mo., U.S. C3 132
Batesburg, S.C., U.S. D4 147
Batesland, S.D., U.S. D3 148
Batesville, Ar., U.S. B4 111
Batesville, In., U.S. F7 121
Batesville, Ms., U.S. A4 131
Batesville, Tx., U.S. E3 150
Bath, N.B., Can. C2 101
Bath, Ont., Can. C8 103
Bath, Eng., U.K. J11 8
Bath, Il., U.S. C3 120
Bath, Me., U.S. E3 126
Bath, Mi., U.S. F6 129
Bath, N.H., U.S. B3 136
Bath, N.Y., U.S. C3 139
Bath, Pa., U.S. E11 145
Bath, S.C., U.S. D4 147
Bath, S.D., U.S. B7 148
Bath, co., Ky., U.S. B6 124
Bath, co., Va., U.S. B3 153
Bathinda, India E6 44
Bathsheba, Barb. H15 94
Bathurst, Austl. I8 70
Bathurst, N.B., Can. B4 101
Bathurst, S. Afr. I8 66
Bathurst, Cape, c., N.W. Ter., Can. B7 96
Bathurst see Banjul, Gam. E1 64
Bathurst Inlet, b., N.W. Ter., Can. C11 96
Bathurst Island, i., Austl. B6 68
Bathurst Island, i., N.W. Ter., Can. A12 96
Batia, Benin F10 64
Batié, Burkina G8 64
Bāṭin, Wādī al-, val., Asia G9 48
Batiscan, stm., Que., Can. B5 104
Batkanu, S.L. G3 64
Batlow, Austl. J8 70
Batman, Tur. C6 48
Batna, Alg. C14 62
Baṭn al-Ghūl, Jord. I5 50
Baton Rouge, La., U.S. D4 125
Batouri, Cam. H9 54
Batovi, Braz. C2 79
Baṭrā (Petra), hist., Jord. H4 50
Batsto, stm., N.J., U.S. D3 137
Batten Kill, stm., U.S. E2 152
Battery Park, Va., U.S. k14 153
Batticaloa, Sri L. I6 46
Battiest, Ok., U.S. C7 143
Battle, stm., Can. F10 96
Battle, stm., Can. A4 106
Battleboro, N.C., U.S. A5 140
Battle Creek, Ia., U.S. B2 122
Battle Creek, Mi., U.S. F5 129
Battle Creek, Ne., U.S. C8 134
Battleford, Sask., Can. E1 105
Battle Ground, In., U.S. C4 121
Battle Ground, Wa., U.S. D3 154
Battle Lake, Mn., U.S. D3 130
Battlement Mesa, mtn., Co., U.S. B2 113
Battle Mountain, Nv., U.S. C5 135
Battle Mountain, mtn., Wy., U.S. E5 157
Battles, Ms., U.S. D5 131
Battles Wharf, Al., U.S. E2 108
Battonya, Hung. I21 10
Batu, mtn., Eth. G8 56
Batu, Kepulauan, is., Indon. O5 40
Batumi, U.S.S.R. I6 22
Batu Pahat, Malay. N7 40
Baturité, Braz. D11 76
Bat Yam, Isr. D3 50
Baubau, Indon. G7 38
Bauchi, Nig. F14 64
Baud, Fr. E3 14
Baudette, Mn., U.S. B4 130
Baudó, stm., Col. E4 84
Baudó, Serranía de, mts., Col. D4 84
Bauer Coulee, val., Wa., U.S. B7 154
Bauld, Cape, c., Newf., Can. C4 102
Baume-les-Dames, Fr. E13 14
Baures, Bol. E10 82
Baures, stm., Bol. E10 82
Bauru, Braz. G4 79
Baús, Braz. E2 79
Bauska, U.S.S.R. E7 26
Bautzen, Ger. D14 10
Bauxite, Ar., U.S. C3 111
Bavaria, Ks., U.S. D6 123
Bavaria see Bayern, state, Ger. F11 10
Bavispe, Mex. B5 90
Bavispe, stm., Mex. C5 90
Bavleny, U.S.S.R. E22 26
Bawdwin, Burma C4 40
Bawku, Ghana F9 64
Bawlf, Alta., Can. C4 98
Baxian, China D4 32
Baxley, Ga., U.S. E4 117
Baxter, Ia., U.S. C4 122
Baxter, Mn., U.S. D4 130
Baxter, Tn., U.S. C8 149
Baxter, W.V., U.S. B4 155
Baxter, co., Ar., U.S. A3 111
Baxter Springs, Ks., U.S. E9 123
Baxterville, Ms., U.S. D4 131
Bay, Ar., U.S. B5 111
Bay, co., Fl., U.S. u16 116
Bay, co., Mi., U.S. E6 129
Bayamo, Cuba D6 94
Bayamón, P.R. E11 94
Bayan Har Shan, mts., China E6 30
Bayano, Lago, res., Pan. C3 84
Bayan Obo, China C9 30
Bayard, Ia., U.S. C3 122
Bayard, Ne., U.S. C2 134
Bayard, N.M., U.S. E1 138
Bayard, W.V., U.S. B5 155
Bayberry, N.Y., U.S. B4 139
Bayboro, N.C., U.S. B6 140
Bay Bulls, Newf., Can. E5 102
Bayburt, Tur. A6 48
Bay Center, Wa., U.S. C2 154
Bay City, Mi., U.S. E7 129
Bay City, Or., U.S. B3 144
Bay City, Tx., U.S. E5 150
Bay City, Wi., U.S. D1 156
Bay de Verde, Newf., Can. D5 102
Baydhabo, Som. H9 56
Bayerische Alpen, mts., Eur. H11 10
Bayern, state, Ger. F11 10
Bayeux, Fr. C6 14
Bayfield, Ont., Can. D3 103
Bayfield, Co., U.S. D3 113
Bayfield, Wi., U.S. B3 156

Name | Map Ref. | Page

Bayfield, co., Wi., U.S. B2 156
Bayiji, China A6 34
Bayingzi, China B8 32
Bay L'Argent, Newf., Can. E4 102
Baylis, Il., U.S. D3 120
Baylor, co., Tx., U.S. C3 150
Bay Mills Indian Reservation, Mi., U.S. B6 129
Bay Minette, Al., U.S. E2 108
Bayombong, Phil. M19 39b
Bayon, Fr. D13 14
Bayonne, Fr. I5 14
Bayonne, N.J., U.S. B4 137
Bayou Bodcau Reservoir, res., La., U.S. B2 125
Bayou Cane, La., U.S. E5 125
Bayou D'Arbonne Lake, res., La., U.S. B3 125
Bayou George, Fl., U.S. u16 116
Bayou Goula, La., U.S. D4 125
Bayou La Batre, Al., U.S. E1 108
Bayou Pigeon, La., U.S. D4 125
Bayóvar, Peru A1 82
Bay Point, c., S.C., U.S. G7 147
Bayport, N.S., Can. E5 101
Bay Port, Mi., U.S. E7 129
Bayport, Mn., U.S. E6 130
Bayport, N.Y., U.S. n15 139
Bayreuth, Ger. F11 10
Bay Ridge, Md., U.S. C5 127
Bayrischzell, Ger. H12 10
Bay Roberts, Newf., Can. E5 102
Bayrūt (Beirut), Leb. A5 50
Bays, Lake of, l., Ont., Can. B5 103
Bay Saint Louis, Ms., U.S. E4 131
Bay Shore, N.Y., U.S. E7 139
Bayshore Gardens, Fl., U.S. q10 116
Bayside, Wi., U.S. m12 156
Bays Mountain, mtn., Tn., U.S. C10 149
Bay Springs, Ms., U.S. D4 131
Bayt al-Faqīh, Yemen G3 47
Bayt Jinn, Syria B5 50
Bayt Laḥm (Bethlehem), Isr. Occ. E4 50
Bayt Mirī, Leb. A5 50
Baytown, Tx., U.S. E5 150
Bayview, Al., U.S. f7 108
Bayview, Id., U.S. B2 119
Bay View Park, De., U.S. F5 115
Bay Village, Oh., U.S. h9 142
Bayville, De., U.S. G5 115
Bayville, N.J., U.S. D4 137
Bayzo, Niger E12 64
Baza, Spain H9 16
Bazaruto, Ilha do, i., Moz. C12 66
Bazas, Fr. H6 14
Bazdār, Pak. G1 44
Bazi, China K2 34
Bazine, Ks., U.S. D4 123
Be, Nosy, i., Madag. N23 67b
Beach, Il., U.S. h9 120
Beach, N.D., U.S. C1 141
Beachburg, Ont., Can. B8 103
Beach City, Oh., U.S. B4 142
Beach City, Tx., U.S. r15 150
Beach Haven, N.J., U.S. D4 137
Beach Haven Inlet, b., N.J., U.S. D4 137
Beach Pond, res., U.S. C8 114
Beachville, Ont., Can. D4 103
Beachwood, N.J., U.S. D4 137
Beacon, Ia., U.S. C5 122
Beacon, N.Y., U.S. D7 139
Beacon Falls, Ct., U.S. D3 114
Beaconsfield, Austl. M7 70
Beaconsfield, Que., Can. q19 104
Beadle, co., S.D., U.S. C7 148
Beagle Gulf, b., Austl. B6 68
Beagle Reef, rf., Austl. C4 68
Bealanana, Madag. O23 67b
Beale, Cape, c., B.C., Can. E5 99
Beale Air Force Base, mil., Ca., U.S. C3 112
Beals, Me., U.S. D5 126
Bean Lake, Mo., U.S. B3 132
Bean Station, Tn., U.S. C10 149
Bear, De., U.S. B3 115
Bear, stm., U.S. B3 151
Bear Creek, Al., U.S. A2 108
Bear Creek, Wi., U.S. D5 156
Bear Creek, stm., U.S. E2 123
Bear Creek, stm., Al., U.S. A1 108
Bear Creek, stm., Or., U.S. E4 144
Bear Creek, stm., Wy., U.S. E8 157
Bearden, Ar., U.S. D3 111
Beardmore, Ont., Can. o18 103
Beards Fork, W.V., U.S. m13 155
Beardsley, Mn., U.S. E2 130
Beardstown, Il., U.S. C3 120
Bearfort Mountain, mtn., N.J., U.S. A4 137
Bear Inlet, b., N.C., U.S. C5 140
Bear Island, i., Ant. C11 73
Bear Island see Bjørnøya, i., Sval. B2 28
Bear Lake, Mi., U.S. D4 129
Bear Lake, co., Id., U.S. G7 119
Bear Lake, l., Man., Can. B4 100
Bear Lake, l., U.S. A4 151
Bear Lake, l., Wi., U.S. C2 156
Bear Lodge Mountains, mts., Wy., U.S. B8 157
Bear Mountain, mtn., Ar., U.S. f7 111
Bear Mountain, mtn., Ky., U.S. C5 124
Bear Mountain, mtn., Ma., U.S. A3 128
Bear Mountain, mtn., Or., U.S. D4 144
Béarn, hist. reg., Fr. I6 14
Bearpaw Mountains, mts., Mt., U.S. B7 133
Bear Pond Mountain, mtn., Md., U.S. A2 127
Bear River, N.S., Can. E4 101
Bear River City, Ut., U.S. B3 151
Bear Swamp, sw., Ma., U.S. h11 128
Beartooth Pass, Wy., U.S. B3 157
Beartooth Range, mts., U.S. E7 133
Bear Town, Ms., U.S. D3 131
Beartown Mountain, mtn., Va., U.S. f10 153
Beasain, Spain B9 16
Beas de Segura, Spain G9 16
Beason, Il., U.S. C4 120
Beata, Cabo, c., Dom. Rep. F9 94
Beata, Isla, i., Dom. Rep. F9 94
Beatrice, Al., U.S. D2 108
Beatrice, Ne., U.S. D9 134
Beatrice, Zimb. B10 66
Beattie, Ks., U.S. C7 123
Beatty, Sask., Can. E3 105
Beatty, Nv., U.S. G5 135
Beatty, Or., U.S. E5 144
Beattyville, Ky., U.S. C6 124
Beaucaire, Fr. I11 14
Beauce, reg., Fr. D8 14
Beaudesert, Austl. F10 70
Beaufort, Mo., U.S. C6 132
Beaufort, N.C., U.S. C6 140
Beaufort, S.C., U.S. G6 147
Beaufort, co., N.C., U.S. B5 140
Beaufort, co., S.C., U.S. G6 147
Beaufort Marine Corps Air Station, mil., S.C., U.S. F6 147
Beaufort Sea, N.A. B5 86
Beaufort West, S. Afr. I6 66
Beaugency, Fr. E8 14
Beauharnois, Que., Can. D4 104
Beau Lake, l., Me., U.S. A3 126
Beaumont, Alta., Can. C4 98
Beaumont, Newf., Can. D4 102
Beaumont, Fr. C5 14
Beaumont, Ks., U.S. E7 123
Beaumont, Ms., U.S. D5 131
Beaumont, Tx., U.S. D5 150
Beaumont-sur-Sarthe, Fr. D7 14
Beaune, Fr. E11 14
Beauport, Que., Can. n17 104
Beaupré, Que., Can. B7 104
Beaupréau, Fr. E5 14
Beauregard, Ms., U.S. D3 131
Beauregard, co., La., U.S. D2 125
Beaurepaire, Fr. G12 14
Beausejour, Man., Can. D3 100
Beauty, Ky., U.S. C7 124
Beauvais, Fr. C9 14
Beauval, Sask., Can. B2 105
Beauvoir-sur-Mer, Fr. F4 14
Beaver, Ak., U.S. B10 109
Beaver, Ok., U.S. A1 143
Beaver, Pa., U.S. E1 145
Beaver, Ut., U.S. E3 151
Beaver, W.V., U.S. D3 155
Beaver, co., Ok., U.S. e10 143
Beaver, co., Pa., U.S. E1 145
Beaver, co., Ut., U.S. E2 151
Beaver, stm., Can. D7 96
Beaver, stm., Can. F11 96
Beaver, stm., Can. B2 105
Beaver, stm., Can. A5 106
Beaver, stm., U.S. A2 143
Beaver, stm., N.Y., U.S. B6 139
Beaver, stm., R.I., U.S. E2 146
Beaver, stm., Ut., U.S. E2 151
Beaverbank, N.S., Can. E6 101
Beaver Brook, stm., U.S. E4 136
Beaver City, Ne., U.S. D6 134
Beaver Creek, B.C., Can. E5 99
Beavercreek, Oh., U.S. C1 142
Beaver Creek, stm., U.S. E4 134
Beaver Creek, stm., U.S. C8 157
Beaver Creek, stm., Co., U.S. B7 113
Beaver Creek, stm., Ia., U.S. e8 122
Beaver Creek, stm., Ky., U.S. C7 124
Beaver Creek, stm., Md., U.S. A2 127
Beaver Creek, stm., Mo., U.S. E5 132
Beaver Creek, stm., Mt., U.S. B9 133
Beaver Creek, stm., Ne., U.S. C7 134
Beaver Creek, stm., N.D., U.S. C1 141
Beaver Creek, stm., N.D., U.S. C5 141
Beaver Creek, stm., Ok., U.S. C3 143
Beaver Creek, stm., Tn., U.S. m13 149
Beaver Creek, stm., Wy., U.S. D4 157
Beaver Creek Mountains, mts., Al., U.S. B3 108
Beaver Crossing, Ne., U.S. D8 134
Beaverdale, Pa., U.S. F4 145
Beaver Dam, Ky., U.S. C3 124
Beaver Dam, Wi., U.S. E5 156
Beaverdam Branch, stm., De., U.S. F3 115
Beaverdam Lake, res., Wi., U.S. E5 156
Beaverdell, B.C., Can. E8 99
Beaver Falls, Pa., U.S. E1 145
Beaverhead, co., Mt., U.S. E3 133
Beaverhead, stm., Mt., U.S. E4 133
Beaverhead Mountains, mts., U.S. D5 119
Beaverhill Lake, l., Alta., Can. C4 98
Beaver Hill Lake, l., Man., Can. B4 100
Beaver Island, i., Mi., U.S. C5 129
Beaver Lake, res., Ar., U.S. A2 111
Beaverlodge, Alta., Can. B1 98
Beaver Meadows, Pa., U.S. E10 145
Beaver Ridge, mtn., Tn., U.S. D9 149
Beaver Run Reservoir, res., Pa., U.S. F2 145
Beaver Springs, Pa., U.S. E7 145
Beavertail Point, c., R.I., U.S. F4 146
Beaverton, Al., U.S. B1 108
Beaverton, Mi., U.S. E6 129
Beaverton, Or., U.S. B4 144
Beavertown, Pa., U.S. E7 145
Beaverville, Il., U.S. C6 120
Beāwar, India G6 44
Beazley, Arg. G5 80
Bebedouro, Braz. F4 79
Bebeji, Nig. F14 64
Becal, Mex. G14 90
Bécancour, Que., Can. C5 104
Bécancour, stm., Que., Can. C6 104
Bečej, Yugo. D4 20
Beceni, Rom. D10 20
Becerro, Cayos, is., Hond. B11 92
Béchar, Alg. E9 62
Becharof Lake, l., Ak., U.S. D8 109
Bechater, Tun. L4 18
Bechyně, Czech. F14 10
Beckemeyer, Il., U.S. E4 120
Becker, Mn., U.S. E5 130
Becker, Ms., U.S. B5 131
Becker, co., Mn., U.S. D3 130
Beckham, co., Ok., U.S. B2 143
Beckley, W.V., U.S. D3 155
Beckum, Ger. D8 10
Beckville, Tx., U.S. C5 150
Beckwith Creek, stm., La., U.S. D2 125
Becky Peak, mtn., Nv., U.S. D7 135
Bédarieux, Fr. I10 14
Bedele, Eth. M9 60
Bedford, N.S., Can. E6 101
Bedford, Que., Can. D5 104
Bedford, In., U.S. G5 121
Bedford, Ia., U.S. D3 122
Bedford, Ky., U.S. B4 124
Bedford, Ma., U.S. B5 128
Bedford, N.H., U.S. E3 136
Bedford, Oh., U.S. A4 142
Bedford, Pa., U.S. F4 145
Bedford, Va., U.S. C3 153
Bedford, Wy., U.S. D2 157
Bedford, co., Pa., U.S. G4 145
Bedford, co., Tn., U.S. B5 149
Bedford, co., Va., U.S. C3 153
Bedford Hills, N.Y., U.S. D7 139
Bedfordshire, co., Eng., U.K. I13 8
Bedias, Tx., U.S. D5 150
Bednodemjanovsk, U.S.S.R. H26 26
Bee, Ne., U.S. C8 134
Bee, co., Tx., U.S. E4 150
Beebe, Que., Can. D5 104
Beebe, Ar., U.S. B4 111
Beebe Plain, Vt., U.S. A4 152
Beebe River, N.H., U.S. C3 136
Bee Branch, Ar., U.S. B3 111
Beech Bluff, Tn., U.S. B3 149
Beech Bottom, W.V., U.S. f8 155
Beech Creek, Ky., U.S. C2 124
Beech Creek, Pa., U.S. D6 145
Beecher, Il., U.S. B6 120
Beecher, Mi., U.S. E7 129
Beecher City, Il., U.S. D5 120
Beech Fork, stm., Ky., U.S. C4 124
Beech Grove, In., U.S. E5 121
Beech Grove, Ky., U.S. C2 124
Beechgrove, Tn., U.S. B5 149
Beech Island, S.C., U.S. E4 147
Beechwood, N.B., Can. C2 101
Beechworth, Austl. K7 70
Beechy, Sask., Can. G2 105
Beecroft Head, c., Austl. J9 70
Beedeville, Ar., U.S. B4 111
Beef Island, i., Tn., U.S. e8 149
Beemer, Ne., U.S. C9 134
Beenleigh, Austl. F10 70
Bee Ridge, Fl., U.S. q11 116
Beersheba see Be'ér Sheva', Isr. F3 50
Beersheba Springs, Tn., U.S. D8 149
Be'ér Sheva (Beersheba), Isr. F3 50
Beersville, N.B., Can. C4 101
Beesleys Point, N.J., U.S. E3 137
Beestekraal, S. Afr. E8 66
Beethoven Peninsula, pen., Ant. C12 73
Beeton, Ont., Can. C5 103
Beeville, Tx., U.S. E4 150
Befale, Zaire A4 58
Befandriana, Madag. O23 67b
Befasy, Madag. R21 67b
Befotaka, Madag. S22 67b
Bega, Austl. K8 70
Bega (Begej), stm., Eur. D5 20
Begej (Bega), stm., Eur. D4 20
Beggs, Ok., U.S. B5 143
Begičevskij, U.S.S.R. H21 26
Begoml', U.S.S.R. G11 26
Begoro, Ghana H9 64
Begunicy, U.S.S.R. B12 26
Begusarai, India H12 44
Behbahān, Iran F11 48
Behm Canal, strt., Ak., U.S. n24 109
Behshahr, Iran C12 48
Bei, stm., China K2 34
Bei'an, China B12 30
Beida see Al-Bayḍā', Libya B5 56
Beidaihe, China D7 32
Beidun, China I7 34
Beigi, Eth. M8 60
Beihai, China D10 40
Beijing (Peking), China D4 32
Beijing Shi (Peking Shih), China C10 30
Beikan, China C10 34
Beiling, China K4 34
Beinwil, Switz. D8 13
Beipan, stm., China F8 30
Beipiao, China B8 32
Beiqi, China C10 32
Beira, Moz. B12 66
Beira Baixa, hist. reg., Port. F4 16
Beira Litoral, hist. reg., Port. E3 16
Beirne, Ar., U.S. D2 111
Beirut see Bayrūt, Leb. A5 50
Beiseker, Alta., Can. D4 98
Beishan, China B10 40
Bei Shan, mts., China C6 30
Beisu, China E2 32
Beitang, China D5 32
Beitbridge, Zimb. D10 66
Beixinzhen, China D10 34
Beizhen, China B9 32
Beja, Port. G4 16
Béja, Tun. M4 18
Bejaïa (Bougie), Alg. B13 62
Béjar, Spain E6 16
Bejuco, Pan. C3 84
Bejuma, Ven. B8 84
Bekabad, U.S.S.R. I11 22
Bekdaš, U.S.S.R. I8 22
Békés, Hung. I21 10
Békés, co., Hung. I20 10
Békéscsaba, Hung. I21 10
Bekilli, Tur. K13 20
Bekily, Madag. T21 67b
Bekitro, Madag. T21 67b
Bekkaria, Alg. N3 18
Bekkevoort, Bel. G6 12
Bekodoka, Madag. P21 67b
Bekoji, Eth. N10 60
Bela, India H9 44
Bela, Pak. G2 44
Belabolo, Sud. M3 60
Bela Crkva, Yugo. E5 20
Bel Air, Md., U.S. A5 127
Bel Aire, Ks., U.S. g12 123
Belaja, stm., U.S.S.R. G9 22
Belaja Ber'ozka, U.S.S.R. I16 26
Belaja Cerkov', U.S.S.R. H4 22
Bel'ajevka, U.S.S.R. C14 20
Bel Alton, Md., U.S. D4 127
Bélanger, stm., Man., Can. C3 100
Bélanger, stm., Sask., Can. B2 105
Bela Palanka, Yugo. F6 20
Belau see Palau, dep., T.T.P.I. E9 38
Belavenona, Madag. T22 67b
Bela Vista, Braz. B10 80
Bela Vista, Moz. F11 66
Bela Vista de Goiás, Braz. D4 79
Bela Vista do Paraíso, Braz. G3 79
Belawan, Indon. M5 40
Belbubulo, Sud. M8 60
Belcamp, Md., U.S. B5 127
Bełchatów, Pol. D19 10
Belcher, Ky., U.S. C7 124
Belcherāgh, Afg. C1 44
Belcher Islands, is., N.W. Ter., Can. E17 96
Belchertown, Ma., U.S. B3 128
Bel'cy, U.S.S.R. H3 22
Belden, Ms., U.S. A5 131
Belden, Ne., U.S. B8 134
Belding, Mi., U.S. E5 129
Beled Weyne, Som. H10 56
Belém, Braz. D9 76
Belén, Arg. D5 80
Belén, Chile H7 82
Belén, Col. G5 84
Belén, Col. D6 84
Belén, Nic. F9 92
Belén, Para. B10 80
Belen, Ms., U.S. A3 131
Belen, N.M., U.S. C3 138
Belén, Ur. F10 80
Belén, stm., Arg. D5 80
Belén de Escobar, Arg. H9 80
Belfair, Wa., U.S. B3 154
Belfast, S. Afr. E10 66
Belfast, N. Ire., U.K. G8 8
Belfast, Me., U.S. D3 126
Belfast, N.Y., U.S. C2 139
Belfast, N.C., U.S. B5 140
Belfast, Tn., U.S. B5 149
Belfield, N.D., U.S. C2 141
Belford, N.J., U.S. C4 137
Belfort, Fr. E13 14
Belfry, Ky., U.S. C7 124
Belfry, Mt., U.S. E8 133
Belgaum, India E3 46
Belgium, Il., U.S. C6 120
Belgium, Wi., U.S. E6 156
Belgium, ctry., Eur. E8 4
Belgorod, U.S.S.R. G5 22
Belgorod-Dnestrovskij, U.S.S.R. H4 22
Belgrade, Mn., U.S. E3 130
Belgrade, Mo., U.S. D7 132
Belgrade, Mt., U.S. E5 133
Belgrade, Ne., U.S. C7 134
Belgrade see Beograd, Yugo. E4 20
Belgrade Lakes, Me., U.S. D3 126
Belgreen, Al., U.S. A2 108
Belhaven, N.C., U.S. B6 140
Beli Drim, stm., Eur. G4 20
Beli Manastir, Yugo. D2 20
Belington, W.V., U.S. B5 155
Belitung, i., Indon. F4 38
Belize, ctry., N.A. I15 90
Belize, stm., Belize I15 90
Belize City, Belize I15 90
Belk, Al., U.S. B2 108
Belknap, co., N.H., U.S. C3 136
Belknap Crater, crat., Or., U.S. C5 144
Belknap Mountain, mtn., N.H., U.S. C4 136
Bell, co., Ky., U.S. D6 124
Bell, co., Tx., U.S. D4 150
Bellac, Fr. F8 14
Bella Coola, B.C., Can. C4 99
Bella Coola, stm., B.C., Can. C4 99
Bella Flor, Bol. D8 82
Bellaire, Mi., U.S. D5 129
Bellaire, Oh., U.S. B5 142
Bellaire, Tx., U.S. r14 150
Bellamy, Al., U.S. C1 108
Bellary, India E4 46
Bella Unión, Ur. F10 80
Bella Vista, Arg. E9 80
Bella Vista, Arg. D6 80
Bella Vista, Para. B10 80
Bellavista, Peru A1 82
Bellavista, Peru B3 82
Bella Vista, Ar., U.S. A1 111
Bellbrook, Oh., U.S. C1 142
Bell Buckle, Tn., U.S. B5 149
Bell City, La., U.S. D3 125
Bell City, Mo., U.S. D8 132
Bellé, Sen. D3 64
Belle, Mo., U.S. C6 132
Belle, W.V., U.S. C3 155
Belle, stm., La., U.S. k9 125
Belleair, Fl., U.S. p10 116
Belle Bay, b., Newf., Can. E4 102
Belle Center, Oh., U.S. B2 142
Belle Chasse, La., U.S. E5 125
Belle Creek, Mt., U.S. E11 133
Belledune, N.B., Can. B4 101
Bellefleur, N.B., Can. B2 101
Bellefontaine, Ms., U.S. B4 131
Bellefontaine, Oh., U.S. B2 142
Bellefonte, Ar., U.S. A2 111
Bellefonte, Pa., U.S. E6 145
Belle Fourche, S.D., U.S. C2 148
Belle Fourche, stm., U.S. C3 148
Belle Fourche Reservoir, res., S.D., U.S. C2 148
Bellegarde, Fr. F12 14
Belle Glade, Fl., U.S. F6 116
Belle Haven, Va., U.S. C7 153
Belle-Île, i., Fr. E3 14
Belle Isle, Fl., U.S. D5 116
Belle Isle, i., Newf., Can. C4 102
Belle Isle, Strait of, strt., Newf., Can. C3 102
Belleisle Creek, N.B., Can. D4 101
Bellême, Fr. D7 14
Belle Meade, Tn., U.S. g10 149
Belle Mina, Al., U.S. A3 108
Belleoram, Newf., Can. E4 102
Belle-Plaine, Sask., Can. G3 105
Belle Plaine, Ia., U.S. C5 122
Belle Plaine, Ks., U.S. E6 123
Belle Plaine, Mn., U.S. F5 130
Belle Rive, Il., U.S. E5 120
Belle River, Ont., Can. E2 103
Belle Rose, La., U.S. D4 125
Belle Vernon, Pa., U.S. F2 145
Belleview, Fl., U.S. C4 116
Belleview, Fl., U.S. *u14 116
Belleview, Mo., U.S. D7 132
Belle View, Va., U.S. g12 153
Belleville, N.S., Can. F4 101
Belleville, Ont., Can. C7 103
Belleville, Ar., U.S. B2 111
Belleville, Il., U.S. E4 120
Belleville, Ks., U.S. C6 123
Belleville, Mi., U.S. p15 129
Belleville, N.J., U.S. B4 137
Belleville, Pa., U.S. E6 145
Belleville, Wi., U.S. F4 156
Belleville Pond, l., R.I., U.S. E4 146
Belleville-sur-Saône, Fr. F11 14
Bellevue, Id., U.S. F4 119
Bellevue, Ia., U.S. B7 122
Bellevue, Ky., U.S. h13 124
Bellevue, Mi., U.S. F5 129
Bellevue, Ne., U.S. C10 134
Bellevue, Oh., U.S. A3 142
Bellevue, Pa., U.S. F1 145
Bellevue, Wa., U.S. e11 154
Belley, Fr. G12 14
Bellflower, Ca., U.S. n12 112
Bellflower, Il., U.S. C5 120
Bellflower, Mo., U.S. B6 132
Bellingen, Austl. H10 70
Bellingham, Eng., U.K. F11 8
Bellingham, Ma., U.S. B5 128
Bellingham, Wa., U.S. A3 154
Bellingshausen, sci., B.A.T. B1 73
Bellingshausen Sea, Ant. C11 73
Bellinzona, Switz. F11 13
Bell-Irving, stm., B.C., Can. A3 99
Bellis, Alta., Can. B4 98
Bell Island, i., Newf., Can. C4 102
Bellmawr, N.J., U.S. D2 137
Bellmont, Il., U.S. E6 120
Bellmore, In., U.S. E3 121
Bello, Col. D5 84
Bellot Strait, strt., N.W. Ter., Can. B14 96
Bellows Falls, Vt., U.S. E4 152
Bell Peninsula, pen., N.W. Ter., Can. D16 96
Bellport, N.Y., U.S. n16 139
Bells, Tn., U.S. B2 149
Bells Creek, stm., W.V., U.S. m13 155
Belltown, De., U.S. F5 115
Belluno, Italy C7 18
Bell Ville, Arg. G7 80
Bellville, Ga., U.S. D5 117
Bellville, Oh., U.S. B3 142
Bellville, Tx., U.S. E4 150
Bellvue, Co., U.S. A5 113
Bellwood, Al., U.S. D4 108
Bellwood, Il., U.S. k9 120
Bellwood, Ne., U.S. C8 134
Bellwood, Pa., U.S. E5 145
Bellwood, Va., U.S. n18 153
Belmar, N.J., U.S. C4 137
Belmond, Ia., U.S. B4 122
Belmont, Man., Can. E2 100
Belmont, N.S., Can. D6 101
Belmont, Ont., Can. E3 103
Belmont, S. Afr. G7 66
Belmont, Ca., U.S. h8 112
Belmont, Ma., U.S. g11 128
Belmont, Ms., U.S. A5 131
Belmont, N.H., U.S. D4 136
Belmont, N.Y., U.S. C2 139
Belmont, N.C., U.S. B1 140
Belmont, Vt., U.S. E3 152
Belmont, W.V., U.S. B3 155
Belmont, Wi., U.S. F3 156
Belmont, co., Oh., U.S. C4 142
Belmonte, Braz. C9 79
Belmonte, Port. E4 16
Belmopan, Belize I15 90
Belmullet, Ire. G3 8
Bel-Nor, Mo., U.S. f13 132
Belo, Madag. Q21 67b
Beloeil, Que., Can. D4 104
Belogorsk, U.S.S.R. G17 24
Belo Horizonte, Braz. E7 79
Beloit, Ks., U.S. C5 123
Beloit, Oh., U.S. B5 142
Beloit, Wi., U.S. F4 156
Beloit North, Wi., U.S. F4 156
Beloje, ozero, l., U.S.S.R. A20 26
Beloje more (White Sea), U.S.S.R. D5 22
Belomorsk, U.S.S.R. E4 22
Belomorsko-Baltijskij kanal, U.S.S.R. I24 6
Beloomut, U.S.S.R. G22 26
Beloozersk, U.S.S.R. I8 26
Belorečensk, U.S.S.R. I5 22
Beloreck, U.S.S.R. G9 22
Belorussia see Belorusskaja Sovetskaja Socialističeskaja Respublika, state, U.S.S.R. H11 26
Belorusskaja Sovetskaja Socialističeskaja Respublika, state, U.S.S.R. H11 26
Belousovo, U.S.S.R. F19 26
Bel'ov, U.S.S.R. H19 26
Belo Vale, Braz. F6 79
Belovo, U.S.S.R. G9 24
Beloz'orsk, U.S.S.R. A20 26
Belpre, Ks., U.S. E4 123
Belpre, Oh., U.S. C4 142
Belspring, Va., U.S. C2 153
Belt, Mt., U.S. C6 133
Belt Creek, stm., Mt., U.S. C6 133
Belted Range, mts., Nv., U.S. F5 135
Belton, Mo., U.S. C3 132
Belton, S.C., U.S. B3 147
Belton, Tx., U.S. D4 150
Belton Lake, res., Tx., U.S. D4 150
Beltrami, co., Mn., U.S. B3 130
Beltrán, Arg. D6 80
Beltsville, Md., U.S. B4 127
Belucha, gora, mtn., U.S.S.R. H15 22
Beluchistān, hist. reg., Asia G17 48
Belūr, India G10 42
Belvedere, S.C., U.S. D4 147
Belvès, Fr. H8 14
Belvidere, Il., U.S. A5 120
Belvidere, Ne., U.S. D8 134
Belvidere, N.J., U.S. B2 137
Belvidere Mountain, mtn., Vt., U.S. B3 152
Belview, Mn., U.S. F3 130
Belvís de la Jara, Spain F7 16
Belvue, Ks., U.S. C7 123
Belwood, Ont., Can. D4 103
Belyando, stm., Austl. C7 70
Belyj, U.S.S.R. F15 26
Belyj, ostrov, i., U.S.S.R. C12 22
Belyje Berega, U.S.S.R. H17 26
Belyje Stolby, U.S.S.R. F20 26
Belyj Gorodok, U.S.S.R. E20 26
Belyj Luch, stm., U.S.S.R. D27 26
Belyniči, U.S.S.R. H12 26
Belynkoviči, U.S.S.R. H15 26
Belzoni, Ms., U.S. B3 131
Bemarivo, Madag. R21 67b
Bemavo, Madag. R21 67b
Bembéréké, Benin F11 64
Bement, Il., U.S. D5 120
Bemidji, Mn., U.S. C4 130
Bemidji, Lake, l., Mn., U.S. C4 130
Bemiss, Ga., U.S. F3 117
Benāb, Iran C9 48
Bena-Dibele, Zaire B4 58
Benagerie, Austl. H4 70
Benahmed, Mor. D7 62
Ben'akoni, U.S.S.R. G8 26
Benalla, Austl. K6 70
Benalto, Alta., Can. C3 98
Benares see Vārānasi, India H10 44
Ben Arous, Tun. B16 62
Benavente, Spain C6 16
Benavides, Tx., U.S. F3 150
Ben Badis, Alg. K11 16
Benbrook, Tx., U.S. n9 150
Benbrook Lake, res., Tx., U.S. n9 150
Bencubbin, Austl. F3 68
Bend, Or., U.S. C5 144
Bendaja, Lib. H4 64
Ben Davis Point, c., N.J., U.S. E2 137
Bende, Nig. I13 64
Bendeleben, Mount, mtn., Ak., U.S. B7 109
Bendemeer, Austl. H9 70
Bendery, U.S.S.R. H3 22
Bendigo, Austl. K6 70
Bendugu, S.L. G4 64
Bene, U.S.S.R. E6 26
Bene Beraq, Isr. D3 50
Benedict, Md., U.S. C4 127
Benedict, Ne., U.S. C8 134
Benedito Leite, Braz. E10 76
Benenitra, Madag. S21 67b
Benešov, Czech. F14 10
Benevento, Italy H9 18
Benevolence, Ga., U.S. E2 117
Benewah, co., Id., U.S. B2 119
Benfeld, Fr. D14 14
Bengal, Bay of, b., Asia J14 44
Ben Gardane, Tun. D16 62
Bengbu, China C6 34
Benghazi see Banghāzī, Libya B5 56
Ben Giang, Viet. G9 40
Bengkalis, Indon. N7 40
Bengkulu, Indon. F3 38
Bengough, Sask., Can. H3 105
Benguela, Ang. D2 58
Benguerir, Mor. D7 62
Benham, Ky., U.S. D7 124
Ben Hill, co., Ga., U.S. E3 117
Beni, Zaire A5 58
Beni, dept., Bol. E9 82
Beni, stm., Bol. D9 82
Béni Abbas, Alg. E9 62
Benicarló, Spain E12 16
Benicia, Ca., U.S. C2 112
Benicito, stm., Bol. D9 82
Benima, Cen. Afr. Rep. O2 60
Beni-Mellal, Mor. D7 62
Benin (Bénin), ctry., Afr. G7 54
Benin, Bight of, Afr. G7 54
Benin City, Nig. H12 64
Beni Saf, Alg. J10 16
Benissa, Spain G12 16
Benito, Man., Can. D1 100
Benito Juárez, Presa, res., Mex. I12 90
Benjamin Aceval, Para. C10 80
Benjamin Constant, Braz. J7 84
Benjamín Hill, Mex. B4 90
Benjamín Zorrilla, Arg. J6 80
Benkelman, Ne., U.S. D4 134
Benld, Il., U.S. D4 120
Ben Lomond, Ar., U.S. D1 111
Ben Mehidi, Alg. M2 18
Bennet, Ne., U.S. D9 134
Bennett, Co., U.S. B6 113
Bennett, Ia., U.S. C7 122
Bennett, co., S.D., U.S. D4 148
Bennetta, ostrov, i., U.S.S.R. B21 24
Bennett Creek, stm., Md., U.S. B3 127
Bennettsville, S.C., U.S. B8 147
Bennington, Id., U.S. G7 119
Bennington, Ks., U.S. C6 123
Bennington, Ne., U.S. g12 134
Bennington, N.H., U.S. D3 136
Bennington, Ok., U.S. C5 143
Bennington, Vt., U.S. F2 152
Bennington, co., Vt., U.S. E2 152
Benniu, China D8 34

Name — Map Ref. — Page

Benoit, Ms., U.S. B2 131
Benoni, S. Afr. F9 66
Bénoué (Benue), stm., Afr. G9 54
Benque Viejo del Carmen, Belize I15 90
Bensenville, Il., U.S. B6 120
Bensheim, Ger. F8 10
Bensley, Va., U.S. C5 153
Ben-Slimane, Mor. D7 62
Ben Smih, Alg. M2 18
Benson, Sask., Can. H4 105
Benson, Az., U.S. F5 110
Benson, Il., U.S. C4 120
Benson, Mn., U.S. E3 130
Benson, N.C., U.S. B4 140
Benson, co., N.D., U.S. A6 141
Bent, co., Co., U.S. D7 113
Bentinck Island, i., Austl. C7 68
Bentiu, Sud. M5 60
Bentley, Alta., Can. C3 98
Bentley, Ks., U.S. E6 123
Bentley, La., U.S. C3 125
Bentleyville, Pa., U.S. F1 145
Bento Gomes, stm., Braz. G13 82
Bento Gonçalves, Braz. E13 80
Benton, N.B., Can. D2 101
Benton, Ar., U.S. C3 111
Benton, Il., U.S. E5 120
Benton, In., U.S. B6 121
Benton, Ks., U.S. E6 123
Benton, Ky., U.S. f9 124
Benton, La., U.S. B2 125
Benton, Ms., U.S. C3 131
Benton, Mo., U.S. D8 132
Benton, Pa., U.S. D9 145
Benton, Tn., U.S. B7 149
Benton, Wi., U.S. F3 156
Benton, co., Ar., U.S. A1 111
Benton, co., In., U.S. C3 121
Benton, co., Ia., U.S. B5 122
Benton, co., Mn., U.S. E4 130
Benton, co., Ms., U.S. A4 131
Benton, co., Mo., U.S. C4 132
Benton, co., Or., U.S. C3 144
Benton, co., Tn., U.S. A3 149
Benton, co., Wa., U.S. C6 154
Benton City, Wa., U.S. C6 154
Bentong, Malay. M6 40
Benton Harbor, Mi., U.S. F4 129
Benton Heights, Mi., U.S. F4 129
Bentonia, Ms., U.S. C3 131
Bentonville, Ar., U.S. A1 111
Bentonville, Va., U.S. B4 153
Ben Tre, Viet. I9 40
Bentree, W.V., U.S. m13 155
Bent's Old Fort National Historic Site, hist., Co., U.S. C7 113
Benue (Bénoué), stm., Afr. G8 54
Benwood, W.V., U.S. f8 155
Benxi (Penhsi), China B11 32
Benzie, co., Mi., U.S. D4 129
Benzonia, Mi., U.S. D4 129
Beograd (Belgrade), Yugo. E4 20
Beowawe, Nv., U.S. C5 135
Beppu, Japan N6 36
Bequia, i., St. Vin. H14 94
Beramanja, Madag. N23 67b
Berat, Alb. I3 20
Berau, Teluk, b., Indon. F9 38
Beravina, Madag. Q21 67b
Berbera, Som. F10 56
Berbérati, Cen. Afr. Rep. H4 56
Berbice, stm., Guy. D14 84
Berchtesgaden, Ger. H13 10
Berd'ansk, U.S.S.R. H5 22
Berdičev, U.S.S.R. H3 22
Berdigest'ach, U.S.S.R. E17 24
Berdsk, U.S.S.R. G8 24
Berea, Ky., U.S. C5 124
Berea, Oh., U.S. A4 142
Berea, S.C., U.S. B3 147
Beregomet, U.S.S.R. A9 20
Beregovo, U.S.S.R. G22 10
Berekua, Dom. G14 94
Berendejevo, U.S.S.R. E22 26
Berens, stm., Can. C3 100
Berens River, Man., Can. C3 100
Beresford, S.D., U.S. D9 148
Berettyó (Barcău), stm., Eur. B5 20
Berevo, Madag. Q21 67b
Berezajka, U.S.S.R. D16 26
Berezino, U.S.S.R. C13 20
Berezino, U.S.S.R. H11 26
Berezino, U.S.S.R. G11 26
Berezniki, U.S.S.R. F9 22
Berg, Nor. G15 6
Berga, Spain C13 16
Bergama, Tur. J11 20
Bergamo, Italy D4 18
Bergantín, Ven. B10 84
Bergara, Spain B9 16
Bergby, Swe. K15 6
Bergen (Mons), Bel. H4 12
Bergen, Ger. C10 10
Bergen, Neth. C6 12
Bergen, Nor. K9 6
Bergen, N.Y., U.S. B3 139
Bergen, co., N.J., U.S. A4 137
Bergen aan Zee, Neth. C6 12
Bergen [auf Rügen], Ger. A13 10
Bergenfield, N.J., U.S. B4 137
Bergen op Zoom, Neth. E5 12
Berger, Mo., U.S. C6 132
Bergerac, Fr. H7 14
Bergholz, Oh., U.S. B5 142
Bergisch, Ger. D7 10
Bergisch Gladbach, Ger. E7 10
Bergland, Mi., U.S. m12 129
Bergman, Ar., U.S. A2 111
Bergoo, W.V., U.S. C4 155
Bergsche Maas, stm., Neth. E6 12
Bergsjö, Swe. K15 6
Bergstrom Air Force Base, mil., Tx., U.S. D4 150
Berguent, Mor. C9 62
Bergues, Fr. B9 14
Berhala, Selat, strt., Indon. O8 40
Beringa, ostrov, i., U.S.S.R. F25 24
Bering Sea C2 86
Bering Strait, strt. m18 106a
Berino, N.M., U.S. E3 138
Berja, Spain I9 16
Berkane, Mor. C9 62
Berkeley, Ont., Can. C4 103
Berkeley, Ca., U.S. D2 112
Berkeley, Mo., U.S. f13 132
Berkeley, R.I., U.S. B4 146
Berkeley, co., S.C., U.S. E8 147
Berkeley, co., W.V., U.S. B6 155
Berkeley Heights, N.J., U.S. B4 137
Berkeley Springs, W.V., U.S. B6 155
Berkley, Mi., U.S. F7 129
Berkner Island, i., Ant. C1 73
Berks, co., Pa., U.S. F9 145
Berkshire, Vt., U.S. B3 152
Berkshire, co., Eng., U.K. J12 8
Berkshire, co., Ma., U.S. B1 128
Berkshire Hills, hills, Ma., U.S. B1 128
Berlaimont, Fr. B10 14
Berland, stm., Alta., Can. C1 98
Berlin, Ger. C13 10
Berlin, S. Afr. I8 66
Berlin, Ct., U.S. C5 114
Berlin, Ga., U.S. E3 117
Berlin, Md., U.S. D7 127
Berlin, N.H., U.S. B4 136
Berlin, N.J., U.S. D3 137
Berlin, N.Y., U.S. C7 139
Berlin, Oh., U.S. B4 142
Berlin, Pa., U.S. G4 145
Berlin, Wi., U.S. E5 156
Berlin, state, Ger. C13 10
Berlin, Mount, mtn., Ant. C10 73
Berlin Corners, Vt., U.S. C3 152
Berlin Heights, Oh., U.S. A3 142
Berlin Lake, res., Oh., U.S. A4 142
Berlin Mountain, mtn., U.S. A1 128
Bermejillo, Mex. E8 90
Bermejo, Arg. F5 80
Bermejo, stm., Arg. F5 80
Bermejo, stm., S.A. C9 80
Bermejo, Paso de, S.A. G3 80
Bermeo, Spain B9 16
Bermuda, dep., N.A. B12 88
Bern (Berne), Switz. E7 13
Bern, Ks., U.S. C8 123
Bern (Berne), state, Switz. E8 13
Bernalda, Italy I11 18
Bernalillo, N.M., U.S. B3 138
Bernalillo, co., N.M., U.S. C3 138
Bernard, Me., U.S. D4 126
Bernardsville, N.J., U.S. B3 137
Bernasconi, Arg. I7 80
Bernau bei Berlin, Ger. C13 10
Bernay, Fr. C7 14
Bernburg, Ger. D11 10
Berne, In., U.S. C8 121
Berner Alpen, mts., Switz. F7 13
Bernice, La., U.S. B3 125
Bernice, Ok., U.S. A7 143
Bernie, Mo., U.S. E8 132
Bernier Bay, b., N.W. Ter., Can. B15 96
Bernina, mts., Eur. F12 13
Bernina, Passo del, Switz. F13 13
Bernina, Piz, mtn., Eur. F16 14
Bernville, Pa., U.S. F9 145
Beromünster, Switz. H8 10
Berón de Astrada, Arg. D10 80
Beroroha, Madag. R21 67b
Ber'ostovica, U.S.S.R. H6 26
Beroun, Czech. F14 10
Berounka, stm., Czech. F13 10
Berovo, Yugo. H6 20
Ber'oza, U.S.S.R. I7 26
Ber'ozovo, U.S.S.R. E11 22
Berrechid, Mor. D7 62
Berri, Austl. J4 70
Berrien, co., Ga., U.S. E3 117
Berrien, co., Mi., U.S. F4 129
Berrien Springs, Mi., U.S. G4 129
Berrigan, Austl. J6 70
Berriyyane, Alg. D12 62
Berry, Al., U.S. B2 108
Berry, Ky., U.S. B5 124
Berry, hist. reg., Fr. E9 14
Berry Creek, stm., Alta., Can. D5 98
Berryessa, Lake, res., Ca., U.S. C2 112
Berry Hill, Tn., U.S. g10 149
Berry Islands, is., Bah. B6 94
Berrys Chapel, Tn., U.S. B5 149
Berryton, Ga., U.S. B1 117
Berryville, Ar., U.S. A2 111
Berryville, Va., U.S. A5 153
Beršad', U.S.S.R. A13 20
Berseba, Nmb. F3 66
Bersenbrück, Ger. C7 10
Bertha, Mn., U.S. D3 130
Berthierville, Que., Can. C4 104
Berthold, N.D., U.S. A4 141
Berthoud, Co., U.S. A5 113
Berthoud Pass, Co., U.S. B5 113
Bertie, co., N.C., U.S. A5 140
Bertoua, Cam. H9 54
Bertram, Tx., U.S. D4 150
Bertrand, Mo., U.S. E8 132
Bertrand, Ne., U.S. D6 134
Beruri, Braz. I12 84
Berwick, N.S., Can. D5 101
Berwick, Il., U.S. C3 120
Berwick, Ia., U.S. e8 122
Berwick, La., U.S. E4 125
Berwick, Me., U.S. E2 126
Berwick, Pa., U.S. D9 145
Berwick-upon-Tweed, Eng., U.K. F11 8
Berwind, W.V., U.S. D3 155
Berwyn, Alta., Can. A2 98
Berwyn, Il., U.S. k9 120
Berwyn, Ne., U.S. C6 134
Berwyn, Pa., U.S. o20 145
Besalampy, Madag. P21 67b
Besançon, Fr. E13 14
Besbes, Alg. M2 18
Bešenkoviči, U.S.S.R. F12 26
Beskid Mountains, mts., Eur. F20 10
Beskra, Alg. C13 62
Beslan, U.S.S.R. I6 22
Besni, Tur. C4 48
Besor, Naḥal, val., Asia F2 50
Bessarabia, hist. reg., U.S.S.R. C12 20
Bessarabka, U.S.S.R. C12 20
Besse, Nig. F12 64
Bessemer, Al., U.S. B3 108
Bessemer, Mi., U.S. n11 129
Bessemer, Pa., U.S. E1 145
Bessemer City, N.C., U.S. B1 140
Bessie, Ok., U.S. B3 143
Best'ach, U.S.S.R. E17 24
Bestobe, U.S.S.R. G12 22
Betafo, Madag. Q22 67b
Betanzos, Bol. H9 82
Betanzos, Spain B3 16
Betaré Oya, Cam. G9 54
Betatakin Ruin, hist., Az., U.S. A5 110
Betbetti, Sud. J3 60
Bete Hor, Eth. L10 60
Bétera, Spain F11 16
Bétérou, Benin G11 64
Bet Guvrin, Isr. E3 50
Bet Ha'arava, Isr. Occ. E5 50
Bethal, S. Afr. F9 66
Bethalto, Il., U.S. E3 120
Bethanien, Nmb. F3 66
Bethany, Ont., Can. C6 103
Bethany, Ct., U.S. D4 114
Bethany, Il., U.S. D5 120
Bethany, Mo., U.S. A3 132
Bethany, Ok., U.S. B4 143
Bethany, W.V., U.S. A4 155
Bethany Beach, De., U.S. F5 115
Bethel, Ak., U.S. C7 109
Bethel, Ct., U.S. D2 114
Bethel, De., U.S. F3 115
Bethel, Ky., U.S. B6 124
Bethel, Me., U.S. D2 126
Bethel, N.C., U.S. B5 140
Bethel, Oh., U.S. D1 142
Bethel, Ok., U.S. C7 143
Bethel, Pa., U.S. F9 145
Bethel, Vt., U.S. D3 152
Bethel Acres, Ok., U.S. C2 143
Bethel Park, Pa., U.S. k14 145
Bethel Springs, Tn., U.S. B3 149
Bethesda, Ar., U.S. B4 111
Bethesda, Md., U.S. C3 127
Bethesda, Oh., U.S. B4 142
Bethlehem, S. Afr. G9 66
Bethlehem, Ct., U.S. C3 114
Bethlehem, Ga., U.S. C3 117
Bethlehem, N.H., U.S. B3 136
Bethlehem, Pa., U.S. E11 145
Bethlehem see Bayt Lahm, Isr. Occ. E4 50
Bethpage, Tn., U.S. A5 149
Bethune, Sask., Can. G3 105
Béthune, Fr. B9 14
Bethune, Co., U.S. B8 113
Bethune, S.C., U.S. C7 147
Beticos, Sistemas, mts., Spain H8 16
Betijoque, Ven. C7 84
Betioky, Madag. S21 67b
Betlica, U.S.S.R. G16 26
Betong, Thai. L6 40
Betoota, Austl. E4 70
Betpak-Dala, des., U.S.S.R. H12 22
Betroka, Madag. S22 67b
Bet She'an, Isr. C5 50
Bet Shemesh, Isr. E4 50
Betsiboka, stm., Madag. P22 67b
Betsie, Point, c., Mi., U.S. D4 129
Betsioky, Madag. R21 67b
Betsy Layne, Ky., U.S. C7 124
Bette, mtn., Libya D4 56
Bettendorf, Ia., U.S. C7 122
Bettsville, Oh., U.S. A2 142
Betül, India J7 44
Betzdorf, Ger. E7 10
Beulah, Al., U.S. C4 108
Beulah, Co., U.S. C6 113
Beulah, Mi., U.S. D4 129
Beulah, Ms., U.S. B3 131
Beulah, N.D., U.S. B4 141
Beulah, Wy., U.S. B8 157
Beulah, Lake, l., Ms., U.S. B3 131
Beulaville, N.C., U.S. C5 140
Bevensen, Ger. B10 10
B. Everett Jordan Lake, res., N.C., U.S. B3 140
Beverley, Austl. F3 68
Beverley, Eng., U.K. H13 8
Beverley Head, c., Newf., Can. D2 102
Beverly, Ks., U.S. C6 123
Beverly, Ma., U.S. A6 128
Beverly, N.J., U.S. C3 137
Beverly, Oh., U.S. C4 142
Beverly, Tn., U.S. m14 149
Beverly, W.V., U.S. C5 155
Beverly Hills, Ca., U.S. m12 112
Beverly Shores, In., U.S. A4 121
Beverwijk, Neth. D6 12
Bewdley, Ont., Can. C6 103
Bexar, co., Tx., U.S. E3 150
Bexley, Oh., U.S. m11 142
Beyçayırı, Tur. I10 20
Beylul, Eth. H3 47
Beypazarı, Tur. G14 4
Beyşehir Gölü, l., Tur. H14 4
Bezaha, Madag. S21 67b
Bežanicy, U.S.S.R. E12 26
Bezau, Aus. H9 10
Bežeck, U.S.S.R. D19 26
Bezerra, stm., Braz. B5 79
Béziers, Fr. I10 14
Bezmein, U.S.S.R. B15 48
Bhadrak, India J12 44
Bhadrāvati, India F3 46
Bhāg, Pak. F2 44
Bhāgalpur, India H12 44
Bhakkar, Pak. E4 44
Bhaktapur, Nepal G11 44
Bhamo, Burma B4 40
Bhandāra, India J8 44
Bharatpur, India G7 44
Bharatpur, Nepal G11 44
Bharūch, India J5 44
Bhātāpāra, India B6 46
Bhātpāra, India I13 44
Bhāvnagar, India J5 44
Bhawānipatna, India C7 46
Bhera, Pak. D5 44
Bhilai, India J9 44
Bhīlwāra, India H6 44
Bhind, India G8 44
Bhiwandi, India C2 46
Bhiwāni, India F7 44
Bhongīr, India D5 46
Bhopāl, India I7 44
Bhubaneshwar, India J11 44
Bhuj, India I3 44
Bhusāwal, India J6 44
Bhutan (Druk-Yul), ctry., Asia D13 42
Bia, stm., Afr. H8 64
Biá, stm., Braz. I9 84
Bia, Phou, mtn., Laos E7 40
Biabo, stm., Peru B3 82
Biafra, Bight of, Afr. H8 54
Biak, i., Indon. F10 38
Biała, Pol. E17 10
Biała Podlaska, Pol. C23 10
Biała Rawska, Pol. D20 10
Białogard, Pol. A16 10
Białystok, Pol. B23 10
Bianco, Monte (Mont Blanc), mtn., Eur. G13 14
Biarritz, Fr. I5 14
Biasca, Switz. F10 13
Bibā, Egypt C6 60
Bibai, Japan D16 36a
Bibala, Ang. D2 58
Bibb, co., Al., U.S. C2 108
Bibb, co., Ga., U.S. D3 117
Bibb City, Ga., U.S. D2 117
Biberach an der Riss, Ger. G9 10
Bibiani, Ghana H8 64
Biblián, Ec. I3 84
Bic, Que., Can. A9 104
Bic, Île du, i., Que., Can. A9 104
Bicas, Braz. F7 79
Bicaz, Rom. C10 20
Bičevinka, U.S.S.R. B20 26
Biche, Lac la, l., Alta., Can. B4 98
Bichena, Eth. L10 60
Bickett Knob, mtn., W.V., U.S. D4 155
Bickle Knob, mtn., W.V., U.S. C5 155
Bicknell, In., U.S. G3 121
Bicknell, Ut., U.S. E4 151
Bicske, Hung. H18 10
Bicudo, stm., Braz. E6 79
Bīd, India C3 46
Bida, Nig. G13 64
Bīdar, India D4 46
Biddeford, Me., U.S. E2 126
Bidian, China C2 34
Bidwell, Mount, mtn., Ca., U.S. B3 112
Bieber, Ca., U.S. B3 112
Biecz, Pol. F21 10
Biedenkopf, Ger. E8 10
Biel (Bienne), Switz. D7 13
Bielawa, Pol. E16 10
Bielefeld, Ger. C8 10
Bielersee, l., Switz. D7 13
Biella, Italy D3 18
Bielsko-Biała, Pol. F19 10
Bielsk Podlaski, Pol. C23 10
Bienfait, Sask., Can. H4 105
Bien Hoa, Viet. I9 40
Bienville, La., U.S. B3 125
Bienville, co., La., U.S. B2 125
Bienville, Lac, l., Que., Can. g12 104
Big, stm., Mo., U.S. c7 132
Biga, Tur. I11 20
Big A Mountain, mtn., Va., U.S. e9 153
Big Arm, Mt., U.S. C2 133
Big Bald, mtn., U.S. f10 140
Big Bald, mtn., Ga., U.S. B2 117
Big Bald Mountain, mtn., N.B., Can. B3 101
Big Baldy, mtn., Id., U.S. E3 119
Big Baldy Mountain, mtn., Mt., U.S. D6 133
Big Bay, Mi., U.S. B3 129
Big Bay De Noc, b., Mi., U.S. C4 129
Big Bayou, stm., Ar., U.S. D4 111
Big Bear City, Ca., U.S. E5 112
Big Beaver, Sask., Can. H3 105
Big Belt Mountains, mts., Mt., U.S. D5 133
Big Bend, Swaz. F10 66
Big Bend, Wi., U.S. n11 156
Big Bend Dam, S.D., U.S. C6 148
Big Bend National Park, Tx., U.S. E1 150
Big Birch Lake, l., Mn., U.S. E4 130
Big Black, stm., Me., U.S. B3 126
Big Black, stm., Ms., U.S. C3 131
Big Blue, stm., In., U.S. E6 121
Big Burro Mountains, mts., N.M., U.S. E1 138
Big Butt, mtn., Tn., U.S. C11 149
Big Cabin, Ok., U.S. A6 143
Big Cabin Creek, stm., Ok., U.S. A6 143
Big Canyon, val., Tx., U.S. D1 150
Big Chino Wash, val., Az., U.S. B3 110
Big Clifty, Ky., U.S. C3 124
Big Coal, stm., W.V., U.S. C3 155
Big Costilla Peak, mtn., N.M., U.S. A4 138
Big Creek, B.C., Can. D6 99
Big Creek, Ca., U.S. D4 112
Big Creek, Ky., U.S. C6 124
Big Creek, W.V., U.S. C2 155
Big Creek, stm., Ar., U.S. C5 111
Big Creek, stm., In., U.S. H2 121
Big Creek, stm., In., U.S. G7 121
Big Creek, stm., Ks., U.S. D4 123
Big Creek, stm., La., U.S. B4 125
Big Creek, stm., Ms., U.S. D5 131
Big Creek, stm., Mo., U.S. C3 132
Big Creek, stm., Tn., U.S. e8 149
Big Creek Lake, res., Al., U.S. E1 108
Big Creek Peak, mtn., Id., U.S. E5 119
Big Cypress Indian Reservation, Fl., U.S. F5 116
Big Cypress Swamp, sw., Fl., U.S. F5 116
Big Darby Creek, stm., Oh., U.S. C2 142
Big Delta, Ak., U.S. C10 109
Big Desert, des., Austl. J4 70
Big Dry Creek, stm., Mt., U.S. C10 133
Big Duke Dam, N.C., U.S. B2 140
Big Eau Pleine, stm., Wi., U.S. D3 156
Big Eau Pleine Reservoir, res., Wi., U.S. D4 156
Big Elk Creek, stm., Md., U.S. A6 127
Bigelow, Ar., U.S. B3 111
Bigelow, Mount, mtn., Me., U.S. C2 126
Big Escambia Creek, stm., U.S. D2 108
Big Falls, Mn., U.S. B5 130
Big Flat Mountain, mtn., Va., U.S. B4 153
Big Flats, N.Y., U.S. C4 139
Bigfork, Mn., U.S. C5 130
Bigfork, Mt., U.S. B2 133
Big Fork, stm., Mn., U.S. B5 130
Big Frog Mountain, mtn., Tn., U.S. D9 149
Biggar, Sask., Can. E1 105
Biggar, Scot., U.K. F10 8
Biggers, Ar., U.S. A5 111
Biggersville, Ms., U.S. A5 131
Biggs, Ca., U.S. C3 112
Biggsville, Il., U.S. C3 120
Big Hatchet Peak, mtn., N.M., U.S. F1 138
Big Hole, stm., Mt., U.S. E4 133
Big Hole National Battlefield, hist., Mt., U.S. E3 133
Big Horn, Wy., U.S. B5 157
Big Horn, co., Mt., U.S. E9 133
Big Horn, co., Wy., U.S. B4 157
Bighorn, stm., U.S. B5 106
Bighorn Canyon National Recreation Area, U.S. F8 133
Bighorn Lake, res., U.S. E8 133
Bighorn Mountains, mts., U.S. B5 157
Big Horn Mountains, mts., Az., U.S. D2 110
Big Island, Va., U.S. C3 153
Big Island, i., N.W. Ter., Can. D18 96
Big Island, i., N.W. Ter., Can. f8 102
Big Kandiyohi Lake, l., Mn., U.S. F4 130
Big Knob, mtn., Pa., U.S. F6 145
Big Knob, mtn., Va., U.S. f9 153
Big Lake, Mn., U.S. E5 130
Big Lake, Tx., U.S. D2 150
Big Lake, l., Me., U.S. C5 126
Biglerville, Pa., U.S. G7 145
Big Lookout Mountain, mtn., Or., U.S. C9 144
Big Lost, stm., Id., U.S. F5 119
Big Mossy Point, c., Man., Can. C2 100
Big Mountain, mtn., Nv., U.S. B2 135
Big Muddy, stm., Il., U.S. F4 120
Big Muddy Creek, stm., Mt., U.S. B12 133
Bignasco, Switz. F10 13
Big Nemaha, stm., Ne., U.S. D10 134
Bignona, Sen. E1 64
Big North Mountain, mts., Va., U.S. B4 153
Big Otter, stm., Va., U.S. C3 153
Big Pine, Ca., U.S. D4 112
Big Pine Creek, stm., In., U.S. D3 121
Big Pine Lake, l., Mn., U.S. D3 130
Big Pine Mountain, mtn., Ca., U.S. E4 112
Big Piney, Wy., U.S. D2 157
Big Piney, stm., Mo., U.S. D5 132
Big Piney Creek, stm., Ar., U.S. B2 111
Big Pipe Creek, stm., Md., U.S. A3 127
Bigpoint, Ms., U.S. E5 131
Big Raccoon Creek, stm., In., U.S. E4 121
Big Rapids, Mi., U.S. E5 129
Big Rib, stm., Wi., U.S. C3 156
Big River, Sask., Can. D2 105
Big River, Ca., U.S. E6 112
Big Rock, Il., U.S. B5 120
Big Rock, Tn., U.S. A4 149
Big Rock Mountain, mtn., Ar., U.S. h10 111
Big Run, Pa., U.S. E4 145
Big Sable Point, c., Mi., U.S. D4 129
Big Sandy, Mt., U.S. B6 133
Big Sandy, Tn., U.S. A3 149
Big Sandy, Tx., U.S. C5 150
Big Sandy, stm., U.S. C2 155
Big Sandy, stm., Az., U.S. C2 110
Big Sandy, stm., Tn., U.S. B3 149
Big Sandy, stm., Wy., U.S. D3 157
Big Sandy Creek, stm., Co., U.S. C8 113
Big Sandy Creek, stm., Mt., U.S. B6 133
Big Sandy Creek, stm., W.V., U.S. C3 155
Big Sandy Lake, l., Mn., U.S. D5 130
Big Sandy Reservoir, res., Wy., U.S. D3 157
Big Satilla Creek, stm., Ga., U.S. E4 117
Big Savage Mountain, mtn., U.S. k12 127
Big Sheep Mountain, mtn., Mt., U.S. C11 133
Big Shiney Mountian, mtn., Pa., U.S. n18 145
Big Sioux, stm., U.S. E9 148
Big Slough, stm., Ga., U.S. F2 117
Big Smoky Valley, val., Nv., U.S. E4 135
Big Snowy Mountains, mts., Mt., U.S. D7 133
Big Southern Butte, mtn., Id., U.S. F5 119
Big South Fork, stm., Ky., U.S. k13 124
Big Spencer Mountain, mtn., Me., U.S. C3 126
Big Spring, Tx., U.S. C2 150
Big Springs, Ne., U.S. C3 134
Big Spruce Knob, mtn., W.V., U.S. C4 155
Big Squaw Mountain, mtn., Me., U.S. C3 126
Big Stone, co., Mn., U.S. E2 130
Bigstone, stm., Man., Can. B4 100
Big Stone City, S.D., U.S. B9 148
Big Stone Gap, Va., U.S. f9 153
Big Stone Lake, l., U.S. E2 130
Big Sunflower, stm., Ms., U.S. B3 131
Big Sur, Ca., U.S. D3 112
Big Thompson, stm., Co., U.S. A5 113
Big Timber, Mt., U.S. E7 133
Big Top, mtn., Tn., U.S. B5 149
Big Trout Lake, l., Ont., Can. n17 103
Biguaçu, Braz. D14 80
Big Valley, Alta., Can. C4 98
Big Walnut Creek, stm., Oh., U.S. m11 142
Big Warrambool, stm., Austl. G8 70
Big Water, Ut., U.S. F4 151
Big Wells, Tx., U.S. E3 150
Big Wills Creek, stm., Al., U.S. A3 108
Bigwood, Ont., Can. A4 103
Big Wood, stm., Id., U.S. F4 119
Bihać, Yugo. E10 18
Bihār, India H11 44
Bihār, state, India H11 44
Bihor, co., Rom. B6 20
Bija, stm., U.S.S.R. G15 22
Bijagós, Arquipélago dos, is., Gui.-B. F1 64
Bījār, Iran D9 48
Bijeljina, Yugo. E3 20
Bijelo Polje, Yugo. F3 20
Bijie, China F8 30
Bijou Creek, stm., Co., U.S. B6 113
Bijsk, U.S.S.R. G9 24
Bīkaner, India F5 44
Bikeqi, China C9 30
Bikin, U.S.S.R. H18 24
Bikin, stm., U.S.S.R. H19 24
Bikini, atoll, Marsh. Is. G20 158
Bikoro, Zaire B3 58
Bilac, Braz. F3 79
Bilāspur, India I10 44
Bilauktaung Range, mts., Asia H5 40
Bilbao, Spain B9 16
Bilian, China G9 34
Bīlimora, India B2 46
Bilin, Burma F4 40
Bílina, Czech. E13 10
Bilk Creek Mountains, mts., Nv., U.S. B3 135
Billabong Creek, stm., Austl. J6 70
Billerica, Ma., U.S. A5 128
Billings, Mo., U.S. D4 132
Billings, Mt., U.S. E8 133
Billings, Ok., U.S. A4 143
Billings, co., N.D., U.S. B2 141
Billings Heights, Mt., U.S. E8 133
Billingsley, Al., U.S. C3 108
Billom, Fr. G10 14
Bill Williams, stm., Az., U.S. C1 110
Bill Williams Mountain, mtn., Az., U.S. B3 110
Bilma, Niger E9 54
Biloela, Austl. E9 70
Biloxi, Ms., U.S. E5 131
Biloxi, stm., Ms., U.S. E4 131
Biloxi Bay, b., Ms., U.S. f8 131
Biltmore Forest, N.C., U.S. f10 140
Bilugyun Island, i., Burma F4 40
Bilwaskarma, Nic. C11 92
Bim, W.V., U.S. n12 155
Bimbān, Egypt E7 60
Bimbila, Ghana G10 64
Bimini Islands, is., Bah. B5 94
Binche, Bel. H5 12
Bindura, Zimb. E6 58
Binéfar, Spain D12 16
Binford, N.D., U.S. B7 141
Binga, Monte, mtn., Afr. B11 66
Bingamon Creek, stm., W.V., U.S. k10 155
Bingara, Austl. G9 70
Bingen, Ger. F7 10
Bingen, Wa., U.S. D4 154
Binger, Ok., U.S. B3 143
Bingham, Me., U.S. C3 126
Bingham, co., Id., U.S. F6 119
Bingham Lake, Mn., U.S. G3 130
Binghamton, N.Y., U.S. C5 139
Bingöl, Tur. B6 48
Binhai (Dongkan), China A8 34
Binjai, Indon. M5 40
Binscarth, Man., Can. D1 100
Bintan, Pulau, i., Indon. N8 40
Bintang, Gam. E1 64
Bintimani, mtn., S.L. G4 64
Bint Jubayl, Leb. B4 50
Bintulu, Malay. E5 38
Binxian, China D8 30
Binyamina, Isr. C3 50
Binyang, China C10 40
Bin Yauri, Nig. F12 64
Biobío, prov., Chile I3 80
Biobío, stm., Chile I2 80
Bioko, i., Eq. Gui. J14 64
Bippus, In., U.S. C6 121
Birāk, Libya C3 56
Bi'r al-Uzam, Libya B2 60
Birao, Cen. Afr. Rep. L2 60
Birātnagar, Nepal F4 30
Birch, stm., W.V., U.S. C4 155
Birch Hills, Sask., Can. E3 105
Birch Island, B.C., Can. D8 99
Birch Island, i., Man., Can. C2 100
Birch Lake, l., Mn., U.S. C7 130
Birch River, Man., Can. C1 100
Birch Rock Hill, mtn., Pa., U.S. F3 145
Birch Run, Mi., U.S. E7 129
Birch Tree, Mo., U.S. E6 132
Birchwood, Ct., U.S. B5 114
Birchwood, Tn., U.S. D9 149
Birchwood, Wi., U.S. C2 156
Birchwood City, Md., U.S. f9 127
Birchy Bay, Newf., Can. D4 102
Bird City, Ks., U.S. C2 123
Bird Creek, stm., Ok., U.S. A6 143
Bird Island, Mn., U.S. F4 130
Bird Island, i., N.C., U.S. D4 140
Bird Island, sci., Falk. Is. A1 73
Bird Islet, i., Austl. D11 68

Name | Map Ref. | Page

Birdsboro, Pa., U.S. F10 145
Birds Creek, Ont., Can. B7 103
Birdseye, In., U.S. H4 121
Birdsong, Ar., U.S. B5 111
Birdsville, Austl. E3 70
Birdtown, N.C., U.S. f9 140
Birdum, Austl. C6 68
Birdwood Creek, stm., Ne., U.S. C4 134
Birecik, Tur. C4 48
Bir el Ater, Alg. C15 62
Bir Enzaran, W. Sah. I3 62
Birigui, Braz. F3 79
Biril'ussy, U.S.S.R. F16 22
Bīrjand, Iran E15 48
Birkenhead, Eng., U.K. H10 8
Birkfeld, Aus. H15 10
Bîrlad, Rom. C11 20
Birmingham, Eng., U.K. I12 8
Birmingham, Al., U.S. B3 108
Birmingham, Ia., U.S. D6 122
Birmingham, Mi., U.S. F7 129
Birmingham, Mo., U.S. h11 132
Birmitrapur, India I11 44
Bîr Mogreïn (Fort-Trinquet), Maur. H5 62
Birnamwood, Wi., U.S. D4 156
Birni, Benin F10 64
Birnie, Man., Can. D2 100
Birni Ngaouré, Niger E11 64
Birnin Gwari, Nig. F13 64
Birni Nkonni, Niger E12 64
Birnin Kudu, Nig. F14 64
Birobidžan, U.S.S.R. H18 24
Biron, Wi., U.S. D4 156
Birrie, stm., Austl. G7 70
Birsay, Sask., Can. F2 105
Birsk, U.S.S.R. F9 22
Birtle, Man., Can. D1 100
Bir'usa, stm., U.S.S.R. F17 22
Biržai, U.S.S.R. E7 26
Bîrzava, stm., Eur. D5 20
Bisbee, Az., U.S. F6 110
Bisbee, N.D., U.S. A6 141
Biscarrosse, Fr. H5 14
Biscay, Bay of, b., Eur. H3 14
Biscayne, Key, i., Fl., U.S. s13 116
Biscayne Bay, b., Fl., U.S. G6 116
Biscayne National Monument, Fl., U.S. G6 116
Biscayne Park, Fl., U.S. s13 116
Bisceglie, Italy H11 18
Bischofswerda, Ger. D14 10
Biscoe, Ar., U.S. C4 111
Biscoe, N.C., U.S. B3 140
Biscoe Islands, is., Ant. B12 73
Biscucuy, Ven. C8 84
Bisha, Eth. J9 60
Bisho, Ciskei I8 66
Bishop, Ca., U.S. D4 112
Bishop, Ga., U.S. C3 117
Bishop, Tx., U.S. F4 150
Bishop Auckland, Eng., U.K. G12 8
Bishop's Falls, Newf., Can. D4 102
Bishops Mills, Ont., Can. C9 103
Bishopton, Que., Can. D6 104
Bishopville, S.C., U.S. C7 147
Bishrah, Ma'tan, well, Libya F2 60
Bislig, Phil. D8 38
Bismarck, Ar., U.S. C2 111
Bismarck, Il., U.S. C6 120
Bismarck, Mo., U.S. D7 132
Bismarck, N.D., U.S. C5 141
Bismarck Archipelago, is., Pap. N. Gui. k16 68a
Bismarck Range, mts., Pap. N. Gui. m15 68a
Bismarck Sea, Pap. N. Gui. I18 158
Bismuna, Laguna, b., Nic. C11 92
Bison, Ks., U.S. D4 123
Bison, S.D., U.S. B3 148
Bison Peak, mtn., Co., U.S. B5 113
Bissau, Gui.-B. F3 54
Bissett, Man., Can. D4 100
Bissikrima, Gui. F4 64
Bissorã, Gui.-B. E2 64
Bistineau, Lake, res., La., U.S. B2 125
Bistrița, Rom. B8 20
Bistrița, stm., Rom. C10 20
Bistrița-Năsăud, co., Rom. B8 20
Bisztynek, Pol. A20 10
Bitam, Gabon A2 58
Bitburg, Ger. F6 10
Bitche, Fr. C14 14
Bitlis, Tur. B7 48
Bitola, Yugo. H5 20
Bitonto, Italy H11 18
Bitter Creek, stm., Wy., U.S. E4 157
Bitterfeld, Ger. D12 10
Bitterfontein, S. Afr. H4 66
Bitter Lake, l., S.D., U.S. B8 148
Bittern Lake, Alta., Can. C4 98
Bitterroot, stm., Mt., U.S. D2 133
Bitterroot Range, mts., U.S. B3 119
Bitti, Italy I4 18
Bitung, Indon. E8 38
Bituruna, Braz. D13 80
Biwabik, Mn., U.S. C6 130
Biwa-ko, l., Japan L11 36
Bixby, Ok., U.S. B6 143
Biyang, China C2 34
Bizana, Transkei H9 66
Bizerte, Tun. L4 18
Bizkaiko, prov., Spain B9 16
Bjala Slatina, Bul. F7 20
Bjelovar, Yugo. D11 18
Bjork Lake, l., Sask., Can. E4 105
Björna, Swe. J16 6
Bjørnøya (Bear Island), i., Sval. B2 28
Bla, Mali E7 64
Black, Al., U.S. D4 108
Black (Lixian) (Da), stm., Asia D8 40
Black, stm., Man., Can. D4 100
Black, stm., Az., U.S. D5 110
Black, stm., Ar., U.S. B4 111
Black, stm., La., U.S. C4 125
Black, stm., Mi., U.S. E8 129
Black, stm., N.Y., U.S. B4 139
Black, stm., N.C., U.S. C4 140
Black, stm., S.C., U.S. D8 147
Black, stm., Vt., U.S. E3 152
Black, stm., Vt., U.S. B4 152
Black, stm., Wi., U.S. D3 156
Black, Bayou, stm., La., U.S. E5 125
Blackall, Austl. E6 70
Black Bear Creek, stm., Ok., U.S. A4 143
Blackbeard Island, i., Ga., U.S. E5 117
Black Bear Island Lake, l., Sask., Can. B3 105
Blackbird, De., U.S. C3 115
Blackburn, Mo., U.S. B4 132
Blackburn, Mount, mtn., Ak., U.S. C11 109
Black Butte, mtn., Mt., U.S. F5 133
Black Butte, mtn., Wy., U.S. B5 157
Black Butte Lake, res., Ca., U.S. C2 112
Black Canyon, val., Co., U.S. C3 113
Black Canyon City, Az., U.S. C3 110
Black Canyon of the Gunnison National Monument, Co., U.S. C3 113
Black Creek, B.C., Can. E5 99
Black Creek, N.C., U.S. B5 140
Black Creek, Wi., U.S. D5 156
Black Creek, stm., U.S. B1 138
Black Creek, stm., Ms., U.S. D4 131
Black Creek, stm., S.C., U.S. B7 147
Black Diamond, Alta., Can. D3 98
Black Diamond, Al., U.S. g6 108
Black Diamond, Wa., U.S. B4 154
Blackduck, Mn., U.S. C4 130
Black Duck, stm., Can. E15 96
Black Eagle, Mt., U.S. C5 133
Black Earth, Wi., U.S. E4 156
Blackey, Ky., U.S. C7 124
Blackfalds, Alta., Can. C4 98
Blackfeet Indian Reservation, Mt., U.S. B4 133
Blackfoot, Alta., Can. C5 98
Blackfoot, Id., U.S. F6 119
Blackfoot, Mt., U.S. B4 133
Blackfoot, stm., Mt., U.S. C3 133
Blackfoot Mountains, mts., Id., U.S. F7 119
Blackfoot Reservoir, res., Id., U.S. G7 119
Blackford, co., In., U.S. D7 121
Black Forest, Co., U.S. C6 113
Black Forest see Schwarzwald, mts., Ger. G8 10
Blackhall Mountain, mtn., Wy., U.S. E6 157
Black Hawk, S.D., U.S. C2 148
Black Hawk, co., Ia., U.S. B5 122
Black Hills, mts., U.S. C2 148
Blackie, Alta., Can. D4 98
Blackjack Mountain, mtn., Ga., U.S. h8 117
Black Lake, Que., Can. C6 104
Black Lake, l., Sask., Can. m7 105
Black Lake, l., Mi., U.S. C6 129
Black Lake, l., N.Y., U.S. f9 139
Black Lake Bayou, stm., La., U.S. B2 125
Black Lick, Pa., U.S. F3 145
Blacklick Estates, Oh., U.S. m11 142
Black Mesa, mtn., Az., U.S. A5 110
Black Mesa, mtn., Ok., U.S. e8 143
Black Mingo Creek, stm., S.C., U.S. D9 147
Blackmore, Mount, mtn., Mt., U.S. E6 133
Black Mountain, N.C., U.S. f10 140
Black Mountain, mtn., U.S. D7 124
Black Mountain, mtn., Az., U.S. E4 110
Black Mountain, mtn., Co., U.S. A5 113
Black Mountain, mtn., Id., U.S. C3 119
Black Mountain, mtn., Mt., U.S. D4 133
Black Mountain, mtn., Or., U.S. B7 144
Black Mountain, mtn., Wy., U.S. B5 157
Black Mountain, mtn., Wy., U.S. D7 157
Black Mountains, mts., Az., U.S. B1 110
Black Oak, Ar., U.S. B5 111
Black Peak, mtn., Az., U.S. C1 110
Black Pine Peak, mtn., Id., U.S. G5 119
Black Pond, l., Me., U.S. B3 126
Blackpool, Eng., U.K. H10 8
Black Range, mts., N.M., U.S. D2 138
Black River, N.Y., U.S. A5 139
Black River Falls, Wi., U.S. D3 156
Black Rock, Ar., U.S. A4 111
Black Rock, N.M., U.S. B1 138
Black Rock, Falk. Is. G8 78
Black Rock Desert, des., Nv., U.S. B3 135
Black Rock Range, mts., Nv., U.S. B3 135
Blacksburg, S.C., U.S. A4 147
Blacksburg, Va., U.S. C2 153
Black Sea G15 4
Blacks Fork, stm., U.S. E3 157
Blacks Harbour, N.B., Can. D3 101
Blackshear, Ga., U.S. E4 117
Blackshear, Lake, res., Ga., U.S. E2 117
Black Squirrel Creek, stm., Co., U.S. C6 113
Blackstock, Ont., Can. C6 103
Blackstone, Ma., U.S. B4 128
Blackstone, Va., U.S. C5 153
Blackstone, stm., R.I., U.S. B4 146
Black Thunder Creek, stm., Wy., U.S. C8 157
Black Tickle, Newf., Can. B4 102
Blackville, N.B., Can. C4 101
Blackville, S.C., U.S. E5 147
Black Volta (Volta Noire), stm., Afr. G6 54
Blackwalnut Point, c., Md., U.S. C5 127
Black Warrior, stm., Al., U.S. C2 108
Blackwater, Mo., U.S. C5 132
Blackwater, stm., Ire. I5 8
Blackwater, stm., Fl., U.S. u15 116
Blackwater, stm., Md., U.S. D5 127
Blackwater, stm., N.H., U.S. D3 136
Blackwater, stm., Va., U.S. D6 153
Blackwater Reservoir, res., N.H., U.S. D3 136
Blackwell, Ar., U.S. B3 111
Blackwell, Ok., U.S. A4 143
Blackwood, N.J., U.S. D2 137
Blackwood Creek, stm., Ne., U.S. D4 134
Bladel, Neth. F7 12
Bladen, Ne., U.S. D7 134
Bladen, co., N.C., U.S. C4 140
Bladenboro, N.C., U.S. C4 140
Bladensburg, Md., U.S. f9 127
Blades, De., U.S. F3 115
Bladgrond, S. Afr. G4 66
Bladon Springs, Al., U.S. D1 108
Bladworth, Sask., Can. F2 105
Blaeberry, stm., B.C., Can. D2 98
Blagodarnyj, U.S.S.R. H6 22
Blagoevgrad, Bul. G7 20
Blagoveščensk, U.S.S.R. G17 24
Blain, Fr. E5 14
Blaine, Me., U.S. B5 126
Blaine, Mn., U.S. m12 130
Blaine, Tn., U.S. C10 149
Blaine, Wa., U.S. A3 154
Blaine, co., Id., U.S. F4 119
Blaine, co., Mt., U.S. B7 133
Blaine, co., Ne., U.S. C6 134
Blaine, co., Ok., U.S. B3 143
Blaine Creek, stm., Ky., U.S. B7 124
Blaine Lake, Sask., Can. E2 105
Blair, Ne., U.S. C9 134
Blair, Ok., U.S. C2 143
Blair, W.V., U.S. n12 155
Blair, Wi., U.S. D2 156
Blair, co., Pa., U.S. E5 145
Blair Athol, Austl. D7 70
Blairsburg, Ia., U.S. B4 122
Blairstown, Ia., U.S. C5 122
Blairstown, Mo., U.S. C4 132
Blairsville, Ga., U.S. B3 117
Blairsville, Pa., U.S. F3 145
Blake Island, i., Wa., U.S. e11 154
Blakely, Ga., U.S. E2 117
Blakely, Pa., U.S. m18 145
Blake Point, c., Mi., U.S. h10 129
Blakesburg, Ia., U.S. D5 122
Blanc, Mont (Monte Bianco), mtn., Eur. G13 14
Blanca, Co., U.S. D5 113
Blanca, Bahía, b., Arg. J7 80
Blanca, Isla, i., Peru C2 82
Blanca, Sierra, mtn., Tx., U.S. o12 150
Blanca Grande, Laguna, l., Arg. J7 80
Blanca Peak, mtn., Co., U.S. D5 113
Blancas, Peñas, mts., Nic. D9 92
Blanchard, Id., U.S. A2 119
Blanchard, La., U.S. B2 125
Blanchard, Mi., U.S. E5 129
Blanchard, Ok., U.S. B4 143
Blanchard, Pa., U.S. D6 145
Blanchard, stm., Oh., U.S. A1 142
Blanchardville, Wi., U.S. F4 156
Blanche, Lake, l., Austl. G3 70
Blanchester, Oh., U.S. C2 142
Blanco, N.M., U.S. A2 138
Blanco, Tx., U.S. D3 150
Blanco, co., Tx., U.S. D3 150
Blanco, stm., Arg. E4 80
Blanco, stm., Bol. E10 82
Blanco, stm., Ec. G3 84
Blanco, stm., Peru A5 82
Blanco, Cabo, c., C.R. H9 92
Blanco, Cape, c., Or., U.S. E2 144
Bland, Mo., U.S. C6 132
Bland, Va., U.S. C1 153
Bland, co., Va., U.S. C1 153
Blandburg, Pa., U.S. E5 145
Blandford, Ma., U.S. B2 128
Blanding, Ut., U.S. F6 151
Blandinsville, Il., U.S. C3 120
Blanes, Spain D14 16
Blanford, In., U.S. E2 121
Blangy-sur-Bresle, Fr. C8 14
Blankenberge, Bel. F3 12
Blankenburg, Ger. D10 10
Blanquilla, Isla, i., Ven. B10 84
Blantyre, Mwi. E7 58
Blarney Castle, hist., Ire. J5 8
Blasdell, N.Y., U.S. C2 139
Blatná, Czech. F13 10
Blaufelden, Ger. F9 10
Blawnox, Pa., U.S. k14 145
Blaye-et-Sainte-Luce, Fr. G6 14
Blayney, Austl. I8 70
Bleckley, co., Ga., U.S. D3 117
Bledsoe, co., Tn., U.S. D8 149
Bleiburg, Aus. I14 10
Blekinge Län, co., Swe. M14 6
Blencoe, Ia., U.S. C1 122
Blende, Co., U.S. C6 113
Blenheim, Ont., Can. E3 103
Blenheim, N.Z. D4 72
Blennerhassett, W.V., U.S. B3 155
Blessing, Tx., U.S. E4 150
Bletterans, Fr. F12 14
Blevins, Ar., U.S. D2 111
Blind, stm., La., U.S. h10 125
Blind River, Ont., Can. A2 103
Bliss, Id., U.S. G4 119
Blissfield, Mi., U.S. G7 129
Blitar, Indon. K16 39a
Blocher, In., U.S. G6 121
Blocker, Ok., U.S. B6 143
Block Island, R.I., U.S. h7 146
Block Island, i., R.I., U.S. h7 146
Block Island Sound, strt., U.S. G2 146
Blockton, Ia., U.S. D3 122
Blodgett, Mo., U.S. D8 132
Bloemfontein, S. Afr. G8 66
Bloemhof, S. Afr. F7 66
Blois, Fr. E8 14
Blönduós, Ice. B3 6a
Blood Mountain, mtn., Ga., U.S. B3 117
Bloodsworth Island, i., Md., U.S. D5 127
Bloodvein, stm., Can. D3 100
Bloomdale, Oh., U.S. A2 142
Bloomer, Ar., U.S. B1 111
Bloomer, Wi., U.S. C2 156
Bloomfield, N.B., Can. D4 101
Bloomfield, Ont., Can. D7 103
Bloomfield, Ct., U.S. B5 114
Bloomfield, In., U.S. F4 121
Bloomfield, Ia., U.S. D5 122
Bloomfield, Ky., U.S. C4 124
Bloomfield, Mo., U.S. E8 132
Bloomfield, Ne., U.S. B8 134
Bloomfield, N.J., U.S. h8 137
Bloomfield, N.M., U.S. A2 138
Bloomfield Hills, Mi., U.S. o15 129
Bloomingburg, Oh., U.S. C2 142
Bloomingdale, Ga., U.S. D5 117
Bloomingdale, Il., U.S. k8 120
Bloomingdale, In., U.S. E3 121
Bloomingdale, Mi., U.S. F5 129
Bloomingdale, N.J., U.S. A4 137
Bloomingdale, Tn., U.S. C11 149
Blooming Grove, Tx., U.S. C4 150
Blooming Prairie, Mn., U.S. G5 130
Bloomington, Id., U.S. G7 119
Bloomington, Il., U.S. C4 120
Bloomington, In., U.S. F4 121
Bloomington, Mn., U.S. F5 130
Bloomington, Ne., U.S. D6 134
Bloomington, Tx., U.S. E4 150
Bloomington, Wi., U.S. F3 156
Bloomington, Lake, res., Il., U.S. C5 120
Bloomsburg, Pa., U.S. E9 145
Bloomsdale, Mo., U.S. C7 132
Bloomville, Oh., U.S. A2 142
Blora, Indon. J15 39a
Blossburg, Al., U.S. f7 108
Blossburg, Pa., U.S. C7 145
Blossom, Tx., U.S. C5 150
Bloumet, Alg. I14 62
Blount, co., Al., U.S. B3 108
Blount, co., Tn., U.S. D10 149
Blountstown, Fl., U.S. B1 116
Blountsville, Al., U.S. A3 108
Blountville, Tn., U.S. C11 149
Blovice, Czech. F13 10
Blowering Reservoir, res., Austl. J8 70
Blowing Rock, N.C., U.S. A1 140
Bloxom, Va., U.S. C7 153
Bludenz, Aus. H9 10
Blue, Ok., U.S. C5 143
Blue, stm., Co., U.S. B4 113
Blue, stm., In., U.S. H5 121
Blue, stm., Mo., U.S. k10 132
Blue, stm., Ok., U.S. C5 143
Blue, Bayou, stm., La., U.S. E5 125
Blue, Mount, mtn., Me., U.S. D2 126
Blue Ash, Oh., U.S. o13 142
Blueberry, stm., B.C., Can. A7 99
Blue Buck Knob, hill, Mo., U.S. E5 132
Blue Buck Point, c., La., U.S. E2 125
Blue Creek, Al., U.S. g6 108
Blue Creek, W.V., U.S. m13 155
Blue Creek, stm., Ne., U.S. C3 134
Blue Creek, stm., W.V., U.S. m13 155
Blue Cypress Lake, l., Fl., U.S. E6 116
Blue Diamond, Nv., U.S. G6 135
Blue Earth, Mn., U.S. G4 130
Blue Earth, co., Mn., U.S. G4 130
Blue Earth, stm., Mn., U.S. G4 130
Bluefield, Va., U.S. C1 153
Bluefield, W.V., U.S. D3 155
Bluefields, Nic. E11 92
Bluefields, Bahía de, b., Nic. F11 92
Blue Grass, Ia., U.S. C7 122
Blue Hill, Me., U.S. D4 126
Blue Hill, Ne., U.S. D7 134
Blue Hill Range, hills, Ma., U.S. h11 128
Blue Hills, Ct., U.S. B5 114
Bluehole, Ky., U.S. C6 124
Blue Island, Il., U.S. B6 120
Bluejoint Lake, l., Or., U.S. E7 144
Blue Knob, mtn., Pa., U.S. F4 145
Blue Lake, Ca., U.S. B2 112
Blue Mesa Reservoir, res., Co., U.S. C3 113
Blue Mound, Il., U.S. D4 120
Blue Mound, Ks., U.S. D8 123
Blue Mountain, Al., U.S. B4 108
Blue Mountain, Ar., U.S. B2 111
Blue Mountain, Ms., U.S. A4 131
Blue Mountain, mtn., Newf., Can. C3 102
Blue Mountain, mtn., Ar., U.S. C1 111
Blue Mountain, mtn., Mt., U.S. C12 133
Blue Mountain, mtn., N.H., U.S. A4 136
Blue Mountain, mtn., N.M., U.S. D2 138
Blue Mountain, mtn., N.Y., U.S. B6 139
Blue Mountain, mtn., Pa., U.S. F6 145
Blue Mountain Lake, res., Ar., U.S. B2 111
Blue Mountain Peak, mtn., Jam. E6 94
Blue Mountains, mts., U.S. B3 106
Blue Nile (Al-Bahr al-Azraq) (Abay), stm., Afr. F7 56
Blue Point, Me., U.S. g7 126
Blue Rapids, Ks., U.S. C7 123
Blue Ridge, Alta., Can. B3 98
Blue Ridge, Ga., U.S. B2 117
Blue Ridge, In., U.S. E6 121
Blue Ridge, Va., U.S. C3 153
Blue Ridge, mts., U.S. D10 106
Blue Ridge Lake, res., Ga., U.S. B2 117
Blue Ridge Summit, Pa., U.S. G7 145
Blue River, B.C., Can. C8 99
Blue River, Or., U.S. C4 144
Blue River, Wi., U.S. E3 156
Bluesky, Alta., Can. A1 98
Blue Springs, Al., U.S. D4 108
Blue Springs, Mo., U.S. h11 132
Blue Springs, Ne., U.S. D9 134
Bluestone, stm., W.V., U.S. D3 155
Bluestone Lake, res., U.S. D4 155
Bluevale, Ont., Can. D3 103
Bluewater, N.M., U.S. B2 138
Bluewell, W.V., U.S. D3 155
Bluff, N.Z. G2 72
Bluff, Ut., U.S. F6 151
Bluff City, Ar., U.S. D2 111
Bluff City, Il., U.S. E4 120
Bluff City, Tn., U.S. C11 149
Bluff Creek, stm., Ks., U.S. E4 123
Bluff Creek, stm., Ok., U.S. A4 143
Bluff Lake, res., Ms., U.S. B5 131
Bluff Mountain, mtn., Vt., U.S. B5 152
Bluff Park, Al., U.S. g7 108
Bluffs, Il., U.S. D3 120
Bluffton, Ga., U.S. E2 117
Bluffton, In., U.S. C7 121
Bluffton, Mn., U.S. D3 130
Bluffton, Oh., U.S. B2 142
Bluffton, S.C., U.S. G6 147
Bluford, Il., U.S. E5 120
Blumberg, Ger. H8 10
Blumenau, Braz. D14 80
Blunt, S.D., U.S. C6 148
Bly, Or., U.S. E5 144
Blying Sound, strt., Ak., U.S. h17 109
Blyth, Ont., Can. D3 103
Blythe, Ca., U.S. F6 112
Blythe, Ga., U.S. C4 117
Blytheville, Ar., U.S. B6 111
Bø, Nor. G14 6
Bø, Nor. L11 6
Bo, S.L. H4 64
Boaco, Nic. E9 92
Boaco, dept., Nic. E9 92
Boa Esperança, Braz. F6 79
Boalsburg, Pa., U.S. E6 145
Boa Nova, Braz. C8 79
Boardman, Oh., U.S. A5 142
Boardman, Or., U.S. B7 144
Boatman, Austl. F7 70
Boa Vista, Braz. D14 80
Boa Vista, Braz. F12 84
Boa Vista, i., C.V. m17 64a
Boavita, Col. D6 84
Boaz, Al., U.S. A3 108
Bobai, China C10 40
Bobbili, India C7 46
Bobbio, Italy E4 18
Bobcaygeon, Ont., Can. C6 103
Böblingen, Ger. G9 10
Bobo Dioulasso, Burkina F7 64
Bobolice, Pol. B16 10
Bobonaza, stm., Ec. I4 84
Bobonong, Bots. C9 66
Bobr, U.S.S.R. G12 26
Bobrujsk, U.S.S.R. H12 26
Bobtown, Pa., U.S. G2 145
Bobures, Ven. C7 84
Boby, Pic, mtn., Madag. S22 67b
Boca Brava, Isla, i., Pan. I12 92
Boca Chica Key, i., Fl., U.S. H5 116
Boca Ciega Bay, b., Fl., U.S. p10 116
Boca del Monte, Pan. I12 92
Boca del Pozo, Ven. B10 84
Bôca do Acre, Braz. C8 82
Boca Grande, Fl., U.S. F4 116
Bocaiúva, Braz. D7 79
Bocanda, I.C. H7 64
Boca Raton, Fl., U.S. F6 116
Bocas del Toro, Pan. C1 84
Bocas del Toro, prov., Pan. I12 92
Bocas del Toro, Archipiélago de, is., Pan. H12 92
Bocay, Nic. C9 92
Bocay, stm., Nic. C9 92
Bochnia, Pol. F20 10
Bocholt, Ger. D6 10
Bochum, Ger. D7 10
Bochum, S. Afr. D9 66
Bocón, Caño, stm., Col. F8 84
Boconó, Ven. C7 84
Bodajbo, U.S.S.R. F14 24
Bodcau Creek, stm., Ar., U.S. D2 111
Bodcaw, Ar., U.S. D2 111
Bode, Ia., U.S. B3 122
Bodega Head, c., Ca., U.S. C2 112
Bodegraven, Neth. D6 12
Bodélé, reg., Chad E4 56
Boden, Swe. I17 6
Bodensee (Lake Constance), l., Eur. E16 14
Bodh Gaya, India E11 42
Bodie Island, i., N.C., U.S. B7 140
Bodināyakkanūr, India G4 46
Bodkin Point, c., Md., U.S. B5 127
Bodo, Alta., Can. C5 98
Bodø, Nor. H14 6
Bodoquena, Serra da, plat., Braz. I13 82
Bodrog, stm., Eur. A5 20
Bodrum, Tur. L11 20
Boelus, Ne., U.S. C7 134
Boende, Zaire B4 58
Boeo, Capo, c., Italy L7 18
Boerne, Tx., U.S. E3 150
Boeuf, stm., La., U.S. C4 125
Boeuf, Bayou, stm., La., U.S. D3 125
Boeuf, Lake, l., La., U.S. k10 125
Bogale, Burma F3 40
Bogalusa, La., U.S. D6 125
Bogan, stm., Austl. H7 70
Bogandé, Burkina E9 64
Bogard, Mo., U.S. B4 132
Bogart, Ga., U.S. C3 117
Bogata, Tx., U.S. C5 150
Boğazlıyan, Tur. B3 48
Bogda Shan, mts., China C4 30
Boger City, N.C., U.S. B1 140
Boggabri, Austl. H9 70
Boggstown, In., U.S. E6 121
Bogo, Phil. C7 38
Bogol'ubovo, U.S.S.R. E23 26
Bogong, Mount, mtn., Austl. K7 70
Bogor, Indon. J13 39a
Bogorodick, U.S.S.R. H21 26
Bogorodsk, U.S.S.R. E26 26
Bogotá, Col. E5 84
Bogota, N.J., U.S. h8 137
Bogota, Tn., U.S. A2 149
Bogotol, U.S.S.R. F9 24
Bogou, Togo F10 64
Bogra, Bngl. H13 44
Bogué, Maur. C2 64
Bogue, Ks., U.S. C4 123
Bogue Chitto, Ms., U.S. D3 131
Bogue Chitto, stm., U.S. D5 125
Bogue Inlet, b., N.C., U.S. C5 140
Bogue Phalia, stm., Ms., U.S. B3 131
Boguševsk, U.S.S.R. G13 26
Bo Hai (Gulf of Chihli), b., China E8 32
Bohai Haixia, strt., China E9 32
Bohain-en-Vermandois, Fr. C10 14
Bohan, Bel. I6 12
Bohemia see Čechy, hist. reg., Czech. F14 10
Bohemian Forest, mts., Eur. F12 10
Bohicon, Benin H11 64
Bohol, i., Phil. D7 38
Bohol Sea, Phil. D7 38
Boiaçu, Braz. H12 84
Boiestown, N.B., Can. C3 101
Boigu Island, i., Austl. A8 68
Boiling Springs, N.C., U.S. B1 140
Boiling Springs, Pa., U.S. F7 145
Boipeba, Ilha de, i., Braz. B9 79
Bois, Rio dos, stm., Braz. E3 79
Bois Blanc Island, i., Mi., U.S. C6 129
Bois Brule, stm., Wi., U.S. B2 156
Boischâtel, Que., Can. C6 104
Boisdale, N.S., Can. C9 101
Bois D'Arc, Mo., U.S. D4 132
Bois-des-Filion, Que., Can. p19 104
Bois de Sioux, stm., Mn., U.S. E2 130
Boise, Id., U.S. F2 119
Boise, co., Id., U.S. F3 119
Boise City, Ok., U.S. e8 143
Bois Fort, Mn., U.S. B5 130
Boissevain, Man., Can. E1 100
Boissevain, Va., U.S. e10 153
Boistfort Peak, mtn., Wa., U.S. C2 154
Boisvert, Pointe au, c., Que., Can. A8 104
Bojayá, stm., Col. D4 84
Bojeador, Cape, c., Phil. L19 39b
Bojnūrd, Iran C14 48
Bojonegoro, Indon. J15 39a
Boju, Nig. H13 64
Bojuru, Braz. F13 80
Bokani, Nig. G12 64
Bokchito, Ok., U.S. C5 143
Boké, Gui. F2 64
Bokeelia, Fl., U.S. F4 116
Bokhara, stm., Austl. G7 70
Bokino, U.S.S.R. I24 26
Bokolako, Sen. E3 64
Bokoshe, Ok., U.S. B7 143
Boksitogorsk, U.S.S.R. B16 26
Bokungu, Zaire B4 58
Bol, Yugo. F11 18
Bolama, Gui.-B. F2 64
Bolaños, stm., Mex. F8 90
Bolaños de Calatrava, Spain G8 16
Bolbec, Fr. C7 14
Bolchov, U.S.S.R. H19 26
Bolckow, Mo., U.S. A3 132
Boles, Ar., U.S. C1 111
Bolesławiec, Pol. D15 10
Boleszkowice, Pol. C14 10
Boley, Ok., U.S. B5 143
Bolgatanga, Ghana F9 64
Bolgrad, U.S.S.R. D12 20
Boli, China B13 30
Boli, Sud. N5 60
Boligee, Al., U.S. C1 108
Boling, Tx., U.S. E5 150
Bolingbrook, Il., U.S. k8 120
Bolinger, Al., U.S. D1 108
Bolívar, Col. E4 84
Bolívar, Col. G4 84
Bolívar, Col. E4 84
Bolívar, Peru B3 82
Bolivar, Mo., U.S. D4 132
Bolivar, N.Y., U.S. C2 139
Bolivar, Oh., U.S. B4 142
Bolivar, Tn., U.S. B3 149
Bolivar, W.V., U.S. B7 155
Bolívar, state, Ven. D11 84
Bolívar, prov., Ec. H3 84
Bolívar, dept., Col. C5 84
Bolivar, co., Ms., U.S. B3 131
Bolívar, Cerro, mtn., Ven. D11 84
Bolivar, Lake, l., Ms., U.S. B3 131
Bolívar, Pico, mtn., Ven. C7 84
Bolivia, ctry., S.A. F8 74
Bollène, Fr. H11 14
Bollinger, co., Mo., U.S. D7 132
Bollnäs, Swe. K15 6
Bollon, Austl. G7 70
Bollullos par del Condado, Spain H5 16
Bolobo, Zaire B3 58
Bolochovo, U.S.S.R. G20 26
Bologna, Italy E6 18
Bolognesi, Peru B5 82
Bologoje, U.S.S.R. D17 26
Bolomba, Zaire A3 58
Bolonchén de Rejón, Mex. G15 90
Bolotino, U.S.S.R. B11 20
Bolotnoje, U.S.S.R. F14 22
Bolovens, Plateau des, plat., Laos G9 40
Bol'šaja Balachn'a, stm., U.S.S.R. C12 24
Bol'šaja Cheta, stm., U.S.S.R. D14 22
Bol'šaja Čuja, stm., U.S.S.R. F14 24
Bol'šaja Ižora, U.S.S.R. B12 26
Bol'šaja Kuonamka, stm., U.S.S.R. D13 24
Bol'šaja Lipovica, U.S.S.R. I24 26
Bol'šaja Murta, U.S.S.R. F16 22
Bol'šaja Višera, U.S.S.R. C15 26
Bol'šakovo, U.S.S.R. G4 26
Bolsena, Italy G6 18
Bolsena, Lago di, l., Italy G6 18
Bol'šereck, U.S.S.R. G23 24
Bol'ševik, U.S.S.R. E21 24
Bol'ševik, U.S.S.R. I13 26

Name | Map Ref. | Page

Bol'ševik, ostrov, i., U.S.S.R. B12 24
Bol'šezemel'skaja Tundra, reg., U.S.S.R. D9 22
Bol'šoj An'uj, stm., U.S.S.R. D24 24
Bol'šoj Begičev, ostrov, i., U.S.S.R. C14 24
Bol'šoje Michajlovskoje, U.S.S.R. E21 26
Bol'šoje Polpino, U.S.S.R. H17 26
Bol'šoj Jenisej, stm., U.S.S.R. G11 24
Bol'šoj Kavkaz (Caucasus), mts., U.S.S.R. I6 22
Bol'šoj L'achovskij, ostrov, i., U.S.S.R. C20 24
Bol'šoj Tal'cy, U.S.S.R. B16 26
Bol'šoj T'uters, ostrov, i., U.S.S.R. B10 26
Bol'šoj Uzen', stm., U.S.S.R. H7 22
Bolton, Ms., U.S. C3 131
Bolton, N.C., U.S. C4 140
Bolton Lakes, l., Ct., U.S. B6 114
Bolton Landing, N.Y., U.S. B7 139
Bolu, Tur. G14 4
Boluntay, China B15 44
Boluochi, China B7 32
Bóly, Hung. J18 10
Bolzano (Bozen), Italy C6 18
Boma, Zaire C2 58
Bomaderry, Austl. J9 70
Bombala, Austl. K8 70
Bombarral, Port. F2 16
Bombay, India C2 46
Bombay Hook Island, i., De., U.S. C4 115
Bomberai, Semenanjung, pen., Indon. F9 38
Bom Despacho, Braz. E6 79
Bomei, China M4 34
Bom Jardim de Goiás, Braz. D2 79
Bom Jesus da Lapa, Braz. B7 79
Bom Jesus de Goiás, Braz. E4 79
Bomoseen, Vt., U.S. D2 152
Bomoseen, Lake, l., Vt., U.S. D2 152
Bom Retiro, Braz. D14 80
Bom Retiro do Sul, Braz. E13 80
Bom Sucesso, Braz. G3 79
Bom Sucesso, Braz. F13 82
Bomu (Mbomou), stm., Afr. H5 56
Bon, Cap, c., Tun. L6 18
Bon Accord, Alta., Can. C4 98
Bon Air, Tn., U.S. D8 149
Bon Air, Va., U.S. C5 153
Bonaire, Ga., U.S. D3 117
Bonaire, i., Neth. Ant. H10 94
Bonampak, hist., Mex. I14 90
Bonanza, Nic. C10 92
Bonanza, Ar., U.S. B1 111
Bonanza, Or., U.S. E5 144
Bonanza Peak, mtn., Wa., U.S. A5 154
Bonao, Dom. Rep. E9 94
Bonaparte, Ia., U.S. D6 122
Bonaparte, Mount, mtn., Wa., U.S. A6 154
Bonaparte Archipelago, is., Austl. B5 68
Bonaparte Lake, l., B.C., Can. D7 99
Bon Aqua, Tn., U.S. B4 149
Bonarbridge, Scot., U.K. D9 8
Bonarcado, Italy I3 18
Bonasila Dome, mtn., Ak., U.S. C7 109
Bonaventure, Que., Can. A4 101
Bonavista, Newf., Can. D5 102
Bonavista, Cape, c., Newf., Can. D5 102
Bonavista Bay, b., Newf., Can. D5 102
Bond, Ky., U.S. C5 124
Bond, Ms., U.S. E4 131
Bond, co., Il., U.S. E4 120
Bondeno, Italy E6 18
Bondo, Zaire H5 56
Bondoukou, I.C. G8 64
Bondsville, Ma., U.S. B3 128
Bonduel, Wi., U.S. D5 156
Bondurant, Ia., U.S. C4 122
Bondurant, Wy., U.S. C2 157
Bondville, Il., U.S. C5 120
Bone, Teluk, b., Indon. F7 38
Bone Gap, Il., U.S. E6 120
Bone Lake, l., Wi., U.S. C1 156
Bonesteel, S.D., U.S. D7 148
Bonete, Cerro, mtn., Arg. D4 80
Bonete Chico, Cerro, mtn., Arg. E4 80
Bonfinópolis, Braz. D4 79
Bonfouca, La., U.S. h12 125
Bonga, Eth. N9 60
Bongak, Sud. N7 60
Bongandanga, Zaire A4 58
Bongo, Massif des, mts., Cen. Afr. Rep. M2 60
Bongor, Chad F4 56
Bongouanou, I.C. H7 64
Bonham, Tx., U.S. C4 150
Bon Homme, co., S.D., U.S. D8 148
Bonhomme, Morne, mtn., Haiti E8 94
Bon Homme Colony, S.D., U.S. E8 148
Bonifacio, Fr. M24 15a
Bonifacio, Strait of, strt., Eur. H4 18
Bonifay, Fl., U.S. u16 116
Bonita, La., U.S. B4 125
Bonita Springs, Fl., U.S. F5 116
Bonito, Braz. I13 82
Bonito, stm., Braz. D3 79
Bonito, Pico, mtn., Hond. B8 92
Bonkoukou, Niger D11 64
Bonn, Ger. E7 10
Bonneau, S.C., U.S. E8 147
Bonneauville, Pa., U.S. G7 145
Bonne Bay (Woody Point), Newf., Can. D3 102
Bonne Bay, b., Newf., Can. D3 102
Bonneia, Eth. O9 60
Bonne Idee, Bayou, stm., La., U.S. B4 125
Bonner, Mt., U.S. D3 133
Bonner, co., Id., U.S. A2 119
Bonners Ferry, Id., U.S. A2 119
Bonner Springs, Ks., U.S. C9 123
Bonnétable, Fr. D7 14
Bonnet Carre Floodway, La., U.S. h11 125
Bonne Terre, Mo., U.S. D7 132
Bonnet Plume, stm., Yukon, Can. C6 96
Bonneval, Fr. D8 14
Bonneville, Fr. F13 14
Bonneville, co., Id., U.S. F7 119
Bonneville Dam, U.S. B4 144
Bonneville Peak, mtn., Id., U.S. F6 119
Bonneville Salt Flats, pl., Ut., U.S. C2 151
Bonney Lake, Wa., U.S. B3 154
Bonnie, Il., U.S. E5 120
Bonnie Doone, N.C., U.S. B4 140
Bonnie Rock, Austl. F3 68
Bonnieville, Ky., U.S. C4 124
Bonnots Mill, Mo., U.S. C6 132
Bonny, Nig. I13 64
Bonny Reservoir, res., Co., U.S. B8 113
Bonnyville, Alta., Can. B5 98
Bono, Ar., U.S. B5 111
Bonorva, Italy I3 18
Bon Secour, Al., U.S. E2 108
Bonsecours, Fr. C8 14
Bonshaw, P.E.I., Can. C6 101
Bonthe, S.L. H3 64
Bontoc, Phil. M19 39b
Bon Wier, Tx., U.S. D6 150
Bonyhád, Hung. I18 10
Booischot, Bel. F6 12
Bookaloo, Austl. H2 70
Book Cliffs, clf, U.S. D6 151
Booker, Tx., U.S. A2 150
Booker T. Washington National Monument, Va., U.S. C3 153
Boola, Gui. G5 64
Boom, Bel. F5 12
Boomarra, Austl. B4 70
Boomer, W.V., U.S. C3 155
Boonah, Austl. G10 70
Boone, Co., U.S. C6 113
Boone, Ia., U.S. B4 122
Boone, N.C., U.S. A1 140
Boone, co., Ar., U.S. A2 111
Boone, co., Il., U.S. A5 120
Boone, co., In., U.S. D4 121
Boone, co., Ia., U.S. B3 122
Boone, co., Ky., U.S. B5 124
Boone, co., Mo., U.S. B5 132
Boone, co., Ne., U.S. C7 134
Boone, co., W.V., U.S. C3 155
Boone, stm., Ia., U.S. B4 122
Boone Lake, res., Tn., U.S. C11 149
Boones Mill, Va., U.S. C3 153
Booneville, Ar., U.S. B2 111
Booneville, Ky., U.S. C6 124
Booneville, Ms., U.S. A5 131
Boonsboro, Md., U.S. A2 127
Boons Pond, l., Ma., U.S. g10 128
Boonton, N.J., U.S. B4 137
Boonville, Ca., U.S. C2 112
Boonville, In., U.S. H3 121
Boonville, Mo., U.S. C5 132
Boonville, N.Y., U.S. B5 139
Boonville, N.C., U.S. A2 140
Boopi, stm., Bol. G8 82
Boorama, Som. G9 56
Boorindal, Austl. H7 70
Boorowa, Austl. J8 70
Boosaaso, Som. F10 56
Booth, Al., U.S. C3 108
Boothbay, Me., U.S. E3 126
Boothbay Harbor, Me., U.S. E3 126
Boothia, Gulf of, b., N.W. Ter., Can. B14 96
Boothia Peninsula, pen., N.W. Ter., Can. B14 96
Booths Creek, stm., W.V., U.S. h11 155
Boothville, La., U.S. E6 125
Booué, Gabon B2 58
Bophuthatswana, ctry., Afr. F7 66
Bopo, Nig. H13 64
Boquerón, Pan. I12 92
Boquerón, dept., Para. B8 80
Boquilla, Presa de la, res., Mex. D7 90
Boquillas del Carmen, Mex. C8 90
Bor, Czech. F12 10
Bor, Sud. N6 60
Bor, Tur. C3 48
Bor, U.S.S.R. E27 26
Bor, Yugo. E6 20
Boraha, Nosy, i., Madag. P23 67b
Borah Peak, mtn., Id., U.S. E5 119
Borås, Swe. M13 6
Borāzjān, Iran G11 48
Borba, Braz. J13 84
Borba, Port. G4 16
Borborema, Braz. F4 79
Borda, Cape, c., Austl. J2 70
Bordeaux, Fr. H6 14
Bordelonville, La., U.S. C4 125
Borden, Sask., Can. E2 105
Borden, In., U.S. H6 121
Borden, co., Tx., U.S. C2 150
Borden Peninsula, pen., N.W. Ter., Can. B16 96
Bordentown, N.J., U.S. C3 137
Borderland, W.V., U.S. D2 155
Borders, prov., Scot., U.K. F10 8
Bordertown, Austl. K4 70
Borđeyri, Ice. B3 6a
Bordighera, Italy F2 18
Bordj Bou Arreridj, Alg. B13 62
Bordj Menaïel, Alg. B12 62
Bordj Omar Idriss, Alg. F14 62
Bordj Sidi Toui, Tun. D16 62
Boreda, Eth. N9 60
Borgå (Porvoo), Fin. K19 6
Borger, Tx., U.S. B2 150
Borgholm, Swe. M15 6
Borghorst, Ger. C7 10
Borgne, Lake, b., La., U.S. D6 125
Borgosesia, Italy D3 18
Boring, Or., U.S. B4 144
Borinskoje, U.S.S.R. I22 26
Borisoglebsk, U.S.S.R. G6 22
Borisoglebskij, U.S.S.R. D22 26
Borisov, U.S.S.R. G11 26
Borja, Peru J4 84
Borken, Ger. D6 10
Borkoviči, U.S.S.R. F11 26
Borkum, i., Ger. B6 10
Borlänge, Swe. K14 6
Bormes-les-Mimosas, Fr. I13 14
Bormio, Italy C5 18
Borna, Ger. D13 10
Borneo (Kalimantan), i., Asia N11 40
Bornholm, i., Den. N14 6
Boro, stm., Sud. M3 60
Borodarou, Benin F11 64
Borodino, U.S.S.R. C13 20
Borodino, U.S.S.R. F18 26
Borogoncy, U.S.S.R. E18 24
Boromo, Burkina F8 64
Boron, Ca., U.S. E5 112
Boroviči, U.S.S.R. C16 26
Borovsk, U.S.S.R. F19 26
Borovucha, U.S.S.R. F11 26
Borrachudo, stm., Braz. E6 79
Borrazópolis, Braz. G3 79
Borrego Springs, Ca., U.S. F5 112
Borriana, Spain F11 16
Borroloola, Austl. C7 68
Borş, Rom. B5 20
Borşa, Rom. B8 20
Borsad, India I5 44
Borsod-Abaúj-Zemplén, co., Hung. G21 10
Borth, Wales, U.K. I9 8
Bort-les-Orgues, Fr. G9 14
Boruca, C.R. H11 92
Borūjen, Iran F11 48
Borūjerd, Iran E10 48
Borz'a, U.S.S.R. G15 24
Bosa, Italy I3 18
Bosanska Dubica, Yugo. D11 18
Bosanska Gradiška, Yugo. D12 18
Bosanski Novi, Yugo. D11 18
Bosanski Šamac, Yugo. D2 20
Bosavi, Mount, mtn., Pap. N. Gui. G11 38
Boscawen, N.H., U.S. D3 136
Boscobel, Wi., U.S. E3 156
Bose, China C9 40
Boshan, China G5 32
Boshoek, S. Afr. E8 66
Boshrūyeh, Iran E14 48
Bosler, Wy., U.S. E7 157
Bosna, stm., Yugo. E13 18
Bosna i Hercegovina (Bosnia-Hercegovina), state, Yugo. E2 20
Bosporus see İstanbul Boğazı, strt., Tur. H13 20
Bosque, N.M., U.S. C3 138
Bosque, co., Tx., U.S. D4 150
Bosque Farms, N.M., U.S. C3 138
Boss, Mo., U.S. D6 132
Bossangoa, Cen. Afr. Rep. G4 56
Bossé Bangou, Niger E10 64
Bossembélé, Cen. Afr. Rep. G4 56
Bossert Estates, N.J., U.S. C3 137
Bossier, co., La., U.S. B2 125
Bossier City, La., U.S. B2 125
Bosso, Dallol, val., Niger E11 64
Bosten Hu, l., China C4 30
Boston, Eng., U.K. I13 8
Boston, Ga., U.S. F3 117
Boston, In., U.S. E8 121
Boston, Ky., U.S. C4 124
Boston, Ma., U.S. B5 128
Boston Bay, b., Ma., U.S. B6 128
Boston Heights, Oh., U.S. h9 142
Boston Mountains, mts., Ar., U.S. B2 111
Bostonnais, stm., Que., Can. B5 104
Bostwick, Fl., U.S. C5 116
Bostwick, Ga., U.S. C3 117
Boswarlos, Newf., Can. D2 102
Boswell, B.C., Can. E9 99
Boswell, In., U.S. C3 121
Boswell, Ok., U.S. C6 143
Boswell, Pa., U.S. F3 145
Bosworth, Mo., U.S. B4 132
Botād, India I4 44
Botany Bay, b., Austl. I9 70
Boteti, stm., Bots. C6 66
Botetourt, co., Va., U.S. C3 153
Botha, Alta., Can. C4 98
Botha's Hill, S. Afr. G10 66
Bothaville, S. Afr. F8 66
Bothell, Wa., U.S. B3 154
Bothnia, Gulf of, b., Eur. J17 6
Bothwell, Ont., Can. E3 103
Bothwell, P.E.I., Can. C7 101
Botkins, Oh., U.S. B1 142
Botoşani, Rom. B10 20
Botoşani, co., Rom. B10 20
Botrange, mtn., Bel. H9 12
Botro, I.C. H7 64
Botsford, Ct., U.S. D2 114
Botswana, ctry., Afr. F4 58
Bottenhavet (Selkämeri), b., Eur. K16 6
Bottenviken (Perämeri), b., Eur. I18 6
Bottineau, N.D., U.S. A5 141
Bottineau, co., N.D., U.S. A4 141
Bottrop, Ger. D6 10
Botucatu, Braz. G4 79
Botwood, Newf., Can. D4 102
Bouaflé, I.C. H7 64
Bou Ahmed, Mor. J6 16
Bouaké, I.C. H7 64
Bouandougou, I.C. G7 64
Bouar, Cen. Afr. Rep. G4 56
Bou Arada, Tun. M4 18
Bouârfa, Mor. D10 62
Bouaye, Fr. E5 14
Bou Bernous, Alg. G9 62
Bouchegouf, Alg. M2 18
Boucherville, Que., Can. D4 104
Bouches-du-Rhône, dept., Fr. I12 14
Bouctouche, N.B., Can. C5 101
Boudreaux, Lake, l., La., U.S. E5 125
Boudry, Switz. E6 13
Boufarik, Alg. B12 62
Bou Ficha, Tun. M5 18
Bougainville, i., Pap. N. Gui. I19 158
Bougouni, Mali F6 64
Bougouriba, stm., Burkina F8 64
Bou Hadjar, Alg. M3 18
Bou Hajar, Tun. N5 18
Bouira, Alg. B12 62
Boujad, Mor. D7 62
Boujdour, Cap, c., W. Sah. G3 62
Bou Kadir, Alg. B11 62
Bou Khadra, Alg. N3 18
Boukombé, Benin F10 64
Boulder, Austl. F4 68
Boulder, Co., U.S. A5 113
Boulder, Mt., U.S. D4 133
Boulder, co., Co., U.S. A5 113
Boulder City, Nv., U.S. H7 135
Boulevard Heights, Md., U.S. f9 127
Bouli, stm., Burkina E9 64
Boulia, Austl. D3 70
Boulogne-Billancourt, Fr. D9 14
Boulogne-sur-Gesse, Fr. I7 14
Boulogne-sur-Mer, Fr. B8 14
Boulouba, Cen. Afr. Rep. N2 60
Boulouli, Mali D5 64
Boulsa, Burkina E9 64
Bouly, Maur. D4 64
Boumalne, Mor. E8 62
Boûmdeïd, Maur. C5 64
Bouna, I.C. G8 64
Boundary, co., Id., U.S. A2 119
Boundary Bald Mountain, mtn., Me., U.S. C2 126
Boundary Bay, b., Wa., U.S. A3 154
Boundary Peak, mtn., Nv., U.S. F3 135
Bound Brook, N.J., U.S. B3 137
Bountiful, Ut., U.S. C4 151
Bounty Islands, is., N.Z. M21 158
Bouqteb, Alg. C11 62
Boura, Mali E7 64
Bourbeuse, stm., Mo., U.S. C6 132
Bourbon, In., U.S. B5 121
Bourbon, Mo., U.S. C6 132
Bourbon, co., Ks., U.S. E9 123
Bourbon, co., Ky., U.S. B5 124
Bourbon-Lancy, Fr. F10 14
Bourbonnais, Il., U.S. B6 120
Bourbonnais, hist. reg., Fr. F9 14
Bourbonne-les-Bains, Fr. E12 14
Bourem, Mali C9 64
Bourg, La., U.S. E5 125
Bourganeuf, Fr. G8 14
Bourg-en-Bresse, Fr. F12 14
Bourges, Fr. E9 14
Bourgogne (Burgundy), hist. reg., Fr. E11 14
Bourgogne, Canal de, Fr. E11 14
Bourgoin, Fr. G12 14
Bourg-Saint-Andéol, Fr. H11 14
Bourg-Saint-Maurice, Fr. G13 14
Bourke, Austl. H6 70
Bourne, Eng., U.K. I13 8
Bourne, Ma., U.S. C6 128
Bournemouth, Eng., U.K. K12 8
Bourzanga, Burkina E9 64
Bou Saâda, Alg. C13 62
Bou Salem, Tun. M3 18
Bouse, Az., U.S. D2 110
Bou Smail, Alg. B12 62
Boussac, Fr. F9 14
Bousso, Chad F4 56
Boussouma, Burkina E9 64
Bouteldja, Alg. M3 18
Boutilimit, Maur. C2 64
Boutte, La., U.S. k11 125
Bouvetøya, i., Ant. A3 73
Bouza, Niger D13 64
Bou Zadjar, Alg. J10 16
Bøverdal, Nor. K11 6
Bovey, Mn., U.S. C5 130
Bovill, Id., U.S. C2 119
Bovina, Tx., U.S. B1 150
Bovril, Arg. F9 80
Bow, N.H., U.S. D3 136
Bow, stm., Alta., Can. D4 98
Bowang, China D7 34
Bowbells, N.D., U.S. A3 141
Bowden, Alta., Can. D4 98
Bowdish Reservoir, res., R.I., U.S. B1 146
Bowdle, S.D., U.S. B6 148
Bowdoinham, Me., U.S. D3 126
Bowdon, Ga., U.S. C1 117
Bowdon, N.D., U.S. B6 141
Bowen, Arg. H5 80
Bowen, Austl. C8 70
Bowen, Il., U.S. C2 120
Bowers, De., U.S. D4 115
Bowersville, Ga., U.S. B3 117
Bowie, Az., U.S. E6 110
Bowie, Md., U.S. B4 127
Bowie, Tx., U.S. C4 150
Bowie, co., Tx., U.S. C5 150
Bowie Creek, stm., Ms., U.S. D4 131
Bow Island, Alta., Can. E5 98
Bow Lake, l., N.H., U.S. D4 136
Bowlegs, Ok., U.S. B5 143
Bowling Green, Fl., U.S. E5 116
Bowling Green, In., U.S. F4 121
Bowling Green, Ky., U.S. D3 124
Bowling Green, Md., U.S. k13 127
Bowling Green, Mo., U.S. B6 132
Bowling Green, Oh., U.S. A2 142
Bowling Green, S.C., U.S. A5 147
Bowling Green, Va., U.S. B5 153
Bowling Green, Cape, c., Austl. B7 70
Bowlus, Mn., U.S. E4 130
Bowman, Ga., U.S. B3 117
Bowman, N.D., U.S. C2 141
Bowman, S.C., U.S. E6 147
Bowman, co., N.D., U.S. C2 141
Bowman Creek, stm., Pa., U.S. m16 145
Bowman-Haley Lake, res., N.D., U.S. C2 141
Bowmanstown, Pa., U.S. E10 145
Bowral, Austl. J9 70
Bowron, stm., B.C., Can. C7 99
Bowser Lake, l., B.C., Can. A3 99
Bowsman, Man., Can. C1 100
Bowstring Lake, l., Mn., U.S. C5 130
Bow Valley, Ne., U.S. B8 134
Box Butte, co., Ne., U.S. B2 134
Box Butte Creek, stm., Ne., U.S. B3 134
Box Butte Reservoir, res., Ne., U.S. B2 134
Box Elder, Mt., U.S. B6 133
Box Elder, S.D., U.S. C2 148
Box Elder, co., Ut., U.S. B2 151
Box Elder Creek, stm., Co., U.S. A6 113
Box Elder Creek, stm., Mt., U.S. C8 133
Boxelder Creek, stm., Mt., U.S. E12 133
Boxford, Ma., U.S. A6 128
Boxholm, Ia., U.S. B3 122
Boxian, China B4 34
Boxmeer, Neth. E8 12
Boxodoi, China A3 32
Boxtel, Neth. E7 12
Boyacá, dept., Col. E6 84
Boyalık, Tur. H12 20
Boyang, China G5 34
Boyce, La., U.S. C3 125
Boyce, Va., U.S. A4 153
Boyceville, Wi., U.S. C1 156
Boyd, Mn., U.S. F3 130
Boyd, Tx., U.S. C4 150
Boyd, Wi., U.S. D2 156
Boyd, co., Ky., U.S. B7 124
Boyd, co., Ne., U.S. B7 134
Boyden, Ia., U.S. A2 122
Boyd Lake, l., Me., U.S. C4 126
Boyd's Cove, Newf., Can. D4 102
Boydton, Va., U.S. D4 153
Boyer, stm., Ia., U.S. C2 122
Boyer Knob, mtn., Md., U.S. k13 127
Boyertown, Pa., U.S. F10 145
Boykin, Ga., U.S. E2 117
Boykins, Va., U.S. D5 153
Boyle, Alta., Can. B4 98
Boyle, Ire. H5 8
Boyle, Ms., U.S. B3 131
Boyle, co., Ky., U.S. C5 124
Boylston, N.S., Can. D8 101
Boylston, Ma., U.S. B4 128
Boyne, stm., Austl. E9 70
Boyne, stm., Ire. H7 8
Boyne City, Mi., U.S. C6 129
Boyne Falls, Mi., U.S. C6 129
Boynton, Ok., U.S. B6 143
Boynton Beach, Fl., U.S. F6 116
Boysen Reservoir, res., Wy., U.S. C4 157
Boys Ranch, Tx., U.S. B1 150
Boys Town, Ne., U.S. g12 134
Boyuibe, Bol. I10 82
Bozel, Fr. G13 14
Bozeman, Mt., U.S. E5 133
Bozeman Pass, Mt., U.S. E6 133
Bozen see Bolzano, Italy C6 18
Bozhen, China E4 32
Bozman, Md., U.S. C5 127
Bozoum, Cen. Afr. Rep. G4 56
Bozovici, Rom. E5 20
Bra, Italy E2 18
Brabant, prov., Bel. G6 12
Brabant Island, i., Ant. B12 73
Brač, Otok, i., Yugo. F11 18
Bracciano, Italy G7 18
Bracciano, Lago di, l., Italy G7 18
Bracebridge, Ont., Can. B5 103
Braceville, Il., U.S. B5 120
Bracken, Sask., Can. H1 105
Bracken, co., Ky., U.S. B5 124
Bracken Lake, l., Man., Can. C2 100
Brackenridge, Pa., U.S. h15 145
Brackettville, Tx., U.S. E2 150
Braço do Norte, Braz. E14 80
Brad, Rom. C6 20
Braddock, Pa., U.S. k14 145
Braddock Heights, Md., U.S. B2 127
Braddock Point, c., S.C., U.S. G6 147
Braddyville, Ia., U.S. D2 122
Braden, Tn., U.S. B2 149
Bradenton, Fl., U.S. E4 116
Bradenville, Pa., U.S. F3 145
Bradford, Ont., Can. C5 103
Bradford, Ar., U.S. B4 111
Bradford, Il., U.S. B4 120
Bradford, N.H., U.S. D3 136
Bradford, Oh., U.S. B1 142
Bradford, Pa., U.S. C4 145
Bradford, R.I., U.S. F2 146
Bradford, Tn., U.S. A3 149
Bradford, Vt., U.S. D4 152
Bradford, co., Fl., U.S. C4 116
Bradford, co., Pa., U.S. C8 145
Bradford Mountain, mtn., Ct., U.S. B2 114
Bradfordsville, Ky., U.S. C4 124
Bradfordwoods, Pa., U.S. h13 145
Bradley, Ar., U.S. D2 111
Bradley, Fl., U.S. E5 116
Bradley, Il., U.S. B6 120
Bradley, Me., U.S. D4 126
Bradley, S.D., U.S. B8 148
Bradley, W.V., U.S. D3 155
Bradley, co., Ar., U.S. D3 111
Bradley, co., Tn., U.S. D9 149
Bradley Beach, N.J., U.S. C4 137
Bradner, Oh., U.S. A2 142
Bradshaw, Md., U.S. B5 127
Bradshaw, Ne., U.S. D8 134
Bradshaw, W.V., U.S. D3 155
Bradshaw Mountains, mts., Az., U.S. C3 110
Bradwell, Sask., Can. F2 105
Brady, Mt., U.S. B5 133
Brady, Ne., U.S. C5 134
Brady, Tx., U.S. D3 150
Braeside, Ont., Can. B8 103
Braga, Port. D3 16
Bragado, Arg. H8 80
Bragança, Braz. D9 76
Bragança, Port. D5 16
Bragança Paulista, Braz. G5 79
Braggadocio, Mo., U.S. E8 132
Braggs, Ok., U.S. B6 143
Braham, Mn., U.S. E5 130
Brāhmanbāria, Bngl. I14 44
Brāhmani, stm., India J11 44
Brahmapur, India C8 46
Brahmaputra (Yarlung), stm., Asia G15 44
Braich y Pwll, c., Wales, U.K. I9 8
Braidwood, Austl. J8 70
Braidwood, Il., U.S. B5 120
Brăila, Rom. D11 20
Brăila, co., Rom. D11 20
Brainard, Ne., U.S. C9 134
Braine-l'Alleud (Eigenbrakel), Bel. G5 12
Braine-le-Comte ('s-Gravenbrakel), Bel. G5 12
Brainerd, Mn., U.S. D4 130
Braintree, Ma., U.S. B5 128
Brake, Ger. B8 10
Brakwater, Nmb. D3 66
Bralorne, B.C., Can. D6 99
Braman, Ok., U.S. A4 143
Brampton, Ont., Can. D5 103
Bramsche, Ger. C7 10
Bramwell, W.V., U.S. D3 155
Branch, Newf., Can. E5 102
Branch, Ar., U.S. B2 111
Branch, co., Mi., U.S. G5 129
Branch, stm., R.I., U.S. B3 146
Branch, stm., Wi., U.S. h10 156
Branch Lake, l., Me., U.S. D4 126
Branchland, W.V., U.S. C2 155
Branch Village, R.I., U.S. B3 146
Branchville, Al., U.S. B3 108
Branchville, Ct., U.S. D2 114
Branchville, S.C., U.S. E6 147
Branco, stm., Braz. C9 82
Branco, stm., Braz. C7 82
Branco, stm., Braz. C11 82
Branco, stm., Braz. B8 82
Branco, stm., Braz. C11 82
Branco, stm., Braz. E11 82
Branco, stm., Braz. I13 82
Branco, stm., Braz. H12 84
Brandberg, mtn., Nmb. C2 66
Brandbu, Nor. K12 6
Brandenburg, Ger. C12 10
Brandenburg, Ky., U.S. C3 124
Brandenburg, state, Ger. C13 10
Brand-Erbisdorf, Ger. E13 10
Brandon, Man., Can. E2 100
Brandon, Fl., U.S. E4 116
Brandon, Ia., U.S. B6 122
Brandon, Mn., U.S. E3 130
Brandon, Ms., U.S. C4 131
Brandon, S.C., U.S. B3 147
Brandon, S.D., U.S. D9 148
Brandon, Vt., U.S. D2 152
Brandon, Wi., U.S. E5 156
Brandsen, Arg. H9 80
Brandsville, Mo., U.S. E6 132
Brandt, S.D., U.S. C9 148
Brandvlei, S. Afr. H5 66
Brandy Peak, mtn., Or., U.S. E3 144
Brandýs nad Labem, Czech. E14 10
Brandy Station, Va., U.S. B5 153
Brandywine, Md., U.S. C4 127
Brandywine, W.V., U.S. C5 155
Brandywine Creek, stm., U.S. A3 115
Branford, Ct., U.S. D4 114
Branford, Fl., U.S. C4 116
Branford Hills, Ct., U.S. D4 114
Braniewo, Pol. A19 10
Branquinho, stm., Braz. A6 82
Bransby, Austl. G5 70
Bransfield Strait, strt., Ant. B12 73
Brańsk, Pol. C22 10
Br'ansk, U.S.S.R. H17 26
Branson, Mo., U.S. E4 132
Brant, Alta., Can. D4 98
Brantford, Ont., Can. D4 103
Brant Lake, N.Y., U.S. B7 139
Brantley, Al., U.S. D3 108
Brantley, co., Ga., U.S. E4 117
Brant Rock, Ma., U.S. B6 128
Brantville, N.B., Can. B5 101
Branxholme, Austl. K4 70
Bras d'Or, N.S., Can. C9 101
Bras d'Or Lake, l., N.S., Can. D9 101
Brashear, Mo., U.S. A5 132
Brasiléia, Braz. D7 82
Brasília, Braz. C5 79
Brasília, Lago de, l., Braz. C5 79
Brasília, Parque Nacional de, Braz. C4 79
Brasília de Minas, Braz. D6 79
Braşov, Rom. D9 20
Braşov, co., Rom. D8 20
Brasstown Bald, mtn., Ga., U.S. B3 117
Brassua Lake, res., Me., U.S. C3 126
Břasy, Czech. F13 10
Bratca, Rom. C6 20
Bratenahl, Oh., U.S. g9 142
Bratislava, Czech. G17 10
Bratsk, U.S.S.R. F12 24
Bratskoje vodochranilišče, res., U.S.S.R. F18 22
Bratt, Fl., U.S. u14 116
Brattleboro, Vt., U.S. F3 152
Braulio Carrillo, Parque Nacional, C.R. G10 92
Braúnas, Braz. E7 79
Braunau [am Inn], Aus. G13 10
Braunschweig (Brunswick), Ger. C10 10
Brava, i., C.V. m16 64a
Brava, Costa, Spain D15 16
Brava, Laguna, l., Arg. E4 80
Brava, Punta, c., Ur. H10 80
Bravičа, U.S.S.R. B12 20
Bravo, Cerro, mtn., Bol. G9 82
Bravo, Cerro, mtn., Peru A2 82
Bravo del Norte (Rio Grande), stm., N.A. F6 106
Brawley, Ca., U.S. F6 112
Brawley Peaks, mts., Nv., U.S. E3 135
Braxton, co., W.V., U.S. C4 155
Bray, Ire. H7 8
Bray, Ok., U.S. C4 143
Braymer, Mo., U.S. B4 132
Brazeau, stm., Alta., Can. C2 98
Brazil, In., U.S. E3 121
Brazil, Tn., U.S. B2 149
Brazil (Brasil), ctry., S.A. F8 76
Brazil Lake, N.S., Can. F4 101

Name — Map Ref. — Page

Brazoria, Tx., U.S. r14 150
Brazoria, co., Tx., U.S. E5 150
Brazos, co., Tx., U.S. D4 150
Brazos, stm., Tx., U.S. D4 150
Brazzaville, Congo B3 58
Brčko, Yugo. E2 20
Brea, Ca., U.S. n13 112
Breadalbane, Austl. D3 70
Bread Loaf Mountain, mtn., Vt., U.S. D3 152
Breakenridge, Mount, mtn., B.C., Can. E7 99
Breakeyville, Que., Can. o17 104
Brea Pozo, Arg. E7 80
Breathitt, co., Ky., U.S. C6 124
Breaux Bridge, La., U.S. D4 125
Breaza, Rom. D9 20
Brécey, Fr. D5 14
Brechin, Ont., Can. C5 103
Brechin, Scot., U.K. E11 8
Breckenridge, Co., U.S. B4 113
Breckenridge, Mi., U.S. E6 129
Breckenridge, Mn., U.S. D2 130
Breckenridge, Mo., U.S. B4 132
Breckenridge, Ok., U.S. A4 143
Breckenridge, Tx., U.S. C3 150
Breckinridge, co., Ky., U.S. C3 124
Brecksville, Oh., U.S. A4 142
Břeclav, Czech. G16 10
Brecon, Wales, U.K. J10 8
Breda, Neth. E6 12
Breda, Ia., U.S. B3 122
Bredasdorp, S. Afr. J5 66
Bredenbury, Sask., Can. G4 105
Breese, Il., U.S. E4 120
Breezand, Neth. C6 12
Breezy Point, Mn., U.S. D4 130
Bregenz, Aus. H9 10
Bréhal, Fr. D5 14
Breiðafjörður, b., Ice. B2 6a
Brejo, Braz. D10 76
Brejões, Braz. B9 79
Brekken, Nor. J12 6
Brekstad, Nor. J11 6
Bremen, Ger. B8 10
Bremen, Ga., U.S. C1 117
Bremen, In., U.S. B5 121
Bremen, Ky., U.S. C2 124
Bremen, Oh., U.S. C3 142
Bremer, co., Ia., U.S. B5 122
Bremerhaven, Ger. B8 10
Bremerton, Wa., U.S. B3 154
Bremervörde, Ger. B9 10
Bremond, Tx., U.S. D4 150
Brenham, Tx., U.S. D4 150
Brenner Pass, Eur. H11 10
Brent, Al., U.S. C2 108
Brent, Fl., U.S. u14 116
Brenton Point, c., R.I., U.S. F5 146
Brentwood, Ca., U.S. h9 112
Brentwood, Md., U.S. f9 127
Brentwood, Mo., U.S. f13 132
Brentwood, N.H., U.S. E4 136
Brentwood, N.Y., U.S. E7 139
Brentwood, N.Y., U.S. n15 139
Brentwood, Pa., U.S. k14 145
Brentwood, S.C., U.S. k11 147
Brentwood, Tn., U.S. A5 149
Brescia, Italy D8 18
Breslau see Wrocław, Pol. D17 10
Bresse, reg., Fr. F12 14
Bressuire, Fr. F6 14
Brest, Fr. D2 14
Brest, U.S.S.R. C23 10
Bretagne (Brittany), hist. reg., Fr. D3 14
Breteuil, Fr. C9 14
Breteuil-sur-Iton, Fr. D7 14
Breton, Alta., Can. C3 98
Breton Islands, is., La., U.S. E6 125
Breton Sound, strt., La., U.S. E6 125
Brett, Cape, c., N.Z. A5 72
Bretten, Ger. F8 10
Bretton Woods, N.H., U.S. B4 136
Breu, Rio do, stm., Braz. I9 84
Breukelen, Neth. D7 12
Brevard, N.C., U.S. f10 140
Brevard, co., Fl., U.S. E6 116
Breves, Braz. D8 76
Brevoort Lake, l., Mi., U.S. B6 129
Brewarrina, Austl. G7 70
Brewer, Me., U.S. D4 126
Brewster, Ks., U.S. C2 123
Brewster, Ma., U.S. C7 128
Brewster, Mn., U.S. G3 130
Brewster, N.Y., U.S. D7 139
Brewster, Oh., U.S. B4 142
Brewster, Wa., U.S. A6 154
Brewster, co., Tx., U.S. E1 150
Brewster, Kap, c., Grnld. B17 86
Brewster, Lake, l., Austl. I7 70
Brewster Islands, is., Ma., U.S. g12 128
Brewton, Al., U.S. D2 108
Brewton, Ga., U.S. D4 117
Brežice, Yugo. D10 18
Brézina, Alg. D11 62
Breznik, Bul. G6 20
Bria, Cen. Afr. Rep. N1 60
Brian Boru Peak, mtn., B.C., Can. B4 99
Briançon, Fr. H13 14
Brian Head, mtn., Ut., U.S. F3 151
Briare, Fr. E9 14
Bričany, U.S.S.R. A11 20
Bricelyn, Mn., U.S. G5 130
Briceville, Tn., U.S. C9 149
Brick [Township], N.J., U.S. C4 137
Bricquebec, Fr. C5 14
Bridal Veil Falls, wtfl, Ut., U.S. C4 151
Bridesville, B.C., Can. E8 99
Bridgeboro, Ga., U.S. E3 117
Bridgehampton, N.Y., U.S. n16 139
Bridgeport, Al., U.S. A4 108
Bridgeport, Ca., U.S. C4 112
Bridgeport, Ct., U.S. E3 114
Bridgeport, Il., U.S. E6 120
Bridgeport, Mi., U.S. E7 129
Bridgeport, Ne., U.S. C2 134
Bridgeport, Oh., U.S. B5 142
Bridgeport, Pa., U.S. o20 145
Bridgeport, Tx., U.S. C4 150
Bridgeport, Wa., U.S. B6 154
Bridgeport, W.V., U.S. B4 155
Bridger, Mt., U.S. E8 133
Bridger Peak, mtn., Wy., U.S. E5 157
Bridger Range, mts., Mt., U.S. E6 133
Bridgeton, In., U.S. E3 121
Bridgeton, Mo., U.S. C7 132
Bridgeton, N.J., U.S. E2 137
Bridgeton, N.C., U.S. B5 140
Bridgetown, Austl. F3 68
Bridgetown, Barb. H15 94
Bridgetown, N.S., Can. E4 101
Bridgeville, N.S., Can. D7 101
Bridgeville, De., U.S. F3 115
Bridgeville, Pa., U.S. k13 145
Bridgewater, Austl. N7 70
Bridgewater, N.S., Can. E5 101
Bridgewater, Ct., U.S. C2 114
Bridgewater, Ia., U.S. C3 122
Bridgewater, Me., U.S. B5 126
Bridgewater, Ma., U.S. C6 128
Bridgewater, N.J., U.S. B3 137
Bridgewater, S.D., U.S. D8 148
Bridgewater, Vt., U.S. D3 152
Bridgewater, Va., U.S. B4 153
Bridgman, Mi., U.S. G4 129
Bridgton, Me., U.S. D2 126
Bridgwater, Eng., U.K. J10 8
Bridport, Vt., U.S. D2 152
Brie, reg., Fr. D10 14
Briec, Fr. D2 14
Brielle, N.J., U.S. C4 137
Brienne-le-Château, Fr. D11 14
Brienz, Switz. E9 13
Brienzersee, l., Switz. E9 13
Brier Creek, stm., Ga., U.S. C5 117
Briercrest, Sask., Can. G3 105
Brierfield, Al., U.S. B3 108
Briery Knob, mtn., W.V., U.S. C4 155
Briey, Fr. C12 14
Brig, Switz. F9 13
Brigantine, N.J., U.S. E4 137
Brigantine Beach, N.J., U.S. E4 137
Brig Bay, Newf., Can. C3 102
Brigden, Ont., Can. E2 103
Briggs Marsh, sw., R.I., U.S. F6 146
Briggsville, Wi., U.S. E4 156
Brigham City, Ut., U.S. B3 151
Brig Harbour Island, i., Newf., Can. A3 102
Bright, Austl. K7 70
Bright, Ont., Can. D4 103
Brighton, Ont., Can. C7 103
Brighton, Eng., U.K. K13 8
Brighton, Al., U.S. B3 108
Brighton, Co., U.S. B6 113
Brighton, Il., U.S. D3 120
Brighton, Ia., U.S. C6 122
Brighton, Mi., U.S. F7 129
Brighton, N.Y., U.S. B3 139
Brighton, Tn., U.S. B2 149
Brighton Downs, Austl. D4 70
Brighton Indian Reservation, Fl., U.S. E5 116
Brignoles, Fr. I13 14
Brikama, Gam. E1 64
Brilhante, stm., Braz. F1 79
Brilliant, B.C., Can. E9 99
Brilliant, Al., U.S. A2 108
Brilliant, Oh., U.S. B5 142
Brillion, Wi., U.S. D5 156
Brilon, Ger. D8 10
Brimfield, Il., U.S. C4 120
Brimhall, N.M., U.S. B1 138
Brimley, Mi., U.S. B6 129
Brindisi, Italy I12 18
Bringhurst, In., U.S. C5 121
Brinje, Yugo. D10 18
Brinkley, Ar., U.S. C4 111
Brinnon, Wa., U.S. B3 154
Brinson, Ga., U.S. F2 117
Brion, Île, i., Que., Can. B8 101
Brioso, stm., Braz. F2 79
Brioude, Fr. G10 14
Briouze, Fr. D6 14
Brisbane, Austl. F10 70
Briscoe, co., Tx., U.S. B2 150
Bristol, N.B., Can. C2 101
Bristol, Eng., U.K. J11 8
Bristol, Co., U.S. C8 113
Bristol, Ct., U.S. C4 114
Bristol, Fl., U.S. B2 116
Bristol, Ga., U.S. E4 117
Bristol, Il., U.S. B5 120
Bristol, In., U.S. A6 121
Bristol, N.H., U.S. C3 136
Bristol, R.I., U.S. D5 146
Bristol, S.D., U.S. B8 148
Bristol, Tn., U.S. C11 149
Bristol, Vt., U.S. C2 152
Bristol, Va., U.S. f9 153
Bristol, Wi., U.S. F5 156
Bristol, co., Ma., U.S. C5 128
Bristol, co., R.I., U.S. D5 146
Bristol Bay, b., Ak., U.S. D7 109
Bristol [Township], Pa., U.S. F12 145
Bristolville, Oh., U.S. A5 142
Bristow, Ne., U.S. B7 134
Bristow, Ok., U.S. B5 143
Britânia, Braz. C3 79
Britannia Beach, B.C., Can. E6 99
Britannia Range, mts., Ant. D8 73
British Antarctic Territory, dep., S.A. B1 73
British Columbia, prov., Can. C6 99
British Honduras see Belize, ctry., N.A. I15 90
British Indian Ocean Territory, dep., Afr. J8 28
British Virgin Islands, dep., N.A. E12 94
Brits, S. Afr. E8 66
Britstown, S. Afr. H6 66
Britt, Ia., U.S. A4 122
Brittany see Bretagne, hist. reg., Fr. D3 14
Britton, Mi., U.S. G7 129
Britton, S.D., U.S. B8 148
Brive-la-Gaillarde, Fr. G8 14
Brixton, Austl. D6 70
Brno, Czech. F16 10
Broa, Ensenada de la, b., Cuba C3 94
Broad, stm., Ga., U.S. B4 117
Broad, stm., S.C., U.S. C5 147
Broadalbin, N.Y., U.S. B6 139
Broadbent, Or., U.S. E2 144
Broad Brook, Ct., U.S. B5 114
Broad Creek, stm., De., U.S. F3 115
Broadford, Scot., U.K. D8 8
Broadford, Va., U.S. f10 153
Broadkill, stm., De., U.S. E4 115
Broadkill Beach, De., U.S. E5 115
Broadlands, Il., U.S. D6 120
Broad Run, stm., Va., U.S. g11 153
Broad Sound, strt., Austl. D8 70
Broad Sound Channel, strt., Austl. D9 70
Broadus, Mt., U.S. E11 133
Broadview, Sask., Can. G4 105
Broadview, Mt., U.S. D8 133
Broadview Heights, Oh., U.S. h9 142
Broadview Park, Fl., U.S. F6 116
Broadwater, Ne., U.S. C3 134
Broadwater, co., Mt., U.S. D5 133
Broadway, N.C., U.S. B3 140
Broadway, Va., U.S. B4 153
Brocēni, U.S.S.R. E5 26
Brochet, Man., Can. f7 100
Brock, Sask., Can. F1 105
Brock, Ne., U.S. D10 134
Brocket, N.D., U.S. A7 141
Brockport, N.Y., U.S. B3 139
Brockton, Ma., U.S. B5 128
Brockton, Mt., U.S. B12 133
Brockton Reservoir, res., Ma., U.S. h11 128
Brockville, Ont., Can. C9 103
Brockway, Pa., U.S. D4 145
Brocton, Il., U.S. D6 120
Brocton, N.Y., U.S. C1 139
Broderick, Sask., Can. F2 105
Brodeur Peninsula, pen., N.W. Ter., Can. B15 96
Brodhead, Ky., U.S. C5 124
Brodhead, Wi., U.S. F4 156
Brodheadsville, Pa., U.S. E11 145
Brodnax, Va., U.S. D4 153
Brodnica, Pol. B19 10
Broken Arrow, Ok., U.S. A6 143
Broken Bay, b., Austl. I9 70
Broken Bow, Ne., U.S. C6 134
Broken Bow, Ok., U.S. C7 143
Broken Bow Lake, res., Ok., U.S. C7 143
Broken Hill, Austl. H4 70
Brokopondo, Sur. B8 76
Brome, Que., Can. D5 104
Brome, Lac, l., Que., Can. D5 104
Bromley Mountain, mtn., Vt., U.S. E3 152
Bromptonville, Que., Can. D6 104
Bronaugh, Mo., U.S. D3 132
Bronnicy, U.S.S.R. F21 26
Bronnoje, U.S.S.R. I13 26
Bronson, Fl., U.S. C4 116
Bronson, Ia., U.S. B1 122
Bronson, Ks., U.S. E8 123
Bronson, Mi., U.S. G5 129
Bronte, Italy L9 18
Bronte, Tx., U.S. D2 150
Bronwood, Ga., U.S. E2 117
Bronx, co., N.Y., U.S. E7 139
Bronxville, N.Y., U.S. h13 139
Brook, In., U.S. C3 121
Brookdale, Man., Can. D2 100
Brooke, co., W.V., U.S. A4 155
Brookfield, N.S., Can. D6 101
Brookfield, Ct., U.S. D2 114
Brookfield, Ga., U.S. E3 117
Brookfield, Il., U.S. k9 120
Brookfield, Ma., U.S. B3 128
Brookfield, Mo., U.S. B4 132
Brookfield, Va., U.S. B5 153
Brookfield, Wi., U.S. m11 156
Brookfield Center, Ct., U.S. D2 114
Brookford, N.C., U.S. B1 140
Brookhaven, Ms., U.S. D3 131
Brookhaven, W.V., U.S. h11 155
Brookings, Or., U.S. E2 144
Brookings, S.D., U.S. C9 148
Brookings, co., S.D., U.S. C9 148
Brookland, Ar., U.S. B5 111
Brooklandville, Md., U.S. g10 127
Brooklawn, N.J., U.S. D2 137
Brooklet, Ga., U.S. D5 117
Brooklin, Me., U.S. D4 126
Brookline, Ma., U.S. B5 128
Brookline, N.H., U.S. E3 136
Brooklyn, N.S., Can. E5 101
Brooklyn, Al., U.S. D3 108
Brooklyn, Ct., U.S. B8 114
Brooklyn, In., U.S. E5 121
Brooklyn, Ia., U.S. C5 122
Brooklyn, Mi., U.S. F6 129
Brooklyn, Ms., U.S. D4 131
Brooklyn, Oh., U.S. h9 142
Brooklyn, S.C., U.S. B6 147
Brooklyn, Wi., U.S. F4 156
Brooklyn Center, Mn., U.S. E5 130
Brooklyn Park, Md., U.S. h11 127
Brooklyn Park, Mn., U.S. m12 130
Brookneal, Va., U.S. C4 153
Brook Park, Oh., U.S. h9 142
Brookport, Il., U.S. F5 120
Brooks, Alta., Can. D5 98
Brooks, Ky., U.S. g11 124
Brooks, Me., U.S. D3 126
Brooks, Mn., U.S. C2 130
Brooks, Or., U.S. h12 144
Brooks, co., Ga., U.S. F3 117
Brooks, co., Tx., U.S. F3 150
Brooks Air Force Base, mil., Tx., U.S. k7 150
Brookshire, Tx., U.S. E5 150
Brookside, Al., U.S. f7 108
Brookside, Co., U.S. C5 113
Brookside, De., U.S. B3 115
Brooks Peninsula, pen., B.C., Can. D4 99
Brooks Range, mts., Ak., U.S. B9 109
Brookston, In., U.S. C4 121
Brooksville, Fl., U.S. D4 116
Brooksville, Ky., U.S. B5 124
Brooksville, Ms., U.S. B5 131
Brookton, Austl. F3 68
Brookton, Me., U.S. C5 126
Brookvale, Co., U.S. B5 113
Brookville, In., U.S. F8 121
Brookville, Ks., U.S. D6 123
Brookville, Oh., U.S. C1 142
Brookville, Pa., U.S. D3 145
Brookville Lake, res., In., U.S. E7 121
Brookwood, Al., U.S. B2 108
Brookwood, N.J., U.S. C4 137
Broomall, Pa., U.S. p20 145
Broome, Austl. C4 68
Broome, co., N.Y., U.S. C5 139
Broomes Island, Md., U.S. D4 127
Broomfield, Co., U.S. B5 113
Broons, Fr. D4 14
Brooten, Mn., U.S. E3 130
Brora, Scot., U.K. C10 8
Brossard, Que., Can. q20 104
Brotas de Macaúbas, Braz. B7 79
Brou, Fr. D8 14
Broughton, Il., U.S. F5 120
Broughty Ferry, Scot., U.K. E11 8
Broussard, La., U.S. D4 125
Brouwersdam, Neth. E4 12
Brouwershaven, Neth. E4 12
Broward, co., Fl., U.S. F6 116
Browardale, Fl., U.S. r13 116
Browerville, Mn., U.S. D4 130
Brown, co., Il., U.S. D3 120
Brown, co., In., U.S. F5 121
Brown, co., Ks., U.S. C8 123
Brown, co., Mn., U.S. F4 130
Brown, co., Ne., U.S. B6 134
Brown, co., Oh., U.S. D2 142
Brown, co., S.D., U.S. B7 148
Brown, co., Tx., U.S. D3 150
Brown, co., Wi., U.S. D6 156
Brown, Point, c., Wa., U.S. C1 154
Brown City, Mi., U.S. E8 129
Brown Deer, Wi., U.S. m12 156
Brownfield, Tx., U.S. C1 150
Browning, Mo., U.S. A4 132
Browning, Mt., U.S. B3 133
Brownlee, Sask., Can. G2 105
Brownlee Dam, U.S. E2 119
Brownlee Reservoir, res., U.S. C10 144
Browns, Il., U.S. E6 120
Browns, stm., Vt., U.S. B2 152
Brownsboro, Ky., U.S. g11 124
Browns Branch, stm., De., U.S. E3 115
Brownsburg, Que., Can. D3 104
Brownsburg, In., U.S. E5 121
Brownsdale, Mn., U.S. G6 130
Browns Inlet, b., N.C., U.S. C5 140
Browns Mills, N.J., U.S. D3 137
Browns Peak, mtn., Az., U.S. D4 110
Brownstown, Il., U.S. E5 120
Brownstown, In., U.S. G5 121
Brownstown, Pa., U.S. F9 145
Browns Valley, Mn., U.S. E2 130
Brownsville, Fl., U.S. s13 116
Brownsville, In., U.S. E8 121
Brownsville, Ky., U.S. C3 124
Brownsville, Mn., U.S. G7 130
Brownsville, Or., U.S. C4 144
Brownsville, Pa., U.S. F2 145
Brownsville, Tn., U.S. B2 149
Brownsville, Tx., U.S. G4 150
Brownton, Mn., U.S. F4 130
Brownton, W.V., U.S. B4 155
Brownvale, Alta., Can. A2 98
Brownville, Al., U.S. B2 108
Brownville, Me., U.S. C3 126
Brownville, Ne., U.S. D10 134
Brownville, N.Y., U.S. A5 139
Brownville Junction, Me., U.S. C3 126
Brownwood, Mo., U.S. D8 132
Brownwood, Tx., U.S. D3 150
Brownwood, Lake, res., Tx., U.S. D3 150
Browse Island, i., Austl. B4 68
Broxton, Ga., U.S. E4 117
Broža, U.S.S.R. I12 26
Bruay-en-Artois, Fr. B9 14
Bruce, Alta., Can. C4 98
Bruce, Ms., U.S. B4 131
Bruce, S.D., U.S. C9 148
Bruce, Wi., U.S. C2 156
Bruce, Mount, mtn., Austl. D3 68
Bruce Crossing, Mi., U.S. m12 129
Brucefield, Ont., Can. D3 103
Bruce National Park, Ont., Can. B3 103
Bruce Peninsula, pen., Ont., Can. B3 103
Bruceton, Tn., U.S. A3 149
Bruceville, In., U.S. G3 121
Bruchsal, Ger. F8 10
Bruck an der Mur, Aus. H15 10
Bruderheim, Alta., Can. C4 98
Bruges (Brugge), Bel. F3 12
Brugg, Switz. D9 13
Brugge (Bruges), Bel. F3 12
Brugge-Gent, Kanaal, Bel. F3 12
Brühl, Ger. E6 10
Bruinisse, Neth. E5 12
Bruin Point, mtn., Ut., U.S. D5 151
Bruja, Cerro, mtn., Pan. H15 92
Brule, Ne., U.S. C4 134
Brule, co., S.D., U.S. D6 148
Brule, stm., U.S. C5 156
Brûlé, Lac, l., Can. F20 96
Brule Lake, l., Mn., U.S. k9 130
Brumadinho, Braz. F6 79
Brumado, Braz. C8 79
Brumath, Fr. D14 14
Brumley Mountain, mtn., Va., U.S. f9 153
Brundidge, Al., U.S. D4 108
Bruneau, Id., U.S. G3 119
Bruneau, stm., U.S. G3 119
Brunei, ctry., Asia E5 38
Brunette Island, i., Newf., Can. E4 102
Bruning, Ne., U.S. D8 134
Brunkild, Man., Can. E3 100
Bruno, Sask., Can. E3 105
Bruno, Ne., U.S. C9 134
Brunson, S.C., U.S. F5 147
Brunswick, Ga., U.S. E5 117
Brunswick, In., U.S. B2 121
Brunswick, Me., U.S. E3 126
Brunswick, Md., U.S. B2 127
Brunswick, Mo., U.S. B4 132
Brunswick, Ne., U.S. B8 134
Brunswick, N.C., U.S. C4 140
Brunswick, Oh., U.S. A4 142
Brunswick, co., N.C., U.S. C4 140
Brunswick, co., Va., U.S. D5 153
Brunswick, Peninsula, pen., Chile G2 78
Brunswick see Braunschweig, Ger. C10 10
Brunswick Naval Air Station, mil., Me., U.S. E3 126
Bruntál, Czech. F17 10
Brus, Laguna de, b., Hond. B10 92
Brush, Co., U.S. A7 113
Brushy Mountain, mtn., Va., U.S. C1 153
Brushy Mountains, mts., N.C., U.S. B1 140
Brus Laguna, Hond. B10 92
Brusly, La., U.S. D4 125
Brusovo, U.S.S.R. D18 26
Brusque, Braz. D14 80
Brussels, Ont., Can. D3 103
Brussels see Bruxelles, Bel. G5 12
Brusy, Pol. B17 10
Bruthen, Austl. K7 70
Bruxelles (Brussel) (Brussels), Bel. G5 12
Bruyères, Fr. D13 14
Bruzual, Ven. C8 84
Bryan, Oh., U.S. A1 142
Bryan, Tx., U.S. D4 150
Bryan, co., Ga., U.S. D5 117
Bryan, co., Ok., U.S. D5 143
Bryansk see Br'ansk, U.S.S.R. H17 26
Bryans Road, Md., U.S. C3 127
Bryant, Ar., U.S. C3 111
Bryant, Fl., U.S. F6 116
Bryant, Il., U.S. C3 120
Bryant, In., U.S. C8 121
Bryant, S.D., U.S. C8 148
Bryant Creek, stm., Mo., U.S. E5 132
Bryant Mountain, mtn., Ma., U.S. B2 128
Bryantown, Md., U.S. C4 127
Bryant Pond, Me., U.S. D2 126
Bryantville, Ma., U.S. B6 128
Bryce Canyon National Park, Ut., U.S. F3 151
Bryn Mawr, Wa., U.S. e11 154
Bryson, Tx., U.S. C3 150
Bryson City, N.C., U.S. f9 140
Brzeg, Pol. E17 10
Brzesko, Pol. F20 10
Brzeziny, Pol. D19 10
B-Say-Tah, Sask., Can. G4 105
Bsharrī, Leb. D4 48
Bua Yai, Thai. G7 40
Buba, Gui.-B. F2 64
Bū Bānī, Jabal, mtn., Afr. F3 60
Bubaque, Gui.-B. F2 64
Būbiyān, i., Kuw. G10 48
Bucaramanga, Col. D6 84
Buccaneer Archipelago, is., Austl. C4 68
Buccino, Italy I10 18
Buchanan, Sask., Can. F4 105
Buchanan, Lib. I4 64
Buchanan, Ga., U.S. C1 117
Buchanan, Mi., U.S. G4 129
Buchanan, Tn., U.S. A3 149
Buchanan, Va., U.S. C3 153
Buchanan, co., Ia., U.S. B6 122
Buchanan, co., Mo., U.S. B3 132
Buchanan, co., Va., U.S. e9 153
Buchanan, Lake, l., Austl. C6 70
Buchans, Newf., Can. D3 102
Buchara, U.S.S.R. J10 22
Buchardo, Arg. H7 80
Bucharest see București, Rom. E10 20
Buchholz, Ger. B9 10
Buchloe, Ger. G10 10
Buchs, Switz. D11 13
Buchtel, Oh., U.S. C3 142
Buchy, Fr. C8 14
Buckatunna, Ms., U.S. D5 131
Buck Creek, In., U.S. D4 121
Buck Creek, stm., Ga., U.S. D2 117
Buck Creek, stm., In., U.S. m11 121
Buck Creek, stm., Ky., U.S. C5 124
Bückeburg, Ger. C9 10
Buckeye, Az., U.S. D3 110
Buckeye, W.V., U.S. C4 155
Buckeye Hills, hills, Az., U.S. m7 110
Buckeye Lake, Oh., U.S. C3 142
Buckfield, Me., U.S. D2 126
Buckhannon, W.V., U.S. C4 155
Buckhaven, Scot., U.K. E10 8
Buckhead, Ga., U.S. C3 117
Buck Hill Falls, Pa., U.S. D11 145
Buckhorn, Ky., U.S. C6 124
Buckhorn Knob, mtn., W.V., U.S. D4 155
Buckhorn Lake, res., Ky., U.S. C6 124
Buckie, Scot., U.K. D11 8
Buckingham, Que., Can. D2 104
Buckingham, co., Va., U.S. C4 153
Buckingham Bay, b., Austl. B7 68
Buckinghamshire, co., Eng., U.K. J13 8
Buckland, Que., Can. C7 104
Buckland, Ak., U.S. B7 109
Bucklands, S. Afr. G6 66
Buckley, Il., U.S. C5 120
Buckley, Mi., U.S. D5 129
Buckley, Wa., U.S. B3 154
Buckley, stm., Austl. C3 70
Bucklin, Ks., U.S. E4 123
Bucklin, Mo., U.S. B5 132
Buck Mountain, mtn., Va., U.S. D1 153
Buck Mountain, mtn., Wa., U.S. A6 154
Buckner, Ar., U.S. D2 111
Buckner, Il., U.S. F4 120
Buckner, Ky., U.S. g12 124
Buckner, Mo., U.S. h11 132
Buckow, Ger. C14 10
Bucks, Al., U.S. D1 108
Bucks, co., Pa., U.S. F11 145
Buckskin, In., U.S. H3 121
Buckskin Mountains, mts., Az., U.S. C2 110
Bucksport, Me., U.S. D4 126
Bucksport, S.C., U.S. D9 147
Bucoda, Wa., U.S. C3 154
Bucun, China G5 32
București (Bucharest), Rom. E10 20
Bucyrus, Ks., U.S. D9 123
Bucyrus, Oh., U.S. B3 142
Bud, W.V., U.S. D3 155
Buda, Il., U.S. B4 120
Buda, Tx., U.S. D4 150
Budalin, Burma C3 40
Budapest, Hung. H19 10
Búðardalur, Ice. B3 6a
Budaun, India F8 44
Budd Lake, l., N.J., U.S. B3 137
Buddu, Sud. L3 60
Bude, Ms., U.S. D3 131
Büdingen, Ger. E9 10
Búðir, Ice. B7 6a
Budogošč', U.S.S.R. B15 26
Bud'onnovsk, U.S.S.R. I6 22
Budweis see České Budějovice, Czech. G14 10
Buea, Cam. I14 64
Buena, N.J., U.S. D3 137
Buena, Wa., U.S. C5 154
Buena Esperanza, Arg. H6 80
Buena Park, Ca., U.S. n12 112
Buenaventura, Col. F4 84
Buenaventura, Mex. C6 90
Buena Vista, Bol. G10 82
Buena Vista, Para. D10 80
Buena Vista, Co., U.S. C4 113
Buena Vista, Fl., U.S. D4 116
Buena Vista, Ga., U.S. D2 117
Buena Vista, N.M., U.S. B4 138
Buena Vista, Va., U.S. C3 153
Buena Vista, co., Ia., U.S. B2 122
Buendia, Embalse de, res., Spain E9 16
Buenolândia, Braz. C3 79
Buenópolis, Braz. D6 79
Buenos Aires, Arg. H9 80
Buenos Aires, Col. F4 84
Buenos Aires, C.R. H11 92
Buenos Aires, prov., Arg. I8 80
Buenos Aires, Lago (Lago General Carrera), l., S.A. F2 78
Buerarema, Braz. C9 79
Buesaco, Col. G4 84
Buffalo, Il., U.S. D4 120
Buffalo, In., U.S. C4 121
Buffalo, Ia., U.S. C7 122
Buffalo, Ks., U.S. E8 123
Buffalo, Mn., U.S. E5 130
Buffalo, Mo., U.S. D4 132
Buffalo, N.Y., U.S. C2 139
Buffalo, N.D., U.S. C8 141
Buffalo, Oh., U.S. C4 142
Buffalo, Ok., U.S. A2 143
Buffalo, S.C., U.S. B4 147
Buffalo, S.D., U.S. B2 148
Buffalo, Tx., U.S. D5 150
Buffalo, W.V., U.S. C3 155
Buffalo, Wi., U.S. D2 156
Buffalo, Wy., U.S. B6 157
Buffalo, co., Ne., U.S. D6 134
Buffalo, co., S.D., U.S. C6 148
Buffalo, co., Wi., U.S. D2 156
Buffalo, stm., Can. E10 96
Buffalo, stm., Ar., U.S. B3 111
Buffalo, stm., Mn., U.S. D2 130
Buffalo, stm., Tn., U.S. B4 149
Buffalo, stm., Wi., U.S. D2 156
Buffalo Bill Reservoir, res., Wy., U.S. B3 157
Buffalo Center, Ia., U.S. A4 122
Buffalo Creek, Co., U.S. B5 113
Buffalo Creek, stm., U.S. f8 155
Buffalo Creek, stm., W.V., U.S. n12 155
Buffalo Creek, stm., W.V., U.S. h10 155
Buffalo Gap, S.D., U.S. D2 148
Buffalo Grove, Il., U.S. h9 120
Buffalo Lake, Mn., U.S. F4 130
Buffalo Lake, l., Alta., Can. C4 98
Buffalo Lake, res., Tx., U.S. B1 150
Buffalo Lake, res., Wi., U.S. E4 156
Buffalo Mountain, mtn., Va., U.S. D2 153
Buffumville Lake, res., Ma., U.S. B4 128
Buford, Ga., U.S. B2 117
Bug, stm., Eur. E12 4
Buga, Col. F4 84
Buga, Nig. G13 64
Bugalagrande, Col. E4 84
Bugeat, Fr. G8 14
Bugojno, Yugo. E12 18
Bugry, U.S.S.R. C18 26
Bugt, China B11 30
Bugt, China A8 32
Bugul'ma, U.S.S.R. G8 22
Buguruslan, U.S.S.R. G8 22
Buhera, Zimb. B10 66
Buhl, Al., U.S. B2 108
Buhl, Id., U.S. G4 119
Buhl, Mn., U.S. C6 130
Buhler, Ks., U.S. D6 123
Buhuşi, Rom. C10 20
Buies Creek, N.C., U.S. B4 140
Builth Wells, Wales, U.K. I10 8
Buin, Chile G3 80
Buin, Piz, mtn., Eur. E13 13
Buir Nuur, l., Asia B10 30
Buj, U.S.S.R. C24 26
Bujalance, Spain H7 16
Buji, China D16 44
Bujnaksk, U.S.S.R. I7 22
Bujumbura, Bdi. B5 58
Bukačača, U.S.S.R. G15 24
Bukama, Zaire C5 58
Būkān, Iran C9 48
Bukavu, Zaire B5 58
Bukittinggi, Indon. O6 40
Bukovina, hist. reg., Eur. B9 20
Bülach, Switz. C10 13
Bulan, Phil. O20 39b
Bulan, Ky., U.S. C6 124
Bulandshahr, India F7 44
Būlāq, Egypt E6 60
Bulawayo, Zimb. C9 66
Buldibuyo, Peru C3 82
Buldir Island, i., Ak., U.S. E3 109

Name	Map Ref.	Page
Bulgan, Mong.	B5	30
Bulgan, Mong.	B7	30
Bulgaria (Bâlgarija), ctry., Eur.	G13	4
Bulki, Eth.	N9	60
Bulkley, stm., B.C., Can.	B4	99
Bulkley Ranges, mts., B.C., Can.	B4	99
Bullard, Ga., U.S.	D3	117
Bullas, Spain	G10	16
Bull Creek, stm., Nv., U.S.	E6	135
Bull Creek, stm., S.D., U.S.	B2	148
Buller, Mount, mtn., Austl.	K7	70
Bullfinch, Austl.	F3	68
Bullfrog Creek, stm., Ut., U.S.	F5	151
Bullhead, S.D., U.S.	B4	148
Bullhead City, Az., U.S.	B1	110
Bull Island, i., S.C., U.S.	G6	147
Bull Island, i., S.C., U.S.	F8	147
Bull Island, i., S.C., U.S.	D9	147
Bullitt, co., Ky., U.S.	C4	124
Bullittsville, Ky., U.S.	h13	124
Bull Mountain, mtn., Mt., U.S.	D4	133
Bulloch, co., Ga., U.S.	D5	117
Bullock, co., Al., U.S.	C4	108
Bullock Creek, Austl.	A6	70
Bullock Creek, Mi., U.S.	E6	129
Bulloo, stm., Austl.	G5	70
Bull Run, stm., Va., U.S.	g11	153
Bull Run Mountains, mts., Va., U.S.	B5	153
Bullrun Ridge, mtn., Tn., U.S.	m13	149
Bullrun Rock, mtn., Or., U.S.	C8	144
Bulls Bay, b., S.C., U.S.	F8	147
Bulls Gap, Tn., U.S.	C10	149
Bull Shoals, Ar., U.S.	A3	111
Bull Shoals Lake, res., U.S.	A3	111
Bull Sluice Lake, res., Ga., U.S.	h8	117
Bully Creek Reservoir, res., Or., U.S.	C9	144
Bulnes, Chile	I2	80
Bultfontein, S. Afr.	G8	66
Bulukumba, Indon.	G7	38
Bulyea, Sask., Can.	G3	105
Bumba, Zaire	A4	58
Bumbuna, S.L.	G4	64
Bumping, stm., Wa., U.S.	C4	154
Bumpus Mills, Tn., U.S.	A4	149
Buna, Tx., U.S.	D6	150
Bunbury, Austl.	F3	68
Bunceton, Mo., U.S.	C5	132
Buncombe, Il., U.S.	F5	120
Buncombe, co., N.C., U.S.	f10	140
Bundaberg, Austl.	E10	70
Bünde, Ger.	C8	10
Būndi, India	H6	44
Bundick Creek, stm., La., U.S.	D2	125
Bungo-suidō, strt., Japan	N7	36
Bunia, Zaire	A6	58
Bunker, Mo., U.S.	D6	132
Bunker Group, is., Austl.	D10	70
Bunker Hill, Il., U.S.	D4	120
Bunker Hill, In., U.S.	C5	121
Bunker Hill, Ks., U.S.	D5	123
Bunker Hill, W.V., U.S.	B6	155
Bunker Hill, W.V., U.S.	m12	155
Bunker Hill, mtn., Nv., U.S.	D4	135
Bunkerville, Nv., U.S.	G7	135
Bunkie, La., U.S.	D3	125
Bunn, N.C., U.S.	B4	140
Bunnell, Fl., U.S.	C5	116
Bunnlevel, N.C., U.S.	B4	140
Buntok, Indon.	F5	38
Bünyan, Tur.	B3	48
Bunyolo, Spain	F11	16
Bunza, Nig.	E11	64
Buon Me Thuot, Viet.	H10	40
Buor-Chaja, guba, b., U.S.S.R.	C18	24
Buor-Chaja, mys, c., U.S.S.R.	C18	24
Buqayq, Sau. Ar.	B6	47
Bura, Kenya	B7	58
Buram, Sud.	L3	60
Burang, China	E3	30
Buranhém, stm., Braz.	D9	79
Buras, La., U.S.	E6	125
Buraydah, Sau. Ar.	H7	48
Burbank, Ca., U.S.	E4	112
Burbank, Il., U.S.	k9	120
Burbank, S.D., U.S.	E9	148
Burbank, Wa., U.S.	C7	154
Burchard, Ne., U.S.	D9	134
Burcher, Austl.	I7	70
Burco, Som.	G10	56
Burdekin, stm., Austl.	B7	70
Burden, Ks., U.S.	E7	123
Burdett, Alta., Can.	E5	98
Burdett, Ks., U.S.	D4	123
Burdette, Ar., U.S.	B6	111
Burdickville, R.I., U.S.	F2	146
Burdur, Tur.	H14	4
Bure, Eth.	L9	60
Bure, Eth.	M8	60
Bureau, Il., U.S.	B4	120
Bureau, co., Il., U.S.	B4	120
Bureinskij chrebet, mts., U.S.S.R.	G18	24
Bureja, stm., U.S.S.R.	G18	24
Büren, Ger.	D8	10
Būr Fu'ād, Egypt	F2	48
Burgas, Bul.	G11	20
Burg [auf Fehmarn], Ger.	A11	10
Burgaw, N.C., U.S.	C5	140
Burg [bei Magdeburg], Ger.	C11	10
Burgdorf, Ger.	C10	10
Burgdorf, Switz.	D8	13
Burgenland, state, Aus.	H16	10
Burgeo, Newf., Can.	E3	102
Burgersdorp, S. Afr.	H8	66
Burgettstown, Pa., U.S.	F1	145
Burgin, China	B4	30
Burgin, Ky., U.S.	C5	124
Burglengenfeld, Ger.	F12	10
Burgos, Mex.	E10	90
Burgos, Spain	C8	16
Burgos, prov., Spain	C8	16
Burgstädt, Ger.	E12	10
Burgundy see Bourgogne, hist. reg., Fr.	E11	14
Burhaniye, Tur.	J10	20
Burhānpur, India	J7	44
Buri, Braz.	G4	79
Burica, Punta, c., N.A.	I12	92
Burila Mare, Rom.	E6	20
Burin, Newf., Can.	E4	102
Burin Peninsula, pen., Newf., Can.	E4	102
Buri Ram, Thai.	G7	40
Buritama, Braz.	F3	79
Buriti, Braz.	D2	79
Buriti, stm., Braz.	E12	82
Buriti Alegre, Braz.	E4	79
Buritizeiro, Braz.	D6	79
Burj al-'Arab, Egypt	B5	60
Burjassot, Spain	F11	16
Burkburnett, Tx., U.S.	B3	150
Burke, S.D., U.S.	D6	148
Burke, co., Ga., U.S.	C4	117
Burke, co., N.C., U.S.	B1	140
Burke, co., N.D., U.S.	A3	141
Burke, stm., Austl.	D3	70
Burke Channel, strt., B.C., Can.	C4	99
Burkesville, Ky., U.S.	D4	124
Burket, In., U.S.	B6	121
Burketown, Austl.	A3	70
Burkeville, Tx., U.S.	D6	150
Burkeville, Va., U.S.	C4	153
Burkina Faso, ctry., Afr.	F6	54
Burkley, Ky., U.S.	f8	124
Burk's Falls, Ont., Can.	B5	103
Burkville, Al., U.S.	C3	108
Burleigh, co., N.D., U.S.	C5	141
Burleson, Tx., U.S.	n9	150
Burleson, co., Tx., U.S.	D4	150
Burley, Id., U.S.	G5	119
Burley, Wa., U.S.	f10	154
Burlingame, Ca., U.S.	h8	112
Burlingame, Ks., U.S.	D8	123
Burlington, Newf., Can.	D3	102
Burlington, Ont., Can.	D5	103
Burlington, Co., U.S.	B8	113
Burlington, Il., U.S.	A5	120
Burlington, In., U.S.	D5	121
Burlington, Ia., U.S.	D6	122
Burlington, Ks., U.S.	D8	123
Burlington, Ky., U.S.	A5	124
Burlington, Me., U.S.	C4	126
Burlington, Ma., U.S.	f11	128
Burlington, N.J., U.S.	C3	137
Burlington, N.C., U.S.	A3	140
Burlington, N.D., U.S.	A4	141
Burlington, Vt., U.S.	C2	152
Burlington, Wa., U.S.	A3	154
Burlington, Wi., U.S.	F5	156
Burlington, Wy., U.S.	B4	157
Burlington, co., N.J., U.S.	D3	137
Burlington Beach, In., U.S.	B3	121
Burlington Junction, Mo., U.S.	A2	132
Burma, ctry., Asia	A2	38
Burmā, Tall, mtn., Jord.	G5	50
Burmakino, U.S.S.R.	D23	26
Burnaby, B.C., Can.	E6	99
Burnaby Island, i., B.C., Can.	C2	99
Burnet, Tx., U.S.	D3	150
Burnet, co., Tx., U.S.	D3	150
Burnett, In., U.S.	E3	121
Burnett, co., Wi., U.S.	C1	156
Burnett, stm., Austl.	E10	70
Burnettown, S.C., U.S.	D4	147
Burnettsville, In., U.S.	C4	121
Burney, Ca., U.S.	B3	112
Burney, In., U.S.	F6	121
Burnham, Me., U.S.	D3	126
Burnham, Pa., U.S.	E6	145
Burnie, Austl.	M6	70
Burning Springs, Ky., U.S.	C6	124
Burnley, Eng., U.K.	H11	8
Burns, Ks., U.S.	D7	123
Burns, Or., U.S.	D7	144
Burns, Tn., U.S.	A4	149
Burns, Wy., U.S.	E8	157
Burns Flat, Ok., U.S.	B2	143
Burnside, Ky., U.S.	D5	124
Burnside, stm., N.W. Ter., Can.	C11	96
Burns Lake, B.C., Can.	B5	99
Burns Paiute Indian Reservation, Or., U.S.	D7	144
Burnsville, N.B., Can.	B4	101
Burnsville, Al., U.S.	C3	108
Burnsville, Mn., U.S.	F5	130
Burnsville, Ms., U.S.	A5	131
Burnsville, N.C., U.S.	f10	140
Burnsville, W.V., U.S.	C4	155
Burnsville Lake, res., W.V., U.S.	C4	155
Burnt Corn, Al., U.S.	D2	108
Burnt Hills, N.Y., U.S.	C7	139
Burnt Islands, Newf., Can.	E2	102
Burnt Mills, Lake, l., Va., U.S.	k14	153
Burnt River, Ont., Can.	C6	103
Burntside Lake, l., Mn., U.S.	C6	130
Burntwood, stm., Man., Can.	B2	100
Burntwood Lake, l., Man., Can.	B1	100
Burnwell, Al., U.S.	f6	108
Burra, Austl.	I3	70
Burragorang, Lake, res., Austl.	I9	70
Burramurra, Austl.	C2	70
Burrendong Reservoir, res., Austl.	I8	70
Burrinjuck Reservoir, res., Austl.	J8	70
Burr Oak, Ks., U.S.	C5	123
Burr Oak, Mi., U.S.	G5	129
Burr Oak Reservoir, res., Oh., U.S.	C3	142
Burroburro, stm., Guy.	E13	84
Burroughs, Ga., U.S.	E5	117
Burrows, In., U.S.	C5	121
Burrton, Ks., U.S.	D6	123
Burruyacú, Arg.	D6	80
Bursa, Tur.	I13	20
Būr Safājah, Egypt	D7	60
Būr Sa'īd (Port Said), Egypt	B7	60
Burstall, Sask., Can.	G1	105
Būr Sūdān (Port Sudan), Sud.	H9	60
Burt, Ia., U.S.	A3	122
Burt, co., Ne., U.S.	C9	134
Būr Tawfīq, Egypt	G2	48
Burt Lake, l., Mi., U.S.	C6	129
Burton, B.C., Can.	D9	99
Burton, Mi., U.S.	E7	129
Burton, Oh., U.S.	A4	142
Burton, Wa., U.S.	f11	154
Burton, W.V., U.S.	B4	155
Burton, Lake, res., Ga., U.S.	B3	117
Burtrum, Mn., U.S.	E4	130
Burtts Corner, N.B., Can.	C3	101
Burtundy, Austl.	I5	70
Buru, i., Indon.	F8	38
Burūm, Yemen	G6	47
Burundi, ctry., Afr.	B6	58
Burun-Šibertuj, gora, mtn., U.S.S.R.	H13	24
Burwell, Ne., U.S.	C6	134
Burwick, Scot., U.K.	C11	8
Bury, Que., Can.	D6	104
Bury Saint Edmunds, Eng., U.K.	I14	8
Busby, Alta., Can.	C4	98
Busby, Mt., U.S.	E10	133
Busca, Italy	E2	18
Bushkill, Pa., U.S.	D11	145
Bush Lot, Guy.	D14	84
Bushnell, Fl., U.S.	D4	116
Bushnell, Il., U.S.	C3	120
Bushnell, Ne., U.S.	C2	134
Bush River, b., Md., U.S.	B5	127
Bushton, Ks., U.S.	D5	123
Buskerud, co., Nor.	K11	6
Busko Zdrój, Pol.	E20	10
Buṣrā al-Ḥarīrī (Bosor), Syria	C6	50
Buṣrá ash-Shām, Syria	C6	50
Busselton, Austl.	F3	68
Bussey, Ia., U.S.	C5	122
Bussum, Neth.	D7	12
Bustamante, Mex.	D9	90
Buşteni, Rom.	D9	20
Busto Arsizio, Italy	D3	18
Buštyna, U.S.S.R.	A7	20
Busu-Djanoa, Zaire	A4	58
Bušuicha, U.S.S.R.	B23	26
Buta, Zaire	H5	56
Butajira, Eth.	M10	60
Buta Ranquil, Arg.	I4	80
Butare, Rw.	B5	58
Bute Inlet, b., B.C., Can.	D5	99
Butera, Italy	L9	18
Butere, Kenya	A6	58
Butha Qi, China	B11	30
Butiá, Braz.	F13	80
Butler, Al., U.S.	C1	108
Butler, Ga., U.S.	D2	117
Butler, In., U.S.	B8	121
Butler, Ky., U.S.	B5	124
Butler, Mo., U.S.	C3	132
Butler, N.J., U.S.	B4	137
Butler, Oh., U.S.	B3	142
Butler, Ok., U.S.	B2	143
Butler, Pa., U.S.	E2	145
Butler, Tn., U.S.	C11	149
Butler, Wi., U.S.	m11	156
Butler, co., Al., U.S.	D3	108
Butler, co., Ia., U.S.	B5	122
Butler, co., Ks., U.S.	E7	123
Butler, co., Ky., U.S.	C3	124
Butler, co., Mo., U.S.	E7	132
Butler, co., Ne., U.S.	C8	134
Butler, co., Oh., U.S.	C1	142
Butler, co., Pa., U.S.	E2	145
Butlerville, In., U.S.	F6	121
Butner, N.C., U.S.	A4	140
Buton, Pulau, i., Indon.	G7	38
Butru, Austl.	C3	70
Buttahatchee, stm., U.S.	B5	131
Butte, Mt., U.S.	E4	133
Butte, Ne., U.S.	B7	134
Butte, N.D., U.S.	B5	141
Butte, co., Ca., U.S.	C3	112
Butte, co., Id., U.S.	F5	119
Butte, co., S.D., U.S.	C2	148
Butte des Morts, Lake, l., Wi., U.S.	D5	156
Butte du Lion, Bel.	G5	12
Butte Falls, Or., U.S.	E4	144
Butte Mountains, mts., Nv., U.S.	D6	135
Butterfield, Ar., U.S.	g8	111
Butterfield, Mn., U.S.	G4	130
Butterfield, Mo., U.S.	E4	132
Butternut, Wi., U.S.	B3	156
Butternut Lake, l., Wi., U.S.	C5	156
Butters, N.C., U.S.	C4	140
Butterworth, Malay.	L6	40
Butterworth, Transkei	I9	66
Button Islands, is., N.W. Ter., Can.	f8	102
Buttonwillow, Ca., U.S.	E4	112
Butts, co., Ga., U.S.	C3	117
Butuan, Phil.	D8	38
Butylicy, U.S.S.R.	F24	26
Butzbach, Ger.	E8	10
Bützow, Ger.	B11	10
Buurgplaatz, mtn., Lux.	H9	12
Buxtehude, Ger.	B9	10
Buxton, Boph.	F7	66
Buxton, Guy.	D13	84
Buxton, N.C., U.S.	B7	140
Buxton, N.D., U.S.	B8	141
Buxy, Fr.	F11	14
Buyo, I.C.	H6	64
Buzançais, Fr.	F8	14
Buzău, Rom.	D10	20
Buzău, co., Rom.	D10	20
Buzău, stm., Rom.	D11	20
Buzen, Japan	N6	36
Búzi, stm., Moz.	B12	66
Búzios, Ponta dos, c., Braz.	G8	79
Buzuluk, U.S.S.R.	G8	22
Buzzard Roost, mtn., N.C., U.S.	B1	140
Buzzards Bay, Ma., U.S.	C6	128
Buzzards Bay, b., Ma., U.S.	C6	128
Byam Martin Channel, strt., N.W. Ter., Can.	A12	96
Byam Martin Island, i., N.W. Ter., Can.	A12	96
Byars, Ok., U.S.	C4	143
Bybee, Tn., U.S.	C10	149
Bychov, U.S.S.R.	H13	26
Bydgoszcz, Pol.	B18	10
Byemoor, Alta., Can.	D4	98
Byers, Co., U.S.	B6	113
Byesville, Oh., U.S.	C4	142
Byfield, Ma., U.S.	A6	128
Bygdin, Nor.	K11	6
Byhalia, Ms., U.S.	A4	131
Bykle, Nor.	L10	6
Bykovec, U.S.S.R.	B12	20
Bylas, Az., U.S.	D5	110
Bylot Island, i., N.W. Ter., Can.	B17	96
Byng, Ok., U.S.	C5	143
Byng Inlet, Ont., Can.	B4	103
Bynum, N.C., U.S.	B3	140
Byram, Ms., U.S.	C3	131
Byrdstown, Tn., U.S.	C8	149
Byromville, Ga., U.S.	D3	117
Byron, Ca., U.S.	h9	112
Byron, Ga., U.S.	D3	117
Byron, Il., U.S.	A4	120
Byron, Mn., U.S.	F6	130
Byron, Ne., U.S.	D8	134
Byron, Wy., U.S.	B4	157
Byron, Cape, c., Austl.	G10	70
Byron Bay, Austl.	G10	70
Byrranga, gory, mts., U.S.S.R.	B12	24
Bystřice, Czech.	F14	10
Bystrzyca Kłodzka, Pol.	E16	10
Bytantaj, stm., U.S.S.R.	D18	24
Bytkov, U.S.S.R.	A8	20
Bytom (Beuthen), Pol.	E18	10
Bytoš', U.S.S.R.	H17	26
Bytów, Pol.	A17	10

C

Name	Map Ref.	Page
Ca, stm., Asia	E8	40
Caacupé, Para.	C10	80
Caaguazú, Para.	C10	80
Caaguazú, dept., Para.	C11	80
Caála, Ang.	D3	58
Caapiranga, Braz.	I12	84
Caapucú, Para.	D10	80
Caazapá, Para.	D10	80
Caazapá, dept., Para.	D10	80
Cabaçal, stm., Braz.	F12	82
Cabaiguán, Cuba	C5	94
Cabaliana, Lago, l., Braz.	I12	84
Caballo, N.M., U.S.	E2	138
Caballo Mountains, mts., N.M., U.S.	E2	138
Caballo Reservoir, res., N.M., U.S.	E2	138
Cabana, Peru	C2	82
Cabanaconde, Peru	F6	82
Cabanatuan, Phil.	N19	39b
Cabano, Que., Can.	B9	104
Cabarrus, co., N.C., U.S.	B2	140
Cabbage Swamp, sw., Fl., U.S.	m9	116
Cabeceiras, Braz.	C5	79
Cabedelo, Braz.	E12	76
Cabell, co., W.V., U.S.	C2	155
Cabery, Il., U.S.	C5	120
Cabeza del Buey, Spain	G6	16
Cabezas, Bol.	H10	82
Cabildo, Arg.	J8	80
Cabildo, Chile	G3	80
Cabimas, Ven.	B7	84
Cabin Creek, W.V., U.S.	m13	155
Cabin Creek, stm., W.V., U.S.	m13	155
Cabinda, Ang.	C2	58
Cabinda, dept., Ang.	C2	58
Cabinet Gorge Reservoir, res., U.S.	B1	133
Cabinet Mountains, mts., Mt., U.S.	B1	133
Cabin John, Md., U.S.	C3	127
Cable, Wi., U.S.	B2	156
Cabo, Braz.	E11	76
Cabo Frio, Braz.	G7	79
Cabo Gracias a Dios, Nic.	C11	92
Cabonga, Réservoir, res., Que., Can.	k11	104
Cabool, Mo., U.S.	D5	132
Caboolture, Austl.	F10	70
Cabora Bassa Dam, Moz.	E6	58
Caborca, Mex.	B3	90
Cabot, Ar., U.S.	C3	111
Cabot, Vt., U.S.	C4	152
Cabot, Mount, mtn., N.H., U.S.	A4	136
Cabot Head, c., Ont., Can.	B3	103
Cabot Strait, strt., Can.	G20	96
Cabo Verde, Braz.	F5	79
Cabra, Spain	H7	16
Cabramurra, Austl.	J8	70
Cabrera, stm., Col.	F5	84
Cabrera, Illa de, i., Spain	F14	16
Cabri, Sask., Can.	G1	105
Cabrillo National Monument, Ca., U.S.	o15	112
Cabrobó, Braz.	E11	76
Cabruta, Ven.	D9	84
Cabure, Ven.	B8	84
Cabuya, C.R.	H9	92
Cabuyal, C.R.	G9	92
Cabuyaro, Col.	E6	84
Caçador, Braz.	D13	80
Čačak, Yugo.	F4	20
Cacaohatán, Mex.	C2	92
Caçapava, Braz.	G6	79
Caçapava do Sul, Braz.	F12	80
Cacapon, stm., W.V., U.S.	B6	155
Caccamo, Italy	L8	18
Cacequi, Braz.	E11	80
Cáceres, Braz.	G13	82
Cáceres, Col.	D5	84
Cáceres, Spain	F5	16
Cacharí, Arg.	I9	80
Cache, Ok., U.S.	C3	143
Cache, co., Ut., U.S.	B4	151
Cache, stm., Ar., U.S.	C4	111
Cache, stm., Il., U.S.	F4	120
Cache Bay, Ont., Can.	A5	103
Cache Creek, B.C., Can.	D7	99
Cache Creek, stm., Ca., U.S.	C2	112
Cache la Poudre, stm., Co., U.S.	A5	113
Cache la Poudre, North Fork, stm., Co., U.S.	A5	113
Cache Mountain, mtn., Ak., U.S.	B10	109
Cache Peak, mtn., Id., U.S.	G5	119
Cacheu, Gui.-B.	E1	64
Cachí, Arg.	C5	80
Cachimbo, Serra do, mts., Braz.	C13	82
Cáchira, stm., Col.	D6	84
Cachoeira, Braz.	B9	79
Cachoeira Alta, Braz.	E3	79
Cachoeira de Goiás, Braz.	D3	79
Cachoeira do Sul, Braz.	F12	80
Cachoeira Paulista, Braz.	G6	79
Cachoeiras de Macacu, Braz.	G7	79
Cachoeiro de Itapemirim, Braz.	F8	79
Cachuela Esperanza, Bol.	D9	82
Cacine, Gui.-B.	F2	64
Cacólo, Ang.	D3	58
Caconda, Ang.	D3	58
Cacra, Peru	E4	82
Cactus, Tx., U.S.	A2	150
Cactus Flat, pl., Nv., U.S.	F5	135
Cactus Peak, mtn., Nv., U.S.	F5	135
Caçu, Braz.	E3	79
Caculé, Braz.	C7	79
Caçumba, Ilha, i., Braz.	D9	79
Čadan, U.S.S.R.	G16	22
Cadariri, stm., Braz.	B13	82
Caddo, Ok., U.S.	C5	143
Caddo, co., La., U.S.	B2	125
Caddo, co., Ok., U.S.	B3	143
Caddo, stm., Ar., U.S.	C2	111
Caddo Creek, stm., Ok., U.S.	C4	143
Caddo Gap, Ar., U.S.	C2	111
Caddo Lake, res., U.S.	B2	125
Caddo Mountains, mtn., Ar., U.S.	C2	111
Caddo Valley, Ar., U.S.	C2	111
Cade, La., U.S.	D4	125
Cadereyta de Jiménez, Mex.	E9	90
Cades, S.C., U.S.	D8	147
Cadet, Mo., U.S.	C7	132
Cadillac, Sask., Can.	H2	105
Cadillac, Mi., U.S.	D5	129
Cadillac Mountain, mtn., Me., U.S.	D4	126
Cádiz, Spain	I5	16
Cadiz, Ky., U.S.	D2	124
Cadiz, Oh., U.S.	B4	142
Cádiz, Golfo de, b., Eur.	I4	16
Čadobec, stm., U.S.S.R.	F11	24
Cadogan, Alta., Can.	C5	98
Cadomin, Alta., Can.	C2	98
Cadott, Wi., U.S.	D2	156
Cadron Creek, stm., Ar., U.S.	B3	111
Cadwell, Ga., U.S.	D3	117
Čadyr-Lunga, U.S.S.R.	C12	20
Cadys Falls, Vt., U.S.	B3	152
Caen, Fr.	C6	14
Caernarfon, Wales, U.K.	H9	8
Caesar Creek Lake, res., Oh., U.S.	C2	142
Cæsarea see Qesari, Ḥorbat, hist., Isr.	C3	50
Caetanópolis, Braz.	E6	79
Caeté, Braz.	E7	79
Caeté, stm., Braz.	C7	82
Caetité, Braz.	C7	79
Cafayate, Arg.	D6	80
Cafelândia do Leste Matogrossense, Braz.	D2	79
Cafuini, stm., Braz.	G14	84
Cagayan, stm., Phil.	L19	39b
Cagayan de Oro, Phil.	D7	38
Çağış, Tur.	J12	20
Cagles Mill Lake, res., In., U.S.	F4	121
Cagli, Italy	F7	18
Cagliari, Italy	J4	18
Cagliari, Golfo di, b., Italy	J4	18
Cagnes, Fr.	I14	14
Čagoda, U.S.S.R.	B18	26
Cagua, Ven.	B9	84
Caguán, stm., Col.	G5	84
Caguas, P.R.	E11	94
Cahaba, stm., Al., U.S.	C2	108
Cahaba Valley, val., Al., U.S.	B3	108
Cahabón, Guat.	B5	92
Cahabón, stm., Guat.	B5	92
Cahokia, Il., U.S.	E3	120
Cahors, Fr.	H8	14
Cahuinari, stm., Col.	H7	84
Cahuita, Punta, c., C.R.	H12	92
Caí, stm., Braz.	E13	80
Caia, stm., Eur.	F4	16
Caiabis, Serra dos, plat., Braz.	D13	82
Caiapó, stm., Braz.	D3	79
Caiapó, Serra do, mts., Braz.	D2	79
Caiapônia, Braz.	D3	79
Caibarién, Cuba	C5	94
Cai Bau, Dao, i., Viet.	D9	40
Caiçara, Braz.	C3	79
Caicara, Ven.	D9	84
Caiçara, stm., Braz.	I10	84
Caicara, Caño, stm., Ven.	D8	84
Caicara de Maturín, Ven.	C11	84
Caicara de Orinoco, Ven.	G11	88
Caicedonia, Col.	E5	84
Caicó, Braz.	E11	76
Caicos Islands, is., T./C. Is.	D9	94
Caicos Passage, strt., N.A.	C8	94
Caigou, China	B3	34
Cailloma, Peru	F6	82
Caillou Bay, b., La., U.S.	E5	125
Caillou Lake, l., La., U.S.	E5	125
Caimanera, Cuba	E7	94
Caine, stm., Bol.	G9	82
Cainsville, Mo., U.S.	A4	132
Caird Coast, Ant.	C2	73
Cairnbrook, Pa., U.S.	F4	145
Cairns, Austl.	A6	70
Cairo, Ga., U.S.	F2	117
Cairo, Il., U.S.	F4	120
Cairo, Mo., U.S.	B5	132
Cairo, Ne., U.S.	D7	134
Cairo, N.Y., U.S.	C6	139
Cairo, W.V., U.S.	B3	155
Cairo see Al-Qāhirah, Egypt	B6	60
Cairo Montenotte, Italy	E3	18
Cairu, Braz.	B9	79
Caiundo, Ang.	E3	58
Caixi, China	J5	34
Caiza, Bol.	I9	82
Cajabamba, Ec.	H3	84
Cajabamba, Peru	B2	82
Cajacay, Peru	D3	82
Cajamarca, Peru	B2	82
Cajamarca, dept., Peru	B2	82
Cajatambo, Peru	D3	82
Cajàzeiras, Braz.	E11	76
Čajek, U.S.S.R.	I12	22
Čajkovskij, U.S.S.R.	F8	22
Cajones, Cayos, rf., Hond.	A11	92
Cajuru, Braz.	F5	79
Çakeni, Ang.	A4	66
Čakovec, Yugo.	C11	18
Cala, Transkei	H8	66
Calabar, Nig.	I14	64
Calabasas, Ca., U.S.	m11	112
Calabozo, Ven.	C9	84
Calabozo, Ensenada de, b., Ven.	B7	84
Calabria, prov., Italy	J11	18
Calafate, Arg.	G2	78
Calahorra, Spain	C10	16
Calais, Fr.	B8	14
Calais, Me., U.S.	C5	126
Calais, Pas de (Strait of Dover), strt., Eur.	J15	8
Calalaste, Sierra de, mts., Arg.	C5	80
Calama, Braz.	C10	82
Calama, Chile	B4	80
Calamar, Col.	B5	84
Calamar, Col.	G6	84
Calamarca, Bol.	G7	82
Calamus, Ia., U.S.	C7	122
Calamus, stm., Ne., U.S.	B6	134
Calapan, Phil.	O19	39b
Călărași, Rom.	E11	20
Calarcá, Col.	E5	84
Calatayud, Spain	D10	16
Calau, Ger.	D13	10
Calaveras, co., Ca., U.S.	C3	112
Calbayog, Phil.	C7	38
Calca, Peru	E6	82
Calcasieu, co., La., U.S.	D2	125
Calcasieu, stm., La., U.S.	D2	125
Calcasieu Lake, l., La., U.S.	E2	125
Calcasieu Pass, strt., La., U.S.	E2	125
Calceta, Ec.	H2	84
Calcha, Bol.	I8	82
Calchaquí, Arg.	E8	80
Calchaquí, stm., Arg.	C5	80
Calçoene, Braz.	C8	76
Calcutta, India	I13	44
Calcutta, Oh., U.S.	B5	142
Calcutta Lake, l., Nv., U.S.	B2	135
Caldas, Braz.	F5	79
Caldas, Col.	D5	84
Caldas, dept., Col.	E5	84
Caldas Novas, Braz.	D4	79
Calder, Sask., Can.	F5	105
Calder, Id., U.S.	B2	119
Caldera, Chile	D3	80
Calderwood, Tn., U.S.	D10	149
Caldron Falls Reservoir, res., Wi., U.S.	C5	156
Caldwell, Ar., U.S.	B5	111
Caldwell, Id., U.S.	F2	119
Caldwell, Ks., U.S.	E6	123
Caldwell, N.J., U.S.	B4	137
Caldwell, Oh., U.S.	C4	142
Caldwell, Tx., U.S.	D4	150
Caldwell, W.V., U.S.	D4	155
Caldwell, co., Ky., U.S.	C2	124
Caldwell, co., La., U.S.	B3	125
Caldwell, co., Mo., U.S.	B3	132
Caldwell, co., N.C., U.S.	B1	140
Caldwell, co., Tx., U.S.	E4	150
Caledon, Ont., Can.	D5	103
Caledon, stm., Afr.	H8	66
Caledonia, Belize	H15	90
Caledonia, N.S., Can.	E4	101
Caledonia, Il., U.S.	A5	120
Caledonia, Mi., U.S.	F5	129
Caledonia, Mn., U.S.	G7	130
Caledonia, Ms., U.S.	B5	131
Caledonia, N.Y., U.S.	C3	139
Caledonia, N.D., U.S.	B9	141
Caledonia, Oh., U.S.	B3	142
Caledonia, co., Vt., U.S.	C4	152
Calella, Spain	D14	16
Calera, Spain	O23	17b
Calera, Al., U.S.	B3	108
Calera, Ok., U.S.	D5	143
Caleta del Sebo, Spain	N27	17b
Caleufú, Arg.	H6	80
Calexico, Ca., U.S.	F6	112
Calgary, Alta., Can.	D3	98
Calhan, Co., U.S.	B6	113
Calhoun, N.B., Can.	C5	101
Calhoun, Al., U.S.	C3	108
Calhoun, Ga., U.S.	B2	117
Calhoun, Ky., U.S.	C2	124
Calhoun, La., U.S.	B3	125
Calhoun, Mo., U.S.	C4	132
Calhoun, Tn., U.S.	D9	149
Calhoun, co., Al., U.S.	B4	108
Calhoun, co., Ar., U.S.	D3	111
Calhoun, co., Fl., U.S.	B1	116
Calhoun, co., Ga., U.S.	E2	117
Calhoun, co., Il., U.S.	D3	120
Calhoun, co., Ia., U.S.	B3	122
Calhoun, co., Mi., U.S.	F5	129
Calhoun, co., Ms., U.S.	B4	131
Calhoun, co., S.C., U.S.	D6	147
Calhoun, co., Tx., U.S.	E4	150
Calhoun, co., W.V., U.S.	C3	155
Calhoun City, Ms., U.S.	B4	131
Calhoun Falls, S.C., U.S.	C2	147
Cali, Col.	F4	84
Calico Rock, Ar., U.S.	A3	111
Calicut, India	G3	46
Caliente, Nv., U.S.	F7	135
Califon, N.J., U.S.	B3	137
California, Md., U.S.	D4	127
California, Mo., U.S.	C5	132
California, Pa., U.S.	F2	145
California, state, U.S.	D4	112
California, Golfo de, b., Mex.	D4	90
California Aqueduct, Ca., U.S.	E4	112
California City, Ca., U.S.	E5	112
Calilegua, Arg.	B6	80
Calimere, Point, c., India	G5	46
Calindó, stm., Braz.	C6	79

Name — Map Ref. — Page

Calingasta, Arg. F4 80
Calion, Ar., U.S. D3 111
Calipatria, Ca., U.S. F6 112
Calispell Peak, mtn., Wa., U.S. A8 154
Calistoga, Ca., U.S. C2 112
Calitri, Italy I10 18
Callabonna, Lake, l., Austl. G4 70
Callac, Fr. D3 14
Callaghan, Mount, mtn., Nv., U.S. D5 135
Callahan, Fl., U.S. B5 116
Callahan, co., Tx., U.S. C3 150
Callanmarca, Peru E4 82
Callanna, Austl. G2 70
Callao, Peru E3 82
Callao, Mo., U.S. B5 132
Callao, Va., U.S. C6 153
Callaway, Md., U.S. D4 127
Callaway, Ne., U.S. C6 134
Callaway, co., Mo., U.S. C6 132
Callender, Ia., U.S. B3 122
Calling Lake, l., Alta., Can. B4 98
Callosa d'En Sarrià, Spain G11 16
Callosa de Segura, Spain G11 16
Calloway, co., Ky., U.S. f9 124
Calmar, Alta., Can. C4 98
Calmar, Ia., U.S. A6 122
Calobre, Pan. I14 92
Caloosahatchee, stm., Fl., U.S. F5 116
Caloundra, Austl. F10 70
Calp, Spain G12 16
Caltagirone, Italy L9 18
Caltanissetta, Italy L9 18
Calumet, Que., Can. D3 104
Calumet, Mi., U.S. A2 129
Calumet, Mn., U.S. C5 130
Calumet, Ok., U.S. B3 143
Calumet, co., Wi., U.S. D5 156
Calumet, Lake, l., Il., U.S. k9 120
Calumet City, Il., U.S. B6 120
Calumet Sag Channel, Il., U.S. k9 120
Calunda, Ang. D4 58
Caluula, Som. F11 56
Calvados, dept., Fr. C6 14
Calvary, Ga., U.S. F2 117
Calvert, Al., U.S. D1 108
Calvert, Tx., U.S. D4 150
Calvert, co., Md., U.S. C4 127
Calvert City, Ky., U.S. e9 124
Calvert Island, i., B.C., Can. D3 99
Calverton, Md., U.S. B4 127
Calverton, N.Y., U.S. n16 139
Calverton Park, Mo., U.S. f13 132
Calvi, Fr. L23 15a
Calvia, Spain F14 16
Calvillo, Mex. G8 90
Calvin, Ok., U.S. C5 143
Calvinia, S. Afr. H4 66
Calw, Ger. G8 10
Calypso, N.C., U.S. B4 140
Calzada, Peru B3 82
Camabatela, Ang. C3 58
Camaçari, Braz. B9 79
Camacupa, Ang. D3 58
Camaguán, Ven. C9 84
Camagüey, Cuba D6 94
Camaiore, Italy F5 18
Camaiú, stm., Braz. B12 82
Camajuaní, Cuba C5 94
Camak, Ga., U.S. C4 117
Camamu, Braz. B9 79
Camaná, Peru G5 82
Camaná, stm., Peru G5 82
Camananaú, stm., Braz. H12 84
Camanche, Ia., U.S. C7 122
Camano Island, i., Wa., U.S. A3 154
Camapuã, Braz. E1 79
Camaquã, Braz. F13 80
Camaquã, stm., Braz. F12 80
Camará, Braz. I11 84
Camararé, stm., Braz. E12 82
Camarès, Fr. I9 14
Camargo, Bol. I9 82
Camargo, Mex. D7 90
Camargo, Il., U.S. D5 120
Camargue, reg., Fr. I11 14
Camarillo, Ca., U.S. E4 112
Camarón, Cabo, c., Hond. A9 92
Camarones, Arg. E3 78
Camas, Spain H5 16
Camas, Wa., U.S. D3 154
Camas, co., Id., U.S. F4 119
Camas Valley, Or., U.S. D3 144
Ca Mau, Viet. J8 40
Ca Mau, Mui, c., Viet. J8 40
Cambados, Spain C3 16
Cambará, Braz. G3 79
Cambodia, ctry., Asia C4 38
Camboon, Austl. E9 70
Camboriú, Braz. D14 80
Camboriú, Ponta, c., Braz. C15 80
Cambrai, Fr. B10 14
Cambria, Ca., U.S. E3 112
Cambria, Wi., U.S. E4 156
Cambria, co., Pa., U.S. E4 145
Cambrian Mountains, mts., Wales, U.K. I10 8
Cambridge, Ont., Can. D4 103
Cambridge, N.Z. B5 72
Cambridge, Eng., U.K. I14 8
Cambridge, Id., U.S. E2 119
Cambridge, Il., U.S. B3 120
Cambridge, Ia., U.S. C4 122
Cambridge, Md., U.S. C5 127
Cambridge, Ma., U.S. B5 128
Cambridge, Mn., U.S. E5 130
Cambridge, Ne., U.S. D5 134
Cambridge, N.Y., U.S. B7 139
Cambridge, Oh., U.S. B4 142
Cambridge, Vt., U.S. B3 152
Cambridge, Wi., U.S. E4 156
Cambridge Bay, N.W. Ter., Can. C11 96
Cambridge City, In., U.S. E7 121
Cambridge Reservoir, res., Ma., U.S. g10 128
Cambridgeshire, co., Eng., U.K. I13 8
Cambridge Springs, Pa., U.S. C1 145
Cambuci, Braz. F8 79
Cambuí, Braz. G5 79
Cambundi-Catembo, Ang. D3 58
Camden, Austl. J9 70
Camden, Al., U.S. D2 108
Camden, Ar., U.S. D3 111
Camden, De., U.S. D3 115
Camden, In., U.S. C4 121
Camden, Me., U.S. D3 126
Camden, Mi., U.S. G6 129
Camden, Ms., U.S. C4 131
Camden, Mo., U.S. B3 132
Camden, N.J., U.S. D2 137
Camden, N.Y., U.S. B5 139
Camden, N.C., U.S. A6 140
Camden, Oh., U.S. C1 142
Camden, S.C., U.S. C6 147
Camden, Tn., U.S. A3 149
Camden, co., Ga., U.S. F5 117
Camden, co., Mo., U.S. C5 132
Camden, co., N.J., U.S. D3 137
Camden, co., N.C., U.S. A6 140
Camdenton, Mo., U.S. D5 132
Camelback Mountain, mtn., Az., U.S. k9 110
Camels Hump, mtn., Vt., U.S. C3 152
Cameron, Az., U.S. B4 110
Cameron, La., U.S. E2 125
Cameron, Mo., U.S. B3 132
Cameron, Ok., U.S. B7 143
Cameron, S.C., U.S. D6 147
Cameron, Tx., U.S. D4 150
Cameron, W.V., U.S. B4 155
Cameron, Wi., U.S. C2 156
Cameron, co., La., U.S. E2 125
Cameron, co., Pa., U.S. D5 145
Cameron, co., Tx., U.S. F4 150
Cameron Hills, hills, Can. E9 96
Cameroon (Cameroun), ctry., Afr. G9 54
Cameroon Mountain, mtn., Cam. I14 64
Cametá, Braz. D9 76
Camiling, Phil. N19 39b
Camilla, Ga., U.S. E2 117
Camiña, Chile H7 82
Camino, Ca., U.S. C3 112
Camiranga, Braz. D9 76
Camiri, Bol. I10 82
Camissombo, Ang. C4 58
Camlachie, Ont., Can. D2 103
Cammack Village, Ar., U.S. C3 111
Camoapa, Nic. E9 92
Camocim, Braz. D10 76
Camooweal, Austl. B3 70
Camorta Island, i., India J2 40
Camp, co., Tx., U.S. C5 150
Campaign, Tn., U.S. D8 149
Campamento, Hond. C8 92
Campana, Arg. H9 80
Campana, Isla, i., Chile I7 74
Campanario, Spain G6 16
Campanario, Cerro de, mtn., Peru A3 82
Campanero, Cerro, mtn., Ven. E10 84
Campania, prov., Italy I9 18
Campania Island, i., B.C., Can. C3 99
Campbell, Ca., U.S. k8 112
Campbell, Fl., U.S. D5 116
Campbell, Mo., U.S. E7 132
Campbell, Ne., U.S. D7 134
Campbell, Oh., U.S. A5 142
Campbell, co., Ky., U.S. B5 124
Campbell, co., S.D., U.S. B5 148
Campbell, co., Tn., U.S. C9 149
Campbell, co., Va., U.S. C3 153
Campbell, co., Wy., U.S. B7 157
Campbell, Cape, c., N.Z. D5 72
Campbellford, Ont., Can. C7 103
Campbell Hill, Il., U.S. F4 120
Campbell Hill, hill, Oh., U.S. B2 142
Campbell Island, i., N.Z. N20 158
Campbell Lake, l., Or., U.S. E7 144
Campbellsburg, In., U.S. G5 121
Campbellsburg, Ky., U.S. B4 124
Campbells Creek, stm., W.V., U.S. m13 155
Campbellsport, Wi., U.S. E5 156
Campbell Station, Ar., U.S. B4 111
Campbellsville, Ky., U.S. C4 124
Campbellton, N.B., Can. A3 101
Campbellton, Newf., Can. D4 102
Campbellton, P.E.I., Can. C5 101
Campbelltown, Austl. J9 70
Campbell Town, Austl. M7 70
Camp Crook, S.D., U.S. B2 148
Camp Douglas, Wi., U.S. E3 156
Campeche, Mex. H14 90
Campeche, state, Mex. H14 90
Campeche, Bahía de, b., Mex. H12 90
Campechuela, Cuba D6 94
Camperdown, Austl. L5 70
Camperville, Man., Can. D1 100
Cam Pha, Viet. D9 40
Camp Hill, Al., U.S. C4 108
Camp Hill, Pa., U.S. F8 145
Camp H. M. Smith Marine Corps Base, mil., Hi., U.S. g10 118
Camp Howard Ridge, mtn., Id., U.S. D2 119
Campillos, Spain H7 16
Campina Grande, Braz. E11 74
Campina Grande, Braz. E11 76
Campinas, Braz. G5 79
Campina Verde, Braz. E4 79
Campion, Co., U.S. A5 113
Camp Lejeune Marine Corps Base, mil., N.C., U.S. C5 140
Campo, Co., U.S. D8 113
Campoalegre, Col. F5 84
Campo Alegre de Goiás, Braz. D5 79
Campobasso, Italy H9 18
Campobello, S.C., U.S. A3 147
Campobello Island, i., N.B., Can. E3 101
Campo Belo, Braz. F6 79
Campo de Criptana, Spain F8 16
Campo de la Cruz, Col. B5 84
Campo Erê, Braz. D12 80
Campo Florido, Braz. E4 79
Campo Gallo, Arg. D7 80
Campo Grande, Arg. D11 80
Campo Grande, Braz. F1 79
Campo Largo, Arg. D8 80
Campo Largo, Braz. C14 80
Campo Maior, Braz. D10 76
Campo Mourão, Braz. H2 79
Campo Nôvo, Braz. D12 80
Campo Quijano, Arg. C6 80
Camporredondo, Peru B2 82
Campos, Braz. F8 79
Campos Altos, Braz. E5 79
Campo Santo, Arg. C6 80
Campos Belos, Braz. B5 79
Campos do Jordão, Braz. G6 79
Campos Gerais, Braz. F6 79
Campos Novos, Braz. D13 80
Camp Pendleton Marine Corps Base, mil., Ca., U.S. F5 112
Camp Point, Il., U.S. C2 120
Camp Springs, Md., U.S. f9 127
Campti, La., U.S. C2 125
Campton, Ga., U.S. C3 117
Campton, Ky., U.S. C6 124
Campton, N.H., U.S. C3 136
Campuya, stm., Peru H5 84
Camp Verde, Az., U.S. C4 110
Camp Verde Indian Reservation, Az., U.S. C4 110
Camp Wood, Tx., U.S. E2 150
Cam Ranh, Viet. I10 40
Cam Ranh, Vinh, b., Viet. I10 40
Camrose, Alta., Can. C4 98
Camu, stm., Braz. G14 84
Canaan, N.B., Can. C4 101
Canaan, Ct., U.S. A2 114
Canaan, Me., U.S. D3 126
Canaan, N.H., U.S. C2 136
Canaan, Vt., U.S. A5 152
Canaan, stm., N.B., Can. C4 101
Canaan Center, N.H., U.S. C2 136
Canaan Street, N.H., U.S. C2 136
Cana Brava, stm., Braz. B4 79
Cana Brava, stm., Braz. B4 79
Canaçarí, Lago, l., Braz. I13 84
Canada, ctry., N.A. D13 96
Canada Bay, b., Newf., Can. C3 102
Cañada de Gómez, Arg. G8 80
Canada Falls Lake, res., Me., U.S. C2 126
Cañada Honda, Arg. F4 80
Canadensis, Pa., U.S. D11 145
Canadian, Ok., U.S. B6 143
Canadian, Tx., U.S. B2 150
Canadian, co., Ok., U.S. B3 143
Canadian, stm., U.S. D6 106
Canaguá, stm., Ven. C7 84
Canaima, Ven. D11 84
Canaima, Parque Nacional, Ven. E11 84
Canajoharie, N.Y., U.S. C6 139
Çanakkale, Tur. I10 20
Çanakkale Boğazı (Dardanelles), strt., Tur. I10 20
Canal Flats, B.C., Can. D10 99
Canal Fulton, Oh., U.S. B4 142
Canalou, Mo., U.S. E8 132
Canal Point, Fl., U.S. F6 116
Canals, Arg. G7 80
Canal Winchester, Oh., U.S. C3 142
Canandaigua, N.Y., U.S. C3 139
Canandaigua Lake, l., N.Y., U.S. C3 139
Cananea, Mex. B4 90
Cananéia, Braz. C15 80
Cananguchal, Col. G5 84
Canápolis, Braz. E4 79
Cañar, Ec. I3 84
Cañar, prov., Ec. I3 84
Canarias, Islas (Canary Islands), is., Spain O25 17b
Canarreos, Archipiélago de los, is., Cuba D4 94
Canary Islands see Canarias, Islas, is., Spain C3 54
Cañas, C.R. G9 92
Cañasgordas, Col. D4 84
Canastota, N.Y., U.S. B5 139
Canastra, Serra da, hills, Braz. G9 76
Canatlán, Mex. E7 90
Canaveral, Cape, c., Fl., U.S. D6 116
Canaveral National Seashore, Fl., U.S. D6 116
Canavieiras, Braz. C9 79
Cañazas, Pan. C2 84
Canberra, Austl. J8 70
Canby, Ca., U.S. B3 112
Canby, Mn., U.S. F2 130
Canby, Or., U.S. B4 144
Cancale, Fr. D5 14
Canchaque, Peru A2 82
Cancún, Mex. G16 90
Cancún, Punta, c., Mex. D1 94
Candarave, Peru G6 82
Candás, Spain B6 16
Candé, Fr. E5 14
Candeias, Braz. B9 79
Candeias, Braz. F6 79
Candeias, stm., Braz. C10 82
Candela, Mex. D9 90
Candela, stm., Mex. D9 90
Candelaria, Arg. D11 80
Candelaria, Arg. G6 80
Candelária, Braz. E12 80
Candelaria, Col. F4 84
Candelaria, Cuba C3 94
Candelaria, stm., Mex. H14 90
Candeleda, Spain E6 16
Candia, N.H., U.S. D4 136
Candiac, Que., Can. q19 104
Candia see Iráklion, Grc. N9 20
Candia Village, N.H., U.S. D4 136
Cándido Aguilar, Mex. E10 90
Cândido de Abreu, Braz. C13 80
Candle Lake, l., Sask., Can. D3 105
Candlemas Islands, is., Falk. Is. A2 73
Candlemas Islands, is., Falk. Is. J12 74
Candler, Fl., U.S. C5 116
Candler, co., Ga., U.S. D4 117
Candlewood, Lake, l., Ct., U.S. D1 114
Candlewood Isle, Ct., U.S. D2 114
Candlewood Shores, Ct., U.S. D2 114
Cando, Sask., Can. E1 105
Cando, N.D., U.S. A6 141
Candor, N.Y., U.S. C4 139
Candor, N.C., U.S. B3 140
Cane, stm., La., U.S. C2 125
Canea see Khaniá, Grc. N8 20
Canehill, Ar., U.S. B1 111
Canela, Braz. E13 80
Canelas, Mex. E6 90
Canelli, Italy E3 18
Canelones, Ur. H10 80
Canendiyu, dept., Para. C11 80
Cañete, Chile I2 80
Cañete, Spain E10 16
Cane Valley, Ky., U.S. C4 124
Caney, Ks., U.S. E8 123
Caney, Ky., U.S. C6 124
Caney, stm., Ok., U.S. A5 143
Caney Creek, stm., Tx., U.S. r14 150
Caney Fork, stm., Tn., U.S. C8 149
Caneyville, Ky., U.S. C3 124
Canfield, Oh., U.S. A5 142
Cangallo, Peru E4 82
Cangas, Braz. G13 82
Cangkuang, Tanjung, c., Indon. J12 39a
Cangombe, Ang. D3 58
Canguçu, Braz. F12 80
Cangzhou, China E4 32
Caniapiscau, stm., Que., Can. g13 104
Canicattì, Italy L8 18
Canimã, stm., Braz. D12 82
Canim Lake, l., B.C., Can. D7 99
Canistear Reservoir, res., N.J., U.S. A4 137
Canisteo, N.Y., U.S. C3 139
Canisteo, stm., N.Y., U.S. C3 139
Canistota, S.D., U.S. D8 148
Cañitas de Felipe Pescador, Mex. F8 90
Canjilon, N.M., U.S. A3 138
Cankton, La., U.S. D3 125
Canmer, Ky., U.S. C4 124
Canmore, Alta., Can. D3 98
Cannanore, India G3 46
Cannel City, Ky., U.S. C6 124
Cannelton, In., U.S. I4 121
Cannelton, W.V., U.S. m13 155
Cannes, Fr. I14 14
Cannes, Bayou des, stm., La., U.S. D3 125
Canning, N.S., Can. D5 101
Cannon, De., U.S. F3 115
Cannon, co., Tn., U.S. B5 149
Cannon, stm., Mn., U.S. F5 130
Cannon Air Force Base, mil., N.M., U.S. C6 138
Cannonball, N.D., U.S. C5 141
Cannonball, stm., N.D., U.S. C5 141
Cannon Beach, Or., U.S. B3 144
Cannondale, Ct., U.S. E2 114
Cannon Falls, Mn., U.S. F6 130
Cannonsburg, Ky., U.S. B7 124
Cannonsville Reservoir, res., N.Y., U.S. C5 139
Cann River, Austl. K8 70
Caño, Isla del, i., C.R. I11 92
Canoas, Braz. E13 80
Canoas, stm., Braz. D13 80
Canoe, Al., U.S. D2 108
Canoinhas, Braz. D13 80
Canon, Ga., U.S. B3 117
Canon City, Co., U.S. C5 113
Caño Negro, C.R. G10 92
Canonsburg, Pa., U.S. F1 145
Canoochee, stm., Ga., U.S. D5 117
Canora, Sask., Can. F4 105
Canosa [di Puglia], Italy H11 18
Canossa, hist., Italy E5 18
Canouan, i., St. Vin. H14 94
Canova, S.D., U.S. D8 148
Canowindra, Austl. I8 70
Cansado, Maur. J2 62
Canso, N.S., Can. D8 101
Canta, Peru D3 82
Cantabria, prov., Spain B7 16
Cantábrica, Cordillera, mts., Spain B6 16
Cantagalo, Braz. F7 79
Cantal, dept., Fr. G9 14
Cantanhede, Port. E3 16
Cantário, stm., Braz. D9 82
Cantaura, Ven. C10 84
Canterbury, N.B., Can. D2 101
Canterbury, Eng., U.K. J15 8
Canterbury, De., U.S. D3 115
Canterbury, N.H., U.S. D3 136
Canterbury Bight, N.Z. F4 72
Can Tho, Viet. I8 40
Canton, Ct., U.S. B4 114
Canton, Ga., U.S. B2 117
Canton, Il., U.S. C3 120
Canton, In., U.S. G5 121
Canton, Ks., U.S. D6 123
Canton, Me., U.S. D2 126
Canton, Ma., U.S. B5 128
Canton, Mn., U.S. G7 130
Canton, Ms., U.S. C3 131
Canton, Mo., U.S. A6 132
Canton, N.Y., U.S. f9 139
Canton, N.C., U.S. f10 140
Canton, Oh., U.S. B4 142
Canton, Ok., U.S. A3 143
Canton, Pa., U.S. C8 145
Canton, S.D., U.S. D9 148
Canton, Tx., U.S. C5 150
Canton Center, Ct., U.S. B4 114
Canton see Guangzhou, China L2 34
Canton Lake, res., Ok., U.S. A3 143
Cantonment, Fl., U.S. u14 116
Cantril, Ia., U.S. D5 122
Cantù, Italy D4 18
Cantu, stm., Braz. C12 80
Cantwell, Ak., U.S. C10 109
Cañuelas, Arg. H9 80
Canumã, Braz. J13 84
Canumã, stm., Braz. J13 84
Canutama, Braz. B9 82
Canute, Ok., U.S. B2 143
Canutillo, Tx., U.S. o11 150
Canwood, Sask., Can. D2 105
Čany, ozero, l., U.S.S.R. G13 22
Cany-Barville, Fr. C7 14
Canyon, Tx., U.S. B2 150
Canyon, co., Id., U.S. F2 119
Canyon City, Or., U.S. C8 144
Canyon Creek, Alta., Can. B3 98
Canyon de Chelly National Monument, Az., U.S. A6 110
Canyon Ferry Lake, res., Mt., U.S. D5 133
Canyon Lake, Tx., U.S. E3 150
Canyon Lake, res., Tx., U.S. E3 150
Canyonlands National Park, Ut., U.S. E6 151
Canyonville, Or., U.S. E3 144
Cao Bang, Viet. C9 40
Caojun, China F5 34
Caomaji, China I4 32
Caoping, China G7 34
Caoqiao, China D8 34
Caota, China F9 34
Caoxian, China I3 32
Caoyangxi, China I7 34
Cap, Pointe du, c., St. Luc. G14 94
Capac, Mi., U.S. F8 129
Čapajevsk, U.S.S.R. G7 22
Cap-à-l'Aigle, Que., Can. B7 104
Capanaparo, stm., S.A. D9 84
Capanema, Braz. C12 80
Capão Bonito, Braz. H4 79
Capão Doce, Morro do, mtn., Braz. D13 80
Caparaó, Parque Nacional do, Braz. F8 79
Caparo, stm., Ven. D7 84
Capatárida, Ven. B7 84
Cap-aux-Meules, Que., Can. B8 101
Cap aux Meules, Île du, i., Que., Can. B8 101
Cap-de-la-Madeleine, Que., Can. C5 104
Cape, stm., Austl. C7 70
Cape Arid National Park, Austl. F4 68
Cape Barren Island, i., Austl. M8 70
Cape Breton Highlands National Park, N.S., Can. C9 101
Cape Breton Island, i., N.S., Can. C9 101
Cape Broyle, Newf., Can. E5 102
Cape Canaveral, Fl., U.S. D6 116
Cape Charles, Va., U.S. C6 153
Cape Coast, Ghana I9 64
Cape Cod Bay, b., Ma., U.S. C7 128
Cape Cod Canal, Ma., U.S. C6 128
Cape Cod National Seashore, Ma., U.S. C7 128
Cape Coral, Fl., U.S. F5 116
Cape Dorset, N.W. Ter., Can. D17 96
Cape Elizabeth, Me., U.S. E2 126
Cape Fair, Mo., U.S. E4 132
Cape Fear, stm., N.C., U.S. C4 140
Cape Girardeau, Mo., U.S. D8 132
Cape Girardeau, co., Mo., U.S. D8 132
Cape Hatteras National Seashore, N.C., U.S. B7 140
Cape Horn Mountain, mtn., Id., U.S. E3 119
Cape Island, i., S.C., U.S. E9 147
Capelinha, Braz. D7 79
Capel'ka, U.S.S.R. C11 26
Capelle [aan den IJssel], Neth. E6 12
Capelongo, Ang. D3 58
Cape Lookout National Seashore, N.C., U.S. C6 140
Capels, W.V., U.S. D3 155
Cape May, N.J., U.S. F3 137
Cape May, co., N.J., U.S. E3 137
Cape May Court House, N.J., U.S. E3 137
Cape Neddick, Me., U.S. E2 126
Cape Porpoise, Me., U.S. E2 126
Cape Ray, Newf., Can. E2 102
Capernaum see Kefar Naḥum, hist., Isr. C5 50
Capers Inlet, b., S.C., U.S. k12 147
Capers Island, i., S.C., U.S. G6 147
Capers Island, i., S.C., U.S. F8 147
Cape Sable Island, i., N.S., Can. F4 101
Cape Tormentine, N.B., Can. C6 101
Cape Town (Kaapstad), S. Afr. I4 66
Cape Verde (Cabo Verde), ctry., Afr. E2 54
Cape York Peninsula, pen., Austl. B8 68
Cap-Haïtien, Haiti E8 94
Capilla de Farruco, Ur. G11 80
Capilla del Monte, Arg. F6 80
Capim, stm., Braz. D9 76
Capinópolis, Braz. E4 79
Capinota, Bol. G8 82
Capinzal, Braz. D13 80
Capira, Pan. C3 84
Capitan, N.M., U.S. D4 138
Capitán Arturo Prat, sci., B.A.T. B1 73
Capitán Bado, Para. B11 80
Capitán Bermúdez, Arg. G8 80
Capitán Meza, Para. D11 80
Capitan Mountains, mts., N.M., U.S. D4 138
Capitan Peak, mtn., N.M., U.S. D4 138
Capitán Sarmiento, Arg. H9 80
Capitari, Braz. G12 84
Capitol Heights, Ia., U.S. e8 122
Capitol Heights, Md., U.S. C4 127
Capitol Peak, mtn., Nv., U.S. B4 135
Capitol Reef National Park, Ut., U.S. E4 151
Capivari, Braz. G5 79
Capivari, stm., Braz. B8 79
Capivari, stm., Braz. H13 82
Capleville, Tn., U.S. e9 149
Caplina, stm., Peru G6 82
Čaplygin, U.S.S.R. H22 26
Capon Springs, W.V., U.S. B6 155
Capote Knob, mtn., Tx., U.S. k8 150
Cap-Pelé, N.B., Can. C5 101
Capreol, Ont., Can. p19 103
Capri, Isola di, i., Italy I9 18
Capricorn, Cape, c., Austl. D9 70
Capricorn Channel, strt., Austl. D10 70
Capricorn Group, is., Austl. D10 70
Caprivi Zipfel (Caprivi Strip), hist. reg., Nmb. A6 66
Capron, Il., U.S. A5 120
Cap-Rouge, Que., Can. n17 104
Cap-Saint-Ignace, Que., Can. B7 104
Capshaw, Al., U.S. A3 108
Captain Cook, Hi., U.S. D6 118
Captains Flat, Austl. J8 70
Captiva, Fl., U.S. F4 116
Captiva Island, i., Fl., U.S. F4 116
Capua, Italy H9 18
Capuça I, Ang. A5 66
Capucapu, stm., Braz. H13 84
Capulin Volcano National Monument, N.M., U.S. A6 138
Caquetá, ter., Col. G5 84
Caquetá (Japurá), stm., S.A. H7 84
Caquiaviri, Bol. G7 82
Cara, Eth. O9 60
Čara, stm., U.S.S.R. E16 24
Carabaya, stm., Peru F7 82
Carabaya, Cordillera de, mts., Peru E6 82
Carabinani, stm., Braz. I11 84
Carabobo, state, Ven. J10 94
Caracal, Rom. E8 20
Caracaraí, Braz. G12 84
Caracas, Ven. B9 84
Carache, Ven. C7 84
Caracol, Braz. B10 80
Caracollo, Bol. G8 82
Caraguatatuba, Braz. G6 79
Caraguatay, Para. C10 80
Caraí, Braz. D8 79
Caraibamba, Peru F5 82
Caraigres, Cerro, mtn., C.R. H10 92
Caraíva, stm., Braz. D9 79
Carajás, Serra dos, mts., Braz. E8 76
Caraná, stm., Braz. E12 82
Caranavi, Bol. F8 82
Carandaí, Braz. F7 79
Carandaiti, Bol. I10 82
Carangola, Braz. F7 79
Caransebeș, Rom. D6 20
Carapá, stm., Para. C11 80
Cara-Paraná, stm., Col. H6 84
Carapari, Bol. I10 82
Carapeguá, Para. C10 80
Carapó, Braz. G1 79
Carapo, stm., Ven. D11 84
Caraquet, N.B., Can. B5 101
Carare, stm., Col. D5 84
Caras, Peru C3 82
Caraș-Severin, co., Rom. D5 20
Caratasca, Laguna de, b., Hond. B11 92
Caratinga, Braz. E7 79
Carauari, Braz. J9 84
Caravaca, Spain G10 16
Caravaggio, Italy D4 18
Caravelas, Braz. D9 79
Caravelí, Peru F5 82
Caraway, Ar., U.S. B5 111
Carayaó, Para. C10 80
Caràzinho, Braz. E12 80
Carazo, dept., Nic. F8 92
Carballiño, Spain C3 16
Carballo, Spain B3 16
Carberry, Man., Can. E2 100
Carbo, Mex. C4 90
Carbon, Alta., Can. D4 98
Carbon, In., U.S. E3 121
Carbon, W.V., U.S. m13 155
Carbon, co., Mt., U.S. E7 133
Carbon, co., Pa., U.S. E10 145
Carbon, co., Ut., U.S. D5 151
Carbon, co., Wy., U.S. E5 157
Carbonado, Wa., U.S. B3 154
Carbondale, Alta., Can. C4 98
Carbondale, Co., U.S. B3 113
Carbondale, Il., U.S. F4 120
Carbondale, Ks., U.S. D8 123
Carbondale, Pa., U.S. C10 145
Carbonear, Newf., Can. E5 102
Carbon Hill, Al., U.S. B2 108
Carbon Hill, Il., U.S. B5 120
Carbonia, Italy J3 18
Carbonville, Ut., U.S. D5 151
Carcaixent, Spain F11 16
Carcarañá, Arg. G8 80
Carcarañá, stm., Arg. G8 80
Carcassonne, Fr. I9 14
Carchi, prov., Ec. G3 84
Carcross, Yukon, Can. D6 96
Cardale, Man., Can. D1 100
Čardarinskoje vodochranilišče, res., U.S.S.R. I11 22
Cárdenas, Cuba C4 94
Cárdenas, Mex. F10 90
Cárdenas, Mex. I13 90
Cárdenas, Nic. F9 92
Cárdenas, Bahía de, b., Cuba C4 94
Çardi, Tur. J13 20
Cardiel, Lago, l., Arg. F2 78
Cardiff, Wales, U.K. J10 8
Cardiff, Md., U.S. A5 127
Cardigan, P.E.I., Can. C7 101
Cardigan, Mount, mtn., N.H., U.S. C3 136
Cardigan Bay, b., P.E.I., Can. C7 101
Cardigan Bay, b., Wales, U.K. I9 8
Cardinal, Ont., Can. C9 103
Cardington, Oh., U.S. B3 142
Cardón, Punta, c., Ven. B7 84
Cardona, Ur. G10 80
Cardonal, Punta, c., Mex. C4 90
Cardoso, Braz. F4 79
Cardozo, Ur. G10 80
Cardston, Alta., Can. E4 98
Cardwell, Austl. B7 70
Cardwell, Mo., U.S. E7 132
Cardwell Mountain, mtn., Tn., U.S. D8 149
Čardžou, U.S.S.R. J10 22

Name — Map Ref. — Page

Carei, Rom. B6 20
Careiro, Braz. I13 84
Careiro, Ilha do, i., Braz. I13 84
Carén, Chile F3 80
Carencro, La., U.S. D3 125
Carentan, Fr. C5 14
Cares, stm., Spain B7 16
Caretta, W.V., U.S. D3 155
Carey, Id., U.S. F5 119
Carey, Oh., U.S. B2 142
Carey, Lake, l., Austl. E4 68
Careysburg, Lib. H4 64
Carhaix-Plouguer, Fr. D3 14
Carhuamayo, Peru D3 82
Carhuanca, Peru E5 82
Carhuás, Peru C3 82
Carhué, Arg. I7 80
Cariacica, Braz. F8 79
Cariaco, Ven. B11 84
Cariaco, Golfo de, b., Ven. B10 84
Cariamanga, Ec. J3 84
Caribana, Punta, c., Col. C4 84
Caribbean Sea G8 94
Cariboo Mountains, mts., B.C., Can. C7 99
Caribou, Me., U.S. B5 126
Caribou, co., Id., U.S. G7 119
Caribou Island, i., N.S., Can. D7 101
Caribou Lake, l., Me., U.S. C3 126
Caribou Mountain, mtn., Id., U.S. F7 119
Caribou Mountain, mtn., Me., U.S. C2 126
Caribou Mountains, mts., Alta., Can. f7 98
Caribou Range, mts., Id., U.S. F7 119
Carichic, Mex. D6 90
Carievale, Sask., Can. H5 105
Carignan, Fr. C12 14
Carinhanha, Braz. C7 79
Carinhanha, stm., Braz. C6 79
Carini, Italy K8 18
Caripe, Ven. B11 84
Caripito, Ven. B11 84
Carl Blackwell, Lake, res., Ok., U.S. A4 143
Carleton, Mi., U.S. F7 129
Carleton, Ne., U.S. D8 134
Carleton, Mount, mtn., N.B., Can. B3 101
Carleton Place, Ont., Can. B8 103
Carlin, Nv., U.S. C5 135
Carlinville, Il., U.S. D4 120
Carlisle, Eng., U.K. G11 8
Carlisle, Ar., U.S. C4 111
Carlisle, In., U.S. G3 121
Carlisle, Ia., U.S. C4 122
Carlisle, Ky., U.S. B5 124
Carlisle, Oh., U.S. C1 142
Carlisle, Pa., U.S. F7 145
Carlisle, S.C., U.S. B5 147
Carlisle, co., Ky., U.S. f8 124
Carl Junction, Mo., U.S. D3 132
Carlock, Il., U.S. C4 120
Carlópolis, Braz. G4 79
Carlos, Mn., U.S. E3 130
Carlos Barbosa, Braz. E13 80
Carlos Casares, Arg. H8 80
Carlos Chagas, Braz. D8 79
Carlos Forseca Amador, Nic. F8 92
Carlos Pellegrini, Arg. G8 80
Carlos Reyles, Ur. G10 80
Carlos Tejedor, Arg. H7 80
Carlotta, Ca., U.S. B1 112
Carlow, Ire. I7 8
Carlow, co., Ire. I7 8
Carlowville, Al., U.S. C2 108
Carlsbad, Ca., U.S. F5 112
Carlsbad, N.M., U.S. E5 138
Carlsbad, Tx., U.S. D2 150
Carlsbad Caverns National Park, N.M., U.S. E5 138
Carlsbad see Karlovy Vary, Czech. E12 10
Carlsbad Springs, Ont., Can. h13 103
Carlsborg, Wa., U.S. A2 154
Carlstadt, N.J., U.S. h8 137
Carlton, Sask., Can. E2 105
Carlton, Ga., U.S. B3 117
Carlton, Mn., U.S. D6 130
Carlton, Or., U.S. B3 144
Carlton, co., Mn., U.S. D6 130
Carlyle, Sask., Can. H4 105
Carlyle, Il., U.S. E4 120
Carlyle Lake, res., Il., U.S. E4 120
Carmacks, Yukon, Can. D5 96
Carmagnola, Italy E2 18
Carman, Man., Can. E2 100
Carmangay, Alta., Can. D4 98
Carmanville, Newf., Can. D4 102
Carmaux, Fr. H9 14
Carmel, Sask., Can. E3 105
Carmel, Ca., U.S. D3 112
Carmel, In., U.S. E5 121
Carmel, Me., U.S. D3 126
Carmel, N.Y., U.S. D7 139
Carmel, Mount see Karmel, Har, mtn., Isr. C4 50
Carmelo, Ur. H9 80
Carmen, Az., U.S. F4 110
Carmen, Ok., U.S. A3 143
Carmen, Ur. G10 80
Carmen, Isla, i., Mex. E4 90
Carmen, Isla del, i., Mex. H14 90
Carmen, Río del, stm., Chile E3 80
Carmen Alto, Chile B4 80
Carmen de Apicalá, Col. E5 84
Carmen de Areco, Arg. H9 80
Carmen de Patagones, Arg. E4 78
Carmer Hill, hill, Pa., U.S. C6 145
Carmi, Il., U.S. E5 120
Carmi, Lake, l., Vt., U.S. B3 152
Carmo, Braz. F7 79
Carmo do Paranaíba, Braz. E5 79
Carmo do Rio Verde, Braz. C4 79
Carmona, Spain H6 16
Carmópolis de Minas, Braz. F6 79
Carnarvon, Austl. D2 68
Carnarvon, S. Afr. H6 66
Carnatic, hist. reg., India G10 42
Carnation, Wa., U.S. B4 154
Carnduff, Sask., Can. H5 105
Carnegie, Ga., U.S. E2 117
Carnegie, Ok., U.S. B3 143
Carnegie, Pa., U.S. F1 145
Carnegie, Lake, l., Austl. E4 68
Carnes, Ms., U.S. E4 131
Carnesville, Ga., U.S. B3 117
Carney, Md., U.S. B4 127
Carney, Ok., U.S. B4 143
Carneys Point, N.J., U.S. D2 137
Carniche, Alpi, mts., Eur. C8 18
Car Nicobar Island, i., India J2 40
Carnot, Cape, c., Austl. J1 70
Carnoustie, Scot., U.K. E11 8
Carnsore Point, c., Ire. I7 8
Carnuel, N.M., U.S. B3 138
Caro, Mi., U.S. E7 129
Carol City, Fl., U.S. s13 116
Caroleen, N.C., U.S. B1 140
Carolina, Braz. E9 76
Carolina, Col. D5 84
Carolina, El Sal. D6 92
Carolina, Al., U.S. D3 108
Carolina, R.I., U.S. F2 146
Carolina, W.V., U.S. k10 155
Carolina Beach, N.C., U.S. C5 140
Caroline, Alta., Can. C3 98
Caroline, Wi., U.S. D5 156
Caroline, co., Md., U.S. C6 127
Caroline, co., Va., U.S. C5 153
Caroline Islands, is., Oc. H18 158
Caron, Sask., Can. G3 105
Carona, Ks., U.S. E9 123
Caroní, stm., Ven. C11 84
Carora, Ven. B7 84
Carouge, Switz. F5 13
Carp, Ont., Can. B8 103
Carpathian Mountains, mts., Eur. F12 4
Carpații Meridionali, mts., Rom. D8 20
Carpentaria, Gulf of, b., Austl. B7 68
Carpenter, Wy., U.S. E8 157
Carpenter Dam, Ar., U.S. g7 111
Carpentersville, Il., U.S. A5 120
Carpentras, Fr. H12 14
Carpi, Italy E5 18
Carpinteria, Ca., U.S. E4 112
Carpio, N.D., U.S. A4 141
Carp Lake, Mi., U.S. C6 129
Carpolac, Austl. K4 70
Carrabelle, Fl., U.S. C2 116
Carragana, Sask., Can. E4 105
Carrancas, Braz. F6 79
Carranza, Cabo, c., Chile H2 80
Carrao, stm., Ven. D11 84
Carrara, Italy E5 18
Carrauntoohil, mtn., Ire. J4 8
Carrboro, N.C., U.S. B3 140
Carreria, Para. A9 80
Carreta, Punta, c., Peru F3 82
Carretas, Punta, c., Peru F7 74
Carriacou, i., Gren. H14 94
Carrick on Shannon, Ire. H5 8
Carrick on Suir, Ire. I6 8
Carrie, Mount, mtn., Wa., U.S. B2 154
Carriere, Ms., U.S. E4 131
Carrier Mills, Il., U.S. F5 120
Carrigan, Mount, mtn., N.H., U.S. B4 136
Carrillo, C.R. H9 92
Carrillo, Mex. D8 90
Carrington, N.D., U.S. B6 141
Carrington Island, i., Ut., U.S. C3 151
Carrión de los Condes, Spain C7 16
Carrizal Bajo, Chile E3 80
Carrizo Creek, stm., U.S. A1 150
Carrizo Mountain, mtn., N.M., U.S. D4 138
Carrizo Mountains, mts., U.S. A6 110
Carrizo Springs, Tx., U.S. E3 150
Carrizo Wash, val., U.S. C6 110
Carrizozo, N.M., U.S. D4 138
Carr Mountain, mtn., N.H., U.S. C3 136
Carroll, Ia., U.S. B3 122
Carroll, Ne., U.S. B8 134
Carroll, Oh., U.S. C3 142
Carroll, co., Ar., U.S. A2 111
Carroll, co., Ga., U.S. C1 117
Carroll, co., Il., U.S. A4 120
Carroll, co., In., U.S. C4 121
Carroll, co., Ia., U.S. B3 122
Carroll, co., Ky., U.S. B4 124
Carroll, co., Md., U.S. A3 127
Carroll, co., Ms., U.S. B4 131
Carroll, co., Mo., U.S. B4 132
Carroll, co., N.H., U.S. C4 136
Carroll, co., Oh., U.S. B4 142
Carroll, co., Tn., U.S. B3 149
Carroll, co., Va., U.S. D2 153
Carrolls, Wa., U.S. C3 154
Carrollton, Al., U.S. B1 108
Carrollton, Ga., U.S. C1 117
Carrollton, Il., U.S. D3 120
Carrollton, Ky., U.S. B4 124
Carrollton, Mi., U.S. E7 129
Carrollton, Ms., U.S. B4 131
Carrollton, Mo., U.S. B4 132
Carrollton, Oh., U.S. B4 142
Carrollton, Tx., U.S. n10 150
Carrolltown, Pa., U.S. E4 145
Carrot, stm., Can. D4 105
Carrot River, Sask., Can. D4 105
Carry Falls Reservoir, res., N.Y., U.S. f10 139
Carrying Place, Ont., Can. C7 103
Čaršanga, U.S.S.R. B1 44
Carseland, Alta., Can. D4 98
Čarsk, U.S.S.R. H14 22
Carson, Ia., U.S. C2 122
Carson, Ms., U.S. D4 131
Carson, N.D., U.S. C4 141
Carson, Wa., U.S. D4 154
Carson, co., Tx., U.S. B2 150
Carson, stm., Nv., U.S. D2 135
Carson City, Mi., U.S. E6 129
Carson City, Nv., U.S. D2 135
Carson Lake, l., Nv., U.S. D3 135
Carson Sink, l., Nv., U.S. D3 135
Carson Spring, Tn., U.S. D10 149
Carsonville, Mi., U.S. E8 129
Carstairs, Alta., Can. D3 98
Carswell Air Force Base, mil., Tx., U.S. n9 150
Cartagena, Chile G3 80
Cartagena, Col. B5 84
Cartagena, Spain H11 16
Cartago, Col. E5 84
Cartago, C.R. H11 92
Cartago, prov., C.R. H11 92
Cartaxo, Port. F3 16
Cartaya, Spain H4 16
Carter, Ky., U.S. B6 124
Carter, Mt., U.S. C6 133
Carter, Ok., U.S. B2 143
Carter, Tn., U.S. C11 149
Carter, co., Ky., U.S. B6 124
Carter, co., Mo., U.S. E7 132
Carter, co., Mt., U.S. E12 133
Carter, co., Ok., U.S. C4 143
Carter, co., Tn., U.S. C11 149
Carter Dome, mtn., N.H., U.S. B4 136
Carteret, N.J., U.S. B4 137
Carteret, co., N.C., U.S. C6 140
Carter Lake, Ia., U.S. C2 122
Carter Mountain, mtn., Wy., U.S. B3 157
Cartersburg, In., U.S. E5 121
Carters Lake, res., Ga., U.S. B2 117
Cartersville, Ga., U.S. B2 117
Carterville, Il., U.S. F4 120
Carterville, Mo., U.S. D3 132
Carthage, Tun. M5 18
Carthage, Ar., U.S. C3 111
Carthage, Il., U.S. C2 120
Carthage, In., U.S. E6 121
Carthage, Ms., U.S. C4 131
Carthage, Mo., U.S. D3 132
Carthage, N.Y., U.S. B5 139
Carthage, N.C., U.S. B3 140
Carthage, S.D., U.S. C8 148
Carthage, Tn., U.S. C8 149
Carthage, Tx., U.S. C5 150
Carthage, hist., Tun. M5 18
Cartier Islands, is., Austl. B4 68
Cartwright, Man., Can. E2 100
Cartwright, Newf., Can. B3 102
Cartwright, Ok., U.S. D5 143
Caruaru, Braz. E11 76
Carumas, Peru G6 82
Carúpano, Ven. B11 84
Carutapera, Braz. D9 76
Caruthersville, Mo., U.S. E8 132
Carver, Ma., U.S. C6 128
Carver, Mn., U.S. F5 130
Carver, co., Mn., U.S. F5 130
Carville, La., U.S. h9 125
Carvin, Fr. B9 14
Carvoeiro, Braz. H12 84
Cary, Ga., U.S. D3 117
Cary, Il., U.S. A5 120
Cary, Ms., U.S. C3 131
Cary, N.C., U.S. B4 140
Caryville, Fl., U.S. u16 116
Caryville, Tn., U.S. C9 149
Casa, Ar., U.S. B2 111
Casablanca (Dar-el-Beida), Mor. D7 62
Casa Blanca, N.M., U.S. B2 138
Casa Branca, Braz. F5 79
Casa Grande, Az., U.S. E4 110
Casa Grande National Monument, Az., U.S. E4 110
Casale Monferrato, Italy D3 18
Casanare, state, Col. E6 84
Casanare, stm., Col. D7 84
Casanay, Ven. B11 84
Casar, N.C., U.S. B1 140
Casas Adobes, Az., U.S. E5 110
Casas Grandes, stm., Mex. B6 90
Casas Ibáñez, Spain F10 16
Casasimarro, Spain F9 16
Casavieja, Spain E7 16
Casbas, Arg. I7 80
Casca, Braz. E13 80
Casca, Rio da, stm., Braz. F14 82
Cascadas Basaseachic, Parque Nacional, Mex. C5 90
Cascade, Co., U.S. C6 113
Cascade, Id., U.S. E2 119
Cascade, Ia., U.S. B6 122
Cascade, Mt., U.S. C5 133
Cascade, N.H., U.S. B4 136
Cascade, Wi., U.S. E5 156
Cascade, co., Mt., U.S. C5 133
Cascade Locks, Or., U.S. B5 144
Cascade Range, mts., N.A. C2 106
Cascade Reservoir, res., Id., U.S. E3 119
Cascade Tunnel, Wa., U.S. B4 154
Cascais, Port. G2 16
Cascalho Rico, Braz. E5 79
Cascavel, Braz. C12 80
Cascina, Italy F5 18
Casco, Me., U.S. D2 126
Casco, Wi., U.S. D6 156
Casco Bay, b., Me., U.S. E3 126
Caserta, Italy H9 18
Caseville, Mi., U.S. E7 129
Casey, Il., U.S. D6 120
Casey, Ia., U.S. C3 122
Casey, co., Ky., U.S. C5 124
Casey, Mount, mtn., Id., U.S. A2 119
Casey Key, i., Fl., U.S. E4 116
Caseyr, c., Som. F11 56
Cash, Ar., U.S. B5 111
Cashel, Ire. I6 8
Cashiers, N.C., U.S. f9 140
Cashion, Az., U.S. m8 110
Cashion, Ok., U.S. B4 143
Cashmere, Wa., U.S. B5 154
Cashton, Wi., U.S. E3 156
Casigua, Ven. C6 84
Casilda, Arg. G8 80
Casillas del Angel, Spain O27 17b
Casimiro de Abreu, Braz. G7 79
Casino, Austl. G10 70
Casiquiare, stm., Ven. F9 84
Čáslav, Czech. F15 10
Casma, Peru C2 82
Čašniki, U.S.S.R. G12 26
Časnočor, gora, mtn., U.S.S.R. H23 6
Caspar, Ca., U.S. C2 112
Caspe, Spain D11 16
Casper, Wy., U.S. D6 157
Casper Mountain, mtn., Wy., U.S. D6 157
Caspian, Mi., U.S. B2 129
Caspian Lake, l., Vt., U.S. B4 152
Caspian Sea I8 22
Cass, In., U.S. F3 121
Cass, co., Il., U.S. D3 120
Cass, co., In., U.S. C5 121
Cass, co., Ia., U.S. C3 122
Cass, co., Mi., U.S. G4 129
Cass, co., Mn., U.S. D4 130
Cass, co., Mo., U.S. C3 132
Cass, co., Ne., U.S. D9 134
Cass, co., N.D., U.S. C8 141
Cass, co., Tx., U.S. C5 150
Cass, stm., Mi., U.S. E7 129
Cassai (Kasai), stm., Afr. C4 58
Cassange, stm., Braz. G13 82
Cassano allo Ionio, Italy J11 18
Cass City, Mi., U.S. E7 129
Casselberry, Fl., U.S. D5 116
Casselman, Ont., Can. B9 103
Casselman, stm., U.S. k12 127
Casselton, N.D., U.S. C8 141
Cássia, Braz. F5 79
Cassia, co., Id., U.S. G5 119
Cassiar, B.C., Can. m17 99
Cassiar Mountains, mts., Can. E7 96
Cassidy, B.C., Can. f12 99
Cassilândia, Braz. E3 79
Cassinga, Ang. E3 58
Cassino, Braz. G12 80
Cassino, Italy H8 18
Cass Lake, Mn., U.S. C4 130
Cass Lake, l., Mn., U.S. C4 130
Cassopolis, Mi., U.S. G4 129
Cassununga, Braz. D2 79
Cassville, Ga., U.S. B2 117
Cassville, In., U.S. C5 121
Cassville, Mo., U.S. E4 132
Cassville, Wi., U.S. F3 156
Castalia, Oh., U.S. A3 142
Castalian Springs, Tn., U.S. A5 149
Castanea, Pa., U.S. D7 145
Castanheira de Pêra, Port. E3 16
Castañones, Punta, c., Nic. E7 92
Castelbuono, Italy L9 18
Castelfiorentino, Italy F5 18
Castelfranco Veneto, Italy D6 18
Casteljaloux, Fr. H7 14
Castella, Ca., U.S. B2 112
Castellammare del Golfo, Italy K7 18
Castellammare [di Stabia], Italy I9 18
Castellaneta, Italy I11 18
Castelli, Arg. I10 80
Castelló, prov., Spain E11 16
Castelló de la Plana, Spain F11 16
Castelmassa, Italy D6 18
Castelnaudary, Fr. I8 14
Castelo, Braz. F8 79
Castelo Branco, Port. F4 16
Castelsarrasin, Fr. H8 14
Castelvetrano, Italy L7 18
Castets, Fr. I5 14
Castile, N.Y., U.S. C2 139
Castilho, Braz. F3 79
Castilla, Peru A1 82
Castilla-La Mancha, prov., Spain F8 16
Castilla la Nueva, hist. reg., Spain F9 16
Castilla la Vieja, hist. reg., Spain D7 16
Castilla-León, prov., Spain D6 16
Castillo del Romeral, Spain P25 17b
Castillo de San Marcos National Monument, Fl., U.S. n9 116
Castillo Incaico de Ingapirca, hist., Ec. I3 84
Castillos, Ur. H12 80
Castillos, Laguna de, l., Ur. H12 80
Castine, Me., U.S. D4 126
Castle Air Force Base, mil., Ca., U.S. D3 112
Castlebar, Ire. H4 8
Castleberry, Al., U.S. D2 108
Castle Dale, Ut., U.S. D4 151
Castle Dome Mountains, mts., Az., U.S. D1 110
Castle Dome Peak, mtn., Az., U.S. D1 110
Castle Douglas, Scot., U.K. G10 8
Castleford, Id., U.S. G4 119
Castlegar, B.C., Can. E9 99
Castle Hayne, N.C., U.S. C5 140
Castle Hills, De., U.S. i7 115
Castlemaine, Austl. K6 70
Castle Mountains, mts., Mt., U.S. D6 133
Castle Peak, mtn., Co., U.S. B4 113
Castle Peak, mtn., Id., U.S. E4 119
Castle Point, Mo., U.S. f13 132
Castlerea, Ire. H5 8
Castlereagh, stm., Austl. H8 70
Castle Rock, Co., U.S. B6 113
Castle Rock, Wa., U.S. C3 154
Castle Rock, mtn., Or., U.S. C8 144
Castle Rock, mtn., Va., U.S. C4 153
Castle Rock Butte, mtn., S.D., U.S. B2 148
Castle Rock Lake, res., Wi., U.S. E4 156
Castleton, Ont., Can. C7 103
Castleton, Vt., U.S. D2 152
Castleton on Hudson, N.Y., U.S. C7 139
Castletown, Scot., U.K. C10 8
Castlewood, S.D., U.S. C8 148
Castlewood, Va., U.S. f9 153
Castor, Alta., Can. C5 98
Castor, stm., Mo., U.S. D7 132
Castor Creek, stm., La., U.S. B3 125
Castres, Fr. I9 14
Castricum, Neth. C6 12
Castries, St. Luc. G14 94
Castro, Braz. C13 80
Castro, Chile E2 78
Castro, co., Tx., U.S. B1 150
Castro Barros, Arg. F6 80
Castro del Río, Spain H7 16
Castro-Urdiales, Spain B8 16
Castro Valley, Ca., U.S. h8 112
Castro Verde, Port. H3 16
Castroville, Tx., U.S. E3 150
Castrovirreyna, Peru E4 82
Castuera, Spain G6 16
Casupá, Ur. H11 80
Caswell, co., N.C., U.S. A3 140
Catacamas, Hond. C9 92
Catacaos, Peru A1 82
Catacocha, Ec. J3 84
Cataguases, Braz. F7 79
Catahoula, La., U.S. D4 125
Catahoula, co., La., U.S. C4 125
Catahoula Lake, l., La., U.S. C3 125
Catalão, Braz. E5 79
Çatalca, Tur. H12 20
Catalina, Newf., Can. D5 102
Catalina, Chile C4 80
Catalonia see Catalunya, prov., Spain D13 16
Catalunya, prov., Spain D13 16
Catamarca, prov., Arg. D5 80
Catamayo, Ec. I3 84
Catamayo, stm., Ec. J3 84
Catanduva, Braz. F4 79
Catania, Italy L10 18
Catania, Golfo di, b., Italy L10 18
Catanzaro, Italy K11 18
Cataouatche, Lake, l., La., U.S. k11 125
Cataract Canyon, val., Ut., U.S. F5 151
Catarama, Ec. H3 84
Cataricahua, Bol. H8 82
Catarman, Phil. C7 38
Catarroja, Spain F11 16
Catasauqua, Pa., U.S. E11 145
Catatumbo, stm., Ven. C7 84
Cataula, Ga., U.S. D2 117
Cataumet, Ma., U.S. C6 128
Catawba, N.C., U.S. B1 140
Catawba, S.C., U.S. B6 147
Catawba, W.V., U.S. h10 155
Catawba, co., N.C., U.S. B1 140
Catawba, stm., S.C., U.S. B6 147
Catawba, South Fork, stm., N.C., U.S. B1 140
Catawissa, Pa., U.S. E9 145
Cat Ba, Dao, i., Viet. D9 40
Catbalogan, Phil. C7 38
Catchabutan, Punta, c., Hond. B8 92
Cateechee, S.C., U.S. B2 147
Caterino Rodriguez, Mex. E9 90
Cates, In., U.S. E3 121
Catete, Ang. C2 58
Cathance, Lake, l., Me., U.S. D5 126
Catharine, Ks., U.S. D4 123
Cathcart, S. Afr. I8 66
Cathedral Bluffs, clf, Co., U.S. B2 113
Cathedral Caverns, Al., U.S. A3 108
Cathedral City, Ca., U.S. F5 112
Cathedral Mountain, mtn., Tx., U.S. o13 150
Cathedral of the Pines, N.H., U.S. E3 136
Catherine, Al., U.S. C2 108
Catherine, Lake, res., Ar., U.S. C3 111
Cathlamet, Wa., U.S. C2 154
Ca' Tiepolo, Italy E7 18
Cat Island, i., Bah. B7 94
Cat Island, i., Ma., U.S. f12 128
Cat Island, i., Ms., U.S. E4 131
Cat Island, i., S.C., U.S. E9 147
Catlettsburg, Ky., U.S. B7 124
Catlin, Il., U.S. C6 120
Catnip Mountain, mtn., Nv., U.S. B2 135
Catoche, Cabo, c., Mex. G16 90
Catoctin Mountain, mtn., U.S. B2 127
Cato Island, i., Austl. D11 70
Catonsville, Md., U.S. B4 127
Catoosa, Ok., U.S. A6 143
Catoosa, co., Ga., U.S. B1 117
Catorce, Mex. F9 90
Catriló, Arg. I7 80
Catrimani, Braz. G12 84
Catrimani, stm., Braz. G11 84
Catron, co., N.M., U.S. D1 138
Catskill, N.Y., U.S. C7 139
Catskill Mountains, mts., N.Y., U.S. C6 139
Catt, Mount, mtn., B.C., Can. B3 99
Cattaraugus, N.Y., U.S. C2 139
Cattaraugus, co., N.Y., U.S. C2 139
Cattaraugus Creek, stm., N.Y., U.S. C2 139
Cattaraugus Indian Reservation, N.Y., U.S. C2 139
Cattolica, Italy F7 18
Catu, Braz. B9 79
Catwick, Îles, is., Viet. I10 40
Cauaburi, stm., Braz. G9 84
Caubvick, Mount (Mont d'Iberville), mtn., Can. f9 102
Cauca, dept., Col. F4 84
Cauca, stm., Col. D5 84
Caucasia, Col. C5 84
Caucasus see Bol'šoj Kavkaz, mts., U.S.S.R. I6 22
Caucete, Arg. F4 80
Cauchari, Salar de, pl., Arg. B5 80
Cauchon Lake, l., Man., Can. B3 100
Caucomgomoc Lake, l., Me., U.S. B3 126
Caudry, Fr. B10 14
Caulonia, Italy K11 18
Caúngula, Ang. C3 58
Čaunskaja guba, b., U.S.S.R. D25 24
Cauquenes, Chile H2 80
Caura, stm., Ven. D10 84
Caurés, stm., Braz. H11 84
Caussade, Fr. H8 14
Čausy, U.S.S.R. H13 26
Cauto, stm., Cuba D6 94
Caux, Pays de, reg., Fr. C7 14
Cavaillon, Fr. I12 14
Cavalaire-sur-Mer, Fr. I13 14
Cavalcante, Braz. B5 79
Cavalheiro, Braz. D4 79
Cavalier, N.D., U.S. A8 141
Cavalier, co., N.D., U.S. A7 141
Cavalla (Cavally), stm., Afr. G5 54
Cavan, Ire. G6 8
Cavan, co., Ire. H6 8
Cavarzere, Italy D7 18
Cave City, Ar., U.S. B4 111
Cave City, Ky., U.S. C4 124
Cave Creek, Az., U.S. D4 110
Cave In Rock, Il., U.S. F5 120
Caveiras, stm., Braz. D13 80
Cave Junction, Or., U.S. E3 144
Cavelo, Ang. A4 66
Cavendish, Austl. K5 70
Cavendish, Alta., Can. D5 98
Cavendish, Vt., U.S. E3 152
Cave Point, c., Wi., U.S. D6 156
Cave Run Lake, res., Ky., U.S. B6 124
Cave Spring, Ga., U.S. B1 117
Cave Spring, Va., U.S. C2 153
Cave Springs, Ar., U.S. A1 111
Cavetown, Md., U.S. A2 127
Caviana, Ilha, i., Braz. D9 74
Caviana, Ilha, i., Braz. C8 76
Cavite, Phil. N19 39b
Cavour, S.D., U.S. C7 148
Cawker City, Ks., U.S. C5 123
Cawood, Ky., U.S. D6 124
Cawston, B.C., Can. E8 99
Caxambu, Braz. F6 79
Caxias, Braz. D10 76
Caxias do Sul, Braz. E13 80
Caxinas, Punta, c., Hond. A8 92
Caxito, Ang. C2 58
Cayambe, Ec. G3 84
Cayambe, vol., Ec. G4 84
Cayce, Ky., U.S. f8 124
Cayce, S.C., U.S. D5 147
Cayenne, Fr. Gu. C8 76
Cayey, P.R. E11 94
Cayley, Alta., Can. D4 98
Cayman Brac, i., Cay. Is. E5 94
Cayman Islands, dep., N.A. E4 94
Cayman Trench H11 86
Cayna, Peru D3 82
Cayo Agua, Isla, i., Pan. H12 92
Cayuga, In., U.S. E3 121
Cayuga, co., N.Y., U.S. C4 139
Cayuga Heights, N.Y., U.S. C4 139
Cayuga Lake, l., N.Y., U.S. C4 139
Cazenovia, N.Y., U.S. C5 139
Cazères, Fr. I8 14
Cazin, Yugo. E10 18
Cazombo, Ang. D4 58
Cazorla, Spain H8 16
Cazorla, Ven. C9 84
Ccapi, Peru E5 82
Cchinvali, U.S.S.R. I6 22
Ceanannus Mór, Ire. H7 8
Ceará-Mirim, Braz. E11 76
Cébaco, Isla, i., Pan. D2 84
Ceballos, Mex. D7 90
Čeboksary, U.S.S.R. F7 22
Cebolla, N.M., U.S. A3 138
Cebolla Creek, stm., Co., U.S. C3 113
Cebollar, Arg. E5 80
Cebollas, Mex. F7 90
Cebollatí, Ur. G12 80
Cebollatí, stm., Ur. G11 80
Céboruco, Volcán, vol., Mex. G7 90
Čebrikovo, U.S.S.R. B14 20
Čebsara, U.S.S.R. B21 26
Cebu, Phil. C7 38
Cebu, i., Phil. C7 38
Ceccano, Italy H8 18
Čecerleg, Mong. B7 30
Čečersk, U.S.S.R. I13 26
Čečevići, U.S.S.R. H12 26
Čechov, U.S.S.R. F20 26
Čechtice, Czech. F15 10
Čechy, hist. reg., Czech. F14 10
Cecil, Al., U.S. C3 108
Cecil, Ga., U.S. E3 117
Cecil, Pa., U.S. F1 145
Cecil, Wi., U.S. D5 156
Cecil, co., Md., U.S. A6 127
Cecil Field Naval Air Station, mil., Fl., U.S. B5 116
Cecilia, Ky., U.S. C4 124
Cecilton, Md., U.S. B6 127
Cecina, Italy F5 18
Cedar, co., Ia., U.S. C6 122
Cedar, co., Mo., U.S. D4 132
Cedar, co., Ne., U.S. B8 134
Cedar, stm., U.S. C6 122
Cedar, stm., Ne., U.S. B7 134
Cedar, stm., Wa., U.S. B4 154
Cedar Bluff, Al., U.S. A4 108
Cedarbluff, Ms., U.S. B5 131
Cedar Bluff Reservoir, res., Ks., U.S. D4 123
Cedar Bluffs, Ne., U.S. C9 134
Cedar Bluff Two, Tn., U.S. D9 149
Cedar Breaks National Monument, Ut., U.S. F3 151
Cedarburg, Wi., U.S. E6 156
Cedar City, Mo., U.S. C5 132
Cedar City, Ut., U.S. F2 151
Cedar Creek, Az., U.S. D5 110
Cedar Creek, Ne., U.S. C9 134
Cedarcreek, Tn., U.S. C11 149
Cedar Creek, stm., Co., U.S. A7 113
Cedar Creek, stm., In., U.S. B7 121
Cedar Creek, stm., Ia., U.S. D6 122
Cedar Creek, stm., Mo., U.S. C5 132
Cedar Creek, stm., N.J., U.S. D4 137
Cedar Creek, stm., N.D., U.S. C3 141
Cedar Creek, stm., Oh., U.S. e7 142
Cedar Creek Lake, res., Tx., U.S. C4 150
Cedar Crest, N.M., U.S. k8 138
Cedaredge, Co., U.S. C3 113
Cedar Falls, Ia., U.S. B5 122
Cedar Grove, In., U.S. F8 121
Cedar Grove, N.J., U.S. B4 137
Cedar Grove, W.V., U.S. C3 155
Cedar Grove, Wi., U.S. E6 156
Cedar Hill, Mo., U.S. g12 132
Cedar Hill, Tn., U.S. A5 149
Cedar Hill, Tx., U.S. n10 150

Name	Map Ref.	Page
Cedarhurst, N.Y., U.S.	k13	139
Cedar Island, N.C., U.S.	C6	140
Cedar Island, i., N.C., U.S.	C6	140
Cedar Island, i., S.C., U.S.	E9	147
Cedar Island, i., Va., U.S.	C7	153
Cedar Key, Fl., U.S.	C3	116
Cedar Keys, is., Fl., U.S.	C3	116
Cedar Lake, In., U.S.	B3	121
Cedar Lake, res., Man., Can.	C1	100
Cedar Lake, res., Il., U.S.	F4	120
Cedar Mountain, mtn., Ca., U.S.	B3	112
Cedar Mountains, mts., Ut., U.S.	C2	151
Cedar Park, Tx., U.S.	D4	150
Cedar Point, Il., U.S.	B4	120
Cedar Point, c., Md., U.S.	D5	127
Cedar Point, c., Oh., U.S.	A3	142
Cedar Point, c., Oh., U.S.	e7	142
Cedar Rapids, Ia., U.S.	C6	122
Cedar Rapids, Ne., U.S.	C7	134
Cedar Springs, Ont., Can.	E2	103
Cedar Springs, Ga., U.S.	E1	117
Cedar Springs, Mi., U.S.	E5	129
Cedar Swamp, sw., Ma., U.S.	f11	128
Cedartown, Ga., U.S.	B1	117
Cedarvale, B.C., Can.	B3	99
Cedar Vale, Ks., U.S.	E7	123
Cedar Valley, Ut., U.S.	C3	151
Cedarville, Ar., U.S.	B1	111
Cedarville, Ca., U.S.	B3	112
Cedarville, Il., U.S.	A4	120
Cedarville, In., U.S.	B7	121
Cedarville, N.J., U.S.	E2	137
Cedarville, Oh., U.S.	C2	142
Cedillo, Embalse de, res., Eur.	F4	16
Cedros, Hond.	C7	92
Cedros, Mex.	E9	90
Cedros, Isla, i., Mex.	C2	90
Ceduna, Austl.	F6	68
Ceerigaabo, Som.	F10	56
Cefalù, Italy	K9	18
Čegdomyn, U.S.S.R.	G18	24
Cegléd, Hung.	H19	10
Cehegín, Spain	G10	16
Cehu-Silvaniei, Rom.	B7	20
Čekalin, U.S.S.R.	G19	26
Čekujevo, U.S.S.R.	J26	6
Čel'abinsk, U.S.S.R.	F10	22
Celano, Italy	G8	18
Celaya, Mex.	G9	90
Celebes Sea, Asia	E7	38
Celebes see Sulawesi, i., Indon.	F7	38
Čeleken, U.S.S.R.	J8	22
Celendín, Peru	B2	82
Celestine, In., U.S.	H4	121
Celestún, Mex.	G14	90
Celica, Ec.	J3	84
Celina, Oh., U.S.	B1	142
Celina, Tn., U.S.	C8	149
Celina, Tx., U.S.	C4	150
Celinograd, U.S.S.R.	G12	22
Celje, Yugo.	C10	18
Čelkar, U.S.S.R.	H9	22
Celle, Ger.	C10	10
Celorico da Beira, Port.	E4	16
Celoron, N.Y., U.S.	C1	139
Celriver, S.C., U.S.	B6	147
Celtic Sea, Eur.	J7	8
Čel'uskin, mys, c., U.S.S.R.	B18	22
Cement, Ok., U.S.	C3	143
Cement City, Mi., U.S.	F6	129
Čementon, Pa., U.S.	E10	145
Čemerno, Yugo.	F13	18
Cenderawasih, Teluk, b., Indon.	F10	38
Cenepa, stm., Peru	J3	84
Centenario, Arg.	J4	80
Centenário do Sul, Braz.	G3	79
Centenary, S.C., U.S.	C9	147
Centennial, Wy., U.S.	E6	157
Centennial Mountains, mts., Id., U.S.	E7	119
Center, Co., U.S.	D4	113
Center, Ga., U.S.	B3	117
Center, In., U.S.	D5	121
Center, Mo., U.S.	B6	132
Center, Ne., U.S.	B8	134
Center, N.D., U.S.	B4	141
Center, Tx., U.S.	D5	150
Center Barnstead, N.H., U.S.	D4	136
Centerbrook, Ct., U.S.	D6	114
Centerburg, Oh., U.S.	B3	142
Center City, Mn., U.S.	E6	130
Center Conway, N.H., U.S.	C4	136
Center Creek, Ut., U.S.	C4	151
Centereach, N.Y., U.S.	n15	139
Center Effingham, N.H., U.S.	C4	136
Centerfield, Ut., U.S.	D4	151
Center Harbor, N.H., U.S.	C4	136
Center Hill, Fl., U.S.	D5	116
Center Hill Lake, res., Tn., U.S.	C8	149
Center Moriches, N.Y., U.S.	n16	139
Center Mountain, mtn., Id., U.S.	D3	119
Center Ossipee, N.H., U.S.	C4	136
Center Point, Al., U.S.	f7	108
Center Point, Ar., U.S.	C2	111
Centerpoint, In., U.S.	F3	121
Center Point, Ia., U.S.	B6	122
Center Point, Tx., U.S.	E3	150
Center Ridge, Ar., U.S.	B3	111
Center Rutland, Vt., U.S.	D2	152
Center Sandwich, N.H., U.S.	C4	136
Center Star, Al., U.S.	A2	108
Center Strafford, N.H., U.S.	D4	136
Centerton, Ar., U.S.	A1	111
Centerton, In., U.S.	E5	121
Centertown, Ky., U.S.	C3	124
Centertown, Mo., U.S.	C5	132
Centertown, Tn., U.S.	D8	149
Center Tuftonboro, N.H., U.S.	C4	136
Centerview, Mo., U.S.	C4	132
Centerville, Ar., U.S.	B2	111
Centerville, De., U.S.	A3	115
Centerville, In., U.S.	E8	121
Centerville, Ia., U.S.	D5	122
Centerville, Ks., U.S.	D8	123
Centerville, La., U.S.	E4	125
Centerville, Ma., U.S.	C7	128
Centerville, Oh., U.S.	C1	142
Centerville, Pa., U.S.	F2	145
Centerville, S.D., U.S.	D9	148
Centerville, Tn., U.S.	B4	149
Centerville, Tx., U.S.	D5	150
Centerville, Ut., U.S.	C4	151
Cento, Italy	E6	18
Central, Az., U.S.	E6	110
Central, N.M., U.S.	E1	138
Central, S.C., U.S.	B2	147
Central, prov., Scot., U.K.	E9	8
Central, dept., Bots.	C8	66
Central, dept., Para.	C10	80
Central, Cordillera, mts., Col.	E5	84
Central, Cordillera, mts., C.R.	G10	92
Central, Cordillera, mts., Pan.	I13	92
Central, Cordillera, mts., Peru	B3	82
Central, Cordillera, mts., P.R.	E11	94
Central, Massif, mts., Fr.	G10	14
Central, Planalto, plat., Braz.	G9	76
Central, Sistema, mts., Spain	E6	16
Central African Republic, ctry., Afr.	G5	56
Central Barren, In., U.S.	H5	121
Central Brāhui Range, mts., Pak.	F2	44
Central Bridge, N.Y., U.S.	C6	139
Central Butte, Sask., Can.	G2	105
Central City, Co., U.S.	B5	113
Central City, Il., U.S.	E4	120
Central City, Ia., U.S.	B6	122
Central City, Ky., U.S.	C2	124
Central City, Ne., U.S.	C7	134
Central City, Pa., U.S.	F4	145
Central City, S.D., U.S.	C2	148
Central Falls, R.I., U.S.	B4	146
Centralhatchee, Ga., U.S.	C1	117
Central Heights, Az., U.S.	D5	110
Centralia, Ont., Can.	D3	103
Centralia, Il., U.S.	E4	120
Centralia, Ks., U.S.	C7	123
Centralia, Mo., U.S.	B5	132
Centralia, Wa., U.S.	C3	154
Centralina, Braz.	E4	79
Central Islip, N.Y., U.S.	n15	139
Central Kalahari Game Reserve, Bots.	D6	66
Central Lake, Mi., U.S.	C5	129
Central Makrān Range, mts., Pak.	G1	44
Central'nyj, U.S.S.R.	H22	26
Central Park, Wa., U.S.	C2	154
Central Point, Or., U.S.	E4	144
Central Range, mts., Leso.	G9	66
Central Square, N.Y., U.S.	B4	139
Central Valley, Ca., U.S.	B2	112
Central Valley, N.Y., U.S.	D6	139
Central Village, Ct., U.S.	C8	114
Centre, Al., U.S.	A4	108
Centre, co., Pa., U.S.	E6	145
Centre, Canal du, Fr.	F11	14
Centre City, N.J., U.S.	D2	137
Centre Hall, Pa., U.S.	E6	145
Centreville, N.B., Can.	C2	101
Centreville, N.S., Can.	E3	101
Centreville, Al., U.S.	C2	108
Centreville, Il., U.S.	E3	120
Centreville, Md., U.S.	B5	127
Centreville, Mi., U.S.	G5	129
Centreville, Ms., U.S.	D2	131
Centropolis, Ks., U.S.	D8	123
Centuria, Wi., U.S.	C1	156
Century, Fl., U.S.	u14	116
Century, W.V., U.S.	B4	155
Cenxi, China	C11	40
Cepu, Indon.	J15	39a
Ceram Sea see Seram, Laut, Indon.	F8	38
Ceram see Seram, i., Indon.	F8	38
Cerbat Mountains, mts., Az., U.S.	B1	110
Čerčany, Czech.	F14	10
Cerdas, Bol.	I8	82
Cère, stm., Fr.	H9	14
Cereal, Alta., Can.	D5	98
Cereales, Arg.	I7	80
Ceredo, W.V., U.S.	C2	155
Čeremchovo, U.S.S.R.	G18	22
Čerepanovo, U.S.S.R.	G14	22
Čerepet', U.S.S.R.	G19	26
Čerepovec, U.S.S.R.	B20	26
Ceres, Arg.	E8	80
Ceres, Braz.	C4	79
Ceres, S. Afr.	I4	66
Ceres, Ca., U.S.	D3	112
Ceresco, Ne., U.S.	C9	134
Ceresole Reale, Italy	D2	18
Céret, Fr.	J9	14
Cereté, Col.	C5	84
Cerf Island, i., Sey.	C10	58
Cerignola, Italy	H10	18
Čerikov, U.S.S.R.	H14	26
Čerkassy, U.S.S.R.	H4	22
Čerkessk, U.S.S.R.	I6	22
Cerknica, Yugo.	D9	18
Čerlak, U.S.S.R.	G12	22
Cermei, Rom.	C5	20
Čern', U.S.S.R.	H19	26
Čern'achovsk (Insterburg), U.S.S.R.	G4	26
Černaja, U.S.S.R.	B13	20
Černavčicy, U.S.S.R.	I6	26
Cernavodă, Rom.	E12	20
Cernay, Fr.	E14	14
Černigov, U.S.S.R.	G4	22
Černobyl' (Chernobyl), U.S.S.R.	G4	22
Černogorsk, U.S.S.R.	G10	24
Černovcy, U.S.S.R.	A9	20
Čern'ovo, U.S.S.R.	C11	26
Černyševskij, U.S.S.R.	E14	24
Cerralvo, Mex.	D10	90
Cerralvo, Isla, i., Mex.	E5	90
Cerrillos, Arg.	C6	80
Cerrillos, N.M., U.S.	B3	138
Cerritos, Mex.	F9	90
Cerro, N.M., U.S.	A4	138
Cerro Alto Mountain, mtn., Tx., U.S.	o12	150
Cerro Azul, Arg.	D11	80
Cêrro Azul, Braz.	C14	80
Cerro Azul, Mex.	G11	90
Cerro Azul, Peru	E3	82
Cerro Chato, Ur.	G11	80
Cerro Colorado, Ur.	G11	80
Cerro de las Mesas, hist., Mex.	H11	90
Cerro de Pasco, Peru	D3	82
Cerro Gordo, Il., U.S.	D5	120
Cerro Gordo, co., Ia., U.S.	A4	122
Cêrro Largo, Braz.	E11	80
Cerro Moreno, Chile	B3	80
Cerrón, Cerro, mtn., Ven.	B7	84
Cerrón Grande, Embalse, res., Hond.	C5	92
Cerros Colorados, Embalse, res., Arg.	J4	80
Cerro Vera, Ur.	G10	80
Čerskogo, chrebet, mts., U.S.S.R.	E21	24
Cerulean, Ky., U.S.	D2	124
Čerusti, U.S.S.R.	F23	26
Červen', U.S.S.R.	H11	26
Červen Brjag, Bul.	F8	20
Cervera, Spain	D13	16
Cerveteri, Italy	G7	18
Cervia, Italy	E7	18
Cervione, Fr.	L24	15a
Červonoarmejskoje, U.S.S.R.	D12	20
Červonograd, U.S.S.R.	G2	22
Cesar, dept., Col.	C6	84
César, stm., Col.	B6	84
Cesena, Italy	E7	18
Cesenatico, Italy	E7	18
Cēsis, U.S.S.R.	D8	26
Česká Lípa, Czech.	E14	10
Česká Socialistická Republika, state, Czech.	F15	10
České Budějovice, Czech.	G14	10
Českomoravská vrchovina, plat., Czech.	F15	10
Český Brod, Czech.	E14	10
Český Krumlov, Czech.	G14	10
Cessford, Alta., Can.	D5	98
Češskaja guba, b., U.S.S.R.	D7	22
Cessnock, Austl.	I9	70
Cestos, stm., Lib.	I5	64
Cesvaine, U.S.S.R.	E9	26
Cetinje, Yugo.	G2	20
Ceuta, Sp. N. Afr.	C8	62
Ceva, Italy	E3	18
Cévennes, reg., Fr.	H10	14
Ceyhan, Tur.	C3	48
Ceylon, Ont., Can.	C4	103
Ceylon, Sask., Can.	H3	105
Ceylon, Mn., U.S.	G4	130
Chaanling, China	F2	34
Chabanais, Fr.	G7	14
Chabarovsk, U.S.S.R.	H19	24
Chabás, Arg.	G8	80
Chablais, reg., Fr.	F13	14
Chablis, Fr.	E10	14
Chacabuco, Arg.	H8	80
Chacanilla, Peru	B3	82
Chacayán, Peru	D3	82
Chachani, Nevado, mtn., Peru	G6	82
Chachas, Peru	F5	82
Chachoengsao, Thai.	H6	40
Chachu, China	D9	44
Chaco, prov., Arg.	D8	80
Chaco, dept., Para.	H11	82
Chaco, stm., N.M., U.S.	A1	138
Chaco Austral, reg., Arg.	D7	80
Chaco Boreal, reg., Para.	B8	80
Chaco Central, reg., Arg.	C8	80
Chaco Culture National Historic Park, N.M., U.S.	A2	138
Chacon, N.M., U.S.	A4	138
Chacon, Cape, c., Ak., U.S.	n24	109
Chacuaco Creek, stm., Co., U.S.	D7	113
Chad (Tchad), ctry., Afr.	E4	56
Chad, Lake (Lac Tchad), l., Afr.	F3	56
Chadbourn, N.C., U.S.	C4	140
Chadds Ford, Pa., U.S.	G10	145
Chadron, Ne., U.S.	B3	134
Chadwick, Il., U.S.	A4	120
Chadwicks, N.Y., U.S.	B5	139
Chaeryŏng, N. Kor.	E13	32
Chafe, Nig.	F13	64
Chaffee, Mo., U.S.	D8	132
Chaffee, N.D., U.S.	C8	141
Chaffee, co., Co., U.S.	C4	113
Chaffin, Ma., U.S.	B4	128
Chafurray, Col.	F6	84
Chāgai Hills, hills, Asia	G18	48
'Chaghcharān, Afg.	C1	44
Chagny, Fr.	F11	14
Chagos Archipelago, is., B.I.O.T.	J8	28
Chagrin Falls, Oh., U.S.	A4	142
Chaguaramas, Ven.	C9	84
Chaguaya, Bol.	I9	82
Chahal, Guat.	B5	92
Chahār Borjak, Afg.	F17	48
Chahe, China	B8	34
Chāībāsa, India	I11	44
Chaigou, China	G7	32
Chai Nat, Thai.	G6	40
Chaiqiao, China	F10	34
Chaiyaphum, Thai.	G7	40
Chajarí, Arg.	F10	80
Chajian, China	C7	34
Chajiaqiao, China	A9	34
Chajul, Guat.	B3	92
Chakachamna Lake, l., Ak., U.S.	g15	109
Chākdaha, India	I13	44
Chakradharpur, India	I11	44
Chakwāl, Pak.	D5	44
Chala, Peru	F4	82
Chalatenango, El Sal.	C6	92
Chalchuapa, El Sal.	D5	92
Chalcis see Khalkís, Grc.	K7	20
Chalengkou, China	B15	44
Chaleur Bay, b., Can.	B4	101
Chalfonte, De., U.S.	h7	115
Chalhuanca, Peru	F5	82
Chaling, China	I2	34
Chālisgaon, India	B3	46
Chalk River, Ont., Can.	A7	103
Challapata, Bol.	H8	82
Challenger Deep	G18	158
Challis, Id., U.S.	E4	119
Challviri, Salar de, pl., Bol.	J8	82
Chalmers, In., U.S.	C4	121
Chalmette, La., U.S.	E6	125
Châlons-sur-Marne, Fr.	D11	14
Chalon-sur-Saône, Fr.	F11	14
Chalosse, reg., Fr.	I6	14
Chaltel, Cerro (Monte Fitzroy), mtn., S.A.	F2	78
Chālūs, Iran	C11	48
Chalybeate, Ms., U.S.	A5	131
Cham, Ger.	F12	10
Chama, Co., U.S.	D5	113
Chama, N.M., U.S.	A3	138
Chama, stm., Ven.	C7	84
Chama, Rio, stm., N.M., U.S.	A3	138
Chamaicó, Arg.	H6	80
Chaman, Pak.	E2	44
Chamaya, stm., Peru	A2	82
Chambal, stm., India	G7	44
Chamberino, N.M., U.S.	E3	138
Chamberlain, Sask., Can.	G3	105
Chamberlain, S.D., U.S.	D6	148
Chamberlain Lake, l., Me., U.S.	B3	126
Chamberlin, Mount, mtn., Ak., U.S.	B10	109
Chambers, Az., U.S.	B6	110
Chambers, La., U.S.	C3	125
Chambers, Ne., U.S.	B7	134
Chambers, co., Al., U.S.	C4	108
Chambers, co., Tx., U.S.	E5	150
Chambersburg, Pa., U.S.	G6	145
Chambers Island, i., Wi., U.S.	C6	156
Chambéry, Fr.	G12	14
Chambi, Jebel, mtn., Tun.	C15	62
Chambira, stm., Peru	I5	84
Chambira, stm., Peru	I5	84
Chamblee, Ga., U.S.	h8	117
Chambly, Que., Can.	D4	104
Chamcook, N.B., Can.	D2	101
Chame, Pan.	I15	92
Chame, Punta, c., Pan.	I15	92
Chamelecón, Hond.	B6	92
Chamelecón, stm., Hond.	B6	92
Chamical, Arg.	F5	80
Chamisal, N.M., U.S.	A4	138
Chamo, Lake, l., Eth.	O9	60
Chamois, Mo., U.S.	C6	132
Chamonix-Mont-Blanc, Fr.	G13	14
Chāmpa, India	I10	44
Champagne, hist. reg., Fr.	D11	14
Champagne Castle, mtn., Afr.	G9	66
Champagnole, Fr.	F12	14
Champaign, Il., U.S.	C5	120
Champaign, co., Il., U.S.	C5	120
Champaign, co., Oh., U.S.	B2	142
Champaquí, Cerro, mtn., Arg.	H8	74
Champaquí, Cerro, mtn., Arg.	F6	80
Champasak, Laos	G8	40
Champeix, Fr.	G10	14
Champerico, Guat.	C3	92
Champéry, Switz.	F6	13
Champion, Alta., Can.	D4	98
Champion, Mi., U.S.	B3	129
Champion, Ne., U.S.	D4	134
Champion, Oh., U.S.	A5	142
Champlain, N.Y., U.S.	f11	139
Champlin, Mn., U.S.	m12	130
Champlitte-et-le-Prélot, Fr.	E12	14
Champney's West, Newf., Can.	D5	102
Champotón, Mex.	H14	90
Chamusca, Port.	F3	16
Chana, Il., U.S.	B4	120
Chañar, Arg.	F6	80
Chañaral, Chile	D3	80
Chañaral, Isla, i., Chile	E3	80
Chancay, Peru	D3	82
Chancay, stm., Peru	D3	82
Chance, Md., U.S.	D6	127
Chancellor, Al., U.S.	D4	108
Chancellor, S.D., U.S.	D8	148
Chanch, Mong.	A7	30
Chan Chan, hist., Peru	C2	82
Chanchelulla Peak, mtn., Ca., U.S.	B2	112
Chanco, Chile	H2	80
Chandalar, stm., Ak., U.S.	B10	109
Chandausi, India	F8	44
Chandeleur Islands, is., La., U.S.	E7	125
Chandeleur Sound, strt., La., U.S.	E6	125
Chandīgarh, India	E7	44
Chandler, Que., Can.	k14	104
Chandler, Az., U.S.	D4	110
Chandler, In., U.S.	H3	121
Chandler, Mn., U.S.	G3	130
Chandler, Ok., U.S.	B5	143
Chandler, Tx., U.S.	C5	150
Chandler Heights, Az., U.S.	m9	110
Chandlerville, Il., U.S.	C3	120
Chandless, stm., S.A.	C6	82
Chāndpur, Bngl.	I14	44
Chāndpur, India	F8	44
Chandrapur, India	C5	46
Chandyga, U.S.S.R.	E19	24
Chang (Yangtze), stm., China	E10	30
Chang, Ko, i., Thai.	H7	40
Changanācheri, India	H4	46
Changane, stm., Moz.	D11	66
Changbai Shan, mts., Asia	B15	32
Chang Cheng (Great Wall), hist., China	C4	32
Chang Chenmo, stm., Asia	C8	44
Changchou see Zhangzhou, China	K6	34
Changchow see Changzhou, China	D8	34
Changchun, China	C12	30
Changdao (Sihou), China	F8	32
Changde, China	F9	30
Change Islands, Newf., Can.	D4	102
Changguandian, China	C4	34
Changhua, Tai.	K9	34
Changhŭng, S. Kor.	I14	32
Changji, China	C4	30
Changjiang, China	J2	34
Changli, China	D7	32
Changlingzi, China	D10	32
Ch'angnyŏng, S. Kor.	H16	32
Changsha, China	G2	34
Changshan, China	G7	34
Changshoujie, China	G2	34
Changshu, China	D9	34
Changsŏng, S. Kor.	H14	32
Changsu, S. Kor.	H15	32
Changting, China	J5	34
Changuinola, Pan.	H12	92
Changuinola, stm., Pan.	H12	92
Changxing, China	D8	34
Changyŏn, N. Kor.	E13	32
Changzhi, China	D9	30
Changzhou (Changchow), China	D8	34
Chanhassen, Mn., U.S.	n11	130
Chanino, U.S.S.R.	G19	26
Chanka, ozero (Xingkai Hu), l., Asia	B13	30
Channahon, Il., U.S.	B5	120
Channel Country, reg., Austl.	E4	70
Channel Islands, is., Eur.	L11	8
Channel Islands, is., Ca., U.S.	F4	112
Channel Islands National Park, Ca., U.S.	F4	112
Channel Lake, Il., U.S.	H8	120
Channel-Port-aux-Basques, Newf., Can.	E2	102
Channelview, Tx., U.S.	r14	150
Channing, Mi., U.S.	B2	129
Chantajskoje, ozero, l., U.S.S.R.	D10	24
Chantajskoje vodochranilišče, res., U.S.S.R.	D15	22
Chantang, China	B6	34
Chanthaburi, Thai.	H7	40
Chantilly, Fr.	C9	14
Chantilly, Va., U.S.	g12	153
Chantrey Inlet, b., N.W. Ter., Can.	C13	96
Chanty-Mansijsk, U.S.S.R.	E11	22
Chanute, Ks., U.S.	E8	123
Chanute Air Force Base, mil., Il., U.S.	C5	120
Chao, Isla, i., Peru	C2	82
Chao'an, China	L5	34
Ch'aochou, Tai.	M9	34
Chao Hu, l., China	E10	30
Chao Phraya, stm., Thai.	G6	40
Chaoshui, China	F8	32
Chaouen, Mor.	C8	62
Chaoyang, China	B8	32
Chaoyang, China	L5	34
Chaoyangchuan, China	A17	32
Chapada dos Guimarães, Braz.	F14	82
Chapala, Mex.	G8	90
Chapala, Laguna de, l., Mex.	G8	90
Chaparé, stm., Bol.	G9	82
Chaparral, Col.	F5	84
Chaparral, N.M., U.S.	E3	138
Chapčeranga, U.S.S.R.	H14	24
Chapecó, Braz.	D12	80
Chapel Hill, Ky., U.S.	D3	124
Chapel Hill, N.C., U.S.	B3	140
Chapel Hill, Tn., U.S.	B5	149
Chapicuy, Ur.	F10	80
Chapimarca, Peru	E5	82
Chapin, Il., U.S.	D3	120
Chaplin, Sask., Can.	G2	105
Chaplin, Ky., U.S.	C4	124
Chaplin, stm., Ky., U.S.	C4	124
Chaplin Lake, l., Sask., Can.	G2	105
Chapman, Al., U.S.	D3	108
Chapman, Ks., U.S.	D6	123
Chapman, Ne., U.S.	C7	134
Chapman, Cape, c., N.W. Ter., Can.	C15	96
Chapman Pond, l., R.I., U.S.	F1	146
Chapman's (Okwa), stm., Afr.	D4	66
Chapmanville, W.V., U.S.	D2	155
Chappaquiddick Island, i., Ma., U.S.	D7	128
Chappell, Ne., U.S.	C3	134
Chaptico Creek, stm., Md., U.S.	D4	127
Chaqui, Bol.	H9	82
Chaquiago, Arg.	E5	80
Charadai, Arg.	D9	80
Charagua, Bol.	H10	82
Charalá, Col.	D6	84
Charaña, Bol.	G7	82
Charata, Arg.	D8	80
Charcana, Peru	F5	82
Charcas, Mex.	F9	90
Charco Azul, Bahía de, b., Pan.	I12	92
Charcos de Figueroa, Mex.	D8	90
Charcos de Risa, Mex.	D8	90
Chardon, Oh., U.S.	A4	142
Charente, dept., Fr.	G7	14
Charente, stm., Fr.	G6	14
Charente-Maritime, dept., Fr.	G6	14
Charenton, La., U.S.	E4	125
Chari, stm., Afr.	F4	56
Chārīkār, Afg.	C3	44
Chariton, Ia., U.S.	C4	122
Chariton, co., Mo., U.S.	B4	132
Chariton, stm., U.S.	A5	132
Charity, Guy.	D13	84
Char'kov, U.S.S.R.	G5	22
Charleroi, Bel.	H5	12
Charleroi, Pa., U.S.	F2	145
Charles, co., Md., U.S.	C3	127
Charles, stm., Ma., U.S.	B5	128
Charles, Cape, c., Va., U.S.	C6	153
Charles A. Goodwin Dam, Ct., U.S.	B3	114
Charlesbourg, Que., Can.	n17	104
Charles City, Ia., U.S.	A5	122
Charles City, co., Va., U.S.	C5	153
Charles Island, i., N.W. Ter., Can.	D18	96
Charles Mill Lake, res., Oh., U.S.	B3	142
Charles Mix, co., S.D., U.S.	D7	148
Charles Mound, hill, Il., U.S.	A3	120
Charleston, Ar., U.S.	B1	111
Charleston, Il., U.S.	D5	120
Charleston, Me., U.S.	C3	126
Charleston, Ms., U.S.	A3	131
Charleston, Mo., U.S.	E8	132
Charleston, Or., U.S.	D2	144
Charleston, S.C., U.S.	F8	147
Charleston, Tn., U.S.	D9	149
Charleston, Ut., U.S.	C4	151
Charleston, W.V., U.S.	C3	155
Charleston, co., S.C., U.S.	F8	147
Charleston Air Force Base, mil., S.C., U.S.	k11	147
Charleston Naval Shipyard, mil., S.C., U.S.	k12	147
Charleston Peak, mtn., Nv., U.S.	G6	135
Charlestown, St. K./N.	F13	94
Charlestown, S. Afr.	F9	66
Charlestown, In., U.S.	H6	121
Charlestown, Md., U.S.	A6	127
Charlestown, N.H., U.S.	D2	136
Charlestown, R.I., U.S.	F2	146
Charles Town, W.V., U.S.	B7	155
Charleville, Austl.	F7	70
Charleville-Mézières, Fr.	C11	14
Charlevoix, Mi., U.S.	C5	129
Charlevoix, co., Mi., U.S.	C5	129
Charlevoix, Lake, l., Mi., U.S.	C5	129
Charlie Lake, B.C., Can.	A7	99
Charlieu, Fr.	F11	14
Charlo, N.B., Can.	B3	101
Charlo, Mt., U.S.	C2	133
Charlotte, Ia., U.S.	C7	122
Charlotte, Mi., U.S.	F6	129
Charlotte, N.C., U.S.	B2	140
Charlotte, Tn., U.S.	A4	149
Charlotte, Tx., U.S.	E3	150
Charlotte, Vt., U.S.	C2	152
Charlotte, co., Fl., U.S.	F5	116
Charlotte, co., Va., U.S.	C4	153
Charlotte Amalie, V.I.U.S.	E12	94
Charlotte Court House, Va., U.S.	C4	153
Charlotte Hall, Md., U.S.	D4	127
Charlotte Harbor, Fl., U.S.	F4	116
Charlotte Harbor, b., Fl., U.S.	F4	116
Charlottesville, In., U.S.	E6	121
Charlottesville, Va., U.S.	B4	153
Charlottetown, Newf., Can.	B3	102
Charlottetown, P.E.I., Can.	C6	101
Charlton, co., Ga., U.S.	F4	117
Charlton City, Ma., U.S.	B4	128
Charlton Island, i., N.W. Ter., Can.	n20	103
Charlu, U.S.S.R.	K22	6
Charmco, W.V., U.S.	C4	155
Charmes, Fr.	D13	14
Charny, Que., Can.	C6	104
Charouine, Alg.	F10	62
Charovsk, U.S.S.R.	B23	26
Chārsadda, Pak.	C4	44
Charter Oak, Ia., U.S.	B2	122
Charters Towers, Austl.	C7	70
Chartres, Fr.	D8	14
Chasavjurt, U.S.S.R.	G17	4
Chascomús, Arg.	H9	80
Chase, B.C., Can.	D8	99
Chase, Ks., U.S.	D5	123
Chase, Md., U.S.	B5	127
Chase, co., Ks., U.S.	D7	123
Chase, co., Ne., U.S.	D4	134
Chase, Mount, mtn., Me., U.S.	B4	126
Chaseburg, Wi., U.S.	E2	156
Chase City, Va., U.S.	D4	153
Chase Field Naval Air Station, mil., Tx., U.S.	E4	150
Chaska, Mn., U.S.	F5	130
Chasŏng, N. Kor.	B14	32
Chassahowitzka Bay, b., Fl., U.S.	D4	116
Chassell, Mi., U.S.	A2	129
Chasuta, Peru	B3	82
Chataignier, La., U.S.	D3	125
Chatanbulag, Mong.	C8	30
Chatanga, stm., U.S.S.R.	C12	24
Chatangskij zaliv, b., U.S.S.R.	C13	24
Chatawa, Ms., U.S.	D3	131
Châteaubriant, Fr.	E5	14
Château-Chinon, Fr.	E10	14
Château d'Oex, Switz.	F7	13
Château-du-Loir, Fr.	E7	14
Châteaudun, Fr.	D8	14
Chateaugay, N.Y., U.S.	f10	139
Château-Gontier, Fr.	E6	14
Châteauguay, Que., Can.	D4	104
Châteaulin, Fr.	D2	14
Châteauneuf-sur-Charente, Fr.	G6	14
Châteauneuf-sur-Loire, Fr.	E9	14
Château-Renault, Fr.	E7	14
Château-Richer, Que., Can.	C6	104
Châteauroux, Fr.	F8	14
Château-Salins, Fr.	D13	14
Château-Thierry, Fr.	C10	14
Châtellerault, Fr.	F7	14
Châtel-sur-Moselle, Fr.	D13	14
Chatfield, Mn., U.S.	G6	130
Chatgal, Mong.	A7	30
Chatham, N.B., Can.	B4	101
Chatham, Ont., Can.	E2	103
Chatham, Il., U.S.	D4	120
Chatham, La., U.S.	B3	125
Chatham, Ma., U.S.	C8	128
Chatham, N.J., U.S.	B4	137
Chatham, N.Y., U.S.	C7	139
Chatham, Va., U.S.	D3	153
Chatham, co., Ga., U.S.	E5	117
Chatham, co., N.C., U.S.	B3	140
Chatham Islands, is., N.Z.	M22	158
Chatham Strait, strt., Ak., U.S.	m22	109
Châtillon, Italy	D2	18
Châtillon-sur-Chalaronne, Fr.	F11	14
Châtillon-sur-Indre, Fr.	F8	14
Châtillon-sur-Seine, Fr.	E11	14
Chatom, Al., U.S.	D1	108
Chatsworth, Ont., Can.	C4	103
Chatsworth, Ga., U.S.	B2	117
Chatsworth, Il., U.S.	C5	120
Chatsworth, Zimb.	B10	66

Name — Map Ref. — Page

Chatsworth Reservoir, res., Ca., U.S. m11 112
Chattahoochee, Fl., U.S. B2 116
Chattahoochee, co., Ga., U.S. D2 117
Chattahoochee, stm., U.S. E1 117
Chattanooga, Ok., U.S. C3 143
Chattanooga, Tn., U.S. D8 149
Chattaroy, Wa., U.S. B8 154
Chattaroy, W.V., U.S. D2 155
Chattooga, co., Ga., U.S. B1 117
Chattooga, stm., U.S. B1 147
Chatuge Lake, res., U.S. g9 140
Chaudière, stm., Que., Can. C7 104
Chau Doc, Viet. I8 40
Chauk, Burma D3 40
Chaullay, Peru E5 82
Chaumont, Fr. D12 14
Chaumont-en-Vexin, Fr. C8 14
Chauncey, Ga., U.S. D3 117
Chauncey, Oh., U.S. C3 142
Chauncy Lake, l., Ma., U.S. g9 128
Chaungwabyin, Burma H5 40
Chauny, Fr. C10 14
Chaussin, Fr. F12 14
Chautauqua, Ks., U.S. E7 123
Chautauqua, N.Y., U.S. C1 139
Chautauqua, co., Ks., U.S. E7 123
Chautauqua, co., N.Y., U.S. C1 139
Chautauqua Lake, l., N.Y., U.S. C1 139
Chauvigny, Fr. F7 14
Chauvin, Alta., Can. C5 98
Chauvin, La., U.S. E5 125
Chavakkad, India G4 46
Chavarría, Arg. E9 80
Chaves, co., N.M., U.S. D5 138
Chavies, Ky., U.S. C6 124
Chaviña, Peru F5 82
Cháviva, Col. E6 84
Chayanta, Bol. H8 82
Chazy, N.Y., U.S. f11 139
Cheadle, Alta., Can. D4 98
Cheaha Mountain, mtn., Al., U.S. B4 108
Cheapside, Va., U.S. h16 153
Cheat, Shavers Fork, stm., W.V., U.S. B5 155
Cheatham, co., Tn., U.S. A4 149
Cheat Mountain, mtn., W.V., U.S. C5 155
Cheb, Czech. E12 10
Chebacco Lake, l., Ma., U.S. f12 128
Chebanse, Il., U.S. C6 120
Chebba, Tun. C16 62
Chebeague Island, Me., U.S. E2 126
Cheboygan, Mi., U.S. C6 129
Cheboygan, co., Mi., U.S. C6 129
Chech, Erg, des., Afr. D6 54
Chech'on, S. Kor. F16 32
Chęciny, Pol. E20 10
Checotah, Ok., U.S. B6 143
Chedabucto Bay, b., N.S., Can. D8 101
Cheduba Island, i., Burma E2 40
Cheektowaga, N.Y., U.S. C2 139
Cheeseman Lake, res., Co., U.S. B5 113
Chegutu, Zimb. B10 66
Chegutu Safari Park, Zimb. A9 66
Chehalem Mountains, mts., Or., U.S. h12 144
Chehalis, Wa., U.S. C3 154
Chehalis, stm., Wa., U.S. C2 154
Chehe, China B9 40
Cheju, S. Kor. E12 30
Chekiang see Zhejiang, prov., China F11 30
Chelan, Sask., Can. E4 105
Chelan, Wa., U.S. B5 154
Chelan, co., Wa., U.S. B4 154
Chelan, Lake, l., Wa., U.S. A5 154
Chelan Falls, Wa., U.S. B5 154
Chelan Mountains, mts., Wa., U.S. A5 154
Chelelektu, Eth. N10 60
Chelforó, Arg. J5 80
Chelghoum el Aïd, Alg. B14 62
Chéliff, Oued, stm., Alg. B11 62
Chełm, Pol. D23 10
Chełmno, Pol. B18 10
Chelmsford, Ma., U.S. A5 128
Chełmża, Pol. B18 10
Chelsea, Que., Can. D2 104
Chelsea, Al., U.S. g7 108
Chelsea, Ia., U.S. C5 122
Chelsea, Me., U.S. D3 126
Chelsea, Ma., U.S. B5 128
Chelsea, Mi., U.S. F6 129
Chelsea, Ok., U.S. A6 143
Chelsea, Vt., U.S. D4 152
Cheltenham, Md., U.S. C4 127
Chelyabinsk see Čel'abinsk, U.S.S.R. F10 22
Chelyan, W.V., U.S. C3 155
Chelyuskintsy Ice Tongue, Ant. B5 73
Chemaïa, Mor. D6 62
Chemax, Mex. G16 90
Chemehuevi Indian Reservation, Ca., U.S. E6 112
Chemnitz, Ger. E12 10
Chemquasabamticook Lake (Ross Lake), l., Me., U.S. B3 126
Chemult, Or., U.S. D5 144
Chemung, Il., U.S. A5 120
Chemung, co., N.Y., U.S. C4 139
Chemung, stm., Pa., U.S. C8 145
Chemung Lake, l., Ont., Can. C6 103
Chenāb, stm., Asia E5 44
Chenachane, Alg. G8 62
Chenango, co., N.Y., U.S. C5 139
Chenango, stm., N.Y., U.S. C5 139
Chenango Bridge, N.Y., U.S. C5 139
Chenārān, Iran C15 48
Chene, Bayou, stm., La., U.S. k9 125
Chenequa, Wi., U.S. m11 156
Chenes, River Aux, b., La., U.S. k12 125
Chénéville, Que., Can. D2 104
Cheney, Ks., U.S. E6 123
Cheney, Wa., U.S. B8 154
Cheney Reservoir, res., Ks., U.S. E6 123
Cheneyville, La., U.S. C3 125
Chengde, China C5 32
Chengdu, China E7 30
Chenghai, China L5 34
Chengjiang, China B7 40
Chengshan Jiao, c., China F10 32
Chengtu see Chengdu, China E7 30
Chengzitan, China D10 32
Chenoa, Il., U.S. C5 120
Chenoweth, Or., U.S. B5 144
Chenxian, China J1 34
Cheo Reo, Viet. H10 40
Chepachet, R.I., U.S. B2 146
Chepachet, stm., R.I., U.S. B2 146
Chepén, Peru B2 82
Chepes, Arg. F5 80
Chepo, Pan. C3 84
Chequamegon Bay, b., Wi., U.S. B3 156
Cher, dept., Fr. E9 14
Cher, stm., Fr. E8 14
Cheraw, Co., U.S. C7 113
Cheraw, S.C., U.S. B8 147
Cherbourg, Fr. C5 14
Cherchell, Alg. B12 62
Chergui, Chott ech, l., Alg. C11 62
Cherhill, Alta., Can. C3 98
Cheriton, Va., U.S. C7 153
Cherkassy see Čerkassy, U.S.S.R. H4 22
Chernobyl see Černobyl', U.S.S.R. G4 22
Cherokee, Al., U.S. A2 108
Cherokee, Ia., U.S. B2 122
Cherokee, Ks., U.S. E9 123
Cherokee, Ok., U.S. A3 143
Cherokee, co., Al., U.S. A4 108
Cherokee, co., Ga., U.S. B2 117
Cherokee, co., Ia., U.S. B2 122
Cherokee, co., Ks., U.S. E9 123
Cherokee, co., N.C., U.S. f8 140
Cherokee, co., Ok., U.S. B6 143
Cherokee, co., S.C., U.S. A4 147
Cherokee, co., Tx., U.S. D5 150
Cherokee Indian Reservation, N.C., U.S. f9 140
Cherokee Lake, res., Tn., U.S. C10 149
Cherokees, Lake O' The, res., Ok., U.S. A7 143
Cherokee Village, Ar., U.S. A4 111
Cherquenco, Chile J2 80
Cherrapunji, India H14 44
Cherry, Il., U.S. B4 120
Cherry, co., Ne., U.S. B4 134
Cherry Creek, S.D., U.S. C4 148
Cherry Creek, stm., Co., U.S. B6 113
Cherry Creek, stm., S.D., U.S. C3 148
Cherryfield, Me., U.S. D5 126
Cherry Grove, Or., U.S. g11 144
Cherry Hill, N.J., U.S. D2 137
Cherry Point, c., Va., U.S. C6 153
Cherry Point Marine Corps Air Station, mil., N.C., U.S. C6 140
Cherryvale, Ks., U.S. E8 123
Cherry Valley, Ont., Can. D7 103
Cherry Valley, Ar., U.S. B5 111
Cherry Valley, Il., U.S. A5 120
Cherry Valley, Ma., U.S. B4 128
Cherryville, N.C., U.S. B1 140
Cherson, U.S.S.R. H4 22
Chesaning, Mi., U.S. E6 129
Chesapeake, Oh., U.S. D3 142
Chesapeake, Va., U.S. D6 153
Chesapeake, W.V., U.S. C3 155
Chesapeake and Delaware Canal, U.S. B3 115
Chesapeake Bay, b., U.S. D11 106
Chesapeake Bay Bridge-Tunnel, Va., U.S. D7 153
Chesapeake Beach, Md., U.S. C4 127
Chesapeake City, Md., U.S. A6 127
Chesapeake Ranch Estates, Md., U.S. D5 127
Chesdin, Lake, res., Va., U.S. C5 153
Cheseaux, Switz. E6 13
Chesham, N.H., U.S. E2 136
Cheshire, Ct., U.S. D4 114
Cheshire, Ma., U.S. A1 128
Cheshire, co., Eng., U.K. H11 8
Cheshire, co., N.H., U.S. E2 136
Cheshire Reservoir, res., Ma., U.S. A1 128
Chesilhurst, N.J., U.S. D3 137
Chesley, Ont., Can. C3 103
Chesnee, S.C., U.S. A4 147
Chester, Eng., U.K. H11 8
Chester, Ar., U.S. B1 111
Chester, Ca., U.S. B3 112
Chester, Ct., U.S. D6 114
Chester, Ga., U.S. D3 117
Chester, Id., U.S. F7 119
Chester, Il., U.S. F4 120
Chester, Md., U.S. C5 127
Chester, Mt., U.S. B6 133
Chester, Ne., U.S. D8 134
Chester, N.H., U.S. E4 136
Chester, N.J., U.S. B3 137
Chester, N.Y., U.S. D6 139
Chester, Pa., U.S. G11 145
Chester, S.C., U.S. B5 147
Chester, S.D., U.S. D9 148
Chester, Vt., U.S. E3 152
Chester, Va., U.S. C5 153
Chester, W.V., U.S. A4 155
Chester, co., Pa., U.S. G10 145
Chester, co., S.C., U.S. B5 147
Chester, co., Tn., U.S. B3 149
Chester, stm., Md., U.S. B5 127
Chester Basin, N.S., Can. E5 101
Chester Depot, Vt., U.S. E3 152
Chesterfield, Il., U.S. D3 120
Chesterfield, In., U.S. D6 121
Chesterfield, Mo., U.S. f12 127
Chesterfield, N.H., U.S. E2 136
Chesterfield, S.C., U.S. B7 147
Chesterfield, Tn., U.S. B3 149
Chesterfield, Va., U.S. C5 153
Chesterfield, co., S.C., U.S. B7 147
Chesterfield, co., Va., U.S. C5 153
Chesterfield, Île, i., Madag. E8 58
Chesterfield, Îles, is., N. Cal. C11 68
Chesterfield Inlet, N.W. Ter., Can. D14 96
Chesterfield Inlet, b., N.W. Ter., Can. D14 96
Chester-le-Street, Eng., U.K. G12 8
Chesterton, In., U.S. A3 121
Chesterton Range, mts., Austl. E7 70
Chestertown, Md., U.S. B5 127
Chestertown, N.Y., U.S. B7 139
Chesterville, Ont., Can. B9 103
Chestnut, Il., U.S. C4 120
Chestnut Knoll, De., U.S. E4 115
Chesuncook Lake, l., Me., U.S. C3 126
Cheswick, Pa., U.S. h14 145
Cheswold, De., U.S. D3 115
Cheta, stm., U.S.S.R. C11 24
Chetac, Lake, l., Wi., U.S. C2 156
Chetaïbi, Alg. L2 18
Chetco, stm., Or., U.S. E2 144
Chetek, Wi., U.S. C2 156
Chetek, Lake, l., Wi., U.S. C2 156
Chéticamp, N.S., Can. C8 101
Chetopa, Ks., U.S. E8 123
Chetumal, Mex. H15 90
Chetumal, Bahía, b., N.A. H15 90
Chetwynd, B.C., Can. B7 99
Chevak, Ak., U.S. C6 109
Chevelon Creek, stm., Az., U.S. C5 110
Cheverie, N.S., Can. D5 101
Cheviot, Oh., U.S. C1 142
Chevreuil, Bayou, stm., La., U.S. k10 125
Chevreuil, Point, c., La., U.S. E4 125
Chevy Chase, Md., U.S. C3 127
Chewack, stm., Wa., U.S. A5 154
Chewalla, Tn., U.S. B3 149
Chew Bahir (Lake Stefanie), l., Afr. H8 56
Chewelah, Wa., U.S. A8 154
Cheyenne, Ok., U.S. B2 143
Cheyenne, Wy., U.S. E8 157
Cheyenne, co., Co., U.S. C8 113
Cheyenne, co., Ks., U.S. C2 123
Cheyenne, co., Ne., U.S. C2 134
Cheyenne, stm., U.S. C4 148
Cheyenne, Dry Fork, stm., Wy., U.S. C7 157
Cheyenne River Indian Reservation, S.D., U.S. B4 148
Cheyenne Wells, Co., U.S. C8 113
Chezhen, China F5 32
Chhapra, India H11 44
Chhātak, Bngl. H14 44
Chhatarpur, India H8 44
Chhatrapur, India C8 46
Chhêb Kândal, Camb. H8 40
Chhindwāra, India I8 44
Chhukha Dzong, Bhu. G13 44
Chi, stm., Thai. G8 40
Chia, Col. E5 84
Chiai, Tai. L9 34
Chiali, Tai. L9 34
Chiang Kham, Thai. E6 40
Chiang Khan, Thai. F6 40
Chiang Mai, Thai. E5 40
Chiang Rai, Thai. E5 40
Chiapa, Chile H7 82
Chiapa de Corzo, Mex. I13 90
Chiapas, state, Mex. I14 90
Chiari, Italy D4 18
Chiasso, Switz. G11 13
Chiautla de Tapia, Mex. H10 90
Chiavari, Italy E4 18
Chiavenna, Italy C4 18
Chiba, Japan L15 36
Chiblow Lake, l., Ont., Can. A1 103
Chibougamau, Que., Can. k12 104
Chibuto, Moz. E11 66
Chicago, Il., U.S. B6 120
Chicago Heights, Il., U.S. B6 120
Chicago Sanitary and Ship Canal, Il., U.S. k8 120
Chicama, stm., Peru B2 82
Chicamacomico, stm., Md., U.S. D6 127
Chicapa, stm., Afr. C4 58
Chichagof Island, i., Ak., U.S. m22 109
Chichas, Cordillera de, mts., Bol. I8 82
Chicheng, China C3 32
Chichén Itzá, hist., Mex. G15 90
Chichester, Eng., U.K. K13 8
Chichester, N.H., U.S. D4 136
Chichi, Tai. L9 34
Chichibu, Japan L14 36
Chichica, Pan. I13 92
Chichicastenango, Guat. C3 92
Chichigalpa, Nic. E7 92
Chichimilá, Mex. G15 90
Chichiriviche, Ven. B8 84
Chickahominy, stm., Va., U.S. C5 153
Chickamauga, Ga., U.S. B1 117
Chickamauga and Chattanooga National Military Park, U.S. k11 149
Chickamauga Dam, Tn., U.S. h11 149
Chickamauga Lake, res., Tn., U.S. D8 149
Chickasaw, Al., U.S. E1 108
Chickasaw, co., Ia., U.S. A5 122
Chickasaw, co., Ms., U.S. B5 131
Chickasawhay, stm., Ms., U.S. D5 131
Chickasaw National Recreation Area, Ok., U.S. C5 143
Chickasha, Ok., U.S. B4 143
Chickasha, Lake, res., Ok., U.S. B3 143
Chickwolnepy Stream, stm., N.H., U.S. A4 136
Chiclana de la Frontera, Spain I5 16
Chiclayo, Peru B2 82
Chico, Ca., U.S. C3 112
Chico, Tx., U.S. C4 150
Chico, Wa., U.S. B3 154
Chico, stm., Arg. F3 78
Chico, stm., Arg. E3 78
Chico, stm., Pan. I14 92
Chico Creek, stm., Co., U.S. C6 113
Chicomo, Moz. E12 66
Chicomuselo, Mex. J13 90
Chicopee, Ga., U.S. B3 117
Chicopee, Ks., U.S. E9 123
Chicopee, Ma., U.S. B2 128
Chicora, Pa., U.S. E2 145
Chicot, Lake, l., Ar., U.S. D4 111
Chicot Island, i., La., U.S. E6 125
Chicoutimi, Que., Can. A6 104
Chicoutimi, stm., Que., Can. A6 104
Chicú, Cerro, mtn., Pan. I14 92
Chicxulub, Mex. G15 90
Chidambaram, India G5 46
Chidester, Ar., U.S. D2 111
Chiefland, Fl., U.S. C4 116
Chiemsee, l., Ger. H12 10
Chien, Bayou de, stm., Ky., U.S. f8 124
Chieri, Italy D2 18
Chiers, stm., Eur. I7 12
Chifeng (Ulanhad), China A7 32
Chigasaki, Japan L14 36
Chignahuapan, Mex. H10 90
Chignecto, Cape, c., N.S., Can. D5 101
Chignecto Bay, b., Can. D5 101
Chignik, Ak., U.S. D8 109
Chigorodó, Col. D4 84
Chigyŏng, N. Kor. D15 32
Chihli, Gulf of see Bo Hai, b., China E8 32
Chihsi see Jixi, China B13 30
Chihuahua, Mex. C6 90
Chihuahua, state, Mex. C6 90
Chihuahuan Desert, des., N.A. F9 86
Chikaskia, stm., U.S. A4 143
Chik Ballāpur, India F4 46
Chikindzonot, Mex. G15 90
Chikmagalūr, India F3 46
Chikou, China E6 34
Chilakalūrupet, India D6 46
Chilapa de Álvarez, Mex. I10 90
Chilās, Pak. C6 44
Chilca, Peru E3 82
Chilca, Cordillera de, mts., Peru F6 82
Chilca, Punta, c., Peru E3 82
Chilcott Island, i., Austl. A8 70
Childers, Austl. E10 70
Childersburg, Al., U.S. B3 108
Childress, Tx., U.S. B2 150
Childress, co., Tx., U.S. B2 150
Chile, ctry., S.A. C2 78
Chile Chico, Chile F2 78
Chilecito, Arg. E5 80
Chilecito, Arg. G4 80
Chilete, Peru B2 82
Chilhowee, Mo., U.S. C4 132
Chilhowee Mountain, mtn., Tn., U.S. n14 149
Chilhowie, Va., U.S. f10 153
Chili, In., U.S. C5 121
Chili, stm., Peru G6 82
Chilika Lake, l., India C8 46
Chililabombwe (Bancroft), Zam. D5 58
Chilko, stm., B.C., Can. D6 99
Chilko Lake, l., B.C., Can. D5 99
Chillagoe, Austl. A6 70
Chillán, Chile I2 80
Chillar, Arg. I9 80
Chillicothe, Il., U.S. C4 120
Chillicothe, Mo., U.S. B4 132
Chillicothe, Oh., U.S. C3 142
Chillicothe, Tx., U.S. B3 150
Chilliwack, B.C., Can. E7 99
Chillón, stm., Peru D3 82
Chillon, hist., Switz. F6 13
Chillum, Md., U.S. f9 127
Chiloé, Isla de, i., Chile E2 78
Chilok, U.S.S.R. G14 24
Chilok, stm., U.S.S.R. G13 24
Chilón, Mex. I13 90
Chiloquin, Or., U.S. E5 144
Chilpancingo de los Bravo, Mex. I10 90
Chilton, Tx., U.S. D4 150
Chilton, Wi., U.S. D5 156
Chilton, co., Al., U.S. C3 108
Chiluage, Ang. C4 58
Chilung, Tai. J10 34
Chilwa, Lake, l., Afr. E7 58
Chimacum, Wa., U.S. A3 154
Chimaltenango, Guat. C4 92
Chimaltenango, dept., Guat. C4 92
Chimán, Pan. C3 84
Chimayo, N.M., U.S. A4 138
Chimbarongo, Chile H3 80
Chimbas, Arg. F4 80
Chimborazo, prov., Ec. H3 84
Chimborazo, mtn., Nic. D9 92
Chimborazo, vol., Ec. H3 84
Chimbote, Peru C2 82
Chimichagua, Col. C6 84
Chimkent see Čimkent, U.S.S.R. I11 22
Chimki, U.S.S.R. F20 26
Chimney Rock, mtn., Ky., U.S. D5 124
Chimney Rock, mtn., Ne., U.S. C2 134
Chimneytop, mtn., Tn., U.S. C11 149
Chimoio, Moz. B11 66
Chimpay, Arg. J5 80
Chin, Cape, c., Ont., Can. B3 103
China, Mex. E10 90
China, Me., U.S. D3 126
China (Zhongguo), ctry., Asia D8 30
Chinácota, Col. D6 84
China Grove, N.C., U.S. B2 140
China Lake, Ca., U.S. E5 112
China Lake, l., Me., U.S. D3 126
Chinameca, El Sal. D6 92
Chinandega, Nic. E7 92
Chinandega, dept., Nic. E8 92
Chinati Peak, mtn., Tx., U.S. p12 150
Chincha Alta, Peru E3 82
Chinchaga, stm., Can. E9 96
Chincheros, Peru E5 82
Chinchilla, Austl. F9 70
Chinchiná, Col. E5 84
Chinch'ŏn, S. Kor. G15 32
Chinchón, Spain E8 16
Chinchorro, Banco, Mex. H16 90
Chincolco, Chile G3 80
Chincoteague, Va., U.S. C7 153
Chincoteague Bay, b., U.S. D7 127
Chinde, Moz. B13 66
Chindo, S. Kor. I14 32
Chindwinn, stm., Burma C3 40
Chingleput, India F5 46
Chingola, Zam. D5 58
Chinguetti, Maur. A3 64
Chinhae, S. Kor. H16 32
Chinhae-man, b., S. Kor. H16 32
Chin Hills, hills, Burma C2 40
Chinhoyi, Zimb. E6 58
Chiniot, Pak. E5 44
Chinitna Point, c., Ak., U.S. h15 109
Chinju, S. Kor. H16 32
Chinkiang see Zhenjiang, China E10 30
Chinko, stm., Cen. Afr. Rep. G5 56
Chinle, Az., U.S. A6 110
Chinle Wash, val., U.S. A6 110
Chinmen, China K7 34
Chinmen Tao, i., Tai. K7 34
Chino, Ca., U.S. F5 112
Chinook, Alta., Can. D5 98
Chinook, Mt., U.S. B7 133
Chinook, Wa., U.S. C2 154
Chinook, Lake, res., Or., U.S. C5 144
Chinook Cove, B.C., Can. D7 99
Chino Valley, Az., U.S. C3 110
Chinquapin, N.C., U.S. C5 140
Chinsali, Zam. D6 58
Chintāmani, India F5 46
Chinú, Col. C5 84
Chiny, Bel. I7 12
Chioggia, Italy D7 18
Chios see Khíos, Grc. K10 20
Chipao, Peru F5 82
Chipata, Zam. D6 58
Chipewyan, stm., Alta., Can. A4 98
Chipinge, Zimb. C11 66
Chipita Park, Co., U.S. C6 113
Chipley, Fl., U.S. u16 116
Chipman, Alta., Can. C4 98
Chipman, N.B., Can. C4 101
Chipola, stm., Fl., U.S. B1 116
Chippewa, co., Mi., U.S. B6 129
Chippewa, co., Mn., U.S. E3 130
Chippewa, co., Wi., U.S. C2 156
Chippewa, stm., Mn., U.S. E3 130
Chippewa, stm., Wi., U.S. D2 156
Chippewa, East Branch, stm., Mn., U.S. E3 130
Chippewa, East Fork, stm., Wi., U.S. C3 156
Chippewa, Lake, l., Wi., U.S. C2 156
Chippewa Falls, Wi., U.S. D2 156
Chipuxet, stm., R.I., U.S. F3 146
Chiquián, Peru D3 82
Chiquimula, Guat. C5 92
Chiquimula, dept., Guat. C5 92
Chiquimulilla, Guat. C4 92
Chiquinata, Bahía, b., Chile I6 82
Chiquinquirá, Col. E6 84
Chiquintirca, Peru E5 82
Chiquito, stm., Mex. H9 90
Chira, stm., S.A. J2 84
Chira, Isla, i., C.R. G9 92
Chirfa, Niger D9 54
Chiricahua Mountains, mts., Az., U.S. E6 110
Chiricahua National Monument, Az., U.S. F6 110
Chiricahua Peak, mtn., Az., U.S. F6 110
Chiriguaná, Col. C6 84
Chirikof Island, i., Ak., U.S. D8 109
Chirilagua, El Sal. D6 92
Chirinos, Peru A2 82
Chiriquí, Pan. I12 92
Chiriquí, prov., Pan. I12 92
Chiriquí, Golfo de, b., Pan. I12 92
Chiriquí, Laguna de, b., Pan. H12 92
Chiriquí Grande, Pan. C1 84
Chiriquí Viejo, stm., Pan. I12 92
Chiromo, Mwi. E7 58
Chirripó, stm., C.R. G11 92
Chirripó, Cerro, mtn., C.R. H11 92
Chirripó, Parque Nacional, C.R. H11 92
Chisago, co., Mn., U.S. E6 130
Chisago City, Mn., U.S. E6 130
Chiscas, Col. D6 84
Chisec, Guat. B4 92
Ch'ishan, Tai. M9 34
Chisholm, Alta., Can. B3 98
Chisholm, Me., U.S. D2 126
Chisholm, Mn., U.S. C6 130
Chishtiān Mandi, Pak. F5 44
Chislaviči, U.S.S.R. G15 26
Chisos Mountains, mts., Tx., U.S. E1 150
Chist'akovo see Torez, U.S.S.R. F15 4
Chita, Col. D6 84
Chitado, Ang. A1 66
Chitagá, Col. D6 84
Chitato, Ang. C4 58
Chitembo, Ang. D3 58
Chitina, stm., Ak., U.S. g19 109
Chitipa, Mwi. C6 58
Chitradurga, India E4 46
Chitrāl, Pak. C4 44
Chitré, Pan. D2 84
Chittagong, Bngl. I14 44
Chittaurgarh, India H6 44
Chittenango, N.Y., U.S. B5 139
Chittenden, Vt., U.S. D3 152
Chittenden, co., Vt., U.S. C2 152
Chittenden Reservoir, res., Vt., U.S. D3 152
Chittoor, India F5 46
Chittūr, India G4 46
Chitu, Eth. M9 60
Chíuchíu, Chile B4 80
Chiumbe, stm., Afr. C4 58
Chiusi, Italy F6 18
Chiuta, Lake, l., Afr. D7 58
Chiva, U.S.S.R. I10 22
Chivacoa, Ven. B8 84
Chivapuri, stm., Ven. D9 84
Chivasso, Italy D2 18
Chivato, Punta, c., Mex. D4 90
Chivay, Peru F6 82
Chivhu, Zimb. B10 66
Chivilcoy, Arg. H8 80
Chixoy (Salinas), stm., N.A. J14 90
Chixoy, Embalse, res., Guat. B4 92
Chlevnoje, U.S.S.R. I22 26
Chloride, Az., U.S. B1 110
Chmel'nickij, U.S.S.R. H3 22
Chŏâm Khsant, Camb. G8 40
Choapa, stm., Chile F3 80
Chobe, dept., Bots. B7 66
Chobe, stm., Afr. A7 66
Chobe National Park, Bots. B7 66
Choccolocco, Al., U.S. B4 108
Choccolocco Creek, stm., Al., U.S. B3 108
Chochis, Cerro, mtn., Bol. H11 82
Choch'iwŏn, S. Kor. G15 32
Chocó, dept., Col. D4 84
Chocolate Mountains, mts., U.S. F6 112
Chocontá, Col. E6 84
Chocope, Peru B2 82
Chocorua, N.H., U.S. C4 136
Chocorua, Mount, mtn., N.H., U.S. C4 136
Chocowinity, N.C., U.S. B5 140
Choctaw, Ar., U.S. B3 111
Choctaw, Ok., U.S. B4 143
Choctaw, co., Al., U.S. C1 108
Choctaw, co., Ms., U.S. B4 131
Choctaw, co., Ok., U.S. C6 143
Choctawhatchee, East Fork, stm., Al., U.S. D4 108
Choctawhatchee, West Fork, stm., Al., U.S. D4 108
Choctawhatchee Bay, b., Fl., U.S. u15 116
Choctaw Indian Reservation, Ms., U.S. C4 131
Chodecz, Pol. C19 10
Chodžakala, U.S.S.R. B14 48
Chodžejli, U.S.S.R. I9 22
Chodžent, U.S.S.R. I11 22
Chodzież, Pol. C16 10
Choele-Choel, Arg. J6 80
Choiceland, Sask., Can. D3 105
Choiseul, i., Sol.Is. I19 158
Choix, Mex. D5 90
Chojnice, Pol. B17 10
Chojnów, Pol. D15 10
Chokio, Mn., U.S. E2 130
Chokoloskee, Fl., U.S. G5 116
Cholet, Fr. E6 14
Cholm, U.S.S.R. D14 26
Cholmec, U.S.S.R. E16 26
Cholmsk, U.S.S.R. H20 24
Choloma, Hond. B7 92
Ch'ŏlsan, N. Kor. D12 32
Choluj, U.S.S.R. E24 26
Cholula [de Rivadabia], Mex. H10 90
Choluteca, Hond. D7 92
Choluteca, dept., Hond. D7 92
Choluteca, stm., Hond. D8 92
Choma, Zam. E5 58
Chomo Lhāri, mtn., Asia G13 44
Chomūm, India G6 44
Chomutov, Czech. E13 10
Chomutovo, U.S.S.R. I20 26
Ch'ŏnan, S. Kor. G15 32
Chon Buri, Thai. H6 40
Chone, Ec. H2 84
Chone, stm., Ec. H2 84
Ch'ŏngdan, N. Kor. F13 32
Ch'ŏngjin, N. Kor. B17 32
Chŏngju, N. Kor. D13 32
Ch'ŏngju, S. Kor. G15 32
Chongos Bajo, Peru E4 82
Chongoyape, Peru B2 82
Chongqing, China F8 30
Chongru, China H9 34
Ch'ŏngsong, N. Kor. B17 32
Chongzuo, China G8 30
Chŏnju, S. Kor. H15 32
Chonos, Archipiélago de los, is., Chile F2 78
Chontaleña, Cordillera, mts., Nic. F10 92
Chontales, dept., Nic. E9 92
Chopda, India B3 46
Chopim, stm., Braz. D12 80
Chopinzinho, Braz. C12 80
Chop'or, stm., U.S.S.R. G6 22
Choptank, stm., Md., U.S. C6 127
Chopu, mtn., Asia F12 44
Chor, stm., U.S.S.R. H19 24
Chorlovo, U.S.S.R. F21 26
Choro, stm., Bol. G9 82
Chorog, U.S.S.R. J12 22
Chorolque, Cerro, mtn., Bol. I8 82
Choros, Isla, i., Chile E3 80
Chorreras, Mex. C7 90
Ch'ŏrwŏn, S. Kor. E15 32
Chorzele, Pol. H3 26
Ch'osan, N. Kor. C13 32
Chōshi, Japan L15 36
Choshui, stm., Tai. L9 34
Chosica, Peru D3 82
Chos Malal, Arg. I3 80
Choszczno, Pol. B15 10
Chota, Peru B2 82
Choteau, Mt., U.S. C4 133
Chotěboř, Czech. F15 10
Chotimsk, U.S.S.R. H15 26
Chotin, U.S.S.R. A10 20
Chot'kovo, U.S.S.R. E21 26
Chotynec, U.S.S.R. H18 26
Choudrant, La., U.S. B3 125
Choûm, Maur. J4 62
Chouteau, Ok., U.S. A6 143
Chouteau, co., Mt., U.S. C6 133
Chovd, Mong. B5 30
Chövsgöl Nuur, l., Mong. A7 30
Chowan, co., N.C., U.S. A6 140
Chowan, stm., N.C., U.S. A6 140
Chowchilla, Ca., U.S. D3 112

Name — Map Ref. — Page

Choya, Arg. E6 80
Chrisman, Il., U.S. D6 120
Chrisney, In., U.S. H3 121
Christchurch, N.Z. E4 72
Christian, co., Il., U.S. D4 120
Christian, co., Ky., U.S. D2 124
Christian, co., Mo., U.S. E4 132
Christian, Cape, c., N.W. Ter., Can. B19 96
Christiana, S. Afr. F7 66
Christiana, De., U.S. B3 115
Christiana, Pa., U.S. G9 145
Christiana, Tn., U.S. B5 149
Christian Island, i., Ont., Can. C4 103
Christiansburg, Oh., U.S. B1 142
Christiansburg, Va., U.S. C2 153
Christian Sound, strt., Ak., U.S. n22 109
Christiansted, V.I.U.S. F12 94
Christie Bay, b., N.W. Ter., Can. D10 96
Christina, stm., Alta., Can. A5 98
Christina, stm., De., U.S. B3 115
Christina, Lake, l., Mn., U.S. D3 130
Christina Peak, mtn., Nv., U.S. D6 135
Christine, N.D., U.S. C9 141
Christmas, Fl., U.S. D5 116
Christmas Island, dep., Oc. H4 38
Christmas Lake, l., Or., U.S. D6 144
Christopher, Il., U.S. F4 120
Christoval, Tx., U.S. D2 150
Chromtau, U.S.S.R. G9 22
Chrudim, Czech. F15 10
Chrzanów, Pol. E19 10
Chu (Xam), stm., Asia E8 40
Chuanliao, China G9 34
Chubbuck, Id., U.S. G6 119
Chubut, stm., Arg. I8 74
Chubut, stm., Arg. E3 78
Chucuito, Peru F7 82
Chucunaque, stm., Pan. C4 84
Chugach Islands, is., Ak., U.S. h16 109
Chugach Mountains, mts., Ak., U.S. g18 109
Chugwater, Wy., U.S. E8 157
Chugwater Creek, stm., Wy., U.S. E8 157
Chuhuichupa, Mex. C5 90
Chuí, Braz. G12 80
Chuichu, Az., U.S. E4 110
Chukai, Malay. L7 40
Chukchi Sea C2 86
Chula, Ga., U.S. E3 117
Chula, Mo., U.S. B4 132
Chula Vista, Ca., U.S. F5 112
Chulucanas, Peru A1 82
Chulumani, Bol. G8 82
Chuma, Bol. F7 82
Chumbicha, Arg. E5 80
Chumphon, Thai. I5 40
Chumpi, Peru F5 82
Chum Saeng, Thai. G6 40
Chunan, Tai. K9 34
Chunchi, Ec. I3 84
Ch'unch'ŏn, S. Kor. F15 32
Chunchula, Al., U.S. E1 108
Chunghwa, N. Kor. E13 32
Ch'ungju, S. Kor. G15 32
Chungking see Chongqing, China F8 30
Chungli, Tai. K10 34
Ch'ungmu, S. Kor. I16 32
Chŭngsan, N. Kor. D13 32
Chungyang Shanmo, mts., Tai. L10 34
Chunhuhux, Mex. H15 90
Chunky, Ms., U.S. C5 131
Chuntuquí, Guat. I14 90
Chuŏr Phnum Krâvanh, mts., Asia H7 40
Chupaca, Peru E4 82
Chupadera Mesa, mtn., N.M., U.S. D3 138
Chuquibamba, Peru F5 82
Chuquibambilla, Peru F5 82
Chuquicamata, Chile B4 80
Chuquisaca, dept., Bol. H9 82
Chur, Switz. E12 13
Churcampa, Peru E4 82
Churchbridge, Sask., Can. G5 105
Church Hill, Md., U.S. B6 127
Church Hill, Tn., U.S. C11 149
Churchill, Man., Can. f9 100
Churchill, co., Nv., U.S. D3 135
Churchill, stm., Can. E13 96
Churchill, stm., Newf., Can. h9 102
Churchill, Cape, c., Man., Can. f9 100
Churchill, Mount, mtn., B.C., Can. E6 99
Churchill Falls, wtfl, Newf., Can. h8 102
Churchill Lake, l., Sask., Can. m7 105
Churchill Lake, l., Me., U.S. B3 126
Church Point, N.S., Can. E3 101
Church Point, La., U.S. D3 125
Church Rock, N.M., U.S. B1 138
Churchs Ferry, N.D., U.S. A6 141
Churchton, Md., U.S. C4 127
Churchville, N.Y., U.S. B3 139
Churchville, Va., U.S. B3 153
Churdan, Ia., U.S. B3 122
Chūru, India F6 44
Churubusco, In., U.S. B7 121
Churuguara, Ven. B8 84
Chushan, Tai. L9 34
Chuska Mountains, mts., Az., U.S. A6 110
Chust, U.S.S.R. H2 22
Chutag, Mong. B7 30
Chutung, Tai. K10 34
Chuwang, China G2 32
Chuxiong, China B6 40
Chuy, Ur. G12 80
Chvalynsk, U.S.S.R. G7 22
Chvojnaja, U.S.S.R. C17 26
Ch'wiya-ri, N. Kor. E13 32
Chyrov, U.S.S.R. F22 10
Cianjur, Indon. J13 39a
Cianorte, Braz. G2 79
Cibecue, Az., U.S. C5 110
Cibola, co., N.M., U.S. C1 138
Cibolo Creek, stm., Tx., U.S. h7 150
Cicero, Il., U.S. B6 120
Cicero, In., U.S. D5 121
Čichačovo, U.S.S.R. D12 26
Ciechanów, Pol. C20 10
Ciechocinek, Pol. C18 10
Ciego de Ávila, Cuba D5 94
Ciempozuelos, Spain E8 16
Ciénaga, Col. B5 84
Ciénaga de Oro, Col. C5 84
Cienfuegos, Cuba C4 94
Čierna [nad Tisou], Czech. G22 10
Cieszyn, Pol. F18 10
Cieza, Spain G10 16
Čiganak, U.S.S.R. H12 22
Cigüela, stm., Spain F8 16
Cihanbeyli, Tur. B2 48
Čiili, U.S.S.R. I11 22
Čikoj, stm., Asia G19 22
Cikou, China F3 34
Cilacap, Indon. J14 39a
Čilik, U.S.S.R. I13 22
Cimarron, Ks., U.S. E3 123
Cimarron, N.M., U.S. A5 138
Cimarron, co., Ok., U.S. e8 143
Cimarron, stm., U.S. D7 106
Cimarron, North Fork, stm., U.S. E2 123
Čimbaj, U.S.S.R. I9 22
Čimišlija, U.S.S.R. C12 20
Čimkent, U.S.S.R. I11 22
Ciml'anskoje vodochranilišče, res., U.S.S.R. H6 22
Cîmpina, Rom. D9 20
Cîmpulung, Rom. D9 20
Cîmpulung Moldovenesc, Rom. B9 20
Činadijevo, U.S.S.R. A6 20
Cinaruco, stm., Ven. D9 84
Cincinnati, Ia., U.S. D5 122
Cincinnati, Oh., U.S. C1 142
Cinco, Canal Numero, Arg. I10 80
Cinco Pinos, Nic. D8 92
Cinco Saltos, Arg. J4 80
Çine, Tur. L12 20
Cingoli, Italy F8 18
Činišeucy, U.S.S.R. B12 20
Cinnaminson, N.J., U.S. D3 137
Cintalapa, Mex. I13 90
Cinto, Monte, mtn., Fr. L23 15a
Cinzas, Rio das, stm., Braz. C13 80
Cipa, stm., U.S.S.R. F15 24
Cipó, stm., Braz. E6 79
Cipolândia, Braz. F1 79
Cipolletti, Arg. J5 80
Čirčik, U.S.S.R. I11 22
Circle, Mt., U.S. C11 133
Circle Pines, Mn., U.S. m12 130
Circleville, Ks., U.S. C8 123
Circleville, Oh., U.S. C3 142
Circleville, Ut., U.S. E3 151
Cirebon, Indon. J14 39a
Ciremay, Gunung, mtn., Indon. J14 39a
Cirey-sur-Vezouze, Fr. D13 14
Ciriè, Italy D2 18
Ciriquiri, stm., Braz. C9 82
Čirpan, Bul. G9 20
Cisco, Ga., U.S. B2 117
Cisco, Il., U.S. C5 120
Cisco, Tx., U.S. C3 150
Ciskei, ctry., Afr. I8 66
Cisne, Il., U.S. E5 120
Cisneros, Col. D5 84
Cispus, stm., Wa., U.S. C4 154
Cissna Park, Il., U.S. C6 120
Cistern Point, c., Bah. C6 94
Čistoje, U.S.S.R. E26 26
Čistopol', U.S.S.R. F8 22
Čita, U.S.S.R. G14 24
Citac, Nevado, mtn., Peru E4 82
Citra, Fl., U.S. C4 116
Citronelle, Al., U.S. D1 108
Citrus, co., Fl., U.S. D4 116
Cittadella, Italy D6 18
Città di Castello, Italy F7 18
Cittanova, Italy K11 18
City of Refuge National Historical Park, Hi., U.S. D5 118
City Point, Fl., U.S. D6 116
City View, S.C., U.S. B3 147
Ciudad Acuña, Mex. C9 90
Ciudad Altamirano, Mex. H9 90
Ciudad Barrios, El Sal. D6 92
Ciudad Bolívar, Ven. C11 84
Ciudad Bolivia, Ven. C7 84
Ciudad Camargo, Mex. D10 90
Ciudad Constitución, Mex. E4 90
Ciudad Cortés, C.R. I11 92
Ciudad Darío, Nic. E8 92
Ciudad del Carmen, Mex. H14 90
Ciudad del Maíz, Mex. F10 90
Ciudad de México (Mexico City), Mex. H10 90
Ciudad de Nutrias, Ven. C8 84
Ciudad Guayana, Ven. C11 84
Ciudad Guzmán, Mex. H8 90
Ciudad Hidalgo, Mex. H9 90
Ciudad Juárez, Mex. B6 90
Ciudad Lerdo, Mex. E8 90
Ciudad Madero, Mex. F11 90
Ciudad Mante, Mex. F10 90
Ciudad Manuel Doblado, Mex. G9 90
Ciudad Miguel Alemán, Mex. D10 90
Ciudad Morelos, Mex. A2 90
Ciudad Obregón, Mex. D5 90
Ciudad Ojeda (Lagunillas), Ven. B7 84
Ciudad Piar, Ven. D11 84
Ciudad Real, Spain G8 16
Ciudad Rodrigo, Spain E5 16
Ciudad Sandino, Nic. D8 92
Ciudad Tecún Umán, Guat. C2 92
Ciudad Trujillo see Santo Domingo, Dom. Rep. E10 94
Ciudad Valles, Mex. G10 90
Ciudad Victoria, Mex. F10 90
Ciudad Vieja, Guat. C4 92
Ciutadella, Spain E15 16
Civitanova Marche, Italy F8 18
Civitavecchia, Italy G6 18
Civray, Fr. F7 14
Cizre, Tur. C7 48
C.J. Strike Reservoir, res., Id., U.S. G3 119
Čkalovsk, U.S.S.R. E26 26
Clackamas, Or., U.S. h12 144
Clackamas, co., Or., U.S. B4 144
Clacton-on-Sea, Eng., U.K. J15 8
Claflin, Ks., U.S. D5 123
Claiborne, Al., U.S. D2 108
Claiborne, co., La., U.S. B2 125
Claiborne, co., Ms., U.S. D3 131
Claiborne, co., Tn., U.S. C10 149
Claiborne, Lake, res., La., U.S. B3 125
Clair, N.B., Can. B1 101
Claire, Lake, l., Alta., Can. f8 98
Claire City, S.D., U.S. B8 148
Clair Engle Lake, res., Ca., U.S. B2 112
Clairfield, Tn., U.S. C10 149
Clairmont, Alta., Can. B1 98
Clairton, Pa., U.S. F2 145
Clairvaux-les-Lacs, Fr. F12 14
Clallam, co., Wa., U.S. B1 154
Clallam Bay, Wa., U.S. A1 154
Clam Lake, l., Wi., U.S. C1 156
Clan Alpine Mountains, mts., Nv., U.S. D4 135
Clancy, Mt., U.S. D5 133
Clandeboye, Ont., Can. D3 103
Clandonald, Alta., Can. C5 98
Clanton, Al., U.S. C3 108
Clanwilliam, Man., Can. D2 100
Clanwilliam, S. Afr. I4 66
Clapperton Island, i., Ont., Can. A2 103
Clara, Arg. F9 80
Clara, Ms., U.S. D5 131
Clara, stm., Austl. B4 70
Clara City, Mn., U.S. F3 130
Clara Peak, mtn., Az., U.S. C2 110
Claraz, Arg. I9 80
Clare, Austl. I3 70
Clare, Mi., U.S. E6 129
Clare, co., Ire. I4 8
Clare, co., Mi., U.S. E6 129
Claremont, Ca., U.S. m13 112
Claremont, Il., U.S. E6 120
Claremont, Mn., U.S. F6 130
Claremont, N.H., U.S. D2 136
Claremont, N.C., U.S. B1 140
Claremont, S.D., U.S. B7 148
Claremont, Va., U.S. C6 153
Claremont, mtn., Ca., U.S. C3 112
Claremore, Ok., U.S. A6 143
Clarence, Ia., U.S. C6 122
Clarence, La., U.S. C2 125
Clarence, Mo., U.S. B5 132
Clarence, Pa., U.S. D6 145
Clarence, stm., Austl. G10 70
Clarence Island, i., B.A.T. B1 73
Clarence Strait, strt., Austl. B6 68
Clarence Strait, strt., Ak., U.S. n23 109
Clarence Town, Bah. C7 94
Clarendon, Ar., U.S. C4 111
Clarendon, Pa., U.S. C3 145
Clarendon, Tx., U.S. B2 150
Clarendon, Vt., U.S. D3 152
Clarendon, co., S.C., U.S. D7 147
Clarendon, stm., Vt., U.S. E2 152
Clarendon Hills, Il., U.S. k9 120
Clarendon Springs, Vt., U.S. D2 152
Clarenville, Newf., Can. D4 102
Claresholm, Alta., Can. D4 98
Claridge, Pa., U.S. F2 145
Clarie Coast, Ant. B7 73
Clarinda, Ia., U.S. D2 122
Clarines, Ven. C10 84
Clarion, Ia., U.S. B4 122
Clarion, Pa., U.S. D3 145
Clarion, co., Pa., U.S. D3 145
Clarion, stm., Pa., U.S. D3 145
Clarión, Isla, i., Mex. H2 90
Clarissa, Mn., U.S. D4 130
Clark, Co., U.S. A4 113
Clark, Mo., U.S. B5 132
Clark, N.J., U.S. B4 137
Clark, S.D., U.S. C8 148
Clark, co., Ar., U.S. C2 111
Clark, co., Id., U.S. E6 119
Clark, co., Il., U.S. D6 120
Clark, co., In., U.S. H6 121
Clark, co., Ks., U.S. E4 123
Clark, co., Ky., U.S. C5 124
Clark, co., Mo., U.S. A6 132
Clark, co., Nv., U.S. G6 135
Clark, co., Oh., U.S. C2 142
Clark, co., S.D., U.S. C8 148
Clark, co., Wa., U.S. D3 154
Clark, co., Wi., U.S. D3 156
Clark, Lake, l., Ak., U.S. C9 109
Clark, Point, c., Ont., Can. C3 103
Clark Colony, S.D., U.S. *C8 148
Clarkdale, Az., U.S. C3 110
Clarkdale, Ga., U.S. h7 117
Clarke, co., Al., U.S. D2 108
Clarke, co., Ga., U.S. C3 117
Clarke, co., Ia., U.S. D4 122
Clarke, co., Ms., U.S. C5 131
Clarke, co., Va., U.S. A4 153
Clarke, stm., Austl. B6 70
Clarke Island, i., Austl. M8 70
Clarke Lake, l., Sask., Can. C2 105
Clarke Range, mts., Austl. C8 70
Clarkesville, Ga., U.S. B3 117
Clarkfield, Mn., U.S. F3 130
Clark Fork, Id., U.S. A2 119
Clark Fork, stm., U.S. C1 133
Clarkia, Id., U.S. B2 119
Clark Mountain, mtn., Mo., U.S. D7 132
Clarkrange, Tn., U.S. C8 149
Clarks, La., U.S. B3 125
Clarks, Ne., U.S. C8 134
Clarks, stm., Ky., U.S. f9 124
Clarks, West Fork, stm., Ky., U.S. f9 124
Clarksburg, Ont., Can. C4 103
Clarksburg, In., U.S. F7 121
Clarksburg, Md., U.S. B3 127
Clarksburg, Mo., U.S. C5 132
Clarksburg, Oh., U.S. C2 142
Clarksburg, Tn., U.S. B3 149
Clarksburg, W.V., U.S. B4 155
Clarksdale, Ms., U.S. A3 131
Clarksdale, Mo., U.S. B3 132
Clarks Grove, Mn., U.S. G5 130
Clark's Harbour, N.S., Can. F4 101
Clarks Hill, In., U.S. D4 121
Clarks Hill Lake, res., U.S. E10 106
Clarkson, Ky., U.S. C3 124
Clarkson, Ne., U.S. C8 134
Clarks Summit, Pa., U.S. m18 145
Clarkston, Ga., U.S. h8 117
Clarkston, Mi., U.S. F7 129
Clarkston, Ut., U.S. B3 151
Clarkston, Wa., U.S. C8 154
Clarksville, N.S., Can. D6 101
Clarksville, Ar., U.S. B2 111
Clarksville, De., U.S. F5 115
Clarksville, In., U.S. H6 121
Clarksville, Ia., U.S. B5 122
Clarksville, Md., U.S. B4 127
Clarksville, Mi., U.S. F5 129
Clarksville, Mo., U.S. B7 132
Clarksville, Tn., U.S. A4 149
Clarksville, Tx., U.S. C5 150
Clarksville, Va., U.S. D4 153
Clarkton, Mo., U.S. E8 132
Clarkton, N.C., U.S. C4 140
Claro, stm., Braz. C3 79
Claro, stm., Braz. E5 79
Claro, stm., Braz. E3 79
Clatonia, Ne., U.S. D9 134
Clatskanie, Or., U.S. A3 144
Clatsop, co., Or., U.S. A3 144
Claude, Tx., U.S. B2 150
Clavet, Sask., Can. F2 105
Clawson, Mi., U.S. o15 129
Claxton, Ga., U.S. D5 117
Clay, Al., U.S. f7 108
Clay, Ky., U.S. C2 124
Clay, W.V., U.S. C3 155
Clay, co., Al., U.S. B4 108
Clay, co., Ar., U.S. A5 111
Clay, co., Fl., U.S. B5 116
Clay, co., Ga., U.S. E2 117
Clay, co., Il., U.S. E5 120
Clay, co., In., U.S. F3 121
Clay, co., Ia., U.S. A2 122
Clay, co., Ks., U.S. C6 123
Clay, co., Ky., U.S. C6 124
Clay, co., Mn., U.S. D2 130
Clay, co., Ms., U.S. B5 131
Clay, co., Mo., U.S. B3 132
Clay, co., Ne., U.S. D7 134
Clay, co., N.C., U.S. f9 140
Clay, co., S.D., U.S. E8 148
Clay, co., Tn., U.S. C8 149
Clay, co., Tx., U.S. C3 150
Clay, co., W.V., U.S. C3 155
Clay Center, Ks., U.S. C6 123
Clay Center, Ne., U.S. D7 134
Clay City, Il., U.S. E5 120
Clay City, In., U.S. F3 121
Clay City, Ky., U.S. C6 124
Clay Creek, stm., Co., U.S. D8 113
Clay Creek, stm., S.D., U.S. D8 148
Clayhatchee, Al., U.S. D4 108
Claymont, De., U.S. A4 115
Clayoquot Sound, strt., B.C., Can. E4 99
Claypool, Az., U.S. D5 110
Claypool, In., U.S. B6 121
Claysburg, Pa., U.S. F5 145
Clay Springs, Az., U.S. C5 110
Claysville, Pa., U.S. F1 145
Clayton, Ont., Can. B8 103
Clayton, Al., U.S. D4 108
Clayton, Ca., U.S. h9 112
Clayton, De., U.S. C3 115
Clayton, Ga., U.S. B3 117
Clayton, Il., U.S. C3 120
Clayton, In., U.S. E4 121
Clayton, La., U.S. C4 125
Clayton, Mo., U.S. f13 132
Clayton, N.J., U.S. D2 137
Clayton, N.M., U.S. A6 138
Clayton, N.Y., U.S. A4 139
Clayton, N.C., U.S. B4 140
Clayton, Ok., U.S. C6 143
Clayton, Wa., U.S. B8 154
Clayton, Wi., U.S. C1 156
Clayton, co., Ga., U.S. C2 117
Clayton, co., Ia., U.S. B6 122
Clayton, stm., Austl. G3 70
Claytor Lake, res., Va., U.S. C2 153
Clear, stm., Alta., Can. A1 98
Clear, stm., R.I., U.S. B2 146
Clear Boggy Creek, stm., Ok., U.S. C5 143
Clearbrook, Mn., U.S. C3 130
Clear Creek, In., U.S. F4 121
Clear Creek, W.V., U.S. n13 155
Clear Creek, co., Co., U.S. B5 113
Clear Creek, stm., Az., U.S. C4 110
Clear Creek, stm., Ne., U.S. C6 134
Clear Creek, stm., Tn., U.S. C9 149
Clear Creek, stm., Wy., U.S. B6 157
Cleare, Cape, c., Ak., U.S. D10 109
Clearfield, Ia., U.S. D3 122
Clearfield, Ky., U.S. B6 124
Clearfield, Pa., U.S. D5 145
Clearfield, Ut., U.S. B3 151
Clearfield, co., Pa., U.S. D5 145
Clear Fork, W.V., U.S. D3 155
Clear Fork, stm., W.V., U.S. D3 155
Clear Fork, stm., W.V., U.S. n13 155
Clearlake, Ca., U.S. C2 112
Clear Lake, Ia., U.S. A4 122
Clear Lake, Mn., U.S. E5 130
Clear Lake, S.D., U.S. C9 148
Clearlake, Wa., U.S. A3 154
Clear Lake, Wi., U.S. C1 156
Clear Lake, l., Ia., U.S. A4 122
Clear Lake, l., Ut., U.S. D3 151
Clear Lake, res., Ca., U.S. C2 112
Clear Lake Reservoir, res., Ca., U.S. B3 112
Clear Lake Shores, Tx., U.S. r15 150
Clearmont, Mo., U.S. A2 132
Clearmont, Wy., U.S. B6 157
Clear Spring, Md., U.S. A2 127
Clear Stream, stm., N.H., U.S. g7 136
Clearview City, Ks., U.S. g12 123
Clearwater, B.C., Can. D7 99
Clearwater, Man., Can. E2 100
Clearwater, Fl., U.S. E4 116
Clearwater, Ks., U.S. E6 123
Clearwater, Mn., U.S. E4 130
Clearwater, Ne., U.S. B7 134
Clearwater, S.C., U.S. E4 147
Clearwater, Wa., U.S. B1 154
Clearwater, co., Id., U.S. C3 119
Clearwater, co., Mn., U.S. C3 130
Clearwater, stm., Can. A5 98
Clearwater, stm., Alta., Can. D3 98
Clearwater, stm., Id., U.S. C2 119
Clearwater, stm., Mn., U.S. C3 130
Clearwater Lake, Wi., U.S. C4 156
Clearwater Lake, res., Mo., U.S. D7 132
Clearwater Mountains, mts., Id., U.S. C2 119
Cleaton, Ky., U.S. C2 124
Cleburne, Tx., U.S. C4 150
Cleburne, co., Al., U.S. B4 108
Cleburne, co., Ar., U.S. B3 111
Cle Elum, Wa., U.S. B5 154
Cle Elum, stm., Wa., U.S. B4 154
Cle Elum Lake, res., Wa., U.S. B4 154
Clefmont, Fr. D12 14
Cleghorn, Ia., U.S. B2 122
Clem, Ga., U.S. C1 117
Clementon, N.J., U.S. D3 137
Clements, Mn., U.S. F3 130
Clementsport, N.S., Can. E4 101
Clementsvale, N.S., Can. E4 101
Clemmons, N.C., U.S. A2 140
Clemson, S.C., U.S. B2 147
Clendenin, W.V., U.S. C3 155
Clendening Lake, res., Oh., U.S. B4 142
Cleona, Pa., U.S. F9 145
Cleo Springs, Ok., U.S. A3 143
Clermont, Austl. D7 70
Clermont, Que., Can. B7 104
Clermont, Fr. C9 14
Clermont, Fl., U.S. D5 116
Clermont, Ga., U.S. B3 117
Clermont, Ia., U.S. A6 122
Clermont, Ky., U.S. C4 124
Clermont, co., Oh., U.S. C1 142
Clermont-en-Argonne, Fr. C12 14
Clermont-Ferrand, Fr. G10 14
Clermont Harbor, Ms., U.S. E4 131
Cles, Italy C6 18
Cleveland, Al., U.S. A3 108
Cleveland, Ga., U.S. B3 117
Cleveland, Il., U.S. B3 120
Cleveland, Mn., U.S. F5 130
Cleveland, Ms., U.S. B3 131
Cleveland, Mo., U.S. C3 132
Cleveland, N.M., U.S. A4 138
Cleveland, N.C., U.S. B2 140
Cleveland, N.D., U.S. C6 141
Cleveland, Oh., U.S. A4 142
Cleveland, Ok., U.S. A5 143
Cleveland, Tn., U.S. D9 149
Cleveland, Tx., U.S. D5 150
Cleveland, Ut., U.S. D5 151
Cleveland, Va., U.S. f9 153
Cleveland, Wi., U.S. k10 156
Cleveland, co., Ar., U.S. D3 111
Cleveland, co., N.C., U.S. B1 140
Cleveland, co., Ok., U.S. B4 143
Cleveland, Cape, c., Austl. B7 70
Cleveland, Mount, mtn., Mt., U.S. B3 133
Cleveland Heights, Oh., U.S. A4 142
Clevelândia, Braz. D12 80
Clever, Mo., U.S. D4 132
Cleves, Oh., U.S. o12 142
Clew Bay, b., Ire. H4 8
Clewiston, Fl., U.S. F6 116
Cliff, N.M., U.S. E1 138
Cliff Island, i., Me., U.S. g7 126
Clifford, Ont., Can. D4 103
Clifford, In., U.S. F6 121
Clifford, Mi., U.S. E7 129
Cliffside, N.C., U.S. B1 140
Cliffside Park, N.J., U.S. h9 137
Clifton, Az., U.S. D6 110
Clifton, Co., U.S. B2 113
Clifton, Id., U.S. G7 119
Clifton, Il., U.S. C6 120
Clifton, Ks., U.S. C6 123
Clifton, N.J., U.S. B4 137
Clifton, S.C., U.S. B4 147
Clifton, Tn., U.S. B4 149
Clifton, Tx., U.S. D4 150
Clifton Forge, Va., U.S. C3 153
Clifton Knolls, N.Y., U.S. C7 139
Clifton Springs, N.Y., U.S. C3 139
Climax, Sask., Can. H1 105
Climax, Ga., U.S. F2 117
Climax, Mi., U.S. F5 129
Climax, Mn., U.S. C2 130
Clinch, co., Ga., U.S. F4 117
Clinch, stm., U.S. D9 149
Clinchco, Va., U.S. e9 153
Clinchfield, Ga., U.S. D3 117
Clinch Mountain, mtn., U.S. C10 149
Clingmans Dome, mtn., U.S. D10 149
Clint, Tx., U.S. o11 150
Clinton, B.C., Can. D7 99
Clinton, Ont., Can. D3 103
Clinton, Al., U.S. C2 108
Clinton, Ar., U.S. B3 111
Clinton, Ct., U.S. D5 114
Clinton, Il., U.S. C5 120
Clinton, In., U.S. E3 121
Clinton, Ia., U.S. C7 122
Clinton, Ky., U.S. f9 124
Clinton, La., U.S. D4 125
Clinton, Me., U.S. D3 126
Clinton, Md., U.S. C4 127
Clinton, Ma., U.S. B4 128
Clinton, Mi., U.S. F7 129
Clinton, Mn., U.S. E2 130
Clinton, Ms., U.S. C3 131
Clinton, Mo., U.S. C4 132
Clinton, Mt., U.S. D3 133
Clinton, N.H., U.S. D3 136
Clinton, N.J., U.S. B3 137
Clinton, N.Y., U.S. B5 139
Clinton, N.C., U.S. C4 140
Clinton, Ok., U.S. B3 143
Clinton, S.C., U.S. C4 147
Clinton, Tn., U.S. C9 149
Clinton, Ut., U.S. B3 151
Clinton, Wa., U.S. B3 154
Clinton, Wi., U.S. F5 156
Clinton, co., Il., U.S. E4 120
Clinton, co., In., U.S. D4 121
Clinton, co., Ia., U.S. C7 122
Clinton, co., Ky., U.S. D4 124
Clinton, co., Mi., U.S. F6 129
Clinton, co., Mo., U.S. B3 132
Clinton, co., N.Y., U.S. f11 139
Clinton, co., Oh., U.S. C2 142
Clinton, co., Pa., U.S. D6 145
Clinton, Cape, c., Austl. D9 70
Clinton, Lake, res., Il., U.S. C5 120
Clinton Lake, res., Ks., U.S. m15 123
Clinton Reservoir, res., N.J., U.S. A4 137
Clintonville, Wi., U.S. D5 156
Clintwood, Va., U.S. e9 153
Clio, Al., U.S. D4 108
Clio, Mi., U.S. E7 129
Clio, S.C., U.S. B8 147
Clio, W.V., U.S. C3 155
Clipperton, Île, atoll, Oc. F3 88
Clisson, Fr. E5 14
Clive, Alta., Can. C4 98
Clive, Ia., U.S. e8 122
Cliza, Bol. G9 82
Clodomira, Arg. D6 80
Cloncurry, Austl. C4 70
Cloncurry, stm., Austl. B4 70
Clonmel, Ire. I6 8
Clontarf, Mn., U.S. E3 130
Cloppenburg, Ger. C8 10
Clopton, Al., U.S. D4 108
Cloquet, Mn., U.S. D6 130
Cloquet, stm., Mn., U.S. C6 130
Clorinda, Arg. C10 80
Closter, N.J., U.S. B5 137
Clothier, W.V., U.S. n12 155
Cloud, co., Ks., U.S. C6 123
Cloudcroft, N.M., U.S. E4 138
Cloud Peak, mtn., Wy., U.S. B5 157
Cloudy Mountain, mtn., Ar., U.S. C8 109
Clover, S.C., U.S. A5 147
Cloverdale, Al., U.S. A2 108
Cloverdale, Ca., U.S. C2 112
Cloverdale, In., U.S. E4 121
Cloverdale, Or., U.S. B3 144
Cloverport, Ky., U.S. C3 124
Clovis, Ca., U.S. D4 112
Clovis, N.M., U.S. C6 138
Cluj-Napoca, Rom. C7 20
Cluj-Napoca, co., Rom. C7 20
Clunes, Austl. K5 70
Cluny, Alta., Can. D4 98
Cluny, Fr. F11 14
Cluses, Fr. F13 14
Clusone, Italy D4 18
Cluster Springs, Va., U.S. D4 153
Clute, Tx., U.S. r14 150
Clutier, Ia., U.S. B5 122
Clwyd, co., Wales, U.K. H10 8
Clyattville, Ga., U.S. F3 117
Clyde, Alta., Can. B4 98
Clyde, Ks., U.S. C6 123
Clyde, N.Y., U.S. B4 139
Clyde, N.C., U.S. f10 140
Clyde, Oh., U.S. A3 142
Clyde, Tx., U.S. C3 150
Clyde, stm., Scot., U.K. F10 8
Clyde, Firth of, est., Scot., U.K. F8 8
Clyde Park, Mt., U.S. E6 133
Clyde River, N.W. Ter., Can. B19 96
Clymer, Pa., U.S. E3 145
Clyo, Ga., U.S. D5 117
Cna, stm., U.S.S.R. G25 26
Coachella, Ca., U.S. F5 112
Coachella Canal, Ca., U.S. F6 112
Coacoyole, Mex. E6 90
Coahoma, Ms., U.S. A3 131
Coahoma, Tx., U.S. C2 150
Coahoma, co., Ms., U.S. A3 131
Coahuila, state, Mex. C8 90
Coal, co., Ok., U.S. C5 143
Coal, stm., W.V., U.S. C3 155
Coal Branch, N.B., Can. C4 101
Coal City, Il., U.S. B5 120
Coal City, In., U.S. F3 121
Coalcomán de Matamoros, Mex. H8 90
Coal Creek, Co., U.S. C5 113
Coal Creek, stm., In., U.S. E3 121
Coal Creek, stm., Ok., U.S. B6 143
Coaldale, Alta., Can. E4 98
Coaldale, Co., U.S. C5 113
Coalfield, Tn., U.S. C9 149
Coal Fork, W.V., U.S. C3 155
Coal Fork, stm., W.V., U.S. m13 155
Coalgate, Ok., U.S. C5 143
Coalgood, Ky., U.S. D6 124
Coal Grove, Oh., U.S. D3 142
Coal Harbour, B.C., Can. D4 99
Coal Hill, Ar., U.S. B2 111
Coalhurst, Alta., Can. E4 98
Coaling, Al., U.S. B2 108
Coalinga, Ca., U.S. D3 112
Coalmont, B.C., Can. E7 99
Coalmont, In., U.S. F3 121
Coalmont, Tn., U.S. D8 149
Coalton, Il., U.S. D4 120
Coalton, Oh., U.S. C3 142
Coalville, Ia., U.S. B3 122
Coalville, Ut., U.S. C4 151
Coalwood, W.V., U.S. D3 155
Coamo, P.R. E11 94
Coaraci, Braz. C9 79
Coari, Braz. J11 84
Coari, stm., Braz. J11 84
Coari, Lago de, l., Braz. J11 84
Coasters Harbor Island, i., R.I., U.S. E5 146
Coast Mountains, mts., N.A. E6 96
Coast Ranges, mts., U.S. C2 106
Coatán, stm., N.A. C2 92
Coatbridge, Scot., U.K. F9 8
Coatepeque, Guat. C3 92
Coatepeque, Lago de, l., El Sal. D5 92
Coatesville, In., U.S. E4 121
Coatesville, Pa., U.S. G10 145
Coaticook, Que., Can. D6 104
Coatney Hill, mtn., Ct., U.S. B7 114
Coats, Ks., U.S. E5 123
Coats, N.C., U.S. B4 140
Coatsburg, Il., U.S. C2 120

Name — Map Ref. — Page

Coats Island, i., N.W. Ter., Can. D16 96
Coats Land, reg., Ant. C2 73
Coatzacoalcos, Mex. H12 90
Coayllo, Peru E3 82
Cobá, hist., Mex. G16 90
Cobadin, Rom. E12 20
Coballo Cocha, Peru I7 84
Cobalt, Ont., Can. p19 103
Cobalt, Ct., U.S. C5 114
Cobalt, Id., U.S. D4 119
Cobán, Guat. B4 92
Cobar, Austl. H6 70
Cobb, Ga., U.S. E3 117
Cobb, Wi., U.S. F3 156
Cobb, co., Ga., U.S. C2 117
Cobb, stm., Mn., U.S. G5 130
Cobberas, Mount, mtn., Austl. K8 70
Cobb Island, Md., U.S. D4 127
Cobble Hill, B.C., Can. g12 99
Cobble Mountain Reservoir, res., Ma., U.S. B2 128
Cobbosseecontee Lake, l., Me., U.S. D3 126
Cobbtown, Ga., U.S. D4 117
Cobden, Ont., Can. B8 103
Cobden, Il., U.S. F4 120
Cobequid Mountains, mts., N.S., Can. D5 101
Cobh, Ire. J5 8
Cobham, stm., Can. C4 100
Cobija, Bol. D7 82
Cobija, Chile B3 80
Cobleskill, N.Y., U.S. C6 139
Coboconk, Ont., Can. C6 103
Cobourg, Ont., Can. D6 103
Cobourg Peninsula, pen., Austl. B6 68
Cobquecura, Chile I2 80
Cobram, Austl. J6 70
Cobre, stm., Pan. I13 92
Cobre, Barranca del, val., Mex. D6 90
Cóbuè, Moz. D6 58
Cobun Creek, stm., W.V., U.S. h11 155
Coburg, Ger. E10 10
Coburg, Or., U.S. C3 144
Coburn Mountain, mtn., Me., U.S. C2 126
Coca, stm., Ec. H4 84
Cocachacra, Peru G6 82
Cocentaina, Spain G11 16
Cochabamba, Bol. G8 82
Cochabamba, dept., Bol. G9 82
Cochagual, Arg. F4 80
Coche, Isla, i., Ven. B11 84
Cocheco, stm., N.H., U.S. D5 136
Cochetopa Creek, stm., Co., U.S. C4 113
Cochetopa Hills, mts., Co., U.S. C4 113
Cochin, India H10 42
Cochinos, Cayos, is., Hond. B8 92
Cochise, Az., U.S. E6 110
Cochise, co., Az., U.S. F5 110
Cochise Head, mtn., Az., U.S. E6 110
Cochiti, N.M., U.S. h8 138
Cochiti Indian Reservation, N.M., U.S. h8 138
Cochiti Reservoir, res., N.M., U.S. B3 138
Cochituate, Ma., U.S. g10 128
Cochituate, Lake, l., Ma., U.S. g10 128
Cochran, Ga., U.S. D3 117
Cochran, co., Tx., U.S. C1 150
Cochrane, Alta., Can. D3 98
Cochrane, Ont., Can. o19 103
Cochrane, Wi., U.S. D2 156
Cochrane, stm., Can. E12 96
Cochrane, Lago (Lago Pueyrredón), l., S.A. F2 78
Cochranton, Pa., U.S. C1 145
Cocke, co., Tn., U.S. D10 149
Cockeysville, Md., U.S. B4 127
Cockrell Hill, Tx., U.S. n10 150
Coclé, prov., Pan. I14 92
Coclé del Norte, stm., Pan. I14 92
Coco, stm., N.A. G3 94
Coco, Cayo, i., Cuba C5 94
Coco, Isla del, i., C.R. G7 88
Cocoa, Fl., U.S. D6 116
Cocoa Beach, Fl., U.S. D6 116
Coco Channel, strt., Asia C1 38
Coco Islands, is., Burma G2 40
Coconino, co., Az., U.S. B3 110
Coconino Plateau, plat., Az., U.S. B3 110
Cocopah Indian Reservation, Az., U.S. E1 110
Cocorocuma, Cayos, rf., Hond. B11 92
Côcos, Braz. C6 79
Cocos (Keeling) Islands, dep., Oc. K10 28
Cocuiza, stm., Ven. B7 84
Cocula, Mex. G8 90
Cod, Cape, c., Ma., U.S. C7 128
Codăeşti, Rom. C11 20
Codajás, Braz. I11 84
Coden, Al., U.S. E1 108
Codera, Cabo, c., Ven. B10 84
Coderre, Sask., Can. G2 105
Codette, Sask., Can. D3 105
Codington, co., S.D., U.S. C8 148
Cod Island, i., Newf., Can. g9 102
Codó, Braz. D10 76
Codogno, Italy D4 18
Codpa, Chile H7 82
Codroy, Newf., Can. E2 102
Cody, Ne., U.S. B4 134
Cody, Wy., U.S. B3 157
Codys, N.B., Can. D4 101
Coeburn, Va., U.S. f9 153
Coe Hill, Ont., Can. C7 103
Coelemu, Chile I2 80
Coen, Austl. B8 68
Coén, stm., C.R. H11 92
Coeroeni, stm., S.A. F14 84
Coetivy Island, i., Sey. C11 58
Coeur d'Alene, Id., U.S. B2 119
Coeur d'Alene, stm., Id., U.S. B2 119
Coeur d'Alene Indian Reservation, Id., U.S. B2 119
Coeur d'Alene Lake, res., Id., U.S. B2 119
Coeur d'Alene Mountains, mts., Id., U.S. B2 119
Coevorden, Neth. C10 12
Coffee, co., Al., U.S. D3 108
Coffee, co., Ga., U.S. E4 117
Coffee, co., Tn., U.S. B5 149
Coffeen, Il., U.S. D4 120
Coffee Springs, Al., U.S. D4 108
Coffeeville, Al., U.S. D1 108
Coffeeville, Ms., U.S. B4 131
Coffey, co., Ks., U.S. D8 123
Coffeyville, Ks., U.S. E8 123
Coffin, Île, i., Que., Can. B8 101
Coffin Bay, b., Austl. F7 68
Coffs Harbour, Austl. H10 70
Cofield, N.C., U.S. A6 140
Cofradía, Hond. B6 92
Cofre de Perote, Cerro, mtn., Mex. H11 90
Cofre de Perote, Parque Nacional, Mex. H11 90
Cogdell, Ga., U.S. E4 117
Coggon, Ia., U.S. B6 122
Cognac, Fr. G6 14
Cogolin, Fr. I13 14
Cogoon, stm., Austl. F8 70
Cogswell, N.D., U.S. C8 141
Cohansey, stm., N.J., U.S. E2 137
Cohasset, Ma., U.S. B6 128
Cohasset, Mn., U.S. C5 130
Cohenga, stm., Peru D5 82
Cohocton, N.Y., U.S. C3 139
Cohocton, stm., N.Y., U.S. C3 139
Cohoe, Ak., U.S. g16 109
Cohoes, N.Y., U.S. C7 139
Cohoni, Bol. G8 82
Cohoon, Lake, res., Va., U.S. k14 153
Cohuna, Austl. J6 70
Cohutta, Ga., U.S. B2 117
Cohutta Mountain, mtn., Ga., U.S. B2 117
Coiba, Isla de, i., Pan. D2 84
Coig, stm., Arg. G2 78
Coihaique, Chile F2 78
Coils Creek, stm., Nv., U.S. D5 135
Coimbatore, India G4 46
Coimbra, Braz. F7 79
Coimbra, Braz. H13 82
Coimbra, Port. E3 16
Coín, Spain I7 16
Coin, Ia., U.S. D2 122
Coinjock, N.C., U.S. A7 140
Coipasa, Lago, l., Bol. H7 82
Coipasa, Salar de, pl., S.A. H7 82
Čojbalsan, Mong. B9 30
Cojedes, Ven. C8 84
Cojedes, state, Ven. C8 84
Cojutepeque, El Sal. D6 92
Cokato, Mn., U.S. E4 130
Coke, co., Tx., U.S. D2 150
Coker, Al., U.S. B2 108
Cokeville, Wy., U.S. D2 157
Colac, Austl. L5 70
Colalao del Valle, Arg. D6 80
Colatina, Braz. E8 79
Colbeck, Cape, c., Ant. C9 73
Colbert, Ga., U.S. B3 117
Colbert, Ok., U.S. D5 143
Colbert, co., Al., U.S. A2 108
Colbert Heights, Al., U.S. A2 108
Colborne, Ont., Can. C7 103
Colbún, Chile H3 80
Colburn, In., U.S. C4 121
Colby, Ks., U.S. C2 123
Colby, Wi., U.S. D3 156
Colca, Peru E4 82
Colca, stm., Peru F5 82
Colcamar, Peru B3 82
Colcapirhua, Bol. G8 82
Colchester, Eng., U.K. J14 8
Colchester, Ct., U.S. C6 114
Colchester, Il., U.S. C3 120
Colchester, Vt., U.S. B2 152
Colcord, Ok., U.S. A7 143
Cold, stm., N.H., U.S. C4 136
Cold, stm., N.H., U.S. D2 136
Cold Bay, Ak., U.S. E7 109
Cold Hollow Mountains, mts., Vt., U.S. B3 152
Cold Lake, Alta., Can. B5 98
Cold Spring, Ky., U.S. A5 124
Cold Spring, Mn., U.S. E4 130
Coldspring, Tx., U.S. D5 150
Coldstream, Scot., U.K. F11 8
Cold Stream Pond, l., Me., U.S. C4 126
Coldwater, Ont., Can. C5 103
Coldwater, Ks., U.S. E4 123
Coldwater, Mi., U.S. G5 129
Coldwater, Ms., U.S. A4 131
Coldwater, Oh., U.S. B1 142
Coldwater, stm., Ms., U.S. A3 131
Coldwater Creek, stm., U.S. e9 143
Cole, Ok., U.S. B4 143
Cole, co., Mo., U.S. C5 132
Colebrook, Ct., U.S. B3 114
Colebrook, N.H., U.S. g7 136
Colebrook River Lake, res., Ct., U.S. A3 114
Cole Camp, Mo., U.S. C4 132
Coleen, stm., Ak., U.S. B11 109
Coleharbor, N.D., U.S. B4 141
Coleman, P.E.I., Can. C5 101
Coleman, Fl., U.S. D4 116
Coleman, Ga., U.S. E2 117
Coleman, Mi., U.S. E6 129
Coleman, Tx., U.S. D3 150
Coleman, Wi., U.S. C5 156
Coleman, co., Tx., U.S. D3 150
Coleman, stm., Austl. B8 68
Colenso, S. Afr. G9 66
Coleraine, Austl. K4 70
Coleraine, Mn., U.S. C5 130
Coleridge, Ne., U.S. B8 134
Coles, co., Il., U.S. D5 120
Coles, Punta, c., Peru G6 82
Colesberg, S. Afr. H7 66
Colesburg, Ia., U.S. B6 122
Colesburg, Ky., U.S. C4 124
Coleville, Sask., Can. F1 105
Colfax, Ca., U.S. C3 112
Colfax, Il., U.S. C5 120
Colfax, In., U.S. D4 121
Colfax, Ia., U.S. C4 122
Colfax, La., U.S. C3 125
Colfax, N.D., U.S. C9 141
Colfax, Wa., U.S. C8 154
Colfax, Wi., U.S. D2 156
Colfax, co., Ne., U.S. C8 134
Colfax, co., N.M., U.S. A5 138
Colhué Huapi, Lago, l., Arg. F3 78
Colico, Italy C4 18
Colima, Mex. H8 90
Colima, state, Mex. H8 90
Colima, Nevado de, mtn., Mex. H8 90
Colimes, stm., Ec. H2 84
Colina, Chile G3 80
Colinas, Braz. E10 76
Colinas, Braz. C4 79
Colinet, Newf., Can. E5 102
Colinton, Alta., Can. B4 98
Collarenebri, Austl. G8 70
Collbran, Co., U.S. B3 113
College, Ak., U.S. B10 109
Collegedale, Tn., U.S. h11 149
College Grove, Tn., U.S. B5 149
College Park, Ga., U.S. C2 117
College Park, Md., U.S. C4 127
College Place, Wa., U.S. C7 154
College Springs, Ia., U.S. D2 122
College Station, Ar., U.S. C3 111
College Station, Tx., U.S. D4 150
Collegeville, In., U.S. C3 121
Collegeville, Pa., U.S. F11 145
Collerina, Austl. G7 70
Colleton, co., S.C., U.S. F6 147
Collie, Austl. F3 68
Collier, co., Fl., U.S. F5 116
Collier Bay, b., Austl. C4 68
Collier Range National Park, Austl. D3 68
Colliers, W.V., U.S. f8 155
Collierville, Tn., U.S. B2 149
Collin, co., Tx., U.S. C4 150
Collingdale, Pa., U.S. p20 145
Collingswood, N.J., U.S. D2 137
Collingsworth, co., Tx., U.S. B2 150
Collingwood, Ont., Can. C4 103
Collins, Ga., U.S. D4 117
Collins, Ia., U.S. C4 122
Collins, Ms., U.S. D4 131
Collins Park, De., U.S. B3 115
Collinston, La., U.S. B4 125
Collinsville, Austl. C7 70
Collinsville, Al., U.S. A4 108
Collinsville, Ct., U.S. B4 114
Collinsville, Il., U.S. E4 120
Collinsville, Ms., U.S. C5 131
Collinsville, Ok., U.S. A6 143
Collinsville, Va., U.S. D3 153
Collinwood, Tn., U.S. B4 149
Collipulli, Chile I2 80
Collyer, Ks., U.S. C3 123
Colman, S.D., U.S. D9 148
Colmar, Fr. D14 14
Colmar Manor, Md., U.S. f9 127
Colmenar de Oreja, Spain E8 16
Colmenar Viejo, Spain E8 16
Colmeneros, Mex. H9 90
Colmesneil, Tx., U.S. D5 150
Colnett, Cabo, c., Mex. B1 90
Colo, Ia., U.S. B4 122
Cologne, Mn., U.S. F5 130
Cologne, N.J., U.S. D3 137
Cologne see Köln, Ger. E6 10
Cololo, Nevado, mtn., Bol. F7 82
Coloma, Mi., U.S. F4 129
Coloma, Wi., U.S. D4 156
Colombey-les-Belles, Fr. D12 14
Colômbia, Braz. F4 79
Colombia, Col. F5 84
Colombia, ctry., S.A. C4 76
Colombo, Braz. C14 80
Colombo, Sri L. I5 46
Colome, S.D., U.S. D6 148
Colón, Arg. G8 80
Colón, Arg. G9 80
Colón, Cuba C4 94
Colón, Pan. C3 84
Colon, Mi., U.S. G5 129
Colon, Ne., U.S. g11 134
Colón, Ur. G11 80
Colón, prov., Pan. I14 92
Colón, dept., Hond. B9 92
Colón, Archipiélago de (Galapagos Islands), is., Ec. J13 84a
Colón, Isla, i., Pan. H12 92
Colón, Montañas de, mts., Hond. C10 92
Colônia, stm., Braz. C9 79
Colonia Agrícola de Turén, Ven. C8 84
Colonia Alvear, Arg. H5 80
Colonia Caroya, Arg. F6 80
Colonia del Sacramento, Ur. H10 80
Colonia Dora, Arg. E7 80
Colonia Elisa, Arg. D9 80
Colonia José Mármol, Arg. D8 80
Colonia Lavalleja, Ur. F10 80
Colonial Beach, Va., U.S. B6 153
Colonial Heights, Tn., U.S. C11 149
Colonial Heights, Va., U.S. C5 153
Colonial National Historical Park, Va., U.S. C6 153
Colonias Unidas, Arg. D9 80
Colonia Vicente Guerrero, Mex. B1 90
Colonia Villafañe, Arg. D9 80
Colonie, N.Y., U.S. C7 139
Colonsay, Sask., Can. F3 105
Colony, Al., U.S. B3 108
Colony, Ks., U.S. D8 123
Colorado, C.R. G11 92
Colorado, Hond. B7 92
Colorado, co., Tx., U.S. E4 150
Colorado, state, U.S. B5 113
Colorado, stm., Arg. J7 80
Colorado, stm., Braz. E10 82
Colorado, stm., N.A. E4 106
Colorado, stm., Tx., U.S. D3 150
Colorado City, Az., U.S. A3 110
Colorado City, Co., U.S. D6 113
Colorado City, Tx., U.S. C2 150
Colorado City, Lake, res., Tx., U.S. C2 150
Colorado National Monument, Co., U.S. B2 113
Colorado Plateau, plat., U.S. B4 110
Colorado River Aqueduct, Ca., U.S. F6 112
Colorado River Indian Reservation, U.S. D1 110
Colorado Springs, Co., U.S. C6 113
Colotepec, stm., Mex. J11 90
Colotlán, Mex. F8 90
Colquechaca, Bol. H8 82
Colquencha, Bol. G7 82
Colquiri, Bol. G8 82
Colquitt, Ga., U.S. E2 117
Colquitt, co., Ga., U.S. E3 117
Colstrip, Mt., U.S. E10 133
Colt, Ar., U.S. B5 111
Colta, Peru F5 82
Coltauco, Chile H3 80
Colton, Or., U.S. B4 144
Colton, S.D., U.S. D9 148
Colton, Wa., U.S. C8 154
Colton Hill, mtn., Vt., U.S. D4 152
Coltons Point, Md., U.S. D4 127
Columbia, Al., U.S. D4 108
Columbia, Ca., U.S. C3 112
Columbia, Ct., U.S. C6 114
Columbia, Il., U.S. E3 120
Columbia, Ky., U.S. C4 124
Columbia, La., U.S. B3 125
Columbia, Md., U.S. B4 127
Columbia, Ms., U.S. D4 131
Columbia, Mo., U.S. C5 132
Columbia, N.C., U.S. B6 140
Columbia, Pa., U.S. F9 145
Columbia, S.C., U.S. C5 147
Columbia, S.D., U.S. B7 148
Columbia, Tn., U.S. B4 149
Columbia, co., Ar., U.S. D2 111
Columbia, co., Fl., U.S. B4 116
Columbia, co., Ga., U.S. C4 117
Columbia, co., N.Y., U.S. C7 139
Columbia, co., Or., U.S. B3 144
Columbia, co., Pa., U.S. D9 145
Columbia, co., Wa., U.S. C7 154
Columbia, co., Wi., U.S. E4 156
Columbia, stm., N.A. B2 106
Columbia, Cape, c., N.W. Ter., Can. A12 86
Columbia, Mount, mtn., Can. C2 98
Columbia Basin, Wa., U.S. C6 154
Columbia City, In., U.S. B7 121
Columbia City, Or., U.S. B4 144
Columbia Falls, Me., U.S. D5 126
Columbia Falls, Mt., U.S. B2 133
Columbia Heights, Mn., U.S. m12 130
Columbia Lake, res., Ct., U.S. C6 114
Columbia Mountains, mts., B.C., Can. C7 99
Columbiana, Al., U.S. B3 108
Columbiana, Oh., U.S. B5 142
Columbiana, co., Oh., U.S. B5 142
Columbiaville, Mi., U.S. E7 129
Columbus, Ar., U.S. D2 111
Columbus, Ga., U.S. D2 117
Columbus, In., U.S. F6 121
Columbus, Ks., U.S. E9 123
Columbus, Ky., U.S. f8 124
Columbus, Ms., U.S. B5 131
Columbus, Mt., U.S. E7 133
Columbus, Ne., U.S. C8 134
Columbus, N.M., U.S. F2 138
Columbus, N.C., U.S. f10 140
Columbus, N.D., U.S. A3 141
Columbus, Oh., U.S. C2 142
Columbus, Pa., U.S. C2 145
Columbus, Tx., U.S. E4 150
Columbus, Wi., U.S. E4 156
Columbus, co., N.C., U.S. C4 140
Columbus Air Force Base, mil., Ms., U.S. B5 131
Columbus City, Ia., U.S. C6 122
Columbus Grove, Oh., U.S. B1 142
Columbus Junction, Ia., U.S. C6 122
Columbus Lake, res., Ms., U.S. B5 131
Columbus Point, c., Bah. B7 94
Coluna, Braz. E7 79
Colusa, Ca., U.S. C2 112
Colusa, co., Ca., U.S. C2 112
Colver, Pa., U.S. E4 145
Colville, Wa., U.S. A8 154
Colville, stm., Ak., U.S. B9 109
Colville, stm., Wa., U.S. A8 154
Colville Indian Reservation, Wa., U.S. A6 154
Colvin Mountain, mtn., Al., U.S. B4 108
Colvos Passage, strt., Wa., U.S. f10 154
Colwich, Ks., U.S. E6 123
Colwood, B.C., Can. h12 99
Colyell Creek, stm., La., U.S. h10 125
Comacchio, Italy E7 18
Comal, co., Tx., U.S. E3 150
Comala, Mex. H8 90
Comalapa, Guat. C4 92
Comalapa, Nic. E9 92
Comalcalco, Mex. H13 90
Coman, Mount, mtn., Ant. C12 73
Comanche, Ok., U.S. C4 143
Comanche, Tx., U.S. D3 150
Comanche, co., Ks., U.S. E4 123
Comanche, co., Ok., U.S. C3 143
Comanche, co., Tx., U.S. D3 150
Comandante Ferraz, sci., B.A.T. B1 73
Comandante Fontana, Arg. C9 80
Comandante Leal, Arg. F6 80
Comandante Nicanor Otamendi, Arg. J10 80
Comarapa, Bol. G9 82
Comas, Peru D4 82
Comayagua, Hond. C7 92
Comayagua, dept., Hond. C7 92
Comayagua, Montañas de, mts., Hond. C7 92
Combahee, stm., S.C., U.S. F6 147
Combarbalá, Chile F3 80
Combeaufontaine, Fr. E12 14
Comber, Ont., Can. E2 103
Combermere, Ont., Can. B7 103
Combined Locks, Wi., U.S. h9 156
Combourg, Fr. D5 14
Comboyne, Austl. H10 70
Combronde, Fr. G10 14
Combs, Ar., U.S. B2 111
Combs, Ky., U.S. C6 124
Comendador, Dom. Rep. E9 94
Comendador Gomes, Braz. E4 79
Comer, Ga., U.S. B3 117
Comercinho, Braz. D8 79
Comfort, Tx., U.S. E3 150
Comfort, W.V., U.S. m12 155
Comfrey, Mn., U.S. F4 130
Comilla, Bngl. I14 44
Comiso, Italy M9 18
Comitan de Dominguez, Mex. I13 90
Comite, stm., La., U.S. D4 125
Commentry, Fr. F9 14
Commerce, Ga., U.S. B3 117
Commerce, Mo., U.S. D8 132
Commerce, Ok., U.S. A7 143
Commerce, Tx., U.S. C5 150
Commerce City, Co., U.S. B6 113
Commercy, Fr. D12 14
Comminges, reg., Fr. I7 14
Committee Bay, b., N.W. Ter., Can. C15 96
Common Fence Point, R.I., U.S. D6 146
Como, Italy D4 18
Como, Ms., U.S. A4 131
Como, Tn., U.S. A3 149
Como, Lago di, l., Italy C4 18
Comobabi, Az., U.S. E4 110
Comodoro Py, Arg. H8 80
Comodoro Rivadavia, Arg. F3 78
Comores, Archipel des, is., Afr. D8 58
Comorin, Cape, c., India H4 46
Comoros (Comores), ctry., Afr. D8 58
Comox, B.C., Can. E5 99
Compeer, Alta., Can. D5 98
Compiègne, Fr. C9 14
Compostela, Mex. G7 90
Comprida, Ilha, i., Braz. C15 80
Comptche, Ca., U.S. C2 112
Compton, Que., Can. D6 104
Compton, Ca., U.S. n12 112
Compton, Il., U.S. B4 120
Comstock, Mi., U.S. F5 129
Comstock, Ne., U.S. C6 134
Čona, stm., U.S.S.R. E13 24
Conakry, Gui. G3 64
Conambo, stm., Ec. H4 84
Conanicut Island, i., R.I., U.S. E5 146
Conanicut Point, c., R.I., U.S. E5 146
Conasauga, Tn., U.S. D9 149
Concarán, Arg. G6 80
Concarneau, Fr. E3 14
Conceição, Braz. B12 82
Conceição, Cachoeira, wtfl, Braz. C9 82
Conceição da Aparecida, Braz. F5 79
Conceição da Barra, Braz. E9 79
Conceição das Alagoas, Braz. E4 79
Conceição de Ipanema, Braz. E8 79
Conceição do Almeida, Braz. B9 79
Conceição do Araguaia, Braz. E9 76
Conceição do Mato Dentro, Braz. E7 79
Conceição do Maú, Braz. F13 84
Conceição do Norte, Braz. B5 79
Concepción, Arg. E10 80
Concepción, Arg. D6 80
Concepción, Bol. D8 82
Concepción, Bol. G10 82
Concepción, Chile I2 80
Concepción, Col. D6 84
Concepción, Para. B10 80
Concepción, Peru D4 82
Concepción, dept., Para. B10 80
Concepción, Bahía, b., Mex. D4 90
Concepción, Laguna, l., Bol. G11 82
Concepción, Volcán, vol., Nic. F9 92
Concepción de Ataco, El Sal. D5 92
Concepción de la Sierra, Arg. D11 80
Concepcion del Oro, Mex. E9 90
Concepción del Uruguay, Arg. G9 80
Concepción Huista, Guat. B3 92
Concepción Quezaltepeque, El Sal. C6 92
Conception, Point, c., Ca., U.S. E3 112
Conception Bay, b., Newf., Can. E5 102
Conception Bay, b., Nmb. D2 66
Conception Bay South, Newf., Can. E5 102
Conception Junction, Mo., U.S. A3 132
Conchagua, El Sal. D7 92
Conchagua, Volcán, vol., El Sal. D7 92
Conchas Dam, N.M., U.S. B5 138
Conchas Lake, res., N.M., U.S. B5 138
Conche, Newf., Can. C4 102
Conches-en-Ouche, Fr. D7 14
Conchi, Chile B4 80
Concho, Az., U.S. C6 110
Concho, co., Tx., U.S. D3 150
Concho, stm., Tx., U.S. D2 150
Conchos, stm., Mex. C7 90
Conchos, stm., Mex. E10 90
Concise, Switz. E6 13
Concón, Chile G3 80
Concord, Ar., U.S. B4 111
Concord, Ca., U.S. h8 112
Concord, Ga., U.S. C2 117
Concord, Ma., U.S. B5 128
Concord, Mi., U.S. F6 129
Concord, Ne., U.S. B9 134
Concord, N.H., U.S. D3 136
Concord, N.C., U.S. B2 140
Concord, Tn., U.S. D9 149
Concord, Vt., U.S. C5 152
Concord, Va., U.S. C4 153
Concord, stm., Ma., U.S. A5 128
Concordia, Arg. F9 80
Concórdia, Braz. D12 80
Concórdia, Braz. J9 84
Concordia, Mex. F6 90
Concordia, Peru J5 84
Concordia, Ks., U.S. C6 123
Concordia, Mo., U.S. C4 132
Concordia, co., La., U.S. C4 125
Concrete, Wa., U.S. A4 154
Conda, Id., U.S. G7 119
Conde, Braz. A10 79
Condé, Fr. D6 14
Conde, S.D., U.S. B7 148
Condega, Nic. D8 92
Condeúba, Braz. C8 79
Condobolin, Austl. I7 70
Condom, Fr. I7 14
Condon, Or., U.S. B6 144
Condoto, Col. E4 84
Conecuh, co., Al., U.S. D2 108
Conecuh, stm., U.S. D3 108
Conegliano, Italy D7 18
Conehatta, Ms., U.S. C4 131
Conejos, Co., U.S. D4 113
Conejos, co., Co., U.S. D4 113
Conejos, stm., Co., U.S. D4 113
Conejos Peak, mtn., Co., U.S. D4 113
Conemaugh, Pa., U.S. F4 145
Conemaugh River Lake, res., Pa., U.S. F3 145
Conestee, S.C., U.S. B3 147
Conesville, Ia., U.S. C6 122
Coney Island (part of New York), N.Y., U.S. k13 139
Confluence, Pa., U.S. G3 145
Confolens, Fr. F7 14
Confusion Range, mts., Ut., U.S. D2 151
Confuso, stm., Para. C9 80
Congamond, Ma., U.S. B2 128
Congamond Lakes, l., U.S. A4 114
Congaree, stm., S.C., U.S. D6 147
Congaree Swamp National Monument, S.C., U.S. D6 147
Congo, ctry., Afr. B3 58
Congo (Zaire) (Zaïre), stm., Afr. C2 58
Congo Basin, Afr. H9 52
Congonhinhas, Braz. G3 79
Congress, Sask., Can. H2 105
Congress, Az., U.S. C3 110
Conimicut Point, c., R.I., U.S. D5 146
Conitaca, Mex. E6 90
Conjeeveram see Kānchipuram, India G10 42
Conklin, Alta., Can. B5 98
Conklin, N.Y., U.S. C5 139
Connaught, hist. reg., Ire. H4 8
Conneaut, Oh., U.S. A5 142
Conneaut Creek, stm., Oh., U.S. A5 142
Conneaut Lake, Pa., U.S. C1 145
Conneaut Lake, l., Pa., U.S. C1 145
Conneautville, Pa., U.S. C1 145
Connecticut, state, U.S. C5 114
Connecticut, stm., U.S. C12 106
Connell, Wa., U.S. C7 154
Connellsville, Pa., U.S. F2 145
Connemara, reg., Ire. H4 8
Connersville, In., U.S. E7 121
Connerville, Ok., U.S. C5 143
Connors, N.B., Can. B1 101
Connors Range, mts., Austl. C8 70
Conococheague Creek, stm., Md., U.S. A2 127
Cononaco, stm., Ec. H4 84
Conorochite, stm., Ven. F9 84
Conover, N.C., U.S. B1 140
Conowingo, Md., U.S. A5 127
Conowingo Dam, Md., U.S. A5 127
Conquest, Sask., Can. F2 105
Conquista, Braz. E5 79
Conrad, Ia., U.S. B5 122
Conrad, Mt., U.S. B5 133
Conroe, Tx., U.S. D5 150
Conroy, Ia., U.S. C6 122
Consecon, Ont., Can. C7 103
Conselheiro Lafaiete, Braz. F7 79
Conselheiro Pena, Braz. E8 79
Conshohocken, Pa., U.S. F11 145
Consolación del Sur, Cuba C3 94
Con Son, is., Viet. J9 40
Consort, Alta., Can. C5 98
Constance, Lake see Bodensee, l., Eur. E16 14
Constanţa, Rom. E12 20
Constanţa, co., Rom. E12 20
Constantia, N.Y., U.S. B5 139
Constantina, Spain H6 16
Constantine, Mi., U.S. G5 129
Constantine, Cape, c., Ak., U.S. D8 109
Constantine see Qacentina, Alg. B14 62
Constantinople see İstanbul, Tur. H12 20
Constitución, Chile H2 80
Constitución, Ur. F10 80
Consuegra, Spain F8 16
Consul, Sask., Can. H1 105
Contamana, Peru B4 82
Contas, Rio de, stm., Braz. C9 79
Contendas do Sincorá, Braz. B8 79
Content Keys, is., Fl., U.S. H5 116
Continental, Oh., U.S. A1 142
Continental Divide, N.M., U.S. B1 138
Continental Peak, mtn., Wy., U.S. D4 157
Continental Reservoir, res., Co., U.S. D3 113
Contoocook, N.H., U.S. D3 136
Contoocook, stm., N.H., U.S. D3 136
Contraalmirante Cordero, Arg. J4 80
Contra Costa, co., Ca., U.S. D3 112
Contratación, Col. D6 84
Contrecoeur, Que., Can. D4 104
Contumazá, Peru B2 82

Name | Map Ref. | Page

Contwoyto Lake, l., N.W. Ter., Can. C10 96
Conty, Fr. C9 14
Convención, Col. C6 84
Convent, La., U.S. D5 125
Convento, C.R. H11 92
Conversano, Italy I12 18
Converse, In., U.S. C6 121
Converse, La., U.S. C2 125
Converse, S.C., U.S. B4 147
Converse, co., Wy., U.S. C7 157
Convoy, Oh., U.S. B1 142
Conway, P.E.I., Can. C6 101
Conway, Ar., U.S. B3 111
Conway, Fl., U.S. D5 116
Conway, Mo., U.S. D5 132
Conway, N.H., U.S. C4 136
Conway, N.C., U.S. A5 140
Conway, Pa., U.S. E1 145
Conway, S.C., U.S. D9 147
Conway, co., Ar., U.S. B3 111
Conway, Lake, res., Ar., U.S. B3 111
Conway Lake, l., N.H., U.S. C4 136
Conway Springs, Ks., U.S. E6 123
Conyers, Ga., U.S. C2 117
Cook, Mn., U.S. C6 130
Cook, Ne., U.S. D9 134
Cook, co., Ga., U.S. E3 117
Cook, co., Il., U.S. B6 120
Cook, co., Mn., U.S. k9 130
Cook, Cape, c., B.C., Can. D4 99
Cook, Mount, mtn., N.Z. E3 72
Cooke, co., Tx., U.S. C4 150
Cooke City, Mt., U.S. E7 133
Cookes Peak, mtn., N.M., U.S. E2 138
Cookeville, Tn., U.S. C8 149
Cookhouse, S. Afr. I7 66
Cook Inlet, b., Ak., U.S. D9 109
Cook Islands, dep., Oc. H2 2
Cook Mountain, mtn., W.V., U.S. n12 155
Cook Point, c., Md., U.S. C5 127
Cook's Harbour, Newf., Can. C4 102
Cookshire, Que., Can. D6 104
Cookson, Ok., U.S. B7 143
Cook Strait, strt., N.Z. D5 72
Cooksville, Il., U.S. C5 120
Cooktown, Austl. C9 68
Coolah, Austl. H8 70
Coolamon, Austl. J7 70
Coolangatta, Austl. G10 70
Cooleemee, N.C., U.S. B2 140
Coolgardie, Austl. F4 68
Coolidge, Az., U.S. E4 110
Coolidge, Ga., U.S. E3 117
Coolidge, Tx., U.S. D4 150
Coolidge, Mount, mtn., S.D., U.S. D2 148
Coolin, Id., U.S. A2 119
Cool Ridge, W.V., U.S. D3 155
Coolville, Oh., U.S. C4 142
Cooma, Austl. K8 70
Coonabarabran, Austl. H8 70
Coonamble, Austl. H8 70
Coonoor, India G4 46
Coon Rapids, Ia., U.S. C3 122
Coon Rapids, Mn., U.S. E5 130
Coon Valley, Wi., U.S. E2 156
Cooper, Tx., U.S. C5 150
Cooper, co., Mo., U.S. C5 132
Cooper, stm., S.C., U.S. F8 147
Cooper, East Branch, stm., S.C., U.S. E8 147
Cooper, West Branch, stm., S.C., U.S. E8 147
Co Operative, Ky., U.S. D5 124
Cooper Creek, stm., Austl. G3 70
Cooper Mountain, mtn., Ak., U.S. g17 109
Coopers, Al., U.S. C3 108
Coopersburg, Pa., U.S. F11 145
Coopers Mills, Me., U.S. D3 126
Cooperstown, N.Y., U.S. C6 139
Cooperstown, N.D., U.S. B7 141
Coopersville, Mi., U.S. E5 129
Cooroy, Austl. F10 70
Coos, co., N.H., U.S. A4 136
Coos, co., Or., U.S. D2 144
Coos, stm., Or., U.S. D2 144
Coosa, Ga., U.S. B1 117
Coosa, co., Al., U.S. C3 108
Coosa, stm., U.S. C3 108
Coosada, Al., U.S. C3 108
Coosawattee, stm., Ga., U.S. B2 117
Coosawhatchie, S.C., U.S. F6 147
Coosawhatchie, stm., S.C., U.S. F5 147
Coos Bay, Or., U.S. D2 144
Cootamundra, Austl. J8 70
Cooter, Mo., U.S. E8 132
Čop, U.S.S.R. A6 20
Copacabana, Arg. E5 80
Copacabana, Bol. G7 82
Copainalá, Mex. I13 90
Copake, N.Y., U.S. C7 139
Copalis Beach, Wa., U.S. B1 154
Copalis Crossing, Wa., U.S. B1 154
Copán, Hond. C5 92
Copan, Ok., U.S. A6 143
Copán, dept., Hond. C6 92
Copán, hist., Hond. C5 92
Copan Reservoir, res., Ok., U.S. A6 143
Copatana, Braz. I9 84
Cope, Co., U.S. B8 113
Copeá, Paraná, mth., Braz. I11 84
Copeland, Fl., U.S. G5 116
Copeland, Ks., U.S. E3 123
Copenhagen, N.Y., U.S. B5 139
Copenhagen see København, Den. N13 6
Copertino, Italy I13 18
Copetonas, Arg. J8 80
Copiah, co., Ms., U.S. D3 131
Copiapó, Chile D3 80
Copiapó, stm., Chile D3 80
Coplay, Pa., U.S. E10 145
Copley, Austl. H3 70
Coporito, Ven. C11 84
Copparo, Italy E6 18
Copper, stm., Ak., U.S. C11 109
Copperas Cove, Tx., U.S. D4 150
Copper Butte, mtn., Wa., U.S. A7 154
Copper Canyon see Cobre, Barranca del, val., Mex. D6 90
Copper Center, Ak., U.S. C10 109
Copper Harbor, Mi., U.S. A3 129
Copperhill, Tn., U.S. D9 149
Coppermine, N.W. Ter., Can. C9 96
Coppermine, stm., N.W. Ter., Can. C10 96
Copper Mountain, mtn., Wy., U.S. C5 157
Copper Mountains, mts., Az., U.S. E2 110
Copper Ridge, mtn., Tn., U.S. m13 149
Copper Ridge, mtn., Va., U.S. f9 153
Coppet, Switz. F5 13
Coquille, Or., U.S. D2 144
Coquimbo, Chile E3 80
Coquimbo, prov., Chile F3 80
Corabia, Rom. F8 20
Coração de Jesus, Braz. D6 79
Coração de Maria, Braz. B9 79
Coracora, Peru F5 82
Coral, Pa., U.S. F3 145
Coralaque, stm., Peru G6 82
Coral Gables, Fl., U.S. G6 116
Coral Harbour, N.W. Ter., Can. D16 96
Coral Sea, Oc. J19 158
Coral Sea Islands Territory, ter., Austl. B9 70
Coralville, Ia., U.S. C6 122
Coralville Lake, res., Ia., U.S. C5 122
Coram, Mt., U.S. B2 133
Corangamite, Lake, l., Austl. L5 70
Coraopolis, Pa., U.S. E1 145
Corato, Italy H11 18
Corbeil-Essonnes, Fr. D9 14
Corbeta Uruguay, sci., B.A.T. A2 73
Corbetton, Ont., Can. C4 103
Corbin, Ky., U.S. D5 124
Corcoran, Ca., U.S. D4 112
Corcoran, Mn., U.S. m11 130
Corcovado, Golfo, b., Chile E2 78
Corcovado, Parque Nacional, C.R. I11 92
Corcovado, Volcán, vol., Chile I7 74
Cord, Ar., U.S. B4 111
Cordaville, Ma., U.S. g9 128
Cordeiro, Braz. G7 79
Cordele, Ga., U.S. E3 117
Cordell, Ok., U.S. B3 143
Cordell Hull Lake, res., Tn., U.S. C8 149
Corder, Mo., U.S. B4 132
Cordillera, dept., Para. C10 80
Cordillo Downs, Austl. F4 70
Cordisburgo, Braz. E6 79
Córdoba, Arg. F6 80
Córdoba, Mex. H11 90
Córdoba, Spain H7 16
Córdoba, prov., Arg. F7 80
Córdoba, dept., Col. C5 84
Córdova, Peru F4 82
Cordova, Al., U.S. B2 108
Cordova, Ak., U.S. C10 109
Cordova, Il., U.S. B3 120
Cordova, Md., U.S. C6 127
Cordova, N.M., U.S. A4 138
Cordova, N.C., U.S. C3 140
Cordova, Tn., U.S. B2 149
Cordova Mines, Ont., Can. C7 103
Cordova Peak, mtn., Ak., U.S. C10 109
Corea, Me., U.S. D5 126
Corentyne (Corantijn), stm., S.A. E14 84
Corerepe, Mex. E5 90
Corfu see Kérkira, Grc. J3 20
Corfu see Kérkira, i., Grc. J3 20
Coria, Spain F5 16
Coria del Río, Spain H5 16
Coribe, Braz. B6 79
Corigliano Calabro, Italy J11 18
Corinda, Austl. A3 70
Corinna, Me., U.S. D3 126
Corinne, Ut., U.S. B3 151
Corinne Key, i., Fl., U.S. G6 116
Corinth, Ga., U.S. C2 117
Corinth, Ms., U.S. A5 131
Corinth, N.Y., U.S. B7 139
Corinth, W.V., U.S. B5 155
Corinth, Gulf of see Korinthiakós Kólpos, b., Grc. K6 20
Corinth Canal see Korínthou, Dhiórix, Grc. L6 20
Corinth see Kórinthos, Grc. L6 20
Corinto, Braz. E6 79
Corinto, El Sal. D7 92
Corinto, Nic. E7 92
Coripata, Bol. G8 82
Corire, Peru G5 82
Coris, Peru C3 82
Corixao, stm., Braz. H13 82
Cork, N.B., Can. D3 101
Cork, Ire. J5 8
Cork, co., Ire. I5 8
Corlay, Fr. D3 14
Corleone, Italy L8 18
Çorlu, Tur. H11 20
Cormeilles, Fr. C7 14
Cormorant, Man., Can. B1 100
Cormorant Lake, l., Man., Can. B1 100
Corn, Ok., U.S. B3 143
Cornelia, Ga., U.S. B3 117
Cornélio Procópio, Braz. G3 79
Cornelius, N.C., U.S. B2 140
Cornelius, Or., U.S. g11 144
Cornell, Il., U.S. C5 120
Cornell, Wi., U.S. C2 156
Corner Brook, Newf., Can. D3 102
Cornerstone, Ar., U.S. C4 111
Cornersville, Tn., U.S. B5 149
Corneta, Punta, c., Mex. J11 90
Cornfield Point, c., Ct., U.S. D6 114
Cornhill, N.B., Can. D4 101
Cornie Bayou, stm., U.S. D3 111
Corning, Ar., U.S. A5 111
Corning, Ca., U.S. C2 112
Corning, Ia., U.S. D3 122
Corning, Ks., U.S. C7 123
Corning, N.Y., U.S. C3 139
Corning, Oh., U.S. C3 142
Cornish, Me., U.S. E2 126
Cornish, Ut., U.S. B4 151
Cornish Center, N.H., U.S. D2 136
Cornish Flat, N.H., U.S. D2 136
Cornishville, Ky., U.S. C5 124
Corno Grande, mtn., Italy G8 18
Cornville, Az., U.S. C4 110
Cornwall, Ont., Can. B10 103
Cornwall, Ct., U.S. B2 114
Cornwall, Pa., U.S. F9 145
Cornwall, co., Eng., U.K. K9 8
Cornwallis Island, i., N.W. Ter., Can. A14 96
Cornwall on Hudson, N.Y., U.S. D6 139
Coro, Ven. B8 84
Coro, Golfete de, b., Ven. I10 84
Coroaci, Braz. E7 79
Corocoro, Bol. G7 82
Corocoro Island, i., S.A. C12 84
Coroico, Bol. G8 82
Coroico, stm., Bol. F8 82
Coromandel, Braz. E5 79
Coromandel Coast, India F6 46
Coromandel Peninsula, pen., N.Z. B5 72
Corona, Al., U.S. B2 108
Corona, Ca., U.S. F5 112
Corona, N.M., U.S. C4 138
Corona, S.D., U.S. B9 148
Coronach, Sask., Can. H3 105
Coronado, Mex. F9 90
Coronado, Ca., U.S. F5 112
Coronado, Bahía de, b., C.R. H11 92
Coronado National Memorial, Az., U.S. F5 110
Coronation, Alta., Can. C5 98
Coronation Gulf, b., N.W. Ter., Can. C10 96
Coronation Island, i., B.A.T. B1 73
Coronation Island, i., Ak., U.S. n22 109
Coronda, Arg. F8 80
Coronel, Chile I2 80
Coronel Bogado, Para. D10 80
Coronel Dorrego, Arg. J8 80
Coronel Du Graty, Arg. D8 80
Coronel Eugenio del Busto, Arg. J6 80
Coronel Fabriciano, Braz. E7 79
Coronel Moldes, Arg. C6 80
Coronel Moldes, Arg. G6 80
Coronel Murta, Braz. D7 79
Coronel Oviedo, Para. C10 80
Coronel Ponce, Braz. C1 79
Coronel Pringles, Arg. I8 80
Coronel Suárez, Arg. I8 80
Coronel Vidal, Arg. I10 80
Coronel Vivida, Braz. C12 80
Corongo, Peru C3 82
Coronie, dept., Sur. E14 84
Coropuna, Nevado, mtn., Peru F5 82
Corowa, Austl. K7 70
Corozal, Belize H15 90
Corozal, Col. C5 84
Corozal, Hond. B8 92
Corps, Fr. H12 14
Corpus, Arg. D11 80
Corpus Christi, Tx., U.S. F4 150
Corpus Christi Naval Air Station, mil., Tx., U.S. F4 150
Corque, Bol. H8 82
Corquín, Hond. C6 92
Corral, Chile D2 78
Corral de Almaguer, Spain F8 16
Corral de Bustos, Arg. G7 80
Corralejo, Spain O27 17b
Corrales, N.M., U.S. k7 138
Correctionville, Ia., U.S. B2 122
Correggio, Italy E5 18
Córrego do Ouro, Braz. D3 79
Córrego Rico, Braz. C5 79
Corrente, stm., Braz. E3 79
Corrente, stm., Braz. B6 79
Correntes, stm., Braz. D1 79
Correntina, Braz. B6 79
Corrèze, dept., Fr. G8 14
Corrib, Lough, l., Ire. H4 8
Corrientes, Arg. D9 80
Corrientes, prov., Arg. E10 80
Corrientes, stm., Arg. E9 80
Corrientes, stm., S.A. I5 84
Corrientes, Bahía de, b., Cuba D2 94
Corrientes, Cabo, c., Arg. J10 80
Corrientes, Cabo, c., Col. E4 84
Corrientes, Cabo, c., Cuba D2 94
Corrientes, Cabo, c., Mex. G7 90
Corrigan, Tx., U.S. D5 150
Corriganville, Md., U.S. k13 127
Corry, Pa., U.S. C2 145
Corse (Corsica), i., Fr. L24 15a
Corse, Cap, c., Fr. K24 15a
Corse-du-Sud, dept., Fr. M24 15a
Corsica, S.D., U.S. D7 148
Corsica see Corse, i., Fr. L24 15a
Corsicana, Tx., U.S. C4 150
Corson, co., S.D., U.S. B4 148
Corson Inlet, b., N.J., U.S. E3 137
Cortaderas, Arg. G6 80
Cortazar, Mex. G9 90
Corte, Fr. G4 18
Cortegana, Spain H5 16
Cortés, dept., Hond. B6 92
Cortez, Co., U.S. D2 113
Cortez, Fl., U.S. q10 116
Cortez, Sea of see California, Golfo de, b., Mex. D4 90
Cortez Mountains, mts., Nv., U.S. C5 135
Cortina d'Ampezzo, Italy C7 18
Cortland, Il., U.S. B5 120
Cortland, In., U.S. G6 121
Cortland, Ne., U.S. D9 134
Cortland, N.Y., U.S. C4 139
Cortland, Oh., U.S. A5 142
Cortland, co., N.Y., U.S. C4 139
Cortona, Italy F6 18
Corubal (Koliba), stm., Afr. F2 64
Çoruh, stm., Asia A6 48
Çorum, Tur. J12 20
Corumbá, Braz. H13 82
Corumbá, stm., Braz. E4 79
Corumbá de Goiás, Braz. C4 79
Corumbaíba, Braz. E4 79
Corumbataí, stm., Braz. C13 80
Corumbaú, Ponta de, c., Braz. D9 79
Corumbiara Antigo, stm., Braz. E11 82
Corumo, stm., Ven. D12 84
Corunna, In., U.S. B7 121
Corunna, Mi., U.S. F6 129
Coruripe, Braz. F11 76
Corvallis, Mt., U.S. D2 133
Corvallis, Or., U.S. C3 144
Corwith, Ia., U.S. B4 122
Cory, In., U.S. F3 121
Corydon, In., U.S. H5 121
Corydon, Ia., U.S. D4 122
Corydon, Ky., U.S. C2 124
Coryell, co., Tx., U.S. D4 150
Corzuela, Arg. D8 80
Cosamaloapan [de Carpio], Mex. H12 90
Cosapa, Bol. H7 82
Cosby, Tn., U.S. D10 149
Cosenza, Italy J11 18
Coshocton, Oh., U.S. B4 142
Coshocton, co., Oh., U.S. B4 142
Cosigüina, Punta, c., Nic. E7 92
Cosigüina, Volcán, vol., Nic. E7 92
Cosmoledo Island, i., Sey. C9 58
Cosmopolis, Wa., U.S. C2 154
Cosmorama, Braz. F4 79
Cosmos, Mn., U.S. F4 130
Cosne-Cours-sur-Loire, Fr. E9 14
Cospán, Peru B2 82
Cosquín, Arg. F6 80
Cossatot, stm., Ar., U.S. C1 111
Cossatot Mountains, mtn., Ar., U.S. C2 111
Cossonay, Switz. E6 13
Costa Mesa, Ca., U.S. n13 112
Costa Rica, Mex. E6 90
Costa Rica, ctry., N.A. G10 92
Costilla, N.M., U.S. A4 138
Costilla, co., Co., U.S. D5 113
Coswig, Ger. D12 10
Cotabambas, Peru E5 82
Cotabato, Phil. D7 38
Cotacajes, stm., Bol. G8 82
Cotagaita, Bol. I9 82
Cotagaita, stm., Bol. I9 82
Cotahuasi, Peru F5 82
Coteau-Landing, Que., Can. D3 104
Coteaux, Haiti E7 94
Côte-d'Or, dept., Fr. E11 14
Cotegipe, Braz. B6 79
Cotentin, pen., Fr. C5 14
Côtes-d'Armor, dept., Fr. D4 14
Coti, stm., Braz. C9 82
Cotija de la Paz, Mex. H8 90
Cotingo, stm., Braz. E12 84
Cotoca, Bol. G10 82
Cotonou, Benin H11 64
Cotopaxi, Co., U.S. C5 113
Cotopaxi, prov., Ec. H3 84
Cotopaxi, vol., Ec. H3 84
Cotovêlo, Cachoeira do, wtfl, Braz. B12 82
Cotswold Hills, hills, Eng., U.K. J11 8
Cottage Grove, Mn., U.S. n13 130
Cottage Grove, Or., U.S. D3 144
Cottage Grove Reservoir, res., Or., U.S. D3 144
Cottageville, S.C., U.S. F7 147
Cottageville, W.V., U.S. C3 155
Cottam, Ont., Can. E2 103
Cottbus, Ger. D14 10
Cotter, Ar., U.S. A3 111
Cottiennes, Alpes (Alpi Cozie), mts., Eur. E1 18
Cottle, co., Tx., U.S. B2 150
Cottle Knob, mtn., W.V., U.S. C4 155
Cottleville, Mo., U.S. f12 132
Cotton, Ga., U.S. E2 117
Cotton, Mn., U.S. C6 130
Cotton, co., Ok., U.S. C3 143
Cottondale, Al., U.S. B2 108
Cottondale, Fl., U.S. B1 116
Cotton Plant, Ar., U.S. B4 111
Cottonport, La., U.S. C3 125
Cottonton, Al., U.S. C4 108
Cottontown, Tn., U.S. A5 149
Cotton Valley, La., U.S. B2 125
Cottonwood, Al., U.S. D4 108
Cottonwood, Az., U.S. C3 110
Cottonwood, Ca., U.S. B2 112
Cottonwood, Id., U.S. C2 119
Cottonwood, Mn., U.S. F3 130
Cottonwood, Ok., U.S. C5 143
Cottonwood, co., Mn., U.S. F3 130
Cottonwood, stm., Ks., U.S. D7 123
Cottonwood, stm., Mn., U.S. F3 130
Cottonwood Cove, Nv., U.S. H7 135
Cottonwood Creek, stm., Wy., U.S. C4 157
Cottonwood Falls, Ks., U.S. D7 123
Cottonwood Wash, val., Ut., U.S. F6 151
Cotuhé, stm., Col. I7 84
Cotui, Dom. Rep. E9 94
Cotuit, Ma., U.S. C7 128
Cotulla, Tx., U.S. E3 150
Coudersport, Pa., U.S. C5 145
Cougar Reservoir, res., Or., U.S. C4 144
Couhé, Fr. F7 14
Coulee City, Wa., U.S. B6 154
Coulee Creek, stm., Wa., U.S. g13 154
Coulee Dam, Wa., U.S. B7 154
Coulee Dam National Recreation Area, Wa., U.S. A7 154
Coulommiers, Fr. D10 14
Coulter, Ia., U.S. B4 122
Coulterville, Ca., U.S. D2 112
Coulterville, Il., U.S. E4 120
Counce, Tn., U.S. B3 149
Council, Id., U.S. E2 119
Council Bluffs, Ia., U.S. C2 122
Council Grove, Ks., U.S. D7 123
Council Grove Lake, res., Ks., U.S. D7 123
Council Mountain, mtn., Id., U.S. E2 119
Country Homes, Wa., U.S. B8 154
Countyline, Ok., U.S. C4 143
Coupeville, Wa., U.S. A3 154
Courcelles, Bel. H5 12
Courcelles, Que., Can. D7 104
Courland see Kurzeme, hist. reg., U.S.S.R. E5 26
Couronnement, Île du see Coronation Island, i., B.A.T. B1 73
Courtalain, Fr. D8 14
Courtenay, B.C., Can. E5 99
Courte Oreilles, Lac, l., Wi., U.S. C2 156
Courtland, Ont., Can. E4 103
Courtland, Al., U.S. A2 108
Courtland, Ks., U.S. C6 123
Courtland, Mn., U.S. F4 130
Courtland, Ms., U.S. A4 131
Courtland, Va., U.S. D5 153
Courtrai (Kortrijk), Bel. G3 12
Coushatta, La., U.S. B2 125
Coutances, Fr. C5 14
Couto de Magalhães, stm., Braz. B2 79
Coutts, Alta., Can. E5 98
Couvin, Bel. H5 12
Covasna, co., Rom. D9 20
Cove, Ar., U.S. C1 111
Cove, Or., U.S. B9 144
Cove City, N.C., U.S. B5 140
Cove Creek, stm., Ut., U.S. E3 151
Covedale, Oh., U.S. o12 142
Covelo, Ca., U.S. C2 112
Coventry, Eng., U.K. I12 8
Coventry, Ct., U.S. B6 114
Coventry, R.I., U.S. D3 146
Coventry, Vt., U.S. B4 152
Cove Point, Md., U.S. D5 127
Cove Point, c., Md., U.S. D5 127
Coverdales Crossroads, De., U.S. F3 115
Covered Wells, Az., U.S. E3 110
Covert, Mi., U.S. F4 129
Covesville, Va., U.S. C4 153
Covilhã, Port. E4 16
Covina, Ca., U.S. m13 112
Covington, Ga., U.S. C3 117
Covington, In., U.S. D3 121
Covington, Ky., U.S. A5 124
Covington, La., U.S. D5 125
Covington, Mi., U.S. B2 129
Covington, Oh., U.S. B1 142
Covington, Ok., U.S. A4 143
Covington, Pa., U.S. C7 145
Covington, Tn., U.S. B2 149
Covington, Va., U.S. C3 153
Covington, Wa., U.S. f11 154
Covington, co., Al., U.S. D3 108
Covington, co., Ms., U.S. D4 131
Covunco, Arroyo, stm., Arg. J4 80
Cowal, Lake, l., Austl. I7 70
Cowan, In., U.S. D7 121
Cowan, Tn., U.S. B5 149
Cowan, Lake, l., Austl. F4 68
Cowan Knob, mtn., Ar., U.S. B2 111
Cowan Lake, l., Sask., Can. C2 105
Cowansville, Que., Can. D5 104
Coward, S.C., U.S. D8 147
Coward Springs, Austl. G2 70
Cowarie, Austl. F3 70
Cowarts, Al., U.S. D4 108
Cow Creek, stm., Ks., U.S. D5 123
Cow Creek, stm., Wa., U.S. C7 154
Cowden, Il., U.S. D5 120
Cowdenbeath, Scot., U.K. E10 8
Cowee Mountains, mts., N.C., U.S. f9 140
Cowell, Austl. I2 70
Cowen, W.V., U.S. C4 155
Cowen, Mount, mtn., Mt., U.S. E6 133
Coweta, Ok., U.S. B6 143
Coweta, co., Ga., U.S. C2 117
Cowgill, Mo., U.S. B4 132
Cow Head, Newf., Can. D3 102
Cowichan Bay, B.C., Can. g12 99
Cowiche, Wa., U.S. C5 154
Cow Knob, mtn., W.V., U.S. C5 155
Cow Lakes, l., Or., U.S. D9 144
Cowley, Austl. F6 70
Cowley, Alta., Can. E3 98
Cowley, Wy., U.S. B4 157
Cowley, co., Ks., U.S. E7 123
Cowlic, Az., U.S. F4 110
Cowlington, Ok., U.S. B7 143
Cowlitz, co., Wa., U.S. C2 154
Cowlitz, stm., Wa., U.S. C3 154
Cowpasture, stm., Va., U.S. B3 153
Cowpen Mountain, mtn., Ga., U.S. B2 117
Cowpens, S.C., U.S. A4 147
Cowra, Austl. I8 70
Cowskin Creek, stm., Ks., U.S. g11 123
Coxá, stm., Braz. C6 79
Coxim, Braz. E1 79
Coxim, stm., Braz. E1 79
Coxipó da Ponte, Braz. F13 82
Coxsackie, N.Y., U.S. C7 139
Cox's Bāzār, Bngl. J14 44
Cox's Cove, Newf., Can. D2 102
Coy, Al., U.S. D2 108
Coy, Ar., U.S. C4 111
Coyaguaima, Cerro, mtn., Arg. B5 80
Coyame, Mex. C7 90
Coyanosa Draw, val., Tx., U.S. D1 150
Coya Sur, Chile B4 80
Coyle, Ok., U.S. B4 143
Coyote, N.M., U.S. A3 138
Coyote Basin, Co., U.S. A2 113
Coyuca de Benítez, Mex. I9 90
Coyuca de Catalán, Mex. H9 90
Cozad, Ne., U.S. D6 134
Cozie, Alpi (Alpes Cottiennes), mts., Eur. E2 18
Cozumel, Mex. G16 90
Cozumel, Isla, i., Mex. G16 90
Crab Creek, stm., Wa., U.S. C6 154
Crab Creek, stm., Wa., U.S. B7 154
Crab Orchard, Ky., U.S. C5 124
Crab Orchard, Tn., U.S. D9 149
Crab Orchard, W.V., U.S. n13 155
Crab Orchard Lake, res., Il., U.S. F4 120
Crab Orchard Mountains, mts., Tn., U.S. D9 149
Crabtree, Or., U.S. C4 144
Crabtree, Pa., U.S. F3 145
Crabtree Mills, Que., Can. D4 104
Cracking, stm., Sask., Can. D4 105
Cradock, S. Afr. I7 66
Crafton, Pa., U.S. k13 145
Craftsbury, Vt., U.S. B4 152
Craftsbury Common, Vt., U.S. B4 152
Cragford, Al., U.S. B4 108
Craig, Ak., U.S. D13 109
Craig, Co., U.S. A3 113
Craig, Mo., U.S. A2 132
Craig, Mt., U.S. C5 133
Craig, Ne., U.S. C9 134
Craig, co., Ok., U.S. A6 143
Craig, co., Va., U.S. C2 153
Craig Air Force Base, mil., Al., U.S. C3 108
Craig Creek, stm., Va., U.S. C2 153
Craigellachie, B.C., Can. D8 99
Craighead, co., Ar., U.S. B5 111
Craigmont, Id., U.S. C2 119
Craigmyle, Alta., Can. D4 98
Craignure, Scot., U.K. E8 8
Craigsville, Va., U.S. B3 153
Craigsville, W.V., U.S. C4 155
Craik, Sask., Can. F3 105
Crailsheim, Ger. F10 10
Craiova, Rom. E7 20
Cramerton, N.C., U.S. B1 140
Cranberry Lake, l., N.Y., U.S. A6 139
Cranberry Portage, Man., Can. B1 100
Cranbrook, B.C., Can. E10 99
Crandall, Ga., U.S. B2 117
Crandall, Tx., U.S. n10 150
Crandon, Wi., U.S. C5 156
Crane, Az., U.S. E1 110
Crane, In., U.S. G4 121
Crane, Mo., U.S. E4 132
Crane, Tx., U.S. D1 150
Crane, co., Tx., U.S. D1 150
Crane Creek, stm., Oh., U.S. e7 142
Crane Creek Reservoir, res., Id., U.S. E2 119
Crane Hill, Al., U.S. A2 108
Crane Lake, Mn., U.S. B6 130
Crane Lake, l., Sask., Can. G1 105
Crane Lake, l., Il., U.S. C3 120
Crane Lake, l., Mn., U.S. B6 130
Crane Mountain, mtn., Or., U.S. E6 144
Crane Prairie Reservoir, res., Or., U.S. D5 144
Crane Valley, Sask., Can. H3 105
Cranfield, Ms., U.S. D2 131
Cranford, N.J., U.S. B4 137
Cranston, R.I., U.S. C4 146
Craon, Fr. E6 14
Craonne, Fr. C10 14
Crapaud, P.E.I., Can. C6 101
Craponne, Fr. G10 14
Crary, N.D., U.S. A7 141
Crasna, Rom. C11 20
Crasna (Kraszna), stm., Eur. B6 20
Crater Lake, Or., U.S. E4 144
Crater Lake, l., Or., U.S. E4 144
Crater Lake National Park, Or., U.S. E4 144
Craters of the Moon National Monument, Id., U.S. F5 119
Crateús, Braz. E10 76
Crauford, Cape, c., N.W. Ter., Can. B16 96
Cravari, stm., Braz. E13 82
Craven, Sask., Can. G3 105
Craven, co., N.C., U.S. B5 140
Cravo Norte, Col. D7 84
Cravo Norte, stm., Col. D7 84
Cravo Sur, stm., Col. E7 84
Crawford, Co., U.S. C3 113
Crawford, Ga., U.S. C3 117
Crawford, Ms., U.S. B5 131
Crawford, Ne., U.S. B2 134
Crawford, co., Ar., U.S. B1 111
Crawford, co., Ga., U.S. D3 117
Crawford, co., Il., U.S. D6 120
Crawford, co., In., U.S. H4 121
Crawford, co., Ia., U.S. B2 122
Crawford, co., Ks., U.S. E9 123
Crawford, co., Mi., U.S. D6 129
Crawford, co., Mo., U.S. D6 132
Crawford, co., Oh., U.S. B3 142
Crawford, co., Pa., U.S. C1 145
Crawford, co., Wi., U.S. E3 156
Crawford Bay, B.C., Can. E9 99
Crawford Lake, l., Me., U.S. C5 126
Crawford Notch State Park, N.H., U.S. B4 136
Crawfordsville, Ar., U.S. B5 111
Crawfordsville, In., U.S. D4 121
Crawfordsville, Ia., U.S. C6 122
Crawfordville, Fl., U.S. B2 116
Crawfordville, Ga., U.S. C4 117
Crayne, Ky., U.S. e9 124
Crazy Mountains, mts., Mt., U.S. D6 133
Crazy Peak, mtn., Mt., U.S. D6 133
Crazy Woman Creek, stm., Wy., U.S. B6 157
Creal Springs, Il., U.S. F5 120
Crécy-en-Brie, Fr. D9 14
Creede, Co., U.S. D4 113
Creedmoor, N.C., U.S. A4 140
Creek, co., Ok., U.S. B5 143
Creel, Mex. D6 90
Cree Lake, l., Sask., Can. m7 105
Creelman, Sask., Can. H4 105
Creemore, Ont., Can. C4 103
Creighton, Sask., Can. C5 105
Creighton, Mo., U.S. C3 132
Creighton, Ne., U.S. B8 134
Creighton, Pa., U.S. h14 145

Name — Map Ref. — Page

Creil, Fr. C9 14
Crema, Italy D4 18
Cremona, Alta., Can. D3 98
Cremona, Italy D5 18
Crenshaw, Ms., U.S. A3 131
Crenshaw, co., Al., U.S. D3 108
Creola, Al., U.S. E1 108
Crepori, stm., Braz. A13 82
Cres, Otok, i., Yugo. E9 18
Cresaptown, Md., U.S. k13 127
Cresbard, S.D., U.S. B7 148
Crescent, Ga., U.S. E5 117
Crescent, Mo., U.S. f12 132
Crescent, Ok., U.S. B4 143
Crescent, Or., U.S. D5 144
Crescent, Lake, l., Wa., U.S. A2 154
Crescent City, Ca., U.S. B1 112
Crescent City, Fl., U.S. C5 116
Crescent City, Il., U.S. C6 120
Crescent Lake, l., Fl., U.S. C5 116
Crescent Lake, l., Or., U.S. D5 144
Crescent Range, mtn., N.H., U.S. B4 136
Crescent Springs, Ky., U.S. h13 124
Cresco, Ia., U.S. A5 122
Crespo, Arg. G8 80
Cresskill, N.J., U.S. h9 137
Cresson, Pa., U.S. F4 145
Cressona, Pa., U.S. E9 145
Crested Butte, Co., U.S. C4 113
Crest Hill, Il., U.S. k8 120
Crestline, Oh., U.S. B3 142
Creston, B.C., Can. E9 99
Creston, Il., U.S. B5 120
Creston, Ia., U.S. C3 122
Creston, Ne., U.S. C8 134
Creston, Oh., U.S. B4 142
Creston, Wa., U.S. B7 154
Crestone Peak, mtn., Co., U.S. D5 113
Crestview, Fl., U.S. u15 116
Crestview, Hi., U.S. g10 118
Crestwood, Ky., U.S. B4 124
Crestwood Village, N.J., U.S. D4 137
Creswell, N.C., U.S. B6 140
Creswell, Or., U.S. D3 144
Creswick, Austl. K5 70
Crete, Il., U.S. B6 120
Crete, Ne., U.S. D9 134
Crete see Kríti, i., Grc. N8 20
Crétéville, Tun. M5 18
Creus, Cap de, c., Spain C15 16
Creuse, dept., Fr. F9 14
Creve Coeur, Il., U.S. C4 120
Crevillent, Spain G11 16
Crewe, Eng., U.K. H11 8
Crewe, Va., U.S. C4 153
Crewkerne, Eng., U.K. K11 8
Cricamola, stm., Pan. I13 92
Criciúma, Braz. E14 80
Cricket, N.C., U.S. A1 140
Cricket Mountains, mts., Ut., U.S. E3 151
Cridersville, Oh., U.S. B1 142
Crieff, Scot., U.K. E10 8
Crikvenica, Yugo. D9 18
Crimea see Krymskij poluostrov, pen., U.S.S.R. H4 22
Crimmitschau, Ger. E12 10
Crîngeni, Rom. E8 20
Cripple Creek, Co., U.S. C5 113
Cripple Creek, Va., U.S. D1 153
Crisfield, Md., U.S. E6 127
Crisp, co., Ga., U.S. E3 117
Crissiumal, Braz. D11 80
Cristalândia, Braz. F9 76
Cristalina, Braz. D5 79
Cristalino, stm., Braz. B3 79
Cristianópolis, Braz. D4 79
Cristóbal, Pan. C3 84
Cristóbal Colón, Pico, mtn., Col. B6 84
Crişul Alb, stm., Eur. C5 20
Crişul Negru, stm., Eur. C5 20
Crişul Repede (Sebes Körös), stm., Eur. B6 20
Crittenden, Ky., U.S. B5 124
Crittenden, co., Ar., U.S. B5 111
Crittenden, co., Ky., U.S. e9 124
Crivitz, Wi., U.S. C6 156
Crixalândia, Braz. C5 79
Crixás, Braz. C4 79
Crixás Açu, stm., Braz. B3 79
Crixás Mirim, stm., Braz. C3 79
Crna Gora, state, Yugo. G2 20
Črnomelj, Yugo. D10 18
Croatia see Hrvatska, state, Yugo. D10 18
Crocker, Mo., U.S. D5 132
Crockett, Ca., U.S. g8 112
Crockett, Tx., U.S. D5 150
Crockett, co., Tn., U.S. B2 149
Crockett, co., Tx., U.S. D2 150
Crockett Mills, Tn., U.S. B2 149
Crofton, Ky., U.S. C2 124
Crofton, Md., U.S. B4 127
Crofton, Ne., U.S. B8 134
Croix, Lac la, l., Mn., U.S. B6 130
Croker, Cape, c., Austl. B6 68
Croker, Cape, c., Ont., Can. C4 103
Croker Island, i., Austl. B6 68
Cromarty, Scot., U.K. D9 8
Cromer, Man., Can. E1 100
Cromínia, Braz. D4 79
Cromona, Ky., U.S. C7 124
Cromwell, N.Z. F2 72
Cromwell, Al., U.S. C1 108
Cromwell, Ct., U.S. C5 114
Cromwell, In., U.S. B6 121
Cromwell, Ky., U.S. C3 124
Cromwell, Ok., U.S. B5 143
Crook, Co., U.S. A8 113
Crook, co., Or., U.S. C6 144
Crook, co., Wy., U.S. B8 157
Crooked, stm., Or., U.S. C6 144
Crooked Creek, Ak., U.S. C8 109
Crooked Creek, stm., U.S. E3 123
Crooked Creek, stm., Ar., U.S. A3 111
Crooked Creek, stm., In., U.S. k10 121
Crooked Creek, stm., Pa., U.S. C7 145
Crooked Creek Lake, res., Pa., U.S. E3 145
Crooked Island, i., Bah. C7 94
Crooked Island Passage, strt., Bah. C7 94
Crooked Lake, l., Fl., U.S. E5 116
Crooked Lake, l., Mn., U.S. B7 130
Crooked River, Sask., Can. E4 105
Crooks, S.D., U.S. D9 148
Crooks Lake, l., Nv., U.S. B2 135
Crookston, Mn., U.S. C2 130
Crooksville, Oh., U.S. C3 142
Crookwell, Austl. J8 70
Cropper, Ky., U.S. B4 124
Cropsey, Il., U.S. C5 120
Crosby, Mn., U.S. D5 130
Crosby, Ms., U.S. D2 131
Crosby, N.D., U.S. A2 141
Crosby, Tx., U.S. r14 150
Crosby, co., Tx., U.S. C2 150
Crosby, Mount, mtn., Wy., U.S. C3 157
Crosbyton, Tx., U.S. C2 150
Crosland, Ga., U.S. E3 117
Cross, co., Ar., U.S. B5 111
Cross, stm., Afr. I14 64
Cross Anchor, S.C., U.S. B4 147
Cross Bay, b., Man., Can. C2 100
Cross City, Fl., U.S. C3 116
Cross Creek, N.B., Can. C3 101
Cross Creek, stm., W.V., U.S. f8 155
Crossett, Ar., U.S. D4 111
Crossfield, Alta., Can. D3 98
Cross Hill, S.C., U.S. C4 147
Cross Island, i., Me., U.S. D5 126
Cross Lake, Man., Can. B3 100
Crosslake, Mn., U.S. D4 130
Cross Lake, l., Me., U.S. A4 126
Cross Lake, res., La., U.S. B2 125
Cross Lanes, W.V., U.S. C3 155
Crossman Peak, mtn., Az., U.S. C1 110
Cross Mill, N.C., U.S. f10 140
Cross Mountains, mtn., Ar., U.S. C1 111
Cross Plains, In., U.S. G7 121
Cross Plains, Tn., U.S. A5 149
Cross Plains, Tx., U.S. C3 150
Cross Plains, Wi., U.S. E4 156
Cross Roads Ohio, N.S., Can. D7 101
Cross Sound, strt., Ak., U.S. k21 109
Cross Timbers, Mo., U.S. C4 132
Crossville, Al., U.S. A4 108
Crossville, Il., U.S. E5 120
Crossville, Tn., U.S. D8 149
Croswell, Mi., U.S. E8 129
Crothersville, In., U.S. G6 121
Crotone, Italy J12 18
Croton-on-Hudson, N.Y., U.S. D7 139
Crouse, N.C., U.S. B1 140
Crouseville, Me., U.S. B4 126
Crow, stm., Mn., U.S. F4 130
Crow, North Fork, stm., Mn., U.S. E4 130
Crow Agency, Mt., U.S. E9 133
Crow Creek, stm., U.S. A6 113
Crow Creek Indian Reservation, S.D., U.S. C6 148
Crowder, Ms., U.S. A3 131
Crowder, Ok., U.S. B6 143
Crowdy Head, c., Austl. H10 70
Crowell, Tx., U.S. C3 150
Crow Indian Reservation, Mt., U.S. E9 133
Crowley, Co., U.S. C7 113
Crowley, La., U.S. D3 125
Crowley, Tx., U.S. n9 150
Crowley, co., Co., U.S. C7 113
Crowley, Lake, res., Ca., U.S. D4 112
Crowleys Ridge, mtn., U.S. B5 111
Crown Point, In., U.S. B3 121
Crown Point, La., U.S. k11 125
Crownpoint, N.M., U.S. B1 138
Crown Point, N.Y., U.S. B7 139
Crow Peak, mtn., Mt., U.S. D5 133
Crowsnest Pass, Alta., Can. E3 98
Crowsnest Pass, Can. E3 98
Crows Nest Peak, mtn., S.D., U.S. C2 148
Crow Wing, co., Mn., U.S. D4 130
Crow Wing, stm., Mn., U.S. D4 130
Croydon, Austl. B5 70
Croydon, Pa., U.S. F12 145
Croydon Peak, mtn., N.H., U.S. D2 136
Crozet, Va., U.S. B4 153
Crozet, Îles, is., F.S.A.T. M9 158
Crucero, Peru F6 82
Cruces, Cuba C4 94
Crucible, Pa., U.S. G1 145
Crucilândia, Braz. F6 79
Cruger, Ms., U.S. B3 131
Cruillas, Mex. E10 90
Crum, W.V., U.S. D2 155
Crump, Tn., U.S. B3 149
Crump Lake, l., Or., U.S. E7 144
Crumpton, Md., U.S. B6 127
Crutwell, Sask., Can. D2 105
Cruz, Cabo, c., Cuba E6 94
Cruz Alta, Arg. G8 80
Cruz Alta, Braz. E12 80
Cruz del Eje, Arg. F6 80
Cruzeiro, Braz. G6 79
Cruzeiro do Oeste, Braz. G2 79
Cruzeiro do Sul, Braz. B5 82
Cruz Grande, Chile E3 80
Cruzília, Braz. F6 79
Cruz Machado, Braz. D13 80
Crysler, Ont., Can. B9 103
Crystal, Mi., U.S. E6 129
Crystal, Mn., U.S. m12 130
Crystal, N.D., U.S. A8 141
Crystal, stm., Co., U.S. B3 113
Crystal Bay, Nv., U.S. D1 135
Crystal Bay, b., Fl., U.S. D4 116
Crystal Beach, Fl., U.S. D4 116
Crystal City, Man., Can. E2 100
Crystal City, Mo., U.S. C7 132
Crystal City, Tx., U.S. E3 150
Crystal Falls, Mi., U.S. B2 129
Crystal Lake, Ct., U.S. B6 114
Crystal Lake, Fl., U.S. u16 116
Crystal Lake, Il., U.S. A5 120
Crystal Lake, Ia., U.S. A4 122
Crystal Lake, l., Ct., U.S. B6 114
Crystal Lake, l., Mi., U.S. D4 129
Crystal Lake, l., N.H., U.S. D4 136
Crystal Lake, l., Vt., U.S. B4 152
Crystal Lawns, Il., U.S. k8 120
Crystal Mountain, mtn., N.H., U.S. g7 136
Crystal Pond, res., Ct., U.S. B7 114
Crystal River, Fl., U.S. D4 116
Crystal Springs, Ar., U.S. C2 111
Crystal Springs, Fl., U.S. D4 116
Crystal Springs, Ms., U.S. D3 131
Csongrád, Hung. I20 10
Csongrád, co., Hung. I20 10
Csurgó, Hung. I17 10
Ču, U.S.S.R. I12 22
Ču, stm., U.S.S.R. I12 22
Cúa, Ven. B9 84
Cuadro Nacional, Arg. H4 80
Cuajinicuilapa, Mex. I10 90
Cuajone, Peru G6 82
Cuamba, Moz. D7 58
Cuando (Kwando), stm., Afr. D4 58
Cuangar, Ang. A4 66
Cuango, Ang. C3 58
Cuango (Kwango), stm., Afr. C3 58
Cuanza, stm., Ang. C3 58
Cuao, stm., Ven. E9 84
Cuaró, Ur. F10 80
Cuarto, stm., Arg. G7 80
Cuary, stm., S.A. G8 84
Cuatrociénegas, Mex. D8 90
Cuauhtémoc, Mex. C6 90
Cuautitlán [de Romero Rubio], Mex. H10 90
Cuba, Port. G4 16
Cuba, Al., U.S. C1 108
Cuba, Il., U.S. C3 120
Cuba, Ks., U.S. C6 123
Cuba, Mo., U.S. C6 132
Cuba, N.M., U.S. A3 138
Cuba, N.Y., U.S. C2 139
Cuba, ctry., N.A. C5 94
Cuba City, Wi., U.S. F3 156
Cubagua, Isla, i., Ven. B10 84
Cubango (Okavango), stm., Afr. E3 58
Cubero, N.M., U.S. B2 138
Cub Run, Ky., U.S. C3 124
Cuchara, Co., U.S. D5 113
Cucharas, stm., Co., U.S. D6 113
Cuchilla Alta, Cerro, mtn., Hond. B6 92
Cuchillo-Có, Arg. J6 80
Cuchivero, stm., Ven. D10 84
Čuchloma, U.S.S.R. C25 26
Cuchumatanes, Sierra los, mts., Guat. B3 92
Čučkovo, U.S.S.R. G24 26
Čučkovo, U.S.S.R. B24 26
Cucuí, Braz. G9 84
Čučuleny, U.S.S.R. B12 20
Cucurpe, Mex. B4 90
Cúcuta, Col. D6 84
Cudahy, Wi., U.S. F6 156
Cuddalore, India G5 46
Cuddapah, India E5 46
Cuddy Mountain, mtn., Id., U.S. E2 119
Čudovo, U.S.S.R. B14 26
Čudskoje ozero (Peipsi järv), l., U.S.S.R. C10 26
Cudworth, Sask., Can. E3 105
Cue, Austl. E3 68
Cuéllar, Spain D7 16
Cuenca, Ec. I3 84
Cuenca, Spain E9 16
Cuencamé [de Ceniceros], Mex. E8 90
Cuernavaca, Mex. H10 90
Cuero, Tx., U.S. E4 150
Cuers, Fr. I13 14
Cueto, Cuba D7 94
Cuetzalan del Progreso, Mex. G11 90
Cuevas, Ms., U.S. f7 131
Cuevo, Bol. I10 82
Cugir, Rom. D7 20
Cuglieri, Italy I3 18
Cuiabá, Braz. F13 82
Cuiabá, stm., Braz. G13 82
Cuiari, Braz. G8 84
Cuicatlán, Mex. I11 90
Cuieiras, stm., Braz. I12 84
Cuijk, Neth. E8 12
Cuilapa, Guat. C4 92
Cuilco, Guat. B3 92
Cuilco (Grijalva), stm., N.A. B3 92
Cuilo (Kwilu), stm., Afr. C3 58
Cuiseaux, Fr. F12 14
Cuíto, stm., Ang. B5 66
Cuíto-Cuanavale, Ang. E3 58
Cuitzeo, Laguna de, l., Mex. H9 90
Cuiuni, stm., Braz. H11 84
Cuivre, West Fork, stm., Mo., U.S. B6 132
Čukotskij, mys, c., U.S.S.R. E29 24
Čukotskij poluostrov, pen., U.S.S.R. D28 24
Çukurca, Tur. C7 48
Culberson, co., Tx., U.S. o12 150
Culbertson, Mt., U.S. B12 133
Culbertson, Ne., U.S. D5 134
Culcairn, Austl. J7 70
Culdesac, Id., U.S. C2 119
Culebra, Isla de, i., P.R. E12 94
Culebra Peak, mtn., Co., U.S. D5 113
Culemborg, Neth. E7 12
Culgoa, stm., Austl. G7 70
Culiacán, Mex. E6 90
Culiacán, Mex. E6 90
Culiacancito, Mex. E6 90
Cullen, La., U.S. B2 125
Culleoka, Tn., U.S. B5 149
Cullera, Spain F11 16
Cullinan, S. Afr. E9 66
Cullison, Ks., U.S. E5 123
Cullman, Al., U.S. A3 108
Cullman, co., Al., U.S. A3 108
Culloden, Ga., U.S. D2 117
Culloden, W.V., U.S. C2 155
Cullom, Il., U.S. C5 120
Cullomburg, Al., U.S. D1 108
Cullowhee, N.C., U.S. f9 140
Cully, Switz. F6 13
Čul'man, U.S.S.R. F16 24
Culpeper, Va., U.S. B5 153
Culpeper, co., Va., U.S. B5 153
Culpina, Bol. I9 82
Cultus Lake, B.C., Can. f14 99
Culuene, stm., Braz. B2 79
Culver, In., U.S. B5 121
Culver, Ks., U.S. D6 123
Culver, Or., U.S. C5 144
Culver City, Ca., U.S. m12 112
Culvers Lake, l., N.J., U.S. A3 137
Čulym, U.S.S.R. F14 22
Čulym, stm., U.S.S.R. F9 24
Cumaná, Ven. B10 84
Cumanacoa, Ven. B11 84
Cumare, Cerro, hill, Col. G6 84
Cumari, Braz. E4 79
Cumbal, Col. G4 84
Cumbal, Nevado de, mtn., Col. G4 84
Cumberland, B.C., Can. E5 99
Cumberland, Ont., Can. g13 103
Cumberland, Ia., U.S. C3 122
Cumberland, Ky., U.S. D7 124
Cumberland, Md., U.S. k13 127
Cumberland, N.C., U.S. B4 140
Cumberland, Va., U.S. C4 153
Cumberland, Wi., U.S. C1 156
Cumberland, co., Il., U.S. D5 120
Cumberland, co., Ky., U.S. D4 124
Cumberland, co., Me., U.S. E2 126
Cumberland, co., N.J., U.S. E2 137
Cumberland, co., N.C., U.S. B4 140
Cumberland, co., Pa., U.S. F7 145
Cumberland, co., Tn., U.S. D8 149
Cumberland, co., Va., U.S. C4 153
Cumberland, stm., U.S. D9 106
Cumberland, Lake, res., Ky., U.S. D5 124
Cumberland, South Fork, stm., U.S. D5 124
Cumberland Center, Me., U.S. g7 126
Cumberland City, Tn., U.S. A4 149
Cumberland Foreside, Me., U.S. E2 126
Cumberland Furnace, Tn., U.S. A4 149
Cumberland Gap, Tn., U.S. C10 149
Cumberland Gap, U.S. D6 124
Cumberland Gap National Historical Park, U.S. D6 124
Cumberland Hill, R.I., U.S. B4 146
Cumberland House, Sask., Can. D4 105
Cumberland Island National Seashore, Ga., U.S. F5 117
Cumberland Islands, is., Austl. C8 70
Cumberland Lake, l., Sask., Can. C4 105
Cumberland Mountain, mtn., Tn., U.S. C9 149
Cumberland Peninsula, pen., N.W. Ter., Can. C19 96
Cumberland Plateau, plat., U.S. D8 149
Cumberland Sound, strt., N.W. Ter., Can. C19 96
Cumbres Pass, Co., U.S. D4 113
Cumbria, co., Eng., U.K. G11 8
Cuming, co., Ne., U.S. C9 134
Cumming, Ga., U.S. B2 117
Cummins, Austl. J1 70
Cumpas, Mex. B5 90
Çumra, Tur. C2 48
Cumuripa, Mex. C5 90
Čumyš, stm., U.S.S.R. G8 24
Čun'a, stm., U.S.S.R. E17 22
Čuna, stm., U.S.S.R. F11 24
Cunani, Braz. C8 76
Cunard, W.V., U.S. m13 155
Cunauaru, stm., Braz. I11 84
Cunaviche, Ven. D9 84
Cunco, Chile J2 80
Cuncumén, Chile F3 80
Cundiff, Ky., U.S. D4 124
Cundinamarca, dept., Col. E5 84
Cundys Harbor, Me., U.S. g8 126
Cunene (Kunene), stm., Afr. E2 58
Cuneo, Italy E2 18
Cunha, Braz. G6 79
Cunha Porã, Braz. D12 80
Cunhuã, Igarapé, stm., Braz. B9 82
Cunnamulla, Austl. G6 70
Cunningham, Ks., U.S. E5 123
Cunningham, Ky., U.S. f9 124
Cunucunuma, stm., Ven. F10 84
Cupar, Sask., Can. G3 105
Cupica, Golfo de, b., Col. D4 84
Cupins, Braz. E3 79
Cuquenán, stm., Ven. E12 84
Curaçao, i., Neth. Ant. H10 94
Curacautín, Chile J3 80
Curacaví, Chile G3 80
Curacó, stm., Arg. J6 80
Curahuara, Bol. G7 82
Curanilahue, Chile I2 80
Curanipe, Chile H2 80
Čuranja, stm., Peru D6 82
Čurapča, U.S.S.R. E18 24
Curaray, stm., S.A. H5 84
Curdsville, Ky., U.S. C2 124
Curecanti National Recreation Area, Co., U.S. C3 113
Curepipe, Mrts. V18 67c
Curepto, Chile H2 80
Curequetê, stm., Braz. C9 82
Curiapo, Ven. C12 84
Curicó, Chile H3 80
Curicuriari, stm., Braz. H9 84
Curicuriari, Serra, hill, Braz. H9 84
Curisevo, stm., Braz. B2 79
Curitiba, Braz. C14 80
Curitibanos, Braz. D13 80
Curiuaú, stm., Braz. H12 84
Curiúva, Braz. H3 79
Curiúva, Braz. C13 80
Curlew, Wa., U.S. A7 154
Curlew Creek, stm., Wa., U.S. A7 154
Curlewis, Austl. H9 70
Curlew Lake, l., Wa., U.S. A7 154
Curnamona, Austl. H3 70
Currais Novos, Braz. E11 76
Curralinho, Braz. D9 76
Curran, Ont., Can. B10 103
Curran, Mi., U.S. D7 129
Currant Creek, stm., Co., U.S. C5 113
Currant Mountain, mtn., Nv., U.S. E6 135
Current, stm., U.S. A5 111
Currie, Austl. L5 70
Currie, Mn., U.S. F3 130
Currituck, N.C., U.S. A6 140
Currituck, co., N.C., U.S. A6 140
Curry, co., N.M., U.S. C6 138
Curry, co., Or., U.S. E2 144
Curryville, Mo., U.S. B6 132
Curtea de Argeş, Rom. D8 20
Curtice, Oh., U.S. A2 142
Curtin, Or., U.S. D3 144
Curtina, Ur. G10 80
Curtis, Ar., U.S. D2 111
Curtis, Mi., U.S. B5 129
Curtis, Ne., U.S. D5 134
Curtis, Port, Austl. D9 70
Curtis Channel, strt., Austl. D9 70
Curtis Island, i., Austl. D9 70
Curtisville, Pa., U.S. E2 145
Curuá, stm., Braz. D8 76
Curuá, stm., Braz. C3 79
Curuá, stm., Braz. B14 82
Curuá, Ilha, i., Braz. C8 76
Curubandé, C.R. G9 92
Curuçá, stm., Braz. J7 84
Čurug, Yugo. D4 20
Curuguaty, Para. C11 80
Curupayty, Riacho, stm., Para. I12 82
Curupira, Sierra de, mts., S.A. G10 84
Cururu, stm., Braz. B13 82
Cururupu, Braz. D10 76
Curutu, stm., Ven. E11 84
Curuzú Cuatiá, Arg. E9 80
Curve, Tn., U.S. B2 149
Curvelo, Braz. G10 76
Curvelo, Braz. E6 79
Curwensville, Pa., U.S. E4 145
Curwensville Lake, res., Pa., U.S. E4 145
Curwood, Mount, mtn., Mi., U.S. B2 129
Cushabatay, stm., Peru B4 82
Cushing, Ia., U.S. B2 122
Cushing, Ok., U.S. B5 143
Cushing, Tx., U.S. D5 150
Cushman, Ar., U.S. B4 111
Cushman, Lake, res., Wa., U.S. B2 154
Cusiana, stm., Col. E6 84
Cusihuiriáchic, Mex. C6 90
Čusovoj, U.S.S.R. F9 22
Cusseta, Al., U.S. C4 108
Cusseta, Ga., U.S. D2 117
Custer, Mi., U.S. E4 129
Custer, Mt., U.S. D9 133
Custer, S.D., U.S. D2 148
Custer, Wa., U.S. A3 154
Custer, co., Co., U.S. C5 113
Custer, co., Id., U.S. E4 119
Custer, co., Mt., U.S. D11 133
Custer, co., Ne., U.S. C6 134
Custer, co., Ok., U.S. B2 143
Custer, co., S.D., U.S. D2 148
Custer Battlefield National Monument, Mt., U.S. E9 133
Custer City, Ok., U.S. B3 143
Custer Peak, mtn., S.D., U.S. C2 148
Cut Bank, Mt., U.S. B4 133
Cutbank, stm., Alta., Can. B1 98
Cut Bank Creek, stm., N.D., U.S. A4 141
Cutchogue, N.Y., U.S. m16 139
Cutervo, Peru B2 82
Cuthbert, Ga., U.S. E2 117
Cut Knife, Sask., Can. E1 105
Cutler, Il., U.S. E4 120
Cutler, In., U.S. C5 121
Cutler, Me., U.S. D5 126
Cutler Ridge, Fl., U.S. s13 116
Cut Off, La., U.S. E5 125
Cutral-Có, Arg. J4 80
Cutro, Italy J11 18
Cuttack, India J11 44
Cut Throat Island, i., Newf., Can. A3 102
Cuttyhunk Island, i., Ma., U.S. D6 128
Cutzamala, stm., Mex. H9 90
Cuvo, stm., Ang. D2 58
Cuxhaven, Ger. B8 10
Cuyahoga, co., Oh., U.S. A4 142
Cuyahoga, stm., Oh., U.S. A4 142
Cuyahoga Falls, Oh., U.S. A4 142
Cuyama, stm., Ca., U.S. E4 112
Cuyamaca Peak, mtn., Ca., U.S. F5 112
Cuyamel, Hond. B6 92
Cuyubini, stm., Ven. C12 84
Cuyuna, Mn., U.S. D5 130
Cuyuni, stm., S.A. D13 84
Cuzco, Peru E6 82
Cuzco, dept., Peru E5 82
C.W. McConaughy, Lake, res., Ne., U.S. C4 134
Cyangugu, Rw. B5 58
Cyclades see Kikládhes, is., Grc. L9 20
Cygnet, Oh., U.S. A2 142
Cynthiana, In., U.S. H2 121
Cynthiana, Ky., U.S. B5 124
Cypress, Al., U.S. C2 108
Cypress, Il., U.S. F4 120
Cypress, Tx., U.S. r14 150
Cypress Bayou, stm., Ar., U.S. B3 111
Cypress Creek, stm., Tx., U.S. r14 150
Cypress Hills Provincial Park, Alta., Can. E5 98
Cypress Hills Provincial Park, Sask., Can. H1 105
Cypress Inn, Tn., U.S. B4 149
Cypress Lake, l., Fl., U.S. D5 116
Cypress Quarters, Fl., U.S. E6 116
Cypress River, Man., Can. E2 100
Cypress Swamp, sw., U.S. F4 115
Cyprus, ctry., Asia H14 4
Cyprus, North, ctry., Asia H14 4
Cyril, Ok., U.S. C3 143
Cyrus, Mn., U.S. E3 130
Czar, Alta., Can. C5 98
Czarna Woda, Pol. B18 10
Czechoslovakia (Československo), ctry., Eur. F11 4
Częstochowa, Pol. E19 10
Człuchów, Pol. B17 10

D

Dabajuro, Ven. B7 84
Dabat, Eth. K9 60
Dabeiba, Col. D4 84
Daberas, Nmb. E4 66
Dabhoi, India I5 44
Dabie Shan, mts., China D4 34
Dabnou, Niger D12 64
Dabola, Gui. F4 64
Dąbrowa Tarnowska, Pol. E21 10
Dacca see Dhaka, Bngl. I14 44
Dachau, Ger. G11 10
Dac Lac, Cao Nguyen, plat., Viet. H10 40
Dacono, Co., U.S. A6 113
Dacula, Ga., U.S. C3 117
Dadanawa, Guy. F13 84
Dade, co., Fl., U.S. G6 116
Dade, co., Ga., U.S. B1 117
Dade, co., Mo., U.S. D4 132
Dade City, Fl., U.S. D4 116
Dadeville, Al., U.S. C4 108
Dadeville, Mo., U.S. D4 132
Dādra and Nagar Haveli, ter., India B2 46
Dādu, Pak. G2 44
Dadu, stm., China E7 30
Daet, Phil. N20 39b
Dagana, Sen. C2 64
Dagang, China M2 34
Daga Post, Sud. M7 60
Dagash, Sud. H7 60
Dagda, U.S.S.R. E10 26
Daggett, Ca., U.S. E5 112
Daggett, co., Ut., U.S. C6 151
Daghfalī, Sud. H7 60
Dagsboro, De., U.S. F5 115
Dagu, China E5 32
Dagua, Col. F4 84
Dagua, Pap. N. Gui. F11 38
Dagupan, Phil. M19 39b
Dahei, India B2 46
Dahinda, Il., U.S. C3 120
Da Hinggan Ling, mts., China B11 30
Dahlak Archipelago, is., Eth. G2 47
Dahlgren, Il., U.S. E5 120
Dahlgren, Va., U.S. B5 153
Dahlonega, Ga., U.S. B3 117
Dahmani, Tun. N3 18
Dāhod, India I6 44
Dahomey see Benin, ctry., Afr. G7 54
Dahra, Libya C4 56
Dahūk, Iraq C7 48
Dahy, Nafūd ad-, des., Sau. Ar. D4 47
Dailekh, Nepal F9 44
Dailey, W.V., U.S. C5 155
Daimiel, Spain F8 16
Daingerfield, Tx., U.S. C5 150
Daireaux, Arg. I8 80
Dairen see Dalian, China E9 32
Daisetta, Tx., U.S. D5 150
Daisy, Ar., U.S. C2 111
Daisy, Ga., U.S. D5 117
Dajabón, Dom. Rep. E9 94
Dājal, Pak. F4 44
Dajarra, Austl. C3 70
Dajian Shan, mtn., China A7 40
Dakar, Sen. D1 64
Dakeng, China I4 34
Dak Gle, Viet. G9 40
Dakhla, W. Sah. I3 62
Dakingari, Nig. F12 64
Dakoro, Niger D13 64
Dakota, Il., U.S. A4 120
Dakota, Mn., U.S. G7 130
Dakota, co., Mn., U.S. F5 130
Dakota, co., Ne., U.S. B9 134
Dakota City, Ia., U.S. B3 122
Dakota City, Ne., U.S. B9 134
Đakovica, Yugo. G4 20
Dakshin Gangotri, sci., Ant. C3 73
Dalaba, Gui. F3 64
Dalan Dzadgad, Mong. C7 30
Dalao, Gui. F3 64
Dalark, Ar., U.S. C3 111
Da Lat, Viet. I10 40
Dalbana, stm., Sur. E14 84
Dālbandin, Pak. G18 48
Dalby, Austl. F9 70
Dale, Nor. K9 6
Dale, Nor. K9 6
Dale, In., U.S. H4 121
Dale, co., Al., U.S. D4 108
Dale City, Va., U.S. B5 153
Dale Hollow Lake, res., U.S. C8 149
Dalemead, Alta., Can. D4 98
Dalen, Nor. L11 6
Dalet, Burma E2 40
Daleville, Al., U.S. D4 108
Daleville, In., U.S. D6 121
Dalhart, Tx., U.S. A1 150
Dalhousie, N.B., Can. A3 101
Dalhousie, Cape, c., N.W. Ter., Can. B7 96
Dali, China B6 40
Dalian (Dairen), China E9 32
Daliang Shan, mts., China F7 30
Daliuzhuang, China B3 34
Daliyat el Karmil, Isr. C4 50
Dalj, Yugo. D2 20
Daljā', Egypt D6 60
Dall, Mount, mtn., Ak., U.S. f15 109
Dallam, co., Tx., U.S. A1 150
Dallas, Al., U.S. B3 108
Dallas, Ga., U.S. C2 117
Dallas, N.C., U.S. B1 140
Dallas, Or., U.S. C3 144
Dallas, Pa., U.S. D10 145
Dallas, S.D., U.S. D6 148

Name — Map Ref. — Page

Dallas, Tx., U.S. C4 150
Dallas, W.V., U.S. f8 155
Dallas, Wi., U.S. C2 156
Dallas, co., Al., U.S. C2 108
Dallas, co., Ar., U.S. D3 111
Dallas, co., Ia., U.S. C3 122
Dallas, co., Mo., U.S. D4 132
Dallas, co., Tx., U.S. C4 150
Dallas Center, Ia., U.S. C4 122
Dallas City, Il., U.S. C2 120
Dallas Naval Air Station, mil., Tx., U.S. n9 150
Dallastown, Pa., U.S. G8 145
Dall Island, i., Ak., U.S. n23 109
Dalmacija, hist. reg., Yugo. F11 18
Dalmacio Vélez Sarsfield, Arg. G7 80
Dalmatia, Pa., U.S. E8 145
Dalmatia see Dalmacija, hist. reg., Yugo. F11 18
Dalmeny, Sask., Can. E2 105
Dal'negorsk, U.S.S.R. I19 24
Dal'nerečensk, U.S.S.R. H18 24
Daloa, I.C. H6 64
Dalqū, Sud. G6 60
Dalrymple, Mount, mtn., Austl. C8 70
Dāltenganj, India H11 44
Dalton, Ga., U.S. B2 117
Dalton, Ma., U.S. B1 128
Dalton, Ne., U.S. C3 134
Dalton, Oh., U.S. B4 142
Dalton, Pa., U.S. C10 145
Dalton, Wi., U.S. E4 156
Dalton City, Il., U.S. D5 120
Dalton Gardens, Id., U.S. B2 119
Dalton Iceberg Tongue, Ant. B7 73
Dalvík, Ice. B4 6a
Dalwallinu, Austl. F3 68
Daly, stm., Austl. B6 68
Daly City, Ca., U.S. h8 112
Daly Waters, Austl. C6 68
Dalzell, Il., U.S. B4 120
Dalzell, S.C., U.S. C7 147
Dāmā, Syria C6 50
Damān, India B2 46
Damān, ter., India B2 46
Damanhūr, Egypt B6 60
Damar, Ks., U.S. C4 123
Damar, Pulau, i., Indon. G8 38
Damaraland, dept., Nmb. C2 66
Damaraland, hist. reg., Nmb. D3 66
Damariscotta, Me., U.S. D3 126
Damariscotta Lake, l., Me., U.S. D3 126
Damascus, Ar., U.S. B3 111
Damascus, Ga., U.S. E2 117
Damascus, Ga., U.S. B2 117
Damascus, Md., U.S. B3 127
Damascus, Va., U.S. f10 153
Damascus see Dimashq, Syria A6 50
Damāvand, Qolleh-ye, mtn., Iran D12 48
Damba, Ang. C3 58
Dam Gamad, Sud. K4 60
Dāmghān, Iran C13 48
Damianópolis, Braz. C5 79
Damietta see Dumyāṭ, Egypt B6 60
Dammartin-en-Goële, Fr. C9 14
Damoh, India I8 44
Damon, Tx., U.S. r14 150
Damongo, Ghana G9 64
Dampier, Austl. D3 68
Dampier, Selat, strt., Indon. F9 38
Dampier Archipelago, is., Austl. D3 68
Dan, stm., U.S. D3 153
Dana, In., U.S. E3 121
Dana, N.C., U.S. f10 140
Da Nang, Viet. F10 40
Danburg, Ga., U.S. C4 117
Danbury, Ct., U.S. D2 114
Danbury, Ia., U.S. B2 122
Danbury, Ne., U.S. D5 134
Danbury, N.H., U.S. C3 136
Danbury, Tx., U.S. r14 150
Danbury, Wi., U.S. B1 156
Danby, Vt., U.S. E3 152
Dandenong, Austl. K6 70
Dandong, China C12 32
Dandridge, Tn., U.S. C10 149
Dan Dume, Nig. F13 64
Dane, Wi., U.S. E4 156
Dane, co., Wi., U.S. E4 156
Danforth, Il., U.S. C6 120
Danforth, Me., U.S. C5 126
Danforth Hills, mts., Co., U.S. A2 113
Dang, stm., China D6 30
Dangba, China C6 32
Danggali Conservation Park, Austl. I4 70
Dangila, Eth. L9 60
Dango, Sud. L3 60
Dangriga, Belize I15 90
Dangtu, China D7 34
Dan Gulbi, Nig. F13 64
Dania, Fl., U.S. F6 116
Daniel, Wy., U.S. D2 157
Daniels, co., Mt., U.S. B11 133
Daniel's Harbour, Newf., Can. C3 102
Danielson, Ct., U.S. B8 114
Daniels Pass, Ut., U.S. C4 151
Danielsville, Ga., U.S. B3 117
Danilov, U.S.S.R. C23 26
Ḍank, Oman C10 47
Dankov, U.S.S.R. H22 26
Danlí, Hond. C8 92
Dannebrog, Ne., U.S. C7 134
Dannemora, N.Y., U.S. f11 139
Dannenberg, Ger. B11 10
Dannevirke, N.Z. D6 72
Dannhauser, S. Afr. G10 66
Dans Mountain, mtn., Md., U.S. k13 127
Dansville, N.Y., U.S. C3 139
Dante, S.D., U.S. D7 148
Dante, Tn., U.S. m14 149
Dante, Va., U.S. f9 153
Danube, Mn., U.S. F3 130
Danube, stm., Eur. G13 4
Danube, Mouths of the, mth., Eur. D13 20
Danubyu, Burma F3 40
Danvers, Il., U.S. C4 120
Danvers, Ma., U.S. A6 128
Danville, Que., Can. D5 104
Danville, Al., U.S. A2 108
Danville, Ar., U.S. B2 111
Danville, Ca., U.S. h9 112
Danville, Ga., U.S. D3 117
Danville, Il., U.S. C6 120
Danville, In., U.S. E4 121
Danville, Ia., U.S. D6 122
Danville, Ky., U.S. C5 124
Danville, N.H., U.S. E4 136
Danville, Oh., U.S. B3 142
Danville, Pa., U.S. E8 145
Danville, Vt., U.S. C4 152
Danville, Va., U.S. D3 153
Danville, W.V., U.S. C3 155
Danyang, China C8 34
Danzig see Gdańsk, Pol. A18 10
Daocheng, China F7 30
Daolin, China H1 34
Daoukro, I.C. H8 64
Daoulas, Fr. D2 14
Daoura, Oued, val., Afr. F9 62
Dapango, Togo F10 64
Daphne, Al., U.S. E2 108
Dapp, Alta., Can. B4 98
Da Qaidam, China B16 44
Daqing, China D6 32
Daqqāq, Sud. K4 60
Dara, Sen. D2 64
Dar'ā, Syria C6 50
Dārāb, Iran G13 48
Darabani, Rom. A10 20
Daraina, Madag. N23 67b
Darāw, Egypt E7 60
Dārayyā, Syria B6 50
Darbhanga, India G11 44
D'Arbonne, Bayou, stm., La., U.S. B3 125
Darby, Mt., U.S. D2 133
Darby, Pa., U.S. G11 145
Darbydale, Oh., U.S. m10 142
Darchan, Mong. B8 30
Dardanelle, Ar., U.S. B2 111
Dardanelle Lake, res., Ar., U.S. B2 111
Dardanelles see Çanakkale Boğazı, strt., Tur. I10 20
Dardara, Mor. J6 16
Darden, Tn., U.S. B3 149
Dardenne Creek, stm., Mo., U.S. f12 132
Dare, co., N.C., U.S. B7 140
Dar-el-Beida see Casablanca, Mor. D7 62
Darende, Tur. B4 48
Dares Beach, Md., U.S. C4 127
Dar es Salaam, Tan. C7 58
Dargai, Pak. C4 44
Dargan-Ata, U.S.S.R. I10 22
Dargaville, N.Z. A4 72
Dargol, Niger E10 64
Darién, Col. F4 84
Darien, Ct., U.S. E2 114
Darien, Ga., U.S. E5 117
Darien, Wi., U.S. F5 156
Darién, Serranía del, mts. C4 84
Dariense, Cordillera, mts., Nic. E9 92
Dariganga, Mong. B9 30
Dārjiling, India G13 44
Darke, co., Oh., U.S. B1 142
Darkesville, W.V., U.S. B6 155
Darlag, China E6 30
Darley Woods, De., U.S. h8 115
Darling, S. Afr. I4 66
Darling, Ms., U.S. A3 131
Darling, stm., Austl. I5 70
Darling, Lake, res., N.D., U.S. A4 141
Darling Downs, reg., Austl. F9 70
Darlingford, Man., Can. E2 100
Darling Range, mts., Austl. F3 68
Darlington, Al., U.S. D2 108
Darlington, In., U.S. D4 121
Darlington, Md., U.S. A5 127
Darlington, S.C., U.S. C8 147
Darlington, Wi., U.S. F3 156
Darlington, co., S.C., U.S. C8 147
Darłowo, Pol. A16 10
Darmstadt, Ger. F8 10
Darnah, Libya B5 56
Darnestown, Md., U.S. B3 127
Darnétal, Fr. C8 14
Darney, Fr. D13 14
Darnley, Cape, c., Ant. B5 73
Darnley Bay, b., N.W. Ter., Can. C8 96
Daroca, Spain D10 16
Dar-Ould-Zidouh, Mor. D7 62
Darou Mousti, Sen. D1 64
Darrah, Mount, mtn., Can. E3 98
Darregueira, Arg. I7 80
Darreh Gaz, Iran C15 48
Darrington, Wa., U.S. A4 154
Darrow, La., U.S. h10 125
Dart, Cape, c., Ant. C10 73
Dartmoor, for., Eng., U.K. K9 8
Dartmouth, N.S., Can. E6 101
Dartmouth, Eng., U.K. K10 8
Dartmouth, Lake, l., Austl. F6 70
Daru, Pap. N. Gui. A8 68
Daru, S.L. H4 64
Daruvar, Yugo. D12 18
Darwin, Arg. J6 80
Darwin, Austl. B6 68
Darwin, Mn., U.S. E4 130
Dās, i., U.A.E. B8 47
Dashaping, China F2 34
Dasht, stm., Pak. I16 48
Dashwood, Ont., Can. D3 103
Dasiji, China B4 34
Dašinčilen, Mong. B7 30
Daškovka, U.S.S.R. H13 26
Dassel, Mn., U.S. E4 130
Date, Japan E15 36a
Dateland, Az., U.S. E2 110
Datia, India H8 44
Datian, China K5 34
Datil, N.M., U.S. C2 138
Datil Mountains, mts., N.M., U.S. C2 138
D'at'kovo, U.S.S.R. H17 26
D'atlovo, U.S.S.R. H8 26
Datong, China C9 30
Datong, stm., China D7 30
Datoushan, China B5 32
Datto, Ar., U.S. A5 111
Datu, Tanjung, c., Asia M10 40
Daua (Dawa), stm., Afr. H9 56
Daufuskie Island, i., S.C., U.S. G6 147
Daugai, U.S.S.R. G7 26
Daugava (Zapadnaja Dvina), stm., U.S.S.R. E7 26
Daugavpils, U.S.S.R. F9 26
Daule, Ec. G2 84
Daule, Ec. H3 84
Daule, stm., Ec. H2 84
Daun, Ger. E6 10
Dauphin, Man., Can. D1 100
Dauphin, co., Pa., U.S. F8 145
Dauphin, stm., Man., Can. D2 100
Dauphiné, hist. reg., Fr. H12 14
Dauphin Island, Al., U.S. E1 108
Dauphin Island, i., Al., U.S. E1 108
Dauphin Lake, l., Man., Can. D2 100
Daura, Nig. E14 64
Daus, Tn., U.S. D8 149
Dāvangere, India E3 46
Davao, Phil. D8 38
Davao Gulf, b., Phil. D8 38
Dāvar Panāh, Iran H17 48
Davel, S. Afr. F9 66
Daveluyville, Que., Can. C5 104
Davenport, Fl., U.S. D5 116
Davenport, Ia., U.S. C7 122
Davenport, Ne., U.S. D8 134
Davenport, N.D., U.S. C8 141
Davenport, Ok., U.S. B5 143
Davenport, Wa., U.S. B7 154
Davey, Ne., U.S. h11 134
Davey, Port, b., Austl. N6 70
David, Pan. C1 84
David, Ky., U.S. C7 124
David City, Ne., U.S. C8 134
Davidson, N.C., U.S. B2 140
Davidson, Ok., U.S. C2 143
Davidson, co., N.C., U.S. B2 140
Davidson, co., Tn., U.S. A5 149
Davie, Fl., U.S. F6 116
Davie, co., N.C., U.S. B2 140
Daviess, co., In., U.S. G3 121
Daviess, co., Ky., U.S. C2 124
Daviess, co., Mo., U.S. B3 132
Davin, Sask., Can. G3 105
Davinópolis, Braz. C3 79
Davis, Ca., U.S. C3 112
Davis, Il., U.S. A4 120
Davis, N.C., U.S. C6 140
Davis, Ok., U.S. C4 143
Davis, S.D., U.S. D9 148
Davis, W.V., U.S. B5 155
Davis, co., Ia., U.S. D5 122
Davis, co., Ut., U.S. C3 151
Davis, Mount, mtn., Pa., U.S. G3 145
Davisboro, Ga., U.S. D4 117
Davis City, Ia., U.S. D4 122
Davis Creek, stm., W.V., U.S. m12 155
Davis Dam, Az., U.S. B1 110
Davis Dam, U.S. H7 135
Davis Inlet, Newf., Can. g9 102
Davis Islands, is., Fl., U.S. p11 116
Davis Junction, Il., U.S. A4 120
Davis Lake, l., Or., U.S. E5 144
Davis-Monthan Air Force Base, mil., Az., U.S. E5 110
Davis Mountains, mts., Tx., U.S. o12 150
Davison, Mi., U.S. E7 129
Davison, co., S.D., U.S. D7 148
Davis Strait, strt., N.A. C21 96
Daviston, Al., U.S. B4 108
Davisville, R.I., U.S. E4 146
Davlekanovo, U.S.S.R. G9 22
Davos, Switz. E12 13
Davutlar, Tur. L11 20
Davy, W.V., U.S. D3 155
Dawa (Daua), stm., Afr. H9 56
Dawāsir, Wādī ad-, val., Sau. Ar. D4 47
Dawei (Tavoy), Burma G5 40
Dawes, co., Ne., U.S. B2 134
Dawn, Mo., U.S. B4 132
Dawna Range, mts., Burma F5 40
Dawqah, Sau. Ar. E2 47
Dawrah, Sud. K3 60
Daws Island, i., S.C., U.S. G6 147
Dawson, Yukon, Can. D5 96
Dawson, Ga., U.S. E2 117
Dawson, Mn., U.S. F2 130
Dawson, Ne., U.S. D10 134
Dawson, N.D., U.S. C6 141
Dawson, Tx., U.S. D4 150
Dawson, co., Ga., U.S. B2 117
Dawson, co., Mt., U.S. C11 133
Dawson, co., Ne., U.S. D6 134
Dawson, co., Tx., U.S. C1 150
Dawson, stm., Austl. E8 70
Dawson, Isla, i., Chile G2 78
Dawson, Mount, mtn., B.C., Can. D9 99
Dawson Creek, B.C., Can. B7 99
Dawson Range, mts., Austl. E8 70
Dawson Springs, Ky., U.S. C2 124
Dawsonville, Ga., U.S. B2 117
Dawusi, China D5 30
Dax, Fr. I5 14
Daxian, China E8 30
Daxing, China D4 32
Daxue Shan, mts., China E7 30
Day, co., S.D., U.S. B8 148
Daye, China E3 34
Daying, China D1 32
Daying (Taping), stm., Asia B5 40
Daykin, Ne., U.S. D8 134
Daylesford, Austl. K6 70
Daymán, stm., Ur. F10 80
Daym Zubayr, Sud. N4 60
Dayr Abū Sa'īd, Jord. C5 50
Dayr 'Alī, Syria B6 50
Dayr az-Zawr, Syria D6 48
Dayr Qānūn, Syria A6 50
Dayrūṭ, Egypt D6 60
Daysland, Alta., Can. C4 98
Dayton, Id., U.S. G7 119
Dayton, In., U.S. D4 121
Dayton, Ia., U.S. B3 122
Dayton, Ky., U.S. h14 124
Dayton, Md., U.S. B4 127
Dayton, Mn., U.S. m12 130
Dayton, Mt., U.S. C2 133
Dayton, Nv., U.S. D2 135
Dayton, N.J., U.S. C3 137
Dayton, Oh., U.S. C1 142
Dayton, Or., U.S. B3 144
Dayton, Tn., U.S. D8 149
Dayton, Tx., U.S. D5 150
Dayton, Va., U.S. B4 153
Dayton, Wa., U.S. C8 154
Dayton, Wy., U.S. B5 157
Daytona Beach, Fl., U.S. C5 116
Dayu, China J3 34
Dayu Ling, mts., China J3 34
Da Yunhe (Grand Canal), China E10 30
Dayville, Ct., U.S. B8 114
Dazey, N.D., U.S. B7 141
Dazui, China E3 34
Dcheïra, Mor. E6 62
De Aar, S. Afr. H7 66
Dead, North Branch, stm., Me., U.S. C2 126
Dead, South Branch, stm., Me., U.S. C2 126
Dead Creek, stm., Vt., U.S. C2 152
Dead Diamond, stm., N.H., U.S. g7 136
Dead Indian Peak, mtn., Wy., U.S. B3 157
Dead Lake, l., Mn., U.S. D3 130
Dead Lakes, l., Fl., U.S. B1 116
Deadman Bay, b., Fl., U.S. C3 116
Deadman Creek, stm., Wa., U.S. g14 154
Deadman's Cay, Bah. C7 94
Dead Sea (Al-Baḥr al-Mayyit) (Yam HaMelaḥ), l., Asia F4 50
Deadwood, S.D., U.S. C2 148
Deadwood Reservoir, res., Id., U.S. E3 119
Deaf Smith, co., Tx., U.S. B1 150
Deakin, Austl. F5 68
Deal, Eng., U.K. J15 8
Deal, N.J., U.S. C4 137
Deale, Md., U.S. C4 127
Deal Island, Md., U.S. D6 127
Deal Island, i., Md., U.S. D6 127
Dean, stm., B.C., Can. C4 99
Dean Channel, strt., B.C., Can. C4 99
Deán Funes, Arg. F6 80
Deanville, W.V., U.S. B4 155
Dearborn, Mi., U.S. F7 129
Dearborn, Mo., U.S. B3 132
Dearborn, co., In., U.S. F7 121
Dearborn Heights, Mi., U.S. p15 129
Dearing, Ga., U.S. C4 117
Dearing, Ks., U.S. E8 123
De Armanville, Al., U.S. B4 108
Deary, Id., U.S. C2 119
Dease Arm, b., N.W. Ter., Can. C8 96
Dease Lake, B.C., Can. m16 99
Dease Strait, strt., N.W. Ter., Can. C11 96
Death Valley, val., Ca., U.S. D5 112
Death Valley National Monument, U.S. D5 112
Deatsville, Al., U.S. C3 108
Deauville, Fr. C7 14
Deaver, Wy., U.S. B4 157
De Baca, co., N.M., U.S. C5 138
Debar, Yugo. H4 20
De Bary, Fl., U.S. D5 116
Debauch Mountain, mtn., Ak., U.S. C8 109
Debden, Sask., Can. D2 105
Debec, N.B., Can. C2 101
De Beque, Co., U.S. B2 113
Dębica, Pol. E21 10
Dęblin, Pol. D21 10
De Borgia, Mt., U.S. C1 133
Deboullie Mountain, mtn., Me., U.S. B4 126
Debrecen, Hung. H21 10
Debre Markos, Eth. L9 60
Debre May, Eth. L9 60
Debre Tabor, Eth. L10 60
Debre Zebit, Eth. L10 60
Debre Zeyit, Eth. M10 60
Debrzno, Pol. B17 10
De Cade, Lake, l., La., U.S. E5 125
Decatur, Al., U.S. A3 108
Decatur, Ar., U.S. A1 111
Decatur, Ga., U.S. C2 117
Decatur, Il., U.S. D5 120
Decatur, In., U.S. C8 121
Decatur, Mi., U.S. F5 129
Decatur, Ms., U.S. C4 131
Decatur, Ne., U.S. B9 134
Decatur, Tn., U.S. D9 149
Decatur, Tx., U.S. C4 150
Decatur, co., Ga., U.S. F2 117
Decatur, co., In., U.S. F6 121
Decatur, co., Ia., U.S. D4 122
Decatur, co., Ks., U.S. C3 123
Decatur, co., Tn., U.S. B3 149
Decatur, Lake, res., Il., U.S. D5 120
Decaturville, Tn., U.S. B3 149
Decazeville, Fr. H9 14
Deccan, plat., India D5 46
Deception, stm., Bots. C6 66
Deception, Mount, mtn., Wa., U.S. B2 154
Deception Island, i., B.A.T. B12 73
Decherd, Tn., U.S. B5 149
Děčín, Czech. E14 10
Decize, Fr. F10 14
Decker, Man., Can. D1 100
Decker, In., U.S. G2 121
Decker Lake, B.C., Can. B5 99
Deckers, Co., U.S. B5 113
Deckerville, Mi., U.S. E8 129
Declo, Id., U.S. G5 119
De Cocksdorp, Neth. B6 12
Decorah, Ia., U.S. A6 122
Decota, W.V., U.S. m13 155
Decs, Hung. I18 10
Deda, Rom. C8 20
Dedham, Ia., U.S. C3 122
Dedham, Ma., U.S. B5 128
De Doorns, S. Afr. I4 66
Dédougou, Burkina E8 64
Dedovsk, U.S.S.R. F20 26
Dee, stm., U.K. H10 8
Dee, stm., Scot., U.K. D11 8
Deep, stm., N.C., U.S. B3 140
Deep Brook, N.S., Can. E4 101
Deep Creek, stm., De., U.S. F3 115
Deep Creek, stm., Mt., U.S. C4 133
Deep Creek, stm., Ut., U.S. B3 151
Deep Creek, stm., Ut., U.S. C2 151
Deep Creek, stm., Ut., U.S. F3 151
Deep Creek, stm., Wa., U.S. g13 154
Deep Creek Lake, res., Md., U.S. K12 127
Deep Creek Mountains, mts., Id., U.S. G6 119
Deep Creek Range, mts., Ut., U.S. D2 151
Deep Fork, stm., Ok., U.S. B5 143
Deep Gap, N.C., U.S. A1 140
Deep Inlet, b., Newf., Can. g10 102
Deep Red Creek, stm., Ok., U.S. C3 143
Deep River, Ont., Can. A7 103
Deep River, Ct., U.S. D6 114
Deep River, Ia., U.S. C5 122
Deepstep, Ga., U.S. C4 117
Deepwater, Mo., U.S. C4 132
Deep Water, W.V., U.S. m13 155
Deer, Ar., U.S. B2 111
Deer Creek, Il., U.S. C4 120
Deer Creek, In., U.S. C5 121
Deer Creek, Mn., U.S. D3 130
Deer Creek, stm., In., U.S. C5 121
Deer Creek, stm., Md., U.S. A5 127
Deer Creek, stm., Ms., U.S. B3 131
Deer Creek, stm., Oh., U.S. C2 142
Deer Creek Indian Reservation, Mn., U.S. C5 130
Deerfield, Il., U.S. h9 120
Deerfield, Ks., U.S. E2 123
Deerfield, Ma., U.S. A2 128
Deerfield, Mi., U.S. G7 129
Deerfield, N.H., U.S. D4 136
Deerfield, Wi., U.S. E4 156
Deerfield, stm., U.S. A2 128
Deerfield Beach, Fl., U.S. F6 116
Deering, Ak., U.S. B7 109
Deering, N.D., U.S. A4 141
Deer Island, pen., Ma., U.S. g12 128
Deer Island, i., Ms., U.S. f8 131
Deer Isle, Me., U.S. D4 126
Deer Isle, i., Me., U.S. D4 126
Deer Lake, Newf., Can. D3 102
Deer Lake, l., Newf., Can. D3 102
Deer Lake, l., Mn., U.S. C5 130
Deer Lodge, Mt., U.S. D4 133
Deer Lodge, Tn., U.S. C9 149
Deer Lodge, co., Mt., U.S. E3 133
Deer Mountain, mtn., Me., U.S. C2 126
Deer Park, Al., U.S. D1 108
Deer Park, Md., U.S. m12 127
Deer Park, N.Y., U.S. n15 139
Deer Park, Oh., U.S. o13 142
Deer Park, Tx., U.S. r14 150
Deer Park, Wa., U.S. B8 154
Deer Peak, mtn., Co., U.S. C5 113
Deer River, Mn., U.S. C5 130
Deer Trail, Co., U.S. B6 113
Deerwood, Mn., U.S. D5 130
Deeth, Nv., U.S. B6 135
Defiance, Ia., U.S. C2 122
Defiance, Mo., U.S. f12 132
Defiance, Oh., U.S. A1 142
Defiance, co., Oh., U.S. A1 142
Defiance, Mount, mtn., Or., U.S. B5 144
De Forest, Wi., U.S. E4 156
De Funiak Springs, Fl., U.S. u15 116
Dêgê, China E6 30
Degeh Bur, Eth. G9 56
Dégelis, Que., Can. B9 104
Degerfors, Swe. L14 6
Deggendorf, Ger. G12 10
Degh, stm., Asia D6 44
Degoma, Eth. K9 60
De Graff, Oh., U.S. B2 142
De Gray Lake, res., Ar., U.S. C2 111
De Grey, stm., Austl. D4 68
Dehalak Deset, i., Eth. E9 56
Deh Bīd, Iran F12 48
Dehibat, Tun. D16 62
Dehiwala-Mount Lavinia, Sri L. I5 46
Deh Kord, Iran E10 48
Dehlorān, Iran E9 48
Dehra Dūn, India E8 44
Dehri, India H11 44
Dehua, China J7 34
Dehui, China C12 30
Dej, Rom. B7 20
Dejnau, U.S.S.R. J10 22
De Kalb, Il., U.S. B5 120
De Kalb, Ms., U.S. C5 131
De Kalb, Mo., U.S. B3 132
De Kalb, Tx., U.S. C5 150
De Kalb, co., Al., U.S. A4 108
De Kalb, co., Ga., U.S. C2 117
De Kalb, co., Il., U.S. B5 120
De Kalb, co., In., U.S. B7 121
De Kalb, co., Mo., U.S. B3 132
De Kalb, co., Tn., U.S. D8 149
Dekemhare, Eth. J10 60
Dekese, Zaire B4 58
Dekina, Nig. H13 64
Delacroix, La., U.S. k12 125
Delafield, Wi., U.S. m11 156
De Lamere, N.D., U.S. C8 141
Delanco, N.J., U.S. C3 137
De Land, Fl., U.S. C5 116
De Land, Il., U.S. C5 120
Delano, Ca., U.S. E4 112
Delano, Mn., U.S. E5 130
Delano, Tn., U.S. D9 149
Delano Peak, mtn., Ut., U.S. E3 151
Delaplaine, Ar., U.S. A5 111
Delārām, Afg. E17 48
Delareyville, S. Afr. F7 66
Delaronde Lake, l., Sask., Can. C2 105
Del'atin, U.S.S.R. A8 20
Delavan, Il., U.S. C4 120
Delavan, Ks., U.S. D7 123
Delavan, Wi., U.S. F5 156
Delaware, Ont., Can. E3 103
Delaware, Ar., U.S. B2 111
Delaware, Oh., U.S. B2 142
Delaware, Ok., U.S. A6 143
Delaware, co., In., U.S. D7 121
Delaware, co., Ia., U.S. B6 122
Delaware, co., N.Y., U.S. C5 139
Delaware, co., Oh., U.S. B2 142
Delaware, co., Ok., U.S. A7 143
Delaware, co., Pa., U.S. G11 145
Delaware, state, U.S. D3 115
Delaware, stm., U.S. E2 137
Delaware, stm., Ks., U.S. C8 123
Delaware, East Branch, stm., N.Y., U.S. C5 139
Delaware, West Branch, stm., U.S. C5 139
Delaware Bay, b., U.S. D11 106
Delaware City, De., U.S. B3 115
Delaware Lake, res., Oh., U.S. B3 142
Delaware Mountains, mts., Tx., U.S. o12 150
Delaware Water Gap, Pa., U.S. E11 145
Delaware Water Gap, N.J., U.S. B2 137
Delaware Water Gap National Recreation Area, U.S. B2 137
Delbarton, W.V., U.S. D2 155
Delburne, Alta., Can. C4 98
Delcambre, La., U.S. E4 125
Del Campillo, Arg. H6 80
Del City, Ok., U.S. B4 143
Delco, N.C., U.S. C4 140
Delegate, Austl. K8 70
Délembé, Cen. Afr. Rep. M2 60
Delémont, Switz. D7 13
De Leon, Tx., U.S. C3 150
De Leon Springs, Fl., U.S. C5 116
Delevan, N.Y., U.S. C2 139
Delfinópolis, Braz. F5 79
Delft, Neth. D5 12
Delfzijl, Neth. B10 12
Delgado, El Sal. D5 92
Delgado, Cabo, c., Moz. D8 58
Delhi, India F7 44
Delhi, Ia., U.S. B6 122
Delhi, La., U.S. B4 125
Delhi, N.Y., U.S. C6 139
Delhi, ter., India F7 44
Delia, Alta., Can. D4 98
Delia, Ks., U.S. C8 123
Delicias, Mex. C7 90
Delight, Ar., U.S. C2 111
Delingde, U.S.S.R. C14 24
Delingha, China D6 30
Delisle, Sask., Can. F2 105
De Lisle, Ms., U.S. E4 131
Delitzsch, Ger. D12 10
Dell, Ar., U.S. B5 111
Dell City, Tx., U.S. o12 150
Delle, Fr. E14 14
Dellenbaugh, Mount, mtn., Az., U.S. A2 110
Delles, Alg. B12 62
Dell Rapids, S.D., U.S. D9 148
Dellslow, W.V., U.S. h11 155
Delmar, Al., U.S. A2 108
Del Mar, Ca., U.S. o15 112
Delmar, De., U.S. G3 115
Delmar, Ia., U.S. C7 122
Delmar, Md., U.S. D6 127
Delmar, N.Y., U.S. C7 139
Delmarva Peninsula, pen., U.S. D11 106
Delmas, Sask., Can. E1 105
Delmenhorst, Ger. B8 10
Delmont, S.D., U.S. D7 148
Del Norte, Co., U.S. D4 113
Del Norte, co., Ca., U.S. B2 112
Deloit, Ia., U.S. B2 122
Delong, In., U.S. B5 121
De-Longa, ostrova, is., U.S.S.R. B22 24
Deloraine, Austl. M7 70
Deloraine, Man., Can. E1 100
Deloro, Ont., Can. C7 103
Del Park Manor, De., U.S. i7 115
Delphi, In., U.S. C4 121
Delphi see Dhelfoí, hist., Grc. K6 20
Delphos, Ks., U.S. C6 123
Delphos, Oh., U.S. B1 142
Delran, N.J., U.S. C3 137
Delray Beach, Fl., U.S. F6 116
Del Rio, Tx., U.S. E2 150
Delson, Que., Can. q19 104
Delta, Ont., Can. C8 103
Delta, Al., U.S. B4 108
Delta, Co., U.S. C2 113
Delta, Ia., U.S. C5 122
Delta, Mo., U.S. D8 132
Delta, Oh., U.S. A1 142
Delta, Pa., U.S. G9 145
Delta, Ut., U.S. D3 151
Delta, co., Co., U.S. C3 113
Delta, co., Mi., U.S. C3 129
Delta, co., Tx., U.S. C5 150
Delta, reg., Ms., U.S. B3 131
Delta Amacuro, ter., Ven. C12 84
Delta Beach, Man., Can. D2 100
Delta City, Ms., U.S. B3 131
Delta Downs, Austl. A4 70
Delta Junction, Ak., U.S. C10 109
Delta Peak, mtn., B.C., Can. A3 99
Delta Reservoir, res., N.Y., U.S. B5 139
Deltaville, Va., U.S. C6 153
Delton, Mi., U.S. F5 129
Deltona, Fl., U.S. D5 116
Demaine, Sask., Can. G2 105
Dem'ansk, U.S.S.R. D15 26
Demarest, N.J., U.S. h9 137
Demba, Zaire C4 58
Dembecha, Eth. L9 60
Dembéni, Com. K15 67a
Dembi, Eth. M9 60
Dembi Dolo, Eth. M8 60
Demerara, stm., Guy. D13 84
Demidov, U.S.S.R. F14 26
Deming, N.M., U.S. E2 138
Deming, Wa., U.S. A3 154
Demini, stm., Braz. H11 84
Demirci, Tur. J12 20
Demirtaş, Tur. I13 20

Name — Map Ref. — Page

Demjanka, stm., U.S.S.R. F6 24
Demjanskoje, U.S.S.R. F11 22
Demmin, Ger. B13 10
Demnate, Mor. E7 62
Demopolis, Al., U.S. C2 108
Demopolis Lock and Dam, Al., U.S. C2 108
Demorest, Ga., U.S. B3 117
Demorestville, Ont., Can. C7 103
Demotte, In., U.S. B3 121
Dempster, S.D., U.S. C9 148
Denain, Fr. B10 14
Denakil, reg., Eth. F9 56
Denali National Park, Ak., U.S. C9 109
Denare Beach, Sask., Can. C4 105
Denau, U.S.S.R. J11 22
Denbigh, Wales, U.K. H10 8
Dender (Dendre), stm., Bel. G4 12
Dendermonde (Termonde), Bel. F5 12
Dendron, S. Afr. D9 66
Dendron, Va., U.S. C6 153
Deneba, Eth. M10 60
Dengcheng, China B3 34
Dêngqên, China E6 30
Dengshahe, China D10 32
Denham, Austl. E2 68
Denham, In., U.S. B4 121
Denham, Mount, mtn., Jam. E6 94
Denham Island, i., Austl. A3 70
Denham Range, mts., Austl. C7 70
Denham Springs, La., U.S. D5 125
Den Helder, Neth. C6 12
Denhoff, N.D., U.S. B5 141
Denholm, Sask., Can. E1 105
Dénia, Spain G12 16
Déniè, Mali F6 64
Deniliquin, Austl. J6 70
Denison, Ia., U.S. B2 122
Denison, Ks., U.S. k14 123
Denison, Tx., U.S. C4 150
Denison Dam, U.S. D5 143
Denizli, Tur. L13 20
Denmark, Austl. F3 68
Denmark, N.S., Can. D6 101
Denmark, Ia., U.S. D6 122
Denmark, S.C., U.S. E5 147
Denmark, Wi., U.S. D6 156
Denmark (Danmark), ctry., Eur. D10 4
Denmark Strait, strt. B4 52
Dennard, Ar., U.S. B3 111
Dennehotso, Az., U.S. A6 110
Denning, Ar., U.S. B2 111
Dennis, Ks., U.S. E8 123
Dennis, Ma., U.S. C7 128
Dennis, Ms., U.S. A5 131
Dennis Hill, mtn., Ct., U.S. B3 114
Dennison, Mn., U.S. F5 130
Dennison, Oh., U.S. B4 142
Dennis Port, Ma., U.S. C7 128
Denny Terrace, S.C., U.S. C5 147
Denpasar, Indon. G6 38
Dent, Mn., U.S. D3 130
Dent, co., Mo., U.S. D6 132
Denton, Ga., U.S. E4 117
Denton, Ks., U.S. C8 123
Denton, Md., U.S. C6 127
Denton, Mi., U.S. p14 129
Denton, Mt., U.S. C7 133
Denton, Ne., U.S. D9 134
Denton, N.C., U.S. B2 140
Denton, Tx., U.S. C4 150
Denton, co., Tx., U.S. C4 150
D'Entrecasteaux, Point, c., Austl. F3 68
D'Entrecasteaux Islands, is., Pap. N. Gui. A10 68
Dentsville, S.C., U.S. C6 147
Denver, Co., U.S. B6 113
Denver, In., U.S. C5 121
Denver, Ia., U.S. B5 122
Denver, N.C., U.S. B1 140
Denver, Pa., U.S. F9 145
Denver, Tn., U.S. A4 149
Denver, co., Co., U.S. B6 113
Denver City, Tx., U.S. C1 150
Denville, N.J., U.S. B4 137
Denzil, Sask., Can. E1 105
Deoghar, India H12 44
Deolāli, India C2 46
Deoria, India G10 44
Depauw, In., U.S. H5 121
De Pere, Wi., U.S. D5 156
Depew, N.Y., U.S. C2 139
Depew, Ok., U.S. B5 143
Depoe Bay, Or., U.S. C2 144
Depok, Indon. J13 39a
Deport, Tx., U.S. C5 150
Deposit, N.Y., U.S. C5 139
Depósito, Braz. F12 84
Depue, Il., U.S. B4 120
Deputy, In., U.S. G6 121
Dêqên, China F6 30
De Queen, Ar., U.S. C1 111
De Queen Reservoir, res., Ar., U.S. C1 111
De Quincy, La., U.S. D2 125
Dera, Lach, val., Afr. A8 58
Dera Ghāzi Khān, Pak. E4 44
Dera Ismāīl Khān, Pak. E4 44
Derbent, U.S.S.R. I7 22
Derby, Austl. M7 70
Derby, N.B., Can. C4 101
Derby, Eng., U.K. I12 8
Derby, Ct., U.S. D3 114
Derby, Ks., U.S. E6 123
Derby, Ms., U.S. E4 131
Derby, N.Y., U.S. C2 139
Derby, Vt., U.S. B4 152
Derby, Va., U.S. f9 153
Derby Junction, N.B., Can. C4 101
Derby Line, Vt., U.S. A4 152
Derbyshire, co., Eng., U.K. H12 8
Derdepoort, S. Afr. E8 66
Derecho, stm., Col. I8 84
Derecske, Hung. H21 10
Derev'anka, U.S.S.R. K24 6
De Ridder, La., U.S. D2 125
Derik, Tur. C6 48
Derma, Ms., U.S. B4 131
Dermott, Ar., U.S. D4 111
Dernieres, Isles, is., La., U.S. E5 125
Déroute, Passage de la, strt., Eur. L11 8
Derrieusseaux Creek, stm., Ar., U.S. C3 111
Derry, N.H., U.S. E4 136
Derry, N.M., U.S. E2 138
Derry, Pa., U.S. F3 145
Derry see Londonderry, N. Ire., U.K. F6 8
Derudeb, Sud. I9 60
De Rust, S. Afr. I6 66
Derval, Fr. E5 14
Derventa, Yugo. E1 20
Derwent, Alta., Can. C5 98
Derwent, stm., Austl. N7 70
Derwood, Md., U.S. B3 127
Deržavinsk, U.S.S.R. G11 22
Desaguadero, stm., Arg. G5 80
Desaguadero, stm., Bol. G7 82
Des Allemands, La., U.S. E5 125
Des Arc, Ar., U.S. C4 111
Des Arc, Mo., U.S. D7 132
Desbiens, Que., Can. A6 104
Desboro, Ont., Can. C3 103
Descabezado Grande, Volcán, vol., Chile H3 80
Descanso, Braz. D12 80
Descartes, Fr. F7 14
Deschaillons [-sur-Saint-Laurent], Que., Can. C5 104
Deschambault, Que., Can. C6 104
Deschambault Lake, Sask., Can. C4 105
Deschambault Lake, l., Sask., Can. C4 105
Deschutes, co., Or., U.S. D5 144
Deschutes, stm., Or., U.S. B6 144
Desdunes, Haiti E8 94
Dese, Eth. F8 56
Deseado, stm., Arg. F3 78
Desengaño, Punta, c., Arg. F3 78
Desenzano del Garda, Italy D5 18
Deseret, Ut., U.S. D3 151
Deseret Peak, mtn., Ut., U.S. C3 151
Deseronto, Ont., Can. C7 103
Desert, Mount, mtn., W.V., U.S. m13 155
Desertas, Ilhas, is., Port. M21 17a
Desert Creek Peak, mtn., Nv., U.S. E2 135
Desert Hot Springs, Ca., U.S. F5 112
Desert Peak, mtn., Ut., U.S. B2 151
Desert Valley, val., Nv., U.S. B3 135
Desha, Ar., U.S. B4 111
Desha, co., Ar., U.S. D4 111
Desheng, China B10 40
Deshler, Ne., U.S. D8 134
Deshler, Oh., U.S. A2 142
Desiderio Tello, Arg. F5 80
Des Lacs, N.D., U.S. A4 141
Des Lacs, stm., N.D., U.S. A4 141
Desloge, Mo., U.S. D7 132
Desmarais, Alta., Can. B4 98
Desmet, Id., U.S. B2 119
De Smet, S.D., U.S. C8 148
Des Moines, Ia., U.S. C4 122
Des Moines, N.M., U.S. A6 138
Des Moines, Wa., U.S. B3 154
Des Moines, co., Ia., U.S. D6 122
Des Moines, stm., U.S. D5 122
Des Moines, East Fork, stm., U.S. A3 122
Desna, stm., U.S.S.R. G4 22
Desolación, Isla, i., Chile J7 74
Desolation Canyon, val., Ut., U.S. D5 151
De Soto, Ga., U.S. E2 117
De Soto, Il., U.S. F4 120
De Soto, Ia., U.S. C3 122
De Soto, Ks., U.S. D9 123
De Soto, Mo., U.S. C7 132
De Soto, Tx., U.S. n10 150
De Soto, Wi., U.S. E2 156
De Soto, co., Fl., U.S. E5 116
De Soto, co., La., U.S. B2 125
De Soto, co., Ms., U.S. A3 131
De Soto City, Fl., U.S. E5 116
Despard, W.V., U.S. k10 155
Des Peres, Mo., U.S. f13 132
Des Plaines, Il., U.S. A6 120
Des Plaines, stm., U.S. k8 120
Desroches, Île, i., Sey. C10 58
Dessau, Ger. D12 10
Destin, Fl., U.S. u15 116
Destrehan, La., U.S. E5 125
Desvres, Fr. B8 14
Deta, Rom. D5 20
Detčino, U.S.S.R. G19 26
Dete, Zimb. B8 66
Detlor, Ont., Can. B7 103
Detmold, Ger. D8 10
Detour, Point, c., Mi., U.S. C4 129
De Tour Village, Mi., U.S. C7 129
Detroit, Al., U.S. A1 108
Detroit, Ks., U.S. D6 123
Detroit, Me., U.S. D3 126
Detroit, Mi., U.S. F7 129
Detroit, Or., U.S. C4 144
Detroit, Tx., U.S. C5 150
Detroit Lake, res., Or., U.S. C4 144
Detroit Lakes, Mn., U.S. D3 130
Deuel, co., Ne., U.S. C3 134
Deuel, co., S.D., U.S. C9 148
Deurne, Bel. F5 12
Deurne, Neth. F8 12
Deutsche Bucht, b., Ger. A7 10
Deux-Montagnes, Que., Can. p19 104
Deux Montagnes, Lac des, l., Que., Can. q19 104
Deux-Sèvres, dept., Fr. F6 14
Deva, Rom. D6 20
Devakottai, India H5 46
De Valls Bluff, Ar., U.S. C4 111
Dev'atiny, U.S.S.R. K25 6
Dévaványa, Hung. H20 10
Devecser, Hung. H17 10
Deventer, Neth. D9 12
Devereux, Ga., U.S. C3 117
DeView, Bayou, stm., Ar., U.S. B4 111
Devil's Island see Diable, Île du, i., Fr. Gu. B8 76
Devils Lake, N.D., U.S. A7 141
Devils Lake, l., N.D., U.S. A6 141
Devils Paw, mtn., Ak., U.S. k23 109
Devils Postpile National Monument, Ca., U.S. D4 112
Devils Tower, Wy., U.S. B8 157
Devils Tower National Monument, Wy., U.S. B8 157
Devil Track Lake, l., Mn., U.S. k9 130
Devine, Tx., U.S. E3 150
Devola, Oh., U.S. C4 142
Devon, Alta., Can. C4 98
Devon, Ks., U.S. E9 123
Devon, co., Eng., U.K. K10 8
Devon Island, i., N.W. Ter., Can. B11 86
Devonport, Austl. M7 70
Devonport, N.Z. B5 72
Devonshire, De., U.S. h7 115
Devoto, Arg. F7 80
Dewar, Ok., U.S. B6 143
Dewās, India I7 44
Dewberry, Alta., Can. C5 98
Dewees Inlet, b., S.C., U.S. k12 147
Dewees Island, i., S.C., U.S. F8 147
Dewetsdorp, S. Afr. G8 66
Dewey, Az., U.S. C3 110
Dewey, Ok., U.S. A6 143
Dewey, co., Ok., U.S. B2 143
Dewey, co., S.D., U.S. B4 148
Dewey Beach, De., U.S. F5 115
Dewey Lake, res., Ky., U.S. C7 124
Deweyville, Tx., U.S. D6 150
Deweyville, Ut., U.S. B3 151
De Winton, Alta., Can. D3 98
De Witt, Ar., U.S. C4 111
De Witt, Ia., U.S. C7 122
De Witt, Mi., U.S. F6 129
De Witt, Ne., U.S. D9 134
De Witt, N.Y., U.S. B4 139
De Witt, co., Il., U.S. C4 120
De Witt, co., Tx., U.S. E4 150
Dexter, Ga., U.S. D3 117
Dexter, Ia., U.S. C3 122
Dexter, Ks., U.S. E7 123
Dexter, Ky., U.S. f9 124
Dexter, Me., U.S. C3 126
Dexter, Mi., U.S. F7 129
Dexter, Mn., U.S. G6 130
Dexter, Mo., U.S. E8 132
Dexter, N.M., U.S. D5 138
Dexter, N.Y., U.S. A4 139
Dexter, Or., U.S. D4 144
Dexter, Lake, l., Fl., U.S. C5 116
Deyhūk, Iran E14 48
Deyyer, Iran H11 48
Dezfūl, Iran E10 48
Dezhou, China F4 32
Dežneva, mys, c., U.S.S.R. D30 24
Dháfni, Grc. L6 20
Dhahab, Egypt C8 60
Dhahabān, Sau. Ar. D1 47
Dhahran see Az-Zahrān, Sau. Ar. A7 47
Dhaka, Bngl. I14 44
Dhamār, Yemen G4 47
Dhamtari, India B6 46
Dhanbād, India I12 44
Dhangadhī, Nepal F9 44
D'Hanis, Tx., U.S. E3 150
Dhār, India I6 44
Dharangaon, India B3 46
Dhārāpuram, India G4 46
Dharmavaram, India E4 46
Dharmshāla, India D7 44
Dhaulpur, India G7 44
Dhawlāgiri, mtn., Nepal F10 44
Dhelfoí, hist., Grc. K6 20
Dhībān, Jord. E5 50
Dhodhekánisos (Dodecanese), is., Grc. M10 20
Dholka, India I5 44
Dhorāji, India J4 44
Dhuburi, India G13 44
Dhule, India J6 44
Diable, Île du, i., Fr. Gu. B8 76
Diablo, Canyon, val., Az., U.S. C4 110
Diablo, Mount, mtn., Ca., U.S. h9 112
Diablo, Pico del, mtn., Mex. B2 90
Diablo Dam, Wa., U.S. A4 154
Diablo Lake, res., Wa., U.S. A4 154
Diablo Range, mts., Ca., U.S. D3 112
Diablotins, Morne, mtn., Dom. G14 94
Diagonal, Ia., U.S. D3 122
Diaka, mth., Mali D7 64
Dialakoto, Sen. E3 64
Diamante, Arg. G8 80
Diamante, stm., Arg. H5 80
Diamantina, Braz. E7 79
Diamantina, stm., Austl. F3 70
Diamantino, Braz. F13 82
Diamantino, stm., Braz. D2 79
Diamond, W.V., U.S. m12 155
Diamond City, Alta., Can. E4 98
Diamond City, Ar., U.S. A3 111
Diamond Harbour, India I13 44
Diamond Head, crat., Hi., U.S. B4 118
Diamond Hill, R.I., U.S. B4 146
Diamond Hill Reservoir, res., R.I., U.S. A4 146
Diamond Islets, is., Austl. A9 70
Diamond Lake, Il., U.S. h9 120
Diamond Lake, l., Or., U.S. D4 144
Diamond Mountains, mts., Nv., U.S. D6 135
Diamond Peak, mtn., Co., U.S. A2 113
Diamond Peak, mtn., Id., U.S. E5 119
Diamond Peak, mtn., Or., U.S. D4 144
Diamond Peak, mtn., Wa., U.S. C8 154
Diamond Springs, Ca., U.S. C3 112
Diamondville, Wy., U.S. E2 157
Diana, W.V., U.S. C4 155
Diana Bay, b., Can. D19 96
Dian Chi, l., China B7 40
Diangounté Kamara, Mali D5 64
Dianhu, China B8 34
Dianópolis, Braz. F9 76
Diapaga, Burkina E10 64
Diaz, Ar., U.S. B4 111
Dibaya, Zaire C4 58
Dibble Iceberg Tongue, Ant. B7 73
Dibeng, S. Afr. F6 66
D'Iberville, Ms., U.S. E5 131
Dibete, Bots. D8 66
Diboll, Tx., U.S. D5 150
Dibrell, Tn., U.S. D8 149
Dibrugarh, India G16 44
Dickens, co., Tx., U.S. C2 150
Dickenson, co., Va., U.S. e9 153
Dickerson, Md., U.S. B3 127
Dickey, co., N.D., U.S. C7 141
Dickeyville, Wi., U.S. F3 156
Dickinson, Al., U.S. D2 108
Dickinson, N.D., U.S. C3 141
Dickinson, co., Ia., U.S. A2 122
Dickinson, co., Ks., U.S. D6 123
Dickinson, co., Mi., U.S. B3 129
Dickinson Dam, N.D., U.S. C3 141
Dickson, Ok., U.S. C5 143
Dickson, Tn., U.S. A4 149
Dickson, co., Tn., U.S. A4 149
Dickson City, Pa., U.S. D10 145
Didimbo, Ang. A5 66
Didsbury, Alta., Can. D3 98
Die, Fr. H12 14
Diébougou, Burkina F8 64
Dieciocho de Julio, Ur. G12 80
Diefenbaker, Lake, res., Sask., Can. F2 105
Diego de Almagro, Chile D3 80
Diego de Ocampo, Pico, mtn., Dom. Rep. E9 94
Diego Garcia, i., B.I.O.T. J8 28
Diego Ramírez, Islas, is., Chile H3 78
Diembéring, Sen. E1 64
Dien Bien Phu, Viet. D7 40
Dieppe, N.B., Can. C5 101
Dieppe, Fr. L15 8
Dieren, Neth. D9 12
Dierks, Ar., U.S. C1 111
Diessenhofen, Switz. C10 13
Dieterich, Il., U.S. D5 120
Dietikon, Switz. D9 13
Dietrich, Id., U.S. G4 119
Dieulefit, Fr. H12 14
Dieuze, Fr. D13 14
Diez de Octubre, Mex. E7 90
Dif, Kenya A8 58
Difang, China H5 32
Differdange, Lux. I8 12
Difficult, Tn., U.S. C8 149
Digboi, India G16 44
Digby, N.S., Can. E4 101
Digges Islands, is., N.W. Ter., Can. D17 96
Dighton, Ks., U.S. D3 123
Dighton, Ma., U.S. C5 128
Digne, Fr. H13 14
Digoin, Fr. F10 14
Digras, India B4 46
Digri, Pak. H3 44
Digul, stm., Indon. G11 38
Dijon, Fr. E12 14
Dikaja, U.S.S.R. B22 26
Dike, Ia., U.S. B5 122
Dikhil, Dji. F9 56
Dikili, Tur. J10 20
Dikodougou, I.C. G7 64
Diksmuide (Dixmude), Bel. F2 12
Dikson, U.S.S.R. C8 24
Dikwa, Nig. F9 54
Dila, Eth. N10 60
Dili, Indon. G8 38
Dilke, Sask., Can. G3 105
Dilkon, Az., U.S. B5 110
Dillard, Ga., U.S. B3 117
Dillard, Or., U.S. D3 144
Dill City, Ok., U.S. B2 143
Dille, W.V., U.S. C4 155
Diller, Ne., U.S. D9 134
Dilley, Tx., U.S. E3 150
Dilling, Sud. K5 60
Dillingen, Ger. F6 10
Dillingen [an der Donau], Ger. G10 10
Dillingham, Ak., U.S. D8 109
Dillon, Co., U.S. B4 113
Dillon, Mt., U.S. E4 133
Dillon, S.C., U.S. C9 147
Dillon, co., S.C., U.S. C9 147
Dillon Lake, res., Oh., U.S. B3 142
Dillon Reservoir, res., Co., U.S. B4 113
Dillonvale, Oh., U.S. B5 142
Dillsboro, In., U.S. F7 121
Dillsburg, Pa., U.S. F7 145
Dillwyn, Va., U.S. C4 153
Dilly, Mali D6 64
Dilolo, Zaire D4 58
Dilworth, Mn., U.S. D2 130
Dimāpur, India H15 44
Dimashq (Damascus), Syria A6 50
Dimboola, Austl. K5 70
Dîmbovița, co., Rom. E9 20
Dîmbovița, stm., Rom. E9 20
Dime, Eth. N9 60
Dimitrovgrad, Bul. G9 20
Dimitrovgrad, U.S.S.R. G7 22
Dimlang, mtn., Nig. G9 54
Dimmit, co., Tx., U.S. E3 150
Dimmitt, Tx., U.S. B1 150
Dimock, S.D., U.S. D8 148
Dimona, Isr. F4 50
Dimondale, Mi., U.S. F6 129
Dinājpur, Bngl. H13 44
Dinan, Fr. D4 14
Dinant, Bel. H6 12
Dinara, mts., Yugo. F11 18
Dinard, Fr. D4 14
Dinaric Alps see Dinara, mts., Yugo. F11 18
Dindar, Nahr ad- (Dinder), stm., Afr. K8 60
Dindigul, India G4 46
Dindima, Nig. F15 64
Dingalan Bay, b., Phil. N19 39b
Dingess, W.V., U.S. D2 155
Dinggyê, China F4 30
Dinghai, China E11 34
Dingle, Id., U.S. G7 119
Dingle Bay, b., Ire. I3 8
Dingmans Ferry, Pa., U.S. D12 145
Dingnan, China K3 34
Dingolfing, Ger. G12 10
Dingshuzhen, China D8 34
Dinguiraye, Gui. F4 64
Dingwall, N.S., Can. C9 101
Dingxi, China D7 30
Dingxian, China E2 32
Dingyuan, China C6 34
Dinh Lap, Viet. D9 40
Dinkelsbühl, Ger. F10 10
Dinner Point, c., Fl., U.S. D4 116
Dinokwe, Bots. D8 66
Dinosaur, Co., U.S. A1 113
Dinosaur National Monument, U.S. C6 151
Dinsmore, Sask., Can. F2 105
Dinuba, Ca., U.S. D4 112
Dinwiddie, co., Va., U.S. C5 153
Dioïla, Mali E6 64
Dionísio, Braz. E7 79
Dionísio Cerqueira, Braz. D12 80
Diorama, Braz. D3 79
Diouloulou, Sen. E1 64
Dioundiou, Niger E11 64
Dioura, Mali D7 64
Diourbel, Sen. D1 64
Dipkarpaz, N. Cyp. D3 48
Dipolog, Phil. D7 38
Dipper Harbour West, N.B., Can. D3 101
Dippoldiswalde, Ger. E13 10
Dīr, Pak. C4 44
Dire Dawa, Eth. G9 56
Diriamba, Nic. F8 92
Dirico, Ang. A5 66
Diriomo, Nic. F8 92
Dirj, Libya E16 62
Dirk Hartog Island, i., Austl. E2 68
Dirrah, Sud. K4 60
Dirranbandi, Austl. G8 70
Ḍirs, Sau. Ar. E3 47
Dirty Devil, stm., Ut., U.S. E5 151
Disappointment, Cape, c., Falk. Is. J11 74
Disappointment, Cape, c., Wa., U.S. C1 154
Disappointment, Lake, l., Austl. D4 68
Disappointment Creek, stm., Co., U.S. D2 113
Disaster Bay, b., Austl. K9 70
Discovery Bay, b., Austl. L4 70
Disentis, Switz. E10 13
Dishman, Wa., U.S. g14 154
Dishnā, Egypt D7 60
Disko, i., Grnld. C14 86
Disley, Sask., Can. G3 105
Dismal, stm., Ne., U.S. C5 134
Dismal Peak, mtn., Va., U.S. C2 153
Disna, U.S.S.R. F11 26
Disney, Ok., U.S. A6 143
Disputanta, Va., U.S. C5 153
Disraëli, Que., Can. D6 104
Distant, Pa., U.S. E3 145
District of Columbia, dept., U.S. f8 127
Distrito Federal, dept., Braz. C5 79
Distrito Federal, dept., Ven. B9 84
Disūq, Egypt B6 60
Diu, India J4 44
Divalá, Pan. I12 92
Divenskaja, U.S.S.R. B13 26
Divernon, Il., U.S. D4 120
Divide, co., N.D., U.S. A2 141
Divide Peak, mtn., Wy., U.S. E5 157
Dividing Creek, stm., Md., U.S. D6 127
Divin, U.S.S.R. J7 26
Divinhe, Moz. C12 66
Divino, Braz. F7 79
Divinópolis, Braz. F6 79
Divisões, Serra das, hills, Braz. D3 79
Divisor, Serra do (Cordillera Ultraoriental), plat., S.A. C5 82
Divizija, U.S.S.R. D13 20
Divnoje, U.S.S.R. H6 22
Divriği, Tur. B5 48
Dix, Il., U.S. E5 120
Dix, Ne., U.S. C2 134
Dix, stm., Ky., U.S. C5 124
Dix Dam, Ky., U.S. C5 124
Dixfield, Me., U.S. D2 126
Dixiana, Al., U.S. B3 108
Dixie, Ga., U.S. F3 117
Dixie, Wa., U.S. C7 154
Dixie, W.V., U.S. C3 155
Dixie, co., Fl., U.S. C3 116
Dixie Inn, La., U.S. B2 125
Dixie Union, Ga., U.S. E4 117
Dixie Valley, val., Nv., U.S. D4 135
Dix Mountain, mtn., N.Y., U.S. A7 139
Dixmude (Diksmuide), Bel. F2 12
Dixon, Ca., U.S. C3 112
Dixon, Il., U.S. B4 120
Dixon, Ia., U.S. C7 122
Dixon, Ky., U.S. C2 124
Dixon, Mo., U.S. D5 132
Dixon, Mt., U.S. C2 133
Dixon, N.M., U.S. A4 138
Dixon, Wy., U.S. E5 157
Dixon, co., Ne., U.S. B9 134
Dixons Mills, Al., U.S. C2 108
Dixonville, Alta., Can. A2 98
Dixonville, Pa., U.S. E3 145
Dixville, Que., Can. D6 104
Dixville Notch, N.H., U.S. g7 136
Dixville Notch, N.H., U.S. g7 136
Dixville Peak, mtn., N.H., U.S. g7 136
Diyālā (Sīrvān), stm., Asia E8 48
Diyarbakır, Tur. C6 48
Dizhou, China C9 40
Dja, stm., Afr. H9 54
Djakarta see Jakarta, Indon. J13 39a
Djamâa, Alg. D13 62
Djambala, Congo B2 58
Djanet, Alg. H15 62
Djedi, Oued, val., Alg. C13 62
Djema, Cen. Afr. Rep. N3 60
Djemila, hist., Alg. B13 62
Djénné, Mali E7 64
Djérem, stm., Cam. G9 54
Djibo, Burkina D9 64
Djibouti, Dji. F9 56
Djibouti, ctry., Afr. F9 56
Djokupunda, Zaire C4 58
Djougou, Benin G10 64
Djúpivogur, Ice. B6 6a
Djurås, Swe. K14 6
D'Lo, Ms., U.S. D4 131
Dmitrija Lapteva, proliv, strt., U.S.S.R. C20 24
Dmitrijevka, U.S.S.R. I23 26
Dmitrijev-L'govskij, U.S.S.R. I18 26
Dmitrov, U.S.S.R. E20 26
Dmitrovskij Pogost, U.S.S.R. F22 26
Dmitrovsk-Orlovskij, U.S.S.R. I18 26
Dnepr, stm., U.S.S.R. H4 22
Dneprodzeržinsk, U.S.S.R. H4 22
Dnepropetrovsk, U.S.S.R. H4 22
Dneprovsko-Bugskij kanal, U.S.S.R. I7 26
Dnestr, stm., U.S.S.R. H3 22
Dnestrovskij liman, l., U.S.S.R. C14 20
Dnieper see Dnepr, stm., U.S.S.R. H4 22
Dniester see Dnestr, stm., U.S.S.R. H3 22
Dno, U.S.S.R. D12 26
Doaktown, N.B., Can. C3 101
Doany, Madag. O23 67b
Doba, Chad E4 56
Dobane, Cen. Afr. Rep. N3 60
Dobbiaco, Italy C7 18
Dobbins Air Force Base, mil., Ga., U.S. h7 117
Dobbs Ferry, N.Y., U.S. g13 139
Dobczyce, Pol. F20 10
Dobele, U.S.S.R. E6 26
Döbeln, Ger. D13 10
Doberai, Jazirah, pen., Indon. F9 38
Doboj, Yugo. E2 20
Doboy Sound, b., Ga., U.S. E5 117
Dobr'anka, U.S.S.R. F9 22
Dobrinka, U.S.S.R. I23 26
Dobříš, Czech. F14 10
Dobromil', U.S.S.R. F22 10
Dobrudžansko plato, plat., Bul. F11 20
Dobruja, reg., Eur. E12 20
Dobruš, U.S.S.R. I14 26
Dobson, N.C., U.S. A2 140
Doce, stm., Braz. E8 79
Doce, stm., Braz. E3 79
Docena, Al., U.S. f7 108
Dock Junction, Ga., U.S. E5 117
Dockton, Wa., U.S. f11 154
Doctor Arroyo, Mex. F9 90
Doctor Cecilio Báez, Para. C10 80
Doctor Pedro P. Peña, Para. B7 80
Doctors Inlet, Fl., U.S. m8 116
Doctors Lake, l., Fl., U.S. m8 116
Dod Ballāpur, India F4 46
Doddridge, Ar., U.S. D2 111
Doddridge, co., W.V., U.S. B4 155
Dodecanese see Dhodhekánisos, is., Grc. M10 20
Dodge, Ne., U.S. C9 134
Dodge, N.D., U.S. B3 141
Dodge, co., Ga., U.S. D3 117
Dodge, co., Mn., U.S. G6 130
Dodge, co., Ne., U.S. C9 134
Dodge, co., Wi., U.S. E5 156
Dodge Center, Mn., U.S. F6 130
Dodge City, Ks., U.S. E3 123
Dodgeville, Wi., U.S. F3 156
Dodola, Eth. N10 60
Dodoma, Tan. C7 58
Dodsland, Sask., Can. F1 105
Dodson, La., U.S. B3 125
Dodson, Mt., U.S. B8 133
Doerun, Ga., U.S. E3 117
Doe Run, Mo., U.S. D7 132
Doetinchem, Neth. E9 12
Dog, stm., Vt., U.S. C3 152
Dogai Coring, l., China C13 44
Dog Island, i., Anguilla E13 94
Dog Island, i., Fl., U.S. C2 116
Dog Keys Pass, strt., Ms., U.S. g8 131
Dog Lake, l., Man., Can. D2 100
Dōgo, i., Japan K8 36
Do Gonbadān, Iran F11 48
Dogondoutchi, Niger E12 64
Doğubayazıt, Tur. B8 48
Doha see Ad-Dawḥah, Qatar B7 47
Doiran, Lake, l., Eur. H6 20
Dois de Novembro, Cachoeira, wtfl, Braz. C10 82
Dokka, Nor. K12 6
Dokšicy, U.S.S.R. G10 26
Doksy, Czech. E14 10
Doland, S.D., U.S. C7 148
Dolbeau, Que., Can. k12 104
Dol-de-Bretagne, Fr. D5 14
Dole, Fr. E12 14
Dolega, Pan. C1 84
Doles, Ga., U.S. E3 117
Dolgeville, N.Y., U.S. B6 139
Dolgoje, U.S.S.R. I20 26
Dolgorukovo, U.S.S.R. I21 26
Dolinsk, U.S.S.R. H20 24
Dolisie, Congo B2 58
Dolj, co., Rom. E7 20
Dollar Bay, Mi., U.S. A2 129
Dollard, Sask., Can. H1 105
Dollard, b., Eur. B11 12
Dolmatovskij, U.S.S.R. D25 26
Dolomite, Al., U.S. B3 108
Dolomites see Dolomiti, mts., Italy C6 18
Dolomiti, mts., Italy C6 18
Dolores, Arg. I10 80
Dolores, Col. F5 84
Dolores, Guat. I15 90
Dolores, Co., U.S. D2 113
Dolores, Ur. G9 80
Dolores, Ven. C8 84
Dolores, co., Co., U.S. D2 113
Dolores, stm., U.S. E7 151
Dolores Hidalgo, Mex. G9 90
Dolphin and Union Strait, strt., N.W. Ter., Can. C9 96
Dolphin Island, i., Ut., U.S. B3 151
Dolton, Il., U.S. k9 120
Dolžak, U.S.S.R. A10 20
Dom Aquino, Braz. C1 79

Name — Map Ref. — Page

Domažlice, Czech. F12 10
Dombarovskij, U.S.S.R. G9 22
Dombås, Nor. J11 6
Dombrád, Hung. G21 10
Dom Cavati, Braz. E7 79
Dome Mountain, mtn., Az., U.S. k9 110
Dome Peak, mtn., Co., U.S. B3 113
Domeyko, Chile E3 80
Domeyko, Cordillera, mts., Chile B4 80
Domfront, Fr. D6 14
Domiciano Ribeiro, Braz. D5 79
Domíngo M. Irala, Para. C11 80
Domingos Martins, Braz. F8 79
Dominica, ctry., N.A. G14 94
Dominical, C.R. H11 92
Dominican Republic (República Dominicana), ctry., N.A. E9 94
Dominica Passage, strt., N.A. G14 94
Dominion, N.S., Can. C9 101
Dominion, Cape, c., N.W. Ter., Can. C18 96
Dominion City, Man., Can. E3 100
Dom Joaquim, Braz. E7 79
Domo, Eth. G10 56
Domodedovo, U.S.S.R. F20 26
Domodossola, Italy C3 18
Domoni, Com. L16 67a
Dom Pedrito, Braz. F11 80
Domremy, Sask., Can. E3 105
Dom Silvério, Braz. F7 79
Domuyo, Volcán, vol., Arg. I3 80
Don, stm., U.S.S.R. H6 22
Don, stm., Scot., U.K. D11 8
Dona Ana, N.M., U.S. E3 138
Dona Ana, co., N.M., U.S. E2 138
Donadeu, Arg. D7 80
Donald, Austl. K5 70
Donald, Or., U.S. h12 144
Donalda, Alta., Can. C4 98
Donalds, S.C., U.S. C3 147
Donaldson, Ar., U.S. C3 111
Donaldsonville, La., U.S. D4 125
Donalsonville, Ga., U.S. E2 117
Doñana, Parque Nacional de, Spain H5 16
Donaueschingen, Ger. H8 10
Donauwörth, Ger. G10 10
Don Benito, Spain G6 16
Doncaster, Eng., U.K. H12 8
Dondo, Ang. C2 58
Dondo, Moz. B12 66
Dondra Head, c., Sri L. J6 46
Dond'ušany, U.S.S.R. A11 20
Doneck, U.S.S.R. H5 22
Donegal, Ire. G5 8
Donegal, co., Ire. G5 8
Donegal Bay, b., Ire. G5 8
Doneraile, S.C., U.S. C8 147
Donetsk see Doneck, U.S.S.R. H5 22
Dong, stm., China L6 34
Donga, stm., Nig. G15 64
Dong'an, China B3 34
Dongara, Austl. E2 68
Dongba, China D8 34
Dongchuan, China A7 40
Dongdaoan, China E5 32
Dong'ezhen, China G4 32
Dongfang (Basuo), China E10 40
Dongfeng, China A13 32
Donggu, China I4 34
Dongguan, China L2 34
Dongguanyingzi, China B8 32
Donghai Dao, i., China D11 40
Dong Hoi, Viet. F9 40
Dongmen, China G3 34
Dong Nai, stm., Viet. I9 40
Dongola, Il., U.S. F4 120
Dongshi, China K7 34
Dongtai, China C9 34
Dongting Hu, l., China G1 34
Dongyang, China F9 34
Dongzhi, China E5 34
Doniphan, Mo., U.S. E7 132
Doniphan, Ne., U.S. D7 134
Doniphan, co., Ks., U.S. C8 123
Donji Vakuf, Yugo. E12 18
Donkey Creek, stm., Wy., U.S. B7 157
Donkin, N.S., Can. C10 101
Donley, co., Tx., U.S. B2 150
Don Matías, Col. D5 84
Donna, Tx., U.S. F3 150
Donnacona, Que., Can. C6 104
Donnellson, Ia., U.S. D6 122
Donnelly, Alta., Can. B2 98
Donnelly, Id., U.S. E2 119
Donner Pass, Ca., U.S. C3 112
Donnybrook, N.D., U.S. A4 141
Donora, Pa., U.S. F2 145
Donostia (San Sebastián), Spain B10 16
Donovan, Il., U.S. C6 120
Don Peninsula, pen., B.C., Can. C3 99
Donskoj, U.S.S.R. H21 26
Donskoje, U.S.S.R. I22 26
Doolittle, Mo., U.S. D6 132
Doolow, Som. H9 56
Dooly, co., Ga., U.S. D3 117
Doomadgee, Austl. A3 70
Doon, Ia., U.S. A1 122
Doonerak, Mount, mtn., Ak., U.S. B9 109
Door, co., Wi., U.S. D6 156
Doornik (Tournai), Bel. G3 12
Dora, Al., U.S. B2 108
Dora, N.M., U.S. D6 138
Doraville, Ga., U.S. h8 117
Dorcheat, Bayou, stm., U.S. B2 125
Dorchester, N.B., Can. D5 101
Dorchester, Eng., U.K. K11 8
Dorchester, Ga., U.S. E5 117
Dorchester, Ne., U.S. D8 134
Dorchester, S.C., U.S. E7 147
Dorchester, Wi., U.S. C3 156
Dorchester, co., Md., U.S. D5 127
Dorchester, co., S.C., U.S. E7 147
Dorchester, Cape, c., N.W. Ter., Can. C17 96
Dorchester Estates, S.C., U.S. k11 147
Dorcyville, La., U.S. h9 125
Dordogne, dept., Fr. G7 14
Dordogne, stm., Fr. H8 14
Dordrecht, Neth. E6 12
Dordrecht, S. Afr. H8 66
Doré, stm., Sask., Can. C2 105
Doré Lake, Sask., Can. C2 105
Doré Lake, l., Sask., Can. C2 105
Dorena, Or., U.S. D4 144
Dorena Lake, res., Or., U.S. D3 144
Dores do Indaiá, Braz. E6 79
Dorion-Vaudreuil, Que., Can. q18 104
Dormont, Pa., U.S. k13 145
Dornach, Switz. D8 13
Dornbirn, Aus. H9 10
Doro, Mali C9 64
Dorochovo, U.S.S.R. F19 26
Dorog, Hung. H18 10
Dorogobuž, U.S.S.R. G16 26
Dorohoi, Rom. B10 20
Dorothy, N.J., U.S. E3 137
Dorothy, W.V., U.S. n13 155
Dorothy Pond, Ma., U.S. B4 128
Dorr, Mi., U.S. F5 129
Dorrance, Ks., U.S. D5 123
Dorre Island, i., Austl. E2 68
Dorrigo, Austl. H10 70
Dorris, Ca., U.S. B3 112
Dorris Heights, Il., U.S. F5 120
Dorset, Ont., Can. B6 103
Dorset, Vt., U.S. E2 152
Dorset, co., Eng., U.K. K11 8
Dorset Peak, mtn., Vt., U.S. E2 152
Dorsey, Md., U.S. B4 127
Dorsey, Ms., U.S. A5 131
Dortmund, Ger. D7 10
Dorton, Ky., U.S. C7 124
Dörtyol, Tur. C4 48
Do Rūd, Iran E10 48
Doruma, Zaire H6 56
Dorval, Que., Can. q19 104
Dos, Canal Numero, Arg. I10 80
Dosatuj, U.S.S.R. G15 24
Dos Bahías, Cabo, c., Arg. E3 78
Doščatoje, U.S.S.R. F25 26
Dos Hermanas, Spain H6 16
Dos Palos, Ca., U.S. D3 112
Dos Quebradas, Col. E5 84
Dosquet, Que., Can. C6 104
Dossor, U.S.S.R. H8 22
Dothan, Al., U.S. D4 108
Dothan, W.V., U.S. n13 155
Dotnuva, U.S.S.R. F6 26
Doty, Wa., U.S. C2 154
Douai, Fr. B10 14
Douala, Cam. I14 64
Douarnenez, Fr. D2 14
Double Beach, Ct., U.S. D4 114
Double Island Point, c., Austl. E10 70
Double Mountain, mtn., Al., U.S. g7 108
Double Oak Mountain, mtn., Al., U.S. g7 108
Double Point, c., Austl. A7 70
Doublespring Pass, Id., U.S. E5 119
Double Springs, Al., U.S. A2 108
Doubletop Peak, mtn., Wy., U.S. C2 157
Doubs, dept., Fr. E13 14
Doubs, stm., Eur. E12 14
Doubs, Saut de, wtfl, Eur. D6 13
Doucette, Tx., U.S. D5 150
Doudeville, Fr. C7 14
Douds, Ia., U.S. D5 122
Douentza, Mali D8 64
Dougherty, co., Ga., U.S. E2 117
Douglas, Ont., Can. B8 103
Douglas, I. of Man G9 8
Douglas, Az., U.S. F6 110
Douglas, Ga., U.S. E4 117
Douglas, Mi., U.S. F4 129
Douglas, Ne., U.S. D9 134
Douglas, N.D., U.S. B4 141
Douglas, Wy., U.S. D7 157
Douglas, co., Co., U.S. B6 113
Douglas, co., Ga., U.S. C2 117
Douglas, co., Il., U.S. D5 120
Douglas, co., Ks., U.S. D8 123
Douglas, co., Mn., U.S. E3 130
Douglas, co., Mo., U.S. E5 132
Douglas, co., Ne., U.S. C9 134
Douglas, co., Nv., U.S. E2 135
Douglas, co., Or., U.S. D3 144
Douglas, co., S.D., U.S. D7 148
Douglas, co., Wa., U.S. B6 154
Douglas, co., Wi., U.S. B2 156
Douglas, Mount, mtn., Ak., U.S. D9 109
Douglas Channel, strt., B.C., Can. C3 99
Douglas Creek, stm., Co., U.S. B2 113
Douglas Lake, B.C., Can. D7 99
Douglas Lake, l., Mi., U.S. C6 129
Douglas Lake, res., Tn., U.S. D10 149
Douglass, Ks., U.S. E7 123
Douglas Station, Man., Can. E2 100
Douglastown, N.B., Can. B4 101
Douglasville, Ga., U.S. C2 117
Doulaincourt, Fr. D12 14
Doulevant-le-Château, Fr. D11 14
Doullens, Fr. B9 14
Doumanaba, Mali F7 64
Doura, Mali E7 64
Dourada, Serra, mts., Braz. D3 79
Dourada, Serra, plat., Braz. D4 79
Dourado, stm., Braz. F4 79
Dourados, Braz. G1 79
Dourados, stm., Braz. G1 79
Dourdan, Fr. D9 14
Dourkoulé, Chad J2 60
Douro (Duero), stm., Eur. D4 16
Doushanhe, China D3 34
Dousman, Wi., U.S. E5 156
Douz, Tun. D15 62
Dove Creek, Co., U.S. D2 113
Dover, Austl. N7 70
Dover, Eng., U.K. J15 8
Dover, Ar., U.S. B2 111
Dover, De., U.S. D3 115
Dover, Fl., U.S. D4 116
Dover, Id., U.S. A2 119
Dover, Ks., U.S. D8 123
Dover, Ky., U.S. B6 124
Dover, Ma., U.S. h10 128
Dover, Mn., U.S. G6 130
Dover, N.H., U.S. D5 136
Dover, N.J., U.S. B3 137
Dover, N.C., U.S. B5 140
Dover, Oh., U.S. B4 142
Dover, Ok., U.S. B4 143
Dover, Pa., U.S. F8 145
Dover, Tn., U.S. A4 149
Dover, Strait of (Pas de Calais), strt., Eur. J15 8
Dover Air Force Base, mil., De., U.S. D4 115
Dover-Foxcroft, Me., U.S. C3 126
Dover Plains, N.Y., U.S. D7 139
Dovre, Nor. K11 6
Dovsk, U.S.S.R. H13 26
Dowagiac, Mi., U.S. G4 129
Dow City, Ia., U.S. C2 122
Dowell, Il., U.S. F4 120
Dowelltown, Tn., U.S. C8 149
Dowlatābād, Afg. B2 44
Dowlatābād, Afg. B1 44
Dowlat Yār, Afg. C1 44
Dowling Lake, l., Alta., Can. D4 98
Downers Grove, Il., U.S. B5 120
Downey, Ca., U.S. n12 112
Downey, Id., U.S. G6 119
Downieville, Ca., U.S. C3 112
Downing, Mo., U.S. A5 132
Downingtown, Pa., U.S. F10 145
Downs, Il., U.S. C5 120
Downs, Ks., U.S. C5 123
Downs Mountain, mtn., Wy., U.S. C3 157
Downsville, N.Y., U.S. C6 139
Downton, Mount, mtn., B.C., Can. C5 99
Dows, Ia., U.S. B4 122
Dowshī, Afg. C3 44
Doyle, Ca., U.S. B3 112
Doyle, Tn., U.S. D8 149
Doyles, Newf., Can. E2 102
Doylestown, Oh., U.S. B4 142
Doylestown, Pa., U.S. F11 145
Doyline, La., U.S. B2 125
Dōzen, is., Japan K8 36
Dozier, Al., U.S. D3 108
Dra'a, Hamada du, des., Alg. F7 62
Drâa, Oued, val., Afr. F5 62
Dracena, Braz. F3 79
Dracut, Ma., U.S. A5 128
Drăgăşani, Rom. E8 20
Dragons Mouth, strt. B12 84
Dragoon, Az., U.S. E5 110
Draguignan, Fr. I13 14
Drain, Or., U.S. D3 144
Drake, Sask., Can. F3 105
Drake, Co., U.S. A5 113
Drake, N.D., U.S. B5 141
Drakensberg, mts., Afr. F9 66
Drake Passage, strt. J8 74
Drake Peak, mtn., Or., U.S. E6 144
Drakesboro, Ky., U.S. C2 124
Drakes Branch, Va., U.S. D4 153
Drakes Creek, stm., Ky., U.S. D3 124
Drakes Creek, West Fork, stm., Ky., U.S. D3 124
Draketown, Ga., U.S. C1 117
Dráma, Grc. H8 20
Drammen, Nor. L12 6
Drang, stm., Asia H9 40
Draper, S.D., U.S. D5 148
Draper, Ut., U.S. C4 151
Drasco, Ar., U.S. B4 111
Drau (Drava) (Dráva), stm., Eur. C8 18
Drava (Drau) (Dráva), stm., Eur. D13 18
Drawno, Pol. B15 10
Drayton, Ont., Can. D4 103
Drayton, N.D., U.S. A8 141
Drayton, S.C., U.S. B4 147
Drayton Plains, Mi., U.S. F7 129
Drayton Valley, Alta., Can. C3 98
Drean, Alg. M2 18
Drenthe, prov., Neth. C10 12
Dresden, Ont., Can. E2 103
Dresden, Ger. D13 10
Dresden, Oh., U.S. B3 142
Dresden, Tn., U.S. A3 149
Dresser, In., U.S. F3 121
Dresser, Wi., U.S. C1 156
Dresslerville, Nv., U.S. E2 135
Dretun, U.S.S.R. F12 26
Dreux, Fr. D8 14
Drew, Ms., U.S. B3 131
Drew, co., Ar., U.S. D4 111
Drewryville, Va., U.S. D5 153
Drews Reservoir, res., Or., U.S. E6 144
Drewsville, N.H., U.S. D2 136
Drexel, Mo., U.S. C3 132
Drexel, N.C., U.S. B1 140
Drexel, Oh., U.S. C1 142
Drift, Ky., U.S. C7 124
Drifton, Pa., U.S. D10 145
Driftpile, Alta., Can. B3 98
Driftpile, stm., Alta., Can. B3 98
Driftwood Creek, stm., Ne., U.S. D4 134
Driggs, Id., U.S. F7 119
Drin, stm., Alb. H3 20
Drina, stm., Yugo. E3 20
Drinit, Gjiri i, b., Alb. H3 20
Drinkwater, Sask., Can. G3 105
Dripping Springs, Tx., U.S. D3 150
Driscoll, N.D., U.S. C5 141
Driscoll, Tx., U.S. F4 150
Driskill Mountain, hill, La., U.S. B3 125
Drobeta-Turnu Severin, Rom. E6 20
Drogheda, Ire. H7 8
Drogičin, U.S.S.R. I8 26
Drogobyč, U.S.S.R. H2 22
Drohiczyn, Pol. C22 10
Drokija, U.S.S.R. A11 20
Drôme, dept., Fr. H12 14
Droskovo, U.S.S.R. I20 26
Druja, U.S.S.R. F10 26
Drumbo, Ont., Can. D4 103
Drumheller, Alta., Can. D4 98
Drum Island, i., S.C., U.S. k12 147
Drummond, Mt., U.S. D3 133
Drummond, Ok., U.S. A3 143
Drummond, Wi., U.S. B2 156
Drummond, Lake, l., Va., U.S. D6 153
Drummond Island, Mi., U.S. B7 129
Drummond Island, i., Mi., U.S. C7 129
Drummond Range, mts., Austl. E7 70
Drummondville, Que., Can. D5 104
Drumright, Ok., U.S. B5 143
Druskininkai, U.S.S.R. G6 26
Družba, U.S.S.R. H14 22
Drvar, Yugo. E11 18
Dry Branch, Ga., U.S. D3 117
Drybranch, W.V., U.S. m13 155
Dry Cimarron, stm., U.S. A6 138
Dry Creek, stm., Ks., U.S. g12 123
Dry Creek Mountain, mtn., Nv., U.S. B5 135
Dryden, Ont., Can. o16 103
Dryden, Me., U.S. D2 126
Dryden, Mi., U.S. F7 129
Dryden, N.Y., U.S. C4 139
Dryden, Wa., U.S. B5 154
Dry Fork, stm., Mo., U.S. D6 132
Dry Fork, stm., W.V., U.S. D3 155
Dry Fork, stm., W.V., U.S. B5 155
Dry Mills, Me., U.S. E2 126
Dry Prong, La., U.S. C3 125
Dry Ridge, Ky., U.S. B5 124
Drysdale, stm., Austl. C5 68
Drysdale River National Park, Austl. B5 68
Dry Tortugas, is., Fl., U.S. H5 116
Dschang, Cam. I15 64
Du, Ghana F9 64
Duarte, Pico, mtn., Dom. Rep. E9 94
Duartina, Braz. G4 79
Dubā, Sau. Ar. H3 48
Dubach, La., U.S. B3 125
Dubai see Dubayy, U.A.E. B9 47
Dubawnt, stm., N.W. Ter., Can. D12 96
Dubawnt Lake, l., N.W. Ter., Can. D12 96
Du Bay, Lake, res., Wi., U.S. D4 156
Dubayy (Dubai), U.A.E. B9 47
Dubberly, La., U.S. B2 125
Dubbo, Austl. I8 70
Dübendorf, Switz. D10 13
Dublin, Ont., Can. D3 103
Dublin (Baile Átha Cliath), Ire. H7 8
Dublin, Al., U.S. C3 108
Dublin, Ga., U.S. D4 117
Dublin, In., U.S. E7 121
Dublin, Md., U.S. A5 127
Dublin, Ms., U.S. A3 131
Dublin, N.H., U.S. E2 136
Dublin, Oh., U.S. k10 142
Dublin, Pa., U.S. F11 145
Dublin, Tx., U.S. C3 150
Dublin, Va., U.S. C2 153
Dublin, co., Ire. H7 8
Dublin Shore, N.S., Can. E5 101
Dubna, U.S.S.R. E20 26
Dubois, Id., U.S. E6 119
Dubois, Il., U.S. E4 120
Dubois, In., U.S. H4 121
Du Bois, Ne., U.S. D9 134
Du Bois, Pa., U.S. D4 145
Dubois, Wy., U.S. C3 157
Dubois, co., In., U.S. H4 121
Duboistown, Pa., U.S. D7 145
Dubossarskoje vodochranilišče, res., U.S.S.R. B13 20
Dubossary, U.S.S.R. B13 20
Dubossary, U.S.S.R. B13 20
Dubovka, U.S.S.R. H6 22
Dubréka, Gui. G3 64
Dubrovka, U.S.S.R. H16 26
Dubrovka, U.S.S.R. B13 26
Dubrovnik, Yugo. G2 20
Dubrovno, U.S.S.R. G13 26
Dubuc, Sask., Can. G4 105
Dubuque, Ia., U.S. B7 122
Dubuque, co., Ia., U.S. B7 122
Duchcov, Czech. E13 10
Duchesne, Ut., U.S. C5 151
Duchesne, co., Ut., U.S. C5 151
Duchesne, stm., Ut., U.S. C5 151
Duchess, Austl. C3 70
Duchess, Alta., Can. D5 98
Duchovščina, U.S.S.R. F15 26
Duck, stm., Tn., U.S. B4 149
Duck Bay, Man., Can. C1 100
Duck Creek, stm., De., U.S. C4 115
Duck Creek, stm., Nv., U.S. D7 135
Duck Creek, stm., Oh., U.S. C4 142
Duck Creek, stm., Wi., U.S. h9 156
Duck Hill, Ms., U.S. B4 131
Duck Lake, Sask., Can. E2 105
Duck Lake, l., Me., U.S. C4 126
Duck Mountain, hills, Man., Can. D1 100
Duck Mountain Provincial Park, Sask., Can. F5 105
Ducktown, Tn., U.S. D9 149
Duck Valley Indian Reservation, U.S. B5 135
Duckwater Indian Reservation, Nv., U.S. E6 135
Duckwater Peak, mtn., Nv., U.S. E6 135
Du Couedic, Cape, c., Austl. K2 70
Duda, stm., Col. F5 84
Dudelange, Lux. J9 12
Duderstadt, Ger. D10 10
Dudinka, U.S.S.R. D9 24
Dudley, Ga., U.S. D3 117
Dudley, Ma., U.S. B4 128
Dudley, Mo., U.S. E7 132
Dudorovskij, U.S.S.R. H18 26
Duékoué, I.C. H6 64
Duenweg, Mo., U.S. D3 132
Duerna, stm., Spain C5 16
Duero (Douro), stm., Eur. D5 16
Due West, S.C., U.S. C3 147
Duff, Sask., Can. G4 105
Duff, Tn., U.S. C9 149
Duffer Peak, mtn., Nv., U.S. B3 135
Duffield, Alta., Can. C3 98
Dufourspitze, mtn., Eur. G14 14
Dufrost, Man., Can. E3 100
Dufur, Or., U.S. B5 144
Duga-Zapadnaja, mys, c., U.S.S.R. F21 24
Dugdemona, stm., La., U.S. B3 125
Dugger, In., U.S. F3 121
Dug Hill Ridge, mtn., Md., U.S. A4 127
Dugi Otok, i., Yugo. E10 18
Duhi, Sud. N5 60
Duida, Cerro, mtn., Ven. F10 84
Duisburg, Ger. D6 10
Duitama, Col. E6 84
Duiwelskloof, S. Afr. D10 66
Dukambiya, Eth. J9 60
Duke, Al., U.S. B4 108
Duke, Ok., U.S. C2 143
Duke Center, Pa., U.S. C5 145
Duke Island, i., Ak., U.S. n24 109
Dukes, co., Ma., U.S. D6 128
Duk Fadiat, Sud. N6 60
Duk Faiwil, Sud. N6 60
Dukhān, Qatar B7 47
Duki, Pak. E3 44
Dukla Pass, Eur. F21 10
Dūkštas, U.S.S.R. F9 26
Duku, Nig. F12 64
Dulac, La., U.S. E5 125
Dulan, China D6 30
Dul'apino, U.S.S.R. D23 26
Dulce, N.M., U.S. A2 138
Dulce, stm., Arg. F7 80
Dulce, Golfo, b., C.R. I11 92
Dulce Nombre de Culmí, Hond. B9 92
Dul'durga, U.S.S.R. G14 24
Dulkaninna, Austl. G3 70
Dulovka, U.S.S.R. D11 26
Dulovo, Bul. F11 20
Duluth, Ga., U.S. B2 117
Duluth, Mn., U.S. D6 130
Duma, Bots. B6 66
Dūmā, Syria A6 50
Dumaguete, Phil. D7 38
Dumaresq, stm., Austl. G9 70
Dumaring, Indon. E6 38
Dumas, Ar., U.S. D4 111
Dumas, Ms., U.S. A5 131
Dumas, Tx., U.S. B2 150
Dumayr, Syria A7 50
Dumbarton, Scot., U.K. F9 8
Dumei, China K6 34
Dumfries, Scot., U.K. F10 8
Dumfries, Va., U.S. B5 153
Dumfries and Galloway, prov., Scot., U.K. F9 8
Duminiči, U.S.S.R. H18 26
Dumka, India H12 44
Dumont, Ia., U.S. B5 122
Dumont, N.J., U.S. B5 137
Dumraon, India H11 44
Dumyāt, Egypt B6 60
Dumyāṭ, Maṣabb, mth., Egypt F1 48
Dunaföldvár, Hung. I18 10
Dunaharaszti, Hung. H19 10
Dunajec, stm., Eur. E20 10
Dunakeszi, Hung. H19 10
Dunaújváros, Hung. I18 10
Dunbar, Ky., U.S. C3 124
Dunbar, Ne., U.S. D9 134
Dunbar, Pa., U.S. G2 145
Dunbar, W.V., U.S. C3 155
Dunbarton, N.H., U.S. D3 136
Duncan, B.C., Can. E6 99
Duncan, Az., U.S. E6 110
Duncan, Ms., U.S. A3 131
Duncan, Ne., U.S. C8 134
Duncan, Ok., U.S. C4 143
Duncan, S.C., U.S. B3 147
Duncan, stm., B.C., Can. D9 99
Duncan Falls, Oh., U.S. C4 142
Duncan Lake, res., B.C., Can. D9 99
Duncannon, Pa., U.S. F7 145
Duncan Passage, strt., India I2 40
Duncansby Head, c., Scot., U.K. C10 8
Duncansville, Pa., U.S. F5 145
Duncanville, Al., U.S. B2 108
Duncanville, Tx., U.S. n10 150
Duncombe, Ia., U.S. B4 122
Dundaga, U.S.S.R. D5 26
Dundalk, Ont., Can. C4 103
Dundalk, Ire. G7 8
Dundalk, Md., U.S. B4 127
Dundas, Ont., Can. D5 103
Dundas, Il., U.S. E5 120
Dundas, Mn., U.S. F5 130
Dundas Island, i., B.C., Can. B2 99
Dundas Peninsula, pen., N.W. Ter., Can. B10 96
Dundee, S. Afr. G10 66
Dundee, Scot., U.K. E11 8
Dundee, Fl., U.S. D5 116
Dundee, Il., U.S. A5 120
Dundee, Ky., U.S. C3 124
Dundee, Mi., U.S. G7 129
Dundee, Ms., U.S. A3 131
Dundee, N.Y., U.S. C4 139
Dundee, Or., U.S. h11 144
Dundurn, Sask., Can. F2 105
Dundy, co., Ne., U.S. D4 134
Dunedin, N.Z. F3 72
Dunedin, Fl., U.S. D4 116
Dunedoo, Austl. I8 70
Duneland Beach, In., U.S. A4 121
Dunellen, N.J., U.S. B4 137
Dunfermline, Scot., U.K. E10 8
Dunfermline, Il., U.S. C3 120
Dungannon, Ont., Can. D3 103
Dungannon, Va., U.S. f9 153
Dungas, Niger E14 64
Dungeness, stm., Wa., U.S. A2 154
Dungog, Austl. I9 70
Dungun, Malay. L7 40
Dunham, Que., Can. D5 104
Dunhua, China C12 30
Dunhuang, China C5 30
Dunilovo, U.S.S.R. D21 26
Dunkard Creek, stm., U.S. B4 155
Dunkerque, Fr. A9 14
Dunkerton, Ia., U.S. B5 122
Dunkirk, In., U.S. D7 121
Dunkirk, Md., U.S. C4 127
Dunkirk, N.Y., U.S. C1 139
Dunkirk, Oh., U.S. B2 142
Dunkirk see Dunkerque, Fr. A9 14
Dunklin, co., Mo., U.S. E7 132
Dunkuj, Sud. K7 60
Dunkwa, Ghana I9 64
Dún Laoghaire, Ire. H7 8
Dunlap, Il., U.S. C4 120
Dunlap, In., U.S. A6 121
Dunlap, Ia., U.S. C2 122
Dunlap, Tn., U.S. D8 149
Dunleary see Dún Laoghaire, Ire. H7 8
Dunleith, De., U.S. i7 115
Dunlo, Pa., U.S. F4 145
Dunloup Creek, stm., W.V., U.S. n13 155
Dunmor, Ky., U.S. C2 124
Dunmore, Pa., U.S. D10 145
Dunmore, Lake, l., Vt., U.S. D2 152
Dunmore Town, Bah. B6 94
Dunn, N.C., U.S. B4 140
Dunn, co., N.D., U.S. B3 141
Dunn, co., Wi., U.S. D2 156
Dunn Center, N.D., U.S. B3 141
Dunnell, Mn., U.S. G4 130
Dunnellon, Fl., U.S. C4 116
Dunning, Ne., U.S. C5 134
Dunnottar, Man., Can. D3 100
Dunnville, Ont., Can. E5 103
Dunnville, Ky., U.S. C5 124
Dunqulah, Sud. H6 60
Dunqulah al-Qadīmah, Sud. H6 60
Dunqunāb, Sud. G9 60
Dunrea, Man., Can. E2 100
Dunrobin, Ont., Can. B8 103
Duns, Scot., U.K. F11 8
Dunseith, N.D., U.S. A5 141
Dunsmuir, Ca., U.S. B2 112
Dun-sur-Auron, Fr. F9 14
Dun-sur-Meuse, Fr. C12 14
Duntroon, Ont., Can. C4 103
Dunville, Newf., Can. E5 102
Dunwoody, Ga., U.S. h8 117
Duolun (Dolonnur), China A4 32
Duolundabohuer, China D15 44
Duomaer, China E2 30
Duomula, China E3 30
Duozhu, China M3 34
Du Page, co., Il., U.S. B5 120
Du Page, stm., Il., U.S. k8 120
Duplessis, La., U.S. h10 125
Duplin, co., N.C., U.S. C5 140
Dupont, Co., U.S. B6 113
Du Pont, Ga., U.S. F4 117
Dupont, In., U.S. G6 121
Dupont, Pa., U.S. n18 145
Du Pont, Wa., U.S. B3 154
Dupont, Bayou, stm., La., U.S. k11 125
Dupont City, W.V., U.S. m12 155
Dupont Manor, De., U.S. D3 115
Dupree, S.D., U.S. B4 148
Dupuyer, Mt., U.S. B4 133
Duque de Caxias, Braz. G7 79
Duquesne, Pa., U.S. F2 145
Du Quoin, Il., U.S. E4 120
Durack Ranges, mts., Austl. C5 68
Duran, N.M., U.S. C4 138
Durance, stm., Fr. I12 14
Durand, Ga., U.S. D2 117
Durand, Il., U.S. A4 120
Durand, Mi., U.S. F6 129
Durand, Wi., U.S. D2 156
Durango, Mex. E7 90
Durango, Spain B9 16
Durango, Co., U.S. D3 113
Durango, state, Mex. E7 90
Durant, Ia., U.S. C7 122
Durant, Ms., U.S. B4 131
Durant, Ok., U.S. D5 143
Durazno, Ur. G10 80
Durban, Man., Can. D1 100
Durban, S. Afr. G10 66
Durbe, U.S.S.R. E4 26
Durbin, W.V., U.S. C5 155
Durbin Creek, stm., Fl., U.S. m8 116
Đurđevac, Yugo. C12 18
Düren, Ger. E6 10
Durg, India J9 44
Durgāpur, India I12 44
Durham, Ont., Can. C4 103
Durham, Ca., U.S. C3 112
Durham, Ct., U.S. D5 114
Durham, Ks., U.S. D6 123
Durham, Mo., U.S. B6 132
Durham, N.H., U.S. D5 136
Durham, N.C., U.S. B4 140
Durham, co., Eng., U.K. G12 8
Durham, co., N.C., U.S. A4 140
Durham Bridge, N.B., Can. C3 101
Durlešty, U.S.S.R. B12 20
Durmitor, mtn., Yugo. F3 20
Durness, Scot., U.K. C9 8
Dürnkrut, Aus. G16 10
Durrell, Newf., Can. D4 102
Durrës, Alb. H3 20
Dursunbey, Tur. J12 20
D'Urville, Tanjung, c., Indon. F10 38
D'Urville Island, i., N.Z. D4 72
Duryea, Pa., U.S. D10 145
Dušak, U.S.S.R. C16 48
Dušanbe, U.S.S.R. J11 22
Dusetos, U.S.S.R. F8 26
Dushan, China B9 40
Dushanzi, China C3 30
Dusheng, China E4 32
Dushore, Pa., U.S. C9 145
Duson, La., U.S. D3 125
Düsseldorf, Ger. D6 10
Dustin, Ok., U.S. B5 143
Dutch Creek, stm., Ar., U.S. C2 111
Dutchess, co., N.Y., U.S. D7 139
Dutch Harbor, Ak., U.S. E6 109
Dutch Island, i., R.I., U.S. F4 146
Dutch John, Ut., U.S. C6 151
Dutchtown, Mo., U.S. D8 132
Dutlwe, Bots. D6 66
Dutou, China M4 34
Dutton, Ont., Can. E3 103
Dutton, Al., U.S. A4 108
Dutton, Mt., U.S. C5 133
Dutton, stm., Austl. C5 70
Dutton, Mount, mtn., Ut., U.S. E3 151
Dutzow, Mo., U.S. C7 132
Duval, Sask., Can. F3 105
Duval, co., Fl., U.S. B5 116

Name — Map Ref. — Page

Duval, co., Tx., U.S. F3 150
Duxbury, Ma., U.S. B6 128
Duxbury, Vt., U.S. C3 152
Duyun, China A9 40
Duze, China F7 34
Dvinskaja guba, b., U.S.S.R. I26 6
Dvuch Cirkov, gora, mtn., U.S.S.R. D25 24
Dvůr Králové [nad Labem], Czech. E15 10
Dwārka, India I3 44
Dwight, Il., U.S. B5 120
Dwight, Ks., U.S. D7 123
Dwight, Ne., U.S. C8 134
Dwight, N.D., U.S. C9 141
Dwight D. Eisenhower Lock, N.Y., U.S. f9 139
Dworshak Reservoir, res., Id., U.S. C3 119
Dyckesville, Wi., U.S. D6 156
Dyer, Ar., U.S. B1 111
Dyer, In., U.S. A2 121
Dyer, Nv., U.S. F3 135
Dyer, Tn., U.S. A3 149
Dyer, co., Tn., U.S. A2 149
Dyer, Cape, c., N.W. Ter., Can. C20 96
Dyer Island, i., R.I., U.S. E5 146
Dyersburg, Tn., U.S. A2 149
Dyersville, Ia., U.S. B6 122
Dyess, Ar., U.S. B5 111
Dyess Air Force Base, mil., Tx., U.S. C3 150
Dyfed, co., Wales, U.K. J9 8
Dyje (Thaya), stm., Eur. G16 10
Dynów, Pol. F22 10
Dysart, Sask., Can. G3 105
Dysart, Ia., U.S. B5 122
Džalal-Abad, U.S.S.R. I12 22
Džalinda, U.S.S.R. G16 24
Džambejty, U.S.S.R. G8 22
Džambul, U.S.S.R. I12 22
Džanga, U.S.S.R. A12 48
Džankoj, U.S.S.R. H4 22
Džanybek, U.S.S.R. H7 22
Dzaoudzi, May. L16 67a
Dzavchan, stm., Mong. B5 30
Džebel, U.S.S.R. B13 48
Dzemul, Mex. G15 90
Dzeržinsk, U.S.S.R. E26 26
Dzeržinsk, U.S.S.R. H10 26
Dzeržinskoje, U.S.S.R. H14 22
Džetygara, U.S.S.R. G10 22
Džezkazgan, U.S.S.R. H11 22
Dzibalchén, Mex. H15 90
Dzibilchaltun, hist., Mex. G15 90
Dzierżoniów (Reichenbach), Pol. E16 10
Dzilam González, Mex. G15 90
Dzioua, Alg. D13 62
Dzitás, Mex. G15 90
Dzitbalché, Mex. G14 90
Džizak, U.S.S.R. I11 22
Džugdžur, chrebet, mts., U.S.S.R. F19 24
Džul'fa, U.S.S.R. J7 22
Dzungarian Basin see Junggar Pendi, China B4 30
Džungarskij Alatau, chrebet, mts., Asia H8 24
Džurin, U.S.S.R. A12 20
Džusaly, U.S.S.R. H10 22
Dzüün Charaa, Mong. B8 30
Dzuunmod, Mong. B8 30
Dzygovka, U.S.S.R. A12 20

E

Eads, Co., U.S. C8 113
Eagan, Mn., U.S. n12 130
Eagan, Tn., U.S. C10 149
Eagar, Az., U.S. C6 110
Eagle, Ak., U.S. C11 109
Eagle, Co., U.S. B4 113
Eagle, Id., U.S. F2 119
Eagle, Ne., U.S. h12 134
Eagle, Wi., U.S. F5 156
Eagle, co., Co., U.S. B4 113
Eagle, stm., Newf., Can. B2 102
Eagle Bend, Mn., U.S. D3 130
Eagle Butte, S.D., U.S. C4 148
Eagle Cave, Wi., U.S. E3 156
Eagle Cliff, mtn., U.S. B3 119
Eagle Creek, stm., In., U.S. D5 121
Eagle Creek, stm., Ky., U.S. B5 124
Eagle Creek Reservoir, res., In., U.S. E5 121
Eagle Dam, In., U.S. E4 121
Eagle Grove, Ia., U.S. B4 122
Eaglehawk, Austl. K6 70
Eagle Key, i., Fl., U.S. G6 116
Eagle Lake, Me., U.S. A4 126
Eagle Lake, Mn., U.S. F5 130
Eagle Lake, Tx., U.S. E4 150
Eagle Lake, l., Ca., U.S. B3 112
Eagle Lake, l., Me., U.S. B3 126
Eagle Lake, l., Me., U.S. A4 126
Eagle Lake, l., Ms., U.S. C3 131
Eagle Lake, l., Wi., U.S. C4 156
Eagle Mountain, mtn., Mn., U.S. k9 130
Eagle Mountain Lake, res., Tx., U.S. m9 150
Eagle Nest, N.M., U.S. A4 138
Eagle Nest Butte, mtn., S.D., U.S. D4 148
Eagle Nest Lake, l., N.M., U.S. A4 138
Eagle Pass, Tx., U.S. E2 150
Eagle Peak, mtn., Ca., U.S. B3 112
Eagle Peak, mtn., Tx., U.S. o12 150
Eagle Point, Or., U.S. E4 144
Eagle River, Wi., U.S. C4 156
Eagle Rock, Va., U.S. C3 153
Eaglesham, Alta., Can. B2 98
Eagle Springs, N.C., U.S. B3 140
Eagletail Mountains, mts., Az., U.S. D2 110
Eagletail Peak, mtn., Az., U.S. D2 110
Eagletown, Ok., U.S. C7 143
Eagleville, Mo., U.S. A4 132
Eagleville, Tn., U.S. B5 149
Eakly, Ok., U.S. B3 143
Earle, Ar., U.S. B5 111
Earl Grey, Sask., Can. G3 105
Earlham, Ia., U.S. C3 122
Earlimart, Ca., U.S. E4 112
Earling, Ia., U.S. C2 122
Earling, W.V., U.S. n12 155
Earlington, Ky., U.S. C2 124
Earl Park, In., U.S. C3 121
Earlsboro, Ok., U.S. B5 143
Earlville, Il., U.S. B5 120
Earlville, Ia., U.S. B6 122
Earlville, N.Y., U.S. C5 139
Early, Ia., U.S. B2 122
Early, co., Ga., U.S. E2 117
Earth, Tx., U.S. B1 150
Easley, S.C., U.S. B2 147
East, stm., Ct., U.S. D5 114
East, stm., N.Y., U.S. k13 139
East, stm., Wi., U.S. h9 156
Eastaboga, Al., U.S. B3 108
Eastabuchie, Ms., U.S. D4 131
East Acton, Ma., U.S. g10 128
East Alstead, N.H., U.S. D2 136
East Alton, Il., U.S. E3 120
East Andover, N.H., U.S. D3 136
East Angus, Que., Can. D6 104
East Arlington, Vt., U.S. E2 152
East Aurora, N.Y., U.S. C2 139
East Baldwin, Me., U.S. E2 126
East Bangor, Pa., U.S. E11 145
East Bank, W.V., U.S. m13 155
East Barre, Vt., U.S. C4 152
East Baton Rouge, co., La., U.S. D4 125
East Bay, b., Fl., U.S. u16 116
East Bay, b., Tx., U.S. R15 150
East Beckwith Mountain, mtn., Co., U.S. C3 113
East Bend, N.C., U.S. A2 140
East Berbice-Corentyne, dept., Guy. E13 84
East Berlin, Ct., U.S. C5 114
East Berlin, Pa., U.S. G8 145
East Bernard, Tx., U.S. E4 150
East Bernstadt, Ky., U.S. C5 124
East Bethel, Mn., U.S. E5 130
East Bethel, Vt., U.S. D3 152
East Billerica, Ma., U.S. f11 128
East Blue Hill, Me., U.S. D4 126
East Bonne Terre, Mo., U.S. D7 132
East Boothbay, Me., U.S. E3 126
Eastborough, Ks., U.S. g12 123
East Brady, Pa., U.S. E2 145
East Branch Clarion River Lake, res., Pa., U.S. C4 145
East Brewton, Al., U.S. D2 108
East Bridgewater, Ma., U.S. B6 128
East Brimfield Lake, res., Ma., U.S. B3 128
East Brookfield, Ma., U.S. B3 128
East Brooklyn, Ct., U.S. B8 114
East Broughton, Que., Can. C6 104
East Brunswick, N.J., U.S. C4 137
East Burke, Vt., U.S. B5 152
East Butler, Pa., U.S. E2 145
East Butte, mtn., Mt., U.S. B5 133
East Cache Creek, stm., Ok., U.S. C3 143
East Caicos, i., T./C. Is. D9 94
East Calais, Vt., U.S. C4 152
East Camden, Ar., U.S. D3 111
East Canaan, Ct., U.S. A2 114
East Candia, N.H., U.S. D4 136
East Cape, c., N.Z. B7 72
East Cape, c., Fl., U.S. G5 116
East Carbon, Ut., U.S. D5 151
East Carroll, co., La., U.S. B4 125
East Chain, Mn., U.S. G3 130
East Chicago, In., U.S. A3 121
East China Sea, Asia R3 37b
East Chop, c., Ma., U.S. D6 128
East Cleveland, Oh., U.S. g9 142
East Concord, Vt., U.S. C5 152
East Corinth, Me., U.S. D3 126
East Cote Blanche Bay, b., La., U.S. E4 125
East Coulee, Alta., Can. D4 98
East Demerara-West Coast Berbice, dept., Guy. D13 84
East Dennis, Ma., U.S. C7 128
East Derry, N.H., U.S. E4 136
East Detroit, Mi., U.S. p16 129
East Dorset, Vt., U.S. E2 152
East Douglas, Ma., U.S. B4 128
East Dover, Vt., U.S. F3 152
East Dubuque, Il., U.S. A3 120
East Dummerston, Vt., U.S. F3 152
East Eddington, Me., U.S. D4 126
East Ellijay, Ga., U.S. B2 117
Eastend, Sask., Can. H1 105
Easter, Mount, mtn., Ct., U.S. B2 114
Easter Island see Pascua, Isla de, i., Chile G4 74
Eastern Bay, b., Md., U.S. C5 127
Eastern Ghāts, mts., India F5 46
Eastern Neck Island, i., Md., U.S. B5 127
Eastern Point, c., Ma., U.S. f13 128
Easterville, Man., Can. C2 100
East Fairfield, Vt., U.S. B3 152
East Fairview, N.D., U.S. B1 141
East Falkland, i., Falk. Is. G5 78
East Falmouth, Ma., U.S. C6 128
East Farmington Heights, Ct., U.S. C4 114
East Feliciana, co., La., U.S. D4 125
East Flat Rock, N.C., U.S. f10 140
Eastford, Ct., U.S. B7 114
East Fork, stm., Wy., U.S. D3 157
East Fork Lake, res., Oh., U.S. C1 142
East Foxboro, Ma., U.S. B5 128
East Frisian Islands see Ostfriesische Inseln, is., Ger. B7 10
East Fultonham, Oh., U.S. C3 142
East Gaffney, S.C., U.S. A4 147
East Galesburg, Il., U.S. C3 120
East Glacier Park, Mt., U.S. B3 133
East Glastonbury, Ct., U.S. C5 114
East Granby, Ct., U.S. B5 114
East Grand Forks, Mn., U.S. C2 130
East Grand Rapids, Mi., U.S. F5 129
East Greenville, Pa., U.S. F10 145
East Greenwich, R.I., U.S. D4 146
East Gwillimbury, Ont., Can. C5 103
East Haddam, Ct., U.S. D6 114
Eastham, Ma., U.S. C8 128
East Hampstead, N.H., U.S. E4 136
East Hampton, Ct., U.S. C5 114
Easthampton, Ma., U.S. B2 128
East Hampton, N.Y., U.S. n16 139
East Hanover, N.J., U.S. B4 137
East Hardwick, Vt., U.S. B4 152
East Hartford, Ct., U.S. B5 114
East Hartland, Ct., U.S. B4 114
East Haven, Ct., U.S. D4 114
East Haverhill, N.H., U.S. B3 136
East Helena, Mt., U.S. D5 133
East Holden, Me., U.S. D4 126
East Jordan, N.S., Can. F4 101
East Jordan, Mi., U.S. C5 129
East Juliette, Ga., U.S. C3 117
East Kilbride, Scot., U.K. F9 8
East Killingly, Ct., U.S. B8 114
East Kingston, N.H., U.S. E4 136
Eastlake, Mi., U.S. D4 129
Eastlake, Oh., U.S. A4 142
East Lake, l., Ont., Can. C5 100
East Lake Tohopekaliga, l., Fl., U.S. D5 116
Eastland, Tx., U.S. C3 150
Eastland, co., Tx., U.S. C3 150
East Lansing, Mi., U.S. F6 129
East Las Vegas, Nv., U.S. G6 135
East Laurinburg, N.C., U.S. C3 140
East Lempster, N.H., U.S. D2 136
East Liverpool, Oh., U.S. B5 142
East London (Oos-Londen), S. Afr. I8 66
East Longmeadow, Ma., U.S. B2 128
East Los Angeles, Ca., U.S. m12 112
East Lyme, Ct., U.S. D7 114
East Lynn, Il., U.S. C6 120
East Lynn, W.V., U.S. C2 155
East Lynne, Mo., U.S. C3 132
East Lynn Lake, res., W.V., U.S. C2 155
East Machias, Me., U.S. D5 126
East Madison, Me., U.S. D3 126
Eastmain-Opinaca, Réservoir, res., Que., Can. h11 104
Eastman, Que., Can. D5 104
Eastman, Ga., U.S. D3 117
Eastman, Wi., U.S. E2 156
East Marion, N.Y., U.S. m16 139
East Matunuck, R.I., U.S. F3 146
East Middlebury, Vt., U.S. D2 152
East Millbury, Ma., U.S. B4 128
East Millinocket, Me., U.S. C4 126
East Moline, Il., U.S. B3 120
East Montpelier, Vt., U.S. C4 152
East Naples, Fl., U.S. F5 116
East Newark, N.J., U.S. k8 137
East Newnan, Ga., U.S. C2 117
East Nishnabotna, stm., Ia., U.S. C2 122
East Norriton, Pa., U.S. o20 145
East Olympia, Wa., U.S. C3 154
Easton, Il., U.S. C4 120
Easton, Ks., U.S. k15 123
Easton, Me., U.S. B5 126
Easton, Md., U.S. C5 127
Easton, Mo., U.S. B3 132
Easton, Pa., U.S. E11 145
Easton, Wa., U.S. B4 154
Easton Reservoir, res., Ct., U.S. E2 114
East Orange, N.J., U.S. B4 137
East Orleans, Ma., U.S. C8 128
Eastover, S.C., U.S. D6 147
East Palatka, Fl., U.S. C5 116
East Palestine, Oh., U.S. B5 142
East Parsonfield, Me., U.S. E2 126
East Pass, strt., Fl., U.S. C2 116
East Pea Ridge, W.V., U.S. C2 155
East Peoria, Il., U.S. C4 120
East Pepperell, Ma., U.S. A4 128
East Petersburg, Pa., U.S. F9 145
East Pittsburgh, Pa., U.S. k14 145
Eastpoint, Fl., U.S. C2 116
East Point, Ga., U.S. C2 117
East Point, c., P.E.I., Can. C8 101
East Point, c., Ma., U.S. B6 128
East Point, c., N.J., U.S. E2 137
Eastport, Newf., Can. D5 102
Eastport, Me., U.S. D6 126
Eastport, N.Y., U.S. n16 139
East Poultney, Vt., U.S. D2 152
East Prairie, Mo., U.S. E8 132
East Providence, R.I., U.S. C4 146
East Pryor Mountain, mtn., Mt., U.S. E8 133
East Quogue, N.Y., U.S. n16 139
East Range, mts., Nv., U.S. C4 135
East Ridge, Tn., U.S. h11 149
East Rindge, N.H., U.S. E3 136
East River, Ct., U.S. D5 114
East River Mountain, mts., U.S. C1 153
East Rochester, N.Y., U.S. B3 139
East Rockingham, N.C., U.S. C3 140
East Rutherford, N.J., U.S. h8 137
East Saint Johnsbury, Vt., U.S. C5 152
East Saint Louis, Il., U.S. E3 120
East Salt Creek, stm., Co., U.S. B2 113
East Sandwich, Ma., U.S. C7 128
East Sebago, Me., U.S. E2 126
East Selkirk, Man., Can. D3 100
East Siberian Sea see Vostočno-Sibirskoje more, U.S.S.R. C23 24
East Sioux Falls, S.D., U.S. D9 148
Eastsound, Wa., U.S. A3 154
East Sparta, Oh., U.S. B4 142
East Spencer, N.C., U.S. B2 140
East Stroudsburg, Pa., U.S. D11 145
East Sullivan, Me., U.S. D4 126
East Sullivan, N.H., U.S. E2 136
East Swanzey, N.H., U.S. E2 136
East Tawas, Mi., U.S. D7 129
East Templeton, Ma., U.S. A3 128
East Thermopolis, Wy., U.S. C4 157
East Thompson, Ct., U.S. A8 114
East Troy, Wi., U.S. F5 156
East Vestal, N.Y., U.S. C5 139
East View, W.V., U.S. k10 155
East Walker, stm., U.S. E2 135
East Wallingford, Vt., U.S. E3 152
East Walpole, Ma., U.S. h11 128
East Wareham, Ma., U.S. C6 128
East Washington, Pa., U.S. F1 145
East Waterboro, Me., U.S. E2 126
East Wenatchee, Wa., U.S. B5 154
East Wilton, Me., U.S. D6 126
East Windsor, N.J., U.S. C3 137
Eastwood, Ky., U.S. g12 124
East York, Ont., Can. D5 103
Eaton, Co., U.S. A6 113
Eaton, In., U.S. D7 121
Eaton, Oh., U.S. C1 142
Eaton, co., Mi., U.S. F6 129
Eatonia, Sask., Can. F1 105
Eaton Rapids, Mi., U.S. F6 129
Eatonton, Ga., U.S. C3 117
Eatontown, N.J., U.S. C4 137
Eatonville, Wa., U.S. C3 154
Eau Claire, Mi., U.S. G4 129
Eau Claire, Wi., U.S. D2 156
Eau Claire, co., Wi., U.S. D2 156
Eau Claire, stm., Wi., U.S. D2 156
Eau Claire, Lac à l', l., Que., Can. g11 104
Eauze, Fr. I7 14
Eban, Nig. G12 64
Ebano, Mex. F10 90
Ebb and Flow Lake, l., Man., Can. D2 100
Ebbw Vale, Wales, U.K. J10 8
Ebenezer, Sask., Can. F4 105
Eben Junction, Mi., U.S. B4 129
Ebensburg, Pa., U.S. F4 145
Ebensee, Aus. H13 10
Eberbach, Ger. F8 10
Ebermannstadt, Ger. F11 10
Eberndorf, Aus. I14 10
Ebersbach, Ger. D14 10
Ebersberg, Ger. G11 10
Eberstein, Aus. I14 10
Eberswalde, Ger. C13 10
Ebetsu, Japan D16 36a
Ebinur Hu, l., China C3 30
Ebnat, Switz. D11 13
Eboli, Italy I10 18
Ebolowa, Cam. H9 54
Ebony, Nmb. D2 66
Ebro (Ebre), stm., Spain E12 16
Ebro, Embalse del, res., Spain B8 16
Eccles, W.V., U.S. n13 155
Echaporã, Braz. G3 79
Ech Cheliff (Orléansville), Alg. B11 62
Echeconnee Creek, stm., Ga., U.S. D3 117
Echo, Al., U.S. D4 108
Echo, La., U.S. C3 125
Echo, Mn., U.S. F3 130
Echo, Or., U.S. B7 144
Echo Bay, Nv., U.S. G7 135
Echoing Lake, l., Ont., Can. B5 100
Echo Lake, l., Me., U.S. D3 126
Echo Lake, l., Vt., U.S. B5 152
Echols, co., Ga., U.S. F4 117
Echt, Neth. F8 12
Echuca, Austl. K6 70
Écija, Spain H6 16
Eckernförde, Ger. A9 10
Eckerty, In., U.S. H4 121
Eckhart Mines, Md., U.S. k13 127
Eckley, Co., U.S. A8 113
Eckville, Alta., Can. C3 98
Eclectic, Al., U.S. C3 108
Eclipse Sound, strt., N.W. Ter., Can. B17 96
Ečmiadzin, U.S.S.R. I6 22
Econfina, stm., Fl., U.S. B3 116
Economy, N.S., Can. D6 101
Economy, In., U.S. E7 121
Economy, Pa., U.S. h13 145
Écorces, Rivière aux, stm., Que., Can. A6 104
Ecorse, Mi., U.S. p15 129
Écrins, Barre des, mtn., Fr. H13 14
Ecru, Ms., U.S. A4 131
Ector, co., Tx., U.S. D1 150
Ecuador, ctry., S.A. D3 76
Ecum Secum, N.S., Can. E7 101
Ecum Secum Bridge, N.S., Can. E7 101
Ed, Eth. H2 47
Edam, Sask., Can. D1 105
Edam, Neth. C7 12
Edberg, Alta., Can. C4 98
Edcouch, Tx., U.S. F4 150
Eddiceton, Ms., U.S. D3 131
Eddy, co., N.M., U.S. E5 138
Eddy, co., N.D., U.S. B7 141
Eddystone, Pa., U.S. p20 145
Eddystone Point, c., Austl. M8 70
Eddyville, Ia., U.S. C5 122
Eddyville, Ky., U.S. e9 124
Eddyville, Ne., U.S. C6 134
Ede, Nig. H12 64
Edéa, Cam. H9 54
Edéia, Braz. D4 79
Edelény, Hung. G20 10
Eden, Austl. K8 70
Eden, Man., Can. D2 100
Eden, Az., U.S. E6 110
Eden, Ga., U.S. D5 117
Eden, Id., U.S. G4 119
Eden, Md., U.S. D6 127
Eden, N.Y., U.S. C2 139
Eden, N.C., U.S. A3 140
Eden, S.D., U.S. B8 148
Eden, Tx., U.S. D3 150
Eden, Ut., U.S. B4 151
Eden, Wi., U.S. E5 156
Eden, Wy., U.S. D3 157
Edenburg, S. Afr. G7 66
Eden Hill, hill, Ct., U.S. D2 114
Eden Prairie, Mn., U.S. n12 130
Edenton, N.C., U.S. A6 140
Eden Valley, Mn., U.S. E4 130
Edenville, S. Afr. F8 66
Edenville, Mi., U.S. E6 129
Edenwold, Sask., Can. G3 105
Edeowie, Austl. H3 70
Eder, stm., Ger. D8 10
Edfu see Idfū, Egypt E7 60
Edgar, Ne., U.S. D8 134
Edgar, Wi., U.S. D4 156
Edgar, co., Il., U.S. D6 120
Edgard, La., U.S. D5 125
Edgar Springs, Mo., U.S. D6 132
Edgartown, Ma., U.S. D6 128
Edgecombe, co., N.C., U.S. B5 140
Edgecumbe, Cape, c., Ak., U.S. m21 109
Edgefield, S.C., U.S. D4 147
Edgefield, co., S.C., U.S. D4 147
Edgeley, N.D., U.S. C7 141
Edgemere, Md., U.S. B5 127
Edgemont, S.D., U.S. D2 148
Edgemoor, De., U.S. A3 115
Edgemoor, S.C., U.S. B5 147
Edgemoor, Tn., U.S. m13 149
Edgeøya, i., Sval. B3 28
Edgerly, La., U.S. D2 125
Edgerton, Alta., Can. C5 98
Edgerton, Ks., U.S. D8 123
Edgerton, Mn., U.S. G2 130
Edgerton, Mo., U.S. B3 132
Edgerton, Oh., U.S. A1 142
Edgerton, Wi., U.S. F4 156
Edgerton, Wy., U.S. C6 157
Edgewater, Al., U.S. f7 108
Edgewater, Fl., U.S. D6 116
Edgewater, Md., U.S. C4 127
Edgewater, N.J., U.S. h9 137
Edgewater Park, N.J., U.S. C3 137
Edgewood, B.C., Can. E8 99
Edgewood, Il., U.S. E5 120
Edgewood, In., U.S. D6 121
Edgewood, Ia., U.S. B6 122
Edgewood, Ky., U.S. h13 124
Edgewood, Md., U.S. B5 127
Edgewood, Md., U.S. B5 127
Edgewood, N.M., U.S. B3 138
Edgewood, Oh., U.S. A5 142
Edgewood, Pa., U.S. k14 145
Edgewood, Wa., U.S. f11 154
Edgeworth, Pa., U.S. h13 145
Edhessa, Grc. I6 20
Edina, Mn., U.S. F5 130
Edina, Mo., U.S. A5 132
Edinboro, Pa., U.S. C1 145
Edinburg, Il., U.S. D4 120
Edinburg, N.D., U.S. A8 141
Edinburg, Tx., U.S. F3 150
Edinburg, Va., U.S. B4 153
Edinburgh, Scot., U.K. F10 8
Edinburgh, In., U.S. F6 121
Edinburgh, Arrecife, rf., Nic. C12 92
Edinburgh Channel, strt., Nic. C12 92
Edincik, Tur. I11 20
Edirne, Tur. H10 20
Edison, Ga., U.S. E2 117
Edison, Ne., U.S. D6 134
Edison, N.J., U.S. B4 137
Edison, Wa., U.S. A3 154
Edisto, stm., S.C., U.S. E6 147
Edisto, North Fork, stm., S.C., U.S. D5 147
Edisto, South Fork, stm., S.C., U.S. E5 147
Edisto Island, i., S.C., U.S. F7 147
Edith, Mount, mtn., Mt., U.S. D5 133
Edjeleh, Alg. G15 62
Edmond, Ok., U.S. B4 143
Edmonds, Wa., U.S. B3 154
Edmondson, Ar., U.S. B5 111
Edmondson Heights, Md., U.S. g10 127
Edmonson, co., Ky., U.S. C3 124
Edmonton, Austl. A6 70
Edmonton, Alta., Can. C4 98
Edmonton, Ky., U.S. D4 124
Edmore, Mi., U.S. E5 129
Edmore, N.D., U.S. A7 141
Edmunds, co., S.D., U.S. B6 148
Edmundston, N.B., Can. B1 101
Edna, Ks., U.S. E8 123
Edna, Tx., U.S. E4 150
Edolo, Italy C5 18
Edon, Oh., U.S. A1 142
Édouard, Lac, l., Que., Can. B5 104
Edremit, Tur. J11 20
Edsbro, Swe. L16 6
Edsbyn, Swe. K14 6
Edson, Alta., Can. C2 98
Edson Butte, mtn., Or., U.S. E2 144
Eduardo Castex, Arg. H6 80
Edward, Lake, l., Afr. B5 58
Edwards, Co., U.S. B4 113
Edwards, Il., U.S. C4 120
Edwards, Ms., U.S. C3 131
Edwards, co., Il., U.S. E5 120
Edwards, co., Ks., U.S. E4 123
Edwards, co., Tx., U.S. E2 150
Edwards Air Force Base, mil., Ca., U.S. E5 112
Edwardsburg, Mi., U.S. G4 129
Edwards Butte, mtn., Or., U.S. B3 144
Edwards Plateau, plat., Tx., U.S. D2 150
Edwardsport, In., U.S. G3 121
Edwardsville, Al., U.S. B4 108
Edwardsville, Il., U.S. E4 120
Edwardsville, Ks., U.S. k16 123
Edwardsville, Pa., U.S. n17 145
Edward VII Peninsula, pen., Ant. C9 73
Edwin, Al., U.S. D4 108
Eek, Ak., U.S. C7 109
Eeklo, Bel. F4 12
Eel, stm., Ca., U.S. B2 112
Eel, stm., In., U.S. F3 121
Eel, stm., In., U.S. C6 121
Effigy Mounds National Monument, Ia., U.S. A6 122
Effingham, Il., U.S. D5 120
Effingham, Ks., U.S. C8 123
Effingham, S.C., U.S. D5 117
Effingham, co., Ga., U.S. D5 117
Effingham, co., Il., U.S. D5 120
Efland, N.C., U.S. A3 140
Ega, stm., Spain C9 16
Egadi, Isole, is., Italy L7 18
Egan, S.D., U.S. D9 148
Egaña, Arg. I9 80
Egan Range, mts., Nv., U.S. E7 135
Eganville, Ont., Can. B7 103
Egegik, Ak., U.S. D8 109
Egeland, N.D., U.S. A6 141
Eger, Hung. H20 10
Eger see Cheb, Czech. E12 10
Egersund, Nor. L10 6
Eggenburg, Aus. G15 10
Egg Harbor City, N.J., U.S. D3 137
Egg Island Point, c., N.J., U.S. E2 137
Egilsstaðir, Ice. B6 6a
Eglin Air Force Base, mil., Fl., U.S. u15 116
Egmont, Mount, mtn., N.Z. C4 72
Egmont Bay, b., P.E.I., Can. C5 101
Egmont Channel, strt., Fl., U.S. p10 116
Egmont Key, i., Fl., U.S. p10 116
Egremont, Alta., Can. B4 98
Éguas, Rio das, stm., Braz. B6 79
Egypt, Ar., U.S. B5 111
Egypt, Ga., U.S. D5 117
Egypt, Ma., U.S. B6 128
Egypt (Miṣr), ctry., Afr. C7 56
Egypt, Lake of, res., Il., U.S. F5 120
Ehrenberg, Az., U.S. D1 110
Ehrhardt, S.C., U.S. E5 147
Eibar, Spain B9 16
Eichstätt, Ger. G11 10
Eidsvåg, Nor. J11 6
Eidsvold, Austl. E9 70
Eielson Air Force Base, mil., Ak., U.S. C10 109
Eifel, mts., Ger. E6 10
Eiger, mtn., Switz. E9 13
Eight Degree Channel, strt., Asia I2 46
Eightmile Creek, stm., Ks., U.S. h12 123
Eights Coast, Ant. C11 73
Eighty Eight, Ky., U.S. D4 124
Eighty Mile Beach, Austl. C4 68
Eildon, Austl. K6 70
Eildon, Lake, res., Austl. K6 70
Eilenburg, Ger. D12 10
Einasleigh, Austl. B6 70
Einasleigh, stm., Austl. A5 70
Einbeck, Ger. D9 10
Eindhoven, Neth. F7 12
Einsiedeln, Switz. D10 13
Eiru, stm., Braz. B6 82
Eirunepé, Braz. B7 82
Eisden, Bel. G8 12
Eisenach, Ger. E10 10
Eisenberg, Ger. E11 10
Eisenerz, Aus. H14 10
Eisenhower, Mount, mtn., N.H., U.S. B4 136
Eisenhüttenstadt, Ger. C14 10
Eisenkappel, Aus. I14 10
Eisenstadt, Aus. H16 10
Eišiškės, U.S.S.R. G8 26
Eisleben, Ger. D11 10
Eitorf, Ger. E7 10
Eivissa, Spain G13 16
Eivissa (Ibiza), i., Spain G13 16
Ejea de los Caballeros, Spain C10 16
Ejeda, Madag. T21 67b
Ejido, Ven. C7 84
Ejido Jaboncillos, Mex. C8 90
Ejin Qi, China C7 30
Ejutla de Crespo, Mex. I11 90
Ekalaka, Mt., U.S. E12 133
Eket, Nig. I13 64
Ekibastuz, U.S.S.R. G7 24
Ekpoma, Nig. H13 64
Eksjö, Swe. M14 6
Ela, Burma E4 40
El Aaiún (La'youn), W. Sah. G4 62
El Abiadh Sidi Cheikh, Alg. D11 62
El Adeb Larache, Alg. G15 62
El Adelanto, Guat. C5 92
El Agreb, Alg. E13 62
El Aguilar, Arg. B6 80
Elaine, Ar., U.S. C5 111
El Alamein see Al-'Alamayn, Egypt B5 60
El Alia, Tun. L5 18
El Alto, Peru J2 84
El Amparo de Apure, Ven. D7 84
Elamville, Al., U.S. D4 108
Elandsvlei, S. Afr. I4 66
El Angel, Ec. G4 84
El Aouinet, Alg. N2 18
El Arahal, Spain H6 16
El Arco, Mex. C3 90
El Aricha, Alg. C10 62
El Aroussa, Tun. M4 18
Elat, Isr. I3 50
El Ávila, Parque Nacional, Ven. B9 84
Elazığ, Tur. B5 48
Elba, Al., U.S. D3 108
Elba, Ne., U.S. C7 134
Elba, Isola d', i., Italy G5 18
El Banco, Col. C6 84
El Barco de Valdeorras, Spain C5 16
Elbasan, Alb. H4 20
El Baúl, Ven. C8 84
El Baúl, Cerro, mtn., Mex. I12 90
El Baúl, Cerro, mtn., Mex. I9 90
Elbe (Labe), stm., Eur. B9 10
Elberfeld, In., U.S. H3 121
Elberon, Ia., U.S. B5 122
Elbert, Co., U.S. B6 113
Elbert, co., Co., U.S. B6 113
Elbert, co., Ga., U.S. B4 117
Elbert, Mount, mtn., Co., U.S. B4 113
Elberta, Al., U.S. E2 108
Elberta, Ga., U.S. D3 117
Elberta, Mi., U.S. D4 129
Elberton, Ga., U.S. B4 117
Elbeuf, Fr. C8 14
El Beyyadh, Alg. D11 62
Elbing, Ks., U.S. f12 123
Elbistan, Tur. B4 48
Elbląg (Elbing), Pol. A19 10
El Bluff, Nic. F11 92
El Bordo, Col. F4 84
El-Borouj, Mor. D7 62
El Boulaïda, Alg. B12 62
Elbow, Sask., Can. F2 105
Elbow, stm., Alta., Can. D3 98
Elbow Cay, i., Bah. C4 94
Elbow Lake, Mn., U.S. E3 130

Name | Map Ref. | Page

El'brus, gora, mtn., U.S.S.R. I6 22
Elbrus, Mount see El'brus, gora, mtn., U.S.S.R. I6 22
Elburn, Il., U.S. B5 120
El Cabezo, Arrecife, rf., Mex. H12 90
El Caburé, Arg. D7 80
El Caimanero, Laguna, b., Mex. F6 90
El Cajon, Ca., U.S. F5 112
El Cajón, Embalse, res., Hond. B7 92
El Callao, Ven. D12 84
El Calvario, Col. E6 84
El Calverio, Ven. C9 84
El Campo, Tx., U.S. E4 150
El Capitan, mtn., Mt., U.S. D2 133
El Capitan Reservoir, res., Ca., U.S. o16 112
El Carmen, Arg. C6 80
El Carmen, Bol. H12 82
El Carmen, Col. C6 84
El Carmen, Peru E3 82
El Carmen, stm., Mex. B6 90
El Carmen de Bolívar, Col. C5 84
El Carricito, Mex. C8 90
El Carril, Arg. C6 80
El Castillo de La Concepción, Nic. F10 92
El Cedral, Guat. A4 92
El Cedrito, Mex. C9 90
El Centro, Ca., U.S. F6 112
El Cerrito, Col. F4 84
El Cerrito, Ca., U.S. h8 112
El Cerro, Bol. G11 82
El Chile, Montaña, mtn., Hond. C8 92
Elcho, Wi., U.S. C4 156
El Cholar, Arg. I3 80
El Chorrillo, Arg. G5 80
El Cocuy, Col. D6 84
El Colorado, Arg. D9 80
El Cóndor, Cerro, mtn., Arg. D4 80
El Congo, El Sal. D5 92
El Corazón, Ec. H3 84
El Corpus, Hond. D7 92
El Coyote, stm., Mex. B3 90
El Cozón, Mex. B3 90
El Cuco, El Sal. D6 92
El Cuervo, Laguna, l., Mex. C7 90
El Cuervo Butte, mtn., N.M., U.S. k9 138
Elda, Spain G11 16
El Dátil, Mex. B3 90
Eldersburg, Md., U.S. B4 127
Eldersley, Sask., Can. E4 105
El Desemboque, Mex. C3 90
El Desemboque, Mex. B3 90
El'dikan, U.S.S.R. E19 24
El Diviso, Col. G3 84
El Djazaïr (Algiers), Alg. B12 62
El Djelfa, Alg. C12 62
Eldon, P.E.I., Can. C7 101
Eldon, Ia., U.S. D5 122
Eldon, Mo., U.S. C5 132
Eldora, Ia., U.S. B4 122
Eldorado, Arg. D11 80
Eldorado, Braz. C14 80
Eldorado, Ont., Can. C7 103
El Dorado, Mex. E6 90
El Dorado, Ar., U.S. D3 111
Eldorado, Ga., U.S. E3 117
Eldorado, Il., U.S. F5 120
El Dorado, Ks., U.S. E7 123
Eldorado, Oh., U.S. C1 142
Eldorado, Ok., U.S. C2 143
Eldorado, Tx., U.S. D2 150
El Dorado, Ven. D12 84
El Dorado, co., Ca., U.S. C3 112
Eldorado Peak, mtn., Wa., U.S. A4 154
Eldorado Springs, Co., U.S. B5 113
El Dorado Springs, Mo., U.S. D3 132
Eldorendo, Ga., U.S. E2 117
Eldoret, Kenya A7 58
Eldred, Il., U.S. D3 120
Eldred, Pa., U.S. C5 145
Eldridge, Al., U.S. B2 108
Eldridge, Ia., U.S. C7 122
Eleanor, W.V., U.S. C3 155
Electra, Tx., U.S. B3 150
Electra Lake, res., Co., U.S. D3 113
Electric Peak, mtn., Co., U.S. C5 113
Electric Peak, mtn., Mt., U.S. E6 133
Elefante, Isla del see Elephant Island, i., B.A.T. B1 73
Elefantes, Rio dos (Olifants), stm., Afr. E11 66
Elei, Wādī, val., Afr. G8 60
Eleja, U.S.S.R. E6 26
Elektrogorsk, U.S.S.R. F21 26
Elektrostal', U.S.S.R. F21 26
El Encanto, Col. H6 84
El Encanto, Guat. I15 90
Elephant Butte Reservoir, res., N.M., U.S. D2 138
Elephant Island, i., B.A.T. K9 74
Elephant Mountain, mtn., Me., U.S. D2 126
El Estor, Guat. B5 92
El Eulma, Alg. B13 62
Eleuthera, i., Bah. B6 94
Eleuthera Point, c., Bah. B6 94
Eleva, Wi., U.S. D2 156
Eleven Mile Canyon Reservoir, res., Co., U.S. C5 113
Eleven Point, stm., U.S. A4 111
Elevsís, Grc. K7 20
El Fahs, Tun. M4 18
El Ferrol del Caudillo, Spain B3 16
Elfrida, Az., U.S. F6 110
Elfros, Sask., Can. F4 105
El Fuerte, Mex. D5 90
El Galpón, Arg. C6 80
El Ghazawet, Alg. C10 62
Elgin, Man., Can. E1 100
Elgin, N.B., Can. D4 101
Elgin, Scot., U.K. D10 8
Elgin, Al., U.S. A2 108
Elgin, Il., U.S. A5 120
Elgin, Ia., U.S. B6 122
Elgin, Ks., U.S. E7 123
Elgin, Mn., U.S. F6 130
Elgin, Ne., U.S. C7 134
Elgin, N.D., U.S. C4 141
Elgin, Ok., U.S. C3 143
Elgin, Or., U.S. B9 144
Elgin, S.C., U.S. B6 147
Elgin, Tx., U.S. D4 150
El Golfete, l., Guat. B6 92
Elgon, Mount, mtn., Afr. A6 58
El Grara, Alg. D13 62
El Grove, Spain C3 16
El Guaje, Mex. D8 90
El Guaje, Laguna, l., Mex. C8 90
El Guamo, Col. B5 84
El Guapo, Ven. B10 84
El Guayabo, Ven. C6 84
El Guayabo de Abajo, Mex. D6 90
El Hadjar, Alg. M2 18
El Hank, clf, Afr. D5 54
El Haouaria, Tun. L6 18
Elhovo, Bul. G10 20
El Huecú, Arg. I3 80
El Huisache, Mex. F9 90
Elida, N.M., U.S. D6 138
Elida, Oh., U.S. B1 142
El Ídolo, Isla, i., Mex. G11 90
El Idrissia, Alg. C12 62
Elim, Ak., U.S. C7 109
El Infiernillo, Canal, strt., Mex. C3 90
Eliot, Me., U.S. E2 126
Élisabethville see Lubumbashi, Zaire D5 58
Elisenvaara, U.S.S.R. K21 6
Elista, U.S.S.R. H6 22
Elizabeth, Austl. J3 70
Elizabeth, Co., U.S. B6 113
Elizabeth, Il., U.S. A3 120
Elizabeth, In., U.S. H6 121
Elizabeth, La., U.S. D3 125
Elizabeth, Mn., U.S. D2 130
Elizabeth, Ms., U.S. B3 131
Elizabeth, N.J., U.S. B4 137
Elizabeth, W.V., U.S. B3 155
Elizabeth, Cape, c., Wa., U.S. B1 154
Elizabeth City, N.C., U.S. A6 140
Elizabeth Islands, is., Ma., U.S. D6 128
Elizabethton, Tn., U.S. C11 149
Elizabethtown, Il., U.S. F5 120
Elizabethtown, In., U.S. F6 121
Elizabethtown, Ky., U.S. C4 124
Elizabethtown, N.Y., U.S. A7 139
Elizabethtown, N.C., U.S. C4 140
Elizabethtown, Pa., U.S. F8 145
Elizabethville, Pa., U.S. E8 145
El-Jadida (Mazagan), Mor. E6 62
El Jaralito, Mex. D7 90
El Jebel, Co., U.S. B3 113
El-Jebha, Mor. J7 16
El Jem, Tun. N5 18
El Jicaro, stm., Nic. D8 92
Ełk, Pol. B22 10
Elk, co., Ks., U.S. E7 123
Elk, co., Pa., U.S. D4 145
Elk, stm., B.C., Can. D10 99
Elk, stm., U.S. A2 108
Elk, stm., Co., U.S. A4 113
Elk, stm., Ks., U.S. E7 123
Elk, stm., W.V., U.S. C3 155
Elk, stm., Wi., U.S. C3 156
Elkader, Ia., U.S. B6 122
El Kantara, Tun. D16 62
El-Karafab, Sud. H6 60
Elk City, Id., U.S. D3 119
Elk City, Ks., U.S. E8 123
Elk City, Ok., U.S. B2 143
Elk City Lake, res., Ks., U.S. E7 123
Elk Creek, Ne., U.S. D9 134
Elk Creek, stm., Ok., U.S. B2 143
Elk Creek, stm., S.D., U.S. C3 148
El Kef, Tun. M3 18
El-Kelâa-des-Srarhna, Mor. D7 62
El Kerma, Alg. J11 16
Elk Falls, Ks., U.S. E7 123
Elkford, B.C., Can. D10 99
Elk Garden, W.V., U.S. B5 155
Elk Grove, Ca., U.S. C3 112
Elk Grove Village, Il., U.S. h9 120
Elkhart, Il., U.S. C4 120
Elkhart, In., U.S. A6 121
Elkhart, Ia., U.S. e8 122
Elkhart, Ks., U.S. E2 123
Elkhart, Tx., U.S. D5 150
Elkhart, co., In., U.S. A6 121
Elkhart, stm., In., U.S. B6 121
Elkhart Lake, Wi., U.S. E5 156
Elkhead Mountains, mts., Co., U.S. A3 113
Elkhorn, Man., Can. E1 100
Elk Horn, Ia., U.S. C2 122
Elkhorn, Ne., U.S. g12 134
Elkhorn, Wi., U.S. F5 156
Elkhorn, stm., Ne., U.S. B7 134
Elkhorn, North Fork, stm., Ne., U.S. B8 134
Elkhorn, South Fork, stm., Ne., U.S. B7 134
Elkhorn City, Ky., U.S. C7 124
Elkhorn Peaks, mts., Id., U.S. F7 119
Elkin, N.C., U.S. A2 140
Elkins, Ar., U.S. A1 111
Elkins, W.V., U.S. C5 155
Elkland, Pa., U.S. C7 145
Elk Mills, Md., U.S. A6 127
Elkmont, Al., U.S. A3 108
Elk Mound, Wi., U.S. D2 156
Elk Mountain, Wy., U.S. E6 157
Elk Mountain, mtn., N.M., U.S. D1 138
Elk Mountain, mtn., Wy., U.S. E6 157
Elk Mountains, mts., U.S. D1 148
Elk Mountains, mts., Co., U.S. B3 113
Elko, B.C., Can. E10 99
Elko, Ga., U.S. D3 117
Elko, Nv., U.S. C6 135
Elko, co., Nv., U.S. B6 135
El Kouif, Alg. N3 18
Elk Park, N.C., U.S. A1 140
Elk Peak, mtn., Mt., U.S. D6 133
Elk Point, Alta., Can. C5 98
Elk Point, S.D., U.S. E9 148
Elk Rapids, Mi., U.S. D5 129
El Krib, Tun. M4 18
Elkridge, Md., U.S. B4 127
Elkridge, W.V., U.S. m13 155
Elk River, Id., U.S. C2 119
Elk River, Mn., U.S. E5 130
Elkton, Ky., U.S. D2 124
Elkton, Md., U.S. A6 127
Elkton, Mi., U.S. E7 129
Elkton, S.D., U.S. C9 148
Elkton, Tn., U.S. B5 149
Elkton, Va., U.S. B4 153
Elkview, W.V., U.S. m13 155
Elkville, Il., U.S. F4 120
Ellabell, Ga., U.S. D5 117
Ellaville, Ga., U.S. D2 117
Ellef Ringnes Island, i., N.W. Ter., Can. B9 86
Ellen, Mount, mtn., Ut., U.S. E5 151
Ellen, Mount, mtn., Vt., U.S. C3 152
Ellenboro, N.C., U.S. B1 140
Ellenboro, W.V., U.S. B3 155
Ellendale, De., U.S. E4 115
Ellendale, Mn., U.S. G5 130
Ellendale, N.D., U.S. C7 141
Ellensburg, Wa., U.S. C5 154
Ellenton, Fl., U.S. E4 116
Ellenton, Ga., U.S. E3 117
Ellenville, N.Y., U.S. D6 139
Ellenwood, Ga., U.S. h8 117
Ellerbe, N.C., U.S. B3 140
Ellershouse, N.S., Can. E6 101
Ellerslie, Ga., U.S. D2 117
Ellerslie, Md., U.S. k13 127
Ellès, Tun. N4 18
Ellesmere Island, i., N.W. Ter., Can. A11 86
Ellettsville, In., U.S. F4 121
Ellice, stm., N.W. Ter., Can. C12 96
Ellice Islands see Tuvalu, ctry., Oc. G24 2
Ellichpur see Achalpur, India J7 44
Ellicott City, Md., U.S. B4 127
Ellijay, Ga., U.S. B2 117
El Limón de Teachi, Mex. E6 90
Ellington, Ct., U.S. B6 114
Ellington, Mo., U.S. D7 132
Ellinwood, Ks., U.S. D5 123
Elliot, S. Afr. H8 66
Elliotdale, Transkei H9 66
Elliot Lake, Ont., Can. A2 103
Elliott, Il., U.S. C5 120
Elliott, Ia., U.S. C2 122
Elliott, Ms., U.S. B4 131
Elliott, S.C., U.S. C7 147
Elliott, co., Ky., U.S. B6 124
Elliott Bay, b., Wa., U.S. e11 154
Elliott Key, i., Fl., U.S. G6 116
Elliott Knob, mtn., Va., U.S. B3 153
Ellis, Ks., U.S. D4 123
Ellis, S.D., U.S. D9 148
Ellis, co., Ks., U.S. D4 123
Ellis, co., Ok., U.S. A2 143
Ellis, co., Tx., U.S. C4 150
Ellis, stm., N.H., U.S. B4 136
Ellis Grove, Il., U.S. E4 120
Ellison Bay, Wi., U.S. C6 156
Ellis Pond, l., Me., U.S. D2 126
Ellisras, S. Afr. D8 66
Elliston, Newf., Can. D5 102
Elliston, Mt., U.S. D4 133
Elliston, Va., U.S. C2 153
Ellisville, Ms., U.S. D4 131
Ellisville, Mo., U.S. f12 132
Elloree, S.C., U.S. D6 147
Ellore see Elūru, India F11 42
Ellport, Pa., U.S. E1 145
Ellsinore, Mo., U.S. E7 132
Ellsworth, Il., U.S. C5 120
Ellsworth, Ia., U.S. B4 122
Ellsworth, Ks., U.S. D5 123
Ellsworth, Me., U.S. D4 126
Ellsworth, Mi., U.S. C5 129
Ellsworth, Mn., U.S. G2 130
Ellsworth, Pa., U.S. F1 145
Ellsworth, Wi., U.S. D1 156
Ellsworth, co., Ks., U.S. D5 123
Ellsworth Air Force Base, mil., S.D., U.S. C2 148
Ellsworth Hill, mtn., Ct., U.S. B2 114
Ellsworth Land, reg., Ant. C12 73
Ellsworth Mountains, mts., Ant. C12 73
Ellwangen, Ger. G10 10
Ellwood City, Pa., U.S. E1 145
Elm, Switz. E11 13
Elm, stm., N.D., U.S. B8 141
Elma, Ia., U.S. A5 122
Elma, Wa., U.S. C2 154
El Mahdia, Tun. C16 62
El Malah, Alg. J10 16
El Maneadero, Mex. B1 90
El Manteco, Ven. D11 84
El Marsa el Kebir, Alg. C10 62
Elm City, N.C., U.S. B5 140
Elm Creek, Man., Can. E2 100
Elm Creek, Ne., U.S. D6 134
Elm Creek, stm., Mn., U.S. G4 130
El Médano, Mex. E4 90
Elmendorf, Tx., U.S. k7 150
Elmendorf Air Force Base, mil., Ak., U.S. C10 109
El Menia, Alg. E12 62
Elmer, N.J., U.S. D2 137
El Mghayyar, Alg. D13 62
Elm Grove, Wi., U.S. m11 156
Elmhurst, Il., U.S. B6 120
Elmhurst, Pa., U.S. D10 145
El Milagro, Arg. F6 80
El Miliyya, Alg. B14 62
Elmina, Ghana I9 64
Elmira, P.E.I., Can. C7 101
Elmira, N.Y., U.S. C4 139
Elmira, Or., U.S. C3 144
El Mirage, Az., U.S. k8 110
Elmira Heights, N.Y., U.S. C4 139
Elmo, Mo., U.S. A2 132
Elmo, Mt., U.S. C2 133
Elmo, Ut., U.S. D5 151
El Mochito, Hond. C6 92
El Mohammadia, Alg. C11 62
El Molinillo, Spain F7 16
Elmont, Ks., U.S. k14 123
Elmont, N.Y., U.S. k13 139
Elmont, Va., U.S. C5 153
El Monte, Chile G3 80
El Monte, Ca., U.S. e4 112
Elmora, Pa., U.S. E4 145
Elmore, Austl. K6 70
Elmore, Al., U.S. C3 108
Elmore, Mn., U.S. G4 130
Elmore, Oh., U.S. A2 142
Elmore, co., Al., U.S. C3 108
Elmore, co., Id., U.S. F3 119
Elmore City, Ok., U.S. C4 143
El Morro National Monument, N.M., U.S. B1 138
Elmsdale, N.S., Can. E6 101
Elmshorn, Ger. B9 10
Elm Springs, Ar., U.S. A1 111
Elm Springs Colony, S.D., U.S. D8 148
Elmsville, N.B., Can. D3 101
El Multe, Mex. I14 90
Elmvale, Ont., Can. C5 103
Elmville, Ct., U.S. B8 114
Elmwood, Ont., Can. C3 103
Elmwood, Il., U.S. C3 120
Elmwood, Ne., U.S. D9 134
Elmwood, Wi., U.S. D1 156
Elmwood Park, Il., U.S. k9 120
Elmwood Park, N.J., U.S. h8 137
Elmwood Place, Oh., U.S. o13 142
El Naranjo, Arg. C6 80
Elne, Fr. J9 14
El Negrito, Hond. B7 92
El Nevado, Cerro, mtn., Arg. H4 80
El Nevado, Cerro, mtn., Col. C4 76
El Nihuil, Arg. H4 80
El Nopal, Cerro, mtn., Mex. C6 90
Elnora, Alta., Can. D4 98
Elnora, In., U.S. G3 121
El Ocote, Cerro, mtn., Mex. E6 90
Eloise, Fl., U.S. E5 116
Elon College, N.C., U.S. A3 140
Elora, Ont., Can. D4 103
Elora, Tn., U.S. B5 149
El Oro, prov., Ec. I3 84
Elortondo, Arg. G8 80
Elorza, Ven. D8 84
El Oso, Ven. E10 84
Eloy, Az., U.S. E4 110
El Pacayal, Mex. J13 90
El Palmar, Bol. I10 82
El Palmar, Ven. D12 84
El Palqui, Chile F3 80
El Pao, Ven. C11 84
El Pao, Ven. C8 84
El Paradero, Ven. B8 84
El Paraíso, Hond. D8 92
El Paraíso, dept., Hond. C8 92
El Paso, Spain O23 17b
El Paso, Ar., U.S. B3 111
El Paso, Il., U.S. C4 120
El Paso, Tx., U.S. o11 150
El Paso, co., Co., U.S. C6 113
El Paso, co., Tx., U.S. o11 150
El Pato, Col. F5 84
El Peñuelo, Mex. E9 90
El Perú, Ven. D12 84
Elphinstone, Man., Can. D1 100
El Pilar, Ven. B11 84
El Piñón, Col. B5 84
El Pintado, Arg. C8 80
El Piquete, Arg. C6 80
El Pital, Cerro, mtn., N.A. C5 92
El Portal, Ca., U.S. D4 112
El Portal, Fl., U.S. s13 116
El Port de Pollença, Spain F15 16
El Porvenir, N.M., U.S. B4 138
El Potro, Cerro, mtn., S.A. E4 80
El Prado, N.M., U.S. A4 138
El Prat de Llobregat, Spain D14 16
El Progreso, Guat. C5 92
El Progreso, Hond. B7 92
El Progreso, dept., Guat. C4 92
El Puerto de Santa María, Spain I5 16
El Puesto, Arg. D5 80
El Qala, Alg. B15 62
El Qoll, Alg. B14 62
El Quebrachal, Arg. C6 80
El Quelite, Mex. F6 90
Elqui, stm., Chile E3 80
Elrama, Pa., U.S. F2 145
El Rastro, Ven. C9 84
El Real de Santa María, Pan. C4 84
El Reno, Ok., U.S. B4 143
El Rito, N.M., U.S. A3 138
El Roble, Mesa, mtn., Mex. B2 90
Elrod, Al., U.S. B2 108
El Rom, Isr. Occ. B5 50
El Rosarito, Mex. C2 90
Elrose, Sask., Can. F1 105
Elroy, Wi., U.S. E3 156
Elsa, Yukon, Can. D5 96
Elsa, Tx., U.S. F4 150
Elsah, Il., U.S. E3 120
El Salado, Chile D3 80
El Salto, Mex. F7 90
El Salvador, ctry., N.A. D6 92
El Samán de Apure, Ven. D8 84
El Sauz, Mex. C6 90
El Sauzal, Mex. B1 90
Elsberry, Mo., U.S. B7 132
El Seibo, Dom. Rep. E10 94
Elsie, Mi., U.S. E6 129
Elsie, Ne., U.S. D4 134
Elsinore, Ut., U.S. E3 151
Elsmere, De., U.S. B3 115
Elsmere, Ky., U.S. B5 124
El Socorro, Ven. C10 84
El Sombrero, Ven. C9 84
Elst, Neth. E8 12
Elsterwerda, Ger. D13 10
Elstow, Sask., Can. F2 105
El Sueco, Mex. C6 90
El Tagarete, Cerro, mtn., Mex. D7 90
El Tajín, hist., Mex. G11 90
El Tala, Arg. D6 80
El Tamarindo, El Sal. D7 92
El Tambo, Col. G4 84
El Tarf, Alg. M3 18
El Tecuán, Mex. E6 90
El Tigre, Col. F8 84
El Tigre, Ven. C10 84
El Tigre, Isla, i., Hond. D7 92
Eltmann, Ger. F10 10
El Tocuyo, Ven. C8 84
El Tofo, Chile E3 80
Elton, La., U.S. D3 125
Eltopia, Wa., U.S. C7 154
El Toro, Ca., U.S. n13 112
El Toro Marine Corps Air Station, mil., Ca., U.S. n13 112
El Tránsito, Chile E3 80
El Tránsito, El Sal. D6 92
El Trapiche, Col. F4 84
El Trébol, Arg. G8 80
El Triunfo, Hond. D7 92
El Triunfo, Mex. F4 90
El Triunfo, Cerro, mtn., Mex. B2 92
El Triunfo de la Cruz, Hond. B7 92
El Tunal, Arg. C6 80
El Turbio, Arg. G2 78
Elūru, India D6 46
Elva, Man., Can. E1 100
Elva, U.S.S.R. C9 26
El Vado Reservoir, res., N.M., U.S. A3 138
El Valle, Pan. C2 84
Elvas, Port. G4 16
El Vendrell, Spain D13 16
El Viejo, Nic. E7 92
El Vigía, Ven. C7 84
El Vigía, Cerro, mtn., Mex. G7 90
Elvins, Mo., U.S. D7 132
Elvira, Arg. H9 80
El Volcán, Arg. G5 80
El Volcán, Chile G3 80
El Wad, Alg. D14 62
El Wanza, Alg. C15 62
Elwell, Lake, res., Mt., U.S. B5 133
Elwha, stm., Wa., U.S. A2 154
Elwood, In., U.S. D6 121
Elwood, Ks., U.S. C9 123
Elwood, Ne., U.S. D6 134
Elwood, N.J., U.S. D3 137
Elwood, Ut., U.S. B3 151
Elwood Park, Fl., U.S. E4 116
Elx, Spain G11 16
Ely, Ia., U.S. C6 122
Ely, Mn., U.S. C7 130
Ely, Nv., U.S. D7 135
El Yagual, Ven. D8 84
Elyria, Oh., U.S. A3 142
Elysburg, Pa., U.S. E8 145
Elysian, Mn., U.S. F5 130
Emāmshahr (Shāhrūd), Iran C13 48
Emanuel, co., Ga., U.S. D4 117
Emas, Parque Nacional das, Braz. E2 79
Emba, U.S.S.R. H9 22
Emba, stm., U.S.S.R. H9 22
Embarcación, Arg. B6 80
Embarras, stm., Il., U.S. E6 120
Embarrass, Wi., U.S. D5 156
Embarrass, stm., Wi., U.S. D5 156
Embden Pond, l., Me., U.S. D3 126
Embira, stm., Braz. B6 82
Embreeville, Tn., U.S. C11 149
Embro, Ont., Can. D4 103
Embrun, Fr. H13 14
Emden, Ger. B7 10
Emden, Il., U.S. C4 120
Emerado, N.D., U.S. B8 141
Emerald, Austl. D8 70
Emero, stm., Bol. E8 82
Emerson, Man., Can. E3 100
Emerson, Ar., U.S. D2 111
Emerson, Ga., U.S. B2 117
Emerson, Ia., U.S. C2 122
Emerson, Ne., U.S. B9 134
Emerson, N.J., U.S. h8 137
Emery, S.D., U.S. D8 148
Emery, Ut., U.S. E4 151
Emery, co., Ut., U.S. E5 151
Emery Mills, Me., U.S. E2 126
Emet, Tur. J13 20
Emida, Id., U.S. B2 119
Emiliano Zapata, Mex. I14 90
Emiliano Zapata, Bahía, b., Mex. H16 90
Emilia-Romagna, prov., Italy E6 18
Emily, Mn., U.S. D5 130
Emily, Lake, l., Mn., U.S. E3 130
Emine, nos, c., Bul. G11 20
Eminence, In., U.S. F4 121
Eminence, Ky., U.S. B4 124
Eminence, Mo., U.S. D6 132
Emlembe, mtn., Afr. E10 66
Emlenton, Pa., U.S. D2 145
Emlyn, Ky., U.S. D5 124
Emma, Mo., U.S. C4 132
Emma Lake, l., Sask., Can. D3 105
Emmaus, Pa., U.S. E11 145
Emmaville, Austl. G9 70
Emmeline Lake, l., Sask., Can. C2 105
Emmeloord, Neth. C8 12
Emmen, Neth. C10 12
Emmenbrücke, Switz. D9 13
Emmendingen, Ger. G7 10
Emmer-Compascuum, Neth. C11 12
Emmerich, Ger. D6 10
Emmet, Ar., U.S. D2 111
Emmet, co., Ia., U.S. A3 122
Emmet, co., Mi., U.S. C6 129
Emmetsburg, Ia., U.S. A3 122
Emmett, Id., U.S. F2 119
Emmett, Ks., U.S. C7 123
Emmiganūru, India E4 46
Emmitsburg, Md., U.S. A3 127
Emmonak, Ak., U.S. C7 109
Emmons, Mn., U.S. G5 130
Emmons, co., N.D., U.S. C5 141
Emory, Tx., U.S. E5 150
Emory Peak, mtn., Tx., U.S. E1 150
Empalme, Mex. D4 90
Empangeni, S. Afr. G10 66
Empedrado, Arg. D9 80
Empedrado, Chile H2 80
Empire, Al., U.S. B2 108
Empire, Co., U.S. B5 113
Empire, Ga., U.S. D3 117
Empire, La., U.S. E6 125
Empire, Mi., U.S. D4 129
Empire, Nv., U.S. C2 135
Empoli, Italy F5 18
Emporia, Ks., U.S. D7 123
Emporia, Va., U.S. D5 153
Emporium, Pa., U.S. D5 145
Empress, Alta., Can. D5 98
Empty Quarter see Ar-Rub'al-Khālī, des., Asia E5 47
Ems, stm., Eur. C7 10
Emsdale, Ont., Can. B5 103
Emsdetten, Ger. C7 10
Emsworth, Pa., U.S. h13 145
Emure-Ekiti, Nig. H12 64
En (Inn), stm., Eur. F17 14
Encampment, Wy., U.S. E6 157
Encantado, Braz. E13 80
Encarnación, Para. D11 80
Enchant, Alta., Can. D4 98
Encinal, Tx., U.S. E3 150
Encinitas, Ca., U.S. F5 112
Encino, N.M., U.S. C4 138
Encino, Tx., U.S. F3 150
Encontrados, Ven. C6 84
Encounter Bay, b., Austl. J3 70
Encruzilhada, Braz. C8 79
Encruzilhada do Sul, Braz. F12 80
Encs, Hung. G21 10
Endako, B.C., Can. B5 99
Endako, stm., B.C., Can. B5 99
Ende, Indon. G7 38
Endeavor, Wi., U.S. E4 156
Endeavour, Sask., Can. E4 105
Endeavour Strait, strt., Austl. B8 68
Enderby, B.C., Can. D8 99
Enderby Land, reg., Ant. B4 73
Enderlin, N.D., U.S. C8 141
Enders Reservoir, res., Ne., U.S. D4 134
Endiang, Alta., Can. D4 98
Endicott, Ne., U.S. D8 134
Endicott, N.Y., U.S. C4 139
Endicott, Wa., U.S. C8 154
Endicott Mountains, mts., Ak., U.S. B9 109
Endimari, stm., Braz. D8 82
Endless Lake, l., Me., U.S. C4 126
Endola, Nmb. A2 66
Endwell, N.Y., U.S. C4 139
Ene, stm., Peru D4 82
Enewetak, atoll, Marsh. Is. G20 158
Enez, Tur. I10 20
Enfida, Tun. M5 18
Enfield, N.S., Can. E6 101
Enfield (Thompsonville), Ct., U.S. B5 114
Enfield, Il., U.S. E5 120
Enfield, Me., U.S. C4 126
Enfield, N.H., U.S. C2 136
Enfield, N.C., U.S. A5 140
Enfield Center, N.H., U.S. C2 136
Engadine, Mi., U.S. B5 129
Engaño, Cabo, c., Dom. Rep. E10 94
Engcobo, Transkei H9 66
'En Gedi, Isr. F4 50
Engelberg, Switz. E9 13
Engelhard, N.C., U.S. B7 140
Engel's, U.S.S.R. G7 22
Engenho, Braz. F13 82
'En Gev, Isr. C5 50
Enggano, Pulau, i., Indon. G3 38
England, Ar., U.S. C4 111
England, ter., U.K. I12 8
England Air Force Base, mil., La., U.S. C3 125
Englee, Newf., Can. C3 102
Englefeld, Sask., Can. E3 105
Englefield, Cape, c., N.W. Ter., Can. C15 96
Engleside, Va., U.S. g12 153
Englewood, Co., U.S. B6 113
Englewood, Fl., U.S. F4 116
Englewood, N.J., U.S. B5 137
Englewood, Oh., U.S. C1 142
Englewood, Tn., U.S. D9 149
Englewood Cliffs, N.J., U.S. h9 137
English, In., U.S. H5 121
English Bay, Ak., U.S. h16 109
English Channel (La Manche), strt., Eur. K12 8
English Coast, Ant. C12 73
Englishtown, N.J., U.S. C4 137
Énguera, Spain G11 16
Engure, U.S.S.R. D6 26
Engwilen, Switz. C11 13
'En Harod, Isr. C4 50
Enid, Ok., U.S. A4 143
Enid Lake, res., Ms., U.S. A4 131
Enigma, Ga., U.S. E3 117
Enilda, Alta., Can. B2 98
eNjesuthi, mtn., Afr. G9 66
Enka, N.C., U.S. f10 140
Enkhuizen, Neth. C7 12
Enmedio, Cerro de, mtn., Mex. H9 90
Enmore, Guy. D14 84
Enna, Italy L9 18
Ennedi, plat., Chad E5 56
Ennis, Mt., U.S. E5 133
Ennis, Tx., U.S. C4 150
Enniskillen, N. Ire., U.K. G6 8
Enns, Aus. G14 10
Enns, stm., Aus. G14 10
Enoch, Ut., U.S. F3 151
Enola, Ar., U.S. B3 111
Enola, Pa., U.S. F8 145
Enon, Oh., U.S. C2 142
Enoree, S.C., U.S. B4 147
Enoree, stm., S.C., U.S. B3 147
Enosburg Falls, Vt., U.S. B3 152
Enrique Urien, Arg. D8 80
Enriquillo, Dom. Rep. F9 94
Enriquillo, Lago, l., Dom. Rep. E9 94
Enschede, Neth. D10 12
Ensenada, Arg. H10 80
Ensenada, Mex. B1 90
Ensenada, N.M., U.S. A3 138
Enshi, China E8 30
Ensign, Alta., Can. D4 98
Ensign, Ks., U.S. E3 123
Ensley, Fl., U.S. u14 116
Entebbe, Ug. A6 58
Enterprise, Ont., Can. C8 103
Enterprise, Guy. D13 84
Enterprise, Al., U.S. D4 108
Enterprise, Ks., U.S. D6 123
Enterprise, Ms., U.S. C5 131
Enterprise, Or., U.S. B9 144
Enterprise, Ut., U.S. F2 151
Enterprise, W.V., U.S. B4 155
Entiat, Wa., U.S. B5 154
Entiat, stm., Wa., U.S. B5 154
Entiat, Lake, l., Wa., U.S. B5 154
Entiat Mountains, mts., Wa., U.S. B5 154

Name	Map Ref.	Page
Entrance, Alta., Can.	C2	98
Entre Ríos, Bol.	I9	82
Entre Rios, Braz.	A9	79
Entre Ríos, prov., Arg.	F9	80
Entre Ríos, Cordillera, mts., Hond.	C9	92
Entre Rios de Minas, Braz.	F6	79
Entroncamento, Port.	F3	16
Entwistle, Alta., Can.	C3	98
Enugu, Nig.	H13	64
Enumclaw, Wa., U.S.	B4	154
Envalira, Port d', Eur.	C13	16
Envermeu, Fr.	C8	14
Envigado, Col.	D5	84
Enville, Tn., U.S.	B3	149
Envira, Braz.	B6	82
Eo, stm., Spain	B4	16
Eola Hills, hills, Or., U.S.	h11	144
Eolia, Mo., U.S.	B6	132
Eolie, Isole, is., Italy	K9	18
Epe, Nig.	H11	64
Epecuén, Lago, l., Arg.	I7	80
Épéhy, Fr.	H3	12
Épernay, Fr.	C10	14
Epes, Al., U.S.	C1	108
Ephesus, Ga., U.S.	C1	117
Ephesus, hist., Tur.	L11	20
Ephraim, Ut., U.S.	D4	151
Ephrata, Pa., U.S.	F9	145
Ephrata, Wa., U.S.	B6	154
Épinal, Fr.	D13	14
Epirus see Ípeiros, hist. reg., Grc.	J4	20
Epokiro, Nmb.	C4	66
Epping, Eng., U.K.	J14	8
Epping, N.H., U.S.	D4	136
Epps, La., U.S.	B4	125
Epsom, Eng., U.K.	J13	8
Epsom, N.H., U.S.	D4	136
Epukiro, stm., Afr.	C5	66
Epworth, Ia., U.S.	B7	122
Eqlīd, Iran	F12	48
Equality, Al., U.S.	C3	108
Equality, Il., U.S.	F5	120
Equatorial Guinea, ctry., Afr.	H8	54
Erath, La., U.S.	E3	125
Erath, co., Tx., U.S.	C3	150
Erba, Italy	D4	18
Erbacon, W.V., U.S.	C4	155
Erciş, Tur.	B7	48
Erciyes Dağı, mtn., Tur.	B3	48
Érd, Hung.	H18	10
Erdaoliangzi, China	C7	32
Erdene, Mong.	C9	30
Erding, Ger.	G11	10
Erebato, stm., Ven.	E10	84
Erebus, Mount, mtn., Ant.	C8	73
Erechim, Braz.	D12	80
Ereğli, Tur.	C3	48
Erenhot, China	C9	30
Erepecu, Lago do, l., Braz.	H14	84
Eressós, Grc.	J9	20
Erétria, Grc.	K7	20
Erfoud, Mor.	E8	62
Erft, stm., Ger.	D6	10
Erfurt, Ger.	E11	10
Erges (Erjas), stm., Eur.	F5	16
Ergli, U.S.S.R.	E8	26
Ergun (Argun'), stm., Asia	A11	30
Er Hai, l., China	B6	40
Erhard, Mn., U.S.	D2	130
Erhlin, Tai.	L9	34
Erial, N.J., U.S.	D2	137
Eriba, Sud.	I9	60
Erice, Italy	K7	18
Erick, Ok., U.S.	B2	143
Erickson, B.C., Can.	E9	99
Erickson, Man., Can.	D2	100
Ericson, Ne., U.S.	C7	134
Erie, Co., U.S.	A5	113
Erie, Il., U.S.	B3	120
Erie, Ks., U.S.	E8	123
Erie, Mi., U.S.	G7	129
Erie, N.D., U.S.	B8	141
Erie, Pa., U.S.	B1	145
Erie, co., N.Y., U.S.	C2	139
Erie, co., Oh., U.S.	A3	142
Erie, co., Pa., U.S.	C1	145
Erie, Lake, l., N.A.	C10	106
Erieau, Ont., Can.	E3	103
Erie Canal, N.Y., U.S.	B5	139
Eriksdale, Man., Can.	D2	100
Erimo-misaki, c., Japan	F18	36a
Erin, Ont., Can.	D4	103
Erin, Tn., U.S.	A4	149
Eritrea, hist. reg., Eth.	E5	56
Erjas (Erges), stm., Eur.	F5	16
Erjiazhen, China	C10	34
Erkelenz, Ger.	D6	10
Erkowit, Sud.	H9	60
Erlangen, Ger.	F11	10
Erlanger, Ky., U.S.	A5	124
Erling, Lake, res., Ar., U.S.	D2	111
Erma, N.J., U.S.	F3	137
Ermelo, Neth.	D8	12
Ermelo, S. Afr.	F9	66
Ermenek, Tur.	C2	48
Ermoúpolis, Grc.	L8	20
Erne, Lower Lough, l., N. Ire., U.K.	G6	8
Erne, Upper Lough, l., Eur.	G6	8
Ernée, Fr.	D6	14
Ernfold, Sask., Can.	G2	105
Erode, India	G4	46
Eromanga, Austl.	F5	70
Erongo, Nmb.	C2	66
Erota, Eth.	I9	60
Er-Rachidia, Mor.	E8	62
Errol, N.H., U.S.	A4	136
Erskine, Alta., Can.	C4	98
Erskine, Mn., U.S.	C3	130
Erstein, Fr.	D14	14
Ertai, China	B5	30
Ertil', U.S.S.R.	J23	26
Ertix (Irtyš), stm., Asia	H9	24
Ertuğrul, Tur.	J11	20
Erudina, Austl.	H3	70
Eruwa, Nig.	H11	64
Erval, Braz.	G12	80
Erwin, N.C., U.S.	B4	140
Erwin, Tn., U.S.	C11	149
Erwinville, La., U.S.	D4	125
Erwood, Sask., Can.	E4	105
Eryuan, China	A5	40
Erzgebirge (Krušné hory), mts., Eur.	E13	10
Erzin, U.S.S.R.	G17	22
Erzincan, Tur.	B5	48
Erzurum, Tur.	B6	48
Esa'ala, Pap. N. Gui.	A10	68
Esashi, Japan	F15	36
Esashi, Japan	H16	36
Esbjerg, Den.	N11	6
Esbon, Ks., U.S.	C5	123
Esca, stm., Spain	J5	14
Escalante, Ut., U.S.	F4	151
Escalante, stm., Ut., U.S.	F4	151
Escalante, stm., Ven.	C7	84
Escalante Creek, stm., Co., U.S.	C2	113
Escalante Desert, des., Ut., U.S.	F2	151
Escalón, Mex.	D7	90
Escalon, Ca., U.S.	D3	112
Escambia, co., Al., U.S.	D2	108
Escambia, co., Fl., U.S.	u14	116
Escambia, stm., Fl., U.S.	u14	116
Escanaba, Mi., U.S.	C3	129
Escanaba, stm., Mi., U.S.	B3	129
Escárcega, Mex.	H14	90
Escarpada Point, c., Phil.	L20	39b
Escatawpa, Ms., U.S.	E5	131
Escatawpa, stm., U.S.	D5	131
Escaut (Schelde), stm., Eur.	E3	10
Esch-sur-Alzette, Lux.	I8	12
Eschwege, Ger.	D10	10
Eschweiler, Ger.	E6	10
Escobal, Pan.	H15	92
Escobedo, Mex.	C8	90
Escocesa, Bahía, b., Dom. Rep.	E10	94
Escondido, Ca., U.S.	F5	112
Escondido, stm., Nic.	E11	92
Escoumins, Rivière des, stm., Que., Can.	A8	104
Escudo de Veraguas, Isla, i., Pan.	H13	92
Escuinapa de Hidalgo, Mex.	F7	90
Escuintla, Guat.	C4	92
Escuintla, Mex.	J13	90
Escuintla, dept., Guat.	C3	92
Escuminac, Point, c., N.B., Can.	B5	101
Escurial, Serra do, mtn., Braz.	F10	76
Eşfahān (Isfahan), Iran	E11	48
Esfarāyen, Iran	C14	48
Eshkāshem, Afg.	B4	44
Eshowe, S. Afr.	G10	66
Esigodini, Zimb.	C9	66
Esk, Austl.	F10	70
Eskdale, W.V., U.S.	C3	155
Eskifjörður, Ice.	B7	6a
Eskilstuna, Swe.	L15	6
Eskimo Lakes, l., N.W. Ter., Can.	C6	96
Eskimo Point, N.W. Ter., Can.	D14	96
Eskişehir, Tur.	H14	4
Esko, Mn., U.S.	D6	130
Eskridge, Ks., U.S.	D7	123
Esla, stm., Spain	C6	16
Eslāmābād, Iran	D9	48
Eslāmshahr, Iran	D11	48
Eşme, Tur.	K12	20
Esmeralda, Austl.	B5	70
Esmeralda, Cuba	D5	94
Esmeralda, co., Nv., U.S.	F4	135
Esmeraldas, Ec.	G3	84
Esmeraldas, prov., Ec.	G3	84
Esmeraldas, stm., Ec.	G3	84
Esmond, N.D., U.S.	A6	141
Esmond, R.I., U.S.	B4	146
Esneux, Bel.	G8	12
Esom Hill, Ga., U.S.	C1	117
Espada, Punta, c., Col.	A7	84
Espalion, Fr.	H9	14
Espanola, Ont., Can.	A3	103
Espanola, Fl., U.S.	C5	116
Espanola, N.M., U.S.	B3	138
Esparto, Ca., U.S.	C2	112
Esparza, C.R.	H10	92
Espejo, Spain	H7	16
Espera Feliz, Braz.	F8	79
Esperança, Braz.	J8	84
Esperance, Austl.	F4	68
Esperance Bay, b., Austl.	F4	68
Esperanza, Arg.	F8	80
Esperanza, Mex.	D5	90
Espinal, Col.	E5	84
Espinar, Peru	F6	82
Espinhaço, Serra do, mts., Braz.	C7	79
Espinho, Port.	D3	16
Espinillo, Arg.	C9	80
Espino, Ven.	C9	84
Espinosa, Braz.	C7	79
Espírito Santo, state, Braz.	E8	79
Espíritu Santo, Isla, i., Mex.	E4	90
Espita, Mex.	G15	90
Esplanada, Braz.	A10	79
Espoo (Esbo), Fin.	K19	6
Espumoso, Braz.	E12	80
Espungabera, Moz.	C11	66
Espy, Pa., U.S.	D9	145
Esquatzel Coulee, val., Wa., U.S.	C6	154
Esquel, Arg.	E2	78
Esquimalt, B.C., Can.	E6	99
Esquina, Arg.	F9	80
Esquina Negra, Arg.	H9	80
Esquipulas, Guat.	C5	92
Esquipulas, Nic.	E9	92
Esquiú, Arg.	E6	80
Essaouira (Mogador), Mor.	E6	62
Es-Sekhira, Tun.	C16	62
Essen, Bel.	F5	12
Essen, Ger.	D7	10
Essequibo, stm., Guy.	E13	84
Es Sers, Tun.	M4	18
Essex, Ont., Can.	E2	103
Essex, Ct., U.S.	D6	114
Essex, Il., U.S.	B5	120
Essex, Ia., U.S.	D2	122
Essex, Md., U.S.	B5	127
Essex, Ma., U.S.	A6	128
Essex, Mo., U.S.	E8	132
Essex, Vt., U.S.	B2	152
Essex, co., Eng., U.K.	J14	8
Essex, co., Ma., U.S.	A5	128
Essex, co., N.J., U.S.	B4	137
Essex, co., N.Y., U.S.	B7	139
Essex, co., Vt., U.S.	B5	152
Essex, co., Va., U.S.	C6	153
Essex Junction, Vt., U.S.	C2	152
Essexville, Mi., U.S.	E7	129
Esslingen, Ger.	G9	10
Es Smala es Souassi, Tun.	N5	18
Essonne, dept., Fr.	D9	14
Essoyes, Fr.	D11	14
Es-Suki, Sud.	K7	60
Est, Île de l', i., Que., Can.	B8	101
Est, Pointe de l', c., Que., Can.	B8	101
Estacada, Or., U.S.	B4	144
Estacado, Llano, pl., U.S.	C1	150
Estados, Isla de los, i., Arg.	J8	74
Eşţahbān, Iran	G13	48
Estaire, Ont., Can.	A4	103
Estância, Braz.	F11	76
Estancia, N.M., U.S.	C3	138
Estanislao del Campo, Arg.	C8	80
Estanzuelas, El Sal.	D6	92
Estats, Pique d', mtn., Eur.	C13	16
Estcourt, S. Afr.	G9	66
Este, Italy	D6	18
Esteio, Braz.	E13	80
Estelí, Nic.	D8	92
Estelí, dept., Nic.	D8	92
Estella, Spain	C9	16
Estelline, S.D., U.S.	C9	148
Estell Manor, N.J., U.S.	E3	137
Estepa, Spain	H7	16
Estepona, Spain	I6	16
Esterhazy, Sask., Can.	G4	105
Estero, Fl., U.S.	F5	116
Estero Bay, b., Ca., U.S.	E3	112
Estero Bay, b., Fl., U.S.	F5	116
Estero Island, i., Fl., U.S.	F5	116
Esteros, Arg.	D7	80
Estes Park, Co., U.S.	A5	113
Este Sudeste, Cayos del, is., Col.	E13	92
Estevan, Sask., Can.	H4	105
Estherville, Ia., U.S.	A3	122
Estherwood, La., U.S.	D3	125
Estill, S.C., U.S.	F5	147
Estill, co., Ky., U.S.	C6	124
Estillfork, Al., U.S.	A3	108
Estill Springs, Tn., U.S.	B5	149
Estonia see Estonskaja Sovetskaja Socialističeskaja Respublika, state, U.S.S.R.	C8	26
Estonskaja Sovetskaja Socialističeskaja Respublika, state, U.S.S.R.	C8	26
Estrêla, Braz.	E13	80
Estrela, mtn., Port.	E4	16
Estrêla do Indaiá, Braz.	E6	79
Estrêla do Leste, Braz.	D2	79
Estrêla do Norte, Braz.	B4	79
Estrêla do Sul, Braz.	E5	79
Estremadura, hist. reg., Port.	F3	16
Esztergom, Hung.	H18	10
Étables, Fr.	D4	14
Etadunna, Austl.	G3	70
Etah, Grnld.	B12	86
Etah, India	G8	44
Étain, Fr.	C12	14
Étampes, Fr.	D9	14
Étang-du-Nord, Que., Can.	B8	101
Étaples, Fr.	B8	14
Etāwah, India	G8	44
Etchojoa, Mex.	D5	90
Eten, Peru	E2	82
Eternity Range, mts., Ant.	B12	73
Ethan, S.D., U.S.	D8	148
Ethel, Ont., Can.	D3	103
Ethel, Ms., U.S.	B4	131
Ethel, W.V., U.S.	n12	155
Ethelbert, Man., Can.	D1	100
Ether, N.C., U.S.	B3	140
Ethete, Wy., U.S.	C4	157
Ethiopia (Ityopiya), ctry., Afr.	G8	56
Ethridge, Tn., U.S.	B4	149
Etna, Ca., U.S.	B2	112
Etna, N.H., U.S.	C2	136
Etna, Pa., U.S.	k14	145
Etna, Wy., U.S.	C1	157
Etna, Monte, vol., Italy	L10	18
Etna Green, In., U.S.	B5	121
Etobicoke, Ont., Can.	D5	103
Etolin Island, i., Ak., U.S.	m23	109
Etolin Strait, strt., Ak., U.S.	C6	109
Eton, Ga., U.S.	B2	117
Etosha Pan, pl., Nmb.	B3	66
Etowah, Ar., U.S.	B5	111
Etowah, Tn., U.S.	D9	149
Etowah, co., Al., U.S.	A3	108
Etowah, stm., Ga., U.S.	B2	117
Étretat, Fr.	C7	14
Etta, Ms., U.S.	A4	131
Ettelbruck, Lux.	I9	12
Et Tîdra, i., Maur.	B1	64
Ettlingen, Ger.	G8	10
Ettrick, Va., U.S.	C5	153
Ettrick, Wi., U.S.	D2	156
Etzikom, Alta., Can.	E5	98
Etzikom Coulee, stm., Alta., Can.	E5	98
Etzná, hist., Mex.	H14	90
Eu, Fr.	B8	14
Eucla, Austl.	F5	68
Euclid, Mn., U.S.	C2	130
Euclid, Oh., U.S.	A4	142
Eucumbene, Lake, res., Austl.	K8	70
Eudora, Ar., U.S.	D4	111
Eudora, Ks., U.S.	D8	123
Eudunda, Austl.	J3	70
Eufaula, Al., U.S.	D4	108
Eufaula, Ok., U.S.	B6	143
Eufaula Lake, res., Ok., U.S.	B6	143
Eugene, In., U.S.	E3	121
Eugene, Or., U.S.	C3	144
Eugenio Bustos, Arg.	G4	80
Eugenópolis, Braz.	F7	79
Eugowra, Austl.	I8	70
Eulonia, Ga., U.S.	E5	117
Eumungerie, Austl.	H8	70
Eunice, La., U.S.	D3	125
Eunice, N.M., U.S.	E6	138
Eunola, Al., U.S.	D4	108
Eupen, Bel.	G9	12
Euphrates (Fırat) (Nahr al-Furāt), stm., Asia	F9	48
Eupora, Ms., U.S.	B4	131
Eure, dept., Fr.	C7	14
Eure, stm., Fr.	D8	14
Eure-et-Loir, dept., Fr.	D8	14
Eureka, Ca., U.S.	B1	112
Eureka, Il., U.S.	C4	120
Eureka, Ks., U.S.	E7	123
Eureka, Mo., U.S.	f12	132
Eureka, Mt., U.S.	B1	133
Eureka, Nv., U.S.	D6	135
Eureka, S.C., U.S.	B5	147
Eureka, S.D., U.S.	B6	148
Eureka, Ut., U.S.	D3	151
Eureka, Wi., U.S.	D5	156
Eureka, co., Nv., U.S.	D5	135
Eureka Springs, Ar., U.S.	A2	111
Euroa, Austl.	K6	70
Europa, Île, i., Reu.	F8	58
Europa, Picos de, mts., Spain	B7	16
Europa Point, c., Gib.	I6	16
Europe	C9	52
Europoort, Neth.	E5	12
Euskal Herriko, prov., Spain	B9	16
Euskirchen, Ger.	E6	10
Eustis, Fl., U.S.	D5	116
Eustis, Ne., U.S.	D5	134
Eutaw, Al., U.S.	C2	108
Eutawville, S.C., U.S.	E7	147
Eutsuk Lake, l., B.C., Can.	C4	99
Eva, Al., U.S.	A3	108
Eva, Tn., U.S.	A3	149
Evangeline, La., U.S.	D3	125
Evangeline, co., La., U.S.	D3	125
Evans, Co., U.S.	A6	113
Evans, Ga., U.S.	C4	117
Evans, W.V., U.S.	C3	155
Evans, co., Ga., U.S.	D5	117
Evans, Mount, mtn., Co., U.S.	B5	113
Evansburg, Alta., Can.	C3	98
Evans City, Pa., U.S.	E1	145
Evansdale, Ia., U.S.	B5	122
Evans Head, c., Austl.	G10	70
Evans Strait, strt., N.W. Ter., Can.	D16	96
Evanston, Co., U.S.	A6	113
Evanston, Il., U.S.	A6	120
Evanston, Wy., U.S.	E2	157
Evansville, Ar., U.S.	B1	111
Evansville, Il., U.S.	E4	120
Evansville, In., U.S.	I2	121
Evansville, Mn., U.S.	D3	130
Evansville, Wi., U.S.	F4	156
Evansville, Wy., U.S.	D6	157
Evart, Mi., U.S.	E5	129
Evarts, Ky., U.S.	D6	124
Eveleth, Mn., U.S.	C6	130
Evening Shade, Ar., U.S.	A4	111
Everard, Lake, l., Austl.	F7	68
Everest, Ks., U.S.	C8	123
Everest, Mount (Qomolangma Feng), mtn., Asia	G12	44
Everett, Ont., Can.	C5	103
Everett, Ga., U.S.	E5	117
Everett, Ma., U.S.	g11	128
Everett, Pa., U.S.	F5	145
Everett, Wa., U.S.	B3	154
Everett, Mount, mtn., Ma., U.S.	B1	128
Everett Lake, res., N.H., U.S.	D3	136
Everettville, W.V., U.S.	h10	155
Everglades National Park, Fl., U.S.	G5	116
Evergreen, Al., U.S.	D3	108
Evergreen, Co., U.S.	B5	113
Evergreen, La., U.S.	D3	125
Evergreen, Ms., U.S.	A5	131
Evergreen, N.C., U.S.	C4	140
Evergreen Park, Il., U.S.	k9	120
Everly, Ia., U.S.	A2	122
Everman, Volcán, vol., Mex.	H4	90
Everson, Pa., U.S.	F2	145
Everson, Wa., U.S.	A3	154
Everton, Ar., U.S.	A3	111
Everton, Mo., U.S.	D4	132
Evesham, Sask., Can.	E1	105
Évian-les-Bains, Fr.	F13	14
Evionnaz, Switz.	F7	13
Evisa, Fr.	G3	18
Évora, Port.	G4	16
Évreux, Fr.	C8	14
Évros (Marica) (Meriç), stm., Eur.	H10	20
Évry, Fr.	D9	14
E.V. Spence Reservoir, res., Tx., U.S.	D2	150
Évvoia, i., Grc.	K7	20
Ewa, Hi., U.S.	B3	118
Ewa Beach, Hi., U.S.	B3	118
Ewa Beach, Hi., U.S.	g9	118
Ewen, Mi., U.S.	m12	129
Ewing, Il., U.S.	E5	120
Ewing, Ky., U.S.	B6	124
Ewing, Mo., U.S.	A6	132
Ewing, Ne., U.S.	B7	134
Ewing, Va., U.S.	f8	153
Ewing Township, N.J., U.S.	C3	137
Ewo, Congo	B2	58
Exaltación, Bol.	E9	82
Excel, Al., U.S.	D2	108
Excelsior Mountain, mtn., Ca., U.S.	C4	112
Excelsior Mountains, mts., Nv., U.S.	E3	135
Excelsior Springs, Mo., U.S.	B3	132
Exeter, Ont., Can.	D3	103
Exeter, Eng., U.K.	K10	8
Exeter, Ca., U.S.	D4	112
Exeter, Mo., U.S.	E4	132
Exeter, Ne., U.S.	D8	134
Exeter, N.H., U.S.	E5	136
Exeter, Pa., U.S.	D10	145
Exeter, stm., N.H., U.S.	E5	136
Exira, Ia., U.S.	C3	122
Exmore, Va., U.S.	C7	153
Exmouth, Austl.	D2	68
Exmouth, Eng., U.K.	K10	8
Exmouth Gulf, b., Austl.	D2	68
Expedition Range, mts., Austl.	E8	70
Experiment, Ga., U.S.	C2	117
Exploits, stm., Newf., Can.	D3	102
Exploits, Bay of, b., Newf., Can.	D4	102
Export, Pa., U.S.	F2	145
Exshaw, Alta., Can.	D3	98
Extension, B.C., Can.	f12	99
Extrema, Braz.	G5	79
Extremadura, prov., Spain	F5	16
Exuma Cays, is., Bah.	B6	94
Exuma Sound, strt., Bah.	B6	94
Eyak, Ak., U.S.	C10	109
Eyebrow, Sask., Can.	G2	105
Eyl, Som.	G10	56
Eylar Mountain, mtn., Ca., U.S.	D3	112
Eymoutiers, Fr.	G8	14
Eyota, Mn., U.S.	G6	130
Eyrarbakki, Ice.	C3	6a
Eyre, Austl.	F5	68
Eyre North, Lake, l., Austl.	G2	70
Eyre Peninsula, pen., Austl.	I1	70
Eyre South, Lake, l., Austl.	G2	70
Eysturoy, i., Faer. Is.	D8	6b
Ezine, Tur.	J10	20

F

Name	Map Ref.	Page
Fabens, Tx., U.S.	o11	150
Fabius, stm., Mo., U.S.	A6	132
Fábrega, Cerro, mtn., Pan.	H12	92
Fabriano, Italy	F7	18
Fabyan, Ct., U.S.	A8	114
Facatativá, Col.	E5	84
Fackler, Al., U.S.	A4	108
Factoryville, Pa., U.S.	C10	145
Fada, Chad	E5	56
Fada Ngourma, Burkina	E10	64
Fadd, Hung.	I18	10
Faddeja, zaliv, b., U.S.S.R.	B13	24
Fadit, Sud.	M7	60
Faenza, Italy	E6	18
Faeroe Islands (Føroyar), dep., Eur.	D8	6b
Fafa, Mali	D10	64
Fafakourou, Sen.	E2	64
Fafen, stm., Eth.	G9	56
Faga, stm., Burkina	E10	64
Făgăraş, Rom.	D8	20
Fagernes, Nor.	K11	6
Făget, Rom.	D6	20
Faguibine, Lac, l., Mali	C8	64
Fagurhólsmýri, Ice.	C5	6a
Fagus, Mo., U.S.	E7	132
Faido, Switz.	F10	13
Fairacres, N.M., U.S.	E3	138
Fairbairn Reservoir, res., Austl.	D8	70
Fairbank, Ia., U.S.	B5	122
Fairbanks, Ak., U.S.	C10	109
Fairbanks, Fl., U.S.	C4	116
Fairbanks, Me., U.S.	D2	126
Fair Bluff, N.C., U.S.	C3	140
Fairborn, Oh., U.S.	C1	142
Fairburn, Ga., U.S.	C2	117
Fairbury, Il., U.S.	C5	120
Fairbury, Ne., U.S.	D8	134
Fairchance, Pa., U.S.	G2	145
Fairchild, Wi., U.S.	D3	156
Fairchild Air Force Base, mil., Wa., U.S.	g13	154
Fairdale, Ky., U.S.	B4	124
Fairdale, N.D., U.S.	A7	141
Fairfax, Ca., U.S.	C2	112
Fairfax, De., U.S.	A3	115
Fairfax, Ia., U.S.	C6	122
Fairfax, Mn., U.S.	F4	130
Fairfax, Mo., U.S.	A2	132
Fairfax, Ok., U.S.	A5	143
Fairfax, S.C., U.S.	F5	147
Fairfax, S.D., U.S.	D7	148
Fairfax, Vt., U.S.	B2	152
Fairfax, Va., U.S.	B5	153
Fairfax, co., Va., U.S.	B5	153
Fairfax Station, Va., U.S.	g12	153
Fairfield, Al., U.S.	B3	108
Fairfield, Ca., U.S.	C2	112
Fairfield, Ct., U.S.	E2	114
Fairfield, Id., U.S.	F4	119
Fairfield, Il., U.S.	E5	120
Fairfield, Ia., U.S.	C6	122
Fairfield, Me., U.S.	D3	126
Fairfield, Mt., U.S.	C5	133
Fairfield, Ne., U.S.	D7	134
Fairfield, N.C., U.S.	B6	140
Fairfield, Oh., U.S.	n12	142
Fairfield, Tx., U.S.	D4	150
Fairfield, Wa., U.S.	B8	154
Fairfield, co., Ct., U.S.	D2	114
Fairfield, co., Oh., U.S.	C3	142
Fairfield, co., S.C., U.S.	C5	147
Fairfield Bay, Ar., U.S.	B3	111
Fairfield Pond, l., Vt., U.S.	B3	152
Fairgrove, Mi., U.S.	E7	129
Fair Grove, Mo., U.S.	D4	132
Fair Grove, N.C., U.S.	B2	140
Fairhaven, Ma., U.S.	C6	128
Fair Haven, Mi., U.S.	F8	129
Fairhaven, Mn., U.S.	E4	130
Fair Haven, N.J., U.S.	C4	137
Fair Haven, N.Y., U.S.	B4	139
Fair Haven, Vt., U.S.	D2	152
Fairhope, Al., U.S.	E2	108
Fairland, In., U.S.	E6	121
Fairland, Ok., U.S.	A7	143
Fair Lawn, N.J., U.S.	h8	137
Fairlawn, Va., U.S.	C2	153
Fairlea, W.V., U.S.	D4	155
Fairlee, Vt., U.S.	D4	152
Fairlie, N.Z.	F3	72
Fairlight, Sask., Can.	H5	105
Fairmont, Il., U.S.	C6	120
Fairmont, Mn., U.S.	G4	130
Fairmont, Ne., U.S.	D8	134
Fairmont, N.C., U.S.	C3	140
Fairmont, W.V., U.S.	B4	155
Fairmount, Ga., U.S.	B2	117
Fairmount, Il., U.S.	C6	120
Fairmount, In., U.S.	D6	121
Fairmount, N.D., U.S.	C9	141
Fairmount Heights, Md., U.S.	f9	127
Fair Oaks, Ar., U.S.	B4	111
Fair Oaks, Ga., U.S.	h7	117
Fair Oaks, In., U.S.	B3	121
Fairoaks, Pa., U.S.	h13	145
Fair Plain, Mi., U.S.	F4	129
Fairplain, W.V., U.S.	C3	155
Fairplay, Co., U.S.	B5	113
Fair Play, Mo., U.S.	D4	132
Fair Play, S.C., U.S.	B2	147
Fairport, Ia., U.S.	C7	122
Fairport, N.Y., U.S.	B3	139
Fair Port, Va., U.S.	C6	153
Fairport Harbor, Oh., U.S.	A4	142
Fairton, N.J., U.S.	E2	137
Fairvale, N.B., Can.	D4	101
Fairview, Alta., Can.	A1	98
Fairview, Il., U.S.	C3	120
Fairview, Ks., U.S.	C8	123
Fairview, Ky., U.S.	D2	124
Fairview, Mi., U.S.	D6	129
Fairview, Mo., U.S.	E3	132
Fairview, Mt., U.S.	C12	133
Fairview, N.J., U.S.	h8	137
Fairview, Ok., U.S.	A3	143
Fairview, Pa., U.S.	B1	145
Fairview, Tn., U.S.	B4	149
Fairview, Ut., U.S.	D4	151
Fairview, W.V., U.S.	B4	155
Fairview, Wy., U.S.	D2	157
Fairview Heights, Il., U.S.	E3	120
Fairview Park, In., U.S.	E3	121
Fairview Park, Oh., U.S.	g9	142
Fairview Peak, mtn., Nv., U.S.	D3	135
Fairview Peak, mtn., Or., U.S.	D4	144
Fair Water, Wi., U.S.	E5	156
Fairway, Ks., U.S.	k16	123
Faisalabad, Pak.	E5	44
Faison, N.C., U.S.	B4	140
Faith, N.C., U.S.	B2	140
Faith, S.D., U.S.	B3	148
Faiyum see Al-Fayyūm, Egypt	C6	60
Faizābād, India	G10	44
Fajardo, P.R.	E12	94
Fakfak, Indon.	F9	38
Fakrinkotti, Sud.	H6	60
Faku, China	A11	32
Falaise, Fr.	D6	14
Falam, Burma	C2	40
Falāvarjān, Iran	E11	48
Fălciu, Rom.	C12	20
Falcon, Co., U.S.	C6	113
Falcon, Ms., U.S.	A3	131
Falcón, state, Ven.	B8	84
Falconara Marittima, Italy	F8	18
Falconer, N.Y., U.S.	C1	139
Falcon Heights, Mn., U.S.	n12	130
Falcon Heights, Or., U.S.	E5	144
Falémé, stm., Afr.	F4	54
Faleşty, U.S.S.R.	B11	20
Falfurrias, Tx., U.S.	F3	150
Falher, Alta., Can.	B2	98
Falkensee, Ger.	C13	10
Falkenstein, Ger.	E12	10
Falkirk, Scot., U.K.	E10	8
Falkland, B.C., Can.	D8	99
Falkland Islands, dep., S.A.	G5	78
Falkland Sound, strt., Falk. Is.	G5	78
Falkner, Ms., U.S.	A5	131
Falkville, Al., U.S.	A3	108
Fall, stm., Ks., U.S.	E7	123
Fallais, Bel.	G7	12
Fall Branch, Tn., U.S.	C11	149
Fallbrook, Ca., U.S.	F5	112
Fall City, Wa., U.S.	B4	154
Fall Creek, Wi., U.S.	D2	156
Fall Creek, stm., In., U.S.	k10	121
Falling Creek, stm., Va., U.S.	n17	153
Falling Rock Creek, stm., W.V., U.S.	m13	155
Falling Waters, W.V., U.S.	B6	155
Fall Mountain Lake, Ct., U.S.	C4	114
Fallon, Mt., U.S.	D11	133
Fallon, Nv., U.S.	D3	135
Fallon, co., Mt., U.S.	D12	133
Fallon Indian Reservation, Nv., U.S.	D3	135
Fallon Naval Air Station, mil., Nv., U.S.	D3	135
Fall River, Ks., U.S.	E7	123
Fall River, Ma., U.S.	C5	128
Fall River, Wi., U.S.	E4	156
Fall River, co., S.D., U.S.	D2	148
Fall River Lake, res., Ks., U.S.	E7	123
Fall River Mills, Ca., U.S.	B3	112
Falls, co., Tx., U.S.	D4	150
Falls Church, Va., U.S.	g12	153
Falls City, Ne., U.S.	D10	134
Falls City, Or., U.S.	C3	144
Falls Creek, Pa., U.S.	D4	145
Falls of Rough, Ky., U.S.	C3	124
Fallston, Md., U.S.	A5	127
Fallston, N.C., U.S.	B1	140
Falls Village, Ct., U.S.	B2	114
Falmouth, N.S., Can.	E5	101
Falmouth, Jam.	E6	94
Falmouth, Eng., U.K.	K8	8
Falmouth, Ky., U.S.	B5	124
Falmouth, Me., U.S.	E2	126
Falmouth, Ma., U.S.	C6	128
Falmouth, Va., U.S.	B5	153
Falsa, Punta, c., Mex.	D2	90
False Cape, c., Fl., U.S.	D6	116
False Cape, c., Va., U.S.	D7	153
False Divi Point, c., India	E6	46
Falso, Cabo, c., Dom. Rep.	F9	94
Falso, Cabo, c., Hond.	B11	92
Falster, i., Den.	N12	6
Fălticeni, Rom.	B10	20
Falun, Swe.	K14	6
Famaillá, Arg.	D6	80
Famatina, Arg.	E5	80
Famatina, Sierra de, mts., Arg.	E5	80
Family Lake, l., Man., Can.	D4	100
Fana, Mali	E6	64
Fanado, stm., Braz.	D7	79
Fanambana, Madag.	N24	67b
Fanchon, Pointe, c., Haiti	E7	94
Fanchuan, China	C8	34
Fancy Farm, Ky., U.S.	f9	124
Fandriana, Madag.	R22	67b
Fang, Thai.	E5	40
Fangak, Sud.	M6	60
Fangcheng, China	B1	34
Fangdao, China	H7	34
Fangxi, China	G3	34

Name	Map Ref.	Page
Fanipol', U.S.S.R.	H10	26
Fannettsburg, Pa., U.S.	F6	145
Fannin, co., Ga., U.S.	B2	117
Fannin, co., Tx., U.S.	C4	150
Fanny, Mount, mtn., Or., U.S.	B9	144
Fanny Bay, B.C., Can.	E5	99
Fannystelle, Man., Can.	E3	100
Fano, Italy	F8	18
Fan Si Pan, mtn., Viet.	C7	40
Fanxian, China	H3	32
Faraday, sci., B.A.T.	B12	73
Faradje, Zaire	H6	56
Faradofay, Madag.	T22	67b
Farafangana, Madag.	S22	67b
Farāh, Afg.	E17	48
Farahalana, Madag.	O24	67b
Farā'id, Jabal al-, mtn., Egypt	J3	48
Faramana, Burkina	E7	64
Faranah, Gui.	F4	64
Farasān, Jazā'ir, is., Sau. Ar.	F2	47
Faratsiho, Madag.	Q22	67b
Farber, Mo., U.S.	B6	132
Farewell, Cape, c., N.Z.	D4	72
Fargo, Ar., U.S.	C4	111
Fargo, Ga., U.S.	F4	117
Fargo, N.D., U.S.	C9	141
Fargo, Ok., U.S.	A2	143
Faribault, Mn., U.S.	F5	130
Faribault, co., Mn., U.S.	G4	130
Farīdkot, India	E6	44
Farīdpur, Bngl.	I13	44
Farīmān, Iran	D15	48
Farina, Il., U.S.	E5	120
Fāriskūr, Egypt	B6	60
Farley, Ia., U.S.	B6	122
Farley, Mo., U.S.	B3	132
Farmer City, Il., U.S.	C5	120
Farmers, Ky., U.S.	B6	124
Farmers Branch, Tx., U.S.	n10	150
Farmersburg, In., U.S.	F3	121
Farmersburg, Ia., U.S.	B6	122
Farmersville, Al., U.S.	C3	108
Farmersville, Il., U.S.	D4	120
Farmerville, La., U.S.	B3	125
Farmingdale, Me., U.S.	D3	126
Farmington, Ar., U.S.	A1	111
Farmington, Ct., U.S.	C4	114
Farmington, De., U.S.	E3	115
Farmington, Il., U.S.	C3	120
Farmington, Ia., U.S.	D6	122
Farmington, Me., U.S.	D2	126
Farmington, Mi., U.S.	p15	129
Farmington, Mn., U.S.	F5	130
Farmington, Mo., U.S.	D7	132
Farmington, N.H., U.S.	D4	136
Farmington, N.M., U.S.	A1	138
Farmington, Ut., U.S.	C4	151
Farmington, W.V., U.S.	h10	155
Farmington, stm., Ct., U.S.	B4	114
Farmington, West Branch, stm., U.S.	B4	114
Farmington Hills, Mi., U.S.	o15	129
Farmland, In., U.S.	D7	121
Farm Pond, l., Ma., U.S.	h10	128
Farmville, N.C., U.S.	B5	140
Farmville, Va., U.S.	C4	153
Farnam, Ne., U.S.	D5	134
Farner, Tn., U.S.	D9	149
Farnham, Que., Can.	D5	104
Farnham, Va., U.S.	C6	153
Farnhamville, Ia., U.S.	B3	122
Faro, Braz.	I14	84
Faro, Port.	H4	16
Faro, stm., Afr.	G9	54
Faro, Punta, c., Col.	B5	84
Farquhar Group, is., Sey.	D10	58
Farragut, Ia., U.S.	D2	122
Farrāshband, Iran	G12	48
Farrell, Ms., U.S.	A3	131
Farrell, Pa., U.S.	D1	145
Farrukhābād, India	G8	44
Fārsī, Afg.	E17	48
Farson, Wy., U.S.	D3	157
Farsund, Nor.	L10	6
Fartak, Ra's, c., Yemen	G8	47
Farvel, Kap, c., Grnld.	D15	86
Farwell, Mi., U.S.	E6	129
Farwell, Ne., U.S.	C7	134
Farwell, Tx., U.S.	B1	150
Fasā, Iran	G12	48
Fasano, Italy	I12	18
Fatehpur, India	G6	44
Fathai, Sud.	M6	60
Fatick, Sen.	D1	64
Fátima, Braz.	G14	82
Fátima, Port.	F3	16
Fatoto, Gam.	E3	64
Fat'ož, U.S.S.R.	I18	26
Faucett, Mo., U.S.	B3	132
Faulk, co., S.D., U.S.	B6	148
Faulkland Heights, De., U.S.	i7	115
Faulkner, co., Ar., U.S.	B3	111
Faulkton, S.D., U.S.	B6	148
Faulquemont, Fr.	C13	14
Fauquier, B.C., Can.	E8	99
Fauquier, co., Va., U.S.	B5	153
Fauske, Nor.	H14	6
Faust, Alta., Can.	B3	98
Fauvillers, Bel.	I8	12
Faux-Cap, Madag.	T21	67b
Favara, Italy	L8	18
Faverges, Fr.	G13	14
Fawcett, Alta., Can.	B3	98
Fawcett Lake, l., Alta., Can.	B4	98
Fawnie Nose, mtn., B.C., Can.	C5	99
Fawnie Range, mts., B.C., Can.	C5	99
Faxaflói, b., Ice.	B2	6a
Faxinal, Braz.	G3	79
Faxinal do Soturno, Braz.	E12	80
Fay, Ok., U.S.	B3	143
Faya, Chad	E4	56
Fayd, Sau. Ar.	H7	48
Fayette, Al., U.S.	B2	108
Fayette, Ia., U.S.	B6	122
Fayette, Ms., U.S.	D2	131
Fayette, Mo., U.S.	B5	132
Fayette, Oh., U.S.	A1	142
Fayette, co., Al., U.S.	B3	108
Fayette, co., Ga., U.S.	C2	117
Fayette, co., Il., U.S.	D5	120
Fayette, co., In., U.S.	E7	121
Fayette, co., Ia., U.S.	B6	122
Fayette, co., Ky., U.S.	B5	124
Fayette, co., Oh., U.S.	C2	142
Fayette, co., Pa., U.S.	G2	145
Fayette, co., Tn., U.S.	B2	149
Fayette, co., Tx., U.S.	E4	150
Fayette, co., W.V., U.S.	C3	155
Fayetteville, Al., U.S.	B3	108
Fayetteville, Ar., U.S.	A1	111
Fayetteville, Ga., U.S.	C2	117
Fayetteville, N.Y., U.S.	B5	139
Fayetteville, N.C., U.S.	B4	140
Fayetteville, Pa., U.S.	G6	145
Fayetteville, Tn., U.S.	B5	149
Fayetteville, W.V., U.S.	C3	155
Fayl-Billot, Fr.	E12	14
Fayville, Ma., U.S.	g9	128
Fazenda de Cima, Braz.	F13	82
Fazenda Nova, Braz.	D3	79
Fāzilka, India	E6	44
Fāzilpur, Pak.	F4	44
Fazzān (Fezzan), hist. reg., Libya	C3	56
Fdérik, Maur.	I4	62
Fear, Cape, c., N.C., U.S.	D5	140
Feather, stm., Ca., U.S.	C3	112
Feather, Middle Fork, stm., Ca., U.S.	C3	112
Featherston, Ok., U.S.	B6	143
Feathertop, Mount, mtn., Austl.	K7	70
Fécamp, Fr.	C7	14
Federación, Arg.	F10	80
Federal, Arg.	F9	80
Federalsburg, Md., U.S.	C6	127
Fedora, S.D., U.S.	C8	148
Fedscreek, Ky., U.S.	C7	124
Feeding Hills, Ma., U.S.	B2	128
Fehérgyarmat, Hung.	H22	10
Fehmarn, i., Ger.	A11	10
Fehmarn Belt, strt., Eur.	A11	10
Feia, Lagoa, b., Braz.	G8	79
Feijó, Braz.	C6	82
Feio, stm., Braz.	F3	79
Feira, Zam.	E6	58
Feira de Santana, Braz.	B9	79
Feixiang, China	G2	32
Fejaj, Chott, sw., Tun.	D15	62
Fejér, co., Hung.	H18	10
Felanitx, Spain	F15	16
Feldbach, Aus.	I15	10
Feldkirch, Aus.	H9	10
Felhit, Eth.	I10	60
Feliciano, Arroyo, stm., Arg.	F9	80
Felicity, Oh., U.S.	D1	142
Felix, Cape, c., N.W. Ter., Can.	C13	96
Felixlândia, Braz.	E6	79
Felixstowe, Eng., U.K.	J15	8
Felixton, S. Afr.	G10	66
Félix U. Gómez, Mex.	C4	90
Fellbach, Ger.	G9	10
Felletin, Fr.	G9	14
Fellsmere, Fl., U.S.	E6	116
Felton, Ca., U.S.	D2	112
Felton, De., U.S.	D3	115
Felton, Ga., U.S.	C1	117
Feltre, Italy	C6	18
Fêmeas, Rio das, stm., Braz.	B6	79
Femund, l., Nor.	J12	6
Femundsenden, Nor.	K12	6
Fen, stm., China	D9	30
Fence, stm., Mi., U.S.	B2	129
Fence Lake, l., Wi., U.S.	C4	156
Fenelon Falls, Ont., Can.	C6	103
Fengcheng, China	C12	32
Fengcheng, China	G4	34
Fengdu, China	F8	30
Fengfeng, China	G2	32
Fenghuanjing, China	D6	34
Fengjia, China	F9	32
Fenglin, Tai.	L10	34
Fengxin, China	G4	34
Fengyang, China	E10	30
Fengyüan, Tai.	K9	34
Fengzhen, China	C9	30
Feni, Bngl.	I14	44
Fenimore Pass, strt., Ak., U.S.	E4	109
Fennimore, Wi., U.S.	F3	156
Fennville, Mi., U.S.	F4	129
Fenoarivo Atsinanana, Madag.	P23	67b
Fenshui'ao, China	J3	34
Fenton, Ia., U.S.	A3	122
Fenton, La., U.S.	D3	125
Fenton, Mi., U.S.	F7	129
Fentress, co., Tn., U.S.	C9	149
Fenwick, W.V., U.S.	C4	155
Fenwick Island, De., U.S.	G5	115
Fenwick Island, i., S.C., U.S.	k11	147
Fenwood, Sask., Can.	G4	105
Fenyang, China	D9	30
Feodosija, U.S.S.R.	H5	22
Fer, Point au, c., La., U.S.	E4	125
Ferdinand, Id., U.S.	C2	119
Ferdinand, In., U.S.	H4	121
Ferdows, Iran	D15	48
Fergana, U.S.S.R.	I12	22
Fergus, Ont., Can.	D4	103
Fergus, co., Mt., U.S.	C7	133
Fergus Falls, Mn., U.S.	D2	130
Ferguson, Ky., U.S.	C5	124
Ferguson, Mo., U.S.	C7	132
Fériana, Tun.	C15	62
Ferintosh, Alta., Can.	C4	98
Ferkéssédougou, I.C.	G7	64
Ferlo, Vallée du, val., Sen.	D2	64
Ferme-Neuve, Que., Can.	C2	104
Fermeuse, Newf., Can.	E5	102
Fermo, Italy	F8	18
Fermont, Que., Can.	h13	104
Fernández, Arg.	D7	80
Fernandina, Isla, i., Ec.	J13	84a
Fernandina Beach, Fl., U.S.	B5	116
Fernando de la Mora, Para.	C10	80
Fernando de Noronha, Ilha, i., Braz.	D12	76
Fernandópolis, Braz.	F3	79
Fernando Póo see Bioko, i., Eq. Gui.	J14	64
Fernán-Núñez, Spain	H7	16
Fern Creek, Ky., U.S.	g11	124
Fern Creek, stm., Ky., U.S.	g11	124
Ferndale, Ar., U.S.	h9	111
Ferndale, Ca., U.S.	B1	112
Ferndale, Ky., U.S.	D6	124
Ferndale, Md., U.S.	B4	127
Ferndale, Mi., U.S.	P15	129
Ferndale, Pa., U.S.	F4	145
Ferndale, Wa., U.S.	A3	154
Fernie, B.C., Can.	E10	99
Fernley, Nv., U.S.	D2	135
Fern Ridge Lake, res., Or., U.S.	C3	144
Fernwood, Id., U.S.	B2	119
Fernwood, Ms., U.S.	D3	131
Ferrara, Italy	E6	18
Ferrellsburg, W.V., U.S.	C2	155
Ferrelo, Cape, c., Or., U.S.	E2	144
Ferreñafe, Peru	B2	82
Ferreyra, Arg.	F6	80
Ferriday, La., U.S.	C4	125
Ferrières, Fr.	D9	14
Ferris, Tx., U.S.	C4	150
Ferrisburg, Vt., U.S.	C2	152
Ferris Mountains, mts., Wy., U.S.	D5	157
Ferro, stm., Braz.	B1	79
Ferrol, Península de, pen., Peru	C2	82
Ferron, Ut., U.S.	D4	151
Ferros, Braz.	E7	79
Ferrum, Va., U.S.	D2	153
Ferry, co., Wa., U.S.	A7	154
Ferry Farms, Va., U.S.	B5	153
Ferryland, Newf., Can.	E5	102
Ferry Point, c., N.J., U.S.	k7	137
Fertile, Ia., U.S.	A4	122
Fertile, Mn., U.S.	C2	130
Fès, Mor.	C8	62
Feshi, Zaire	C3	58
Fessenden, N.D., U.S.	B6	141
Festus, Mo., U.S.	C7	132
Fété Bowé, Sen.	D3	64
Fetești, Rom.	E11	20
Fethiye, Tur.	M13	20
Feuchtwangen, Ger.	F10	10
Feuet, Libya	H16	62
Feuilles, Rivière aux, stm., Que., Can.	g12	104
Feversham, Ont., Can.	C4	103
Feyzābād, Afg.	B4	44
Fez see Fès, Mor.	C8	62
Fiambalá, Arg.	D5	80
Fianarantsoa, Madag.	R22	67b
Fiantsonana, Madag.	Q22	67b
Fiche, Eth.	M10	60
Fichtelberg, mtn., Ger.	E12	10
Fichtelgebirge, mts., Eur.	E11	10
Ficksburg, S. Afr.	G8	66
Fidalgo Island, i., Wa., U.S.	A3	154
Fidenza, Italy	E5	18
Fidler Lake, l., Man., Can.	A3	100
Field, B.C., Can.	D9	99
Fieldale, Va., U.S.	D3	153
Fielding, Ut., U.S.	B3	151
Fieldon, Il., U.S.	D3	120
Fields, Lake, l., Fl., U.S.	B3	116
Fields, Lake, l., La., U.S.	k10	125
Fier, Alb.	I3	20
Fiesch, Switz.	F9	13
Fiesole, Italy	F6	18
Fife, prov., Scot., U.K.	E10	8
Fife Lake, Sask., Can.	H3	105
Fife Lake, Mi., U.S.	D5	129
Fife Lake, l., Sask., Can.	H3	105
Fifield, Wi., U.S.	C3	156
Fifteenmile Creek, stm., Wy., U.S.	B4	157
Fifteen Mile Falls Reservoir, res., U.S.	C5	152
Fifty Lakes, Mn., U.S.	D4	130
Fifty-Six, Ar., U.S.	B3	111
Figueira da Foz, Port.	E3	16
Figueres, Spain	C14	16
Figuig, Mor.	D10	62
Fiji, ctry., Oc.	H24	2
Filabusi, Zimb.	C9	66
Filadelfia, C.R.	G9	92
Filchner Ice Shelf, Ant.	C1	73
File Lake, l., Man., Can.	B1	100
Filer, Id., U.S.	G4	119
Filer City, Mi., U.S.	D4	129
Filingué, Niger	D11	64
Filley, Ne., U.S.	D9	134
Fillmore, Sask., Can.	H4	105
Fillmore, Ca., U.S.	E4	112
Fillmore, Il., U.S.	D4	120
Fillmore, In., U.S.	E4	121
Fillmore, Mo., U.S.	A3	132
Fillmore, Ut., U.S.	E3	151
Fillmore, co., Mn., U.S.	G6	130
Fillmore, co., Ne., U.S.	D8	134
Finale Ligure, Italy	E3	18
Finarwa, Eth.	K10	60
Finca El Rey, Parque Nacional, Arg.	C6	80
Fincastle, Va., U.S.	C3	153
Finch, Ont., Can.	B9	103
Findlater, Sask., Can.	G3	105
Findlay, Il., U.S.	D5	120
Findlay, Oh., U.S.	A2	142
Fingal, N.D., U.S.	C8	141
Finger, Tn., U.S.	B3	149
Finger Lake, l., Ont., Can.	C5	100
Fingerville, S.C., U.S.	A3	147
Fingoè, Moz.	E6	58
Finistère, dept., Fr.	D2	14
Finisterre, Cabo de, c., Spain	C2	16
Finke, Austl.	E6	68
Finke, stm., Austl.	E7	68
Finksburg, Md., U.S.	B4	127
Finland, Mn., U.S.	C7	130
Finland (Suomi), ctry., Eur.	C13	4
Finland, Gulf of, b., Eur.	L20	6
Finley, Austl.	J6	70
Finley, N.D., U.S.	B8	141
Finley, Tn., U.S.	A2	149
Finleyson, Ga., U.S.	D3	117
Finly, In., U.S.	E6	121
Finn, stm., Eur.	G6	8
Finney, co., Ks., U.S.	D3	123
Finnmark, co., Nor.	F19	6
Finn Mountain, mtn., Ak., U.S.	C8	109
Fins, Oman	C11	47
Finsteraarhorn, mtn., Switz.	E9	13
Finsterwalde, Ger.	D13	10
Fiora, stm., Italy	G6	18
Fīq, Isr. Occ.	C5	50
Firavitoba, Col.	E6	84
Fircrest, Wa., U.S.	f10	154
Firebaugh, Ca., U.S.	D3	112
Firenze (Florence), Italy	F6	18
Firestone, Co., U.S.	A6	113
Firmat, Arg.	G8	80
Firminópolis, Braz.	D3	79
Firminy, Fr.	G11	14
Firovo, U.S.S.R.	D16	26
Fīrozābād, India	G8	44
Fīrozpur, India	E6	44
First Connecticut Lake, l., N.H., U.S.	f7	136
First Roach Pond, l., Me., U.S.	C3	126
Firth, Id., U.S.	F6	119
Firth, Ne., U.S.	D9	134
Firth, stm., N.A.	C4	96
Fīrūzābād, Iran	G12	48
Fīrūz Kūh, Iran	D12	48
Fish (Vis), stm., Nmb.	F3	66
Fish, stm., Al., U.S.	E2	108
Fish, stm., Me., U.S.	A4	126
Fish Creek, stm., W.V., U.S.	g8	155
Fisheating Creek, stm., Fl., U.S.	F5	116
Fisher, Ar., U.S.	B5	111
Fisher, Il., U.S.	C5	120
Fisher, La., U.S.	C2	125
Fisher, Mn., U.S.	C2	130
Fisher, co., Tx., U.S.	C2	150
Fisher Bay, b., Man., Can.	D3	100
Fisher Branch, Man., Can.	D3	100
Fisher Lake, l., N.S., Can.	E4	101
Fishermans Island, i., Va., U.S.	h15	153
Fishers, In., U.S.	E5	121
Fishers Island, i., N.Y., U.S.	m16	139
Fishers Peak, mtn., Co., U.S.	D6	113
Fisher Strait, strt., N.W. Ter., Can.	D16	96
Fishersville, Va., U.S.	B4	153
Fishertown, Pa., U.S.	F4	145
Fish Haven, Id., U.S.	G7	119
Fishing Bay, b., Md., U.S.	D5	127
Fishing Creek, Md., U.S.	D5	127
Fishing Creek, stm., N.C., U.S.	A5	140
Fishing Creek, stm., S.C., U.S.	B5	147
Fishing Creek, stm., W.V., U.S.	B4	155
Fishing Creek, North Fork, stm., W.V., U.S.	h9	155
Fishing Creek, South Fork, stm., W.V., U.S.	h9	155
Fishing Creek Reservoir, res., S.C., U.S.	B6	147
Fishkill, N.Y., U.S.	D7	139
Fish River Lake, l., Me., U.S.	B4	126
Fish Springs Range, mts., Ut., U.S.	D2	151
Fishtail, Mt., U.S.	E7	133
Fishtrap Lake, res., Ky., U.S.	C7	124
Fisk, Mo., U.S.	E7	132
Fiskdale, Ma., U.S.	B3	128
Fiske, Sask., Can.	F1	105
Fismes, Fr.	C10	14
Fitchburg, Ma., U.S.	A4	128
Fitchville, Ct., U.S.	C7	114
Fithian, Il., U.S.	C6	120
Fittstown, Ok., U.S.	C5	143
Fitzgerald, Ga., U.S.	E3	117
Fitzgerald River National Park, Austl.	F3	68
Fitzroy, stm., Austl.	C4	68
Fitzroy, stm., Austl.	D9	70
Fitzroy, Monte (Cerro Chaltel), mtn., S.A.	F2	78
Fitzroy Crossing, Austl.	C5	68
Fitzwilliam, N.H., U.S.	E2	136
Fitzwilliam Depot, N.H., U.S.	E2	136
Fitzwilliam Island, i., Ont., Can.	B3	103
Fiume see Rijeka, Yugo.	D9	18
Fiumicino, Italy	H7	18
Five Island Lake, l., Ia., U.S.	A3	122
Five Islands, N.S., Can.	D5	101
Fivemile Creek, stm., Wy., U.S.	C4	157
Five Points, Al., U.S.	B4	108
Five Points, N.M., U.S.	B3	138
Fizi, Zaire	B5	58
Fizuli, U.S.S.R.	B9	48
Fjällåsen, Swe.	H17	6
Fkih-Ben-Salah, Mor.	D7	62
Flag Knob, mtn., Ky., U.S.	C7	124
Flagler, Co., U.S.	B7	113
Flagler, co., Fl., U.S.	C5	116
Flagler Beach, Fl., U.S.	C5	116
Flag Mountain, hill, Al., U.S.	C3	108
Flagstaff, Az., U.S.	B4	110
Flagstaff Lake, l., Or., U.S.	E7	144
Flambeau, stm., Wi., U.S.	C3	156
Flambeau, South Fork, stm., Wi., U.S.	C3	156
Fläming, reg., Ger.	D12	10
Flaming Gorge Dam, Ut., U.S.	C6	151
Flaming Gorge National Recreation Area, U.S.	E3	157
Flaming Gorge Reservoir, res., U.S.	E3	157
Flanagan, Il., U.S.	C5	120
Flanders (Flandre), hist. reg., Eur.	G2	12
Flandes, Col.	E5	84
Flandreau, S.D., U.S.	C9	148
Flandreau Indian Reservation, S.D., U.S.	C9	148
Flasher, N.D., U.S.	C4	141
Flat, stm., Mi., U.S.	E5	129
Flat, stm., N.C., U.S.	A4	140
Flat, stm., R.I., U.S.	E2	146
Flat Bay, Newf., Can.	D2	102
Flat Brook, stm., N.J., U.S.	A3	137
Flatbush, Alta., Can.	B3	98
Flat Creek, Tn., U.S.	B5	149
Flatey, Ice.	B2	6a
Flateyri, Ice.	B2	6a
Flathead, co., Mt., U.S.	B2	133
Flathead, South Fork, stm., Mt., U.S.	C3	133
Flathead Indian Reservation, Mt., U.S.	C2	133
Flathead Lake, l., Mt., U.S.	C2	133
Flathead Valley, val., Mt., U.S.	C2	133
Flat Lake, l., Alta., Can.	B4	98
Flat Lake, l., La., U.S.	k9	125
Flatlands, N.B., Can.	B3	101
Flat Lick, Ky., U.S.	D6	124
Flatonia, Tx., U.S.	E4	150
Flat River, P.E.I., Can.	C7	101
Flat River, Mo., U.S.	D7	132
Flat River Reservoir, res., R.I., U.S.	D3	146
Flat Rock, Al., U.S.	A4	108
Flat Rock, Il., U.S.	E6	120
Flat Rock, In., U.S.	F6	121
Flat Rock, Mi., U.S.	F7	129
Flat Rock, N.C., U.S.	f10	140
Flatrock, stm., In., U.S.	F6	121
Flattery, Cape, c., Wa., U.S.	A1	154
Flatwoods, Ky., U.S.	B7	124
Flatwoods, Tn., U.S.	B4	149
Flaxcombe, Sask., Can.	F1	105
Flaxton, N.D., U.S.	A3	141
Flaxville, Mt., U.S.	B11	133
Fleet, Alta., Can.	C5	98
Fleetwood, Pa., U.S.	F10	145
Fleming, Sask., Can.	G5	105
Fleming, Co., U.S.	A8	113
Fleming, Ga., U.S.	E5	117
Fleming, co., Ky., U.S.	B6	124
Fleming-Neon, Ky., U.S.	C7	124
Flemingsburg, Ky., U.S.	B6	124
Flemington, Ga., U.S.	E5	117
Flemington, N.J., U.S.	B3	137
Flemington, Pa., U.S.	D7	145
Flemington, W.V., U.S.	k10	155
Flensburg, Ger.	A9	10
Flesherton, Ont., Can.	C4	103
Fletcher, Ont., Can.	E2	103
Fletcher, N.C., U.S.	f10	140
Fletcher, Oh., U.S.	B1	142
Fletcher, Ok., U.S.	C3	143
Fleurance, Fr.	I7	14
Fleur-de-Lys, Newf., Can.	C3	102
Fleurier, Switz.	E6	13
Flevoland, prov., Neth.	D7	12
Flinders, stm., Austl.	A4	70
Flinders Island, i., Austl.	M8	70
Flinders Reefs, rf., Austl.	A8	70
Flin Flon, Man., Can.	B1	100
Flint, Mi., U.S.	E7	129
Flint, stm., Ga., U.S.	E2	117
Flint City, Al., U.S.	A3	108
Flint Creek, stm., Al., U.S.	A3	108
Flint Creek Range, mts., Mt., U.S.	D3	133
Flinthill, Mo., U.S.	C7	132
Flint Hill, Va., U.S.	B4	153
Flint Hills, hills, Ks., U.S.	D7	123
Flinton, Ont., Can.	C7	103
Flint Run, stm., W.V., U.S.	k9	155
Flintstone, Md., U.S.	k13	127
Flintville, Tn., U.S.	B5	149
Flippin, Ar., U.S.	A3	111
Flisa, Nor.	K13	6
Flize, Fr.	C11	14
Flomaton, Al., U.S.	D2	108
Floodwood, Mn., U.S.	D6	130
Flora, Il., U.S.	E5	120
Flora, In., U.S.	C4	121
Flora, Ms., U.S.	C3	131
Florac, Fr.	H10	14
Florahome, Fl., U.S.	C5	116
Florala, Al., U.S.	D3	108
Flora Vista, N.M., U.S.	A1	138
Florence, Al., U.S.	A2	108
Florence, Az., U.S.	D4	110
Florence, Co., U.S.	C5	113
Florence, In., U.S.	G8	121
Florence, Ks., U.S.	D7	123
Florence, Ky., U.S.	A5	124
Florence, Ms., U.S.	C3	131
Florence, Mt., U.S.	D2	133
Florence, N.J., U.S.	C3	137
Florence, Or., U.S.	D2	144
Florence, S.C., U.S.	C8	147
Florence, S.D., U.S.	B8	148
Florence, Tx., U.S.	D4	150
Florence, Wi., U.S.	C5	156
Florence, co., S.C., U.S.	C8	147
Florence, co., Wi., U.S.	C5	156
Florence see Firenze, Italy	F6	18
Florenceville, N.B., Can.	C2	101
Florencia, Col.	G5	84
Florencio Sánchez, Ur.	G10	80
Flores, Braz.	E11	76
Flores, i., Indon.	G7	38
Flores, i., Port.	k18	62a
Flores, Cachoeira das, wtfl, Braz.	C2	79
Flores, Laut (Flores Sea), Indon.	G7	38
Flores da Cunha, Braz.	E13	80
Flôres de Goiás, Braz.	C5	79
Floresta Azul, Braz.	C9	79
Florestina, Braz.	E4	79
Florešty, U.S.S.R.	B12	20
Floresville, Tx., U.S.	E3	150
Florham Park, N.J., U.S.	B4	137
Floriano, Braz.	E10	76
Floriano Peixoto, Braz.	C8	82
Florianópolis, Braz.	D14	80
Florida, Col.	F4	84
Florida, Cuba	D5	94
Florida, Hond.	B6	92
Florida, Peru	A3	82
Florida, N.M., U.S.	C3	138
Florida, N.Y., U.S.	D6	139
Florida, Ur.	H10	80
Florida, state, U.S.	E5	116
Florida, Cape, c., Fl., U.S.	G6	116
Florida, Straits of, strt., N.A.	B4	94
Florida Bay, b., Fl., U.S.	H6	116
Floridablanca, Col.	D6	84
Florida City, Fl., U.S.	G6	116
Florida Keys, is., Fl., U.S.	H6	116
Florida Mountains, mts., N.M., U.S.	E2	138
Florida State Indian Reservation, Fl., U.S.	F5	116
Floridia, Italy	L10	18
Florido, stm., Mex.	D7	90
Florien, La., U.S.	C2	125
Flórina, Grc.	I5	20
Florissant, Co., U.S.	C5	113
Florissant, Mo., U.S.	f13	132
Florissant Fossil Beds National Monument, Co., U.S.	C5	113
Florø, Nor.	K9	6
Flossmoor, Il., U.S.	k9	120
Flourtown, Pa., U.S.	o21	145
Flovilla, Ga., U.S.	C3	117
Flower Brook, stm., Vt., U.S.	E2	152
Flower's Cove, Newf., Can.	C3	102
Flower Station, Ont., Can.	B8	103
Flowery Branch, Ga., U.S.	B3	117
Flowood, Ms., U.S.	C3	131
Floyd, Ia., U.S.	A5	122
Floyd, N.M., U.S.	C6	138
Floyd, Va., U.S.	D2	153
Floyd, co., Ga., U.S.	B1	117
Floyd, co., In., U.S.	H6	121
Floyd, co., Ia., U.S.	A5	122
Floyd, co., Ky., U.S.	C7	124
Floyd, co., Tx., U.S.	B2	150
Floyd, co., Va., U.S.	D2	153
Floyd, stm., Ia., U.S.	B1	122
Floydada, Tx., U.S.	C2	150
Floydsburg, Ky., U.S.	g12	124
Floyds Fork, stm., Ky., U.S.	B4	124
Floyds Knobs, In., U.S.	H6	121
Fluchthorn, mtn., Eur.	E13	13
Flushing, Mi., U.S.	E7	129
Flushing, Oh., U.S.	B4	142
Fluvanna, co., Va., U.S.	C4	153
Fly, stm.	m15	68a
Foam Lake, Sask., Can.	F4	105
Foard, co., Tx., U.S.	B3	150
Foça, Tur.	K10	20
Foča, Yugo.	F2	20
Focșani, Rom.	D11	20
Fodé, Cen. Afr. Rep.	O2	60
Fodécontea, Gui.	F2	64
Foggaret el Arab, Alg.	G12	62
Foggaret ez Zoua, Alg.	G12	62
Foggia, Italy	H10	18
Fogland Point, c., R.I., U.S.	E6	146
Fogo, Newf., Can.	D4	102
Fogo, i., C.V.	m16	64a
Fogo, Cape, c., Newf., Can.	D5	102
Fogo Island, i., Newf., Can.	D4	102
Fogolawa, Nig.	E14	64
Fohnsdorf, Aus.	H14	10
Foix, Fr.	J8	14
Foix, hist. reg., Fr.	J8	14
Fokino, U.S.S.R.	H17	26
Folakara, Madag.	Q21	67b
Foley, Al., U.S.	E2	108
Foley, Mn., U.S.	E5	130
Foley, Mo., U.S.	B7	132
Foligno, Italy	G7	18
Folkestone, Eng., U.K.	J15	8
Folkston, Ga., U.S.	F4	117
Follansbee, W.V., U.S.	A4	155
Follonica, Italy	G5	18
Follonica, Golfo di, b., Italy	G5	18
Folly Beach, S.C., U.S.	F8	147
Folly Island, i., S.C., U.S.	F8	147
Folly Lake, N.S., Can.	D6	101
Folsom, Ca., U.S.	C3	112
Folsom, La., U.S.	D5	125
Folsom, N.J., U.S.	D3	137
Folsom, W.V., U.S.	B4	155
Fomboni, Com.	L15	67a
Fonda, Ia., U.S.	B3	122
Fonda, N.Y., U.S.	C6	139
Fond du Lac, Wi., U.S.	E5	156
Fond du Lac, co., Wi., U.S.	E5	156
Fond du Lac Indian Reservation, Mn., U.S.	D6	130
Fondi, Italy	H8	18
Fondouk el Aouareb, Tun.	N4	18
Fonni, Italy	I4	18
Fonseca, Col.	B6	84
Fonseca, Golfo de, b., N.A.	D7	92
Fontainebleau, Fr.	D9	14
Fontana, Arg.	D9	80
Fontana, Ca., U.S.	m14	112
Fontana, Ks., U.S.	D9	123
Fontana, Wi., U.S.	F5	156
Fontana Lake, res., N.C., U.S.	f9	140
Fontanelle, Ia., U.S.	C3	122
Fontanet, In., U.S.	E3	121
Fontas, stm., Can.	E8	96
Fonte Boa, Braz.	I9	84
Fontenelle Reservoir, res., Wy., U.S.	D2	157
Fontibón, Col.	E5	84
Fontur, c., Ice.	A6	6a
Fonyód, Hung.	I17	10
Foochow see Fuzhou, China	I8	34
Footville, Wi., U.S.	F4	156
Forada, Mn., U.S.	E3	130
Foraker, Mount, mtn., Ak., U.S.	f16	109
Forbach, Fr.	C13	14
Forbes, Austl.	I8	70
Forbes, Mount, mtn., Alta., Can.	D2	98
Force, Pa., U.S.	D4	145
Forchheim, Ger.	F11	10
Ford, Ks., U.S.	E4	123
Ford, Ky., U.S.	C5	124
Ford, co., Il., U.S.	C5	120
Ford, co., Ks., U.S.	E4	123
Ford, stm., Mi., U.S.	C3	129
Ford City, Ca., U.S.	E4	112
Ford City, Pa., U.S.	E2	145
Fordland, Mo., U.S.	D5	132
Fordoche, La., U.S.	D4	125
Ford Ranges, mts., Ant.	C10	73
Fords, N.J., U.S.	B4	137
Fords Prairie, Wa., U.S.	C2	154
Fordsville, Ky., U.S.	C3	124
Fordville, N.D., U.S.	A8	141
Fordwich, Ont., Can.	D3	103
Fordyce, Ar., U.S.	D3	111
Fordyce, Ne., U.S.	B8	134
Forel, Mont, mtn., Grnld.	C16	86
Foreman, Ar., U.S.	D1	111
Foremost, Alta., Can.	E5	98
Forest, Ont., Can.	D2	103
Forest, In., U.S.	D5	121
Forest, Ms., U.S.	C4	131
Forest, Oh., U.S.	B2	142

Name — Map Ref. — Page

Forest, Va., U.S. C3 153
Forest, co., Pa., U.S. C3 145
Forest, co., Wi., U.S. C5 156
Forest, stm., N.D., U.S. A8 141
Forest Acres, S.C., U.S. C6 147
Forestburg, Alta., Can. C4 98
Forestburg, S.D., U.S. C7 148
Forest City, Il., U.S. C4 120
Forest City, Ia., U.S. A4 122
Forest City, Mo., U.S. B2 132
Forest City, N.C., U.S. B1 140
Forest City, Pa., U.S. C11 145
Forestdale, Al., U.S. B3 108
Forestdale, R.I., U.S. B3 146
Forest Dale, Vt., U.S. D2 152
Forest Glen, La., U.S. h12 125
Forest Grove, Or., U.S. B3 144
Forest Hill, La., U.S. C3 125
Forest Hill, Md., U.S. A5 127
Forest Hill, Tx., U.S. n9 150
Forest Hills, Pa., U.S. k14 145
Forest Hills, Tn., U.S. A5 149
Forest Home, Al., U.S. D3 108
Forest Knolls, Ca., U.S. g7 112
Forest Lake, Mn., U.S. E6 130
Foreston, Mn., U.S. E5 130
Forest Park, Ga., U.S. h8 117
Forest Park, Il., U.S. k9 120
Forest Park, La., U.S. B3 125
Forest Park, Oh., U.S. n12 142
Forestport, N.Y., U.S. B5 139
Forest River, N.D., U.S. A8 141
Forestville, Wi., U.S. D6 156
Forfar, Scot., U.K. E11 8
Forgan, Ok., U.S. A1 143
Forget, Sask., Can. H4 105
Forillon, Parc National de, Que., Can. k14 104
Fork Creek, stm., W.V., U.S. m12 155
Forked Deer, stm., Tn., U.S. B2 149
Forked Deer, Middle Fork, stm., Tn., U.S. D3 149
Forked Deer, North Fork, stm., Tn., U.S. B3 149
Forked Deer, South Fork, stm., Tn., U.S. B2 149
Forked Island, La., U.S. E3 125
Forked River, N.J., U.S. D4 137
Forkland, Al., U.S. C2 108
Fork River, Man., Can. D1 100
Forks, Wa., U.S. B1 154
Fork Union, Va., U.S. C4 153
Forkville, Ms., U.S. C4 131
Forlì, Italy E7 18
Forman, N.D., U.S. C8 141
Formentera, i., Spain G13 16
Formia, Italy H8 18
Formiga, Braz. F6 79
Formosa, Arg. D9 80
Formosa, Braz. C5 79
Formosa, Ont., Can. C3 103
Formosa, Ar., U.S. B3 111
Formosa, prov., Arg. C9 80
Formosa, Serra, plat., Braz. D14 82
Formosa see Taiwan, ctry., Asia L9 34
Formoso, Ks., U.S. C6 123
Formoso, stm., Braz. E2 79
Formoso, stm., Braz. D6 79
Formoso, stm., Braz. B6 79
Forney, Tx., U.S. C4 150
Fornosovo, U.S.S.R. B13 26
Forres, Arg. D7 80
Forrest, Austl. F5 68
Forrest, Il., U.S. C5 120
Forrest, co., Ms., U.S. D4 131
Forrest City, Ar., U.S. B5 111
Forrester Island, i., Ak., U.S. n23 109
Forreston, Il., U.S. A4 120
Forsayth, Austl. B5 70
Forst, Ger. D14 10
Forster, Austl. I10 70
Forsyth, Ga., U.S. C3 117
Forsyth, Il., U.S. D5 120
Forsyth, Mo., U.S. E4 132
Forsyth, Mt., U.S. D10 133
Forsyth, co., Ga., U.S. B2 117
Forsyth, co., N.C., U.S. A2 140
Forsyth Range, mts., Austl. D5 70
Fort Adams, Ms., U.S. D2 131
Fortaleza, Braz. D11 76
Fortaleza, stm., Peru D3 82
Fortaleza de Santa Teresa, Ur. G12 80
Fortaleza do Ituxi, Braz. B8 82
Fort Apache, Az., U.S. D6 110
Fort Apache Indian Reservation, Az., U.S. D5 110
Fort Ashby, W.V., U.S. B6 155
Fort Assiniboine, Alta., Can. B3 98
Fort Atkinson, Ia., U.S. A6 122
Fort Atkinson, Wi., U.S. F5 156
Fort Barnwell, N.C., U.S. B5 140
Fort Beaufort, S. Afr. I8 66
Fort Belknap Agency, Mt., U.S. B8 133
Fort Belknap Indian Reservation, Mt., U.S. B8 133
Fort Belvoir, mil., Va., U.S. g12 153
Fort Bend, co., Tx., U.S. E5 150
Fort Benjamin Harrison, mil., In., U.S. k10 121
Fort Benning, mil., Ga., U.S. D2 117
Fort Benton, Mt., U.S. C6 133
Fort Berthold Indian Reservation, N.D., U.S. B3 141
Fort Bidwell Indian Reservation, Ca., U.S. B3 112
Fort Blackmore, Va., U.S. f9 153
Fort Bliss, mil., Tx., U.S. o11 150
Fort Bragg, Ca., U.S. C2 112
Fort Bragg, mil., N.C., U.S. B3 140
Fort Branch, In., U.S. H2 121
Fort Bridger, Wy., U.S. E2 157
Fort Calhoun, Ne., U.S. C9 134
Fort Campbell, mil., U.S. A4 149
Fort-Carnot, Madag. R22 67b
Fort Carson, mil., Co., U.S. C6 113
Fort Chipewyan, Alta., Can. f8 98
Fort Clatsop National Memorial, hist., Or., U.S. A3 144
Fort Cobb, Ok., U.S. B3 143
Fort Cobb Reservoir, res., Ok., U.S. B3 143
Fort Collins, Co., U.S. A5 113
Fort Coulonge, Que., Can. B8 103
Fort Covington, N.Y., U.S. f10 139
Fort Davis, Al., U.S. C4 108
Fort Davis, Tx., U.S. o13 150
Fort Davis National Historic Site, hist., Tx., U.S. o13 150
Fort Defiance, Az., U.S. B6 110
Fort-de-France, Mart. G14 94
Fort Deposit, Al., U.S. D3 108
Fort Detrick, mil., Md., U.S. B3 127
Fort Devens, mil., Ma., U.S. f9 128
Fort Dix, mil., N.J., U.S. C3 137
Fort Dodge, Ia., U.S. B3 122
Fort Dodge, Ks., U.S. D4 123
Fort Donelson National Battlefield, Tn., U.S. A4 149
Fort Duchesne, Ut., U.S. C6 151
Forteau, Newf., Can. C3 102
Fort Edward, N.Y., U.S. B7 139
Fort Erie, Ont., Can. E6 103
Fortescue, stm., Austl. D3 68
Fort Eustis, mil., Va., U.S. h14 153
Fortezza, Italy C6 18
Fort Fairfield, Me., U.S. B5 126
Fort Frances, Ont., Can. o16 103
Fort Franklin, N.W. Ter., Can. C8 96
Fort Fraser, B.C., Can. B5 99
Fort Frederica National Monument, Ga., U.S. E5 117
Fort Gaines, Ga., U.S. E1 117
Fort Garland, Co., U.S. D5 113
Fort Gay, W.V., U.S. C2 155
Fort Gibson, Ok., U.S. B6 143
Fort Gibson Lake, res., Ok., U.S. A6 143
Fort Good Hope, N.W. Ter., Can. C7 96
Fort Gordon, mil., Ga., U.S. C4 117
Fort Greely, mil., Ak., U.S. C10 109
Forth, Firth of, b., Scot., U.K. E11 8
Fort Hall, Id., U.S. F6 119
Fort Hall Indian Reservation, Id., U.S. F6 119
Fort Hancock, Tx., U.S. o12 150
Fort Hood, mil., Tx., U.S. D4 150
Fort Howard, Md., U.S. B5 127
Fort Huachuca, mil., Az., U.S. F5 110
Fortierville, Que., Can. C5 104
Fortín Ayacucho, Para. H12 82
Fortín Coroneles Sanchez, Para. H12 82
Fortine, Mt., U.S. B2 133
Fortín Florida, Para. I12 82
Fortín Garrapatal, Para. I11 82
Fortín Teniente Montanía, Para. B9 80
Fortín Uno, Arg. J6 80
Fort Jackson, mil., S.C., U.S. C6 147
Fort Jefferson National Monument, Fl., U.S. H4 116
Fort Jones, Ca., U.S. B2 112
Fort Kent, Alta., Can. B5 98
Fort Kent, Me., U.S. A4 126
Fort Kent Mills, Me., U.S. A4 126
Fort Knox, mil., Ky., U.S. B4 124
Fort-Lamy see N'Djamena, Chad F4 56
Fort Laramie, Wy., U.S. D8 157
Fort Laramie National Historic Site, hist., Wy., U.S. D8 157
Fort Lauderdale, Fl., U.S. F6 116
Fort Lawn, S.C., U.S. B6 147
Fort Leavenworth, mil., Ks., U.S. C9 123
Fort Lee, N.J., U.S. B5 137
Fort Lee, mil., Va., U.S. C5 153
Fort Leonard Wood, mil., Mo., U.S. D5 132
Fort Lewis, mil., Wa., U.S. B3 154
Fort Liard, N.W. Ter., Can. D8 96
Fort-Liberté, Haiti E9 94
Fort Loramie, Oh., U.S. B1 142
Fort Loudon, Pa., U.S. G6 145
Fort Loudoun Lake, res., Tn., U.S. D9 149
Fort Lupton, Co., U.S. A6 113
Fort MacArthur, mil., Ca., U.S. n12 112
Fort MacKay, Alta., Can. f8 98
Fort Macleod, Alta., Can. E4 98
Fort Madison, Ia., U.S. D6 122
Fort Matanzas National Monument, Fl., U.S. C5 116
Fort McClellan, mil., Al., U.S. B4 108
Fort McDermitt Indian Reservation, U.S. B4 135
Fort McDowell, Az., U.S. k9 110
Fort McDowell Indian Reservation, Az., U.S. D4 110
Fort McHenry National Monument And Historic Shrine, Md., U.S. g11 127
Fort McMurray, Alta., Can. A5 98
Fort McPherson, N.W. Ter., Can. C6 96
Fort Meade, Fl., U.S. E5 116
Fort Meade, mil., Md., U.S. B4 127
Fort Meadow Reservoir, res., Ma., U.S. g9 128
Fort Mill, S.C., U.S. A6 147
Fort Mitchell, Al., U.S. C4 108
Fort Mitchell, Ky., U.S. h13 124
Fort Mojave Indian Reservation, U.S. C1 110
Fort Monmouth, mil., N.J., U.S. C4 137
Fort Monroe, mil., Va., U.S. h15 153
Fort Morgan, Co., U.S. A7 113
Fort Myer, mil., Va., U.S. g12 153
Fort Myers, Fl., U.S. F5 116
Fort Myers Beach, Fl., U.S. F5 116
Fort Nelson, B.C., Can. m18 99
Fort Norman, N.W. Ter., Can. D7 96
Fort Ogden, Fl., U.S. E5 116
Fort Oglethorpe, Ga., U.S. B1 117
Fort Ord, mil., Ca., U.S. D3 112
Fort Payne, Al., U.S. A4 108
Fort Peck, Mt., U.S. B10 133
Fort Peck Dam, Mt., U.S. B10 133
Fort Peck Indian Reservation, Mt., U.S. B11 133
Fort Peck Lake, res., Mt., U.S. C9 133
Fort Pierce, Fl., U.S. E6 116
Fort Pierce Inlet, b., Fl., U.S. E6 116
Fort Pierre, S.D., U.S. C5 148
Fort Plain, N.Y., U.S. C6 139
Fort Polk, mil., La., U.S. C2 125
Fort Portal, Ug. A6 58
Fort Providence, N.W. Ter., Can. D9 96
Fort Qu'Appelle, Sask., Can. G4 105
Fort Randall Dam, S.D., U.S. D7 148
Fort Ransom, N.D., U.S. C8 141
Fort Recovery, Oh., U.S. B1 142
Fort Resolution, N.W. Ter., Can. D10 96
Fortress Mountain, mtn., Wy., U.S. B3 157
Fort Richardson, mil., Ak., U.S. C10 109
Fort Riley, mil., Ks., U.S. C7 123
Fort Ritchie, mil., Md., U.S. A3 127
Fort Rucker, mil., Al., U.S. D4 108
Fort Saint James, B.C., Can. B5 99
Fort Saint John, B.C., Can. A7 99
Fort Sam Houston, mil., Tx., U.S. k7 150
Fort Saskatchewan, Alta., Can. C4 98
Fort Scott, Ks., U.S. E9 123
Fort-Ševčenko, U.S.S.R. I8 22
Fort Severn, Ont., Can. n18 103
Fort Shafter, mil., Hi., U.S. g10 118
Fort Shaw, Mt., U.S. C5 133
Fort Shawnee, Oh., U.S. B1 142
Fort Sheridan, mil., Il., U.S. h9 120
Fort Sill, mil., Ok., U.S. C3 143
Fort Simpson, N.W. Ter., Can. D8 96
Fort Smith, N.W. Ter., Can. D10 96
Fort Smith, Ar., U.S. B1 111
Fort Stanton, N.M., U.S. D4 138
Fort Steele, B.C., Can. E10 99
Fort Stewart, mil., Ga., U.S. D5 117
Fort Stockton, Tx., U.S. D1 150
Fort Sumner, N.M., U.S. C5 138
Fort Sumter National Monument, S.C., U.S. k12 147
Fort Supply, Ok., U.S. A2 143
Fort Supply Lake, res., Ok., U.S. A2 143
Fort Thomas, Az., U.S. D6 110
Fort Thomas, Ky., U.S. h14 124
Fort Thompson, S.D., U.S. C6 148
Fort Totten, N.D., U.S. B7 141
Fort Totten Indian Reservation, N.D., U.S. B7 141
Fort Towson, Ok., U.S. C6 143
Fortuna, Arg. H6 80
Fortuna, C.R. G10 92
Fortuna, Ca., U.S. B1 112
Fortuna, Mo., U.S. C5 132
Fortuna, Río de la, stm., Bol. G12 82
Fortune, Newf., Can. E4 102
Fortune Bay, b., Newf., Can. E4 102
Fortune Harbour, Newf., Can. D4 102
Fort Union National Monument, N.M., U.S. B5 138
Fort Valley, Ga., U.S. D3 117
Fort Vermilion, Alta., Can. f7 98
Fortville, In., U.S. E6 121
Fort Wainwright, mil., Ak., U.S. C10 109
Fort Walton Beach, Fl., U.S. u15 116
Fort Washakie, Wy., U.S. C4 157
Fort Washington, Pa., U.S. o21 145
Fort Washington Forest, Md., U.S. C4 127
Fort Wayne, In., U.S. B7 121
Fort Wellington, Guy. D14 84
Fort William, Scot., U.K. E8 8
Fort Wingate, N.M., U.S. B1 138
Fort Worth, Tx., U.S. C4 150
Fort Wright, Ky., U.S. h13 124
Fort Yates, N.D., U.S. C5 141
Forty Fort, Pa., U.S. D10 145
Fort Yukon, Ak., U.S. B10 109
Fort Yuma Indian Reservation, Ca., U.S. F6 112
Foshan, China L2 34
Fossano, Italy E2 18
Fossil, Or., U.S. B6 144
Fossil Butte National Monument, Wy., U.S. E2 157
Fossil Lake, l., Or., U.S. D6 144
Foss Reservoir, res., Ok., U.S. B2 143
Fosston, Sask., Can. E4 105
Fosston, Mn., U.S. C3 130
Foster, Austl. L7 70
Foster, Mo., U.S. C3 132
Foster, Or., U.S. C4 144
Foster, co., N.D., U.S. B6 141
Foster Brook, Pa., U.S. C4 145
Foster City, Ca., U.S. h8 112
Foster City, Mi., U.S. C3 129
Fosters, Al., U.S. B2 108
Fosters Pond, l., Ma., U.S. f11 128
Foster Village, Hi., U.S. g10 118
Fosterville, Tn., U.S. B5 149
Fostoria, Al., U.S. C3 108
Fostoria, Ia., U.S. A2 122
Fostoria, Mi., U.S. E7 129
Fostoria, Oh., U.S. A2 142
Fouesnant, Fr. E2 14
Fougamou, Gabon B2 58
Fougères, Fr. D5 14
Fouke, Ar., U.S. D2 111
Foul Bay, b., Egypt J3 48
Foulpointe, Madag. P23 67b
Foulwind, Cape, c., N.Z. D3 72
Foumban, Cam. G9 54
Foumbouni, Com. K15 67a
Foum-el-Hisn, Mor. F6 62
Foum-Zguid, Mor. E7 62
Foundiougne, Sen. D1 64
Fountain, Al., U.S. D2 108
Fountain, Co., U.S. C6 113
Fountain, Fl., U.S. B1 116
Fountain, Mn., U.S. G6 130
Fountain, N.C., U.S. B5 140
Fountain, co., In., U.S. D3 121
Fountain City, In., U.S. E8 121
Fountain City, Wi., U.S. D2 156
Fountain Creek, stm., Co., U.S. C6 113
Fountain Green, Ut., U.S. D4 151
Fountain Hill, Ar., U.S. D4 111
Fountain Hill, Pa., U.S. E11 145
Fountain Inn, S.C., U.S. B3 147
Fountain Lake, Ar., U.S. f8 111
Fountain Peak, mtn., Ca., U.S. E6 112
Fountain Place, La., U.S. D4 125
Fountain Run, Ky., U.S. D4 124
Fountaintown, In., U.S. E6 121
Fourche Creek, stm., Ar., U.S. k10 111
Fourche LaFave, stm., Ar., U.S. C2 111
Fourche Maline, stm., Ok., U.S. C6 143
Fourche Mountain, mtn., Ar., U.S. C2 111
Fouriesburg, S. Afr. G9 66
Four Lakes, Wa., U.S. B8 154
Fourmies, Fr. B11 14
Fourmile, Ky., U.S. D6 124
Fourmile Creek, stm., Ia., U.S. e8 122
Four Mountains, Islands of, is., Ak., U.S. E6 109
Fournier, Ont., Can. B10 103
Four Oaks, N.C., U.S. B4 140
Fouta Djalon, reg., Gui. F3 64
Foux, Cap à, c., Haiti E8 94
Foveaux Strait, strt., N.Z. G1 72
Fowler, Ca., U.S. D4 112
Fowler, Co., U.S. C6 113
Fowler, Il., U.S. C2 120
Fowler, In., U.S. C3 121
Fowler, Ks., U.S. E3 123
Fowler, Mi., U.S. E6 129
Fowlerton, In., U.S. D6 121
Fowlerville, Mi., U.S. F6 129
Fowlkes, Tn., U.S. B2 149
Fowlstown, Ga., U.S. F2 117
Fowman, Iran C10 48
Fox, Ar., U.S. B3 111
Fox, Ok., U.S. C4 143
Fox, stm., Man., Can. B4 100
Fox, stm., U.S. B5 120
Fox, stm., U.S. A6 132
Fox, stm., Mi., U.S. B4 129
Fox, stm., Wi., U.S. D5 156
Foxboro, Ont., Can. C7 103
Foxboro, Ma., U.S. B5 128
Fox Creek, Alta., Can. B2 98
Foxe Basin, b., N.W. Ter., Can. C17 96
Foxe Channel, strt., N.W. Ter., Can. D16 96
Foxe Peninsula, pen., N.W. Ter., Can. D17 96
Fox Harbour, Newf., Can. E5 102
Fox Island, i., R.I., U.S. E4 146
Fox Island, i., Wa., U.S. f10 154
Fox Islands, is., Ak., U.S. E6 109
Fox Lake, Il., U.S. A5 120
Fox Lake, Wi., U.S. E5 156
Fox Lake, l., Il., U.S. h8 120
Fox Mountain, mtn., Nv., U.S. B2 135
Foxpark, Wy., U.S. E6 157
Fox Point, Wi., U.S. E6 156
Fox River Grove, Il., U.S. h8 120
Fox Valley, Sask., Can. G1 105
Foxville, Vt., U.S. C4 152
Foxwarren, Man., Can. D1 100
Foxworth, Ms., U.S. D4 131
Foyle, Lough, b., Eur. F6 8
Foz do Cunene, Ang. E2 58
Foz do Iguaçu, Braz. C11 80
Foz do Jordão, Braz. C6 82
Foz Giraldo, Port. E4 16
Foziling, China D5 34
Frackville, Pa., U.S. E9 145
Fraga, Arg. G6 80
Fraile Muerto, Ur. G11 80
Framingham, Ma., U.S. B5 128
Frampol, Pol. E22 10
Franca, Braz. F5 79
Franca-Iosifa, Zeml'a (Franz Josef Land), is., U.S.S.R. A6 28
Francavilla Fontana, Italy I12 18
France, ctry., Eur. F8 4
Francestown, N.H., U.S. E3 136
Francés Viejo, Cabo, c., Dom. Rep. E10 94
Francesville, In., U.S. C4 121
Franceville, Gabon B2 58
Franche-Comté, hist. reg., Fr. F12 14
Francia, Ur. G10 80
Francis, Sask., Can. G4 105
Francis, Ok., U.S. C5 143
Francis, Ut., U.S. C4 151
Francis, Lake, l., N.H., U.S. f7 136
Francis Case, Lake, res., S.D., U.S. D6 148
Francisco, In., U.S. H3 121
Francisco Beltrão, Braz. D12 80
Francisco I. Madero, Mex. E8 90
Francisco I. Madero, Mex. E7 90
Francisco Morazán, dept., Hond. C7 92
Francisco Murguía, Mex. E8 90
Francisco Sá, Braz. D7 79
Francis Creek, Wi., U.S. h10 156
Francistown, Bots. C8 66
Francofonte, Italy L9 18
François, Newf., Can. E3 102
Franconia, N.H., U.S. B3 136
Franconia Notch, N.H., U.S. B3 136
Francs Peak, mtn., Wy., U.S. C3 157
Frangy, Fr. F12 14
Frankenmuth, Mi., U.S. E7 129
Frankford, Ont., Can. C7 103
Frankford, De., U.S. F5 115
Frankford, Mo., U.S. B6 132
Frankford, W.V., U.S. D4 155
Frankfort, S. Afr. F9 66
Frankfort, S. Afr. I8 66
Frankfort, Il., U.S. m9 120
Frankfort, In., U.S. D4 121
Frankfort, Ks., U.S. C7 123
Frankfort, Ky., U.S. B5 124
Frankfort, Me., U.S. D4 126
Frankfort, Mi., U.S. D4 129
Frankfort, N.Y., U.S. B5 139
Frankfort, Oh., U.S. C2 142
Frankfort, S.D., U.S. C7 148
Frankfurt am Main, Ger. E8 10
Frankfurt an der Oder, Ger. C14 10
Franklin, Man., Can. D2 100
Franklin, Al., U.S. C4 108
Franklin, Al., U.S. D2 108
Franklin, Az., U.S. E6 110
Franklin, Ar., U.S. A4 111
Franklin, Ga., U.S. C1 117
Franklin, Id., U.S. G7 119
Franklin, Il., U.S. D3 120
Franklin, In., U.S. F5 121
Franklin, Ks., U.S. E9 123
Franklin, Ky., U.S. D3 124
Franklin, La., U.S. E4 125
Franklin, Me., U.S. D4 126
Franklin, Ma., U.S. B5 128
Franklin, Mn., U.S. F4 130
Franklin, Mo., U.S. B5 132
Franklin, Ne., U.S. D7 134
Franklin, N.H., U.S. D3 136
Franklin, N.J., U.S. A3 137
Franklin, N.C., U.S. f9 140
Franklin, Oh., U.S. C1 142
Franklin, Pa., U.S. D2 145
Franklin, Tn., U.S. B5 149
Franklin, Tx., U.S. D4 150
Franklin, Va., U.S. D6 153
Franklin, W.V., U.S. C5 155
Franklin, Wi., U.S. n11 156
Franklin, co., Al., U.S. A2 108
Franklin, co., Ar., U.S. B2 111
Franklin, co., Fl., U.S. C2 116
Franklin, co., Ga., U.S. B3 117
Franklin, co., Id., U.S. G7 119
Franklin, co., Il., U.S. E4 120
Franklin, co., In., U.S. F7 121
Franklin, co., Ia., U.S. B4 122
Franklin, co., Ks., U.S. D8 123
Franklin, co., Ky., U.S. B5 124
Franklin, co., La., U.S. B4 125
Franklin, co., Me., U.S. C2 126
Franklin, co., Ma., U.S. A2 128
Franklin, co., Ms., U.S. D3 131
Franklin, co., Mo., U.S. C6 132
Franklin, co., Ne., U.S. D7 134
Franklin, co., N.Y., U.S. f10 139
Franklin, co., N.C., U.S. A4 140
Franklin, co., Oh., U.S. B2 142
Franklin, co., Pa., U.S. G6 145
Franklin, co., Tn., U.S. B5 149
Franklin, co., Tx., U.S. C5 150
Franklin, co., Vt., U.S. B2 152
Franklin, co., Va., U.S. D3 153
Franklin, co., Wa., U.S. C6 154
Franklin, Point, c., Ak., U.S. A8 109
Franklin Bay, b., N.W. Ter., Can. C7 96
Franklin D. Roosevelt Lake, res., Wa., U.S. B7 154
Franklin Falls Reservoir, res., N.H., U.S. C3 136
Franklin Grove, Il., U.S. B4 120
Franklin Harbor, b., Austl. I2 70
Franklin Island, i., Ont., Can. B4 103
Franklin Lake, l., Nv., U.S. C6 135
Franklin Mine, Mi., U.S. A2 129
Franklin Mountains, mts., N.W. Ter., Can. D8 96
Franklin Park, Il., U.S. k9 120
Franklin Park, Pa., U.S. h13 145
Franklin Strait, strt., N.W. Ter., Can. B13 96
Franklinton, La., U.S. D5 125
Franklinton, N.C., U.S. A4 140
Franklinville, N.J., U.S. D2 137
Franklinville, N.Y., U.S. C2 139
Franklinville, N.C., U.S. B3 140
Frankston, Tx., U.S. C5 150
Franksville, Wi., U.S. n12 156
Frankton, In., U.S. D6 121
Franktown, Co., U.S. B6 113
Frankville, N.S., Can. D8 101
Frankville, Al., U.S. D1 108
Frannie, Wy., U.S. B4 157
Franz Josef Land see Franca-Iosifa, Zeml'a, is., U.S.S.R. A6 28
Frascati, Italy H7 18
Fraser, Co., U.S. B5 113
Fraser, stm., B.C., Can. E7 99
Fraser, stm., Newf., Can. g9 102
Fraser, Mount, mtn., Can. C8 99
Fraserburg, S. Afr. H5 66
Fraser Island, i., Austl. E10 70
Fraser Lake, B.C., Can. B5 99
Fraser Plateau, plat., B.C., Can. D6 99
Fraserwood, Man., Can. D3 100
Frauenfeld, Switz. C10 13
Fray Bentos, Ur. G9 80
Fray Luis Beltrán, Arg. J6 80
Fray Marcos, Ur. H11 80
Frazee, Mn., U.S. D3 130
Frazer, Mt., U.S. B10 133
Frazeysburg, Oh., U.S. B3 142
Frazier Park, Ca., U.S. E4 112
Fr'azino, U.S.S.R. F21 26
Frederic, Mi., U.S. D6 129
Frederic, Wi., U.S. C1 156
Frederica, De., U.S. D4 115
Fredericia, Den. N11 6
Frederick, Co., U.S. A6 113
Frederick, Md., U.S. B3 127
Frederick, Ok., U.S. C2 143
Frederick, S.D., U.S. B7 148
Frederick, co., Md., U.S. B3 127
Frederick, co., Va., U.S. A4 153
Frederick Reef, rf., Austl. C11 70
Fredericksburg, In., U.S. H5 121
Fredericksburg, Ia., U.S. B5 122
Fredericksburg, Oh., U.S. B4 142
Fredericksburg, Pa., U.S. F9 145
Fredericksburg, Tx., U.S. D3 150
Fredericksburg, Va., U.S. B5 153
Frederick Sound, strt., Ak., U.S. m23 109
Fredericktown, Mo., U.S. D7 132
Fredericktown, Oh., U.S. B3 142
Fredericktown, Pa., U.S. F1 145
Frederico Westphalen, Braz. D12 80
Fredericton, N.B., Can. D3 101
Fredericton Junction, N.B., Can. D3 101
Frederikshavn, Den. M12 6
Frederiksted, V.I.U.S. F12 94
Frederik Willem IV Vallen, wtfl, Sur. F14 84
Fredonia, Col. E5 84
Fredonia, Az., U.S. A3 110
Fredonia, Ia., U.S. C6 122
Fredonia, Ks., U.S. E8 123
Fredonia, Ky., U.S. C1 124
Fredonia, N.Y., U.S. C1 139
Fredonia, Pa., U.S. D1 145
Fredonia, Wi., U.S. E6 156
Fredrikstad, Nor. L12 6
Freeborn, Mn., U.S. G5 130
Freeborn, co., Mn., U.S. G5 130
Freeburg, Il., U.S. E4 120
Freeburg, Mo., U.S. C6 132
Freeburg, Pa., U.S. E8 145
Freedom, In., U.S. F4 121
Freedom, N.H., U.S. C4 136
Freedom, Ok., U.S. A2 143
Freedom, Pa., U.S. E1 145
Freedom, Wi., U.S. h9 156
Freedom, Wy., U.S. D2 157
Freehold, N.J., U.S. C4 137
Freeland, Mi., U.S. E6 129
Freeland, Pa., U.S. D10 145
Freelandville, In., U.S. G3 121
Freel Peak, mtn., Ca., U.S. C4 112
Freels, Cape, c., Newf., Can. D5 102
Freels, Cape, c., Newf., Can. E5 102
Freeman, Mo., U.S. C3 132
Freeman, S.D., U.S. D8 148
Freeman, Lake, l., In., U.S. C4 121
Freemansburg, Pa., U.S. E11 145
Freemanville, Al., U.S. D2 108
Freemason Island, i., La., U.S. E7 125
Freeport, Bah. A5 94
Freeport, N.S., Can. E3 101
Freeport, Fl., U.S. u15 116
Freeport, Il., U.S. A4 120
Freeport, Me., U.S. E2 126
Freeport, Mi., U.S. F5 129
Freeport, Mn., U.S. E4 130
Freeport, N.Y., U.S. n15 139
Freeport, Pa., U.S. E2 145
Freeport, Tx., U.S. E5 150
Freer, Tx., U.S. F3 150
Freestone, co., Tx., U.S. D4 150
Freetown, P.E.I., Can. C6 101
Freetown, S.L. G3 64
Freetown, In., U.S. G5 121
Freezeout Mountains, mts., Wy., U.S. D6 157
Fregenal de la Sierra, Spain G5 16
Freiberg, Ger. E13 10
Freiburg [im Breisgau], Ger. H7 10
Freirina, Chile E3 80
Freising, Ger. G11 10
Freistadt, Aus. G14 10
Freital, Ger. D13 10
Fréjus, Fr. I13 14
Fremantle, Austl. F3 68
Fremont, Ca., U.S. D2 112
Fremont, In., U.S. A8 121
Fremont, Ia., U.S. C5 122
Fremont, Mi., U.S. E5 129
Fremont, Mo., U.S. E6 132
Fremont, Ne., U.S. C9 134
Fremont, N.H., U.S. E4 136
Fremont, N.C., U.S. B5 140
Fremont, Oh., U.S. A2 142
Fremont, Ut., U.S. E4 151
Fremont, Wi., U.S. D5 156
Fremont, co., Co., U.S. C5 113
Fremont, co., Id., U.S. E7 119
Fremont, co., Ia., U.S. D2 122
Fremont, co., Wy., U.S. C4 157
Fremont, stm., Ut., U.S. E4 151
Fremont Island, i., Ut., U.S. B3 151
Fremont Lake, l., Wy., U.S. D3 157
Fremont Peak, mtn., Wy., U.S. C3 157
French Broad, stm., U.S. D10 149
Frenchburg, Ky., U.S. C6 124
French Camp, Ms., U.S. B4 131
French Creek, stm., Pa., U.S. C2 145
French Frigate Shoals, rf., Hi., U.S. m14 118
French Guiana (Guyane française), dep., S.A. C8 76
French Gulch, Ca., U.S. B2 112
French Island, i., Austl. L6 70
French Lick, In., U.S. G4 121
Frenchman Bay, b., Me., U.S. D4 126
Frenchman Butte, Sask., Can. D1 105
Frenchman Creek, stm., U.S. D4 134
Frenchman Hills, hills, Wa., U.S. C6 154
Frenchman Knob, mtn., Ky., U.S. C4 124
Frenchman Lake, l., Nv., U.S. G6 135
Frenchmans Cap, mtn., Austl. N6 70
Frenchman's Cove, Newf., Can. D2 102
Frenchman's Cove, Newf., Can. E4 102
French Polynesia, dep., Oc. H3 2
French River, Mn., U.S. D7 130
French Settlement, La., U.S. D5 125
French Southern and Antarctic Territories, dep., Afr. M10 158
Frenchtown, Mt., U.S. C2 133
Frenchtown, N.J., U.S. B2 137
French Village, N.S., Can. E6 101
Frenchville, Me., U.S. A4 126
Frenda, Alg. C11 62
Fresco, stm., Braz. E8 76
Freshfield, Mount, mtn., Can. D2 98
Fresne-Saint-Mamès, Fr. E12 14

Name	Map Ref.	Page
Fresnes-en-Woëvre, Fr.	C12	14
Fresnillo, Mex.	F8	90
Fresno, Col.	E5	84
Fresno, Ca., U.S.	D4	112
Fresno, co., Ca., U.S.	D4	112
Fresno Reservoir, res., Mt., U.S.	B6	133
Frewsburg, N.Y., U.S.	C1	139
Freycinet Peninsula, pen., Austl.	N8	70
Freyre, Arg.	F7	80
Fria, Cape, c., Nmb.	E2	58
Friant, Ca., U.S.	D4	112
Friars Point, Ms., U.S.	A3	131
Frías, Arg.	E6	80
Frías, Peru	A2	82
Fribourg (Freiburg), Switz.	E7	13
Fribourg (Freiburg), state, Switz.	E7	13
Friday Harbor, Wa., U.S.	A2	154
Fridley, Mn., U.S.	m12	130
Fridtjof Nansen, Mount, mtn., Ant.	D9	73
Friedberg, Aus.	H16	10
Friedberg, Ger.	E8	10
Friedberg, Ger.	G10	10
Friedland, Ger.	B13	10
Friedrichshafen, Ger.	H9	10
Friedrichsort, Ger.	A10	10
Friedrichstadt, Ger.	A9	10
Friend, Ne., U.S.	D8	134
Friendship, Ar., U.S.	C3	111
Friendship, Me., U.S.	E3	126
Friendship, N.Y., U.S.	C2	139
Friendship, Oh., U.S.	D2	142
Friendship, Tn., U.S.	B2	149
Friendship, Wi., U.S.	E4	156
Friendsville, Md., U.S.	k12	127
Friendsville, Tn., U.S.	D9	149
Friendswood, Tx., U.S.	r14	150
Fries, Va., U.S.	D2	153
Friesach, Aus.	I14	10
Friesland, prov., Neth.	B8	12
Friguia, Gui.	E4	64
Frio, co., Tx., U.S.	E3	150
Frio, stm., N.A.	G10	92
Frio, stm., Tx., U.S.	E3	150
Frio, Cabo, c., Braz.	G7	79
Frio Draw, val., U.S.	C6	138
Friona, Tx., U.S.	B1	150
Fripps Island, i., S.C., U.S.	G7	147
Frisco, Co., U.S.	B4	113
Frisco, N.C., U.S.	B7	140
Frisco City, Al., U.S.	D2	108
Frisco Peak, mtn., Ut., U.S.	E2	151
Frisian Islands, is., Eur.	E9	4
Frissell, Mount, mtn., U.S.	A2	114
Fritch, Tx., U.S.	B2	150
Friuli-Venezia-Giulia, prov., Italy	C7	18
Friza, proliv, strt., U.S.S.R.	H21	24
Frobisher, Sask., Can.	H4	105
Frobisher Bay, b., N.W. Ter., Can.	D19	96
Frobisher Lake, l., Sask., Can.	m7	105
Frohna, Mo., U.S.	D8	132
Frohnleiten, Aus.	H15	10
Froid, Mt., U.S.	B12	133
Frolovo, U.S.S.R.	H6	22
Fromberg, Mt., U.S.	E8	133
Frombork, Pol.	A19	10
Frome, stm., Austl.	G3	70
Frome, Lake, l., Austl.	H3	70
Frontenac, Ks., U.S.	E9	123
Frontenac, Mn., U.S.	F6	130
Frontera, Mex.	D9	90
Frontera, Mex.	H13	90
Frontier, Sask., Can.	H1	105
Frontier, Wy., U.S.	E2	157
Frontier, co., Ne., U.S.	D5	134
Frontino, Col.	D4	84
Frontino, Páramo, mtn., Col.	D4	84
Front Range, mts., Co., U.S.	A5	113
Front Royal, Va., U.S.	B4	153
Frosinone, Italy	H8	18
Frost, Tx., U.S.	C4	150
Frostburg, Md., U.S.	k13	127
Frostproof, Fl., U.S.	E5	116
Frøya, i., Nor.	J11	6
Fruges, Fr.	B9	14
Fruita, Co., U.S.	B2	113
Fruitdale, Al., U.S.	D1	108
Fruit Heights, Ut., U.S.	B4	151
Fruithurst, Al., U.S.	B4	108
Fruitland, Id., U.S.	F2	119
Fruitland, Ia., U.S.	C6	122
Fruitland, Md., U.S.	D6	127
Fruitland, N.M., U.S.	A1	138
Fruitland, Tn., U.S.	B3	149
Fruitland Park, Fl., U.S.	D5	116
Fruitport, Mi., U.S.	E4	129
Fruitvale, B.C., Can.	E9	99
Fruitvale, Co., U.S.	B2	113
Fruitvale, Id., U.S.	E2	119
Fruitvale, Wa., U.S.	C5	154
Fruitville, Fl., U.S.	E4	116
Frunze, U.S.S.R.	I12	22
Frunzovka, U.S.S.R.	B13	20
Frutal, Braz.	F4	79
Frutigen, Switz.	E8	13
Frýdek-Místek, Czech.	F18	10
Fryeburg, Me., U.S.	D2	126
Fuchang, China	E2	34
Fuchū, Japan	M8	36
Fuchun, stm., China	F8	34
Fuding, China	H9	34
Fuego, Volcán de, vol., Guat.	C4	92
Fuencaliente de la Palma, Spain	O23	17b
Fuensalida, Spain	E7	16
Fuente de Cantos, Spain	G5	16
Fuente de Oro, Col.	F6	84
Fuentesaúco, Spain	D6	16
Fuerte, stm., Mex.	D5	90
Fuerte Olimpo, Para.	I13	82
Fuerteventura, i., Spain	O26	17b
Fufeng, China	E8	30
Fuhe, China	L2	34
Fuhu, China	F7	34
Fuji, Japan	L13	36
Fujian (Fukien), prov., China	F10	30
Fujieda, Japan	M13	36
Fujin, China	B13	30
Fujinomiya, Japan	L13	36
Fuji-san (Fujiyama), vol., Japan	L13	36
Fujisawa, Japan	L14	36
Fujiyama see Fuji-san, vol., Japan	L13	36
Fuji-yoshida, Japan	L13	36
Fukagawa, Japan	D17	36a
Fukou, China	I6	34
Fukuchiyama, Japan	L10	36
Fukue-jima, i., Japan	O3	36
Fukui, Japan	K11	36
Fukuoka, Japan	N5	36
Fukushima, Japan	J15	36
Fukuyama, Japan	M8	36
Fulacunda, Gui.-B.	F2	64
Fūlādī, Kūh-e, mtn., Afg.	C2	44
Fulda, Ger.	E9	10
Fulda, In., U.S.	H4	121
Fulda, Mn., U.S.	G3	130
Fulda, stm., Ger.	D9	10
Fulechang, China	B8	40
Fuling, China	F8	30
Fullarton, Ont., Can.	D3	103
Fullerton, Ca., U.S.	n13	112
Fullerton, Ne., U.S.	C8	134
Fullerton, N.D., U.S.	C7	141
Fulpmes, Aus.	H11	10
Fulshear, Tx., U.S.	r14	150
Fulton, Al., U.S.	D2	108
Fulton, Ar., U.S.	D2	111
Fulton, Il., U.S.	B3	120
Fulton, In., U.S.	C5	121
Fulton, Ks., U.S.	D9	123
Fulton, Ky., U.S.	f9	124
Fulton, Md., U.S.	B4	127
Fulton, Mi., U.S.	A2	129
Fulton, Ms., U.S.	A5	131
Fulton, Mo., U.S.	C6	132
Fulton, N.Y., U.S.	B4	139
Fulton, co., Ar., U.S.	A4	111
Fulton, co., Ga., U.S.	C2	117
Fulton, co., Il., U.S.	C3	120
Fulton, co., In., U.S.	B5	121
Fulton, co., Ky., U.S.	f8	124
Fulton, co., N.Y., U.S.	B6	139
Fulton, co., Oh., U.S.	A1	142
Fulton, co., Pa., U.S.	G5	145
Fultondale, Al., U.S.	f7	108
Fultz, Ky., U.S.	B6	124
Fumay, Fr.	C11	14
Fumel, Fr.	H7	14
Fumintun, China	A14	32
Funabashi, Japan	L14	36
Funchal, Port.	M21	17a
Fundación, Col.	B5	84
Fundão, Braz.	E8	79
Fundy, Bay of, b., Can.	D4	101
Fundy National Park, N.B., Can.	D4	101
Funhalouro, Moz.	D12	66
Funing, China	B8	34
Funk, Ne., U.S.	D6	134
Funkstown, Md., U.S.	A2	127
Funtua, Nig.	F13	64
Fuqikou, China	F6	34
Fuquay-Varina, N.C., U.S.	B4	140
Furano, Japan	D17	36a
Fūrg, Iran	G13	48
Furman, Al., U.S.	C3	108
Furmanov, U.S.S.R.	D24	26
Furnace Brook, stm., Vt., U.S.	D3	152
Furnas, co., Ne., U.S.	D6	134
Furnas, Represa de, res., Braz.	F5	79
Furneaux Group, is., Austl.	L8	70
Furnes (Veurne), Bel.	F2	12
Furness, Sask., Can.	D1	105
Furqlus, Syria	D4	48
Fürstenfeldbruck, Ger.	G11	10
Fürstenwalde, Ger.	C14	10
Fürth, Ger.	F10	10
Furth im Wald, Ger.	F12	10
Furudal, Swe.	K14	6
Furukawa, Japan	K12	36
Furukawa, Japan	I15	36
Fury and Hecla Strait, strt., N.W. Ter., Can.	C15	96
Fusagasugá, Col.	E5	84
Fushan, China	D9	34
Fushuigang, China	D2	34
Fushun, China	B11	32
Fusui, China	G8	30
Futianpu, China	H1	34
Future City, Il., U.S.	F4	120
Futuyu, China	D2	32
Fuwah, Egypt	B6	60
Fuxi, China	J2	34
Fuxian, China	D8	30
Fuxian (Wafangdian), China	D10	32
Fuxian Hu, l., China	B7	40
Fuxin, China	A9	32
Fuyang, China	C4	34
Fuyu, China	B11	30
Fuzhai, China	F9	34
Fuzhou, China	G5	34
Fuzhou (Foochow), China	I8	34
Fuzhuang, China	I6	32
Fyffe, Al., U.S.	A4	108
Fyn, i., Den.	N12	6

G

Name	Map Ref.	Page
Gaalkacyo, Som.	G10	56
Gaastra, Mi., U.S.	B2	129
Gabarus, N.S., Can.	D9	101
Gabas, stm., Fr.	I6	14
Gabbs, Nv., U.S.	E4	135
Gabela, Ang.	D2	58
Gabès, Tun.	D16	62
Gabès, Golfe de, b., Tun.	C16	62
Gabiarra, Braz.	D9	79
Gabir, Sud.	M3	60
Gabon, ctry., Afr.	B2	58
Gaborone, Bots.	E7	66
Gabriel Strait, strt., N.W. Ter., Can.	D19	96
Gabriola, B.C., Can.	f12	99
Gabrovo, Bul.	G9	20
Gacé, Fr.	D7	14
Gachetá, Col.	E6	84
Gachsārān, Iran	F11	48
Gackle, N.D., U.S.	C6	141
Gadag, India	E3	46
Gadamai, Sud.	I9	60
Gäddede, Swe.	I14	6
Gadiloviči, U.S.S.R.	H13	26
Gadsby, Alta., Can.	C4	98
Gadsden, Al., U.S.	A3	108
Gadsden, Az., U.S.	E1	110
Gadsden, Tn., U.S.	B3	149
Gadsden, co., Fl., U.S.	B2	116
Gaeta, Italy	H8	18
Gaeta, Golfo di, b., Italy	H8	18
Gaffney, S.C., U.S.	A4	147
Gafour, Tun.	M4	18
Gafsa, Tun.	C15	62
Gagarin, U.S.S.R.	F18	26
Gage, Ok., U.S.	A2	143
Gage, co., Ne., U.S.	D9	134
Gagetown, N.B., Can.	D3	101
Gagetown, Mi., U.S.	E7	129
Gaggenau, Ger.	G8	10
Gaghamni, Sud.	L5	60
Gagnoa, I.C.	H7	64
Gagra, U.S.S.R.	I6	22
Gahanna, Oh., U.S.	k11	142
Gaibandha, Bngl.	H13	44
Gaillac, Fr.	I8	14
Gaillard, Lake, l., Ct., U.S.	D5	114
Gaillon, Fr.	C8	14
Gaines, Mi., U.S.	F7	129
Gaines, co., Tx., U.S.	C1	150
Gainesboro, Tn., U.S.	C8	149
Gaines Creek, stm., Ok., U.S.	C6	143
Gainesville, Al., U.S.	C1	108
Gainesville, Fl., U.S.	C4	116
Gainesville, Ga., U.S.	B3	117
Gainesville, Mo., U.S.	E5	132
Gainesville, Tx., U.S.	C4	150
Gainesville, Va., U.S.	g11	153
Gainsborough, Sask., Can.	H5	105
Gairdner, Lake, l., Austl.	F7	68
Gaital, Cerro, mtn., Pan.	I14	92
Gaithersburg, Md., U.S.	B3	127
Gaixian, China	C10	32
Gajny, U.S.S.R.	E8	22
Gajutino, U.S.S.R.	C21	26
Gajvoron, U.S.S.R.	A13	20
Galaassija, U.S.S.R.	B18	48
Galahad, Alta., Can.	C5	98
Galán, Cerro, mtn., Arg.	G8	74
Galán, Cerro, mtn., Arg.	C5	80
Galapagos Islands see Colón, Archipiélago de, is., Ec.	J13	84a
Galashiels, Scot., U.K.	F11	8
Galaţi, Rom.	D12	20
Galaţi, co., Rom.	D11	20
Galatia, Il., U.S.	F5	120
Galatina, Italy	I13	18
Galax, Va., U.S.	D2	153
Gáldar, Spain	O25	17b
Galeana, Mex.	B6	90
Galeana, Mex.	E9	90
Galela, Indon.	E8	38
Galena, Ak., U.S.	C8	109
Galena, Il., U.S.	A3	120
Galena, Ks., U.S.	E9	123
Galena, Mo., U.S.	E4	132
Galeota Point, c., Trin.	I14	94
Galera, stm., Braz.	F12	82
Galera, Punta, c., Ec.	G2	84
Galera Point, c., Trin.	I14	94
Galesburg, Il., U.S.	C3	120
Galesburg, Ks., U.S.	E8	123
Galesburg, Mi., U.S.	F5	129
Galesburg, N.D., U.S.	B8	141
Gales Ferry, Ct., U.S.	D7	114
Galesville, Md., U.S.	C4	127
Galesville, Wi., U.S.	D2	156
Galeton, Co., U.S.	A6	113
Galeton, Pa., U.S.	C6	145
Galheirão, stm., Braz.	B6	79
Galheiros, Braz.	B5	79
Galiano Island, i., B.C., Can.	E6	99
Galič, U.S.S.R.	C25	26
Galicia, prov., Spain	C3	16
Galicia, hist. reg., Eur.	F12	4
Galien, Mi., U.S.	G4	129
Galilee, R.I., U.S.	F3	146
Galilee, Lake, l., Austl.	D6	70
Galilee, Sea of see Kinneret, Yam, l., Isr.	C5	50
Galiléia, Braz.	E8	79
Galion, Oh., U.S.	B3	142
Galisteo Creek, stm., N.M., U.S.	k8	138
Galiuro Mountains, mts., Az., U.S.	E5	110
Gallant, Al., U.S.	B3	108
Gallarate, Italy	D3	18
Gallatin, Mo., U.S.	B4	132
Gallatin, Tn., U.S.	A5	149
Gallatin, co., Il., U.S.	F5	120
Gallatin, co., Ky., U.S.	B5	124
Gallatin, co., Mt., U.S.	E5	133
Gallatin, stm., Mt., U.S.	E5	133
Gallatin Gateway, Mt., U.S.	E5	133
Gallatin Range, mts., Mt., U.S.	E5	133
Gallaway, Tn., U.S.	B2	149
Galle, Sri L.	I6	46
Gallia, co., Oh., U.S.	D3	142
Galliano, La., U.S.	E5	125
Galliate, Italy	D3	18
Gallina, N.M., U.S.	A3	138
Gallinas, Punta, c., Col.	A7	84
Gallinas Mountains, mts., N.M., U.S.	C2	138
Gallion, Al., U.S.	C2	108
Gallipoli, Austl.	B2	70
Gallipoli, Italy	I12	18
Gallipoli see Gelibolu, Tur.	I10	20
Gallipoli Peninsula see Gelibolu Yarımadası, pen., Tur.	I10	20
Gallipolis, Oh., U.S.	D3	142
Gallipolis Ferry, W.V., U.S.	C2	155
Gallitzin, Pa., U.S.	F4	145
Gällivare, Swe.	H17	6
Gallo Mountains, mts., N.M., U.S.	C1	138
Galloo Island, i., N.Y., U.S.	B4	139
Galloway, W.V., U.S.	B4	155
Galloway, Mull of, c., Scot., U.K.	G9	8
Gallup, N.M., U.S.	B1	138
Galougo, Mali	E4	64
Galt, Ca., U.S.	C3	112
Galt, Mo., U.S.	A4	132
Galtat Zemmour, W. Sah.	H4	62
Galty Mountains, mts., Ire.	I5	8
Galva, Il., U.S.	B3	120
Galva, Ia., U.S.	B2	122
Galva, Ks., U.S.	D6	123
Galvarino, Chile	J2	80
Galveston, In., U.S.	C5	121
Galveston, Tx., U.S.	E5	150
Galveston, co., Tx., U.S.	E5	150
Galveston Bay, b., Tx., U.S.	E5	150
Galveston Island, i., Tx., U.S.	E5	150
Gálvez, Arg.	G8	80
Galway, Ire.	H4	8
Galway, co., Ire.	H5	8
Galway Bay, b., Ire.	H4	8
Gamagōri, Japan	M12	36
Gamaliel, Ar., U.S.	A3	111
Gamaliel, Ky., U.S.	D4	124
Gamarra, Col.	C6	84
Gambaga, Ghana	F9	64
Gambela, Eth.	M8	60
Gambell, Ak., U.S.	C5	109
Gambia, ctry., Afr.	F3	54
Gambia (Gambie), stm., Afr.	F3	54
Gambi Aṭrash, Sud.	L7	60
Gambier, Oh., U.S.	B3	142
Gambier, Îles, is., Fr. Poly.	K26	158
Gambo, Newf., Can.	D4	102
Gamboa, Pan.	C3	84
Gamboma, Congo	B3	58
Gambrills, Md., U.S.	B4	127
Gamerco, N.M., U.S.	B1	138
Gamoep, S. Afr.	G4	66
Gamon, Sen.	E3	64
Gan, stm., China	A11	30
Gan, stm., China	G4	34
Ganado, Az., U.S.	B6	110
Ganado, Tx., U.S.	E4	150
Gananoque, Ont., Can.	C8	103
Ganāveh, Iran	G11	48
Ganceviči, U.S.S.R.	I9	26
Gand (Gent), Bel.	F4	12
Ganda, Ang.	D2	58
Gandak (Nārāyani), stm., Asia	G11	44
Gander, Newf., Can.	D4	102
Gander, stm., Newf., Can.	D4	102
Ganderkesee, Ger.	B8	10
Gander Lake, l., Newf., Can.	D4	102
Gāndhi Sāgar, res., India	H6	44
Gandi, Nig.	E12	64
Gandía, Spain	G11	16
Gandu, Braz.	B9	79
Ganfang, China	G3	34
Gangānagar, India	F5	44
Gangāpur, India	G7	44
Gangaw, Burma	C3	40
Gangdisê Shan, mts., China	E9	44
Ganges, B.C., Can.	g12	99
Ganges, Fr.	I10	14
Ganges (Ganga) (Padma), stm., Asia	I13	44
Ganghu, China	D12	44
Gangi, Italy	L9	18
Gangkou, China	F4	34
Gang Mills, N.Y., U.S.	C3	139
Gangotri, India	E8	44
Gangotri, India	E8	44
Gangou, China	C7	32
Gangoumen, China	B4	32
Gangtok, India	G13	44
Gangu, China	E8	30
Gannett Peak, mtn., Wy., U.S.	C3	157
Gannvalley, S.D., U.S.	C7	148
Ganq, China	B15	44
Gans, Ok., U.S.	B7	143
Gänserndorf, Aus.	G16	10
Ganso Azul, Peru	C4	82
Gansu (Kansu), prov., China	D7	30
Gantt, Al., U.S.	D3	108
Gantt, S.C., U.S.	B3	147
Gantt Lake, res., Al., U.S.	D3	108
Ganxi, China	G7	34
Ganzê, China	E7	30
Ganzhou, China	J3	34
Gao, Mali	C9	64
Gaobu, China	H6	34
Gaocun, China	F10	32
Gaohe, China	M1	34
Gaokeng, China	H2	34
Gaoling, China	C5	32
Gaona, Arg.	C6	80
Gaoqiaozhen, China	C9	32
Gaoshan, China	J8	34
Gaotan, China	E6	34
Gaotingsi, China	I1	34
Gaoua, Burkina	F8	64
Gaoxinji, China	A4	34
Gaoya, China	G6	32
Gaoyou, China	C8	34
Gaoyou Hu, l., China	C8	34
Gap, Fr.	H13	14
Gap, Pa., U.S.	G9	145
Gap Mills, W.V., U.S.	D4	155
Gar, China	E3	30
Garachiné, Pan.	C3	84
Garachiné, Punta, c., Pan.	C3	84
Garagoa, Col.	E6	84
Garanhuns, Braz.	E11	76
Garara, Pap. N. Gui.	A9	68
Garber, Ok., U.S.	A4	143
Garberville, Ca., U.S.	B2	112
Garça, Braz.	G4	79
Garças, Rio das, stm., Braz.	C2	79
García, Mex.	C5	90
García de Sola, Embalse de, res., Spain	F6	16
Garcias, Braz.	F2	79
Gard, dept., Fr.	I11	14
Garda, Italy	D5	18
Garda, Lago di, l., Italy	D5	18
Gardelegen, Ger.	C11	10
Garden, co., Ne., U.S.	C3	134
Gardena, Ca., U.S.	n12	112
Garden City, Al., U.S.	A3	108
Garden City, Ga., U.S.	D5	117
Garden City, Id., U.S.	F2	119
Garden City, In., U.S.	F6	121
Garden City, Ks., U.S.	E3	123
Garden City, Mi., U.S.	p15	129
Garden City, Mn., U.S.	F4	130
Garden City, Mo., U.S.	C3	132
Garden City, S.D., U.S.	C8	148
Gardendale, Al., U.S.	B3	108
Garden Grove, Ca., U.S.	n13	112
Garden Grove, Ia., U.S.	D4	122
Garden Island, i., Mi., U.S.	C5	129
Garden Plain, Ks., U.S.	E6	123
Garden Prairie, Il., U.S.	A5	120
Garden Reach, India	I13	44
Gardenton, Man., Can.	E3	100
Garden Valley, Id., U.S.	E3	119
Gardey, Arg.	I9	80
Gardeyz, Afg.	D3	44
Gardi, Ga., U.S.	E5	117
Gardiner, Me., U.S.	D3	126
Gardiner, Mt., U.S.	E6	133
Gardiner, Or., U.S.	D2	144
Gardiners Island, i., N.Y., U.S.	m16	139
Gardner, Ar., U.S.	D3	111
Gardner, Il., U.S.	B5	120
Gardner, Ks., U.S.	D9	123
Gardner, Ma., U.S.	A4	128
Gardner, N.D., U.S.	B9	141
Gardner, Tn., U.S.	A3	149
Gardner Canal, strt., B.C., Can.	C3	99
Gardner Lake, l., Ct., U.S.	C6	114
Gardner Lake, l., Me., U.S.	D5	126
Gardner Mountain, mtn., N.H., U.S.	B3	136
Gardner Pinnacles, Hi., U.S.	k14	118
Gardnerville, Nv., U.S.	E2	135
Gardone Val Trompia, Italy	D5	18
Garešnica, Yugo.	D11	18
Garfield, Ar., U.S.	A2	111
Garfield, Ga., U.S.	D4	117
Garfield, Ks., U.S.	D4	123
Garfield, N.J., U.S.	h8	137
Garfield, N.M., U.S.	E2	138
Garfield, Wa., U.S.	B8	154
Garfield, co., Co., U.S.	B2	113
Garfield, co., Mt., U.S.	C9	133
Garfield, co., Ne., U.S.	C6	134
Garfield, co., Ok., U.S.	A4	143
Garfield, co., Ut., U.S.	F4	151
Garfield, co., Wa., U.S.	C8	154
Garfield Heights, Oh., U.S.	h9	142
Garfield Mountain, mtn., Mt., U.S.	F4	133
Garfield Peak, mtn., Wy., U.S.	D5	157
Gargouna, Mali	D10	64
Gargždai, U.S.S.R.	F4	26
Garibaldi, Braz.	E13	80
Garibaldi, Or., U.S.	B3	144
Garibaldi, Mount, mtn., B.C., Can.	E6	99
Garies, S. Afr.	H4	66
Garissa, Kenya	B7	58
Garita Palmera, El Sal.	D5	92
Garko, Nig.	F14	64
Garland, Ar., U.S.	D2	111
Garland, Ks., U.S.	E9	123
Garland, Ne., U.S.	D9	134
Garland, N.C., U.S.	C4	140
Garland, Tn., U.S.	B2	149
Garland, Tx., U.S.	n10	150
Garland, Ut., U.S.	B3	151
Garland, co., Ar., U.S.	C2	111
Garlasco, Italy	D3	18
Garliava, U.S.S.R.	G6	26
Garlin, Fr.	I6	14
Garm, U.S.S.R.	J12	22
Garmisch-Partenkirchen, Ger.	H11	10
Garnavillo, Ia., U.S.	B6	122
Garner, Ar., U.S.	B4	111
Garner, Ia., U.S.	A4	122
Garner, Ky., U.S.	C7	124
Garner, N.C., U.S.	B4	140
Garnet Range, mts., Mt., U.S.	D3	133
Garnett, Ks., U.S.	D8	123
Garnish, Newf., Can.	E4	102
Garonne, stm., Eur.	H6	14
Garoua, Cam.	G9	54
Garrard, co., Ky., U.S.	C5	124
Garretson, S.D., U.S.	D9	148
Garrett, In., U.S.	B7	121
Garrett, Ky., U.S.	C7	124
Garrett, co., Md., U.S.	k12	127
Garrett Park, Md., U.S.	B3	127
Garrettsville, Oh., U.S.	A4	142
Garrick, Sask., Can.	D3	105
Garrison, Ia., U.S.	B5	122
Garrison, Ky., U.S.	B6	124
Garrison, Md., U.S.	B4	127
Garrison, N.Y., U.S.	D7	139
Garrison, N.D., U.S.	B4	141
Garrison, Tx., U.S.	D5	150
Garrison Dam, N.D., U.S.	B4	141
Garrovillas, Spain	F5	16
Garry Lake, l., N.W. Ter., Can.	C12	96
Garson Quarry, Man., Can.	D3	100
Garth, Al., U.S.	A3	108
Garthby Station (Beaulac), Que., Can.	D6	104
Garub, Nmb.	F3	66
Garut, Indon.	J13	39a
Garvin, co., Ok., U.S.	C4	143
Garwin, Ia., U.S.	B5	122
Garwolin, Pol.	D21	10
Garwood, Tx., U.S.	E4	150
Gary, In., U.S.	A3	121
Gary, S.D., U.S.	C9	148
Gary, W.V., U.S.	D3	155
Garyarsa, China	E9	44
Garysburg, N.C., U.S.	A5	140
Garyville, La., U.S.	D5	125
Garza, Arg.	E7	80
Garza, co., Tx., U.S.	C2	150
Garza-Little Elm Reservoir, res., Tx., U.S.	C4	150
Garzón, Col.	F5	84
Garzón, Ur.	H11	80
Gas, Ks., U.S.	E8	123
Gas City, In., U.S.	D6	121
Gascogne, hist. reg., Fr.	H6	14
Gasconade, Mo., U.S.	C6	132
Gasconade, co., Mo., U.S.	C6	132
Gasconade, stm., Mo., U.S.	C6	132
Gasconade, Osage Fork, stm., Mo., U.S.	D5	132
Gascoyne, stm., Austl.	E2	68
Gash (Nahr al-Qāsh), stm., Afr.	F8	56
Gashaka, Nig.	G9	54
Gas Hills, Wy., U.S.	D5	157
Gaspar, Braz.	D14	80
Gasparilla Island, i., Fl., U.S.	F4	116
Gaspé, Que., Can.	k14	104
Gaspésie, Péninsule de la, pen., Que., Can.	k13	104
Gasport, N.Y., U.S.	B2	139
Gassaway, W.V., U.S.	C4	155
Gassville, Ar., U.S.	A3	111
Gaston, In., U.S.	D7	121
Gaston, N.C., U.S.	A5	140
Gaston, Or., U.S.	h11	144
Gaston, S.C., U.S.	D5	147
Gaston, co., N.C., U.S.	B1	140
Gaston, Lake, res., U.S.	A5	140
Gaston Dam, N.C., U.S.	A5	140
Gastonia, N.C., U.S.	B1	140
Gastre, Arg.	E3	78
Gata, Cabo de, c., Spain	I9	16
Gátas, Akrotírion, c., Cyp.	D2	48
Gatčina, U.S.S.R.	B13	26
Gate City, Va., U.S.	f9	153
Gates, N.Y., U.S.	B3	139
Gates, N.C., U.S.	A6	140
Gates, Or., U.S.	C4	144
Gates, Tn., U.S.	B2	149
Gates, co., N.C., U.S.	A6	140
Gateshead, Eng., U.K.	G12	8
Gates of the Arctic National Park, Ak., U.S.	B9	109
Gatesville, N.C., U.S.	A6	140
Gatesville, Tx., U.S.	D4	150
Gateway, Co., U.S.	C2	113
Gatineau, Que., Can.	D2	104
Gatineau, stm., Que., Can.	D2	104
Gatineau, Parc de la, Que., Can.	D2	104
Gatliff, Ky., U.S.	D5	124
Gatlinburg, Tn., U.S.	D10	149
Gattinara, Italy	D3	18
Gatton, Austl.	F10	70
Gatún, Esclusas de, Pan.	H15	92
Gatún, Lago, res., Pan.	H15	92
Gauley, stm., W.V., U.S.	C3	155
Gauley Bridge, W.V., U.S.	C3	155
Gaurama, Braz.	D12	80
Gaurīśaṅkar, mtn., Asia	G12	44
Gause, Tx., U.S.	D4	150
Gautier, Ms., U.S.	f8	131
Gauting, Ger.	G11	10
Gavà, Spain	D14	16
Gávdhos, i., Grc.	O8	20
Gavião, stm., Braz.	C8	79
Gavins Point Dam, U.S.	B8	134
Gävle, Swe.	K15	6
Gävleborgs Län, co., Swe.	K15	6
Gavrilov-Jam, U.S.S.R.	D22	26
Gavrilov Posad, U.S.S.R.	E23	26
Gawler, Austl.	J3	70
Gawler Ranges, mts., Austl.	F7	68
Gaxun Nur, l., China	C7	30
Gay, Ga., U.S.	C2	117
Gaya, India	H11	44
Gay Head, c., Ma., U.S.	D6	128
Gaylesville, Al., U.S.	A4	108
Gaylord, Ks., U.S.	C5	123
Gaylord, Mi., U.S.	C6	129
Gaylord, Mn., U.S.	F4	130
Gaylordsville, Ct., U.S.	C2	114
Gayndah, Austl.	E9	70
Gays, Il., U.S.	D5	120
Gays Mills, Wi., U.S.	E3	156
Gaysville, Vt., U.S.	D3	152
Gayville, S.D., U.S.	E8	148
Gaza see Ghazzah, Isr. Occ.	F3	48
Gaza Strip, hist. reg., Isr. Occ.	F2	50
Gaziantep, Tur.	C4	48
Gazimağusa (Famagusta), N. Cyp.	D2	48
Gbangbatok, S.L.	H3	64
Gbanhala, stm., Afr.	G5	64
Gbarnga, Lib.	H5	64
Gbongan, Nig.	H12	64
Gcoverega, Bots.	B7	66
Gdańsk (Danzig), Pol.	A18	10
Gdańsk, Gulf of, b., Eur.	A19	10
Gdov, U.S.S.R.	C10	26
Gdyel, Alg.	J11	16
Gdynia, Pol.	A18	10
Gearhart, Or., U.S.	A3	144
Gearhart Mountain, mtn., Or., U.S.	E6	144
Geary, N.B., Can.	D3	101
Geary, Ok., U.S.	B3	143
Geary, co., Ks., U.S.	D7	123
Geauga, co., Oh., U.S.	A4	142
Geba, stm., Afr.	F4	54
Gebeit Mine, Sud.	G9	60
Gebze, Tur.	I13	20
Gecha, Eth.	N8	60
Geddes, S.D., U.S.	D7	148
Gedera, Isr.	E3	50
Gediz, Tur.	J13	20
Gedo, Eth.	M9	60
Geduan, China	H7	34
Geel, Bel.	F7	12
Geelong, Austl.	L6	70
Geesthacht, Ger.	B10	10
Geeveston, Austl.	N7	70
Geff, Il., U.S.	E5	120
Gegong, China	E6	34
Geiger, Al., U.S.	C1	108
Geilo, Nor.	K11	6
Geiranger, Nor.	J10	6
Geislingen, Ger.	G9	10
Geistown, Pa., U.S.	F4	145
Geist Reservoir, res., In., U.S.	E6	121
Geithain, Ger.	D12	10
Gejiatun, China	C7	32
Gejiu (Kokiu), China	C7	40
Gela, Italy	L9	18
Gelderland, prov., Neth.	D8	12
Geldermalsen, Neth.	E7	12
Geldrop, Neth.	F7	12
Gelenbe, Tur.	J11	20
Gelert, Ont., Can.	C6	103
Gelgaudiškis, U.S.S.R.	F6	26
Gelibolu, Tur.	I10	20
Gelibolu Yarımadası (Gallipoli Peninsula), pen., Tur.	I10	20
Gelsenkirchen, Ger.	D7	10
Geltsa, Eth.	N9	60
Gem, Ks., U.S.	C3	123
Gem, co., Id., U.S.	E2	119

Name — Map Ref. — Page

Gemena, Zaire H4 56
Gemlik, Tur. I13 20
Gemsbok National Park, Bots. E5 66
Gemünden, Ger. E9 10
Gem Village, Co., U.S. D3 113
Gen, stm., China A11 30
Genale (Jubba), stm., Afr. G9 56
Gençay, Fr. F7 14
General, stm., C.R. H11 92
General Acha, Arg. I6 80
General Alvear, Arg. I8 80
General Alvear, Arg. H5 80
General Aquino, Para. C10 80
General Arenales, Arg. H8 80
General Belgrano, Arg. H9 80
General Bravo, Mex. E10 90
General Cabrera, Arg. G7 80
General Câmara, Braz. E13 80
General Campos, Arg. F9 80
General Carneiro, Braz. C2 79
General Carrera, Lago (Lago Buenos Aires), l., S.A. F2 78
General Cepeda, Mex. E9 90
General Conesa, Arg. I10 80
General Daniel Cerri, Arg. J7 80
General Elizardo Aquino, Para. D10 80
General Enrique Martínez, Ur. G12 80
General Enrique Mosconi, Arg. B7 80
General Escobedo, Mex. E7 90
General Eugenio A. Garay, Para. C10 80
General Eugenio A. Garay, Para. I10 82
General Galarza, Arg. G9 80
General Güemes, Arg. C6 80
General Guido, Arg. I10 80
General Gutiérrez, Arg. G4 80
General José de San Martín, Arg. D9 80
General Juan José Ríos, Mex. E5 90
General Juan Madariaga, Arg. I10 80
General La Madrid, Arg. I8 80
General Lavalle, Arg. I10 80
General Levalle, Arg. H7 80
General Manuel Belgrano, Cerro, mtn., Arg. E5 80
General O'Brien, Arg. H8 80
General Paz, Arg. H9 80
General Paz, Arg. D10 80
General Pico, Arg. H7 80
General Pinedo, Arg. D8 80
General Pinto, Arg. H8 80
General Pizarro, Arg. C6 80
General Plaza (Limón), Ec. I3 84
General Roca, Arg. J5 80
General Rojo, Arg. G8 80
General Saavedra, Bol. G10 82
General San Martín, Arg. H9 80
General San Martín, Arg. I7 80
General Santos, Phil. D8 38
General Terán, Mex. E10 90
General Vargas, Braz. E11 80
General Viamonte (Los Toldos), Arg. H8 80
General Villegas, Arg. H7 80
Genesee, Id., U.S. C2 119
Genesee, Mi., U.S. E7 129
Genesee, co., Mi., U.S. E7 129
Genesee, co., N.Y., U.S. B2 139
Genesee, stm., N.Y., U.S. C2 139
Genesee Depot, Wi., U.S. n11 156
Geneseo, Il., U.S. B3 120
Geneseo, Ks., U.S. D5 123
Geneseo, N.Y., U.S. C3 139
Geneseo, N.D., U.S. C8 141
Geneva, Al., U.S. D4 108
Geneva, Ga., U.S. D2 117
Geneva, Il., U.S. B5 120
Geneva, In., U.S. C8 121
Geneva, Ky., U.S. C2 124
Geneva, Ne., U.S. D8 134
Geneva, N.Y., U.S. C4 139
Geneva, Oh., U.S. A5 142
Geneva, co., Al., U.S. D4 108
Geneva, Lake, l., Eur. F13 14
Geneva, Lake, l., Wi., U.S. F5 156
Geneva see Genève, Switz. F13 14
Geneva-on-the-Lake, Oh., U.S. A5 142
Genève (Geneva), Switz. F5 13
Genève, state, Switz. F5 13
Gengma, China C5 40
Genk, Bel. G8 12
Genlis, Fr. E12 14
Genoa, Ar., U.S. D2 111
Genoa, Co., U.S. B7 113
Genoa, Il., U.S. A5 120
Genoa, Ne., U.S. C8 134
Genoa, Nv., U.S. D2 135
Genoa, Oh., U.S. A2 142
Genoa City, Wi., U.S. F5 156
Genoa see Genova, Italy E3 18
Genola, Ut., U.S. D4 151
Genova (Genoa), Italy E3 18
Genova, Golfo di, b., Italy E3 18
Genrijetty, ostrov, i., U.S.S.R. B23 24
Gent (Gand), Bel. F4 12
Genthin, Ger. C12 10
Gentry, Ar., U.S. A1 111
Gentry, co., Mo., U.S. A3 132
Gentryville, In., U.S. H3 121
Geographe Bay, b., Austl. F3 68
Geographe Channel, strt., Austl. D2 68
Geokčaj, U.S.S.R. I7 22
Geok-Tepe, U.S.S.R. B14 48
George, S. Afr. I6 66
George, Ia., U.S. A2 122
George, co., Ms., U.S. E5 131
George, stm., Que., Can. g13 104
George, Cape, c., N.S., Can. D8 101
George, Lake, l., Austl. J8 70
George, Lake, l., N.S., Can. E3 101
George, Lake, l., Ug. B6 58
George, Lake, l., Fl., U.S. C5 116
George, Lake, l., N.Y., U.S. B7 139
George Air Force Base, mil., Ca., U.S. E5 112
George B. Stevenson Reservoir, res., Pa., U.S. D6 145
George Hill, mtn., Md., U.S. k12 127
George Peak, mtn., Ut., U.S. B2 151
Georges Bank E13 86
Georges Mills, N.H., U.S. D2 136
George Town, Austl. M7 70
Georgetown, P.E.I., Can. C7 101
George Town, Cay. Is. E4 94
Georgetown, Gam. E2 64
Georgetown, Guy. D13 84
George Town (Pinang), Malay. L6 40
Georgetown, St. Vin. H14 94
Georgetown, Ar., U.S. B4 111
Georgetown, Ca., U.S. C3 112
Georgetown, Co., U.S. B5 113
Georgetown, Ct., U.S. D2 114
Georgetown, De., U.S. F4 115
Georgetown, Fl., U.S. C5 116
Georgetown, Ga., U.S. E1 117
Georgetown, Id., U.S. G7 119
Georgetown, Il., U.S. D6 120
Georgetown, In., U.S. H6 121
Georgetown, Ky., U.S. B5 124
Georgetown, La., U.S. C3 125
Georgetown, Ma., U.S. A6 128
Georgetown, Ms., U.S. D3 131
Georgetown, Oh., U.S. D2 142
Georgetown, S.C., U.S. E9 147
Georgetown, Tx., U.S. D4 150
Georgetown, co., S.C., U.S. E9 147
George V Coast, Ant. B7 73
George VI Sound, strt., Ant. C12 73
George Washington Birthplace National Monument, Va., U.S. B6 153
George Washington Carver National Monument, Mo., U.S. E3 132
George West, Tx., U.S. E3 150
Georgia, state, U.S. D3 117
Georgia see Gruzinskaja Sovetskaja Socialističeskaja Respublika, state, U.S.S.R. I6 22
Georgiana, Al., U.S. D3 108
Georgian Bay, b., Ont., Can. B3 103
Georgijevsk, U.S.S.R. I6 22
Georgina, stm., Austl. D3 70
Georgiu-Dež, U.S.S.R. G5 22
Gera, Ger. E12 10
Gerais, Chapada dos, plat., Braz. D6 79
Geral, Serra, clf, Braz. D14 80
Gerald, Sask., Can. G5 105
Gerald, Mo., U.S. C6 132
Geral de Goiás, Serra, clf, Braz. B5 79
Geraldine, Al., U.S. A4 108
Geraldine, Mt., U.S. C6 133
Geraldton, Austl. E2 68
Geraldton, Ont., Can. o18 103
Gérardmer, Fr. D13 14
Gerber, Ca., U.S. B2 112
Gerber Reservoir, res., Or., U.S. E5 144
Gerdine, Mount, mtn., Ak., U.S. C9 109
Gereshk, Afg. E1 44
Gering, Ne., U.S. C2 134
Gerlach, Nv., U.S. C2 135
Gerlachovský štít, mtn., Czech. F20 10
Germantown, N.B., Can. D5 101
Germantown, Il., U.S. E4 120
Germantown, Ky., U.S. B6 124
Germantown, Md., U.S. B3 127
Germantown, Oh., U.S. C1 142
Germantown, Tn., U.S. B2 149
Germantown, Wi., U.S. E5 156
Germany, ctry., Eur. E9 4
Germiston, S. Afr. F9 66
Gernika-Lumo (Guernica y Luno), Spain B9 16
Geronimo, Ok., U.S. C3 143
Gerrardstown, W.V., U.S. B6 155
Gers, dept., Fr. I7 14
Gerufa, Bots. B8 66
Gervais, Or., U.S. B4 144
Gêrzê, China D11 44
Gesher HaZiw, Isr. B4 50
Getafe, Spain E8 16
Gettysburg, Oh., U.S. B1 142
Gettysburg, Pa., U.S. G7 145
Gettysburg, S.D., U.S. C6 148
Getulina, Braz. F4 79
Getúlio Vargas, Braz. D12 80
Geuda Springs, Ks., U.S. E6 123
Gevgelija, Yugo. H6 20
Gévora, stm., Eur. F4 16
Gex, Fr. F13 14
Geyikli, Tur. J10 20
Geyser, Mt., U.S. C6 133
Geyserville, Ca., U.S. C2 112
Ghaapplato, plat., Afr. F7 66
Ghadāmis, Libya E15 62
Ghāghara, stm., Asia G10 44
Ghana, ctry., Afr. G6 54
Ghanzi, Bots. C5 66
Ghanzi, dept., Bots. D6 66
Gharbi, Oued el, val., Alg. D11 62
Gharbīyah, Aṣ-Ṣaḥrā' al- (Western Desert), des., Egypt D4 60
Ghardaïa, Alg. D12 62
Ghardimaou, Tun. M3 18
Gharig, Sud. L4 60
Gharyān, Libya B3 56
Ghaṣm, Syria C6 50
Ghāt, Libya H16 62
Ghātāl, India I12 44
Għawdex (Gozo), i., Malta M9 18
Ghawr ash-Sharqīyah, Qanāt al- (East Ghor Canal), Jord. D5 50
Ghayth, Wādī, val., Jord. G5 50
Ghazāl, Bahr al-, stm., Sud. M5 60
Ghazal, Bahr el, val., Chad F4 56
Ghāziābād, India F7 44
Ghāzīpur, India H10 44
Ghazlūna, Pak. E2 44
Ghaznī, Afg. D3 44
Ghazzah (Gaza), Isr. Occ. F3 48
Ghedi, Italy D5 18
Gheen, Mn., U.S. C6 130
Ghent, Ky., U.S. B4 124
Ghent, Mn., U.S. F3 130
Ghent see Gent, Bel. F4 12
Gheorghe Gheorghiu-Dej, Rom. C10 20
Gheorgheni, Rom. C9 20
Gherla, Rom. B7 20
Ghilizane, Alg. C11 62
Ghisonaccia, Fr. L24 15a
Ghudāf, Wādī al-, val., Iraq E7 48
Ghūrīān, Afg. D16 48
Giant Mountain, mtn., N.Y., U.S. A7 139
Giant's Castle, mtn., Afr. G9 66
Giants Neck, Ct., U.S. D7 114
Giarre, Italy L10 18
Gibara, Cuba D6 94
Gibbon, Mn., U.S. F4 130
Gibbon, Ne., U.S. D7 134
Gibbons, Alta., Can. C4 98
Gibbonsville, Id., U.S. D5 119
Gibbstown, N.J., U.S. D2 137
Gibeon, Nmb. E3 66
Gibraleón, Spain H5 16
Gibraltar, Gib. I6 16
Gibraltar, dep., Eur. H6 4
Gibraltar, Strait of (Estrecho de Gibraltar), strt. J6 16
Gibsland, La., U.S. B2 125
Gibson, Ga., U.S. C4 117
Gibson, La., U.S. E5 125
Gibson, N.C., U.S. C3 140
Gibson, Tn., U.S. B3 149
Gibson, co., In., U.S. H2 121
Gibson, co., Tn., U.S. A3 149
Gibsonburg, Oh., U.S. A2 142
Gibson City, Il., U.S. C5 120
Gibson Desert, des., Austl. D5 68
Gibsonia, Pa., U.S. h14 145
Gibson Island, i., Md., U.S. B5 127
Gibsons, B.C., Can. E6 99
Gibsonton, Fl., U.S. p11 116
Gibsonville, N.C., U.S. A3 140
Gidami, Eth. M8 60
Gidda, Eth. M8 60
Giddings, Tx., U.S. D4 150
Gideon, Mo., U.S. E8 132
Gidole, Eth. O9 60
Gidrotorf, U.S.S.R. E26 26
Gien, Fr. E9 14
Giessen, Ger. E8 10
Gifford, Ar., U.S. g8 111
Gifford, Fl., U.S. E6 116
Gifford, Il., U.S. C5 120
Gifhorn, Ger. C10 10
Gifu, Japan L11 36
Giganta, Sierra de la, mts., Mex. E4 90
Gigante, Col. F5 84
Gig Harbor, Wa., U.S. B3 154
Gihon, stm., Vt., U.S. B3 152
Gijón, Spain B6 16
Gila, N.M., U.S. E1 138
Gila, co., Az., U.S. D5 110
Gila, stm., U.S. E4 106
Gila Bend, Az., U.S. E3 110
Gila Bend Indian Reservation, Az., U.S. D3 110
Gila Bend Mountains, mts., Az., U.S. D2 110
Gila Cliff Dwellings National Monument, N.M., U.S. D1 138
Gila Mountains, mts., Az., U.S. D6 110
Gila Peak, mtn., Az., U.S. D6 110
Gila River Indian Reservation, Az., U.S. D4 110
Gilbert, Az., U.S. D4 110
Gilbert, Ia., U.S. B4 122
Gilbert, La., U.S. B4 125
Gilbert, Mn., U.S. C6 130
Gilbert, S.C., U.S. D5 147
Gilbert, W.V., U.S. D3 155
Gilbert, stm., Austl. A4 70
Gilbert, stm., Newf., Can. B3 102
Gilbertown, Al., U.S. D1 108
Gilbert Peak, mtn., Wa., U.S. C4 154
Gilbert Plains, Man., Can. D1 100
Gilbertsville, Ky., U.S. f9 124
Gilbertsville, Pa., U.S. F10 145
Gilbertville, Ia., U.S. B5 122
Gilbertville, Ma., U.S. B3 128
Gilboa', Haré, hills, Asia D4 50
Gilbués, Braz. E9 76
Gilby, N.D., U.S. A8 141
Gilchrist, Or., U.S. D5 144
Gilchrist, co., Fl., U.S. C4 116
Gilcrest, Co., U.S. A6 113
Gildford, Mt., U.S. B6 133
Giles, co., Tn., U.S. B4 149
Giles, co., Va., U.S. C2 153
Gilford, N.H., U.S. C4 136
Gilford Island, i., B.C., Can. D4 99
Gilgandra, Austl. H8 70
Gilgit, Pak. C6 44
Gilgit, stm., Pak. B5 44
Gill, Co., U.S. A6 113
Gillam, Man., Can. A4 100
Gilles, Lake, l., Austl. I2 70
Gillespie, Il., U.S. D4 120
Gillespie, co., Tx., U.S. D3 150
Gillespie Dam, Az., U.S. D3 110
Gillett, Ar., U.S. C4 111
Gillett, Wi., U.S. D5 156
Gillette, Wy., U.S. B7 157
Gillham, Ar., U.S. C1 111
Gilliam, Mo., U.S. B4 132
Gilliam, co., Or., U.S. B6 144
Gilman, Co., U.S. B4 113
Gilman, Il., U.S. C5 120
Gilman, Ia., U.S. C5 122
Gilman, Mn., U.S. E5 130
Gilman, Vt., U.S. C5 152
Gilman, Wi., U.S. C3 156
Gilman City, Mo., U.S. A4 132
Gilmanton, N.H., U.S. D4 136
Gilmanton Iron Works, N.H., U.S. D4 136
Gilmer, Tx., U.S. C5 150
Gilmer, co., Ga., U.S. B2 117
Gilmer, co., W.V., U.S. C4 155
Gilmore, Ar., U.S. B5 111
Gilmore City, Ia., U.S. B3 122
Gilpin, co., Co., U.S. B5 113
Gilroy, Ca., U.S. D3 112
Gilson, Il., U.S. C3 120
Gilsum, N.H., U.S. D2 136
Gilt Edge, Tn., U.S. B2 149
Giltner, Ne., U.S. D7 134
Giluwe, Mount, mtn., Pap. N. Gui. m15 68a
Gimbi, Eth. M8 60
Gimie, Mount, mtn., St. Luc. H14 94
Gimli, Man., Can. D3 100
Gimoly, U.S.S.R. J23 6
Gimont, Fr. I7 14
Gin Gin, Austl. E9 70
Ginir, Eth. G9 56
Ginosa, Italy I11 18
Gioia del Colle, Italy I11 18
Gioia Tauro, Italy K10 18
Gipuzkoako, prov., Spain B9 16
Girard, Ga., U.S. C5 117
Girard, Il., U.S. D4 120
Girard, Ks., U.S. E9 123
Girard, Oh., U.S. A5 142
Girard, Pa., U.S. B1 145
Girardot, Col. E5 84
Girardville, Pa., U.S. E9 145
Girbovu, Rom. E7 20
Girdletree, Md., U.S. D7 127
Girgarre, Austl. K6 70
Girīdīh, India H12 44
Girne, N. Cyp. D2 48
Giromagny, Fr. E13 14
Girón, Ec. I3 84
Girona, Spain D14 16
Gironde, dept., Fr. G6 14
Gironde, est., Fr. G6 14
Giroux, Man., Can. E3 100
Girouxville, Alta., Can. B2 98
Giru, Austl. B7 70
Giruá, Braz. E11 80
Girvas, U.S.S.R. J23 6
Gisborne, N.Z. C7 72
Giscome, B.C., Can. B6 99
Gisenyi, Rw. B5 58
Gisors, Fr. C8 14
Giswil, Switz. E9 13
Gitega, Bdi. B5 58
Giugliano [in Campania], Italy I9 18
Giulianova, Italy G8 18
Giurgiu, Rom. F9 20
Giv'atayim, Isr. D3 50
Givet, Fr. B11 14
Givors, Fr. G11 14
Givry, Fr. F11 14
Giyon, Eth. M9 60
Giza see Al-Jīzah, Egypt B6 60
Gīzāb, Afg. D2 44
Gižduvan, U.S.S.R. I10 22
Gizen, Sud. L8 60
Gižiginskaja guba, b., U.S.S.R. E23 24
Giżycko, Pol. A21 10
Gjandža, U.S.S.R. I7 22
Gjirokastër, Alb. I4 20
Gjoa Haven, N.W. Ter., Can. C13 96
Gjøvik, Nor. K12 6
Gjuhëzës, Kep i, c., Alb. I3 20
Glace Bay, N.S., Can. C10 101
Glacier, Wa., U.S. A4 154
Glacier, co., Mt., U.S. B3 133
Glacier Bay, b., Ak., U.S. k21 109
Glacier Bay National Park, Ak., U.S. D12 109
Glacier National Park, B.C., Can. D9 99
Glacier National Park, Mt., U.S. B2 133
Glacier Peak, mtn., Wa., U.S. A4 154
Gladbach see Mönchengladbach, Ger. D6 10
Gladbeck, Ger. D6 10
Gladbrook, Ia., U.S. B5 122
Glade, Ks., U.S. C4 123
Glade Creek, stm., Wa., U.S. C6 154
Glade Creek, stm., W.V., U.S. n14 155
Glade Creek, stm., W.V., U.S. n13 155
Glade Park, Co., U.S. B2 113
Glades, co., Fl., U.S. F5 116
Glade Spring, Va., U.S. f10 153
Gladeville, Tn., U.S. A5 149
Gladewater, Tx., U.S. C5 150
Gladmar, Sask., Can. H3 105
Gladstone, Austl. I3 70
Gladstone, Austl. D9 70
Gladstone, Man., Can. D2 100
Gladstone, Il., U.S. C3 120
Gladstone, Mi., U.S. C4 129
Gladstone, Mo., U.S. h10 132
Gladstone, N.J., U.S. B3 137
Gladstone, N.D., U.S. C3 141
Gladstone, Or., U.S. B4 144
Gladwin, Mi., U.S. E6 129
Gladwin, co., Mi., U.S. D6 129
Gladys, Va., U.S. C3 153
Glåma, stm., Nor. K12 6
Glandorf, Oh., U.S. A1 142
Glarner Alpen, mts., Switz. E10 13
Glarus, Switz. D11 13
Glarus, state, Switz. E11 13
Glasco, Ks., U.S. C6 123
Glasco, N.Y., U.S. C7 139
Glascock, co., Ga., U.S. C4 117
Glasford, Il., U.S. C4 120
Glasgow, Scot., U.K. F9 8
Glasgow, Ky., U.S. C4 124
Glasgow, Mo., U.S. B5 132
Glasgow, Mt., U.S. B10 133
Glasgow, Va., U.S. C3 153
Glasgow, W.V., U.S. m13 155
Glaslyn, Sask., Can. D1 105
Glassboro, N.J., U.S. D2 137
Glasscock, co., Tx., U.S. D2 150
Glass Mountains, mts., Tx., U.S. D1 150
Glassport, Pa., U.S. F2 145
Glastenbury Mountain, mtn., Vt., U.S. F2 152
Glastonbury, Ct., U.S. C5 114
Glattfelden, Switz. C10 13
Glauchau, Ger. E12 10
Glaževo, U.S.S.R. B15 26
Glazier Lake, l., Me., U.S. A3 126
Glazov, U.S.S.R. F8 22
Glazunovka, U.S.S.R. I19 26
Glazypeau Mountain, mtn., Ar., U.S. f7 111
Gleason, Tn., U.S. A3 149
Gleichen, Alta., Can. D4 98
Gleisdorf, Aus. H15 10
Glen, N.H., U.S. B4 136
Glen Allan, Ms., U.S. B2 131
Glen Allen, Al., U.S. B2 108
Glen Allen, Va., U.S. C5 153
Glen Alpine, N.C., U.S. B1 140
Glenavon, Sask., Can. G4 105
Glenbeulah, Wi., U.S. k9 156
Glenboro, Man., Can. E2 100
Glenbrook, Nv., U.S. D2 135
Glenburn, N.D., U.S. A4 141
Glen Burnie, Md., U.S. B4 127
Glen Canyon, val., U.S. G4 151
Glen Canyon Dam, Az., U.S. A4 110
Glen Canyon National Recreation Area, U.S. F5 151
Glencoe, Austl. K4 70
Glencoe, Ont., Can. E3 103
Glencoe, Al., U.S. B4 108
Glencoe, Il., U.S. A6 120
Glencoe, Ky., U.S. B5 124
Glencoe, Mn., U.S. F4 130
Glencoe, Mo., U.S. f12 132
Glencoe, Ok., U.S. A5 143
Glen Cove, N.Y., U.S. h13 139
Glendale, Az., U.S. D3 110
Glendale, Ca., U.S. m12 112
Glendale, Ky., U.S. C4 124
Glendale, Ms., U.S. D4 131
Glendale, Oh., U.S. C1 142
Glendale, Or., U.S. E3 144
Glendale, R.I., U.S. B2 146
Glendale, S.C., U.S. B4 147
Glendale, Ut., U.S. F3 151
Glen Dale, W.V., U.S. B4 155
Glendale, Wi., U.S. m12 156
Glendale Colony, S.D., U.S. C7 148
Glendale Heights, W.V., U.S. g8 155
Glendive, Mt., U.S. C12 133
Glendo, Wy., U.S. D7 157
Glendola, N.J., U.S. C4 137
Glendon, Alta., Can. B5 98
Glendora, Ca., U.S. m13 112
Glendora, Ms., U.S. B3 131
Glendo Reservoir, res., Wy., U.S. D8 157
Glen Elder, Ks., U.S. C5 123
Glenelg, Md., U.S. B4 127
Glenella, Man., Can. D2 100
Glen Ellis Falls, wtfl, N.H., U.S. B4 136
Glen Ellyn, Il., U.S. k8 120
Glen Ewen, Sask., Can. H4 105
Glenfield, N.D., U.S. B7 141
Glen Gardner, N.J., U.S. B3 137
Glenham, N.Y., U.S. D7 139
Glenham, S.D., U.S. B5 148
Glen Haven, Co., U.S. A5 113
Glen Innes, Austl. G9 70
Glen Jean, W.V., U.S. D3 155
Glen Lake, l., Mi., U.S. D5 129
Glen Lyon, Pa., U.S. D9 145
Glenmora, La., U.S. D3 125
Glenmorgan, Austl. F8 70
Glenn, co., Ca., U.S. C2 112
Glennallen, Ak., U.S. f19 109
Glenns Ferry, Id., U.S. G3 119
Glennville, Ga., U.S. E5 117
Glenolden, Pa., U.S. p20 145
Glenoma, Wa., U.S. C3 154
Glenormiston, Austl. D3 70
Glenpool, Ok., U.S. B5 143
Glen Raven, N.C., U.S. A3 140
Glenreagh, Austl. H10 70
Glen Ridge, N.J., U.S. h8 137
Glen Robertson, Ont., Can. B10 103
Glen Rock, N.J., U.S. h8 137
Glen Rock, Pa., U.S. G8 145
Glenrock, Wy., U.S. D7 157
Glen Rose, Tx., U.S. C4 150
Glen Saint Mary, Fl., U.S. B4 116
Glens Falls, N.Y., U.S. B7 139
Glenside, Sask., Can. F2 105
Glenside, Pa., U.S. F11 145
Glenties, Ire. G5 8
Glentworth, Sask., Can. H2 105
Glen Ullin, N.D., U.S. C4 141
Glenview, Il., U.S. h9 120
Glenview Naval Air Station, mil., Il., U.S. h9 120
Glenvil, Ne., U.S. D7 134
Glenville, Mn., U.S. G5 130
Glenville, N.C., U.S. f9 140
Glenville, W.V., U.S. C4 155
Glen White, W.V., U.S. D3 155
Glen Wilton, Va., U.S. C3 153
Glenwood, Newf., Can. D4 102
Glenwood, Al., U.S. D3 108
Glenwood, Ar., U.S. C2 111
Glenwood, Fl., U.S. C5 116
Glenwood, Ga., U.S. D4 117
Glenwood, In., U.S. E7 121
Glenwood, Ia., U.S. C2 122
Glenwood, Mn., U.S. E3 130
Glenwood, Mo., U.S. A5 132
Glenwood, N.M., U.S. D1 138
Glenwood, Ut., U.S. E4 151
Glenwood, Va., U.S. D3 153
Glenwood, Wa., U.S. C4 154
Glenwood City, Wi., U.S. C1 156
Glenwood Springs, Co., U.S. B3 113
Glenwoodville, Alta., Can. E4 98
Glidden, Sask., Can. F1 105
Glidden, Ia., U.S. B3 122
Glidden, Wi., U.S. B3 156
Glide, Or., U.S. D3 144
Glinka, U.S.S.R. G15 26
Glittertinden, mtn., Nor. K11 6
Gliwice (Gleiwitz), Pol. E18 10
Globe, Az., U.S. D5 110
Globe, Ky., U.S. B6 124
Gloggnitz, Aus. H15 10
Głogów, Pol. D16 10
Glória de Dourados, Braz. G1 79
Glorieta, N.M., U.S. B4 138
Glorieuses, Îles, is., Reu. D9 58
Gloster, Ms., U.S. D2 131
Gloucester, Austl. H9 70
Gloucester, Ont., Can. h12 103
Gloucester, Eng., U.K. J11 8
Gloucester, Ma., U.S. A6 128
Gloucester, Va., U.S. C6 153
Gloucester, co., N.J., U.S. D2 137
Gloucester, co., Va., U.S. C6 153
Gloucester City, N.J., U.S. D2 137
Gloucester Island, i., Austl. C8 70
Gloucester Point, Va., U.S. C6 153
Gloucestershire, co., Eng., U.K. J11 8
Glouster, Oh., U.S. C3 142
Glover, Vt., U.S. B4 152
Glover Island, i., Newf., Can. D3 102
Glovers Reef, rf., Belize I16 90
Gloversville, N.Y., U.S. B6 139
Glovertown, Newf., Can. D4 102
Gloverville, S.C., U.S. E4 147
Głowno, Pol. D19 10
Głubczyce, Pol. E17 10
Glubokoje, U.S.S.R. F10 26
Głuchołazy, Pol. E17 10
Gluck, S.C., U.S. C2 147
Glückstadt, Ger. B9 10
Gluša, U.S.S.R. H11 26
Glusk, U.S.S.R. I11 26
Glybokaja, U.S.S.R. A9 20
Glyndon, Md., U.S. B4 127
Glyndon, Mn., U.S. D2 130
Glynn, co., Ga., U.S. E5 117
Gmünd, Aus. G15 10
Gmunden, Aus. H13 10
Gnadenhutten, Oh., U.S. B4 142
Gnalta, Austl. H5 70
Gnezdovo, U.S.S.R. G14 26
Gniew, Pol. B18 10
Gniewkowo, Pol. C18 10
Gniezno, Pol. C17 10
Gnjilane, Yugo. G5 20
Gnowangerup, Austl. F3 68
Goa, state, India E2 46
Goalen Head, c., Austl. K9 70
Goālpāra, India G14 44
Goan, Mali E7 64
Goascorán, Hond. D7 92
Goascorán, stm., N.A. D7 92
Goat Island, i., R.I., U.S. F5 146
Goat Mountain, mtn., Mt., U.S. C3 133
Goat Rock Dam, U.S. C4 108
Goba, Eth. G9 56
Gobabis, Nmb. D4 66
Gobabis, dept., Nmb. D4 66
Gobernador Gregores, Arg. F2 78
Gobernador Ingeniero Valentín Virasoro, Arg. E10 80
Gobernador Juan E. Martínez, Arg. E9 80
Gobernador Racedo, Arg. F8 80
Gobi, des., Asia C7 30
Gobles, Mi., U.S. F5 129
Gobō, Japan N10 36
Goce Delčev, Bul. H7 20
Goch, Ger. D6 10
Gochas, Nmb. E4 66
Godāvari, stm., India D6 46
Goddard, Ks., U.S. E6 123
Goderich, Ont., Can. D3 103
Goderville, Fr. C7 14
Godfrey, Ga., U.S. C3 117
Godfrey, Il., U.S. E3 120
Godhavn, Grnld. C14 86
Godhra, India I5 44
Godinne, Bel. H6 12
Godley, Tx., U.S. n9 150
Godoy Cruz, Arg. G4 80
Gods, stm., Man., Can. A5 100
Gods Lake, l., Man., Can. B4 100
Gods Mercy, Bay of, b., N.W. Ter., Can. D15 96
Godthåb, Grnld. C14 86
Godwin Austen see K2, mtn., Asia C7 44
Goehner, Ne., U.S. D8 134
Goélands, Lac aux, l., Que., Can. g8 102
Goes, Neth. E4 12
Goessel, Ks., U.S. D6 123
Goff, Ks., U.S. C8 123
Goff Creek, stm., Ok., U.S. e9 143
Goffstown, N.H., U.S. D3 136
Gogebic, co., Mi., U.S. n12 129
Gogebic, Lake, l., Mi., U.S. m12 129
Gogebic Range, hills, U.S. B3 156
Gogland, ostrov, i., U.S.S.R. A10 26
Gogonou, Benin F11 64
Gohad, India G8 44
Gohitafla, I.C. H7 64
Goiana, Braz. E12 76
Goianápolis, Braz. D4 79
Goiandira, Braz. E4 79
Goianésia, Braz. C4 79
Goiânia, Braz. D4 79
Goianira, Braz. D4 79
Goiás, Braz. C3 79
Goiás, state, Braz. B4 79
Goiatuba, Braz. E4 79
Goio-Erê, Braz. C12 80
Goio-Erê, stm., Braz. B12 80
Goito, Italy D5 18
Gojō, Japan M10 36
Gokāk, India D3 46
Gol, Nor. K11 6
Golāghāt, India G15 44
Golan Heights, clf, Isr. Occ. C5 50
Golbāf, Iran G14 48
Golconda, Il., U.S. F5 120
Golconda, Nv., U.S. C4 135
Gölcük, Tur. J11 20
Gołdap, Pol. A22 10
Gold Bar, Wa., U.S. B4 154
Gold Beach, Or., U.S. E2 144
Goldboro, N.S., Can. D8 101
Gold Coast, Ghana I9 64
Golden, B.C., Can. D9 99
Golden, Co., U.S. B5 113
Golden, Il., U.S. C2 120
Golden, Ms., U.S. A5 131
Golden Beach, Md., U.S. D4 127
Golden City, Mo., U.S. D3 132
Goldendale, Wa., U.S. D5 154
Golden Gate Bridge, Ca., U.S. h7 112
Golden Gate National Recreation Area, Ca., U.S. h7 112

Name | Map Ref. | Page

Golden Hinde, mtn., B.C., Can. E5 99
Golden Lake, Ont., Can. B7 103
Golden Meadow, La., U.S. E5 125
Golden Prairie, Sask., Can. G1 105
Golden Spike National Historic Site, hist., Ut., U.S. B3 151
Golden Valley, Mn., U.S. n12 130
Goldenvalley, N.D., U.S. B3 141
Golden Valley, co., Mt., U.S. D7 133
Golden Valley, co., N.D., U.S. B2 141
Goldfield, Ia., U.S. B4 122
Goldfield, Nv., U.S. F4 135
Gold Hill, N.C., U.S. B2 140
Gold Hill, Or., U.S. E3 144
Goldonna, La., U.S. B3 125
Goldsboro, N.C., U.S. B5 140
Goldsby, Ok., U.S. B4 143
Goldsmith, In., U.S. D5 121
Goldsworthy, Austl. D3 68
Goldthwaite, Tx., U.S. D3 150
Golela, S. Afr. F10 66
Goleniów, Pol. B14 10
Goleta, Ca., U.S. E4 112
Golfito, C.R. I11 92
Golf Manor, Oh., U.S. o13 142
Golfo de Santa Clara, Mex. B2 90
Goliad, Tx., U.S. E4 150
Goliad, co., Tx., U.S. E4 150
Golicyno, U.S.S.R. F19 26
Golmud, China D5 30
Golo, stm., Fr. J16 14
Golovanevsk, U.S.S.R. A14 20
Golovin, Ak., U.S. C7 109
Golpāyegān, Iran E11 48
Goltry, Ok., U.S. A3 143
Golva, N.D., U.S. C2 141
Golynki, U.S.S.R. G14 26
Golyšmanovo, U.S.S.R. F11 22
Goma, Zaire B5 58
Gomel', U.S.S.R. I14 26
Gomera, i., Spain O23 17b
Gómez Farías, Mex. C6 90
Gómez Palacio, Mex. E8 90
Gómez Plata, Col. D5 84
Gonābād, Iran D15 48
Gonaïves, Haiti E8 94
Gonâve, Golfe de la, b., Haiti E8 94
Gonâve, Île de la, i., Haiti E8 94
Gonbad-e Qābūs, Iran C13 48
Gonda, India G9 44
Gondal, India J4 44
Gondarbal, India C6 44
Gonder, Eth. K9 60
Gondia, India J9 44
Gondrecourt-le-Château, Fr. D12 14
Gönen, Tur. I11 20
Gongbo'gyamda, China F5 30
Gongchenqiao, China E9 34
Gongchuan, China I6 34
Gongdian, China G5 34
Gongga Shan, mtn., China F7 30
Gongkou, China H7 32
Gongogi, Braz. C9 79
Gongola, stm., Nig. F9 54
Gongpingxu, China I1 34
Gongxian, China E9 30
Gongyingzi, China C7 32
Goñi, Ur. G10 80
Goniądz, Pol. B22 10
Gonvick, Mn., U.S. C3 130
Gonzales, Ca., U.S. D3 112
Gonzales, La., U.S. D5 125
Gonzales, Tx., U.S. E4 150
Gonzales, co., Tx., U.S. E4 150
Gonzalez, Mex. F10 90
Gonzalez, Fl., U.S. u14 116
González, Riacho, stm., Para. B9 80
González Chaves, Arg. J8 80
González Moreno, Arg. H7 80
Gonzanamá, Ec. J3 84
Goochland, Va., U.S. C5 153
Goochland, co., Va., U.S. C5 153
Goode, Mount, mtn., Ak., U.S. g18 109
Goodell, Ia., U.S. B4 122
Gooderham, Ont., Can. C6 103
Goodeve, Sask., Can. F4 105
Goodfellow Air Force Base, mil., Tx., U.S. D2 150
Goodfield, Il., U.S. C4 120
Good Hope, S. Afr. H5 66
Good Hope, Al., U.S. A3 108
Good Hope, Ga., U.S. C3 117
Good Hope, Il., U.S. C3 120
Good Hope, Cape of, c., S. Afr. J4 66
Good Hope Mountain, mtn., B.C., Can. D5 99
Goodhue, Mn., U.S. F6 130
Goodhue, co., Mn., U.S. F6 130
Gooding, Id., U.S. G4 119
Gooding, co., Id., U.S. F4 119
Goodland, Fl., U.S. G5 116
Goodland, In., U.S. C3 121
Goodland, Ks., U.S. C2 123
Goodlands, Man., Can. E1 100
Goodlettsville, Tn., U.S. g10 149
Goodman, Ms., U.S. C4 131
Goodman, Mo., U.S. E3 132
Goodman, Wi., U.S. C5 156
Goodnews Bay, Ak., U.S. D7 109
Good Pine, La., U.S. C3 125
Goodrich, N.D., U.S. B5 141
Goodsprings, Al., U.S. B2 108
Goodsprings, Nv., U.S. H6 135
Good Thunder, Mn., U.S. F4 130
Goodview, Mn., U.S. F7 130
Goodwater, Al., U.S. B3 108
Goodway, Al., U.S. D2 108
Goodwell, Ok., U.S. e9 143
Goodwin, Ar., U.S. C4 111
Goodwin, S.D., U.S. C9 148
Goodyear, Az., U.S. D3 110
Goolgowi, Austl. I6 70
Goombalie, Austl. G6 70
Goondiwindi, Austl. G9 70
Goose, stm., Newf., Can. h9 102
Goose, stm., N.D., U.S. B8 141
Goose Bay, b., Newf., Can. B1 102
Goose Bay see Happy Valley-Goose Bay, Newf., Can. B1 102
Gooseberry Creek, stm., Wy., U.S. B4 157
Goose Creek, S.C., U.S. F7 147
Goose Creek, stm., U.S. G5 119
Goose Creek, stm., Ne., U.S. B5 134
Goose Creek, stm., Va., U.S. C3 153
Goose Creek Reservoir, res., S.C., U.S. k11 147
Goose Lake, Ia., U.S. C7 122
Goose Lake, l., U.S. B3 112
Goose Pond, l., N.H., U.S. C2 136
Gooty, India E4 46
Gopichettipālaiyam, India G4 46
Goppenstein, Switz. F8 13
Göppingen, Ger. G9 10
Goqên, China F6 30
Góra, Pol. D16 10
Goradit, Eth. L10 60
Gorakhpur, India G10 44
Gor'any, U.S.S.R. F12 26
Goražde, Yugo. F2 20
Gorbatov, U.S.S.R. E26 26
Gorbatovka, U.S.S.R. E26 26
Gorboviči, U.S.S.R. H13 26
Gorčucha, U.S.S.R. D26 26
Gorda, Punta, c., Chile H6 82
Gorda, Punta, c., Cuba C3 94
Gorda, Punta, c., Nic. F11 92
Gorda, Punta, c., Nic. C11 92
Gordo, Al., U.S. B2 108
Gordon, Al., U.S. D4 108
Gordon, Ga., U.S. D3 117
Gordon, Ne., U.S. B3 134
Gordon, Wi., U.S. B2 156
Gordon, co., Ga., U.S. B2 117
Gordon, Lake, res., Austl. N7 70
Gordon Creek, stm., Ne., U.S. B5 134
Gordonsville, Tn., U.S. C8 149
Gordonsville, Va., U.S. B4 153
Gordonvale, Austl. A6 70
Gordonville, Mo., U.S. D8 132
Gore, N.S., Can. D6 101
Gore, Eth. M8 60
Gore, N.Z. G2 72
Gore, Ok., U.S. B6 143
Gore Bay, Ont., Can. B2 103
Gore Mountain, mtn., Vt., U.S. B5 152
Gore Point, c., Austl. A3 70
Gore Point, c., Ak., U.S. h16 109
Gore Range, mts., Co., U.S. B4 113
Goreville, Il., U.S. F5 120
Gorgān, Iran C13 48
Gorgas, Al., U.S. B2 108
Gorge High Dam, Wa., U.S. A4 154
Gorgona, Isla, i., Col. F3 84
Gorgor, Peru D3 82
Gorgora, Eth. K9 60
Gorham, Il., U.S. F4 120
Gorham, Ks., U.S. D4 123
Gorham, Me., U.S. E2 126
Gorham, N.H., U.S. B4 136
Gorham, N.Y., U.S. C3 139
Gori, U.S.S.R. I6 22
Goricy, U.S.S.R. D19 26
Gorinchem, Neth. E7 12
Goris, U.S.S.R. B9 48
Gorizia, Italy D8 18
Gorj, co., Rom. E7 20
Gorkhā, Nepal F11 44
Gorki, U.S.S.R. G13 26
Gor'kovskoje vodochranilišče, res., U.S.S.R. D26 26
Gorky see Nižnij Novgorod, U.S.S.R. E27 26
Gorlice, Pol. F21 10
Görlitz, Ger. D14 10
Gorlovka, U.S.S.R. H5 22
Gorlovo, U.S.S.R. H22 26
Gorman, Tx., U.S. C3 150
Gormania, W.V., U.S. B5 155
Gorn'ackij, U.S.S.R. D10 22
Gorn'ak, U.S.S.R. H22 26
Gornji Milanovac, Yugo. E4 20
Gorno-Altajsk, U.S.S.R. G9 24
Gornozavodsk, U.S.S.R. H20 24
Gorochovec, U.S.S.R. E25 26
Gorodec, U.S.S.R. E26 26
Gorodec, U.S.S.R. C12 26
Gorodeja, U.S.S.R. H9 26
Gorodenka, U.S.S.R. A9 20
Gorodišče, U.S.S.R. H9 26
Gorodišče, U.S.S.R. H12 26
Gorodkovka, U.S.S.R. A12 20
Gorodok, U.S.S.R. F12 26
Goroka, Pap. N. Gui. G12 38
Gorontalo, Indon. E7 38
Gorouol, stm., Afr. D10 64
Gorrie, Ont., Can. D3 103
Gorutuba, stm., Braz. C7 79
Gorzów Wielkopolski (Landsberg an der Warthe), Pol. C15 10
Gosford, Austl. I9 70
Goshabi, Sud. I6 60
Goshen, N.S., Can. D8 101
Goshen, Al., U.S. D3 108
Goshen, Ct., U.S. B3 114
Goshen, In., U.S. A6 121
Goshen, Ky., U.S. g11 124
Goshen, N.H., U.S. D2 136
Goshen, N.Y., U.S. D6 139
Goshen, Oh., U.S. C1 142
Goshen, Ut., U.S. D4 151
Goshen, Va., U.S. C3 153
Goshen, co., Wy., U.S. D8 157
Goshen Hole, Wy., U.S. D8 157
Goshute Indian Reservation, U.S. D7 135
Goshute Lake, l., Nv., U.S. C7 135
Goshute Mountains, mts., Nv., U.S. C7 135
Goslar, Ger. D10 10
Gosnell, Ar., U.S. B6 111
Gosper, co., Ne., U.S. D6 134
Gosport, In., U.S. F4 121
Gossas, Sen. D1 64
Gossi, Mali D9 64
Gossville, N.H., U.S. D4 136
Gostivar, Yugo. H4 20
Gostyń, Pol. D17 10
Gostynin, Pol. C19 10
Göta älv, stm., Swe. M13 6
Gotebo, Ok., U.S. B3 143
Göteborg (Gothenburg), Swe. M12 6
Göteborgs Och Bohus län, co., Swe. L12 6
Gotemba, Japan L13 36
Goteşty, U.S.S.R. C12 20
Gotha, Ger. E10 10
Gotham, Wi., U.S. E3 156
Gothenburg, Ne., U.S. D5 134
Gothenburg see Göteborg, Swe. M12 6
Gothèye, Niger E10 64
Gotland, i., Swe. M16 6
Gotlands Län, co., Swe. M16 6
Gotō-rettō, is., Japan O3 36
Göttingen, Ger. D9 10
Gottwaldov, Czech. F17 10
Gouarec, Fr. D3 14
Gouda, Neth. D6 12
Goudge, Arg. H4 80
Goudiry, Sen. D3 64
Gough, Ga., U.S. C4 117
Gough Island, i., St. Hel. M6 52
Gouin, Réservoir, res., Que., Can. k12 104
Goulburn, Austl. J8 70
Goulburn Islands, is., Austl. B6 68
Gould, Ar., U.S. D4 111
Gould, Ok., U.S. C2 143
Goulding, Fl., U.S. u14 116
Gould Island, i., R.I., U.S. E5 146
Goulds, Fl., U.S. s13 116
Gouldsboro, Me., U.S. D4 126
Goulimime, Mor. F5 62
Gounamitz, stm., N.B., Can. B2 101
Goundam, Mali C8 64
Gourdon, Fr. H8 14
Gouré, Niger E15 64
Gourin, Fr. D3 14
Gourma Rharous, Mali C9 64
Gournay-en-Bray, Fr. C8 14
Gouvêa, Braz. E7 79
Gouverneur, N.Y., U.S. f9 139
Gouyadong, China J1 34
Govan, Sask., Can. F3 105
Gove, Ks., U.S. D3 123
Gove, co., Ks., U.S. D3 123
Govena, mys, c., U.S.S.R. F25 24
Governador Valadares, Braz. E8 79
Government Camp, Or., U.S. B5 144
Governor's Harbour, Bah. B6 94
Govind Ballabh Pant Sāgar, res., India H10 44
Govind Sāgar, res., India E7 44
Gowanda, N.Y., U.S. C2 139
Gowan Range, mts., Austl. E6 70
Gowen, Mi., U.S. E5 129
Gowen, Ok., U.S. C6 143
Gower, Mo., U.S. B3 132
Gowmal (Gumal), stm., Asia D3 44
Gowrie, Ia., U.S. B3 122
Goya, Arg. E9 80
Gozo see Għawdex, i., Malta M9 18
Graaff-Reinet, S. Afr. I7 66
Grabill, In., U.S. B8 121
Grabo, I.C. I6 64
Grabowiec, Pol. E23 10
Gračanica, Yugo. E2 20
Grace, Id., U.S. G7 119
Grace, Ms., U.S. C3 131
Grace, Mount, mtn., Ma., U.S. A3 128
Grace City, N.D., U.S. B7 141
Gracemont, Ok., U.S. B3 143
Graceville, Fl., U.S. u16 116
Graceville, Mn., U.S. E2 130
Gracewood, Ga., U.S. C4 117
Gracey, Ky., U.S. D2 124
Gracias, Hond. C6 92
Gracias a Dios, dept., Hond. B10 92
Gracias a Dios, Cabo, c., N.A. B11 92
Gradačac, Yugo. E2 20
Gradaús, Braz. E8 76
Gradaús, Serra dos, plat., Braz. E8 76
Grado, Italy D8 18
Grady, Ar., U.S. C4 111
Grady, N.M., U.S. C6 138
Grady, co., Ga., U.S. F2 117
Grady, co., Ok., U.S. C4 143
Graettinger, Ia., U.S. A3 122
Grafenau, Ger. G13 10
Gräfenhainichen, Ger. D12 10
Grafing [bei München], Ger. G11 10
Graford, Tx., U.S. C3 150
Grafton, Austl. G10 70
Grafton, Ont., Can. D6 103
Grafton, Il., U.S. E3 120
Grafton, Ia., U.S. A4 122
Grafton, Ma., U.S. B4 128
Grafton, Ne., U.S. D8 134
Grafton, N.H., U.S. C3 136
Grafton, N.D., U.S. A8 141
Grafton, Oh., U.S. A3 142
Grafton, Vt., U.S. E3 152
Grafton, Va., U.S. h15 153
Grafton, W.V., U.S. B4 155
Grafton, Wi., U.S. E6 156
Grafton, co., N.H., U.S. C3 136
Grafton, Cape, c., Austl. A6 70
Graham, Ky., U.S. C2 124
Graham, Mo., U.S. A2 132
Graham, N.C., U.S. A3 140
Graham, Ok., U.S. C4 143
Graham, Tx., U.S. C3 150
Graham, co., Az., U.S. E5 110
Graham, co., Ks., U.S. C4 123
Graham, co., N.C., U.S. f9 140
Graham, Lake, res., Tx., U.S. C3 150
Graham, Mount, mtn., Az., U.S. E6 110
Graham Creek, stm., In., U.S. G6 121
Graham Island, i., B.C., Can. C1 99
Graham Lake, l., Me., U.S. D4 126
Graham Land, reg., Ant. B12 73
Graham Moore, Cape, c., N.W. Ter., Can. B17 96
Graham Moore Bay, b., N.W. Ter., Can. A12 96
Grahamstown, S. Afr. I8 66
Grahamsville, N.Y., U.S. D6 139
Grahn, Ky., U.S. B6 124
Grain Coast, Lib. I5 64
Grainfield, Ks., U.S. C3 123
Grainger, co., Tn., U.S. C10 149
Grain Valley, Mo., U.S. B3 132
Grajaú, Braz. E9 76
Grajaú, stm., Braz. D9 76
Grajewo, Pol. B22 10
Gramada, Bul. F6 20
Gramado, Braz. E13 80
Gramalote, Col. D6 84
Grambling, La., U.S. B3 125
Gramercy, La., U.S. h10 125
Gramilla, Arg. D6 80
Gramling, S.C., U.S. A3 147
Grammer, In., U.S. F6 121
Grammichele, Italy L9 18
Grampian, prov., Scot., U.K. D11 8
Grampian Mountains, mts., Scot., U.K. E9 8
Grampians National Park, Austl. K5 70
Granada, Col. F6 84
Granada, Nic. F9 92
Granada, Spain H8 16
Granada, Co., U.S. C8 113
Granada, Mn., U.S. G4 130
Granada, dept., Nic. F8 92
Granadilla de Abona, Spain O24 17b
Granbury, Tx., U.S. C4 150
Granby, Que., Can. D5 104
Granby, Co., U.S. A5 113
Granby, Ct., U.S. B4 114
Granby, Ma., U.S. B2 128
Granby, Mo., U.S. E3 132
Granby, Lake, res., Co., U.S. A5 113
Gran Canaria, i., Spain O25 17b
Gran Chaco, pl., S.A. C8 80
Grand, co., Co., U.S. A4 113
Grand, co., Ut., U.S. E6 151
Grand, stm., Ont., Can. D4 103
Grand, stm., Mi., U.S. E5 129
Grand, stm., Mo., U.S. A3 132
Grand, stm., Oh., U.S. A4 142
Grand, stm., S.D., U.S. B4 148
Grand, North Fork, stm., U.S. B2 148
Grand, South Fork, stm., S.D., U.S. B3 148
Grand Bahama, i., Bah. A5 94
Grand Bank, Newf., Can. E4 102
Grand Banks of Newfoundland E14 86
Grand-Bassam, I.C. I8 64
Grand Bay, N.B., Can. D3 101
Grand Bay, Al., U.S. E1 108
Grand Bayou, stm., La., U.S. h9 125
Grand Bayou, stm., La., U.S. k10 125
Grand Bend, Ont., Can. D3 103
Grand Blanc, Mi., U.S. F7 129
Grand Bruit, Newf., Can. E2 102
Grand Caillou, La., U.S. E5 125
Grand Canal, Ire. H6 8
Grand Canal see Da Yunhe, China E10 30
Grand Canyon, Az., U.S. A3 110
Grand Canyon, val., Az., U.S. A3 110
Grand Canyon National Park, Az., U.S. B3 110
Grand Cayman, i., Cay. Is. E4 94
Grand Centre, Alta., Can. B5 98
Grand Cess, Lib. I5 64
Grand Chenier, La., U.S. E3 125
Grand Codroy, stm., Newf., Can. E2 102
Grand Combin, mtn., Switz. G7 13
Grand Coteau, La., U.S. D3 125
Grand Coulee, Wa., U.S. B6 154
Grand Coulee Dam, Wa., U.S. B6 154
Grand-Couronne, Fr. C8 14
Grande, stm., Arg. I4 80
Grande, stm., Arg. C6 80
Grande, stm., Bol. G9 82
Grande, stm., Braz. F10 76
Grande, stm., Braz. E3 79
Grande, stm., Chile F3 80
Grande, stm., Nic. E8 92
Grande, stm., Pan. I14 92
Grande, stm., Peru F4 82
Grande, Arroyo, stm., Ur. G10 80
Grande, Bahía, Arg. G3 78
Grande, Boca, mth., Ven. C12 84
Grande, Cerro, mtn., Mex. C6 90
Grande, Cerro, mtn., Mex. G8 90
Grande, Corixa, stm., S.A. G7 76
Grande, Corixa (Curiche Grande), sw., S.A. G12 82
Grande, Cuchilla, mtn., Ur. G11 80
Grande, Ilha, i., Braz. G6 79
Grande, Ilha, i., Braz. B11 80
Grande, Ponta, c., Braz. D9 79
Grande, Punta, c., Chile C3 80
Grande, Rio (Bravo del Norte), stm., N.A. F7 106
Grande-Anse, N.B., Can. B4 101
Grande Cache, Alta., Can. C1 98
Grande Cayemite, i., Haiti E8 94
Grand Ecore, La., U.S. C2 125
Grande da Botija, Ilha, i., Braz. J11 84
Grande de Lipez, stm., Bol. I8 84
Grande de Manacapuru, Lago, l., Braz. I12 84
Grande de Matagalpa, stm., Nic. D11 92
Grande de Santa Marta, Ciénaga, b., Col. B5 84
Grande de Santiago, stm., Mex. G7 90
Grande de Tarija, stm., S.A. J9 82
Grande de Térraba, stm., C.R. I11 92
Grande-Digue, N.B., Can. C5 101
Grande do Gurupá, Ilha, i., Braz. D8 76
Grand-Entrée, Que., Can. B8 101
Grande Prairie, Alta., Can. B1 98
Grand Erg de Bilma, des., Niger E9 54
Grand Erg Occidental, des., Alg. E11 62
Grand Erg Oriental, des., Alg. E14 62
Grande rivière de la Baleine, stm., Que., Can. g11 104
Grande Ronde, stm., U.S. C8 154
Grandes, Salinas, pl., Arg. B6 80
Grandes, Salinas, pl., Arg. F6 80
Grandes-Bergeronnes, Que., Can. A8 104
Grand-Étang, N.S., Can. C8 101
Grande-Terre, i., Guad. F14 94
Grand Falls (Grand-Sault), N.B., Can. B2 101
Grand Falls, Newf., Can. D4 102
Grandfalls, Tx., U.S. D1 150
Grand Falls, wtfl, Me., U.S. C5 126
Grandfather Mountain, mtn., N.C., U.S. A1 140
Grandfield, Ok., U.S. C3 143
Grand Forks, B.C., Can. E8 99
Grand Forks, N.D., U.S. B8 141
Grand Forks, co., N.D., U.S. B8 141
Grand Forks Air Force Base, mil., N.D., U.S. B8 141
Grand Gorge, N.Y., U.S. C6 139
Grand Harbour, N.B., Can. E3 101
Grand Haven, Mi., U.S. E4 129
Grand Hers, stm., Fr. I8 14
Grand Hogback, mtn., Co., U.S. B3 113
Grandiči, U.S.S.R. H6 26
Grandin, Mo., U.S. E7 132
Grandin, N.D., U.S. B9 141
Grand Island, Ne., U.S. D7 134
Grand Island, i., La., U.S. D6 125
Grand Island, i., Mi., U.S. B4 129
Grand Isle, La., U.S. E6 125
Grand Isle, Me., U.S. A4 126
Grand Isle, Vt., U.S. B2 152
Grand Isle, co., Vt., U.S. B2 152
Grand Isle, i., La., U.S. E6 125
Grand Junction, Co., U.S. B2 113
Grand Junction, Ia., U.S. B3 122
Grand Junction, Tn., U.S. B2 149
Grand lac Bostonnais, l., Que., Can. B5 104
Grand-Lahou, I.C. I7 64
Grand Lake, Co., U.S. A5 113
Grand Lake, l., N.B., Can. D3 101
Grand Lake, l., Newf., Can. D3 102
Grand Lake, l., Newf., Can. B1 102
Grand Lake, l., La., U.S. E3 125
Grand Lake, l., La., U.S. E6 125
Grand Lake, l., Mi., U.S. C7 129
Grand Lake, l., Oh., U.S. B1 142
Grand Lake Matagamon, l., Me., U.S. B4 126
Grand Lake Seboeis, l., Me., U.S. B4 126
Grand Lake Stream, Me., U.S. C5 126
Grand Ledge, Mi., U.S. F6 129
Grand Manan Island, i., N.B., Can. E3 101
Grand Marais, Mi., U.S. B5 129
Grand Marais, Mn., U.S. k9 130
Grand Marsh, Wi., U.S. E4 156
Grand Meadow, Mn., U.S. G6 130
Grand-Mère, Que., Can. C5 104
Grand Mesa, mtn., Co., U.S. C2 113
Grand Mound, Ia., U.S. C7 122
Grand-Popo, Benin H10 64
Grand Portage, Mn., U.S. k10 130
Grand Portage Indian Reservation, Mn., U.S. k10 130
Grand Portage National Monument, Mn., U.S. h10 130
Grand Prairie, Tx., U.S. n10 150
Grand Pré, N.S., Can. D5 101
Grand Rapids, Mi., U.S. F5 129
Grand Rapids, Mn., U.S. C5 130
Grand Rapids, Oh., U.S. f6 142
Grand Ridge, Fl., U.S. B1 116
Grand Ridge, Il., U.S. B5 120
Grandrieu, Bel. H5 12
Grand River, N.S., Can. D9 101
Grand Rivers, Ky., U.S. f9 124
Grand Ronde, Or., U.S. B3 144
Grand-Saint-Bernard, Col du, Eur. G7 13
Grand-Saint-Bernard, Tunnel du, Eur. G14 14
Grand Saline, Tx., U.S. C5 150
Grand Terre Islands, is., La., U.S. E6 125
Grand Teton, mtn., Wy., U.S. C2 157
Grand Teton National Park, Wy., U.S. C2 157
Grand Tower, Il., U.S. F4 120
Grand Traverse, co., Mi., U.S. D5 129
Grand Traverse Bay, b., Mi., U.S. C5 129
Grand Traverse Bay, East Arm, b., Mi., U.S. D5 129
Grand Traverse Bay, West Arm, b., Mi., U.S. D5 129
Grand Turk, T./C. Is. D9 94
Grand Valley, Ont., Can. D4 103
Grand Valley, val., Co., U.S. B2 113
Grandview, Man., Can. D1 100
Grand View, Id., U.S. G2 119
Grandview, In., U.S. I4 121
Grandview, Ia., U.S. C6 122
Grandview, Mo., U.S. C3 132
Grandview, Tn., U.S. D9 149
Grandview, Wa., U.S. C6 154
Grandview Heights, Oh., U.S. m10 142
Grandville, Mi., U.S. F5 129
Grand Wash Cliffs, clf, Az., U.S. B2 110
Grandy, Mn., U.S. E5 130
Grandy, N.C., U.S. A7 140
Graneros, Chile H3 80
Granger, In., U.S. A5 121
Granger, Ia., U.S. C4 122
Granger, Tx., U.S. D4 150
Granger, Wa., U.S. C5 154
Granger, Wy., U.S. E3 157
Grangeville, Id., U.S. D2 119
Gran Guardia, Arg. C9 80
Granisle, B.C., Can. B4 99
Granite, Ok., U.S. C2 143
Granite, co., Mt., U.S. D3 133
Granite Canon, Wy., U.S. E7 157
Granite City, Il., U.S. E3 120
Granite Falls, Mn., U.S. F3 130
Granite Falls, N.C., U.S. B1 140
Granite Falls, Wa., U.S. A4 154
Granite Lake, res., Newf., Can. D3 102
Granite Mountain, mtn., Ak., U.S. B7 109
Granite Mountains, mts., Az., U.S. E2 110
Granite Mountains, mts., Wy., U.S. D5 157
Granite Pass, Wy., U.S. B5 157
Granite Peak, mtn., Mt., U.S. E7 133
Granite Peak, mtn., Nv., U.S. C2 135
Granite Peak, mtn., Nv., U.S. B4 135
Granite Peak, mtn., Ut., U.S. C2 151
Granite Peak, mtn., Ut., U.S. E3 151
Granite Peak, mtn., Wy., U.S. D4 157
Granite Quarry, N.C., U.S. B2 140
Granite Range, mts., Nv., U.S. C2 135
Graniteville, Ma., U.S. f10 128
Graniteville, S.C., U.S. D4 147
Graniteville, Vt., U.S. C4 152
Grannis, Ar., U.S. C1 111
Granollers, Spain D14 16
Gran Pajonal, mts., Peru D4 82
Gran Paradiso, mtn., Italy D2 18
Gran Sasso d'Italia, mts., Italy G8 18
Grant, Al., U.S. A3 108
Grant, Fl., U.S. E6 116
Grant, Mi., U.S. E5 129
Grant, Ne., U.S. D4 134
Grant, Ok., U.S. D6 143
Grant, co., Ar., U.S. C3 111
Grant, co., In., U.S. D6 121
Grant, co., Ks., U.S. E2 123
Grant, co., Ky., U.S. B5 124
Grant, co., La., U.S. C3 125
Grant, co., Mn., U.S. E2 130
Grant, co., Ne., U.S. C4 134
Grant, co., N.M., U.S. E1 138
Grant, co., N.D., U.S. C4 141
Grant, co., Ok., U.S. A4 143
Grant, co., Or., U.S. C7 144
Grant, co., S.D., U.S. B8 148
Grant, co., Wa., U.S. B6 154
Grant, co., W.V., U.S. B5 155
Grant, co., Wi., U.S. F3 156
Grant, Mount, mtn., Nv., U.S. E3 135
Gran Tarajal, Spain O26 17b
Grant City, Mo., U.S. A3 132
Grantham, N.H., U.S. D2 136
Granton, Ont., Can. D3 103
Granton, Wi., U.S. D3 156
Grant Park, Il., U.S. B6 120
Grant Range, mts., Nv., U.S. E6 135
Grants, N.M., U.S. B2 138
Grantsboro, N.C., U.S. B6 140
Grantsburg, In., U.S. H5 121
Grantsburg, Wi., U.S. C1 156
Grantsdale, Mt., U.S. D2 133
Grants Pass, Or., U.S. E3 144
Grantsville, Md., U.S. k12 127
Grantsville, Ut., U.S. C3 151
Grantsville, W.V., U.S. C3 155
Grant Town, W.V., U.S. B4 155
Grantville, Ga., U.S. C2 117
Grantville, Ks., U.S. k14 123
Granum, Alta., Can. E4 98
Granville, Fr. D5 14
Granville, Il., U.S. B4 120
Granville, Ia., U.S. B2 122
Granville, N.Y., U.S. B7 139
Granville, N.D., U.S. A5 141
Granville, Oh., U.S. B3 142
Granville, Vt., U.S. D3 152
Granville, W.V., U.S. h11 155
Granville, co., N.C., U.S. A4 140
Granville Centre, N.S., Can. E4 101
Granville Ferry, N.S., Can. E4 101
Granville Lake, l., Man., Can. A1 100
Granvin, Nor. K10 6
Grão Mogol, Braz. D7 79
Grapeland, Tx., U.S. D5 150
Grapeview, Wa., U.S. B3 154
Grapevine, Tx., U.S. C4 150
Grapevine Lake, res., Tx., U.S. n9 150
Grapevine Peak, mtn., Nv., U.S. G4 135
Grasmere, S. Afr. F8 66
Grasonville, Md., U.S. C5 127
Grass, stm., Man., Can. B2 100
Grass, stm., N.Y., U.S. f9 139
Grass Creek, In., U.S. C5 121
Grasse, Fr. I13 14
Grassflat, Pa., U.S. D5 145
Grass Lake, Il., U.S. h8 120
Grass Lake, Mi., U.S. F6 129
Grass Lake, l., Il., U.S. h8 120
Grassrange, Mt., U.S. C8 133
Grass Valley, Ca., U.S. C3 112
Grassy, Austl. M6 70
Grassy Brook, stm., Vt., U.S. E3 152
Grassy Lake, Alta., Can. E5 98
Grassy Lake, l., La., U.S. k9 125
Grates Cove, Newf., Can. D5 102
Grates Point, c., Newf., Can. D5 102
Gratiot, co., Mi., U.S. E6 129
Gratis, Oh., U.S. C1 142
Gratz, Pa., U.S. E8 145
Graubünden (Grischun), state, Switz. E11 13
Gravatá, Braz. E11 76
Gravatá, stm., Braz. D7 79
Grave Creek, stm., W.V., U.S. g8 155

Name | Map Ref. | Page

Gravelines, Fr. B9 14
Gravell Point, c., N.W. Ter., Can. C17 96
Gravelly, Ar., U.S. C2 111
Gravelly Branch, stm., De., U.S. F4 115
Gravelly Range, mts., Mt., U.S. E4 133
Gravel Ridge, Ar., U.S. h10 111
Gravenhurst, Ont., Can. C5 103
Grave Peak, mtn., Id., U.S. C4 119
Graves, co., Ky., U.S. f9 124
Gravette, Ar., U.S. A1 111
Gravina in Puglia, Italy I11 18
Gravity, Ia., U.S. D3 122
Gray, Sask., Can. G3 105
Gray, Fr. E12 14
Gray, Ga., U.S. C3 117
Gray, Ky., U.S. D5 124
Gray, La., U.S. k10 125
Gray, Me., U.S. g7 126
Gray, co., Ks., U.S. E3 123
Gray, co., Tx., U.S. B2 150
Grayback Mountain, mtn., Or., U.S. E3 144
Gray Court, S.C., U.S. B3 147
Grayland, Wa., U.S. C1 154
Grayling, Ak., U.S. C7 109
Grayling, Mi., U.S. D6 129
Graylyn Crest, De., U.S. A3 115
Grays Harbor, co., Wa., U.S. B2 154
Grays Harbor, b., Wa., U.S. C1 154
Grayslake, Il., U.S. A5 120
Grays Lake, sw., Id., U.S. F7 119
Grayson, Sask., Can. G4 105
Grayson, Al., U.S. A2 108
Grayson, Ga., U.S. C3 117
Grayson, Ky., U.S. B7 124
Grayson, La., U.S. B3 125
Grayson, co., Ky., U.S. C3 124
Grayson, co., Tx., U.S. C4 150
Grayson, co., Va., U.S. D1 153
Grayson Lake, res., Ky., U.S. B7 124
Grays Peak, mtn., Co., U.S. B5 113
Grays River, Wa., U.S. C2 154
Gray Summit, Mo., U.S. g12 132
Graysville, Al., U.S. f7 108
Graysville, Tn., U.S. D8 149
Grayville, Il., U.S. E5 120
Graz, Aus. H15 10
Grazalema, Spain I6 16
Gr'azi, U.S.S.R. I22 26
Gr'aznoje, U.S.S.R. G22 26
Gr'azovec, U.S.S.R. C23 26
Greasewood, Az., U.S. B6 110
Great Artesian Basin, Austl. E5 70
Great Australian Bight, Austl. F5 68
Great Averill Pond, l., Vt., U.S. B5 152
Great Barrier Island, i., N.Z. B5 72
Great Barrier Reef, rf., Austl. C9 68
Great Barrier Reef Marine Park, Austl. C9 68
Great Barrington, Ma., U.S. B1 128
Great Basin, U.S. C3 106
Great Basin National Park, Nv., U.S. E7 135
Great Bay, b., N.H., U.S. D5 136
Great Bay, b., N.J., U.S. D4 137
Great Bear Lake, l., N.W. Ter., Can. C8 96
Great Bend, Ks., U.S. D5 123
Great Bend, N.D., U.S. C9 141
Great Bend, Pa., U.S. C10 145
Great Blue Hill, hill, Ma., U.S. B5 128
Great Britain, i., U.K. E7 4
Great Burnt Lake, l., Newf., Can. D3 102
Great Cacapon, W.V., U.S. B6 155
Great Captain Island, i., Ct., U.S. F1 114
Great Channel, strt., Asia K3 40
Great Dismal Swamp, sw., U.S. D6 153
Great Divide Basin, Wy., U.S. E4 157
Great Dividing Range, mts., Austl. E9 68
Great Duck Island, i., Ont., Can. B2 103
Great East Lake, l., U.S. C5 136
Great Egg Harbor, stm., N.J., U.S. D3 137
Greater Antilles, is., N.A. D7 94
Greater Cincinnati Airport, Ky., U.S. h13 124
Greater Khingan Range see Da Hinggan Ling, mts., China B11 30
Greater Sunda Islands, is., Asia F5 38
Great Exuma, i., Bah. C7 94
Great Falls, Man., Can. D3 100
Great Falls, Mt., U.S. C5 133
Great Falls, S.C., U.S. B6 147
Great Falls, wtfl, Md., U.S. B3 127
Great Falls Dam, Tn., U.S. D6 149
Great Guana Cay, i., Bah. B6 94
Greathouse Peak, mtn., Mt., U.S. D7 133
Great Inagua, i., Bah. D8 94
Great Indian Desert (Thar Desert), des., Asia G4 44
Great Island, spit, Ma., U.S. C7 128
Great Island, i., N.C., U.S. B6 140
Great Karroo, plat., S. Afr. I6 66
Great Lake, l., Austl. M7 70
Great Lakes Naval Training Center, mil., Il., U.S. h9 120
Great Miami, stm., U.S. C1 142
Great Misery Island, i., Ma., U.S. f12 128
Great Moose Lake, l., Me., U.S. D3 126
Great Namaqualand, hist. reg., Nmb. E3 66
Great Neck, N.Y., U.S. h13 139
Great Nicobar, i., India K2 40
Great North Mountain, mtn., U.S. C6 155
Great Palm Island, i., Austl. B7 70
Great Pee Dee, stm., U.S. D9 147
Great Plain of the Koukdjuak, pl., N.W. Ter., Can. C18 96
Great Plains, pl., N.A. E9 86
Great Point, c., Ma., U.S. D7 128
Great Pond, l., Me., U.S. D3 126
Great Pond, l., Ma., U.S. h11 128
Great Pond, l., Ma., U.S. h12 128
Great Quittacas Pond, l., Ma., U.S. C6 128
Great Ruaha, stm., Tan. C7 58
Great Sacandaga Lake, l., N.Y., U.S. C6 139
Great Saint Bernard Pass see Grand-Saint-Bernard, Col du, Eur. G7 13
Great Salt Lake, l., Ut., U.S. B3 151
Great Salt Lake Desert, des., Ut., U.S. C2 151
Great Salt Plains Lake, res., Ok., U.S. A3 143
Great Salt Pond, b., R.I., U.S. h7 146
Great Sand Dunes National Monument, Co., U.S. D5 113
Great Sand Hills, hills, Sask., Can. G1 105
Great Sandy Desert, des., Austl. D4 68
Great Scarcies (Kolenté), stm., Afr. G3 64
Great Seneca Creek, stm., Md., U.S. B3 127
Great Slave Lake, l., N.W. Ter., Can. D10 96
Great Smoky Mountains, mts., U.S. B8 149
Great Smoky Mountains National Park, U.S. B8 149
Great Swamp, sw., R.I., U.S. F3 146
Great Valley, val., U.S. C2 153
Great Victoria Desert, des., Austl. E5 68
Great Village, N.S., Can. D6 101
Great Wall, sci., B.A.T. B1 73
Great Wall see Chang Cheng, hist., China C4 32
Great Wass Island, i., Me., U.S. D5 126
Great Yarmouth, Eng., U.K. I15 8
Great Zab (Büyükzap) (Az-Zāb al-Kabīr), stm., Asia C7 48
Gréboun, mtn., Niger A14 64
Grecia, C.R. G10 92
Greco, Ur. G10 80
Greece, N.Y., U.S. B3 139
Greece, N.Y., U.S. B3 139
Greece (Ellás), ctry., Eur. H12 4
Greeley, Co., U.S. A6 113
Greeley, Ia., U.S. B6 122
Greeley, Ks., U.S. D8 123
Greeley, Ne., U.S. C7 134
Greeley, Pa., U.S. D12 145
Greeley, co., Ks., U.S. D2 123
Greeley, co., Ne., U.S. C7 134
Greeleyville, S.C., U.S. D8 147
Green, Ks., U.S. C6 123
Green, Or., U.S. D3 144
Green, co., Ky., U.S. C4 124
Green, co., Wi., U.S. F4 156
Green, stm., N.B., Can. B1 101
Green, stm., U.S. D5 106
Green, stm., U.S. A1 113
Green, stm., U.S. F3 152
Green, stm., Il., U.S. B4 120
Green, stm., Ky., U.S. C2 124
Green, stm., Wa., U.S. B3 154
Green Acres, De., U.S. h8 115
Greenacres, Wa., U.S. B8 154
Greenacres City, Fl., U.S. F6 116
Greenback, Tn., U.S. D9 149
Greenbackville, Va., U.S. C7 153
Green Bank, W.V., U.S. C5 155
Green Bay, Wi., U.S. D6 156
Green Bay, b., U.S. D3 129
Greenbelt, Md., U.S. C4 127
Greenbriar, Va., U.S. g12 153
Greenbrier, Al., U.S. A3 108
Greenbrier, Ar., U.S. B3 111
Green Brier, Tn., U.S. A5 149
Greenbrier, co., W.V., U.S. D4 155
Greenbrier, stm., W.V., U.S. D4 155
Greenbush, Me., U.S. C4 126
Greenbush, Mn., U.S. B2 130
Greencastle, In., U.S. E4 121
Green Castle, Mo., U.S. A5 132
Greencastle, Pa., U.S. G6 145
Green City, Mo., U.S. A5 132
Green Court, Alta., Can. B3 98
Green Cove Springs, Fl., U.S. C5 116
Green Creek, N.J., U.S. E3 137
Greendale, In., U.S. F8 121
Greendale, Wi., U.S. F6 156
Greene, Ia., U.S. B5 122
Greene, Me., U.S. D2 126
Greene, N.Y., U.S. C5 139
Greene, co., Al., U.S. C1 108
Greene, co., Ar., U.S. A5 111
Greene, co., Ga., U.S. C3 117
Greene, co., Il., U.S. D3 120
Greene, co., In., U.S. F4 121
Greene, co., Ia., U.S. B3 122
Greene, co., Ms., U.S. D5 131
Greene, co., Mo., U.S. D4 132
Greene, co., N.Y., U.S. C6 139
Greene, co., N.C., U.S. B5 140
Greene, co., Oh., U.S. C2 142
Greene, co., Pa., U.S. G1 145
Greene, co., Tn., U.S. C11 149
Greene, co., Va., U.S. B4 153
Greeneville, Tn., U.S. C11 149
Green Fall, stm., U.S. F1 146
Greenfield, Ar., U.S. B5 111
Greenfield, Ca., U.S. D3 112
Greenfield, Il., U.S. D3 120
Greenfield, In., U.S. E6 121
Greenfield, Ia., U.S. C3 122
Greenfield, Ma., U.S. A2 128
Greenfield, Mo., U.S. D4 132
Greenfield, N.H., U.S. E3 136
Greenfield, N.M., U.S. D5 138
Greenfield, Oh., U.S. C2 142
Greenfield, Ok., U.S. B3 143
Greenfield, Tn., U.S. A3 149
Greenfield, Wi., U.S. n11 156
Greenfield Plaza, Ia., U.S. e8 122
Green Forest, Ar., U.S. A2 111
Green Harbor, Ma., U.S. B6 128
Green Head, c., Austl. F2 68
Greenhill, Al., U.S. A2 108
Green Hill Pond, l., R.I., U.S. G3 146
Greenhills, Oh., U.S. n12 142
Greenhorn Creek, stm., Co., U.S. D6 113
Green Lake, Sask., Can. C2 105
Green Lake, Wi., U.S. E5 156
Green Lake, co., Wi., U.S. E4 156
Green Lake, l., Me., U.S. D4 126
Green Lake, l., Wi., U.S. E5 156
Greenland, Ar., U.S. B1 111
Greenland, Mi., U.S. B1 129
Greenland, N.H., U.S. D5 136
Greenland (Kalaallit Nunaat), dep., N.A. B15 86
Greenland Sea B20 86
Greenleaf, Ks., U.S. C7 123
Greenleaf, Wi., U.S. D5 156
Greenlee, co., Az., U.S. D6 110
Green Lookout Mountain, mtn., Wa., U.S. D3 154
Greenmount, Md., U.S. A4 127
Green Mountain, Ia., U.S. B5 122
Green Mountain, mtn., Wy., U.S. D5 157
Green Mountain Reservoir, res., Co., U.S. B4 113
Green Mountains, mts., Vt., U.S. F2 152
Greenock, Pa., U.S. F2 145
Green Peter Lake, res., Or., U.S. C4 144
Green Pond, Al., U.S. B2 108
Green Pond, l., N.J., U.S. A4 137
Green Pond Mountain, mtn., N.J., U.S. B3 137
Greenport, N.Y., U.S. m16 139
Green Ridge, Mo., U.S. C4 132
Green River, Ut., U.S. E5 151
Green River, Wy., U.S. E3 157
Green River Lake, res., Ky., U.S. C4 124
Green River Lock and Dam, U.S. I2 121
Green River Reservoir, res., Vt., U.S. B3 152
Green Rock, Il., U.S. B3 120
Greensboro, Al., U.S. C2 108
Greensboro, Fl., U.S. B2 116
Greensboro, Ga., U.S. C3 117
Greensboro, In., U.S. E7 121
Greensboro, Md., U.S. C6 127
Greensboro, N.C., U.S. A3 140
Greensboro, Vt., U.S. B4 152
Greensboro Bend, Vt., U.S. B4 152
Greensburg, In., U.S. F7 121
Greensburg, Ks., U.S. E4 123
Greensburg, Ky., U.S. C4 124
Greensburg, La., U.S. D5 125
Greensburg, Pa., U.S. F2 145
Greens Fork, In., U.S. E7 121
Greens Peak, mtn., Az., U.S. C6 110
Greenspond, Newf., Can. D5 102
Green Spring, W.V., U.S. B6 155
Green Springs, Oh., U.S. A2 142
Greensville, co., Va., U.S. D5 153
Green Swamp, sw., N.C., U.S. C4 140
Greentop, Mo., U.S. A5 132
Greentown, In., U.S. D6 121
Greenup, Il., U.S. D5 120
Greenup, Ky., U.S. B7 124
Greenup, co., Ky., U.S. B7 124
Greenvale, Austl. B6 70
Green Valley, Az., U.S. F5 110
Green Valley, Il., U.S. C4 120
Green Valley, val., Tx., U.S. p13 150
Greenview, Il., U.S. C4 120
Greenview, W.V., U.S. n12 155
Greenville, Lib. I5 64
Greenville, Al., U.S. D3 108
Greenville, Ca., U.S. B3 112
Greenville, De., U.S. A3 115
Greenville, Fl., U.S. B3 116
Greenville, Ga., U.S. C2 117
Greenville, Il., U.S. E4 120
Greenville, In., U.S. H6 121
Greenville, Ky., U.S. C2 124
Greenville, Me., U.S. C3 126
Greenville, Mi., U.S. E5 129
Greenville, Ms., U.S. B2 131
Greenville, Mo., U.S. D7 132
Greenville, N.H., U.S. E3 136
Greenville, N.C., U.S. B5 140
Greenville, Oh., U.S. B1 142
Greenville, Pa., U.S. D1 145
Greenville, R.I., U.S. C3 146
Greenville, S.C., U.S. B3 147
Greenville, Tx., U.S. C4 150
Greenville, Va., U.S. B3 153
Greenville, co., S.C., U.S. B3 147
Greenville Creek, stm., Oh., U.S. B1 142
Greenville Junction, Me., U.S. C3 126
Greenway, Ar., U.S. A5 111
Greenwich, Ct., U.S. E1 114
Greenwich, N.Y., U.S. B7 139
Greenwich, Oh., U.S. A3 142
Greenwich Bay, b., R.I., U.S. D4 146
Greenwich Hill, N.B., Can. D3 101
Greenwich Point, c., Ct., U.S. E1 114
Greenwood, B.C., Can. E8 99
Greenwood, Ar., U.S. B1 111
Greenwood, De., U.S. E3 115
Greenwood, Fl., U.S. B1 116
Greenwood, In., U.S. E5 121
Greenwood, La., U.S. B2 125
Greenwood, Ms., U.S. B3 131
Greenwood, Mo., U.S. k11 132
Greenwood, Ne., U.S. D9 134
Greenwood, Pa., U.S. E5 145
Greenwood, S.C., U.S. C3 147
Greenwood, S.D., U.S. E7 148
Greenwood, Wi., U.S. D3 156
Greenwood, co., Ks., U.S. E7 123
Greenwood, co., S.C., U.S. C3 147
Greenwood, Lake, res., In., U.S. G4 121
Greenwood, Lake, res., S.C., U.S. C4 147
Greenwood Lake, N.Y., U.S. D6 139
Greenwood Lake, l., U.S. A4 137
Greenwood Lake, l., Mn., U.S. C7 130
Greer, S.C., U.S. B3 147
Greer, co., Ok., U.S. C2 143
Greers Ferry, Ar., U.S. B3 111
Greers Ferry Lake, res., Ar., U.S. B3 111
Greeson, Lake, res., Ar., U.S. C2 111
Gregg, co., Tx., U.S. C5 150
Gregoire Lake, l., Alta., Can. A5 98
Gregório, stm., Braz. B6 82
Gregory, Ar., U.S. B4 111
Gregory, Mi., U.S. F6 129
Gregory, S.D., U.S. D6 148
Gregory, co., S.D., U.S. D6 148
Gregory, stm., Austl. B3 70
Gregory, Lake, l., Austl. G3 70
Gregory Bald, mtn., U.S. D10 149
Gregory Range, mts., Austl. B5 70
Greifswald, Ger. A13 10
Greilickville, Mi., U.S. D5 129
Greiz, Ger. E12 10
Grem'ačinsk, U.S.S.R. F9 22
Grenada, Ca., U.S. B2 112
Grenada, Ms., U.S. B4 131
Grenada, co., Ms., U.S. B4 131
Grenada, ctry., N.A. H14 94
Grenada Lake, res., Ms., U.S. B4 131
Grenadines, is., N.A. H14 94
Grenchen, Switz. D7 13
Grenfell, Austl. I8 70
Grenfell, Sask., Can. G4 105
Grenoble, Fr. G12 14
Grenola, Ks., U.S. E7 123
Grenora, N.D., U.S. A2 141
Grenville, Que., Can. D3 104
Grenville, Cape, c., Austl. B8 68
Grenville, Point, c., Wa., U.S. B1 154
Gréoux-les-Bains, Fr. I12 14
Gresham, Ne., U.S. C8 134
Gresham, Or., U.S. B4 144
Gresham, Wi., U.S. D5 156
Gresik, Indon. J16 39a
Gresten, Aus. G15 10
Gretna, Man., Can. E3 100
Gretna, Fl., U.S. B2 116
Gretna, La., U.S. E5 125
Gretna, Ne., U.S. C9 134
Gretna, Va., U.S. D3 153
Greven, Ger. C7 10
Grevená, Grc. I5 20
Grevenbroich, Ger. D6 10
Grey, stm., Newf., Can. E3 102
Greybull, Wy., U.S. B4 157
Greybull, stm., Wy., U.S. B4 157
Grey Eagle, Mn., U.S. E4 130
Greylock, Mount, mtn., Ma., U.S. A1 128
Greymouth, N.Z. E3 72
Grey Range, mts., Austl. G5 70
Greys, stm., Wy., U.S. C2 157
Greytown, S. Afr. G10 66
Gribanovskij, U.S.S.R. G6 22
Gridley, Ca., U.S. C3 112
Gridley, Il., U.S. C5 120
Gridley, Ks., U.S. D8 123
Gridley Mountain, mtn., Ct., U.S. A2 114
Griesbach, Ger. G13 10
Griesheim, Ger. F8 10
Griffin, Sask., Can. H4 105
Griffin, Ga., U.S. C2 117
Griffin, In., U.S. H2 121
Griffiss Air Force Base, mil., N.Y., U.S. B5 139
Griffith, Austl. J7 70
Griffith, In., U.S. A3 121
Griffith Island, i., Ont., Can. C4 103
Griffithsville, W.V., U.S. C3 155
Griffithville, Ar., U.S. B4 111
Grifton, N.C., U.S. B5 140
Griggs, co., N.D., U.S. B7 141
Griggsville, Il., U.S. D3 120
Grignan, Fr. H11 14
Grigoriopol', U.S.S.R. B13 20
Grijalva, stm., Mex. I13 90
Grijalva (Cuilco), stm., N.A. B3 92
Grijpskerk, Neth. B9 12
Grim, Cape, c., Austl. M6 70
Grimes, Al., U.S. D4 108
Grimes, Ia., U.S. C4 122
Grimes, co., Tx., U.S. D4 150
Grimesland, N.C., U.S. B5 140
Grimma, Ger. D12 10
Grimsby, Ont., Can. D5 103
Grimsby, Eng., U.K. H13 8
Grimselpass, Switz. E9 13
Grimshaw, Alta., Can. A2 98
Grimsley, Tn., U.S. C9 149
Grímsstaðir, Ice. B5 6a
Grimstad, Nor. L11 6
Grímsvötn, mtn., Ice. B5 6a
Grin'ava, U.S.S.R. B8 20
Grindall Creek, Va., U.S. n18 153
Grindelwald, Switz. E9 13
Grinnell, Ia., U.S. C5 122
Grinnell, Ks., U.S. C3 123
Grinnell Peninsula, pen., N.W. Ter., Can. A13 96
Gris-Nez, Cap, c., Fr. B8 14
Grissom Air Force Base, mil., In., U.S. C5 121
Griswold, Man., Can. E1 100
Griswold, Ia., U.S. C2 122
Grizzly Bear Mountain, mtn., N.W. Ter., Can. C8 96
Grizzly Mountain, mtn., Id., U.S. B2 119
Grizzly Mountain, mtn., Or., U.S. C6 144
Grizzly Mountain, mtn., Wa., U.S. A7 154
Groais Island, i., Newf., Can. C4 102
Grobiņa, U.S.S.R. E4 26
Groblersdal, S. Afr. E9 66
Groblershoop, S. Afr. G5 66
Grodków, Pol. E17 10
Grodno, U.S.S.R. H6 26
Grodzisk Mazowiecki, Pol. C20 10
Groede, Neth. F4 12
Groenlo, Neth. D10 12
Groesbeck, Tx., U.S. D4 150
Groesbeek, Neth. E8 12
Groix, Fr. E3 14
Grójec, Pol. D20 10
Grombalia, Tun. M5 18
Gronau, Ger. C7 10
Groningen, Neth. B10 12
Groningen, prov., Neth. B10 12
Gronlid, Sask., Can. D3 105
Groom, Tx., U.S. B2 150
Groom Lake, l., Nv., U.S. F6 135
Groom Range, mts., Nv., U.S. F6 135
Groot-Brakrivier, S. Afr. J5 66
Groote Eylandt, i., Austl. B7 68
Grootfontein, Nmb. B4 66
Groot Karasberge, mts., Nmb. F4 66
Groot-Kei, stm., Afr. I9 66
Groot Laagte, stm., Afr. C5 66
Groot-Marico, S. Afr. E8 66
Groot-Vis, stm., Afr. I8 66
Gros-Mécatina, Île du, i., Que., Can. C2 102
Gros Morne, mtn., Newf., Can. D3 102
Gros Morne National Park, Newf., Can. D3 102
Grosse Île, i., Que., Can. B8 101
Grosse Isle Naval Air Station, mil., Mi., U.S. p15 129
Grossenhain, Ger. D13 10
Grosse Pointe, Mi., U.S. p16 129
Grosse Pointe Park, Mi., U.S. p16 129
Grosse Pointe Woods, Mi., U.S. p16 129
Grosse Tete, La., U.S. D4 125
Grosseto, Italy G6 18
Gross-Gerau, Ger. F8 10
Grossglockner, mtn., Aus. H12 10
Grosshöchstetten, Switz. E8 13
Grossmont, Ca., U.S. o16 112
Grossräschen, Ger. D14 10
Grosvenor Dale, Ct., U.S. B8 114
Gros Ventre, stm., Wy., U.S. C2 157
Gros Ventre Range, mts., Wy., U.S. C2 157
Groton, Ct., U.S. D7 114
Groton, Ma., U.S. A4 128
Groton, N.H., U.S. C3 136
Groton, N.Y., U.S. C4 139
Groton, S.D., U.S. B7 148
Groton, Vt., U.S. C4 152
Groton Long Point, Ct., U.S. D7 114
Grottaglie, Italy I12 18
Grottoes, Va., U.S. B4 153
Grouard Mission, Alta., Can. B2 98
Grouse Creek, stm., Ks., U.S. E7 123
Grouse Creek, stm., Ut., U.S. B2 151
Grouse Creek Mountain, mtn., Id., U.S. E5 119
Grouse Creek Mountains, mts., Ut., U.S. B2 151
Grovania, Ga., U.S. D3 117
Grove, Ok., U.S. A7 143
Grove City, Fl., U.S. F4 116
Grove City, Mn., U.S. E4 130
Grove City, Oh., U.S. C2 142
Grove City, Pa., U.S. D1 145
Grove Hill, Al., U.S. D2 108
Groveland, Fl., U.S. D5 116
Groveland, Ga., U.S. D5 117
Groveland, Ma., U.S. A5 128
Grove Point, c., Md., U.S. B5 127
Groveport, Oh., U.S. C3 142
Grover, Co., U.S. A6 113
Grover, N.C., U.S. B1 140
Grover, Wy., U.S. D2 157
Grover City, Ca., U.S. E3 112
Grover Hill, Oh., U.S. A1 142
Groves, Tx., U.S. E6 150
Grovespring, Mo., U.S. D5 132
Groveton, N.H., U.S. A3 136
Groveton, Tx., U.S. D5 150
Groveton, Va., U.S. g12 153
Groveton Gardens, Va., U.S. B5 153
Grovetown, Ga., U.S. C4 117
Groveville, N.J., U.S. C3 137
Growler Peak, mtn., Az., U.S. E2 110
Groznyj, U.S.S.R. I7 22
Grubbs, Ar., U.S. B4 111
Grudziądz, Pol. B18 10
Gruetli-Laager, Tn., U.S. D8 149
Gruitrode, Bel. F8 12
Grulla, Tx., U.S. F3 150
Grünau, Nmb. F4 66
Grünau [im Almtal], Aus. H13 10
Grundy, Va., U.S. e9 153
Grundy, co., Il., U.S. B5 120
Grundy, co., Ia., U.S. B5 122
Grundy, co., Mo., U.S. A4 132
Grundy, co., Tn., U.S. D8 149
Grundy Center, Ia., U.S. B5 122
Grunthal, Man., Can. E3 100
Gruver, Tx., U.S. A2 150
Gruzinskaja Sovetskaja Socialističeskaja Respublika (Georgia), state, U.S.S.R. I6 22
Grybów, Pol. F20 10
Gryfice, Pol. B15 10
Gstaad, Switz. F7 13
Guabito, Pan. H12 92
Guacanayabo, Golfo de, b., Cuba D6 94
Guacara, Ven. B9 84
Guacarí, Col. F4 84
Gu Achi, Az., U.S. E3 110
Guachiría, stm., Col. E7 84
Guachochi, Mex. D6 90
Guaçuí, Braz. F8 79
Guadalajara, Mex. G8 90
Guadalajara, Spain E8 16
Guadalcanal, i., Sol.Is. I20 158
Guadalén, stm., Spain G8 16
Guadalén, Embalse de, res., Spain G8 16
Guadalmena, stm., Spain G9 16
Guadalquivir, stm., Spain H6 16
Guadalupe, Bol. H9 82
Guadalupe, Col. F5 84
Guadalupe, C.R. H10 92
Guadalupe, Mex. F8 90
Guadalupe, Mex. E9 90
Guadalupe, Peru B2 82
Guadalupe, Az., U.S. m9 110
Guadalupe, Ca., U.S. E3 112
Guadalupe, Co., U.S. D4 113
Guadalupe, co., N.M., U.S. C5 138
Guadalupe, co., Tx., U.S. E4 150
Guadalupe [Bravos], Mex. B6 90
Guadalupe Mountains, mts., U.S. E5 138
Guadalupe Mountains National Park, Tx., U.S. o12 150
Guadalupe Peak, mtn., Tx., U.S. o12 150
Guadalupe Victoria, Mex. E7 90
Guadalupita, N.M., U.S. A4 138
Guadarrama, Sierra de, mts., Spain E7 16
Guadeloupe, dep., N.A. F14 94
Guadeloupe Passage, strt., N.A. F14 94
Guadiana, stm., Eur. H4 16
Guadix, Spain H8 16
Guaíba, Braz. F13 80
Guaíba, est., Braz. F13 80
Guaihe, China B1 34
Guaimaca, Hond. C8 92
Guaimoreto, Laguna de, b., Hond. B9 92
Guainía, dept., Col. F8 84
Guainía, stm., S.A. F9 84
Guaiquinima, Cerro, mtn., Ven. E11 84
Guaíra, Braz. F4 79
Guaíra, Braz. C11 80
Guairá, dept., Para. C10 80
Guáitara, stm., Col. G4 84
Guajaba, Cayo, i., Cuba D6 94
Guajará-Mirim, Braz. D9 82
Gualaca, Pan. C1 84
Gualaceo, Ec. I3 84
Gualala, Ca., U.S. C2 112
Gualán, Guat. B5 92
Gualaquiza, Ec. I3 84
Gualdo Tadino, Italy F7 18
Gualeguay, Arg. G9 80
Gualeguay, stm., Arg. G9 80
Gualeguaychú, Arg. G9 80
Gualicho, Salina del, pl., Arg. E3 78
Guam, dep., Oc. F22 2
Guamal, Col. C5 84
Guamal, Col. F6 84
Guaminí, Arg. I7 80
Guamo, Col. E5 84
Guamote, Ec. H3 84
Guamúchil, Mex. E5 90
Guamués, stm., Col. G4 84
Guanacaste, prov., C.R. G9 92
Guanacaste, Cordillera de, mts., C.R. G9 92
Guanacaste, Parque Nacional, C.R. G9 92
Guanacaure, Cerro, mtn., Hond. D7 92
Guanaceví, Mex. E7 90
Guanache, stm., Peru B4 82
Guanahacabibes, Golfo de, b., Cuba C2 94
Guanaja, Hond. A9 92
Guanaja, Isla de, i., Hond. A9 92
Guanajay, Cuba C3 94
Guanajuato, Mex. G9 90
Guanajuato, state, Mex. G9 90
Guanambi, Braz. C7 79
Guañape, Isla, i., Peru C2 82
Guanare, Ven. C8 84
Guanare, stm., Ven. C8 84
Guanare Viejo, stm., Ven. C8 84
Guanarito, Ven. C8 84
Guanay, Bol. F8 82
Guanay, Cerro, mtn., Ven. E9 84
Guanbuqiao, China F3 34
Guandacol, Arg. E4 80
Guandanghu, China E2 34
Guandian, China C7 34
Guane, Cuba C2 94
Guang'an, China E8 30
Guangde, China E8 34
Guangdong (Kwangtung), prov., China G9 30
Guanghua, China E9 30
Guangnan, China G8 30
Guangrao, China F6 32
Guangxi Zhuangzu Zizhiqu (Kwangsi Chuang), prov., China G8 30
Guangyuan, China E8 30
Guangzhou (Canton), China L2 34
Guanhães, Braz. E7 79
Guanipa, stm., Ven. C11 84
Guankou, China E4 34
Guano, Ec. H3 84
Guano Lake, l., Or., U.S. E7 144
Guanqian, China E6 34
Guanqiaopu, China D1 34
Guanta, Ven. B10 84
Guantánamo, Cuba D7 94
Guantao (Nanguantao), China G3 32
Guantou, China G9 34
Guanxian, China E7 30
Guanyintang, China D1 34
Guanzhuang, China F2 32
Guanzhuang, China C3 34
Guapí, Col. F4 84
Guapiara, Braz. H4 79
Guápiles, C.R. G11 92
Guapó, Braz. D4 79
Guaporé, Braz. E13 80
Guaporé, stm., Braz. E12 80
Guaporé (Iténez), stm., S.A. E10 82
Guaqui, Bol. G7 82
Guará, stm., Braz. B6 79
Guarabira, Braz. E11 76
Guaraçaí, Braz. F3 79
Guaraci, Braz. G3 79
Guaraci, Braz. F4 79
Guaraciama, Braz. D7 79

Name — Map Ref. — Page

Guaramirim, Braz. D14 80
Guaranda, Ec. H3 84
Guaraniaçu, Braz. C12 80
Guarani das Missões, Braz. E11 80
Guarani de Goiás, Braz. B5 79
Guarapari, Braz. F8 79
Guarapuava, Braz. C13 80
Guaraqueçaba, Braz. C14 80
Guararé, Pan. D2 84
Guaratinguetá, Braz. G6 79
Guaratuba, Braz. C14 80
Guarda, Port. E4 16
Guardafui, Cape see Caseyr, c., Som. F11 56
Guardavalle, Italy K11 18
Guardia Escolta, Arg. E7 80
Guardiagrele, Italy G9 18
Guardo, Spain C7 16
Guareí, stm., Braz. G2 79
Guareim (Quaraí), stm., S.A. F10 80
Guareña, Spain G5 16
Guarenas, Ven. B9 84
Guariba, stm., Braz. C11 82
Guarico, Ven. C8 84
Guárico, state, Ven. C9 84
Guárico, stm., Ven. C9 84
Guárico, Embalse del, res., Ven. C9 84
Guariquito, stm., Ven. D9 84
Guarizama, Hond. C8 92
Guarulhos, Braz. G5 79
Guasare, stm., Ven. B6 84
Guasave, Mex. E5 90
Guasdualito, Ven. D7 84
Guasipati, Ven. D12 84
Guastalla, Italy E5 18
Guastatoya, Guat. C4 92
Guatajiagua, El Sal. D6 92
Guatemala, Guat. C4 92
Guatemala, dept., Guat. C4 92
Guatemala, ctry., N.A. E6 88
Guateque, Col. E6 84
Guatimozín, Arg. G7 80
Guatire, Ven. B9 84
Guatopo, Parque Nacional, Ven. C9 84
Guatraché, Arg. I7 80
Guaviare, ter., Col. F6 84
Guaviare, stm., Col. F8 84
Guaxupé, Braz. F5 79
Guayabal, Cuba D6 94
Guayabal, Ven. C9 84
Guayabero, stm., Col. F6 84
Guayacán, Chile E3 80
Guayama, P.R. F11 94
Guayambre, stm., Hond. C8 92
Guayape, Hond. C8 92
Guayape, stm., Hond. C9 92
Guayapo, stm., Ven. E9 84
Guayaquil, Ec. I3 84
Guayaquil, Golfo de, b., S.A. I2 84
Guayaramerín, Bol. D9 82
Guayas, prov., Ec. H2 84
Guayas, stm., Col. G5 84
Guayas, stm., Ec. I3 84
Guayatayoc, Laguna de, l., Arg. B6 80
Guaycora, Mex. C5 90
Guaymas, Mex. D4 90
Guayquiraró, stm., Arg. F9 80
Guayuriba, stm., Col. F6 84
Guazacapán, Guat. C4 92
Guazapares, Mex. D5 90
Guazárachi, Mex. D6 90
Guba, Eth. L8 60
Gubacha, U.S.S.R. F9 22
Gubbio, Italy F7 18
Guben, Ger. D14 10
Gubin, Pol. D14 10
Gubkin, U.S.S.R. G5 22
Gucheng, China C7 34
Güdalür, India H4 46
Gudermes, U.S.S.R. I7 22
Gudianzi, China D5 34
Gudiyāttam, India F5 46
Güdür, India E5 46
Guebwiller, Fr. E14 14
Güéjar, stm., Col. F6 84
Guelma, Alg. B14 62
Guelph, Ont., Can. D4 103
Guéméné-sur-Scorff, Fr. D3 14
Guené, Benin F11 64
Guérande, Fr. E4 14
Guercif, Mor. C9 62
Güere, stm., Ven. C10 84
Guéréda, Chad J2 60
Guéret, Fr. F8 14
Guernsey, Sask., Can. F3 105
Guernsey, Wy., U.S. D8 157
Guernsey, co., Oh., U.S. B4 142
Guernsey, dep., Eur. F7 4
Guerrero, Mex. C6 90
Guerrero, state, Mex. I9 90
Guerzim, Alg. F10 62
Guessou-Sud, Benin F11 64
Gueydan, La., U.S. D3 125
Gugang, China G2 34
Guge, mtn., Eth. N9 60
Guia, Braz. F13 82
Guía de Isora, Spain O24 17b
Guia Lopes da Laguna, Braz. I13 82
Guibes, Nmb. F3 66
Güicán, Col. D6 84
Guichen, Fr. E5 14
Guichón, Ur. G10 80
Guidan Roumji, Niger E13 64
Guide, China D7 30
Guide Rock, Ne., U.S. D7 134
Guidigri, Niger E14 64
Guidimouni, Niger E14 64
Guiding, China A9 40
Guifujie, China H9 34
Guiglo, I.C. H6 64
Güija, Lago de, l., N.A. C5 92
Guild, N.H., U.S. D2 136
Guildford, Eng., U.K. J13 8
Guilford, Ct., U.S. D5 114
Guilford, Me., U.S. C3 126
Guilford, Vt., U.S. F3 152
Guilford, co., N.C., U.S. A3 140
Guilin (Kweilin), China B11 40
Guillaumes, Fr. H13 14
Güimar, Spain O24 17b
Guimarães, Port. D3 16
Guin, Al., U.S. B2 108
Guinea (Guinée), ctry., Afr. F4 54
Guinea, Gulf of, b., Afr. H7 52
Guinea-Bissau (Guiné-Bissau), ctry., Afr. F3 54
Güines, Cuba C3 94
Guînes, Fr. B8 14
Guingamp, Fr. D3 14
Güinope, Hond. D8 92
Guiones, Punta, c., C.R. H9 92
Guiping, China C11 40
Guir, Hammada du, des., Afr. E9 62
Guir, Oued, val., Afr. E9 62
Güira de Melena, Cuba C3 94
Guiratinga, Braz. D2 79
Güiria, Ven. B11 84
Guiricema, Braz. F7 79
Guise, Fr. C10 14
Güisisil, mtn., Nic. E8 92
Guist Creek, stm., Ky., U.S. B4 124
Guita Koulouba, Cen. Afr. Rep. O2 60
Guitou, China K2 34
Guîtres, Fr. G6 14
Guiuan, Phil. C8 38
Guixi, China G6 34
Guixian, China C10 40
Guiyang (Kweiyang), China A9 40
Güiza, stm., Col. G3 84
Guizhou (Kweichow), prov., China F8 30
Gujarāt, state, India I4 44
Gujrānwāla, Pak. D6 44
Gujrāt, Pak. D6 44
Gulbarga, India D4 46
Gulbene, U.S.S.R. D9 26
Guledagudda, India D3 46
Guleitou, China L6 34
Gulf, co., Fl., U.S. C1 116
Gulf Gate Estates, Fl., U.S. E4 116
Gulf Hammock, Fl., U.S. C4 116
Gulf Islands National Seashore, U.S. E5 131
Gulfport, Fl., U.S. E4 116
Gulf Port, Il., U.S. C2 120
Gulfport, Ms., U.S. E4 131
Gulf Shores, Al., U.S. E2 108
Gulgong, Austl. I8 70
Gulistān, Pak. E2 44
Gulistan, U.S.S.R. I11 22
Gulkana, Ak., U.S. C10 109
Gull Island, i., N.C., U.S. B7 140
Gullivan Bay, b., Fl., U.S. G5 116
Gull Lake, Sask., Can. G1 105
Gull Lake, l., Alta., Can. C4 98
Gull Lake, l., Mn., U.S. D4 130
Güllük, Tur. L11 20
Gulnam, Sud. N5 60
Gülpınar, Tur. J10 20
Guluy, Eth. J9 60
Gumal (Gowmal), stm., Asia D3 44
Gumare, Bots. B6 66
Gumboro, De., U.S. G4 115
Gumiao, China C2 34
Gummersbach, Ger. D7 10
Gummi, Nig. E12 64
Gum Spring Mountain, mtn., Tn., U.S. D8 149
Gum Springs, Ar., U.S. C2 111
Gum Swamp Creek, stm., Ga., U.S. D3 117
Gümüşhane, Tur. A5 48
Guna, India H7 44
Gundagai, Austl. J8 70
Gungu, Zaire C3 58
Gunisao, stm., Man., Can. C3 100
Gunisao Lake, l., Man., Can. C3 100
Gunnbjørn Fjeld, mtn., Grnld. C17 86
Gunnedah, Austl. H9 70
Gunnison, Co., U.S. C4 113
Gunnison, Ms., U.S. B3 131
Gunnison, Ut., U.S. D4 151
Gunnison, co., Co., U.S. C3 113
Gunnison, stm., Co., U.S. C2 113
Gunnison, Mount, mtn., Co., U.S. C3 113
Gunpowder Creek, stm., Ky., U.S. k13 124
Gunpowder Neck, c., Md., U.S. B5 127
Gunpowder River, b., Md., U.S. B5 127
Guntakal, India E4 46
Gunter Air Force Base, mil., Al., U.S. C3 108
Guntersville, Al., U.S. A3 108
Guntersville Dam, Al., U.S. A3 108
Guntersville Lake, res., Al., U.S. A3 108
Gunton, Man., Can. D3 100
Guntown, Ms., U.S. A5 131
Guntūr, India D6 46
Gunungsitoli, Indon. N4 40
Gunzenhausen, Ger. F10 10
Guolutan, China C4 34
Guozhuang, China H5 32
Gupei, China I5 32
Guraferda, Eth. N8 60
Gura-Galbena, U.S.S.R. C12 20
Gurara, stm., Nig. G13 64
Gurdāspur, India D6 44
Gurdon, Ar., U.S. D2 111
Güre, Tur. K13 20
Gurguéia, stm., Braz. E10 76
Guri, Embalse, res., Ven. D11 84
Gurjev, U.S.S.R. H8 22
Gurjevsk, U.S.S.R. G15 22
Gurjevsk, U.S.S.R. G3 26
Gurley, Al., U.S. A3 108
Gurley, Ne., U.S. C3 134
Gurnee, Il., U.S. h9 120
Gurnet Point, c., Ma., U.S. B6 128
Gurupá, Braz. D8 76
Gurupi, Braz. F9 76
Gurupi, stm., Braz. D9 76
Gusau, Nig. E13 64
Gus'-Chrustal'nyj, U.S.S.R. F23 26
Gusev, U.S.S.R. G5 26
Gusevskij, U.S.S.R. F23 26
Gushanzi, China C8 32
Gushi, China C4 34
Gushikawa, Japan U2 37b
Gusino, U.S.S.R. G14 26
Gusinoozersk, U.S.S.R. G13 24
Guspini, Italy J3 18
Gustavus, Ak., U.S. D12 109
Gustine, Ca., U.S. D3 112
Güstrow, Ger. B12 10
Gus'-Železnyj, U.S.S.R. F24 26
Gütersloh, Ger. D8 10
Guthrie, Ky., U.S. D2 124
Guthrie, Ok., U.S. B4 143
Guthrie, W.V., U.S. m12 155
Guthrie, co., Ia., U.S. C3 122
Guthrie Center, Ia., U.S. C3 122
Gutian, China I7 34
Gutiérrez, Bol. H10 82
Gutiérrez Zamora, Mex. G11 90
Guttenberg, Ia., U.S. B6 122
Guttenberg, N.J., U.S. h8 137
Gutu, Zimb. B10 66
Gu Vo, Az., U.S. E3 110
Guwāhāti, India G14 44
Guxian, China F9 32
Guxiansi, China C5 34
Guy, Ar., U.S. B3 111
Guyana, ctry., S.A. B7 76
Guyandotte, stm., W.V., U.S. C2 155
Guyandotte Mountain, mtn., W.V., U.S. n12 155
Guyi, China J7 34
Guymon, Ok., U.S. e9 143
Guyot, Mount, mtn., U.S. D10 149
Guyra, Austl. H9 70
Guys, Tn., U.S. B3 149
Guysborough, N.S., Can. D8 101
Guyton, Ga., U.S. D5 117
Guyuan, China D8 30
Guzar, U.S.S.R. J11 22
Guzhu, China I5 34
Guzmán, Mex. B6 90
Guzmán, Laguna, l., Mex. B6 90
Gvardejsk, U.S.S.R. G4 26
Gvozdec, U.S.S.R. A9 20
Gwa, Burma F3 40
Gwadabawa, Nig. E12 64
Gwādar, Pak. I17 48
Gwai, Zimb. B8 66
Gwāl Haidarzai, Pak. E3 44
Gwalior, India G8 44
Gwanda, Zimb. C9 66
Gwandu, Nig. E12 64
Gwātar Bay, b., Asia I16 48
Gwent, co., Wales, U.K. J11 8
Gweru, Zimb. B9 66
Gweta, Bots. C7 66
Gwinhurst, De., U.S. h8 115
Gwinn, Mi., U.S. B3 129
Gwinner, N.D., U.S. C8 141
Gwinnett, co., Ga., U.S. C2 117
Gwydyr Bay, b., Ak., U.S. A10 109
Gwynedd, U.S. H9 8
Gwynedd, co., Wales, U.K. H9 8
Gwynn, Va., U.S. C6 153
Gwynne, Alta., Can. C4 98
Gwynneville, In., U.S. E6 121
Gwynns Falls, stm., Md., U.S. g10 127
Gy, Fr. E12 14
Gyangzê, China F4 30
Gyaring Co, l., China E13 44
Gyaring Hu, l., China E6 30
Gydanskaja guba, b., U.S.S.R. C13 22
Gydanskij poluostrov, pen., U.S.S.R. C13 22
Gyirong, China F11 44
Gympie, Austl. F10 70
Gyobingauk, Burma E3 40
Gyoma, Hung. I20 10
Gyöngyös, Hung. H19 10
Győr, Hung. H17 10
Győr-Sopron, co., Hung. H17 10
Gypsum, Co., U.S. B4 113
Gypsum, Ks., U.S. D6 123
Gypsum Point, c., N.W. Ter., Can. D10 96
Gypsumville, Man., Can. D2 100
Gyula, Hung. I21 10

H

Haag in Oberbayern, Ger. G12 10
Haakon, co., S.D., U.S. C4 148
Haalenberg, Nmb. F2 66
Haaltert, Bel. G5 12
Haapajärvi, Fin. J19 6
Haapamäki, Fin. J19 6
Haapsalu, U.S.S.R. C6 26
Ha'Arava (Wādī al-Jayb), val., Asia H4 50
Ha'Arava (Wādī al-'Arabah), val., Asia G4 50
Haarlem, Neth. D6 12
Habarūt, Yemen F8 47
Habbān, Yemen G5 47
Habbūsh, Leb. B4 50
Habermehl Peak, mtn., Ant. C3 73
Habersham, co., Ga., U.S. B3 117
Habiganj, Bngl. H14 44
Habomai-shotō see Malaja Kuril'skaja Gr'ada, is., U.S.S.R. D21 36a
Hachijō-jima, i., Japan E14 30
Hachinohe, Japan G16 36
Hachiōji, Japan L14 36
Hacienda Miravalles, C.R. G9 92
Hacienda Murciélago, C.R. G9 92
Hackberry, La., U.S. E2 125
Hackberry Creek, stm., Ks., U.S. D3 123
Hackensack, N.J., U.S. B4 137
Hackensack, stm., N.J., U.S. h8 137
Hacker Valley, W.V., U.S. C4 155
Hackett, Ar., U.S. B1 111
Hackettstown, N.J., U.S. B3 137
Hackleburg, Al., U.S. A2 108
Hack Point, Md., U.S. B6 127
Hadalīya, Sud. I9 60
Hadar, Ne., U.S. B8 134
Hadd, Ra's al-, c., Oman C11 47
Haddam, Ct., U.S. D5 114
Haddam, Ks., U.S. C6 123
Haddington, Scot., U.K. F11 8
Haddix, Ky., U.S. C6 124
Haddock, Ga., U.S. C3 117
Haddonfield, N.J., U.S. D2 137
Haddon Heights, N.J., U.S. D2 137
Hadejia, Nig. E14 64
Hadejia, stm., Nig. E14 64
Hadera, Isr. D3 50
Hadera, stm., Asia D3 50
Hadley, Ma., U.S. B2 128
Hadley, N.Y., U.S. B7 139
Hadley Bay, b., N.W. Ter., Can. B11 96
Hadley Lake, l., Me., U.S. D5 126
Hadlock, Wa., U.S. A3 154
Hadlyme, Ct., U.S. D6 114
Ha Dong, Viet. D8 40
Hadramawt, reg., Yemen G6 47
Haeju, N. Kor. E13 32
Haenam, S. Kor. I14 32
Hafford, Sask., Can. E2 105
Haffouz, Tun. N4 18
Hafīrat al-'Ayda, Sau. Ar. H5 48
Hafnarfjördur, Ice. B3 6a
Haft Gel, Iran F10 48
Hafun, Ras, c., Som. F11 56
Hagan, Ga., U.S. D5 117
Hagarville, Ar., U.S. B2 111
Hagemeister Island, i., Ak., U.S. D7 109
Hagen, Ger. D7 10
Hagensborg, B.C., Can. C4 99
Hagere Hiywet, Eth. M9 60
Hagere Selam, Eth. N10 60
Hagerman, Id., U.S. G4 119
Hagerman, N.M., U.S. D5 138
Hagerstown, In., U.S. E7 121
Hagerstown, Md., U.S. A2 127
Hagetmau, Fr. I6 14
Haggin, Mount, mtn., Mt., U.S. D3 133
Ha Giang, Viet. C8 40
Hagondange, Fr. C13 14
Hague, Sask., Can. E2 105
Hague, N.D., U.S. C6 141
Hague, Cap de la, c., Fr. C5 14
Haguenau, Fr. D14 14
Hagues Peak, mtn., Co., U.S. A5 113
Ha90 Ha90, Baie des, b., Que., Can. C2 102
Hahaïa, Com. K15 67a
Hahira, Ga., U.S. F3 117
Hahnville, La., U.S. E5 125
Haian Shanmo, mts., Tai. L10 34
Haicheng, China C10 32
Haïdra, Tun. N3 18
Hai Duong, Viet. D9 40
Haifa see Hefa, Isr. C4 50
Haifeng, China M4 34
Haig, Austl. F5 68
Haigler, Ne., U.S. D4 134
Hailar (Leizhou), China D11 40
Haikou, China D11 40
Haiku, Hi., U.S. C5 118
Hā'il, Sau. Ar. H6 48
Hailākāndi, India H15 44
Hailar, China B10 30
Hailar, stm., China B11 30
Hailey, Id., U.S. F4 119
Haileybury, Ont., Can. p20 103
Haileyville, Ok., U.S. C6 143
Hailong (Meihekou), China A13 32
Hailun, China B12 30
Haimen, China G10 34
Haimen, China L5 34
Hainan, prov., China H8 30
Hainan Dao, i., China E10 40
Hainaut, prov., Bel. G4 12
Hainaut, hist. reg., Eur. H4 12
Haines, Ak., U.S. D12 109
Haines, Or., U.S. C9 144
Haines City, Fl., U.S. D5 116
Haines Falls, N.Y., U.S. C6 139
Haines Junction, Yukon, Can. D5 96
Hainesport, N.J., U.S. D3 137
Hainfeld, Aus. G15 10
Hai Phong, Viet. D9 40
Hairy Hill, Alta., Can. C5 98
Haiti (Haïti), ctry., N.A. E8 94
Haitou, China I7 32
Haiyaopu, China A6 40
Haizhou, China A8 34
Hajdú-Bihar, co., Hung. H21 10
Hajdúböszörmény, Hung. H21 10
Hajdúnánás, Hung. H21 10
Hajeb el Ayoun, Tun. N4 18
Haji Langar, China C8 44
Hājīpur, India H11 44
Hajjah, Yemen G3 47
Hajnówka, Pol. C23 10
Hakalau, Hi., U.S. D6 118
Hakīm, Abyār al-, well, Libya B2 60
Hakkâri, Tur. C7 48
Hakodate, Japan F15 36a
Hakui, Japan K11 36
Halab (Aleppo), Syria C4 48
Halabjah, Iraq D8 48
Halachó, Mex. G14 90
Halā'ib, Egypt F9 60
Halaula, Hi., U.S. C6 118
Halawa, Cape, c., Hi., U.S. B5 118
Halawa Heights, Hi., U.S. g10 118
Halawotelake, China B14 44
Halberstadt, Ger. D11 10
Halbrite, Sask., Can. H4 105
Halbur, Ia., U.S. C3 122
Haldeman, Ky., U.S. B6 124
Haldimand, Ont., Can. E5 103
Haldwāni, India F8 44
Hale, Mi., U.S. D7 129
Hale, Mo., U.S. B4 132
Hale, co., Al., U.S. C2 108
Hale, co., Tx., U.S. B2 150
Haleakala Crater, crat., Hi., U.S. C5 118
Haleakala National Park, Hi., U.S. C6 118
Hale Center, Tx., U.S. B2 150
Haleiwa, Hi., U.S. B3 118
Hales Corners, Wi., U.S. n11 156
Halethorpe, Md., U.S. B4 127
Haleyville, Al., U.S. A2 108
Half Moon Bay, Ca., U.S. k8 112
Halfway, Md., U.S. A2 127
Half Way, Mo., U.S. D4 132
Halfway, Or., U.S. C9 144
Haliburton, Ont., Can. B6 103
Halibut Point, c., Ma., U.S. A6 128
Halifax, Austl. B7 70
Halifax, N.S., Can. E6 101
Halifax, Ma., U.S. C6 128
Halifax, N.C., U.S. A5 140
Halifax, Pa., U.S. F8 145
Halifax, Va., U.S. D4 153
Halifax, co., N.C., U.S. A5 140
Halifax, co., Va., U.S. D4 153
Halifax Bay, b., Austl. B7 70
Haliimaile, Hi., U.S. C5 118
Halkirk, Alta., Can. C4 98
Hall, Mt., U.S. D3 133
Hall, co., Ga., U.S. B3 117
Hall, co., Ne., U.S. D7 134
Hall, co., Tx., U.S. B2 150
Hallam, Ne., U.S. D9 134
Hallam Peak, mtn., B.C., Can. C8 99
Hallandale, Fl., U.S. G6 116
Hallands Län, co., Swe. M13 6
Halla-san, mtn., S. Kor. E12 30
Halle (Hal), Bel. G5 12
Halle, Ger. D11 10
Hallein, Aus. H13 10
Hallettsville, Tx., U.S. E4 150
Halley, Ar., U.S. D4 111
Halliday, N.D., U.S. B3 141
Hallie, Wi., U.S. D2 156
Hall in Tirol, Aus. H11 10
Hall Island, i., Ak., U.S. C5 109
Hall Meadow Brook, stm., Ct., U.S. B3 114
Hall Meadow Brook Reservoir, res., Ct., U.S. B3 114
Hall Mountain, mtn., Wa., U.S. A8 154
Hällnäs, Swe. I16 6
Hallock, Mn., U.S. B2 130
Hallowell, Ks., U.S. E9 123
Hallowell, Me., U.S. D3 126
Hall Peninsula, pen., N.W. Ter., Can. D19 96
Halls, Tn., U.S. B2 149
Hallsberg, Swe. L14 6
Hallsboro, N.C., U.S. C4 140
Halls Creek, Austl. C5 68
Halls Creek, stm., Ut., U.S. F5 151
Halls Crossroads, Tn., U.S. m14 149
Halls Harbour, N.S., Can. D5 101
Halls Stream, stm., N.H., U.S. f7 136
Hallstavik, Swe. K16 6
Hallstead, Pa., U.S. C10 145
Hallsville, Mo., U.S. B5 132
Hallsville, Tx., U.S. C5 150
Hall Top, mtn., Tn., U.S. D10 149
Halltown, Mo., U.S. D4 132
Hallwood, Va., U.S. C7 153
Halma, Bel. H7 12
Halmahera, i., Indon. E8 38
Halmahera, Laut (Halmahera Sea), Indon. F8 38
Halmstad, Swe. M13 6
Halsell, Al., U.S. C1 108
Halsey, Ne., U.S. C5 134
Halsey, Or., U.S. C3 144
Hälsingborg see Helsingborg, Swe. M13 6
Halstad, Mn., U.S. C2 130
Halstead, Ks., U.S. E6 123
Haltern, Ger. D7 10
Haltiatunturi, mtn., Eur. G17 6
Halton Hills, Ont., Can. D5 103
Hamad, Sud. J7 60
Hamada, Japan M7 36
Hamadān, Iran D10 48
Hamāh, Syria D4 48
Hamale, Ghana F8 64
Hamamatsu, Japan M12 36
Hamar, Nor. K12 6
Hamātah, Jabal, mtn., Egypt I3 48
Hamblen, co., Tn., U.S. C10 149
Hamburg, Ger. B9 10
Hamburg, Ar., U.S. D4 111
Hamburg, Ia., U.S. D2 122
Hamburg, N.J., U.S. A3 137
Hamburg, N.Y., U.S. C2 139
Hamburg, Pa., U.S. E10 145
Hamburg Mountains, mts., N.J., U.S. A3 137
Hamdānah, Sau. Ar. E2 47
Hamden, Ct., U.S. D4 114
Hamden, Oh., U.S. C3 142
Hämeen lääni, prov., Fin. K19 6
Hämeenlinna, Fin. K19 6
Hamel, Mn., U.S. m11 130
Hameln, Ger. C9 10
Hamer, S.C., U.S. C9 147
Hamersley Range, mts., Austl. D3 68
Hamersley Range National Park, Austl. D3 68
Hamersville, Oh., U.S. D2 142
Hamhŭng, N. Kor. D15 32
Hami, China C5 30
Hamill, S.D., U.S. D6 148
Hamilton, Austl. K5 70
Hamilton, Ber. B12 88
Hamilton, Ont., Can. D5 103
Hamilton, N.Z. B5 72
Hamilton, Scot., U.K. F9 8
Hamilton, Al., U.S. A2 108
Hamilton, Ga., U.S. D2 117
Hamilton, Il., U.S. C2 120
Hamilton, In., U.S. A8 121
Hamilton, Ks., U.S. E7 123
Hamilton, Ma., U.S. A6 128
Hamilton, Mi., U.S. F4 129
Hamilton, Ms., U.S. B5 131
Hamilton, Mo., U.S. B3 132
Hamilton, Mt., U.S. D2 133
Hamilton, N.Y., U.S. C5 139
Hamilton, N.C., U.S. B5 140
Hamilton, Oh., U.S. C1 142
Hamilton, Tx., U.S. D3 150
Hamilton, Va., U.S. A5 153
Hamilton, Wa., U.S. A4 154
Hamilton, co., Fl., U.S. B3 116
Hamilton, co., Il., U.S. E5 120
Hamilton, co., In., U.S. D5 121
Hamilton, co., Ia., U.S. B4 122
Hamilton, co., Ks., U.S. E2 123
Hamilton, co., Ne., U.S. D7 134
Hamilton, co., N.Y., U.S. B6 139
Hamilton, co., Oh., U.S. C1 142
Hamilton, co., Tn., U.S. D8 149
Hamilton, co., Tx., U.S. D3 150
Hamilton, stm., Austl. D4 70
Hamilton, Lake, res., Ar., U.S. C2 111
Hamilton, Mount, mtn., Ak., U.S. C8 109
Hamilton, Mount, mtn., Ca., U.S. k9 112
Hamilton, Mount, mtn., Nv., U.S. D6 135
Hamilton City, Ca., U.S. C2 112
Hamilton Dome, Wy., U.S. C4 157
Hamilton Hotel, Austl. D4 70
Hamilton Inlet, b., Newf., Can. A2 102
Hamilton Mountain, mtn., N.Y., U.S. B6 139
Hamilton Reservoir, res., Ma., U.S. B3 128
Hamilton Sound, strt., Newf., Can. D4 102
Hamilton Square, N.J., U.S. C3 137
Hamina, Fin. K20 6
Hamiota, Man., Can. D1 100
Hāmir, Wādī, val., Asia F7 48
Hamīrpur, India H9 44
Hamler, Oh., U.S. A1 142
Hamlet, In., U.S. B4 121
Hamlet, N.C., U.S. C3 140
Hamlet, Mount, mtn., Ak., U.S. B6 109
Hamlin, Pa., U.S. D11 145
Hamlin, Tx., U.S. C2 150
Hamlin, W.V., U.S. C2 155
Hamlin, co., S.D., U.S. C8 148
Hamlin Lake, l., Mi., U.S. D4 129
Hamm, Ger. D7 10
Hammamet, Alg. N2 18
Hammamet, Tun. M5 18
Hammamet, Golfe de, b., Tun. M5 18
Hammam Lif, Tun. M5 18
Hammār, Hawr al-, l., Iraq F9 48
Hamme, Bel. F5 12
Hammerdal, Swe. J14 6
Hammerfest, Nor. F18 6
Hammett, Id., U.S. G3 119
Hammon, Ok., U.S. B2 143
Hammonasset, stm., Ct., U.S. D5 114
Hammonasset Point, c., Ct., U.S. E5 114
Hammond, Il., U.S. D5 120
Hammond, In., U.S. A2 121
Hammond, La., U.S. D5 125
Hammond, Or., U.S. A3 144
Hammond, Wi., U.S. D1 156
Hammond Bay, b., Mi., U.S. C6 129
Hammondsport, N.Y., U.S. C3 139
Hammonton, N.J., U.S. D3 137
Ham-Nord, Que., Can. D6 104
Hamoyet, Jabal, mtn., Afr. I10 60
Hampden, Newf., Can. D3 102
Hampden, Me., U.S. D4 126
Hampden, Ma., U.S. B3 128
Hampden, N.D., U.S. A7 141
Hampden, co., Ma., U.S. B2 128
Hampden Highlands, Me., U.S. D4 126
Hampshire, Il., U.S. A5 120
Hampshire, Tn., U.S. B4 149
Hampshire, co., Eng., U.K. J12 8
Hampshire, co., Ma., U.S. B2 128
Hampshire, co., W.V., U.S. B6 155
Hampstead, N.B., Can. D3 101
Hampstead, Md., U.S. A4 127
Hampstead, N.H., U.S. E4 136
Hampstead, N.C., U.S. C5 140
Hampton, N.B., Can. D4 101
Hampton, Ar., U.S. D3 111
Hampton, Ct., U.S. B7 114
Hampton, Ga., U.S. C2 117
Hampton, Ia., U.S. B4 122
Hampton, Mn., U.S. F5 130
Hampton, Ne., U.S. D8 134
Hampton, N.H., U.S. E5 136
Hampton, N.J., U.S. B3 137
Hampton, S.C., U.S. F5 147
Hampton, Tn., U.S. C11 149
Hampton, Va., U.S. C6 153
Hampton, co., S.C., U.S. F5 147
Hampton Bays, N.Y., U.S. n16 139
Hampton Beach, N.H., U.S. E5 136
Hampton Butte, mtn., Or., U.S. D6 144
Hampton Falls, N.H., U.S. E5 136
Hampton Roads, Va., U.S. k15 153
Hampton Roads Bridge-Tunnel, Va., U.S. k15 153
Hamra, As Saquia al, val., W. Sah. G4 62
Hams Fork, stm., Wy., U.S. E2 157
Hamtramck, Mi., U.S. p15 129
Hamyang, S. Kor. H15 32
Han, stm., China E9 30
Hana, Hi., U.S. C6 118
Hanahan, S.C., U.S. F7 147
Hanalei, Hi., U.S. A2 118
Hanalei Bay, b., Hi., U.S. A2 118
Hanamaki, Japan H16 36
Hanamaulu, Hi., U.S. B2 118
Hanapepe, Hi., U.S. B2 118
Hanau, Ger. E8 10
Hanbury, stm., N.W. Ter., Can. D11 96
Hanceville, B.C., Can. D6 99
Hanceville, Al., U.S. A3 108
Hancheng, China D9 30
Hancock, Ia., U.S. C2 122
Hancock, Me., U.S. D4 126
Hancock, Md., U.S. A1 127
Hancock, Mi., U.S. A2 129
Hancock, Mn., U.S. E3 130
Hancock, N.H., U.S. E3 136
Hancock, N.Y., U.S. D5 139
Hancock, Vt., U.S. D3 152
Hancock, Wi., U.S. D4 156
Hancock, co., Ga., U.S. C3 117
Hancock, co., Il., U.S. C2 120
Hancock, co., In., U.S. E6 121
Hancock, co., Ia., U.S. A4 122
Hancock, co., Ky., U.S. C3 124
Hancock, co., Me., U.S. D4 126
Hancock, co., Ms., U.S. E4 131
Hancock, co., Oh., U.S. A2 142
Hancock, co., Tn., U.S. C10 149
Hancock, co., W.V., U.S. A4 155
Hancock Pond, l., Me., U.S. E2 126
Hancocks Bridge, N.J., U.S. D2 137

Name | Map Ref. | Page

Hand, co., S.D., U.S. C6 148
Handa, Japan M11 36
Handa, Som. F11 56
Handan, China G2 32
Handley, W.V., U.S. m13 155
Handub, Sud. H9 60
HaNegev (Negev Desert), reg., Isr. G3 50
Hanford, Ca., U.S. D4 112
Han'gang, China I2 32
Han-gang, stm., Asia F14 32
Hangchow see Hangzhou, China E9 34
Hanggin Houqi, China C8 30
Hanggin Qi, China D8 30
Hangman Creek, stm., Wa., U.S. B8 154
Hangö (Hanko), Fin. L18 6
Hangu, China D5 32
Hangu, Pak. D4 44
Hangzhou (Hangchow), China E9 34
Hangzhou Wan (Hangchow Bay), b., China E10 34
Hani, Tur. B6 48
Ḥanīsh, is., Yemen H3 47
Ḥanita, Isr. B4 50
Hanjiang, China J8 34
Hankey, S. Afr. I7 66
Hankinson, N.D., U.S. C9 141
Hanko see Hangö, Fin. D12 4
Hankow see Wuhan, China E3 34
Hanksville, Ut., U.S. E5 151
Hanley, Sask., Can. F2 105
Hanna, Alta., Can. D5 98
Hanna, In., U.S. B4 121
Hanna, Wy., U.S. E6 157
Hanna City, Il., U.S. C4 120
Hannaford, N.D., U.S. B7 141
Hannahville Indian Reservation, Mi., U.S. C3 129
Hannibal, Mo., U.S. B6 132
Hannibal, Oh., U.S. C5 142
Hannover, Ger. C9 10
Ha Noi, Viet. D8 40
Hanover, Ont., Can. C3 103
Hanover, Ct., U.S. C7 114
Hanover, Il., U.S. A3 120
Hanover, In., U.S. G7 121
Hanover, Ks., U.S. C7 123
Hanover, Me., U.S. D2 126
Hanover, Ma., U.S. B6 128
Hanover, Mi., U.S. F6 129
Hanover, Mn., U.S. m11 130
Hanover, N.H., U.S. C2 136
Hanover, N.M., U.S. E1 138
Hanover, Oh., U.S. B3 142
Hanover, Pa., U.S. G8 145
Hanover, Va., U.S. C5 153
Hanover, co., Va., U.S. C5 153
Hanover Center, Ma., U.S. h12 128
Hanover see Hannover, Ger. C9 10
Hanover Park, Il., U.S. k8 120
Hansen, Id., U.S. G4 119
Hansford, co., Tx., U.S. A2 150
Hānsi, India F6 44
Hanska, Mn., U.S. F4 130
Hanson, Ky., U.S. C2 124
Hanson, Ma., U.S. B6 128
Hanson, co., S.D., U.S. D8 148
Hanston, Ks., U.S. D4 123
Hant's Harbour, Newf., Can. D5 102
Hantsport, N.S., Can. D5 101
Hanumangarh, India F6 44
Hanušovice, Czech. E16 10
Hanwood, Austl. J7 70
Hanzhong, China E8 30
Hanzhuang, China I5 32
Haohekou, China G1 34
Hāora, India I13 44
Hapeville, Ga., U.S. C2 117
Happy, Tx., U.S. B2 150
Happy Jack, Az., U.S. C4 110
Happy Valley, N.M., U.S. E5 138
Happy Valley-Goose Bay, Newf., Can. B1 102
Hāpur, India F7 44
Haquira, Peru F5 82
Ḥaraḍ, Sau. Ar. B6 47
Ḥarad, Jabal al-, mtn., Jord. I5 50
Harahan, La., U.S. k11 125
Haralson, co., Ga., U.S. C1 117
Harare (Salisbury), Zimb. A10 66
Ḥarash, Bi'r al-, well, Libya E2 60
Harbeson, De., U.S. F4 115
Harbin, China B12 30
Harbinger, N.C., U.S. A7 140
Harbor, Or., U.S. E2 144
Harbor Beach, Mi., U.S. E8 129
Harborcreek, Pa., U.S. B2 145
Harbor Springs, Mi., U.S. C6 129
Harborton, Va., U.S. C7 153
Harbour Breton, Newf., Can. E4 102
Harbour Grace, Newf., Can. E5 102
Harbour Mille, Newf., Can. E4 102
Harbourville, N.S., Can. D5 101
Harcourt, N.B., Can. C4 101
Harcourt, Ia., U.S. B3 122
Harcuvar Mountains, mts., Az., U.S. D2 110
Harda, India I7 44
Hardangerfjorden, Nor. K10 6
Hardaway, Al., U.S. C4 108
Hardee, co., Fl., U.S. E5 116
Hardeeville, S.C., U.S. G5 147
Hardeman, co., Tn., U.S. B2 149
Hardeman, co., Tx., U.S. B3 150
Harderwijk, Neth. D8 12
Hardesty, Ok., U.S. e9 143
Hardin, Il., U.S. D3 120
Hardin, Ky., U.S. f9 124
Hardin, Mo., U.S. B4 132
Hardin, Mt., U.S. E9 133
Hardin, co., Il., U.S. F5 120
Hardin, co., Ia., U.S. B4 122
Hardin, co., Ky., U.S. C4 124
Hardin, co., Oh., U.S. B2 142
Hardin, co., Tn., U.S. B3 149
Hardin, co., Tx., U.S. D5 150
Harding, S. Afr. H9 66
Harding, co., N.M., U.S. B5 138
Harding, co., S.D., U.S. B2 148
Harding, Lake, res., U.S. C4 108
Hardinsburg, In., U.S. H5 121
Hardinsburg, Ky., U.S. C3 124
Hardisty, Alta., Can. C5 98
Hardoi, India G9 44
Hardshell, Ky., U.S. C6 124
Hardtner, Ks., U.S. E5 123
Hardwick, Ga., U.S. C3 117
Hardwick, Vt., U.S. B4 152
Hardwicke, N.B., Can. B5 101
Hardwood Ridge, mtn., Pa., U.S. D11 145
Hardy, Ar., U.S. A4 111
Hardy, Ne., U.S. D8 134
Hardy, co., W.V., U.S. B6 155
Hardy Lake, res., In., U.S. G6 121
Hare Bay, Newf., Can. D4 102
Hare Bay, b., Newf., Can. C4 102
Harer, Eth. G9 56
Hareto, Eth. M9 60
Harford, co., Md., U.S. A5 127
Hargeysa, Som. G9 56
Harghita, co., Rom. C9 20
Hargill, Tx., U.S. F3 150
Har Hu, l., China D6 30
Hari, stm., Indon. F3 38
Haría, Spain N27 17b
Haridwār, India F8 44
Harihar, India E3 46
Haringvliet, strt., Neth. E5 12
Harīrūd (Tedžen), stm., Asia C16 48
Harkers Island, N.C., U.S. C6 140
Harlan, In., U.S. B8 121
Harlan, Ia., U.S. C2 122
Harlan, Ky., U.S. D6 124
Harlan, co., Ky., U.S. D6 124
Harlan, co., Ne., U.S. D6 134
Harlan County Lake, res., Ne., U.S. E6 134
Harlem, Fl., U.S. F6 116
Harlem, Ga., U.S. C4 117
Harlem, Mt., U.S. B8 133
Harleyville, S.C., U.S. E7 147
Harlingen, Neth. B7 12
Harlingen, Tx., U.S. F4 150
Harlowton, Mt., U.S. D7 133
Harman, Va., U.S. e9 153
Harmanli, Bul. H9 20
Harmon, co., Ok., U.S. C2 143
Harmon Creek, stm., W.V., U.S. f8 155
Harmony, In., U.S. E3 121
Harmony, Me., U.S. D3 126
Harmony, Mn., U.S. G6 130
Harmony, N.C., U.S. B2 140
Harmony, Pa., U.S. E1 145
Harmony, R.I., U.S. B3 146
Harmony Grove, Ar., U.S. D3 111
Harned, Ky., U.S. C3 124
Harnett, co., N.C., U.S. B4 140
Harney, co., Or., U.S. D7 144
Harney Lake, l., Fl., U.S. D5 116
Harney Lake, l., Or., U.S. D7 144
Harney Peak, mtn., S.D., U.S. D2 148
Härnösand, Swe. J15 6
Haro, Spain C9 16
Haro, Cabo, c., Mex. D4 90
Haro Strait, strt., Wa., U.S. A2 154
Harper, Lib. I6 64
Harper, Ks., U.S. E5 123
Harper, Wa., U.S. e10 154
Harper, co., Ks., U.S. E5 123
Harper, co., Ok., U.S. A2 143
Harper, Mount, mtn., Ak., U.S. C11 109
Harpers Ferry, Ia., U.S. A6 122
Harpers Ferry, W.V., U.S. B7 155
Harpers Ferry National Historical Park, W.V., U.S. B7 155
Harpersville, Al., U.S. B3 108
Harperville, Ms., U.S. C4 131
Harpeth, stm., Tn., U.S. A5 149
Harqin Qi (Jinshan), China B6 32
Harquahala Mountain, mtn., Az., U.S. D2 110
Harquahala Mountains, mts., Az., U.S. D2 110
Harrah, Ok., U.S. B4 143
Harrah, Wa., U.S. C5 154
Harrān al-'Awāmīd, Syria B7 50
Harrell, Ar., U.S. D3 111
Harricana, stm., Can. F17 96
Harricana, stm., Can. A11 106
Harriman, Tn., U.S. D9 149
Harriman Reservoir, res., Vt., U.S. F3 152
Harrington, De., U.S. E3 115
Harrington, Me., U.S. D5 126
Harrington, Wa., U.S. B7 154
Harrington Park, N.J., U.S. h9 137
Harrington Pond, l., Me., U.S. C3 126
Harris, Sask., Can. F2 105
Harris, Mn., U.S. E6 130
Harris, R.I., U.S. D3 146
Harris, co., Ga., U.S. D2 117
Harris, co., Tx., U.S. E5 150
Harris, Lake, l., Fl., U.S. D5 116
Harrisburg, Ar., U.S. B5 111
Harrisburg, Il., U.S. F5 120
Harrisburg, Mo., U.S. B5 132
Harrisburg, Or., U.S. C3 144
Harrisburg, Pa., U.S. F8 145
Harrisburg, S.D., U.S. D9 148
Harris Hill, hill, Ma., U.S. A3 128
Harrismith, S. Afr. G9 66
Harrison, Ar., U.S. A2 111
Harrison, Ga., U.S. D4 117
Harrison, Id., U.S. B2 119
Harrison, Il., U.S. F4 120
Harrison, Me., U.S. D2 126
Harrison, Mi., U.S. D6 129
Harrison, Mt., U.S. E5 133
Harrison, Ne., U.S. B2 134
Harrison, N.J., U.S. k8 137
Harrison, N.Y., U.S. h13 139
Harrison, Oh., U.S. C1 142
Harrison, Tn., U.S. h11 149
Harrison, co., In., U.S. H5 121
Harrison, co., Ia., U.S. C2 122
Harrison, co., Ky., U.S. B5 124
Harrison, co., Ms., U.S. E4 131
Harrison, co., Mo., U.S. A3 132
Harrison, co., Oh., U.S. B4 142
Harrison, co., Tx., U.S. C5 150
Harrison, co., W.V., U.S. B4 155
Harrison, Cape, c., Newf., Can. g10 102
Harrison Bay, b., Ak., U.S. A9 109
Harrisonburg, La., U.S. C4 125
Harrisonburg, Va., U.S. B4 153
Harrison Hot Springs, B.C., Can. f14 99
Harrison Lake, l., B.C., Can. E7 99
Harrisonville, Mo., U.S. C3 132
Harriston, Ont., Can. D4 103
Harriston, Ms., U.S. D2 131
Harristown, Il., U.S. D4 120
Harrisville, Mi., U.S. D7 129
Harrisville, Ms., U.S. D3 131
Harrisville, N.H., U.S. E2 136
Harrisville, Pa., U.S. D1 145
Harrisville, R.I., U.S. B2 146
Harrisville, Ut., U.S. B4 151
Harrisville, W.V., U.S. B3 155
Harrod, Oh., U.S. B2 142
Harrodsburg, In., U.S. F4 121
Harrodsburg, Ky., U.S. C5 124
Harrods Creek, stm., Ky., U.S. g11 124
Harrogate, Eng., U.K. G12 8
Harrold, S.D., U.S. C6 148
Harrow, Ont., Can. E2 103
Harrowsmith, Ont., Can. C8 103
Harry S. Truman Reservoir, res., Mo., U.S. C4 132
Harry Strunk Lake, res., Ne., U.S. D5 134
Harsīn, Iran D9 48
Hart, Mi., U.S. E4 129
Hart, Tx., U.S. B1 150
Hart, co., Ga., U.S. B4 117
Hart, co., Ky., U.S. C4 124
Hart, Lake, l., Austl. H2 70
Hart, Lake, l., Fl., U.S. D5 116
Hartberg, Aus. H15 10
Hartford, Al., U.S. D4 108
Hartford, Ar., U.S. B1 111
Hartford, Ct., U.S. B5 114
Hartford, Il., U.S. E3 120
Hartford, Ia., U.S. C4 122
Hartford, Ks., U.S. D8 123
Hartford, Ky., U.S. C3 124
Hartford, Mi., U.S. F4 129
Hartford, S.D., U.S. D9 148
Hartford, Vt., U.S. D4 152
Hartford, W.V., U.S. C3 155
Hartford, Wi., U.S. E5 156
Hartford, co., Ct., U.S. B4 114
Hartford City, In., U.S. D7 121
Hartington, Ne., U.S. B8 134
Hart Lake, l., Or., U.S. E7 144
Hartland, N.B., Can. C2 101
Hartland, Me., U.S. D3 126
Hartland, Mi., U.S. F7 129
Hartland, Mn., U.S. G5 130
Hartland, Vt., U.S. D4 152
Hartland, Wi., U.S. E5 156
Hartland Four Corners, Vt., U.S. D4 152
Hartlepool, Eng., U.K. G12 8
Hartley, Ia., U.S. A2 122
Hartley, co., Tx., U.S. B1 150
Hartly, De., U.S. D3 115
Hartman, Ar., U.S. B2 111
Hartman, Co., U.S. C8 113
Hart Mountain, mtn., Man., Can. C1 100
Hartney, Man., Can. E1 100
Harts, stm., Afr. G7 66
Hartsburg, Il., U.S. C4 120
Hartselle, Al., U.S. A3 108
Hartsfield, Ga., U.S. E3 117
Hartshorn, Mo., U.S. D6 132
Hartshorne, Ok., U.S. C6 143
Hartsville, In., U.S. F6 121
Hartsville, S.C., U.S. C7 147
Hartsville, Tn., U.S. A5 149
Hartville, Mo., U.S. D5 132
Hartville, Oh., U.S. B4 142
Hartville, Wy., U.S. D8 157
Hartwell, Ga., U.S. B4 117
Hartwell Lake, res., U.S. B1 147
Harvard, Il., U.S. A5 120
Harvard, Ma., U.S. B4 128
Harvard, Ne., U.S. D7 134
Harvard, Mount, mtn., Co., U.S. C4 113
Harvel, Il., U.S. D4 120
Harvest, Al., U.S. A3 108
Harvey, N.B., Can. D5 101
Harvey, N.B., Can. D3 101
Harvey, Il., U.S. B6 120
Harvey, Ia., U.S. C5 122
Harvey, La., U.S. E5 125
Harvey, Mi., U.S. B3 129
Harvey, N.D., U.S. B6 141
Harvey, W.V., U.S. n13 155
Harvey, co., Ks., U.S. D6 123
Harvey Lake, res., Pa., U.S. m16 145
Harvey Mountain, mtn., U.S. B1 128
Harveys Creek, stm., Pa., U.S. n16 145
Harveyville, Ks., U.S. D8 123
Harviell, Mo., U.S. E7 132
Harwich, Eng., U.K. J15 8
Harwich, Ma., U.S. C7 128
Harwich Port, Ma., U.S. C7 128
Harwinton, Ct., U.S. B3 114
Harwood, Ont., Can. C6 103
Harwood, Ma., U.S. f9 128
Harwood, N.D., U.S. C9 141
Haryāna, state, India F7 44
Harz, mts., Eur. D10 10
Ḥaṣā, Bi'r al-, well, Egypt J3 48
Ḥasan Kīādeh, Iran C10 48
Ḥāṣbānī, Nahr al-, stm., Asia B5 50
Hasbrouck Heights, N.J., U.S. h8 137
Hasenkamp, Arg. F9 80
Hashā', Jabal al-, mtn., Yemen H4 47
Hāsilpur, Pak. F5 44
Haskell, Ar., U.S. C3 111
Haskell, Ok., U.S. B6 143
Haskell, Tx., U.S. C3 150
Haskell, co., Ks., U.S. E3 123
Haskell, co., Ok., U.S. B6 143
Haskell, co., Tx., U.S. C3 150
Haskins, Oh., U.S. A2 142
Haskovo, Bul. H9 20
Haslet, Tx., U.S. n9 150
Hassan, India F4 46
Hassayampa, stm., Az., U.S. D3 110
Hasselt, Bel. G7 12
Hassi Bel Guebbour, Alg. F14 62
Hassi el Ghella, Alg. J10 16
Hassi Mameche, Alg. J12 16
Hassi Messaoud, Alg. E13 62
Hassi Zehana, Alg. J11 16
Hässleholm, Swe. M13 6
Hastings, Ont., Can. C7 103
Hastings, N.Z. C6 72
Hastings, Eng., U.K. K14 8
Hastings, Fl., U.S. C5 116
Hastings, Mi., U.S. F5 129
Hastings, Mn., U.S. F6 130
Hastings, Ne., U.S. D7 134
Hastings, Pa., U.S. E4 145
Hastings-on-Hudson, N.Y., U.S. h13 139
Hasty, Co., U.S. C8 113
Hatch, N.M., U.S. E2 138
Hatchechubbee, Al., U.S. C4 108
Hatchet Creek, stm., Al., U.S. B3 108
Hatchet Lake, N.S., Can. E6 101
Hatchie, stm., Tn., U.S. B2 149
Hatchineha, Lake, l., Fl., U.S. D5 116
Hatch Wash, val., Ut., U.S. E6 151
Hat Creek, stm., S.D., U.S. E2 148
Hatfield, Ar., U.S. C1 111
Hatfield, In., U.S. I3 121
Hatfield, Ma., U.S. B2 128
Hatfield, Pa., U.S. F11 145
Hāthras, India G8 44
Ha Tien, Viet. I8 40
Ha Tinh, Viet. E8 40
Hatley, Ms., U.S. B5 131
Hat Mountain, mtn., Az., U.S. E3 110
Hato Mayor [del Rey], Dom. Rep. E10 94
Hatteras, N.C., U.S. B7 140
Hatteras, Cape, c., N.C., U.S. B7 140
Hatteras Inlet, b., N.C., U.S. B7 140
Hattiesburg, Ms., U.S. D4 131
Hattieville, Ar., U.S. B3 111
Hatton, Al., U.S. A2 108
Hatton, Ar., U.S. C1 111
Hatton, N.D., U.S. B8 141
Hatvan, Hung. H19 10
Hat Yai, Thai. K6 40
Haubstadt, In., U.S. H2 121
Haugan, Mt., U.S. C1 133
Hauge, Nor. L10 6
Haugen, Wi., U.S. C2 156
Haugesund, Nor. L9 6
Haughton, La., U.S. B2 125
Haugsdorf, Aus. G16 10
Haunstetten, Ger. G10 10
Hauraki Gulf, b., N.Z. B5 72
Hauser, Or., U.S. D2 144
Hauser Dam, Mt., U.S. D5 133
Haut, Isle au, i., Me., U.S. D4 126
Haut Atlas, mts., Mor. E7 62
Haute-Corse, dept., Fr. L24 15a
Haute-Garonne, dept., Fr. I8 14
Haute-Loire, dept., Fr. G10 14
Haute-Marne, dept., Fr. D12 14
Hautes-Alpes, dept., Fr. H13 14
Haute-Saône, dept., Fr. E13 14
Haute-Savoie, dept., Fr. F13 14
Hautes Fagnes, mts., Eur. E6 10
Hautes-Pyrénées, dept., Fr. I7 14
Haute-Vienne, dept., Fr. G8 14
Haut-Folin, mtn., Fr. E11 14
Hautmont, Fr. B10 14
Haut-Rhin, dept., Fr. E14 14
Hauula, Hi., U.S. B4 118
Havana, Ar., U.S. B2 111
Havana, Fl., U.S. B2 116
Havana, Il., U.S. C3 120
Havana, Ks., U.S. E8 123
Havana, N.D., U.S. D8 141
Havana see La Habana, Cuba C3 94
Havana Nakya, Az., U.S. E4 110
Havasu, Lake, res., U.S. C1 110
Havasupai Indian Reservation, Az., U.S. A3 110
Havelock, N.B., Can. D4 101
Havelock, Ont., Can. C7 103
Havelock, Ia., U.S. B3 122
Havelock, N.C., U.S. C6 140
Haven, Ks., U.S. E6 123
Havensville, Ks., U.S. C7 123
Haverford [Township], Pa., U.S. o20 145
Haverhill, Ma., U.S. A5 128
Haverhill, N.H., U.S. B2 136
Hāveri, India E3 46
Haverstraw, N.Y., U.S. D7 139
Haviland, Ks., U.S. E4 123
Havířov, Czech. F18 10
Havlíčkův Brod, Czech. F15 10
Havre, Mt., U.S. B7 133
Havre-Aubert, Que., Can. B8 101
Havre Boucher, N.S., Can. D8 101
Havre de Grace, Md., U.S. A5 127
Havre North, Mt., U.S. B7 133
Havsa, Tur. H10 20
Haw, stm., N.C., U.S. B3 140
Hawaii, co., Hi., U.S. D6 118
Hawaii, state, U.S. C5 118
Hawaii, i., Hi., U.S. D6 118
Hawaiian Islands, is., Hi., U.S. m14 118
Hawaiian Ridge F22 158
Hawaii Volcanoes National Park, Hi., U.S. D6 118
Hawarden, Sask., Can. F2 105
Hawarden, Ia., U.S. A1 122
Hawera, N.Z. C5 72
Hawesville, Ky., U.S. C3 124
Hawi, Hi., U.S. C6 118
Hawick, Scot., U.K. F11 8
Hawke, Cape, c., Austl. I10 70
Hawke Bay, b., N.Z. C6 72
Hawker, Austl. H3 70
Hawkes, Mount, mtn., Ant. D1 73
Hawkesbury, Ont., Can. B10 103
Hawkesbury Island, i., B.C., Can. C3 99
Hawkeye, Ia., U.S. B6 122
Hawkins, Wi., U.S. C3 156
Hawkins, co., Tn., U.S. C11 149
Hawkinsville, Ga., U.S. D3 117
Haw Knob, mtn., U.S. D9 149
Hawk Point, Mo., U.S. C6 132
Hawk Run, Pa., U.S. E5 145
Hawksbill, mtn., Va., U.S. B4 153
Hawks Nest Point, c., Bah. B7 94
Hawk Springs, Wy., U.S. E8 157
Hawley, Mn., U.S. D2 130
Hawley, Pa., U.S. D11 145
Hawley, Tx., U.S. C3 150
Hawleyville, Ct., U.S. D2 114
Haworth, N.J., U.S. h9 137
Haworth, Ok., U.S. D7 143
Haw River, N.C., U.S. A3 140
Hawthorne, Ca., U.S. n12 112
Hawthorne, Fl., U.S. C4 116
Hawthorne, Nv., U.S. E3 135
Hawthorne, N.J., U.S. B4 137
Hawwārah, Jord. C5 50
Hawza, W. Sah. G5 62
Hawzen, Eth. K10 60
Haxtun, Co., U.S. A8 113
Hay, Austl. J6 70
Hay, stm., Austl. D2 70
Hay, stm., Can. E9 96
Hay, Cape, c., N.W. Ter., Can. B10 96
Hayange, Fr. C13 14
Haybān, Sud. L6 60
Hayden, Al., U.S. B3 108
Hayden, Az., U.S. E5 110
Hayden, Co., U.S. A3 113
Hayden, In., U.S. G6 121
Hayden Lake, l., Id., U.S. B2 119
Haydenville, Oh., U.S. C3 142
Hayes, La., U.S. D3 125
Hayes, co., Ne., U.S. D4 134
Hayes, stm., Man., Can. B5 100
Hayes, Mount, mtn., Ak., U.S. C10 109
Hayes Center, Ne., U.S. D4 134
Hayfield, Mn., U.S. G6 130
Hayford Peak, mtn., Nv., U.S. G6 135
Hayfork, Ca., U.S. B2 112
Haykota, Eth. J9 60
Hay Lakes, Alta., Can. C4 98
Haymana, Tur. B2 48
Haymarket, Va., U.S. B5 153
Haymock Lake, l., Me., U.S. B3 126
Haynes, Alta., Can. C4 98
Haynes, Ar., U.S. C5 111
Haynesville, La., U.S. B2 125
Hayneville, Al., U.S. C3 108
Hay River, N.W. Ter., Can. D9 96
Hays, Ks., U.S. D4 123
Hays, Mt., U.S. C8 133
Hays, N.C., U.S. A1 140
Hays, co., Tx., U.S. D3 150
Hays Canyon Peak, mtn., Nv., U.S. B2 135
Haysi, Va., U.S. e9 153
Hay Springs, Ne., U.S. B3 134
Haystack Mountain, mtn., Ct., U.S. B3 114
Haystack Mountain, mtn., Nv., U.S. B6 135
Haysville, In., U.S. H4 121
Haysville, Ks., U.S. g12 123
Hayter, Alta., Can. C5 98
Hayti, Mo., U.S. E8 132
Hayti, S.D., U.S. C8 148
Hayti Heights, Mo., U.S. E8 132
Hayward, Ca., U.S. h8 112
Hayward, Wi., U.S. B2 156
Haywood, Man., Can. E2 100
Haywood, Ok., U.S. C6 143
Haywood, co., N.C., U.S. f9 140
Haywood, co., Tn., U.S. B2 149
Hazard, Ky., U.S. C6 124
Hazardville, Ct., U.S. B5 114
Hazārībāg, India I11 44
Hazebrouck, Fr. B9 14
Hazel, Ky., U.S. f9 124
Hazel, S.D., U.S. C8 148
Hazel Crest, Il., U.S. k9 120
Hazel Dell, Wa., U.S. D3 154
Hazel Green, Al., U.S. A3 108
Hazel Green, Ky., U.S. C6 124
Hazel Green, Wi., U.S. F3 156
Hazelhurst, Wi., U.S. C4 156
Hazel Park, Mi., U.S. p15 129
Hazelton, B.C., Can. B4 99
Hazelton, Id., U.S. G4 119
Hazelton, Ks., U.S. E5 123
Hazelton, N.D., U.S. C5 141
Hazelton Pyramid, mtn., Wy., U.S. B5 157
Hazelwood, N.C., U.S. f9 140
Hazen, Ar., U.S. C4 111
Hazen, N.D., U.S. B4 141
Hazen Bay, b., Ak., U.S. C6 109
Hazenmore, Sask., Can. H2 105
Hazlehurst, Ga., U.S. E4 117
Hazlehurst, Ms., U.S. D3 131
Hazlet, Sask., Can. G1 105
Hazlet, N.J., U.S. C4 137
Hazleton, In., U.S. H2 121
Hazleton, Ia., U.S. B6 122
Hazleton, Pa., U.S. E10 145
Ḥaẓor HaGelilit, Isr. C5 50
Head Harbor Island, i., Me., U.S. D5 126
Headland, Al., U.S. D4 108
Headley, Mount, mtn., Mt., U.S. C1 133
Head of Island, La., U.S. h10 125
Headquarters, Id., U.S. C3 119
Healdsburg, Ca., U.S. C2 112
Healdton, Ok., U.S. C4 143
Healesville, Austl. K6 70
Healy, Ak., U.S. C10 109
Healy, Ks., U.S. D3 123
Heany Junction, Zimb. C9 66
Heard, co., Ga., U.S. C1 117
Heard Island, i., Austl. N11 158
Hearne, Tx., U.S. D4 150
Hearst, Ont., Can. o19 103
Hearst Island, i., Ant. B12 73
Heart, stm., Alta., Can. B2 98
Heart, stm., N.D., U.S. C3 141
Heart Butte, Mt., U.S. B4 133
Heart Butte Dam, N.D., U.S. C4 141
Hearthstone Mountain, mtn., Md., U.S. A2 127
Heart Lake, l., Alta., Can. B5 98
Heart Lake, l., Wy., U.S. B2 157
Heart's Content, Newf., Can. E5 102
Heath, Al., U.S. D3 108
Heath, Oh., U.S. B3 142
Heath, stm., S.A. E7 82
Heathcote, Austl. K6 70
Heatherton, N.S., Can. D8 101
Heath Springs, S.C., U.S. B6 147
Heathsville, Va., U.S. C6 153
Heavener, Ok., U.S. C7 143
Hebbronville, Tx., U.S. F3 150
Hebei (Hopeh), prov., China D10 30
Heber, Az., U.S. C5 110
Heber City, Ut., U.S. C4 151
Heber Springs, Ar., U.S. B3 111
Hébertville, Que., Can. A6 104
Hebgen Lake, res., Mt., U.S. F5 133
Hebi, China H2 32
Hebo, Or., U.S. B3 144
Hebrides, is., Scot., U.K. D6 4
Hebron, N.S., Can. F3 101
Hebron, Ct., U.S. C6 114
Hebron, Il., U.S. A5 120
Hebron, In., U.S. B3 121
Hebron, Ky., U.S. h13 124
Hebron, Me., U.S. D2 126
Hebron, Md., U.S. D6 127
Hebron, Ne., U.S. D8 134
Hebron, N.H., U.S. C3 136
Hebron, N.D., U.S. C3 141
Hebron, Oh., U.S. C3 142
Hebron see Al-Khalīl, Isr. Occ. E4 50
Hebu, China H4 34
Hecate Strait, strt., B.C., Can. C2 99
Hecelchakán, Mex. G14 90
Heceta Island, i., Ak., U.S. n23 109
Hechi, China B10 40
Hechingen, Ger. G8 10
Hechuan, China E8 30
Hecker, Il., U.S. E4 120
Hecla, S.D., U.S. B7 148
Hecla Island, i., Man., Can. D3 100
Hectanooga, N.S., Can. E3 101
Hector, Ar., U.S. B3 111
Hector, Mn., U.S. F4 130
Hédé, Fr. D5 14
He Devil, mtn., Id., U.S. D2 119
Hedgehog Hill, hill, Ct., U.S. B7 114
Hedges, Fl., U.S. k8 116
Hedgesville, W.V., U.S. B7 155
Hedian, China C3 34
Hedley, B.C., Can. E7 99
Hedmark, co., Nor. K12 6
Hedrick, Ia., U.S. C5 122
Heerenveen, Neth. C8 12
Heerlen, Neth. G8 12
Ḥefa (Haifa), Isr. C4 50
Hefei, China D6 34
Heflin, Al., U.S. B4 108
Heflin, La., U.S. B2 125
Hefner, Lake, res., Ok., U.S. B4 143
Hegang, China B13 30
Hegins, Pa., U.S. E9 145
Heho, Burma D4 40
Heichengzi, China A9 32
Heide, Ger. A9 10
Heidelberg, Ger. F8 10
Heidelberg, S. Afr. J5 66
Heidelberg, S. Afr. F9 66
Heidelberg, Ms., U.S. D5 131
Heidenheim, Ger. F10 10
Heidenreichstein, Aus. G15 10
Heidrick, Ky., U.S. D6 124
Heilbron, S. Afr. F8 66
Heilbronn, Ger. F9 10
Heiligenstadt, Ger. D10 10
Heilin, China H6 32
Heilong (Amur), stm., Asia A12 30
Heilongjiang (Heilungkiang), prov., China B12 30
Heilwood, Pa., U.S. E4 145
Heimaey, i., Ice. C3 6a
Heimdal, N.D., U.S. B6 141
Heinsburg, Alta., Can. C5 98
Heinkut, Burma H16 44
Heishan, China B10 32
Heishantou, China A13 32
Heiskell, Tn., U.S. m13 149
Heisler, Alta., Can. C4 98
Heizer, Ks., U.S. D5 123
Hejian, China E4 32
Hekla, vol., Ice. C4 6a
Hekou, China C7 40
Hel, Pol. A18 10
Helen, Mount, mtn., Austl. C4 70
Helena, Al., U.S. B3 108
Helena, Ar., U.S. C5 111
Helena, Ga., U.S. D4 117
Helena, Mt., U.S. D4 133
Helena, Ok., U.S. A3 143
Helensburgh, Scot., U.K. E9 8
Helenwood, Tn., U.S. C9 149
Helgoland, i., Ger. A7 10
Helgoländer Bucht, b., Ger. A8 10
Heliuji, China B5 34
Hellam, Pa., U.S. G8 145
Hellertown, Pa., U.S. E11 145
Hellín, Spain G10 16
Hells Canyon, val., U.S. B10 144
Hells Canyon National Recreation Area, U.S. B10 144
Hell-Ville, Madag. N23 67b
Helmand, stm., Asia D1 44
Helmetta, N.J., U.S. C4 137
Helmond, Neth. F8 12
Helmsburg, In., U.S. F5 121
Helmstedt, Ger. C11 10
Helmville, Mt., U.S. D4 133
Helotes, Tx., U.S. h7 150
Helper, Ut., U.S. D5 151
Helsingborg, Swe. M13 6
Helsingfors see Helsinki, Fin. K19 6
Helsingør (Elsinore), Den. M13 6
Helsinki (Helsingfors), Fin. K19 6
Helska, Mierzeja, spit, Pol. A18 10
Heltonville, In., U.S. G5 121
Helvecia, Arg. F8 80
Hematite, Mo., U.S. C7 132
Hemau, Ger. F11 10

Name Map Ref. Page

Hemel Hempstead, Eng., U.K. J13 8
Hemet, Ca., U.S. F5 112
Hemford, N.S., Can. E5 101
Hemingford, Ne., U.S. B2 134
Hemingway, S.C., U.S. D9 147
Hemlock, In., U.S. D5 121
Hemlock, Mi., U.S. E6 129
Hemlock Reservoir, res., Ct., U.S. E2 114
Hemmingford, Que., Can. D4 104
Hemphill, Tx., U.S. D6 150
Hemphill, co., Tx., U.S. B2 150
Hempstead, N.Y., U.S. n15 139
Hempstead, Tx., U.S. D4 150
Hempstead, co., Ar., U.S. D2 111
Hemujing, China F3 32
Henagar, Al., U.S. A4 108
Henan (Honan), prov., China E9 30
Henderson, Arg. I8 80
Henderson, Co., U.S. B6 113
Henderson, Ia., U.S. C2 122
Henderson, Ky., U.S. C2 124
Henderson, La., U.S. D4 125
Henderson, Mn., U.S. F5 130
Henderson, Ne., U.S. D8 134
Henderson, Nv., U.S. G7 135
Henderson, N.C., U.S. A4 140
Henderson, Tn., U.S. B3 149
Henderson, Tx., U.S. C5 150
Henderson, W.V., U.S. C2 155
Henderson, co., Il., U.S. C3 120
Henderson, co., Ky., U.S. C2 124
Henderson, co., N.C., U.S. f10 140
Henderson, co., Tn., U.S. B3 149
Henderson, co., Tx., U.S. C5 150
Henderson Island, i., Pit. K27 158
Henderson's Point, Ms., U.S. g7 131
Hendersonville, N.C., U.S. f10 140
Hendersonville, Tn., U.S. A5 149
Hendījān, Iran F10 48
Hendon, Sask., Can. E4 105
Hendricks, Mn., U.S. F2 130
Hendricks, W.V., U.S. B5 155
Hendricks, co., In., U.S. E4 121
Hendrum, Mn., U.S. C2 130
Hendry, co., Fl., U.S. F5 116
Henefer, Ut., U.S. C4 151
Hengdaohe, China A11 32
Hengelo, Neth. D10 12
Henggang, China F4 34
Hengshan, China D8 30
Hengshan, China H1 34
Hengshui, China F3 32
Hengxian, China C10 40
Hengyang, China F9 30
Henlawson, W.V., U.S. n12 155
Henlopen, Cape, c., De., U.S. E5 115
Henlopen Acres, De., U.S. F5 115
Hennaya, Alg. K10 16
Hennebont, Fr. E3 14
Hennef, Ger. E7 10
Hennenman, S. Afr. F8 66
Hennepin, Il., U.S. B4 120
Hennepin, Ok., U.S. C4 143
Hennepin, co., Mn., U.S. E5 130
Hennessey, Ok., U.S. A4 143
Hennigsdorf, Ger. C13 10
Henniker, N.H., U.S. D3 136
Henning, Il., U.S. C6 120
Henning, Mn., U.S. D3 130
Henning, Tn., U.S. B2 149
Henribourg, Sask., Can. D3 105
Henri-Chapelle (Hendrik-Kapelle), Bel. G8 12
Henrico, co., Va., U.S. C5 153
Henrietta, Mo., U.S. B4 132
Henrietta, N.Y., U.S. B3 139
Henrietta, N.C., U.S. B1 140
Henrietta, Tx., U.S. C3 150
Henrietta Maria, Cape, c., Ont., Can. n19 103
Henry, Il., U.S. B4 120
Henry, Ne., U.S. C1 134
Henry, S.D., U.S. C8 148
Henry, Tn., U.S. A3 149
Henry, Va., U.S. D3 153
Henry, co., Al., U.S. D4 108
Henry, co., Ga., U.S. C2 117
Henry, co., Il., U.S. B3 120
Henry, co., In., U.S. E7 121
Henry, co., Ia., U.S. C6 122
Henry, co., Ky., U.S. B4 124
Henry, co., Mo., U.S. C4 132
Henry, co., Oh., U.S. A1 142
Henry, co., Tn., U.S. A3 149
Henry, co., Va., U.S. D3 153
Henry, Mount, mtn., Mt., U.S. B1 133
Henryetta, Ok., U.S. B6 143
Henry Kater, Cape, c., N.W. Ter., Can. C19 96
Henry Mountains, mts., Ut., U.S. E5 151
Henry Pittier, Parque Nacional, Ven. B9 84
Henrys Fork, stm., U.S. E2 157
Henryville, Que., Can. D4 104
Henryville, In., U.S. G6 121
Hensall, Ont., Can. D3 103
Hensley, Ar., U.S. C3 111
Henson Creek, stm., Md., U.S. f9 127
Hentiesbaai, Nmb. D2 66
Henty, Austl. J7 70
Henzada, Burma F3 40
Hepburn, Sask., Can. E2 105
Hephzibah, Ga., U.S. C4 117
Heping, China K3 34
Hepler, Ks., U.S. E9 123
Heppenheim, Ger. F8 10
Heppner, Or., U.S. B7 144
Hepu (Lianzhou), China D10 40
Hepworth, Ont., Can. C3 103
Heqiao, China D8 34
Herāt, Afg. D17 48
Hérault, dept., Fr. I10 14
Herbert, Sask., Can. G2 105
Herbert, stm., Austl. B6 70
Herberton, Austl. A6 70
Herbes, Isle aux, i., Al., U.S. E1 108
Herbignac, Fr. E4 14
Herceg-Novi, Yugo. G2 20
Herculaneum, Mo., U.S. C7 132
Hércules, Mex. C8 90
Heredia, C.R. G10 92
Heredia, prov., C.R. G10 92
Hereford, Az., U.S. F5 110
Hereford, Md., U.S. A4 127
Hereford, Tx., U.S. B1 150
Hereford and Worcester, co., Eng., U.K. I11 8
Hereford Inlet, b., N.J., U.S. E3 137
Herencia, Spain F8 16
Herentals, Bel. F6 12
Hereroland Oos, dept., Nmb. C5 66
Hereroland Wes, dept., Nmb. C4 66
Herford, Ger. C8 10
Hergla, Tun. M5 18
Herington, Ks., U.S. D7 123
Herisau, Switz. D11 13
Herkimer, Ks., U.S. C7 123
Herkimer, N.Y., U.S. B6 139
Herkimer, co., N.Y., U.S. B5 139
Herleshausen, Ger. D10 10
Herman, Mn., U.S. E2 130
Herman, Ne., U.S. C9 134
Hermann, Mo., U.S. C6 132
Hermano Peak, mtn., Co., U.S. D2 113
Hermansville, Mi., U.S. C3 129
Hermantown, Mn., U.S. D6 130
Hermanus, S. Afr. J4 66
Hermanville, Ms., U.S. D3 131
Herminie, Pa., U.S. F2 145
Hermiston, Or., U.S. B7 144
Hermitage, Newf., Can. E4 102
Hermitage, Ar., U.S. D3 111
Hermitage, La., U.S. D4 125
Hermitage, Mo., U.S. D4 132
Hermitage Bay, b., Newf., Can. E3 102
Hermon, Mount see Shaykh, Jabal ash-, mtn., Asia B5 50
Hermosa, S.D., U.S. D2 148
Hermosillo, Mex. C4 90
Hermoso, Cerro, mtn., Ec. H3 84
Hernád, stm., Eur. G21 10
Hernandarias, Para. C11 80
Hernandez, N.M., U.S. A3 138
Hernando, Arg. G7 80
Hernando, Fl., U.S. D4 116
Hernando, Ms., U.S. A4 131
Hernando, co., Fl., U.S. D4 116
Herndon, Ks., U.S. C3 123
Herndon, Ky., U.S. D2 124
Herndon, Va., U.S. B5 153
Herndon, W.V., U.S. D3 155
Herne, Ger. D7 10
Heroica Zitácuaro, Mex. H9 90
Heron, Mt., U.S. B1 133
Heron Bay, Al., U.S. E1 108
Heron Island, i., Austl. D9 70
Heron Lake, Mn., U.S. G3 130
Herradura, Arg. D9 80
Herreid, S.D., U.S. B5 148
Herrera, Arg. E7 80
Herrera, prov., Pan. I14 92
Herrick, Il., U.S. D5 120
Herrick, S.D., U.S. D6 148
Herrick Mountain, mtn., Vt., U.S. D2 152
Herrin, Il., U.S. F4 120
Herring Bay, b., Md., U.S. C4 127
Herring Cove, N.S., Can. E6 101
Herring Run, stm., Md., U.S. g11 127
Herrington Lake, res., Ky., U.S. C5 124
Herschel, Sask., Can. F1 105
Herschel Island, i., Yukon, Can. C5 96
Herscher, Il., U.S. B5 120
Hersey, Mi., U.S. E5 129
Hershey, Ne., U.S. C5 134
Hershey, Pa., U.S. F8 145
Herstal, Bel. G8 12
Hertford, N.C., U.S. A6 140
Hertford, co., N.C., U.S. A5 140
Hertfordshire, co., Eng., U.K. J13 8
Hervel d'Oeste, Braz. D13 80
Hervey Bay, b., Austl. E10 70
Herzberg, Ger. D13 10
Herzberg [am Harz], Ger. D10 10
Herzliyya, Isr. D3 50
Herzogenburg, Aus. G15 10
Hesdin, Fr. B9 14
Heshangqiao, China A2 34
Heshi, China J7 34
Heshuijian, China E5 34
Hesperia, Ca., U.S. E5 112
Hesperia, Mi., U.S. E4 129
Hesperus, Co., U.S. D2 113
Hesperus Mountain, mtn., Co., U.S. D2 113
Hessen, state, Ger. E9 10
Hessmer, La., U.S. C3 125
Hesston, Ks., U.S. D6 123
Hetang, China I8 34
Hetou, China K2 34
Hettick, Il., U.S. D3 120
Hettinger, N.D., U.S. D3 141
Hettinger, co., N.D., U.S. C3 141
Hettstedt, Ger. D11 10
Hetupu, China E5 34
Heves, Hung. H20 10
Heves, co., Hung. H20 10
Ḥevron, Naḥal, val., Asia F3 50
Hewitt, Mn., U.S. D3 130
Hewitt, Tx., U.S. D4 150
Hewitt, Wi., U.S. D3 156
Hexi, China K6 34
Hexian, China G9 30
Heyang, China H6 32
Heyburn, Id., U.S. G5 119
Heywood, Austl. L4 70
Heyworth, Il., U.S. C5 120
Heze (Caozhou), China H3 32
Hezhen, China F9 34
Hialeah, Fl., U.S. G6 116
Hiattville, Ks., U.S. E9 123
Hiawassee, Ga., U.S. B3 117
Hiawatha, Ia., U.S. B6 122
Hiawatha, Ks., U.S. C8 123
Hibbing, Mn., U.S. C6 130
Hibbs, Point, c., Austl. N6 70
Hibernia Reef, rf., Austl. B4 68
Hickam Air Force Base, mil., Hi., U.S. g10 118
Hickman, De., U.S. E3 115
Hickman, Ky., U.S. f8 124
Hickman, Ne., U.S. D9 134
Hickman, co., Ky., U.S. f8 124
Hickman, co., Tn., U.S. B4 149
Hickman's Harbour, Newf., Can. D5 102
Hickory, Ky., U.S. f9 124
Hickory, Ms., U.S. C4 131
Hickory, N.C., U.S. B1 140
Hickory, co., Mo., U.S. D4 132
Hickory Flat, Ms., U.S. A4 131
Hickory Plains, Ar., U.S. C4 111
Hickory Ridge, Ar., U.S. B5 111
Hickory Valley, Tn., U.S. B2 149
Hicks, Point, c., Austl. K8 70
Hickson, Ont., Can. D4 103
Hicksville, N.Y., U.S. E7 139
Hicksville, Oh., U.S. A1 142
Hico, Tx., U.S. D3 150
Hico, W.V., U.S. C3 155
Hidalgo, Mex. E9 90
Hidalgo, Mex. E10 90
Hidalgo, Mex. F8 90
Hidalgo, Mex. D10 90
Hidalgo, Tx., U.S. F3 150
Hidalgo, state, Mex. G10 90
Hidalgo, co., N.M., U.S. F1 138
Hidalgo, co., Tx., U.S. F3 150
Hidalgo del Parral, Mex. D7 90
Hida-sammyaku, mts., Japan K12 36
Hiddenite, N.C., U.S. B1 140
Hidrolândia, Braz. D4 79
Hidrolina, Braz. C4 79
Hieflau, Aus. H14 10
Hieroglyphic Mountains, mts., Az., U.S. k8 110
Hierro (Ferro), i., Spain P22 17b
Higashine, Japan I15 36
Higashiōsaka, Japan M10 36
Higbee, Mo., U.S. B5 132
Higdon, Al., U.S. A4 108
Higganum, Ct., U.S. D5 114
Higgins Lake, Mi., U.S. D6 129
Higgins Lake, l., Mi., U.S. D6 129
Higgins Millpond, res., Md., U.S. C6 127
Higginson, Ar., U.S. B4 111
Higginsville, Mo., U.S. B4 132
High Bluff, Man., Can. D2 100
High Bridge, N.J., U.S. B3 137
High Falls Reservoir, res., Wi., U.S. C5 156
Highfield, Md., U.S. A3 127
Highgate, Ont., Can. E3 103
Highgate Falls, Vt., U.S. B2 152
High Hill, Mo., U.S. C6 132
High Island, Tx., U.S. E5 150
High Island, i., Mi., U.S. C5 129
High Knob, mtn., U.S. A4 153
High Knob, mtn., W.V., U.S. C5 155
Highland, Il., U.S. E4 120
Highland, In., U.S. A3 121
Highland, Ks., U.S. C8 123
Highland, Mi., U.S. o14 129
Highland, N.Y., U.S. D7 139
Highland, Wi., U.S. E3 156
Highland, prov., Scot., U.K. D8 8
Highland, co., Oh., U.S. C2 142
Highland, co., Va., U.S. B3 153
Highland Grove, Ont., Can. B6 103
Highland Home, Al., U.S. D3 108
Highland Lake, l., Me., U.S. g7 126
Highland Lakes, N.J., U.S. A4 137
Highland Park, Il., U.S. A6 120
Highland Park, Mi., U.S. p15 129
Highland Park, Tx., U.S. n10 150
Highland Peak, mtn., Ca., U.S. C4 112
Highland Point, c., Fl., U.S. G5 116
Highlands, N.J., U.S. C5 137
Highlands, N.C., U.S. f9 140
Highlands, Tx., U.S. r14 150
Highlands, co., Fl., U.S. E5 116
Highland Springs, Va., U.S. C5 153
High Level, Alta., Can. F7 98
Highmore, S.D., U.S. C6 148
High Point, N.C., U.S. B2 140
High Point, Wa., U.S. e12 154
High Prairie, Alta., Can. B2 98
High Ridge, Mo., U.S. g12 132
High River, Alta., Can. D4 98
High Rock, mtn., Md., U.S. k12 127
Highrock Lake, l., Man., Can. B1 100
High Rock Lake, res., N.C., U.S. B2 140
High Shoals, Ga., U.S. C3 117
High Shoals, N.C., U.S. B1 140
High Spire, Pa., U.S. F8 145
High Springs, Fl., U.S. C4 116
High Top, mtn., W.V., U.S. C5 155
Hightstown, N.J., U.S. C3 137
Highwood, Il., U.S. A6 120
Highwood, Mt., U.S. C6 133
Highwood Baldy, mtn., Mt., U.S. C6 133
Highwood Mountains, mts., Mt., U.S. C6 133
High Wycombe, Eng., U.K. J13 8
Higley, Az., U.S. D4 110
Higuera de Abuya, Mex. E6 90
Higuera de Zaragoza, Mex. E5 90
Higüero, Punta, c., P.R. E11 94
Higuerote, Ven. B9 84
Higüey, Dom. Rep. E10 94
Higuito, stm., Hond. C6 92
Hiiumaa, i., U.S.S.R. C5 26
Hiko, Nv., U.S. F6 135
Hikone, Japan L11 36
Hiko Range, mts., Nv., U.S. F6 135
Hilbert, Wi., U.S. D5 156
Hilda, Alta., Can. D5 98
Hilda, S.C., U.S. E5 147
Hildale, Ut., U.S. F3 151
Hildburghausen, Ger. E10 10
Hilden, N.S., Can. D6 101
Hildesheim, Ger. C9 10
Hildreth, Ne., U.S. D6 134
Hill, N.H., U.S. C3 136
Hill, co., Mt., U.S. B6 133
Hill, co., Tx., U.S. D4 150
Hillaby, Mount, mtn., Barb. H15 94
Hill Bank, Belize I15 90
Hill City, Ga., U.S. B2 117
Hill City, Ks., U.S. C4 123
Hill City, Mn., U.S. D5 130
Hill City, S.D., U.S. D2 148
Hillcrest, Il., U.S. B4 120
Hillcrest, Mi., U.S. n11 129
Hillcrest Heights, Md., U.S. C4 127
Hilli, Bngl. H13 44
Hilliard, Alta., Can. C4 98
Hilliard, Fl., U.S. B5 116
Hilliard, Oh., U.S. k10 142
Hillier, Ont., Can. D7 103
Hillisburg, In., U.S. D5 121
Hill Lake, l., Ar., U.S. h10 111
Hillman, Mi., U.S. C7 129
Hillrose, Co., U.S. A7 113
Hills, Ia., U.S. C6 122
Hills, Mn., U.S. G2 130
Hillsboro, Ont., Can. D4 103
Hillsboro, Al., U.S. A2 108
Hillsboro, Ga., U.S. C3 117
Hillsboro, Il., U.S. D4 120
Hillsboro, In., U.S. D3 121
Hillsboro, Ks., U.S. D6 123
Hillsboro, Ky., U.S. B6 124
Hillsboro, Md., U.S. C6 127
Hillsboro, Mo., U.S. C7 132
Hillsboro, N.H., U.S. D3 136
Hillsboro, N.M., U.S. E2 138
Hillsboro, N.D., U.S. B8 141
Hillsboro, Oh., U.S. C2 142
Hillsboro, Or., U.S. B4 144
Hillsboro, Tn., U.S. D8 149
Hillsboro, Tx., U.S. C4 150
Hillsboro, Wi., U.S. E3 156
Hillsboro Canal, Fl., U.S. F6 116
Hillsborough, N.B., Can. D5 101
Hillsborough, N.C., U.S. A3 140
Hillsborough, co., Fl., U.S. E4 116
Hillsborough, co., N.H., U.S. E3 136
Hillsborough, Cape, c., Austl. C8 70
Hillsborough Bay, b., P.E.I., Can. C6 101
Hillsborough Lower Village, N.H., U.S. D3 136
Hillsborough Upper Village, N.H., U.S. D3 136
Hillsburgh, Ont., Can. D4 103
Hills Creek Lake, res., Or., U.S. D4 144
Hillsdale, Ont., Can. C5 103
Hillsdale, Il., U.S. B3 120
Hillsdale, In., U.S. E3 121
Hillsdale, Ks., U.S. D9 123
Hillsdale, Mi., U.S. G6 129
Hillsdale, N.J., U.S. g8 137
Hillsdale, Wy., U.S. E8 157
Hillsdale, co., Mi., U.S. G6 129
Hillside, N.J., U.S. k8 137
Hillspring, Alta., Can. E4 98
Hillston, Austl. I6 70
Hillsville, Pa., U.S. D1 145
Hillsville, Va., U.S. D2 153
Hilltonia, Ga., U.S. D5 117
Hillview, Il., U.S. D3 120
Hilo, Hi., U.S. D6 118
Hilo Bay, b., Hi., U.S. D6 118
Hilton, N.Y., U.S. B3 139
Hilton Head Island, S.C., U.S. G6 147
Hilton Head Island, i., S.C., U.S. G6 147
Hilversum, Neth. D7 12
Hima, Ky., U.S. C6 124
Himāchal Pradesh, state, India E7 44
Himalayas, mts., Asia F11 44
Himeji, Japan M9 36
Himi, Japan K11 36
Hims (Homs), Syria D4 48
Hinche, Haiti E8 94
Hinchinbrook Island, i., Austl. B7 70
Hinchinbrook Island, i., Ak., U.S. g18 109
Hinch Mountain, mtn., Tn., U.S. D9 149
Hinckley, Il., U.S. B5 120
Hinckley, Me., U.S. D3 126
Hinckley, Mn., U.S. D6 130
Hinckley, Oh., U.S. A4 142
Hinckley, Ut., U.S. D3 151
Hinckley Reservoir, res., N.Y., U.S. B5 139
Hindaun, India G7 44
Hindman, Ky., U.S. C7 124
Hindmarsh, Lake, l., Austl. K4 70
Hinds, co., Ms., U.S. C3 131
Hindsboro, Il., U.S. D5 120
Hinds Lake, l., Newf., Can. D3 102
Hindu Kush, mts., Asia B4 44
Hindupur, India F4 46
Hines, Or., U.S. D7 144
Hinesburg, Vt., U.S. C2 152
Hines Creek, Alta., Can. A1 98
Hineston, La., U.S. C3 125
Hinesville, Ga., U.S. E5 117
Hinganghāt, India B5 46
Hingham, Ma., U.S. B6 128
Hingham, Mt., U.S. B6 133
Hingham Bay, b., Ma., U.S. g12 128
Hingol, stm., Pak. H1 44
Hingoli, India C4 46
Hınıs, Tur. B6 48
Hinkle, Ms., U.S. A5 131
Hinkley, Ca., U.S. E5 112
Hinnøya, i., Nor. G14 6
Hinojosa del Duque, Spain G6 16
Hinsdale, Il., U.S. k9 120
Hinsdale, Ma., U.S. B1 128
Hinsdale, Mt., U.S. B9 133
Hinsdale, N.H., U.S. E2 136
Hinsdale, N.Y., U.S. C2 139
Hinsdale, co., Co., U.S. D3 113
Hinterrhein, stm., Switz. E11 13
Hinton, Alta., Can. C2 98
Hinton, Ia., U.S. B1 122
Hinton, Ok., U.S. B3 143
Hinton, W.V., U.S. D4 155
Hipólito, Mex. E9 90
Hipólito Yrigoyen, Arg. G5 80
Hirado, Japan N4 36
Hirākud Reservoir, res., India B7 46
Hiram, Ga., U.S. C2 117
Hiram, Me., U.S. E2 126
Hiram, Oh., U.S. A4 142
Hirata, Japan L7 36
Hiratsuka, Japan L14 36
Hirhafok, Alg. I13 62
Hirjillah, Syria B6 50
Hirosaki, Japan G15 36
Hiroshima, Japan M7 36
Hirson, Fr. C11 14
Hisār, India F6 44
Hisbān, Jord. E5 50
Hiseville, Ky., U.S. C4 124
Ḥiṣn al-Qarn, Yemen G6 47
Hispaniola, i., N.A. E9 94
Hita, Japan N5 36
Hitachi, Japan K15 36
Hitchcock, Sask., Can. H4 105
Hitchcock, S.D., U.S. C7 148
Hitchcock, Tx., U.S. r14 150
Hitchcock, co., Ne., U.S. D4 134
Hitchcock Lake, Ct., U.S. C4 114
Hitchins, Ky., U.S. B7 124
Hitoyoshi, Japan O5 36
Hitra, i., Nor. J11 6
Hiva Oa, i., Fr. Poly. I26 158
Hiwannee, Ms., U.S. D5 131
Hiwassee, stm., Tn., U.S. D9 149
Hiwassee Lake, res., N.C., U.S. f8 140
Hixon, B.C., Can. C6 99
Hixton, Wi., U.S. D2 156
Hkakabo Razi, mtn., Burma F6 30
Hkok (Kok), stm., Asia D5 40
Hlatikulu, Swaz. F10 66
Hlegu, Burma F4 40
Hlinsko, Czech. F15 10
Hlobane, S. Afr. F10 66
Hlohovec, Czech. G17 10
Hluboká nad Vltavou, Czech. F14 10
Hlučín, Czech. F18 10
Hmawbi, Burma F4 40
Ho, Ghana H10 64
Hoa Binh, Viet. D8 40
Hoagland, In., U.S. C8 121
Hoback, stm., Wy., U.S. C2 157
Hobart, Austl. N7 70
Hobart, In., U.S. A3 121
Hobart, Ok., U.S. B2 143
Hobbema, Alta., Can. C4 98
Hobbs, In., U.S. D6 121
Hobbs, N.M., U.S. E6 138
Hobe Sound, Fl., U.S. E6 116
Hobgood, N.C., U.S. A5 140
Hobo, Col. F5 84
Hoboken, Bel. F5 12
Hoboken, Ga., U.S. E4 117
Hoboken, N.J., U.S. k8 137
Hobson, Mt., U.S. D7 133
Hobucken, N.C., U.S. B6 140
Hobyo, Som. G10 56
Hochalmspitze, mtn., Aus. H13 10
Hochkönig, mtn., Aus. H13 10
Höchstadt an der Aisch, Ger. F10 10
Hockenheim, Ger. F8 10
Hockessin, De., U.S. A3 115
Hocking, co., Oh., U.S. C3 142
Hocking, stm., Oh., U.S. C3 142
Hockley, Tx., U.S. q14 150
Hockley, co., Tx., U.S. C1 150
Hodeida see Al-Ḥudaydah, Yemen G3 47
Hodgdon, Me., U.S. B5 126
Hodge, La., U.S. B3 125
Hodgeman, co., Ks., U.S. D4 123
Hodgen, Ok., U.S. C7 143
Hodgenville, Ky., U.S. C4 124
Hodges, Al., U.S. A2 108
Hodges Village Reservoir, res., Ma., U.S. B4 128
Hodgeville, Sask., Can. G2 105
Hodgson, Man., Can. D3 100
Hódmezővásárhely, Hung. I20 10
Hodna, Chott el, l., Alg. C13 62
Hodonín, Czech. G17 10
Hoehne, Co., U.S. D6 113
Hoek van Holland, Neth. E5 12
Hoeryŏng, N. Kor. A17 32
Hoey, Sask., Can. E3 105
Hoeyang, N. Kor. E15 32
Hof, Ger. E11 10
Hof, Ice. B6 6a
Hoffman, Mn., U.S. E3 130
Hoffman, N.C., U.S. B3 140
Hoffman Estates, Il., U.S. h8 120
Hoffmeyr, S. Afr. H7 66
Höfn, Ice. B6 6a
Hofors, Swe. K15 6
Hōfu, Japan M6 36
Hofuf see Al-Hufūf, Sau. Ar. I10 48
Hogansville, Ga., U.S. C2 117
Hogback Mountain, mtn., Mt., U.S. F4 133
Hogback Mountain, mtn., Ne., U.S. C2 134
Hogback Mountain, mtn., S.C., U.S. A3 147
Hoggar see Ahaggar, mts., Alg. I13 62
Hog Island, i., Fl., U.S. C3 116
Hog Island, i., Mi., U.S. C5 129
Hog Island, i., N.C., U.S. B6 140
Hog Island, i., R.I., U.S. D5 146
Hog Island, i., Va., U.S. C7 153
Högsby, Swe. M15 6
Hogup Mountains, mts., Ut., U.S. B2 151
Hoh, stm., Wa., U.S. B1 154
Hohenau, Para. D11 80
Hohenau an der March, Aus. G16 10
Hohenlimburg, Ger. D7 10
Hohenthurn, Aus. I13 10
Hohenwald, Tn., U.S. B4 149
Hoher Dachstein, mtn., Aus. H13 10
Hohe Tauern, mts., Aus. H12 10
Hoh Head, c., Wa., U.S. B1 154
Hohhot, China C9 30
Hohoe, Ghana H10 64
Ho-Ho-Kus, N.J., U.S. h8 137
Hoh Xil Shan, mts., China C13 44
Hoi An, Viet. G10 40
Hoisington, Ks., U.S. D5 123
Hojāi, India G15 44
Hokah, Mn., U.S. G7 130
Hoke, co., N.C., U.S. B3 140
Hokes Bluff, Al., U.S. B4 108
Hokitika, N.Z. E3 72
Hokkaidō, i., Japan D17 36a
Holbrook, Austl. J7 70
Holbrook, Az., U.S. C5 110
Holbrook, Id., U.S. G6 119
Holbrook, Ma., U.S. B5 128
Holbrook, Ne., U.S. D5 134
Holcomb, Ks., U.S. E3 123
Holcomb, Ms., U.S. B4 131
Holcomb, Mo., U.S. E7 132
Holcombe, Wi., U.S. C2 156
Holden, Alta., Can. C4 98
Holden, La., U.S. g10 125
Holden, Ma., U.S. B4 128
Holden, Mo., U.S. C4 132
Holden, Ut., U.S. D3 151
Holden, W.V., U.S. D2 155
Holden Heights, Fl., U.S. D5 116
Holdenville, Ok., U.S. B5 143
Holder, Fl., U.S. D4 116
Holderness, N.H., U.S. C3 136
Holdfast, Sask., Can. G3 105
Holdingford, Mn., U.S. E4 130
Holdrege, Ne., U.S. D6 134
Hole in the Mountain Peak, mtn., Nv., U.S. C6 135
Holgate, Oh., U.S. A1 142
Holguín, Cuba D6 94
Holič, Czech. G17 10
Hollabrunn, Aus. G16 10
Holladay, Ut., U.S. C4 151
Holland, Man., Can. E2 100
Holland, In., U.S. H3 121
Holland, Ia., U.S. B5 122
Holland, Ky., U.S. D3 124
Holland, Mi., U.S. F4 129
Holland, Mo., U.S. E8 132
Holland, Ne., U.S. D9 134
Holland, N.Y., U.S. C2 139
Holland, Oh., U.S. A2 142
Holland, Tx., U.S. D4 150
Hollandale, Ms., U.S. B3 131
Holland Centre, Ont., Can. C4 103
Holland Island, i., Md., U.S. D5 127
Holland see Netherlands, ctry., Eur. E9 4
Holland Point, c., Md., U.S. C4 127
Hollandsbird Island, i., S. Afr. E2 66
Hollandsch Diep, strt., Neth. E5 12
Holland Straits, strt., Md., U.S. D5 127
Holley, N.Y., U.S. B2 139
Holliday, Tx., U.S. C3 150
Hollidaysburg, Pa., U.S. F5 145
Hollins, Al., U.S. B3 108
Hollins, Va., U.S. C3 153
Hollis, N.H., U.S. E3 136
Hollis, Ok., U.S. C2 143
Hollis Center, Me., U.S. E2 126
Hollister, Ca., U.S. D3 112
Hollister, Id., U.S. G4 119
Hollister, Mo., U.S. E4 132
Hollister, N.C., U.S. A5 140
Holliston, Ma., U.S. B5 128
Holloman Air Force Base, mil., N.M., U.S. E3 138
Hollow Rock, Tn., U.S. A3 149
Hollowtop Mountain, mtn., Mt., U.S. E4 133
Hollsopple, Pa., U.S. F4 145
Holly, Co., U.S. C8 113
Holly, Mi., U.S. F7 129
Holly Bluff, Ms., U.S. C3 131
Holly Grove, Ar., U.S. C4 111
Holly Hill, Fl., U.S. C5 116
Holly Hill, S.C., U.S. E7 147
Holly Pond, Al., U.S. A3 108
Holly Ridge, N.C., U.S. C5 140
Holly Shelter Swamp, sw., N.C., U.S. C5 140
Holly Springs, Ga., U.S. B2 117
Holly Springs, Ms., U.S. A4 131
Holly Springs, N.C., U.S. B4 140
Hollywood, Al., U.S. A4 108
Hollywood, Az., U.S. E6 110
Hollywood (part of Los Angeles), Ca., U.S. m12 112
Hollywood, Fl., U.S. F6 116
Hollywood, Ga., U.S. B3 117
Hollywood, Md., U.S. D4 127
Hollywood, S.C., U.S. k11 147
Hollywood Indian Reservation, Fl., U.S. r3 116
Hollywood Park, Tx., U.S. h7 150
Holman, N.W. Ter., Can. B9 96
Holman, N.M., U.S. A4 138
Holmen, Wi., U.S. E2 156
Holmes, co., Fl., U.S. u16 116
Holmes, co., Ms., U.S. B3 131
Holmes, co., Oh., U.S. B4 142
Holmes, Mount, mtn., Wy., U.S. B2 157
Holmestrand, Nor. L12 6
Holmesville, Ne., U.S. D9 134
Holmia, Guy. E13 84
Holod, Rom. C6 20
Holoit, Punta, c., Mex. G15 90
Ḥolon, Isr. D3 50
Holoog, Nmb. F3 66
Holstebro, Den. M11 6
Holstein, Ont., Can. C4 103
Holstein, Ia., U.S. B2 122
Holstein, Ne., U.S. D7 134
Holston, stm., Tn., U.S. C11 149
Holston, Middle Fork, stm., Va., U.S. f10 153
Holston High Knob, mtn., Tn., U.S. C11 149
Holt, Al., U.S. B2 108
Holt, Fl., U.S. u15 116
Holt, Mi., U.S. F6 129
Holt, Mo., U.S. B3 132
Holt, co., Mo., U.S. A2 132
Holt, co., Ne., U.S. B7 134
Holt Creek, stm., Ne., U.S. B6 134
Holt Knob, mtn., Tn., U.S. g10 149
Holt Lake, res., Al., U.S. B2 108
Holton, In., U.S. F7 121
Holton, Ks., U.S. C8 123
Holton, Mi., U.S. E4 129
Holtville, Al., U.S. C3 108
Holtville, Ca., U.S. F6 112
Holualoa, Hi., U.S. D6 118
Holy Cross, Ak., U.S. C8 109
Holy Cross, Ia., U.S. B7 122
Holy Cross, Mountain of the, mtn., Co., U.S. B4 113
Holyoke, Co., U.S. A8 113

Name — Map Ref. — Page

Holyoke, Ma., U.S. B2 128
Holyoke Range, hills, Ma., U.S. B2 128
Holyrood, Ks., U.S. D5 123
Holy Trinity, Al., U.S. C4 108
Holzkirchen, Ger. H11 10
Holzminden, Ger. D9 10
Homalin, Burma B3 40
Homathko, stm., B.C., Can. D5 99
Homberg, Ger. D9 10
Hombori Tondo, mtn., Mali D9 64
Hombre Muerto, Salar del, pl., Arg. C5 80
Homburg, Ger. F7 10
Homburg see Bad Homburg vor der Höhe, Ger. E8 10
Home, Ks., U.S. C7 123
Home Corner, In., U.S. C6 121
Homecroft, In., U.S. m10 121
Homedale, Id., U.S. F2 119
Home Gardens, Ca., U.S. n14 112
Home Hill, Austl. B7 70
Homelake, Co., U.S. D4 113
Homeland, Fl., U.S. E5 116
Homeland, Ga., U.S. F4 117
Home Place, In., U.S. E5 121
Homer, Ak., U.S. D9 109
Homer, Ga., U.S. B3 117
Homer, Il., U.S. C6 120
Homer, In., U.S. E6 121
Homer, La., U.S. B2 125
Homer, Mi., U.S. F6 129
Homer, Ne., U.S. B9 134
Homer, N.Y., U.S. C4 139
Homer City, Pa., U.S. E3 145
Homerville, Ga., U.S. E4 117
Homer Youngs Peak, mtn., Mt., U.S. E3 133
Homestead, Fl., U.S. G6 116
Homestead, Ia., U.S. C6 122
Homestead, Pa., U.S. k14 145
Homestead Air Force Base, mil., Fl., U.S. G6 116
Homestead National Monument of America, Ne., U.S. D9 134
Homewood, Al., U.S. g7 108
Homewood, Ca., U.S. C3 112
Homewood, Il., U.S. B6 120
Homewood, Oh., U.S. C1 142
Hominy, Ok., U.S. A5 143
Hominy Creek, stm., Ok., U.S. A5 143
Homme Dam, N.D., U.S. A8 141
Homochitto, stm., Ms., U.S. D2 131
Homosassa, Fl., U.S. D4 116
Homs see Al-Khums, Libya B3 56
Homs see Ḥims, Syria D4 48
Honaker, Va., U.S. e10 153
Honan see Henan, prov., China E9 30
Honaunau, Hi., U.S. D6 118
Honaz, Tur. L13 20
Honda, Col. E5 84
Honda, Bahía, b., Col. A7 84
Hondeklipbaai, S. Afr. H3 66
Hondo, N.M., U.S. D4 138
Hondo, Tx., U.S. E3 150
Hondo, stm., N.A. H15 90
Hondo, Rio, stm., N.M., U.S. D4 138
Hondsrug, hills, Neth. C10 12
Honduras, ctry., N.A. B8 92
Honduras, Cabo de, c., Hond. A8 92
Honduras, Gulf of, b., N.A. E7 88
Honduras, Port, b., Belize A6 92
Honea Path, S.C., U.S. C3 147
Hønefoss, Nor. K12 6
Honeoye Falls, N.Y., U.S. C3 139
Honesdale, Pa., U.S. C11 145
Honey Brook, Pa., U.S. F10 145
Honey Creek, Wi., U.S. n11 156
Honey Grove, Tx., U.S. C5 150
Honey Lake, l., Ca., U.S. B3 112
Honeymoon Bay, B.C., Can. E5 99
Honeypot Glen, Ct., U.S. C4 114
Honeyville, Ut., U.S. B3 151
Honfleur, Fr. C7 14
Hon Gai, Viet. D9 40
Hong'an, China D3 34
Honga River, b., Md., U.S. D5 127
Hongch'ŏn, S. Kor. F15 32
Hongcun, China H5 34
Honghu, China F2 34
Hongjiang, China F8 30
Hong Kong, dep., Asia G9 30
Honglai, China J7 34
Hongliuyuan, China C6 30
Honglu, China J8 34
Hongmendu, China A7 40
Hong Ngu, Viet. I8 40
Hong see Red, stm., Asia C8 40
Hongshi, China B7 32
Hongshui, stm., China C10 40
Hongshuyangzi, China C4 32
Hongsŏng, S. Kor. G14 32
Hongtong, China D9 30
Hongwŏn, N. Kor. C15 32
Hongxingqiao, China E8 34
Hongyang, China L5 34
Hongze Hu, l., China B7 34
Honiara, Sol.Is. I19 158
Honobia, Ok., U.S. C7 143
Honokaa, Hi., U.S. C6 118
Honokahua, Hi., U.S. B5 118
Honokohau, Hi., U.S. D6 118
Honolulu, Hi., U.S. B4 118
Honolulu, co., Hi., U.S. B3 118
Honolulu International Airport, Hi., U.S. g10 118
Honomu, Hi., U.S. D6 118
Honouliuli, Hi., U.S. g9 118
Hon Quan, Viet. I9 40
Honshū, i., Japan K13 36
Honuapo Bay, b., Hi., U.S. D6 118
Hood, co., Tx., U.S. C4 150
Hood, Mount, mtn., Or., U.S. B5 144
Hood Canal, b., Wa., U.S. B2 154
Hoodoo Peak, mtn., Wa., U.S. A5 154
Hood Point, c., Austl. F3 68
Hood River, Or., U.S. B5 144
Hood River, co., Or., U.S. B5 144
Hoodsport, Wa., U.S. B2 154
Hoods Range, mts., Austl. G6 70
Hooker, Ok., U.S. e9 143
Hooker, co., Ne., U.S. C4 134
Hookerton, N.C., U.S. B5 140
Hookina, Austl. H3 70
Hook Island, i., Austl. C8 70
Hooks, Tx., U.S. C5 150
Hooksett, N.H., U.S. D4 136
Hoolehua, Hi., U.S. B4 118
Hoonah, Ak., U.S. D12 109
Hoopa Valley Indian Reservation, Ca., U.S. B2 112
Hooper, Co., U.S. D5 113
Hooper, Ne., U.S. C9 134
Hooper, Ut., U.S. B3 151
Hooper Bay, Ak., U.S. C6 109
Hooper Creek, stm., Ne., U.S. h12 134
Hooper Islands, is., Md., U.S. D5 127
Hooper Strait, strt., Md., U.S. D5 127
Hoopes Reservoir, res., De., U.S. A3 115
Hoopeston, Il., U.S. C6 120
Hoople, N.D., U.S. A8 141
Hoosac Range, mts., U.S. A1 128
Hoosic, stm., U.S. C7 139
Hoosick Falls, N.Y., U.S. C7 139
Hoosuc Range, mts., U.S. D1 126
Hoover, Al., U.S. B3 108
Hoover Dam, U.S. G7 135
Hoover Reservoir, res., Oh., U.S. B3 142
Hooverson Heights, W.V., U.S. f8 155
Hooversville, Pa., U.S. F4 145
Hopatcong, N.J., U.S. B3 137
Hopatcong, Lake, l., N.J., U.S. A3 137
Hope, B.C., Can. E7 99
Hope, Ak., U.S. C10 109
Hope, Ar., U.S. D2 111
Hope, In., U.S. F6 121
Hope, Ks., U.S. D6 123
Hope, Mn., U.S. G5 130
Hope, N.M., U.S. E5 138
Hope, N.D., U.S. B8 141
Hope, R.I., U.S. D3 146
Hope, Point, c., Ak., U.S. B6 109
Hopedale, Newf., Can. g9 102
Hopedale, Il., U.S. C4 120
Hopedale, La., U.S. E6 125
Hopedale, Ma., U.S. B4 128
Hopedale, Oh., U.S. B5 142
Hopefield, S. Afr. I4 66
Hope Hull, Al., U.S. C3 108
Hope Island, i., R.I., U.S. E5 146
Hopelchén, Mex. H15 90
Hope Mills, N.C., U.S. C4 140
Hopes Advance, Cap, c., Que., Can. f13 104
Hopetoun, Austl. F4 68
Hopetoun, Austl. J5 70
Hopetown, S. Afr. G7 66
Hope Valley, R.I., U.S. E2 146
Hopewell, N.S., Can. D7 101
Hopewell, N.J., U.S. C3 137
Hopewell, Oh., U.S. C3 142
Hopewell, Va., U.S. C5 153
Hopewell Cape, N.B., Can. D5 101
Hopewell Junction, N.Y., U.S. D7 139
Hopi Buttes, mtn., Az., U.S. B5 110
Hopi Indian Reservation, Az., U.S. A5 110
Hopkins, Mi., U.S. F5 129
Hopkins, Mn., U.S. n12 130
Hopkins, Mo., U.S. A3 132
Hopkins, S.C., U.S. D6 147
Hopkins, co., Ky., U.S. C2 124
Hopkins, co., Tx., U.S. C5 150
Hopkinsville, Ky., U.S. D2 124
Hopkinton, Ia., U.S. B6 122
Hopkinton, Ma., U.S. B4 128
Hopkinton, N.H., U.S. D3 136
Hopkinton, R.I., U.S. F1 146
Hopkinton Lake, res., N.H., U.S. D3 136
Hopland, Ca., U.S. C2 112
Hopwood, Pa., U.S. G2 145
Hopwood, Mount, mtn., Austl. C6 70
Hoquiam, Wa., U.S. C2 154
Horace, Ks., U.S. D2 123
Horace, N.D., U.S. C9 141
Horace Mountain, mtn., Ak., U.S. B10 109
Horancia, Eth. N10 60
Horatio, Ar., U.S. D1 111
Horatio, S.C., U.S. C6 147
Horconcitos, Pan. I12 92
Hordaland, co., Nor. K10 6
Hordville, Ne., U.S. C8 134
Horezu, Rom. D7 20
Horgen, Switz. D10 13
Horicon, Wi., U.S. E5 156
Horine, Mo., U.S. C7 132
Horizontina, Braz. D11 80
Horlick Mountains, mts., Ant. D10 73
Hormuz, Strait of, strt., Asia H14 48
Horn, Aus. G15 10
Horn, c., Ice. A2 6a
Horn, Cape see Hornos, Cabo de, c., Chile H3 78
Hornbeak, Tn., U.S. A2 149
Hornbeck, La., U.S. C2 125
Hornell, N.Y., U.S. C3 139
Hornersville, Mo., U.S. E7 132
Hornick, Ia., U.S. B1 122
Horning's Mills, Ont., Can. C4 103
Horn Island, i., Ms., U.S. E5 131
Horn Island Pass, strt., Ms., U.S. g8 131
Hornito, Cerro, mtn., Pan. I12 92
Horn Lake, Ms., U.S. A3 131
Horn Mountain, mtn., Al., U.S. B3 108
Hornos, Cabo de (Cape Horn), c., Chile H3 78
Horn Pond, l., Ma., U.S. g11 128
Hornsby, Tn., U.S. B3 149
Hornsbyville, Va., U.S. h15 153
Horqin Youyi Qianqi, China B11 30
Horqueta, Para. B10 80
Horry, co., S.C., U.S. D10 147
Horse, stm., Ct., U.S. C6 114
Horseback Knob, hill, Oh., U.S. C2 142
Horse Branch, Ky., U.S. C3 124
Horse Cave, Ky., U.S. C4 124
Horse Creek, Wy., U.S. E7 157
Horse Creek, stm., U.S. E8 157
Horse Creek, stm., Co., U.S. C7 113
Horse Creek, stm., Mo., U.S. D4 132
Horse Creek Reservoir, res., Co., U.S. C7 113
Horsefly, B.C., Can. C7 99
Horsefly Lake, l., B.C., Can. C7 99
Horsehead Lake, l., N.D., U.S. B6 141
Horseheads, N.Y., U.S. C4 139
Horse Heaven Hills, hills, Wa., U.S. C6 154
Horsens, Den. N11 6
Horse Peak, mtn., N.M., U.S. D1 138
Horseshoe Bend, Ar., U.S. A4 111
Horseshoe Bend, Id., U.S. F2 119
Horseshoe Bend National Military Park, Al., U.S. C4 108
Horseshoe Cove, b., Fl., U.S. C3 116
Horseshoe Point, c., Fl., U.S. C3 116
Horse Shoe Reef, rf., Br. Vir. Is. E12 94
Horseshoe Reservoir, res., Az., U.S. C4 110
Horsham, Austl. K5 70
Horsham, Eng., U.K. J13 8
Horst, Neth. F9 12
Hortense, Ga., U.S. E5 117
Horton, Al., U.S. A3 108
Horton, In., U.S. D5 121
Horton, Ks., U.S. C8 123
Hortonia, Lake, l., Vt., U.S. D2 152
Hortonville, Wi., U.S. D5 156
Hosaina, Eth. N9 60
Hoschton, Ga., U.S. B3 117
Hosére Vokré, mtn., Cam. G9 54
Hosford, Fl., U.S. B2 116
Hoshangābād, India I7 44
Hoshiārpur, India E6 44
Hoskins, Ne., U.S. B8 134
Hoskinston, Ky., U.S. C6 124
Hosmer, B.C., Can. E10 99
Hosmer, S.D., U.S. B6 148
Hospers, Ia., U.S. A2 122
Hospet, India E4 46
Hossegor, Fr. I5 14
Hosston, La., U.S. B2 125
Hosta Butte, mtn., N.M., U.S. B1 138
Hoste, Isla, i., Chile H3 78
Hot, Thai. E5 40
Hotan, China D2 30
Hotan, stm., China D3 30
Hotazel, S. Afr. F6 66
Hotchkiss, Co., U.S. C3 113
Hotchkissville, Ct., U.S. C3 114
Hot Creek Range, mts., Nv., U.S. E5 135
Hot Creek Valley, val., Nv., U.S. E5 135
Hotevilla, Az., U.S. B5 110
Hot Spring, co., Ar., U.S. C2 111
Hot Springs, Mt., U.S. C2 133
Hot Springs, N.C., U.S. f10 140
Hot Springs, S.D., U.S. D2 148
Hot Springs, Va., U.S. C3 153
Hot Springs, co., Wy., U.S. C4 157
Hot Springs National Park, Ar., U.S. C2 111
Hot Springs National Park, Ar., U.S. C2 111
Hot Springs Peak, mtn., Ca., U.S. B3 112
Hot Springs Peak, mtn., Nv., U.S. B4 135
Hot Springs see Truth or Consequences, N.M., U.S. D2 138
Hot Springs Village, Ar., U.S. C2 111
Hot Sulphur Springs, Co., U.S. A4 113
Hottentotbaai, b., Nmb. F2 66
Houbao, China B13 32
Houck, Az., U.S. B6 110
Houdan, Fr. D8 14
Houghton, Mi., U.S. A2 129
Houghton, N.Y., U.S. C2 139
Houghton, co., Mi., U.S. B2 129
Houghton Lake, Mi., U.S. D6 129
Houghton Lake, l., Mi., U.S. D6 129
Houghton Lake Heights, Mi., U.S. D6 129
Houjie, China M2 34
Houlka, Ms., U.S. A4 131
Houlton, Me., U.S. B5 126
Houma, China D9 30
Houma, La., U.S. E5 125
Houndé, Burkina F8 64
Housatonic, Ma., U.S. B1 128
Housatonic, stm., U.S. D3 114
House, stm., Alta., Can. B4 98
House Range, mts., Ut., U.S. D2 151
House Springs, Mo., U.S. g12 132
Houston, Al., U.S. A2 108
Houston, Ak., U.S. g16 109
Houston, Ar., U.S. B3 111
Houston, De., U.S. E3 115
Houston, Mn., U.S. G7 130
Houston, Ms., U.S. B4 131
Houston, Mo., U.S. D6 132
Houston, Pa., U.S. F1 145
Houston, Tx., U.S. E5 150
Houston, co., Al., U.S. D4 108
Houston, co., Ga., U.S. D3 117
Houston, co., Mn., U.S. G7 130
Houston, co., Tn., U.S. A4 149
Houston, co., Tx., U.S. D5 150
Houston, stm., La., U.S. D2 125
Houston, Lake, res., Tx., U.S. r14 150
Houstonia, Mo., U.S. C4 132
Houston Intercontinental Airport, Tx., U.S. r14 150
Houtman Abrolhos, is., Austl. E2 68
Houtzdale, Pa., U.S. E5 145
Houxijie, China G7 34
Houxinqiu, China A10 32
Hoven, S.D., U.S. B6 148
Hovenweep National Monument, Ut., U.S. F6 151
Hovland, Mn., U.S. k10 130
Howar, Wādī (Ouadi Howa), val., Afr. I3 60
Howard, Austl. E10 70
Howard, Co., U.S. C5 113
Howard, Ga., U.S. D2 117
Howard, Ks., U.S. E7 123
Howard, N.Y., U.S. C3 139
Howard, Pa., U.S. D6 145
Howard, S.D., U.S. C8 148
Howard, Wi., U.S. D5 156
Howard, co., Ar., U.S. C2 111
Howard, co., In., U.S. C5 121
Howard, co., Ia., U.S. A5 122
Howard, co., Md., U.S. B4 127
Howard, co., Mo., U.S. B5 132
Howard, co., Ne., U.S. C7 134
Howard, co., Tx., U.S. C2 150
Howard City, Mi., U.S. E5 129
Howard Hanson Reservoir, res., Wa., U.S. B4 154
Howard Lake, Mn., U.S. E4 130
Howard Prairie Lake, res., Or., U.S. E4 144
Howards Grove-Millersville, Wi., U.S. E6 156
Howardville, Mo., U.S. E8 132
Howe, In., U.S. A7 121
Howe, Ok., U.S. C7 143
Howe, Cape, c., Austl. K8 70
Howeke, Lib. I6 64
Howell, Mi., U.S. F7 129
Howell, Ut., U.S. B3 151
Howell, co., Mo., U.S. E6 132
Howells, Ne., U.S. C8 134
Howe Sound, strt., B.C., Can. E6 99
Howick, Que., Can. D4 104
Howick, S. Afr. G10 66
Howitt, Mount, mtn., Austl. K7 70
Howland, Me., U.S. C4 126
Howland Island, i., Oc. H22 158
Howley, Newf., Can. D3 102
Hoxie, Ar., U.S. A5 111
Hoxie, Ks., U.S. C3 123
Höxter, Ger. D9 10
Høyanger, Nor. K10 6
Hoyerswerda, Ger. D14 10
Hoyleton, Il., U.S. E4 120
Hoyt, N.B., Can. D3 101
Hoyt, Ks., U.S. C8 123
Hoyt Lakes, Mn., U.S. C6 130
Hradec Králové, Czech. E15 10
Hranice, Czech. F17 10
Hron, stm., Czech. G18 10
Hronov, Czech. E16 10
Hrubieszów, Pol. E23 10
Hrvatska (Croatia), state, Yugo. D10 18
Hsihu, Tai. L9 34
Hsilo, Tai. L9 34
Hsinchu, Tai. K9 34
Hsinchuang, Tai. J10 34
Hsinhua, Tai. L9 34
Hsintien, Tai. K10 34
Hsipaw, Burma C4 40
Hsüehchia, Tai. L9 34
Hua'an, China J6 34
Huacaña, Peru F4 82
Huacaraje, Bol. E10 82
Huachacalla, Bol. H7 82
Huacheng, China K4 34
Huachi, Laguna, l., Bol. F10 82
Huacho, Peru D3 82
Huachón, Peru D4 82
Huachos, Peru E4 82
Huachuca City, Az., U.S. F5 110
Huaco, Arg. F4 80
Huacrachuco, Peru C3 82
Huadian, China C12 30
Hua Hin, Thai. H5 40
Huai, stm., China C6 34
Huai'an, China B8 34
Huaibin, China C4 34
Huaide, China C11 30
Huailai, China C3 32
Huaillati, Peru F5 82
Huainan, China C6 34
Huaining, China E5 34
Huaiyang, China B3 34
Huaiyuan, China C6 34
Huajuapan de León, Mex. I11 90
Huakou, China J6 34
Hualahuises, Mex. E10 90
Hualalai, vol., Hi., U.S. D6 118
Hualañé, Chile H3 80
Hualapai Indian Reservation, Az., U.S. B2 110
Hualapai Mountains, mts., Az., U.S. C2 110
Hualapai Peak, mtn., Az., U.S. B2 110
Hualfín, Arg. D5 80
Hualgayoc, Peru B2 82
Hualien, Tai. L10 34
Hualla, Peru E5 82
Huallaga, stm., Peru A4 82
Huallanca, Peru C3 82
Huallanca, Peru C3 82
Huamachuco, Peru B2 82
Huamanquiquia, Peru E4 82
Huambo (Nova Lisboa), Ang. D3 58
Huambo, Peru F5 82
Huambo, stm., Peru B3 82
Huambos, Peru B2 82
Huancabamba, Peru D4 82
Huancabamba, Peru A2 82
Huancané, Peru F7 82
Huancapi, Peru E4 82
Huancarama, Peru E5 82
Huancarqui, Peru G5 82
Huancavelica, Peru E4 82
Huancavelica, dept., Peru E4 82
Huancaybamba, Peru C3 82
Huancayo, Peru E4 82
Huanchaca, Bol. I8 82
Huanchaca, Serranía de, mts., S.A. F11 82
Huando, Peru E4 82
Huang, stm., Asia F6 40
Huang (Yellow), stm., China D10 30
Huang'an, China H3 32
Huangbai, China B14 32
Huangchuan, China C4 34
Huangdu, China D10 34
Huanggang, China E3 34
Huangguoshu, China A8 40
Huanghua, China E5 32
Huangkeng, China H6 34
Huangling, China D8 30
Huangmao, China G3 34
Huangnihe, China D6 34
Huangqi, China I8 34
Huangqiao, China C9 34
Huangshapu, China J1 34
Huangshatuo, China B10 32
Huangshi, China E4 34
Huangshiguan, China I4 34
Huangtankou, China G7 34
Huangtianfan, China F9 34
Huangtugang, China D4 34
Huanguelén, Arg. I8 80
Huangyan, China G10 34
Huangyuan, China D7 30
Huangzhuang, China A1 34
Huanjiang, China B10 40
Huanta, Peru E4 82
Huántar, Peru C3 82
Huánuco, Peru C3 82
Huánuco, dept., Peru C4 82
Huanuni, Bol. H8 82
Huanxi, China I2 34
Huanzo, Cordillera de, mts., Peru F5 82
Huapí, Serranías, mts., Nic. E10 92
Huara, Chile H7 82
Huaral, Peru D3 82
Huaraz, Peru C3 82
Huari, Bol. H8 82
Huari, Peru C3 82
Huariaca, Peru D3 82
Huaribamba, Peru E4 82
Huarina, Bol. G7 82
Huarmey, Peru D2 82
Huarochirí, Peru E3 82
Huarocondo, Peru E5 82
Huasaga, stm., S.A. I4 84
Huascarán, Nevado, mtn., Peru C3 82
Huasco, Chile E3 80
Huasco, stm., Chile E3 80
Huashan, China I4 32
Huashi, China D9 34
Huatabampo, Mex. D5 90
Huatong, China C9 32
Huatunas, Lagunas, l., Bol. E8 82
Huauchinango, Mex. G10 90
Huaura, Peru D3 82
Huaura, stm., Peru D3 82
Huautla, Mex. H11 90
Huaxian, China L2 34
Huayllay, Peru D3 82
Huayna Potosí, Nevado, mtn., Bol. G7 82
Huaytará, Peru E4 82
Huayuanzui, China B7 34
Huayunca, Nevado, mtn., Peru F5 82
Huayuri, Pampa de, pl., Peru F4 82
Huazhou, China D11 40
Hubbard, Sask., Can. F4 105
Hubbard, Ia., U.S. B4 122
Hubbard, Ne., U.S. B9 134
Hubbard, Oh., U.S. A5 142
Hubbard, Or., U.S. B4 144
Hubbard, Tx., U.S. D4 150
Hubbard, co., Mn., U.S. C4 130
Hubbard Creek Lake, res., Tx., U.S. C3 150
Hubbard Lake, l., Mi., U.S. D7 129
Hubbards, N.S., Can. E5 101
Hubbardston, Mi., U.S. E6 129
Hubbardton, stm., Vt., U.S. D2 152
Hubbell, Mi., U.S. A2 129
Hubei (Hupeh), prov., China E9 30
Huberdeau, Que., Can. D3 104
Hubli-Dhārwār, India E3 46
Huch'ang, N. Kor. B15 32
Huchi, China D6 34
Huckleberry Hill, Ct., U.S. B4 114
Huckleberry Mountain, mtn., Or., U.S. D4 144
Huddersfield, Eng., U.K. H12 8
Huddleston Knob, mtn., Tn., U.S. C8 149
Huddy, Ky., U.S. C7 124
Hudgens Creek, stm., Ar., U.S. D3 111
Hūdī, Sud. I8 60
Hudiksvall, Swe. K15 6
Hudson, Que., Can. D3 104
Hudson, Co., U.S. A6 113
Hudson, Fl., U.S. D4 116
Hudson, Il., U.S. C5 120
Hudson, In., U.S. A7 121
Hudson, Ia., U.S. B5 122
Hudson, Ks., U.S. D5 123
Hudson, Ma., U.S. B4 128
Hudson, Mi., U.S. G6 129
Hudson, N.H., U.S. E4 136
Hudson, N.Y., U.S. C7 139
Hudson, N.C., U.S. B1 140
Hudson, Oh., U.S. A4 142
Hudson, S.D., U.S. D9 148
Hudson, Wi., U.S. D1 156
Hudson, Wy., U.S. D4 157
Hudson, co., N.J., U.S. B4 137
Hudson, stm., U.S. E7 139
Hudson, stm., Ga., U.S. B3 117
Hudson, Lake, res., Ok., U.S. A6 143
Hudson Bay, Sask., Can. E4 105
Hudson Bay, b., Can. D15 96
Hudson Falls, N.Y., U.S. B7 139
Hudson Hope, B.C., Can. A6 99
Hudson Lake, In., U.S. A4 121
Hudson Mountain, mtn., Me., U.S. B3 126
Hudson Strait, strt., Can. D18 96
Hudsonville, Mi., U.S. F5 129
Hudspeth, co., Tx., U.S. o12 150
Hue, Viet. F9 40
Huehuetán, Mex. B2 92
Huehuetenango, Guat. B3 92
Huehuetenango, dept., Guat. B3 92
Huejutla de Reyes, Mex. G10 90
Huelgoat, Fr. D3 14
Huelva, Spain H5 16
Huenque, stm., Peru G7 82
Huentelauquén, Chile F3 80
Huércal-Overa, Spain H10 16
Huerfano, co., Co., U.S. D5 113
Huerfano, stm., Co., U.S. D6 113
Huerfano Mountain, mtn., N.M., U.S. A2 138
Huerva, stm., Spain D10 16
Huesca, Spain C11 16
Huéscar, Spain H9 16
Huetamo de Núñez, Mex. H9 90
Hueytown, Al., U.S. g6 108
Huffakers, Nv., U.S. D2 135
Huggins, Mount, mtn., Ant. C8 73
Hugh Butler Lake, res., Ne., U.S. D5 134
Hughenden, Austl. C6 70
Hughenden, Alta., Can. C5 98
Hughes, Ar., U.S. C5 111
Hughes, co., Ok., U.S. B5 143
Hughes, co., S.D., U.S. C5 148
Hughes, North Fork, stm., W.V., U.S. B3 155
Hughes, South Fork, stm., W.V., U.S. B3 155
Hughesville, Md., U.S. C4 127
Hughesville, Mo., U.S. C4 132
Hughesville, Pa., U.S. D8 145
Hughson, Ca., U.S. D3 112
Hugh Town, Eng., U.K. L7 8
Hugli, stm., India J12 44
Hugo, Co., U.S. B7 113
Hugo, Mn., U.S. m13 130
Hugo, Ok., U.S. C6 143
Hugo Lake, res., Ok., U.S. C6 143
Hugoton, Ks., U.S. E2 123
Hugou, China B6 34
Huichang, China J4 34
Huichapan, Mex. G10 90
Hŭich'ŏn, N. Kor. C14 32
Huicungo, Peru B3 82
Huidong, China A7 40
Huila, dept., Col. F5 84
Huila, Nevado del, mtn., Col. F4 84
Huili, China A7 40
Huillapima, Arg. E6 80
Huilong, China K2 34
Huimin, China F5 32
Huinan (Chaoyang), China A14 32
Huinca Renancó, Arg. H6 80
Huisduinen, Neth. C6 12
Huiting, China I4 32
Huitzo, Mex. I11 90
Huitzuco de los Figueroa, Mex. H10 90
Huixtla, Mex. J13 90
Huiyang, China A5 38
Huize, China A7 40
Huizen, Neth. D7 12
Huizhou, China L3 34
Hukeng, China H3 34
Hukūmah, Sud. K9 60
Hukuntsi, Bots. E5 66
Hulah Lake, res., Ok., U.S. A5 143
Hulan, China B12 30
Hulan Ergi, China B11 30
Hulbert, Mi., U.S. B5 129
Hulbert, Ok., U.S. B6 143
Hulen, Ky., U.S. D6 124
Hulett, Wy., U.S. B8 157
Hulin, China B13 30
Hull, Que., Can. D2 104
Hull, Il., U.S. D2 120
Hull, Ia., U.S. A1 122
Hull, Ma., U.S. B6 128
Hull see Kingston upon Hull, Eng., U.K. H13 8
Hulls Cove, Me., U.S. D4 126
Hulun Nur, l., China B10 30
Ḥulwān, Egypt C6 60
Huma, China A12 30
Huma, stm., China A11 30
Humacao, P.R. E12 94
Humahuaca, Arg. B6 80
Humaitá, Braz. B10 82
Humaitá, Para. D9 80
Humaitá, stm., Braz. C5 82
Humansdorp, S. Afr. J7 66
Humansville, Mo., U.S. D4 132
Humayingzi, China B4 32
Humbe, Ang. E2 58
Humber, stm., Eng., U.K. H13 8
Humberside, co., Eng., U.K. H13 8
Humberto Primo, Arg. F8 80
Humble, Tx., U.S. E5 150
Humboldt, Sask., Can. E3 105
Humboldt, Az., U.S. C3 110
Humboldt, Il., U.S. D5 120
Humboldt, Ia., U.S. B3 122
Humboldt, Ks., U.S. E8 123
Humboldt, Ne., U.S. D10 134
Humboldt, S.D., U.S. D8 148
Humboldt, Tn., U.S. B3 149
Humboldt, co., Ca., U.S. B2 112
Humboldt, co., Ia., U.S. B3 122
Humboldt, co., Nv., U.S. B3 135
Humboldt, stm., Nv., U.S. C3 135
Humboldt, North Fork, stm., Nv., U.S. B6 135
Humboldt Range, mts., Nv., U.S. C3 135
Hume, Il., U.S. D6 120
Hume, Mo., U.S. C3 132
Hume, Lake, res., Austl. K7 70
Humeburn, Austl. F6 70
Humenné, Czech. G21 10
Humeston, Ia., U.S. D4 122
Hummels Wharf, Pa., U.S. E8 145
Humnoke, Ar., U.S. C4 111
Humphrey, Ar., U.S. C4 111
Humphrey, Ne., U.S. C8 134
Humphreys, co., Ms., U.S. B3 131
Humphreys, co., Tn., U.S. A4 149
Humphreys, Mount, mtn., Ca., U.S. D4 112
Humphreys Peak, mtn., Az., U.S. B4 110
Humptulips, Wa., U.S. B2 154
Humpty Doo, Austl. B6 68
Humuya, stm., Hond. C7 92
Húnaflói, b., Ice. B3 6a
Hunan, prov., China F9 30
Hunchun, China A18 32

Name Map Ref. Page

Hundred, W.V., U.S. B4 155
Hundred Acre Pond, l., R.I., U.S. E3 146
Hunedoara, Rom. D6 20
Hunedoara, co., Rom. D6 20
Hünfeld, Ger. E9 10
Hungary (Magyarország), ctry., Eur. F12 4
Hŭngnam, N. Kor. D15 32
Hungry Horse, Mt., U.S. B2 133
Hungry Horse Reservoir, res., Mt., U.S. B3 133
Hung Yen, Viet. D9 40
Huningue, Fr. E14 14
Hunjiang (Badaojiang), China B14 32
Hunkurāb, Ra's, c., Egypt I3 48
Hunnewell, Mo., U.S. B6 132
Hunsberge, mts., Nmb. F3 66
Hunsrück, mts., Ger. F6 10
Hunt, co., Tx., U.S. C4 150
Hunt, stm., R.I., U.S. D4 146
Hunter, Ar., U.S. B4 111
Hunter, Ks., U.S. C5 123
Hunter, N.D., U.S. B8 141
Hunter, Ok., U.S. A4 143
Hunterdon, co., N.J., U.S. B3 137
Hunter Island, i., Austl. M6 70
Hunter Island, i., B.C., Can. D3 99
Hunter Mountain, mtn., N.Y., U.S. C6 139
Hunter River, P.E.I., Can. C6 101
Huntersfield Mountain, mtn., N.Y., U.S. C6 139
Hunters Road, Zimb. B9 66
Huntertown, In., U.S. B7 121
Huntingburg, In., U.S. H4 121
Hunting Creek, stm., Md., U.S. C4 127
Huntingdon, B.C., Can. f13 99
Huntingdon, Que., Can. D3 104
Huntingdon, Pa., U.S. F6 145
Huntingdon, Tn., U.S. A3 149
Huntingdon, co., Pa., U.S. F5 145
Hunting Island, i., S.C., U.S. G7 147
Huntington, Ar., U.S. B1 111
Huntington, In., U.S. C7 121
Huntington, Ma., U.S. B2 128
Huntington, N.Y., U.S. E7 139
Huntington, Or., U.S. C9 144
Huntington, Tx., U.S. D5 150
Huntington, Ut., U.S. D5 151
Huntington, Vt., U.S. C3 152
Huntington, W.V., U.S. C2 155
Huntington, co., In., U.S. C6 121
Huntington Beach, Ca., U.S. F4 112
Huntington Creek, stm., Nv., U.S. C6 135
Huntington Lake, res., In., U.S. C7 121
Huntington Woods, Mi., U.S. p15 129
Huntingtown, Md., U.S. C4 127
Huntland, Tn., U.S. B5 149
Huntley, Il., U.S. A5 120
Huntley, Mt., U.S. E8 133
Huntley, Wy., U.S. E8 157
Huntly, N.Z. B5 72
Hunt Mountain, mtn., Wy., U.S. B5 157
Hunts Point, N.S., Can. F5 101
Huntsville, Ont., Can. B5 103
Huntsville, Al., U.S. A3 108
Huntsville, Ar., U.S. A2 111
Huntsville, In., U.S. E6 121
Huntsville, Ky., U.S. C3 124
Huntsville, Mo., U.S. B5 132
Huntsville, Tn., U.S. C9 149
Huntsville, Tx., U.S. D5 150
Huntsville, Ut., U.S. B4 151
Hunucmá, Mex. G15 90
Hunyani, stm., Afr. E6 58
Hunyuan, China D1 32
Huon Gulf, b., Pap. N. Gui. m16 68a
Huonville, Austl. N7 70
Huoqiu, China C5 34
Huotong, China I8 34
Hupeh see Hubei, prov., China E9 30
Huraymilā, Sau. Ar. B5 47
Hurd, Cape, c., Ont., Can. B3 103
Hurdland, Mo., U.S. A5 132
Hurdsfield, N.D., U.S. B6 141
Hure Qi, China A9 32
Huriel, Fr. F9 14
Hurley, Ms., U.S. E5 131
Hurley, N.M., U.S. E1 138
Hurley, N.Y., U.S. D6 139
Hurley, S.D., U.S. D8 148
Hurley, Va., U.S. e9 153
Hurley, Wi., U.S. B3 156
Hurlock, Md., U.S. C6 127
Huron, Ca., U.S. D3 112
Huron, In., U.S. G4 121
Huron, Oh., U.S. A3 142
Huron, S.D., U.S. C7 148
Huron, co., Mi., U.S. E7 129
Huron, co., Oh., U.S. A3 142
Huron, stm., Mi., U.S. p14 129
Huron, Lake, l., N.A. C10 106
Huron Mountains, hills, Mi., U.S. B3 129
Hurricane, Ms., U.S. A4 131
Hurricane, Ut., U.S. F2 151
Hurricane, W.V., U.S. C2 155
Hurricane Cliffs, clf, U.S. A2 110
Hurricane Creek, stm., Ar., U.S. C3 111
Hurricane Creek, stm., Ga., U.S. E4 117
Hurricane Mountain, mtn., Tn., U.S. C9 149
Hurst, Il., U.S. F4 120
Hurstbridge, Austl. K6 70
Hurt, Va., U.S. C3 153
Hurtado, stm., Chile F3 80
Hurtsboro, Al., U.S. C4 108
Húsavik, Faer. Is. E8 6b
Húsavík, Ice. A5 6a
Husheib, Sud. J8 60
Hushiha, China C4 32
Huşi, Rom. C12 20
Huslia, Ak., U.S. B8 109
Hussar, Alta., Can. D4 98
Hustisford, Wi., U.S. E5 156
Hustonville, Ky., U.S. C5 124
Husum, Ger. A9 10
Husum, Swe. J16 6
Husum, Wa., U.S. D4 154
Hutanopan, Indon. N5 40
Hutchins, Tx., U.S. n10 150
Hutchinson, S. Afr. H6 66
Hutchinson, Ks., U.S. D6 123
Hutchinson, Mn., U.S. F4 130
Hutchinson, co., S.D., U.S. D8 148
Hutchinson, co., Tx., U.S. B2 150
Hutchinson Island, i., Fl., U.S. E6 116
Hutchinson Island, i., S.C., U.S. k11 147
Hutch Mountain, mtn., Az., U.S. C4 110
Hutouya, China F7 32
Hutsonville, Il., U.S. D6 120
Huttig, Ar., U.S. D3 111
Hutto, Tx., U.S. D4 150
Huttonsville, W.V., U.S. C5 155
Huttwil, Switz. D8 13
Huwei, Tai. L9 34
Ḩuwwārah, Isr. Occ. D4 50
Huxford, Al., U.S. D2 108
Huxley, Alta., Can. D4 98
Huxley, Ia., U.S. C4 122
Huyangzhen, China C1 34
Hūzgān, Iran F10 48
Huzhou, China E9 34
Hvannadalshnúkur, mtn., Ice. B5 6a
Hvar, Yugo. F11 18
Hvar, Otok, i., Yugo. F11 18
Hveragerði, Ice. B3 6a
Hvolsvöllur, Ice. C3 6a
Hwange, Zimb. B8 66
Hwang Ho see Huang, stm., China D10 30
Hwangju, N. Kor. E13 32
Hyannis, Ma., U.S. C7 128
Hyannis, Ne., U.S. C4 134
Hyannis Port, Ma., U.S. C7 128
Hyas, Sask., Can. F4 105
Hyattsville, Md., U.S. C4 127
Hyattville, Wy., U.S. B5 157
Hybart, Al., U.S. D2 108
Hybla Valley, Va., U.S. g12 153
Hyco, stm., Va., U.S. D3 153
Hyco Lake, res., N.C., U.S. A3 140
Hydaburg, Ak., U.S. D13 109
Hyde, Pa., U.S. D5 145
Hyde, co., N.C., U.S. B6 140
Hyde, co., S.D., U.S. C6 148
Hyden, Austl. F3 68
Hyden, Ky., U.S. C6 124
Hyde Park, Guy. D13 84
Hyde Park, N.Y., U.S. D7 139
Hyde Park, Ut., U.S. B4 151
Hyde Park, Vt., U.S. B3 152
Hyderābād, India D5 46
Hyderābād, Pak. H3 44
Hydetown, Pa., U.S. C2 145
Hydeville, Vt., U.S. D2 152
Hydra see Ídhra, i., Grc. L7 20
Hydro, Ok., U.S. B3 143
Hydrographers Passage, strt., Austl. C8 70
Hyères, Fr. I13 14
Hyères, Îles d', is., Fr. B18 16
Hyesan, N. Kor. B16 32
Hygiene, Co., U.S. A5 113
Hyland, stm., Can. D7 96
Hylo, Alta., Can. B4 98
Hymaya, stm., Mex. E6 90
Hymera, In., U.S. F3 121
Hyndman, Pa., U.S. G4 145
Hyndman Peak, mtn., Id., U.S. F4 119
Hyŏpch'ŏn, S. Kor. H16 32
Hyrra Banda, Cen. Afr. Rep. O2 60
Hyrum, Ut., U.S. B4 151
Hysham, Mt., U.S. D9 133
Hythe, Alta., Can. B1 98

I

Iacanga, Braz. F4 79
Iaciara, Braz. C5 79
Iaco (Yaco), stm., S.A. C7 82
Iaçu, Braz. B8 79
Iaeger, W.V., U.S. D3 155
Ialomița, co., Rom. E11 20
Ialomița, stm., Rom. E11 20
Iamonia, Lake, l., Fl., U.S. B2 116
Ianakafy, Madag. S21 67b
Iantha, Mo., U.S. D3 132
Iapó, stm., Braz. C13 80
Iapu, Braz. E7 79
Iași, Rom. B11 20
Iași, co., Rom. B11 20
Iatt, Lake, res., La., U.S. C3 125
Iauaretê, Braz. G8 84
Ibadan, Nig. H11 64
Ibagué, Col. E5 84
Ibaiti, Braz. G3 79
Ibans, Laguna de, b., Hond. B10 92
Ibapah Peak, mtn., Ut., U.S. D2 151
Ibarra, Ec. G3 84
Ibarreta, Arg. C9 80
Ibb, Yemen G4 47
Ibbenbüren, Ger. C7 10
Iberia, Mo., U.S. C5 132
Iberia, co., La., U.S. E4 125
Ibérico, Sistema, mts., Spain D9 16
Iberville, Que., Can. D4 104
Iberville, La., U.S. D4 125
Iberville, co., La., U.S. D4 125
Iberville, Mont d' (Mount Caubvick), mtn., Can. g14 104
Ibeto, Nig. F12 64
Ibiá, Braz. E5 79
Ibicaraí, Braz. C9 79
Ibicuí, Braz. C9 79
Ibicuí, stm., Braz. E10 80
Ibicuy, Arg. G9 80
Ibiquera, Braz. B8 79
Ibirá, Braz. F5 79
Ibiraçu, Braz. E8 79
Ibirama, Braz. D14 80
Ibirapuã, Braz. D8 79
Ibirapuitã, stm., Braz. F11 80
Ibirataia, Braz. C9 79
Ibirubá, Braz. E12 80
Ibitiara, Braz. B7 79
Ibitinga, Braz. F4 79
Ibo, Moz. D8 58
Ibotirama, Braz. B7 79
'Ibrī, Oman C10 47
Ibshawāy, Egypt C6 60
Ibusuki, Japan P5 36
Ica, Peru F4 82
Ica, dept., Peru F4 82
Ica, stm., Peru F4 82
Içá (Putumayo), stm., S.A. I8 84
Icabarú, stm., Ven. E11 84
Icamaquã, stm., Braz. E11 80
Içana, Braz. G9 84
Içana (Isana), stm., S.A. G9 84
Icaño, Arg. E6 80
Icaño, Arg. E7 80
Ice Harbor Dam, Wa., U.S. C7 154
İçel, Tur. C3 48
Iceland (Ísland), ctry., Eur. B4 4
Icém, Braz. F4 79
Ichaikaronji, India D3 46
Ichikawa, Japan L14 36
Ichilo, stm., Bol. G9 82
Ichinomiya, Japan L11 36
Ichinoseki, Japan I16 36
Ichkeul, Lac, l., Tun. L4 18
Ichoa, stm., Bol. F9 82
Ichoca, Bol. G8 82
Ich'on, N. Kor. E14 32
Ich'ŏn, S. Kor. F15 32
Icicle Creek, stm., Wa., U.S. B5 154
Ičinskaja Sopka, vulkan, vol., U.S.S.R. F23 24
Icó, Braz. E11 76
Iconha, Braz. F8 79
Icoraci, Braz. D9 76
Icy Cape, c., Ak., U.S. A7 109
Icy Strait, strt., Ak., U.S. k22 109
Ida, La., U.S. A2 125
Ida, Mi., U.S. G7 129
Ida, co., Ia., U.S. B2 122
Ida, Lake, l., Mn., U.S. D3 130
Idabel, Ok., U.S. D7 143
Ida Grove, Ia., U.S. B2 122
Idah, Nig. H13 64
Idaho, co., Id., U.S. D3 119
Idaho, state, U.S. E3 119
Idaho City, Id., U.S. F3 119
Idaho Falls, Id., U.S. F6 119
Idaho Springs, Co., U.S. B5 113
Idalia, Co., U.S. B8 113
Idalou, Tx., U.S. C2 150
Idamay, W.V., U.S. k10 155
Idana, Ks., U.S. C6 123
Idanha, Or., U.S. C4 144
Idanre, Nig. H12 64
Idappādi, India G4 46
Idar-Oberstein, Ger. F7 10
Idaville, In., U.S. C4 121
Ideal, Ga., U.S. D2 117
Idelès, Alg. I13 62
Ider, Al., U.S. A4 108
Idfū, Egypt E7 60
Ídhi Óros, mtn., Grc. N8 20
Ídhra, i., Grc. L7 20
Idi, Indon. L4 40
Idiofa, Zaire C3 58
Idlewild, Tn., U.S. A3 149
Idleyld Park, Or., U.S. D3 144
Idlib, Syria D4 48
Idre, Swe. K13 6
Idrica, U.S.S.R. E11 26
Idrija, Yugo. C9 18
Idutywa, Transkei I9 66
Iecava, U.S.S.R. E7 26
Iepê, Braz. G3 79
Ieper (Ypres), Bel. G2 12
Ierisós, Grc. I7 20
Ife, Nig. H12 64
Iferouâne, Niger B14 64
Ifni, hist. reg., Mor. F5 62
Ifôghas, Adrar des, mts., Afr. E7 54
Ifon-Oshogbo, Nig. H12 64
Igal, Hung. I17 10
Iganna, Nig. H11 64
Igaporã, Braz. B7 79
Igara Paraná, stm., Col. H6 84
Igarka, U.S.S.R. D9 24
Igbasa-Odo, Nig. H11 64
Iğdır, Tur. B8 48
Igharghar, Oued, val., Afr. J14 62
Igizyar, China A7 44
Iglesia, Arg. F4 80
Iglesias, Italy J3 18
Igli, Alg. E9 62
Igloolik, N.W. Ter., Can. C16 96
Ignacej, U.S.S.R. B12 20
Ignacio, Co., U.S. D3 113
Ignacio Zaragoza, Mex. C6 90
Ignalina, U.S.S.R. F9 26
İğneada, Tur. H11 20
Iguaçu, stm., S.A. C12 80
Iguaçu, Saltos do, wtfl, S.A. C11 80
Iguaí, Braz. C8 79
Iguala, Mex. H10 90
Igualada, Spain D13 16
Iguana, stm., Ven. C10 84
Iguape, Braz. C15 80
Iguaraçu, Braz. G3 79
Iguassu Falls see Iguaçu, Saltos do, wtfl, S.A. C11 80
Iguatemi, Braz. G1 79
Iguatemi, stm., Braz. G1 79
Iguatu, Braz. E11 76
Iguazú (Iguaçu), Parque Nacional, S.A. C11 80
Iguéla, Gabon B1 58
Iguîdi, 'Erg, dunes, Afr. C5 54
Igžej, U.S.S.R. G12 24
Iheya-shima, i., Japan T2 37b
Ihiala, Nig. I13 64
Ihosy, Madag. S22 67b
Ihtiman, Bul. G7 20
Iida, Japan L12 36
Iisaku, U.S.S.R. B10 26
Ii-shima, i., Japan F12 30
Iiyama, Japan K13 36
Iizuka, Japan N5 36
Ijâfene, des., Afr. D5 54
Ijaji, Eth. M9 60
Ijebu-Igbo, Nig. H12 64
IJmuiden, Neth. D6 12
IJssel, stm., Neth. C8 12
IJsselmeer (Zuiderzee), Neth. C7 12
IJsselstein, Neth. D7 12
Ijuí, Braz. E12 80
Ijuí, stm., Braz. E11 80
Ikalamavony, Madag. R22 67b
Ikang, Nig. I14 64
Ikaría, i., Grc. L10 20
Ikeja, Nig. H11 64
Ikela, Zaire B4 58
Ikirun, Nig. H12 64
Ikot Ekpene, Nig. I13 64
Ikša, U.S.S.R. E20 26
Ila, Ga., U.S. B3 117
Ilabaya, Peru G6 82
Ilagan, Phil. M19 39b
Ilaka, Madag. Q23 67b
Īlām, Iran E9 48
Ilām, Nepal G12 44
Ilan, Tai. K10 34
Ilanskij, U.S.S.R. F17 22
Ilanz, Switz. E11 13
Ilaro, Nig. H11 64
Iława, Pol. B19 10
Ilbenge, U.S.S.R. E16 24
Ilchester, Md., U.S. B4 127
Ilderton, Ont., Can. D3 103
Île-à-la-Crosse, Sask., Can. m7 105
Île-à-la-Crosse, Lac, l., Sask., Can. B2 105
Ilebo, Zaire B4 58
Île-de-France, hist. reg., Fr. C9 14
Ilek, stm., U.S.S.R. G8 22
Île-Perrot, Que., Can. q19 104
Ilesha, Nig. H12 64
Ilesha Ibarida, Nig. G11 64
Ilford, Man., Can. A4 100
Ilfov, co., Rom. E10 20
Ilfracombe, Austl. D6 70
Ilhabela, Braz. G6 79
Ilha Grande, Braz. H10 84
Ilha Grande, Baía da, b., Braz. G6 79
Ilhéus, Braz. C9 79
Ili, stm., Asia H12 22
Iliamna Lake, l., Ak., U.S. D8 109
Iliamna Volcano, vol., Ak., U.S. C9 109
Ilicínea, Braz. F6 79
Iliff, Co., U.S. A7 113
Iligan, Phil. D7 38
Ilimsk, U.S.S.R. F12 24
Ilion, N.Y., U.S. B5 139
Ilio Point, c., Hi., U.S. B4 118
Ilizi, Alg. G15 62
Iljinskij, U.S.S.R. K23 6
Iljinskij, U.S.S.R. H20 24
Iljinskoje, U.S.S.R. E20 26
Iljinskoje, U.S.S.R. D21 26
Iljinskoje-Chovanskoje, U.S.S.R. E22 26
Ilkal, India E4 46
Il'kino, U.S.S.R. F24 26
Illampu, Nevado, mtn., Bol. F7 82
Illapel, Chile F3 80
Ille-et-Vilaine, dept., Fr. D5 14
Illéla, Niger D12 64
Iller, stm., Ger. H10 10
Illescas, Mex. F8 90
Illescas, Spain E8 16
Illiers, Fr. D8 14
Illimani, Nevado, mtn., Bol. G8 82
Illimo, Peru B2 82
Illiniza, mtn., Ec. H3 84
Illinois, state, U.S. C4 120
Illinois, stm., U.S. A7 143
Illinois, stm., Il., U.S. B5 120
Illinois, stm., Or., U.S. E3 144
Illinois City, Il., U.S. B3 120
Illinois Peak, mtn., Id., U.S. B3 119
Illiopolis, Il., U.S. D4 120
Illmo, Mo., U.S. D8 132
Il'men', ozero, l., U.S.S.R. C14 26
Ilmenau, Ger. E10 10
Ilo, Peru G6 82
Ilobasco, El Sal. D6 92
Iloilo, Phil. C7 38
Ilopango, Lago de, l., El Sal. D5 92
Ilora, Nig. H11 64
Ilorin, Nig. G12 64
Ilūkste, U.S.S.R. F9 26
Ilwaco, Wa., U.S. C1 154
Ilwaki, Indon. G8 38
Imabari, Japan M8 36
Imabu, stm., Braz. H14 84
Imandra, ozero, l., U.S.S.R. H23 6
Imari, Japan N4 36
Imaruí, Braz. E14 80
Imaruí, Lagoa, b., Braz. E14 80
Imatra, Fin. K21 6
Imaza, stm., Peru A2 82
Imbabura, prov., Ec. G3 84
Imbituba, Braz. E14 80
Imbituva, Braz. C13 80
Imbler, Or., U.S. B9 144
Imboden, Ar., U.S. A4 111
Imeni Babuškina, U.S.S.R. B26 26
Imeni 0206 Bakinskich Komissarov, U.S.S.R. B10 48
Imeni C'urupy, U.S.S.R. F21 26
Imeni Vorovskogo, U.S.S.R. F24 26
Imeni Žel'abova, U.S.S.R. C19 26
Imerimandroso, Madag. P23 67b
Imi, Eth. G9 56
Imías, Cuba D7 94
Imilac, Chile C4 80
Imi-n'Tanout, Mor. E6 62
Imišli, U.S.S.R. B10 48
Imjin-gang, stm., Asia F14 32
Imlay, Nv., U.S. C3 135
Imlay City, Mi., U.S. E7 129
Immingham Dock, Eng., U.K. H13 8
Immokalee, Fl., U.S. F5 116
Imnaha, stm., Or., U.S. B10 144
Imola, Italy E6 18
Imotski, Yugo. F12 18
Imperatriz, Braz. E9 76
Imperia, Italy F3 18
Imperial, Sask., Can. F3 105
Imperial, Peru E3 82
Imperial, Ca., U.S. F6 112
Imperial, Mo., U.S. C7 132
Imperial, Ne., U.S. D4 134
Imperial, Pa., U.S. k13 145
Imperial, Tx., U.S. D1 150
Imperial, co., Ca., U.S. F6 112
Imperial, stm., Chile J2 80
Imperial Beach, Ca., U.S. o15 112
Imperial Dam, U.S. E1 110
Imperial Mills, Alta., Can. B5 98
Imperial Reservoir, res., U.S. E1 110
Imperial Valley, val., Ca., U.S. F6 112
Impfondo, Congo A3 58
Imphāl, India H15 44
Impilachti, U.S.S.R. K22 6
Imsil, S. Kor. H15 32
Imuris, Mex. B4 90
Ina, Japan L12 36
Ina, Il., U.S. E5 120
Inambari, stm., Peru E7 82
In Amguel, Alg. I13 62
In Amnas, Alg. F15 62
Iñapari, Peru D7 82
In'aptuk, gora, mtn., U.S.S.R. F14 24
Inari, Fin. G20 6
Inarijärvi, l., Fin. G20 6
Inauini, stm., Braz. C8 82
Inavale, Ne., U.S. D7 134
Inawashiro-ko, l., Japan J15 36
In Belbel, Alg. G11 62
Inca, Spain F14 16
Inca de Oro, Chile D4 80
Incaguasi, Chile E3 80
İncesu, Tur. B3 48
Inchelium, Wa., U.S. A7 154
Inch'ŏn, S. Kor. F14 32
Incline Village, Nv., U.S. D2 135
Incomáti (Komati), stm., Afr. E11 66
Indaiá, stm., Braz. E6 79
Inda Silase, Eth. J10 60
Indaw, Burma C3 40
Indé, Mex. E7 90
Independence, Ca., U.S. D4 112
Independence, In., U.S. D3 121
Independence, Ia., U.S. B6 122
Independence, Ks., U.S. E8 123
Independence, Ky., U.S. B5 124
Independence, La., U.S. D5 125
Independence, Ms., U.S. A4 131
Independence, Mo., U.S. B3 132
Independence, Or., U.S. C3 144
Independence, Va., U.S. D1 153
Independence, Wi., U.S. D2 156
Independence, co., Ar., U.S. B4 111
Independence, stm., N.Y., U.S. B5 139
Independence Mountains, mts., Nv., U.S. C5 135
Independence National Historical Park, Pa., U.S. p21 145
Independence Rock, mtn., Wy., U.S. D5 157
Independencia, Bol. G8 82
Independencia, Isla, i., Peru F3 82
India (Bhārat), ctry., Asia E10 42
Indiahoma, Ok., U.S. C3 143
Indian, stm., Ont., Can. B7 103
Indian, stm., De., U.S. F4 115
Indian, stm., Mi., U.S. B4 129
Indian, stm., N.Y., U.S. A5 139
Indiana, Pa., U.S. E3 145
Indiana, co., Pa., U.S. E3 145
Indiana, state, U.S. E5 121
Indiana Dunes National Lakeshore, In., U.S. A3 121
Indianapolis, In., U.S. E5 121
Indian Bay, b., Fl., U.S. D4 116
Indian Brook, N.S., Can. C9 101
Indian Cedar Swamp, sw., R.I., U.S. F2 146
Indian Church, Belize I15 90
Indian Creek, stm., In., U.S. H5 121
Indian Creek, stm., Md., U.S. C4 127
Indian Creek, stm., Oh., U.S. C1 142
Indian Creek, stm., S.D., U.S. B2 148
Indian Creek, stm., Tn., U.S. B3 149
Indian Creek, stm., W.V., U.S. D4 155
Indian Creek, stm., W.V., U.S. k9 155
Indian Grave Mountain, hill, Ga., U.S. C2 117
Indian Head, Sask., Can. G4 105
Indian Head, Md., U.S. C3 127
Indian Island, i., N.C., U.S. B6 140
Indian Lake, l., Mi., U.S. C4 129
Indian Lake, l., N.Y., U.S. B6 139
Indian Lake, l., Oh., U.S. B2 142
Indian Lake, l., R.I., U.S. F4 146
Indian Mound, Tn., U.S. A4 149
Indian Mound Beach, Ma., U.S. C6 128
Indian Mountain, mtn., Ct., U.S. B2 114
Indian Neck, Ct., U.S. D4 114
Indian Ocean J11 158
Indianola, Il., U.S. D6 120
Indianola, Ia., U.S. C4 122
Indianola, Ms., U.S. B3 131
Indianola, Ne., U.S. D5 134
Indianópolis, Braz. E5 79
Indian Peak, mtn., Ut., U.S. E2 151
Indian Peak, mtn., Wy., U.S. B3 157
Indian Pond, l., Me., U.S. D3 126
Indian Pond, l., Me., U.S. B3 126
Indian Pond, l., Me., U.S. C3 126
Indian Prairie Canal, Fl., U.S. E5 116
Indian Ridge Estates, Az., U.S. E5 110
Indian River, Ont., Can. C6 103
Indian River, Mi., U.S. C6 129
Indian River, co., Fl., U.S. E6 116
Indian River, b., Fl., U.S. D6 116
Indian River Bay, b., De., U.S. F5 115
Indian Rock, mtn., Wa., U.S. D5 154
Indian Rocks Beach, Fl., U.S. p10 116
Indian Springs, Ga., U.S. C3 117
Indian Springs, Nv., U.S. G6 135
Indian Stream, stm., N.H., U.S. f7 136
Indiantown, Fl., U.S. E6 116
Indian Trail, N.C., U.S. B2 140
Indian Village, Ks., U.S. E8 123
Indian Village, La., U.S. D3 125
Indiaporã, Braz. E3 79
Indibir, Eth. M9 60
Indigirka, stm., U.S.S.R. D21 24
Indio, Ca., U.S. F5 112
Indio, stm., Nic. F10 92
Indio, stm., Pan. H14 92
Indira Gandhi Canal, India F5 44
Indispensable Reefs, rf., Sol.Is. B12 68
Indochina, reg., Asia H11 28
Indonesia, ctry., Asia G7 38
Indore, India I6 44
Indragiri, stm., Indon. O7 40
Indrāvati, stm., India C6 46
Indre, dept., Fr. F8 14
Indre-et-Loire, dept., Fr. E7 14
Indrio, Fl., U.S. E6 116
Indura, U.S.S.R. H6 26
Indus, stm., Asia H2 44
Industry, Il., U.S. C3 120
Indwe, S. Afr. H8 66
İnece, Tur. H11 20
In Ecker, Alg. H13 62
İnegöl, Tur. I13 20
Inez, Ky., U.S. C7 124
Inez, Tx., U.S. E4 150
Inferior, Laguna, b., Mex. I12 90
Infiernillo, Presa del, res., Mex. H9 90
Ingaí, stm., Braz. F6 79
Ingal, Niger C13 64
Ingalls, In., U.S. E6 121
Ingalls, Ks., U.S. E3 123
Ingalls Park, Il., U.S. B5 120
Ingelheim, Ger. F8 10
Ingelmunster, Bel. G3 12
Ingende, Zaire B3 58
Ingeniero Luiggi, Arg. H6 80
Ingeniero Luis A. Huergo, Arg. J5 80
Ingeniero White, Arg. J7 80
Ingenio La Esperanza, Arg. C6 80
Ingenio Santa Ana, Arg. D6 80
Ingersoll, Ont., Can. D4 103
Ingham, Austl. B7 70
Ingham, co., Mi., U.S. F6 129
Ingleside, Tx., U.S. F4 150
Inglewood, Austl. G9 70
Inglewood, Ca., U.S. n12 112
Inglewood, Ne., U.S. C9 134
Inglis, Man., Can. D1 100
Ingoda, stm., U.S.S.R. G14 24
Ingoldsby, Ont., Can. C6 103
Ingolstadt, Ger. G11 10
Ingomar, Ms., U.S. A4 131
Ingonish, N.S., Can. C9 101
Ingonish Beach, N.S., Can. C9 101
Ingraham, Lake, l., Fl., U.S. G5 116
Ingrāj Bāzār, India H13 44
Ingram, Pa., U.S. k13 145
Ingram, Tx., U.S. D3 150
In Guezzam, Alg. B12 64
Ingwiller, Fr. D14 14
Inhaca, Ilha da, i., Moz. F11 66
Inhafenga, Moz. C11 66
Inhambane, Moz. D12 66
Inhambupe, Braz. A9 79
Inhaminga, Moz. B12 66
Inhapim, Braz. E7 79
Inharrime, Moz. E12 66
Inhaúma, Braz. E6 79
Inhobi, stm., Braz. G1 79
Inhumas, Braz. D4 79
Inimutaba, Braz. E6 79
Inírida, stm., Col. F8 84
Inisa, Nig. H12 64
Inishmore, i., Ire. H4 8
Injibara, Eth. L9 60
Injune, Austl. E8 70
Inkerman, N.B., Can. B5 101
Inkom, Id., U.S. G6 119
Inkster, Mi., U.S. p15 129
Inkster, N.D., U.S. A8 141
Inland Sea see Seto-naikai, Japan M7 36
Inle Lake, l., Burma D4 40
Inman, Ga., U.S. C2 117
Inman, Ks., U.S. D6 123
Inman, Ne., U.S. B7 134
Inman, S.C., U.S. A3 147
Inn (En), stm., Eur. D20 14
Innamincka, Austl. F4 70
Inner Channel, strt., Belize I15 90
Inner Hebrides, is., Scot., U.K. E7 8
Inner Mongolia see Nei Monggol Zizhiqu, prov., China C10 30
Innertkirchen, Switz. E9 13
Innisfail, Austl. A7 70
Innisfail, Alta., Can. C4 98
Innisfree, Alta., Can. C5 98
Innsbruck, Aus. H11 10
Inocência, Braz. E3 79
Inola, Ok., U.S. A6 143
Inongo, Zaire B3 58
Inowrocław, Pol. C18 10
In Rhar, Alg. G11 62
In Salah, Alg. G12 62
Inscription House Ruin, hist., Az., U.S. A5 110
Ińsko, Pol. B15 10
Institute, W.V., U.S. m12 155
Inta, U.S.S.R. D10 22
Intendente Alvear, Arg. H7 80
İntepe, Tur. I10 20
Intercession City, Fl., U.S. D5 116
Interlachen, Fl., U.S. C5 116
Interlaken, Switz. E8 13
Interlândia, Braz. D4 79
International Falls, Mn., U.S. B5 130
Intervale, N.H., U.S. B4 136
Inthanon, Doi, mtn., Thai. E5 40
Intibucá, Hond. C6 92
Intibucá, dept., Hond. C6 92
Intipucá, El Sal. D6 92
Intiyaco, Arg. E8 80
Intracoastal Waterway, U.S. E4 125
Intuto, Peru I5 84
Inukjuak, Que., Can. g11 104
Inuvik, N.W. Ter., Can. C6 96
Inuya, stm., Peru D5 82
Invercargill, N.Z. G2 72
Inverell, Austl. G9 70
Invergordon, Scot., U.K. D9 8
Inver Grove Heights, Mn., U.S. n12 130
Invermay, Sask., Can. F4 105

Name — Map Ref. — Page

Invermere, B.C., Can. D9 99
Inverness, Que., Can. C6 104
Inverness, Scot., U.K. D9 8
Inverness, Ca., U.S. C2 112
Inverness, Fl., U.S. D4 116
Inverness, Ms., U.S. B3 131
Inverness, Mt., U.S. B6 133
Investigator Group, is., Austl. F6 68
Investigator Strait, strt., Austl. J2 70
Invisible Mountain, mtn., Id., U.S. F5 119
Inwood, Man., Can. D3 100
Inwood, Ont., Can. E3 103
Inwood, In., U.S. B5 121
Inwood, Ia., U.S. A1 122
Inwood, N.Y., U.S. k13 139
Inwood, W.V., U.S. B6 155
Inyangani, mtn., Zimb. B11 66
Inyan Kara Creek, stm., Wy., U.S. B8 157
Inyan Kara Mountain, mtn., Wy., U.S. B8 157
Inyantue, Zimb. B8 66
Inyati, Zimb. B9 66
Inyo, co., Ca., U.S. D5 112
Inyo, Mount, mtn., Ca., U.S. D5 112
Inyo Mountains, mts., Ca., U.S. D4 112
Inywa, Burma C4 40
Inza, U.S.S.R. G7 22
Inzana Lake, l., B.C., Can. B5 99
Inžavino, U.S.S.R. I25 26
Ioánnina, Grc. J4 20
Iō-jima, i., Japan F18 158
Iola, Ks., U.S. E8 123
Iola, Wi., U.S. D4 156
Iolotan', U.S.S.R. J10 22
Iona, N.S., Can. D9 101
Iona, Id., U.S. F7 119
Iona, Mn., U.S. G3 130
Ione, Ca., U.S. C3 112
Ione, Or., U.S. B7 144
Ione, Wa., U.S. A8 154
Ionia, Ia., U.S. A5 122
Ionia, Mi., U.S. F5 129
Ionia, co., Mi., U.S. F5 129
Ionian Islands see Iónioi Nísoi, is., Grc. K4 20
Ionian Sea, Eur. H11 4
Iónioi Nísoi, is., Grc. K4 20
Íos, i., Grc. M9 20
Iosco, co., Mi., U.S. D7 129
Iosegun, stm., Alta., Can. B2 98
Iota, La., U.S. D3 125
Iowa, La., U.S. D2 125
Iowa, co., Ia., U.S. C5 122
Iowa, co., Wi., U.S. E3 156
Iowa, state, U.S. C4 122
Iowa, stm., Ia., U.S. C6 122
Iowa, West Branch, stm., Ia., U.S. B4 122
Iowa City, Ia., U.S. C6 122
Iowa Falls, Ia., U.S. B4 122
Iowa Indian Reservation, U.S. C8 123
Iowa Lake, l., U.S. A3 122
Iowa Park, Tx., U.S. C3 150
Ipameri, Braz. D4 79
Ipatinga, Braz. E7 79
Ipava, Il., U.S. C3 120
Ipeiros, hist. reg., Grc. J4 20
Ipel' (Ipoly), stm., Eur. G19 10
Iphigenia Bay, b., Ak., U.S. n22 109
Ipiales, Col. G4 84
Ipiaú, Braz. C9 79
Ipirá, Braz. B9 79
Ipiranga, Braz. C13 80
Ipiranga, Braz. I9 84
Ipitá, Bol. H10 82
Ipixuna, stm., Braz. B5 82
Ipixuna, stm., Braz. B10 82
Ipixuna, stm., Braz. B10 82
Ipoh, Malay. L6 40
Ipoly (Ipel'), stm., Eur. G18 10
Iporá, Braz. D3 79
Iporã, Braz. G2 79
Ipoti-Ekiti, Nig. H12 64
Ipswich, Austl. F10 70
Ipswich, Eng., U.K. I15 8
Ipswich, Ma., U.S. A6 128
Ipswich, S.D., U.S. B6 148
Ipswich, stm., Ma., U.S. A5 128
Ipu, Braz. D10 76
Ipupiara, Braz. A7 79
Iqaluit, N.W. Ter., Can. D19 96
Iquique, Chile G7 74
Iquique, Chile I6 82
Iquitos, Peru I6 84
Iraan, Tx., U.S. D2 150
Iraí, Braz. D12 80
Iráklion, Grc. N9 20
Iran (Īrān), ctry., Asia C5 42
Iran, Pegunungan, mts., Asia E5 38
Īrānshahr, Iran H16 48
Irapa, Ven. B11 84
Irapuato, Mex. G9 90
Iraq (Al-'Irāq), ctry., Asia C3 42
Irará, Braz. B9 79
Irasburg, Vt., U.S. B4 152
Irati, Braz. C13 80
Irazú, Volcán, vol., C.R. H11 92
Irbeni väin (Irves šaurums), strt., U.S.S.R. D5 26
Irbid, Jord. C5 50
Irbīl, Iraq C8 48
Irbit, U.S.S.R. F10 22
Iredell, co., N.C., U.S. B2 140
Ireland, In., U.S. H3 121
Ireland (Eire), ctry., Eur. E6 4
Irene, S. Afr. E9 66
Irene, S.D., U.S. D8 148
Ireng (Maú), stm., S.A. E13 84
Ireton, Ia., U.S. B1 122
Irgiz, U.S.S.R. H10 22
Iri, S. Kor. H14 32
Iriba, Chad J2 60
Irīgui, reg., Afr. C7 64
Iringa, Tan. C7 58
Irion, co., Tx., U.S. D2 150
Iriona, Hond. B9 92
Iriri, stm., Braz. D8 76
Irish, Mount, mtn., Nv., U.S. F6 135
Irish Sea, Eur. H8 8
Irkutsk, U.S.S.R. G12 24
Irma, Alta., Can. C5 98
Irmo, S.C., U.S. C5 147
Iron, co., Mi., U.S. B2 129
Iron, co., Mo., U.S. D7 132
Iron, co., Ut., U.S. F2 151
Iron, co., Wi., U.S. B3 156
Iron Belt, Wi., U.S. B3 156
Iron City, Ga., U.S. E2 117
Iron City, Tn., U.S. B4 149
Irondale, Al., U.S. f7 108
Irondale, Mo., U.S. D7 132
Irondequoit, N.Y., U.S. B3 139
Iron Gate, Va., U.S. C3 153
Iron Gate, val., Eur. E6 20
Iron Gate Reservoir, res., Eur. E6 20
Iron Gate Reservoir, res., Ca., U.S. B2 112
Ironia, N.J., U.S. B3 137
Iron Knob, Austl. I2 70
Iron Mountain, Mi., U.S. C2 129
Iron Mountain, Mo., U.S. D7 132
Iron Mountain, mtn., Az., U.S. D4 110
Iron Mountains, mts., U.S. D1 153
Iron Range, Austl. B8 68
Iron Ridge, Wi., U.S. E5 156
Iron River, Mi., U.S. B2 129
Iron River, Wi., U.S. B2 156
Ironton, Mn., U.S. D5 130
Ironton, Mo., U.S. D7 132
Ironton, Oh., U.S. D3 142
Ironwood, Mi., U.S. n11 129
Iroquois, Ont., Can. C9 103
Iroquois, S.D., U.S. C8 148
Iroquois, co., Il., U.S. C6 120
Iroquois, stm., U.S. C6 120
Iroquois, Lake, l., Vt., U.S. B2 152
Iroquois Falls, Ont., Can. o19 103
Irrawaddy see Ayeyarwady, stm., Burma F3 40
Irricana, Alta., Can. D4 98
Irrigon, Or., U.S. B7 144
Irševa, U.S.S.R. A7 20
Irtyš (Ertix), stm., Asia E11 22
Irtyš (Ertix), stm., Asia A3 30
Irtyšsk, U.S.S.R. G13 22
Irumu, Zaire A5 58
Irún, Spain B10 16
Irupana, Bol. G8 82
Irurzun, Spain C10 16
Irú Tepuy, mtn., Ven. E12 84
Irves šaurums (Irbeni väin), strt., U.S.S.R. D5 26
Irvine, Alta., Can. E5 98
Irvine, Scot., U.K. F9 8
Irvine, Ca., U.S. n13 112
Irvine, Ky., U.S. C6 124
Irving, Il., U.S. D4 120
Irving, Tx., U.S. n10 150
Irvington, Al., U.S. E1 108
Irvington, Il., U.S. E4 120
Irvington, Ky., U.S. C3 124
Irvington, Ne., U.S. g12 134
Irvington, N.J., U.S. k8 137
Irvington, N.Y., U.S. g13 139
Irvington, Va., U.S. C6 153
Irvona, Pa., U.S. E4 145
Irwin, Id., U.S. F7 119
Irwin, Ia., U.S. C2 122
Irwin, Pa., U.S. F2 145
Irwin, co., Ga., U.S. E3 117
Irwinton, Ga., U.S. D3 117
Irwinville, Ga., U.S. E3 117
Isaac, stm., Austl. D8 70
Isaac Lake, l., B.C., Can. C7 99
Isabel, Ks., U.S. E5 123
Isabel, S.D., U.S. B4 148
Isabel, Mount, mtn., Wy., U.S. D2 157
Isabela, Phil. D7 38
Isabela, Cabo, c., Dom. Rep. E9 94
Isabela, Isla, i., Ec. J13 84a
Isabela, Isla, i., Mex. G7 90
Isabelia, Cordillera, mts., Nic. D9 92
Isabella, Ga., U.S. E3 117
Isabella, Mo., U.S. E5 132
Isabella, Tn., U.S. D9 149
Isabella, co., Mi., U.S. E6 129
Isabella Indian Reservation, Mi., U.S. E6 129
Isabella Lake, l., Mn., U.S. C7 130
Isaccea, Rom. D12 20
Ísafjördur, Ice. A2 6a
Isahaya, Japan O5 36
Īsa Khel, Pak. D4 44
Işalniţa, Rom. E7 20
Isana (Içana), stm., S.A. G8 84
Isanti, Mn., U.S. E5 130
Isanti, co., Mn., U.S. E5 130
Isar, stm., Eur. G11 10
Isara, Nig. H11 64
Ischia, Italy I8 18
Ischia, Isola d', i., Italy I8 18
Iscuandé, stm., Col. F4 84
Ise (Uji-yamada), Japan M11 36
Iselin, N.J., U.S. B4 137
Iseo, Lago d', l., Italy D5 18
Isère, dept., Fr. G12 14
Isère, stm., Fr. G12 14
Iserlohn, Ger. D7 10
Isernia, Italy H9 18
Isesaki, Japan K14 36
Iset', stm., U.S.S.R. F11 22
Iseyin, Nig. H11 64
Isherton, Guy. F13 84
Ishinomaki, Japan I16 36
Ishioka, Japan K15 36
Ishpeming, Mi., U.S. B3 129
Isigny, Fr. C5 14
Isil'kul', U.S.S.R. G12 22
Išim, U.S.S.R. F11 22
Išim, stm., U.S.S.R. F12 22
Išimbaj, U.S.S.R. G9 22
Isinglass, stm., N.H., U.S. D4 136
Isiolo, Kenya A7 58
Isipingo, S. Afr. G10 66
Isiro, Zaire H6 56
Isisford, Austl. E6 70
Iskăr, stm., Bul. F8 20
Iskăr, jazovir, res., Bul. G7 20
İskele, N. Cyp. D2 48
İskenderun, Tur. C4 48
İskenderun Körfezi, b., Tur. H15 4
Iskitim, U.S.S.R. G8 24
Isla, Mex. H12 90
Isla, Salar de la, pl., Chile C4 80
Isla Cristina, Spain H4 16
Isla de Maipo, Chile G3 80
Islāmābād, Pak. D5 44
Islāmkot, Pak. H4 44
Islamorada, Fl., U.S. H6 116
Islāmpur, India D3 46
Isla Mujeres, Mex. G16 90
Island, Ky., U.S. C2 124
Island, co., Wa., U.S. A3 154
Island Beach, N.J., U.S. D4 137
Island City, Or., U.S. B8 144
Island Falls, Me., U.S. B4 126
Island Heights, N.J., U.S. D4 137
Island Lagoon, l., Austl. H2 70
Island Lake, l., Man., Can. C4 100
Island Lake, stm., Man., Can. B4 100
Island Park, Id., U.S. E7 119
Island Park, R.I., U.S. E6 146
Island Park Reservoir, res., Id., U.S. E7 119
Island Pond, Vt., U.S. B5 152
Island Pond, l., N.H., U.S. E4 136
Islands, Bay of, b., Newf., Can. D2 102
Isla Patrulla, Ur. G11 80
Islas de la Bahía, dept., Hond. A8 92
Isla Verde, Arg. G7 80
Isla Vista, Ca., U.S. E4 112
Islay, Alta., Can. C5 98
Islay, i., Scot., U.K. F7 8
Islay, Punta, c., Peru G5 82
Isle, Mn., U.S. D5 130
Isle-aux-Morts, Newf., Can. E2 102
Isle of Man, dep., Eur. E7 4
Isle of Palms, S.C., U.S. k12 147
Isle of Wight, co., Eng., U.K. K12 8
Isle of Wight, co., Va., U.S. D6 153
Isle of Wight Bay, b., Md., U.S. D7 127
Isle Royale National Park, Mi., U.S. h9 129
Islesboro Island, i., Me., U.S. D4 126
Isleta, N.M., U.S. C3 138
Isleta Indian Reservation, N.M., U.S. C3 138
Isleton, Ca., U.S. C3 112
Islington, Ma., U.S. h11 128
Islón, Chile E3 80
Ismael Cortinas, Ur. G10 80
Ismailia see Al-Ismā'īlīyah, Egypt B7 60
İsmailli, Tur. K11 20
Isnā, Egypt E7 60
Isojoki, Fin. J17 6
Isola, Ms., U.S. B3 131
Isone, Switz. F10 13
Isparta, Tur. H14 4
İspir, Tur. A6 48
Israel (Yisra'el), ctry., Asia C2 42
Israel, stm., N.H., U.S. B3 136
Issano, Guy. E13 84
Issaquah, Wa., U.S. B3 154
Issaquena, co., Ms., U.S. C2 131
Issoire, Fr. G10 14
Issoudun, Fr. F9 14
Is-sur-Tille, Fr. E12 14
Issyk-Kul', ozero, l., U.S.S.R. I13 22
İstanbul, Tur. H12 20
İstanbul Boğazı (Bosporus), strt., Tur. H13 20
Istmina, Col. E4 84
Isto, Mount, mtn., Ak., U.S. B11 109
Istokpoga, Lake, l., Fl., U.S. E5 116
Istra, U.S.S.R. F19 26
Istra, pen., Yugo. D8 18
Istria see Istra, pen., Yugo. D8 18
Itá, Para. C10 80
Itabaiana, Braz. E11 76
Itabaiana, Braz. F11 76
Itabapoana, Braz. F8 79
Itaberá, Braz. G4 79
Itaberaba, Braz. B8 79
Itaberaí, Braz. D4 79
Itabira, Braz. E7 79
Itabuna, Braz. C9 79
Itacambiruçu, stm., Braz. D7 79
Itacaré, Braz. C9 79
Itacoatiara, Braz. I13 84
Itacuaí, stm., Braz. J7 84
Itacurubí del Rosario, Para. C10 80
Itaeté, Braz. B8 79
Itagi, Braz. C8 79
Itaguaçu, Braz. E8 79
Itaguaí, Braz. G7 79
Itaguajé, Braz. G3 79
Itaguara, Braz. F6 79
Itaguari, stm., Braz. C6 79
Itaguaru, Braz. C6 79
Itagüí, Col. D5 84
Itaí, Braz. G4 79
Itá-Ibaté, Arg. D10 80
Itaiópolis, Braz. D14 80
Itaituba, Braz. D7 76
Itajá, Braz. E3 79
Itajaí, Braz. D14 80
Itajaí do Sul, stm., Braz. D14 80
Itajubá, Braz. G6 79
Itaju do Colônia, Braz. C9 79
Itajuípe, Braz. C9 79
Italy, Tx., U.S. C4 150
Italy (Italia), ctry., Eur. G10 4
Italy Cross, N.S., Can. E5 101
Itamaraju, Braz. D9 79
Itamarandiba, Braz. D7 79
Itamarandiba, stm., Braz. D7 79
Itamari, Braz. B9 79
Itambacuri, Braz. E8 79
Itambé, Braz. C8 79
Itami, Japan M10 36
Itanhaém, Braz. H5 79
Itanhauã, stm., Braz. A9 82
Itanhém, Braz. D8 79
Itanhém, stm., Braz. D9 79
Itanhomi, Braz. E8 79
Itaobim, Braz. D8 79
Itapaci, Braz. C4 79
Itapagipe, Braz. E4 79
Itaparaná, stm., Braz. B10 82
Itaparica, Ilha de, i., Braz. B9 79
Itapaya, Bol. G8 82
Itapé, Braz. C9 79
Itapebi, Braz. C9 79
Itapecerica, Braz. F6 79
Itapecuru, stm., Braz. D10 76
Itapecuru-Mirim, Braz. D10 76
Itapemirim, Braz. F8 79
Itaperuna, Braz. F8 79
Itapetinga, Braz. C8 79
Itapetininga, Braz. G4 79
Itapetininga, stm., Braz. G5 79
Itapeva, Braz. G4 79
Itapicuru, stm., Braz. F11 76
Itapira, Braz. G5 79
Itapiranga, Braz. D12 80
Itapiranga, Braz. I13 84
Itapirapuã, Braz. C3 79
Itapitanga, Braz. C9 79
Itápolis, Braz. F4 79
Itaporã, Braz. G1 79
Itaporanga, Braz. G4 79
Itapúa, dept., Para. D11 80
Itapuranga, Braz. C4 79
Itaquara, Braz. B9 79
Itaquari, Braz. F8 79
Itaqui, Braz. E10 80
Itaquyry, Para. C11 80
Itarantim, Braz. C8 79
Itararé, Braz. H4 79
Itararé, stm., Braz. B14 80
Itārsi, India I7 44
Itarumã, Braz. E3 79
Itasca, Il., U.S. k8 120
Itasca, Tx., U.S. C4 150
Itasca, co., Mn., U.S. C5 130
Itasca, Lake, l., Mn., U.S. C3 130
Itata, stm., Chile I2 80
Itatí, Arg. D9 80
Itatiaia, Parque Nacional do, Braz. G6 79
Itatiba, Braz. G5 79
Itatinga, Braz. G4 79
Itauçu, Braz. D4 79
Itaúna, Braz. F6 79
Itawamba, co., Ms., U.S. A5 131
Ité, stm., Col. D5 84
Iténez (Guaporé), stm., S.A. E10 82
Ithaca, Mi., U.S. E6 129
Ithaca, Ne., U.S. g11 134
Ithaca, N.Y., U.S. C4 139
Itháki, Grc. K4 20
Itháki, i., Grc. K4 20
Itinga, Braz. D8 79
Itinga, stm., Braz. D8 79
Itiquira, Braz. D1 79
Itiquira, stm., Braz. G14 82
Itirapina, Braz. G5 79
Itiruçu, Braz. B8 79
Itō, Japan M14 36
Itoigawa, Japan J12 36
Itonamas, stm., Bol. E9 82
Itororó, Braz. C8 79
Itsā, Egypt C6 60
Itta Bena, Ms., U.S. B3 131
Itu, Braz. G5 79
Itu, stm., Braz. E11 80
Ituaçu, Braz. B8 79
Ituberá, Braz. B9 79
Itucumã, stm., Braz. B7 82
Itueta, Braz. E8 79
Ituí, stm., Braz. J7 84
Ituim, stm., Braz. E13 80
Ituiutaba, Braz. E4 79
Itumbiara, Braz. E4 79
Ituna, Sask., Can. F4 105
Ituni, Guy. E13 84
Ituporanga, Braz. D14 80
Iturama, Braz. E3 79
Iturbe, Para. D10 80
Iturbide, Mex. H15 90
Iturup, ostrov (Etorofu-tō), i., U.S.S.R. C22 36a
Ituverava, Braz. F5 79
Ituxi, stm., Braz. B9 82
Ituzaingó, Arg. D10 80
Itzehoe, Ger. B9 10
Iuka, Il., U.S. E5 120
Iuka, Ks., U.S. E5 123
Iuka, Ms., U.S. A5 131
Iúna, Braz. F8 79
Iva, S.C., U.S. C2 147
Ivacevići, U.S.S.R. I8 26
Ivahona, Madag. S22 67b
Ivaí, stm., Braz. G2 79
Ivaiporã, Braz. C13 80
Ivane-Puste, U.S.S.R. A10 20
Ivangorod, U.S.S.R. B11 26
Ivangrad, Yugo. G3 20
Ivanhoe, Austl. I6 70
Ivanhoe, Mn., U.S. F2 130
Ivanhoe, Va., U.S. D2 153
Ivan'kovo, U.S.S.R. G20 26
Ivan'kovskij, U.S.S.R. E23 26
Ivan'kovskoje vodochranilišče, res., U.S.S.R. E19 26
Ivano-Frankovsk, U.S.S.R. H2 22
Ivanovo, U.S.S.R. D23 26
Ivanovo, U.S.S.R. I8 26
Ivato, Madag. R22 67b
Ivatuva, Braz. G2 79
Ivdel', U.S.S.R. E10 22
Ivenec, U.S.S.R. H9 26
Ivesdale, Il., U.S. D5 120
Ivinheima, stm., Braz. G2 79
Ivins, Ut., U.S. F2 151
Ivje, U.S.S.R. H8 26
Ivo, Bol. I10 82
Ivon, stm., Bol. D8 82
Ivor, Va., U.S. D6 153
Ivorogbo, Nig. I13 64
Ivory Coast (Côte d'Ivoire), ctry., Afr. G5 54
Ivory Coast, I.C. I7 64
Ivoryton, Ct., U.S. D6 114
Ivrea, Italy D2 18
İvrindi, Tur. J11 20
Ivujivik, Que., Can. f11 104
Ivy, Va., U.S. B4 153
Ivydale, W.V., U.S. C3 155
Ivy Mountain, mtn., Ct., U.S. B3 114
Iwaki (Taira), Japan J15 36
Iwakuni, Japan M7 36
Iwamizawa, Japan D16 36a
Iwanai, Japan E15 36a
Iwo, Nig. H12 64
Iwo Jima see Iō-jima, i., Japan F18 158
Iwŏn, N. Kor. C16 32
Ixcán, stm., N.A. B3 92
Ixchiguán, Guat. B3 92
Ixiamas, Bol. E7 82
Iximché, hist., Guat. C4 92
Ixmiquilpan, Mex. G10 90
Ixopo, S. Afr. H10 66
Ixtahuacán, Guat. B3 92
Ixtapa, Mex. I9 90
Ixtepec, Mex. I12 90
Ixtlán de Juárez, Mex. I11 90
Ixtlán del Río, Mex. G7 90
'Iyāl Bakhīt, Sud. K5 60
Iyo-mishima, Japan N8 36
Izabal, Guat. B5 92
Izabal, dept., Guat. B5 92
Izabal, Lago de, l., Guat. B5 92
Īzad Khvāst, Iran F12 48
Izalco, El Sal. D5 92
Izamal, Mex. G15 90
Izapa, hist., Mex. J13 90
Izard, co., Ar., U.S. A4 111
'Izbat Abū Suql, Egypt F1 50
Izberbaš, U.S.S.R. I7 22
Izbica, Pol. A17 10
Izd'oškovo, U.S.S.R. F16 26
Izegem, Bel. G3 12
Īzeh, Iran F10 48
Iževsk, U.S.S.R. F8 22
Izkī, Oman C10 47
Izma, stm., U.S.S.R. E8 22
Izmail, U.S.S.R. H3 22
Izmalkovo, U.S.S.R. I20 26
İzmir (Smyrna), Tur. K11 20
İzmit, Tur. G13 4
Iznajar, Embalse de, res., Spain H7 16
Izoplit, U.S.S.R. E19 26
Izopo, Punta, c., Hond. B7 92
Izozog, Bañados de, sw., Bol. H10 82
Izra', Syria C6 50
Izsák, Hung. I19 10
Iztaccíhuatl, Volcán, vol., Mex. H10 90
Iztaccíhuatl y Popocatéptl, Parques Nacionales, Mex. H10 90
Iztapa, Guat. D4 92
Izucar de Matamoros, Mex. H10 90
Izuhara, Japan M4 36
Iz'um, U.S.S.R. H5 22
Izumi, Japan O5 36
Izumi, Japan I15 36
Izumi, Japan M10 36
Izumo, Japan L7 36
Izu-shotō, is., Japan E15 30
Izvestij CIK, ostrova, is., U.S.S.R. B14 22

J

Jaba, Eth. N8 60
Jabal al-Awliyā', Sud. J7 60
Jabalpur, India I8 44
Jabālyah, Isr. Occ. E2 50
Jabiru, Austl. B6 68
Jabjabah, Wādī, val., Afr. G7 60
Jablah, Syria D3 48
Jablonec nad Nisou, Czech. E15 10
Jabłonka, Pol. F19 10
Jablonov, U.S.S.R. A8 20
Jablonovyj chrebet, mts., U.S.S.R. G14 24
Jaboatão, Braz. E11 76
Jaborandi, Braz. F4 79
Jaboticabal, Braz. F4 79
Jabung, Tanjung, c., Indon. O8 40
Jaca, Spain C11 16
Jacala, Mex. G10 90
Jacaleapa, Hond. C8 92
Jacaltenango, Guat. B3 92
Jacaraci, Braz. C7 79
Jacaré, stm., Braz. B8 79
Jacaré, stm., Braz. B10 82
Jacareí, Braz. G6 79
Jacarèzinho, Braz. G4 79
Jaceel, val., Som. F11 56
Jáchal, stm., Arg. F4 80
Jachin, Al., U.S. C1 108
Jachroma, U.S.S.R. E20 26
Jaciara, Braz. C1 79
Jacinto, Braz. D8 79
Jacinto, Ms., U.S. A5 131
Jacinto Aráuz, Arg. J7 80
Jacinto City, Tx., U.S. r14 150
Jacinto Machado, Braz. E14 80
Jaci Paraná, Braz. C9 82
Jaciparaná, stm., Braz. D9 82
Jack, co., Tx., U.S. C3 150
Jackfish Lake, l., Sask., Can. D1 105
Jackman, Me., U.S. C2 126
Jackman Station, Me., U.S. C2 126
Jack Mountain, mtn., Mt., U.S. D4 133
Jack Mountain, mtn., Va., U.S. B3 153
Jack Mountain, mtn., Wa., U.S. A5 154
Jackpot, Nv., U.S. B7 135
Jacksboro, Tn., U.S. C9 149
Jacksboro, Tx., U.S. C3 150
Jacks Creek, Tn., U.S. B3 149
Jacks Mountain, mtn., Pa., U.S. E6 145
Jackson, Al., U.S. D2 108
Jackson, Ca., U.S. C3 112
Jackson, Ga., U.S. C3 117
Jackson, Ky., U.S. C6 124
Jackson, La., U.S. D4 125
Jackson, Mi., U.S. F6 129
Jackson, Mn., U.S. G4 130
Jackson, Ms., U.S. C3 131
Jackson, Mo., U.S. D8 132
Jackson, Mt., U.S. E3 133
Jackson, Ne., U.S. B9 134
Jackson, N.H., U.S. B4 136
Jackson, N.C., U.S. A5 140
Jackson, Oh., U.S. C3 142
Jackson, S.C., U.S. E4 147
Jackson, Tn., U.S. B3 149
Jackson, Wi., U.S. E5 156
Jackson, Wy., U.S. C2 157
Jackson, co., Al., U.S. A3 108
Jackson, co., Ar., U.S. B4 111
Jackson, co., Co., U.S. A4 113
Jackson, co., Fl., U.S. B1 116
Jackson, co., Ga., U.S. B3 117
Jackson, co., Il., U.S. F4 120
Jackson, co., In., U.S. G5 121
Jackson, co., Ia., U.S. B7 122
Jackson, co., Ks., U.S. C8 123
Jackson, co., Ky., U.S. C5 124
Jackson, co., La., U.S. B3 125
Jackson, co., Mi., U.S. F6 129
Jackson, co., Mn., U.S. G3 130
Jackson, co., Ms., U.S. E5 131
Jackson, co., Mo., U.S. B3 132
Jackson, co., N.C., U.S. f9 140
Jackson, co., Oh., U.S. C3 142
Jackson, co., Ok., U.S. C2 143
Jackson, co., Or., U.S. E4 144
Jackson, co., S.D., U.S. D4 148
Jackson, co., Tn., U.S. C8 149
Jackson, co., Tx., U.S. E4 150
Jackson, co., W.V., U.S. C3 155
Jackson, co., Wi., U.S. D3 156
Jackson, stm., Va., U.S. C3 153
Jackson, Lake, l., Fl., U.S. E5 116
Jackson, Lake, l., Fl., U.S. B2 116
Jackson, Mount, mtn., Ant. C12 73
Jackson, Mount, mtn., N.H., U.S. B4 136
Jacksonboro, S.C., U.S. F7 147
Jacksonburg, W.V., U.S. B4 155
Jackson Center, Oh., U.S. B1 142
Jackson Dam, Al., U.S. D2 108
Jackson Lake, res., Ga., U.S. C3 117
Jackson Lake, res., Wy., U.S. C2 157
Jackson Mountain, mtn., Me., U.S. D2 126
Jackson Mountains, mts., Nv., U.S. B3 135
Jacksonport, Ar., U.S. B4 111
Jackson's Arm, Newf., Can. D3 102
Jacksons Gap, Al., U.S. C4 108
Jacksonville, Al., U.S. B4 108
Jacksonville, Ar., U.S. C3 111
Jacksonville, Fl., U.S. B5 116
Jacksonville, Ga., U.S. E4 117
Jacksonville, Il., U.S. D3 120
Jacksonville, Me., U.S. D5 126
Jacksonville, N.C., U.S. C5 140
Jacksonville, Oh., U.S. C3 142
Jacksonville, Or., U.S. E4 144
Jacksonville, Tx., U.S. D5 150
Jacksonville, Vt., U.S. F3 152
Jacksonville Beach, Fl., U.S. B5 116
Jacksonville Naval Air Station, mil., Fl., U.S. B5 116
Jacks Peak, mtn., Ut., U.S. E3 151
Jacmel, Haiti E8 94
Jaco, Mex. D7 90
Jacobābād, Pak. F3 44
Jacobina, Braz. F10 76
Jacobsdal, S. Afr. G7 66
Jacques-Cartier, stm., Que., Can. B6 104
Jacques-Cartier, Détroit de, strt., Que., Can. h8 102
Jacquet, stm., N.B., Can. B3 101
Jacquet River, N.B., Can. B4 101
Jacqueville, I.C. I7 64
Jacuba, stm., Braz. E2 79
Jacuí, stm., Braz. F12 80
Jacuípe, Braz. B9 79
Jacuípe, stm., Braz. B9 79
Jacumba, Ca., U.S. F5 112
Jacupiranga, Braz. C14 80
Jaén, Peru A2 82
Jaén, Spain H8 16
Jāfarābād, India B1 46
Jaffa, Cape, c., Austl. K3 70
Jaffa, Tel Aviv- see Tel Aviv-Yafo, Isr. D3 50
Jaffna, Sri L. H6 46
Jaffrey, N.H., U.S. E2 136
Jaffrey Center, N.H., U.S. E2 136
Jafr, Qā'al-, depr., Jord. H6 50
Jagādhri, India E7 44
Jagdalpur, India C7 46
Jagersfontein, S. Afr. G7 66
Jagodnoje, U.S.S.R. E21 24
Jagraon, India E6 44
Jagtiāl, India C5 46
Jaguaquara, Braz. B9 79
Jaguarão, Braz. G12 80
Jaguarão (Yaguarón), stm., S.A. G12 80
Jaguari, Braz. E11 80
Jaguariaíva, Braz. C14 80
Jaguaribe, stm., Braz. E11 76
Jaguaripe, Braz. B9 79
Jaguaruna, Braz. E14 80
Jagüé, Arg. E4 80
Jagüey Grande, Cuba C4 94
Jahānābād, India H11 44
Jahrom, Iran G12 48
Jailolo, Indon. E8 38
Jaipur, India G6 44
Jaisalmer, India G4 44
Jaja, U.S.S.R. F15 22
Jājapur, India J12 44
Jajce, Yugo. E12 18
Jakarta, Indon. J13 39a
Jakestown, Tn., U.S. C8 149
Jakin, Ga., U.S. E2 117
Jakobstad (Pietarsaari), Fin. J18 6
Jakša, U.S.S.R. E9 22
Jakutsk, U.S.S.R. E17 24
Jal, N.M., U.S. E6 138
Jalālābād, Afg. C4 44
Jalāmīd, Sau. Ar. B10 60
Jalán, stm., Hond. C8 92
Jalandhar, India E6 44
Jalapa, Guat. C5 92
Jalapa, Nic. D8 92
Jalapa, dept., Guat. C5 92
Jālgaon, India J6 44
Jalisco, state, Mex. G7 90
Jālna, India C3 46
Jālor, India H5 44
Jalostotitlán, Mex. G8 90
Jalpa, Mex. G8 90
Jalpāiguri, India G13 44
Jalpan, Mex. G10 90
Jalta, U.S.S.R. I4 22
Jaltepec, stm., Mex. I12 90
Jalūlā', Iraq D8 48

Name — Map Ref. — Page

Jalutorovsk, U.S.S.R. F11 22
Jamaame, Som. A8 58
Jamaica, Ia., U.S. C3 122
Jamaica, Vt., U.S. E3 152
Jamaica, ctry., N.A. E6 94
Jamaica Bay, b., N.Y., U.S. k13 139
Jamaica Channel, strt., N.A. E7 94
Jamal, poluostrov, pen., U.S.S.R. C12 22
Jamālpur, Bngl. H13 44
Jamālpur, India H12 44
Jamanari, stm., Braz. I8 84
Jamantau, gora, mtn., U.S.S.R. G9 22
Jamanxim, stm., Braz. A13 82
Jamari, stm., Braz. C10 82
Jamari, Lago, l., Braz. H14 84
Jamarovka, U.S.S.R. G14 24
Jambelí, Canal de, strt., Ec. I2 84
Jambi, Indon. F3 38
Jambol, Bul. G10 20
James, Ga., U.S. D3 117
James, stm., Alta., Can. D3 98
James, stm., U.S. C7 106
James, stm., Mo., U.S. E4 132
James, stm., Va., U.S. C5 153
James, Lake, l., In., U.S. A7 121
James, Lake, res., N.C., U.S. B1 140
James Bay, b., Can. F16 96
James Bay, b., Can. A10 106
James Branch, stm., De., U.S. F3 115
Jamesburg, N.J., U.S. C4 137
James City, N.C., U.S. B5 140
James City, co., Va., U.S. C6 153
James Craik, Arg. G7 80
James Island, S.C., U.S. k12 147
James Island, i., Md., U.S. C5 127
James Island, i., S.C., U.S. F8 147
Jamesport, Mo., U.S. B4 132
James River Bridge, Va., U.S. k15 153
James Ross, Cape, c., N.W. Ter., Can. B10 96
James Ross Strait, strt., N.W. Ter., Can. C13 96
Jamestown, Austl. I3 70
Jamestown, S. Afr. H8 66
Jamestown, Ca., U.S. D3 112
Jamestown, Co., U.S. A5 113
Jamestown, In., U.S. E4 121
Jamestown, Ks., U.S. C6 123
Jamestown, Ky., U.S. D4 124
Jamestown, Mo., U.S. C5 132
Jamestown, N.Y., U.S. C1 139
Jamestown, N.C., U.S. B3 140
Jamestown, N.D., U.S. C7 141
Jamestown, Oh., U.S. C2 142
Jamestown, Pa., U.S. D1 145
Jamestown, R.I., U.S. F5 146
Jamestown, Tn., U.S. C9 149
James Town, Wy., U.S. E3 157
Jamestown Dam, N.D., U.S. C7 141
Jamestown Reservoir, res., N.D., U.S. C7 141
Jamesville, N.C., U.S. B6 140
Jaminauá, stm., Braz. C6 82
Jamkhandi, India D3 46
Jamm, U.S.S.R. C11 26
Jammu, India D6 44
Jammu and Kashmīr, dep., Asia C10 42
Jamnagar, India I4 44
Jampol', U.S.S.R. A12 20
Jamsah, Egypt D7 60
Jamshedpur, India I12 44
Jamsk, U.S.S.R. F22 24
Jämtlands Län, co., Swe. J13 6
Jamūi, India H12 44
Jamuna, stm., Bngl. H13 44
Jamundí, Col. F4 84
Jana, stm., U.S.S.R. C19 24
Janauacá, Lago, l., Braz. I12 84
Janaúba, Braz. C7 79
Janaucu, Ilha, i., Braz. C8 76
Jand, Pak. D5 44
Jandaia, Braz. D3 79
Jandaia do Sul, Braz. G3 79
Jandaq, Iran D13 48
Jandiāla, India E6 44
Jandiatuba, stm., Braz. J8 84
Janeiro, Rio de, stm., Braz. A6 79
Jane Lew, W.V., U.S. B4 155
Janesville, Ca., U.S. B3 112
Janesville, Ia., U.S. B5 122
Janesville, Mn., U.S. F5 130
Janesville, Wi., U.S. F4 156
Janeville, N.B., Can. B4 101
Jangijul', U.S.S.R. I11 22
Jangīpur, India H13 44
Janīn, Isr. Occ. D4 50
Janjina, Madag. R21 67b
Jan Kempdorp (Andalusia), S. Afr. F7 66
Jan Mayen, i., Sval. A6 52
Janos, Mex. B5 90
Jánoshalma, Hung. I19 10
Jánosháza, Hung. H17 10
Janoviči, U.S.S.R. F13 26
Jansen, Sask., Can. F3 105
Jansen, Co., U.S. D6 113
Jansen, Ne., U.S. D8 134
Janskij zaliv, b., U.S.S.R. C19 24
Jantarnyj, U.S.S.R. G2 26
Januária, Braz. C6 79
Janzé, Fr. E5 14
Jaora, India I6 44
Japan (Nihon), ctry., Asia D14 30
Japan, Sea of (Nihon-kai), Asia K7 36
Japiim, Braz. B5 82
Japurá, Braz. H9 84
Japurá (Caquetá), stm., S.A. H8 84
Jaqué, Pan. D3 84
Jaqui, Peru F4 82
Jarābulus, Syria C5 48
Jarad, Sau. Ar. E2 47
Jaraguá, Braz. C4 79
Jaraguá do Sul, Braz. D14 80
Jaraiz de la Vera, Spain E6 16
Jarales, N.M., U.S. C3 138
Jarama, stm., Spain E8 16
Jaramānah, Syria B6 50
Jaransk, U.S.S.R. F7 22
Jarash, Jord. D5 50
Jarbalo, Ks., U.S. k15 123
Jarcevo, U.S.S.R. F15 26
Jardim, Braz. I13 82
Jardín América, Arg. D11 80
Jardine River National Park, Austl. B8 68
Jardines de la Reina, Archipiélago de los, is., Cuba D5 94
Jardinópolis, Braz. F5 79
Jaredi, Nig. E12 64
Jaremča, U.S.S.R. A8 20
Jarensk, U.S.S.R. E7 22
Jargara, U.S.S.R. C12 20
Jargeau, Fr. E9 14
Jari, stm., Braz. E9 74
Jari, stm., Braz. A10 82
Jari, Lago, l., Braz. J11 84
Jaridih, India I12 44
Jarmen, Ger. B13 10
Jarnac, Fr. G6 14
Jarocin, Pol. D17 10
Jaroměř, Czech. E15 10
Jaroslavl', U.S.S.R. D22 26
Jarosław, Pol. E22 10
Jarratt, Va., U.S. D5 153
Jarrettsville, Md., U.S. A5 127
Jaru, Braz. D10 82
Jaru, stm., Braz. D10 82
Järva-Jaani, U.S.S.R. B8 26
Järvenpää, Fin. K19 6
Jarvie, Alta., Can. B4 98
Jarvis Island, i., Oc. I23 158
Jaša Tomić, Yugo. D4 20
Jasikan, Ghana H10 64
Jasin'a, U.S.S.R. A8 20
Jāsk, Iran I14 48
Jasło, Pol. F21 10
Jasmine Estates, Fl., U.S. D4 116
Jasnogorsk, U.S.S.R. G20 26
Jason Islands, is., Falk. Is. G4 78
Jasonville, In., U.S. F3 121
Jasper, Ont., Can. C9 103
Jasper, Al., U.S. B2 108
Jasper, Ar., U.S. B2 111
Jasper, Fl., U.S. B4 116
Jasper, Ga., U.S. B2 117
Jasper, In., U.S. H4 121
Jasper, Mn., U.S. G2 130
Jasper, Mo., U.S. D3 132
Jasper, Tn., U.S. D8 149
Jasper, Tx., U.S. D6 150
Jasper, co., Ga., U.S. C3 117
Jasper, co., Il., U.S. D5 120
Jasper, co., In., U.S. B3 121
Jasper, co., Ia., U.S. C4 122
Jasper, co., Ms., U.S. C4 131
Jasper, co., Mo., U.S. D3 132
Jasper, co., S.C., U.S. G5 147
Jasper, co., Tx., U.S. D5 150
Jasper Lake, l., Alta., Can. C1 98
Jasper National Park, Alta., Can. C1 98
Jászapáti, Hung. H20 10
Jászberény, Hung. H19 10
Jataí, Braz. D3 79
Jatapu, stm., Braz. H13 84
Jataté, stm., Mex. I14 90
Jatni, India J11 44
Jatobá, stm., Braz. B1 79
Jaú, Braz. G4 79
Jaú, stm., Braz. H12 84
Jauaperi, stm., Braz. H12 84
Jauja, Peru D4 82
Jaúna, stm., Braz. B12 82
Jaungulbene, U.S.S.R. D9 26
Jaunjelgava, U.S.S.R. E8 26
Jaunpiebalga, U.S.S.R. D9 26
Jaunpur, India H10 44
Jaupaci, Braz. D3 79
Jauquara, stm., Braz. F13 82
Jauru, stm., Braz. E1 79
Jauru, stm., Braz. G13 82
Java, S.D., U.S. B6 148
Java see Jawa, i., Indon. J15 39a
Javari (Yavarí), stm., S.A. D4 76
Javas, U.S.S.R. G25 26
Java Sea see Jawa, Laut, Indon. G5 38
Java Trench J11 28
Jawa (Java), i., Indon. J15 39a
Jawa, Laut (Java Sea), Indon. G5 38
Jawbar, Syria A6 50
Jawor, Pol. D16 10
Jaworzno, Pol. E19 10
Jay, Fl., U.S. u14 116
Jay, Me., U.S. D2 126
Jay, Ok., U.S. A7 143
Jay, co., In., U.S. D7 121
Jaya, Puncak, mtn., Indon. F10 38
Jayanca, Peru B2 82
Jayapura (Sukarnapura), Indon. F11 38
Jayb, Wādī al- (Ha'Arava), val., Asia H4 50
Jay Peak, mtn., Vt., U.S. B3 152
Jaypur, India C7 46
Jayton, Tx., U.S. C2 150
Jaželbicy, U.S.S.R. C15 26
J. B. Thomas, Lake, res., Tx., U.S. C2 150
Jean, Nv., U.S. H6 135
Jeanerette, La., U.S. E4 125
Jean Lafitte, La., U.S. k11 125
Jean Lafitte National Historical Park, La., U.S. k12 125
Jeannette, Pa., U.S. F2 145
Jebba, Nig. G12 64
Jebeniana, Tun. C16 62
Jeberos, Peru A3 82
Jechegnadzor, U.S.S.R. B8 48
Jedburg, Mo., U.S. f12 132
Jeddore Lake, res., Newf., Can. D3 102
Jędrzejów, Pol. E20 10
Jefawa, Sud. L2 60
Jeff, Ky., U.S. C6 124
Jeffara (Al-Jifārah), pl., Afr. D16 62
Jeff Davis, co., Ga., U.S. E4 117
Jeff Davis, co., Tx., U.S. o12 150
Jeffers, Mn., U.S. F3 130
Jeffers, Mt., U.S. E5 133
Jefferson, Al., U.S. C2 108
Jefferson, Ar., U.S. C3 111
Jefferson, Co., U.S. B5 113
Jefferson, Ga., U.S. B3 117
Jefferson, In., U.S. D4 121
Jefferson, Ia., U.S. B3 122
Jefferson, La., U.S. k11 125
Jefferson, Me., U.S. D3 126
Jefferson, Ma., U.S. B4 128
Jefferson, N.H., U.S. B4 136
Jefferson, N.C., U.S. A1 140
Jefferson, Oh., U.S. A5 142
Jefferson, Or., U.S. C3 144
Jefferson, S.C., U.S. B7 147
Jefferson, S.D., U.S. E9 148
Jefferson, Tx., U.S. C5 150
Jefferson, Wi., U.S. E5 156
Jefferson, co., Al., U.S. B3 108
Jefferson, co., Ar., U.S. C3 111
Jefferson, co., Co., U.S. B5 113
Jefferson, co., Fl., U.S. B3 116
Jefferson, co., Ga., U.S. C4 117
Jefferson, co., Id., U.S. F6 119
Jefferson, co., Il., U.S. E5 120
Jefferson, co., In., U.S. G6 121
Jefferson, co., Ia., U.S. C5 122
Jefferson, co., Ks., U.S. C8 123
Jefferson, co., Ky., U.S. B4 124
Jefferson, co., La., U.S. E5 125
Jefferson, co., Ms., U.S. D2 131
Jefferson, co., Mo., U.S. C7 132
Jefferson, co., Mt., U.S. D4 133
Jefferson, co., Ne., U.S. D8 134
Jefferson, co., N.Y., U.S. A5 139
Jefferson, co., Oh., U.S. B5 142
Jefferson, co., Ok., U.S. C4 143
Jefferson, co., Or., U.S. C5 144
Jefferson, co., Pa., U.S. D3 145
Jefferson, co., Tn., U.S. C10 149
Jefferson, co., Tx., U.S. E5 150
Jefferson, co., Wa., U.S. B1 154
Jefferson, co., W.V., U.S. B7 155
Jefferson, co., Wi., U.S. E5 156
Jefferson, stm., Mt., U.S. E5 133
Jefferson, Mount, mtn., Id., U.S. E7 119
Jefferson, Mount, mtn., Nv., U.S. E5 135
Jefferson, Mount, mtn., Or., U.S. C5 144
Jefferson City, Mo., U.S. C5 132
Jefferson City, Mt., U.S. D5 133
Jefferson City, Tn., U.S. C10 149
Jefferson Davis, co., La., U.S. D3 125
Jefferson Davis, co., Ms., U.S. D4 131
Jefferson Farms, De., U.S. i7 115
Jefferson Heights, Md., U.S. A2 127
Jefferson Hill, hill, Ky., U.S. g11 124
Jefferson Proving Ground, mil., In., U.S. G7 121
Jeffersontown, Ky., U.S. B4 124
Jeffersonville, Ga., U.S. D3 117
Jeffersonville, In., U.S. H6 121
Jeffersonville, Ky., U.S. C6 124
Jeffersonville, Oh., U.S. C2 142
Jeffersonville, Vt., U.S. B3 152
Jeffrey, W.V., U.S. D3 155
Jeffrey City, Wy., U.S. D5 157
Jeffries Creek, stm., S.C., U.S. C8 147
Jefimovskij, U.S.S.R. L24 6
Jefremov, U.S.S.R. G5 22
Jega, Nig. E12 64
Jegenstorf, Switz. D8 13
Jegorjevsk, U.S.S.R. F22 26
Jehossee Island, i., S.C., U.S. k11 147
Jejsk, U.S.S.R. H5 22
Jēkabpils, U.S.S.R. E8 26
Jekateriny, proliv, strt., U.S.S.R. I21 24
Jekimoviči, U.S.S.R. G16 26
Jekyll Island, i., Ga., U.S. E5 117
Jelabuga, U.S.S.R. F8 22
Jelancy, U.S.S.R. G13 24
Jel'cy, U.S.S.R. E16 26
Jelec, U.S.S.R. I21 26
Jelenia Góra (Hirschberg), Pol. E15 10
Jelenskij, U.S.S.R. H18 26
Jelgava, U.S.S.R. E6 26
Jelizarovo, U.S.S.R. C27 26
Jelizavety, mys, c., U.S.S.R. G20 24
Jelizovo, U.S.S.R. H12 26
Jellico, Tn., U.S. C9 149
Jelm Mountain, mtn., Wy., U.S. E7 157
Jel'n'a, U.S.S.R. G16 26
Jelnat', U.S.S.R. D25 26
Jeloguj, stm., U.S.S.R. E15 22
Jelšava, Czech. G20 10
Jemanželinsk, U.S.S.R. G10 22
Jember, Indon. G5 38
Jemca, U.S.S.R. J27 6
Jemez, stm., N.M., U.S. k7 138
Jemez Canyon Dam, N.M., U.S. k7 138
Jemez Indian Reservation, N.M., U.S. h7 138
Jemez Pueblo, N.M., U.S. B3 138
Jemez Springs, N.M., U.S. B3 138
Jemison, Al., U.S. C3 108
Jemmal, Tun. N5 18
Jemseg, N.B., Can. D3 101
Jena, Ger. E11 10
Jena, La., U.S. C3 125
Jenašimskij Polkan, gora, mtn., U.S.S.R. F16 22
Jenbach, Aus. H11 10
Jendouba (Souk el Arba), Tun. M3 18
Jenisej (Yenisey), stm., U.S.S.R. D15 22
Jenisejsk, U.S.S.R. F10 24
Jenisejskij kr'až, mts., U.S.S.R. F16 22
Jenisejskij zaliv, b., U.S.S.R. C8 24
Jenkins, Ky., U.S. C7 124
Jenkins, Mn., U.S. D4 130
Jenkins, co., Ga., U.S. D5 117
Jenkinsburg, Ga., U.S. C2 117
Jenkintown, Pa., U.S. o21 145
Jenks, Ok., U.S. A6 143
Jenner, Alta., Can. D5 98
Jenners, Pa., U.S. F3 145
Jennersdorf, Aus. I16 10
Jennette, Ar., U.S. B5 111
Jennie, Ar., U.S. D4 111
Jennings, Fl., U.S. B3 116
Jennings, Ks., U.S. C3 123
Jennings, La., U.S. D3 125
Jennings, Mo., U.S. f13 132
Jennings, Ok., U.S. A5 143
Jennings, co., In., U.S. G6 121
Jenny Jump Mountain, mtn., N.J., U.S. B3 137
Jenny Lind, Ar., U.S. B1 111
Jensen, Ut., U.S. C6 151
Jensen Beach, Fl., U.S. E6 116
Jeparit, Austl. K4 70
Jepelacio, Peru B3 82
Jepifan', U.S.S.R. H21 26
Jeptha Knob, hill, Ky., U.S. B4 124
Jequeri, Braz. F7 79
Jequetepeque, stm., Peru B2 82
Jequié, Braz. B8 79
Jequitaí, Braz. D6 79
Jequitinhonha, Braz. D8 79
Jequitinhonha, stm., Braz. D9 79
Jerada, Mor. C9 62
Jeradou, Tun. M5 18
Jerauld, co., S.D., U.S. C7 148
Jerba, Île de, i., Tun. D16 62
Jerécuaro, Mex. G9 90
Jérémie, Haiti E7 94
Jeremoabo, Braz. F11 76
Jerevan, U.S.S.R. I6 22
Jerez de García Salinas, Mex. F8 90
Jerez de la Frontera, Spain I5 16
Jerez de los Caballeros, Spain G5 16
Jergeni, hills, U.S.S.R. H6 22
Jericho, Ar., U.S. B5 111
Jericho, Vt., U.S. B3 152
Jericho see Arīḥā, Isr. Occ. E4 50
Jericó, Col. E5 84
Jerico Springs, Mo., U.S. D4 132
Jerid, Chott, sw., Tun. D15 62
Jerilderie, Austl. J6 70
Jerimoth Hill, hill, R.I., U.S. C1 146
Jermiš', U.S.S.R. G25 26
Jermolino, U.S.S.R. F19 26
Jermyn, Pa., U.S. C10 145
Jeroaquara, Braz. C3 79
Jerofej Pavlovič, U.S.S.R. G16 24
Jerome, Az., U.S. C3 110
Jerome, Fl., U.S. F5 116
Jerome, Id., U.S. G4 119
Jerome, Mo., U.S. D6 132
Jerome, Pa., U.S. F4 145
Jerome, co., Id., U.S. G4 119
Jeromesville, Oh., U.S. B3 142
Jerônimo Monteiro, Braz. F8 79
Jersey, Ga., U.S. C3 117
Jersey, co., Il., U.S. D3 120
Jersey, dep., Eur. F7 4
Jersey City, N.J., U.S. B4 137
Jersey Mountain, mtn., Id., U.S. E3 119
Jersey Shore, Pa., U.S. D7 145
Jersey Village, Tx., U.S. r14 150
Jerseyville, Il., U.S. D3 120
Jeršov, U.S.S.R. G7 22
Jerusalem, Ar., U.S. B3 111
Jerusalem see Yerushalayim, Isr. E4 50
Jervis, Cape, c., Austl. J3 70
Jervis Bay, b., Austl. J9 70
Jervis Inlet, b., B.C., Can. D6 99
Jesenice, Czech. E13 10
Jesi, Italy F8 18
Jesil', U.S.S.R. G11 22
Jessamine, co., Ky., U.S. C5 124
Jessentuki, U.S.S.R. I6 22
Jessieville, Ar., U.S. C2 111
Jessore, Bngl. I13 44
Jessup, Md., U.S. B4 127
Jessup, Pa., U.S. m18 145
Jesup, Ga., U.S. E5 117
Jesup, Ia., U.S. B5 122
Jesup, Lake, l., Fl., U.S. D5 116
Jesús, Para. D11 80
Jésus, Île, i., Que., Can. p19 104
Jesús Carranza, Mex. I12 90
Jesús de Otoro, Hond. C7 92
Jesús María, Arg. F6 80
Jesús María, Mex. E6 90
Jesús María, stm., Mex. F7 90
Jesús Menéndez, Cuba D6 94
Jet, Ok., U.S. A3 143
Jetmore, Ks., U.S. D4 123
Jetpur, India J4 44
Jette, Bel. G5 12
Jeumont, Fr. B11 14
Jever, Ger. B7 10
Jevlach, U.S.S.R. I7 22
Jevpatorija, U.S.S.R. H4 22
Jewel Cave National Monument, S.D., U.S. D2 148
Jewell, Ia., U.S. B4 122
Jewell, Ks., U.S. C5 123
Jewell, co., Ks., U.S. C5 123
Jewell Ridge, Va., U.S. e10 153
Jewett, Oh., U.S. B4 142
Jewett, Tx., U.S. D4 150
Jewett City, Ct., U.S. C8 114
Jewett Lake, l., Sask., Can. A3 105
Jezerce, mtn., Alb. G3 20
Jezerišče, U.S.S.R. F12 26
Jeziorany, Pol. B20 10
Jhābua, India I6 44
Jhālāwār, India H7 44
Jhal Jhao, Pak. G1 44
Jhang Sadar, Pak. E5 44
Jhānsi, India H8 44
Jharia, India I12 44
Jhārsuguda, India B8 46
Jhelum, Pak. D5 44
Jhelum, stm., Asia E5 44
Jhok Rind, Pak. E4 44
Jhunjhunūn, India F6 44
Jiaban, China B9 40
Jiading, China D10 34
Jiāganj, India H13 44
Jiakou, China E8 34
Jiali, China E5 30
Jialing, stm., China E8 30
Jiamusi, China B13 30
Ji'an, China H3 34
Jianchang, China B12 32
Jianchuan, China A5 40
Jiangbeixu, China I4 34
Jiangbianzhai, China C6 40
Jiangcun, China G6 34
Jiangdihe, China B6 40
Jiangduo, China C9 34
Jianggezhuang, China D7 32
Jiangji, China C4 34
Jiangjin, China F8 30
Jiangkou, China G9 30
Jiangkou, China H7 34
Jiangkouji, China C5 34
Jiangliadian, China A5 32
Jiangmen, China M2 34
Jiangsu (Kiangsu), prov., China E10 30
Jiangtun, China B10 32
Jiangxi (Kiangsi), prov., China F10 30
Jiangxiang, China C6 34
Jiangyin, China D9 34
Jiangzhasiji, China E13 44
Jianli, China F1 34
Jianning, China I5 34
Jian'ou, China H7 34
Jianshan, China F9 34
Jianshui, China C7 40
Jiantouji, China I5 32
Jiaohe, China C12 30
Jiaomei, China K6 34
Jiaoshanhe, China F1 34
Jiaoxian, China G7 32
Jiaozuo, China D9 30
Jiashan, China C7 34
Jiashun Hu, l., China C12 44
Jiawang, China A6 34
Jiaxian, China B2 34
Jiaxing, China E9 34
Jiayu, China F2 34
Jiazi, China M5 34
Jibiya, Nig. E13 64
Jiboa, stm., El Sal. D5 92
Jicarilla Apache Indian Reservation, N.M., U.S. A2 138
Jicarón, Isla, i., Pan. D2 84
Jicatuyo, stm., Hond. C6 92
Jiddah (Jeddah), Sau. Ar. D1 47
Jidingxilin, China D15 44
Jiedong, China I2 34
Jiehe, China H5 32
Jieji, China B7 34
Jiepai, China E8 34
Jiesheng, China M4 34
Jieshou, China B4 34
Jieshou, China B8 34
Jieyang, China L5 34
Jieznas, U.S.S.R. G7 26
Jigongzhen, China A4 34
Jiguaní, Cuba D6 94
Jiguanshan, China A12 32
Jigüey, Bahía de, b., Cuba C5 94
Jihlava, Czech. F15 10
Jijel, Alg. B13 62
Jijiadianzi, China H6 32
Jikawo, Eth. M7 60
Jikawo, stm., Afr. M8 60
Jilib, Som. A8 58
Jili Hu, l., China B4 30
Jilin, China C12 30
Jilin (Kirin), prov., China C12 30
Jill, Kediet ej, mtn., Maur. I4 62
Jima, Eth. N9 60
Jimbolia, Rom. D4 20
Jiménez, Mex. C9 90
Jiménez, Mex. D7 90
Jiménez del Téul, Mex. F7 90
Jim Hogg, co., Tx., U.S. F3 150
Jim Lake, res., N.D., U.S. B7 141
Jimo, China G8 32
Jim Thorpe, Pa., U.S. E10 145
Jim Wells, co., Tx., U.S. F3 150
Jin (Gam), stm., Asia C8 40
Jināh, Egypt E6 60
Jinan (Tsinan), China G4 32
Jinbang, China J7 34
Jincheng, China D9 30
Jīnd, India F7 44
Jindřichův Hradec, Czech. F15 10
Jingangtou, China H2 34
Jingcheng, China K6 34
Jingdezhen (Kingtechen), China F6 34
Jinggang, China G1 34
Jinggangshan (Ciping), China I3 34
Jinghai, China E4 32
Jinghaiwei, China G10 32
Jinghong, China C6 40
Jingning, China H8 34
Jingoutun, China B5 32
Jingxi, China C9 40
Jingxian, China F4 32
Jingyu, China A14 32
Jingzhi, China G7 32
Jinhua, China F8 34
Jining, China C9 30
Jining, China H4 32
Jinja, Ug. A6 58
Jinjiang, China A6 40
Jinjing, China G2 34
Jinkeng, China H6 34
Jinkou, China G8 32
Jinlingzhen, China G6 32
Jinning, China B7 40
Jinotega, Nic. D8 92
Jinotega, dept., Nic. D9 92
Jinotepe, Nic. F8 92
Jinping, China A10 40
Jinrui, China H3 34
Jinsha, stm., China F6 30
Jinshan, China E10 34
Jinshi, China F9 30
Jintian, China H3 34
Jinxi, China C8 32
Jinxian, China D9 32
Jinyun, China G9 34
Jinzhaizhen, China D4 34
Jinzhou (Chinchou), China B9 32
Jiparaná, stm., Braz. C10 82
Jipijapa, Ec. H2 84
Jiquilisco, El Sal. D6 92
Jiquilisco, Bahía de, b., El Sal. D6 92
Jiquiriçá, Braz. B9 79
Jiquiriçá, stm., Braz. B8 79
Jirāfī, Wādī al- (Naḥal Paran), val. I3 50
Jirbān, Sud. L6 60
Jirjā, Egypt D6 60
Jirkov, Czech. E13 10
Jīroft, Iran G14 48
Jisr ash-Shughūr, Syria D4 48
Jitan, China K4 34
Jitaúna, Braz. C9 79
Jiu, stm., Rom. F7 20
Jiubao, China J4 34
Jiucheng, China E5 32
Jiuguan, China F9 32
Jiuhu, China F5 32
Jiuhuaxian, China L2 34
Jiujiang, China F4 34
Jiukou, China E1 34
Jiulian Shan, mts., China K3 34
Jiuling Shan, mts., China G3 34
Jiulong, China K1 34
Jiumianyang, China E2 34
Jiuningyang, China J6 34
Jiuquan, China D6 30
Jiushangshui, China B3 34
Jiutai, China C12 30
Jiuxian, China B2 34
Jiuxiangcheng, China B3 34
Jixi, China B13 30
Jixian, China H2 32
Jixian, China C5 32
Jixingji, China C5 34
Jiyang, China G5 32
Jīzān, Sau. Ar. F3 47
Joaçaba, Braz. D13 80
Joaíma, Braz. D8 79
Joanésia, Braz. E7 79
Joanna, S.C., U.S. C4 147
João de Tiba, stm., Braz. D9 79
João Neiva, Braz. E8 79
João Pessoa, Braz. E12 76
João Pinheiro, Braz. D5 79
Joaquim Távora, Braz. G4 79
Joaquín V. González, Arg. C6 80
Job Peak, mtn., Nv., U.S. D3 135
Jocassee, Lake, res., U.S. B1 147
Jocolí, Arg. G4 80
Jocón, Hond. B8 92
Jocoro, El Sal. D6 92
Jocotán, Guat. C5 92
Jódar, Spain H8 16
Jo Daviess, co., Il., U.S. A3 120
Jodhpur, India G5 44
Jodie, W.V., U.S. m13 155
Joe Batt's Arm [-Barr'd Islands-Shoal Bay], Newf., Can. D4 102
Joensuu, Fin. J21 6
Joes Brook, stm., Vt., U.S. C4 152
Joes Creek, stm., W.V., U.S. m12 155
Joetsu, Japan J13 36
Joffre, Mount, mtn., Can. D3 98
Jõgeva, U.S.S.R. C9 26
Jog Falls, wtfl, India E3 46
Joggins, N.S., Can. D5 101
Johannesburg, S. Afr. F9 66
John, Cape, c., N.S., Can. D6 101
John Day, Or., U.S. C8 144
John Day, stm., Or., U.S. B6 144
John Day, North Fork, stm., Or., U.S. C7 144
John Day Dam, U.S. D5 154
John Day Fossil Beds National Monument, Or., U.S. C6 144
John F. Kennedy Space Center, sci., Fl., U.S. D6 116
John H. Kerr Dam, Va., U.S. D4 153
John H. Kerr Reservoir, res., U.S. D4 153
John Martin Reservoir, res., Co., U.S. C7 113
John Muir National Historical Site, hist., Ca., U.S. h8 112
John O'Groats, Scot., U.K. C10 8
John Redmond Reservoir, res., Ks., U.S. D8 123
Johnsburg, Il., U.S. h8 120
John Sevier, Tn., U.S. m14 149
Johns Island, S.C., U.S. F7 147
Johns Island, i., S.C., U.S. F7 147
Johnson, Ar., U.S. A1 111
Johnson, Ks., U.S. E2 123
Johnson, Ne., U.S. D10 134
Johnson, Vt., U.S. B3 152
Johnson, co., Ar., U.S. B2 111
Johnson, co., Ga., U.S. D4 117
Johnson, co., Il., U.S. F5 120
Johnson, co., In., U.S. F5 121
Johnson, co., Ia., U.S. C6 122
Johnson, co., Ks., U.S. D9 123
Johnson, co., Ky., U.S. C7 124
Johnson, co., Mo., U.S. C4 132
Johnson, co., Ne., U.S. D9 134
Johnson, co., Tn., U.S. C12 149
Johnson, co., Tx., U.S. C4 150
Johnson, co., Wy., U.S. B6 157
Johnsonburg, Pa., U.S. D4 145
Johnson City, N.Y., U.S. C5 139
Johnson City, Tn., U.S. C11 149
Johnson City, Tx., U.S. D3 150
Johnson Creek, Wi., U.S. E5 156
Johnsonville, S.C., U.S. D9 147
Johns Pass, strt., Fl., U.S. p10 116
Johnston, Ia., U.S. e8 122
Johnston, R.I., U.S. C4 146
Johnston, S.C., U.S. D4 147
Johnston, co., N.C., U.S. B4 140
Johnston, co., Ok., U.S. C5 143
Johnston Atoll, atoll, Oc. G23 158
Johnston City, Il., U.S. F5 120
Johnstone Strait, strt., B.C., Can. D4 99
Johnston Key, i., Fl., U.S. H5 116
Johnstown, Co., U.S. A6 113
Johnstown, N.Y., U.S. B6 139
Johnstown, Oh., U.S. B3 142
Johnstown, Pa., U.S. F4 145
Johnsville, Md., U.S. A3 127
John W. Flannagan Reservoir, res., Va., U.S. e9 153
Johor Baharu, Malay. N7 40
Joice, Ia., U.S. A4 122
Joigny, Fr. E10 14
Joiner, Ar., U.S. B5 111
Joinvile, Braz. D14 80
Joinville, Fr. D12 14
Joinville Island, i., Ant. B1 73
Jokkmokk, Swe. H16 6

Name	Map Ref.	Page
Jolārpettai, India	F5	46
Jolfā, Iran	B8	48
Joliet, Il., U.S.	B5	120
Joliet, Mt., U.S.	E8	133
Joliette, Que., Can.	C4	104
Jolo, Phil.	D7	38
Jomda, China	E6	30
Jonava, U.S.S.R.	F7	26
Jones, Al., U.S.	C3	108
Jones, Ok., U.S.	B4	143
Jones, co., Ga., U.S.	C3	117
Jones, co., Ia., U.S.	B6	122
Jones, co., Ms., U.S.	D4	131
Jones, co., N.C., U.S.	B5	140
Jones, co., S.D., U.S.	D5	148
Jones, co., Tx., U.S.	C3	150
Jonesboro, Ar., U.S.	B5	111
Jonesboro, Ga., U.S.	C2	117
Jonesboro, Il., U.S.	F4	120
Jonesboro, In., U.S.	D6	121
Jonesboro, La., U.S.	B3	125
Jonesboro, Me., U.S.	D5	126
Jonesborough, Tn., U.S.	C11	149
Jonesburg, Mo., U.S.	C6	132
Jones Creek, Tx., U.S.	s14	150
Jones Mill, Ar., U.S.	C3	111
Jonesport, Me., U.S.	D5	126
Jones Sound, strt., N.W. Ter., Can.	A15	96
Jonestown, Ms., U.S.	C3	131
Jonestown, Ms., U.S.	A3	131
Jonestown, Pa., U.S.	F9	145
Jonesville, In., U.S.	F6	121
Jonesville, La., U.S.	C4	125
Jonesville, Mi., U.S.	G6	129
Jonesville, N.C., U.S.	A2	140
Jonesville, S.C., U.S.	B4	147
Jonesville, Vt., U.S.	C3	152
Jonesville, Va., U.S.	f8	153
Joniškėlis, U.S.S.R.	E7	26
Joniškis, U.S.S.R.	E6	26
Jönköping, Swe.	M14	6
Jonquière, Que., Can.	A6	104
Jonuta, Mex.	H13	90
Joplin, Mo., U.S.	D3	132
Joplin, Mt., U.S.	B6	133
Joppa, Al., U.S.	A3	108
Joppa, Il., U.S.	F5	120
Joppatowne, Md., U.S.	B5	127
Jordan, Al., U.S.	D1	108
Jordan, Mn., U.S.	F5	130
Jordan, Mt., U.S.	C10	133
Jordan, N.Y., U.S.	B4	139
Jordan (Al-Urdunn), ctry., Asia	C2	42
Jordan (Nahr al-Urdunn) (HaYarden), stm., Asia	E5	50
Jordan, stm., Ut., U.S.	C4	151
Jordan Creek, stm., U.S.	E9	144
Jordânia, Braz.	C8	79
Jordan Lake, l., N.S., Can.	E4	101
Jordan Lake, res., Al., U.S.	C3	108
Jordanów, Pol.	F19	10
Jordan Valley, Or., U.S.	D9	144
Jordão, stm., Braz.	C13	80
Jordet, Nor.	K13	6
Jorhāt, India	G16	44
Jornado del Muerto, des., N.M., U.S.	D3	138
Jos, Nig.	G14	64
José Batlle y Ordóñez, Ur.	G11	80
José Bonifácio, Braz.	F4	79
José Francisco Vergara, Chile	B4	80
Joselândia, Braz.	G13	82
José María Blanco (Tres Lomas), Arg.	I7	80
José Pedro Varela, Ur.	G11	80
Joseph, Or., U.S.	B9	144
Joseph, Lac, l., Newf., Can.	h8	102
Joseph Bonaparte Gulf, b., Austl.	B5	68
Joseph City, Az., U.S.	C5	110
Josephine, co., Or., U.S.	E3	144
Josephville, Mo., U.S.	f12	132
Joshua, Tx., U.S.	n9	150
Joshua Tree, Ca., U.S.	E5	112
Joshua Tree National Monument, Ca., U.S.	F6	112
Joškar-Ola, U.S.S.R.	F7	22
Josselin, Fr.	E4	14
Joubertina, S. Afr.	I6	66
Jourdanton, Tx., U.S.	E3	150
Joussard, Alta., Can.	B3	98
Jovellanos, Cuba	C4	94
Joviânia, Braz.	D4	79
Jowhar, Som.	H10	56
Joy, Il., U.S.	B3	120
Joyce, La., U.S.	C3	125
Józefów, Pol.	C21	10
J. Percy Priest Lake, res., Tn., U.S.	A5	149
Juab, co., Ut., U.S.	D2	151
Juami, stm., Braz.	H9	84
Juan Aldama, Mex.	E8	90
Juan B. Arruabarrena, Arg.	F9	80
Juan de Fuca, Strait of, strt., N.A.	A1	154
Juan de Mena, Para.	C10	80
Juan de Nova, Île, i., Reu.	E8	58
Juan E. Barra, Arg.	I8	80
Juan Eugenio, Mex.	E8	90
Juan Fernández, Archipiélago, is., Chile	C1	78
Juangriego, Ven.	B11	84
Juan Guerra, Peru	B3	82
Juan Jorba, Arg.	G6	80
Juan José Castelli, Arg.	C8	80
Juanjuí, Peru	B3	82
Juan L. Lacaze, Ur.	H10	80
Juan N. Fernández, Arg.	J9	80
Juan Viñas, C.R.	H11	92
Juárez, Arg.	I9	80
Juárez, Mex.	B5	90
Juárez, Mex.	D9	90
Juárez, Sierra de, mts., Mex.	B2	90
Juárez see Ciudad Juárez, Mex.	B6	90
Juatinga, Ponta de, c., Braz.	G6	79
Juàzeiro, Braz.	E10	76
Juàzeiro do Norte, Braz.	E11	76
Jūbā, Sud.	H7	56
Juba, stm., Braz.	F12	82
Jūbāl, Maḍīq, strt., Egypt	D7	60
Jubal, Strait of see Jūbāl, Maḍīq, strt., Egypt	D7	60
Jubaysho, Eth.	O9	60
Jubayt, Sud.	H9	60
Jubba (Genale), stm., Afr.	H9	56
Jubbah, Sau. Ar.	G6	48
Jubones, stm., Ec.	I3	84
Juby, Cap, c., Mor.	G4	62
Júcar (Xúquer), stm., Spain	F10	16
Juçara, Braz.	C3	79
Júcaro, Cuba	D5	94
Juchipila, Mex.	G8	90
Juchitán de Zaragoza, Mex.	I12	90
Juchnov, U.S.S.R.	G18	26
Juchoviči, U.S.S.R.	E11	26
Jucuapa, El Sal.	D6	92
Jucurucu, stm., Braz.	D9	79
Jud, N.D., U.S.	C7	141
Juda, Wi., U.S.	F4	156
Judaea, hist. reg., Asia	E4	50
Judas, Punta, c., C.R.	H10	92
Judenburg, Aus.	H14	10
Judique, N.S., Can.	D8	101
Judith, stm., Mt., U.S.	C7	133
Judith, Point, c., R.I., U.S.	G4	115
Judith Basin, co., Mt., U.S.	C6	133
Judith Gap, Mt., U.S.	D7	133
Judith Island, i., N.C., U.S.	B6	140
Judith Mountains, mts., Mt., U.S.	C7	133
Judith Peak, mtn., Mt., U.S.	C7	133
Judson, Mn., U.S.	F4	130
Judson, N.D., U.S.	C4	141
Judsonia, Ar., U.S.	B4	111
Juexi, China	F10	34
Jufari, stm., Braz.	H11	84
Jugon, Fr.	D4	14
Juḥā, Sau. Ar.	F3	47
Juidongshan, China	L6	34
Juigalpa, Nic.	E9	92
Juiná, stm., Braz.	E12	82
Juiz de Fora, Braz.	F7	79
Jujuy, prov., Arg.	B5	80
Jukagirskoje ploskogorje, plat., U.S.S.R.	D23	24
Julesburg, Co., U.S.	A8	113
Juli, Peru	G7	82
Juliaca, Peru	F6	82
Julia Creek, Austl.	C4	70
Juliaetta, Id., U.S.	C2	119
Julian, Ca., U.S.	F5	112
Julian, W.V., U.S.	C3	155
Julianakanaal, Neth.	F8	12
Julian Alps, mts., Eur.	C8	18
Juliana Top, mtn., Sur.	F14	84
Julianehåb, Grnld.	C15	86
Jülich, Ger.	E6	10
Juliette, Ga., U.S.	C3	117
Julimes, Mex.	C7	90
Júlio de Castilhos, Braz.	E12	80
Julu, China	F3	32
Juma, U.S.S.R.	I23	6
Juma, stm., Braz.	A9	82
Jumay, Volcán, vol., Guat.	C5	92
Jumbilla, Peru	A3	82
Jumboo, Som.	B8	58
Jumbo Peak, mtn., Nv., U.S.	G7	135
Jumentos Cays, is., Bah.	C7	94
Jumet, Bel.	H5	12
Jumilla, Spain	G10	16
Jump, stm., Wi., U.S.	C3	156
Jump, North Fork, stm., Wi., U.S.	C3	156
Jump, South Fork, stm., Wi., U.S.	C3	156
Jumping Branch, W.V., U.S.	D4	155
Jumping Lake, l., Sask., Can.	E3	105
Jūnāgadh, India	J4	44
Junaynah, Ra's al-, mtn., Egypt	G2	48
Junction, Il., U.S.	F5	120
Junction, Tx., U.S.	D3	150
Junction City, Ar., U.S.	D3	111
Junction City, Ga., U.S.	D2	117
Junction City, Il., U.S.	E4	120
Junction City, Ks., U.S.	C7	123
Junction City, Ky., U.S.	C5	124
Junction City, La., U.S.	A3	125
Junction City, Oh., U.S.	C3	142
Junction City, Or., U.S.	C3	144
Junction City, Wi., U.S.	D4	156
Jundiaí, Braz.	G5	79
Jundiaí do Sul, Braz.	G3	79
Juneau, Ak., U.S.	D13	109
Juneau, Wi., U.S.	E5	156
Juneau, co., Wi., U.S.	E3	156
Junee, Austl.	J7	70
June in Winter, Lake, l., Fl., U.S.	E5	116
June Lake, Ca., U.S.	D4	112
Jungar Qi, China	D9	30
Jungfrau, mtn., Switz.	E8	13
Junggar Pendi, China	B4	30
Jungshāhi, Pak.	H2	44
Juniata, Ne., U.S.	D7	134
Juniata, co., Pa., U.S.	F7	145
Juniata, stm., Pa., U.S.	F7	145
Juniata, Raystown Branch, stm., Pa., U.S.	F5	145
Junín, Arg.	H8	80
Junín, Ec.	H2	84
Junín, Peru	D3	82
Junín, dept., Peru	D4	82
Junín, Lago, l., Peru	D3	82
Junior, W.V., U.S.	C5	155
Junior Lake, l., Me., U.S.	C4	126
Juniper, N.B., Can.	C2	101
Juniper Mountains, mts., Az., U.S.	B2	110
Junipero Serra Peak, mtn., Ca., U.S.	D3	112
Juniville, Fr.	C11	14
Junqueirópolis, Braz.	F3	79
Juntas, C.R.	G9	92
Junxian, China	E9	30
Juparanã, Lagoa, l., Braz.	E8	79
Jupilingo, stm., Guat.	C5	92
Jupiter, Fl., U.S.	F6	116
Jupiter Inlet, b., Fl., U.S.	F6	116
Jupiter Island, i., Fl., U.S.	E6	116
Juquiá, Braz.	C15	80
Jur, Czech.	G17	10
Jur, stm., Sud.	M5	60
Jura, state, Switz.	D7	13
Jura, dept., Fr.	F12	14
Jura, mts., Eur.	F13	14
Jura, i., Scot., U.K.	E8	8
Juramento, Braz.	D7	79
Juratiški, U.S.S.R.	G8	26
Jurbarkas, U.S.S.R.	F5	26
Jurf ad-Darāwīsh, Jord.	G5	50
Jurga, U.S.S.R.	F8	24
Jurjevec, U.S.S.R.	D26	26
Jurjev-Pol'skij, U.S.S.R.	E22	26
Jūrmala, U.S.S.R.	E6	26
Jurty, U.S.S.R.	F17	22
Juruá, Braz.	I9	84
Juruá, stm., S.A.	D5	76
Juruá Mirim, stm., Braz.	C5	82
Juruena, stm., Braz.	B12	82
Jurupari, stm., Braz.	C7	82
Jur'uzan', U.S.S.R.	G9	22
Juscelândia, Braz.	C3	79
Jusepín, Ven.	C11	84
Juskatla, B.C., Can.	C1	99
Jussey, Fr.	E12	14
Justin, Tx., U.S.	C4	150
Justiniano Posse, Arg.	G7	80
Justo Daract, Arg.	G6	80
Jutaí, Braz.	A7	82
Jutaí, stm., Braz.	D5	76
Jüterbog, Ger.	D13	10
Juti, Braz.	G1	79
Jutiapa, Guat.	C5	92
Jutiapa, dept., Guat.	C5	92
Juticalpa, Hond.	C8	92
Jutiquile, Hond.	C8	92
Jutland see Jylland, pen., Den.	M11	6
Juva, Fin.	K20	6
Juventud, Isla de la (Isla de Pinos), i., Cuba	D3	94
Juxi, China	H8	34
Juža, U.S.S.R.	E25	26
Južno-Sachalinsk, U.S.S.R.	H20	24
Južno-Ural'sk, U.S.S.R.	G10	22
Južnyj, mys, c., U.S.S.R.	F23	24
Južnyj Bug, stm., U.S.S.R.	H4	22
Jwayyā, Leb.	B4	50
Jylland, pen., Den.	M11	6
Jyväskylä, Fin.	J19	6
K		
K2 (Qogir Feng), mtn., Asia	C7	44
Kaaawa, Hi., U.S.	f10	118
Kaachka, U.S.S.R.	J9	22
Kaachka, U.S.S.R.	C15	48
Kaala, mtn., Hi., U.S.	f9	118
Kaalualu Bay, b., Hi., U.S.	E6	118
Kaapstad see Cape Town, S. Afr.	I4	66
Kaaumakua, Puu, mtn., Hi., U.S.	f10	118
Kabah, hist., Mex.	G15	90
Kabale, Ug.	B5	58
Kabalega Falls, wtfl, Ug.	H7	56
Kabalo, Zaire	C5	58
Kabambare, Zaire	B5	58
Kabba, Nig.	H13	64
Kabetogama Lake, l., Mn., U.S.	B5	130
Kabinda, Zaire	C4	58
Kabīr Kūh, mts., Iran	E9	48
Kabkābīyah, Sud.	K3	60
Kabna, Sud.	H7	60
Kābol, Afg.	C3	44
Kābol, stm., Asia	C4	44
Kabompo, stm., Zam.	D4	58
Kabongo, Zaire	C5	58
Kabot, Gui.	F2	64
Kabou, Togo	G10	64
Kabr, Sud.	L4	60
Kābul see Kābol, Afg.	C3	44
Kaburuang, Pulau, i., Indon.	E8	38
Kabwe (Broken Hill), Zam.	D5	58
Kačanik, Yugo.	G5	20
Kačerginė, U.S.S.R.	G6	26
Kachchh, Gulf of, b., India	I3	44
Kachemak, Ak., U.S.	D9	109
Kachess Lake, res., Wa., U.S.	B4	154
Kachisi, Eth.	M9	60
Kachovskoje vodochranilišče, res., U.S.S.R.	H4	22
K'achta, U.S.S.R.	G13	24
Kačug, U.S.S.R.	G13	24
Kadaiyanallūr, India	H4	46
Kadanai (Kadaney), stm., Asia	E2	44
Kadaney (Kadanai), stm., Asia	E2	44
Kadan Kyun, i., Burma	H5	40
Kade, Ghana	H9	64
Kadéï, stm., Afr.	H4	56
Kadi, India	I5	44
Kadiana, Mali	F6	64
Kadina, Austl.	I2	70
Kadiri, India	E5	46
Kadirli, Tur.	C4	48
Kadja, Ouadi (Wādī Kaja), val., Afr.	L3	60
Kadnikov, U.S.S.R.	B23	26
Kadnikovskij, U.S.S.R.	A23	26
Kado, Nig.	H14	64
Kadodo, Sud.	L5	60
Kadoka, S.D., U.S.	D4	148
Kadom, U.S.S.R.	G25	26
Kadoma, Zimb.	B9	66
Kaduj, U.S.S.R.	B20	26
Kaduna, Nig.	F13	64
Kaduna, stm., Nig.	G12	64
Kāduqlī, Sud.	L5	60
Kadyj, U.S.S.R.	D26	26
Kadykčan, U.S.S.R.	E21	24
Kadžerom, U.S.S.R.	E9	22
Kaech'ŏn, N. Kor.	D13	32
Kaédi, Maur.	C3	64
Kaena Point, c., Hi., U.S.	B3	118
Kaesŏng, N. Kor.	F14	32
Kāf, Sau. Ar.	F4	48
Kafan, U.S.S.R.	B9	48
Kafanchan, Nig.	G14	64
Kaffraria, hist. reg., Transkei	H9	66
Kaffrine, Sen.	D2	64
Kafia Kingi, Sud.	M3	60
Kafin Madaki, Nig.	F14	64
Kafirévs, Ákra, c., Grc.	K8	20
Kafr ad-Dawwār, Egypt	B6	60
Kafr ash-Shaykh, Egypt	B6	60
Kafue, stm., Zam.	E5	58
Kagan, U.S.S.R.	J10	22
Kagawong, Ont., Can.	B2	103
Kagaznagar, India	C5	46
Kagelike, China	B12	44
Kagera, stm., Afr.	B6	58
Kağızman, Tur.	A7	48
Kagmar, Sud.	J6	60
Kagoshima, Japan	P5	36
Kagoshima-wan, b., Japan	P5	36
Kagul, U.S.S.R.	H3	22
Kahakuloa, Hi., U.S.	B5	118
Kahaluu, Hi., U.S.	D6	118
Kahaluu, Hi., U.S.	g10	118
Kahana, Hi., U.S.	B4	118
Kahana Bay, b., Hi., U.S.	f10	118
Kahayan, stm., Indon.	F5	38
Kahemba, Zaire	C3	58
Kahnūj, Iran	H14	48
Kahoka, Mo., U.S.	A6	132
Kahoolawe, i., Hi., U.S.	C5	118
Kahramanmaraş, Tur.	C4	48
Kahuku, Hi., U.S.	B4	118
Kahuku Point, c., Hi., U.S.	B4	118
Kahului, Hi., U.S.	C5	118
Kahului Bay, b., Hi., U.S.	C5	118
Kai, Kepulauan, is., Indon.	G9	38
Kaiama, Nig.	G11	64
Kaiapoi, N.Z.	E4	72
Kaibab Indian Reservation, Az., U.S.	A3	110
Kaibab Plateau, plat., Az., U.S.	A3	110
Kaibito, Az., U.S.	A4	110
Kaibito Plateau, plat., Az., U.S.	A4	110
Kaidu, stm., China	C4	30
Kaieteur Fall, wtfl, Guy.	E13	84
Kaifeng, China	I2	32
Kaikoura, N.Z.	E4	72
Kailahun, S.L.	G4	64
Kaili, China	A9	40
Kailu, China	C11	30
Kailua, Hi., U.S.	B4	118
Kailua Bay, b., Hi., U.S.	g11	118
Kailua Kona, Hi., U.S.	D6	118
Kai Malino, Hi., U.S.	D6	118
Kainaliu, Hi., U.S.	D6	118
Kainan, Japan	M10	36
Kaipara Harbour, b., N.Z.	B5	72
Kaiparowits Plateau, plat., Ut., U.S.	F4	151
Kaiping, China	G9	30
Kaipokok Bay, b., Newf., Can.	g10	102
Kairāna, India	F7	44
Kairouan, Tun.	N5	18
Kaiserslautern, Ger.	F7	10
Kaishantun, China	A17	32
Kaišiadorys, U.S.S.R.	G7	26
Kaitangata, N.Z.	G2	72
Kaithal, India	F7	44
Kaituma, stm., Guy.	D13	84
Kaiwi Channel, strt., Hi., U.S.	B4	118
Kaiyuan, China	A12	32
Kaja, Wādī (Ouadi Kadja), val., Afr.	L3	60
Kajaani, Fin.	I20	6
Kajang, Malay.	M6	40
Kajnar, U.S.S.R.	H13	22
Kaka, Cen. Afr. Rep.	N4	60
Kākā, Sud.	L7	60
Kakadu National Park, Austl.	B6	68
Kakamas, S. Afr.	G5	66
Kaka Point, c., Hi., U.S.	C5	118
Kake, Ak., U.S.	D13	109
Kakegawa, Japan	M13	36
Kākināda, India	D7	46
Kako, stm., Guy.	E12	84
Kakoaka, Bots.	B7	66
Kakogawa, Japan	M9	36
Kaktovik, Ak., U.S.	A11	109
Kalaa Kebira, Tun.	N5	18
Kalaallit Nunaat see Greenland, dep., N.A.	B15	86
Kalaa Sghira, Tun.	N5	18
Kālābagh, Pak.	D4	44
Kalabo, Zam.	D4	58
Kalač, U.S.S.R.	G6	22
Kalačinsk, U.S.S.R.	F12	22
Kalač-na-Donu, U.S.S.R.	H6	22
Kaladan, stm., Asia	D2	40
Kaladar, Ont., Can.	C7	103
Ka Lae, c., Hi., U.S.	E6	118
Kalagwe, Burma	C4	40
Kalahari Desert, des., Afr.	E5	66
Kalaheo, Hi., U.S.	B2	118
Kalai-Chumb, U.S.S.R.	A4	44
Kalai-Mor, U.S.S.R.	D17	48
Kalajoki, Fin.	I18	6
Kalakamate, Bots.	C8	66
Kalām, Pak.	C5	44
Kalama, Wa., U.S.	C3	154
Kalámai, Grc.	L6	20
Kalamariá, Grc.	I6	20
Kalamazoo, Mi., U.S.	F5	129
Kalamazoo, co., Mi., U.S.	F5	129
Kalamazoo, stm., Mi., U.S.	F5	129
Kalampáka, Grc.	J5	20
Kalaoa Homesteads, Hi., U.S.	D6	118
Kalaraš, U.S.S.R.	B12	20
Kalasin, Thai.	F7	40
Kalašnikovo, U.S.S.R.	D18	26
Kalāt, Pak.	F2	44
Kalaupapa, Hi., U.S.	B5	118
Kalaupapa Peninsula, pen., Hi., U.S.	B5	118
Kalaw, Burma	D4	40
Kalawao, co., Hi., U.S.	B5	118
Kal'azin, U.S.S.R.	D20	26
Kalb, Ra's al-, c., Yemen	G6	47
Kalbā', U.A.E.	B10	47
Kalbarri, Austl.	E2	68
Kale, Tur.	L12	20
Kaleden, B.C., Can.	E8	99
Kalemie (Albertville), Zaire	C5	58
Kalemyo, Burma	C3	40
Kalena, Puu, mtn., Hi., U.S.	g9	118
Kaletwa, Burma	D2	40
Kaleva, Mi., U.S.	D4	129
Kalevala, U.S.S.R.	D4	22
Kalewa, Burma	C3	40
Kálfafell, Ice.	C5	6a
Kalgan see Zhangjiakou, China	C2	32
Kalgin Island, i., Ak., U.S.	g16	109
Kalgoorlie, Austl.	F4	68
Kali, Mali	E4	64
Kaliakra, nos, c., Bul.	F12	20
Kalibo, Phil.	C7	38
Kalima, Zaire	B5	58
Kalimantan see Borneo, i., Asia	E5	38
Kálimnos, Grc.	M10	20
Kālimpang, India	G13	44
Kaliningrad (Königsberg), U.S.S.R.	G3	26
Kalinkoviči, U.S.S.R.	I12	26
Kalinovik, Yugo.	F2	20
Kalispel Indian Reservation, Wa., U.S.	A8	154
Kalispell, Mt., U.S.	B2	133
Kalisz, Pol.	D18	10
Kalkaska, Mi., U.S.	D5	129
Kalkaska, co., Mi., U.S.	D5	129
Kalkfontein, Bots.	D5	66
Kallaste, U.S.S.R.	C10	26
Kallavesi, l., Fin.	J20	6
Kallnach, Switz.	D7	13
Kalmar, Swe.	M15	6
Kālna, India	I13	44
Kalnciems, U.S.S.R.	E6	26
Kalohi Channel, strt., Hi., U.S.	C4	118
Kālol, India	I5	44
Kaloli Point, c., Hi., U.S.	D7	118
Kalomo, Zam.	E5	58
Kalona, Ia., U.S.	C6	122
Kalone Peak, mtn., B.C., Can.	C4	99
Kalpeni Island, i., India	G2	46
Kalskag, Ak., U.S.	C7	109
Kaltag, Ak., U.S.	C8	109
Kaltan, U.S.S.R.	G15	22
Kaluga, U.S.S.R.	G19	26
Kalundborg, Den.	N12	6
Kałuszyn, Pol.	C21	10
Kalutara, Sri L.	I5	46
Kalvarija, U.S.S.R.	G6	26
Kalyān, India	C2	46
Kama, stm., U.S.S.R.	F8	22
Kamaishi, Japan	H16	36
Kamakou, mtn., Hi., U.S.	B5	118
Kamakura, Japan	L14	36
Kamamaung, Burma	F4	40
Kamananui Stream, stm., Hi., U.S.	f9	118
Kamanjab, Nmb.	B2	66
Kamarān, i., Yemen	G3	47
Kamarang, stm., S.A.	E12	84
Kamas, Ut., U.S.	C4	151
Kamatsi Lake, l., Sask., Can.	A4	105
Kamba, Nig.	F11	64
Kambam, India	H4	46
Kambar, Pak.	G3	44
Kambarka, U.S.S.R.	F8	22
Kambia, S.L.	G3	64
Kamčatka, poluostrov (Kamchatka), pen., U.S.S.R.	F24	24
Kamčatskij zaliv, b., U.S.S.R.	F24	24
Kamchatka see Kamčatka, poluostrov, pen., U.S.S.R.	F24	24
Kâmchay Méa, Camb.	I8	40
Kamčija, stm., Bul.	F11	20
Kamen', U.S.S.R.	F11	26
Kamen', gora, mtn., U.S.S.R.	D16	22
Kamenec, U.S.S.R.	I6	26
Kamenec-Podol'skij, U.S.S.R.	H3	22
Kamenjak, Rt, c., Yugo.	E8	18
Kamenka, U.S.S.R.	A12	20
Kamenka, U.S.S.R.	G6	22
Kamen'-na-Obi, U.S.S.R.	G8	24
Kamennogorsk, U.S.S.R.	K21	6
Kamensk-Ural'skij, U.S.S.R.	F10	22
Kameškovo, U.S.S.R.	E24	26
Kāmet, mtn., Asia	E8	44
Kamiah, Id., U.S.	C2	119
Kamiak Butte, mtn., Wa., U.S.	C8	154
Kamienna Góra, Pol.	E16	10
Kamieńsk, Pol.	D19	10
Kamina, Zaire	C5	58
Kaminaljuyú, hist., Guat.	J14	90
Kaminaljuyú, hist., Guat.	C4	92
Kaminoyama, Japan	I15	36
Kaminskij, U.S.S.R.	D24	26
Kamisunagawa, Japan	D17	36a
Kamloops, B.C., Can.	D7	99
Kamo, U.S.S.R.	A8	48
Kamoa Mountains, mts., Guy.	G13	84
Kamooloa, Hi., U.S.	f9	118
Kamouraska, Que., Can.	B8	104
Kampala, Ug.	A6	58
Kampar, Malay.	L6	40
Kampar, stm., Indon.	N7	40
Kampen, Neth.	C8	12
Kampeska, Lake, l., S.D., U.S.	C8	148
Kamphaeng Phet, Thai.	F5	40
Kamp'o, S. Kor.	H17	32
Kâmpóng Cham, Camb.	H8	40
Kâmpóng Chhnăng, Camb.	H8	40
Kâmpóng Saôm, Camb.	I7	40
Kâmpóng Saôm, Chhâk, b., Camb.	I7	40
Kâmpóng Thum, Camb.	H8	40
Kâmpôt, Camb.	I8	40
Kampsville, Il., U.S.	D3	120
Kâmpŭchéa see Cambodia, ctry., Asia	C4	38
Kamrar, Ia., U.S.	B4	122
Kamsack, Sask., Can.	F5	105
Kamskoje vodochranilišče, res., U.S.S.R.	F9	22
Kāmthi, India	B5	46
Kamuela (Waimea), Hi., U.S.	C6	118
Kámuk, Cerro, mtn., C.R.	H11	92
Kamyšin, U.S.S.R.	G7	22
Kamyšlov, U.S.S.R.	F10	22
Kanab, Ut., U.S.	F3	151
Kanab Creek, stm., U.S.	A3	110
Kanabec, co., Mn., U.S.	E5	130
Kanafis, Sud.	M3	60
Kanaga Island, i., Ak., U.S.	E4	109
Kanairiktok, stm., Newf., Can.	g9	102
Kananga (Luluabourg), Zaire	C4	58
Kanapou Bay, b., Hi., U.S.	C5	118
Kanarraville, Ut., U.S.	F2	151
Kanaš, U.S.S.R.	F7	22
Kanata, Ont., Can.	B9	103
Kanauga, Oh., U.S.	D3	142
Kanawha, Ia., U.S.	B4	122
Kanawha, co., W.V., U.S.	C3	155
Kanawha, stm., W.V., U.S.	C3	155
Kanazawa, Japan	K11	36
Kanchanaburi, Thai.	G5	40
Kānchenjunga, mtn., Asia	G13	44
Kānchipuram, India	F5	46
Kandalakša, U.S.S.R.	D4	22
Kandalakšskaja guba, b., U.S.S.R.	H23	6
Kandangan, Indon.	F6	38
Kandava, U.S.S.R.	D5	26
Kandersteg, Switz.	E8	13
Kandi, Benin	F11	64
Kandi, India	I13	44
Kandiāro, Pak.	G3	44
Kandiyohi, Mn., U.S.	E4	130
Kandiyohi, co., Mn., U.S.	E3	130
Kandos, Austl.	I8	70
Kandrāch, Pak.	H1	44
Kandy, Sri L.	I6	46
Kane, Il., U.S.	D3	120
Kane, Pa., U.S.	C4	145
Kane, co., Il., U.S.	B5	120
Kane, co., Ut., U.S.	F3	151
Kaneohe, Hi., U.S.	B4	118
Kaneohe Bay, b., Hi., U.S.	g10	118
Kaneohe Bay Marine Corps Air Station, mil., Hi., U.S.	g10	118
Kang, Bots.	D6	66
Kangal, Tur.	B4	48
Kangalassy, U.S.S.R.	E17	24
Kangar, Malay.	K6	40
Kangaroo Island, i., Austl.	J2	70
Kangāvar, Iran	D9	48
Kangaz, U.S.S.R.	C12	20
Kangding, China	E7	30
Kangdong, N. Kor.	D14	32
Kangean, Kepulauan, is., Indon.	G6	38
Kanggye, N. Kor.	C14	32
Kanghwa, S. Kor.	F14	32
Kanghwa-man, b., S. Kor.	F14	32
Kangiqsualujjuaq, Que., Can.	f8	102
Kangiqsujuaq, Que., Can.	f12	104
Kangirsuk, Que., Can.	f12	104
Kangjin, S. Kor.	I14	32
Kangley, Il., U.S.	B5	120
Kangnichumike, China	D9	44
Kangnŭng, S. Kor.	F16	32
Kango, Gabon	A2	58
Kangping, China	A11	32
Kangrinboqê Feng, mtn., China	E9	44
Kangshan, Tai.	M9	34
Kangsŏ, N. Kor.	E13	32
Kangto, mtn., Asia	G15	44
Kangyidaung, Burma	F3	40
Kani, Burma	C3	40
Kaniama, Zaire	C4	58
Kanin, poluostrov, pen., U.S.S.R.	D7	22
Kanin Nos, mys, c., U.S.S.R.	D6	22
Kaniva, Austl.	K4	70
Kanjiža, Yugo.	C4	20
Kankakee, Il., U.S.	B6	120
Kankakee, co., Il., U.S.	B6	120
Kankakee, stm., U.S.	B5	120
Kankan, Gui.	F5	64
Kankéla, Mali	F6	64
Kankossa, Maur.	D4	64
Kanmaw Kyun, i., Burma	I5	40
Kannapolis, N.C., U.S.	B2	140
Kannauj, India	G8	44
Kano, Nig.	E14	64
Kanonji, Japan	M8	36
Kanopolis, Ks., U.S.	D5	123
Kanopolis Lake, res., Ks., U.S.	D5	123
Kanorado, Ks., U.S.	C1	123
Kanosh, Ut., U.S.	E3	151
Kanoya, Japan	P5	36
Kānpur, India	G9	44
Kansas, Al., U.S.	B2	108
Kansas, Il., U.S.	D6	120
Kansas, Ok., U.S.	A7	143
Kansas, state, U.S.	D5	123
Kansas, stm., Ks., U.S.	C7	123
Kansas City, Ks., U.S.	C9	123
Kansas City, Mo., U.S.	B3	132
Kansau, Burma	C2	40
Kanshan, China	E9	34
Kansk, U.S.S.R.	F11	24
Kansu see Gansu, prov., China	D7	30
Kant, U.S.S.R.	I12	22
Kantang, Thai.	K5	40
Kantché, Niger	E14	64
Kantō-sanchi, mts., Japan	K13	36
Kantunilkin, Mex.	G16	90
Kanuku Mountains, mts., Guy.	F13	84
Kanuma, Japan	K14	36
Kanus, Nmb.	F4	66
Kan'utino, U.S.S.R.	F16	26
Kanye, Bots.	E7	66
Kanyu, Bots.	C7	66
Kaohsiung, Tai.	M9	34
Kaohsiunghsien, Tai.	M9	34
Kaokoland, dept., Nmb.	A1	66
Kaoko Veld, plat., Nmb.	B1	66
Kaolack, Sen.	D1	64
Kaoma, Zam.	D4	58
Kaoshanpu, China	E3	34
Kapaa, Hi., U.S.	A2	118
Kapaau, Hi., U.S.	C6	118
Kapadvanj, India	I5	44
Kapanga, Zaire	C4	58
Kapapa Island, i., Hi., U.S.	g10	118
Kapčagaj, U.S.S.R.	I13	22
Kapčagajskoje vodochranilišče, res., U.S.S.R.	I13	22
Kapfenberg, Aus.	H15	10
Kaplan, La., U.S.	D3	125
Kapoe, Thai.	J5	40
Kaposvár, Hung.	I17	10

Name	Map Ref.	Page
Kapowsin, Wa., U.S.	C3	154
Kappeln, Ger.	A9	10
Kapps, Nmb.	D3	66
Kaprun, Aus.	H12	10
Kapsan, N. Kor.	B16	32
Kapsukas, U.S.S.R.	G6	26
Kapuas, stm., Indon.	F4	38
Kapuas Hulu, Pegunungan, mts., Asia	E5	38
Kapulena, Hi., U.S.	C6	118
Kapunda, Austl.	J3	70
Kapūrthala, India	E6	44
Kapuskasing, Ont., Can.	o19	103
Kapuvár, Hung.	H17	10
Kara, stm., Afr.	G10	64
Kara-Balta, U.S.S.R.	I12	22
Karabanovo, U.S.S.R.	E21	26
Karabaš, U.S.S.R.	F10	22
Karabekaul, U.S.S.R.	B18	48
Kara-Bogaz-Gol, zaliv, b., U.S.S.R.	I8	22
Karabük, Tur.	G14	4
Karacabey, Tur.	I12	20
Karacadağ, Tur.	H11	20
Karačev, U.S.S.R.	H18	26
Karāchi, Pak.	H2	44
Karād, India	D3	46
Karaganda, U.S.S.R.	H12	22
Karaginskij, ostrov, i., U.S.S.R.	F24	24
Karaginskij zaliv, b., U.S.S.R.	F24	24
Karagoš, gora, mtn., U.S.S.R.	G15	22
Kāraikāl, India	G5	46
Kāraikkudi, India	G5	46
Karaj, Iran	D11	48
Karakax, stm., China	B8	44
Karakelong, Pulau, i., Indon.	E8	38
Karakoram Pass, Asia	C7	44
Karakoram Range, mts., Asia	C7	44
Karakoro, stm., Afr.	D4	64
Karakumskij kanal, U.S.S.R.	C16	48
Karakumy, des., U.S.S.R.	J9	22
Karaman, Tur.	L13	20
Karaman, Tur.	C2	48
Karamay, China	B3	30
Karamea Bight, N.Z.	D3	72
Karamürsel, Tur.	I13	20
Karamyševo, U.S.S.R.	D11	26
Kāranja, India	B4	46
Karapınar, Tur.	C2	48
Karasburg, Nmb.	G4	66
Karasburg, dept., Nmb.	G4	66
Kara Sea see Karskoje more, U.S.S.R.	C11	22
Karasjok, Nor.	G19	6
Karasu, stm., Tur.	B5	48
Karasuk, U.S.S.R.	G7	24
Karatau, U.S.S.R.	I12	22
Karatau, chrebet, mts., U.S.S.R.	I12	22
Karaton, U.S.S.R.	H8	22
Karatsu, Japan	N4	36
Karauli, India	G7	44
Karawang, Indon.	J13	39a
Karawang, Tanjung, c., Indon.	I13	39a
Karawanken, mts., Eur.	C9	18
Karaye, Nig.	F14	64
Karažal, U.S.S.R.	H12	22
Karbalā', Iraq	E8	48
Karcag, Hung.	H20	10
Kardhítsa, Grc.	J5	20
Kärdla, U.S.S.R.	B5	26
Kardymovo, U.S.S.R.	G15	26
Kârdžali, Bul.	H9	20
Karelia, hist. reg., Eur.	J22	6
Karesuando, Swe.	G18	6
Kargopol', U.S.S.R.	E5	22
Karia-Ba-Mohammed, Mor.	C8	62
Kariba, Zimb.	E5	58
Kariba, Lake, res., Afr.	E5	58
Karibib, Nmb.	C2	66
Karigasniemi, Fin.	G19	6
Karimata, Kepulauan, is., Indon.	F4	38
Karimata, Selat (Karimata Strait), strt., Indon.	F4	38
Karīmnagar, India	C5	46
Karimunjawa, Kepulauan, is., Indon.	G5	38
Karin, Som.	F10	56
Karis (Karjaa), Fin.	K18	6
Karisimbi, Volcan, vol., Afr.	B5	58
Kariya, Japan	M11	36
Kārīz, Iran	D16	48
Karkaralinsk, U.S.S.R.	H13	22
Karl-Marx-Stadt see Chemnitz, Ger.	E12	10
Karloske, stm., Man., Can.	B4	100
Karlovac, Yugo.	D10	18
Karlovo, Bul.	G8	20
Karlovy Vary, Czech.	E12	10
Karlsborg, Swe.	I18	6
Karlskoga, Swe.	L14	6
Karlskrona, Swe.	M14	6
Karlsruhe, Ger.	F8	10
Karlsruhe, N.D., U.S.	A5	141
Karlstad, Mn., U.S.	B2	130
Karlstadt, Ger.	F9	10
Karma, Niger	E10	64
Karmah, Sud.	H6	60
Karmel, Har (Mount Carmel), mtn., Isr.	C4	50
Karmiyya, Isr.	E3	50
Karnak, Il., U.S.	F5	120
Karnak see Al-Karnak, Egypt	E7	60
Karnāl, India	F7	44
Karṇālī, stm., Asia	F9	44
Karnātaka, state, India	E3	46
Karnes, co., Tx., U.S.	E4	150
Karnes City, Tx., U.S.	E4	150
Karnobat, Bul.	G10	20
Karns, Tn., U.S.	n13	149
Kärnten, state, Aus.	I13	10
Karonga, Mwi.	C6	58
Karora, Sud.	I10	60
Kárpathos, i., Grc.	N11	20
Karpenísion, Grc.	K5	20
Karpinsk, U.S.S.R.	F10	22
Karpogory, U.S.S.R.	E6	22
Karratha, Austl.	D3	68
Kars, Tur.	A7	48
Karsakpaj, U.S.S.R.	H11	22
Kärsämäki, Fin.	J19	6
Kārsava, U.S.S.R.	E10	26
Karši, U.S.S.R.	J11	22
Karsin, Pol.	B17	10
Karskije Vorota, proliv, strt., U.S.S.R.	C9	22
Karskoje more (Kara Sea), U.S.S.R.	C11	22
Kartaly, U.S.S.R.	G10	22
Kartuzy, Pol.	A18	10
Karukuwisa, Nmb.	B4	66
Karūr, India	G5	46
Karval, Co., U.S.	C7	113
Karviná, Czech.	F18	10
Kārwār, India	E3	46
Karymskoje, U.S.S.R.	G14	24
Kas, Sud.	K3	60
Kasai (Cassai), stm., Afr.	B3	58
Kasaji, Zaire	D4	58
Kasama, Zam.	D6	58
Kasan, U.S.S.R.	B18	48
Kasane, Bots.	A7	66
Kasanga, Tan.	C6	58
Kasaoka, Japan	M8	36
Kāsaragod, India	F3	46
Kasba Lake, l., N.W. Ter., Can.	D12	96
Kasba-Tadla, Mor.	D7	62
Kaseda, Japan	P5	36
Kasempa, Zam.	D5	58
Kasenga, Zaire	D5	58
Kasese, Zaire	B5	58
Kāsganj, India	G8	44
Kāshān, Iran	K8	22
Kashgar see Kashi, China	D2	30
Kashi, China	F8	28
Kashi, China	D2	30
Kashihara, Japan	M10	36
Kashima, Japan	N5	36
Kāshīpur, India	F8	44
Kashiwazaki, Japan	J13	36
Kāshmar, Iran	D15	48
Kashmor, Pak.	F3	44
Kasigluk, Ak., U.S.	C7	109
Kasilof, Ak., U.S.	C9	109
Kasimov, U.S.S.R.	G24	26
Kašin, U.S.S.R.	D20	26
Kasinka, Bots.	B7	66
Kašira, U.S.S.R.	G21	26
Kasiruta, Pulau, i., Indon.	F8	38
Kaskaskia, Il., U.S.	F4	120
Kaskaskia, stm., Il., U.S.	D5	120
Kaskö (Kaskinen), Fin.	J17	6
Kasli, U.S.S.R.	F10	22
Kaslo, B.C., Can.	E9	99
Kasn'a, U.S.S.R.	F17	26
Kasongo, Zaire	B5	58
Kasongo-Lunda, Zaire	C3	58
Kásos, i., Grc.	N10	20
Kasota, Mn., U.S.	F5	130
Kaspijsk, U.S.S.R.	I7	22
Kaspijskij, U.S.S.R.	H7	22
Kasr, Ra's, c., Afr.	H10	60
Kassalā, Sud.	J9	60
Kassándra, pen., Grc.	I7	20
Kassándras, Kólpos, b., Grc.	I7	20
Kassel, Ger.	D9	10
Kasserine, Tun.	C15	62
Kassikaityu, stm., Guy.	G13	84
Kassinger, Sud.	H6	60
Kasson, Mn., U.S.	F6	130
Kastamonu, Tur.	G14	4
Kastoría, Grc.	I5	20
Kastrávion, Tekhnití Límni, res., Grc.	K5	20
Kasūr, Pak.	E6	44
Kataeregi, Nig.	G13	64
Katahdin, Mount, mtn., Me., U.S.	C4	126
Katanga, hist. reg., Zaire	D5	58
Katanga, stm., U.S.S.R.	F12	24
Katanning, Austl.	F3	68
Katchall Island, i., India	K2	40
Katélé, Mali	F7	64
Katepwa Beach, Sask., Can.	G4	105
Kateríni, Grc.	I6	20
Kates Needle, mtn., Ak., U.S.	m24	109
Katha, Burma	B4	40
Katherine, Austl.	B6	68
Kāthiāwār Peninsula, pen., India	I4	44
Kathleen, Fl., U.S.	D4	116
Kāṭhmāṇḍau, Nepal	G11	44
Kathrabbā, Jord.	F5	50
Katihār, India	F4	30
Katiola, I.C.	G7	64
Katmai, Mount, mtn., Ak., U.S.	D9	109
Katmai National Park, Ak., U.S.	D9	109
Kātmāndu see Kāṭhmāṇḍau, Nepal	G11	44
Katoomba, Austl.	I9	70
Katoúna, Grc.	K5	20
Katowice, Pol.	E19	10
Kātrīnā, Jabal, mtn., Egypt	C7	60
Katsepe, Madag.	O22	67b
Katsina, Nig.	E13	64
Katsina Ala, Nig.	H14	64
Katsina Ala, stm., Afr.	G8	54
Katsuta, Japan	K15	36
Katsuura, Japan	L15	36
Katsuyama, Japan	K11	36
Kattakurgan, U.S.S.R.	J11	22
Kattaviá, Grc.	N11	20
Kattegat, strt., Eur.	M12	6
Katun', stm., U.S.S.R.	G9	24
Katunki, U.S.S.R.	E26	26
Kātwa, India	I13	44
Katwijk aan Zee, Neth.	D5	12
Katy, Tx., U.S.	r14	150
Kauai, co., Hi., U.S.	B1	118
Kauai, i., Hi., U.S.	A2	118
Kauai Channel, strt., Hi., U.S.	B3	118
Kau Desert, des., Hi., U.S.	D6	118
Kaufbeuren, Ger.	H10	10
Kaufman, Tx., U.S.	C4	150
Kaufman, co., Tx., U.S.	C4	150
Kauiki Head, c., Hi., U.S.	C6	118
Kaukauna, Wi., U.S.	D5	156
Kaukau Veld, plat., Afr.	B5	66
Kaula Island, i., Hi., U.S.	m15	118
Kaulakahi Channel, strt., Hi., U.S.	A2	118
Kauliranta, Fin.	H18	6
Kaumakani, Hi., U.S.	B2	118
Kaumalapau, Hi., U.S.	C5	118
Kaunakakai, Hi., U.S.	B4	118
Kauna Point, c., Hi., U.S.	D6	118
Kaunas, U.S.S.R.	G6	26
Kaura Namoda, Nig.	E13	64
Kauru, Nig.	F14	64
Kaušany, U.S.S.R.	C13	20
Kaustinen, Fin.	J18	6
Kautokeino, Nor.	G18	6
Kavacık, Tur.	J12	20
Kavajë, Alb.	H3	20
Kavála, Grc.	I8	20
Kavalerovo, U.S.S.R.	I19	24
Kāvali, India	E5	46
Kavaratti Island, i., India	G2	46
Kāveri, stm., India	G5	46
Kāveri Falls, wtfl, India	F4	46
Kaverino, U.S.S.R.	G24	26
Kavieng, Pap. N. Gui.	k17	68a
Kavimba, Bots.	B7	66
Kavīr, Dasht-e, des., Iran	D13	48
Kawagoe, Japan	L14	36
Kawaguchi, Japan	L14	36
Kawaihae, Hi., U.S.	C6	118
Kawaihoa Point, c., Hi., U.S.	B1	118
Kawaikini, mtn., Hi., U.S.	A2	118
Kawailoa, Hi., U.S.	f9	118
Kawailoa Beach, Hi., U.S.	f9	118
Kawambwa, Zam.	C5	58
Kawara Débé, Niger	E11	64
Kawasaki, Japan	L14	36
Kaw City, Ok., U.S.	A5	143
Kawdut, Burma	G4	40
Kaweenakumik Lake, l., Man., Can.	C2	100
Kawela, Hi., U.S.	f9	118
Kawich Peak, mtn., Nv., U.S.	F5	135
Kawich Range, mts., Nv., U.S.	F5	135
Kaw Lake, res., Ok., U.S.	A5	143
Kawludo, Burma	E4	40
Kawm Umbū, Egypt	E7	60
Kawthaung, Burma	J5	40
Kaxgar, stm., China	D2	30
Kay, co., Ok., U.S.	A4	143
Kaya, Burkina	E9	64
Kayan, Burma	F4	40
Kayan, stm., Indon.	E6	38
Kāyankulam, India	H4	46
Kaycee, Wy., U.S.	C6	157
Kayenta, Az., U.S.	A5	110
Kayes, Congo	B2	58
Kayes, Mali	D4	64
Kayford, W.V., U.S.	C3	155
Kayjay, Ky., U.S.	D6	124
Kaylor, S.D., U.S.	D8	148
Kayser Gebergte, mts., Sur.	F14	84
Kayseri, Tur.	B3	48
Kaysville, Ut., U.S.	B4	151
Kayville, Sask., Can.	H3	105
Kazachskaja Sovetskaja Socialističeskaja Respublika (Kazakhstan), state, U.S.S.R.	H11	22
Kazachskij melkosopočnik, hills, U.S.S.R.	H12	22
Kazačinskoje, U.S.S.R.	F16	22
Kazakhstan see Kazachskaja Sovetskaja Socialističeskaja Respublika, state, U.S.S.R.	H11	22
Kazaki, U.S.S.R.	I21	26
Kazaklija, U.S.S.R.	C12	20
Kazalinsk, U.S.S.R.	H10	22
Kazan', U.S.S.R.	F7	22
Kazan, stm., N.W. Ter., Can.	D13	96
Kazandžik, U.S.S.R.	J9	22
Kazanlâk, Bul.	G9	20
Kazanovka, U.S.S.R.	H21	26
Kazbek, gora, mtn., U.S.S.R.	I6	22
Kāzerūn, Iran	G11	48
Kazi-Magomed, U.S.S.R.	I7	22
Kazimierza Wielka, Pol.	E20	10
Kazincbarcika, Hung.	G20	10
Kazinka, U.S.S.R.	I22	26
Kazlų Rūda, U.S.S.R.	G6	26
Kazungula, Zam.	A7	66
Kazym, stm., U.S.S.R.	E5	24
Kazyr, stm., U.S.S.R.	G17	22
Kcynia, Pol.	B17	10
Kdyně, Czech.	F13	10
Kéa, i., Grc.	L8	20
Keaau, Hi., U.S.	D6	118
Keahiakahoe, Puu, mtn., Hi., U.S.	g10	118
Keahole Point, c., Hi., U.S.	D5	118
Kealaikahiki Channel, strt., Hi., U.S.	C5	118
Kealaikahiki Point, c., Hi., U.S.	C5	118
Kealakekua, Hi., U.S.	D6	118
Kealia, Hi., U.S.	A2	118
Keams Canyon, Az., U.S.	B5	110
Keanae, Hi., U.S.	C5	118
Keanapapa Point, c., Hi., U.S.	C4	118
Keansburg, N.J., U.S.	C4	137
Kearney, Ont., Can.	B5	103
Kearney, Mo., U.S.	B3	132
Kearney, Ne., U.S.	D6	134
Kearney, co., Ne., U.S.	D7	134
Kearneysville, W.V., U.S.	B7	155
Kearns, Ut., U.S.	C4	151
Kearny, Az., U.S.	D5	110
Kearny, N.J., U.S.	h8	137
Kearny, co., Ks., U.S.	D2	123
Kearsarge, N.H., U.S.	B4	136
Kearsarge, Mount, mtn., N.H., U.S.	D3	136
Kearsarge North, mtn., N.H., U.S.	B4	136
Keatchie, La., U.S.	B2	125
Keaton, Ky., U.S.	C7	124
Keats, Ks., U.S.	C7	123
Keauhou, Hi., U.S.	D6	118
Kebeiti, China	B8	44
Kébémer, Sen.	D1	64
Kebili, Tun.	D15	62
Kebnekaise, mtn., Swe.	H16	6
Kebri Dehar, Eth.	G9	56
Kecel, Hung.	I19	10
Kech, stm., Pak.	H17	48
Kecskemét, Hung.	I19	10
Kėdainiai, U.S.S.R.	F7	26
Kedges Straits, strt., Md., U.S.	D5	127
Kedgwick, N.B., Can.	B2	101
Kediri, Indon.	J16	39a
Kédougou, Sen.	E3	64
Kędzierzyn Kozle, Pol.	E18	10
Keedysville, Md., U.S.	B2	127
Keegan, Me., U.S.	A5	126
Keego Harbor, Mi., U.S.	o15	129
Keei, Hi., U.S.	D6	118
Keele Peak, mtn., Yukon, Can.	D6	96
Keeling Islands see Cocos Islands, dep., Oc.	K10	28
Keels, Newf., Can.	D5	102
Keene, Ont., Can.	C6	103
Keene, Ky., U.S.	C5	124
Keene, N.H., U.S.	E2	136
Keene, Tx., U.S.	n9	150
Keenesburg, Co., U.S.	A6	113
Keeney Knob, mtn., W.V., U.S.	D4	155
Keensburg, Il., U.S.	E6	120
Keerbergen, Bel.	F6	12
Keeseville, N.Y., U.S.	f11	139
Keesler Air Force Base, mil., Ms., U.S.	E5	131
Keetmanshoop, Nmb.	F4	66
Keet Seel Ruin, hist., Az., U.S.	A5	110
Keewatin, Ont., Can.	E4	100
Keewatin, Mn., U.S.	C5	130
Keewatin, stm., Man., Can.	A1	100
Keezletown, Va., U.S.	B4	153
Kefallinía, i., Grc.	K4	20
Kefar Blum, Isr.	B5	50
Kefar 'Eẕyon, Isr. Occ.	E4	50
Kefar Naḥum (Capernaum), hist., Isr.	C5	50
Kefar Sava, Isr.	D3	50
Keffi, Nig.	G13	64
Keffin Hausa, Nig.	E14	64
Keflavík, Ice.	B2	6a
Keftya, Eth.	K9	60
Ke Ga, Mui, c., Viet.	H10	40
Kegonsa, Lake, l., Wi., U.S.	F4	156
Kegums, U.S.S.R.	E7	26
Kehra, U.S.S.R.	B8	26
Ke-hsi Mānsām, Burma	D4	40
Keila, U.S.S.R.	B7	26
Keimoes, S. Afr.	G5	66
Keiser, Ar., U.S.	B5	111
Keith, Scot., U.K.	D11	8
Keith, co., Ne., U.S.	C4	134
Keith Arm, b., N.W. Ter., Can.	C8	96
Keithsburg, Il., U.S.	B3	120
Keizer, Or., U.S.	C3	144
Kejimkujik National Park, N.S., Can.	E4	101
Kekaha, Hi., U.S.	B2	118
Kékes, mtn., Hung.	H20	10
Kekexili, China	D5	30
Kelafo, Eth.	G9	56
Kelang, Malay.	M6	40
Kelantan, stm., Malay.	L7	40
Kelegou, China	B6	32
Kelibia, Tun.	M6	18
Kell, Il., U.S.	E5	120
Keller, Tx., U.S.	n9	150
Keller, Va., U.S.	C7	153
Keller, Wa., U.S.	A7	154
Kellerberrin, Austl.	F3	68
Kellerman, Al., U.S.	B2	108
Kellerton, Ia., U.S.	D3	122
Kellett, Cape, c., N.W. Ter., Can.	B7	96
Kelley, Ia., U.S.	C4	122
Kelleys Island, i., Oh., U.S.	A3	142
Kelliher, Sask., Can.	F4	105
Kelliher, Mn., U.S.	C4	130
Kellnersville, Wi., U.S.	D6	156
Kellogg, Id., U.S.	B2	119
Kellogg, Ia., U.S.	C5	122
Kellogg, Mn., U.S.	F6	130
Kelly, Wy., U.S.	C2	157
Kelly Air Force Base, mil., Tx., U.S.	k7	150
Kelly Brook Mountain, mtn., Me., U.S.	A3	126
Kelly Island, i., De., U.S.	D4	115
Kelly Lake, B.C., Can.	B7	99
Kellyton, Al., U.S.	C3	108
Kellyville, N.H., U.S.	D2	136
Kellyville, Ok., U.S.	B5	143
Kelmė, U.S.S.R.	F5	26
Kel'mency, U.S.S.R.	A10	20
Kelmet, Eth.	I10	60
Kelo, Chad	G4	56
Kelolokan, Indon.	E6	38
Kelowna, B.C., Can.	E8	99
Kelsey Lake, l., Man., Can.	C1	100
Kelseyville, Ca., U.S.	C2	112
Kelso, Mo., U.S.	D8	132
Kelso, Wa., U.S.	C3	154
Keluang, Malay.	M7	40
Kelvington, Sask., Can.	E4	105
Kelwood, Man., Can.	D2	100
Kem', U.S.S.R.	E4	22
Kemalpaşa, Tur.	K11	20
Kemano, B.C., Can.	C4	99
Kemer Barajı, res., Tur.	L12	20
Kemerovo, U.S.S.R.	F9	24
Kemi, Fin.	I19	6
Kemijärvi, Fin.	H20	6
Kemijoki, stm., Fin.	H19	6
Kemmerer, Wy., U.S.	E2	157
Kemnath, Ger.	F11	10
Kemnay, Man., Can.	E1	100
Kemp, Tx., U.S.	C4	150
Kemp, Lake, res., Tx., U.S.	C3	150
Kemparana, Mali	E7	64
Kempele, Fin.	I19	6
Kempen, Ger.	D6	10
Kemper, co., Ms., U.S.	C5	131
Kemps Bay, Bah.	B6	94
Kempsey, Austl.	H10	70
Kempshall Mountain, mtn., N.Y., U.S.	A6	139
Kempten [Allgäu], Ger.	H10	10
Kempton, Il., U.S.	C5	120
Kempton, In., U.S.	D5	121
Kemptville, Ont., Can.	B9	103
Kenai, Ak., U.S.	C9	109
Kenai Fjords National Park, Ak., U.S.	D10	109
Kenai Mountains, mts., Ak., U.S.	h16	109
Kenai Peninsula, pen., Ak., U.S.	h16	109
Kenansville, Fl., U.S.	E6	116
Kenansville, N.C., U.S.	C5	140
Kenaston, Sask., Can.	F2	105
Kenbridge, Va., U.S.	D4	153
Kendal, Sask., Can.	G4	105
Kendal, S. Afr.	F9	66
Kendall, Fl., U.S.	s13	116
Kendall, Ks., U.S.	E2	123
Kendall, Wi., U.S.	E3	156
Kendall, co., Il., U.S.	B5	120
Kendall, co., Tx., U.S.	E3	150
Kendall, Cape, c., N.W. Ter., Can.	D15	96
Kendall Park, N.J., U.S.	C3	137
Kendallville, In., U.S.	B7	121
Kendari, Indon.	F7	38
Kendrāparha, India	J12	44
Kendrick, Id., U.S.	C2	119
Kenduskeag, Me., U.S.	D4	126
Kenedy, Tx., U.S.	E4	150
Kenedy, co., Tx., U.S.	F4	150
Kenel, S.D., U.S.	B5	148
Kenema, S.L.	H4	64
Kenesaw, Ne., U.S.	D7	134
Kenge, Zaire	B3	58
Kengtian, China	J8	34
Kēng Tung, Burma	D5	40
Kenhardt, S. Afr.	G5	66
Kenilworth, Il., U.S.	h9	120
Kenilworth, Ut., U.S.	D5	151
Kenitra, Mor.	C7	62
Kenly, N.C., U.S.	B4	140
Kenmare, N.D., U.S.	A3	141
Kenmore, N.Y., U.S.	C2	139
Kenna, W.V., U.S.	C3	155
Kennaday Peak, mtn., Wy., U.S.	E6	157
Kennard, In., U.S.	E6	121
Kennard, Ne., U.S.	C9	134
Kennebago Lake, l., Me., U.S.	C2	126
Kennebec, S.D., U.S.	D5	148
Kennebec, co., Me., U.S.	D3	126
Kennebec, stm., Me., U.S.	D3	126
Kennebunk, Me., U.S.	E2	126
Kennebunkport, Me., U.S.	E2	126
Kennedy, Sask., Can.	G4	105
Kennedy, Al., U.S.	B2	108
Kennedy, Mn., U.S.	B2	130
Kennedy, Zimb.	B8	66
Kennedy, Mount, mtn., Yukon, Can.	D5	96
Kennedy Entrance, strt., Ak., U.S.	D9	109
Kenner, La., U.S.	E5	125
Kennesaw, Ga., U.S.	B2	117
Kennesaw Mountain, mtn., Ga., U.S.	C2	117
Kennesaw Mountain National Battlefield Park, Ga., U.S.	h7	117
Kennetcook, N.S., Can.	D6	101
Kennett, Mo., U.S.	E7	132
Kennett Square, Pa., U.S.	G10	145
Kennewick, Wa., U.S.	C6	154
Kenney, Il., U.S.	C4	120
Kenn Reef, rf., Austl.	D11	68
Kennydale, Wa., U.S.	e11	154
Keno, Or., U.S.	E5	144
Kénogami, Lac, l., Que., Can.	A6	104
Kenora, Ont., Can.	o16	103
Kenosha, Wi., U.S.	F6	156
Kenosha, co., Wi., U.S.	F5	156
Kenova, W.V., U.S.	C2	155
Kensal, N.D., U.S.	B7	141
Kensett, Ar., U.S.	B4	111
Kensett, Ia., U.S.	A4	122
Kensico Reservoir, res., N.Y., U.S.	g13	139
Kensington, P.E.I., Can.	C6	101
Kensington, Ct., U.S.	C4	114
Kensington, Ks., U.S.	C4	123
Kensington, Md., U.S.	B3	127
Kensington, Mn., U.S.	E3	130
Kensington, N.H., U.S.	E5	136
Kent, S.L.	G3	64
Kent, Al., U.S.	C4	108
Kent, Ct., U.S.	C2	114
Kent, Oh., U.S.	A4	142
Kent, Wa., U.S.	B3	154
Kent, co., Eng., U.K.	J14	8
Kent, co., De., U.S.	D3	115
Kent, co., Md., U.S.	B5	127
Kent, co., Mi., U.S.	E5	129
Kent, co., R.I., U.S.	D2	146
Kent, co., Tx., U.S.	C2	150
Kentau, U.S.S.R.	I11	22
Kent Bridge, Ont., Can.	E2	103
Kent City, Mi., U.S.	E5	129
Kent Group, is., Austl.	L7	70
Kent Island, i., De., U.S.	D4	115
Kent Island, i., Md., U.S.	C5	127
Kent Junction, N.B., Can.	C4	101
Kentland, In., U.S.	C3	121
Kenton, Man., Can.	E1	100
Kenton, De., U.S.	D3	115
Kenton, Ky., U.S.	k14	124
Kenton, Oh., U.S.	B2	142
Kenton, Tn., U.S.	A2	149
Kenton, co., Ky., U.S.	B5	124
Kent Peninsula, pen., N.W. Ter., Can.	C11	96
Kent Point, c., Md., U.S.	C5	127
Kentucky, state, U.S.	C4	124
Kentucky, stm., Ky., U.S.	B5	124
Kentucky, Middle Fork, stm., Ky., U.S.	C6	124
Kentucky, North Fork, stm., Ky., U.S.	C6	124
Kentucky, South Fork, stm., Ky., U.S.	C6	124
Kentucky Dam, Ky., U.S.	e9	124
Kentucky Lake, res., U.S.	D9	106
Kentucky Ridge, mtn., Ky., U.S.	D6	124
Kentville, N.S., Can.	D5	101
Kentwood, La., U.S.	D5	125
Kentwood, Mi., U.S.	F5	129
Kenvil, N.J., U.S.	B3	137
Kenville, Man., Can.	D1	100
Kenvir, Ky., U.S.	D6	124
Kenya, ctry., Afr.	B7	58
Kenya, Mount see Kirinyaga, mtn., Kenya	B7	58
Kenyon, Mn., U.S.	F6	130
Kenyon, R.I., U.S.	F2	146
Keo, Ar., U.S.	C3	111
Keokea, Hi., U.S.	C5	118
Keokuk, Ia., U.S.	D6	122
Keokuk, co., Ia., U.S.	C5	122
Keokuk Lock and Dam, U.S.	D6	122
Keoma, Alta., Can.	D4	98
Keo Neua, Col de, Asia	E8	40
Keosauqua, Ia., U.S.	D6	122
Keota, Ia., U.S.	C6	122
Keota, Ok., U.S.	B7	143
Keowee, Lake, res., S.C., U.S.	B2	147
Kępice, Pol.	A16	10
Kępno, Pol.	D17	10
Keppel Bay, b., Austl.	D9	70
Kequan, China	G2	32
Kerala, state, India	G4	46
Kerang, Austl.	J5	70
Kerby, Or., U.S.	E3	144
Kerč', U.S.S.R.	H5	22
Keremeos, B.C., Can.	E8	99
Keren, Eth.	J10	60
Kerend, Iran	D9	48
Kerens, Tx., U.S.	C4	150
Keret', ozero, l., U.S.S.R.	I23	6
Kerewan, Gam.	E1	64
Kerguélen, Îles, is., F.S.A.T.	M10	158
Kerhonkson, N.Y., U.S.	D6	139
Kericho, Kenya	B7	58
Keri Kera, Sud.	K7	60
Kerinci, Gunung, mtn., Indon.	F3	38
Keriya, stm., China	B9	44
Kerkebet, Eth.	I9	60
Kerkenna, Îles, is., Tun.	C16	62
Kerkhoven, Mn., U.S.	E3	130
Kerki, U.S.S.R.	J11	22
Kérkira (Corfu), Grc.	J3	20
Kérkira, i., Grc.	J3	20
Kerkrade, Neth.	G9	12
Kermadec Islands, is., N.Z.	K22	158
Kermān, Iran	F14	48
Kerman, Ca., U.S.	D3	112
Kermit, Tx., U.S.	D1	150
Kermit, W.V., U.S.	D2	155
Kermode, Mount, mtn., B.C., Can.	C2	99
Kern, co., Ca., U.S.	E4	112
Kern, stm., Ca., U.S.	E4	112
Kernersville, N.C., U.S.	A2	140
Kernville, Ca., U.S.	E4	112
Kérou, Benin	F11	64
Kerpinen', U.S.S.R.	C12	20
Kerr, co., Tx., U.S.	D3	150
Kerr, Lake, l., Fl., U.S.	C5	116
Kerrobert, Sask., Can.	F1	105
Kerrville, Tx., U.S.	D3	150
Kerry, co., Ire.	I4	8
Kersey, Co., U.S.	A6	113
Kersey, Pa., U.S.	D4	145
Kershaw, S.C., U.S.	B6	147
Kershaw, co., S.C., U.S.	C6	147
Kersley, B.C., Can.	C6	99
Kerulen (Cherlen) (Herlen), stm., Asia	B10	30
Kerzaz, Alg.	F10	62
Kerzers, Switz.	E7	13
Keşan, Tur.	I10	20
Kesennuma, Japan	I16	36
Keshena, Wi., U.S.	D5	156
Keshendeh, Afg.	B2	44
Keshod, India	J4	44
Keskin, Tur.	B2	48
Keski-Suomen lääni, prov., Fin.	J19	6
Keskozero, U.S.S.R.	K23	6
Kes'ma, U.S.S.R.	C20	26
Kesova Gora, U.S.S.R.	D20	26
Kesra, Tun.	N4	18
Kesten'ga, U.S.S.R.	I22	6
Keswick, Ia., U.S.	C5	122
Keszthely, Hung.	I17	10
Ket', stm., U.S.S.R.	F8	24
Keta, Ghana	I10	64
Keta, ozero, l., U.S.S.R.	D10	24
Ketama, Mor.	K7	16
Ketang, China	M4	34
Ketchikan, Ak., U.S.	D13	109
Ketchum, Id., U.S.	F4	119
Ketchum, Ok., U.S.	A6	143
Kete Krachi, Ghana	H9	64
Kétou, Benin	H11	64
Kętrzyn (Rastenburg), Pol.	A21	10
Kettering, Eng., U.K.	I13	8
Kettering, Oh., U.S.	C1	142
Kettle, stm., Mn., U.S.	D6	130
Kettle Creek, stm., Pa., U.S.	D6	145
Kettle Creek Lake, res., Pa., U.S.	D6	145
Kettle Falls, Wa., U.S.	A7	154
Kettleman City, Ca., U.S.	E4	112
Kettle River, Mn., U.S.	D6	130
Keuka Lake, l., N.Y., U.S.	C3	139
Kevil, Ky., U.S.	e9	124
Kevin, Mt., U.S.	B5	133
Kew, T./C. Is.	D8	94
Kewanee, Il., U.S.	B4	120
Kewanee, Mo., U.S.	E8	132
Kewanna, In., U.S.	B5	121
Kewaskum, Wi., U.S.	E5	156
Kewaunee, Wi., U.S.	D6	156
Kewaunee, co., Wi., U.S.	D6	156
Keweenaw, co., Mi., U.S.	A2	129
Keweenaw Bay, b., Mi., U.S.	B2	129
Keweenaw Peninsula, pen., Mi., U.S.	A3	129
Keweenaw Point, c., Mi., U.S.	A3	129
Keya Paha, co., Ne., U.S.	B6	134
Keya Paha, stm., U.S.	A5	134
Keyes, Ok., U.S.	e8	143
Keyesport, Il., U.S.	E4	120
Keyhole Reservoir, res., Wy., U.S.	B8	157
Key Largo, Fl., U.S.	G6	116

Name — Map Ref. — Page

Keymar, Md., U.S. A3 127
Keyport, N.J., U.S. C4 137
Keyser, W.V., U.S. B6 155
Keystone, In., U.S. C7 121
Keystone, Ia., U.S. C5 122
Keystone, S.D., U.S. D2 148
Keystone, W.V., U.S. D3 155
Keystone Heights, Fl., U.S. C4 116
Keystone Lake, res., Ok., U.S. A5 143
Keystone Peak, mtn., Az., U.S. F4 110
Keysville, Ga., U.S. C4 117
Keysville, Va., U.S. C4 153
Keytesville, Mo., U.S. B5 132
Key West, Fl., U.S. H5 116
Key West, Ia., U.S. B7 122
Key West Naval Air Station, mil., Fl., U.S. H5 116
Kezar Falls, Me., U.S. E2 126
Kezar Lake, l., Me., U.S. D2 126
Kezar Pond, l., Me., U.S. D2 126
Kežmarok, Czech. F20 10
Kgalagadi, dept., Bots. E5 66
Kgatleng, dept., Bots. E8 66
Khābūr, Nahr al-, stm., Asia D6 48
Khadki (Kirkee), India C2 46
Khairpur, Pak. G3 44
Khajrāho, India H8 44
Khakhea, Bots. E6 66
Khalkhalah, Syria B7 50
Khalkidhikí, hist. reg., Grc. I7 20
Khalkís, Grc. K7 20
Khalūf, Oman D11 47
Khambhāliya, India I3 44
Khambhāt, India I5 44
Khambhāt, Gulf of, b., India J5 44
Khāmgaon, India B4 46
Khamir, Yemen F3 47
Khamīs Mushayṭ, Sau. Ar. E3 47
Khamkeut, Laos E8 40
Khammam, India D6 46
Khānābād, Afg. B3 44
Khān al-Baghdādī, Iraq E7 48
Khānaqīn, Iraq D8 48
Khancoban, Austl. K8 70
Khandwa, India J7 44
Khānewāl, Pak. E4 44
Khāngarh, Pak. F4 44
Khaniá, Grc. N8 20
Khānpur, Pak. F4 44
Khān Yūnus, Isr. Occ. F2 50
Kharagpur, India I12 44
Kharānoq, Iran E13 48
Kharg Island see Khārk, Jazīreh-ye, i., Iran G11 48
Khargon, India J6 44
Khāriān Cantonment, Pak. D5 44
Khārk, Jazīreh-ye, i., Iran G11 48
Kharkov see Char'kov, U.S.S.R. E15 4
Khartoum see Al-Kharṭūm, Sud. J7 60
Khartoum North see Al-Kharṭūm Baḥrī, Sud. J7 60
Khartum see Al-Kharṭūm, Sud. J7 60
Khasebake, Bots. C7 66
Khāsh, Afg. F17 48
Khāsh, Iran G16 48
Khashm al-Qirbah, Sud. J8 60
Khatt, Oued al, val., W. Sah. G4 62
Khawsa, Burma G4 40
Khemis, Alg. B12 62
Khemmarat, Thai. F8 40
Khenchla, Alg. C14 62
Khenifra, Mor. D8 62
Kherrata, Alg. B13 62
Khíos, Grc. K10 20
Khíos, i., Grc. K10 20
Khirbat 'Awwād, Syria D7 50
Khlong Thom, Thai. K5 40
Kholm, Afg. B2 44
Khomeyn, Iran E11 48
Khomeynīshahr, Iran E11 48
Khomodimo, Bots. D6 66
Khon Kaen, Thai. F7 40
Khóra, Grc. L5 20
Khorramābād, Iran E10 48
Khorramshahr, Iran F10 48
Khossanto, Sen. E4 64
Khouribga, Mor. D7 62
Khowst, Afg. D3 44
Khuff, Sau. Ar. B4 47
Khugaung, Burma A5 40
Khuis, Bots. F5 66
Khu Khan, Thai. G8 40
Khulna, Bngl. I13 44
Khūnjerāb Pass, Asia B6 44
Khurai, India H8 44
Khurīyā Murīyā, Jazā'ir, is., Oman F10 47
Khurja, India F7 44
Khuzdār, Pak. G2 44
Khvāf, Iran D16 48
Khvor, Iran E13 48
Khvormūj, Iran G11 48
Khvoy, Iran B8 48
Khwae Noi, stm., Thai. G5 40
Khyber Pass, Asia C4 44
Kiama, Austl. J9 70
Kiamichi, stm., Ok., U.S. C6 143
Kiamika, stm., Que., Can. C2 104
Kiana, Ak., U.S. B7 109
Kiangarow, Mount, mtn., Austl. F9 70
Kiangsi see Jiangxi, prov., China F10 30
Kiangsu see Jiangsu, prov., China E10 30
Kiawah Island, i., S.C., U.S. F7 147
Kibangou, Congo B2 58
Kibombo, Zaire B5 58
Kibre Mengist, Eth. O10 60
Kičevo, Yugo. H4 20
Kickamuit, stm., R.I., U.S. D5 146
Kickany, U.S.S.R. C13 20
Kickapoo, stm., Wi., U.S. E3 156
Kickapoo, Lake, res., Tx., U.S. C3 150
Kickapoo Creek, stm., Il., U.S. C4 120
Kickapoo Indian Reservation, Ks., U.S. C8 123
Kicking Horse Pass, Can. D2 98
Kicman', U.S.S.R. A9 20

Kidal, Mali B10 64
Kidder, Mo., U.S. B3 132
Kidder, S.D., U.S. B8 148
Kidder, co., N.D., U.S. C6 141
Kidira, Sen. D3 64
Kiefer, Ok., U.S. B5 143
Kiel, Ger. A10 10
Kiel, Wi., U.S. E5 156
Kiel Canal see Nord-Ostsee-Kanal, Ger. A9 10
Kielce, Pol. E20 10
Kieler Bucht, b., Ger. A10 10
Kiester, Mn., U.S. G5 130
Kiev see Kijev, U.S.S.R. G4 22
Kiffa, Maur. C4 64
Kifisiá, Grc. K7 20
Kifrī, Iraq D8 48
Kigali, Rw. B6 58
Kigille, Sud. M8 60
Kigoma, Tan. B5 58
Kihei, Hi., U.S. C5 118
Kihniö, Fin. J18 6
Kihnu, i., U.S.S.R. C7 26
Kiholo Bay, b., Hi., U.S. D5 118
Kii-suidō, strt., Japan N9 36
Kijev (Kiev), U.S.S.R. G4 22
Kijevskoje vodochranilišče, res., U.S.S.R. G4 22
Kikerino, U.S.S.R. B12 26
Kikinda, Yugo. D4 20
Kikládhes (Cyclades), is., Grc. L9 20
Kikori, Pap. N. Gui. G11 38
Kikwit, Zaire C3 58
Kila, Mt., U.S. B2 133
Kilambé, Cerro, mtn., Nic. D9 92
Kilauea, Hi., U.S. A2 118
Kilauea Crater, crat., Hi., U.S. D6 118
Kilauea Point, c., Hi., U.S. A2 118
Kilbourne, Il., U.S. C4 120
Kilbourne, La., U.S. B4 125
Kilburn, N.B., Can. C2 101
Kilchu, N. Kor. C17 32
Kilcoy, Austl. F10 70
Kildare, Ire. H7 8
Kildare, co., Ire. H7 8
Kil'din, ostrov, i., U.S.S.R. G24 6
Kil'dinstroj, U.S.S.R. G23 6
Kilgore, Tx., U.S. C5 150
Kilibo, Benin G11 64
Kilija, U.S.S.R. D13 20
Kilikollūr, India H4 46
Kilimanjaro, mtn., Tan. B7 58
Kilimavony, Madag. S20 67b
Kilingi-Nõmme, U.S.S.R. C7 26
Kilis, Tur. C4 48
Kilkenny, Ire. I6 8
Kilkenny, Mn., U.S. F5 130
Kilkenny, co., Ire. I6 8
Kilkís, Grc. H6 20
Killaloe, Ire. I5 8
Killaloe Station, Ont., Can. B7 103
Killaly, Sask., Can. G4 105
Killam, Alta., Can. C5 98
Killarney, Man., Can. E2 100
Killarney, Ire. I4 8
Killarney Provincial Park, Ont., Can. A3 103
Killbuck, Oh., U.S. B4 142
Killdeer, N.D., U.S. B3 141
Killdeer Mountains, mts., N.D., U.S. B3 141
Killeen, Tx., U.S. D4 150
Killen, Al., U.S. A2 108
Killian, La., U.S. h10 125
Killik, stm., Ak., U.S. B9 109
Killington Peak, mtn., Vt., U.S. D3 152
Killinkoski, Fin. J18 6
Killona, La., U.S. h11 125
Kilmarnock, Scot., U.K. F9 8
Kilmarnock, Va., U.S. C6 153
Kilmichael, Ms., U.S. B4 131
Kiln, Ms., U.S. E4 131
Kilomines, Zaire A6 58
Kilosa, Tan. C7 58
Kilpisjärvi, Fin. G17 6
Kilrush, Ire. I4 8
Kiltān Island, i., India G2 46
Kilwa, Zaire C5 58
Kim, stm., Cam. G9 54
Kimba, Austl. I2 70
Kimball, Mn., U.S. E4 130
Kimball, Ne., U.S. C2 134
Kimball, S.D., U.S. D7 148
Kimball, W.V., U.S. D3 155
Kimball, co., Ne., U.S. C2 134
Kimball, Mount, mtn., Ak., U.S. C11 109
Kimballton, Ia., U.S. C2 122
Kimberley, B.C., Can. E9 99
Kimberley, S. Afr. G7 66
Kimberley Plateau, plat., Austl. C5 68
Kimberling City, Mo., U.S. E4 132
Kimberlin Heights, Tn., U.S. n14 149
Kimberly, Al., U.S. B3 108
Kimberly, Id., U.S. G4 119
Kimberly, W.V., U.S. m13 155
Kimberly, Wi., U.S. h9 156
Kimble, co., Tx., U.S. D3 150
Kimbrough, Al., U.S. C1 108
Kimch'aek (Sŏngjin), N. Kor. C17 32
Kimch'ŏn, S. Kor. G16 32
Kimito (Kemiö), Fin. K18 6
Kimiwan Lake, l., Alta., Can. B2 98
Kimje, S. Kor. H14 32
Kimmell, In., U.S. B6 121
Kimovsk, U.S.S.R. H21 26
Kimry, U.S.S.R. E20 26
Kinabalu, Gunong, mtn., Malay. D6 38
Kinbasket Lake, res., B.C., Can. D8 99
Kinburn, Ont., Can. B8 103
Kincaid, Sask., Can. H2 105
Kincaid, Il., U.S. D4 120
Kincaid, Ks., U.S. D8 123
Kincaid, W.V., U.S. m13 155
Kincaid, Lake, res., Il., U.S. D4 120
Kincaid Knob, mtn., W.V., U.S. k11 155
Kincardine, Ont., Can. C3 103
Kinchafoonee Creek, stm., Ga., U.S. E2 117

Kincheloe Air Force Base, mil., Mi., U.S. B6 129
Kindberg, Aus. H15 10
Kinde, Mi., U.S. E8 129
Kinder, La., U.S. D3 125
Kinderhook, Il., U.S. D2 120
Kinderhook, N.Y., U.S. C7 139
Kindersley, Sask., Can. F1 105
Kindia, Gui. F3 64
Kindred, N.D., U.S. C9 141
Kindu, Zaire B5 58
Kinel', U.S.S.R. G8 22
Kineo, Mount, mtn., Me., U.S. C3 126
Kinešma, U.S.S.R. D25 26
King, N.C., U.S. A2 140
King, Wi., U.S. D4 156
King, co., Tx., U.S. C2 150
King, co., Wa., U.S. B3 154
King and Queen, co., Va., U.S. C6 153
Kingaroy, Austl. F9 70
King City, Ca., U.S. D3 112
King City, Mo., U.S. A3 132
King Cove, Ak., U.S. E7 109
Kingfield, Me., U.S. D2 126
Kingfisher, Ok., U.S. B4 143
Kingfisher, co., Ok., U.S. B3 143
King George, Va., U.S. B5 153
King George, co., Va., U.S. B5 153
King George Island, i., B.A.T. B1 73
King George Islands, is., N.W. Ter., Can. E17 96
King Hill, Id., U.S. F3 119
King Island, i., Austl. L6 70
King Island, i., B.C., Can. C4 99
King Lear Peak, mtn., Nv., U.S. B3 135
King Leopold Ranges, mts., Austl. C5 68
Kingman, Alta., Can. C4 98
Kingman, Az., U.S. B1 110
Kingman, In., U.S. E3 121
Kingman, Ks., U.S. E5 123
Kingman, Me., U.S. C4 126
Kingman, co., Ks., U.S. E5 123
Kingman Reef, rf., Oc. H23 158
King Mountain, mtn., Ok., U.S. C2 143
King Mountain, mtn., Or., U.S. D8 144
King Mountain, mtn., Or., U.S. E3 144
King of Prussia, Pa., U.S. F11 145
King Peak, mtn., Ca., U.S. B1 112
Kings, Il., U.S. A4 120
Kings, Ms., U.S. C3 131
Kings, co., Ca., U.S. D4 112
Kings, co., N.Y., U.S. E7 139
Kings, stm., Ar., U.S. A2 111
Kings, stm., Ca., U.S. D4 112
Kings, stm., Nv., U.S. B3 135
King Salmon, Ak., U.S. D8 109
Kingsburg, Ca., U.S. D4 112
Kingsbury, In., U.S. A4 121
Kingsbury, co., S.D., U.S. C8 148
Kings Canyon National Park, Ca., U.S. D4 112
Kingsclear, N.B., Can. D3 101
Kingscote, Austl. J2 70
Kingsdown, Ks., U.S. E4 123
Kingsey-Falls, Que., Can. D5 104
Kingsford, Mi., U.S. C2 129
Kingsgate, B.C., Can. E9 99
Kingsland, Ar., U.S. D3 111
Kingsland, Ga., U.S. F5 117
Kingsland, Tx., U.S. D3 150
Kingsley, Ia., U.S. B2 122
Kingsley, Mi., U.S. D5 129
Kingsley Dam, Ne., U.S. C4 134
King's Lynn, Eng., U.K. I14 8
Kings Mills, Oh., U.S. C1 142
Kings Mountain, N.C., U.S. B1 140
King Solomon's Mines see Mikhrot Shelomo Hamelekh, hist., Isr. I3 50
King Sound, strt., Austl. C4 68
Kings Park West, Va., U.S. B5 153
Kings Peak, mtn., Ut., U.S. C5 151
King's Point, Newf., Can. D3 102
Kingsport, Tn., U.S. C11 149
Kingston, Ont., Can. C8 103
Kingston, Jam. E6 94
Kingston, N.Z. F2 72
Kingston, Ar., U.S. A2 111
Kingston, Ga., U.S. B2 117
Kingston, Id., U.S. B2 119
Kingston, Il., U.S. A5 120
Kingston, Ky., U.S. C5 124
Kingston, Ma., U.S. C6 128
Kingston, Mi., U.S. E7 129
Kingston, Mo., U.S. B3 132
Kingston, N.H., U.S. E4 136
Kingston, N.J., U.S. C3 137
Kingston, N.Y., U.S. D6 139
Kingston, Oh., U.S. C3 142
Kingston, Ok., U.S. D5 143
Kingston, Pa., U.S. D10 145
Kingston, R.I., U.S. F3 146
Kingston, Tn., U.S. D9 149
Kingston, Wi., U.S. E4 156
Kingston Southeast, Austl. K3 70
Kingston Springs, Tn., U.S. A4 149
Kingston upon Hull, Eng., U.K. H13 8
Kingstown, St. Vin. H14 94
Kingstown, Md., U.S. B5 127
Kingstree, S.C., U.S. D8 147
Kingsville, Ont., Can. E2 103
Kingsville, Md., U.S. B5 127
Kingsville, Mo., U.S. C3 132
Kingsville (North Kingsville), Oh., U.S. A5 142
Kingsville, Tx., U.S. F4 150
Kingsville Naval Air Station, mil., Tx., U.S. F4 150
Kingswood, Ky., U.S. C3 124
King William, co., Va., U.S. C5 153
King William Island, i., N.W. Ter., Can. C13 96
King William's Town, S. Afr. I8 66
Kingwood, Tx., U.S. q14 150
Kingwood, W.V., U.S. B5 155
Kinistino, Sask., Can. E3 105
Kinkaid Lake, res., Il., U.S. F4 120
Kinkony, Lac, l., Madag. P21 67b

Kinkora, P.E.I., Can. C6 101
Kinley, Sask., Can. E2 105
Kin-Li-Chee, Az., U.S. B6 110
Kinloch, Mo., U.S. f13 132
Kinmount, Ont., Can. C6 103
Kinmundy, Il., U.S. E5 120
Kinnaird Head, c., Scot., U.K. D11 8
Kinnear, Wy., U.S. C4 157
Kinnelon, N.J., U.S. B4 137
Kinneret, Yam (Sea of Galilee), l., Isr. C5 50
Kinney, co., Tx., U.S. E2 150
Kinross, P.E.I., Can. C7 101
Kinsale, Va., U.S. B6 153
Kinsale, Old Head of, c., Ire. J5 8
Kinsella, Alta., Can. C5 98
Kinsey, Al., U.S. D4 108
Kinshasa (Léopoldville), Zaire B3 58
Kinsley, Ks., U.S. E4 123
Kinsman, Oh., U.S. A5 142
Kinston, Al., U.S. D3 108
Kinston, N.C., U.S. B5 140
Kinta, Ok., U.S. B6 143
Kintampo, Ghana G9 64
Kintyre, pen., Scot., U.K. F8 8
Kintyre, Mull of, c., Scot., U.K. F8 8
Kinuso, Alta., Can. B3 98
Kinyeti, mtn., Sud. H7 56
Kinzua, Or., U.S. C6 144
Kiosk, Ont., Can. A6 103
Kiowa, Co., U.S. B6 113
Kiowa, Ks., U.S. E5 123
Kiowa, Ok., U.S. C6 143
Kiowa, co., Co., U.S. C8 113
Kiowa, co., Ks., U.S. E4 123
Kiowa, co., Ok., U.S. C2 143
Kiowa Creek, stm., Co., U.S. B6 113
Kiowa Creek, stm., Ok., U.S. A1 143
Kipapa Stream, stm., Hi., U.S. g9 118
Kipengere Range, mts., Tan. C6 58
Kiperčeny, U.S.S.R. B12 20
Kipling, Sask., Can. G4 105
Kipling, Mi., U.S. C3 129
Kipnuk, Ak., U.S. C7 109
Kipp, Ks., U.S. D6 123
Kipushi, Zaire D5 58
Kirane, Mali D4 64
Kirazlı, Tur. I10 20
Kirby, Ar., U.S. C2 111
Kirby, Wy., U.S. C4 157
Kirbyville, Tx., U.S. D6 150
Kirchberg, Ger. F9 10
Kirchheim, Ger. G10 10
Kirchheimbolanden, Ger. F8 10
Kirchmöser, Ger. C12 10
Kirchschlag in der Buckligen Welt, Aus. H16 10
Kirejevsk, U.S.S.R. H20 26
Kirenga, stm., U.S.S.R. F13 24
Kirensk, U.S.S.R. F13 24
Kirghizia see Kirgizskaja Sovetskaja Socialističeskaja Respublika, state, U.S.S.R. I13 22
Kirgizskaja Sovetskaja Socialističeskaja Respublika, state, U.S.S.R. I13 22
Kirgizskij chrebet, mts., U.S.S.R. I12 22
Kiri, Zaire B3 58
Kiribati, ctry., Oc. F24 2
Kırıkhan, Tur. C4 48
Kırıkkale, Tur. B2 48
Kirillov, U.S.S.R. B21 26
Kirillovskoje, U.S.S.R. A12 26
Kirin see Jilin, China C12 30
Kirin see Jilin, prov., China C12 30
Kirinyaga, mtn., Kenya B7 58
Kiriši, U.S.S.R. B15 26
Kiriwina Islands, is., Pap. N. Gui. A10 68
Kirk, Co., U.S. B8 113
Kırkağaç, Tur. J11 20
Kirkcaldy, Scot., U.K. E10 8
Kirkcudbright, Scot., U.K. G9 8
Kirkenes, Nor. G22 6
Kirkersville, Oh., U.S. C3 142
Kirkfield, Ont., Can. C5 103
Kirkjubæjarklaustur, Ice. C4 6a
Kirkland, Az., U.S. D2 108
Kirkland, Il., U.S. A5 120
Kirkland, Wa., U.S. B3 154
Kirkland Lake, Ont., Can. o19 103
Kırklareli, Tur. H11 20
Kirklin, In., U.S. D5 121
Kirkpatrick, Mount, mtn., Ant. D8 73
Kirksey, Ky., U.S. f9 124
Kirksville, Ky., U.S. C5 124
Kirksville, Mo., U.S. A5 132
Kirkton, Ont., Can. D3 103
Kirkūk, Iraq D8 48
Kirkwall, Scot., U.K. C11 8
Kirkwood, S. Afr. I7 66
Kirkwood, De., U.S. B3 115
Kirkwood, Il., U.S. C3 120
Kirkwood, Mo., U.S. f13 132
Kirn, Ger. F7 10
Kirov, U.S.S.R. B22 112
Kirov, U.S.S.R. F7 22
Kirov, U.S.S.R. G17 26
Kirovakan, U.S.S.R. I6 22
Kirovgrad, U.S.S.R. F10 22
Kirovograd, U.S.S.R. H4 22
Kirovsk, U.S.S.R. D4 22
Kirovsk, U.S.S.R. B14 26
Kirovsk, U.S.S.R. H12 26
Kirovskij, U.S.S.R. I7 22
Kirovskij, U.S.S.R. I13 22
Kirs, U.S.S.R. F8 22
Kirsanov, U.S.S.R. I25 26
Kırşehir, Tur. B3 48
Kīrthar Range, mts., Pak. G2 44
Kirtland, N.M., U.S. A1 138
Kirtland Air Force Base, mil., N.M., U.S. k7 138
Kiruna, Swe. H17 6
Kirwin, Ks., U.S. C4 123

Kirwin Reservoir, res., Ks., U.S. C4 123
Kiryū, Japan K14 36
Kiržač, U.S.S.R. E21 26
Kisa, Swe. M14 6
Kisangani (Stanleyville), Zaire A5 58
Kisarazu, Japan L14 36
K.I. Sawyer Air Force Base, mil., Mi., U.S. B3 129
Kisbey, Sask., Can. H4 105
Kisel'ovsk, U.S.S.R. G9 24
Kishanganj, India G12 44
Kishangarh Bās, India G6 44
Kishi, Nig. G11 64
Kishiwada, Japan M10 36
Kishorganj, Bngl. H14 44
Kishwaukee, stm., Il., U.S. A5 120
Kisii, Kenya B6 58
Kišin'ov, U.S.S.R. H3 22
Kisiwa Creek, stm., Ks., U.S. g11 123
Kiska Island, i., Ak., U.S. E3 109
Kiskittogisu Lake, l., Man., Can. B2 100
Kiskunfélegyháza, Hung. I19 10
Kiskunhalas, Hung. I19 10
Kiskunmajsa, Hung. I19 10
Kislovodsk, U.S.S.R. I6 22
Kismaayo, Som. B8 58
Kismet, Ks., U.S. E3 123
Kiso-sammyaku, mts., Japan L12 36
Kissee Mills, Mo., U.S. E4 132
Kissidougou, Gui. G4 64
Kissimmee, Fl., U.S. D5 116
Kissimmee, stm., Fl., U.S. E5 116
Kissimmee, Lake, l., Fl., U.S. E5 116
Kissimmee Park, Fl., U.S. D5 116
Kississing Lake, l., Man., Can. B1 100
Kistler, W.V., U.S. D3 155
Kisújszállás, Hung. H20 10
Kisumu, Kenya B6 58
Kisvárda, Hung. G22 10
Kita, Mali E5 64
Kita-Daitō-jima, i., Japan F13 30
Kitaibaraki, Japan K15 36
Kitakata, Japan J14 36
Kitakyūshū, Japan N5 36
Kitale, Kenya A7 58
Kitami, Japan D18 36a
Kitami-sanchi, mts., Japan C17 36a
Kit Carson, Co., U.S. C8 113
Kit Carson, co., Co., U.S. B8 113
Kitchener, Ont., Can. D4 103
Kite, Ga., U.S. D4 117
Kiteiyab, Sud. I7 60
Kíthira, Grc. M7 20
Kíthira, i., Grc. M6 20
Kíthnos, i., Grc. L8 20
Kitimat, B.C., Can. B3 99
Kitsap, co., Wa., U.S. B3 154
Kitscoty, Alta., Can. C5 98
Kittanning, Pa., U.S. E2 145
Kittatinny Mountain, mtn., U.S. B2 137
Kittery, Me., U.S. E2 126
Kittery Point, Me., U.S. E2 126
Kittilä, Fin. H19 6
Kittitas, Wa., U.S. C5 154
Kittitas, co., Wa., U.S. B4 154
Kittitas Valley, val., Wa., U.S. B5 154
Kitts, Ky., U.S. D6 124
Kitts Hummock, De., U.S. D4 115
Kittson, co., Mn., U.S. B2 130
Kitty Hawk, N.C., U.S. A7 140
Kitty Hawk Bay, b., N.C., U.S. A7 140
Kitui, Kenya B7 58
Kitwanga, B.C., Can. B3 99
Kitwe, Zam. D5 58
Kitwitwi, Nmb. A4 66
Kitzbühel, Aus. H12 10
Kitzingen, Ger. F10 10
Kiukiang see Jiujiang, China F4 34
Kivalina, Ak., U.S. B7 109
Kiviõli, U.S.S.R. B9 26
Kivu, Lac, l., Afr. B5 58
Kıyıköy, Tur. H12 20
Kizel, U.S.S.R. F9 22
Kızıl, stm., Tur. A2 48
Kızıltepe, Tur. C6 48
Kizl'ar, U.S.S.R. I7 22
Kizyl-Arvat, U.S.S.R. J9 22
Kizyl-Atrek, U.S.S.R. J8 22
Kizyl-Su, U.S.S.R. B12 48
Kjustendil, Bul. G6 20
Kladanj, Yugo. E2 20
Kladno, Czech. E14 10
Klagenfurt, Aus. I14 10
Klagetoh, Az., U.S. B6 110
Klaipėda (Memel), U.S.S.R. F4 26
Klaksvík, Faer. Is. D8 6b
Klamath, Ca., U.S. B1 112
Klamath, co., Or., U.S. E5 144
Klamath, stm., U.S. B2 112
Klamath Falls, Or., U.S. E5 144
Klamath Glen, Ca., U.S. B2 112
Klamath Mountains, mts., U.S. E2 144
Klangpi, Burma C2 40
Klarälven, stm., Eur. K13 6
Kl'asticy, U.S.S.R. F11 26
Klatovy, Czech. F13 10
Klawer, S. Afr. H4 66
Klawock, Ak., U.S. D13 109
Kl'az'ma, stm., U.S.S.R. E25 26
Kleberg, co., Tx., U.S. F4 150
Kleck, U.S.S.R. H9 26
Kleena Kleene, B.C., Can. D5 99
Klemme, Ia., U.S. A4 122
Klerksdorp, S. Afr. F8 66
Klet', mtn., Czech. G14 10
Kletn'a, U.S.S.R. H16 26
Kleve, Ger. D6 10
Kličev, U.S.S.R. H12 26
Klickitat, Wa., U.S. D4 154
Klickitat, co., Wa., U.S. D4 154
Klickitat, stm., Wa., U.S. C4 154
Klimoviči, U.S.S.R. H14 26
Klimovo, U.S.S.R. I15 26
Klimovsk, U.S.S.R. F20 26
Klin, U.S.S.R. E19 26
Klincy, U.S.S.R. I15 26

Klipplaat, S. Afr. I7 66
Kliškovcy, U.S.S.R. A10 20
Kłobuck, Pol. E18 10
Kłodzko, Pol. E16 10
Klondike, hist. reg., Yukon, Can. D5 96
Klondike Gold Rush National Historical Park, Ak., U.S. k22 109
Klosterneuburg, Aus. G16 10
Klosters, Switz. E12 13
Kloten, Switz. D10 13
Klötze, Ger. C11 10
Klotzville, La., U.S. h9 125
Klouto, Togo H10 64
Kluane Lake, l., Yukon, Can. D5 96
Kl'učevskaja Sopka, vulkan, vol., U.S.S.R. F24 24
Kl'uči, U.S.S.R. F24 24
Kluczbork, Pol. E18 10
Klukwan, Ak., U.S. k22 109
Klutina Lake, l., Ak., U.S. g19 109
Knapp, Wi., U.S. D1 156
Knapp Creek, stm., W.V., U.S. C5 155
Knäred, Swe. M13 6
Kn'ažji Gory, U.S.S.R. E18 26
Knee Lake, l., Man., Can. B4 100
Knevicy, U.S.S.R. D15 26
Kneža, Bul. F8 20
Knić, Yugo. F4 20
Knife, stm., N.D., U.S. B3 141
Knife River, Mn., U.S. D7 130
Knifley, Ky., U.S. C4 124
Knightdale, N.C., U.S. B4 140
Knight Inlet, b., B.C., Can. D5 99
Knight Island, i., Ak., U.S. g18 109
Knights Landing, Ca., U.S. C3 112
Knightstown, In., U.S. E6 121
Knightsville, In., U.S. E3 121
Knightville Reservoir, res., Ma., U.S. B2 128
Knin, Yugo. E11 18
Knittelfeld, Aus. H14 10
Knob Creek, stm., Ky., U.S. g11 124
Knobel, Ar., U.S. A5 111
Knobly Mountain, mtn., W.V., U.S. B5 155
Knob Noster, Mo., U.S. C4 132
Knokke-Heist, Bel. F3 12
Knollwood, Ct., U.S. D6 114
Knollwood, W.V., U.S. m12 155
Knops Pond, l., Ma., U.S. f9 128
Knott, co., Ky., U.S. C6 124
Knotts Island, N.C., U.S. A7 140
Knottsville, Ky., U.S. C3 124
Knox, In., U.S. B4 121
Knox, Pa., U.S. D2 145
Knox, co., Il., U.S. B3 120
Knox, co., In., U.S. G3 121
Knox, co., Ky., U.S. D6 124
Knox, co., Me., U.S. D4 126
Knox, co., Mo., U.S. A5 132
Knox, co., Ne., U.S. B8 134
Knox, co., Oh., U.S. B3 142
Knox, co., Tn., U.S. C10 149
Knox, co., Tx., U.S. C3 150
Knox, Cape, c., B.C., Can. B1 99
Knox City, Mo., U.S. A5 132
Knox City, Tx., U.S. C3 150
Knox Coast, Ant. B6 73
Knoxville, Ar., U.S. B2 111
Knoxville, Ga., U.S. D3 117
Knoxville, Il., U.S. C3 120
Knoxville, Ia., U.S. C4 122
Knoxville, Tn., U.S. D10 149
Knysna, S. Afr. J6 66
Knyszyn, Pol. B22 10
Kobar Sink, depr., Eth. F9 56
Kobayashi, Japan P5 36
Kōbe, Japan M10 36
København (Copenhagen), Den. N13 6
Koblenz, Ger. E7 10
Koboža, U.S.S.R. C18 26
Kobrin, U.S.S.R. I7 26
Kobrinskoje, U.S.S.R. B13 26
Kobuk, stm., Ak., U.S. B8 109
Kobuk Valley National Park, Ak., U.S. B8 109
Kobylin, Pol. D17 10
Kočani, Yugo. H6 20
Kočečum, stm., U.S.S.R. D12 24
Kočetovka, U.S.S.R. I23 26
Kočevje, Yugo. D9 18
Kŏch'ang, S. Kor. H14 32
Kochanovo, U.S.S.R. G13 26
Koch Bihār, India G13 44
Kōchi, Japan N8 36
Kochma, U.S.S.R. E24 26
Koch Peak, mtn., Mt., U.S. E5 133
Kodaikānal, India G4 46
Kodak, Ky., U.S. C6 124
Kodāri, Nepal G11 44
Kodiak, Ak., U.S. D9 109
Kodiak Island, i., Ak., U.S. D9 109
Kodino, U.S.S.R. J26 6
Kodok, Sud. M7 60
Kodyma, U.S.S.R. A13 20
Koekelare, Bel. F2 12
Koersel, Bel. F7 12
Koes, Nmb. E4 66
Kofa Mountains, mts., Az., U.S. D2 110
Köflach, Aus. H15 10
Koforidua, Ghana H9 64
Kōfu, Japan L13 36
Koga, Japan K14 36
Kogaluk, stm., Newf., Can. g9 102
Kogan, Austl. F9 70
Køge, Den. N13 6
Kogoni, Mali D6 64
Kohala Mountains, mts., Hi., U.S. C6 118
Kohāt, Pak. D4 44
Kohila, U.S.S.R. B7 26
Kohīma, India H16 44
Kohler, Wi., U.S. E6 156
Kohtla-Järve, U.S.S.R. B10 26
Kohŭng, S. Kor. I15 32
Kohunlich, hist., Mex. H15 90
Koidu, S.L. G4 64
Koigi, U.S.S.R. C8 26
Koimbani, Com. K15 67a
Kojgorodok, U.S.S.R. E8 22
Kojŏ, N. Kor. E15 32

Name | Map Ref. | Page

Kok (Hkok), stm., Asia D5 40
Kokand, U.S.S.R. I12 22
Kokanee Glacier Provincial Park, B.C., Can. E9 99
Kokčetav, U.S.S.R. G11 22
Koki, Sen. D2 64
Kokka, Sud. G6 60
Kokkola (Karleby), Fin. J18 6
Koknese, U.S.S.R. E8 26
Koko, Nig. F12 64
Kokoda, Pap. N. Gui. A9 68
Koko Head, c., Hi., U.S. B4 118
Kokolik, stm., Ak., U.S. B7 109
Kokomo, Hi., U.S. C5 118
Kokomo, In., U.S. D5 121
Kokomo, Ms., U.S. D3 131
Kokong, Bots. E6 66
Koko Nor see Qinghai Hu, l., China D7 30
Kokopo, Pap. N. Gui. k17 68a
Kokorevka, U.S.S.R. I17 26
Kokosing, stm., Oh., U.S. B3 142
Kokšaalatau, chrebet, mts., Asia I13 22
Koksan, N. Kor. E14 32
Koksilah, B.C., Can. g12 99
Koksŏng, S. Kor. H15 32
Kokstad, S. Afr. H9 66
Kola, U.S.S.R. G23 6
Kolahun, Lib. G4 64
Kola Peninsula see Kol'skij poluostrov, pen., U.S.S.R. D5 22
Kolār, India F5 46
Kolār Gold Fields, India F5 46
Kolárovo, Czech. H18 10
Kolbasna, U.S.S.R. B13 20
Kolbio, Kenya B8 58
Kolchozabad, U.S.S.R. B3 44
Kol'čugino, U.S.S.R. E22 26
Kolda, Sen. E2 64
Kolenté (Great Scarcies), stm., Afr. G3 64
Kolgujev, ostrov, i., U.S.S.R. D7 22
Kolhāpur, India D3 46
Kolia, I.C. G6 64
Koliba (Corubal), stm., Afr. E3 64
Koliganek, Ak., U.S. D8 109
Kolimbine, stm., Afr. D4 64
Kolín, Czech. E15 10
Kolka, U.S.S.R. D5 26
Kolkasrags, c., U.S.S.R. D5 26
Kollegāl, India F4 46
Köln (Cologne), Ger. E6 10
Kolno, Pol. B21 10
Kolo, Niger E11 64
Koło, Pol. C18 10
Koloa, Hi., U.S. B2 118
Kolob Canyon, val., Ut., U.S. F2 151
Kolobovo, U.S.S.R. E24 26
Kołobrzeg, Pol. A15 10
Kolodn'a, U.S.S.R. G15 26
Kologriv, U.S.S.R. C27 26
Koloko, Burkina F7 64
Kolola Springs, Ms., U.S. B5 131
Kolomna, U.S.S.R. F21 26
Kolomyja, U.S.S.R. H3 22
Kol'osnoje, U.S.S.R. C13 20
Kolpaševo, U.S.S.R. F8 24
Kolpino, U.S.S.R. B13 26
Kolpny, U.S.S.R. I20 26
Kol'skij poluostrov (Kola Peninsula), pen., U.S.S.R. D5 22
Kol'ubakino, U.S.S.R. F19 26
Kolwezi, Zaire D5 58
Kolyma, stm., U.S.S.R. D23 24
Kolymskaja nizmennost', pl., U.S.S.R. D22 24
Koma, Eth. M9 60
Komadugu Gana, stm., Nig. F9 54
Komadugu Yobe, stm., Afr. F9 54
Komandorskije ostrova, is., U.S.S.R. F25 24
Komariči, U.S.S.R. I17 26
Komarniki, U.S.S.R. F23 10
Komarno, Man., Can. D3 100
Komárno, Czech. H18 10
Komárom, Hung. H18 10
Komárom, co., Hung. H18 10
Komarovo, U.S.S.R. C16 26
Komati (Incomáti), stm., Afr. E10 66
Komatipoort, S. Afr. E10 66
Komatke, Az., U.S. D3 110
Komatsu, Japan K11 36
Komatsushima, Japan M9 36
Kombone, Cam. I14 64
Komin Yanga, Burkina F10 64
Komló, Hung. I18 10
Kommunarsk, U.S.S.R. H5 22
Kommunizma, pik, mtn., U.S.S.R. J12 22
Komodo, Pulau, i., Indon. G6 38
Komoé, stm., Afr. G6 54
Komotiní, Grc. H9 20
Komrat, U.S.S.R. C12 20
Komsomolec, U.S.S.R. G10 22
Komsomolec, ostrov, i., U.S.S.R. A17 22
Komsomolec, zaliv, b., U.S.S.R. H8 22
Komsomol'sk, U.S.S.R. D23 26
Komsomol'sk, U.S.S.R. B17 48
Komsomol'sk-na-Amure, U.S.S.R. G19 24
Komsomol'skoj Pravdy, ostrova, is., U.S.S.R. B13 24
Kona, Mali D8 64
Konahuanui, Puu, mtn., Hi., U.S. g10 118
Konakovo, U.S.S.R. E19 26
Konakpınar, Tur. J11 20
Konar, stm., Asia C4 44
Konārak, India K12 44
Konawa, Ok., U.S. C5 143
Konceba, U.S.S.R. A13 20
Konch, India H8 44
Konda, stm., U.S.S.R. E5 24
Kondoa, Tan. B7 58
Kondopoga, U.S.S.R. E4 22
Kondratjevo, U.S.S.R. A11 26
Kondrovo, U.S.S.R. G18 26
Kondūz, Afg. B3 44
Konfara, Gui. F5 64
Kông, stm., Asia H9 40
Kongcheng, China D6 34
Kongfang, China H5 34
Kongju, S. Kor. G15 32
Konglong, China F4 34
Kongolo, Zaire C5 58
Kongor, Sud. N6 60
Kongsvinger, Nor. K13 6
Kongur Shan, mtn., China D2 30
Kongzhen, China D8 34
Konice, Czech. F16 10
Königswinter, Ger. E7 10
Konin, Pol. C18 10
Köniz, Switz. E7 13
Konjic, Yugo. F1 20
Könkämäälven, stm., Eur. G17 6
Kon'-Kolodez', U.S.S.R. I22 26
Konkouré, stm., Gui. F3 64
Konnur, India D3 46
Konomoc, Lake, res., Ct., U.S. D7 114
Konoša, U.S.S.R. E6 22
Konotop, U.S.S.R. G4 22
Kon'ovo, U.S.S.R. J26 6
Konqi, stm., China C4 30
Końskie, Pol. D20 10
Konstantinovka, U.S.S.R. H5 22
Konstantinovskij, U.S.S.R. D22 26
Konstanz, Ger. H9 10
Kontagora, Nig. F12 64
Kontejevo, U.S.S.R. C24 26
Kontich, Bel. F5 12
Kontiomäki, Fin. I21 6
Kon Tum, Viet. G10 40
Kontum, Plateau du, plat., Viet. H10 40
Konya, Tur. C2 48
Konza, Kenya B7 58
Konžakovskij Kamen', gora, mtn., U.S.S.R. F9 22
Koochiching, co., Mn., U.S. B4 130
Koolamarra, Austl. C4 70
Koolau Range, mts., Hi., U.S. f10 118
Kooloonong, Austl. J5 70
Koondrook, Austl. J6 70
Koontz Lake, In., U.S. B5 121
Koosharem, Ut., U.S. E4 151
Kooskia, Id., U.S. C3 119
Koossa, Gui. G5 64
Kootenai, co., Id., U.S. B2 119
Kootenay Lake, l., B.C., Can. E9 99
Kootenay National Park, B.C., Can. D9 99
Kootjieskolk, S. Afr. H5 66
Kopargaon, India C3 46
Kópasker, Ice. A5 6a
Kopcevìči, U.S.S.R. I11 26
Kopejsk, U.S.S.R. F10 22
Koper, Yugo. D8 18
Kopetdag, chrebet, mts., Asia C15 48
Koppal, India E4 46
Kopparbergs Län, co., Swe. K14 6
Koppel, Pa., U.S. E1 145
Koprivnica, Yugo. C11 18
Kopt'ovo, U.S.S.R. E23 26
Kopyl', U.S.S.R. H10 26
Kopys', U.S.S.R. G13 26
Korab, mts., Eur. H4 20
Korablino, U.S.S.R. H23 26
Kor'akskaja Sopka, vulkan, vol., U.S.S.R. G23 24
Korāput, India C7 46
Korba, Tun. M5 18
Korbach, Ger. D8 10
Korbous, Tun. M5 18
Korçë, Alb. I4 20
Korčula, Otok, i., Yugo. G11 18
Kord Kūy, Iran C13 48
Korea, North, ctry., Asia C12 30
Korea, South, ctry., Asia D12 30
Korea Bay, b., Asia E11 32
Korea Strait, strt., Asia I16 32
Korekozevo, U.S.S.R. G19 26
Koreliči, U.S.S.R. H9 26
Korfovskij, U.S.S.R. H19 24
Korgus, Sud. H7 60
Korhogo, I.C. G7 64
Korinthiakós Kólpos, b., Grc. K6 20
Kórinthos (Corinth), Grc. L6 20
Korínthou, Dhiórix, Grc. L6 20
Kōriyama, Japan J15 36
Korkino, U.S.S.R. G10 22
Korla, China C4 30
Korněšty, U.S.S.R. B11 20
Korneuburg, Aus. G16 10
Koro, Mali D8 64
Korogwe, Tan. C7 58
Koroit, Austl. L5 70
Korol'ovo, U.S.S.R. A7 20
Koróni, Grc. M5 20
Koronis, Lake, l., Mn., U.S. E4 130
Koronowo, Pol. B17 10
Körös, stm., Hung. I21 10
Korosten', U.S.S.R. G3 22
Korotovo, U.S.S.R. C20 26
Korovin Volcano, vol., Ak., U.S. E5 109
Korpilahti, Fin. J19 6
Korpo (Korppoo), Fin. K17 6
Korsakov, U.S.S.R. H20 24
Korsør, Den. N12 6
Korsze, Pol. A21 10
Kortrijk (Courtrai), Bel. G3 12
Koruçam Burnu, c., N. Cyp. D2 48
Korumburra, Austl. L6 70
Koryŏng, S. Kor. H16 32
Kos, Grc. M11 20
Kos, i., Grc. M11 20
Kosa, Eth. N9 60
Kosa, U.S.S.R. F8 22
Koš-Agač, U.S.S.R. G15 22
Kosaja Gora, U.S.S.R. G20 26
Koščagyl, U.S.S.R. H8 22
Kościan, Pol. C16 10
Kościerzyna, Pol. A18 10
Kosciusko, Ms., U.S. B4 131
Kosciusko, co., In., U.S. B6 121
Kosciusko, Mount, mtn., Austl. K8 70
Kosciusko National Park, Austl. K8 70
Koshikijima-rettō, is., Japan P4 36
Koshkonong, Mo., U.S. E6 132
Koshkonong, Lake, l., Wi., U.S. F5 156
Košice, Czech. G21 10
Köşk, Tur. L12 20
Koski, Fin. K18 6
Koslan, U.S.S.R. E7 22
Kosmynino, U.S.S.R. D23 26
Kosŏng, N. Kor. E16 32
Kosov, U.S.S.R. A9 20
Kosse, Tx., U.S. D4 150
Kossuth, Ms., U.S. A5 131
Kossuth, co., Ia., U.S. A3 122
Koster, S. Afr. E8 66
Kosterevo, U.S.S.R. F22 26
Kostešty, U.S.S.R. C12 20
Kostešty-Stynka, vodochranilišče (Lacul Stînca-Costeşti), res., Eur. B11 20
Kostriževka, U.S.S.R. A9 20
Kostroma, U.S.S.R. D23 26
Kostroma, stm., U.S.S.R. C23 26
Kostrzyn, Pol. C14 10
Kost'ukoviči, U.S.S.R. H15 26
Kost'ukovka, U.S.S.R. I13 26
Koszalin (Köslin), Pol. A16 10
Kőszeg, Hung. H16 10
Kota, India H6 44
Kota Baharu, Malay. K7 40
Kotabaru, Indon. F6 38
Kotabumi, Indon. F3 38
Kotadabok, Indon. O8 40
Kotel'nič, U.S.S.R. F7 22
Kotel'nikovo, U.S.S.R. H6 22
Kotel'nyj, ostrov, i., U.S.S.R. B19 24
Köthen, Ger. D11 10
Kotka, Fin. K20 6
Kot Kapūra, India E6 44
Kotlas, U.S.S.R. E7 22
Kotli, Pak. D5 44
Kotlik, Ak., U.S. C7 109
Kotlin, ostrov, i., U.S.S.R. A12 26
Kotly, U.S.S.R. B11 26
Koton-Karifi, Nig. G13 64
Kotonkoro, Nig. F12 64
Kotor, Yugo. G2 20
Kotoriba, Yugo. C11 18
Kotorovo, U.S.S.R. G24 26
Kotouba, I.C. G8 64
Kotovsk, U.S.S.R. C12 20
Kotovsk, U.S.S.R. H3 22
Kotovsk, U.S.S.R. I24 26
Kottagūdem, India D6 46
Kottayam, India H4 46
Kotto, stm., Cen. Afr. Rep. G5 56
Kotuj, stm., U.S.S.R. C12 24
Kot'užen', U.S.S.R. B12 20
Kotzebue, Ak., U.S. B7 109
Kotzebue Sound, strt., Ak., U.S. B7 109
Kötzting, Ger. F12 10
Kou'an, China C8 34
Kouandé, Benin F10 64
Kouchibouguac National Park, N.B., Can. C5 101
Koudougou, Burkina E8 64
Kouéré, Burkina F8 64
Koukdjuak, stm., N.W. Ter., Can. C18 96
Koulamoutou, Gabon B2 58
Koulikoro, Mali E6 64
Koulouguidi, Mali E4 64
Koulountou, stm., Afr. E3 64
Koumbakara, Sen. E2 64
Koumbal, Cen. Afr. Rep. M2 60
Koumpentoum, Sen. E2 64
Koumra, Chad G4 56
Koundara, Gui. E3 64
Koungheul, Sen. E2 64
Kounradskij, U.S.S.R. H13 22
Kountze, Tx., U.S. D5 150
Koupéla, Burkina E9 64
Kouroukoto, Mali E4 64
Kouroussa, Gui. F5 54
Koussanar, Sen. E2 64
Koussané, Mali D4 64
Koussane, Sen. D3 64
Koussi, Emi, mtn., Chad E4 56
Koussili, Mali E4 64
Koutia Ba, Sen. D2 64
Koutiala, Mali E7 64
Kouto, I.C. G6 64
Koutou, China E2 32
Kouts, In., U.S. B3 121
Kovarskas, U.S.S.R. F7 26
Kovdor, U.S.S.R. H22 6
Kovel', U.S.S.R. G2 22
Kovernino, U.S.S.R. D26 26
Kovilpatti, India H4 46
Kovrov, U.S.S.R. F6 22
Kovvur, India D6 46
Kowalewo Pomorskie, Pol. B18 10
Kowloon (Jiulong), H.K. M3 34
Kowŏn, N. Kor. D15 32
Koyna Reservoir, res., India D2 46
Koyuk, Ak., U.S. C7 109
Koyukuk, Ak., U.S. C8 109
Koyukuk, stm., Ak., U.S. B8 109
Kozan, Tur. C3 48
Kozáni, Grc. I5 20
Kozel'sk, U.S.S.R. G18 26
Kozlov Bereg, U.S.S.R. C10 26
Kozlovo, U.S.S.R. E19 26
Kozlovščina, U.S.S.R. H8 26
Kpandae, Ghana G9 64
Kpandu, Ghana H10 64
Kra, Isthmus of, Asia I5 40
Krabi, Thai. J5 40
Krâchéh, Camb. H9 40
Kraemer, La., U.S. k10 125
Kragerø, Nor. L11 6
Kragujevac, Yugo. E4 20
Krajenka, Pol. B17 10
Krakatoa see Rakata, Pulau, i., Indon. J12 39a
Krâkôr, Camb. H8 40
Kraków, Pol. E19 10
Kralendijk, Neth. Ant. H10 94
Kraljevo, Yugo. F4 20
Kralovice, Czech. F13 10
Kramatorsk, U.S.S.R. H5 22
Kranj, Yugo. C9 18
Kranzberg, Nmb. C2 66
Kranzburg, S.D., U.S. C9 148
Kraskino, U.S.S.R. A18 32
Krāslava, U.S.S.R. F10 26
Krasnaja Gorbatka, U.S.S.R. F24 26
Krasnaja Gorka, U.S.S.R. E26 26
Krasnaja Zar'a, U.S.S.R. I20 26
Kraśnik, Pol. E22 10
Krasnoarmejsk, U.S.S.R. E21 26
Krasnodar, U.S.S.R. H5 22
Krasnofarfornyj, U.S.S.R. B14 26
Krasnogorsk, U.S.S.R. H20 24
Krasnogorsk, U.S.S.R. F20 26
Krasnoil'sk, U.S.S.R. A9 20
Krasnojarsk, U.S.S.R. F10 24
Krasnojarskoje vodochranilišče, res., U.S.S.R. F16 22
Krasnoje, U.S.S.R. C13 20
Krasnoje, U.S.S.R. G10 26
Krasnoje Echo, U.S.S.R. F23 26
Krasnoje-na-Volge, U.S.S.R. D24 26
Krasnoje Selo, U.S.S.R. B13 26
Krasnoje Znam'a, U.S.S.R. C17 48
Krasnokamsk, U.S.S.R. F9 22
Krasnolesje, U.S.S.R. G5 26
Krasnoslobodsk, U.S.S.R. H6 22
Krasnoturjinsk, U.S.S.R. F10 22
Krasnoufimsk, U.S.S.R. D19 4
Krasnoural'sk, U.S.S.R. F10 22
Krasnovišersk, U.S.S.R. E9 22
Krasnovodsk, U.S.S.R. I8 22
Krasnovodskij poluostrov, pen., U.S.S.R. A12 48
Krasnovodskij zaliv, b., U.S.S.R. B12 48
Krasnozavodsk, U.S.S.R. E21 26
Krasnoznamenskij, U.S.S.R. G11 22
Krasnoz'orskoje, U.S.S.R. G13 22
Krasnyj Bogatyr', U.S.S.R. E24 26
Krasnyj Cholm, U.S.S.R. C20 26
Krasnyje Okny, U.S.S.R. B13 20
Krasnyje Tkači, U.S.S.R. D22 26
Krasnyj Kut, U.S.S.R. G7 22
Krasnyj Luč, U.S.S.R. H5 22
Krasnyj Luč, U.S.S.R. D13 26
Krasnyj Okt'abr', U.S.S.R. E21 26
Krasnyj Profintern, U.S.S.R. D23 26
Krasnyj Rog, U.S.S.R. I16 26
Krasnyj Tkač, U.S.S.R. F22 26
Krasnystaw, Pol. E23 10
Kraszna (Crasna), stm., Eur. A6 20
Krebs, Ok., U.S. C6 143
Krečetovo, U.S.S.R. K26 6
Krečevicy, U.S.S.R. C14 26
Krefeld, Ger. D6 10
Kremastón, Tekhnití Límni, res., Grc. K5 20
Kremenčug, U.S.S.R. H4 22
Kremenčugskoje vodochranilišče, res., U.S.S.R. H4 22
Kremlin, Mt., U.S. B6 133
Kremlin, Ok., U.S. A4 143
Kremmling, Co., U.S. A4 113
Krems an der Donau, Aus. G15 10
Kress, Tx., U.S. B2 150
Kresta, zaliv, b., U.S.S.R. D28 24
Krestcy, U.S.S.R. C15 26
Kretinga, U.S.S.R. F4 26
Kribi, Cam. H8 54
Kričov, U.S.S.R. H14 26
Kriens, Switz. D9 13
Kriljon, mys, c., U.S.S.R. B17 36a
Křimice, Czech. F13 10
Kriničnoje, U.S.S.R. D12 20
Krishna, stm., India D5 46
Krishnagiri, India F5 46
Krishnanagar, India I13 44
Krishnarāja Sāgara, res., India F4 46
Kristdala, Swe. M15 6
Kristiansand, Nor. L11 6
Kristianstad, Swe. M14 6
Kristiansund, Nor. J10 6
Kristineberg, Swe. I16 6
Kríti (Crete), i., Grc. N8 20
Kritikón Pélagos (Sea of Crete), Grc. N8 20
Kriva Palanka, Yugo. G6 20
Kriviči, U.S.S.R. G10 26
Krivodol, Bul. F7 20
Krivoje Ozero, U.S.S.R. B14 20
Krivoj Rog, U.S.S.R. H4 22
Križevci, Yugo. C11 18
Krk, Otok, i., Yugo. D9 18
Krnov, Czech. E17 10
Krobia, Pol. D16 10
Krokek, Swe. L15 6
Kroken, Nor. I14 6
Krokowa, Pol. A18 10
Krombi Pits, Bots. B7 66
Kroměříž, Czech. F17 10
Kromy, U.S.S.R. I18 26
Kronau, Sask., Can. G3 105
Krŏng Kaôh Kŏng, Camb. I7 40
Krŏng Kêb, Camb. I8 40
Kronobergs Län, co., Swe. M14 6
Kronoby (Kruunupyy), Fin. J18 6
Kronockij zaliv, b., U.S.S.R. G24 24
Kronštadt, U.S.S.R. B12 26
Kroonstad, S. Afr. F8 66
Kropotkin, U.S.S.R. H6 22
Krosno, Pol. F21 10
Krotoszyn, Pol. D17 10
Krotz Springs, La., U.S. D4 125
Kr'učkovo, U.S.S.R. D18 26
Krugersdorp, S. Afr. F8 66
Kruidfontein, S. Afr. I5 66
Kruisfontein, S. Afr. J7 66
Krukira, Laguna de, b., Nic. D11 92
Kr'ukovo, U.S.S.R. F20 26
Krulevščina, U.S.S.R. F10 26
Krumbach [Schwaben], Ger. G10 10
Krung Thep (Bangkok), Thai. H6 40
Krupka, Czech. E13 10
Krupki, U.S.S.R. G12 26
Kruševac, Yugo. F5 20
Kruševo, Yugo. H5 20
Krušné hory (Erzgebirge), mts., Eur. B19 14
Kruszwica, Pol. C18 10
Krutoje, U.S.S.R. I20 26
Kruzenšterna, proliv, strt., U.S.S.R. H22 24
Kruzof Island, i., Ak., U.S. m21 109
Krydor, Sask., Can. E2 105
Krymskij poluostrov (Crimea), pen., U.S.S.R. H4 22
Krynica, Pol. F20 10
Kryžopol', U.S.S.R. A12 20
Ksar Chellala, Alg. C12 62
Ksar el Barka, Maur. B3 64
Ksar-el-Kebir, Mor. J6 16
Ksar-el-Seghir, Mor. J6 16
Ksar Hellal, Tun. N5 18
Ksenjevka, U.S.S.R. G15 24
Ksour, Monts des, mts., Alg. D10 62
Ksour Essaf, Tun. N6 18
Kuala Kangsar, Malay. L6 40
Kualakapuas, Indon. F5 38
Kuala Lipis, Malay. L7 40
Kuala Lumpur, Malay. M6 40
Kuala Pilah, Malay. M7 40
Kualapuu, Hi., U.S. B4 118
Kuala Terengganu, Malay. L7 40
Kuancheng, China C6 32
Kuantan, Malay. M7 40
Kuba, U.S.S.R. I7 22
Kuban', stm., U.S.S.R. H5 22
Kubbum, Sud. L2 60
Kubenskoje, U.S.S.R. B22 26
Kubenskoje, ozero, l., U.S.S.R. B22 26
Kučevo, Yugo. E5 20
Kuchāman, India G6 44
Kuching, Malay. N11 40
Kudirkos Naumiestis, U.S.S.R. G5 26
Kudus, Indon. J15 39a
Kudymkar, U.S.S.R. F8 22
Kuee Ruins, hist., Hi., U.S. D6 118
Kufstein, Aus. H12 10
Kuga, China C3 30
Kūhdasht, Iran E9 48
Kūhpāyeh, Iran E12 48
Kuidesu, China B7 32
Kuidou, China J7 34
Kuiseb, stm., Afr. D2 66
Kuito, Ang. D3 58
Kuiu Island, i., Ak., U.S. m23 109
Kujang, N. Kor. D14 32
Kujbyšev, U.S.S.R. F13 22
Kujbyšev see Samara, U.S.S.R. G8 22
Kujbyševskij, U.S.S.R. J11 22
Kujbyševskoje vodochranilišče, res., U.S.S.R. G7 22
Kujman', U.S.S.R. I22 26
Kukalaya, stm., Nic. D11 92
Kukawa, Nig. F9 54
Kukawa, Nig. F3 56
Kukkola, Fin. I19 6
Kukuihaele, Hi., U.S. C6 118
Kukuiula, Hi., U.S. B2 118
Kula, Hi., U.S. C5 118
Kula, Yugo. D3 20
Kul'ab, U.S.S.R. J11 22
Kula Kangri, mtn., Bhu. F14 44
Kulākh, Sau. Ar. D2 47
Kulautuva, U.S.S.R. G6 26
Kulaykilī, Sud. L3 60
Kuldīga, U.S.S.R. E4 26
Kule, Bots. D5 66
Kulebaki, U.S.S.R. F25 26
Kulikovo, U.S.S.R. I22 26
Kulim, Malay. L6 40
Kulm, N.D., U.S. C7 141
Kulmbach, Ger. E11 10
Kuloj, U.S.S.R. E6 22
Kulongshan, China B4 32
Kulotino, U.S.S.R. C16 26
Kulpmont, Pa., U.S. E9 145
Kul'sary, U.S.S.R. H8 22
Kulti, India I12 44
Kulumadau, Pap. N. Gui. A10 68
Kulundinskaja step', pl., U.S.S.R. G7 24
Kuma, stm., U.S.S.R. I7 22
Kumagaya, Japan K14 36
Kumamoto, Japan O5 36
Kumanovo, Yugo. G5 20
Kumārapālaiyam, India G4 46
Kumasi, Ghana H9 64
Kumba, Cam. I14 64
Kumbakonam, India G5 46
Kumba Pits, Bots. B7 66
Kŭmch'ŏn, N. Kor. E14 32
Kum-Dag, U.S.S.R. J8 22
Kume-jima, i., Japan U1 37b
Kumertau, U.S.S.R. E19 4
Kŭmhwa, S. Kor. E15 32
Kumla, Swe. L14 6
Kumo, Nig. F9 54
Kumukahi, Cape, c., Hi., U.S. D7 118
Kumukuli, China B13 44
Kumzār, Oman A10 47
Kuna, Id., U.S. F2 119
Kunašir, ostrov (Kunashiri-tō), i., U.S.S.R. C21 36a
Kunchhā, Nepal F11 44
Kunda, U.S.S.R. B9 26
Kundar, stm., Asia E3 44
Kunene (Cunene), stm., Afr. E2 58
Kunghit Island, i., B.C., Can. C2 99
Kungrad, U.S.S.R. I9 22
Kungsbacka, Swe. M13 6
Kungur, U.S.S.R. F9 22
Kunhegyes, Hung. H20 10
Kunia, Hi., U.S. g9 118
Kunja, U.S.S.R. E13 26
Kunjāh, Pak. D5 44
Kunlong, Burma C5 40
Kunlun Shan, mts., China B12 44
Kunming, China B7 40
Kunsan, S. Kor. H14 32
Kunshan, China D9 34
Kunszentmárton, Hung. I20 10
Kuntair, Gam. E1 64
Kuntaur, Gam. E2 64
Kunting, China F10 34
Kununurra, Austl. C5 68
Kunwi, S. Kor. G16 32
Kuokegan, China B13 44
Kuopio, Fin. J20 6
Kuopion lääni, prov., Fin. J20 6
Kupang, Indon. H7 38
Kup'ansk, U.S.S.R. H5 22
Kupanskoje, U.S.S.R. E21 26
Kupino, U.S.S.R. G7 24
Kupiškis, U.S.S.R. F7 26
Küplü, Tur. H10 20
Kupreanof Island, i., Ak., U.S. m23 109
Kura, stm., Asia B10 48
Kurashiki, Japan M8 36
Kuraymah, Sud. H6 60
Kurayyimah, Jord. D5 50
Kurba, U.S.S.R. D22 26
K'urdamir, U.S.S.R. A10 48
Kurdistan, hist. reg., Asia B4 42
Kure, Japan M7 36
Kure Island, i., Hi., U.S. k12 118
Kurejka, stm., U.S.S.R. D9 24
Kuressaare, U.S.S.R. B11 26
Kuressaare, U.S.S.R. C5 26
Kurgan, U.S.S.R. F11 22
Kurgan-T'ube, U.S.S.R. J11 22
Kuria Muria Islands see Khurīyā Murīyā, is., Oman F10 47
Kuridala, Austl. C4 70
Kurīgrām, Bngl. H13 44
Kuril Islands see Kuril'skije ostrova, is., U.S.S.R. H22 24
Kuril'skije ostrova (Kuril Islands), is., U.S.S.R. H22 24
Kuril Strait see Pervyj Kuril'skij proliv, strt., U.S.S.R. G23 24
Kuril Trench D19 158
Kurinskaja kosa, spit, U.S.S.R. B10 48
Kurinwás, stm., Nic. E11 92
Kurkino, U.S.S.R. H21 26
Kurlovskij, U.S.S.R. F23 26
Kurmuk, Sud. L8 60
Kurnool, India E5 46
Kuroki, Sask., Can. F4 105
Kurovskoje, U.S.S.R. F21 26
Kurow, N.Z. F3 72
Kuršėnai, U.S.S.R. E5 26
Kursk, U.S.S.R. G5 22
Kurskaja kosa, spit, U.S.S.R. F4 26
Kurskij zaliv, b., U.S.S.R. F3 26
Kūrtī, Sud. H6 60
Kurtistown, Hi., U.S. D6 118
Kuru, Sud. N4 60
Kuruman, S. Afr. F6 66
Kuruman, stm., Afr. F5 66
Kurumanheuwels, hills, Afr. F6 66
Kurume, Japan N5 36
Kurumkan, U.S.S.R. G14 24
Kurun, stm., Afr. O8 60
Kurunegala, Sri L. I6 46
Kurzeme, hist. reg., U.S.S.R. E5 26
Kusa, U.S.S.R. F9 22
Kušalino, U.S.S.R. D19 26
Kusel, Ger. F7 10
Kushaka, Nig. F13 64
Kushiro, Japan E19 36a
Kushtia, Bngl. I13 44
Kushui, China C5 30
Kuška, U.S.S.R. J10 22
Kuška, stm., Asia C17 48
Kuskokwim, stm., Ak., U.S. C8 109
Kuskokwim Bay, b., Ak., U.S. D7 109
Kuskokwim Mountains, mts., Ak., U.S. C8 109
Kušmurun, U.S.S.R. G10 22
Küsnacht, Switz. D10 13
Kušnica, U.S.S.R. A7 20
Kusŏng, N. Kor. D13 32
Kussharo-ko, l., Japan D19 36a
Küssnacht am Rigi, Switz. D9 13
Kustanaj, U.S.S.R. G10 22
Kustar'ovka, U.S.S.R. G25 26
Kūstī, Sud. K7 60
Kušva, U.S.S.R. F9 22
Kut, Ko, i., Thai. I7 40
Kuta, Nig. G13 64
Kütahya, Tur. H13 4
Kutaisi, U.S.S.R. I6 22
Kutch, Rann of (Rann of Kachchh), reg., Asia H4 44
Kutina, Yugo. D11 18
Kutná Hora, Czech. F15 10
Kutno, Pol. C19 10
Kutse Game Reserve, Bots. D7 66
Kuttawa, Ky., U.S. e9 124
Kuttura, Fin. G20 6
Kuttusoja, Fin. H21 6
Kutu, Zaire B3 58
Kutum, Sud. J3 60
Kuty, U.S.S.R. A9 20
Kutztown, Pa., U.S. E10 145
Kuujjuaq, Que., Can. g13 104
Kuusamo, Fin. I21 6
Kuusankoski, Fin. K20 6
Kuvandyk, U.S.S.R. G9 22
Kuvango, Ang. D3 58
Kuvšinovo, U.S.S.R. D17 26
Kuwait (Al-Kuwayt), ctry., Asia D4 42
Kuwait see Al-Kuwayt, Kuw. G9 48
Kuwana, Japan L11 36
Kuwayt, Jūn al- (Kuwait Bay), b., Kuw. G10 48
Kuybyshev see Samara, U.S.S.R. G8 22
Kūysanjaq, Iraq C8 48
Kuyuwini, stm., Guy. F13 84
Kuženkino, U.S.S.R. D16 26
Kuzneck, U.S.S.R. G7 22
Kuzneckij Alatau, mts., U.S.S.R. G9 24
Kvaløy, i., Nor. G16 6
Kwai see Khwae Noi, stm., Thai. G5 40
Kwajok, Sud. M4 60
Kwakoegron, Sur. B7 76
Kwando (Cuando), stm., Afr. E4 58
Kwangchow see Guangzhou, China L2 34
Kwangju, S. Kor. H14 32
Kwango (Cuango), stm., Afr. B3 58
Kwangtung see Guangdong, prov., China G9 30
Kwangyang, S. Kor. I15 32
Kweisui see Hohhot, China C9 30
Kwekwe, Zimb. B9 66
Kweneng, dept., Bots. E7 66
Kwenge, stm., Afr. C3 58
Kwethluk, Ak., U.S. C7 109
Kwidzyn, Pol. B18 10
Kwigillingok, Ak., U.S. D7 109
Kwilu (Cuilo), stm., Afr. B3 58

Name	Map Ref.	Page
Kwitaro, stm., Guy.	F13	84
Kwolla, Nig.	G14	64
Kyabra, Austl.	F5	70
Kyabram, Austl.	K6	70
Kyaiklat, Burma	F3	40
Kyaikto, Burma	F4	40
Kyaukhnyat, Burma	E4	40
Kyaukpyu, Burma	E2	40
Kyaukse, Burma	D4	40
Kyauktaw, Burma	D2	40
Kyaunggon, Burma	F3	40
Kybartai, U.S.S.R.	G5	26
Kyeikdon, Burma	F5	40
Kyindwe, Burma	D2	40
Kyle, Sask., Can.	G1	105
Kyle, S.D., U.S.	D3	148
Kyle, Tx., U.S.	E4	150
Kyle of Lochalsh, Scot., U.K.	D8	8
Kymen lääni, prov., Fin.	K20	6
Kyneton, Austl.	K6	70
Kyoga, Lake, l., Ug.	A6	58
Kyogle, Austl.	G10	70
Kyŏnggi-man, b., Asia	F13	32
Kyŏngju, S. Kor.	H17	32
Kyŏngsan, S. Kor.	H16	32
Kyŏngsŏng, N. Kor.	B17	32
Kyŏngwŏn, N. Kor.	A18	32
Kyōto, Japan	L10	36
Kyren, U.S.S.R.	G12	24
Kyritz, Ger.	C12	10
Kyštovka, U.S.S.R.	F13	22
Kyštym, U.S.S.R.	F10	22
Kyunhla, Burma	C3	40
Kyuquot, B.C., Can.	D4	99
Kyuquot Sound, strt., B.C., Can.	E4	99
Kyūshū, i., Japan	O5	36
Kywebwe, Burma	E4	40
Kywong, Austl.	J7	70
Kyyjärvi, Fin.	J19	6
Kyzyl, U.S.S.R.	G10	24
Kyzyl-Kija, U.S.S.R.	I12	22
Kyzylkum, des., U.S.S.R.	I10	22
Kzyl-Orda, U.S.S.R.	I11	22
Kzyltu, U.S.S.R.	G12	22

L

Name	Map Ref.	Page
Laa an der Thaya, Aus.	G16	10
La Aguja, Cabo de, c., Col.	B5	84
La Alcarria, reg., Spain	E9	16
La Algaba, Spain	H5	16
La Antigua, Salina, pl., Arg.	E5	80
La Araucanía, prov., Chile	J2	80
La Arena, Pan.	J14	92
Laas Caanood, Som.	G10	56
La Ascención, Mex.	E10	90
La Asunción, Ven.	B11	84
La Atravesada, Loma, hill, Mex.	C3	90
Laau Point, c., Hi., U.S.	B4	118
La Babia, Mex.	C8	90
Labadie, Mo., U.S.	C7	132
Labadieville, La., U.S.	E5	125
La Banda, Arg.	D6	80
La Bandera, Cerro, mtn., Mex.	E7	90
La Bañeza, Spain	C6	16
La Barca, Mex.	G8	90
La Barge, Wy., U.S.	D2	157
La Barge Creek, stm., Wy., U.S.	D2	157
La Barra, Nic.	E11	92
La Barrita, Guat.	C3	92
La Bassée, Fr.	B9	14
La Baule-Escoublac, Fr.	E4	14
Labé, Gui.	F3	64
Labe (Elbe), stm., Eur.	B9	10
La Belle, Fl., U.S.	F5	116
La Belle, Mo., U.S.	A6	132
Labette, co., Ks., U.S.	E8	123
Labette Creek, stm., Ks., U.S.	E8	123
Labin, Yugo.	D9	18
Labinsk, U.S.S.R.	I6	22
La Bisbal, Spain	D15	16
Labná, hist., Mex.	G15	90
Laboe, Ger.	A10	10
Laborde, Arg.	G7	80
Labouheyre, Fr.	H6	14
Laboulaye, Arg.	H7	80
Labrador, reg., Newf., Can.	g9	102
Labrador City, Newf., Can.	h8	102
Labrador Sea, N.A.	E22	96
Lábrea, Braz.	E6	76
Labrea, Braz.	B9	82
Labrit, Fr.	H6	14
La Broquerie, Man., Can.	E3	100
Labutta, Burma	F3	40
Labytnangi, U.S.S.R.	D11	22
Lača, ozero, l., U.S.S.R.	K26	6
Laca Jahuira, stm., Bol.	H8	82
La Cal, stm., Bol.	G12	82
La Calera, Chile	G3	80
La Campana, Spain	H6	16
La Canada Flintridge, Ca., U.S.	m12	112
La Candelaria, Arg.	D6	80
Lacantún, stm., Mex.	I14	90
La Capelle [-en-Thierache], Fr.	C10	14
Lacapelle-Marival, Fr.	H8	14
La Carlota, Arg.	G7	80
La Carolina, Spain	G8	16
Lacaune, Fr.	I9	14
Lac-Baker, N.B., Can.	B1	101
Lac-Bouchette, Que., Can.	A5	104
Lac-Brome, Que., Can.	D5	104
Laccadive Islands see Lakshadweep, is., India	G2	46
Lac-Carré, Que., Can.	C3	104
Lac Courte Oreilles Indian Reservation, Wi., U.S.	C2	156
Lac du Bonnet, Man., Can.	D3	100
Lac du Flambeau, Wi., U.S.	C4	156
Lac du Flambeau Indian Reservation, Wi., U.S.	C3	156
La Ceiba, Hond.	B8	92
La Ceiba, Ven.	C7	84
La Center, Ky., U.S.	e9	124
Lac-Etchemin, Que., Can.	C7	104
Lacey, Wa., U.S.	B3	154
Laceys Spring, Al., U.S.	A3	108
La Chambre, Fr.	G13	14
La Chapelle-d'Angillon, Fr.	E9	14
La Chartre-sur-le-Loir, Fr.	E7	14
La Châtaigneraie, Fr.	F6	14
La Chaux-de-Fonds, Switz.	D6	13
Lachay, Punta, c., Peru	D3	82
Lachdenpochja, U.S.S.R.	K22	6
Lachen, Switz.	D10	13
Lachhmangarh Sīkar, India	G6	44
Lachine, Que., Can.	D4	104
Lachlan, stm., Austl.	J6	70
La Chorrera, Col.	H6	84
La Chorrera, Pan.	C3	84
L'achoviči, U.S.S.R.	H9	26
L'achovskije ostrova, is., U.S.S.R.	C20	24
Lachute, Que., Can.	D3	104
Lachva, U.S.S.R.	I10	26
La Ciénaga, Arg.	D5	80
La Cienega, N.M., U.S.	h8	138
La Ciotat, Fr.	I12	14
La Citadelle, hist., Haiti	E8	94
La Ciudad, Mex.	F7	90
Lackawanna, N.Y., U.S.	C2	139
Lackawanna, co., Pa., U.S.	D10	145
Lackawaxen, Pa., U.S.	D12	145
Lackland Air Force Base, mil., Tx., U.S.	k7	150
Lac La Biche, Alta., Can.	B5	98
Lac la Hache, B.C., Can.	D7	99
Laclede, Id., U.S.	A2	119
Laclede, Mo., U.S.	B4	132
Laclede, co., Mo., U.S.	D5	132
La Clotilde, Arg.	D8	80
Lac-Mégantic, Que., Can.	D7	104
La Cocha, Arg.	D6	80
Lacolle, Que., Can.	D4	104
La Colorada, Mex.	C4	90
La Coma, Mex.	E10	90
Lacombe, Alta., Can.	C4	98
Lacombe, La., U.S.	D6	125
Lacombe Bayou, stm., La., U.S.	h12	125
Lacon, Il., U.S.	B4	120
Lacona, Ia., U.S.	C4	122
La Concepción, Pan.	C1	84
La Concepción, Ven.	B7	84
Laconia, N.H., U.S.	C4	136
La Conner, Wa., U.S.	A3	154
La Consulta, Arg.	G4	80
Lacoochee, Fl., U.S.	D4	116
La Coruña, Spain	B3	16
Lac qui Parle, co., Mn., U.S.	F2	130
Lac qui Parle, stm., Mn., U.S.	F2	130
Lac qui Parle, West Branch, stm., Mn., U.S.	F2	130
La Creek Lake, l., S.D., U.S.	D4	148
La Crescent, Mn., U.S.	G7	130
La Crete, Alta., Can.	f7	98
La Crosse, In., U.S.	B4	121
La Crosse, Ks., U.S.	D4	123
La Crosse, Va., U.S.	D4	153
Lacrosse, Wa., U.S.	C8	154
La Crosse, Wi., U.S.	E2	156
La Crosse, co., Wi., U.S.	E2	156
La Crosse, stm., Wi., U.S.	E3	156
La Cruz, Arg.	E10	80
La Cruz, Col.	G4	84
La Cruz, C.R.	F9	92
La Cruz, Ur.	G10	80
La Cruz, Cerro, mtn., Mex.	I9	90
La Cruz de Río Grande, Nic.	D10	92
Lac-Saguay, Que., Can.	C2	104
La Cuesta, C.R.	I12	92
La Cumbre, Arg.	F6	80
Lac-Vert, Sask., Can.	E3	105
La Cygne, Ks., U.S.	D9	123
Ladainha, Braz.	D8	79
Ladākh Range, mts., Asia	C7	44
Ladário, Braz.	H13	82
Ladd, Il., U.S.	B4	120
Ladder Creek, stm., Ks., U.S.	D2	123
Laddonia, Mo., U.S.	B6	132
La Désirade, i., Guad.	F14	94
Ladies Island, i., S.C., U.S.	G6	147
La Digue, i., Sey.	B11	58
Ladismith, S. Afr.	I5	66
Lādīz, Iran	G16	48
Lādnūn, India	G6	44
Ladoga, In., U.S.	E4	121
Ladoga, Lake see Ladožskoje ozero, l., U.S.S.R.	E4	22
Ladonia, Tx., U.S.	C5	150
Ladora, Ia., U.S.	C5	122
La Dorada, Col.	E5	84
La Dormida, Arg.	G5	80
Ladožskoje Ozero, U.S.S.R.	A14	26
Ladožskoje ozero (Lake Ladoga), l., U.S.S.R.	E4	22
Ladson, S.C., U.S.	F7	147
Laduškin, U.S.S.R.	G3	26
Ladva-Vetka, U.S.S.R.	K24	6
L'ady, U.S.S.R.	C11	26
Lady Ann Strait, strt., N.W. Ter., Can.	A16	96
Ladybrand, S. Afr.	G8	66
Lady Elliot Island, i., Austl.	E10	70
Lady Lake, Fl., U.S.	D5	116
Lady Laurier, Mount, mtn., B.C., Can.	A6	99
Ladysmith, B.C., Can.	E6	99
Ladysmith, S. Afr.	G9	66
Ladysmith, Wi., U.S.	C2	156
Lae, Pap. N. Gui.	m16	68a
La Encantada, Mex.	E9	90
La Esmeralda, Mex.	D8	90
La Esmeralda, Para.	B7	80
La Esmeralda, Ven.	F10	84
La Esperanza, Cuba	C3	94
La Esperanza, Hond.	C6	92
La Estrella, Bol.	G10	82
La Falda, Arg.	F6	80
La Farge, Wi., U.S.	E3	156
Lafayette, Al., U.S.	C4	108
Lafayette, Ca., U.S.	h8	112
Lafayette, Co., U.S.	B5	113
Lafayette, Ga., U.S.	B1	117
La Fayette, Il., U.S.	B4	120
Lafayette, In., U.S.	D4	121
Lafayette, La., U.S.	D3	125
Lafayette, Mn., U.S.	F4	130
Lafayette, N.C., U.S.	B4	140
Lafayette, Or., U.S.	B3	144
La Fayette, R.I., U.S.	E4	146
Lafayette, Tn., U.S.	A5	149
Lafayette, co., Ar., U.S.	D2	111
Lafayette, co., Fl., U.S.	C3	116
Lafayette, co., La., U.S.	D3	125
Lafayette, co., Ms., U.S.	A4	131
Lafayette, co., Mo., U.S.	B4	132
Lafayette, co., Wi., U.S.	F3	156
Lafayette, Mount, mtn., N.H., U.S.	B3	136
La Fé, Cuba	D3	94
Lafe, Ar., U.S.	A5	111
La Fère, Fr.	C10	14
La Feria, Tx., U.S.	F4	150
La Ferté-Bernard, Fr.	D7	14
La Ferté-Gaucher, Fr.	D10	14
La Ferté-Macé, Fr.	D6	14
La Ferté-Saint-Aubin, Fr.	E8	14
Lafferty, Oh., U.S.	B4	142
Lafia, Nig.	G14	64
Lafitte, La., U.S.	k11	125
Laflèche, Sask., Can.	H2	105
La Flèche, Fr.	E6	14
La Florida, Guat.	I14	90
Lafnitz, stm., Eur.	H16	10
La Follette, Tn., U.S.	C9	149
La Fontaine, In., U.S.	C6	121
Lafontaine, Ks., U.S.	E8	123
Lafourche, La., U.S.	E5	125
Lafourche, co., La., U.S.	E5	125
Lafourche, Bayou, stm., La., U.S.	E5	125
La Fragua, Arg.	D6	80
La France, S.C., U.S.	B2	147
La Francia, Arg.	F7	80
La Fría, Ven.	C6	84
La Galite, i., Tun.	L3	18
La Gallareta, Arg.	E8	80
Lagangzong, China	F14	44
Lagarto, C.R.	G10	92
Lagawe, Phil.	M19	39b
Lage, China	F11	44
Lågen, stm., Nor.	K11	6
Lågen, stm., Nor.	K12	6
Lage Zwaluwe, Neth.	E6	12
Laghouat, Alg.	D12	62
La Gleize, Bel.	H8	12
La Gloria, Col.	C6	84
Lago, Mount, mtn., Wa., U.S.	A5	154
Lagoa da Prata, Braz.	F6	79
Lagoa Dourada, Braz.	F6	79
Lagoa Formosa, Braz.	E5	79
Lagoa Santa, Braz.	E7	79
Lagoa Vermelha, Braz.	E13	80
Lagolândia, Braz.	C4	79
Lagos, Nig.	H11	64
Lagos, Port.	H3	16
Lagos de Moreno, Mex.	G9	90
La Gouèra, W. Sah.	J2	62
La Goulette, Tun.	M5	18
La Grand'Combe, Fr.	H11	14
La Grande, Or., U.S.	B8	144
La Grande, stm., Que., Can.	h11	104
La Grande Deux, Réservoir, res., Que., Can.	h11	104
La Grange, Austl.	C4	68
La Grange, Ar., U.S.	C5	111
La Grange, Ga., U.S.	C1	117
La Grange, Il., U.S.	B6	120
Lagrange, In., U.S.	A7	121
La Grange, Ky., U.S.	B4	124
La Grange, Mo., U.S.	A6	132
La Grange, N.C., U.S.	B5	140
Lagrange, Oh., U.S.	A3	142
La Grange, Tn., U.S.	B2	149
La Grange, Tx., U.S.	E4	150
Lagrange, Wy., U.S.	E8	157
Lagrange, co., In., U.S.	A7	121
La Grange Park, Il., U.S.	k9	120
La Gran Sabana, pl., Ven.	E12	84
La Grita, Ven.	C7	84
Lagro, In., U.S.	C6	121
La Grue Bayou, stm., Ar., U.S.	C4	111
Lagu, China	A6	40
La Guadeloupe (Saint-Evariste), Que., Can.	D7	104
La Guaira, Ven.	B9	84
La Guajira, dept., Col.	B6	84
La Guajira, Península de, pen., S.A.	A7	84
La Guardia, Arg.	E6	80
La Guardia, Bol.	G10	82
La Guardia, Spain	D3	16
La Guerche-de-Bretagne, Fr.	E5	14
La Guerche-sur-l'Aubois, Fr.	F9	14
Laguna, Braz.	E14	80
Laguna, N.M., U.S.	B2	138
Laguna, Ilha da, i., Braz.	D8	76
Laguna Beach, Ca., U.S.	F5	112
Laguna Carapã, Braz.	G1	79
Laguna Dam, U.S.	E1	110
Laguna Indian Reservation, N.M., U.S.	C2	138
Laguna Larga, Arg.	F7	80
Laguna Limpia, Arg.	D9	80
Laguna Paiva, Arg.	F8	80
Lagunas, Peru	A4	82
Lagunas de Chacagua, Parque Nacional, Mex.	I11	90
Lagunas de Montebello, Parque Nacional, Mex.	A3	92
Lagunillas, Bol.	H10	82
Lagunillas, Ven.	C7	84
Lagunillás, Laguna, l., Peru	F6	82
Laguntara, b., Hond.	B10	92
La Habana (Havana), Cuba	C3	94
La Habra, Ca., U.S.	n13	112
Lahaina, Hi., U.S.	C5	118
La Harpe, Il., U.S.	C3	120
La Harpe, Ks., U.S.	E8	123
Lahat, Indon.	F3	38
La Have, stm., N.S., Can.	E5	101
La Have Island, N.S., Can.	E5	101
La Haye-du-Puits, Fr.	C5	14
La Higuera, Chile	E3	80
Lahij, Yemen	H4	47
Lāhījān, Iran	C11	48
Lahnstein, Ger.	E7	10
Lahoma, Ok., U.S.	A3	143
Lahontan Reservoir, res., Nv., U.S.	D2	135
Lahore, Pak.	E6	44
La Horqueta, Col.	F6	84
Lahr, Ger.	G7	10
Lahri, Pak.	F3	44
Lahti, Fin.	K19	6
La Huaca, Peru	A1	82
La Huacana, Mex.	H9	90
Laibin, China	C10	40
Lai Chau, Viet.	C7	40
Laie, Hi., U.S.	B4	118
Laifang, China	J5	34
L'Aigle, Fr.	D7	14
L'Aigle Creek, stm., Ar., U.S.	D3	111
Laignes, Fr.	E11	14
La Independencia, Bahía de, b., Peru	F3	82
Laingsburg, S. Afr.	I5	66
Laingsburg, Mi., U.S.	F6	129
La Inmaculada, Mex.	C4	90
Laird, Sask., Can.	E2	105
Laird, Co., U.S.	A8	113
Laishan, China	F9	32
Laishui, China	D3	32
Laiwu, China	G5	32
Laiyang, China	G8	32
Laizhou Wan (Laichow Bay), b., China	F7	32
Laja, stm., Chile	I3	80
Laja, Laguna de la, l., Chile	I3	80
Laja, Salto del, wtfl, Chile	I3	80
La Jalca, Peru	B3	82
La Jara, Co., U.S.	D5	113
Lajas, Cuba	C4	94
Laje, Braz.	B9	79
Lajeado, Braz.	E13	80
Lajes, Braz.	E11	76
Lajes, Braz.	D13	80
Lajinha, Braz.	F8	79
La Jolla, Point, c., Ca., U.S.	o15	112
Lajosmizse, Hung.	H19	10
La Joya, Peru	G6	82
Lajoya, N.M., U.S.	C3	138
La Joya, Tx., U.S.	F3	150
La Junta, Co., U.S.	D7	113
Lakamané, Mali	D5	64
Lake, Mi., U.S.	E5	129
Lake, Ms., U.S.	C4	131
Lake, co., Ca., U.S.	C2	112
Lake, co., Co., U.S.	B4	113
Lake, co., Fl., U.S.	D5	116
Lake, co., Il., U.S.	A6	120
Lake, co., In., U.S.	B3	121
Lake, co., Mi., U.S.	E5	129
Lake, co., Mn., U.S.	C7	130
Lake, co., Mt., U.S.	C2	133
Lake, co., Oh., U.S.	A4	142
Lake, co., Or., U.S.	E6	144
Lake, co., S.D., U.S.	C8	148
Lake, co., Tn., U.S.	A2	149
Lake Alfred, Fl., U.S.	D5	116
Lake Alma, Sask., Can.	H3	105
Lake Andes, S.D., U.S.	D7	148
Lake Ariel, Pa., U.S.	D11	145
Lake Arrowhead, Ca., U.S.	E5	112
Lake Arthur, La., U.S.	D3	125
Lake Arthur, N.M., U.S.	D5	138
Lake Barcroft, Va., U.S.	B5	153
Lake Benton, Mn., U.S.	F2	130
Lake Beseck, Ct., U.S.	C5	114
Lake Beulah, Wi., U.S.	n11	156
Lake Bluff, Il., U.S.	A6	120
Lake Bronson, Mn., U.S.	B2	130
Lake Butler, Fl., U.S.	B4	116
Lake Cargelligo, Austl.	I7	70
Lake Charles, La., U.S.	D2	125
Lake Chelan National Recreation Area, Wa., U.S.	A5	154
Lake City, Ar., U.S.	B5	111
Lake City, Co., U.S.	C3	113
Lake City, Fl., U.S.	B4	116
Lake City, Ia., U.S.	B3	122
Lake City, Mi., U.S.	D5	129
Lake City, Mn., U.S.	F6	130
Lake City, Pa., U.S.	B1	145
Lake City, S.C., U.S.	D8	147
Lake City, Tn., U.S.	C9	149
Lake Clark National Park, Ak., U.S.	C9	109
Lake Cormorant, Ms., U.S.	A3	131
Lake Cowichan, B.C., Can.	g11	99
Lake Creek, stm., Wa., U.S.	B7	154
Lake Crystal, Mn., U.S.	F4	130
Lake Delta, N.Y., U.S.	B5	139
Lake Delton, Wi., U.S.	E4	156
Lake Elsinore, Ca., U.S.	F5	112
Lake Erie Beach, N.Y., U.S.	C1	139
Lakefield, Ont., Can.	C6	103
Lakefield, Mn., U.S.	G3	130
Lakefield National Park, Austl.	C8	68
Lake Forest, Il., U.S.	A6	120
Lake Fork, stm., Co., U.S.	C3	113
Lake Fork, stm., Ut., U.S.	C5	151
Lake Geneva, Wi., U.S.	F5	156
Lake George, Co., U.S.	C5	113
Lake George, Mi., U.S.	E6	129
Lake George, N.Y., U.S.	B7	139
Lake Hamilton, Ar., U.S.	g7	111
Lake Harbour, N.W. Ter., Can.	D19	96
Lake Havasu City, Az., U.S.	C1	110
Lake Helen, Fl., U.S.	D5	116
Lake Hubert, Mn., U.S.	D4	130
Lake Hughes, Ca., U.S.	E4	112
Lakehurst, N.J., U.S.	C4	137
Lakehurst Naval Air Station, mil., N.J., U.S.	C4	137
Lake in the Hills, Il., U.S.	h8	120
Lake Isabella, Ca., U.S.	E4	112
Lake Itasca, Mn., U.S.	C3	130
Lake Jackson, Tx., U.S.	E5	150
Lake Katrine, N.Y., U.S.	D7	139
Lakeland, Fl., U.S.	D5	116
Lakeland, Ga., U.S.	E3	117
Lakeland, Tn., U.S.	B2	149
Lake Leelanau, Mi., U.S.	D5	129
Lake Lenore, Sask., Can.	E3	105
Lake Linden, Mi., U.S.	A2	129
Lake Louise, Alta., Can.	D2	98
Lake Luzerne, N.Y., U.S.	B7	139
Lake Magdalene, Fl., U.S.	o11	116
Lake Mary, Fl., U.S.	D5	116
Lake Mead National Recreation Area, U.S.	H7	135
Lake Meredith National Recreation Area, Tx., U.S.	B2	150
Lake Metigoshe, N.D., U.S.	A5	141
Lake Mills, Ia., U.S.	A4	122
Lake Mills, Wi., U.S.	E5	156
Lakemore, Oh., U.S.	A4	142
Lake Mountain, mtn., Wy., U.S.	E6	157
Lakenan, Mo., U.S.	B5	132
Lake Nash, Austl.	C2	70
Lake Nebagamon, Wi., U.S.	B2	156
Lake Norden, S.D., U.S.	C8	148
Lake Odessa, Mi., U.S.	F5	129
Lake Of The Woods, co., Mn., U.S.	B4	130
Lake Orion, Mi., U.S.	F7	129
Lake Oswego, Or., U.S.	B4	144
Lake Ozark, Mo., U.S.	C5	132
Lake Park, Fl., U.S.	F6	116
Lake Park, Ga., U.S.	F3	117
Lake Park, Ia., U.S.	A2	122
Lake Park, Mn., U.S.	D2	130
Lake Placid, Fl., U.S.	E5	116
Lake Placid, N.Y., U.S.	A7	139
Lake Pontchartrain Causeway, La., U.S.	h11	125
Lakeport, Ca., U.S.	C2	112
Lake Preston, S.D., U.S.	C8	148
Lake Providence, La., U.S.	B4	125
Lake Range, mts., Nv., U.S.	C2	135
Lake Ridge, Va., U.S.	B5	153
Lake Shore, Md., U.S.	B5	127
Lakeshore, Ms., U.S.	E4	131
Lakeside, N.S., Can.	E6	101
Lakeside, Ca., U.S.	F5	112
Lakeside, Ct., U.S.	D3	114
Lakeside, Ct., U.S.	C3	114
Lakeside, Ia., U.S.	B2	122
Lakeside, Mt., U.S.	B2	133
Lakeside, Oh., U.S.	A3	142
Lakeside, Or., U.S.	D2	144
Lakeside Mountains, mts., Ut., U.S.	B3	151
Lakeside Park, Ky., U.S.	h13	124
Lakeside-Pinetop, Az., U.S.	C6	110
Lakesite, Tn., U.S.	D8	149
Lake Station, In., U.S.	A3	121
Lake Station, Ok., U.S.	A5	143
Lake Stevens, Wa., U.S.	A3	154
Lake Superior Provincial Park, Ont., Can.	p18	103
Lake Swamp, stm., S.C., U.S.	D8	147
Lake Tansi Village, Tn., U.S.	D8	149
Lake Telemark, N.J., U.S.	B4	137
Lake Tomahawk, Wi., U.S.	C4	156
Laketon, In., U.S.	C6	121
Laketown, Ut., U.S.	B4	151
Lake Valley, Sask., Can.	G2	105
Lake Valley, val., Nv., U.S.	E7	135
Lakeview, Al., U.S.	A4	108
Lake View, Ar., U.S.	C5	111
Lake View, Ia., U.S.	B2	122
Lakeview, Mi., U.S.	E5	129
Lake View, N.Y., U.S.	C2	139
Lakeview, Oh., U.S.	B2	142
Lakeview, Or., U.S.	E6	144
Lake View, S.C., U.S.	C9	147
Lake Villa, Il., U.S.	h8	120
Lake Village, Ar., U.S.	D4	111
Lake Village, In., U.S.	B3	121
Lakeville, Ct., U.S.	B2	114
Lakeville, In., U.S.	A5	121
Lakeville, Ma., U.S.	C6	128
Lakeville, Mn., U.S.	F5	130
Lakeville, N.Y., U.S.	C3	139
Lake Waccamaw, N.C., U.S.	C4	140
Lake Wales, Fl., U.S.	E5	116
Lake Wilson, Mn., U.S.	G3	130
Lakewood, Ca., U.S.	n12	112
Lakewood, Co., U.S.	B5	113
Lakewood, Il., U.S.	D5	120
Lakewood, Ia., U.S.	f8	122
Lakewood, N.J., U.S.	C4	137
Lakewood, N.Y., U.S.	C1	139
Lakewood, Oh., U.S.	A4	142
Lakewood, Tn., U.S.	A5	149
Lakewood, Wa., U.S.	A3	154
Lakewood Center, Wa., U.S.	B3	154
Lake Worth, Fl., U.S.	F6	116
Lake Worth Inlet, b., Fl., U.S.	F7	116
Lake Zurich, Il., U.S.	h8	120
Lakhīmpur, India	G9	44
Lakhish, val., Asia	E3	50
Lakin, Ks., U.S.	E2	123
Lakinsk, U.S.S.R.	E22	26
Lakonikós Kólpos, b., Grc.	M6	20
Lakota, Ia., U.S.	A3	122
Lakota, N.D., U.S.	A7	141
Lakshadweep, ter., India	H2	46
Lakshadweep, is., India	G2	46
Lakshadweep Sea, Asia	H3	46
La Lajilla, Mex.	D10	90
L'Albufera, l., Spain	F11	16
La Leonesa, Arg.	D9	80
Lalibela, Eth.	K10	60
La Libertad, El Sal.	D5	92
La Libertad, Guat.	I14	90
La Libertad, Hond.	C7	92
La Libertad, Nic.	E9	92
La Libertad, dept., Peru	B2	82
La Ligua, Chile	G3	80
La Lima, Hond.	B7	92
La Línea, Spain	I6	16
Lalitpur, India	H8	44
Lālmanir Hāt, Bngl.	H13	44
La Loche, Sask., Can.	m7	105
La Loupe, Fr.	D8	14
Lalupon, Nig.	H12	64
La Luz, Mex.	E11	90
La Luz, Nic.	D10	92
La Luz, N.M., U.S.	D4	138
Lama, ozero, l., U.S.S.R.	D16	22
La Macarena, Serranía de, mts., Col.	F6	84
La Maddalena, Italy	H4	18
La Madera, N.M., U.S.	A3	138
Lamadong, China	C7	32
La Madrid, Arg.	D6	80
La Malbaie, Que., Can.	B7	104
Lamaline, Newf., Can.	E4	102
La Mancha, reg., Spain	G8	16
La Manche (English Channel), strt., Eur.	K12	8
Lamar, Ar., U.S.	B2	111
Lamar, Co., U.S.	C8	113
Lamar, Mo., U.S.	D3	132
Lamar, Pa., U.S.	D7	145
Lamar, S.C., U.S.	C7	147
Lamar, co., Al., U.S.	B1	108
Lamar, co., Ga., U.S.	C2	117
Lamar, co., Ms., U.S.	D4	131
Lamar, co., Tx., U.S.	C5	150
Lamar, stm., Wy., U.S.	B2	157
Lamarche, Fr.	D12	14
La Mariscala, Ur.	H11	80
Lamarque, Arg.	J6	80
La Marsa, Tun.	M5	18
Lamas, Peru	B3	82
Lamasco, Ky., U.S.	f10	124
La Masica, Hond.	B7	92
Lamastre, Fr.	H11	14
La Mauricie, Parc National de, Que., Can.	C5	104
Lamb, co., Tx., U.S.	B1	150
Lamballe, Fr.	D4	14
Lambaréné, Gabon	B2	58
Lambari, stm., Braz.	F6	79
Lambayeque, Peru	B2	82
Lambayeque, dept., Peru	B1	82
Lambayeque, stm., Peru	B2	82
Lambert, Ms., U.S.	A3	131
Lambert, Mt., U.S.	C12	133
Lambert Glacier, Ant.	C5	73
Lamberton, Mn., U.S.	F3	130
Lambert's Bay, S. Afr.	I4	66
Lambertville, Mi., U.S.	G7	129
Lambertville, N.J., U.S.	C3	137
Lambomakondro, Madag.	S21	67b
Lambrama, Peru	E5	82
Lambrook, Ar., U.S.	C5	111
Lambton, Cape, c., N.W. Ter., Can.	B8	96
Lame Deer, Mt., U.S.	E10	133
La Media Luna, Arrecifes de, rf., Hond.	B12	92
La Mendieta, Arg.	C6	80
Lamèque, N.B., Can.	B5	101
Lamèque, Île, i., N.B., Can.	B5	101
La Merced, Arg.	E6	80
La Merced, Arg.	C6	80
La Merced, Peru	D4	82
La Mesa, Pan.	I13	92
La Mesa, Ca., U.S.	F5	112
La Mesa, N.M., U.S.	E3	138
Lamesa, Tx., U.S.	C2	150
Lamía, Grc.	K6	20
L'amin, stm., U.S.S.R.	E12	22
La Minerve, Que., Can.	C3	104
La Moille, Il., U.S.	B4	120
Lamoille, Nv., U.S.	C6	135
Lamoille, co., Vt., U.S.	B3	152
Lamoille, stm., Vt., U.S.	B3	152
Lamoille, North Branch, stm., Vt., U.S.	B3	152
La Moine, stm., Il., U.S.	C3	120
Lamon Bay, b., Phil.	N19	39b
Lamoni, Ia., U.S.	D4	122
Lamont, Alta., Can.	C4	98
Lamont, Ca., U.S.	E4	112
Lamont, Ia., U.S.	B6	122
Lamont, Ok., U.S.	A4	143
La Monte, Mo., U.S.	C4	132
La Mosquitia, hist. reg., Hond.	B11	92
La Mothe-Achard, Fr.	F5	14
La Motte, Ia., U.S.	B7	122
La Motte, Isle, i., Vt., U.S.	B2	152
Lamotte-Beuvron, Fr.	E9	14
La Moure, N.D., U.S.	C7	141
La Moure, co., N.D., U.S.	C7	141
Lampa, Peru	F6	82
Lampang, Thai.	E5	40
Lampasas, Tx., U.S.	D3	150
Lampasas, co., Tx., U.S.	D3	150
Lampazos de Naranjo, Mex.	D9	90
Lampedusa, Isola di, i., Italy	N7	18
Lamphun, Thai.	E5	40
Lampman, Sask., Can.	H4	105
Lamprey, stm., N.H., U.S.	D4	136
Lamud, Peru	B3	82
La Muerte, Cerro, mtn., C.R.	H11	92
Lana, Italy	C6	18
Lanagan, Mo., U.S.	E3	132
Lanai, i., Hi., U.S.	C4	118
Lanai City, Hi., U.S.	C5	118
Lanaihale, mtn., Hi., U.S.	C5	118
Lanalhue, Lago, l., Chile	I2	80
Lanare, Ca., U.S.	D4	112
Lanark, Ont., Can.	C8	103
Lanark, Il., U.S.	A4	120
Lanark, W.V., U.S.	D3	155
Lanark Village, Fl., U.S.	C2	116
Lanbi Kyun, i., Burma	I5	40
Lancashire, co., Eng., U.K.	H11	8
Lancaster, Ont., Can.	B10	103
Lancaster, Eng., U.K.	G11	8
Lancaster, Ca., U.S.	E4	112
Lancaster, Ks., U.S.	C8	123
Lancaster, Ky., U.S.	C5	124
Lancaster, Ma., U.S.	B4	128
Lancaster, Mn., U.S.	B2	130
Lancaster, Mo., U.S.	A5	132
Lancaster, N.H., U.S.	B3	136
Lancaster, N.Y., U.S.	C2	139
Lancaster, Oh., U.S.	C3	142
Lancaster, Pa., U.S.	F9	145
Lancaster, S.C., U.S.	B6	147
Lancaster, Tn., U.S.	C8	149
Lancaster, Tx., U.S.	n10	150
Lancaster, Wi., U.S.	F3	156
Lancaster, co., Ne., U.S.	D9	134
Lancaster, co., Pa., U.S.	G9	145
Lancaster, co., S.C., U.S.	B6	147
Lancaster, co., Va., U.S.	C6	153
Lancaster Sound, strt., N.W. Ter., Can.	B16	96
Lance, Point, c., Newf., Can.	E4	102
Lance Creek, Wy., U.S.	C8	157
Lance Creek, stm., Wy., U.S.	C8	157
Lancer, Sask., Can.	G1	105
Lanciano, Italy	G9	18
Lančin, U.S.S.R.	A8	20
Lancing, Tn., U.S.	C8	149
Lancones, Peru	J2	84
Lancun, China	G8	32
Łańcut, Pol.	E22	10
Lancy, Switz.	F5	13
Landau, Ger.	F8	10
Landau an der Isar, Ger.	G12	10

Name | Map Ref. | Page

Land Between the Lakes, U.S. f9 124
Landeck, Aus. H10 10
Landen, Bel. G7 12
Lander, Wy., U.S. D4 157
Lander, co., Nv., U.S. C4 135
Landerneau, Fr. D2 14
Landes, dept., Fr. H6 14
Landess, In., U.S. C6 121
Landete, Spain F10 16
Landing Lake, l., Man., Can. B3 100
Landis, Sask., Can. E1 105
Landis, N.C., U.S. B2 140
Landivisiau, Fr. D2 14
Lando, S.C., U.S. B5 147
Land O' Lakes, Wi., U.S. B4 156
Landquart, Switz. E12 13
Landrum, S.C., U.S. A3 147
Landsberg [am Lech], Ger. G10 10
Land's End, c., Eng., U.K. K8 8
Lands End, c., R.I., U.S. F5 146
Landshut, Ger. G12 10
Landskrona, Swe. N13 6
Landsman Creek, stm., Co., U.S. B8 113
Lane, Ks., U.S. D8 123
Lane, Ok., U.S. C6 143
Lane, S.C., U.S. D8 147
Lane, co., Ks., U.S. D3 123
Lane, co., Or., U.S. C4 144
Laneburg, Ar., U.S. D2 111
La Negra, Chile B3 80
Lanesboro, Ma., U.S. A1 128
Lanesboro, Mn., U.S. G7 130
Lanesboro, Pa., U.S. C10 145
Lanesville, In., U.S. H6 121
Lanett, Al., U.S. C4 108
Lang, Sask., Can. H3 105
Langano, Lake, l., Eth. N10 60
Langarūd, Iran C11 48
Lang Bay, B.C., Can. E5 99
Langdon, Alta., Can. D4 98
Langdon, N.H., U.S. D2 136
Langdon, N.D., U.S. A7 141
Langeac, Fr. G10 14
Langeais, Fr. E7 14
Langeloth, Pa., U.S. F1 145
Langenburg, Sask., Can. G5 105
Langenhagen, Ger. C9 10
Langenthal, Switz. D8 13
Langford, S.D., U.S. B8 148
Langham, Sask., Can. E2 105
Langholm, Scot., U.K. F10 8
Langhorne, Pa., U.S. F12 145
Langlade, co., Wi., U.S. C4 156
Langley, B.C., Can. f13 99
Langley, Ky., U.S. C7 124
Langley, Ok., U.S. A6 143
Langley, S.C., U.S. E4 147
Langley, Wa., U.S. A3 154
Langley Air Force Base, mil., Va., U.S. h15 153
Langley Park, Md., U.S. f9 127
Langleyville, Il., U.S. D4 120
Langlo, stm., Austl. E6 70
Langnau, Switz. E8 13
Langogne, Fr. H10 14
Langon, Fr. H6 14
Langøya, i., Nor. G14 6
Langqiao, China E7 34
Langres, Fr. E12 14
Langruth, Man., Can. D2 100
Langsa, Indon. L4 40
Lang Son, Viet. D9 40
Langston, Ok., U.S. B4 143
Langtian, China J2 34
Langton, Ont., Can. E4 103
Langue, Hond. D7 92
Languedoc, hist. reg., Fr. I9 14
L'Anguille, stm., Ar., U.S. B5 111
Langui y Layo, Laguna de, l., Peru F6 82
Langxi, China D8 34
Langzhong, China E8 30
Lanham, Md., U.S. C4 127
Lanier, co., Ga., U.S. E3 117
Lanigan, Sask., Can. F3 105
Lankin, N.D., U.S. A8 141
Lankou, China L4 34
Lannemezan, Fr. I7 14
Lannilis, Fr. D2 14
Lannion, Fr. D3 14
Lannon, Wi., U.S. m11 156
L'Annonciation, Que., Can. C3 104
Lanoka Harbor, N.J., U.S. D4 137
Lanquín, Guat. B5 92
Lansdale, Pa., U.S. F11 145
Lansdowne, Ont., Can. C8 103
Lansdowne, Md., U.S. B4 127
L'Anse, Mi., U.S. B2 129
L'Anse-au-Clair, Newf., Can. C3 102
L'Anse-au-Loup, Newf., Can. C3 102
L'Anse-aux-Meadows, Newf., Can. C4 102
L'Anse Indian Reservation, Mi., U.S. B2 129
Lansford, N.D., U.S. A4 141
Lansford, Pa., U.S. E10 145
Lansing, Il., U.S. B6 120
Lansing, Ia., U.S. A6 122
Lansing, Ks., U.S. C9 123
Lansing, Mi., U.S. F6 129
Lansing, N.Y., U.S. C4 139
Lansing, W.V., U.S. m13 155
Lanslebourg, Fr. G13 14
Lantana, Fl., U.S. F6 116
Lantang, China L3 34
Lantau Island, i., H.K. M2 34
Lantern Hill, hill, Ct., U.S. D8 114
Lantsch, Switz. E12 13
Lanusei, Italy J4 18
Lanxi, China F8 34
Lanzarote, i., Spain N27 17b
Lanzhou, China D7 30
Laoag, Phil. L19 39b
Lao Cai, Viet. C7 40
Laochang, China B8 40
Laoge, China C8 34
Laoha, stm., China A7 32
Laois, co., Ire. I6 8
Laojie, China B5 40
La Oliva, Spain O27 17b
Laon, Fr. C10 14
Laona, Wi., U.S. C5 156
La Orchila, Isla, i., Ven. I11 94
La Orotava, Spain O24 17b
La Oroya, Peru D4 82
Laos (Lao), ctry., Asia B3 38
Laotto, In., U.S. B7 121
Laoxinkou, China E1 34
Laoyingpan, China I4 34
Laozishan, China B7 34
Lapa, Braz. C14 80
Lapalisse, Fr. F10 14
La Palma, Col. E5 84
La Palma, El Sal. C5 92
La Palma, Pan. C3 84
La Palma, Pan. D2 84
La Palma, Az., U.S. E4 110
La Palma, i., Spain O23 17b
La Palma del Condado, Spain H5 16
La Paloma, Ur. H11 80
La Pampa, prov., Arg. I5 80
La Paragua, Ven. D11 84
La Pasión, Río de, stm., Guat. I14 90
La Passe, Ont., Can. B8 103
La Patrie, Que., Can. D6 104
La Paz, Arg. F9 80
La Paz, Arg. G5 80
La Paz, Bol. G7 82
La Paz, Col. B6 84
La Paz, Hond. C7 92
La Paz, Mex. F9 90
La Paz, Mex. E4 90
Lapaz, In., U.S. B5 121
La Paz, Ur. H10 80
La Paz, dept., Bol. F7 82
La Paz, dept., Hond. C7 92
La Paz, co., Az., U.S. D2 110
La Paz, Bahía, b., Mex. E4 90
La Paz, Río de, stm., Bol. G8 82
La Paz Centro, Nic. E8 92
La Pedrera, Col. H8 84
Lapeer, Mi., U.S. E7 129
Lapeer, co., Mi., U.S. E7 129
Lapel, In., U.S. D6 121
La Perla, Mex. C7 90
La Perouse Strait (Sōya-kaikyō), strt., Asia B17 36a
La Pesca, Mex. F11 90
La Piedad de Cabadas, Mex. G8 90
Lapine, Al., U.S. D3 108
La Pine, Or., U.S. D5 144
Lapin lääni, prov., Fin. H20 6
Lapinlahti, Fin. J20 6
La Pintada, Pan. I14 92
La Place, Il., U.S. D5 120
La Place, La., U.S. h11 125
Lapland, hist. reg., Eur. H18 6
La Plata, Arg. H10 80
La Plata, Col. F5 84
La Plata, Md., U.S. C4 127
La Plata, Mo., U.S. A5 132
La Plata, co., Co., U.S. D3 113
La Plata Mountains, mts., Co., U.S. D3 113
La Plata Peak, mtn., Co., U.S. B4 113
La Platte, Ne., U.S. g13 134
La Platte, stm., Vt., U.S. C2 152
La Pobla de Segur, Spain C12 16
La Pocatière, Que., Can. B7 104
La Poile Bay, b., Newf., Can. E2 102
Lapoint, Ut., U.S. C6 151
Laporte, Co., U.S. A5 113
La Porte, In., U.S. A4 121
La Porte, Tx., U.S. r14 150
La Porte, co., In., U.S. A4 121
La Porte City, Ia., U.S. B5 122
La Porteña, Salinas, pl., Arg. J7 80
La Poza Grande, Mex. E3 90
Lappeenranta, Fin. K21 6
Lappfjärd (Lapväärtti), Fin. J17 6
La Prairie, Que., Can. D4 104
La Prairie, Mn., U.S. C5 130
La Presa, stm., Mex. E4 90
Laprida, Arg. I8 80
Laprida, Arg. E6 80
La Pryor, Tx., U.S. E3 150
Lâpseki, Tur. I10 20
Laptev Sea see Laptevych, more, U.S.S.R. B17 24
Laptevych, more (Laptev Sea), U.S.S.R. B17 24
La Puebla de Cazalla, Spain H6 16
La Puebla de Montalbán, Spain F7 16
La Puerta, Arg. E6 80
La Purísima, Mex. D3 90
Lāpuş, Rom. B8 20
La Push, Wa., U.S. B1 154
Lapwai, Id., U.S. C2 119
La Quiaca, Arg. B6 80
La Quiaca, Arg. J9 82
L'Aquila, Italy G8 18
Lār, Iran H13 48
Lara, state, Ven. B8 84
Larache, Mor. J5 16
Laragne-Montéglin, Fr. H12 14
Laramate, Peru F4 82
Laramie, Wy., U.S. E7 157
Laramie, co., Wy., U.S. E8 157
Laramie, stm., U.S. E7 157
Laramie Mountains, mts., Wy., U.S. D7 157
Laramie Peak, mtn., Wy., U.S. D7 157
Laranjal, Braz. F7 79
Laranjal, stm., Braz. G1 79
Laranjeiras do Sul, Braz. C12 80
Laraos, Peru E4 82
Larap, Phil. N20 39b
La Raya, Abra, Peru F6 82
L'Arbresle, Fr. G11 14
Larche, Col de, Eur. H13 14
Larchmont, N.Y., U.S. h13 139
Larchwood, Ia., U.S. A1 122
Lardeau, B.C., Can. D9 99
L'Ardoise, N.S., Can. D9 101
Laredo, Spain B8 16
Laredo, Mo., U.S. A4 132
Laredo, Tx., U.S. F3 150
La Reforma, Mex. E5 90
La Réole, Fr. H6 14
Lares, Peru E5 82
La Restinga, Spain P23 17b
Largo, Fl., U.S. E4 116
Largo, Cañon, val., N.M., U.S. A2 138
Largo, Cayo, i., Cuba D4 94
Largo, Key, i., Fl., U.S. G6 116
Largs, Scot., U.K. F9 8
Lari, Peru F6 82
Larimer, co., Co., U.S. A5 113
Larimore, N.D., U.S. B8 141
Larino, Italy H9 18
La Rioja, Arg. E5 80
La Rioja, prov., Arg. E5 80
La Rioja, prov., Spain C9 16
Lárisa, Grc. J6 20
La Rivière, Man., Can. E2 100
Lark, Ut., U.S. C3 151
Lārkāna, Pak. G3 44
Lark Harbour, Newf., Can. D2 102
Larkinsville, Al., U.S. A3 108
Larkspur, Ca., U.S. h7 112
Larkspur, Co., U.S. B6 113
Larksville, Pa., U.S. n17 145
Lárnax (Larnaca), Cyp. D2 48
Larned, Ks., U.S. D4 123
La Rochefoucauld, Fr. G7 14
La Rochelle, Fr. F5 14
La Roche-sur-Yon, Fr. F5 14
La Roda, Spain F9 16
La Romana, Dom. Rep. E10 94
La Ronge, Sask., Can. B3 105
Larose, La., U.S. E5 125
La Rosita, Nic. D10 92
Larreynaga, Nic. E8 92
Larrys River, N.S., Can. D8 101
Larsen Bay, Ak., U.S. D9 109
Larsen Ice Shelf, Ant. B12 73
Larteh Aheneasi, Ghana I10 64
La Rubia, Arg. F8 80
La Rue, Oh., U.S. B2 142
Larue, co., Ky., U.S. C4 124
Laruns, Fr. J6 14
Larvik, Nor. L12 6
Larwill, In., U.S. B6 121
La Sabana, Arg. D9 80
La Sal, Ut., U.S. E6 151
LaSalle, Que., Can. q19 104
La Salle, Co., U.S. A6 113
La Salle, Il., U.S. B4 120
La Salle, co., Il., U.S. B4 120
La Salle, co., La., U.S. C3 125
La Salle, co., Tx., U.S. E3 150
Las Almejas, Bahía, b., Mex. E4 90
La Sal Mountains, mts., Ut., U.S. E6 151
Las Animas, Co., U.S. C7 113
Las Animas, co., Co., U.S. D6 113
La Sarraz, Switz. E6 13
La Sarre, Que., Can. k11 104
Las Arrias, Arg. F7 80
Las Ballenas, Canal de, strt., Mex. C3 90
Las Bonitas, Ven. D10 84
Las Breñas, Arg. D8 80
Las Cabezas de San Juan, Spain I6 16
Las Cabras, Chile H3 80
Lascano, Ur. G11 80
Lascar, Volcán, vol., Chile B5 80
Las Casuarinas, Arg. F4 80
Las Catitas, Arg. G4 80
Lascaux, Grotte de, Fr. G8 14
Las Cejas, Arg. D6 80
Las Choapas, Mex. I12 90
La Scie, Newf., Can. D4 102
Las Cruces, N.M., U.S. E3 138
Las Cuevas, Mex. C9 90
Las Delicias, Mex. J14 90
La Selle, Morne, mtn., Haiti E9 94
La Serena, Chile E3 80
La Seyne, Fr. I12 14
Las Flores, Arg. I9 80
Las Flores, Arg. F4 80
Las Flores, Arroyo, stm., Arg. H9 80
Las Flores, Cerro, mtn., Mex. I12 90
Las Garcitas, Arg. D9 80
Las Guayabas, Mex. E11 90
Lashburn, Sask., Can. D1 105
Lāsh-e Joveyn, Afg. F16 48
Las Heras, Arg. G4 80
Lashio, Burma C4 40
Las Hormigas, Mex. E10 90
La Sierra, Montaña, mts., Hond. C7 92
Las Iglesias, Cerro, mtn., Mex. D6 90
Łasin, Pol. B19 10
Łask, Pol. D19 10
L'askel'a, U.S.S.R. K22 6
Las Lajas, Arg. J3 80
Las Lajas, Pan. C2 84
Las Lajitas, Arg. C6 80
Las Lomas, Peru J2 84
Las Lomitas, Arg. C8 80
Lašma, U.S.S.R. G24 26
Las Malvinas, Arg. H4 80
Las Margaritas, Mex. I14 90
Las Marianas, Arg. H9 80
Las Mercedes, Ven. C9 84
Las Minas, Cerro, mtn., Hond. C6 92
Las Nieves, Mex. D7 90
Las Nopaleras, Cerro, mtn., Mex. E8 90
La Solana, Spain G8 16
La Soledad, Cerro, mtn., Mex. D6 90
Las Ovejas, Arg. I3 80
Las Palmas, Arg. D9 80
Las Palmas, Pan. C2 84
Las Palmas, prov., Spain O26 17b
Las Palmas de Gran Canaria, Spain O25 17b
La Spezia, Italy E4 18
Las Piedras, Bol. D8 82
Las Piedras, Ur. H10 80
Las Piedras, Río de, stm., Peru E7 82
Las Plumas, Arg. E3 78
Las Ramas, Ec. H3 84
Las Rosas, Arg. G8 80
Las Rosas, Mex. I13 90
Las Salinas de Zipaquirá, Col. E6 84
Lassance, Braz. D6 79
Lassay, Fr. D6 14
Lassen, co., Ca., U.S. B3 112
Lassen Peak, vol., Ca., U.S. B3 112
Lassen Volcanic National Park, Ca., U.S. B3 112
L'Assomption, Que., Can. D4 104
Las Tablas, Pan. D2 84
Las Taperas, Bol. G11 82
Las Tinajas, Arg. D7 80
Last Mountain Lake, l., Sask., Can. F3 105
Las Tórtolas, Cerro, mtn., S.A. E4 80
Las Toscas, Arg. E9 80
Lastoursville, Gabon B2 58
Las Tunas, Cuba D6 94
Las Tunas Grandes, Laguna, l., Arg. I7 80
La Suze, Fr. E7 14
Las Varas, Mex. C5 90
Las Varas, Mex. G7 90
Las Varillas, Arg. F7 80
Las Vegas, Nv., U.S. G6 135
Las Vegas, N.M., U.S. B4 138
Las Vegas, Ven. C8 84
Las Vírgenes, Volcán, vol., Mex. D3 90
Latacunga, Ec. H3 84
Latady Island, i., Ant. C12 73
La Tagua, Col. H5 84
Latah, co., Id., U.S. C2 119
Latakia see Al-Lādhiqīyah, Syria D3 48
La Teste-de-Buch, Fr. H5 14
La Tetilla, Cerro, mtn., Mex. G7 90
Latham, Il., U.S. D4 120
Latham, Ks., U.S. E7 123
Lathrop, Ca., U.S. h10 112
Lathrop, Mo., U.S. B3 132
Lathrop Wells, Nv., U.S. G5 135
Latimer, Ia., U.S. B4 122
Latimer, co., Ok., U.S. C6 143
Latina, Italy H7 18
Latisana, Italy D8 18
La Toma, Arg. G6 80
Laton, Ca., U.S. D4 112
Latorica, stm., Eur. G22 10
La Tortuga, Isla, i., Ven. B10 84
Latouche Treville, Cape, c., Austl. C4 68
La Tour-du-Pin, Fr. G12 14
Latour Peak, mtn., Id., U.S. B2 119
Latowicz, Pol. C21 10
La Tremblade, Fr. G5 14
La Trimouille, Fr. F8 14
La Trinidad, Arg. D6 80
La Trinidad, Nic. E8 92
La Trinidad de Orichuna, Ven. D8 84
La Trinitaria, Mex. I13 90
La Trinité, Mart. G14 94
Latrobe, Austl. M7 70
Latrobe, Pa., U.S. F3 145
Latta, S.C., U.S. C9 147
Lattimer Mines, Pa., U.S. E10 145
La Tuque, Que., Can. B5 104
Lātūr, India C4 46
Latvia see Latvijskaja Sovetskaja Socialističeskaja Respublika, state, U.S.S.R. D8 26
Latvijskaja Sovetskaja Socialističeskaja Respublika, state, U.S.S.R. D8 26
Lauca, stm., Bol. H7 82
Lauchhammer, Ger. D13 10
Lauder, Man., Can. E1 100
Lauder, Scot., U.K. F11 8
Lauderdale, Ms., U.S. C5 131
Lauderdale, co., Al., U.S. A2 108
Lauderdale, co., Ms., U.S. C5 131
Lauderdale, co., Tn., U.S. B2 149
Lauderdale Lakes, Fl., U.S. r13 116
Lauf an der Pegnitz, Ger. F11 10
Läufelfingen, Switz. D8 13
Laufen, Switz. D8 13
Laughery Creek, stm., In., U.S. F7 121
Laughlin, Nv., U.S. H7 135
Laughlin Air Force Base, mil., Tx., U.S. E2 150
Laughlin Peak, mtn., N.M., U.S. A5 138
Laughlintown, Pa., U.S. F3 145
Laukuva, U.S.S.R. F5 26
Launceston, Austl. M7 70
Launceston, Eng., U.K. K9 8
Launching Point, c., P.E.I., Can. C7 101
La Unión, Chile E2 78
La Unión, Col. G4 84
La Unión, El Sal. D7 92
La Unión, Mex. I9 90
La Unión, Peru C3 82
La Unión, Peru A1 82
La Unión, Spain H11 16
La Union, N.M., U.S. F3 138
La Unión, Ven. C9 84
Laupahoehoe, Hi., U.S. D6 118
Laura, Austl. C8 68
La Urbana, Ven. D9 84
Laurel, Ont., Can. D4 103
Laurel, De., U.S. F3 115
Laurel, Fl., U.S. E4 116
Laurel, In., U.S. F7 121
Laurel, Ia., U.S. C5 122
Laurel, Md., U.S. B4 127
Laurel, Ms., U.S. D4 131
Laurel, Mt., U.S. E8 133
Laurel, Ne., U.S. B8 134
Laurel, Va., U.S. C5 153
Laurel, co., Ky., U.S. C5 124
Laurel, stm., Ky., U.S. D5 124
Laurel Bay, S.C., U.S. G6 147
Laurel Bloomery, Tn., U.S. C12 149
Laurel Creek, stm., W.V., U.S. n14 155
Laurel Creek, stm., W.V., U.S. m12 155
Laureldale, Pa., U.S. F10 145
Laureles, Ur. F11 80
Laurel Fork, stm., W.V., U.S. C5 155
Laurel Hill, Fl., U.S. u15 116
Laurel Hill, N.C., U.S. C3 140
Laurel Mountain, mtn., W.V., U.S. B5 155
Laurel River Lake, res., Ky., U.S. D5 124
Laurel Run, Pa., U.S. n17 145
Laurelville, Oh., U.S. C3 142
Laurence G. Hanscom Air Force Base, mil., Ma., U.S. g10 128
Laurence Harbor, N.J., U.S. C4 137
Laurens, Ia., U.S. B3 122
Laurens, S.C., U.S. C3 147
Laurens, co., Ga., U.S. D4 117
Laurens, co., S.C., U.S. C4 147
Laurentides, Que., Can. D4 104
Laurentides, Parc Provincial des, Que., Can. B6 104
Lauria, Italy I10 18
Laurie Island, i., B.A.T. B1 73
Laurie Island, i., B.A.T. K10 74
Laurier, Man., Can. D2 100
Laurier, Que., Can. C6 104
Laurière, Fr. F8 14
Laurierville, Que., Can. C6 104
Laurinburg, N.C., U.S. C3 140
Laurium, Mi., U.S. A2 129
Lauro Müller, Braz. E14 80
Lausanne, Switz. E6 13
Laut, Pulau, i., Indon. F6 38
Lauta, Ger. D14 10
Lautaro, Chile J2 80
Lauterbach, Ger. E9 10
Lauterbrunnen, Switz. E8 13
Lauter [Sachsen], Ger. E12 10
Laut Kecil, Kepulauan, is., Indon. F6 38
Lauzon, Que., Can. C6 104
Lava (Łyna), stm., Eur. G4 26
Lava, Nosy, i., Madag. O22 67b
Lava Beds National Monument, Ca., U.S. B3 112
Lavaca, Al., U.S. C1 108
Lavaca, Ar., U.S. B1 111
Lavaca, co., Tx., U.S. E4 150
Lava Hot Springs, Id., U.S. G6 119
Lavaisse, Arg. G6 80
Laval, Que., Can. D4 104
Laval, Fr. D6 14
La Vale, Md., U.S. k13 127
La Vall d'Uixo, Spain F11 16
Lavalle, Arg. E9 80
Lavalle, Arg. E6 80
La Valle, Wi., U.S. E3 156
Lavallette, N.J., U.S. D4 137
La Valley, Co., U.S. D5 113
Lavaltrie, Que., Can. D4 104
Lavapié, Punta, c., Chile I2 80
Lávara, Grc. H10 20
Lavardac, Fr. H7 14
Lava Tudo, stm., Braz. E13 80
Laveen, Az., U.S. m8 110
La Vega, Dom. Rep. E9 94
La Vela, Cabo de, c., Col. A6 84
La Vela de Coro, Ven. B8 84
Lavelanet, Fr. J8 14
Lavello, Italy H10 18
L'Avenir, Que., Can. D5 104
La Venta, hist., Mex. H12 90
La Ventura, Mex. E9 90
La Verde, Arg. D9 80
La Vergne, Tn., U.S. A5 149
La Verkin, Ut., U.S. F2 151
La Verne, Ca., U.S. m13 112
Laverne, Ok., U.S. A2 143
La Vernia, Tx., U.S. E3 150
Laverton, Austl. E4 68
La Veta, Co., U.S. D5 113
La Victoria, Ven. B9 84
La Vila Joiosa, Spain G11 16
La Villa, stm., Pan. J14 92
Lavillette, N.B., Can. B4 101
La Viña, Arg. C6 80
Lavina, Mt., U.S. D8 133
La Virginia, Col. E5 84
La Vista, Ga., U.S. h8 117
La Vista, Ne., U.S. g12 134
Lavonia, Ga., U.S. B3 117
Lavon Lake, res., Tx., U.S. m10 150
La Voulte-sur-Rhône, Fr. H11 14
Lavoy, Alta., Can. C5 98
Lavras, Braz. F6 79
Lavras do Sul, Braz. F12 80
Lavumisa, Swaz. F10 66
Lawai, Hi., U.S. B2 118
Lawdar, Yemen H4 47
Lawford Lake, l., Man., Can. B3 100
Lawksawk, Burma D4 40
Lawler, Ia., U.S. A5 122
Lawn, Newf., Can. E4 102
Lawndale, N.C., U.S. B1 140
Lawn Hill, Austl. B3 70
Lawrence, In., U.S. E5 121
Lawrence, Ks., U.S. D8 123
Lawrence, Ma., U.S. A5 128
Lawrence, Mi., U.S. F4 129
Lawrence, Ms., U.S. C4 131
Lawrence, Ne., U.S. D7 134
Lawrence, N.Y., U.S. k13 139
Lawrence, Pa., U.S. F1 145
Lawrence, co., Al., U.S. A2 108
Lawrence, co., Ar., U.S. A4 111
Lawrence, co., Il., U.S. E6 120
Lawrence, co., In., U.S. G4 121
Lawrence, co., Ky., U.S. B7 124
Lawrence, co., Ms., U.S. D3 131
Lawrence, co., Mo., U.S. D4 132
Lawrence, co., Oh., U.S. D3 142
Lawrence, co., Pa., U.S. E1 145
Lawrence, co., Tn., U.S. B4 149
Lawrenceburg, In., U.S. F8 121
Lawrenceburg, Ky., U.S. B5 124
Lawrenceburg, Tn., U.S. B4 149
Lawrence Park, Pa., U.S. B1 145
Lawrence Station, N.B., Can. D2 101
Lawrencetown, N.S., Can. E4 101
Lawrenceville, Que., Can. D5 104
Lawrenceville, Ga., U.S. C3 117
Lawrenceville, Il., U.S. E6 120
Lawrenceville, N.J., U.S. C3 137
Lawrenceville, Va., U.S. D5 153
Lawson, Ar., U.S. D3 111
Lawson, Mo., U.S. B3 132
Lawsonia, Md., U.S. E6 127
Lawtell, La., U.S. D3 125
Lawtey, Fl., U.S. B4 116
Lawton, Ia., U.S. B1 122
Lawton, Mi., U.S. F5 129
Lawton, Ok., U.S. C3 143
Lawz, Jabal al-, mtn., Sau. Ar. G3 48
Laxå, Swe. L14 6
Lay Dam, Al., U.S. C3 108
Laylā, Sau. Ar. C5 47
Lay Lake, res., Al., U.S. B3 108
Layland, W.V., U.S. n14 155
Laysan Island, i., Hi., U.S. k13 118
Laysville, Ct., U.S. D6 114
Layton, Ut., U.S. B4 151
Laytonville, Ca., U.S. C2 112
La Zarca, Mex. E7 90
Lázaro Cárdenas, Mex. B2 90
Lázaro Cárdenas, Mex. I8 90
Lázaro Cárdenas, Presa, res., Mex. E7 90
Lazdijai, U.S.S.R. G6 26
Lazhulong, China C9 44
Lazio, prov., Italy G7 18
Lea, co., N.M., U.S. D6 138
Léach, Camb. H7 40
Leachville, Ar., U.S. B5 111
Lead, S.D., U.S. C2 148
Leadbetter Point, c., Wa., U.S. C1 154
Leader, Sask., Can. G1 105
Lead Hill, Ar., U.S. A3 111
Lead Hill, hill, Mo., U.S. D5 132
Lead Mountain, mtn., Me., U.S. D4 126
Lead Mountain Ponds, l., Me., U.S. D4 126
Leadville, Co., U.S. B4 113
Leadwood, Mo., U.S. D7 132
Leaf, stm., Ms., U.S. D5 131
Leaf Rapids, Man., Can. A1 100
Leaf River, Il., U.S. A4 120
League City, Tx., U.S. r14 150
Leake, co., Ms., U.S. C4 131
Leakesville, Ms., U.S. D5 131
Lealman, Fl., U.S. p10 116
Leamington, Ont., Can. E2 103
Leamington, Ut., U.S. D3 151
Leán, stm., Hond. B7 92
Leandro N. Alem, Arg. D11 80
Leary, Ga., U.S. E2 117
Leasburg, Mo., U.S. C6 132
Leask, Sask., Can. E2 105
Leatherman Peak, mtn., Id., U.S. E5 119
Leatherwood, Ky., U.S. C6 124
L'Eau Frais Creek, stm., Ar., U.S. C3 111
Leavenworth, In., U.S. H5 121
Leavenworth, Ks., U.S. C9 123
Leavenworth, Wa., U.S. B5 154
Leavenworth, co., Ks., U.S. C8 123
Leavittsburg, Oh., U.S. A5 142
Leawood, Ks., U.S. D9 123
Lebak, Phil. D7 38
Lebam, Wa., U.S. C2 154
Lebanon, Ct., U.S. C7 114
Lebanon, De., U.S. D4 115
Lebanon, Il., U.S. E4 120
Lebanon, In., U.S. D5 121
Lebanon, Ks., U.S. C5 123
Lebanon, Ky., U.S. C4 124
Lebanon, Mo., U.S. D5 132
Lebanon, N.H., U.S. C2 136
Lebanon, N.J., U.S. B3 137
Lebanon, Oh., U.S. C1 142
Lebanon, Ok., U.S. D5 143
Lebanon, Or., U.S. C4 144
Lebanon, Pa., U.S. F9 145
Lebanon, S.D., U.S. B6 148
Lebanon, Tn., U.S. A5 149
Lebanon, Va., U.S. f9 153
Lebanon, co., Pa., U.S. F8 145
Lebanon (Al-Lubnān), ctry., Asia C2 42
Lebanon Junction, Ky., U.S. C4 124
Leb'ažje, U.S.S.R. G13 22
Lebec, Ca., U.S. E4 112
Lebed'an', U.S.S.R. H22 26
Le Blanc, Fr. F8 14
Lebo, Ks., U.S. D8 123
Lebombo Mountains, hills, Afr. E10 66
Lebon Régis, Braz. D13 80
Lębork, Pol. A17 10
Lebret, Sask., Can. G4 105
Lebrija, Spain I5 16
Lebrija, stm., Col. D6 84
Lebu, Chile I2 80
Le Cannet, Fr. I14 14
Le Cateau, Fr. B10 14
Lecce, Italy I13 18
Lecco, Italy D4 18
Le Center, Mn., U.S. F5 130
Lech, stm., Eur. G10 10
Le Châble, Switz. F7 13
Le Chesne, Fr. C11 14
Le Cheylard, Fr. H11 14
Lechiguanas, Islas de las, is., Arg. G9 80
Lechtaler Alpen, mts., Aus. H10 10
Lechuguilla, Cerro, mtn., Mex. F7 90
Le Claire, Ia., U.S. C7 122
Leclercville, Que., Can. C6 104
Lecompte, La., U.S. C3 125
Lecompton, Ks., U.S. C8 123
Leconte, Mount, mtn., Tn., U.S. D10 149
Le Creusot, Fr. F11 14
Łęczyca, Pol. C19 10
Led'anaja, gora, mtn., U.S.S.R. E26 24
Lede, Bel. G4 12
Ledford, Il., U.S. F5 120
Ledgewood, N.J., U.S. B3 137
Ledo, India D14 42
Ledong, China E10 40
Ledoux, N.M., U.S. B4 138
Ledu, China D7 30
Leduc, Alta., Can. C4 98
Lee, Il., U.S. B5 120
Lee, Me., U.S. C4 126
Lee, Ma., U.S. B1 128
Lee, co., Al., U.S. C4 108
Lee, co., Ar., U.S. C5 111
Lee, co., Fl., U.S. F5 116
Lee, co., Ga., U.S. E2 117
Lee, co., Il., U.S. B4 120

Name	Map Ref.	Page
Lee, co., Ia., U.S.	D6	122
Lee, co., Ky., U.S.	C6	124
Lee, co., Ms., U.S.	A5	131
Lee, co., N.C., U.S.	B3	140
Lee, co., S.C., U.S.	C7	147
Lee, co., Tx., U.S.	D4	150
Lee, co., Va., U.S.	f8	153
Lee, Lake, l., Ms., U.S.	B3	131
Lee Center, Il., U.S.	B4	120
Leechburg, Pa., U.S.	E2	145
Leech Lake, l., Mn., U.S.	C4	130
Leech Lake Indian Reservation, Mn., U.S.	C4	130
Lee Creek, stm., U.S.	B1	111
Leedey, Ok., U.S.	B2	143
Leeds, Eng., U.K.	H12	8
Leeds, Al., U.S.	B3	108
Leeds, N.D., U.S.	A6	141
Leeds, Ut., U.S.	F2	151
Leek, Neth.	B9	12
Leelanau, co., Mi., U.S.	D5	129
Leelanau, Lake, l., Mi., U.S.	C5	129
Leende, Neth.	F8	12
Lee Park, Pa., U.S.	n17	145
Leeper, Mo., U.S.	D7	132
Leer, Ger.	B7	10
Leesburg, Al., U.S.	A4	108
Leesburg, Fl., U.S.	D5	116
Leesburg, Ga., U.S.	E2	117
Leesburg, In., U.S.	B6	121
Leesburg, Oh., U.S.	C2	142
Leesburg, Va., U.S.	A5	153
Lees Summit, Mo., U.S.	C3	132
Leesville, La., U.S.	C2	125
Leesville, S.C., U.S.	D4	147
Leesville Lake, res., Va., U.S.	C3	153
Leeton, Austl.	J7	70
Leeton, Mo., U.S.	C4	132
Leetonia, Oh., U.S.	B5	142
Leetsdale, Pa., U.S.	h13	145
Leeuwarden, Neth.	B8	12
Leeuwin, Cape, c., Austl.	F3	68
Lee Vining, Ca., U.S.	D4	112
Leeward Islands, is., N.A.	F13	94
Leffingwell, Ct., U.S.	C7	114
Leflore, co., Ms., U.S.	B3	131
Le Flore, co., Ok., U.S.	C7	143
Lefor, N.D., U.S.	C3	141
Lefors, Tx., U.S.	B2	150
Leftrook Lake, l., Man., Can.	A2	100
Legal, Alta., Can.	C4	98
Leganés, Spain	E8	16
Legaspi, Phil.	O20	39b
Leggett, Ca., U.S.	C2	112
Leghorn see Livorno, Italy	F5	18
Legion Mine, Zimb.	C9	66
Legionowo, Pol.	C20	10
Legnago, Italy	D6	18
Legnano, Italy	D3	18
Legnica (Liegnitz), Pol.	D16	10
Le Grand, Ca., U.S.	D3	112
Le Grand, Ia., U.S.	B5	122
Le Grand-Lucé, Fr.	E7	14
Le Grau-du-Roi, Fr.	I11	14
Leh, India	C7	44
Le Havre, Fr.	C7	14
Lehi, Ut., U.S.	C4	151
Lehigh, Ia., U.S.	B3	122
Lehigh, Ks., U.S.	D6	123
Lehigh, Ok., U.S.	C5	143
Lehigh, co., Pa., U.S.	E10	145
Lehigh, stm., Pa., U.S.	E10	145
Lehigh Acres, Fl., U.S.	F5	116
Lehighton, Pa., U.S.	E10	145
Leho, Sud.	N7	60
Lehr, N.D., U.S.	C6	141
Lehrte, Ger.	C9	10
Lehtse, U.S.S.R.	B8	26
Lehua Island, i., Hi., U.S.	A1	118
Lehututu, Bots.	D5	66
Leiah, Pak.	E4	44
Leibnitz, Aus.	I15	10
Leicester, Eng., U.K.	I12	8
Leicester, Ma., U.S.	B4	128
Leicestershire, co., Eng., U.K.	I12	8
Leichhardt, stm., Austl.	A3	70
Leichhardt Range, mts., Austl.	C7	70
Leiden, Neth.	D6	12
Leie (Lys), stm., Eur.	B10	14
Leigh, Ne., U.S.	C8	134
Leigh Creek, Austl.	H3	70
Leighton, Al., U.S.	A2	108
Leikanger, Nor.	K10	6
Leinster, hist. reg., Ire.	H6	8
Leipers Fork, Tn., U.S.	B5	149
Leipsic, De., U.S.	D3	115
Leipsic, Oh., U.S.	A2	142
Leipsic, stm., De., U.S.	C3	115
Leipzig, Ger.	D12	10
Leisure City, Fl., U.S.	s13	116
Leitches Creek, N.S., Can.	C9	101
Leitchfield, Ky., U.S.	C3	124
Leitersburg, Md., U.S.	A2	127
Leiters Ford, In., U.S.	B5	121
Leitha, stm., Eur.	H16	10
Leitrim, co., Ire.	H6	8
Leiva, Col.	E6	84
Leiyang, China	I1	34
Leizhou Bandao, pen., China	D11	40
Leizhuang, China	D6	32
Lejunior, Ky., U.S.	D6	124
Lek, stm., Neth.	E6	12
Le Kreider, Alg.	C11	62
Leksand, Swe.	K14	6
Leksozero, ozero, l., U.S.S.R.	J22	6
Le Lamentin, Mart.	G14	94
Leland, Il., U.S.	B5	120
Leland, Ia., U.S.	A4	122
Leland, Mi., U.S.	C5	129
Leland, Ms., U.S.	B3	131
Leleiwi Point, c., Hi., U.S.	D7	118
Leleque, Arg.	E2	78
Le Limbé, Haiti	E8	94
Leli Shan, mtn., China	D9	44
Le Locle, Switz.	D6	13
Leloup, Ks., U.S.	D8	123
Le Lude, Fr.	E7	14
Lelystad, Neth.	C7	12
Lema, Nig.	E12	64
Le Maire, Estrecho de, strt., Arg.	G4	78
Le Mans, Fr.	D7	14
Le Mars, Ia., U.S.	B1	122
Lemberg, Sask., Can.	G4	105
Lemdiyya, Alg.	B12	62
Leme, Braz.	G5	79
Lemesós (Limassol), Cyp.	D2	48
Lemgo, Ger.	C8	10
Lemhi, co., Id., U.S.	E4	119
Lemhi, stm., Id., U.S.	E5	119
Lemhi Pass, Id., U.S.	E5	119
Lemhi Range, mts., Id., U.S.	E5	119
Lemieux Islands, is., N.W. Ter., Can.	D20	96
Lemin, China	D10	40
Lemitar, N.M., U.S.	C3	138
Lemmon, S.D., U.S.	B3	148
Lemmon, Mount, mtn., Az., U.S.	E5	110
Léros, i., Grc.	L10	20
Lemmon Valley, Nv., U.S.	F4	105
Lemnos see Límnos, i., Grc.	J9	20
Lemon, Lake, l., In., U.S.	F5	121
Lemon Fair, stm., Vt., U.S.	C2	152
Lemon Grove, Ca., U.S.	o15	112
Lemon Island, i., S.C., U.S.	G6	147
Lemont, Il., U.S.	B5	120
Lemont, Pa., U.S.	E6	145
Le Mont-Saint-Michel, Fr.	D5	14
Lemonweir, stm., Wi., U.S.	D3	156
Lemoore, Ca., U.S.	D4	112
Lemoore Naval Air Station, mil., Ca., U.S.	D4	112
Le Moule, Guad.	F14	94
Lemoyne, Ne., U.S.	C4	134
Lempa, stm., N.A.	D6	92
Lem Peak, mtn., Id., U.S.	E5	119
Lempira, dept., Hond.	C6	92
Lempster, N.H., U.S.	D2	136
Lemsid, W. Sah.	G4	62
Lena, Il., U.S.	A4	120
Lena, La., U.S.	C3	125
Lena, Ms., U.S.	C4	131
Lena, Wi., U.S.	D5	156
Lena, stm., U.S.S.R.	C17	24
Lenapah, Ok., U.S.	A6	143
Lenawee, co., Mi., U.S.	G6	129
Lençóis, Braz.	B8	79
Lendery, U.S.S.R.	J22	6
Lenexa, Ks., U.S.	D9	123
Lenghu, China	D5	30
Lenhovda, Swe.	M14	6
Lenina, pik, mtn., U.S.S.R.	J12	22
Leninakan, U.S.S.R.	I6	22
Leningrad (Saint Petersburg), U.S.S.R.	B13	26
Leningradskaja, sci., Ant.	B8	73
Leninogorsk, U.S.S.R.	G8	22
Leninogorsk, U.S.S.R.	G8	24
Leninsk, U.S.S.R.	H10	22
Leninsk, U.S.S.R.	I12	22
Leninsk-Kuzneckij, U.S.S.R.	G9	24
Lenk, Switz.	F7	13
Lenkoran', U.S.S.R.	J7	22
Lennox, S.D., U.S.	D9	148
Lennox, Isla, i., Chile	H3	78
Lennoxville, Que., Can.	D6	104
Lenoir, N.C., U.S.	B1	140
Lenoir, co., N.C., U.S.	B5	140
Lenoir City, Tn., U.S.	D9	149
Lenora, Ks., U.S.	C4	123
Lenore, Man., Can.	E1	100
Lenore, Id., U.S.	C2	119
Lenore Lake, l., Sask., Can.	E3	105
Lenore Lake, l., Wa., U.S.	B6	154
Lenox, Ga., U.S.	E3	117
Lenox, Ia., U.S.	D3	122
Lenox, Ma., U.S.	B1	128
Lenox, Tn., U.S.	A2	149
Lens, Fr.	B9	14
Lensk, U.S.S.R.	E14	24
Lenti, Hung.	I16	10
Lentini, Italy	L10	18
Lentner, Mo., U.S.	B5	132
Lentvaris, U.S.S.R.	G8	26
Lenzburg, Switz.	D9	13
Léo, Burkina	F8	64
Leo, In., U.S.	B7	121
Leoben, Aus.	H15	10
Léogâne, Haiti	E8	94
Leola, Ar., U.S.	C3	111
Leola, S.D., U.S.	B7	148
Leoma, Tn., U.S.	B4	149
Leominster, Ma., U.S.	A4	128
Léon, Fr.	I5	14
León, Nic.	E8	92
León, Spain	C6	16
Leon, Ia., U.S.	D4	122
Leon, Ks., U.S.	E7	123
León, dept., Nic.	E8	92
Leon, co., Fl., U.S.	B2	116
Leon, co., Tx., U.S.	D4	150
León, hist. reg., Spain	D6	16
Leona, Punta, c., C.R.	H10	92
Leonard, Ont., Can.	h13	103
Leonard, Mi., U.S.	F7	129
Leonard, N.D., U.S.	C8	141
Leonard, Ok., U.S.	B6	143
Leonard, Tx., U.S.	C4	150
Leonardo, N.J., U.S.	C4	137
Leonardtown, Md., U.S.	D4	127
Leonardville, N.B., Can.	E3	101
Leonardville, Ks., U.S.	C7	123
León [de los Aldamas], Mex.	G9	90
Leones, Arg.	G7	80
Leonforte, Italy	L9	18
Leongatha, Austl.	L6	70
Leonia, N.J., U.S.	h9	137
Leonora, Austl.	E4	68
León Rougés, Arg.	D6	80
Leonville, La., U.S.	D4	125
Leopold, Mo., U.S.	D8	132
Leopold and Astrid Coast, Ant.	B5	73
Leopoldina, Braz.	F7	79
Leopoldo de Bulhões, Braz.	D4	79
Léopoldville see Kinshasa, Zaire	B3	58
Leota, Mn., U.S.	G2	130
Leoti, Ks., U.S.	D2	123
Leoville, Sask., Can.	D2	105
Leovo, U.S.S.R.	C12	20
Le Palais, Fr.	E3	14
Lepanto, C.R.	H9	92
Lepanto, Ar., U.S.	B5	111
Lepe, Spain	H4	16
Lepel', U.S.S.R.	G11	26
Le Pellerin, Fr.	E5	14
Lephepe, Bots.	D7	66
Leping, China	G6	34
L'Epiphanie, Que., Can.	D4	104
Le Pont-de-Beauvoisin, Fr.	G12	14
Lepontine, Alpi, mts., Eur.	F15	14
Le Port, Reu.	V17	67c
Lepreau, N.B., Can.	D3	101
Lepsy, U.S.S.R.	H13	22
Le Puy, Fr.	G10	14
Lequeitio, Spain	I4	14
Lequire, Ok., U.S.	B6	143
Léraba, stm., Afr.	G7	64
Lere, Nig.	F14	64
Lerici, Italy	E4	18
Lérida, Col.	G7	84
Lerma, stm., Mex.	G9	90
Lerna, Il., U.S.	D5	120
Léros, i., Grc.	L10	20
Leross, Sask., Can.	F4	105
Leroux Wash, val., Az., U.S.	B5	110
Leroy, Sask., Can.	F3	105
Leroy, Al., U.S.	D2	108
Le Roy, Il., U.S.	C5	120
Leroy, In., U.S.	B3	121
Le Roy, Ks., U.S.	D8	123
Le Roy, Mn., U.S.	G6	130
Le Roy, N.Y., U.S.	C3	139
Lerwick, Scot., U.K.	A12	8
Léry, Que., Can.	q19	104
Lery, Lake, l., La., U.S.	k12	125
Les Andelys, Fr.	C8	14
Les Borges Blanques, Spain	D12	16
Lesbos see Lésvos, i., Grc.	J10	20
Les Cayes, Haiti	E8	94
Leshan, China	F7	30
Leshara, Ne., U.S.	g12	134
Les Haudères, Switz.	F8	13
Lesjaskog, Nor.	J11	6
Lesko, Pol.	F22	10
Leskovac, Yugo.	G5	20
Leskov Island, i., Falk. Is.	A2	73
Leskov Island, i., Falk. Is.	J12	74
Leslie, Sask., Can.	F4	105
Leslie, S. Afr.	F9	66
Leslie, Ar., U.S.	B3	111
Leslie, Ga., U.S.	E2	117
Leslie, Mi., U.S.	F6	129
Leslie, S.C., U.S.	B6	147
Leslie, W.V., U.S.	C4	155
Leslie, co., Ky., U.S.	C6	124
Leslieville, Alta., Can.	C3	98
Les Mosses, Switz.	F7	13
Lesnaja, U.S.S.R.	I8	26
Lesnoj, U.S.S.R.	G23	26
Lesogorskij, U.S.S.R.	K21	6
Lesosibirsk, U.S.S.R.	F10	24
Lesotho, ctry., Afr.	G5	58
Lesozavodsk, U.S.S.R.	H18	24
Les Pieux, Fr.	C5	14
Les Riceys, Fr.	E11	14
Les Sables-d'Olonne, Fr.	F5	14
Les Saintes, is., Guad.	G14	94
Lessay, Fr.	C5	14
Lessen (Lessines), Bel.	G4	12
Lesser Antilles, is.	H14	94
Lesser Khingan Range see Xiao Hinggan Ling, mts., China	B12	30
Lesser Slave Lake, l., Alta., Can.	B3	98
Lesser Sunda Islands see Tenggara, Nusa, is., Indon.	G7	38
Lessines (Lessen), Bel.	G4	12
Lester, Ia., U.S.	A1	122
Lester, W.V., U.S.	n13	155
Lester Prairie, Mn., U.S.	F4	130
Lesterville, Mo., U.S.	D7	132
Lesterville, S.D., U.S.	D8	148
Lestock, Sask., Can.	F3	105
Le Sueur, Mn., U.S.	F5	130
Le Sueur, co., Mn., U.S.	F5	130
Lešukonskoje, U.S.S.R.	E7	22
Les Vans, Fr.	H11	14
Lésvos, i., Grc.	J10	20
Leszno, Pol.	D16	10
Letcher, S.D., U.S.	D7	148
Letcher, co., Ky., U.S.	C7	124
Letellier, Man., Can.	E3	100
Letenye, Hung.	I16	10
Letha, Id., U.S.	F2	119
Lethbridge, Alta., Can.	E4	98
Lethbridge, Newf., Can.	D5	102
Lethem, Guy.	F13	84
Le Thillot, Fr.	E13	14
Leti, Kepulauan, is., Indon.	G8	38
Leticia, Col.	J8	84
Leting, China	D6	32
Letjiesbos, S. Afr.	I6	66
Letlhakane, Bots.	C7	66
Letlhakeng, Bots.	E7	66
Letnerečenskij, U.S.S.R.	I24	6
Letohatchee, Al., U.S.	C3	108
Letona, Ar., U.S.	B4	111
Le Tourneau, Ms., U.S.	C3	131
Letpadan, Burma	F3	40
Le Trayas, Fr.	I13	14
Le Tréport, Fr.	B8	14
Letsôk-aw Kyun, i., Burma	I5	40
Letterkenny, Ire.	G6	8
Letts, In., U.S.	F6	121
Letts, Ia., U.S.	C6	122
Leu, Rom.	E8	20
Leuk, Switz.	F8	13
Leuna, Ger.	D12	10
Leuser, Gunung, mtn., Indon.	M4	40
Leutkirch, Ger.	H10	10
Leuven (Louvain), Bel.	G6	12
Leuze, Bel.	G4	12
Levádhia, Grc.	K6	20
Levan, Ut., U.S.	D4	151
Levant, Me., U.S.	D4	126
Levanto, Italy	E4	18
Leveaux Mountain, mtn., Mn., U.S.	k9	130
Levelland, Tx., U.S.	C1	150
Leveque, Cape, c., Austl.	C4	68
Levering, Mi., U.S.	C6	129
Leverkusen, Ger.	D6	10
Levice, Czech.	G18	10
Levie, Fr.	H4	18
Levier, Fr.	F13	14
Le Vigan, Fr.	I10	14
Levin, N.Z.	D5	72
Lévis, Que., Can.	C6	104
Levisa Fork, stm., U.S.	C7	124
Levittown, N.Y., U.S.	E7	139
Levittown, Pa., U.S.	F12	145
Levkás, Grc.	K4	20
Levkás, i., Grc.	K4	20
Levkímmi, Grc.	J4	20
Levroux, Fr.	F8	14
Lev Tolstoj, U.S.S.R.	H22	26
Levy, co., Fl., U.S.	C4	116
Levy Lake, l., Fl., U.S.	C4	116
Lewe, Burma	E4	40
Lewellen, Ne., U.S.	C3	134
Lewes, Eng., U.K.	K14	8
Lewes, De., U.S.	E5	115
Lewes and Rehoboth Canal, De., U.S.	F5	115
Lewis, In., U.S.	F3	121
Lewis, Ia., U.S.	C2	122
Lewis, Ks., U.S.	E4	123
Lewis, co., Id., U.S.	C2	119
Lewis, co., Ky., U.S.	B6	124
Lewis, co., Mo., U.S.	A6	132
Lewis, co., N.Y., U.S.	B5	139
Lewis, co., Tn., U.S.	B4	149
Lewis, co., Wa., U.S.	C3	154
Lewis, co., W.V., U.S.	C4	155
Lewis, stm., Wa., U.S.	C4	154
Lewis, stm., Wy., U.S.	B2	157
Lewis, Butt of, c., Scot., U.K.	C7	8
Lewis, Isle of, i., Scot., U.K.	C7	8
Lewis, Mount, mtn., Nv., U.S.	C5	135
Lewis and Clark, co., Mt., U.S.	C4	133
Lewis and Clark Cavern, Mt., U.S.	D5	133
Lewis and Clark Lake, res., U.S.	E8	148
Lewisburg, Ky., U.S.	D3	124
Lewisburg, La., U.S.	D3	125
Lewisburg, Oh., U.S.	C1	142
Lewisburg, Pa., U.S.	E8	145
Lewisburg, Tn., U.S.	B5	149
Lewisburg, W.V., U.S.	D4	155
Lewis Creek, stm., Vt., U.S.	C2	152
Lewis Hills, hills, Newf., Can.	D2	102
Lewis Lake, l., Wy., U.S.	B2	157
Lewisport, Ky., U.S.	C3	124
Lewisporte, Newf., Can.	D4	102
Lewis Smith Lake, res., Al., U.S.	B2	108
Lewiston, Id., U.S.	C1	119
Lewiston, Me., U.S.	D2	126
Lewiston, Mi., U.S.	D6	129
Lewiston, Mn., U.S.	G7	130
Lewiston, N.Y., U.S.	B1	139
Lewiston, Ut., U.S.	B4	151
Lewiston Peak, mtn., Ut., U.S.	C3	151
Lewiston Woodville, N.C., U.S.	A5	140
Lewistown, Il., U.S.	C3	120
Lewistown, Mo., U.S.	A6	132
Lewistown, Mt., U.S.	C7	133
Lewistown, Pa., U.S.	E6	145
Lewisville, Ar., U.S.	D2	111
Lewisville, Id., U.S.	F6	119
Lewisville, In., U.S.	E7	121
Lewisville, Mn., U.S.	G4	130
Lewisville, Tx., U.S.	C4	150
Lewisville Lake, res., Tx., U.S.	C4	150
Lexa, Ar., U.S.	C5	111
Lexington, Al., U.S.	A2	108
Lexington, Ga., U.S.	C3	117
Lexington, Il., U.S.	C5	120
Lexington, In., U.S.	G6	121
Lexington, Ky., U.S.	B5	124
Lexington, Ma., U.S.	B5	128
Lexington, Mi., U.S.	E8	129
Lexington, Ms., U.S.	B3	131
Lexington, Mo., U.S.	B4	132
Lexington, Ne., U.S.	D6	134
Lexington, N.C., U.S.	B2	140
Lexington, Oh., U.S.	B3	142
Lexington, Ok., U.S.	B4	143
Lexington, Or., U.S.	B7	144
Lexington, S.C., U.S.	D5	147
Lexington, Tn., U.S.	B3	149
Lexington, Tx., U.S.	D4	150
Lexington, Va., U.S.	C3	153
Lexington, co., S.C., U.S.	D5	147
Lexington Park, Md., U.S.	D5	127
Leyte, i., Phil.	C7	38
Leyte Gulf, b., Phil.	C8	38
Leža, U.S.S.R.	C23	26
Leżajsk, Pol.	E22	10
Lezama, Ven.	C9	84
Ležn'ovo, U.S.S.R.	E23	26
L'gov, U.S.S.R.	G5	22
Lhasa, China	F14	44
Lhazê, China	F12	44
Lhokseumawe, Indon.	L4	40
Lhorong, China	E6	30
L'Hospitalet de Llobregat, Spain	D14	16
Lhozhag, China	F14	44
Lhuntsi Dzong, Bhu.	G14	44
Li, stm., China	F9	30
Liangcheng, China	H7	32
Lianghe, China	B5	40
Liangjiadian, China	D9	32
Liangjiang, China	C10	40
Liangkou, China	L2	34
Liangmentou, China	G10	34
Liangtian, China	J2	34
Liangying, China	L5	34
Lianhe, China	A13	32
Lianjiang, China	I8	34
Lianpu, China	I7	34
Lianshui, China	B8	34
Lianxian, China	G9	30
Lianyungang, China	I7	32
Lianyungang (Xinpu), China	I7	32
Liao, stm., China	C11	30
Liaocheng, China	G3	32
Liaodong Bandao (Liaotung Peninsula), pen., China	D10	32
Liaodong Wan, b., China	C11	30
Liaojiangshi, China	I2	34
Liaoning, prov., China	C11	30
Liaoyang, China	B11	32
Liaoyuan, China	C12	30
Liaozhong, China	B10	32
Liard, stm., Can.	D8	96
Líbano, Col.	E5	84
Libau, Man., Can.	D3	100
Libby, Mt., U.S.	B1	133
Libenge, Zaire	H4	56
Liberal, Ks., U.S.	E3	123
Liberal, Mo., U.S.	D3	132
Liberdade, Braz.	G6	79
Liberdade, Riozinho da, stm., Braz.	B6	82
Liberec, Czech.	E15	10
Liberia, C.R.	G9	92
Liberia, ctry., Afr.	G5	54
Libertad, Ur.	H10	80
Libertad, Ven.	C8	84
Libertad, Ven.	C8	84
Libertador General Bernardo O'Higgins, prov., Chile	H3	80
Libertador General San Martín, Arg.	B6	80
Liberty, Sask., Can.	F3	105
Liberty, Id., U.S.	G7	119
Liberty, Il., U.S.	D2	120
Liberty, In., U.S.	E8	121
Liberty, Ks., U.S.	E8	123
Liberty, Ky., U.S.	C5	124
Liberty, Me., U.S.	D3	126
Liberty, Ms., U.S.	D3	131
Liberty, Mo., U.S.	B3	132
Liberty, N.Y., U.S.	D6	139
Liberty, N.C., U.S.	B3	140
Liberty, S.C., U.S.	B2	147
Liberty, Tn., U.S.	C8	149
Liberty, Tx., U.S.	D5	150
Liberty, co., Fl., U.S.	B2	116
Liberty, co., Ga., U.S.	E5	117
Liberty, co., Mt., U.S.	B5	133
Liberty, co., Tx., U.S.	D5	150
Liberty Center, In., U.S.	C7	121
Liberty Center, Oh., U.S.	A1	142
Liberty Lake, res., Md., U.S.	B4	127
Liberty Mills, In., U.S.	B6	121
Libertytown, Md., U.S.	B3	127
Libertyville, Al., U.S.	D3	108
Libertyville, Il., U.S.	A6	120
Libertyville, Ia., U.S.	D5	122
Lībīyah, Aṣ-Ṣaḥrā' al- (Libyan Desert), des., Afr.	D6	56
Libourne, Fr.	H6	14
Libramont, Bel.	I7	12
Libres, Mex.	H11	90
Libreville, Gabon	A1	58
Libu, China	C11	40
Libuse, La., U.S.	C3	125
Libya (Lībīyā), ctry., Afr.	C4	56
Libyan Desert see Lībīyah, Aṣ-Ṣaḥrā' al-, des., Afr.	D6	56
Libyan Plateau see Aḍ-Ḍiffah, plat., Afr.	B3	60
Licantén, Chile	H2	80
Licata, Italy	L8	18
Lice, Tur.	B6	48
Lichinga, Moz.	D7	58
Lichoslavl', U.S.S.R.	D18	26
Lichtenfels, Ger.	E11	10
Lichuan, China	H5	34
Lick Creek, stm., Tn., U.S.	C11	149
Lickershamn, Swe.	M16	6
Licking, Mo., U.S.	D6	132
Licking, co., Oh., U.S.	B3	142
Licking, stm., Ky., U.S.	B6	124
Licking, North Fork, stm., Ky., U.S.	B5	124
Licking, South Fork, stm., Ky., U.S.	B5	124
Lida, U.S.S.R.	H8	26
Lida, Lake, l., Mn., U.S.	D3	130
Lidao, China	F10	32
Lidderdale, Ia., U.S.	B3	122
Liden, Swe.	J15	6
Lidesi, China	B4	34
Lidgerwood, N.D., U.S.	C8	141
Lidice, Pan.	C3	84
Lidköping, Swe.	L13	6
Lidzbark, Pol.	B19	10
Lidzbark Warmiński, Pol.	A20	10
Liebenthal, Ks., U.S.	D4	123
Liechtenstein, ctry., Eur.	F9	4
Liège (Luik), Bel.	G8	12
Liège, prov., Bel.	G8	12
Liegnitz see Legnica, Pol.	D16	10
Lielvārde, U.S.S.R.	E7	26
Lienz, Aus.	I12	10
Liepāja, U.S.S.R.	E4	26
Lier (Lierre), Bel.	F6	12
Lierre (Lier), Bel.	F6	12
Lieshout, Neth.	E8	12
Liestal, Switz.	D8	13
Liévin, Fr.	B9	14
Lièvre, Rivière du, stm., Que., Can.	D2	104
Liezen, Aus.	H14	10
Liffré, Fr.	D5	14
Līgatne, U.S.S.R.	D8	26
Lighthouse Inlet, b., S.C., U.S.	k12	147
Lighthouse Point, c., Fl., U.S.	C2	116
Lighthouse Point, c., La., U.S.	E3	125
Lighthouse Point, c., Mi., U.S.	C5	129
Lighthouse Reef, rf., Belize	I16	90
Lightning Creek, stm., Wy., U.S.	C8	157
Lignières, Fr.	F9	14
Lignite, N.D., U.S.	A3	141
Ligny-en-Barrois, Fr.	D12	14
Ligonha, stm., Moz.	E7	58
Ligonier, In., U.S.	B6	121
Ligonier, Pa., U.S.	F3	145
Ligui, Mex.	E4	90
Liguria, prov., Italy	E3	18
Ligurian Sea, Eur.	F4	18
Lihue, Hi., U.S.	B2	118
Lihula, U.S.S.R.	C6	26
Lijia, China	F6	32
Lijiang, China	F7	30
Lijiawobao, China	B10	32
Likasi (Jadotville), Zaire	D5	58
Likely, B.C., Can.	C7	99
Likino-Dulevo, U.S.S.R.	F21	26
Liknes, Nor.	L10	6
Likoma Island, i., Mwi.	D6	58
Likou, China	F6	34
Likus, stm., Nic.	C11	92
Lilburn, Mo., U.S.	E8	132
Lilburn, Ga., U.S.	h8	117
L'Île-Rousse, Fr.	J15	14
Lilesville, N.C., U.S.	C3	140
Lilienfeld, Aus.	G15	10
Liling, China	H2	34
Lille, Fr.	B10	14
Lille, Me., U.S.	A4	126
Lillebonne, Fr.	C7	14
Lillehammer, Nor.	K12	6
Lillers, Fr.	B9	14
Lillesand, Nor.	L11	6
Lillestrøm, Nor.	L12	6
Lillian, Al., U.S.	E2	108
Lillington, N.C., U.S.	B4	140
Lillinonah, Lake, l., Ct., U.S.	C2	114
Lillooet, B.C., Can.	D7	99
Lillooet, stm., B.C., Can.	D6	99
Lillooet Lake, l., B.C., Can.	D6	99
Lillooet Range, mts., B.C., Can.	E7	99
Lilly, Ga., U.S.	D3	117
Lilly, Pa., U.S.	F4	145
Lilly Fork, stm., W.V., U.S.	m13	155
Lilly Grove, W.V., U.S.	D3	155
Lilongwe, Mwi.	D6	58
Lilo Viejo, Arg.	D7	80
Liloy, Phil.	D7	38
Lily, Ky., U.S.	C5	124
Lilydale, Austl.	M7	70
Lima, Para.	B10	80
Lima, Peru	E3	82
Lima, Mt., U.S.	F4	133
Lima, N.Y., U.S.	C3	139
Lima, Oh., U.S.	B1	142
Lima, dept., Peru	D3	82
Lima (Limia), stm., Eur.	D3	16
Limache, Chile	G3	80
Liman, U.S.S.R.	D13	20
Limanowa, Pol.	F20	10
Limanskoje, U.S.S.R.	C14	20
Lima Reservoir, res., Mt., U.S.	F4	133
Limarí, stm., Chile	F3	80
Limay, stm., Arg.	J4	80
Limay Mahuida, Arg.	I5	80
Limbani, Peru	F7	82
Limbaži, U.S.S.R.	D7	26
Līmbdi, India	I4	44
Limburg, prov., Bel.	G7	12
Limburg, prov., Neth.	F8	12
Limburg an der Lahn, Ger.	E8	10
Limeira, Braz.	G5	79
Limen, China	H8	34
Limerick, Sask., Can.	H2	105
Limerick, Ire.	I5	8
Limerick, Me., U.S.	E2	126
Limerick, co., Ire.	I5	8
Lime Springs, Ia., U.S.	A5	122
Limestone, Me., U.S.	B5	126
Limestone, Tn., U.S.	C11	149
Limestone, co., Al., U.S.	A2	108
Limestone, co., Tx., U.S.	D4	150
Limestone Bay, b., Man., Can.	C2	100
Limestone Point, pen., Man., Can.	C2	100
Limfjorden, strt., Den.	M11	6
Limia (Lima), stm., Eur.	D3	16
Limington, Me., U.S.	E2	126
Liminka, Fin.	I19	6
Limmen Bight, Austl.	B7	68
Límnos, i., Grc.	J9	20
Limoeiro, Braz.	E11	76
Limoges, Ont., Can.	B9	103
Limoges, Fr.	G8	14
Limogne, Fr.	H8	14
Limón, C.R.	A2	76
Limón, Hond.	B9	92
Limon, Co., U.S.	B7	113
Limón, prov., C.R.	H11	92
Limoux, Fr.	I9	14
Limpopo, stm., Afr.	E11	66
Limu, China	B11	40
Linachamari, U.S.S.R.	G22	6
Līnah, Sau. Ar.	G7	48
Lin'an, China	E8	34
Linares, Chile	H3	80
Linares, Col.	G4	84
Linares, Mex.	E10	90
Linares, Spain	G8	16
Lincang, China	C7	40
Linch, Wy., U.S.	C6	157
Lincoln, Arg.	H8	80
Lincoln, Ont., Can.	D5	103
Lincoln, Eng., U.K.	H13	8
Lincoln, Al., U.S.	B3	108
Lincoln, Ar., U.S.	B1	111
Lincoln, Ca., U.S.	C3	112
Lincoln, De., U.S.	E4	115
Lincoln, Id., U.S.	F7	119
Lincoln, Il., U.S.	C4	120
Lincoln, Ks., U.S.	C5	123
Lincoln, Me., U.S.	C4	126
Lincoln, Ma., U.S.	g10	128
Lincoln, Mi., U.S.	D7	129
Lincoln, Mo., U.S.	C4	132
Lincoln, Mt., U.S.	D4	133
Lincoln, Ne., U.S.	D9	134
Lincoln, N.H., U.S.	B3	136
Lincoln, N.M., U.S.	D4	138
Lincoln, Tn., U.S.	B5	149
Lincoln, Vt., U.S.	C3	152
Lincoln, Va., U.S.	A5	153
Lincoln, co., Ar., U.S.	D4	111
Lincoln, co., Co., U.S.	C7	113
Lincoln, co., Ga., U.S.	C4	117
Lincoln, co., Id., U.S.	G4	119
Lincoln, co., Ks., U.S.	C5	123
Lincoln, co., Ky., U.S.	C5	124
Lincoln, co., La., U.S.	B3	125
Lincoln, co., Me., U.S.	D3	126
Lincoln, co., Mn., U.S.	F2	130
Lincoln, co., Ms., U.S.	D3	131
Lincoln, co., Mo., U.S.	B7	132
Lincoln, co., Mt., U.S.	B1	133
Lincoln, co., Ne., U.S.	D5	134
Lincoln, co., Nv., U.S.	F6	135
Lincoln, co., N.M., U.S.	D4	138
Lincoln, co., N.C., U.S.	B1	140
Lincoln, co., Ok., U.S.	B5	143
Lincoln, co., Or., U.S.	C3	144
Lincoln, co., S.D., U.S.	D9	148
Lincoln, co., Tn., U.S.	B5	149
Lincoln, co., Wa., U.S.	B7	154
Lincoln, co., W.V., U.S.	C2	155

Name — Map Ref. — Page

Lincoln, co., Wi., U.S. C4 156
Lincoln, co., Wy., U.S. D2 157
Lincoln, Mount, mtn., Co., U.S. B4 113
Lincoln Acres, Ca., U.S. o15 112
Lincoln Center, Me., U.S. C4 126
Lincoln City, In., U.S. H4 121
Lincoln City, Or., U.S. C3 144
Lincoln Heights, Oh., U.S. o13 142
Lincoln Park, Co., U.S. C5 113
Lincoln Park, Ga., U.S. D2 117
Lincoln Park, Mi., U.S. p15 129
Lincoln Park, N.J., U.S. B4 137
Lincoln Sea, N.A. A14 86
Lincolnshire, Il., U.S. h9 120
Lincolnshire, co., Eng., U.K. H13 8
Lincoln Tomb State Memorial, hist., Il., U.S. D4 120
Lincolnton, Ga., U.S. C4 117
Lincolnton, N.C., U.S. B1 140
Lincolnville, Ks., U.S. D7 123
Lincolnville, Me., U.S. D3 126
Lincolnville, S.C., U.S. h11 147
Lincolnwood, Il., U.S. h9 120
Lincroft, N.J., U.S. C4 137
Lind, Wa., U.S. C7 154
Linda, U.S.S.R. E27 26
Lindale, Ga., U.S. B1 117
Lindale, Tx., U.S. C5 150
Lindau, Ger. H9 10
Lindbergh, Alta., Can. C5 98
Linde, stm., U.S.S.R. D16 24
Linden, Alta., Can. D4 98
Linden, Guy. D13 84
Linden, Al., U.S. C2 108
Linden, In., U.S. D4 121
Linden, Ia., U.S. C3 122
Linden, Mi., U.S. F7 129
Linden, N.J., U.S. k8 137
Linden, Tn., U.S. B4 149
Linden, Tx., U.S. C5 150
Linden, Wi., U.S. F3 156
Lindenhurst, Il., U.S. h8 120
Lindenhurst, N.Y., U.S. n15 139
Lindenwold, N.J., U.S. D3 137
Lindi, Tan. D7 58
Lindley, S. Afr. G8 66
Lindon, Ut., U.S. C4 151
Lindong, China I7 34
Lindsay, Ont., Can. C6 103
Lindsay, Ca., U.S. D4 112
Lindsay, Ne., U.S. C8 134
Lindsay, Ok., U.S. C4 143
Lindsborg, Ks., U.S. D6 123
Lindsey, Oh., U.S. A2 142
Lindstrom, Mn., U.S. E6 130
Linefork, Ky., U.S. C7 124
Line Islands, is., Oc. H24 158
Linesville, Pa., U.S. C1 145
Lineville, Al., U.S. B4 108
Lineville, Ia., U.S. D4 122
Linfen, China D9 30
Linganamakki Reservoir, res., India F3 46
Linganore Creek, stm., Md., U.S. B3 127
Lingao, China E10 40
Lingayen, Phil. M19 39b
Lingbi, China B6 34
Lingen, Ger. C7 10
Lingfengwei, China K4 34
Lingga, Kepulauan, is., Indon. O8 40
Lingga, Pulau, i., Indon. O8 40
Linghu, China E9 34
Lingle, Wy., U.S. D8 157
Linglestown, Pa., U.S. F8 145
Lingling, China A11 40
Linglongta, China C7 32
Lingqiu, China D2 32
Lingshan, China G8 32
Lingshui, China E11 40
Linguère, Sen. D2 64
Lingxiazhu, China F8 34
Lingyuan, China B7 32
Linh, Ngoc, mtn., Viet. G9 40
Linhai, China G10 34
Linhares, Braz. E8 79
Linhe, China C8 30
Linhuaiguan, China C6 34
Linière, Que., Can. C7 104
Linjiang, China B14 32
Linjianghu, China G6 34
Linköping, Swe. L14 6
Linkou, China B13 30
Linksmakalnis, U.S.S.R. G6 26
Linkuva, U.S.S.R. E6 26
Linn, Ks., U.S. C6 123
Linn, Mo., U.S. C6 132
Linn, co., Ia., U.S. B6 122
Linn, co., Ks., U.S. D9 123
Linn, co., Mo., U.S. B4 132
Linn, co., Or., U.S. C4 144
Linnancang, China D5 32
Linn Creek, Mo., U.S. C5 132
Linneus, Me., U.S. B5 126
Linneus, Mo., U.S. B4 132
Linn Grove, In., U.S. C7 121
Lino Lakes, Mn., U.S. m12 130
Linqing, China G3 32
Linqu, China G6 32
Linquan, China B4 34
Linru, China A1 34
Linruzhen, China A1 34
Lins, Braz. F4 79
Linshanhe, China E3 34
Lintao, China D7 30
Linthal, Switz. E11 13
Linthicum Heights, Md., U.S. B4 127
Lintlaw, Sask., Can. E4 105
Linton, In., U.S. F3 121
Linton, N.D., U.S. C5 141
Linwood, Ont., Can. D4 103
Linwood, Ga., U.S. B1 117
Linwood, Ks., U.S. m15 123
Linwood, Mi., U.S. E7 129
Linwood, N.J., U.S. E3 137
Linworth, Oh., U.S. k10 142
Linxi, China C10 30
Linxia, China D7 30
Linxiang, China F2 34
Linyanti, Nmb. B7 66
Linyanti, stm., Afr. B7 66
Linyi, China H6 32
Linying, China B2 34
Linz, Aus. G14 10
Linzhai, China K4 34
Linzikou, China G1 34
Lion, Golfe du, b., Fr. I11 14
Lion's Head, Ont., Can. C3 103
Liozno, U.S.S.R. F13 26
Lipari, Isola, i., Italy K9 18
Lipeck, U.S.S.R. I22 26
Lipeckoje Vtoroje, U.S.S.R. B13 20
Lipetsk see Lipeck, U.S.S.R. I22 26
Lipez, Cerro, mtn., Bol. I8 82
Lipin Bor, U.S.S.R. A20 26
Lipkany, U.S.S.R. A10 20
Lipki, U.S.S.R. H20 26
Lipno, Pol. C19 10
Lipno, údolní nádrž, res., Czech. G14 10
Lipova, Rom. C5 20
Lippe, stm., Ger. D8 10
Lippstadt, Ger. D8 10
Lipscomb, Al., U.S. B3 108
Lipscomb, co., Tx., U.S. A2 150
Lipton, Sask., Can. G4 105
Liptovský Mikuláš, Czech. F19 10
Liptrap, Cape, c., Austl. L6 70
Lira, Ug. H7 56
Lircay, Peru E4 82
Liren, China B7 34
Lisala, Zaire A4 58
Lisboa (Lisbon), Port. G2 16
Lisbon, Il., U.S. B5 120
Lisbon, Ia., U.S. C6 122
Lisbon, Me., U.S. D2 126
Lisbon, Md., U.S. B3 127
Lisbon, N.H., U.S. B3 136
Lisbon, N.D., U.S. C8 141
Lisbon, Oh., U.S. B5 142
Lisbon Center, Me., U.S. f7 126
Lisbon Falls, Me., U.S. E2 126
Lisbon see Lisboa, Port. G2 16
Lisburn, N. Ire., U.K. G7 8
Lisburne, Cape, c., Ak., U.S. B6 109
Lisco, Ne., U.S. C3 134
Liscomb, N.S., Can. D7 101
Liscomb, Ia., U.S. B5 122
Lishe, China F10 34
Lishui, China G8 34
Lisianski Island, i., Hi., U.S. k13 118
Lisičansk, U.S.S.R. H5 22
Lisieux, Fr. C7 14
Lisle, Ont., Can. C5 103
Lisle, Il., U.S. k8 120
L'Isle Jourdain, Fr. F7 14
L'Isle-sur-le-Doubs, Fr. E13 14
L'Islet-sur-Mer, Que., Can. B7 104
L'Isle-Verte, Que., Can. A8 104
Lisman, Al., U.S. C1 108
Lismore, Austl. G10 70
Lismore, N.S., Can. D7 101
Lišov, Czech. F14 10
Lister, B.C., Can. E9 99
Listie, Pa., U.S. F3 145
Listowel, Ont., Can. D4 103
Lita, China H5 34
Litang, China E7 30
Litang, China G8 30
Litang, stm., China F7 30
Litchfield, Ct., U.S. C3 114
Litchfield, Il., U.S. D4 120
Litchfield, Mi., U.S. F6 129
Litchfield, Mn., U.S. E4 130
Litchfield, Ne., U.S. C6 134
Litchfield, co., Ct., U.S. B2 114
Litchfield Park, Az., U.S. m8 110
Litchville, N.D., U.S. C7 141
Lithgow, Austl. I9 70
Lithia Springs, Ga., U.S. h7 117
Líthinon, Ákra, c., Grc. O8 20
Lithonia, Ga., U.S. C2 117
Lithuania see Litovskaja Sovetskaja Socialističeskaja Respublika, state, U.S.S.R. F6 26
Litian, China I3 34
Lititz, Pa., U.S. F9 145
Litoměřice, Czech. E14 10
Litomyšl, Czech. F16 10
Litovko, U.S.S.R. H19 24
Litovskaja Sovetskaja Socialističeskaja Respublika, state, U.S.S.R. F6 26
Little, stm., U.S. B5 111
Little, stm., U.S. D7 143
Little, stm., Ct., U.S. C7 114
Little, stm., Ga., U.S. C4 117
Little, stm., Ga., U.S. E3 117
Little, stm., Ga., U.S. C3 117
Little, stm., Ky., U.S. D2 124
Little, stm., La., U.S. C3 125
Little, stm., N.C., U.S. B3 140
Little, stm., Ok., U.S. B5 143
Little, stm., S.C., U.S. C2 147
Little, stm., Tn., U.S. n14 149
Little, stm., Vt., U.S. C3 152
Little, stm., Va., U.S. D2 153
Little Abaco, i., Bah. A6 94
Little Acres, Az., U.S. D5 110
Little America, Wy., U.S. E3 157
Little Andaman, i., India I2 40
Little Arkansas, stm., Ks., U.S. D6 123
Little Bay Islands, Newf., Can. D4 102
Little Beaver Creek, stm., Ks., U.S. C2 123
Little Belt Mountains, mts., Mt., U.S. D6 133
Little Bighorn, stm., U.S. E9 133
Little Black, stm., Me., U.S. A3 126
Little Blue, stm., U.S. C6 123
Little Blue, stm., In., U.S. H5 121
Little Boars Head, N.H., U.S. E5 136
Little Bow, stm., Alta., Can. D4 98
Little Britain, Ont., Can. C6 103
Little Brook, N.S., Can. E3 101
Little Buffalo, stm., Can. D10 96
Little Cacapon, stm., W.V., U.S. B6 155
Little Catalina, Newf., Can. D5 102
Little Cayman, i., Cay. Is. E4 94
Little Cedar, stm., Ia., U.S. A5 122
Little Churchill, stm., Man., Can. A4 100
Little Chute, Wi., U.S. D5 156
Little Coal, stm., W.V., U.S. C3 155
Little Colorado, stm., Az., U.S. B4 110
Little Compton, R.I., U.S. E6 146
Little Creek, De., U.S. D4 115
Little Creek Naval Amphibious Base, mil., Va., U.S. k15 153
Little Creek Peak, mtn., Ut., U.S. F3 151
Little Current, Ont., Can. B3 103
Little Desert, des., Austl. K4 70
Little Diomede Island, i., Ak., U.S. B6 109
Little Dry Creek, stm., Mt., U.S. C10 133
Little Eagle, S.D., U.S. B5 148
Little Egg Harbor, b., N.J., U.S. D4 137
Little Egg Inlet, b., N.J., U.S. E4 137
Little Exuma, i., Bah. C7 94
Little Falls, Mn., U.S. E4 130
Little Falls, N.J., U.S. B4 137
Little Falls, N.Y., U.S. B6 139
Little Ferry, N.J., U.S. h8 137
Littlefield, Tx., U.S. C1 150
Little Fishing Creek, stm., W.V., U.S. h9 155
Littlefork, Mn., U.S. B5 130
Little Fork, stm., Mn., U.S. B5 130
Little Frog Mountain, mtn., Tn., U.S. D9 149
Little Goose Creek, stm., Wy., U.S. B6 157
Little Gunpowder Falls, stm., Md., U.S. A4 127
Little Hocking, Oh., U.S. C4 142
Little Humboldt, stm., Nv., U.S. B4 135
Little Humboldt, North Fork, stm., Nv., U.S. B4 135
Little Humboldt, South Fork, stm., Nv., U.S. B5 135
Little Inagua, i., Bah. D8 94
Little Kanawha, stm., W.V., U.S. C4 155
Little Kanawha, West Fork, stm., W.V., U.S. B3 155
Little Lake, Mi., U.S. B3 129
Little Lake, l., La., U.S. E5 125
Little Lynches, stm., S.C., U.S. C7 147
Little Manatee, stm., Fl., U.S. p11 116
Little Mazarn Creek, stm., Ar., U.S. g7 111
Little Mecatina, stm., Can. h9 102
Little Mexico, Tx., U.S. D1 150
Little Miami, stm., Oh., U.S. C1 142
Little Miami, East Fork, stm., Oh., U.S. C1 142
Little Miami, Todd Fork, stm., Oh., U.S. C1 142
Little Missouri, stm., U.S. B6 106
Little Missouri, stm., Ar., U.S. D2 111
Little Moose Mountain, mtn., N.Y., U.S. B6 139
Little Muddy, stm., Il., U.S. E4 120
Little Muddy, stm., N.D., U.S. A2 141
Little Nicobar, i., India K2 40
Little Osage, stm., U.S. E9 123
Little Otter Creek, stm., Vt., U.S. C2 152
Little Owyhee, stm., U.S. B5 135
Little Pee Dee, stm., S.C., U.S. C9 147
Little Pigeon Creek, stm., In., U.S. I3 121
Little Pipe Creek, stm., Md., U.S. A3 127
Little Powder, stm., U.S. F11 133
Little Rann of Kachchh, pl., India I4 44
Little Red, stm., Ar., U.S. B4 111
Little Red, Middle Fork, stm., Ar., U.S. B3 111
Little River, N.S., Can. E3 101
Little River, Ks., U.S. D5 123
Little River, S.C., U.S. D10 147
Little River, co., Ar., U.S. D1 111
Little River Inlet, b., S.C., U.S. D10 147
Little Rock, Ar., U.S. C3 111
Little Rock, Ia., U.S. A2 122
Little Rock, S.C., U.S. C9 147
Littlerock, Wa., U.S. C2 154
Little Rock, stm., U.S. A1 122
Little Rock Air Force Base, mil., Ar., U.S. C3 111
Little Sable Point, c., Mi., U.S. E4 129
Little Saint Bernard Pass see Petit-Saint-Bernard, Col du, Eur. G13 14
Little Salt Lake, l., Ut., U.S. F3 151
Little Sand Creek, stm., Mn., U.S. D6 130
Little Sandy, stm., Ky., U.S. B6 124
Little Sandy Creek, stm., Wy., U.S. D3 157
Little Scarcies, stm., Afr. G4 54
Little Sebago Lake, l., Me., U.S. g7 126
Little Silver, N.J., U.S. C4 137
Little Sioux, Ia., U.S. C1 122
Little Sioux, stm., U.S. B2 122
Little Sioux, West Fork, stm., Ia., U.S. B2 122
Little Smoky, stm., Alta., Can. B2 98
Little Snake, stm., U.S. A2 113
Little Spokane, stm., Wa., U.S. B8 154
Littlestown, Pa., U.S. G7 145
Little Tallapoosa, stm., U.S. B4 108
Little Tenmile Creek, stm., W.V., U.S. k10 155
Little Tennessee, stm., U.S. D9 149
Littleton, Co., U.S. B6 113
Littleton, Me., U.S. B5 126
Littleton, Ma., U.S. f10 128
Littleton, N.H., U.S. B3 136
Littleton, N.C., U.S. A5 140
Little Valley, N.Y., U.S. C2 139
Littleville, Al., U.S. A2 108
Little Wabash, stm., Il., U.S. E5 120
Little Walnut, stm., Ks., U.S. g13 123
Little West Fork, stm., Tn., U.S. A4 149
Little White, stm., S.D., U.S. D5 148
Little Wolf, stm., Wi., U.S. D4 156
Little Wood, stm., Id., U.S. F4 119
Little York, Il., U.S. B3 120
Little York, In., U.S. G6 121
Little Zab (Zāb-e Kūchek) (Az-Zāb aṣ-Ṣaghīr), stm., Asia D7 48
Litvínov, Czech. E13 10
Liuchen, China C11 40
Liucheng, China B10 40
Liucura, Chile J3 80
Liudaogou, China B15 32
Liufangling, China E3 34
Liuguan, China F2 34
Liuhe, China A13 32
Liuhe, China C7 34
Liujia, China B9 40
Liujiadu, China C9 34
Liujiahe, China C2 34
Liuku, China B5 40
Liulongtai, China B8 32
Liuquan, China I5 32
Liurenba, China F3 34
Liushilipu, China C4 34
Liushuigou, China D1 34
Liutai, China B1 32
Liuwanglou, China I4 32
Liuyang, China G2 34
Liuyuan, China G2 32
Liuzhou, China B10 40
Liuzhuang, China B9 34
Līvāni, U.S.S.R. E9 26
Livelong, Sask., Can. D1 105
Live Oak, Ca., U.S. C3 112
Live Oak, Fl., U.S. B4 116
Live Oak, co., Tx., U.S. E3 150
Livermore, Ca., U.S. h9 112
Livermore, Ia., U.S. B3 122
Livermore, Ky., U.S. C2 124
Livermore, Me., U.S. D2 126
Livermore, Mount, mtn., Tx., U.S. o12 150
Livermore Falls, Me., U.S. D2 126
Liverpool, N.S., Can. E5 101
Liverpool, Eng., U.K. H11 8
Liverpool, Pa., U.S. E7 145
Livingston, Guat. B6 92
Livingston, Al., U.S. C1 108
Livingston, Ca., U.S. D3 112
Livingston, Il., U.S. E4 120
Livingston, Ky., U.S. C5 124
Livingston, La., U.S. D5 125
Livingston, Mt., U.S. E6 133
Livingston, N.J., U.S. B4 137
Livingston, Tn., U.S. C8 149
Livingston, Tx., U.S. D5 150
Livingston, Wi., U.S. F3 156
Livingston, co., Il., U.S. C5 120
Livingston, co., Ky., U.S. e9 124
Livingston, co., La., U.S. D5 125
Livingston, co., Mi., U.S. F7 129
Livingston, co., Mo., U.S. B4 132
Livingston, co., N.Y., U.S. C3 139
Livingston, Lake, res., Tx., U.S. D5 150
Livingstone, Zam. A7 66
Livingstone, Chutes de, wtfl, Afr. B2 58
Livingstone Cove, N.S., Can. D8 101
Livingstone Falls see Livingstone, Chutes de, wtfl, Afr. B2 58
Livingstonia, Mwi. D6 58
Livingston Island, i., B.A.T. B12 73
Livingston Manor, N.Y., U.S. D6 139
Livno, Yugo. F12 18
Livny, U.S.S.R. I20 26
Livonia, La., U.S. D4 125
Livonia, Mi., U.S. F7 129
Livonia, N.Y., U.S. C3 139
Livorno (Leghorn), Italy F5 18
Livramento do Brumado, Braz. B8 79
Lixi, China F3 34
Lixian, China E3 32
Lixing, China B4 34
Liyang, China D8 34
Liyuanbao, China J1 34
Liyujiang, China J2 34
Lizard Creek, stm., Ia., U.S. B3 122
Lizard Head Pass, Co., U.S. D3 113
Lizard Head Peak, mtn., Wy., U.S. D3 157
Lizard Point, c., Eng., U.K. L8 8
Lizella, Ga., U.S. D3 117
Lizhu, China F9 34
Lizton, In., U.S. E4 121
Ljubija, Yugo. E11 18
Ljubljana, Yugo. C9 18
Ljubuški, Yugo. F12 18
Ljungby, Swe. M13 6
Ljusdal, Swe. K15 6
Llaima, Volcán, vol., Chile J3 80
Llallagua, Bol. H8 82
Llamara, Salar de, pl., Chile I7 82
Llancanelo, Laguna, l., Arg. H4 80
Llandrindod Wells, Wales, U.K. I10 8
Llangefni, Wales, U.K. H9 8
Llangollen, Wales, U.K. I10 8
Llanidloes, Wales, U.K. I10 8
Llano, N.M., U.S. A4 138
Llano, Tx., U.S. D3 150
Llano, co., Tx., U.S. D3 150
Llano, stm., Tx., U.S. D3 150
Llanos, pl., S.A. E7 84
Llanquera, Bol. H8 82
Llanta, Chile D4 80
Llanwrtyd Wells, Wales, U.K. I10 8
Llata, Peru C3 82
Lleida, Spain D12 16
Llera de Canales, Mex. F10 90
Lleulleu, Lago, l., Chile J2 80
Llica, Bol. H7 82
Llico, Chile H2 80
Lliria, Spain F11 16
Llorona, Punta, c., C.R. I11 92
Lloyd, Ky., U.S. B7 124
Lloydminster, Alta., Can. C5 98
Lloydminster (Alta. and Sask.), Sask., Can. D1 105
Lloyds, stm., Newf., Can. D3 102
Llucmajor, Spain F14 16
Llullaillaco, Volcán, vol., S.A. C4 80
Llusco, Peru F5 82
Lluta, stm., Chile H7 82
Lo (Panlong), stm., Asia C8 40
Loa, Ut., U.S. E4 151
Loa, stm., Chile I7 82
Loachapoka, Al., U.S. C4 108
Loami, Il., U.S. D4 120
Loanda, Braz. G2 79
Loange (Luangue), stm., Afr. C3 58
Lobanovo, U.S.S.R. H21 26
Lobatse, Bots. E7 66
Lobaye, stm., Cen. Afr. Rep. H4 56
Lobelville, Tn., U.S. B4 149
Lobería, Arg. J9 80
Lobito, Ang. D2 58
Lobitos, Peru J2 84
Lobn'a, U.S.S.R. E20 26
Lobos, Arg. H9 80
Lobos, Cay, i., Bah. C6 94
Lobos, Isla, i., Mex. D4 90
Lobos, Punta, c., Chile I6 82
Lobos de Afuera, Islas, is., Peru B1 82
Lobos de Tierra, Isla, i., Peru B1 82
Lobster Lake, l., Me., U.S. C3 126
Locarno, Switz. F10 13
Lochearn, Md., U.S. g10 127
Loches, Fr. E8 14
Loch Lomond, Va., U.S. B5 153
Loch Lynn Heights, Md., U.S. m12 127
Lochmaben, Scot., U.K. F10 8
Lochmere, N.H., U.S. D3 136
Loch Raven Reservoir, res., Md., U.S. B4 127
Lochsa, stm., Id., U.S. C3 119
Lock, Austl. I1 70
Locke Mills, Me., U.S. D2 126
Lockeport, N.S., Can. F4 101
Lockerbie, Scot., U.K. F10 8
Lockesburg, Ar., U.S. D1 111
Lockhart, Austl. J7 70
Lockhart, Al., U.S. D3 108
Lockhart, Tx., U.S. E4 150
Lock Haven, Pa., U.S. D7 145
Lockland, Oh., U.S. o13 142
Lockney, Tx., U.S. B2 150
Löcknitz, Ger. B14 10
Lockport, Man., Can. D3 100
Lockport, Il., U.S. B5 120
Lockport, La., U.S. E5 125
Lockport, N.Y., U.S. B2 139
Lockridge, Ia., U.S. C6 122
Lockwood, Mo., U.S. D4 132
Lockwood, Mt., U.S. E8 133
Loc Ninh, Viet. I9 40
Loco Hills, N.M., U.S. E6 138
Locri, Italy K11 18
Locroja, Peru E4 82
Locumba, Peru G6 82
Locumba, stm., Peru G6 82
Locust, N.C., U.S. B2 140
Locust Bayou, Ar., U.S. D3 111
Locust Creek, stm., Mo., U.S. B4 132
Locust Fork, stm., Al., U.S. B3 108
Locust Grove, Ga., U.S. C2 117
Locust Grove, Md., U.S. B2 127
Locust Grove, Ok., U.S. A6 143
Lod (Lydda), Isr. E3 50
Loda, Il., U.S. C5 120
Lodejnoje Pole, U.S.S.R. A16 26
Lodève, Fr. I10 14
Lodge, Newf., Can. B4 102
Lodge Grass, Mt., U.S. E9 133
Lodgepole, Alta., Can. C3 98
Lodge Pole, Mt., U.S. B8 133
Lodgepole, Ne., U.S. C3 134
Lodgepole Creek, stm., U.S. C3 134
Lodi, Italy D4 18
Lodi, Ca., U.S. C3 112
Lodi, N.J., U.S. h8 137
Lodi, Oh., U.S. A3 142
Lodi, Wi., U.S. E4 156
Lodja, Zaire B4 58
Lodore, Canyon of, val., Co., U.S. A2 113
Lodwar, Kenya H8 56
Łódź, Pol. D19 10
Loei, Thai. F6 40
Loeriesfontein, S. Afr. H4 66
Lofa, stm., Afr. G4 54
Lofoten, is., Nor. G13 6
Logan, Niger E11 64
Logan, Il., U.S. F5 120
Logan, Ia., U.S. C2 122
Logan, Ks., U.S. C4 123
Logan, Mt., U.S. E5 133
Logan, N.M., U.S. B6 138
Logan, N.D., U.S. A4 141
Logan, Oh., U.S. C3 142
Logan, Ut., U.S. B4 151
Logan, W.V., U.S. D3 155
Logan, co., Ar., U.S. B2 111
Logan, co., Co., U.S. A7 113
Logan, co., Il., U.S. C4 120
Logan, co., Ks., U.S. D2 123
Logan, co., Ky., U.S. D3 124
Logan, co., Ne., U.S. C5 134
Logan, co., N.D., U.S. C6 141
Logan, co., Oh., U.S. B2 142
Logan, co., Ok., U.S. B4 143
Logan, co., W.V., U.S. D3 155
Logan, Mount, mtn., Yukon, Can. D4 96
Logan, Mount, mtn., Wa., U.S. A5 154
Logan Creek, stm., Ne., U.S. B9 134
Logandale, Nv., U.S. G7 135
Logan Lake, B.C., Can. D7 99
Logan Martin Lake, res., Al., U.S. B3 108
Logan Pass, Mt., U.S. B2 133
Logansport, In., U.S. C5 121
Logansport, La., U.S. C2 125
Loganville, Ga., U.S. C3 117
Loganville, Pa., U.S. G8 145
Loggieville, N.B., Can. B4 101
Log Lane Village, Co., U.S. A7 113
Logojsk, U.S.S.R. G10 26
Logone, stm., Afr. F4 56
Logroño, Spain C9 16
Løgstør, Den. M11 6
Lohiniva, Fin. H19 6
Lohit, stm., Asia G16 44
Lohja, Fin. K19 6
Lohne, Ger. C8 10
Lohr, Ger. E9 10
Lohrville, Ia., U.S. B3 122
Loi, stm., Asia D6 40
Loi-kaw, Burma E4 40
Loimaa, Fin. K18 6
Loire, dept., Fr. G11 14
Loire, stm., Fr. E5 14
Loire-Atlantique, dept., Fr. E5 14
Loiret, dept., Fr. D9 14
Loir-et-Cher, dept., Fr. E8 14
Loitz, Ger. B13 10
Loja, Ec. E7 74
Loja, Ec. I3 84
Loja, Ec. J12 86
Loja, Spain H7 16
Loja, prov., Ec. J3 84
Lokandu, Zaire B5 58
Lokan tekojärvi, res., Fin. H20 6
Lokbatan, U.S.S.R. A10 48
Lokka, Fin. H20 6
Løkken, Den. M11 6
Lokn'a, U.S.S.R. E13 26
Loko, Nig. G13 64
Lokoja, Nig. H13 64
Lokolama, Zaire B3 58
Lokossa, Benin H10 64
Lokot', U.S.S.R. I17 26
Lol, Sud. N5 60
Lol, stm., Sud. M4 60
Lola, Gui. H5 64
Lola, Ky., U.S. e9 124
Lola, Mount, mtn., Ca., U.S. C3 112
Lolo, Mt., U.S. D2 133
Lolo Pass, U.S. C4 119
Lolotique, El Sal. D6 92
Lom, Bul. F7 20
Lom, U.S.S.R. D22 26
Lom, stm., Afr. G9 54
Loma, Eth. N9 60
Loma, Co., U.S. B2 113
Loma, Mt., U.S. C6 133
Lomas, Peru F4 82
Lomas de Zamora, Arg. H9 80
Lomax, Al., U.S. C3 108
Lomax, Il., U.S. C2 120
Lombard, Il., U.S. k8 120
Lombardia, prov., Italy D4 18
Lomblen, Pulau, i., Indon. G7 38
Lombok, i., Indon. G6 38
Lomé, Togo H10 64
Lomela, Zaire B4 58
Lometa, Tx., U.S. D3 150
Lomira, Wi., U.S. E5 156
Lo Miranda, Chile H3 80
Lommel, Bel. F7 12
Lomond, Alta., Can. D4 98
Lomond, Loch, l., Scot., U.K. E9 8
Lomonosov, U.S.S.R. B12 26
Lomonosovskij, U.S.S.R. G11 22
Lompoc, Ca., U.S. E3 112
Lom Sak, Thai. F6 40
Łomża, Pol. B22 10
Lonaconing, Md., U.S. k13 127
Loncoche, Chile D2 78
Loncopué, Arg. J3 80
Londesborough, Ont., Can. D3 103
Londinières, Fr. C8 14
London, Ont., Can. E3 103
London, Eng., U.K. J13 8
London, Ar., U.S. B2 111
London, Ky., U.S. C5 124
London, Oh., U.S. C2 142
Londonderry, N.S., Can. D6 101
Londonderry, N. Ire., U.K. F6 8
Londonderry, N.H., U.S. E4 136
Londonderry, Vt., U.S. E3 152
Londonderry, Cape, c., Austl. B5 68
London Mills, Il., U.S. C3 120
Londontown, Md., U.S. C4 127
Londres, Arg. D5 80
Londrina, Braz. G3 79
Lone Grove, Ok., U.S. C4 143
Lone Jack, Mo., U.S. C3 132
Lone Mountain, Tn., U.S. C10 149
Lone Mountain, mtn., Nv., U.S. E4 135
Lone Oak, Ky., U.S. e9 124
Lone Oak, Tx., U.S. C5 150
Lone Pine, Ca., U.S. D4 112
Lone Rock, Sask., Can. D1 105
Lone Rock, Wi., U.S. E3 156
Lone Tree, Ia., U.S. C6 122
Lone Tree Creek, stm., Co., U.S. A6 113
Lone Wolf, Ok., U.S. C2 143
Long, co., Ga., U.S. E5 117
Longa, stm., Ang. D2 58
Longa, proliv, strt., U.S.S.R. C27 24
Long'an, China B10 40
Longaví, Chile H3 80
Long Bar Harbor, Md., U.S. B5 127
Long Beach, Ca., U.S. F4 112
Long Beach, In., U.S. A4 121
Long Beach, Md., U.S. D5 127
Long Beach, Ms., U.S. g7 131
Long Beach, N.Y., U.S. E7 139
Long Beach, Wa., U.S. C1 154
Long Beach Naval Shipyard, mil., Ca., U.S. n12 112
Longboat Key, Fl., U.S. q10 116
Longboat Key, i., Fl., U.S. E4 116
Longboat Pass, strt., Fl., U.S. q10 116
Long Branch, N.J., U.S. C5 137
Longbranch, Wa., U.S. B3 154
Long Cay, i., Bah. C7 94
Longchang, China F8 30
Longchuan, China K4 34
Longchuan (Shweli), stm., Asia B4 40

Name	Map Ref.	Page
Long Creek Mountain, mtn., Wy., U.S.	D5	157
Longcun, China	L4	34
Longdale, Ok., U.S.	A3	143
Longdou, China	H6	34
Longeau, Fr.	E12	14
Longford, Austl.	L7	70
Longford, Ont., Can.	C5	103
Longford, co., Ire.	H6	8
Long Grove, Ia., U.S.	C7	122
Long Harbour [-Mount Arlington Heights], Newf., Can.	E5	102
Longhua, China	B5	32
Long Island, Ks., U.S.	C4	123
Long Island, i., Austl.	D8	70
Long Island, i., Bah.	C7	94
Long Island, i., N.S., Can.	E3	101
Long Island, i., Me., U.S.	g7	126
Long Island, i., Ma., U.S.	g12	128
Long Island, i., N.Y., U.S.	E7	139
Long Island Sound, strt., U.S.	E7	139
Longitudinal, Valle, val., Chile	H3	80
Longjiang, China	B11	30
Longjin, China	G5	34
Longka, China	D8	44
Longkangji, China	B5	34
Long Key, i., Fl., U.S.	H6	116
Longkou, China	D11	30
Longkou, China	I4	34
Long Lake, Il., U.S.	h8	120
Long Lake, l., Me., U.S.	A4	126
Long Lake, l., Me., U.S.	D2	126
Long Lake, l., Mi., U.S.	C7	129
Long Lake, l., Mi., U.S.	D5	129
Long Lake, l., Mn., U.S.	D4	130
Long Lake, l., N.Y., U.S.	B6	139
Long Lake, l., N.D., U.S.	C6	141
Long Lake, l., Wa., U.S.	f10	154
Long Lake, l., Wi., U.S.	C2	156
Long Lake Colony, S.D., U.S.	*B7	148
Longleaf, La., U.S.	C3	125
Longli, China	F8	30
Longling, China	B5	40
Longmeadow, Ma., U.S.	B2	128
Longmensuo, China	C3	32
Longming, China	C9	40
Longmont, Co., U.S.	A5	113
Long Mountain, mtn., Mo., U.S.	E5	132
Long Mountain, mtn., N.H., U.S.	A4	136
Longnan, China	K3	34
Longnawan, Indon.	E5	38
Longny, Fr.	M14	8
Long Pine, Ne., U.S.	B6	134
Long Point, N.S., Can.	D8	101
Long Point, Ont., Can.	E4	103
Long Point, Il., U.S.	B5	120
Long Point, c., Man., Can.	C2	100
Long Point, c., Newf., Can.	D2	102
Long Point, pen., Ont., Can.	E4	103
Long Pond, l., Me., U.S.	C3	126
Long Pond, l., Me., U.S.	C2	126
Long Pond, l., Ma., U.S.	C6	128
Long Pond, l., Ma., U.S.	C6	128
Long Pond, res., Fl., U.S.	C4	116
Longport, N.J., U.S.	E3	137
Long Prairie, Mn., U.S.	E4	130
Longquan, China	G8	34
Longquanguan, China	E1	32
Long Range Mountains, mts., Newf., Can.	D3	102
Longreach, Austl.	D6	70
Longshansuo, China	E10	34
Longsheng, China	B11	40
Longs Peak, mtn., Co., U.S.	A5	113
Longtian, China	J8	34
Longton, Ks., U.S.	E7	123
Longtoupu, China	H2	34
Longueuil, Que., Can.	D4	104
Longuyon, Fr.	C12	14
Long Valley, N.J., U.S.	B3	137
Longview, Alta., Can.	D3	98
Long View, Ky., U.S.	C4	124
Longview, Ms., U.S.	B5	131
Long View, N.C., U.S.	B1	140
Longview, Tx., U.S.	C5	150
Longview, Wa., U.S.	C3	154
Longwangmiao, China	G3	32
Longwy, Fr.	C12	14
Longxi, China	E7	30
Long Xuyen, Viet.	I8	40
Longyan, China	J6	34
Longyuanba, China	K3	34
Longzhou, China	C9	40
Lonigo, Italy	D6	18
Löningen, Ger.	C7	10
Lonoke, Ar., U.S.	C4	111
Lonoke, co., Ar., U.S.	C4	111
Lonsdale, Ont., Can.	C7	103
Lonsdale, Ar., U.S.	C3	111
Lonsdale, Mn., U.S.	F5	130
Lonsdale, R.I., U.S.	B4	146
Lons-le-Saunier, Fr.	F12	14
Lonton, Burma	B4	40
Lontra, Ribeirão, stm., Braz.	F2	79
Loogootee, In., U.S.	G4	121
Lookout, Ky., U.S.	C7	124
Lookout, W.V., U.S.	C4	155
Lookout, Cape, c., N.C., U.S.	C6	140
Lookout, Point, c., Mi., U.S.	d7	129
Lookout Mountain, Tn., U.S.	h11	149
Lookout Mountain, mtn., U.S.	D8	149
Lookout Mountain, mtn., Or., U.S.	C6	144
Lookout Pass, U.S.	B3	119
Lookout Point Lake, res., Or., U.S.	D4	144
Loomis, Ne., U.S.	D6	134
Loomis, Wa., U.S.	A6	154
Loon Bay, Newf., Can.	D4	102
Loon Lake, Wa., U.S.	A8	154
Loon Lake, l., Me., U.S.	B3	126
Loon op Zand, Neth.	E7	12
Loop, Tx., U.S.	C1	150
Loop Creek, stm., W.V., U.S.	m13	155
Loosahatchie, stm., Tn., U.S.	B2	149
Loose Creek, Mo., U.S.	C6	132
Lop, China	B9	44
Lopar'ovo, U.S.S.R.	C25	26
Lopatina, gora, mtn., U.S.S.R.	G20	24
Lopatka, mys, c., U.S.S.R.	G23	24
Lop Buri, Thai.	G6	40
López, Mex.	D7	90
Lopez, Cap, c., Gabon	B1	58
Lopez Island, i., Wa., U.S.	A3	154
Lop Nur (Lop Nor), l., China	C5	30
Łopuszno, Pol.	E20	10
Lora, stm., Ven.	C6	84
Lora, Hāmūn-i-, l., Asia	F1	44
Lora del Río, Spain	H6	16
Lorado, W.V., U.S.	D3	155
Lorain, Oh., U.S.	A3	142
Lorain, co., Oh., U.S.	A3	142
Loraine, Il., U.S.	C2	120
Loraine, Tx., U.S.	C2	150
Loramie, Lake, res., Oh., U.S.	B1	142
Loranger, La., U.S.	D5	125
Lorca, Spain	H10	16
Lord Howe Island, i., Austl.	F11	68
Lordsburg, N.M., U.S.	E1	138
Loreauville, La., U.S.	D4	125
Loreburn, Sask., Can.	F2	105
Loreley, Ger.	E7	10
Lorena, Braz.	G6	79
Lorentz, W.V., U.S.	B4	155
Lorenzo, Tx., U.S.	C2	150
Lorenzo Geyres (Queguay), Ur.	G10	80
Loreto, Arg.	D10	80
Loreto, Bol.	F9	82
Loreto, Braz.	E9	76
Loreto, Col.	I7	84
Loreto, Mex.	D4	90
Loreto, Mex.	F9	90
Loreto, Para.	B10	80
Loreto, dept., Peru	I5	84
Lorette, Man., Can.	E3	100
Loretteville, Que., Can.	C6	104
Loretto, Ky., U.S.	C4	124
Loretto, Mi., U.S.	C3	129
Loretto, Pa., U.S.	F4	145
Loretto, Tn., U.S.	B4	149
Lorica, Col.	C5	84
Lorida, Fl., U.S.	E5	116
Lorient, Fr.	E3	14
L'Orignal, Ont., Can.	B10	103
Lorimor, Ia., U.S.	C3	122
Loring Air Force Base, mil., Me., U.S.	B5	126
Loriol, Fr.	H11	14
Loris, S.C., U.S.	C10	147
Lorman, Ms., U.S.	D2	131
Lorne, Austl.	L5	70
Lorne, N.B., Can.	B3	101
Lorneville, Ont., Can.	C5	103
Lörrach, Ger.	H7	10
Lorraine, Ks., U.S.	D5	123
Lorraine, hist. reg., Fr.	D13	14
Lorris, Fr.	E9	14
Losada, stm., Col.	F5	84
Los Alamos, Ca., U.S.	E3	112
Los Alamos, N.M., U.S.	B3	138
Los Alamos, co., N.M., U.S.	B3	138
Los Aldamas, Mex.	D10	90
Los Altos, Ca., U.S.	k8	112
Los Amates, Guat.	B5	92
Los Americanos, Barra, i., Mex.	E11	90
Los Andes, Chile	G3	80
Los Ángeles, Chile	I2	80
Los Angeles, Ca., U.S.	E4	112
Los Angeles, co., Ca., U.S.	E4	112
Los Angeles Aqueduct, Ca., U.S.	E4	112
Losantville, In., U.S.	D7	121
Los Arroyos, Laguna de, l., Bol.	E9	82
Los Banos, Ca., U.S.	D3	112
Los Berros, Arg.	F4	80
Los Blancos, Arg.	B7	80
Los Bolones, Cerro, mtn., Mex.	I13	90
Los Cerrillos, Arg.	F6	80
Los Chacos, Bol.	F10	82
Los Chiles, C.R.	F10	92
Los Conquistadores, Arg.	F9	80
Los Cristianos, Spain	O24	17b
Los Esclavos, stm., Guat.	D4	92
Los Frentones, Arg.	D8	80
Los Fresnos, Tx., U.S.	F4	150
Los Gatos, Ca., U.S.	D2	112
Los Hermanos, Islas, is., Ven.	B10	84
Łosice, Pol.	C22	10
Los Juríes, Arg.	E7	80
Los Lagos, Chile	D2	78
Los Llanos de Aridane, Spain	O23	17b
Los Lunas, N.M., U.S.	C3	138
Los Maribios, Cordillera, mts., Nic.	E8	92
Los Micos, Laguna de, b., Hond.	B7	92
Los Mochis, Mex.	E5	90
Los Molinos, Ca., U.S.	B2	112
Lošnica, U.S.S.R.	G11	26
Los Ojos, N.M., U.S.	A3	138
Los Padillas, N.M., U.S.	m7	138
Los Palacios, Arg.	E4	80
Los Palacios, Cuba	C3	94
Los Palacios y Villafranca, Spain	H6	16
Los Pinos, stm., Co., U.S.	D3	113
Los Quirquinchos, Arg.	G8	80
Los Ranchos de Albuquerque, N.M., U.S.	B3	138
Los Ríos, prov., Ec.	H3	84
Los Rodríguez, Mex.	D9	90
Los Roques, Islas, is., Ven.	B9	84
Los Santos, Pan.	D2	84
Los Santos, prov., Pan.	J14	92
Los Santos de Maimona, Spain	G5	16
Los Sauces, Chile	I2	80
Los Sauces, Spain	O23	17b
Lossiemouth, Scot., U.K.	D10	8
Lost, stm., In., U.S.	G4	121
Lost, stm., Wa., U.S.	A5	154
Lost, stm., W.V., U.S.	B6	155
Lostant, Il., U.S.	B4	120
Los Taques, Ven.	B7	84
Lost Creek, W.V., U.S.	B4	155
Lost Creek, stm., Ar., U.S.	C3	111
Lost Creek, stm., Wy., U.S.	D4	157
Los Telares, Arg.	E7	80
Los Teques, Ven.	B9	84
Los Testigos, Islas, is., Ven.	B11	84
Lost Hills, Ca., U.S.	E4	112
Lost Nation, Ia., U.S.	C7	122
Lost Peak, mtn., Ut., U.S.	F2	151
Lost Ranger Peak, mtn., Co., U.S.	A4	113
Lost River Glacial Caverns, N.H., U.S.	B3	136
Lost River Range, mts., Id., U.S.	E5	119
Los Trujillos, N.M., U.S.	C3	138
Lost Springs, Ks., U.S.	D7	123
Lost Trail Pass, U.S.	D5	119
Losuia, Pap. N. Gui.	A10	68
Los Vidrios, Mex.	B3	90
Los Vilos, Chile	F3	80
Lot, dept., Fr.	H8	14
Lot, stm., Fr.	H7	14
Lota, Chile	I2	80
Lotawana, Lake, res., Mo., U.S.	k11	132
Lotbinière, Que., Can.	C6	104
Lot-et-Garonne, dept., Fr.	H7	14
Lothair, S. Afr.	F10	66
Lothian, prov., Scot., U.K.	F10	8
Lotsane, stm., Bots.	D8	66
Lott, Tx., U.S.	D4	150
Lotung, Tai.	K10	34
Louang Namtha, Laos	D6	40
Louangphrabang, Laos	E7	40
Louann, Ar., U.S.	D3	111
Louchi, U.S.S.R.	D4	22
Loudéac, Fr.	D4	14
Loudon, Tn., U.S.	D9	149
Loudon, co., Tn., U.S.	D9	149
Loudonville, Oh., U.S.	B3	142
Loudoun, co., Va., U.S.	A5	153
Loudun, Fr.	E7	14
Loué, Fr.	D6	14
Louga, Sen.	D1	64
Louge, Arg.	I8	80
Lougheed, Alta., Can.	C5	98
Loughman, Fl., U.S.	D5	116
Louhans, Fr.	F12	14
Louin, Ms., U.S.	C4	131
Louisa, Ky., U.S.	B7	124
Louisa, Va., U.S.	B4	153
Louisa, co., Ia., U.S.	C6	122
Louisa, co., Va., U.S.	C5	153
Louisa, Lake, l., Fl., U.S.	D5	116
Louisbourg, N.S., Can.	D10	101
Louisburg, Ks., U.S.	D9	123
Louisburg, N.C., U.S.	A4	140
Louisdale, N.S., Can.	D8	101
Louise, Ga., U.S.	C2	117
Louise, Ms., U.S.	C3	131
Louise, Tx., U.S.	E4	150
Louise, Lake, l., Ak., U.S.	f18	109
Louise Island, i., B.C., Can.	C2	99
Louiseville, Que., Can.	C5	104
Louisiade Archipelago, is., Pap. N. Gui.	B10	68
Louisiana, Mo., U.S.	B6	132
Louisiana, state, U.S.	C3	125
Louisiana Point, c., La., U.S.	E2	125
Louis Trichardt, S. Afr.	D9	66
Louisville, Al., U.S.	D4	108
Louisville, Co., U.S.	B5	113
Louisville, Ga., U.S.	C4	117
Louisville, Il., U.S.	E5	120
Louisville, Ks., U.S.	C7	123
Louisville, Ky., U.S.	B4	124
Louisville, Ms., U.S.	B4	131
Louisville, Ne., U.S.	D9	134
Louisville, Oh., U.S.	B4	142
Louisville, Tn., U.S.	D9	149
Louis-XIV, Pointe, c., Que., Can.	h11	104
Loujiaying, China	A4	32
Loup, co., Ne., U.S.	C6	134
Loup, stm., Ne., U.S.	C8	134
Loup, Rivière du, stm., Que., Can.	C4	104
Loup, Rivière du, stm., Que., Can.	B8	104
Loup City, Ne., U.S.	C7	134
Lourdes, Newf., Can.	D2	102
Lourdes, Fr.	I6	14
Lourenço Marques see Maputo, Moz.	E11	66
Lousana, Alta., Can.	C4	98
Louta, Burkina	E8	64
Louth, co., Ire.	H7	8
Loutre, Bayou de, stm., La., U.S.	B3	125
Louvain (Leuven), Bel.	G6	12
Louvale, Ga., U.S.	D2	117
Louviers, Fr.	C8	14
Louviers, Co., U.S.	B6	113
Lovat', stm., U.S.S.R.	D14	26
Love, Sask., Can.	D3	105
Love, co., Ok., U.S.	D4	143
Loveč, Bul.	F8	20
Lovelaceville, Ky., U.S.	f9	124
Lovelady, Tx., U.S.	D5	150
Loveland, Co., U.S.	A5	113
Loveland, Oh., U.S.	n13	142
Loveland Park, Oh., U.S.	C1	142
Loveland Pass, Co., U.S.	B5	113
Lovell, Me., U.S.	D2	126
Lovell, Wy., U.S.	B4	157
Lovelock, Nv., U.S.	C3	135
Lovely, Ky., U.S.	C7	124
Lovenia, Mount, mtn., Ut., U.S.	C5	151
Love Point, c., Md., U.S.	B5	127
Lovere, Italy	D5	18
Loves Park, Il., U.S.	A4	120
Lovettsville, Va., U.S.	A5	153
Lovewell Pond, l., Me., U.S.	D2	126
Lovick, Al., U.S.	f7	108
Lovilia, Ia., U.S.	C5	122
Loving, N.M., U.S.	E5	138
Loving, co., Tx., U.S.	D1	150
Lovingston, Va., U.S.	C4	153
Lovington, Il., U.S.	D5	120
Lovington, Ia., U.S.	e8	122
Lovington, N.M., U.S.	E6	138
Lovosice, Czech.	E14	10
Lovozero, U.S.S.R.	G24	6
Lovozero, ozero, l., U.S.S.R.	H24	6
Lövstabruk, Swe.	K15	6
Low, Cape, c., N.W. Ter., Can.	D15	96
Lowden, Ia., U.S.	C7	122
Lowe Farm, Man., Can.	E3	100
Lowell, Ar., U.S.	A1	111
Lowell, In., U.S.	B3	121
Lowell, Ma., U.S.	A5	128
Lowell, Mi., U.S.	F5	129
Lowell, N.C., U.S.	B1	140
Lowell, Oh., U.S.	C4	142
Lowell, Or., U.S.	D4	144
Lowell, Vt., U.S.	B4	152
Lowell, Wi., U.S.	E5	156
Lowell, Lake, res., Id., U.S.	F2	119
Lowelli, Sud.	O7	60
Lowell Mountains, mts., Vt., U.S.	B4	152
Lowellville, Oh., U.S.	A5	142
Löwenberg, Ger.	C13	10
Lower Arrow Lake, res., B.C., Can.	E8	99
Lower Brule, S.D., U.S.	C6	148
Lower Brule Indian Reservation, S.D., U.S.	C6	148
Lower California see Baja California, pen., Mex.	C3	90
Lower East Pubnico, N.S., Can.	F4	101
Lower Hutt, N.Z.	D5	72
Lower Island Cove, Newf., Can.	D5	102
Lower Klamath Lake, l., Ca., U.S.	B3	112
Lower Matecumbe Key, i., Fl., U.S.	H6	116
Lower Monumental Lake, res., Wa., U.S.	C7	154
Lower New York Bay, b., N.J., U.S.	B4	137
Lower Otay Lake, res., Ca., U.S.	o16	112
Lower Paia, Hi., U.S.	C5	118
Lower Peach Tree, Al., U.S.	D2	108
Lower Red Lake, l., Mn., U.S.	C3	130
Lower Rice Lake, l., Mn., U.S.	C3	130
Lower Salmon Dam, Id., U.S.	G4	119
Lower Village, Vt., U.S.	C3	152
Lower West Pubnico, N.S., Can.	F4	101
Lower Wilson Pond, l., Me., U.S.	C3	126
Lower Woods Harbour, N.S., Can.	F4	101
Lowes, Ky., U.S.	f9	124
Lowestoft, Eng., U.K.	I15	8
Łowicz, Pol.	C19	10
Lowmansville, Ky., U.S.	C7	124
Low Moor, Ia., U.S.	C7	122
Lowmoor, Va., U.S.	C3	153
Lowndes, co., Al., U.S.	C3	108
Lowndes, co., Ga., U.S.	F3	117
Lowndes, co., Ms., U.S.	B5	131
Lowndesboro, Al., U.S.	C3	108
Lowrah (Pishīn Lora), stm., Asia	G18	48
Low Rocky Point, c., Austl.	N6	70
Lowry Air Force Base, mil., Co., U.S.	B6	113
Lowry City, Mo., U.S.	C4	132
Lowville, N.Y., U.S.	B5	139
Loxley, Al., U.S.	E2	108
Loxton, Austl.	J4	70
Loxton, S. Afr.	H6	66
Loyal, Wi., U.S.	D3	156
Loyall, Ky., U.S.	D6	124
Loyalsock Creek, stm., Pa., U.S.	D8	145
Loyalton, Ca., U.S.	C3	112
Lozère, dept., Fr.	H10	14
Loznica, Yugo.	E3	20
Lualaba, stm., Zaire	B5	58
Lua Makika, crat., Hi., U.S.	C5	118
Lu'an, China	D5	34
Luan, stm., China	C10	30
Luanda, Ang.	C2	58
Luando, stm., Ang.	D3	58
Luang, Thale, b., Thai.	K6	40
Luang Prabang Range, mts., Asia	E6	40
Luangue (Loange), stm., Afr.	C3	58
Luanguinga, stm., Afr.	D4	58
Luangwa, stm., Afr.	D6	58
Luanhaizi, China	C15	44
Luanshishan, China	A11	32
Luanshya, Zam.	D5	58
Luán Toro, Arg.	I6	80
Luapula, stm., Afr.	D5	58
Luau, Ang.	D4	58
Luba, Eq. Gui.	H8	54
Lubaantun, hist., Belize	I15	90
Lubań, Pol.	D15	10
L'uban', U.S.S.R.	B14	26
L'uban', U.S.S.R.	I10	26
Lubāna, U.S.S.R.	E9	26
Lubango, Ang.	D2	58
Lubao, China	L1	34
L'ubašovka, U.S.S.R.	B14	20
Lubawa, Pol.	B19	10
Lübbenau, Ger.	D13	10
Lubbock, Tx., U.S.	C2	150
Lubbock, co., Tx., U.S.	C2	150
L'ubča, U.S.S.R.	H9	26
Lubec, Me., U.S.	D6	126
Lübeck, Ger.	B10	10
Lubefu, Zaire	B4	58
L'ubercy, U.S.S.R.	F20	26
L'ubim, U.S.S.R.	C23	26
Lubin, Pol.	D16	10
Lublin, Pol.	D22	10
Lubliniec, Pol.	E18	10
Lubnān, Jabal (Lebanon Mountains), mts., Leb.	A5	50
L'ubnica, U.S.S.R.	D15	26
Lubny, U.S.S.R.	G4	22
L'ubochna, U.S.S.R.	H17	26
Luboń, Pol.	C16	10
L'ubotin, U.S.S.R.	H5	22
Lubraniec, Pol.	C18	10
Lubsko, Pol.	D14	10
Lubudi, Zaire	C5	58
Lubumbashi (Élisabethville), Zaire	D5	58
Lubutu, Zaire	B5	58
L'ubytino, U.S.S.R.	C16	26
Lübz, Ger.	B12	10
Lucama, N.C., U.S.	B4	140
Lucan, Ont., Can.	D3	103
Lucanas, Peru	F4	82
Lucania, Mount, mtn., Yukon, Can.	D4	96
Lucas, Ia., U.S.	C4	122
Lucas, Ks., U.S.	C5	123
Lucas, Oh., U.S.	B3	142
Lucas, co., Ia., U.S.	C4	122
Lucas, co., Oh., U.S.	A2	142
Lucas González, Arg.	G9	80
Lucasville, Oh., U.S.	D3	142
Lucca, Italy	F5	18
Luce, co., Mi., U.S.	B5	129
Lucedale, Ms., U.S.	E5	131
Lucena, Phil.	O19	39b
Lucena, Spain	H7	16
Lučenec, Czech.	G19	10
Lucera, Italy	H10	18
Lucerne, Ca., U.S.	C2	112
Lucerne, Co., U.S.	A6	113
Lucerne, In., U.S.	C5	121
Lucerne, Lake see Vierwaldstätter See, l., Switz.	D9	13
Lucerne see Luzern, Switz.	D9	13
Lucernemines, Pa., U.S.	E3	145
Lucerne Valley, Ca., U.S.	E5	112
Luceville, Que., Can.	A9	104
Luch, stm., U.S.S.R.	E25	26
Lucheng, China	B9	40
Luchovicy, U.S.S.R.	G22	26
Lüchow, Ger.	C11	10
Luchow see Luzhou, China	F8	30
Luchuan, China	C11	40
Luci, China	F8	34
Lucie, stm., Sur.	F14	84
Lucile, Id., U.S.	D2	119
Lucindale, Austl.	K4	70
Lucira, Ang.	D2	58
Luck, U.S.S.R.	G3	22
Luck, Wi., U.S.	C1	156
Luckau, Ger.	D13	10
Luckenwalde, Ger.	C13	10
Luckey, Oh., U.S.	A2	142
Luckhoff, S. Afr.	G7	66
Lucknow, Ont., Can.	D3	103
Lucknow, India	G9	44
Lucky, La., U.S.	B3	125
Lucky Lake, Sask., Can.	G2	105
Lucky Peak Lake, res., Id., U.S.	F3	119
Luçon, Fr.	F5	14
Lucun, China	G6	32
Lucy, La., U.S.	h10	125
Lucy, Tn., U.S.	B2	149
Lüda see Dalian, China	E9	32
Lüdenscheid, Ger.	D7	10
Lüderitz, Nmb.	F2	66
Ludhiāna, India	E6	44
Lüdinghausen, Ger.	D7	10
Ludington, Mi., U.S.	E4	129
L'udinovo, U.S.S.R.	H17	26
L'udkovo, U.S.S.R.	G17	26
Ludlow, N.B., Can.	C3	101
Ludlow, Il., U.S.	C5	120
Ludlow, Ky., U.S.	h13	124
Ludlow, Ma., U.S.	B3	128
Ludlow, Ms., U.S.	C4	131
Ludlow, Pa., U.S.	C4	145
Ludlow, Vt., U.S.	E3	152
Ludlow Mountain, mtn., Vt., U.S.	E3	152
Ludowici, Ga., U.S.	E5	117
Ludvika, Swe.	K14	6
Ludwigsburg, Ger.	G9	10
Ludwigsfelde, Ger.	C13	10
Ludwigshafen, Ger.	F8	10
Ludwigslust, Ger.	B11	10
Ludza, U.S.S.R.	E10	26
Luebo, Zaire	C4	58
Luena, Ang.	D3	58
Luena, Zaire	C5	58
Luena, stm., Ang.	D4	58
Luepa, Ven.	E12	84
Lufeng, China	M4	34
Lufeng, China	B7	40
Lufkin, Tx., U.S.	D5	150
Luga, U.S.S.R.	C12	26
Lugano, Switz.	F10	13
Lugano, Lago di, l., Eur.	C4	18
Lugansk, U.S.S.R.	H5	22
Lugenda, stm., Moz.	D7	58
Lugnaquillia Mountain, mtn., Ire.	I7	8
Lugo, Italy	E6	18
Lugo, Spain	B4	16
Lugoff, S.C., U.S.	C6	147
Lugoj, Rom.	D5	20
Lühedian, China	C3	34
Luik (Liège), Bel.	G8	12
Luino, Italy	C3	18
Luís Alves, Braz.	D14	80
Luishia, Zaire	D5	58
Luisiânia, Braz.	F3	79
Luis Lopez, N.M., U.S.	D3	138
Luiza, Zaire	C4	58
Luján, Arg.	G4	80
Luján, Arg.	G6	80
Lujiao, China	F1	34
Lukachukai, Az., U.S.	A6	110
Lukang, Tai.	K9	34
Lukanga Swamp, sw., Zam.	D5	58
Luke Air Force Base, mil., Az., U.S.	D3	110
Luknovo, U.S.S.R.	E25	26
Lukolela, Zaire	B3	58
Lukou, China	H3	34
Lukoupu, China	F2	34
Łuków, Pol.	D22	10
Lukulu, Zam.	D4	58
Lula, Ga., U.S.	B3	117
Lula, Ms., U.S.	A3	131
Luleå, Swe.	I18	6
Lüleburgaz, Tur.	H11	20
Lules, Arg.	D6	80
Luliang, China	B7	40
Lüliang Shan, mts., China	D9	30
Luling, La., U.S.	k11	125
Luling, Tx., U.S.	E4	150
Lumaling, China	F15	44
Lumbala N'guimbo, Ang.	D4	58
Lumber, stm., U.S.	C9	147
Lumber City, Ga., U.S.	E4	117
Lumberport, W.V., U.S.	B4	155
Lumberton, Ms., U.S.	D4	131
Lumberton, N.J., U.S.	D3	137
Lumberton, N.M., U.S.	A3	138
Lumberton, N.C., U.S.	C3	140
Lumberton, Tx., U.S.	D5	150
Lumbres, Fr.	B9	14
Lumby, B.C., Can.	D8	99
Lumding, India	H15	44
Luminárias, Braz.	F6	79
Lummi Indian Reservation, Wa., U.S.	A3	154
Lumpkin, Ga., U.S.	D2	117
Lumpkin, co., Ga., U.S.	B2	117
Lumsden, Newf., Can.	D5	102
Lumsden, Sask., Can.	G3	105
Lumut, Malay.	L6	40
Luna, N.M., U.S.	D1	138
Luna, co., N.M., U.S.	E2	138
Luna, stm., Braz.	J12	84
Luna Pier, Mi., U.S.	G7	129
Lūnāvāda, India	I5	44
Lund, Swe.	N13	6
Lund, Nv., U.S.	E6	135
Lundale, W.V., U.S.	n12	155
Lundar, Man., Can.	D2	100
Lundazi, Zam.	D6	58
Lundbreck, Alta., Can.	E3	98
Lundi, stm., Zimb.	C10	66
Lüneburg, Ger.	B10	10
Lüneburger Heide, reg., Ger.	B10	10
Lunel, Fr.	I11	14
Lünen, Ger.	D7	10
Lunenburg, N.S., Can.	E5	101
Lunenburg, Ma., U.S.	A4	128
Lunenburg, Vt., U.S.	C5	152
Lunenburg, co., Va., U.S.	D4	153
Lunéville, Fr.	D13	14
Lunga, stm., Zam.	D5	58
Lunge'nake, China	E11	44
Lungi, S.L.	G3	64
Lungué-Bungo, stm., Afr.	D4	58
Lunin, U.S.S.R.	I9	26
Luninec, U.S.S.R.	I9	26
Lunjiao, China	M2	34
Lunno, U.S.S.R.	H7	26
Luo, stm., China	E9	30
Luochanghe, China	D6	34
Luoci, China	B7	40
Luofang, China	H4	34
Luogang, China	K4	34
Luohe, China	B3	34
Luoheya, China	H6	32
Luoji, China	C6	34
Luokeng, China	K2	34
Luoqiao, China	I8	34
Luoshuihe, China	D2	32
Luotuodian, China	C2	34
Luoyang, China	E9	30
Lupala, Nmb.	A4	66
Lupani, Zimb.	B8	66
Lupeni, Rom.	D7	20
Luqu, China	E7	30
Luray, Ks., U.S.	C5	123
Luray, Va., U.S.	B4	153
Lure, Fr.	E13	14
Lure, Lake, res., N.C., U.S.	f10	140
Luremo, Ang.	C3	58
Luribay, Bol.	G8	82
Lurín, Peru	E3	82
Lúrio, Moz.	D8	58
Lúrio, stm., Moz.	D7	58
Lusaka, Zam.	E5	58
Lusambo, Zaire	B4	58
Lusanga, Zaire	B3	58
Lusby, Md., U.S.	D5	127
Luseland, Sask., Can.	E1	105
Lushan, China	E7	30
Lu Shan, mtn., China	F10	30
Lushanguanliju, China	F4	34
Lushnje, Alb.	I3	20
Lushoto, Tan.	B7	58
Lushui, China	A5	40
Lüshun (Port Arthur), China	E9	32
Lüsi, China	C10	34
Lusignan, Fr.	F7	14
L'usino, U.S.S.R.	I9	26
Lusk, Wy., U.S.	D8	157
Lustenau, Aus.	H9	10
Lūt, Dasht-e, des., Iran	E15	48
Lutai, China	B4	34
Lutang, China	J1	34
Lutcher, La., U.S.	D5	125
Luther, Mi., U.S.	D5	129
Luther, Ok., U.S.	B4	143
Luthersville, Ga., U.S.	C2	117
Lutherville-Timonium, Md., U.S.	B4	127
Lutian, China	I3	34
Luton, Eng., U.K.	J13	8
Lutong, Malay.	E5	38
Lutou, China	C1	34
Lutsen, Mn., U.S.	k9	130
Luttrell, Tn., U.S.	C10	149
Lutts, Tn., U.S.	B4	149
Lutz, Fl., U.S.	D4	116
Lützow-Holm Bay, b., Ant.	B4	73
Lutzputs, S. Afr.	G5	66
Lutzville, S. Afr.	H4	66
Luuq, Som.	H9	56
Luverne, Al., U.S.	D3	108
Lu Verne, Ia., U.S.	B3	122
Luverne, Mn., U.S.	G2	130
Luvuvhu, stm., Afr.	D10	66
Luxapallila Creek, stm., U.S.	B5	131
Luxembourg (Luxemburg), Lux.	I9	12
Luxembourg, prov., Bel.	I7	12
Luxembourg, ctry., Eur.	F9	4
Luxemburg, Ia., U.S.	B6	122
Luxemburg, Wi., U.S.	D6	156
Luxeuil-les-Bains, Fr.	E13	14
Luxi (Mangshi), China	B5	40
Lüxia, China	I9	34
Luxomni, Ga., U.S.	h8	117
Luxora, Ar., U.S.	B6	111
Luxor see Al-Uqṣur, Egypt	E7	60
Lüyang, China	B9	32
Luz, Braz.	E6	79
Luza, U.S.S.R.	E7	22
Luzarches, Fr.	C9	14
Luzern, Switz.	D9	13
Luzern, state, Switz.	D9	13
Luzerne, Mi., U.S.	D6	129
Luzerne, Pa., U.S.	n17	145

Name — Map Ref. — Page

Luzerne, co., Pa., U.S. D9 145
Luzhou, China F8 30
Luziânia, Braz. D5 79
Lužnice, stm., Eur. G14 10
Luzon, i., Phil. N19 39b
Luzon Strait, strt., Asia N9 34
Luzy, Fr. F10 14
L'vov, U.S.S.R. H2 22
L'vovskij, U.S.S.R. F20 26
Lwówek, Pol. C16 10
Lybster, Scot., U.K. C10 8
Lyčkovo, U.S.S.R. D15 26
Lycksele, Swe. I16 6
Lycoming, co., Pa., U.S. D7 145
Lycoming Creek, stm., Pa., U.S. D7 145
Lydenburg, S. Afr. E10 66
Lydia, S.C., U.S. C7 147
Lyell, Mount, mtn., Can. D2 98
Lyell Island, i., B.C., Can. C2 99
Lyerly, Ga., U.S. B1 117
Lyford, In., U.S. E3 121
Lyford, Tx., U.S. F4 150
Lykens, Pa., U.S. E8 145
Lykošino, U.S.S.R. C16 26
Lyle, Mn., U.S. G6 130
Lyle, Wa., U.S. D4 154
Lyles, Tn., U.S. B4 149
Lyleton, Man., Can. E1 100
Lyman, Ms., U.S. E4 131
Lyman, Ne., U.S. C1 134
Lyman, S.C., U.S. B3 147
Lyman, Wa., U.S. A3 154
Lyman, Wy., U.S. E2 157
Lyman, co., S.D., U.S. D6 148
Lyman Lake, res., Az., U.S. C6 110
Lyme, Ct., U.S. D6 114
Lyme, N.H., U.S. C2 136
Lyme Center, N.H., U.S. C2 136
Lyme Regis, Eng., U.K. K11 8
Łyna (Lava), stm., Eur. G3 26
Lynch, Ky., U.S. D7 124
Lynch, Ne., U.S. B7 134
Lynchburg, Oh., U.S. C2 142
Lynchburg, S.C., U.S. C7 147
Lynchburg, Tn., U.S. B5 149
Lynchburg, Va., U.S. C3 153
Lynches, stm., S.C., U.S. D8 147
Lynch Heights, De., U.S. E4 115
Lynch Station, Va., U.S. C3 153
Lynd, Mn., U.S. F3 130
Lynden, Wa., U.S. A3 154
Lynde Point, c., Ct., U.S. D6 114
Lyndhurst, Austl. H3 70
Lyndhurst, Ont., Can. C8 103
Lyndhurst, N.J., U.S. h8 137
Lyndhurst, Oh., U.S. g10 142
Lyndon, Il., U.S. B4 120
Lyndon, Ks., U.S. D8 123
Lyndon, Ky., U.S. g11 124
Lyndon, Vt., U.S. B4 152
Lyndon B. Johnson National Historical Site, hist., Tx., U.S. D3 150
Lyndon B. Johnson Space Center, sci., Tx., U.S. r14 150
Lyndon Center, Vt., U.S. B4 152
Lyndon Station, Wi., U.S. E4 156
Lyndonville, N.Y., U.S. B2 139
Lyndonville, Vt., U.S. B4 152
Lyndora, Pa., U.S. E2 145
Lyngdal, Nor. L10 6
Lyngen, Nor. G17 6
Lyngør, Nor. L11 6
Lynn, Al., U.S. A2 108
Lynn, Ar., U.S. A4 111
Lynn, In., U.S. D8 121
Lynn, Ma., U.S. B6 128
Lynn, co., Tx., U.S. C2 150
Lynn, Lake, res., W.V., U.S. B5 155
Lynn Canal, b., Ak., U.S. k22 109
Lynne, Fl., U.S. C5 116
Lynne Acres, Md., U.S. B4 127
Lynnfield, Ma., U.S. f11 128
Lynn Garden, Tn., U.S. C11 149
Lynn Garden, Tn., U.S. A9 149
Lynn Grove, Ky., U.S. f9 124
Lynn Haven, Fl., U.S. u16 116
Lynnhaven Roads, b., Va., U.S. k15 153
Lynnville, In., U.S. H3 121
Lynnville, Ia., U.S. C5 122
Lynnville, Tn., U.S. B4 149
Lynnwood, Wa., U.S. B3 154
Lyntupy, U.S.S.R. F9 26
Lynwood, Ca., U.S. n12 112
Lyon, Fr. G11 14
Lyon, Ms., U.S. A3 131
Lyon, co., Ia., U.S. A1 122
Lyon, co., Ks., U.S. D7 123
Lyon, co., Ky., U.S. C1 124
Lyon, co., Mn., U.S. F3 130
Lyon, co., Nv., U.S. D2 135
Lyon Creek, stm., Ks., U.S. D7 123
Lyon Mountain, N.Y., U.S. f11 139
Lyon Mountain, mtn., N.Y., U.S. f11 139
Lyonnais, Monts du, mts., Fr. G11 14
Lyons, Co., U.S. A5 113
Lyons, Ga., U.S. D4 117
Lyons, Il., U.S. k9 120
Lyons, In., U.S. G3 121
Lyons, Ks., U.S. D5 123
Lyons, Mi., U.S. F6 129
Lyons, Ne., U.S. C9 134
Lyons, N.Y., U.S. B3 139
Lyons, Oh., U.S. A1 142
Lyons, Or., U.S. C4 144
Lyons, S.D., U.S. D9 148
Lyons, Wi., U.S. n11 156
Lyons, stm., Austl. D3 68
Lyons Plains, Ct., U.S. E2 114
Lys (Leie), stm., Eur. B9 14
Lysite, Wy., U.S. C5 157
Lyster Station, Que., Can. C6 104
Lys'va, U.S.S.R. F9 22
Lytle, Tx., U.S. E3 150
Lytton, B.C., Can. D7 99
Lytton, Ia., U.S. B3 122

M

Ma, stm., Asia D8 40
Maalaea Bay, b., Hi., U.S. C5 118
Ma'alot-Tarshiḥa, Isr. B4 50
Ma'ān, Jord. H5 50
Ma'anshan, China D7 34
Maardu, U.S.S.R. B8 26
Ma'arrat an-Nu'mān, Syria D4 48
Maas (Meuse), stm., Eur. D5 10
Maaseik, Bel. F8 12
Maasmechelen, Bel. G8 12
Maastricht, Neth. G8 12
Maave, Moz. C12 66
Maba, China C7 34
Mababe Depression, depr., Bots. B7 66
Mabank, Tx., U.S. C4 150
Mabaruma, Guy. C13 84
Mabel, Mn., U.S. G7 130
Mabeleapodi, Bots. C6 66
Maben, Ms., U.S. B4 131
Mabeul, Tun. M5 18
Mableton, Ga., U.S. h7 117
Mabou, N.S., Can. C8 101
Mabrūk, Sud. M5 60
Mabscott, W.V., U.S. D3 155
Mabton, Wa., U.S. C5 154
Mabuasehube Game Reserve, Bots. E6 66
Mabuguai, China F1 34
Macachín, Arg. I7 80
Macaé, Braz. G8 79
Macajuba, Braz. B8 79
Macalister, stm., Austl. K6 70
Macalister, Mount, mtn., Austl. J8 70
Macão, Port. F3 16
Macapá, Braz. C8 76
Macará, Ec. J3 84
Macarani, Braz. C8 79
Macareo, Caño, mth., Ven. C12 84
Macas, Ec. I3 84
Macau, Braz. E11 76
Macau (Aomen), Macao M2 34
Macau, dep., Asia G9 30
Macauã, stm., Braz. C7 82
Macaúbas, Braz. B7 79
Macaya, Pic, mtn., Haiti E7 94
Maccan, N.S., Can. D5 101
MacClenny, Fl., U.S. B4 116
Macclesfield, Eng., U.K. H11 8
MacClesfield, N.C., U.S. B5 140
Macdhui, Ben, mtn., Afr. H8 66
MacDill Air Force Base, mil., Fl., U.S. E4 116
Macdonald, Man., Can. D2 100
Macdonald, W.V., U.S. D3 155
Macdonald Range, mts., B.C., Can. E10 99
MacDonnell Ranges, mts., Austl. D6 68
MacDowell Reservoir, res., N.H., U.S. E2 136
Macduff, Scot., U.K. D11 8
Macdui, Ben, mtn., Scot., U.K. D10 8
Mace, In., U.S. D4 121
Macedon, N.Y., U.S. B3 139
Macedonia, Ia., U.S. C2 122
Macedonia, Oh., U.S. A4 142
Macedonia, hist. reg., Eur. H6 20
Macedonia see Makedonija, state, Yugo. H5 20
Maceió, Braz. E11 76
Macenta, Gui. G5 64
Maceo, Col. D5 84
Maceo, Ky., U.S. C3 124
Macerata, Italy F8 18
Maces Bay, b., N.B., Can. D3 101
Macfarlane, Lake, l., Austl. H2 70
MacGregor, Man., Can. E2 100
Macha, Bol. H8 82
Machacamarca, Bol. H8 82
Machachi, Ec. H3 84
Machačkala, U.S.S.R. I7 22
Machadinho, stm., Braz. C10 82
Machado, Braz. F6 79
Machagai, Arg. D8 80
Machakos, Kenya B7 58
Machala, Ec. I3 84
Machalí, Chile H3 80
Machaneng, Bots. D8 66
Machang, China A7 32
Machangfu, China B7 40
Machaquilá, stm., Guat. A5 92
Machattie, Lake, l., Austl. E3 70
Machecoul, Fr. E5 14
Machias, Me., U.S. D5 126
Machias, N.Y., U.S. C2 139
Machias, stm., Me., U.S. D5 126
Machias, stm., Me., U.S. B4 126
Machias Bay, b., Me., U.S. D5 126
Machias Lakes, l., Me., U.S. C5 126
Machiasport, Me., U.S. D5 126
Machico, Port. M21 17a
Machilīpatnam (Bandar), India D6 46
Machiques, Ven. B6 84
Macho, Arroyo del, val., N.M., U.S. C4 138
Machupicchu, Peru E5 82
Machupicchu, hist., Peru E5 82
Machupo, stm., Bol. E9 82
Machynlleth, Wales, U.K. I10 8
Maciá, Arg. G9 80
Macintyre, stm., Austl. G8 70
Macintyre, stm., Austl. G9 70
Mack, Co., U.S. B2 113
Mackay, Austl. C8 70
Mackay, Id., U.S. F5 119
MacKay, stm., Alta., Can. A4 98
Mackay, Lake, l., Austl. D5 68
MacKenzie, B.C., Can. B6 99
Mackenzie, Guy. D13 84
Mackenzie, stm., N.W. Ter., Can. C6 96
Mackenzie Bay, b., Can. C5 96
Mackenzie Mountains, mts., Can. D7 96
Mackinac, co., Mi., U.S. B5 129
Mackinac, Straits of, strt., Mi., U.S. C6 129
Mackinac Bridge, Mi., U.S. C6 129
Mackinac Island, Mi., U.S. C6 129
Mackinac Island, i., Mi., U.S. C6 129
Mackinaw, Il., U.S. C4 120
Mackinaw, stm., Il., U.S. C4 120
Mackinaw City, Mi., U.S. C6 129
Mackinnon Road, Kenya B7 58
Macklin, Sask., Can. E1 105
Macks Creek, Mo., U.S. D5 132
Macksville, Austl. H10 70
Macksville, Ks., U.S. E5 123
Mackville, Ky., U.S. C4 124
Maclean, Austl. G10 70
Macleod, Lake, l., Austl. D2 68
Maclovia Herrera, Mex. C7 90
Macmillan, stm., Yukon, Can. D6 96
MacNutt, Sask., Can. F5 105
Macomb, Il., U.S. C3 120
Macomb, co., Mi., U.S. F8 129
Macomer, Italy I3 18
Mâcon, Fr. F11 14
Macon, Ar., U.S. C3 111
Macon, Ga., U.S. D3 117
Macon, Il., U.S. D5 120
Macon, Ms., U.S. B5 131
Macon, Mo., U.S. B5 132
Macon, Tn., U.S. B2 149
Macon, co., Al., U.S. C4 108
Macon, co., Ga., U.S. D2 117
Macon, co., Il., U.S. D4 120
Macon, co., Mo., U.S. B5 132
Macon, co., N.C., U.S. f9 140
Macon, co., Tn., U.S. A5 149
Macon, Bayou, stm., U.S. B4 125
Macorís, Cabo, c., Dom. Rep. E9 94
Macoun, Sask., Can. H4 105
Macoupin, co., Il., U.S. D4 120
Macoupin Creek, stm., Il., U.S. D3 120
Macquarie, stm., Austl. H7 70
Macquarie, stm., Austl. M7 70
Macquarie Harbour, b., Austl. N6 70
Macquarie Island, i., Austl. A8 73
Mac. Robertson Land, reg., Ant. B5 73
Macroom, Ire. J5 8
Macrorie, Sask., Can. F2 105
MacTier, Ont., Can. B5 103
Macuelizo, Hond. B6 92
Macujer, Col. G6 84
Macungie, Pa., U.S. E10 145
Macunqiao, China B5 34
Macuro, Ven. B12 84
Macusani, Peru F6 82
Macuspana, Mex. I13 90
Macusse, Ang. A5 66
Macy, In., U.S. C5 121
Macy, Ne., U.S. B9 134
Mad, stm., Ca., U.S. B2 112
Mad, stm., Ct., U.S. B3 114
Mad, stm., N.H., U.S. C3 136
Mad, stm., Oh., U.S. C2 142
Mad, stm., Vt., U.S. C3 152
Ma'dabā, Jord. E5 50
Madagascar (Madagasikara), ctry., Afr. E9 58
Madā'in Ṣāliḥ, Sau. Ar. H4 48
Madame, Isle, i., N.S., Can. D9 101
Madanapalle, India F5 46
Madang, Pap. N. Gui. m16 68a
Mādārīpur, Bngl. I14 44
Madawaska, Ont., Can. B7 103
Madawaska, Me., U.S. A4 126
Madawaska, stm., Can. B9 104
Madawaska, stm., Ont., Can. B7 103
Madawaska Lake, l., Me., U.S. A4 126
Maddaloni, Italy H9 18
Madden, Ms., U.S. C4 131
Maddock, N.D., U.S. B6 141
Madeira, Oh., U.S. o13 142
Madeira, i., Port. M21 17a
Madeira, stm., S.A. E6 76
Madeira, Arquipélago da, is., Port. M21 17a
Madeirinha, stm., Braz. C11 82
Madeirinha, Paraná, mth., Braz. I13 84
M'adel', U.S.S.R. G9 26
Mädelegabel, mtn., Eur. E17 14
Madeleine, Îles de la, is., Que., Can. B8 101
Madelia, Mn., U.S. F4 130
Madeline Island, i., Wi., U.S. B3 156
Maden, Tur. B5 48
Madera, Mex. C5 90
Madera, Ca., U.S. D3 112
Madera, Pa., U.S. E5 145
Madera, co., Ca., U.S. D4 112
Maderas, Volcán, vol., Nic. F9 92
Madhubani, India G12 44
Madhya Pradesh, state, India I8 44
Madibogo, S. Afr. F7 66
Madidi, stm., Bol. E8 82
Madill, Ok., U.S. C5 143
Madimba, Zaire B3 58
Madina do Boé, Gui.-B. F2 64
Madinani, I.C. G6 64
Madīnat ash-Sha'b (Al-Ittiḥad), Yemen H4 47
Madingou, Congo B2 58
Madirobe, Madag. P22 67b
Madison, Al., U.S. A3 108
Madison, Ar., U.S. B5 111
Madison, Ct., U.S. D5 114
Madison, Fl., U.S. B3 116
Madison, Ga., U.S. C3 117
Madison, Il., U.S. E3 120
Madison, In., U.S. G7 121
Madison, Ks., U.S. D7 123
Madison, Me., U.S. D3 126
Madison, Mn., U.S. E2 130
Madison, Ms., U.S. C3 131
Madison, Mo., U.S. B5 132
Madison, Ne., U.S. C8 134
Madison, N.H., U.S. C4 136
Madison, N.J., U.S. B4 137
Madison, N.C., U.S. A3 140
Madison, Oh., U.S. A4 142
Madison, S.D., U.S. C8 148
Madison, Va., U.S. B4 153
Madison, W.V., U.S. C3 155
Madison, Wi., U.S. E4 156
Madison, co., Al., U.S. A3 108
Madison, co., Ar., U.S. B2 111
Madison, co., Fl., U.S. B3 116
Madison, co., Ga., U.S. B3 117
Madison, co., Id., U.S. F7 119
Madison, co., Il., U.S. E4 120
Madison, co., In., U.S. D6 121
Madison, co., Ia., U.S. C3 122
Madison, co., Ky., U.S. C5 124
Madison, co., La., U.S. B4 125
Madison, co., Ms., U.S. C4 131
Madison, co., Mo., U.S. D7 132
Madison, co., Mt., U.S. E5 133
Madison, co., Ne., U.S. C8 134
Madison, co., N.Y., U.S. C5 139
Madison, co., N.C., U.S. f10 140
Madison, co., Oh., U.S. C2 142
Madison, co., Tn., U.S. B3 149
Madison, co., Tx., U.S. D5 150
Madison, co., Va., U.S. B4 153
Madison, stm., Mt., U.S. E5 133
Madison Heights, Mi., U.S. o15 129
Madison Heights, Va., U.S. C3 153
Madison Lake, Mn., U.S. F5 130
Madison Range, mts., Mt., U.S. E5 133
Madisonville, Ky., U.S. C2 124
Madisonville, La., U.S. D5 125
Madisonville, Tn., U.S. D9 149
Madisonville, Tx., U.S. D5 150
Madiun, Indon. J15 39a
Madoc, Ont., Can. C7 103
Madoi, China E6 30
Madol, Sud. M4 60
Madona, U.S.S.R. E9 26
Madougou, Mali D8 64
Madrakah, Sau. Ar. D1 47
Madrakah, Ra's al-, c., Oman E10 47
Madras, India G11 42
Madras, Or., U.S. C5 144
Madras see Tamil Nādu, state, India G5 46
Madre, Laguna, b., Mex. E11 90
Madre, Laguna, b., Tx., U.S. F4 150
Madre, Sierra, mts., Phil. M20 39b
Madre de Chiapas, Sierra, mts., N.A. B2 92
Madre de Dios, dept., Peru D6 82
Madre de Dios, stm., S.A. D8 82
Madre de Dios, Isla, i., Chile A12 73
Madre de Dios, Isla, i., Chile J7 74
Madre del Sur, Sierra, mts., Mex. I10 90
Madre Occidental, Sierra, mts., Mex. E6 90
Madre Oriental, Sierra, mts., Mex. F9 90
Madre Vieja, stm., Guat. C3 92
Madrid, Col. E5 84
Madrid, Spain E8 16
Madrid, Al., U.S. D4 108
Madrid, Ia., U.S. C4 122
Madrid, Ne., U.S. D4 134
Madrid, N.Y., U.S. f9 139
Madrid, prov., Spain E8 16
Madridejos, Spain F8 16
Madriz, dept., Nic. D8 92
Madura, i., Indon. J16 39a
Madurai, India H5 46
Maebashi, Japan K14 36
Mae Hong Son, Thai. E4 40
Mae Klong, stm., Thai. G5 40
Maengsan, N. Kor. D14 32
Mae Sariang, Thai. E4 40
Maeser, Ut., U.S. C6 151
Mae Sot, Thai. F5 40
Maesteg, Wales, U.K. J10 8
Maestra, Sierra, mts., Cuba D6 94
Maevatanana, Madag. P22 67b
Mafeking, Man., Can. C1 100
Mafeteng, Leso. G8 66
Maffra, Austl. K7 70
Mafia Island, i., Tan. C7 58
Mafikeng, Boph. G5 58
Mafikeng, S. Afr. E7 66
Mafra, Braz. D14 80
Magadan, U.S.S.R. F22 24
Magadi, Kenya B7 58
Magalia, Ca., U.S. C3 112
Magallanes, Phil. O20 39b
Magallanes, Estrecho de (Strait of Magellan), strt., S.A. G3 78
Magangué, Col. C5 84
Magazine, Ar., U.S. B2 111
Magazine Mountain, mtn., Ar., U.S. B2 111
Magburaka, S.L. G4 64
Magdagači, U.S.S.R. G17 24
Magdalena, Arg. H10 80
Magdalena, Bol. E9 82
Magdalena, Mex. G8 90
Magdalena, Peru B3 82
Magdalena, N.M., U.S. C2 138
Magdalena, dept., Col. B5 84
Magdalena, stm., Col. C5 84
Magdalena, stm., Mex. B4 90
Magdalena, Bahía, b., Mex. E3 90
Magdalena, Isla, i., Chile E2 78
Magdalena, Isla, i., Mex. E3 90
Magdalena, Punta, c., Col. F4 84
Magdalena de Kino, Mex. B4 90
Magdalena Mountains, mts., N.M., U.S. D2 138
Magdeburg, Ger. C11 10
Magé, Braz. G7 79
Magee, Ms., U.S. D4 131
Magelang, Indon. J15 39a
Magellan, Strait of see Magallanes, Estrecho de, strt., S.A. G3 78
Magenta, Italy D3 18
Maggia, Switz. F10 13
Maggie Creek, stm., Nv., U.S. C5 135
Maggiore, Lago, l., Eur. C3 18
Maghāghah, Egypt C6 60
Maghama, Maur. D3 64
Maghniyya, Alg. C10 62
Magic Reservoir, res., Id., U.S. F4 119
Magione, Italy F7 18
Maglaj, Yugo. E2 20
Magna, Ut., U.S. C3 151
Magness, Ar., U.S. B4 111
Magnetawan, Ont., Can. B5 103
Magnetawan, stm., Ont., Can. B4 103
Magnet Cove, Ar., U.S. C3 111
Magnitogorsk, U.S.S.R. G9 22
Magnolia, Ar., U.S. D2 111
Magnolia, De., U.S. D4 115
Magnolia, Il., U.S. B4 120
Magnolia, Ia., U.S. C2 122
Magnolia, Ky., U.S. C4 124
Magnolia, Mn., U.S. G2 130
Magnolia, Ms., U.S. D3 131
Magnolia, N.C., U.S. C4 140
Magnolia, Oh., U.S. B4 142
Magnolia, Tx., U.S. D5 150
Magnolia Springs, Al., U.S. E2 108
Magoffin, co., Ky., U.S. C6 124
Magog, Que., Can. D5 104
Magothy River, b., Md., U.S. B4 127
Magozal, Mex. G11 90
Magpie, stm., Que., Can. h8 102
Magrath, Alta., Can. E4 98
Magruder Mountain, mtn., Nv., U.S. F4 135
Maguari, Cabo, c., Braz. D9 76
Maguzhan, China E13 44
Magway, Burma D3 40
Mahābād, Iran C8 48
Mahābaleshwar, India F9 42
Mahabe, Madag. P21 67b
Mahābhārat Lek, mts., Nepal F10 44
Mahabo, Madag. S22 67b
Mahabo, Madag. R21 67b
Mahaicony Village, Guy. D14 84
Mahajamba, Helodranon' i, b., Madag. O22 67b
Mahajanga, Madag. O22 67b
Mahākālī (Sārda), stm., Asia F9 44
Mahakam, stm., Indon. E6 38
Mahalatswe, Bots. D8 66
Mahallāt, Iran E11 48
Mahanoro, Madag. Q23 67b
Mahanoy City, Pa., U.S. E9 145
Mahārāshtra, state, India C3 46
Maha Sarakham, Thai. F7 40
Mahaska, co., Ia., U.S. C5 122
Mahasoa, Madag. S22 67b
Mahasolo, Madag. Q22 67b
Mahates, Col. B5 84
Mahatsinjo, Madag. R21 67b
Mahaṭṭat al-Hafīf, Jord. D8 50
Mahbūbnagar, India D4 46
Mahd adh-Dhahab, Sau. Ar. C2 47
Mahdia, Tun. N6 18
Mahe, India G3 46
Mahébourg, Mrts. V18 67c
Mahé Island, i., Sey. B11 58
Mahendra Giri, mtn., India C8 46
Mahesāna, India I5 44
Mahia Peninsula, pen., N.Z. C7 72
Mahned, Ms., U.S. D4 131
Mahnomen, Mn., U.S. C3 130
Mahnomen, co., Mn., U.S. C3 130
Mahoba, India H8 44
Mahogany Mountain, mtn., Or., U.S. D9 144
Mahomet, Il., U.S. C5 120
Mahone Bay, N.S., Can. E5 101
Mahoning, co., Oh., U.S. B5 142
Mahoning, stm., U.S. A5 142
Mahoosuc Range, mts., N.H., U.S. B4 136
Mahopac, N.Y., U.S. D7 139
Mahres, Tun. C16 62
Mahtowa, Mn., U.S. D6 130
Mahuva, India B1 46
Mahwah, N.J., U.S. A4 137
Mai Aini, Eth. J10 60
Maicao, Col. B6 84
Maîche, Fr. E13 14
Maici, stm., Braz. B11 82
Maicurú, stm., Braz. D8 76
Maiden, N.C., U.S. B1 140
Maidenhead, Eng., U.K. J13 8
Maidstone, Sask., Can. D1 105
Maidstone, Eng., U.K. J14 8
Maidstone Lake, l., Vt., U.S. B5 152
Maidsville, W.V., U.S. B5 155
Maiduguri, Nig. F9 54
Maienfeld, Switz. D12 13
Maigatari, Nig. E14 64
Maignelay, Fr. C9 14
Maili, Hi., U.S. g9 118
Maili Point, c., Hi., U.S. g9 118
Maillezais, Fr. F6 14
Mai Mefales, Eth. J10 60
Main, stm., Ger. F9 10
Main-à-Dieu, N.S., Can. C10 101
Mainart, stm., Braz. F7 79
Main Channel, strt., Ont., Can. B3 103
Mai-Ndombe, Lac, l., Zaire B3 58
Maine, N.Y., U.S. C4 139
Maine, hist. reg., Fr. D6 14
Maine, state, U.S. C3 126
Maine, Gulf of, b., N.A. C13 106
Maine-et-Loire, dept., Fr. E6 14
Mainhardt, Ger. F9 10
Mainland, i., Scot., U.K. B10 8
Mainland, i., Scot., U.K. A12 8
Main Pass, strt., La., U.S. E6 125
Mainpuri, India G8 44
Maintenon, Fr. D8 14
Maintirano, Madag. Q21 67b
Main Topsail, mtn., Newf., Can. D3 102
Mainz, Ger. E8 10
Maio, i., C.V. m17 64a
Maipo, stm., Chile G3 80
Maipo, Volcán, vol., S.A. H4 80
Maipú, Arg. I10 80
Maipú, Arg. G4 80
Maipú, Chile G3 80
Maiquetía, Ven. B9 84
Mairipotaba, Braz. D4 79
Maisonnette, N.B., Can. B4 101
Maitengwe, Bots. C8 66
Maitengwe, stm., Afr. C8 66
Maitland, Austl. J2 70
Maitland, Austl. I9 70
Maitland, N.S., Can. D6 101
Maitland, Ont., Can. C9 103
Maitland, Mo., U.S. A2 132
Maíz, stm., Nic. F10 92
Maíz, Islas del, is., Nic. E11 92
Maize, Ks., U.S. g12 123
Maizuru, Japan L10 36
Maja, stm., U.S.S.R. F18 24
Majagual, Col. C5 84
Majaki, U.S.S.R. C14 20
Majari, stm., Braz. F12 84
Majestic, Ky., U.S. C7 124
Maji, Eth. N8 60
Majia, China C7 34
Majie, China B7 40
Majja, U.S.S.R. E18 24
Majkain, U.S.S.R. G13 22
Majkop, U.S.S.R. I6 22
Major, Sask., Can. F1 105
Major, co., Ok., U.S. A3 143
Majorca see Mallorca, i., Spain F15 16
Maka, Sen. E2 64
Makabana, Congo B2 58
Makaha, Hi., U.S. g9 118
Makaha Point, c., Hi., U.S. A2 118
Makah Indian Reservation, Wa., U.S. A1 154
Makahuena Point, c., Hi., U.S. B2 118
Makakilo City, Hi., U.S. g9 118
Makalamabedi, Bots. C6 66
Makallé, Arg. D9 80
Makālu, mtn., Asia G12 44
Makanda, Il., U.S. F4 120
Makanza, Zaire A3 58
Makapala, Hi., U.S. C6 118
Makapuu Head, c., Hi., U.S. B4 118
Makarjev, U.S.S.R. D26 26
Makarov, U.S.S.R. H20 24
Makarska, Yugo. F12 18
Makasar, Selat (Makassar Strait), strt., Indon. F6 38
Makassar Strait see Makasar, Selat, strt., Indon. F6 38
Makat, U.S.S.R. H8 22
Makawao, Hi., U.S. C5 118
Makaweli, Hi., U.S. B2 118
Makedonija, state, Yugo. H5 20
Makejevka, U.S.S.R. H5 22
Makeni, S.L. G3 64
Makgadikgadi, pl., Bots. C7 66
Makgadikgadi Pans Game Reserve, Bots. C7 66
Makhfar al-Quwayrah, Jord. I4 50
Makhfar Ramn, Jord. I4 50
Makhrūq, Wādī al-, val., Asia F7 50
Makindu, Kenya B7 58
Makinsk, U.S.S.R. G12 22
M'akiševo, U.S.S.R. E11 26
M'akit, U.S.S.R. E22 24
Makkah (Mecca), Sau. Ar. D1 47
Makkovik, Newf., Can. g10 102
Makó, Hung. I20 10
Makokou, Gabon A2 58
Makoti, N.D., U.S. B4 141
Makoua, Congo A3 58
Makrāna, India G6 44
Makran Coast, Asia I16 48
M'aksa, U.S.S.R. C21 26
Maksaticha, U.S.S.R. D18 26
Makthar, Tun. N4 18
Mākū, Iran B8 48
Makumbi, Zaire C4 58
Makung (P'enghu), Tai. L8 34
Makurdi, Nig. H14 64
Makushin Volcano, vol., Ak., U.S. E6 109
Makwassie, S. Afr. F8 66
Mal, Maur. C3 64
Mala, Peru E3 82
Mala, stm., Peru E3 82
Mala, Punta, c., Pan. D3 84
Malabang, Phil. D7 38
Malabar, Fl., U.S. D6 116
Malabar Coast, India F3 46
Malabo, Eq. Gui. J14 64
Malacacheta, Braz. D7 79
Malacca, Strait of, strt., Asia M6 40
Malacky, Czech. G17 10
Malad City, Id., U.S. G6 119
Málaga, Col. D6 84
Málaga, Spain I7 16
Malaga, N.J., U.S. D2 137
Malaga, N.M., U.S. E5 138
Malagash, N.S., Can. D6 101
Malagasy Republic see Madagascar, ctry., Afr. E9 58
Malagón, Spain F8 16
Malaimbandy, Madag. R21 67b
Malaja Kuril'skaja Gr'ada (Habomai-Shotō), is., U.S.S.R. D21 36a
Malaja Višera, U.S.S.R. C15 26
Malakāl, Sud. M6 60
Malakoff, Tx., U.S. C4 150
Malān, Burma B4 40
Malang, Indon. J16 39a
Malanggwā, Nepal G11 44
Malanje, Ang. C3 58
Malanville, Benin F11 64
Malanzán, Arg. F5 80
Mälaren, l., Swe. L15 6
Malargüe, Arg. H4 80
Malartic, Que., Can. k11 104
Malaspina Glacier, Ak., U.S. D11 109
Malatya, Tur. B5 48
Malaut, India E6 44
Malawi, ctry., Afr. D6 58
Malawi, Lake see Nyasa, Lake, l., Afr. D6 58
Malaybalay, Phil. D8 38
Malāyer, Iran D10 48
Malay Peninsula, pen., Asia K6 40
Malay Reef, rf., Austl. A8 70
Malaysia, ctry., Asia E3 38
Malazgirt, Tur. B7 48
Malbaie, stm., Que., Can. B7 104
Malbork, Pol. A19 10
Malbrán, Arg. E7 80
Malcolm, Austl. E4 68
Malcolm, Ne., U.S. D9 134
Malcom, Ia., U.S. C5 122
Maldegem, Bel. F3 12
Malden, Il., U.S. B4 120
Malden, Ma., U.S. B5 128
Malden, Mo., U.S. E8 132
Malden, W.V., U.S. m12 155
Maldive Islands, is., Mald. I2 46
Maldives, ctry., Asia I8 28
Maldonado, Ur. H11 80
Malé, Italy C5 18
Male, Mald. I8 28
Maléa, Ákra, c., Grc. M7 20
Mālegaon, India B3 46
Malek, Sud. N6 60

Name — Map Ref. — Page

Malek Sīāh, Kūh-e, mtn., Asia G16 48
Malema, Moz. D7 58
Malen'ga, U.S.S.R. J25 6
Māler Kotla, India E6 44
Malesherbes, Fr. D9 14
Malestroit, Fr. E4 14
Malha Wells, Sud. J4 60
Malheur, co., Or., U.S. D9 144
Malheur, stm., Or., U.S. D9 144
Malheur Lake, l., Or., U.S. D8 144
Mali, ctry., Afr. E6 54
Mali, stm., Burma A4 40
Malibu, Ca., U.S. m11 112
Malik, Wādī al-, val., Sud. I6 60
Mali Kyun, i., Burma H5 40
Malin, Or., U.S. E5 144
Malinalco, hist., Mex. H10 90
Malinaltepec, Mex. I10 90
Malines (Mechelen), Bel. F5 12
Malin Head, c., Ire. F6 8
Maliwun, Burma I5 40
Maljamar, N.M., U.S. E6 138
Malka, U.S.S.R. G23 24
Malkāpur, India B4 46
Malkara, Tur. I10 20
Mallāh, Syria C7 50
Mallaig, Alta., Can. B5 98
Mallaig, Scot., U.K. D8 8
Mallala, Austl. J3 70
Mallaoua, Niger E14 64
Mallard, Ia., U.S. B3 122
Mallawī, Egypt D6 60
Mallet, Braz. C13 80
Malletts Bay, b., Vt., U.S. B2 152
Malligasta, Arg. E5 80
Mallnitz, Aus. I13 10
Mallorca, i., Spain F15 16
Mallow, Ire. I5 8
Malmédy, Bel. H9 12
Malmesbury, S. Afr. I4 66
Malmö, Swe. N13 6
Malmo, Ne., U.S. C9 134
Malmöhus Län, co., Swe. N13 6
Malmstrom Air Force Base, mil., Mt., U.S. C5 133
Maloarchangel'sk, U.S.S.R. I19 26
Maloja, Switz. F12 13
Malojaroslavec, U.S.S.R. F19 26
Maloje Kozino, U.S.S.R. E26 26
Maloje Skuratovo, U.S.S.R. H20 26
Malolos, Phil. N19 39b
Malone, Fl., U.S. B1 116
Malone, N.Y., U.S. f10 139
Malone, Wa., U.S. C2 154
Maloney Reservoir, res., Ne., U.S. C5 134
Malonga, Zaire D4 58
Małopolska, reg., Pol. E21 10
Malošujka, U.S.S.R. E5 22
Malott, Wa., U.S. A6 154
Måløy, Nor. K9 6
Malpaisillo, Nic. E8 92
Malpas, Austl. J4 70
Malpelo, Isla de, i., Col. C2 76
Malpeque Bay, b., P.E.I., Can. C6 101
Malta, U.S.S.R. E10 26
Malta, Id., U.S. G5 119
Malta, Il., U.S. B5 120
Malta, Mt., U.S. B9 133
Malta, Oh., U.S. C4 142
Malta, ctry., Eur. H10 4
Malta, i., Malta N9 18
Malta Bend, Mo., U.S. B4 132
Malta Channel, strt., Eur. M9 18
Maltahöhe, Nmb. E3 66
Maltepe, Tur. I11 20
Maluku (Moluccas), is., Indon. F8 38
Maluku, Laut (Molucca Sea), Indon. F7 38
Malumfashi, Nig. F13 64
Malvern, Al., U.S. D4 108
Malvern, Ar., U.S. C3 111
Malvern, Ia., U.S. D2 122
Malvern, Oh., U.S. B4 142
Malvern, Pa., U.S. o19 145
Malverne, N.Y., U.S. k13 139
Malvinas, Arg. E9 80
Malwal, Sud. M6 60
Malý Dunaj, stm., Czech. H17 10
Malyj, ostrov, i., U.S.S.R. A11 26
Malyj An'uj, stm., U.S.S.R. D24 24
Malyj Jenisej, stm., U.S.S.R. G11 24
Malyj Kavkaz, mts., U.S.S.R. I6 22
Malyj Tajmyr, ostrov, i., U.S.S.R. B13 24
Malyj T'uters, ostrov, i., U.S.S.R. B9 26
Malyj Uzen', stm., U.S.S.R. H7 22
Malyševo, U.S.S.R. D18 26
Mamala Bay, b., Hi., U.S. g10 118
Mamara, Peru F5 82
Mamaroneck, N.Y., U.S. h13 139
Mambaí, Braz. C5 79
Mamberamo, stm., Indon. F10 38
Mambéré, stm., Cen. Afr. Rep. H4 56
Ma-Me-O Beach, Alta., Can. C4 98
Mamers, Fr. D7 14
Mamfe, Cam. G8 54
Mamiá, Lago, l., Braz. J11 84
Mamiña, Chile I7 82
Mammoth, Az., U.S. E5 110
Mammoth, W.V., U.S. C3 155
Mammoth Cave National Park, Ky., U.S. C4 124
Mammoth Lakes, Ca., U.S. D4 112
Mammoth Spring, Ar., U.S. A4 111
Mamonovo, U.S.S.R. G2 26
Mamoré, stm., S.A. D9 82
Mamori, Lago, l., Braz. I12 84
Mamoriá, stm., Braz. B8 82
Mamoritanas, stm., Braz. H9 84
Mamou, Gui. F3 64
Mamou, La., U.S. D3 125
Mamoutzou, May. L16 67a
Mampikony, Madag. P22 67b
Mamry, Jezioro, l., Pol. A21 10
Mamuchi, China H6 32
Ma'mūn, Sud. K2 60
Mamuno, Bots. D5 66
Mamuru, stm., Braz. I14 84
Man, I.C. H6 64
Man, W.V., U.S. D3 155
Mana, stm., Fr. Gu. B8 76
Manabí, prov., Ec. H2 84
Manacá, stm., Braz. I11 84
Manacacías, stm., Col. F6 84
Manacapuru, Braz. I12 84
Manacor, Spain F15 16
Manado, Indon. E7 38
Managua, Nic. E8 92
Managua, dept., Nic. E8 92
Managua, Lago de, l., Nic. E8 92
Manahawkin, N.J., U.S. D4 137
Manakara, Madag. S23 67b
Manakin, Va., U.S. C5 153
Manāli, India C10 42
Manama see Al-Manāmah, Bahr. H11 48
Manambato, Madag. N23 67b
Manambolosy, Madag. P23 67b
Mánamo, Caño, mth., Ven. C11 84
Manana Island, i., Hi., U.S. g11 118
Mananara, Madag. P23 67b
Mananjary, Madag. R23 67b
Manantenina, Madag. T22 67b
Manantico Creek, stm., N.J., U.S. E3 137
Manapiare, stm., Ven. E9 84
Manapire, stm., Ven. C9 84
Mana Point, c., Hi., U.S. A2 118
Manaquiri, Lago, l., Braz. I12 84
Manaravolo, Madag. S21 67b
Manas, China C4 30
Manās, stm., Asia G14 44
Manas Hu, l., China B4 30
Manāslu, mtn., Nepal F11 44
Manasquan, N.J., U.S. C4 137
Manasquan, stm., N.J., U.S. C4 137
Manassa, Co., U.S. D5 113
Manassas, Ga., U.S. D4 117
Manassas, Va., U.S. B5 153
Manassas National Battlefield Park, Va., U.S. g11 153
Manassas Park, Va., U.S. B5 153
Manatee, co., Fl., U.S. E4 116
Manatee, stm., Fl., U.S. E4 116
Manatí, Col. B5 84
Manatí, P.R. E11 94
Manaung, Burma E2 40
Manaus, Braz. I12 84
Manawa, Wi., U.S. D5 156
Manbij, Syria C4 48
Mancelona, Mi., U.S. D5 129
Manchac, Bayou, stm., La., U.S. h10 125
Mancha Real, Spain H8 16
Manchaug, Ma., U.S. B4 128
Manche, dept., Fr. C5 14
Manchester, Eng., U.K. H11 8
Manchester, Ct., U.S. B5 114
Manchester, Ga., U.S. D2 117
Manchester, Il., U.S. D3 120
Manchester, Ia., U.S. B6 122
Manchester, Ky., U.S. C6 124
Manchester, Me., U.S. D3 126
Manchester, Md., U.S. A4 127
Manchester, Ma., U.S. A6 128
Manchester, Mi., U.S. F6 129
Manchester, Mo., U.S. f12 132
Manchester, N.H., U.S. E4 136
Manchester, N.Y., U.S. C3 139
Manchester, Oh., U.S. D2 142
Manchester, Pa., U.S. F8 145
Manchester, Tn., U.S. B5 149
Manchester, Vt., U.S. E2 152
Manchester Center, Vt., U.S. E2 152
Manchón, Guat. C2 92
Manchuria, hist. reg., China B12 30
Máncora, Peru J2 84
Mancos, Co., U.S. D2 113
Mancos, stm., U.S. D2 113
Mandabe, Madag. R21 67b
Mandaguaçu, Braz. G2 79
Mandaguari, Braz. G3 79
Mandal, Nor. L10 6
Mandala, Puncak, mtn., Indon. F11 38
Mandalay, Burma C4 40
Mandalgov', Mong. B8 30
Mandalī, Iraq E8 48
Mandan, N.D., U.S. C5 141
Mandara Mountains, mts., Afr. F9 54
Mandaree, N.D., U.S. B3 141
Mandas, Italy J4 18
Mandeb, Bab el, strt. H3 47
Mandel, Afg. E16 48
Manderson, S.D., U.S. D3 148
Manderson, Wy., U.S. B5 157
Mandeville, Jam. E6 94
Mandeville, Ar., U.S. D2 111
Mandeville, La., U.S. D5 125
Mandi, India E7 44
Mandiana, Gui. F5 64
Mandimba, Moz. D7 58
Mandinga, Pan. C3 84
Mandioli, Pulau, i., Indon. F8 38
Mandioré, Lagoa, l., S.A. H13 82
Mandla, India A6 46
Mandoto, Madag. Q22 67b
Mandouri, Togo F10 64
Mandra, Pak. D5 44
Mandritsara, Madag. O23 67b
Mandronarivo, Madag. R21 67b
Mandsaur, India H6 44
Manduri, Braz. G4 79
Manduria, Italy I12 18
Māndvi, India I3 44
Mandya, India F4 46
Manfalūt, Egypt D6 60
Manfredonia, Italy H10 18
Manfredonia, Golfo di, b., Italy H11 18
Manga, Braz. C7 79
Manga, Burkina F9 64
Mangabeiras, Chapada das, hills, Braz. F9 76
Mangalagiri, India D6 46
Mangalore, India F3 46
Mangaoka, Madag. N23 67b
Mangchang, China F8 30
Mange, China D10 44
Mange, S.L. G3 64
Mangham, La., U.S. B4 125
Manglares, Cabo, c., Col. G3 84
Mangochi, Mwi. D7 58
Mangoky, stm., Madag. R21 67b
Mangole, Pulau, i., Indon. F8 38
Mangoupa, Cen. Afr. Rep. O3 60
Mangrol, India J4 44
Mangrove Cay, i., Bah. B6 94
Mangueira, Lagoa, b., Braz. G12 80
Mangueirinha, Braz. C12 80
Mangulile, Hond. B8 92
Mangum, Ok., U.S. C2 143
Mangya, China D5 30
Manhattan, Ks., U.S. C7 123
Manhattan, Mt., U.S. E5 133
Manhattan Beach, Ca., U.S. n12 112
Manhattan Island, i., N.Y., U.S. h13 139
Manheim, Pa., U.S. F9 145
Manhuaçu, Braz. F7 79
Manhuaçu, stm., Braz. E8 79
Manhumirim, Braz. F8 79
Maniago, Italy C7 18
Maniamba, Moz. D7 58
Manicauá-Miçu, stm., Braz. A1 79
Manicoré, Braz. A11 82
Manicoré, stm., Braz. B11 82
Manicouagan, Réservoir, res., Que., Can. h13 104
Manignan, I.C. F6 64
Manigotagan, Man., Can. D3 100
Manila, Phil. N19 39b
Manila, Ar., U.S. B5 111
Manila, Ut., U.S. C6 151
Manila Bay, b., Phil. N19 39b
Manilla, Austl. H9 70
Manilla, In., U.S. E6 121
Manilla, Ia., U.S. C2 122
Manily, U.S.S.R. E25 24
Manimpé, Mali D7 64
Manino, U.S.S.R. H17 26
Manipur, state, India H15 44
Manipur, stm., Asia C2 40
Manisa, Tur. K11 20
Manistee, Mi., U.S. D4 129
Manistee, co., Mi., U.S. D4 129
Manistee, stm., Mi., U.S. D5 129
Manistique, Mi., U.S. C4 129
Manistique, stm., Mi., U.S. B4 129
Manistique Lake, l., Mi., U.S. B5 129
Manito, Il., U.S. C4 120
Manitoba, prov., Can. C3 100
Manitoba, Lake, l., Man., Can. D2 100
Manitou, Man., Can. E2 100
Manitou, Ok., U.S. C3 143
Manitou, stm., Ont., Can. E5 100
Manitou, Lake, l., Ont., Can. B3 103
Manitou Beach, Sask., Can. F3 105
Manitou Island, i., Mi., U.S. A3 129
Manitou Lake, l., Ont., Can. A6 103
Manitou Lake, l., Sask., Can. E1 105
Manitoulin Island, i., Ont., Can. B2 103
Manitou Springs, Co., U.S. C6 113
Manitowaning, Ont., Can. B3 103
Manitowoc, Wi., U.S. D6 156
Manitowoc, co., Wi., U.S. D6 156
Manitowoc, stm., Wi., U.S. h10 156
Manitowoc, North Branch, stm., Wi., U.S. h9 156
Manitowoc, South Branch, stm., Wi., U.S. k9 156
Maniwaki, Que., Can. C2 104
Manizales, Col. E5 84
Manja, Madag. R21 67b
Manjacaze, Moz. E11 66
Manjakandriana, Madag. Q22 67b
Manjimup, Austl. F3 68
Mankato, Ks., U.S. C5 123
Mankato, Mn., U.S. F5 130
Mankayane, Swaz. F10 66
Mankota, Sask., Can. H2 105
Manley, Ne., U.S. h12 134
Manlius, Il., U.S. B4 120
Manlius, N.Y., U.S. C5 139
Manlleu, Spain C14 16
Manly, Ia., U.S. A4 122
Manmād, India B3 46
Mannahill, Austl. I3 70
Mannar, Gulf of, b., Asia H5 46
Mannārgudi, India G5 46
Männedorf, Switz. D10 13
Mannford, Ok., U.S. A5 143
Mannheim, Ger. F8 10
Manni, China C12 44
Manning, Alta., Can. A2 98
Manning, Ia., U.S. C2 122
Manning, S.C., U.S. D7 147
Mannington, Ky., U.S. C2 124
Mannington, W.V., U.S. B4 155
Manns Creek, stm., W.V., U.S. n14 155
Manns Harbor, N.C., U.S. B7 140
Mannsville, Ok., U.S. C5 143
Mannum, Austl. J3 70
Mannville, Alta., Can. C5 98
Mano, stm., Afr. H4 64
Manoa, Bol. C9 82
Manokin, stm., Md., U.S. D6 127
Manokotak, Ak., U.S. D8 109
Manombo, Madag. S20 67b
Manomet, Ma., U.S. C6 128
Manomet Hill, hill, Ma., U.S. C6 128
Manomet Point, c., Ma., U.S. C6 128
Manono, Zaire C5 58
Manor, Sask., Can. H4 105
Manor, Ga., U.S. E4 117
Manor, Tx., U.S. D4 150
Manosque, Fr. I12 14
Manouane, Lac, l., Que., Can. h12 104
Manp'o, N. Kor. B14 32
Manresa, Spain D13 16
Mānsa, India F6 44
Mansa, Zam. D5 58
Manseau, Que., Can. C5 104
Mansel Island, i., N.W. Ter., Can. D17 96
Mansfield, Austl. K7 70
Mansfield, Ar., U.S. B1 111
Mansfield, Ga., U.S. C3 117
Mansfield, Il., U.S. C5 120
Mansfield, La., U.S. B2 125
Mansfield, Ma., U.S. B5 128
Mansfield, Mo., U.S. D5 132
Mansfield, Oh., U.S. B3 142
Mansfield, Pa., U.S. C7 145
Mansfield, S.D., U.S. B7 148
Mansfield, Tn., U.S. A3 149
Mansfield, Tx., U.S. n9 150
Mansfield, Wa., U.S. B6 154
Mansfield, Mount, mtn., Vt., U.S. B3 152
Mansfield Center, Ct., U.S. B7 114
Mansfield Depot, Ct., U.S. B6 114
Mansfield Hollow Lake, res., Ct., U.S. B7 114
Mansión, C.R. G9 92
Mansle, Fr. G7 14
Manso, stm., Braz. B5 79
Manso, stm., Braz. F13 82
Manson, Ia., U.S. B3 122
Manson, Wa., U.S. B5 154
Manson Creek, B.C., Can. B5 99
Mansonville, Que., Can. D5 104
Mansura, La., U.S. C3 125
Mansura see Al-Manṣūrah, Egypt B6 60
Manta, Ec. H2 84
Manta, Bahía de, b., Ec. H2 84
Mantachie, Ms., U.S. A5 131
Mantador, N.D., U.S. C9 141
Mantaro, stm., Peru E4 82
Manteca, Ca., U.S. D3 112
Mantecal, Ven. D8 84
Manteno, Il., U.S. B6 120
Manteo, N.C., U.S. B7 140
Manter, Ks., U.S. E2 123
Mantes-la-Jolie, Fr. D8 14
Manti, Ut., U.S. D4 151
Mantiqueira, Serra da, mts., Braz. G6 79
Manton, Mi., U.S. D5 129
Mantorville, Mn., U.S. F6 130
Mantos Blancos, Chile B3 80
Mantova, Italy D5 18
Mantua, Cuba C2 94
Mantua, N.J., U.S. D2 137
Mantua, Oh., U.S. A4 142
Mantua, Ut., U.S. B4 151
Mantua see Mantova, Italy D5 18
Manturovo, U.S.S.R. C27 26
Mäntyharju, Fin. K20 6
Manu, Peru E6 82
Manú, stm., Peru E6 82
Manua Islands, is., Am. Sam. J23 158
Manuel, Mex. F10 90
Manuel Antonio, Parque Nacional, C.R. H10 92
Manuel Benavides, Mex. C8 90
Manuel Derqui, Arg. D9 80
Manuel Ribas, Braz. C13 80
Manuel Urbano, Braz. C7 82
Manumuskin, stm., N.J., U.S. E3 137
Manupari, stm., Bol. D8 82
Manurimi, stm., Bol. E8 82
Manuripe (Manuripi), stm., S.A. D8 82
Manus Island, i., Pap. N. Gui. k16 68a
Manvel, N.D., U.S. A8 141
Manvel, Tx., U.S. r14 150
Manville, N.J., U.S. B3 137
Manville, R.I., U.S. B4 146
Manville, Wy., U.S. D8 157
Many, La., U.S. C2 125
Manyana, Bots. D5 66
Manyara, Lake, l., Tan. B7 58
Manyberries, Alta., Can. E5 98
Manyč, stm., U.S.S.R. H6 22
Many Farms, Az., U.S. A6 110
Manzanares, Spain F8 16
Manzanillo, Cuba D6 94
Manzanillo, Mex. H7 90
Manzanillo, Punta, c., Pan. H15 92
Manzanillo Bay, b., N.A. E9 94
Manzanita, Or., U.S. B3 144
Manzanola, Co., U.S. C7 113
Manzano Mountains, mts., N.M., U.S. C3 138
Manzano Peak, mtn., N.M., U.S. C3 138
Manzhouli, China B10 30
Manzini, Swaz. F10 66
Mao, Chad F4 56
Mao, Dom. Rep. E9 94
Maó, Spain F16 16
Maoke, Pegunungan, mts., Indon. F10 38
Maoming, China G9 30
Maouri, Dallol, val., Niger E11 64
Mapastepec, Mex. J13 90
Mapaville, Mo., U.S. C7 132
Mapia, Kepulauan, is., Indon. E9 38
Mapimí, Mex. E8 90
Mapimí, Bolsón de, des., Mex. D8 90
Maping, China D2 34
Mapinhane, Moz. D12 66
Mapire, Ven. D10 84
Mapiri, Bol. F7 82
Mapiri, stm., Bol. D8 82
Mapixari, Ilha, i., Braz. I10 84
Maple, stm., U.S. A7 148
Maple, stm., Ia., U.S. B2 122
Maple, stm., N.D., U.S. C8 141
Maple Bluff, Wi., U.S. E4 156
Maple Creek, Sask., Can. H1 105
Maple Creek, stm., Ne., U.S. C9 134
Maple Falls, Wa., U.S. A3 154
Maple Grove, Mn., U.S. m12 130
Maple Heights, Oh., U.S. h9 142
Maple Hill, Ks., U.S. C7 123
Maple Island, Mn., U.S. G5 130
Maple Lake, Mn., U.S. E5 130
Maple Mount, Ky., U.S. C2 124
Maple Plain, Mn., U.S. m11 130
Maple Rapids, Mi., U.S. E6 129
Maple Shade, N.J., U.S. D2 137
Maplesville, Al., U.S. C3 108
Mapleton, Ia., U.S. B2 122
Mapleton, Me., U.S. B4 126
Mapleton, Mn., U.S. G5 130
Mapleton, N.D., U.S. C8 141
Mapleton, Or., U.S. C3 144
Mapleton, Ut., U.S. C4 151
Maple Valley, Wa., U.S. f11 154
Mapleville, R.I., U.S. B2 146
Maplewood, Mn., U.S. n12 130
Maplewood, Mo., U.S. f13 132
Maplewood, N.J., U.S. B4 137
Mapuera, stm., Braz. H14 84
Mapulanguene, Moz. E11 66
Mapulau, stm., Braz. G11 84
Maputo, Moz. E11 66
Maputo, stm., Afr. F11 66
Maqna, Sau. Ar. G3 48
Maquela do Zombo, Ang. C3 58
Maquinchao, Arg. E3 78
Maquoketa, Ia., U.S. B7 122
Maquoketa, stm., Ia., U.S. B6 122
Maquoketa, North Fork, stm., Ia., U.S. B7 122
Maquon, Il., U.S. C3 120
Mar, Serra do, clf, Braz. C14 80
Mara, Peru F5 82
Mara, stm., Afr. B6 58
Maraã, Braz. H10 84
Marabá, Braz. E9 76
Maracá, Ilha de, i., Braz. F12 84
Maracaí, Braz. G3 79
Maracaibo, Ven. B7 84
Maracaibo, Lago de, l., Ven. C7 84
Maracaju, Braz. F1 79
Maracaju, Serra de, hills, S.A. F1 79
Maracanã, stm., Braz. C12 82
Maracás, Braz. B8 79
Maracay, Ven. B9 84
Marādah, Libya C4 56
Maradi, Niger E13 64
Maradi, Goulbin, stm., Afr. E13 64
Marāgheh, Iran C9 48
Maragogipe, Braz. F11 76
Maragogipe, Braz. B9 79
Marahuaca, Cerro, mtn., Ven. F10 84
Marais des Cygnes, stm., U.S. D8 123
Marajó, Baía de, b., Braz. D9 76
Marajó, Ilha de, i., Braz. D9 76
Marakabei, Leso. G9 66
Maralal, Kenya A7 58
Maralaleng, Bots. E6 66
Marambaia, Ilha da, i., Braz. G7 79
Marampa, S.L. G3 64
Maramureș, co., Rom. B8 20
Maran, Malay. M7 40
Marana, Az., U.S. E4 110
Marand, Iran B8 48
Marangani, Peru F6 82
Maranguape, Braz. D11 76
Maranhão, stm., Braz. C4 79
Maranoa, stm., Austl. E9 68
Marañón, stm., Peru D3 76
Marapanim, Braz. D9 76
Marapi, stm., Braz. G14 84
Maras, Peru E5 82
Marathon, Austl. C5 70
Marathón, Grc. K7 20
Marathon, Fl., U.S. H5 116
Marathon, Ia., U.S. B3 122
Marathon, N.Y., U.S. C4 139
Marathon, Tx., U.S. D1 150
Marathon, Wi., U.S. D4 156
Marathon, co., Wi., U.S. D4 156
Maraú, Braz. C9 79
Marau, Braz. E12 80
Marauiá, stm., Braz. H10 84
Maravilha, Braz. D12 80
Maravillas, Mex. D7 90
Marawī, Sud. H6 60
Marayes, Arg. F5 80
Marbach, Switz. E8 13
Marbella, Spain I7 16
Marble, Ar., U.S. A2 111
Marble, Mn., U.S. C5 130
Marble, N.C., U.S. f9 140
Marble Bar, Austl. D3 68
Marble Canyon, Az., U.S. A4 110
Marble Canyon, val., Az., U.S. A4 110
Marble City, Ok., U.S. B7 143
Marble Cliff, Oh., U.S. m10 142
Marbledale, Tn., U.S. n14 149
Marble Falls, Tx., U.S. D3 150
Marble Hall, S. Afr. E9 66
Marblehead, Ma., U.S. B6 128
Marblehead, Oh., U.S. A3 142
Marblehill, Ga., U.S. B2 117
Marble Hill, Mo., U.S. D8 132
Marblemount, Wa., U.S. A4 154
Marble Mountain, N.S., Can. D8 101
Marble Rock, Ia., U.S. B5 122
Marbleton, Que., Can. D6 104
Marbleton, Wy., U.S. D2 157
Marburg, Ger. E8 10
Marbury, Al., U.S. C3 108
Marbury, Md., U.S. C3 127
Marcaconga, Peru E6 82
Marcala, Hond. C6 92
Marcali, Hung. I17 10
Marcaria, Italy D5 18
Marcelin, Sask., Can. E2 105
Marceline, Mo., U.S. B5 132
Marcelino Ramos, Braz. D13 80
Marcellus, Mi., U.S. F5 129
March (Morava), stm., Eur. G16 10
Marcha, stm., U.S.S.R. E15 24
March Air Force Base, mil., Ca., U.S. F5 112
Marchand, Man., Can. E3 100
Marche, prov., Italy F8 18
Marche, hist. reg., Fr. F8 14
Marche-en-Famenne, Bel. H7 12
Marchegg, Aus. G16 10
Marchena, Spain H6 16
Mar Chiquita, Laguna, b., Arg. I10 80
Mar Chiquita, Laguna, l., Arg. F7 80
Marchwell, Sask., Can. G5 105
Marcigny, Fr. F11 14
Marco, Fl., U.S. G5 116
Marcola, Or., U.S. C4 144
Marcona, Peru F4 82
Marcos Juárez, Arg. G7 80
Marcos Paz, Arg. H9 80
Marcus, Ia., U.S. B2 122
Marcus Baker, Mount, mtn., Ak., U.S. g18 109
Marcus Hook, Pa., U.S. G11 145
Marcy, Mount, mtn., N.Y., U.S. A7 139
Mardān, Pak. C5 44
Mardarovka, U.S.S.R. B13 20
Mar del Plata, Arg. J10 80
Mardin, Tur. C6 48
Marea de Portillo, Cuba E6 94
Marechal Cândido Rondon, Braz. C11 80
Mareeba, Austl. A6 70
Marengo, Sask., Can. F1 105
Marengo, Il., U.S. A5 120
Marengo, In., U.S. H5 121
Marengo, Ia., U.S. C5 122
Marengo, co., Al., U.S. C2 108
Marenisco, Mi., U.S. n12 129
Marfa, Tx., U.S. o12 150
Marganec, U.S.S.R. H4 22
Margaree, N.S., Can. C8 101
Margaree Harbour, N.S., Can. C8 101
Margaret, Al., U.S. B3 108
Margaretsville, N.S., Can. D4 101
Margarita, Isla, i., Col. C5 84
Margarita, Isla de, i., Ven. B10 84
Margarita Belén, Arg. D9 80
Margate, S. Afr. H10 66
Margate, Eng., U.K. J15 8
Margate, Fl., U.S. F6 116
Margate City, N.J., U.S. E3 137
Margecany, Czech. G21 10
Margherita Peak, mtn., Afr. A5 58
Marghī, Afg. C2 44
Margilan, U.S.S.R. I12 22
Margo, Sask., Can. F4 105
Margos, Peru D3 82
Margow, Dasht-e, des., Afg. F17 48
Margrethe, Lake, l., Mi., U.S. D6 129
Margua, stm., Col. D6 84
Marguerite Bay, b., Ant. B12 73
Mari, stm., Braz. B9 82
María Cleofas, Isla, i., Mex. G6 90
María Elena, Chile B4 80
Maria Gail, Aus. I13 10
Mariah Hill, In., U.S. H4 121
María Ignacia (Vela), Arg. I9 80
Maria Island, i., Austl. N8 70
María la Baja, Col. C5 84
María Madre, Isla, i., Mex. G6 90
María Magdalena, Isla, i., Mex. G6 90
Marian, Lake, l., Fl., U.S. E5 116
Mariana, Braz. F7 79
Mariana Islands, is., Oc. G18 158
Mariana Trench G18 158
Mariāni, India G16 44
Marianna, Ar., U.S. C5 111
Marianna, Fl., U.S. B1 116
Mariano I. Loza, Arg. E9 80
Mariano Moreno, Arg. J3 80
Mariánské Lázně, Czech. F12 10
Mariapolis, Man., Can. E2 100
Mariara, Ven. B9 84
Marias, stm., Mt., U.S. B4 133
Marías, Islas, is., Mex. G6 90
Marias Pass, Mt., U.S. B3 133
María Teresa, Arg. H8 80
Mariato, Punta, c., Pan. D2 84
Mā'rib, Yemen G4 47
Maribel, Wi., U.S. h10 156
Maribor, Yugo. C10 18
Maricá, Braz. G7 79
Marica (Évros) (Meriç), stm., Eur. H10 20
Marico, stm., Afr. E8 66
Maricopa, Az., U.S. E3 110
Maricopa, Ca., U.S. E4 112
Maricopa, co., Az., U.S. D3 110
Maricopa Mountains, mts., Az., U.S. m7 110
Maricunga, Salar de, pl., Chile D4 80
Marie, Ar., U.S. B5 111
Marié, stm., Braz. H9 84
Marie Byrd Land, reg., Ant. C10 73
Marie-Galante, i., Guad. G14 94
Mariehamn, Fin. K16 6
Mariemont, Oh., U.S. o13 142
Marienbad see Mariánské Lázně, Czech. F12 10
Marienburg see Malbork, Pol. A19 10
Mariental, Nmb. E3 66
Marienthal, Ks., U.S. D2 123
Marienville, Pa., U.S. D3 145
Marie-Reine, Alta., Can. A2 98
Maries, co., Mo., U.S. C6 132
Mariestad, Swe. L13 6
Marieta, stm., Ven. E9 84
Marietta, Ga., U.S. C2 117
Marietta, In., U.S. F6 121
Marietta, Ms., U.S. A5 131
Marietta, Oh., U.S. C4 142
Marietta, Ok., U.S. D4 143
Marietta, S.C., U.S. A2 147
Marietta, Wa., U.S. A3 154
Marieville, Que., Can. D4 104
Mariga, stm., Nig. F13 64
Marignane, Fr. I12 14
Marigot, Dom. G14 94
Marigot, Guad. E13 94
Mariinsk, U.S.S.R. F9 24
Marikana, S. Afr. E8 66
Mari Lake, l., Sask., Can. B4 105
Marília, Braz. G4 79
Marimari, stm., Braz. J13 84
Marimba, Ang. C3 58
Marín, Spain C3 16
Marin, co., Ca., U.S. C2 112
Marina, Ca., U.S. D3 112
Marina di Ravenna, Italy E7 18
Marina Fall, wtfl, Guy. E13 84
Marine, Il., U.S. E4 120
Marine City, Mi., U.S. F8 129
Marine On St. Croix, Mn., U.S. E6 130
Marinette, Wi., U.S. C6 156
Marinette, co., Wi., U.S. C5 156
Maringá, Braz. G3 79
Maringouin, La., U.S. D4 125
Marínguè, Moz. A12 66
Marino, Italy H7 18
Marion, Al., U.S. C2 108
Marion, Ar., U.S. B5 111
Marion, Ct., U.S. C4 114
Marion, Il., U.S. F5 120
Marion, In., U.S. C6 121
Marion, Ia., U.S. B6 122
Marion, Ks., U.S. D6 123

Name Map Ref. Page

Marion, Ky., U.S. e9 124
Marion, La., U.S. B3 125
Marion, Ma., U.S. C6 128
Marion, Mi., U.S. D5 129
Marion, Ms., U.S. C5 131
Marion, Mt., U.S. B2 133
Marion, N.Y., U.S. B3 139
Marion, N.C., U.S. B1 140
Marion, N.D., U.S. C7 141
Marion, Oh., U.S. B2 142
Marion, Pa., U.S. G6 145
Marion, S.C., U.S. C9 147
Marion, S.D., U.S. D8 148
Marion, Va., U.S. f10 153
Marion, Wi., U.S. D5 156
Marion, co., Al., U.S. A2 108
Marion, co., Ar., U.S. A3 111
Marion, co., Fl., U.S. C4 116
Marion, co., Ga., U.S. D2 117
Marion, co., Il., U.S. E4 120
Marion, co., In., U.S. E5 121
Marion, co., Ia., U.S. C4 122
Marion, co., Ks., U.S. D6 123
Marion, co., Ky., U.S. C4 124
Marion, co., Ms., U.S. D4 131
Marion, co., Mo., U.S. B6 132
Marion, co., Oh., U.S. B2 142
Marion, co., Or., U.S. C4 144
Marion, co., S.C., U.S. C9 147
Marion, co., Tn., U.S. D8 149
Marion, co., Tx., U.S. C5 150
Marion, co., W.V., U.S. B4 155
Marion, Lake, res., S.C., U.S. E7 147
Marion Heights, In., U.S. F3 121
Marion Junction, Al., U.S. C2 108
Marion Reef, rf., Austl. B10 70
Marion Station, Md., U.S. D6 127
Marionville, Mo., U.S. D4 132
Mariópolis, Braz. D12 80
Maripa, Ven. D10 84
Mariposa, Ca., U.S. D4 112
Mariposa, co., Ca., U.S. D3 112
Mariquita, Col. E5 84
Mariscal Estigarribia, Para. B8 80
Marissa, Il., U.S. E4 120
Maritime Alps, mts., Eur. H14 14
Mariupol' (Ždanov), U.S.S.R. H5 22
Mariusa, Caño, mth., Ven. C12 84
Marīvān, Iran D9 48
Märjamaa, U.S.S.R. C7 26
Marjina Gorka, U.S.S.R. H11 26
Marjinsko, U.S.S.R. C11 26
Mark, Il., U.S. B4 120
Marka, Som. H9 56
Markala, Mali E6 64
Markdale, Ont., Can. C4 103
Marked Tree, Ar., U.S. B5 111
Markesan, Wi., U.S. E5 156
Markham, Ont., Can. D5 103
Markham, Il., U.S. k9 120
Markham, Tx., U.S. E4 150
Markham, Mount, mtn., Ant. D8 73
Markinch, Sask., Can. G3 105
Markland Lock and Dam, U.S. B5 124
Markle, In., U.S. C7 121
Markleville, In., U.S. E6 121
Markovo, U.S.S.R. E26 24
Markovo, U.S.S.R. D23 26
Marks, U.S.S.R. G7 22
Marks, Ms., U.S. A3 131
Marksville, La., U.S. C3 125
Marktheidenfeld, Ger. F9 10
Marktoberdorf, Ger. H10 10
Marktredwitz, Ger. E12 10
Mark Twain Lake, res., Mo., U.S. B6 132
Markundi, Sud. L2 60
Marland, Ok., U.S. A4 143
Marlbank, Ont., Can. C7 103
Marlboro, Alta., Can. C2 98
Marlboro, N.Y., U.S. D6 139
Marlboro, Vt., U.S. F3 152
Marlboro, Va., U.S. n17 153
Marlboro, co., S.C., U.S. B8 147
Marlborough, Austl. D8 70
Marlborough, Guy. D13 84
Marlborough, Eng., U.K. J12 8
Marlborough, Ct., U.S. C6 114
Marlborough, Ma., U.S. B4 128
Marlborough, N.H., U.S. E2 136
Marle, Fr. C10 14
Marlette, Mi., U.S. E7 129
Marley, Md., U.S. B4 127
Marlin, Tx., U.S. D4 150
Marlinton, W.V., U.S. C4 155
Marlow, Al., U.S. E2 108
Marlow, Ga., U.S. D5 117
Marlow, N.H., U.S. D2 136
Marlow, Ok., U.S. C4 143
Marlowe, W.V., U.S. B7 155
Marlton, N.J., U.S. D3 137
Marmaduke, Ar., U.S. A5 111
Marmande, Fr. H7 14
Marmara Denizi (Sea of Marmara), Tur. I12 20
Marmara Ereğlisi, Tur. I11 20
Marmaris, Tur. M12 20
Marmarth, N.D., U.S. C2 141
Marmelos, Braz. B11 82
Marmelos, Rio dos, stm., Braz. B11 82
Marmet, W.V., U.S. C3 155
Marmora, Ont., Can. C7 103
Mar Muerto, Laguna, b., Mex. I12 90
Marnay, Fr. E12 14
Marne, Mi., U.S. E5 129
Marne, dept., Fr. D11 14
Marne, stm., Fr. C10 14
Marne au Rhin, Canal de la, Fr. D13 14
Maroa, Il., U.S. C5 120
Maroa, Ven. F9 84
Maroala, Madag. O22 67b
Maroantsetra, Madag. O23 67b
Maroelaboom, Nmb. B4 66
Marolambo, Madag. R23 67b
Maromme, Fr. C8 14
Maromokotro, mtn., Madag. O23 67b
Marondera, Zimb. B10 66
Maroni, stm., S.A. C8 76
Maro Reef, rf., Hi., U.S. k13 118
Maros (Mureş), stm., Eur. C4 20
Maroseranana, Madag. Q23 67b
Maroua, Cam. F9 54
Marovato, Madag. O23 67b
Marovoay, Madag. P22 67b
Marquand, Mo., U.S. D7 132
Marquesas Islands see Marquises, Îles, is., Fr. Poly. I26 158
Marquesas Keys, is., Fl., U.S. H4 116
Marquette, Man., Can. D3 100
Marquette, Ia., U.S. A6 122
Marquette, Ks., U.S. D6 123
Marquette, Mi., U.S. B3 129
Marquette, Ne., U.S. D8 134
Marquette, co., Mi., U.S. B3 129
Marquette, co., Wi., U.S. E4 156
Marquette Heights, Il., U.S. C4 120
Marquis, Sask., Can. G3 105
Marquise, Fr. B8 14
Marquises, Îles (Marquesas Islands), is., Fr. Poly. I26 158
Marrah, Jabal, mtn., Sud. K3 60
Marrakech, Mor. E6 62
Marrawah, Austl. M6 70
Marree, Austl. G3 70
Marrero, La., U.S. E5 125
Marromeu, Moz. B12 66
Mars, Pa., U.S. E1 145
Marsā al-Burayqah, Libya B4 56
Marsabit, Kenya H8 56
Marsala, Italy L7 18
Marsā Maṭrūḥ, Egypt B4 56
Marsden, Austl. I7 70
Marsden, Sask., Can. E1 105
Marseille, Fr. I12 14
Marseille-en-Beauvaisis, Fr. C8 14
Marseilles, Il., U.S. B5 120
Marshall, Sask., Can. D1 105
Marshall, Lib. G4 54
Marshall, Lib. H4 64
Marshall, Ak., U.S. C7 109
Marshall, Ar., U.S. B3 111
Marshall, Il., U.S. D6 120
Marshall, In., U.S. E3 121
Marshall, Mi., U.S. F6 129
Marshall, Mn., U.S. F3 130
Marshall, Mo., U.S. B4 132
Marshall, N.C., U.S. f10 140
Marshall, Ok., U.S. A4 143
Marshall, Tx., U.S. C5 150
Marshall, Va., U.S. B5 153
Marshall, Wi., U.S. E4 156
Marshall, co., Al., U.S. A3 108
Marshall, co., Il., U.S. B4 120
Marshall, co., In., U.S. B5 121
Marshall, co., Ia., U.S. C4 122
Marshall, co., Ks., U.S. C7 123
Marshall, co., Ky., U.S. f9 124
Marshall, co., Mn., U.S. B2 130
Marshall, co., Ms., U.S. A4 131
Marshall, co., Ok., U.S. C5 143
Marshall, co., S.D., U.S. B8 148
Marshall, co., Tn., U.S. B5 149
Marshall, co., W.V., U.S. B4 155
Marshallberg, N.C., U.S. C6 140
Marshall Islands, ctry., Oc. H20 158
Marshallton, De., U.S. B3 115
Marshalltown, Ia., U.S. B5 122
Marshallville, Ga., U.S. D3 117
Marshallville, Oh., U.S. B4 142
Marshes Siding, Ky., U.S. D5 124
Marshfield, Ma., U.S. B6 128
Marshfield, Mo., U.S. D5 132
Marshfield, Vt., U.S. C4 152
Marshfield, Wi., U.S. D3 156
Marshfield Hills, Ma., U.S. B6 128
Marsh Fork, stm., W.V., U.S. n13 155
Marsh Harbour, Bah. A6 94
Mars Hill, Me., U.S. B5 126
Mars Hill, N.C., U.S. f10 140
Mars Hill, mtn., Me., U.S. B5 126
Marsh Island, i., La., U.S. E4 125
Marsh Lake, res., Mn., U.S. E2 130
Marsh Peak, mtn., Ut., U.S. C6 151
Marshville, N.C., U.S. C2 140
Marshyhope Creek, stm., Md., U.S. C6 127
Marsing, Id., U.S. F2 119
Marston, Mo., U.S. E8 132
Marstons Mills, Ma., U.S. C7 128
Mart, Tx., U.S. D4 150
Martaban, Burma F4 40
Martaban, Gulf of, b., Burma F4 40
Martapura, Indon. F5 38
Martell, Ne., U.S. D9 134
Martelle, Ia., U.S. B6 122
Martensdale, Ia., U.S. C4 122
Marte R. Gómez, Presa, res., Mex. D10 90
Martha, Ok., U.S. C2 143
Marthasville, Mo., U.S. C6 132
Martha's Vineyard, i., Ma., U.S. D6 128
Marthaville, La., U.S. C2 125
Martí, Cuba D6 94
Martigny, Switz. F7 13
Martigues, Fr. I12 14
Martil, Mor. J6 16
Martin, Czech. F18 10
Martin, Ga., U.S. B3 117
Martin, Ky., U.S. C7 124
Martin, La., U.S. B2 125
Martin, Mi., U.S. F5 129
Martin, N.D., U.S. B5 141
Martin, S.D., U.S. D4 148
Martin, Tn., U.S. A3 149
Martin, Ut., U.S. D5 151
Martin, co., Fl., U.S. E6 116
Martin, co., In., U.S. G4 121
Martin, co., Ky., U.S. C7 124
Martin, co., Mn., U.S. G4 130
Martin, co., N.C., U.S. B5 140
Martin, co., Tx., U.S. C2 150
Martina Franca, Italy I12 18
Martin City, Mt., U.S. B3 133
Martindale, Tx., U.S. h8 150
Martinez, Ca., U.S. C2 112
Martinez, Ga., U.S. C4 117
Martínez de la Torre, Mex. G11 90
Martinho Campos, Braz. E6 79
Martinique, dep., N.A. G14 94
Martinique Passage, strt., N.A. G14 94
Martin Lake, res., Al., U.S. C4 108
Martinniemi, Fin. I19 6
Martin Point, c., Ak., U.S. A11 109
Martinsberg, Aus. G15 10
Martinsburg, In., U.S. H5 121
Martinsburg, Mo., U.S. B6 132
Martinsburg, Pa., U.S. F5 145
Martinsburg, W.V., U.S. B7 155
Martins Ferry, Oh., U.S. B5 142
Martins Pond, l., Ma., U.S. f11 128
Martinsville, Il., U.S. D6 120
Martinsville, In., U.S. F5 121
Martinsville, Ms., U.S. D3 131
Martinsville, Va., U.S. D3 153
Martinton, Il., U.S. C5 120
Martin Vaz, Ilhas, is., Braz. G12 74
Martisovo, U.S.S.R. E14 26
Martos, Spain H8 16
Martre, Lac la, l., N.W. Ter., Can. D9 96
Martti, Fin. H21 6
Marty, S.D., U.S. E7 148
Maru, Nig. E13 64
Marugame, Japan M8 36
Marula, Zimb. C9 66
Marumsco Creek, stm., Md., U.S. D6 127
Marunga, Ang. A5 66
Marungu, mts., Zaire C5 58
Ma'rūt, Afg. E2 44
Marv Dasht, Iran G12 48
Marvejols, Fr. H10 14
Marvel, Al., U.S. B2 108
Marvel, Co., U.S. D2 113
Marvell, Ar., U.S. C5 111
Marvine, Mount, mtn., Ut., U.S. E4 151
Marwayne, Alta., Can. C5 98
Mary, U.S.S.R. J10 22
Mary, Lake, l., Mn., U.S. E3 130
Mary, Lake, l., Ms., U.S. D2 131
Maryborough, Austl. E10 70
Maryborough, Austl. K5 70
Marydale, S. Afr. G6 66
Marydel, De., U.S. D3 115
Maryfield, Sask., Can. H5 105
Mary Kathleen, Austl. C3 70
Maryland, state, U.S. B4 127
Maryland City, Md., U.S. B4 127
Maryland Heights, Mo., U.S. f13 132
Maryland Point, c., Md., U.S. D3 127
Marys, stm., Nv., U.S. B6 135
Mary's Harbour, Newf., Can. B4 102
Mary's Igloo, Ak., U.S. B6 109
Marys Peak, mtn., Or., U.S. C3 144
Marystown, Newf., Can. E4 102
Marysvale, Ut., U.S. E3 151
Marysville, Ca., U.S. C3 112
Marysville, Id., U.S. E7 119
Marysville, Ks., U.S. C7 123
Marysville, Mi., U.S. F8 129
Marysville, Oh., U.S. B2 142
Marysville, Pa., U.S. F8 145
Marysville, Wa., U.S. A3 154
Maryville, Mo., U.S. A3 132
Maryville, Tn., U.S. D10 149
Marzagão, Braz. D4 79
Marzo, Punta, c., Col. D4 84
Marzūq, Libya C3 56
Marzūq, Ṣaḥrā', des., Libya D3 56
Masachapa, Nic. F8 92
Masada see Meẓada, Horvot, hist., Isr. F4 50
Masagua, Guat. C4 92
Masai Steppe, plat., Tan. B7 58
Masaka, Ug. B6 58
Masally, U.S.S.R. B10 48
Masan, S. Kor. H16 32
Masaryktown, Fl., U.S. D4 116
Masasi, Tan. D7 58
Masatepe, Nic. F8 92
Masaya, Nic. F8 92
Masaya, dept., Nic. E8 92
Masbate, Phil. C7 38
Mascarene Islands, is., Afr. F11 58
Mascasín, Arg. F5 80
Mascoma, stm., N.H., U.S. C2 136
Mascoma Lake, l., N.H., U.S. C2 136
Mascot, Tn., U.S. C10 149
Mascota, Mex. G7 90
Mascouche, Que., Can. D4 104
Mascoutah, Il., U.S. E4 120
Maseru, Leso. G8 66
Mashaba Mountains, mts., Zimb. B10 66
Mashābih, i., Sau. Ar. I4 48
Mashapaug Pond, l., Ct., U.S. A7 114
Mashar, Sud. M4 60
Mashhad, Iran C15 48
Mashīz, Iran G14 48
Māshkel, Hāmūn-i-, l., Pak. G17 48
Māshkel, Rūd-i- (Māshkīd), stm., Asia G17 48
Mashra'ur-Raqq, Sud. M5 60
Masi Manimba, Zaire B3 58
Maṣīrah, Khalīj, b., Oman E11 47
Masisea, Peru C4 82
Masjed-e Soleymān, Iran F10 48
Mask, Lough, l., Ire. H4 8
Maska, Nig. F13 64
Maskanah, Syria C5 48
Maskin, Oman C10 47
Maskinongé, Que., Can. C4 104
Masoala, Madag. O24 67b
Masoala, Cap, c., Madag. O24 67b
Masoala, Presqu'île de, pen., Madag. O24 67b
Masoarivo, Madag. Q21 67b
Masomeloka, Madag. R23 67b
Mason, Il., U.S. E5 120
Mason, Mi., U.S. F6 129
Mason, Nv., U.S. E2 135
Mason, N.H., U.S. E3 136
Mason, Oh., U.S. C1 142
Mason, Tn., U.S. B2 149
Mason, Tx., U.S. D3 150
Mason, W.V., U.S. B2 155
Mason, co., Il., U.S. C4 120
Mason, co., Ky., U.S. B6 124
Mason, co., Mi., U.S. D4 129
Mason, co., Tx., U.S. D3 150
Mason, co., Wa., U.S. B2 154
Mason, co., W.V., U.S. C3 155
Mason City, Il., U.S. C4 120
Mason City, Ia., U.S. A4 122
Mason City, Ne., U.S. C6 134
Masonhall, Tn., U.S. A2 149
Masontown, Pa., U.S. G2 145
Masontown, W.V., U.S. B5 155
Masonville, Co., U.S. A5 113
Masqaṭ (Muscat), Oman C11 47
Massa, Italy E5 18
Massabesic Lake, l., N.H., U.S. E4 136
Massac, co., Il., U.S. F5 120
Massachusetts, state, U.S. B4 128
Massachusetts Bay, b., Ma., U.S. B6 128
Massacre Lake, l., Nv., U.S. B2 135
Massaemett Mountain, mtn., Ma., U.S. A2 128
Massafra, Italy I12 18
Massa Marittima, Italy F5 18
Massangena, Moz. C11 66
Massanutten Mountain, mts., Va., U.S. B4 153
Massapoag Lake, l., Ma., U.S. h11 128
Massarosa, Italy F5 18
Massasecum, Lake, l., N.H., U.S. D3 136
Massena, Ia., U.S. C3 122
Massena, N.Y., U.S. f10 139
Massenya, Chad F4 56
Masset, B.C., Can. C1 99
Masseube, Fr. I7 14
Massey, Ont., Can. A2 103
Massillon, Oh., U.S. B4 142
Massina, reg., Mali D7 64
Massinga, Moz. D12 66
Massive, Mount, mtn., Co., U.S. B4 113
Mastābah, Sau. Ar. D1 47
Maštaga, U.S.S.R. I8 22
Masterton, N.Z. D5 72
Mastic Beach, N.Y., U.S. n16 139
Mastung, Pak. F2 44
Mastūrah, Sau. Ar. C1 47
Masuda, Japan M6 36
Masury, Oh., U.S. A5 142
Masvingo, Zimb. C10 66
Matachewan, Ont., Can. p19 103
Matacuni, stm., Ven. F10 84
Mata de São João, Braz. B9 79
Matadi, Zaire C2 58
Matador, Tx., U.S. B2 150
Matagalpa, Nic. E9 92
Matagalpa, dept., Nic. E9 92
Matagorda, Tx., U.S. E5 150
Matagorda, co., Tx., U.S. E5 150
Matagorda Bay, b., Tx., U.S. E4 150
Matagorda Island, i., Tx., U.S. E4 150
Matagorda Peninsula, pen., Tx., U.S. E5 150
Matale, Sri L. I6 46
Matam, Sen. D3 64
Matama, Cerro, mtn., C.R. H11 92
Matamoras, Pa., U.S. D12 145
Matamoros, Mex. E11 90
Matamoros, Mex. E8 90
Matane, Que., Can. k13 104
Matanuska, stm., Ak., U.S. g18 109
Matanzas, Cuba C4 94
Matanzas, Mex. G9 90
Matanzas Inlet, b., Fl., U.S. C5 116
Matapalo, Cabo, c., C.R. I11 92
Matape, stm., Mex. C4 90
Mataquito, stm., Chile H3 80
Matará, Peru B2 82
Matara, Sri L. J6 46
Mataram, Indon. G6 38
Matarani, Peru G5 82
Matarca, Col. H6 84
Mataró, Spain D14 16
Matatiele, S. Afr. H9 66
Matauá, stm., Braz. B11 82
Matawan, N.J., U.S. C4 137
Mateare, Nic. E8 92
Matehuala, Mex. F9 90
Matera, Italy I11 18
Mátészalka, Hung. H22 10
Mateur, Tun. L4 18
Matewan, W.V., U.S. D2 155
Mather, Man., Can. E2 100
Mather, Pa., U.S. G1 145
Mather Air Force Base, mil., Ca., U.S. C3 112
Mather Peaks, mts., Wy., U.S. B5 157
Matherville, Il., U.S. B3 120
Matheson, Co., U.S. B7 113
Matheson Island, Man., Can. D3 100
Mathews, Al., U.S. C3 108
Mathews, La., U.S. E5 125
Mathews, Va., U.S. C6 153
Mathews, co., Va., U.S. C6 153
Mathews, Lake, l., Ca., U.S. n14 112
Mathias, W.V., U.S. C6 155
Mathis, Tx., U.S. E4 150
Mathiston, Ms., U.S. B4 131
Mathura, India G7 44
Matiacoali, Burkina E10 64
Matias Barbosa, Braz. F7 79
Matías Romero, Mex. I12 90
Matícora, stm., Ven. B7 84
Matignon, Fr. D4 14
Matiguás, Nic. E9 92
Matinenda Lake, l., Ont., Can. A2 103
Matinicus Island, i., Me., U.S. E3 126
Matipó, Braz. F7 79
Matipó, stm., Braz. F7 79
Matiyure, stm., Ven. D8 84
Matlamanyane, Bots. B7 66
M'atlevo, U.S.S.R. G18 26
Matmata, Tun. D15 62
Mato, stm., Ven. D10 84
Mato, Cerro, mtn., Ven. D10 84
Matoaca, Va., U.S. n18 153
Matoaka, W.V., U.S. D3 155
Matočkin Šar, proliv, strt., U.S.S.R. C8 22
Mato Grosso, Braz. F12 82
Mato Grosso, state, Braz. D13 82
Mato Grosso, Planalto do, plat., Braz. G7 76
Matopo Hills, hills, Zimb. C9 66
Matos, stm., Bol. F9 82
Matosinhos, Port. D3 16
Matou, Tai. L9 34
Matoury, Fr. Gu. C8 76
Matouying, China D6 32
Mato Verde, Braz. C7 79
Matozinhos, Braz. E6 79
Maṭraḥ, Oman C11 47
Matrei in Osttirol, Aus. H12 10
Matru, S.L. H3 64
Matsapha, Swaz. F10 66
Matsqui, B.C., Can. f13 99
Matsudo, Japan L14 36
Matsue, Japan L8 36
Matsumae, Japan F15 36
Matsumoto, Japan K12 36
Matsu Tao, i., Tai. I8 34
Matsuyama, Japan N7 36
Mattamiscontis Lake, l., Me., U.S. C4 126
Mattamuskeet, Lake, l., N.C., U.S. B6 140
Mattapoisett, Ma., U.S. C6 128
Mattaponi, stm., Va., U.S. C5 153
Mattawa, Ont., Can. A6 103
Mattawamkeag, Me., U.S. C4 126
Mattawamkeag, stm., Me., U.S. C4 126
Mattawamkeag, East Branch, stm., Me., U.S. C4 126
Mattawamkeag, West Branch, stm., Me., U.S. C4 126
Mattawamkeag Lake, l., Me., U.S. C4 126
Mattawoman Creek, stm., Md., U.S. C3 127
Matterhorn, mtn., Eur. G14 14
Matterhorn, mtn., Nv., U.S. B6 135
Mattersburg, Aus. H16 10
Matteson, Il., U.S. k9 120
Matthews, Ga., U.S. C4 117
Matthews, In., U.S. D7 121
Matthews, Mo., U.S. E8 132
Matthews, N.C., U.S. B2 140
Matthews Mountain, mtn., Mo., U.S. D6 132
Matthews Ridge, Guy. D12 84
Matthew Town, Bah. D8 94
Maṭṭī, Sabkhat, l., Asia J12 48
Mattighofen, Aus. G13 10
Mattituck, N.Y., U.S. n16 139
Mattoon, Il., U.S. D5 120
Mattoon, Wi., U.S. C4 156
Mattoon, Lake, res., Il., U.S. D5 120
Mattydale, N.Y., U.S. B4 139
Matuba, Moz. E11 66
Matucana, Peru D3 82
Matunuck, R.I., U.S. G3 146
Maturín, Ven. C11 84
Maturino, U.S.S.R. B20 26
Matutina, Braz. E6 79
Maú (Ireng), stm., S.A. E13 84
Maúa, Moz. D7 58
Maubeuge, Fr. B10 14
Maud, Oh., U.S. n13 142
Maud, Ok., U.S. B5 143
Maude, Austl. J6 70
Maués, Braz. I14 84
Maués-Açu, stm., Braz. I14 84
Maugansville, Md., U.S. A2 127
Maugerville, N.B., Can. D3 101
Maui, co., Hi., U.S. B5 118
Maui, i., Hi., U.S. C6 118
Mauk, Ga., U.S. D2 117
Mauldin, S.C., U.S. B3 147
Maule, prov., Chile H2 80
Maule, stm., Chile H2 80
Maule, Laguna del, l., Chile I3 80
Mauléon, Fr. F6 14
Maumee, Oh., U.S. A2 142
Maumee, stm., U.S. A2 142
Maumee Bay, b., U.S. G7 129
Maumelle, Ar., U.S. h10 111
Maumelle, Lake, res., Ar., U.S. C3 111
Maun, Bots. C6 66
Mauna Kea, vol., Hi., U.S. D6 118
Maunaloa, Hi., U.S. B4 118
Mauna Loa, vol., Hi., U.S. D6 118
Maunalua Bay, b., Hi., U.S. g10 118
Maunath Bhanjan, India H10 44
Maunatlala, Bots. D8 66
Maunawili, Hi., U.S. g10 118
Maungdaw, Burma D2 40
Maupin, Or., U.S. B5 144
Mau Rānīpur, India H8 44
Maure-de-Bretagne, Fr. E5 14
Maurepas, Lake, l., La., U.S. D5 125
Maurertown, Va., U.S. B4 153
Mauri, stm., Bol. G7 82
Mauriac, Fr. G9 14
Maurice, Ia., U.S. B1 122
Maurice, La., U.S. D3 125
Maurice, stm., N.J., U.S. E2 137
Mauritania (Mauritanie), ctry., Afr. D4 54
Mauritius, ctry., Afr. F11 58
Mauritius, i., Mrts. V18 67c
Mauron, Fr. D4 14
Maury, N.C., U.S. B5 140
Maury, co., Tn., U.S. B4 149
Maury City, Tn., U.S. B2 149
Maury Island, i., Wa., U.S. f11 154
Mauston, Wi., U.S. E3 156
Mauterndorf, Aus. H13 10
Mauthausen, Aus. G14 10
Mauvezin, Fr. I7 14
Mauwee Peak, mtn., Ct., U.S. C2 114
Mavá, stm., Col. G8 84
Mavaca, stm., Ven. F10 84
Maverick, co., Tx., U.S. E2 150
Mavinga, Ang. E4 58
Mawchi, Burma E4 40
Maw-daung Pass, Asia I5 40
Mawkhi, Burma F5 40
Mawlaik, Burma C3 40
Mawlamyine (Moulmein), Burma F4 40
Maw Taung, mtn., Asia I5 40
Max, Ne., U.S. D4 134
Max, N.D., U.S. B4 141
Maxbass, N.D., U.S. A4 141
Maxcanú, Mex. G15 90
Maxeys, Ga., U.S. C3 117
Maxinkuckee, Lake, l., In., U.S. B5 121
Maxixe, Moz. D12 66
Max Meadows, Va., U.S. D2 153
Maxton, N.C., U.S. C3 140
Maxville, Ont., Can. B10 103
Maxwell, Ca., U.S. C2 112
Maxwell, In., U.S. E6 121
Maxwell, Ia., U.S. C4 122
Maxwell, Ne., U.S. C5 134
Maxwell, N.M., U.S. A5 138
Maxwell, Tn., U.S. B5 149
Maxwell Acres, W.V., U.S. g8 155
Maxwell Air Force Base, mil., Al., U.S. C3 108
May, Id., U.S. E5 119
Maya, Mesa de, mtn., Co., U.S. D7 113
Mayaguana, i., Bah. C8 94
Mayaguana Passage, strt., Bah. C8 94
Mayagüez, P.R. E11 94
Mayales, Punta, c., Nic. F9 92
Maya Mountains, mts., N.A. I15 90
Mayapan, hist., Mex. G15 90
Mayarí, Cuba D7 94
Maybee, Mi., U.S. F7 129
Maybell, Co., U.S. A2 113
Maybole, Scot., U.K. F9 8
Mayenne, Fr. M13 8
Mayenne, dept., Fr. D6 14
Mayer, Az., U.S. C3 110
Mayersville, Ms., U.S. C2 131
Mayerthorpe, Alta., Can. C3 98
Mayes, co., Ok., U.S. A6 143
Mayesville, S.C., U.S. D7 147
Mayetta, Ks., U.S. C8 123
Mayfair, Sask., Can. E2 105
Mayfield, Ks., U.S. E6 123
Mayfield, Ky., U.S. f9 124
Mayfield, N.Y., U.S. B4 139
Mayfield, Pa., U.S. C10 145
Mayfield, Ut., U.S. D4 151
Mayfield Heights, Oh., U.S. A4 142
Mayfield Lake, res., Wa., U.S. C3 154
Mayflower, Ar., U.S. C3 111
Mayhill, N.M., U.S. E4 138
May Jirgui, Niger E14 64
Mayking, Ky., U.S. C7 124
Mayland, Tn., U.S. C8 149
Maymont, Sask., Can. E2 105
Maymyo, Burma C4 40
Maynard, Ar., U.S. A5 111
Maynard, Ia., U.S. B6 122
Maynard, Ma., U.S. B5 128
Maynard, Mn., U.S. F3 130
Maynardville, Tn., U.S. C10 149
Mayne, B.C., Can. g12 99
Mayne, stm., Austl. D4 70
Mayne Island, i., B.C., Can. g12 99
Maynooth, Ont., Can. B7 103
Mayo, Yukon, Can. D5 96
Mayo, Fl., U.S. B3 116
Mayo, Md., U.S. C4 127
Mayo, S.C., U.S. A4 147
Mayo, co., Ire. H4 8
Mayo, stm., Col. G4 84
Mayo, stm., Mex. D5 90
Mayo, stm., Peru B3 82
Mayodan, N.C., U.S. A3 140
Mayon Volcano, vol., Phil. O20 39b
Mayor Buratovich, Arg. J7 80
Mayor Pablo Lagerenza, Para. H11 82
Mayotte, dep., Afr. D9 58
May Park, Or., U.S. B8 144
May Pen, Jam. F6 94
Mayport Naval Station, mil., Fl., U.S. B5 116
Mayrhofen, Aus. H11 10
Mays, In., U.S. E7 121
Mays Landing, N.J., U.S. E3 137
Mays Lick, Ky., U.S. B6 124
Maysville, Al., U.S. A3 108
Maysville, Ar., U.S. A1 111
Maysville, Ga., U.S. B3 117
Maysville, Ky., U.S. B6 124
Maysville, Mo., U.S. B3 132
Maysville, N.C., U.S. C5 140
Maysville, Ok., U.S. C4 143
Mayumba, Gabon B2 58
Māyūram, India G5 46
Mayview, Mo., U.S. B4 132
Mayville, Mi., U.S. E7 129
Mayville, N.Y., U.S. C1 139
Mayville, N.D., U.S. B8 141
Mayville, Wi., U.S. E5 156
Maywood, Il., U.S. k9 120
Maywood, Mo., U.S. B6 132
Maywood, Ne., U.S. D5 134
Maywood, N.J., U.S. h8 137
Maywood Park, Or., U.S. B4 144
Maza, Arg. I7 80
Mazabuka, Zam. E5 58
Mazagan see El-Jadida, Mor. D6 62
Mazagão, Braz. D8 76
Mazamet, Fr. I9 14
Mazán, stm., Peru I6 84
Mazār, Jabal, mtn., Asia A6 50
Mazara del Vallo, Italy L7 18
Mazār-e Sharīf, Afg. B2 44
Mazarn Creek, stm., Ar., U.S. g7 111
Mazaruni, stm., Guy. E13 84
Mazaruni-Potaro, dept., Guy. D12 84
Mazatenango, Guat. C3 92
Mazatlán, Mex. F6 90
Mazatzal Mountains, mts., Az., U.S. C4 110
Mazatzal Peak, mtn., Az., U.S. C4 110
Mažeikiai, U.S.S.R. E5 26
Mazeppa, Mn., U.S. F6 130
Mazhuang, China C3 34
Mazirbe, U.S.S.R. D5 26
Mazoe, stm., Afr. E6 58
Mazomanie, Wi., U.S. E4 156
Mazon, Il., U.S. B5 120
Mazsalaca, U.S.S.R. D8 26
Mazunga, Zimb. C9 66
Mazury, reg., Pol. B20 10
Mbabane, Swaz. F10 66
Mbacké, Sen. D2 64
Mbage, Cen. Afr. Rep. O3 60
Mbaïki, Cen. Afr. Rep. H4 56
Mbala, Zam. C6 58

Name | Map Ref. | Page

Mbale, Ug. A6 58
Mbalmayo, Cam. H9 54
Mbamba Bay, Tan. D6 58
Mbandaka (Coquilhatville), Zaire A3 58
Mbanga, Cam. I14 64
M'banza Congo, Ang. C2 58
Mbanza-Ngungu, Zaire C2 58
Mbarara, Ug. B6 58
Mbari, stm., Cen. Afr. Rep. G5 56
Mbashe, stm., Afr. I9 66
M'bengué, I.C. F7 64
Mbeya, Tan. C6 58
Mbinda, Congo B2 58
Mbini, Eq. Gui. H8 54
Mbomou (Bomu), stm., Afr. H5 56
Mbonge, Cam. I14 64
Mboro, Sud. N5 60
Mbour, Sen. D1 64
Mbout, Maur. C3 64
Mbuji-Mayi (Bakwanga), Zaire C4 58
Mburucuyá, Arg. E9 80
McAdam, N.B., Can. D2 101
McAdams, Ms., U.S. B4 131
McAdoo, Pa., U.S. E9 145
McAfee Peak, mtn., Nv., U.S. B6 135
McAlester, Ok., U.S. C6 143
McAlester, Lake, res., Ok., U.S. B6 143
McAlisterville, Pa., U.S. E7 145
McAllen, Tx., U.S. F3 150
McAlmont, Ar., U.S. h10 111
McAlpine, Md., U.S. B4 127
McAlpine Lock and Dam, U.S. H6 121
McAndrews, Ky., U.S. C7 124
McArthur, Oh., U.S. C3 142
McAuley, Man., Can. D1 100
McBain, Mi., U.S. D5 129
McBee, S.C., U.S. C7 147
McBride, B.C., Can. C7 99
McCall, Id., U.S. E2 119
McCalla, Al., U.S. g6 108
McCallsburg, Ia., U.S. B4 122
McCamey, Tx., U.S. D1 150
McCammon, Id., U.S. G6 119
McCandless, Pa., U.S. h13 145
McCartney Mountain, mtn., Mt., U.S. E4 133
McCartys, N.M., U.S. B2 138
McCauley Island, i., B.C., Can. C2 99
McCaysville, Ga., U.S. B2 117
McChord Air Force Base, mil., Wa., U.S. f11 154
McClain, co., Ok., U.S. C4 143
McClave, Co., U.S. C8 113
McCleary, Wa., U.S. B2 154
McClellan Air Force Base, mil., Ca., U.S. C3 112
McClellandville, De., U.S. B2 115
McClellanville, S.C., U.S. E9 147
McClintock, Mount, mtn., Ant. D8 73
McCloud, Ca., U.S. B2 112
McClure, Il., U.S. F4 120
McClure, Oh., U.S. A2 142
McClure, Pa., U.S. E7 145
McClure, Va., U.S. e9 153
McClusky, N.D., U.S. B5 141
McColl, S.C., U.S. B8 147
McCollum, Al., U.S. B2 108
McComas, W.V., U.S. D3 155
McComb, Ms., U.S. D3 131
McComb, Oh., U.S. A2 142
McCone, co., Mt., U.S. C11 133
McConnell, Il., U.S. A4 120
McConnell Air Force Base, mil., Ks., U.S. g12 123
McConnellsburg, Pa., U.S. G6 145
McConnelstown, Pa., U.S. F5 145
McConnelsville, Oh., U.S. C4 142
McCook, Ne., U.S. D5 134
McCook, co., S.D., U.S. D8 148
McCook Lake, S.D., U.S. E9 148
McCool, Ms., U.S. B4 131
McCool Junction, Ne., U.S. D8 134
McCordsville, In., U.S. E6 121
McCormick, S.C., U.S. D3 147
McCormick, co., S.C., U.S. D3 147
McCracken, Ks., U.S. D4 123
McCracken, co., Ky., U.S. e9 124
McCreary, Man., Can. D2 100
McCreary, co., Ky., U.S. D5 124
McCrory, Ar., U.S. B4 111
McCulloch, co., Tx., U.S. D3 150
McCullough, Al., U.S. D2 108
McCullough Mountain, mtn., Nv., U.S. H6 135
McCune, Ks., U.S. E8 123
McCurtain, Ok., U.S. B7 143
McCurtain, co., Ok., U.S. C7 143
McDermitt, Nv., U.S. B4 135
McDermott, Oh., U.S. D2 142
McDonald, Ks., U.S. C2 123
McDonald, Tn., U.S. h12 149
McDonald, co., Mo., U.S. E3 132
McDonald Creek, stm., Mt., U.S. C8 133
McDonough, Ga., U.S. C2 117
McDonough, co., Il., U.S. C3 120
McDougal, Ar., U.S. A5 111
McDougall, Mount, mtn., Wy., U.S. D2 157
McDowell, Ky., U.S. C7 124
McDowell, co., N.C., U.S. f10 140
McDowell, co., W.V., U.S. D3 155
McDowell Mountains, mts., Az., U.S. k9 110
McDowell Peak, mtn., Az., U.S. k9 110
McDuffie, co., Ga., U.S. C4 117
McElroy Creek, stm., W.V., U.S. k9 155
Mcensk, U.S.S.R. H19 26
McEwen, Tn., U.S. A4 149
McFadden, Wy., U.S. E6 157
McFarland, Ca., U.S. E4 112
McFarland, Ks., U.S. C7 123
McFarland, Wi., U.S. E4 156
McGaheysville, Va., U.S. B4 153
McGehee, Ar., U.S. D4 111
McGill, Nv., U.S. D7 135
McGivney, N.B., Can. C3 101
McGrath, Ak., U.S. C8 109
McGraw, N.Y., U.S. C4 139
McGraws, W.V., U.S. D3 155
McGregor, Ia., U.S. A6 122
McGregor, Mn., U.S. D5 130
McGregor, N.D., U.S. A3 141
McGregor, Tx., U.S. D4 150
McGregor, stm., B.C., Can. B7 99
McGregor Lake, l., Alta., Can. D4 98
McGregor Range, mts., Austl. F5 70
McGuffey, Oh., U.S. B2 142
McGuire, Mount, mtn., Id., U.S. D4 119
McGuire Air Force Base, mil., N.J., U.S. C3 137
McHenry, Il., U.S. A5 120
McHenry, Ky., U.S. C3 124
McHenry, Md., U.S. k12 127
McHenry, Ms., U.S. E4 131
McHenry, N.D., U.S. B7 141
McHenry, co., Il., U.S. A5 120
McHenry, co., N.D., U.S. A5 141
Mchinji, Mwi. D6 58
McIndoe Falls, Vt., U.S. C4 152
McIntosh, Al., U.S. D1 108
McIntosh, Fl., U.S. C4 116
McIntosh, Ga., U.S. E5 117
McIntosh, Mn., U.S. C3 130
McIntosh, S.D., U.S. B4 148
McIntosh, co., Ga., U.S. E5 117
McIntosh, co., N.D., U.S. C6 141
McIntosh, co., Ok., U.S. B6 143
McIntosh Lake, l., Sask., Can. B3 105
McIntosh Run, stm., Md., U.S. D4 127
McIntyre, Ga., U.S. D3 117
McKean, co., Pa., U.S. C4 145
McKee, Ky., U.S. C6 124
McKee City, N.J., U.S. E3 137
McKeesport, Pa., U.S. F2 145
McKees Rocks, Pa., U.S. F1 145
McKenney, Va., U.S. D5 153
McKenzie, Al., U.S. D3 108
McKenzie, Tn., U.S. A3 149
McKenzie, co., N.D., U.S. B2 141
McKenzie, stm., Or., U.S. C4 144
McKerrow, Ont., Can. A3 103
McKinley, co., N.M., U.S. B1 138
McKinley, Mount, mtn., Ak., U.S. C9 109
McKinley Park, Ak., U.S. C10 109
McKinleyville, Ca., U.S. B1 112
McKinney, Ky., U.S. C5 124
McKinney, Tx., U.S. C4 150
McKinney, Lake, l., Ks., U.S. E2 123
McKittrick Summit, mtn., Ca., U.S. E4 112
McLain, Ms., U.S. D5 131
McLaughlin, Alta., Can. C5 98
McLaughlin, S.D., U.S. B5 148
McLaurin, Ms., U.S. D4 131
McLean, Sask., Can. G3 105
McLean, Il., U.S. C4 120
McLean, Tx., U.S. B2 150
McLean, Va., U.S. g12 153
McLean, co., Il., U.S. C4 120
McLean, co., Ky., U.S. C2 124
McLean, co., N.D., U.S. B4 141
McLean Lake, l., Sask., Can. A6 98
McLean Mountain, mtn., Me., U.S. A4 126
McLeansboro, Il., U.S. E5 120
McLemoresville, Tn., U.S. B3 149
McLennan, Alta., Can. B2 98
McLennan, co., Tx., U.S. D4 150
McLeod, N.D., U.S. C8 141
McLeod, co., Mn., U.S. F4 130
McLeod, stm., Alta., Can. C2 98
McLeod Bay, b., N.W. Ter., Can. D10 96
McLeod Lake, B.C., Can. B6 99
M'Clintock Channel, strt., N.W. Ter., Can. B12 96
McLoud, Ok., U.S. B4 143
McLoughlin, Mount, mtn., Or., U.S. D4 144
McLouth, Ks., U.S. C8 123
M'Clure Strait, strt., N.W. Ter., Can. B9 96
McMechen, W.V., U.S. B4 155
McMillan, Lake, res., N.M., U.S. E5 138
McMillin, Wa., U.S. f11 154
McMinn, co., Tn., U.S. D9 149
McMinnville, Or., U.S. B3 144
McMinnville, Tn., U.S. D8 149
McMullen, Al., U.S. B1 108
McMullen, co., Tx., U.S. E3 150
McMurdo, sci., Ant. C8 73
McMurdo Sound, strt., Ant. C8 73
McNabb, Il., U.S. B4 120
McNairy, co., Tn., U.S. B3 149
McNary, Az., U.S. C6 110
McNary Dam, U.S. B7 144
McNeil, Ar., U.S. D2 111
McNeil, Mount, mtn., B.C., Can. B2 99
McNeil Island, i., Wa., U.S. f10 154
McNeill, Ms., U.S. E4 131
McPherson, Ks., U.S. D6 123
McPherson, co., Ks., U.S. D6 123
McPherson, co., Ne., U.S. C4 134
McPherson, co., S.D., U.S. B6 148
McPherson Range, mts., Austl. G10 70
McQueeney, Tx., U.S. h7 150
McRae, Ar., U.S. B4 111
McRae, Ga., U.S. D4 117
McRoberts, Ky., U.S. C7 124
McSherrystown, Pa., U.S. G7 145
McTaggart, Sask., Can. H3 105
McTavish, Man., Can. E3 100
McVeigh, Ky., U.S. C7 124
McVille, N.D., U.S. B7 141
McWilliams, Al., U.S. D2 108
M'Daourouch, Alg. M2 18
Meacham, Sask., Can. E3 105
Mead, Co., U.S. A6 113
Mead, Ne., U.S. C9 134
Mead, Wa., U.S. B8 154
Mead, Lake, res., U.S. A1 110
Meade, Ks., U.S. E3 123
Meade, co., Ks., U.S. E3 123
Meade, co., Ky., U.S. C3 124
Meade, co., S.D., U.S. C3 148
Meade, stm., Ak., U.S. B8 109
Meaden Peak, mtn., Co., U.S. A3 113
Meade Peak, mtn., Id., U.S. G7 119
Meadow, Tx., U.S. C1 150
Meadow, Ut., U.S. E3 151
Meadow, stm., W.V., U.S. C4 155
Meadow Bridge, W.V., U.S. D4 155
Meadowbrook, W.V., U.S. k10 155
Meadow Creek, W.V., U.S. D4 155
Meadow Creek, stm., W.V., U.S. n14 155
Meadow Grove, Ne., U.S. B8 134
Meadow Lake, Sask., Can. n7 105
Meadow Lands, Pa., U.S. F1 145
Meadow Mountain, mtn., U.S. k12 127
Meadows, Id., U.S. E2 119
Meadow Valley Wash, val., Nv., U.S. F7 135
Meadowview, Va., U.S. f10 153
Meadville, Ms., U.S. D3 131
Meadville, Mo., U.S. B4 132
Meadville, Pa., U.S. C1 145
Meaford, Ont., Can. C4 103
Meagher, co., Mt., U.S. D6 133
Meaghers Grant, N.S., Can. E6 101
Mealy Mountains, mts., Newf., Can. h9 102
Méan, Bel. H7 12
Meana, U.S.S.R. C16 48
Meandarra, Austl. F8 70
Meander Creek Reservoir, res., Oh., U.S. A5 142
Means, Ky., U.S. C6 124
Mears, Mi., U.S. E4 129
Meath, co., Ire. H7 8
Meath, hist. reg., Ire. H6 8
Meath Park, Sask., Can. D3 105
Meaux, Fr. D9 14
Mebane, N.C., U.S. A3 140
Mecaya, stm., Col. G5 84
Mecca, Ca., U.S. F5 112
Mecca, In., U.S. E3 121
Mecca see Makkah, Sau. Ar. D1 47
Mechanic Falls, Me., U.S. D2 126
Mechanicsburg, In., U.S. D5 121
Mechanicsburg, Oh., U.S. B2 142
Mechanicsburg, Pa., U.S. F7 145
Mechanicsville, Ia., U.S. C6 122
Mechanicsville, Md., U.S. D4 127
Mechanicsville, Va., U.S. C5 153
Mechanicville, N.Y., U.S. C7 139
Mechant, Lake, l., La., U.S. E4 125
Mechelen (Malines), Bel. F5 12
Mechita, Arg. H8 80
Mechra Safsaf, Mor. K9 16
Mechriyya, Alg. D10 62
Mechroha, Alg. M2 18
Mecklenburg, co., N.C., U.S. B2 140
Mecklenburg, co., Va., U.S. D4 153
Mecklenburg, hist. reg., Ger. B12 10
Mecklenburger Bucht, b., Ger. A11 10
Mecklenburg-Vorpommern, state, Ger. B12 10
Meckling, S.D., U.S. E8 148
Mecosta, Mi., U.S. E5 129
Mecosta, co., Mi., U.S. E5 129
Meda, Port. E4 16
Medan, Indon. M5 40
Medanales, N.M., U.S. A3 138
Médanos, Arg. J7 80
Medanosa, Punta, c., Arg. F3 78
Medaryville, In., U.S. B4 121
Meddybumps Lake, l., Me., U.S. C5 126
Mede, Italy D3 18
Medeiros Neto, Braz. D8 79
Medellín, Col. D5 84
Médenine, Tun. D16 62
Mederdra, Maur. C2 64
Medfield, Ma., U.S. h10 128
Medford, Ma., U.S. B5 128
Medford, Mn., U.S. F5 130
Medford, N.J., U.S. D3 137
Medford, Ok., U.S. A4 143
Medford, Or., U.S. E4 144
Medford, Wi., U.S. C3 156
Medford Lakes, N.J., U.S. D3 137
Medgidia, Rom. E12 20
Media, Pa., U.S. G11 145
Mediapolis, Ia., U.S. C6 122
Mediaș, Rom. C8 20
Medical Lake, Wa., U.S. B8 154
Medicina, Italy E6 18
Medicine Bow, Wy., U.S. E6 157
Medicine Bow, stm., Wy., U.S. E6 157
Medicine Bow Mountains, mts., U.S. E6 157
Medicine Bow Peak, mtn., Wy., U.S. E6 157
Medicine Creek, stm., Mo., U.S. B4 132
Medicine Creek, stm., Ne., U.S. D5 134
Medicine Hat, Alta., Can. D5 98
Medicine Lake, Mt., U.S. B12 133
Medicine Lodge, Ks., U.S. E5 123
Medicine Lodge, stm., U.S. E4 123
Medicine Park, Ok., U.S. C3 143
Medina, Braz. D8 79
Medina, N.Y., U.S. B2 139
Medina, N.D., U.S. C6 141
Medina, Oh., U.S. A4 142
Medina, Tn., U.S. B3 149
Medina, Wa., U.S. e11 154
Medina, co., Oh., U.S. A4 142
Medina, co., Tx., U.S. E3 150
Medina, stm., Tx., U.S. k7 150
Medina see Al-Madīnah, Sau. Ar. B1 47
Medina del Campo, Spain D7 16
Medininkai, U.S.S.R. G8 26
Medinīpur, India I12 44
Mediterranean Sea E9 52
Medjerda, Monts de la, mts., Afr. M3 18
Mednogorsk, U.S.S.R. G9 22
Mednoje, U.S.S.R. E18 26
Mednyj, ostrov, i., U.S.S.R. G25 24
Médoc, reg., Fr. G6 14
Medora, Man., Can. E1 100
Medora, Il., U.S. D3 120
Medora, In., U.S. G5 121
Medora, N.D., U.S. C2 141
Médouneu, Gabon A2 58
Medstead, Sask., Can. D1 105
Meductic, N.B., Can. D2 101
Medveđa, Yugo. G5 20
Medvedevskoje, U.S.S.R. C18 26
Medvedica, stm., U.S.S.R. G6 22
Medvežjegorsk, U.S.S.R. E4 22
Medvežji ostrova, is., U.S.S.R. C24 24
Medway, Me., U.S. C4 126
Medway, Ma., U.S. B5 128
Medway, stm., N.S., Can. E5 101
Medyn', U.S.S.R. G18 26
Meekatharra, Austl. E3 68
Meeker, Co., U.S. A3 113
Meeker, Ok., U.S. B5 143
Meeker, co., Mn., U.S. E4 130
Meelpaeg Lake, res., Newf., Can. D3 102
Meer, Bel. F6 12
Meerane, Ger. E12 10
Meerut, India F7 44
Meeteetse, Wy., U.S. B4 157
Meeting Creek, Alta., Can. C4 98
Mega, Eth. H8 56
Mégantic, Lac, l., Que., Can. D7 104
Mégantic, Mont, mtn., Que., Can. D6 104
Mégara, Grc. K7 20
Megargel, Al., U.S. D2 108
Meggett, S.C., U.S. F7 147
Meghālaya, state, India H14 44
Meghna, stm., Bngl. H14 44
Megunticook, Mount, mtn., Me., U.S. D3 126
Mehadia, Rom. E6 20
Mehar, Pak. G2 44
Mehdia, Alg. C11 62
Mehedinți, co., Rom. E6 20
Meherrin, stm., U.S. A4 140
Mehlville, Mo., U.S. f13 132
Mehrān, Iran E9 48
Meia Ponte, stm., Braz. D4 79
Meigs, Ga., U.S. E2 117
Meigs, co., Oh., U.S. C3 142
Meigs, co., Tn., U.S. D9 149
Meiktila, Burma D3 40
Meilie, China I6 34
Meiningen, Ger. E10 10
Meio, Rio do, stm., Braz. D9 79
Meiringen, Switz. E9 13
Meissen, Ger. D13 10
Meixian, China K5 34
Meiyino, Sud. N8 60
Meizhai, China B10 40
Mejerda, Oued (Oued Medjerda), stm., Afr. M4 18
Mejez el Bab, Tun. M4 18
Mejicanos, El Sal. D5 92
Mejillones, Chile B3 80
Mejillones, Península, pen., Chile B3 80
Mejillones del Sur, Bahía de, b., Chile B3 80
Mékambo, Gabon A2 58
Mekele, Eth. K10 60
Mekinock, N.D., U.S. A8 141
Meknès, Mor. D8 62
Mekong, stm., Asia H8 40
Mekoryuk, Ak., U.S. C6 109
Mékrou, stm., Afr. F7 54
Melado, stm., Chile H3 80
Melaka, Malay. M7 40
Melanesia, is., Oc. I19 158
Melba, Id., U.S. F2 119
Melber, Ky., U.S. f9 124
Melbeta, Ne., U.S. C2 134
Melbourne, Austl. K6 70
Melbourne, Ont., Can. E3 103
Melbourne, Ar., U.S. A4 111
Melbourne, Fl., U.S. D6 116
Melbourne, Ia., U.S. C4 122
Melbourne, Ky., U.S. h14 124
Melbourne Beach, Fl., U.S. D6 116
Melby House, Scot., U.K. A12 8
Melcher, Ia., U.S. C4 122
Melchor Múzquiz, Mex. D9 90
Meldorf, Ger. A9 10
Meldrim, Ga., U.S. D5 117
Melechovo, U.S.S.R. E24 26
Melegnano, Italy D4 18
Melenki, U.S.S.R. F24 26
Meleuz, U.S.S.R. G9 22
Mélèzes, Rivière aux, stm., Que., Can. g12 104
Melfi, Chad F4 56
Melfi, Italy H10 18
Melfort, Sask., Can. E3 105
Melgaço, Port. C3 16
Melgar, Col. E5 84
Melghir, Chott, l., Alg. C14 62
Melhus, Nor. J12 6
Meli, stm., Afr. G4 64
Meliane, Oued, stm., Tun. M5 18
Melide, Switz. G10 13
Melilla, Sp. N. Afr. C9 62
Melincué, Arg. G8 80
Melipilla, Chile G3 80
Melita, Man., Can. E1 100
Melitopol', U.S.S.R. F15 4
Mellègue, Oued, stm., Afr. M3 18
Mellen, Wi., U.S. B3 156
Mellette, S.D., U.S. B7 148
Mellette, co., S.D., U.S. D5 148
Mellott, In., U.S. D3 121
Mellwood, Ar., U.S. C5 111
Mel'nica-Podol'skaja, U.S.S.R. A10 20
Mělník, Czech. E14 10
Melo, Ur. G11 80
Melo, stm., Para. I12 82
Melocheville, Que., Can. q19 104
Melong, Cam. I14 64
Melos see Mílos, i., Grc. M8 20
Melrose, N.B., Can. C6 101
Melrose, N.S., Can. D7 101
Melrose, Ct., U.S. B5 114
Melrose, Fl., U.S. C4 116
Melrose, Ma., U.S. B5 128
Melrose, Mn., U.S. E4 130
Melrose, N.M., U.S. C6 138
Melrose, Wi., U.S. D3 156
Melrose Park, Fl., U.S. r13 116
Melstone, Mt., U.S. D9 133
Melton Hill Lake, res., Tn., U.S. D9 149
Melton Mowbray, Eng., U.K. I13 8
Melúa, Col. F6 84
Melun, Burma D2 40
Melun, Fr. D9 14
Melvern, Ks., U.S. D8 123
Melvern Lake, res., Ks., U.S. D8 123
Melville, Sask., Can. G4 105
Melville, La., U.S. D4 125
Melville, Lake, l., Newf., Can. B2 102
Melville Bugt, b., Grnld. B13 86
Melville Island, i., Austl. B6 68
Melville Island, i., N.W. Ter., Can. B8 86
Melville Peninsula, pen., N.W. Ter., Can. C16 96
Melville Sound, strt., N.W. Ter., Can. C11 96
Melvin, Al., U.S. D1 108
Melvin, Il., U.S. C5 120
Melvin, Ia., U.S. A2 122
Melvin, Ky., U.S. C7 124
Melvin, Lough, l., Eur. G5 8
Melvin Village, N.H., U.S. C4 136
Melyana, Alg. B12 62
Melzo, Italy D4 18
Memel, S. Afr. F9 66
Memel see Nemunas, stm., U.S.S.R. F6 26
Memmingen, Ger. H10 10
Memo, stm., Ven. C9 84
Mémót, Camb. I9 40
Mempawah, Indon. N10 40
Memphis, Fl., U.S. p10 116
Memphis, In., U.S. H6 121
Memphis, Mi., U.S. F8 129
Memphis, Mo., U.S. A5 132
Memphis, Ne., U.S. g12 134
Memphis, Tn., U.S. B1 149
Memphis, Tx., U.S. B2 150
Memphis Naval Air Station, mil., Tn., U.S. B2 149
Memramcook, N.B., Can. C5 101
Mena, Ar., U.S. C1 111
Menahga, Mn., U.S. D3 130
Ménaka, Mali D11 64
Menaldum, Neth. B8 12
Menan, Id., U.S. F7 119
Menands, N.Y., U.S. C7 139
Menard, Tx., U.S. D3 150
Menard, co., Il., U.S. C4 120
Menard, co., Tx., U.S. D3 150
Menasha, Wi., U.S. D5 156
Menawashei, Sud. K3 60
Mendawai, stm., Indon. F5 38
Mende, Fr. H10 14
Menden, Ger. D7 10
Mendenhall, Ms., U.S. D4 131
Mendes, Ga., U.S. E5 117
Méndez, Ec. I3 84
Méndez, Mex. E10 90
Mendham, Sask., Can. G1 105
Mendham, N.J., U.S. B3 137
Mendi, Eth. M8 60
Mendi, Pap. N. Gui. G11 38
Mendocino, Ca., U.S. C2 112
Mendocino, co., Ca., U.S. C2 112
Mendon, Il., U.S. C2 120
Mendon, Ma., U.S. h9 128
Mendon, Mi., U.S. F5 129
Mendon, Mo., U.S. B4 132
Mendon, Oh., U.S. B1 142
Mendon, Ut., U.S. B4 151
Mendota, Ca., U.S. D3 112
Mendota, Il., U.S. B4 120
Mendota, Lake, l., Wi., U.S. E4 156
Mendoza, Arg. G4 80
Mendoza, Peru B3 82
Mendoza, prov., Arg. H4 80
Mendoza, stm., Arg. G4 80
Ménéac, Fr. D4 14
Mene de Mauroa, Ven. B7 84
Mene Grande, Ven. C7 84
Menemen, Tur. K11 20
Menen (Menin), Bel. G3 12
Menfi, Italy L7 18
Mengcheng, China E10 30
Menggala, Indon. F4 38
Menggu, China A7 40
Menghai, China C6 40
Mengla, China D6 40
Mengzhi, China B5 40
Mengzi, China C7 40
Menifee, Ar., U.S. B3 111
Menifee, co., Ky., U.S. C6 124
Menindee, Austl. I5 70
Menindee Lake, l., Austl. I5 70
Menlo, Ga., U.S. B1 117
Menlo, Ia., U.S. C3 122
Menlo, Wa., U.S. C2 154
Menlo Park, Ca., U.S. k8 112
Menno, S.D., U.S. D8 148
Menominee, Mi., U.S. C3 129
Menominee, co., Mi., U.S. C3 129
Menominee, co., Wi., U.S. C5 156
Menominee, stm., U.S. C6 156
Menominee Indian Reservation, Wi., U.S. C5 156
Menomonee, stm., Wi., U.S. m11 156
Menomonee Falls, Wi., U.S. E5 156
Menomonie, Wi., U.S. D2 156
Menongue, Ang. D3 58
Menorca, i., Spain F16 16
Mens, Fr. H12 14
Mentawai, Kepulauan, is., Indon. F2 38
Mentawai, Selat, strt., Indon. F3 38
Mentmore, N.M., U.S. B1 138
Menton, Fr. I14 14
Mentone, Al., U.S. A4 108
Mentone, In., U.S. B5 121
Mentor, Ky., U.S. k14 124
Mentor, Oh., U.S. A4 142
Mentor, Tn., U.S. n13 149
Mentor-on-the-Lake, Oh., U.S. A4 142
Menzel Bourguiba, Tun. L4 18
Menzel Bou Zelfa, Tun. M5 18
Menzel Djemil, Tun. L4 18
Menzel Temime, Tun. M5 18
Menzies, Austl. E4 68
Menzies, Mount, mtn., Ant. C5 73
Meoqui, Mex. C7 90
Meota, Sask., Can. D1 105
Meppel, Neth. C9 12
Meppen, Ger. C7 10
Meqerghane, Sebkha, pl., Alg. G11 62
Mequon, Wi., U.S. E6 156
Mer, Fr. E8 14
Meramec, stm., Mo., U.S. C7 132
Merano (Meran), Italy C6 18
Merasheen Island, i., Newf., Can. E4 102
Merate, Italy D4 18
Merauke, Indon. G11 38
Meraux, La., U.S. k12 125
Mercaderes, Col. G4 84
Mercāra, India F3 46
Merced, Ca., U.S. D3 112
Merced, co., Ca., U.S. D3 112
Merced, stm., Ca., U.S. D3 112
Mercedario, Cerro, mtn., Arg. F3 80
Mercedes, Arg. H9 80
Mercedes, Arg. G6 80
Mercedes, Arg. E9 80
Mercedes, Tx., U.S. F4 150
Mercedes, Ur. G9 80
Mercer, Mo., U.S. A4 132
Mercer, N.D., U.S. B5 141
Mercer, Pa., U.S. D1 145
Mercer, Tn., U.S. B2 149
Mercer, Wi., U.S. B3 156
Mercer, co., Il., U.S. B3 120
Mercer, co., Ky., U.S. C5 124
Mercer, co., Mo., U.S. A4 132
Mercer, co., N.J., U.S. C3 137
Mercer, co., N.D., U.S. B4 141
Mercer, co., Oh., U.S. B1 142
Mercer, co., Pa., U.S. D1 145
Mercer, co., W.V., U.S. D3 155
Mercer Island, Wa., U.S. B3 154
Mercer Island, i., Wa., U.S. e11 154
Mercersburg, Pa., U.S. G6 145
Mercerville, N.J., U.S. C3 137
Merchtem, Bel. G5 12
Mercier, Que., Can. D4 104
Mercy, Cape, c., N.W. Ter., Can. D20 96
Meredith, N.H., U.S. C3 136
Meredith, Lake, l., Co., U.S. C7 113
Meredith, Lake, res., Tx., U.S. B2 150
Meredith Center, N.H., U.S. C3 136
Meredosia, Il., U.S. D3 120
Meredosia Lake, l., Il., U.S. D3 120
Mereeg, Som. H10 56
Merenkurkku (Norra Kvarken), strt., Eur. J17 6
Merevari, stm., Ven. E10 84
Merewa, Eth. N9 60
Mergui (Myeik), Burma H5 40
Mergui Archipelago, is., Burma H5 40
Meriç (Marica) (Évros), stm., Eur. H10 20
Mérida, Mex. G15 90
Mérida, Spain G5 16
Mérida, Ven. C7 84
Mérida, state, Ven. C7 84
Mérida, Cordillera de, mts., Ven. C7 84
Meriden, Ct., U.S. C4 114
Meriden, Ks., U.S. C8 123
Meriden, N.H., U.S. C2 136
Meriden, Wy., U.S. E8 157
Meridian, Ga., U.S. E5 117
Meridian, Id., U.S. F2 119
Meridian, Ms., U.S. C5 131
Meridian, Pa., U.S. E2 145
Meridian, Tx., U.S. D4 150
Meridian Hills, In., U.S. k10 121
Meridian Naval Air Station, mil., Ms., U.S. C5 131
Meridianville, Al., U.S. A3 108
Mérignac, Fr. H6 14
Merigold, Ms., U.S. B3 131
Merigomish, N.S., Can. D7 101
Merimbula, Austl. K8 70
Merín, Laguna (Lagoa Mirim), b., S.A. G12 80
Merino, Co., U.S. A7 113
Merinos, Ur. G10 80
Meriwether, co., Ga., U.S. C2 117
Merkel, Tx., U.S. C2 150
Merkendorf, Ger. F10 10
Merkinė, U.S.S.R. G7 26
Merkulovići, U.S.S.R. I13 26
Merlin, Ont., Can. E2 103
Merlin, Or., U.S. E3 144
Merlo, Arg. G6 80
Mermentau, La., U.S. D3 125
Mermentau, stm., La., U.S. E3 125
Merna, Ne., U.S. C6 134
Mernye, Hung. I17 10
Merom, In., U.S. F2 121
Meron, Hare, mtn., Isr. C4 50
Merredin, Austl. F3 68
Merriam, Ks., U.S. k16 123
Merrick, co., Ne., U.S. C7 134
Merrick Brook, stm., Ct., U.S. C7 114
Merrickville, Ont., Can. C9 103
Merrifield, Mn., U.S. D4 130
Merrill, Ia., U.S. B1 122
Merrill, Mi., U.S. E6 129
Merrill, Or., U.S. E5 144
Merrill, Wi., U.S. C4 156
Merrillan, Wi., U.S. D3 156
Merrillville, In., U.S. B3 121
Merrimac, Ma., U.S. A5 128
Merrimac, Wi., U.S. E4 156
Merrimack, N.H., U.S. E4 136
Merrimack, co., N.H., U.S. D3 136
Merrimack, stm., U.S. A5 128
Merriman, Ne., U.S. B4 134
Merritt, B.C., Can. D7 99
Merritt Island, Fl., U.S. D6 116
Merritt Reservoir, res., Ne., U.S. B5 134
Merriwa, Austl. I9 70
Mer Rouge, La., U.S. B4 125
Merrymeeting Lake, l., N.H., U.S. D4 136
Merryville, La., U.S. D2 125
Mersch, Lux. I9 12

Name | Map Ref. | Page

Merseburg, Ger. D11 10
Mersey, stm., Austl. M7 70
Mershon, Ga., U.S. E4 117
Mersing, Malay. M7 40
Mērsrags, U.S.S.R. D6 26
Merthyr Tydfil, Wales, U.K. J10 8
Mértola, Port. H4 16
Merton, Wi., U.S. m11 156
Mertzon, Tx., U.S. D2 150
Méru, Fr. C9 14
Meru, Kenya A7 58
Meru, Mount, mtn., Tan. B7 58
Mervin, Sask., Can. D1 105
Merwin Lake, res., Wa., U.S. C3 154
Méry, Fr. D10 14
Merzig, Ger. F6 10
Mesa, Az., U.S. D4 110
Mesa, Co., U.S. B2 113
Mesa, co., Co., U.S. C2 113
Mesa, stm., Spain D10 16
Mesabi Range, hills, Mn., U.S. C6 130
Mesagne, Italy I12 18
Mesa Mountain, mtn., Co., U.S. D4 113
Mesa Verde National Park, Co., U.S. D2 113
Mescalero, N.M., U.S. D4 138
Mescalero Indian Reservation, N.M., U.S. D4 138
Meschede, Ger. D8 10
Meščovsk, U.S.S.R. G18 26
Mesena, Ga., U.S. C4 117
Meservey, Ia., U.S. B4 122
Mesfinto, Eth. K9 60
Meshgīn Shahr, Iran B9 48
Meshomasic Mountain, mtn., Ct., U.S. C5 114
Mesick, Mi., U.S. D5 129
Mesilla, N.M., U.S. E3 138
Mesita, N.M., U.S. C2 138
Meskiana, Alg. C14 62
Meslay-du-Maine, Fr. E6 14
Mesocco, Switz. F11 13
Mesolóngion, Grc. K5 20
Mesopotamia, hist. reg., Asia D8 48
Mesquita, Braz. E7 79
Mesquite, Nv., U.S. G7 135
Mesquite, N.M., U.S. E3 138
Mesquite, Tx., U.S. n10 150
Messalo, stm., Moz. D7 58
Messalonskee Lake, l., Me., U.S. D3 126
Messina, Italy K10 18
Messina, S. Afr. D10 66
Messina, Stretto di, strt., Italy K10 18
Messini, Grc. L6 20
Messiniakós Kólpos, b., Grc. M6 20
Messojacha, stm., U.S.S.R. D13 22
Mestá, Grc. K9 20
Mesta (Néstos), stm., Eur. H7 20
Mestasa, Mor. C8 62
Mestghanem, Alg. C11 62
Mestre, Italy D7 18
Meta, Mo., U.S. C5 132
Meta, dept., Col. F6 84
Meta, stm., S.A. D9 84
Métabetchouan, Que., Can. A6 104
Métabetchouane, stm., Que., Can. A5 104
Meta Incognita Peninsula, pen., N.W. Ter., Can. D19 96
Metairie, La., U.S. k11 125
Metaline, Wa., U.S. A8 154
Metaline Falls, Wa., U.S. A8 154
Metamora, Il., U.S. C4 120
Metamora, In., U.S. F7 121
Metamora, Mi., U.S. F7 129
Metamora, Oh., U.S. A2 142
Metán, Arg. C6 80
Metapán, El Sal. C5 92
Meta Pond, l., Newf., Can. D4 102
Metcalf, Ga., U.S. F3 117
Metcalf, Il., U.S. D6 120
Metcalfe, Ont., Can. B9 103
Metcalfe, Ms., U.S. B2 131
Metcalfe, co., Ky., U.S. C4 124
Metedeconk, North Branch, stm., N.J., U.S. C4 137
Metedeconk, South Branch, stm., N.J., U.S. C3 137
Meteghan, N.S., Can. E3 101
Meteghan River, N.S., Can. E3 101
Meteghan Station, N.S., Can. E3 101
Metema, Eth. K9 60
Meteor Crater, crat., Az., U.S. C4 110
Methóni, Grc. M5 20
Methow, stm., Wa., U.S. A5 154
Methuen, Ma., U.S. A5 128
Metiskow, Alta., Can. C5 98
Metković, Yugo. F12 18
Metlakatla, Ak., U.S. D13 109
Metlaoui, Tun. C15 62
Metlatonoc, Mex. I10 90
Meto, Bayou, stm., Ar., U.S. C4 111
Metolius, Or., U.S. C5 144
Metonga, Lake, l., Wi., U.S. C5 156
Metropolis, Il., U.S. F5 120
Metropolitana, prov., Chile G3 80
Metsematluku, Bots. E7 66
Mettawee, stm., U.S. E2 152
Metter, Ga., U.S. D4 117
Mettmann, Ger. D6 10
Mettuppālaiyam, India G4 46
Mettūr, India G4 46
Metu, Eth. M8 60
Metuchen, N.J., U.S. B4 137
Metulla, Isr. B5 50
Metz, Fr. C13 14
Metzger, Or., U.S. h12 144
Meulan, Fr. C8 14
Meureudu, Indon. L4 40
Meurthe, stm., Fr. D13 14
Meurthe-et-Moselle, dept., Fr. D13 14
Meuse, dept., Fr. D12 14
Meuse (Maas), stm., Eur. E5 10
Meuselwitz, Ger. D12 10
Mexia, Al., U.S. D2 108
Mexia, Tx., U.S. D4 150
Mexia, Lake, res., Tx., U.S. D4 150
Mexiana, Ilha, i., Braz. D9 76
Mexicali, Mex. A2 90
Mexican Springs, N.M., U.S. B1 138
Mexico, In., U.S. C5 121
Mexico, Me., U.S. D2 126
Mexico, Mo., U.S. B6 132
Mexico, N.Y., U.S. B4 139
México, state, Mex. H10 90
Mexico (México), ctry., N.A. F9 90
Mexico, Gulf of, b., N.A. C6 88
Mexico City see Ciudad de México, Mex. H10 90
Meximieux, Fr. G12 14
Meycauayan, Phil. N19 39b
Meyersdale, Pa., U.S. G3 145
Meyisti, i., Grc. H13 4
Meymac, Fr. G9 14
Meymaneh, Afg. C1 44
Meymeh, stm., Asia E9 48
Meyrargues, Fr. I12 14
Meẓada, Ḥorvot (Masada), hist., Isr. F4 50
Mezapa, Hond. B7 92
Mezcala, Mex. I10 90
Mezcalapa, stm., Mex. I13 90
Meždurečensk, U.S.S.R. G9 24
Mèze, Fr. I10 14
Mezen', U.S.S.R. D6 22
Mezen', stm., U.S.S.R. D6 22
Mežgorje, U.S.S.R. A7 20
Mézin, Fr. H7 14
Mezinovskij, U.S.S.R. F23 26
Mezőberény, Hung. I21 10
Mezőcsát, Hung. H20 10
Mezőkovácsháza, Hung. I20 10
Mezőkövesd, Hung. H20 10
Mezőtúr, Hung. H20 10
Mezquital, Mex. F7 90
Mezquital, stm., Mex. F7 90
Mglin, U.S.S.R. H15 26
M'goun, Irhil, mtn., Mor. E7 62
Mhow, India I6 44
Miahuatlán de Porfirio Díaz, Mex. I11 90
Miajadas, Spain F6 16
Miami, Man., Can. E2 100
Miami, Az., U.S. D5 110
Miami, Fl., U.S. G6 116
Miami, In., U.S. C5 121
Miami, N.M., U.S. A5 138
Miami, Ok., U.S. A7 143
Miami, Tx., U.S. B2 150
Miami, W.V., U.S. m13 155
Miami, co., In., U.S. C5 121
Miami, co., Ks., U.S. D9 123
Miami, co., Oh., U.S. B1 142
Miami Beach, Fl., U.S. G6 116
Miami Canal, Fl., U.S. F6 116
Miami International Airport, Fl., U.S. G6 116
Miamisburg, Oh., U.S. C1 142
Miami Shores, Fl., U.S. G6 116
Miami Springs, Fl., U.S. G6 116
Miamitown, Oh., U.S. o12 142
Miāndoāb, Iran C9 48
Miandrivazo, Madag. Q21 67b
Miāneh, Iran C9 48
Miangas, Pulau, i., Indon. D8 38
Mianhu, China L5 34
Mianus Reservoir, res., U.S. E1 114
Miānwāli, Pak. D4 44
Mianyang, China E7 30
Mianyang, China E2 34
Miaoli, Tai. K9 34
Miarinavaratra, Madag. R22 67b
Miass, U.S.S.R. G10 22
Miastko, Pol. A17 10
Mica Creek, B.C., Can. C8 99
Mica Mountain, mtn., Az., U.S. E5 110
Micanopy, Fl., U.S. C4 116
Micaúne, Moz. B13 66
Micco, Fl., U.S. E6 116
Miccosukee, Lake, res., Fl., U.S. B2 116
Michajlov, U.S.S.R. G22 26
Michajlovka, U.S.S.R. G6 22
Michanoviči, U.S.S.R. H10 26
Michaud, Point, c., N.S., Can. D9 101
Michelson, Mount, mtn., Ak., U.S. B11 109
Miches, Dom. Rep. E10 94
Michichi, Alta., Can. D4 98
Michie, Tn., U.S. B3 149
Michigamme, Mi., U.S. B2 129
Michigamme, Lake, l., Mi., U.S. B2 129
Michigamme Reservoir, res., Mi., U.S. B2 129
Michigan, N.D., U.S. A7 141
Michigan, state, U.S. E6 129
Michigan, stm., Co., U.S. A4 113
Michigan, Lake, l., U.S. C9 106
Michigan Center, Mi., U.S. F6 129
Michigan City, In., U.S. A4 121
Michigan City, Ms., U.S. A4 131
Michigan Island, i., Wi., U.S. B3 156
Michigan Prairie, reg., Wa., U.S. C7 154
Michigantown, In., U.S. D5 121
Michnevo, U.S.S.R. F20 26
Michoacán, state, Mex. H9 90
Mico, stm., Nic. E10 92
Mico, Montañas del, mts., Guat. B6 92
Micro, N.C., U.S. B4 140
Micronesia, is., Oc. G19 158
Micronesia, Federated States of, ctry., Oc. H19 158
Mičurinsk, U.S.S.R. I23 26
Midale, Sask., Can. H4 105
Midar, Mor. C9 62
Mid-Atlantic Ridge F9 160
Middelburg, Neth. E4 12
Middelburg, S. Afr. H7 66
Middelburg, S. Afr. E9 66
Middelfart, Den. N11 6
Middelharnis, Neth. E5 12
Middelpos, S. Afr. H5 66
Middelwater, S. Afr. D10 66
Middenmeer, Neth. C7 12
Middle, Ia., U.S. C6 122
Middle, stm., Ia., U.S. C3 122
Middle, stm., Mn., U.S. B2 130
Middle America Trench H10 86
Middle Andaman, i., India H2 40
Middleboro (Middleborough Center), Ma., U.S. C6 128
Middlebourne, W.V., U.S. B4 155
Middlebranch, Oh., U.S. B4 142
Middlebro, Man., Can. E4 100
Middlebrook, Va., U.S. B3 153
Middleburg, Fl., U.S. B5 116
Middleburg, Ky., U.S. C5 124
Middleburg, Pa., U.S. E7 145
Middleburg, Va., U.S. B5 153
Middleburgh, N.Y., U.S. C6 139
Middleburg Heights, Oh., U.S. h9 142
Middlebury, Ct., U.S. C3 114
Middlebury, In., U.S. A6 121
Middlebury, Vt., U.S. C2 152
Middle Caicos, i., T./C. Is. D9 94
Middlefield, Ct., U.S. C5 114
Middlefield, Oh., U.S. A4 142
Middle Haddam, Ct., U.S. C5 114
Middle Island Creek, stm., W.V., U.S. B3 155
Middle Lake, Sask., Can. E3 105
Middle Loup, stm., Ne., U.S. C5 134
Middle Musquodoboit, N.S., Can. D6 101
Middle Nodaway, stm., Ia., U.S. C3 122
Middle Park, val., Co., U.S. A4 113
Middle Patuxent, stm., Md., U.S. B4 127
Middle Point, Oh., U.S. B1 142
Middleport, N.Y., U.S. B2 139
Middleport, Oh., U.S. C3 142
Middle Raccoon, stm., Ia., U.S. C3 122
Middle River, Md., U.S. B5 127
Middle River, Mn., U.S. B2 130
Middlesboro, Ky., U.S. D6 124
Middlesbrough, Eng., U.K. G12 8
Middlesex, Belize I15 90
Middlesex, N.J., U.S. B4 137
Middlesex, N.C., U.S. B4 140
Middlesex, Vt., U.S. C3 152
Middlesex, co., Ct., U.S. D5 114
Middlesex, co., Ma., U.S. A5 128
Middlesex, co., N.J., U.S. C4 137
Middlesex, co., Va., U.S. C6 153
Middlesex Fells Reservation, Ma., U.S. g11 128
Middle Stewiacke, N.S., Can. D6 101
Middleton, N.S., Can. E4 101
Middleton, Id., U.S. F2 119
Middleton, Ma., U.S. A5 128
Middleton, Mi., U.S. E6 129
Middleton, N.H., U.S. D4 136
Middleton, Tn., U.S. B3 149
Middleton, Wi., U.S. E4 156
Middletown, Ca., U.S. C2 112
Middletown, Ct., U.S. C5 114
Middletown, De., U.S. C3 115
Middletown, Il., U.S. C4 120
Middletown, In., U.S. D6 121
Middletown, Ia., U.S. D6 122
Middletown, Ky., U.S. g11 124
Middletown, Md., U.S. B2 127
Middletown, Mo., U.S. B6 132
Middletown, N.J., U.S. C4 137
Middletown, N.Y., U.S. D6 139
Middletown, Oh., U.S. C1 142
Middletown, Pa., U.S. F8 145
Middletown, R.I., U.S. E5 146
Middletown, Va., U.S. A4 153
Middletown Springs, Vt., U.S. E2 152
Middleville, Mi., U.S. F5 129
Midelt, Mor. D8 62
Midfield, Al., U.S. g7 108
Midgic, N.B., Can. D5 101
Mid Glamorgan, co., Wales, U.K. J10 8
Midhurst, Ont., Can. C5 103
Midi, Canal du, Fr. I9 14
Midi de Bigorre, Pic du, mtn., Fr. J7 14
Midkiff, W.V., U.S. C2 155
Midland, Ont., Can. C5 103
Midland, Ar., U.S. B1 111
Midland, In., U.S. F3 121
Midland, La., U.S. D3 125
Midland, Md., U.S. k13 127
Midland, Mi., U.S. E6 129
Midland, N.C., U.S. B2 140
Midland, Pa., U.S. E1 145
Midland, S.D., U.S. C4 148
Midland, Tx., U.S. D1 150
Midland, co., Mi., U.S. E6 129
Midland, co., Tx., U.S. D1 150
Midland Basin, Co., U.S. A2 113
Midland City, Al., U.S. D4 108
Midland Park, Ks., U.S. g12 123
Midland Park, N.J., U.S. B4 137
Midland Park, S.C., U.S. k11 147
Midlothian, Il., U.S. k9 120
Midlothian, Md., U.S. k13 127
Midlothian, Tx., U.S. C4 150
Midlothian, Va., U.S. m17 153
Midnight, Ms., U.S. B3 131
Midongy Sud, Madag. S22 67b
Miduzhen, China B6 40
Midvale, Id., U.S. E2 119
Midvale, Oh., U.S. B4 142
Midvale, Ut., U.S. C4 151
Midville, Ga., U.S. D4 117
Midway, B.C., Can. E8 99
Midway, Al., U.S. C4 108
Midway, De., U.S. F5 115
Midway, Fl., U.S. B2 116
Midway, Ky., U.S. B5 124
Midway, Pa., U.S. G7 145
Midway, Tn., U.S. C11 149
Midway, Ut., U.S. C4 151
Midway Islands, dep., Oc. E1 2
Midway Range, mts., B.C., Can. E8 99
Midwest, Wy., U.S. C6 157
Midwest City, Ok., U.S. B4 143
Midyat, Tur. C6 48
Midžor (Midžur), mtn., Eur. F6 20
Miechów, Pol. E20 10
Międzychód, Pol. C15 10
Międzyrzec Podlaski, Pol. C22 10
Międzyrzecz, Pol. C15 10
Miélan, Fr. I7 14
Mielec, Pol. E21 10
Mier, Mex. D10 90
Mier, In., U.S. C6 121
Miercurea-Ciuc, Rom. C9 20
Mieres, Spain B6 16
Mier y Noriega, Mex. F9 90
Miesbach, Ger. H11 10
Mifflin, Pa., U.S. E7 145
Mifflin, co., Pa., U.S. E6 145
Mifflinburg, Pa., U.S. E7 145
Mifflintown, Pa., U.S. E7 145
Mifflinville, Pa., U.S. D9 145
Migdal, Isr. C5 50
Migennes, Fr. E10 14
Miguel Alemán, Presa, res., Mex. H11 90
Miguel Auza, Mex. E8 90
Miguel de la Borda, Pan. H14 92
Miguel Hidalgo, Presa, res., Mex. D5 90
Miguelópolis, Braz. F4 79
Miguel Riglos, Arg. I7 80
Mihajlovgrad, Bul. F7 20
Mihara, Japan M8 36
Mijdahah, Yemen G6 47
Mikado, Sask., Can. F4 105
Mikana, Wi., U.S. C2 156
Mikaševiči, U.S.S.R. I10 26
Mikhrot Shelomo Hamelekh (Timna') (King Solomon's Mines), hist., Isr. I3 50
Mikkeli, Fin. K20 6
Mikkelin lääni, prov., Fin. J20 6
Mikołajki, Pol. B21 10
Mikołów, Pol. E18 10
Míkonos, Grc. L9 20
Mikun', U.S.S.R. E8 22
Milaca, Mn., U.S. E5 130
Milagro, Ec. I3 84
Milam, co., Tx., U.S. D4 150
Milan, Ga., U.S. D3 117
Milan, Il., U.S. B3 120
Milan, In., U.S. F7 121
Milan, Ks., U.S. E6 123
Milan, Mi., U.S. F7 129
Milan, Mn., U.S. E3 130
Milan, Mo., U.S. A4 132
Milan, N.H., U.S. A4 136
Milan, N.M., U.S. B2 138
Milan, Oh., U.S. A3 142
Milan, Tn., U.S. B3 149
Milan see Milano, Italy D4 18
Milano (Milan), Italy D4 18
Milanoa, Madag. N23 67b
Milazzo, Italy K10 18
Milbank, S.D., U.S. B9 148
Milbridge, Me., U.S. D5 126
Milburn, Ky., U.S. f9 124
Milburn, Ok., U.S. C5 143
Milden, Sask., Can. F2 105
Mildmay, Ont., Can. C3 103
Mildred, Pa., U.S. D9 145
Mildura, Austl. J5 70
Mile, China B7 40
Miles, Austl. F9 70
Miles, Ia., U.S. B7 122
Miles, Tx., U.S. D2 150
Milesburg, Pa., U.S. E6 145
Miles City, Mt., U.S. D11 133
Miles Mountain, mtn., Vt., U.S. C5 152
Milestone, Sask., Can. G3 105
Milevsko, Czech. F14 10
Milford, Ct., U.S. E3 114
Milford, De., U.S. E4 115
Milford, Il., U.S. C6 120
Milford, In., U.S. B6 121
Milford, Ia., U.S. A2 122
Milford, Ks., U.S. C7 123
Milford, Me., U.S. D4 126
Milford, Ma., U.S. B4 128
Milford, Mi., U.S. F7 129
Milford, Ne., U.S. D8 134
Milford, N.H., U.S. E3 136
Milford, N.J., U.S. B2 137
Milford, Oh., U.S. C1 142
Milford, Pa., U.S. D12 145
Milford, Ut., U.S. E2 151
Milford, Va., U.S. B5 153
Milford Center, Oh., U.S. B2 142
Milford Haven, Wales, U.K. J8 8
Milford Lake, res., Ks., U.S. C6 123
Milford Station, N.S., Can. D6 101
Milḥ, Baḥr al-, l., Iraq E7 48
Milicz, Pol. D17 10
Mililani Town, Hi., U.S. g9 118
Milk Creek, stm., Co., U.S. A3 113
Mil'kovo, U.S.S.R. G23 24
Milk River, Alta., Can. E4 98
Mill, stm., Ma., U.S. h9 128
Milladore, Wi., U.S. D4 156
Millard, co., Ut., U.S. D2 151
Millau, Fr. H10 14
Millbank, Ont., Can. D4 103
Millboro, Va., U.S. C3 153
Millbrae, Ca., U.S. h8 112
Millbrook, Ont., Can. C6 103
Millbrook, Al., U.S. C3 108
Millbrook, N.Y., U.S. D7 139
Mill Brook, stm., Vt., U.S. B5 152
Millburn, N.J., U.S. B4 137
Millbury, Ma., U.S. B4 128
Millbury, Oh., U.S. e7 142
Mill City, Or., U.S. C4 144
Mill Creek, In., U.S. A4 121
Mill Creek, Ok., U.S. C5 143
Millcreek, Ut., U.S. C4 151
Mill Creek, W.V., U.S. C5 155
Mill Creek, stm., In., U.S. F4 121
Mill Creek, stm., Ks., U.S. C6 123
Mill Creek, stm., Ks., U.S. C7 123
Mill Creek, stm., N.J., U.S. D4 137
Mill Creek, stm., Oh., U.S. B2 142
Mill Creek, stm., Tn., U.S. g10 149
Mill Creek, stm., W.V., U.S. m13 155
Mill Creek, stm., W.V., U.S. C3 155
Millcreek Township, Pa., U.S. B1 145
Milldale, Ct., U.S. C4 114
Milledgeville, Ga., U.S. C3 117
Milledgeville, Il., U.S. B4 120
Milledgeville, Tn., U.S. B3 149
Mille Îles, Rivière des, stm., Que., Can. p19 104
Mille Lacs, co., Mn., U.S. E5 130
Mille Lacs Indian Reservation, Mn., U.S. D5 130
Mille Lacs Lake, l., Mn., U.S. D5 130
Millen, Ga., U.S. D5 117
Miller, Ne., U.S. D6 134
Miller, S.D., U.S. C7 148
Miller, co., Ar., U.S. D2 111
Miller, co., Ga., U.S. E2 117
Miller, co., Mo., U.S. C5 132
Miller, Mount, mtn., Ak., U.S. C11 109
Miller Creek, stm., De., U.S. F5 115
Millerovo, U.S.S.R. H6 22
Miller Peak, mtn., Az., U.S. F5 110
Miller Run, stm., Vt., U.S. B4 152
Millers, stm., Ma., U.S. A3 128
Millersburg, In., U.S. A6 121
Millersburg, Ky., U.S. B5 124
Millersburg, Oh., U.S. B4 142
Millersburg, Pa., U.S. E8 145
Millers Falls, Ma., U.S. A3 128
Millers Ferry, Al., U.S. C2 108
Millers Ferry Dam, Al., U.S. C2 108
Millersport, Oh., U.S. C3 142
Millerstown, Pa., U.S. E7 145
Millersville, Pa., U.S. F9 145
Millerton, N.B., Can. C4 101
Millerton, N.Y., U.S. D7 139
Millerton, Ok., U.S. D6 143
Millertown, Newf., Can. D3 102
Millerville, Al., U.S. B4 108
Millet, Alta., Can. C4 98
Millevaches, Plateau de, plat., Fr. G9 14
Mill Grove, In., U.S. D7 121
Mill Hall, Pa., U.S. D7 145
Millheim, Pa., U.S. E7 145
Millhousen, In., U.S. F7 121
Millicent, Austl. K4 70
Milligan, Fl., U.S. u15 116
Milligan, Ne., U.S. D8 134
Milliken, Co., U.S. A6 113
Millington, Mi., U.S. E7 129
Millington, Or., U.S. D2 144
Millington, Tn., U.S. B2 149
Millinocket, Me., U.S. C4 126
Millinocket Lake, l., Me., U.S. C4 126
Millinocket Lake, l., Me., U.S. B4 126
Millis, Ma., U.S. B5 128
Millmerran, Austl. F9 70
Millport, Al., U.S. B1 108
Mill Run, Pa., U.S. G3 145
Millry, Al., U.S. D1 108
Mills, Wy., U.S. D6 157
Mills, co., Ia., U.S. C2 122
Mills, co., Tx., U.S. D3 150
Millsboro, De., U.S. F4 115
Millsboro, Pa., U.S. G1 145
Mill Shoals, Il., U.S. E5 120
Mill Spring, Mo., U.S. D7 132
Millstadt, Il., U.S. E3 120
Millstatt, Aus. I13 10
Millstone, stm., N.J., U.S. C4 137
Millstream Chichester Range National Park, Austl. D3 68
Milltown, In., U.S. H5 121
Milltown, Ky., U.S. C4 124
Milltown, Mt., U.S. D3 133
Milltown, N.J., U.S. C4 137
Milltown, Wi., U.S. C1 156
Milltown [-Head of Bay d'Espoir], Newf., Can. E4 102
Millvale, Pa., U.S. k14 145
Mill Valley, Ca., U.S. D2 112
Mill Village, N.S., Can. E5 101
Millville, N.B., Can. C2 101
Millville, De., U.S. F5 115
Millville, Ky., U.S. B5 124
Millville, Ma., U.S. B4 128
Millville, N.J., U.S. E2 137
Millville, Oh., U.S. n12 142
Millville, Pa., U.S. D9 145
Millville, Ut., U.S. B4 151
Millville, W.V., U.S. B7 155
Millville Lake, N.H., U.S. E4 136
Millwood, Ga., U.S. E4 117
Millwood, Va., U.S. A4 153
Millwood, Wa., U.S. g14 154
Millwood Lake, res., Ar., U.S. D1 111
Milne Bay, b., Pap. N. Gui. B10 68
Milner, Co., U.S. A3 113
Milner, Ga., U.S. C2 117
Milner Dam, Id., U.S. G5 119
Milnor, N.D., U.S. C8 141
Milo, Alta., Can. D4 98
Milo, Ia., U.S. C4 122
Milo, Me., U.S. C4 126
Milo, Or., U.S. E3 144
Mílos, Grc. M8 20
Mílos, i., Grc. M8 20
Miloslavskoje, U.S.S.R. H22 26
Milparinka, Austl. G4 70
Milpitas, Ca., U.S. k9 112
Milroy, In., U.S. F7 121
Milroy, Mn., U.S. F3 130
Milroy, Pa., U.S. E6 145
Milstead, Al., U.S. C4 108
Milstead, Ga., U.S. C3 117
Miltenberg, Ger. F9 10
Milton, Ont., Can. D5 103
Milton, N.Z. G2 72
Milton, De., U.S. E4 115
Milton, Fl., U.S. u14 116
Milton, Il., U.S. D3 120
Milton, In., U.S. E7 121
Milton, Ia., U.S. D5 122
Milton, Ky., U.S. B4 124
Milton, La., U.S. D3 125
Milton, Ma., U.S. B5 128
Milton, N.H., U.S. D5 136
Milton, N.Y., U.S. D7 139
Milton, N.D., U.S. A7 141
Milton, Pa., U.S. D8 145
Milton, Vt., U.S. B2 152
Milton, Wa., U.S. f11 154
Milton, W.V., U.S. C2 155
Milton, Wi., U.S. F5 156
Milton, Lake, l., Oh., U.S. A4 142
Miltona, Mn., U.S. D3 130
Miltona, Lake, l., Mn., U.S. D3 130
Milton-Freewater, Or., U.S. B8 144
Milton Mills, N.H., U.S. C5 136
Milton Reservoir, res., Co., U.S. A6 113
Miltonvale, Ks., U.S. C6 123
Milverton, Ont., Can. D4 103
Milwaukee, Wi., U.S. E6 156
Milwaukee, co., Wi., U.S. E6 156
Milwaukee, stm., Wi., U.S. m12 156
Milwaukie, Or., U.S. B4 144
Mim, Ghana H8 64
Mimoso, Braz. C4 79
Mimoso, Braz. G14 82
Mimoso do Sul, Braz. F8 79
Mims, Fl., U.S. D6 116
Min, stm., China E7 30
Min, stm., China I7 34
Mina, Nv., U.S. E3 135
Mīnāb, Iran H14 48
Mina El Limón, Nic. E8 92
Minahasa, pen., Indon. E7 38
Minamata, Japan O5 36
Minami-Daitō-jima, i., Japan F13 30
Mina Pirquitas, Arg. B5 80
Minas, Cuba D6 94
Minas, Ur. H11 80
Minas, Sierra de las, mts., Guat. B5 92
Minas Basin, b., N.S., Can. D5 101
Minas Channel, strt., N.S., Can. D5 101
Minas de Barroterán, Mex. D9 90
Minas de Corrales, Ur. F11 80
Minas de Matahambre, Cuba C3 94
Minas de Oro, Hond. C7 92
Minas Gerais, state, Braz. E6 79
Minas Novas, Braz. D7 79
Minatare, Ne., U.S. C2 134
Minatitlán, Mex. I12 90
Minbu, Burma D3 40
Minburn, Alta., Can. C5 98
Minburn, Ia., U.S. C3 122
Minco, Ok., U.S. B4 143
Mindanao, i., Phil. D8 38
Mindelo, C.V. k16 64a
Mindemoya, Ont., Can. B2 103
Minden, Ont., Can. C6 103
Minden, Ger. C8 10
Minden, Ia., U.S. C2 122
Minden, La., U.S. B2 125
Minden, Ne., U.S. D7 134
Minden, Nv., U.S. E2 135
Minden, W.V., U.S. D3 155
Mindenmines, Mo., U.S. D3 132
Mindon, Burma E3 40
Mindoro, i., Phil. C7 38
Mindoro Strait, strt., Phil. C7 38
Mine Centre, Ont., Can. E5 100
Minechoag Mountain, hill, Ma., U.S. B3 128
Mine Hill, N.J., U.S. B3 137
Mineiros, Braz. D2 79
Mineola, N.Y., U.S. E7 139
Mineola, Tx., U.S. C5 150
Miner, Mo., U.S. E8 132
Miner, co., S.D., U.S. D8 148
Mineral, Il., U.S. B4 120
Mineral, Va., U.S. B5 153
Mineral, Wa., U.S. C3 154
Mineral, co., Co., U.S. D4 113
Mineral, co., Mt., U.S. C1 133
Mineral, co., Nv., U.S. E3 135
Mineral, co., W.V., U.S. B6 155
Mineral City, Oh., U.S. B4 142
Mineral de Cucharas, Mex. F7 90
Mineral Mountains, mts., Ut., U.S. E3 151
Mineral'nyje Vody, U.S.S.R. I6 22
Mineral Point, Mo., U.S. D7 132
Mineral Point, Wi., U.S. F3 156
Mineral Springs, Ar., U.S. D2 111
Mineral Wells, Ms., U.S. A4 131
Mineral Wells, Tx., U.S. C3 150
Minersville, Pa., U.S. E9 145
Minersville, Ut., U.S. E3 151
Minerva, Oh., U.S. B4 142
Minervino Murge, Italy H11 18
Minetto, N.Y., U.S. B4 139
Mineville, N.Y., U.S. A7 139
Minfeng, China D3 30
Mingečaur, U.S.S.R. I7 22
Mingela, Austl. B7 70
Minggang, China C3 34
Mingo, Ia., U.S. C4 122
Mingo, co., W.V., U.S. D2 155
Mingo Junction, Oh., U.S. B5 142
Minhang, China D10 34
Minhla, Burma F3 40
Minho, hist. reg., Port. D3 16
Minho (Miño), stm., Eur. D3 16
Minhou, China I8 34
Minicoy Island, i., India H2 46
Minidoka, co., Id., U.S. G5 119
Minidoka Dam, Id., U.S. G5 119
Minier, Il., U.S. C4 120
Minīn, Syria A6 50
Miniota, Man., Can. D1 100
Minipi Lake, l., Newf., Can. h9 102
Minisink Island, i., N.J., U.S. A3 137
Minitonas, Man., Can. C1 100
Minjar, U.S.S.R. F9 22
Min'kovo, U.S.S.R. B26 26
Minlaton, Austl. J2 70
Minle, China D7 30
Minna, Nig. G13 64
Minneapolis, Ks., U.S. C6 123
Minneapolis, Mn., U.S. F5 130
Minnedosa, Man., Can. D2 100
Minnedosa, stm., Man., Can. D1 100
Minnehaha, co., S.D., U.S. D9 148
Minneola, Ks., U.S. E3 123
Minneota, Mn., U.S. F3 130
Minnesota, state, U.S. E4 130
Minnesota, stm., Mn., U.S. F2 130
Minnesota Lake, Mn., U.S. G5 130
Minnetonka, Mn., U.S. n12 130
Minnetonka, Lake, l., Mn., U.S. n11 130
Minnewaska, Lake, l., Mn., U.S. E3 130
Minnewaukan, N.D., U.S. A6 141
Mino, Japan L11 36
Miño (Minho), stm., Eur. D3 16
Minocqua, Wi., U.S. C4 156
Minonk, Il., U.S. C4 120
Minooka, Il., U.S. B5 120
Minor Hill, Tn., U.S. B4 149
Minot, Ma., U.S. h12 128
Minot, N.D., U.S. A4 141

Name — Map Ref. — Page

Minot Air Force Base, mil., N.D., U.S. A4 141
Minquadale, De., U.S. i7 115
Minsk, U.S.S.R. H10 26
Mińsk Mazowiecki, Pol. C21 10
Minster, Oh., U.S. B1 142
Mintaka Pass, Asia B6 44
Minter City, Ms., U.S. B3 131
Mint Hill, N.C., U.S. B2 140
Minto, Man., Can. E1 100
Minto, N.B., Can. C3 101
Minto, Ak., U.S. C10 109
Minto, N.D., U.S. A8 141
Minto Inlet, b., N.W. Ter., Can. B9 96
Minton, Sask., Can. H3 105
Minturn, Ar., U.S. B4 111
Minturn, Co., U.S. B4 113
Minturno, Italy H8 18
Minusinsk, U.S.S.R. G10 24
Minute Man National Historical Park, Ma., U.S. g10 128
Minxian, China E7 30
Minya see Al-Minyā, Egypt C6 60
Minya Konka see Gongga Shan, mtn., China F7 30
Mio, Mi., U.S. D6 129
Miory, U.S.S.R. F10 26
Mir, U.S.S.R. H9 26
Mira, Port. E3 16
Mira, stm., Col. G3 84
Mirabel, Que., Can. D3 104
Miracema do Norte, Braz. E9 76
Mirador, Braz. E10 76
Miradouro, Braz. F7 79
Miraflores, Arg. E6 80
Miraflores, Col. E6 84
Miraflores, Col. G6 84
Miraflores, Esclusas de, Pan. I15 92
Mira Gut, N.S., Can. C10 101
Mīrah, Wādī al-, val., Asia B11 60
Miraj, India D3 46
Miramar, Arg. J10 80
Miramar, Arg. F7 80
Miramar, C.R. G10 92
Miramar, Fl., U.S. s13 116
Miramar Naval Air Station, mil., Ca., U.S. F5 112
Miramas, Fr. I12 14
Miramichi Bay, b., N.B., Can. B5 101
Miranda, Braz. I13 82
Miranda, Col. F4 84
Miranda, state, Ven. B9 84
Miranda, stm., Braz. H13 82
Miranda de Ebro, Spain C9 16
Miranda do Douro, Port. D5 16
Mirande, Fr. I7 14
Mirandela, Port. D4 16
Mirandola, Italy E6 18
Mirante do Paranapanema, Braz. G3 79
Mirapuxi, stm., Braz. B3 79
Mira Taglio, Italy D7 18
Miravalles, Volcán, vol., C.R. G9 92
Mirbāt, Oman F9 47
Mirebeau-sur-Bèze, Fr. E12 14
Mirecourt, Fr. D13 14
Miri, Malay. E5 38
Miriam Vale, Austl. E9 70
Mirim, Lagoa, b., S.A. H9 74
Mirim, Lagoa (Laguna Merín), b., S.A. G12 80
Miriñay, stm., Arg. E10 80
Miriti, Braz. B12 82
Miritiparaná, stm., Col. H7 84
Mirjāveh, Iran G16 48
Mirnyj, U.S.S.R. E14 24
Mirnyy, sci., Ant. B6 73
Mirow, Ger. B12 10
Mirpur, Pak. D5 44
Mirpur Khās, Pak. H3 44
Mirria, Niger E14 64
Mirror, Alta., Can. C4 98
Mirror Lake, N.H., U.S. C4 136
Mirror Lake, l., N.H., U.S. C4 136
Mirzāpur, India H10 44
Misāhah, Bi'r, well, Egypt F4 60
Misantla, Mex. H11 90
Miscoe Hill, hill, Ma., U.S. h9 128
Miscou Centre, N.B., Can. B5 101
Miscouche, P.E.I., Can. C6 101
Miscou Island, i., N.B., Can. B5 101
Miscou Point, c., N.B., Can. A5 101
Misenheimer, N.C., U.S. B2 140
Mishan, China B13 30
Mishansha, stm., Peru D5 82
Mishawaka, In., U.S. A5 121
Mishbih, Jabal, mtn., Egypt J3 48
Misheguk Mountain, mtn., Ak., U.S. B7 109
Mishicot, Wi., U.S. D6 156
Misikan, China C13 44
Misilmeri, Italy K8 18
Misiones, prov., Arg. D11 80
Misiones, dept., Para. D10 80
Misión San Francisco de Laishí, Arg. D9 80
Misión San Vicente, Mex. B1 90
Miskī, Sud. J3 60
Miskito Channel, strt., Nic. C11 92
Miskitos, Cayos, is., Nic. C12 92
Miskitos Reef, rf., Nic. C12 92
Miskolc, Hung. G20 10
Mislata, Spain A10 62
Misool, Pulau, i., Indon. F9 38
Mispillion, stm., De., U.S. E4 115
Misrātah, Libya B4 56
Missaukee, co., Mi., U.S. D5 129
Missaukee, Lake, l., Mi., U.S. D5 129
Mission, Ks., U.S. m16 123
Mission, S.D., U.S. D5 148
Mission, Tx., U.S. F3 150
Mission Hill, S.D., U.S. E8 148
Mission Mountain, mtn., Ok., U.S. A7 145
Mission Range, mts., Mt., U.S. C3 133
Mission Viejo, Ca., U.S. n13 112
Missisquoi, stm., Vt., U.S. B3 152
Missisquoi Bay, b., Vt., U.S. A2 152
Mississauga, Ont., Can. D5 103
Mississinewa, stm., U.S. D7 121
Mississinewa Lake, res., In., U.S. C6 121
Mississippi, co., Ar., U.S. B5 111
Mississippi, co., Mo., U.S. E8 132
Mississippi, state, U.S. C4 131
Mississippi, stm., U.S. E8 106
Mississippi Delta, La., U.S. E6 125
Mississippi Lake, l., Ont., Can. B8 103
Mississippi Sound, strt., U.S. E5 131
Mississippi State, Ms., U.S. B5 131
Missoula, Mt., U.S. D2 133
Missoula, co., Mt., U.S. D2 133
Missouri, state, U.S. C5 132
Missouri, stm., U.S. C7 106
Missouri Buttes, mtn., Wy., U.S. B8 157
Missouri City, Mo., U.S. h11 132
Missouri City, Tx., U.S. r14 150
Missouri Valley, Ia., U.S. C2 122
Mistaken Point, c., Newf., Can. E5 102
Mistassini, Que., Can. h12 104
Mistassini, Lac, l., Que., Can. h12 104
Mistastin Lake, l., Newf., Can. g9 102
Mistatim, Sask., Can. E4 105
Mistelbach, Aus. G16 10
Misterbianco, Italy L10 18
Misterei, Sud. K2 60
Misti, Volcán, vol., Peru G6 82
Mistretta, Italy L9 18
Mita, Punta, c., Mex. G7 90
Mitchell, Austl. F7 70
Mitchell, Ont., Can. D3 103
Mitchell, Ga., U.S. C4 117
Mitchell, Il., U.S. E3 120
Mitchell, In., U.S. G5 121
Mitchell, Ne., U.S. C2 134
Mitchell, S.D., U.S. D7 148
Mitchell, co., Ga., U.S. E2 117
Mitchell, co., Ia., U.S. A5 122
Mitchell, co., Ks., U.S. C5 123
Mitchell, co., N.C., U.S. e10 140
Mitchell, co., Tx., U.S. C2 150
Mitchell, stm., Austl. K7 70
Mitchell, Lake, l., Mi., U.S. D5 129
Mitchell, Lake, res., Al., U.S. C3 108
Mitchell, Mount, mtn., N.C., U.S. f10 140
Mitchell Island, i., La., U.S. E6 125
Mitchellsburg, Ky., U.S. C5 124
Mitchellville, Ar., U.S. D4 111
Mitchellville, Ia., U.S. C4 122
Mitchellville, Tn., U.S. A5 149
Mitilíni, Grc. J10 20
Mitkof Island, i., Ak., U.S. m23 109
Mitla, hist., Mex. I11 90
Mito, Japan K15 36
Mitsamiouli, Com. K15 67a
Mitsinjo, Madag. P21 67b
Mitsio, Nosy, i., Madag. N23 67b
Mitsiwa (Massawa), Eth. J10 60
Mittellandkanal, Ger. C9 10
Mittenwald, Ger. H11 10
Mittersill, Aus. H12 10
Mitú, Col. G7 84
Mitumba, Monts, mts., Zaire B5 58
Mitwaba, Zaire C5 58
Mitzic, Gabon A2 58
Miura, Japan L14 36
Mixco Viejo, hist., Guat. C4 92
Miyake-jima, i., Japan M14 36
Miyako, Japan H16 36
Miyakonojō, Japan P6 36
Miyazaki, Japan P6 36
Miyazu, Japan L10 36
Miyun, China C4 32
Mizan Teferi, Eth. N8 60
Mizdah, Libya B3 56
Mize, Ms., U.S. D4 131
Mizen Head, c., Ire. J4 8
Mizoram, state, India I15 44
Mizpah, N.J., U.S. E3 137
Mizpah Creek, stm., Mt., U.S. E11 133
Mizpé Ramon, Isr. G3 50
Mizque, Bol. G9 82
Mizque, stm., Bol. H9 82
Mjøsa, l., Nor. K12 6
Mladá Boleslav, Czech. E14 10
Mladenovac, Yugo. E4 20
Mlanje Peak see Sapitwa, mtn., Mwi. E7 58
Mława, Pol. B20 10
Mmabatho, Boph. E7 66
Mmadinare, Bots. C8 66
Mo, Nor. H14 6
Mo, stm., Afr. G10 64
Moa, stm., Afr. G4 54
Moa, stm., Braz. B5 82
Moab, Ut., U.S. E6 151
Moaco, stm., Braz. C7 82
Moa Island, i., Austl. B8 68
Moama, Austl. K6 70
Moanda, Gabon B2 58
Moapa, Nv., U.S. G7 135
Moapa River Indian Reservation, Nv., U.S. G7 135
Moark, Ar., U.S. A5 111
Mobara, Japan L15 36
Mobaye, Cen. Afr. Rep. H5 56
Moberly, Mo., U.S. B5 132
Moberly Lake, B.C., Can. B7 99
Mobile, Newf., Can. E5 102
Mobile, Al., U.S. E1 108
Mobile, co., Al., U.S. E1 108
Mobile, stm., Al., U.S. E1 108
Mobile Bay, b., Al., U.S. E1 113
Mobridge, S.D., U.S. B5 148
Moca, Dom. Rep. E9 94
Mocal, stm., N.A. C6 92
Moçambique, Moz. E8 58
Mocanal, Spain P23 17b
Mocanaqua, Pa., U.S. D9 145
Moccasin, Az., U.S. A3 110
Moccasin, Mt., U.S. C7 133
Mocha, Isla, i., Chile J2 80
Mocha see Al-Mukhā', Yemen H3 47
Moche, stm., Peru C2 82
Mochudi, Bots. E8 66
Mocímboa da Praia, Moz. D8 58
Mocksville, N.C., U.S. B2 140
Moclips, Wa., U.S. B1 154
Mocó, stm., Braz. I9 84
Môco, Serra, mtn., Ang. D3 58
Mocoa, Col. G4 84
Mococa, Braz. F5 79
Mocoduene, Moz. D12 66
Mocomoco, Bol. F7 82
Mocoretá, Arg. F10 80
Mocorito, Mex. E6 90
Moctezuma, Mex. C5 90
Moctezuma, stm., Mex. C5 90
Moctezuma, stm., Mex. G10 90
Mocuba, Moz. E7 58
Modale, Ia., U.S. C2 122
Modane, Fr. G13 14
Modderrivier, S. Afr. G7 66
Model Reservoir, res., Co., U.S. D6 113
Modena, Italy E5 18
Modena, N.Y., U.S. D6 139
Modesto, Ca., U.S. D3 112
Modesto, Il., U.S. D4 120
Modica, Italy M9 18
Mödling, Aus. G16 10
Modoc, In., U.S. D7 121
Modoc, co., Ca., U.S. B3 112
Moe, Austl. L7 70
Moeda, Braz. F6 79
Moema, Braz. E6 79
Moengo, Sur. B8 76
Moenkopi, Az., U.S. A4 110
Moenkopi Plateau, plat., Az., U.S. B4 110
Moenkopi Wash, val., Az., U.S. A5 110
Moers, Ger. D6 10
Moffat, co., Co., U.S. A2 113
Moffat Tunnel, Co., U.S. B5 113
Moffett, Ok., U.S. B7 143
Moffett Field Naval Air Station, mil., Ca., U.S. k8 112
Moffit, N.D., U.S. C5 141
Moga, India E6 44
Mogadiscio see Muqdisho, Som. H10 56
Mogadishu see Muqdisho, Som. H10 56
Mogadore, Oh., U.S. A4 142
Mogán, Spain P25 17b
Mogapinyana, Bots. D8 66
Mogaung, Burma B4 40
Mogi das Cruzes, Braz. G5 79
Mogil'ov, U.S.S.R. H13 26
Mogil'ov-Podol'skij, U.S.S.R. H3 22
Mogi-Mirim, Braz. G5 79
Mogincual, Moz. E8 58
Mogliano Veneto, Italy D7 18
Mogoča, U.S.S.R. G15 24
Mogogh, Sud. M6 60
Mogok, Burma C4 40
Mogollon Mesa, mtn., Az., U.S. C4 110
Mogollon Mountains, mts., N.M., U.S. D1 138
Mogollon Rim, clf, Az., U.S. C5 110
Mogote, Co., U.S. D4 113
Mogotes, Col. D6 84
Mogotón, mtn., N.A. D8 92
Moguer, Spain H5 16
Mogzon, U.S.S.R. G14 24
Mohács, Hung. J18 10
Mohall, N.D., U.S. A4 141
Mohammedia (Fedala), Mor. D7 62
Mohave, co., Az., U.S. B1 110
Mohave, Lake, res., U.S. H7 135
Mohave Mountains, mts., Az., U.S. C1 110
Mohave Valley, Az., U.S. C1 110
Mohawk, Mi., U.S. A2 129
Mohawk, N.Y., U.S. C5 139
Mohawk, stm., N.H., U.S. g7 136
Mohawk, stm., N.Y., U.S. C6 139
Mohawk Lake, l., N.J., U.S. A3 137
Mohawk Mountain, mtn., Ct., U.S. B2 114
Mohawk Mountains, mts., Az., U.S. E2 110
Mohe, China A11 30
Mohican, stm., Oh., U.S. B3 142
Mohican, Black Fork, stm., Oh., U.S. B3 142
Mohican, Clear Fork, stm., Oh., U.S. B3 142
Mohnton, Pa., U.S. F10 145
Moho, stm., Belize A6 92
Moinești, Rom. C10 20
Mointy, U.S.S.R. H12 22
Moiporá, Braz. D3 79
Mõisaküla, U.S.S.R. C8 26
Moisés Ville, Arg. F8 80
Moisie, Que., Can. h8 102
Moissac, Fr. H8 14
Moitaco, Ven. C10 84
Mojana, Caño, mth., Col. C5 84
Mojave, Ca., U.S. E4 112
Mojave, stm., Ca., U.S. E5 112
Mojave Desert, des., Ca., U.S. E5 112
Moji-Guaçu, stm., Braz. F5 79
Mojjero, stm., U.S.S.R. D12 24
Mojo, Eth. M10 60
Mokāma, India H11 44
Mokane, Mo., U.S. C6 132
Mokapu Peninsula, pen., Hi., U.S. g10 118
Mokapu Point, c., Hi., U.S. g11 118
Mokelumne, stm., Ca., U.S. C3 112
Mokelumne Hill, Ca., U.S. C3 112
Mokena, Il., U.S. k9 120
Moknine, Tun. N5 18
Mokp'o, S. Kor. I14 32
Mokrisset, Mor. K6 16
Mokša, stm., U.S.S.R. G24 26
Moku Manu, i., Hi., U.S. g11 118
Mokwa, Nig. G12 64
Mol, Bel. F7 12
Mola di Bari, Italy H12 18
Molalla, Or., U.S. B4 144
Molasses Pond, l., Me., U.S. D4 126
Moldau see Vltava, stm., Czech. F14 10
Moldavia, hist. reg., Rom. B11 20
Moldavia see Moldavskaja Sovetskaja Socialističeskaja Respublika, state, U.S.S.R. H3 22
Moldavskaja Sovetskaja Socialističeskaja Respublika, state, U.S.S.R. H3 22
Molde, Nor. J10 6
Moldoveanu, Vîrful, mtn., Rom. D8 20
Môle, Cap du, c., Haiti E8 94
Molena, Ga., U.S. C2 117
Molepolole, Bots. E7 66
Molėtai, U.S.S.R. F8 26
Molfetta, Italy H11 18
Molina, Chile H3 80
Molina de Segura, Spain G10 16
Moline, Il., U.S. B3 120
Moline, Ks., U.S. E7 123
Moline, Mi., U.S. F5 129
Molino, Fl., U.S. u14 116
Molinos, Arg. C5 80
Molins de Rei, Spain D14 16
Molise, prov., Italy H9 18
Mollendo, Peru G5 82
Mollepata, Peru E5 82
Mölln, Ger. B10 10
Mölndal, Swe. M13 6
Moločnoje, U.S.S.R. B22 26
Molodečno, U.S.S.R. G9 26
Mologa, stm., U.S.S.R. C19 26
Molokai, i., Hi., U.S. B5 118
Molokini, i., Hi., U.S. C5 118
Molong, Austl. I8 70
Molopo, stm., Afr. F5 66
Molotov see Perm', U.S.S.R. F9 22
Molou, Chad K1 60
Molsheim, Fr. D14 14
Molson, stm., Man., Can. C3 100
Molson Lake, l., Man., Can. B3 100
Molteno, S. Afr. H8 66
Molucca Sea see Maluku, Laut, Indon. F7 38
Moluccas see Maluku, is., Indon. F8 38
Molus, Ky., U.S. D6 124
Moma, Moz. E7 58
Moma, stm., U.S.S.R. D20 24
Momanga, Nmb. B5 66
Mombachito, Cerro, mtn., Nic. E9 92
Mombacho, Volcán, vol., Nic. F9 92
Mombasa, Kenya B7 58
Mombetsu, Japan C18 36a
Momence, Il., U.S. B6 120
Momotombo, Volcán, vol., Nic. E8 92
Mompós, Col. C5 84
Mona, Ut., U.S. D4 151
Mona, Canal de la, strt., N.A. E11 94
Mona, Isla de, i., P.R. E11 94
Mona, Punta, c., C.R. H12 92
Monaca, Pa., U.S. E1 145
Monaco, Mon. I14 14
Monaco, ctry., Eur. G9 4
Monadnock, Mount, mtn., N.H., U.S. E2 136
Monadnock Mountain, mtn., Vt., U.S. B5 152
Monagas, state, Ven. C11 84
Monaghan, co., Ire. G6 8
Monagrillo, Pan. D2 84
Monahans, Tx., U.S. D1 150
Monarch, Alta., Can. E4 98
Monarch, Mt., U.S. C6 133
Monarch Mills, S.C., U.S. B4 147
Monarch Pass, Co., U.S. C4 113
Monashee Mountains, mts., B.C., Can. D8 99
Monastir, Tun. N5 18
Monastir see Bitola, Yugo. H5 20
Monastyrščina, U.S.S.R. G14 26
Moncalieri, Italy D2 18
Monção, Braz. D9 76
Mončegorsk, U.S.S.R. D4 22
Mönchengladbach, Ger. D6 10
Moncks Corner, S.C., U.S. E7 147
Monclo, W.V., U.S. D3 155
Monclova, Mex. D9 90
Moncontour, Fr. D4 14
Moncoutant, Fr. F6 14
Moncton, N.B., Can. C5 101
Moncure, N.C., U.S. B3 140
Mondaí, Braz. D12 80
Mondamin, Ia., U.S. C1 122
Monday, stm., Para. C11 80
Mondoro, Mali D9 64
Mondoubleau, Fr. E7 14
Mondovi, Wi., U.S. D2 156
Mondragone, Italy H8 18
Monee, Il., U.S. B6 120
Moneron, ostrov, i., U.S.S.R. A16 36a
Monessen, Pa., U.S. F2 145
Monesterio, Spain G5 16
Monett, Mo., U.S. E4 132
Monette, Ar., U.S. B5 111
Monfalcone, Italy D8 18
Monflanquin, Fr. H7 14
Monforte, Port. F4 16
Monforte de Lemos, Spain C4 16
Monfort Heights, Oh., U.S. o12 142
Mongaguá, Braz. H5 79
Mongalla, Sud. G7 56
Mong Cai, Viet. D9 40
Mongers Lake, l., Austl. E3 68
Möng Hsat, Burma D5 40
Möng Mit, Burma C4 40
Mongo, Chad F4 56
Mongo, In., U.S. A7 121
Mongo, stm., Afr. G4 64
Mongol Altajn nuruu, mts., Asia H16 22
Mongolia (Mongol Ard Uls), ctry., Asia B8 30
Mongororo, Chad K2 60
Möng Pai, Burma E4 40
Mongu, Zam. E4 58
Möng Yawng, Burma D6 40
Monhegan Island, i., Me., U.S. E3 126
Monheim, Ger. G10 10
Monida Pass, U.S. E6 119
Monino, U.S.S.R. F21 26
Moniquirá, Col. E6 84
Monistrol-sur-Loire, Fr. G11 14
Moniteau, co., Mo., U.S. C5 132
Monitor, Alta., Can. D5 98
Monitor Range, mts., Nv., U.S. E5 135
Monitor Valley, val., Nv., U.S. D5 135
Monkey River, Belize A6 92
Mońki, Pol. B22 10
Monkira, Austl. E4 70
Monkton, Ont., Can. D3 103
Monkton, Vt., U.S. C2 152
Mon Louis, Al., U.S. E1 108
Monmouth, Il., U.S. C3 120
Monmouth, Me., U.S. D2 126
Monmouth, Or., U.S. C3 144
Monmouth, co., N.J., U.S. C4 137
Monmouth Beach, N.J., U.S. C5 137
Monmouth Junction, N.J., U.S. C3 137
Monmouth Mountain, mtn., B.C., Can. D6 99
Mono, co., Ca., U.S. D4 112
Mono, stm., Afr. G7 54
Mono, Caño, stm., Col. E8 84
Mono, Punta, c., Nic. F11 92
Monocacy, stm., Md., U.S. B3 127
Mono Lake, l., Ca., U.S. D4 112
Monomonac, Lake, l., U.S. E3 136
Monomoy Island, i., Ma., U.S. C7 128
Monomoy Point, c., Ma., U.S. C7 128
Monon, In., U.S. C4 121
Monona, Ia., U.S. A6 122
Monona, Wi., U.S. E4 156
Monona, co., Ia., U.S. B1 122
Monona, Lake, l., Wi., U.S. E4 156
Monongah, W.V., U.S. B4 155
Monongahela, Pa., U.S. F2 145
Monongahela, stm., U.S. G2 145
Monongalia, co., W.V., U.S. B4 155
Monopoli, Italy I12 18
Monóver, Spain G11 16
Monreale, Italy K8 18
Monroe, Ar., U.S. C4 111
Monroe, Ct., U.S. D3 114
Monroe, Ga., U.S. C3 117
Monroe, In., U.S. C8 121
Monroe, Ia., U.S. C4 122
Monroe, La., U.S. B3 125
Monroe, Mi., U.S. G7 129
Monroe, Ne., U.S. C8 134
Monroe, N.H., U.S. B2 136
Monroe, N.Y., U.S. D6 139
Monroe, N.C., U.S. C2 140
Monroe, Oh., U.S. C1 142
Monroe, Ok., U.S. C7 143
Monroe, Or., U.S. C3 144
Monroe, S.D., U.S. D8 148
Monroe, Ut., U.S. E3 151
Monroe, Va., U.S. C3 153
Monroe, Wa., U.S. B4 154
Monroe, Wi., U.S. F4 156
Monroe, co., Al., U.S. D2 108
Monroe, co., Ar., U.S. C4 111
Monroe, co., Fl., U.S. G5 116
Monroe, co., Ga., U.S. D3 117
Monroe, co., Il., U.S. E3 120
Monroe, co., In., U.S. F4 121
Monroe, co., Ia., U.S. D5 122
Monroe, co., Ky., U.S. D4 124
Monroe, co., Mi., U.S. G7 129
Monroe, co., Ms., U.S. B5 131
Monroe, co., Mo., U.S. B5 132
Monroe, co., N.Y., U.S. B3 139
Monroe, co., Oh., U.S. C4 142
Monroe, co., Pa., U.S. D11 145
Monroe, co., Tn., U.S. D9 149
Monroe, co., W.V., U.S. D4 155
Monroe, co., Wi., U.S. E3 156
Monroe Center, Ct., U.S. D3 114
Monroe Center, Il., U.S. A5 120
Monroe City, In., U.S. G3 121
Monroe City, Mo., U.S. B6 132
Monroe Lake, res., In., U.S. F5 121
Monroe Park, De., U.S. h7 115
Monroeville, Al., U.S. D2 108
Monroeville, In., U.S. C8 121
Monroeville, Oh., U.S. A3 142
Monroeville, Pa., U.S. k14 145
Monrovia, Lib. H4 64
Monrovia, Ca., U.S. m13 112
Monrovia, In., U.S. E5 121
Mons (Bergen), Bel. H4 12
Monsarás, Ponta do, c., Braz. E9 79
Monsefú, Peru B2 82
Monselice, Italy D6 18
Monson, Me., U.S. C3 126
Monson, Ma., U.S. B3 128
Montabaur, Ger. E7 10
Montagnana, Italy D6 18
Montagu, S. Afr. I5 66
Montague, P.E.I., Can. C7 101
Montague, Ca., U.S. B2 112
Montague, Mi., U.S. E4 129
Montague, co., Tx., U.S. C4 150
Montague, Isla, i., Mex. B2 90
Montague Island, i., Ak., U.S. D10 109
Montague Peak, mtn., Ak., U.S. g18 109
Montague Strait, strt., Ak., U.S. h18 109
Montagu Island, i., Falk. Is. A2 73
Montaigu, Fr. F5 14
Montalcino, Italy F6 18
Montalegre, Port. D4 16
Mont Alto, Pa., U.S. G6 145
Montana, Switz. F7 13
Montana, state, U.S. D7 133
Montandon, Pa., U.S. E8 145
Montargis, Fr. D9 14
Montauban, Fr. H8 14
Montbard, Fr. E11 14
Montbarrey, Fr. E12 14
Montbéliard, Fr. E13 14
Mont Belvieu, Tx., U.S. E5 150
Mont Blanc, Tunnel du, Eur. G6 13
Montbrison, Fr. G11 14
Montbron, Fr. G7 14
Montcalm, co., Mi., U.S. E5 129
Montceau [-les-Mines], Fr. F11 14
Montchanin, Fr. F11 14
Montchanin, De., U.S. h7 115
Montclair, Ca., U.S. m13 112
Montclair, N.J., U.S. B4 137
Mont Clare, Pa., U.S. o19 145
Montcoal, W.V., U.S. D3 155
Mont-de-Marsan, Fr. I6 14
Montdidier, Fr. C9 14
Monte, Laguna del, l., Arg. I7 80
Monteagle, Tn., U.S. D8 149
Monteagudo, Bol. H10 82
Monte Albán, hist., Mex. I11 90
Monte Alegre, Braz. D8 76
Monte Alegre de Goiás, Braz. B5 79
Monte Alegre de Minas, Braz. E4 79
Monte Azul, Braz. C7 79
Monte Azul Paulista, Braz. F4 79
Montebello, Que., Can. D3 104
Montebello, Ca., U.S. m12 112
Monte Bello Islands, is., Austl. D3 68
Monte Buey, Arg. G7 80
Montecarlo, Arg. D11 80
Monte Caseros, Arg. F10 80
Montecassino, Abbazia di, Italy H8 18
Montecatini-Terme, Italy F5 18
Montecillos, Cordillera de, mts., Hond. C7 92
Monte Comán, Arg. H5 80
Monte Cristi, Dom. Rep. E9 94
Montecristi, Ec. H2 84
Monte Cristo, Bol. F11 82
Monte Escobedo, Mex. F8 90
Montego Bay, Jam. E6 94
Monte Grande, Chile F3 80
Montegut, La., U.S. E5 125
Montelíbano, Col. C5 84
Montélimar, Fr. H11 14
Montelindo, stm., Para. B9 80
Montellano, Spain H6 16
Montello, Nv., U.S. B7 135
Montello, Wi., U.S. E4 156
Monte Maíz, Arg. G7 80
Montemorelos, Mex. E10 90
Montemor-o-Novo, Port. G3 16
Montemor-o-Vehlo, Port. E3 16
Montendre, Fr. G6 14
Montenegro, Braz. E13 80
Montenegro see Crna Gora, state, Yugo. G2 20
Monte Pascoal, Parque Nacional de, Braz. D9 79
Monte Patria, Chile F3 80
Montepuez, Moz. D7 58
Montepulciano, Italy F6 18
Monte Quemado, Arg. C7 80
Montereau-Faut-Yonne, Fr. D9 14
Monterey, Ca., U.S. D3 112
Monterey, In., U.S. B4 121
Monterey, Ky., U.S. B5 124
Monterey, Tn., U.S. C8 149
Monterey, Va., U.S. B3 153
Monterey, co., Ca., U.S. D3 112
Monterey Bay, b., Ca., U.S. D2 112
Monterey Park, Ca., U.S. m12 112
Montería, Col. C5 84
Montero, Bol. G10 82
Monteros, Arg. D6 80
Monterotondo, Italy G7 18
Monterrey, Mex. E9 90
Montesano, Italy I10 18
Montesano, Wa., U.S. C2 154
Monte Sano Mountain, mtn., Al., U.S. A3 108
Monte Sant'Angelo, Italy H10 18
Montesarchio, Italy H9 18
Montes Claros, Braz. F10 74
Montes Claros, Braz. D7 79
Montevallo, Al., U.S. B3 108
Montevarchi, Italy F6 18
Montevideo, Mn., U.S. F3 130
Montevideo, Ur. H10 80
Monte Vista, Co., U.S. D4 113
Montezuma, Ga., U.S. D2 117
Montezuma, In., U.S. E3 121
Montezuma, Ia., U.S. C5 122
Montezuma, Ks., U.S. E3 123
Montezuma, N.M., U.S. B4 138
Montezuma, co., Co., U.S. D2 113
Montezuma Canyon, val., Ut., U.S. F6 151
Montezuma Castle National Monument, Az., U.S. C4 110
Montezuma Creek, Ut., U.S. F6 151
Montezuma Peak, mtn., Az., U.S. D3 110
Montfort, Fr. D5 14
Montfort, Wi., U.S. F3 156
Montgomery, Al., U.S. C3 108
Montgomery, Ga., U.S. E5 117
Montgomery, Il., U.S. B5 120
Montgomery, In., U.S. G3 121
Montgomery, La., U.S. C3 125
Montgomery, Mi., U.S. G6 129
Montgomery, Mn., U.S. F5 130
Montgomery, N.Y., U.S. D6 139
Montgomery, Oh., U.S. o13 142
Montgomery, Pa., U.S. D8 145
Montgomery, Vt., U.S. B3 152
Montgomery, W.V., U.S. C3 155
Montgomery, co., Al., U.S. C3 108
Montgomery, co., Ar., U.S. C2 111
Montgomery, co., Ga., U.S. D4 117
Montgomery, co., Il., U.S. D4 120
Montgomery, co., In., U.S. D4 121
Montgomery, co., Ia., U.S. C2 122
Montgomery, co., Ks., U.S. E8 123
Montgomery, co., Ky., U.S. B6 124
Montgomery, co., Md., U.S. B3 127
Montgomery, co., Ms., U.S. B4 131
Montgomery, co., Mo., U.S. C6 132
Montgomery, co., N.Y., U.S. C6 139
Montgomery, co., N.C., U.S. B3 140
Montgomery, co., Oh., U.S. C1 142
Montgomery, co., Pa., U.S. F11 145
Montgomery, co., Tn., U.S. A4 149
Montgomery, co., Tx., U.S. D5 150
Montgomery, co., Va., U.S. C2 153
Montgomery Center, Vt., U.S. B3 152
Montgomery City, Mo., U.S. C6 132

Name | Map Ref. | Page

Montgomery Creek, Ca., U.S. B3 112
Monthermé, Fr. C11 14
Monthey, Switz. F6 13
Monthois, Fr. C11 14
Monticello, P.E.I., Can. C7 101
Monticello, Ar., U.S. D4 111
Monticello, Fl., U.S. B3 116
Monticello, Ga., U.S. C3 117
Monticello, Il., U.S. C5 120
Monticello, In., U.S. C4 121
Monticello, Ia., U.S. B6 122
Monticello, Ky., U.S. D5 124
Monticello, Me., U.S. B5 126
Monticello, Mn., U.S. E5 130
Monticello, Ms., U.S. D3 131
Monticello, N.Y., U.S. D6 139
Monticello, Ut., U.S. F6 151
Monticello, Wi., U.S. F4 156
Montichiari, Italy D5 18
Montier, Mo., U.S. D6 132
Montignac, Fr. G8 14
Montigny-le-Roi, Fr. D12 14
Montigny-sur-Aube, Fr. E11 14
Montijo, Pan. D2 84
Montijo, Port. G3 16
Montijo, Spain G5 16
Montijo, Golfo de, b., Pan. D2 84
Montilla, Spain H7 16
Montividiu, Braz. D3 79
Montivilliers, Fr. C7 14
Mont-Joli, Que., Can. A9 104
Mont-Laurier, Que., Can. C2 104
Mont-Louis, Fr. J9 14
Montluçon, Fr. F9 14
Montluel, Fr. G12 14
Montmagny, Que., Can. C7 104
Montmartre, Sask., Can. G4 105
Montmédy, Fr. C12 14
Montmirail, Fr. D10 14
Montmorenci, In., U.S. D3 121
Montmorenci, S.C., U.S. D4 147
Montmorency, co., Mi., U.S. C6 129
Montmorillon, Fr. F7 14
Monto, Austl. E9 70
Montoro, Spain G7 16
Montour, Ia., U.S. C5 122
Montour, co., Pa., U.S. D8 145
Montour Falls, N.Y., U.S. C4 139
Montoursville, Pa., U.S. D8 145
Montpelier, Id., U.S. G7 119
Montpelier, In., U.S. C7 121
Montpelier, Ia., U.S. C7 122
Montpelier, Oh., U.S. A1 142
Montpelier, Vt., U.S. C3 152
Montpellier, Que., Can. D2 104
Montpellier, Fr. I10 14
Montpon-Ménesterol, Fr. G7 14
Montréal, Que., Can. D4 104
Montreal, Wi., U.S. B3 156
Montréal, Île de, i., Que., Can. q19 104
Montreal Lake, l., Sask., Can. C3 105
Montréal-Nord, Que., Can. p19 104
Montreat, N.C., U.S. f10 140
Montreuil, Fr. B8 14
Montreux, Switz. F6 13
Montrevel [-en-Bresse], Fr. F12 14
Mont-Rolland, Que., Can. D3 104
Montrose, B.C., Can. E9 99
Montrose, Scot., U.K. E11 8
Montrose, Al., U.S. E2 108
Montrose, Ar., U.S. D4 111
Montrose, Co., U.S. C3 113
Montrose, Ga., U.S. D3 117
Montrose, Il., U.S. D5 120
Montrose, Ia., U.S. D6 122
Montrose, Mi., U.S. E7 129
Montrose, Mo., U.S. C4 132
Montrose, Pa., U.S. C10 145
Montrose, S.D., U.S. D8 148
Montrose, Va., U.S. m18 153
Montrose, co., Co., U.S. C2 113
Montross, Va., U.S. B6 153
Mont-Royal, Que., Can. p19 104
Mont-Saint-Michel see Le Mont-Saint-Michel, Fr. D5 14
Montserrat, Mo., U.S. C4 132
Montserrat, dep., N.A. F13 94
Mont-Tremblant, Parc Provincial du, Que., Can. C3 104
Montvale, N.J., U.S. A4 137
Montvale, Va., U.S. C3 153
Mont Vernon, N.H., U.S. E3 136
Montville, Ct., U.S. D7 114
Montville, N.J., U.S. B4 137
Montz, La., U.S. h11 125
Monument, Co., U.S. B6 113
Monument, N.M., U.S. E6 138
Monument Beach, Ma., U.S. C6 128
Monument Peak, mtn., Co., U.S. B3 113
Monument Peak, mtn., Id., U.S. G4 119
Monument Valley, val., Az., U.S. A5 110
Monywa, Burma C3 40
Monza, Italy D4 18
Monzón, Peru C3 82
Monzón, Spain D12 16
Moodus, Ct., U.S. D6 114
Moodus Reservoir, res., Ct., U.S. C6 114
Moody, Me., U.S. E2 126
Moody, Tx., U.S. D4 150
Moody, co., S.D., U.S. C9 148
Moody Air Force Base, mil., Ga., U.S. F3 117
Mooirivier, S. Afr. G9 66
Mookane, Bots. E7 66
Moolawatana, Austl. G3 70
Moonie, stm., Austl. F8 70
Moon Lake, l., Ms., U.S. A3 131
Moon Run, Pa., U.S. k13 145
Moonta, Austl. J2 70
Moora, Austl. F3 68
Moorcroft, Wy., U.S. B8 157
Moore, Id., U.S. F5 119
Moore, Mt., U.S. D7 133
Moore, Ok., U.S. B4 143
Moore, co., N.C., U.S. B3 140
Moore, co., Tn., U.S. B5 149
Moore, co., Tx., U.S. B2 150
Moore, Lake, l., Austl. E3 68
Moore Dam, U.S. B3 136
Moorefield, Ont., Can. D4 103
Moorefield, Ky., U.S. B6 124
Moorefield, W.V., U.S. B6 155
Moore Haven, Fl., U.S. F5 116
Mooreland, In., U.S. E7 121
Mooreland, Ok., U.S. A2 143
Moore Mill, N.B., Can. D2 101
Moore Reservoir, res., U.S. B3 136
Mooresburg, Tn., U.S. C10 149
Moores Creek National Military Park, N.C., U.S. C4 140
Moores Hill, In., U.S. F7 121
Moorestown, N.J., U.S. D3 137
Mooresville, In., U.S. E5 121
Mooresville, N.C., U.S. B2 140
Mooreton, N.D., U.S. C9 141
Mooreville, Ms., U.S. A5 131
Moorhead, Ia., U.S. C2 122
Moorhead, Mn., U.S. D2 130
Moorhead, Ms., U.S. B3 131
Mooringsport, La., U.S. B2 125
Moorland, Ia., U.S. B3 122
Moorman, Ky., U.S. C2 124
Moornanyah Lake, l., Austl. I5 70
Moorreesburg, S. Afr. I4 66
Moosburg, Ger. G11 10
Moose, Wy., U.S. C2 157
Moose, stm., N.H., U.S. B4 136
Moose, stm., N.Y., U.S. B5 139
Moose, stm., Vt., U.S. B5 152
Moose Creek, Ont., Can. B10 103
Moosehead Lake, l., Me., U.S. C3 126
Mooseheart, Il., U.S. B5 120
Moose Hill, hill, Ma., U.S. h11 128
Moosehorn, Man., Can. D2 100
Moose Jaw, Sask., Can. G3 105
Moose Jaw, stm., Sask., Can. G3 105
Moose Lake, Man., Can. C1 100
Moose Lake, Mn., U.S. D6 130
Moose Lake, l., B.C., Can. C1 98
Moose Lake, l., Wi., U.S. B2 156
Mooseleuk Stream, stm., Me., U.S. B4 126
Mooselookmeguntic Lake, l., Me., U.S. D2 126
Moose Mountain, mtn., Sask., Can. H4 105
Moose Mountain, mtn., N.H., U.S. C2 136
Moose Mountain Creek, stm., Sask., Can. H4 105
Moose Mountain Provincial Park, Sask., Can. H4 105
Moose River, Me., U.S. C2 126
Moosic, Pa., U.S. m18 145
Moosilauke, Mount, mtn., N.H., U.S. B3 136
Moosomin, Sask., Can. G5 105
Moosonee, Ont., Can. o19 103
Moosup, Ct., U.S. C8 114
Moosup, stm., U.S. C1 146
Mopane, S. Afr. D9 66
Mopang Lake, l., Me., U.S. D5 126
Mopipi, Bots. C7 66
Mopti, Mali D7 64
Moquegua, Peru G6 82
Moquegua, dept., Peru G6 82
Mór, Hung. H18 10
Mora, Spain F8 16
Mora, Swe. K14 6
Mora, Mn., U.S. E5 130
Mora, N.M., U.S. B4 138
Mora, co., N.M., U.S. A5 138
Mora, stm., N.M., U.S. B5 138
Morādābād, India F8 44
Morada Nova de Minas, Braz. E6 79
Moradel, Montaña de, mtn., Hond. B8 92
Mora de Rubielos, Spain E11 16
Morado Primero, Cerro, mtn., Arg. B6 80
Morafenobe, Madag. P21 67b
Mórahalom, Hung. I19 10
Mor'akovskij Zaton, U.S.S.R. F14 22
Moraleda, Canal de, strt., Chile E2 78
Morales, Guat. B6 92
Morales, Peru B3 82
Morales, Laguna, b., Mex. F11 90
Moran, Ks., U.S. E8 123
Morant Bay, Jam. F6 94
Morant Cays, is., Jam. F7 94
Morant Point, c., Jam. F6 94
Moratalla, Spain G10 16
Morattico, Va., U.S. C6 153
Moratuwa, Sri L. I5 46
Morava, hist. reg., Czech. F17 10
Morava (March), stm., Eur. G16 10
Moravia, C.R. H11 92
Moravia, Ia., U.S. D5 122
Moravia, N.Y., U.S. C4 139
Moravia see Morava, hist. reg., Czech. F17 10
Morawhanna, Guy. C13 84
Moraya, Bol. I9 82
Moray Firth, est., Scot., U.K. D10 8
Morazán, Guat. C4 92
Morazán, Hond. B7 92
Morbegno, Italy C4 18
Morbi, India I4 44
Morbihan, dept., Fr. E4 14
Morcenx, Fr. H6 14
Morden, Man., Can. E2 100
Morden, N.S., Can. D5 101
Mordovo, U.S.S.R. I23 26
Mordves, U.S.S.R. G21 26
Moreau, stm., S.D., U.S. B3 148
Moreau, North Fork, stm., S.D., U.S. B2 148
Moreau, South Fork, stm., S.D., U.S. B2 148
Moreau Peak, mtn., S.D., U.S. B2 148
Moreauville, La., U.S. C4 125
Moree, Austl. G8 70
Morée, Fr. E8 14
Morehead, Ky., U.S. B6 124
Morehead City, N.C., U.S. C6 140
Morehouse, Mo., U.S. E8 132
Morehouse, co., La., U.S. B4 125
Moreland, Ar., U.S. B3 111
Moreland, Ga., U.S. C2 117
Moreland, Id., U.S. F6 119
Morelia, Mex. H9 90
Morell, P.E.I., Can. C7 101
Morelos, Mex. D6 90
Morelos, state, Mex. H10 90
Moremi Wildlife Reserve, Bots. B6 66
Morena, India G8 44
Morena, Sierra, mts., Spain G6 16
Morenci, Az., U.S. D6 110
Morenci, Mi., U.S. G6 129
Moreno, Bahía, b., Chile B3 80
Møre og Romsdal, co., Nor. J10 6
Moresby Island, i., B.C., Can. C2 99
Mores Island, i., Bah. A6 94
Moresnet, Bel. G8 12
Moreton Island, i., Austl. F10 70
Moretown, Vt., U.S. C3 152
Moreuil, Fr. C9 14
Morewood, Ont., Can. B9 103
Morey, Lake, l., Vt., U.S. D4 152
Morey Peak, mtn., Nv., U.S. E5 135
Morez, Fr. F13 14
Morgan, Ga., U.S. E2 117
Morgan, Mn., U.S. F4 130
Morgan, Ut., U.S. B4 151
Morgan, co., Al., U.S. A3 108
Morgan, co., Co., U.S. A7 113
Morgan, co., Ga., U.S. C3 117
Morgan, co., Il., U.S. D3 120
Morgan, co., In., U.S. F5 121
Morgan, co., Ky., U.S. C6 124
Morgan, co., Mo., U.S. C5 132
Morgan, co., Oh., U.S. C4 142
Morgan, co., Tn., U.S. C9 149
Morgan, co., Ut., U.S. B4 151
Morgan, co., W.V., U.S. B6 155
Morgan Center, Vt., U.S. B5 152
Morgan City, La., U.S. E4 125
Morganfield, Ky., U.S. C2 124
Morgan Hill, Ca., U.S. D3 112
Morgan Island, i., S.C., U.S. G6 147
Morganito, Ven. E9 84
Morgan Point, c., Ct., U.S. E4 114
Morganton, Ga., U.S. B2 117
Morganton, N.C., U.S. B1 140
Morgantown, In., U.S. F5 121
Morgantown, Ky., U.S. C3 124
Morgantown, Ms., U.S. D2 131
Morgantown, Ms., U.S. D4 131
Morgantown, Pa., U.S. F10 145
Morgantown, Tn., U.S. D8 149
Morgantown, W.V., U.S. B5 155
Morganville, Ks., U.S. C6 123
Morganville, N.J., U.S. C4 137
Morganza, La., U.S. D4 125
Morgenzon, S. Afr. F9 66
Morghāb (Murgab), stm., Asia B16 48
Moriah, Mount, mtn., Nv., U.S. D7 135
Moriah, Mount, mtn., N.H., U.S. B4 136
Moriarty, N.M., U.S. C3 138
Moribaya, Gui. G5 64
Morice Lake, l., B.C., Can. B4 99
Morichal Largo, stm., Ven. C11 84
Moriki, Nig. E13 64
Moringen, Ger. D9 10
Morino, U.S.S.R. D13 26
Morinville, Alta., Can. C4 98
Morioka, Japan H16 36
Morisset, Austl. I9 70
Morkiny Gory, U.S.S.R. D19 26
Morkoka, stm., U.S.S.R. D14 24
Morlaix, Fr. D3 14
Morland, Ks., U.S. C3 123
Morley, Mi., U.S. E5 129
Morley, Mo., U.S. D8 132
Mormal', U.S.S.R. I12 26
Mormon Lake, Az., U.S. C4 110
Mormon Peak, mtn., Nv., U.S. G7 135
Morney, Austl. E4 70
Morningdale, Ma., U.S. B4 128
Morningside, S.D., U.S. C7 148
Morning Sun, Ia., U.S. C6 122
Mornington, Austl. L6 70
Mornington, Isla, i., Chile F1 78
Mornington Island, i., Austl. A3 70
Morning View, Ky., U.S. k14 124
Moro, Ar., U.S. C5 111
Moro, Or., U.S. B6 144
Moro, stm., Afr. H4 64
Morobe, Pap. N. Gui. m16 68a
Morocco, In., U.S. C3 121
Morocco (Al-Magreb), ctry., Afr. B5 54
Morococala, Bol. H8 82
Morococha, Peru D3 82
Moro Creek, stm., Ar., U.S. D3 111
Morogoro, Tan. C7 58
Moro Gulf, b., Phil. D7 38
Moroleón, Mex. G9 90
Morombe, Madag. R20 67b
Morón, Arg. H9 80
Morón, Cuba C5 94
Mörön, Mong. B7 30
Morón, Ven. B8 84
Morona, stm., Peru I4 84
Morona-Santiago, prov., Ec. I3 84
Morondava, Madag. R21 67b
Morón de la Frontera, Spain H6 16
Moroni, Com. K15 67a
Moroni, Ut., U.S. D4 151
Morotai, i., Indon. E8 38
Morozovsk, U.S.S.R. H6 22
Morpeth, Ont., Can. E3 103
Morretes, Braz. C14 80
Morrill, Ks., U.S. C8 123
Morrill, Ne., U.S. C2 134
Morrill, co., Ne., U.S. C2 134
Morrilton, Ar., U.S. B3 111
Morrin, Alta., Can. D4 98
Morrinhos, Braz. D4 79
Morrinsville, N.Z. B5 72
Morris, Man., Can. E3 100
Morris, Al., U.S. B3 108
Morris, Ga., U.S. E2 117
Morris, Il., U.S. B5 120
Morris, In., U.S. F7 121
Morris, Mn., U.S. E3 130
Morris, Ok., U.S. B6 143
Morris, co., Ks., U.S. D7 123
Morris, co., N.J., U.S. B3 137
Morris, co., Tx., U.S. C5 150
Morris, Mount, mtn., N.Y., U.S. A6 139
Morrisburg, Ont., Can. C9 103
Morrisdale, Pa., U.S. E5 145
Morris Island, i., S.C., U.S. F8 147
Morris Jesup, Kap, c., Grnld. A16 86
Morrison, Arg. G7 80
Morrison, Co., U.S. B5 113
Morrison, Il., U.S. B4 120
Morrison, Mo., U.S. C6 132
Morrison, Ok., U.S. A4 143
Morrison, Tn., U.S. D8 149
Morrison, co., Mn., U.S. D4 130
Morrison City, Tn., U.S. C11 149
Morrisonville, Il., U.S. D4 120
Morrisonville, N.Y., U.S. f11 139
Morris Plains, N.J., U.S. B4 137
Morristown, Az., U.S. D3 110
Morristown, In., U.S. E6 121
Morristown, Mn., U.S. F5 130
Morristown, N.J., U.S. B4 137
Morristown, Tn., U.S. C10 149
Morristown National Historical Park, N.J., U.S. B3 137
Morrisville, Mo., U.S. D4 132
Morrisville, N.Y., U.S. C5 139
Morrisville, Pa., U.S. F12 145
Morrisville, Vt., U.S. B3 152
Morrito, Nic. F9 92
Morro, Ec. I2 84
Morro, Punta, c., Chile D3 80
Morro, Punta, c., Mex. H14 90
Morro Bay, Ca., U.S. E3 112
Morro del Jable, Spain O26 17b
Morro do Chapéu, Braz. F10 76
Morro do Pilar, Braz. E7 79
Morropón, Peru A1 82
Morrosquillo, Golfo de, b., Col. C5 84
Morrow, Ga., U.S. C2 117
Morrow, La., U.S. D3 125
Morrow, Oh., U.S. C1 142
Morrow, co., Oh., U.S. B3 142
Morrow, co., Or., U.S. B7 144
Morrowville, Ks., U.S. C6 123
Morrumbene, Moz. D12 66
Moršansk, U.S.S.R. H24 26
Morse, Sask., Can. G2 105
Morse, La., U.S. D3 125
Morse Bluff, Ne., U.S. C9 134
Morse Mill, Mo., U.S. g12 132
Morse Reservoir, res., In., U.S. D5 121
Morses Creek, stm., N.J., U.S. k8 137
Mortagne, Fr. D7 14
Mortagne-sur-Sèvre, Fr. E6 14
Mortain, Fr. D6 14
Mortara, Italy D3 18
Morteau, Fr. E13 14
Morteros, Arg. F7 80
Mortes, Rio das, stm., Braz. B3 79
Mortesoro, Sud. L8 60
Mortlach, Sask., Can. G2 105
Mortlake, Austl. L5 70
Morton, Il., U.S. C4 120
Morton, Mn., U.S. F4 130
Morton, Ms., U.S. C4 131
Morton, Tx., U.S. C1 150
Morton, Wa., U.S. C3 154
Morton, co., Ks., U.S. E2 123
Morton, co., N.D., U.S. C4 141
Morton Grove, Il., U.S. h9 120
Morton Pass, Wy., U.S. E7 157
Mortons Gap, Ky., U.S. C2 124
Moruya, Austl. J9 70
Morven, Austl. F7 70
Morven, Ga., U.S. F3 117
Morven, N.C., U.S. C2 140
Morwell, Austl. L7 70
Morženga, U.S.S.R. B23 26
Mosal'sk, U.S.S.R. G17 26
Mosby, Mo., U.S. h11 132
Moščnyj, ostrov, i., U.S.S.R. A10 26
Moscow, Ar., U.S. C4 111
Moscow, Id., U.S. C2 119
Moscow, Ia., U.S. C6 122
Moscow, Ks., U.S. E2 123
Moscow, Pa., U.S. m18 145
Moscow, Tn., U.S. B2 149
Moscow, Vt., U.S. C3 152
Moscow Mills, Mo., U.S. C7 132
Moscow see Moskva, U.S.S.R. F20 26
Mosel (Moselle), stm., Eur. C13 14
Moselle, Ms., U.S. D4 131
Moselle, dept., Fr. D13 14
Moselle (Mosel), stm., Eur. D13 14
Mosers River, N.S., Can. E7 101
Moses Coulee, val., Wa., U.S. B6 154
Moses Lake, Wa., U.S. B6 154
Moses Lake, l., Wa., U.S. B6 154
Mosetse, Bots. C8 66
Moshaweng, stm., Afr. F6 66
Mosheim, Tn., U.S. C11 149
Mosherville, N.S., Can. D6 101
Moshi, Tan. B7 58
Mosina, Pol. C16 10
Mosinee, Wi., U.S. D4 156
Mosjøen, Nor. I13 6
Moskva (Moscow), U.S.S.R. F20 26
Moskva, stm., U.S.S.R. F21 26
Moskvy, kanal imeni, U.S.S.R. E20 26
Mošok, U.S.S.R. F24 26
Mosolovo, U.S.S.R. G23 26
Mosomane, Bots. E8 66
Mosonmagyaróvár, Hung. H17 10
Mosopa, Bots. E7 66
Mosquera, Col. F3 84
Mosquero, N.M., U.S. B6 138
Mosquito, Punta, c., Pan. C4 84
Mosquito, Riacho, stm., Para. B9 80
Mosquito Creek, stm., Ia., U.S. C2 122
Mosquito Creek Lake, res., Oh., U.S. A5 142
Mosquito Lagoon, b., Fl., U.S. D6 116
Mosquitos, Costa de, hist. reg., Nic. D11 92
Mosquitos, Golfo de los, b., Pan. H13 92
Moss, Nor. L12 6
Moss, Ms., U.S. D4 131
Moss, Tn., U.S. C8 149
Mossaka, Congo B3 58
Mossâmedes, Braz. D3 79
Mossbank, Sask., Can. H3 105
Moss Bluff, La., U.S. D2 125
Mosselbaai, S. Afr. J6 66
Mossendjo, Congo B2 58
Mosses, Al., U.S. C3 108
Mossleigh, Alta., Can. D4 98
Moss Mountain, mtn., Ar., U.S. C3 111
Mossoró, Braz. E11 76
Moss Point, Ms., U.S. E5 131
Moss Vale, Austl. J9 70
Mossyrock, Wa., U.S. C3 154
Most, Czech. E13 10
Mosta, U.S.S.R. E25 26
Mostar, Yugo. F12 18
Mostardas, Braz. F13 80
Mostiska, U.S.S.R. F23 10
Mostok, U.S.S.R. H13 26
Mosty, U.S.S.R. H7 26
Mosul see Al-Mawṣil, Iraq C7 48
Moswansicut Pond, l., R.I., U.S. C3 146
Mota, Eth. L9 60
Motagua, stm., N.A. B6 92
Motala, Swe. L14 6
Motatán, Ven. C7 84
Motherwell, Scot., U.K. F9 8
Motīhāri, India G11 44
Motley, Mn., U.S. D4 130
Motley, co., Tx., U.S. B2 150
Motloutse, Bots. C8 66
Motozintla de Mendoza, Mex. J13 90
Motril, Spain I8 16
Motru, Rom. E7 20
Mott, N.D., U.S. C3 141
Mottola, Italy I12 18
Motueka, N.Z. D4 72
Motul [de Felipe Carrillo Puerto], Mex. G15 90
Motupe, Peru B2 82
Mouaskar, Alg. C11 62
Mouchoir Passage, strt., N.A. D9 94
Moudjéria, Maur. C3 64
Moudon, Switz. E6 13
Mouila, Gabon B2 58
Mouit, Maur. C3 64
Mouka, Cen. Afr. Rep. N1 60
Moulamein, Austl. J6 70
Moulay-Idriss, Mor. C8 62
Moulins, Fr. F10 14
Moulins-la-Marche, Fr. D7 14
Moulmeingyun, Burma F3 40
Moulmein see Mawlamyine, Burma F4 40
Moulouya, Oued, stm., Mor. C9 62
Moulton, Al., U.S. A2 108
Moulton, Ia., U.S. D5 122
Moultonboro, N.H., U.S. C4 136
Moultrie, Ga., U.S. E3 117
Moultrie, co., Il., U.S. D5 120
Moultrie, Lake, res., S.C., U.S. E7 147
Mound, Mn., U.S. n11 130
Mound Bayou, Ms., U.S. B3 131
Mound City, Il., U.S. F4 120
Mound City, Ks., U.S. D9 123
Mound City, Mo., U.S. A2 132
Mound City, S.D., U.S. B5 148
Mound City Group National Monument, Oh., U.S. C2 142
Moundou, Chad G4 56
Moundridge, Ks., U.S. D6 123
Mounds, Il., U.S. F4 120
Mounds, Ok., U.S. B5 143
Mounds View, Mn., U.S. m12 130
Moundsville, W.V., U.S. B4 155
Mound Valley, Ks., U.S. E8 123
Moundville, Al., U.S. C2 108
Mounlapamôk, Laos G8 40
Mountain, N.D., U.S. A8 141
Mountainair, N.M., U.S. C3 138
Mountainaire, Az., U.S. B4 110
Mountainboro, Al., U.S. A3 108
Mountain Brook, Al., U.S. g7 108
Mountainburg, Ar., U.S. B1 111
Mountain City, Ga., U.S. B3 117
Mountain City, Nv., U.S. B6 135
Mountain City, Tn., U.S. C12 149
Mountain Fork, stm., U.S. C7 143
Mountain Grove, Ont., Can. C8 103
Mountain Grove, Mo., U.S. D5 132
Mountain Home, Ar., U.S. A3 111
Mountain Home, Id., U.S. F3 119
Mountainhome, Pa., U.S. D11 145
Mountain Home Air Force Base, mil., Id., U.S. F3 119
Mountain Iron, Mn., U.S. C6 130
Mountain Lake, Mn., U.S. G4 130
Mountain Lake Park, Md., U.S. m12 127
Mountain Nile (Baḥr al-Jabal), stm., Sud. M6 60
Mountain Park, Ok., U.S. C3 143
Mountain Pine, Ar., U.S. C2 111
Mountainside, N.J., U.S. B4 137
Mountain Valley, Ar., U.S. C2 111
Mountain View, Alta., Can. E4 98
Mountain View, Ar., U.S. B3 111
Mountain View, Ca., U.S. k8 112
Mountainview, Hi., U.S. D6 118
Mountain View, Mo., U.S. D6 132
Mountain View, N.M., U.S. C3 138
Mountain View, Ok., U.S. B3 143
Mountain View, Wy., U.S. E2 157
Mountain View, Wy., U.S. D6 157
Mountain Village, Ak., U.S. C7 109
Mount Airy, Ga., U.S. B3 117
Mount Airy, Md., U.S. B3 127
Mount Airy, N.C., U.S. A2 140
Mount Albert, Ont., Can. C5 103
Mount Alida, S. Afr. G10 66
Mount Angel, Or., U.S. B4 144
Mount Arlington, N.J., U.S. B3 137
Mount Auburn, Il., U.S. D4 120
Mount Ayr, In., U.S. C3 121
Mount Ayr, Ia., U.S. D3 122
Mount Barker, Austl. F3 68
Mount Barker, Austl. J3 70
Mount Berry, Ga., U.S. B1 117
Mount Calvary, Wi., U.S. E5 156
Mount Carmel, Al., U.S. C3 108
Mount Carmel, Il., U.S. E6 120
Mount Carmel, Oh., U.S. o13 142
Mount Carmel, Pa., U.S. E9 145
Mount Carmel [-Mitchell's Brook-Saint Catherine's], Newf., Can. E5 102
Mount Carroll, Il., U.S. A4 120
Mount Clare, W.V., U.S. B4 155
Mount Clemens, Mi., U.S. F8 129
Mount Crawford, Va., U.S. B4 153
Mount Desert Island, i., Me., U.S. D4 126
Mount Dora, Fl., U.S. D5 116
Mount Eden, Ky., U.S. B4 124
Mount Elgin, Ont., Can. E4 103
Mount Enterprise, Tx., U.S. D5 150
Mount Forest, Ont., Can. D4 103
Mount Freedom, N.J., U.S. B3 137
Mount Gambier, Austl. K4 70
Mount Garnet, Austl. A6 70
Mount Gay, W.V., U.S. D2 155
Mount Gilead, N.C., U.S. B3 140
Mount Gilead, Oh., U.S. B3 142
Mount Hagen, Pap. N. Gui. G11 38
Mount Healthy, Oh., U.S. o12 142
Mount Holly, Ar., U.S. D3 111
Mount Holly, N.J., U.S. D3 137
Mount Holly, N.C., U.S. B1 140
Mount Holly, Vt., U.S. E3 152
Mount Holly Springs, Pa., U.S. F7 145
Mount Hope, Austl. J1 70
Mount Hope, Al., U.S. A2 108
Mount Hope, Ks., U.S. E6 123
Mount Hope, W.V., U.S. D3 155
Mount Hope, stm., Ct., U.S. B7 114
Mount Hope Bay, b., U.S. D6 146
Mount Horeb, Wi., U.S. E4 156
Mount Ida, Ar., U.S. C2 111
Mount Isa, Austl. C3 70
Mount Jackson, Va., U.S. B4 153
Mount Jewett, Pa., U.S. C4 145
Mount Joy, Ia., U.S. h10 122
Mount Joy, Pa., U.S. F9 145
Mount Juliet, Tn., U.S. A5 149
Mount Kisco, N.Y., U.S. D7 139
Mount Lebanon, Pa., U.S. F1 145
Mount Lemmon, Az., U.S. E5 110
Mount Lookout, W.V., U.S. C4 155
Mount Magnet, Austl. E3 68
Mount Manara, Austl. I5 70
Mount Meigs, Al., U.S. C3 108
Mount Morgan, Austl. D9 70
Mount Morris, Il., U.S. A4 120
Mount Morris, Mi., U.S. E7 129
Mount Morris, N.Y., U.S. C3 139
Mount Morris, Pa., U.S. G1 145
Mount Mulligan, Austl. A6 70
Mount Olive, Al., U.S. B3 108
Mount Olive, Il., U.S. D4 120
Mount Olive, Ms., U.S. D4 131
Mount Olive, N.C., U.S. B4 140
Mount Olive, Tn., U.S. n14 149
Mount Olivet, Ky., U.S. B5 124
Mount Orab, Oh., U.S. C2 142
Mount Pearl, Newf., Can. E5 102
Mount Penn, Pa., U.S. F10 145
Mount Perry, Austl. E9 70
Mount Pleasant, Ar., U.S. B4 111
Mount Pleasant, Ia., U.S. D6 122
Mount Pleasant, Mi., U.S. E6 129
Mount Pleasant, Ms., U.S. A4 131
Mount Pleasant, N.C., U.S. B2 140
Mount Pleasant, Pa., U.S. F2 145
Mount Pleasant, S.C., U.S. F8 147
Mount Pleasant, Tn., U.S. B4 149
Mount Pleasant, Tx., U.S. C5 150
Mount Pleasant, Ut., U.S. D4 151
Mount Pocono, Pa., U.S. D11 145
Mount Prospect, Il., U.S. A6 120
Mount Pulaski, Il., U.S. C4 120
Mountrail, co., N.D., U.S. A3 141
Mount Rainier, Md., U.S. f9 127
Mount Rainier National Park, Wa., U.S. C4 154
Mount Revelstoke National Park, B.C., Can. D8 99
Mount Rogers National Recreation Area, Va., U.S. D1 153
Mount Rushmore National Memorial, hist., S.D., U.S. D2 148
Mount Savage, Md., U.S. k13 127
Mount Shasta, Ca., U.S. B2 112
Mount Sidney, Va., U.S. B4 153
Mount Sterling, Il., U.S. D3 120
Mount Sterling, Ky., U.S. B6 124
Mount Sterling, Oh., U.S. C2 142
Mount Stewart, P.E.I., Can. C7 101
Mount Stewart, S. Afr. I7 66
Mount Storm, W.V., U.S. B5 155
Mount Summit, In., U.S. D7 121
Mount Sunapee, N.H., U.S. D2 136
Mount Surprise, Austl. B6 70
Mount Uniacke, N.S., Can. E6 101
Mount Union, Pa., U.S. F6 145
Mount Vernon, Al., U.S. D1 108
Mount Vernon, Ar., U.S. B3 111
Mount Vernon, Ga., U.S. D4 117
Mount Vernon, Il., U.S. E5 120
Mount Vernon, In., U.S. I2 121
Mount Vernon, Ia., U.S. C6 122
Mount Vernon, Ky., U.S. C5 124
Mount Vernon, Me., U.S. D3 126
Mount Vernon, Mo., U.S. D4 132
Mount Vernon, N.Y., U.S. h13 139
Mount Vernon, Oh., U.S. B3 142
Mount Vernon, Or., U.S. C7 144
Mount Vernon, S.D., U.S. D7 148
Mount Vernon, Tn., U.S. D9 149
Mount Vernon, Tx., U.S. C5 150
Mount Vernon, Wa., U.S. A3 154
Mount Victory, Oh., U.S. B2 142
Mount View, R.I., U.S. D4 146
Mountville, Ga., U.S. C2 117
Mount Washington, Ky., U.S. B4 124
Mount Wolf, Pa., U.S. F8 145
Mount Zion, Ga., U.S. C1 117
Mount Zion, Il., U.S. D5 120
Moura, Austl. E8 70
Moura, Braz. H12 84
Moura, Port. G4 16
Mourdi, Dépression du, depr., Chad E5 56
Mourdiah, Mali D6 64

Name — Map Ref. — Page

Mourne Mountains, mts., N. Ire., U.K. G7 8
Mousie, Ky., U.S. C7 124
Moussoro, Chad F4 56
Moutier, Switz. D7 13
Moûtiers, Fr. G13 14
Mouzon, Fr. C12 14
Moville, Ire. F6 8
Moville, Ia., U.S. B1 122
Moweaqua, Il., U.S. D4 120
Mower, co., Mn., U.S. G6 130
Moxee City, Wa., U.S. C5 154
Moxie Pond, l., Me., U.S. C3 126
Moya, Com. L16 67a
Moya, Peru E4 82
Moyahua, Mex. G8 90
Moyamba, S.L. G3 64
Moyen Atlas, mts., Mor. D8 62
Moyeuvre-Grande, Fr. C13 14
Moyie, B.C., Can. E10 99
Moyie Springs, Id., U.S. A2 119
Moyobamba, Peru B3 82
Moyock, N.C., U.S. A6 140
Moyogalpa, Nic. F9 92
Moyuta, Volcán, vol., Guat. C4 92
Možajsk, U.S.S.R. F19 26
Mozambique (Moçambique), ctry., Afr. E7 58
Mozambique Channel, strt., Afr. E8 58
Mozarlândia, Braz. C3 79
Mozart, Sask., Can. F3 105
Mozdok, U.S.S.R. I6 22
Mozelle, Ky., U.S. D6 124
Možga, U.S.S.R. F8 22
Mozyr', U.S.S.R. G3 22
Mphoengs, Zimb. C8 66
Mpika, Zam. D6 58
Mpraeso, Ghana H9 64
Mpwapwa, Tan. C7 58
Mqanduli, Transkei H9 66
Mrągowo, Pol. B21 10
M'Ramani, Com. L16 67a
Mrkopalj, Yugo. D9 18
M'Saken, Tun. N5 18
M'Sila, Alg. C13 62
Mšinskaja, U.S.S.R. B12 26
Msta, U.S.S.R. D17 26
Msta, stm., U.S.S.R. C14 26
Mstera, U.S.S.R. E24 26
Mstislavl', U.S.S.R. G14 26
Mszczonów, Pol. D20 10
Mtamvuna, stm., Afr. H9 66
Mtwara, Tan. D8 58
Mu, Cerro, mtn., S.A. C6 84
Muanda, Zaire C2 58
Muang Hôngsa, Laos E6 40
Muang Huang, Laos E7 40
Muang Khammouan, Laos F8 40
Muang Khi, Laos E6 40
Muang Không, Laos G8 40
Muang Khôngxédôn, Laos G8 40
Muang Long, Laos D6 40
Muang Ngoy, Laos D7 40
Muang Ou Nua, Laos C6 40
Muang Ou Tai, Laos C6 40
Muang Pak-Lay, Laos E6 40
Muang Pakxan, Laos E7 40
Muang Phiang, Laos E6 40
Muang Phoun, Laos E7 40
Muang Sing, Laos D6 40
Muang Souy, Laos E7 40
Muang Thadua, Laos E6 40
Muang Vangviang, Laos E7 40
Muang Vapi, Laos G8 40
Muang Xaignabouri, Laos E6 40
Muang Xay, Laos D6 40
Muang Xépôn, Laos F9 40
Muang Xon, Laos D7 40
Muang You, Laos E7 40
Muar (Bandar Maharani), Malay. M7 40
Muarasiberut, Indon. F2 38
Mucajaí, stm., Braz. F12 84
Muchanovo, U.S.S.R. E21 26
Muchinga Mountains, mts., Zam. D6 58
Muchtolovo, U.S.S.R. F26 26
Muckadilla, Austl. F8 70
Muckalee Creek, stm., Ga., U.S. D2 117
Mučkapskij, U.S.S.R. J25 26
Muckleshoot Indian Reservation, Wa., U.S. f11 154
Muconda, Ang. D4 58
Mucuchíes, Ven. C7 84
Mucucuaú, stm., Braz. H12 84
Mucugê, Braz. B8 79
Mucuim, stm., Braz. B9 82
Muçum, Braz. E13 80
Mucupia, Moz. B13 66
Mucupina, Monte, mtn., Hond. B8 92
Mucur, Tur. B3 48
Mucuri, Braz. E9 79
Mucuri, stm., Braz. E9 79
Mucusso, Ang. B5 66
Mud, stm., Ky., U.S. C3 124
Mud, stm., Mn., U.S. B3 130
Mud, stm., W.V., U.S. C2 155
Mudan, stm., China B12 30
Mudanjiang, China C12 30
Mud Creek, stm., Al., U.S. g6 108
Mud Creek, stm., Co., U.S. D8 113
Mud Creek, stm., Ia., U.S. e9 122
Mud Creek, stm., Ne., U.S. C6 134
Mud Creek, stm., Ok., U.S. C4 143
Muddy Boggy Creek, stm., Ok., U.S. C6 143
Muddy Creek, stm., Co., U.S. A4 113
Muddy Creek, stm., Ks., U.S. k14 123
Muddy Creek, stm., Ut., U.S. E4 151
Muddy Creek, stm., Wy., U.S. E2 157
Muddy Creek, stm., Wy., U.S. E5 157
Muddy Creek, stm., Wy., U.S. D6 157
Muddy Creek, stm., Wy., U.S. C4 157
Muddy Mountains, mts., Nv., U.S. G7 135
Muddy Peak, mtn., Nv., U.S. G7 135
Mudgee, Austl. I8 70
Mudjuga, U.S.S.R. J26 6
Mud Lake, Id., U.S. F6 119
Mud Lake, l., Me., U.S. A4 126
Mud Lake, l., Nv., U.S. F4 135
Mud Lick Creek, stm., Ky., U.S. k13 124
Mudon, Burma F4 40
Mudu, China D9 34
Muelle de los Bueyes, Nic. E10 92
Muenster, Sask., Can. E3 105
Muenster, Tx., U.S. C4 150
Muerto, stm., Arg. B7 80
Mufulira, Zam. D5 58
Mu Gia, Deo, Asia F8 40
Muğla, Tur. L12 20
Mugron, Fr. I6 14
Muhammad, Ra's, c., Egypt D8 60
Muhammad Qawl, Sud. G9 60
Mühlacker, Ger. G8 10
Mühldorf, Ger. G12 10
Muhlenberg, co., Ky., U.S. C2 124
Mühlhausen, Ger. D10 10
Mühlig-Hofmann Mountains, mts., Ant. C3 73
Muhu, i., U.S.S.R. C6 26
Muhu väin, strt., U.S.S.R. C6 26
Muir, Mi., U.S. E6 129
Muirkirk, Md., U.S. B4 127
Muiron Islands, is., Austl. D2 68
Muir Woods National Monument, Ca., U.S. h7 112
Muisne, Ec. G2 84
Mujang-ni, S. Kor. H14 32
Mujezerskij, U.S.S.R. J22 6
Mujnak, U.S.S.R. I9 22
Muju, S. Kor. G15 32
Mukačevo, U.S.S.R. H2 22
Mukah, Malay. E5 38
Mukdahan, Thai. F8 40
Mukden see Shenyang, China B11 32
Mukilteo, Wa., U.S. B3 154
Mukry, U.S.S.R. J11 22
Muktsar, India E6 44
Mukwonago, Wi., U.S. F5 156
Mula, Spain G10 16
Mulanje, Mwi. E7 58
Mulas, Punta de, c., Cuba D7 94
Mulatos, Mex. C5 90
Mulatupo, Pan. C4 84
Mulberry, Ar., U.S. B1 111
Mulberry, Fl., U.S. E4 116
Mulberry, In., U.S. D4 121
Mulberry, Ks., U.S. E9 123
Mulberry, N.C., U.S. A1 140
Mulberry, Oh., U.S. C1 142
Mulberry, Tn., U.S. B5 149
Mulberry, stm., Ar., U.S. B1 111
Mulberry Fork, stm., Al., U.S. B3 108
Mulberry Grove, Il., U.S. E4 120
Mulberry Mountain, mtn., Ar., U.S. B3 111
Mulchén, Chile I2 80
Mulde, stm., Ger. D12 10
Muldraugh, Ky., U.S. C4 124
Muldrow, Ok., U.S. B7 143
Mulegé, Mex. D3 90
Mulegns, Switz. E12 13
Muleshoe, Tx., U.S. B1 150
Mulga, Al., U.S. B3 108
Mulgowie, Austl. F10 70
Mulgrave, N.S., Can. D8 101
Mulhacén, mtn., Spain H8 16
Mulhouse, Fr. E14 14
Mulino, Or., U.S. B4 144
Mull, Island of, i., Scot., U.K. E7 8
Mullan, Id., U.S. B3 119
Mullan Pass, Mt., U.S. D4 133
Mullen, Ne., U.S. B4 134
Mullengudgery, Austl. H7 70
Mullens, W.V., U.S. D3 155
Muller, Pegunungan, mts., Indon. E5 38
Mullet Key, i., Fl., U.S. p10 116
Mullett Lake, l., Mi., U.S. C6 129
Mullewa, Austl. E3 68
Mullica, stm., N.J., U.S. D3 137
Mullica Hill, N.J., U.S. D2 137
Mulligan, stm., Austl. D3 70
Mulliken, Mi., U.S. F6 129
Mullingar, Ire. H6 8
Mullins, S.C., U.S. C9 147
Mullinville, Ks., U.S. E4 123
Mullumbimby, Austl. G10 70
Multān, Pak. E4 44
Multnomah, co., Or., U.S. B4 144
Mulvane, Ks., U.S. E6 123
Mulvihill, Man., Can. D2 100
Mulyah Mountain, mtn., Austl. H6 70
Mumbwa, Zam. D5 58
Mummy Range, mts., Co., U.S. A5 113
Mumu, Sud. K2 60
Mumungwe, Bots. C8 66
Mun, stm., Thai. G8 40
Muna, Mex. G15 90
Munā, Sau. Ar. D1 47
Muna, stm., U.S.S.R. D15 24
Münchberg, Ger. E11 10
München (Munich), Ger. G11 10
München-Gladbach see Mönchengladbach, Ger. D6 10
Münchenstein, Switz. C8 13
Munchique, Cerro, mtn., Col. F4 84
Munch'ŏn, N. Kor. D15 32
Muncie, In., U.S. D7 121
Muncy, Pa., U.S. D8 145
Mundare, Alta., Can. C4 98
Munday, Tx., U.S. C3 150
Mundelein, Il., U.S. A5 120
Münden, Ger. D9 10
Munden, Ks., U.S. C6 123
Mundo Novo, Braz. A8 79
Mundubbera, Austl. E9 70
Munene, Zimb. C10 66
Munford, Al., U.S. B4 108
Munford, Tn., U.S. B2 149
Munfordville, Ky., U.S. C4 124
Mungallala, Austl. F7 70
Mungbere, Zaire H6 56
Munger, India H12 44
Mungindi, Austl. G8 70
Munhall, Pa., U.S. k14 145
Munhango, Ang. D3 58
Munich, N.D., U.S. A7 141
Munich see München, Ger. G11 10
Munising, Mi., U.S. B4 129
Munith, Mi., U.S. F6 129
Muniz Freire, Braz. F8 79
Munjor, Ks., U.S. D4 123
Munku-Sardyk, gora, mtn., Asia G12 24
Munsan, S. Kor. F14 32
Münsingen, Switz. E8 13
Munson, Alta., Can. D4 98
Munsonville, N.H., U.S. D2 136
Munster, Fr. D14 14
Münster, Ger. D7 10
Munster, Ger. C10 10
Munster, In., U.S. A2 121
Munster, hist. reg., Ire. I5 8
Munsungan Lake, l., Me., U.S. B3 126
Munuscong Lake, l., Mi., U.S. B6 129
Muong Saiapoun, Laos E6 40
Muonio, Fin. H18 6
Muoro, Italy I4 18
Muqayshiṭ, i., U.A.E. B8 47
Muqdisho (Mogadishu), Som. H10 56
Muqi, China B12 32
Muqui, Braz. F8 79
Mur (Mura), stm., Eur. I15 10
Mura (Mur), stm., Eur. I16 10
Muradiye, Tur. B7 48
Murakami, Japan I14 36
Muraši, U.S.S.R. F7 22
Murat, stm., Tur. B5 48
Murauaú, stm., Braz. G12 84
Muravjovo, U.S.S.R. E17 26
Murča, Port. D4 16
Mürcheh Khvort, Iran E11 48
Murchison, Austl. K6 70
Murchison, stm., Austl. E3 68
Murchison Falls see Kabalega Falls, wtfl, Ug. H7 56
Murcia, Spain H10 16
Murcia, prov., Spain G10 16
Murciélago, Islas, is., C.R. G9 92
Murderkill, stm., De., U.S. D4 115
Murdo, S.D., U.S. D5 148
Murdock, Mn., U.S. E3 130
Murdock, Ne., U.S. h12 134
Mureck, Aus. I15 10
Mureș, co., Rom. C8 20
Mureș (Maros), stm., Eur. C5 20
Muret, Fr. I8 14
Murfreesboro, Ar., U.S. C2 111
Murfreesboro, N.C., U.S. A5 140
Murfreesboro, Tn., U.S. B5 149
Murgab, U.S.S.R. J12 22
Murgab (Morghāb), stm., Asia B16 48
Murgha Kibzai, Pak. E3 44
Murgon, Austl. F9 70
Muri, Switz. E7 13
Muriaé, Braz. F7 79
Muriaé, stm., Braz. F8 79
Muritiba, Braz. B9 79
Müritz, l., Ger. B12 10
Murmansk, U.S.S.R. D4 22
Murmino, U.S.S.R. G23 26
Murnei, Sud. K2 60
Murom, U.S.S.R. F25 26
Muroran, Japan E15 36a
Muroto, Japan N9 36
Murphy, Ga., U.S. E3 117
Murphy, Id., U.S. F2 119
Murphy, Mo., U.S. g13 132
Murphy, N.C., U.S. f8 140
Murphy, Or., U.S. E3 144
Murphy Island, i., S.C., U.S. E9 147
Murphy Lake, l., B.C., Can. C7 99
Murphys, Ca., U.S. C3 112
Murphysboro, Il., U.S. F4 120
Murphytown, W.V., U.S. B3 155
Murray, Id., U.S. B3 119
Murray, Ia., U.S. C4 122
Murray, Ky., U.S. f9 124
Murray, Ne., U.S. D10 134
Murray, Ut., U.S. C4 151
Murray, co., Ga., U.S. B2 117
Murray, co., Mn., U.S. F3 130
Murray, co., Ok., U.S. C4 143
Murray, stm., Austl. J3 70
Murray, stm., B.C., Can. B7 99
Murray, Lake, l., Pap. N. Gui. G11 38
Murray, Lake, res., Ok., U.S. C4 143
Murray, Lake, res., S.C., U.S. C5 147
Murray Bridge, Austl. J3 70
Murray Harbour, P.E.I., Can. D7 101
Murray Head, c., P.E.I., Can. C7 101
Murray River, P.E.I., Can. C7 101
Murraysburg, S. Afr. H6 66
Murrayville, Ga., U.S. B3 117
Murrayville, Il., U.S. D3 120
Murree, Pak. D5 44
Murrells Inlet, S.C., U.S. D9 147
Murrells Inlet, b., S.C., U.S. D10 147
Murrhardt, Ger. G9 10
Murrī, stm., Col. D4 84
Murrumbidgee, stm., Austl. J6 70
Murrumburrah, Austl. J8 70
Murrurundi, Austl. H9 70
Murska Sobota, Yugo. C11 18
Murtajāpur, India B4 46
Murtaugh, Id., U.S. G4 119
Murten, Switz. E7 13
Murtoa, Austl. K5 70
Murtosa, Port. E3 16
Muru, stm., Braz. C6 82
Murud, Gunong, mtn., Malay. E6 38
Murupara, N.Z. C6 72
Murutinga, Braz. I13 84
Murwāra, India I9 44
Murwillumbah, Austl. G10 70
Mürzzuschlag, Aus. H15 10
Muş, Tur. B6 48
Mūsā, Jabal (Mount Sinai), mtn., Egypt C7 60
Musaid, Libya B3 60
Musala, mtn., Bul. G7 20
Musan, N. Kor. A17 32
Musandam Peninsula, pen., Oman A10 47
Mūsā Qal'eh, Afg. D1 44
Musay'īd, Qatar D11 56
Muscatatuck, stm., In., U.S. G5 121
Muscatatuck, Vernon Fork, stm., In., U.S. G6 121
Muscatine, Ia., U.S. C6 122
Muscatine, co., Ia., U.S. C6 122
Muscat see Masqaṭ, Oman C11 47
Mus-Chaja, gora, mtn., U.S.S.R. E20 24
Muscle Shoals, Al., U.S. A2 108
Musclow, Mount, mtn., B.C., Can. C4 99
Muscoda, Wi., U.S. E3 156
Muscogee, co., Ga., U.S. D2 117
Musconetcong, stm., N.J., U.S. B4 137
Musconetcong Mountain, mtn., N.J., U.S. B2 137
Muscooten Bay, l., Il., U.S. C3 120
Muscotah, Ks., U.S. C8 123
Muse, Ok., U.S. C7 143
Muse, Pa., U.S. F1 145
Müsgebi, Tur. L11 20
Musgrave, Austl. B8 68
Musgrave Harbour, Newf., Can. D5 102
Musgravetown, Newf., Can. D5 102
Mushandike Sanctuary, Zimb. C10 66
Mushie, Zaire B3 58
Mushin, Nig. H11 64
Muskeg Bay, b., Mn., U.S. B3 130
Muskeget Channel, strt., Ma., U.S. D7 128
Muskeget Island, i., Ma., U.S. D7 128
Muskego, Wi., U.S. F5 156
Muskego Lake, l., Wi., U.S. n11 156
Muskegon, Mi., U.S. E4 129
Muskegon, co., Mi., U.S. E4 129
Muskegon, stm., Mi., U.S. E4 129
Muskegon Heights, Mi., U.S. E4 129
Muskegon Lake, l., Mi., U.S. E4 129
Muskingum, co., Oh., U.S. B4 142
Muskingum, stm., Oh., U.S. C4 142
Muskogee, Ok., U.S. B6 143
Muskogee, co., Ok., U.S. B6 143
Muslimbāgh, Pak. E2 44
Musoma, Tan. B6 58
Musquacook Lakes, l., Me., U.S. B3 126
Musquash, N.B., Can. D3 101
Musquash Mountain, mtn., Me., U.S. C5 126
Musquodoboit Harbour, N.S., Can. E6 101
Musselshell, Mt., U.S. D9 133
Musselshell, co., Mt., U.S. D8 133
Musselshell, stm., Mt., U.S. D9 133
Mussomeli, Italy L8 18
Mussuma, Ang. D4 58
Mustafakemalpaşa, Tur. I12 20
Mustang, Ok., U.S. B4 143
Mustinka, stm., Mn., U.S. E2 130
Mustla, U.S.S.R. C8 26
Mustvee, U.S.S.R. C9 26
Muswellbrook, Austl. I9 70
Mūt, Egypt E5 60
Mut, Tur. C2 48
Mutá, Ponta do, c., Braz. B9 79
Mutambara, Zimb. B11 66
Mutare, Zimb. B11 66
Mutlu (Rezovska), stm., Eur. H11 20
Mutsamudu, Com. L16 67a
Mutsu, Japan F16 36
Mutsu-wan, b., Japan F15 36
Muttaburra, Austl. D6 70
Muttenz, Switz. C8 13
Mutton Mountains, mts., Or., U.S. C5 144
Mutuípe, Braz. B9 79
Mutum, Braz. E8 79
Mutum, stm., Braz. J8 84
Mutunópolis, Braz. B4 79
Muxima, Ang. C2 58
Muymanu, stm., S.A. D7 82
Muy Muy, Nic. E9 92
Muyua Island, i., Pap. N. Gui. A10 68
Muyua Island, i., Pap. N. Gui. m17 68a
Muyumba, Zaire C5 58
Muzaffarābād, Pak. C5 44
Muzaffarnagar, India F7 44
Muzaffarpur, India G11 44
Muzat, stm., China C3 30
Muzon, Cape, c., Ak., U.S. n23 109
Muztag, mtn., China B9 44
Muztag, mtn., China B12 44
Mvolo, Sud. N5 60
Mvuma, Zimb. B10 66
Mwali (Mohéli), i., Com. L15 67a
Mwanza, Tan. B6 58
Mweka, Zaire B4 58
Mwenezi, Zimb. C10 66
Mweru, Lake, l., Afr. C5 58
Mwinilunga, Zam. D4 58
Myaing, Burma D3 40
Myakka, stm., Fl., U.S. E4 116
Myanaung, Burma E3 40
Myanmar see Burma, ctry., Asia A2 38
Myaungmya, Burma F3 40
Myebon, Burma D2 40
Myerstown, Pa., U.S. F9 145
Myersville, Md., U.S. A2 127
Myingyan, Burma D3 40
Myitkyinā, Burma B4 40
Myittha, Burma D4 40
Myjava, Czech. G17 10
Myllymäki, Fin. J19 6
Mymensingh, Bngl. H14 44
Mynämäki, Fin. K18 6
Mynard, Ne., U.S. h13 134
Mynfontein, S. Afr. H6 66
Myrnam, Alta., Can. C5 98
Myrskylä (Mörskom), Fin. K19 6
Myrtle, Ms., U.S. A4 131
Myrtle Beach, S.C., U.S. D10 147
Myrtle Beach Air Force Base, mil., S.C., U.S. D10 147
Myrtle Grove, Fl., U.S. u14 116
Myrtle Point, Or., U.S. D2 144
Myrtlewood, Al., U.S. C2 108
Myski, U.S.S.R. G9 24
Myškino, U.S.S.R. D21 26
Myślenice, Pol. F19 10
Mysłowice, Pol. E19 10
Mysore, India F4 46
Mystic, Ct., U.S. D8 114
Mystic, Ga., U.S. E3 117
Mystic, Ia., U.S. D5 122
Mystic Lakes, l., Ma., U.S. g11 128
Myszków, Pol. E19 10
Myt, U.S.S.R. E25 26
My Tho, Viet. I9 40
Mytišči, U.S.S.R. F20 26
Myton, Ut., U.S. C5 151
Mzimba, Mwi. D6 58
Mzimvubu, stm., Afr. H9 66
Mzuzu, Mwi. D6 58

N

Na (Tengtiao), stm., Asia C7 40
Naalehu, Hi., U.S. D6 118
Naas, Ire. H7 8
Nabā, Jabal an- (Mount Nebo), mtn., Jord. E5 50
Nabalat Al-Hajanah, Sud. K5 60
Nabburg, Ger. F12 10
Nabereżnyje Čelny, U.S.S.R. F8 22
Nabeul, Tun. M5 18
Nābha, India E7 44
Nabileque, stm., Braz. I13 82
Nabī Shu'ayb, Jabal an-, mtn., Yemen G3 47
Nabnasset, Ma., U.S. A5 128
Nabogame, Mex. D6 90
Naboomspruit, S. Afr. E9 66
Nabq, Egypt C8 60
Nābulus, Isr. Occ. D4 50
Nacala-Velha, Moz. D8 58
Nacaome, Hond. D7 92
Naches, Wa., U.S. C5 154
Naches, stm., Wa., U.S. C5 154
Nachičevan', U.S.S.R. J7 22
Náchod, Czech. E16 10
Nachodka, U.S.S.R. I18 24
Nacimiento, Chile I2 80
Nacimiento, Lake, res., Ca., U.S. E3 112
Nacmine, Alta., Can. D4 98
Naco, Mex. B5 90
Naco, Az., U.S. F6 110
Nacogdoches, Tx., U.S. D5 150
Nacogdoches, co., Tx., U.S. D5 150
Nácori Chico, Mex. C5 90
Nacozari de García, Mex. B5 90
Ñacunday, Para. D11 80
Nadiād, India I5 44
Nădlac, Rom. C4 20
Nador, Mor. C9 62
Nadvoicy, U.S.S.R. J24 6
Nadvornaja, U.S.S.R. A8 20
Nadym, U.S.S.R. D12 22
Nadym, stm., U.S.S.R. D12 22
Nafadji, Sen. E4 64
Näfels, Switz. D11 13
Nafī, Sau. Ar. I7 48
Naga, Phil. O20 39b
Nâga, Kreb en, clf, Afr. I7 62
Naga Hills, mts., Asia B3 40
Nāgāland, state, India H16 44
Nagano, Japan K13 36
Nagaoka, Japan J13 36
Nagaon, India G15 44
Nāgappattinam, India G5 46
Nāgārjuna Sāgar, res., India D5 46
Nagarote, Nic. E8 92
Nagar Pārkar, Pak. H4 44
Nagasaki, Japan O4 36
Nāgaur, India G5 44
Nagda, India I6 44
Nāgercoil, India H4 46
Nagīna, India F8 44
Nagog Pond, l., Ma., U.S. f10 128
Nagold, Ger. G8 10
Nagornoje, U.S.S.R. D12 20
Nagornyj, U.S.S.R. F16 24
Nagoya, Japan L11 36
Nāgpur, India J8 44
Nagqu, China E5 30
Nags Head, N.C., U.S. B7 140
Nagua, Dom. Rep. E10 94
Nagyatád, Hung. I17 10
Nagybajom, Hung. I17 10
Nagyecsed, Hung. H22 10
Nagykálló, Hung. H21 10
Nagykanizsa, Hung. I17 10
Nagykőrös, Hung. H19 10
Naha, Japan U2 37b
Nāhan, India E7 44
Nahang (Nihing), stm., Asia H17 48
Nahant, Ma., U.S. g12 128
Nahariyya, Isr. B4 50
Nahāvand, Iran D10 48
Nahe, China B11 30
Nahmakanta Lake, l., Me., U.S. C3 126
Nahualate, stm., Guat. C3 92
Nahuel Huapí, Lago, l., Arg. E2 78
Nahunta, Ga., U.S. E5 117
Naica, Mex. D7 90
Naicam, Sask., Can. E3 105
Nailin, China B7 32
Nain, Newf., Can. g9 102
Nā'īn, Iran E12 48
Naini Tāl, India F8 44
Nairn, La., U.S. E6 125
Nairobi, Kenya B7 58
Naissaar, i., U.S.S.R. B7 26
Naivasha, Kenya B7 58
Najafābād, Iran E11 48
Najasa, stm., Cuba D6 94
Nájera, Spain C9 16
Naj'Hammādī, Egypt D7 60
Najībābād, India F8 44
Najin, N. Kor. A18 32
Najstenjarvi, U.S.S.R. J23 6
Naju, S. Kor. H14 32
Nakadōri-shima, i., Japan O4 36
Nakaminato, Japan K15 36
Nakano-shima, i., Japan R4 37b
Nakape, Sud. O5 60
Nakatsu, Japan N6 36
Nakfa, Eth. I10 60
Nakhon Nayok, Thai. G6 40
Nakhon Pathom, Thai. H6 40
Nakhon Phanom, Thai. F8 40
Nakhon Ratchasima, Thai. G7 40
Nakhon Sawan, Thai. G6 40
Nakhon Si Thammarat, Thai. J5 40
Nakina, Ont., Can. o18 103
Nakło nad Notecią, Pol. B17 10
Naknek, Ak., U.S. D8 109
Naknek Lake, l., Ak., U.S. D8 109
Nakskov, Den. N12 6
Nakuru, Kenya B7 58
Nakusp, B.C., Can. D9 99
Nalajch, Mong. B8 30
Nālanda, India D12 42
Nal'čik, U.S.S.R. I6 22
Nalgonda, India D5 46
Nallen, W.V., U.S. m14 155
Nālūt, Libya E16 62
Nam, stm., Asia D5 40
Namaacha, Moz. E11 66
Namak, Daryācheh-ye, l., Iran D11 48
Namaka, Alta., Can. D4 98
Namaksār, Kowl-e, l., Asia D18 48
Namangan, U.S.S.R. I12 22
Namanock Island, i., N.J., U.S. A3 137
Namapa, Moz. D7 58
Namatanai, Pap. N. Gui. k17 68a
Nambe, N.M., U.S. B4 138
Nambour, Austl. F10 70
Nambucca Heads, Austl. H10 70
Nam Can, Viet. J8 40
Nam Co, l., China E14 44
Nam Dinh, Viet. D9 40
Namekagon, stm., Wi., U.S. B2 156
Namekagon Lake, l., Wi., U.S. B2 156
Namen (Namur), Bel. H6 12
Namhkam, Burma C4 40
Namib Desert, des., Afr. D2 66
Namibe, Ang. E2 58
Namibia, ctry., Afr. F3 58
Namjagbarwa Feng, mtn., China F16 44
Namoi, stm., Austl. H8 70
Namounou, Burkina F10 64
Nampa, Alta., Can. A2 98
Nampa, Id., U.S. F2 119
Nampawng, Burma C4 40
Namp'o, N. Kor. E13 32
Nampula, Moz. E7 58
Namsang, Burma D4 40
Namsos, Nor. I12 6
Namtu, Burma A2 38
Namur (Namen), Bel. H6 12
Namur, prov., Bel. H6 12
Namutoni, Nmb. B3 66
Namwŏn, S. Kor. H15 32
Namyang, N. Kor. A17 32
Namyit Island, i., Asia C5 38
Namysłów, Pol. D17 10
Nan, Thai. E6 40
Nan, stm., Thai. F6 40
Nanafalia, Al., U.S. C2 108
Nanaimo, B.C., Can. E5 99
Nanakuli, Hi., U.S. B3 118
Nanam, N. Kor. B17 32
Nanango, Austl. F10 70
Nanao, Japan J11 36
Nanay, stm., Peru I6 84
Nance, co., Ne., U.S. C7 134
Nanchang, China G4 34
Nancheng, China H5 34
Nanchong, China E8 30
Nancowry Island, i., India K2 40
Nancun, China G8 32
Nancy, Fr. D13 14
Nancy, Ky., U.S. C5 124
Nancy Creek, stm., Ga., U.S. h8 117
Nanda Devi, mtn., India E8 44
Nandaime, Nic. F8 92
Nānded, India C4 46
Nanding, stm., Asia C5 40
N'andoma, U.S.S.R. E6 22
Nandu, stm., China E11 40
Nandurbār, India J6 44
Nandyāl, India E5 46
Nanga Parbat, mtn., Pak. C6 44
Nangin, Burma I5 40
Nangnim, N. Kor. C15 32
Nangola, Mali E6 64
Nang Rong, Thai. G7 40
Nanjangūd, India F4 46
Nanjiang, China C9 34
Nanjing (Nanking), China C7 34
Nankang, China J3 34
Nanking see Nanjing, China C7 34
Nankou, China I6 34
Nan Ling, mts., China J2 34
Nanlinqiao, China F3 34
Nannine, Austl. E3 68
Nanning, China C10 40
Nanoose Bay, B.C., Can. f11 99
Nanpi, China E4 32
Nanping, China I7 34
Nanpu, China D6 32
Nansa, stm., Spain B7 16
Nansei-shotō (Ryukyu Islands), is., Japan S4 37b
Nansemond, stm., Va., U.S. k14 153
Nanshan Island, i., Asia C6 38
Nanshan see Qilian Shan, mts., China D6 30
Nant, Fr. H10 14
Nantang, China I4 34
Nantes, Fr. E5 14
Nanticoke, Ont., Can. E4 103
Nanticoke, Md., U.S. D6 127
Nanticoke, Pa., U.S. D10 145
Nanticoke, stm., U.S. D6 127
Nanton, Alta., Can. D4 98
Nantong, China C9 34
Nant'ou, Tai. L9 34
Nantua, Fr. F12 14
Nantucket, Ma., U.S. D7 128
Nantucket, co., Ma., U.S. D7 128
Nantucket Island, i., Ma., U.S. D7 128
Nantucket Sound, strt., Ma., U.S. C7 128

Name — Map Ref. — Page

Nantuxent Point, c., N.J., U.S. E2 137
Nanty Glo, Pa., U.S. F4 145
Nanuet, N.Y., U.S. g12 139
Nanuque, Braz. D8 79
Nanwan, China C2 34
Nanxiang, China D10 34
Nanxiong, China J3 34
Nanyang, China B1 34
Nanzhao, China B1 34
Naoma, W.V., U.S. n13 155
Não-me-Toque, Braz. E12 80
Naomi Peak, mtn., Ut., U.S. B4 151
Náousa, Grc. I6 20
Napa, Ca., U.S. C2 112
Napa, co., Ca., U.S. C2 112
Napadogan, N.B., Can. C3 101
Napakiak, Ak., U.S. C7 109
Napaktok Bay, b., Newf., Can. f9 102
Napanee, Ont., Can. C8 103
Napanoch, N.Y., U.S. D6 139
Napaskiak, Ak., U.S. C7 109
Napatree Point, c., R.I., U.S. G1 146
Napavine, Wa., U.S. C3 154
Napé, Laos E8 40
Napenay, Arg. D8 80
Naper, Ne., U.S. B6 134
Naperville, Il., U.S. B5 120
Napier, N.Z. C6 72
Napier, S. Afr. J4 66
Napier Mountains, mts., Ant. B4 73
Napierville, Que., Can. D4 104
Napinka, Man., Can. E1 100
Naplate, Il., U.S. B5 120
Naples, Fl., U.S. F5 116
Naples, Id., U.S. A2 119
Naples, Me., U.S. E2 126
Naples, N.Y., U.S. C3 139
Naples, Tx., U.S. C5 150
Naples, Ut., U.S. C6 151
Naples see Napoli, Italy I9 18
Napo, prov., Ec. H4 84
Napo, stm., S.A. I6 84
Napoleon, In., U.S. F7 121
Napoleon, Mo., U.S. B3 132
Napoleon, N.D., U.S. C6 141
Napoleon, Oh., U.S. A1 142
Napoleonville, La., U.S. E4 125
Napoli (Naples), Italy I9 18
Nappanee, In., U.S. B5 121
Naqādah, Egypt E7 60
Naqadeh, Iran C8 48
Nara, Japan M10 36
Nara, Mali D6 64
Naracoorte, Austl. K4 70
Naradhan, Austl. I7 70
Naramata, B.C., Can. E8 99
Naranja, Fl., U.S. G6 116
Naranjal, Ec. I3 84
Naranjito, Hond. C6 92
Naranjo, C.R. G10 92
Naranjo, stm., Guat. C3 92
Narasapur, India D6 46
Narasaraopet, India D6 46
Narathiwat, Thai. K6 40
Nara Visa, N.M., U.S. B6 138
Nārāyanganj, Bngl. I14 44
Nārāyani (Gandak), stm., Asia G11 44
Nārāyanpet, India D4 46
Narberth, Pa., U.S. p20 145
Narbonne, Fr. I10 14
Nardò, Italy I13 18
Nare, stm., Col. D5 84
Nares Strait, strt., N.A. A13 86
Narew, stm., Eur. C21 10
Narinda, Baie de, b., Madag. O22 67b
Nariño, dept., Col. G3 84
Narita, Japan L15 36
Nar'jan-Mar, U.S.S.R. D8 22
Narka, Ks., U.S. C6 123
Narmada, stm., India J5 44
Nārnaul, India F7 44
Narni, Italy G7 18
Naro, Italy L8 18
Narodnaja, gora, mtn., U.S.S.R. D10 22
Naro-Fominsk, U.S.S.R. F19 26
Narol, Man., Can. D3 100
Narol, Pol. E23 10
Narooma, Austl. K9 70
Narrabri, Austl. H8 70
Narragansett, R.I., U.S. F4 146
Narragansett Bay, b., R.I., U.S. E5 146
Narraguagus, stm., Me., U.S. D5 126
Narran, stm., Austl. G7 70
Narrandera, Austl. J7 70
Narrogin, Austl. F3 68
Narromine, Austl. I8 70
Narrows, Va., U.S. C2 153
Narsimhapur, India I8 44
Narsīpatnam, India D7 46
Naruna, Va., U.S. C3 153
Narva, U.S.S.R. B11 26
Narva, stm., U.S.S.R. B10 26
Narvik, Nor. G15 6
Narvskij zaliv (Narva laht), b., U.S.S.R. B10 26
Narvskoje vodochranilišče, res., U.S.S.R. B11 26
Naryn, U.S.S.R. I13 22
Naryn, stm., U.S.S.R. I12 22
Naryškino, U.S.S.R. I18 26
Na San, Thai. J5 40
Nasarawa, Nig. G13 64
Naschel, Arg. G6 80
Naselle, Wa., U.S. C2 154
Nash, Ok., U.S. A3 143
Nash, Tx., U.S. C5 150
Nash, co., N.C., U.S. A4 140
Nashawena Island, i., Ma., U.S. D6 128
Nash Creek, N.B., Can. B3 101
Nāshik, India C2 46
Nashoba Hill, hill, Ma., U.S. f10 128
Nash Stream, stm., N.H., U.S. A4 136
Nashua, Ia., U.S. B5 122
Nashua, Mt., U.S. B10 133
Nashua, N.H., U.S. E4 136
Nashua, stm., U.S. E3 136
Nashville, Ar., U.S. D2 111
Nashville, Ga., U.S. E3 117
Nashville, Il., U.S. E4 120
Nashville, In., U.S. F5 121
Nashville, Ks., U.S. E5 123
Nashville, Mi., U.S. F5 129
Nashville, N.C., U.S. B5 140
Nashville, Tn., U.S. A5 149
Nashwaaksis, N.B., Can. D3 101
Nashwauk, Mn., U.S. C5 130
Nasielsk, Pol. C20 10
Näsijärvi, l., Fin. K18 6
Nāṣir, Sud. M7 60
Nāṣir, Buhayrat, res., Afr. D7 56
Nasīrābād, India G6 44
Nasīrābād, Pak. F3 44
Naskaupi, stm., Newf., Can. g9 102
Nason, Il., U.S. E5 120
Nassau, Bah. B6 94
Nassau, De., U.S. E5 115
Nassau, N.Y., U.S. C7 139
Nassau, co., Fl., U.S. B5 116
Nassau, co., N.Y., U.S. E7 139
Nassau, stm., Fl., U.S. k8 116
Nassau Sound, b., Fl., U.S. B5 116
Nassawadox, Va., U.S. C7 153
Nassawango Creek, stm., Md., U.S. D7 127
Nasser, Lake see Nāṣir, Buhayrat, res., Afr. D7 56
Nassereith, Aus. H10 10
Nässjö, Swe. M14 6
Nastapoka Islands, is., N.W. Ter., Can. E17 96
Nasukoin Mountain, mtn., Mt., U.S. B2 133
Nasva, U.S.S.R. E13 26
Nata, Bots. C8 66
Natá, Pan. C2 84
Nata, stm., Afr. B8 66
Natagaima, Col. F5 84
Natal, Braz. E11 76
Natal, Indon. E2 38
Natalbany, La., U.S. D5 125
Natalia, Tx., U.S. E3 150
Natanes Plateau, plat., Az., U.S. D5 110
Natash, Wādī, val., Egypt I2 48
Natashquan, Que., Can. h9 102
Natashquan, stm., Can. h9 102
Natchaug, stm., Ct., U.S. B7 114
Natchez, La., U.S. C2 125
Natchez, Ms., U.S. D2 131
Natchitoches, La., U.S. C2 125
Natchitoches, co., La., U.S. C2 125
Nathrop, Co., U.S. C4 113
Natick, Ma., U.S. B5 128
Natimuk, Austl. K4 70
Nation, stm., B.C., Can. B6 99
National City, Ca., U.S. F5 112
Natitingou, Benin F10 64
Nativity, Church of the, Isr. Occ. E4 50
Natl, Jord. E5 50
Natoma, Ks., U.S. C4 123
Natong, China C9 40
Natron, Lake, l., Afr. B7 58
Natrona, co., Wy., U.S. D5 157
Natrona Heights, Pa., U.S. E2 145
Natuna Besar, i., Indon. L10 40
Natuna Besar, Kepulauan, is., Indon. L10 40
Natural Bridge, Al., U.S. A2 108
Natural Bridge, Va., U.S. C3 153
Natural Bridge, Ut., U.S. F3 151
Natural Bridge, Va., U.S. C3 153
Natural Bridges National Monument, Ut., U.S. F6 151
Naturaliste, Cape, c., Austl. F3 68
Naturaliste Channel, strt., Austl. E2 68
Naturita, Co., U.S. C2 113
Nau, Cap de la, c., Spain G12 16
Nauders, Aus. I10 10
Nauen, Ger. C12 10
Naugatuck, Ct., U.S. D3 114
Naugatuck, stm., Ct., U.S. D3 114
Naujamiestis, U.S.S.R. F7 26
Naujoji Akmenė, U.S.S.R. E5 26
Naumburg, Ger. D11 10
Naungpale, Burma E4 40
Ñaupe, Peru A2 82
Nauroz Kalāt, Pak. F1 44
Nauru, ctry., Oc. G24 2
Naushon Island, i., Ma., U.S. D6 128
Nauta, Peru J6 84
Nautilus Park, Ct., U.S. D7 114
Nautla, Mex. G11 90
Nauvoo, Al., U.S. B2 108
Nauvoo, Il., U.S. C2 120
Nauwigewauk, N.B., Can. D4 101
Nava, Mex. C9 90
Navadwip, India I13 44
Navahermosa, Spain F7 16
Navajo, Az., U.S. B6 110
Navajo, N.M., U.S. B1 138
Navajo, co., Az., U.S. B5 110
Navajo Dam, N.M., U.S. A2 138
Navajo Indian Reservation, U.S. A4 110
Navajo Mountain, mtn., Ut., U.S. F5 151
Navajo National Monument, Az., U.S. A5 110
Navajo Reservoir, res., U.S. A2 138
Navalmoral de la Mata, Spain F6 16
Navan, Ont., Can. B9 103
Navarin, mys, c., U.S.S.R. E27 24
Navarino, Isla, i., Chile H3 78
Navarra, prov., Spain C10 16
Navarre, Oh., U.S. B4 142
Navarro, Arg. H9 80
Navarro, co., Tx., U.S. D4 150
Navašino, U.S.S.R. F25 26
Navasota, Tx., U.S. D4 150
Navassa, N.C., U.S. C4 140
Navassa Island, i., N.A. E7 94
Navesink, N.J., U.S. C4 137
Navia, Arg. H5 80
Navidad, Chile G3 80
Naviraí, Braz. G1 79
Navl'a, U.S.S.R. I17 26
Nāvodari, Rom. E12 20
Navoi, U.S.S.R. I11 22
Navojoa, Mex. D5 90
Navolato, Mex. E6 90
Navoloki, U.S.S.R. D24 26
Návpaktos, Grc. K5 20
Návplion, Grc. L6 20
Navsāri, India J5 44
Nawābganj, Bngl. H13 44
Nawābshāh, Pak. G3 44
Nāwah, Afg. D2 44
Nawalgarh, India G6 44
Nawiliwili Bay, b., Hi., U.S. B2 118
Náxos, Grc. L9 20
Náxos, i., Grc. L9 20
Nayarit, state, Mex. F7 90
Nāy Band, Iran E14 48
Naylor, Ga., U.S. F3 117
Naylor, Mo., U.S. E7 132
Nayoro, Japan C17 36a
Nazaré, Braz. B9 79
Nazaré, Port. F2 16
Nazaré da Mata, Braz. E11 76
Nazareth, Ky., U.S. C4 124
Nazareth, Pa., U.S. E11 145
Nazareth see Naẓerat, Isr. C4 50
Nazário, Braz. D4 79
Nazarovo, U.S.S.R. F10 24
Nazas, Mex. E7 90
Nazas, stm., Mex. E7 90
Nazca, Peru F4 82
Naze, Japan S4 37b
N'azepetrovsk, U.S.S.R. F9 22
Naẓerat (Nazareth), Isr. C4 50
Naẓerat 'Illit, Isr. C4 50
Nazija, U.S.S.R. B14 26
Nazilli, Tur. L12 20
Nazko, stm., B.C., Can. C6 99
Nazlini, Az., U.S. B6 110
Nazret, Eth. M10 60
Nazyvajevsk, U.S.S.R. F12 22
N'dalatando, Ang. C2 58
Ndali, Benin G11 64
Ndélé, Cen. Afr. Rep. G5 56
Ndendé, Gabon B2 58
N'Djamena, Chad F4 56
Ndjolé, Gabon B2 58
Ndola, Zam. D5 58
Neagh, Lough, l., N. Ire., U.K. G7 8
Neah Bay, Wa., U.S. A1 154
Neamț, co., Rom. C10 20
Néa Páfos (Paphos), Cyp. D2 48
Near Islands, is., Ak., U.S. E2 109
Nebaj, Guat. B3 92
Nebit-Dag, U.S.S.R. J8 22
Neblina, Pico da, mtn., S.A. G9 84
Nebo, Il., U.S. D3 120
Nebo, Ky., U.S. C2 124
Nebo, Mount, mtn., Ut., U.S. D4 151
Nebolči, U.S.S.R. B16 26
Nebraska, state, U.S. C6 134
Nebraska City, Ne., U.S. D10 134
Necedah, Wi., U.S. D3 156
Nechako, stm., B.C., Can. C5 99
Nechako Range, mts., B.C., Can. C5 99
Neche, N.D., U.S. A8 141
Neches, stm., Tx., U.S. D5 150
Nechí, Col. C5 84
Nechí, stm., Col. D5 84
Nechmeya, Alg. M2 18
Neckar, stm., Ger. F9 10
Neckarsulm, Ger. F9 10
Necker Island, i., Hi., U.S. m15 118
Necochea, Arg. J9 80
Nectar, Al., U.S. B3 108
Nederland, Co., U.S. B5 113
Nederland, Tx., U.S. E6 150
Neder Rijn, mth., Neth. E8 12
Nêdong, China F5 30
Nédroma, Alg. C10 62
Nedrow, N.Y., U.S. C4 139
Needham, Ma., U.S. g11 128
Needle Mountain, mtn., Wy., U.S. B3 157
Needles, Ca., U.S. E6 112
Needmore, In., U.S. G4 121
Needville, Tx., U.S. r14 150
Neels Gap, Ga., U.S. B3 117
Neely, Ms., U.S. D5 131
Neelyville, Mo., U.S. E7 132
Ñeembucú, dept., Para. D9 80
Neenah, Wi., U.S. D5 156
Neepawa, Man., Can. D2 100
Neeses, S.C., U.S. D5 147
Neffs, Oh., U.S. B5 142
Neffsville, Pa., U.S. F9 145
Nefta, Tun. D14 62
Nefza, Tun. M4 18
Negage, Ang. C3 58
Négala, Mali E5 64
Negaunee, Mi., U.S. B3 129
Negele, Eth. G8 56
Negev Desert see HaNegev, reg., Isr. G3 50
Negley, Oh., U.S. B5 142
Negombo, Sri L. I5 46
Negoreloje, U.S.S.R. H10 26
Negotin, Yugo. E6 20
Negra, Laguna, l., Ur. H12 80
Negra, Punta, c., Belize A6 92
Negra, Punta, c., Peru B1 82
Negreira, Spain C3 16
Negrești, Rom. C11 20
Negrine, Alg. C14 62
Negritos, Peru J2 84
Negro, stm., Arg. E4 78
Negro, stm., Bol. F10 82
Negro, stm., Bol. D9 82
Negro, stm., Braz. C13 80
Negro, stm., Braz. H13 82
Negro, stm., Braz. A6 82
Negro, stm., Col. E5 84
Negro, stm., N.A. E7 92
Negro, stm., Para. C10 80
Negro, stm., S.A. G10 80
Negro, stm., S.A. H13 84
Negro, stm., Ven. C6 84
Negro Mountain, mtn., Md., U.S. k12 127
Negros, i., Phil. C7 38
Neguac, N.B., Can. B4 101
Nehalem, stm., Or., U.S. A3 144
Nehawka, Ne., U.S. D10 134
Nehbandān, Iran F16 48
Neiba, Dom. Rep. E9 94
Neiges, Piton des, mtn., Reu. V17 67c
Neihuang, China H2 32
Neijiang, China F8 30
Neilburg, Sask., Can. E1 105
Neill Point, c., Wa., U.S. f11 154
Neillsville, Wi., U.S. D3 156
Nei Monggol Zizhiqu (Inner Mongolia), prov., China C10 30
Neira, Col. E5 84
Neisse (Nysa Łużycka) (Nisa), stm., Eur. D14 10
Neiva, Col. F5 84
Neixpa, stm., Mex. H8 90
Neja, U.S.S.R. C26 26
Nejapa de Madero, Mex. I12 90
Nejdek, Czech. E12 10
Nejo, Eth. M8 60
Nekemte, Eth. M9 60
Nekoosa, Wi., U.S. D4 156
Nekrasovskoje, U.S.S.R. D23 26
Neksø, Den. N14 6
Nelidovo, U.S.S.R. E15 26
Neligh, Ne., U.S. B7 134
Nellikuppam, India G5 46
Nellis Air Force Base, mil., Nv., U.S. G6 135
Nellore, India E5 46
Nel'ma, U.S.S.R. H19 24
Nelson, B.C., Can. E9 99
Nelson, N.Z. D4 72
Nelson, Ga., U.S. B2 117
Nelson, Il., U.S. B4 120
Nelson, Mn., U.S. E3 130
Nelson, Mo., U.S. B4 132
Nelson, Ne., U.S. D7 134
Nelson, N.H., U.S. E2 136
Nelson, Wi., U.S. D1 156
Nelson, co., Ky., U.S. C4 124
Nelson, co., N.D., U.S. B7 141
Nelson, co., Va., U.S. C4 153
Nelson, stm., Man., Can. A4 100
Nelson, Cape, c., Austl. L4 70
Nelsonville, Oh., U.S. C3 142
Nelspoort, S. Afr. I6 66
Nelspruit, S. Afr. E10 66
Néma, Maur. C6 64
Nemacolin, Pa., U.S. G2 145
Nemadji, stm., U.S. B1 156
Nemaha, Ne., U.S. D10 134
Nemaha, co., Ks., U.S. C7 123
Nemaha, co., Ne., U.S. D10 134
Neman, U.S.S.R. F5 26
Neman (Nemunas), stm., U.S.S.R. F5 26
Nemeiben Lake, l., Sask., Can. B3 105
Nemenčinė, U.S.S.R. G8 26
Nemiscau, Que., Can. h11 104
Nemours, Fr. D9 14
Nemuna, Bjeshkët e, mts., Eur. G3 20
Nemunas (Neman), stm., U.S.S.R. F6 26
Nemuro, Japan D20 36a
Nemuro Strait, strt., Asia C20 36a
Nen, stm., China B11 30
Nenagh, Ire. I5 8
Nenana, Ak., U.S. C10 109
Nenaševo, U.S.S.R. G20 26
Nentón, stm., N.A. B3 92
Neodesha, Ks., U.S. E8 123
Neoga, Il., U.S. D5 120
Neola, Ia., U.S. C2 122
Neola, Ut., U.S. C5 151
Neopit, Wi., U.S. D5 156
Neosho, Mo., U.S. E3 132
Neosho, Wi., U.S. E5 156
Neosho, co., Ks., U.S. E8 123
Neosho, stm., Ok., U.S. A6 143
Neosho Falls, Ks., U.S. D8 123
Neosho Rapids, Ks., U.S. D8 123
Neotsu, Or., U.S. B3 144
Nepa, stm., U.S.S.R. F13 24
Nepal (Nepāl), ctry., Asia D11 42
Nepālganj, Nepal F9 44
Nepaug Reservoir, res., Ct., U.S. B3 114
Nepean, Ont., Can. h12 103
Nepeña, Peru C2 82
Nepewassi Lake, l., Ont., Can. A4 103
Nephi, Ut., U.S. D4 151
Nephton, Ont., Can. C7 103
Nepisiguit, stm., N.B., Can. B3 101
Nepisiguit Bay, b., N.B., Can. B4 101
Neponset, Il., U.S. B4 120
Neponset, stm., Ma., U.S. h11 128
Nepton, Ky., U.S. B6 124
Neptune, N.J., U.S. C4 137
Neptune Beach, Fl., U.S. B5 116
Neptune City, N.J., U.S. C4 137
Nera, stm., Eur. E5 20
Nerča, stm., U.S.S.R. G15 24
Nerčinsk, U.S.S.R. G15 24
Nerčinskij Zavod, U.S.S.R. G15 24
Nerechta, U.S.S.R. D23 26
Nereta, U.S.S.R. E8 26
Neringa, U.S.S.R. F4 26
Neriquinha, Ang. E4 58
Nerja, Spain I8 16
Nerl', U.S.S.R. E23 26
Nerl', stm., U.S.S.R. E23 26
Nerópolis, Braz. D4 79
Nerussa, stm., U.S.S.R. I17 26
Nerva, Spain H5 16
Nesbit, Ms., U.S. A3 131
Nesbitt, Man., Can. E2 100
Nescopeck, Pa., U.S. D9 145
Neshanic, stm., N.J., U.S. C3 137
Nesher, Isr. C4 50
Neshkoro, Wi., U.S. E4 156
Neshoba, Ms., U.S. C4 131
Neshoba, co., Ms., U.S. C4 131
Nesika Beach, Or., U.S. E2 144
Nesle, Fr. C9 14
Nesowadnehunk, l., Me., U.S. B3 126
Nesquehoning, Pa., U.S. E10 145
Ness, co., Ks., U.S. D4 123
Ness, Loch, l., Scot., U.K. D9 8
Ness City, Ks., U.S. D4 123
Nesselwang, Ger. H10 10
Nesslau, Switz. D11 13
Nesterov, U.S.S.R. G5 26
Nestoita, U.S.S.R. B13 20
Néstos (Mesta), stm., Eur. H8 20
Nesviž, U.S.S.R. H9 26
Nes Ẕiyyona, Isr. E3 50
Netanya, Isr. D3 50
Netawaka, Ks., U.S. C8 123
Netcong, N.J., U.S. B3 137
Netherdale, Austl. C8 70
Netherhill, Sask., Can. F1 105
Netherlands (Nederland), ctry., Eur. E9 4
Netherlands Antilles (Nederlandse Antillen), dep., N.A. H10 94
Netrakona, Bngl. H14 44
Nettie, W.V., U.S. C4 155
Nettilling Lake, l., N.W. Ter., Can. C18 96
Nett Lake, Mn., U.S. B5 130
Nett Lake, l., Mn., U.S. B5 130
Nett Lake Indian Reservation, Mn., U.S. B6 130
Nettleton, Ms., U.S. A5 131
Nettuno, Italy H7 18
Neubrandenburg, Ger. B13 10
Neuburg an der Donau, Ger. G11 10
Neuchâtel, Switz. E6 13
Neuchâtel, state, Switz. E6 13
Neuchâtel, Lac de, l., Switz. E6 13
Neudorf, Sask., Can. G4 105
Neuenhagen, Ger. C13 10
Neuf-Brisach, Fr. D14 14
Neufchâteau, Bel. I7 12
Neufchâteau, Fr. D12 14
Neufchâtel-en-Bray, Fr. C8 14
Neuhausen, Switz. C10 13
Neu-Isenburg, Ger. E8 10
Neumarkt [im Hausruckkreis], Aus. G13 10
Neumarkt in der Oberpfalz, Ger. F11 10
Neumarkt in Steiermark, Aus. H14 10
Neumarkt-Sankt Veit, Ger. G12 10
Neumünster, Ger. A9 10
Neunburg vorm Wald, Ger. F12 10
Neunkirchen/Saar, Ger. F7 10
Neuquén, Arg. J4 80
Neuquén, prov., Arg. J4 80
Neuquén, stm., Arg. J4 80
Neurara, Chile C4 80
Neuruppin, Ger. C12 10
Neuschwanstein, Schloss, Ger. C14 13
Neuse, stm., N.C., U.S. B6 140
Neusiedl am See, Aus. H16 10
Neusiedler See, l., Eur. H16 10
Neustadt, Ont., Can. C4 103
Neustadt [an der Aisch], Ger. F10 10
Neustadt an der Waldnaab, Ger. F12 10
Neustadt an der Weinstrasse, Ger. F8 10
Neustadt bei Coburg, Ger. E11 10
Neustadt in Holstein, Ger. A10 10
Neustrelitz, Ger. B13 10
Neu-Ulm, Ger. G10 10
Neuville, Que., Can. C6 104
Neuville-sur-Saône, Fr. G11 14
Neuwied, Ger. E7 10
Neva, stm., U.S.S.R. B13 26
Nevada, Ia., U.S. B4 122
Nevada, Mo., U.S. D3 132
Nevada, Oh., U.S. B2 142
Nevada, co., Ar., U.S. D2 111
Nevada, co., Ca., U.S. C3 112
Nevada, state, U.S. D5 135
Nevada, Sierra, mts., Spain H8 16
Nevada, Sierra, mts., Ca., U.S. D4 112
Nevada City, Ca., U.S. C3 112
Nevado, Cerro, mtn., Col. F5 84
Nevado de Colima, Parque Nacional del, Mex. H8 90
Nevado de Toluca, Parque Nacional, Mex. H9 90
Nevel', U.S.S.R. E12 26
Nevel'sk, U.S.S.R. H20 24
Never, U.S.S.R. G16 24
Nevers, Fr. E10 14
Neversink, stm., N.Y., U.S. D6 139
Nevertire, Austl. H7 70
Nevesinje, Yugo. F2 20
Neville, Sask., Can. H2 105
Nevils, Ga., U.S. D5 117
Nevinnomyssk, U.S.S.R. I6 22
Nevis, Mn., U.S. D4 130
Nevis, i., St. K./N. F13 94
Nevis, Ben, mtn., Scot., U.K. E9 8
Nevjansk, U.S.S.R. F10 22
Nevşehir, Tur. B3 48
New, stm., Belize H15 90
New, stm., Guy. F14 84
New, stm., U.S. C3 155
New, stm., Az., U.S. k8 110
New, stm., N.C., U.S. C5 140
New Albany, In., U.S. H6 121
New Albany, Ms., U.S. A4 131
New Albany, Oh., U.S. k11 142
New Albin, Ia., U.S. A6 122
New Alfa, Sud. J8 60
New Alsace, In., U.S. F8 121
New Amsterdam, Guy. D14 84
Newark, Ar., U.S. B4 111
Newark, Ca., U.S. h8 112
Newark, De., U.S. B3 115
Newark, Il., U.S. B5 120
Newark, N.J., U.S. B4 137
Newark, N.Y., U.S. B3 139
Newark, Oh., U.S. B3 142
Newark, Tx., U.S. m9 150
Newark Bay, b., N.J., U.S. k8 137
Newark Lake, l., Nv., U.S. D6 135
Newark-on-Trent, Eng., U.K. H13 8
Newark Valley, N.Y., U.S. C4 139
New Athens, Il., U.S. E4 120
New Auburn, Mn., U.S. F4 130
New Auburn, Wi., U.S. C2 156
New Augusta, Ms., U.S. D4 131
Newaygo, Mi., U.S. E5 129
Newaygo, co., Mi., U.S. E5 129
New Baden, Il., U.S. E4 120
New Baltimore, Mi., U.S. F8 129
New Baltimore, N.Y., U.S. C7 139
New Bedford, Ma., U.S. C6 128
New Bedford, Pa., U.S. D1 145
Newberg, Or., U.S. B4 144
New Berlin, Il., U.S. D4 120
New Berlin, N.Y., U.S. C5 139
New Berlin, Pa., U.S. E7 145
New Berlin, Wi., U.S. n11 156
Newbern, Al., U.S. C2 108
New Bern, N.C., U.S. B5 140
Newbern, Tn., U.S. A2 149
Newberry, Fl., U.S. C4 116
Newberry, In., U.S. G3 121
Newberry, Mi., U.S. B5 129
Newberry, S.C., U.S. C4 147
Newberry, co., S.C., U.S. C4 147
Newberry Springs, Ca., U.S. E5 112
New Bethlehem, Pa., U.S. D3 145
New Bight, Bah. B7 94
New Blaine, Ar., U.S. B2 111
New Bloomfield, Mo., U.S. C5 132
New Bloomfield, Pa., U.S. F7 145
Newborn, Ga., U.S. C3 117
Newboro, Ont., Can. C8 103
New Boston, Il., U.S. B3 120
New Boston, Mi., U.S. p15 129
New Boston, N.H., U.S. E3 136
New Boston, Oh., U.S. D3 142
New Boston, Tx., U.S. C5 150
New Braunfels, Tx., U.S. E3 150
New Bremen, Oh., U.S. B1 142
New Brighton, Mn., U.S. m12 130
New Brighton, Pa., U.S. E1 145
New Britain, Ct., U.S. C4 114
New Britain, i., Pap. N. Gui. m17 68a
New Brockton, Al., U.S. D4 108
Newbrook, Alta., Can. B4 98
New Brunswick, N.J., U.S. C4 137
New Brunswick, prov., Can. C3 101
New Buffalo, Mi., U.S. G4 129
Newburg, Md., U.S. D4 127
Newburg, Mo., U.S. D6 132
Newburg, N.D., U.S. A5 141
Newburg, W.V., U.S. B5 155
Newburg, Wi., U.S. E5 156
Newburgh, Ont., Can. C8 103
Newburgh, In., U.S. I3 121
Newburgh, Me., U.S. D4 126
Newburgh, N.Y., U.S. D6 139
Newburgh Heights, Oh., U.S. h9 142
New Burnside, Il., U.S. F5 120
Newbury, Ont., Can. E3 103
Newbury, Eng., U.K. J12 8
Newbury, Ma., U.S. A6 128
Newbury, N.H., U.S. D2 136
Newbury, Vt., U.S. C4 152
Newburyport, Ma., U.S. A6 128
New Caledonia, dep., Oc. H24 2
New Cambria, Ks., U.S. D6 123
New Cambria, Mo., U.S. B5 132
New Canaan, Ct., U.S. E2 114
New Canton, Il., U.S. D2 120
New Carlisle, In., U.S. A4 121
New Carlisle, Oh., U.S. C1 142
New Carrollton, Md., U.S. C4 127
Newcastle, Austl. I9 70
Newcastle, N.B., Can. C4 101
Newcastle, Ont., Can. D6 103
Newcastle, S. Afr. F9 66
New Castle, Al., U.S. B3 108
New Castle, Co., U.S. B3 113
New Castle, De., U.S. B3 115
New Castle, In., U.S. E7 121
New Castle, Ky., U.S. B4 124
Newcastle, Me., U.S. D3 126
Newcastle, Ne., U.S. B9 134
New Castle, N.H., U.S. D5 136
Newcastle, Ok., U.S. B4 143
New Castle, Pa., U.S. D1 145
Newcastle, Tx., U.S. C3 150
Newcastle, Ut., U.S. F2 151
Newcastle, Wy., U.S. C8 157
New Castle, co., De., U.S. B3 115
Newcastle Creek, N.B., Can. C3 101
Newcastle-under-Lyme, Eng., U.K. H11 8
Newcastle upon Tyne, Eng., U.K. G12 8
Newcastle Waters, Austl. C6 68
New City, N.Y., U.S. D6 139
Newcomb, N.M., U.S. A1 138
Newcomb, Tn., U.S. A7 149
Newcomerstown, Oh., U.S. B4 142
New Concord, Oh., U.S. C4 142
New Cumberland, Pa., U.S. F8 145
New Cumberland, W.V., U.S. A4 155
Newdale, Man., Can. D1 100
Newdale, Id., U.S. F7 119
New Dayton, Alta., Can. E4 98
Newdegate, Austl. F3 68
New Delhi, India F7 44
New Denmark, N.B., Can. C2 101
New Denver, B.C., Can. D9 99
New Durham, N.H., U.S. D4 136
New Edinburg, Ar., U.S. D3 111
New Effington, S.D., U.S. B9 148
New Egypt, N.J., U.S. C3 137
Newell, Ia., U.S. B2 122
Newell, S.D., U.S. C2 148
Newell, W.V., U.S. A4 155
New Ellenton, S.C., U.S. E4 147
Newellton, La., U.S. B4 125
New England, N.D., U.S. C3 141
New England Range, mts., Austl. H9 70
Newenham, Cape, c., Ak., U.S. D7 109
New Era, Mi., U.S. E4 129
New Fairfield, Ct., U.S. D2 114
Newfane, N.Y., U.S. B2 139
Newfane, Vt., U.S. F3 152
Newfield, Me., U.S. E2 126
Newfield, N.J., U.S. D2 137
Newfields, N.H., U.S. D5 136
New Florence, Mo., U.S. C6 132
New Florence, Pa., U.S. F3 145
Newfolden, Mn., U.S. B2 130
Newfound Gap, U.S. f9 140
Newfound Lake, l., N.H., U.S. C3 136
Newfoundland, N.J., U.S. A4 137
Newfoundland, Pa., U.S. D11 145
Newfoundland, prov., Can. D4 102
Newfoundland, i., Newf., Can. D3 102
Newfoundland Mountains, mts., Ut., U.S. B2 151
New Franklin, Mo., U.S. B5 132

Name — Map Ref. — Page

New Freedom, Pa., U.S. G8 145
New Galloway, Scot., U.K. F9 8
New Georgia, i., Sol.Is. A11 68
New Germany, N.S., Can. E5 101
New Glarus, Wi., U.S. F4 156
New Glasgow, N.S., Can. D7 101
New Gloucester, Me., U.S. E2 126
New Goshen, In., U.S. E3 121
New Guinea, i. m15 68a
Newhalem, Wa., U.S. A4 154
Newhall, Ia., U.S. C6 122
Newhall, Me., U.S. g7 126
Newhall, W.V., U.S. D3 155
New Hampshire, state, U.S. C3 136
New Hampton, Ia., U.S. A5 122
New Hampton, Mo., U.S. A3 132
New Hampton, N.H., U.S. C3 136
New Hanover, co., N.C., U.S. C5 140
New Hanover, i., Pap. N. Gui. k17 68a
New Harbor, Me., U.S. E3 126
New Harbour, Newf., Can. E5 102
New Harmony, In., U.S. H2 121
New Hartford, Ct., U.S. B4 114
New Hartford, Ia., U.S. B5 122
Newhaven, Eng., U.K. K14 8
New Haven, Ct., U.S. D4 114
New Haven, Il., U.S. F5 120
New Haven, In., U.S. B7 121
New Haven, Ky., U.S. C4 124
New Haven, Mi., U.S. F8 129
New Haven, Mo., U.S. C6 132
New Haven, W.V., U.S. C3 155
New Haven, co., Ct., U.S. D4 114
New Haven, stm., Vt., U.S. C2 152
New Haven Harbor, b., Ct., U.S. E4 114
New Hazelton, B.C., Can. B4 99
New Hebrides Trench K21 158
New Hebrides see Vanuatu, ctry., Oc. H24 2
Newhebron, Ms., U.S. D4 131
New Holland, Ga., U.S. B3 117
New Holland, Il., U.S. C4 120
New Holland, Oh., U.S. C2 142
New Holland, Pa., U.S. F9 145
New Holland, S.D., U.S. D7 148
New Holstein, Wi., U.S. E5 156
New Hope, Al., U.S. A3 108
Newhope, Ar., U.S. C2 111
New Hope, Ky., U.S. C4 124
New Hope, Mn., U.S. m12 130
New Hope, Pa., U.S. F12 145
New Hope, Tn., U.S. D8 149
New Hope Mountain, mtn., Al., U.S. g7 108
New Hudson, Mi., U.S. o14 129
New Iberia, La., U.S. D4 125
Newington, Ct., U.S. C5 114
Newington, Ga., U.S. D5 117
New Inlet, b., N.C., U.S. D5 140
New Ipswich, N.H., U.S. E3 136
New Ireland, i., Pap. N. Gui. k17 68a
New Jersey, state, U.S. C4 137
New Johnsonville, Tn., U.S. A4 149
New Kensington, Pa., U.S. E2 145
New Kent, co., Va., U.S. C5 153
Newkirk, Ok., U.S. A4 143
New Knoxville, Oh., U.S. B1 142
New Laguna, N.M., U.S. B2 138
New Lake, l., N.C., U.S. B6 140
Newland, N.C., U.S. A1 140
Newlands, Austl. C7 70
New Lebanon, In., U.S. F3 121
New Lebanon, N.Y., U.S. C7 139
New Leipzig, N.D., U.S. C4 141
New Lenox, Il., U.S. B6 120
New Lexington, Oh., U.S. C3 142
New Liberty, Ky., U.S. B5 124
New Lisbon, In., U.S. E7 121
New Lisbon, Wi., U.S. E3 156
New Liskeard, Ont., Can. p20 103
Newllano, La., U.S. C2 125
New London, Ct., U.S. D7 114
New London, In., U.S. D5 121
New London, Ia., U.S. D6 122
New London, Mn., U.S. E4 130
New London, Mo., U.S. B6 132
New London, N.H., U.S. D3 136
New London, N.C., U.S. B2 140
New London, Oh., U.S. A3 142
New London, Wi., U.S. D5 156
New London, co., Ct., U.S. C7 114
New London Submarine Base, mil., Ct., U.S. D7 114
New Lothrop, Mi., U.S. E7 129
New Lowell, Ont., Can. C5 103
New Madison, Oh., U.S. C1 142
New Madrid, Mo., U.S. E8 132
New Madrid, co., Mo., U.S. E8 132
Newman, Austl. D3 68
Newman, Ca., U.S. D3 112
Newman, Il., U.S. D6 120
New Manchester, W.V., U.S. e8 155
Newman Grove, Ne., U.S. C8 134
Newman Lake, l., Wa., U.S. B8 154
Newmanstown, Pa., U.S. F9 145
Newmarket, Ont., Can. C5 103
Newmarket, Ire. I4 8
Newmarket, Eng., U.K. I14 8
New Market, Al., U.S. A3 108
New Market, In., U.S. E4 121
New Market, Ia., U.S. D3 122
Newmarket, N.H., U.S. D5 136
New Market, Tn., U.S. C10 149
New Market, Va., U.S. B4 153
New Martinsville, W.V., U.S. B4 155
New Matamoras, Oh., U.S. C4 142
New Meadows, Id., U.S. D2 119
New Melle, Mo., U.S. C7 132
New Mexico, state, U.S. C3 138
New Miami, Oh., U.S. C1 142
New Milford, Ct., U.S. C2 114
New Milford, N.J., U.S. h8 137
New Milford, Pa., U.S. C10 145
New Mills, N.B., Can. B3 101
New Minden, Il., U.S. E4 120
New Munich, Mn., U.S. E4 130
New Munster, Wi., U.S. n11 156
Newnan, Ga., U.S. C2 117
Newnans Lake, l., Fl., U.S. C4 116
New Norfolk, Austl. N7 70
New Norway, Alta., Can. C4 98
New Offenburg, Mo., U.S. D7 132
New Orleans, La., U.S. E5 125
New Orleans Naval Air Station, mil., La., U.S. k11 125
New Oxford, Pa., U.S. G7 145
New Palestine, In., U.S. E6 121
New Paltz, N.Y., U.S. D6 139
New Paris, In., U.S. B6 121
New Paris, Oh., U.S. C1 142
New Perlican, Newf., Can. E5 102
New Philadelphia, Oh., U.S. B4 142
New Philadelphia, Pa., U.S. E9 145
New Plymouth, N.Z. C5 72
New Plymouth, Id., U.S. F2 119
New Point, In., U.S. F7 121
New Point Comfort, c., Va., U.S. C6 153
Newport, Scot., U.K. E11 8
Newport, Wales, U.K. I9 8
Newport, Ar., U.S. B4 111
Newport, De., U.S. B3 115
Newport, In., U.S. E3 121
Newport, Ky., U.S. A5 124
Newport, Me., U.S. D3 126
Newport, Mi., U.S. G7 129
Newport, Mn., U.S. n13 130
Newport, Ne., U.S. B6 134
Newport, N.H., U.S. D2 136
Newport, N.C., U.S. C6 140
Newport, Oh., U.S. C4 142
Newport, Or., U.S. C2 144
Newport, Pa., U.S. F7 145
Newport, R.I., U.S. F5 146
Newport, Tn., U.S. D10 149
Newport, Vt., U.S. B4 152
Newport, Wa., U.S. A8 154
Newport, co., R.I., U.S. E5 146
Newport Beach, Ca., U.S. n13 112
New Portland, Me., U.S. D2 126
Newport News, Va., U.S. D6 153
New Port Richey, Fl., U.S. D4 116
Newport Station, N.S., Can. E5 101
New Prague, Mn., U.S. F5 130
New Preston, Ct., U.S. C2 114
New Providence, Ia., U.S. B4 122
New Providence, N.J., U.S. B4 137
New Providence, i., Bah. B6 94
New Richland, Mn., U.S. G5 130
New Richmond, Que., Can. A4 101
New Richmond, In., U.S. D4 121
New Richmond, Oh., U.S. D1 142
New Richmond, Wi., U.S. C1 156
New River, Az., U.S. D3 110
New River, Tn., U.S. C9 149
New River Gorge, val., W.V., U.S. m13 155
New River Inlet, b., N.C., U.S. C5 140
New Roads, La., U.S. D4 125
New Rochelle, N.Y., U.S. E7 139
New Rockford, N.D., U.S. B6 141
New Ross, N.S., Can. E5 101
New Ross, Ire. I7 8
New Ross, In., U.S. E4 121
Newry, N. Ire., U.K. G7 8
Newry, Me., U.S. D2 126
Newry, S.C., U.S. B2 147
New Salem, Il., U.S. D3 120
New Salem, In., U.S. E7 121
New Salem, N.D., U.S. C4 141
New Salisbury, In., U.S. H5 121
New Sarepta, Alta., Can. C4 98
New Sarpy, La., U.S. k11 125
New Schwabenland, reg., Ant. C2 73
New Sharon, Ia., U.S. C5 122
New Sharon, Me., U.S. D2 126
New Siberian Islands see Novosibirskije ostrova, is., U.S.S.R. B20 24
New Site, Al., U.S. B4 108
New Site, Ms., U.S. A5 131
New Smyrna Beach, Fl., U.S. C6 116
Newsoms, Va., U.S. D5 153
New South Wales, state, Austl. F9 68
New Straitsville, Oh., U.S. C3 142
New Tazewell, Tn., U.S. C10 149
Newtok, Ak., U.S. C7 109
Newton, Al., U.S. D4 108
Newton, Ga., U.S. E2 117
Newton, Il., U.S. E5 120
Newton, Ia., U.S. C4 122
Newton, Ks., U.S. D6 123
Newton, Ma., U.S. B5 128
Newton, Ms., U.S. C4 131
Newton, N.H., U.S. E4 136
Newton, N.J., U.S. A3 137
Newton, N.C., U.S. B1 140
Newton, Tx., U.S. D6 150
Newton, Ut., U.S. B4 151
Newton, co., Ar., U.S. B2 111
Newton, co., Ga., U.S. C3 117
Newton, co., In., U.S. B3 121
Newton, co., Ms., U.S. C4 131
Newton, co., Mo., U.S. E3 132
Newton, co., Tx., U.S. D6 150
Newton Abbot, Eng., U.K. K10 8
Newton Falls, Oh., U.S. A5 142
Newton Grove, N.C., U.S. B4 140
Newton Junction, N.H., U.S. E4 136
Newton Lake, res., Il., U.S. E5 120
Newton Stewart, Scot., U.K. G9 8
Newtonville, N.J., U.S. D3 137
Newtown, Newf., Can. D5 102
Newtown, Ct., U.S. D2 114
Newtown, In., U.S. D3 121
New Town, N.D., U.S. B3 141
Newtown, Oh., U.S. C1 142
Newtownabbey, N. Ire., U.K. G8 8
Newtown Square, Pa., U.S. p20 145
New Trenton, In., U.S. F8 121
New Ulm, Mn., U.S. F4 130
New Underwood, S.D., U.S. C3 148
New Vienna, Ia., U.S. B6 122
New Vienna, Oh., U.S. C2 142
Newville, Al., U.S. D4 108
Newville, Pa., U.S. F7 145
New Vineyard, Me., U.S. D2 126
New Virginia, Ia., U.S. C4 122
New Washington, In., U.S. G6 121
New Washington, Oh., U.S. B3 142
New Waterford, N.S., Can. C9 101
New Waterford, Oh., U.S. B5 142
New Waverly, Tx., U.S. D5 150
New Westminster, B.C., Can. E6 99
New Whiteland, In., U.S. E5 121
New Wilmington, Pa., U.S. D1 145
New Windsor, Il., U.S. B3 120
New Windsor, Md., U.S. A3 127
New Windsor, N.Y., U.S. D6 139
New World Island, i., Newf., Can. D4 102
New York, N.Y., U.S. E7 139
New York, co., N.Y., U.S. k13 139
New York, state, U.S. C6 139
New York Mills, Mn., U.S. D3 130
New Zealand, ctry., Oc. D4 72
Neyrīz, Iran G13 48
Neyshābūr, Iran C15 48
Nezahualcóyotl, Mex. H10 90
Nezahualcóyotl, Presa, res., Mex. I13 90
Nežin, U.S.S.R. G4 22
Neznanovo, U.S.S.R. G23 26
Nez Perce, co., Id., U.S. C2 119
Nez Perce Indian Reservation, Id., U.S. C2 119
Nezpique, Bayou, stm., La., U.S. D3 125
Ngami, Lake, l., Bots. C6 66
Ngamiland, dept., Bots. B6 66
Ngamo, Zimb. B8 66
Ngangla Ringco, l., China E10 44
Nganglong Kangri, mts., China D10 44
Ngaoundéré, Cam. G9 54
Ngezi Recreational Park, Zimb. B10 66
Ngoko, stm., Afr. A3 58
Ngolo, Cen. Afr. Rep. M2 60
Ngoring Hu, l., China E6 30
Ngotwane, stm., Afr. E8 66
Nguigmi, Niger F9 54
Nguiroungou, Cen. Afr. Rep. N2 60
Nguru, Nig. F9 54
Nhamundá, Braz. I14 84
Nhamundá, stm., Braz. H14 84
Nhandeara, Braz. F3 79
Nha Trang, Viet. H10 40
Nhecolândia, Braz. H13 82
Nhill, Austl. K4 70
Niafounké, Mali D7 64
Niagara, Wi., U.S. C6 156
Niagara, co., N.Y., U.S. B2 139
Niagara Falls, Ont., Can. D5 103
Niagara Falls, N.Y., U.S. B1 139
Niagara-on-the-Lake, Ont., Can. D5 103
Niamey, Niger E11 64
Niangara, Zaire H6 56
Niangoloko, Burkina F7 64
Niangua, stm., Mo., U.S. D5 132
Niantic, Ct., U.S. D7 114
Niaro, Sud. L6 60
Nias, Pulau, i., Indon. N4 40
Nibley, Ut., U.S. B4 151
Nica, stm., U.S.S.R. F10 22
Nicaragua, ctry., N.A. E9 92
Nicaragua, Lago de, l., Nic. F9 92
Nicastro, Italy K11 18
Nicatous Lake, l., Me., U.S. C4 126
Nice, Fr. I14 14
Niceville, Fl., U.S. u15 116
Nichicun, Lac, l., Que., Can. h12 104
Nichinan, Japan P6 36
Nicholas, co., Ky., U.S. B6 124
Nicholas, co., W.V., U.S. C4 155
Nicholas Channel, strt., N.A. C4 94
Nicholasville, Ky., U.S. C5 124
Nicholls, Ga., U.S. E4 117
Nicholl's Town, Bah. B5 94
Nichols, Ia., U.S. C6 122
Nichols, S.C., U.S. C9 147
Nichols Hills, Ok., U.S. B4 143
Nicholson, Ms., U.S. E4 131
Nicholson, Pa., U.S. C10 145
Nicholson, stm., Austl. A2 70
Nickajack Lake, res., Tn., U.S. D8 149
Nickel Centre, Ont., Can. p19 103
Nickelsville, Va., U.S. f9 153
Nickerie, dept., Sur. E14 84
Nickerie, stm., Sur. E14 84
Nickerson, Ks., U.S. D5 123
Nickerson, Ne., U.S. C9 134
Nickerson Hill, hill, Ct., U.S. D6 114
Nicobar Islands, is., India J2 40
Nicodemus, Ks., U.S. C4 123
Nicolet, Que., Can. C5 104
Nicolet, stm., Que., Can. C5 104
Nicolet, Lake, l., Mi., U.S. B6 129
Nicollet, Mn., U.S. F4 130
Nicollet, co., Mn., U.S. F4 130
Nicoma Park, Ok., U.S. B4 143
Nicosia, Cyp. D2 48
Nicosia, Italy L9 18
Nicotera, Italy K10 18
Nicoya, C.R. G9 92
Nicoya, Golfo de, b., C.R. H10 92
Nicoya, Península de, pen., C.R. H9 92
Nictaux Falls, N.S., Can. E4 101
Nictheroy see Niterói, Braz. H10 76
Nidzica, Pol. B20 10
Niederbronn-les-Bains, Fr. D14 14
Niedermarsberg, Ger. D8 10
Niederösterreich, state, Aus. G15 10
Niedersachsen, state, Ger. C8 10
Niedu, China J3 34
Niekerkshoop, S. Afr. G6 66
Niellé, I.C. F7 64
Niemodlin, Pol. E17 10
Niéna, Mali F6 64
Nienburg, Ger. C9 10
Niers, stm., Eur. E9 12
Niesky, Ger. D14 10
Nieszawa, Pol. C18 10
Nieu Bethesda, S. Afr. H7 66
Nieuw Amsterdam, Sur. B7 76
Nieuwegein, Neth. D7 12
Nieuweschans, Neth. B11 12
Nieuwe Tonge, Neth. E5 12
Nieuw Nickerie, Sur. E14 84
Nieuwolda, Neth. B10 12
Nieuwoudtville, S. Afr. H4 66
Nieuwpoort (Nieuport), Bel. F2 12
Nieuw-Schoonebeek, Neth. C10 12
Nieva, stm., Peru J4 84
Nièvre, dept., Fr. E10 14
Niga, Mali E7 64
Nigadoo, N.B., Can. B4 101
Niğde, Tur. C3 48
Niger, ctry., Afr. E8 54
Niger, stm., Afr. G8 54
Nigeria, ctry., Afr. F8 54
Nigríta, Grc. I7 20
Nihing (Nahang), stm., Asia H17 48
Nihoa, i., Hi., U.S. m15 118
Nihuil, Embalse del, res., Arg. H4 80
Niigata, Japan J14 36
Niihama, Japan N8 36
Niihau, i., Hi., U.S. B1 118
Nii-jima, i., Japan M14 36
Nijil, Jord. G5 50
Nijkerk, Neth. D8 12
Nijmegen, Neth. E8 12
Nijvel (Nivelles), Bel. G5 12
Nijverdal, Neth. D9 12
Nikel', U.S.S.R. G22 6
Nikishka, Ak., U.S. g16 109
Nikki, Benin G11 64
Nikkō, Japan K14 36
Nikolajev, U.S.S.R. H4 22
Nikolajevka, U.S.S.R. C13 20
Nikolajevo, U.S.S.R. C12 26
Nikolajevsk-na-Amure, U.S.S.R. G20 24
Nikol'sk, U.S.S.R. G7 22
Nikol'sk, U.S.S.R. F7 22
Nikol'skij, U.S.S.R. K24 6
Nikopol', U.S.S.R. H4 22
Nīkshahr, Iran H16 48
Nikšić, Yugo. G2 20
Nikulino, U.S.S.R. C27 26
Niland, Ca., U.S. F6 112
Nile (Nahr an-Nīl), stm., Afr. C7 56
Niles, Il., U.S. h9 120
Niles, Mi., U.S. G4 129
Niles, Oh., U.S. A5 142
Nilo Peçanha, Braz. B9 79
Nilwood, Il., U.S. D4 120
Nīmach, India H6 44
Nimba, Mont, mtn., Afr. G5 54
Nimba Range, mts., Afr. G5 54
Nîmes, Fr. I11 14
Nimmitabel, Austl. K8 70
Nimrod Lake, res., Ar., U.S. C2 111
Nimule, Sud. H7 56
Nindigully, Austl. G8 70
Nindirí, Nic. E8 92
Nine Degree Channel, strt., India H2 46
Ninemile Creek, stm., Ks., U.S. k15 123
Nine Mile Creek, stm., Ut., U.S. D5 151
Nine Mile Falls, Wa., U.S. g13 154
Ninemile Point, c., Mi., U.S. C6 129
Ninette, Man., Can. E2 100
Ninety Mile Beach, Austl. L7 70
Ninety Six, S.C., U.S. C3 147
Ninga, Man., Can. E2 100
Ningari, Mali D8 64
Ningbo, China F10 34
Ningcheng (Tianyi), China B7 32
Ningdu, China I4 34
Ninghai, China F10 34
Ningi, Nig. F14 64
Ningming, China C9 40
Ningshan, China E8 30
Ningsia see Yinchuan, China D8 30
Ningwu, China D9 30
Ningxia Huizu Zizhiqu (Ningsia Hui), prov., China D8 30
Ningxiang, China G1 34
Ninh Binh, Viet. D8 40
Ninhue, Chile I2 80
Ninigret Pond, l., R.I., U.S. G2 146
Ninilchik, Ak., U.S. C9 109
Ninnekah, Ok., U.S. C4 143
Ninnescah, stm., Ks., U.S. E6 123
Ninnescah, North Fork, stm., Ks., U.S. E5 123
Ninnescah, South Fork, stm., Ks., U.S. E5 123
Ninole, Hi., U.S. D6 118
Nioaque, Braz. I14 82
Nioaque, stm., Braz. I14 82
Niobrara, Ne., U.S. B7 134
Niobrara, co., Wy., U.S. C8 157
Niobrara, stm., U.S. B7 134
Nioki, Zaire B3 58
Niono, Mali D6 64
Nioro du Sahel, Mali D5 64
Niort, Fr. F6 14
Niota, Il., U.S. C2 120
Niota, Tn., U.S. D9 149
Nipan, Austl. E9 70
Nipāni, India D3 46
Nipawin, Sask., Can. D4 105
Nipe, Bahía de, b., Cuba D7 94
Nipekamew Lake, l., Sask., Can. C3 105
Nipew Lake, l., Sask., Can. C2 105
Nipigon, Lake, l., Ont., Can. o17 103
Nipishish Lake, l., Newf., Can. g9 102
Nipissing, Lake, l., Ont., Can. A5 103
Nipomo, Ca., U.S. E3 112
Nippers Harbour, Newf., Can. D4 102
Nipple Mountain, mtn., Co., U.S. D2 113
Niquelândia, Braz. C4 79
Niquero, Cuba D6 94
Niquivil, Arg. F4 80
Nirgua, Ven. B8 84
Nirmal, India C5 46
Niš, Yugo. F5 20
Nisa (Neisse) (Nysa Łużycka), stm., Eur. E15 10
Nişāb, Sau. Ar. G8 48
Niscemi, Italy L9 18
Nishio, Japan M12 36
Niskayuna, N.Y., U.S. C7 139
Nisland, S.D., U.S. C2 148
Nisqually, stm., Wa., U.S. C3 154
Nisswa, Mn., U.S. D4 130
Niterói, Braz. G7 79
Nitra, Czech. G18 10
Nitro, W.V., U.S. C3 155
Niubu, China D6 34
Niue, dep., Oc. H1 2
Niut, Gunung, mtn., Indon. N10 40
Niutuo, China D4 32
Niuzhuang, China C10 32
Nive, stm., Austl. E7 70
Nivelles (Nijvel), Bel. G5 12
Nivernais, hist. reg., Fr. E10 14
Niverville, Man., Can. E3 100
Nivskij, U.S.S.R. H23 6
Niwot, Co., U.S. A5 113
Nixa, Mo., U.S. D4 132
Nixburg, Al., U.S. C3 108
Nixon, Nv., U.S. D2 135
Nixon, Tn., U.S. B3 149
Nixon, Tx., U.S. E4 150
Nizāmābād, India C5 46
Nizām Sāgar, res., India C4 46
Nižankoviči, U.S.S.R. F22 10
Nizip, Tur. C4 48
Nízke Tatry, mts., Czech. G19 10
Nižn'aja Pojma, U.S.S.R. F11 24
Nižn'aja Tunguska, stm., U.S.S.R. E10 24
Nižn'aja Tura, U.S.S.R. F9 22
Nižneudinsk, U.S.S.R. G11 24
Nižnevartovsk, U.S.S.R. E13 22
Nižnij Novgorod (Gorky), U.S.S.R. E27 26
Nižnij P'andž, U.S.S.R. J11 22
Nižnij Tagil, U.S.S.R. F9 22
Nizwā, Oman C10 47
Niẓẓana, Isr. G2 50
Njazidja (Grande Comore), i., Com. K15 67a
Njombe, Tan. C6 58
Nkhata Bay, Mwi. D6 58
Nkhotakota, Mwi. D6 58
Nkongsamba, Cam. H8 54
Nkurenkuru, Nmb. A4 66
Nmai, stm., Burma B4 40
Noākhāli, Bngl. I14 44
Noank, Ct., U.S. D8 114
Noatak, Ak., U.S. B7 109
Noatak, stm., Ak., U.S. B7 109
Nobel, Ont., Can. B4 103
Nobeoka, Japan O6 36
Noble, Ga., U.S. B1 117
Noble, Il., U.S. E5 120
Noble, Ok., U.S. B4 143
Noble, co., In., U.S. B7 121
Noble, co., Oh., U.S. C4 142
Noble, co., Ok., U.S. A4 143
Nobleford, Alta., Can. E4 98
Nobles, co., Mn., U.S. G3 130
Noblesville, In., U.S. D6 121
Noboribetsu, Japan E16 36a
Nobres, Braz. F13 82
Nobsa, Col. E6 84
Nobscot Hill, hill, Ma., U.S. B5 128
Nocatee, Fl., U.S. E5 116
Nocera [Inferiore], Italy I9 18
Noci, Italy I12 18
Nockatunga, Austl. F5 70
Nocona, Tx., U.S. C4 150
Nocupétaro, Mex. H9 90
Nodaway, co., Mo., U.S. A3 132
Nodaway, stm., U.S. A2 132
Noel, Mo., U.S. E3 132
Noelville, Ont., Can. A4 103
Noetinger, Arg. G7 80
Nogal, N.M., U.S. D4 138
Nogales, Chile G3 80
Nogales, Mex. B4 90
Nogales, Az., U.S. F5 110
Nogara, Eth. K9 60
Nogaro, Fr. I6 14
Nōgata, Japan N5 36
Nogent-le-Rotrou, Fr. D7 14
Noginsk, U.S.S.R. F21 26
Nogoa, stm., Austl. D7 70
Nogoyá, Arg. G9 80
Nógrád, co., Hung. H19 10
Noirmoutier, Île de, i., Fr. E4 14
Nokaneng, Bots. B6 66
Nokesville, Va., U.S. B5 153
Nokomis, Sask., Can. F3 105
Nokomis, Fl., U.S. E4 116
Nokomis, Il., U.S. D4 120
Nokomis, Lake, res., Wi., U.S. C4 156
Nola, Italy I9 18
Nolan, W.V., U.S. D2 155
Nolan, co., Tx., U.S. C2 150
Nolichucky, stm., Tn., U.S. C10 149
Nolin, stm., Ky., U.S. C3 124
Nolin Lake, res., Ky., U.S. C3 124
Nolinsk, U.S.S.R. F7 22
Nomans Land, i., Ma., U.S. D6 128
Nombre de Dios, Mex. F7 90
Nombre de Dios, Pan. C3 84
Nombre de Dios, Cordillera, mts., Hond. B8 92
Nome, Ak., U.S. C6 109
Nomgon, Mong. C8 30
Nominingue, Que., Can. C2 104
Nonacho Lake, l., N.W. Ter., Can. D11 96
Nondalton, Ak., U.S. C8 109
Nondweni, S. Afr. G10 66
Nonesuch, stm., Me., U.S. g7 126
Nong'an, China C12 30
Nong Khai, Thai. F7 40
Nongoma, S. Afr. F10 66
Nono, Eth. M9 60
Nonoai, Braz. D12 80
Nonoava, Mex. D6 90
Nonogasta, Arg. E5 80
Nonquit Pond, l., R.I., U.S. E6 146
Nonsan, S. Kor. G15 32
Nonthaburi, Thai. H6 40
Nontron, Fr. G7 14
Nooksack, Wa., U.S. A3 154
Nooksack, North Fork, stm., Wa., U.S. A4 154
Nooksack, South Fork, stm., Wa., U.S. A3 154
Noonan, N.D., U.S. A2 141
Noone, N.H., U.S. E3 136
Noord-Brabant, prov., Neth. E6 12
Noord-Holland, prov., Neth. C6 12
Noordoewer, Nmb. G3 66
Noordoostpolder, reg., Neth. C8 12
Noordwijk aan Zee, Neth. D5 12
Noordzeekanaal, Neth. D5 12
Noorvik, Ak., U.S. B7 109
Nootka Sound, strt., B.C., Can. E4 99
No Point, Point, c., Md., U.S. D5 127
Noquebay, Lake, l., Wi., U.S. C6 156
Nóqui, Ang. C2 58
Nora Islands, is., Eth. E9 56
Noranda, Que., Can. k11 104
Nora Springs, Ia., U.S. A5 122
Norberto de la Riestra, Arg. H9 80
Norbertville, Que., Can. C6 104
Norborne, Mo., U.S. B4 132
Norcatur, Ks., U.S. C3 123
Norcia, Italy G8 18
Norco, Ca., U.S. n13 112
Norco, La., U.S. E5 125
Norcross, Ga., U.S. C2 117
Nord, dept., Fr. B10 14
Nordaustlandet, i., Sval. B3 28
Nordegg, Alta., Can. C2 98
Nordegg, stm., Alta., Can. C3 98
Norden, Ger. B7 10
Nordenham, Ger. B8 10
Nordenšel'da, archipelag, is., U.S.S.R. B11 24
Norderstedt, Ger. B10 10
Nordhausen, Ger. D10 10
Nordhorn, Ger. C7 10
Nordkapp, c., Nor. F19 6
Nordland, Wa., U.S. A3 154
Nordland, co., Nor. H14 6
Nördlingen, Ger. G10 10
Nordman, Id., U.S. A2 119
Nordostrundingen, c., Grnld. A18 86
Nord-Ostsee-Kanal, Ger. A9 10
Nordreisa, Nor. G17 6
Nordrhein-Westfalen, state, Ger. D7 10
Nord-Trøndelag, co., Nor. I12 6
Nore, Nor. K11 6
Norfolk, Ct., U.S. B3 114
Norfolk, Ne., U.S. B8 134
Norfolk, N.Y., U.S. f9 139
Norfolk, Va., U.S. D6 153
Norfolk, co., Eng., U.K. I15 8
Norfolk, co., Ma., U.S. B5 128
Norfolk Island, dep., Oc. K20 158
Norfolk Naval Base, mil., Va., U.S. k15 153
Norfolk Naval Shipyard, mil., Va., U.S. k15 153
Norfork, Ar., U.S. A3 111
Norfork Dam, Ar., U.S. A3 111
Norfork Lake, res., U.S. A3 111
Noril'sk, U.S.S.R. D9 24
Norland, Ont., Can. C6 103
Norland, Fl., U.S. s13 116
Norlina, N.C., U.S. A4 140
Norma, N.J., U.S. E2 137
Normal, Il., U.S. C5 120
Norman, Ar., U.S. C2 111
Norman, Ok., U.S. B4 143
Norman, co., Mn., U.S. C2 130
Norman, stm., Austl. B4 70
Norman, Lake, res., N.C., U.S. B2 140
Normandie, hist. reg., Fr. D6 14
Normandie, Collines de, hills, Fr. D6 14
Normandy, Mo., U.S. f13 132
Normandy see Normandie, hist. reg., Fr. D6 14
Normangee, Tx., U.S. D4 150
Norman Park, Ga., U.S. E3 117
Normanton, Austl. A4 70
Norman Wells, N.W. Ter., Can. C7 96
Norogachi, Mex. D6 90
Norphlet, Ar., U.S. D3 111
Norquay, Sask., Can. F4 105
Norra Kvarken (Merenkurkku), strt., Eur. J17 6
Norrbottens Län, co., Swe. H16 6
Norridge, Il., U.S. k9 120
Norridgewock, Me., U.S. D3 126
Norris, Il., U.S. C3 120
Norris, S.C., U.S. B2 147
Norris, S.D., U.S. D4 148
Norris, Tn., U.S. C9 149
Norris Arm, Newf., Can. D4 102
Norris City, Il., U.S. F5 120
Norris Dam, Tn., U.S. C9 149
Norris Lake, res., Tn., U.S. C10 149
Norris Point, Newf., Can. D3 102
Norristown, Pa., U.S. F11 145
Norrköping, Swe. L15 6
Norrtälje, Swe. L16 6
Norseman, Austl. F4 68
Norsk, U.S.S.R. G17 24
Norte, Canal do, strt., Braz. C8 76
Norte, Punta, c., Arg. I10 80
Norte, Serra do, plat., Braz. D12 82
Norte de Santander, dept., Col. C6 84
Nortelândia, Braz. F13 82
North, S.C., U.S. D5 147
North, stm., Al., U.S. B2 108
North, stm., Ia., U.S. f8 122
North, stm., Ma., U.S. h12 128
North, stm., W.V., U.S. B6 155
North, Cape, c., N.S., Can. B9 101
North Acton, Ma., U.S. f10 128
North Adams, Ma., U.S. A1 128
North Adams, Mi., U.S. G6 129
North Albany, Or., U.S. k11 144
Northam, Austl. F3 68
North America E9 86
North Amherst, Ma., U.S. B2 128
Northampton, Austl. E2 68
Northampton, Eng., U.K. I13 8
Northampton, Ma., U.S. B2 128
Northampton, Pa., U.S. E11 145
Northampton, co., N.C., U.S. A5 140
Northampton, co., Pa., U.S. E11 145
Northampton, co., Va., U.S. C7 153
Northamptonshire, co., Eng., U.K. I13 8
North Andaman, i., India H2 40
North Andover, Ma., U.S. A5 128
North Andrews Gardens, Fl., U.S. r13 116
North Anna, stm., Va., U.S. B5 153
North Anson, Me., U.S. D3 126
North Apollo, Pa., U.S. E2 145

Name | Map Ref. | Page

North Arapaho Peak, mtn., Co., U.S. A5 113
North Arlington, N.J., U.S. h8 137
North Atlanta, Ga., U.S. h8 117
North Attleboro, Ma., U.S. C5 128
North Augusta, Ont., Can. C9 103
North Augusta, S.C., U.S. D4 147
North Aulatsivik Island, i., Newf., Can. f9 102
North Aurora, Il., U.S. k8 120
North Baltimore, Oh., U.S. A2 142
North Battleford, Sask., Can. E1 105
North Bay, Ont., Can. A5 103
North Beach, Md., U.S. C4 127
North Belmont, N.C., U.S. B1 140
North Bend, B.C., Can. E7 99
North Bend, Ne., U.S. C9 134
North Bend, Oh., U.S. o12 142
North Bend, Or., U.S. D2 144
North Bend, Pa., U.S. D6 145
North Bend, Wa., U.S. B4 154
North Bennington, Vt., U.S. F2 152
North Bergen, N.J., U.S. h8 137
North Berwick, Scot., U.K. E11 8
North Berwick, Me., U.S. E2 126
North Billerica, Ma., U.S. A5 128
North Bloomfield, Oh., U.S. A5 142
North Bonneville, Wa., U.S. D4 154
Northborough, Ma., U.S. B4 128
North Bourke, Austl. H6 70
North Branch, Mi., U.S. E7 129
North Branch, Mn., U.S. E6 130
North Branch, N.H., U.S. D3 136
North Branch, N.J., U.S. B3 137
North Branford, Ct., U.S. D4 114
Northbridge, Ma., U.S. B4 128
North Bridgton, Me., U.S. D2 126
Northbrook, Ont., Can. C7 103
Northbrook, Il., U.S. h9 120
North Brookfield, Ma., U.S. B3 128
North Brother, mtn., Me., U.S. C4 126
North Brunswick, N.J., U.S. C4 137
North Caicos, i., T./C. Is. D9 94
North Caldwell, N.J., U.S. B4 137
North Canadian, stm., Ok., U.S. A5 143
North Canton, Ga., U.S. B2 117
North Canton, Oh., U.S. B4 142
North Cape, c., P.E.I., Can. B6 101
North Cape, c., N.Z. A4 72
North Cape May, N.J., U.S. F3 137
North Cape see Nordkapp, c., Nor. F19 6
North Carolina, state, U.S. B3 140
North Carrollton, Ms., U.S. B4 131
North Cascades National Park, Wa., U.S. A4 154
North Channel, strt., Ont., Can. A2 103
North Channel, strt., U.K. F8 8
North Charleston, S.C., U.S. F8 147
North Chicago, Il., U.S. A6 120
North Chichester, N.H., U.S. D4 136
North Clarendon, Vt., U.S. D3 152
North Cohasset, Ma., U.S. g12 128
North College Hill, Oh., U.S. o12 142
North Collins, N.Y., U.S. C2 139
North Conway, N.H., U.S. B4 136
North Corbin, Ky., U.S. D5 124
North Creek, N.Y., U.S. B7 139
North Crossett, Ar., U.S. D4 111
North Dakota, state, U.S. B5 141
North Dartmouth, Ma., U.S. C6 128
North Dighton, Ma., U.S. C5 128
North Druid Hills, Ga., U.S. h8 117
North Eagle Butte, S.D., U.S. B4 148
North East, Md., U.S. A6 127
North East, Pa., U.S. B2 145
North-East, dept., Bots. C8 66
Northeast, stm., Md., U.S. A6 127
Northeast Cape, c., Ak., U.S. C6 109
Northeast Cape Fear, stm., N.C., U.S. C5 140
North Eastham, Ma., U.S. C8 128
Northeast Harbor, Me., U.S. D4 126
Northeast Henrietta, N.Y., U.S. B3 139
North Easton, Ma., U.S. B5 128
North East Point, c., Bah. D8 94
North East Point, c., Bah. C8 94
Northeast Pond, l., N.H., U.S. D5 136
Northeast Providence Channel, strt., Bah. B6 94
North Edisto, stm., S.C., U.S. k11 147
Northeim, Ger. D10 10
North English, Ia., U.S. C5 122
North English, stm., Ia., U.S. C5 122
North Enid, Ok., U.S. A4 143
Northern Arm, Newf., Can. D4 102
Northern Cheyenne Indian Reservation, Mt., U.S. E10 133
Northern Dvina see Severnaja Dvina, stm., U.S.S.R. E6 22
Northern Head, c., N.B., Can. E3 101
Northern Indian Lake, l., Man., Can. A3 100
Northern Ireland, ter., U.K. G7 8
Northern Mariana Islands, ctry., Oc. G19 158
Northern Territory, ter., Austl. C6 68
North Fairfield, Oh., U.S. A3 142
North Falmouth, Ma., U.S. C6 128
Northfield, Ct., U.S. C3 114
Northfield, Ma., U.S. A3 128
Northfield, Mn., U.S. F5 130
Northfield, N.H., U.S. D3 136
Northfield, N.J., U.S. E3 137
Northfield, Oh., U.S. h9 142
Northfield, Vt., U.S. C3 152
Northfield Center, Vt., U.S. C3 152
Northfield Falls, Vt., U.S. C3 152
Northfield Mountains, mts., Vt., U.S. C3 152
North Flinders Range, mts., Austl. H3 70
North Fond du Lac, Wi., U.S. E5 156
Northford, Ct., U.S. D4 114
North Foreland, c., Eng., U.K. J15 8
North Fork, Ca., U.S. D4 112
North Fork, Id., U.S. D5 119
North Fork Reservoir, res., Or., U.S. B4 144
North Fort Myers, Fl., U.S. F5 116
North Fox Island, i., Mi., U.S. C5 129
North Freedom, Wi., U.S. E4 156
North Frisian Islands, is., Eur. A8 10
Northglenn, Co., U.S. B6 113
North Gorham, Me., U.S. g7 126
North Gower, Ont., Can. B9 103
North Grafton, Ma., U.S. B4 128
North Grosvenordale, Ct., U.S. B8 114
North Gulfport, Ms., U.S. E4 131
North Halawa Stream, stm., Hi., U.S. g10 118
North Haledon, N.J., U.S. B4 137
North Hampton, N.H., U.S. E5 136
North Hanover, Ma., U.S. h12 128
North Harpswell, Me., U.S. g8 126
North Hartland, Vt., U.S. D4 152
North Hartland Reservoir, res., Vt., U.S. D4 152
North Hatley, Que., Can. D6 104
North Haven, Ct., U.S. D4 114
North Haven, Me., U.S. D4 126
North Haverhill, N.H., U.S. B2 136
North Head, N.B., Can. E3 101
North Hero, Vt., U.S. B2 152
North Hero Island, i., Vt., U.S. B2 152
North Horn Lake, l., Tn., U.S. e8 149
North Hyde Park, Vt., U.S. B3 152
North Industry, Oh., U.S. B4 142
North Inlet, b., S.C., U.S. E9 147
North Island, i., N.Z. B4 72
North Island, i., S.C., U.S. E9 147
North Island Naval Air Station, mil., Ca., U.S. o15 112
North Islands, is., La., U.S. E7 125
North Jay, Me., U.S. D2 126
North Judson, In., U.S. B4 121
North Kansas City, Mo., U.S. h10 132
North Kingstown, R.I., U.S. E4 146
North Kingsville, Oh., U.S. A5 142
North La Junta, Co., U.S. C7 113
Northlake, Il., U.S. k9 120
North Lake, Wi., U.S. m11 156
North Lakhimpur, India G16 44
North Laramie, stm., Wy., U.S. D7 157
North Las Vegas, Nv., U.S. G6 135
North La Veta Pass, Co., U.S. D5 113
North Lewisburg, Oh., U.S. B2 142
North Liberty, In., U.S. A5 121
North Liberty, Ia., U.S. C6 122
North Lima, Oh., U.S. B5 142
North Little Rock, Ar., U.S. C3 111
North Logan, Ut., U.S. B4 151
North Loon Mountain, mtn., Id., U.S. D3 119
North Loup, Ne., U.S. C7 134
North Loup, stm., Ne., U.S. B5 134
North Magnetic Pole B9 86
North Mamm Peak, mtn., Co., U.S. B3 113
North Manchester, In., U.S. C6 121
North Manitou Island, i., Mi., U.S. C4 129
North Mankato, Mn., U.S. F4 130
North Merrydale, La., U.S. D4 125
North Miami, Fl., U.S. G6 116
North Miami, Ok., U.S. A7 143
North Miami Beach, Fl., U.S. s13 116
North Middletown, Ky., U.S. B5 124
North Monmouth, Me., U.S. D2 126
North Montpelier, Vt., U.S. C4 152
Northmoor, Mo., U.S. h10 132
North Moose Lake, l., Man., Can. B1 100
North Mountain, mtn., Pa., U.S. D9 145
North Muskegon, Mi., U.S. E4 129
North Myrtle Beach, S.C., U.S. D10 147
North Naples, Fl., U.S. F5 116
North Newport, N.H., U.S. D2 136
North New Portland, Me., U.S. D2 126
North New River Canal, Fl., U.S. F6 116
North Ogden, Ut., U.S. B4 151
North Olmsted, Oh., U.S. h9 142
Northome, Mn., U.S. C4 130
North Oxford, Ma., U.S. B4 128
North Palisade, mtn., Ca., U.S. D4 112
North Park, Il., U.S. A4 120
North Park, val., Co., U.S. A4 113
North Pass, strt., La., U.S. E7 125
North Pembroke, Ma., U.S. B6 128
North Plainfield, N.J., U.S. B4 137
North Plains, Or., U.S. B4 144
North Plains, pl., N.M., U.S. C1 138
North Platte, Ne., U.S. C5 134
North Platte, stm., U.S. C6 106
North Point, c., Md., U.S. B5 127
North Point, c., Mi., U.S. C7 129
North Pole, Ak., U.S. C10 109
North Pole A4 86
North Pond, l., Me., U.S. D3 126
North Pond, l., Ma., U.S. h9 128
Northport, Al., U.S. B2 108
Northport, Mi., U.S. C5 129
Northport, Wa., U.S. A8 154
North Portal, Sask., Can. H4 105
North Powder, Or., U.S. B9 144
North Pownal, Vt., U.S. F2 152
North Prairie, Wi., U.S. F5 156
North Providence, R.I., U.S. C4 146
North Raccoon, stm., Ia., U.S. C3 122
North Range Corner, N.S., Can. E4 101
North Reading, Ma., U.S. f11 128
North Richland Hills, Tx., U.S. n9 150
Northridge, Oh., U.S. C2 142
North Ridgeville, Oh., U.S. A3 142
North River Bridge, N.S., Can. C9 101
Northrop, Mn., U.S. G4 130
North Rose, N.Y., U.S. B4 139
North Royalton, Oh., U.S. h9 142
North Rustico, P.E.I., Can. C6 101
North Salem, In., U.S. E4 121
North Salem, N.H., U.S. E4 136
North Salt Lake, Ut., U.S. C4 151
North Sanbornton, N.H., U.S. C3 136
North Santee, stm., S.C., U.S. E9 147
North Saskatchewan, stm., Can. F10 96
North Schell Peak, mtn., Nv., U.S. D7 135
North Scituate, Ma., U.S. h12 128
North Scituate, R.I., U.S. C3 146
North Sea, Eur. D8 4
North Shores, De., U.S. F5 115
North Shoshone Peak, mtn., Nv., U.S. D4 135
North Siberian Lowland see Severo-Sibirskaja nizmennost', pl., U.S.S.R. C18 22
North Sioux City, S.D., U.S. E9 148
North Skunk, stm., Ia., U.S. C5 122
North Solitary Island, i., Austl. G10 70
North Spot, i., Belize A6 92
North Springfield, Vt., U.S. E3 152
North Springfield Reservoir, res., Vt., U.S. E4 152
North Star, De., U.S. A3 115
North Star, Mi., U.S. E6 129
North Stonington, Ct., U.S. D8 114
North St. Paul, Mn., U.S. m13 130
North Stradbroke Island, i., Austl. F10 70
North Stratford, N.H., U.S. A3 136
North Sudbury, Ma., U.S. g10 128
North Sutton, N.H., U.S. D3 136
North Swansea, Ma., U.S. C5 128
North Swanzey, N.H., U.S. E2 136
North Sydney, N.S., Can. C9 101
North Syracuse, N.Y., U.S. B4 139
North Taranaki Bight, N.Z. C5 72
North Tarrytown, N.Y., U.S. D7 139
North Terre Haute, In., U.S. E3 121
North Tewksbury, Ma., U.S. A5 128
North Thompson, stm., B.C., Can. D8 99
North Tonawanda, N.Y., U.S. B2 139
North Troy, Vt., U.S. B4 152
North Tunica, Ms., U.S. A3 131
North Turner Mountain, mtn., Me., U.S. C4 126
North Twin Lake, l., Wi., U.S. B4 156
North Uist, i., Scot., U.K. D6 8
Northumberland, Pa., U.S. E8 145
Northumberland, co., Eng., U.K. F11 8
Northumberland, co., Pa., U.S. D8 145
Northumberland, co., Va., U.S. C6 153
Northumberland Isles, is., Austl. C9 70
Northumberland Strait, strt., Can. C6 101
North Umpqua, stm., Or., U.S. D3 144
North Uxbridge, Ma., U.S. B4 128
Northvale, N.J., U.S. g9 137
North Vancouver, B.C., Can. E6 99
North Vassalboro, Me., U.S. D3 126
North Vernon, In., U.S. F6 121
Northview, Mo., U.S. D4 132
Northville, Ct., U.S. C2 114
Northville, Mi., U.S. p15 129
Northville, N.Y., U.S. B6 139
Northville, S.D., U.S. B7 148
North Waldoboro, Me., U.S. D3 126
North Wales, Pa., U.S. F11 145
North Walpole, N.H., U.S. D2 136
North Warren, Pa., U.S. C3 145
North Waterford, Me., U.S. D2 126
Northway, Ak., U.S. C11 109
North Webster, In., U.S. B6 121
North West, dept., Guy. D13 84
North West Cape, c., Austl. D2 68
North Westchester, Ct., U.S. C6 114
North Westminster, Vt., U.S. E4 152
Northwest Miramichi, stm., N.B., Can. B3 101
Northwest Providence Channel, strt., Bah. A5 94
North West River, Newf., Can. B1 102
Northwest Territories, prov., Can. C12 96
North Wildwood, N.J., U.S. E3 137
North Wilkesboro, N.C., U.S. A1 140
North Windham, Ct., U.S. C7 114
North Windham, Me., U.S. E2 126
Northwood, Ia., U.S. A4 122
Northwood, N.H., U.S. D4 136
Northwood, N.D., U.S. B8 141
Northwood Center, N.H., U.S. D4 136
Northwood Ridge, N.H., U.S. D4 136
North Woodstock, N.H., U.S. B3 136
North York, Ont., Can. D5 103
North York, Pa., U.S. G8 145
North Yorkshire, co., Eng., U.K. G12 8
North Zulch, Tx., U.S. D4 150
Norton, N.B., Can. D4 101
Norton, Ks., U.S. C4 123
Norton, Ma., U.S. C5 128
Norton, Oh., U.S. A4 142
Norton, Va., U.S. f9 153
Norton, W.V., U.S. C5 155
Norton, co., Ks., U.S. C4 123
Norton Air Force Base, mil., Ca., U.S. E5 112
Norton Bay, b., Ak., U.S. C7 109
Norton Creek, stm., Al., U.S. B1 108
Norton Pond, l., Vt., U.S. B5 152
Norton Reservoir, res., Ks., U.S. C3 123
Nortons Corner, Az., U.S. D4 110
Norton Shores, Mi., U.S. E4 129
Norton Sound, strt., Ak., U.S. C6 109
Nortonville, Ks., U.S. C8 123
Nortonville, Ky., U.S. C2 124
Nortorf, Ger. A9 10
Norvegia, Cape, c., Ant. C2 73
Norwalk, Ca., U.S. n12 112
Norwalk, Ct., U.S. E2 114
Norwalk, Ia., U.S. C4 122
Norwalk, Oh., U.S. A3 142
Norwalk, Wi., U.S. E3 156
Norwalk, stm., Ct., U.S. E2 114
Norwalk Islands, is., Ct., U.S. E2 114
Norway, In., U.S. C4 121
Norway, Ia., U.S. C6 122
Norway, Me., U.S. D2 126
Norway, Mi., U.S. C3 129
Norway, S.C., U.S. E5 147
Norway (Norge), ctry., Eur. C10 4
Norway House, Man., Can. C3 100
Norway Lake, l., Mn., U.S. E3 130
Norwegian Sea, Eur. C1 28
Norwell, Ma., U.S. h12 128
Norwich, Eng., U.K. I15 8
Norwich, Ct., U.S. C7 114
Norwich, Ks., U.S. E6 123
Norwich, N.Y., U.S. C5 139
Norwich, N.D., U.S. A5 141
Norwich, Vt., U.S. D4 152
Norwood, Ont., Can. C7 103
Norwood, Co., U.S. C2 113
Norwood, Ga., U.S. C4 117
Norwood, La., U.S. D4 125
Norwood, Ma., U.S. B5 128
Norwood, Mn., U.S. F5 130
Norwood, Mo., U.S. D5 132
Norwood, N.J., U.S. h9 137
Norwood, N.Y., U.S. f10 139
Norwood, N.C., U.S. B2 140
Norwood, Oh., U.S. o13 142
Norwood, Pa., U.S. p20 145
Norwoodville, Ia., U.S. e8 122
Norwottock, Mount, mtn., Ma., U.S. B3 128
Noshiro, Japan G15 36
Nosop (Nossob), stm., Afr. E5 66
Nossa Senhora do Livramento, Braz. F13 82
Nossob (Nosop), stm., Afr. E5 66
Nosy Varika, Madag. R23 67b
Notasulga, Al., U.S. C4 108
Notch Mountain, mtn., Ma., U.S. A3 128
Notch Peak, mtn., Ut., U.S. D2 151
Noteć, stm., Pol. C15 10
Notikewin, Alta., Can. A2 98
Noto, Italy M10 18
Notodden, Nor. L11 6
Noto-hantō, pen., Japan J11 36
Notozero, ozero, l., U.S.S.R. H23 6
Notre Dame, Monts, mts., Que., Can. k13 104
Notre Dame Bay, b., Newf., Can. D4 102
Notre Dame de Lourdes, Man., Can. E2 100
Notre-Dame-des-Bois, Que., Can. D6 104
Notre-Dame-du-Lac, Que., Can. B9 104
Notre-Dame-du-Laus, Que., Can. C2 104
Nottawa, Ont., Can. C4 103
Nottawasaga Bay, b., Ont., Can. C4 103
Nottaway, stm., Que., Can. h11 104
Nottely Lake, res., Ga., U.S. B2 117
Nottingham, Eng., U.K. I12 8
Nottingham, N.H., U.S. D4 136
Nottingham Island, i., N.W. Ter., Can. D17 96
Nottinghamshire, co., Eng., U.K. H12 8
Nottoway, co., Va., U.S. C4 153
Nottoway, stm., Va., U.S. D5 153
Notus, Id., U.S. F2 119
Nouâdhibou, Maur. J2 62
Nouâdhibou, Râs, c., Afr. J2 62
Nouakchott, Maur. B2 64
Nouâmghâr, Maur. B1 64
Nouméa, N. Cal. H24 2
Nouna, Burkina E8 64
Noupoort, S. Afr. H7 66
Nova América, Braz. C4 79
Nova Andradina, Braz. G2 79
Nova Aurora, Braz. E4 79
Nova Caipemba, Ang. C2 58
Nova Era, Braz. E7 79
Nova Esperança, Braz. G2 79
Nova Fátima, Braz. G3 79
Nova Friburgo, Braz. G7 79
Nova Gradiška, Yugo. D12 18
Nova Granada, Braz. F4 79
Nova Iguaçu, Braz. G7 79
Novaja Ivanovka, U.S.S.R. D13 20
Novaja Kachovka, U.S.S.R. H4 22
Novaja Kazanka, U.S.S.R. H7 22
Novaja Ladoga, U.S.S.R. A15 26
Novaja Sibir', ostrov, i., U.S.S.R. B21 24
Novaja Zeml'a, is., U.S.S.R. C9 22
Nova Lamego, Gui.-B. E2 64
Nova Lima, Braz. E7 79
Nova Mambone, Moz. C12 66
Nova Olinda do Norte, Braz. I13 84
Nova Ponte, Braz. E5 79
Nova Prata, Braz. E13 80
Novar, Ont., Can. B5 103
Novara, Italy D3 18
Nova Resende, Braz. F5 79
Nova Roma, Braz. B5 79
Nova Scotia, prov., Can. D6 101
Nova Sofala, Moz. C12 66
Novato, Ca., U.S. C2 112
Nova Varoš, Yugo. F3 20
Nova Venécia, Braz. E8 79
Nova Veneza, Braz. E14 80
Nova Vida, Braz. D10 82
Nova Vida, Cachoeira, wtfl, Braz. C10 82
Nova Zagora, Bul. G10 20
Novelda, Spain G11 16
Nové Zámky, Czech. H18 10
Novgorod, U.S.S.R. C14 26
Novi, Mi., U.S. p15 129
Novi Bečej, Yugo. D4 20
Novigrad, Yugo. E10 18
Novi Ligure, Italy E3 18
Novinger, Mo., U.S. A5 132
Novi Pazar, Bul. F11 20
Novi Pazar, Yugo. F4 20
Novi Sad, Yugo. D3 20
Novki, U.S.S.R. E24 26
Novl'anka, U.S.S.R. F24 26
Novlenskoje, U.S.S.R. B22 26
Nôvo, stm., Braz. A6 82
Nôvo Acôrdo, Braz. B5 79
Novoaltajsk, U.S.S.R. G8 24
Novoanninskij, U.S.S.R. G6 22
Novo Aripuanã, Braz. J12 84
Novo Brasil, Braz. D3 79
Novočerkassk, U.S.S.R. H6 22
Nôvo Cruzeiro, Braz. D8 79
Novodugino, U.S.S.R. F17 26
Novodvinsk, U.S.S.R. E6 22
Novograd-Volynskij, U.S.S.R. G3 22
Novogrudok, U.S.S.R. H8 26
Novo Hamburgo, Braz. E13 80
Novo Horizonte, Braz. F4 79
Novoizborsk, U.S.S.R. D10 26
Novoje Leušino, U.S.S.R. E23 26
Novojel'n'a, U.S.S.R. H8 26
Novokaširsk, U.S.S.R. G21 26
Novokazalinsk, U.S.S.R. H10 22
Novokujbyševsk, U.S.S.R. G7 22
Novokuzneck, U.S.S.R. G9 24
Novol'vovsk, U.S.S.R. H21 26
Novo Mesto, Yugo. D10 18
Novomoskovsk, U.S.S.R. H5 22
Novomoskovsk, U.S.S.R. G21 26
Novopetrovskoje, U.S.S.R. F19 26
Novopiscovo, U.S.S.R. D24 26
Novopolock, U.S.S.R. F11 26
Novorossijsk, U.S.S.R. I5 22
Novorybnoje, U.S.S.R. C13 24
Novoržev, U.S.S.R. D12 26
Novošachtinsk, U.S.S.R. H5 22
Novoselica, U.S.S.R. A10 20
Novosel'skoje, U.S.S.R. D12 20
Novosibirsk, U.S.S.R. F8 24
Novosibirskije ostrova, is., U.S.S.R. B20 24
Novosibirskoje vodochranilišče, res., U.S.S.R. G14 22
Novosil', U.S.S.R. I20 26
Novosokol'niki, U.S.S.R. E13 26
Novos'olki, U.S.S.R. G22 26
Novotroick, U.S.S.R. G9 22
Novouzensk, U.S.S.R. G7 22
Novov'atsk, U.S.S.R. F7 22
Novov'azniki, U.S.S.R. E25 26
Novovolynsk, U.S.S.R. G2 22
Novozavidovskij, U.S.S.R. E19 26
Novozybkov, U.S.S.R. I14 26
Novska, Yugo. D11 18
Nový Bohumín, Czech. F18 10
Nový Jičín, Czech. F18 10
Novyj Nekouz, U.S.S.R. D21 26
Novyj Ropsk, U.S.S.R. I15 26
Nowa Ruda, Pol. E16 10
Nowa Sól (Neusalz), Pol. D15 10
Nowata, Ok., U.S. A6 143
Nowata, co., Ok., U.S. A6 143
Nowogród, Pol. H4 26
Nowogrodziec, Pol. D15 10
Nowood, stm., Wy., U.S. B5 157
Nowra, Austl. J9 70
Nowshāk, mtn., Asia B4 44
Nowshera, Pak. C4 44
Nowy Dwór Mazowiecki, Pol. C20 10
Nowy Sącz, Pol. F20 10
Nowy Targ, Pol. F20 10
Noxapater, Ms., U.S. C4 131
Noxen, Pa., U.S. D9 145
Noxon, Mt., U.S. C1 133
Noxon Reservoir, res., Mt., U.S. C1 133
Noxontown Lake, res., De., U.S. C3 115
Noxubee, co., Ms., U.S. B5 131
Noxubee, stm., U.S. B5 131
Noyes Island, i., Ak., U.S. n22 109
Noyon, Fr. C10 14
Nsanje, Mwi. E7 58
Nsawam, Ghana I9 64
Nsukka, Nig. H13 64
Ntakat, Maur. C4 64
Ntem, stm., Afr. H9 54
N'Tsaoueni, Com. K15 67a
Ntwetwe Pan, pl., Bots. C7 66
Nuanetsi, stm., Afr. C10 66
Nuanli, China C6 40
Nūbah, Jibāl an-, mts., Sud. L6 60
Nubanusit Lake, l., N.H., U.S. E2 136
Nuberg, Ga., U.S. B4 117
Nubian Desert, des., Sud. G8 60
Ñuble, stm., Chile I3 80
Nucet, Rom. C6 20
N'uchča, U.S.S.R. E7 22
Nuckolls, co., Ne., U.S. D7 134
Nucla, Co., U.S. C2 113
Nucuray, stm., Peru J5 84
Nueces, co., Tx., U.S. F4 150
Nueces, stm., Tx., U.S. E3 150
Nueltin Lake, l., Can. D13 96
Nuestra Señora de las Lajas, Col. G4 84
Nuestra Señora de Talavera, Arg. C7 80
Nueva, Isla, i., Chile H3 78
Nueva Antioquia, Col. D8 84
Nueva Asunción, dept., Para. I11 82
Nueva California, Arg. G4 80
Nueva Ciudad Guerrero, Mex. D10 90
Nueva Concepción, El Sal. C5 92
Nueva Esparta, state, Ven. B10 84
Nueva Francia, Arg. E6 80
Nueva Galia, Arg. H6 80
Nueva Germania, Para. B10 80
Nueva Gerona, Cuba D3 94
Nueva Helvecia, Ur. H10 80
Nueva Imperial, Chile J2 80
Nueva Italia de Ruiz, Mex. H8 90
Nueva Ocotepeque, Hond. C5 92
Nueva Palmira, Ur. G9 80
Nueva Rosita, Mex. D9 90
Nueva San Salvador, El Sal. D5 92
Nueva Segovia, dept., Nic. D8 92
Nueva Venecia, Guat. C3 92
Nueve, Canal Numero, Arg. I9 80
Nueve de Julio, Arg. H8 80
Nuevitas, Cuba D6 94
Nuevo, Bajo, Col. G5 94
Nuevo, Cayo, i., Mex. G13 90
Nuevo Berlín, Ur. G9 80
Nuevo Casas Grandes, Mex. B6 90
Nuevo Chagres, Pan. H14 92
Nuevo Delicias, Mex. D8 90
Nuevo Laredo, Mex. D10 90
Nuevo León, state, Mex. D9 90
Nuevo Progreso, Mex. H13 90
Nuevo Rocafuerte, Ec. H5 84
Nuia, U.S.S.R. C8 26
Nuits-Saint-Georges, Fr. E11 14
N'uja, stm., U.S.S.R. E14 24
N'uk, ozero, l., U.S.S.R. I22 6
Nukey Bluff, clf, Austl. I1 70
Nukus, U.S.S.R. I9 22
Nulato, Ak., U.S. C8 109
Nulhegan, stm., Vt., U.S. B5 152
Nullagine, Austl. D4 68
Nullarbor National Park, Austl. F6 68
Nullarbor Plain, pl., Austl. F5 68
Numazu, Japan L13 36
Numila, Hi., U.S. B2 118
Numurkah, Austl. K6 70
Nunda, N.Y., U.S. C3 139
Nunez, Ga., U.S. D4 117
Nunica, Mi., U.S. E4 129
Nunivak Island, i., Ak., U.S. D6 109
Nunjiang, China B12 30
Nunkini, Mex. G14 90
Nunn, Co., U.S. A6 113
Nunnelly, Tn., U.S. B4 149
Nuomin, stm., China B11 30
Nuon, stm., Afr. H5 64
Nuoro, Italy I4 18
Nuquí, Col. E4 84
Nura, stm., U.S.S.R. G12 22
N'urba, U.S.S.R. E15 24
Nürburgring, Ger. H10 12
Nurek, U.S.S.R. A3 44
Nuremberg, Pa., U.S. E9 145
Nuremberg see Nürnberg, Ger. F11 10
Nürnberg (Nuremberg), Ger. F11 10
Nurri, Italy J4 18
Nurri, Mount, hill, Austl. H7 70
Nürtingen, Ger. G9 10
Nusah, Yemen G5 47
Nusaybin, Tur. C6 48
Nu Shan, mts., China F6 30
Nushki, Pak. F2 44
Nutley, N.J., U.S. B4 137
Nutrioso, Az., U.S. D6 110
Nutter Fort, W.V., U.S. k10 155
Nutting Lake, Ma., U.S. f10 128
Nuuanu Pali, Hi., U.S. g10 118
Nuwaybi' al-Muzayyinah, Egypt C8 60
Nuwerus, S. Afr. H4 66
Nxainxai, Bots. B5 66
Nxai Pan National Park, Bots. B7 66
Nxaunxau, Bots. B5 66
Nyaake, Lib. I6 64
Nyabing, Austl. F3 68
Nyack, N.Y., U.S. D7 139
Nyah West, Austl. J5 70
Nyainqêntanglha Shan, mts., China E13 44
Nyakrom, Ghana I9 64
Nyala, Sud. K3 60
Nyamandhlovu, Zimb. B9 66
Nyamina, Mali E6 64
Nyamlell, Sud. M4 60
Nyanza, Rw. B5 58
Nyasa, Lake (Lake Malawi), l., Afr. D6 58
Nyasaland see Malawi, ctry., Afr. D6 58
Nyaunglebin, Burma F4 40
Nybergsund, Nor. K13 6
Nye, co., Nv., U.S. E5 135
Nyiel, Sud. N6 60
Nyíradony, Hung. H21 10
Nyírbátor, Hung. H22 10
Nyíregyháza, Hung. H21 10
Nykøbing, Den. M11 6
Nykøbing, Den. N12 6
Nyköping, Swe. L15 6
Nylstroom, S. Afr. E9 66
Nymburk, Czech. E15 10
Nynäshamn, Swe. L15 6
Nyngan, Austl. H7 70
Nyon, Switz. F5 13
Nyong, stm., Cam. H9 54
Nýrsko, Czech. F13 10
Nysa, Pol. E17 10
Nysa Łużycka (Neisse) (Nisa), stm., Eur. D14 10
Nyssa, Or., U.S. D9 144
Nytva, U.S.S.R. F9 22
Nzébéla, Gui. G5 64
Nzérékoré, Gui. H5 64
N'zeto, Ang. C2 58
Nzi, stm., I.C. H7 64
Nzwani (Anjouan), i., Com. L16 67a

O

Oacoma, S.D., U.S. D6 148
Oahe, Lake, res., U.S. B6 106
Oahe Dam, S.D., U.S. C5 148
Oahu, i., Hi., U.S. B4 118
Oakbank, Austl. I4 70
Oak Bay, B.C., Can. h12 99
Oak Bay, N.B., Can. D2 101
Oak Bluffs, Ma., U.S. D6 128
Oakboro, N.C., U.S. B2 140
Oakburn, Man., Can. D1 100

Name	Map Ref.	Page
Oak City, Ut., U.S.	D3	151
Oak Creek, Co., U.S.	A4	113
Oak Creek, Wi., U.S.	n12	156
Oakdale, Ca., U.S.	D3	112
Oakdale, Ct., U.S.	D7	114
Oakdale, Ga., U.S.	h8	117
Oakdale, La., U.S.	D3	125
Oakdale, Ne., U.S.	B8	134
Oakdale, Pa., U.S.	k13	145
Oakdale, Tn., U.S.	D9	149
Oakes, N.D., U.S.	C7	141
Oakesdale, Wa., U.S.	B8	154
Oakey, Austl.	F9	70
Oakfield, Ga., U.S.	E3	117
Oakfield, Me., U.S.	B4	126
Oakfield, N.Y., U.S.	B2	139
Oakfield, Wi., U.S.	E5	156
Oakford, Il., U.S.	C4	120
Oakford, In., U.S.	D5	121
Oak Forest, Il., U.S.	k9	120
Oak Grove, Al., U.S.	B3	108
Oak Grove, Ar., U.S.	A2	111
Oak Grove, Ky., U.S.	D2	124
Oak Grove, La., U.S.	B4	125
Oak Grove, Mo., U.S.	B3	132
Oak Grove, Or., U.S.	B4	144
Oak Grove Heights, Ar., U.S.	A5	111
Oak Harbor, Oh., U.S.	A2	142
Oak Harbor, Wa., U.S.	A3	154
Oak Hill, Fl., U.S.	D6	116
Oak Hill, Mi., U.S.	D4	129
Oak Hill, Oh., U.S.	D3	142
Oak Hill, Tn., U.S.	A5	149
Oak Hill, W.V., U.S.	D3	155
Oak Hill, mtn., Ma., U.S.	f9	128
Oakhurst, N.J., U.S.	C4	137
Oakhurst, Ok., U.S.	A5	143
Oak Island, i., Wi., U.S.	B3	156
Oak Lake, Man., Can.	E1	100
Oak Lake, l., Man., Can.	E1	100
Oakland, Ont., Can.	D4	103
Oakland, Al., U.S.	A2	108
Oakland, Ca., U.S.	D2	112
Oakland, Il., U.S.	D5	120
Oakland, Ia., U.S.	C2	122
Oakland, Ky., U.S.	C3	124
Oakland, Me., U.S.	D3	126
Oakland, Md., U.S.	m12	127
Oakland, Ms., U.S.	A4	131
Oakland, Ne., U.S.	C9	134
Oakland, N.J., U.S.	A4	137
Oakland, Ok., U.S.	C5	143
Oakland, Or., U.S.	D3	144
Oakland, Pa., U.S.	C10	145
Oakland, R.I., U.S.	B2	146
Oakland, Tn., U.S.	B2	149
Oakland, co., Mi., U.S.	F7	129
Oakland City, In., U.S.	H3	121
Oakland Park, Fl., U.S.	r13	116
Oak Lawn, Il., U.S.	B6	120
Oaklawn, Ks., U.S.	g12	123
Oaklawn, La., U.S.	h12	125
Oakley, Id., U.S.	G5	119
Oakley, Ks., U.S.	C3	123
Oakley, Mi., U.S.	E6	129
Oakley, Ms., U.S.	C3	131
Oakley, Ut., U.S.	C4	151
Oakman, Al., U.S.	B2	108
Oakman, Ga., U.S.	B2	117
Oakmont, Pa., U.S.	E2	145
Oak Mountain, mtn., Ga., U.S.	D2	117
Oak Mountain, mtn., Tn., U.S.	h11	149
Oak Orchard, De., U.S.	F5	115
Oak Park, Ga., U.S.	D4	117
Oak Park, Il., U.S.	B6	120
Oak Park, Mi., U.S.	p15	129
Oak Point, Man., Can.	D3	100
Oak Ridge, Mo., U.S.	D8	132
Oak Ridge, N.C., U.S.	A3	140
Oakridge, Or., U.S.	D4	144
Oak Ridge, Tn., U.S.	C9	149
Oak Ridge Reservoir, res., N.J., U.S.	A3	137
Oak River, Man., Can.	D1	100
Oaks, Ok., U.S.	A7	143
Oaks, Pa., U.S.	o20	145
Oakton, Ky., U.S.	f8	124
Oakton, Va., U.S.	g12	153
Oaktown, In., U.S.	G3	121
Oak Vale, Ms., U.S.	D4	131
Oak Valley, N.J., U.S.	D2	137
Oakville, Man., Can.	E2	100
Oakville, Ont., Can.	D5	103
Oakville, Ct., U.S.	C3	114
Oakville, In., U.S.	D7	121
Oakville, Ia., U.S.	C6	122
Oakville, Mo., U.S.	g13	132
Oakville, Wa., U.S.	C2	154
Oakwood, Ga., U.S.	B3	117
Oakwood, Il., U.S.	C6	120
Oakwood, N.D., U.S.	A8	141
Oakwood, Oh., U.S.	A1	142
Oakwood, Oh., U.S.	C1	142
Oakwood, Tx., U.S.	D5	150
Oakwood, Va., U.S.	e9	153
Oamaru, N.Z.	F3	72
Oancea, Rom.	D12	20
Oark, Ar., U.S.	B2	111
Oatlands, Austl.	N7	70
Oatman, Az., U.S.	C1	110
Oaxaca, state, Mex.	I11	90
Oaxaca [de Juárez], Mex.	I11	90
Ob', stm., U.S.S.R.	D11	22
Obama, Japan	L10	36
Oban, Austl.	C3	70
Oban, Nig.	I14	64
Oban, Scot., U.K.	E8	8
Obed, Alta., Can.	C2	98
Obed, stm., Tn., U.S.	C9	149
Obeliai, U.S.S.R.	F8	26
Oberá, Arg.	D11	80
Oberdrauburg, Aus.	I12	10
Obergurgl, Aus.	I11	10
Oberhausen, Ger.	D6	10
Oberlin, Ks., U.S.	C3	123
Oberlin, La., U.S.	D3	125
Oberlin, Oh., U.S.	A3	142
Obernai, Fr.	D14	14
Obernburg am Main, Ger.	F9	10
Oberon, Austl.	I8	70
Oberon, N.D., U.S.	B6	141
Oberösterreich, state, Aus.	G13	10
Oberpullendorf, Aus.	H16	10
Obertin, U.S.S.R.	A9	20
Oberursel, Ger.	E8	10
Obervellach, Aus.	I13	10
Oberwart, Aus.	H16	10
Obetz, Oh., U.S.	C3	142
Obi, Nig.	G14	64
Obi, Kepulauan, is., Indon.	F8	38
Obiaruku, Nig.	I13	64
Óbidos, Braz.	D7	76
Obihiro, Japan	E18	36a
Obilatu, Pulau, i., Indon.	F8	38
Obing, Ger.	G12	10
Obion, Tn., U.S.	A2	149
Obion, co., Tn., U.S.	A2	149
Obion, stm., Tn., U.S.	A2	149
Obion, Middle Fork, stm., Tn., U.S.	A3	149
Obion, Rutherford Fork, stm., Tn., U.S.	A3	149
Obion, South Fork, stm., Tn., U.S.	A3	149
Obion Creek, stm., Ky., U.S.	f9	124
Oblong, Il., U.S.	D6	120
Oblučje, U.S.S.R.	H18	24
Obninsk, U.S.S.R.	F19	26
Obock, Dji.	F9	56
Obol', U.S.S.R.	F12	26
Oborniki, Pol.	C16	10
Oboz'orskij, U.S.S.R.	J27	6
O'Brien, Or., U.S.	E3	144
O'Brien, co., Ia., U.S.	A2	122
Obščij Syrt, mtn., U.S.S.R.	G8	22
Observation Peak, mtn., Ca., U.S.	B3	112
Obskaja guba, b., U.S.S.R.	D12	22
Obuasi, Ghana	H9	64
Obuchova, U.S.S.R.	E15	26
Obžericha, U.S.S.R.	D25	26
Ocala, Fl., U.S.	C4	116
Ocallí, Peru	B2	82
Ocamo, stm., Ven.	F10	84
Ocampo, Mex.	C5	90
Ocampo, Mex.	D8	90
Ocaña, Col.	C6	84
Occidental, Cordillera, mts., Col.	E4	84
Occidental, Cordillera, mts., Peru	C3	82
Occoquan, Va., U.S.	B5	153
Ocean, co., N.J., U.S.	D4	137
Oceana, W.V., U.S.	D3	155
Oceana, co., Mi., U.S.	E4	129
Oceana Naval Air Station, mil., Va., U.S.	k15	153
Ocean Bluff, Ma., U.S.	B6	128
Ocean City, Fl., U.S.	u15	116
Ocean City, Md., U.S.	D7	127
Ocean City, N.J., U.S.	E3	137
Ocean City, Wa., U.S.	B1	154
Ocean Gate, N.J., U.S.	D4	137
Ocean Grove, Ma., U.S.	C5	128
Ocean Grove, N.J., U.S.	C4	137
Ocean Park, Wa., U.S.	C1	154
Ocean Pines, Md., U.S.	D7	127
Ocean Port, N.J., U.S.	C4	137
Oceanside, Ca., U.S.	F5	112
Ocean Springs, Ms., U.S.	E5	131
Ocean [Township], N.J., U.S.	C4	137
Ocean View, De., U.S.	F5	115
Oceanville, N.J., U.S.	E4	137
Ocha, U.S.S.R.	G20	24
Ocheda Lake, l., Mn., U.S.	G3	130
Ochelata, Ok., U.S.	A6	143
Ocheyedan, Ia., U.S.	A2	122
Ocheyedan, stm., Ia., U.S.	A2	122
Ochiltree, co., Tx., U.S.	A2	150
Ochlocknee, Ga., U.S.	F2	117
Ochlockonee, stm., Fl., U.S.	B2	116
Ochoco Lake, res., Or., U.S.	C6	144
Ochopee, Fl., U.S.	G5	116
Ocho Rios, Jam.	E6	94
Ochota, stm., U.S.S.R.	F20	24
Ochotsk, U.S.S.R.	F20	24
Ochre River, Man., Can.	D2	100
Ochsenfurt, Ger.	F10	10
Ochvat, U.S.S.R.	E15	26
Ocilla, Ga., U.S.	E3	117
Ocmulgee, stm., Ga., U.S.	D3	117
Ocmulgee National Monument, Ga., U.S.	D3	117
Ocoa, Bahía de, b., Dom. Rep.	E9	94
Ocoee, Fl., U.S.	D5	116
Ocoee, Tn., U.S.	D9	149
Ocoee, Lake, res., Tn., U.S.	D9	149
Ocoña, Peru	G5	82
Ocoña, stm., Peru	G5	82
Oconee, Ga., U.S.	D4	117
Oconee, Il., U.S.	D4	120
Oconee, co., Ga., U.S.	C3	117
Oconee, co., S.C., U.S.	B1	147
Oconee, stm., Ga., U.S.	C3	117
Oconee, Lake, res., Ga., U.S.	C3	117
Ocongate, Peru	E6	82
Oconomowoc, Wi., U.S.	E5	156
Oconto, Ne., U.S.	C6	134
Oconto, Wi., U.S.	D6	156
Oconto, co., Wi., U.S.	D5	156
Oconto, stm., Wi., U.S.	D5	156
Oconto Falls, Wi., U.S.	D5	156
Ocós, Guat.	C2	92
Ocosingo, Mex.	I13	90
Ocotal, Nic.	D8	92
Ocotepeque, dept., Hond.	C5	92
Ocotillo, Az., U.S.	m9	110
Ocotlán, Mex.	G8	90
Ocotlán de Morelos, Mex.	I11	90
Ocozocoautla [de Espinosa], Mex.	I13	90
Ocracoke, N.C., U.S.	B7	140
Ocracoke Inlet, b., N.C., U.S.	B6	140
Ocracoke Island, i., N.C., U.S.	B7	140
Ocros, Peru	D3	82
Octavia, Ne., U.S.	C8	134
Octoraro Creek, stm., U.S.	A5	127
Ocú, Pan.	J14	92
Ocumare del Tuy, Ven.	B9	84
Ocurí, Bol.	H9	82
Ocussi, Indon.	A4	68
Oda, Ghana	I9	64
Oda, Jabal, mtn., Sud.	G9	60
Odanakumadona, Bots.	C7	66
Ōdate, Japan	G15	36
Odawara, Japan	L14	36
Odda, Nor.	K10	6
Odebolt, Ia., U.S.	B2	122
Odei, stm., Man., Can.	A3	100
Odell, Il., U.S.	B5	120
Odell, Ne., U.S.	D9	134
Odell, Or., U.S.	B5	144
Odell Lake, l., Or., U.S.	E5	144
Odem, Tx., U.S.	F4	150
Ödemiş, Tur.	K11	20
Oden, Ar., U.S.	C2	111
Odendaalsrus, S. Afr.	F8	66
Odense, Den.	N12	6
Odenton, Md., U.S.	B4	127
Odenville, Al., U.S.	B3	108
Oder (Odra), stm., Eur.	C14	10
Oderberg, Ger.	C14	10
Oderhaff (Zalew Szczeciński), b., Eur.	B14	10
Oderzo, Italy	D7	18
Odessa, Ont., Can.	C8	103
Odessa, Sask., Can.	G4	105
Odessa, U.S.S.R.	H4	22
Odessa, De., U.S.	C3	115
Odessa, Mn., U.S.	E2	130
Odessa, Mo., U.S.	C4	132
Odessa, Ne., U.S.	D6	134
Odessa, N.Y., U.S.	C4	139
Odessa, Tx., U.S.	D1	150
Odessa, Wa., U.S.	B7	154
Odesskoje, U.S.S.R.	G12	22
Odiakwe, Bots.	C7	66
Odib, Wādī, val., Afr.	F9	60
Odienné, I.C.	G6	64
Odin, Il., U.S.	E4	120
Odin, Ks., U.S.	D5	123
Odincovo, U.S.S.R.	F20	26
Odojev, U.S.S.R.	H19	26
Odon, In., U.S.	G4	121
O'Donnell, Tx., U.S.	C2	150
Odorheiu Secuiesc, Rom.	C9	20
Odum, Ga., U.S.	E4	117
Odzi, Zimb.	B11	66
Oebisfelde, Ger.	C10	10
Oeiras, Braz.	E10	76
Oelde, Ger.	D8	10
Oelrichs, S.D., U.S.	D2	148
Oelsnitz, Ger.	E12	10
Oelwein, Ia., U.S.	B6	122
Oesterdam, Neth.	F5	12
Oettingen in Bayern, Ger.	G10	10
Oetz, Aus.	H10	10
Ofahoma, Ms., U.S.	C4	131
O'Fallon, Il., U.S.	E4	120
O'Fallon, Mo., U.S.	f12	132
O'Fallon Creek, stm., Mt., U.S.	D12	133
Ofaqim, Isr.	F3	50
Offa, Nig.	G12	64
Offaly, co., Ire.	H6	8
Offenbach, Ger.	E8	10
Offenburg, Ger.	G7	10
Offerle, Ks., U.S.	E4	123
Offerman, Ga., U.S.	E4	117
Offutt Air Force Base, mil., Ne., U.S.	g3	134
Oficina Alianza, Chile	I7	82
Oficina Chile, Chile	C4	80
Oficina Pedro de Valdivia, Chile	B4	80
Oficina Victoria, Chile	I7	82
Ōfunato, Japan	H16	36
Oga, Japan	H14	36
Ogaden, reg., Afr.	G9	56
Ōgaki, Japan	L11	36
Ogallah, Ks., U.S.	D4	123
Ogallala, Ne., U.S.	C4	134
Ogbomosho, Nig.	G12	64
Ogden, Ar., U.S.	D1	111
Ogden, Il., U.S.	C6	120
Ogden, Ia., U.S.	B3	122
Ogden, Ks., U.S.	C7	123
Ogden, Ut., U.S.	B4	151
Ogden, Mount, mtn., N.A.	k23	109
Ogdensburg, N.J., U.S.	A3	137
Ogdensburg, N.Y., U.S.	f9	139
Ogeechee, stm., Ga., U.S.	D5	117
Ogema, Sask., Can.	H3	105
Ogema, Mn., U.S.	C3	130
Ogemaw, co., Mi., U.S.	D6	129
Ogilvie, Mn., U.S.	E5	130
Ogilvie Mountains, mts., Yukon, Can.	D5	96
Oglala, S.D., U.S.	D3	148
Ogle, co., Il., U.S.	A4	120
Oglesby, Il., U.S.	B4	120
Oglethorpe, Ga., U.S.	D2	117
Oglethorpe, co., Ga., U.S.	C3	117
Oglethorpe, Mount, mtn., Ga., U.S.	B2	117
Oglio, stm., Italy	D5	18
Ogmore, Austl.	D8	70
Ognon, stm., Fr.	E12	14
Ogoja, Nig.	H14	64
Ogoki, stm., Ont., Can.	o18	103
Ogooué, stm., Afr.	B1	58
Ogorodnoje, U.S.S.R.	D12	20
Ogr, Sud.	K4	60
Ogre, U.S.S.R.	E7	26
Ogulin, Yugo.	D10	18
Ogunquit, Me., U.S.	E2	126
Ogurčinskij, ostrov, i., U.S.S.R.	B12	48
Oğuzeli, Tur.	C4	48
Ogwashi-Uku, Nig.	H13	64
Ohanet, Alg.	F15	62
O'Hanly, stm., Man., Can.	D4	100
Ōhara, Japan	L15	36
Ohatchee, Al., U.S.	B3	108
Ohaton, Alta., Can.	C4	98
O'Higgins, Lago (Lago San Martín), l., S.A.	F2	78
Ohio, Il., U.S.	B4	120
Ohio, co., In., U.S.	G7	121
Ohio, co., Ky., U.S.	C3	124
Ohio, co., W.V., U.S.	A4	155
Ohio, state, U.S.	B3	142
Ohio, stm., U.S.	D9	106
Ohio Brush Creek, stm., Oh., U.S.	D2	142
Ohio City, Oh., U.S.	B1	142
Ohio Peak, mtn., Co., U.S.	C3	113
Ohioville, Pa., U.S.	E1	145
Ohiowa, Ne., U.S.	D8	134
Ohoopee, stm., Ga., U.S.	D4	117
Ohře, stm., Eur.	E13	10
Ohrid, Yugo.	H4	20
Ohrid, Lake, l., Eur.	H4	20
Öhringen, Ger.	F9	10
Ohuira, Bahía, b., Mex.	E5	90
Oiapoque, Braz.	C8	76
Oiapoque (Oyapock), stm., S.A.	C8	76
Oil Center, N.M., U.S.	E6	138
Oil City, La., U.S.	B2	125
Oil City, Pa., U.S.	D2	145
Oil Creek, stm., Pa., U.S.	C2	145
Oildale, Ca., U.S.	E4	112
Oil Springs, Ont., Can.	E2	103
Oilton, Ok., U.S.	A5	143
Oil Trough, Ar., U.S.	B4	111
Oise, dept., Fr.	C9	14
Oise, stm., Eur.	C9	14
Oisemont, Fr.	C8	14
Ōita, Japan	N6	36
Ojai, Ca., U.S.	E4	112
Ojat', stm., U.S.S.R.	A16	26
Ojinaga, Mex.	C7	90
Ojocaliente, Mex.	F8	90
Ojo Caliente, N.M., U.S.	A3	138
Ojo del Carrizo, Mex.	C7	90
Ojo de Liebre, Laguna, b., Mex.	D2	90
Ojo Sarco, N.M., U.S.	A4	138
Ojos del Salado, Nevado, mtn., S.A.	D4	80
Ojos Negros, Mex.	B1	90
Oju, Nig.	H14	64
Oka, stm., U.S.S.R.	G12	24
Oka, stm., U.S.S.R.	E26	26
Okahandja, Nmb.	C3	66
Okaloosa, co., Fl., U.S.	u15	116
Okamanpeedan Lake, l., U.S.	A3	122
Okanagan Centre, B.C., Can.	D8	99
Okanagan Falls, B.C., Can.	E8	99
Okanagan Lake, l., B.C., Can.	D8	99
Okanagan Landing, B.C., Can.	D8	99
Okanogan, Wa., U.S.	A6	154
Okanogan, co., Wa., U.S.	A5	154
Okapilco Creek, stm., Ga., U.S.	E3	117
Okaputa, Nmb.	C3	66
Okāra, Pak.	E5	44
Okarche, Ok., U.S.	B4	143
Okatibee Reservoir, res., Ms., U.S.	C5	131
Okatoma Creek, stm., Ms., U.S.	D4	131
Okauchee Lake, Wi., U.S.	E5	156
Okaukuejo, Nmb.	B2	66
Okavango (Cubango), stm., Afr.	E3	58
Okavango Delta, Bots.	B6	66
Okawville, Il., U.S.	E4	120
Okay, Ok., U.S.	B6	143
Okaya, Japan	K13	36
Okayama, Japan	M8	36
Okazaki, Japan	M12	36
O'Kean, Ar., U.S.	A5	111
Okeechobee, Fl., U.S.	E6	116
Okeechobee, co., Fl., U.S.	E6	116
Okeechobee, Lake, l., Fl., U.S.	F6	116
Okeene, Ok., U.S.	A3	143
Okefenokee Swamp, sw., U.S.	F4	117
Okeigbo, Nig.	H12	64
Okemah, Ok., U.S.	B5	143
Okene, Nig.	H13	64
Oke-Ode, Nig.	G12	64
Oketo, Ks., U.S.	C7	123
Okfuskee, co., Ok., U.S.	B5	143
Okhotsk, Sea of, Asia	C19	36a
Okiep, S. Afr.	G3	66
Okinawa, Japan	U2	37b
Okinawa-jima, i., Japan	U2	37b
Okinawa-shotō, is., Japan	U2	37b
Okino-Daitō-jima, i., Japan	G13	30
Okino-Erabu-shima, i., Japan	T3	37b
Okino-Tori-shima (Parece Vela), i., Japan	G14	30
Oki-shotō, is., Japan	K8	36
Okladnevo, U.S.S.R.	C16	26
Oklahoma, co., Ok., U.S.	B4	143
Oklahoma, state, U.S.	B4	143
Oklahoma City, Ok., U.S.	B4	143
Oklawaha, Fl., U.S.	C5	116
Oklawaha, stm., Fl., U.S.	C5	116
Oklawaha, Lake, res., Fl., U.S.	C5	116
Oklee, Mn., U.S.	C3	130
Okmulgee, Ok., U.S.	B6	143
Okmulgee, co., Ok., U.S.	B5	143
Oknica, U.S.S.R.	A11	20
Okno, U.S.S.R.	A9	20
Okoboji, Ia., U.S.	A2	122
Okobojo Creek, stm., S.D., U.S.	C5	148
Okolona, Ar., U.S.	D2	111
Okolona, Ky., U.S.	g11	124
Okolona, Ms., U.S.	B5	131
Okombahe, Nmb.	C2	66
Okotoks, Alta., Can.	D4	98
Okpara, stm., Afr.	H11	64
Okreek, S.D., U.S.	D5	148
Okrika, Nig.	I13	64
Okt'abr', U.S.S.R.	D20	26
Okt'abr'skij, U.S.S.R.	G8	22
Okt'abr'skij, U.S.S.R.	D23	26
Okt'abr'skij, U.S.S.R.	C27	26
Okt'abr'skij, U.S.S.R.	G21	26
Okt'abr'skij, U.S.S.R.	I11	26
Okt'abr'skoje, U.S.S.R.	I22	26
Okt'abr'skoj Revol'ucii, ostrov, i., U.S.S.R.	B17	22
Oktaha, Ok., U.S.	B6	143
Oktibbeha, co., Ms., U.S.	B5	131
Okulovka, U.S.S.R.	C16	26
Okushiri-tō, i., Japan	E14	36a
Okuta, Nig.	G11	64
Okwa (Chapman's), stm., Afr.	D5	66
Okwoga, Nig.	H13	64
Olá, Pan.	I14	92
Ola, Ar., U.S.	B2	111
Ólafsfjörður, Ice.	A4	6a
Olalla, Wa., U.S.	f10	154
Olamon, Me., U.S.	C4	126
Olancha, Ca., U.S.	D5	112
Olancha Peak, mtn., Ca., U.S.	D4	112
Olanchito, Hond.	B8	92
Olancho, dept., Hond.	C9	92
Öland, i., Swe.	M15	6
Olanta, S.C., U.S.	D8	147
Olar, S.C., U.S.	E5	147
Olary, Austl.	I4	70
Olascoaga, Arg.	H8	80
Olathe, Co., U.S.	C3	113
Olathe, Ks., U.S.	D9	123
Olavarría, Arg.	I8	80
Oława, Pol.	E17	10
Olberg, Az., U.S.	D4	110
Olbia, Italy	I4	18
Olca, Volcán, vol., S.A.	I7	82
Olcott, N.Y., U.S.	B2	139
Olcott, W.V., U.S.	C3	155
Old Bahama Channel, strt., N.A.	C5	94
Old Bennington, Vt., U.S.	F2	152
Old Bridge, N.J., U.S.	C4	137
Old Crow, Yukon, Can.	C5	96
Old Crow, stm., N.A.	C4	96
Olden, Tx., U.S.	C3	150
Oldenburg, In., U.S.	F7	121
Oldenburg, hist. reg., Ger.	B8	10
Oldenburg [in Holstein], Ger.	A10	10
Oldenzaal, Neth.	D10	12
Old Faithful Geyser, Wy., U.S.	B2	157
Old Forge, N.Y., U.S.	B6	139
Old Forge, Pa., U.S.	D10	145
Old Fort, N.C., U.S.	f10	140
Oldham, S.D., U.S.	C8	148
Oldham, co., Ky., U.S.	B4	124
Oldham, co., Tx., U.S.	B1	150
Old Harbor, Ak., U.S.	D9	109
Old Hickory Lake, res., Tn., U.S.	A5	149
Oldman, stm., Alta., Can.	E4	98
Old Man of the Mountain, N.H., U.S.	B3	136
Oldmans Creek, stm., N.J., U.S.	D2	137
Oldmeldrum, Scot., U.K.	D11	8
Old Monroe, Mo., U.S.	C7	132
Old Mystic, Ct., U.S.	D8	114
Old Northwood, N.H., U.S.	D4	136
Old Orchard Beach, Me., U.S.	E2	126
Old Perlican, Newf., Can.	D5	102
Old Point Comfort, c., Va., U.S.	h15	153
Old Rhodes Key, i., Fl., U.S.	G6	116
Old River Lake, l., Ar., U.S.	k10	111
Olds, Alta., Can.	D3	98
Olds, Ia., U.S.	C6	122
Old Saybrook, Ct., U.S.	D6	114
Oldsmar, Fl., U.S.	o10	116
Old Speck Mountain, mtn., Me., U.S.	D2	126
Old Tampa Bay, b., Fl., U.S.	p10	116
Old Tappan, N.J., U.S.	g9	137
Old Tate, Bots.	C8	66
Old Topsail Inlet, b., N.C., U.S.	C5	140
Old Town, Fl., U.S.	C4	116
Old Town, Id., U.S.	A1	119
Old Town, Me., U.S.	D4	126
Oldtown, Md., U.S.	k13	127
Olduvai Gorge, val., Tan.	B7	58
Old Wives Lake, l., Sask., Can.	G2	105
Olean, N.Y., U.S.	C2	139
O'Leary, P.E.I., Can.	C5	101
Olecko, Pol.	A22	10
Olen, Bel.	F6	12
Ølen, Nor.	L9	6
Olenegorsk, U.S.S.R.	D4	22
Olenij, ostrov, i., U.S.S.R.	C13	22
Olenino, U.S.S.R.	E16	26
Olen'ok, stm., U.S.S.R.	C16	24
Olen'okskij zaliv, b., U.S.S.R.	C16	24
Olentangy, stm., Oh., U.S.	B3	142
Oléron, Île d', i., Fr.	G5	14
Oleśnica, Pol.	D17	10
Olesno, Pol.	E18	10
Oley, Pa., U.S.	F10	145
Ol'ga, U.S.S.R.	I19	24
Olga, Mount, mtn., Vt., U.S.	F3	152
Ölgij, Mong.	B4	30
Ol'gopol', U.S.S.R.	A13	20
Olhão, Port.	H4	16
Oli, stm., Afr.	G12	64
Olifants (Rio dos Elefantes), stm., Afr.	E10	66
Ólimbos, mtn., Cyp.	D2	48
Ólimbos, mtn., Grc.	I6	20
Olímpia, Braz.	F4	79
Olin, Ia., U.S.	B6	122
Olinalá, Mex.	I10	90
Olinda, Braz.	E12	76
Olio, Austl.	C5	70
Oliva, Arg.	G7	80
Oliva, Spain	G11	16
Oliva de la Frontera, Spain	G5	16
Olivare, Cerro de, mtn., S.A.	F4	80
Olive Branch, Il., U.S.	F4	120
Olive Branch, Ms., U.S.	A4	131
Olive Hill, Ky., U.S.	B6	124
Olivehurst, Ca., U.S.	C3	112
Oliveira, Braz.	F6	79
Oliveira dos Brejinhos, Braz.	B7	79
Olivenza, Spain	G4	16
Oliver, B.C., Can.	E8	99
Oliver, Al., U.S.	A2	108
Oliver, Ga., U.S.	D5	117
Oliver, Pa., U.S.	G2	145
Oliver, co., N.D., U.S.	B4	141
Oliver Dam, U.S.	C5	108
Oliver Springs, Tn., U.S.	C9	149
Olivet, Il., U.S.	D6	120
Olivet, Mi., U.S.	F6	129
Olivia, Mn., U.S.	F4	130
Olivia, N.C., U.S.	B3	140
Olla, La., U.S.	C3	125
Ollagüe, Chile	I7	82
Ollagüe, Volcán, vol., S.A.	I7	82
Ollantaytambo, Peru	E5	82
Ollie, Ia., U.S.	C5	122
Olmito, Tx., U.S.	F4	150
Olmitz, Ks., U.S.	D5	123
Olmos, Peru	A2	82
Olmos Park, Tx., U.S.	k7	150
Olmsted, Il., U.S.	F4	120
Olmsted, co., Mn., U.S.	G6	130
Olmsted Falls, Oh., U.S.	h9	142
Olney, Il., U.S.	E5	120
Olney, Md., U.S.	B3	127
Olney, Mt., U.S.	B2	133
Olney, Tx., U.S.	C3	150
Olney Springs, Co., U.S.	C7	113
Ol'okma, stm., U.S.S.R.	F16	24
Ol'okminsk, U.S.S.R.	E16	24
Olomega, Laguna, l., El Sal.	D6	92
Olomouc, Czech.	F17	10
Olonec, U.S.S.R.	E4	22
Olongapo, Phil.	N19	39b
Oloron-Sainte-Marie, Fr.	I6	14
Olot, Spain	C14	16
Olov'annaja, U.S.S.R.	G15	24
Olowalu, Hi., U.S.	C5	118
Olpe, Ger.	D7	10
Olpe, Ks., U.S.	D7	123
Olsburg, Ks., U.S.	C7	123
Olsztyn (Allenstein), Pol.	B20	10
Olsztynek, Pol.	B20	10
Olt, co., Rom.	E8	20
Olt, stm., Rom.	F8	20
Olta, Arg.	F5	80
Olten, Switz.	D8	13
Oltenița, Rom.	E10	20
Olton, Tx., U.S.	B1	150
Oltu, Tur.	A6	48
Oluan Pi, c., Tai.	N9	34
Olukonda, Nmb.	B3	66
Olustee, Fl., U.S.	B4	116
Olustee, Ok., U.S.	C2	143
Ol'utorskij, mys, c., U.S.S.R.	F26	24
Ol'utorskij zaliv, b., U.S.S.R.	E25	24
Olvera, Spain	I6	16
Olympia, Wa., U.S.	B3	154
Olympic Mountains, mts., Wa., U.S.	B2	154
Olympic National Park, Wa., U.S.	B2	154
Olympus, Mount, mtn., Ky., U.S.	B6	124
Olympus, Mount, mtn., Wa., U.S.	B2	154
Olympus, Mount see Ólimbos, mtn., Grc.	I6	20
Olyphant, Pa., U.S.	D10	145
Om', stm., U.S.S.R.	F7	24
Omagh, N. Ire., U.K.	G6	8
Omaguas, Peru	J6	84
Omaha, Ar., U.S.	A2	111
Omaha, Ga., U.S.	D1	117
Omaha, Il., U.S.	F5	120
Omaha, Ne., U.S.	C10	134
Omaha Indian Reservation, Ne., U.S.	B9	134
Omak, Wa., U.S.	A6	154
Omak Lake, l., Wa., U.S.	A6	154
Oman ('Umān), ctry., Asia	E6	42
Oman, Gulf of, b., Asia	B10	47
Omar, W.V., U.S.	D3	155
Omarama, N.Z.	F2	72
Omaruru, Nmb.	C2	66
Omas, Peru	E3	82
Omatako, stm., Nmb.	B5	66
Omate, Peru	G6	82
Ombombo, Nmb.	B1	66
Omboué, Gabon	B1	58
Omčak, U.S.S.R.	E21	24
Omdurman see Umm Durmān, Sud.	J7	60
Omega, Ga., U.S.	E3	117
Omega, Ok., U.S.	B3	143
Omegna, Italy	D3	18
Omemee, Ont., Can.	C6	103
Omeo, Austl.	K7	70
Omer, Mi., U.S.	D7	129
Omerville, Que., Can.	D5	104
Ometepe, Isla de, i., Nic.	F9	92
Ometepec, Mex.	I10	90
Om Hajer, Eth.	J9	60
Omineca, stm., B.C., Can.	B5	99
Omineca Mountains, mts., B.C., Can.	A4	99
Ōmiya, Japan	L14	36
Ommaney, Cape, c., Ak., U.S.	D12	109
Ommanney Bay, b., N.W. Ter., Can.	B12	96
Omo, stm., Afr.	G8	56
Omoa, Bahía de, b., N.A.	B6	92
Omoloj, stm., U.S.S.R.	C18	24
Omolon, stm., U.S.S.R.	D23	24
Ompompanoosuc, stm., Vt., U.S.	D4	152
Ompompanoosuc, West Branch, stm., Vt., U.S.	D4	152
Omro, Wi., U.S.	D5	156
Omsk, U.S.S.R.	F6	24
Omsukčan, U.S.S.R.	E23	24
Omu-Aran, Nig.	G12	64
Ōmuta, Japan	N5	36
Omutninsk, U.S.S.R.	F8	22
On, Viet.	D9	40
Onabas, Mex.	C5	90
Onaga, Ks., U.S.	C7	123
Onalaska, Wa., U.S.	C3	154
Onalaska, Wi., U.S.	E2	156
Onamia, Mn., U.S.	D5	130
Onancock, Va., U.S.	C7	153
Onanole, Man., Can.	D2	100
Onarga, Il., U.S.	C6	120
Onawa, Ia., U.S.	B1	122
Onawa, Lake, l., Me., U.S.	C3	126
Onaway, Mi., U.S.	C6	129
Oncativo, Arg.	F7	80
Once, Canal Numero, Arg.	I9	80
Onda, Spain	F11	16
Ondangwa, Nmb.	A3	66
Ondas, Rio das, stm., Braz.	B6	79
Onderdijk, Neth.	C7	12
Ondjiva, Ang.	E3	58
Ondo, Nig.	H12	64
Öndörchaan, Mong.	B9	30
Ondozero, ozero, l., U.S.S.R.	J23	6
Oneco, Ct., U.S.	C8	114
Oneco, Fl., U.S.	E4	116
Onega, U.S.S.R.	E5	22
Onega, stm., U.S.S.R.	J26	6

Name	Map Ref.	Page
Onega, Lake see Onežskoje ozero, l., U.S.S.R.	E5	22
One Hundred Fifty Mile House, B.C., Can.	C7	99
One Hundred Mile House, B.C., Can.	D7	99
Oneida, Ar., U.S.	C5	111
Oneida, Il., U.S.	B3	120
Oneida, Ky., U.S.	C6	124
Oneida, N.Y., U.S.	B5	139
Oneida, Oh., U.S.	C1	142
Oneida, Tn., U.S.	C9	149
Oneida, co., Id., U.S.	G6	119
Oneida, co., N.Y., U.S.	B5	139
Oneida, co., Wi., U.S.	C4	156
Oneida Lake, l., N.Y., U.S.	B5	139
O'Neill, Ne., U.S.	B7	134
Onekama, Mi., U.S.	D4	129
Onekotan, ostrov, i., U.S.S.R.	H22	24
Oneonta, Al., U.S.	B3	108
Oneonta, N.Y., U.S.	C5	139
Onežskaja guba, b., U.S.S.R.	I25	6
Onežskij poluostrov, pen., U.S.S.R.	I25	6
Onežskoje ozero, l., U.S.S.R.	E5	22
Ongjin, N. Kor.	F13	32
Ongole, India	E6	46
Onida, S.D., U.S.	C5	148
Onitsha, Nig.	H13	64
Onley, Va., U.S.	C7	153
Ōno, Japan	L11	36
Onoda, Japan	N6	36
Onomichi, Japan	M8	36
Onon, stm., Asia	A9	30
Onondaga, co., N.Y., U.S.	C4	139
Onondaga Indian Reservation, N.Y., U.S.	C4	139
Onota Lake, l., Ma., U.S.	B1	128
Onoto, Ven.	C10	84
Onoway, Alta., Can.	C3	98
Onseepkans, S. Afr.	G4	66
Onset, Ma., U.S.	C6	128
Onslow, Austl.	D3	68
Onslow, Ia., U.S.	B6	122
Onslow, co., N.C., U.S.	C5	140
Onslow Bay, b., N.C., U.S.	C5	140
Onsted, Mi., U.S.	F6	129
Ontario, Ca., U.S.	E5	112
Ontario, N.Y., U.S.	B3	139
Ontario, Oh., U.S.	B3	142
Ontario, Or., U.S.	C10	144
Ontario, Wi., U.S.	E3	156
Ontario, co., N.Y., U.S.	C3	139
Ontario, prov., Can.	C6	103
Ontario, Lake, l., N.A.	C11	106
Ontinyent (Onteniente), Spain	G11	16
Ontonagon, Mi., U.S.	m12	129
Ontonagon, co., Mi., U.S.	m12	129
Ontonagon Indian Reservation, Mi., U.S.	B1	129
Onverwacht, Sur.	B7	76
Ōnyang, S. Kor.	G15	32
Oodnadatta, Austl.	E7	68
Ookala, Hi., U.S.	C6	118
Ooldea, Austl.	F6	68
Oolitic, In., U.S.	G4	121
Oologah, Ok., U.S.	A6	143
Oologah Lake, res., Ok., U.S.	A6	143
Ooltewah, Tn., U.S.	D8	149
Oostburg, Wi., U.S.	E6	156
Oostelijk Flevoland, reg., Neth.	C8	12
Oostende (Ostende), Bel.	F2	12
Oosterend, Neth.	B6	12
Oosterhout, Neth.	E6	12
Oosterschelde, b., Neth.	E4	12
Oosterscheldedam, Neth.	E4	12
Oosterwolde, Neth.	C9	12
Oostflakkee, Neth.	E5	12
Oost-Vlaanderen, prov., Bel.	G4	12
Oostvleteren, Bel.	G2	12
Ootsa Lake, B.C., Can.	C4	99
Ootsa Lake, l., B.C., Can.	C4	99
Ootsi, Bots.	E7	66
Opal, Wy., U.S.	E2	157
Opala, Zaire	B4	58
Opalaca, Cordillera, mts., Hond.	C6	92
Opa-Locka, Fl., U.S.	s13	116
Oparino, U.S.S.R.	F7	22
Opatów, Pol.	E21	10
Opava, Czech.	F17	10
Opava, stm., Eur.	F17	10
Opdyke, Il., U.S.	E5	120
Opelika, Al., U.S.	C4	108
Opelousas, La., U.S.	D3	125
Opequon Creek, stm., W.V., U.S.	B6	155
Opheim, Mt., U.S.	B10	133
Opobo, Nig.	I13	64
Opočka, U.S.S.R.	E11	26
Opoczno, Pol.	D20	10
Opole (Oppeln), Pol.	E17	10
Opono, Lake, l., Nmb.	B2	66
Oporto see Porto, Port.	D3	16
Opotiki, N.Z.	B6	72
Opp, Al., U.S.	D3	108
Oppelo, Ar., U.S.	B3	111
Oppland, co., Nor.	K11	6
Opportunity, Wa., U.S.	B8	154
Opsa, U.S.S.R.	F9	26
Optima Reservoir, res., Ok., U.S.	e9	143
Opuwo, Nmb.	B1	66
Oquawka, Il., U.S.	C3	120
Oquossoc, Me., U.S.	D2	126
Ora, Italy	C6	18
Ora, In., U.S.	B4	121
Ora, Ms., U.S.	D4	131
Oracle, Az., U.S.	E5	110
Oradea, Rom.	B5	20
Oradell, N.J., U.S.	h8	137
Oradell Reservoir, res., N.J., U.S.	h9	137
Orai, India	H8	44
Oraibi, Az., U.S.	B5	110
Oraibi Wash, val., Az., U.S.	A5	110
Oral, S.D., U.S.	D2	148
Oran, Ia., U.S.	B5	122
Oran, Mo., U.S.	D8	132
Orange, Austl.	I8	70
Orange, Fr.	H11	14
Orange, Ca., U.S.	n13	112
Orange, Ct., U.S.	D3	114
Orange, In., U.S.	E7	121
Orange, Ma., U.S.	A3	128
Orange, N.J., U.S.	B4	137
Orange, Tx., U.S.	D6	150
Orange, Va., U.S.	B4	153
Orange, co., Ca., U.S.	F5	112
Orange, co., Fl., U.S.	D5	116
Orange, co., In., U.S.	G4	121
Orange, co., N.Y., U.S.	D6	139
Orange, co., N.C., U.S.	A3	140
Orange, co., Tx., U.S.	D6	150
Orange, co., Vt., U.S.	D3	152
Orange, co., Va., U.S.	B4	153
Orange (Oranje), stm., Afr.	G4	66
Orange, Cabo, c., Braz.	D9	74
Orange, Cabo, c., Braz.	C8	76
Orange Beach, Al., U.S.	E2	108
Orangeburg, S.C., U.S.	E6	147
Orangeburg, co., S.C., U.S.	E6	147
Orange City, Fl., U.S.	D5	116
Orange City, Ia., U.S.	B1	122
Orangedale, N.S., Can.	D8	101
Orange Grove, Ms., U.S.	E5	131
Orange Grove, Tx., U.S.	F4	150
Orange Lake, Fl., U.S.	C4	116
Orange Lake, l., Fl., U.S.	C4	116
Orange Park, Fl., U.S.	B5	116
Orangeville, Ont., Can.	D4	103
Orangeville, Il., U.S.	A4	120
Orangeville, Ut., U.S.	D4	151
Orange Walk, Belize	H15	90
Oranienburg, Ger.	C13	10
Oranjefontein, S. Afr.	D8	66
Oranjemund, Nmb.	G3	66
Oranjerivier, S. Afr.	G7	66
Oranjestad, Aruba	H9	94
Oran see Wahran, Alg.	A6	54
Or 'Aqiva, Isr.	C3	50
Orarak, Sud.	N7	60
Orăştie, Rom.	D7	20
Oravais (Oravainen), Fin.	J18	6
Orbe, Switz.	E6	13
Orbetello, Italy	G6	18
Orbost, Austl.	K8	70
Orcadas, sci., B.A.T.	B1	73
Orcas Island, i., Wa., U.S.	A3	154
Orcera, Spain	G9	16
Orchard, Co., U.S.	A6	113
Orchard, Ne., U.S.	B7	134
Orchard City, Co., U.S.	C3	113
Orchard Farm, Mo., U.S.	f13	132
Orchard Homes, Mt., U.S.	D2	133
Orchard Park, N.Y., U.S.	C2	139
Orchards, Wa., U.S.	D3	154
Orchard Valley, Wy., U.S.	E8	157
Orchies, Fr.	B10	14
Orchila, Isla, i., Ven.	B10	84
Orchon, stm., Mong.	B7	30
Orcotuna, Peru	D4	82
Orcutt, Ca., U.S.	E3	112
Ord, Ne., U.S.	C7	134
Ord, stm., Austl.	C5	68
Ord, Mount, mtn., Austl.	C5	68
Orderville, Ut., U.S.	F3	151
Ordoqui, Arg.	H8	80
Ordu, Tur.	G15	4
Ordway, Co., U.S.	C7	113
Ore, Nig.	H12	64
Oreana, Il., U.S.	D5	120
Oreana, Nv., U.S.	C3	135
Örebro, Swe.	L14	6
Orechovo-Zujevo, U.S.S.R.	F21	26
Orechovsk, U.S.S.R.	G13	26
Ore City, Tx., U.S.	C5	150
Oredež, U.S.S.R.	C13	26
Oregon, Il., U.S.	A4	120
Oregon, Mo., U.S.	B2	132
Oregon, Oh., U.S.	A2	142
Oregon, Wi., U.S.	F4	156
Oregon, co., Mo., U.S.	E6	132
Oregon, state, U.S.	C6	144
Oregon Caves National Monument, Or., U.S.	E2	144
Oregon City, Or., U.S.	B4	144
Oregon Inlet, b., N.C., U.S.	B7	140
Orellana, Peru	B4	82
Orel see Or'ol, U.S.S.R.	I19	26
Orem, Ut., U.S.	C4	151
Orenburg, U.S.S.R.	G9	22
Örencik, Tur.	J13	20
Orense, Arg.	J9	80
Orense, Spain	C4	16
Orestes, In., U.S.	D6	121
Orestes Pereyra, Mex.	D7	90
Orestiás, Grc.	H10	20
Orfanoú, Kólpos, b., Grc.	I7	20
Orford, N.H., U.S.	C2	136
Orford, Mont, mtn., Que., Can.	D5	104
Orfordville, N.H., U.S.	C2	136
Orfordville, Wi., U.S.	F4	156
Organ, N.M., U.S.	E3	138
Organ Cave, W.V., U.S.	D4	155
Organ Mountains, mts., N.M., U.S.	E3	138
Organ Pipe Cactus National Monument, Az., U.S.	E3	110
Orgejev, U.S.S.R.	B12	20
Orgelet, Fr.	F12	14
Orgtrud, U.S.S.R.	E23	26
Orgūn, Afg.	D3	44
Orhanlar, Tur.	J11	20
Orica, Hond.	C8	92
Orichuna, stm., Ven.	D8	84
Orick, Ca., U.S.	B1	112
Orient, Il., U.S.	F5	120
Orient, Ia., U.S.	C3	122
Orient, N.Y., U.S.	m16	139
Oriental, N.C., U.S.	B6	140
Oriental, Cordillera, mts., Col.	E6	84
Oriental, Cordillera, mts., Peru	C4	82
Oriente, Arg.	J8	80
Orillia, Ont., Can.	C5	103
Orinduik, Guy.	E12	84
Orinoco, stm., S.A.	C11	84
Orinoco, Delta del, Ven.	C12	84
Oriola (Orihuela), Spain	G11	16
Orion, Il., U.S.	B3	120
Oripää, Fin.	K18	6
Oriska, N.D., U.S.	C8	141
Oriskany, N.Y., U.S.	B5	139
Orissa, state, India	B7	46
Orissaare, U.S.S.R.	C6	26
Oristano, Italy	J3	18
Orituco, stm., Ven.	C9	84
Oriximiná, Braz.	D7	76
Orizaba, Mex.	H11	90
Orizaba, Pico de (Volcán Citlaltépetl), vol., Mex.	H11	90
Orizona, Braz.	D4	79
Orkney, S. Afr.	F8	66
Orkney, prov., Scot., U.K.	B10	8
Orkney Islands, is., Scot., U.K.	B10	8
Orland, Ca., U.S.	C2	112
Orland, In., U.S.	A7	121
Orland, Me., U.S.	D4	126
Orlândia, Braz.	F5	79
Orlando, Fl., U.S.	D5	116
Orland Park, Il., U.S.	k9	120
Orleães, Braz.	E14	80
Orléanais, hist. reg., Fr.	E8	14
Orléans, Fr.	E8	14
Orleans, Ca., U.S.	B2	112
Orleans, In., U.S.	G5	121
Orleans, In., U.S.	G5	121
Orleans, Ia., U.S.	A2	122
Orleans, Ma., U.S.	C7	128
Orleans, Ne., U.S.	D6	134
Orleans, Vt., U.S.	B4	152
Orleans, co., La., U.S.	E6	125
Orleans, co., N.Y., U.S.	B2	139
Orleans, co., Vt., U.S.	B4	152
Orléans, Île d', i., Que., Can.	C6	104
Orlinda, Tn., U.S.	A5	149
Orlová, Czech.	F18	10
Orman Dam, S.D., U.S.	C2	148
Ormāra, Pak.	I18	48
Ormiston, Sask., Can.	H3	105
Ormoc, Phil.	C7	38
Ormond Beach, Fl., U.S.	C5	116
Ormsby, Mn., U.S.	G4	130
Ormstown, Que., Can.	D3	104
Ornans, Fr.	E13	14
Orne, dept., Fr.	D7	14
Orne, stm., Fr.	D6	14
Örnsköldsvik, Swe.	J16	6
Oro, N. Kor.	C15	32
Orocué, Col.	E7	84
Orocuina, Hond.	D7	92
Orodara, Burkina	F7	64
Orofino, Id., U.S.	C2	119
Oro Grande, Ca., U.S.	E5	112
Or'ol, U.S.S.R.	I19	26
Oromocto, N.B., Can.	D3	101
Oromocto Lake, l., N.B., Can.	D2	101
Oron, Nig.	I14	64
Orono, Me., U.S.	D4	126
Oronoco, Mn., U.S.	F6	130
Oronogo, Mo., U.S.	D3	132
Oronoque, stm., Guy.	F14	84
Orosháza, Hung.	I20	10
Orosí, Volcán, vol., C.R.	G9	92
Oroville, Ca., U.S.	C3	112
Oroville, Wa., U.S.	A6	154
Oroville, Lake, res., Ca., U.S.	C3	112
Orr, Mn., U.S.	B6	130
Orrick, Mo., U.S.	B3	132
Orrington, Me., U.S.	D4	126
Orroroo, Austl.	I3	70
Orrs Island, Me., U.S.	E3	126
Orrville, Ont., Can.	B5	103
Orrville, Al., U.S.	C2	108
Orrville, Oh., U.S.	B4	142
Orša, U.S.S.R.	G13	26
Orsières, Switz.	F7	13
Orsk, U.S.S.R.	G9	22
Orta Nova, Italy	H10	18
Ortega, Col.	F5	84
Ortegal, Cabo, c., Spain	B4	16
Orteguaza, stm., Col.	G5	84
Orthez, Fr.	I6	14
Orthon, stm., Bol.	D8	82
Ortigueira, Braz.	C13	80
Orting, Wa., U.S.	B3	154
Ortisei, Italy	C6	18
Ortiz, Mex.	C4	90
Ortiz, Co., U.S.	D4	113
Ortiz, Ven.	C9	84
Ortles (Otler), mtn., Italy	E14	13
Ortona, Italy	G9	18
Ortonville, Mi., U.S.	F7	129
Ortonville, Mn., U.S.	E2	130
Orūmīyeh (Reẕā'īyeh), Iran	C8	48
Orūmīyeh, Daryācheh-ye (Lago Urmia), l., Iran	C8	48
Oruro, Bol.	G8	82
Oruro, dept., Bol.	H8	82
Orvieto, Italy	G7	18
Orwell, Oh., U.S.	A5	142
Orwell, Vt., U.S.	D2	152
Orwigsburg, Pa., U.S.	E9	145
Orxon, stm., China	B10	30
Or Yehuda, Isr.	D3	50
Orzinuovi, Italy	D4	18
Orzola, Spain	N27	17b
Orzysz, Pol.	B21	10
Oš, U.S.S.R.	I12	22
Osa, Península de, pen., C.R.	I11	92
Osage, Ia., U.S.	A5	122
Osage, Mn., U.S.	D3	130
Osage, Wy., U.S.	C8	157
Osage, co., Ks., U.S.	D8	123
Osage, co., Mo., U.S.	C6	132
Osage, co., Ok., U.S.	A5	143
Osage, stm., Mo., U.S.	C3	132
Osage Beach, Mo., U.S.	C5	132
Osage City, Ks., U.S.	D8	123
Osage Creek, stm., Ar., U.S.	A2	111
Ōsaka, Japan	M10	36
Ōsaka-wan, b., Japan	M10	36
Osakis, Mn., U.S.	E3	130
Osakis, Lake, l., Mn., U.S.	E3	130
Osan, S. Kor.	F15	32
Osawatomie, Ks., U.S.	D9	123
Osborn, Mo., U.S.	B3	132
Osborne, Ks., U.S.	C5	123
Osborne, co., Ks., U.S.	C5	123
Osburn, Id., U.S.	B3	119
Osceola, Ar., U.S.	B6	111
Osceola, In., U.S.	A5	121
Osceola, Ia., U.S.	C4	122
Osceola, Mo., U.S.	C4	132
Osceola, Ne., U.S.	C8	134
Osceola, Wi., U.S.	C1	156
Osceola, co., Fl., U.S.	E5	116
Osceola, co., Ia., U.S.	A2	122
Osceola, co., Mi., U.S.	E5	129
Osceola Mills, Pa., U.S.	E5	145
Oschatz, Ger.	D13	10
Oschersleben, Ger.	C11	10
Oscoda, Mi., U.S.	D7	129
Oscoda, co., Mi., U.S.	D6	129
Oscura Mountains, mts., N.M., U.S.	D3	138
Osgood, In., U.S.	F7	121
O'Shanassy, stm., Austl.	B3	70
Oshawa, Ont., Can.	D6	103
Oshigambo, Nmb.	A3	66
Ō-shima, i., Japan	M14	36
Ō-shima, i., Japan	F14	36a
Oshkosh, Ne., U.S.	C3	134
Oshkosh, Wi., U.S.	D5	156
Oshnovīyeh, Iran	C8	48
Oshogbo, Nig.	H12	64
Oshwe, Zaire	B3	58
Osi, Nig.	G12	64
Osich'ŏn-ni, N. Kor.	B16	32
Osijek, Yugo.	D2	20
Osimo, Italy	F8	18
Osinniki, U.S.S.R.	G9	24
Osipoviči, U.S.S.R.	H11	26
Osire, Nmb.	C3	66
Oskaloosa, Ia., U.S.	C5	122
Oskaloosa, Ks., U.S.	C8	123
Oskarshamn, Swe.	M15	6
Oskū, Iran	C9	48
Osler, Sask., Can.	E2	105
Oslo, Nor.	L12	6
Oslo, Mn., U.S.	B1	130
Osmānābād, India	C4	46
Osmaniye, Tur.	C4	48
Ošm'any, U.S.S.R.	G8	26
Osmond, Ne., U.S.	B8	134
Osmore, Río de, stm., Peru	G6	82
Osnabrock, N.D., U.S.	A7	141
Osnabrück, Ger.	C8	10
Osório, Braz.	B6	78
Osório Fonseca, Braz.	I13	84
Osorno, Chile	E2	78
Osoyoos, B.C., Can.	E8	99
Osoyoos Lake, l., Wa., U.S.	A6	154
Ospino, Ven.	C8	84
Osprey, Fl., U.S.	E4	116
Ossa, Mount, mtn., Austl.	M7	70
Ossabaw Island, i., Ga., U.S.	E5	117
Ossabaw Sound, strt., Ga., U.S.	E6	117
Osse, stm., Nig.	H12	64
Osseo, Mn., U.S.	m12	130
Osseo, Wi., U.S.	D2	156
Ossian, In., U.S.	C7	121
Ossian, Ia., U.S.	A6	122
Ossining, N.Y., U.S.	D7	139
Ossipee, N.H., U.S.	C4	136
Ossipee, stm., U.S.	C5	136
Ossipee Lake, l., N.H., U.S.	C4	136
Ossipee Mountains, mts., N.H., U.S.	C4	136
Ossora, U.S.S.R.	F24	24
Ošta, U.S.S.R.	K24	6
Ostaškov, U.S.S.R.	D16	26
Osteen, Fl., U.S.	D5	116
Ostende (Oostende), Bel.	F2	12
Osterburg, Ger.	C11	10
Östergötlands Län, co., Swe.	L14	6
Osterholz-Scharmbeck, Ger.	B8	10
Osterode, Ger.	D10	10
Östersund, Swe.	J14	6
Osterville, Ma., U.S.	C7	128
Osterwieck, Ger.	D10	10
Østfold, co., Nor.	L12	6
Ostfriesische Inseln, is., Ger.	B7	10
Ostfriesland, hist. reg., Ger.	B7	10
Ost'or, U.S.S.R.	G15	26
Ostrander, Mn., U.S.	G6	130
Ostrava, Czech.	F18	10
Ostróda, Pol.	B19	10
Ostrogožsk, U.S.S.R.	G5	22
Ostrołęka, Pol.	B21	10
Ostrošickij Gorodok, U.S.S.R.	G10	26
Ostrov, Czech.	E12	10
Ostrov, U.S.S.R.	D11	26
Ostrov, i., Czech.	H17	10
Ostrovno, U.S.S.R.	F12	26
Ostrovskoje, U.S.S.R.	D25	26
Ostrowiec Świętokrzyski, Pol.	E21	10
Ostrów Mazowiecka, Pol.	C21	10
Ostrów Wielkopolski, Pol.	D17	10
Ostrzeszów, Pol.	D17	10
Ostúa, stm., N.A.	C5	92
Ostuni, Italy	I12	18
Ōsumi-kaikyō, strt., Japan	Q5	36
Ōsumi-shotō, is., Japan	Q5	37b
Osuna, Spain	H6	16
Osvaldo Cruz, Braz.	F3	79
Osveja, U.S.S.R.	E11	26
Oswegatchie, stm., N.Y., U.S.	f9	139
Oswego, Il., U.S.	B5	120
Oswego, Ks., U.S.	E8	123
Oswego, N.Y., U.S.	B4	139
Oswego, co., N.Y., U.S.	B4	139
Oswego, stm., N.J., U.S.	D4	137
Oswego, stm., N.Y., U.S.	B4	139
Oświęcim, Pol.	E19	10
Osyka, Ms., U.S.	D3	131
Otaki, N.Z.	D5	72
Otanmäki, Fin.	I20	6
Otaru, Japan	D16	36a
Otava, Fin.	K20	6
Otava, stm., Czech.	F13	10
Otavalo, Ec.	G3	84
Otavi, Nmb.	B3	66
Oteen, N.C., U.S.	f10	140
Otego, N.Y., U.S.	C5	139
Otepää, U.S.S.R.	C9	26
Otero, co., Co., U.S.	D7	113
Otero, co., N.M., U.S.	E3	138
Oteros, stm., Mex.	D5	90
Othello, Wa., U.S.	C6	154
Óthiris, Óros, mts., Grc.	J6	20
Otho, Ia., U.S.	B3	122
Oti, stm., Afr.	G7	54
Otinapa, Mex.	E7	90
Otis, Co., U.S.	A8	113
Otis, In., U.S.	A4	121
Otis, Ks., U.S.	D4	123
Otisco, In., U.S.	G6	121
Otis Orchards, Wa., U.S.	g14	154
Otis Reservoir, res., Ma., U.S.	B1	128
Otisville, Mi., U.S.	E7	129
Otjimbingue, Nmb.	D3	66
Otjiwarongo, Nmb.	C3	66
Otley, Ia., U.S.	C4	122
Otočac, Yugo.	E10	18
Otoe, Ne., U.S.	D9	134
Otoe, co., Ne., U.S.	D9	134
Otoque, Isla, i., Pan.	I15	92
Otoro, stm., Hond.	C6	92
Otra, stm., Nor.	L10	6
Otradnyj, U.S.S.R.	G8	22
Otranto, Italy	I13	18
Otranto, Strait of, strt., Eur.	I2	20
Otsego, Mi., U.S.	F5	129
Otsego, co., Mi., U.S.	C6	129
Otsego, co., N.Y., U.S.	C5	139
Otsego Lake, l., N.Y., U.S.	C6	139
Ōtsu, Japan	L10	36
Otta, Nor.	K11	6
Ottauquechee, stm., Vt., U.S.	D4	152
Ottawa, Ont., Can.	B9	103
Ottawa, Il., U.S.	B5	120
Ottawa, Ks., U.S.	D8	123
Ottawa, Oh., U.S.	A1	142
Ottawa, W.V., U.S.	n12	155
Ottawa, co., Ks., U.S.	C6	123
Ottawa, co., Mi., U.S.	F4	129
Ottawa, co., Oh., U.S.	A2	142
Ottawa, co., Ok., U.S.	A7	143
Ottawa, stm., Can.	G17	96
Ottawa, stm., Can.	B11	106
Ottawa, stm., Oh., U.S.	e6	142
Ottawa Hills, Oh., U.S.	e6	142
Ottawa Islands, is., N.W. Ter., Can.	E16	96
Otter, stm., Alta., Can.	A2	98
Otterbein, In., U.S.	D3	121
Otter Brook, stm., N.H., U.S.	E2	136
Otter Brook Lake, res., N.H., U.S.	E2	136
Otterburne, Man., Can.	E3	100
Otter Creek, Me., U.S.	D4	126
Otter Creek, stm., Ut., U.S.	E4	151
Otter Creek, stm., Vt., U.S.	C2	152
Otter Creek Reservoir, res., Ut., U.S.	E4	151
Otter Islands, is., S.C., U.S.	m11	147
Otter Lake, Mi., U.S.	E7	129
Ottertail, Mn., U.S.	D3	130
Otter Tail, co., Mn., U.S.	D3	130
Otter Tail, stm., Mn., U.S.	D2	130
Otter Tail Lake, l., Mn., U.S.	D3	130
Otterville, Ont., Can.	E4	103
Otterville, Mo., U.S.	C4	132
Otthon, Sask., Can.	F4	105
Otto, Wy., U.S.	B4	157
Ottoville, Oh., U.S.	B1	142
Ottumwa, Ia., U.S.	C5	122
Ottweiler, Ger.	F7	10
Otu, Nig.	G11	64
Otumpa, Arg.	D7	80
Otuquis, Bañados de, sw., Bol.	H12	82
Oturkpo, Nig.	H14	64
Otuzco, Peru	B2	82
Otway, Cape, c., Austl.	L5	70
Otwell, Ar., U.S.	B5	111
Otwell, In., U.S.	H3	121
Otwock, Pol.	C21	10
Otyn'a, U.S.S.R.	A8	20
Ötztaler Alpen, mts., Eur.	C5	18
Ou, stm., China	J2	34
Ou, stm., Laos	D7	40
Ouachita, co., Ar., U.S.	D3	111
Ouachita, co., La., U.S.	B3	125
Ouachita, Lake, res., Ar., U.S.	C2	111
Ouachita Mountains, mts., U.S.	E8	106
Ouadâne, Maur.	J5	62
Ouadda, Cen. Afr. Rep.	M2	60
Ouagadougou, Burkina	E9	64
Ouahigouya, Burkina	F6	54
Ouahigouya, Burkina	E8	64
Ouaka, stm., Cen. Afr. Rep.	G5	56
Oualâta, Maur.	C6	64
Oualé, stm., Afr.	F10	64
Oualidia, Mor.	D6	62
Ouallam, Niger	D11	64
Ouallene, Alg.	H11	62
Ouanda Djallé, Cen. Afr. Rep.	M2	60
Ouaninou, I.C.	G6	64
Ouan Taredert, Alg.	G15	62
Ouarane, reg., Maur.	A4	64
Ouarkziz, Jbel, mts., Afr.	F6	62
Ouarzazate, Mor.	E7	62
Ouassoulou, stm., Afr.	F5	64
Ouatcha, Niger	E14	64
Oubangui (Ubangi), stm., Afr.	H8	52
Oud-Beijerland, Neth.	E5	12
Ouddorp, Neth.	F4	12
Oudenaarde (Audenarde), Bel.	G4	12
Oude Pekela, Neth.	B10	12
Oudtshoorn, S. Afr.	I6	66
Oudyoumoudi, Burkina	D9	64
Oued Cheham, Alg.	M2	18
Oued Meliz, Tun.	M3	18
Oued Tlelat, Alg.	J11	16
Oued Zarga, Tun.	M4	18
Oued-Zem, Mor.	D7	62
Ouémé, stm., Benin	H11	64
Ouenza, Alg.	N3	18
Ouessant, Île d' (Ushant), i., Fr.	D1	14
Ouesso, Congo	A3	58
Ouezzane, Mor.	C8	62
Ouham, stm., Afr.	G4	56
Ouidah, Benin	H11	64
Ouistreham, Fr.	C6	14
Oujda, Mor.	C10	62
Oulainen, Fin.	I19	6
Oulu, Fin.	I19	6
Oulujärvi, l., Fin.	I20	6
Oulujoki, stm., Fin.	I20	6
Oulun lääni, prov., Fin.	I20	6
Oum-Chalouba, Chad	E5	56
Oum El Bouagui, Alg.	C14	62
Oum er Rbia, Oued, stm., Mor.	D7	62
Ounara, Mor.	E6	62
Ounianga Kébir, Chad	E5	56
Ouray, Co., U.S.	C3	113
Ouray, co., Co., U.S.	C3	113
Ouray, Mount, mtn., Co., U.S.	C4	113
Ourinhos, Braz.	G4	79
Ouro, Paraná do, stm., Braz.	C6	82
Ouro Fino, Braz.	G5	79
Ouro Prêto, Braz.	F7	79
Ouro Prêto, stm., Braz.	D9	82
Oursi, Burkina	D9	64
Ourthe, stm., Bel.	H8	12
Ōu-sammyaku, mts., Japan	I15	36
Ouse, stm., Eng., U.K.	H12	8
Outagamie, co., Wi., U.S.	D5	156
Outardes Quatre, Réservoir, res., Que., Can.	h13	104
Outer Hebrides, is., Scot., U.K.	D6	8
Outer Island, i., Wi., U.S.	A3	156
Outer Santa Barbara Passage, strt., Ca., U.S.	F4	112
Outjo, Nmb.	C3	66
Outlook, Sask., Can.	F2	105
Outlook, Mt., U.S.	B12	133
Outlook, Wa., U.S.	C5	154
Outpost Mountain, mtn., Ak., U.S.	B9	109
Outremont, Que., Can.	p19	104
Ouvidor, Braz.	E5	79
Ouyen, Austl.	J5	70
Ouzinkie, Ak., U.S.	D9	109
Ouzouer-le-Marché, Fr.	E8	14
Ouzzal, Oued i-n-, val., Alg.	J12	62
Ovalle, Chile	F3	80
Ovamboland, hist. reg., Nmb.	A3	66
Ovana, Cerro, mtn., Ven.	E9	84
Ovando, Mt., U.S.	C3	133
Ovejas, Col.	C5	84
Overbrook, Ks., U.S.	D8	123
Overflakkee, i., Neth.	E5	12
Overgaard, Az., U.S.	C5	110
Overhalla, Nor.	I12	6
Overijssel, prov., Neth.	D9	12
Overland, Mo., U.S.	f13	132
Overland Park, Ks., U.S.	m16	123
Overlea, Md., U.S.	B4	127
Overpelt, Bel.	F7	12
Overton, Ne., U.S.	D6	134
Overton, Nv., U.S.	G7	135
Overton, Tx., U.S.	C5	150
Overton, co., Tn., U.S.	C8	149
Övertorneå, Swe.	H18	6
Ovett, Ms., U.S.	D4	131
Ovid, Co., U.S.	A8	113
Ovid, Id., U.S.	G7	119
Ovid, Mi., U.S.	E6	129
Oviedo, Spain	B6	16
Ovino, U.S.S.R.	B16	26
Ovstug, U.S.S.R.	H16	26
Owando, Congo	B3	58
Owaneco, Il., U.S.	D4	120
Owasco Lake, l., N.Y., U.S.	C4	139
Owasso, Ok., U.S.	A6	143
Owatonna, Mn., U.S.	F5	130
Owbeh, Afg.	D17	48
Owego, N.Y., U.S.	C4	139
Owen, Wi., U.S.	D3	156
Owen, co., In., U.S.	F4	121
Owen, co., Ky., U.S.	B5	124
Owen, Lake, l., Wi., U.S.	B2	156
Owen, Mount, mtn., Co., U.S.	C3	113
Owens, stm., Ca., U.S.	D4	112
Owensboro, Ky., U.S.	C2	124
Owensburg, In., U.S.	G4	121
Owens Creek, stm., Md., U.S.	A3	127
Owens Cross Roads, Al., U.S.	A3	108
Owens Lake, l., Ca., U.S.	D5	112
Owen Sound, Ont., Can.	C4	103
Owen Sound, b., Ont., Can.	C4	103
Owen Stanley Range, mts., Pap. N. Gui.	m16	68a
Owensville, Ar., U.S.	C3	111
Owensville, In., U.S.	H2	121
Owensville, Mo., U.S.	C6	132
Owensville, Oh., U.S.	C1	142
Owenton, Ky., U.S.	B5	124
Owerri, Nig.	I13	64
Owings, Md., U.S.	C4	127
Owings Mills, Md., U.S.	B4	127
Owingsville, Ky., U.S.	B6	124
Owl Creek, stm., Wy., U.S.	C4	157
Owl Creek Mountains, mts., Wy., U.S.	C4	157
Owls Head, Me., U.S.	D3	126
Owo, Nig.	H12	64
Owosso, Mi., U.S.	E6	129
Owsley, co., Ky., U.S.	C6	124
Owyhee, Nv., U.S.	B5	135
Owyhee, co., Id., U.S.	G2	119
Owyhee, stm., U.S.	E9	144
Owyhee, Lake, res., Or., U.S.	D9	144
Owyhee, North Fork, stm., U.S.	E9	144
Owyhee, South Fork, stm., U.S.	G2	119
Owyhee Dam, Or., U.S.	D9	144
Owyhee Mountains, mts., U.S.	G2	119
Oxapampa, Peru	D4	82
Oxbow, Sask., Can.	H4	105
Oxbow Dam, U.S.	E2	119
Oxford, N.S., Can.	D6	101
Oxford, Eng., U.K.	J12	8
Oxford, Al., U.S.	B4	108
Oxford, Ar., U.S.	A4	111
Oxford, Ct., U.S.	D3	114
Oxford, Fl., U.S.	D4	116
Oxford, Ga., U.S.	C3	117
Oxford, In., U.S.	C3	121
Oxford, Ia., U.S.	C6	122
Oxford, Ks., U.S.	E6	123
Oxford, Me., U.S.	D2	126
Oxford, Md., U.S.	C5	127
Oxford, Ma., U.S.	B4	128
Oxford, Mi., U.S.	F7	129
Oxford, Ms., U.S.	A4	131
Oxford, Ne., U.S.	D6	134

Name	Map Ref.	Page
Oxford, N.J., U.S.	B3	137
Oxford, N.Y., U.S.	C5	139
Oxford, N.C., U.S.	A4	140
Oxford, Oh., U.S.	C1	142
Oxford, Pa., U.S.	G10	145
Oxford, Wi., U.S.	E4	156
Oxford, co., Me., U.S.	D2	126
Oxford Junction, N.S., Can.	D6	101
Oxford Junction, Ia., U.S.	C7	122
Oxford Lake, l., Man., Can.	B4	100
Oxford Peak, mtn., Id., U.S.	G6	119
Oxfordshire, co., Eng., U.K.	J12	8
Oxkutzcab, Mex.	G15	90
Oxley, Austl.	J6	70
Oxly, Mo., U.S.	E7	132
Oxnard, Ca., U.S.	E4	112
Oxon Hill, Md., U.S.	f9	127
Oyama, B.C., Can.	D8	99
Oyama, Japan	K14	36
Oyem, Gabon	A2	58
Oyen, Alta., Can.	D5	98
Oyo, Nig.	H11	64
Oyón, Peru	D3	82
Oyonnax, Fr.	F12	14
Oyotún, Peru	B2	82
Oyster Bay, N.Y., U.S.	E7	139
Oyster Creek, Tx., U.S.	r14	150
Oyster Keys, is., Fl., U.S.	G6	116
Ozamiz, Phil.	D7	38
Ozariči, U.S.S.R.	I12	26
Ozark, Al., U.S.	D4	108
Ozark, Ar., U.S.	B2	111
Ozark, Mo., U.S.	D4	132
Ozark, co., Mo., U.S.	E5	132
Ozark Escarpment, clf, U.S.	B4	111
Ozark Plateau, plat., U.S.	D8	106
Ozark Reservoir, res., Ar., U.S.	B1	111
Ozarks, Lake of the, res., Mo., U.S.	C5	132
Ozaukee, co., Wi., U.S.	E6	156
Ozawkie, Ks., U.S.	k15	123
Ózd, Hung.	G20	10
Ožerelje, U.S.S.R.	G21	26
Ozernovskij, U.S.S.R.	G23	24
Ozery, U.S.S.R.	G21	26
Ozette Lake, l., Wa., U.S.	A1	154
Ozieri, Italy	I4	18
Ozimek, Pol.	E18	10
Ozona, Fl., U.S.	o10	116
Ozona, Ms., U.S.	E4	131
Ozona, Tx., U.S.	D2	150
Ozone, Ar., U.S.	B2	111
Ozorków, Pol.	D19	10
Oz'ornyj, U.S.S.R.	D23	26
Oz'ory, U.S.S.R.	H7	26
Ozubulu, Nig.	I13	64
Ozuluama, Mex.	G11	90
P		
Paarl, S. Afr.	I4	66
Paauhau, Hi., U.S.	C6	118
Paauilo, Hi., U.S.	C6	118
Pabellones, Ensenada, b., Mex.	E6	90
Pabianice, Pol.	D19	10
Pablo, Mt., U.S.	C2	133
Pābna, Bngl.	H13	44
Pabradė, U.S.S.R.	G8	26
Pacaás Novos, stm., Braz.	D9	82
Pacaás Novos, Serra dos, mts., Braz.	D10	82
Pacaembu, Braz.	F3	79
Pacahuaras, stm., Bol.	D8	82
Pacaltsdorp, S. Afr.	J6	66
Pacarán, Peru	E3	82
Pacaraos, Peru	D3	82
Pacasmayo, Peru	B2	82
Paccha, stm., Peru	C3	82
Pace, Fl., U.S.	u14	116
Pace, Ms., U.S.	B3	131
Pachacamac, Peru	E3	82
Pachacamac, hist., Peru	E3	82
Pachaug Pond, l., Ct., U.S.	C8	114
Pachino, Italy	M10	18
Pachitea, stm., Peru	C4	82
Pachiza, Peru	B3	82
Pachmarhi, India	I8	44
Pacho, Col.	E5	84
Pachuca [de Soto], Mex.	G10	90
Pachuta, Ms., U.S.	C5	131
Pacific, Mo., U.S.	C7	132
Pacific, Wa., U.S.	f11	154
Pacific, co., Wa., U.S.	C2	154
Pacifica, Ca., U.S.	h8	112
Pacific Beach, Wa., U.S.	B1	154
Pacific City, Or., U.S.	B3	144
Pacific Creek, stm., Wy., U.S.	D3	157
Pacific Grove, Ca., U.S.	D3	112
Pacific Junction, Ia., U.S.	C2	122
Pacific Ocean	J24	158
Pacific Palisades, Hi., U.S.	g10	118
Pacific Ranges, mts., B.C., Can.	D4	99
Pacific Rim National Park, B.C., Can.	E5	99
Packard Mountain, hill, Ma., U.S.	B3	128
Pack Monadnock Mountain, mtn., N.H., U.S.	E3	136
Packwaukee, Wi., U.S.	E4	156
Packwood, Ia., U.S.	C5	122
Packwood, Wa., U.S.	C4	154
Pacllón, Peru	D3	82
Pacolet, S.C., U.S.	B4	147
Pacolet, stm., S.C., U.S.	A4	147
Pacolet Mills, S.C., U.S.	B4	147
Pácora, Col.	E5	84
Pacora, Pan.	C3	84
Pacquet, Newf., Can.	D4	102
Pactola Reservoir, res., S.D., U.S.	C2	148
Pacuare, stm., C.R.	G11	92
Pacuí, stm., Braz.	D6	79
Pacuneiro, stm., Braz.	B2	79
Padamo, stm., Ven.	F10	84
Padang, Indon.	O6	40
Padang Endau, Malay.	M7	40
Padangpanjang, Indon.	O6	40
Padangsidempuan, Indon.	N5	40
Padauiri, stm., Braz.	G10	84
Padcaya, Bol.	I9	82
Paddle Prairie, Alta., Can.	f7	98
Paddock Lake, Wi., U.S.	n11	156
Paddockwood, Sask., Can.	D3	105
Paddy Knob, mtn., U.S.	C5	155
Paden, Ok., U.S.	B5	143
Paden City, W.V., U.S.	B4	155
Paderborn, Ger.	D8	10
Padilla, Bol.	H9	82
Padova, Italy	D6	18
Padre Bernardo, Braz.	C4	79
Padre Island, i., Tx., U.S.	F4	150
Padre Island National Seashore, Tx., U.S.	F4	150
Padre Paraíso, Braz.	D8	79
Padroni, Co., U.S.	A7	113
Padua see Padova, Italy	D6	18
Paduari, stm., Braz.	I12	84
Paducah, Ky., U.S.	e9	124
Paducah, Tx., U.S.	B2	150
Paektu-san, mtn., Asia	A16	32
Páez, stm., Col.	F4	84
Pafúri, Moz.	D10	66
Pag, Yugo.	E10	18
Pag, Otok, i., Yugo.	E10	18
Pagadian, Phil.	D7	38
Pagai Selatan, Pulau, i., Indon.	F3	38
Pagai Utara, Pulau, i., Indon.	F3	38
Pagan, Burma	D3	40
Pagancillo, Arg.	E4	80
Pagasitikós Kólpos, b., Grc.	J6	20
Page, Az., U.S.	A4	110
Page, Ne., U.S.	B7	134
Page, N.D., U.S.	B8	141
Page, W.V., U.S.	C3	155
Page, co., Ia., U.S.	D2	122
Page, co., Va., U.S.	B4	153
Pagėgiai, U.S.S.R.	F4	26
Pageland, S.C., U.S.	B7	147
Pagoda Peak, mtn., Co., U.S.	A3	113
Pagoda Point, c., Burma	G3	40
Pagon, Bukit, mtn., Asia	E6	38
Pagosa Springs, Co., U.S.	D3	113
Pagouda, Togo	G10	64
Paguate, N.M., U.S.	B2	138
Pahala, Hi., U.S.	D6	118
Pahang, stm., Malay.	M7	40
Páhara, Laguna, b., Nic.	C11	92
Pahoa, Hi., U.S.	D7	118
Pahokee, Fl., U.S.	F6	116
Pahrump, Nv., U.S.	G6	135
Pahute Mesa, mtn., Nv., U.S.	F5	135
Pai, stm., Asia	E5	40
Paia, Hi., U.S.	C5	118
Paico, Peru	F5	82
Paide, U.S.S.R.	C8	26
Paignton, Eng., U.K.	K10	8
Paiguano, Chile	F3	80
Paiján, Peru	B2	82
Päijänne, l., Fin.	K19	6
Paila, stm., Bol.	G10	82
Pailin, Camb.	H7	40
Pailitas, Col.	C6	84
Pailolo Channel, strt., Hi., U.S.	B5	118
Paimpol, Fr.	D3	14
Paincourt, Ont., Can.	E2	103
Paincourtville, La., U.S.	k9	125
Painesdale, Mi., U.S.	A2	129
Painesville, Oh., U.S.	A4	142
Pains, Braz.	F6	79
Paint, stm., Mi., U.S.	B2	129
Paint Creek, stm., Oh., U.S.	C2	142
Paint Creek, stm., W.V., U.S.	m13	155
Paint Creek, North Fork, stm., Oh., U.S.	C2	142
Paint Creek Lake, res., Oh., U.S.	C2	142
Painted Desert, des., Az., U.S.	B4	110
Painted Post, N.Y., U.S.	C3	139
Painted Rock Reservoir, res., Az., U.S.	D3	110
Painter, Va., U.S.	C7	153
Paint Lick, Ky., U.S.	C5	124
Paint Mountain, mtn., W.V., U.S.	n13	155
Paint Rock, Al., U.S.	A3	108
Paintsville, Ky., U.S.	C7	124
Paisley, Ont., Can.	C3	103
Paisley, Scot., U.K.	F9	8
Paisley, Fl., U.S.	D5	116
Paisley, Or., U.S.	E6	144
Paita, Peru	A1	82
Paita, Bahía de, b., Peru	A1	82
Paizhou, China	E2	34
Pajala, Swe.	H18	6
Paján, Ec.	H2	84
Pájara, Spain	O26	17b
Pajjer, gora, mtn., U.S.S.R.	D10	22
Pakaraima Mountains, mts., S.A.	D8	74
Pakaraima Mountains, mts., S.A.	E12	84
Pakaraima Mountains, mts., S.A.	H7	160
Pak Ban, Laos	D7	40
Pakch'ŏn, N. Kor.	D13	32
Pakeng, Sud.	N6	60
Pakenham, Ont., Can.	B8	103
Pakhoi see Beihai, China	G8	30
Pakistan (Pākistān), ctry., Asia	C9	42
Pakokku, Burma	D3	40
Pakouabo, I.C.	H7	64
Pakowki Lake, l., Alta., Can.	E5	98
Pākpattan, Pak.	E5	44
Pak Phanang, Thai.	J6	40
Pak Phraek, Thai.	J6	40
Pakrac, Yugo.	D12	18
Pakruojis, U.S.S.R.	F6	26
Paks, Hung.	I18	10
P'akupur, stm., U.S.S.R.	E7	24
Pakxé, Laos	G8	40
Pala, Chad	G3	56
Palacca Point, c., Bah.	D8	94
Palacios, Tx., U.S.	E4	150
Palacios, stm., Bol.	G10	82
Palagonia, Italy	L9	18
Palagruža, Otoci, is., Yugo.	G11	18
Pālakodu, India	D6	46
Palamós, Spain	D15	16
Palana, U.S.S.R.	F23	24
Palanga, U.S.S.R.	F4	26
Palangkaraya, Indon.	F5	38
Palani, India	G4	46
Pālanpur, India	H5	44
Palaoa Point, c., Hi., U.S.	C4	118
Palapye, Bots.	D8	66
Palatine, Il., U.S.	A5	120
Palatka, U.S.S.R.	E22	24
Palatka, Fl., U.S.	C5	116
Palau (Belau), dep., T.T.P.I.	D9	38
Palauk, Burma	H5	40
Palawan, i., Phil.	D6	38
Pālayankottai, India	H4	46
Palca, Bol.	G8	82
Palca, Peru	D4	82
Palcamayo, Peru	D4	82
Pal'co, U.S.S.R.	H17	26
Palco, Ks., U.S.	C4	123
Paldiski, U.S.S.R.	B7	26
Palech, U.S.S.R.	E24	26
Palembang, Indon.	F3	38
Palena, Italy	H9	18
Palencia, Spain	C7	16
Palenque, Mex.	I14	90
Palenque, hist., Mex.	I13	90
Palenque, Punta, c., Dom. Rep.	E9	94
Palenville, N.Y., U.S.	C6	139
Palermo, Col.	F5	84
Palermo, Italy	K8	18
Palermo, N.J., U.S.	E3	137
Palermo, N.D., U.S.	A3	141
Palermo, Ur.	G11	80
Palestina, Braz.	F4	79
Palestine, Ar., U.S.	C5	111
Palestine, Il., U.S.	D6	120
Palestine, Tx., U.S.	D5	150
Palestine, hist. reg., Asia	D4	50
Palestine, Lake, res., Tx., U.S.	C5	150
Palestrina, Italy	H7	18
Paletwa, Burma	D2	40
Pālghāt, India	G4	46
Pāli, India	H5	44
Palikea, mtn., Hi., U.S.	g9	118
Palín, Guat.	C4	92
Palisade, Co., U.S.	B2	113
Palisade, Ne., U.S.	D4	134
Palisades Park, N.J., U.S.	h8	137
Palisades Reservoir, res., U.S.	F7	119
Paliseul, Bel.	I7	12
Pālitāna, India	B1	46
Palivere, U.S.S.R.	C6	26
Palizada, Mex.	H13	90
Palk Bay, b., Asia	H5	46
Palk Strait, strt., Asia	H5	46
Palla Bianca (Weisskugel), mtn., Eur.	E14	13
Pallasca, Peru	C2	82
Palling, B.C., Can.	B5	99
Palliser, Cape, c., N.Z.	D5	72
Palma, Braz.	F7	79
Palma, Moz.	D8	58
P'al'ma, U.S.S.R.	J24	6
Palma, stm., Braz.	B5	79
Palma del Río, Spain	H6	16
Palma [de Mallorca], Spain	F14	16
Palma di Montechiaro, Italy	L8	18
Palmar, stm., Ven.	B6	84
Palmar Camp, Belize	I15	90
Palmar de los Sepúlveda, Mex.	E6	90
Palmar de Varela, Col.	B5	84
Palmares, Braz.	E11	76
Palmares, C.R.	G10	92
Palmares, C.R.	H11	92
Palmares do Sul, Braz.	F13	80
Palmarito, Ven.	D7	84
Palmar Sur, C.R.	I11	92
Palmas, Braz.	D12	80
Palmas Bellas, Pan.	C2	84
Palmas de Monte Alto, Braz.	C7	79
Palma Soriano, Cuba	D6	94
Palm Bay, Fl., U.S.	D6	116
Palm Beach, Fl., U.S.	F6	116
Palm Beach, co., Fl., U.S.	F6	116
Palm Beach Gardens, Fl., U.S.	F6	116
Palmdale, Ca., U.S.	E4	112
Palm Desert, Ca., U.S.	F5	112
Palmeira, Braz.	C13	80
Palmeira, C.V.	k17	64a
Palmeira das Missões, Braz.	D12	80
Palmeira d'Oeste, Braz.	F3	79
Palmeira dos Índios, Braz.	E11	76
Palmeiras, Braz.	B8	79
Palmeiras, stm., Braz.	C3	79
Palmelo, Braz.	D4	79
Palmer, Sask., Can.	H2	105
Palmer, Ak., U.S.	C10	109
Palmer, Il., U.S.	D4	120
Palmer, Ia., U.S.	B3	122
Palmer, Ks., U.S.	C6	123
Palmer, Ma., U.S.	B3	128
Palmer, Mi., U.S.	B3	129
Palmer, Ms., U.S.	D4	131
Palmer, Ne., U.S.	C7	134
Palmer, Tn., U.S.	D8	149
Palmer, Tx., U.S.	n10	150
Palmer, Wa., U.S.	f12	154
Palmer, sci., B.A.T.	B12	73
Palmer Lake, Co., U.S.	B6	113
Palmer Land, reg., Ant.	C12	73
Palmerston, Ont., Can.	D4	103
Palmerston, N.Z.	F3	72
Palmerston, Cape, c., Austl.	C8	70
Palmerston North, N.Z.	D5	72
Palmerton, Pa., U.S.	E10	145
Palmetto, Fl., U.S.	E4	116
Palmetto, Ga., U.S.	C2	117
Palm Harbor, Fl., U.S.	o10	116
Palmi, Italy	K10	18
Palminópolis, Braz.	D3	79
Palmira, Arg.	G4	80
Palmira, Col.	F4	84
Palmira, Cuba	C4	94
Palmira, Ec.	I3	84
Palmitas, Ur.	G10	80
Palmitos, Braz.	D12	80
Palms, Isle of, i., S.C., U.S.	F8	147
Palm Springs, Ca., U.S.	F5	112
Palm Springs, Fl., U.S.	F6	116
Palm Valley, Fl., U.S.	m9	116
Palmyra, Il., U.S.	D4	120
Palmyra, In., U.S.	H5	121
Palmyra, Mo., U.S.	B6	132
Palmyra, Ne., U.S.	D9	134
Palmyra, N.J., U.S.	C2	137
Palmyra, N.Y., U.S.	B3	139
Palmyra, Pa., U.S.	F8	145
Palmyra, Va., U.S.	C4	153
Palmyra, Wi., U.S.	F5	156
Palmyra, hist., Syria	D5	48
Palmyra Atoll, atoll, Oc.	H23	158
Palmyra see Tudmur, Syria	D5	48
Palo, Ia., U.S.	B6	122
Palo Alto, Ca., U.S.	D2	112
Palo Alto, co., Ia., U.S.	A3	122
Palo Duro Canyon, val., Tx., U.S.	B2	150
Paloich, Sud.	L7	60
Palomar Mountain, mtn., Ca., U.S.	F5	112
Palomas Mountains, mts., Az., U.S.	D2	110
Palomas Viejo, Mex.	B6	90
Palo Negro, Ven.	B9	84
Palo Pinto, Tx., U.S.	C3	150
Palo Pinto, co., Tx., U.S.	C3	150
Palopo, Indon.	F7	38
Palora, stm., Ec.	H3	84
Palos, Cabo de, c., Spain	H11	16
Palo Santo, Arg.	C9	80
Palos de la Frontera, Spain	H5	16
Palos see Palos de la Frontera, Spain	H5	16
Palos Park, Il., U.S.	k9	120
Palos Verdes Estates, Ca., U.S.	n12	112
Palourde, Lake, l., La., U.S.	k9	125
Palouse, Wa., U.S.	C8	154
Palouse, stm., Wa., U.S.	C7	154
Palo Verde, Az., U.S.	D3	110
Palo Verde, Ca., U.S.	F6	112
Palo Verde, Parque Nacional, C.R.	G9	92
Palpa, Peru	F4	82
Palpalá, Arg.	C6	80
Palu, Indon.	F6	38
Palwal, India	F7	44
Pama, Burkina	F10	64
Pāmban Island, i., India	H5	46
Pambeguwa, Nig.	F14	64
Pambrun, Sask., Can.	H2	105
Pamekasan, Indon.	J16	39a
Pamiers, Fr.	I8	14
Pamir, mts., Asia	B5	44
Pamlico, co., N.C., U.S.	B6	140
Pamlico, stm., N.C., U.S.	B6	140
Pamlico Sound, strt., N.C., U.S.	B6	140
Pampa, Tx., U.S.	B2	150
Pampã, stm., Braz.	D8	79
Pampa, reg., Arg.	I6	80
Pampa Almirón, Arg.	D9	80
Pampacolca, Peru	F5	82
Pampa del Chañar, Arg.	F4	80
Pampa del Indio, Arg.	D9	80
Pampa del Infierno, Arg.	D8	80
Pampa de los Guanacos, Arg.	D8	80
Pampa Grande, Bol.	H9	82
Pampas, Peru	E4	82
Pampas, stm., Peru	E5	82
Pamplico, S.C., U.S.	D8	147
Pamplin, Va., U.S.	C4	153
Pamplona, Col.	D6	84
Pamplona, Spain	C10	16
Pampoenpoort, S. Afr.	H6	66
Pamunkey, stm., Va., U.S.	C5	153
Pana, Il., U.S.	D4	120
Panabá, Mex.	G15	90
Panaca, Nv., U.S.	F7	135
Panacachi, Bol.	H8	82
Panacea, Fl., U.S.	B2	116
Panache, Lake, l., Ont., Can.	A3	103
Panaji (Panjim), India	E2	46
Panamá, Braz.	E4	79
Panamá, Pan.	C3	84
Panama, Il., U.S.	D4	120
Panama, Ia., U.S.	C2	122
Panama, Ne., U.S.	D9	134
Panama, Ok., U.S.	B7	143
Panamá, prov., Pan.	I15	92
Panama (Panamá), ctry., N.A.	G8	88
Panamá, Bahía de, b., Pan.	C3	84
Panamá, Canal de, Pan.	H15	92
Panamá, Golfo de, b., Pan.	C3	84
Panamá, Istmo de, Pan.	C2	84
Panama City, Fl., U.S.	u16	116
Panama City Beach, Fl., U.S.	u16	116
Panamá Vieja, hist., Pan.	H15	92
Panambi, Braz.	E12	80
Panamint Range, mts., Ca., U.S.	D5	112
Panao, Peru	C3	82
Pancake Range, mts., Nv., U.S.	E6	135
Pančevo, Yugo.	E4	20
Pandamatenga, Bots.	B7	66
Pan de Azúcar, Ur.	H11	80
Pandėlys, U.S.S.R.	E8	26
Pandharpur, India	D3	46
Pāndhurna, India	B5	46
Pando, Ur.	H11	80
Pando, dept., Bol.	D8	82
Pandora, Oh., U.S.	B2	142
P'andž (Panj), stm., Asia	A4	44
Panevėžys, U.S.S.R.	F7	26
Panfang, China	H4	34
Panfilov, U.S.S.R.	I14	22
Pangala, Congo	B2	58
Pangalanes, Canal des, Madag.	Q23	67b
Pangani, Tan.	C7	58
Pangburn, Ar., U.S.	B4	111
Pangfou see Bengbu, China	E10	30
Pangi, Zaire	B5	58
Pangkalanbuun, Indon.	F5	38
Pangkalpinang, Indon.	F4	38
Pangman, Sask., Can.	H3	105
Pangnirtung, N.W. Ter., Can.	C19	96
Pangong Tso, l., Asia	D8	44
Panguitch, Ut., U.S.	F3	151
Panhandle, Tx., U.S.	B2	150
Paniau, mtn., Hi., U.S.	B1	118
Panino, U.S.S.R.	E17	26
Pānīpat, India	F7	44
Panj (P'andž), stm., Asia	B4	44
Panjāb, Afg.	C2	44
Panjgūr, Pak.	H18	48
Panjim see Panaji, India	E2	46
Pankeyville, Il., U.S.	F5	120
Pankshin, Nig.	G14	64
Panlong (Lo), stm., Asia	C8	40
P'anmunjŏm, N. Kor.	F14	32
Panna, India	H9	44
Pannawonica, Austl.	D3	68
Panola, Al., U.S.	C1	108
Panola, co., Ms., U.S.	A3	131
Panola, co., Tx., U.S.	C5	150
Panora, Ia., U.S.	C3	122
Panorama, Braz.	F3	79
Pansik, Rápido, wtfl, N.A.	C9	92
Pantelleria, Isola di, i., Italy	M7	18
Pantha, Burma	C3	40
Pánuco, Mex.	F10	90
Pánuco, stm., Mex.	G10	90
Panxian, China	B8	40
Panxidu, China	H3	32
Panyam, Nig.	G14	64
Panyang, Sud.	L5	60
Panyu, China	M2	34
Panzós, Guat.	B5	92
Pao, stm., Ven.	C8	84
Pao, stm., Ven.	C10	84
Paola, Italy	J11	18
Paola, Ks., U.S.	D9	123
Paoli, In., U.S.	G5	121
Paoli, Ok., U.S.	C4	143
Paoli, Pa., U.S.	o20	145
Paonia, Co., U.S.	C3	113
Paotow see Baotou, China	C8	30
P'aozero, ozero, l., U.S.S.R.	H22	6
Paozi, China	A10	32
Pápa, Hung.	H17	10
Papaaloa, Hi., U.S.	D6	118
Papagaio, stm., Braz.	I11	84
Papagayo, Golfo de, b., C.R.	G9	92
Papago Indian Reservation, Az., U.S.	E3	110
Papaikou, Hi., U.S.	D6	118
Papantla [de Olarte], Mex.	G11	90
Papawai Point, c., Hi., U.S.	C5	118
Papayacu, Lago, l., Peru	A3	82
Papenburg, Ger.	B7	10
Paper Mill Village, Vt., U.S.	F2	152
Papilė, U.S.S.R.	E5	26
Papillion, Ne., U.S.	C9	134
Papineauville, Que., Can.	D2	104
Paposo, Chile	C3	80
Papua, Gulf of, b., Pap. N. Gui.	m15	68a
Papua New Guinea, ctry., Oc.	m15	68a
Papudo, Chile	G3	80
Papun, Burma	E4	40
Papunava, stm., Col.	G7	84
Papurí, stm., S.A.	G7	84
Paquera, C.R.	H10	92
Paquetville, N.B., Can.	B4	101
Paquica, Cabo, c., Chile	A3	80
Pará, state, Braz.	B13	82
Pará, stm., Braz.	E9	74
Pará, stm., Braz.	E6	79
Paraburdoo, Austl.	D3	68
Paracari, stm., Braz.	A13	82
Paracas, Bahía de, b., Peru	E3	82
Paracas, Península, pen., Peru	E3	82
Paracatu, Braz.	D5	79
Paracatu, stm., Braz.	D6	79
Paracatu, stm., Braz.	D6	79
Paracel Islands see Xisha Qundao, is., China	B5	38
Parachilna, Austl.	H3	70
Paracho de Verduzco, Mex.	H8	90
Parachute, Co., U.S.	B2	113
Paraćin, Yugo.	F5	20
Parád, Hung.	H20	10
Parada, Punta, c., Peru	F4	82
Paradas, Spain	H6	16
Paradis, La., U.S.	k11	125
Paradise, Ca., U.S.	C3	112
Paradise, Mt., U.S.	C2	133
Paradise, Nv., U.S.	G6	135
Paradise, Ut., U.S.	B4	151
Paradise, stm., Newf., Can.	B3	102
Paradise Hill, Sask., Can.	D1	105
Paradise Hills, N.M., U.S.	B3	138
Paradise River, Newf., Can.	B3	102
Paradise Valley, Alta., Can.	C5	98
Paradise Valley, Az., U.S.	k9	110
Paradise Valley, Nv., U.S.	B4	135
Parado, stm., Braz.	D14	82
Paradox, Co., U.S.	C2	113
Paragon, In., U.S.	F4	121
Paragonah, Ut., U.S.	F3	151
Paragould, Ar., U.S.	A5	111
Paraguá, stm., Bol.	E11	82
Paragua, stm., Ven.	D11	84
Paraguaçu, stm., Braz.	F10	74
Paraguaçu, stm., Braz.	B9	79
Paraguaçu Paulista, Braz.	G3	79
Paraguaipoa, Ven.	B7	84
Paraguaná, Península de, pen., Ven.	B8	84
Paraguarí, Para.	C10	80
Paraguarí, dept., Para.	D10	80
Paraguay, ctry., S.A.	A5	78
Paraguay (Paraguai), stm., S.A.	G9	74
Paraíba do Sul, stm., Braz.	F7	79
Paraibuna, Braz.	G6	79
Paraíso, Braz.	E2	79
Paraíso, C.R.	H11	92
Paraíso, Mex.	H13	90
Paraiso, Pan.	C3	84
Paraíso do Norte, Braz.	G2	79
Paraisópolis, Braz.	G6	79
Paraitinga, stm., Braz.	G6	79
Parakou, Benin	G11	64
Paramakkudi, India	H5	46
Paramaribo, Sur.	B7	76
Paramillo, Nudo de, mtn., Col.	D5	84
Paramirim, Braz.	B7	79
Paramirim, stm., Braz.	B7	79
Paramonga, Peru	D3	82
Paramount, Md., U.S.	A2	127
Paramus, N.J., U.S.	h8	137
Paramušir, ostrov, i., U.S.S.R.	G23	24
Paran, Naḥal (Wādī al-Jirāfī), val.	H3	50
Paraná, Arg.	F8	80
Paranã, Braz.	B5	79
Paraná, state, Braz.	C13	80
Paranã, stm., Braz.	B5	79
Paraná, stm., S.A.	H9	74
Paranaguá, Braz.	C14	80
Paranaguá, Baía, b., Braz.	C14	80
Paranaíba, Braz.	E3	79
Paranaíba, stm., Braz.	E3	79
Paranaíta, stm., Braz.	C13	82
Paranam, Sur.	B7	76
Paranapanema, stm., Braz.	G3	79
Paranapiacaba, Serra do, mts., Braz.	C14	80
Paranavaí, Braz.	G2	79
Paranhos, Braz.	G1	79
Paraopeba, Braz.	E6	79
Parapara, Ven.	C9	84
Parapetí, stm., Bol.	H10	82
Paras, Peru	E4	82
Paratinga, Braz.	B7	79
Parauari, stm., Braz.	J13	84
Paraúna, Braz.	D3	79
Paray-le-Monial, Fr.	F11	14
Pārbati, stm., India	H7	44
Pārbatipur, Bngl.	H13	44
Parbhani, India	C4	46
Parchment, Mi., U.S.	F5	129
Parczew, Pol.	D22	10
Pardeeville, Wi., U.S.	E4	156
Pardes Hanna-Karkur, Isr.	D3	50
Pardo, stm., Braz.	F2	79
Pardo, stm., Braz.	C6	79
Pardo, stm., Braz.	F4	79
Pardo, stm., Braz.	G4	79
Pardo, stm., Braz.	C9	79
Pardo, stm., Braz.	E12	80
Pardubice, Czech.	E15	10
Parecis, Braz.	F13	82
Parecis, stm., Braz.	E13	82
Parecis, Chapada dos, mts., Braz.	F12	82
Paredón, Mex.	E9	90
Paren', stm., U.S.S.R.	E24	24
Parent, Que., Can.	k12	104
Parepare, Indon.	F6	38
Parera, Arg.	H6	80
Parfino, U.S.S.R.	D14	26
Pargolovo, U.S.S.R.	A13	26
Paria, stm., U.S.	A4	110
Paria, Gulf of, b.	B11	84
Paria, Península de, pen., Ven.	B11	84
Pariaguán, Ven.	C10	84
Pariaman, Indon.	O6	40
Pariamanu, stm., Peru	E6	82
Paria Plateau, plat., Az., U.S.	A4	110
Paricá, Lago, l., Braz.	H10	84
Pariči, U.S.S.R.	I12	26
Paricutín, vol., Mex.	H8	90
Parida, Isla, i., Pan.	I12	92
Parika, Guy.	D13	84
Parima, stm., Braz.	F11	84
Parima, Sierra, mts., S.A.	F10	84
Pariñas, Punta, c., Peru	J2	84
Parîngu Mare, Vîrful, mtn., Rom.	D7	20
Parintins, Braz.	I14	84
Pariquera-Açu, Braz.	C15	80
Paris, Ont., Can.	D4	103
Paris, Fr.	D9	14
Paris, Ar., U.S.	B2	111
Paris, Id., U.S.	G7	119
Paris, Il., U.S.	D6	120
Paris, Ky., U.S.	B5	124
Paris, Me., U.S.	D2	126
Paris, Mo., U.S.	B5	132
Paris, Tn., U.S.	A3	149
Paris, Tx., U.S.	C5	150
Parismina, C.R.	G11	92
Parismina, stm., C.R.	G11	92
Paris Peak, mtn., Id., U.S.	G7	119
Parita, Bahía de, b., Pan.	I14	92
Parit Buntar, Malay.	L6	40
Park, Ks., U.S.	C3	123
Park, co., Co., U.S.	B5	113
Park, co., Mt., U.S.	E6	133
Park, co., Wy., U.S.	B3	157
Park, stm., N.D., U.S.	A8	141
Parkano, Fin.	J18	6
Park City, Ks., U.S.	g12	123
Park City, Ky., U.S.	C3	124
Park City, Mt., U.S.	E8	133
Park City, Ut., U.S.	C4	151
Parkdale, P.E.I., Can.	C6	101
Parkdale, Ar., U.S.	D4	111
Parkdale, Mi., U.S.	D4	129
Parkdale, Or., U.S.	B5	144
Parke, co., In., U.S.	E3	121
Parker, Az., U.S.	C1	110
Parker, Co., U.S.	B6	113
Parker, Fl., U.S.	u16	116
Parker, Id., U.S.	F7	119
Parker, Ks., U.S.	D9	123
Parker, Pa., U.S.	D2	145
Parker, S.D., U.S.	D8	148
Parker, Wa., U.S.	C5	154
Parker, co., Tx., U.S.	C4	150
Parker, Cape, c., N.W. Ter., Can.	A17	96
Parker City, In., U.S.	D7	121
Parker Dam, U.S.	C1	110
Parker Peak, mtn., S.D., U.S.	D2	148
Parkersburg, Il., U.S.	E5	120
Parkersburg, Ia., U.S.	B5	122
Parkersburg, W.V., U.S.	B3	155
Parkers Prairie, Mn., U.S.	D3	130
Parkes, Austl.	I8	70
Parkesburg, Pa., U.S.	G10	145
Park Falls, Wi., U.S.	C3	156
Park Forest, Il., U.S.	B6	120
Park Hall, Md., U.S.	D5	127
Park Head, Ont., Can.	C3	103
Parkhill, Ont., Can.	D3	103
Park Hill, Ok., U.S.	B7	143
Park Hills, Ky., U.S.	h13	124
Parkin, Ar., U.S.	B5	111
Parkland, Alta., Can.	D4	98
Parkland, Wa., U.S.	f11	154
Park Layne, Oh., U.S.	C1	142
Parkman, Oh., U.S.	A4	142
Park Place, Or., U.S.	h12	144

Name	Map Ref.	Page
Park Plateau, plat., Co., U.S.	D6	113
Park Range, mts., Co., U.S.	A4	113
Park Rapids, Mn., U.S.	D3	130
Park Ridge, Il., U.S.	B6	120
Park Ridge, N.J., U.S.	g8	137
Park River, N.D., U.S.	A8	141
Parkrose, Or., U.S.	B4	144
Parks, Ar., U.S.	C2	111
Parks, La., U.S.	D4	125
Parkside, Sask., Can.	D2	105
Parksley, Va., U.S.	C7	153
Parkston, S.D., U.S.	D8	148
Parksville, B.C., Can.	E5	99
Parkville, Md., U.S.	B4	127
Parkville, Mo., U.S.	B3	132
Parkwater, Wa., U.S.	g14	154
Parkwood, N.C., U.S.	B4	140
Parla, Spain	E8	16
Parlākimidi, India	C8	46
Parle, Lac qui, l., Mn., U.S.	E3	130
Parli, India	C4	46
Parlier, Ca., U.S.	D4	112
Parma, Italy	E5	18
Parma, Id., U.S.	F2	119
Parma, Mi., U.S.	F6	129
Parma, Mo., U.S.	E8	132
Parma, Oh., U.S.	A4	142
Parmachenee Lake, l., Me., U.S.	C2	126
Parma Heights, Oh., U.S.	h9	142
Parmelee, S.D., U.S.	D4	148
Parmer, co., Tx., U.S.	B1	150
Parnaguá, Braz.	F10	76
Parnaíba, Braz.	D10	76
Parnaíba, stm., Braz.	D10	76
Parnassós, mtn., Grc.	K6	20
Parnell, Ia., U.S.	C6	122
Parnell, Mo., U.S.	A3	132
Pärnu, U.S.S.R.	C7	26
Pärnu-Jaagupi, U.S.S.R.	C7	26
Paro, Bhu.	G13	44
Paromaj, U.S.S.R.	G20	24
Paron, Ar., U.S.	C3	111
Paroo, stm., Austl.	H5	70
Páros, i., Grc.	L9	20
Parowan, Ut., U.S.	F3	151
Parpaillon, mts., Fr.	H13	14
Parpan, Switz.	E12	13
Par Pond, res., S.C., U.S.	D5	147
Parral, Chile	I3	80
Parral, stm., Mex.	D7	90
Parral see Hidalgo del Parral, Mex.	D7	90
Parramatta, Austl.	I9	70
Parramore Island, i., Va., U.S.	C7	153
Parras de la Fuente, Mex.	E8	90
Parrish, Al., U.S.	B2	108
Parrish, Fl., U.S.	E4	116
Parrita, C.R.	H10	92
Parrita, stm., C.R.	H10	92
Parrott, Ga., U.S.	E2	117
Parrott, Va., U.S.	C2	153
Parrsboro, N.S., Can.	D5	101
Parrs Ridge, mtn., Md., U.S.	B3	127
Parry, Cape, c., N.W. Ter., Can.	B8	96
Parry, Mount, mtn., B.C., Can.	C3	99
Parry Channel, strt., N.W. Ter., Can.	B9	86
Parry Sound, Ont., Can.	B4	103
Parsberg, Ger.	F11	10
Parseier Spitze, mtn., Aus.	D13	13
Parshall, Co., U.S.	A4	113
Parshall, N.D., U.S.	B3	141
Parsons, Ks., U.S.	E8	123
Parsons, Tn., U.S.	B3	149
Parsons, W.V., U.S.	B5	155
Parsonsburg, Md., U.S.	D7	127
Parson's Pond, Newf., Can.	C3	102
Pärsti, U.S.S.R.	C8	26
Partanna, Italy	L7	18
Parthenay, Fr.	F6	14
Partinico, Italy	K8	18
Partizansk, U.S.S.R.	I18	24
Partridge, Ks., U.S.	E5	123
Partridge Point, c., Newf., Can.	C3	102
Paru, stm., Braz.	D8	76
Parú, stm., Ven.	E10	84
Parucito, stm., Ven.	E9	84
Paru de Oeste, stm., Braz.	D7	76
Paruro, Peru	E6	82
Pārvatīpuram, India	C7	46
Paryang, China	E10	44
Pasaco, Guat.	D4	92
Pasadena, Newf., Can.	D3	102
Pasadena, Ca., U.S.	E4	112
Pasadena, Md., U.S.	B4	127
Pasadena, Tx., U.S.	r14	150
Pasado, Cabo, c., Ec.	H2	84
Pasaje, Ec.	I3	84
Pasaje, stm., Arg.	C6	80
Pa Sak, stm., Thai.	G6	40
Pasawng, Burma	E4	40
Pascagoula, Ms., U.S.	E5	131
Pascagoula, stm., Ms., U.S.	E5	131
Pascagoula Bay, b., Ms., U.S.	f8	131
Pașcani, Rom.	B10	20
Pasco, Wa., U.S.	C6	154
Pasco, dept., Peru	D4	82
Pasco, co., Fl., U.S.	D4	116
Pascoag, R.I., U.S.	B2	146
Pascoag Reservoir, res., R.I., U.S.	B2	146
Pascua, Isla de (Easter Island), i., Chile	G4	74
Pas-de-Calais, dept., Fr.	B9	14
Pasewalk, Ger.	B14	10
Pasig, Phil.	N19	39b
P'asina, stm., U.S.S.R.	C9	24
Pasinler, Tur.	B6	48
P'asino, ozero, l., U.S.S.R.	D9	24
P'asinskij zaliv, b., U.S.S.R.	C14	22
Pasir Puteh, Malay.	L7	40
Pasmore, stm., Austl.	H3	70
Pasni, Pak.	I17	48
Paso del Cerro, Ur.	F11	80
Paso de los Libres, Arg.	E10	80
Paso de los Toros, Ur.	G10	80
Paso de Patria, Para.	D9	80
Paso Hondo, Mex.	J13	90
Pasorapa, Bol.	H9	82
Paso Robles, Ca., U.S.	E3	112
Pasque Island, i., Ma., U.S.	D6	128
Pasquel, Punta, c., Mex.	E4	90
Pasquia Hills, hills, Sask., Can.	D4	105
Pasquotank, co., N.C., U.S.	A6	140
Pasrūr, Pak.	D6	44
Passaconaway, Mount, mtn., N.H., U.S.	C4	136
Passadumkeag Mountain, mtn., Me., U.S.	C4	126
Passage Point, c., N.W. Ter., Can.	B9	96
Passaic, N.J., U.S.	B4	137
Passaic, co., N.J., U.S.	A4	137
Passaic, stm., N.J., U.S.	h8	137
Passamaquoddy Bay, b., Me., U.S.	C6	126
Passau, Ger.	G13	10
Pass Christian, Ms., U.S.	E4	131
Passekeag, N.B., Can.	D4	101
Passero, Capo, c., Italy	M10	18
Pašškij Perevoz, U.S.S.R.	A15	26
Passo Fundo, Braz.	E12	80
Passo Fundo, stm., Braz.	D12	80
Passos, Braz.	F5	79
Passumpsic, Vt., U.S.	C4	152
Passumpsic, stm., Vt., U.S.	C4	152
Pastaza, prov., Ec.	H4	84
Pastaza, stm., S.A.	J4	84
Pasto, Col.	G4	84
Pastora Peak, mtn., Az., U.S.	A6	110
Pasuruan, Indon.	J16	39a
Pasvalys, U.S.S.R.	E7	26
Pásztó, Hung.	H19	10
Patacamaya, Bol.	G8	82
Patagonia, Az., U.S.	F5	110
Patagonia, reg., Arg.	F3	78
Pātan, India	I5	44
Patapsco, stm., Md., U.S.	B4	127
Patapsco, North Branch, stm., Md., U.S.	A4	127
Patargān, Daqq-e, sw., Asia	E16	48
Pataskala, Oh., U.S.	C3	142
Pataz, Peru	B3	82
Patchet Brook Reservoir, res., R.I., U.S.	E6	146
Patchewollock, Austl.	J5	70
Patchogue, N.Y., U.S.	n15	139
Patea, N.Z.	C5	72
Pategi, Nig.	G12	64
Pate Island, i., Kenya	B8	58
Patensie, S. Afr.	I7	66
Paterna, Spain	F11	16
Paternion, Aus.	I13	10
Paternò, Italy	L9	18
Pateros, Wa., U.S.	A6	154
Paterson, S. Afr.	I7	66
Paterson, N.J., U.S.	B4	137
Pathānkot, India	D6	44
Pathein (Bassein), Burma	F3	40
Pathfinder Reservoir, res., Wy., U.S.	D6	157
Pathfork, Ky., U.S.	D6	124
Pathiong, Sud.	N6	60
Pati, stm., Braz.	I8	84
Patía, Col.	F4	84
Patía, stm., Col.	F3	84
Patiāla, India	E7	44
Patience Island, i., R.I., U.S.	D5	146
P'atigorsk, U.S.S.R.	I6	22
Pātīrlagele, Rom.	D10	20
Pativilca, Peru	D3	82
Pativilca, stm., Peru	D3	82
Pātkai Range, mts., Asia	G16	44
Patman, Lake, res., Tx., U.S.	C5	150
Patna, India	H11	44
Pato Branco, Braz.	D12	80
Patoka, Il., U.S.	E4	120
Patoka, In., U.S.	H2	121
Patoka, stm., In., U.S.	H2	121
Patoka Lake, res., In., U.S.	H4	121
Paton, Ia., U.S.	B3	122
Patos, Braz.	E11	76
Patos, Cachoeira dos, wtfl, Braz.	C11	82
Patos, Lagoa dos, b., Braz.	F13	80
Patos, Río de los, stm., Arg.	F4	80
Patos, Rio dos, stm., Braz.	C4	79
Patos, Rio dos, stm., Braz.	E13	82
Patos de Minas, Braz.	E5	79
P'atovskij, U.S.S.R.	G19	26
Patquía, Arg.	F5	80
Pátrai, Grc.	K5	20
Patraïkós Kólpos, b., Grc.	K5	20
Patras see Pátrai, Grc.	K5	20
Patricia, Alta., Can.	D5	98
Patrick, S.C., U.S.	B7	147
Patrick, co., Va., U.S.	D2	153
Patrick Air Force Base, mil., Fl., U.S.	D6	116
Patricksburg, In., U.S.	F4	121
Patrick Springs, Va., U.S.	D2	153
Patriot, In., U.S.	G8	121
Patrocínio, Braz.	E5	79
Patrocínio Paulista, Braz.	F5	79
Patsaliga Creek, stm., Al., U.S.	D3	108
Pattada, Italy	I4	18
Pattani, Thai.	K6	40
Pattaquattic Hill, hill, Ma., U.S.	B3	128
Patten, Me., U.S.	C4	126
Patterson, Ar., U.S.	B4	111
Patterson, Ga., U.S.	E4	117
Patterson, La., U.S.	E4	125
Patterson, Mo., U.S.	D7	132
Patterson, N.Y., U.S.	D7	139
Patterson, Va., U.S.	e10	153
Patterson Creek, stm., W.V., U.S.	B5	155
Patti, Italy	K9	18
Pattison, Ms., U.S.	D3	131
Patton, Mo., U.S.	D7	132
Patton, Pa., U.S.	E4	145
Pattonsburg, Mo., U.S.	A3	132
Patuca, stm., Hond.	B10	92
Patuca, Punta, c., Hond.	B10	92
Patul, mtn., Ec.	I3	84
Patulul, Guat.	C3	92
Patuxent, stm., Md., U.S.	D4	127
Patuxent Naval Air Test Center, mil., Md., U.S.	D5	127
Pátzcuaro, Mex.	H9	90
Patzicía, Guat.	C4	92
Patzún, Guat.	C3	92
Pau, Fr.	I6	14
Pau Brasil, Braz.	C9	79
Paucarbamba, Peru	E4	82
Paucarpata, Peru	G6	82
Paucartambo, Peru	E6	82
Pauini, Braz.	B8	82
Pauini, stm., Braz.	B8	82
Pauini, stm., Braz.	H11	84
Pauk, Burma	D3	40
Paul, Id., U.S.	G5	119
Paula Lima, Braz.	F7	79
Paulaya, stm., Hond.	B9	92
Paulding, Ms., U.S.	C4	131
Paulding, Oh., U.S.	A1	142
Paulding, co., Ga., U.S.	C2	117
Paulding, co., Oh., U.S.	A1	142
Paulhan, Fr.	I10	14
Paulicéia, Braz.	F3	79
Paulina, La., U.S.	h10	125
Paulina Mountains, mts., Or., U.S.	D5	144
Paulina Peak, mtn., Or., U.S.	E5	144
Pauline, S.C., U.S.	B4	147
Paulins Kill, stm., N.J., U.S.	A3	137
Paul Island, i., Newf., Can.	g9	102
Paulistana, Braz.	E10	76
Paulistas, Braz.	E7	79
Paullina, Ia., U.S.	B2	122
Paulo Afonso, Braz.	E11	76
Paulo de Faria, Braz.	F4	79
Paulpietersburg, S. Afr.	F10	66
Paulsboro, N.J., U.S.	D2	137
Paul Stream, stm., Vt., U.S.	B5	152
Pauls Valley, Ok., U.S.	C4	143
Paungbyin, Burma	B3	40
Paungde, Burma	E3	40
Paupack, Pa., U.S.	D11	145
Pausa, Peru	F5	82
Pausania, Italy	I4	18
Paute, Ec.	I3	84
Paute, stm., Ec.	I3	84
Pauto, stm., Col.	E7	84
Pauwela, Hi., U.S.	C5	118
Pavant Range, mts., Ut., U.S.	E3	151
Pāveh, Iran	D9	48
Pavelec, U.S.S.R.	H22	26
Pavia, Italy	D4	18
Pavilion Key, i., Fl., U.S.	G5	116
Pavillion, Wy., U.S.	C4	157
Pavilly, Fr.	C7	14
Pāvilosta, U.S.S.R.	E4	26
Pavlikeni, Bul.	F9	20
Pavlodar, U.S.S.R.	G7	24
Pavlof Volcano, vol., Ak., U.S.	D7	109
Pavlovo, U.S.S.R.	F26	26
Pavlovsk, U.S.S.R.	B13	26
Pavlovskij Posad, U.S.S.R.	F21	26
Pavo, Ga., U.S.	F3	117
Pavón, Col.	F6	84
Pawcatuck, Ct., U.S.	D8	114
Pawcatuck, stm., R.I., U.S.	G1	146
Paw Creek, N.C., U.S.	B2	140
Pawhuska, Ok., U.S.	A5	143
Pawlet, Vt., U.S.	E2	152
Pawling, N.Y., U.S.	D7	139
Pawnee, Il., U.S.	D4	120
Pawnee, Ok., U.S.	A5	143
Pawnee, co., Ks., U.S.	D4	123
Pawnee, co., Ne., U.S.	D9	134
Pawnee, co., Ok., U.S.	A5	143
Pawnee, stm., Ks., U.S.	D3	123
Pawnee City, Ne., U.S.	D9	134
Pawnee Creek, stm., Co., U.S.	A7	113
Pawnee Rock, Ks., U.S.	D5	123
Pawpaw, Il., U.S.	B5	120
Paw Paw, Mi., U.S.	F5	129
Paw Paw, W.V., U.S.	B6	155
Paw Paw, stm., Mi., U.S.	F4	129
Pawpaw Creek, stm., W.V., U.S.	h10	155
Pawtuckaway Pond, l., N.H., U.S.	D4	136
Pawtucket, R.I., U.S.	C4	146
Pawtuxet, stm., R.I., U.S.	C4	146
Pawtuxet, North Branch, stm., R.I., U.S.	D3	146
Pawtuxet, South Branch, stm., R.I., U.S.	D3	146
Paxico, Ks., U.S.	C7	123
Paxton, Fl., U.S.	u15	116
Paxton, Il., U.S.	C5	120
Paxton, In., U.S.	F3	121
Paxton, Ma., U.S.	B4	128
Paxton, Ne., U.S.	C4	134
Paya, Hond.	B9	92
Payakumbuh, Indon.	O6	40
Payas, Cerro, mtn., Hond.	B9	92
Payerne, Switz.	E6	13
Payette, Id., U.S.	E2	119
Payette, co., Id., U.S.	E2	119
Payette, North Fork, stm., Id., U.S.	E2	119
Payette, South Fork, stm., Id., U.S.	E3	119
Payette Lake, res., Id., U.S.	E3	119
Payne, Ga., U.S.	D3	117
Payne, Oh., U.S.	A1	142
Payne, co., Ok., U.S.	A4	143
Payne, Lac, l., Que., Can.	g12	104
Payne Bay, b., Can.	D19	96
Paynesville, Mn., U.S.	E4	130
Payneville, Ky., U.S.	C3	124
Paynton, Sask., Can.	D1	105
Paysandú, Ur.	H9	74
Paysandú, Ur.	G9	80
Payson, Az., U.S.	C4	110
Payson, Il., U.S.	D2	120
Payson, Ut., U.S.	C4	151
Payún, Cerro, mtn., Arg.	I4	80
Paz, stm., N.A.	D4	92
Pazardžik, Bul.	G8	20
Pazarköy, Tur.	J11	20
Paz de Ariporo, Col.	E7	84
Paz de Río, Col.	E6	84
P'ažijeva Sel'ga, U.S.S.R.	K24	6
Pazin, Yugo.	D8	18
Pazña, Bol.	H8	82
Pea, stm., Al., U.S.	D3	108
Peabody, Ks., U.S.	D6	123
Peabody, Ma., U.S.	A6	128
Peabody, stm., N.H., U.S.	B4	136
Peace, stm., Can.	E10	96
Peace, stm., Fl., U.S.	E5	116
Peace Dale, R.I., U.S.	F3	146
Peace River, Alta., Can.	A2	98
Peach, co., Ga., U.S.	D3	117
Peacham, Vt., U.S.	C4	152
Peacham Pond, res., Vt., U.S.	C4	152
Peach Creek, W.V., U.S.	D5	155
Peach Orchard, Ar., U.S.	A5	111
Peach Orchard Knob, mtn., Ky., U.S.	C3	124
Peach Point, c., Ma., U.S.	f12	128
Peach Springs, Az., U.S.	B2	110
Peaked Mountain, mtn., Me., U.S.	B4	126
Peak Hill, Austl.	E3	68
Peak Hill, Austl.	I8	70
Peaks Island, i., Me., U.S.	g7	126
Peale, Mount, mtn., Ut., U.S.	E6	151
Pea Patch Island, i., De., U.S.	B3	115
Pearcy, Ar., U.S.	C2	111
Pea Ridge, Ar., U.S.	A1	111
Pea Ridge National Military Park, Ar., U.S.	A1	111
Pearisburg, Va., U.S.	C2	153
Pearl, Ms., U.S.	C3	131
Pearl, stm., U.S.	D3	131
Pearland, Tx., U.S.	r14	150
Pearl and Hermes Reef, rf., Hi., U.S.	k12	118
Pearl City, Hi., U.S.	B4	118
Pearl City, Il., U.S.	A4	120
Pearl Harbor, b., Hi., U.S.	B3	118
Pearl Harbor Naval Station, mil., Hi., U.S.	g10	118
Pearlington, Ms., U.S.	E4	131
Pearl River, La., U.S.	D6	125
Pearl River, N.Y., U.S.	g12	139
Pearl River, co., Ms., U.S.	E4	131
Pearsall, Tx., U.S.	E3	150
Pearsoll Peak, mtn., Or., U.S.	E3	144
Pearson, Ga., U.S.	E4	117
Pearston, S. Afr.	I7	66
Peary Land, reg., Grnld.	A16	86
Pease, Mn., U.S.	E5	130
Pease, stm., Tx., U.S.	B3	150
Pease Air Force Base, mil., N.H., U.S.	D5	136
Pebane, Moz.	E7	58
Pebas, Peru	I7	84
Peć, Yugo.	G4	20
Peçanha, Braz.	E7	79
Peças, Ilha das, i., Braz.	C14	80
Pecatonica, Il., U.S.	A4	120
Pecatonica, stm., U.S.	A4	120
Pecatonica, East Branch, stm., Wi., U.S.	F4	156
Pečenežin, U.S.S.R.	A8	20
Pečenga, U.S.S.R.	D4	22
Pechora see Pečora, stm., U.S.S.R.	D8	22
Pecica, Rom.	C5	20
Peck, Id., U.S.	C2	119
Peck, Ks., U.S.	E6	123
Peck, Mi., U.S.	E8	129
Peckerwood Lake, res., Ar., U.S.	C4	111
Pečora, U.S.S.R.	D9	22
Pečora, stm., U.S.S.R.	D8	22
Pečorskaja guba, b., U.S.S.R.	D8	22
Pečorskoje more, U.S.S.R.	D8	22
Pečory, U.S.S.R.	D10	26
Pecos, N.M., U.S.	B4	138
Pecos, Tx., U.S.	D1	150
Pecos, co., Tx., U.S.	D1	150
Pecos, stm., U.S.	E6	106
Pecos National Monument, N.M., U.S.	B4	138
Pécs, Hung.	I18	10
Peculiar, Mo., U.S.	C3	132
Pedasí, Pan.	D2	84
Peddāpuram, India	D7	46
Pedder, Lake, res., Austl.	N7	70
Peddocks Island, i., Ma., U.S.	g12	128
Pedernales, Arg.	H9	80
Pedernales, Dom. Rep.	E9	94
Pedernales, Ven.	C11	84
Pedernales, Salar de, pl., Chile	D4	80
Pedra Azul, Braz.	D8	79
Pedra Grande, Recifes da, rf., Braz.	D9	79
Pedra Lume, C.V.	k17	64a
Pedras, Braz.	I14	84
Pedras, Rio das, stm., Braz.	B6	79
Pedras Negras, Braz.	E10	82
Pedraza, Col.	B5	84
Pedregal, Pan.	C1	84
Pedregal, Ven.	B7	84
Pedregulho, Braz.	F5	79
Pedreiras, Braz.	D10	76
Pedriceña, Mex.	E8	90
Pedricktown, N.J., U.S.	D2	137
Pedro Afonso, Braz.	E9	76
Pedro Cays, is., Jam.	F6	94
Pedrógão Grande, Port.	F3	16
Pedro Gomes, Braz.	E1	79
Pedro González, Isla, i., Pan.	C3	84
Pedro II, Braz.	D10	76
Pedro II, Ilha, i., S.A.	G9	84
Pedro Juan Caballero, Para.	B11	80
Pedro Leopoldo, Braz.	E6	79
Pedro Luro, Arg.	J7	80
Pedro Muñoz, Spain	F9	16
Pedro Osório, Braz.	F12	80
Pedro R. Fernández, Arg.	E9	80
Peebinga, Austl.	J4	70
Peebles, Oh., U.S.	D2	142
Peekaboo Mountain, hill, Me., U.S.	C5	126
Peekskill, N.Y., U.S.	D7	139
Peel, N.B., Can.	C2	101
Peel, I. of Man	G9	8
Peel, stm., Can.	C5	96
Pe Ell, Wa., U.S.	C2	154
Peel Point, c., N.W. Ter., Can.	B10	96
Peel Sound, strt., N.W. Ter., Can.	B13	96
Peene, stm., Ger.	B13	10
Peerless, Mt., U.S.	B11	133
Peers, Alta., Can.	C3	98
Peetz, Co., U.S.	A7	113
Peever, S.D., U.S.	B9	148
Pegan Hill, hill, Ma., U.S.	g10	128
Pegasus Bay, b., N.Z.	E4	72
Pegnitz, Ger.	F11	10
Pegnitz, stm., Ger.	F11	10
Pego, Spain	G11	16
Pegram, Tn., U.S.	A4	149
Pegu see Bago, Burma	F4	40
Pegu Yoma, mts., Burma	E3	40
Pehčevo, Yugo.	H6	20
Pehuajó, Arg.	H8	80
Peikang, Tai.	L9	34
Peine, Ger.	C10	10
Peipus, Lake see Čudskoje ozero, l., U.S.S.R.	C10	26
Peissenberg, Ger.	H11	10
Peixe, Braz.	B4	79
Peixe, Rio do, stm., Braz.	C3	79
Peixe, Rio do, stm., Braz.	G3	79
Peixian, China	E10	30
Peiziyan, China	H3	32
Pejepscot, Me., U.S.	E2	126
Pekalongan, Indon.	J14	39a
Pekanbaru, Indon.	N6	40
Pekin, Il., U.S.	C4	120
Pekin, In., U.S.	G5	121
Pekin, N.D., U.S.	B7	141
Peking see Beijing, China	D4	32
Peklino, U.S.S.R.	H16	26
Pelabuhan Kelang, Malay.	M6	40
Pelagie, Isole, is., Italy	N7	18
Pelahatchie, Ms., U.S.	C4	131
Pełczyce, Pol.	B15	10
Peleaga, Vîrful, mtn., Rom.	D6	20
Pelechuco, Bol.	F7	82
Pelée, Montagne, mtn., Mart.	G14	94
Pelee Island, i., Ont., Can.	F2	103
Pelham, Ont., Can.	D5	103
Pelham, Al., U.S.	B3	108
Pelham, Ga., U.S.	E2	117
Pelham, N.H., U.S.	E4	136
Pelham, S.C., U.S.	B3	147
Pelham, Tn., U.S.	D8	149
Pelham Manor, N.Y., U.S.	h13	139
Pelhřimov, Czech.	F15	10
Pelican, Ak., U.S.	m21	109
Pelican Bay, b., Man., Can.	C1	100
Pelican Lake, l., Man., Can.	C1	100
Pelican Lake, l., Mn., U.S.	D3	130
Pelican Lake, l., Mn., U.S.	D4	130
Pelican Lake, l., Mn., U.S.	B6	130
Pelican Lake, l., Mn., U.S.	E5	130
Pelican Lake, l., Wi., U.S.	C4	156
Pelican Mountain, mtn., Alta., Can.	B4	98
Pelican Narrows, Sask., Can.	B4	105
Pelican Rapids, Man., Can.	C1	100
Pelican Rapids, Mn., U.S.	D2	130
Pelileo, Ec.	H3	84
Pelion, S.C., U.S.	D5	147
Pelister, mtn., Yugo.	H5	20
Pelkosenniemi, Fin.	H20	6
Pella, Ia., U.S.	C5	122
Pell City, Al., U.S.	B3	108
Pellegrini, Arg.	I7	80
Pellegrini, Lago, l., Arg.	J4	80
Pell Lake, Wi., U.S.	n11	156
Pello, Fin.	H19	6
Pellston, Mi., U.S.	C6	129
Pelly, Sask., Can.	F5	105
Pelly, stm., Yukon, Can.	D6	96
Pelly Bay, b., N.W. Ter., Can.	C14	96
Pelly Crossing, Yukon, Can.	D5	96
Pelly Mountains, mts., Yukon, Can.	D6	96
Pelón, Cerro, mtn., Mex.	G10	90
Peloncillo Mountains, mts., U.S.	E1	138
Peloponnesos see Pelopónnisos, pen., Grc.	L6	20
Pelopónnisos, pen., Grc.	L6	20
Pelotas, Braz.	F12	80
Pelotas, stm., Braz.	D13	80
Pelton, Lake, l., La., U.S.	E5	125
Pel'ušn'a, U.S.S.R.	C15	26
Pemadumcook Lake, l., Me., U.S.	C3	126
Pemalang, Indon.	J14	39a
Pematangsiantar, Indon.	M5	40
Pemba, Moz.	D8	58
Pemba, i., Tan.	C7	58
Pemberton, Austl.	F3	68
Pemberton, B.C., Can.	D6	99
Pemberton, N.J., U.S.	D3	137
Pemberville, Oh., U.S.	A2	142
Pembina, N.D., U.S.	A8	141
Pembina, co., N.D., U.S.	A8	141
Pembina, stm., Alta., Can.	C3	98
Pembine, Wi., U.S.	C6	156
Pembroke, Ont., Can.	B7	103
Pembroke, Wales, U.K.	J9	8
Pembroke, Ga., U.S.	D5	117
Pembroke, Ky., U.S.	D2	124
Pembroke, Me., U.S.	D5	126
Pembroke, Ma., U.S.	B6	128
Pembroke, N.C., U.S.	C3	140
Pembroke, Va., U.S.	C2	153
Pembroke, Cape, c., N.W. Ter., Can.	D16	96
Pembroke Pines, Fl., U.S.	r13	116
Pemigewasset, stm., N.H., U.S.	C3	136
Pemigewasset, East Branch, stm., N.H., U.S.	B3	136
Pemiscot, co., Mo., U.S.	E8	132
Pemmican Portage, Sask., Can.	D4	105
Pemuco, Chile	I2	80
Peña Blanca, Pan.	I13	92
Pena Blanca, N.M., U.S.	B3	138
Penafiel, Port.	D3	16
Peña Gorda, Cerro, mtn., Mex.	G7	90
Peña Negra, Punta, c., Peru	J2	84
Penápolis, Braz.	F3	79
Peñaranda de Bracamonte, Spain	E6	16
Pen Argyl, Pa., U.S.	E11	145
Peñarroya-Pueblonuevo, Spain	G6	16
Penas, Golfo de, b., Chile	F2	78
Penasco, N.M., U.S.	A4	138
Peñasco, Rio, stm., N.M., U.S.	E4	138
Penbrook, Pa., U.S.	F8	145
Pencahue, Chile	H3	80
Pendembu, S.L.	G3	64
Pender, Ne., U.S.	B9	134
Pender, co., N.C., U.S.	C4	140
Pendergrass, Ga., U.S.	B3	117
Pendjari, stm., Afr.	F7	54
Pendleton, In., U.S.	E6	121
Pendleton, Or., U.S.	B8	144
Pendleton, S.C., U.S.	B2	147
Pendleton, co., Ky., U.S.	B5	124
Pendleton, co., W.V., U.S.	C5	155
Pendley Hills, Ga., U.S.	h8	117
Pend Oreille, co., Wa., U.S.	A8	154
Pend Oreille, Lake, l., Id., U.S.	A2	119
Pend Oreille, Mount, mtn., Id., U.S.	A2	119
Penedo, Braz.	F11	76
Penedono, Port.	E4	16
Penetanguishene, Ont., Can.	C5	103
Penfield, Ga., U.S.	C3	117
Penfield, Il., U.S.	C6	120
Penfield, Pa., U.S.	D4	145
Penganga, stm., India	C5	46
Penge, S. Afr.	E10	66
P'enghu Ch'üntao (Pescadores), is., Tai.	L8	34
P'enghu Shuitao, strt., Tai.	L8	34
Pengkou, China	J5	34
Penglai (Dengzhou), China	F8	32
Pengshui, China	F8	30
Penguin, Austl.	M7	70
Pengxian, China	E7	30
Penha, Braz.	D14	80
Penhold, Alta., Can.	C4	98
Peniche, Port.	F2	16
Peninsula, Oh., U.S.	A4	142
Penitentiary Mountain, hill, Al., U.S.	A2	108
Penjamillo [de Degollado], Mex.	G9	90
Pennant Point, c., N.S., Can.	E6	101
Pennant Station, Sask., Can.	G1	105
Pennask Mountain, mtn., B.C., Can.	E7	99
Penne, Italy	G8	18
Pennell, Mount, mtn., Ut., U.S.	F5	151
Penney Farms, Fl., U.S.	C5	116
Pennfield, N.B., Can.	D3	101
Penn Hills, Pa., U.S.	k14	145
Penniac, N.B., Can.	C3	101
Pennines, mts., Eng., U.K.	G11	8
Pennines, Alpes, mts., Eur.	C2	18
Pennington, Al., U.S.	C1	108
Pennington, N.J., U.S.	C3	137
Pennington, co., Mn., U.S.	B2	130
Pennington, co., S.D., U.S.	D2	148
Pennington Gap, Va., U.S.	f8	153
Pennock, Mn., U.S.	E3	130
Pennsauken, N.J., U.S.	D2	137
Pennsboro, W.V., U.S.	B4	155
Pennsburg, Pa., U.S.	F11	145
Penns Grove, N.J., U.S.	D2	137
Pennsville, N.J., U.S.	D1	137
Pennsylvania, state, U.S.	E7	145
Pennville, In., U.S.	D7	121
Penny, B.C., Can.	C7	99
Penn Yan, N.Y., U.S.	C3	139
Pennycutaway, stm., Man., Can.	A5	100
Penny Ice Cap, N.W. Ter., Can.	C19	96
Penny Strait, strt., N.W. Ter., Can.	A13	96
Peno, U.S.S.R.	E15	26
Penobscot, co., Me., U.S.	C4	126
Penobscot, stm., Me., U.S.	C4	126
Penobscot, East Branch, stm., Me., U.S.	C4	126
Penobscot, North Branch, stm., Me., U.S.	B2	126
Penobscot, West Branch, stm., Me., U.S.	C3	126
Penobscot Bay, b., Me., U.S.	D3	126
Penobscot Lake, l., Me., U.S.	C2	126
Penokee, Ks., U.S.	C4	123
Penola, Austl.	K4	70
Peñón Blanco, Mex.	E7	90
Penong, Austl.	F6	68
Penonomé, Pan.	C2	84
Penrith, Austl.	I9	70
Pensacola, Fl., U.S.	u14	116
Pensacola Bay, b., Fl., U.S.	u14	116
Pensacola Dam, Ok., U.S.	A6	143
Pensacola Mountains, mts., Ant.	D1	73
Pensacola Naval Air Station, mil., Fl., U.S.	u14	116
Pense, Sask., Can.	G3	105
Pensilvania, Col.	E5	84
Pentagon Mountain, mtn., Mt., U.S.	C3	133
Penticton, B.C., Can.	E8	99
Pentland, Austl.	C6	70
Pentland Firth, strt., Scot., U.K.	C10	8
Pentwater, Mi., U.S.	E4	129
Pènwègon, Burma	E4	40
Penza, U.S.S.R.	G7	22
Penzance, Sask., Can.	F3	105
Penzance, Eng., U.K.	K8	8
Penzberg, Ger.	H11	10
Penžina, stm., U.S.S.R.	E25	24
Penžinskaja guba, b., U.S.S.R.	E24	24
Peonan Point, c., Man., Can.	D2	100
Peoria, Az., U.S.	D3	110
Peoria, Il., U.S.	C4	120
Peoria, co., Il., U.S.	C4	120
Peoria Heights, Il., U.S.	C4	120
Peotone, Il., U.S.	B6	120
Pepacton Reservoir, res., N.Y., U.S.	C6	139
Pepeekeo, Hi., U.S.	D6	118
Pepel, S.L.	G3	64
Peper, Sud.	N7	60

Name	Map Ref.	Page
Pepin, Wi., U.S.	D1	156
Pepin, co., Wi., U.S.	D2	156
Pepin, Lake, l., U.S.	D1	156
Pepper Creek, stm., De., U.S.	F5	115
Pepperell, Ma., U.S.	A4	128
Pequannock, N.J., U.S.	B4	137
Pequeri, stm., Braz.	G14	82
Pequest, stm., N.J., U.S.	B2	137
Pequop Mountains, mts., Nv., U.S.	C7	135
Pequot Lakes, Mn., U.S.	D4	130
Perabumulih, Indon.	F3	38
Perak, stm., Malay.	L6	40
Peralillo, Chile	H3	80
Perämeri (Bottenviken), b., Eur.	I18	6
Perchtoldsdorf, Aus.	G16	10
Percy, Il., U.S.	E4	120
Percy Isles, is., Austl.	C9	70
Perdeberg, S. Afr.	G7	66
Perdido, Al., U.S.	D2	108
Perdido, stm., Braz.	I13	82
Perdido, stm., U.S.	E2	108
Perdido, Monte, mtn., Spain	C12	16
Perdido Bay, b., Al., U.S.	E2	108
Perdizes, Braz.	E5	79
Perdue, Sask., Can.	E2	105
Perečin, U.S.S.R.	G22	10
Peregonovka, U.S.S.R.	A14	20
Pereira, Col.	E5	84
Pereira Barreto, Braz.	F3	79
Pere Marquette, stm., Mi., U.S.	E4	129
Peremyšl', U.S.S.R.	G19	26
Perené, stm., Peru	D4	82
Pereslavl'-Zalesskij, U.S.S.R.	E21	26
Peresypkino Pervoje, U.S.S.R.	I25	26
Pérez, Arg.	G8	80
Perg, Aus.	G14	10
Pergamino, Arg.	G8	80
Pergine Valsugana, Italy	C6	18
Pergola, Italy	F7	18
Perham, Mn., U.S.	D3	130
Perico, Arg.	C6	80
Pericos, Mex.	E6	90
Peridot, Az., U.S.	D5	110
Périers, Fr.	C5	14
Périgord, hist. reg., Fr.	G7	14
Périgueux, Fr.	G7	14
Perijá, Sierra de, mts., S.A.	B6	84
Periyakulam, India	G4	46
Perkasie, Pa., U.S.	F11	145
Perkins, Que., Can.	D2	104
Perkins, Ga., U.S.	D5	117
Perkins, Mi., U.S.	C3	129
Perkins, Ok., U.S.	B4	143
Perkins, co., Ne., U.S.	D4	134
Perkins, co., S.D., U.S.	B3	148
Perkinston, Ms., U.S.	E4	131
Perla, Ar., U.S.	C3	111
Perlas, Archipiélago de las, is., Pan.	C3	84
Perlas, Laguna de, b., Nic.	E11	92
Perlas, Punta de, c., Nic.	E11	92
Perleberg, Ger.	B11	10
Perm', U.S.S.R.	F9	22
Pernatty Lagoon, l., Austl.	H2	70
Pernell, Ok., U.S.	C4	143
Pernik, Bul.	G7	20
Péronne, Fr.	C9	14
Perot, Bayou, stm., La., U.S.	k11	125
Perote, Mex.	H11	90
Perotó, Bol.	F9	82
Perpignan, Fr.	J9	14
Perquimans, co., N.C., U.S.	A6	140
Perrine, Fl., U.S.	G6	116
Perris, Ca., U.S.	F5	112
Perro, Laguna del, l., N.M., U.S.	C4	138
Perros, Bahía de, b., Cuba	C5	94
Perrot, Île, i., Que., Can.	q19	104
Perry, Ar., U.S.	B3	111
Perry, Fl., U.S.	B3	116
Perry, Ga., U.S.	D3	117
Perry, Il., U.S.	D3	120
Perry, Ia., U.S.	C3	122
Perry, Ks., U.S.	C8	123
Perry, Mi., U.S.	F6	129
Perry, Mo., U.S.	B6	132
Perry, N.Y., U.S.	C2	139
Perry, Oh., U.S.	A4	142
Perry, Ok., U.S.	A4	143
Perry, Ut., U.S.	B3	151
Perry, co., Al., U.S.	C2	108
Perry, co., Ar., U.S.	C3	111
Perry, co., Il., U.S.	E4	120
Perry, co., In., U.S.	H4	121
Perry, co., Ky., U.S.	C6	124
Perry, co., Ms., U.S.	D4	131
Perry, co., Mo., U.S.	D8	132
Perry, co., Oh., U.S.	C3	142
Perry, co., Pa., U.S.	F7	145
Perry, co., Tn., U.S.	B4	149
Perry Hall, Md., U.S.	B5	127
Perry Lake, res., Ks., U.S.	C8	123
Perryman, Md., U.S.	B5	127
Perry Peak, mtn., Ma., U.S.	B1	128
Perry Point, Md., U.S.	A5	127
Perrysburg, Oh., U.S.	A2	142
Perrysburg Heights, Oh., U.S.	e6	142
Perry Stream, stm., N.H., U.S.	f7	136
Perry's Victory and International Peace Memorial, hist., Oh., U.S.	A2	142
Perrysville, In., U.S.	D3	121
Perrysville, Oh., U.S.	B3	142
Perryton, Tx., U.S.	A2	150
Perryville, Ak., U.S.	D8	109
Perryville, Ar., U.S.	B3	111
Perryville, Ky., U.S.	C5	124
Perryville, Md., U.S.	A5	127
Perryville, Mo., U.S.	D8	132
Perryville, Tn., U.S.	B3	149
Peršaj, U.S.S.R.	G9	26
Perseverancia, Bol.	F10	82
Pershing, In., U.S.	E7	121
Pershing, Ia., U.S.	C5	122
Pershing, co., Nv., U.S.	C3	135
Persia, Ia., U.S.	C2	122
Persia see Iran, ctry., Asia	C5	42
Persian Gulf (Arabian Gulf), b., Asia	H11	48
Persimmon Grove, Ky., U.S.	k14	124
Person, co., N.C., U.S.	A3	140
Pertek, Tur.	B5	48
Perth, Austl.	F3	68
Perth, Ont., Can.	C8	103
Perth, Scot., U.K.	E10	8
Perth Amboy, N.J., U.S.	B4	137
Perth-Andover, N.B., Can.	D10	101
Pertokar, Eth.	I9	60
Peru, Il., U.S.	B4	120
Peru, In., U.S.	C5	121
Peru, Ks., U.S.	E7	123
Peru, Ne., U.S.	D10	134
Peru, N.Y., U.S.	f11	139
Peru, Vt., U.S.	E3	152
Peru (Perú), ctry., S.A.	E3	76
Peruaçu, stm., Braz.	C6	79
Peru-Chile Trench	G7	74
Perugia, Italy	F7	18
Perugorría, Arg.	E9	80
Peruíbe, Braz.	C15	80
Peruípe, stm., Braz.	D9	79
Pervoavgustovskij, U.S.S.R.	I18	26
Pervomajsk, U.S.S.R.	H4	22
Pervomajskij, U.S.S.R.	H23	26
Pervomajskij, U.S.S.R.	H8	26
Pervoural'sk, U.S.S.R.	F9	22
Pervyj Kuril'skij proliv, strt., U.S.S.R.	G23	24
Pes', U.S.S.R.	C17	26
Pesaro, Italy	F7	18
Pesca, Col.	E6	84
Pescadero, Ca., U.S.	D2	112
Pescadores, Punta, c., Mex.	F5	90
Pescadores, Punta, c., Peru	G5	82
Pescadores see P'enghu Ch'üntao, is., Tai.	L8	34
Peščanaja, U.S.S.R.	A13	20
Peščanka, U.S.S.R.	A12	20
Peščanoje, U.S.S.R.	J24	6
Pescara, Italy	G9	18
Pescia, Italy	F5	18
Pesé, Pan.	D2	84
Peseux, Switz.	E6	13
Peshastin, Wa., U.S.	B5	154
Peshāwar, Pak.	C4	44
Peshtigo, Wi., U.S.	C6	156
Peshtigo, stm., Wi., U.S.	C5	156
Peski, U.S.S.R.	F21	26
Pesmes, Fr.	E12	14
Pesočenskij, U.S.S.R.	G19	26
Pesočnoje, U.S.S.R.	C22	26
Pesočnyj, U.S.S.R.	A13	26
Peso da Régua, Port.	D4	16
Pesotum, Il., U.S.	D5	120
Pespire, Hond.	D7	92
Pesqueira, Braz.	E11	76
Pessac, Fr.	H6	14
Pest, co., Hung.	H19	10
Pest'aki, U.S.S.R.	E25	26
Peštera, Bul.	G8	20
Pestovo, U.S.S.R.	C18	26
Petacalco, Bahía, b., Mex.	I8	90
Petaḥ Tiqwa, Isr.	D3	50
Petal, Ms., U.S.	D4	131
Petalcingo, Mex.	I13	90
Petalión, Kólpos, b., Grc.	L8	20
Petaluma, Ca., U.S.	C2	112
Pétange, Lux.	I8	12
Petare, Ven.	B9	84
Petatlán, Mex.	I9	90
Petawawa, Ont., Can.	B7	103
Petawawa, stm., Ont., Can.	A6	103
Petén, dept., Guat.	A5	92
Petén Itzá, Lago, l., Guat.	I15	90
Petenwell Lake, res., Wi., U.S.	D4	156
Peterborough, Austl.	I3	70
Peterborough, Ont., Can.	C6	103
Peterborough, Eng., U.K.	I13	8
Peterborough, N.H., U.S.	E3	136
Peterculter, Scot., U.K.	D11	8
Peter Dana Point, Me., U.S.	C5	126
Peterhead, Scot., U.K.	D12	8
Peter I Island, i., Ant.	B11	73
Peterman, Al., U.S.	D2	108
Peter Pond Lake, l., Sask., Can.	m7	105
Petersburg, Ak., U.S.	D13	109
Petersburg, De., U.S.	D3	115
Petersburg, Il., U.S.	C4	120
Petersburg, In., U.S.	H3	121
Petersburg, Ky., U.S.	h13	124
Petersburg, Mi., U.S.	G7	129
Petersburg, Ne., U.S.	C7	134
Petersburg, N.D., U.S.	A8	141
Petersburg, Oh., U.S.	B5	142
Petersburg, Tn., U.S.	B5	149
Petersburg, Tx., U.S.	C2	150
Petersburg, Va., U.S.	C5	153
Petersburg, W.V., U.S.	B5	155
Peters Creek, stm., W.V., U.S.	m14	155
Petersfield, Man., Can.	D3	100
Peters Mountain, mtn., U.S.	D4	155
Peterson, Al., U.S.	B2	108
Peterson, Ia., U.S.	B2	122
Peterson, Mn., U.S.	G7	130
Peterson Field, mil., Co., U.S.	C6	113
Peterstown, W.V., U.S.	D4	155
Petersville, Al., U.S.	A2	108
Pétervására, Hung.	G20	10
Petilia Policastro, Italy	J11	18
Pétionville, Haiti	E8	94
Petit Bois Island, i., Ms., U.S.	E5	131
Petitcodiac, N.B., Can.	D4	101
Petitcodiac, stm., N.B., Can.	C5	101
Petit-de-Grat, N.S., Can.	D9	101
Petite Amite, stm., La., U.S.	h10	125
Petite Rivière, N.S., Can.	E5	101
Petite-Rivière-de-l'Île, N.B., Can.	B5	101
Petite Rivière Noire, Piton de la, mtn., Mrts.	V18	67c
Petit-Étang, N.S., Can.	C9	101
Petit-Goâve, Haiti	E8	94
Petit Jean, stm., Ar., U.S.	B2	111
Petit Lac Des Allemands, l., La., U.S.	k11	125
Petit Lake, l., La., U.S.	k12	125
Petitot, stm., Can.	E8	96
Petit-Rocher, N.B., Can.	B4	101
Petit-Saint-Bernard, Col du, Eur.	G13	14
Petitsikapau Lake, l., Newf., Can.	g8	102
Petlād, India	I5	44
Petlalcingo, Mex.	H11	90
Peto, Mex.	G15	90
Petorca, Chile	G3	80
Petoskey, Mi., U.S.	C6	129
Petra see Baträ, hist., Jord.	H4	50
Petra Velikogo, zaliv, b., U.S.S.R.	I18	24
Petrified Forest National Park, Az., U.S.	B6	110
Petrikov, U.S.S.R.	I11	26
Petrila, Rom.	D7	20
Petrinja, Yugo.	D11	18
Petrodvorec, U.S.S.R.	B12	26
Petrokrepost', U.S.S.R.	B14	26
Petrólea, Col.	C6	84
Petroleum, In., U.S.	C7	121
Petroleum, co., Mt., U.S.	C8	133
Petrolia, Ont., Can.	E2	103
Petrolia, Ks., U.S.	E8	123
Petrolia, Tx., U.S.	B3	150
Petrolina, Braz.	E10	76
Petrolina de Goiás, Braz.	D4	79
Petropavlovsk, U.S.S.R.	G11	22
Petropavlovsk-Kamčatskij, U.S.S.R.	G23	24
Petrópolis, Braz.	G7	79
Petros, Tn., U.S.	C9	149
Petroşani, Rom.	D7	20
Petrovsk, U.S.S.R.	G7	22
Petrovskoje, U.S.S.R.	I23	26
Petrovskoje, U.S.S.R.	D22	26
Petrovsk-Zabajkal'skij, U.S.S.R.	G13	24
Petrozavodsk, U.S.S.R.	E4	22
Petrusburg, S. Afr.	G7	66
Petrus Steyn, S. Afr.	F9	66
Petrusville, S. Afr.	H7	66
Pettaquamscutt Lake Shores, R.I., U.S.	F4	146
Petten, Neth.	C6	12
Pettibone, N.D., U.S.	B6	141
Pettigrew, Ar., U.S.	B2	111
Pettingell Peak, mtn., Co., U.S.	B5	113
Pettis, co., Mo., U.S.	C4	132
Pettisville, Oh., U.S.	A1	142
Pettus, Tx., U.S.	E4	150
Petuchovo, U.S.S.R.	F11	22
Petuški, U.S.S.R.	F22	26
Peuerbach, Aus.	G13	10
Pevek, U.S.S.R.	D26	24
Pevely, Mo., U.S.	g13	132
Pewamo, Mi., U.S.	E6	129
Pewaukee, Wi., U.S.	E5	156
Pewaukee Lake, l., Wi., U.S.	m11	156
Pewee Valley, Ky., U.S.	B4	124
Peykjahlíð, Ice.	B5	6a
Peyton, Co., U.S.	B6	113
Pézenas, Fr.	I10	14
Pezinok, Czech.	G17	10
Pfäffikon, Switz.	D10	13
Pfarrkirchen, Ger.	G12	10
Pfeifer, Ks., U.S.	D4	123
Pforzheim, Ger.	G8	10
Pfronten, Ger.	H10	10
Pfungstadt, Ger.	F8	10
Pha-an, Burma	F4	40
Phagwāra, India	E6	44
Phala, Bots.	D8	66
Phalaborwa, S. Afr.	D10	66
Phalodi, India	G5	44
Phalsbourg, Fr.	D14	14
Phaltan, India	D3	46
Phan, Thai.	E5	40
Phangan, Ko, i., Thai.	J6	40
Phangnga, Thai.	J5	40
Phanom Dongrak, Thiu Khao, mts., Asia	G7	40
Phan Rang, Viet.	I10	40
Phan Thiet, Viet.	I10	40
Phariāro, Pak.	G3	44
Pharr, Tx., U.S.	F3	150
Phatthalung, Thai.	K6	40
Phayao, Thai.	E5	40
Pheba, Ms., U.S.	B5	131
Phelps, Ky., U.S.	C7	124
Phelps, N.Y., U.S.	C3	139
Phelps, Wi., U.S.	B4	156
Phelps, co., Mo., U.S.	D6	132
Phelps, co., Ne., U.S.	D6	134
Phelps Lake, l., N.C., U.S.	B6	140
Phenix, Va., U.S.	C4	153
Phenix City, Al., U.S.	C4	108
Phepane, stm., Afr.	E6	66
Phetchabun, Thai.	F6	40
Phetchabun, Thiu Khao, mts., Thai.	F6	40
Phetchaburi, Thai.	H5	40
Phichit, Thai.	F6	40
Philadelphia, Ms., U.S.	C4	131
Philadelphia, Mo., U.S.	B6	132
Philadelphia, N.Y., U.S.	A5	139
Philadelphia, Pa., U.S.	G11	145
Philadelphia, Tn., U.S.	D9	149
Philadelphia, co., Pa., U.S.	G12	145
Philadelphia Naval Shipyard, mil., Pa., U.S.	P21	145
Phil Campbell, Al., U.S.	A2	108
Philip, S.D., U.S.	C4	148
Philipp, Ms., U.S.	B3	131
Philippeville, Bel.	H6	12
Philippi, W.V., U.S.	B4	155
Philippi, Lake, l., Austl.	E3	70
Philippines (Pilipinas), ctry., Asia	C7	38
Philippine Sea	G17	158
Philippine Trench	H16	158
Philippolis, S. Afr.	H7	66
Philipsburg, Que., Can.	D4	104
Philipsburg, Neth. Ant.	F13	94
Philipsburg, Mt., U.S.	D3	133
Philipsburg, Pa., U.S.	E5	145
Philipstown, S. Afr.	H7	66
Philipsville, Ont., Can.	C8	103
Philleo Lake, l., Wa., U.S.	h14	154
Phillip Island, i., Austl.	L6	70
Phillips, Me., U.S.	D2	126
Phillips, Ne., U.S.	D7	134
Phillips, Tx., U.S.	B2	150
Phillips, Wi., U.S.	C3	156
Phillips, co., Ar., U.S.	C5	111
Phillips, co., Co., U.S.	A8	113
Phillips, co., Ks., U.S.	C4	123
Phillips, co., Mt., U.S.	B8	133
Phillips Brook, stm., N.H., U.S.	A4	136
Phillipsburg, Ks., U.S.	C4	123
Phillipsburg, Mo., U.S.	D5	132
Phillipsburg, N.J., U.S.	B2	137
Philmont, N.Y., U.S.	C7	139
Philo, Il., U.S.	C5	120
Philo, Oh., U.S.	C4	142
Philomath, Ga., U.S.	C4	117
Philomath, Or., U.S.	C3	144
Philpott Reservoir, res., Va., U.S.	D2	153
Phimai, Thai.	G7	40
Phippsburg, Co., U.S.	A4	113
Phitsanulok, Thai.	F6	40
Phnom Penh see Phnum Pénh, Camb.	I8	40
Phnum Pénh, Camb.	I8	40
Phoenicia, N.Y., U.S.	C6	139
Phoenix, Az., U.S.	D3	110
Phoenix, Il., U.S.	k9	120
Phoenix, La., U.S.	E6	125
Phoenix, Md., U.S.	A4	127
Phoenix, N.Y., U.S.	B4	139
Phoenix, Or., U.S.	E4	144
Phoenix Islands, is., Kir.	I22	158
Phoenixville, Pa., U.S.	F10	145
Phon, Thai.	G7	40
Phôngsali, Laos	D7	40
Phrae, Thai.	E6	40
Phra Nakhon Si Ayutthaya, Thai.	G6	40
Phuket, Thai.	K5	40
Phuket, Ko, i., Thai.	J5	40
Phu Ly, Viet.	D8	40
Phumĭ Béng, Camb.	H8	40
Phumĭ Chhuk, Camb.	I8	40
Phumĭ Kâmpóng Trâbêk, Camb.	H8	40
Phumĭ Kaôh Kōng, Camb.	I7	40
Phumĭ Sâmraông, Camb.	G7	40
Phumĭ Srê Rônéam, Camb.	H9	40
Phuoc Binh, Viet.	I9	40
Phu Quoc, Dao, i., Viet.	I8	40
Phu Tho, Viet.	D8	40
Phutthaisong, Thai.	G7	40
Phu Yen, Viet.	D8	40
Piacatu, Braz.	F3	79
Piacenza, Italy	D4	18
Pialba, Austl.	E10	70
Piana, Fr.	L23	15a
Pianoro, Italy	E6	18
Piapot, Sask., Can.	H1	105
Piaseczno, Pol.	C21	10
Piatã, Braz.	B8	79
Piatra-Neamț, Rom.	C10	20
Piatt, co., Il., U.S.	D5	120
Piauí, stm., Braz.	D8	79
Piaus, Rio dos, stm., Braz.	B4	79
Piave, stm., Italy	D7	18
Piaxtla, Mex.	E7	90
Piazza Armerina, Italy	L9	18
Pibor, stm., Afr.	G7	56
Pibor Post, Sud.	N7	60
Pibroch, Alta., Can.	B4	98
Pica, Chile	I7	82
Picabo, Id., U.S.	F4	119
Picacho, Az., U.S.	E4	110
Picacho, N.M., U.S.	D4	138
Picardie, hist. reg., Fr.	C9	14
Picayune, Ms., U.S.	E4	131
Piccadilly, Newf., Can.	D2	102
Piceance Creek, stm., Co., U.S.	B2	113
Pichana, stm., Peru	I7	84
Pichanal, Arg.	B6	80
Picher, Ok., U.S.	A7	143
Pichilemu, Chile	H2	80
Pichimá, Col.	E4	84
Pichi-Mahuida, Arg.	J6	80
Pichincha, prov., Ec.	H3	84
Pichis, stm., Peru	D4	82
Pichucalco, Mex.	I13	90
Pickardville, Alta., Can.	B4	98
Pickaway, co., Oh., U.S.	C2	142
Pick City, N.D., U.S.	B4	141
Pickens, Ar., U.S.	D4	111
Pickens, Ms., U.S.	C4	131
Pickens, S.C., U.S.	B2	147
Pickens, co., Al., U.S.	B1	108
Pickens, co., Ga., U.S.	B2	117
Pickens, co., S.C., U.S.	B2	147
Pickensville, Al., U.S.	B1	108
Pickerel, Wi., U.S.	C5	156
Pickerel Lake, l., Wi., U.S.	C5	156
Pickering, Ont., Can.	D5	103
Pickering, Mo., U.S.	A3	132
Pickerington, Oh., U.S.	C3	142
Pickett, co., Tn., U.S.	C8	149
Pickford, Mi., U.S.	B6	129
Pickrell, Ne., U.S.	D9	134
Pickstown, S.D., U.S.	D7	148
Pickwick, Mn., U.S.	G7	130
Pickwick Lake, res., U.S.	A6	131
Pickworth Point, c., Ma., U.S.	f12	128
Pico, i., Port.	k19	62a
Pico, Ponta do, mtn., Port.	k19	62a
Pico de Orizaba, Parque Nacional, Mex.	H11	90
Pico Rivera, Ca., U.S.	n12	112
Picos, Braz.	E10	76
Picos, Riacho dos, stm., Braz.	B8	79
Picota, Peru	B3	82
Picton, Austl.	J9	70
Picton, Ont., Can.	D7	103
Picton, N.Z.	D5	72
Picton, Isla, i., Chile	H3	78
Pictou, N.S., Can.	D7	101
Pictou Island, i., N.S., Can.	D7	101
Pictou Landing, N.S., Can.	D7	101
Picture Butte, Alta., Can.	E4	98
Pictured Rocks National Lakeshore, Mi., U.S.	B4	129
Picture Rocks, Pa., U.S.	D8	145
Pidálion, Akrotírion, c., Cyp.	D3	48
Pidurutalagala, mtn., Sri L.	I6	46
Piedecuesta, Col.	D6	84
Piedicroce, Fr.	L24	15a
Piedmont, Al., U.S.	B4	108
Piedmont, Ca., U.S.	h8	112
Piedmont, Ks., U.S.	E7	123
Piedmont, Mo., U.S.	D7	132
Piedmont, Ok., U.S.	B4	143
Piedmont, S.C., U.S.	B3	147
Piedmont, S.D., U.S.	C2	148
Piedmont, W.V., U.S.	B5	155
Piedmont Lake, res., Oh., U.S.	B4	142
Piedra, C.R.	H11	92
Piedra, Ca., U.S.	D4	112
Piedra, stm., Co., U.S.	D3	113
Piedra Roja, Pan.	I13	92
Piedras, Punta, c., Arg.	H10	80
Piedras, Punta, c., Ven.	B12	84
Piedras Blancas, Arg.	F9	80
Piedras Blancas, Point, c., Ca., U.S.	E3	112
Piedras Coloradas, Ur.	G10	80
Piedras de Tunja, Col.	E5	84
Piedras Negras, Guat.	I14	90
Piedras Negras, Mex.	C9	90
Piedras Negras, hist., Guat.	I14	90
Piedra Sola, Ur.	G10	80
Pieksämäki, Fin.	J20	6
Pielavesi, Fin.	J20	6
Pielinen, l., Fin.	J21	6
Piemonte, prov., Italy	E2	18
Piendamó, Col.	F4	84
Pienza, Italy	F6	18
Pierce, Co., U.S.	A6	113
Pierce, Id., U.S.	C3	119
Pierce, Ne., U.S.	B8	134
Pierce, co., Ga., U.S.	E4	117
Pierce, co., Ne., U.S.	B8	134
Pierce, co., N.D., U.S.	A5	141
Pierce, co., Wa., U.S.	C3	154
Pierce, co., Wi., U.S.	D1	156
Pierce, Lake, l., Fl., U.S.	E5	116
Pierce City, Mo., U.S.	E3	132
Pierce Pond, l., Me., U.S.	C2	126
Pierceton, In., U.S.	B6	121
Pierceville, In., U.S.	F7	121
Pierceville, Ks., U.S.	E3	123
Piermont, N.H., U.S.	C2	136
Pierpont, S.D., U.S.	B8	148
Pierre, S.D., U.S.	C5	148
Pierre, Bayou, stm., Ms., U.S.	D3	131
Pierrefonds, Que., Can.	q19	104
Pierre Part, La., U.S.	k9	125
Pierreville, Que., Can.	C5	104
Pierron, Il., U.S.	E4	120
Pierson, Man., Can.	E1	100
Pierson, Fl., U.S.	C5	116
Pierson, Ia., U.S.	B2	122
Pierz, Mn., U.S.	E4	130
Piešt'any, Czech.	G17	10
Pietermaritzburg, S. Afr.	G10	66
Pietersburg, S. Afr.	D9	66
Pietrasanta, Italy	F5	18
Piet Retief, S. Afr.	F10	66
Pigeon, Mi., U.S.	E7	129
Pigeon, stm., U.S.	f9	140
Pigeon, stm., In., U.S.	A6	121
Pigeon, stm., Mn., U.S.	h10	130
Pigeon, stm., Wi., U.S.	k10	156
Pigeon Cove, Ma., U.S.	A6	128
Pigeon Creek, stm., Al., U.S.	D3	108
Pigeon Creek, stm., In., U.S.	H3	121
Pigeon Forge, Tn., U.S.	D10	149
Pigeon Mountain, mtn., U.S.	B1	117
Pigeon Point, c., Mn., U.S.	h10	130
Pigg, stm., Va., U.S.	D3	153
Piggott, Ar., U.S.	A5	111
Piggs Peak, Swaz.	E10	66
Pigna, Italy	F2	18
Pigs, Bay of, b., Cuba	C4	94
Pigüé, Arg.	I7	80
Pihtipudas, Fin.	J19	6
P'ihyŏn, N. Kor.	C12	32
Pijijiapan, Mex.	J13	90
Pijol, Pico, mtn., Hond.	B7	92
Pikal'ovo, U.S.S.R.	B17	26
Pike, N.H., U.S.	B2	136
Pike, co., Al., U.S.	D4	108
Pike, co., Ar., U.S.	C2	111
Pike, co., Ga., U.S.	C2	117
Pike, co., Il., U.S.	D2	120
Pike, co., In., U.S.	H3	121
Pike, co., Ky., U.S.	C7	124
Pike, co., Ms., U.S.	D3	131
Pike, co., Mo., U.S.	B6	132
Pike, co., Oh., U.S.	C2	142
Pike, co., Pa., U.S.	D11	145
Pike, stm., Wi., U.S.	C6	156
Pike City, Ar., U.S.	C2	111
Pike Island Dam, U.S.	f8	155
Pike Lake, Mn., U.S.	D6	130
Pikes Peak, mtn., Co., U.S.	C5	113
Pikes Rocks, mtn., Pa., U.S.	C3	145
Pikesville, Md., U.S.	B4	127
Piketberg, S. Afr.	I4	66
Piketon, Oh., U.S.	C2	142
Pikeville, Ky., U.S.	C7	124
Pikeville, N.C., U.S.	B5	140
Pikeville, Tn., U.S.	D8	149
Pikwitonei, Man., Can.	B3	100
Pila, Arg.	I9	80
Piła (Schneidemühl), Pol.	B16	10
Pilar, Arg.	F7	80
Pilar, Arg.	F8	80
Pilar, Para.	D9	80
Pilar de Goiás, Braz.	C4	79
Pilar do Sul, Braz.	G5	79
Piława, Pol.	D21	10
Pilaya, stm., Bol.	I9	82
Pilcomayo, stm., S.A.	G8	74
Pilcomayo, Brazo Norte, stm., Para.	C9	80
Pilcomayo, Brazo Sur, stm., S.A.	C9	80
Pilger, Sask., Can.	E3	105
Pilger, Ne., U.S.	B8	134
Pilgrim, Ky., U.S.	C7	124
Pīlībhīt, India	F8	44
Pilica, stm., Pol.	D21	10
Pillager, Mn., U.S.	D4	130
Píllaro, Ec.	H3	84
Pillar Point, c., Ca., U.S.	k7	112
Pilley's Island, Newf., Can.	D4	102
Pillo, mtn., Austl.	K8	70
Pilot Butte, Sask., Can.	G3	105
Pilot Grove, Mo., U.S.	C5	132
Pilot Knob, Mo., U.S.	D7	132
Pilot Knob, mtn., Ar., U.S.	B2	111
Pilot Knob, mtn., Ar., U.S.	C1	111
Pilot Knob, mtn., Id., U.S.	D3	119
Pilot Mound, Man., Can.	E2	100
Pilot Mountain, N.C., U.S.	A2	140
Pilot Peak, mtn., Nv., U.S.	E4	135
Pilot Peak, mtn., Nv., U.S.	B7	135
Pilot Peak, mtn., Wy., U.S.	B3	157
Pilot Point, Tx., U.S.	C4	150
Pilot Range, mts., Nv., U.S.	B7	135
Pilot Range, mts., N.H., U.S.	A4	136
Pilot Rock, Or., U.S.	B8	144
Pilot Station, Ak., U.S.	C7	109
Pilpah Range, mts., Austl.	C3	70
Pilsen see Plzeň, Czech.	F13	10
Piltene, U.S.S.R.	D4	26
Pim, stm., U.S.S.R.	E6	24
Pima, Az., U.S.	E6	110
Pima, co., Az., U.S.	E3	110
Pimba, Austl.	H2	70
Pimentel, Peru	B2	82
Pimmit Hills, Va., U.S.	g12	153
Pina, Spain	D11	16
Pinal, co., Az., U.S.	E4	110
Pinaleno Mountains, mts., Az., U.S.	E5	110
Pinal Mountains, mts., Az., U.S.	D5	110
Pinalón, Cerro, mtn., Guat.	B5	92
Pinang, Pulau, i., Malay.	L6	40
Pinang see George Town, Malay.	L6	40
Pınarbaşı, Tur.	B4	48
Pinar del Río, Cuba	C3	94
Pinardville, N.H., U.S.	E3	136
Pınarhisar, Tur.	H11	20
Pinas, Arg.	F6	80
Piñas, Ec.	I3	84
Piñas, Cerro, mtn., Hond.	B9	92
Pincher Creek, Alta., Can.	E4	98
Pincher Station, Alta., Can.	E4	98
Pinckard, Al., U.S.	D4	108
Pinckney, Mi., U.S.	F7	129
Pinckney Island, i., S.C., U.S.	G6	147
Pinckneyville, Il., U.S.	E4	120
Pinconning, Mi., U.S.	E7	129
Pińczów, Pol.	E20	10
Pindaíba, Ribeirão, stm., Braz.	C3	79
Pindall, Ar., U.S.	A3	111
Pindamonhangaba, Braz.	G6	79
Píndhos Óros, mts., Grc.	J5	20
Pindoyacu, stm., Ec.	H4	84
Pinduši, U.S.S.R.	J24	6
Pindus Mountains see Píndhos Óros, mts., Grc.	J5	20
Pine, Az., U.S.	C4	110
Pine, Co., U.S.	B5	113
Pine, co., Mn., U.S.	D6	130
Pine, stm., Mi., U.S.	D7	129
Pine, stm., Mi., U.S.	D5	129
Pine, stm., N.H., U.S.	C4	136
Pine, stm., Wi., U.S.	C5	156
Pine, stm., Wi., U.S.	C4	156
Pine Apple, Al., U.S.	D3	108
Pine Barrens, reg., N.J., U.S.	D3	137
Pine Bluff, Ar., U.S.	C3	111
Pinebluff, N.C., U.S.	B3	140
Pine Bluffs, Wy., U.S.	E8	157
Pine Bridge, Ct., U.S.	D3	114
Pine Bush, N.Y., U.S.	D6	139
Pine Castle, Fl., U.S.	D5	116
Pine City, Mn., U.S.	E6	130
Pine Creek, Austl.	B6	68
Pine Creek, stm., Nv., U.S.	C5	135
Pine Creek, stm., Pa., U.S.	C6	145
Pine Creek, stm., Wa., U.S.	B8	154
Pine Creek Lake, res., Ok., U.S.	C6	143
Pinedale, Al., U.S.	C3	108
Pinedale, Az., U.S.	C5	110
Pinedale, Wy., U.S.	D3	157
Pine Falls, Man., Can.	D3	100
Pinefield, Md., U.S.	C4	127
Pine Forest Range, mts., Nv., U.S.	B3	135
Pinega, stm., U.S.S.R.	E7	22
Pine Grove, La., U.S.	D5	125
Pine Grove, Pa., U.S.	E9	145
Pine Grove Mills, Pa., U.S.	E6	145
Pine Haven, Wy., U.S.	B8	157
Pine Hill, Al., U.S.	D2	108
Pine Hill, N.J., U.S.	D3	137
Pine Hills, Fl., U.S.	D5	116
Pinehouse Lake, Sask., Can.	B2	105
Pinehouse Lake, l., Sask., Can.	B2	105
Pinehurst, Ga., U.S.	D3	117
Pinehurst, Ma., U.S.	f11	128
Pinehurst, N.J., U.S.	E3	137
Pinehurst, N.C., U.S.	B3	140
Pinehurst Lake, l., Alta., Can.	B5	98
Pine Island, Mn., U.S.	F6	130
Pine Island, N.Y., U.S.	D6	139
Pine Island, i., Fl., U.S.	F4	116
Pine Island Bay, b., Ant.	C11	73
Pine Island Sound, strt., Fl., U.S.	F4	116
Pine Key, i., Fl., U.S.	p10	116
Pine Knot, Ky., U.S.	D5	124
Pine Lake, Ga., U.S.	h8	117
Pine Lake, l., In., U.S.	A4	121
Pine Lake, l., Wi., U.S.	C5	156
Pine Lawn, Mo., U.S.	f13	132
Pine Level, Al., U.S.	C3	108
Pine Level, N.C., U.S.	B4	140
Pinellas, co., Fl., U.S.	D4	116
Pinellas, Point, c., Fl., U.S.	p10	116
Pinellas Park, Fl., U.S.	E4	116
Pine Mountain, Ga., U.S.	D2	117
Pine Mountain, mtn., U.S.	D6	124
Pine Mountain, mtn., Ct., U.S.	B4	114
Pine Mountain, mtn., Ga., U.S.	D2	117
Pine Mountain, mtn., Or., U.S.	D6	144
Pine Mountain, mtn., Tn., U.S.	C9	149
Pine Mountain, mtn., Wy., U.S.	E3	157
Pine Mountain, hills, Ok., U.S.	C6	143
Pineora, Ga., U.S.	D5	117

Name	Map Ref.	Page

Pine Orchard, Ct., U.S. D4 114
Pine Park, Ga., U.S. F2 117
Pine Plains, N.Y., U.S. D7 139
Pine Point, N.W. Ter., Can. D10 96
Pine Point, Me., U.S. E2 126
Pine Prairie, La., U.S. D3 125
Pine Ridge, Ky., U.S. C6 124
Pine Ridge, S.D., U.S. D3 148
Pine Ridge, mtn., Ne., U.S. B2 134
Pine Ridge Indian Reservation, S.D., U.S. D3 148
Pine River, Man., Can. D1 100
Pine River, Mn., U.S. D4 130
Pinerolo, Italy E2 18
Pines, Lake O' the, res., Tx., U.S. C5 150
Pinesdale, Mt., U.S. D2 133
Pine Swamp Knob, mtn., W.V., U.S. B5 155
Pinetops, N.C., U.S. B5 140
Pinetown, S. Afr. G10 66
Pine Tree Corners, De., U.S. C3 115
Pine Valley, Ca., U.S. F5 112
Pine Valley, N.H., U.S. E3 136
Pine Valley, val., Ut., U.S. E2 151
Pine Valley Mountains, mts., Ut., U.S. F2 151
Pineview, Ga., U.S. D3 117
Pineville, Ky., U.S. D6 124
Pineville, La., U.S. C3 125
Pineville, Mo., U.S. E3 132
Pineville, N.C., U.S. B2 140
Pineville, W.V., U.S. D3 155
Pinewald, N.J., U.S. D4 137
Pinewood, Fl., U.S. s13 116
Pinewood, S.C., U.S. D7 147
Piney, Man., Can. E4 100
Piney, Fr. D11 14
Piney Creek, stm., W.V., U.S. n13 155
Piney Flats, Tn., U.S. C11 149
Piney Fork, Oh., U.S. B5 142
Piney Fork, stm., W.V., U.S. h9 155
Piney Point, Md., U.S. D4 127
Piney View, W.V., U.S. n13 155
Piney Woods, Ms., U.S. C3 131
Ping, stm., Thai. F5 40
Ping'anbu, China B4 32
Pingdingshan, China B2 34
Pingdu, China G7 32
Pinghe, China K6 34
Pinghu, China E10 34
Pingjiang, China G2 34
Pingliang, China D8 30
Pingquan, China C6 32
Pingree, Id., U.S. F6 119
Pingshui, China F9 34
P'ingtung, Tai. M9 34
Pingwu, China E7 30
Pingxiang, China H2 34
Pingxiang, China C9 40
Pingyao, China D9 30
Pingyi, China H5 32
Pinhal, Braz. G5 79
Pinhal Novo, Port. G3 16
Pinheiro, Braz. D9 76
Pinheiro Machado, Braz. F12 80
Pinhel, Port. E4 16
Pinhuã, stm., Braz. B9 82
Pini, Pulau, i., Indon. N5 40
Pinillos, Col. C5 84
Piniós, stm., Grc. J6 20
Pinjarra, Austl. F3 68
Pink Cliffs, clf, Ut., U.S. F3 151
Pinkham Notch, N.H., U.S. B4 136
Pink Hill, N.C., U.S. B5 140
Pinlebu, Burma B3 40
Pinnacle, Ar., U.S. C3 111
Pinnacle, N.C., U.S. A2 140
Pinnacle, mtn., N.Y., U.S. B6 139
Pinnacle Buttes, mtn., Wy., U.S. C3 157
Pinnacles National Monument, Ca., U.S. D3 112
Pinnaroo, Austl. J4 70
Pinneberg, Ger. B9 10
Pinole, Ca., U.S. h8 112
Pinon, Az., U.S. A5 110
Pinopolis Dam, S.C., U.S. E8 147
Pinos, Mex. F9 90
Pinos, Mount, mtn., Ca., U.S. E4 112
Pinos Altos, N.M., U.S. E1 138
Pinos-Puente, Spain H8 16
Pinrang, Indon. F6 38
Pins, Pointe aux, c., Ont., Can. E3 103
Pinsk, U.S.S.R. I9 26
Pinson, Al., U.S. f7 108
Pinson, Tn., U.S. B3 149
Pinta, Sierra, mts., Az., U.S. E2 110
Pintado, stm., Braz. B4 79
Pintados, Chile I7 82
Pintados, Salar de, pl., Chile I7 82
Pinto, Arg. E7 80
Pinto Butte, mtn., Sask., Can. H2 105
Pintoyacu, stm., Peru I5 84
Pintwater Range, mts., Nv., U.S. G6 135
Pin'ug, U.S.S.R. E7 22
Pinware, stm., Newf., Can. C3 102
Pioche, Nv., U.S. F7 135
Piombino, Italy G5 18
Pioneer, Oh., U.S. A1 142
Pioneer Mountains, mts., Id., U.S. F5 119
Pioneer Mountains, mts., Mt., U.S. E3 133
Pioner, ostrov, i., U.S.S.R. B16 22
Pionerskij, U.S.S.R. G3 26
Pionki, Pol. D21 10
Piorini, stm., Braz. I11 84
Piorini, Lago, l., Braz. I11 84
Piotrków Trybunalski, Pol. D19 10
Pipanaco, Salar de, pl., Arg. D5 80
Pipe Creek, stm., In., U.S. D6 121
Piper, Ks., U.S. k16 123
Piper City, Il., U.S. C5 120
Pipe Spring National Monument, Az., U.S. A3 110
Pipestem Creek, stm., N.D., U.S. B6 141
Pipestone, Man., Can. E1 100
Pipestone, Mn., U.S. G2 130
Pipestone, co., Mn., U.S. F2 130
Pipestone National Monument, Mn., U.S. G2 130
Pipestone Pass, Mt., U.S. E4 133
Pipinas, Arg. H10 80
Pipmuacan, Réservoir, res., Que., Can. k12 104
Piqua, Ks., U.S. E8 123
Piqua, Oh., U.S. B1 142
Piquiri, stm., Braz. C12 80
Pira, Benin G10 64
Piracanjuba, Braz. D4 79
Piracanjuba, stm., Braz. D4 79
Piracanjuba, stm., Braz. D4 79
Piracicaba, Braz. G5 79
Piracicaba, stm., Braz. G5 79
Piraeus see Piraiévs, Grc. L7 20
Piraí do Sul, Braz. C14 80
Piraiévs (Piraeus), Grc. L7 20
Piraju, Braz. G4 79
Pirajuba, Braz. E4 79
Pirajuí, Braz. F4 79
Piran, Yugo. D8 18
Pirané, Arg. C9 80
Piranga, Braz. F7 79
Piranhas, Braz. D3 79
Pīrān Shahr, Iran C8 48
Pirapó, stm., Braz. G2 79
Pirapora, Braz. D6 79
Piraputanga, Braz. F1 79
Piraquara, Braz. C14 80
Pirarajá, Ur. G11 80
Piraras, Cachoeira de, wtfl, Braz. C2 79
Pirassununga, Braz. F5 79
Piratinga, stm., Braz. C5 79
Piratini, Braz. F12 80
Piratini, stm., Braz. E11 80
Piratuba, Braz. D13 80
Piratucu, stm., Braz. I14 84
Piray, stm., Bol. G10 82
Pirenópolis, Braz. C4 79
Pires do Rio, Braz. D4 79
Pírgos, Grc. L5 20
Piriápolis, Ur. H11 80
Piribebuy, Para. C10 80
Píritu, Ven. B8 84
Píritu, Ven. C8 84
Pirmasens, Ger. F7 10
Pirna, Ger. E13 10
Pirot, Yugo. F6 20
Pirovano, Arg. I8 80
Pīr Panjāl Range, mts., Asia D6 44
Pirtleville, Az., U.S. F6 110
Pisa, Italy F5 18
Pisac, hist., Peru E6 82
Pisagua, Chile H6 82
Piscataqua, stm., N.H., U.S. D5 136
Piscataquis, co., Me., U.S. C3 126
Piscataquis, stm., Me., U.S. C3 126
Piscataquog, stm., N.H., U.S. D3 136
Piscataway, N.J., U.S. B4 137
Piscataway Creek, stm., Md., U.S. C4 127
Pisco, Peru E3 82
Pisco, stm., Peru E4 82
Piscovo, U.S.S.R. D23 26
Piseco Lake, l., N.Y., U.S. B6 139
Písek, Czech. F14 10
Pisek, N.D., U.S. A8 141
Pisgah, Al., U.S. A4 108
Pisgah, Ia., U.S. C2 122
Pisgah, Oh., U.S. n13 142
Pisgah, Mount, mtn., Ct., U.S. B3 114
Pisgah, Mount, mtn., Vt., U.S. F3 152
Pisgah, Mount, mtn., Wy., U.S. B8 157
Pisgah Forest, N.C., U.S. f10 140
Pishan, China B8 44
Pishīn, Pak. E2 44
Pishīn Lora (Lowrah), stm., Asia G18 48
Pisinemo, Az., U.S. E3 110
Pismo Beach, Ca., U.S. E3 112
Pisqui, stm., Peru B4 82
Pisticci, Italy I11 18
Pistoia, Italy F5 18
Pistolet Bay, b., Newf., Can. C4 102
Pisz, Pol. B21 10
Pit, stm., Ca., U.S. B3 112
Pital, Col. F5 84
Pitalito, Col. G4 84
Pitanga, Braz. C13 80
Pitangueiras, Braz. F4 79
Pitangui, Braz. E6 79
Pitcairn, Pa., U.S. k14 145
Pitcairn, dep., Oc. K27 158
Piteå, Swe. I17 6
Pitelino, U.S.S.R. G24 26
Pitești, Rom. E8 20
Pithapuram, India D7 46
Pithiviers, Fr. D9 14
Pitigliano, Italy G6 18
Pitiquito, Mex. B3 90
Pitk'aranta, U.S.S.R. K22 6
Pitkin, La., U.S. D3 125
Pitkin, co., Co., U.S. B4 113
Pitman, N.J., U.S. D2 137
Pitt, co., N.C., U.S. B5 140
Pitt Island, i., B.C., Can. C3 99
Pittman Center, Tn., U.S. D10 149
Pitts, Ga., U.S. E3 117
Pittsboro, In., U.S. E5 121
Pittsboro, Ms., U.S. B4 131
Pittsboro, N.C., U.S. B3 140
Pittsburg, Ca., U.S. g9 112
Pittsburg, Il., U.S. F5 120
Pittsburg, In., U.S. C4 121
Pittsburg, Ks., U.S. E9 123
Pittsburg, Ky., U.S. C5 124
Pittsburg, Ok., U.S. C6 143
Pittsburg, Tx., U.S. C5 150
Pittsburg, co., Ok., U.S. C6 143
Pittsburgh, Pa., U.S. F1 145
Pittsfield, Il., U.S. D3 120
Pittsfield, Me., U.S. D3 126
Pittsfield, Ma., U.S. B1 128
Pittsfield, N.H., U.S. D4 136
Pittsford, Mi., U.S. G6 129
Pittsford, Vt., U.S. D2 152
Pittston, Pa., U.S. D10 145
Pittsview, Al., U.S. C4 108
Pittsville, Md., U.S. D7 127
Pittsville, Wi., U.S. D3 156
Pittsworth, Austl. F9 70
Pittsylvania, co., Va., U.S. D3 153
Pituil, Arg. E5 80
Pitumarca, Peru E6 82
Pium, Braz. F9 76
Piura, Peru A1 82
Piura, dept., Peru A1 82
Piura, stm., Peru A1 82
Piute, co., Ut., U.S. E3 151
Piute Peak, mtn., Ca., U.S. E4 112
Piute Reservoir, res., Ut., U.S. E3 151
Pivan', U.S.S.R. G19 24
Pivijay, Col. B5 84
Pixley, Ca., U.S. E4 112
Pizzo, Italy K11 18
Placentia, Newf., Can. E5 102
Placentia Bay, b., Newf., Can. E4 102
Placer, co., Ca., U.S. C3 112
PLacer Mountain, mtn., N.M., U.S. k8 138
Placerville, Ca., U.S. C3 112
Placerville, Co., U.S. C2 113
Placetas, Cuba C5 94
Plachtejevka, U.S.S.R. C13 20
Placid, Lake, l., Fl., U.S. E5 116
Placid, Lake, l., N.Y., U.S. f11 139
Placida, Fl., U.S. F4 116
Plácido de Castro, Braz. D8 82
Plácido Rosas, Ur. G12 80
Placitas, N.M., U.S. B3 138
Plain, Wi., U.S. E3 156
Plain City, Oh., U.S. B2 142
Plain City, Ut., U.S. B3 151
Plain Dealing, La., U.S. B2 125
Plainfield, Ct., U.S. C8 114
Plainfield, Il., U.S. B5 120
Plainfield, In., U.S. E5 121
Plainfield, Ia., U.S. B5 122
Plainfield, N.H., U.S. C2 136
Plainfield, N.J., U.S. B4 137
Plainfield, Vt., U.S. C4 152
Plainfield, Wi., U.S. D4 156
Plainfield Heights, Mi., U.S. E5 129
Plains, Ga., U.S. D2 117
Plains, Ks., U.S. E3 123
Plains, Mt., U.S. C2 133
Plains, Pa., U.S. n17 145
Plains, Tx., U.S. C1 150
Plainsboro, N.J., U.S. C3 137
Plainview, Ar., U.S. C2 111
Plainview, Mn., U.S. F6 130
Plainview, Ne., U.S. B8 134
Plainview, Tx., U.S. B2 150
Plainville, Ct., U.S. C4 114
Plainville, Ga., U.S. D3 117
Plainville, Il., U.S. D2 120
Plainville, In., U.S. G3 121
Plainville, Ks., U.S. C4 123
Plainville, Ma., U.S. B5 128
Plainwell, Mi., U.S. F5 129
Plaistow, N.H., U.S. E4 136
Plamondon, Alta., Can. B4 98
Planalto, Braz. C8 79
Planalto, Braz. D12 80
Planeta Rica, Col. C5 84
Plankinton, S.D., U.S. D7 148
Plano, Il., U.S. B5 120
Plano, Tx., U.S. C4 150
Plantagenet, Ont., Can. B9 103
Plantation, Fl., U.S. r13 116
Plant City, Fl., U.S. D4 116
Plantersville, Al., U.S. C3 108
Plantersville, Ms., U.S. A5 131
Plantsite, Az., U.S. D6 110
Plantsville, Ct., U.S. C4 114
Plaquemine, La., U.S. D4 125
Plaquemines, co., La., U.S. E6 125
Plasencia, Spain E5 16
Plast, U.S.S.R. G10 22
Plaster Rock, N.B., Can. C2 101
Plata, Isla de la, i., Ec. H2 84
Plata, Río de la, est., S.A. H10 80
Plateau, N.S., Can. C8 101
Plateau Creek, stm., Co., U.S. B3 113
Plate Cove West, Newf., Can. D5 102
Plato, Col. C5 84
Platonovka, U.S.S.R. I24 26
Platta, Switz. E10 13
Platte, S.D., U.S. D7 148
Platte, co., Mo., U.S. B3 132
Platte, co., Ne., U.S. C8 134
Platte, co., Wy., U.S. D7 157
Platte, stm., U.S. B3 132
Platte, stm., Mn., U.S. E4 130
Platte, stm., Ne., U.S. D6 134
Platte Center, Ne., U.S. C8 134
Platte City, Mo., U.S. B3 132
Plattenville, La., U.S. k9 125
Platter, Ok., U.S. D5 143
Platteville, Co., U.S. A6 113
Platteville, Wi., U.S. F3 156
Plattsburg, Mo., U.S. B3 132
Plattsburgh, N.Y., U.S. f11 139
Plattsburgh Air Force Base, mil., N.Y., U.S. f11 139
Plattsmouth, Ne., U.S. D10 134
Plattsville, Ont., Can. D4 103
Platveld, Nmb. B3 66
Plau, Ger. B12 10
Plauen, Ger. E12 10
Plav, Yugo. G3 20
Plaviņas, U.S.S.R. E8 26
Plavsk, U.S.S.R. H20 26
Playa Azul, Mex. I8 90
Playa Bonita, C.R. H10 92
Playa del Carmen, Mex. G16 90
Playa Noriega, Laguna, l., Mex. C4 90
Playas, N.M., U.S. F1 138
Playas Lake, l., N.M., U.S. F2 138
Playa Vicente, Mex. I12 90
Play Cu, Viet. H10 40
Playgreen Lake, l., Man., Can. B2 100
Playon Grande, Pan. C3 84
Plaza, N.D., U.S. A4 141
Plaza de Caisán, Pan. I12 92
Plaza Huincul, Arg. J4 80
Pleasant, stm., Me., U.S. C3 126
Pleasant, Lake, res., Az., U.S. D3 110
Pleasant, Mount, mtn., Va., U.S. C3 153
Pleasant Bay, N.S., Can. C9 101
Pleasantdale, Sask., Can. E3 105
Pleasant Dale, Ne., U.S. D9 134
Pleasant Gap, Pa., U.S. E6 145
Pleasant Garden, N.C., U.S. B3 140
Pleasant Grove, Al., U.S. g7 108
Pleasant Grove, Ut., U.S. C4 151
Pleasant Hill, Ca., U.S. h8 112
Pleasant Hill, Il., U.S. D3 120
Pleasant Hill, Ia., U.S. e8 122
Pleasant Hill, La., U.S. C2 125
Pleasant Hill, Me., U.S. g7 126
Pleasant Hill, Ms., U.S. A4 131
Pleasant Hill, Mo., U.S. C3 132
Pleasant Hill, Oh., U.S. B1 142
Pleasant Hills, Md., U.S. A5 127
Pleasant Hope, Mo., U.S. D4 132
Pleasant Lake, In., U.S. A7 121
Pleasant Lake, l., Me., U.S. C5 126
Pleasant Lake, l., N.H., U.S. D4 136
Pleasant Mills, In., U.S. C8 121
Pleasanton, Ca., U.S. h9 112
Pleasanton, Ks., U.S. D9 123
Pleasanton, Ne., U.S. D6 134
Pleasanton, Tx., U.S. E3 150
Pleasant Plains, Ar., U.S. B4 111
Pleasant Plains, Il., U.S. D4 120
Pleasant Pond, l., Me., U.S. C3 126
Pleasant Prairie, Wi., U.S. n12 156
Pleasants, co., W.V., U.S. B3 155
Pleasant Shade, Tn., U.S. C8 149
Pleasant Valley, Ia., U.S. g11 122
Pleasant Valley, Mo., U.S. h11 132
Pleasant Valley, N.Y., U.S. D7 139
Pleasant Valley, Oh., U.S. C2 142
Pleasant View, In., U.S. m11 121
Pleasant View, Ky., U.S. D5 124
Pleasant View, Tn., U.S. A4 149
Pleasant View, Ut., U.S. B3 151
Pleasant View, Wi., U.S. D3 156
Pleasantville, In., U.S. G3 121
Pleasantville, Ia., U.S. C4 122
Pleasantville, N.J., U.S. E3 137
Pleasantville, N.Y., U.S. D7 139
Pleasantville, Oh., U.S. C3 142
Pleasure Beach, Ct., U.S. D7 114
Pleasure Ridge Park, Ky., U.S. g11 124
Pleasureville, Ky., U.S. B4 124
Plechanovo, U.S.S.R. G20 26
Pléneuf, Fr. D4 14
Plenty, Sask., Can. F1 105
Plenty, Bay of, b., N.Z. B6 72
Plentywood, Mt., U.S. B12 133
Pleščenicy, U.S.S.R. G10 26
Pleseck, U.S.S.R. E6 22
Plessisville, Que., Can. C6 104
Pleszew, Pol. D17 10
Pleven, Bul. F8 20
Plevna, Ks., U.S. E5 123
Plevna, Mt., U.S. D12 133
Pliny Range, mts., N.H., U.S. B4 136
Pljevlja, Yugo. F3 20
Ploaghe, Italy I3 18
Płock, Pol. C19 10
Plöckenpass, Eur. I12 10
Ploërmel, Fr. E4 14
Ploești see Ploiești, Rom. E10 20
Ploiești, Rom. E10 20
Plomárion, Grc. K10 20
Plomosa Mountains, mts., Az., U.S. D1 110
Plön, Ger. A10 10
Plonge, Lac la, l., Sask., Can. B2 105
Płońsk, Pol. C20 10
Pl'os, U.S.S.R. D24 26
Ploskoje, U.S.S.R. I21 26
Plottier, Arg. J4 80
Plouay, Fr. E3 14
Ploudalmézeau, Fr. D2 14
Plouguenast, Fr. D4 14
Plouha, Fr. D4 14
Plovdiv, Bul. G8 20
Plover, Wi., U.S. D4 156
Plover, stm., Wi., U.S. D4 156
Plum, Pa., U.S. k14 145
Pluma, S.D., U.S. C2 148
Plumas, Man., Can. D2 100
Plumas, co., Ca., U.S. B3 112
Plum Bayou, stm., Ar., U.S. k10 111
Plum Beach, R.I., U.S. E4 146
Plum City, Wi., U.S. D1 156
Plum Coulee, Man., Can. E3 100
Plum Creek, stm., Ne., U.S. D6 134
Plumerville, Ar., U.S. B3 111
Plum Island, i., Ma., U.S. A6 128
Plummer, Id., U.S. B2 119
Plummer, Mn., U.S. C2 130
Plum Point, Md., U.S. C4 127
Plumsteadville, Pa., U.S. F11 145
Plumtree, Zimb. C8 66
Plungė, U.S.S.R. F4 26
Plunkett, Sask., Can. F3 105
Pl'ussa, U.S.S.R. C12 26
Pl'ussa, stm., U.S.S.R. C11 26
Plutarco Elías Calles, Presa, res., Mex. C5 90
Plymouth, Monts. F13 94
Plymouth, Eng., U.K. K9 8
Plymouth, Ct., U.S. C3 114
Plymouth, Fl., U.S. D5 116
Plymouth, Il., U.S. C3 120
Plymouth, In., U.S. B5 121
Plymouth, Ia., U.S. A4 122
Plymouth, Ks., U.S. D7 123
Plymouth, Me., U.S. D3 126
Plymouth, Ma., U.S. C6 128
Plymouth, Mi., U.S. p15 129
Plymouth, Mn., U.S. m12 130
Plymouth, Ne., U.S. D9 134
Plymouth, N.H., U.S. C3 136
Plymouth, N.C., U.S. B6 140
Plymouth, Oh., U.S. A3 142
Plymouth, Pa., U.S. D10 145
Plymouth, Ut., U.S. B3 151
Plymouth, Vt., U.S. E3 152
Plymouth, Wi., U.S. E6 156
Plymouth, co., Ia., U.S. B1 122
Plymouth, co., Ma., U.S. C6 128
Plymouth Bay, b., Ma., U.S. C6 128
Plympton, N.S., Can. E4 101
Plzeň, Czech. F13 10
Pô, Burkina F9 64
Po, stm., Italy E7 18
Po, stm., Va., U.S. B5 153
Poamoho Stream, stm., Hi., U.S. f9 118
Poana, stm., Braz. G14 84
Poás, Volcán, vol., C.R. G10 92
Pobé, Benin H11 64
Pobeda, gora, mtn., U.S.S.R. D21 24
Pobeda Ice Island, i., Ant. B6 73
Pobedino, U.S.S.R. H20 24
Pobedy, pik, mtn., Asia I14 22
Pocahontas, Ar., U.S. A5 111
Pocahontas, Il., U.S. E4 120
Pocahontas, Ia., U.S. B3 122
Pocahontas, Tn., U.S. B3 149
Pocahontas, Va., U.S. e10 153
Pocahontas, co., Ia., U.S. B3 122
Pocahontas, co., W.V., U.S. C4 155
Pocasset, Ma., U.S. C6 128
Pocasset, Ok., U.S. B4 143
Pocatalico, W.V., U.S. C3 155
Pocatalico, stm., W.V., U.S. C3 155
Pocatello, Id., U.S. G6 119
Počep, U.S.S.R. I16 26
Pöchlarn, Aus. G15 10
Pochvistnevo, U.S.S.R. G8 22
Počinok, U.S.S.R. G15 26
Pocitos, Salar, pl., Arg. C5 80
Pocoata, Bol. H8 82
Poções, Braz. C8 79
Poço Fundo, Braz. A16 80
Pocola, Ok., U.S. B7 143
Pocomoke, stm., Md., U.S. D7 127
Pocomoke City, Md., U.S. D6 127
Pocomoke Sound, strt., Md., U.S. E6 127
Pocona, Bol. G9 82
Poconé, Braz. G13 82
Pocono Mountains, hills, Pa., U.S. E11 145
Pocono Pines, Pa., U.S. D11 145
Poços de Caldas, Braz. F5 79
Pocotopaug Lake, res., Ct., U.S. C6 114
Pocrane, Braz. E8 79
Pocrí, Pan. I14 92
Pocumtuck Mountain, mtn., Ma., U.S. A2 128
Podberezje, U.S.S.R. E13 26
Podborovje, U.S.S.R. B18 26
Poddorje, U.S.S.R. D14 26
Poděbrady, Czech. E15 10
Podkamennaja Tunguska, stm., U.S.S.R. E11 24
Podol'sk, U.S.S.R. F20 26
Podor, Maur. C2 64
Podoz'orskij, U.S.S.R. D23 26
Podporožje, U.S.S.R. E4 22
Podravska Slatina, Yugo. D1 20
Podsvilje, U.S.S.R. F10 26
Podujevo, Yugo. G5 20
Podu Turcului, Rom. C11 20
Pofadder, S. Afr. G4 66
Pogan, China G5 34
Pogar, U.S.S.R. I16 26
Poge, Cape, c., Ma., U.S. D7 128
Poggibonsi, Italy F6 18
Pogoanele, Rom. E11 20
Pogoreloje Gorodišče, U.S.S.R. E17 26
Pogost, U.S.S.R. H12 26
Pograničnyj, U.S.S.R. I18 24
P'ohang, S. Kor. G17 32
Pohénégamook, Que., Can. B8 104
Pohjois-Karjalan lääni, prov., Fin. J21 6
Pohue Bay, b., Hi., U.S. E6 118
Poinsett, co., Ar., U.S. B5 111
Poinsett, Cape, c., Ant. B6 73
Poinsett, Lake, l., Fl., U.S. D6 116
Poinsett, Lake, l., S.D., U.S. C8 148
Point Arena, Ca., U.S. C2 112
Point Clear, Al., U.S. E2 108
Pointe a la Hache, La., U.S. E6 125
Pointe-à-Pitre, Guad. F14 94
Pointe au Baril Station, Ont., Can. B4 103
Pointe-au-Pic, Que., Can. B7 104
Pointe-Calumet, Que., Can. p19 104
Pointe-Claire, Que., Can. D4 104
Pointe Coupee, co., La., U.S. D4 125
Pointe-des-Cascades, Que., Can. q19 104
Pointe du Bois, Man., Can. D4 100
Pointe-du-Chêne, N.B., Can. C5 101
Point Edward, Ont., Can. D2 103
Pointe-Noire, Congo B2 58
Pointe-Verte, N.B., Can. B4 101
Point Fortin, Trin. I14 94
Point Hope, Ak., U.S. B6 109
Point Imperial, mtn., Az., U.S. A4 110
Point Judith Pond, l., R.I., U.S. F4 146
Point Lake, l., N.W. Ter., Can. C10 96
Point Leamington, Newf., Can. D4 102
Point Marion, Pa., U.S. G2 145
Point Mugu Naval Air Station, mil., Ca., U.S. E4 112
Point of Rocks, Md., U.S. B2 127
Point of Rocks, Wy., U.S. E4 157
Point Pelee National Park, Ont., Can. F2 103
Point Pleasant, N.J., U.S. C4 137
Point Pleasant, W.V., U.S. C2 155
Point Pleasant Beach, N.J., U.S. C4 137
Point Reyes National Seashore, Ca., U.S. C2 112
Point Roberts, Wa., U.S. A2 154
Point Sapin, N.B., Can. C5 101
Poipu, Hi., U.S. B2 118
Poison Creek, stm., Wy., U.S. C5 157
Poisson Blanc, Lac du, res., Que., Can. C2 104
Poissy, Fr. D9 14
Poitiers, Fr. F7 14
Poix, Fr. C8 14
Pojarkovo, U.S.S.R. H17 24
Pojo, Bol. G9 82
Pojuca, stm., Braz. B9 79
Pokegama Lake, l., Mn., U.S. C5 130
Pokegama Lake, l., Wi., U.S. C2 156
Pokharā, Nepal F10 44
Pokrov, U.S.S.R. F22 26
Pokrovsk, U.S.S.R. E17 24
Pokrovskoje, U.S.S.R. I19 26
Pola, U.S.S.R. D14 26
Polacca, Az., U.S. B5 110
Pola de Lena, Spain B6 16
Polān, Iran I16 48
Polanco, Ur. G11 80
Poland, In., U.S. F4 121
Poland (Polska), ctry., Eur. E11 4
Poland Spring, Me., U.S. D2 126
Polanów, Pol. A16 10
Polar Bear Provincial Park, Ont., Can. n18 103
Pol'arnyj, U.S.S.R. D4 22
Polatlı, Tur. B2 48
Polcura, Chile I3 80
Polecat Creek, stm., Ok., U.S. B5 143
Pol-e Khomrī, Afg. C3 44
Polesje, reg., U.S.S.R. G3 22
Polessk [Labiau], U.S.S.R. G4 26
Polevskoj, U.S.S.R. F10 22
Polgár, Hung. H21 10
Pŏlgyo, S. Kor. I15 32
Police, Pol. B14 10
Poligny, Fr. F12 14
Pólis, Cyp. D2 48
Polish Mountain, mtn., U.S. k13 127
Polistena, Italy K11 18
Políyiros, Grc. I7 20
Polk, Ne., U.S. C8 134
Polk, Pa., U.S. D2 145
Polk, co., Ar., U.S. C1 111
Polk, co., Fl., U.S. E5 116
Polk, co., Ga., U.S. C1 117
Polk, co., Ia., U.S. C4 122
Polk, co., Mn., U.S. C2 130
Polk, co., Mo., U.S. D4 132
Polk, co., Ne., U.S. C8 134
Polk, co., N.C., U.S. f10 140
Polk, co., Or., U.S. C3 144
Polk, co., Tn., U.S. D9 149
Polk, co., Tx., U.S. D5 150
Polk, co., Wi., U.S. C1 156
Polk City, Fl., U.S. D5 116
Polk City, Ia., U.S. C4 122
Polkton, N.C., U.S. B2 140
Polla, Italy I10 18
Pollāchi, India G4 46
Pollard, Al., U.S. D2 108
Pollard, Ar., U.S. A5 111
Pollards Point, Newf., Can. D3 102
Pöllau, Aus. H15 10
Pollock, La., U.S. C3 125
Pollock, S.D., U.S. B5 148
Pol'noje-Jaltunovo, U.S.S.R. H24 26
Polo, Il., U.S. B4 120
Polo, Mo., U.S. B3 132
Polochic, stm., Guat. B5 92
Polock, U.S.S.R. F11 26
Polonio, Cabo, c., Ur. H12 80
Polonnaruwa, Sri L. I6 46
Polotn'anyj, U.S.S.R. G19 26
Polson, Mt., U.S. C2 133
Poltava, U.S.S.R. H4 22
Põltsamaa, U.S.S.R. C8 26
Poluj, stm., U.S.S.R. D11 22
Polunočnoje, U.S.S.R. E10 22
Polvadera, N.M., U.S. C3 138
Polynesia, is., Oc. I24 158
Polysajevo, U.S.S.R. G15 22
Pomabamba, Peru C3 82
Pomacanchi, Peru F6 82
Pomata, Peru G7 82
Pombal, Port. F3 16
Pombas, Rio das, stm., Braz. B11 82
Pomene, Moz. D12 66
Pomerania, hist. reg., Pol. A16 10
Pomeranian Bay, b., Eur. A14 10
Pomerene, Az., U.S. E5 110
Pomerode, Braz. D14 80
Pomeroon, stm., Guy. D13 84
Pomeroy, Ia., U.S. B3 122
Pomeroy, Oh., U.S. C3 142
Pomeroy, Wa., U.S. C8 154
Pomfret, Ct., U.S. B8 114
Pomfret, Md., U.S. C3 127
Pomfret Center, Ct., U.S. B8 114
Pomme de Terre, stm., Mn., U.S. E3 130
Pomme de Terre, stm., Mo., U.S. D4 132
Pomme de Terre Lake, res., Mo., U.S. D4 132
Pomoho, Hi., U.S. f9 118
Pomona, Ca., U.S. E5 112
Pomona, Ks., U.S. D8 123
Pomona, Mo., U.S. E6 132
Pomona, N.J., U.S. E3 137
Pomona Lake, res., Ks., U.S. D7 123
Pomona Park, Fl., U.S. C5 116
Pompano Beach, Fl., U.S. F6 116
Pompei, Italy I9 18
Pompei, hist., Italy I9 18
Pompéia, Braz. G3 79
Pompéu, Braz. E6 79
Pompton Lakes, N.J., U.S. A4 137
Pomquet, N.S., Can. D8 101
Ponaganset, stm., R.I., U.S. C2 146
Ponaganset Reservoir, res., R.I., U.S. B2 146
Ponca, Ne., U.S. B9 134
Ponca City, Ok., U.S. A4 143
Ponca Creek, stm., U.S. A6 134
Ponca Indian Reservation, Ne., U.S. B7 134
Ponce, P.R. E11 94
Ponce de Leon, Fl., U.S. u16 116
Ponce de Leon Bay, b., Fl., U.S. G5 116
Ponce de Leon Inlet, b., Fl., U.S. C6 116
Poncha Pass, Co., U.S. C4 113
Poncha Springs, Co., U.S. C4 113
Ponchatoula, La., U.S. D5 125
Pond, stm., Ky., U.S. C2 124
Pond, West Fork, stm., Ky., U.S. C2 124
Pond Creek, Ok., U.S. A3 143
Pond Creek, stm., Co., U.S. C7 113
Pond Creek, stm., Ky., U.S. g11 124

Name — Map Ref. — Page

Pondera, co., Mt., U.S. B4 133
Ponderay, Id., U.S. A2 119
Ponderosa, N.M., U.S. B3 138
Pond Fork, stm., W.V., U.S. D3 155
Pond Fork, West Fork, stm., W.V., U.S. n12 155
Pondicherry, India G5 46
Pondicherry, ter., India G5 46
Pond Inlet, N.W. Ter., Can. B17 96
Pond Inlet, b., N.W. Ter., Can. B17 96
Pondoland, hist. reg., Transkei H9 66
Ponds, Island of, i., Newf., Can. B4 102
Pone Island, i., Md., U.S. D5 127
Poneto, In., U.S. C7 121
Ponferrada, Spain C5 16
Ponkapog Pond, l., Ma., U.S. h11 128
Ponnūru Nidubrolu, India D6 46
Ponoj, stm., U.S.S.R. D5 22
Ponoka, Alta., Can. C4 98
Ponorogo, Indon. J15 39a
Pons, Fr. G6 14
Ponsford, Mn., U.S. D3 130
Ponta do Sol, Port. M20 17a
Ponta Grossa, Braz. C13 80
Pontalina, Braz. D4 79
Ponta Porã, Braz. G1 79
Pontarlier, Fr. F13 14
Pontassieve, Italy F6 18
Pont-Audemer, Fr. C7 14
Pont-Aven, Fr. E3 14
Pont Canavese, Italy D2 18
Pontchartrain, Lake, l., La., U.S. D5 125
Pont-d'Ain, Fr. F12 14
Pont-de-Vaux, Fr. F11 14
Ponte Alta do Bom Jesus, Braz. B5 79
Ponte Branca, Braz. D2 79
Pontedera, Italy F5 18
Ponteix, Sask., Can. H2 105
Ponte Nova, Braz. F7 79
Ponte Serrada, Braz. D13 80
Pontevedra, Spain C3 16
Ponte Vedra Beach, Fl., U.S. B5 116
Pontiac, Il., U.S. C5 120
Pontiac, Mi., U.S. F7 129
Pontianak, Indon. F4 38
Pontivy, Fr. D4 14
Pont-l'Abbé, Fr. E2 14
Pont-l'Évêque, Fr. C7 14
Pontoise, Fr. C9 14
Pontoosuc Lake, l., Ma., U.S. B1 128
Pontorson, Fr. D5 14
Pontotoc, Ms., U.S. A4 131
Pontotoc, co., Ms., U.S. A4 131
Pontotoc, co., Ok., U.S. C5 143
Pontremoli, Italy E4 18
Pontresina, Switz. F12 13
Pont-Rouge, Que., Can. C6 104
Ponts, Spain D13 16
Pont-sur-Yonne, Fr. D10 14
Pontypool, Ont., Can. C6 103
Pontypridd, Wales, U.K. J10 8
Pony, Mt., U.S. E5 133
Ponyri, U.S.S.R. I19 26
Ponziane, Isole, is., Italy I7 18
Poole, Eng., U.K. K12 8
Poole, Ky., U.S. C2 124
Pooler, Ga., U.S. D5 117
Pooles Island, i., Md., U.S. B5 127
Poolesville, Md., U.S. B3 127
Poona see Pune, India C2 46
Poopó, Bol. H8 82
Poopó, Lago, l., Bol. H8 82
Popa, Isla, i., Pan. H12 92
Popayán, Col. F4 84
Pope, Ms., U.S. A4 131
Pope, co., Ar., U.S. B2 111
Pope, co., Il., U.S. F5 120
Pope, co., Mn., U.S. E3 130
Pope Air Force Base, mil., N.C., U.S. B3 140
Poperinge, Bel. G2 12
Popigaj, stm., U.S.S.R. C14 24
Popiltah Lake, l., Austl. I4 70
Poplar, Mt., U.S. B11 133
Poplar, Wi., U.S. B2 156
Poplar, stm., Can. C3 100
Poplar, stm., Mn., U.S. C2 130
Poplar, West Fork, stm., U.S. B11 133
Poplar Bluff, Mo., U.S. E7 132
Poplar Branch, N.C., U.S. A7 140
Poplarfield, Man., Can. D3 100
Poplar Grove, Ar., U.S. C5 111
Poplar Grove, Il., U.S. A5 120
Poplar Island, i., Md., U.S. C5 127
Poplar Mountain, mtn., Ky., U.S. D5 124
Poplarville, Ms., U.S. E4 131
Poplevinskij, U.S.S.R. H22 26
Popocatépetl, Volcán, vol., Mex. H10 90
Popokabaka, Zaire C3 58
Popoli, Italy G8 18
Popondetta, Pap. N. Gui. m16 68a
Popovo, Bul. F10 20
Poppel, Bel. F7 12
Poppi, Italy F6 18
Popple, stm., Wi., U.S. C5 156
Poprad, Czech. F20 10
Poprad, stm., Eur. F20 10
Pŏptong, N. Kor. E15 32
Poptún, Guat. A5 92
Poquonock, Ct., U.S. B5 114
Poquonock Bridge, Ct., U.S. D7 114
Poquoson, Va., U.S. C6 153
Porangatu, Braz. B4 79
Porbandar, India J3 44
Porce, stm., Col. D5 84
Porcher Island, i., B.C., Can. C2 99
Porchov, U.S.S.R. D12 26
Porciúncula, Braz. F7 79
Porco, Bol. H9 82
Porcos, Rio dos, stm., Braz. B6 79
Porcuna, Spain H7 16
Porcupine, S.D., U.S. D3 148
Porcupine Mountains, mts., Mi., U.S. m12 129
Porcupine Plain, Sask., Can. E4 105
Pordenone, Italy D7 18
Porecatu, Braz. G3 79
Porečje, U.S.S.R. H7 26
Porečje Rybnoje, U.S.S.R. D22 26
Pori, Fin. K17 6
Porlamar, Ven. B11 84
Poroma, Bol. H9 82
Poronajsk, U.S.S.R. H20 24
Poroškovo, U.S.S.R. G22 10
Porosozero, U.S.S.R. J23 6
Porozovo, U.S.S.R. I7 26
Porpoise Bay, b., Ant. B7 73
Porrentruy, Switz. D7 13
Portachuelo, Bol. G10 82
Port Adelaide, Austl. J3 70
Portadown, N. Ire., U.K. G7 8
Portage, In., U.S. A3 121
Portage, Me., U.S. B4 126
Portage, Mi., U.S. F5 129
Portage, Pa., U.S. F4 145
Portage, Ut., U.S. B3 151
Portage, Wi., U.S. E4 156
Portage, co., Oh., U.S. A4 142
Portage, co., Wi., U.S. D4 156
Portage, stm., Oh., U.S. B2 142
Portage, North Branch, stm., Oh., U.S. f7 142
Portage Bay, b., Man., Can. D2 100
Portage Des Sioux, Mo., U.S. f13 132
Portage Head, c., Wa., U.S. A1 154
Portage Island, i., N.B., Can. B4 101
Portage Lake, l., Me., U.S. B4 126
Portage Lakes, Oh., U.S. B4 142
Portage la Prairie, Man., Can. E2 100
Portageville, Mo., U.S. E8 132
Portal, Az., U.S. F6 110
Portal, Ga., U.S. D5 117
Portal, N.D., U.S. A3 141
Port Alberni, B.C., Can. E5 99
Portal del Infierno, wtfl, Hond. C9 92
Portales, N.M., U.S. C6 138
Port Alexander, Ak., U.S. D13 109
Port Alfred (Kowie), S. Afr. I8 66
Port Alice, B.C., Can. D4 99
Port Allegany, Pa., U.S. C5 145
Port Allen, La., U.S. D4 125
Port Amherst, W.V., U.S. m12 155
Port Angeles, Wa., U.S. A2 154
Port Anson, Newf., Can. D4 102
Port Antonio, Jam. E6 94
Port Aransas, Tx., U.S. F4 150
Port Arthur, Austl. N7 70
Port Arthur, Tx., U.S. E6 150
Port Arthur see Lüshun, China E9 32
Port Augusta, Austl. I2 70
Port au Port Bay, b., Newf., Can. D2 102
Port au Port [West-Aguathuna-Felix Cove], Newf., Can. D2 102
Port-au-Prince, Haiti E8 94
Port-au-Prince, Baie de, b., Haiti E8 94
Port au Prince Peninsula, pen., Newf., Can. D2 102
Port Austin, Mi., U.S. D7 129
Port Barre, La., U.S. D4 125
Port-Bergé, Madag. O22 67b
Port Birmingham, Al., U.S. B2 108
Port Blair, India I2 40
Port Blandford, Newf., Can. D4 102
Port Bolivar, Tx., U.S. E5 150
Port-Bouët, I.C. I8 64
Port Broughton, Austl. I2 70
Port Burwell, Ont., Can. E4 103
Port Byron, Il., U.S. B3 120
Port Byron, N.Y., U.S. B4 139
Port Canning, India I13 44
Port Carbon, Pa., U.S. E9 145
Port Carling, Ont., Can. B5 103
Port-Cartier-Ouest, Que., Can. k13 104
Port Chalmers, N.Z. F3 72
Port Charlotte, Fl., U.S. F4 116
Port Chester, N.Y., U.S. E7 139
Port Clements, B.C., Can. C1 99
Port Clinton, Oh., U.S. A3 142
Port Clyde, N.S., Can. F4 101
Port Clyde, Me., U.S. E3 126
Port Colborne, Ont., Can. E5 103
Port Coquitlam, B.C., Can. E6 99
Port-de-Paix, Haiti E8 94
Port Deposit, Md., U.S. A5 127
Port Dickinson, N.Y., U.S. C5 139
Port Dickson, Malay. M6 40
Porte Crayon, Mount, mtn., W.V., U.S. C5 155
Port Edward, B.C., Can. B2 99
Port Edward, S. Afr. H10 66
Port Edwards, Wi., U.S. D4 156
Portegolpe, C.R. G9 92
Porteirinha, Braz. C7 79
Portel, Braz. D8 76
Port Elgin, N.B., Can. C5 101
Port Elgin, Ont., Can. C3 103
Port Elizabeth, S. Afr. I7 66
Port Elizabeth, N.J., U.S. E3 137
Porteña, Arg. F7 80
Port-en-Bessin, Fr. C6 14
Porter, Al., U.S. B2 108
Porter, In., U.S. A3 121
Porter, Me., U.S. E2 126
Porter, Ok., U.S. B6 143
Porter, Tx., U.S. D5 150
Porter, co., In., U.S. B3 121
Porter Creek, stm., W.V., U.S. m13 155
Porterdale, Ga., U.S. C3 117
Porterville, Ca., U.S. D4 112
Portete, Bahía de, b., Col. A6 84
Port Ewen, N.Y., U.S. D7 139
Port Fairy, Austl. L5 70
Port Gamble, Wa., U.S. B3 154
Port Gamble Indian Reservation, Wa., U.S. B3 154
Port Gentil, Gabon B1 58
Port George, N.S., Can. D4 101
Port Germein, Austl. I3 70
Port Gibson, Ms., U.S. D3 131
Port Graham, Ak., U.S. D9 109
Port Greville, N.S., Can. D5 101
Port Harcourt, Nig. I13 64
Port Hastings, N.S., Can. D8 101
Port Hawkesbury, N.S., Can. D8 101
Port Hedland, Austl. D3 68
Port Heiden, Ak., U.S. D8 109
Port Henry, N.Y., U.S. A7 139
Port Hill, P.E.I., Can. C6 101
Port Hood, N.S., Can. C8 101
Port Hope, Ont., Can. D6 103
Port Hope, Mi., U.S. E8 129
Port Hope Simpson, Newf., Can. B3 102
Port Howe, Bah. B7 94
Port Hueneme, Ca., U.S. E4 112
Port Huron, Mi., U.S. F8 129
Portia, Ar., U.S. A4 111
Port-Iljič, U.S.S.R. B10 48
Portimão, Port. H3 16
Portis, Ks., U.S. C5 123
Port Isabel, Tx., U.S. F4 150
Port Jefferson, N.Y., U.S. n15 139
Port Jervis, N.Y., U.S. D6 139
Port Kembla, Austl. J9 70
Portland, Austl. I9 70
Portland, Austl. L4 70
Portland, Ont., Can. C8 103
Portland, Ar., U.S. D4 111
Portland, Ct., U.S. C5 114
Portland, In., U.S. D8 121
Portland, Me., U.S. E2 126
Portland, Mi., U.S. F6 129
Portland, Mo., U.S. C6 132
Portland, N.Y., U.S. C1 139
Portland, N.D., U.S. B8 141
Portland, Or., U.S. B4 144
Portland, Tn., U.S. A5 149
Portland, Tx., U.S. F4 150
Portland, Bill of, c., Eng., U.K. K11 8
Portland, Cape, c., Austl. M7 70
Portland Bay, b., Austl. L4 70
Portland Bight, Jam. F6 94
Portland Creek Pond, l., Newf., Can. C3 102
Portland Inlet, b., B.C., Can. B2 99
Portland Point, c., Jam. F6 94
Port Laoise, Ire. H6 8
Port Lavaca, Tx., U.S. E4 150
Port Lincoln, Austl. J1 70
Port Lions, Ak., U.S. D9 109
Port Loko, S.L. G3 64
Port Loring, Ont., Can. B4 103
Port-Louis, Fr. E3 14
Port Louis, Mrts. V18 67c
Port Ludlow, Wa., U.S. B3 154
Port Macquarie, Austl. H10 70
Port Madison Indian Reservation, Wa., U.S. B3 154
Port Maitland, N.S., Can. F3 101
Port Maria, Jam. E6 94
Port Matilda, Pa., U.S. E5 145
Port McNeil, B.C., Can. D4 99
Port McNicoll, Ont., Can. C5 103
Port Medway, N.S., Can. E5 101
Port Monmouth, N.J., U.S. C4 137
Port Moresby, Pap. N. Gui. m16 68a
Port Morien, N.S., Can. C10 101
Port Mouton, N.S., Can. F5 101
Port Neches, Tx., U.S. E6 150
Portneuf, Que., Can. C6 104
Port Nolloth, S. Afr. G3 66
Port Norris, N.J., U.S. E2 137
Porto, Port. D3 16
Porto Acre, Braz. C8 82
Porto Alegre, Braz. F13 80
Porto Amazonas, Braz. C14 80
Porto Amboim, Ang. D2 58
Porto Belo, Braz. D14 80
Portobelo, Pan. C3 84
Port O'Connor, Tx., U.S. E4 150
Porto de Moz, Braz. D8 76
Porto de Pedras, Braz. E11 76
Porto Empedocle, Italy L8 18
Porto Esperança, Braz. H13 82
Porto Esperidião, Braz. F12 82
Porto Farina, Tun. L5 18
Porto Feliz, Braz. G5 79
Porto Ferreira, Braz. F5 79
Port of Spain, Trin. I14 94
Portogruaro, Italy D7 18
Porto Inglês, C.V. m17 64a
Portola, Ca., U.S. C3 112
Porto Lucena, Braz. D11 80
Pörtom (Pirttikylä), Fin. J17 6
Porto Mendes, Braz. C11 80
Porto Murtinho, Braz. I13 82
Porto Nacional, Braz. F9 76
Porto-Novo, Benin H11 64
Port Orange, Fl., U.S. C6 116
Port Orchard, Wa., U.S. B3 154
Porto Recanati, Italy F8 18
Port Orford, Or., U.S. E2 144
Porto San Giorgio, Italy F8 18
Porto Sant'Elpidio, Italy F8 18
Porto Santo, i., Port. L21 17a
Porto São José, Braz. G2 79
Porto Seguro, Braz. D9 79
Porto-Séguro, Togo H10 64
Porto Torres, Italy I3 18
Porto União, Braz. D13 80
Porto Válter, Braz. C5 82
Porto-Vecchio, Fr. M24 15a
Porto Velho, Braz. C10 82
Portoviejo, Ec. H2 84
Port Penn, De., U.S. B3 115
Port Phillip Bay, b., Austl. L6 70
Port Pirie, Austl. I3 70
Port Reading, N.J., U.S. k8 137
Port Renfrew, B.C., Can. E5 99
Port Republic, N.J., U.S. D4 137
Port Rexton, Newf., Can. D5 102
Port Richey, Fl., U.S. D4 116
Port Rowan, Ont., Can. E4 103
Port Royal, Ky., U.S. B4 124
Port Royal, Pa., U.S. E7 145
Port Royal, S.C., U.S. G6 147
Port Royal, Va., U.S. B5 153
Port Royal Island, i., S.C., U.S. G6 147
Port Royal Sound, strt., S.C., U.S. G6 147
Port Said see Būr Sa'īd, Egypt B7 60
Port Saint Joe, Fl., U.S. C1 116
Port Saint Johns, Transkei H9 66
Port Saint Lucie, Fl., U.S. E6 116
Port Salerno, Fl., U.S. E6 116
Port Sanilac, Mi., U.S. E8 129
Port Saunders, Newf., Can. C3 102
Portsea, Austl. L6 70
Port Sewall, Fl., U.S. E6 116
Port Shepstone, S. Afr. H10 66
Portsmouth, Eng., U.K. K12 8
Portsmouth, N.H., U.S. D5 136
Portsmouth, Oh., U.S. D3 142
Portsmouth, R.I., U.S. E6 146
Portsmouth, Va., U.S. D6 153
Portsmouth Naval Shipyard, mil., Me., U.S. D5 136
Portsoy, Scot., U.K. D11 8
Port Stanley, Ont., Can. E3 103
Port Sudan see Būr Sūdān, Sud. H9 60
Port Sulphur, La., U.S. E6 125
Port Talbot, Wales, U.K. J10 8
Port Taufiq see Būr Tawfīq, Egypt G2 48
Porttipahdan tekojärvi, res., Fin. G20 6
Port Townsend, Wa., U.S. A3 154
Portugal, ctry., Eur. H6 4
Portugal, Cachoeira, wtfl, Braz. C9 82
Portugal Cove South, Newf., Can. E5 102
Portugalete, Spain B8 16
Portuguesa, state, Ven. C8 84
Portuguesa, stm., Ven. C9 84
Portuguese Guinea see Guinea-Bissau, ctry., Afr. F3 54
Port Union, Newf., Can. D5 102
Port-Vendres, Fr. J10 14
Portville, N.Y., U.S. C2 139
Port Vincent, La., U.S. D5 125
Port Wakefield, Austl. J3 70
Port Washington, N.Y., U.S. h13 139
Port Washington, Oh., U.S. B4 142
Port Washington, Wi., U.S. E6 156
Port Wentworth, Ga., U.S. D5 117
Porum, Ok., U.S. B6 143
Porvenir, Chile G2 78
Porvenir, Mex. B7 90
Porz, Ger. E7 10
Porzuna, Spain F7 16
Posada, Italy I4 18
Posadas, Arg. D11 80
Posadas, Spain H6 16
Poschiavo, Switz. F13 13
Pošechonje-Volodarsk, U.S.S.R. C22 26
Posen, Il., U.S. k9 120
Posen see Poznań, Pol. C16 10
Posey, co., In., U.S. H2 121
Poseyville, In., U.S. H2 121
Positano, Italy I9 18
Posjet, U.S.S.R. I18 24
Posse, Braz. C5 79
Possession Islands, is., Ant. C8 73
Pössneck, Ger. E11 10
Post, Tx., U.S. C2 150
Postavy, U.S.S.R. F9 26
Poste Ramartina, Madag. Q21 67b
Post Falls, Id., U.S. B2 119
Post Mills, Vt., U.S. D4 152
Postojna, Yugo. D9 18
P'ostraja Dresva, U.S.S.R. E23 24
Postrevalle, Bol. H10 82
Postville, Newf., Can. g10 102
Postville, Ia., U.S. A6 122
Pótam, Mex. D4 90
Potaro, stm., Guy. E13 84
Potaro Landing, Guy. E13 84
Potawatomi Indian Reservation, Ks., U.S. C8 123
Poté, Braz. D8 79
Poteau, Ok., U.S. B7 143
Poteau, stm., U.S. B7 143
Poteau Mountain, mtn., U.S. C1 111
Poteet, Tx., U.S. E3 150
Potenza, Italy I10 18
Potes, Spain B7 16
Potgietersrus, S. Afr. E9 66
Poth, Tx., U.S. E3 150
Potholes Reservoir, res., Wa., U.S. B6 154
Poti, U.S.S.R. I6 22
Poti, stm., Braz. E10 76
Potiraguá, Braz. C9 79
Potirendaba, Braz. F4 79
Potiskum, Nig. F9 54
Potlatch, Id., U.S. C2 119
Potomac, Il., U.S. C6 120
Potomac, Md., U.S. B3 127
Potomac, stm., U.S. D4 127
Potomac, North Branch, stm., U.S. m12 127
Potomac, South Branch, stm., U.S. B6 155
Potomac, South Branch, North Fork, stm., W.V., U.S. C5 155
Potomac, South Branch, South Fork, stm., U.S. B6 155
Potomac Heights, Md., U.S. C3 127
Potomac Park, Md., U.S. k13 127
Potosí, Bol. F8 74
Potosí, Bol. H9 82
Potosi, Mo., U.S. D7 132
Potosi, Wi., U.S. F3 156
Potosí, dept., Bol. I8 82
Potrerillos, Chile D4 80
Potrerillos, Hond. B7 92
Potrerillos Arriba, Pan. I12 92
Potrero, C.R. G9 92
Potrero Grande, C.R. H11 92
Potsdam, Ger. C13 10
Potsdam, N.Y., U.S. f10 139
Pottawatomie, co., Ks., U.S. C7 123
Pottawatomie, co., Ok., U.S. B4 143
Pottawatomie Creek, stm., Ks., U.S. D8 123
Pottawattamie, co., Ia., U.S. C2 122
Potter, Ks., U.S. C8 123
Potter, Ne., U.S. C2 134
Potter, co., Pa., U.S. C6 145
Potter, co., S.D., U.S. B6 148
Potter, co., Tx., U.S. B2 150
Potter Place, N.H., U.S. D3 136
Potter Valley, Ca., U.S. C2 112
Potterville, Ga., U.S. D2 117
Potts Camp, Ms., U.S. A4 131
Potts Creek, stm., U.S. C2 153
Pottstown, Pa., U.S. F10 145
Pottsville, Ar., U.S. B2 111
Pottsville, Pa., U.S. E9 145
Potwin, Ks., U.S. E6 123
P'otzu, Tai. L9 34
Pouancé, Fr. E5 14
Pouce Coupe, B.C., Can. B7 99
Pouch Cove, Newf., Can. E5 102
Poughkeepsie, N.Y., U.S. D7 139
Poulan, Ga., U.S. E3 117
Poulsbo, Wa., U.S. B3 154
Poultney, Vt., U.S. D2 152
Poultney, stm., Vt., U.S. D2 152
Poŭn, S. Kor. G15 32
Pound, Va., U.S. e9 153
Pound, Wi., U.S. C5 156
Pound Gap, U.S. C7 124
Pouso Alegre, Braz. G6 79
Pouso Redondo, Braz. D14 80
Poŭthĭsăt, Camb. H7 40
Považská Bystrica, Czech. F18 10
Povenec, U.S.S.R. J24 6
Póvoa de Varzim, Port. D3 16
Povorino, U.S.S.R. G6 22
Povungnituk, Que., Can. f11 104
Powassan, Ont., Can. A5 103
Poway, Ca., U.S. F5 112
Powder, stm., U.S. B5 106
Powder, stm., Or., U.S. C9 144
Powder, Middle Fork, stm., Wy., U.S. C6 157
Powder, North Fork, stm., Wy., U.S. C6 157
Powder, South Fork, stm., Wy., U.S. C6 157
Powder River, Wy., U.S. C6 157
Powder River, co., Mt., U.S. E11 133
Powder River Pass, Wy., U.S. B5 157
Powder Springs, Ga., U.S. h8 117
Powell, Oh., U.S. B2 142
Powell, Tn., U.S. m13 149
Powell, Wy., U.S. B4 157
Powell, co., Ky., U.S. C6 124
Powell, co., Mt., U.S. D4 133
Powell, stm., U.S. C10 149
Powell, Lake, res., U.S. F5 151
Powell, Mount, mtn., Co., U.S. B4 113
Powell, Mount, mtn., N.M., U.S. B1 138
Powell Butte, Or., U.S. C5 144
Powell Mountain, mtn., U.S. C10 149
Powell Park, reg., Co., U.S. A2 113
Powell River, B.C., Can. E5 99
Powell's Crossroads, Al., U.S. A4 108
Powells Crossroads, Tn., U.S. D8 149
Powellton, W.V., U.S. C3 155
Power, Mt., U.S. C5 133
Power, co., Id., U.S. G5 119
Powers, Or., U.S. E2 144
Powers Lake, N.D., U.S. A3 141
Powerview, Man., Can. D3 100
Poweshiek, co., Ia., U.S. C5 122
Powhatan, Va., U.S. C5 153
Powhatan, co., Va., U.S. C5 153
Powhatan Point, Oh., U.S. C5 142
Powhattan, Ks., U.S. C8 123
Pownal, Vt., U.S. F2 152
Pownal Center, Vt., U.S. F2 152
Powys, co., Wales, U.K. I10 8
Poxoréu, Braz. C1 79
Poyang Hu, l., China F5 34
Poyen, Ar., U.S. C3 111
Poygan, Lake, l., Wi., U.S. D5 156
Poynette, Wi., U.S. E4 156
Poynor, Mo., U.S. E7 132
Poy Sippi, Wi., U.S. D4 156
Požarevac, Yugo. E5 20
Poza Rica, Mex. G11 90
Poznań, Pol. C16 10
Pozo Almonte, Chile I7 82
Pozoblanco, Spain G7 16
Pozo Colorado, Para. B9 80
Pozo del Molle, Arg. G7 80
Pozo del Tigre, Arg. C8 80
Pozo Hondo, Arg. D6 80
Pozo Negro, Spain O27 17b
Pozo Redondo Mountains, mts., Az., U.S. E3 110
Pozuelo de Alarcón, Spain E8 16
Pozuelos, Ven. B10 84
Pozuelos, Laguna de, l., Arg. B6 80
Pozuzo, Peru D4 82
Pozuzo, stm., Peru C4 82
Pozzallo, Italy M9 18
Pozzuoli, Italy I9 18
Prachin Buri, Thai. G6 40
Prachuap Khiri Khan, Thai. I5 40
Praco, Al., U.S. f6 108
Pradera, Col. F4 84
Prades, Fr. J9 14
Prado, Braz. D9 79
Prado Flood Control Basin, Ca., U.S. n13 112
Prados, Braz. F6 79
Prague, Ne., U.S. C9 134
Prague, Ok., U.S. B5 143
Prague see Praha, Czech. E14 10
Praha (Prague), Czech. E14 10
Prahova, co., Rom. D10 20
Praia, C.V. m17 64a
Praia Grande, Braz. E14 80
Prainha, Braz. B11 82
Prairie, Ms., U.S. B5 131
Prairie, co., Ar., U.S. C4 111
Prairie, co., Mt., U.S. D11 133
Prairie, stm., Mn., U.S. C5 130
Prairie, stm., Wi., U.S. C4 156
Prairie Bayou, stm., Ar., U.S. g7 111
Prairie City, Il., U.S. C3 120
Prairie City, Ia., U.S. C4 122
Prairie City, Or., U.S. C8 144
Prairie Creek, In., U.S. F3 121
Prairie Creek Reservoir, res., In., U.S. D7 121
Prairie Dog Creek, stm., U.S. C3 123
Prairie du Chien, Wi., U.S. E2 156
Prairie Du Rocher, Il., U.S. E3 120
Prairie du Sac, Wi., U.S. E4 156
Prairie Farm, Wi., U.S. C2 156
Prairie Grove, Ar., U.S. B1 111
Prairie Home, Mo., U.S. C5 132
Prairie River, Sask., Can. E4 105
Prairies, Rivière des, stm., Que., Can. p19 104
Prairieton, In., U.S. F3 121
Prairie View, Ar., U.S. B2 111
Prairie View, Ks., U.S. C4 123
Prairie View, Tx., U.S. D5 150
Prairie Village, Ks., U.S. m16 123
Prairieville, La., U.S. h10 125
Prampram, Ghana I10 64
Pran Buri, Thai. H5 40
Praslin Island, i., Sey. B11 58
Prata, Braz. E4 79
Prata, Rio da, stm., Braz. D5 79
Prata, Rio da, stm., Braz. E4 79
Prata, Rio da, stm., Braz. E2 79
Pratāpgarh, India H6 44
Pratápolis, Braz. F5 79
Pratas Island see Tungsha Tao, i., Tai. G10 30
Prater Mountain, mtn., Wy., U.S. C2 157
Pratinha, Braz. E5 79
Prato, Italy F6 18
Pratt, Ks., U.S. E5 123
Pratt, co., Ks., U.S. E5 123
Prattsburg, N.Y., U.S. C3 139
Prattsville, Ar., U.S. C3 111
Prattville, Al., U.S. C3 108
Pratudão, stm., Braz. B6 79
Pravdinsk, U.S.S.R. G4 26
Pravdinsk, U.S.S.R. E26 26
Pravdinskij, U.S.S.R. E20 26
Praya, Indon. G6 38
Pr'aža, U.S.S.R. K23 6
Preble, In., U.S. C7 121
Preble, co., Oh., U.S. C1 142
Prečistoje, U.S.S.R. F15 26
Prečistoje, U.S.S.R. C23 26
Preda, Switz. E12 13
Predazzo, Italy C6 18
Predeal, Rom. D9 20
Predești, Rom. E7 20
Predlitz [-Turrach], Aus. H13 10
Preeceville, Sask., Can. F4 105
Pré-en-Pail, Fr. D6 14
Preetz, Ger. A10 10
Pregarten, Aus. G14 10
Pregol'a, stm., U.S.S.R. G4 26
Pregonero, Ven. C7 84
Preila, U.S.S.R. F4 26
Preiļi, U.S.S.R. E9 26
Prelate, Sask., Can. G1 105
Prémery, Fr. E10 14
Premnitz, Ger. C12 10
Premont, Tx., U.S. F3 150
Prenter, W.V., U.S. C3 155
Prentice, Wi., U.S. C3 156
Prentiss, Ms., U.S. D4 131
Prentiss, co., Ms., U.S. A5 131
Prenzlau, Ger. B13 10
Preparis Island, i., Burma G2 40
Preparis North Channel, strt., Burma G3 40
Preparis South Channel, strt., Burma G3 40
Přerov, Czech. F17 10
Prescott, Ont., Can. C9 103
Prescott, Az., U.S. C3 110
Prescott, Ar., U.S. D2 111
Prescott, Ia., U.S. C3 122
Prescott, Ks., U.S. D9 123
Prescott, Mi., U.S. D7 129
Prescott, Wa., U.S. C7 154
Prescott, Wi., U.S. D1 156
Preševo, Yugo. G5 20
Presho, S.D., U.S. D5 148
Presidencia de la Plaza, Arg. D9 80
Presidencia Roca, Arg. D9 80
Presidencia Roque Sáenz Peña, Arg. D8 80
Presidente Epitácio, Braz. F2 79
Presidente Getúlio, Braz. D14 80
Presidente Hayes, dept., Para. C9 80
Presidente Olegário, Braz. E5 79
Presidente Prudente, Braz. G3 79
Presidente Venceslau, Braz. F3 79
Presidential Range, mts., N.H., U.S. B4 136
Presidents Island, i., Tn., U.S. e8 149
Presidio, Tx., U.S. p12 150
Presidio, co., Tx., U.S. o12 150
Presidio, stm., Mex. F7 90
Presidio of San Francisco, mil., Ca., U.S. h8 112
Prešov, Czech. F21 10
Prespa, Lake, l., Eur. I5 20
Presque Isle, Me., U.S. B5 126
Presque Isle, co., Mi., U.S. C6 129
Presto, Bol. H9 82
Preston, Eng., U.K. H11 8
Preston, Ga., U.S. D2 117
Preston, Id., U.S. G7 119
Preston, Ia., U.S. B7 122
Preston, Ks., U.S. E5 123
Preston, Ky., U.S. B6 124
Preston, Md., U.S. C6 127
Preston, Mn., U.S. G6 130
Preston, Ok., U.S. B6 143
Preston, Wa., U.S. e12 154
Preston, co., W.V., U.S. B5 155
Preston Peak, mtn., Ca., U.S. B2 112
Prestonsburg, Ky., U.S. C7 124
Prestonville, Ky., U.S. B4 124
Prestwick, Scot., U.K. F9 8
Presumpscot, stm., Me., U.S. g7 126
Prêto, stm., Braz. E3 79
Prêto, stm., Braz. E8 79
Prêto, stm., Braz. F4 79
Prêto, stm., Braz. B4 79
Prêto, stm., Braz. D5 79
Prêto, stm., Braz. E8 79
Prêto, stm., Braz. C10 82
Prêto, stm., Braz. H10 84
Prêto, Igarapé, stm., Braz. J8 84
Prêto do Igapó-Açu, stm., Braz. J12 84

Name	Map Ref.	Page
Pretoria, S. Afr.	E9	66
Prettyboy Reservoir, res., Md., U.S.	A4	127
Pretty Prairie, Ks., U.S.	E5	123
Préveza, Grc.	K4	20
Prewitt, N.M., U.S.	B1	138
Prewitt Reservoir, res., Co., U.S.	A7	113
Prey Vêng, Camb.	I8	40
Pribilof Islands, is., Ak., U.S.	D5	109
Priboj, Yugo.	F3	20
Příbram, Czech.	F14	10
Price, Tx., U.S.	C5	150
Price, Ut., U.S.	D5	151
Price, co., Wi., U.S.	C3	156
Price, stm., Ut., U.S.	D5	151
Price Inlet, b., S.C., U.S.	k12	147
Priceville, Ont., Can.	C4	103
Priceville, Al., U.S.	A3	108
Prichard, Al., U.S.	E1	108
Prichard, W.V., U.S.	C2	155
Priego de Córdoba, Spain	H7	16
Priekule, U.S.S.R.	E4	26
Priekule, U.S.S.R.	F4	26
Prienai, U.S.S.R.	G6	26
Prieska, S. Afr.	G6	66
Priest Lake, l., Id., U.S.	A2	119
Priest Rapids Dam, Wa., U.S.	C6	154
Priest Rapids Lake, res., Wa., U.S.	C6	154
Priest River, Id., U.S.	A2	119
Prievidza, Czech.	G18	10
Prijedor, Yugo.	E11	18
Prijutovo, U.S.S.R.	G8	22
Prikaspijskaja nizmennost', pl., U.S.S.R.	H7	22
Prilep, Yugo.	H5	20
Priluki, U.S.S.R.	G4	22
Prim, Point, c., P.E.I., Can.	C6	101
Primate, Sask., Can.	E1	105
Primeiro de Maio, Braz.	G3	79
Primero, stm., Arg.	F7	80
Primghar, Ia., U.S.	A2	122
Primorje [Warnicken], U.S.S.R.	G3	26
Primorsk, U.S.S.R.	G3	26
Primorsk, U.S.S.R.	A11	26
Primorsk, U.S.S.R.	A10	48
Primorsko, Bul.	G11	20
Primrose, R.I., U.S.	B3	146
Prince, Sask., Can.	E1	105
Prince, Lake, res., Va., U.S.	k14	153
Prince Albert, Sask., Can.	D3	105
Prince Albert, S. Afr.	I6	66
Prince Albert Mountains, mts., Ant.	C8	73
Prince Albert National Park, Sask., Can.	C2	105
Prince Albert Sound, strt., N.W. Ter., Can.	B9	96
Prince Charles Island, i., N.W. Ter., Can.	C17	96
Prince Charles Mountains, mts., Ant.	C5	73
Prince Edward, co., Va., U.S.	C4	153
Prince Edward Island, prov., Can.	C6	101
Prince Edward Island National Park, P.E.I., Can.	C6	101
Prince Edward Islands, is., S. Afr.	M7	158
Prince Frederick, Md., U.S.	C4	127
Prince George, B.C., Can.	C6	99
Prince George, co., Va., U.S.	C5	153
Prince Georges, co., Md., U.S.	C4	127
Prince of Wales, Cape, c., Ak., U.S.	B6	109
Prince of Wales Island, i., Austl.	B8	68
Prince of Wales Island, i., N.W. Ter., Can.	B13	96
Prince of Wales Island, i., Ak., U.S.	n23	109
Prince of Wales Strait, strt., N.W. Ter., Can.	B9	96
Prince Olav Coast, Ant.	B4	73
Prince Patrick Island, i., N.W. Ter., Can.	B8	86
Prince Regent Inlet, b., N.W. Ter., Can.	B14	96
Prince Rupert, B.C., Can.	B2	99
Princes Lakes, In., U.S.	F5	121
Princess Anne, Md., U.S.	D6	127
Princess Astrid Coast, Ant.	C3	73
Princess Martha Coast, Ant.	C2	73
Princess Ragnhild Coast, Ant.	C3	73
Princess Royal Channel, strt., B.C., Can.	C3	99
Princess Royal Island, i., B.C., Can.	C3	99
Princes Town, Trin.	I14	94
Princeton, B.C., Can.	E7	99
Princeton, Newf., Can.	D5	102
Princeton, Ont., Can.	D4	103
Princeton, Al., U.S.	A3	108
Princeton, Ca., U.S.	C2	112
Princeton, Fl., U.S.	G6	116
Princeton, Id., U.S.	C2	119
Princeton, Il., U.S.	B4	120
Princeton, In., U.S.	H2	121
Princeton, Ia., U.S.	C7	122
Princeton, Ks., U.S.	D8	123
Princeton, Ky., U.S.	C2	124
Princeton, Me., U.S.	C5	126
Princeton, Ma., U.S.	B4	128
Princeton, Mn., U.S.	E5	130
Princeton, Mo., U.S.	A4	132
Princeton, N.J., U.S.	C3	137
Princeton, N.C., U.S.	B4	140
Princeton, W.V., U.S.	D3	155
Princeton, Wi., U.S.	E4	156
Princeton, Mount, mtn., Co., U.S.	C4	113
Princeton Junction, N.J., U.S.	C3	137
Princeville, Que., Can.	C6	104
Princeville, Il., U.S.	C4	120
Princeville, N.C., U.S.	B5	140
Prince William, co., Va., U.S.	B5	153
Prince William Sound, strt., Ak., U.S.	g18	109
Príncipe, i., S. Tom./P.	A1	58
Principe Channel, strt., B.C., Can.	C3	99
Príncipe da Beira, Braz.	E9	82
Prineville, Or., U.S.	C6	144
Prineville Reservoir, res., Or., U.S.	C6	144
Pringle, S.D., U.S.	D2	148
Prinsburg, Mn., U.S.	F3	130
Prinzapolka, Nic.	D11	92
Prinzapolka, stm., Nic.	D11	92
Prior, Cabo, c., Spain	B3	16
Prior Lake, Mn., U.S.	F5	130
Prioz'orsk, U.S.S.R.	K22	6
Prip'at', stm., U.S.S.R.	G3	22
Pripet Marshes see Polesje, reg., U.S.S.R.	G3	22
Prišib, U.S.S.R.	B10	48
Priština, Yugo.	G5	20
Pritchards Island, i., S.C., U.S.	G6	147
Pritchett, Co., U.S.	D8	113
Pritzwalk, Ger.	B12	10
Privas, Fr.	H11	14
Priverno, Italy	H8	18
Privolžsk, U.S.S.R.	D24	26
Privolžskaja vozvyšennost', plat., U.S.S.R.	G7	22
Privolžskij, U.S.S.R.	G7	22
Prizren, Yugo.	G4	20
Prizzi, Italy	L8	18
Prnjavor, Yugo.	E12	18
Probolinggo, Indon.	J16	39a
Probstzella, Ger.	E11	10
Prochladnyj, U.S.S.R.	I6	22
Procter, B.C., Can.	E9	99
Proctor, Mn., U.S.	D6	130
Proctor, Vt., U.S.	D2	152
Proctor Lake, res., Tx., U.S.	C3	150
Proctorsville, Vt., U.S.	E3	152
Proctorville, Oh., U.S.	D3	142
Proddatūr, India	E5	46
Progreso, Mex.	G15	90
Progreso, Ur.	H10	80
Prokopjevsk, U.S.S.R.	G9	24
Prokuplje, Yugo.	F5	20
Proletarij, U.S.S.R.	C14	26
Proletarskij, U.S.S.R.	F20	26
Prome (Pyè), Burma	E3	40
Promissão, Braz.	F4	79
Promontogno, Switz.	F12	13
Promontory Mountains, mts., Ut., U.S.	B3	151
Pronsk, U.S.S.R.	G22	26
Prophetstown, Il., U.S.	B4	120
Propriá, Braz.	F11	76
Propriano, Fr.	M23	15a
Proserpine, Austl.	C8	70
Prospect, N.S., Can.	E6	101
Prospect, Ct., U.S.	C4	114
Prospect, In., U.S.	G4	121
Prospect, Ky., U.S.	g11	124
Prospect, Oh., U.S.	B2	142
Prospect, Or., U.S.	E4	144
Prospect, Pa., U.S.	E1	145
Prospect, Tn., U.S.	B4	149
Prospect, Va., U.S.	C4	153
Prospect Harbor, Me., U.S.	D4	126
Prospect Hill, mtn., Or., U.S.	k11	144
Prospect Hill, hill, Ma., U.S.	g10	128
Prospect Hill, hill, Ma., U.S.	D6	128
Prospect Park, N.J., U.S.	B4	137
Prospect Park, Pa., U.S.	p20	145
Prosperity, S.C., U.S.	C4	147
Prosperity, W.V., U.S.	n13	155
Prosser, Wa., U.S.	C6	154
Prostějov, Czech.	F17	10
Proston, Austl.	F9	70
Protection, Ks., U.S.	E4	123
Protem, S. Afr.	J5	66
Protivin, Ia., U.S.	A5	122
Proton Station, Ont., Can.	C4	103
Protville, Tun.	M5	18
Provadija, Bul.	F11	20
Provencal, La., U.S.	C2	125
Provence, hist. reg., Fr.	I13	14
Providence, Al., U.S.	C2	108
Providence, Ky., U.S.	C2	124
Providence, R.I., U.S.	C4	146
Providence, Ut., U.S.	B4	151
Providence, co., R.I., U.S.	C2	146
Providence, stm., R.I., U.S.	C5	146
Providence, Cape, c., N.Z.	F1	72
Providence Bay, Ont., Can.	B2	103
Providence Forge, Va., U.S.	C5	153
Providence Island, i., Sey.	C10	58
Providence Point, c., R.I., U.S.	D5	146
Providencia, Isla de, i., Col.	H8	94
Providenciales, i., T./C. Is.	D8	94
Providenija, U.S.S.R.	E29	24
Province Lake, l., N.H., U.S.	C5	136
Provincetown, Ma., U.S.	B7	128
Provins, Fr.	D10	14
Provo, S.D., U.S.	D2	148
Provo, Ut., U.S.	C4	151
Provo, stm., Ut., U.S.	C4	151
Provost, Alta., Can.	C5	98
Prowers, co., Co., U.S.	D8	113
Pruden, Tn., U.S.	C10	149
Prudence Island, i., R.I., U.S.	E5	146
Prudentópolis, Braz.	C13	80
Prudenville, Mi., U.S.	D6	129
Prudhoe Bay, b., Ak., U.S.	A10	109
Prudhoe Island, i., Austl.	C8	70
Prud'homme, Sask., Can.	E3	105
Prudnik, Pol.	E17	10
Prudy, U.S.S.R.	H9	26
Prue, Ok., U.S.	A5	143
Prüm, Ger.	E6	10
Pruszków, Pol.	C20	10
Prut, stm., Eur.	D12	20
Prutz, Aus.	H10	10
Pružany, U.S.S.R.	I7	26
Prydz Bay, b., Ant.	B5	73
Pryor, Mt., U.S.	E8	133
Pryor, Ok., U.S.	A6	143
Pryor Mountains, mts., Mt., U.S.	E8	133
Przasnysz, Pol.	B20	10
Przedbórz, Pol.	D19	10
Przemyśl, Pol.	F22	10
Prževal'sk, U.S.S.R.	I13	22
Przeworsk, Pol.	E22	10
Pskov, U.S.S.R.	D11	26
Pskovskoje ozero, l., U.S.S.R.	C11	26
Pszczyna, Pol.	F18	10
Ptarmigan, Cape, c., N.W. Ter., Can.	B9	96
Ptolemaïs, Grc.	I5	20
Ptuj, Yugo.	C10	18
Puán, Arg.	I7	80
Puan, S. Kor.	H14	32
Pucallpa, Peru	C4	82
Pucará, Bol.	H9	82
Pucarani, Bol.	G7	82
Pučež, U.S.S.R.	E26	26
Pucheng, China	H7	34
Pucheta, Arg.	E10	80
Puchoviči, U.S.S.R.	H11	26
Puck, Pol.	A18	10
Puckaway Lake, l., Wi., U.S.	E4	156
Puckett, Ms., U.S.	C4	131
Pudož, U.S.S.R.	E5	22
Puduhe, China	B7	40
Pudukkottai, India	G5	46
Puebla, state, Mex.	H10	90
Puebla [de Zaragoza], Mex.	H10	90
Pueblo, Co., U.S.	C6	113
Pueblo, co., Co., U.S.	C6	113
Pueblo Colorado Wash, val., Az., U.S.	B6	110
Pueblo Hundido, Chile	B2	78
Pueblo Ledesma, Arg.	B6	80
Pueblo Libertador, Arg.	F9	80
Pueblo Mountain, mtn., Or., U.S.	E8	144
Pueblo Mountains, mts., Or., U.S.	E8	144
Pueblonuevo, Col.	C5	84
Pueblo Nuevo, Nic.	D8	92
Pueblo Nuevo, Ven.	B8	84
Pueblo Nuevo Tiquisate, Guat.	C3	92
Pueblo of Acoma, N.M., U.S.	C2	138
Pueblo Reservoir, res., Co., U.S.	C6	113
Puebloviejo, Ec.	H3	84
Pueblo Viejo, Laguna, b., Mex.	F11	90
Pueblo Yaqui, Mex.	D4	90
Puelches, Arg.	J6	80
Puente Alto, Chile	G3	80
Puente-Genil, Spain	H7	16
Pueo Point, c., Hi., U.S.	B1	118
Puerco, stm., U.S.	C6	110
Puerco, Rio, stm., N.M., U.S.	B2	138
Puerto Acosta, Bol.	F7	82
Puerto Adela, Para.	C11	80
Puerto Aisén, Chile	F2	78
Puerto Alegre, Bol.	E11	82
Puerto Alfonso, Col.	I7	84
Puerto Ángel, Mex.	J11	90
Puerto Arista, Mex.	J13	90
Puerto Armuelles, Pan.	C1	84
Puerto Asís, Col.	G4	84
Puerto Ayacucho, Ven.	E9	84
Puerto Bahía Negra, Para.	I12	82
Puerto Baquerizo Moreno, Ec.	J14	84a
Puerto Barrios, Guat.	B6	92
Puerto Belgrano, Arg.	J7	80
Puerto Bermejo, Arg.	D9	80
Puerto Bermúdez, Peru	D4	82
Puerto Berrío, Col.	D5	84
Puerto Bolívar, Ec.	I3	84
Puerto Boyacá, Col.	E5	84
Puerto Busch, Bol.	I13	82
Puerto Cabello, Ven.	B8	84
Puerto Cabezas, Nic.	C11	92
Puerto Carreño, Col.	D9	84
Puerto Casado, Para.	B10	80
Puerto Castilla, Hond.	A8	92
Puerto Chicama, Peru	B2	82
Puerto Colombia, Col.	B5	84
Puerto Cortés, Hond.	B7	92
Puerto Cumarebo, Ven.	B8	84
Puerto de la Cruz, Spain	O24	17b
Puerto Delicia, Arg.	D11	80
Puerto Delón, Hond.	C9	92
Puerto del Rosario, Spain	O27	17b
Puerto de Luna, N.M., U.S.	C5	138
Puerto de Nutrias, Ven.	B5	76
Puerto El Triunfo, El Sal.	D6	92
Puerto Escondido, Mex.	J11	90
Puerto Esperanza, Arg.	D11	80
Puerto Fonciere, Para.	B10	80
Puerto Francisco de Orellana, Ec.	H4	84
Puerto Guaraní, Para.	I13	82
Puerto Heath, Bol.	E7	82
Puerto Iguazú, Arg.	C11	80
Puerto Inírida, Col.	F9	84
Puerto Jiménez, C.R.	I11	92
Puerto Juárez, Mex.	G16	90
Puerto la Cruz, Ven.	B10	84
Puerto Leda, Para.	I12	82
Puerto Leguízamo, Col.	H5	84
Puerto Lempira, Hond.	B11	92
Puerto Libertad, Arg.	C11	80
Puerto Libertad, Mex.	C3	90
Puerto Limón, Col.	F6	84
Puerto Limón, C.R.	G11	92
Puertollano, Spain	G7	16
Puerto López, Col.	E6	84
Puerto Madero, Mex.	C2	92
Puerto Maldonado, Peru	E7	82
Puerto Manatí, Cuba	D6	94
Puerto Mihanovich, Para.	I13	82
Puerto Montt, Chile	E2	78
Puerto Morazán, Nic.	E7	92
Puerto Morelos, Mex.	G16	90
Puerto Nariño, Col.	E9	84
Puerto Natales, Chile	G2	78
Puerto Padre, Cuba	D6	94
Puerto Páez, Ven.	D9	84
Puerto Peñasco, Mex.	B3	90
Puerto Pilón, Pan.	H15	92
Puerto Pinasco, Para.	B10	80
Puerto Piray, Arg.	D11	80
Puerto Píritu, Ven.	B10	84
Puerto Plata, Dom. Rep.	E9	94
Puerto Portillo, Peru	C5	82
Puerto Presidente Stroessner, Para.	C11	80
Puerto Princesa, Phil.	D6	38
Puerto Real, Spain	I5	16
Puerto Reyes, Col.	H6	84
Puerto Rico, Arg.	D11	80
Puerto Rico, Bol.	D8	82
Puerto Rico, Col.	G5	84
Puerto Rico, dep., N.A.	E11	94
Puerto Rico Trench	G13	86
Puerto Rondón, Col.	D7	84
Puerto Saavedra, Chile	J2	80
Puerto Salgar, Col.	E5	84
Puerto Sandino, Nic.	E8	92
Puerto San José, Guat.	D4	92
Puerto Sastre, Para.	B10	80
Puerto Siles, Bol.	E9	82
Puerto Suárez, Bol.	H13	82
Puerto Supe, Peru	D3	82
Puerto Tejada, Col.	F4	84
Puerto Toledo, Col.	H5	84
Puerto Umbría, Col.	G4	84
Puerto Vallarta, Mex.	G7	90
Puerto Varas, Chile	E2	78
Puerto Victoria, Arg.	D11	80
Puerto Victoria, Peru	C4	82
Puerto Viejo, C.R.	G11	92
Puerto Viejo, C.R.	H12	92
Puerto Villamizar, Col.	C6	84
Puerto Villaroel, Bol.	G9	82
Puerto Wilches, Col.	D6	84
Puerto Ybapobó, Para.	B10	80
Pueyrredón, Lago (Lago Cochrane), l., S.A.	F2	78
Pugačov, U.S.S.R.	G7	22
Puget Sound, strt., Wa., U.S.	B3	154
Puget Sound Naval Shipyard, mil., Wa., U.S.	e10	154
Puget-Théniers, Fr.	I13	14
Puglia, prov., Italy	I11	18
Pugwash, N.S., Can.	D6	101
Puhi, Hi., U.S.	B2	118
Puica, Peru	F5	82
Puigcerdá, Spain	C13	16
Puigmal, mtn., Eur.	C14	16
Puinahua, Canal de, mth., Peru	A4	82
Pujehun, S.L.	H4	64
Pujiang, China	F8	34
Pujilí, Ec.	H3	84
Pukalani, Hi., U.S.	C5	118
Pukaskwa National Park, Ont., Can.	o18	103
Pukch'ang, N. Kor.	D14	32
Pukch'ŏng, N. Kor.	C16	32
Pukeashun Mountain, mtn., B.C., Can.	D8	99
Pukekohe, N.Z.	B5	72
Pukhan-gang, stm., Asia	F15	32
Pukou, China	C7	34
Puksoozero, U.S.S.R.	J27	6
Pukwana, S.D., U.S.	D6	148
Pula, Yugo.	E8	18
Pulacayo, Bol.	I8	82
Púlar, Cerro, mtn., Chile	C4	80
Pulaski, Ga., U.S.	D5	117
Pulaski, Il., U.S.	F4	120
Pulaski, In., U.S.	C4	121
Pulaski, Ia., U.S.	D5	122
Pulaski, N.Y., U.S.	B4	139
Pulaski, Tn., U.S.	B4	149
Pulaski, Va., U.S.	C2	153
Pulaski, Wi., U.S.	D5	156
Pulaski, co., Ar., U.S.	C3	111
Pulaski, co., Ga., U.S.	D3	117
Pulaski, co., Il., U.S.	F4	120
Pulaski, co., In., U.S.	B4	121
Pulaski, co., Ky., U.S.	C5	124
Pulaski, co., Mo., U.S.	D5	132
Pulaski, co., Va., U.S.	C2	153
Puławy, Pol.	D21	10
Pulgaon, India	B5	46
Puli, Tai.	L9	34
Puliyangudi, India	H4	46
Pullman, Mi., U.S.	F4	129
Pullman, Wa., U.S.	C8	154
Pullo, Peru	F5	82
Pully, Switz.	E6	13
Pulog, Mount, mtn., Phil.	M19	39b
Pulsano, Italy	I12	18
Pułtusk, Pol.	C21	10
Pumphrey, Md., U.S.	h11	127
Pumpkin Buttes, mtn., Wy., U.S.	C7	157
Pumpkin Creek, stm., Mt., U.S.	E11	133
Pumpkin Creek, stm., Ne., U.S.	C2	134
Puna, Bol.	H9	82
Puná, Isla, i., Ec.	I2	84
Punakha, Bhu.	G13	44
Punata, Bol.	G9	82
Pünch, India	D6	44
Punduga, U.S.S.R.	A23	26
Pune (Poona), India	C2	46
Pŭngoë, stm., Afr.	B11	66
Pungo Lake, l., N.C., U.S.	B6	140
P'ungsan, N. Kor.	C16	32
Punia, Zaire	B5	58
Punilla, Sierra de la, mts., Arg.	E4	80
Puning, China	L5	34
Punitaqui, Chile	C2	78
Punitaqui, Chile	F3	80
Punjab, state, India	E6	44
Punnichy, Sask., Can.	F3	105
Puno, Peru	F6	82
Puno, dept., Peru	F6	82
Punta, Cerro de, mtn., P.R.	E11	94
Punta Alta, Arg.	J7	80
Punta Arenas, Chile	G2	78
Punta Banda, Cabo, c., Mex.	B1	90
Punta Cardón, Ven.	B7	84
Punta Colnett, Mex.	B1	90
Punta de Bombón, Peru	G6	82
Punta de Díaz, Chile	E3	80
Punta del Cobre, Chile	D3	80
Punta del Este, Ur.	H11	80
Punta de los Llanos, Arg.	F5	80
Punta de Mata, Ven.	C11	84
Punta Gorda, Belize	I15	90
Punta Gorda, Nic.	F11	92
Punta Gorda, Fl., U.S.	F4	116
Punta Gorda, stm., Nic.	F11	92
Punta Gorda, Bahía de, b., Nic.	F11	92
Punta Moreno, Peru	B2	82
Punta Negra, Salar de, pl., Chile	C4	80
Punta Piedras, Ven.	B10	84
Punta Porá, Arg.	C9	80
Punta Prieta, Mex.	C2	90
Puntarenas, C.R.	H10	92
Puntarenas, prov., C.R.	I11	92
Puntas del Sauce, Ur.	G10	80
Punto Fijo, Ven.	B7	84
Punxsutawney, Pa., U.S.	E4	145
Puolanka, Fin.	I20	6
Puqi, China	F9	30
Puquio, Peru	F4	82
Pur, stm., U.S.S.R.	D7	24
Puracé, Volcán, vol., Col.	F4	84
Purcell, Mo., U.S.	D3	132
Purcell, Ok., U.S.	B4	143
Purcellville, Va., U.S.	A5	153
Purdham Hill, mtn., Ar., U.S.	h10	111
Purdin, Mo., U.S.	B4	132
Purdy, Mo., U.S.	E4	132
Purgatoire, stm., Co., U.S.	D7	113
Purgatoire Peak, mtn., Co., U.S.	D5	113
Puri, India	K11	44
Purificación, Col.	F5	84
Purificación, Mex.	H7	90
Purificación, stm., Mex.	E10	90
Purikari neem, c., U.S.S.R.	B8	26
Purmerend, Neth.	C6	12
Pūrnia, India	H12	44
Purple Springs, Alta., Can.	E5	98
Purros, Nmb.	B1	66
Pursglove, W.V., U.S.	B4	155
Puruê, stm., Braz.	H8	84
Puruliya, India	I12	44
Puruni, stm., Guy.	D13	84
Purus (Purús), stm., S.A.	D6	76
Purvis, Ms., U.S.	D4	131
Purwakarta, Indon.	J13	39a
Purwokerto, Indon.	J14	39a
Puryear, Tn., U.S.	A3	149
Pusan, S. Kor.	H17	32
Pushaw Lake, l., Me., U.S.	D4	126
Pushkar, India	G6	44
Pushmataha, Al., U.S.	C1	108
Pushmataha, co., Ok., U.S.	C6	143
Puškin, U.S.S.R.	B13	26
Puškino, U.S.S.R.	E20	26
Puškinskije Gory, U.S.S.R.	D11	26
Püspökladány, Hung.	H21	10
Püssi, U.S.S.R.	B10	26
Pustoška, U.S.S.R.	E12	26
Putaendo, Chile	G3	80
Putao, Burma	G17	44
Put'atino, U.S.S.R.	G24	26
Putian, China	J8	34
Putila, U.S.S.R.	A9	20
Putina, Peru	F7	82
Puting, Tanjung, c., Indon.	F5	38
Putnam, Al., U.S.	C1	108
Putnam, Ct., U.S.	B8	114
Putnam, co., Fl., U.S.	C5	116
Putnam, co., Ga., U.S.	C3	117
Putnam, co., Il., U.S.	B4	120
Putnam, co., In., U.S.	E4	121
Putnam, co., Mo., U.S.	A4	132
Putnam, co., N.Y., U.S.	D7	139
Putnam, co., Oh., U.S.	B1	142
Putnam, co., Tn., U.S.	C8	149
Putnam, co., W.V., U.S.	C3	155
Putnamville, In., U.S.	E4	121
Putney, Ga., U.S.	E2	117
Putney, Vt., U.S.	F3	152
Putorana, plato, plat., U.S.S.R.	D17	22
Putre, Chile	H7	82
Puttalam, Sri L.	H5	46
Puttgarden, Ger.	A11	10
Putú, Chile	H2	80
Putumayo, ter., Col.	G4	84
Putumayo (Içá), stm., S.A.	I7	84
Putuo, China	F11	34
Puukohola Heiau National Historic Site, hist., Hi., U.S.	D6	118
Puukolii, Hi., U.S.	C5	118
Puula, l., Fin.	K20	6
Puumala, Fin.	K21	6
Puunene, Hi., U.S.	C5	118
Puurmani, U.S.S.R.	C9	26
Puxi, China	J8	34
Puxico, Mo., U.S.	E7	132
Puyallup, Wa., U.S.	B3	154
Puyallup, stm., Wa., U.S.	C3	154
Puyang, China	H2	32
Puyango (Tumbes), stm., S.A.	I3	84
Puy-de-Dôme, dept., Fr.	G10	14
Puylaurens, Fr.	I9	14
Puyo, Ec.	H4	84
Puyŏ, S. Kor.	G14	32
Pweto, Zaire	C5	58
Pyapon, Burma	F3	40
Pyatt, Ar., U.S.	A3	111
Pyaye, Burma	E3	40
Pyhäjoki, Fin.	I19	6
Pyhäselkä, l., Fin.	J21	6
Pyinmana, Burma	E4	40
Pyles Fork, stm., W.V., U.S.	h10	155
Pymatuning Reservoir, res., U.S.	C1	145
Pyŏktong, N. Kor.	C13	32
P'yŏlch'ang-ni, N. Kor.	D14	32
P'yŏngch'ang, S. Kor.	F16	32
P'yŏngsan, N. Kor.	E14	32
P'yŏngt'aek, S. Kor.	F15	32
P'yŏngyang, N. Kor.	D13	32
Pyramid Lake, l., Nv., U.S.	C2	135
Pyramid Lake Indian Reservation, Nv., U.S.	D2	135
Pyramid Mountains, mts., N.M., U.S.	E1	138
Pyramid Peak, mtn., N.M., U.S.	E1	138
Pyramid Peak, mtn., Wy., U.S.	C2	157
Pyrenees, mts., Eur.	C13	16
Pyrénées-Atlantiques, dept., Fr.	I6	14
Pyrénées-Orientales, dept., Fr.	J9	14
Pyrmont, In., U.S.	D4	121
Pyrzyce, Pol.	B14	10
Pytalovo, U.S.S.R.	D10	26
Pyu, Burma	E4	40
Pyuntaza, Burma	F4	40
Q		
Qacentina (Constantine), Alg.	B14	62
Qā'emshahr, Iran	C12	48
Qā'en, Iran	E15	48
Qaidam Pendi, China	B16	44
Qalāt, Afg.	D2	44
Qal'at ash-Shaqīf (Beaufort Castle), hist., Leb.	B5	50
Qal'at Bīshah, Sau. Ar.	D3	47
Qal'at Ṣāliḥ, Iraq	F9	48
Qal'at Sukkar, Iraq	F9	48
Qal'eh-ye Now, Afg.	C2	44
Qallābāt, Sud.	K9	60
Qalqīlīya, Isr. Occ.	D3	50
Qamar, Ghubbat al-, b., Yemen	F8	47
Qamdo, China	E6	30
Qānā, Leb.	B4	50
Qanā, Sau. Ar.	H6	48
Qandahār, Afg.	E1	44
Qandala, Som.	F10	56
Qantur, Sud.	M3	60
Qārah, Sau. Ar.	G6	48
Qardho, Som.	G10	56
Qarqan, stm., China	D4	30
Qārūn, Birkat, l., Egypt	C6	60
Qāsh, Nahr al- (Gash), stm., Afr.	E8	56
Qaṣr al-Farāfirah, Egypt	D4	60
Qasr el-Boukhari, Alg.	C12	62
Qaṣr-e Shīrīn, Iran	D8	48
Qa'ṭabah, Yemen	H4	47
Qaṭanā, Syria	B6	50
Qatar (Qaṭar), ctry., Asia	D5	42
Qattara Depression see Qaṭṭārah, Munkhafaḍ al-, depr., Egypt	B4	60
Qaṭṭārah, Munkhafaḍ al- (Qattara Depression), depr., Egypt	B4	60
Qazvīn, Iran	C11	48
Qesari, Ḥorbat (Cæsarea), hist., Isr.	C3	50
Qeshm, Iran	H14	48
Qeshm, Jazīreh-ye, i., Iran	H13	48
Qetura, Isr.	I4	50
Qezel Owzan, stm., Iran	C10	48
Qianfang, China	G5	34
Qianqi, China	H9	34
Qianyang, China	F9	30
Qiaogou, China	C4	34
Qiddīsah Kātrīnā, Dayr al- (Monastery of Saint Catherine), Egypt	G3	48
Qidong, China	D10	34
Qidu, China	E6	34
Qiemo, China	A11	44
Qift (Coptos), Egypt	D7	60
Qijiang, China	F8	30
Qijiawan, China	E3	34
Qila Lādgasht, Pak.	H17	48
Qilian Shan, mtn., China	D6	30
Qilian Shan, mts., China	D6	30
Qimen, China	J2	34
Qinā, Egypt	D7	60
Qinā, Wādī, val., Egypt	H2	48
Qingchengzi, China	C11	32
Qingdao (Tsingtao), China	G8	32
Qinghai (Tsinghai), prov., China	D6	30
Qinghai Hu, l., China	D7	30
Qinghezhen, China	F5	32
Qingjiang, China	G4	34
Qingjiang, China	B8	34
Qinglian, China	K1	34
Qinglong, China	B8	40
Qingpu, China	D10	34
Qingshan, China	E3	34
Qingshui, stm., China	D8	30
Qingshui, stm., China	F8	30
Qingtang, China	K2	34
Qingyang, China	D8	30
Qingyangzhen, China	D9	34
Qingyuan, China	G8	30
Qingyuan, China	L2	34
Qingzhou, China	L5	34
Qinhuangdao (Chinwangtao), China	D7	32
Qin Ling, mts., China	E8	30
Qinzhou, China	D10	40
Qionglai, China	E7	30
Qiongzhong, China	E10	40
Qiongzhou Haixia, strt., China	D11	40
Qipanshan, China	A5	32
Qiqian, China	A11	30
Qiqihar (Tsitsihar), China	B11	30
Qiryat Ata, Isr.	C4	50
Qiryat Bialik, Isr.	C4	50
Qiryat Gat, Isr.	E3	50
Qiryat Mal'akhi, Isr.	E3	50
Qiryat Motzkin, Isr.	C4	50
Qiryat Ono, Isr.	D3	50
Qiryat Shemona, Isr.	B5	50
Qiryat Yam, Isr.	C4	50
Qishn, Yemen	G7	47
Qishon, stm., Asia	C4	50
Qishuyan, China	D9	34
Qitai, China	C4	30
Qiyang, China	A11	40
Qnadsa, Alg.	E9	62
Qogir Feng (K2), mtn., Asia	C7	44
Qom, Iran	D11	48
Qomsheh, Iran	E11	48
Qondūz, Afg.	J11	22
Qondūz, stm., Afg.	B3	44
Qonggyai, China	F5	30
Qorveh, Iran	D9	48
Quabbin Reservoir, res., Ma., U.S.	B3	128
Quaco Head, c., N.B., Can.	D4	101
Quaddick, Ct., U.S.	B8	114
Quaddick Reservoir, res., Ct., U.S.	B8	114
Quadros, Lagoa dos, b., Braz.	E13	80
Quail Oaks, Va., U.S.	n18	153
Quakenbrück, Ger.	C7	10
Quaker City, Oh., U.S.	C4	142
Quaker Hill, Ct., U.S.	D7	114
Quakertown, Pa., U.S.	F11	145
Qualicum Beach, B.C., Can.	E5	99
Quanah, Tx., U.S.	B3	150
Quangang, China	G4	34
Quang Ngai, Viet.	G10	40

Name | Map Ref. | Page

Quang Trach, Viet. F9 40
Quannapowitt, Lake, l., Ma., U.S. f11 128
Quantico, Va., U.S. B5 153
Quantico Marine Corps Air Station, mil., Va., U.S. B5 153
Quanzhou (Chuanchou), China K7 34
Quapaw, Ok., U.S. A7 143
Qu'Appelle, Sask., Can. G4 105
Qu'Appelle, stm., Can. G4 105
Quaraí, Braz. F10 80
Quaraí (Guareim), stm., S.A. F10 80
Quarryville, N.B., Can. C4 101
Quarryville, Ct., U.S. B6 114
Quarryville, Pa., U.S. G9 145
Quartu Sant'Elena, Italy J4 18
Quartz Mountain, mtn., Or., U.S. D4 144
Quartzsite, Az., U.S. D1 110
Quasqueton, Ia., U.S. B6 122
Quassapaug, Lake, l., Ct., U.S. C3 114
Quatá, Braz. G3 79
Quatsino Sound, strt., B.C., Can. D3 99
Quay, co., N.M., U.S. C6 138
Qūchān, Iran C15 48
Queanbeyan, Austl. J8 70
Québec, Que., Can. C6 104
Quebec, prov., Can. C5 104
Quebra-Anzol, stm., Braz. E5 79
Quebracho, Ur. F10 80
Quechee, Vt., U.S. D4 152
Quechee Gorge, val., Vt., U.S. D4 152
Quedas, Moz. B11 66
Quedlinburg, Ger. D11 10
Queen, stm., R.I., U.S. E3 146
Queen Alexandra Range, mts., Ant. D8 73
Queen Annes, co., Md., U.S. B5 127
Queen Bess, Mount, mtn., B.C., Can. D5 99
Queen Charlotte, B.C., Can. C1 99
Queen Charlotte Islands, is., B.C., Can. C1 99
Queen Charlotte Mountains, mts., B.C., Can. C1 99
Queen Charlotte Sound, strt., B.C., Can. n17 99
Queen Charlotte Strait, strt., B.C., Can. D4 99
Queen City, Mo., U.S. A5 132
Queen City, Tx., U.S. C5 150
Queen Creek, Az., U.S. m9 110
Queen Elizabeth Islands, is., N.W. Ter., Can. B9 86
Queen Mary Coast, Ant. B6 73
Queen Maud Gulf, b., N.W. Ter., Can. C12 96
Queen Maud Land, reg., Ant. C3 73
Queen Maud Mountains, mts., Ant. D9 73
Queens, co., N.Y., U.S. E7 139
Queensborough, Ont., Can. C7 103
Queenscliff, Austl. L6 70
Queensland, Ga., U.S. E3 117
Queensland, state, Austl. D9 68
Queenstown, Austl. N6 70
Queenstown, N.B., Can. D3 101
Queenstown, Guy. D13 84
Queenstown, N.Z. F2 72
Queenstown, S. Afr. H8 66
Queenstown, Md., U.S. C5 127
Queets, Wa., U.S. B1 154
Queguay Grande, stm., Ur. G10 80
Queimados, Braz. G7 79
Quelimane, Moz. A13 66
Quemado, N.M., U.S. C1 138
Quemado, Tx., U.S. E2 150
Quemado, Punta de, c., Cuba D7 94
Quemado de Güines, Cuba C4 94
Quemoy see Chinmen Tao, i., Tai. K7 34
Quemú Quemú, Arg. I7 80
Quenemo, Ks., U.S. D8 123
Quepos, C.R. H10 92
Quequén, Arg. J9 80
Querary, stm., Col. G7 84
Quercy, hist. reg., Fr. H8 14
Querecotillo, Peru A1 82
Querência do Norte, Braz. G2 79
Querétaro, Mex. G9 90
Querétaro, state, Mex. G10 90
Querobabi, Mex. B4 90
Querobamba, Peru E5 82
Quesada, C.R. G10 92
Quesada, Spain H8 16
Queshan, China C3 34
Quesnel, B.C., Can. C6 99
Quesnel, stm., B.C., Can. C6 99
Quesnel Lake, l., B.C., Can. C7 99
Questa, N.M., U.S. A4 138
Quetena, Bol. J8 82
Quetico Provincial Park, Ont., Can. o17 103
Quetta, Pak. E2 44
Quettehou, Fr. C5 14
Quetzaltenango, Guat. C3 92
Quetzaltenango, dept., Guat. C3 92
Quevedo, Ec. H3 84
Quevedo, stm., Ec. H3 84
Quezaltepeque, El Sal. D5 92
Quezaltepeque, Guat. C5 92
Quezon City, Phil. N19 39b
Qufu, China H5 32
Quiabaya, Bol. F7 82
Quibdó, Col. E4 84
Quiberon, Fr. E3 14
Quíbor, Ven. C8 84
Quiches, Peru C3 82
Quicksand Pond, l., R.I., U.S. E6 146
Quidnessett, R.I., U.S. E4 146
Quidnick, R.I., U.S. D3 146
Quidnick Reservoir, res., R.I., U.S. D2 146
Quiindy, Para. C10 80
Quila, Mex. E6 90
Quilalí, Nic. D8 92
Quilcene, Wa., U.S. B3 154
Quileute Indian Reservation, Wa., U.S. B1 154
Quilimarí, Chile G3 80
Quilino, Arg. F6 80
Quillabamba, Peru E5 82
Quillacas, Bol. H8 82
Quillacollo, Bol. G8 82
Quillagua, Chile I7 82
Quillan, Fr. J9 14
Quill Lake, Sask., Can. E3 105
Quillota, Chile G3 80
Quilon, India H4 46
Quilpie, Austl. F6 70
Quilpué, Chile G3 80
Quimarí, Alto de, mtn., Col. C4 84
Quimbaya, Col. E5 84
Quimby, Ia., U.S. B2 122
Quime, Bol. G8 82
Quimilí, Arg. D7 80
Quimper, Fr. D2 14
Quimperlé, Fr. E3 14
Quimpitirique, Peru E5 82
Quinault, Wa., U.S. B2 154
Quinault, stm., Wa., U.S. B1 154
Quinault, Lake, l., Wa., U.S. B2 154
Quinault Indian Reservation, Wa., U.S. B1 154
Quincemil, Peru E6 82
Quinches, Peru E3 82
Quincy, Ca., U.S. C3 112
Quincy, Fl., U.S. B2 116
Quincy, Il., U.S. D2 120
Quincy, In., U.S. F4 121
Quincy, Ky., U.S. B6 124
Quincy, Ma., U.S. B5 128
Quincy, Mi., U.S. G6 129
Quincy, Ms., U.S. B5 131
Quincy, Oh., U.S. B2 142
Quincy, Wa., U.S. B6 154
Quincy Bay, b., Ma., U.S. g12 128
Quindío, dept., Col. E5 84
Quinebaug, Ct., U.S. A8 114
Quinebaug, stm., Ct., U.S. C8 114
Quines, Arg. G6 80
Quinga, Moz. E8 58
Quinhagak, Ak., U.S. D7 109
Qui Nhon, Viet. H10 40
Quinlan, Tx., U.S. C4 150
Quinn, stm., Nv., U.S. B3 135
Quinn Canyon Range, mts., Nv., U.S. F6 135
Quinnesec, Mi., U.S. C3 129
Quinnipiac, stm., Ct., U.S. D4 114
Quintanar de la Orden, Spain F8 16
Quintana Roo, state, Mex. H15 90
Quinter, Ks., U.S. C3 123
Quintero, Chile G3 80
Quintin, Fr. D4 14
Quinto, stm., Arg. H6 80
Quinto de Noviembre, Presa, El Sal. D6 92
Quinton, Sask., Can. F3 105
Quinton, Ok., U.S. B6 143
Quinwood, W.V., U.S. C4 155
Quirauk Mountain, mtn., Md., U.S. A2 127
Quiriguá, hist., Guat. B5 92
Quirihue, Chile I2 80
Quirindi, Austl. H9 70
Quirinópolis, Braz. E3 79
Quiriquire, Ven. C11 84
Quiroga, Mex. H9 90
Quiroga, Spain C4 16
Quirós, Arg. E6 80
Quiruvilca, Peru B2 82
Quissanga, Moz. D8 58
Quitaque, Tx., U.S. B2 150
Quitéria, stm., Braz. E3 79
Quitilipi, Arg. D8 80
Quitman, Ar., U.S. B3 111
Quitman, Ga., U.S. F3 117
Quitman, Ms., U.S. C5 131
Quitman, Tx., U.S. C5 150
Quitman, co., Ga., U.S. E1 117
Quitman, co., Ms., U.S. A3 131
Quitman Mountains, mts., Tx., U.S. o12 150
Quito, Ec. H3 84
Quivilla, Peru C3 82
Quixadá, Braz. D11 76
Quixito, stm., Braz. J7 84
Qujiang, China K2 34
Qujing, China B7 40
Qulin, Mo., U.S. E7 132
Qumar, stm., China D5 30
Qumarlêb, China E6 30
Quonnipaug Lake, l., Ct., U.S. D5 114
Quonochontaug, R.I., U.S. G2 146
Quonochontaug Pond, l., R.I., U.S. G2 146
Quonset Point, c., R.I., U.S. E4 146
Quorn, Austl. I3 70
Qurayyāt, Oman C11 47
Qurdūd, Sud. L5 60
Qūṣ, Egypt E7 60
Quthing, Leso. H8 66
Quxi, China L5 34
Quxian, China G7 34
Quyquyó, Para. D10 80
Quzhou, China G2 32

R

Raab (Rába), stm., Eur. H15 10
Raahe, Fin. I19 6
Raalte, Neth. D9 12
Ra'ananna, Isr. D3 50
Raasiku, U.S.S.R. B8 26
Raba, Indon. G6 38
Rába (Raab), stm., Eur. H17 10
Rabak, Sud. K7 60
Rabat (Victoria), Malta M9 18
Rabat, Mor. C7 62
Rabaul, Pap. N. Gui. k17 68a
Rabbit Creek, stm., S.D., U.S. B3 148
Rabbit Ears Pass, Co., U.S. A4 113
Rabbit Lake, Sask., Can. D2 105
Rābigh, Sau. Ar. C1 47
Rābigh, Sau. Ar. J5 48
Rabinal, Guat. B4 92
Rabka, Pol. F19 10
Rabkavi Banhatti, India D3 46
Raboćeostrovsk, U.S.S.R. I24 6
Rabun, Al., U.S. D2 108
Rabun, co., Ga., U.S. B3 117
Rabun Bald, mtn., Ga., U.S. B3 117
Rabyānah, Ṣaḥrā', des., Libya D5 56
Raccoon Creek, stm., Oh., U.S. D3 142
Raccourci Island, i., La., U.S. D4 125
Race, Cape, c., Newf., Can. E5 102
Raceland, Ky., U.S. B7 124
Raceland, La., U.S. E5 125
Race Point, c., Ma., U.S. B7 128
Race Pond, Ga., U.S. F4 117
Rach'a, U.S.S.R. A13 26
Rach Gia, Viet. I8 40
Rachov, U.S.S.R. A8 20
Racibórz (Ratibor), Pol. E18 10
Racine, Mn., U.S. G6 130
Racine, Mo., U.S. E3 132
Racine, Oh., U.S. D4 142
Racine, W.V., U.S. C3 155
Racine, Wi., U.S. F6 156
Racine, co., Wi., U.S. F5 156
Racine Dam, U.S. C3 155
Ráckeve, Hung. H18 10
Rădăuţi, Rom. B9 20
Radcliff, Ky., U.S. C4 124
Radcliffe, Ia., U.S. B4 122
Radeberg, Ger. D13 10
Radebeul, Ger. D13 10
Rades, Tun. B16 62
Radford, Va., U.S. C2 153
Rādhanpur, India I4 44
Radisson, Sask., Can. E2 105
Radium Hot Springs, B.C., Can. D9 99
Radium Springs, N.M., U.S. E3 138
Radofinnikovo, U.S.S.R. B13 26
Radolfzell, Ger. H8 10
Radom, Pol. D21 10
Radomsko, Pol. D19 10
Radoškoviči, U.S.S.R. G10 26
Radoviš, Yugo. H6 20
Radun', U.S.S.R. G8 26
Radviliškis, U.S.S.R. F6 26
Radville, Sask., Can. H3 105
Raḍwā, Jabal, mtn., Sau. Ar. E10 60
Radway, Alta., Can. B4 98
Rae, N.W. Ter., Can. D9 96
Rāe Bareli, India G9 44
Raeford, N.C., U.S. C3 140
Rae Isthmus, N.W. Ter., Can. C15 96
Rae Strait, strt., N.W. Ter., Can. C13 96
Raetihi, N.Z. C5 72
Rafael, Cachoeira do, wtfl, Braz. D10 82
Rafaela, Arg. F8 80
Rafah, Isr. Occ. F2 50
Raffadali, Italy L8 18
Rafḥā', Sau. Ar. G7 48
Rafsanjān, Iran F14 48
Raft, stm., Id., U.S. G5 119
Raft River Mountains, mts., Ut., U.S. B2 151
Rafz, Switz. C10 13
Raga, Sud. M3 60
Ragged Island, i., Bah. C7 94
Ragged Island, i., Me., U.S. E4 126
Ragged Island Range, is., Bah. C7 94
Ragged Lake, l., Me., U.S. C3 126
Ragged Top Mountain, mtn., Wy., U.S. E7 157
Ragland, Al., U.S. B3 108
Ragusa, Italy M9 18
Raguva, U.S.S.R. F7 26
Rahad, Nahr ar-, stm., Afr. F8 56
Rahad al-Bardī, Sud. L2 60
Rahīmyār Khān, Pak. F4 44
Rahway, N.J., U.S. B4 137
Rahway, stm., N.J., U.S. k7 137
Rāichūr, India D4 46
Raiganj, India H13 44
Raigarh, India J10 44
Railroad Valley, val., Nv., U.S. E6 135
Railton, Austl. M7 70
Rainbow Bridge National Monument, Ut., U.S. F5 151
Rainbow City, Al., U.S. A3 108
Rainbow Falls, wtfl, Tn., U.S. D10 149
Rainbow Flowage, res., Wi., U.S. C4 156
Rainbow Lake, l., Me., U.S. C3 126
Rainelle, W.V., U.S. D4 155
Rainier, Or., U.S. A4 144
Rainier, Wa., U.S. C3 154
Rainier, Mount, mtn., Wa., U.S. C4 154
Rains, co., Tx., U.S. C5 150
Rainsville, Al., U.S. A4 108
Rainy Lake, l., Mn., U.S. B5 130
Rainy River, Ont., Can. o16 103
Raipur, India J9 44
Ra'īs, Sau. Ar. C1 47
Raitī, Nic. C9 92
Rājahmundry, India D6 46
Rājāj, Sud. L3 60
Rajang, stm., Malay. E5 38
Rājapālaiyam, India H4 46
Rājasthān, state, India G5 44
Rajčichinsk, U.S.S.R. H17 24
Rajka, Hung. G17 10
Rājkot, India I4 44
Rāj Nāndgaon, India J9 44
Rājpipla, India B2 46
Rājshāhi, Bngl. H13 44
Rakamaz, Hung. G21 10
Rakaposhi, mtn., Pak. B6 44
Rakata, Pulau, i., Indon. J12 39a
Rake, Ia., U.S. A4 122
Rakops, Bots. C7 66
Rakovník, Czech. E13 10
Rakvere, U.S.S.R. B9 26
Raleigh, Newf., Can. C4 102
Raleigh, Il., U.S. F5 120
Raleigh, Ms., U.S. C4 131
Raleigh, N.C., U.S. B4 140
Raleigh, W.V., U.S. n13 155
Raleigh, co., W.V., U.S. D3 155
Raleigh Bay, b., N.C., U.S. C6 140
Ralls, Tx., U.S. C2 150
Ralls, co., Mo., U.S. B6 132
Ralph, Al., U.S. B2 108
Ralston, Ne., U.S. g12 134
Ralston, Ok., U.S. A5 143
Ralston, Wy., U.S. B4 157
Ralston Valley, val., Nv., U.S. E4 135
Rama, Sask., Can. F4 105
Rama, Isr. C4 50
Rama, Nic. E10 92
Rama, stm., Nic. F10 92
Ramacca, Italy L9 18
Ramah, N.M., U.S. B1 138
Ramah Indian Reservation, N.M., U.S. C1 138
Ramalho, Serra do, mts., Braz. B6 79
Rām Allāh, Isr. Occ. E4 50
Rāmanāthapuram, India H5 46
Ramapo, stm., N.J., U.S. A4 137
Ramapo Mountains, mts., N.J., U.S. A4 137
Ramasucha, U.S.S.R. I16 26
Ramat Gan, Isr. D3 50
Ramat HaSharon, Isr. D3 50
Ramathlabama, Bots. E7 66
Rambervillers, Fr. D13 14
Ramblewood, N.J., U.S. D3 137
Rambouillet, Fr. D8 14
Ramea, Newf., Can. E3 102
Ramenskoje, U.S.S.R. F21 26
Ramer, Al., U.S. C3 108
Ramer, Tn., U.S. B3 149
Rameški, U.S.S.R. D19 26
Rāmeswaram, India H10 42
Rāmhormoz, Iran F10 48
Ramingstein, Aus. H13 10
Ramiriquí, Col. E6 84
Ramla, Isr. E3 50
Ramlu, mtn., Eth. F9 56
Ramm, Jabal, mtn., Jord. I4 50
Ramona, Ca., U.S. F5 112
Ramona, Ks., U.S. D6 123
Ramona, Ok., U.S. A6 143
Ramona, S.D., U.S. C8 148
Ramos, Mex. F9 90
Ramos, stm., Mex. E7 90
Ramot, Isr. Occ. C5 50
Ramotswa, Bots. E7 66
Rampart Range, mts., Co., U.S. B5 113
Rāmpur, India F8 44
Rāmpur Hāt, India H12 44
Ramree Island, i., Burma E2 40
Ramsay, Mi., U.S. n12 129
Ramseur, N.C., U.S. B3 140
Ramsey, I. of Man G9 8
Ramsey, Il., U.S. D4 120
Ramsey, Mn., U.S. E5 130
Ramsey, N.J., U.S. A4 137
Ramsey, co., Mn., U.S. E5 130
Ramsey, co., N.D., U.S. A7 141
Rāmshīr, Iran F10 48
Ramshorn Peak, mtn., Mt., U.S. E5 133
Ramshorn Peak, mtn., Wy., U.S. C3 157
Ramu, stm., Pap. N. Gui. m16 68a
Ramygala, U.S.S.R. F7 26
Rānāghāt, India I13 44
Ranburne, Al., U.S. B4 108
Rancagua, Chile H3 80
Rance, stm., Fr. D4 14
Rancevo, U.S.S.R. E17 26
Rancharia, Braz. G3 79
Ranchería, stm., Col. B6 84
Rancheria Rock, mtn., Or., U.S. C6 144
Ranchester, Wy., U.S. B5 157
Rānchi, India I11 44
Ranchillos, Arg. D6 80
Ranchito, N.M., U.S. A4 138
Rancho California, Ca., U.S. F5 112
Rancho Palos Verdes, Ca., U.S. n12 112
Ranchos de Taos, N.M., U.S. A4 138
Rancocas Creek, stm., N.J., U.S. C3 137
Rancocas Creek, South Branch, stm., N.J., U.S. D3 137
Rancocas Woods, N.J., U.S. D3 137
Rancul, Arg. H6 80
Rand, W.V., U.S. C3 155
Randall, Mn., U.S. D4 130
Randall, co., Tx., U.S. B2 150
Randallstown, Md., U.S. B4 127
Randers, Den. M12 6
Randle, Wa., U.S. C4 154
Randleman, N.C., U.S. B3 140
Randlett, Ok., U.S. C3 143
Randolph, Al., U.S. C3 108
Randolph, Az., U.S. E4 110
Randolph, Ia., U.S. D2 122
Randolph, Me., U.S. D3 126
Randolph, Ma., U.S. B5 128
Randolph, Ms., U.S. A4 131
Randolph, Ne., U.S. B8 134
Randolph, N.H., U.S. B4 136
Randolph, N.Y., U.S. C2 139
Randolph, Oh., U.S. A4 142
Randolph, Ut., U.S. B4 151
Randolph, Vt., U.S. D3 152
Randolph, Wi., U.S. E4 156
Randolph, co., Al., U.S. B4 108
Randolph, co., Ar., U.S. A4 111
Randolph, co., Ga., U.S. E2 117
Randolph, co., Il., U.S. E4 120
Randolph, co., In., U.S. D7 121
Randolph, co., Mo., U.S. B5 132
Randolph, co., N.C., U.S. B3 140
Randolph, co., W.V., U.S. C5 155
Randolph Air Force Base, mil., Tx., U.S. h7 150
Randolph Center, Vt., U.S. D3 152
Randolph Hills, Md., U.S. B3 127
Random Island, i., Newf., Can. D5 102
Random Lake, Wi., U.S. E6 156
Råneå, Swe. I18 6
Ranfurly, Alta., Can. C5 98
Rāngāmāti, Bngl. I15 44
Rangeley, Me., U.S. D2 126
Rangeley Lake, l., Me., U.S. D2 126
Rangely, Co., U.S. A2 113
Ranger, Ga., U.S. B2 117
Ranger, Tx., U.S. C3 150
Ranger, W.V., U.S. C2 155
Ranger Lake, l., N.M., U.S. D6 138
Rangoon see Yangon, Burma B2 38
Rangpur, Bngl. H13 44
Ranguana Cay, i., Belize A6 92
Ranguana Entrance, strt., Belize A6 92
Rānībennur, India E3 46
Ranier, Mn., U.S. B5 130
Rānīganj, India I12 44
Rānikhet, India F8 44
Ranken, stm., Austl. C2 70
Ranken Store, Austl. B2 70
Rankin, Il., U.S. C6 120
Rankin, Pa., U.S. k14 145
Rankin, Tx., U.S. D2 150
Rankin, co., Ms., U.S. C4 131
Rankin Inlet, N.W. Ter., Can. D14 96
Ranohira, Madag. S21 67b
Ranomafana, Madag. T22 67b
Ranong, Thai. J5 40
Ranopiso, Madag. T22 67b
Ranotsara Nord, Madag. S22 67b
Ransom, Il., U.S. B5 120
Ransom, Ks., U.S. D4 123
Ransom, co., N.D., U.S. C8 141
Ransomville, N.Y., U.S. B2 139
Ranson, W.V., U.S. B7 155
Rantauprapat, Indon. M5 40
Rantekombola, Bulu, mtn., Indon. F7 38
Rantoul, Il., U.S. C5 120
Rantoul, Ks., U.S. D8 123
Rantowles, S.C., U.S. k11 147
Ranua, Fin. I20 6
Ranwanalenaus, Bots. B6 66
Raoping, China L6 34
Raoul, Ga., U.S. B3 117
Rapa, Ponta do, c., Braz. D14 80
Rapallo, Italy E4 18
Rapel, stm., Chile G3 80
Rapelje, Mt., U.S. E7 133
Rapelli, Arg. D6 80
Raphine, Va., U.S. C3 153
Rapid, stm., Mn., U.S. B4 130
Rapid, North Branch, stm., Mn., U.S. B4 130
Rapid City, Man., Can. D1 100
Rapid City, Mi., U.S. D5 129
Rapid City, S.D., U.S. C2 148
Rapides, co., La., U.S. C3 125
Rapid River, Mi., U.S. C4 129
Rapids City, Il., U.S. B3 120
Räpina, U.S.S.R. C10 26
Rapla, U.S.S.R. B7 26
Rappahannock, co., Va., U.S. B4 153
Rappahannock, stm., Va., U.S. B5 153
Rapperswil, Switz. D10 13
Rāpti, stm., Asia G10 44
Rápulo, stm., Bol. F8 82
Raquette, stm., N.Y., U.S. f10 139
Raquette Lake, l., N.Y., U.S. B6 139
Raritan, N.J., U.S. B3 137
Raritan, stm., N.J., U.S. C4 137
Raritan, South Branch, stm., N.J., U.S. B3 137
Raritan Bay, b., N.J., U.S. C4 137
Raron, Switz. F8 13
Ra's al-'Ayn, Syria C6 48
Ra's al-Khaymah, U.A.E. B9 47
Ra's an-Naqb, Egypt I3 50
Ra's an-Naqb, Jord. H4 50
Ras Dashen Terara, mtn., Eth. K10 60
Raseiniai, U.S.S.R. F6 26
Râs el Aïoun, Alg. N3 18
Ras el Ma, Alg. C10 62
Rashād, Sud. L6 60
Rashīd, Egypt B6 60
Rasht, Iran C10 48
Rāsipuram, India G5 46
Raška, Yugo. F4 20
Raškov, U.S.S.R. B12 20
Raspberry Peak, mtn., Ar., U.S. C1 111
Rass Jebel, Tun. L5 18
Rasskazovo, U.S.S.R. I24 26
Rasšua, ostrov, i., U.S.S.R. H22 24
Ra's Tannūrah, Sau. Ar. H11 48
Rastatt, Ger. G8 10
Rastede, Ger. B8 10
Rasūl, Pak. D5 44
Rātangarh, India F6 44
Rätansbyn, Swe. J14 6
Ratcliff, Ar., U.S. B2 111
Rāth, India H8 44
Rathbun Lake, res., Ia., U.S. D5 122
Rathdrum, Id., U.S. B2 119
Rathenow, Ger. C12 10
Rathwell, Man., Can. E2 100
Ratingen, Ger. D6 10
Rat Islands, is., Ak., U.S. E3 109
Rat Lake, l., Man., Can. B4 100
Ratlām, India I6 44
Ratnāgiri, India D2 46
Ratnapura, Sri L. I6 46
Ratomka, U.S.S.R. H10 26
Raton, N.M., U.S. A5 138
Raton Pass, N.M., U.S. A5 138
Rattan, Ok., U.S. C6 143
Rattlesnake Creek, stm., Ks., U.S. E4 123
Rattlesnake Creek, stm., Oh., U.S. C2 142
Rattlesnake Creek, stm., Wa., U.S. C6 154
Rattlesnake Flat, pl., Wa., U.S. C7 154
Rattlesnake Hills, hills, Wa., U.S. C6 154
Rattlesnake Mountain, mtn., Ct., U.S. C4 114
Rattling Brook, Newf., Can. D3 102
Ratzeburg, Ger. B10 10
Raub, Malay. M6 40
Rauch, Arg. I9 80
Raul Soares, Braz. F7 79
Rauma, Fin. K17 6
Raurkela, India I11 44
Ravalli, Mt., U.S. C2 133
Ravalli, co., Mt., U.S. D2 133
Ravanusa, Italy L8 18
Rāvar, Iran F14 48
Ravelo, Bol. H9 82
Raven, Va., U.S. e10 153
Ravena, N.Y., U.S. C7 139
Ravenden, Ar., U.S. A4 111
Ravenden Springs, Ar., U.S. A4 111
Ravenel, S.C., U.S. k11 147
Ravenna, Italy E7 18
Ravenna, Ky., U.S. C6 124
Ravenna, Mi., U.S. E5 129
Ravenna, Ne., U.S. C7 134
Ravenna, Oh., U.S. A4 142
Raven Park, reg., Co., U.S. A2 113
Ravensburg, Ger. H9 10
Ravenscroft, Tn., U.S. D8 149
Ravensdale, Wa., U.S. f12 154
Ravenshoe, Austl. A6 70
Ravensthorpe, Austl. F4 68
Ravenswood, In., U.S. k10 121
Ravenswood, W.V., U.S. C3 155
Ravenwood, Mo., U.S. A3 132
Rāvi, stm., Asia E5 44
Ravia, Ok., U.S. C5 143
Ravinia, S.D., U.S. D7 148
Ravnina, U.S.S.R. C17 48
Rāwalpindi, Pak. D5 44
Rawa Mazowiecka, Pol. D20 10
Rawāndūz, Iraq C8 48
Rawdon, Que., Can. C4 104
Rawhide Creek, stm., Wy., U.S. D8 157
Rawicz, Pol. D16 10
Rawlings, Md., U.S. k13 127
Rawlinna, Austl. F5 68
Rawlins, Wy., U.S. E5 157
Rawlins, co., Ks., U.S. C2 123
Rawson, Arg. E3 78
Rawson, Arg. H8 80
Raxāul, India D11 42
Ray, In., U.S. A8 121
Ray, N.D., U.S. A2 141
Ray, co., Mo., U.S. B3 132
Ray, Cape, c., Newf., Can. E2 102
Raya, Bukit, mtn., Indon. F5 38
Rāyadurg, India E4 46
Ray City, Ga., U.S. E3 117
Rayle, Ga., U.S. C4 117
Raymond, Alta., Can. E4 98
Raymond, Ca., U.S. D4 112
Raymond, Ga., U.S. C2 117
Raymond, Il., U.S. D4 120
Raymond, Ks., U.S. D5 123
Raymond, Me., U.S. E2 126
Raymond, Mn., U.S. E3 130
Raymond, Ms., U.S. C3 131
Raymond, Ne., U.S. D9 134
Raymond, N.H., U.S. D4 136
Raymond, S.D., U.S. C8 148
Raymond, Wa., U.S. C2 154
Raymond Terrace, Austl. I9 70
Raymondville, Mo., U.S. D6 132
Raymondville, Tx., U.S. F4 150
Raymore, Sask., Can. F3 105
Raymore, Mo., U.S. C3 132
Rayne, La., U.S. D3 125
Raynham, Ma., U.S. C5 128
Raynham Center, Ma., U.S. C5 128
Rayón, Mex. C4 90
Rayones, Mex. E9 90
Rayong, Thai. H6 40
Raytown, Mo., U.S. h11 132
Rayville, La., U.S. B4 125
Rayville, Mo., U.S. B3 132
Razan, Iran D10 48
R'azan', U.S.S.R. G22 26
R'azancevo, U.S.S.R. E22 26
Ražanj, Yugo. F5 20
Razdan, U.S.S.R. A8 48
Razdel'naja, U.S.S.R. C14 20
Razgrad, Bul. F10 20
R'ažsk, U.S.S.R. H23 26
Ré, Île de, i., Fr. F5 14
Reader, W.V., U.S. B4 155
Reader Lake, l., Man., Can. C1 100
Readfield, Me., U.S. D3 126
Reading, Eng., U.K. J13 8
Reading, Ks., U.S. D8 123
Reading, Ma., U.S. A5 128
Reading, Mi., U.S. G6 129
Reading, Oh., U.S. C1 142
Reading, Pa., U.S. F10 145
Reading, Vt., U.S. E3 152
Readland, Ar., U.S. D4 111
Readlyn, Ia., U.S. B5 122
Readsboro, Vt., U.S. F3 152
Readstown, Wi., U.S. E3 156
Readyville, Tn., U.S. B5 149
Reagan, Tn., U.S. B3 149
Reagan, co., Tx., U.S. D2 150
Real, co., Tx., U.S. E3 150
Real, Cordillera, mts., S.A. H9 82
Real, Estero, stm., Nic. E7 92
Real del Padre, Arg. H5 80
Realicó, Arg. H6 80
Reamstown, Pa., U.S. F9 145
Reardan, Wa., U.S. B8 154
Reata, Mex. D9 90
Reay, Scot., U.K. C10 8
Rebecca, Ga., U.S. E3 117
Rebersburg, Pa., U.S. E7 145
Reboly, U.S.S.R. J22 6
Rebouças, Braz. C13 80
Rebun-tō, i., Japan B16 36a
Recalde, Arg. I8 80
Recanati, Italy F8 18
Rečane, U.S.S.R. E14 26
Recherche, Archipelago of the, is., Austl. F4 68
Rečica, U.S.S.R. I13 26
Recife, Braz. E12 76
Recinto, Chile I3 80
Recklinghausen, Ger. D7 10
Reconquista, Arg. E9 80
Recreio, Braz. F7 79
Recreio, Braz. C12 82
Recreo, Arg. E6 80
Rector, Ar., U.S. A5 111
Recuay, Peru C3 82
Red (Hong) (Yuan), stm., Asia C8 40
Red, stm., N.A. B7 106
Red, stm., U.S. E8 106
Red, stm., Ky., U.S. C6 124
Red, stm., Tn., U.S. A4 149
Red, Elm Fork, stm., U.S. B2 143

Name Map Ref. Page

Red, North Fork, stm., U.S. B1 143
Red, Salt Fork, stm., U.S. C2 143
Red, South Fork, stm., U.S. A5 149
Red, West Fork, stm., U.S. A4 149
Redange, Lux. I8 12
Red Bank, N.J., U.S. C4 137
Red Bank, S.C., U.S. D5 147
Red Bank, Tn., U.S. D8 149
Red Banks, Ms., U.S. A4 131
Red Bay, Newf., Can. C3 102
Red Bay, Al., U.S. A1 108
Redberry Lake, l., Sask., Can. E2 105
Redbird, Oh., U.S. A4 142
Red Bird, stm., Ky., U.S. C6 124
Red Bluff, Ca., U.S. B2 112
Red Bluff Lake, res., U.S. o12 150
Red Bluff Reservoir, res., U.S. B8 90
Red Boiling Springs, Tn., U.S. C8 149
Red Bud, Il., U.S. E4 120
Red Butte, mtn., Ut., U.S. B2 151
Red Buttes Village, Wy., U.S. D6 157
Redby, Mn., U.S. C4 130
Red Cedar, stm., Wi., U.S. C2 156
Red Cedar Lake, l., Wi., U.S. C2 156
Redcliff, Alta., Can. D5 98
Redcliff, Co., U.S. B4 113
Redcliff, Zimb. B9 66
Redcliffe, Austl. F10 70
Red Cliff Indian Reservation, Wi., U.S. B2 156
Red Cliffs, Austl. J5 70
Red Cloud, Ne., U.S. D7 134
Redcloud Peak, mtn., Co., U.S. D3 113
Red Creek, stm., Ms., U.S. E4 131
Red Cross Lake, l., Man., Can. B5 100
Red Deer, Alta., Can. C4 98
Red Deer, stm., Can. D4 98
Red Deer, stm., Can. E4 105
Reddell, La., U.S. D3 125
Reddick, Fl., U.S. C4 116
Reddick, Il., U.S. B5 120
Redding, Ca., U.S. B2 112
Redding, Ct., U.S. D2 114
Redding Ridge, Ct., U.S. D2 114
Reddish Knob, mtn., U.S. C5 155
Redeye, stm., Mn., U.S. D3 130
Red Feather Lakes, Co., U.S. A5 113
Redfield, Ar., U.S. C3 111
Redfield, Ia., U.S. C3 122
Redfield, Ks., U.S. E9 123
Redfield, S.D., U.S. C7 148
Redford, Mi., U.S. F7 129
Redgranite, Wi., U.S. D4 156
Red Hook, N.Y., U.S. C7 139
Red House, W.V., U.S. C3 155
Red Indian Lake, l., Newf., Can. D3 102
Red Jacket, W.V., U.S. D2 155
Redkey, In., U.S. D7 121
Redkino, U.S.S.R. E19 26
Redlake, Mn., U.S. C3 130
Red Lake, co., Mn., U.S. C2 130
Red Lake, l., Az., U.S. B1 110
Red Lake, stm., Mn., U.S. C2 130
Red Lake Falls, Mn., U.S. C2 130
Red Lake Indian Reservation, Mn., U.S. B3 130
Redlands, S. Afr. G6 66
Redlands, Ca., U.S. E5 112
Red Level, Al., U.S. D3 108
Red Lick, Ms., U.S. D3 131
Red Lion, Pa., U.S. G8 145
Red Lodge, Mt., U.S. E7 133
Red Mill Pond, l., De., U.S. E5 115
Redmon, Il., U.S. D6 120
Redmond, Or., U.S. C5 144
Redmond, Ut., U.S. E4 151
Redmond, Wa., U.S. e11 154
Red Mountain, mtn., Al., U.S. B3 108
Red Mountain, mtn., Ca., U.S. B2 112
Red Mountain, mtn., Mt., U.S. C4 133
Red Mountain Pass, Co., U.S. D3 113
Red Oak, Ga., U.S. h7 117
Red Oak, Ia., U.S. D2 122
Red Oak, Ok., U.S. C6 143
Red Oak, Tx., U.S. n10 150
Red Oaks, La., U.S. h9 125
Redon, Fr. E4 14
Redonda, i., Antig. F13 94
Redondo, Port. G4 16
Redondo, Wa., U.S. f11 154
Redondo Beach, Ca., U.S. n12 112
Redoubt Volcano, vol., Ak., U.S. g15 109
Red Peak, mtn., Co., U.S. B4 113
Red Rapids, N.B., Can. C2 101
Red River, N.M., U.S. A4 138
Red River, co., La., U.S. B2 125
Red River, co., Tx., U.S. C5 150
Red Rock, B.C., Can. C6 99
Red Rock, Az., U.S. E4 110
Red Rock, Ok., U.S. A4 143
Red Rock, stm., Mt., U.S. F4 133
Red Rock, Lake, res., Ia., U.S. C4 122
Red Scaffold, S.D., U.S. C4 148
Red Sea D8 56
Red Springs, N.C., U.S. C3 140
Redstone, Co., U.S. B3 113
Redstone, N.H., U.S. B4 136
Red Sucker, stm., Man., Can. B5 100
Red Table Mountain, mts., Co., U.S. B4 113
Redvale, Co., U.S. C2 113
Redvers, Sask., Can. H5 105
Redwater, Alta., Can. C4 98
Redwater, stm., Mt., U.S. C11 133
Red Willow, Alta., Can. C4 98
Red Willow, co., Ne., U.S. D5 134
Redwillow, stm., Can. B7 99
Red Willow Creek, stm., Ne., U.S. D5 134
Red Wing, Mn., U.S. F6 130
Redwood, Ms., U.S. C3 131
Redwood, co., Mn., U.S. F3 130
Redwood, stm., Mn., U.S. F3 130
Redwood City, Ca., U.S. D2 112
Redwood Falls, Mn., U.S. F3 130
Redwood National Park, Ca., U.S. B2 112
Redwood Valley, Ca., U.S. C2 112
Ree, Lough, l., Ire. H5 8
Reed, Ar., U.S. D4 111
Reed City, Mi., U.S. E5 129
Reeder, N.D., U.S. C3 141
Reed Lake, l., Man., Can. B1 100
Reedley, Ca., U.S. D4 112
Reedpoint, Mt., U.S. E7 133
Reedsburg, Wi., U.S. E3 156
Reeds Peak, mtn., N.M., U.S. D2 138
Reedsport, Or., U.S. D2 144
Reeds Spring, Mo., U.S. E4 132
Reedsville, Pa., U.S. E6 145
Reedsville, W.V., U.S. B5 155
Reedsville, Wi., U.S. D6 156
Reedville, Va., U.S. C6 153
Reedy, W.V., U.S. C3 155
Reedy, stm., S.C., U.S. C3 147
Reedy Lake, l., Fl., U.S. E5 116
Reefton, N.Z. E3 72
Ree Heights, S.D., U.S. C6 148
Reelfoot Lake, l., Tn., U.S. A2 149
Reelsville, In., U.S. E4 121
Reese, Mi., U.S. E7 129
Reese, stm., Nv., U.S. C4 135
Reese Air Force Base, mil., Tx., U.S. C1 150
Reese Station, Oh., U.S. m11 142
Reeseville, Wi., U.S. E5 156
Reeves, co., Tx., U.S. o13 150
Reform, Al., U.S. B1 108
Refugio, Tx., U.S. E4 150
Refugio, co., Tx., U.S. E4 150
Regaïa, Mor. J6 16
Regencia, Braz. E9 79
Regensburg, Ger. F12 10
Regent, N.D., U.S. C3 141
Reggâne, Alg. G11 62
Reggello, Italy F6 18
Reggio di Calabria, Italy K10 18
Reggio nell'Emilia, Italy E5 18
Reghin, Rom. C8 20
Regina, Sask., Can. G3 105
Régina, Fr. Gu. C8 76
Regina Beach, Sask., Can. G3 105
Register, Ga., U.S. D5 117
Registro, Braz. C15 80
Registro do Araguaia, Braz. C3 79
Regnéville, Fr. C5 14
Reguengos de Monsaraz, Port. G4 16
Rehau, Ger. E12 10
Rehoboth, Nmb. D3 66
Rehoboth, N.M., U.S. B1 138
Rehoboth Bay, b., De., U.S. F5 115
Rehoboth Beach, De., U.S. F5 115
Reḥovot, Isr. E3 50
Reichenau, Switz. E11 13
Reichenbach, Ger. E12 10
Reid, Mount, mtn., Ak., U.S. n24 109
Reidland, Ky., U.S. e9 124
Reidsville, Ga., U.S. D4 117
Reidsville, N.C., U.S. A3 140
Reidville, S.C., U.S. B3 147
Reigate, Eng., U.K. J13 8
Reigoldswil, Switz. D8 13
Reims, Fr. C11 14
Reina Adelaida, Archipiélago, is., Chile G2 78
Reinach, Switz. D9 13
Reinach, Switz. C8 13
Reinbeck, Ia., U.S. B5 122
Reindeer Island, i., Man., Can. C3 100
Reindeer Lake, l., Can. m8 105
Reinga, Cape, c., N.Z. A4 72
Reinosa, Spain B7 16
Reisdorf, Lux. I9 12
Reisterstown, Md., U.S. B4 127
Reitz, S. Afr. F9 66
Reliance, De., U.S. F3 115
Reliance, S.D., U.S. D6 148
Reliance, Tn., U.S. D9 149
Reliance, Wy., U.S. E3 157
Remada, Tun. D16 62
Remagen, Ger. B14 14
Remanso, Braz. E10 76
Rembang, Indon. J15 39a
Rembert, S.C., U.S. C6 147
Rembrandt, Ia., U.S. B2 122
Remecó, Arg. I7 80
Remedios, Col. D5 84
Remedios, Pan. C2 84
Remedios, Punta, c., El Sal. D5 92
Remer, Mn., U.S. C5 130
Remerton, Ga., U.S. F3 117
Remeshk, Iran H15 48
Remington, In., U.S. C3 121
Remington, Va., U.S. B5 153
Remiremont, Fr. D13 14
Remlap, Al., U.S. B3 108
Remmel Dam, Ar., U.S. g8 111
Remoulins, Fr. I11 14
Remscheid, Ger. D7 10
Remsen, Ia., U.S. B2 122
Remus, Mi., U.S. E5 129
Renaix (Ronse), Bel. G4 12
Rena Lara, Ms., U.S. A3 131
Renascença, Braz. I9 84
Renault, Il., U.S. E3 120
Renčeni, U.S.S.R. D8 26
Rencontre East, Newf., Can. E4 102
Rende, Italy J11 18
Rend Lake, res., Il., U.S. E5 120
Rendsburg, Ger. A9 10
Renens, Switz. E6 13
Renews [-Cappahayden], Newf., Can. E5 102
Renforth, N.B., Can. D4 101
Renfrew, Ont., Can. B8 103
Rengat, Indon. O7 40
Rengo, Chile H3 80
Reng Tlāng, mtn., Asia J15 44
Renhua, China J2 34
Reni, U.S.S.R. D12 20
Renick, Mo., U.S. B5 132
Renmark, Austl. J4 70
Rennell, i., Sol.Is. B12 68
Renner, S.D., U.S. D9 148
Rennes, Fr. D5 14
Rennick Glacier, Ant. C8 73
Rennie, Man., Can. E4 100
Reno, Nv., U.S. D2 135
Reno, Oh., U.S. C4 142
Reno, co., Ks., U.S. E5 123
Reno, stm., Italy E6 18
Reno, Lake, l., Mn., U.S. E3 130
Reno Hill, mtn., Wy., U.S. D6 157
Renous, N.B., Can. C4 101
Renovo, Pa., U.S. D6 145
Renshou, China H6 34
Rensselaer, In., U.S. C3 121
Rensselaer, N.Y., U.S. C7 139
Rensselaer, co., N.Y., U.S. C7 139
Rentería, Spain B10 16
Renton, Wa., U.S. B3 154
Rentz, Ga., U.S. D4 117
Renville, Mn., U.S. F3 130
Renville, co., Mn., U.S. F4 130
Renville, co., N.D., U.S. A4 141
Renwick, Ia., U.S. B4 122
Répce, stm., Eur. H16 10
Repentigny, Que., Can. D4 104
Repetek, U.S.S.R. J10 22
Repino, U.S.S.R. A12 26
Repton, Al., U.S. D2 108
Republic, Ks., U.S. C6 123
Republic, Mi., U.S. B3 129
Republic, Mo., U.S. D4 132
Republic, Oh., U.S. A2 142
Republic, Pa., U.S. G2 145
Republic, Wa., U.S. A7 154
Republic, co., Ks., U.S. C6 123
Republican, stm., U.S. C6 123
Republican, North Fork, stm., U.S. A8 113
Republican, South Fork, stm., U.S. E4 134
Republican City, Ne., U.S. D6 134
Repulse Bay, N.W. Ter., Can. C15 96
Repulse Bay, b., Austl. C8 70
Requena, Peru A5 82
Requena, Spain F10 16
Réquista, Fr. H9 14
Reschenpass, Eur. F17 14
Rescue, Va., U.S. k14 153
Resen, Yugo. H5 20
Reserva, Braz. C13 80
Reserve, Ks., U.S. C8 123
Reserve, La., U.S. h10 125
Reserve, Mt., U.S. B12 133
Reserve, N.M., U.S. D1 138
Reservoir Pond, l., Ma., U.S. h11 128
Rešetnikovo, U.S.S.R. E19 26
Resistencia, Arg. D9 80
Reşiţa, Rom. D5 20
Rešma, U.S.S.R. D25 26
Resolute, N.W. Ter., Can. B14 96
Resolution Island, i., N.W. Ter., Can. D19 96
Resolution Island, i., N.Z. F1 72
Resplendor, Braz. E8 79
Restinga, Mor. J6 16
Restinga Sêca, Braz. E12 80
Reston, Man., Can. E1 100
Reston, Va., U.S. B5 153
Restrepo, Col. E6 84
Restrepo, Col. F4 84
Retalhuleu, Guat. C3 92
Retalhuleu, dept., Guat. C3 92
Retamosa, Ur. G11 80
Rethel, Fr. C11 14
Réthimnon, Grc. N8 20
Reunion (Réunion), dep., Afr. F11 58
Reus, Spain D13 16
Reuss, stm., Switz. D9 13
Reuterstadt Stavenhagen, Ger. B12 10
Reutlingen, Ger. G9 10
Rev'akino, U.S.S.R. G20 26
Revda, U.S.S.R. F9 22
Revelo, Ky., U.S. D5 124
Revelstoke, B.C., Can. D8 99
Revelstoke, Lake, res., B.C., Can. D8 99
Reventazón, Peru B1 82
Reventazón, stm., C.R. G11 92
Revere, Ma., U.S. g11 128
Revigny-sur-Ornain, Fr. D11 14
Revillagigedo, Islas, is., Mex. H4 90
Revillagigedo Island, i., Ak., U.S. n24 109
Revillo, S.D., U.S. B9 148
Revin, Fr. C11 14
Revloc, Pa., U.S. F4 145
Revol'ucii, pik, mtn., U.S.S.R. A5 44
Revolución Mexicana, Mex. A1 92
Revuè, stm., Afr. B11 66
Rewa, India H9 44
Rewa, stm., Guy. F13 84
Rewāri, India F7 44
Rex, Ga., U.S. h8 117
Rexburg, Id., U.S. F7 119
Rexford, Ks., U.S. C3 123
Rexford, Mt., U.S. B1 133
Rexton, N.B., Can. C5 101
Rey, Isla del, i., Pan. C3 84
Rey, Laguna del, l., Mex. D8 90
Reydon, Ok., U.S. B2 143
Reyes, Bol. F8 82
Reyes, Point, c., Ca., U.S. C2 112
Reyhanlı, Tur. C4 48
Reykjanes, pen., Ice. C2 6a
Reykjavík, Ice. B3 6a
Reyno, Ar., U.S. A5 111
Reynolds, Ga., U.S. D2 117
Reynolds, Il., U.S. B3 120
Reynolds, In., U.S. C4 121
Reynolds, Mo., U.S. D6 132
Reynolds, Ne., U.S. D8 134
Reynolds, N.D., U.S. B8 141
Reynolds, co., Mo., U.S. D6 132
Reynoldsburg, Oh., U.S. C3 142
Reynoldsville, Pa., U.S. D4 145
Reynosa, Mex. D10 90
Rež, U.S.S.R. F10 22
Reza, gora (Kūh-e Rīzeh), mtn., Asia C15 48
Rezé, Fr. E5 14
Rēzekne, U.S.S.R. E10 26
Rezeny, U.S.S.R. C12 20
Rezina, U.S.S.R. B12 20
Rezovska (Mutlu), stm., Eur. G11 20
Rhaetian Alps, mts., Eur. F16 14
Rhame, N.D., U.S. C2 141
Rhea, co., Tn., U.S. D9 149
Rheda-Wiedenbrück, Ger. D8 10
Rheims see Reims, Fr. C11 14
Rhein, Sask., Can. F4 105
Rheine, Ger. C7 10
Rheinfelden, Ger. H7 10
Rheinland-Pfalz, state, Ger. E6 10
Rhein see Rhine, stm., Eur. D6 10
Rhine, Ga., U.S. E3 117
Rhine (Rhein) (Rhin), stm., Eur. D6 10
Rhinebeck, N.Y., U.S. D7 139
Rhineland, Mo., U.S. C6 132
Rhinelander, Wi., U.S. C4 156
Rhir, Cap, c., Mor. E6 62
Rho, Italy D4 18
Rhode Island, state, U.S. D3 146
Rhode Island, i., R.I., U.S. E5 146
Rhode Island Sound, strt., U.S. F5 146
Rhodell, W.V., U.S. D3 155
Rhodesia see Zimbabwe, ctry., Afr. E5 58
Rhodes Peak, mtn., Id., U.S. C4 119
Rhodes see Ródhos, i., Grc. M12 20
Rhodhiss, N.C., U.S. B1 140
Rhodope Mountains, mts., Eur. H8 20
Rhome, Tx., U.S. m9 150
Rhön, mts., Ger. E9 10
Rhône, dept., Fr. G11 14
Rhône, stm., Eur. H11 14
Rhône au Rhin, Canal du, Fr. H7 10
Rhourde-El-Baguel, Alg. E14 62
Riaba, Eq. Gui. J14 64
Riachão, Braz. E9 76
Riacho de Santana, Braz. B7 79
Rialma, Braz. C4 79
Rialto, Ca., U.S. m14 112
Rianápolis, Braz. C4 79
Riangnom, Sud. M6 60
Riaño, Spain C6 16
Riau, Kepulauan, is., Indon. N8 40
Ribas do Rio Pardo, Braz. F2 79
Ribeauvillé, Fr. D14 14
Ribeira, Braz. C14 80
Ribeira de Iguape, stm., Braz. C14 80
Ribeira Grande, C.V. k16 64a
Ribeirão do Pinhal, Braz. G3 79
Ribeirão Prêto, Braz. F5 79
Ribeirão Vermelho, Braz. F6 79
Ribeirãozinho, Braz. D2 79
Ribemont, Fr. C10 14
Ribera, Italy L8 18
Ribera, N.M., U.S. B4 138
Riberalta, Bol. D8 82
Rib Lake, Wi., U.S. C3 156
Rib Mountain, mtn., Wi., U.S. D4 156
Ribnica, Yugo. D9 18
Ribnitz-Damgarten, Ger. A12 10
Ribstone, Alta., Can. C5 98
Ricardo Flores Magón, Mex. C6 90
Ricaurte, Col. G4 84
Riccia, Italy H9 18
Riccione, Italy F7 18
Rice, Mn., U.S. E4 130
Rice, Va., U.S. C4 153
Rice, co., Ks., U.S. D5 123
Rice, co., Mn., U.S. F5 130
Riceboro, Ga., U.S. E5 117
Rice Creek, stm., Mn., U.S. m12 130
Rice Lake, Wi., U.S. C2 156
Rice Lake, l., Ont., Can. C6 103
Rice Lake, l., Mn., U.S. D5 130
Riceton, Sask., Can. G3 105
Riceville, Ia., U.S. A5 122
Riceville, Tn., U.S. D9 149
Rich, co., Ut., U.S. B4 151
Rich, Cape, c., Ont., Can. C4 103
Richard Collinson Inlet, b., N.W. Ter., Can. B10 96
Richard's Bay, S. Afr. G11 66
Richard's Bay, b., S. Afr. G11 66
Richards-Gebaur Air Force Base, mil., Mo., U.S. C3 132
Richards Island, i., N.W. Ter., Can. C6 96
Richardson, Tx., U.S. n10 150
Richardson, co., Ne., U.S. D10 134
Richardson, stm., Can. E10 96
Richardson Lakes, l., Me., U.S. D2 126
Richardson Mountains, mts., Can. C5 96
Richardton, N.D., U.S. C3 141
Richburg, S.C., U.S. B5 147
Rich Creek, Va., U.S. C2 153
Riche, Pointe, c., Newf., Can. C3 102
Richelieu, Fr. E7 14
Richer, Man., Can. E3 100
Richey, Mt., U.S. C11 133
Richfield, Id., U.S. F4 119
Richfield, Mn., U.S. F5 130
Richfield, N.C., U.S. B2 140
Richfield, Pa., U.S. E7 145
Richfield, Ut., U.S. E3 151
Richfield, Wi., U.S. m11 156
Richfield Springs, N.Y., U.S. C5 139
Richford, Vt., U.S. B3 152
Rich Fountain, Mo., U.S. C6 132
Rich Hill, Mo., U.S. C3 132
Richibucto, N.B., Can. C5 101
Richisau, Switz. D10 13
Richland, Ga., U.S. D2 117
Richland, In., U.S. I3 121
Richland, Ia., U.S. C6 122
Richland, Mi., U.S. F5 129
Richland, Mo., U.S. D5 132
Richland, N.J., U.S. E3 137
Richland, Wa., U.S. C6 154
Richland, co., Il., U.S. E5 120
Richland, co., La., U.S. B4 125
Richland, co., Mt., U.S. C12 133
Richland, co., N.D., U.S. C8 141
Richland, co., Oh., U.S. B3 142
Richland, co., S.C., U.S. D6 147
Richland, co., Wi., U.S. E3 156
Richland Balsam, mtn., N.C., U.S. f10 140
Richland Center, Wi., U.S. E3 156
Richland Creek, stm., Tn., U.S. B5 149
Richlands, N.C., U.S. C5 140
Richlands, Va., U.S. e10 153
Richlandtown, Pa., U.S. F11 145
Richmond, Austl. C5 70
Richmond, Austl. I9 70
Richmond, B.C., Can. E6 99
Richmond, P.E.I., Can. C6 101
Richmond, Que., Can. D5 104
Richmond, N.Z. D4 72
Richmond, S. Afr. G10 66
Richmond, S. Afr. H6 66
Richmond, Ca., U.S. D2 112
Richmond, Il., U.S. A5 120
Richmond, In., U.S. E8 121
Richmond, Ks., U.S. D8 123
Richmond, Ky., U.S. C5 124
Richmond, Me., U.S. D3 126
Richmond, Mi., U.S. F8 129
Richmond, Mn., U.S. E4 130
Richmond, Mo., U.S. B4 132
Richmond, Tx., U.S. E5 150
Richmond, Ut., U.S. B4 151
Richmond, Vt., U.S. C3 152
Richmond, Va., U.S. C5 153
Richmond, co., Ga., U.S. C4 117
Richmond, co., N.Y., U.S. E6 139
Richmond, co., N.C., U.S. B3 140
Richmond, co., Va., U.S. C6 153
Richmond Beach, Wa., U.S. B3 154
Richmond Dale, Oh., U.S. C3 142
Richmond Heights, Fl., U.S. s13 116
Richmond Heights, Mo., U.S. f13 132
Richmond Highlands, Wa., U.S. B3 154
Richmond Hill, Ont., Can. D5 103
Richmond Hill, Ga., U.S. E5 117
Richmond National Battlefield Park, Va., U.S. n18 153
Richmondville, N.Y., U.S. C6 139
Richmound, Sask., Can. G1 105
Rich Mountain, mtn., U.S. C1 111
Rich Mountain, mtn., Va., U.S. C1 153
Rich Mountain, mtn., W.V., U.S. C5 155
Rich Square, N.C., U.S. A5 140
Richthofen, Mount, mtn., Co., U.S. A5 113
Richton, Ms., U.S. D5 131
Richview, Il., U.S. E4 120
Richville, Mi., U.S. E7 129
Richwood, La., U.S. B3 125
Richwood, Oh., U.S. B2 142
Richwood, Tx., U.S. r14 150
Richwood, W.V., U.S. C4 155
Richwoods, Mo., U.S. C7 132
Rickenbacker Air Force Base, mil., Oh., U.S. m11 142
Rickman, Tn., U.S. C8 149
Riddle, Or., U.S. E3 144
Riddle Mountain, mtn., Or., U.S. D8 144
Rideau, stm., Ont., Can. B9 103
Riderwood, Al., U.S. C1 108
Ridgecrest, Ca., U.S. E5 112
Ridgecrest, La., U.S. C4 125
Ridgecrest, N.C., U.S. f10 140
Ridgecrest, Wa., U.S. B3 154
Ridgedale, Sask., Can. E3 105
Ridgedale, Mo., U.S. E4 132
Ridge Farm, Il., U.S. D6 120
Ridgefield, Ct., U.S. D2 114
Ridgefield, N.J., U.S. h8 137
Ridgefield, Wa., U.S. D3 154
Ridgefield Park, N.J., U.S. B4 137
Ridgeland, Ms., U.S. C3 131
Ridgeland, S.C., U.S. G6 147
Ridgeley, W.V., U.S. B6 155
Ridgely, Md., U.S. C6 127
Ridgely, Tn., U.S. A2 149
Ridgeside, Tn., U.S. h11 149
Ridge Spring, S.C., U.S. D4 147
Ridgetop, Tn., U.S. A5 149
Ridgetown, Ont., Can. E3 103
Ridgeview, W.V., U.S. C3 155
Ridgeville, Man., Can. E3 100
Ridgeville, Ga., U.S. E5 117
Ridgeville, In., U.S. D7 121
Ridgeville, S.C., U.S. E7 147
Ridgeville Corners, Oh., U.S. A1 142
Ridgeway, Ia., U.S. A6 122
Ridgeway, Mo., U.S. A4 132
Ridgeway, S.C., U.S. C6 147
Ridgeway, Va., U.S. D3 153
Ridgeway, Wi., U.S. E4 156
Ridgewood, N.J., U.S. B4 137
Ridgewood Park, Ct., U.S. D7 114
Ridgway, Co., U.S. C3 113
Ridgway, Il., U.S. F5 120
Ridgway, Pa., U.S. D4 145
Riding Mountain, hills, Man., Can. D1 100
Riding Mountain National Park, Man., Can. D1 100
Ridley Park, Pa., U.S. p20 145
Ried im Innkreis, Aus. G13 10
Rienzi, Ms., U.S. A5 131
Riesa, Ger. D13 10
Riesco, Isla, i., Chile G2 78
Riesi, Italy L9 18
Rietavas, U.S.S.R. F4 26
Rietfontein, Nmb. C5 66
Rieti, Italy G7 18
Rif, mts., Mor. C8 62
Riffe Lake, res., Wa., U.S. C3 154
Rifle, Co., U.S. B3 113
Rifle, stm., Mi., U.S. D6 129
Rift Valley, val., Afr. I9 52
Rīga, U.S.S.R. E7 26
Riga, Gulf of see Rižskij zaliv, b., U.S.S.R. D6 26
Rigacikun, Nig. F13 64
Rīgān, Iran G15 48
Rigaud, Que., Can. D3 104
Rigby, Id., U.S. F7 119
Rīgestān, reg., Afg. E1 44
Riggins, Id., U.S. D2 119
Rigi, mtn., Switz. D10 13
Rigo, Pap. N. Gui. A9 68
Rigolet, Newf., Can. A2 102
Riiser-Larsen Peninsula, pen., Ant. B4 73
Rijeka, Yugo. D9 18
Rijswijk, Neth. D5 12
Riley, In., U.S. F3 121
Riley, Ks., U.S. C7 123
Riley, co., Ks., U.S. C7 123
Riley, Mount, mtn., N.M., U.S. F2 138
Rillito, Az., U.S. E4 110
Rima, stm., Nig. E12 64
Rímac, stm., Peru D3 82
Rimachi, Lago, l., Peru J4 84
Rimavská Sobota, Czech. G20 10
Rimbey, Alta., Can. C3 98
Rimersburg, Pa., U.S. D3 145
Rimi, Nig. E13 64
Rimini, Italy E7 18
Rîmnicu Sărat, Rom. D11 20
Rîmnicu Vîlcea, Rom. D8 20
Rimouski, Que., Can. A9 104
Rimouski, stm., Que., Can. A9 104
Rimouski-Est, Que., Can. A9 104
Rimrock, Az., U.S. C4 110
Rimrock Lake, res., Wa., U.S. C4 154
Rincón, C.R. I11 92
Rincon, Ga., U.S. D5 117
Rincon, N.M., U.S. E2 138
Rinconada, Arg. B5 80
Rincón de la Vieja, Parque Nacional, C.R. G9 92
Rincón del Bonete, Lago Artificial, res., Ur. G11 80
Rincón del Ocote, Cerro, mtn., Hond. D7 92
Rincón de Romos, Mex. F8 90
Rincon Mountains, mts., Az., U.S. E5 110
Rindal, Nor. J11 6
Rindge, N.H., U.S. E2 136
Riner, Va., U.S. C2 153
Rineyville, Ky., U.S. C4 124
Ringebu, Nor. K12 6
Ringgold, Ga., U.S. B1 117
Ringgold, La., U.S. B2 125
Ringgold, Va., U.S. D3 153
Ringgold, co., Ia., U.S. D3 122
Ringim, Nig. E14 64
Ringling, Ok., U.S. C4 143
Ringoes, N.J., U.S. C3 137
Ringsted, Ia., U.S. A3 122
Ringwood, N.J., U.S. A4 137
Ringwood, Ok., U.S. A3 143
Rinjani, Gunung, mtn., Indon. G6 38
Rinteln, Ger. C9 10
Rio, Fl., U.S. E6 116
Rio, Il., U.S. B3 120
Rio, Wi., U.S. E4 156
Rio Arriba, co., N.M., U.S. A2 138
Rio Azul, Braz. C13 80
Riobamba, Ec. H3 84
Río Blanco, Chile G3 80
Rio Blanco, co., Co., U.S. B2 113
Rio Branco, Braz. C8 82
Rio Branco, Ur. G12 80
Río Bravo, Mex. E10 90
Rio Brilhante, Braz. F1 79
Río Caribe, Ven. B11 84
Rio Casca, Braz. F7 79
Río Ceballos, Arg. F6 80
Río Chico, Ven. B10 84
Rio Claro, Braz. G5 79
Rio Claro, Trin. I14 94
Río Colorado, Arg. J6 80
Río Cuarto, Arg. G6 80
Rio das Antas, Braz. D13 80
Rio das Flores, Braz. G7 79
Rio de Contas, Braz. B8 79
Rio de Janeiro, Braz. G7 79
Rio de Janeiro, state, Braz. G7 79
Río de Jesús, Pan. J13 92
Rio Dell, Ca., U.S. B1 112
Río de Oro, Col. C6 84
Rio d'Oeste, Braz. D14 80
Rio do Prado, Braz. D8 79
Rio do Sul, Braz. D14 80
Rio Espera, Braz. F7 79
Rio Fortuna, Braz. E14 80
Río Gallegos, Arg. G3 78
Rio Grande, Braz. G12 80
Río Grande, Mex. F8 90
Río Grande, Nic. E8 92
Rio Grande, N.J., U.S. E3 137
Rio Grande, Oh., U.S. D3 142
Rio Grande, co., Co., U.S. D4 113
Rio Grande City, Tx., U.S. F3 150
Rio Grande do Sul, state, Braz. E11 80
Rio Grande see Grande, Rio, stm., N.A. F7 106
Rio Grande Reservoir, res., Co., U.S. D3 113
Ríohacha, Col. B6 84
Río Hato, Pan. C2 84
Rio Hondo, Tx., U.S. F4 150
Rioja, Peru B3 82
Río Lagartos, Mex. G15 90
Riolândia, Braz. E4 79
Rio Largo, Braz. E11 76
Riom, Fr. G10 14
Río Mulatos, Bol. H8 82
Riondel, B.C., Can. E9 99
Rio Negrinho, Braz. D14 80
Rio Negro, Braz. E1 79
Rio Negro, Braz. D14 80
Rionegro, Col. D5 84
Rionegro, Col. D6 84
Río Negro, prov., Arg. J6 80
Rio Negro, Pantanal do, sw., Braz. H13 82
Rionero in Vulture, Italy I10 18
Rio Novo do Sul, Braz. F8 79
Rio Pardo, Braz. E12 80
Rio Pardo de Minas, Braz. C7 79
Río Piedras, Arg. C6 80
Río Pilcomayo, Parque Nacional, Arg. C9 80
Rio Piracicaba, Braz. E7 79
Rio Pomba, Braz. F7 79
Rio Prêto, Braz. G7 79
Rio Rancho, N.M., U.S. B3 138
Río San Juan, dept., Nic. F10 92
Río Segundo, Arg. F7 80

Name — Map Ref. — Page

Río Sucio, Col. E5 84
Ríosucio, Col. D4 84
Rio Tercero, Arg. G6 80
Rio Tinto, Braz. E11 76
Rio Verde, Braz. D3 79
Ríoverde, Mex. G10 90
Rio Verde de Mato Grosso, Braz. E1 79
Rio Vermelho, Braz. E7 79
Rio Vista, Ca., U.S. C3 112
Rioz, Fr. E13 14
Riozinho, stm., Braz. I9 84
Ripley, Ont., Can. C3 103
Ripley, Ca., U.S. F6 112
Ripley, Ms., U.S. A5 131
Ripley, N.Y., U.S. C1 139
Ripley, Oh., U.S. D2 142
Ripley, Ok., U.S. A5 143
Ripley, Tn., U.S. B2 149
Ripley, W.V., U.S. C3 155
Ripley, co., In., U.S. F7 121
Ripley, co., Mo., U.S. E7 132
Ripogenus Pond, l., Me., U.S. C3 126
Ripoll, Spain C14 16
Ripon, Que., Can. D2 104
Ripon, Eng., U.K. G12 8
Ripon, Wi., U.S. E5 156
Riposto, Italy L10 18
Rippey, Ia., U.S. C3 122
Ripples, N.B., Can. D3 101
Rippowam, stm., Ct., U.S. E1 114
Ririe, Id., U.S. F7 119
Ririe Lake, res., Id., U.S. F7 119
Risaralda, dept., Col. E4 84
Riscle, Fr. I6 14
Risco, Mo., U.S. E8 132
Rishiri-tō, i., Japan B16 36a
Rishmayyā, Leb. A5 50
Rishon LeZiyyon, Isr. E3 50
Rising City, Ne., U.S. C8 134
Rising Star, Tx., U.S. C3 150
Rising Sun, De., U.S. D3 115
Rising Sun, In., U.S. G8 121
Rising Sun, Md., U.S. A5 127
Risingsun, Oh., U.S. A2 142
Rison, Ar., U.S. D3 111
Rison, Md., U.S. C3 127
Risør, Nor. L11 6
Rissani, Mor. E8 62
Risti, U.S.S.R. C7 26
Ritchie, co., W.V., U.S. B3 155
Ritter, Mount, mtn., Ca., U.S. D4 112
Rittman, Oh., U.S. B4 142
Ritzville, Wa., U.S. B7 154
Riva, Italy D5 18
Rivadavia, Arg. H7 80
Rivadavia, Arg. G4 80
Rivadavia, Arg. C7 80
Rivadavia, Arg. F4 80
Rivadavia, Chile E3 80
Rivanna, stm., Va., U.S. C4 153
Rivas, Nic. F9 92
Rivas, dept., Nic. F8 92
Rive-de-Gier, Fr. G11 14
Rivera, Arg. I7 80
Rivera, Col. F5 84
Rivera, Ur. F11 80
Riverbank, Ca., U.S. D3 112
River Bourgeois, N.S., Can. D9 101
River Cess, Lib. I5 64
Riverdale, Ca., U.S. D4 112
Riverdale, Il., U.S. k9 120
Riverdale, Ia., U.S. g11 122
Riverdale, Md., U.S. C4 127
Riverdale, Ne., U.S. D6 134
Riverdale, N.J., U.S. B4 137
Riverdale, N.D., U.S. B4 141
Riverdale, Va., U.S. D4 153
River Edge, N.J., U.S. h8 137
River Falls, Al., U.S. D3 108
River Falls, Wi., U.S. D1 156
River Forest, Il., U.S. k9 120
Rivergaro, Italy E4 18
River Grove, Il., U.S. k9 120
Riverhaven, In., U.S. B7 121
Riverhead, N.Y., U.S. n16 139
River Hebert, N.S., Can. D5 101
River Heights, Ut., U.S. B4 151
River Hills, Wi., U.S. m12 156
Riverhurst, Sask., Can. G2 105
Riverina, reg., Austl. J6 70
River John, N.S., Can. D6 101
River Jordan, B.C., Can. h11 99
River of Ponds, Newf., Can. C3 102
River Pines, Ma., U.S. f10 128
Riverport, N.S., Can. E5 101
River Ridge, La., U.S. k11 125
River Road, Or., U.S. C3 144
River Rouge, Mi., U.S. p15 129
Rivers, Man., Can. D1 100
Riversdale, S. Afr. J5 66
Riverside, Al., U.S. B3 108
Riverside, Ca., U.S. F5 112
Riverside, Il., U.S. k9 120
Riverside, Ia., U.S. C6 122
Riverside, N.J., U.S. C3 137
Riverside, Pa., U.S. E8 145
Riverside, Ut., U.S. B3 151
Riverside, Wa., U.S. A6 154
Riverside, Wy., U.S. E6 157
Riverside, co., Ca., U.S. F5 112
Riverside-Albert, N.B., Can. D5 101
Riverside Reservoir, res., Co., U.S. A6 113
Riverton, Man., Can. D3 100
Riverton, N.Z. G2 72
Riverton, Ct., U.S. B3 114
Riverton, Il., U.S. D4 120
Riverton, Ia., U.S. D2 122
Riverton, Ks., U.S. E9 123
Riverton, Ne., U.S. D7 134
Riverton, N.J., U.S. C3 137
Riverton, Ut., U.S. C4 151
Riverton, Vt., U.S. C3 152
Riverton, Va., U.S. B4 153
Riverton, Wy., U.S. C4 157
Riverton Heights, Wa., U.S. f11 154
River Vale, N.J., U.S. h8 137
Riverview, Fl., U.S. p11 116
Riverview, Mi., U.S. p15 129
Rives, Tn., U.S. A2 149
Rivesaltes, Fr. J9 14
Rives Junction, Mi., U.S. F6 129
Rivesville, W.V., U.S. B4 155
Riviera, Tx., U.S. F4 150
Riviera Beach, Fl., U.S. F6 116
Riviera Beach, Md., U.S. B4 127
Rivière-à-Pierre, Que., Can. B5 104
Rivière-du-Loup, Que., Can. B8 104
Rivière-Trois-Pistoles, Que., Can. A8 104
Rivière-Verte, N.B., Can. B1 101
Riviersonderend, S. Afr. J4 66
Rivoli, Italy D2 18
Riyadh see Ar-Riyāḍ, Sau. Ar. B5 47
Rize, Tur. G16 4
Rizhao, China H7 32
Rīžskij zaliv (Rīgas Jūras līcis) (Gulf of Riga), b., U.S.S.R. D6 26
Roa, Nor. K12 6
Roachdale, In., U.S. E4 121
Road Town, Br. Vir. Is. E12 94
Roan Cliffs, clf, U.S. B1 113
Roan Creek, stm., Co., U.S. B2 113
Roane, co., Tn., U.S. D9 149
Roane, co., W.V., U.S. C3 155
Roan High Knob, mtn., U.S. C11 149
Roan Mountain, Tn., U.S. C11 149
Roann, In., U.S. C6 121
Roanne, Fr. F11 14
Roanoke, Al., U.S. B4 108
Roanoke, Il., U.S. C4 120
Roanoke, In., U.S. C7 121
Roanoke, La., U.S. D3 125
Roanoke, Tx., U.S. m9 150
Roanoke, Va., U.S. C3 153
Roanoke, co., Va., U.S. C2 153
Roanoke, stm., U.S. A5 140
Roanoke Island, i., N.C., U.S. B7 140
Roanoke Rapids, N.C., U.S. A5 140
Roanoke Rapids Lake, res., U.S. A5 140
Roan Plateau, plat., U.S. B2 113
Roaring Fork, stm., Co., U.S. C4 113
Roaring Spring, Pa., U.S. F5 145
Roark, Ky., U.S. C6 124
Roatán, Hond. A8 92
Roatán, Isla de, i., Hond. A8 92
Robāa Oued Yahia, Tun. M4 18
Robards, Ky., U.S. C2 124
Robāṭ Karīm, Iran D11 48
Robb, Alta., Can. C2 98
Robbins, Il., U.S. k9 120
Robbins, N.C., U.S. B3 140
Robbins, Tn., U.S. C9 149
Robbinsdale, Mn., U.S. m12 130
Robbins Island, i., Austl. M6 70
Robbinston, Me., U.S. C5 126
Robbinsville, N.C., U.S. f9 140
Röbel, Ger. B12 10
Robersonville, N.C., U.S. B5 140
Roberta, Ga., U.S. D2 117
Robert Lee, Tx., U.S. D2 150
Roberts, Id., U.S. F6 119
Roberts, Il., U.S. C5 120
Roberts, Mt., U.S. E7 133
Roberts, Wi., U.S. C1 156
Roberts, co., S.D., U.S. B8 148
Roberts, co., Tx., U.S. B2 150
Roberts, Point, c., Wa., U.S. A2 154
Robert's Arm, Newf., Can. D4 102
Roberts Creek Mountain, mtn., Nv., U.S. D5 135
Robertsdale, Al., U.S. E2 108
Robertsdale, Pa., U.S. F5 145
Robertsfield, Lib. H4 64
Robert S. Kerr Reservoir, res., Ok., U.S. B6 143
Roberts Mountain, mtn., Ak., U.S. C6 109
Roberts Mountain, mtn., Wy., U.S. D3 157
Robertson, S. Afr. I4 66
Robertson, co., Ky., U.S. B5 124
Robertson, co., Tn., U.S. A5 149
Robertson, co., Tx., U.S. D4 150
Robertsonville, Que., Can. C6 104
Robertsport, Lib. H4 64
Robertstown, Ga., U.S. B3 117
Robertville, N.B., Can. B4 101
Roberval, Que., Can. A5 104
Robeson, co., N.C., U.S. C3 140
Robins, Ia., U.S. B6 122
Robins Air Force Base, mil., Ga., U.S. D3 117
Robinson, Il., U.S. D6 120
Robinson, Ks., U.S. C8 123
Robinson, Me., U.S. B5 126
Robinson, N.D., U.S. B6 141
Robinson, Pa., U.S. F3 145
Róbinson Crusoe, Isla, i., Chile H7 74
Robinson Fork, stm., W.V., U.S. m14 155
Robinson Fork, stm., W.V., U.S. k9 155
Robinson Mountain, mtn., Ar., U.S. A1 111
Robinson Range, mts., Austl. E3 68
Robinsons, Newf., Can. D2 102
Robinsonville, Ms., U.S. A3 131
Robinvale, Austl. J5 70
Roblin, Man., Can. D1 100
Roboré, Bol. H12 82
Robson, Mount, mtn., B.C., Can. C8 99
Robstown, Tx., U.S. F4 150
Roby, Tx., U.S. C2 150
Roca, Cabo da, c., Port. G2 16
Rocafuerte, Ec. H2 84
Rocanville, Sask., Can. G5 105
Roca Partida, Isla, i., Mex. H3 90
Roca Partida, Punta, c., Mex. H12 90
Rocas, Atol das, atoll, Braz. D12 76
Roccastrada, Italy F6 18
Rocciamelone, mtn., Italy D2 18
Rocha, Ur. H9 74
Rocha, Ur. H11 80
Rochdale, Ma., U.S. B4 128
Rochedinho, Braz. F1 79
Rochedinho, Braz. I14 82
Rochedo, Braz. E1 79
Rochefort, Bel. H7 12
Rochefort, Fr. G6 14
Roche Harbor, Wa., U.S. A2 154
Rochelle, Ga., U.S. E3 117
Rochelle, Il., U.S. B4 120
Rochelle Park, N.J., U.S. h8 137
Roche-Percée, Sask., Can. H4 105
Rocheport, Mo., U.S. C5 132
Rochester, Austl. K6 70
Rochester, Alta., Can. B4 98
Rochester, Il., U.S. D4 120
Rochester, In., U.S. B5 121
Rochester, Ky., U.S. C3 124
Rochester, Mi., U.S. F7 129
Rochester, Mn., U.S. F6 130
Rochester, N.H., U.S. D5 136
Rochester, N.Y., U.S. B3 139
Rochester, Pa., U.S. E1 145
Rochester, Vt., U.S. D3 152
Rochester, Wa., U.S. C2 154
Rochester, Wi., U.S. n11 156
Rochester Mountain, mtn., Vt., U.S. D3 152
Rochfort Bridge, Alta., Can. C3 98
Rochlitz, Ger. D12 10
Rock, Mi., U.S. B3 129
Rock, co., Mn., U.S. G2 130
Rock, co., Ne., U.S. B6 134
Rock, co., Wi., U.S. F4 156
Rock, stm., U.S. B3 120
Rock, stm., U.S. A1 122
Rockall, i., Scot., U.K. D5 4
Rockaway, N.J., U.S. B3 137
Rockaway, Or., U.S. B3 144
Rockaway Beach, Mo., U.S. E4 132
Rockbridge, Il., U.S. D3 120
Rockbridge, co., Va., U.S. C3 153
Rockcastle, co., Ky., U.S. C5 124
Rockcastle, stm., Ky., U.S. C5 124
Rockcliffe Park, Ont., Can. h12 103
Rock Creek, B.C., Can. E8 99
Rock Creek, Mn., U.S. E6 130
Rock Creek, Oh., U.S. A5 142
Rock Creek, stm., U.S. B3 127
Rock Creek, stm., U.S. h14 154
Rock Creek, stm., Il., U.S. B4 120
Rock Creek, stm., Ks., U.S. g10 123
Rock Creek, stm., Ne., U.S. g11 134
Rock Creek, stm., Nv., U.S. C5 135
Rock Creek, stm., Or., U.S. B6 144
Rock Creek, stm., Wa., U.S. D5 154
Rock Creek, stm., Wa., U.S. B8 154
Rock Creek, stm., Wy., U.S. E6 157
Rock Creek Butte, mtn., Or., U.S. C8 144
Rockdale, Il., U.S. B5 120
Rockdale, Md., U.S. B4 127
Rockdale, Tx., U.S. D4 150
Rockdale, co., Ga., U.S. C3 117
Rockefeller Plateau, plat., Ant. D10 73
Rockenhausen, Ger. F7 10
Rockfall, Ct., U.S. C5 114
Rock Falls, Il., U.S. B4 120
Rockfield, In., U.S. C4 121
Rockfield, Ky., U.S. D3 124
Rockford, Al., U.S. C3 108
Rockford, Il., U.S. A4 120
Rockford, Ia., U.S. A5 122
Rockford, Mi., U.S. E5 129
Rockford, Mn., U.S. E5 130
Rockford, Oh., U.S. B1 142
Rockford, Tn., U.S. D10 149
Rockford, Wa., U.S. B8 154
Rockglen, Sask., Can. H3 105
Rock Hall, Md., U.S. B5 127
Rockhampton, Austl. D9 70
Rock Hill, S.C., U.S. B5 147
Rockholds, Ky., U.S. D5 124
Rockingham, N.C., U.S. C3 140
Rockingham, co., N.H., U.S. D4 136
Rockingham, co., N.C., U.S. A3 140
Rockingham, co., Va., U.S. B4 153
Rockingham Bay, b., Austl. B7 70
Rock Island, Que., Can. D5 104
Rock Island, Il., U.S. B3 120
Rock Island, Ok., U.S. B7 143
Rock Island, Wa., U.S. B5 154
Rock Island, co., Il., U.S. B3 120
Rock Island, i., Fl., U.S. C3 116
Rock Island, i., Wi., U.S. C7 156
Rocklake, N.D., U.S. A6 141
Rock Lake, l., Man., Can. E2 100
Rock Lake, l., Wa., U.S. B8 154
Rockland, Ont., Can. B9 103
Rockland, Id., U.S. G6 119
Rockland, Me., U.S. D3 126
Rockland, Ma., U.S. B6 128
Rockland, Mi., U.S. m12 129
Rockland, co., N.Y., U.S. D6 139
Rocklands Reservoir, res., Austl. K5 70
Rockledge, Fl., U.S. D6 116
Rockledge, Ga., U.S. D4 117
Rockledge, Pa., U.S. o20 145
Rocklin, Ca., U.S. C3 112
Rockmart, Ga., U.S. B1 117
Rock Mountain, mtn., Al., U.S. B2 108
Rock Mountain, mtn., Co., U.S. D3 113
Rock Point, Az., U.S. A6 110
Rockport, Ar., U.S. g8 111
Rockport, Il., U.S. D2 120
Rockport, In., U.S. I3 121
Rockport, Ky., U.S. C3 124
Rockport, Me., U.S. D3 126
Rockport, Ma., U.S. A6 128
Rock Port, Mo., U.S. A2 132
Rockport, Tx., U.S. E4 150
Rockport, Wa., U.S. A4 154
Rock Rapids, Ia., U.S. A1 122
Rock River, Wy., U.S. E7 157
Rock Run, Al., U.S. A4 108
Rock Sound, Bah. B6 94
Rocksprings, Tx., U.S. D2 150
Rock Springs, Wi., U.S. E4 156
Rock Springs, Wy., U.S. E3 157
Rockstone, Guy. E13 84
Rockton, Il., U.S. A4 120
Rockvale, Co., U.S. C5 113
Rockvale, Tn., U.S. B5 149
Rock Valley, Ia., U.S. A1 122
Rockville, In., U.S. E3 121
Rockville, Md., U.S. B3 127
Rockville, Mn., U.S. E4 130
Rockville, Mo., U.S. C3 132
Rockville Centre, N.Y., U.S. n15 139
Rockwall, Tx., U.S. C4 150
Rockwall, co., Tx., U.S. C4 150
Rockwell, Ia., U.S. B4 122
Rockwell, N.C., U.S. B2 140
Rockwell City, Ia., U.S. B3 122
Rockwell Park, N.C., U.S. B2 140
Rockwood, Me., U.S. C3 126
Rockwood, Mi., U.S. F7 129
Rockwood, Pa., U.S. G3 145
Rockwood, Tn., U.S. D9 149
Rocky, stm., N.C., U.S. B2 140
Rocky, stm., S.C., U.S. C2 147
Rocky, East Branch, stm., Oh., U.S. h9 142
Rocky, West Branch, stm., Oh., U.S. h9 142
Rocky Boy, Mt., U.S. B7 133
Rocky Boys Indian Reservation, Mt., U.S. B7 133
Rocky Comfort, Mo., U.S. E3 132
Rocky Coulee, val., Wa., U.S. B6 154
Rockyford, Alta., Can. D4 98
Rocky Ford, Co., U.S. C7 113
Rocky Ford, Ga., U.S. D5 117
Rocky Fork Lake, l., Oh., U.S. C2 142
Rocky Gap, Va., U.S. C1 153
Rocky Harbour, Newf., Can. D3 102
Rocky Hill, Ct., U.S. C5 114
Rocky Hill, Ky., U.S. C3 124
Rocky Lake, l., Man., Can. B1 100
Rocky Lake, l., Me., U.S. D5 126
Rocky Mount, N.C., U.S. B5 140
Rocky Mount, Va., U.S. D3 153
Rocky Mountain, mtn., Mt., U.S. C4 133
Rocky Mountain House, Alta., Can. C3 98
Rocky Mountain National Park, Co., U.S. A5 113
Rocky Mountains, mts., N.A. E8 86
Rocky Point, N.C., U.S. C5 140
Rocky Ripple, In., U.S. k10 121
Rocky River, Oh., U.S. A4 142
Rocky Top, mtn., Or., U.S. C4 144
Roda, Va., U.S. f9 153
Rodalben, Ger. F7 10
Rødbyhavn, Den. N12 6
Roddickton, Newf., Can. C3 102
Roddy, Tn., U.S. D9 149
Rodeio, Braz. D14 80
Rodeo, Arg. F4 80
Rodeo, Mex. E7 90
Rodeo, N.M., U.S. F1 138
Roderfield, W.V., U.S. D3 155
Roderick Island, i., B.C., Can. C3 99
Rodessa, La., U.S. B2 125
Rodewisch, Ger. E12 10
Rodey, N.M., U.S. E2 138
Rodez, Fr. H9 14
Ródhos (Rhodes), Grc. M12 20
Ródhos (Rhodes), i., Grc. M12 20
Rodi Garganico, Italy H10 18
Roding, Ger. F12 10
Rodney, Ont., Can. E3 103
Rodney, Cape, c., Ak., U.S. C6 109
Rodney Pond, l., Newf., Can. D4 102
Rodney Village, De., U.S. D3 115
Rodniki, U.S.S.R. D24 26
Rodolfo Iselín, Arg. H4 80
Rodrigues, i., Mrts. K7 28
Roe, Ar., U.S. C4 111
Roebling, N.J., U.S. C3 137
Roebourne, Austl. D3 68
Roebuck, S.C., U.S. B4 147
Roeland Park, Ks., U.S. k16 123
Roelofarendsveen, Neth. D6 12
Roer (Rur), stm., Eur. F9 12
Roermond, Neth. F9 12
Roes Welcome Sound, strt., N.W. Ter., Can. D15 96
Roff, Ok., U.S. C5 143
Rogačevo, U.S.S.R. E20 26
Rogačov, U.S.S.R. H13 26
Rogagua, Laguna, l., Bol. E8 82
Rogaguado, Laguna, l., Bol. E9 82
Rogaland, co., Nor. L10 6
Rogatica, Yugo. F3 20
Roger Mills, co., Ok., U.S. B2 143
Rogers, Ar., U.S. A1 111
Rogers, Ct., U.S. B8 114
Rogers, Mn., U.S. E5 130
Rogers, Tx., U.S. D4 150
Rogers, co., Ok., U.S. A6 143
Rogers, Mount, mtn., Va., U.S. f10 153
Rogers City, Mi., U.S. C7 129
Rogers Lake, res., Ct., U.S. D6 114
Rogers Pass, Mt., U.S. C4 133
Rogersville, N.B., Can. C4 101
Rogersville, Al., U.S. A2 108
Rogersville, Mo., U.S. D4 132
Rogersville, Tn., U.S. C10 149
Roggen, Co., U.S. A6 113
Rogliano, Fr. J16 14
Rogoźno, Pol. C17 10
Rogue, stm., Or., U.S. E2 144
Rogue River, Or., U.S. E3 144
Rohnert Park, Ca., U.S. C2 112
Rohtak, India F7 44
Rohunta, Laguna, b., Hond. B11 92
Roi Et, Thai. F7 40
Roisel, Fr. C10 14
Roja, U.S.S.R. D5 26
Rojas, Arg. H8 80
Rojl'anka, U.S.S.R. C13 20
Rojo, Cabo, c., Mex. G11 90
Rojo, Cabo, c., P.R. F11 94
Rokeby National Park, Austl. B8 68
Rokiškis, U.S.S.R. F8 26
Rokycany, Czech. F13 10
Roland, Man., Can. E3 100
Roland, Ar., U.S. C3 111
Roland, Ia., U.S. B4 122
Roland, Ok., U.S. B7 143
Roland, Lake, res., Md., U.S. g11 127
Rolândia, Braz. G3 79
Røldal, Nor. L10 6
Roldán, Arg. G8 80
Roldanillo, Col. E4 84
Rolesville, N.C., U.S. B4 140
Rolette, N.D., U.S. A6 141
Rolette, co., N.D., U.S. A6 141
Rolfe, Ia., U.S. B3 122
Roll, Az., U.S. E2 110
Rolla, B.C., Can. B7 99
Rolla, Ks., U.S. E2 123
Rolla, Mo., U.S. D6 132
Rolla, N.D., U.S. A6 141
Rolle, Switz. F5 13
Rolleston, Austl. E8 70
Rollingbay, Wa., U.S. e10 154
Rolling Fork, Ms., U.S. C3 131
Rolling Fork, stm., Ar., U.S. C1 111
Rolling Fork, stm., Ky., U.S. C4 124
Rolling Hills, Wy., U.S. D7 157
Rolling Meadows, Il., U.S. h8 120
Rollingstone, Austl. B7 70
Rollingstone, Mn., U.S. F7 130
Rollins, Mt., U.S. C2 133
Rollinsford, N.H., U.S. D5 136
Roma, Austl. F8 70
Roma (Rome), Italy H7 18
Roma, Tx., U.S. F3 150
Romagna, hist. reg., Italy H18 14
Romain, Cape, c., S.C., U.S. F9 147
Romaine, stm., Can. A14 106
Roman, Rom. C10 20
Romania (România), ctry., Eur. F13 4
Roman-Koš, gora, mtn., U.S.S.R. I4 22
Romankovcy, U.S.S.R. A11 20
Roman Nose Mountain, mtn., Md., U.S. m12 127
Roman Nose Mountain, mtn., Or., U.S. D3 144
Romano, Cape, c., Fl., U.S. G5 116
Romano, Cayo, i., Cuba C6 94
Romanshorn, Switz. C11 13
Romans [-sur-Isère], Fr. G12 14
Romanzof, Cape, c., Ak., U.S. C6 109
Romanzof Mountains, mts., Ak., U.S. B11 109
Romayor, Tx., U.S. D5 150
Rombauer, Mo., U.S. E7 132
Rome, Ga., U.S. B1 117
Rome, Il., U.S. C4 120
Rome, Ms., U.S. B3 131
Rome, N.Y., U.S. B5 139
Rome, Oh., U.S. D3 142
Rome City, In., U.S. B7 121
Romeo, Co., U.S. D4 113
Romeo, Mi., U.S. F7 129
Romeoville, Il., U.S. k8 120
Rome see Roma, Italy H7 18
Rometan, U.S.S.R. B18 48
Romilly-sur-Seine, Fr. D10 14
Rommani, Mor. C7 62
Romney, In., U.S. D4 121
Romney, W.V., U.S. B6 155
Romny, U.S.S.R. G4 22
Romont, Switz. E6 13
Romorantin-Lanthenay, Fr. E8 14
Romulus, Mi., U.S. p15 129
Ron, Mui, c., Viet. E9 40
Ronald, Wa., U.S. B4 154
Ronan, Mt., U.S. C2 133
Roncador, Serra do, plat., Braz. F9 74
Roncador, Serra do, plat., Braz. F8 76
Ronceverte, W.V., U.S. D4 155
Ronchamp, Fr. E13 14
Ronda, Spain I6 16
Rønde, Den. M12 6
Rondo, Ar., U.S. C5 111
Rondon, Braz. G2 79
Rondônia, Braz. D11 82
Rondônia, state, Braz. D10 82
Rondonópolis, Braz. D1 79
Ronge, Lac la, l., Sask., Can. B3 105
Rongshui, China B10 40
Rõngu, U.S.S.R. C9 26
Rønne, Den. N14 6
Ronneby, Swe. M14 6
Ronne Entrance, b., Ant. C12 73
Ronne Ice Shelf, Ant. C12 73
Ronse (Renaix), Bel. G4 12
Ronuro, stm., Braz. B1 79
Roodhouse, Il., U.S. D3 120
Roof Butte, mtn., Az., U.S. A6 110
Rooiboklaagte, stm., Nmb. C5 66
Rooks, co., Ks., U.S. C4 123
Roopville, Ga., U.S. C1 117
Roorkee, India F7 44
Roosendaal, Neth. E5 12
Roosevelt, Az., U.S. D4 110
Roosevelt, Mn., U.S. B3 130
Roosevelt, Ok., U.S. C2 143
Roosevelt, Ut., U.S. C5 151
Roosevelt, co., Mt., U.S. B11 133
Roosevelt, co., N.M., U.S. C6 138
Roosevelt, stm., Braz. B11 82
Roosevelt Island, i., Ant. C9 73
Roosevelt Park, Mi., U.S. E4 129
Root, stm., Mn., U.S. G7 130
Root, stm., Wi., U.S. n12 156
Rootstown, Oh., U.S. A4 142
Roper, N.C., U.S. B6 140
Roper, stm., Austl. B6 68
Roquefort, Fr. H6 14
Roque Pérez, Arg. H9 80
Roraima, ter., Braz. G12 84
Roraima, Mount, mtn., S.A. E12 84
Rorketon, Man., Can. D2 100
Røros, Nor. J12 6
Rorschach, Switz. D12 13
Rørvik, Nor. I12 6
Rosa, Lake, l., Bah. D8 94
Rosa, Monte, mtn., Eur. G8 13
Rošal', U.S.S.R. F22 26
Rosales, Mex. C7 90
Rosalia, Ks., U.S. E7 123
Rosalia, Wa., U.S. B8 154
Rosalie, Ne., U.S. B9 134
Rosalind, Alta., Can. C4 98
Rosamond, Ca., U.S. E4 112
Rosamond, Il., U.S. D4 120
Rosamorada, Mex. F7 90
Rosana, Braz. B12 80
Rosario, Arg. G8 80
Rosário, Braz. D10 76
Rosario, Mex. D5 90
Rosario, Mex. F7 90
Rosario, Para. C10 80
Rosario, Ur. H10 80
Rosario, Ven. B6 84
Rosario, stm., Arg. C6 80
Rosario, Bahía, b., Mex. C2 90
Rosario, Islas del, is., Col. B5 84
Rosario de Arriba, Mex. B2 90
Rosario de la Frontera, Arg. C6 80
Rosario de Lerma, Arg. C6 80
Rosario del Tala, Arg. G9 80
Rosário do Sul, Braz. F11 80
Rosário Oeste, Braz. F13 82
Rosarito, Mex. D4 90
Rosarno, Italy K10 18
Roščino, U.S.S.R. A12 26
Roscoe, Il., U.S. A5 120
Roscoe, N.Y., U.S. D6 139
Roscoe, Pa., U.S. F2 145
Roscoe, S.D., U.S. B6 148
Roscoe, Tx., U.S. C2 150
Roscommon, Ire. H5 8
Roscommon, Mi., U.S. D6 129
Roscommon, co., Ire. H5 8
Roscommon, co., Mi., U.S. D6 129
Roscrea, Ire. I6 8
Rose, Mount, mtn., Nv., U.S. D2 135
Roseau, Dom. G14 94
Roseau, Mn., U.S. B3 130
Roseau, co., Mn., U.S. B3 130
Roseau, South Fork, stm., Mn., U.S. B3 130
Rosebery, Austl. M6 70
Rose-Blanche [-Harbour le Cou], Newf., Can. E2 102
Roseboro, N.C., U.S. C4 140
Rosebud, Alta., Can. D4 98
Rose Bud, Ar., U.S. B3 111
Rosebud, Mo., U.S. C6 132
Rosebud, Mt., U.S. D10 133
Rosebud, S.D., U.S. D5 148
Rosebud, Tx., U.S. D4 150
Rosebud, co., Mt., U.S. D10 133
Rosebud, stm., Alta., Can. D4 98
Rosebud Creek, stm., Mt., U.S. E10 133
Rosebud Indian Reservation, S.D., U.S. D5 148
Roseburg, Or., U.S. D3 144
Rosebush, Mi., U.S. E6 129
Rose City, Mi., U.S. D6 129
Rose Creek, Mn., U.S. G6 130
Rosedale, Austl. E9 70
Rosedale, Alta., Can. D4 98
Rosedale, In., U.S. E3 121
Rosedale, Md., U.S. g11 127
Rosedale, Ms., U.S. B2 131
Rosedale, Wa., U.S. f10 154
Rose Hall, Guy. D14 84
Rosehearty, Scot., U.K. D11 8
Rose-Hill, Mrts. V18 67c
Rose Hill, Ks., U.S. E6 123
Rose Hill, Ms., U.S. C4 131
Rose Hill, N.C., U.S. C4 140
Rose Hill, Va., U.S. f8 153
Roseisle, Man., Can. E2 100
Roseland, Fl., U.S. E6 116
Roseland, In., U.S. A5 121
Roseland, La., U.S. D5 125
Roseland, Ne., U.S. D7 134
Roseland, Oh., U.S. B3 142
Roselawn, In., U.S. B3 121
Roselle, Il., U.S. k8 120
Roselle, N.J., U.S. k7 137
Roselle Park, N.J., U.S. k7 137
Rosemary, Alta., Can. D4 98
Rosemère, Que., Can. p19 104
Rosemont, W.V., U.S. k10 155
Rosemount, Mn., U.S. F5 130
Rosenberg, Tx., U.S. E5 150
Rosendal, Nor. L10 6
Rosendale, Mo., U.S. A3 132
Rosendale, Wi., U.S. E5 156
Roseneath, Ont., Can. C6 103
Rosenfeld, Man., Can. E3 100
Rosenheim, Ger. H12 10
Rose Peak, mtn., Az., U.S. D6 110
Rosepine, La., U.S. D2 125
Rose Point, c., B.C., Can. B2 99
Roseto, Pa., U.S. E11 145
Rosetown, Sask., Can. F1 105
Rosetta see Rashīd, Egypt B6 60
Rose Valley, Sask., Can. E4 105
Roseville, Ca., U.S. C3 112
Roseville, Il., U.S. C3 120
Roseville, Mi., U.S. o16 129
Roseville, Mn., U.S. m12 130
Roseville, Oh., U.S. C3 142
Rosewood, Austl. F10 70
Rosewood Heights, Il., U.S. E3 120
Rosharon, Tx., U.S. r14 150
Rosh Ha'Ayin, Isr. D3 50
Rosholt, S.D., U.S. B9 148
Rosholt, Wi., U.S. D4 156
Rosh Pinna, Isr. C5 50
Rosiclare, Il., U.S. F5 120
Rosignano Marittimo, Italy F5 18
Rosignol, Guy. D14 84
Roșiori de Vede, Rom. E9 20
Roskilde, Den. N13 6
Rosl'akovo, U.S.S.R. G23 6
Rosl'atino, U.S.S.R. B27 26
Roslavl', U.S.S.R. H15 26
Roslyn, S.D., U.S. B8 148
Roslyn, Wa., U.S. B4 154
Roslyn Heights, N.Y., U.S. h13 139
Rosporden, Fr. E3 14
Ross, Austl. N7 70
Ross, N.Z. E3 72
Ross, Oh., U.S. C1 142
Ross, co., Oh., U.S. C2 142
Rossano, Italy J11 18
Ross Barnett Reservoir, res., Ms., U.S. C3 131
Rossburn, Man., Can. D1 100
Ross Dam, Wa., U.S. A4 154
Rosseau, Ont., Can. B5 103
Rossell y Rius, Ur. G11 80
Rossendale, Man., Can. E2 100
Rossford, Oh., U.S. A2 142
Ross Ice Shelf, Ant. D9 73
Rossignol, Lake, l., N.S., Can. E4 101

Name | Map Ref. | Page

Rossijskaja Sovetskaja Federativnaja Socialističeskaja Respublika (Russian Soviet Federative Socialist Republic),state, U.S.S.R. E14 22
Ross Island, i., Ant. C8 73
Ross Island, i., Man., Can. B3 100
Rossiter, Pa., U.S. E4 145
Ross Lake National Recreation Area, Wa., U.S. A5 154
Rossland, B.C., Can. E9 99
Rosslare, Ire. I7 8
Rosslau, Ger. D12 10
Rosso, Maur. C2 64
Ross-on-Wye, Eng., U.K. J11 8
Rossony, U.S.S.R. F11 26
Rossoš', U.S.S.R. G5 22
Ross River, Yukon, Can. D6 96
Ross Sea, Ant. C9 73
Rosston, Ar., U.S. D2 111
Rossville, Ga., U.S. B1 117
Rossville, Il., U.S. C6 120
Rossville, In., U.S. D4 121
Rossville, Ks., U.S. C8 123
Rossville, Tn., U.S. B2 149
Rossway, N.S., Can. E4 101
Rosthern, Sask., Can. E2 105
Rostock, Ger. A12 10
Rostov, U.S.S.R. D22 26
Rostov-na-Donu, U.S.S.R. H5 22
Roswell, Ga., U.S. B2 117
Roswell, Id., U.S. F2 119
Roswell, N.M., U.S. D5 138
Rota, Spain I5 16
Rotan, Tx., U.S. C2 150
Rotenburg, Ger. B9 10
Rotenburg, Ger. D9 10
Roth, Ger. F11 10
Rothaargebirge, mts., Ger. D8 10
Rothbury, Mi., U.S. E4 129
Rothenburg ob der Tauber, Ger. F10 10
Rothesay, N.B., Can. D4 101
Rothsay, Mn., U.S. D2 130
Rothschild, Wi., U.S. D4 156
Rothsville, Pa., U.S. F9 145
Roti, Pulau, i., Indon. H7 38
Roto, Austl. I6 70
Rotondella, Italy I11 18
Rotorua, N.Z. C6 72
Rott am Inn, Ger. H12 10
Rottenburg, Ger. G8 10
Rottenmann, Aus. H14 10
Rotterdam, Neth. E5 12
Rotterdam, N.Y., U.S. C6 139
Rottweil, Ger. G8 10
Roubaix, Fr. B10 14
Roubideau Creek, stm., Co., U.S. C2 113
Roudnice, Czech. E14 10
Rouen, Fr. C8 14
Rougé, Fr. E5 14
Rouge, stm., Que., Can. D3 104
Rougemont, Fr. E13 14
Rougemont, N.C., U.S. A4 140
Rough, stm., Ky., U.S. C3 124
Rough River Lake, res., Ky., U.S. C3 124
Rougon, La., U.S. D4 125
Rouillac, Fr. G6 14
Rouleau, Sask., Can. G3 105
Roulette, Pa., U.S. C5 145
Round Harbour, Newf., Can. D4 102
Round Hill, Alta., Can. C4 98
Round Hill, N.S., Can. E4 101
Round Hill, Va., U.S. A5 153
Round Hill Head, c., Austl. E9 70
Round Island, i., Ms., U.S. g8 131
Round Lake, Il., U.S. h8 120
Round Lake, Mn., U.S. G3 130
Round Lake, l., Ont., Can. B7 103
Round Lake, l., Sask., Can. G4 105
Round Lake Beach, Il., U.S. h8 120
Round Mound, hill, Ks., U.S. D4 123
Round Mountain, Nv., U.S. E4 135
Round Mountain, mtn., Austl. H10 70
Round Oak, Ga., U.S. C3 117
Round Pond, Ar., U.S. B5 111
Round Pond, Me., U.S. E3 126
Round Rock, Az., U.S. A6 110
Round Rock, Tx., U.S. D4 150
Round Top Hill, mtn., Ma., U.S. B2 128
Roundup, Mt., U.S. D8 133
Round Valley Indian Reservation, Ca., U.S. C2 112
Round Valley Reservoir, res., N.J., U.S. B3 137
Rouses Point, N.Y., U.S. f11 139
Roussillon, hist. reg., Fr. J9 14
Routt, co., Co., U.S. A3 113
Rouxville, S. Afr. H8 66
Rouyn, Que., Can. k11 104
Rouzerville, Pa., U.S. G6 145
Rovaniemi, Fin. H19 6
Rovato, Italy D5 18
Rover, Ar., U.S. C2 111
Rover, Tn., U.S. B5 149
Rovereto, Italy D6 18
Roversi, Arg. D8 80
Rovigo, Italy D6 18
Rovira, Col. E5 84
Rovno, U.S.S.R. G3 22
Rovuma (Ruvuma), stm., Afr. D7 58
Rowan, co., Ky., U.S. B6 124
Rowan, co., N.C., U.S. B2 140
Rowan Lake, l., Ont., Can. E5 100
Rowe, N.M., U.S. B4 138
Rowland, N.C., U.S. C3 140
Rowlesburg, W.V., U.S. B5 155
Rowletts, Ky., U.S. C4 124
Rowley, Ia., U.S. B6 122
Rowley, Ma., U.S. A6 128
Rowley Island, i., N.W. Ter., Can. C17 96
Rowley Shoals, rf., Austl. C3 68
Roxana, De., U.S. G5 115
Roxas, Phil. C7 38
Roxboro, N.C., U.S. A4 140
Roxburgh, N.Z. F2 72
Roxbury, Ks., U.S. D6 123
Roxbury, Vt., U.S. C3 152
Roxie, Ms., U.S. D2 131
Roxo, Cap, c., Afr. E1 64
Roxton, Tx., U.S. C5 150
Roxton Falls, Que., Can. D5 104
Roxton Pond, Que., Can. D5 104
Roy, Mt., U.S. C8 133
Roy, N.M., U.S. B5 138
Roy, Ut., U.S. B3 151
Roy, Wa., U.S. C3 154
Royal, Ar., U.S. C2 111
Royal, Ia., U.S. A2 122
Royal, Tn., U.S. B5 149
Royal, stm., Me., U.S. g7 126
Royal Canal, Ire. H6 8
Royal Center, In., U.S. C4 121
Royale, Isle, i., Mi., U.S. h9 129
Royal Gorge, val., Co., U.S. C5 113
Royal Leamington Spa, Eng., U.K. I12 8
Royal Oak, Md., U.S. C5 127
Royal Oak, Mi., U.S. F7 129
Royal Pines, N.C., U.S. f10 140
Royalton, Il., U.S. F4 120
Royalton, Ky., U.S. C6 124
Royalton, Mn., U.S. E4 130
Royal Tunbridge Wells, Eng., U.K. J14 8
Royan, Fr. G5 14
Roye, Fr. C9 14
Royersford, Pa., U.S. F10 145
Royerton, In., U.S. D7 121
Royse City, Tx., U.S. C4 150
Royston, B.C., Can. E5 99
Royston, Ga., U.S. B3 117
Rožaj, Yugo. G4 20
Roždestvo, U.S.S.R. D16 26
Rozel, Ks., U.S. D4 123
Rozet, Wy., U.S. B7 157
Rožňava, Czech. G20 10
Roznov, Rom. C10 20
Roztocze, hills, Eur. E22 10
Rtiščevo, U.S.S.R. G6 22
Ruacaná, Nmb. A2 66
Ruacana Falls, wtfl, Afr. A2 66
Ruapehu, Mount, mtn., N.Z. L21 158
Rub' al Khali see Ar-Rub' al-Khālī, des., Asia D7 47
Rubcovsk, U.S.S.R. G8 24
Rubežnoje, U.S.S.R. H5 22
Rubiataba, Braz. C4 79
Rubidoux, Ca., U.S. n14 112
Rubim, Braz. D8 79
Rubinéia, Braz. F3 79
Rubino, I.C. H7 64
Rubio, Ven. D6 84
Ruboani, Sud. M6 60
Rubonia, Fl., U.S. p10 116
Ruby, Ak., U.S. C8 109
Ruby, S.C., U.S. B7 147
Ruby Dome, mtn., Nv., U.S. C6 135
Ruby Lake, l., Nv., U.S. C6 135
Ruby Mountains, mts., Nv., U.S. C6 135
Ruby Range, mts., Co., U.S. C3 113
Ruby Range, mts., Mt., U.S. E4 133
Rucava, U.S.S.R. E4 26
Rudall, Austl. I2 70
Rudall River National Park, Austl. D4 68
Ruda Śląska, Pol. E18 10
Rūdbār, Afg. F17 48
Rudd, Ia., U.S. A5 122
Ruddels Mills, Ky., U.S. B5 124
Rudensk, U.S.S.R. H10 26
Rüdersdorf, Ger. C13 10
Rüdesheim, Ger. F7 10
Rūdiškės, U.S.S.R. G7 26
Rudn'a, U.S.S.R. G14 26
Rudnica, U.S.S.R. A12 20
Rudnyj, U.S.S.R. G10 22
Rudo, Yugo. F3 20
Rudolf, Lake (Lake Turkana), l., Afr. H8 56
Rudolph, Oh., U.S. A2 142
Rudolstadt, Ger. E11 10
Rudong, China C10 34
Rūdsar, Iran C11 48
Rudyard, Mi., U.S. B6 129
Rudyard, Mt., U.S. B6 133
Rue, Fr. B8 14
Ruen, mtn., Eur. G6 20
Rufā'ah, Sud. J7 60
Ruffieux, Fr. G12 14
Ruffin, S.C., U.S. E6 147
Rufino, Arg. H7 80
Rufisque, Sen. D1 64
Rufus, Or., U.S. B6 144
Rufus Woods Lake, res., Wa., U.S. A6 154
Rugao, China C9 34
Rugby, Eng., U.K. I12 8
Rugby, N.D., U.S. A6 141
Rügen, i., Ger. A13 10
Ruhr, stm., Ger. F10 12
Rui'an, China H9 34
Ruidoso, N.M., U.S. D4 138
Ruidoso Downs, N.M., U.S. D4 138
Ruijin, China J5 34
Ruivo, Pico, mtn., Port. M21 17a
Ruiz, Mex. G7 90
Ruiz de Montoya, Arg. D11 80
Rūjiena, U.S.S.R. D8 26
Rukwa, Lake, l., Tan. C6 58
Rule, Tx., U.S. C3 150
Rule Creek, stm., Co., U.S. D7 113
Ruleville, Ms., U.S. B3 131
Rulo, Ne., U.S. D10 134
Rum, stm., Mn., U.S. D5 130
Ruma, Il., U.S. E3 120
Ruma, Yugo. D3 20
Rumbek, Sud. N5 60
Rumbeke, Bel. G3 12
Rum Cay, i., Bah. C7 94
Rum Creek, stm., W.V., U.S. n12 155
Rumford, Me., U.S. D2 126
Rumia, Pol. A18 10
Rumigny, Fr. C11 14
Rum Jungle, Austl. B6 68
Rummānah, Egypt B7 60
Rumney, N.H., U.S. C3 136
Rumney Depot, N.H., U.S. C3 136
Rumoi, Japan D16 36a
Rump Mountain, mtn., Me., U.S. C1 126
Rumsey, Alta., Can. D4 98
Rumsey, Ky., U.S. C2 124
Rumson, N.J., U.S. C4 137
Rumstick Point, c., R.I., U.S. D5 146
Runan, China B3 34
Runanga, N.Z. E3 72
Rundu, Nmb. A4 66
Runge, Tx., U.S. E4 150
Rungwa, Tan. C6 58
Rungwa, stm., Tan. C6 58
Runnells, Ia., U.S. C4 122
Runnels, co., Tx., U.S. D3 150
Runnemede, N.J., U.S. D2 137
Ruo, stm., China C6 30
Ruoqiang, China D4 30
Ruoxi, China F4 34
Rupea, Rom. C9 20
Rupert, Id., U.S. G5 119
Rupert, W.V., U.S. D4 155
Rupert, Rivière de, stm., Que., Can. h11 104
Rupununi, dept., Guy. F13 84
Rupununi, stm., Guy. F13 84
Ruqqād, Wādī ar-, val., Asia C5 50
Rur (Roer), stm., Eur. F9 12
Rural Hall, N.C., U.S. A2 140
Rural Retreat, Va., U.S. D1 153
Rurrenabaque, Bol. F8 82
Rurstausee, res., Ger. G9 12
Rusagonis, N.B., Can. D3 101
Rušan, U.S.S.R. B4 44
Rusape, Zimb. B11 66
Ruşayriş, Khazzān ar-, res., Afr. L8 60
Ruse, Bul. F9 20
Rush, Ky., U.S. B7 124
Rush, co., In., U.S. E6 121
Rush, co., Ks., U.S. D4 123
Rush, stm., Mn., U.S. F4 130
Rush, stm., Wi., U.S. D1 156
Rush Center, Ks., U.S. D4 123
Rush City, Mn., U.S. E6 130
Rush Creek, stm., Co., U.S. C7 113
Rush Creek, stm., Ne., U.S. C3 134
Rush Creek, stm., Oh., U.S. B2 142
Rush Creek, stm., Ok., U.S. C4 143
Rushford, Mn., U.S. G7 130
Rush Lake, Sask., Can. G2 105
Rush Lake, l., Mn., U.S. E5 130
Rush Lake, l., Mn., U.S. D3 130
Rush Lake, l., Wi., U.S. E5 156
Rushmere, Va., U.S. h14 153
Rushmore, Mn., U.S. G3 130
Rush Springs, Ok., U.S. C4 143
Rushsylvania, Oh., U.S. B2 142
Rush Valley, Ut., U.S. C3 151
Rushville, Il., U.S. C3 120
Rushville, In., U.S. E7 121
Rushville, Mo., U.S. B2 132
Rushville, Ne., U.S. B3 134
Rusk, Tx., U.S. D5 150
Rusk, co., Tx., U.S. C5 150
Rusk, co., Wi., U.S. C2 156
Ruskin, Fl., U.S. E4 116
Ruskin, Ne., U.S. D8 134
Russas, Braz. D11 76
Russell, Man., Can. D1 100
Russell, Ont., Can. B9 103
Russell, Ar., U.S. B4 111
Russell, Ia., U.S. D4 122
Russell, Ks., U.S. D5 123
Russell, Ky., U.S. B7 124
Russell, Ma., U.S. B2 128
Russell, Mn., U.S. F3 130
Russell, Pa., U.S. C3 145
Russell, co., Al., U.S. C4 108
Russell, co., Ks., U.S. D5 123
Russell, co., Ky., U.S. D4 124
Russell, co., Va., U.S. f9 153
Russell, Cape, c., N.W. Ter., Can. A9 96
Russell, Mount, mtn., Ak., U.S. f16 109
Russell Cave National Monument, Al., U.S. A4 108
Russell Fork, stm., U.S. C7 124
Russell Island, i., N.W. Ter., Can. B13 96
Russell Lake, l., Alta., Can. A3 98
Russell Springs, Ky., U.S. C4 124
Russellville, Al., U.S. A2 108
Russellville, Ar., U.S. B2 111
Russellville, In., U.S. E4 121
Russellville, Ky., U.S. D3 124
Russellville, Mo., U.S. C5 132
Russellville, Tn., U.S. C10 149
Rüsselsheim, Ger. E8 10
Russian, stm., Ca., U.S. C2 112
Russian Soviet Federative Socialist Republic see Rossijskaja Sovetskaja Federativnaja Socialističeskaja Respublika, state, U.S.S.R. E14 22
Russiaville, In., U.S. D5 121
Russkij, ostrov, i., U.S.S.R. B17 22
Rust, Aus. H16 10
Rustavi, U.S.S.R. I7 22
Rustburg, Va., U.S. C3 153
Rustenburg, S. Afr. E8 66
Ruston, La., U.S. B3 125
Ruston, Wa., U.S. B3 154
Rute, Spain H7 16
Ruteng, Indon. G7 38
Rutenga, Zimb. C10 66
Ruth, Ms., U.S. D3 131
Ruth, Nv., U.S. D6 135
Ruth, W.V., U.S. m12 155
Rutherford, N.J., U.S. B4 137
Rutherford, Tn., U.S. A3 149
Rutherford, co., N.C., U.S. B1 140
Rutherford, co., Tn., U.S. B5 149
Rutherfordton, N.C., U.S. B1 140
Rutherglen, Ont., Can. A5 103
Rutheron, N.M., U.S. A3 138
Ruthton, Mn., U.S. F2 130
Ruthven, Ia., U.S. A3 122
Rüti, Switz. D10 13
Rutland, Il., U.S. C4 120
Rutland, Ma., U.S. B4 128
Rutland, N.D., U.S. C8 141
Rutland, S.D., U.S. C9 148
Rutland, Vt., U.S. D3 152
Rutland, co., Vt., U.S. D2 152
Rutledge, Al., U.S. D3 108
Rutledge, Ga., U.S. C3 117
Rutledge, Mn., U.S. D6 130
Rutledge, Tn., U.S. C10 149
Rutog, China D8 44
Rutshuru, Zaire B5 58
Ruvuma (Rovuma), stm., Afr. D7 58
Ruy Barbosa, Braz. B8 79
Ruza, U.S.S.R. F19 26
Ruzajevka, U.S.S.R. G6 22
Ružany, U.S.S.R. I7 26
Ružomberok, Czech. F19 10
Rwanda, ctry., Afr. B6 58
Ryan, Ia., U.S. B6 122
Ryan, Ok., U.S. C4 143
Ryan Creek, stm., Al., U.S. A3 108
Ryan Peak, mtn., Id., U.S. F4 119
Rybačij, poluostrov, pen., U.S.S.R. G23 6
Rybačje, U.S.S.R. I13 22
Rybačje, U.S.S.R. H8 24
Rybinsk, U.S.S.R. C21 26
Rybinskoje vodochranilišče, res., U.S.S.R. C21 26
Rybnica, U.S.S.R. B13 20
Rybnik, Pol. E18 10
Rybnoje, U.S.S.R. G22 26
Rycroft, Alta., Can. B1 98
Ryd, Swe. M14 6
Ryde, Eng., U.K. K12 8
Ryder, N.D., U.S. B4 141
Ryderwood, Wa., U.S. C2 154
Rye, Co., U.S. D6 113
Rye, N.H., U.S. D5 136
Rye, N.Y., U.S. h13 139
Rye Beach, N.H., U.S. E5 136
Ryegate, Mt., U.S. D7 133
Rye Patch Dam, Nv., U.S. C3 135
Rye Patch Reservoir, res., Nv., U.S. C3 135
Ryes, Fr. C6 14
Ryley, Alta., Can. C4 98
Rymanów, Pol. F21 10
Rypin, Pol. B19 10
Ryškany, U.S.S.R. B11 20
Rysy, mtn., Eur. F20 10
Ryukyu Islands see Nansei-shotō, is., Japan F12 30
Ryukyu Trench F16 158
Ržaksa, U.S.S.R. I25 26
Ržanica, U.S.S.R. H16 26
Rzeszów, Pol. E22 10
Ržev, U.S.S.R. E17 26

S

Saale, stm., Ger. D11 10
Saales, Fr. D14 14
Saalfeld, Ger. E11 10
Saar, stm., Eur. J10 12
Saarbrücken, Ger. F6 10
Saarburg, Ger. F6 10
Sääre, U.S.S.R. D5 26
Saaremaa, i., U.S.S.R. C5 26
Saarland, state, Ger. F6 10
Saarlouis, Ger. F6 10
Saar see Saarland, state, Ger. F6 10
Saas Grund, Switz. F8 13
Saatly, U.S.S.R. B10 48
Saavedra, Arg. I7 80
Saba, i., Neth. Ant. F13 94
Šabac, Yugo. E3 20
Sabadell, Spain D14 16
Sabae, Japan L11 36
Sabana, Archipiélago de, is., Cuba C4 94
Sabana de La Mar, Dom. Rep. E10 94
Sabana de Mendoza, Ven. C7 84
Sabanagrande, Hond. D7 92
Sabanalarga, Col. B5 84
Sabancuy, Mex. H14 90
Sabaneta, Dom. Rep. E9 94
Sabaneta, Ven. C8 84
Sabang, Indon. E6 38
Sabang, Indon. L3 40
Sabanillas, Mex. E9 90
Sabará, Braz. E7 79
Sabasṭīyah (Samaria), Isr. Occ. D4 50
Sabattus, Me., U.S. D2 126
Sabattus Pond, l., Me., U.S. D2 126
Sabaudia, Italy H8 18
Sabaya, Bol. H7 82
Şabāyā, Jabal, i., Sau. Ar. E2 47
Sabbathday Pond, l., Me., U.S. g7 126
Sāberī, Hāmūn-e, l., Asia F16 48
Sabetha, Ks., U.S. C8 123
Sabhā, Libya C3 56
Sabi (Save), stm., Afr. C11 66
Sābiē, stm., Afr. E11 66
Sabile, U.S.S.R. D5 26
Sabillasville, Md., U.S. A3 127
Sabin, Mn., U.S. D2 130
Sabina, Oh., U.S. C2 142
Sabinal, Tx., U.S. E3 150
Sabinal, Cayo, i., Cuba D6 94
Sabiñánigo, Spain C11 16
Sabinas, Mex. D9 90
Sabinas, stm., Mex. D9 90
Sabinas, stm., Mex. D10 90
Sabinas Hidalgo, Mex. D9 90
Sabine, W.V., U.S. D3 155
Sabine, co., La., U.S. C2 125
Sabine, co., Tx., U.S. D6 150
Sabine, stm., U.S. D6 150
Sabine, Mount, mtn., Ant. C8 73
Sabine Bay, b., N.W. Ter., Can. A11 96
Sabine Lake, l., U.S. E2 125
Sabine Pass, Tx., U.S. E6 150
Sabine Pass, strt., U.S. E2 125
Sabine Peninsula, pen., N.W. Ter., Can. A11 96
Sabinópolis, Braz. E7 79
Sabinosa, Spain P22 17b
Sabirabad, U.S.S.R. A10 48
Sable, Cape, c., Fl., U.S. G5 116
Sable, Île de, i., N. Cal. C11 68
Sable Island, i., N.S., Can. F10 101
Sable River, N.S., Can. F4 101
Sablé-sur-Sarthe, Fr. E6 14
Sabogal, stm., C.R. G10 92
Sabonkafi, Niger D14 64
Sabou, Burkina E8 64
Sabres, Fr. H6 14
Sabrina Coast, Ant. B7 73
Sabula, Ia., U.S. B7 122
Şabyā, Sau. Ar. F3 47
Sabzevār, Iran C14 48
Sac, co., Ia., U.S. B2 122
Sac, stm., Mo., U.S. D4 132
Sacaba, Bol. G8 82
Sacaca, Bol. H8 82
Sacajawea, Lake, res., Wa., U.S. C7 154
Sacajawea Peak, mtn., Or., U.S. B9 144
Sacanche, Peru B3 82
Sacandaga Lake, l., N.Y., U.S. B6 139
Sac and Fox Indian Reservation, Ia., U.S. C5 122
Sacaton, Az., U.S. D4 110
Sac City, Ia., U.S. B2 122
Săcele, Rom. D9 20
Sachalin, ostrov (Sakhalin), i., U.S.S.R. G20 24
Sachalinskij zaliv, b., U.S.S.R. G20 24
Sachayoj, Arg. D8 80
Šachbuz, U.S.S.R. B8 48
Sachem Head, Ct., U.S. E5 114
Sachigo Lake, l., Ont., Can. C5 100
Šachovskaja, U.S.S.R. E18 26
Šachrisabz, U.S.S.R. J11 22
Sachse, Tx., U.S. n10 150
Sachsen, state, Ger. D13 10
Sachsen-Anhalt, state, Ger. C11 10
Sachs Harbour, N.W. Ter., Can. B7 96
Šachty, U.S.S.R. H6 22
Sachuest Point, c., R.I., U.S. F6 146
Šachunja, U.S.S.R. F7 22
Šack, U.S.S.R. G24 26
Sackets Harbor, N.Y., U.S. B4 139
Sackville, N.B., Can. D5 101
Saco, Me., U.S. E2 126
Saco, Mt., U.S. B9 133
Saco, stm., U.S. E2 126
Saco, East Branch, stm., N.H., U.S. B4 136
Sacramento, Braz. E5 79
Sacramento, Ca., U.S. C3 112
Sacramento, Ky., U.S. C2 124
Sacramento, N.M., U.S. E4 138
Sacramento, co., Ca., U.S. C3 112
Sacramento, stm., Ca., U.S. C3 112
Sacramento, stm., N.M., U.S. E4 138
Sacramento, Pampa del, pl., Peru C4 82
Sacramento Mountains, mts., N.M., U.S. E4 138
Sacramento Valley, val., Az., U.S. B1 110
Sacramento Valley, val., Ca., U.S. C2 112
Sacre, stm., Braz. E12 82
Sacré-Coeur-Saguenay, Que., Can. A8 104
Sacred Heart, Mn., U.S. F3 130
Sacupana, Ven. C12 84
Sacuriuiná, stm., Braz. E13 82
Sada, Spain B3 16
Şa'dah, Yemen F3 47
Saddle (Burnt), stm., Alta., Can. B1 98
Saddle, stm., N.J., U.S. h8 137
Saddleback Mountain, mtn., Az., U.S. k8 110
Saddleback Mountain, mtn., Me., U.S. B4 126
Saddleback Mountain, mtn., Me., U.S. D2 126
Saddle Ball Mountain, mtn., Ma., U.S. A1 128
Saddle Brook, N.J., U.S. h8 137
Saddlebunch Keys, is., Fl., U.S. H5 116
Saddle Mountain, mtn., Or., U.S. B3 144
Saddle Mountains, mts., Wa., U.S. C5 154
Saddle River, N.J., U.S. A4 137
Sa Dec, Viet. I8 40
Sadêng, China E16 44
Sadieville, Ky., U.S. B5 124
Sadiola, Mali E4 64
Sadiya, India D14 42
Sado, i., Japan I13 36
Şadorus, Il., U.S. D5 120
Šadrinsk, U.S.S.R. F10 22
Sädvaluspen, Swe. H15 6
Saegertown, Pa., U.S. C1 145
Safad see Ẕefat, Isr. C5 50
Safājah, Jazīrat, i., Egypt H2 48
Safety Harbor, Fl., U.S. E4 116
Saffell, Ar., U.S. B4 111
Safford, Al., U.S. C2 108
Safford, Az., U.S. E6 110
Safi, Mor. D6 62
Safonovo, U.S.S.R. F4 22
Saga, China F4 30
Saga, Japan N5 36
Sagadahoc, co., Me., U.S. E3 126
Sagaing, Burma D3 40
Sagamihara, Japan L14 36
Sagami-nada, b., Japan L14 36
Sagamore, Ma., U.S. C6 128
Sagamore, Pa., U.S. E3 145
Sagamore Hills, Oh., U.S. h9 142
Saganaga Lake, l., Mn., U.S. B7 130
Saganthit Kyun, i., Burma I5 40
Šagany, ozero, l., U.S.S.R. D13 20
Sāgar, India I8 44
Sag Harbor, N.Y., U.S. m16 139
Saginaw, Al., U.S. B3 108
Saginaw, Mi., U.S. E7 129
Saginaw, Tx., U.S. n9 150
Saginaw, co., Mi., U.S. E6 129
Saginaw Bay, b., Mi., U.S. E7 129
Sagle, Id., U.S. A2 119
Sagleipie, Lib. H5 64
Saglek Bay, b., Newf., Can. f9 102
Šagonar, U.S.S.R. G16 22
Saguache, Co., U.S. C4 113
Saguache, co., Co., U.S. C4 113
Saguache Creek, stm., Co., U.S. C4 113
Sagua de Tánamo, Cuba D7 94
Sagua la Grande, Cuba C4 94
Saguaro Lake, res., Az., U.S. k10 110
Saguaro National Monument (Tucson Mountain Section), Az., U.S. E4 110
Saguaro National Monument, Az., U.S. E5 110
Saguenay, stm., Que., Can. A7 104
Sagunt, Spain F11 16
Sa'gya, China F13 44
Sahāb, Jord. E6 50
Sahaba, Sud. H6 60
Sahagún, Col. C5 84
Sahara, des., Afr. F7 52
Sahāranpur, India F7 44
Sahaswān, India F8 44
Sahel see Sudan, reg., Afr. F11 54
Sāhibganj, India H12 44
Şahin, Tur. H10 20
Sāhīwal, Pak. E5 44
Sahuaripa, Mex. C5 90
Sahuarita, Az., U.S. F5 110
Sahuayo de José María Morelos, Mex. G8 90
Sai Buri, Thai. K6 40
Saïda, Alg. C11 62
Saïdia, Mor. C9 62
Saidpur, Bngl. H13 44
Saidu, Pak. C5 44
Saignelégier, Switz. D7 13
Saigon see Thanh Pho Ho Chi Minh, Viet. I9 40
Saijō, Japan N8 36
Saiki, Japan O6 36
Saimaa, l., Fin. K20 6
Saín Alto, Mex. F8 90
Saint Adolphe, Man., Can. E3 100
Saint-Affrique, Fr. I9 14
Saint Agatha, Me., U.S. A4 126
Sainte Agathe, Man., Can. E3 100
Sainte-Agathe, Que., Can. C6 104
Sainte-Agathe-des-Monts, Que., Can. C3 104
Saint-Aimé (Massueville), Que., Can. D5 104
Saint-Alban, Que., Can. C5 104
Saint Alban's, Newf., Can. E4 102
Saint Albans, Eng., U.K. J13 8
Saint Albans, Me., U.S. D3 126
Saint Albans, Vt., U.S. B2 152
Saint Albans, W.V., U.S. C3 155
Saint Albans Bay, b., Vt., U.S. B2 152
Saint Albert, Alta., Can. C4 98
Saint-Alexandre, Que., Can. D4 104
Saint-Amand-Montrond, Fr. F9 14
Saint Amant, La., U.S. h10 125
Saint-Ambroise, Que., Can. A6 104
Saint-Amour, Fr. F12 14
Saint-Anaclet, Que., Can. A9 104
Saint-André, Reu. V17 67c
Saint-André, Cap, c., Madag. P21 67b
Saint-André-Avellin, Que., Can. D2 104
Saint-André-Est, Que., Can. D3 104
Saint Andrew Bay, b., Fl., U.S. u16 116
Saint Andrews, N.B., Can. D2 101
Saint Andrew's, Newf., Can. E2 102
Saint Andrews, Scot., U.K. E11 8
Saint Andrews, S.C., U.S. C5 147
Saint Andrews, S.C., U.S. F7 147
Saint Andrews, Tn., U.S. D8 149
Saint Andrew Sound, strt., Ga., U.S. F5 117
Saint Anne, Il., U.S. B6 120
Sainte-Anne, stm., Que., Can. B6 104
Sainte-Anne, Lac, l., Alta., Can. C3 98
Sainte-Anne-de-Beaupré, Que., Can. B7 104
Sainte-Anne [-de-Bellevue], Que., Can. q19 104
Sainte Anne-de-Madawaska, N.B., Can. B1 101
Sainte-Anne-des-Chênes, Man., Can. E3 100
Sainte-Anne-du-Lac, Que., Can. k11 104
Sainte-Anne du Nord, stm., Que., Can. B7 104
Saint Anne's, Eng., U.K. H10 8
Saint Anns, N.S., Can. C9 101
Saint Ann's Bay, Jam. E6 94
Saint-Anselme, Que., Can. C7 104
Saint Ansgar, Ia., U.S. A5 122
Saint Anthony, Newf., Can. C4 102
Saint Anthony, Id., U.S. F7 119
Saint Anthony, In., U.S. H4 121
Saint Anthony, N.D., U.S. C5 141
Saint Antoine, N.B., Can. C5 101
Saint-Antoine [-sur-Richelieu], Que., Can. D4 104
Saint-Apollinaire, Que., Can. C6 104
Saint Arnaud, Austl. K5 70
Saint-Arsène, Que., Can. B8 104
Saint Arthur, N.B., Can. B3 101
Saint-Athanase, Que., Can. B8 104
Saint-Aubert, Que., Can. B7 104
Saint Augustin, stm., Can. C2 102
Saint Augustine, Fl., U.S. C5 116
Saint-Augustin-Nord-Ouest, stm., Que., Can. C2 102
Saint-Avold, Fr. C13 14
Saint-Barthélemy, i., Guad. F13 94
Saint Basile, N.B., Can. B1 101
Saint-Basile [-Sud], Que., Can. C6 104
Saint-Béat, Fr. J7 14
Saint Benedict, Sask., Can. E3 105
Saint-Benoît-Labre, Que., Can. C7 104
Saint-Bernard, Que., Can. C6 104
Saint Bernard, Al., U.S. A3 108
Saint Bernard, La., U.S. E6 125
Saint Bernard, Oh., U.S. o13 142
Saint Bernard, co., La., U.S. E6 125

Name	Map Ref.	Page
Saint Bernice, In., U.S.	E2	121
Saint Bethlehem, Tn., U.S.	A4	149
Saint-Blaise, Switz.	D6	13
Saint-Bonaventure, Que., Can.	D5	104
Saint-Bonnet, Fr.	H13	14
Saint-Bonnet-de-Joux, Fr.	F11	14
Saint Brendan's, Newf., Can.	D5	102
Saint Bride, Mount, mtn., Alta., Can.	D3	98
Saint Bride's, Newf., Can.	E4	102
Saint-Brieuc, Fr.	D4	14
Saint Brieux, Sask., Can.	E3	105
Saint-Bruno, Que., Can.	A6	104
Saint-Calais, Fr.	E7	14
Saint-Camille [-de-Bellechasse], Que., Can.	C7	104
Saint-Casimir, Que., Can.	C5	104
Saint Catharine, Ky., U.S.	C4	124
Saint Catharines, Ont., Can.	D5	103
Saint Catherine, Lake, l., Vt., U.S.	E2	152
Saint Catherines Island, i., Ga., U.S.	E5	117
Saint Catherines Sound, strt., Ga., U.S.	E5	117
Saint-Célestin (Annaville), Que., Can.	C5	104
Saint-Cergue, Switz.	F5	13
Saint-Césaire, Que., Can.	D4	104
Saint-Chamond, Fr.	G11	14
Saint-Charles, Que., Can.	C7	104
Saint Charles, Ar., U.S.	C4	111
Saint Charles, Id., U.S.	G7	119
Saint Charles, Il., U.S.	B5	120
Saint Charles, Ia., U.S.	C4	122
Saint Charles, Ky., U.S.	C2	124
Saint Charles, Md., U.S.	C4	127
Saint Charles, Mi., U.S.	E6	129
Saint Charles, Mn., U.S.	G6	130
Saint Charles, Mo., U.S.	C7	132
Saint Charles, Va., U.S.	f8	153
Saint Charles, co., La., U.S.	E5	125
Saint Charles, co., Mo., U.S.	C7	132
Saint Christopher (Saint Kitts), i., St. K./N.	F13	94
Saint Christopher-Nevis see Saint Kitts and Nevis, ctry., N.A.	F13	94
Saint-Chrysostome, Que., Can.	D4	104
Saint Clair, Mi., U.S.	F8	129
Saint Clair, Mn., U.S.	F5	130
Saint Clair, Mo., U.S.	C6	132
Saint Clair, Pa., U.S.	E9	145
Saint Clair, co., Al., U.S.	B3	108
Saint Clair, co., Il., U.S.	E3	120
Saint Clair, co., Mi., U.S.	F8	129
Saint Clair, co., Mo., U.S.	C4	132
Saint Clair Shores, Mi., U.S.	p16	129
Saint Clairsville, Oh., U.S.	B5	142
Saint Claude, Man., Can.	E2	100
Saint-Claude, Fr.	F12	14
Saint Clements Creek, stm., Md., U.S.	D4	127
Sainte-Clothilde, Que., Can.	D5	104
Saint Cloud, Fl., U.S.	D5	116
Saint Cloud, Mn., U.S.	E4	130
Saint Cloud, Wi., U.S.	E5	156
Saint-Coeur-de-Marie, Que., Can.	A6	104
Saint-Constant, Que., Can.	q19	104
Saint Croix, N.B., Can.	D2	101
Sainte-Croix, Que., Can.	C6	104
Sainte-Croix, Switz.	E6	13
Saint Croix, co., Wi., U.S.	C1	156
Saint Croix, i., V.I.U.S.	F12	94
Saint Croix, stm., U.S.	C1	156
Saint Croix, Lake, l., U.S.	D1	156
Saint Croix Falls, Wi., U.S.	C1	156
Saint Croix Stream, stm., Me., U.S.	B4	126
Saint-Damase, Que., Can.	D4	104
Saint-Damase-des-Aulnaies, Que., Can.	B7	104
Saint David, Az., U.S.	F5	110
Saint David, Il., U.S.	C3	120
Saint-David-de-l'Auberivière, Que., Can.	n17	104
Saint David's, Newf., Can.	D2	102
Saint David's Head, c., Wales, U.K.	J8	8
Saint-Denis, Que., Can.	D4	104
Saint-Denis, Fr.	D9	14
Saint-Denis, Reu.	V17	67c
Saint-Denis [-de-la-Bouteillerie], Que., Can.	B8	104
Saint-Dié, Fr.	D13	14
Saint-Dizier, Fr.	D11	14
Saint-Dominique, Que., Can.	D5	104
Saint Edward, Ne., U.S.	C8	134
Saint Eleanor's, P.E.I., Can.	C6	101
Saint Elias, Cape, c., Ak., U.S.	D11	109
Saint Elias, Mount, mtn., N.A.	D4	96
Saint-Élie, Fr. Gu.	C8	76
Saint Elizabeth, Mo., U.S.	C5	132
Saint Elmo, Al., U.S.	E1	108
Saint Elmo, Il., U.S.	D5	120
Saint-Éloi, Que., Can.	A8	104
Saint-Émile [-de-Suffolk], Que., Can.	D3	104
Saint-Éphrem [-de-Tring], Que., Can.	C7	104
Saint-Étienne, Fr.	G11	14
Saint-Eusèbe, Que., Can.	B9	104
Saint-Eustache, Que., Can.	D4	104
Saint-Félicien, Que., Can.	A5	104
Saint-Félix-de-Valois, Que., Can.	C4	104
Saint-Ferdinand (Bernierville), Que., Can.	C6	104
Saint-Ferréol [-les-Neiges], Que., Can.	B7	104
Saint Fintan's, Newf., Can.	D2	102
Saint-Flavien, Que., Can.	C6	104
Saint-Florent, Fr.	L24	15a
Saint Florian, Al., U.S.	A2	108
Saint-Flour, Fr.	G10	14
Sainte-Foy, Que., Can.	n17	104
Sainte-Foy-la-Grande, Fr.	H7	14
Saint Francis, Ks., U.S.	C2	123
Saint Francis, Me., U.S.	A4	126
Saint Francis, Mn., U.S.	E5	130
Saint Francis, S.D., U.S.	D5	148
Saint Francis, Wi., U.S.	n12	156
Saint Francis, co., Ar., U.S.	B5	111
Saint Francis, stm., U.S.	A5	111
Saint Francis, Cape, c., Newf., Can.	E5	102
Saint Francisville, Il., U.S.	E6	120
Saint Francisville, La., U.S.	D4	125
Saint Francois, co., Mo., U.S.	D7	132
Saint-François, stm., Que., Can.	D5	104
Saint-François, Lac, l., Que., Can.	D6	104
Saint Francois Mountains, hills, Mo., U.S.	D7	132
Saint-Frédéric, Que., Can.	C7	104
Saint Froid Lake, l., Me., U.S.	B4	126
Saint-Fulgence, Que., Can.	A7	104
Saint-Gabriel, Que., Can.	C4	104
Saint Gabriel, La., U.S.	h9	125
Saint-Gaudens, Fr.	I7	14
Saint-Gédéon, Que., Can.	D7	104
Sainte Genevieve, Mo., U.S.	D7	132
Sainte Genevieve, co., Mo., U.S.	D7	132
Saint George, Austl.	G8	70
Saint George, N.B., Can.	D3	101
Saint George, Ont., Can.	D4	103
Saint George, Ga., U.S.	F4	117
Saint George, Ks., U.S.	C7	123
Saint George, Me., U.S.	D3	126
Saint George, S.C., U.S.	E6	147
Saint George, Ut., U.S.	F2	151
Saint George, Cape, c., Newf., Can.	D2	102
Saint George, Cape, c., Fl., U.S.	C1	116
Saint George Island, i., Ak., U.S.	D6	109
Saint George Island, i., Fl., U.S.	C2	116
Saint George's, Newf., Can.	D2	102
Saint-Georges, Que., Can.	C5	104
Saint-Georges, Fr. Gu.	C8	76
Saint George's, Gren.	H14	94
Saint Georges, De., U.S.	B3	115
Saint George's Bay, b., Newf., Can.	D2	102
Saint Georges Bay, b., N.S., Can.	D8	101
Saint George's Channel, strt., Eur.	J7	8
Saint-Georges [-de-Windsor], Que., Can.	D6	104
Saint Georges Head, c., Austl.	J9	70
Saint-Georges-Ouest, Que., Can.	C7	104
Saint-Gérard, Que., Can.	D6	104
Saint-Germain, Fr.	D9	14
Saint Germain, Wi., U.S.	C4	156
Saint-Germain-du-Bois, Fr.	F12	14
Saint-Gervais, Que., Can.	C7	104
Saint-Gervais-les-Bains, Fr.	G13	14
Saint-Géry, Fr.	H8	14
Saint-Gilles (Sint-Gillis), Bel.	G5	12
Saint-Gilles, Que., Can.	C6	104
Saint-Gingolph, Switz.	F6	13
Saint-Girons, Fr.	J8	14
Saint-Grégoire (Larochelle), Que., Can.	C5	104
Saint Gregor, Sask., Can.	E3	105
Saint Gregory, Mount, mtn., Newf., Can.	D2	102
Saint-Guénolé, Fr.	E2	14
Saint-Guillaume-d'Upton, Que., Can.	D5	104
Saint Hedwig, Tx., U.S.	k7	150
Saint Helen, Lake, l., Mi., U.S.	D6	129
Saint Helena, Ca., U.S.	C2	112
Saint Helena, co., La., U.S.	D5	125
Saint Helena, dep., Afr.	J6	52
Saint Helena Island, i., S.C., U.S.	G6	147
Saint Helena Sound, strt., S.C., U.S.	G7	147
Sainte-Hélène [-de-Kamouraska], Que., Can.	B8	104
Saint Helens, Austl.	M8	70
Saint Helens, Or., U.S.	B4	144
Saint Helens, Mount, vol., Wa., U.S.	C3	154
Saint Helier, Jersey	L11	8
Sainte-Hénédine, Que., Can.	C7	104
Saint Henry, Oh., U.S.	B1	142
Saint Hilaire, Mn., U.S.	B2	130
Saint-Hilaire-du-Harcouët, Fr.	D5	14
Saint-Hilarion, Que., Can.	B7	104
Saint-Hippolyte, Fr.	E13	14
Saint-Hippolyte-du-Fort, Fr.	I10	14
Saint-Honoré, Que., Can.	D7	104
Saint-Honoré-de-Témiscouata, Que., Can.	B8	104
Saint-Hubert, Que., Can.	q20	104
Saint-Hubert-de-Témiscouata, Que., Can.	B8	104
Saint-Hyacinthe, Que., Can.	D5	104
Saint Ignace, N.B., Can.	C4	101
Saint Ignace, Mi., U.S.	C6	129
Saint Ignatius, Guy.	F13	84
Saint Ignatius, Mt., U.S.	C2	133
Saint-Imier, Switz.	D7	13
Saint Inigoes, Md., U.S.	D5	127
Saint Isidore, N.B., Can.	B4	101
Saint Isidore de Prescott, Ont., Can.	B10	103
Saint Jacob, Il., U.S.	E4	120
Saint Jacobs, Ont., Can.	D4	103
Saint Jacques, N.B., Can.	B1	101
Saint-Jacques, Que., Can.	D4	104
Saint James, La., U.S.	k10	125
Saint James, Mi., U.S.	C5	129
Saint James, Mn., U.S.	G4	130
Saint James, Mo., U.S.	D6	132
Saint James, co., La., U.S.	D5	125
Saint James, Cape, c., B.C., Can.	D2	99
Saint James City, Fl., U.S.	F4	116
Saint-Jean, stm., Que., Can.	A7	104
Saint-Jean, Lac, l., Que., Can.	A5	104
Saint Jean Baptiste, Man., Can.	E3	100
Saint-Jean-Chrysostome, Que., Can.	o17	104
Saint-Jean-d'Angély, Fr.	G6	14
Saint-Jean-de-Losne, Fr.	E12	14
Saint-Jean-de-Luz, Fr.	I5	14
Saint-Jean-Pied-de-Port, Fr.	I5	14
Saint-Jean-sur-Richelieu, Que., Can.	D4	104
Saint-Jérôme, Que., Can.	D3	104
Saint Jo, Tx., U.S.	C4	150
Saint-Joachim, Que., Can.	B7	104
Saint Joe, Ar., U.S.	A3	111
Saint Joe, In., U.S.	B8	121
Saint Joe, stm., Id., U.S.	B3	119
Saint John, N.B., Can.	D3	101
Saint John, In., U.S.	B3	121
Saint John, Ks., U.S.	E5	123
Saint John, N.D., U.S.	A6	141
Saint John, Wa., U.S.	B8	154
Saint John, i., V.I.U.S.	E12	94
Saint John, Cape, c., Newf., Can.	D4	102
Saint John Bay, b., Newf., Can.	C3	102
Saint John's, Antig.	F14	94
Saint John's, Newf., Can.	E5	102
Saint Johns, Az., U.S.	C6	110
Saint Johns, Il., U.S.	E4	120
Saint Johns, Mi., U.S.	F6	129
Saint Johns, co., Fl., U.S.	C5	116
Saint Johns, stm., Fl., U.S.	B5	116
Saint Johnsbury, Vt., U.S.	C4	152
Saint Johnsbury Center, Vt., U.S.	C4	152
Saint Johnsville, N.Y., U.S.	B6	139
Saint John the Baptist, co., La., U.S.	D5	125
Saint Jones, stm., De., U.S.	D4	115
Saint Joseph, N.B., Can.	D5	101
Saint Joseph, Il., U.S.	C5	120
Saint Joseph, La., U.S.	C4	125
Saint Joseph, Mi., U.S.	F4	129
Saint Joseph, Mn., U.S.	E4	130
Saint Joseph, Mo., U.S.	B3	132
Saint Joseph, Tn., U.S.	B4	149
Saint Joseph, co., In., U.S.	A5	121
Saint Joseph, co., Mi., U.S.	G5	129
Saint Joseph, stm., U.S.	F5	129
Saint-Joseph, Lac, l., Que., Can.	n16	104
Saint Joseph, Lake, l., Ont., Can.	o17	103
Saint Joseph Bay, b., Fl., U.S.	C1	116
Saint-Joseph-de-Beauce, Que., Can.	C7	104
Saint-Joseph-de-la-Rive, Que., Can.	B7	104
Saint Joseph Point, c., Fl., U.S.	v16	116
Saint Joseph's, Newf., Can.	E5	102
Saint Joseph Sound, strt., Fl., U.S.	o10	116
Saint-Jovite, Que., Can.	C3	104
Saint-Julien-en-Born, Fr.	H5	14
Saint-Julien-en-Genevois, Fr.	F13	14
Sainte-Julie-Station, Que., Can.	C6	104
Saint-Junien, Fr.	G7	14
Saint-Just-en-Chaussée, Fr.	C9	14
Sainte-Justine [-de-Newton], Que., Can.	C5	104
Saint Kilda, i., Scot., U.K.	D5	8
Saint Kitts and Nevis, ctry., N.A.	F13	94
Saint Kitts see Saint Christopher, i., St. K./N.	F13	94
Saint-Lambert, Que., Can.	p19	104
Saint Landry, La., U.S.	D3	125
Saint Landry, co., La., U.S.	D3	125
Saint Laurent, Man., Can.	D3	100
Saint-Laurent, Que., Can.	p19	104
Saint-Laurent-du-Maroni, Fr. Gu.	B8	76
Saint Lawrence, Austl.	D8	70
Saint Lawrence, Newf., Can.	E4	102
Saint Lawrence, S.D., U.S.	C7	148
Saint Lawrence, co., N.Y., U.S.	A5	139
Saint Lawrence, stm., N.A.	G19	96
Saint Lawrence, Cape, c., N.S., Can.	B9	101
Saint Lawrence, Gulf of, b., Can.	G20	96
Saint Lawrence Island, i., Ak., U.S.	C5	109
Saint Lawrence Islands National Park, Ont., Can.	C9	103
Saint Lazare, Man., Can.	D1	100
Saint-Lazare, Que., Can.	q18	104
Saint Leo, Fl., U.S.	D4	116
Saint Leon, In., U.S.	F8	121
Saint Léonard, N.B., Can.	B2	101
Saint-Léonard [-d'Aston], Que., Can.	C5	104
Saint Lewis, stm., Newf., Can.	B3	102
Saint-Liboire, Que., Can.	D5	104
Saint Libory, Ne., U.S.	C7	134
Saint-Lô, Fr.	C5	14
Saint Louis, P.E.I., Can.	C5	101
Saint Louis, Sask., Can.	E3	105
Saint-Louis, Reu.	V17	67c
Saint-Louis, Sen.	C1	64
Saint Louis, Mi., U.S.	E6	129
Saint Louis, Mo., U.S.	C7	132
Saint Louis, co., Mn., U.S.	C6	130
Saint Louis, co., Mo., U.S.	C7	132
Saint Louis, stm., U.S.	D6	130
Saint-Louis, Lac, l., Que., Can.	q19	104
Saint Louis Bay, b., Ms., U.S.	f7	131
Saint-Louis-de-Gonzague, Que., Can.	D3	104
Saint-Louis-de-Kent, N.B., Can.	C5	101
Saint-Louis-du-Ha! Ha!, Que., Can.	B8	104
Sainte-Louise, Que., Can.	B7	104
Saint Louis Park, Mn., U.S.	n12	130
Saint-Loup-sur-Semouse, Fr.	E13	14
Saint-Luc, Que., Can.	D4	104
Saint Lucia, ctry., N.A.	H14	94
Saint Lucia Channel, strt., N.A.	G14	94
Sainte-Lucie, Fr.	M24	15a
Saint Lucie, Fl., U.S.	E6	116
Saint Lucie, co., Fl., U.S.	E6	116
Saint Lucie Canal, Fl., U.S.	F6	116
Sainte-Lucie-de-Beauregard, Que., Can.	C7	104
Saint Lucie Inlet, b., Fl., U.S.	E6	116
Saint-Ludger, Que., Can.	D7	104
Sainte-Madeleine, Que., Can.	D4	104
Saint-Magloire, Que., Can.	C7	104
Saint-Malachie, Que., Can.	C7	104
Saint Malo, Man., Can.	E3	100
Saint-Malo, Fr.	D4	14
Saint-Malo, Golfe de, b., Fr.	D4	14
Saint-Marc, Haiti	E8	94
Saint-Marc, Canal de, strt., Haiti	E8	94
Saint-Marc [-des-Carrières], Que., Can.	C5	104
Saint Margaret Bay, b., Newf., Can.	C3	102
Sainte-Marguerite, stm., Que., Can.	A7	104
Sainte-Marguerite-de-Dorchester, Que., Can.	C7	104
Sainte-Marie, Que., Can.	C6	104
Sainte Marie, Il., U.S.	E5	120
Sainte-Marie, Cap, c., Madag.	T21	67b
Sainte-Marie-aux-Mines, Fr.	D14	14
Saint Maries, Id., U.S.	B2	119
Sainte Marie-sur-Mer, N.B., Can.	B5	101
Saint Mark, Ks., U.S.	g11	123
Sainte-Marthe, Que., Can.	D3	104
Saint Martin, co., La., U.S.	D4	125
Saint-Martin (Sint Maarten), i., N.A.	E13	94
Saint Martin, Lake, l., Man., Can.	D2	100
Saint Martin Island, i., Mi., U.S.	C4	129
Saint Martins, N.B., Can.	D4	101
Saint Martin Station, Man., Can.	D2	100
Saint Martinville, La., U.S.	D4	125
Saint Mary, Ky., U.S.	C4	124
Saint Mary, Mo., U.S.	D8	132
Saint Mary, co., La., U.S.	E4	125
Saint Mary-of-the-Woods, In., U.S.	E3	121
Saint Mary Peak, mtn., Austl.	H3	70
Saint Mary Reservoir, res., Alta., Can.	E4	98
Saint Marys, Austl.	M8	70
Saint Mary's, Newf., Can.	E5	102
Saint Mary's, Ont., Can.	D3	103
Saint Marys, Ak., U.S.	C7	109
Saint Marys, Ga., U.S.	F5	117
Saint Marys, In., U.S.	A5	121
Saint Marys, Ks., U.S.	C7	123
Saint Marys, Oh., U.S.	B1	142
Saint Marys, Pa., U.S.	D4	145
Saint Marys, W.V., U.S.	B3	155
Saint Marys, co., Md., U.S.	D4	127
Saint Marys, stm., N.S., Can.	D8	101
Saint Marys, stm., U.S.	F5	117
Saint Marys, stm., U.S.	C8	121
Saint Marys, stm., Md., U.S.	D5	127
Saint Mary's, Cape, c., Newf., Can.	E4	102
Saint Mary's Bay, b., Newf., Can.	E5	102
Saint Marys Bay, b., N.S., Can.	E3	101
Saint Marys City, Md., U.S.	D5	127
Saint Marys Entrance, strt., Ga., U.S.	F5	117
Saint-Mathieu, Fr.	G7	14
Saint Matthew Island, i., Ak., U.S.	C5	109
Saint Matthews, Ky., U.S.	B4	124
Saint Matthews, S.C., U.S.	D6	147
Saint-Maur [-des-Fossés], Fr.	D9	14
Saint-Maurice, Que., Can.	C5	104
Saint-Maurice, stm., Que., Can.	C5	104
Sainte-Maxime, Fr.	I13	14
Saint-Méen-le-Grand, Fr.	D4	14
Saint Meinrad, In., U.S.	H4	121
Sainte-Menehould, Fr.	C11	14
Sainte-Mère-Église, Fr.	C5	14
Saint-Méthode [-de-Frontenac], Que., Can.	C6	104
Saint Michael, Alta., Can.	C4	98
Saint Michael, Ak., U.S.	C7	109
Saint Michael, Mn., U.S.	E5	130
Saint Michaels, Az., U.S.	B6	110
Saint Michaels, Md., U.S.	C5	127
Saint-Michel [-de-Bellechasse], Que., Can.	C7	104
Saint-Mihiel, Fr.	D12	14
Sainte-Monique [-de-Nicolet], Que., Can.	C5	104
Saint-Moritz see Sankt Moritz, Switz.	F16	14
Saint-Nazaire, Fr.	E4	14
Saint-Nazaire [-de-Buckland], Que., Can.	C7	104
Saint Nazianz, Wi., U.S.	D6	156
Saint-Nicolas, Que., Can.	o17	104
Saint-Nicolas see Sint-Niklaas, Bel.	F5	12
Saint-Odilon, Que., Can.	C7	104
Saint-Omer, Fr.	B9	14
Saint Onge, S.D., U.S.	C2	148
Saintonge, hist. reg., Fr.	G6	14
Saint-Ours, Que., Can.	D4	104
Saint-Pacôme, Que., Can.	B8	104
Saint-Pamphile, Que., Can.	C8	104
Saint Paris, Oh., U.S.	B2	142
Saint-Pascal, Que., Can.	B8	104
Saint Paul, Alta., Can.	B5	98
Saint-Paul, Fr.	I14	14
Saint-Paul, Reu.	V17	67c
Saint Paul, Ak., U.S.	D5	109
Saint Paul, In., U.S.	F6	121
Saint Paul, Ks., U.S.	E8	123
Saint Paul, Mn., U.S.	F5	130
Saint Paul, Mo., U.S.	f12	132
Saint Paul, Ne., U.S.	C7	134
Saint Paul, Or., U.S.	h12	144
Saint Paul, Va., U.S.	f9	153
Saint Paul, stm., Lib.	H4	64
Saint-Paul, Île, i., F.S.A.T.	L11	158
Saint-Paulin, Que., Can.	C4	104
Saint Paul Island, i., Ak., U.S.	D5	109
Saint Paul Park, Mn., U.S.	n12	130
Saint Pauls, N.C., U.S.	C4	140
Sainte-Perpétue-de-L'Islet, Que., Can.	B8	104
Saint Peter, Il., U.S.	E5	120
Saint Peter, Mn., U.S.	F5	130
Saint Peter Island, i., Austl.	F6	68
Saint Peter Port, Guernsey	C4	14
Saint Peters, N.S., Can.	D9	101
Saint Peters, Mo., U.S.	C7	132
Saint Petersburg, Fl., U.S.	E4	116
Saint Petersburg Beach, Fl., U.S.	p10	116
Saint Petersburg see Leningrad, U.S.S.R.	B13	26
Saint-Philémon, Que., Can.	C7	104
Saint Philip, In., U.S.	I2	121
Saint Phillips Island, i., S.C., U.S.	G6	147
Saint-Pie, Que., Can.	D5	104
Saint-Pierre, Mart.	G14	94
Saint-Pierre, Reu.	V17	67c
Saint-Pierre, St. P./M.	E3	102
Saint-Pierre, Lac, l., Que., Can.	C5	104
Saint Pierre and Miquelon, dep., N.A.	E3	102
Saint-Pierre-Église, Fr.	C5	14
Saint Pierre Island, i., Sey.	C10	58
Saint Pierre-Jolys, Man., Can.	E3	100
Saint-Pierre-Montmagny, Que., Can.	C7	104
Saint-Placide, Que., Can.	p18	104
Saint-Pol-de-Léon, Fr.	D3	14
Saint-Pol-sur-Ternoise, Fr.	B9	14
Saint-Pons, Fr.	I9	14
Saint-Prime, Que., Can.	A5	104
Saint Quentin, N.B., Can.	B2	101
Saint-Quentin, Fr.	C10	14
Saint-Raphaël, Que., Can.	C7	104
Saint-Raphaël, Fr.	I13	14
Saint Raphaël-sur-Mer, N.B., Can.	B5	101
Saint-Raymond, Que., Can.	C6	104
Saint-Rédempteur, Que., Can.	o17	104
Saint Regis, Mt., U.S.	C1	133
Saint Regis, West Branch, stm., N.Y., U.S.	f10	139
Saint Regis Falls, N.Y., U.S.	f10	139
Saint-Rémi, Que., Can.	D4	104
Saint-Rémy-de-Provence, Fr.	I11	14
Saint-Romuald, Que., Can.	C6	104
Saint Rose, La., U.S.	k11	125
Sainte Rose du Lac, Man., Can.	D2	100
Saintes, Fr.	G6	14
Sainte-Sabine-de-Bellechasse, Que., Can.	C7	104
Saint Samuel, Que., Can.	D7	104
Saint Sauveur, N.B., Can.	B4	101
Saint-Sauveur-des-Monts, Que., Can.	D3	104
Saint-Seine-l'Abbaye, Fr.	E11	14
Saint-Séverin-de-Beauce, Que., Can.	C6	104
Saint Shotts, Newf., Can.	E5	102
Saint-Siméon, Que., Can.	B8	104
Saint Simons Island, Ga., U.S.	E5	117
Saint Simons Island, i., Ga., U.S.	E5	117
Saint Simons Sound, strt., Ga., U.S.	E5	117
Saintes-Maries-de-la-Mer, Fr.	I11	14
Sainte-Sophie [-de-Lévrard], Que., Can.	C5	104
Sainte-Sophie [-de-Mégantic], Que., Can.	C6	104
Saint Stephen, N.B., Can.	D2	101
Saint Stephen, S.C., U.S.	E8	147
Saint Stephens, Al., U.S.	D1	108
Saint-Sylvestre, Que., Can.	C6	104
Saint Tammany, co., La., U.S.	D5	125
Sainte-Thècle, Que., Can.	C5	104
Saint-Théophile, Que., Can.	D7	104
Sainte-Thérèse, Que., Can.	D4	104
Saint Thomas, Ont., Can.	E3	103
Saint Thomas, Mo., U.S.	C5	132
Saint Thomas, N.D., U.S.	A8	141
Saint Thomas, Pa., U.S.	G6	145
Saint Thomas, i., V.I.U.S.	E12	94
Saint Timothée, Que., Can.	q18	104
Saint-Tite, Que., Can.	C5	104
Saint-Trond see Sint-Truiden, Bel.	G7	12
Saint-Tropez, Fr.	I13	14
Saint-Valéry-en-Caux, Fr.	C7	14
Saint-Valéry-sur-Somme, Fr.	B8	14
Saint-Vallier, Que., Can.	C7	104
Saint-Vallier-de-Thiey, Fr.	I13	14
Sainte-Véronique, Que., Can.	C3	104
Saint-Victor, Que., Can.	C7	104
Saint Vincent, i., St. Vin.	H14	94
Saint Vincent, Cape see São Vicente, Cabo de, c., Port.	H2	16
Saint Vincent, Gulf, b., Austl.	J3	70
Saint Vincent and the Grenadines, ctry., N.A.	H14	94
Saint-Vincent-de-Tyrosse, Fr.	I5	14
Saint Vincent Island, i., Fl., U.S.	C1	116
Saint Vincent Passage, strt., N.A.	H14	94
Saint Vincent's [-Saint Stephens-Peter's River], Newf., Can.	E5	102
Saint-Vith (Sankt Vith), Bel.	H9	12
Saint Walburg, Sask., Can.	D1	105
Saint Wendells, In., U.S.	H2	121
Saint Williams, Ont., Can.	E4	103
Saint Xavier, Mt., U.S.	E9	133
Saint-Zacharie, Que., Can.	C7	104
Sairecábur, Cerro, mtn., S.A.	J8	82
Saitula, China	D2	30
Sai Yok, Thai.	G5	40
Sajama, Bol.	H7	82
Sajama, Nevado, mtn., Bol.	H7	82
Sajano-Sušenskoje vodochranilišče, res., U.S.S.R.	G16	22
Sajat, U.S.S.R.	B17	48
Šajmak', U.S.S.R.	B6	44
Sajnšand, Mong.	C9	30
Sajó, stm., Eur.	G20	10
Sajószentpéter, Hung.	G20	10
Sa Kaeo, Thai.	H7	40
Sakai, Japan	M10	36
Sakaiminato, Japan	L8	36
Sakākah, Sau. Ar.	G6	48
Sakakawea, Lake, res., N.D., U.S.	B3	141
Sakania, Zaire	D5	58
Sakaraha, Madag.	S21	67b
Sakarya, stm., Tur.	G14	4
Sakata, Japan	I14	36
Sakchu, N. Kor.	C13	32
Sakété, Benin	H11	64
Sakhalin see Sachalin, ostrov, i., U.S.S.R.	G20	24
Şakhrīyāt, Jabal aş-, mtn., Jord.	F6	50
Sakht Sar, Iran	C11	48
Šakiai, U.S.S.R.	G6	26
Sakiet Sidi Youssef, Tun.	M3	18
Sakon Nakhon, Thai.	F8	40
Sakonnet, stm., R.I., U.S.	E6	146
Sakonnet Point, c., R.I., U.S.	F6	146
Sakrand, Pak.	G3	44
Sakrivier, S. Afr.	H5	66
Sal, i., C.V.	k17	64a
Sal, stm., U.S.S.R.	H6	22
Sal, Cay, i., Bah.	C4	94
Sal, Point, c., Ca., U.S.	E3	112
Sal, Punta, c., Hond.	B7	92
Sala, Swe.	L15	6
Salaberry-de-Valleyfield, Que., Can.	D3	104
Salacgrīva, U.S.S.R.	D7	26
Salada, Laguna, l., Mex.	A2	90
Saladas, Arg.	E9	80
Saladillo, Arg.	H9	80
Saladillo, stm., Arg.	E7	80
Saladillo Dulce, Arroyo, stm., Arg.	F8	80
Salado, Arg.	E5	80
Salado, stm., Arg.	H9	80
Salado, stm., Arg.	H5	80
Salado, stm., Arg.	E5	80
Salado, stm., Arg.	F8	80
Salado, stm., Cuba	D6	94
Salado, stm., Mex.	D10	90
Salado, Rio, stm., N.M., U.S.	C2	138
Sălaj, co., Rom.	B7	20
Šalakuša, U.S.S.R.	J27	6
Salala, Chile	F3	80
Salala, Lib.	H4	64
Şalālah, Oman	F9	47
Salamá, Guat.	B4	92
Salamá, Hond.	C8	92
Salamanca, Chile	F3	80
Salamanca, Mex.	G9	90
Salamanca, Peru	F5	82
Salamanca, Spain	E6	16
Salamanca, N.Y., U.S.	C2	139
Salamat, Bahr, stm., Chad	F4	56
Salamina, Col.	E5	84
Salamís, Grc.	L7	20
Salamís, i., Grc.	L7	20
Salamonie, stm., In., U.S.	C6	121
Salamonie Lake, res., In., U.S.	C6	121
Salantai, U.S.S.R.	E4	26
Salaquí, Col.	D4	84
Salaquí, stm., Col.	D4	84
Salas, Peru	B2	82
Salatiga, Indon.	J15	39a
Salavat, U.S.S.R.	G9	22
Salaverry, Peru	C2	82
Salavina, Arg.	E7	80
Sala y Gómez, Isla, i., Chile	K29	158
Salcajá, Guat.	C3	92
Salcantay, Nevado, mtn., Peru	E5	82
Salcedo, Dom. Rep.	E9	94
Šalčininkai, U.S.S.R.	G8	26
Saldaña, stm., Col.	F5	84
Saldanha, S. Afr.	I3	66
Saldungaray, Arg.	J8	80
Saldus, U.S.S.R.	E5	26
Sale, Austl.	L7	70
Salé, Mor.	C7	62
Salebabu, Pulau, i., Indon.	E8	38
Salechard, U.S.S.R.	D5	24
Sale City, Ga., U.S.	E2	117
Sale Creek, Tn., U.S.	D8	149
Salem, India	G5	46
Salem, Al., U.S.	C4	108
Salem, Ar., U.S.	A4	111
Salem, Il., U.S.	E5	120
Salem, In., U.S.	G5	121
Salem, Ia., U.S.	D6	122
Salem, Ky., U.S.	e9	124
Salem, Ma., U.S.	A6	128
Salem, Mi., U.S.	p14	129
Salem, Mo., U.S.	D6	132
Salem, Ne., U.S.	D10	134
Salem, N.H., U.S.	E4	136
Salem, N.J., U.S.	D2	137
Salem, N.M., U.S.	E2	138
Salem, N.Y., U.S.	B7	139
Salem, Oh., U.S.	B5	142
Salem, Or., U.S.	C4	144
Salem, S.D., U.S.	D8	148
Salem, Ut., U.S.	C4	151
Salem, Va., U.S.	C2	153
Salem, W.V., U.S.	B4	155
Salem, Wi., U.S.	n11	156
Salem, co., N.J., U.S.	D2	137
Salem, stm., N.J., U.S.	D2	137
Salem, Lake, l., Vt., U.S.	B4	152
Salemburg, N.C., U.S.	B4	140
Salemi, Italy	L7	18

Name	Map Ref.	Page
Salentina, Penisola, pen., Italy	I13	18
Salerno, Italy	I9	18
Salerno, Golfo di, b., Italy	I9	18
Salesville, Ar., U.S.	A3	111
Salgar, Col.	E5	84
Salgótarján, Hung.	G19	10
Sali, Alg.	G10	62
Salí, stm., Arg.	D6	80
Salida, Co., U.S.	C5	113
Salies-de-Béarn, Fr.	I6	14
Salihli, Tur.	K12	20
Salim, Sud.	K5	60
Salima, Mwi.	D6	58
Salimani, Com.	K15	67a
Salina, Az., U.S.	A6	110
Salina, Ks., U.S.	D6	123
Salina, Ok., U.S.	A6	143
Salina, Ut., U.S.	E4	151
Salina Cruz, Mex.	I12	90
Salina Point, c., Bah.	C7	94
Salinas, Braz.	D7	79
Salinas, Ec.	I2	84
Salinas, Ca., U.S.	D3	112
Salinas, stm., Braz.	D7	79
Salinas, stm., Ca., U.S.	D3	112
Salinas, Pampa de las, pl., Arg.	G5	80
Salinas de Garci Mendoza, Bol.	H8	82
Salinas de Hidalgo, Mex.	F9	90
Salinas Peak, mtn., N.M., U.S.	D3	138
Salinas Pueblo Missions National Monument, N.M., U.S.	C3	138
Saline, La., U.S.	B3	125
Saline, Mi., U.S.	F7	129
Saline, co., Ar., U.S.	C3	111
Saline, co., Il., U.S.	F5	120
Saline, co., Ks., U.S.	D6	123
Saline, co., Mo., U.S.	B4	132
Saline, co., Ne., U.S.	D8	134
Saline, stm., Ar., U.S.	C1	111
Saline, stm., Ar., U.S.	D4	111
Saline, stm., Ks., U.S.	C3	123
Saline, North Fork, stm., Il., U.S.	F5	120
Saline, South Fork, stm., Ar., U.S.	f8	111
Saline Bayou, stm., La., U.S.	B3	125
Saline Lake, res., La., U.S.	C3	125
Salineville, Oh., U.S.	B5	142
Salingyi, Burma	D3	40
Salisbury, Austl.	J3	70
Salisbury, N.B., Can.	C4	101
Salisbury, Eng., U.K.	J12	8
Salisbury, Ct., U.S.	B2	114
Salisbury, Md., U.S.	D6	127
Salisbury, Ma., U.S.	A6	128
Salisbury, Mo., U.S.	B5	132
Salisbury, N.H., U.S.	D3	136
Salisbury, N.C., U.S.	B2	140
Salisbury, Pa., U.S.	G3	145
Salisbury, Vt., U.S.	D2	152
Salisbury see Harare, Zimb.	A10	66
Salisbury Island, i., N.W. Ter., Can.	D17	96
Salisbury Plain, pl., Eng., U.K.	J12	8
Salish Mountains, mts., Mt., U.S.	B2	133
Salitpa, Al., U.S.	D1	108
Salix, Ia., U.S.	B1	122
Saljany, U.S.S.R.	J7	22
Salkehatchie, stm., S.C., U.S.	E5	147
Şalkhad, Syria	D7	50
Salkum, Wa., U.S.	C3	154
Sallanches, Fr.	G13	14
Salley, S.C., U.S.	D5	147
Salliqueló, Arg.	I7	80
Sallisaw, Ok., U.S.	B7	143
Salluit, Que., Can.	f11	104
Sallūm, Khalīj as-, b., Afr.	B3	60
Salluyo, Nevado, mtn., S.A.	F7	82
Salmās, Iran	B8	48
Salmi, U.S.S.R.	K22	6
Salmo, B.C., Can.	E9	99
Salmon, Id., U.S.	D5	119
Salmon, stm., N.B., Can.	C4	101
Salmon, stm., Id., U.S.	D3	119
Salmon, Middle Fork, stm., Id., U.S.	E4	119
Salmon, South Fork, stm., Id., U.S.	E3	119
Salmon Creek, Wa., U.S.	D3	154
Salmon Creek Reservoir, res., Id., U.S.	G4	119
Salmon Falls, stm., U.S.	D5	136
Salmon Falls Creek, stm., U.S.	G4	119
Salmon Mountain, mtn., N.H., U.S.	f7	136
Salmon Mountains, mts., Ca., U.S.	B2	112
Salmon Peak, mtn., Tx., U.S.	E2	150
Salmon Point, c., Ont., Can.	D7	103
Salmon River Mountains, mts., Id., U.S.	E3	119
Salmon River Reservoir, res., N.Y., U.S.	B5	139
Salo, Fin.	K18	6
Salò, Italy	D5	18
Salobra, stm., Braz.	I13	82
Salome, Az., U.S.	D2	110
Salon-de-Provence, Fr.	I12	14
Salonika see Thessaloníki, Grc.	I6	20
Salonta, Rom.	C5	20
Saloum, stm., Sen.	D2	64
Sal Rei, C.V.	k17	64a
Salsacate, Arg.	F6	80
Salsilgo, Qawz, dunes, Afr.	L2	60
Salsipuedes, Canal, strt., Mex.	C3	90
Salsipuedes, Punta, c., C.R.	I11	92
Salsipuedes, Punta, c., Mex.	A1	90
Sal'sk, U.S.S.R.	H6	22
Salsomaggiore Terme, Italy	E4	18
Salt, stm., Az., U.S.	D4	110
Salt, stm., Ky., U.S.	C4	124
Salt, stm., Mo., U.S.	B6	132
Salt, Middle Fork, stm., Mo., U.S.	B5	132
Salt, North Fork, stm., Mo., U.S.	B5	132
Salt, South Fork, stm., Mo., U.S.	B5	132
Salta, Arg.	C6	80
Salta, prov., Arg.	C5	80
Saltcoats, Sask., Can.	F4	105
Salt Creek, stm., Il., U.S.	C4	120
Salt Creek, stm., Ks., U.S.	f10	123
Salt Creek, stm., Ne., U.S.	h11	134
Salt Creek, stm., N.M., U.S.	D5	138
Salt Creek, stm., Oh., U.S.	C3	142
Salt Creek, stm., Wy., U.S.	C6	157
Salter Path, N.C., U.S.	C6	140
Salt Fork Lake, res., Oh., U.S.	B4	142
Saltillo, Mex.	E9	90
Saltillo, Ms., U.S.	A5	131
Saltillo, Tn., U.S.	B3	149
Salt Lake, co., Ut., U.S.	C3	151
Salt Lake, l., Hi., U.S.	g10	118
Salt Lake, l., N.M., U.S.	E6	138
Salt Lake City, Ut., U.S.	C4	151
Salt Lick, Ky., U.S.	B6	124
Salto, Arg.	H8	80
Salto, Braz.	G5	79
Salto, Ur.	F10	80
Salto da Divisa, Braz.	D9	79
Salto de las Rosas, Arg.	H4	80
Salto Grande, Braz.	G4	79
Salton Sea, l., Ca., U.S.	F5	112
Saltonstall, Lake, l., Ct., U.S.	D4	114
Saltos del Guaira, Para.	C11	80
Salt Point, c., Ca., U.S.	C2	112
Salt River Indian Reservation, Az., U.S.	k9	110
Salt River Range, mts., Wy., U.S.	D2	157
Salt Rock, W.V., U.S.	C2	155
Saltsburg, Pa., U.S.	F3	145
Saltspring Island, i., B.C., Can.	E6	99
Salt Springs, Fl., U.S.	C5	116
Saltville, Va., U.S.	f10	153
Salt Wells Creek, stm., Wy., U.S.	E4	157
Saluda, N.C., U.S.	f10	140
Saluda, S.C., U.S.	C4	147
Saluda, Va., U.S.	C6	153
Saluda, co., S.C., U.S.	C4	147
Saluda, stm., S.C., U.S.	C4	147
Saluda Dam, S.C., U.S.	C5	147
Sālūr, India	C7	46
Saluzzo, Italy	E2	18
Salvador, Braz.	B9	79
Salvador, Sask., Can.	E1	105
Salvador, El see El Salvador, ctry., N.A.	D6	92
Salvador, Lake, l., La., U.S.	E5	125
Salvador Mazza, Arg.	B7	80
Salvage, Newf., Can.	D5	102
Salvaterra de Magos, Port.	F3	16
Salvatierra, Mex.	G9	90
Salvisa, Ky., U.S.	C5	124
Salwā, Dawḥat, b., Asia	I11	48
Salwā Baḥrī, Egypt	E7	60
Salween (Nu) (Thanlwin), stm., Asia	D5	40
Salyān, Nepal	F10	44
Salyer, Ca., U.S.	B2	112
Salyersville, Ky., U.S.	C6	124
Salzach, stm., Eur.	G12	10
Salzburg, Aus.	H13	10
Salzburg, state, Aus.	H13	10
Salzgitter, Ger.	C10	10
Salzkammergut, reg., Aus.	H13	10
Salzwedel, Ger.	C11	10
Samā, Jord.	D6	50
Sama, stm., Peru	G6	82
Samacá, Col.	E6	84
Sama [de Langreo], Spain	B6	16
Samaipata, Bol.	H10	82
Samalá, stm., Guat.	C3	92
Sāmalkot, India	D7	46
Samālūṭ, Egypt	C6	60
Samambaia, stm., Braz.	G2	79
Samaná, Dom. Rep.	E10	94
Samaná, Bahía de, b., Dom. Rep.	E10	94
Samaná, Cabo, c., Dom. Rep.	E10	94
Samana Cay, i., Bah.	C8	94
Samandağı, Tur.	C3	48
Samaniego, Col.	G4	84
Samar, Isr.	I4	50
Samara, U.S.S.R.	G8	22
Samara, stm., U.S.S.R.	G8	22
Samarai, Pap. N. Gui.	n17	68a
Samaria, Id., U.S.	G6	119
Samariapo, Ven.	E9	84
Samarinda, Indon.	F6	38
Samarkand, U.S.S.R.	J11	22
Sāmarrā', Iraq	D7	48
Samastīpur, India	H11	44
Sambalpur, India	J10	44
Sambas, Indon.	N10	40
Sambava, Madag.	O24	67b
Sambawizi, Zimb.	B8	66
Sambhal, India	F8	44
Sāmbhar, India	G6	44
Sâmbor, Camb.	H8	40
Sambor, U.S.S.R.	F23	10
Samborombón, stm., Arg.	H10	80
Samborombón, Bahía, b., Arg.	I10	80
Samborondón, Ec.	H3	84
Sambre, stm., Eur.	B11	14
Sambú, stm., Pan.	C3	84
Samburg, Tn., U.S.	A2	149
Sambusu, Nmb.	A4	66
Samch'ŏk, S. Kor.	F17	32
Samch'ŏnp'o, S. Kor.	I16	32
Samedan, Switz.	E12	13
Samho, N. Kor.	D15	32
Samiria, stm., Peru	J5	84
Sammamish Lake, l., Wa., U.S.	e11	154
Samnaungruppe, mts., Eur.	D13	13
Samnye, S. Kor.	H15	32
Samoa, Ca., U.S.	B1	112
Samoa Islands, is., Oc.	J22	158
Samo Alto, Chile	F3	80
Samoded, U.S.S.R.	E6	22
Sámos, Grc.	L11	20
Sámos, i., Grc.	L10	20
Samoset, Fl., U.S.	q10	116
Samosir, Pulau, i., Indon.	M5	40
Samothrace see Samothráki, i., Grc.	I9	20
Samothráki, i., Grc.	I9	20
S'amozero, U.S.S.R.	K23	6
Sampacho, Arg.	G6	80
Sampit, Indon.	F5	38
Sampit, stm., S.C., U.S.	E9	147
Sampson, co., N.C., U.S.	B4	140
Sampués, Col.	C5	84
Sampur, U.S.S.R.	I24	26
Sam Rayburn Reservoir, res., Tx., U.S.	D5	150
Samre, Eth.	K10	60
Samreboi, Ghana	I8	64
Samson, Al., U.S.	D3	108
Samsun, Tur.	G15	4
Samtown, La., U.S.	C3	125
Samuels, Id., U.S.	A2	119
Samuhú, Arg.	D8	80
Samui, Ko, i., Thai.	J6	40
Samut Prakan, Thai.	H6	40
Samut Sakhon, Thai.	H6	40
Samut Songkhram, Thai.	H6	40
S'amža, U.S.S.R.	A24	26
San, Mali	E7	64
San (Xan), stm., Asia	H9	40
San, stm., Eur.	E22	10
Saña, Peru	B2	82
Şan'ā', Yemen	G4	47
Sanaba, stm., Afr.	D4	64
San Acacia, N.M., U.S.	C3	138
Sanaduva, Braz.	D13	80
Sanaga, stm., Cam.	J14	64
San Agustín, Arg.	J9	80
San Agustín, Arg.	F6	80
San Agustín, Col.	G4	84
San Agustin, Plains of, pl., N.M., U.S.	C2	138
San Agustín de Valle Fértil, Arg.	F5	80
Sanak Islands, is., Ak., U.S.	E7	109
San Alejo, El Sal.	D7	92
Sanalona, Presa, res., Mex.	E6	90
San Ambrosio, Isla, i., Chile	B1	78
Sanana, Pulau, i., Indon.	F8	38
Sanandaj, Iran	D9	48
Sanandita, Bol.	I10	82
San Andreas, Ca., U.S.	C3	112
San Andrés, Col.	H4	94
San Andrés, Mex.	D2	90
San Andrés, Pan.	I12	92
San Andrés, Isla de, i., Col.	H4	94
San Andrés de Giles, Arg.	H9	80
San Andres Mountains, mts., N.M., U.S.	E3	138
San Andres Peak, mtn., N.M., U.S.	E3	138
San Andrés Sajcabajá, Guat.	B4	92
San Andrés Tuxtla, Mex.	H12	90
San Andrés y Providencia, ter., Col.	H4	94
San Angelo, Tx., U.S.	D2	150
San Anselmo, Ca., U.S.	h7	112
San Antero, Col.	C5	84
San Antonio, Arg.	C6	80
San Antonio, Arg.	E6	80
San Antonio, Belize	A5	92
San Antonio, Chile	D3	80
San Antonio, Chile	G3	80
San Antonio, Col.	F5	84
San Antonio, C.R.	G9	92
San Antonio, Peru	B3	82
San Antonio, Fl., U.S.	D4	116
San Antonio, N.M., U.S.	D3	138
San Antonio, Tx., U.S.	E3	150
San Antonio, Ur.	F10	80
San Antonio, stm., Mex.	B2	90
San Antonio, Cabo, c., Arg.	I10	80
San Antonio, Cabo de, c., Cuba	D2	94
San Antonio, Punta, c., Mex.	C2	90
San Antonio, Punta, c., Mex.	D4	90
San Antonio Bay, b., Tx., U.S.	E4	150
San Antonio de Areco, Arg.	H9	80
San Antonio del Golfo, Ven.	B11	84
San Antonio de los Baños, Cuba	C3	94
San Antonio de los Cobres, Arg.	C5	80
San Antonio del Táchira, Ven.	D6	84
San Antônio de Pádua, Braz.	F7	79
San Antonio de Tamanaco, Ven.	C9	84
San Antonio El Bravo, Mex.	B7	90
San Antonio Mountain, mtn., N.M., U.S.	A3	138
San Antonio Suchitepéquez, Guat.	C3	92
San Ardo, Ca., U.S.	D3	112
Sanatorium, Ms., U.S.	D4	131
San Augustine, Tx., U.S.	D5	150
San Augustine, co., Tx., U.S.	D5	150
San Bartolomé, Spain	N27	17b
San Benedetto del Tronto, Italy	G8	18
San Benedicto, Isla, i., Mex.	H4	90
San Benito, Bol.	G9	82
San Benito, Guat.	I15	90
San Benito, Peru	B2	82
San Benito, Tx., U.S.	F4	150
San Benito, co., Ca., U.S.	D3	112
San Benito Mountain, mtn., Ca., U.S.	D3	112
San Bernardino, Switz.	F11	13
San Bernardino, Ca., U.S.	E5	112
San Bernardino, co., Ca., U.S.	E5	112
San Bernardo, Arg.	D8	80
San Bernardo, Chile	G3	80
San Bernardo, Mex.	E7	90
San Bernardo, Isla, i., Nic.	F9	92
San Bernardo, Islas de, is., Col.	C4	84
San Bernardo del Viento, Col.	C5	84
San Blas, Mex.	G7	90
San Blas, Mex.	D5	90
San Blas, Cape, c., Fl., U.S.	v16	116
San Blas, Cordillera de, mts., Pan.	C3	84
San Blas, Golfo de, b., Pan.	C3	84
San Blas de los Sauces, Arg.	E5	80
San Borja, Bol.	F8	82
Sanborn, Ia., U.S.	A2	122
Sanborn, Mn., U.S.	F3	130
Sanborn, N.D., U.S.	C7	141
Sanborn, co., S.D., U.S.	D7	148
Sanbornton, N.H., U.S.	D3	136
Sanbornville, N.H., U.S.	C4	136
San Bruno, Ca., U.S.	D2	112
San Buena Ventura, Bol.	F8	82
San Buenaventura, Mex.	D9	90
Sancang, China	C9	34
San Carlos, Arg.	G4	80
San Carlos, Arg.	D11	80
San Carlos, Arg.	C6	80
San Carlos, Chile	I3	80
San Carlos, Mex.	E10	90
San Carlos, Mex.	C9	90
San Carlos, Nic.	F10	92
San Carlos, Pan.	C3	84
San Carlos, Para.	B10	80
San Carlos, Phil.	C7	38
San Carlos, Phil.	N19	39b
San Carlos, Az., U.S.	D5	110
San Carlos, Ca., U.S.	k8	112
San Carlos, Ur.	H11	80
San Carlos, Ven.	C8	84
San Carlos, stm., C.R.	G10	92
San Carlos, stm., Ven.	C8	84
San Carlos, Riacho, stm., Para.	B9	80
San Carlos Centro, Arg.	F8	80
San Carlos de Bariloche, Arg.	E2	78
San Carlos de Bolívar, Arg.	I8	80
San Carlos de Guaroa, Col.	F6	84
San Carlos del Zulia, Ven.	C7	84
San Carlos de Río Negro, Ven.	G9	84
San Carlos Indian Reservation, Az., U.S.	D5	110
San Carlos Lake, res., Az., U.S.	D5	110
San Cataldo, Italy	L8	18
San Cayetano, Arg.	J9	80
Sancerre, Fr.	E9	14
Sánchez, Dom. Rep.	E10	94
Sanch'ŏng, S. Kor.	H15	32
San Ciro de Acosta, Mex.	G10	90
San Clemente, Spain	F9	16
San Clemente, Ca., U.S.	F5	112
San Clemente Island, i., Ca., U.S.	F4	112
San Cosme, Arg.	D9	80
San Cristóbal, Arg.	F8	80
San Cristóbal, Dom. Rep.	E9	94
San Cristóbal, N.M., U.S.	A4	138
San Cristóbal, Ven.	D6	84
San Cristóbal, Bahía, b., Mex.	D2	90
San Cristóbal, Isla, i., Ec.	J14	84a
San Cristóbal, Volcán, vol., Nic.	E7	92
San Cristóbal de la Laguna, Spain	O24	17b
San Cristóbal de las Casas, Mex.	I13	90
San Cristóbal Totonicapán, Guat.	C3	92
San Cristóbal Verapaz, Guat.	B4	92
Sancti Spíritus, Cuba	D5	94
Sancy, Puy de, mtn., Fr.	G9	14
Sand, stm., Alta., Can.	B5	98
San Damián, Peru	E3	82
Sandaré, Mali	D4	64
Sandborn, In., U.S.	G3	121
Sand Coulee, Mt., U.S.	C5	133
Sand Creek, stm., In., U.S.	F6	121
Sand Creek, stm., Ks., U.S.	g12	123
Sand Creek, stm., Wy., U.S.	C7	157
Sanders, Az., U.S.	B6	110
Sanders, Ky., U.S.	B5	124
Sanders, co., Mt., U.S.	C1	133
Sanderson, Tx., U.S.	D1	150
Sandersville, Ga., U.S.	D4	117
Sandersville, Ms., U.S.	D4	131
Sandfly Lake, l., Sask., Can.	B2	105
Sandford, In., U.S.	E2	121
Sandgate, Austl.	F10	70
Sand Hill, Ma., U.S.	h13	128
Sandhill, Ms., U.S.	C4	131
Sand Hill, Ms., U.S.	D5	131
Sand Hill, stm., Newf., Can.	B3	102
Sand Hill, stm., Mn., U.S.	C2	130
Sandia, Peru	F7	82
Sandia Crest, mtn., N.M., U.S.	k8	138
Sandia Indian Reservation, N.M., U.S.	k7	138
Sandia Mountains, mts., N.M., U.S.	k8	138
Sandia Park, N.M., U.S.	k8	138
San Diego, Ca., U.S.	F5	112
San Diego, Tx., U.S.	F3	150
San Diego, co., Ca., U.S.	F5	112
San Diego, stm., Ca., U.S.	o15	112
San Diego, Cabo, c., Arg.	G3	78
San Diego de la Unión, Mex.	G9	90
San Diego Naval Station, mil., Ca., U.S.	o15	112
San Diego Naval Training Center, mil., Ca., U.S.	o15	112
Sandilands, Man., Can.	E3	100
San Dionisio, Nic.	E9	92
Sand Island, i., Hi., U.S.	g10	118
Sand Island, i., Wi., U.S.	B3	156
Sand Key, i., Fl., U.S.	E4	116
Sand Lake, Mi., U.S.	E5	129
Sandlick Creek, stm., W.V., U.S.	n13	155
Sand Mountain, mtn., U.S.	A3	108
Sandoa, Zaire	C4	58
Sandomierz, Pol.	E21	10
Sandoná, Col.	G4	84
San Donà di Piave, Italy	D7	18
Sandoval, Il., U.S.	E4	120
Sandoval, co., N.M., U.S.	B2	138
Sandovalina, Braz.	G3	79
Sandovo, U.S.S.R.	C19	26
Sandoway, Burma	E3	40
Sandown, N.H., U.S.	E4	136
Sand Point, Ont., Can.	B8	103
Sand Point, Ak., U.S.	D7	109
Sandpoint, Id., U.S.	A2	119
Sandringham, Eng., U.K.	I13	8
Sands Key, i., Fl., U.S.	s3	116
Sandspit, B.C., Can.	C2	99
Sand Springs, Ok., U.S.	A5	143
Sandston, Va., U.S.	m18	153
Sandstone, Austl.	E3	68
Sandstone, Mn., U.S.	D6	130
Sandstone, W.V., U.S.	D4	155
Sandtown, De., U.S.	D3	115
Sandu Ao, b., China	I8	34
Sandusky, Mi., U.S.	E8	129
Sandusky, Oh., U.S.	A3	142
Sandusky, co., Oh., U.S.	A2	142
Sandusky, stm., Oh., U.S.	B2	142
Sandusky Bay, b., Oh., U.S.	A3	142
Sandvika, Nor.	L12	6
Sandviken, Swe.	K15	6
Sandwich, Il., U.S.	B5	120
Sandwich, Ma., U.S.	C7	128
Sandwich Bay, b., Newf., Can.	B3	102
Sandwich Range, mts., N.H., U.S.	C3	136
Sandwīp Island, i., Bngl.	I14	44
Sandy, Or., U.S.	B4	144
Sandy, Ut., U.S.	C4	151
Sandy, stm., Me., U.S.	D2	126
Sandy Bay, b., Nic.	C11	92
Sandy Bay Mountain, mtn., Me., U.S.	C2	126
Sandy Brook, stm., Ct., U.S.	A3	114
Sandy Cape, c., Austl.	E10	70
Sandy Creek, stm., Oh., U.S.	B4	142
Sandy Creek, stm., Ok., U.S.	C2	143
Sandy Hook, Ct., U.S.	D2	114
Sandy Hook, Ky., U.S.	B6	124
Sandy Hook, spit, N.J., U.S.	C5	137
Sandy Island, i., S.C., U.S.	D9	147
Sandykači, U.S.S.R.	J10	22
Sandy Lake, Man., Can.	D1	100
Sandy Lake, l., Newf., Can.	D3	102
Sandy Lake, l., Ont., Can.	n16	103
Sandy Lake, l., Sask., Can.	B2	105
Sandy Neck, pen., Ma., U.S.	C7	128
Sandy Point, c., R.I., U.S.	h7	146
Sandy Point Town, St. K./N.	F13	94
Sandy Pond, l., Ma., U.S.	g10	128
Sandy Ridge, Al., U.S.	C3	108
Sandy Ridge, mtn., Va., U.S.	e9	153
Sandy Springs, Ga., U.S.	h8	117
Sandy Springs, S.C., U.S.	B2	147
Sandyville, Md., U.S.	A4	127
Sandyville, W.V., U.S.	C3	155
San Enrique, Arg.	H8	80
San Estanislao, Col.	B5	84
San Estanislao, Para.	C10	80
San Esteban, Hond.	B9	92
San Esteban, Isla, i., Mex.	C3	90
San Felipe, Chile	G3	80
San Felipe, Col.	G9	84
San Felipe, Mex.	B2	90
San Felipe, Mex.	G9	90
San Felipe, Phil.	N19	39b
San Felipe, Ven.	B8	84
San Felipe, Castillo de, hist., Guat.	B5	92
San Felipe, Cayos de, is., Cuba	D3	94
San Felipe de Vichayal, Peru	A1	82
San Felipe Indian Reservation, N.M., U.S.	k8	138
San Felipe Nuevo Mercurio, Mex.	E8	90
San Felipe Pueblo, N.M., U.S.	B3	138
San Félix, stm., Pan.	I13	92
San Félix, Isla, i., Chile	K31	158
San Fernando, Chile	H3	80
San Fernando, Mex.	E10	90
San Fernando, Phil.	M19	39b
San Fernando, Phil.	N19	39b
San Fernando, Spain	I5	16
San Fernando, Trin.	I14	94
San Fernando, Ca., U.S.	m12	112
San Fernando de Apure, Ven.	D9	84
San Fernando de Atabapo, Ven.	E9	84
San Fernando del Valle de Catamarca, Arg.	E6	80
Sanford, Al., U.S.	D3	108
Sanford, Co., U.S.	D5	113
Sanford, Fl., U.S.	D5	116
Sanford, Me., U.S.	E2	126
Sanford, Mi., U.S.	E6	129
Sanford, N.C., U.S.	B3	140
Sanford, Mount, mtn., Ak., U.S.	C11	109
San Francisco, Arg.	F7	80
San Francisco, Col.	G4	84
San Francisco, C.R.	H9	92
San Francisco, El Sal.	D6	92
San Francisco, Pan.	I14	92
San Francisco, Ca., U.S.	D2	112
San Francisco, co., Ca., U.S.	D2	112
San Francisco, stm., Arg.	B6	80
San Francisco, stm., U.S.	D6	110
San Francisco, Paso de, S.A.	D4	80
San Francisco Bay, b., Ca., U.S.	h8	112
San Francisco de Borja, Mex.	D6	90
San Francisco de la Paz, Hond.	C8	92
San Francisco del Chañar, Arg.	E7	80
San Francisco del Monte de Oro, Arg.	G5	80
San Francisco del Oro, Mex.	D7	90
San Francisco del Rincón, Mex.	G9	90
San Francisco de Macorís, Dom. Rep.	E9	94
San Francisco de Mostazal, Chile	G3	80
San Francisco Libre, Nic.	E8	92
San Francisco Mountains, mts., Ut., U.S.	E2	151
San Franco, Cerro, mtn., Hond.	B7	92
San Gabriel, Ec.	G4	84
San Gabriel, Ca., U.S.	m12	112
San Gabriel Chilac, Mex.	H11	90
San Gabriel Mountains, mts., Ca., U.S.	m12	112
San Gallán, Isla, i., Peru	E3	82
Sangamner, India	C3	46
Sangamon, co., Il., U.S.	D4	120
Sangamon, stm., Il., U.S.	C3	120
Sanga Puitã, Braz.	G1	79
Sangay, Volcán, vol., Ec.	H3	84
Sangchungshih, Tai.	J10	34
Sang-e Māsheh, Afg.	D2	44
Sanger, Ca., U.S.	D4	112
Sanger, Tx., U.S.	C4	150
Sangerhausen, Ger.	D11	10
San Germán, Cuba	D6	94
San Germán, P.R.	E11	94
Sangerville, Me., U.S.	C3	126
Sanggan, stm., China	C9	30
Sangha, stm., Afr.	A3	58
Sangihe, Kepulauan, is., Indon.	E8	38
Sangihe, Pulau, i., Indon.	E8	38
San Gil, Col.	D6	84
San Gimignano, Italy	F6	18
San Giovanni in Fiore, Italy	J11	18
San Giovanni in Persiceto, Italy	E6	18
San Giovanni Rotondo, Italy	H10	18
San Giovanni Valdarno, Italy	F6	18
Sangju, S. Kor.	G16	32
Sāngli, India	D3	46
Sangolquí, Ec.	H3	84
San Gorgonio Mountain, mtn., Ca., U.S.	E5	112
San Gottardo, Passo del, Switz.	E10	13
San Gregorio, Arg.	H7	80
San Gregorio, Ur.	G11	80
Sangre Grande, Trin.	I14	94
Sangrūr, India	E6	44
Sanguandian, China	D7	34
Sangudo, Alta., Can.	C3	98
Sangue, Rio do, stm., Braz.	D12	82
Sanhecun, China	A17	32
San Hipólito, Punta, c., Mex.	D3	90
Sanibel, Fl., U.S.	F4	116
Sanibel Island, i., Fl., U.S.	F4	116
San Ignacio, Arg.	D11	80
San Ignacio, Bol.	F9	82
San Ignacio, Bol.	G11	82
San Ignacio, C.R.	H10	92
San Ignacio, Hond.	C7	92
San Ignacio, Mex.	D3	90
San Ignacio, Mex.	F9	90
San Ignacio, Para.	D10	80
San Ignacio, Isla, i., Mex.	E5	90
San Ignacio, Laguna, l., Mex.	D3	90
Sanilac, co., Mi., U.S.	E8	129
San Ildefonso, Cerro, mtn., Hond.	B6	92
San Isidro, Arg.	H9	80
San Isidro, Arg.	E6	80
San Isidro, C.R.	H11	92
San Isidro, Nic.	E8	92
San Isidro, Tx., U.S.	F3	150
San Jacinto, Col.	C5	84
San Jacinto, Ca., U.S.	F5	112
San Jacinto, co., Tx., U.S.	D5	150
San Jacinto, stm., Tx., U.S.	r14	150
San Javier, Arg.	F9	80
San Javier, Arg.	D11	80
San Javier, Bol.	F8	82
San Javier, Bol.	G10	82
San Javier, Ur.	G9	80
San Javier, stm., Arg.	E9	80
San Javier de Loncomilla, Chile	H3	80
Sanjāwi, Pak.	E3	44
San Jerónimo, Guat.	B4	92
San Jerónimo Norte, Arg.	F8	80
Sanjō, Japan	J13	36
San Joaquín, Bol.	E9	82
San Joaquín, Para.	C10	80
San Joaquin, Ca., U.S.	D3	112
San Joaquin, co., Ca., U.S.	D3	112
San Joaquín, stm., Bol.	E10	82
San Joaquin, stm., Ca., U.S.	D3	112
San Joaquin Valley, val., Ca., U.S.	D3	112
San Jon, N.M., U.S.	B6	138
San Jorge, Arg.	F8	80
San Jorge, El Sal.	D6	92
San Jorge, Nic.	F9	92
San Jorge, stm., Col.	C5	84
San Jorge, Bahía, b., Mex.	B3	90
San Jorge, Golfo, b., Arg.	F3	78
San José, Arg.	D11	80
San José, Bol.	F7	82
San José, C.R.	H10	92
San José, Ec.	H3	84
San José, Para.	C10	80
San Jose, Phil.	N19	39b
San Jose, Az., U.S.	E6	110
San Jose, Ca., U.S.	D3	112
San Jose, Il., U.S.	C4	120
San Jose, N.M., U.S.	B4	138
San José, prov., C.R.	H11	92
San José, Isla, i., Mex.	E4	90
San José, Isla, i., Pan.	C3	84
San José Batuc, Mex.	C5	90
San José Buena Vista, Guat.	D4	92
San José de Bácum, Mex.	D4	90
San José de Chiquitos, Bol.	G11	82
San José de Copán, Hond.	C6	92
San José de Feliciano, Arg.	F9	80
San José de Guaribe, Ven.	C10	84
San José de Guanipa, Ven.	C10	84
San José de Jáchal, Arg.	F4	80
San José de la Esquina, Arg.	G8	80
San José de las Lajas, Cuba	C3	94

Name	Map Ref.	Page
San José de las Raíces, Mex.	E9	90
San José del Cabo, Mex.	F5	90
San José del Guaviare, Col.	F6	84
San José de los Molinos, Peru	E4	82
San José de Mayo, Ur.	H10	80
San José de Ocuné, Col.	E7	84
San José de Sisa, Peru	B3	82
San José de Tiznados, Ven.	C9	84
San Jose Island, i., Tx., U.S.	E4	150
San Juan, Arg.	F4	80
San Juan, Guat.	B6	92
San Juan, Peru	F4	82
San Juan, P.R.	E11	94
San Juan, Tx., U.S.	F3	150
San Juan, prov., Arg.	F4	80
San Juan, co., Co., U.S.	D3	113
San Juan, co., N.M., U.S.	A1	138
San Juan, co., Ut., U.S.	F5	151
San Juan, co., Wa., U.S.	A2	154
San Juan, stm., Arg.	G5	80
San Juan, stm., Col.	E4	84
San Juan, stm., Mex.	E10	90
San Juan, stm., N.A.	G10	92
San Juan, stm., Peru	E4	82
San Juan, stm., S.A.	G3	84
San Juan, stm., U.S.	D5	106
San Juan, stm., Ven.	B11	84
San Juan, Pico, mtn., Cuba	D4	94
San Juan Bautista, Para.	D10	80
San Juan Capistrano, Ca., U.S.	F5	112
San Juan Cotzal, Guat.	B3	92
San Juan de Abajo, Mex.	G7	90
San Juan de Colón, Ven.	C6	84
San Juan de Guadalupe, Mex.	E8	90
San Juan [de la Maguana], Dom. Rep.	E9	94
San Juan del César, Col.	B6	84
San Juan del Norte, Nic.	G11	92
San Juan del Oro, stm., Bol.	I9	82
San Juan de los Cayos, Ven.	B8	84
San Juan de los Morros, Ven.	C9	84
San Juan del Piray, Bol.	I9	82
San Juan del Río, Mex.	E7	90
San Juan del Río, Mex.	G9	90
San Juan del Sur, Nic.	F9	92
San Juan de Micay, stm., Col.	F4	84
San Juan de Payara, Ven.	D9	84
San Juan Evangelista, Mex.	I12	90
San Juanico, Mex.	D3	90
San Juanillo, C.R.	G9	92
San Juan Island, i., Wa., U.S.	A2	154
San Juanito, Isla, i., Mex.	G6	90
San Juan Mountains, mts., Co., U.S.	D3	113
San Juan Nepomuceno, Col.	C5	84
San Juan Nepomuceno, Para.	D11	80
San Juan Sacatepéquez, Guat.	C4	92
San Juan Teotihuacán, Mex.	H10	90
San Julián, Arg.	F3	78
San Justo, Arg.	F8	80
Sankarani, stm., Afr.	F5	64
Sankosh, stm., Asia	G14	44
Sankt Aegyd am Neuwalde, Aus.	H15	10
Sankt Anton [am Arlberg], Aus.	H10	10
Sankt Gallen, Aus.	H14	10
Sankt Gallen, Switz.	D11	13
Sankt Gallen, state, Switz.	D11	13
Sankt Gilgen, Aus.	H13	10
Sankt Goar, Ger.	E7	10
Sankt Goarshausen, Ger.	E7	10
Sankt Ingbert, Ger.	F7	10
Sankt Johann im Pongau, Aus.	H13	10
Sankt Johann in Tirol, Aus.	H12	10
Sankt Moritz, Switz.	E12	13
Sankt Niklaus, Switz.	F8	13
Sankt Paul [im Lavanttal], Aus.	I14	10
Sankt Peter, Ger.	A8	10
Sankt Pölten, Aus.	G15	10
Sankt Valentin, Aus.	G14	10
Sankt Veit an der Glan, Aus.	I14	10
Sankt Vith (Saint-Vith), Bel.	H9	12
Sankt Wendel, Ger.	F7	10
San Lázaro, Para.	B10	80
San Lázaro, Cabo, c., Mex.	E3	90
San Leandro, Ca., U.S.	h8	112
Sanlicheng, China	D3	34
San Lope, Col.	D7	84
San Lorenzo, Arg.	G8	80
San Lorenzo, Arg.	E9	80
San Lorenzo, Bol.	I9	82
San Lorenzo, Ec.	G3	84
San Lorenzo, Hond.	D7	92
San Lorenzo, Mex.	E8	90
San Lorenzo, Nic.	E9	92
San Lorenzo, N.M., U.S.	E2	138
San Lorenzo, Ven.	C7	84
San Lorenzo, stm., Mex.	E6	90
San Lorenzo, Bahía de, b., Hond.	D7	92
San Lorenzo, Cabo, c., Ec.	H2	84
San Lorenzo, Isla, i., Mex.	C3	90
San Lorenzo, Isla, i., Peru	E3	82
San Lorenzo de El Escorial, Spain	E7	16
Sanlúcar de Barrameda, Spain	I5	16
Sanlúcar la Mayor, Spain	H5	16
San Lucas, Bol.	I9	82
San Lucas, Ec.	I3	84
San Lucas, Mex.	F5	90
San Lucas, Cabo, c., Mex.	F5	90
San Luis, Arg.	G5	80
San Luis, Cuba	D7	94
San Luis, Guat.	A5	92
San Luis, Az., U.S.	E1	110
San Luis, Co., U.S.	D5	113
San Luis, Ven.	B8	84
San Luis, prov., Arg.	H5	80
San Luis, Laguna, l., Bol.	E9	82
San Luis, Point, c., Ca., U.S.	E3	112
San Luis, Sierra de, mts., Arg.	G6	80
San Luis Creek, stm., Co., U.S.	C5	113
San Luis de la Paz, Mex.	G9	90
San Luis del Cordero, Mex.	E7	90
San Luis del Palmar, Arg.	D9	80
San Luis Gonzaga, Mex.	E4	90
San Luis Gonzaga, Bahía, b., Mex.	C2	90
San Luis Jilotepeque, Guat.	C5	92
San Luis Obispo, Ca., U.S.	E3	112
San Luis Obispo, co., Ca., U.S.	E3	112
San Luis Pass, strt., Tx., U.S.	r14	150
San Luis Peak, mtn., Co., U.S.	D4	113
San Luis Potosí, Mex.	F9	90
San Luis Potosí, state, Mex.	F9	90
San Luis Río Colorado, Mex.	A2	90
San Luis Valley, val., Co., U.S.	D4	113
Sanluri, Italy	J3	18
San Manuel, Arg.	I9	80
San Manuel, Az., U.S.	E5	110
San Marcial, stm., Mex.	C4	90
San Marcos, Chile	F3	80
San Marcos, Col.	C5	84
San Marcos, C.R.	H10	92
San Marcos, El Sal.	D5	92
San Marcos, Guat.	C3	92
San Marcos, Hond.	C6	92
San Marcos, Hond.	B6	92
San Marcos, Mex.	I10	90
San Marcos, Tx., U.S.	E4	150
San Marcos, dept., Guat.	B3	92
San Marcos, stm., Tx., U.S.	h8	150
San Marcos, Isla, i., Mex.	D3	90
San Marcos de Colón, Hond.	D8	92
San Marino, S. Mar.	F7	18
San Marino, Ca., U.S.	m12	112
San Marino, ctry., Eur.	G10	4
San Martín, Arg.	E6	80
San Martín, Arg.	G4	80
San Martín, Col.	F6	84
San Martín, dept., Peru	B3	82
San Martín, stm., Bol.	E10	82
San Martín, Lago (Lago O'Higgins), l., S.A.	F2	78
San Martín de los Andes, Arg.	E2	78
San Martín Texmelucan, Mex.	H10	90
San Mateo, Ca., U.S.	D2	112
San Mateo, Fl., U.S.	C5	116
San Mateo, N.M., U.S.	B2	138
San Mateo, Ven.	C10	84
San Mateo, co., Ca., U.S.	D2	112
San Mateo Ixtatán, Guat.	B3	92
San Mateo Mountains, mts., N.M., U.S.	B2	138
San Mateo Mountains, mts., N.M., U.S.	D2	138
San Matías, Bol.	G12	82
San Matías, Golfo, b., Arg.	E4	78
Sanmenxia, China	E9	30
San Miguel, Arg.	E10	80
San Miguel, Bol.	G11	82
San Miguel, Ec.	H3	84
San Miguel, El Sal.	D6	92
San Miguel, Mex.	C9	90
San Miguel, Pan.	C3	84
San Miguel, Peru	E5	82
San Miguel, Spain	O24	17b
San Miguel, Ca., U.S.	E3	112
San Miguel, N.M., U.S.	E3	138
San Miguel, co., Co., U.S.	D2	113
San Miguel, co., N.M., U.S.	B5	138
San Miguel, stm., Bol.	F10	82
San Miguel (Cuilco), stm., N.A.	B2	92
San Miguel, stm., S.A.	H11	82
San Miguel, stm., Co., U.S.	C2	113
San Miguel, Cerro, hill, Bol.	H11	82
San Miguel, Golfo de, b., Pan.	C3	84
San Miguel, Volcán de, vol., El Sal.	D6	92
San Miguel de Allende, Mex.	G9	90
San Miguel de Cruces, Mex.	E7	90
San Miguel del Monte, Arg.	H9	80
San Miguel de Pallaques, Peru	B2	82
San Miguel de Salcedo, Ec.	H3	84
San Miguel de Tucumán, Arg.	D6	80
San Miguel el Alto, Mex.	G8	90
San Miguel Island, i., Ca., U.S.	E3	112
San Miguelito, Nic.	F10	92
San Miguel Ixtahuacán, Guat.	B3	92
San Miguel Mountains, mts., Co., U.S.	D2	113
San Miniato, Italy	F5	18
Sannār, Sud.	K7	60
Sannicandro Garganico, Italy	H10	18
San Nicolás, Hond.	B6	92
San Nicolás, Peru	F4	82
San Nicolás, Spain	P25	17b
San Nicolás, stm., Mex.	H7	90
San Nicolás de los Arroyos, Arg.	G8	80
San Nicolás de los Garza, Mex.	E9	90
San Nicolas Island, i., Ca., U.S.	F4	112
Sannikova, proliv, strt., U.S.S.R.	C20	24
Sanniquellie, Lib.	H5	64
Sano, Japan	K14	36
Sañogasta, Arg.	E5	80
Sanok, Pol.	F22	10
San Onofre, Col.	C5	84
San Pablo, Col.	G4	84
San Pablo, Phil.	N19	39b
San Pablo, Ca., U.S.	h8	112
San Pablo, Co., U.S.	D5	113
San Pablo, stm., Bol.	F10	82
San Pablo, stm., Pan.	I13	92
San Pablo Bay, b., Ca., U.S.	g8	112
San Pablo de Tiquina, Bol.	G7	82
San Patricio, N.M., U.S.	D4	138
San Patricio, co., Tx., U.S.	E4	150
San Patricio, Bayou, stm., La., U.S.	C2	125
San Pedro, Arg.	C6	80
San Pedro, Arg.	G9	80
San Pedro, Arg.	D6	80
San Pedro, Bol.	F9	82
San Pedro, Chile	A4	80
San Pedro, Chile	G3	80
San Pedro, Col.	C5	84
San Pedro, C.R.	H10	92
San Pédro, I.C.	I6	64
San Pedro, Para.	C10	80
San Pedro, Ven.	C7	84
San Pedro, dept., Para.	C10	80
San Pedro, stm., Mex.	B5	90
San Pedro, stm., N.A.	I14	90
San Pedro, stm., Az., U.S.	E5	110
San Pedro, Punta, c., Chile	C3	80
San Pedro, Volcán, vol., Chile	A4	80
San Pedro Ayampuc, Guat.	C4	92
San Pedro Bay, b., Ca., U.S.	n12	112
San Pedro Carchá, Guat.	B4	92
San Pedro de Atacama, Chile	B4	80
San Pedro de Buena Vista, Bol.	H9	82
San Pedro de la Cueva, Mex.	C5	90
San Pedro de las Colonias, Mex.	E8	90
San Pedro del Gallo, Mex.	E7	90
San Pedro de Lloc, Peru	B2	82
San Pedro del Norte, Nic.	D10	92
San Pedro del Paraná, Para.	D10	80
San Pedro de Macorís, Dom. Rep.	E10	94
San Pedro Peaks, mts., N.M., U.S.	A3	138
San Pedro Pinula, Guat.	C5	92
San Pedro Pochutla, Mex.	J11	90
San Pedro Sacatepéquez, Guat.	C3	92
San Pedro Sula, Hond.	B6	92
San Pedro Tabasco, Mex.	I14	90
San Pelayo, Col.	C5	84
Sanpete, co., Ut., U.S.	D4	151
San Pierre, In., U.S.	B4	121
San Pitch Mountains, mts., Ut., U.S.	D4	151
Sanpoil, stm., Wa., U.S.	A7	154
Sanpoil, West Fork, stm., Wa., U.S.	A7	154
San Quintín, Cabo, c., Mex.	B1	90
San Rafael, Arg.	H4	80
San Rafael, Chile	H3	80
San Rafael, Mex.	E9	90
San Rafael, Ca., U.S.	D2	112
San Rafael, N.M., U.S.	B2	138
San Rafael, Ven.	B7	84
San Rafael, stm., Bol.	H12	82
San Rafael, stm., Ut., U.S.	D5	151
San Rafael del Norte, Nic.	D8	92
San Rafael del Sur, Nic.	F8	92
San Rafael Desert, des., Ut., U.S.	E5	151
San Rafael Knob, mtn., Ut., U.S.	E5	151
San Rafael Mountains, mts., Ca., U.S.	E4	112
San Rafael Oriente, El Sal.	D6	92
San Rafael Swell, plat., Ut., U.S.	E5	151
San Rafael Tasajera, El Sal.	D6	92
San Ramón, Arg.	D6	80
San Ramón, Bol.	E9	82
San Ramón, C.R.	G10	92
San Ramón, Hond.	C10	92
San Ramón, Peru	D4	82
San Ramon, Ca., U.S.	h9	112
San Ramón, Ur.	H11	80
San Ramón de la Nueva Orán, Arg.	B6	80
Sanrao, China	L5	34
San Remo, Italy	F2	18
San Román, stm., Guat.	A4	92
San Román, Cabo, c., Ven.	A7	84
San Roque, Arg.	E9	80
San Roque, Arg.	F4	80
San Roque, Spain	I6	16
San Roque, Punta, c., Mex.	D2	90
San Rosendo, Chile	I2	80
San Saba, Tx., U.S.	D3	150
San Saba, co., Tx., U.S.	D3	150
San Salvador, Arg.	E10	80
San Salvador, Arg.	F9	80
San Salvador, El Sal.	D5	92
San Salvador (Watling Island), i., Bah.	B7	94
San Salvador, Isla, i., Ec.	J13	84a
San Salvador, Volcán de, vol., El Sal.	D5	92
San Salvador de Jujuy, Arg.	C6	80
Sansanné-Mango, Togo	F10	64
Sans Bois Mountains, mts., Ok., U.S.	B6	143
San Sebastián, El Sal.	D6	92
San Sebastián, Guat.	C3	92
San Sebastián, Hond.	C6	92
San Sebastián de la Gomera, Spain	O23	17b
San Sebastián de Yalí, Nic.	D8	92
Sansepolcro, Italy	F7	18
San Severo, Italy	H10	18
Sanshui, China	L1	34
San Simon, Az., U.S.	E6	110
San Simón, stm., Bol.	E10	82
San Simon, stm., Az., U.S.	E6	110
Sanso, Mali	F6	64
San Solano, Arg.	F6	80
Sans-Souci, hist., Haiti	E8	94
Santa, Peru	C2	82
Santa, Id., U.S.	B2	119
Santa, stm., Peru	C2	82
Santa, Isla de, i., Peru	C2	82
Santa Adélia, Braz.	F4	79
Santa Albertina, Braz.	F3	79
Santa Ana, Arg.	D11	80
Santa Ana, Bol.	H12	82
Santa Ana, Bol.	F8	82
Santa Ana, Bol.	E9	82
Santa Ana, Col.	C5	84
Santa Ana, Ec.	H2	84
Santa Ana, El Sal.	D5	92
Santa Ana, Mex.	E9	90
Santa Ana, Mex.	B4	90
Santa Ana, Ca., U.S.	F5	112
Santa Ana, Ven.	C10	84
Santa Ana, stm., Ca., U.S.	n13	112
Santa Ana, Volcán de, vol., El Sal.	D5	92
Santa Ana Indian Reservation, N.M., U.S.	h7	138
Santa Ana Mountains, mts., Ca., U.S.	n13	112
Santa Ana Pueblo, N.M., U.S.	B3	138
Santa Anna, Tx., U.S.	D3	150
Santa Bábara, Braz.	A9	79
Santa Bárbara, Chile	I2	80
Santa Bárbara, Col.	E5	84
Santa Bárbara, Hond.	C6	92
Santa Bárbara, Mex.	D7	90
Santa Barbara, Ca., U.S.	E4	112
Santa Bárbara, Ven.	F9	84
Santa Bárbara, Ven.	D7	84
Santa Bárbara, dept., Hond.	B6	92
Santa Barbara, co., Ca., U.S.	E3	112
Santa Bárbara, stm., Bol.	G11	82
Santa Barbara Channel, strt., Ca., U.S.	E3	112
Santa Bárbara do Sul, Braz.	E12	80
Santa Barbara Island, i., Ca., U.S.	F4	112
Santa Branca, Braz.	G6	79
Santa Catalina, Arg.	A5	80
Santa Catalina, Gulf of, b., Ca., U.S.	F5	112
Santa Catalina, Isla, i., Mex.	E4	90
Santa Catalina Island, i., Ca., U.S.	F4	112
Santa Catalina Mountains, mts., Az., U.S.	E5	110
Santa Catalina o Calovébora, Pan.	I13	92
Santa Catarina, Mex.	E9	90
Santa Catarina, state, Braz.	D13	80
Santa Catarina, Ilha de, i., Braz.	D14	80
Santa Cecília, Braz.	D13	80
Santa Clara, Arg.	E4	80
Santa Clara, Col.	I8	84
Santa Clara, Cuba	C5	94
Santa Clara, Mex.	C6	90
Santa Clara, Ca., U.S.	D2	112
Santa Clara, Ut., U.S.	F2	151
Santa Clara, co., Ca., U.S.	D3	112
Santa Clara, stm., Ca., U.S.	E4	112
Santa Clara de Olimar, Ur.	G11	80
Santa Claus, In., U.S.	H4	121
Santa Clotilde, Peru	I6	84
Santa Coloma de Farners, Spain	D14	16
Santa Comba Dão, Port.	E3	16
Santa Cruz, Arg.	G3	78
Santa Cruz, Bol.	G10	82
Santa Cruz, Braz.	E8	79
Santa Cruz, Chile	H3	80
Santa Cruz, C.R.	G9	92
Santa Cruz, Peru	B2	82
Santa Cruz, Phil.	N19	39b
Santa Cruz, Phil.	O20	39b
Santa Cruz, Port.	M21	17a
Santa Cruz, Ca., U.S.	D2	112
Santa Cruz, N.M., U.S.	B3	138
Santa Cruz, Ven.	C7	84
Santa Cruz, dept., Bol.	G11	82
Santa Cruz, co., Az., U.S.	F5	110
Santa Cruz, co., Ca., U.S.	D2	112
Santa Cruz, stm., Arg.	G2	78
Santa Cruz, stm., Az., U.S.	E4	110
Santa Cruz, Isla, i., Ec.	J13	84a
Santa Cruz, Sierra de, mts., Guat.	B5	92
Santa Cruz Cabrália, Braz.	D9	79
Santa Cruz da Vitória, Braz.	C9	79
Santa Cruz de Goiás, Braz.	D4	79
Santa Cruz de la Palma, Spain	O23	17b
Santa Cruz del Quiché, Guat.	B3	92
Santa Cruz del Sur, Cuba	D5	94
Santa Cruz de Tenerife, Spain	O24	17b
Santa Cruz de Tenerife, prov., Spain	O23	17b
Santa Cruz do Rio Pardo, Braz.	G4	79
Santa Cruz do Sul, Braz.	E12	80
Santa Cruz Island, i., Ca., U.S.	F4	112
Santa Cruz Islands, is., Sol.Is.	J20	158
Santa Elena, Arg.	F9	80
Santa Elena, Ec.	I2	84
Santa Elena, El Sal.	D6	92
Santa Elena, Mex.	D8	90
Santa Elena, stm., Bol.	G8	82
Santa Elena, Bahía de, b., Ec.	I2	84
Santa Elena, Golfo de, b., C.R.	G9	92
Santa Elena, Punta, c., C.R.	G9	92
Santa Elena, Punta, c., Ec.	I2	84
Santa Elena de Uairén, Ven.	E12	84
Santa Eugenia, Spain	C2	16
Santa Eulalia, Guat.	B3	92
Santa Eulària del Riu, Spain	G13	16
Santa Fe, Arg.	F8	80
Santa Fé, Braz.	C3	79
Santa Fé, Braz.	G3	79
Santa Fe, Hond.	B8	92
Santa Fé, Pan.	I13	92
Santa Fe, Spain	H8	16
Santa Fe, N.M., U.S.	B4	138
Santa Fe, Tn., U.S.	B4	149
Santa Fe, Tx., U.S.	r14	150
Santa Fe, prov., Arg.	F8	80
Santa Fe, co., N.M., U.S.	B3	138
Santa Fe, stm., N.M., U.S.	h8	138
Santa Fe Baldy, mtn., N.M., U.S.	B4	138
Santa Fé do Sul, Braz.	F3	79
Santa Filomena, Braz.	E9	76
Santa Helena de Goiás, Braz.	D3	79
Santai, China	E8	30
Santa Inês, Braz.	B9	79
Santa Inés, Bahía, b., Mex.	D4	90
Santa Inés, Isla, i., Chile	G2	78
Santa Isabel, Arg.	I5	80
Santa Isabel, Arg.	G8	80
Santa Isabel, Ec.	I3	84
Santa Isabel, i., Sol.Is.	I19	158
Santa Isabel, stm., Guat.	B5	92
Santa Isabel de Sihuas, Peru	G5	82
Santa Juliana, Braz.	E5	79
Santa Leopoldina, Braz.	F8	79
Santa Lucía, Arg.	E9	80
Santa Lucía, Arg.	F4	80
Santa Lucía, Cuba	D6	94
Santa Lucía, Ur.	H10	80
Santa Lucía, Ven.	C8	84
Santa Lucía Cotzumalguapa, Guat.	C3	92
Santa Lucia Range, mts., Ca., U.S.	E3	112
Santa Luzia, i., C.V.	E2	54
Santa Magdalena, Arg.	H7	80
Santa Margarita, Ca., U.S.	E3	112
Santa Margarita, Isla, i., Mex.	E4	90
Santa Margherita Ligure, Italy	E4	18
Santa María, Arg.	D5	80
Santa Maria, Braz.	E12	80
Santa Maria, C.V.	k17	64a
Santa María, C.R.	H11	92
Santa María, Pan.	I14	92
Santa Maria, Switz.	E13	13
Santa Maria, Switz.	F11	13
Santa Maria, Ca., U.S.	E3	112
Santa Maria, stm., Braz.	F11	80
Santa Maria, stm., Braz.	A11	80
Santa María, stm., Mex.	G10	90
Santa María, stm., Mex.	B6	90
Santa María, stm., Pan.	I14	92
Santa Maria, stm., Az., U.S.	C2	110
Santa María, Bahía, b., Mex.	E5	90
Santa María, Cabo, c., Ur.	H11	80
Santa Maria, Cabo de, c., Ang.	D2	58
Santa Maria, Cape, c., Bah.	C7	94
Santa María, Isla, i., Chile	I2	80
Santa María, Isla, i., Ec.	J13	84a
Santa María, Laguna, l., Mex.	B6	90
Santa María, Volcán, vol., Guat.	C3	92
Santa Maria Asunción Tlaxiaco, Mex.	I11	90
Santa Maria Capua Vetere, Italy	H9	18
Santa María Colotepec, Mex.	J11	90
Santa Maria da Vitória, Braz.	B6	79
Santa María de Huazamota, Mex.	F7	90
Santa María de Ipire, Ven.	C10	84
Santa Maria de Itabira, Braz.	E7	79
Santa María del Oro, Mex.	E7	90
Santa María del Río, Mex.	G9	90
Santa Mariá de Mohovano, Mex.	D8	90
Santa Maria di Leuca, Capo, c., Italy	J13	18
Santa Maria do Suaçuí, Braz.	E7	79
Santa Maria Madalena, Braz.	F7	79
Santa Maria Mountains, mts., Az., U.S.	C3	110
Santa-Maria-Siché, Fr.	M23	15a
Santa Marinella, Italy	G6	18
Santa Marta, Col.	B5	84
Santa Marta, Guat.	D3	92
Santa Marta, Cerro, mtn., Mex.	H12	90
Santa Marta Grande, Cabo de, c., Braz.	E14	80
Santa Monica, Ca., U.S.	m12	112
Santan, Az., U.S.	m9	110
Santana, Braz.	B6	79
Santana, Port.	M21	17a
Santana, stm., Braz.	E3	79
Santana, Cachoeira, wtfl, Braz.	C4	79
Santana, Coxilha de, hills, S.A.	F11	80
Santana da Boa Vista, Braz.	F12	80
Santana do Livramento, Braz.	F11	80
Santander, Col.	F4	84
Santander, Spain	B8	16
Santander, dept., Col.	D6	84
Santander, Norte de, state, Col.	J8	94
Santander Jiménez, Mex.	E10	90
Santanilla, Islas, is., Hond.	F3	94
Santanoni Peak, mtn., N.Y., U.S.	A6	139
Sant Antoni de Portmany, Spain	G13	16
Santa Paula, Ca., U.S.	E4	112
Santaquin, Ut., U.S.	D4	151
Santarém, Braz.	D8	76
Santarém, Port.	F3	16
Santaren Channel, strt., Bah.	C5	94
Santa Rita, Col.	G6	84
Santa Rita, Hond.	B7	92
Santa Rita, Mex.	C4	90
Santa Rita, Mt., U.S.	B4	133
Santa Rita, Ven.	B7	84
Santa Rita, Riacho, stm., Braz.	B7	79
Santa Rita de Catuna, Arg.	F5	80
Santa Rita do Araguaia, Braz.	D2	79
Santa Rita do Weil, Braz.	I8	84
Santa Rosa, Arg.	E5	80
Santa Rosa, Arg.	I6	80
Santa Rosa, Arg.	B6	80
Santa Rosa, Arg.	G6	80
Santa Rosa, Bol.	F8	82
Santa Rosa, Bol.	D8	82
Santa Rosa, Bol.	G10	82
Santa Rosa, Braz.	B6	78
Santa Rosa, Braz.	C5	79
Santa Rosa, Braz.	D11	80
Santa Rosa, Col.	F8	84
Santa Rosa, C.R.	G9	92
Santa Rosa, Ec.	I3	84
Santa Rosa, Para.	D10	80
Santa Rosa, Para.	I11	82
Santa Rosa, Ca., U.S.	C2	112
Santa Rosa, N.M., U.S.	C5	138
Santa Rosa, Ven.	C8	84
Santa Rosa, dept., Guat.	C4	92
Santa Rosa, co., Fl., U.S.	u14	116
Santa Rosa, Parque Nacional, C.R.	G9	92
Santa Rosa Beach, Fl., U.S.	u15	116
Santa Rosa de Aguán, Hond.	B9	92
Santa Rosa de Amanadona, Ven.	G9	84
Santa Rosa de Cabal, Col.	E5	84
Santa Rosa [de Copán], Hond.	C6	92
Santa Rosa de la Roca, Bol.	G11	82
Santa Rosa de Leales, Arg.	D6	80
Santa Rosa de Lima, El Sal.	D7	92
Santa Rosa del Palmar, Bol.	G10	82
Santa Rosa de Osos, Col.	D5	84
Santa Rosa de Río Primero, Arg.	F7	80
Santa Rosa de Sucumbíos, Ec.	G4	84
Santa Rosa de Viterbo, Col.	E6	84
Santa Rosa Island, i., Ca., U.S.	F3	112
Santa Rosa Island, i., Fl., U.S.	u14	116
Santa Rosalía, Mex.	D3	90
Santa Rosalía, Ven.	C8	84
Santa Rosa Range, mts., Nv., U.S.	B4	135
Šantarskije ostrova, is., U.S.S.R.	F19	24
Santa Sylvina, Arg.	D8	80
Santa Teresa, Arg.	G8	80
Santa Teresa, Braz.	E8	79
Santa Teresa, Mex.	E11	90
Santa Teresa, N.M., U.S.	F3	138
Santa Teresa, stm., Braz.	B4	79
Santa Teresa, Embalse de, res., Spain	E6	16
Santa Teresa de Goiás, Braz.	B4	79
Santa Teresa del Tuy, Ven.	B9	84
Santa Teresinha, Braz.	B9	79
Santa Vitória, Braz.	E3	79
Santa Vitória do Palmar, Braz.	G12	80
Santa Ynez, Ca., U.S.	E3	112
Sant Carles de la Ràpita, Spain	E12	16
Santee, Ca., U.S.	o16	112
Santee, Ne., U.S.	B8	134
Santee, stm., S.C., U.S.	E8	147
Santee Dam, S.C., U.S.	E7	147
Santee Indian Reservation, Ne., U.S.	B8	134
Sant Feliu de Guíxols, Spain	D15	16
Santhià, Italy	D3	18
Santiago, Bol.	H12	82
Santiago, Braz.	E11	80
Santiago, Chile	G3	80
Santiago, Mex.	F5	90
Santiago, Pan.	C2	84
Santiago, Para.	D10	80
Santiago, Peru	F4	82
Santiago, i., C.V.	G4	52
Santiago, i., C.V.	m17	64a
Santiago, stm., Mex.	E7	90
Santiago, stm., S.A.	I4	84
Santiago, Cerro, mtn., Pan.	I13	92
Santiago, Serranía de, mts., Bol.	H12	82
Santiago Atitlán, Guat.	C3	92
Santiago Choapan, Mex.	I12	90
Santiago de Cao, Peru	B2	82
Santiago de Chocorvos, Peru	E4	82
Santiago de Chuco, Peru	C2	82
Santiago de Compostela, Spain	C3	16
Santiago de Cuba, Cuba	D7	94
Santiago de Huata, Bol.	G7	82
Santiago del Estero, Arg.	D6	80
Santiago del Estero, prov., Arg.	E7	80
Santiago [de los Caballeros], Dom. Rep.	E9	94
Santiago de Machaca, Bol.	G7	82
Santiago Ixcuintla, Mex.	G7	90
Santiago Jamiltepec, Mex.	I11	90
Santiago Larre, Arg.	H9	80
Santiago Papasquiaro, Mex.	E7	90
Santiago Peak, mtn., Ca., U.S.	n13	112
Santiago Reservoir, res., Ca., U.S.	n13	112
Santiaguillo, Laguna, l., Mex.	E7	90
Santiam Pass, Or., U.S.	C4	144
San Timoteo, Ven.	C7	84
Säntis, mtn., Switz.	D11	13
Sant Jordi, Golf de, b., Spain	E13	16
Santo, Tx., U.S.	B3	150
Santo Amaro, Braz.	B9	79
Santo Anastácio, Braz.	F3	79
Santo Anastácio, stm., Braz.	G3	79
Santo André, Braz.	G5	79
Santo Ângelo, Braz.	E11	80
Santo Antão, i., C.V.	k16	64a
Santo Antônio, Braz.	E13	80
Santo António, S. Tom./P.	A1	58
Santo Antônio, stm., Braz.	E6	79
Santo Antônio, Cachoeira, wtfl, Braz.	C11	82
Santo Antônio, Igarapé, stm., Braz.	H12	84
Santo Antônio da Boa Vista, Braz.	C6	79
Santo Antônio de Jesus, Braz.	B9	79

Name	Map Ref.	Page
Santo Antônio do Amparo, Braz.	F6	79
Santo Antônio do Içá, Braz.	I9	84
Santo Antônio do Leverger, Braz.	F13	82
Santo Antônio do Rio Verde, Braz.	D5	79
Santo Antônio do Sudoeste, Braz.	D12	80
Santo Augusto, Braz.	D12	80
Santo Corazón, Bol.	G12	82
Santo Cristo, Braz.	D11	80
Santo Domingo, Arg.	E7	80
Santo Domingo, Dom. Rep.	E10	94
Santo Domingo, Mex.	E3	90
Santo Domingo, Nic.	E9	92
Santo Domingo, stm., Mex.	A3	92
Santo Domingo de los Colorados, Ec.	H3	84
Santo Domingo Indian Reservation, N.M., U.S.	h8	138
Santo Domingo Pueblo, N.M., U.S.	B3	138
Santo Domingo Tehuantepec, Mex.	I12	90
Santo Domingo Zanatepec, Mex.	I12	90
Santo Estevão, Braz.	B9	79
San Tomé, Ven.	C10	84
Santoña, Spain	B8	16
Santo Onofre, stm., Braz.	B7	79
Santorini see Thíra, i., Grc.	M9	20
Santos, Braz.	G5	79
Santos Dumont, Braz.	F7	79
Santos Tomás del Norte, Nic.	D8	92
Santo Tomás, Col.	B5	84
Santo Tomás, Mex.	B1	90
Santo Tomás, Nic.	E9	92
Santo Tomás, Peru	B3	82
Santo Tomás, Peru	F5	82
Santo Tomás, Ven.	C10	84
Santo Tomás, stm., Peru	F5	82
Santo Tomás, Punta, c., Mex.	B1	90
Santo Tomé, Arg.	E10	80
Santo Tomé, Arg.	F8	80
Santunying, China	C6	32
San Ubaldo, Nic.	F9	92
San Valentín, Cerro, mtn., Chile	F2	78
San Vicente, Arg.	E6	80
San Vicente, El Sal.	D6	92
San Vicente, Volcán de, vol., El Sal.	D6	92
San Vicente de Cañete, Peru	E3	82
San Vicente de Chucurí, Col.	D6	84
San Vicente del Caguán, Col.	F5	84
San Vicente de Tagua-Tagua, Chile	H3	80
San Vicente Reservoir, res., Ca., U.S.	o16	112
San Vincenzo, Italy	F5	18
San Vito, C.R.	I12	92
San Vito, Italy	J4	18
San Vito dei Normanni, Italy	I12	18
San Xavier Indian Reservation, Az., U.S.	E4	110
San Ygnacio, Tx., U.S.	F3	150
San Ysidro, N.M., U.S.	B3	138
Sanyuan, China	E8	30
Sanza Pombo, Ang.	C3	58
Sanzha, China	B2	32
São Benedito, stm., Braz.	C13	82
São Bento, Braz.	D10	76
São Bento, Braz.	F12	84
São Bento do Sul, Braz.	D14	80
São Borja, Braz.	E10	80
São Caetano do Sul, Braz.	G5	79
São Carlos, Braz.	G5	79
São Carlos, Braz.	D12	80
São Cristóvão, Braz.	F11	76
São Domingos, Braz.	B5	79
São Domingos, Braz.	D12	80
São Domingos, Gui.-B.	E1	64
São Domingos, stm., Braz.	B5	79
São Domingos, stm., Braz.	E3	79
São Domingos, stm., Braz.	E2	79
São Domingos, stm., Braz.	E9	82
São Filipe, Braz.	C8	79
São Filipe, C.V.	m16	64a
São Francisco, Braz.	C6	79
São Francisco, stm., Braz.	E11	76
São Francisco, stm., Braz.	B7	79
São Francisco, stm., Braz.	C8	79
São Francisco, Baía de, b., Braz.	D14	80
São Francisco, Ilha de, i., Braz.	D14	80
São Francisco de Assis, Braz.	E11	80
São Francisco de Goiás, Braz.	C4	79
São Francisco de Paula, Braz.	E13	80
São Francisco do Sul, Braz.	D14	80
São Gabriel, Braz.	F11	80
São Gabriel da Palha, Braz.	E8	79
São Gabriel de Goiás, Braz.	C5	79
São Gonçalo do Abaeté, Braz.	E6	79
São Gonçalo do Pará, Braz.	E6	79
São Gonçalo do Sapucaí, Braz.	F6	79
São Gonçalo dos Campos, Braz.	B9	79
Sao Hill, Tan.	C7	58
São Jerônimo, Braz.	E13	80
São Jerônimo, Serra de, plat., Braz.	D1	79
São Jerônimo da Serra, Braz.	G3	79
São João, stm., Braz.	B3	79
São João da Aliança, Braz.	C5	79
São João da Barra, Braz.	F8	79
São João da Boa Vista, Braz.	F5	79
São João da Madeira, Port.	E3	16
São João da Ponte, Braz.	C6	79
São João del Rei, Braz.	F6	79
São João do Araguaia, Braz.	E9	76
São João do Caiuá, Braz.	G2	79
São João do Paraíso, Braz.	C7	79
São João do Triunfo, Braz.	C13	80
São João Evangelista, Braz.	E7	79
São Joaquim, Braz.	E14	80
São Joaquim, Parque Nacional de, Braz.	E14	80
São Joaquim da Barra, Braz.	F5	79
São Jorge, Braz.	G2	79
São José, Braz.	D14	80
São José, stm., Braz.	E8	79
São José de Anauá, Braz.	G12	84
São José do Calçado, Braz.	F8	79
São José do Cedro, Braz.	D12	80
São José do Goiabal, Braz.	E7	79
São José do Norte, Braz.	G12	80
São José do Rio Prêto, Braz.	F4	79
São José dos Campos, Braz.	G6	79
São José dos Pinhais, Braz.	C14	80
São Leopoldo, Braz.	E13	80
São Lourenço, Braz.	G6	79
São Lourenço, stm., Braz.	G14	82
São Lourenço, Pantanal de, sw., Braz.	G13	82
São Lourenço d'Oeste, Braz.	D12	80
São Lourenço do Sul, Braz.	F13	80
São Luís, Braz.	D10	76
São Luís de Montes Belos, Braz.	D3	79
São Luís do Tocantins, Braz.	C5	79
São Luís Gonzaga, Braz.	E11	80
São Manuel, Braz.	G4	79
São Manuel, stm., Braz.	C13	82
São Marcos, stm., Braz.	D5	79
São Mateus, Braz.	E9	79
São Mateus, stm., Braz.	B5	79
São Mateus, Braço Norte, stm., Braz.	E8	79
São Mateus, Braço Sul, stm., Braz.	E8	79
São Mateus do Sul, Braz.	C13	80
São Miguel, i., Port.	m21	62a
São Miguel, stm., Braz.	D8	79
São Miguel do Anta, Braz.	F7	79
São Miguel do Araguaia, Braz.	B3	79
São Miguel d'Oeste, Braz.	D12	80
Saona, Isla, i., Dom. Rep.	E10	94
Saône, stm., Fr.	F11	14
Saône-et-Loire, dept., Fr.	F11	14
São Nicolau, i., C.V.	k16	64a
São Paulo, Braz.	G5	79
São Paulo, state, Braz.	G4	79
São Paulo de Olivença, Braz.	I8	84
São Pedro, Braz.	E3	79
São Pedro, stm., Braz.	D8	79
São Pedro do Ivaí, Braz.	G3	79
São Pedro do Sul, Braz.	E11	80
São Pedro do Sul, Port.	E3	16
São Raimundo Nonato, Braz.	E10	76
São Romão, Braz.	D6	79
São Roque, Braz.	G5	79
São Roque, Cabo de, c., Braz.	E11	76
São Roque do Paraguaçu, Braz.	B9	79
São Sebastião, Braz.	G6	79
São Sebastião, Ilha de, i., Braz.	G6	79
São Sebastião, Ponta, c., Moz.	D12	66
São Sebastião do Maranhão, Braz.	E7	79
São Sebastião do Paraíso, Braz.	F5	79
São Sebastião do Rio Claro, Braz.	C3	79
São Sepé, Braz.	F12	80
São Simão, Braz.	E3	79
São Simão, Braz.	F5	79
São Simão, stm., Braz.	E10	82
São Tiago, Braz.	F6	79
São Timóteo, Braz.	B7	79
São Tomé, S. Tom./P.	A1	58
São Tomé, i., S. Tom./P.	A1	58
São Tomé, stm., Braz.	C13	82
São Tomé, Cabo de, c., Braz.	F8	79
Sao Tome and Principe (São Tomé e Príncipe), ctry., Afr.	A1	58
Saoura, Oued, val., Alg.	F10	62
São Valério, stm., Braz.	A4	79
São Vicente, Braz.	G5	79
São Vicente, i., C.V.	k16	64a
São Vicente, Cabo de (Cape Saint Vincent), c., Port.	H2	16
São Vicente de Minas, Braz.	F6	79
Sapallanga, Peru	E4	82
Sapé, Braz.	E11	76
Sapeaçu, Braz.	B9	79
Sapele, Nig.	I12	64
Sapello, N.M., U.S.	B4	138
Sapelo Island, i., Ga., U.S.	E5	117
Sapelo Sound, strt., Ga., U.S.	E5	117
Şaphane, Tur.	J13	20
Sapitwa, mtn., Mwi.	E7	58
Šapki, U.S.S.R.	B14	26
Sa Pobla, Spain	F15	16
Sapodilla Cays, i., Belize	A6	92
Saponé, Burkina	E9	64
Saposoa, Peru	B3	82
Sapožok, U.S.S.R.	H23	26
Sappa Creek, stm., U.S.	E5	134
Sappa Creek, Middle Fork, stm., Ks., U.S.	C2	123
Sappa Creek, South Fork, stm., Ks., U.S.	C3	123
Sapphire Mountains, mts., Mt., U.S.	D3	133
Sapporo, Japan	D16	36a
Sapri, Italy	I10	18
Saptakoší, stm., Nepal	G12	44
Sapucaia, Braz.	G7	79
Sapulpa, Ok., U.S.	B5	143
Sāqiat al-'Abd, Sud.	G6	60
Saqqez, Iran	C9	48
Saquarema, Braz.	G7	79
Saquena, Peru	A5	82
Saquisilí, Ec.	H3	84
Sarāb, Iran	C9	48
Saraburi, Thai.	G6	40
Saracura, stm., Braz.	B8	79
Saragossa, Al., U.S.	B2	108
Saragossa see Zaragoza, Spain	D11	16
Saraguro, Ec.	I3	84
Sarah, Ms., U.S.	A3	131
Sarai, U.S.S.R.	H24	26
Sarajevo, Yugo.	F2	20
Sarakhs, Iran	C16	48
Saraland, Al., U.S.	E1	108
Saramacca, dept., Sur.	E14	84
Saran', U.S.S.R.	H12	22
Saranac, Mi., U.S.	F5	129
Saranac, stm., N.Y., U.S.	F11	139
Saranac Lake, N.Y., U.S.	f10	139
Saranac Lakes, l., N.Y., U.S.	f10	139
Sarandi, Braz.	D12	80
Sarandí del Yi, Ur.	G11	80
Sarandí Grande, Ur.	G10	80
Saransk, U.S.S.R.	G7	22
Sarapiquí, stm., C.R.	G11	92
Sarapul, U.S.S.R.	F8	22
Sarare, Ven.	C8	84
Sara Sara, Nevado, mtn., Peru	F5	82
Sarasota, Fl., U.S.	E4	116
Sarasota, co., Fl., U.S.	E4	116
Sarasota Bay, b., Fl., U.S.	E4	116
Sarata, U.S.S.R.	C13	20
Saratoga, Ar., U.S.	D2	111
Saratoga, Ca., U.S.	k8	112
Saratoga, In., U.S.	D8	121
Saratoga, Tx., U.S.	D5	150
Saratoga, Wy., U.S.	E6	157
Saratoga, co., N.Y., U.S.	B7	139
Saratoga Lake, l., N.Y., U.S.	C7	139
Saratoga National Historical Park, N.Y., U.S.	B7	139
Saratoga Springs, N.Y., U.S.	B7	139
Saratov, U.S.S.R.	G7	22
Saratovskoje vodochranilišče, res., U.S.S.R.	G7	22
Sararcu, mtn., Ec.	H4	84
Saravan, Laos	G9	40
Saraya, Gui.	F4	64
Sarayköy, Tur.	L12	20
Sarbāz, Iran	H16	48
Sárbogárd, Hung.	I18	10
Sarcoxie, Mo., U.S.	D3	132
Sārda (Mahākālī), stm., Asia	F9	44
Sardārshahr, India	F6	44
Sardegna, prov., Italy	I4	18
Sardegna (Sardinia), i., Italy	I4	18
Sardina, Col.	F9	84
Sardinal, C.R.	G9	92
Sardinata, Col.	C6	84
Sardinia, In., U.S.	F6	121
Sardinia, Oh., U.S.	C2	142
Sardinia see Sardegna, i., Italy	I4	18
Sardis, Al., U.S.	C2	108
Sardis, Ga., U.S.	D5	117
Sardis, Ky., U.S.	B6	124
Sardis, Ms., U.S.	A4	131
Sardis, Oh., U.S.	C5	142
Sardis, Ok., U.S.	C6	143
Sardis, Tn., U.S.	B3	149
Sardis Lake, res., Ms., U.S.	A4	131
Sar-e Pol, Afg.	B1	44
Sarepta, La., U.S.	B2	125
Sargans, Switz.	D11	13
Sargasso Sea	B8	74
Sargent, Ga., U.S.	C2	117
Sargent, Ne., U.S.	C6	134
Sargent, co., N.D., U.S.	C8	141
Sargodha, Pak.	D5	44
Sarh, Chad	G4	56
Sārī, Iran	C12	48
Saric, Mex.	B4	90
Şarif, Yemen	F7	47
Sarıkamış, Tur.	A7	48
Sarina, Austl.	C8	70
Sariñena, Spain	D11	16
Sarīr, Libya	D2	60
Sariwŏn, N. Kor.	E13	32
Šarja, U.S.S.R.	F7	22
Sark, i., Guernsey	L11	8
Sarkad, Hung.	I21	10
Şarkışla, Tur.	B4	48
Šarkovščina, U.S.S.R.	F10	26
Şarköy, Tur.	I11	20
Šarlauk, U.S.S.R.	B13	48
Sarles, N.D., U.S.	A6	141
Sármellék, Hung.	I17	10
Sarmiento, Cerro, mtn., Chile	G2	78
Särna, Swe.	K13	6
Sarnen, Switz.	E9	13
Sarnia, Ont., Can.	E2	103
Sarno, Italy	I9	18
Saron, S. Afr.	I4	66
Saronikós Kólpos, b., Grc.	L7	20
Saronno, Italy	D4	18
Sárospatak, Hung.	G21	10
Sarpsborg, Nor.	L12	6
Sarpy, co., Ne., U.S.	C9	134
Sarralbe, Fr.	C14	14
Sarrebourg, Fr.	D14	14
Sarreguemines, Fr.	C14	14
Sarre-Union, Fr.	D14	14
Sarro, Mali	E7	64
Sarsfield, Ont., Can.	h13	103
Sarstoon (Sarstún), stm., N.A.	B5	92
Sarstún (Sarstoon), stm., N.A.	B5	92
Sartang, stm., U.S.S.R.	D18	24
Sartell, Mn., U.S.	E4	130
Sartène, Fr.	H3	18
Sarthe, dept., Fr.	D7	14
Sartilly, Fr.	D5	14
Saruhanlı, Tur.	K11	20
Sarūr, Oman	C11	47
Sárvár, Hung.	H16	10
Sarvestān, Iran	G12	48
Saryg-Sep, U.S.S.R.	G17	22
Sarykol'skij chrebet, mts., Asia	A6	44
Saryozek, U.S.S.R.	I13	22
Sarysu, stm., U.S.S.R.	H11	22
Sary-Taš, U.S.S.R.	J12	22
Sarzana, Italy	E4	18
Sāsarām, India	H11	44
Sásd, Hung.	I18	10
Sasebo, Japan	N4	36
Saskatchewan, prov., Can.	E3	105
Saskatchewan, stm., Can.	F12	96
Saskatoon, Sask., Can.	E2	105
Saslaya, Cerro, mtn., Nic.	H2	94
Sasolburg, S. Afr.	F8	66
Sasovo, U.S.S.R.	G24	26
Sassafras, stm., Md., U.S.	B5	127
Sassafras Mountain, mtn., U.S.	A2	147
Sassandra, I.C.	I6	64
Sassandra, stm., I.C.	I6	64
Sassari, Italy	I3	18
Sasser, Ga., U.S.	E2	117
Sassoferrato, Italy	F7	18
Sasso Marconi, Italy	E6	18
S'as'stroj, U.S.S.R.	A15	26
Sassuolo, Italy	E5	18
Sastown, Lib.	I5	64
Sastre, Arg.	F8	80
Sasyk, ozero, l., U.S.S.R.	D13	20
Satah Mountain, mtn., B.C., Can.	C5	99
Šatalovo, U.S.S.R.	G15	26
Sata-misaki, c., Japan	Q5	36
Satanta, Ks., U.S.	E3	123
Sātāra, India	D2	46
Satara, S. Afr.	E10	66
Satélite, Mex.	B6	90
Satilla, stm., Ga., U.S.	E5	117
Satipo, Peru	D4	82
Satīt (Tekeze), stm., Afr.	J9	60
Satka, U.S.S.R.	F9	22
Satna, India	H9	44
Sátoraljaújhely, Hung.	G21	10
Sātpura Range, mts., India	J7	44
Satsop, Wa., U.S.	B2	154
Satsuma, Al., U.S.	E1	108
Satsuma, Fl., U.S.	C5	116
Satsunan-shotō, is., Japan	R4	37b
Sattahip, Thai.	H6	40
Satthwa, Burma	F3	40
Satu Mare, Rom.	B6	20
Satu Mare, co., Rom.	B6	20
Şatun, Thai.	K6	40
Šatura, U.S.S.R.	F22	26
Saturna Island, i., B.C., Can.	E6	99
Saturnino M. Laspiur, Arg.	F7	80
Šāturtorf, U.S.S.R.	F22	26
Satus Creek, stm., Wa., U.S.	C5	154
Sauce, Arg.	F9	80
Sauce, Peru	B3	82
Sauce, Ur.	H10	80
Sauce Chico, stm., Arg.	J7	80
Sauce Corto, Arroyo, stm., Arg.	I8	80
Sauceda Mountains, mts., Az., U.S.	E3	110
Sauce Grande, stm., Arg.	J8	80
Saucier, Ms., U.S.	E4	131
Saucillo, Mex.	C7	90
Sauda, Nor.	L10	6
Saudi Arabia (Al-'Arabīyah as-Su'ūdīyah), ctry., Asia	D4	42
Sauer (Sûre), stm., Eur.	I10	12
Sauêruiná, stm., Braz.	E12	82
Sauêuiná, stm., Braz.	E12	82
Saufley Field Naval Air Station, mil., Fl., U.S.	u14	116
Saugatuck, Mi., U.S.	F4	129
Saugatuck, stm., Ct., U.S.	D2	114
Saugatucket, stm., R.I., U.S.	F4	146
Saugatuck Reservoir, res., Ct., U.S.	D2	114
Saugerties, N.Y., U.S.	C7	139
Saugus, Ma., U.S.	B5	128
Saugus, stm., Ma., U.S.	g11	128
Saujil, Arg.	E5	80
Sauk, co., Wi., U.S.	E4	156
Sauk, stm., Mn., U.S.	E4	130
Sauk, stm., Wa., U.S.	A4	154
Sauk Centre, Mn., U.S.	E4	130
Sauk City, Wi., U.S.	E4	156
Sauk Rapids, Mn., U.S.	E4	130
Saukville, Wi., U.S.	E6	156
Saül, Fr. Gu.	C8	76
Saulgau, Ger.	G9	10
Saulieu, Fr.	E11	14
Saulkrasti, U.S.S.R.	D7	26
Saulnierville, N.S., Can.	E3	101
Sault-au-Mouton, Que., Can.	A8	104
Sault Sainte Marie, Ont., Can.	p18	103
Sault Sainte Marie, Mi., U.S.	B6	129
Saumarez Reef, rf., Austl.	C10	70
Saumur, Fr.	E6	14
Saunders, co., Ne., U.S.	C9	134
Saunders Island, i., Falk. Is.	A2	73
Saunders Island, i., Falk. Is.	J12	74
Saunderstown, R.I., U.S.	E4	146
Saunemin, Il., U.S.	C5	120
Saurimo, Ang.	C4	58
Sausalito, Ca., U.S.	D2	112
Sauveterre-de-Béarn, Fr.	I6	14
Sauvo, Fin.	K18	6
Sava, Italy	I12	18
Sava, stm., Yugo.	F11	4
Savage, Md., U.S.	B4	127
Savage, Ms., U.S.	A3	131
Savage, Mt., U.S.	C12	133
Savage, stm., Md., U.S.	k12	127
Savage River Reservoir, res., Md., U.S.	k12	127
Savai'i, i., W. Sam.	J22	158
Savalou, Benin	H10	64
Savanna, Il., U.S.	A3	120
Savanna, Ok., U.S.	C6	143
Savannah, Ga., U.S.	D5	117
Savannah, Mo., U.S.	B3	132
Savannah, Tn., U.S.	B3	149
Savannah, stm., U.S.	F5	147
Savannah River Plant, sci., S.C., U.S.	E4	147
Savannakhét, Laos	F8	40
Savanna Lake, l., Md., U.S.	D6	127
Savanna-la-Mar, Jam.	E5	94
Savé, Benin	G11	64
Save (Sabi), stm., Afr.	C12	66
Sāveh, Iran	D11	48
Savelli, Italy	J11	18
Saverdun, Fr.	I8	14
Saverne, Fr.	D14	14
Savigliano, Italy	E2	18
Saville Dam, Ct., U.S.	B4	114
Savino, U.S.S.R.	E24	26
Savinskij, U.S.S.R.	J27	6
Šavnik, Yugo.	G3	20
Savognin, Switz.	E12	13
Savoie, dept., Fr.	G13	14
Savona, B.C., Can.	D7	99
Savona, Italy	E3	18
Savona, N.Y., U.S.	C3	139
Savoonga, Ak., U.S.	C5	109
Savoy, Il., U.S.	C5	120
Savran', U.S.S.R.	A14	20
Savu Sea see Sawu, Laut, Indon.	G7	38
Sawahlunto, Indon.	O6	40
Sawāi Mādhopur, India	H7	44
Sawākin, Sud.	H9	60
Sawankhalok, Thai.	F5	40
Sawatch Range, mts., Co., U.S.	B4	113
Sawdā', Jabal, mtn., Sau. Ar.	E3	47
Sawdā', Jabal as-, hills, Libya	C4	56
Sawdā', Qurnat as-, mtn., Leb.	D4	48
Sawdirī, Sud.	J5	60
Sawhāj, Egypt	D6	60
Sawknah, Libya	C4	56
Sawmill, Az., U.S.	B6	110
Sawnee Mountain, mtn., Ga., U.S.	B2	117
Sawqirah, Ghubbat, b., Oman	E10	47
Sawtooth Mountains, mts., Id., U.S.	F4	119
Sawtooth National Recreation Area, Id., U.S.	E3	119
Sawtooth Ridge, mtn., Wa., U.S.	A5	154
Sawu, Laut (Savu Sea), Indon.	G7	38
Sawu, Pulau, i., Indon.	H7	38
Sawyer, Ks., U.S.	E5	123
Sawyer, Mi., U.S.	G4	129
Sawyer, Mn., U.S.	D6	130
Sawyer, N.D., U.S.	A4	141
Sawyer, co., Wi., U.S.	C2	156
Sawyerville, Que., Can.	D6	104
Saxapahaw, N.C., U.S.	B3	140
Saxby, stm., Austl.	B4	70
Saxis, Va., U.S.	C7	153
Saxman, Ak., U.S.	n24	109
Saxon, Switz.	F7	13
Saxonburg, Pa., U.S.	E2	145
Saxton, Pa., U.S.	F5	145
Saxtons, stm., Vt., U.S.	E3	152
Saxtons River, Vt., U.S.	E3	152
Say, Niger	E11	64
Sayán, Peru	D3	82
Sayan Mountains (Sajany), mts., Asia	G11	24
Sayaxché, Guat.	I14	90
Saybrook, Il., U.S.	C5	120
Saybrook Manor, Ct., U.S.	D6	114
Saybrook Point, Ct., U.S.	D6	114
Saydā (Sidon), Leb.	A4	50
Saydel, Ia., U.S.	e8	122
Sayhūt, Yemen	G7	47
Sayil, hist., Mex.	G15	90
Saylesville, R.I., U.S.	B4	146
Saylorsburg, Pa., U.S.	E11	145
Saylorville, Ia., U.S.	e8	122
Saylorville Lake, res., Ia., U.S.	C4	122
Saylūn, Khirbat (Shiloh), hist., Isr. Occ.	D4	50
Sayner, Wi., U.S.	B4	156
Sayre, Al., U.S.	B3	108
Sayre, Ok., U.S.	B2	143
Sayre, Pa., U.S.	C8	145
Sayreville, N.J., U.S.	C4	137
Sayula, Mex.	H8	90
Sayville, N.Y., U.S.	n15	139
Sayward, B.C., Can.	D5	99
Saywūn, Yemen	G6	47
Şazonovo, U.S.S.R.	B18	26
Šazud, U.S.S.R.	B5	44
Sba, Alg.	F10	62
Sbeïtla, Tun.	N4	18
Sbiba, Tun.	N4	18
Scafell Pikes, mtn., Eng., U.K.	G10	8
Scalea, Italy	J10	18
Scales Mound, Il., U.S.	A3	120
Scalp Level, Pa., U.S.	F4	145
Scaly Mountain, N.C., U.S.	f9	140
Scammon, Ks., U.S.	E9	123
Scammon Bay, Ak., U.S.	C6	109
Scandia, Alta., Can.	D4	98
Scandia, Ks., U.S.	C6	123
Scanlon, Mn., U.S.	D6	130
Scanterbury, Man., Can.	D3	100
Scantic, Ct., U.S.	B5	114
Scapa Flow, b., Scot., U.K.	C10	8
Scapegoat Mountain, mtn., Mt., U.S.	C3	133
Ščapino, U.S.S.R.	F23	24
Scappoose, Or., U.S.	B4	144
Scarborough, Ont., Can.	m15	103
Scarborough, Trin.	I14	94
Scarborough, Eng., U.K.	G13	8
Scarborough, Me., U.S.	E2	126
Scarbro, W.V., U.S.	n13	155
Scarsdale, N.Y., U.S.	h13	139
Scawfell Island, i., Austl.	C8	70
Ščelkovo, U.S.S.R.	F21	26
Scenic, S.D., U.S.	D3	148
Sceptre, Sask., Can.	G1	105
Ščerbinka, U.S.S.R.	F20	26
Schaefferstown, Pa., U.S.	F9	145
Schaerbeek (Schaarbeek), Bel.	G5	12
Schaffhausen, Switz.	C10	13
Schaffhausen, state, Switz.	C10	13
Schaller, Ia., U.S.	B2	122
Schärding, Aus.	G13	10
Schaumburg, Il., U.S.	h8	120
Schefferville, Que., Can.	h13	104
Scheibbs, Aus.	G15	10
Scheinfeld, Ger.	F10	10
Schelde (Escaut), stm., Eur.	D4	10
Schell City, Mo., U.S.	C3	132
Schell Creek Range, mts., Nv., U.S.	D7	135
Schenectady, N.Y., U.S.	C7	139
Schenectady, co., N.Y., U.S.	C6	139
Scherer, Lake, res., Ga., U.S.	C3	117
Schererville, In., U.S.	B3	121
Schertz, Tx., U.S.	h7	150
Schesslitz, Ger.	F11	10
Scheveningen, Neth.	D5	12
Schiedam, Neth.	E5	12
Schiermonnikoog, Neth.	B9	12
Schiermonnikoog, i., Neth.	B9	12
Schiller Park, Il., U.S.	k9	120
Schiltigheim, Fr.	D14	14
Schio, Italy	D6	18
Schipbeek, stm., Eur.	D9	12
Schkeuditz, Ger.	D12	10
Schladming, Aus.	H13	10
Schlater, Ms., U.S.	B3	131
Schleicher, co., Tx., U.S.	D2	150
Schleswig, Ger.	A9	10
Schleswig, Ia., U.S.	B2	122
Schleswig-Holstein, state, Ger.	A9	10
Schleusingen, Ger.	E10	10
Schley, co., Ga., U.S.	D2	117
Schlieren, Switz.	D9	13
Schlitz, Ger.	E9	10
Schlüchtern, Ger.	E9	10
Schmalkalden, Ger.	E10	10
Schmidmühlen, Ger.	F11	10
Schmölln, Ger.	E12	10
Schneider, In., U.S.	B3	121
Schneverdingen, Ger.	B9	10
Schodn'a, U.S.S.R.	F20	26
Schoenchen, Ks., U.S.	D4	123
Schofield, Wi., U.S.	D4	156
Schofield Barracks, mil., Hi., U.S.	g9	118
Schoharie, N.Y., U.S.	C6	139
Schoharie, co., N.Y., U.S.	C6	139
Schoharie Creek, stm., N.Y., U.S.	C6	139
Schönebeck, Ger.	C11	10
Schongau, Ger.	H10	10
Schoodic Lake, l., Me., U.S.	C4	126
Schoolcraft, Mi., U.S.	F5	129
Schoolcraft, co., Mi., U.S.	B4	129
Schooleys Mountain, mtn., N.J., U.S.	B3	137
Schopfheim, Ger.	H7	10
Schorndorf, Ger.	G9	10
Schouten Island, i., Austl.	N8	70
Schouwen, i., Neth.	E4	12
Schramberg, Ger.	G8	10
Schram City, Il., U.S.	D4	120
Schriever, La., U.S.	E5	125
Schroeder, Mn., U.S.	C8	130
Schroffenstein, mtn., Nmb.	F4	66
Schroon Lake, N.Y., U.S.	B7	139
Schroon Lake, l., N.Y., U.S.	B7	139
Schruns, Aus.	H9	10
Schulenburg, Tx., U.S.	E4	150
Schuler, Alta., Can.	D5	98
Schulter, Ok., U.S.	B6	143
Schultz Lake, l., N.W. Ter., Can.	D13	96
Schüpfheim, Switz.	E9	13
Schurz, Nv., U.S.	E3	135
Schuyler, Ne., U.S.	C8	134
Schuyler, Va., U.S.	C4	153
Schuyler, co., Il., U.S.	C3	120
Schuyler, co., Mo., U.S.	A5	132
Schuyler, co., N.Y., U.S.	C4	139
Schuylerville, N.Y., U.S.	B7	139
Schuylkill, co., Pa., U.S.	E9	145
Schuylkill, stm., Pa., U.S.	F10	145
Schuylkill Haven, Pa., U.S.	E9	145
Schwabach, Ger.	F11	10
Schwaben, hist. reg., Ger.	G10	10
Schwäbische Alb, mts., Ger.	G9	10
Schwäbisch Gmünd, Ger.	G9	10
Schwäbisch Hall, Ger.	F9	10
Schwabmünchen, Ger.	G10	10
Schwanden, Switz.	D11	13
Schwandorf, Ger.	F12	10
Schwaner, Pegunungan, mts., Indon.	F5	38
Schwarza, Ger.	E11	10
Schwarzach im Pongau, Aus.	H13	10
Schwarzenburg, Switz.	E7	13
Schwarzwald (Black Forest), mts., Ger.	G8	10
Schwaz, Aus.	H11	10
Schwedt, Ger.	B14	10
Schweinfurt, Ger.	E10	10
Schweizer Nationalpark, Switz.	E13	13
Schwerin, Ger.	B11	10
Schwyz, Switz.	D10	13
Schwyz, state, Switz.	D10	13
Sciacca, Italy	L8	18
Scicli, Italy	M9	18
Science Hill, Ky., U.S.	C5	124
Scilla, Italy	K10	18
Scilly, Isles of, is., Eng., U.K.	L7	8
Scio, Oh., U.S.	B4	142
Scio, Or., U.S.	C4	144
Scioto, co., Oh., U.S.	D3	142
Scioto, stm., Oh., U.S.	B2	142
Scipio, In., U.S.	F6	121
Scipio, Ut., U.S.	D3	151
Scircleville, In., U.S.	D5	121
Scituate, Ma., U.S.	B6	128
Scituate Reservoir, res., R.I., U.S.	C3	146
Scobey, Mt., U.S.	B11	133
Scofield Reservoir, res., Ut., U.S.	D4	151
Ščokino, U.S.S.R.	G20	26
Scone, Austl.	I9	70
Scooba, Ms., U.S.	C5	131
Scordia, Italy	L9	18
Scotch Plains, N.J., U.S.	B4	137
Scotia, Ont., Can.	B5	103
Scotia, Ca., U.S.	B1	112
Scotia, Ne., U.S.	C7	134
Scotia, N.Y., U.S.	C7	139
Scotia Sea, S.A.	A1	73
Scotland, Ont., Can.	D4	103
Scotland, Ar., U.S.	B3	111
Scotland, Ct., U.S.	C7	114

Name — Map Ref. — Page

Scotland, Ga., U.S. D4 117
Scotland, In., U.S. G4 121
Scotland, Pa., U.S. G6 145
Scotland, S.D., U.S. D8 148
Scotland, co., Mo., U.S. A5 132
Scotland, co., N.C., U.S. C3 140
Scotland, ter., U.K. D9 8
Scotland Neck, N.C., U.S. A5 140
Scotlandville, La., U.S. D4 125
Scotrun, Pa., U.S. D11 145
Scotsburn, N.S., Can. D7 101
Scotstown, Que., Can. D6 104
Scott, Sask., Can. E1 105
Scott, Ar., U.S. C3 111
Scott, Ga., U.S. D4 117
Scott, La., U.S. D3 125
Scott, Ms., U.S. B2 131
Scott, co., Ar., U.S. C1 111
Scott, co., Il., U.S. D3 120
Scott, co., In., U.S. G6 121
Scott, co., Ia., U.S. C7 122
Scott, co., Ks., U.S. D3 123
Scott, co., Ky., U.S. B5 124
Scott, co., Mn., U.S. F5 130
Scott, co., Ms., U.S. C4 131
Scott, co., Mo., U.S. D8 132
Scott, co., Tn., U.S. C9 149
Scott, co., Va., U.S. f9 153
Scott, Cape, c., B.C., Can. D3 99
Scott, Mount, mtn., Ok., U.S. C3 143
Scott, Mount, mtn., Or., U.S. E4 144
Scott Air Force Base, mil., Il., U.S. E4 120
Scott Base, sci., Ant. C8 73
Scottburgh, S. Afr. H10 66
Scott City, Ks., U.S. D3 123
Scott City, Mo., U.S. D8 132
Scottdale, Ga., U.S. h8 117
Scottdale, Pa., U.S. F2 145
Scott Islands, is., B.C., Can. D3 99
Scott Mountain, mtn., Id., U.S. E3 119
Scott Peak, mtn., Id., U.S. E6 119
Scott Reef, rf., Austl. B4 68
Scott Reservoir, res., N.C., U.S. A1 140
Scotts, Mi., U.S. F5 129
Scottsbluff, Ne., U.S. C2 134
Scotts Bluff, co., Ne., U.S. C2 134
Scotts Bluff National Monument, Ne., U.S. C2 134
Scottsboro, Al., U.S. A3 108
Scottsburg, In., U.S. G6 121
Scottsdale, Austl. M7 70
Scottsdale, Az., U.S. D4 110
Scotts Hill, Tn., U.S. B3 149
Scotts Mills, Or., U.S. B4 144
Scotts Mountain, mtn., N.J., U.S. B2 137
Scottsville, Ky., U.S. D3 124
Scottsville, N.Y., U.S. B3 139
Scottsville, Va., U.S. C4 153
Scottville, Mi., U.S. E4 129
Scow Bay, Ak., U.S. m23 109
Scraggly Lake, l., Me., U.S. B4 126
Scranton, Ar., U.S. B2 111
Scranton, Ia., U.S. B3 122
Scranton, Ks., U.S. D8 123
Scranton, N.D., U.S. C2 141
Scranton, Pa., U.S. D10 145
Scranton, S.C., U.S. D8 147
Screven, Ga., U.S. E4 117
Screven, co., Ga., U.S. D5 117
Scribner, Ne., U.S. C9 134
Ščučin, U.S.S.R. H7 26
Ščučinsk, U.S.S.R. G12 22
Scugog, Lake, l., Ont., Can. C6 103
Scuol (Schuls), Switz. E13 13
Scurry, co., Tx., U.S. C2 150
Scutari, Lake, l., Eur. G3 20
Seaboard, N.C., U.S. A5 140
Seabreeze, De., U.S. F5 115
Sea Bright, N.J., U.S. C5 137
Seabrook, N.H., U.S. E5 136
Seabrook, N.J., U.S. E2 137
Seabrook, Tx., U.S. r14 150
Seabrook Island, i., S.C., U.S. F7 147
Seadrift, Tx., U.S. E4 150
Seaford, De., U.S. F3 115
Seaford, Va., U.S. h15 153
Seaforth, Ont., Can. D3 103
Sea Girt, N.J., U.S. C4 137
Seagoville, Tx., U.S. n10 150
Seagrave, Ont., Can. C6 103
Seagraves, Tx., U.S. C1 150
Seahorse Point, c., N.W. Ter., Can. D16 96
Sea Islands, is., U.S. E10 106
Sea Isle City, N.J., U.S. E3 137
Seal, stm., Man., Can. f8 100
Sea Lake, Austl. J5 70
Seal Cays, is., T./C. Is. D9 94
Seal Cove, N.B., Can. E3 101
Seal Cove, Newf., Can. D3 102
Seale, Al., U.S. C4 108
Seal Harbor, Me., U.S. D4 126
Seal Point, c., P.E.I., Can. C5 101
Seal Rock, Or., U.S. C2 144
Sealy, Tx., U.S. E4 150
Seama, N.M., U.S. B2 138
Seaman, Oh., U.S. D2 142
Seaman Range, mts., Nv., U.S. F6 135
Seara, Braz. D12 80
Searchlight, Nv., U.S. H7 135
Searcy, Ar., U.S. B4 111
Searcy, co., Ar., U.S. B3 111
Searles, Al., U.S. B2 108
Searles, Mn., U.S. F4 130
Searles Lake, l., Ca., U.S. E5 112
Sears Falls, wtfl, Ne., U.S. B5 134
Searsmont, Me., U.S. D3 126
Searsport, Me., U.S. D4 126
Searston, Newf., Can. E2 102
Seaside, Or., U.S. B3 144
Seaside Heights, N.J., U.S. D4 137
Seaside Park, N.J., U.S. D4 137
Seaton, Il., U.S. B3 120
Seat Pleasant, Md., U.S. C4 127
Seattle, Wa., U.S. B3 154
Seattle-Tacoma International Airport, Wa., U.S. f11 154
Seaview, Wa., U.S. C1 154
Seaville, N.J., U.S. E3 137
Seba Beach, Alta., Can. C3 98
Sébaco, Nic. E8 92
Sebago Lake, Me., U.S. E2 126
Sebakwe Recreational Area, Zimb. B10 66
Šebalino, U.S.S.R. G15 22
Sebasco Estates, Me., U.S. g8 126
Sebastian, Fl., U.S. E6 116
Sebastian, co., Ar., U.S. B1 111
Sebastian, Cape, c., Or., U.S. E2 144
Sebastian Inlet, b., Fl., U.S. E6 116
Sebastián Vizcaíno, Bahía, b., Mex. C2 90
Sebasticook Lake, l., Me., U.S. D3 126
Sebastopol, Ms., U.S. C4 131
Sebderat, Eth. J9 60
Sebec Lake, l., Me., U.S. C3 126
Sebeka, Mn., U.S. D3 130
Seberi, Braz. D12 80
Sebeş, Rom. D7 20
Sebes Körös (Crişul Repede), stm., Eur. B5 20
Sebewaing, Mi., U.S. E7 129
Sebež, U.S.S.R. E11 26
Şebinkarahisar, Tur. A5 48
Sebiş, Rom. C6 20
Sebnitz, Ger. E14 10
Seboeis, stm., Me., U.S. B4 126
Seboeis Lake, l., Me., U.S. C4 126
Seboomook Lake, l., Me., U.S. C3 126
Seboyeta, N.M., U.S. B2 138
Sebree, Ky., U.S. C2 124
Sebring, Fl., U.S. E5 116
Sebring, Oh., U.S. B4 142
Sebringville, Ont., Can. D3 103
Secas, Islas, is., Pan. J12 92
Secaucus, N.J., U.S. h8 137
Sechelt, B.C., Can. E6 99
Sechura, Peru A1 82
Sechura, Bahía de, b., Peru A1 82
Sechura, Desierto de, des., Peru A1 82
Seclantas, Arg. C5 80
Seco, Ky., U.S. C7 124
Seco, stm., Arg. B7 80
Second Lake, l., N.H., U.S. f7 136
Second Mesa, Az., U.S. B5 110
Secor, Il., U.S. C4 120
Sečovce, Czech. G21 10
Secretary, Md., U.S. C6 127
Secret Lake, l., R.I., U.S. E4 146
Section, Al., U.S. A4 108
Sécure, stm., Bol. F9 82
Security, Co., U.S. C6 113
Seda, China E7 30
Seda, U.S.S.R. D8 26
Seda, U.S.S.R. E5 26
Sedalia, Co., U.S. B6 113
Sedalia, Ky., U.S. f9 124
Sedalia, Mo., U.S. C4 132
Sedan, Fr. C11 14
Sedan, Ks., U.S. E7 123
Sedano, Spain C8 16
Sedel'nikovo, U.S.S.R. F13 22
Sederot, Isr. E3 50
Sedgewick, Alta., Can. C5 98
Sedgewick, Mount, mtn., N.M., U.S. B1 138
Sedgwick, Co., U.S. A8 113
Sedgwick, Ks., U.S. E6 123
Sedgwick, Me., U.S. D4 126
Sedgwick, co., Co., U.S. A8 113
Sedgwick, co., Ks., U.S. E6 123
Sedini, Italy I3 18
Sedlčany, Czech. F14 10
Sedley, Sask., Can. G3 105
Sedley, Va., U.S. D6 153
Sedom (Sodom), hist., Isr. F4 50
Sedona, Az., U.S. C4 110
Sedot Yam, Isr. D3 50
Sedova, pik, mtn., U.S.S.R. C8 22
Sedrata, Alg. M2 18
Sedro Woolley, Wa., U.S. A3 154
Šeduva, U.S.S.R. F6 26
Seebe, Alta., Can. D3 98
Seeberg, Switz. D8 13
Seefeld in Tirol, Aus. H11 10
Seehausen, Ger. C11 10
Seeheim, Nmb. F3 66
Seeis, Nmb. D3 66
Seekonk, Ma., U.S. C5 128
Seekonk, stm., R.I., U.S. C4 146
Seeley, Ca., U.S. F6 112
Seeley Lake, Mt., U.S. C3 133
Seeleys Bay, Ont., Can. C8 103
Seelow, Ger. C14 10
Seelyville, In., U.S. F3 121
Seengen, Switz. D9 13
Sées, Fr. D7 14
Seesen, Ger. D10 10
Sefadu, S.L. G4 64
Sefar, hist., Alg. H15 62
Sefare, Bots. D8 66
Sefīd Ābeh, Iran F16 48
Sefrou, Mor. D8 62
Segamat, Malay. M7 40
Şegarcea, Rom. E7 20
Segbana, Benin F11 64
Segbwema, S.L. G4 64
Segeža, U.S.S.R. E4 22
Segni, Italy H8 18
Segorbe, Spain F11 16
Ségou, Mali E6 64
Segovia, Col. D5 84
Segovia, Spain E7 16
Segozero, ozero, l., U.S.S.R. J23 6
Segre, stm., Eur. D12 16
Seguam Island, i., Ak., U.S. E5 109
Seguam Pass, strt., Ak., U.S. E5 109
Séguédine, Niger D9 54
Séguéla, I.C. H6 64
Séguéla, Mali D6 64
Seguí, Arg. F8 80
Seguin, Tx., U.S. E4 150
Segundo, Co., U.S. D6 113
Segundo, stm., Arg. F7 80
Segura, Port. F5 16
Segura, stm., Spain G11 16
Sehithwa, Bots. C6 66
Seia, Port. E4 16
Seibert, Co., U.S. B8 113
Seiling, Ok., U.S. A3 143
Seilo, Sud. K2 60
Sein, Île de, i., Fr. D2 14
Seinäjoki, Fin. J18 6
Seine, stm., Fr. C7 14
Seine, Baie de la, b., Fr. C6 14
Seine-et-Marne, dept., Fr. D10 14
Seine-Maritime, dept., Fr. C8 14
Seixal, Port. G2 16
Sejm, stm., U.S.S.R. G4 22
Sejmčan, U.S.S.R. E22 24
Seke, Eth. M10 60
Seki, Japan L11 36
Seki, Tur. M13 20
Şeki (Nucha), U.S.S.R. I7 22
Sekiu, Wa., U.S. A1 154
Sekoma, Bots. E6 66
Sekondi-Takoradi, Ghana I9 64
Sekota, Eth. K10 60
Šeksna, U.S.S.R. B21 26
Šelagskij, mys, c., U.S.S.R. C26 24
Selah, Wa., U.S. C5 154
Selaru, Pulau, i., Indon. G9 38
Selatan, Tanjung, c., Indon. F5 38
Selawik, Ak., U.S. B7 109
Selawik Lake, l., Ak., U.S. B7 109
Selayar, Pulau, i., Indon. G7 38
Selb, Ger. E12 10
Selbu, Nor. J12 6
Selby, S.D., U.S. B5 148
Selbyville, De., U.S. G5 115
Sel'co, U.S.S.R. H17 26
Selden, Ks., U.S. C3 123
Seldovia, Ak., U.S. D9 109
Selebi Phikwe, Bots. D8 66
Selenga (Selenge), stm., Asia G19 22
Selenge (Selenga), stm., Asia B7 30
Selenn'ach, stm., U.S.S.R. D20 24
Sélestat, Fr. D14 14
Selezn'ovo, U.S.S.R. A11 26
Selfridge, N.D., U.S. C5 141
Sélibaby, Maur. D3 64
Šelichova, zaliv, b., U.S.S.R. F23 24
Seliger, ozero, l., U.S.S.R. D16 26
Seligman, Az., U.S. B3 110
Seligman, Mo., U.S. E4 132
Selinsgrove, Pa., U.S. E8 145
Selišče, U.S.S.R. E16 26
Seližarovo, U.S.S.R. E16 26
Selje, Nor. J9 6
Seljord, Nor. L11 6
Selkirk, Man., Can. D3 100
Selkirk, Scot., U.K. F11 8
Selleck, Wa., U.S. B4 154
Sellers, Al., U.S. C3 108
Sellers, S.C., U.S. C9 147
Sellersburg, In., U.S. H6 121
Sellersville, Pa., U.S. F11 145
Sells, Az., U.S. F4 110
Selm, Ger. D7 10
Selma, N.S., Can. D6 101
Selma, Al., U.S. C2 108
Selma, Ca., U.S. D4 112
Selma, In., U.S. D7 121
Selma, N.C., U.S. B4 140
Selmer, Tn., U.S. B3 149
Seltz, Fr. D15 14
Selva, Arg. E7 80
Selvas, for., Braz. E6 76
Selvin, In., U.S. H3 121
Selway, stm., Id., U.S. C3 119
Selwyn, Austl. C4 70
Selwyn Mountains, mts., Can. D6 96
Selwyn Range, mts., Austl. C4 70
Selz, N.D., U.S. B6 141
Šemacha, U.S.S.R. A10 48
Seman, stm., Alb. I3 20
Semans, Sask., Can. F3 105
Semarang, Indon. J15 39a
Semeru, Gunung, mtn., Indon. K16 39a
Semeževo, U.S.S.R. I10 26
Semibratovo, U.S.S.R. D22 26
Seminary, Ms., U.S. D4 131
Seminoe Mountains, mts., Wy., U.S. D6 157
Seminoe Reservoir, res., Wy., U.S. D6 157
Seminole, Al., U.S. E2 108
Seminole, Ok., U.S. B5 143
Seminole, Tx., U.S. C1 150
Seminole, co., Fl., U.S. D5 116
Seminole, co., Ga., U.S. F2 117
Seminole, co., Ok., U.S. B5 143
Seminole, Lake, res., U.S. F2 117
Semipalatinsk, U.S.S.R. G8 24
Semisopochnoi Island, i., Ak., U.S. E3 109
Semmes, Al., U.S. E1 108
Semnān, Iran D12 48
Semois, stm., Eur. I7 12
Šemonaicha, U.S.S.R. G14 22
Sem'onov, U.S.S.R. F6 22
Sem'onovka, U.S.S.R. I15 26
Semporna, Malay. E6 38
Semuliki, stm., Afr. A5 58
Semur-en-Auxois, Fr. E11 14
Sena, Bol. D8 82
Sena, Moz. E7 58
Sena, N.M., U.S. B4 138
Senachwine Lake, l., Il., U.S. B4 120
Senador Canedo, Braz. D4 79
Senador Firmino, Braz. F7 79
Senador Pompeu, Braz. E11 76
Senahú, Guat. B5 92
Sena Madureira, Braz. C7 82
Senanga, Zam. E4 58
Senath, Mo., U.S. E7 132
Senatobia, Ms., U.S. A4 131
Sendafa, Eth. M10 60
Sendai, Japan I15 36
Sêndo, China E15 44
Seneca, Il., U.S. B5 120
Seneca, Ks., U.S. C7 123
Seneca, Mo., U.S. E3 132
Seneca, Pa., U.S. D2 145
Seneca, S.C., U.S. B2 147
Seneca, S.D., U.S. B6 148
Seneca, co., N.Y., U.S. C4 139
Seneca, co., Oh., U.S. A2 142
Seneca Falls, N.Y., U.S. C4 139
Seneca Lake, l., N.Y., U.S. C4 139
Senecaville Lake, res., Oh., U.S. C4 142
Senegal (Sénégal), ctry., Afr. F4 54
Sénégal, stm., Afr. E4 54
Senekal, S. Afr. G8 66
Senftenberg, Ger. D14 10
Sengés, Braz. H4 79
Senhora do Pôrto, Braz. E7 79
Senhor do Bonfim, Braz. F10 76
Senica, Czech. G17 10
Senigallia, Italy F8 18
Senise, Italy I11 18
Senj, Yugo. E9 18
Senja, i., Nor. G15 6
Senkursk, U.S.S.R. E6 22
Senlac, Sask., Can. E1 105
Senlis, Fr. C9 14
Senmonorom, Camb. H9 40
Senneterre, Que., Can. k11 104
Sennori, Italy I3 18
Senoia, Ga., U.S. C2 117
Senqu see Orange, stm., Afr. G4 66
Sens, Fr. D10 14
Sensuntepeque, El Sal. D6 92
Senta, Yugo. D4 20
Sentinel, Ok., U.S. B2 143
Sentinel Butte, N.D., U.S. C2 141
Sentinel Butte, mtn., N.D., U.S. C2 141
Seo de Urgel, Spain C13 16
Seoni, India I8 44
Seoul see Sŏul, S. Kor. F14 32
Sepatini, stm., Braz. B9 82
Sepetiba, Baía de, b., Braz. G7 79
Šepetovka, U.S.S.R. G3 22
Sepik, stm., Pap. N. Gui. k15 68a
Sepólno Krajeńskie, Pol. B17 10
Sepopa, Bots. B6 66
Sepoti, stm., Braz. B11 82
Sepotuba, stm., Braz. F13 82
Sept-Îles (Seven Islands), Que., Can. h13 104
Sepulga, stm., Al., U.S. D3 108
Sequatchie, Tn., U.S. D8 149
Sequatchie, co., Tn., U.S. D8 149
Sequatchie, stm., Tn., U.S. D8 149
Sequeros, Spain E5 16
Sequim, Wa., U.S. A2 154
Sequoia National Park, Ca., U.S. D4 112
Sequoyah, co., Ok., U.S. B7 143
Šerabad, U.S.S.R. B2 44
Serachs, U.S.S.R. C16 48
Serafimovič, U.S.S.R. H6 22
Seraidi, Alg. M2 18
Seraing, Bel. G7 12
Seram (Ceram), i., Indon. F8 38
Seram, Laut (Ceram Sea), Indon. F8 38
Serang, Indon. J13 39a
Serbia see Srbija, state, Yugo. F4 20
Serdobsk, U.S.S.R. G6 22
Serebr'anyje Prudy, U.S.S.R. G21 26
Sered', Czech. G17 10
Seredejskij, U.S.S.R. G18 26
Seredina-Buda, U.S.S.R. I17 26
Seredžius, U.S.S.R. F6 26
Seremban, Malay. M6 40
Serengeti Plain, pl., Tan. B6 58
Serenje, Zam. D6 58
Šereševo, U.S.S.R. I7 26
Sergeant Bluff, Ia., U.S. B1 122
Sergeja Kirova, ostrova, is., U.S.S.R. B15 22
Sergejevka, U.S.S.R. I18 24
Seria, Bru. E5 38
Serian, Malay. N11 40
Sérifos, i., Grc. L8 20
Serkhe, Cerro, mtn., Bol. G7 82
Šerlovaja Gora, U.S.S.R. G15 24
Serowe, Bots. ...

Name | Map Ref. | Page

Sharon, W.V., U.S. m13 155
Sharon, Wi., U.S. F5 156
Sharon Hill, Pa., U.S. p20 145
Sharon Park, Oh., U.S. n12 142
Sharon Springs, Ks., U.S. D2 123
Sharonville, Oh., U.S. n13 142
Sharp, co., Ar., U.S. A4 111
Sharpe, Lake, res., S.D., U.S. C6 148
Sharpes, Fl., U.S. D6 116
Sharples, W.V., U.S. D3 155
Sharpley, De., U.S. h7 115
Sharpsburg, Ky., U.S. B6 124
Sharpsburg, Md., U.S. B2 127
Sharpsburg, N.C., U.S. B5 140
Sharpsburg, Pa., U.S. k14 145
Sharpsville, In., U.S. D5 121
Sharpsville, Pa., U.S. D1 145
Sharp Top Mountain, mtn., Ar., U.S. C2 111
Sharptown, Md., U.S. C6 127
Sharqī, Al-Jabal ash- (Anti-Lebanon), mts., Asia A6 50
Sharqīyah, Aṣ-Ṣaḥrā' ash- (Arabian Desert), des., Egypt D7 60
Shasha, Eth. N8 60
Shashe, stm., Afr. C9 66
Shashemene, Eth. N10 60
Shashi, China E9 30
Shasta, co., Ca., U.S. B3 112
Shasta, Mount, vol., Ca., U.S. B2 112
Shasta Lake, res., Ca., U.S. B2 112
Shaṭawī, Sud. J7 60
Shatney Mountain, mtn., N.H., U.S. f7 136
Shattuck, Ok., U.S. A2 143
Shatuji, China H3 32
Shaunavon, Sask., Can. H1 105
Shaw, Ms., U.S. B3 131
Shaw Air Force Base, mil., S.C., U.S. D7 147
Shawangunk Mountains, mts., N.Y., U.S. D6 139
Shawano, Wi., U.S. D5 156
Shawano, co., Wi., U.S. D5 156
Shawano Lake, l., Wi., U.S. D5 156
Shawboro, N.C., U.S. A6 140
Shawhan, Ky., U.S. B5 124
Shawinigan, Que., Can. C5 104
Shawinigan Lake, B.C., Can. g12 99
Shawinigan-Sud, Que., Can. C5 104
Shawnee, Co., U.S. B5 113
Shawnee, Ga., U.S. D5 117
Shawnee, Ks., U.S. k16 123
Shawnee, Oh., U.S. C3 142
Shawnee, Ok., U.S. B5 143
Shawnee, co., Ks., U.S. D8 123
Shawneetown, Il., U.S. F5 120
Shawo, China G3 34
Shawsheen, stm., Ma., U.S. f11 128
Shawsville, Va., U.S. C2 153
Shaybārā, i., Sau. Ar. I4 48
Shay Gap, Austl. D4 68
Shaykh, Jabal ash- (Mount Hermon), mtn., Asia B5 50
Shaykh 'Uthmān, Yemen H4 47
Shayuan, China H9 34
Shebele (Shabeelle), stm., Afr. G9 56
Shebelē Wenz, stm., Afr. H3 42
Sheberghān, Afg. B1 44
Sheboygan, Wi., U.S. E6 156
Sheboygan, co., Wi., U.S. E6 156
Sheboygan, stm., Wi., U.S. k10 156
Sheboygan Falls, Wi., U.S. E6 156
Shechem see Nābulus, Isr. Occ. D4 50
Shedden, Ont., Can. E3 103
Shediac, N.B., Can. C5 101
Sheenjek, stm., Ak., U.S. B11 109
Sheep Mountain, mtn., Az., U.S. E1 110
Sheep Mountain, mtn., Wy., U.S. C2 157
Sheep Mountain, mtn., Wy., U.S. B5 157
Sheep Peak, mtn., Nv., U.S. G6 135
Sheep Range, mts., Nv., U.S. G6 135
Sheeps Heaven Mountain, mtn., Ma., U.S. A1 128
Sheerness, Alta., Can. D5 98
Sheet Harbour, N.S., Can. E7 101
Shefar'am, Isr. C4 50
Sheffield, N.Z. E4 72
Sheffield, Eng., U.K. H12 8
Sheffield, Al., U.S. A2 108
Sheffield, Il., U.S. B4 120
Sheffield, Ia., U.S. B4 122
Sheffield, Ma., U.S. B1 128
Sheffield, Pa., U.S. C3 145
Sheffield, Vt., U.S. B4 152
Sheffield Lake, Oh., U.S. A3 142
Shegaon, India B4 46
Sheguiandah, Ont., Can. B3 103
Sheho, Sask., Can. F4 105
Sheikh Hasan, Eth. K8 60
Sheila, N.B., Can. B5 101
Shekhūpura, Pak. E5 44
Shelagyote Peak, mtn., B.C., Can. B4 99
Shelbiana, Ky., U.S. C7 124
Shelbina, Mo., U.S. B5 132
Shelburn, In., U.S. F3 121
Shelburne, N.S., Can. F4 101
Shelburne, Ont., Can. C4 103
Shelburne, Vt., U.S. C2 152
Shelburne Falls, Ma., U.S. A2 128
Shelburne Pond, l., Vt., U.S. C2 152
Shelby, Al., U.S. B3 108
Shelby, In., U.S. B3 121
Shelby, Ia., U.S. C2 122
Shelby, Mi., U.S. E4 129
Shelby, Ms., U.S. B3 131
Shelby, Mt., U.S. B5 133
Shelby, Ne., U.S. C8 134
Shelby, N.C., U.S. B1 140
Shelby, Oh., U.S. B3 142
Shelby, co., Al., U.S. B3 108
Shelby, co., Il., U.S. D5 120
Shelby, co., In., U.S. E6 121
Shelby, co., Ia., U.S. C2 122
Shelby, co., Ky., U.S. B4 124
Shelby, co., Mo., U.S. B5 132
Shelby, co., Oh., U.S. B1 142
Shelby, co., Tn., U.S. B2 149
Shelby, co., Tx., U.S. D5 150
Shelbyville, Il., U.S. D5 120
Shelbyville, In., U.S. F6 121
Shelbyville, Ky., U.S. B4 124
Shelbyville, Mo., U.S. B5 132
Shelbyville, Tn., U.S. B5 149
Shelbyville, Lake, res., Il., U.S. D5 120
Sheldahl, Ia., U.S. e8 122
Sheldon, Il., U.S. C6 120
Sheldon, Ia., U.S. A2 122
Sheldon, Mo., U.S. D3 132
Sheldon, N.D., U.S. C8 141
Sheldon, Tx., U.S. r14 150
Sheldon, Vt., U.S. B3 152
Sheldon Springs, Vt., U.S. B3 152
Shelikof Strait, strt., Ak., U.S. D9 109
Shell, Wy., U.S. B5 157
Shell, stm., Man., Can. D1 100
Shellbrook, Sask., Can. D2 105
Shell Creek, Tn., U.S. C11 149
Shell Creek, stm., U.S. A2 113
Shell Creek, stm., Wy., U.S. B5 157
Shelley, B.C., Can. C6 99
Shelley, Id., U.S. F6 119
Shellharbour, Austl. J9 70
Shell Lake, Sask., Can. D2 105
Shell Lake, Wi., U.S. C2 156
Shell Lake, l., Mn., U.S. D3 130
Shell Lake, l., Wi., U.S. C2 156
Shellman, Ga., U.S. E2 117
Shellman Bluff, Ga., U.S. E5 117
Shellmouth, Man., Can. D1 100
Shellpot Creek, stm., De., U.S. h7 115
Shell Rock, Ia., U.S. B5 122
Shell Rock, stm., Ia., U.S. B5 122
Shell Rock, West Fork, stm., Ia., U.S. B5 122
Shellsburg, Ia., U.S. B6 122
Shelly Mountain, mtn., Id., U.S. F5 119
Shelter Island, N.Y., U.S. m16 139
Shelton, Ct., U.S. D3 114
Shelton, Ne., U.S. D7 134
Shelton, Wa., U.S. B2 154
Shemogue, N.B., Can. C5 101
Shemya Air Force Base, mil., Ak., U.S. E2 109
Shenandoah, Ia., U.S. D2 122
Shenandoah, Pa., U.S. E9 145
Shenandoah, Va., U.S. B4 153
Shenandoah, co., Va., U.S. B4 153
Shenandoah, stm., U.S. A5 153
Shenandoah, North Fork, stm., Va., U.S. B4 153
Shenandoah, South Fork, stm., Va., U.S. B4 153
Shenandoah Mountain, mtn., U.S. B3 153
Shenandoah National Park, Va., U.S. B4 153
Shenandoah Valley, val., U.S. B4 153
Shenango River Lake, res., U.S. D1 145
Shendam, Nig. G14 64
Shengang, China H5 34
Shengtian, China H2 34
Shengze, China E9 34
Shenipsit Lake, l., Ct., U.S. B6 114
Shenqiu, China B4 34
Shensi see Shaanxi, prov., China D8 30
Shenyang (Mukden), China B11 32
Sheopur, India H7 44
Shepard, Alta., Can. D4 98
Shepardsville, In., U.S. E3 121
Shepaug, stm., Ct., U.S. C2 114
Shepaug Dam, Ct., U.S. D2 114
Shepaug Reservoir, res., Ct., U.S. C2 114
Shepherd, Mi., U.S. E6 129
Shepherd, Mt., U.S. E8 133
Shepherd, Tx., U.S. D5 150
Shepherdstown, W.V., U.S. B7 155
Shepherdsville, Ky., U.S. C4 124
Sheppard Air Force Base, mil., Tx., U.S. C3 150
Shepparton, Austl. K6 70
Sheppton, Pa., U.S. E9 145
Sheqi, China B1 34
Sherab, Sud. L3 60
Sherada, Eth. N9 60
Sherard, Ms., U.S. A3 131
Sherard, Cape, c., N.W. Ter., Can. B16 96
Sherborn, Ma., U.S. h10 128
Sherbro Island, i., S.L. H3 64
Sherbrooke, N.S., Can. D8 101
Sherbrooke, Que., Can. D6 104
Sherburn, Mn., U.S. G4 130
Sherburne, N.Y., U.S. C5 139
Sherburne, co., Mn., U.S. E5 130
Sheridan, Ar., U.S. C3 111
Sheridan, Il., U.S. B5 120
Sheridan, In., U.S. D5 121
Sheridan, Me., U.S. B4 126
Sheridan, Mi., U.S. E5 129
Sheridan, Mo., U.S. A3 132
Sheridan, Mt., U.S. E4 133
Sheridan, Or., U.S. B3 144
Sheridan, Wy., U.S. B6 157
Sheridan, co., Ks., U.S. C3 123
Sheridan, co., Mt., U.S. B12 133
Sheridan, co., Ne., U.S. B3 134
Sheridan, co., N.D., U.S. B5 141
Sheridan, co., Wy., U.S. B5 157
Sheridan, Mount, mtn., Wy., U.S. B2 157
Sherman, Ms., U.S. A5 131
Sherman, Tx., U.S. C4 150
Sherman, co., Ks., U.S. C2 123
Sherman, co., Ne., U.S. C6 134
Sherman, co., Or., U.S. B6 144
Sherman, co., Tx., U.S. A2 150
Sherman Mills, Me., U.S. C4 126
Sherman Mountain, mtn., Ar., U.S. A2 111
Sherman Reservoir, res., Ne., U.S. C7 134
Sherman Station, Me., U.S. C4 126
Sherpur, Bngl. H14 44
Sherrard, Il., U.S. B3 120
Sherrelwood, Co., U.S. B6 113
Sherridon, Man., Can. B1 100
Sherrill, N.Y., U.S. B5 139
Shertallai, India H4 46
's-Hertogenbosch, Neth. E7 12
Sherwood, P.E.I., Can. C6 101
Sherwood, Ar., U.S. C3 111
Sherwood, N.D., U.S. A4 141
Sherwood, Oh., U.S. A1 142
Sherwood, Or., U.S. h12 144
Sherwood, Tn., U.S. D8 149
Sherwood, Wi., U.S. h9 156
Sherwood Manor, Ct., U.S. A5 114
Sherwood Park, De., U.S. i7 115
Sheshea, stm., Peru C5 82
Shetek, Lake, l., Mn., U.S. G3 130
Shetland, prov., Scot., U.K. A12 8
Shetland Islands, is., Scot., U.K. A12 8
Shetucket, stm., Ct., U.S. C7 114
Shevlin, Mn., U.S. C3 130
Shewa Gimira, Eth. N8 60
Shexian, China F7 34
Sheyenne, N.D., U.S. B6 141
Sheyenne, stm., N.D., U.S. C8 141
Sheyenne Lake, res., N.D., U.S. B5 141
Sheykhābād, Afg. C3 44
Shhīm, Leb. A4 50
Shiawassee, co., Mi., U.S. F6 129
Shiba, China C7 34
Shibām, Yemen G6 47
Shibarni, Sud. J3 60
Shibata, Japan J14 36
Shibetsu, Japan C17 36a
Shibīn al-Kawm, Egypt B6 60
Shicheng, China I5 34
Shickley, Ne., U.S. D8 134
Shickshinny, Pa., U.S. D9 145
Shidao, China G10 32
Shideler, In., U.S. D7 121
Shidler, Ok., U.S. A5 143
Shifodian, China C4 34
Shigaib, Sud. J2 60
Shigezhuang, China E4 32
Shihan, Wādī, val., Asia E8 47
Shihe, China D9 32
Shijiazhuang, China E2 32
Shijing, China K7 34
Shikārpur, Pak. G3 44
Shikohābād, India G8 44
Shikoku, i., Japan N8 36
Shiliguri, India G13 44
Shillelagh, Ire. I7 8
Shillington, Pa., U.S. F10 145
Shillong, India H14 44
Shiloh, Ga., U.S. D2 117
Shiloh, Oh., U.S. B3 142
Shiloh, Tn., U.S. B3 149
Shiloh National Military Park, Tn., U.S. B3 149
Shiloh see Saylūn, Khirbat, hist., Isr. Occ. D4 50
Shilong, China L2 34
Shimabara, Japan O5 36
Shimada, Japan M13 36
Shimber Berris, mtn., Som. F10 56
Shimen, China D6 32
Shimian, China F7 30
Shimiaozi, China C11 32
Shimizu, Japan L13 36
Shimla, India E7 44
Shimodate, Japan K14 36
Shimoga, India F3 46
Shimokita-hantō, pen., Japan F16 36
Shimonoseki, Japan N5 36
Shinall Mountain, mtn., Ar., U.S. h10 111
Shināṣ, Oman B10 47
Shīndand, Afg. E17 48
Shiner, Tx., U.S. E4 150
Shingbwiyang, Burma A4 40
Shinglehouse, Pa., U.S. C5 145
Shingleton, Mi., U.S. B4 129
Shingū, Japan M9 36
Shingū, Japan N10 36
Shingwidzi (Singuédeze), stm., Afr. D10 66
Shinjō, Japan I15 36
Shinkolobwe, Zaire D5 58
Shinnston, W.V., U.S. B4 155
Shinyanga, Tan. B6 58
Shiocton, Wi., U.S. D5 156
Shiogama, Japan I16 36
Shiojiri, Japan K12 36
Shiono-misaki, c., Japan N10 36
Ship Bottom, N.J., U.S. D4 137
Ship Harbour, N.S., Can. E7 101
Shiping, China C7 40
Ship Island, i., Ms., U.S. E5 131
Ship Island Pass, strt., Ms., U.S. g7 131
Shipman, Il., U.S. D4 120
Shipman, Va., U.S. C4 153
Shippegan, N.B., Can. B5 101
Shippensburg, Pa., U.S. F6 145
Shiprock, N.M., U.S. A1 138
Ship Rock, mtn., N.M., U.S. A1 138
Shipshewana, In., U.S. A6 121
Shipu, China F10 34
Shirakami-misaki, c., Japan F15 36a
Shiraoi, Japan E16 36a
Shīrāz, Iran G12 48
Shire, stm., Afr. E6 58
Shiretoko-misaki, c., Japan C20 36a
Shirley, Ar., U.S. B3 111
Shirley, In., U.S. E6 121
Shirley, Ma., U.S. A4 128
Shirley, W.V., U.S. k9 155
Shirley Basin, Wy., U.S. D6 157
Shirley Mills, Me., U.S. C3 126
Shirley Mountains, mts., Wy., U.S. D6 157
Shiroishi, Japan I15 36
Shirpur, India B3 46
Shīrvān, Iran C14 48
Shishaldin Volcano, vol., Ak., U.S. E7 109
Shishmaref, Ak., U.S. B6 109
Shitan, China L2 34
Shively, Ky., U.S. B4 124
Shivpuri, India H7 44
Shivwits Plateau, plat., Az., U.S. A2 110
Shixia, China C2 32
Shizheng, China K4 34
Shizuoka, Japan M13 36
Shkodër, Alb. G3 20
Shoal, stm., Man., Can. C1 100
Shoal Creek, stm., U.S. B4 149
Shoal Harbour, Newf., Can. D4 102
Shoal Lake, Man., Can. D1 100
Shoals, In., U.S. G4 121
Shoals, Isles of, is., Me., U.S. E2 126
Shoalwater, Cape, c., Wa., U.S. C1 154
Shoalwater Bay, b., Austl. D9 70
Shobonier, Il., U.S. E4 120
Shōdo-shima, i., Japan M9 36
Shoe Cove, Newf., Can. D4 102
Shoemakersville, Pa., U.S. F10 145
Shongopovi, Az., U.S. B5 110
Shonto, Az., U.S. A5 110
Shop Springs, Tn., U.S. A5 149
Shoreacres, B.C., Can. E9 99
Shore Acres, Ma., U.S. h13 128
Shoreham, Mi., U.S. F4 129
Shores Acres, R.I., U.S. E4 146
Shoreview, Mn., U.S. m12 130
Shorewood, Il., U.S. k8 120
Shorewood, Mn., U.S. n11 130
Shorewood, Wi., U.S. E6 156
Short Beach, Ct., U.S. D4 114
Shorter, Al., U.S. C4 108
Shorterville, Al., U.S. D4 108
Short Mountain, mtn., Tn., U.S. D8 149
Shortsville, N.Y., U.S. C3 139
Shoshone, Id., U.S. G4 119
Shoshone, co., Id., U.S. B2 119
Shoshone, stm., Wy., U.S. B4 157
Shoshone, North Fork, stm., Wy., U.S. B3 157
Shoshone, South Fork, stm., Wy., U.S. B3 157
Shoshone Falls, wtfl, Id., U.S. G4 119
Shoshone Lake, l., Wy., U.S. B2 157
Shoshone Mountains, mts., Nv., U.S. E4 135
Shoshone Peak, mtn., Nv., U.S. G5 135
Shoshone Range, mts., Nv., U.S. C5 135
Shoshong, Bots. D8 66
Shoshoni, Wy., U.S. C4 157
Shouning, China H8 34
Shouns, Tn., U.S. C12 149
Shoup, Id., U.S. D4 119
Shouxian, China C5 34
Show Low, Az., U.S. C5 110
Shreve, Oh., U.S. B3 142
Shreveport, La., U.S. B2 125
Shrewsbury, Eng., U.K. I11 8
Shrewsbury, Ma., U.S. B4 128
Shrewsbury, N.J., U.S. C4 137
Shrewsbury, Pa., U.S. G8 145
Shri Dūngargarh, India F6 44
Shrīrangapattana, India F4 46
Shropshire, co., Eng., U.K. I11 8
Shuajingsi, China E7 30
Shuangcheng, China B12 30
Shuanghe, China D5 34
Shuangjiangqiao, China B5 40
Shuangliao, China C11 30
Shuangmiaozi, China A10 32
Shuangyashan, China B13 30
Shubenacadie, N.S., Can. D6 101
Shubert, Ne., U.S. D10 134
Shubrā al-Khaymah, Egypt B6 60
Shubuta, Ms., U.S. D5 131
Shuhong, China G9 34
Shuijing, China A5 40
Shuikouguan, China C9 40
Shuitouwei, China I4 34
Shuksan, Mount, mtn., Wa., U.S. A4 154
Shule, stm., China C6 30
Shulerville, S.C., U.S. E8 147
Shullsburg, Wi., U.S. F3 156
Shumagin Islands, is., Ak., U.S. E7 109
Shumway, Il., U.S. D5 120
Shunchang, China I6 34
Shunde, China M2 34
Shungnak, Ak., U.S. B8 109
Shuqualak, Ms., U.S. C5 131
Shurugwi, Zimb. B10 66
Shūsh, Iran E10 48
Shūshtar, Iran E10 48
Shuswap Lake, l., B.C., Can. D8 99
Shuwak, Sud. J8 60
Shwebo, Burma C3 40
Shweli (Longchuan), stm., Asia C4 40
Shyok, stm., Asia C7 44
Siālkot, Pak. D6 44
Siam, Gulf of see Thailand, Gulf of, b., Asia I6 40
Siam see Thailand, ctry., Asia B3 38
Si'an, China E8 34
Sian see Xi'an, China E8 30
Šiapa, stm., Ven. G10 84
Šiaškotan, ostrov, i., U.S.S.R. H22 24
Šiauliai, U.S.S.R. F6 26
Sibā'ī, Jabal as-, mtn., Egypt I3 48
Sibaj, U.S.S.R. E19 4
Sibasa, Venda D10 66
Sibbald, Alta., Can. D5 98
Šibenik, Yugo. F10 18
Siberia, In., U.S. H4 121
Siberia see Sibir', reg., U.S.S.R. D14 24
Sibert, Ky., U.S. C6 124
Siberut, Pulau, i., Indon. F2 38
Sibi, Pak. F2 44
Sibir' (Siberia), reg., U.S.S.R. D14 24
Sibir'akova, ostrov, i., U.S.S.R. C13 22
Sibiti, Congo B2 58
Sibiu, Rom. D8 20
Sibiu, co., Rom. D8 20
Sibley, Il., U.S. C5 120
Sibley, Ia., U.S. A2 122
Sibley, La., U.S. B2 125
Sibley, Ms., U.S. D2 131
Sibley, Mo., U.S. h11 132
Sibley, co., Mn., U.S. F4 130
Sibolga, Indon. N5 40
Sibsāgar, India G16 44
Sibuyan Island, i., Phil. C7 38
Sibuyan Sea, Phil. C7 38
Sicamous, B.C., Can. D8 99
Sicasica, Bol. G8 82
Siccus, stm., Austl. H3 70
Sichomovi, Az., U.S. B5 110
Sichote-Alin', mts., U.S.S.R. H19 24
Sichuan (Szechwan), prov., China E7 30
Sichuanzhai, China C6 40
Sicilia, prov., Italy L9 18
Sicilia (Sicily), i., Italy L9 18
Sicily, Strait of, strt. L6 18
Sicily Island, La., U.S. C4 125
Sicily see Sicilia, i., Italy L9 18
Sicklerville, N.J., U.S. D3 137
Sico Tinto, stm., Hond. B9 92
Sicuani, Peru F6 82
Šid, Yugo. D3 20
Siddhapur, India I5 44
Siddipet, India C5 46
Sideling Hill, mtn., U.S. A1 127
Sideling Hill Creek, stm., Md., U.S. A1 127
Sidell, Il., U.S. D6 120
Sidéradougou, Burkina F7 64
Siderópolis, Braz. E14 80
Sídheros, Ákra, c., Grc. N10 20
Sidhi, India H9 44
Sīdī 'Abd ar-Raḥmān, Egypt B5 60
Sidi Aïssa, Alg. C12 62
Sidi Ali Ben Nasrallah, Tun. N4 18
Sīdī Barrānī, Egypt B3 60
Sidi bel Abbès, Alg. C10 62
Sidi Bennour, Mor. D6 62
Sidi Bou Zid, Tun. C15 62
Sidi Daoud, Tun. L5 18
Sīdī Hunaysh, Egypt B4 60
Sidi Ifni, Mor. F5 62
Sidi Kacem, Mor. C8 62
Sidikalang, Indon. M5 40
Sidi Moussa, Oued, val., Alg. G13 62
Sidi Okba, Alg. C13 62
Sidi Slimane, Mor. C8 62
Sidi Smaïl, Mor. D6 62
Sidley, Mount, mtn., Ant. C10 73
Sidmouth, Eng., U.K. K10 8
Sidney, B.C., Can. E6 99
Sidney, Man., Can. E2 100
Sidney, Ar., U.S. A4 111
Sidney, Il., U.S. C5 120
Sidney, In., U.S. B6 121
Sidney, Ia., U.S. D2 122
Sidney, Mt., U.S. C12 133
Sidney, Ne., U.S. C3 134
Sidney, N.Y., U.S. C5 139
Sidney, Oh., U.S. B1 142
Sidney Center, N.Y., U.S. C5 139
Sidney Lanier, Lake, res., Ga., U.S. B2 117
Sido, Mali F6 64
Sidon, Ms., U.S. B3 131
Sidonia, Tn., U.S. A3 149
Sidon see Ṣaydā, Leb. A4 50
Sidra, Gulf of see Surt, Khalīj, b., Libya B4 56
Sidrolândia, Braz. F1 79
Siedlce, Pol. C22 10
Siegburg, Ger. E7 10
Siegen, Ger. E8 10
Siemianowice Śląskie, Pol. E19 10
Siemiatycze, Pol. C22 10
Siĕmréab, Camb. H7 40
Siena, Italy F6 18
Sieradz, Pol. D18 10
Sierck-les-Bains, Fr. C13 14
Sierpc, Pol. C19 10
Sierra, co., Ca., U.S. C3 112
Sierra, co., N.M., U.S. D2 138
Sierra Blanca, Tx., U.S. o12 150
Sierra Blanca Peak, mtn., N.M., U.S. D4 138
Sierra Chica, Arg. I8 80
Sierra City, Ca., U.S. C3 112
Sierra Colorada, Arg. E3 78
Sierra de Agua, Belize I15 90
Sierra de Outes, Spain C3 16
Sierra Estrella, mts., Az., U.S. m8 110
Sierra Gorda, Chile B4 80
Sierra Leone, ctry., Afr. G4 54
Sierra Madre, Ca., U.S. m12 112
Sierra Nevada, Parque Nacional, Ven. C7 84
Sierras Bayas, Arg. I8 80
Sierra Vista, Az., U.S. F5 110
Sierre, Switz. F8 13
Siesta Key, i., Fl., U.S. E4 116
Siete Puntas, stm., Para. B9 80
Sífnos, i., Grc. M8 20
Sifton, Man., Can. D1 100
Sig, Alg. J11 16
Sig, U.S.S.R. I24 6
Sigean, Fr. I9 14
Sigel, Il., U.S. D5 120
Sighetu Marmaţiei, Rom. B7 20
Sighişoara, Rom. C8 20
Sigli, Indon. L3 40
Siglufjördur, Ice. A4 6a
Sigmaringen, Ger. G9 10
Signal Mountain, Tn., U.S. D8 149
Signal Mountain, mtn., Tn., U.S. C9 149
Signal Mountain, mtn., Vt., U.S. C4 152
Signal Mountain, mtn., Va., U.S. g11 153
Signal Peak, mtn., Az., U.S. D1 110
Signal Peak, mtn., Ut., U.S. F2 151
Signy, sci., B.A.T. B1 73
Signy-l'Abbaye, Fr. C11 14
Sigourney, Ia., U.S. C5 122
Sigre, stm., Hond. B10 92
Sigsig, Ec. I3 84
Siguanea, Ensenada de la, b., Cuba D3 94
Siguas, stm., Peru G5 82
Siguatepeque, Hond. C7 92
Sigüenza, Spain D9 16
Siguiri, Gui. F5 64
Sigulda, U.S.S.R. D7 26
Sigurd, Ut., U.S. E4 151
Sihanoukville see Kâmpóng Saôm, Camb. I7 40
Sihu, China I5 32
Sihuas, Peru C3 82
Siirt, Tur. C6 48
Sijiazi, China B8 32
Sikandarābād, India F7 44
Sīkar, India G6 44
Sikasso, Mali F7 64
Sikéai, Grc. M6 20
Sikensi, I.C. I7 64
Sikeston, Mo., U.S. E8 132
Sikkim, state, India G13 44
Sikosi, Nmb. A6 66
Šikotan, ostrov (Shikotan-tō), i., U.S.S.R. D21 36a
Silacayoapan, Mex. I10 90
Šilalė, U.S.S.R. F5 26
Silandro, Italy C5 18
Silao, Mex. G9 90
Silas, Al., U.S. D1 108
Sīlat az-Zahr, Isr. Occ. D4 50
Silay, Phil. C7 38
Silchar, India H15 44
Şile, Tur. H13 20
Siler City, N.C., U.S. B3 140
Silesia, hist. reg., Pol. D16 10
Silet, Alg. I13 62
Siletz, Or., U.S. C3 144
Silex, Mo., U.S. B6 132
Silgadhī, Nepal F9 44
Silhouette, i., Sey. B11 58
Siliana, Tun. M4 18
Silifke, Tur. C2 48
Siling Co, l., China E13 44
Silistra, Bul. E11 20
Silivri, Tur. H12 20
Šilka, U.S.S.R. G15 24
Šilka, stm., U.S.S.R. G15 24
Sillamäe, U.S.S.R. B10 26
Sillery, Que., Can. n17 104
Sillian, Aus. I12 10
Sillustani, hist., Peru F6 82
Siloam, Ga., U.S. C3 117
Siloam Springs, Ar., U.S. A1 111
Šilovo, U.S.S.R. G23 26
Silsbee, Tx., U.S. D5 150
Silt, Co., U.S. B3 113
Silton, Sask., Can. G3 105
Šiluko, Nig. H12 64
Šilutė, U.S.S.R. F4 26
Silva, Mo., U.S. D7 132
Silva Jardim, Braz. G7 79
Silvan (Miyafarkin), Tur. B6 48
Silvânia, Braz. D4 79
Silvaplana, Switz. F12 13
Silver Bank Passage, strt., N.A. D9 94
Silver Bay, Mn., U.S. C7 130
Silver Bow, co., Mt., U.S. E4 133
Silver City, Ia., U.S. C2 122
Silver City, Ms., U.S. B3 131
Silver City, Nv., U.S. D2 135
Silver City, N.M., U.S. E1 138
Silver Cliff, Co., U.S. C5 113
Silver Creek, Ga., U.S. B1 117
Silver Creek, Ms., U.S. D3 131
Silver Creek, Ne., U.S. C8 134
Silver Creek, N.Y., U.S. C1 139
Silver Creek, stm., U.S. H6 121
Silver Creek, stm., Ne., U.S. g11 134
Silver Creek, stm., Or., U.S. D7 144
Silverdale, Wa., U.S. B3 154
Silver Grove, Ky., U.S. h14 124
Silverhill, Al., U.S. E2 108
Silver Hill, Md., U.S. f9 127
Silver Island Mountains, mts., Ut., U.S. C2 151
Silver Lake, In., U.S. B6 121
Silver Lake, Ks., U.S. C8 123
Silver Lake, Ma., U.S. f11 128
Silver Lake, Mn., U.S. F4 130
Silver Lake, N.H., U.S. C4 136
Silver Lake, Wi., U.S. F5 156
Silver Lake, l., De., U.S. D3 115
Silver Lake, l., Ia., U.S. A3 122
Silver Lake, l., Me., U.S. C3 126
Silver Lake, l., N.H., U.S. E2 136
Silver Lake, l., N.H., U.S. C4 136
Silver Lake, l., Or., U.S. D7 144
Silver Lake, l., Wa., U.S. g13 154
Silverpeak, Nv., U.S. F4 135
Silver Peak Range, mts., Nv., U.S. F4 135
Silver Point, Tn., U.S. C8 149
Silver Spring, Md., U.S. C3 127
Silver Springs, Fl., U.S. C4 116
Silver Springs, Nv., U.S. D2 135
Silver Star Mountain, mtn., Wa., U.S. A5 154
Silverthrone Mountain, mtn., B.C., Can. D4 99
Silvertip Mountain, mtn., Mt., U.S. C3 133
Silverton, B.C., Can. E9 99
Silverton, Co., U.S. D3 113
Silverton, Id., U.S. B3 119
Silverton, N.J., U.S. C4 137
Silverton, Oh., U.S. o13 142
Silverton, Or., U.S. C4 144
Silverton, Tx., U.S. B2 150
Silvi, Italy G9 18
Silvia, Col. F4 84
Silvies, stm., Or., U.S. D7 144
Silview, De., U.S. B3 115
Silvis, Il., U.S. B3 120
Silvretta Gruppe, mts., Eur. E13 13
Sima, Com. L16 67a
Şima, U.S.S.R. E22 26
Šimanovsk, U.S.S.R. G17 24
Simao, China G7 30
Simav, Tur. J12 20
Simbal, Peru B2 82
Simcoe, Ont., Can. E4 103
Simcoe, Lake, l., Ont., Can. C5 103
Simeria, Rom. D7 20
Simeulue, Pulau, i., Indon. M4 40
Simferopol', U.S.S.R. I4 22
Sími, i., Grc. M11 20
Simikot, Nepal F9 44
Simiri, Niger D11 64
Simití, Col. D6 84
Simi Valley, Ca., U.S. E4 112
Simla, Co., U.S. B6 113
Simmern, Ger. F7 10
Simmesport, La., U.S. D4 125
Simmie, Sask., Can. H1 105

Name — Map Ref. — Page

Simms, Mt., U.S. C5 133
Simms Stream, stm., N.H., U.S. g7 136
Simnas, U.S.S.R. G6 26
Simoca, Arg. D6 80
Simojovel, Mex. I13 90
Simonette, stm., Alta., Can. B1 98
Simon's Town, S. Afr. J4 66
Šimorskoje, U.S.S.R. F25 26
Simpang-kiri, stm., Indon. M4 40
Simplon Pass, Switz. F9 13
Simplon Tunnel, Eur. F9 13
Simpson, Sask., Can. F3 105
Simpson, Ks., U.S. C6 123
Simpson, La., U.S. C3 125
Simpson, N.C., U.S. B5 140
Simpson, Pa., U.S. C11 145
Simpson, W.V., U.S. k10 155
Simpson, co., Ky., U.S. D3 124
Simpson, co., Ms., U.S. D4 131
Simpson Creek, stm., W.V., U.S. k10 155
Simpson Desert, des., Austl. D7 68
Simpson Desert National Park, Austl. E3 70
Simpson Strait, strt., N.W. Ter., Can. C13 96
Simpsonville, Ky., U.S. B4 124
Simpsonville, S.C., U.S. B3 147
Sims, Il., U.S. E5 120
Sims, In., U.S. D6 121
Simsboro, La., U.S. B3 125
Simsbury, Ct., U.S. B4 114
Šimsk, U.S.S.R. C13 26
Simušir, ostrov, i., U.S.S.R. H22 24
Sīnā', Shibh Jazīrat (Sinai Peninsula), pen., Egypt C7 60
Sinai, S.D., U.S. C8 148
Sinai, Mount see Mūsā, Jabal, mtn., Egypt C7 60
Sinaia, Rom. D9 20
Sinai Peninsula see Sīnā', Shibh Jazīrat, pen., Egypt C7 60
Sin'aja, stm., U.S.S.R. E16 24
Sinaloa, state, Mex. F6 90
Sinaloa, stm., Mex. E5 90
Sinalunga, Italy F6 18
Sinamaica, Ven. B7 84
Sinan, China F8 30
Sinanju, N. Kor. D13 32
Sin'avka, U.S.S.R. I9 26
Sīnāwin, Libya E16 62
Sinbo, Burma B4 40
Sincé, Col. C5 84
Sincelejo, Col. C5 84
Sinch'ang, N. Kor. C16 32
Sinch'ŏn, N. Kor. E13 32
Sinclair, Man., Can. E1 100
Sinclair, Me., U.S. A4 126
Sinclair, Wy., U.S. E5 157
Sinclair, Lake, res., Ga., U.S. C3 117
Sindara, Gabon B2 58
Sindelfingen, Ger. G9 10
Sindi, U.S.S.R. C7 26
Sındırgı, Tur. J12 20
Sindri, India I12 44
Sine, val., Sen. D2 64
Şinekçi, Tur. I11 20
Sinendé, Benin F11 64
Sinevir, U.S.S.R. A7 20
Sinez'orki, U.S.S.R. H17 26
Singapore, Sing. N7 40
Singapore, ctry., Asia E3 38
Singapore Strait, strt., Asia N8 40
Singaraja, Indon. G6 38
Sing Buri, Thai. G6 40
Singen [Hohentwiel], Ger. H8 10
Singhampton, Ont., Can. C4 103
Singida, Tan. B6 58
Singkaling Hkāmti, Burma A3 40
Singkang, Indon. F7 38
Singkawang, Indon. N10 40
Singkep, Pulau, i., Indon. O8 40
Singleton, Austl. I9 70
Singuédeze (Shingwidzi), stm., Afr. D10 66
Sinhŭng, N. Kor. C15 32
Sinj, Yugo. F11 18
Sinjah, Sud. K7 60
Sinjai, Indon. G7 38
Sinkāt, Sud. H9 60
Sinkiang see Xinjiang Uygur Zizhiqu, prov., China C3 30
Sinking Creek, stm., Ky., U.S. C3 124
Sinmak, N. Kor. E14 32
Sinnai, Italy J4 18
Sinnamary, Fr. Gu. B8 76
Sinnar, India C3 46
Sinnemahoning Creek, stm., Pa., U.S. D5 145
Sinnemahoning Creek, First Fork, stm., Pa., U.S. D5 145
Sinnes, Nor. L10 6
Sînnicolau Mare, Rom. C4 20
Sinnūris, Egypt C6 60
Sinop, Tur. G15 4
Sinp'o, N. Kor. C16 32
Sinsheim, Ger. C15 14
Sintaluta, Sask., Can. G4 105
Sint-Amandsberg, Bel. F4 12
Sintang, Indon. E5 38
Sint Annaland, Neth. E5 12
Sint Annaparochie, Neth. B8 12
Sint Eustatius, i., Neth. Ant. F13 94
Sint Maarten (Saint-Martin), i., N.A. E13 94
Sint-Michiels, Bel. F3 12
Sint-Niklaas (Saint-Nicolas), Bel. F5 12
Sinton, Tx., U.S. E4 150
Sintra, Port. G2 16
Sint-Truiden (Saint-Trond), Bel. G7 12
Sinú, stm., Col. C5 84
Sinŭiju, N. Kor. C12 32
Siocon, Phil. D7 38
Siófok, Hung. I18 10
Sion (Sitten), Switz. F7 13
Sioux, co., Ia., U.S. A1 122
Sioux, co., Ne., U.S. B2 134
Sioux, co., N.D., U.S. C4 141
Sioux Center, Ia., U.S. A1 122
Sioux City, Ia., U.S. B1 122
Sioux Falls, S.D., U.S. D9 148
Sioux Lookout, Ont., Can. o17 103
Sioux Rapids, Ia., U.S. B2 122
Sipaliwini, stm., Sur. F14 84
Sipapo, stm., Ven. E9 84
Siparia, Trin. I14 94
Siping, China C11 30
Sipiwesk Lake, l., Man., Can. B3 100
Siple, sci., Ant. C12 73
Siple, Mount, mtn., Ant. C10 73
Sipsey, Al., U.S. B2 108
Sipsey, stm., Al., U.S. B2 108
Sipsey Fork, stm., Al., U.S. A2 108
Sipu, China C1 32
Šipunskij, mys, c., U.S.S.R. G24 24
Siqueira Campos, Braz. G4 79
Siquia, stm., Nic. E10 92
Siquirres, C.R. G11 92
Siquisique, Ven. B8 84
Si Racha, Thai. H6 40
Siracuas, Para. I11 82
Siracusa, Italy L10 18
Šir'ajevo, U.S.S.R. B14 20
Sirājganj, Bngl. H13 44
Sirasso, I.C. G6 64
Sirba, stm., Afr. E10 64
Sirdar, B.C., Can. E9 99
Sir Douglas, Mount, mtn., Can. D3 98
Sire, Eth. M9 60
Sir Edward Pellew Group, is., Austl. C7 68
Širega, U.S.S.R. A24 26
Siren, Wi., U.S. C1 156
Siret, stm., Eur. D11 20
Sirevåg, Nor. L9 6
Sirḥān, Wādī as-, val., Sau. Ar. F5 48
Siriya-zaki, c., Japan F16 36
Sir James MacBrien, Mount, mtn., N.W. Ter., Can. D7 96
Sīrjān, Iran G13 48
Sir Joseph Banks Group, is., Austl. J2 70
Sirohi, India H5 44
Sironj, India H7 44
Síros, i., Grc. L8 20
Sirotino, U.S.S.R. F12 26
Sir Sandford, Mount, mtn., B.C., Can. D9 99
Sirsi, India E3 46
Sirte, Gulf of see Surt, Khalīj, b., Libya B4 56
Sirupa, stm., Mex. C5 90
Sīrvān (Diyālā), stm., Asia E8 48
Širvintos, U.S.S.R. F7 26
Sir-Wilfrid, Mont, mtn., Que., Can. C2 104
Sir Wilfrid Laurier, Mount, mtn., B.C., Can. C8 99
Sís, stm., Guat. C3 92
Sisak, Yugo. D11 18
Si Sa Ket, Thai. G8 40
Sishen, S. Afr. F6 66
Sishui, China H5 32
Šišicy, U.S.S.R. H10 26
Siskiyou, co., Ca., U.S. B2 112
Siskiyou Mountains, mts., U.S. F3 144
Siskiyou Pass, Or., U.S. E4 144
Sissach, Switz. D8 13
Sisseton, S.D., U.S. B8 148
Sisseton Indian Reservation, U.S. B8 148
Sissiboo, stm., N.S., Can. E4 101
Sissili, stm., Afr. F9 64
Sisson Branch Reservoir, res., N.B., Can. B2 101
Sissonne, Fr. C10 14
Sissonville, W.V., U.S. C3 155
Sīstān, reg., Asia F17 48
Sister Bay, Wi., U.S. C6 156
Sisters, Or., U.S. C5 144
Sistersville, W.V., U.S. B4 155
Sitabamba, Peru C3 82
Sitakili, Mali E4 64
Sītāmarhi, India G11 44
Sitampiky, Madag. P22 67b
Sītāpur, India G9 44
Siteki, Swaz. F10 66
Sítio da Abadia, Braz. C5 79
Sitionuevo, Col. B5 84
Sitka, Ak., U.S. D12 109
Sitka National Historical Park, Ak., U.S. m22 109
Sitka Sound, strt., Ak., U.S. m22 109
Sitona, Eth. J9 60
Sitrah, Bahr. H11 48
Sittard, Neth. F8 12
Sittoung, stm., Burma E4 40
Sittwe (Akyab), Burma D2 40
Siuna, Nic. D10 92
Siuri, India I12 44
Sivakāsi, India H4 46
Sivas, Tur. B4 48
Sivé, Maur. D3 64
Šiveluč, vulkan, vol., U.S.S.R. F24 24
Siverek, Tur. C5 48
Siverskij, U.S.S.R. B13 26
Sīwah, Egypt C3 60
Siwān, India G11 44
Sixaola, stm., N.A. H12 92
Sixitou, China H8 34
Six Mile, S.C., U.S. B2 147
Sixmile Creek, stm., Fl., U.S. n8 116
Siyāl, Jazā'ir, is., Egypt J4 48
Siyeteb, Sud. H8 60
Sizun, Fr. D2 14
Sjælland, i., Den. N12 6
Sjenica, Yugo. F4 20
Skærbæk, Den. N11 6
Skaftung, Fin. J17 6
Skagen, Den. M12 6
Skagerrak, strt., Eur. M11 6
Skagit, co., Wa., U.S. A4 154
Skagway, Ak., U.S. D12 109
Skaidi, Nor. F19 6
Skaistkalne, U.S.S.R. E7 26
Skalino, U.S.S.R. C23 26
Skalistyj Golec, gora, mtn., U.S.S.R. F15 24
Skamania, co., Wa., U.S. D3 154
Skamokawa, Wa., U.S. C2 154
Skanderborg, Den. M11 6
Skaneateles, N.Y., U.S. C4 139
Skaneateles Lake, l., N.Y., U.S. C4 139
Skaraborgs Län, co., Swe. L13 6
Skard, Ice. B4 6a
Skārdu, Pak. C6 44
Skarżysko-Kamienna, Pol. D20 10
Skaudvilė, U.S.S.R. F5 26
Skawina, Pol. F19 10
Skei, Nor. K10 6
Skeldon, Guy. E14 84
Skeleton Coast, Nmb. B1 66
Skeleton Lake, l., Ont., Can. B5 103
Skellefteå, Swe. I17 6
Skellytown, Tx., U.S. B2 150
Skelton, W.V., U.S. n13 155
Skene, Swe. M13 6
Skene, Ms., U.S. B3 131
Skiatook, Ok., U.S. A5 143
Skiatook Reservoir, res., Ok., U.S. A5 143
Skidel', U.S.S.R. H7 26
Skidmore, Mo., U.S. A2 132
Skidmore, Tx., U.S. E4 150
Skien, Nor. L11 6
Skierniewice, Pol. D20 10
Skihist Mountain, mtn., B.C., Can. D7 99
Skikda (Philippeville), Alg. B14 62
Skillet Fork, stm., Il., U.S. E5 120
Skipton, Austl. K5 70
Skíros, Grc. K8 20
Skive, Den. M11 6
Šklov, U.S.S.R. G13 26
Škofja Loka, Yugo. C9 18
Skokie, Il., U.S. A6 120
Skokomish Indian Reservation, Wa., U.S. B2 154
Skopin, U.S.S.R. H22 26
Skopje, Yugo. H5 20
Skövde, Swe. L13 6
Skovorodino, U.S.S.R. G16 24
Skowhegan, Me., U.S. D3 126
Skownan, Man., Can. D2 100
Skrīveri, U.S.S.R. E8 26
Skrudaļiena, U.S.S.R. F9 26
Skrunda, U.S.S.R. E5 26
Skukuza, S. Afr. E10 66
Skull Valley, Az., U.S. C3 110
Skull Valley, val., Ut., U.S. C3 151
Skull Valley Indian Reservation, Ut., U.S. C3 151
Skuna, stm., Ms., U.S. B4 131
Skunk, stm., Ia., U.S. D6 122
Skuodas, U.S.S.R. E4 26
Skuratovskij, U.S.S.R. G20 26
Skwentna, stm., Ak., U.S. g15 109
Skye, Island of, i., Scot., U.K. D7 8
Skykomish, Wa., U.S. B4 154
Skykomish, stm., Wa., U.S. B4 154
Skyland, Nv., U.S. D2 135
Skyland, N.C., U.S. f10 140
Skylight Mountain, mtn., Ar., U.S. B1 111
Skyline, Al., U.S. A3 108
Skyring, Seno, strt., Chile G2 78
Slade, Ky., U.S. C6 124
Slagovišči, U.S.S.R. H18 26
Slamet, Gunung, mtn., Indon. J14 39a
Slancy, U.S.S.R. B11 26
Slaný, Czech. E14 10
Slater, Ia., U.S. C4 122
Slater, Mo., U.S. B4 132
Slater, S.C., U.S. A3 147
Slatersville, R.I., U.S. A3 146
Slatersville Reservoir, res., R.I., U.S. B3 146
Slatina, Rom. E8 20
Slatington, Pa., U.S. E10 145
Slaton, Tx., U.S. C2 150
Slaughter, La., U.S. D4 125
Slaughter Beach, De., U.S. E4 115
Slaughters, Ky., U.S. C2 124
Slav'ansk, U.S.S.R. H5 22
Slav'ansk-na-Kubani, U.S.S.R. H5 22
Slave, stm., Can. D10 96
Slave Coast, Afr. I11 64
Slave Lake, Alta., Can. B3 98
Slavgorod, U.S.S.R. G7 24
Slavgorod, U.S.S.R. H13 26
Slavkov u Brna, Czech. F16 10
Slavonija, hist. reg., Yugo. D12 18
Slavonska Požega, Yugo. D12 18
Slavonski Brod, Yugo. D13 18
Slavsk, U.S.S.R. F4 26
Sławno, Pol. A16 10
Slayton, Mn., U.S. G3 130
Sledge, Ms., U.S. A3 131
Sled'uki, U.S.S.R. H13 26
Sleeping Bear Dunes National Lakeshore, Mi., U.S. D4 129
Sleeping Bear Point, c., Mi., U.S. D4 129
Sleepy Eye, Mn., U.S. F4 130
Sleetmute, Ak., U.S. C8 109
Slemp, Ky., U.S. C6 124
Slickville, Pa., U.S. F2 145
Slidell, La., U.S. D6 125
Slide Mountain, mtn., N.Y., U.S. D6 139
Sliderock Mountain, mtn., Mt., U.S. D3 133
Sliedrecht, Neth. E6 12
Sligo, Ire. G5 8
Sligo, Pa., U.S. D3 145
Sligo, co., Ire. G5 8
Slim Buttes, mtn., S.D., U.S. B2 148
Slinger, Wi., U.S. E5 156
Slippery Rock, Pa., U.S. D1 145
Sliven, Bul. G10 20
Slivnica, Bul. G7 20
Sloan, Ia., U.S. B1 122
Sloan, Nv., U.S. H6 135
Sloan, N.Y., U.S. C2 139
Sloans Valley, Ky., U.S. D5 124
Slobodka, U.S.S.R. B13 20
Slobodskoj, U.S.S.R. F8 22
Slobodzeja, U.S.S.R. C13 20
Slobozia, Rom. E11 20
Slobozia, Rom. F9 20
Slocan, B.C., Can. E9 99
Slocomb, Al., U.S. D4 108
Slonim, U.S.S.R. H8 26
Slope, co., N.D., U.S. C2 141
Slovak, Ar., U.S. C4 111
Slovakia see Slovensko, hist. reg., Czech. G19 10
Slovan, Pa., U.S. F1 145
Slovenia see Slovenija, state, Yugo. C9 18
Slovenija, state, Yugo. C9 18
Slovenska Bistrica, Yugo. C10 18
Slovenská Socialistická Republika, state, Czech. G20 10
Slovensko, hist. reg., Czech. G19 10
Sluck, U.S.S.R. H10 26
Sl'ud'anka, U.S.S.R. G12 24
Slunj, Yugo. D10 18
Słupca, Pol. C17 10
Słupsk (Stolp), Pol. A17 10
Slurry, S. Afr. E7 66
Smackover, Ar., U.S. D3 111
Smackover Creek, stm., Ar., U.S. D3 111
Smalininkai, U.S.S.R. F5 26
Small Point, c., Me., U.S. g8 126
Smallwood Reservoir, res., Newf., Can. g8 102
Smara, W. Sah. G5 62
Smarr, Ga., U.S. D3 117
Smarts Mountain, mtn., N.H., U.S. C2 136
Smartt, Tn., U.S. D8 149
Smeaton, Sask., Can. D3 105
Smederevo, Yugo. E4 20
Smela, U.S.S.R. H4 22
Smelterville, Id., U.S. B2 119
Smethport, Pa., U.S. C5 145
Šmidovič, U.S.S.R. H18 24
Šmidta, ostrov, i., U.S.S.R. A16 22
Smiley, Sask., Can. F1 105
Smiloviči, U.S.S.R. H11 26
Smiltene, U.S.S.R. D8 26
Smirnovskij, U.S.S.R. G11 22
Smith, Alta., Can. B3 98
Smith, Nv., U.S. E2 135
Smith, co., Ks., U.S. C5 123
Smith, co., Ms., U.S. C4 131
Smith, co., Tn., U.S. A5 149
Smith, co., Tx., U.S. C5 150
Smith, stm., U.S. D3 153
Smith, stm., Mt., U.S. D5 133
Smith and Sayles Reservoir, res., R.I., U.S. B2 146
Smith Arm, b., N.W. Ter., Can. C8 96
Smith Bay, b., Ak., U.S. A9 109
Smithboro, Il., U.S. E4 120
Smith Canyon, val., Co., U.S. D7 113
Smith Center, Ks., U.S. C5 123
Smithers, B.C., Can. B4 99
Smithers, W.V., U.S. C3 155
Smithfield, S. Afr. H8 66
Smithfield, Il., U.S. C3 120
Smithfield, Me., U.S. D3 126
Smithfield, Mo., U.S. D3 132
Smithfield, N.C., U.S. B4 140
Smithfield, Oh., U.S. B5 142
Smithfield, Pa., U.S. G2 145
Smithfield, Ut., U.S. B4 151
Smithfield, Va., U.S. D6 153
Smithfield, W.V., U.S. k9 155
Smith Island, i., B.A.T. B12 73
Smith Island, i., U.S. D5 127
Smith Island, i., Va., U.S. C7 153
Smithland, Ia., U.S. B2 122
Smithland, Ky., U.S. e9 124
Smithmill, Pa., U.S. E5 145
Smith Mills, Ky., U.S. C2 124
Smith Mountain Lake, res., Va., U.S. C3 153
Smith Peak, mtn., Id., U.S. A2 119
Smith Point, c., Ma., U.S. D7 128
Smith Point, c., Va., U.S. C6 153
Smith River, Ca., U.S. B1 112
Smiths, Al., U.S. C4 108
Smithsburg, Md., U.S. A2 127
Smiths Cove, N.S., Can. E4 101
Smiths Falls, Ont., Can. C8 103
Smiths Grove, Ky., U.S. C3 124
Smithshire, Il., U.S. C3 120
Smithton, Austl. M6 70
Smithton, Il., U.S. E4 120
Smithton, Mo., U.S. C4 132
Smith Town, Ky., U.S. D5 124
Smithtown, N.Y., U.S. n15 139
Smithville, Ga., U.S. E2 117
Smithville, In., U.S. F4 121
Smithville, Ms., U.S. A5 131
Smithville, Mo., U.S. B3 132
Smithville, Oh., U.S. B4 142
Smithville, Tn., U.S. D8 149
Smithville, Tx., U.S. D4 150
Smithville, W.V., U.S. B3 155
Smithville Lake, res., Mo., U.S. B3 132
Smoke Creek Desert, des., Nv., U.S. C2 135
Smokey, Cape, c., N.S., Can. C9 101
Smokey Dome, mtn., Id., U.S. F4 119
Smoky, stm., Alta., Can. B1 98
Smoky Cape, c., Austl. H10 70
Smoky Hill, stm., U.S. D5 123
Smoky Hill, North Fork, stm., U.S. C2 123
Smoky Lake, Alta., Can. B4 98
Smoky Mountains, mts., Id., U.S. F4 119
Smolan, Ks., U.S. D6 123
Smol'anica, U.S.S.R. I7 26
Smolensk, U.S.S.R. G15 26
Smoleviči, U.S.S.R. G11 26
Smoljan, Bul. H8 20
Smoot, Wy., U.S. D2 157
Smooth Rock Falls, Ont., Can. o19 103
Smoothstone Lake, l., Sask., Can. C2 105
Smoots Creek, stm., Ks., U.S. g11 123
Smorgon', U.S.S.R. G9 26
Smyrna, De., U.S. C3 115
Smyrna, Ga., U.S. C2 117
Smyrna, Tn., U.S. B5 149
Smyrna, stm., De., U.S. C3 115
Smyrna see İzmir, Tur. K11 20
Smyrna Mills, Me., U.S. B4 126
Smyth, co., Va., U.S. f10 153
Snake, stm., U.S. B3 106
Snake, stm., U.S. D5 130
Snake, stm., Mn., U.S. B1 130
Snake, stm., Ne., U.S. B4 134
Snake Creek, stm., Ne., U.S. B2 134
Snake Falls, wtfl, Ne., U.S. B5 134
Snake Indian, stm., Alta., Can. C1 98
Snake Mountain, mtn., U.S. A10 149
Snake Mountain, mtn., Vt., U.S. C2 152
Snake Range, mts., Nv., U.S. E7 135
Snake River Plain, pl., Id., U.S. F2 119
Snake River Range, mts., U.S. C2 157
Snake Valley, val., U.S. D2 151
Snares Islands, is., N.Z. M20 158
Sn'atyn, U.S.S.R. A9 20
Snead, Al., U.S. A3 108
Sneads, Fl., U.S. B2 116
Sneads Ferry, N.C., U.S. C5 140
Sneedville, Tn., U.S. C10 149
Sneek, Neth. B8 12
Śniardwy, Jezioro, l., Pol. B21 10
Snina, Czech. G22 10
Snipe Keys, is., Fl., U.S. H5 116
Snohomish, Wa., U.S. B3 154
Snohomish, co., Wa., U.S. A4 154
Snoqualmie, Wa., U.S. B4 154
Snoqualmie, stm., Wa., U.S. B4 154
Snoqualmie Pass, Wa., U.S. B4 154
Snøtinden, mtn., Nor. H14 6
Snover, Mi., U.S. E8 129
Snowbank Lake, l., Mn., U.S. B7 130
Snowdon, mtn., Wales, U.K. H9 8
Snowdoun, Al., U.S. C3 108
Snowdrift, N.W. Ter., Can. D10 96
Snowflake, Man., Can. E2 100
Snowflake, Az., U.S. C5 110
Snow Hill, Al., U.S. C2 108
Snow Hill, Md., U.S. D7 127
Snow Hill, N.C., U.S. B5 140
Snowking Mountain, mtn., Wa., U.S. A4 154
Snow Lake, Man., Can. B1 100
Snowmass Mountain, mtn., Co., U.S. B3 113
Snow Mountain, mtn., Me., U.S. C2 126
Snow Peak, mtn., Wa., U.S. A7 154
Snow Shoe, Pa., U.S. D6 145
Snowshoe Lake, l., Me., U.S. B4 126
Snowshoe Peak, mtn., Mt., U.S. B1 133
Snowville, Ut., U.S. B3 151
Snow Water Lake, l., Nv., U.S. C7 135
Snowy, stm., Austl. K8 70
Snowy Mountain, mtn., N.Y., U.S. B6 139
Snowy Mountains, mts., Austl. K8 70
Snowyside Peak, mtn., Id., U.S. F4 119
Snyder, Co., U.S. A7 113
Snyder, Ne., U.S. C9 134
Snyder, Ok., U.S. C3 143
Snyder, Tx., U.S. C2 150
Snyder, co., Pa., U.S. E7 145
Snyder Knob, mtn., W.V., U.S. C5 155
Soacha, Col. E5 84
Soahany, Madag. Q21 67b
Soalala, Madag. P21 67b
Soamanonga, Madag. S21 67b
Soanindrariny, Madag. Q22 67b
Soap Lake, Wa., U.S. B6 154
Soatá, Col. D6 84
Soavinandriana, Madag. Q22 67b
Sobaek-sanmaek, mts., S. Kor. G15 32
Sobat, stm., Sud. M7 60
Sobernheim, Ger. F7 10
Sobieski, Mn., U.S. E4 130
Sobinka, U.S.S.R. F23 26
Soboko, Cen. Afr. Rep. N3 60
Sobolevka, U.S.S.R. A13 20
Sobradinho, Braz. E12 80
Sobrado, Port. D3 16
Sobral, Braz. D10 76
Socaire, Chile B5 80
Socastee, S.C., U.S. D9 147
Soc Giang, Viet. C9 40
Sochaczew, Pol. C20 10
Sochi see Soči, U.S.S.R. G15 4
Sŏch'ŏn, S. Kor. G14 32
Soči, U.S.S.R. I5 22
Social Circle, Ga., U.S. C3 117
Société, Îles de la (Society Islands), is., Fr. Poly. J24 158
Society Hill, S.C., U.S. C8 147
Soco, stm., Dom. Rep. E10 94
Socoltenango, Mex. I13 90
Socompa, Paso, S.A. C4 80
Socorro, Col. D6 84
Socorro, N.M., U.S. C3 138
Socorro, Tx., U.S. o11 150
Socorro, co., N.M., U.S. D2 138
Socorro, Isla, i., Mex. H4 90
Sócota, Peru B2 82
Socotra see Suquṭrā, i., Yemen G5 42
Soc Trang, Viet. J8 40
Socuéllamos, Spain F9 16
Soda Springs, Id., U.S. G7 119
Soddy-Daisy, Tn., U.S. D8 149
Söderhamn, Swe. K15 6
Södermanlands Län, co., Swe. L15 6
Södertälje, Swe. L15 6
Sodo, Eth. N9 60
Södra Kvarken, strt., Eur. K16 6
Sodus, N.Y., U.S. B3 139
Sodus Point, N.Y., U.S. B4 139
Soe, Indon. G7 38
Soekmekaar, S. Afr. D9 66
Soela väin, strt., U.S.S.R. C5 26
Soest, Ger. D8 10
Sofia, stm., Madag. O22 67b
Sofia see Sofija, Bul. G7 20
Sofija (Sofia), Bul. G7 20
Sofrino, U.S.S.R. E20 26
Sogakofe, Ghana H10 64
Sogamoso, Col. E6 84
Sogamoso, stm., Col. D6 84
Sognafjorden, Nor. K9 6
Søgne, Nor. L10 6
Sogn og Fjordane, co., Nor. K10 6
Sogo Nur, l., China C7 30
Söğütalan, Tur. I12 20
Sogxian, China E5 30
Soham, N.M., U.S. B4 138
Soin, Burkina E8 64
Sointula, B.C., Can. D4 99
Soissons, Fr. C10 14
Sojat, India H5 44
Sokal'skogo, proliv, strt., U.S.S.R. B12 24
Sokch'o, S. Kor. E16 32
Söke, Tur. L11 20
Sokir'any, U.S.S.R. A11 20
Sokodé, Togo G10 64
Sokol, U.S.S.R. F6 22
Sokółka, Pol. B23 10
Sokolov, Czech. E12 10
Sokolovo, U.S.S.R. I17 26
Sokołów, Pol. E22 10
Sokołów Podlaski, Pol. C22 10
Sokoto, Nig. E12 64
Sol, Costa del, Spain I7 16
Sol, Rio do, stm., Braz. B8 82
Solacolu, Rom. E10 20
Solana, Fl., U.S. F5 116
Solana Beach, Ca., U.S. F5 112
Solano, Phil. M19 39b
Solano, co., Ca., U.S. C3 112
Solāpur, India D3 46
Solca, Arg. F5 80
Sol'cy, U.S.S.R. C13 26
Soldados, Cerro, mtn., Ec. I3 84
Sol de Julio, Arg. E7 80
Soldier, Ia., U.S. C2 122
Soldier, Ks., U.S. C8 123
Soldier, Ky., U.S. B6 124
Soldier, stm., Ia., U.S. C2 122
Soldier Creek, stm., Ks., U.S. C8 123
Soldier Key, i., Fl., U.S. s3 116
Soldier Pond, Me., U.S. A4 126
Soldiers Grove, Wi., U.S. E3 156
Soldotna, Ak., U.S. g16 109
Soledad, Col. B5 84
Soledad, Ca., U.S. D3 112
Soledad, Ven. C11 84
Soledad Díez Gutiérrez, Mex. F9 90
Soledade, Braz. E12 80
Soleduck, stm., Wa., U.S. B1 154
Solen, N.D., U.S. C5 141
Solentiname, Archipiélago de, is., Nic. F9 92
Solenzara, Fr. M24 15a
Soligalič, U.S.S.R. B25 26
Soligorsk, U.S.S.R. I10 26
Solikamsk, U.S.S.R. F9 22
Solila, Madag. R22 67b
Sol'-Ileck, U.S.S.R. G8 22
Soliman, Tun. M5 18
Solimões see Amazon, stm., S.A. D7 76
Solingen, Ger. D7 10
Solís, Ur. H11 80
Sollefteå, Swe. J15 6
Sóller, Spain F14 16
Solnečnogorsk, U.S.S.R. E19 26
Sologne, reg., Fr. E9 14
Solok, Indon. O6 40
Sololá, Guat. C3 92
Sololá, dept., Guat. C3 92
Solomon, Az., U.S. E6 110
Solomon, Ks., U.S. D6 123
Solomon, stm., Ks., U.S. C6 123
Solomon, North Fork, stm., Ks., U.S. C4 123
Solomon, South Fork, stm., Ks., U.S. C4 123
Solomon Islands, ctry., Oc. G23 2
Solomons, Md., U.S. D5 127
Solomon Sea, Oc. I19 158
Solomon's Pools see Sulaymān, Birak, hist., Isr. Occ. E4 50
Solon, China B11 30
Solon, Ia., U.S. C6 122
Solon, Me., U.S. D3 126
Solon, Oh., U.S. A4 142
Solon Mills, Il., U.S. h8 120
Solon Springs, Wi., U.S. B2 156
Solopaca, Italy H9 18
Solotča, U.S.S.R. G22 26
Solothurn, Switz. D8 13
Solothurn, state, Switz. D7 13
Solotvin, U.S.S.R. A8 20
Solotvina, U.S.S.R. B7 20
Soloveckije ostrova, is., U.S.S.R. I24 6
Solovjevsk, U.S.S.R. H15 24
Solovjovka, U.S.S.R. A13 26
Solovjovsk, U.S.S.R. H21 22
Solsberry, In., U.S. F4 121
Solsona, Spain D13 16
Solt, Hung. I19 10
Solvay, N.Y., U.S. B4 139
Sol'vyčegodsk, U.S.S.R. E7 22
Solway Firth, est., U.K. G10 8
Solwezi, Zam. D5 58
Soly, U.S.S.R. G9 26
Sōma, Japan J15 36
Soma, Tur. J11 20
Somalia (Somaliya), ctry., Afr. G10 56
Somali Republic see Somalia, ctry., Afr. G10 56
Sombor, Yugo. D3 20
Sombra, Ont., Can. E2 103
Sombrerete, Mex. F8 90
Sombrero, i., St. K./N. E13 94
Sombrero Channel, strt., India K2 40
Sombrio, Braz. E14 80
Sombrio, Lagoa do, b., Braz. E14 80
Somerdale, N.J., U.S. D2 137
Sõmerpalu, U.S.S.R. D9 26
Somers, Ct., U.S. B6 114

Name — Map Ref. — Page

Somers, Mt., U.S. B2 133
Somers, Wi., U.S. F6 156
Somerset, Austl. M6 70
Somerset, Man., Can. E2 100
Somerset, Co., U.S. C3 113
Somerset, In., U.S. C6 121
Somerset, Ky., U.S. C5 124
Somerset, Ma., U.S. C5 128
Somerset, N.J., U.S. B3 137
Somerset, Oh., U.S. C3 142
Somerset, Pa., U.S. F3 145
Somerset, Tx., U.S. k7 150
Somerset, Wi., U.S. C1 156
Somerset, co., Eng., U.K. J11 8
Somerset, co., Me., U.S. C2 126
Somerset, co., Md., U.S. D6 127
Somerset, co., N.J., U.S. B3 137
Somerset, co., Pa., U.S. G3 145
Somerset East, S. Afr. I7 66
Somerset Island, i., N.W. Ter., Can. B14 96
Somerset Reservoir, res., Vt., U.S. E3 152
Somerset West, S. Afr. J4 66
Somers Point, N.J., U.S. E3 137
Somersville, Ct., U.S. B6 114
Somersworth, N.H., U.S. D5 136
Somerton, Az., U.S. E1 110
Somervell, co., Tx., U.S. C4 150
Somerville, Al., U.S. A3 108
Somerville, In., U.S. H3 121
Somerville, Ma., U.S. B5 128
Somerville, N.J., U.S. B3 137
Somerville, Tn., U.S. B2 149
Somerville, Tx., U.S. D4 150
Somerville Lake, res., Tx., U.S. D4 150
Someș (Szamos), stm., Eur. B7 20
Somino, U.S.S.R. B17 26
Somme, dept., Fr. C9 14
Somme, stm., Fr. C9 14
Sömmerda, Ger. D11 10
Somogy, co., Hung. I17 10
Somonauk, Il., U.S. B5 120
Somotillo, Nic. D8 92
Somoto, Nic. D8 92
Somport, Puerto de, Eur. C11 16
Sompuis, Fr. D11 14
Son, stm., India H10 44
Soná, Pan. C2 84
Sonaguera, Hond. B8 92
Sonceboz, Switz. D7 13
Sŏnch'ŏn, N. Kor. D12 32
Sønderborg, Den. N11 6
Sondershausen, Ger. D10 10
Sondheimer, La., U.S. B4 125
Sondrio, Italy C4 18
Sonepur, India B7 46
Songbu, China D3 34
Sŏngbyŏn-ni, N. Kor. E13 32
Song Cau, Viet. H10 40
Songea, Tan. D7 58
Songhua, stm., China B13 30
Songhua Hu, res., China C12 30
Songhwa, N. Kor. E13 32
Songjiang, China D10 34
Songjiangzhen, China A14 32
Songjŏng, S. Kor. H14 32
Sŏngju, S. Kor. H16 32
Songkhla, Thai. K6 40
Songlinba, China K4 34
Sŏngnam, S. Kor. F15 32
Songnim, N. Kor. E13 32
Songshu, China D10 32
Šonguj, U.S.S.R. G23 6
Sonid Youqi, China C9 30
Sonīpat, India F7 44
Sonkovo, U.S.S.R. D20 26
Son La, Viet. D7 40
Sonmiāni, Pak. H2 44
Sonneberg, Ger. E11 10
Sonningdale, Sask., Can. E2 105
Sono, Rio do, stm., Braz. D6 79
Sonoma, Ca., U.S. C2 112
Sonoma, co., Ca., U.S. C2 112
Sonoma Peak, mtn., Nv., U.S. C4 135
Sonoma Range, mts., Nv., U.S. C4 135
Sonora, Ca., U.S. D3 112
Sonora, Ky., U.S. C4 124
Sonora, Tx., U.S. D2 150
Sonora, state, Mex. C4 90
Sonora, stm., Mex. C4 90
Sonoran Desert, des., N.A. F8 86
Sonoyta, Mex. B3 90
Sonqor, Iran D9 48
Sŏnsan, S. Kor. G16 32
Sonseca, Spain F8 16
Sonskyn, S. Afr. H8 66
Sonsón, Col. E5 84
Sonsonate, El Sal. D5 92
Sontag, Ms., U.S. D3 131
Son Tay, Viet. D8 40
Sonthofen, Ger. H10 10
Soochow see Suzhou, China D9 34
Sopachuy, Bol. H9 82
Soper, Ok., U.S. C6 143
Soperton, Ga., U.S. D4 117
Sopetrán, Col. D5 84
Sop Hao, Laos D8 40
Sophia, W.V., U.S. D3 155
Sopot, Pol. A18 10
Sopron, Hung. H16 10
Sopur, India C6 44
Sora, Italy H8 18
Soras, Peru F5 82
Sorata, Bol. F7 82
Soraya, Peru F5 82
Sorel, Que., Can. C4 104
Sorell, Austl. N7 70
Sorell, Cape, c., Austl. N6 70
Sorento, Il., U.S. E4 120
Sørfold, Nor. H14 6
Sorgono, Italy I4 18
Soria, Spain D9 16
Soriano, Ur. G9 80
Sørli, Nor. I13 6
Sorocaba, Braz. G5 79
Soročinsk, U.S.S.R. G8 22
Soroki, U.S.S.R. A12 20
Sorong, Indon. F9 38
Soroti, Ug. H7 56
Sørøya, i., Nor. F18 6
Sorrento, Italy I9 18
Sorrento, Fl., U.S. D5 116
Sorrento, La., U.S. D5 125
Sorris Sorris, Nmb. C2 66
Sør Rondane Mountains, mts., Ant. C3 73
Sorsele, Swe. I15 6
Sorsogon, Phil. O21 39b
Sortavala, U.S.S.R. E4 22
Sortland, Nor. G14 6
Sør-Trøndelag, co., Nor. J12 6
Sõrve neem, c., U.S.S.R. D5 26
Sŏsan, S. Kor. G14 32
Sosneado, Cerro, mtn., Arg. H4 80
Sosnogorsk, U.S.S.R. E8 22
Sosnovec, U.S.S.R. I24 6
Sosnovo, U.S.S.R. A13 26
Sosnovo-Oz'orskoje, U.S.S.R. G14 24
Sosnovskoje, U.S.S.R. F26 26
Sosnovyj Bor, U.S.S.R. B12 26
Sosnovyj Bor, U.S.S.R. I12 26
Sosnowiec, Pol. E19 10
Șoso, Ms., U.S. D4 131
Šostka, U.S.S.R. G4 22
Sos'va, U.S.S.R. F10 22
Sotério, stm., Braz. D9 82
Sotkamo, Fin. I21 6
Soto la Marina, Mex. F10 90
Soto la Marina, Barra, i., Mex. E11 90
Sotomayor, Bol. H9 82
Sotteville, Fr. C8 14
Soucook, stm., N.H., U.S. D4 136
Soudan, Mn., U.S. C6 130
Souderton, Pa., U.S. F11 145
Soufrière, mtn., Guad. F14 94
Soufrière, mtn., St. Vin. H14 94
Souguer, Alg. C11 62
Souhegan, stm., N.H., U.S. E3 136
Souilly, Fr. C12 14
Souk-el-Arba-des-Beni-Hassan, Mor. J6 16
Souk-Khemis-du-Sahel, Mor. J5 16
Sŏul (Seoul), S. Kor. F14 32
Soulougou, Burkina E10 64
Soúnion, Ákra, c., Grc. L8 20
Souq Ahras, Alg. B14 62
Sources, Mont aux, mtn., Afr. G9 66
Soure, Port. E3 16
Sour el Ghozlane, Alg. B12 62
Souris, Man., Can. E1 100
Souris, P.E.I., Can. C7 101
Souris, N.D., U.S. A5 141
Souris, stm., N.A. B6 106
Sourland Mountain, hill, N.J., U.S. C3 137
Sourou, stm., Afr. E8 64
Sousa, Braz. E11 76
Sousânia, Braz. D4 79
Sousel, Port. G4 16
Sousse, Tun. N5 18
South, stm., Ga., U.S. h8 117
South, stm., Ia., U.S. C4 122
South, stm., N.C., U.S. C4 140
South Acton, Ma., U.S. g10 128
South Acworth, N.H., U.S. D2 136
South Addison, Me., U.S. D5 126
South Africa (Suid-Afrika), ctry., Afr. H4 58
South Amboy, N.J., U.S. C4 137
South America F8 74
South Amherst, Ma., U.S. B2 128
South Amherst, Oh., U.S. A3 142
Southampton, N.B., Can. D2 101
Southampton, N.S., Can. D5 101
Southampton, Ont., Can. C3 103
Southampton, Eng., U.K. K12 8
Southampton, N.Y., U.S. n16 139
Southampton, co., Va., U.S. D5 153
Southampton, Cape, c., N.W. Ter., Can. D16 96
Southampton Island, i., N.W. Ter., Can. D16 96
South Andaman, i., India I2 40
South Anna, stm., Va., U.S. C5 153
South Ashburnham, Ma., U.S. A4 128
South Australia, state, Austl. F7 68
Southaven, Ms., U.S. A3 131
South Bald Mountain, mtn., Co., U.S. A5 113
South Baldy, mtn., N.M., U.S. D2 138
South Barnstead, N.H., U.S. D4 136
South Barre, Vt., U.S. C3 152
South Bay, Fl., U.S. F6 116
Southbeach, Or., U.S. C2 144
South Belmar, N.J., U.S. C4 137
South Beloit, Il., U.S. A4 120
South Bend, In., U.S. A5 121
South Bend, Wa., U.S. C2 154
South Berwick, Me., U.S. E2 126
South Bethany, De., U.S. F5 115
South Bloomfield, Oh., U.S. C3 142
Southborough, Ma., U.S. B4 128
South Boston, Va., U.S. D4 153
South Bound Brook, N.J., U.S. B3 137
South Branch, Newf., Can. E2 102
South Branch Lake, l., Me., U.S. C4 126
South Branch Mountain, mtn., W.V., U.S. B6 155
Southbridge, Ma., U.S. B3 128
South Bristol, Me., U.S. E3 126
South Britain, Ct., U.S. D3 114
South Broadway, Wa., U.S. C5 154
South Brookfield, N.S., Can. E5 101
South Bruny Island, i., Austl. N7 70
South Burlington, Vt., U.S. C2 152
Southbury, Ct., U.S. D3 114
South Carolina, state, U.S. D6 147
South Carthage, Tn., U.S. C8 149
South Carver, Ma., U.S. C6 128
South Charleston, Oh., U.S. C2 142
South Charleston, W.V., U.S. C3 155
South Chatham, Ma., U.S. C7 128
South Chicago Heights, Il., U.S. m9 120
South China, Me., U.S. D3 126
South China Sea, Asia M7 34
South Cle Elum, Wa., U.S. B5 154
South Coffeyville, Ok., U.S. A6 143
South Colby, Wa., U.S. e10 154
South Congaree, S.C., U.S. D5 147
South Connellsville, Pa., U.S. G2 145
South Corning, N.Y., U.S. C3 139
South Dakota, state, U.S. C5 148
South Danville, N.H., U.S. E4 136
South Dartmouth, Ma., U.S. C6 128
South Daytona, Fl., U.S. C5 116
South Deerfield, Ma., U.S. B2 128
South Dennis, Ma., U.S. C7 128
South Dorset, Vt., U.S. E2 152
South Duxbury, Ma., U.S. B6 128
South East, dept., Bots. E7 66
South East Cape, c., Austl. N7 70
Southeast Cape, c., Ak., U.S. C6 109
South Easton, Ma., U.S. B5 128
Southeast Pass, strt., La., U.S. E7 125
South East Point, c., Austl. L7 70
Southeast Point, c., R.I., U.S. h7 146
South Elgin, Il., U.S. B5 120
Southend-on-Sea, Eng., U.K. J14 8
South English, Ia., U.S. C5 122
Southern, dept., Bots. E7 66
Southern Alps, mts., N.Z. E3 72
Southern Cross, Austl. F3 68
Southern Ghāts, mts., India H4 46
Southern Indian Lake, l., Man., Can. f8 100
Southern Pines, N.C., U.S. B3 140
Southern Ute Indian Reservation, Co., U.S. D2 113
South Esk, stm., Austl. M7 70
South Euclid, Oh., U.S. g9 142
Southey, Sask., Can. G3 105
South Fabius, stm., Mo., U.S. A5 132
South Fallsburg, N.Y., U.S. D6 139
Southfield, Mi., U.S. o15 129
South Foreland, c., Eng., U.K. J15 8
South Fork, Co., U.S. D4 113
South Fork, Pa., U.S. F4 145
South Fox Island, i., Mi., U.S. C5 129
South Freeport, Me., U.S. g7 126
South Fulton, Tn., U.S. A3 149
South Gastonia, N.C., U.S. B1 140
South Gate, Ca., U.S. n12 112
Southgate, Ky., U.S. h14 124
Southgate, Mi., U.S. p15 129
South Georgia, i., Falk. Is. J11 74
South Glamorgan, co., Wales, U.K. J10 8
South Glastonbury, Ct., U.S. C5 114
South Glens Falls, N.Y., U.S. B7 139
South Grafton, Ma., U.S. B4 128
South Grand, stm., Mo., U.S. C3 132
South Hadley, Ma., U.S. B2 128
South Hadley Falls, Ma., U.S. B2 128
South Hamilton, Ma., U.S. A6 128
South Hanover, Ma., U.S. h12 128
South Harpswell, Me., U.S. g7 126
South Harwich, Ma., U.S. C7 128
South Hātia Island, i., Bngl. I14 44
South Haven, In., U.S. A3 121
South Haven, Ks., U.S. E6 123
South Haven, Mi., U.S. F4 129
South Heart, N.D., U.S. C3 141
South Heart, stm., Alta., Can. B2 98
South Hero, Vt., U.S. B2 152
South Hero Island, i., Vt., U.S. B2 152
South Hill, Va., U.S. D4 153
South Hingham, Ma., U.S. h12 128
South Holland, Il., U.S. k9 120
South Holston Lake, res., U.S. A9 149
South Hooksett, N.H., U.S. D4 136
South Hopkinton, R.I., U.S. F1 146
South Houston, Tx., U.S. r14 150
South Hutchinson, Ks., U.S. f11 123
South Indian Lake, Man., Can. A2 100
Southington, Ct., U.S. C4 114
South International Falls, Mn., U.S. B5 130
South Island, i., N.Z. E2 72
South Island, i., S.C., U.S. E9 147
South Jacksonville, Il., U.S. D3 120
South Jordan, Ut., U.S. C3 151
South Junction, Man., Can. E4 100
South Kenosha, Wi., U.S. F6 156
South Lake Tahoe, Ca., U.S. C4 112
South Lancaster, Ma., U.S. B4 128
South Laurel, Md., U.S. B4 127
South Lebanon, Me., U.S. E2 126
South Lebanon, Oh., U.S. C1 142
South Londonderry, Vt., U.S. E3 152
South Loup, stm., Ne., U.S. C6 134
South Lyme, Ct., U.S. D6 114
South Lyndeborogh, N.H., U.S. E3 136
South Lyon, Mi., U.S. F7 129
South Magnetic Pole, Ant. B7 73
South Manitou Island, i., Mi., U.S. C4 129
South Mansfield, La., U.S. B2 125
South Marsh Island, i., Md., U.S. D5 127
South Merrimack, N.H., U.S. E3 136
South Miami, Fl., U.S. G6 116
South Miami Heights, Fl., U.S. s13 116
South Milford, In., U.S. A7 121
South Mills, N.C., U.S. A6 140
South Milwaukee, Wi., U.S. F6 156
South Molton, Eng., U.K. J10 8
Southmont, N.C., U.S. B2 140
South Moose Lake, l., Man., Can. C1 100
South Mountain, Pa., U.S. G7 145
South Mountain, mtn., U.S. B2 127
South Mountain, mtn., Id., U.S. G2 119
South Mountain, mtn., N.M., U.S. k8 138
South Mountains, mts., Az., U.S. m8 110
South Mountains, mts., N.C., U.S. B1 140
South Nahanni, stm., N.W. Ter., Can. D7 96
South Naknek, Ak., U.S. D8 109
South Negril Point, c., Jam. E5 94
South New River Canal, Fl., U.S. r3 116
South Ogden, Ut., U.S. B4 151
Southold, N.Y., U.S. m16 139
South Orange, N.J., U.S. B4 137
South Orkney Islands, is., B.A.T. B1 73
South Orrington, Me., U.S. D4 126
South Paris, Me., U.S. D2 126
South Park, val., Co., U.S. B5 113
South Pass, Wy., U.S. D4 157
South Pass, strt., La., U.S. F6 125
South Patrick Shores, Fl., U.S. D6 116
South Pekin, Il., U.S. C4 120
South Pittsburg, Tn., U.S. D8 149
South Plainfield, N.J., U.S. B4 137
South Platte, stm., U.S. C6 106
South Point, c., Mi., U.S. D7 129
South Pole, Ant. D4 73
South Pomfret, Vt., U.S. D3 152
Southport, Austl. F10 70
Southport, Eng., U.K. H10 8
Southport, Fl., U.S. u16 116
Southport, In., U.S. E5 121
Southport, N.Y., U.S. C4 139
Southport, N.C., U.S. D4 140
South Portland, Me., U.S. E2 126
South Portsmouth, Ky., U.S. B6 124
South Range, Mi., U.S. A2 129
South River, Ont., Can. B5 103
South River, N.J., U.S. C4 137
South River, b., Md., U.S. C4 127
South Royalton, Vt., U.S. D3 152
South Rustico, P.E.I., Can. C6 101
South Ryegate, Vt., U.S. C4 152
South Saint Paul, Mn., U.S. n12 130
South Sandwich Islands, is., Falk. Is. A2 73
South San Francisco, Ca., U.S. h8 112
South Saskatchewan, stm., Can. F11 96
South Shetland Islands, is., B.A.T. B1 73
South Shore, Mo., U.S. f12 132
South Shore, S.D., U.S. B9 148
Southside, Al., U.S. B3 108
Southside, Tn., U.S. A4 149
Southside Place, Tx., U.S. r14 150
South Sioux City, Ne., U.S. B9 134
South Skunk, stm., Ia., U.S. C4 122
South Slocan, B.C., Can. E9 99
South Stony Brook, N.Y., U.S. n15 139
South Streator, Il., U.S. B5 120
South Sutton, N.H., U.S. D3 136
South Swansea, Ma., U.S. C5 128
South Tamworth, N.H., U.S. C4 136
South Taranaki Bight, N.Z. C5 72
South Toms River, N.J., U.S. D4 137
South Torrington, Wy., U.S. D8 157
South Tucson, Az., U.S. E5 110
South Tunnel, Tn., U.S. A5 149
South Twin Mountain, mtn., N.H., U.S. B3 136
South Uist, i., Scot., U.K. D6 8
South Valley Stream, N.Y., U.S. n15 139
South Van Buren, Mo., U.S. E6 132
South Venice, Fl., U.S. E4 116
South Ventana Cone, vol., Ca., U.S. D3 112
South Vienna, Oh., U.S. C2 142
South Wabasca Lake, l., Alta., Can. B4 98
South Wallingford, Vt., U.S. E3 152
South Walpole, Ma., U.S. h10 128
South Waverly, Pa., U.S. C8 145
South Wayne, Wi., U.S. F4 156
South Webster, Oh., U.S. D3 142
South Wellfleet, Ma., U.S. C8 128
South Wellington, B.C., Can. f12 99
Southwest, Pa., U.S. F3 145
South West Africa see Namibia, dep., Afr. F3 58
South Westbury, N.Y., U.S. n15 139
South West Cape, c., Austl. N7 70
Southwest Channel, strt., Fl., U.S. E4 116
South West City, Mo., U.S. E3 132
Southwest Harbor, Me., U.S. D4 126
Southwest Head, c., N.B., Can. E3 101
Southwest Miramichi, stm., N.B., Can. C3 101
Southwest Mountains, mts., Va., U.S. B4 153
Southwest National Park, Austl. N7 70
Southwest Pass, strt., La., U.S. F6 125
Southwest Pass, strt., La., U.S. E3 125
Southwest Point, c., Bah. B6 94
Southwest Point, c., R.I., U.S. h7 146
South Weymouth Naval Air Station, mil., Ma., U.S. h12 128
South Whitley, In., U.S. B6 121
Southwick, Ma., U.S. B2 128
South Williamson, Ky., U.S. C7 124
South Williamsport, Pa., U.S. D7 145
South Wilmington, Il., U.S. B5 120
South Windham, Ct., U.S. C7 114
South Windham, Me., U.S. E2 126
South Windsor, Ct., U.S. B5 114
South Wolfeboro, N.H., U.S. C4 136
Southwood, Co., U.S. B6 113
Southwood Acres, Ct., U.S. A5 114
South Woodstock, Ct., U.S. B8 114
South Yarmouth, Ma., U.S. C7 128
South Zanesville, Oh., U.S. C3 142
Soutpan, S. Afr. G8 66
Soutpansberg, mts., Afr. D9 66
Souvigny, Fr. F10 14
Sovereign, Sask., Can. F2 105
Sovetsk, U.S.S.R. F2 22
Sovetsk, U.S.S.R. F7 22
Sovetsk, U.S.S.R. H20 26
Sovetskaja Gavan', U.S.S.R. H20 24
Sovetskij, U.S.S.R. A11 26
Soviet Union see Union of Soviet Socialist Republics, ctry., Eur. E14 22
Søvik, Nor. J10 6
Soweto, S. Afr. F8 66
Soyapango, El Sal. D5 92
Soyo, Ang. C2 58
Spa, Bel. G8 12
Spadra, Ar., U.S. B2 111
Spain (España), ctry., Eur. G7 4
Spakenburg, Neth. D7 12
Spalding, Sask., Can. E3 105
Spalding, Eng., U.K. I13 8
Spalding, Id., U.S. C2 119
Spalding, Ne., U.S. C7 134
Spalding, co., Ga., U.S. C2 117
Spanaway, Wa., U.S. B3 154
Spangle, Wa., U.S. B8 154
Spangler, Pa., U.S. E4 145
Spaniard's Bay, Newf., Can. E5 102
Spanishburg, W.V., U.S. D3 155
Spanish Fork, Ut., U.S. C4 151
Spanish Fort, Al., U.S. E2 108
Spanish Lake, Mo., U.S. f13 132
Spanish North Africa, dep., Afr. J6 16
Spanish Peak, mtn., Or., U.S. C7 144
Spanish Sahara see Western Sahara, dep., Afr. D4 54
Spanish Town, Jam. F6 94
Sparkman, Ar., U.S. D3 111
Sparks, Ga., U.S. E3 117
Sparks, Nv., U.S. D2 135
Sparks, Ok., U.S. B5 143
Sparland, Il., U.S. B4 120
Sparr, Fl., U.S. C4 116
Sparrows Point, Md., U.S. B5 127
Sparta, Ga., U.S. C4 117
Sparta, Il., U.S. E4 120
Sparta, Mi., U.S. E5 129
Sparta, Mo., U.S. D4 132
Sparta (Lake Mohawk), N.J., U.S. A3 137
Sparta, N.C., U.S. A1 140
Sparta, Tn., U.S. D8 149
Sparta, Wi., U.S. E3 156
Sparta Mountains, mts., N.J., U.S. B3 137
Spartanburg, In., U.S. D8 121
Spartanburg, S.C., U.S. B4 147
Spartanburg, co., S.C., U.S. B3 147
Sparta see Spárti, Grc. L6 20
Spárti (Sparta), Grc. L6 20
Spartivento, Capo, c., Italy K3 18
Sparwood, B.C., Can. E10 99
Spas-Demensk, U.S.S.R. G17 26
Spas-Klepiki, U.S.S.R. F23 26
Spassk-Dal'nij, U.S.S.R. I18 24
Spátha, Ákra, c., Grc. N7 20
Spavinaw, Ok., U.S. A6 143
Spavinaw Creek, stm., Ok., U.S. A7 143
Spear, Cape, c., Newf., Can. E5 102
Spearfish, S.D., U.S. C2 148
Spearman, Tx., U.S. A2 150
Spearville, Ks., U.S. E4 123
Spectacle Pond, l., Me., U.S. D4 126
Spedden, Alta., Can. B5 98
Speed, In., U.S. H6 121
Speedway, In., U.S. E5 121
Speedwell, Va., U.S. D1 153
Speers, Sask., Can. E2 105
Speigener, Al., U.S. C3 108
Speight, Ky., U.S. C7 124
Speightstown, Barb. H15 94
Spello, Italy G7 18
Spelter, W.V., U.S. k10 155
Spence Bay, N.W. Ter., Can. C14 96
Spencer, In., U.S. F4 121
Spencer, Ia., U.S. A2 122
Spencer, Ma., U.S. B4 128
Spencer, Ne., U.S. B7 134
Spencer, N.Y., U.S. C4 139
Spencer, N.C., U.S. B2 140
Spencer, Oh., U.S. A3 142
Spencer, S.D., U.S. D8 148
Spencer, Tn., U.S. D8 149
Spencer, W.V., U.S. C3 155
Spencer, Wi., U.S. D3 156
Spencer, co., In., U.S. H4 121
Spencer, co., Ky., U.S. B4 124
Spencer, Cape, c., Austl. J2 70
Spencer, Cape, c., Ak., U.S. k21 109
Spencer Gulf, b., Austl. J2 70
Spencer Lake, l., Me., U.S. C2 126
Spencerport, N.Y., U.S. B3 139
Spencers Island, N.S., Can. D5 101
Spencerville, In., U.S. B8 121
Spencerville, Md., U.S. B4 127
Spencerville, Oh., U.S. B1 142
Spences Bridge, B.C., Can. D7 99
Sperling, Man., Can. E3 100
Sperry, Ok., U.S. A6 143
Sperryville, Va., U.S. B4 153
Spesutie Island, i., Md., U.S. B5 127
Speyer, Ger. F8 10
Speyside, Trin. I14 94
Spezia see La Spezia, Italy E4 18
Spiceland, In., U.S. E7 121
Spicer, Mn., U.S. E4 130
Spickard, Mo., U.S. A4 132
Spider Lake, l., Wi., U.S. B2 156
Spiez, Switz. E8 13
Spijkenisse, Neth. F5 12
Spillville, Ia., U.S. A6 122
Spinazzola, Italy I11 18
Spincourt, Fr. C12 14
Spindale, N.C., U.S. B1 140
Spink, co., S.D., U.S. C7 148
Spink Colony, S.D., U.S. C7 148
Spirit Lake, Id., U.S. B2 119
Spirit Lake, Ia., U.S. A2 122
Spirit Lake, l., Ia., U.S. A2 122
Spirit Lake, l., Wa., U.S. C3 154
Spirit River, Alta., Can. B1 98
Spirit River Flowage, res., Wi., U.S. C4 156
Spiritwood, Sask., Can. D2 105
Spiro, Ok., U.S. B7 143
Spirovo, U.S.S.R. D17 26
Spišská Nová Ves, Czech. G20 10
Spitsbergen, i., Sval. B2 28
Spittal an der Drau, Aus. I13 10
Spitz, Aus. G15 10
Split, Yugo. F11 18
Split, Cape, c., N.S., Can. D5 101
Split Lake, l., Man., Can. A4 100
Split Rock Creek, stm., U.S. G2 130
Spluga, Passo della (Splügenpass), Eur. E11 13
Splügen, Switz. E11 13
Spofford, N.H., U.S. E2 136
Spofford Lake, l., N.H., U.S. E2 136
Spoği, U.S.S.R. E9 26
Spokane, Wa., U.S. B8 154
Spokane, co., Wa., U.S. B8 154
Spokane, stm., U.S. B8 154
Spokane, Mount, mtn., Wa., U.S. B8 154
Spokane Indian Reservation, Wa., U.S. B8 154
Spoleto, Italy G7 18
Spoon, stm., Il., U.S. C3 120
Spooner, Wi., U.S. C2 156
Spooner Lake, l., Wi., U.S. C2 156
Spornoje, U.S.S.R. E22 24
Spotswood, N.J., U.S. C4 137
Spotsylvania, Va., U.S. B5 153
Spotsylvania, co., Va., U.S. B5 153
Spottsville, Ky., U.S. C2 124
Spragge, Ont., Can. A2 103
Sprague, Man., Can. E4 100
Sprague, Al., U.S. C3 108
Sprague, Ne., U.S. D9 134
Sprague, Wa., U.S. B8 154
Sprague, W.V., U.S. n13 155
Sprague, stm., Or., U.S. E5 144
Sprague Lake, l., Wa., U.S. B7 154
Sprague River, Or., U.S. E5 144
Spratly Islands, is., Asia D5 38
Spremberg, Ger. D14 10
Sprigg, W.V., U.S. D2 155
Spring, Tx., U.S. q14 150
Spring, stm., Ar., U.S. A4 111
Spring, South Fork, stm., U.S. A4 111
Spring, South Fork, stm., U.S. E6 132
Spring Arbor, Mi., U.S. F6 129
Spring Bay, b., Ut., U.S. B3 151
Springbok, S. Afr. G3 66
Springboro, Oh., U.S. C1 142
Springbrook, Ont., Can. C7 103
Spring Brook, stm., Pa., U.S. n18 145
Spring City, Pa., U.S. F10 145
Spring City, Tn., U.S. D9 149
Spring City, Ut., U.S. D4 151
Spring Coulee, Alta., Can. E4 98
Spring Creek, Tn., U.S. B3 149
Spring Creek, stm., U.S. D4 134
Spring Creek, stm., Co., U.S. B8 113
Spring Creek, stm., Ga., U.S. F2 117
Spring Creek, stm., Nv., U.S. C4 135
Spring Creek, stm., N.D., U.S. B3 141
Springdale, Newf., Can. D3 102
Springdale, Ar., U.S. A1 111
Springdale, Oh., U.S. n13 142
Springdale, Or., U.S. B4 144
Springdale, Pa., U.S. E2 145
Springdale, S.C., U.S. D5 147
Springdale, Ut., U.S. F3 151
Springdale, Wa., U.S. A8 154
Spring Dale, W.V., U.S. D4 155
Springe, Ger. C9 10
Springer, N.M., U.S. A5 138
Springer, Ok., U.S. C4 143
Springerville, Az., U.S. C6 110
Springfield, N.B., Can. D4 101
Springfield, N.S., Can. E5 101
Springfield, Ont., Can. E4 103
Springfield, Ar., U.S. B3 111
Springfield, Co., U.S. D8 113
Springfield, Fl., U.S. u16 116
Springfield, Ga., U.S. D5 117
Springfield, Id., U.S. F6 119
Springfield, Il., U.S. D4 120
Springfield, Ky., U.S. C4 124
Springfield, La., U.S. D5 125
Springfield, Ma., U.S. B2 128
Springfield, Mn., U.S. F4 130
Springfield, Mo., U.S. D4 132
Springfield, Ne., U.S. C9 134
Springfield, N.J., U.S. B4 137
Springfield, Oh., U.S. C2 142
Springfield, Or., U.S. C4 144
Springfield, Pa., U.S. p20 145
Springfield, S.C., U.S. E5 147
Springfield, S.D., U.S. E8 148
Springfield, Tn., U.S. A5 149
Springfield, Vt., U.S. E4 152
Springfield, Va., U.S. g12 153
Springfield, W.V., U.S. B6 155
Springfield, Lake, res., Il., U.S. D4 120
Springfontein, S. Afr. H7 66
Spring Garden, Guy. D13 84
Spring Garden, Al., U.S. B4 108
Spring Glen, Ut., U.S. D5 151
Spring Green, Wi., U.S. E3 156
Spring Grove, Il., U.S. h8 120
Spring Grove, In., U.S. E8 121
Spring Grove, Mn., U.S. G7 130
Spring Grove, Pa., U.S. G8 145
Springhill, N.S., Can. D5 101
Spring Hill, Ar., U.S. D2 111
Spring Hill, Fl., U.S. D4 116
Spring Hill, Ks., U.S. D9 123
Springhill, La., U.S. A2 125
Spring Hill, Tn., U.S. B5 149

Name — Map Ref. — Page

Springhill Junction, N.S., Can. D5 101
Spring Hope, N.C., U.S. B4 140
Springhouse, B.C., Can. D6 99
Spring Island, i., S.C., U.S. G6 147
Spring Lake, Mi., U.S. E4 129
Spring Lake, N.J., U.S. C4 137
Spring Lake, N.C., U.S. B4 140
Spring Lake, Ut., U.S. C4 151
Spring Lake, l., Me., U.S. C2 126
Spring Lake, res., U.S. B3 120
Spring Lake Heights, N.J., U.S. C4 137
Spring Mills, Pa., U.S. E6 145
Spring Mountains, mts., Nv., U.S. G6 135
Spring Place, Ga., U.S. B2 117
Springport, In., U.S. D7 121
Springport, Mi., U.S. F6 129
Springs, S. Afr. F9 66
Springside, Sask., Can. F4 105
Springsure, Austl. E8 70
Springvale, Austl. D4 70
Springvale, Me., U.S. E2 126
Spring Valley, Al., U.S. A2 108
Spring Valley, Ca., U.S. o16 112
Spring Valley, Ca., U.S. F5 112
Spring Valley, Il., U.S. B4 120
Spring Valley, Mn., U.S. G6 130
Spring Valley, N.Y., U.S. g12 139
Spring Valley, Oh., U.S. C1 142
Spring Valley, Wi., U.S. D1 156
Springview, Ne., U.S. B6 134
Springville, Al., U.S. B3 108
Springville, In., U.S. G4 121
Springville, Ia., U.S. B6 122
Springville, N.Y., U.S. C2 139
Springville, Ut., U.S. C4 151
Sprucedale, Ont., Can. B5 103
Spruce Fork, stm., W.V., U.S. m12 155
Spruce Grove, Alta., Can. C4 98
Spruce Knob, mtn., W.V., U.S. C6 155
Spruce Knob-Seneca Rocks National Recreation Area, W.V., U.S. C5 155
Spruce Lake, Sask., Can. D1 105
Spruce Mountain, mtn., Az., U.S. C3 110
Spruce Mountain, mtn., Nv., U.S. C7 135
Spruce Pine, Al., U.S. A2 108
Spruce Pine, N.C., U.S. f10 140
Spruce Run Reservoir, res., N.J., U.S. B3 137
Spur, Tx., U.S. C2 150
Spurr, Mount, mtn., Ak., U.S. g15 109
Spy Hill, Sask., Can. G5 105
Squam Lake, l., N.H., U.S. C4 136
Squam Mountains, mts., N.H., U.S. C3 136
Squapan Lake, l., Me., U.S. B4 126
Square Lake, l., Me., U.S. A4 126
Squatec, Que., Can. B9 104
Squaw Cap Mountain, mtn., N.B., Can. B3 101
Squaw Hill, mtn., Wy., U.S. E7 157
Squaw Peak, mtn., Mt., U.S. C2 133
Squibnocket Point, c., Ma., U.S. D6 128
Squinzano, Italy I13 18
Squire, W.V., U.S. D3 155
Srbija (Serbia), state, Yugo. F4 20
Srbobran, Yugo. D3 20
Sredinnyj chrebet, mts., U.S.S.R. F24 24
Sredna Gora, mts., Bul. G8 20
Sredneje Kujto, ozero, l., U.S.S.R. I22 6
Srednekolymsk, U.S.S.R. D22 24
Srednerusskaja vozvyšennost', plat., U.S.S.R. G5 22
Srednesibirskoje ploskogorje, plat., U.S.S.R. D13 24
Srem, Pol. C17 10
Srê Moât, Camb. H9 40
Sremska Mitrovica, Yugo. E3 20
Sremski Karlovci, Yugo. D3 20
Sretensk, U.S.S.R. G15 24
Sri Jayawardenepura (Kotte), Sri L. I5 46
Srīkākulam, India C7 46
Sri Kālahasti, India F5 46
Sri Lanka, ctry., Asia H11 42
Srīnagar, India C6 44
Srīrampur, India C3 46
Srīrangam, India G5 46
Srīvilliputtūr, India H4 46
Środa Wielkopolski, Pol. C17 10
Staaten, stm., Austl. C8 68
Staaten River National Park, Austl. C8 68
Staatsburg, N.Y., U.S. D7 139
Stachanov, U.S.S.R. H5 22
Stack Reservoir, res., R.I., U.S. C3 146
Stacyville, Ia., U.S. A5 122
Stade, Ger. B9 10
Staden, Bel. G3 12
Stadl-Paura, Aus. G13 10
Stadskanaal, Neth. B10 12
Stadt Haag, Aus. G14 10
Staffelstein, Ger. E11 10
Stafford, Eng., U.K. I11 8
Stafford, Ct., U.S. B6 114
Stafford, Ks., U.S. E5 123
Stafford, Va., U.S. B5 153
Stafford, co., Ks., U.S. D5 123
Stafford, co., Va., U.S. B5 153
Stafford Pond, l., R.I., U.S. D6 146
Staffordshire, co., Eng., U.K. I11 8
Stafford Springs, Ct., U.S. B6 114
Staffordsville, Ky., U.S. C7 124
Staffordville, Ct., U.S. B6 114
Staicele, U.S.S.R. D7 26
Staines, Eng., U.K. J13 8
Stairs Mountain, mtn., N.H., U.S. B4 136
Stalden, Switz. F8 13
Stalheim, Nor. K10 6
Stalin (Kuçovë), Alb. I3 20
Stalingrad see Volgograd, U.S.S.R. H6 22
Stalowa Wola, Pol. E22 10
Stambaugh, Mi., U.S. B2 129
Stamford, Austl. C5 70
Stamford, Ct., U.S. E1 114
Stamford, Ne., U.S. D6 134
Stamford, N.Y., U.S. C6 139
Stamford, Tx., U.S. C3 150
Stamford, Vt., U.S. F2 152
Stamford, Lake, res., Tx., U.S. C3 150
Stamping Ground, Ky., U.S. B5 124
Stamps, Ar., U.S. D2 111
Stanaford, W.V., U.S. D3 155
Stanardsville, Va., U.S. B4 153
Stanberry, Mo., U.S. A3 132
Stanchfield, Mn., U.S. E5 130
Standard, Alta., Can. D4 98
Standard, Il., U.S. B4 120
Standerton, S. Afr. F9 66
Standing Rock, Al., U.S. B4 108
Standing Rock Indian Reservation, U.S. B4 148
Standish, Me., U.S. E2 126
Standish, Mi., U.S. E7 129
Stanfield, Az., U.S. E3 110
Stanfield, Or., U.S. B7 144
Stanford, Il., U.S. C4 120
Stanford, Ky., U.S. C5 124
Stanford, Mt., U.S. C6 133
Stanhope, Ia., U.S. B4 122
Stanhope, N.J., U.S. B3 137
Stanislaus, co., Ca., U.S. D3 112
Stanke Dimitrov, Bul. G7 20
Stanley, N.B., Can. C3 101
Stanley, Falk. Is. G5 78
Stanley, Ks., U.S. D9 123
Stanley, Ky., U.S. C2 124
Stanley, N.M., U.S. B4 138
Stanley, N.C., U.S. B1 140
Stanley, N.D., U.S. A3 141
Stanley, Va., U.S. B4 153
Stanley, Wi., U.S. D3 156
Stanley, co., S.D., U.S. C5 148
Stanley Reservoir, res., India G4 46
Stanleytown, Va., U.S. D3 153
Stanleyville, N.C., U.S. A2 140
Stanleyville see Kisangani, Zaire A5 58
Stanly, co., N.C., U.S. B2 140
Stanovoj chrebet, mts., U.S.S.R. F17 24
Stanovoje nagorje (Stanovoy Mountains), mts., U.S.S.R. F14 24
Stans, Switz. E9 13
Stansbury Mountains, mts., Ut., U.S. C3 151
Stanstead, Que., Can. D5 104
Stanthorpe, Austl. G9 70
Stanton, Al., U.S. C3 108
Stanton, Ia., U.S. D2 122
Stanton, Ky., U.S. C6 124
Stanton, Mi., U.S. E5 129
Stanton, Mo., U.S. C6 132
Stanton, Ne., U.S. C8 134
Stanton, N.D., U.S. B4 141
Stanton, Tn., U.S. B2 149
Stanton, Tx., U.S. C2 150
Stanton, co., Ks., U.S. E2 123
Stanton, co., Ne., U.S. C8 134
Stantonsburg, N.C., U.S. B5 140
Stantonville, Tn., U.S. B3 149
Stanwood, Ia., U.S. C6 122
Stanwood, Wa., U.S. A3 154
Staplehurst, Ne., U.S. D8 134
Staples, Mn., U.S. D4 130
Stapleton, Al., U.S. E2 108
Stapleton, Ga., U.S. C4 117
Stapleton, Ne., U.S. C5 134
Star, Id., U.S. F2 119
Star, Ms., U.S. C3 131
Star, N.C., U.S. B3 140
Stará Boleslav, Czech. E14 10
Starachowice, Pol. D21 10
Staraja Russa, U.S.S.R. C14 26
Staraja Toropa, U.S.S.R. E14 26
Staraja Ušica, U.S.S.R. A11 20
Staraja Vičuga, U.S.S.R. D24 26
Stara Pazova, Yugo. E4 20
Stara Planina (Balkan Mountains), mts., Eur. G8 20
Stara Zagora, Bul. G9 20
Starbuck, Man., Can. E3 100
Starbuck, Mn., U.S. E3 130
Star City, Sask., Can. E3 105
Star City, Ar., U.S. D4 111
Star City, In., U.S. C4 121
Star City, W.V., U.S. B5 155
Stargard Szczeciński (Stargard in Pommern), Pol. B15 10
Stargo, Az., U.S. D6 110
Starica, U.S.S.R. E17 26
Stark, N.H., U.S. A4 136
Stark, co., Il., U.S. B4 120
Stark, co., N.D., U.S. C3 141
Stark, co., Oh., U.S. B4 142
Starke, Fl., U.S. C4 116
Starke, co., In., U.S. B4 121
Starks, La., U.S. D2 125
Starkville, Co., U.S. D6 113
Starkville, Ms., U.S. B5 131
Starkweather, N.D., U.S. A7 141
Star Lake, l., Mn., U.S. D3 130
Starnberg, Ger. G11 10
Starnberger See, l., Ger. H11 10
Starobin, U.S.S.R. I10 26
Starodub, U.S.S.R. I15 26
Starogard Gdański, Pol. B18 10
Staroje Selo, U.S.S.R. F12 26
Staroje Ustje, U.S.S.R. H24 26
Starokazačje, U.S.S.R. C13 20
Staroseslavino, U.S.S.R. H23 26
Starožilovo, U.S.S.R. G22 26
Star Peak, mtn., Nv., U.S. C3 135
Star Prairie, Wi., U.S. C1 156
Starr, co., Tx., U.S. F3 150
Starr Mountain, mtn., Tn., U.S. D9 149
Startex, S.C., U.S. B3 147
Startup, Wa., U.S. B4 154
Starye Dorogi, U.S.S.R. H11 26
Staryje Popel'uchi, U.S.S.R. A12 20
Staryj Oskol, U.S.S.R. G5 22
Staryj Sambor, U.S.S.R. F22 10
Stassfurt, Ger. D11 10
Staszów, Pol. E21 10
State Center, Ia., U.S. B4 122
State College, Pa., U.S. E6 145
State Line, In., U.S. D2 121
State Line, Ms., U.S. D5 131
Stateline, Nv., U.S. E2 135
State Line, Pa., U.S. G6 145
Staten Island, i., N.Y., U.S. k12 139
Statenville, Ga., U.S. F4 117
State Road, N.C., U.S. A2 140
Statesboro, Ga., U.S. D5 117
Statesville, N.C., U.S. B2 140
Statham, Ga., U.S. C3 117
Statue of Liberty National Monument, N.J., U.S. k8 137
Staunton, Il., U.S. D4 120
Staunton, In., U.S. F3 121
Staunton, Va., U.S. B3 153
Stavanger, Nor. L9 6
Stavely, Alta., Can. D4 98
Stavnoje, U.S.S.R. G22 10
Stavropol', U.S.S.R. H6 22
Stawell, Austl. K5 70
Stawell, stm., Austl. C5 70
Stawiszyn, Pol. D18 10
Stayner, Ont., Can. C4 103
Stayton, Or., U.S. C4 144
Steamboat, Nv., U.S. D2 135
Steamboat Canyon, Az., U.S. B6 110
Steamboat Mountain, mtn., Mt., U.S. C4 133
Steamboat Mountain, mtn., Wy., U.S. E4 157
Steamboat Rock, Ia., U.S. B4 122
Steamboat Springs, Co., U.S. A4 113
Stearns, Ky., U.S. D5 124
Stearns, co., Mn., U.S. E4 130
Stearns Brook, stm., N.H., U.S. A4 136
Stebbins, Ak., U.S. C7 109
Steckborn, Switz. C10 13
Steele, Al., U.S. B3 108
Steele, Mo., U.S. E8 132
Steele, N.D., U.S. C6 141
Steele, co., Mn., U.S. F5 130
Steele, co., N.D., U.S. B8 141
Steele, Mount, mtn., Wy., U.S. E6 157
Steele City, Ne., U.S. D8 134
Steeleville, Il., U.S. E4 120
Steelton, Pa., U.S. F8 145
Steelville, Mo., U.S. D6 132
Steen, Mn., U.S. G2 130
Steens, Ms., U.S. B5 131
Steens Mountain, mts., Or., U.S. E8 144
Steep Falls, Me., U.S. E2 126
Steep Rock, Man., Can. D2 100
Stefansson Island, i., N.W. Ter., Can. B11 96
Steffisburg, Switz. E8 13
Steger, Il., U.S. B6 120
Steiermark, state, Aus. H15 10
Steilacoom, Wa., U.S. f10 154
Stein, Switz. C8 13
Steinach, Aus. H11 10
Steinbach, Man., Can. E3 100
Steinhatchee, Fl., U.S. C3 116
Steinhatchee, stm., Fl., U.S. C3 116
Steinhausen, Nmb. C4 66
Steinkjer, Nor. I12 6
Steksovo, U.S.S.R. F26 26
Stella, Ont., Can. C8 103
Stella, Ky., U.S. f9 124
Stella, Ne., U.S. D10 134
Stellarton, N.S., Can. D7 101
Stellenbosch, S. Afr. I4 66
Stenay, Fr. C12 14
Stendal, Ger. C11 10
Stendal, In., U.S. H3 121
Stende, U.S.S.R. D5 26
Stenen, Sask., Can. F4 105
Stepanakert, U.S.S.R. J7 22
Stephen, Mn., U.S. B2 130
Stephens, Ar., U.S. D2 111
Stephens, co., Ga., U.S. B3 117
Stephens, co., Ok., U.S. C4 143
Stephens, co., Tx., U.S. C3 150
Stephens, Port, b., Austl. I10 70
Stephens City, Va., U.S. A4 153
Stephens Knob, hill, Ky., U.S. D5 124
Stephens Lake, res., Man., Can. A4 100
Stephenson, Mi., U.S. C3 129
Stephenson, co., Il., U.S. A4 120
Stephens Passage, strt., Ak., U.S. m23 109
Stephensport, Ky., U.S. C3 124
Stephenville, Newf., Can. D2 102
Stephenville, Tx., U.S. C3 150
Stephenville Crossing, Newf., Can. D2 102
Stepn'ak, U.S.S.R. G12 22
Sterkstroom, S. Afr. H8 66
Sterling, Ak., U.S. g16 109
Sterling, Co., U.S. A7 113
Sterling, Ct., U.S. C8 114
Sterling, Ga., U.S. E5 117
Sterling, Il., U.S. B4 120
Sterling, Ks., U.S. D5 123
Sterling, Ma., U.S. B4 128
Sterling, Mi., U.S. D6 129
Sterling, Ne., U.S. D9 134
Sterling, N.D., U.S. C5 141
Sterling, Ok., U.S. C3 143
Sterling, Va., U.S. A5 153
Sterling, co., Tx., U.S. D2 150
Sterling City, Tx., U.S. D2 150
Sterling Heights, Mi., U.S. o15 129
Sterling Reservoir, res., Co., U.S. A7 113
Sterlington, La., U.S. B3 125
Sterlitamak, U.S.S.R. G9 22
Sterrett, Al., U.S. B3 108
Stetson Mountain, mtn., Me., U.S. C4 126
Stetsonville, Wi., U.S. C3 156
Stettin see Szczecin, Pol. B14 10
Stettler, Alta., Can. C4 98
Steuben, co., In., U.S. A7 121
Steuben, co., N.Y., U.S. C3 139
Steubenville, Oh., U.S. B5 142
Stevens, co., Ks., U.S. E2 123
Stevens, co., Mn., U.S. E3 130
Stevens, co., Wa., U.S. A7 154
Stevens Creek Dam, U.S. C4 117
Stevenson, Al., U.S. A4 108
Stevenson, Ct., U.S. D3 114
Stevenson, Wa., U.S. D4 154
Stevenson Lake, l., Man., Can. C4 100
Stevenson Mountain, mtn., Ar., U.S. B1 111
Stevens Pass, Wa., U.S. B4 154
Stevens Peak, mtn., Id., U.S. B3 119
Stevens Point, Wi., U.S. D4 156
Stevens Pottery, Ga., U.S. D3 117
Stevens Village, Ak., U.S. B10 109
Stevensville, Md., U.S. C5 127
Stevensville, Mi., U.S. F4 129
Stevensville, Mt., U.S. D2 133
Steward, Il., U.S. B4 120
Stewardson, Il., U.S. D5 120
Stewart, B.C., Can. B3 99
Stewart, Mn., U.S. F4 130
Stewart, Ms., U.S. B4 131
Stewart, Tn., U.S. A4 149
Stewart, co., Ga., U.S. D2 117
Stewart, co., Tn., U.S. A4 149
Stewart, stm., Yukon, Can. D5 96
Stewart Island, i., N.Z. G1 72
Stewart Mountain, mtn., Az., U.S. k9 110
Stewarton, Scot., U.K. F9 8
Stewarts Point, Nv., U.S. G7 135
Stewartstown, N.H., U.S. f6 136
Stewartstown, Pa., U.S. G8 145
Stewartsville, Al., U.S. B3 108
Stewartsville, In., U.S. H2 121
Stewartsville, Mo., U.S. B3 132
Stewart Valley, Sask., Can. G2 105
Stewartville, Mn., U.S. G6 130
Stewiacke, N.S., Can. D6 101
Steynsburg, S. Afr. H7 66
Steyr, Aus. G14 10
Steytlerville, S. Afr. I7 66
Stickney, S.D., U.S. D7 148
Stif, Alg. B13 62
Stigler, Ok., U.S. B6 143
Stikine, stm., Ak., U.S. D13 109
Stilbaai, S. Afr. J5 66
Stilesville, In., U.S. E4 121
Stilfontein, S. Afr. F8 66
Stilís, Grc. K6 20
Still, Alg. C13 62
Still, stm., Ct., U.S. B3 114
Stillaguamish, North Fork, stm., Wa., U.S. A4 154
Stillaguamish, South Fork, stm., Wa., U.S. A4 154
Stillhouse Hollow Lake, res., Tx., U.S. D4 150
Stillman Valley, Il., U.S. A4 120
Stillmore, Ga., U.S. D4 117
Stillwater, Mn., U.S. E6 130
Stillwater, N.Y., U.S. C7 139
Stillwater, Ok., U.S. A4 143
Stillwater, co., Mt., U.S. E7 133
Stillwater Range, mts., Nv., U.S. D3 135
Stillwater Reservoir, res., N.Y., U.S. B5 139
Stillwater Reservoir, res., R.I., U.S. B3 146
Stillwell, In., U.S. A4 121
Stilson, Ga., U.S. D5 117
Stilwell, Ks., U.S. D9 123
Stilwell, Ok., U.S. B7 143
Stimson, Mount, mtn., Mt., U.S. B3 133
Stînca-Costeşti, Lacul (vodochranilišče Kostešty-Stynka), res., Eur. B11 20
Stine Mountain, mtn., Mt., U.S. E3 133
Stinesville, In., U.S. F4 121
Stinking Lake, l., N.M., U.S. A3 138
Stinnett, Tx., U.S. B2 150
Štip, Yugo. H6 20
Stirling, Alta., Can. E4 98
Stirling, Ont., Can. C7 103
Stirling, Scot., U.K. E10 8
Stirling, N.J., U.S. B4 137
Stites, Id., U.S. C3 119
Stockach, Ger. H9 10
Stöckalp, Switz. E9 13
Stockbridge, Ga., U.S. C2 117
Stockbridge, Ma., U.S. B1 128
Stockbridge, Mi., U.S. F6 129
Stockbridge, Wi., U.S. D5 156
Stockbridge-Munsee Indian Reservation, Wi., U.S. D5 156
Stockdale, Tx., U.S. E4 150
Stockerau, Aus. G16 10
Stockertown, Pa., U.S. E11 145
Stockett, Mt., U.S. C5 133
Stockholm, Sask., Can. G4 105
Stockholm, Swe. L16 6
Stockholm, Me., U.S. A4 126
Stockholm, N.J., U.S. A3 137
Stockholm, S.D., U.S. B9 148
Stockport, Ia., U.S. D6 122
Stockton, Al., U.S. E2 108
Stockton, Ca., U.S. D3 112
Stockton, Ga., U.S. F4 117
Stockton, Il., U.S. A3 120
Stockton, Ks., U.S. C4 123
Stockton, Md., U.S. D7 127
Stockton, Mo., U.S. D4 132
Stockton, Ut., U.S. C3 151
Stockton Island, i., Wi., U.S. B3 156
Stockton Lake, res., Mo., U.S. D4 132
Stockton [-on-Tees], Eng., U.K. G12 8
Stockton Plateau, plat., Tx., U.S. D1 150
Stockton Springs, Me., U.S. D4 126
Stockwell, In., U.S. D4 121
Stoddard, N.H., U.S. D2 136
Stoddard, Wi., U.S. E2 156
Stoddard, co., Mo., U.S. E8 132
Stodolišče, U.S.S.R. G15 26
Stœng Trêng, Camb. H8 40
Stoke-on-Trent, Eng., U.K. H11 8
Stokes, co., N.C., U.S. A2 140
Stokesdale, N.C., U.S. A3 140
Stolac, Yugo. F12 18
Stolbcy, U.S.S.R. H9 26
Stolberg, Ger. E6 10
Stolbovoj, ostrov, i., U.S.S.R. C19 24
Stollings, W.V., U.S. n12 155
Stolp see Słupsk, Pol. A17 10
Stone, Ky., U.S. C7 124
Stone, co., Ar., U.S. B3 111
Stone, co., Ms., U.S. E4 131
Stone, co., Mo., U.S. E4 132
Stonebluff, In., U.S. D3 121
Stoneboro, Pa., U.S. D1 145
Stone Corral Lake, l., Or., U.S. E7 144
Stonefort, Il., U.S. F5 120
Stonega, Va., U.S. f9 153
Stoneham, Ma., U.S. g11 128
Stone Harbor, N.J., U.S. E3 137
Stonehaven, N.B., Can. B4 101
Stonehenge, Austl. E5 70
Stone Lake, Wi., U.S. C2 156
Stone Mountain, Ga., U.S. C2 117
Stone Mountain, mtn., Ga., U.S. C2 117
Stone Mountain, mtn., Vt., U.S. B5 152
Stone Mountains, mts., U.S. A1 140
Stones River National Battlefield, hist., Tn., U.S. B4 149
Stoneville, Ms., U.S. B3 131
Stoneville, N.C., U.S. A3 140
Stonewall, Man., Can. D3 100
Stonewall, La., U.S. B2 125
Stonewall, Ms., U.S. C5 131
Stonewall, Ok., U.S. C5 143
Stonewall, co., Tx., U.S. C2 150
Stonewood, W.V., U.S. k10 155
Stoney Creek, Ont., Can. D5 103
Stonington, Ct., U.S. D8 114
Stonington, Il., U.S. D4 120
Stonington, Me., U.S. D4 126
Stono, stm., S.C., U.S. k11 147
Stono Inlet, b., S.C., U.S. F8 147
Stony Brook, N.Y., U.S. n15 139
Stony Brook, stm., N.J., U.S. C3 137
Stony Creek, Ct., U.S. D5 114
Stony Creek, Va., U.S. D5 153
Stony Creek, stm., Va., U.S. C5 153
Stony Island, i., Newf., Can. B4 102
Stony Island, i., N.Y., U.S. B4 139
Stony Plain, Alta., Can. C3 98
Stony Point, N.C., U.S. B1 140
Stony Rapids, Sask., Can. m7 105
Storby, Fin. K16 6
Storden, Mn., U.S. F3 130
Storey, co., Nv., U.S. D2 135
Storkerson Peninsula, pen., N.W. Ter., Can. B11 96
Storla, S.D., U.S. D7 148
Storlien, Swe. J13 6
Storm Bay, b., Austl. N7 70
Storm Lake, Ia., U.S. B2 122
Storm Lake, l., Ia., U.S. B2 122
Storm Mountain, mtn., Ak., U.S. h16 109
Stormsrivier, S. Afr. I6 66
Stornoway, Scot., U.K. C7 8
Storožinec, U.S.S.R. A9 20
Storrs, Ct., U.S. B7 114
Storthoaks, Sask., Can. H5 105
Storuman, Swe. I15 6
Story, Ar., U.S. C2 111
Story, Wy., U.S. B6 157
Story, co., Ia., U.S. B4 122
Story City, Ia., U.S. B4 122
Stotts City, Mo., U.S. D4 132
Stottville, N.Y., U.S. C7 139
Stoughton, Sask., Can. H4 105
Stoughton, Ma., U.S. B5 128
Stoughton, Wi., U.S. F4 156
Stoutland, Mo., U.S. D5 132
Stoutsville, Oh., U.S. C3 142
Stovall, Ga., U.S. D2 117
Stovall, N.C., U.S. A4 140
Stover, Mo., U.S. C5 132
Stow, Ma., U.S. B4 128
Stow, Oh., U.S. A4 142
Stow Creek, stm., N.J., U.S. E2 137
Stowe, Pa., U.S. F10 145
Stowe, Vt., U.S. C3 152
Stoyoma Mountain, mtn., B.C., Can. E7 99
Strabane, Pa., U.S. F1 145
Stradeč, U.S.S.R. J6 26
Stradella, Italy D4 18
Strafford, Mo., U.S. D4 132
Strafford, N.H., U.S. D4 136
Strafford, co., N.H., U.S. D4 136
Straffordville, Ont., Can. E4 103
Strahan, Austl. N6 70
Strakonice, Czech. F13 10
Stralsund, Ger. A13 10
Strand, S. Afr. J4 66
Stranger Creek, stm., Ks., U.S. k15 123
Strangford Lough, l., N. Ire., U.K. G8 8
Stranraer, Scot., U.K. G8 8
Strasbourg, Sask., Can. F3 105
Strasbourg, Fr. D14 14
Strasburg, Co., U.S. B6 113
Strasburg, Il., U.S. D5 120
Strasburg, N.D., U.S. C5 141
Strasburg, Oh., U.S. B4 142
Strasburg, Pa., U.S. G9 145
Strasburg, Va., U.S. B4 153
Stratford, Ont., Can. D3 103
Stratford, N.Z. C5 72
Stratford, Ca., U.S. D4 112
Stratford, Ct., U.S. E3 114
Stratford, Ia., U.S. B4 122
Stratford, N.H., U.S. A3 136
Stratford, N.J., U.S. D2 137
Stratford, Ok., U.S. C5 143
Stratford, S.D., U.S. B7 148
Stratford, Tx., U.S. A1 150
Stratford, Wi., U.S. D3 156
Stratford Centre, Que., Can. D6 104
Stratford Point, c., Ct., U.S. E3 114
Stratford-upon-Avon, Eng., U.K. I12 8
Strathalbyn, Austl. J3 70
Stratham, N.H., U.S. D5 136
Strathclair, Man., Can. D1 100
Strathclyde, prov., Scot., U.K. F8 8
Strathcona, Ont., Can. C8 103
Strathlorne, N.S., Can. C8 101
Strathmore, Alta., Can. D4 98
Strathmore, Ca., U.S. D4 112
Strathmore, N.J., U.S. C4 137
Strathroy, Ont., Can. E3 103
Stratton, Co., U.S. B8 113
Stratton, Me., U.S. C2 126
Stratton, Ne., U.S. D4 134
Stratton Mountain, mtn., Vt., U.S. E3 152
Straubing, Ger. G12 10
Straughn, In., U.S. E7 121
Strausberg, Ger. C13 10
Strawberry, Ar., U.S. B4 111
Strawberry, stm., Ar., U.S. A4 111
Strawberry, stm., Ut., U.S. C5 151
Strawberry Mountain, mtn., Or., U.S. C8 144
Strawberry Plains, Tn., U.S. C10 149
Strawberry Point, Ia., U.S. B6 122
Strawberry Point, c., Ma., U.S. B6 128
Strawberry Range, mts., Or., U.S. C8 144
Strawberry Reservoir, res., Ut., U.S. C4 151
Strawn, Ks., U.S. D8 123
Strawn, Tx., U.S. C3 150
Streamstown, Alta., Can. C5 98
Streator, Il., U.S. B5 120
Streeter, N.D., U.S. C6 141
Strel'na, U.S.S.R. B13 26
Strenči, U.S.S.R. D8 26
Stresa, Italy D3 18
Strešin, U.S.S.R. I13 26
Streymoy, i., Faer. Is. D8 6b
Strickland, stm., Pap. N. Gui. m15 68a
Strimón (Struma), stm., Eur. I7 20
Stringer, Ms., U.S. D4 131
Stringtown, Co., U.S. B4 113
Stringtown, Ky., U.S. B5 124
Stringtown, Ms., U.S. B3 131
Stringtown, Ok., U.S. C5 143
Strobel, Arg. G8 80
Stroh, In., U.S. A7 121
Stromboli, Isola, i., Italy K10 18
Strome, Alta., Can. C4 98
Stromeferry, Scot., U.K. D8 8
Stromness, Scot., U.K. C10 8
Stromsburg, Ne., U.S. C8 134
Strömsund, Swe. J14 6
Strong, Ar., U.S. D3 111
Strong, Me., U.S. D2 126
Strong, stm., Ms., U.S. C4 131
Strong City, Ks., U.S. D7 123
Strongfield, Sask., Can. F2 105
Stronghurst, Il., U.S. C3 120
Strongs, Mi., U.S. B6 129
Strongsville, Oh., U.S. A4 142
Stroud, Austl. I9 70
Stroud, Ok., U.S. B5 143
Stroudsburg, Pa., U.S. E11 145
Stroudwater, stm., Me., U.S. g7 126
Struer, Den. M11 6
Struga, Yugo. H4 20
Strugi-Krasnyje, U.S.S.R. C12 26
Strum, Wi., U.S. D2 156
Struma (Strimón), stm., Eur. H7 20
Strumica, Yugo. H6 20
Strunino, U.S.S.R. E21 26
Strunk, Ky., U.S. D5 124
Struthers, Oh., U.S. A5 142
Stryj, U.S.S.R. H2 22
Stryker, Oh., U.S. A1 142
Strzegom, Pol. E16 10
Strzelce Opolskie, Pol. E18 10
Strzelecki Creek, stm., Austl. G4 70
Strzelecki Desert, des., Austl. F4 70
Strzelin, Pol. E17 10
Stuart, Fl., U.S. E6 116
Stuart, Ia., U.S. C3 122
Stuart, Ne., U.S. B6 134
Stuart, Ok., U.S. C5 143
Stuart, Va., U.S. D2 153
Stuart, stm., B.C., Can. B5 99
Stuart, Mount, mtn., Wa., U.S. B5 154
Stuart Lake, l., B.C., Can. B5 99
Stuarts Draft, Va., U.S. B3 153
Stub Hill, mtn., N.H., U.S. f7 136
Stučka, U.S.S.R. E8 26
Studen Kladenec, jazovir, res., Bul. H9 20
Stull, stm., Can. B5 100
Stump Lake, l., N.D., U.S. B7 141
Stump Pond, res., R.I., U.S. D2 146
Stupino, U.S.S.R. G21 26
Sturbridge, Ma., U.S. B3 128
Sturgeon, Mo., U.S. B5 132
Sturgeon, stm., Mi., U.S. B4 129
Sturgeon Bay, Wi., U.S. D6 156
Sturgeon Bay, b., Man., Can. C3 100
Sturgeon Falls, Ont., Can. A5 103
Sturgeon Lake, l., Ont., Can. C6 103
Sturgeon-weir, stm., Sask., Can. C4 105
Sturgis, Sask., Can. F4 105
Sturgis, Ky., U.S. e10 124
Sturgis, Mi., U.S. G5 129
Sturgis, Ms., U.S. B4 131
Sturgis, S.D., U.S. C2 148
Sturtevant, Wi., U.S. F6 156
Sturt National Park, Austl. G4 70
Sturt Stony Desert, des., Austl. G4 70
Stutsman, co., N.D., U.S. B6 141
Stutterheim, S. Afr. I8 66
Stuttgart, Ger. G9 10
Stuttgart, Ar., U.S. C4 111
Stykkishólmur, Ice. B2 6a
Suaçuí Grande, stm., Braz. E7 79
Suaita, Col. D6 84
Suakin Archipelago, is., Sud. H10 60
Su'ao, China J8 34
Suaqui Grande, Mex. C5 90
Subačius, U.S.S.R. F7 26

Name — Map Ref. — Page

Subansiri, stm., Asia F16 44
Subarnarekha, stm., India I12 44
Subata, U.S.S.R. E8 26
Subiaco, Italy H8 18
Subiaco, Ar., U.S. B2 111
Sublette, Il., U.S. B4 120
Sublette, Ks., U.S. E3 123
Sublette, co., Wy., U.S. D2 157
Sublett Range, mts., Id., U.S. G6 119
Sublimity, Or., U.S. C4 144
Subotica, Yugo. C3 20
Suca, Eth. N10 60
Sucarnoochee, stm., Al., U.S. C1 108
Succasunna, N.J., U.S. B3 137
Success, Sask., Can. G1 105
Success, Ar., U.S. A5 111
Success, Mount, mtn., N.H., U.S. B4 136
Suceava, Rom. B10 20
Suceava, co., Rom. B9 20
Sucha [Beskidzka], Pol. F19 10
Sūchbaatar, Mong. A8 30
Suches, Ga., U.S. B2 117
Suchiapa, stm., Mex. I13 90
Súchil, Mex. F8 90
Suchiniči, U.S.S.R. G18 26
Suchitepéquez, dept., Guat. C3 92
Suchitoto, El Sal. D5 92
Suchodol'skij, U.S.S.R. H21 26
Suchona, stm., U.S.S.R. E6 22
Suchotinka, U.S.S.R. I24 26
Suchou see Suzhou, China E11 30
Suchoverkovo, U.S.S.R. E18 26
Suchumi, U.S.S.R. I6 22
Sucio, stm., Col. D4 84
Sucre, Bol. H9 82
Sucre, Col. C5 84
Sucre, Ec. H2 84
Sucre, state, Ven. B11 84
Sucre, dept., Col. C5 84
Sucúa, Ec. I3 84
Sucuaro, Col. E8 84
Sucunduri, stm., Braz. B12 82
Sucuriú, stm., Braz. F3 79
Sud, Canal du, strt., Haiti E8 94
Suda, U.S.S.R. B20 26
Sudan, Tx., U.S. B1 150
Sudan (As-Sūdān), ctry., Afr. E7 56
Sudan, reg., Afr. F9 54
Sudbury, Ont., Can. A4 103
Sudbury, Ma., U.S. B5 128
Sudbury, stm., Ma., U.S. B5 128
Sudbury Center, Ma., U.S. g10 128
Sudbury Reservoir, res., Ma., U.S. g10 128
Suddie, Guy. D13 84
Sudeten see Sudety, mts., Eur. E16 10
Sudety, mts., Eur. E16 10
Sudislavl', U.S.S.R. D24 26
Sudlersville, Md., U.S. B6 127
Sudogda, U.S.S.R. F23 26
Suđuroy, i., Faer. Is. E8 6b
Sue, stm., Sud. N5 60
Sueca, Spain F11 16
Suez, Gulf of see Suways, Khalīj as-, b., Egypt C7 60
Suez see As-Suways, Egypt C7 60
Suez Canal see Suways, Qanāt as-, Egypt C7 60
Şufaynah, Sau. Ar. C2 47
Suffern, N.Y., U.S. D6 139
Suffield, Alta., Can. D5 98
Suffield, Ct., U.S. B5 114
Suffolk, Va., U.S. D6 153
Suffolk, co., Eng., U.K. I15 8
Suffolk, co., Ma., U.S. B5 128
Suffolk, co., N.Y., U.S. n15 139
Sufu see Kashi, China D2 30
Sugar, stm., U.S. F4 156
Sugar, stm., N.H., U.S. D2 136
Sugar, North Branch, stm., N.H., U.S. D2 136
Sugar City, Co., U.S. C7 113
Sugar City, Id., U.S. F7 119
Sugar Creek, Mo., U.S. h11 132
Sugarcreek, Pa., U.S. D2 145
Sugar Creek, stm., In., U.S. E3 121
Sugar Creek, stm., In., U.S. F6 121
Sugar Creek, stm., Oh., U.S. C2 142
Sugar Creek, stm., Pa., U.S. C8 145
Sugargrove, Pa., U.S. C3 145
Sugar Grove, Va., U.S. D1 153
Sugar Hill, Ga., U.S. B2 117
Sugar Hill, N.H., U.S. B3 136
Sugar Island, i., Mi., U.S. B6 129
Sugar Land, Tx., U.S. E5 150
Sugarland Run, Va., U.S. A5 153
Sugar Loaf, Va., U.S. C3 153
Sugarloaf, mtn., N.H., U.S. A4 136
Sugarloaf, hill, Oh., U.S. A4 142
Sugarloaf Mountain, mtn., Me., U.S. C2 126
Sugar Loaf Mountain, mtn., Md., U.S. B3 127
Sugarloaf Mountain, mtn., Mt., U.S. C4 133
Sugar Loaf Mountain, mtn., Ok., U.S. B7 143
Sugarloaf Point, c., Austl. I10 70
Sugar Mountain, mtn., Mi., U.S. k9 129
Sugar Notch, Pa., U.S. n17 145
Sugar Valley, Ga., U.S. B1 117
Suggi Lake, l., Sask., Can. C4 105
Suggsville, Al., U.S. D2 108
Sugoj, stm., U.S.S.R. E23 24
Şuḥār, Oman B10 47
Suhl, Ger. E10 10
Suhr, Switz. D9 13
Suia-Miçu, stm., Braz. A2 79
Suiattle, stm., Wa., U.S. A4 154
Suichuan, China I3 34
Suide, China D9 30
Suifenhe, China C13 30
Suihua, China B12 30
Suining, China E8 30
Suipacha, Arg. H9 80
Suiping, China B2 34
Suippes, Fr. C11 14
Suitland, Md., U.S. C4 127
Suixian, China D2 34
Suiyangdian, China C1 34
Suizhong, China C8 32
Šuja, U.S.S.R. K24 6
Šuja, U.S.S.R. E24 26
Sujāngarh, India G6 44
Sujiatun, China B11 32
Sukabumi, Indon. J13 39a
Sukagawa, Japan J15 36
Sukch'ŏn, N. Kor. D13 32
Sukhothai, Thai. F5 40
Sukkozero, U.S.S.R. E4 22
Sukkur, Pak. G3 44
Sukumo, Japan O7 36
Sukunka, stm., B.C., Can. B7 99
Sul, Baía do, b., Braz. D14 80
Sul, Canal do, strt., Braz. D9 76
Sula, Kepulauan, is., Indon. F8 38
Sulaco, stm., Hond. B7 92
Sulaimān Range, mts., Pak. F3 44
Sulawesi (Celebes), i., Indon. F7 38
Sulaymān, Birak (Solomon's Pools), hist., Isr. Occ. E4 50
Sulechów, Pol. C15 10
Sulejówek, Pol. C21 10
Sulima, S.L. H4 64
Sulingen, Ger. C8 10
Sulitelma, mtn., Eur. H15 6
Sullana, Peru A1 82
Sulligent, Al., U.S. B1 108
Sullivan, Il., U.S. D5 120
Sullivan, In., U.S. F3 121
Sullivan, Ky., U.S. C2 124
Sullivan, Mo., U.S. C6 132
Sullivan, Wi., U.S. E5 156
Sullivan, co., In., U.S. F3 121
Sullivan, co., Mo., U.S. A4 132
Sullivan, co., N.H., U.S. D2 136
Sullivan, co., N.Y., U.S. D6 139
Sullivan, co., Pa., U.S. D9 145
Sullivan, co., Tn., U.S. C11 149
Sullivan Lake, l., Alta., Can. D5 98
Sullivans Island, S.C., U.S. k12 147
Sully, Fr. E9 14
Sully, Ia., U.S. C5 122
Sully, co., S.D., U.S. C5 148
Sulmona, Italy G8 18
Sulphide, Ont., Can. C7 103
Sulphur, Ky., U.S. B4 124
Sulphur, La., U.S. D2 125
Sulphur, Ok., U.S. C5 143
Sulphur, stm., U.S. D2 111
Sulphur Rock, Ar., U.S. B4 111
Sulphur Spring Range, mts., Nv., U.S. C5 135
Sulphur Springs, Ar., U.S. A1 111
Sulphur Springs, In., U.S. D7 121
Sulphur Springs, Tx., U.S. C5 150
Sulphur Springs Valley, val., Az., U.S. E6 110
Sultan, Wa., U.S. B4 154
Sultānpur, India G10 44
Sulu Archipelago, is., Phil. D7 38
Sululta, Eth. M10 60
Sulūq, Libya B5 56
Sulu Sea, Asia D6 38
Sulzbach-Rosenberg, Ger. F11 10
Sumampa, Arg. E7 80
Sumas, Wa., U.S. A3 154
Sumatera (Sumatra), i., Indon. F3 38
Sumatra see Sumatera, i., Indon. F3 38
Sumaúma, Braz. B11 82
Sumava Resorts, In., U.S. B3 121
Sumayh, Sud. K6 60
Sumba, Faer. Is. E8 6b
Sumba, i., Indon. G7 38
Sumbawa, i., Indon. G6 38
Sumbawa Besar, Indon. G6 38
Sumbawanga, Tan. C6 58
Sumbay, Peru F6 82
Sumbe, Ang. D2 58
Sümber, Mong. B8 30
Sumbilla, Spain B10 16
Sumbuya, S.L. H4 64
Sümeg, Hung. I17 10
Šumen, Bul. F10 20
Sumenep, Indon. J16 39a
Šumerl'a, U.S.S.R. F7 22
Sumgait, U.S.S.R. I7 22
Šumicha, U.S.S.R. F10 22
Šumilino, U.S.S.R. F12 26
Sumisu-jima, i., Japan E15 30
Sumiswald, Switz. D8 13
Sumiton, Al., U.S. B2 108
Summerdale, Al., U.S. E2 108
Summerfield, Fl., U.S. C4 116
Summerfield, Ks., U.S. C7 123
Summerfield, N.C., U.S. A3 140
Summerford, Newf., Can. D4 102
Summer Island, i., Mi., U.S. C4 129
Summer Lake, l., Or., U.S. E6 144
Summerland, B.C., Can. E8 99
Summerland Key, Fl., U.S. H5 116
Summers, co., W.V., U.S. D4 155
Summer Shade, Ky., U.S. D4 124
Summerside, P.E.I., Can. C6 101
Summersville, Ky., U.S. C4 124
Summersville, Mo., U.S. D6 132
Summersville, W.V., U.S. C4 155
Summersville Lake, res., W.V., U.S. C4 155
Summerton, S.C., U.S. D7 147
Summertown, Ga., U.S. D4 117
Summertown, Tn., U.S. B4 149
Summertown, Tn., U.S. B4 149
Summerville, Ga., U.S. B1 117
Summerville, Pa., U.S. D3 145
Summerville, S.C., U.S. E7 147
Summit, Ar., U.S. A3 111
Summit, Il., U.S. k9 120
Summit, Ms., U.S. D3 131
Summit, N.J., U.S. B4 137
Summit, S.D., U.S. B8 148
Summit, Tn., U.S. h11 149
Summit, co., Co., U.S. B4 113
Summit, co., Oh., U.S. A4 142
Summit, co., Ut., U.S. C5 151
Summit Hill, Pa., U.S. E10 145
Summit Lake, B.C., Can. B6 99
Summit Lake, l., Ia., U.S. C3 122
Summit Lake Indian Reservation, Nv., U.S. B2 135
Summit Mountain, mtn., Nv., U.S. D5 135
Summit Peak, mtn., Co., U.S. D4 113
Summit Point, W.V., U.S. B7 155
Summit Station, Oh., U.S. k11 142
Summitville, In., U.S. D6 121
Summitville, Tn., U.S. D8 149
Summum, Il., U.S. C3 120
Sumner, Ga., U.S. E3 117
Sumner, Il., U.S. E6 120
Sumner, Ia., U.S. B5 122
Sumner, Ms., U.S. B3 131
Sumner, Ne., U.S. D6 134
Sumner, Ok., U.S. A4 143
Sumner, Wa., U.S. B3 154
Sumner, co., Ks., U.S. E6 123
Sumner, co., Tn., U.S. A5 149
Sumner, Lake, res., N.M., U.S. C5 138
Sumner Dam, N.M., U.S. C5 138
Sumner Strait, strt., Ak., U.S. m23 109
Sumoto, Japan M9 36
Šumperk, Czech. F16 10
Sumprabum, Burma A4 40
Sumrall, Ms., U.S. D4 131
Šumšu, ostrov, i., U.S.S.R. G23 24
Sumter, S.C., U.S. D7 147
Sumter, co., Al., U.S. C1 108
Sumter, co., Fl., U.S. D4 116
Sumter, co., Ga., U.S. D2 117
Sumter, co., S.C., U.S. D7 147
Sumterville, Al., U.S. C1 108
Sumy, U.S.S.R. G4 22
Sumzom, China F17 44
Sun, La., U.S. D6 125
Sun, stm., Mt., U.S. C4 133
Suna, stm., U.S.S.R. J23 6
Sunan, N. Kor. D13 32
Sunapee, N.H., U.S. D2 136
Sunapee Lake, l., N.H., U.S. D2 136
Sunapee Mountain, mtn., N.H., U.S. D2 136
Sunbright, Tn., U.S. C9 149
Sunburst, Mt., U.S. B5 133
Sunbury, Austl. K6 70
Sunbury, N.C., U.S. A6 140
Sunbury, Oh., U.S. B3 142
Sunbury, Pa., U.S. E8 145
Sunchales, Arg. F8 80
Sunch'ang, S. Kor. H15 32
Suncho Corral, Arg. D7 80
Sunch'ŏn, N. Kor. D13 32
Sunch'ŏn, S. Kor. I15 32
Sun City, Az., U.S. k8 110
Sun City, Fl., U.S. p10 116
Suncook, N.H., U.S. D4 136
Suncook, stm., N.H., U.S. D4 136
Suncook Lakes, l., N.H., U.S. D4 136
Sunda, Selat, strt., Indon. G4 38
Sundance, Wy., U.S. B8 157
Sundance Mountain, mtn., Wy., U.S. B8 157
Sundarbans, reg., Asia J13 44
Sunda Strait see Sunda, Selat, strt., Indon. G4 38
Sunderland, Ont., Can. C5 103
Sunderland, Md., U.S. C4 127
Sunderland, Ma., U.S. B2 128
Sunderland, Vt., U.S. E2 152
Sundown, Man., Can. E3 100
Sundown, Tx., U.S. C1 150
Sundre, Alta., Can. D3 98
Sundridge, Ont., Can. B5 103
Sundsvall, Swe. J15 6
Sunfield, Mi., U.S. F5 129
Sunflower, Ms., U.S. B3 131
Sunflower, co., Ms., U.S. B3 131
Sunflower, Mount, mtn., Ks., U.S. C2 123
Sungaipenuh, Indon. F3 38
Sungai Petani, Malay. L6 40
Sunjiabu, China C4 34
Sunjikāy, Sud. K5 60
Sunland Park, N.M., U.S. F3 138
Sunlight Creek, stm., Wy., U.S. B3 157
Sunman, In., U.S. F7 121
Sunnybrae, N.S., Can. D7 101
Sunnybrook, Alta., Can. C3 98
Sunnyland, Fl., U.S. q11 116
Sunnyside, Newf., Can. E5 102
Sunnyside, Fl., U.S. u16 116
Sunnyside, Ut., U.S. D5 151
Sunnyside, Wa., U.S. C5 154
Sunny South, Al., U.S. D2 108
Sunnyvale, Ca., U.S. k8 112
Sunol, Ca., U.S. h9 112
Sun Prairie, Wi., U.S. E4 156
Sunray, Ok., U.S. C4 143
Sunray, Tx., U.S. A2 150
Sunrise, Wy., U.S. D8 157
Sunrise Manor, Nv., U.S. G6 135
Sunrise Mountain, mtn., N.J., U.S. A3 137
Sun River, Mt., U.S. C5 133
Sunset, La., U.S. D3 125
Sunset, Me., U.S. D4 126
Sunset, Tx., U.S. C4 150
Sunset, Ut., U.S. B4 151
Sunset Beach, Hi., U.S. f9 118
Sunset Country, reg., Austl. J4 70
Sunset Crater National Monument, Az., U.S. B4 110
Sunset Hill, hill, Ct., U.S. B7 114
Sunset Lake, l., Vt., U.S. D2 152
Sunshine, Austl. K6 70
Sunshine, Ak., U.S. f16 109
Suntaug Lake, l., Ma., U.S. f11 128
Suntu, Eth. M9 60
Sun Valley, Id., U.S. F4 119
Sun Valley, Nv., U.S. D2 135
Sunyani, Ghana H8 64
Sunzom, China F6 30
Suojarvi, U.S.S.R. J23 6
Suonenjoki, Fin. J20 6
Supamo, stm., Ven. D11 84
Supe, Eth. M8 60
Superior, Az., U.S. D4 110
Superior, Co., U.S. B5 113
Superior, Mt., U.S. C2 133
Superior, Ne., U.S. D7 134
Superior, Wi., U.S. B1 156
Superior, Wy., U.S. E4 157
Superior, Laguna, b., Mex. I12 90
Superior, Lake, l., N.A. B9 106
Superstition Mountains, mts., Az., U.S. m10 110
Suphan Buri, Thai. G6 40
Supi Oidak, Az., U.S. F4 110
Suponevo, U.S.S.R. H17 26
Supply, N.C., U.S. C4 140
Sup'ung-chŏsuji, res., Asia C13 32
Sūq ash-Shuyūkh, Iraq F9 48
Suq'at al-Jamal, Sud. K4 60
Suqian, China B7 34
Sūq Suwayq, Sau. Ar. I5 48
Suquamish, Wa., U.S. B3 154
Suquṭrā (Socotra), i., Yemen G5 42
Şūr (Tyre), Leb. B4 50
Şūr, Oman C11 47
Sur, Point, c., Ca., U.S. D3 112
Sur, Punta, c., Arg. I10 80
Sura, stm., U.S.S.R. G7 22
Surabaya, Indon. J16 39a
Surakarta, Indon. J15 39a
Sūrat, India J5 44
Surat Thani (Ban Don), Thai. J5 40
Suraž, U.S.S.R. H15 26
Suraž, U.S.S.R. F13 26
Surdulica, Yugo. G6 20
Sûre (Sauer), stm., Eur. I9 12
Surendranagar, India I4 44
Suretka, C.R. H12 92
Surettes Island, N.S., Can. F4 101
Surf City, N.J., U.S. D4 137
Surfers Paradise, Austl. G10 70
Surfside, Fl., U.S. s13 116
Surfside Beach, S.C., U.S. D10 147
Surgoinsville, Tn., U.S. C11 149
Surgut, U.S.S.R. E6 24
Suriāpet, India D5 46
Surigao, Phil. D8 38
Surin, Thai. G7 40
Suriname, ctry., S.A. C7 76
Suring, Wi., U.S. D5 156
Sūrmaq, Iran F12 48
Surprise, Az., U.S. k8 110
Surrency, Ga., U.S. E4 117
Surrey, N.D., U.S. A4 141
Surrey, co., Eng., U.K. J13 8
Surry, Me., U.S. D4 126
Surry, co., N.C., U.S. A2 140
Surry, co., Va., U.S. C6 153
Surry Mountain Lake, res., N.H., U.S. D2 136
Sursee, Switz. D9 13
Surt, Libya B4 56
Surt, Khalīj, b., Libya B4 56
Surtsey, i., Ice. C3 6a
Sürüç, Tur. C5 48
Surumu, stm., Braz. F12 84
Surveyor, W.V., U.S. n13 155
Susa, Italy D2 18
Susaki, Japan N8 36
Susanino, U.S.S.R. C24 26
Susanville, Ca., U.S. B3 112
Susch, Switz. E13 13
Šušenskoje, U.S.S.R. G16 22
Sušice, Czech. F13 10
Susitna, stm., Ak., U.S. C10 109
Susoh, Indon. M4 40
Susquehanna, Pa., U.S. C10 145
Susquehanna, co., Pa., U.S. C10 145
Susquehanna, stm., U.S. A5 127
Susquehanna, West Branch, stm., Pa., U.S. D5 145
Susques, Arg. B5 80
Sussex, N.B., Can. D4 101
Sussex, N.J., U.S. A3 137
Sussex, Wi., U.S. m11 156
Sussex, co., De., U.S. F4 115
Sussex, co., N.J., U.S. A3 137
Sussex, co., Va., U.S. D5 153
Sussex, East, co., Eng., U.K. K14 8
Susuman, U.S.S.R. E21 24
Susurluk, Tur. J12 20
Susz, Pol. H11 20
Susuzmüsellim, Tur. H11 20
Sutcliffe, Nv., U.S. D2 135
Sutherland, S. Afr. I5 66
Sutherland, Ia., U.S. B2 122
Sutherland, Ne., U.S. C4 134
Sutherland Springs, Tx., U.S. k7 150
Sutherlin, Or., U.S. D3 144
Sutlej (Satluj) (Langqên), stm., Asia F4 44
Sutter, co., Ca., U.S. C3 112
Sutter Creek, Ca., U.S. C3 112
Sutton, Que., Can. D5 104
Sutton, Ak., U.S. g17 109
Sutton, Ne., U.S. D8 134
Sutton, N.H., U.S. D3 136
Sutton, N.D., U.S. B7 141
Sutton, W.V., U.S. C4 155
Sutton, co., Tx., U.S. D2 150
Sutton in Ashfield, Eng., U.K. H12 8
Sutton Lake, res., W.V., U.S. C4 155
Suttons Bay, Mi., U.S. D5 129
Suttor, stm., Austl. C7 70
Sutwik Island, i., Ak., U.S. D8 109
Suurbraak, S. Afr. J5 66
Suure-Jaani, U.S.S.R. C8 26
Suva, Fiji H24 2
Suvainiškis, U.S.S.R. E8 26
Suvorov, U.S.S.R. G19 26
Suvorovo, U.S.S.R. D12 20
Suwa, Eth. G2 47
Suwa, Japan K13 36
Suwałki, Pol. A22 10
Suwanee, Ga., U.S. B2 117
Suwannee, co., Fl., U.S. B3 116
Suwannee, stm., U.S. C4 116
Suwannee Sound, strt., Fl., U.S. C3 116
Suwanose-jima, i., Japan R4 37b
Şuwaylih, Jord. D5 50
Suways, Khalīj as- (Gulf of Suez), b., Egypt C7 60
Suways, Qanāt as- (Suez Canal), Egypt C7 60
Suwŏn, S. Kor. F15 32
Suxi, China F9 34
Suxian, China B5 34
Suyo, Peru J2 84
Suzak, U.S.S.R. I11 22
Suzdal', U.S.S.R. E23 26
Suzhou (Soochow), China D9 34
Suzigou, China C11 32
Suzuka, Japan M11 36
Sval'ava, U.S.S.R. A6 20
Svalbard, dep., Eur. B2 28
Svappavaara, Swe. H17 6
Svataj, U.S.S.R. D22 24
Sv'atoj Nos, mys, c., U.S.S.R. G26 6
Sv'atoj Nos, mys, c., U.S.S.R. C20 24
Svay Riĕng, Camb. I8 40
Svėdasai, U.S.S.R. F8 26
Svelgen, Nor. K9 6
Svelvik, Nor. L12 6
Šven', U.S.S.R. H17 26
Švenčionėliai, U.S.S.R. F9 26
Švenčionys, U.S.S.R. F9 26
Svensen, Or., U.S. A3 144
Sverdlovsk, U.S.S.R. H5 22
Sverdlovsk, U.S.S.R. F10 22
Sverdrup, ostrov, i., U.S.S.R. C13 22
Svetlogorsk, U.S.S.R. I12 26
Svetlogorsk, U.S.S.R. G3 26
Svetlograd, U.S.S.R. H6 22
Svetlyj, U.S.S.R. G3 26
Svetogorsk, U.S.S.R. K21 6
Svilajnac, Yugo. E5 20
Svilengrad, Bul. H10 20
Svindal, Nor. L10 6
Svir', U.S.S.R. G9 26
Svir', stm., U.S.S.R. A16 26
Svirica, U.S.S.R. A15 26
Svirsk, U.S.S.R. G12 24
Svir'stroj, U.S.S.R. A16 26
Svisloč', U.S.S.R. B24 10
Svisloč', U.S.S.R. H7 26
Svištov, Bul. F9 20
Svobodnyj, U.S.S.R. G17 24
Svolvær, Nor. G14 6
Swain, co., N.C., U.S. f9 140
Swain Mountain, mtn., Ar., U.S. A2 111
Swain Reefs, rf., Austl. C10 70
Swainsboro, Ga., U.S. D4 117
Swakop, stm., Afr. D2 66
Swakopmund, Nmb. D2 66
Swalwell, Alta., Can. D4 98
Swampscott, Ma., U.S. B6 128
Swan, stm., Can. C1 100
Swan Creek, stm., Oh., U.S. e6 142
Swan Falls, wtfl, Id., U.S. F2 119
Swan Hill, Austl. J5 70
Swan Hills, Alta., Can. B3 98
Swan Islands see Santanilla, Islas, is., Hond. F3 94
Swan Lake, Man., Can. E2 100
Swanlake, Id., U.S. G6 119
Swan Lake, Ms., U.S. B3 131
Swan Lake, Mt., U.S. C3 133
Swan Lake, l., Man., Can. C1 100
Swan Lake, l., Me., U.S. D4 126
Swan Lake, l., Ne., U.S. C3 134
Swannanoa, N.C., U.S. f10 140
Swan Peak, mtn., Mt., U.S. C3 133
Swanquarter, N.C., U.S. B6 140
Swan Range, mts., Mt., U.S. C3 133
Swan River, Man., Can. C1 100
Swansboro, N.C., U.S. C5 140
Swansea, Austl. N8 70
Swansea, Wales, U.K. J10 8
Swansea, Il., U.S. E4 120
Swansea, Ma., U.S. C5 128
Swansea, S.C., U.S. D5 147
Swans Island, Me., U.S. D4 126
Swanson Lake, res., Ne., U.S. D4 134
Swanton, Ne., U.S. D8 134
Swanton, Oh., U.S. A2 142
Swanton, Vt., U.S. B2 152
Swan Valley, Id., U.S. F7 119
Swanville, Mn., U.S. E4 130
Swanzey Center, N.H., U.S. E2 136
Swarthmore, Pa., U.S. p20 145
Swartswood Lake, l., N.J., U.S. A3 137
Swartz, La., U.S. B4 125
Swartz Creek, Mi., U.S. F7 129
Swarzędz, Pol. C17 10
Swatow see Shantou, China L5 34
Swayzee, In., U.S. C6 121
Swaziland, ctry., Afr. G6 58
Swea City, Ia., U.S. A3 122
Swedeborg, Mo., U.S. D5 132
Sweden (Sverige), ctry., Eur. C11 4
Swedesboro, N.J., U.S. D2 137
Swedru, Ghana I9 64
Sweeny, Tx., U.S. r14 150
Sweet Briar, Va., U.S. C3 153
Sweetgrass, Mt., U.S. B5 133
Sweet Grass, co., Mt., U.S. E7 133
Sweet Home, Or., U.S. C4 144
Sweetser, In., U.S. C6 121
Sweet Springs, Mo., U.S. C4 132
Sweet Springs, W.V., U.S. D4 155
Sweet Water, Al., U.S. C2 108
Sweetwater, Tn., U.S. D9 149
Sweetwater, Tx., U.S. C2 150
Sweetwater, co., Wy., U.S. E3 157
Sweetwater, stm., Wy., U.S. D4 157
Sweetwater Creek, Fl., U.S. p10 116
Sweetwater Creek, stm., Ok., U.S. B1 143
Swellendam, S. Afr. J5 66
Swepsonville, N.C., U.S. A3 140
Świdnica (Schweidnitz), Pol. E16 10
Świdnik, Pol. D22 10
Świdwin, Pol. B15 10
Świebodzice, Pol. E16 10
Świebodzin, Pol. C15 10
Świecie, Pol. B18 10
Swift, co., Mn., U.S. E3 130
Swift, stm., N.H., U.S. B4 136
Swift Creek, stm., N.C., U.S. B5 140
Swift Creek, stm., Va., U.S. n17 153
Swift Creek Reservoir, res., Wa., U.S. C3 154
Swift Current, Sask., Can. G2 105
Swiftcurrent Creek, stm., Sask., Can. H1 105
Swift Diamond, stm., N.H., U.S. g7 136
Swifton, Ar., U.S. B4 111
Swilly, Lough, b., Ire. F6 8
Swinburne, Cape, c., N.W. Ter., Can. B13 96
Swindon, Eng., U.K. J12 8
Swink, Co., U.S. C7 113
Swink, Ok., U.S. C6 143
Swinomish Indian Reservation, Wa., U.S. A3 154
Świnoujście (Swinemünde), Pol. B14 10
Swisher, Ia., U.S. C6 122
Swisher, co., Tx., U.S. B2 150
Swiss, W.V., U.S. C3 155
Swissvale, Pa., U.S. k14 145
Switz City, In., U.S. F3 121
Switzer, W.V., U.S. D3 155
Switzerland, Fl., U.S. m8 116
Switzerland, co., In., U.S. G7 121
Switzerland, ctry., Eur. F9 4
Swords Range, mts., Austl. C4 70
Swoyerville, Pa., U.S. D10 145
Sycamore, Al., U.S. B3 108
Sycamore, Ga., U.S. E3 117
Sycamore, Il., U.S. B5 120
Sycamore, Ks., U.S. E8 123
Sycamore, Oh., U.S. B2 142
Sycamore Creek, stm., W.V., U.S. m13 155
Syčovka, U.S.S.R. F17 26
Sydenham, Ont., Can. C8 103
Sydney, Austl. I9 70
Sydney, N.S., Can. C9 101
Sydney Mines, N.S., Can. C9 101
Syke, Ger. C8 10
Sykeston, N.D., U.S. B6 141
Sykesville, Md., U.S. B4 127
Sykesville, Pa., U.S. D4 145
Syktyvkar, U.S.S.R. E8 22
Sylacauga, Al., U.S. B3 108
Sylhet, Bngl. H14 44
Sylt, i., Ger. A8 10
Sylva, N.C., U.S. f9 140
Sylvan Beach, N.Y., U.S. B5 139
Sylvan Grove, Ks., U.S. C5 123
Sylvania, Sask., Can. E3 105
Sylvania, Al., U.S. A4 108
Sylvania, Ga., U.S. D5 117
Sylvania, Oh., U.S. A2 142
Sylvan Lake, Alta., Can. C3 98
Sylvan Lake, Mi., U.S. o15 129
Sylvan Lake, l., In., U.S. B7 121
Sylvan Pass, Wy., U.S. B2 157
Sylvester, Ga., U.S. E3 117
Sylvia, Ks., U.S. E5 123
Symmes Creek, stm., Oh., U.S. D3 142
Symsonia, Ky., U.S. f9 124
Syntul, U.S.S.R. F24 26
Synžereja, U.S.S.R. B12 20
Syracuse, In., U.S. B6 121
Syracuse, Ks., U.S. E2 123
Syracuse, Mo., U.S. C5 132
Syracuse, Ne., U.S. D9 134
Syracuse, N.Y., U.S. B4 139
Syracuse, Oh., U.S. D4 142
Syracuse, Ut., U.S. B3 151
Syracuse see Siracusa, Italy L10 18
Syrdarja, U.S.S.R. I11 22
Syrdarja (Syr Darya), stm., U.S.S.R. H10 22
Syria (As-Sūrīyah), ctry., Asia B2 42
Syriam, Burma F4 40
Syrskij, U.S.S.R. I22 26
Sysert', U.S.S.R. F10 22
Sysladobsis Lake, l., Me., U.S. C4 126
Syzran', U.S.S.R. G7 22
Szabolcs-Szatmár, co., Hung. G22 10
Szamos (Someș), stm., Eur. B6 20
Szamotuły, Pol. C16 10
Szarvas, Hung. I20 10
Szczecin (Stettin), Pol. B14 10
Szczecinek (Neustettin), Pol. B16 10
Szczeciński, Zalew (Oderhaff), b., Eur. B14 10
Szczuczyn, Pol. B22 10
Szczytno, Pol. B21 10
Szechwan see Sichuan, prov., China E7 30
Szécsény, Hung. G19 10
Szeged, Hung. I20 10
Szeghalom, Hung. H21 10
Székesfehérvár, Hung. H18 10
Szekszárd, Hung. I18 10
Szentendre, Hung. H19 10
Szentes, Hung. I20 10
Szentgotthárd, Hung. I16 10
Szerencs, Hung. G21 10
Szob, Hung. H18 10
Szolnok, Hung. H20 10
Szolnok, co., Hung. H20 10
Szombathely, Hung. H16 10
Szprotawa, Pol. D15 10
Szubin, Pol. B17 10

T

Tabacal, Arg. B6 80
Tabaco, Phil. O20 39b
Tabacundo, Ec. G3 84
Tabalosos, Peru B3 82
Tabarka, Tun. M3 18
Ţabas, Iran E14 48
Tabasará, stm., Pan. I13 92
Tabasco, state, Mex. I13 90
Ţabas Masīnā, Iran E16 48
Tabatinga, stm., Braz. D7 79
Tabbys Peak, mtn., Ut., U.S. C3 151
Tabelbala, Alg. C6 54
Taber, Alta., Can. E4 98
Tabernash, Co., U.S. B5 113
Tabla, Niger E11 64
Table Bay, b., Newf., Can. B3 102
Table Bay, b., S. Afr. I4 66
Table Grove, Il., U.S. C3 120
Table Head, c., Newf., Can. B4 102
Table Mountain, mtn., Az., U.S. E5 110
Table Rock, Ne., U.S. D9 134

Name | Map Ref. | Page

Table Rock Lake, res., U.S. E4 132
Table Top, mtn., Az., U.S. E3 110
Tabligbo, Togo H10 64
Taboco, stm., Braz. I14 82
Taboga, Pan. I15 92
Tábor, Czech. F14 10
Tabor, Ia., U.S. D2 122
Tabor, S.D., U.S. E8 148
Tabora, Tan. C6 58
Tabor City, N.C., U.S. C4 140
Tabou, I.C. I6 64
Tabrīz, Iran B9 48
Tabūk, Sau. Ar. G4 48
Tacámbaro de Codallos, Mex. H9 90
Tacaná, Guat. B2 92
Tacaná, Volcán, vol., N.A. B2 92
Tacañitas, Arg. E7 80
T'ačev, U.S.S.R. A7 20
Tacheng, China B3 30
Tachiataš, U.S.S.R. I9 22
Tachikawa, Japan L14 36
Táchira, state, Ven. D6 84
Tachov, Czech. F12 10
Tachtamygda, U.S.S.R. G16 24
Taciuã, Lago, stm., Braz. J12 84
Tacna, Peru H6 82
Tacna, Az., U.S. E1 110
Tacna, dept., Peru G6 82
Tacoma, Wa., U.S. B3 154
Taconic, Ct., U.S. A2 114
Taconic Range, mts., U.S. A1 128
Taconite, Mn., U.S. C5 130
Taco Pozo, Arg. C7 80
Tacotalpa, stm., Mex. I13 90
Tacuarembó, Ur. F11 80
Tacuarembó, stm., Ur. F11 80
Tacuarí, stm., Ur. G11 80
Tacuatí, Para. B10 80
Tacutu (Takutu), stm., S.A. F12 84
Tad, W.V., U.S. m13 155
Tademaït, Plateau du, plat., Alg. F12 62
Tādepallegūdem, India D6 46
Tadía, Ciénaga de, l., Col. D4 84
Tadjemout, Alg. H12 62
Tadjoura, Dji. F9 56
Tadoussac, Que., Can. A8 104
Tādpatri, India E5 46
Tadžikskaja Sovetskaja Socialističeskaja Respublika, state, U.S.S.R. J12 22
T'aebaek-sanmaek, mts., Asia F16 32
Taech'ŏn, S. Kor. G14 32
Taedong, N. Kor. D13 32
Taegu, S. Kor. H16 32
Taegwan, N. Kor. C13 32
T'aein, S. Kor. H14 32
Taejŏn, S. Kor. G15 32
Ta'erwan, China D2 34
Tafalla, Spain C10 16
Ţafas, Syria C6 50
Tafassâsset, Oued, val., Afr. D8 54
Tafiré, I.C. G7 64
Tafí Viejo, Arg. D6 80
Tafraoute, Mor. F6 62
Taft, Ca., U.S. E4 112
Taft, Ok., U.S. B6 143
Taft, Tn., U.S. B5 149
Taft, Tx., U.S. F4 150
Taftsville, Vt., U.S. D4 152
Taganrog, U.S.S.R. F15 4
Tagawa, Japan N5 36
Tagaytay, Phil. N19 39b
Taghit, Alg. E9 62
Tagish Lake, l., Can. E6 96
Taguatinga, Braz. B5 79
Taguke, China E3 30
Taguke, China D11 44
Tagula Island, i., Pap. N. Gui. B10 68
Tagus (Tejo) (Tajo), stm., Eur. F3 16
Tah, Sebkha, l., Afr. G4 62
Tahakopa, N.Z. G2 72
Tahala, Mor. C8 62
Tahanaoute, Mor. E7 62
Tahart, Alg. I13 62
Tahat, mtn., Alg. I13 62
Tahifet, Alg. I13 62
Tahiti, i., Fr. Poly. J25 158
Tahkuna neem, c., U.S.S.R. B5 26
Tāhlāb (Tālāb), stm., Asia G17 48
Tahlequah, Ok., U.S. B7 143
Tahoe, Lake, l., U.S. E1 135
Tahoe City, Ca., U.S. C3 112
Tahoka, Tx., U.S. C2 150
Taholah, Wa., U.S. B1 154
Tahoua, Niger D12 64
Tahquamenon, stm., Mi., U.S. B5 129
Tahsis, B.C., Can. E4 99
Ţahţā, Egypt D6 60
Tahtsa Peak, mtn., B.C., Can. C4 99
Tahuamanú, stm., S.A. D7 82
Tahuna, Indon. E8 38
Tahuya, Wa., U.S. B2 154
Tai'an, China G5 32
Taibai Shan, mtn., China D2 30
T'aichung, Tai. K9 34
Taif see Aţ-Ţā'if, Sau. Ar. D2 47
Taihang Shan, mts., China D9 30
Taihape, N.Z. C5 72
Taihe, China B4 34
Tai Hu, l., China D9 34
Taijiang, China A10 40
Taikkyi, Burma F3 40
Tailai, China B11 30
Tailem Bend, Austl. J3 70
T'ainan, Tai. L9 34
Taínaron, Ákra, c., Grc. M6 20
Taining, China I6 34
Taiobeiras, Braz. C7 79
Taipas, Braz. B5 79
T'aipei, Tai. J10 34
T'aipeihsien, Tai. J10 34
Taiping, China M2 34
Taiping, Malay. L6 40
Taishun, China H8 34
Taitao, Península de, pen., Chile F1 78
Taitouying, China C7 32
T'aitung, Tai. M10 34
Taiwan (T'aiwan), ctry., Asia G11 30
Taiwan Strait, strt., Asia K8 34
Taixian, China C9 34
Taixing, China C9 34
Taiyiba, Isr. D4 50
Taiyuan, China D9 30
Taizhou, China C8 34
Ta'izz, Yemen H4 47
Tajerouine, Tun. N3 18
Tajga, U.S.S.R. F9 24
Tajgonos, mys, c., U.S.S.R. E24 24
Tajikistan see Tadžikskaja Sovetskaja Socialističeskaja Respublika, state, U.S.S.R. J12 22
Tajimi, Japan L12 36
Tajique, N.M., U.S. C3 138
Tajitos, Mex. B3 90
Tajmura, stm., U.S.S.R. E17 22
Tajmyr, ozero, l., U.S.S.R. C18 22
Tajmyr, poluostrov, pen., U.S.S.R. B18 22
Tajšet, U.S.S.R. F11 24
Tajumulco, Volcán, vol., Guat. B3 92
Tak, Thai. F5 40
Takāb, Iran C9 48
Takachu, Bots. D5 66
Takahashi, Japan M8 36
Takahe, Mount, mtn., Ant. C11 73
Takaka, N.Z. D4 72
Takamatsu, Japan M9 36
Takaoka, Japan K12 36
Takapuna, N.Z. B5 72
Takasaki, Japan K14 36
Takatsuki, Japan M10 36
Takayama, Japan K12 36
Takefu, Japan L11 36
Takenake, China C9 44
Takengon, Indon. L4 40
Take-shima, i., Japan Q5 37b
Take-shima (Tok-to), is., Asia J6 36
Tākestān, Iran C10 48
Takêv, Camb. I8 40
Takhli, Thai. G6 40
Takijuk Lake, l., N.W. Ter., Can. C10 96
Takikawa, Japan D16 36a
Takilma, Or., U.S. E3 144
Takla Lake, l., B.C., Can. B5 99
Taklimakan Shamo, des., China D3 30
Takoma Park, Md., U.S. f8 127
Takrouna, Tun. M5 18
Takua Pa, Thai. J5 40
Taku Glacier, Ak., U.S. k22 109
Takum, Nig. H14 64
Takutu (Tacutu), stm., S.A. F13 84
Tala, Mex. G8 90
Tala, Ur. H11 80
Talagang, Pak. D5 44
Talagante, Chile G3 80
Talala, Ok., U.S. A6 143
Talamanca, Cordillera de, mts., C.R. H11 92
Talara, Peru J2 84
Talas, U.S.S.R. I12 22
Talasea, Pap. N. Gui. m17 68a
Talata Mafara, Nig. E13 64
Talaud, Kepulauan, is., Indon. E8 38
Talavera de la Reina, Spain F7 16
Talawdī, Sud. L6 60
Talbert, Ky., U.S. C6 124
Talbot, co., Ga., U.S. D2 117
Talbot, co., Md., U.S. C5 127
Talbot Island, i., Fl., U.S. B5 116
Talbot Lake, l., Man., Can. B2 100
Talbotton, Ga., U.S. D2 117
Talbragar, stm., Austl. I8 70
Talca, Chile H3 80
Talcahuano, Chile I2 80
Talchichitle, Isla, i., Mex. E5 90
Talco, Tx., U.S. C5 150
Talcott, W.V., U.S. D4 155
Taldom, U.S.S.R. E20 26
Taldy-Kurgan, U.S.S.R. H13 22
Talent, Or., U.S. E4 144
Tālesh, Iran C10 48
Talgar, U.S.S.R. I13 22
Taliabu, Pulau, i., Indon. F7 38
Taliaferro, co., Ga., U.S. C4 117
Talica, U.S.S.R. F10 22
Talickij Čamlyk, U.S.S.R. I23 26
Talihina, Ok., U.S. C6 143
Taliouine, Mor. E7 62
Tali Post, Sud. O6 60
Talisheek, La., U.S. D6 125
Talish Mountains (Kūhhā-ye Ţavālesh, mts., Asia B10 48
Tal'ka, U.S.S.R. H11 26
Talkeetna, Ak., U.S. C10 109
Talkeetna Mountains, mts., Ak., U.S. f17 109
Talladega, Al., U.S. B3 108
Talladega, co., Al., U.S. B3 108
Talladega Springs, Al., U.S. B3 108
Tall 'Afar, Iraq C7 48
Tallah, Egypt C6 60
Tallahala Creek, stm., Ms., U.S. D4 131
Tallahassee, Fl., U.S. B2 116
Tallahatchie, co., Ms., U.S. B3 131
Tallahatchie, stm., Ms., U.S. B3 131
Tallangatta, Austl. K7 70
Tallapoosa, Ga., U.S. C1 117
Tallapoosa, Mo., U.S. E8 132
Tallapoosa, co., Al., U.S. C4 108
Tallapoosa, stm., Al., U.S. C3 108
Tallassee, Al., U.S. C4 108
Talleyville, De., U.S. A3 115
Tallinn, U.S.S.R. B7 26
Tall Kalakh, Syria D4 48
Tallmadge, Oh., U.S. A4 142
Tallula, Il., U.S. D4 120
Tallulah, La., U.S. B4 125
Talmage, Ks., U.S. C6 123
Talmage, Ne., U.S. D9 134
Tal'menka, U.S.S.R. G14 22
Talmont, Fr. F5 14
Talo, mtn., Eth. L9 60
Taloga, Ok., U.S. A3 143
Talowah, Ms., U.S. D4 131
Talquin, Lake, res., Fl., U.S. B2 116
Talsi, U.S.S.R. D5 26
Taltal, Chile C3 80
Talwood, Austl. G8 70
Tama, Arg. F5 80
Tama, Ia., U.S. C5 122
Tama, co., Ia., U.S. B5 122
Tamacuarí, Pico, mtn., S.A. G10 84
Tamadjert, Alg. H14 62
Tamalameque, Col. C6 84
Tamale, Ghana G9 64
Tamalpais, Mount, mtn., Ca., U.S. h7 112
Tamana, Japan O5 36
Tamanā, Cerro, mtn., Col. E4 84
Tamanaco, stm., Ven. C10 84
Tamaniquá, Braz. I10 84
Tamano, Japan M8 36
Tamapatz, Mex. G10 90
Tamaqua, Pa., U.S. E10 145
Tamaquari, Ilha, i., Braz. H10 84
Tamar, stm., Austl. M7 70
Támara, Col. E6 84
Tamaroa, Il., U.S. E4 120
Tamarugal, Pampa del, pl., Chile I7 82
Tamási, Hung. I18 10
Tamaské, Niger D12 64
Tamaulipas, state, Mex. F10 90
Tamaya, stm., Peru C4 82
Tamazula, Mex. E6 90
Tamazula de Gordiano, Mex. H8 90
Tamazulapan del Progreso, Mex. I11 90
Tamazunchale, Mex. G10 90
Tambacounda, Sen. E3 64
Tamba Dabatou, Gui. F4 64
Tāmbaram, India F6 46
Tambelan, Kepulauan, is., Indon. N9 40
Tamberías, Arg. F4 80
Tambo, Austl. E7 70
Tambo, Peru E4 82
Tambo, stm., Austl. K7 70
Tambo, stm., Peru D5 82
Tambo, stm., Peru G6 82
Tamboara, Braz. G2 79
Tambo Grande, Peru A1 82
Tambohorano, Madag. P20 67b
Tambopata, stm., S.A. E7 82
Tambor, C.R. H9 92
Tamboritha, Mount, mtn., Austl. K7 70
Tambov, U.S.S.R. I24 26
Tambo Yacu, stm., Peru H5 84
Tambura, Sud. O4 60
Tamchaket, Maur. C4 64
Tame, Col. D7 84
Tameapa, Mex. E6 90
Tameghza, Tun. C14 62
Tamel Aike, Arg. F2 78
Tamelelt, Mor. E7 62
Tamenghest, Alg. I13 62
Tamenghest, Oued, val., Alg. I11 62
Tamiahua, Mex. G11 90
Tamiahua, Laguna de, b., Mex. G11 90
Tamiami Canal, Fl., U.S. G6 116
Tamil Nādu, state, India G5 46
Tamina, Tx., U.S. D5 150
Tamiš (Timiş), stm., Eur. D4 20
Tamitatoala, stm., Braz. B2 79
Tam Ky, Viet. G10 40
Tamms, Il., U.S. F4 120
Tamnum, Yemen G7 47
Tampa, Fl., U.S. E4 116
Tampa, Ks., U.S. D6 123
Tampa Bay, b., Fl., U.S. E4 116
Tampaón, stm., Mex. G10 90
Tampere, Fin. K18 6
Tampico, Mex. F11 90
Tampico, Il., U.S. B4 120
Tampico, In., U.S. G6 121
Tampin, Malay. M7 40
Tam Quan, Viet. G10 40
Tamri, Mor. E6 62
Tamsagbulag, Mong. B10 30
Tamsalu, U.S.S.R. B9 26
Tamshiyacu, Peru J6 84
Tamsweg, Aus. H13 10
Tamworth, Austl. H9 70
Tamworth, Ont., Can. C8 103
Tamworth, N.H., U.S. C4 136
Tamyang, S. Kor. H14 32
Tana, Chile H7 82
Tana (Teno), stm., Eur. F20 6
Tana, Lake, l., Eth. K9 60
Tanabe, Japan N10 36
Tanabi, Braz. F4 79
Tanacross, Ak., U.S. C11 109
Tanaga Island, i., Ak., U.S. E4 109
Tanahbala, Pulau, i., Indon. O5 40
Tanahmasa, Pulau, i., Indon. O5 40
Tanami Desert, des., Austl. C5 68
Tan An, Viet. I9 40
Tanana, Ak., U.S. B9 109
Tanana, stm., Ak., U.S. C10 109
Tananarive see Antananarivo, Madag. Q22 67b
Tancheng, China I6 32
Tanchoj, U.S.S.R. G13 24
Tanch'ŏn, N. Kor. C16 32
Tancítaro, Pico de, mtn., Mex. H8 90
Tancook Island, N.S., Can. E5 101
Tānda, India G10 44
Tandaltī, Sud. K6 60
Tandil, Arg. I9 80
Tandou Lake, l., Austl. I5 70
Tanega-shima, i., Japan Q6 37b
Tan Emellel, Alg. G15 62
Taney, co., Mo., U.S. E4 132
Taneycomo, Lake, res., Mo., U.S. E4 132
Taneytown, Md., U.S. A3 127
Taneyville, Mo., U.S. E4 132
Tanezrouft, des., Afr. D6 54
Tanga, Tan. C7 58
Tangail, Bngl. H13 44
Tangainony, Madag. S22 67b
Tangalla, Sri L. I6 46
Tanganyika, Lake, l., Afr. C5 58
Tangarā, Braz. D13 80
Tangarana, stm., Peru I5 84
Tangcun, China J2 34
Tangent, Or., U.S. C3 144
Tanger (Tangier), Mor. C8 62
Tangermünde, Ger. C11 10
Tanggou, China B7 34
Tanggu, China D5 32
Tanggula Shan, mts., China D13 44
Tangier, N.S., Can. E7 101
Tangier, Va., U.S. C7 153
Tangier Island, i., Va., U.S. C6 153
Tangier Sound, strt., Md., U.S. D6 127
Tangier see Tanger, Mor. C8 62
Tangipahoa, La., U.S. D5 125
Tangipahoa, co., La., U.S. D5 125
Tangipahoa, stm., La., U.S. D5 125
Tangjiagou, China E6 34
Tangjin, S. Kor. G14 32
Tangra Yumco, l., China E12 44
Tangsanying, China B5 32
Tangshan, China D6 32
Tanguiéta, Benin F10 64
Tanguro, stm., Braz. B2 79
Tangxian, China E2 32
Tanimbar, Kepulauan, is., Indon. G9 38
Taninges, Fr. F13 14
Tanjiafang, China G6 32
Tanjiang, China K5 34
Tanjungbalai, Indon. M5 40
Tanjungpandan, Indon. F4 38
Tanjungpinang, Indon. N8 40
Tanjungselor, Indon. E6 38
Tānk, Pak. D4 44
Tan Kena, Alg. G15 62
Tännäs, Swe. J13 6
Tanner, Al., U.S. A3 108
Tannu-Ola, chrebet, mts., Asia G10 24
Tannūrah, Ra's, c., Sau. Ar. H11 48
Tano, stm., Afr. I8 64
Tânout, Niger D14 64
Tanquinho, Braz. A9 79
Tanshui, Tai. J10 34
Tânsin, Isle de, i., Hond. B11 92
Tânsin, Laguna de, b., Hond. B11 92
Ţanţā, Egypt B6 60
Tantallon, Sask., Can. G5 105
Tan-Tan, Mor. F5 62
Tantoyuca, Mex. G10 90
Tanuku, India D6 46
Tanyang, S. Kor. G16 32
Tanzania, ctry., Afr. C6 58
Tao, stm., China E7 30
Taochong, China D7 34
Tao'er, stm., China B11 30
Taolakepa, China D11 44
Taoling, China E7 34
Taormina, Italy L10 18
Taos, Mo., U.S. C5 132
Taos, N.M., U.S. A4 138
Taos, co., N.M., U.S. A4 138
Taos Pueblo, N.M., U.S. A4 138
Taoudenni, Mali I8 62
Taounate, Mor. C8 62
Taoura, Alg. M3 18
Taourirt, Mor. C9 62
Taoussa, Mali C9 64
Taoyuan, China J6 34
Tapa, U.S.S.R. B8 26
Tapacarí, Bol. G8 82
Tapachula, Mex. J13 90
Tapah, Malay. L6 40
Tapaje, stm., Col. F3 84
Tapajós, stm., Braz. D7 76
Tapalquén, Arg. I8 80
Tapanahony, stm., Sur. C7 76
Tapauá, Braz. A10 82
Tapauá, stm., Braz. A9 82
Tapejara, Braz. E12 80
Tapera, Braz. E12 80
Taperoá, Braz. B9 79
Tapes, Braz. F13 80
Tapeta, Lib. H5 64
Taphan Hin, Thai. F6 40
Tāpi, stm., India B2 46
Tapiche, stm., Peru A5 82
Taping (Daying), stm., Asia B4 40
Tapirai, Braz. E5 79
Tāplejung, Nepal G12 44
Tapoa, stm., Afr. E11 64
Tapolca, Hung. I17 10
Tappahannock, Va., U.S. C6 153
Tappan, N.Y., U.S. g13 139
Tappan, Lake, res., N.J., U.S. g9 137
Tappan Lake, res., Oh., U.S. B4 142
Tappen, N.D., U.S. C6 141
Tappi-zaki, c., Japan F15 36
Tappo, Ghana F8 64
Tapurucuara, Braz. H10 84
Taqātu' Hayyā, Sud. H9 60
Taquara, Braz. E13 80
Taquaral, Braz. D4 79
Taquaras, Ponta das, c., Braz. D14 80
Taquari, Braz. D2 79
Taquari, Braz. E13 80
Taquari, stm., Braz. E13 80
Taquari, stm., Braz. H13 82
Taquari, Pantanal do, sw., Braz. H13 82
Taquaritinga, Braz. F4 79
Taquaruçu, stm., Braz. F2 79
Tar, stm., N.C., U.S. B5 140
Tara, Austl. F9 70
Tara, Ont., Can. C3 103
Tara, U.S.S.R. F6 24
Taraba, stm., Nig. G9 54
Tarabine, Oued ti-n-, val., Afr. J14 62
Tarabuco, Bol. H9 82
Tarābulus (Tripoli), Leb. D3 48
Tarābulus (Tripoli), Libya B3 56
Tarābulus (Tripolitania), hist. reg., Libya B3 56
Tarago, Austl. J8 70
Taraira (Traíra), stm., S.A. H8 84
Tarakan, Indon. E6 38
Taraklija, U.S.S.R. D12 20
Tarancón, Spain E8 16
Taranto, Italy I12 18
Taranto, Golfo di, b., Italy I12 18
Tarapacá, Col. I8 84
Tarapoto, Peru B3 82
Taraquá, Braz. G8 84
Tarare, Fr. G11 14
Tarariras, Ur. H10 80
Tarāsa Dwīp, i., India J2 40
Tarascon, Fr. J8 14
Tarascon, Fr. I11 14
Tarat, Alg. G15 62
Tarata, Bol. G8 82
Tarata, Peru G6 82
Tarauacá, Braz. C6 82
Tarauacá, stm., Braz. B6 82
Tarawa, atoll, Kir. H21 158
Tarawera, N.Z. C6 72
Tarazona, Spain D10 16
Tarazona de la Mancha, Spain F10 16
Tarbagataj, chrebet, mts., Asia H8 24
Tarbes, Fr. I7 14
Tarboro, Ga., U.S. E5 117
Tarboro, N.C., U.S. B5 140
Tarbū, Libya C4 56
Tarcento, Italy C8 18
Tarcoola, Austl. F6 68
Tardajos, Spain C8 16
Tardoki-Jani, gora, mtn., U.S.S.R. H19 24
Taree, Austl. H10 70
Tärendö, Swe. H18 6
Tarentum, Pa., U.S. E2 145
Ţarfā', Ra's at-, c., Sau. Ar. F3 47
Ţarfā', Wādī at-, val., Egypt G1 48
Tarfaya, Mor. G4 62
Targhee Pass, U.S. E7 119
Târgovişte, Bul. F10 20
Targuist, Mor. C8 62
Tarhjijt, Mor. F6 62
Tarhūnah, Libya B3 56
Tari, Pap. N. Gui. G11 38
Tāriba, Ven. D6 84
Tarifa, Spain I6 16
Tarifa, Punta de, c., Spain I6 16
Tariffville, Ct., U.S. B4 114
Tarija, Bol. I9 82
Tarija, dept., Bol. I9 82
Tarīm, Yemen F6 47
Tarim, stm., China C3 30
Tarim Pendi, China A9 44
Taritatu, stm., Indon. F10 38
Tarka, Niger D13 64
Tarkastad, S. Afr. I8 66
Tarkiln Hill, mtn., Me., U.S. g7 126
Tarkio, Mo., U.S. A2 132
Tarkwa, Ghana I9 64
Tarlac, Phil. N19 39b
Tarm, Den. N11 6
Tarma, Peru D4 82
Tarn, dept., Fr. I9 14
Tärnaby, Swe. I14 6
Tarn-et-Garonne, dept., Fr. H8 14
Tarnobrzeg, Pol. E21 10
Tarnów, Pol. E21 10
Tarnowskie Góry, Pol. E18 10
Taroom, Austl. E8 70
Taroudant, Mor. E6 62
Tarpey, Ca., U.S. D4 112
Tarpon, Lake, l., Fl., U.S. o10 116
Tarpon Springs, Fl., U.S. D4 116
Tarqui, Peru H5 84
Tarra, stm., Ven. C6 84
Tarrafal, C.V. k16 64a
Tarrafal, C.V. m17 64a
Tarragona, Spain D13 16
Tarraleah, Austl. N7 70
Tarrant, Al., U.S. B3 108
Tarrant, co., Tx., U.S. C4 150
Tàrrega, Spain D13 16
Tarry, Ar., U.S. C4 111
Tarryall Creek, stm., Co., U.S. B5 113
Tarryall Mountains, mts., Co., U.S. B5 113
Tarrytown, Ga., U.S. D4 117
Tarrytown, N.Y., U.S. D7 139
Tarsus, Tur. C3 48
Tartagal, Arg. B7 80
Tartagal, Arg. E9 80
Tartu, U.S.S.R. C9 26
Ţarţūs, Syria D3 48
Tarumirim, Braz. E8 79
Tarusa, U.S.S.R. G20 26
Tarutino, U.S.S.R. C13 20
Tarutung, Indon. M5 40
Tarvisio, Italy C8 18
Tarvo, stm., S.A. F11 82
Tašauz, U.S.S.R. I9 22
Tasejeva, stm., U.S.S.R. F16 22
Tasejevo, U.S.S.R. F16 22
Taseko Mountain, mtn., B.C., Can. D6 99
Tashi Gang Dzong, Bhu. G14 44
Ţashk, Daryācheh-ye, l., Iran G12 48
Tashkent see Taškent, U.S.S.R. I11 22
Tasikmalaya, Indon. J14 39a
Taškent, U.S.S.R. I11 22
Taškepri, U.S.S.R. J10 22
Tasman Bay, b., N.Z. D4 72
Tasmania, state, Austl. H9 68
Tasmania, i., Austl. N7 70
Tasman Peninsula, pen., Austl. N7 70
Tasman Sea, Oc. L19 158
Tăşnad, Rom. B6 20
Tassara, Niger C12 64
Tasso, Tn., U.S. D9 149
Taštagol, U.S.S.R. G9 24
Tastiota, Mex. C4 90
Taswell, In., U.S. H4 121
Tata, Hung. H18 10
T'at'a, vulkan, vol., U.S.S.R. C21 36a
Tatabánya, Hung. H18 10
Tataouine, Tun. D16 62
Tatarbunary, U.S.S.R. D13 20
Tatarka, U.S.S.R. H11 26
Tatarlar, Tur. H10 20
Tatarsk, U.S.S.R. F7 24
Tatarskij proliv, strt., U.S.S.R. H20 24
Tatar Strait see Tatarskij proliv, strt., U.S.S.R. H20 24
Tate, Ga., U.S. B2 117
Tate, co., Ms., U.S. A4 131
Tate, stm., Austl. A6 70
Tateville, Ky., U.S. D5 124
Tatitlek, Ak., U.S. C10 109
Tatnam, Cape, c., Man., Can. f9 100
Tatrang, China A11 44
Tatta, Pak. H2 44
Tattnall, co., Ga., U.S. D4 117
Tatum, N.M., U.S. D6 138
Tatvan, Tur. B7 48
Taubaté, Braz. G6 79
Tauberbischofsheim, Ger. F9 10
Taučik, U.S.S.R. I8 22
Tauini, stm., Braz. G13 84
Taulabé, Hond. C7 92
Taumarunui, N.Z. C5 72
Taumaturgo, Braz. C5 82
Taum Sauk Mountain, mtn., Mo., U.S. D6 132
Taunay, Braz. I13 82
Taung, Boph. F7 66
Taungdwingyi, Burma D3 40
Taunggyi, Burma D4 40
Taungup, Burma E3 40
Taunton, Eng., U.K. J10 8
Taunton, Ma., U.S. C5 128
Taunton, Mn., U.S. F2 130
Taunton, stm., Ma., U.S. C5 128
Taupo, N.Z. C6 72
Taupo, Lake, l., N.Z. C5 72
Tauragė, U.S.S.R. F5 26
Tauranga, N.Z. B6 72
Taureau, Réservoir, res., Que., Can. C4 104
Taurianova, Italy K11 18
Tauripampa, Peru E3 82
Taurisma, Peru F5 82
Tauroa Point, c., N.Z. A4 72
Taurus Mountains see Toros Dağları, mts., Tur. H14 4
Tauste, Spain D10 16
Tavaí, Para. D11 80
Tavanasa, Switz. E11 13
Tavares, Fl., U.S. D5 116
Tavda, U.S.S.R. F11 22
Tavda, stm., U.S.S.R. F10 22
Tavernes de Valldigna, Spain F11 16
Tavernier, Fl., U.S. G6 116
Tavira, Port. H4 16
Tavolžan, U.S.S.R. G13 22
Tavor, Har (Mount Tabor), mtn., Isr. C4 50
Tavoy see Dawei, Burma G5 40
Tavşanlı, Tur. J13 20
Tawakoni, Lake, res., Tx., U.S. C4 150
Tawas City, Mi., U.S. D7 129
Tawas Lake, l., Mi., U.S. D7 129
Ţawīlah, Juzur, is., Egypt H2 48
Tawkar, Sud. H9 60
Taxco de Alarcón, Mex. H10 90
Taxisco, Guat. C4 92
Taxkorgan, China D2 30
Tay, stm., Scot., U.K. E10 8
Tayabamba, Peru C3 82
Taylor, B.C., Can. A7 99
Taylor, Al., U.S. D4 108
Taylor, Az., U.S. C5 110
Taylor, Ar., U.S. D2 111
Taylor, Mi., U.S. p15 129
Taylor, Ms., U.S. A4 131
Taylor, Ne., U.S. C6 134
Taylor, N.D., U.S. C3 141
Taylor, Pa., U.S. D10 145
Taylor, Tx., U.S. D4 150
Taylor, Wi., U.S. D2 156
Taylor, co., Fl., U.S. B3 116
Taylor, co., Ga., U.S. D2 117
Taylor, co., Ia., U.S. D3 122
Taylor, co., Ky., U.S. C4 124
Taylor, co., Tx., U.S. C3 150
Taylor, co., W.V., U.S. B4 155
Taylor, co., Wi., U.S. C3 156
Taylor, stm., Co., U.S. C4 113
Taylor, Mount, mtn., N.M., U.S. B2 138
Taylor Knob, hll, Tn., U.S. G10 149
Taylor Mill, Ky., U.S. k14 124
Taylor Mountain, mtn., Id., U.S. E4 119
Taylor Park Reservoir, res., Co., U.S. C4 113
Taylor Ridge, mtn., Ga., U.S. B1 117
Taylors, S.C., U.S. B3 147
Taylors Falls, Mn., U.S. E6 130
Taylors Island, Md., U.S. D5 127
Taylors Island, i., Md., U.S. D5 127
Taylor Springs, Il., U.S. D4 120
Taylorsville, Ga., U.S. B2 117
Taylorsville, In., U.S. F6 121
Taylorsville, Ky., U.S. B4 124
Taylorsville, Ms., U.S. D4 131
Taylorsville, N.C., U.S. B1 140
Taylorville, Il., U.S. D4 120
Taymā', Sau. Ar. H5 48
Taymouth, N.B., Can. C3 101
Taymyr Peninsula see Tajmyr, poluostrov, pen., U.S.S.R. B12 24
Tay Ninh, Viet. I9 40
Tayoltita, Mex. E7 90
Tayside, prov., Scot., U.K. E10 8
Taytay, Phil. C6 38
Tayyārah, Sud. K6 60
Taz, stm., U.S.S.R. D8 24
Taza, Mor. C8 62
Tazenakht, Mor. E7 62
Tazewell, Ga., U.S. D2 117
Tazewell, Tn., U.S. C10 149
Tazewell, Va., U.S. e10 153
Tazewell, co., Il., U.S. C4 120
Tazewell, co., Va., U.S. e10 153
Tazin, stm., Can. D10 96
Tazovskaja guba, b., U.S.S.R. D7 24
Tazovskij poluostrov, pen., U.S.S.R. D13 22
Tazrouk, Alg. I14 62
Tazumal, hist., El Sal. D5 92
Tazungdām, Burma F17 44
Tbessa, Alg. C15 62
Tbilisi, U.S.S.R. I6 22
Tchamba, Togo G10 64
Tchaourou, Benin G11 64
Tchefuncta, stm., La., U.S. D5 125
Tchériba, Burkina E8 64
Tchetti, Benin H10 64
Tchibanga, Gabon B2 58
Tchien, Lib. G5 54
Tchin-Tabáradene, Niger D12 64

Name	Map Ref.	Page
Tchula, Ms., U.S.	B3	131
Tczew, Pol.	A18	10
Tea, S.D., U.S.	D9	148
Tea, stm., Braz.	H10	84
Teaca, Rom.	C8	20
Teacapan, Mex.	F7	90
Tea Creek, stm., Sask., Can.	C2	105
Teague, Tx., U.S.	D4	150
Teakean Butte, mtn., Id., U.S.	C2	119
Teaneck, N.J., U.S.	h8	137
Teano, Italy	H9	18
Teapa, Mex.	I13	90
Teasdale, Ut., U.S.	E4	151
Teaticket, Ma., U.S.	C6	128
Te Awamutu, N.Z.	C5	72
Teba, Spain	I7	16
Tebbetts, Mo., U.S.	C6	132
Tebicuary, stm., Para.	D10	80
Tebicuary-Mí, stm., Para.	D10	80
Tebingtinggi, Indon.	M5	40
Tebingtinggi, Pulau, i., Indon.	N7	40
Tébourba, Tun.	M4	18
Téboursouk, Tun.	M4	18
Tecalitlán, Mex.	H8	90
Tecamachalco, Mex.	H11	90
Tecate, Mex.	A1	90
Teche, Bayou, stm., La., U.S.	D4	125
Techirghiol, Rom.	E12	20
Techlé, W. Sah.	J3	62
Tecklenburg, Ger.	C7	10
Tecomán, Mex.	H8	90
Tecpan de Galeana, Mex.	I9	90
Tecpán Guatemala, Guat.	C3	92
Tecuala, Mex.	F7	90
Tecuamburro, Volcán, vol., Guat.	C4	92
Tecuci, Rom.	D11	20
Tecumseh, Ont., Can.	E2	103
Tecumseh, Ks., U.S.	k14	123
Tecumseh, Mi., U.S.	G7	129
Tecumseh, Ne., U.S.	D9	134
Tecumseh, Ok., U.S.	B5	143
Tecumseh, Mount, mtn., N.H., U.S.	C3	136
Tedžen, U.S.S.R.	J10	22
Tedžen (Harīrūd), stm., Asia	C16	48
Teec Nos Pos, Az., U.S.	A6	110
Teegarden, In., U.S.	B5	121
Teeli, U.S.S.R.	G16	22
Tees, Alta., Can.	C4	98
Tees, stm., Eng., U.K.	G12	8
Teesside see Middlesbrough, Eng., U.K.	G12	8
Teeswater, Ont., Can.	C3	103
Tefé, Braz.	I10	84
Tefé, stm., Braz.	D5	76
Tefé, Lago de, l., Braz.	I10	84
Tegal, Indon.	J14	39a
Tegelen, Neth.	F9	12
Tegernsee, Ger.	H11	10
Tegina, Nig.	F13	64
Tegucigalpa, Hond.	C7	92
Teguise, Spain	N27	17b
Tehachapi, Ca., U.S.	E4	112
Tehachapi Mountains, mts., Ca., U.S.	E4	112
Tehama, co., Ca., U.S.	B2	112
Tehamiyam, Sud.	H9	60
Téhini, I.C.	G8	64
Tehrān, Iran	D11	48
Tehrathum, Nepal	G12	44
Tehuacán, Mex.	H11	90
Tehuantepec, Golfo de, b., Mex.	J12	90
Tehuantepec, Istmo de, Mex.	I12	90
Teide, Pico de, mtn., Spain	O24	17b
Teixeira Pinto, Gui.-B.	E3	64
Teixeiras, Braz.	F7	79
Teixeira Soares, Braz.	C13	80
Tejamén, Mex.	E7	90
Tejkovo, U.S.S.R.	E23	26
Tejo see Tagus, stm., Eur.	F3	16
Tejupan, Punta, c., Mex.	H8	90
Tejupilco de Hidalgo, Mex.	H9	90
Tekamah, Ne., U.S.	C9	134
Tekax, Mex.	G15	90
Tekeli, U.S.S.R.	I13	22
Tekeze, stm., Afr.	F8	56
Tekirdağ, Tur.	I11	20
Tekoa, Wa., U.S.	B8	154
Tekonsha, Mi., U.S.	F5	129
Te Kuiti, N.Z.	C5	72
Tela, Hond.	B7	92
Tela, Bahía de, b., Hond.	B7	92
Télagh, Alg.	C10	62
Tel Aviv-Yafo, Isr.	D3	50
Telde, Spain	O25	17b
Telechany, U.S.S.R.	I8	26
Telefomin, Pap. N. Gui.	G11	38
Telemark, co., Nor.	L11	6
Telembí, stm., Col.	G4	84
Telén, Arg.	I6	80
Telenešty, U.S.S.R.	B12	20
Teleorman, co., Rom.	F8	20
Telertheba, Djebel, mtn., Alg.	H14	62
Telescope Peak, mtn., Ca., U.S.	D5	112
Telfair, co., Ga., U.S.	E4	117
Telford, Pa., U.S.	F11	145
Telford, Tn., U.S.	C11	149
Telfs, Aus.	H11	10
Telica, stm., Hond.	C8	92
Telica, Volcán, vol., Nic.	E8	92
Telkwa, B.C., Can.	B4	99
Tell City, In., U.S.	I4	121
Teller, Ak., U.S.	B6	109
Teller, co., Co., U.S.	C5	113
Tellicherry, India	G3	46
Tellico Plains, Tn., U.S.	D9	149
Tello, Col.	F5	84
Telluride, Co., U.S.	D3	113
Tel Megiddo (Armageddon), hist., Isr.	C4	50
Tel Mond, Isr.	D3	50
Telok Anson, Malay.	L6	40
Teloloapan, Mex.	H10	90
Telos Lake, l., Me., U.S.	B3	126
Telpaneca, Nic.	D8	92
Telšiai, U.S.S.R.	F5	26
Telti, Italy	I4	18
Teltow, Ger.	C13	10
Tema, Ghana	I10	64
Temax, Mex.	G15	90
Tembenči, stm., U.S.S.R.	D11	24
Temblador, Ven.	C11	84
Tembleque, Spain	F8	16
Temecula, Ca., U.S.	F5	112
Temera, Mor.	D7	62
Temirtau, U.S.S.R.	G12	22
Témiscouata, Lac, l., Que., Can.	B9	104
Te-Moak Indian Reservation, Nv., U.S.	C6	135
Temora, Austl.	J7	70
Temosachic, Mex.	C6	90
Tempe, Az., U.S.	D4	110
Temperance, Mi., U.S.	G7	129
Temperance, stm., Mn., U.S.	C8	130
Temperanceville, Va., U.S.	C7	153
Tempio Pausania, Italy	I4	18
Tempisque, stm., C.R.	G9	92
Temple, Ga., U.S.	C1	117
Temple, Mi., U.S.	D5	129
Temple, N.H., U.S.	E3	136
Temple, Ok., U.S.	C3	143
Temple, Pa., U.S.	F10	145
Temple, Tx., U.S.	D4	150
Temple Hill, Ky., U.S.	D4	124
Temple Terrace, Fl., U.S.	o11	116
Templeton, Ia., U.S.	C3	122
Templeton, Ma., U.S.	A3	128
Templeton, Pa., U.S.	E3	145
Templeton, stm., Austl.	C3	70
Templin, Ger.	B13	10
Tempoal, stm., Mex.	G10	90
Tempoal de Sánchez, Mex.	G10	90
Tempy, U.S.S.R.	E20	26
Temr'uk, U.S.S.R.	H5	22
Temuco, Chile	J2	80
Tena, Ec.	H4	84
Tenabo, Mex.	G14	90
Tenafly, N.J., U.S.	B5	137
Tenaha, Tx., U.S.	D5	150
Tenāli, India	D6	46
Tenant Mountain, mtn., N.Y., U.S.	B6	139
Tenants Harbor, Me., U.S.	E3	126
Tenasserim, Burma	H5	40
Tendaho, Eth.	F9	56
Tende, Col de, Eur.	H14	14
Ten Degree Channel, strt., India	J2	40
Tendoy, Id., U.S.	E5	119
Tenente Marques, stm., Braz.	D11	82
Tenente Portela, Braz.	D12	80
Ténéré, des., Niger	E9	54
Tenerife, i., Spain	O24	17b
Ténès, Alg.	B11	62
Teng'aopu, China	B10	32
Tengchong, China	B5	40
Tenggara, Nusa (Lesser Sunda Islands), is., Indon.	G7	38
Tengiz, ozero, l., U.S.S.R.	G11	22
Tengtian, China	H4	34
Tengtiao (Na), stm., Asia	C7	40
Tengxian, China	H5	32
Teniente Rodolfo Marsh, sci., B.A.T.	B1	73
Tenino, Wa., U.S.	C3	154
Tenkāsi, India	H4	46
Tenke, Zaire	D5	58
Tenkiller Ferry Lake, res., Ok., U.S.	B6	143
Tenkodogo, Burkina	F9	64
Tenmile, stm., U.S.	B5	146
Tenmile Creek, stm., W.V., U.S.	k10	155
Tenmile Lake, l., Mn., U.S.	D4	130
Tennant Creek, Austl.	C6	68
Tennessee, state, U.S.	B5	149
Tennessee, stm., U.S.	D9	106
Tennessee Pass, Co., U.S.	B4	113
Tennessee Ridge, Tn., U.S.	A4	149
Tennga, Ga., U.S.	B2	117
Tennille, Ga., U.S.	D4	117
Tennyson, In., U.S.	H3	121
Teno, Chile	H3	80
Teno (Tana), stm., Eur.	F20	6
Tenosique, Mex.	I14	90
Tenryū, Japan	M12	36
Tensas, co., La., U.S.	B4	125
Tensas, stm., La., U.S.	B4	125
Tensaw, stm., Al., U.S.	E2	108
Ten Sleep, Wy., U.S.	B5	157
Tenstrike, Mn., U.S.	C4	130
Tenterfield, Austl.	G10	70
Ten Thousand Islands, is., Fl., U.S.	G5	116
Teocaltiche, Mex.	G8	90
Teodelina, Arg.	H8	80
Teófilo Otoni, Braz.	D8	79
Teotihuacán, hist., Mex.	H10	90
Tepalcatepec, Mex.	H8	90
Tepeaca, Mex.	H11	90
Tepehuanes, Mex.	E7	90
Tepehuanes, stm., Mex.	E7	90
Tepeji de Ocampo, Mex.	H10	90
Tepelenë, Alb.	I4	20
Tepi, Eth.	N8	60
Tepic, Mex.	G7	90
Teplice, Czech.	E13	10
Teplovo, U.S.S.R.	F25	26
Tepoca, Bahía, b., Mex.	B3	90
Tepoca, Punta, c., Mex.	C3	90
Tepopa, Cabo, c., Mex.	C3	90
Téra, Niger	D10	64
Tera, stm., Spain	D6	16
Teramo, Italy	G8	18
Terang, Austl.	L5	70
Terborg, Neth.	E9	12
Terbuny, U.S.S.R.	I21	26
Terceira, i., Port.	k21	62a
Tercero, stm., Arg.	G7	80
Terechovka, U.S.S.R.	I14	26
Tereida, Sud.	L6	60
Terek, stm., U.S.S.R.	I7	22
Terenino, U.S.S.R.	G16	26
Terenos, Braz.	F1	79
Teresina, Braz.	E10	76
Teresópolis, Braz.	G7	79
Terespol, Pol.	C23	10
Teresva, U.S.S.R.	A7	20
Terhorne, Neth.	B8	12
Teribe, stm., N.A.	H12	92
Termas de Río Hondo, Arg.	D6	80
Termez, U.S.S.R.	J11	22
Termini Imerese, Italy	L8	18
Términos, Laguna de, b., Mex.	H14	90
Termoli, Italy	G10	18
Ternate, Indon.	E8	38
Ternberg, Aus.	H14	10
Ternej, U.S.S.R.	H19	24
Terneuzen, Neth.	F4	12
Terni, Italy	G7	18
Ternopol', U.S.S.R.	H3	22
Ternovka, U.S.S.R.	A13	20
Teror, Spain	O25	17b
Terpenija, mys, c., U.S.S.R.	H20	24
Terpenija, zaliv, b., U.S.S.R.	H20	24
Terra Alta, W.V., U.S.	B5	155
Terra Boa, Braz.	G2	79
Terrace, B.C., Can.	B3	99
Terracina, Italy	H8	18
Terral, Ok., U.S.	D4	143
Terralba, Italy	J3	18
Terra Nova, Newf., Can.	D4	102
Terra Nova National Park, Newf., Can.	D4	102
Terra Rica, Braz.	G2	79
Terra Roxa d'Oeste, Braz.	C12	80
Terra Santa, Braz.	I14	84
Terrassa, Spain	D14	16
Terrebonne, Que., Can.	D4	104
Terrebonne, Or., U.S.	C5	144
Terrebonne, co., La., U.S.	E5	125
Terrebonne Bay, b., La., U.S.	E5	125
Terre Haute, In., U.S.	F3	121
Terre Hill, Pa., U.S.	F9	145
Terrell, N.C., U.S.	B2	140
Terrell, Tx., U.S.	C4	150
Terrell, co., Ga., U.S.	E2	117
Terrell, co., Tx., U.S.	D1	150
Terrell Hills, Tx., U.S.	k7	150
Terrenceville, Newf., Can.	E4	102
Terreton, Id., U.S.	F6	119
Terril, Ia., U.S.	A3	122
Terry, Ms., U.S.	C3	131
Terry, Mt., U.S.	D11	133
Terry, co., Tx., U.S.	C1	150
Terry Peak, mtn., S.D., U.S.	C2	148
Terrytown, Ne., U.S.	C2	134
Terryville, Ct., U.S.	C3	114
Terschelling, i., Neth.	B7	12
Teruel, Col.	F5	84
Teruel, Spain	E10	16
Tésa, Hung.	G18	10
Teša, U.S.S.R.	F25	26
Tesalia, Col.	F5	84
Tešanj, Yugo.	E2	20
Tes-Chem (Tesijn), stm., Asia	A5	30
Tescott, Ks., U.S.	C6	123
Teseney, Eth.	J9	60
Teshekpuk Lake, l., Ak., U.S.	A9	109
Tesijn (Tes-Chem), stm., Asia	B6	30
Teslić, Yugo.	E1	20
Teslin, Yukon, Can.	D6	96
Teslin, stm., Can.	D6	96
Teslin Lake, l., Can.	D6	96
Tesouras, stm., Braz.	C3	79
Tesouro, Braz.	D2	79
Tessala, Monts du, mts., Alg.	J11	16
Tessalit, Mali	A10	64
Tessaoua, Niger	E13	64
Tessenderlo, Bel.	F7	12
Tessy-sur-Vire, Fr.	D5	14
Testour, Tun.	M4	18
Tesuque, N.M., U.S.	B4	138
Tesuque Pueblo, N.M., U.S.	B4	138
Tete, Moz.	E6	58
Teterow, Ger.	B12	10
Teton, Id., U.S.	F7	119
Teton, co., Id., U.S.	F7	119
Teton, co., Mt., U.S.	C4	133
Teton, co., Wy., U.S.	C2	157
Teton, stm., Mt., U.S.	C5	133
Tetonia, Id., U.S.	F7	119
Teton Pass, Wy., U.S.	C2	157
Teton Range, mts., Wy., U.S.	C2	157
Teton Village, Wy., U.S.	C2	157
Tétouan, Mor.	C8	62
Tetovo, Yugo.	G4	20
Teuco, stm., Arg.	C8	80
Teulada, Italy	K3	18
Teulada, Capo, c., Italy	K3	18
Teúl de González Ortega, Mex.	G8	90
Teulon, Man., Can.	D3	100
Teutopolis, Il., U.S.	D5	120
Teuva, Fin.	J17	6
Tevere (Tiber), stm., Italy	G7	18
Teverya (Tiberias), Isr.	C5	50
Tevli, U.S.S.R.	I7	26
Tewksbury, Ma., U.S.	A5	128
Texada Island, i., B.C., Can.	E5	99
Texarkana, Ar., U.S.	D1	111
Texarkana, Tx., U.S.	C5	150
Texas, Austl.	G9	70
Texas, co., Mo., U.S.	D5	132
Texas, co., Ok., U.S.	e9	143
Texas, state, U.S.	D3	150
Texas City, Tx., U.S.	E5	150
Texel, i., Neth.	B6	12
Texhoma, Ok., U.S.	e9	143
Texico, N.M., U.S.	C6	138
Texoma, Lake, res., U.S.	D5	143
Teyateyaneng, Leso.	G8	66
Teywarah, Afg.	D1	44
Teziutlán, Mex.	H11	90
Tezpur, India	G15	44
Tha-anne, stm., N.W. Ter., Can.	D13	96
Thabana-Ntlenyana, mtn., Leso.	G9	66
Thabazimbi, S. Afr.	E8	66
Thacker, W.V., U.S.	D2	155
Thackerville, Ok., U.S.	D4	143
Thai Binh, Viet.	D9	40
Thailand (Prathet Thai), ctry., Asia	B3	38
Thailand, Gulf of, b., Asia	I6	40
Thai Nguyen, Viet.	D8	40
Thal, Pak.	D4	44
Thala, Tun.	N3	18
Thale, Ger.	D11	10
Thalfang, Ger.	F6	10
Thalwil, Switz.	D10	13
Thamar, Jabal, mtn., Yemen	H4	47
Thames, N.Z.	B5	72
Thames, stm., Ont., Can.	E3	103
Thames, stm., Eng., U.K.	J12	8
Thames, stm., Ct., U.S.	D7	114
Thamesville, Ont., Can.	E3	103
Thāna, India	C2	46
Thanbyuzayat, Burma	G4	40
Thang Binh, Viet.	G10	40
Thanh Hoa, Viet.	E8	40
Thanh Pho Ho Chi Minh (Saigon), Viet.	I9	40
Thanjāvūr, India	G5	46
Thann, Fr.	E14	14
Thar Desert (Great Indian Desert), des., Asia	F4	44
Thargomindah, Austl.	G5	70
Thar Nhom, Sud.	N6	60
Tharrawaddy, Burma	F3	40
Thásos, i., Grc.	I8	20
Thatcher, Az., U.S.	E6	110
Thatcher, Id., U.S.	G7	119
Thaton, Burma	F4	40
Thaungdut, Burma	B3	40
Thaungyin, stm., Asia	F5	40
Thawville, Il., U.S.	C5	120
Thaxton, Ms., U.S.	A4	131
Thaya (Dyje), stm., Eur.	G15	10
Thayer, Il., U.S.	D4	120
Thayer, In., U.S.	B3	121
Thayer, Ks., U.S.	E8	123
Thayer, Mo., U.S.	E6	132
Thayer, co., Ne., U.S.	D8	134
Thayetmyo, Burma	E3	40
Thayne, Wy., U.S.	D1	157
Thazi, Burma	D4	40
Thealka, Ky., U.S.	C7	124
Theba, Az., U.S.	E3	110
The Backway, b., Newf., Can.	A2	102
The Barrens, plat., Tn., U.S.	B5	149
Thebes, Il., U.S.	F4	120
Thebes, hist., Egypt	E7	60
Thebes see Thívai, Grc.	K7	20
The Colony, Tx., U.S.	C4	150
The Coteau, hills, Sask., Can.	F2	105
The Dalles, Or., U.S.	B5	144
The Dells, val., Wi., U.S.	E4	156
Thedford, Ont., Can.	D3	103
Thedford, Ne., U.S.	C5	134
The Dome, mtn., Vt., U.S.	F2	152
The English Companys Islands, is., Austl.	B7	68
The Everglades, sw., Fl., U.S.	G6	116
The Fens, reg., Eng., U.K.	I14	8
The Flat Tops, mts., Co., U.S.	B3	113
The Flume, wtfl, N.H., U.S.	B3	136
The Graves, is., Ma., U.S.	g12	128
The Hague see 's-Gravenhage, Neth.	E5	12
The Heads, c., Or., U.S.	E2	144
The Little Minch, strt., Scot., U.K.	D7	8
Thelon, stm., N.W. Ter., Can.	D12	96
The Lynd, Austl.	B6	70
The Minch, strt., Scot., U.K.	C8	8
The Narrows, strt., Wa., U.S.	f10	154
Thenia, Alg.	B12	62
Theniet el Hadd, Alg.	C12	62
Theodore, Austl.	E9	70
Theodore, Sask., Can.	F4	105
Theodore, Al., U.S.	E1	108
Theodore Roosevelt Lake, res., Az., U.S.	D4	110
Theodore Roosevelt National Park (South Unit), N.D., U.S.	C2	141
Theodore Roosevelt National Park (North Unit), N.D., U.S.	B2	141
Theodosia, Mo., U.S.	E5	132
Theólogos, Grc.	I8	20
The Palisades, clf, N.J., U.S.	h9	137
The Pas, Man., Can.	C1	100
The Peak, mtn., N.C., U.S.	A1	140
The Pinnacle, hill, Ct., U.S.	B4	114
The Pinnacle, hill, Mo., U.S.	B7	132
The Plains, Oh., U.S.	C3	142
The Plains, Va., U.S.	B5	153
The Rand see Witwatersrand, reg., S. Afr.	E8	66
The Range, N.B., Can.	C4	101
Theresa, N.Y., U.S.	A5	139
Theresa, Wi., U.S.	E5	156
Therien, Alta., Can.	B5	98
Thermaïkós Kólpos, b., Grc.	I6	20
Thermopílai, hist., Grc.	K6	20
Thermopolis, Wy., U.S.	C4	157
Thermopylae see Thermopílai, hist., Grc.	K6	20
The Rock, Austl.	J7	70
The Rockies, mts., Wa., U.S.	C3	154
The Sound, strt., Eur.	N13	6
Thessalía, hist. reg., Grc.	J6	20
Thessalon, Ont., Can.	p19	103
Thessaloníki (Salonika), Grc.	I6	20
Theta, Tn., U.S.	B4	149
Thetford Center, Vt., U.S.	D4	152
Thetford Mines, Que., Can.	C6	104
The Thimbles, is., Ct., U.S.	E5	114
The Valley, Anguilla	E13	94
The Village, Ok., U.S.	B4	143
The Wash, b., Eng., U.K.	I14	8
Thibodaux, La., U.S.	E5	125
Thicket Portage, Man., Can.	B3	100
Thickwood Hills, hills, Sask., Can.	E2	105
Thida, Ar., U.S.	B4	111
Thief, stm., Mn., U.S.	B2	130
Thief Lake, l., Mn., U.S.	B3	130
Thief River Falls, Mn., U.S.	B2	130
Thielsen, Mount, mtn., Or., U.S.	D4	144
Thiene, Italy	D6	18
Thiensville, Wi., U.S.	E6	156
Thiers, Fr.	G10	14
Thiès, Sen.	D1	64
Thiesi, Italy	I3	18
Thika, Kenya	B7	58
Thimphu, Bhu.	G13	44
Thingvellir, Ice.	B3	6a
Thingvellir National Park, Ice.	B3	6a
Thionville, Fr.	C13	14
Thíra, i., Grc.	M9	20
Third Lake, l., N.H., U.S.	f7	136
Thiruvārūr, India	G5	46
Thistle Island, i., Austl.	J2	70
Thívai (Thebes), Grc.	K7	20
Thlewiaza, stm., N.W. Ter., Can.	D13	96
Thohoyandou, Venda	D10	66
Thoi Binh, Viet.	J8	40
Thomas, Ok., U.S.	B3	143
Thomas, W.V., U.S.	B5	155
Thomas, co., Ga., U.S.	F3	117
Thomas, co., Ks., U.S.	C2	123
Thomas, co., Ne., U.S.	C5	134
Thomasboro, Il., U.S.	C5	120
Thomas Creek, stm., Fl., U.S.	k8	116
Thomaston, Al., U.S.	C2	108
Thomaston, Ct., U.S.	C3	114
Thomaston, Ga., U.S.	D2	117
Thomaston, Me., U.S.	D3	126
Thomaston Reservoir, res., Ct., U.S.	C3	114
Thomastown, Ms., U.S.	C4	131
Thomasville, Al., U.S.	D2	108
Thomasville, Ga., U.S.	F3	117
Thomasville, N.C., U.S.	B2	140
Thompson, Man., Can.	B3	100
Thompson, Ct., U.S.	B8	114
Thompson, Ia., U.S.	A4	122
Thompson, N.D., U.S.	B8	141
Thompson, stm., U.S.	A4	132
Thompson Creek, stm., Ms., U.S.	D5	131
Thompson Falls, Mt., U.S.	C1	133
Thompson Island, i., Ma., U.S.	g11	128
Thompson Lake, l., U.S.	D2	126
Thompson Peak, mtn., Ca., U.S.	B2	112
Thompson Peak, mtn., N.M., U.S.	h9	138
Thompson Reservoir, res., Or., U.S.	E5	144
Thompsons Station, Tn., U.S.	B5	149
Thompsonville, Il., U.S.	F5	120
Thompsonville, Mi., U.S.	D5	129
Thomson, Ga., U.S.	C4	117
Thomson, Il., U.S.	B3	120
Thomson, stm., Austl.	E5	70
Thon Buri, Thai.	H6	40
Thongwa, Burma	F4	40
Thonon-les-Bains, Fr.	F13	14
Thonotosassa, Fl., U.S.	D4	116
Thonze, Burma	F3	40
Thor, Ia., U.S.	B3	122
Thorburn, N.S., Can.	D7	101
Thoreau, N.M., U.S.	B1	138
Thorhild, Alta., Can.	B4	98
Thorial, Sud.	M5	60
Thornburg, Ar., U.S.	C3	111
Thornbury, Ont., Can.	C4	103
Thorndale, Tx., U.S.	D4	150
Thorndike, Ma., U.S.	B3	128
Thorne Bay, Ak., U.S.	n23	109
Thornhill, Man., Can.	E2	100
Thornton, Ont., Can.	C5	103
Thornton, Ar., U.S.	D3	111
Thornton, Id., U.S.	F7	119
Thornton, Ia., U.S.	B4	122
Thornton, Ms., U.S.	B3	131
Thornton, Tx., U.S.	D4	150
Thornton, W.V., U.S.	k11	155
Thornton Gap, Va., U.S.	B4	153
Thorntonville, Tx., U.S.	D1	150
Thorntown, In., U.S.	D4	121
Thornville, Oh., U.S.	C3	142
Thorny Mountain, mtn., Mo., U.S.	D6	132
Thorofare, N.J., U.S.	D2	137
Thorold, Ont., Can.	D5	103
Thorp, Wa., U.S.	B5	154
Thorp, Wi., U.S.	D3	156
Thorsby, Alta., Can.	C3	98
Thorsby, Al., U.S.	C3	108
Thouars, Fr.	F6	14
Thousand Islands, is., N.Y., U.S.	A4	139
Thousand Lake Mountain, mtn., Ut., U.S.	E4	151
Thousand Springs Creek, stm., U.S.	B7	135
Thrace, hist. reg., Eur.	H10	20
Thrakikón Pélagos, Grc.	I8	20
Thrashers, Ms., U.S.	A5	131
Three Fingered Jack, mtn., Or., U.S.	C5	144
Three Forks, Mt., U.S.	E5	133
Three Hills, Alta., Can.	D4	98
Three Hummock Island, i., Austl.	M6	70
Three Lakes, Wi., U.S.	C4	156
Three Mile Plains, N.S., Can.	E5	101
Three Oaks, Mi., U.S.	G4	129
Three Pagodas Pass, Asia	G5	40
Three Rivers, Ma., U.S.	B3	128
Three Rivers, Mi., U.S.	G5	129
Three Rivers, Ms., U.S.	E5	131
Three Rivers, Tx., U.S.	E3	150
Three Rock Cove, Newf., Can.	D2	102
Three Sisters, S. Afr.	H6	66
Three Sisters, mtn., Or., U.S.	C5	144
Three Springs, Austl.	E3	68
Throckmorton, Tx., U.S.	C3	150
Throckmorton, co., Tx., U.S.	C3	150
Throop, Pa., U.S.	m18	145
Thu Dau Mot, Viet.	I9	40
Thule, Grnld.	B13	86
Thun, Switz.	E8	13
Thunder Bay, Ont., Can.	o17	103
Thunder Bay, b., Mi., U.S.	D7	129
Thunder Bay, stm., Mi., U.S.	D6	129
Thunder Bay, North Branch, stm., Mi., U.S.	C6	129
Thunderbird, Lake, res., Ok., U.S.	B4	143
Thunderbolt, Ga., U.S.	D5	117
Thunder Butte, mtn., S.D., U.S.	B4	148
Thunder Butte Creek, stm., S.D., U.S.	B3	148
Thunersee, l., Switz.	E8	13
Thung Song, Thai.	J5	40
Thur, stm., Switz.	C10	13
Thurgau, state, Switz.	C11	13
Thüringen, state, Ger.	D11	10
Thüringer Wald, mts., Ger.	E10	10
Thurlow Dam, Al., U.S.	C4	108
Thurman, Ia., U.S.	D2	122
Thurmont, Md., U.S.	A3	127
Thursday Island, Austl.	B8	68
Thurso, Que., Can.	D2	104
Thurso, Scot., U.K.	C10	8
Thurston, Oh., U.S.	C3	142
Thurston, co., Ne., U.S.	B9	134
Thurston, co., Wa., U.S.	C2	154
Thurston Island, i., Ant.	C11	73
Thusis, Switz.	E11	13
Thwaites Ice Tongue, Ant.	C11	73
Thyolo, Mwi.	E7	58
Tiahuanacu, Bol.	G7	82
Tía Juana, Ven.	B7	84
Tianchang, China	C8	34
Tiandong, China	C9	40
Tianfanjie, China	F5	34
Tianjiazhen, China	F4	34
Tianjin (Tientsin), China	D5	32
Tianjin Shi, China	D10	30
Tianjun, China	D6	30
Tianlin, China	B9	40
Tianmen, China	E2	34
Tianshui, China	E8	30
Tiantai, China	F10	34
Tiantou, China	I4	34
Tianxiyang, China	I7	34
Tianzhu, China	D7	30
Tianzhuang, China	J2	34
Tiawah, Ok., U.S.	A6	143
Tibagi, Braz.	C13	80
Tibaji, stm., Braz.	B13	80
Tibasti, Sarīr, des., Libya	D4	56
Tibbie, Al., U.S.	D1	108
Tibe, Eth.	M9	60
Tiber see Tevere, stm., Italy	G7	18
Tibesti, mts., Chad	D4	56
Tibet see Xizang Zizhiqu, prov., China	E3	30
Tibiri, Niger	E13	64
Tibiriçá, stm., Braz.	F3	79
Tibiriçá, stm., Braz.	A13	80
Tiburón, Cabo, c.	C4	84
Tiburón, Isla, i., Mex.	C3	90
Tiča, jazovir, res., Bul.	F10	20
Tice, Fl., U.S.	F5	116
Tichborne, Ont., Can.	C8	103
Tîchît, Maur.	B5	64
Tichmenevo, U.S.S.R.	C21	26
Tichoreck, U.S.S.R.	H6	22
Tichvin, U.S.S.R.	B16	26
Ticino, state, Switz.	F10	13
Ticino, stm., Eur.	D3	18
Tickfaw, La., U.S.	D5	125
Tickfaw, stm., La., U.S.	C5	125
Ticonderoga, N.Y., U.S.	B7	139
Ticul, Mex.	G15	90
Tide Head, N.B., Can.	B3	101
Tidikelt, pl., Alg.	G11	62
Tidioute, Pa., U.S.	C3	145
Tidjikja, Maur.	B4	64
Tidore, Indon.	E8	38
Tiekou, China	F9	32
Tieli, China	B12	30
Tieling, China	A11	32
Tielt, Bel.	F3	12
Tielutou, China	H4	34
Tiémé, I.C.	G6	64
T'ienchung, Tai.	L9	34
Tien Shan, mts., Asia	C3	30
Tientsin see Tianjin, China	D5	32
Tie Plant, Ms., U.S.	B4	131
Tierra Amarilla, Chile	D3	80
Tierra Amarilla, N.M., U.S.	A3	138
Tierra Blanca, Mex.	H11	90
Tierra del Fuego, Isla Grande de, i., S.A.	G3	78
Tierralta, Col.	C4	84
Tierras Coloradas, Mex.	F7	90
Tieshanguan, China	L2	34
Tietê, Braz.	G5	79
Tietê, stm., Braz.	F3	79
Tieton, Wa., U.S.	C5	154
Tieton, stm., Wa., U.S.	C4	154
Tieton Dam, Wa., U.S.	C4	154
Tif, Alg.	G11	62
Tiffany Mountain, mtn., Wa., U.S.	A6	154
Tiffin, Ia., U.S.	C6	122
Tiffin, Oh., U.S.	A2	142
Tiffin, stm., Oh., U.S.	A1	142
Tift, co., Ga., U.S.	E3	117
Tifton, Ga., U.S.	E3	117
Tigard, Or., U.S.	h12	144
Tiger, Ga., U.S.	B3	117
Tigerton, Wi., U.S.	D4	156
Tighennif, Alg.	C11	62
Tigil', U.S.S.R.	F23	24
Tiglid, Mor.	F5	62
Tignall, Ga., U.S.	C4	117
Tignish, P.E.I., Can.	C5	101
Tigre, stm., Peru	J5	84
Tigre, stm., Ven.	C11	84
Tigre, Cerro, mtn., C.R.	I11	92
Tigrett, Tn., U.S.	B2	149
Tigris (Dicle) (Dijlah), stm., Asia	F9	48
Tiguabos, Cuba	D7	94
Tiguentourine, Alg.	G15	62
Tihāmah, pl., Asia	H4	48
Tihert, Alg.	C11	62
Tihuatlán, Mex.	G11	90
Tijamuchi, stm., Bol.	F9	82
Tijeras, N.M., U.S.	B3	138
Tijesno, Yugo.	F10	18
Tijuana, Mex.	A1	90
Tijucas, Braz.	D14	80
Tijucas do Sul, Braz.	C14	80
Tijuco, stm., Braz.	E4	79
Tikal, hist., Guat.	I15	90
Tiko, Cam.	I14	64
Tikrīt, Iraq	D7	48
Tikša, U.S.S.R.	I23	6

Name Map Ref. Page

Tikšeozero, ozero, l., U.S.S.R. H22 6
Tilarán, C.R. G10 92
Tilbalakan, Laguna, b., Hond. B10 92
Tilburg, Neth. E7 12
Tilbury, Ont., Can. E2 103
Tilcara, Arg. B6 80
Tilden, Il., U.S. E4 120
Tilden, Ne., U.S. B8 134
Tilemsès, Niger D12 64
Tilemsi, Vallée du, val., Mali B10 64
Tilghman, Md., U.S. C5 127
Tilghman Island, i., Md., U.S. C5 127
Tilhar, India G8 44
Tilimsen, Alg. C10 62
Tiline, Ky., U.S. e9 124
Tilisarao, Arg. G6 80
Tillaberi, Niger D10 64
Tillamook, Or., U.S. B3 144
Tillamook, co., Or., U.S. B3 144
Tillanchāng Dwīp, i., India J2 40
Tillar, Ar., U.S. D4 111
Tillery, Lake, res., N.C., U.S. B2 140
Tilley, Alta., Can. D5 98
Tillia, Niger C12 64
Tillman, co., Ok., U.S. C2 143
Tillmans Corner, Al., U.S. E1 108
Tillson, N.Y., U.S. D6 139
Tillsonburg, Ont., Can. E4 103
Tilpa, Austl. H6 70
Tilrhemt, Alg. D12 62
Tilston, Man., Can. E1 100
Tilting, Newf., Can. D4 102
Tilton, Ga., U.S. B2 117
Tilton, Il., U.S. C6 120
Tilton, N.H., U.S. D3 136
Tiltonsville, Oh., U.S. B5 142
Tīmā, Egypt D6 60
Timaná, Col. G5 84
Timane, stm., Para. I12 82
Timanskij kr'až, mtn., U.S.S.R. D7 22
Timaru, N.Z. F3 72
Timbalier Island, i., La., U.S. E5 125
Timbedgha, Maur. C5 64
Timbered Knob, mtn., Mo., U.S. E5 132
Timber Lake, S.D., U.S. B4 148
Timberlake, Va., U.S. C3 153
Timberville, Va., U.S. B4 153
Timbío, Col. F4 84
Timbó, Braz. D14 80
Timbo, Lib. I5 64
Timboon, Austl. L5 70
Timbuktu see Tombouctou, Mali C8 64
Timétrine, Mali B9 64
Timgad, hist., Alg. C14 62
Timimoun, Alg. F11 62
Timinar, Sud. H6 60
Timir'azevskij, U.S.S.R. F14 22
Timirist, Râs, c., Maur. B1 64
Timiș, co., Rom. D5 20
Timiș (Tamiš), stm., Eur. D5 20
Timișoara, Rom. D5 20
Timmendorfer Strand, Ger. A10 10
Timmins, Ont., Can. o19 103
Timmonsville, S.C., U.S. C8 147
Timms Hill, hill, Wi., U.S. C3 156
Timnath, Co., U.S. A5 113
Timor, i., Indon. G8 38
Timor Sea J16 158
Timotes, Ven. C7 84
Timoudi, Alg. F10 62
Timpanogos Cave National Monument, Ut., U.S. C4 151
Timpas Creek, stm., Co., U.S. D7 113
Timpia, stm., Peru D5 82
Timpson, Tx., U.S. D5 150
Tims Ford Lake, res., Tn., U.S. B5 149
Tina, Mo., U.S. B4 132
Tinaca Point, c., Phil. D8 38
Tinaco, Ven. C8 84
Tīnah, Khalīj aṭ-, b., Egypt F2 48
Tinaja, Punta, c., Peru G5 82
Ti-n-Amzi, val., Afr. B12 64
Tinaquillo, Ven. C8 84
Tindivanam, India F5 46
Tindouf, Alg. G6 62
Tindouf, Hamada de, reg., Afr. F6 62
Tindouf, Sebkha de, pl., Alg. G7 62
Tineo, Spain B5 16
Tinga, mtn., Afr. M2 60
Tingha, Austl. G9 70
Tinghert, Ḥamādat (Plateau du Tinghert), plat., Afr. F15 62
Tinghert, Plateau du (Hamādat Tinghert), plat., Afr. F15 62
Tingmerkpuk Mountain, mtn., Ak., U.S. B7 109
Tingo de Saposoa, Peru B3 82
Tingo María, Peru C4 82
Tingri, China F12 44
Tingsiqiao, China F3 34
Tinguipaya, Bol. H9 82
Tingvoll, Nor. J11 6
Tinharé, Ilha de, i., Braz. B9 79
Tinh Bien, Viet. I8 40
Tinker Air Force Base, mil., Ok., U.S. B4 143
Tinkisso, stm., Gui. F5 64
Tinley Park, Il., U.S. k9 120
Tinnie, N.M., U.S. D4 138
Tinniswood, Mount, mtn., B.C., Can. D6 99
Tinnoset, Nor. L11 6
Tinogasta, Arg. E5 80
Tínos, Grc. L9 20
Tínos, i., Grc. L9 20
Tinrhir, Mor. E8 62
Tinsley, Ms., U.S. C3 131
Tinsukia, India G16 44
Tinte, Cerro, mtn., S.A. J8 82
Tintina, Arg. D7 80
Tinton Falls, N.J., U.S. C4 137
Ti-n-Zaouatene, Alg. B11 64
Tio, Eth. G2 47
Tioga, La., U.S. C3 125
Tioga, N.D., U.S. A3 141
Tioga, Pa., U.S. C7 145
Tioga, W.V., U.S. C4 155
Tioga, co., N.Y., U.S. C4 139
Tioga, co., Pa., U.S. C7 145
Tioga, stm., Pa., U.S. B7 145
Tioga Terrace, N.Y., U.S. C4 139
Tiogue Lake, res., R.I., U.S. D3 146
Tiojala, Fin. K18 6
Tioman, Pulau, i., Malay. M8 40
Tionesta, Pa., U.S. D3 145
Tionesta Creek, stm., Pa., U.S. C3 145
Tionesta Lake, res., Pa., U.S. D3 145
Tior, Sud. N6 60
Tioro, Selat, strt., Indon. F7 38
Tioughnioga, stm., N.Y., U.S. C4 139
Tipitapa, Nic. E8 92
Tippah, co., Ms., U.S. A5 131
Tippah, stm., Ms., U.S. A4 131
Tipp City, Oh., U.S. C1 142
Tippecanoe, In., U.S. B5 121
Tippecanoe, co., In., U.S. D4 121
Tippecanoe, stm., In., U.S. C4 121
Tipperary, Ire. I5 8
Tipperary, co., Ire. I5 8
Tipton, Ca., U.S. D4 112
Tipton, In., U.S. D5 121
Tipton, Ia., U.S. C6 122
Tipton, Ks., U.S. C5 123
Tipton, Mo., U.S. C5 132
Tipton, Ok., U.S. C2 143
Tipton, Tn., U.S. B2 149
Tipton, co., In., U.S. D5 121
Tipton, co., Tn., U.S. B2 149
Tipton, Mount, mtn., Az., U.S. B1 110
Tiptonville, Tn., U.S. A2 149
Tip Top Mountain, mtn., Ont., Can. o18 103
Tiputini, stm., Ec. H4 84
Tīra, Isr. D3 50
Tiracambu, Serra do, plat., Braz. D9 76
Tiradentes, Braz. F6 79
Tīrān, i., Sau. Ar. H3 48
Tīrān, Maḍīq, strt. D8 60
Tiran, Strait of see Tīrān, Maḍīq, strt. D8 60
Tiranë, Alb. H3 20
Tirano, Italy C5 18
Tiraque, Bol. G9 82
Tiraspol', U.S.S.R. H3 22
Tirat Karmel, Isr. C3 50
Tirat Ẕevi, Isr. D5 50
Tire Hill, Pa., U.S. F4 145
Tîrgoviște, Rom. E9 20
Tîrgu Bujor, Rom. D11 20
Tîrgu-Cărbunești, Rom. E7 20
Tîrgu Jiu, Rom. D7 20
Tîrgu Mureș, Rom. C8 20
Tîrgu-Neamț, Rom. B10 20
Tîrgu Ocna, Rom. C10 20
Tîrgusor, Rom. E12 20
Tirich Mīr, mtn., Pak. B4 44
Tirilye, Tur. I12 20
Tiriro, Gui. F5 64
Tîrnăveni, Rom. C8 20
Tírnavos, Grc. J6 20
Tirol, state, Aus. H10 10
Tiros, Braz. E6 79
Tiroungoulou, Cen. Afr. Rep. M2 60
Tirschenreuth, Ger. F12 10
Tiruchchirāppalli, India G5 46
Tiruchengodu, India G4 46
Tiruliai, U.S.S.R. F6 26
Tirunelveli, India H4 46
Tirupati, India F5 46
Tiruppattūr, India F5 46
Tiruppur, India G4 46
Tiruvannāmalai, India F5 46
Tiruvottiyūr, India F6 46
Tisa (Tisza), stm., Eur. C4 20
Tisdale, Sask., Can. E3 105
Tishomingo, Ms., U.S. A5 131
Tishomingo, Ok., U.S. C5 143
Tishomingo, co., Ms., U.S. A5 131
Tisisat Falls, wtfl, Eth. L9 60
Tīsīyah, Syria D6 50
Tiskilwa, Il., U.S. B4 120
Tisma, Nic. E8 92
Tissemsilt, Alg. C11 62
Tīsta, stm., Asia G13 44
Tisza (Tisa), stm., Eur. C4 20
Tiszaföldvár, Hung. I20 10
Tiszafüred, Hung. H20 10
Tiszavasvári, Hung. H21 10
Tit, Alg. I13 62
Titaf, Alg. G10 62
Titicaca, Lago, l., S.A. F7 82
Titograd, Yugo. G3 20
Titonka, Ia., U.S. A3 122
Titova Mitrovica, Yugo. G4 20
Titovo Užice, Yugo. F3 20
Titov Veles, Yugo. H5 20
Titov vrh, mtn., Yugo. G4 20
Titran, Nor. J11 6
Tittmoning, Ger. G12 10
Titule, Zaire H6 56
Titus, co., Tx., U.S. C5 150
Titusville, Fl., U.S. D6 116
Titusville, Pa., U.S. C2 145
Tiverton, N.S., Can. E3 101
Tiverton, Ont., Can. C3 103
Tiverton, R.I., U.S. D6 146
Tivoli, Italy H7 18
Tivoli, N.Y., U.S. C7 139
Tivoli, Tx., U.S. E4 150
Tiwāl, Wādī, val., Afr. L2 60
Tizimín, Mex. G15 90
Tizi-Ouzou, Alg. B13 62
Tiznados, stm., Ven. C9 84
Tiznit, Mor. F6 62
Tjolotjo, Zimb. B8 66
Tlacotalpan, Mex. H12 90
Tlacotepec, Mex. I10 90
Tlahualilo de Zaragoza, Mex. D8 90
Tlalixtaquilla, Mex. I10 90
Tlalnepantla, Mex. H10 90
Tlaltenango de Sánchez Román, Mex. G8 90
Tlapaneco, stm., Mex. I10 90
Tlapeng, Bots. D5 66
Tlaquepaque, Mex. G8 90
Tlaxcala [de Xicoténcatl], Mex. H10 90
Tłuszcz, Pol. C21 10
Toabré, stm., Pan. I14 92
Toachi, stm., Ec. H3 84
Toadlena, N.M., U.S. A1 138
Toahayaná, Mex. D6 90
Toamasina, Madag. Q23 67b
Toano, Va., U.S. C6 153
Toano Range, mts., Nv., U.S. C7 135
Toay, Arg. I6 80
Toba, Japan M11 36
Toba, Mali F6 64
Toba, Danau, l., Indon. M5 40
Tobacco Root Mountains, mts., Mt., U.S. E5 133
Tobago, i., Trin. I14 94
Toba Inlet, b., B.C., Can. D5 99
Toba Kākar Range, mts., Pak. E3 44
Tobas, Arg. E7 80
Toba Tek Singh, Pak. E5 44
Tobejuba, Isla, i., Ven. C12 84
Tobelo, Indon. E8 38
Tobercurry, Ire. G5 8
Tobermory, Austl. F5 70
Tobias, Ne., U.S. D8 134
Tobin, Mount, mtn., Nv., U.S. C4 135
Tobin Lake, l., Sask., Can. D4 105
Tobin Range, mts., Nv., U.S. C4 135
Tobique, stm., N.B., Can. B2 101
Tobol, U.S.S.R. G10 22
Tobol, stm., U.S.S.R. F11 22
Tobol'sk, U.S.S.R. F11 22
Tobré, Benin F11 64
Tobruk see Ṭubruq, Libya A2 60
Toby, Mount, mtn., Ma., U.S. B2 128
Tobyhanna, Pa., U.S. D11 145
Tocaima, Col. E5 84
Tocantínia, Braz. E9 76
Tocantinópolis, Braz. E9 76
Tocantins, stm., Braz. D9 76
Tocantins, stm., Braz. A13 82
Tocantins, Parque Nacional do, Braz. B5 79
Tocantinzinho, stm., Braz. C4 79
Toccoa, Ga., U.S. B3 117
Toccoa, stm., Ga., U.S. B2 117
Toccoa Falls, Ga., U.S. B3 117
Toccopola, Ms., U.S. A4 131
Tochigi, Japan K14 36
Tochtamyš, U.S.S.R. B6 44
Toco, Chile B4 80
Tocoa, Hond. B8 92
Toconao, Chile B4 80
Tocopilla, Chile B3 80
Tocsin, In., U.S. C7 121
Tocumwal, Austl. J6 70
Tocuyo, stm., Ven. B8 84
Tocuyo de la Costa, Ven. B8 84
Todd, co., Ky., U.S. D2 124
Todd, co., Mn., U.S. D4 130
Todd, co., S.D., U.S. D5 148
Toddy Pond, l., Me., U.S. D4 126
Todi, Italy G7 18
Todos Santos, Bol. G9 82
Todos Santos, Mex. F4 90
Todos Santos, Bahía, b., Mex. B1 90
Todtnau, Ger. H7 10
T'oejo, N. Kor. D15 32
Tofield, Alta., Can. C4 98
Tofino, B.C., Can. E5 99
Tofte, Mn., U.S. C8 130
Togiak, Ak., U.S. D7 109
Togian, Kepulauan, is., Indon. F7 38
Togo, Sask., Can. F5 105
Togo, ctry., Afr. G7 54
Togučin, U.S.S.R. F14 22
Togwotee Pass, Wy., U.S. C2 157
Tohakum Peak, mtn., Nv., U.S. C2 135
Tohatchi, N.M., U.S. B1 138
Tohopekaliga, Lake, l., Fl., U.S. D5 116
Toinya, Sud. N5 60
Toiyabe Range, mts., Nv., U.S. D4 135
Tok, Ak., U.S. C11 109
Tokanui, N.Z. G2 72
Tokara-rettō, is., Japan R4 37b
Tokar'ovka, U.S.S.R. J24 26
Tokat, Tur. A4 48
Tokeland, Wa., U.S. C2 154
Tokelau, dep., Oc. G1 2
Tokio, N.D., U.S. B7 141
Tokmak, U.S.S.R. I13 22
Toko Range, mts., Austl. D3 70
Tokoroa, N.Z. C5 72
Toksook Bay, Ak., U.S. C7 109
Toksovo, U.S.S.R. A13 26
Tokuno-shima, i., Japan T3 37b
Tokushima, Japan M9 36
Tokuyama, Japan M6 36
Tōkyō, Japan L14 36
Tokyo Bay see Tōkyō-wan, b., Japan L14 36
Tōkyō-wan, b., Japan L14 36
Tokzār, Afg. C2 44
Tolbuhin, Bul. F11 20
Tolé, Pan. I13 92
Toleak Point, c., Wa., U.S. B1 154
Toledo, Bol. H8 82
Toledo, Braz. C12 80
Toledo, Ont., Can. C8 103
Toledo, Col. D6 84
Toledo, Spain F7 16
Toledo, Il., U.S. D5 120
Toledo, Ia., U.S. B5 122
Toledo, Oh., U.S. A2 142
Toledo, Or., U.S. C3 144
Toledo, Wa., U.S. C3 154
Toledo Bend Reservoir, res., U.S. C2 125
Tolentino, Italy F8 18
Toler, Ky., U.S. C7 124
Tolga, Alg. C13 62
Toliara, Madag. S20 67b
Tolima, dept., Col. F5 84
Tolima, Nevado del, mtn., Col. E5 84
Toljatti, U.S.S.R. G7 22
Tolland, Ct., U.S. B6 114
Tolland, co., Ct., U.S. B6 114
Tollesboro, Ky., U.S. B6 124
Tolleson, Az., U.S. m8 110
Tollette, Ar., U.S. D2 111
Tolley, N.D., U.S. A4 141
Tolloche, Arg. C7 80
Tolmačovo, U.S.S.R. C12 26
Tolmezzo, Italy C8 18
Tolna, Hung. I18 10
Tolna, N.D., U.S. B7 141
Tolna, co., Hung. I18 10
Tolo, Teluk, b., Indon. F7 38
Toločin, U.S.S.R. G12 26
Tolongoina, Madag. R22 67b
Tolono, Il., U.S. D5 120
Tolosa, Spain B9 16
Tolstoi, Man., Can. E3 100
Tolstoj, mys, c., U.S.S.R. F23 24
Toltén, Chile D2 78
Tolt Reservoir, res., Wa., U.S. B4 154
Tolú, Col. C5 84
Tolu, Ky., U.S. e9 124
Toluca, Il., U.S. C4 120
Toluca, Nevado de, vol., Mex. H10 90
Toluca [de Lerdo], Mex. H10 90
Tolwa, Sud. N7 60
Tom', stm., U.S.S.R. F9 24
Tom, Mount, hill, Ct., U.S. C2 114
Tomah, Wi., U.S. E3 156
Tomahawk, Wi., U.S. C4 156
Tomahawk Lake, l., Wi., U.S. C4 156
Tomakomai, Japan E16 36a
Tomar, Port. F3 16
Tomás Barrón (Eucaliptus), Bol. G8 82
Tomás Gomensoro, Ur. F10 80
Tomašpol', U.S.S.R. A12 20
Tomaszów Lubelski, Pol. E23 10
Tomaszów Mazowiecki, Pol. D20 10
Tomatlán, Mex. H7 90
Tomave, Bol. I8 82
Tomazina, Braz. G4 79
Tombador, Serra do, plat., Braz. D13 82
Tomball, Tx., U.S. D5 150
Tombe, Sud. O6 60
Tombigbee, stm., U.S. D1 108
Tombos, Braz. F7 79
Tombouctou (Timbuktu), Mali C8 64
Tombstone, Az., U.S. F5 110
Tombua, Ang. E2 58
Tom Burke, S. Afr. D9 66
Tomé, Chile I2 80
Tome, N.M., U.S. C3 138
Tomelloso, Spain F8 16
Tom Green, co., Tx., U.S. D2 150
Tomichi Creek, stm., Co., U.S. C4 113
Tomini, Teluk, b., Indon. F7 38
Tominian, Mali E7 64
Tomkins Cove, N.Y., U.S. D6 139
Tommot, U.S.S.R. F17 24
Tom Nevers Head, c., Ma., U.S. D8 128
Tomo, stm., Col. E8 84
Tompkins, Newf., Can. E2 102
Tompkins, Sask., Can. G1 105
Tompkins, co., N.Y., U.S. C4 139
Tompkinsville, Ky., U.S. D4 124
Tom Price, Austl. D3 68
Tomra, Nor. J10 6
Toms, stm., N.J., U.S. C4 137
Toms, Ridgeway Branch, stm., N.J., U.S. C4 137
Tomsk, U.S.S.R. F8 24
Toms River, N.J., U.S. D4 137
Tonalá, Mex. I13 90
Tonalea, Az., U.S. A5 110
Tonantins, Braz. I9 84
Tonantins, stm., Braz. I8 84
Tonasket, Wa., U.S. A6 154
Tonawanda, N.Y., U.S. C2 139
Tonawanda, N.Y., U.S. B2 139
Tonawanda Indian Reservation, N.Y., U.S. B2 139
Tonbridge, Eng., U.K. J14 8
Tondano, Indon. E7 38
Tønder, Den. N11 6
Tondoro, Nmb. A4 66
Tonekābon, Iran C11 48
Toney, Al., U.S. A3 108
Tonga, Sud. M6 60
Tonga, ctry., Oc. H1 2
Tongaat, S. Afr. G10 66
Tonganoxie, Ks., U.S. C8 123
Tongcheng, China D5 34
Tongchengzha, China D7 34
Tongchuan, China D8 30
Tonggou, China B13 32
Tongguan, China E9 30
Tongguan, China G1 34
Tonghai, China B7 40
Tonghe, China C1 34
Tonghua, China B13 32
Tongjosŏn-man, b., N. Kor. D16 32
Tongli, China D9 34
Tongliao, China C11 30
Tongling, China E6 34
Tongmu, China H2 34
Tongnae, S. Kor. H17 32
Tongo, Austl. H5 70
Tongobory, Madag. S21 67b
Tongoy, Chile F3 80
Tongren, China F8 30
Tongsa Dzong, Bhu. G14 44
Tongshi, China H5 32
Tongtai, China C9 34
Tongtian, stm., China D17 44
Tongtianheyan, China E5 30
Tongue, Scot., U.K. C9 8
Tongue, stm., Mt., U.S. E10 133
Tongue, stm., Tx., U.S. p13 150
Tongxian, China D4 32
Tongyu, China C11 30
Tongzhaipu, China C1 34
Tongzi, China F8 30
Tonica, Il., U.S. B4 120
Tonj, Sud. N5 60
Tonk, India G6 44
Tonkawa, Ok., U.S. A4 143
Tonkin, Gulf of, b., Asia D10 40
Tônlé Sab, Bœng, l., Camb. H8 40
Tonle Sap see Tônlé Sab, Bœng, l., Camb. H8 40
Tonneins, Fr. H7 14
Tonnerre, Fr. E10 14
Tönning, Ger. A8 10
Tōno, Japan H16 36
Tonoloway Ridge, mtn., Md., U.S. A1 127
Tonopah, Az., U.S. D3 110
Tonopah, Nv., U.S. E4 135
Tonosí, Pan. D2 84
Tonota, Bots. C8 66
Tønsberg, Nor. L12 6
Tontitown, Ar., U.S. A1 111
Tonto Basin, Az., U.S. D4 110
Tonto National Monument, Az., U.S. D4 110
Tonto Natural Bridge, Az., U.S. C4 110
Toobeah, Austl. G8 70
Tooele, Ut., U.S. C3 151
Tooele, co., Ut., U.S. C2 151
Toole, co., Mt., U.S. B5 133
Toombs, co., Ga., U.S. D4 117
Toompine, Austl. F6 70
Toomsboro, Ga., U.S. D3 117
Toomsuba, Ms., U.S. C5 131
Toone, Tn., U.S. B3 149
Tootsi, U.S.S.R. C7 26
Toowoomba, Austl. F9 70
Topawa, Az., U.S. F4 110
Topeka, In., U.S. A6 121
Topeka, Ks., U.S. C8 123
Topia, Mex. E6 90
Topinabee, Mi., U.S. C6 129
Topki, U.S.S.R. F9 24
Topko, gora, mtn., U.S.S.R. F19 24
Topley, B.C., Can. B4 99
Toplița, Rom. C9 20
T'oploje, U.S.S.R. H20 26
Topock, Az., U.S. C1 110
Topol'čany, Czech. G18 10
Topolobampo, Mex. E5 90
Topolog, Rom. E12 20
Topozero, ozero, l., U.S.S.R. I22 6
Toppenish, Wa., U.S. C5 154
Toppenish Ridge, mtn., Wa., U.S. C5 154
Topsfield, Ma., U.S. A6 128
Topsham, Me., U.S. E3 126
Topsham, Vt., U.S. C4 152
Topton, Pa., U.S. F10 145
Toquerville, Ut., U.S. F2 151
Toquima Range, mts., Nv., U.S. E5 135
Tor, Eth. N7 60
Toraya, Peru F5 82
Torbat-e Ḥeydarīyeh, Iran D15 48
Torbat-e Jām, Iran D16 48
Torbay, Newf., Can. E5 102
Torbay see Torquay, Eng., U.K. K10 8
Torbejevo, U.S.S.R. G26 26
Torbert, Mount, mtn., Ak., U.S. g15 109
Torbino, U.S.S.R. C15 26
Torbrook, N.S., Can. E5 101
Torch, stm., Sask., Can. D4 105
Torch Lake, l., Mi., U.S. D5 129
Tordesillas, Spain D6 16
Töre, Swe. I18 6
Torez, U.S.S.R. H5 22
Torgau, Ger. D13 10
Torino (Turin), Italy D2 18
Toriparu, Braz. D2 79
Torit, Sud. H7 56
Torneälven (Tornionjoki), stm., Eur. H18 6
Torngat Mountains, mts., Can. f8 102
Tornillo, Tx., U.S. o11 150
Tornio, Fin. I19 6
Tornionjoki (Torneälven), stm., Eur. H19 6
Tornquist, Arg. J7 80
Toro, Spain D6 16
Toro, Cerro, mtn., Mex. H7 90
Torodi, Niger E10 64
Törökszentmiklós, Hung. H20 10
Torola, stm., N.A. D6 92
Toroni, Nevado, mtn., S.A. H7 82
Toronto, Ont., Can. D5 103
Toronto, Ks., U.S. E8 123
Toronto, Oh., U.S. B5 142
Toronto, S.D., U.S. C9 148
Toronto Lake, res., Ks., U.S. E7 123
Toro Peak, mtn., Ca., U.S. F5 112
Toropec, U.S.S.R. E14 26
Tororo, Ug. A6 58
Toros Dağları, mts., Tur. H14 4
Torošino, U.S.S.R. D11 26
Torotoro, Bol. H9 82
Torquay, Sask., Can. H4 105
Torquay, Eng., U.K. K10 8
Torrance, Ca., U.S. n12 112
Torrance, co., N.M., U.S. C3 138
Torre del Campo, Spain H8 16
Torredonjimeno, Spain H8 16
Torrejón de Ardoz, Spain E8 16
Torrelavega, Spain B7 16
Torremaggiore, Italy H10 18
Torremolinos, Spain I7 16
Torrens, Lake, l., Austl. H2 70
Torrens Creek, Austl. C6 70
Torrent, Arg. E10 80
Torrent, Spain F11 16
Torreón, Mex. E8 90
Torreon, N.M., U.S. C3 138
Torreperogil, Spain G8 16
Tôrres, Braz. E14 80
Torres de Alcalá, Mor. J7 16
Torres Strait, strt., Oc. B8 68
Torrevella, Spain H11 16
Torridon, Scot., U.K. D8 8
Torriglia, Italy E4 18
Torrijos, Spain F7 16
Torrington, Alta., Can. D4 98
Torrington, Ct., U.S. B3 114
Torrington, Wy., U.S. D8 157
Torrinha, Braz. G4 79
Torrox, Spain I8 16
Tors Cove, Newf., Can. E5 102
Tórshavn, Faer. Is. D8 6b
Tortola, i., Br. Vir. Is. E12 94
Tortoli, Italy J4 18
Tortona, Italy E3 18
Tortosa, Spain E12 16
Tortue, Île de la, i., Haiti D8 94
Tortuguero, stm., C.R. G11 92
Tortuguero, Parque Nacional, C.R. G11 92
Toruń, Pol. B18 10
Torunos, Ven. C7 84
Torup, Swe. M13 6
Tõrva, U.S.S.R. C8 26
Tory Hill, Ont., Can. C6 103
Toržok, U.S.S.R. F4 22
T'osan, N. Kor. E14 32
Tosa-shimizu, Japan O7 36
Tosa-wan, b., Japan N8 36
Toscana (Tuscany), prov., Italy F5 18
Toscano, stm., Mex. H8 90
Tosno, U.S.S.R. B13 26
T'osovo-Netyl'skij, U.S.S.R. C14 26
T'osovskij, U.S.S.R. C13 26
Tostado, Arg. E8 80
Tõstamaa, U.S.S.R. C7 26
Tostón, Spain O26 17b
Toston, Mt., U.S. D5 133
Totagatic, stm., Wi., U.S. B2 156
Totana, Spain H10 16
Toteng, Bots. C6 66
Tôtes, Fr. C8 14
Tot'ma, U.S.S.R. B25 26
Totness, Sur. E14 84
Totonicapán, Guat. C3 92
Totonicapán, dept., Guat. B3 92
Totora, Bol. G9 82
Totora, Bol. G7 82
Totora Palca, Bol. H9 82
Totoras, Arg. G8 80
Totos, Peru E4 82
Tototlán, Mex. G8 90
Totowa, N.J., U.S. B4 137
Totson Mountain, mtn., Ak., U.S. C8 109
Tottenham, Austl. I7 70
Tottenham, Ont., Can. C5 103
Tottori, Japan L9 36
Totz, Ky., U.S. D6 124
Touba, I.C. G6 64
Toubkal, Jebel, mtn., Mor. E7 62
Touchet, Wa., U.S. C7 154
Touchet, stm., Wa., U.S. C7 154
Touchwood Lake, l., Man., Can. B4 100
Toudaogou, China A17 32
Tougan, Burkina E8 64
Touggourt, Alg. D13 62
Touisset, Ma., U.S. C5 128
Toukoto, Mali E5 64
Toul, Fr. D12 14
Touliu, Tai. L9 34
Toulon, Fr. I12 14
Toulon, Il., U.S. B4 120
Toulouse, Fr. I8 14
Tounan, Tai. L9 34
Toungoo, Burma E4 40
Touques, stm., Fr. C7 14
Tourakom, Laos E7 40
Tourcoing, Fr. B10 14
Tournai (Doornik), Bel. G3 12
Tourndo, Oued, val., Afr. I16 62
Tournus, Fr. F11 14
Tou Rout, Viet. F9 40
Tours, Fr. E7 14
Tourville, Que., Can. B8 104
Toussaint Creek, stm., Oh., U.S. f7 142
Toussidé, Pic, mtn., Chad D4 56
Toustain, Alg. M3 18
Toutle, North Fork, stm., Wa., U.S. C3 154
Toutuohe, China D5 34
Touwsrivier, S. Afr. I5 66
Tovar, Ven. C7 84
Tovarkovskij, U.S.S.R. H21 26
Tovey, Il., U.S. D4 120
Towaco, N.J., U.S. B4 137
Towanda, Il., U.S. C5 120
Towanda, Ks., U.S. E7 123
Towanda, Pa., U.S. C9 145
Towanda Creek, stm., Pa., U.S. C8 145
Towaoc, Co., U.S. D2 113
Tower, Mi., U.S. C6 129
Tower, Mn., U.S. C6 130
Tower City, N.D., U.S. C8 141
Tower City, Pa., U.S. E8 145
Tower Hill, Il., U.S. D5 120
Town Creek, Al., U.S. A2 108
Towner, N.D., U.S. A5 141
Towner, co., N.D., U.S. A6 141
Town Hill, mtn., U.S. A1 127
Townley, Al., U.S. B2 108
Towns, co., Ga., U.S. B3 117
Townsend, De., U.S. C3 115
Townsend, Ga., U.S. E5 117
Townsend, Ma., U.S. A4 128
Townsend, Mt., U.S. D5 133
Townsend, Tn., U.S. D10 149
Townsend, Va., U.S. C7 153
Townsend, Mount, mtn., Austl. K8 70
Townshend, Vt., U.S. E3 152
Townshend Island, i., Austl. D9 70
Townshend Reservoir, res., Vt., U.S. E3 152
Townsville, Austl. B7 70
Townville, S.C., U.S. B2 147
Towrzī, Afg. E1 44
Towson, Md., U.S. B4 127
Toxey, Al., U.S. D1 108
Toxkan, stm., China C2 30
Toyama, Japan K12 36
Toyama-wan, b., Japan K12 36
Toyohashi, Japan M12 36
Toyokawa, Japan M12 36
Toyonaka, Japan M10 36
Toyosaka, Japan J14 36
Toyota, Japan L12 36
Tozeur, Tun. D15 62
Trabiju, Braz. G4 79
Trabzon, Tur. G15 4
Tracadie, N.B., Can. B5 101
Tracadie, N.S., Can. D8 101
Tracajá, Cachoeira, wtfl, Braz. D9 82
Tracy, N.B., Can. D3 101
Tracy, Que., Can. C4 104

Name — Map Ref. — Page

Tracy, Ca., U.S. D3 112
Tracy, Ia., U.S. C5 122
Tracy, Mn., U.S. F3 130
Tracy, Mo., U.S. B3 132
Tracy City, Tn., U.S. D8 149
Tracys Creek, stm., Md., U.S. C4 127
Tracyton, Wa., U.S. e10 154
Trade, Tn., U.S. C12 149
Tradewater, stm., Ky., U.S. C2 124
Traer, Ia., U.S. B5 122
Trafalgar, In., U.S. F5 121
Trafalgar, Cabo, c., Spain I5 16
Trafford, Pa., U.S. k14 145
Trafford, Lake, l., Fl., U.S. F5 116
Traiguén, Chile J2 80
Trail, B.C., Can. E9 99
Trail, Or., U.S. E4 144
Trail City, S.D., U.S. B5 148
Trail Creek, In., U.S. A4 121
Traill, co., N.D., U.S. B8 141
Trail Ridge, mtn., U.S. F4 117
Traíra (Taraira), stm., S.A. H8 84
Traíras, stm., Braz. C4 79
Trakai, U.S.S.R. G7 26
Tralee, Ire. I4 8
Trammel, Va., U.S. e9 153
Tramore, Ire. I6 8
Trampas, N.M., U.S. A4 138
Tramping Lake, Sask., Can. E1 105
Trancas, Arg. D6 80
Trancoso, Port. E4 16
Tranebjerg, Den. N12 6
Trang, Thai. K5 40
Trangahy, Madag. Q21 67b
Trangie, Austl. I7 70
Trani, Italy H11 18
Tranqueras, Ur. F11 80
Tranquillity, Ca., U.S. D3 112
Transantarctic Mountains, mts., Ant. D9 73
Transfer, Pa., U.S. D1 145
Transkei, ctry., Afr. H9 66
Transylvania, co., N.C., U.S. f10 140
Transylvania, hist. reg., Rom. C7 20
Transylvanian Alps see Carpații Meridionali, mts., Rom. D8 20
Trapani, Italy K7 18
Trap Mountain, mtn., Ar., U.S. g7 111
Trappe, Md., U.S. C5 127
Trappe Creek, stm., Md., U.S. D7 127
Trapper Peak, mtn., Mt., U.S. E2 133
Traralgon, Austl. L7 70
Trasacco, Italy H8 18
Trasimeno, Lago, l., Italy F7 18
Traskwood, Ar., U.S. C3 111
Trás-os-Montes, hist. reg., Port. D4 16
Trat, Thai. H7 40
Traun, Aus. G14 10
Traun, stm., Aus. G14 10
Traunstein, Ger. H12 10
Travelers Rest, S.C., U.S. B3 147
Travellers Lake, l., Austl. I5 70
Traverse, co., Mn., U.S. E2 130
Traverse, Lake, l., U.S. B9 148
Traverse City, Mi., U.S. D5 129
Tra Vinh, Viet. J9 40
Travis, co., Tx., U.S. D4 150
Travis Air Force Base, mil., Ca., U.S. C2 112
Travnik, Yugo. E12 18
Tray Mountain, mtn., Ga., U.S. B3 117
Trbovlje, Yugo. C10 18
Treasure, co., Mt., U.S. D9 133
Treasure Island Naval Station, mil., Ca., U.S. h8 112
Třebíč, Czech. F15 10
Trebinje, Yugo. G2 20
Trebisacce, Italy J11 18
Trebišov, Czech. G21 10
Treblinka, Pol. C22 10
Trebloc, Ms., U.S. B5 131
Trecate, Italy D3 18
Treece, Ks., U.S. E9 123
Treene, stm., Ger. A9 10
Trego, co., Ks., U.S. D4 123
Tregosse Islets, is., Austl. A9 70
Tregubovo, U.S.S.R. C14 26
Tréguier, Fr. D3 14
Treherne, Man., Can. E2 100
Treinta y Tres, Ur. G11 80
Trélazé, Fr. E6 14
Trelew, Arg. E3 78
Trelleborg, Swe. N13 6
Tremblant, Mont, mtn., Que., Can. C3 104
Trembleur Lake, l., B.C., Can. B5 99
Tremedal, Braz. C8 79
Tremont, Il., U.S. C4 120
Tremont, Ms., U.S. A5 131
Tremont, Pa., U.S. E9 145
Tremonton, Ut., U.S. B3 151
Trempealeau, Wi., U.S. D2 156
Trempealeau, co., Wi., U.S. D2 156
Trempealeau, stm., Wi., U.S. D2 156
Trenche, stm., Que., Can. B5 104
Trenčín, Czech. G18 10
Trenel, Arg. H6 80
Trenque Lauquen, Arg. H7 80
Trent, S.D., U.S. D9 148
Trent, stm., Eng., U.K. H13 8
Trent, stm., N.C., U.S. B5 140
Trente et un Milles, Lac des, l., Que., Can. C2 104
Trentino-Alto Adige, prov., Italy C6 18
Trento, Italy C6 18
Trenton, N.S., Can. D7 101
Trenton, Ont., Can. C7 103
Trenton, Al., U.S. A3 108
Trenton, Fl., U.S. C4 116
Trenton, Ga., U.S. B1 117
Trenton, Il., U.S. E4 120
Trenton, Ky., U.S. D2 124
Trenton, Mi., U.S. F7 129
Trenton, Mo., U.S. A4 132
Trenton, Ne., U.S. D4 134
Trenton, N.J., U.S. C3 137
Trenton, N.D., U.S. A2 141
Trenton, Oh., U.S. C1 142
Trenton, S.C., U.S. D4 147
Trenton, Tn., U.S. B3 149
Trenton, Tx., U.S. C4 150
Trenton, Ut., U.S. B4 151
Trent see Trento, Italy C6 18
Trepassey, Newf., Can. E5 102
Trepassey Bay, b., Newf., Can. E5 102
Tres Algarrobos, Arg. H7 80
Tres Árboles, Ur. G10 80
Tres Arroyos, Arg. J8 80
Tresckow, Pa., U.S. E10 145
Três Corações, Braz. F6 79
Três Coroas, Braz. E13 80
Três de Maio, Braz. D11 80
Tres Esquinas, Col. G5 84
Três Fronteiras, Braz. F3 79
Tres Isletas, Arg. D8 80
Três Lagoas, Braz. F3 79
Três Marias, Represa, res., Braz. E6 79
Tres Palos, Laguna, b., Mex. I10 90
Tres Passos, Braz. D12 80
Tres Picos, Cerro, mtn., Arg. J8 80
Tres Piedras, N.M., U.S. A4 138
Três Pontas, Braz. F6 79
Tres Puntas, Cabo, c., Arg. F3 78
Tres Puntas, Cabo, c., Guat. B6 92
Três Ranchos, Braz. E5 79
Três Rios, Braz. G7 79
Tres Ríos, C.R. H11 92
Tres Zapotes, hist., Mex. H12 90
Treuchtlingen, Ger. G10 10
Treuenbrietzen, Ger. C12 10
Treutlen, co., Ga., U.S. D4 117
Treviglio, Italy D4 18
Treviso, Italy D7 18
Trevlac, In., U.S. F5 121
Trevor, Wi., U.S. n11 156
Trevorton, Pa., U.S. E8 145
Trévoux, Fr. G11 14
Treynor, Ia., U.S. C2 122
Treze Quedas, wtfl, Braz. H14 84
Trezevant, Tn., U.S. A3 149
Triabunna, Austl. N7 70
Triadelphia, W.V., U.S. A4 155
Triadelphia Reservoir, res., Md., U.S. B3 127
Triánda, Grc. M12 20
Triangle, Va., U.S. B5 153
Triángulos, Arrecifes, rf., Mex. G13 90
Tribbey, Ok., U.S. B4 143
Tribugá, Golfo de, b., Col. E4 84
Tribune, Sask., Can. H4 105
Tribune, Ks., U.S. D2 123
Tricao Malal, Arg. I3 80
Tricase, Italy J13 18
Trichardt, S. Afr. F9 66
Trichūr, India G4 46
Tri City, Or., U.S. E3 144
Trident Peak, mtn., Nv., U.S. B3 135
Triduby, U.S.S.R. A14 20
Trier, Ger. F6 10
Trieste, Italy D8 18
Trigal, Bol. H9 82
Trigg, co., Ky., U.S. D2 124
Triglav, mtn., Yugo. C8 18
Trigo Mountains, mts., Az., U.S. D1 110
Trigueros, Spain H5 16
Tríkala, Grc. J5 20
Trikhonís, Límni, l., Grc. K5 20
Trikora, Puncak, mtn., Indon. F10 38
Tri Lakes, In., U.S. B7 121
Trilby, Fl., U.S. D4 116
Trilla, Il., U.S. D5 120
Trimble, Mo., U.S. B3 132
Trimble, Tn., U.S. A2 149
Trimble, co., Ky., U.S. B4 124
Trimont, Mn., U.S. G4 130
Trin, Switz. E11 13
Trinchera Creek, stm., Co., U.S. D5 113
Trincheras, Mex. B4 90
Trincomalee, Sri L. H6 46
Trindade, Braz. D4 79
Trindade, i., Braz. G12 74
Třinec, Czech. F18 10
Tring Jonction, Que., Can. C6 104
Trinidad, Bol. F9 82
Trinidad, Col. E7 84
Trinidad, Cuba D5 94
Trinidad, Hond. C6 92
Trinidad, Co., U.S. D6 113
Trinidad, Tx., U.S. C4 150
Trinidad, Ur. G10 80
Trinidad, i., Trin. I14 94
Trinidad, Isla, i., Arg. J8 80
Trinidad and Tobago, ctry., N.A. I14 94
Trinidad Head, c., Ca., U.S. B1 112
Trinity, Newf., Can. D5 102
Trinity, Newf., Can. D5 102
Trinity, Al., U.S. A2 108
Trinity, Tx., U.S. D5 150
Trinity, co., Ca., U.S. B2 112
Trinity, co., Tx., U.S. D5 150
Trinity, stm., Ca., U.S. B2 112
Trinity, stm., Tx., U.S. D5 150
Trinity, East Fork, stm., Tx., U.S. n10 150
Trinity, Elm Fork, stm., Tx., U.S. m10 150
Trinity, South Fork, stm., Ca., U.S. B2 112
Trinity, West Fork, stm., Tx., U.S. n9 150
Trinity Bay, b., Newf., Can. D5 102
Trinity Center, Ca., U.S. B2 112
Trinity Islands, is., Ak., U.S. D9 109
Trinity Mountain, mtn., Id., U.S. F3 119
Trinity Mountains, mts., Ca., U.S. B2 112
Trinity Peak, mtn., Nv., U.S. C3 135
Trinity Range, mts., Nv., U.S. C3 135
Trinkat Island, i., India J2 40
Trinkitat, Sud. H9 60
Trino, Italy D3 18
Trinway, Oh., U.S. B3 142
Trion, Ga., U.S. B1 117
Tripoli, Ia., U.S. B5 122
Trípolis, Grc. L6 20
Tripolis, hist., Tur. L13 20
Tripoli see Tarābulus, Leb. D3 48
Tripoli see Tarābulus, Libya B3 56
Tripp, S.D., U.S. D8 148
Tripp, co., S.D., U.S. D6 148
Tripura, state, India I14 44
Tristan da Cunha Group, is., St. Hel. L5 52
Tristao, Îles, is., Afr. F2 64
Triste, Golfo, b., Ven. B8 84
Triumph, La., U.S. E6 125
Trivandrum, India H4 46
Trnava, Czech. G17 10
Trochu, Alta., Can. D4 98
Trogir, Yugo. F11 18
Troia, Italy H10 18
Troick, U.S.S.R. G10 22
Troickoje, U.S.S.R. B14 20
Troicko-Pečorsk, U.S.S.R. E9 22
Troina, Italy L9 18
Troisdorf, Ger. E7 10
Trois-Pistoles, Que., Can. A8 104
Trois-Rivières, Que., Can. C5 104
Trois-Rivières-Ouest, Que., Can. C5 104
Trojan, Bul. G8 20
Trojekurovo, U.S.S.R. H22 26
Trollhättan, Swe. L13 6
Trombetas, stm., Braz. H14 84
Trombudo Central, Braz. D14 80
Tromelin, Île, i., Reu. E10 58
Trompsburg, S. Afr. H7 66
Troms, co., Nor. G16 6
Tromsø, Nor. G16 6
Trona, Ca., U.S. E5 112
Tronador, Monte, mtn., S.A. E2 78
Troncoso, Mex. F8 90
Trondheim, Nor. J12 6
Troon, Scot., U.K. F9 8
Tropas, Rio das, stm., Braz. B13 82
Tropea, Italy K10 18
Trophy Mountain, mtn., B.C., Can. D8 99
Tropic, Ut., U.S. F3 151
Tropojë, Alb. G4 20
Troškūnai, U.S.S.R. F7 26
Trosna, U.S.S.R. I18 26
Trossachs, Sask., Can. H3 105
Trost'anec, U.S.S.R. A13 20
Trotwood, Oh., U.S. C1 142
Trou-du-Nord, Haiti E8 94
Troup, co., Ga., U.S. C1 117
Trousdale, co., Tn., U.S. A5 149
Trousers Lake, l., N.B., Can. B3 101
Trout, La., U.S. C3 125
Trout, stm., Fl., U.S. m8 116
Trout, stm., Vt., U.S. B3 152
Trout Creek, Ont., Can. B5 103
Trout Creek, Mt., U.S. C1 133
Trout Creek Pass, Co., U.S. C5 113
Trout Lake, Mi., U.S. B6 129
Trout Lake, Wa., U.S. D4 154
Trout Lake, l., B.C., Can. D9 99
Trout Lake, l., Ont., Can. o16 103
Trout Lake, l., Mn., U.S. B6 130
Trout Lake, l., Wi., U.S. B4 156
Troutman, N.C., U.S. B2 140
Trout Peak, mtn., Wy., U.S. B3 157
Trout River, Newf., Can. D2 102
Troutville, Va., U.S. C3 153
Trouville [-sur-Mer], Fr. C7 14
Trowbridge, Eng., U.K. J11 8
Troy, Al., U.S. D4 108
Troy, Id., U.S. C2 119
Troy, Il., U.S. E4 120
Troy, In., U.S. H4 121
Troy, Ks., U.S. C8 123
Troy, Mi., U.S. o15 129
Troy, Ms., U.S. A5 131
Troy, Mo., U.S. C7 132
Troy, Mt., U.S. B1 133
Troy, N.H., U.S. E2 136
Troy, N.Y., U.S. C7 139
Troy, N.C., U.S. B3 140
Troy, Oh., U.S. B1 142
Troy, Pa., U.S. C8 145
Troy, Tn., U.S. A2 149
Troy, Vt., U.S. B4 152
Troy, hist., Tur. J10 20
Troyes, Fr. D11 14
Troy Grove, Il., U.S. B4 120
Troy Mills, Ia., U.S. B6 122
Troy Peak, mtn., Nv., U.S. E6 135
Trstenik, Yugo. F5 20
Trubč'ovsk, U.S.S.R. I16 26
Truchas, N.M., U.S. A4 138
Truchas Peak, mtn., N.M., U.S. B4 138
Truckee, Ca., U.S. C3 112
Truckee, stm., U.S. D2 135
Trujillo, Col. E4 84
Trujillo, Hond. B8 92
Trujillo, Peru C2 82
Trujillo, Spain F6 16
Trujillo, Ven. C7 84
Trujillo, state, Ven. C7 84
Truk Islands, is., Micron. H19 158
Truman, Mn., U.S. G4 130
Trumann, Ar., U.S. B5 111
Trumansburg, N.Y., U.S. C4 139
Trumbull, Ct., U.S. E3 114
Trumbull, Ne., U.S. D7 134
Trumbull, co., Oh., U.S. A5 142
Trumbull, Mount, mtn., Az., U.S. A2 110
Trundle, Austl. I7 70
Truro, N.S., Can. D6 101
Truro, Ia., U.S. C4 122
Truro, Ma., U.S. C7 128
Trussville, Al., U.S. B3 108
Trustom Pond, l., R.I., U.S. G3 146
Trust Territory of the Pacific Islands, dep., Oc. F23 2
Truth or Consequences (Hot Springs), N.M., U.S. D2 138
Trutnov, Czech. E15 10
Truxton, Az., U.S. B2 110
Tryon, Ne., U.S. C5 134
Tryon, N.C., U.S. f10 140
Tryon, Ok., U.S. B5 143
Trzcianka, Pol. B16 10
Trzebież, Pol. B14 10
Trzebinia, Pol. E19 10
Tsala Apopka Lake, l., Fl., U.S. D4 116
Tsarabaria, Madag. N23 67b
Tsaratanana, Madag. P22 67b
Tsaratanana, Massif du, mts., Madag. O23 67b
Tsau, Bots. C6 66
Tsaukaib, Nmb. F2 66
Tsavo, Kenya B7 58
Tschetter Colony, S.D., U.S. D8 148
Tschida, Lake, res., N.D., U.S. C4 141
Tsekanyani, Bots. B8 66
Tsévié, Togo H10 64
Tshabong, Bots. F6 66
Tshane, Bots. E5 66
Tshangalele, Lac, l., Zaire D5 58
Tshela, Zaire B2 58
Tshesebe, Bots. C8 66
Tshidilamolomo, Boph. E7 66
Tshikapa, Zaire C4 58
Tshofa, Zaire C5 58
Tshukudu, Bots. D6 66
Tshwaane, Bots. D6 66
Tsiafajavona, mtn., Madag. Q22 67b
Tsianaloka, Madag. Q21 67b
Tsihombe, Madag. T21 67b
Tsilmamo, Eth. N8 60
Tsimilofo, Madag. T21 67b
Tsineng, Boph. F6 66
Tsingtao see Qingdao, China G8 32
Tsinjomitondraka, Madag. O22 67b
Tsiribihina, stm., Madag. Q21 67b
Tsiroanomandidy, Madag. Q22 67b
Tsitondroina, Madag. R22 67b
Tsivory, Madag. T22 67b
Tsobis, Nmb. B3 66
Tsomo, stm., Afr. H8 66
Tsoying, Tai. M9 34
Tsu, Japan M11 36
Tsuchiura, Japan K15 36
Tsugaru-kaikyō, strt., Japan F15 36a
Tsumeb, Nmb. B3 66
Tsumis Park, Nmb. D3 66
Tsumkwe, Nmb. B5 66
Tsuni see Zunyi, China F8 30
Tsuruga, Japan L11 36
Tsuruoka, Japan I14 36
Tsushima, is., Japan M4 36
Tsushima-kaikyō (Eastern Channel), strt., Japan N4 36
Tsuyama, Japan L9 36
Tua Chau, Viet. D7 40
Tual, Indon. G9 38
Tualatin, stm., Or., U.S. h11 144
Tuam, Ire. H5 8
Tuamotu, Îles, is., Fr. Poly. J26 158
Tuanfeng, China E3 34
Tuanlin, China D7 32
Tuanwang, China G8 32
Tuapse, U.S.S.R. I5 22
Tubac, Az., U.S. F4 110
Tuba City, Az., U.S. A4 110
Tubarão, Braz. E14 80
Tübingen, Ger. G9 10
Tubruq (Tobruk), Libya A2 60
Tucacas, Ven. B8 84
Tucacas, Punta, c., Ven. B8 84
Tucannon, stm., Wa., U.S. C8 154
Tucannon Canyon, val., Wa., U.S. C8 154
Tucano, Braz. F11 76
Tucavaca, stm., Bol. H12 82
Tuchengzi, China C12 32
Tuchola, Pol. B17 10
Tuckahoe, N.J., U.S. E3 137
Tuckahoe, N.Y., U.S. h13 139
Tuckahoe, stm., N.J., U.S. E3 137
Tuckahoe Creek, stm., Md., U.S. C6 127
Tucker, Ar., U.S. C4 111
Tucker, Ga., U.S. h8 117
Tucker, co., W.V., U.S. B5 155
Tucker Island, i., N.J., U.S. E4 137
Tuckerman, Ar., U.S. B4 111
Tuckernuck Island, i., Ma., U.S. D7 128
Tuckerton, N.J., U.S. D4 137
Tučkovo, U.S.S.R. F19 26
Tucson, Az., U.S. E5 110
Tucumã, Paraná, mth., Braz. J9 84
Tucumán, prov., Arg. D6 80
Tucumcari, N.M., U.S. B6 138
Tucumcari Mountain, mtn., N.M., U.S. B6 138
Tucunduva, Braz. D11 80
Tucunuco, Arg. F4 80
Tucuparé, Cachoeira do, wtfl, Braz. A14 82
Tucupido, Ven. C10 84
Tucupita, Ven. C11 84
Tucuruí, Braz. D9 76
Tudcum, Arg. F4 80
Tudela, Spain C10 16
Tudmur (Palmyra), Syria D5 48
Tudu, U.S.S.R. B9 26
Tugaloo Lake, res., U.S. B1 147
Tugaske, Sask., Can. G2 105
Tug Fork, stm., U.S. C2 155
Tuichi, stm., Bol. F8 82
Tuineje, Spain O26 17b
Tujmazy, U.S.S.R. G8 22
T'ukalinsk, U.S.S.R. F12 22
Tukangbesi, Kepulauan, is., Indon. G7 38
Tuktoyaktuk, N.W. Ter., Can. C6 96
Tukums, U.S.S.R. D6 26
Tukwila, Wa., U.S. f11 154
Tula, Mex. F10 90
Tula, U.S.S.R. G20 26
Tulalip Indian Reservation, Wa., U.S. A3 154
Tulancingo, Mex. G10 90
Tulare, Ca., U.S. D4 112
Tulare, S.D., U.S. C7 148
Tulare, co., Ca., U.S. D4 112
Tulare Lake, l., Ca., U.S. D4 112
Tularosa, N.M., U.S. D3 138
Tularosa Mountains, mts., N.M., U.S. D1 138
Tularosa Valley, val., N.M., U.S. E3 138
Tulbagh, S. Afr. I4 66
Tulcán, Ec. G4 84
Tulcea, Rom. D12 20
Tulcea, co., Rom. D12 20
Tule, stm., Nic. F10 92
Tulelake, Ca., U.S. B3 112
Tule Lake, sw., Ca., U.S. B3 112
Tule River Indian Reservation, Ca., U.S. E4 112
Tule Valley, val., Ut., U.S. D2 151
T'ul'gan, U.S.S.R. G9 22
Tuli, Zimb. C9 66
Tulia, Tx., U.S. B2 150
Tuling, China J7 34
Ṭūlkarm, Isr. Occ. D4 50
Tullahoma, Tn., U.S. B5 149
Tullamore, Austl. I7 70
Tullamore, Ire. H6 8
Tulle, Fr. G8 14
Tullibigeal, Austl. I7 70
Tulln, Aus. G16 10
Tullos, La., U.S. C3 125
Tullus, Sud. L3 60
Tully, Austl. A6 70
Tuloma, stm., U.S.S.R. G23 6
Tulsa, Ok., U.S. A6 143
Tulsa, co., Ok., U.S. B6 143
Tuluá, Col. E4 84
Tulum, Mex. G16 90
Tulum, hist., Mex. G16 90
Tulumaya (Lavalle), Arg. G4 80
Tulumayo, stm., Peru D4 82
Tulun, U.S.S.R. G12 24
Tulungagung, Indon. K15 39a
Tuma, U.S.S.R. F23 26
Tuma, stm., Nic. D10 92
Tumacacori, Az., U.S. F4 110
Tumacacori National Monument, Az., U.S. F4 110
Tumaco, Col. G3 84
Tumaco, Ensenada de, b., Col. G3 84
Tumalo, Or., U.S. C5 144
Tumatumari, Guy. E13 84
Tumba, Lac, l., Zaire B3 58
Tumbarumba, Austl. J8 70
Tumbaya, Arg. B6 80
Tumbes, Peru I2 84
Tumbes, prov., Peru F2 84
Tumbes (Puyango), stm., S.A. I2 84
Tumble Mountain, mtn., Mt., U.S. E7 133
Tumbler Ridge, B.C., Can. B7 99
Tumbling Shoals, Ar., U.S. B3 111
Tumbotino, U.S.S.R. F26 26
Tumby Bay, Austl. J2 70
Tumča, stm., Eur. H21 6
Tumen, China A17 32
T'umen', U.S.S.R. F11 22
Tumen (Tuman-gang), stm., Asia A18 32
Tumeremo, Ven. D12 84
Tumiritinga, Braz. E8 79
Tumkūr, India F4 46
Tummo, Libya D3 56
Tumos, stm., Afr. D2 66
Tumpat, Malay. K7 40
Tumsar, India B5 46
Tumtum, Wa., U.S. B8 154
Tumuc-Humac Mountains, mts., S.A. C7 76
Tumupasa, Bol. F8 82
Tumut, Austl. J8 70
Tumwater, Wa., U.S. B3 154
Tuña, stm., Col. G5 84
Tunari, Cerro, mtn., Bol. G8 82
Tunas de Zaza, Cuba D5 94
Tunaydah, Egypt E5 60
Tunçbilek, Tur. J13 20
Tunduru, Tan. D7 58
Tundža, stm., Eur. G10 20
T'ung, stm., U.S.S.R. E16 24
Tungabhadra Reservoir, res., India E4 46
Tungaru, Sud. L6 60
Tungkang, Tai. M9 34
Tungla, Nic. D10 92
Tungsha Tao (Pratas Island), i., Tai. G10 30
Tungshih, Tai. K9 34
Tungurahua, prov., Ec. H3 84
Tuni, India D7 46
Tunia, stm., Col. G6 84
Tunica, Ms., U.S. A3 131
Tunica, co., Ms., U.S. A3 131
Tunis, Tun. M5 18
Tunis, Golfe de, b., Tun. L5 18
Tunisia (Tunisie), ctry., Afr. B8 54
Tunja, Col. E6 84
Tunkás, Mex. G15 90
Tunkhannock, Pa., U.S. C10 145
Tunk Lake, l., Me., U.S. D4 126
Tunnel Hill, Ga., U.S. B1 117
Tunnel Springs, Al., U.S. D2 108
Tunnelton, In., U.S. G5 121
Tunnelton, W.V., U.S. B5 155
Tunp Range, mts., Wy., U.S. D2 157
Tununak, Ak., U.S. C6 109
Tunungayualok Island, i., Newf., Can. g9 102
Tunuyán, Arg. G4 80
Tunuyán, stm., Arg. G5 80
Tunxi, China F7 34
Tuo, stm., China E7 30
Tuocheng, China K4 34
Tuokusidawan Ling, mtn., China B11 44
Tuolumne, Ca., U.S. D3 112
Tuolumne, co., Ca., U.S. C4 112
Tuolumne, stm., Ca., U.S. D3 112
Tupã, Braz. F3 79
Tupaciguara, Braz. E4 79
Tupana, stm., Braz. J12 84
Tupanciretã, Braz. E12 80
Tuparro, stm., Col. E8 84
Tupelo, Ar., U.S. B4 111
Tupelo, Ms., U.S. A5 131
Tupelo, Ok., U.S. C5 143
Tupinambarana, Ilha, i., Braz. I14 84
Tupi Paulista, Braz. F3 79
Tupiraçaba, Braz. C4 79
Tupiza, Bol. I9 82
Tupper, B.C., Can. B7 99
Tupper Lake, N.Y., U.S. A6 139
Tupper Lake, l., N.Y., U.S. A6 139
Tupperville, Ont., Can. E2 103
Tupungato, Arg. G4 80
Tupungato, Cerro, mtn., S.A. G4 80
Túquerres, Col. G4 84
Tura, India H14 44
Tura, stm., U.S.S.R. F10 22
Turabah, Sau. Ar. D2 47
Turayf, Sau. Ar. F5 48
Turbaco, Col. B5 84
Turbacz, mtn., Pol. F20 10
Turbat, Pak. I17 48
Turbeville, S.C., U.S. D7 147
Turbo, Col. C4 84
Turbotville, Pa., U.S. D8 145
Turda, Rom. C7 20
Turdej, U.S.S.R. H21 26
Turek, Pol. C18 10
Turfan Depression see Turpan Pendi, depr., China C4 30
Turfan see Turpan, China C4 30
Turgaj, U.S.S.R. H10 22
Turgaj, stm., U.S.S.R. H10 22
Turgajskaja ložbina, val., U.S.S.R. G10 22
Turgajskoje plato, plat., U.S.S.R. G10 22
Turginovo, U.S.S.R. E19 26
Turgoš, U.S.S.R. B18 26
Turgutlu, Tur. K11 20
Türi, U.S.S.R. C8 26
Turia, stm., Spain F11 16
Turimiquire, Cerro, mtn., Ven. B11 84
Turin, Alta., Can. E4 98
Turin, Ga., U.S. C2 117
Turinsk, U.S.S.R. F10 22
Turin see Torino, Italy D2 18
Turka, U.S.S.R. F23 10
Turkestan, U.S.S.R. I11 22
Túrkeve, Hung. H20 10
Turkey, Tx., U.S. B2 150
Turkey (Türkiye), ctry., Asia H15 4
Turkey, stm., Ia., U.S. B6 122
Turkey Creek, La., U.S. D3 125
Turkey Creek, stm., Ne., U.S. D8 134
Turkey Creek, stm., Ok., U.S. A3 143
Turkey Point, c., Md., U.S. B5 127
Turkish Republic of Northern Cyprus see Cyprus, North, ctry., Asia H14 4
Turkmenistan see Turkmenskaja Sovetskaja Socialističeskaja Respublika, state, U.S.S.R. I9 22
Turkmenskaja Sovetskaja Socialističeskaja Respublika, state, U.S.S.R. I9 22
Turks and Caicos Islands, dep., N.A. D9 94
Turks Island Passage, strt., T./C. Is. D9 94
Turks Islands, is., T./C. Is. D9 94
Turku (Åbo), Fin. K18 6
Turley, Ok., U.S. A6 143
Turlock, Ca., U.S. D3 112
Turmalina, Braz. D7 79
Turmero, Ven. B9 84
Turnbull, Mount, mtn., Az., U.S. D5 110
Turneffe Islands, is., Belize I16 90
Turner, Me., U.S. D2 126
Turner, Mt., U.S. B8 133
Turner, Or., U.S. C4 144
Turner, co., Ga., U.S. E3 117
Turner, co., S.D., U.S. D8 148
Turner Mountain, hill, Ct., U.S. C1 114
Turners Falls, Ma., U.S. A2 128
Turner Valley, Alta., Can. D3 98
Turney, Mo., U.S. B3 132
Turnhout, Bel. F6 12
Türnitz, Aus. H15 10
Turnor Lake, l., Sask., Can. m7 105
Turnu-Măgurele, Rom. F8 20
Turon, Ks., U.S. E5 123
Turpan, China C4 30
Turpan Pendi, depr., China C4 30
Turpin, Ok., U.S. e10 143
Turquino, Pico, mtn., Cuba E6 94
Turrell, Ar., U.S. B5 111
Turret Peak, mtn., Az., U.S. C4 110
Turrialba, C.R. H11 92
Turrialba, Volcán, vol., C.R. G11 92
Turriff, Scot., U.K. D11 8
Turrubares, Cerro, mtn., C.R. H10 92
Turtle Creek, N.B., Can. D5 101
Turtle Creek, Pa., U.S. k14 145
Turtle Flambeau Flowage, res., Wi., U.S. B3 156
Turtleford, Sask., Can. D1 105
Turtle Lake, N.D., U.S. B5 141
Turtle Lake, Wi., U.S. C1 156
Turtle Lake, l., Sask., Can. D1 105
Turtle Mountain Indian Reservation, N.D., U.S. A6 141
Turton, S.D., U.S. B7 148
Turu, stm., U.S.S.R. D12 24
Turuchan, stm., U.S.S.R. D9 24
Turvânia, Braz. D3 79
Turvo, Braz. E14 80
Turvo, stm., Braz. D3 79
Turvo, stm., Braz. F4 79
Tuscaloosa, Al., U.S. B2 108
Tuscaloosa, co., Al., U.S. B2 108
Tuscany see Toscana, prov., Italy F5 18
Tuscarawas, co., Oh., U.S. B4 142
Tuscarawas, stm., Oh., U.S. B4 142
Tuscarora, Nv., U.S. B5 135
Tuscarora Indian Reservation, N.Y., U.S. B2 139
Tuscarora Mountain, mts., Pa., U.S. F6 145
Tuscarora Mountains, mts., Nv., U.S. B5 135
Tuscola, Il., U.S. D5 120
Tuscola, Tx., U.S. C3 150
Tuscola, co., Mi., U.S. E7 129
Tusculum College, Tn., U.S. C11 149

Name — Map Ref. — Page

Tuscumbia, Al., U.S. A2 108
Tushka, Ok., U.S. C5 143
Tuskegee, Al., U.S. C4 108
Tusket, N.S., Can. F4 101
Tusket, stm., N.S., Can. E4 101
Tustumena Lake, l., Ak., U.S. g16 109
Tutajev, U.S.S.R. D22 26
Tutang, China F5 34
Tuticorin, India H5 46
Tutóia, Braz. D10 76
Tutrakan, Bul. E10 20
Tuttle, N.D., U.S. B6 141
Tuttle, Ok., U.S. B4 143
Tuttle Creek Dam, Ks., U.S. C7 123
Tuttle Creek Lake, res., Ks., U.S. C7 123
Tutupaca, Volcán, vol., Peru G6 82
Tututalak Mountain, mtn., Ak., U.S. B7 109
Tutwiler, Ms., U.S. A3 131
Tuurun-Poorin lääni, prov., Fin. K18 6
Tuvalu, ctry., Oc. G24 2
Ṭuwayq, Jabal, mts., Sau. Ar. D4 47
Tuxedo, N.C., U.S. f10 140
Tuxedo Park, De., U.S. i7 115
Tuxford, Sask., Can. G3 105
Tuxpan, Mex. G7 90
Tuxpan, Mex. G11 90
Tuxtepec, Mex. H11 90
Tuxtla Gutiérrez, Mex. I13 90
Tuy, stm., Ven. B9 84
Tuy An, Viet. H10 40
Tuyen Quang, Viet. D8 40
Tuy Hoa, Viet. H10 40
Tuz Gölü, l., Tur. H14 4
Tuzigoot National Monument, Az., U.S. C4 110
Tūz Khurmātū, Iraq D8 48
Tuzla, Yugo. E2 20
Tuzly, U.S.S.R. D14 20
Tver', U.S.S.R. E18 26
Tweed, Ont., Can. C7 103
Tweed Heads, Austl. G10 70
Tweedsmuir Provincial Park, B.C., Can. C4 99
Tweedy Mountain, mtn., Mt., U.S. E4 133
Twee Rivieren, S. Afr. F5 66
Twelve Mile, In., U.S. C5 121
Twelvepole Creek, stm., W.V., U.S. C2 155
Twelvepole Creek, East Fork, stm., W.V., U.S. D2 155
Twelvepole Creek, West Fork, stm., W.V., U.S. D2 155
Twentymile Creek, stm., W.V., U.S. C3 155
Twentynine Palms, Ca., U.S. E5 112
Twentynine Palms Marine Corps Base, mil., Ca., U.S. E5 112
Twiggs, co., Ga., U.S. D3 117
Twillingate, Newf., Can. D4 102
Twin Bridges, Mt., U.S. E4 133
Twin Buttes, mtn., Or., U.S. C4 144
Twin Buttes Reservoir, res., Tx., U.S. D2 150
Twin City, Ga., U.S. D4 117
Twin Creek, stm., Oh., U.S. C1 142
Twin Falls, Id., U.S. G4 119
Twin Falls, co., Id., U.S. G4 119
Twin Knolls, Az., U.S. m9 110
Twin Lakes, Ga., U.S. F3 117
Twin Lakes, In., U.S. B5 121
Twin Lakes, Wi., U.S. F5 156
Twin Lakes, l., Ct., U.S. A2 114
Twin Lakes, l., Ia., U.S. B3 122
Twin Lakes, l., Me., U.S. C4 126
Twin Lakes Mountain, mtn., N.Y., U.S. B6 139
Twin Mountain, N.H., U.S. B3 136
Twin Mountains, mtn., Wy., U.S. E7 157
Twin Peaks, mts., Id., U.S. E4 119
Twin Rivers, N.J., U.S. C4 137
Twin Rocks, Pa., U.S. F4 145
Twinsburg, Oh., U.S. A4 142
Twin Valley, Mn., U.S. C2 130
Twisp, Wa., U.S. A5 154
Two Butte Creek, stm., Co., U.S. D8 113
Twofold Bay, b., Austl. K8 70
Twoforks, stm., Sask., Can. C2 105
Two Harbors, Mn., U.S. C7 130
Two Hills, Alta., Can. C5 98
Two Mile Beach, N.J., U.S. F3 137
Two Prairie, Bayou, stm., Ar., U.S. h11 111
Two Rivers, Wi., U.S. D6 156
Two Rivers, North Branch, stm., Mn., U.S. B2 130
Two Rivers, South Branch, stm., Mn., U.S. B2 130
Tybee Island, Ga., U.S. D6 117
Tychy, Pol. E18 10
Tygart Lake, res., W.V., U.S. B5 155
Tygart River, Falls of the, wtfl, W.V., U.S. k10 155
Tygarts Creek, stm., Ky., U.S. B7 124
Tygart Valley, stm., W.V., U.S. B4 155
Tyger, stm., S.C., U.S. B4 147
Tygh Valley, Or., U.S. B5 144
Tyler, Al., U.S. C3 108
Tyler, Mn., U.S. F2 130
Tyler, Tx., U.S. C5 150
Tyler, co., Tx., U.S. D5 150
Tyler, co., W.V., U.S. B4 155
Tyler, Lake, res., Tx., U.S. C5 150
Tyler Branch, stm., Vt., U.S. B3 152
Tyler Heights, W.V., U.S. C3 155
Tylertown, Ms., U.S. D3 131
Tym, stm., U.S.S.R. E8 24
Tymochtee Creek, stm., Oh., U.S. B2 142
Tyndall, Man., Can. D3 100
Tyndall, S.D., U.S. E8 148
Tyndall Air Force Base, mil., Fl., U.S. u16 116
Tyndinskij, U.S.S.R. F16 24
Tyne, stm., Eng., U.K. G11 8
Tynemouth, Eng., U.K. F12 8
Tyner, In., U.S. B5 121
Tyner, Ky., U.S. C6 124
Tyne Valley, P.E.I., Can. C6 101
Týn nad Vltavou, Czech. F14 10
Tyonek, Ak., U.S. C9 109
Tyre see Şūr, Leb. B4 50
Tyrma, U.S.S.R. G18 24
Tyro, Ks., U.S. E8 123
Tyrone, Ky., U.S. B5 124
Tyrone, N.M., U.S. E1 138
Tyrone, Ok., U.S. e9 143
Tyrone, Pa., U.S. E5 145
Tyronza, Ar., U.S. B5 111
Tyrrell, co., N.C., U.S. B6 140
Tyrrell, Lake, l., Austl. J5 70
Tyrrhenian Sea (Mare Tirreno), Eur. I7 18
Tytuvėnai, U.S.S.R. F6 26
Ty Ty, Ga., U.S. E3 117
Ty Ty Creek, stm., Ga., U.S. E3 117
Tyvan, Sask., Can. G4 105
Tzaneen, S. Afr. D10 66
Tzucacab, Mex. G15 90

U

Uatumã, stm., Braz. I13 84
Uaupés (Vaupés), stm., S.A. G9 84
Uaxactún, hist., Guat. I15 90
Ubá, Braz. F7 79
Ubaíra, Braz. B9 79
Ubaitaba, Braz. C9 79
Ubangi (Oubangui), stm., Afr. H10 54
Ubatã, Braz. C9 79
Ubaté, Col. E6 84
Ubatuba, Braz. G6 79
Ubayyiḍ, Wādī al-, val., Asia B11 60
Ube, Japan N6 36
Úbeda, Spain G8 16
Uberaba, Braz. E5 79
Uberaba, stm., Braz. E4 79
Uberaba, Lagoa, l., S.A. G13 82
Uberlândia, Braz. E4 79
Ubiaja, Nig. H13 64
Ubly, Mi., U.S. E8 129
Ubon Ratchathani, Thai. G8 40
Ubundu, Zaire B5 58
Ucacha, Arg. G7 80
Uč-Adži, U.S.S.R. B17 48
Ucayali, prov., Peru C4 82
Ucayali, stm., Peru A4 82
Uchiura-wan, b., Japan E15 36a
Uchiza, Peru C3 82
Uchoa, Braz. F4 79
Ucholovo, U.S.S.R. H23 26
Uchta, U.S.S.R. E8 22
Uchtoma, U.S.S.R. A21 26
Uckermark, reg., Ger. B13 10
Ucluelet, B.C., Can. E5 99
Ucon, Id., U.S. F7 119
Uda, stm., U.S.S.R. G18 24
Udagamandalam, India G4 46
Udaipur, India H5 44
Udall, Ks., U.S. E6 123
Udamalpet, India G4 46
Udaquiola, Arg. I9 80
Udaypur, Nepal G12 44
Udbina, Yugo. E10 18
Uddevalla, Swe. L12 6
Udgīr, India C4 46
Udine, Italy C8 18
Udoml'a, U.S.S.R. D18 26
Udon Thani, Thai. F7 40
Udskaja guba, b., U.S.S.R. G19 24
Udupi, India F3 46
Udžary, U.S.S.R. A9 48
Ueckermünde, Ger. B14 10
Ueda, Japan K13 36
Uehling, Ne., U.S. C9 134
Uelzen, Ger. C10 10
Ueno, Japan M11 36
Uetersen, Ger. B9 10
Ufa, U.S.S.R. G9 22
Uffenheim, Ger. F10 10
Ufra, U.S.S.R. A12 48
Ugab, stm., Nmb. C1 66
Ugāle, U.S.S.R. D5 26
Uganda, ctry., Afr. A6 58
Ugashik Lakes, l., Ak., U.S. D8 109
Ughaybish, Sud. L6 60
Ugie, S. Afr. H9 66
Uglegorsk, U.S.S.R. H20 24
Uglič, U.S.S.R. D21 26
Uglovka, U.S.S.R. C16 26
Ugodskij Zavod, U.S.S.R. F19 26
Ugoma, mtn., Zaire B5 58
Ugra, U.S.S.R. G17 26
Uh (Už), stm., Eur. G22 10
Uha-dong, N. Kor. C13 32
Uherské Hradiště, Czech. F17 10
Uherský Brod, Czech. F17 10
Uhlenhorst, Nmb. D3 66
Uhlman Lake, l., Man., Can. A2 100
Uhrichsville, Oh., U.S. B4 142
Uíge, Ang. C3 58
Uijŏngbu, S. Kor. F15 32
Uiju, N. Kor. C12 32
Uil, stm., U.S.S.R. H8 22
Uiñaimarca, Lago, l., S.A. G7 82
Uinebona, stm., Ven. E11 84
Uinkaret Plateau, plat., Az., U.S. A2 110
Uinta, co., Wy., U.S. E2 157
Uinta, stm., Ut., U.S. C5 151
Uintah, co., Ut., U.S. D6 151
Uintah and Ouray Indian Reservation, Ut., U.S. C5 151
Uinta Mountains, mts., Ut., U.S. C5 151
Ŭisŏng, S. Kor. G16 32
Uitenhage, S. Afr. I7 66
Uithoorn, Neth. D6 12
Uivak, Cape, c., Newf., Can. f9 102
Uj, stm., U.S.S.R. G10 22
Ujandina, stm., U.S.S.R. D20 24
Ujar, U.S.S.R. F16 22
Ujarrás, hist., C.R. H11 92
Ujemskij, U.S.S.R. I27 6
Újfehértó, Hung. H21 10
Uji-guntō, is., Japan P4 37b
Ujiji, Tan. B5 58
Ujjain, India I6 44
'Ujmān, U.A.E. B9 47
Ujungkulon National Park, Indon. J12 39a
Ujungpandang, Indon. G6 38
Ukiah, Ca., U.S. C2 112
Ukiah, Or., U.S. B8 144
Ukmergė, U.S.S.R. F7 26
Ukraine see Ukrainskaja Sovetskaja Socialističeskaja Respublika, state, U.S.S.R. H3 22
Ukrainskaja Sovetskaja Socialističeskaja Respublika (Ukraine), state, U.S.S.R. H3 22
Ulaanbaatar, Mong. B8 30
Ulaangom, Mong. B5 30
Ulak Island, i., Ak., U.S. E4 109
Ulan, Austl. I8 70
Ulan Bator see Ulaanbaatar, Mong. B8 30
Ulang, stm., Nic. C11 92
Ulan-Ude, U.S.S.R. G13 24
Ułazów, Pol. E23 10
Ulchin, S. Kor. G17 32
Ulcinj, Yugo. H3 20
Ulco, S. Afr. G7 66
Ulcumayo, Peru D4 82
Uldz, stm., Asia H14 24
Ulen, Mn., U.S. C2 130
Ulhāsnagar, India C2 46
Uliastaj, Mong. B6 30
Uljanovka, U.S.S.R. A14 20
Uljanovka, U.S.S.R. B13 26
Uljanovsk, U.S.S.R. G7 22
Ulla, U.S.S.R. F12 26
Ulladulla, Austl. J9 70
Ullapool, Scot., U.K. D8 8
Ullin, Il., U.S. F4 120
Ullún, Arg. F4 80
Ulm, Ger. G10 10
Ulm, Ar., U.S. C4 111
Ulm, Mt., U.S. C5 133
Ulmarra, Austl. G10 70
Ulongué, Moz. D6 58
Ulrum, Neth. B9 12
Ulsan, S. Kor. H17 32
Ulster, co., N.Y., U.S. D6 139
Ulster, hist. reg., Eur. G6 8
Ultraoriental, Cordillera (Serra do Divisor), mts., S.A. C5 82
Ulu, U.S.S.R. E17 24
Ulúa, stm., Hond. B6 92
Ulubey, Tur. K13 20
Ulukışla, Tur. C3 48
Ulungur, stm., China B4 30
Ulungur Hu, l., China B4 30
Uluru National Park, Austl. E6 68
Ulverstone, Austl. M7 70
Ulysses, Ks., U.S. E2 123
Ulysses, Ne., U.S. C8 134
Ulysses, Pa., U.S. C6 145
Ulzë, Alb. H3 20
Umán, Mex. G15 90
Uman', U.S.S.R. H4 22
Umarkot, Pak. H3 44
Umatilla, Fl., U.S. D5 116
Umatilla, Or., U.S. B7 144
Umatilla, co., Or., U.S. B8 144
Umatilla, stm., Or., U.S. B7 144
Umatilla Indian Reservation, Or., U.S. B8 144
Umbagog Lake, l., U.S. A4 136
Umbertide, Italy F7 18
Umboi Island, i., Pap. N. Gui. m16 68a
Umbrail, Pass, Eur. E13 13
Umbria, prov., Italy G7 18
Umbuzero, ozero, l., U.S.S.R. H24 6
Umcolcus Lake, l., Me., U.S. B4 126
Umeå, Swe. J17 6
Umfuli, stm., Zimb. A9 66
Umhlanga Rocks, S. Afr. G10 66
Umkomaas, S. Afr. H10 66
Umm al-Birak, Sau. Ar. C1 47
Umm al-Qaywayn, U.A.E. B9 47
Umm al-Qiṭṭayn, Jord. D7 50
Umm Badr, Sud. J4 60
Umm Dabbī, Sud. J6 60
Umm Dhibbān, Sud. J5 60
Umm Digulgulaya, Sud. L3 60
Umm Durmān (Omdurman), Sud. J7 60
Umm el Faḥm, Isr. C4 50
Umm Jamālah, Sud. L5 60
Umm Kaddādah, Sud. K4 60
Umm Kuwaykah, Sud. K7 60
Umm Lajj, Sau. Ar. I4 48
Umm Mirdi, Sud. H7 60
Umm Qantur, Sud. J6 60
Umm Qaṣr, Iraq F9 48
Umm Quṣayr, Jord. E5 50
Umm Ruwābah, Sud. K6 60
Umm Sayyālah, Sud. J6 60
Umm Shalīl, Sud. L2 60
Umm Shutūr, Sud. N7 60
Umm Walad, Syria C6 50
Umnak Island, i., Ak., U.S. E6 109
Um'ot, U.S.S.R. G25 26
Um'ot, U.S.S.R. I25 26
Umpire, Ar., U.S. C1 111
Umpqua, stm., Or., U.S. D3 144
Umred, India B5 46
Umreth, India I5 44
Umsaskis Lake, l., Me., U.S. B3 126
Ŭmsŏng, S. Kor. G15 32
Umtanum Ridge, mtn., Wa., U.S. C5 154
Umtata, Transkei H9 66
Umtentweni, S. Afr. H10 66
Umuahia, Nig. I13 64
Umuarama, Braz. G2 79
Umzinto, S. Afr. H10 66
Una, Braz. C9 79
Unadilla, Ga., U.S. D3 117
Unadilla, Ne., U.S. h12 134
Unadilla, N.Y., U.S. C5 139
Unadilla, stm., N.Y., U.S. C5 139
Unaí, Braz. D5 79
Unaka Mountains, mts., U.S. C11 149
Unalakleet, Ak., U.S. C7 109
Unalaska, Ak., U.S. E6 109
Unalaska Island, i., Ak., U.S. E6 109
Unare, stm., Ven. C10 84
'Unayzah, Sau. Ar. H7 48
'Unayzah, Jabal, mtn., Asia E5 48
'Unayzah, Jabal, mtn., Jord. G5 50
Uncasville, Ct., U.S. D7 114
Uncia, Bol. H8 82
Uncompahgre, stm., Co., U.S. C3 113
Uncompahgre Butte, mtn., Co., U.S. C2 113
Uncompahgre Mountains, mts., Co., U.S. C3 113
Uncompahgre Peak, mtn., Co., U.S. C3 113
Uncompahgre Plateau, plat., Co., U.S. C2 113
Underhill, Vt., U.S. B3 152
Underhill Center, Vt., U.S. B3 152
Underwood, Al., U.S. B3 108
Underwood, In., U.S. G6 121
Underwood, Ia., U.S. C2 122
Underwood, Mn., U.S. D3 130
Underwood, N.D., U.S. B4 141
Underwood, Wa., U.S. D4 154
Undva nina, c., U.S.S.R. C4 26
Uneča, U.S.S.R. I15 26
Uneiuxi, stm., Braz. H10 84
Ungarie, Austl. I7 70
Ungava, Péninsule d', pen., Que., Can. g12 104
Ungava Bay, b., Can. E19 96
Unggi, N. Kor. A18 32
União, Braz. D10 76
União da Vitória, Braz. D13 80
União dos Palmares, Braz. E11 76
Unicoi, Tn., U.S. C11 149
Unicoi, co., Tn., U.S. C11 149
Unicoi Mountains, mts., U.S. D9 149
Unimak Island, i., Ak., U.S. D7 109
Unimak Pass, strt., Ak., U.S. E6 109
Unini, stm., Braz. H12 84
Unión, Arg. H6 80
Unión, C.R. I11 92
Unión, Para. C10 80
Union, Al., U.S. C2 108
Union, Il., U.S. A5 120
Union, Ia., U.S. B4 122
Union, Ky., U.S. k13 124
Union, La., U.S. h10 125
Union, Me., U.S. D3 126
Union, Ms., U.S. C4 131
Union, Mo., U.S. C6 132
Union, Ne., U.S. D10 134
Union, N.H., U.S. D4 136
Union, Or., U.S. B9 144
Union, S.C., U.S. B4 147
Union, Wa., U.S. B2 154
Union, W.V., U.S. D4 155
Union, co., Ar., U.S. D3 111
Union, co., Fl., U.S. B4 116
Union, co., Ga., U.S. B2 117
Union, co., Il., U.S. F4 120
Union, co., In., U.S. E8 121
Union, co., Ia., U.S. C3 122
Union, co., Ky., U.S. C2 124
Union, co., La., U.S. B3 125
Union, co., Ms., U.S. A4 131
Union, co., N.J., U.S. B4 137
Union, co., N.M., U.S. A6 138
Union, co., N.C., U.S. B2 140
Union, co., Oh., U.S. B2 142
Union, co., Or., U.S. B8 144
Union, co., Pa., U.S. E7 145
Union, co., S.C., U.S. B4 147
Union, co., S.D., U.S. E9 148
Union, co., Tn., U.S. C10 149
Union, West Branch, stm., Me., U.S. D4 126
Union Bay, B.C., Can. E5 99
Union Beach, N.J., U.S. C4 137
Union Bridge, Md., U.S. A3 127
Union City, Ca., U.S. h8 112
Union City, Ga., U.S. C2 117
Union City, In., U.S. D8 121
Union City, Mi., U.S. F5 129
Union City, N.J., U.S. h8 137
Union City, Oh., U.S. B1 142
Union City, Ok., U.S. B4 143
Union City, Pa., U.S. C2 145
Union City, Tn., U.S. A2 149
Uniondale, In., U.S. C7 121
Unión de Reyes, Cuba C4 94
Unión de Tula, Mex. H7 90
Union Flat Creek, stm., Wa., U.S. C8 154
Union Gap, Wa., U.S. C5 154
Union Grove, Wi., U.S. F5 156
Union Lake, l., N.J., U.S. E2 137
Union Mill, Hi., U.S. C6 118
Union Mills, In., U.S. B4 121
Union of Soviet Socialist Republics, ctry., Eur. E14 22
Union Pier, Mi., U.S. G4 129
Union Point, Ga., U.S. C3 117
Union Springs, Al., U.S. C4 108
Union Springs, N.Y., U.S. C4 139
Union Star, Mo., U.S. B3 132
Uniontown, Al., U.S. C2 108
Uniontown, Ks., U.S. E9 123
Uniontown, Ky., U.S. C2 124
Uniontown, Oh., U.S. B4 142
Uniontown, Pa., U.S. G2 145
Uniontown, Wa., U.S. C8 154
Union Village, R.I., U.S. B3 146
Union Village Reservoir, res., Vt., U.S. D4 152
Unionville, Ct., U.S. B4 114
Unionville, In., U.S. F5 121
Unionville, Mi., U.S. E7 129
Unionville, Mo., U.S. A4 132
Unionville, Oh., U.S. A5 142
Unionville, Tn., U.S. B5 149
United, Pa., U.S. F3 145
United Arab Emirates (Al-Imārāt al-'Arabīyah al-Muttaḥidah), ctry., Asia E5 42
United Arab Republic see Egypt, ctry., Afr. C7 56
United Kingdom, ctry., Eur. E7 4
United Nations Headquarters, N.Y., U.S. h12 139
United States, ctry., N.A. D7 106
United States Air Force Academy, mil., Co., U.S. B6 113
United States Military Academy, mil., N.Y., U.S. C6 139
United States Naval Academy, mil., Md., U.S. C4 127
Unity, Sask., Can. E1 105
Unity, Il., U.S. F4 120
Unity, Me., U.S. D3 126
Unity Pond, l., Me., U.S. D3 126
Unity Reservoir, res., Or., U.S. C8 144
Universal, In., U.S. E3 121
University City, Mo., U.S. C7 132
University Heights, Ia., U.S. C6 122
University Heights, Oh., U.S. h9 142
University Park, Ia., U.S. C5 122
University Park, N.M., U.S. E3 138
University Park, Tx., U.S. n10 150
University Place, Wa., U.S. f10 154
Unjha, India I5 44
Unna, Ger. D7 10
Uno, Canal Numero, Arg. I10 80
Ŭnp'a, N. Kor. E13 32
Unquillo, Arg. F6 80
Ŭnsan, N. Kor. D14 32
Unterterzen, Switz. D11 13
Unterwalden, state, Switz. E9 13
Unuli Horog, China C14 44
Unža, U.S.S.R. C27 26
Unža, stm., U.S.S.R. D26 26
Uozu, Japan K12 36
Upala, C.R. G9 92
Upano, stm., Ec. I3 84
Upata, Ven. C11 84
Upatoi Creek, stm., Ga., U.S. D2 117
Upemba, Lac, l., Zaire C5 58
Upham, N.D., U.S. A5 141
Upía, stm., Col. E6 84
Upington, S. Afr. G5 66
Upire, stm., Ven. B8 84
Upland, Ca., U.S. E5 112
Upland, In., U.S. D7 121
Upland, Ne., U.S. D7 134
Upleta, India J4 44
Upolu, i., W. Sam. J22 158
Upolu Point, c., Hi., U.S. C6 118
Upper Ammonoosuc, stm., N.H., U.S. A4 136
Upper Arlington, Oh., U.S. B2 142
Upper Arrow Lake, res., B.C., Can. D9 99
Upper Blackville, N.B., Can. C4 101
Upperco, Md., U.S. A4 127
Upper Darby, Pa., U.S. G11 145
Upper Fairmount, Md., U.S. D6 127
Upper Fraser, B.C., Can. B7 99
Upper Frenchville, Me., U.S. A4 126
Upper Gagetown, N.B., Can. D3 101
Upper Gloucester, Me., U.S. E2 126
Upper Graniteville, Vt., U.S. C4 152
Upper Greenwood Lake, N.J., U.S. A4 137
Upper Humber, stm., Newf., Can. D3 102
Upper Iowa, stm., Ia., U.S. A5 122
Upper Island Cove, Newf., Can. E5 102
Upper Kent, N.B., Can. C2 101
Upper Klamath Lake, l., Or., U.S. E4 144
Upper Marlboro, Md., U.S. C4 127
Upper Musquodoboit, N.S., Can. D7 101
Upper New York Bay, b., U.S. k8 137
Upper Red Lake, l., Mn., U.S. B4 130
Upper Saddle River, N.J., U.S. A4 137
Upper Sandusky, Oh., U.S. B2 142
Upper Sheila, N.B., Can. B5 101
Upperville, Va., U.S. B5 153
Upper Wilson Pond, l., Me., U.S. C3 126
Uppsala, Swe. L15 6
Upright, Cape, c., Ak., U.S. C5 109
Upsala, Mn., U.S. E4 130
Upsala see Uppsala, Swe. L15 6
Upsalquitch, N.B., Can. B3 101
Upshur, co., Tx., U.S. C5 150
Upshur, co., W.V., U.S. C4 155
Upson, co., Ga., U.S. D2 117
Upstart, Cape, c., Austl. B7 70
Upton, Que., Can. D5 104
Upton, Ky., U.S. C4 124
Upton, Ma., U.S. B4 128
Upton, Wy., U.S. B8 157
Upton, co., Tx., U.S. D2 150
Uquía, Cerro, mtn., Ven. E11 84
Urabá, Golfo de, b., Col. C4 84
Uracoa, Ven. C11 84
Uraj, U.S.S.R. E10 22
Ural, stm., U.S.S.R. H8 22
Uralla, Austl. H9 70
Ural Mountains see Ural'skije gory, mts., U.S.S.R. E9 22
Ural'sk, U.S.S.R. G8 22
Ural'skije gory (Ural Mountains), mts., U.S.S.R. E9 22
Urana, Austl. J7 70
Urandangi, Austl. C3 70
Urandi, Braz. C7 79
Urangan, Austl. E10 70
Urania, La., U.S. C3 125
Urariá, Paraná, mth., Braz. I14 84
Uraricaá, stm., Braz. F11 84
Uraricoera, Braz. F12 84
Uraricoera, stm., Braz. F12 84
Ura-T'ube, U.S.S.R. J11 22
Uravan, Co., U.S. C2 113
Urawa, Japan L14 36
Urbana, Ar., U.S. D3 111
Urbana, Il., U.S. C5 120
Urbana, In., U.S. C6 121
Urbana, Ia., U.S. B6 122
Urbana, Mo., U.S. D4 132
Urbana, Oh., U.S. B2 142
Urbancrest, Oh., U.S. m10 142
Urbandale, Ia., U.S. C4 122
Urbania, Italy F7 18
Urbanna, Va., U.S. C6 153
Urbino, Italy F7 18
Urcos, Peru E6 82
Urdinarrain, Arg. G9 80
Uré, Col. D5 84
Urečje, U.S.S.R. I10 26
Urén, stm., C.R. H11 92
Ureña, Ven. D6 84
Ures, Mex. C4 90
Urfa, Tur. C5 48
Urgenč, U.S.S.R. I10 22
Ürgüp, Tur. B3 48
Uri, state, Switz. E10 13
Uriah, Al., U.S. D2 108
Uribante, stm., Ven. D7 84
Uribe, Col. F5 84
Uribia, Col. B6 84
Urich, Mo., U.S. C4 132
Urique, Mex. D6 90
Urique, stm., Mex. D6 90
Urituyacu, stm., Peru J5 84
Urla, Tur. K10 20
Urmia see Orūmīyeh, Iran C8 48
Uroševac, Yugo. G5 20
Urrao, Col. D4 84
Ursa, Il., U.S. C2 120
Uršel'skij, U.S.S.R. F23 26
Uru, stm., Braz. C4 79
Uruaçu, Braz. C4 79
Uruana, Braz. C4 79
Uruapan del Progreso, Mex. H8 90
Urubamba, Peru E5 82
Urubamba, stm., Peru D5 82
Urubaxi, stm., Braz. H10 84
Urubu, stm., Braz. I13 84
Urubu, Cachoeira do, wtfl, Braz. B4 79
Urucará, Braz. I14 84
Urucu, stm., Braz. J10 84
Uruçuca, Braz. C9 79
Urucuia, stm., Braz. D6 79
Urucurituba, Braz. I14 84
Uruguaiana, Braz. E10 80
Uruguay, ctry., S.A. C5 78
Uruguay (Uruguai), stm., S.A. G9 80
Urumchi see Ürümqi, China C4 30
Ürümqi, China C4 30
Urundel, Arg. B6 80
Urup, ostrov, i., U.S.S.R. H22 24
Urupá, stm., Braz. D10 82
Urupadi, stm., Braz. J14 84
Urupês, Braz. F4 79
Ur'upinsk, U.S.S.R. G6 22
Urussanga, Braz. E14 80
Urutaí, Braz. D4 79
Urutaú, Arg. C7 80
Uržum, U.S.S.R. F8 22
Usa, Japan N6 36
Usa, stm., U.S.S.R. D9 22
Ušači, U.S.S.R. F11 26
Uşak, Tur. K13 20
Ušaki, U.S.S.R. B13 26
Usakos, Nmb. D2 66
Usedom, i., Eur. A14 10
'Usfān, Sau. Ar. D1 47
Ushant see Ouessant, Île d', i., Fr. D1 14
'Ushayrah, Sau. Ar. D2 47
Ushuaia, Arg. G3 78
Usingen, Ger. E8 10
Usk, B.C., Can. B3 99
Usk, Wa., U.S. A8 154
Uslar, Ger. D9 10
Usman', U.S.S.R. I22 26
Usolje-Sibirskoje, U.S.S.R. G12 24
Usoro, Nig. I13 64
Uspallata, Arg. G4 80
Uspanapa, stm., Mex. I12 90
Usquepaug, R.I., U.S. F3 146
Ussuri (Wusuli), stm., Asia B13 30
Ussurijsk, U.S.S.R. I18 24
Ustaritz, Fr. I5 14
Ust'-Barguzin, U.S.S.R. G13 24
Ust'-Cil'ma, U.S.S.R. D8 22
Ust'-Čorna, U.S.S.R. A7 20
Ust'-Dolyssy, U.S.S.R. E12 26
Uster, Switz. D10 13
Ust'-Ilimskoje vodochranilišče, res., U.S.S.R. F18 22
Ústí nad Labem, Czech. E14 10
Ústí nad Orlicí, Czech. F16 10
Ust'-Išim, U.S.S.R. F12 22
Ustje, U.S.S.R. D22 26
Ustka, Pol. A16 10
Ust'-Kamčatsk, U.S.S.R. F24 24
Ust'-Kamenogorsk, U.S.S.R. H8 24
Ust'-Katav, U.S.S.R. G9 22
Ust'-Koksa, U.S.S.R. G15 22
Ust'-Kut, U.S.S.R. F13 24
Ust'-Luga, U.S.S.R. B11 26
Ust'-Nera, U.S.S.R. E20 24
Uštobe, U.S.S.R. H13 22
Ust'-Omčug, U.S.S.R. E21 24
Ust'-Ordynskij, U.S.S.R. G12 24
Ust'uckoje, U.S.S.R. C18 26
Ustupo Yantupo, Pan. C3 84
Ust'urt, plato, plat., U.S.S.R. I9 22
Ust'-Usa, U.S.S.R. D9 22
Ust'užna, U.S.S.R. C19 26
Usu, China C3 30
Usulután, El Sal. D6 92
Usumacinta, stm., N.A. I14 90
Ušumun, U.S.S.R. G17 24
Utah, co., Ut., U.S. C4 151
Utah, state, U.S. D4 151
Utah Lake, l., Ut., U.S. C4 151
Utapi, Nmb. A2 66
Utashinai, Japan D17 36a
Ute, Ia., U.S. B2 122
Ute Creek, stm., N.M., U.S. A6 138
Utembo, stm., Ang. E4 58
Ute Mountain Indian Reservation, U.S. D2 113
Utena, U.S.S.R. F8 26
Ute Reservoir, res., N.M., U.S. B6 138
Utete, Tan. C7 58
Uthai Thani, Thai. G6 40
Utiariti, Braz. E12 82
Utica, Il., U.S. B5 120
Utica, In., U.S. H6 121
Utica, Ks., U.S. D3 123
Utica, Ky., U.S. C2 124
Utica, Mi., U.S. F7 129

Name — Map Ref. — Page

Utica, Ms., U.S. C3 131
Utica, Mo., U.S. B4 132
Utica, Ne., U.S. D8 134
Utica, N.Y., U.S. B5 139
Utica, Oh., U.S. B3 142
Utica, S.D., U.S. E8 148
Utiel, Spain F10 16
Utikuma Lake, l., Alta., Can. B3 98
Utila, Hond. A8 92
Utila, Isla de, i., Hond. A8 92
Utinga, stm., Braz. B8 79
Utique, Tun. L5 18
Uto, Japan O5 36
Utopia, Lake, l., N.B., Can. D3 101
Utorgoš, U.S.S.R. C13 26
Utrecht, Neth. D7 12
Utrecht, S. Afr. F10 66
Utrecht, prov., Neth. D7 12
Utrera, Spain H6 16
Utsunomiya, Japan K14 36
Uttaradit, Thai. F6 40
Uttar Pradesh, state, India G9 44
Utuado, P.R. E11 94
Uudenmaan lääni, prov., Fin. K19 6
Uusikaupunki (Nystad), Fin. K17 6
Uvá, Braz. C3 79
Uvá, stm., Col. F8 84
Uvalda, Ga., U.S. D4 117
Uvalde, Tx., U.S. E3 150
Uvalde, co., Tx., U.S. E3 150
Uvaroviči, U.S.S.R. I13 26
Uvarovka, U.S.S.R. F18 26
Uvarovo, U.S.S.R. J25 26
Uvat, U.S.S.R. F11 22
Uvinza, Tan. C6 58
Uvira, Zaire B5 58
Uvs nuur, l., Asia A5 30
Uwajima, Japan N7 36
Uwayl, Sud. M4 60
'Uwaynāt, Jabal al-, mtn., Afr. D5 56
Uwharrie, stm., N.C., U.S. B3 140
Uxbridge, Ma., U.S. B4 128
Uxmal, hist., Mex. G15 90
Uyuni, Bol. I8 82
Uyuni, Salar de, pl., Bol. I8 82
Už (Uh), stm., Eur. G22 10
Užava, U.S.S.R. D4 26
Uzbekistan see Uzbekskaja Sovetskaja Socialističeskaja Respublika, state, U.S.S.R. I10 22
Uzbekskaja Sovetskaja Socialističeskaja Respublika, state, U.S.S.R. I10 22
Uzboj, stm., U.S.S.R. B13 48
Uzda, U.S.S.R. H10 26
Uzdin, Yugo. D4 20
Užgorod, U.S.S.R. H2 22
Uzlovaja, U.S.S.R. H21 26
Uzunköprü, Tur. H10 20
Užur, U.S.S.R. F9 24
Užventis, U.S.S.R. F5 26

V

Vääksy, Fin. K19 6
Vaala, Fin. I20 6
Vaalserberg, mtn., Neth. G9 12
Vaalwater, S. Afr. E9 66
Vaanta (Vanda), Fin. K19 6
Vaasa (Vasa), Fin. J17 6
Vaasan lääni, prov., Fin. J18 6
Vabalninkas, U.S.S.R. F7 26
Vabkent, U.S.S.R. A18 48
Vác, Hung. H19 10
Vača, U.S.S.R. F25 26
Vacacaí, stm., Braz. F11 80
Vaca Key, i., Fl., U.S. H5 116
Vacaria, Braz. E13 80
Vacaria, stm., Braz. D7 79
Vacaria, stm., Braz. F1 79
Vacaville, Ca., U.S. C3 112
Vaccarès, Étang de, b., Fr. I11 14
Vach, stm., U.S.S.R. E7 24
Vache, Île à, i., Haiti E8 94
Vacherie, La., U.S. h10 125
Vachš, stm., U.S.S.R. J11 22
Vacoas, Mrts. V18 67c
Vader, Wa., U.S. C3 154
Vadino, U.S.S.R. F16 26
Vadito, N.M., U.S. A4 138
Vado, N.M., U.S. E3 138
Vadodara, India I5 44
Vado Ligure, Italy E3 18
Vaduz, Liech. E16 14
Vaga, stm., U.S.S.R. E6 22
Vagaj, U.S.S.R. F11 22
Vågåmo, Nor. K11 6
Vágar, i., Faer. Is. D8 6b
Váh, stm., Czech. G17 10
Vaiden, Ms., U.S. B4 131
Vaihingen, Ger. G8 10
Väike-Maarja, U.S.S.R. B9 26
Vail, Az., U.S. E5 110
Vail, Co., U.S. B4 113
Vail, Ia., U.S. B2 122
Vailly-sur-Aisne, Fr. C10 14
Vainode, U.S.S.R. E4 26
Vajgač, ostrov, i., U.S.S.R. C9 22
Valais (Wallis), state, Switz. F7 13
Valašské Meziříčí, Czech. F17 10
Valatie, N.Y., U.S. C7 139
Val-Barrette, Que., Can. C2 104
Val-Bélair, Que., Can. n17 104
Valcheta, Arg. E3 78
Valcourt, Que., Can. D5 104
Valdagno, Italy D6 18
Valdai Hills see Valdajskaja vozvyšennost', hills, U.S.S.R. D15 26
Valdaj, U.S.S.R. D16 26
Valdajskaja vozvyšennost', hills, U.S.S.R. D16 26
Val-David, Que., Can. C3 104
Valdelândia, Braz. C3 79
Valdemārpils, U.S.S.R. D5 26
Valdepeñas, Spain G8 16
Valders, Wi., U.S. D6 156
Valdés, Peninsula, pen., Arg. E4 78
Valdese, N.C., U.S. B1 140
Valdez, Ec. G3 84
Valdez, Ak., U.S. C10 109
Valdez, N.M., U.S. A4 138
Val-d'Isère, Fr. G13 14
Valdivia, Chile D2 78
Valdivia, Col. D5 84
Valdobbiadene, Italy D7 18
Val-d'Oise, dept., Fr. C9 14
Val-d'Or, Que., Can. k11 104
Valdosta, Ga., U.S. F3 117
Vale, Or., U.S. D9 144
Vale, S.D., U.S. C2 148
Valeene, In., U.S. H5 121
Valemount, B.C., Can. C8 99
Valença, Braz. B9 79
Valença, Braz. G7 79
Valença, Port. C3 16
Valençay, Fr. E8 14
Valence, Fr. H11 14
Valencia, Hond. C9 92
Valência, Spain F11 16
Valencia, Az., U.S. m7 110
Valencia, Ven. B8 84
Valência, prov., Spain F11 16
Valencia, co., N.M., U.S. C3 138
València, Golf de, b., Spain F12 16
Valencia, Lago de, l., Ven. B9 84
Valencia de Alcántata, Spain F4 16
Valencia Heights, S.C., U.S. D6 147
Valenciennes, Fr. B10 14
Valentine, Ne., U.S. B5 134
Valenza, Italy D3 18
Valera, Ven. C7 84
Valga, U.S.S.R. D9 26
Valhalla, N.Y., U.S. D7 139
Valhermoso Springs, Al., U.S. A3 108
Valiente, Peninsula, pen., Pan. C2 84
Valiente, Punta, c., Pan. H13 92
Valier, Il., U.S. E4 120
Valier, Mt., U.S. B4 133
Valjevo, Yugo. E3 20
Valka, U.S.S.R. D9 26
Valkininkas, U.S.S.R. G7 26
Valladolid, Ec. J3 84
Valladolid, Mex. G15 90
Valladolid, Spain D7 16
Vallauris, Fr. I14 14
Valldal, Nor. J10 6
Valle, Spain B7 16
Valle, U.S.S.R. E7 26
Valle, dept., Hond. D7 92
Vallecito, Co., U.S. D3 113
Vallecito Reservoir, res., Co., U.S. D3 113
Vallecitos, N.M., U.S. A3 138
Valle d'Aosta, prov., Italy D2 18
Valle de Guanape, Ven. C10 84
Valle de la Pascua, Ven. C9 84
Valle del Cauca, dept., Col. F4 84
Valle de Olivos, Mex. D6 90
Valle de Santiago, Mex. G9 90
Valle de Zaragoza, Mex. D7 90
Valledupar, Col. B6 84
Valle Edén, Ur. F10 80
Vallée-Jonction, Que., Can. C7 104
Vallegrande, Bol. H9 82
Valle Hermoso, Arg. F6 80
Valle Hermoso, Mex. E11 90
Vallehermoso, Spain O23 17b
Vallejo, Ca., U.S. C2 112
Vallenar, Chile E3 80
Valles Mines, Mo., U.S. C7 132
Valletta, Malta N9 18
Valley, Al., U.S. C4 108
Valley, Ne., U.S. C9 134
Valley, Wa., U.S. A8 154
Valley, co., Id., U.S. E3 119
Valley, co., Mt., U.S. B10 133
Valley, co., Ne., U.S. C6 134
Valley, stm., Man., Can. D1 100
Valley Bend, W.V., U.S. C5 155
Valley Center, Ks., U.S. E6 123
Valley City, N.D., U.S. C8 141
Valley Cottage, N.Y., U.S. g13 139
Valley Creek, stm., Al., U.S. g6 108
Valley East, Ont., Can. p19 103
Valley Falls, Ks., U.S. C8 123
Valley Falls, R.I., U.S. B4 146
Valley Farms, Az., U.S. E4 110
Valleyford, Wa., U.S. B8 154
Valley Forge, Pa., U.S. o20 145
Valley Grove, W.V., U.S. A4 155
Valley Head, Al., U.S. A4 108
Valley Head, W.V., U.S. C4 155
Valley Mills, Tx., U.S. D4 150
Valley of the Kings, hist., Egypt E7 60
Valley Park, Ms., U.S. C3 131
Valley Park, Mo., U.S. f12 132
Valley Springs, Ar., U.S. A3 111
Valley Springs, S.D., U.S. D9 148
Valley Station, Ky., U.S. g11 124
Valley Stream, N.Y., U.S. n15 139
Valleyview, Alta., Can. B2 98
Valley View, Ky., U.S. C5 124
Valley View, Pa., U.S. E8 145
Valley View, Tx., U.S. C4 150
Valliant, Ok., U.S. D6 143
Vallimanca, Arroyo, stm., Arg. H8 80
Vallonia, In., U.S. G5 121
Vallorbe, Switz. E5 13
Valls, Spain D13 16
Vallscreek, W.V., U.S. D3 155
Val Marie, Sask., Can. H2 105
Valmaseda, Spain B8 16
Valmeyer, Il., U.S. E3 120
Valmiera, U.S.S.R. D8 26
Valmont, Que., Can. C5 104
Valmy, Nv., U.S. C4 135
Valognes, Fr. C5 14
Valongo, Port. D3 16
Vālpārai, India G4 46
Valparaíso, Braz. F3 79
Valparaíso, Chile G3 80
Valparaiso, Fl., U.S. u15 116
Valparaiso, In., U.S. B3 121
Valparaiso, Ne., U.S. C9 134
Valparaíso, prov., Chile G3 80
Valréas, Fr. H11 14
Vals, Tanjung, c., Indon. G10 38
Valsbaai, b., S. Afr. J4 66
Valsetz, Or., U.S. C3 144
Valtimo, Fin. J21 6
Valujki, U.S.S.R. G5 22
Val Verda, Ut., U.S. C4 151
Val Verde, co., Tx., U.S. E2 150
Valverde del Camino, Spain H5 16
Van, Tur. B7 48
Van, Tx., U.S. C5 150
Van, W.V., U.S. n12 155
Vanadium, N.M., U.S. E1 138
Van Alstyne, Tx., U.S. C4 150
Vananda, B.C., Can. E5 99
Van Buren, Ar., U.S. B1 111
Van Buren, In., U.S. C6 121
Van Buren, Me., U.S. A5 126
Van Buren, Mo., U.S. E6 132
Van Buren, co., Ar., U.S. B3 111
Van Buren, co., Ia., U.S. D6 122
Van Buren, co., Mi., U.S. F4 129
Van Buren, co., Tn., U.S. D8 149
Vanč, U.S.S.R. J12 22
Vance, Ms., U.S. A3 131
Vance, co., N.C., U.S. A4 140
Vance Air Force Base, mil., Ok., U.S. A3 143
Vanceboro, Me., U.S. C5 126
Vanceboro, N.C., U.S. B5 140
Vanceburg, Ky., U.S. B6 124
Vancleave, Ms., U.S. E5 131
Vancouver, B.C., Can. E6 99
Vancouver, Wa., U.S. D3 154
Vancouver, Cape, c., Austl. G3 68
Vancouver Island, i., B.C., Can. E4 99
Vancouver Island Ranges, mts., B.C., Can. D4 99
Vandalia, Il., U.S. E4 120
Vandalia, Mo., U.S. B6 132
Vandenberg Air Force Base, mil., Ca., U.S. E3 112
Vander, N.C., U.S. B4 140
Vanderbijlpark, S. Afr. F8 66
Vanderbilt, Tx., U.S. E4 150
Vanderbilt Peak, mtn., N.M., U.S. E1 138
Vanderburgh, co., In., U.S. H2 121
Vandergrift, Pa., U.S. E2 145
Vanderhoof, B.C., Can. C5 99
Vanderlin Island, i., Austl. C7 68
Vandervoort, Ar., U.S. C1 111
Vanderwagen, N.M., U.S. B1 138
Van Diemen Gulf, b., Austl. B6 68
Vandiver, Al., U.S. B3 108
Vandling, Pa., U.S. C11 145
Vändra, U.S.S.R. C8 26
Vanduser, Mo., U.S. E8 132
Vandyne, Wi., U.S. k9 156
Vanegas, Mex. F9 90
Vänern, l., Swe. L13 6
Vänersborg, Swe. L13 6
Vangaindrano, Madag. S22 67b
Van Gölü, l., Tur. B7 48
Vangsnes, Nor. K10 6
Vanguard, Sask., Can. H2 105
Van Horn, Tx., U.S. o12 150
Van Horne, Ia., U.S. B5 122
Vanier, Ont., Can. h12 103
Vanimo, Pap. N. Gui. F11 38
Vanino, U.S.S.R. H20 24
Vāniyambādi, India F5 46
Vankleek Hill, Ont., Can. B10 103
Van Kull, Kill, stm., N.J., U.S. k8 137
Van Lear, Ky., U.S. C7 124
Vanleer, Tn., U.S. A4 149
Van Meter, Ia., U.S. C4 122
Vanna, Ga., U.S. B3 117
Vanndale, Ar., U.S. B5 111
Vannes, Fr. E4 14
Van Ninh, Viet. H10 40
Van Rees, Pegunungan, mts., Indon. F10 38
Vanrhynsdorp, S. Afr. H4 66
Vansant, Va., U.S. e9 153
Vanscoy, Sask., Can. E2 105
Vanskoje, U.S.S.R. C19 26
Vanstadensrus, S. Afr. G8 66
Vanua Levu, i., Fiji J21 158
Vanuatu, ctry., Oc. H24 2
Van Vleck, Tx., U.S. r14 150
Van Vleet, Ms., U.S. B5 131
Van Wert, Ga., U.S. C1 117
Van Wert, Ia., U.S. D4 122
Van Wert, Oh., U.S. B1 142
Van Wert, co., Oh., U.S. B1 142
Van Wyck, S.C., U.S. B6 147
Van Zandt, co., Tx., U.S. C5 150
Vanzylsrus, S. Afr. F6 66
Vapn'arka, U.S.S.R. A12 20
Var, dept., Fr. I13 14
Var, stm., Fr. I13 14
Varakļāni, U.S.S.R. E9 26
Varallo, Italy D3 18
Vārānasi (Benares), India H10 44
Varangerfjorden, Nor. G22 6
Varangerhalvøya, pen., Nor. F21 6
Varaždin, Yugo. C11 18
Varazze, Italy E3 18
Varberg, Swe. M13 6
Vardaman, Ms., U.S. B4 131
Vardar (Axiós), stm., Eur. H6 20
Vardø, Nor. F22 6
Varegovo, U.S.S.R. D22 26
Varel, Ger. B8 10
Varela, Arg. H5 80
Varėna, U.S.S.R. G7 26
Varennes, Que., Can. D4 104
Vareš, Yugo. E2 20
Varese, Italy D3 18
Varginha, Braz. F6 79
Varina, Va., U.S. C5 153
Varjão, Braz. D4 79
Varkaus, Fin. J20 6
Värmlands Län, co., Swe. L13 6
Varna, Bul. F11 20
Varna, Ont., Can. D3 103
Varna, Il., U.S. B4 120
Varnado, La., U.S. D6 125
Värnamo, Swe. M14 6
Varney, Ont., Can. C4 103
Varnsdorf, Czech. E14 10
Varnville, S.C., U.S. F5 147
Várpalota, Hung. H18 10
Vars, Ont., Can. h13 103
Värska, U.S.S.R. D10 26
Várzea, Rio da, stm., Braz. D12 80
Várzea da Palma, Braz. D6 79
Várzea Grande, Braz. F13 82
Varzeão, Braz. C14 80
Vas, co., Hung. H16 10
Vasalemma, U.S.S.R. B7 26
Vashon, Wa., U.S. B3 154
Vashon, Point, c., Wa., U.S. e11 154
Vashon Island, i., Wa., U.S. f11 154
Vasileviči, U.S.S.R. I12 26
Vasiliká, Grc. I7 20
Vasiljevskij Moch, U.S.S.R. D18 26
Vasiljevskoje, U.S.S.R. E24 26
Vaskelovo, U.S.S.R. A13 26
Vaškovci, U.S.S.R. A11 20
Vaškovcy, U.S.S.R. A9 20
Vaslui, Rom. C11 20
Vaslui, co., Rom. C11 20
Vass, N.C., U.S. B3 140
Vassar, Man., Can. E4 100
Vassar, Ks., U.S. D8 123
Vassar, Mi., U.S. E7 129
Västerås, Swe. L15 6
Västerbottens Län, co., Swe. I15 6
Västernorrlands Län, co., Swe. J15 6
Västervik, Swe. M15 6
Västmanlands Län, co., Swe. L15 6
Vasto, Italy G9 18
Vas'ugan, stm., U.S.S.R. F13 22
Vas'uganje, sw., U.S.S.R. F7 24
Vasvár, Hung. H16 10
Vatan, Fr. E8 14
Vathí, Grc. L10 20
Vatican City (Città del Vaticano), ctry., Eur. H7 18
V'atka, stm., U.S.S.R. F8 22
Vatnajökull, Ice. B5 6a
Vatneyri, Ice. B2 6a
Vatomandry, Madag. Q23 67b
Vatra Dornei, Rom. B9 20
V'atskije Pol'any, U.S.S.R. F8 22
Vättern, l., Swe. L14 6
Vaucluse, S.C., U.S. D4 147
Vaucluse, dept., Fr. I12 14
Vaucouleurs, Fr. D12 14
Vaud, state, Switz. E6 13
Vaudreuil, Que., Can. D3 104
Vaughan, Ont., Can. D5 103
Vaughan, Ms., U.S. C3 131
Vaughn, Mt., U.S. C5 133
Vaughn, N.M., U.S. C4 138
Vaupés, ter., Col. G7 84
Vaupés (Uaupés), stm., S.A. G7 84
Vauvert, Fr. I11 14
Vauxhall, Alta., Can. D4 98
Vavatenina, Madag. P23 67b
Vavoua, I.C. H6 64
Vawn, Sask., Can. D1 105
Växjö, Swe. M14 6
Vazante, Braz. E5 79
Vazante Grande, stm., Braz. H13 82
V'azemskij, U.S.S.R. H18 24
V'az'ma, U.S.S.R. F17 26
V'azniki, U.S.S.R. E25 26
Veazie, Me., U.S. D4 126
Veblen, S.D., U.S. B8 148
Vecht, stm., Eur. C9 12
Vechta, Ger. C8 10
Vecsés, Hung. H19 10
Vedea, Rom. E8 20
Vedia, Arg. H8 80
Veedersburg, In., U.S. D3 121
Veendam, Neth. B10 12
Veenendaal, Neth. D8 12
Vega, Tx., U.S. B1 150
Veghel, Neth. E8 12
Vegreville, Alta., Can. C4 98
Veguita, N.M., U.S. C3 138
Veinticinco de Mayo, Arg. H8 80
Veinticinco de Mayo, Arg. H4 80
Veinticinco de Mayo, Ur. H10 80
Veintiocho de Mayo, Ec. I3 84
Veintisiete de Abril, C.R. G9 92
Veisiejai, U.S.S.R. G6 26
Vejer de la Frontera, Spain I6 16
Vejle, Den. N11 6
Velarde, N.M., U.S. A4 138
Velardeña, Mex. E8 90
Velas, Cabo, c., C.R. G9 92
Velázquez, Ur. H11 80
Velbert, Ger. D7 10
Velda Rose Estates, Az., U.S. D4 110
Velddrif, S. Afr. I4 66
Velden, Ger. G12 10
Veldhoven, Neth. F7 12
Velet'ma, U.S.S.R. F25 26
Velez, Col. D6 84
Velez de la Gomera, Peñón de, i., Sp. N. Afr. J7 16
Vélez-Málaga, Spain I7 16
Vel'gija, U.S.S.R. C16 26
Velhas, Rio das, stm., Braz. D6 79
Velikaja, stm., U.S.S.R. E26 24
Velikaja Kosnica, U.S.S.R. A12 20
Velikaja Michajlovka, U.S.S.R. B13 20
Velika Morava, stm., Yugo. E5 20
Velika Plana, Yugo. E5 20
Velikij Ber'oznyj, U.S.S.R. G22 10
Velikij Byčkov, U.S.S.R. B8 20
Velikije Lučki, U.S.S.R. A6 20
Velikije Luki, U.S.S.R. E13 26
Velikij Ust'ug, U.S.S.R. E7 22
Velikodvorskij, U.S.S.R. F23 26
Veliko Gradište, Yugo. E5 20
Velikoje, U.S.S.R. D22 26
Velikoploskoje, U.S.S.R. B13 20
Veliko Târnovo, Bul. F9 20
Vélingara, Sen. F4 54
Veliž, U.S.S.R. F14 26
Velletri, Italy H7 18
Vellore, India F5 46
Velma, Ok., U.S. C4 143
Velp, Neth. D8 12
Velpen, In., U.S. H3 121
Vel'sk, U.S.S.R. E6 22
Velten, Ger. C13 10
Velva, N.D., U.S. A5 141
Venaco, Fr. G4 18
Venadillo, Col. E5 84
Venado, Isla del, i., Nic. F11 92
Venado Tuerto, Arg. G8 80
Venâncio Aires, Braz. E12 80
Venango, Ne., U.S. D3 134
Venango, co., Pa., U.S. D2 145
Vence, Fr. I14 14
Venceslau Brás, Braz. G4 79
Venda, ctry., Afr. D10 66
Venda Nova, Port. D4 16
Vendas Novas, Port. G3 16
Vendée, dept., Fr. F5 14
Vendeuvre-sur-Barse, Fr. D11 14
Vendičany, U.S.S.R. A11 20
Vendôme, Fr. E8 14
Venecia, C.R. G10 92
Veneta, Or., U.S. C3 144
Venetie, Ak., U.S. B10 109
Veneto, prov., Italy G18 14
Venev, U.S.S.R. G21 26
Venezia (Venice), Italy D7 18
Venezuela, ctry., S.A. B5 76
Venezuela, Golfo de, b., S.A. B7 84
Vengerovo, U.S.S.R. F13 22
Veniaminof, Mount, mtn., Ak., U.S. D8 109
Venice, Fl., U.S. E4 116
Venice, Il., U.S. E3 120
Venice, La., U.S. E6 125
Venice, Ne., U.S. g12 134
Venice, Ut., U.S. E4 151
Venice, Gulf of, b., Eur. D8 18
Venice see Venezia, Italy D7 18
Vénissieux, Fr. G11 14
Venlo, Neth. F9 12
Venosa, Italy I10 18
Vent, Aus. I10 10
Ventanas, Ec. H3 84
Ventersdorp, S. Afr. F8 66
Venterstad, S. Afr. H7 66
Ventimiglia, Italy F2 18
Ventnor, Ont., Can. C9 103
Ventnor City, N.J., U.S. E4 137
Ventspils, U.S.S.R. D4 26
Ventuari, stm., Ven. E9 84
Ventura (San Buenaventura), Ca., U.S. E4 112
Ventura, Ia., U.S. A4 122
Ventura, co., Ca., U.S. E4 112
Venus, Tx., U.S. n9 150
Venustiano Carranza, Mex. I13 90
Venustiano Carranza, Mex. H8 90
Venustiano Carranza, Bahía, b., Mex. H16 90
Venustiano Carranza, Presa, res., Mex. D9 90
Vera, Arg. E8 80
Veracruz, state, Mex. H12 90
Veracruz [Llave], Mex. H11 90
Veraguas, prov., Pan. I13 92
Veranópolis, Braz. E13 80
Verāval, India J4 44
Verbania, Italy D3 18
Verbena, Al., U.S. C3 108
Verbilki, U.S.S.R. E20 26
Verbovskij, U.S.S.R. F25 26
Vercelli, Italy D3 18
Vercel [-Villedieu-le-Camp], Fr. E13 14
Verchères, Que., Can. D4 104
Verchn'aja Inta, U.S.S.R. D10 22
Verchn'aja Salda, U.S.S.R. F10 22
Verchn'aja Tajmyra, stm., U.S.S.R. C11 24
Verchn'aja Troica, U.S.S.R. D20 26
Verchn'aja Tura, U.S.S.R. F9 22
Verchnedneprovskij, U.S.S.R. G16 26
Verchnedvinsk, U.S.S.R. F10 26
Verchnemulomskoje vodochranilišče, res., U.S.S.R. G22 6
Verchnevil'ujsk, U.S.S.R. E16 24
Verchnij Baskunčak, U.S.S.R. H7 22
Verchnij Ufalej, U.S.S.R. F10 22
Verchojansk, U.S.S.R. D18 24
Verchojanskij chrebet, mts., U.S.S.R. D17 24
Verchoturje, U.S.S.R. F10 22
Verchovje, U.S.S.R. I20 26
Vercors, reg., Fr. H12 14
Verda, Ky., U.S. D6 124
Verde, stm., Braz. C4 79
Verde, stm., Braz. D5 79
Verde, stm., Braz. D3 79
Verde, stm., Braz. E3 79
Verde, stm., Braz. E4 79
Verde, stm., Braz. F2 79
Verde, stm., Braz. E12 82
Verde, stm., Braz. E13 82
Verde, stm., Mex. G8 90
Verde, stm., Para. B9 80
Verde, stm., S.A. F11 82
Verde, stm., Az., U.S. C4 110
Verde, Arroyo, stm., Bol. E8 82
Verde, Cape, c., Bah. C7 94
Verde Grande, stm., Braz. C7 79
Verden, Ger. C9 10
Verden, Ok., U.S. B3 143
Verde Pequeno, stm., Braz. C7 79
Verdi, Nv., U.S. D2 135
Verdigre, Ne., U.S. B7 134
Verdigris, Ok., U.S. A6 143
Verdigris, stm., U.S. A6 143
Verdinho, stm., Braz. D3 79
Verdi Peak, mtn., Nv., U.S. C6 135
Verdon, Ne., U.S. D10 134
Verdun, Que., Can. q19 104
Verdun, Fr. I8 14
Verdun-sur-le-Doubs, Fr. F12 14
Verdun-sur-Meuse, Fr. C12 14
Vereeniging, S. Afr. F8 66
Vereja, U.S.S.R. F19 26
Veremejki, U.S.S.R. H14 26
Vereščagino, U.S.S.R. F8 22
Vergara, Ur. G12 80
Vergas, Mn., U.S. D3 130
Vergennes, Il., U.S. F4 120
Vergennes, Vt., U.S. C2 152
Verigin, Sask., Can. F4 105
Verin, Spain D4 16
Veriora, U.S.S.R. C10 26
Verissimo, Braz. E4 79
Verkhoyansk see Verchojansk, U.S.S.R. D18 24
Vermelho, stm., Braz. C3 79
Vermilion, Alta., Can. C5 98
Vermilion, Il., U.S. D6 120
Vermilion, Oh., U.S. A3 142
Vermilion, co., Il., U.S. C6 120
Vermilion, co., La., U.S. E3 125
Vermilion, stm., Alta., Can. C5 98
Vermilion, stm., Il., U.S. C5 120
Vermilion, stm., La., U.S. E3 125
Vermilion, stm., Mn., U.S. B6 130
Vermilion, stm., Oh., U.S. A3 142
Vermilion Bay, Ont., Can. E5 100
Vermilion Bay, b., La., U.S. E3 125
Vermilion Lake, l., Mn., U.S. C6 130
Vermilion Pass, Can. D2 98
Vermilion Range, hills, Mn., U.S. C7 130
Vermillion, Ks., U.S. C7 123
Vermillion, S.D., U.S. E9 148
Vermillion, co., In., U.S. E2 121
Vermillion, East Fork, stm., S.D., U.S. D8 148
Vermillion Bluffs, clf, Co., U.S. A2 113
Vermillion Creek, stm., Co., U.S. A2 113
Vermillon, stm., Que., Can. B4 104
Vermont, Il., U.S. C3 120
Vermont, state, U.S. D3 152
Vermontville, Mi., U.S. F5 129
Vernal, Ut., U.S. C6 151
Vernayaz, Switz. F7 13
Verndale, Mn., U.S. D3 130
Verneuil, Fr. D7 14
Vernon, B.C., Can. D8 99
Vernon, Fr. C8 14
Vernon, Al., U.S. B1 108
Vernon, Az., U.S. C6 110
Vernon, Fl., U.S. u16 116
Vernon, Il., U.S. E4 120
Vernon, In., U.S. G6 121
Vernon, Tx., U.S. B3 150
Vernon, Vt., U.S. F3 152
Vernon, co., La., U.S. C2 125
Vernon, co., Mo., U.S. D3 132
Vernon, co., Wi., U.S. E3 156
Vernon Bridge, P.E.I., Can. C7 101
Vernon Center, Mn., U.S. G4 130
Vernon Hills, Il., U.S. h9 120
Vernonia, Or., U.S. B3 144
Vernon River, P.E.I., Can. C7 101
Verny, Fr. C13 14
Vero Beach, Fl., U.S. E6 116
Véroia, Grc. I6 20
Verona, Ont., Can. C8 103
Verona, Italy D6 18
Verona, Il., U.S. B5 120
Verona, Ky., U.S. k13 124
Verona, Ms., U.S. A5 131
Verona, Mo., U.S. E4 132
Verona, N.J., U.S. B4 137
Verona, N.C., U.S. C5 140
Verona, N.D., U.S. C7 141
Verona, Pa., U.S. k14 145
Verona, Wi., U.S. F4 156
Verónica, Arg. H10 80
Verret, N.B., Can. B1 101
Verret, Lake, l., La., U.S. E4 125
Verrettes, Haiti E8 94
Versailles, Fr. D9 14
Versailles, Ct., U.S. C7 114
Versailles, Il., U.S. D3 120
Versailles, In., U.S. F7 121
Versailles, Ky., U.S. B5 124
Versailles, Mo., U.S. C5 132
Versailles, Oh., U.S. B1 142
Veršino-Darasunskij, U.S.S.R. G15 24
Vert, Cap, c., Sen. D1 64
Vertientes, Cuba D5 94
Vertou, Fr. E5 14
Verviers, Bel. G8 12
Vervins, Fr. C10 14
Vescovato, Fr. G4 18
Vesjegonsk, U.S.S.R. C20 26
Vesoul, Fr. E13 14
Vespasiano, Braz. E7 79
Vesper, Wi., U.S. D4 156
Vesta, C.R. H11 92
Vesta, Mn., U.S. F3 130
Vestaburg, Mi., U.S. E6 129
Vest-Agder, co., Nor. L10 6
Vestal, N.Y., U.S. C4 139
Vestal Center, N.Y., U.S. C4 139
Vestavia Hills, Al., U.S. g7 108
Vesterålen, is., Nor. G14 6
Vestfjorden, Nor. H14 6
Vestfold, co., Nor. L12 6
Vestmannaeyjar, Ice. C3 6a
Vesuvio, vol., Italy I9 18
Vesuvius, Va., U.S. C3 153
Vesuvius see Vesuvio, vol., Italy I9 18
Veszprém, Hung. H17 10
Veszprém, co., Hung. H17 10
Vésztő, Hung. I21 10
Veteran, Alta., Can. C5 98
Veteran, Wy., U.S. E8 157
Vetluga, U.S.S.R. F7 22
Vetralla, Italy G7 18
Vetrino, U.S.S.R. F11 26
Vetrișoaia, Rom. C12 20
Vetschau, Ger. D14 10
Veurne (Furnes), Bel. F2 12
Vevay, In., U.S. G7 121
Vevey, Switz. F6 13
Vézelise, Fr. D13 14
Viacha, Bol. G7 82
Viadana, Italy E5 18
Viadutos, Braz. D12 80
Viale, Arg. F8 80
Viamão, Braz. F13 80
Viamonte, Arg. G7 80
Vian, Ok., U.S. B7 143
Viana, Braz. D9 76
Viana do Alentejo, Port. G3 16
Viana do Castelo, Port. D3 16
Viangchan (Vientiane), Laos F7 40
Viangphoukha, Laos D6 40
Viareggio, Italy F5 18
Vibank, Sask., Can. G4 105
Viborg, Den. M11 6
Viborg, S.D., U.S. D8 148
Vibo Valentia, Italy K11 18
Vibraye, Fr. D7 14
Viburnum, Mo., U.S. D6 132
Vic (Vich), Spain D14 16
Vicam, Mex. D4 90
Vicco, Ky., U.S. C6 124
Vic-en-Bigorre, Fr. I7 14
Vicente, Point, c., Ca., U.S. n12 112
Vicente Guerrero, Mex. F8 90
Vicente López, Arg. H9 80
Vicente Noble, Dom. Rep. E9 94
Vicenza, Italy D6 18

Name	Map Ref.	Page
Vichada, dept., Col.	E8	84
Vichada, stm., Col.	E8	84
Vichadero, Ur.	F11	80
Vichigasta, Arg.	E5	80
Vichuquén, Chile	H2	80
Vichy, Fr.	F10	14
Vichy, Mo., U.S.	C6	132
Vici, Ok., U.S.	A2	143
Vicksburg, In., U.S.	F3	121
Vicksburg, Mi., U.S.	F5	129
Vicksburg, Ms., U.S.	C3	131
Vicksburg National Military Park, Ms., U.S.	C3	131
Vico, Fr.	L23	15a
Viçosa, Braz.	F7	79
Victor, Co., U.S.	C5	113
Victor, Id., U.S.	F7	119
Victor, Ia., U.S.	C5	122
Victor, Mt., U.S.	D2	133
Victor, N.Y., U.S.	C3	139
Victor Harbor, Austl.	J3	70
Victoria, Arg.	G8	80
Victoria, Cam.	I14	64
Victoria, B.C., Can.	E6	99
Victoria, Newf., Can.	E5	102
Victoria, P.E.I., Can.	C6	101
Victoria, Chile	J2	80
Victoria, Gren.	H14	94
Victoria (Xianggang), H.K.	M3	34
Victoria, Malay.	D6	38
Victoria, Sey.	B11	58
Victoria, Ar., U.S.	B5	111
Victoria, Il., U.S.	B3	120
Victoria, Ks., U.S.	D4	123
Victoria, Ms., U.S.	A4	131
Victoria, Mo., U.S.	C7	132
Victoria, Tx., U.S.	E4	150
Victoria, Va., U.S.	D4	153
Victoria, state, Austl.	G9	68
Victoria, co., Tx., U.S.	E4	150
Victoria, stm., Austl.	C6	68
Victoria, Lake, l., Afr.	B6	58
Victoria, Lake, l., Austl.	I4	70
Victoria, Mount, mtn., Burma	D2	40
Victoria, Mount, mtn., Pap. N. Gui.	A9	68
Victoria Beach, Man., Can.	D3	100
Victoria Falls, Zimb.	A7	66
Victoria Falls, wtfl, Afr.	A7	66
Victoria Harbour, Ont., Can.	C5	103
Victoria Island, i., N.W. Ter., Can.	B10	96
Victoria Lake, res., Newf., Can.	D3	102
Victoria Land, reg., Ant.	C8	73
Victoria Nile, stm., Ug.	H7	56
Victoria Peak, mtn., Belize	I15	90
Victoria River Downs, Austl.	C6	68
Victoria Road, Ont., Can.	C6	103
Victoria Strait, strt., N.W. Ter., Can.	C12	96
Victoriaville, Que., Can.	C6	104
Victoria West, S. Afr.	H6	66
Victorica, Arg.	I6	80
Victorino, Ven.	F9	84
Victorino de la Plaza, Arg.	I7	80
Victorville, Ca., U.S.	E5	112
Vičuga, U.S.S.R.	D24	26
Vicuña, Chile	F3	80
Vicuña Mackenna, Arg.	G6	80
Vidalia, Ga., U.S.	D4	117
Vidalia, La., U.S.	C4	125
Vidal Ramos, Braz.	D14	80
Vidauban, Fr.	I13	14
Videira, Braz.	D13	80
Vidette, Ga., U.S.	C4	117
Vidigueira, Port.	G4	16
Vidin, Bul.	F6	20
Vidisha, India	I7	44
Vidlica, U.S.S.R.	K23	6
Vidor, Tx., U.S.	D5	150
Vidzeme, hist. reg., U.S.S.R.	D8	26
Vidzy, U.S.S.R.	F9	26
Viechtach, Ger.	F12	10
Viedma, Arg.	E4	78
Viedma, Lago, l., Arg.	F2	78
Vieja, Sierra, mts., Tx., U.S.	o12	150
Viejo, Cerro, mtn., Peru	J3	84
Viekšniai, U.S.S.R.	E5	26
Viella, Spain	C12	16
Vienna, Ont., Can.	E4	103
Vienna, Ga., U.S.	D3	117
Vienna, Il., U.S.	F5	120
Vienna, La., U.S.	B3	125
Vienna, Mo., U.S.	C6	132
Vienna, S.D., U.S.	C8	148
Vienna, Va., U.S.	B5	153
Vienna, W.V., U.S.	B3	155
Vienna see Wien, Aus.	G16	10
Vienne, Fr.	G11	14
Vienne, dept., Fr.	F7	14
Vienne, stm., Fr.	E7	14
Vientiane see Viangchan, Laos	F7	40
Vieques, P.R.	E12	94
Vieques, Isla de, i., P.R.	E12	94
Vierfontein, S. Afr.	F8	66
Viersen, Ger.	D6	10
Vierwaldstättersee, l., Switz.	D9	13
Vierzon, Fr.	E9	14
Viesca, Mex.	E8	90
Viesīte, U.S.S.R.	E8	26
Vieste, Italy	H11	18
Vietnam, ctry., Asia	B4	38
Viet Tri, Viet.	D8	40
Vieux Desert, Lac, l., Wi., U.S.	B4	156
Vieux Fort, St. Luc.	H14	94
Vievis, U.S.S.R.	G7	26
Vieytes, Arg.	H10	80
Vigan, Phil.	M19	39b
Vigeland, Nor.	L10	6
Vigevano, Italy	D3	18
Vigneulles-lès-Hattonchâtel, Fr.	D12	14
Vignola, Italy	E6	18
Vigo, Spain	C3	16
Vigo, co., In., U.S.	F3	121
Vihowa, Pak.	E4	44
Viitasaari, Fin.	J19	6
Vijāpur, India	I5	44
Vijayawāda, India	D6	46
Vijosë (Aóös), stm., Eur.	I4	20
Viking, Alta., Can.	C5	98
Vikna, i., Nor.	C10	4
Vikramasingapuram, India	H4	46
Vila Brasil, Braz.	J14	82
Vila da Ribeira Brava, C.V.	k16	64a
Vila de Manica, Moz.	B11	66
Vila do Bispo, Port.	H3	16
Vila Fontes, Moz.	A12	66
Vilafranca del Penedès, Spain	D13	16
Vila Gomes da Costa, Moz.	E11	66
Viļaka, U.S.S.R.	D10	26
Vilama, Laguna de, l., Arg.	B5	80
Vila Machado, Moz.	B12	66
Vilanculos, Moz.	D12	66
Viļāni, U.S.S.R.	E9	26
Vila Nova de Foz Côa, Port.	D4	16
Vila Nova de Gaia, Port.	D3	16
Vilanova i la Geltrú, Spain	D13	16
Vila Novo de Ourém, Port.	F3	16
Vila Paiva de Andrada, Moz.	B12	66
Vila Real, Port.	D4	16
Vila Real de Santo António, Port.	H4	16
Vilar Formoso, Port.	E5	16
Vila Rica, Braz.	I12	84
Vilas, Co., U.S.	D8	113
Vilas, co., Wi., U.S.	B4	156
Vila Velha, Braz.	F8	79
Vila Velha de Ródão, Port.	F4	16
Vila Verde, Port.	D3	16
Vîlcea, co., Rom.	E8	20
Vilejka, U.S.S.R.	G9	26
Vilelas, Arg.	D7	80
Vilhelmina, Swe.	I15	6
Vilhena, Braz.	E11	82
Viljandi, U.S.S.R.	C8	26
Viljoenskroon, S. Afr.	F8	66
Vilkaviškis, U.S.S.R.	G6	26
Vil'kickogo, ostrov, i., U.S.S.R.	C13	22
Vil'kickogo, proliv, strt., U.S.S.R.	B18	22
Vilkija, U.S.S.R.	F6	26
Vilkovo, U.S.S.R.	D13	20
Villa Abecia, Bol.	I9	82
Villa Aberastain, Arg.	F4	80
Villa Alberdi, Arg.	D6	80
Villa Alemana, Chile	G3	80
Villa Allende, Arg.	F6	80
Villa Ana, Arg.	E9	80
Villa Ángela, Arg.	D8	80
Villa Atamisqui, Arg.	E7	80
Villa Atuel, Arg.	H5	80
Villa Bella, Bol.	D9	82
Villa Berthet, Arg.	D8	80
Villa Bruzual, Ven.	C8	84
Villa Bustos, Arg.	E5	80
Villa Cañás, Arg.	H8	80
Villacañas, Spain	F8	16
Villa Carlos Paz, Arg.	F6	80
Villacarrillo, Spain	G8	16
Villa Castelli, Arg.	E4	80
Villach, Aus.	I13	10
Villacidro, Italy	J3	18
Villa Comaltitlan, Mex.	B2	92
Villa Concepción del Tío, Arg.	F7	80
Villa Constitución, Arg.	G8	80
Villada, Spain	C7	16
Villa de Arista, Mex.	F9	90
Villa de Arriaga, Mex.	G9	90
Villa de Cos, Mex.	F8	90
Villa de Cura, Ven.	B9	84
Villa del Carmen, Arg.	G6	80
Villa del Rosario, Arg.	F7	80
Villa del Rosario, Arg.	F10	80
Villa de María, Arg.	E7	80
Villa de Nova Sintra, C.V.	m16	64a
Villa de San Antonio, Hond.	C7	92
Villa de San Francisco, Hond.	C8	92
Villa de Soto, Arg.	F6	80
Villa Diego, Arg.	G8	80
Villadiego, Spain	C7	16
Villa Dolores, Arg.	F6	80
Villa El Alto, Arg.	E6	80
Villa Elisa, Arg.	G9	80
Villa Eufronio Viscarra, Bol.	G9	82
Villa Flores, Mex.	I13	90
Villa Florida, Para.	D10	80
Villafranca de los Barros, Spain	G5	16
Villafranca di Verona, Italy	D5	18
Village, Ar., U.S.	D2	111
Village Creek, stm., Al., U.S.	f7	108
Villa General Roca, Arg.	G5	80
Village Springs, Al., U.S.	B3	108
Villagrán, Mex.	E10	90
Villa Grove, Il., U.S.	D5	120
Villaguay, Arg.	F9	80
Villa Guerrero, Mex.	H10	90
Villa Guillermina, Arg.	E9	80
Villa Hayes, Para.	C10	80
Villahermosa, Mex.	I13	90
Villa Hernandarias, Arg.	F9	80
Villa Hidalgo, Mex.	G8	90
Villa Huidobro, Arg.	H6	80
Villaines-la-Juhel, Fr.	D6	14
Villa Insurgentes, Mex.	E4	90
Villa Iris, Arg.	J7	80
Villa Juárez, Mex.	D5	90
Villa Krause, Arg.	F4	80
Villa La Paz, Arg.	G5	80
Villa Larca, Arg.	G6	80
Villa Larroque, Arg.	G9	80
Villaldama, Mex.	D9	90
Villalonga, Arg.	D4	78
Villa Mainero, Mex.	E10	90
Villa María, Arg.	G7	80
Villa María Grande, Arg.	F9	80
Villa Martín, Bol.	I8	82
Villa Matoque, Arg.	C7	80
Villa Mazán, Arg.	E5	80
Villa Media Agua, Arg.	F4	80
Villa Mercedes, Arg.	F4	80
Villamil, Ec.	J13	84a
Villa Montes, Bol.	I10	82
Villa Nueva, Arg.	G7	80
Villa Nueva, Arg.	G4	80
Villanueva, Col.	B6	84
Villa Nueva, Guat.	C4	92
Villanueva, Hond.	B6	92
Villanueva, Mex.	F8	90
Villa Nueva, Nic.	E8	92
Villanueva, N.M., U.S.	B4	138
Villanueva de Córdoba, Spain	G7	16
Villanueva de la Serana, Spain	G6	16
Villanueva del Río y Minas, Spain	H6	16
Villa Ocampo, Arg.	E9	80
Villa Ojo de Agua, Arg.	E7	80
Villa Oliva, Para.	D10	80
Villa Park, Il., U.S.	k8	120
Villapinzón, Col.	E6	84
Villa Quinteros, Arg.	D6	80
Villa Ramírez, Arg.	G8	80
Villarcayo, Spain	C8	16
Villa Regina, Arg.	J5	80
Villa Reynolds, Arg.	G6	80
Villa Rica, Ga., U.S.	C2	117
Villa Ridge, Il., U.S.	F4	120
Villa Ridge, Mo., U.S.	C7	132
Villa Rivero, Bol.	G9	82
Villa Rosario, Col.	D6	84
Villarrica, Chile	D2	78
Villarrica, Col.	F5	84
Villarrica, Para.	C10	80
Villarrobledo, Spain	F9	16
Villas, N.J., U.S.	E3	137
Villa Sandino, Nic.	E10	92
Villa San José, Arg.	G9	80
Villa San Martín, Arg.	E6	80
Villa Santa, Montaña, mtn., Hond.	C8	92
Villa Santo Domingo, Mex.	F9	90
Villasayas, Spain	D9	16
Villa Serrano, Bol.	H9	82
Villasimius, Italy	J4	18
Villasor, Italy	J3	18
Villa Tunari, Bol.	G9	82
Villa Unión, Arg.	E4	80
Villa Unión, Arg.	E7	80
Villa Unión, Mex.	F6	90
Villa Unión, Mex.	C9	90
Villa Vaca Guzmán, Bol.	H10	82
Villa Valeria, Arg.	H6	80
Villavicencio, Col.	E6	84
Villaviciosa, Spain	B6	16
Villazón, Bol.	J9	82
Villa Zorraquín, Arg.	F9	80
Villé, Fr.	D14	14
Villedieu, Fr.	D5	14
Villefort, Fr.	H10	14
Villefranche, Fr.	G11	14
Villena, Spain	G11	16
Villeneuve-d'Aveyron, Fr.	H9	14
Villeneuve-Saint-Georges, Fr.	D9	14
Villeneuve-sur-Lot, Fr.	H7	14
Ville Platte, La., U.S.	D3	125
Villers-Bocage, Fr.	C9	14
Villers-Bocage, Fr.	C6	14
Villersexel, Fr.	E13	14
Villerupt, Fr.	C12	14
Ville Saint-Georges, Que., Can.	C7	104
Villeta, Col.	E5	84
Villeurbanne, Fr.	G11	14
Villiers, S. Afr.	F9	66
Villingen-Schwenningen, Ger.	G8	10
Villisca, Ia., U.S.	D3	122
Vilna, Alta., Can.	B5	98
Vilnius, U.S.S.R.	G8	26
Vilonia, Ar., U.S.	B3	111
Vilshofen, Ger.	G13	10
Vil'uj, stm., U.S.S.R.	E16	24
Vil'ujsk, U.S.S.R.	E16	24
Vil'ujskoje vodochranilišče, res., U.S.S.R.	E20	22
Vimianzo, Spain	B2	16
Vimoutiers, Fr.	D7	14
Vimperk, Czech.	F13	10
Vina, Al., U.S.	A1	108
Vina, Ca., U.S.	C2	112
Vina, stm., Cam.	G9	54
Viñac, Peru	E4	82
Viña del Mar, Chile	G3	80
Vinalhaven, Me., U.S.	D4	126
Vinalhaven Island, i., Me., U.S.	D4	126
Vinaròs, Spain	E12	16
Vincennes, In., U.S.	G2	121
Vincennes Bay, b., Ant.	B6	73
Vincent, Al., U.S.	B3	108
Vincentown, N.J., U.S.	D3	137
Vinces, Ec.	H3	84
Vinces, stm., Ec.	H3	84
Vinchina, Arg.	E4	80
Vinchos, Peru	E4	82
Vindhya Range, mts., India	I7	44
Vine Brook, stm., Ma., U.S.	g11	128
Vinegar Hill, mtn., Or., U.S.	C8	144
Vine Grove, Ky., U.S.	C4	124
Vineland, N.J., U.S.	E2	137
Vinemont, Al., U.S.	A3	108
Vineyard Haven, Ma., U.S.	D6	128
Vineyard Sound, strt., Ma., U.S.	D6	128
Ving Ngün, Burma	C5	40
Vinh, Viet.	E8	40
Vinh Long, Viet.	I8	40
Vinita, Ok., U.S.	A6	143
Vinkovci, Yugo.	D2	20
Vinnica, U.S.S.R.	H3	22
Vinogradov, U.S.S.R.	A7	20
Vinson Massif, mtn., Ant.	C12	73
Vinton, Ia., U.S.	B5	122
Vinton, La., U.S.	D2	125
Vinton, Va., U.S.	C3	153
Vinton, co., Oh., U.S.	C3	142
Viny, U.S.S.R.	C15	26
Viola, Ar., U.S.	A4	111
Viola, De., U.S.	D3	115
Viola, Id., U.S.	C1	119
Viola, Il., U.S.	B3	120
Viola, Ks., U.S.	E6	123
Viola, Wi., U.S.	E3	156
Violet, La., U.S.	k12	125
Violín, Isla, i., C.R.	I11	92
Vipiteno, Italy	C6	18
Vipos, Arg.	D6	80
Virac, Phil.	C7	38
Virac, Phil.	M19	39b
Viradouro, Braz.	F4	79
Viramgām, India	I5	44
Viranşehir, Tur.	C5	48
Virbalis, U.S.S.R.	G5	26
Virden, Man., Can.	E1	100
Virden, Il., U.S.	D4	120
Virden, N.M., U.S.	E1	138
Vire, Fr.	D6	14
Virelles, Bel.	H5	12
Vîrfurile, Rom.	C6	20
Virgem da Lapa, Braz.	D7	79
Virgin, Ut., U.S.	F2	151
Virgin, stm., U.S.	G8	135
Virgin Gorda, i., Br. Vir. Is.	E12	94
Virginia, S. Afr.	G8	66
Virginia, Al., U.S.	g6	108
Virginia, Il., U.S.	D3	120
Virginia, Mn., U.S.	C6	130
Virginia, state, U.S.	C4	153
Virginia Beach, Va., U.S.	D7	153
Virginia City, Mt., U.S.	E5	133
Virginia City, Nv., U.S.	D2	135
Virginia Falls, wtfl, N.W. Ter., Can.	D7	96
Virginia Peak, mtn., Nv., U.S.	D2	135
Virgin Islands, dep., N.A.	E12	94
Virgin Mountains, mts., U.S.	A1	110
Virginópolis, Braz.	E7	79
Virgolândia, Braz.	E7	79
Virôchey, Camb.	H9	40
Virojoki, Fin.	K20	6
Viroqua, Wi., U.S.	E3	156
Virovitica, Yugo.	D12	18
Virrat, Fin.	J18	6
Virtaniemi, Fin.	G21	6
Vîrtopu, Rom.	E7	20
Virtsu, U.S.S.R.	C6	26
Virú, Peru	C2	82
Virudunagar, India	H4	46
Virungu, Zaire	C5	58
Viru-Nigula, U.S.S.R.	B9	26
Vis, Yugo.	F11	18
Vis (Fish), stm., Nmb.	E3	66
Vis, Otok, i., Yugo.	F11	18
Visalia, Ca., U.S.	D4	112
Visalia, Ky., U.S.	k14	124
Visayan Sea, Phil.	C7	38
Visby, Swe.	M16	6
Viscount, Sask., Can.	F3	105
Viscount Melville Sound, strt., N.W. Ter., Can.	B11	96
Visé (Wezet), Bel.	G8	12
Višegrad, Yugo.	F3	20
Viseu, Port.	E4	16
Vishākhapatnam, India	D7	46
Vislinskij zaliv, b., Eur.	A19	10
Visnagar, India	I5	44
Viso, Monte, mtn., Italy	E2	18
Visoko, Yugo.	F2	20
Visokoi Island, i., Falk. Is.	A2	73
Visp, Switz.	F8	13
Visselhövede, Ger.	C9	10
Vista, Man., Can.	D1	100
Vista, Ca., U.S.	F5	112
Vista Alegre, Arg.	J4	80
Vista Flores, Arg.	G4	80
Vistula see Wisła, stm., Pol.	A18	10
Vita, Man., Can.	E3	100
Vita, stm., Col.	E8	84
Vitarte, Peru	E3	82
Vitebsk, U.S.S.R.	F13	26
Viterbo, Italy	G7	18
Vitichi, Bol.	I9	82
Viti Levu, i., Fiji	J21	158
Vitim, stm., U.S.S.R.	F14	24
Vítor, Peru	G6	82
Vitor, stm., Peru	G5	82
Vitória, Braz.	G10	74
Vitória, Braz.	F8	79
Vitoria (Gasteiz), Spain	C9	16
Vitória da Conquista, Braz.	C8	79
Vitré, Fr.	D5	14
Vitry-le-François, Fr.	D11	14
Vittangi, Swe.	H17	6
Vitteaux, Fr.	E11	14
Vittel, Fr.	D12	14
Vittoria, Ont., Can.	E4	103
Vittoria, Italy	M9	18
Vittorio Veneto, Italy	D7	18
Viver, Spain	F11	16
Vivi, stm., U.S.S.R.	D17	22
Vivian, La., U.S.	B2	125
Vivian, S.D., U.S.	D5	148
Vivoratá, Arg.	I10	80
Vivorillo, Cayos, is., Hond.	B11	92
Vizcaíno, Desierto de, des., Mex.	D3	90
Vize, Tur.	H11	20
Vize, ostrov, i., U.S.S.R.	B13	22
Vizianagaram, India	C7	46
Vižnica, U.S.S.R.	A9	20
Vizzini, Italy	L9	18
Vlaardingen, Neth.	E5	12
Vladikavkaz, U.S.S.R.	I6	22
Vladimir, U.S.S.R.	E23	26
Vladimirskij Tupik, U.S.S.R.	F16	26
Vladivostok, U.S.S.R.	I18	24
Vlasenica, Yugo.	E2	20
Vlasotince, Yugo.	G6	20
Vlieland, i., Neth.	B7	12
Vlissingen (Flushing), Neth.	F4	12
Vlonë see Vlorë, Alb.	I3	20
Vlorë, Alb.	I3	20
Vlorës, Gji i, b., Alb.	I3	20
Vltava, stm., Czech.	F14	10
Vnukovo, U.S.S.R.	F20	26
Vochtoga, U.S.S.R.	C24	26
Vodlozero, ozero, l., U.S.S.R.	J25	6
Vodňany, Czech.	F14	10
Vogelsberg, mts., Ger.	E9	10
Voghera, Italy	E4	18
Vohenstrauss, Ger.	F12	10
Vohibinany, Madag.	Q23	67b
Vohilava, Madag.	R23	67b
Vohimarina, Madag.	N24	67b
Vohipeno, Madag.	S22	67b
Võhma, U.S.S.R.	C8	26
Void, Fr.	D12	14
Voinjama, Lib.	G5	64
Voiron, Fr.	G12	14
Voitsberg, Aus.	H15	10
Voj-Vož, U.S.S.R.	E8	22
Volary, Czech.	G13	10
Volcán, Arg.	B6	80
Volcán, Pan.	C1	84
Volcano, Hi., U.S.	D6	118
Volcán Poás, Parque Nacional, C.R.	G10	92
Volchov, U.S.S.R.	B15	26
Volchov, stm., U.S.S.R.	B15	26
Volčje, U.S.S.R.	F22	10
Volga, U.S.S.R.	D21	26
Volga, Ia., U.S.	B6	122
Volga, S.D., U.S.	C9	148
Volga, stm., U.S.S.R.	H7	22
Volgino, U.S.S.R.	C16	26
Volgo-Baltijskij kanal, U.S.S.R.	L26	6
Volgodonsk, U.S.S.R.	H6	22
Volgograd (Stalingrad), U.S.S.R.	H6	22
Volgogradskoje vodochranilišče, res., U.S.S.R.	H7	22
Volin, S.D., U.S.	E8	148
Volkach, Ger.	F10	10
Völkermarkt, Aus.	I14	10
Völklingen, Ger.	F6	10
Volkovysk, U.S.S.R.	H7	26
Volksrust, S. Afr.	F9	66
Volockaja, U.S.S.R.	A25	26
Volodarsk, U.S.S.R.	E26	26
Volodarskoje, U.S.S.R.	G11	22
Vologda, U.S.S.R.	B22	26
Vologda, stm., U.S.S.R.	B22	26
Volokolamsk, U.S.S.R.	E18	26
Volontirovka, U.S.S.R.	C13	20
Vólos, Grc.	J6	20
Volosovo, U.S.S.R.	B12	26
Volot, U.S.S.R.	D13	26
Volovec, U.S.S.R.	A7	20
Volovo, U.S.S.R.	H21	26
Voložin, U.S.S.R.	G9	26
Vol'sk, U.S.S.R.	G7	22
Volta, Lake, res., Ghana	H9	64
Volta Blanche (White Volta), stm., Afr.	F6	54
Volta Grande, Braz.	F7	79
Volta Noire (Black Volta), stm., Afr.	F6	54
Volta Redonda, Braz.	G6	79
Volta Rouge, stm., Afr.	F9	64
Volterra, Italy	F5	18
Voltri, Italy	E3	18
Volusia, co., Fl., U.S.	C5	116
Volyně, Czech.	F13	10
Volžsk, U.S.S.R.	F7	22
Volžskij, U.S.S.R.	H6	22
Vona, Co., U.S.	B8	113
Vonda, Sask., Can.	E2	105
Vondrozo, Madag.	S22	67b
Von Frank Mountain, mtn., Ak., U.S.	C9	109
Vonore, Tn., U.S.	D9	149
Von Ormy, Tx., U.S.	k7	150
Vopnafjörður, Ice.	B6	6a
Vorarlberg, state, Aus.	H9	10
Vorau, Aus.	H15	10
Vorden, Neth.	D9	12
Vorder-Grauspitz, mtn., Eur.	D12	13
Vorderrhein, stm., Switz.	E10	13
Vordingborg, Den.	N12	6
Vorga, U.S.S.R.	H15	26
Voríai Sporádhes, is., Grc.	J7	20
Vorkuta, U.S.S.R.	D10	22
Vormsi, i., U.S.S.R.	B6	26
Vorob'jovo, U.S.S.R.	B23	26
Vorochta, U.S.S.R.	A8	20
Voronež, U.S.S.R.	G5	22
Voronkovo, U.S.S.R.	B13	20
Voronovo, U.S.S.R.	G8	26
Voropajevo, U.S.S.R.	F10	26
Voroshilovsk see Stavropol', U.S.S.R.	H6	22
Vorošilovgrad see Lugansk, U.S.S.R.	H5	22
Vorpommern, hist. reg., Ger.	B13	10
Vorsma, U.S.S.R.	F26	26
Võrtsjärv, l., U.S.S.R.	C9	26
Võru, U.S.S.R.	D10	26
Vosges, dept., Fr.	D13	14
Vosges, mts., Fr.	D14	14
Voskresensk, U.S.S.R.	F21	26
Voskresenskoje, U.S.S.R.	B20	26
Voskresenskoje, U.S.S.R.	D20	26
Voss, Nor.	K10	6
Vossburg, Ms., U.S.	D5	131
Vostočno-Sibirskoje more (East Siberian Sea), U.S.S.R.	C23	24
Vostočnyj Sajan, mts., U.S.S.R.	G11	24
Vostok, sci., Ant.	C6	73
Votkinsk, U.S.S.R.	F8	22
Votuporanga, Braz.	F4	79
Voulou, Cen. Afr. Rep.	M2	60
Vouziers, Fr.	C11	14
Voves, Fr.	D8	14
Voyageurs National Park, Mn., U.S.	B5	130
Vože, ozero, l., U.S.S.R.	K26	6
Vožega, U.S.S.R.	A23	26
Voznesensk, U.S.S.R.	H4	22
Voznesenskoje, U.S.S.R.	G25	26
Vraca, Bul.	F7	20
Vrådal, Nor.	L11	6
Vrancea, co., Rom.	D10	20
Vrangel'a, ostrov, i., U.S.S.R.	C28	24
Vranje, Yugo.	G5	20
Vrbas, Yugo.	D3	20
Vrede, S. Afr.	F9	66
Vredenburg, S. Afr.	I3	66
Vredenburgh, Al., U.S.	D2	108
Vredendal, S. Afr.	H4	66
Vreed en Hoop, Guy.	D13	84
Vrin, Switz.	E11	13
Vrindāvan, India	G7	44
Vrondádhes, Grc.	K10	20
Vršac, Yugo.	D5	20
Vryburg, S. Afr.	F7	66
Vryheid, S. Afr.	F10	66
Vsetín, Czech.	F17	10
Vsevidof, Mount, mtn., Ak., U.S.	E6	109
Vsevoložsk, U.S.S.R.	A13	26
Vtoryje Levyje Lamki, U.S.S.R.	H24	26
Vukovar, Yugo.	D3	20
Vulcan, Alta., Can.	D4	98
Vulcan, Rom.	D7	20
Vulkanešty, U.S.S.R.	D12	20
Vung Tau, Viet.	I9	40
Vuohijärvi, Fin.	K20	6
Vuoksenniska, Fin.	K21	6
Vuotso, Fin.	G20	6
Vuyyūru, India	D6	46
Vyborg, U.S.S.R.	A11	26
Vyborgskij zaliv, b., U.S.S.R.	A11	26
Vyčegda, stm., U.S.S.R.	E7	22
Vygoniči, U.S.S.R.	H17	26
Vygozero, ozero, l., U.S.S.R.	J24	6
Vyksa, U.S.S.R.	F25	26
Vypolzovo, U.S.S.R.	D16	26
Vyrica, U.S.S.R.	B13	26
Vyša, U.S.S.R.	H25	26
Vyšgorodok, U.S.S.R.	D11	26
Vyškov, Czech.	F17	10
Vyškov, U.S.S.R.	I14	26
Vyšnij Voločok, U.S.S.R.	D17	26
Vysock, U.S.S.R.	A11	26
Vysoké Tatry, mts., Eur.	F20	10
Vysokiniči, U.S.S.R.	G19	26
Vysokogornyj, U.S.S.R.	G19	24
Vysokoje, U.S.S.R.	E17	26
Vysokoje, U.S.S.R.	I6	26
Vysokovsk, U.S.S.R.	E19	26
Vyšší Brod, Czech.	G14	10
Vytegra, U.S.S.R.	E5	22
W		
Wa, Ghana	F8	64
Waal, stm., Neth.	E7	12
Waao, China	B8	40
Waawaa, Puu, mtn., Hi., U.S.	D6	118
Wabag, Pap. N. Gui.	G11	38
Wabamun, Alta., Can.	C3	98
Wabana (Bell Island), Newf., Can.	E5	102
Wabasca, Alta., Can.	B4	98
Wabasca, stm., Alta., Can.	f1	98
Wabash, In., U.S.	C6	121
Wabash, co., Il., U.S.	E6	120
Wabash, co., In., U.S.	C6	121
Wabash, stm., U.S.	H2	121
Wabasha, Mn., U.S.	F6	130
Wabasha, co., Mn., U.S.	F6	130
Wabasso, Fl., U.S.	E6	116
Wabasso, Mn., U.S.	F3	130
Wabaunsee, co., Ks., U.S.	D7	123
Wabbaseka, Ar., U.S.	C4	111
Wabeno, Wi., U.S.	C5	156
Wabigoon, Ont., Can.	E5	100
Wabowden, Man., Can.	B2	100
Wąbrzeźno, Pol.	B18	10
Wabush, Newf., Can.	h8	102
Wabuska, Nv., U.S.	D2	135
Waccamaw, stm., U.S.	D9	147
Waccamaw, Lake, l., N.C., U.S.	C4	140
Waccasassa Bay, b., Fl., U.S.	C4	116
Wachapreague, Va., U.S.	C7	153
Wachusett Mountain, mtn., Ma., U.S.	B4	128
Wachusett Reservoir, res., Ma., U.S.	B4	128
Waco, Ga., U.S.	C1	117
Waco, Ne., U.S.	D8	134
Waco, Tx., U.S.	D4	150
Waco Lake, res., Tx., U.S.	D4	150
Waconda Lake, res., Ks., U.S.	C5	123
Waconia, Mn., U.S.	F5	130
Wad Al-Ḥaddād, Sud.	K7	60
Wad Bandah, Sud.	K4	60
Wad Ban Naqa, Sud.	I7	60
Waddell, Az., U.S.	D3	110
Waddenzee, Neth.	B7	12
Waddington, N.Y., U.S.	f9	139
Waddington, Mount, mtn., B.C., Can.	D5	99
Waddy, Ky., U.S.	B4	124
Wade, Mount, mtn., Ant.	D9	73
Wadena, Sask., Can.	F4	105
Wadena, Ia., U.S.	B6	122
Wadena, Mn., U.S.	D3	130
Wadena, co., Mn., U.S.	D4	130
Wädenswil, Switz.	D10	13
Wadesboro, N.C., U.S.	C2	140
Wadesville, In., U.S.	H2	121
Wad Ḥāmid, Sud.	I7	60
Wādī as-Sīr, Jord.	E5	50
Wādī Ḥalfā', Sud.	G6	60
Wading, stm., N.J., U.S.	D3	137
Wading, West Branch, stm., N.J., U.S.	D3	137
Wadley, Al., U.S.	B4	108
Wadley, Ga., U.S.	D4	117
Wad Madanī, Sud.	J7	60
Wadmalaw Island, i., S.C., U.S.	F7	147
Wadowice, Pol.	F19	10
Wadsworth, Il., U.S.	h9	120
Wadsworth, Nv., U.S.	D2	135
Wadsworth, Oh., U.S.	A4	142
Waegwan, S. Kor.	H16	32
Waelder, Tx., U.S.	E4	150
Wafang, China	B6	32
Wafrah, Kuw.	G10	48
Wagarville, Al., U.S.	D1	108
Wagener, S.C., U.S.	D5	147
Wageningen, Neth.	E8	12
Wageningen, Sur.	E14	84
Wager Bay, b., N.W. Ter., Can.	C15	96
Wagga Wagga, Austl.	J7	70
Waggoner, Il., U.S.	D4	120
Wagin, Austl.	F3	68
Waging am See, Ger.	H12	10
Wagner, S.D., U.S.	D7	148
Wagoner, Ok., U.S.	B6	143
Wagoner, co., Ok., U.S.	B6	143
Wagon Mound, N.M., U.S.	A5	138
Wagontire Mountain, mtn., Or., U.S.	D7	144
Wagram, N.C., U.S.	C3	140
Wągrowiec, Pol.	C17	10
Waha, Libya	C4	56
Wāh Cantonment, Pak.	D5	44
Wahiawa, Hi., U.S.	B3	118
Wahiawa Reservoir, res., Hi., U.S.	g9	118
Wahkiakum, co., Wa., U.S.	C2	154
Wahkon, Mn., U.S.	D5	130
Wahoo, Ne., U.S.	C9	134
Wahoo Creek, stm., Ne., U.S.	g11	134
Wahpeton, N.D., U.S.	C9	141

Name | Map Ref. | Page

Wahran (Oran), Alg. C10 62
Wah Wah Mountains, mts., Ut., U.S. E2 151
Wahweap Creek, stm., Ut., U.S. F4 151
Waialua, Hi., U.S. B3 118
Waialua Bay, b., Hi., U.S. B3 118
Waianae, Hi., U.S. B3 118
Waianae Range, mts., Hi., U.S. f9 118
Waiau, N.Z. E4 72
Waiawa Stream, stm., Hi., U.S. g10 118
Waiblingen, Ger. G9 10
Waidhofen an der Thaya, Aus. G15 10
Waidhofen an der Ybbs, Aus. H14 10
Waigeo, Pulau, i., Indon. F9 38
Waihee, Hi., U.S. C5 118
Waihi, N.Z. B5 72
Waikapu, Hi., U.S. C5 118
Waikato, stm., N.Z. C5 72
Waikerie, Austl. J3 70
Waikiki Beach, Hi., U.S. g10 118
Wailea, Hi., U.S. D6 118
Wailua, Hi., U.S. A2 118
Wailuku, Hi., U.S. C5 118
Wailuku, stm., Hi., U.S. D6 118
Waimanalo, Hi., U.S. B4 118
Waimanalo Bay, b., Hi., U.S. g11 118
Waimate, N.Z. F3 72
Waimea, Hi., U.S. f9 118
Waimea, Hi., U.S. B2 118
Wainganga, stm., India C6 46
Waingapu, Indon. G7 38
Waini, stm., Guy. D13 84
Wainwright, Alta., Can. C5 98
Wainwright, Ak., U.S. A8 109
Wainwright, Ok., U.S. B6 143
Waiohinu, Hi., U.S. D6 118
Waipahu, Hi., U.S. B3 118
Waipara, N.Z. E4 72
Waipio Acres, Hi., U.S. g9 118
Waipio Peninsula, pen., Hi., U.S. g10 118
Waipukurau, N.Z. C6 72
Wairoa, N.Z. C6 72
Waitara, N.Z. C5 72
Waite Park, Mn., U.S. E4 130
Waits, stm., Vt., U.S. C4 152
Waitsburg, Wa., U.S. C7 154
Waitsfield, Vt., U.S. C3 152
Waiuku, N.Z. B5 72
Wajima, Japan J11 36
Waka, Eth. N9 60
Wakarusa, In., U.S. A5 121
Wakarusa, Ks., U.S. D8 123
Wakarusa, stm., Ks., U.S. D8 123
Wakatomika Creek, stm., Oh., U.S. B3 142
Wakaw, Sask., Can. E3 105
Wakayama, Japan M10 36
Wake, co., N.C., U.S. B4 140
Wa Keeney, Ks., U.S. C4 123
Wakefield, Que., Can. D2 104
Wakefield, Ks., U.S. C6 123
Wakefield, Ma., U.S. B5 128
Wakefield, Mi., U.S. n12 129
Wakefield, Ne., U.S. B9 134
Wakefield, N.H., U.S. C4 136
Wakefield, R.I., U.S. F3 146
Wakefield, Va., U.S. D6 153
Wake Forest, N.C., U.S. B4 140
Wake Island, dep., Oc. E24 2
Wakema, Burma F3 40
Wakeman, Oh., U.S. A3 142
Wakita, Ok., U.S. A4 143
Wakkanai, Japan B16 36a
Wakonda, S.D., U.S. D8 148
Wakpala, S.D., U.S. B5 148
Wakuach, Lac, l., Que., Can. g8 102
Waku Kundo, Ang. D3 58
Wakulla, co., Fl., U.S. B2 116
Walbridge, Oh., U.S. e6 142
Wałbrzych (Waldenburg), Pol. E16 10
Walcha, Austl. H9 70
Walcheren, i., Neth. E4 12
Walcott, Ar., U.S. A5 111
Walcott, Ia., U.S. C7 122
Walcott, N.D., U.S. C9 141
Walcott, Lake, res., Id., U.S. G5 119
Wałcz, Pol. B16 10
Wald, Switz. D10 13
Waldbillig, Lux. I9 12
Waldeck, Sask., Can. G2 105
Waldeck, Ger. D9 10
Walden, Ont., Can. A3 103
Walden, Co., U.S. A4 113
Walden, N.Y., U.S. D6 139
Waldenburg, Ar., U.S. B5 111
Walden Pond, l., Ma., U.S. g10 128
Walden Ridge, mtn., Tn., U.S. D8 149
Waldheim, Sask., Can. E2 105
Waldkirchen, Ger. G13 10
Waldmünchen, Ger. F12 10
Waldo, Ar., U.S. D2 111
Waldo, Fl., U.S. C4 116
Waldo, co., Me., U.S. D3 126
Waldoboro, Me., U.S. D3 126
Waldo Lake, l., Ma., U.S. h11 128
Waldo Lake, l., Or., U.S. D4 144
Waldport, Or., U.S. C2 144
Waldron, Ar., U.S. C1 111
Waldron, In., U.S. F6 121
Waldron, Mi., U.S. G6 129
Waldron, Mo., U.S. h10 132
Waldshut, Ger. H8 10
Waldviertel, reg., Aus. G15 10
Waldwick, N.J., U.S. A4 137
Walenstadt, Switz. D11 13
Wales, Ak., U.S. B6 109
Wales, ter., U.K. I10 8
Wales Island, i., N.W. Ter., Can. C15 96
Waleska, Ga., U.S. B2 117
Walford Station, Ont., Can. A2 103
Walgett, Austl. H8 70
Walgreen Coast, Ant. C11 73
Walhalla, Mi., U.S. E4 129
Walhalla, N.D., U.S. A8 141
Walhalla, S.C., U.S. B1 147
Walhonding, stm., Oh., U.S. B3 142
Walker, Ia., U.S. B6 122
Walker, La., U.S. g10 125
Walker, Mi., U.S. E5 129
Walker, Mn., U.S. C4 130
Walker, Mo., U.S. D3 132
Walker, co., Al., U.S. B2 108
Walker, co., Ga., U.S. B1 117
Walker, co., Tx., U.S. D5 150
Walker, stm., Nv., U.S. D3 135
Walker Lake, l., Man., Can. B3 100
Walker Lake, l., Nv., U.S. E3 135
Walker Mountain, mtn., Ga., U.S. B3 117
Walker Mountain, mtn., Va., U.S. C1 153
Walker River Indian Reservation, Nv., U.S. D3 135
Walker Springs, Al., U.S. D2 108
Walkersville, Md., U.S. B3 127
Walkerton, Ont., Can. C3 103
Walkerton, In., U.S. B5 121
Walkertown, N.C., U.S. A2 140
Walkerville, Mt., U.S. D4 133
Wall, S.D., U.S. D3 148
Wallace, N.S., Can. D6 101
Wallace, Id., U.S. B3 119
Wallace, Ne., U.S. D4 134
Wallace, N.C., U.S. C5 140
Wallace, S.D., U.S. B8 148
Wallace, W.V., U.S. B4 155
Wallace, co., Ks., U.S. D2 123
Wallaceburg, Ont., Can. E2 103
Wallace Lake, res., La., U.S. B2 125
Wallacetown, Ont., Can. E3 103
Wallachia, hist. reg., Rom. E8 20
Walland, Tn., U.S. D10 149
Wallangarra, Austl. G9 70
Wallaroo, Austl. I2 70
Walla Walla, Wa., U.S. C7 154
Walla Walla, co., Wa., U.S. C7 154
Walla Walla, stm., U.S. C7 154
Walled Lake, Mi., U.S. o15 129
Wallen, In., U.S. B7 121
Wallenpaupack, Lake, l., Pa., U.S. D11 145
Wallen Ridge, mtn., Tn., U.S. C10 149
Waller, Tx., U.S. q14 150
Waller, co., Tx., U.S. E4 150
Wallingford, Ct., U.S. D4 114
Wallingford, Vt., U.S. E3 152
Walling Mountain, mtn., Ma., U.S. B1 128
Wallington, N.J., U.S. h8 137
Wallis, Tx., U.S. E4 150
Wallis and Futuna, dep., Oc. G1 2
Wallisellen, Switz. D10 13
Wallis Sands, N.H., U.S. D5 136
Wallkill, N.Y., U.S. D6 139
Wallkill, stm., N.Y., U.S. D6 139
Wall Lake, Ia., U.S. B2 122
Wall Lake, l., Ia., U.S. B4 122
Walloomsac, stm., U.S. F2 152
Walloon Lake, l., Mi., U.S. C6 129
Wallowa, Or., U.S. B9 144
Wallowa, co., Or., U.S. B9 144
Wallowa Mountains, mts., Or., U.S. B9 144
Walls, Ms., U.S. A3 131
Wallsburg, Ut., U.S. C4 151
Wallula, Lake, res., U.S. C7 154
Wallum Lake, l., U.S. A1 146
Walnut, Il., U.S. B4 120
Walnut, Ia., U.S. C2 122
Walnut, Ks., U.S. E8 123
Walnut, Ms., U.S. A5 131
Walnut, N.C., U.S. f10 140
Walnut, stm., Ks., U.S. E6 123
Walnut Canyon National Monument, Az., U.S. B4 110
Walnut Cove, N.C., U.S. A2 140
Walnut Creek, Ca., U.S. h8 112
Walnut Creek, stm., Ks., U.S. D4 123
Walnut Grove, Al., U.S. A3 108
Walnut Grove, Mn., U.S. F3 130
Walnut Grove, Ms., U.S. C4 131
Walnut Grove, Mo., U.S. D4 132
Walnut Hill, Me., U.S. g7 126
Walnut Hill, hill, Ma., U.S. A2 128
Walnut Mountain, hill, Ct., U.S. B3 114
Walnutport, Pa., U.S. E10 145
Walnut Ridge, Ar., U.S. A5 111
Walpeup, Austl. J5 70
Walpole, Ma., U.S. B5 128
Walpole, N.H., U.S. D2 136
Walsenburg, Co., U.S. D6 113
Walsh, Alta., Can. E5 98
Walsh, Co., U.S. D8 113
Walsh, co., N.D., U.S. A8 141
Walsrode, Ger. C9 10
Walterboro, S.C., U.S. F6 147
Walter F. George Dam, U.S. D4 108
Walter F. George Lake, res., U.S. D4 108
Walterhill, Tn., U.S. B5 149
Walters, Ok., U.S. C3 143
Walters Falls, Ont., Can. C4 103
Waltershausen, Ger. E10 10
Waltersville, Ms., U.S. C3 131
Walterville, Or., U.S. C4 144
Walthall, Ms., U.S. B4 131
Walthall, co., Ms., U.S. D3 131
Waltham, Ma., U.S. B5 128
Waltham, Mn., U.S. G6 130
Walthill, Ne., U.S. B9 134
Walthourville, Ga., U.S. E5 117
Walton, N.S., Can. D6 101
Walton, Ont., Can. D3 103
Walton, In., U.S. C5 121
Walton, Ks., U.S. D6 123
Walton, Ky., U.S. B5 124
Walton, Ne., U.S. h11 134
Walton, N.Y., U.S. C5 139
Walton, W.V., U.S. C3 155
Walton, co., Fl., U.S. u15 116
Walton, co., Ga., U.S. C3 117
Waltonville, Il., U.S. E4 120
Walvisbaai (Walvis Bay), S. Afr. D2 66
Walvis Bay see Walvisbaai, S. Afr. D2 66
Walworth, Wi., U.S. F5 156
Walworth, co., S.D., U.S. B5 148
Walworth, co., Wi., U.S. F5 156
Wamac, Il., U.S. E4 120
Wamba, Nig. G14 64
Wamba, stm., Afr. C3 58
Wamego, Ks., U.S. C7 123
Wamesit, Ma., U.S. A5 128
Wampú, Hond. B9 92
Wampú, stm., Hond. B9 92
Wampum, Pa., U.S. E1 145
Wamsutter, Wy., U.S. E5 157
Wanaaring, Austl. G6 70
Wanaka, N.Z. F2 72
Wanamie, Pa., U.S. D9 145
Wanamingo, Mn., U.S. F6 130
Wan'an, China I3 34
Wanapum Dam, Wa., U.S. C6 154
Wanapum Lake, res., Wa., U.S. B6 154
Wanaque, N.J., U.S. A4 137
Wanaque Reservoir, res., N.J., U.S. A4 137
Wanatah, In., U.S. B4 121
Wanbi, Austl. J4 70
Wanblee, S.D., U.S. D4 148
Wanchese, N.C., U.S. B7 140
Wandering River, Alta., Can. B4 98
Wando, S. Kor. I14 32
Wando, stm., S.C., U.S. F8 147
Wandoan, Austl. F8 70
Wando Woods, S.C., U.S. k11 147
Wanette, Ok., U.S. C4 143
Wanfoxia, China C6 30
Wanganui, N.Z. C5 72
Wangaratta, Austl. K7 70
Wangary, Austl. J1 70
Wangdu Phodrang, Bhu. G13 44
Wanghu, China D1 32
Wanghuzhuang, China E5 32
Wangjiang, China E5 34
Wangpan Yang, b., China E11 30
Wangsi, China E4 32
Wangtuan, China F10 32
Wangzhong, China H4 32
Wangzhuangbu, China D1 32
Wanham, Alta., Can. B1 98
Wani, India B5 46
Wanigela, Pap. N. Gui. A9 68
Wānkāner, India I4 44
Wanli, China D9 34
Wanne-Eickel, Ger. D7 10
Wanneroo, Austl. F3 68
Wanship, Ut., U.S. C4 151
Wanxian, China E8 30
Wanzai, China G3 34
Wanzleben, Ger. C11 10
Wapakoneta, Oh., U.S. B1 142
Wapanucka, Ok., U.S. C5 143
Wapato, Wa., U.S. C5 154
Wapawekka Lake, l., Sask., Can. C3 105
Wapella, Sask., Can. G5 105
Wapella, Il., U.S. C5 120
Wapello, Ia., U.S. C6 122
Wapello, co., Ia., U.S. C5 122
Wapiti, Wy., U.S. B3 157
Wapiti, stm., Can. B1 98
Wapiti Ridge, mtn., Wy., U.S. B3 157
Wappapello, Mo., U.S. E7 132
Wappapello, Lake, res., Mo., U.S. D7 132
Wappingers Falls, N.Y., U.S. D7 139
Wapsipinicon, stm., Ia., U.S. B6 122
Wapske, N.B., Can. C2 101
Waqqāş, Jord. C5 50
War, W.V., U.S. D3 155
Waramaug, Lake, l., Ct., U.S. C2 114
Warangal, India C5 46
Waratah, Austl. M6 70
Warbreccan, Austl. E5 70
Warburg, Alta., Can. C3 98
Warburg, Ger. D9 10
Warburton, Austl. K6 70
Warburton Creek, stm., Austl. E7 68
Ward, Al., U.S. C1 108
Ward, Ar., U.S. B4 111
Ward, co., N.D., U.S. A4 141
Ward, co., Tx., U.S. D1 150
Ward, stm., Austl. E7 70
Wardell, Mo., U.S. E8 132
Warden, Que., Can. D5 104
Warden, Wa., U.S. C6 154
Wardha, India B5 46
Wardha, stm., India C5 46
Wardlow, Alta., Can. D5 98
Ward Mountain, mtn., Mt., U.S. D2 133
Wardner, B.C., Can. E10 99
Wardner, Id., U.S. B2 119
Wardsboro, Vt., U.S. E3 152
Wardsville, Ont., Can. E3 103
Ware, Ma., U.S. B3 128
Ware, co., Ga., U.S. E4 117
Ware, stm., Ma., U.S. B3 128
War Eagle Creek, stm., Ar., U.S. A2 111
War Eagle Mountain, mtn., Id., U.S. G2 119
Waregem, Bel. G3 12
Wareham, Eng., U.K. K11 8
Wareham, Ma., U.S. C6 128
Warehouse Point, Ct., U.S. B5 114
Waremme (Borgworm), Bel. G7 12
Waren, Ger. B12 10
Warendorf, Ger. D7 10
Waresboro, Ga., U.S. E4 117
Ware Shoals, S.C., U.S. C3 147
Waretown, N.J., U.S. D4 137
Warfield, B.C., Can. E9 99
Warfield, Ky., U.S. C7 124
Wargla, Alg. E13 62
Warialda, Austl. G9 70
Warin Chamrap, Thai. G8 40
Warkworth, Ont., Can. C7 103
Warman, Sask., Can. E2 105
Warmbad, Nmb. G4 66
Warmbad, S. Afr. E9 66
Warm Beach, Wa., U.S. A3 154
Warminster, Eng., U.K. J11 8
Warminster, Pa., U.S. F11 145
Warm Springs, Ga., U.S. D2 117
Warm Springs, Or., U.S. C5 144
Warm Springs, Va., U.S. B3 153
Warm Springs Indian Reservation, Or., U.S. C5 144
Warm Springs Reservoir, res., Or., U.S. D8 144
Warner, Alta., Can. E4 98
Warner, N.H., U.S. D3 136
Warner, Ok., U.S. B6 143
Warner, S.D., U.S. B7 148
Warner, stm., N.H., U.S. D3 136
Warner Mountain, mtn., Ma., U.S. B1 128
Warner Mountains, mts., Ca., U.S. B3 112
Warner Peak, mtn., Or., U.S. E7 144
Warner Robins, Ga., U.S. D3 117
Warnes, Arg. H8 80
Warnes, Bol. G10 82
Warracknabeal, Austl. K5 70
Warr Acres, Ok., U.S. B4 143
Warragul, Austl. L6 70
Warrego, stm., Austl. G6 70
Warrego Range, mts., Austl. E7 70
Warren, Austl. H7 70
Warren, Ont., Can. A4 103
Warren, Ar., U.S. D3 111
Warren, Il., U.S. A4 120
Warren, In., U.S. C7 121
Warren, Me., U.S. D3 126
Warren, Ma., U.S. B3 128
Warren, Mi., U.S. F7 129
Warren, Mn., U.S. B2 130
Warren, N.H., U.S. C3 136
Warren, Oh., U.S. A5 142
Warren, Or., U.S. B4 144
Warren, Pa., U.S. C3 145
Warren, R.I., U.S. D5 146
Warren, Tx., U.S. D5 150
Warren, Vt., U.S. C3 152
Warren, co., Ga., U.S. C4 117
Warren, co., Il., U.S. C3 120
Warren, co., In., U.S. D3 121
Warren, co., Ia., U.S. C4 122
Warren, co., Ky., U.S. C3 124
Warren, co., Ms., U.S. C3 131
Warren, co., Mo., U.S. C6 132
Warren, co., N.J., U.S. B3 137
Warren, co., N.Y., U.S. B7 139
Warren, co., N.C., U.S. A4 140
Warren, co., Oh., U.S. C1 142
Warren, co., Pa., U.S. C3 145
Warren, co., Tn., U.S. D8 149
Warren, co., Va., U.S. B4 153
Warren, stm., U.S. D5 146
Warren Park, In., U.S. k10 121
Warren Peaks, mts., Wy., U.S. B8 157
Warrens, Wi., U.S. D3 156
Warrensburg, Il., U.S. D4 120
Warrensburg, Mo., U.S. C4 132
Warrensburg, N.Y., U.S. B7 139
Warrensville Heights, Oh., U.S. h9 142
Warrenton, S. Afr. G7 66
Warrenton, Ga., U.S. C4 117
Warrenton, Mo., U.S. C6 132
Warrenton, N.C., U.S. A4 140
Warrenton, Or., U.S. A3 144
Warrenton, Va., U.S. B5 153
Warrenville, Il., U.S. k8 120
Warrenville, S.C., U.S. D4 147
Warri, Nig. I12 64
Warrick, co., In., U.S. H3 121
Warrington, Fl., U.S. u14 116
Warrior, Al., U.S. B3 108
Warrior Lake, res., Al., U.S. C2 108
Warrior Mountain, mtn., Md., U.S. k13 127
Warrnambool, Austl. L5 70
Warroad, Mn., U.S. B3 130
Warsaw, Ont., Can. C6 103
Warsaw, Il., U.S. C2 120
Warsaw, In., U.S. B6 121
Warsaw, Ky., U.S. B5 124
Warsaw, Mo., U.S. C4 132
Warsaw, N.Y., U.S. C2 139
Warsaw, N.C., U.S. B4 140
Warsaw, N.D., U.S. A8 141
Warsaw, Oh., U.S. B3 142
Warsaw, Va., U.S. C6 153
Warsaw see Warszawa, Pol. C21 10
Warspite, Alta., Can. B4 98
Warszawa (Warsaw), Pol. C21 10
Warta, stm., Pol. C15 10
Wartburg, Tn., U.S. C9 149
Wartburg, hist., Ger. E10 10
Warthen, Ga., U.S. C4 117
Wartrace, Tn., U.S. B5 149
Warud, India B5 46
Warunta, Laguna de, l., Hond. B10 92
Warwick, Austl. G10 70
Warwick, Ont., Can. D3 103
Warwick, Que., Can. D6 104
Warwick, Eng., U.K. I12 8
Warwick, Ga., U.S. E3 117
Warwick, Md., U.S. B6 127
Warwick, N.Y., U.S. D6 139
Warwick, N.D., U.S. B7 141
Warwick, R.I., U.S. D4 146
Warwick Channel, strt., Austl. B7 68
Warwick Dam, Ga., U.S. E3 117
Warwickshire, co., Eng., U.K. I12 8
Wasaga Beach, Ont., Can. C4 103
Wasagu, Nig. F12 64
Wasatch, co., Ut., U.S. C4 151
Wasatch Plateau, plat., Ut., U.S. D4 151
Wascana Creek, stm., Sask., Can. G3 105
Wasco, Ca., U.S. E4 112
Wasco, Or., U.S. B6 144
Wasco, co., Or., U.S. B5 144
Waseca, Sask., Can. D1 105
Waseca, Mn., U.S. F5 130
Waseca, co., Mn., U.S. F5 130
Washademoak Lake, l., N.B., Can. D4 101
Washago, Ont., Can. C5 103
Washakie, co., Wy., U.S. C4 157
Washakie Needles, mts., Wy., U.S. C3 157
Washburn, Il., U.S. C4 120
Washburn, Ia., U.S. B5 122
Washburn, Me., U.S. B4 126
Washburn, Mo., U.S. E4 132
Washburn, N.D., U.S. B5 141
Washburn, Tn., U.S. C10 149
Washburn, Wi., U.S. B3 156
Washburn, co., Wi., U.S. C2 156
Washburn, Mount, mtn., Wy., U.S. B2 157
Washington, Ar., U.S. D2 111
Washington, Ct., U.S. C2 114
Washington, D.C., U.S. C3 127
Washington, Ga., U.S. C4 117
Washington, Il., U.S. C4 120
Washington, In., U.S. G3 121
Washington, Ia., U.S. C6 122
Washington, Ks., U.S. C6 123
Washington, Ky., U.S. B6 124
Washington, La., U.S. D3 125
Washington, Ms., U.S. D2 131
Washington, Mo., U.S. C6 132
Washington, Ne., U.S. g12 134
Washington, N.J., U.S. B3 137
Washington, N.C., U.S. B5 140
Washington, Ok., U.S. B4 143
Washington, Pa., U.S. F1 145
Washington, Tn., U.S. D9 149
Washington, Ut., U.S. F2 151
Washington, Vt., U.S. C4 152
Washington, W.V., U.S. B3 155
Washington, co., Al., U.S. D1 108
Washington, co., Ar., U.S. A1 111
Washington, co., Co., U.S. B7 113
Washington, co., Fl., U.S. u16 116
Washington, co., Ga., U.S. C4 117
Washington, co., Id., U.S. E2 119
Washington, co., Il., U.S. E4 120
Washington, co., In., U.S. G5 121
Washington, co., Ia., U.S. C6 122
Washington, co., Ks., U.S. C6 123
Washington, co., Ky., U.S. C4 124
Washington, co., La., U.S. D5 125
Washington, co., Me., U.S. D5 126
Washington, co., Md., U.S. A2 127
Washington, co., Mn., U.S. E6 130
Washington, co., Ms., U.S. B3 131
Washington, co., Mo., U.S. D7 132
Washington, co., Ne., U.S. C9 134
Washington, co., N.Y., U.S. B7 139
Washington, co., N.C., U.S. B6 140
Washington, co., Oh., U.S. C4 142
Washington, co., Ok., U.S. A6 143
Washington, co., Or., U.S. B3 144
Washington, co., Pa., U.S. F1 145
Washington, co., R.I., U.S. E2 146
Washington, co., Tn., U.S. C11 149
Washington, co., Tx., U.S. D4 150
Washington, co., Ut., U.S. F2 151
Washington, co., Vt., U.S. C3 152
Washington, co., Va., U.S. f9 153
Washington, co., Wi., U.S. E5 156
Washington, state, U.S. B5 154
Washington, Lake, l., Fl., U.S. D6 116
Washington, Lake, l., Mn., U.S. E4 130
Washington, Lake, l., Ms., U.S. B3 131
Washington, Lake, l., Wa., U.S. e11 154
Washington, Mount, mtn., N.H., U.S. B4 136
Washington Court House, Oh., U.S. C2 142
Washington Depot, Ct., U.S. C2 114
Washington Island, i., Wi., U.S. C7 156
Washington Park, Il., U.S. E3 120
Washington Terrace, Ut., U.S. B4 151
Washita, co., Ok., U.S. B2 143
Washita, stm., Ok., U.S. C4 143
Washoe, co., Nv., U.S. C2 135
Washoe City, Nv., U.S. D2 135
Washougal, Wa., U.S. D3 154
Washow Bay, b., Man., Can. D3 100
Washta, Ia., U.S. B2 122
Washtenaw, co., Mi., U.S. F7 129
Washtucna, Wa., U.S. C7 154
Wasilków, Pol. B23 10
Wasilla, Ak., U.S. C10 109
Waskada, Man., Can. E1 100
Waskatenau, Alta., Can. B4 98
Waskesiu Lake, l., Sask., Can. D2 105
Waskom, Tx., U.S. C5 150
Waspam, Nic. C11 92
Waspuk, stm., Nic. C10 92
Wasque Point, c., Ma., U.S. D7 128
Wassaw Sound, strt., Ga., U.S. E6 117
Wassen, Switz. E10 13
Wassenaar, Neth. D5 12
Wasseralfingen, Ger. G10 10
Wasserbillig, Lux. I10 12
Wasserburg am Inn, Ger. G12 10
Wasson, Il., U.S. F5 120
Wassookeag, Lake, l., Me., U.S. C3 126
Wassou, Gui. F3 64
Wassuk Range, mts., Nv., U.S. E3 135
Wassy, Fr. D11 14
Wasta, S.D., U.S. C3 148
Wataga, Il., U.S. B3 120
Watampone, Indon. F7 38
Watapi Lake, l., Sask., Can. B6 98
Watatic, Mount, mtn., Ma., U.S. A4 128
Watauga, Tn., U.S. C11 149
Watauga, co., N.C., U.S. A1 140
Watauga, stm., Tn., U.S. C12 149
Watauga Lake, res., Tn., U.S. C12 149
Watchaug Pond, l., R.I., U.S. F2 146
Watch Hill, R.I., U.S. G1 146
Watch Hill Point, c., R.I., U.S. G1 146
Watchung, N.J., U.S. B4 137
Waterberg, Nmb. C3 66
Waterberg Plateau Park, Nmb. C3 66
Waterboro, Me., U.S. E2 126
Waterbury, Ct., U.S. C3 114
Waterbury, Vt., U.S. C3 152
Waterbury Center, Vt., U.S. C3 152
Waterbury Reservoir, res., Vt., U.S. C3 152
Wateree, stm., S.C., U.S. D6 147
Wateree Lake, res., S.C., U.S. C6 147
Waterflow, N.M., U.S. A1 138
Waterford, Ire. I6 8
Waterford, Ct., U.S. D7 114
Waterford, In., U.S. A4 121
Waterford, Ms., U.S. A4 131
Waterford, N.Y., U.S. C7 139
Waterford, Oh., U.S. C4 142
Waterford, Pa., U.S. C2 145
Waterford, Va., U.S. A5 153
Waterford, Wi., U.S. F5 156
Waterford, co., Ire. I6 8
Waterford Mills, In., U.S. A6 121
Waterford Works, N.J., U.S. D3 137
Waterhen Lake, l., Man., Can. C2 100
Waterloo, Bel. G5 12
Waterloo, Ont., Can. D4 103
Waterloo, Que., Can. D5 104
Waterloo, Al., U.S. A1 108
Waterloo, Il., U.S. E3 120
Waterloo, In., U.S. B7 121
Waterloo, Ia., U.S. B5 122
Waterloo, Ne., U.S. g12 134
Waterloo, N.Y., U.S. C4 139
Waterloo, Wi., U.S. E5 156
Waterman, Il., U.S. B5 120
Waterman Reservoir, res., R.I., U.S. B3 146
Waterproof, La., U.S. C4 125
Watersmeet, Mi., U.S. n12 129
Waterton Lakes National Park, Alta., Can. E3 98
Waterton Park, Alta., Can. E4 98
Watertown, Ct., U.S. C3 114
Watertown, Fl., U.S. B4 116
Watertown, Ma., U.S. g11 128
Watertown, N.Y., U.S. B5 139
Watertown, S.D., U.S. C8 148
Watertown, Tn., U.S. A5 149
Watertown, Wi., U.S. E5 156
Water Valley, Ky., U.S. f9 124
Water Valley, Ms., U.S. A4 131
Water Village, N.H., U.S. C4 136
Waterville, N.S., Can. D5 101
Waterville, Ks., U.S. C7 123
Waterville, Me., U.S. D3 126
Waterville, Mn., U.S. F5 130
Waterville, N.Y., U.S. C5 139
Waterville, Oh., U.S. A2 142
Waterville, Wa., U.S. B5 154
Watervliet, Mi., U.S. F4 129
Watervliet, N.Y., U.S. C7 139
Watford, Ont., Can. E3 103
Watford City, N.D., U.S. B2 141
Wathena, Ks., U.S. C9 123
Watino, Alta., Can. B2 98
Watkins, Mn., U.S. E4 130
Watkins Glen, N.Y., U.S. C4 139
Watkinsville, Ga., U.S. C3 117
Watling Island see San Salvador, i., Bah. B7 94
Watonga, Ok., U.S. B3 143
Watonwan, co., Mn., U.S. F4 130
Watonwan, stm., Mn., U.S. G4 130
Watova, Ok., U.S. A6 143
Watrous, Sask., Can. F3 105
Watrous, N.M., U.S. B5 138
Watseka, Il., U.S. C6 120
Watson, Sask., Can. E3 105
Watson, Ar., U.S. D4 111
Watson, Il., U.S. D5 120
Watson, In., U.S. H6 121
Watson, Ok., U.S. C7 143
Watson Lake, Yukon, Can. D7 96
Watsontown, Pa., U.S. D8 145
Watsonville, Ca., U.S. D3 112
Wattenberg, Co., U.S. A6 113
Wattens, Aus. H11 10
Wattensaw Bayou, stm., Ar., U.S. C4 111
Wattenscheid, Ger. D7 10
Wattenwil, Switz. E8 13
Watts (part of Los Angeles), Ca., U.S. n12 112
Watts, Ok., U.S. A7 143
Watts Bar Dam, Tn., U.S. D9 149
Watts Bar Lake, res., Tn., U.S. D9 149
Wattsville, Al., U.S. B3 108
Wattsville, S.C., U.S. B4 147
Wattwil, Switz. D11 13
Watubela, Kepulauan, is., Indon. F9 38
Watuppa Pond, l., Ma., U.S. C5 128
Watzmann, mtn., Ger. H12 10
Waubaushene, Ont., Can. C5 103
Waubay, S.D., U.S. B8 148
Waubay Lake, l., S.D., U.S. B8 148
Waubun, Mn., U.S. C3 130
Wauchope, Austl. H10 70
Wauchula, Fl., U.S. E5 116
Waucoma, Ia., U.S. A5 122
Wauconda, Il., U.S. h8 120
Waugh Mountain, mtn., Id., U.S. D4 119
Waukaringa, Austl. I3 70
Waukee, Ia., U.S. C4 122
Waukegan, Il., U.S. A6 120
Waukesha, Wi., U.S. F5 156
Waukesha, co., Wi., U.S. E5 156
Waukewan, Lake, l., N.H., U.S. C3 136
Waukomis, Ok., U.S. A4 143
Waukon, Ia., U.S. A6 122
Wauna, Wa., U.S. f10 154
Waunakee, Wi., U.S. E4 156
Wauneta, Ne., U.S. D4 134
Waungumbaug Lake, l., Ct., U.S. B6 114
Waupaca, Wi., U.S. D4 156
Waupaca, co., Wi., U.S. D5 156
Waupun, Wi., U.S. E5 156
Wauregan, Ct., U.S. C8 114
Waurika, Ok., U.S. C4 143
Waurika Lake, res., Ok., U.S. C3 143
Wausa, Ne., U.S. B8 134
Wausau, Wi., U.S. D4 156

Name	Map Ref.	Page
Wausau, Lake, res., Wi., U.S.	D4	156
Wausaukee, Wi., U.S.	C6	156
Wauseon, Oh., U.S.	A1	142
Waushara, co., Wi., U.S.	D4	156
Wautoma, Wi., U.S.	D4	156
Wauwatosa, Wi., U.S.	m12	156
Wauzeka, Wi., U.S.	E3	156
Wave Hill, Austl.	C6	68
Waveland, In., U.S.	E3	121
Waveland, Ms., U.S.	E4	131
Waverley, N.S., Can.	E6	101
Waverly, Al., U.S.	C4	108
Waverly, Ga., U.S.	E5	117
Waverly, Il., U.S.	D4	120
Waverly, In., U.S.	E5	121
Waverly, Ia., U.S.	B5	122
Waverly, Ks., U.S.	D8	123
Waverly, Ky., U.S.	C2	124
Waverly, Mn., U.S.	E5	130
Waverly, Mo., U.S.	B4	132
Waverly, Ne., U.S.	D9	134
Waverly, N.Y., U.S.	C4	139
Waverly, Oh., U.S.	C3	142
Waverly, Tn., U.S.	A4	149
Waverly, Va., U.S.	C5	153
Waverly, W.V., U.S.	B3	155
Waverly Hall, Ga., U.S.	D2	117
Wavre (Waver), Bel.	G6	12
Wāw, Sud.	N4	60
Wawa, Sud.	G6	60
Wawa, stm., Nic.	C11	92
Wawaka, In., U.S.	B7	121
Wāw al-Kabīr, Libya	C4	56
Wawanesa, Man., Can.	E2	100
Wawasee, Lake, l., In., U.S.	B6	121
Wawayanda Lake, l., N.J., U.S.	A4	137
Wawayanda Mountain, mtn., U.S.	A4	137
Wawota, Sask., Can.	H4	105
Waxahachie, Tx., U.S.	C4	150
Waxhaw, N.C., U.S.	C2	140
Wayabula, Indon.	E8	38
Wayagamac, Lac, l., Que., Can.	B5	104
Waycross, Ga., U.S.	E4	117
Wayland, Ia., U.S.	C6	122
Wayland, Ky., U.S.	C7	124
Wayland, Ma., U.S.	g10	128
Wayland, Mi., U.S.	F5	129
Wayland, Mo., U.S.	A6	132
Wayland, N.Y., U.S.	C3	139
Waylyn, S.C., U.S.	k12	147
Waymart, Pa., U.S.	C11	145
Wayne, Alta., Can.	D4	98
Wayne, Mi., U.S.	p15	129
Wayne, Ne., U.S.	B8	134
Wayne, N.J., U.S.	B4	137
Wayne, Oh., U.S.	A2	142
Wayne, Ok., U.S.	C4	143
Wayne, W.V., U.S.	C2	155
Wayne, co., Ga., U.S.	E5	117
Wayne, co., Il., U.S.	E5	120
Wayne, co., In., U.S.	E7	121
Wayne, co., Ia., U.S.	D4	122
Wayne, co., Ky., U.S.	D5	124
Wayne, co., Mi., U.S.	F7	129
Wayne, co., Ms., U.S.	D5	131
Wayne, co., Mo., U.S.	D7	132
Wayne, co., Ne., U.S.	B8	134
Wayne, co., N.Y., U.S.	B3	139
Wayne, co., N.C., U.S.	B4	140
Wayne, co., Oh., U.S.	B4	142
Wayne, co., Pa., U.S.	C11	145
Wayne, co., Tn., U.S.	B4	149
Wayne, co., Ut., U.S.	E4	151
Wayne, co., W.V., U.S.	C2	155
Wayne City, Il., U.S.	E5	120
Waynesboro, Ga., U.S.	C4	117
Waynesboro, Ms., U.S.	D5	131
Waynesboro, Pa., U.S.	G6	145
Waynesboro, Tn., U.S.	B4	149
Waynesboro, Va., U.S.	B4	153
Waynesburg, Ky., U.S.	C5	124
Waynesburg, Oh., U.S.	B4	142
Waynesburg, Pa., U.S.	G1	145
Waynesville, Ga., U.S.	E5	117
Waynesville, Il., U.S.	C4	120
Waynesville, Mo., U.S.	D5	132
Waynesville, N.C., U.S.	f10	140
Waynesville, Oh., U.S.	C1	142
Waynetown, In., U.S.	D3	121
Waynewood, Va., U.S.	g12	153
Waynoka, Ok., U.S.	A3	143
Wayside, Ms., U.S.	B2	131
Wayzata, Mn., U.S.	n11	130
Wāzah Khwāh, Afg.	D3	44
Wāzin, Libya	E16	62
Wazīrābād, Pak.	D6	44
We, Pulau, i., Indon.	L3	40
Weakley, co., Tn., U.S.	A3	149
Weare, N.H., U.S.	D3	136
Weatherford, Ok., U.S.	B3	143
Weatherford, Tx., U.S.	C4	150
Weatherly, Pa., U.S.	E10	145
Weatogue, Ct., U.S.	B4	114
Weaubleau, Mo., U.S.	D4	132
Weaver, Al., U.S.	B4	108
Weaver Mountains, mts., Az., U.S.	C3	110
Weaverville, Ca., U.S.	B2	112
Weaverville, N.C., U.S.	f10	140
Webb, Sask., Can.	G1	105
Webb, Al., U.S.	D4	108
Webb, Ms., U.S.	B3	131
Webb, co., Tx., U.S.	F3	150
Webb City, Mo., U.S.	D3	132
Webbers Falls, Ok., U.S.	B6	143
Webberville, Mi., U.S.	F6	129
Webb Hill, hill, Ma., U.S.	B3	128
Webb Lake, l., Me., U.S.	D2	126
Webbwood, Ont., Can.	A3	103
Weber, co., Ut., U.S.	B4	151
Weber City, Va., U.S.	f9	153
Weberi Bekera, Eth.	M10	60
Webster, Fl., U.S.	D4	116
Webster, In., U.S.	E8	121
Webster, Ma., U.S.	B4	128
Webster, Mn., U.S.	F5	130
Webster, N.Y., U.S.	B3	139
Webster, Pa., U.S.	F2	145
Webster, S.D., U.S.	B8	148
Webster, Wi., U.S.	C1	156
Webster, co., Ga., U.S.	D2	117
Webster, co., Ia., U.S.	B3	122
Webster, co., Ky., U.S.	C2	124
Webster, co., La., U.S.	B2	125
Webster, co., Ms., U.S.	B4	131
Webster, co., Mo., U.S.	D5	132
Webster, co., Ne., U.S.	D7	134
Webster, co., W.V., U.S.	C4	155
Webster City, Ia., U.S.	B4	122
Webster Groves, Mo., U.S.	f13	132
Webster Reservoir, res., Ks., U.S.	C4	123
Webster Springs, W.V., U.S.	C4	155
Websterville, Vt., U.S.	C4	152
Weda, Indon.	E8	38
Weddell Sea, Ant.	B1	73
Wedderburn, Austl.	K5	70
Wedderburn, Or., U.S.	E2	144
Wedel, Ger.	B9	10
Wedgeport, N.S., Can.	F4	101
Wedgewood, Mo., U.S.	f13	132
Wedowee, Al., U.S.	B4	108
Wedron, Il., U.S.	B5	120
Wedweil, Sud.	M4	60
Wedza, Zimb.	B10	66
Weed, Ca., U.S.	B2	112
Weed Heights, Nv., U.S.	E2	135
Weedon, Que., Can.	D6	104
Weed Patch Hill, hill, In., U.S.	F5	121
Weedsport, N.Y., U.S.	B4	139
Weedville, Pa., U.S.	D5	145
Weehawken, N.J., U.S.	h8	137
Weekes, Sask., Can.	E4	105
Weeksbury, Ky., U.S.	C7	124
Weeksville, N.C., U.S.	A6	140
Weems, Va., U.S.	C6	153
Weenen, S. Afr.	G10	66
Weeping Water, Ne., U.S.	D9	134
Weeping Water Creek, stm., Ne., U.S.	h12	134
Weert, Neth.	F8	12
Weesp, Neth.	D7	12
Wee Waa, Austl.	H8	70
Węgrów, Pol.	C22	10
Wei, stm., China	E8	30
Weiden in der Oberpfalz, Ger.	F12	10
Weidman, Mi., U.S.	E6	129
Weifang, China	G7	32
Weihai, China	F10	32
Weilburg, Ger.	E8	10
Weilheim, Ger.	H11	10
Weimar, Ger.	E11	10
Weimar, Tx., U.S.	E4	150
Weinan, China	E8	30
Weiner, Ar., U.S.	B5	111
Weinfelden, Switz.	C11	13
Weinheim, Ger.	F8	10
Weipa, Austl.	B8	68
Weippe, Id., U.S.	C3	119
Weir, Ks., U.S.	E9	123
Weir, Ky., U.S.	C2	124
Weir, Ms., U.S.	B4	131
Weir, stm., Austl.	F9	70
Weir, Lake, l., Fl., U.S.	C5	116
Weirdale, Sask., Can.	D3	105
Weirsdale, Fl., U.S.	D5	116
Weirton, W.V., U.S.	A4	155
Weisburd, Arg.	D7	80
Weiser, Id., U.S.	E2	119
Weiser, stm., Id., U.S.	E2	119
Weishan (Xiazhen), China	I5	32
Weishancheng, China	C2	34
Weisner Mountain, hill, Al., U.S.	A4	108
Weissenburg, Switz.	E7	13
Weissenburg in Bayern, Ger.	F10	10
Weissenfels, Ger.	D11	10
Weisshorn, mtn., Switz.	F8	13
Weisskugel (Palla Bianca), mtn., Eur.	E14	13
Weiss Lake, res., U.S.	A4	108
Weitou, China	K7	34
Weitra, Aus.	G14	10
Weiz, Aus.	H15	10
Weizhen, China	F2	32
Weizhou Wan, b., Asia	K7	34
Wejherowo, Pol.	A18	10
Welaka, Fl., U.S.	C5	116
Welch, Ok., U.S.	A6	143
Welch, W.V., U.S.	D3	155
Welches, Or., U.S.	B5	144
Welcome, La., U.S.	h10	125
Welcome, Mn., U.S.	G4	130
Welcome, S.C., U.S.	B3	147
Weld, Me., U.S.	D2	126
Weld, co., Co., U.S.	A6	113
Welda, Ks., U.S.	D8	123
Weldon, Sask., Can.	D3	105
Weldon, Ar., U.S.	B4	111
Weldon, Il., U.S.	C5	120
Weldon, N.C., U.S.	A5	140
Weldona, Co., U.S.	A7	113
Weldon Spring, Mo., U.S.	f12	132
Weleetka, Ok., U.S.	B5	143
Welkite, Eth.	M9	60
Welkom, S. Afr.	F8	66
Welland, Ont., Can.	E5	103
Wellandport, Ont., Can.	D5	103
Wellborn, Fl., U.S.	B4	116
Wellesley, Ont., Can.	D4	103
Wellesley, Ma., U.S.	B5	128
Wellesley Islands, is., Austl.	A3	70
Wellfleet, Ma., U.S.	C7	128
Wellford, S.C., U.S.	B3	147
Wellington, Austl.	I8	70
Wellington, Ont., Can.	D7	103
Wellington, N.Z.	D5	72
Wellington, S. Afr.	I4	66
Wellington, Eng., U.K.	I11	8
Wellington, Al., U.S.	B4	108
Wellington, Co., U.S.	A5	113
Wellington, Il., U.S.	C6	120
Wellington, Ks., U.S.	E6	123
Wellington, Mo., U.S.	B4	132
Wellington, Nv., U.S.	E2	135
Wellington, Oh., U.S.	A3	142
Wellington, Tx., U.S.	B2	150
Wellington, Ut., U.S.	D5	151
Wellington, Isla, i., Chile	F2	78
Wellington Channel, strt., N.W. Ter., Can.	A14	96
Wellington Station, P.E.I., Can.	C5	101
Wellman, Ia., U.S.	C6	122
Wellpinit, Wa., U.S.	B8	154
Wells, B.C., Can.	C7	99
Wells, Me., U.S.	E2	126
Wells, Mi., U.S.	C3	129
Wells, Mn., U.S.	G5	130
Wells, Nv., U.S.	B7	135
Wells, Tx., U.S.	D5	150
Wells, Vt., U.S.	E2	152
Wells, co., In., U.S.	C7	121
Wells, co., N.D., U.S.	B6	141
Wells, stm., Vt., U.S.	C4	152
Wells Beach, Me., U.S.	E2	126
Wellsboro, In., U.S.	A4	121
Wellsboro, Pa., U.S.	C7	145
Wellsburg, Ia., U.S.	B5	122
Wellsburg, W.V., U.S.	A4	155
Wellsford, N.Z.	B5	72
Wells-next-the-Sea, Eng., U.K.	I14	8
Wells River, Vt., U.S.	C4	152
Wellston, Oh., U.S.	C3	142
Wellston, Ok., U.S.	B4	143
Wellsville, Ks., U.S.	D8	123
Wellsville, Mo., U.S.	B6	132
Wellsville, N.Y., U.S.	C3	139
Wellsville, Oh., U.S.	B5	142
Wellsville, Ut., U.S.	B4	151
Wellton, Az., U.S.	E1	110
Wellwood, Man., Can.	D2	100
Wels, Aus.	G14	10
Welsford, N.B., Can.	D3	101
Welsh, La., U.S.	D3	125
Welwitschia, Nmb.	C2	66
Welwyn, Sask., Can.	G5	105
Wembley, Alta., Can.	B1	98
Wemme, Or., U.S.	B5	144
Wenasoga, Ms., U.S.	A5	131
Wenatchee, Wa., U.S.	B5	154
Wenatchee, stm., Wa., U.S.	B5	154
Wenatchee Lake, l., Wa., U.S.	B5	154
Wenatchee Mountains, mts., Wa., U.S.	B5	154
Wenchow see Wenzhou, China	G9	34
Wendell, Id., U.S.	G4	119
Wendell, Mn., U.S.	D2	130
Wendell, N.C., U.S.	B4	140
Wenden, Az., U.S.	D2	110
Wendeng, China	F10	32
Wendo, Eth.	N10	60
Wendover, Ut., U.S.	C1	151
Wengyang, China	G9	34
Wengyuan, China	K3	34
Wenham, Ma., U.S.	A6	128
Wenham Lake, l., Ma., U.S.	f12	128
Wenham Swamp, sw., Ma., U.S.	f12	128
Wenling, China	G10	34
Wenlock, stm., Austl.	B8	68
Wenona, Il., U.S.	B4	120
Wenonah, N.J., U.S.	D2	137
Wenshan, China	C8	40
Wentworth, Austl.	J4	70
Wentworth, N.S., Can.	D6	101
Wentworth, N.H., U.S.	C3	136
Wentworth, S.D., U.S.	C8	148
Wentworth, Lake, l., N.H., U.S.	C4	136
Wentzville, Mo., U.S.	C7	132
Wenzhou, China	G9	34
Weohyakapka, Lake, l., Fl., U.S.	E5	116
Weott, Ca., U.S.	B2	112
Wequetequock, Ct., U.S.	D8	114
Werda, Bots.	E6	66
Werdau, Ger.	E12	10
Werder, Ger.	C12	10
Werdohl, Ger.	D7	10
Were Ilu, Eth.	L10	60
Werl, Ger.	D7	10
Wernigerode, Ger.	D10	10
Werra, stm., Ger.	E10	10
Werribee, Austl.	K6	70
Werris Creek, Austl.	H9	70
Wertheim, Ger.	F9	10
Wertingen, Ger.	G10	10
Wesel, Ger.	D6	10
Weser, stm., Ger.	B8	10
Weskan, Ks., U.S.	D2	123
Weslaco, Tx., U.S.	F4	150
Weslemkoon Lake, l., Ont., Can.	C7	103
Wesley, Ia., U.S.	A4	122
Wesleyville, Newf., Can.	D5	102
Wesleyville, Pa., U.S.	B2	145
Wessel, Cape, c., Austl.	B7	68
Wessel Islands, is., Austl.	B7	68
Wesserunsett Lake, l., Me., U.S.	D3	126
Wessington, S.D., U.S.	C7	148
Wessington Springs, S.D., U.S.	C7	148
Wesson, Ar., U.S.	D3	111
Wesson, Ms., U.S.	D3	131
West, Ms., U.S.	B4	131
West, Tx., U.S.	D4	150
West, stm., Ct., U.S.	D5	114
West, stm., Ma., U.S.	h9	128
West, stm., Vt., U.S.	E3	152
West Acton, Ma., U.S.	g10	128
West Alexandria, Oh., U.S.	C1	142
West Allis, Wi., U.S.	m11	156
West Alton, Mo., U.S.	f13	132
West Alton, N.H., U.S.	C4	136
West Andover, Ma., U.S.	A5	128
West Arichat, N.S., Can.	D8	101
West Baden Springs, In., U.S.	G4	121
West Baldwin, Me., U.S.	E2	126
West Bank, hist. reg., Isr. Occ.	E4	50
West Barnstable, Ma., U.S.	C7	128
West Baton Rouge, co., La., U.S.	D4	125
West Bay, Newf., Can.	A3	102
West Bay, N.S., Can.	D8	101
West Bay, b., Fl., U.S.	u16	116
West Bay, b., N.C., U.S.	B6	140
West Bay, b., Tx., U.S.	r15	150
West Bend, Ia., U.S.	B3	122
West Bend, Wi., U.S.	E5	156
West Bengal, state, India	I12	44
West Berlin, N.J., U.S.	D3	137
West Bethel, Me., U.S.	D2	126
West Billerica, Ma., U.S.	f10	128
West Blocton, Al., U.S.	B2	108
Westboro, Mo., U.S.	A2	132
Westborough, Ma., U.S.	B4	128
West Bountiful, Ut., U.S.	C4	151
Westbourne, Man., Can.	D2	100
West Boylston, Ma., U.S.	B4	128
West Branch, Ia., U.S.	C6	122
West Branch, Mi., U.S.	D6	129
West Branch Reservoir, res., Ct., U.S.	B3	114
West Brentwood, N.H., U.S.	E4	136
West Bridgewater, Ma., U.S.	B5	128
Westbrook, Ct., U.S.	D6	114
Westbrook, Me., U.S.	E2	126
Westbrook, Mn., U.S.	F3	130
West Brookfield, Ma., U.S.	B3	128
West Burke, Vt., U.S.	B5	152
West Burlington, Ia., U.S.	D6	122
West Butte, mtn., Mt., U.S.	B5	133
West Buxton, Me., U.S.	E2	126
Westby, Mt., U.S.	B12	133
Westby, Wi., U.S.	E3	156
West Cache Creek, stm., Ok., U.S.	C3	143
West Caicos, i., T./C. Is.	D8	94
West Caldwell, N.J., U.S.	B4	137
West Campton, N.H., U.S.	C3	136
West Canada Creek, stm., N.Y., U.S.	B6	139
West Cape May, N.J., U.S.	F3	137
West Carroll, co., La., U.S.	B4	125
West Carrollton, Oh., U.S.	C1	142
West Carry Pond, l., Me., U.S.	C2	126
West Carthage, N.Y., U.S.	B5	139
West Charleston, Vt., U.S.	B4	152
West Chatham, Ma., U.S.	C8	128
West Chazy, N.Y., U.S.	f11	139
Westchester, Il., U.S.	k9	120
West Chester, Oh., U.S.	n13	142
West Chester, Pa., U.S.	G10	145
Westchester, co., N.Y., U.S.	D7	139
West Chesterfield, N.H., U.S.	E1	136
Westchester Station, N.S., Can.	D6	101
West Chicago, Il., U.S.	k8	120
West Chop, c., Ma., U.S.	D6	128
West City, Il., U.S.	F5	120
Westcliffe, Co., U.S.	C5	113
West Coffeyville, Ks., U.S.	E8	123
West College Corner, In., U.S.	E8	121
West Columbia, S.C., U.S.	D5	147
West Columbia, Tx., U.S.	E5	150
West Concord, Ma., U.S.	B5	128
West Concord, Mn., U.S.	F6	130
West Concord, N.C., U.S.	B2	140
Westconnaug Reservoir, res., R.I., U.S.	C2	146
West Cornwall, Ct., U.S.	B2	114
West Cote Blanche Bay, b., La., U.S.	E4	125
West Covina, Ca., U.S.	m13	112
West Creek, N.J., U.S.	D4	137
West Crossett, Ar., U.S.	D4	111
West Cumberland, Me., U.S.	E2	126
West Danville, Vt., U.S.	C4	152
West Decatur, Pa., U.S.	E5	145
West Demerara-Essequibo Coast, dept., Guy.	D13	84
West Dennis, Ma., U.S.	C7	128
West Des Moines, Ia., U.S.	C4	122
West Dover, Vt., U.S.	F3	152
West Dummerston, Vt., U.S.	F3	152
West Elk Mountains, mts., Co., U.S.	C3	113
West Elk Peak, mtn., Co., U.S.	C3	113
West Elwood, In., U.S.	D6	121
West Emma Creek, stm., Ks., U.S.	D6	123
West End, Bah.	A5	94
West End, N.C., U.S.	B3	140
West Enfield, Me., U.S.	C4	126
West Epping, N.H., U.S.	D4	136
Westerlo, Bel.	F6	12
Westerly, R.I., U.S.	F1	146
Western, Ne., U.S.	D8	134
Western, stm., Austl.	D5	70
Western Australia, state, Austl.	E4	68
Western Channel, strt., Asia	I16	32
Western Desert see Gharbīyah, Aṣ-Ṣaḥrā' al-, des., Egypt	D4	60
Western Ghāts, mts., India	D2	46
Western Grove, Ar., U.S.	A3	111
Western Head, c., N.S., Can.	F5	101
Western Island, i., Newf., Can.	C4	102
Western Isles, prov., Scot., U.K.	D6	8
Westernport, Md., U.S.	m12	127
Western Sahara, dep., Afr.	D4	54
Western Samoa, ctry., Oc.	G1	2
Western Springs, Il., U.S.	k9	120
Westerschelde, est., Neth.	F4	12
Westerstede, Ger.	B7	10
Westervelt, Il., U.S.	D5	120
Westerville, Oh., U.S.	B3	142
West Fairlee, Vt., U.S.	D4	152
West Falkland, i., Falk. Is.	G4	78
West Falmouth, Ma., U.S.	C6	128
West Fargo, N.D., U.S.	C9	141
West Farmington, Me., U.S.	D2	126
West Farmington, Oh., U.S.	A5	142
West Feliciana, co., La., U.S.	D4	125
Westfield, N.B., Can.	D3	101
Westfield, Il., U.S.	D6	120
Westfield, In., U.S.	D5	121
Westfield, Me., U.S.	B5	126
Westfield, Ma., U.S.	B2	128
Westfield, N.J., U.S.	B4	137
Westfield, N.Y., U.S.	C1	139
Westfield, Pa., U.S.	C6	145
Westfield, Wi., U.S.	E4	156
Westfield, stm., Ma., U.S.	B2	128
Westfield Center, Oh., U.S.	A4	142
Westfir, Or., U.S.	D4	144
Westford, Ma., U.S.	f10	128
West Fork, Ar., U.S.	B1	111
West Fork, stm., W.V., U.S.	B4	155
West Frankfort, Il., U.S.	F5	120
West Freehold, N.J., U.S.	C4	137
West Friendship, Md., U.S.	B4	127
Westgate, Austl.	F7	70
Westgate, Fl., U.S.	F6	116
Westgate, Ia., U.S.	B6	122
West Glacier, Mt., U.S.	B3	133
West Glamorgan, co., Wales, U.K.	J10	8
West Goshen, Ct., U.S.	B2	114
West Granby, Ct., U.S.	B4	114
West Grand Lake, l., Me., U.S.	C5	126
West Green, Ga., U.S.	E4	117
West Groton, Ma., U.S.	A4	128
West Grove, Pa., U.S.	G10	145
West Hamlin, W.V., U.S.	C2	155
West Hampstead, N.H., U.S.	E4	136
Westhampton Beach, N.Y., U.S.	n16	139
West Hanover, Ma., U.S.	h12	128
West Harrison, In., U.S.	F8	121
West Hartford, Ct., U.S.	B4	114
West Hartford, Vt., U.S.	D4	152
West Hartland, Ct., U.S.	A4	114
West Haven, Ct., U.S.	D4	114
West Hazleton, Pa., U.S.	E9	145
West Helena, Ar., U.S.	C5	111
West Hill Reservoir, res., Ma., U.S.	B4	128
Westhope, N.D., U.S.	A4	141
West Hyannisport, Ma., U.S.	C7	128
West Ice Shelf, Ant.	B5	73
West Indies, is.	E9	94
West Island, i., Ma., U.S.	C6	128
West Jefferson, N.C., U.S.	A1	140
West Jefferson, Oh., U.S.	C2	142
West Jordan, Ut., U.S.	C4	151
West Kennebunk, Me., U.S.	E2	126
West Kingston, R.I., U.S.	F3	146
West Lafayette, In., U.S.	D4	121
West Lafayette, Oh., U.S.	B4	142
Westlake, La., U.S.	D2	125
Westlake, Oh., U.S.	h9	142
West Lake, l., Me., U.S.	C4	126
Westland, Mi., U.S.	F7	129
West Laramie, Wy., U.S.	E7	157
West Lawn, Pa., U.S.	F10	145
West Lebanon, In., U.S.	D3	121
West Leisenring, Pa., U.S.	G2	145
West Liberty, Ia., U.S.	C6	122
West Liberty, Ky., U.S.	C6	124
West Liberty, Oh., U.S.	B2	142
West Liberty, W.V., U.S.	f8	155
West Linn, Or., U.S.	B4	144
Westlock, Alta., Can.	B4	98
West Long Branch, N.J., U.S.	C4	137
West Lorne, Ont., Can.	E3	103
West Louisville, Ky., U.S.	C2	124
West Mansfield, Oh., U.S.	B2	142
West Marion, N.C., U.S.	f10	140
Westmeath, Ont., Can.	B8	103
Westmeath, co., Ire.	H6	8
West Medway, Ma., U.S.	B5	128
West Memphis, Ar., U.S.	B5	111
West Miami, Fl., U.S.	s13	116
West Middlesex, Pa., U.S.	D1	145
West Middleton, In., U.S.	D5	121
West Mifflin, Pa., U.S.	F2	145
West Milford, N.J., U.S.	A4	137
West Milton, Oh., U.S.	C1	142
West Milton, Pa., U.S.	D8	145
West Milwaukee, Wi., U.S.	m12	156
West Mineral, Ks., U.S.	E9	123
Westminster, Ca., U.S.	n12	112
Westminster, Co., U.S.	B5	113
Westminster, La., U.S.	h9	125
Westminster, Md., U.S.	A4	127
Westminster, Ma., U.S.	A4	128
Westminster, S.C., U.S.	B1	147
Westminster, Vt., U.S.	E4	152
West Monroe, La., U.S.	B3	125
Westmont, Ca., U.S.	n12	112
Westmont, Il., U.S.	k9	120
Westmont, N.J., U.S.	D2	137
Westmont, Pa., U.S.	F4	145
Westmoreland, Ks., U.S.	C7	123
Westmoreland, N.H., U.S.	E2	136
Westmoreland, Tn., U.S.	A5	149
Westmoreland, co., Pa., U.S.	F2	145
Westmoreland, co., Va., U.S.	B6	153
Westmorland, Ca., U.S.	F6	112
West Mountain, mtn., Ar., U.S.	f7	111
West Mountain, mtn., N.Y., U.S.	B6	139
West Mountain, mtn., Vt., U.S.	B5	152
West Muncie, In., U.S.	D7	121
West Musquash Lake, l., Me., U.S.	C5	126
West Mystic, Ct., U.S.	D8	114
West Newbury, Ma., U.S.	A6	128
West Newton, Pa., U.S.	F2	145
West New York, N.J., U.S.	h8	137
West Nicholson, Zimb.	C9	66
West Nishnabotna, stm., Ia., U.S.	C2	122
West Norriton, Pa., U.S.	o20	145
West Nottingham, N.H., U.S.	D4	136
Weston, Co., U.S.	D6	113
Weston, Ct., U.S.	E2	114
Weston, Id., U.S.	G7	119
Weston, Ma., U.S.	g10	128
Weston, Mo., U.S.	B3	132
Weston, Ne., U.S.	C9	134
Weston, Oh., U.S.	A2	142
Weston, Or., U.S.	B8	144
Weston, Vt., U.S.	E3	152
Weston, W.V., U.S.	B4	155
Weston, Wi., U.S.	D4	156
Weston, co., Wy., U.S.	C8	157
Weston-super-Mare, Eng., U.K.	J11	8
West Orange, N.J., U.S.	B4	137
West Ossipee, N.H., U.S.	C4	136
Westover, Al., U.S.	B3	108
Westover, Md., U.S.	D6	127
Westover, Tn., U.S.	B3	149
Westover, W.V., U.S.	B5	155
Westover Air Force Base, mil., Ma., U.S.	B2	128
West Palm Beach, Fl., U.S.	F6	116
West Paris, Me., U.S.	D2	126
West Park, N.Y., U.S.	D7	139
West Pawlet, Vt., U.S.	E2	152
West Pearl, stm., La., U.S.	D6	125
West Pelzer, S.C., U.S.	B3	147
West Pensacola, Fl., U.S.	u14	116
West Peoria, Il., U.S.	C4	120
West Peru, Me., U.S.	D2	126
West Peterborough, N.H., U.S.	E3	136
Westphalia, In., U.S.	G3	121
Westphalia, Ks., U.S.	D8	123
Westphalia, Mi., U.S.	F6	129
Westphalia, Mo., U.S.	C5	132
West Pittsburg, Pa., U.S.	E1	145
West Pittston, Pa., U.S.	m17	145
West Plains, Mo., U.S.	E6	132
West Point, Al., U.S.	A3	108
West Point, Ar., U.S.	B4	111
West Point, Ca., U.S.	C3	112
West Point, Ga., U.S.	D1	117
West Point, Il., U.S.	C2	120
Westpoint, In., U.S.	D3	121
West Point, Ia., U.S.	D6	122
West Point, Ky., U.S.	C4	124
West Point, Ms., U.S.	B5	131
West Point, Ne., U.S.	C9	134
West Point, N.Y., U.S.	D7	139
Westpoint, Tn., U.S.	B4	149
West Point, Va., U.S.	C6	153
West Point, mtn., Ak., U.S.	C11	109
West Point, c., Austl.	J2	70
West Point Lake, res., U.S.	C1	117
Westport, Newf., Can.	D3	102
Westport, N.S., Can.	E3	101
Westport, Ont., Can.	C8	103
Westport, N.Z.	D3	72
Westport, Ct., U.S.	E2	114
Westport, In., U.S.	F6	121
Westport, Ky., U.S.	B4	124
Westport, N.H., U.S.	E2	136
Westport, Or., U.S.	A3	144
Westport, S.D., U.S.	B7	148
Westport, Wa., U.S.	C1	154
West Portsmouth, Oh., U.S.	D2	142
West Pubnico, N.S., Can.	F4	101
West Quoddy Head, c., Me., U.S.	D6	126
West Reading, Pa., U.S.	F10	145
West Ridge, Ar., U.S.	B5	111
West Rindge, N.H., U.S.	E2	136
West Rumney, N.H., U.S.	C3	136
West Rupert, Vt., U.S.	E2	152
West Rutland, Vt., U.S.	D2	152
West Rye, N.H., U.S.	D5	136
West Saint Modeste, Newf., Can.	C3	102
West Saint Paul, Mn., U.S.	n12	130
West Salem, Il., U.S.	E5	120
West Salem, Oh., U.S.	B3	142
West Salem, Wi., U.S.	E2	156
West Salt Creek, stm., Co., U.S.	B2	113
West Scarborough, Me., U.S.	E2	126
West Seneca, N.Y., U.S.	C2	139
West Siberian Plain see Zapadno-Sibirskaja ravnina, pl., U.S.S.R.	E13	22
Westside, Ia., U.S.	B2	122
West Simsbury, Ct., U.S.	B4	114
West Slope, Or., U.S.	g12	144
West Spanish Peak, mtn., Co., U.S.	D6	113
West Springfield, Ma., U.S.	B2	128
West Springfield, Va., U.S.	g12	153
West Stafford, Ct., U.S.	B6	114
West Suffield, Ct., U.S.	B5	114
West Sussex, co., Eng., U.K.	K13	8
West Swanzey, N.H., U.S.	E2	136
West Terre Haute, In., U.S.	F3	121
West Thompson Lake, res., Ct., U.S.	B8	114
West Thornton, N.H., U.S.	C3	136
West Townshend, Vt., U.S.	E3	152
West Union, Il., U.S.	D6	120
West Union, Ia., U.S.	B6	122
West Union, Oh., U.S.	D2	142
West Union, W.V., U.S.	B4	155
West Unity, Oh., U.S.	A1	142
West University Place, Tx., U.S.	r14	150
West Upton, Ma., U.S.	B4	128
West Valley City, Ut., U.S.	C4	151
West Vancouver, B.C., Can.	f12	99
West Van Lear, Ky., U.S.	C7	124
West View, Pa., U.S.	h13	145
Westville, N.S., Can.	D7	101
Westville, Il., U.S.	C6	120
Westville, In., U.S.	A4	121
Westville, N.H., U.S.	E4	136
Westville, N.J., U.S.	D2	137
Westville, Ok., U.S.	A7	143
Westville Lake, res., Ma., U.S.	B3	128
West Virginia, state, U.S.	C4	155
West-Vlaanderen, prov., Bel.	F2	12
West Walker, stm., U.S.	E2	135
West Wardsboro, Vt., U.S.	E3	152
West Wareham, Ma., U.S.	C6	128
West Warren, Ma., U.S.	B3	128
West Warwick, R.I., U.S.	D3	146
Westwego, La., U.S.	k11	125
West Willington, Ct., U.S.	B6	114
West Wilton, N.H., U.S.	E3	136
Westwold, B.C., Can.	D8	99
Westwood, Ca., U.S.	B3	112
Westwood, Ks., U.S.	k16	123
Westwood, Ky., U.S.	B7	124
Westwood, Ma., U.S.	B5	128
Westwood, N.J., U.S.	B4	137
Westwood Lakes, Fl., U.S.	s13	116
West Woodstock, Vt., U.S.	D3	152
West Wyalong, Austl.	I7	70
West Wyoming, Pa., U.S.	n17	145
West Yarmouth, Ma., U.S.	C7	128
West Yellowstone, Mt., U.S.	F5	133
West York, Il., U.S.	D6	120
West York, Pa., U.S.	G8	145
Wetar, Pulau, i., Indon.	G8	38
Wetaskiwin, Alta., Can.	C4	98
Wete, Tan.	C7	58
Wethersfield, Ct., U.S.	C5	114
Wetmore, Co., U.S.	C5	113
Wetmore, Ks., U.S.	C8	123

Name	Map Ref.	Page
Wetmore, Mi., U.S.	B4	129
Wet Mountains, mts., Co., U.S.	C5	113
Wetteren, Bel.	F4	12
Wetumka, Ok., U.S.	B5	143
Wetumpka, Al., U.S.	C3	108
Wetzel, co., W.V., U.S.	B4	155
Wetzikon, Switz.	D10	13
Wetzlar, Ger.	E8	10
Wewahitchka, Fl., U.S.	B1	116
Wewak, Pap. N. Gui.	k15	68a
Wewoka, Ok., U.S.	B5	143
Wexford, Ire.	I7	8
Wexford, co., Ire.	I7	8
Wexford, co., Mi., U.S.	D5	129
Weyakwin Lake, l., Sask., Can.	C3	105
Weyauwega, Wi., U.S.	D5	156
Weyburn, Sask., Can.	H4	105
Weyers Cave, Va., U.S.	B4	153
Weymouth, N.S., Can.	E4	101
Weymouth, Eng., U.K.	K11	8
Weymouth, Ma., U.S.	B6	128
Whakatane, N.Z.	B6	72
Whaleysville, Md., U.S.	D7	127
Whalom, Ma., U.S.	A4	128
Whangarei, N.Z.	A5	72
Wharton, N.J., U.S.	B3	137
Wharton, Tx., U.S.	E4	150
Wharton, W.V., U.S.	n12	155
Wharton, co., Tx., U.S.	E4	150
Whataroa, N.Z.	E3	72
What Cheer, Ia., U.S.	C5	122
Whatcom, co., Wa., U.S.	A4	154
Whatcom, Lake, l., Wa., U.S.	A3	154
Whatley, Al., U.S.	D2	108
Wheatcroft, Ky., U.S.	C2	124
Wheatfield, In., U.S.	B3	121
Wheatland, Ca., U.S.	C3	112
Wheatland, In., U.S.	G3	121
Wheatland, Ia., U.S.	C7	122
Wheatland, Mo., U.S.	D4	132
Wheatland, N.D., U.S.	C8	141
Wheatland, Pa., U.S.	D1	145
Wheatland, Wy., U.S.	D8	157
Wheatland, co., Mt., U.S.	D7	133
Wheatland Reservoir, res., Wy., U.S.	E7	157
Wheatley, Ont., Can.	E2	103
Wheatley, Ar., U.S.	C4	111
Wheaton, Il., U.S.	B5	120
Wheaton, Ks., U.S.	C7	123
Wheaton, Md., U.S.	B3	127
Wheaton, Mn., U.S.	E2	130
Wheaton, Mo., U.S.	E3	132
Wheat Ridge, Co., U.S.	B5	113
Wheelbarrow Peak, mtn., Nv., U.S.	F5	135
Wheeler, Al., U.S.	A2	108
Wheeler, In., U.S.	B3	121
Wheeler, Ms., U.S.	A5	131
Wheeler, Or., U.S.	B3	144
Wheeler, Tx., U.S.	B2	150
Wheeler, Wi., U.S.	C2	156
Wheeler, co., Ga., U.S.	D4	117
Wheeler, co., Ne., U.S.	C7	134
Wheeler, co., Or., U.S.	C6	144
Wheeler, co., Tx., U.S.	B2	150
Wheeler Air Force Base, mil., Hi., U.S.	g9	118
Wheeler Dam, Al., U.S.	A2	108
Wheeler Lake, res., Al., U.S.	A2	108
Wheeler Peak, mtn., Ca., U.S.	C4	112
Wheeler Peak, mtn., Nv., U.S.	E7	135
Wheeler Peak, mtn., N.M., U.S.	A4	138
Wheelersburg, Oh., U.S.	D3	142
Wheeling, Il., U.S.	h9	120
Wheeling, Mo., U.S.	B4	132
Wheeling, W.V., U.S.	A4	155
Wheeling Creek, stm., W.V., U.S.	f8	155
Wheelock Mountain, mtn., Vt., U.S.	B4	152
Wheelwright, Arg.	G8	80
Wheelwright, Ky., U.S.	C7	124
Whelen Springs, Ar., U.S.	D2	111
Whetstone, stm., U.S.	E2	130
Whidbey Island, i., Wa., U.S.	A3	154
Whidbey Island Naval Air Station, mil., Wa., U.S.	A3	154
Whigham, Ga., U.S.	F2	117
Whiskey Peak, mtn., Wy., U.S.	D5	157
Whiskeytown-Shasta-Trinity National Recreation Area, Ca., U.S.	B2	112
Whisky Chitto Creek, stm., La., U.S.	C2	125
Whistler, B.C., Can.	D6	99
Whitacres, Ct., U.S.	A5	114
Whitakers, N.C., U.S.	A5	140
Whitbourne, Newf., Can.	E5	102
Whitby, Ont., Can.	D6	103
Whitchurch-Stouffville, Ont., Can.	D5	103
Whitcomb Mountain, mtn., N.H., U.S.	A4	136
White, Ga., U.S.	B2	117
White, S.D., U.S.	C9	148
White, co., Ar., U.S.	B4	111
White, co., Ga., U.S.	B3	117
White, co., Il., U.S.	E5	120
White, co., In., U.S.	C4	121
White, co., Tn., U.S.	D8	149
White, stm., U.S.	D8	106
White, stm., U.S.	C4	111
White, stm., U.S.	D5	148
White, stm., U.S.	C7	151
White, stm., Az., U.S.	D5	110
White, stm., In., U.S.	H2	121
White, stm., Mi., U.S.	E4	129
White, stm., Nv., U.S.	E6	135
White, stm., Tx., U.S.	C2	150
White, stm., Vt., U.S.	D4	152
White, stm., Wa., U.S.	B5	154
White, stm., Wa., U.S.	B4	154
White, East Fork, stm., In., U.S.	G5	121
White Bay, b., Newf., Can.	D3	102
White Bear, stm., Newf., Can.	E3	102
White Bear Lake, Mn., U.S.	E5	130
White Bird, Id., U.S.	D2	119
White Bluff, Tn., U.S.	A4	149
White Breast Creek, stm., Ia., U.S.	C4	122
White Butte, mtn., N.D., U.S.	C2	141
White Cap Mountain, mtn., Me., U.S.	C3	126
White Castle, La., U.S.	D4	125
White Center, Wa., U.S.	e11	154
White City, Fl., U.S.	C1	116
White City, Ks., U.S.	D7	123
White City, Or., U.S.	E4	144
White Clay Creek, stm., U.S.	A3	134
White Clay Creek, stm., De., U.S.	B3	115
White Cliffs, Austl.	H5	70
White Cloud, Ks., U.S.	C8	123
White Cloud, Mi., U.S.	E5	129
Whitecourt, Alta., Can.	B3	98
White Creek, stm., U.S.	E2	152
Whiteday, stm., W.V., U.S.	h10	155
White Deer, Tx., U.S.	B2	150
White Earth, Mn., U.S.	C3	130
White Earth Indian Reservation, Mn., U.S.	C3	130
White Earth Lake, l., Mn., U.S.	C3	130
Whiteface, Tx., U.S.	C1	150
Whiteface, stm., Mn., U.S.	C6	130
Whiteface Mountain, mtn., N.Y., U.S.	f11	139
White Face Mountain, mtn., Vt., U.S.	B3	152
Whitefield, N.H., U.S.	B3	136
Whitefield, Ok., U.S.	B6	143
Whitefish, Mt., U.S.	B2	133
Whitefish Bay, Wi., U.S.	m12	156
Whitefish Bay, b., Mi., U.S.	B6	129
Whitefish Falls, Ont., Can.	A3	103
Whitefish Lake, l., Mn., U.S.	D4	130
Whitefish Range, mts., Mt., U.S.	B2	133
Whiteford, Md., U.S.	A5	127
White Fox, Sask., Can.	D3	105
White Hall, Al., U.S.	C3	108
White Hall, Ar., U.S.	C3	111
White Hall, Ga., U.S.	C3	117
White Hall, Il., U.S.	D3	120
Whitehall, Mi., U.S.	E4	129
Whitehall, Mt., U.S.	E4	133
Whitehall, N.Y., U.S.	B7	139
Whitehall, Oh., U.S.	m11	142
Whitehall, Wi., U.S.	D2	156
Whitehall Reservoir, res., Ma., U.S.	h9	128
White Haven, Pa., U.S.	D10	145
White Heath, Il., U.S.	C5	120
Whitehorn, Point, c., Wa., U.S.	A3	154
Whitehorse, Yukon, Can.	D5	96
White Horse, N.J., U.S.	C3	137
Whitehorse, S.D., U.S.	B5	148
White Horse Beach, Ma., U.S.	C6	128
Whitehouse, Oh., U.S.	A2	142
White House, Tn., U.S.	A5	149
Whitehouse, Tx., U.S.	C5	150
White House Station, N.J., U.S.	B3	137
White Island, i., N.W. Ter., Can.	C16	96
White Island Shores, Ma., U.S.	C6	128
White Knob Mountains, mts., Id., U.S.	F5	119
White Lake, Ont., Can.	B8	103
White Lake, S.D., U.S.	D7	148
White Lake, Wi., U.S.	C5	156
White Lake, l., Ont., Can.	B8	103
White Lake, l., La., U.S.	E3	125
Whitelaw, Alta., Can.	A1	98
Whitelaw, Wi., U.S.	h10	156
Whiteman Air Force Base, mil., Mo., U.S.	C4	132
Whitemark, Austl.	M8	70
White Meadow Lake, N.J., U.S.	B3	137
White Mesa Natural Bridge, Az., U.S.	A4	110
White Mountain, Ak., U.S.	C7	109
White Mountain Peak, mtn., Ca., U.S.	D4	112
White Mountains, mts., U.S.	D4	112
White Mountains, mts., N.H., U.S.	B3	136
Whitemouth, Man., Can.	E4	100
Whitemouth, stm., Man., Can.	E4	100
Whitemouth Lake, l., Man., Can.	E4	100
White Nile (Al-Bahr al-Abyad), stm., Sud.	L7	60
White Oak, Ga., U.S.	E5	117
White Oak, Oh., U.S.	o12	142
White Oak, Tx., U.S.	C5	150
White Oak Creek, stm., Oh., U.S.	D2	142
Whiteoak Creek, stm., Tn., U.S.	A4	149
White Oak Lake, res., Ar., U.S.	D2	111
White Oak Mountain, mtn., Ar., U.S.	C2	111
White Pigeon, Mi., U.S.	G5	129
White Pine, Mi., U.S.	m12	129
White Pine, Tn., U.S.	C10	149
White Pine, co., Nv., U.S.	D6	135
White Plains, Al., U.S.	B4	108
White Plains, Ga., U.S.	C3	117
White Plains, Ky., U.S.	C2	124
White Plains, Md., U.S.	C4	127
White Plains, N.Y., U.S.	D7	139
Whiteriver, Az., U.S.	D6	110
White River, S.D., U.S.	D5	148
White River Junction, Vt., U.S.	D4	152
White River Plateau, plat., Co., U.S.	B3	113
White Rock, B.C., Can.	E6	99
White Rock, N.M., U.S.	B3	138
White Rock, R.I., U.S.	F1	146
White Rock, S.C., U.S.	C5	147
White Rock Creek, stm., Ks., U.S.	C5	123
Whiterocks, Ut., U.S.	C6	151
White Rocks, mtn., Ky., U.S.	D6	124
White Russia see Belorusskaja Sovetskaja Socialističeskaja Respublika, state, U.S.S.R.	H11	26
Whitesail Lake, l., B.C., Can.	C4	99
White Salmon, Wa., U.S.	D4	154
White Salmon, stm., Wa., U.S.	D4	154
White Sands Missile Range, mil., N.M., U.S.	E3	138
White Sands National Monument, N.M., U.S.	E3	138
Whitesboro, N.J., U.S.	E3	137
Whitesboro, N.Y., U.S.	B5	139
Whitesboro, Ok., U.S.	C7	143
Whitesboro, Tx., U.S.	C4	150
Whites Brook, N.B., Can.	B2	101
Whitesburg, Ga., U.S.	C2	117
Whitesburg, Ky., U.S.	C7	124
Whites Creek, stm., Tn., U.S.	g10	149
White Sea see Beloje more, U.S.S.R.	D5	22
Whiteside, Tn., U.S.	D8	149
Whiteside, co., Il., U.S.	B3	120
White Springs, Fl., U.S.	B4	116
Whitestone, Ga., U.S.	B2	117
White Stone, Va., U.S.	C6	153
Whitestown, In., U.S.	C5	121
White Sulphur Springs, Mt., U.S.	D6	133
White Sulphur Springs, W.V., U.S.	D4	155
Whitesville, Ky., U.S.	C3	124
Whitesville, N.Y., U.S.	C3	139
Whitesville, W.V., U.S.	D3	155
White Swan, Wa., U.S.	C5	154
Whitetail, Mt., U.S.	B11	133
White Tank Mountains, mts., Az., U.S.	k7	110
Whiteville, N.C., U.S.	C4	140
Whiteville, Tn., U.S.	B2	149
White Volta (Volta Blanche), stm., Afr.	F6	54
Whitewater, Co., U.S.	C2	113
Whitewater, Ks., U.S.	E6	123
Whitewater, Mt., U.S.	B9	133
Whitewater, Wi., U.S.	F5	156
Whitewater, stm., U.S.	F7	121
Whitewater, stm., Ks., U.S.	E6	123
Whitewater, East Fork, stm., In., U.S.	E8	121
Whitewater, West Branch, stm., Ks., U.S.	g12	123
Whitewater Baldy, mtn., N.M., U.S.	D1	138
Whitewater Bay, b., Fl., U.S.	G6	116
White Woman Creek, stm., Ks., U.S.	D2	123
Whitewood, Austl.	C5	70
Whitewood, Sask., Can.	G4	105
Whitewood, S.D., U.S.	C2	148
Whitewright, Tx., U.S.	C4	150
Whitfield, co., Ga., U.S.	B2	117
Whitfield Estates, Fl., U.S.	q10	116
Whithorn, Scot., U.K.	G9	8
Whiting, In., U.S.	A3	121
Whiting, Ia., U.S.	B1	122
Whiting, Ks., U.S.	C8	123
Whiting, N.J., U.S.	D4	137
Whiting, Wi., U.S.	D4	156
Whiting Field Naval Air Station, mil., Fl., U.S.	u14	116
Whitingham, Vt., U.S.	F3	152
Whitinsville, Ma., U.S.	B4	128
Whitley, co., In., U.S.	B6	121
Whitley, co., Ky., U.S.	D5	124
Whitley City, Ky., U.S.	D5	124
Whitman, Ma., U.S.	B6	128
Whitman, Ne., U.S.	B4	134
Whitman, W.V., U.S.	D2	155
Whitman, co., Wa., U.S.	B8	154
Whitmans Pond, l., Ma., U.S.	h12	128
Whitman Square, N.J., U.S.	D2	137
Whitmer, W.V., U.S.	C5	155
Whitmire, S.C., U.S.	B4	147
Whitmore Lake, Mi., U.S.	p14	129
Whitmore Village, Hi., U.S.	f9	118
Whitney, Pa., U.S.	F3	145
Whitney, S.C., U.S.	B4	147
Whitney, Tx., U.S.	D4	150
Whitney, Lake, res., Tx., U.S.	D4	150
Whitney, Mount, mtn., Ca., U.S.	D4	112
Whitney Point, N.Y., U.S.	C5	139
Whitney Point Lake, res., N.Y., U.S.	C5	139
Whitneyville, Me., U.S.	D5	126
Whitsunday Island, i., Austl.	D8	70
Whittemore, Ia., U.S.	A3	122
Whittemore, Mi., U.S.	D7	129
Whittier, Ak., U.S.	C10	109
Whittier, Ca., U.S.	F4	112
Whittlesea, Austl.	K6	70
Whittlesea, Ciskei	I8	66
Whittlesey, Mount, hill, Wi., U.S.	B3	156
Whitwell, Tn., U.S.	D8	149
Whyalla, Austl.	I2	70
Whycocomagh, N.S., Can.	D8	101
Wiarton, Ont., Can.	C3	103
Wiawso, Ghana	H8	64
Wibaux, Mt., U.S.	D12	133
Wibaux, co., Mt., U.S.	D12	133
Wichita, Ks., U.S.	E6	123
Wichita, co., Ks., U.S.	D2	123
Wichita, co., Tx., U.S.	B3	150
Wichita Falls, Tx., U.S.	C3	150
Wichita Mountains, mts., Ok., U.S.	C3	143
Wick, Scot., U.K.	C10	8
Wickenburg, Az., U.S.	D3	110
Wickes, Ar., U.S.	C1	111
Wickett, Tx., U.S.	D1	150
Wickham, Cape, c., Austl.	L5	70
Wickiup Reservoir, res., Or., U.S.	E5	144
Wickliffe, Ky., U.S.	f8	124
Wickliffe, Oh., U.S.	A4	142
Wicklow, co., Ire.	I7	8
Wicklow Mountains, mts., Ire.	H7	8
Wicomico, co., Md., U.S.	D6	127
Wicomico, stm., Md., U.S.	D6	127
Wiconisco, Pa., U.S.	E8	145
Widefield, Co., U.S.	C6	113
Widen, W.V., U.S.	C4	155
Widener, Ar., U.S.	B5	111
Widerøe, Mount, mtn., Ant.	C3	73
Wide Ruins, Az., U.S.	B6	110
Wiehl, Ger.	E7	10
Wiek, Ger.	A13	10
Wieliczka, Pol.	F20	10
Wielkopolska, reg., Pol.	D17	10
Wieluń, Pol.	D18	10
Wien (Vienna), Aus.	G16	10
Wiener Neustadt, Aus.	H16	10
Wienerwald, mts., Aus.	G16	10
Wieprz, stm., Pol.	D22	10
Wierden, Neth.	D10	12
Wiesbaden, Ger.	E8	10
Wieselburg, Aus.	G15	10
Wiesloch, Ger.	F8	10
Wietze, Ger.	C9	10
Wigan, Eng., U.K.	H11	8
Wiggins, Co., U.S.	A6	113
Wiggins, Ms., U.S.	E4	131
Wiggins Peak, mtn., Wy., U.S.	C3	157
Wigtown, Scot., U.K.	G9	8
Wijalpurā, Nepal	G11	44
Wikieup, Az., U.S.	C2	110
Wikwemikong, Ont., Can.	B3	103
Wil, Switz.	D11	13
Wilbarger, co., Tx., U.S.	B3	150
Wilber, Ne., U.S.	D9	134
Wilberforce, Ont., Can.	B6	103
Wilberforce, Oh., U.S.	C2	142
Wilbraham, Ma., U.S.	B3	128
Wilbur, Or., U.S.	D3	144
Wilbur, Wa., U.S.	B7	154
Wilburn, Ar., U.S.	B4	111
Wilburton, Ok., U.S.	C6	143
Wilcannia, Austl.	H5	70
Wilcox, Sask., Can.	G3	105
Wilcox, Ne., U.S.	D6	134
Wilcox, Pa., U.S.	C4	145
Wilcox, co., Al., U.S.	D2	108
Wilcox, co., Ga., U.S.	E3	117
Wilcox, Mount, mtn., Ma., U.S.	B1	128
Wild, stm., U.S.	B4	136
Wild Ammonoosuc, stm., N.H., U.S.	B3	136
Wild Branch, stm., Vt., U.S.	B4	152
Wildcat Creek, stm., In., U.S.	D4	121
Wildcat Creek, South Fork, stm., In., U.S.	D4	121
Wildcat Top, mtn., Tn., U.S.	D10	149
Wilder, Id., U.S.	F2	119
Wilder, Vt., U.S.	D4	152
Wilder Dam, U.S.	C2	136
Wildersville, Tn., U.S.	B3	149
Wilderville, Or., U.S.	E3	144
Wildhaus, Switz.	D11	13
Wildhay, stm., Alta., Can.	C2	98
Wildhorse Creek, stm., Ok., U.S.	C4	143
Wild Horse Reservoir, res., Nv., U.S.	B6	135
Wildon, Aus.	I15	10
Wildorado, Tx., U.S.	B1	150
Wild Rice, stm., Mn., U.S.	C2	130
Wild Rice, stm., N.D., U.S.	C8	141
Wild Rice, South Branch, stm., Mn., U.S.	C2	130
Wildrose, N.D., U.S.	A2	141
Wild Rose, Wi., U.S.	D4	156
Wildsville, La., U.S.	C4	125
Wildwood, Alta., Can.	C3	98
Wildwood, Fl., U.S.	D4	116
Wildwood, Il., U.S.	h9	120
Wildwood, N.J., U.S.	F3	137
Wildwood Crest, N.J., U.S.	F3	137
Wiley, Co., U.S.	C8	113
Wiley, Wa., U.S.	C5	154
Wilhelm, Mount, mtn., Pap. N. Gui.	m15	68a
Wilhelmina Gebergte, mts., Sur.	F14	84
Wilhelminakanaal, Neth.	E7	12
Wilhelmina Peak see Trikora, Puncak, mtn., Indon.	F10	38
Wilhelm-Pieck-Stadt Guben see Guben, Ger.	D14	10
Wilhelmshaven, Ger.	B8	10
Wilhelmstal, Nmb.	C3	66
Wilhoit, Az., U.S.	C3	110
Wilkes, co., Ga., U.S.	C4	117
Wilkes, co., N.C., U.S.	A1	140
Wilkes-Barre, Pa., U.S.	D10	145
Wilkesboro, N.C., U.S.	A1	140
Wilkes Land, reg., Ant.	C7	73
Wilkeson, Wa., U.S.	B3	154
Wilkie, Sask., Can.	E1	105
Wilkin, co., Mn., U.S.	D2	130
Wilkinsburg, Pa., U.S.	F2	145
Wilkinson, In., U.S.	E6	121
Wilkinson, Ms., U.S.	D2	131
Wilkinson, W.V., U.S.	D3	155
Wilkinson, co., Ga., U.S.	D3	117
Wilkinson, co., Ms., U.S.	D2	131
Will, co., Il., U.S.	B6	120
Willacoochee, Ga., U.S.	E3	117
Willacy, co., Tx., U.S.	F4	150
Willamette, stm., Or., U.S.	C3	144
Willamette, Middle Fork, stm., Or., U.S.	D4	144
Willamette Pass, Or., U.S.	D4	144
Willamina, Or., U.S.	B3	144
Willandra Billabong Creek, stm., Austl.	I6	70
Willapa, Wa., U.S.	C2	154
Willapa Bay, b., Wa., U.S.	C1	154
Willard, Ks., U.S.	C8	123
Willard, Ky., U.S.	B7	124
Willard, Mo., U.S.	D4	132
Willard, N.M., U.S.	C3	138
Willard, N.Y., U.S.	C4	139
Willard, Oh., U.S.	A3	142
Willard, Ut., U.S.	B3	151
Willard, Punta, c., Mex.	C3	90
Willard Bay, b., Ut., U.S.	B3	151
Willards, Md., U.S.	D7	127
Willard Stream, stm., Vt., U.S.	B5	152
Willcox, Az., U.S.	E6	110
Willcox Playa, l., Az., U.S.	E5	110
Willemstad, Neth. Ant.	H10	94
William "Bill" Dannelly Reservoir, res., Al., U.S.	C2	108
William P. Lane, Jr. Memorial Bridge, Md., U.S.	B5	127
Williams, Az., U.S.	B3	110
Williams, Ca., U.S.	C2	112
Williams, In., U.S.	G4	121
Williams, Ia., U.S.	B4	122
Williams, co., N.D., U.S.	A2	141
Williams, co., Oh., U.S.	A1	142
Williams, stm., Austl.	C4	70
Williams, stm., Vt., U.S.	E3	152
Williams, stm., W.V., U.S.	C4	155
Williams Air Force Base, mil., Az., U.S.	D4	110
Williams Bay, Wi., U.S.	F5	156
Williamsburg, Ont., Can.	C9	103
Williamsburg, In., U.S.	E8	121
Williamsburg, Ia., U.S.	C5	122
Williamsburg, Ks., U.S.	D8	123
Williamsburg, Ky., U.S.	D5	124
Williamsburg, Ma., U.S.	B2	128
Williamsburg, N.M., U.S.	D2	138
Williamsburg, Oh., U.S.	C1	142
Williamsburg, Pa., U.S.	F5	145
Williamsburg, Va., U.S.	C6	153
Williamsburg, W.V., U.S.	D4	155
Williamsburg, co., S.C., U.S.	D8	147
Williamsfield, Il., U.S.	C3	120
Williams Fork, stm., Co., U.S.	A3	113
Williams Harbour, Newf., Can.	B4	102
Williams Lake, B.C., Can.	C6	99
Williams Mountain, mtn., Ok., U.S.	C7	143
Williamson, Ga., U.S.	C2	117
Williamson, N.Y., U.S.	B3	139
Williamson, W.V., U.S.	D2	155
Williamson, co., Il., U.S.	F4	120
Williamson, co., Tn., U.S.	B5	149
Williamson, co., Tx., U.S.	D4	150
Williamsport, In., U.S.	D3	121
Williamsport, Md., U.S.	A2	127
Williamsport, Oh., U.S.	C2	142
Williamsport, Pa., U.S.	D7	145
Williamston, Mi., U.S.	F6	129
Williamston, N.C., U.S.	B5	140
Williamston, S.C., U.S.	B3	147
Williamstown, Ont., Can.	B10	103
Williamstown, Ky., U.S.	B5	124
Williamstown, Ma., U.S.	A1	128
Williamstown, Mo., U.S.	A6	132
Williamstown, N.J., U.S.	D3	137
Williamstown, Pa., U.S.	E8	145
Williamstown, Vt., U.S.	C3	152
Williamstown, W.V., U.S.	B3	155
Williamsville, De., U.S.	G5	115
Williamsville, Il., U.S.	D4	120
Williamsville, Ms., U.S.	B4	131
Williamsville, Mo., U.S.	E7	132
Williamsville, N.Y., U.S.	C2	139
Willich, Ger.	A13	14
Willimantic, Ct., U.S.	C7	114
Willimantic, stm., Ct., U.S.	B6	114
Willimantic Reservoir, res., Ct., U.S.	C7	114
Willingboro, N.J., U.S.	C3	137
Willingdon, Alta., Can.	C4	98
Willis, Mi., U.S.	p14	129
Willis, Tx., U.S.	D5	150
Willisau, Switz.	D9	13
Willisburg, Ky., U.S.	C4	124
Willis Group, is., Austl.	C10	68
Williston, S. Afr.	H5	66
Williston, Fl., U.S.	C4	116
Williston, N.D., U.S.	A2	141
Williston, S.C., U.S.	E5	147
Williston, Tn., U.S.	B2	149
Williston, Vt., U.S.	C2	152
Williston Basin, U.S.	B2	141
Williston Lake, res., B.C., Can.	B6	99
Willisville, Ar., U.S.	D2	111
Willisville, Il., U.S.	F4	120
Willis Wharf, Va., U.S.	C7	153
Willits, Ca., U.S.	C2	112
Willmar, Mn., U.S.	E3	130
Willoughby, Oh., U.S.	A4	142
Willoughby, Cape, c., Austl.	J3	70
Willoughby, Lake, l., Vt., U.S.	B4	152
Willoughby Hills, Oh., U.S.	A4	142
Willow, Ak., U.S.	g17	109
Willow Branch, In., U.S.	E6	121
Willowbrook, Sask., Can.	F4	105
Willow Bunch, Sask., Can.	H3	105
Willow City, N.D., U.S.	A5	141
Willow Creek, Mt., U.S.	E5	133
Willow Creek, stm., Nv., U.S.	E5	135
Willow Creek, stm., Ut., U.S.	D6	151
Willow Creek, stm., Wy., U.S.	C6	157
Willow Grove, De., U.S.	D3	115
Willow Grove, Pa., U.S.	F11	145
Willow Grove Naval Air Station, mil., Pa., U.S.	F11	145
Willow Hill, Il., U.S.	E5	120
Willowick, Oh., U.S.	A4	142
Willow Lake, S.D., U.S.	C8	148
Willowmore, S. Afr.	I6	66
Willow Reservoir, res., Wi., U.S.	C3	156
Willow River, B.C., Can.	B6	99
Willow River, Mn., U.S.	D6	130
Willow Run, De., U.S.	i7	115
Willow Run, Mi., U.S.	p14	129
Willows, Ca., U.S.	C2	112
Willow Springs, Il., U.S.	k9	120
Willow Springs, Mo., U.S.	E6	132
Wills, Lake, l., Austl.	D5	68
Willsboro, N.Y., U.S.	f11	139
Wills Hill, hill, Ma., U.S.	f11	128
Willshire, Oh., U.S.	B1	142
Willston, Va., U.S.	B5	153
Willunga, Austl.	J3	70
Wilmar, Ar., U.S.	D4	111
Wilmer, Al., U.S.	E1	108
Wilmerding, Pa., U.S.	k14	145
Wilmette, Il., U.S.	A6	120
Wilmington, Austl.	I3	70
Wilmington, De., U.S.	B3	115
Wilmington, Il., U.S.	B5	120
Wilmington, Ma., U.S.	A5	128
Wilmington, N.C., U.S.	C5	140
Wilmington, Oh., U.S.	C2	142
Wilmington, Vt., U.S.	F3	152
Wilmington Manor, De., U.S.	i7	115
Wilmont, Mn., U.S.	G3	130
Wilmore, Ky., U.S.	C5	124
Wilmot, N.S., Can.	E4	101
Wilmot, Ar., U.S.	D4	111
Wilmot, S.D., U.S.	B9	148
Wilmot Flat, N.H., U.S.	D3	136
Wilno, Ont., Can.	B7	103
Wilsall, Mt., U.S.	E6	133
Wilsey, Ks., U.S.	D7	123
Wilson, Austl.	I3	70
Wilson, Ar., U.S.	B5	111
Wilson, Ks., U.S.	D5	123
Wilson, La., U.S.	D4	125
Wilson, N.Y., U.S.	B2	139
Wilson, N.C., U.S.	B5	140
Wilson, Ok., U.S.	C4	143
Wilson, Pa., U.S.	E11	145
Wilson, Ut., U.S.	B3	151
Wilson, Wy., U.S.	C2	157
Wilson, co., Ks., U.S.	E8	123
Wilson, co., N.C., U.S.	C2	140
Wilson, co., Tn., U.S.	A5	149
Wilson, co., Tx., U.S.	E3	150
Wilson, stm., Austl.	F4	70
Wilson, Cape, c., N.W. Ter., Can.	C16	96
Wilson, Mount, mtn., Az., U.S.	B1	110
Wilson, Mount, mtn., Ca., U.S.	m12	112
Wilson, Mount, mtn., Co., U.S.	D2	113
Wilson, Mount, mtn., Nv., U.S.	E7	135
Wilson, Mount, mtn., Or., U.S.	B5	144
Wilson Creek, stm., Wa., U.S.	B6	154
Wilson Creek, stm., Wa., U.S.	B5	154
Wilson Dam, Al., U.S.	A2	108
Wilson Lake, res., Al., U.S.	A2	108
Wilson Lake, res., Ks., U.S.	D4	123
Wilsons Beach, N.B., Can.	E3	101
Wilsons Mills, N.C., U.S.	B4	140
Wilsons Promontory, c., Austl.	L7	70
Wilsonville, Al., U.S.	B3	108
Wilsonville, Ct., U.S.	A8	114
Wilsonville, Il., U.S.	D4	120
Wilsonville, Ne., U.S.	D5	134
Wilsonville, Or., U.S.	h12	144
Wilton, Al., U.S.	B3	108
Wilton, Ar., U.S.	D1	111
Wilton, Ct., U.S.	E2	114
Wilton, Ia., U.S.	C6	122
Wilton, Me., U.S.	D2	126
Wilton, Mn., U.S.	C3	130
Wilton, N.H., U.S.	E3	136
Wilton, N.D., U.S.	B5	141
Wilton, Wi., U.S.	E3	156
Wilton Center, N.H., U.S.	E3	136
Wiltshire, co., Eng., U.K.	J12	8
Wiluna, Austl.	E4	68
Wimauma, Fl., U.S.	E4	116
Wimbledon, N.D., U.S.	B7	141
Wimborne, Alta., Can.	D4	98
Wimico, Lake, l., Fl., U.S.	C1	116
Winagami Lake, l., Alta., Can.	B2	98
Winamac, In., U.S.	B4	121
Winburg, S. Afr.	G8	66
Wincheck Pond, l., R.I., U.S.	E1	146
Winchell Mountain, mtn., Ma., U.S.	B2	128
Winchendon, Ma., U.S.	A3	128
Winchester, Ont., Can.	B9	103
Winchester, Eng., U.K.	J12	8
Winchester, Ar., U.S.	D4	111
Winchester, Id., U.S.	C2	119
Winchester, Il., U.S.	D3	120
Winchester, In., U.S.	D8	121
Winchester, Ks., U.S.	k15	123
Winchester, Ky., U.S.	C5	124
Winchester, Ma., U.S.	g11	128
Winchester, Nv., U.S.	G6	135
Winchester, N.H., U.S.	E2	136
Winchester, Oh., U.S.	D2	142
Winchester, Tn., U.S.	B5	149
Winchester, Va., U.S.	A4	153
Winchester Bay, Or., U.S.	D2	144
Wind, stm., Wa., U.S.	D4	154
Wind, stm., Wy., U.S.	C4	157
Windber, Pa., U.S.	F4	145
Wind Cave National Park, S.D., U.S.	D2	148
Winder, Ga., U.S.	C3	117
Windermere, B.C., Can.	D10	99
Windfall, In., U.S.	D6	121
Windgap, Pa., U.S.	E11	145
Windham, Ct., U.S.	C7	114
Windham, Oh., U.S.	A4	142
Windham, co., Ct., U.S.	B7	114
Windham, co., Vt., U.S.	F3	152
Windhoek, Nmb.	D3	66
Winding Stair Mountain, mts., Ok., U.S.	C6	143
Windischgarsten, Aus.	H14	10
Wind Lake, Wi., U.S.	F5	156
Wind Lake, l., Wi., U.S.	n11	156
Windmill Point, c., Va., U.S.	C6	153
Windom, Ks., U.S.	D6	123
Windom, Mn., U.S.	G3	130
Windom Peak, mtn., Co., U.S.	D3	113
Windorah, Austl.	E5	70
Window Rock, Az., U.S.	B6	110
Wind Point, Wi., U.S.	n12	156
Wind River Indian Reservation, Wy., U.S.	C4	157
Wind River Peak, mtn., Wy., U.S.	D3	157
Wind River Range, mts., Wy., U.S.	C3	157
Windsor, Austl.	I9	70
Windsor, Newf., Can.	D4	102

Name | Map Ref. | Page

Windsor, N.S., Can. E5 101
Windsor, Ont., Can. E1 103
Windsor, Que., Can. D5 104
Windsor, Eng., U.K. J13 8
Windsor, Co., U.S. A6 113
Windsor, Ct., U.S. B5 114
Windsor, Il., U.S. D5 120
Windsor, Mo., U.S. C4 132
Windsor, N.C., U.S. B6 140
Windsor, Pa., U.S. G8 145
Windsor, Vt., U.S. E4 152
Windsor, Va., U.S. D6 153
Windsor, co., Vt., U.S. D3 152
Windsor Heights, Ia., U.S. e8 122
Windsor Locks, Ct., U.S. B5 114
Windsorville, Ct., U.S. B5 114
Windthorst, Sask., Can. G4 105
Windward Islands, is., N.A. H14 94
Windward Passage, strt., N.A. E7 94
Windy Hill, S.C., U.S. C8 147
Windy Peak, mtn., Wa., U.S. A6 154
Winefred, stm., Alta., Can. B5 98
Winefred Lake, l., Alta., Can. B5 98
Winejok, Sud. M4 60
Winfall, N.C., U.S. A6 140
Winfield, Alta., Can. C3 98
Winfield, Al., U.S. B2 108
Winfield, Ia., U.S. C6 122
Winfield, Ks., U.S. E7 123
Winfield, Mo., U.S. C7 132
Winfield, N.J., U.S. k7 137
Winfield, Tn., U.S. C9 149
Winfield, W.V., U.S. C3 155
Wing, Al., U.S. D3 108
Wing, N.D., U.S. B5 141
Wing, stm., Mn., U.S. D3 130
Wingate, In., U.S. D3 121
Wingate, N.C., U.S. C2 140
Wingene, Bel. F3 12
Winger, Mn., U.S. C3 130
Wingham, Austl. H10 70
Wingham, Ont., Can. D3 103
Wingo, Ky., U.S. f9 124
Winifred, Mt., U.S. C7 133
Winifreda, Arg. I6 80
Winifrede, W.V., U.S. m12 155
Winigan, Mo., U.S. A5 132
Winisk, stm., Ont., Can. n18 103
Winisk Lake, l., Ont., Can. n18 103
Wink, Tx., U.S. D1 150
Winkana, Burma G5 40
Winkelman, Az., U.S. E5 110
Winkler, Man., Can. E3 100
Winkler, co., Tx., U.S. D1 150
Winlaw, B.C., Can. E9 99
Winlock, Wa., U.S. C3 154
Winn, Me., U.S. C4 126
Winn, Mi., U.S. E6 129
Winn, co., La., U.S. C3 125
Winneba, Ghana I9 64
Winnebago, Il., U.S. A4 120
Winnebago, Mn., U.S. G4 130
Winnebago, Ne., U.S. B9 134
Winnebago, Wi., U.S. h8 156
Winnebago, co., Il., U.S. A4 120
Winnebago, co., Ia., U.S. A4 122
Winnebago, co., Wi., U.S. D5 156
Winnebago, stm., Ia., U.S. A4 122
Winnebago, Lake, l., Wi., U.S. E5 156
Winnebago Indian Reservation, Ne., U.S. B9 134
Winneconne, Wi., U.S. D5 156
Winnemucca, Nv., U.S. C4 135
Winnemucca Lake, l., Nv., U.S. C2 135
Winner, S.D., U.S. D6 148
Winneshiek, co., Ia., U.S. A6 122
Winnetka, Il., U.S. A6 120
Winnett, Mt., U.S. C8 133
Winnfield, La., U.S. C3 125
Winnibigoshish, Lake, l., Mn., U.S. C4 130
Winnipeg, Man., Can. E3 100
Winnipeg, stm., Can. D4 100
Winnipeg, Lake, l., Man., Can. C3 100
Winnipeg Beach, Man., Can. D3 100
Winnipegosis, Man., Can. D2 100
Winnipegosis, Lake, l., Man., Can. C2 100
Winnipesaukee, Lake, l., N.H., U.S. C4 136
Winnisquam, N.H., U.S. C3 136
Winnisquam Lake, l., N.H., U.S. C3 136
Winnsboro, La., U.S. B4 125
Winnsboro, S.C., U.S. C5 147
Winnsboro, Tx., U.S. C5 150
Winnsboro Mills, S.C., U.S. C5 147
Winona, Ks., U.S. C2 123
Winona, Mn., U.S. F7 130
Winona, Ms., U.S. B4 131
Winona, Mo., U.S. D6 132
Winona, W.V., U.S. C4 155
Winona, co., Mn., U.S. F7 130
Winona Lake, In., U.S. B6 121
Winona Lake, l., Vt., U.S. C2 152
Winooski, Vt., U.S. C2 152
Winooski, stm., Vt., U.S. C3 152
Winooski, North Branch, stm., Vt., U.S. C3 152
Winschoten, Neth. B11 12
Winside, Ne., U.S. B8 134
Winslow, Az., U.S. C5 110
Winslow, Ar., U.S. B1 111
Winslow, Il., U.S. A4 120
Winslow, In., U.S. H3 121
Winslow, Me., U.S. D3 126
Winslow, Ne., U.S. C9 134
Winsted, Ct., U.S. B3 114
Winsted, Mn., U.S. F4 130
Winston, Fl., U.S. D4 116
Winston, Mo., U.S. B3 132
Winston, Or., U.S. D3 144
Winston, co., Al., U.S. A2 108
Winston, co., Ms., U.S. B4 131
Winston-Salem, N.C., U.S. A2 140
Winstonville, Ms., U.S. B3 131
Winter, Wi., U.S. C2 156
Winter Beach, Fl., U.S. E6 116
Winter Garden, Fl., U.S. D5 116
Winter Harbor, Me., U.S. D4 126
Winter Harbour, B.C., Can. D3 99
Winter Haven, Fl., U.S. D5 116
Wintering Lake, l., Man., Can. B3 100
Winter Park, Co., U.S. B5 113
Winter Park, Fl., U.S. D5 116
Winter Park, N.C., U.S. C5 140
Winterport, Me., U.S. D4 126
Winter Ridge, mtn., Or., U.S. E6 144
Winters, Ca., U.S. C2 112
Winters, Tx., U.S. D3 150
Winterset, Ia., U.S. C4 122
Wintersville, Oh., U.S. B5 142
Winterthur, Switz. C10 13
Winterthur, De., U.S. h7 115
Winterton, Newf., Can. E5 102
Winterville, Ga., U.S. C3 117
Winterville, N.C., U.S. B5 140
Winthrop, Ar., U.S. D1 111
Winthrop, Ia., U.S. B6 122
Winthrop, Me., U.S. D3 126
Winthrop, Ma., U.S. B6 128
Winthrop, Mn., U.S. F4 130
Winthrop, N.Y., U.S. f10 139
Winthrop, Wa., U.S. A5 154
Winthrop, Lake, l., Ma., U.S. h10 128
Winthrop Harbor, Il., U.S. A6 120
Winton, Austl. D5 70
Winton, N.Z. G2 72
Winton, Mn., U.S. C7 130
Winton, N.C., U.S. A6 140
Winton Lake, res., Oh., U.S. o12 143
Winyah Bay, b., S.C., U.S. E9 147
Wipperfürth, Ger. D7 10
Wirātanagar, Nepal G12 44
Wīrgañj, Nepal G11 44
Wirral, N.B., Can. D3 101
Wirral, pen., Eng., U.K. H10 8
Wirraminna, Austl. H2 70
Wirt, co., W.V., U.S. B3 155
Wiscasset, Me., U.S. D3 126
Wisconsin, state, U.S. D4 156
Wisconsin, stm., Wi., U.S. E3 156
Wisconsin, Lake, res., Wi., U.S. E4 156
Wisconsin Dells, Wi., U.S. E4 156
Wisconsin Rapids, Wi., U.S. D4 156
Wisdom, Mt., U.S. E3 133
Wise, N.C., U.S. A4 140
Wise, Va., U.S. f9 153
Wise, co., Tx., U.S. C4 150
Wise, co., Va., U.S. e9 153
Wiseton, Sask., Can. F2 105
Wishart, Sask., Can. F3 105
Wishart, Mo., U.S. D4 132
Wishek, N.D., U.S. C6 141
Wishram, Wa., U.S. D4 154
Wisła, stm., Pol. A18 10
Wismar, Ger. B11 10
Wismar, Guy. D13 84
Wisner, La., U.S. C4 125
Wisner, Ne., U.S. C9 134
Wissembourg, Fr. C14 14
Wissota, Lake, res., Wi., U.S. D2 156
Wister, Ok., U.S. C7 143
Wister Lake, res., Ok., U.S. C7 143
Wisznice, Pol. D23 10
Witbank, S. Afr. E9 66
Witbooisvlei, Nmb. E4 66
Withamsville, Oh., U.S. C1 142
Withee, Wi., U.S. D3 156
Witherbee, N.Y., U.S. A7 139
Witherspoon, Mount, mtn., Ak., U.S. g18 109
Withlacoochee, stm., U.S. B3 116
Withlacoochee, stm., Fl., U.S. C4 116
Witjira National Park, Austl. E7 68
Witless Bay, Newf., Can. E5 102
Witrivier, S. Afr. E10 66
Witsand, S. Afr. J5 66
Witt, Il., U.S. D4 120
Witt, Tn., U.S. C10 149
Witten, Ger. D7 10
Witten, S.D., U.S. D5 148
Wittenberg, Ger. D12 10
Wittenberg, Wi., U.S. D4 156
Wittenberge, Ger. B11 10
Wittenburg, Ger. B11 10
Wittenoom, Austl. D3 68
Wittingen, Ger. C10 10
Wittlich, Ger. F6 10
Wittman, Md., U.S. C5 127
Wittmann, Az., U.S. D3 110
Wittmund, Ger. B7 10
Wittstock, Ger. B12 10
Witwatersrant, reg., S. Afr. E8 66
Witzputz, Nmb. F3 66
Wixom, Mi., U.S. o14 129
Wixom Lake, res., Mi., U.S. E6 129
Wizajny, Pol. A22 10
W. J. van Blommestein Meer, res., Sur. C7 76
Włocławek, Pol. C19 10
Włoszczowa, Pol. E19 10
Woburn, Ma., U.S. B5 128
Woden, Ia., U.S. A4 122
Wodonga, Austl. K7 70
Wohlen, Switz. D9 13
Wohlthat Mountains, mts., Ant. C3 73
Woi, Sud. N6 60
Woking, Eng., U.K. J13 8
Wolbach, Ne., U.S. C7 134
Wolcott, Ct., U.S. C4 114
Wolcott, In., U.S. C3 121
Wolcott, N.Y., U.S. B4 139
Wolcott, Vt., U.S. B4 152
Wolcottville, In., U.S. A7 121
Wolf, stm., Ms., U.S. E4 131
Wolf, stm., Tn., U.S. e9 149
Wolf, stm., Wi., U.S. C5 156
Wolf, North Fork, stm., Tn., U.S. B2 149
Wolfach, Ger. G8 10
Wolf Creek, Mt., U.S. C4 133
Wolf Creek, Or., U.S. E3 144
Wolf Creek, stm., U.S. A2 143
Wolf Creek, stm., Ia., U.S. B5 122
Wolf Creek, stm., Mi., U.S. D7 129
Wolf Creek, stm., Mt., U.S. C7 133
Wolf Creek, stm., W.V., U.S. m13 155
Wolf Creek Pass, Co., U.S. D3 113
Wolfe, co., Ky., U.S. C6 124
Wolfeboro, N.H., U.S. C4 136
Wolfeboro Falls, N.H., U.S. C4 136
Wolfe City, Tx., U.S. C4 150
Wolfen, Ger. D12 10
Wolfenbüttel, Ger. C10 10
Wolfhagen, Ger. D9 10
Wolf Lake, Il., U.S. F4 120
Wolflake, In., U.S. B7 121
Wolf Lake, Mi., U.S. E4 129
Wolf Lake, l., Il., U.S. k9 120
Wolf Mountain, mtn., Ak., U.S. B9 109
Wolf Point, Mt., U.S. B11 133
Wolfratshausen, Ger. H11 10
Wolfsberg, Aus. I14 10
Wolfsburg, Ger. C10 10
Wolf Swamp, sw., N.C., U.S. C5 140
Wolfville, N.S., Can. D5 101
Wolgast, Ger. A13 10
Wolhusen, Switz. D9 13
Wollaston, Islas, is., Chile H3 78
Wollaston Lake, l., Sask., Can. m8 105
Wollaston Peninsula, pen., N.W. Ter., Can. C9 96
Wollemi National Park, Austl. I9 70
Wollogorang, Austl. A2 70
Wollongong, Austl. J9 70
Wolmaransstad, S. Afr. F8 66
Wołomin, Pol. C21 10
Wolseley, Sask., Can. G4 105
Wolseley, S. Afr. I4 66
Wolsey, S.D., U.S. C7 148
Wolsztyn, Pol. C16 10
Wolvega, Neth. C9 12
Wolverhampton, Eng., U.K. I11 8
Wolverton, Mn., U.S. D2 130
Woman Lake, l., Mn., U.S. D4 130
Womelsdorf, Pa., U.S. F9 145
Wondai, Austl. F9 70
Wonder Lake, Il., U.S. A5 120
Wonewoc, Wi., U.S. E3 156
Wŏnju, S. Kor. F15 32
Wonosobo, Indon. J14 39a
Wonotobo Vallen, wtfl, Sur. E14 84
Wonowon, B.C., Can. A7 99
Wŏnsan, N. Kor. D15 32
Wonthaggi, Austl. L6 70
Wood, co., Oh., U.S. A2 142
Wood, co., Tx., U.S. C5 150
Wood, co., W.V., U.S. B3 155
Wood, co., Wi., U.S. D3 156
Wood, stm., Sask., Can. H2 105
Wood, stm., R.I., U.S. F2 146
Wood, stm., Wy., U.S. C3 157
Wood, Mount, mtn., Mt., U.S. E7 133
Woodall Mountain, mtn., Ms., U.S. A5 131
Woodbine, Ga., U.S. F5 117
Woodbine, Ia., U.S. C2 122
Woodbine, Ks., U.S. D7 123
Woodbine, Ky., U.S. D5 124
Woodbine, N.J., U.S. E3 137
Woodbourne, N.Y., U.S. D6 139
Woodbridge, Ct., U.S. D3 114
Woodbridge, Va., U.S. B5 153
Woodbridge [Township], N.J., U.S. B4 137
Woodburn, In., U.S. B8 121
Woodburn, Ia., U.S. C4 122
Woodburn, Ky., U.S. D3 124
Woodburn, Or., U.S. B4 144
Woodbury, Ct., U.S. C3 114
Woodbury, Ga., U.S. D2 117
Woodbury, Mn., U.S. F6 130
Woodbury, N.J., U.S. D2 137
Woodbury, Tn., U.S. B5 149
Woodbury, Vt., U.S. C4 152
Woodbury, co., Ia., U.S. B1 122
Woodbury Mountain, mtn., Vt., U.S. C4 152
Woodcliff, Ga., U.S. D5 117
Woodcliff Lake, N.J., U.S. g8 137
Woodcliff Lake, l., N.J., U.S. g8 137
Wood Dale, Il., U.S. k9 120
Woodenbong, Austl. G10 70
Wood End, spit, Ma., U.S. B7 128
Woodfield, S.C., U.S. C6 147
Woodford, co., Il., U.S. C4 120
Woodford, co., Ky., U.S. B5 124
Woodhull, Il., U.S. B3 120
Woodlake, Ca., U.S. D4 112
Wood Lake, Mn., U.S. F3 130
Woodland, Al., U.S. B4 108
Woodland, Ca., U.S. C3 112
Woodland, Ga., U.S. D2 117
Woodland, Il., U.S. C6 120
Woodland, Me., U.S. C5 126
Woodland, Mi., U.S. F5 129
Woodland, Ms., U.S. B4 131
Woodland, N.C., U.S. A5 140
Woodland, Pa., U.S. E5 145
Woodland, Wa., U.S. D3 154
Woodland Acres, Co., U.S. D6 113
Woodland Beach, De., U.S. C4 115
Woodland Mills, Tn., U.S. A2 149
Woodland Park, Co., U.S. C5 113
Woodlawn, Ont., Can. h11 103
Woodlawn, Il., U.S. E4 120
Woodlawn, Ky., U.S. e9 124
Woodlawn, Md., U.S. g10 127
Woodlawn, Oh., U.S. n13 142
Woodlawn, Tn., U.S. A4 149
Woodlawn, Va., U.S. D2 153
Woodmont, Ct., U.S. E4 114
Woodmoor, Md., U.S. B4 127
Wood Mountain, mtn., Sask., Can. H2 105
Woodridge, Man., Can. E3 100
Woodridge, Il., U.S. k8 120
Wood-Ridge, N.J., U.S. h8 137
Wood River, Il., U.S. E3 120
Wood River, Ne., U.S. D7 134
Woodroffe, stm., Austl. C2 70
Woodroffe, Mount, mtn., Austl. E6 68
Woodrow, Sask., Can. H2 105
Woodruff, Az., U.S. C5 110
Woodruff, S.C., U.S. B3 147
Woodruff, Wi., U.S. C4 156
Woodruff, co., Ar., U.S. B4 111
Woods, co., Ok., U.S. A3 143
Woods, Lake, l., Austl. C6 68
Woods, Lake, res., Tn., U.S. B5 149
Woods, Lake of the, l., N.A. G14 96
Woodsboro, Md., U.S. A3 127
Woodsboro, Tx., U.S. E4 150
Woods Cross, Ut., U.S. C4 151
Woodsfield, Oh., U.S. C4 142
Woods Hole, Ma., U.S. C6 128
Woodside, Austl. L7 70
Woodside, De., U.S. D3 115
Woodson, Ar., U.S. C3 111
Woodson, Il., U.S. D3 120
Woodson, co., Ks., U.S. E8 123
Woodstock, N.B., Can. C2 101
Woodstock, Ont., Can. D4 103
Woodstock, Al., U.S. B2 108
Woodstock, Ct., U.S. B8 114
Woodstock, Ga., U.S. B2 117
Woodstock, Il., U.S. A5 120
Woodstock, Md., U.S. B4 127
Woodstock, Mn., U.S. F2 130
Woodstock, N.H., U.S. C3 136
Woodstock, N.Y., U.S. C6 139
Woodstock, Vt., U.S. D3 152
Woodstock, Va., U.S. B4 153
Woodstock Valley, Ct., U.S. B7 114
Woodston, Ks., U.S. C4 123
Woodstown, N.J., U.S. D2 137
Woodsville, N.H., U.S. B2 136
Woodville, Ont., Can. C5 103
Woodville, N.Z. D5 72
Woodville, Fl., U.S. B2 116
Woodville, Ga., U.S. C3 117
Woodville, Id., U.S. F6 119
Woodville, Ms., U.S. D2 131
Woodville, Oh., U.S. A2 142
Woodville, Tx., U.S. D5 150
Woodville, Wi., U.S. D1 156
Woodward, Al., U.S. B3 108
Woodward, Ia., U.S. C4 122
Woodward, Ok., U.S. A2 143
Woodward, co., Ok., U.S. A2 143
Woodwards Cove, N.B., Can. E3 101
Woodworth, La., U.S. C3 125
Woodworth, N.D., U.S. B6 141
Woody Head, c., Austl. G10 70
Woolgoolga, Austl. H10 70
Woolmarket, Ms., U.S. E5 131
Woolper Creek, stm., Ky., U.S. h13 124
Woolrich, Pa., U.S. D7 145
Woolsey Peak, mtn., Az., U.S. D3 110
Woolstock, Ia., U.S. B4 122
Woolwich, Me., U.S. g8 126
Woomera, Austl. H2 70
Woonsocket, R.I., U.S. A3 146
Woonsocket, S.D., U.S. C7 148
Woonsocket Reservoir Number Three, res., R.I., U.S. B3 146
Woorabinda, Austl. E8 70
Wooramel, stm., Austl. E3 68
Wooster, Ar., U.S. B3 111
Wooster, Oh., U.S. B4 142
Worb, Switz. E8 13
Worcester, S. Afr. I4 66
Worcester, Eng., U.K. I11 8
Worcester, Ma., U.S. B4 128
Worcester, N.Y., U.S. C6 139
Worcester, Vt., U.S. C3 152
Worcester, co., Md., U.S. D7 127
Worcester, co., Ma., U.S. A3 128
Worcester Mountains, mts., Vt., U.S. C3 152
Worden, Il., U.S. E4 120
Worden, Mt., U.S. E8 133
Worden Pond, l., R.I., U.S. F3 146
Wörgl, Aus. H12 10
Workington, Eng., U.K. G10 8
Worksop, Eng., U.K. H12 8
Workum, Neth. C7 12
Worland, Wy., U.S. B5 157
Worley, Id., U.S. B2 119
Wormerveer, Neth. D6 12
Worms, Ger. F8 10
Worth, Il., U.S. k9 120
Worth, co., Ga., U.S. E3 117
Worth, co., Ia., U.S. A4 122
Worth, co., Mo., U.S. A3 132
Wortham, Tx., U.S. D4 150
Worthing, Eng., U.K. K13 8
Worthing, S.D., U.S. D9 148
Worthington, In., U.S. F4 121
Worthington, Ia., U.S. B6 122
Worthington, Ky., U.S. B7 124
Worthington, Mn., U.S. G3 130
Worthington, Oh., U.S. B2 142
Worthington, Pa., U.S. E2 145
Worthington, W.V., U.S. k10 155
Worthington Knob, mtn., Tn., U.S. D8 149
Worthington Peak, mtn., Nv., U.S. F6 135
Worthville, Ky., U.S. B4 124
Woudrichem, Neth. E7 12
Wounded Knee, S.D., U.S. D3 148
Wounta, Nic. D11 92
Wounta, Laguna de, b., Nic. D11 92
Wouw, Neth. E5 12
Wowan, Austl. D9 70
Woy Woy, Austl. I9 70
Wrangel Island see Vrangel'a, ostrov, i., U.S.S.R. C28 24
Wrangell, Ak., U.S. D13 109
Wrangell, Cape, c., Ak., U.S. E2 109
Wrangell, Mount, mtn., Ak., U.S. f19 109
Wrangell Island, i., Ak., U.S. m24 109
Wrangell Mountains, mts., Ak., U.S. C11 109
Wrangell-Saint Elias National Park, Ak., U.S. C11 109
Wrath, Cape, c., Scot., U.K. C8 8
Wray, Co., U.S. A8 113
Wreck Reef, rf., Austl. D11 70
Wrens, Ga., U.S. C4 117
Wrenshall, Mn., U.S. D6 130
Wrentham, Alta., Can. E4 98
Wrentham, Ma., U.S. B5 128
Wrexham, Wales, U.K. H10 8
Wright, Ks., U.S. E4 123
Wright, Wy., U.S. C7 157
Wright, co., Ia., U.S. B4 122
Wright, co., Mn., U.S. E4 130
Wright, co., Mo., U.S. D5 132
Wright, Mount, mtn., Mt., U.S. C4 133
Wright Brothers National Memorial, hist., N.C., U.S. A7 140
Wright City, Mo., U.S. C8 132
Wright City, Ok., U.S. C6 143
Wright-Patterson Air Force Base, mil., Oh., U.S. C1 142
Wrightson, Mount, mtn., Az., U.S. F5 110
Wrightstown, N.J., U.S. C3 137
Wrightstown, Wi., U.S. D5 156
Wrightsville, Ar., U.S. C3 111
Wrightsville, Ga., U.S. D4 117
Wrightsville, Pa., U.S. F8 145
Wrightsville Beach, N.C., U.S. C5 140
Wrightsville Reservoir, res., Vt., U.S. C3 152
Wrightwood, Ca., U.S. E5 112
Wrigley, N.W. Ter., Can. D8 96
Wrigley, Tn., U.S. B4 149
Wrocław (Breslau), Pol. D17 10
Wrong Lake, l., Man., Can. C3 100
Wrottesley, Cape, c., N.W. Ter., Can. B8 96
Wroxeter, Ont., Can. D3 103
Września, Pol. C17 10
Wu, stm., China F8 30
Wucheng, China B2 34
Wuchin see Changzhou, China E10 30
Wuchuan, China D11 40
Wudian, China D1 34
Wudinna, Austl. I1 70
Wudu, China E7 30
Wugang, China F9 30
Wugong Shan, mts., China H2 34
Wuhai, China D8 30
Wuhan, China E3 34
Wuhu, China D7 34
Wuhua, China L4 34
Wuhuanchi, China A9 32
Wuji, China E2 32
Wujiang, China D9 34
Wukari, Nig. H14 64
Wuliang Shan, mts., China B6 40
Wum, Cam. H15 64
Wum Rog, Sud. M5 60
Wunstorf, Ger. C9 10
Wupatki National Monument, Az., U.S. B4 110
Wuping, China J5 34
Wuppertal, Ger. D7 10
Wuppertal, S. Afr. I4 66
Würenlingen, Switz. C9 13
Wurtsboro, N.Y., U.S. D6 139
Wurtsmith Air Force Base, mil., Mi., U.S. D7 129
Würzburg, Ger. F9 10
Wurzen, Ger. D12 10
Wushan, China E8 30
Wusheng, China F8 34
Wushenqi, China D8 30
Wuskwatim Lake, l., Man., Can. B2 100
Wusong, China D10 34
Wutai, China D9 30
Wutai Shan, mtn., China D1 32
Wutangjie, China F11 34
Wutongqiao, China F7 30
Wuustwezel, Bel. F6 12
Wuvulu Island, i., Pap. N. Gui. F11 38
Wuwei, China D7 30
Wuwei, China D6 34
Wuxi (Wuhsi), China D9 34
Wuyi Shan, mts., China I5 34
Wuyuan, China C8 30
Wuzhi Shan, mtn., China E10 40
Wuzhong, China D8 30
Wuzhou (Wuchow), China C11 40
Wyaconda, Mo., U.S. A6 132
Wyaconda, stm., Mo., U.S. A6 132
Wyalusing, Pa., U.S. C9 145
Wyandot, co., Oh., U.S. B2 142
Wyandotte, Mi., U.S. F7 129
Wyandotte, Ok., U.S. A7 143
Wyandotte, co., Ks., U.S. C9 123
Wyandra, Austl. F6 70
Wyanet, Il., U.S. B4 120
Wyangala, Lake, res., Austl. I8 70
Wyatt, In., U.S. A5 121
Wyatt, Mo., U.S. E8 132
Wycheproof, Austl. K5 70
Wye, stm., U.K. J11 8
Wyebridge, Ont., Can. C5 103
Wye Mills, Md., U.S. C5 127
Wyevale, Ont., Can. C5 103
Wykoff, Mn., U.S. G6 130
Wylie, Lake, res., U.S. A5 147
Wylliesburg, Va., U.S. D4 153
Wyman Lake, res., Me., U.S. C3 126
Wymark, Sask., Can. G2 105
Wymore, Ne., U.S. D9 134
Wyndham, Austl. C5 68
Wyndmere, N.D., U.S. C8 141
Wynnburg, Tn., U.S. A2 149
Wynndel, B.C., Can. E9 99
Wynne, Ar., U.S. B5 111
Wynnewood, Ok., U.S. C4 143
Wynniatt Bay, b., N.W. Ter., Can. B10 96
Wynona, Ok., U.S. A5 143
Wynoochee, stm., Wa., U.S. B2 154
Wynot, Ne., U.S. B8 134
Wynyard, Austl. M6 70
Wynyard, Sask., Can. F3 105
Wyocena, Wi., U.S. E4 156
Wyodak, Wy., U.S. B7 157
Wyola, Mt., U.S. E9 133
Wyoming, Ont., Can. E2 103
Wyoming, De., U.S. D3 115
Wyoming, Il., U.S. B4 120
Wyoming, Ia., U.S. B6 122
Wyoming, Mi., U.S. F5 129
Wyoming, Mn., U.S. E6 130
Wyoming, Oh., U.S. o13 142
Wyoming, Pa., U.S. n17 145
Wyoming, R.I., U.S. E2 146
Wyoming, co., N.Y., U.S. C2 139
Wyoming, co., Pa., U.S. D9 145
Wyoming, co., W.V., U.S. D3 155
Wyoming, state, U.S. C5 157
Wyoming Peak, mtn., Wy., U.S. D2 157
Wyoming Range, mts., Wy., U.S. D2 157
Wyomissing, Pa., U.S. F10 145
Wyong, Austl. I9 70
Wysocking Bay, b., N.C., U.S. B7 140
Wysokie Mazowieckie, Pol. C22 10
Wyszków, Pol. C21 10
Wythe, co., Va., U.S. D1 153
Wytheville, Va., U.S. D1 153

X

Xacbal, stm., N.A. B3 92
Xaidulla, China B8 44
Xainza, China E4 30
Xai-Xai, Moz. E11 66
Xalapa, Mex. H11 90
Xam (Chu), stm., Asia E8 40
Xambrê, stm., Braz. G2 79
Xam Nua, Laos D8 40
Xan (San), stm., Asia G9 40
Xangongo, Ang. E3 58
Xánthi, Grc. H8 20
Xanxerê, Braz. D12 80
Xapecó, stm., Braz. D12 80
Xapuri, Braz. D7 82
Xapuri, stm., Braz. D7 82
Xar Moron, stm., China C10 30
Xàtiva (Játiva), Spain G11 16
Xau, Lake, pl., Bots. C7 66
Xavantina, Braz. F2 79
Xaxim, Braz. D12 80
Xcalak, Mex. H16 90
X-Can, Mex. G16 90
Xenia, Il., U.S. E5 120
Xenia, Oh., U.S. C2 142
Xertigny, Fr. D13 14
Xhumo, Bots. C7 66
Xi, stm., China G9 30
Xiagaixin, China C5 40
Xiagezhuang, China G8 32
Xiahe, China D7 30
Xiamen (Amoy), China K7 34
Xiamen Gang, b., Asia K7 34
Xi'an (Sian), China E8 30
Xianfeng, China J6 34
Xiang, stm., China F9 30
Xiangcheng, China B2 34
Xiangfan, China E9 30
Xianggongshi, China G2 34
Xiangheguan, China B2 34
Xiangkhoang, Laos E7 40
Xiangkhoang, Plateau de, plat., Laos E7 40
Xiangride, China D6 30
Xiangtan, China H1 34
Xianinggang, China G1 34
Xianju, China G9 34
Xianxian, China E4 32
Xianyou, China J7 34
Xiaodanyang, China D7 34
Xiaogan, China E2 34
Xiaogushan, China D11 32
Xiao Hinggan Ling, mts., China B12 30
Xiaoji, China C8 34
Xiaojiang, China J3 34
Xiaolan, China M2 34
Xiaolipu, China G4 32
Xiaoshan, China E9 34
Xiaoshi, China H5 34
Xiaoshixiang, China E5 34
Xiaoxi, China J4 34
Xiapu, China I9 34
Xiapu, China H3 34
Xiaying, China F7 32
Xibu, China D7 34
Xichang, China F7 30
Xicoténcatl, Mex. F10 90
Xié, stm., Braz. G9 84
Xielipuke, China E10 44
Xigaotun, China C10 32
Xigazê, China F13 44
Xihua, China B3 34
Xijialong, China C7 40
Xikouxu, China J6 34
Xiliao, stm., China C11 30
Ximiao, China C7 30
Xin'an, China I5 34
Xinavane, Moz. E11 66
Xinba, China I7 32
Xincheng, China J3 34
Xindian, China F2 32
Xindukou, China B6 40
Xing'an, China F9 30
Xingcheng, China C8 32
Xinghua, China C8 34
Xingkai Hu (ozero Chanka), l., Asia B13 30
Xinglong, China C5 32
Xingtai, China F2 32
Xingu, stm., Braz. D8 76
Xinguan, China B7 34
Xingyi, China B8 40
Xinhe, China F3 32
Xinhua, China F9 30
Xinhui, China M2 34
Xining, China D7 30
Xinjiaji, China G4 32
Xinjiang, China D9 30
Xinjiang Uygur Zizhiqu (Sinkiang), prov., China C3 30
Xinle (Dongchangshou), China E2 32
Xinmin, China A10 32
Xinshi, China E9 34
Xinwen (Suncun), China H5 32
Xinxian, China D3 34
Xinxiang, China H1 32
Xinxing, China M1 34
Xinyang, China C3 34
Xinzao, China L2 34
Xinzhangzi, China C5 32
Xiongjiachang, China A8 40
Xipamanu, stm., S.A. D7 82
Xiping, China B3 34
Xique-Xique, Braz. F10 76
Xiruá, stm., Braz. B7 82
Xisha Qundao (Paracel Islands), is., China B5 38
Xishu, China G1 32
Xitole, Gui.-B. F2 64

Name Map Ref. Page

Xiuyan, China C11 32
Xixian, China C3 34
Xiyou, China F7 32
Xizang Zizhiqu (Tibet), prov., China E3 30
Xizhou, China F10 34
Xochicalco, hist., Mex. H10 90
Xochistlahuaca, Mex. I10 90
Xuancheng, China E7 34
Xuanhua, China C3 32
Xuchang, China A2 34
Xueao, China F10 34
Xuecheng, China I5 32
Xuji, China D5 34
Xun, stm., China G9 30
Xushui, China D3 32
Xuwen, China D11 40
Xuyong, China F8 30
Xuzhou (Süchow), China A6 34

Y

Yaan, China E7 30
Yablis, Nic. C11 92
Yablonovy Range see Jablonovyj chrebet, mts., U.S.S.R. G14 24
Yacambu, Parque Nacional, Ven. C8 84
Yacaré Norte, Riacho, stm., Para. B9 80
Yachats, Or., U.S. C2 144
Yaciretá, Isla, i., Para. D10 80
Yaco, Bol. G8 82
Yaco (Iaco), stm., S.A. D6 82
Yacolt, Wa., U.S. D3 154
Yacuiba, Bol. J10 82
Yacuma, stm., Bol. E8 82
Yādgīr, India D4 46
Yadkin, co., N.C., U.S. A2 140
Yadkin, stm., N.C., U.S. B2 140
Yadkinville, N.C., U.S. A2 140
Yad Mordekhay, Isr. E3 50
Yadong, China F4 30
Yafran, Libya B3 56
Yağcılar, Tur. J12 20
Yagoua, Cam. F10 54
Yagradagzê Shan, mtn., China C16 44
Yaguachi, Ec. I3 84
Yaguachi, stm., Ec. I3 84
Yaguajay, Cuba C5 94
Yaguala, stm., Hond. B8 92
Yaguará, Col. F5 84
Yaguaraparo, Ven. B11 84
Yaguarí, Ur. F11 80
Yaguarón (Jaguarão), stm., S.A. G12 80
Yaguas, stm., Peru I7 84
Yahk, B.C., Can. E9 99
Yahongqiao, China D5 32
Yahualica, Mex. G8 90
Yai, Khao, mtn., Asia H5 40
Yainax Butte, mtn., Or., U.S. E5 144
Yaizu, Japan M13 36
Yakima, Wa., U.S. C5 154
Yakima, co., Wa., U.S. C4 154
Yakima, stm., Wa., U.S. C6 154
Yakima Indian Reservation, Wa., U.S. C5 154
Yakima Ridge, mtn., Wa., U.S. C5 154
Yakima Valley, val., Wa., U.S. C5 154
Yako, Burkina E8 64
Yakobi Island, i., Ak., U.S. m21 109
Yakoma, Zaire H5 56
Yaku-shima, i., Japan Q5 37b
Yakutat, Ak., U.S. D12 109
Yakutat Bay, b., Ak., U.S. D11 109
Yakutsk see Jakutsk, U.S.S.R. E17 24
Yala, Thai. K6 40
Yalaha, Fl., U.S. D5 116
Yalahau, Laguna, b., Mex. G16 90
Yale, B.C., Can. E7 99
Yale, Ia., U.S. C3 122
Yale, Mi., U.S. E8 129
Yale, Ok., U.S. A5 143
Yale, S.D., U.S. C8 148
Yale, Mount, mtn., Co., U.S. C5 113
Yale Lake, res., Wa., U.S. D3 154
Yalgoo, Austl. E3 68
Yalinga, Cen. Afr. Rep. N2 60
Yalleroi, Austl. E6 70
Yalobusha, co., Ms., U.S. A4 131
Yalobusha, stm., Ms., U.S. B4 131
Yalong, stm., China E6 30
Yalova, Tur. I13 20
Yalta see Jalta, U.S.S.R. I4 22
Yalu (Amnok-kang), stm., Asia C12 32
Yamachiche, Que., Can. C5 104
Yamagata, Japan I15 36
Yamaguchi, Japan M6 36
Yamaska (Saint-Michel), Que., Can. C5 104
Yamba, Austl. G10 70
Yambio, Sud. H6 56
Yambrasbamba, Peru A3 82
Yamdena, Pulau, i., Indon. G9 38
Yamethin, Burma D4 40
Yamhill, Or., U.S. h11 144
Yamhill, co., Or., U.S. B3 144
Yamia, Niger E15 64
Yamma Yamma, Lake, I., Austl. F4 70
Yamoussoukro, I.C. H7 64
Yampa, Co., U.S. A4 113
Yampa, stm., Co., U.S. A2 113
Yampa Plateau, plat., U.S. A1 113
Yamparáez, Bol. H9 82
Yamsay Mountain, mtn., Or., U.S. E5 144
Yamuna, stm., India H9 44
Yamzho Yumco, I., China F14 44
Yanac, Austl. K4 70
Yanacachi, Bol. G8 82
Yanagawa, Japan N5 36
Yanahuara, Peru G6 82
Yanai, Japan N7 36
Yanam, India D7 46
Yan'an, China D8 30
Yanaoca, Peru F6 82
Yanbu' al-Bahr, Sau. Ar. I5 48
Yanbutou, China F4 34
Yancey, co., N.C., U.S. f10 140
Yanceyville, N.C., U.S. A3 140
Yanchang, China D9 30
Yancheng, China B9 34
Yanchi, China D8 30
Yanco, Austl. J7 70
Yandev, Nig. H14 64
Yandoon, Burma F3 40
Yanfolila, Mali F5 64
Yangcun, China L3 34
Yangguanpu, China C4 34
Yangjia, China I7 32
Yangjiang, China G9 30
Yangkoushi, China G7 34
Yangliuqing, China D5 32
Yanglousi, China F2 34
Yangon (Rangoon), Burma B2 38
Yangp'yŏng, S. Kor. F15 32
Yangquan, China F1 32
Yangsan, S. Kor. H17 32
Yangshuling, China B6 32
Yangtze see Chang, stm., China E10 30
Yangxiaodian, China D5 34
Yangyang, S. Kor. E16 32
Yangzhou, China C8 34
Yanheying, China C7 32
Yanji, China A17 32
Yankdŏk, N. Kor. D14 32
Yankeetown, Fl., U.S. C4 116
Yankeetown, In., U.S. I3 121
Yankton, S.D., U.S. E8 148
Yankton, co., S.D., U.S. D8 148
Yanliumiao, China C5 34
Yanna, Austl. F7 70
Yanqi, China C4 30
Yanqing, China C3 32
Yanque, Peru F6 82
Yantā, Leb. A5 50
Yantabulla, Austl. G6 70
Yantai (Chefoo), China F9 32
Yantian, China H3 34
Yantic, stm., Ct., U.S. C7 114
Yantley, Al., U.S. C1 108
Yanush, Ok., U.S. C6 143
Yanzhou, China H4 32
Yao, Japan M10 36
Yaopi, China I2 34
Yaoundé, Cam. H9 54
Yaoya, stm., Nic. D10 92
Yapacaní, Bol. G9 82
Yapacaní, stm., Bol. G9 82
Yapen, Pulau, i., Indon. F10 38
Yapeyú, Arg. E10 80
Yappar, stm., Austl. B4 70
Ya'qūb, Sud. K3 60
Yaque del Norte, stm., Dom. Rep. E9 94
Yaqui, stm., Mex. C5 90
Yaracuy, state, Ven. B8 84
Yaraka, Austl. E6 70
Yarbasan, Tur. K12 20
Yardea, Austl. I1 70
Yardley, Pa., U.S. F12 145
Yardville, N.J., U.S. C3 137
Yarí, stm., Col. H6 84
Yarīm, Yemen G4 47
Yaring, Thai. K6 40
Yaritagua, Ven. B8 84
Yarkand see Shache, China A7 44
Yarkant (Yarkand), stm., China D2 30
Yarker, Ont., Can. C8 103
Yarlung see Brahmaputra, stm., Asia G15 44
Yarmouth, N.S., Can. F3 101
Yarmouth, Ia., U.S. C6 122
Yarmouth, Me., U.S. E2 126
Yarmouth, Ma., U.S. C7 128
Yarmūk, Nahr al-, stm., Asia C5 50
Yarnell, Az., U.S. C3 110
Yarram, Austl. L7 70
Yarraman, Austl. F9 70
Yarrawonga, Austl. K7 70
Yarumal, Col. D5 84
Yarvicoya, Cerro, mtn., Chile I7 82
Yashiro-jima, i., Japan N7 36
Yasothon, Thai. G8 40
Yass, Austl. J8 70
Yasuní, stm., Ec. H5 84
Yata, Bol. E8 82
Yata, stm., Bol. D9 82
Yatakala, Niger D10 64
Yates, co., N.Y., U.S. C3 139
Yatesboro, Pa., U.S. E3 145
Yates Center, Ks., U.S. E8 123
Yates City, Il., U.S. C3 120
Yatesville, Ga., U.S. D2 117
Yathkyed Lake, I., N.W. Ter., Can. D13 96
Yatsushiro, Japan O5 36
Yaṭṭah, Isr. Occ. F4 50
Yatua, stm., Ven. G9 84
Yauca, Peru F4 82
Yauca, stm., Peru F4 82
Yauco, P.R. E11 94
Yauli, Peru D3 82
Yaupi, Ec. I4 84
Yautepec, Mex. H10 90
Yauyos, Peru E4 82
Yavapai, co., Az., U.S. C3 110
Yavarí (Javari), stm., S.A. D4 76
Yavarí Mirim, stm., Peru J6 84
Yavaros, Mex. D5 90
Yavatmāl, India B5 46
Yavero, stm., Peru E5 82
Yaví, Cerro, mtn., Ven. E10 84
Yavita, Ven. F9 84
Yaviza, Pan. C4 84
Yavne, Isr. E3 50
Yawatahama, Japan N7 36
Yawgoog Pond, I., R.I., U.S. E1 146
Yaxchilán, hist., Mex. I14 90
Yaxian, China E10 40
Yayuan, China B14 32
Yazd, Iran F13 48
Yazmān, Pak. F4 44
Yazoo, co., Ms., U.S. C3 131
Yazoo, stm., Ms., U.S. C3 131
Yazoo City, Ms., U.S. C3 131
Ybbs an der Donau, Aus. G15 10
Ybycuí, Para. D10 80
Ye, Burma G4 40
Yeadon, Pa., U.S. p21 145
Yeagertown, Pa., U.S. E6 145
Yecheng, China B7 44
Yech'ŏn, S. Kor. G16 32
Yecla, Spain G10 16
Yécora, Mex. C5 90
Yeelanna, Austl. J1 70
Yegros, Para. D10 80
Yehud, Isr. D3 50
Yei, stm., Sud. N6 60
Yela Island, i., Pap. N. Gui. B10 68
Yelarbon, Austl. G9 70
Yele, S.L. G4 64
Yélimané, Mali D4 64
Yell, co., Ar., U.S. B2 111
Yellow, stm., U.S. u15 116
Yellow, stm., Ga., U.S. h8 117
Yellow, stm., In., U.S. B4 121
Yellow, stm., Wi., U.S. D3 156
Yellow, stm., Wi., U.S. C3 156
Yellow Creek, Sask., Can. E3 105
Yellow Creek, stm., Tn., U.S. A4 149
Yellow Grass, Sask., Can. H3 105
Yellowhead Pass, Can. C1 98
Yellow see Huang, stm., China D10 30
Yellowjacket Mountains, mts., Id., U.S. D4 119
Yellowknife, N.W. Ter., Can. D10 96
Yellow Lake, I., Wi., U.S. C1 156
Yellow Medicine, co., Mn., U.S. F2 130
Yellow Pine, Al., U.S. D1 108
Yellow Pine, Id., U.S. E3 119
Yellow Sea (Huang Hai), Asia B11 34
Yellow Springs, Md., U.S. B3 127
Yellow Springs, Oh., U.S. C2 142
Yellowstone, co., Mt., U.S. D8 133
Yellowstone, stm., U.S. D10 133
Yellowstone, Clarks Fork, stm., U.S. F7 133
Yellowstone Lake, I., Wy., U.S. B2 157
Yellowstone National Park, Wy., U.S. B2 157
Yellowstone National Park, co., Mt., U.S. E6 133
Yellowstone National Park, U.S. B2 157
Yellville, Ar., U.S. A3 111
Yelm, Wa., U.S. C3 154
Yelvertoft, Austl. C3 70
Yelvington, Ky., U.S. C3 124
Yelwa, Nig. F12 64
Yemaotai, China A10 32
Yemassee, S.C., U.S. F6 147
Yemen (Al-Yaman), ctry., Asia F3 42
Yenangyaung, Burma D3 40
Yen Bai, Viet. D8 40
Yenda, Austl. J7 70
Yende Millimou, Gui. G4 64
Yendéré, Burkina F7 64
Yendi, Ghana G9 64
Yengisar, China D2 30
Yeniköy, Tur. J12 20
Yenisey see Jenisej, stm., U.S.S.R. D15 22
Yenshuichen, Tai. L9 34
Yentna, stm., Ak., U.S. f16 109
Yeola, India B3 46
Yeoval, Austl. I8 70
Yepachic, Mex. C5 90
Yeppoon, Austl. D9 70
Yerba Buena, Montaña, mtn., Hond. C7 92
Yerevan see Jerevan, U.S.S.R. I6 22
Yerington, Nv., U.S. E2 135
Yerington Indian Reservation, Nv., U.S. D2 135
Yermasóyia, Cyp. D2 48
Yermo, Ca., U.S. E5 112
Yerupaja, Nevado, mtn., Peru D3 82
Yerushalayim (Al-Quds) (Jerusalem), Isr. E4 50
Yesa, Embalse de, res., Spain C10 16
Yesan, S. Kor. G14 32
Yeşilhisar, Tur. B3 48
Yeste, Spain G9 16
Yetman, Austl. G9 70
Yetti, reg., Afr. G7 62
Ye-u, Burma C3 40
Yeu, Île d', i., Fr. F4 14
Yexian, China B2 34
Ygatimí, Para. C11 80
Yguazú, stm., Para. C11 80
Yhú, Para. C11 80
Yi, stm., Ur. G10 80
Yi'an, China B12 30
Yiannitsá, Grc. I6 20
Yibin, China F7 30
Yicanghe, China C9 34
Yichang, China E9 30
Yichun, China B12 30
Yichun, China F9 30
Yidu, China G6 32
Yifag, Eth. K9 60
Yijianzhen, China E7 34
Yilan, China B12 30
Yiliang, China B7 40
Yinchuan, China D8 30
Ying, stm., China C5 34
Yingcheng, China E2 34
Yingde, China K2 34
Yingkou, China C10 32
Yingtan, China G6 34
Yingtian, China G1 34
Yining, China C3 30
Yinzhan'ao, China L2 34
Yirba Muda, Eth. N10 60
Yirga Alem, Eth. N10 60
Yirol, Sud. N6 60
Yirwa, Sud. N4 60
Yishan, China B10 40
Yishui, China H6 32
Yíthion, Grc. M6 20
Yitulihe, China A11 30
Yiwu, China F9 34
Yiyang, China F9 30
Ylivieska, Fin. I19 6
Ymir, B.C., Can. E9 99
Yoakum, Tx., U.S. E4 150
Yoakum, co., Tx., U.S. C1 150
Yockanookany, stm., Ms., U.S. C4 131
Yoco, Ven. B11 84
Yocona, stm., Ms., U.S. A4 131
Yoder, In., U.S. C7 121
Yoder, Ks., U.S. g11 123
Yoder, Wy., U.S. E8 157
Yogyakarta, Indon. J15 39a
Yoho National Park, B.C., Can. D9 99
Yoichi, Japan D15 36a
Yojoa, Lago de, I., Hond. C7 92
Yŏju, S. Kor. F15 32
Yokkaichi, Japan M11 36
Yokohama, Japan L14 36
Yokosuka, Japan L14 36
Yokote, Japan H15 36
Yokum Seat, mtn., Ma., U.S. B1 128
Yola, Nig. G9 54
Yolaina, Serranías de, mts., Nic. F10 92
Yolo, co., Ca., U.S. C2 112
Yolombó, Col. D5 84
Yolyn, W.V., U.S. n12 155
Yom, stm., Thai. F6 40
Yomba Indian Reservation, Nv., U.S. D4 135
Yonago, Japan L8 36
Yŏnan, N. Kor. F14 32
Yoncalla, Or., U.S. D3 144
Yonezawa, Japan J15 36
Yŏngam, S. Kor. I14 32
Yongamp'o, N. Kor. D12 32
Yong'an, China J6 34
Yŏngan, N. Kor. B17 32
Yongchang, China F8 34
Yŏngch'ŏn, S. Kor. E15 32
Yŏngch'ŏn, S. Kor. H16 32
Yongdeng, China D7 30
Yongding, China K5 34
Yongding, stm., China K5 34
Yŏngdŏk, S. Kor. G17 32
Yŏngdong, S. Kor. G15 32
Yongfeng, China H4 34
Yŏnghŭng, N. Kor. D15 32
Yŏngju, S. Kor. G16 32
Yongkang, China G9 34
Yŏngmi-dong, N. Kor. D13 32
Yongren, China F7 30
Yongsanp'o, S. Kor. I14 32
Yongshan, China F7 30
Yŏngwŏl, S. Kor. F16 32
Yongxin, China I3 34
Yŏngyu, N. Kor. D13 32
Yonkers, N.Y., U.S. E7 139
Yonne, dept., Fr. E10 14
Yopal, Col. E6 84
Yorba Linda, Ca., U.S. n13 112
York, Austl. F3 68
York, Ont., Can. D5 103
York, Eng., U.K. H12 8
York, Al., U.S. C1 108
York, Me., U.S. E2 126
York, Ne., U.S. D8 134
York, Pa., U.S. G8 145
York, S.C., U.S. B5 147
York, co., Me., U.S. E2 126
York, co., Ne., U.S. D8 134
York, co., Pa., U.S. G8 145
York, co., S.C., U.S. A5 147
York, co., Va., U.S. C6 153
York, stm., Ont., Can. B7 103
York, stm., Va., U.S. C6 153
York, Cape, c., Austl. B8 68
York, Kap, c., Grnld. B13 86
York Beach, Me., U.S. E2 126
Yorke Peninsula, pen., Austl. J2 70
York Harbor, Me., U.S. E2 126
Yorklyn, De., U.S. A3 115
Yorkshire, N.Y., U.S. C2 139
York Sound, strt., Austl. B5 68
Yorkton, Sask., Can. F4 105
Yorktown, In., U.S. D7 121
Yorktown, Tx., U.S. E4 150
Yorktown, Va., U.S. C6 153
Yorktown Manor, R.I., U.S. E4 146
Yorkville, Il., U.S. B5 120
Yorkville, N.Y., U.S. B5 139
Yorkville, Oh., U.S. B5 142
Yorkville, Tn., U.S. A2 149
Yoro, Hond. B7 92
Yoro, Mali D8 64
Yoro, dept., Hond. B7 92
Yoron-jima, i., Japan T3 37b
Yosemite, Ky., U.S. C5 124
Yosemite National Park, Ca., U.S. D4 112
Yosemite National Park, Ca., U.S. D4 112
Yos Sudarso, Pulau, i., Indon. G10 38
Yŏsu, S. Kor. I15 32
Yotala, Bol. H9 82
Yotaú, Bol. G10 82
Yotvata, Isr. I4 50
You, stm., China G8 30
Youbou, B.C., Can. g11 99
Youghiogheny, stm., U.S. F2 145
Youghiogheny River Lake, res., U.S. G3 145
Young, Austl. J8 70
Young, Sask., Can. F3 105
Young, Az., U.S. C5 110
Young, Ur. G10 80
Young, co., Tx., U.S. C3 150
Young America, In., U.S. C5 121
Young Harris, Ga., U.S. B3 117
Younghusband Peninsula, pen., Austl. K3 70
Youngs, Lake, I., Wa., U.S. f11 154
Youngs Point, Ont., Can. C6 103
Youngstown, Alta., Can. D5 98
Youngstown, In., U.S. F3 121
Youngstown, N.Y., U.S. B1 139
Youngstown, Oh., U.S. A5 142
Youngsville, La., U.S. D3 125
Youngsville, N.C., U.S. A4 140
Youngsville, Pa., U.S. C3 145
Youngtown, Az., U.S. k8 110
Youngwood, Pa., U.S. F2 145
Youssoufia, Mor. D6 62
Youxi, China I7 34
Youyang, China F8 30
Yozgat, Tur. B3 48
Ypacaraí, Para. C10 80
Ypané, stm., Para. B10 80
Ypé Jhu, Para. B11 80
Ypres (Ieper), Bel. G2 12
Ypsilanti, Mi., U.S. F7 129
Ypsilanti, N.D., U.S. C7 141
Yreka, Ca., U.S. B2 112
Ystad, Swe. N13 6
Ytambey, stm., Para. C11 80
Yu, stm., China C10 40
Yu'alliq, Jabal, mtn., Egypt F2 48
Yuan, stm., China F9 30
Yüanlin, Tai. L9 34
Yuanling, China F9 30
Yuanmou, China B6 40
Yuba, co., Ca., U.S. C3 112
Yuba, stm., Ca., U.S. C3 112
Yuba City, Ca., U.S. C3 112
Yūbari, Japan D16 36a
Yubdo, Eth. M8 60
Yucatán, state, Mex. G15 90
Yucatán, Canal de, strt., N.A. D2 94
Yucatan Peninsula (Península de Yucatán), pen., N.A. H15 90
Yucca, Az., U.S. C1 110
Yucca Lake, I., Nv., U.S. F5 135
Yucca Mountain, mtn., Nv., U.S. G5 135
Yuci, China D9 30
Yuecheng, China C3 34
Yueyang, China F2 34
Yugoslavia (Jugoslavija), ctry., Eur. G11 4
Yukanbey, Tur. J11 20
Yukon, Ok., U.S. B4 143
Yukon, W.V., U.S. D3 155
Yukon, prov., Can. D5 96
Yukon, stm., N.A. m19 106a
Yukou, China C5 32
Yulee, Fl., U.S. B5 116
Yüli, Tai. L10 34
Yulin, China D8 30
Yulin, China C11 40
Yuma, Az., U.S. E1 110
Yuma, Co., U.S. A8 113
Yuma, co., Az., U.S. E1 110
Yuma, co., Co., U.S. A8 113
Yuma, Bahía de, b., Dom. Rep. E10 94
Yuma Marine Corps Air Station, mil., Az., U.S. E1 110
Yumare, Ven. B8 84
Yumbel, Chile I2 80
Yumbo, Col. F4 84
Yumen, China D6 30
Yuna, stm., Dom. Rep. E9 94
Yuncheng, China D9 30
Yungas, reg., Bol. F8 82
Yungay, Chile I2 80
Yungay, Peru C3 82
Yunhe, China G8 34
Yunnan, prov., China F7 30
Yunta, Austl. I3 70
Yunxian, China E9 30
Yura, Peru G6 82
Yurimaguas, Peru A3 82
Yuriria, Mex. G9 90
Yuriria, Laguna de, I., Mex. G9 90
Yuruarí, stm., Ven. D12 84
Yurubí, Parque Nacional, Ven. B8 84
Yurumanguí, stm., Col. F4 84
Yusala, Laguna, I., Bol. F8 82
Yuscarán, Hond. D8 92
Yushan, China B2 34
Yü Shan, mtn., Tai. L9 34
Yushu, China E6 30
Yutan, Ne., U.S. C9 134
Yutian, China B9 44
Yuty, Para. D10 80
Yuwangcheng, China D3 34
Yuxian, China A2 34
Yuyao, China E10 34
Yvelines, dept., Fr. D8 14
Yverdon, Switz. E6 13
Yvetot, Fr. C7 14

Z

Zabajkal'sk, U.S.S.R. H15 24
Žabari, Yugo. E5 20
Zabarjad, Jazīrat, i., Egypt F2 48
Zabīd, Yemen G3 47
Žabinka, U.S.S.R. I7 26
Žabje, U.S.S.R. A8 20
Ząbkowice Śląskie, Pol. E16 10
Žabljak, Yugo. F3 20
Zābol, Iran F16 48
Zābolī, Iran H16 48
Zabolotov, U.S.S.R. A9 20
Zabory, U.S.S.R. F15 26
Zabré, Burkina F9 64
Zabrze (Hindenburg), Pol. E18 10
Zacapa, Guat. C5 92
Zacapa, dept., Guat. B5 92
Zacapu, Mex. H9 90
Zacatecas, Mex. F8 90
Zacatecas, state, Mex. F8 90
Zacatecoluca, El Sal. D6 92
Zacatlán, Mex. H11 90
Zacharovo, U.S.S.R. G22 26
Zachary, La., U.S. D4 125
Zachmet, U.S.S.R. C17 48
Zacoalco de Torres, Mex. G8 90
Zacualpa, Guat. B4 92
Zacualtipan, Mex. G10 90
Zaculeu, hist., Guat. B3 92
Zadar, Yugo. E10 18
Zadetkyi Kyun, i., Burma J5 40
Zadonsk, U.S.S.R. I21 26
Zafer Burnu, c., N. Cyp. D3 48
Zafir, U.A.E. C8 47
Zafra, Spain G5 16
Żagań, Pol. D15 10
Žagare, U.S.S.R. E6 26
Zaghouan, Tun. M5 18
Zagnanado, Benin H11 64
Zagnitkov, U.S.S.R. A12 20
Zagora, Mor. E8 62
Zagorsk, U.S.S.R. E21 26
Zagreb, Yugo. D10 18
Zāgros, Kūhhā-ye, mts., Iran E9 48
Žagubica, Yugo. E5 20
Zagyva, stm., Hung. H20 10
Zahana, Alg. J11 16
Zāhedān, Iran G16 48
Zahlah, Leb. A5 50
Záhony, Hung. G22 10
Zahrān, Sau. Ar. F3 47
Zaire (Zaïre), ctry., Afr. B4 58
Zaïre see Congo, stm., Afr. C2 58
Zaječar, Yugo. F6 20
Zajkany, U.S.S.R. B11 20
Zajsan, U.S.S.R. H14 22
Zajsan, ozero, I., U.S.S.R. H14 22
Zakamensk, U.S.S.R. G12 24
Zákas, Grc. I5 20
Zākhū, Iraq C7 48
Zákinthos, Grc. L4 20
Zákinthos, i., Grc. L4 20
Zakīyah, Syria B6 50
Zakopane, Pol. F19 10
Zala, Eth. N9 60
Zala, co., Hung. I16 10
Zala, stm., Hung. I16 10
Zalaegerszeg, Hung. I16 10
Zalalövő, Hung. I16 10
Zalanga, Nig. F15 64
Zalaszentgrót, Hung. I17 10
Zalău, Rom. B7 20
Zalegošč', U.S.S.R. I19 26
Zaleščiki, U.S.S.R. A9 20
Zalesje, U.S.S.R. C19 26
Zalim, Sau. Ar. C3 47
Zalingei, Sud. K2 60
Zaltbommel, Neth. E7 12
Žaltyr, U.S.S.R. G11 22
Zamakh, Yemen F5 47
Zambezi (Zambeze), stm., Afr. E6 58
Zambia, ctry., Afr. D5 58
Zamboanga, Phil. D7 38
Zambrano, Col. C5 84
Zambrów, Pol. B22 10
Zamfara, stm., Nig. E12 64
Zamora, Ec. J3 84
Zamora, Spain D6 16
Zamora, stm., Ec. I3 84
Zamora-Chinchipe, prov., Ec. J3 84
Zamora de Hidalgo, Mex. H8 90
Zamość, Pol. E23 10
Zamuro, Punta, c., Ven. B8 84
Zana, hist., Alg. C14 62
Zanaga, Congo B2 58
Zandvoort, Neth. D6 12
Zandvoort, Circuit Autorace, Neth. D6 12
Zanesville, In., U.S. C7 121
Zanesville, Oh., U.S. C4 142
Zangasso, Mali E7 64
Zanggezhuang, China F8 32
Zanjān, Iran C10 48
Zanjón, Arg. D6 80
Zanjón, stm., Arg. F4 80
Žannetty, ostrov, i., U.S.S.R. B23 24
Zanthus, Austl. F4 68
Zanzibar, Tan. C7 58
Zanzibar, i., Tan. C7 58
Zaokskij, U.S.S.R. G20 26
Zaostrovje, U.S.S.R. A16 26
Zaouiet Azmour, Tun. M6 18
Zaouiet el Mgaïz, Tun. M5 18
Zaoxi, China E8 34
Zaozhuang, China I5 32
Zaoz'ornyj, U.S.S.R. F10 24
Zap, N.D., U.S. B4 141
Zapadnaja Dvina, U.S.S.R. E15 26
Zapadnaja Dvina (Daugava), stm., U.S.S.R. F10 26
Zapadno-Sibirskaja ravnina, pl., U.S.S.R. E13 22
Zapadnyj Sajan, mts., U.S.S.R. G10 24
Zapala, Arg. J3 80
Zapata, Tx., U.S. F3 150
Zapata, co., Tx., U.S. F3 150
Zapata, Península de, pen., Cuba C4 94
Zapatera, Isla, i., Nic. F9 92
Zapatoca, Col. D6 84
Zapatosa, Ciénaga de, I., Col. C6 84
Zapl'usje, U.S.S.R. C12 26
Zapol'arnyj, U.S.S.R. G22 6
Zapolje, U.S.S.R. C12 26
Zapopan, Mex. G8 90
Zaporožje, U.S.S.R. H5 22
Zapotal, stm., Ec. H3 84
Zapotillo, Ec. J2 84
Zaprudn'a, U.S.S.R. E20 26
Zara, Tur. B4 48
Zaragoza, Col. D5 84
Zaragoza, Mex. B6 90
Zaragoza, Mex. C9 90
Zaragoza, Mex. F10 90
Zaragoza, Spain D11 16
Zarajsk, U.S.S.R. G21 26
Zarand, Iran F14 48
Zarasai, U.S.S.R. F9 26
Zárate, Arg. H9 80
Zarautz, Spain B9 16
Zaraza, Ven. C10 84
Zarcero, C.R. G10 92
Zard Kūh, mtn., Iran E11 48
Zarečnyj, U.S.S.R. D25 26
Zarembo Island, i., Ak., U.S. m23 109
Zarghūn Shahr, Afg. D3 44
Zaria, Nig. F13 64
Žarkovskij, U.S.S.R. F15 26
Žarma, U.S.S.R. H14 22
Zarqā', Nahr az-, stm., Jord. D5 50
Zarrīn Shahr, Iran E11 48
Zarubino, U.S.S.R. C16 26
Zaruma, Ec. I3 84
Zarumilla, Peru I2 84
Żary (Sorau), Pol. D15 10
Zaryn', U.S.S.R. H16 26
Zarzaïtine, Alg. F15 62
Zarzal, Col. E4 84
Zarzis, Tun. D16 62
Zāskār Mountains, mts., Asia D7 44
Zaslavl', U.S.S.R. G10 26
Zastavna, U.S.S.R. A9 20
Zastron, S. Afr. H8 66
Zatišje, U.S.S.R. B13 20
Zavala, co., Tx., U.S. E3 150
Zavalje, U.S.S.R. A14 20

Name	Map Ref.	Page
Zavalla, Tx., U.S.	D5	150
Zavidovići, Yugo.	E2	20
Zavitinsk, U.S.S.R.	G17	24
Zavodovski Island, i., Falk. Is.	J12	74
Zavolžje, U.S.S.R.	E26	26
Zavolžsk, U.S.S.R.	D25	26
Zavoronežskoje, U.S.S.R.	I23	26
Zawiercie, Pol.	E19	10
Zawiyat Shammās, Egypt	B4	60
Zaza, stm., Cuba	D5	94
Zaza, Presa, res., Cuba	D5	94
Zazafotsy, Madag.	S22	67b
Zbiroh, Czech.	F13	10
Zduńska Wola, Pol.	D18	10
Zealandia, Sask., Can.	F2	105
Zearing, Ia., U.S.	B4	122
Zeballos, B.C., Can.	D4	99
Zebila, Ghana	F9	64
Zebulon, Ga., U.S.	C2	117
Zebulon, Ky., U.S.	C7	124
Zebulon, N.C., U.S.	B4	140
Zeebrugge, Bel.	F3	12
Zeehan, Austl.	M6	70
Zeeland, Mi., U.S.	F5	129
Zeeland, N.D., U.S.	D6	141
Zeeland, prov., Neth.	F4	12
Zeerust, S. Afr.	E8	66
Ẕefat (Safad), Isr.	C5	50
Zege, Eth.	L9	60
Zehdenick, Ger.	C13	10
Zeigler, Il., U.S.	F4	120
Zeil, Mount, mtn., Austl.	D6	68
Zeist, Neth.	D7	12
Zeitz, Ger.	D12	10
Zeja, U.S.S.R.	G17	24
Zeja, stm., U.S.S.R.	G17	24
Zejskoje vodochranilišče, res., U.S.S.R.	G17	24
Zekiah Swamp Run, stm., Md., U.S.	D4	127
Zelaya, dept., Nic.	E10	92
Zele, Bel.	F5	12
Żelechów, Pol.	D21	10
Zelenoborskij, U.S.S.R.	H23	6
Zelenogorsk, U.S.S.R.	A12	26
Zelenograd, U.S.S.R.	E20	26
Zelenogradsk, U.S.S.R.	G3	26
Železnodorožnyj, U.S.S.R.	E8	22
Železnodorožnyj, U.S.S.R.	G4	26
Železnogorsk, U.S.S.R.	I18	26
Železnogorsk-Ilimskij, U.S.S.R.	F12	24
Zelienople, Pa., U.S.	E1	145
Zell, Ger.	E7	10
Zella-Mehlis, Ger.	E10	10
Zell am See, Aus.	H12	10
Zelma, Sask., Can.	F3	105
Zel'onodol'sk, U.S.S.R.	F7	22
Zelów, Pol.	D19	10
Želudok, U.S.S.R.	H7	26
Zel'va, U.S.S.R.	H7	26
Zelzate, Bel.	F4	12
Zemcy, U.S.S.R.	E15	26
Zemetčino, U.S.S.R.	H25	26
Zémio, Cen. Afr. Rep.	G6	56
Zemmour, reg., Afr.	H4	62
Zempoala, hist., Mex.	H11	90
Zemst, Bel.	G5	12
Zendeh Jān, Afg.	D16	48
Zenica, Yugo.	E1	20
Zenith, Wa., U.S.	f11	154
Zenobia Peak, mtn., Co., U.S.	A2	113
Zenon Park, Sask., Can.	D4	105
Zephyr Cove, Nv., U.S.	E2	135
Zephyrhills, Fl., U.S.	D4	116
Zeravšan, stm., U.S.S.R.	J11	22
Zerbst, Ger.	D12	10
Žerdevka, U.S.S.R.	J24	26
Zermatt, Switz.	F8	13
Zernez, Switz.	E13	13
Zernograd, U.S.S.R.	H6	22
Zeulenroda, Ger.	E11	10
Zeven, Ger.	B9	10
Zevenaar, Neth.	E9	12
Zevenbergen, Neth.	E6	12
Zeytindağ, Tur.	K11	20
Zgierz, Pol.	D19	10
Zhagenasongduo, China	D16	44
Zhanggezhuang, China	G7	32
Zhangjiakou (Kalgan), China	C2	32
Zhangjinhe, China	E1	34
Zhangmutou, China	M3	34
Zhangping, China	J6	34
Zhangtaizi, China	B11	32
Zhangye, China	D7	30
Zhangzhou (Longxi), China	K6	34
Zhanjiang, China	D11	40
Zhanjiaqiao, China	F2	34
Zhao'an, China	L6	34
Zhaoqing, China	G9	30
Zhaotong, China	F7	30
Zhaoyuan, China	F8	32
Zhapu, China	E10	34
Zhaxigang, China	D8	44
Zhdanov see Mariupol', U.S.S.R.	H5	22
Zhegu, China	F14	44
Zhejiang (Chekiang), prov., China	F11	30
Zhengding, China	E2	32
Zhengguo, China	L2	34
Zhengyangguan, China	C5	34
Zhengzhou, China	E9	30
Zhenjiang, China	C8	34
Zhenping, China	E9	30
Zhentoushi, China	G2	34
Zhenxing, China	A12	32
Zhenyuan, China	F8	30
Zhidoi, China	E5	30
Zhierling, China	C2	32
Zhixia, China	F8	34
Zhob, Pak.	E3	44
Zhob, stm., Pak.	E3	44
Zhongba, China	F3	30
Zhongbu, China	G6	34
Zhongdian, China	F6	30
Zhongheying, China	C7	40
Zhongmeihe, China	D5	34
Zhongning, China	D8	30
Zhongsha, China	I5	34
Zhongshan (Shiqizhen), China	M2	34
Zhongxiang, China	D1	34
Zhoucun, China	G5	32
Zhouning, China	H8	34
Zhoushan Qundao, is., China	E11	34
Zhoushuizi, China	E9	32
Zhuge, China	G6	32
Zhugouzhen, China	C2	34
Zhujiang Kou, est., Asia	M2	34
Zhulanbu, China	J4	34
Zhumadian, China	C3	34
Zhuotian, China	J5	34
Zhuoxian, China	D3	32
Zhushan, China	E9	30
Zhutian, China	G6	34
Zhuya, China	G6	32
Zhuzhou (Chuchow), China	H2	34
Zi, stm., China	F9	30
Zia Indian Reservation, N.M., U.S.	h7	138
Žiar nad Hronom, Czech.	G18	10
Zibo (Zhangdian), China	G6	32
Zicavo, Fr.	M24	15a
Ziebach, co., S.D., U.S.	C4	148
Ziegenhain, Ger.	E9	10
Zielona Góra (Grünberg), Pol.	D15	10
Zierikzee, Neth.	E4	12
Ziesar, Ger.	C12	10
Žiežmariai, U.S.S.R.	G7	26
Ziftā, Egypt	B6	60
Žigalovo, U.S.S.R.	G13	24
Zigong, China	F7	30
Ziguinchor, Sen.	E1	64
Zihuatanejo, Mex.	I9	90
Zikejevo, U.S.S.R.	H17	26
Zikhron Ya'aqov, Isr.	C3	50
Žilina, Czech.	F18	10
Žilino, U.S.S.R.	G4	26
Zillah, Libya	C4	56
Zillah, Wa., U.S.	C5	154
Zillertaler Alpen, mts., Eur.	I11	10
Žiloj, ostrov, i., U.S.S.R.	A11	48
Žil'ovo, U.S.S.R.	G21	26
Zilupe, U.S.S.R.	E11	26
Zilwaukee, Mi., U.S.	E7	129
Zima, U.S.S.R.	G12	24
Zimapán, Mex.	G10	90
Zimbabwe, ctry., Afr.	E5	58
Zimmerman, Mn., U.S.	E5	130
Zimnicea, Rom.	F9	20
Zinal, Switz.	F8	13
Zinder, Niger	E14	64
Zingwanda, Sud.	N4	60
Zion, Il., U.S.	A6	120
Zion National Park, Ut., U.S.	F3	151
Zion Reservoir, res., Az., U.S.	C6	110
Zionsville, In., U.S.	E5	121
Zipaquirá, Col.	E5	84
Ziqlāb, Wādī, val., Jord.	C5	50
Zirkel, Mount, mtn., Co., U.S.	A4	113
Žitkoviči, U.S.S.R.	I10	26
Žitkovo, U.S.S.R.	A12	26
Žitomir, U.S.S.R.	G3	22
Zittau, Ger.	E14	10
Zitundo, Moz.	F11	66
Ziway, Lake, l., Eth.	M10	60
Ziwuji, China	C4	34
Ziyun, China	F8	30
Žizdra, U.S.S.R.	H17	26
Zizhong, China	F7	30
Žižica, U.S.S.R.	E14	26
Zlatar, Yugo.	C11	18
Zlatica, Bul.	G8	20
Zlatoust, U.S.S.R.	F9	22
Zlīṭan, Libya	B3	56
Žlobin, U.S.S.R.	I13	26
Złotoryja, Pol.	D15	10
Złotów, Pol.	B17	10
Zlynka, U.S.S.R.	I14	26
Zmeinogorsk, U.S.S.R.	G14	22
Zmi'ovka, U.S.S.R.	I19	26
Znamenka, U.S.S.R.	H4	22
Znamensk, U.S.S.R.	G4	26
Znamenskoje, U.S.S.R.	F12	22
Znamenskoje, U.S.S.R.	F6	24
Znob'-Novgorodskoje, U.S.S.R.	I16	26
Znojmo, Czech.	G16	10
Žodino, U.S.S.R.	G11	26
Zofingen, Switz.	D8	13
Zogno, Italy	D4	18
Zolfo Springs, Fl., U.S.	E5	116
Zollikofen, Switz.	D7	13
Zollikon, Switz.	D10	13
Zolotkovo, U.S.S.R.	F24	26
Zolotuchino, U.S.S.R.	I19	26
Žoltyje Vody, U.S.S.R.	H4	22
Žolymbet, U.S.S.R.	G12	22
Zomba, Mwi.	E7	58
Zonguldak, Tur.	G14	4
Zonza, Fr.	M24	15a
Zorgo, Burkina	E9	64
Zorita, Spain	F6	16
Zorkul', ozero, l., Asia	B5	44
Zorritos, Peru	I2	84
Zouar, Chad	D4	56
Zouérat, Maur.	I4	62
Zouping, China	G5	32
Zourma, Burkina	F9	64
Žovten', U.S.S.R.	B14	20
Zrenjanin, Yugo.	D4	20
Zriba, Tun.	M5	18
Zuata, stm., Ven.	C10	84
Zubcov, U.S.S.R.	E17	26
Zubova Pol'ana, U.S.S.R.	G25	26
Zudañez, Bol.	H9	82
Zuénoula, I.C.	H6	64
Zuera, Spain	D11	16
Ẓufār, reg., Oman	F9	47
Zug, Switz.	D10	13
Zug, state, Switz.	D10	13
Zugdidi, U.S.S.R.	I6	22
Zugersee, l., Switz.	D10	13
Zugspitze, mtn., Eur.	H10	10
Zuiderzee see IJsselmeer, Neth.	C7	12
Zuid-Holland, prov., Neth.	D6	12
Zujevka, U.S.S.R.	F8	22
Žukovka, U.S.S.R.	H16	26
Žukovskij, U.S.S.R.	F21	26
Zulia, state, Ven.	B6	84
Zulia, stm., S.A.	C6	84
Zulueta, Cuba	C5	94
Zululand, hist. reg., S. Afr.	F10	66
Zumba, Ec.	J3	84
Zumbo, Moz.	E6	58
Zumbro, stm., Mn., U.S.	F6	130
Zumbrota, Mn., U.S.	F6	130
Zungeru, Nig.	G13	64
Zungur, Nig.	G14	64
Zuni (Zuni Pueblo), N.M., U.S.	B1	138
Zuni, Va., U.S.	k14	153
Zuni, stm., U.S.	C6	110
Zuni Indian Reservation, N.M., U.S.	B1	138
Zuni Mountains, mts., N.M., U.S.	B1	138
Zunyi, China	F8	30
Zuodeng, China	C9	40
Zuoz, Switz.	E12	13
Zūq Muṣbīḥ, Leb.	A5	50
Zurayghiṭ, Sau. Ar.	H6	48
Zurich, Ont., Can.	D3	103
Zurich, Neth.	B7	12
Zürich, Switz.	D10	13
Zurich, Ks., U.S.	C4	123
Zürich, state, Switz.	D10	13
Zürichsee, l., Switz.	D10	13
Zuru, Nig.	F12	64
Zutphen, Neth.	D9	12
Zuwārah, Libya	B3	56
Zuwayzā, Jord.	E5	50
Zvenigorod, U.S.S.R.	F19	26
Zvishavane, Zimb.	C10	66
Zvolen, Czech.	G19	10
Zvornik, Yugo.	E3	20
Zweibrücken, Ger.	F7	10
Zweisimmen, Switz.	E7	13
Zwettl, Aus.	G15	10
Zwickau, Ger.	E12	10
Zwiesel, Ger.	F13	10
Zwijndrecht, Neth.	E6	12
Zwolle, Neth.	C9	12
Zwolle, La., U.S.	C2	125
Zyr'anovsk, U.S.S.R.	H8	24
Żyrardów, Pol.	C20	10
Żywiec, Pol.	F19	10

World Political Information

This table lists the area, population, population density, form of government, political status, and capital for every country in the world.

The populations are estimates for January 1, 1991 made by Rand McNally on the basis of official data, United Nations estimates, and other available information. Area figures include inland water.

The political units listed in the table are categorized by political status, as follows: A–independent countries; B–internally independent political entities which are under the protection of other countries in matters of defense and foreign affairs; C–colonies and other dependent political units; D–the major administrative subdivisions of Australia, Canada, China, the Soviet Union, the United Kingdom, the United States, and Yugoslavia. For comparison, the table also includes the continents and the world.

All footnotes to this table appear on page 260.

Country, Division or Region English (Conventional)	Area in sq. mi.	Area in sq. km.	Estimated Population 1/1/91	Pop. per sq. mi.	Pop. per sq. km.	Form of Government and Political Status	Capital
† Afghanistan	251,826	652,225	16,400,000	65	25	Republic ... A	Kābol
Africa	11,700,000	30,300,000	671,800,000	57	22		
Alabama	51,704	133,913	4,063,000	79	30	State (U.S.) ... D	Montgomery
Alaska	591,004	1,530,693	560,000	0.9	0.4	State (U.S.) ... D	Juneau
† Albania	11,100	28,748	3,318,000	299	115	Socialist republic ... A	Tiranë
Alberta	255,287	661,190	2,473,000	9.7	3.7	Province (Canada) ... D	Edmonton
† Algeria	919,595	2,381,741	26,115,000	28	11	Socialist republic ... A	El Djazaïr (Algiers)
American Samoa	77	199	42,000	545	211	Unincorporated territory (U.S.) ... C	Pago Pago
Andorra	175	453	52,000	297	115	Coprincipality (Spanish and French protection) ... B	Andorra
† Angola	481,354	1,246,700	10,155,000	21	8.1	Socialist republic ... A	Luanda
Anguilla	35	91	7,000	200	77	Dependent territory (U.K. protection) ... B	The Valley
Antarctica	5,400,000	14,000,000	[1]	—	—		
† Antigua and Barbuda	171	443	80,000	468	181	Parliamentary state ... A	St. John's
Anwei (Anhui)	53,668	139,000	56,390,000	1,051	406	Province (China) ... D	Hefei
† Argentina	1,073,400	2,780,092	32,485,000	30	12	Republic ... A	Buenos Aires
Arizona	114,002	295,264	3,700,000	32	13	State (U.S.) ... D	Phoenix
Arkansas	53,191	137,764	2,384,000	45	17	State (U.S.) ... D	Little Rock
Armenia (Arm'anskaja S.S.R.)	11,506	29,800	3,350,000	291	112	Soviet socialist republic (U.S.S.R.) ... D	Jerevan
Aruba	75	193	66,000	880	342	Self-governing territory (Netherlands protection) ... B	Oranjestad
Asia	17,300,000	44,900,000	3,232,000,000	187	72		
† Australia	2,966,155	7,682,300	17,260,000	5.8	2.2	Federal parliamentary state ... A	Canberra
Australian Capital Territory	927	2,400	286,000	309	119	Territory (Australia) ... D	Canberra
† Austria	32,377	83,855	7,681,000	237	92	Federal republic ... A	Wien (Vienna)
Azerbaijan (Azerbajdžanskaja S.S.R.)	33,436	86,600	7,140,000	214	82	Soviet socialist republic (U.S.S.R.) ... D	Baku
† Bahamas	5,380	13,934	256,000	48	18	Parliamentary state ... A	Nassau
† Bahrain	267	691	501,000	1,876	725	Monarchy ... A	Al-Manāmah
† Bangladesh	55,598	143,998	109,540,000	1,970	761	Islamic republic ... A	Dhaka (Dacca)
† Barbados	166	430	259,000	1,560	602	Parliamentary state ... A	Bridgetown
† Belgium	11,783	30,518	9,927,000	842	325	Constitutional monarchy ... A	Bruxelles (Brussels)
† Belize	8,866	22,963	204,000	23	8.9	Parliamentary state ... A	Belmopan
† Belorussia (Belorusskaja S.S.R.)	80,155	207,600	10,370,000	129	50	Soviet socialist republic (U.S.S.R.) ... D	Minsk
† Benin	43,475	112,600	4,819,000	111	43	Republic ... A	Porto-Novo and Cotonou
Bermuda	21	54	60,000	2,857	1,111	Dependent territory (U.K.) ... C	Hamilton
† Bhutan	17,954	46,500	1,580,000	88	34	Monarchy (Indian protection) ... B	Thimphu
† Bolivia	424,165	1,098,581	7,507,000	18	6.8	Republic ... A	La Paz and Sucre
Bophuthatswana[2]	15,641	40,509	2,575,000	165	64	National state (South African protection) ... B	Mmabatho
Bosnia-Hercegovina (Bosna i Hercegovina)	19,741	51,129	4,492,000	228	88	Republic (Yugoslavia) ... D	Sarajevo
† Botswana	224,711	582,000	1,324,000	5.9	2.3	Republic ... A	Gaborone
† Brazil	3,286,488	8,511,965	152,050,000	46	18	Federal republic ... A	Brasília
British Columbia	365,948	947,800	3,075,000	8.4	3.2	Province (Canada) ... D	Victoria
British Indian Ocean Territory	23	60	[1]	—	—	Dependent territory (U.K.) ... C	
British Virgin Islands	59	153	14,000	237	93	Dependent territory (U.K.) ... C	Road Town
† Brunei	2,226	5,765	261,000	117	45	Monarchy ... A	Bandar Seri Begawan
† Bulgaria	42,823	110,912	9,008,000	210	81	Republic ... A	Sofija (Sofia)
† Burkina Faso	105,869	274,200	9,247,000	87	34	Provisional military government ... A	Ouagadougou
† Burma	261,228	676,577	41,690,000	160	62	Provisional military government ... A	Yangon (Rangoon)
† Burundi	10,745	27,830	5,541,000	516	199	Provisional military government ... A	Bujumbura
California	158,704	411,041	29,905,000	188	73	State (U.S.) ... D	Sacramento
† Cambodia	69,898	181,035	8,345,000	119	46	Socialist republic ... A	Phnum Pénh (Phnom Penh)
† Cameroon	183,569	475,442	12,110,000	66	25	Republic ... A	Yaoundé
† Canada	3,849,674	9,970,610	26,710,000	6.9	2.7	Federal parliamentary state ... A	Ottawa
† Cape Verde	1,557	4,033	381,000	245	94	Republic ... A	Praia
Cayman Islands	100	259	26,000	260	100	Dependent territory (U.K.) ... C	George Town
† Central African Republic	240,535	622,984	2,917,000	12	4.7	Republic ... A	Bangui
† Chad	495,755	1,284,000	5,122,000	10	4.0	Republic ... A	N'Djamena
Chekiang (Zhejiang)	39,305	101,800	43,835,000	1,115	431	Province (China) ... D	Hangzhou
† Chile	292,135	756,626	13,270,000	45	18	Republic ... A	Santiago
† China (excl. Taiwan)	3,689,631	9,556,100	1,141,530,000	309	119	Socialist republic ... A	Beijing (Peking)
Christmas Island	52	135	1,500	29	11	External territory (Australia) ... C	
Ciskei[2]	2,996	7,760	1,320,000	441	170	National state (South African protection) ... B	Bisho
Cocos (Keeling) Islands	5.4	14	700	130	50	Part of Australia ... C	
† Colombia	440,831	1,141,748	31,370,000	71	27	Republic ... A	Bogotá
Colorado	104,094	269,602	3,400,000	33	13	State (U.S.) ... D	Denver
† Comoros	863	2,235	498,000	577	223	Federal Islamic republic ... A	Moroni
† Congo	132,047	342,000	2,346,000	18	6.9	Socialist republic ... A	Brazzaville
Connecticut	5,019	12,999	3,285,000	655	253	State (U.S.) ... D	Hartford
Cook Islands	91	236	18,000	198	76	Self-governing territory (New Zealand protection) ... B	Avarua
† Costa Rica	19,730	51,100	3,032,000	154	59	Republic ... A	San José
Croatia (Hrvatska)[10]	21,829	56,538	4,772,000	219	84	Republic (Yugoslavia) ... D	Zagreb
† Cuba	42,804	110,861	10,805,000	252	97	Socialist republic ... A	La Habana (Havana)
† Cyprus (excl. North Cyprus)	2,276	5,896	528,000	232	90	Republic ... A	Nicosia (Levkosía)
Cyprus, North[3]	1,295	3,355	176,000	136	52	Republic ... A	Nicosia (Lefkoşa)
† Czechoslovakia	49,382	127,899	15,690,000	318	123	Federal republic ... A	Praha (Prague)
Delaware	2,045	5,297	677,000	331	128	State (U.S.) ... D	Dover
† Denmark	16,638	43,093	5,138,000	309	119	Constitutional monarchy ... A	København (Copenhagen)
District of Columbia	69	179	577,000	8,362	3,223	Federal district (U.S.) ... D	Washington
† Djibouti	8,958	23,200	341,000	38	15	Republic ... A	Djibouti
† Dominica	305	790	89,000	292	113	Republic ... A	Roseau
† Dominican Republic	18,704	48,442	7,245,000	387	150	Republic ... A	Santo Domingo
† Ecuador	109,484	283,561	10,930,000	100	39	Republic ... A	Quito
† Egypt	386,662	1,001,449	54,910,000	142	55	Socialist republic ... A	Al-Qāhirah (Cairo)
† El Salvador	8,124	21,041	5,363,000	660	255	Republic ... A	San Salvador
England	50,363	130,439	47,820,000	950	367	Administrative division (U.K.) ... D	London
† Equatorial Guinea	10,831	28,051	353,000	33	13	Republic ... A	Malabo
Estonia	17,413	45,100	1,602,000	92	36	Republic ... A	Tallinn
† Ethiopia	483,123	1,251,282	52,206,000	108	42	Socialist republic ... A	Adis Abeba
Europe	3,800,000	9,800,000	693,500,000	183	71		
Faeroe Islands	540	1,399	48,000	89	34	Self-governing territory (Danish protection) ... B	Tórshavn
Falkland Islands[4]	4,700	12,173	2,200	0.5	0.2	Dependent territory (U.K.) ... C	Stanley

Country, Division or Region English (Conventional)	Area in sq. mi.	Area in sq. km.	Estimated Population 1/1/91	Pop. per sq. mi.	Pop. per sq. km.	Form of Government and Political Status	Capital
† Fiji	7,078	*18,333*	732,000	103	*40*	Republic A	Suva
† Finland	130,559	*338,145*	4,984,000	38	*15*	Republic A	Helsinki (Helsingfors)
Florida	58,668	*151,949*	13,150,000	224	*87*	State (U.S.) D	Tallahassee
† France (excl. Overseas Departments)	211,208	*547,026*	56,580,000	268	*103*	Republic A	Paris
French Guiana	35,135	*91,000*	100,000	2.8	*1.1*	Overseas department (France) C	Cayenne
French Polynesia	1,544	*4,000*	199,000	129	*50*	Overseas territory (France) C	Papeete
Fukien (Fujian)	46,332	*120,000*	29,795,000	643	*248*	Province (China) D	Fuzhou
† Gabon	103,347	*267,667*	1,074,000	10	*4.0*	Republic A	Libreville
† Gambia	4,361	*11,295*	831,000	191	*74*	Republic A	Banjul
Georgia	58,914	*152,587*	6,540,000	111	*43*	State (U.S.) D	Atlanta
Georgia (Gruzinskaja S.S.R.)	26,911	*69,700*	5,535,000	206	*79*	Soviet socialist republic (U.S.S.R.) D	Tbilisi
† Germany	108,333	*357,040*	79,220,000	575	*222*	Federal republic A	Berlin and Bonn
† Ghana	92,098	*238,533*	15,550,000	169	*65*	Provisional military government A	Accra
Gibraltar	2.3	*6.0*	33,000	14,348	*5,500*	Dependent territory (U.K.) C	Gibraltar
† Greece	50,962	*131,990*	10,075,000	198	*76*	Republic A	Athínai (Athens)
Greenland	840,004	*2,175,600*	57,000	0.1	—	Self-governing territory (Danish protection) B	Godthåb (Nuuk)
† Grenada	133	*344*	114,000	857	*331*	Parliamentary state A	St. George's
Guadeloupe (incl. Dependencies)	687	*1,780*	350,000	509	*197*	Overseas department (France) C	Basse-Terre
Guam	209	*541*	144,000	689	*266*	Unincorporated territory (U.S.) C	Agana
† Guatemala	42,042	*108,889*	9,324,000	222	*86*	Republic A	Guatemala
Guernsey (incl. Dependencies)	30	*78*	56,000	1,867	*718*	Bailiwick (Channel Islands) C	St. Peter Port
† Guinea	94,926	*245,857*	7,364,000	78	*30*	Provisional military government A	Conakry
† Guinea-Bissau	13,948	*36,125*	1,011,000	72	*28*	Republic A	Bissau
† Guyana	83,000	*214,969*	1,000,000	12	*4.7*	Republic A	Georgetown
Hainan	13,127	*34,000*	6,872,000	524	*202*	Province (China) D	Haikou
† Haiti	10,714	*27,750*	5,745,000	536	*207*	Republic A	Port-au-Prince
Hawaii	6,473	*16,765*	1,140,000	176	*68*	State (U.S.) D	Honolulu
Heilungkiang (Heilongjiang)	181,082	*469,000*	36,300,000	200	*77*	Province (China) D	Harbin
Honan (Henan)	64,479	*167,000*	84,700,000	1,314	*507*	Province (China) D	Zhengzhou
† Honduras	43,277	*112,088*	5,181,000	120	*46*	Republic A	Tegucigalpa
Hong Kong	414	*1,072*	6,009,000	14,514	*5,605*	Chinese territory under British administration C	Hong Kong (Victoria)
Hopeh (Hebei)	73,359	*190,000*	61,070,000	832	*321*	Province (China) D	Shijiazhuang
Hunan	81,081	*210,000*	61,640,000	760	*294*	Province (China) D	Changsha
† Hungary	35,920	*93,033*	10,540,000	293	*113*	Republic A	Budapest
Hupeh (Hubei)	72,356	*187,400*	54,110,000	748	*289*	Province (China) D	Wuhan
† Iceland	39,769	*103,000*	260,000	6.5	*2.5*	Republic A	Reykjavík
Idaho	83,566	*216,435*	1,028,000	12	*4.8*	State (U.S.) D	Boise
Illinois	57,872	*149,888*	11,560,000	200	*77*	State (U.S.) D	Springfield
† India (incl. part of Jammu and Kashmir)	1,237,062	*3,203,975*	836,170,000	676	*261*	Federal republic A	New Delhi
Indiana	36,417	*94,320*	5,618,000	154	*60*	State (U.S.) D	Indianapolis
† Indonesia	741,101	*1,919,443*	193,080,000	261	*101*	Republic A	Jakarta
Inner Mongolia (Nei Monggol)	456,759	*1,183,000*	21,915,000	48	*19*	Autonomous region (China) D	Hohhot
Iowa	56,275	*145,752*	2,765,000	49	*19*	State (U.S.) D	Des Moines
† Iran	636,372	*1,648,196*	56,810,000	89	*34*	Islamic republic A	Tehrān
† Iraq	169,235	*438,317*	18,920,000	112	*43*	Republic A	Baghdād
† Ireland	27,137	*70,285*	3,471,000	128	*49*	Republic A	Dublin (Baile Átha Cliath)
Isle of Man	221	*572*	68,000	308	*119*	Self-governing territory (U.K. protection) B	Douglas
† Israel	8,019	*20,770*	4,518,000	563	*218*	Republic A	Yerushalayim (Jerusalem)
Israeli Occupied Areas[5]	2,947	*7,632*	1,989,000	675	*261*	...	...
† Italy	116,324	*301,277*	57,630,000	495	*191*	Republic A	Roma (Rome)
† Ivory Coast	124,518	*322,500*	12,305,000	99	*38*	Republic A	Abidjan and Yamoussoukro[6]
† Jamaica	4,244	*10,991*	2,425,000	571	*221*	Parliamentary state A	Kingston
† Japan	145,870	*377,801*	123,850,000	849	*328*	Constitutional monarchy A	Tōkyō
Jersey	45	*116*	82,000	1,822	*707*	Bailiwick (Channel Islands) C	St. Helier
† Jordan	35,135	*91,000*	3,112,000	89	*34*	Constitutional monarchy A	'Ammān
Kansas	82,282	*213,109*	2,508,000	30	*12*	State (U.S.) D	Topeka
Kansu (Gansu)	173,746	*450,000*	22,375,000	129	*50*	Province (China) D	Lanzhou
Kazakh (Kazachskaja S.S.R.)	1,049,156	*2,717,300*	16,810,000	16	*6.2*	Soviet socialist republic (U.S.S.R.) D	Alma-Ata
Kentucky	40,414	*104,672*	3,737,000	92	*36*	State (U.S.) D	Frankfort
† Kenya	224,961	*582,646*	26,400,000	117	*45*	Republic A	Nairobi
Kiangsi (Jiangxi)	64,325	*166,600*	38,015,000	591	*228*	Province (China) D	Nanchang
Kiangsu (Jiangsu)	39,614	*102,600*	67,580,000	1,706	*659*	Province (China) D	Nanjing (Nanking)
Kirghizia (Kirgizskaja S.S.R)	76,641	*198,500*	4,370,000	57	*22*	Soviet socialist republic (U.S.S.R.) D	Frunze (Pišpek)
Kiribati	280	*726*	74,000	264	*102*	Republic A	Bairiki
Kirin (Jilin)	72,201	*187,000*	25,115,000	348	*134*	Province (China) D	Changchun
Korea, North	46,540	*120,538*	23,335,000	501	*194*	Socialist republic A	P'yŏngyang
Korea, South	38,230	*99,016*	42,975,000	1,124	*434*	Republic A	Sŏul (Seoul)
† Kuwait	6,880	*17,818*	2,189,000	318	*123*	Constitutional monarchy A	Al-Kuwayt (Kuwait)
Kwangsi Chuang (Guangxi Zhuangzu)	91,236	*236,300*	42,695,000	468	*181*	Autonomous region (China) D	Nanning
Kwangtung (Guangdong)	68,726	*178,000*	61,850,000	900	*347*	Province (China) D	Guangzhou (Canton)
Kweichow (Guizhou)	65,637	*170,000*	32,650,000	497	*192*	Province (China) D	Guiyang
† Laos	91,429	*236,800*	4,069,000	45	*17*	Socialist republic A	Viangchan (Vientiane)
Latvia	24,595	*63,700*	2,738,000	111	*43*	Republic A	Rīga
† Lebanon	4,015	*10,400*	3,360,000	837	*323*	Republic A	Bayrūt (Beirut)
† Lesotho	11,720	*30,355*	1,764,000	151	*58*	Constitutional monarchy A	Maseru
Liaoning	56,255	*145,700*	40,295,000	716	*277*	Province (China) D	Shenyang (Mukden)
† Liberia	38,250	*99,067*	2,689,000	70	*27*	Republic A	Monrovia
† Libya	679,362	*1,759,540*	4,271,000	6.3	*2.4*	Socialist republic A	Ṭarābulus (Tripoli)
† Liechtenstein	62	*160*	31,000	500	*194*	Constitutional monarchy A	Vaduz
Lithuania	25,174	*65,200*	3,760,000	149	*58*	Republic A	Vilnius
Louisiana	47,750	*123,672*	4,180,000	88	*34*	State (U.S.) D	Baton Rouge
† Luxembourg	998	*2,586*	379,000	380	*147*	Constitutional monarchy A	Luxembourg
Macau	6.6	*17*	462,000	70,000	*27,176*	Chinese territory under Portuguese administration C	Macau
Macedonia (Makedonija)	9,928	*25,713*	2,109,000	212	*82*	Republic (Yugoslavia) D	Skopje
† Madagascar	226,658	*587,041*	11,995,000	53	*20*	Republic A	Antananarivo
Maine	33,265	*86,156*	1,254,000	38	*15*	State (U.S.) D	Augusta
† Malawi	45,747	*118,484*	8,432,000	184	*71*	Republic A	Lilongwe
† Malaysia	129,251	*334,758*	17,915,000	139	*54*	Federal constitutional monarchy A	Kuala Lumpur
† Maldives	115	*298*	215,000	1,870	*721*	Republic A	Male
† Mali	478,767	*1,240,000*	8,205,000	17	*6.6*	Republic A	Bamako
† Malta	122	*316*	354,000	2,902	*1,120*	Republic A	Valletta
Manitoba	250,947	*649,950*	1,116,000	4.4	*1.7*	Province (Canada) D	Winnipeg
Marshall Islands	70	*181*	44,000	629	*243*	Republic (U.S. protection) B	Majuro (island)
Martinique	425	*1,100*	341,000	802	*310*	Overseas department (France) C	Fort-de-France
Maryland	10,461	*27,094*	4,900,000	468	*181*	State (U.S.) D	Annapolis
Massachusetts	8,286	*21,461*	6,044,000	729	*282*	State (U.S.) D	Boston
† Mauritania	395,956	*1,025,520*	2,070,000	5.2	*2.0*	Provisional military government A	Nouakchott

Country, Division or Region English (Conventional)	Area in sq. mi.	Area in sq. km.	Estimated Population 1/1/91	Pop. per sq. mi.	Pop. per sq. km.	Form of Government and Political Status	Capital
† Mauritius (incl. Dependencies)	788	*2,040*	1,091,000	1,385	*535*	Parliamentary state A	Port Louis
Mayotte[8]	144	*374*	85,000	590	*227*	Territorial collectivity (France) C	Dzaoudzi and Mamoudzou[6]
† Mexico	756,066	*1,958,201*	86,675,000	115	*44*	Federal republic A	Ciudad de México (Mexico City)
Michigan	97,107	*251,506*	9,180,000	95	*37*	State (U.S.) D	Lansing
Micronesia, Federated States of	271	*702*	94,000	347	*134*	Republic (U.S. protection) B	Kolonia
Midway Islands	2.0	*5.2*	500	250	*96*	Unincorporated territory (U.S.) C	.....
Minnesota	86,614	*224,329*	4,439,000	51	*20*	State (U.S.) D	St. Paul
Mississippi	47,691	*123,519*	2,583,000	54	*21*	State (U.S.) D	Jackson
Missouri	69,697	*180,514*	5,192,000	74	*29*	State (U.S.) D	Jefferson City
Moldavia (Moldavskaja S.S.R.)	13,012	*33,700*	4,400,000	338	*131*	Soviet socialist republic (U.S.S.R.) D	Kišin'ov (Kishinev)
Monaco	0.7	*1.9*	29,000	41,429	*15,263*	Constitutional monarchy A	Monaco
† Mongolia	604,829	*1,566,500*	2,203,000	3.6	*1.4*	Socialist republic A	Ulaanbaatar (Ulan Bator)
Montana	147,045	*380,845*	803,000	5.5	*2.1*	State (U.S.) D	Helena
Montenegro (Crna Gora)	5,333	*13,812*	638,000	120	*66*	Republic (Yugoslavia) D	Titograd
Montserrat	39	*102*	12,000	308	*118*	Dependent territory (U.K.) C	Plymouth
† Morocco (excl. Western Sahara)	172,414	*446,550*	26,575,000	154	*60*	Constitutional monarchy A	Rabat
† Mozambique	308,642	*799,379*	15,785,000	51	*20*	Republic A	Maputo
† Namibia (excl. Walvis Bay)	317,818	*823,144*	1,904,000	6.0	*2.3*	Republic A	Windhoek
Nauru	8.1	*21*	9,000	1,111	*429*	Republic A	Yaren District
Nebraska	77,350	*200,336*	1,605,000	21	*8.0*	State (U.S.) D	Lincoln
† Nepal	56,827	*147,181*	19,390,000	341	*132*	Constitutional monarchy A	Kāṭhmāṇḍau
† Netherlands	16,133	*41,785*	14,980,000	929	*359*	Constitutional monarchy A	Amsterdam and 's-Gravenhage (The Hague)
Netherlands Antilles	309	*800*	194,000	628	*243*	Self-governing territory (Netherlands protection) B	Willemstad
Nevada	110,562	*286,354*	1,400,000	13	*4.9*	State (U.S.) D	Carson City
New Brunswick	28,355	*73,440*	737,000	26	*10*	Province (Canada) D	Fredericton
New Caledonia	7,358	*19,058*	170,000	23	*8.9*	Overseas territory (France) C	Nouméa
Newfoundland	156,649	*405,720*	585,000	3.7	*1.4*	Province (Canada) D	St. John's
New Hampshire	9,278	*24,030*	1,129,000	122	*47*	State (U.S.) D	Concord
New Jersey	7,787	*20,168*	7,775,000	998	*386*	State (U.S.) D	Trenton
New Mexico	121,594	*314,927*	1,550,000	13	*4.9*	State (U.S.) D	Santa Fe
New South Wales	309,500	*801,600*	5,902,000	19	*7.4*	State (Australia) D	Sydney
New York	52,737	*136,588*	17,980,000	341	*132*	State (U.S.) D	Albany
† New Zealand	103,519	*268,112*	3,483,000	34	*13*	Parliamentary state A	Wellington
† Nicaragua	50,054	*129,640*	3,659,000	73	*28*	Republic A	Managua
† Niger	489,191	*1,267,000*	7,848,000	16	*6.2*	Provisional military government A	Niamey
† Nigeria	356,669	*923,768*	112,830,000	316	*122*	Provisional military government A	Lagos and Abuja[6]
Ningsia Hui (Ningxia Huizu)	25,637	*66,400*	4,566,000	178	*69*	Autonomous region (China) D	Yinchuan
Niue	102	*263*	1,800	18	*6.8*	Self-governing territory (New Zealand protection) B	Alofi
Norfolk Island	14	*36*	2,000	143	*56*	External territory (Australia) C	Kingston
North America	9,400,000	*24,400,000*	426,800,000	45	*17*	.....	.....
North Carolina	52,669	*136,412*	6,696,000	127	*49*	State (U.S.) D	Raleigh
North Dakota	70,702	*183,117*	634,000	9.0	*3.5*	State (U.S.) D	Bismarck
Northern Ireland	5,452	*14,121*	1,596,000	293	*113*	Administrative division (U.K.) D	Belfast
Northern Mariana Islands	184	*477*	24,000	130	*50*	Commonwealth (U.S. protection) B	Saipan (island)
Northern Territory	519,771	*1,346,200*	159,000	0.3	*0.1*	Territory (Australia) D	Darwin
Northwest Territories	1,322,910	*3,426,320*	53,000	—	—	Territory (Canada) D	Yellowknife
† Norway (incl. Svalbard and Jan Mayen)	149,412	*386,975*	4,271,000	29	*11*	Constitutional monarchy A	Oslo
Nova Scotia	21,425	*55,490*	911,000	43	*16*	Province (Canada) D	Halifax
Oceania (incl. Australia)	3,300,000	*8,500,000*	26,700,000	8.1	*3.1*	.....	.....
Ohio	44,786	*115,995*	10,770,000	240	*93*	State (U.S.) D	Columbus
Oklahoma	69,957	*181,188*	3,185,000	46	*18*	State (U.S.) D	Oklahoma City
† Oman	82,030	*212,457*	1,366,000	17	*6.4*	Monarchy A	Masqaṭ (Muscat)
Ontario	412,581	*1,068,580*	9,717,000	24	*9.1*	Province (Canada) D	Toronto
Oregon	97,076	*251,426*	2,884,000	30	*11*	State (U.S.) D	Salem
Pacific Islands, Trust Territory of the	196	*508*	15,000	77	*30*	United Nations trusteeship (U.S. administration) B	.....
† Pakistan (incl. part of Jammu and Kashmir)	339,732	*879,902*	114,380,000	337	*130*	Federal Islamic republic A	Islāmābād
Palau (Trust Territory)	196	*508*	15,000	77	*30*	Part of Trust Territory of the Pacific Islands B	Koror
† Panama	29,157	*75,517*	2,445,000	84	*32*	Republic A	Panamá
† Papua New Guinea	178,704	*462,840*	3,641,000	20	*7.9*	Parliamentary state A	Port Moresby
† Paraguay	157,048	*406,752*	4,338,000	28	*11*	Republic A	Asunción
Peking (Beijing)	6,487	*16,800*	10,470,000	1,614	*623*	Autonomous city (China) D	Beijing (Peking)
Pennsylvania	46,047	*119,261*	11,765,000	256	*99*	State (U.S.) D	Harrisburg
† Peru	496,225	*1,285,216*	22,610,000	46	*18*	Republic A	Lima
† Philippines	115,831	*300,000*	62,170,000	537	*207*	Republic A	Manila
Pitcairn (incl. Dependencies)	19	*49*	50	2.6	*1.0*	Dependent territory (U.K.) C	Adamstown
† Poland	120,728	*312,683*	38,,000	315	*122*	Republic A	Warszawa (Warsaw)
† Portugal	35,516	*91,985*	10,560,000	297	*115*	Republic A	Lisboa (Lisbon)
Prince Edward Island	2,185	*5,660*	134,000	61	*24*	Province (Canada) D	Charlottetown
Puerto Rico	3,515	*9,104*	3,604,000	1,025	*396*	Commonwealth (U.S. protection) B	San Juan
† Qatar	4,416	*11,437*	514,000	116	*45*	Monarchy A	Ad-Dawḥah (Doha)
Quebec	594,860	*1,540,680*	6,840,000	11	*4.4*	Province (Canada) D	Québec
Queensland	666,876	*1,727,200*	2,923,000	4.4	*1.7*	State (Australia) D	Brisbane
Reunion	969	*2,510*	600,000	619	*239*	Overseas department (France) C	Saint-Denis
Rhode Island	1,212	*3,139*	1,003,000	828	*320*	State (U.S.) D	Providence
† Romania	91,699	*237,500*	23,325,000	254	*98*	Republic A	București (Bucharest)
Russian Soviet Federative Socialist Republic (Rossijskaja S.F.S.R.)	6,592,849	*17,075,400*	149,730,000	23	*8.8*	Soviet socialist republic (U.S.S.R.) D	Moskva (Moscow)
† Rwanda	10,169	*26,338*	7,748,000	762	*294*	Provisional military government A	Kigali
St. Helena (incl. Dependencies)	121	*314*	7,700	64	*25*	Dependent territory (U.K.) C	Jamestown
† St. Kitts and Nevis	104	*269*	44,000	423	*164*	Parliamentary state A	Basseterre
† St. Lucia	238	*616*	152,000	639	*247*	Parliamentary state A	Castries
St. Pierre and Miquelon	93	*242*	6,800	73	*28*	Territorial collectivity (France) C	Saint-Pierre
† St. Vincent and the Grenadines	150	*388*	115,000	767	*296*	Parliamentary state A	Kingstown
San Marino	24	*61*	24,000	1,000	*393*	Republic A	San Marino
† Sao Tome and Principe	372	*964*	127,000	341	*132*	Republic A	São Tomé
Saskatchewan	251,866	*652,330*	1,042,000	4.1	*1.6*	Province (Canada) D	Regina
† Saudi Arabia	830,000	*2,149,690*	15,285,000	18	*7.1*	Monarchy A	Ar-Riyāḍ (Riyadh)
Scotland	30,414	*78,772*	5,090,000	167	*65*	Administrative division (U.K.) D	Edinburgh
† Senegal	75,951	*196,712*	7,257,000	96	*37*	Republic A	Dakar
Serbia (Srbija)	34,116	*88,361*	9,919,000	290	*112*	Republic (Yugoslavia)) D	Beograd (Belgrade)
† Seychelles	175	*453*	68,000	389	*150*	Republic A	Victoria
Shanghai	2,394	*6,200*	13,240,000	5,530	*2,135*	Autonomous city (China) D	Shanghai

Country, Division or Region English (Conventional)	Area in sq. mi.	Area in sq. km.	Estimated Population 1/1/91	Pop. per sq. mi.	Pop. per sq. km.	Form of Government and Political Status	Capital
Shansi (Shanxi)	60,232	*156,000*	28,765,000	478	*184*	Province (China) D	Taiyuan
Shantung (Shandong)	59,074	*153,000*	84,470,000	1,430	*552*	Province (China) D	Jinan
Shensi (Shaanxi)	79,151	*205,000*	33,105,000	418	*161*	Province (China) D	Xi'an (Sian)
† Sierra Leone	27,925	*72,325*	4,222,000	151	*58*	Republic A	Freetown
† Singapore	246	*636*	2,757,000	11,207	*4,335*	Republic A	Singapore
Sinkiang Uighur (Xinjiang Uygur)	617,764	*1,600,000*	15,070,000	24	*9.4*	Autonomous region (China) D	Ürümqi
Slovenia (Slovenija)(10)	7,819	*20,251*	1,977,000	253	*98*	Republic (Yugoslavia) D	Ljubljana
† Solomon Islands	10,954	*28,370*	322,000	29	*11*	Parliamentary state A	Honiara
† Somalia	246,201	*637,657*	8,499,000	35	*13*	Provisional military government A	Muqdisho (Mogadishu)
† South Africa (incl. Walvis Bay)	433,680	*1,123,226*	40,055,000	92	*36*	Republic A	Pretoria, Cape Town, and Bloemfontein
South America	6,900,000	*17,800,000*	299,200,000	43	*17*		
South Australia	379,925	*984,000*	1,458,000	3.8	*1.5*	State (Australia) D	Adelaide
South Carolina	31,116	*80,590*	3,550,000	114	*44*	State (U.S.) D	Columbia
South Dakota	77,120	*199,740*	702,000	9.1	*3.5*	State (U.S.) D	Pierre
South Georgia and the South Sandwich Islands	1,450	*3,755*	(1)	—	—	Dependent territory (U.K.) C	
† Spain	194,885	*504,750*	40,190,000	206	*80*	Constitutional monarchy A	Madrid
Spanish North Africa(9)	12	*32*	121,000	10,083	*3,781*	Five possessions (Spain) C	
† Sri Lanka	24,962	*64,652*	17,135,000	686	*265*	Socialist republic A	Colombo and Sri Jayawardenepura
† Sudan	967,500	*2,505,813*	25,515,000	26	*10*	Islamic Republic A	Al-Kharṭūm (Khartoum)
† Suriname	63,251	*163,820*	412,000	6.5	*2.5*	Republic A	Paramaribo
† Swaziland	6,704	*17,364*	791,000	118	*46*	Monarchy A	Mbabane and Lobamba
† Sweden	173,732	*449,964*	8,602,000	50	*19*	Constitutional monarchy A	Stockholm
Switzerland	15,943	*41,293*	6,737,000	423	*163*	Federal republic A	Bern (Berne)
† Syria	71,498	*185,180*	12,315,000	172	*67*	Socialist republic A	Dimashq (Damascus)
Szechwan (Sichuan)	220,078	*570,000*	111,640,000	507	*196*	Province (China) D	Chengdu
Taiwan	13,900	*36,002*	20,565,000	1,479	*571*	Republic A	T'aipei
Tajikstan (Tajikskaja S.S.R.)	55,251	*143,100*	5,185,000	94	*36*	Soviet socialist republic (U.S.S.R.) D	Dušanbe
† Tanzania	364,900	*945,087*	26,065,000	71	*28*	Republic A	Dar es Salaam and Dodoma(6)
Tasmania	26,178	*67,800*	461,000	18	*6.8*	State (Australia) D	Hobart
Tennessee	42,143	*109,150*	4,916,000	117	*45*	State (U.S.) D	Nashville
Texas	266,805	*691,022*	17,300,000	65	*25*	State (U.S.) D	Austin
† Thailand	198,115	*513,115*	56,860,000	287	*111*	Constitutional monarchy A	Krung Thep (Bangkok)
Tibet (Xizang)	471,045	*1,220,000*	2,283,000	4.8	*1.9*	Autonomous region (China) D	Lhasa
Tientsin (Tianjin)	4,363	*11,300*	8,790,000	2,015	*778*	Autonomous city (China) D	Tianjin (Tientsin)
† Togo	21,925	*56,785*	3,627,000	165	*64*	Republic A	Lomé
Tokelau	4.6	*12*	1,800	391	*150*	Island territory (New Zealand) C	
Tonga	290	*750*	102,000	352	*136*	Constitutional monarchy A	Nuku'alofa
Transkei(2)	16,816	*43,553*	4,016,000	239	*92*	National state (South African protection) B	Umtata
† Trinidad and Tobago	1,980	*5,128*	1,242,000	627	*242*	Republic A	Port of Spain
Tsinghai (Qinghai)	277,994	*720,000*	4,452,000	16	*6.2*	Province (China) D	Xining
† Tunisia	63,170	*163,610*	8,188,000	130	*50*	Republic A	Tunis
† Turkey	300,948	*779,452*	63,720,000	212	*82*	Republic A	Ankara
Turkmenistan (Turkmenskaja S.S.R.)	188,456	*488,100*	3,585,000	19	*7.3*	Soviet socialist republic (U.S.S.R.) D	Aščhabad
Turks and Caicos Islands	193	*500*	13,000	67	*26*	Dependent territory (U.K.) C	Grand Turk
Tuvalu	10	*26*	8,900	890	*342*	Parliamentary state A	Funafuti
† Uganda	93,104	*241,139*	17,890,000	192	*74*	Republic A	Kampala
† Ukraine (Ukrainskaja S.S.R.)	233,090	*603,700*	52,520,000	225	*87*	Soviet socialist republic (U.S.S.R.) D	Kijev (Kiev)
† Union of Soviet Socialist Republics(7)	8,533,205	*22,100,900*	283,210,000	33	*13*	Federal socialist republic A	Moskva (Moscow)
† United Arab Emirates	32,278	*83,600*	2,321,000	72	*28*	Federation of monarchs A	Abū Ẓaby (Abu Dhabi)
† United Kingdom	94,248	*244,100*	57,380,000	609	*235*	Constitutional monarchy A	London
† United States	3,679,245	*9,529,202*	250,800,000	68	*26*	Federal republic A	Washington
† Uruguay	68,500	*177,414*	3,105,000	45	*18*	Republic A	Montevideo
Utah	84,902	*219,895*	1,765,000	21	*8.0*	State (U.S.) D	Salt Lake City
Uzbekistan (Uzbekskaja S.S.R.)	172,742	*447,400*	20,215,000	117	*45*	Soviet socialist republic (U.S.S.R.) D	Taškent
† Vanuatu	4,707	*12,190*	148,000	31	*12*	Republic A	Port Vila
Vatican City	0.2	*0.4*	800	4,000	*2,000*	Ecclesiastical city-state A	Città del Vaticano (Vatican City)
Venda(2)	2,393	*6,198*	652,000	272	*105*	National state (South African protection) B	Thohoyandou
† Venezuela	352,145	*912,050*	19,995,000	57	*22*	Federal republic A	Caracas
Vermont	9,614	*24,900*	577,000	60	*23*	State (U.S.) D	Montpelier
Victoria	87,877	*227,600*	4,428,000	50	*19*	State (Australia) D	Melbourne
† Vietnam	128,066	*331,689*	67,850,000	530	*205*	Socialist republic A	Ha Noi
Virginia	40,763	*105,576*	6,275,000	154	*59*	State (U.S.) D	Richmond
Virgin Islands	133	*344*	117,000	880	*340*	Unincorporated territory (U.S.) C	Charlotte Amalie
Wake Island	3.0	*7.8*	300	100	*38*	Unincorporated territory (U.S.) C	
Wales	8,019	*20,768*	2,874,000	358	*138*	Administrative division (U.K.) D	Cardiff
Wallis and Futuna	98	*255*	16,000	163	*63*	Overseas territory (France) C	Mata-Utu
Washington	68,139	*176,479*	4,920,000	72	*28*	State (U.S.) D	Olympia
Western Australia	975,101	*2,525,500*	1,643,000	1.7	*0.7*	State (Australia) D	Perth
Western Sahara	102,703	*266,000*	200,000	1.9	*0.8*	Occupied by Morocco	El Aaiún (Laayone)
† Western Samoa	1,093	*2,831*	188,000	172	*66*	Constitutional monarchy A	Apia
West Virginia	24,236	*62,771*	1,831,000	76	*29*	State (U.S.) D	Charleston
Wisconsin	66,213	*171,491*	4,966,000	75	*29*	State (U.S.) D	Madison
Wyoming	97,808	*253,322*	450,000	4.6	*1.8*	State (U.S.) D	Cheyenne
† Yemen	205,356	*531,869*	13,310,000	65	*25*	Republic A	Ṣan'ā'
† Yugoslavia(10)	98,766	*255,804*	23,907,000	242	*93*	Federal socialist republic A	Beograd (Belgrade)
Yukon Territory	186,661	*483,450*	27,000	0.1	*0.1*	Territory (Canada) D	Whitehorse
Yunnan	152,124	*394,000*	37,440,000	246	*95*	Province (China) D	Kunming
† Zaire	905,446	*2,345,095*	36,095,000	40	*15*	Republic A	Kinshasa
† Zambia	290,586	*752,614*	8,226,000	28	*11*	Republic A	Lusaka
† Zimbabwe	150,873	*390,759*	9,491,000	63	*24*	Republic A	Harare (Salisbury)
WORLD	57,800,000	*149,700,000*	5,350,000,000	93	*36*		

† Member of the United Nations (1990).
(1) No permanent population.
(2) Bophuthatswana, Ciskei, Transkei, and Venda are not recognized by the United Nations.
(3) North Cyprus unilaterally declared its independence from Cyprus in 1983.
(4) Claimed by Argentina.
(5) Includes West Bank, Golan Heights, and Gaza Strip.
(6) Future capital.
(7) Late in 1991 Estonia, Latvia, and Lithuania were recognized as independent nations. Other Soviet Republics (S.S.R.s) declared their intentions to secede at that time.
(8) Claimed by Comoros.
(9) Comprises Ceuta, Melilla, and several small islands.
(10) In June, 1991, the republics of Croatia (Hrvatska) and Slovenia (Slovenija) declared independence from Yugoslavia.

General Information

MOVEMENTS OF THE EARTH

The earth makes one complete revolution around the sun every 365 days, 5 hours, 48 minutes, and 46 seconds.

The earth makes one complete rotation on its axis in 23 hours, 56 minutes and 4 seconds.

The earth revolves in its orbit around the sun at a speed of 66,700 miles per hour (107,343 kilometers per hour).

The earth rotates on its axis at an equatorial speed of more than 1,000 miles per hour (1,600 kilometers per hour).

MEASUREMENTS OF THE EARTH

Estimated age of the earth, at least 4.6 billion years.

Equatorial diameter of the earth, 7,926.38 miles *(12,756.27 kilometers).*

Polar diameter of the earth, 7,899.80 miles *(12,713.50 kilometers).*

Mean diameter of the earth, 7,917.52 miles *(12,742.01 kilometers).*

Equatorial circumference of the earth, 24,901.46 miles *(40,075.02 kilometers).*

Polar circumference of the earth, 24,855.34 miles *(40,000.79 kilometers).*

Difference between equatorial and polar circumferences of the earth, 46.12 miles *(74.23 kilometers).*

Weight of the earth, 6,600,000,000,000,000,000,000 tons, or 6,600 billion billion tons *(6,000 billion billion metric tons).*

THE EARTH'S SURFACE

Total area of the earth, 197,000,000 square miles *(510,000,000 square kilometers).*

Total land area of the earth (including inland water and Antarctica), 57,800,000 square miles *(149,700,000 square kilometers).*

Highest point on the earth's surface, Mt. Everest, Asia, 29,028 feet *(8,848 meters).*

Lowest point on the earth's land surface, shores of the Dead Sea, Asia, 1,322 feet *(403 meters)* below sea level.

Greatest known depth of the ocean, the Mariana Trench, southwest of Guam, Pacific Ocean, 35,810 feet *(10,915 meters).*

THE EARTH'S INHABITANTS

Population of the earth is estimated to be 5,350,000,000 *(January 1, 1991).*

Estimated population density of the earth, 93 per square mile *(36 per square kilometer).*

EXTREMES OF TEMPERATURE AND RAINFALL OF THE EARTH

Highest temperature ever recorded, 136° F. *(58° C.)* at Al-ʻAzīzīyah, Libya, Africa, on September 13, 1922.

Lowest temperature ever recorded, -129° F. *(-89° C.)* at Vostok, Antarctica on July 21, 1983.

Highest mean annual temperature, 94° F. *(34° C.)* at Dalol, Ethiopia.

Lowest mean annual temperature, -70° F. *(-50° C.)* at Plateau Station, Antarctica.

The greatest local average annual rainfall is at Waialeale, Kauai, Hawaii, 460 inches *(11,680 millimeters).*

The greatest 24-hour rainfall, 74 inches *(1,880 millimeters),* is at Cilaos, Reunion Island, March 15-16, 1952.

The lowest local average annual rainfall is at Arica, Chile, .03 inches *(8 millimeters).*

The longest dry period, over 14 years, is at Arica, Chile, October 1903 to January 1918.

The Continents

CONTINENT	Area (sq. mi.) (sq. km.)	Estimated Population Jan. 1, 1991	Population per sq. mi. (sq. km.)	Mean Elevation (feet) (m.)	Highest Elevation (Feet) (m.)	Lowest Elevation (Feet) (m.)	Highest Recorded Temperature	Lowest Recorded Temperature
North America	9,400,000 *(24,400,000)*	426,800,000	45 *(17)*	2,000 *(610)*	Mt. McKinley, Alaska, United States 20,320 *(6,194)*	Death Valley, California, United States 282 *(84)* below sea level	Death Valley, California 134° F *(57° C)*	Northice, Greenland -87° F *(-66° C)*
South America	6,900,000 *(17,800,000)*	299,200,000	43 *(17)*	1,800 *(550)*	Cerro Aconcagua, Argentina 22,831 *(6,959)*	Salinas Chicas, Argentina 138 *(42)* below sea level	Rivadavia, Argentina 120° F *(49° C)*	Sarmiento, Argentina -27° F *(-33° C)*
Europe	3,800,000 *(9,800,000)*	693,500,000	183 *(71)*	980 *(300)*	Gora El'brus, U.S.S.R. 18,510 *(5,642)*	Caspian Sea, Soviet Union-Iran 92 *(28) below sea level*	Sevilla, Spain 122° F *(50° C)*	Ust' Ščugor, U.S.S.R. -67° F *(-55° C)*
Asia	17,300,000 *(44,900,000)*	3,232,000,000	187 *(72)*	3,000 *(910)*	Mt. Everest, China-Nepal 29,028 *(8,848)*	Dead Sea, Israel-Jordan 1,322 *(403)* below sea level	Tirat Z̧evi, Israel 129° F *(54° C)*	Ojm'akon and Verchojansk, Soviet Union -90° F *(-68° C)*
Africa	11,700,000 *(30,300,000)*	671,800,000	57 *(22)*	1,900 *(580)*	Kilimanjaro, Tanzania 19,340 *(5,895)*	Lac Assal, Djibouti 509 *(155)* below sea level	Al-ʻAzīzīyah, Libya 136° F *(58° C)*	Ifrane, Morocco -11° F *(-24° C)*
Oceania, incl. Australia	3,300,000 *(8,500,000)*	26,700,000	8.1 *(3.1)*	....	Mt. Wilhelm, Papua New Guinea 14,793 *(4,509)*	Lake Eyre, South Australia, Australia 52 *(16)* below sea level	Cloncurry, Queensland, Australia 128° F *(53° C)*	Charlottes Pass, New South Wales, Australia -8° F *(-22° C)*
Australia	2,966,155 *(7,682,300)*	17,260,000	5.8 *(2.2)*	1,000 *(300)*	Mt. Kosciusko, New South Wales 7,310 *(2,228)*	Lake Eyre, South Australia 52 *(16)* below sea level	Cloncurry, Queensland 128° F *(53° C)*	Charlottes Pass, New South Wales -8° F *(-22° C)*
Antarctica	5,400,000 *(14,000,000)*	....	....	6,000 *(1830)*	Vinson Massif 16,066 *(4,897)*	sea level	Vanda Station 59° F *(15° C)*	Vostok -129° F *(-89° C)*
World	57,800,000 *(149,700,000)*	5,350,000,000	93 *(36)*	....	Mt. Everest, China-Nepal 29,028 *(8,848)*	Dead Sea, Israel-Jordan 1,322 *(403)* below sea level	Al-ʻAzīzīyah, Libya 136° F *(58° C)*	Vostok, Antarctica -129° F *(-89° C)*

Historical Populations *

AREA	1650	1750	1800	1850	1900	1920	1950	1970	1980	1990
North America	*5,000,000*	*5,000,000*	*13,000,000*	*39,000,000*	106,000,000	147,000,000	219,000,000	316,600,000	365,000,000	423,600,000
South America	*8,000,000*	*7,000,000*	*12,000,000*	*20,000,000*	38,000,000	61,000,000	111,000,000	187,400,000	239,000,000	293,700,000
Europe	*100,000,000*	*140,000,000*	*190,000,000*	265,000,000	400,000,000	453,000,000	530,000,000	623,700,000	660,300,000	688,000,000
Asia	*335,000,000*	*476,000,000*	*593,000,000*	*754,000,000*	*932,000,000*	*1,000,000,000*	*1,418,000,000*	2,086,200,000	2,581,000,000	3,156,100,000
Africa	*100,000,000*	*95,000,000*	*90,000,000*	*95,000,000*	*118,000,000*	*140,000,000*	*199,000,000*	346,900,000	463,800,000	648,300,000
Oceania, incl. Australia	*2,000,000*	*2,000,000*	*2,000,000*	*2,000,000*	6,000,000	9,000,000	13,000,000	19,200,000	22,700,000	26,300,000
Australia	*	*	*	*	4,000,000	6,000,000	8,000,000	12,460,000	14,510,000	16,950,000
World	*550,000,000*	*725,000,000*	*900,000,000*	*1,175,000,000*	*1,600,000,000*	*1,810,000,000*	*2,490,000,000*	3,580,000,000	4,332,000,000	5,236,000,000

* Figures prior to 1970 are rounded to the nearest million. Figures in italics represent very rough estimates.

Largest Countries : Population

		Population 1/1/91
1	China (excl. Taiwan)	1,141,530,000
2	India (incl. part of Jammu and Kashmir)	836,170,000
3	Union of Soviet Socialist Republics	283,210,000
4	United States	250,800,000
5	Indonesia	193,080,000
6	Brazil	152,050,000
7	Japan	123,850,000
8	Pakistan (incl. part of Jammu and Kashmir)	114,380,000
9	Nigeria	112,830,000
10	Bangladesh	109,540,000
11	Mexico	86,675,000
12	Germany	79,220,000
13	Vietnam	67,850,000
14	Turkey	63,720,000
15	Philippines	62,170,000
16	Italy	57,630,000
17	United Kingdom	57,380,000
18	Thailand	56,860,000
19	Iran	56,810,000
20	France	56,580,000
21	Egypt	54,910,000
22	Ethiopia	52,206,000
23	Korea, South	42,975,000
24	Burma (Myanmar)	41,690,000
25	Spain	40,190,000
26	South Africa	40,055,000
27	Poland	38,010,000

Largest Countries : Area

		Area (sq. mi.)	Area (sq. km.)
1	Union of Soviet Socialist Republics	8,533,205	*22,100,900*
2	Canada	3,849,674	*9,970,610*
3	China (excl. Taiwan)	3,689,631	*9,556,100*
4	United States	3,679,245	*9,529,202*
5	Brazil	3,286,488	*8,511,965*
6	Australia	2,966,155	*7,682,300*
7	India (incl. part of Jammu and Kashmir)	1,237,062	*3,203,975*
8	Argentina	1,073,400	*2,780,092*
9	Sudan	967,500	*2,505,813*
10	Algeria	919,595	*2,381,741*
11	Zaire	905,446	*2,345,095*
12	Greenland	840,004	*2,175,600*
13	Saudi Arabia	830,000	*2,149,690*
14	Mexico	756,066	*1,958,201*
15	Indonesia	741,101	*1,919,443*
16	Libya	679,362	*1,759,540*
17	Iran	636,372	*1,648,196*
18	Mongolia	604,829	*1,566,500*
19	Peru	496,225	*1,285,216*
20	Chad	495,755	*1,284,000*
21	Niger	489,191	*1,267,000*
22	Ethiopia	483,123	*1,251,282*
23	Angola	481,354	*1,246,700*
24	Mali	478,767	*1,240,000*
25	Colombia	440,831	*1,141,748*
26	South Africa	433,680	*1,123,226*
27	Bolivia	424,165	*1,098,581*
28	Mauritania	395,956	*1,025,520*

Principal Mountains

North America

	Height (feet)	Height (meters)
McKinley, Mt., Δ Alaska (Δ United States; Δ North America)	20,320	6,194
Logan, Mt., Δ Canada (Δ Yukon; Δ St. Elias Mts.)	19,524	5,951
Orizaba, Pico de, Δ Mexico	18,406	5,610
St. Elias, Mt., Alaska-Canada	18,008	5,489
Popocatépetl, Volcán, Mexico	17,930	5,465
Foraker, Mt., Alaska	17,400	5,304
Iztaccíhuatl, Mexico	17,159	5,230
Lucania, Mt., Canada	17,147	5,226
Fairweather, Mt., Alaska-Canada (Δ British Columbia)	15,300	4,663
Whitney, Mt., Δ California,	14,494	4,418
Elbert, Mt., Δ Colorado (Δ Rocky Mts.)	14,433	4,399
Massive, Mt., Colorado	14,421	4,396
Harvard, Mt., Colorado	14,420	4,395
Rainier, Mt., Δ Washington (Δ Cascade Range)	14,410	4,392
Williamson, Mt., California	14,375	4,382
Blanca Pk., Colorado (Δ Sangre de Cristo Mts.)	14,345	4,372
La Plata Pk., Colorado	14,336	4,370
Uncompahgre Pk., Colorado (Δ San Juan Mts.)	14,309	4,361
Grays Pk., Colorado (Δ Front Range)	14,270	4,349
Evans, Mt., Colorado	14,264	4,348
Longs Pk., Colorado	14,255	4,345
Wrangell, Mt., Alaska	14,163	4,317
Shasta, Mt., California	14,162	4,317
Pikes Pk., Colorado	14,110	4,301
Colima, Nevado de, Mexico	13,993	4,240
Tajumulco, Volcán, Δ Guatemala (Δ Central America)	13,846	4,220
Gannett Pk., Δ Wyoming	13,804	4,207
Mauna Kea, Δ Hawaii	13,796	4,205
Grand Teton, Wyoming	13,770	4,197
Mauna Loa, Hawaii	13,679	4,169
Kings Pk., Δ Utah	13,528	4,123
Cloud Pk., Wyoming (Δ Bighorn Mts.)	13,167	4,013
Wheeler Pk., Δ New Mexico	13,161	4,011
Boundary Pk., Δ Nevada	13,143	4,006
Waddington, Mt., Canada (Δ Coast Mts.)	13,104	3,994
Robson, Mt., Canada (Δ Canadian Rockies)	12,972	3,954
Granite Pk., Δ Montana	12,799	3,901
Borah Pk., Δ Idaho	12,662	3,859
Humphreys Pk., Δ Arizona	12,633	3,851
Chirripó, Cerro, Δ Costa Rica	12,533	3,819
Columbia, Mt., Canada (Δ Alberta)	12,294	3,747
Adams, Mt., Washington	12,276	3,742
Gunnbjørn Fjeld, Δ Greenland	12,139	3,700
San Gorgonio Mtn., California	11,499	3,505
Barú, Volcán, Δ Panama	11,411	3,475
Hood, Mt., Δ Oregon	11,235	3,424
Lassen Pk., California	10,457	3,187
Duarte, Pico, Δ Dominican Rep. (Δ West Indies)	10,417	3,175
Haleakala Crater, Hawaii (Δ Maui)	10,023	3,055
Paricutín, Mexico	9,213	2,800
El Pital, Cerro, Δ El Salvador-Honduras	8,957	2,730
La Selle, Morne, Δ Haiti	8,773	2,674
Guadalupe Pk., Δ Texas	8,749	2,667
Olympus, Mt., Washington (Δ Olympic Mts.)	7,965	2,428
Blue Mountain Pk., Δ Jamaica	7,402	2,256
Harney Pk., Δ South Dakota (Δ Black Hills)	7,242	2,207
Mitchell, Mt., Δ North Carolina (Δ Appalachian Mts.)	6,684	2,037
Clingmans Dome, North Carolina-Δ Tennessee (Δ Great Smoky Mts.)	6,643	2,025
Turquino, Pico, Δ Cuba	6,470	1,972
Washington, Mt., Δ New Hampshire (Δ White Mts.)	6,288	1,917
Rogers, Mt., Δ Virginia	5,729	1,746
Marcy, Mt., Δ New York (Δ Adirondack Mts.)	5,344	1,629
Katahdin, Mt., Δ Maine	5,268	1,606
Kawaikini, Hawaii (Δ Kauai)	5,243	1,598
Spruce Knob, Δ West Virginia	4,862	1,482
Pelée, Montagne, Δ Martinique	4,583	1,397
Mansfield, Mt., Δ Vermont (Δ Green Mts.)	4,393	1,339
Punta, Cerro de, Δ Puerto Rico	4,389	1,338
Black Mtn., Δ Kentucky-Virginia	4,145	1,263
Kaala, Hawaii (Δ Oahu)	4,040	1,231

South America

Aconcagua, Cerro, Δ Argentina; Δ Andes; (Δ South America)	22,831	6,959
Ojos del Salado, Nevado, Argentina-Δ Chile	22,615	6,880
Illimani, Nevado, Δ Bolivia	22,579	6,402
Bonete, Cerro, Argentina	22,546	6,872
Huascarán, Nevado, Δ Peru	22,133	6,768
Llullaillaco, Volcán, Argentina-Chile	22,057	6,739
Yerupaja, Nevado, Peru	21,765	6,634
Tupungato, Cerro, Argentina-Chile	21,555	6,550
Sajama, Nevado, Bolivia	21,463	6,542
Illampu, Nevado, Bolivia	20,873	6,362
Chimborazo, Δ Ecuador	20,702	6,310
Antofalla, Volcán, Argentina	20,013	6,100
Cotopaxi, Ecuador	19,347	5,897
Misti, Volcán, Peru	19,101	5,821
Huila, Nevado del, Colombia (Δ Cordillera Central)	16,896	5,150
Bolívar, Pico, Δ Venezuela	16,427	5,007
Fitzroy, Monte (Cerro Chaltel), Argentina-Chile	11,073	3,375
Neblina, Pico da, Δ Brazil-Venezuela	9,888	3,014

Europe

El'brus, gora, U.S.S.R. (Δ Caucasus; Δ Europe)	18,510	5,642
Dychtau, gora, U.S.S.R.	17,073	5,204
Šchara, gora, U.S.S.R.	16,512	5,033
Blanc, Mont (Monte Bianco), Δ France-Δ Italy (Δ Alps)	15,771	4,807
Dufourspitze, Italy-Δ Switzerland	15,203	4,634
Weisshorn, Switzerland	14,783	4,506
Matterhorn, Italy-Switzerland	14,692	4,478
Finsteraarhorn, Switzerland	14,022	4,274
Jungfrau, Switzerland	13,642	4,158
Écrins, Barre des, France	13,458	4,102
Viso, Monte, Italy (Δ Alpes Cottiennes)	12,602	3,841
Grossglockner, Δ Austria	12,457	3,797
Teide, Pico de, Δ Spain (Δ Canary Is.)	12,188	3,715
Mulhacén, Δ Spain (continental)	11,410	3,482
Aneto, Pico de, Spain (Δ Pyrenees)	11,168	3,404
Perdido, Monte, Spain	11,007	3,355
Etna, Monte, Italy (Δ Sicily)	10,902	3,323
Zugspitze, Austria-Δ Germany	9,721	2,963
Musala, Δ Bulgaria	9,596	2,925
Ólimbos (Mount Olympus), Δ Greece	9,570	2,917
Corno Grande, Italy (Δ Apennines)	9,554	2,912
Triglav, Δ Yugoslavia	9,393	2,864
Korab, Δ Albania-Yugoslavia	9,026	2,751
Cinto, Monte, France (Δ Corsica)	8,878	2,710
Gerlachovský Štít, Δ Czechoslovakia (Δ Carpathian Mts.)	8,711	2,655
Moldoveanu, Δ Romania	8,346	2,544
Rysy, Czechoslovakia-Δ Poland	8,199	2,499
Glittertinden, Δ Norway (Δ Scandinavia)	8,110	2,472
Parnassos, Greece	8,061	2,457
Ídhi, Óros, Greece (Δ Crete)	8,057	2,453
Pico, Ponta do, Δ Portugal (Δ Azores Is.)	7,713	2,351
Hvannadalshnúkur, Δ Iceland	6,952	2,119
Kebnekaise, Δ Sweden	6,926	2,111
Estrela, Δ Portugal (continental)	6,539	1,993
Narodnaja, gora, U.S.S.R. (Δ Ural Mts.)	6,213	1,895
Sancy, Puy de, France (Δ Massif Central)	6,184	1,885
La Marmora, Punta, Italy (Δ Sardinia)	6,017	1,834
Hekla, Iceland	4,892	1,491
Nevis, Ben, Δ United Kingdom (Δ Scotland)	4,406	1,343
Haltiatunturi, Δ Finland-Norway	4,357	1,328
Vesuvio, Italy	4,190	1,277
Snowdon, United Kingdom (Δ Wales)	3,560	1,085
Carrauntoohil, Δ Ireland	3,406	1,038
Kékes, Δ Hungary	3,330	1,015
Scafell Pikes, United Kingdom (Δ England)	3,210	978

Asia

Everest, Mount, Δ China-Δ Nepal (Δ Tibet; Δ Himalayas; Δ Asia; Δ World)	29,028	8,848
K2 (Qogir Feng), China-Δ Pakistan (Δ Kashmir; Δ Karakoram Range)	28,250	8,611
Kānchenjunga, Δ India-Nepal	28,208	8,598
Makālu, China-Nepal	27,825	8,481
Dhawlagiri, Nepal	26,810	8,172
Nānga Parbat, Pakistan	26,660	8,126
Annapūrna, Nepal	26,504	8,078
Gasherbrum, China-Pakistan	26,470	8,068
Xixabangma Feng, China	26,286	8,012
Nanda Devi, India	25,645	7,817
Kamet, China-India	25,447	7,756
Namjagbarwa Feng, China	25,442	7,756
Muztag, China (Δ Kunlun Shan)	25,338	7,723
Tirich Mir, Pakistan (Δ Hindu Kush)	25,230	7,690
Gongga Shan, China	24,790	7,556
Kula Kangri, Δ Bhutan	24,784	7,554
Kommunizma, pik, Δ U.S.S.R. (Δ Pamir)	24,590	7,495
Nowshāk, Δ Afghanistan-Pakistan	24,557	7,485
Pobedy, pik, China-U.S.S.R.	24,406	7,439
Chomo Lhari, Bhutan-China	23,997	7,314
Muztag, China	23,891	7,282
Lenina, pik, U.S.S.R.	23,406	7,134
Api, Nepal	23,399	7,132
Kangrinboqê Feng, China	22,028	6,714
Hkakabo Razi, Δ Burma	19,296	5,881
Damāvand, Qollah-ye, Δ Iran	18,386	5,604
Ağrı Dağı (Mount Ararat), Δ Turkey	16,804	5,122
Jaya, Puncak, Δ Indonesia (Δ New Guinea)	16,503	5,030
Fūlādī, Kūh-e, Afghanistan	16,243	5,135
Kl'učevskaja Sopka, vulkan, U.S.S.R. (Δ Puluostrov Kamčatka)	15,584	4,750
Trikora, Puncak, Indonesia	15,584	4,750
Belucha, gora, U.S.S.R.	14,783	4,506
Turgen, Mount, Mongolia	14,311	4,362
Kinabalu, Gunong, Δ Malaysia (Δ Borneo)	13,455	4,101
Yü Shan, Δ Taiwan	13,114	3,997
Erciyes Dağı, Turkey	12,851	3,917
Kerinci, Gunung, Indonesia (Δ Sumatra)	12,467	3,800
Fuji-san, Δ Japan (Δ Honshu)	12,388	3,776
Rinjani, Gunung, Indonesia (Δ Lombok)	12,224	3,726
Semeru, Gunung, Indonesia (Δ Java)	12,060	3,676
Nabī Shu'ayb, Jabal an-, Δ Yemen (Δ Arabian Peninsula)	12,008	3,760
Rantekombola, Bulu, Indonesia (Δ Celebes)	11,335	3,455
Slamet, Gunung, Indonesia	11,247	3,428
Fan Si Pan, Δ Vietnam	10,312	3,143
Shām, Jabal ash-, Δ Oman	9,957	3,035
Apo, Mount, Δ Philippines (Δ Mindanao)	9,692	2,954
Pulog, Mount, Philippines (Δ Luzon)	9,626	2,934
Bia, Phou, Δ Laos	9,249	2,819
Shaykh, Jabal ash-, Lebanon-Δ Syria	9,232	2,814
Paektu-san, Δ North Korea-China	9,003	2,744
Inthanon, Doi, Δ Thailand	8,530	2,600
Pidurutalagala, Δ Sri Lanka	8,281	2,524
Mayon Volcano, Philippines	8,077	2,462
Asahi-dake, Japan (Δ Hokkaidō)	7,513	2,290
Tahan, Gunong, Malaysia (Δ Malaya)	7,174	2,187
Ólimbos, Δ Cyprus	6,401	1,951
Halla-san, Δ South Korea	6,398	1,950
Aôral, Phnum, Δ Cambodia	5,948	1,813
Kujū-san, Japan (Δ Kyūshū)	5,863	1,787
Ramm, Jabal, Δ Jordan	5,755	1,754
Meron, Hare, Δ Israel	3,963	1,208
Karmel, Har (Mount Carmel), Israel	1,791	546

Africa

Kilimanjaro, Δ Tanzania (Δ Africa)	19,340	5,895
Kirinyaga (Mount Kenya), Δ Kenya	17,058	5,199
Margherita Peak, Δ Uganda-Δ Zaire	16,763	5,109
Ras Dashen Terara, Δ Ethiopia	15,158	4,620
Meru, Mount, Tanzania	14,978	4,565
Karisimbi, Volcan, Δ Rwanda-Zaire	14,787	4,507
Elgon, Mount, Kenya-Uganda	14,178	4,321
Toubkal, Jebel, Δ Morocco (Δ Atlas Mts.)	13,665	4,165
Cameroon Mountain, Δ Cameroon	13,451	4,100
Ntlenyana, Thabana, Δ Lesotho	11,425	3,482
eNjesuthi, Δ South Africa	11,306	3,446
Koussi, Emi, Δ Chad (Δ Tibesti)	11,204	3,415
Kinyeti, Δ Sudan	10,456	3,187
Santa Isabel, Pico de, Δ Equatorial Guinea (Δ Bioko)	9,869	3,008
Tahat, Δ Algeria (Δ Ahaggar)	9,541	2,908
Maromokotro, Δ Madagascar	9,436	2,876
Kātrīnā, Jabal, Δ Egypt	8,668	2,642
São Tome, Pico de, Δ Sao Tome	6,640	2,024

Oceania

Wilhelm, Mount, Δ Papua New Guinea	14,793	4,509
Giluwe, Mount, Papua New Guinea	14,330	4,368
Bangeta, Mt., Papua New Guinea	13,520	4,121
Victoria, Mount, Papua New Guinea (Δ Owen Stanley Range)	13,238	4,035
Cook, Mount, Δ New Zealand (Δ South Island)	12,349	3,764
Ruapehu, New Zealand (Δ North Island)	9,177	2,797
Balbi, Papua New Guinea (Δ Solomon Is.)	9,000	2,743
Taranaki, Mount, New Zealand	8,260	2,518
Orohena, Mont, Δ French Polynesia (Δ Tahiti)	7,352	2,241
Kosciusko, Mount, Δ Australia (Δ New South Wales)	7,310	2,218
Silisili, Mauga, Δ Western Samoa	6,096	1,858
Panié, Mont, Δ New Caledonia	5,341	1,628
Bartle Frere, Australia (Δ Queensland)	5,322	1,622
Ossa, Mount, Australia (Δ Tasmania)	5,305	1,617
Woodroffe, Mount, Australia (Δ South Australia)	4,724	1,440
Sinewit, Mt., Papua New Guinea	4,462	1,360
Tomanivi, Δ Fiji (Δ Viti Levu)	4,341	1,323
Meharry, Mt., Australia (Δ Western Australia)	4,104	1,251
Ayers Rock, Australia	2,844	867

Antarctica

Vinson Massif, Δ Antarctica	16,066	4,897
Kirkpatrick, Mount, Antarctica	14,856	4,528
Markham, Mount, Antarctica	14,049	4,350
Jackson, Mount, Antarctica	13,747	4,190
Sidley, Mount, Antarctica	13,717	4,181
Wade, Mount, Antarctica	13,399	4,083

Δ Highest mountain in state, country, range, or region named.

World Oceans, Seas, Gulfs, Lakes, Rivers and Islands

Oceans, Seas and Gulfs

	Area (sq. mi.)	Area (sq. km.)
Pacific Ocean	63,800,000	*165,200,000*
Atlantic Ocean	31,800,000	*82,400,000*
Indian Ocean	28,900,000	*74,900,000*
Arctic Ocean	5,400,000	*14,000,000*
Arabian Sea	1,492,000	*3,864,000*
South China Sea	1,331,000	*3,447,000*
Caribbean Sea	1,063,000	*2,753,000*
Mediterranean Sea	967,000	*2,505,000*
Bering Sea	876,000	*2,269,000*
Bengal, Bay of	839,000	*2,173,000*
Okhotsk, Sea of	619,000	*1,603,000*
Norwegian Sea	597,000	*1,546,000*
Mexico, Gulf of	596,000	*1,544,000*
Hudson Bay	475,000	*1,230,000*
Greenland Sea	465,000	*1,204,000*

Principal Lakes

	Area (sq. mi.)	Area (sq. km.)
Caspian Sea, Iran—U.S.S.R. (Salt)	143,240	*370,990*
Superior, Lake, Canada—U.S.	31,700	*82,100*
Victoria, Lake, Kenya—Tanzania—Uganda	26,820	*69,463*
Aral'skoje more (Aral Sea), U.S.S.R. (Salt)	24,700	*64,100*
Huron, Lake, Canada—U.S.	23,000	*60,000*
Michigan, Lake, U.S.	22,300	*57,800*
Tanganyika, Lake, Africa	12,350	*31,986*
Bajkal, ozero, U.S.S.R.	12,200	*31,500*
Great Bear Lake, Canada	12,095	*31,326*
Malawi, Lake (Lake Nyasa), Malawi—Mozambique—Tanzania	11,150	*28,878*
Great Slave Lake, Canada	11,030	*28,568*
Erie, Lake, Canada—U.S.	9,910	*25,667*
Winnipeg, Lake, Canada	9,416	*24,387*
Ontario, Lake, Canada—U.S.	7,540	*19,529*
Balchaš, ozero, U.S.S.R.	Δ 7,100	*18,300*
Ladožskoje ozero, U.S.S.R.	6,833	*17,700*
Chad, Lake (Lac Tchad), Cameroon—Chad—Nigeria	6,300	*16,300*
Onežskoje ozero, U.S.S.R.	3,753	*9,720*
Eyre, Lake, Australia (Salt)	Δ 3,700	*9,500*
Titicaca, Lago, Bolivia—Peru	3,200	*8,300*
Nicaragua, Lago de, Nicaragua	3,150	*8,158*
Mai-Ndombe, Lac, Zaire	Δ 3,100	*8,000*
Athabasca, Lake, Canada	3,064	*7,935*
Reindeer Lake, Canada	2,568	*6,650*
Tônlé Sab, Bœng, Cambodia	Δ 2,500	*6,500*
Rudolf, Lake, Ethiopia—Kenya (Salt)	2,473	*6,405*
Issyk-Kul', ozero, U.S.S.R. (Salt)	2,425	*6,280*
Torrens, Lake, Australia (Salt)	2,300	*5,900*
Albert, Lake, Uganda—Zaire	2,160	*5,594*
Vänern, Sweden	2,156	*5,584*
Nettilling Lake, Canada	2,140	*5,542*
Winnipegosis, Lake, Canada	2,075	*5,374*
Bangweulu, Lake, Zambia	1,930	*4,999*
Nipigon, Lake, Canada	1,872	*4,848*
Orūmīyeh, Daryācheh-ye, Iran (Salt)	Δ 1,815	*4,701*
Manitoba, Lake, Canada	1,785	*4,624*
Woods, Lake of the, Canada—U.S.	1,727	*4,472*
Kyoga, Lake, Uganda	1,710	*4,429*
Gairdner, Lake, Australia (Salt)	Δ 1,700	*4,300*
Great Salt Lake, U.S. (Salt)	1,680	*4,351*

Δ *Due to seasonal fluctuations in water level, areas of these lakes vary considerably.*

Principal Rivers

	Length (miles)	Length (km.)
Nile, Africa	4,145	*6,671*
Amazon-Ucayali, South America	4,000	*6,400*
Chang (Yangtze), Asia	3,900	*6,300*
Mississippi-Missouri, North America	3,740	*6,019*
Huang (Yellow), Asia	3,395	*5,464*
Ob'-Irtyš, Asia	3,362	*5,410*
Río de la Plata-Paraná, South America	3,030	*4,876*
Congo (Zaïre), Africa	2,900	*4,700*
Paraná, South America	2,800	*4,500*
Amur-Argun', Asia	2,761	*4,444*
Amur (Heilong), Asia	2,744	*4,416*
Lena, Asia	2,700	*4,400*
Mackenzie, North America	2,635	*4,241*
Mekong, Asia	2,600	*4,200*
Niger, Africa	2,600	*4,200*
Jenisej, Asia	2,543	*4,092*
Missouri-Red Rock, North America	2,533	*4,076*
Mississippi, North America	2,348	*3,779*
Murray-Darling, Australia	2,330	*3,750*
Missouri, North America	2,315	*3,726*
Volga, Europe	2,194	*3,531*
Madeira, South America	2,013	*3,240*
São Francisco, South America	1,988	*3,199*
Grande, Rio (Río Bravo), North America	1,885	*3,034*
Purús, South America	1,860	*2,993*
Indus, Asia	1,800	*2,900*
Danube, Europe	1,776	*2,858*
Brahmaputra, Asia	1,770	*2,849*
Yukon, North America	1,770	*2,849*
Salween (Nu), Asia	1,750	*2,816*
Zambezi, Africa	1,700	*2,700*
Vil'uj, Asia	1,647	*2,650*
Tocantins, South America	1,640	*2,639*
Orinoco South America,	1,600	*2,600*
Paraguay, South America	1,610	*2,591*
Amu Darya, Asia	1,578	*2,540*
Murray, Australia	1,566	*2,520*
Ganges, Asia	1,560	*2,511*
Pilcomayo, South America	1,550	*2,494*
Euphrates, Asia	1,510	*2,430*
Ural, Asia	1,509	*2,428*
Arkansas, North America	1,459	*2,348*
Colorado, North America (U.S.-Mexico)	1,450	*2,334*
Aldan, Asia	1,412	*2,273*
Syrdarja, Asia	1,370	*2,205*
Dnepr, Europe	1,400	*2,200*
Araguaia, South America	1,400	*2,200*
Kasai (Cassai), Africa	1,338	*2,153*
Tarim, Asia	1,328	*2,137*
Kolyma, Asia	1,323	*2,129*
Orange, Africa	1,300	*2,100*
Negro, South America	1,300	*2,100*
Ayeyarwady (Irrawaddy), Asia	1,300	*2,100*
Red, North America	1,270	*2,044*
Juruá, South America	1,250	*2,012*
Columbia, North America	1,200	*2,000*
Xingu, South America	1,230	*1,979*
Ucayali, South America	1,220	*1,963*
Saskatchewan-Bow, North America	1,205	*1,939*
Peace, North America	1,195	*1,923*
Tigris, Asia	1,180	*1,899*
Don, Europe	1,162	*1,870*
Songhua, Asia	1,140	*1,835*
Pečora, Europe	1,124	*1,809*
Kama, Europe	1,122	*1,805*
Limpopo, Africa	1,100	*1,800*
Angara, Asia	1,105	*1,779*
Snake, North America	1,038	*1,670*
Uruguay, South America	1,025	*1,650*
Churchill, North America	1,000	*1,600*
Marañón, South America	1,000	*1,600*
Tobol, Asia	989	*1,591*
Ohio, North America	981	*1,579*
Magdalena, South America	950	*1,529*
Roosevelt, South America	950	*1,529*
Oka, Europe	900	*1,500*
Xiang, Asia	930	*1,497*
Godāvari, Asia	930	*1,497*
Canadian, North America	906	*1,458*
Brazos, North America	900	*1,400*
Salado, South America	900	*1,400*
Darling, Australia	864	*1,390*
Fraser, North America	851	*1,370*
Parnaíba, South America	850	*1,368*
Colorado, North America (Texas)	840	*1,352*
Dnestr, Europe	840	*1,352*
Rhine, Europe	820	*1,320*
Narmada, Asia	800	*1,300*
St. Lawrence, North America	800	*1,300*
Ottawa, North America	790	*1,271*
Athabasca, North America	765	*1,231*
Pecos, North America	735	*1,183*
Severskij Donec, Europe	735	*1,183*
Green, North America	730	*1,175*
White, North America (Ar.-Mo.)	720	*1,159*
Cumberland, North America	720	*1,159*
Elbe (Labe), Europe	720	*1,159*
James, North America (N./S. Dakota)	710	*1,143*
Gambia, Africa	680	*1,094*
Yellowstone, North America	671	*1,080*
Tennessee, North America	652	*1,049*
Gila, North America	630	*1,014*
Wisła (Vistula), Europe	630	*1,014*
Tagus (Tejo) (Tajo), Europe	625	*1,006*
Loire, Europe	625	*1,006*
Cimarron, North America	600	*1,000*
North Platte, North America	618	*995*
Albany, North America	610	*982*
Tisza (Tisa), Europe	607	*977*
Back, North America	605	*974*
Ouachita, North America	605	*974*
Sava, Europe	585	*941*
Nemunas (Neman), Europe	582	*937*
Branco, South America	580	*933*
Meuse (Maas), Europe	575	*925*
Oder (Odra), Europe	565	*909*
Rhône, Europe	500	*800*

Principal Islands

	Area (sq. mi.)	Area (sq. km.)
Grønland (Greenland), North America	840,000	*2,175,600*
New Guinea, Asia—Oceania	309,000	*800,000*
Borneo (Kalimantan), Asia	287,300	*744,100*
Madagascar, Africa	226,500	*587,000*
Baffin Island, Canada	195,928	*507,451*
Sumatera (Sumatra), Indonesia	182,860	*473,606*
Honshū, Japan	89,176	*230,966*
Great Britain, United Kingdom	88,795	*229,978*
Victoria Island, Canada	83,897	*217,291*
Ellesmere Island, Canada	75,767	*196,236*
Sulawesi (Celebes), Indonesia	73,057	*189,216*
South Island, New Zealand	57,708	*149,463*
Jawa (Java), Indonesia	51,038	*132,187*
Seram (Ceram), Indonesia	45,801	*118,625*
North Island, New Zealand	44,332	*114,821*
Cuba, North America	42,800	*110,800*
Newfoundland, Canada	42,031	*108,860*
Luzon, Philippines	40,420	*104,688*
Ísland (Iceland), Europe	39,800	*103,000*
Mindanao, Philippines	36,537	*94,630*
Ireland, Europe	32,600	*84,400*
Hokkaidō, Japan	32,245	*83,515*
Novaja Zeml'a (Novaya Zemlya), U.S.S.R.	31,900	*82,600*
Sachalin, ostrov (Sakhalin), U.S.S.R.	29,500	*76,400*
Hispaniola, North America	29,400	*76,200*
Banks Island, Canada	27,038	*70,028*
Tasmania, Australia	26,200	*67,800*
Sri Lanka, Asia	24,900	*64,600*
Devon Island, Canada	21,331	*55,247*
Tierra del Fuego, Isla Grande de, South America	18,600	*48,200*
Kyūshū, Japan	17,129	*44,363*
Melville Island, Canada	16,274	*42,149*
Southampton Island, Canada	15,913	*41,214*
Spitsbergen, Norway	15,260	*39,523*
New Britain, Papua New Guinea	14,093	*36,500*
T'aiwan, Asia	13,900	*36,000*
Hainan Dao, China	13,100	*34,000*
Prince of Wales Island, Canada	12,872	*33,339*
Vancouver Island, Canada	12,079	*31,285*
Sicilia (Sicily), Italy	9,926	*25,709*
Somerset Island, Canada	9,570	*24,786*
Sardegna (Sardinia), Italy	9,301	*24,090*
Shikoku, Japan	7,258	*18,799*
Nordaustlandet (North East Land), Norway	6,350	*16,446*
New Caledonia, Oceania	6,252	*16,192*
Timor, Indonesia	5,743	*14,874*
Flores, Indonesia	5,502	*14,250*
Samar, Philippines	5,100	*13,080*
Negros, Philippines	4,907	*12,710*
Palawan, Philippines	4,550	*11,785*
Panay, Philippines	4,446	*11,515*
Jamaica, North America	4,200	*11,000*
Hawaii, United States	4,034	*10,448*
Cape Breton Island, Canada	3,981	*10,311*
Mindoro, Philippines	3,759	*9,735*
Kodiak Island, United States	3,670	*9,505*
Bougainville, Papua New Guinea	3,600	*9,300*
Cyprus, Asia	3,572	*9,251*
Puerto Rico, North America	3,500	*9,100*
New Ireland, Papua New Guinea	3,500	*9,000*
Corse (Corsica), France	3,367	*8,720*
Kríti (Crete), Greece	3,189	*8,259*
Vrangel'a, ostrov (Wrangel Island), U.S.S.R.	2,800	*7,300*
Leyte, Philippines	2,785	*7,214*
Guadalcanal, Solomon Islands	2,060	*5,336*
Long Island, United States	1,377	*3,566*

World Populations

This table includes every urban center of 50,000 or more population in the world as well as many other important or well-known cities and towns.

The population figures are all from recent censuses (designated C) or official estimates (designated E), except for a few cities for which only unofficial estimates are available (designated U). The date of the census or estimate is specified for each country. Individual exceptions are dated in parentheses.

For many cities, a second population figure is given accompanied by a star (★). The starred population refers to the city's entire metropolitan area, including suburbs. These metropolitan areas have been defined by Rand McNally, following consistent rules to facilitate comparisons among the urban centers of various countries. Where a place is part of the metropolitan area of another city, that city's name is specified in parentheses preceded by (★). A population preceded by a triangle (▲) refers to an entire municipality, commune, or other district, which includes rural areas in addition to the urban center itself. The names of capital cities appear in CAPITALS; the largest city in each country is designated by the symbol (•).

For more recent population totals for countries, see the Rand McNally population estimates in the World Political Information table.

AFGHANISTAN / Afghānestān

1988 E 15,513,000

Herāt 177,300
Jalālābād (1982 E) 58,000
• KĀBOL 1,424,400
Kondūz (1982 E) 57,000
Mazār-e Sharīf 130,600
Qandahār 225,500

ALBANIA / Shqipëri

1989 C 3,182,400

Durrës 82,700
Elbasan 80,700
Korçë 63,600
Shkodër 79,900
• TIRANË 238,100
Vlorë 71,700

ALGERIA / Algérie / Djazaïr

1987 C 23,038,942

Aïn el Beïda 61,997
Aïn Oussera 44,270
Aïn Témouchent 47,479
Annaba (Bône) 305,526
Bab Ezzouar (★ El Djazaïr) 55,211
Barika 56,488
Batna 181,601
Béchar 107,311
Bejaïa (Bougie) 114,534
Beskra 128,281
Bordj Bou Arreridj 84,264
Bordj el Kiffan (★ El Djazaïr) 61,035
Boufarik 41,305
Bou Saâda 66,688
Ech Cheliff (Orléansville) 129,976
El Boulaïda 170,935
• EL DJAZAÏR (ALGIERS) (★ 2,547,983) 1,507,241
El Djelfa 84,207
El Eulma 67,933
El Wad 70,073
Ghardaïa 89,415
Ghilizane 80,091
Guelma 77,821
Jijel 62,793
Khemis 55,335
Khenchla 69,743
Laghouat 67,214
Lemdiyya 85,195
Maghniyya 52,275
Messaad 47,460
Mestghanem 114,037
Mouaskar 64,691
M'Sila 65,805
Qacentina 440,842
Saïda 80,825
Sidi bel Abbès 152,778
Skikda 128,747
Souq Ahras 83,015
Stif 170,182
Tbessa 107,559
Tihert 95,821
Tilimsen 126,882
Tizi-Ouzou 61,163
Touggourt 70,645
Wahran 628,558
Wargla 81,721

AMERICAN SAMOA / Amerika Samoa

1980 C 32,279

• PAGO PAGO 3,075

ANDORRA

1986 C 46,976

• ANDORRA 18,463

ANGOLA

1989 E 9,739,100

Benguela (1983 E) 155,000
Huambo (Nova Lisboa) (1983 E) 203,000
Lobito (1983 E) 150,000
• LUANDA 1,459,900
Lubango (1984 E) 95,915
Namibe (1981 E) 100,000

ANGUILLA

1984 C 6,680

South Hill 961
• THE VALLEY 1,042

ANTIGUA AND BARBUDA

1977 E 72,000

• SAINT JOHN'S 24,359

ARGENTINA

1980 C 27,947,446

Almirante Brown (★ Buenos Aires) 331,919
Avellaneda (★ Buenos Aires) 334,145
Bahía Blanca 223,818
Berazategui (★ Buenos Aires) 201,862
Berisso (★ Buenos Aires) 66,152
• BUENOS AIRES (★ 10,750,000) 2,922,829
Campana (★ Buenos Aires) 54,832
Caseros (Tres de Febrero) (★ Buenos Aires) 345,424
Catamarca (★ 90,000) 78,799
Comodoro Rivadavia 96,817
Concordia 94,222
Córdoba (★ 1,070,000) 993,055
Corrientes 180,612
Esteban Echeverría (★ Buenos Aires) 188,923
Florencio Varela (★ Buenos Aires) 173,452
Formosa 93,603
General San Martín (★ Buenos Aires) 385,625
General Sarmiento (San Miguel) (★ Buenos Aires) 502,926
Godoy Cruz (★ Mendoza) 142,408
Gualeguaychú 51,400
Junín 62,458
Lanús (★ Buenos Aires) 466,980
La Plata (★ Buenos Aires) 477,175
La Rioja 67,043
Las Heras (★ Mendoza) 101,579
Lomas de Zamora (★ Buenos Aires) 510,130
Mar del Plata 414,696
Mendoza (★ 650,000) 119,088
Mercedes 50,992
Merlo (★ Buenos Aires) 292,587
Moreno (★ Buenos Aires) 194,440
Morón (★ Buenos Aires) 598,420
Necochea 51,069
Neuquén 90,089
Olavarría 64,097
Paraná 161,638
Pergamino 68,612
Pilar (★ Buenos Aires) 84,429
Posadas 143,889
Presidencia Roque Sáenz Peña 49,341
Punta Alta 56,620
Quilmes (★ Buenos Aires) 446,587
Rafaela 53,273
Resistencia 220,104
Río Cuarto 110,254
Rosario (★ 1,045,000) 938,120
Salta 260,744
San Carlos de Bariloche 48,980
San Fernando (★ Buenos Aires) 133,624
San Francisco (★ 58,536) 51,932
San Isidro (★ Buenos Aires) 289,170
San Juan (★ 300,000) 118,046
San Justo (★ Buenos Aires) 949,566
San Lorenzo (★ Rosario) 96,891
San Luis 70,999
San Miguel de Tucumán (★ 525,000) 392,888
San Nicolás de los Arroyos 98,495
San Rafael 70,959
San Salvador de Jujuy 124,950
Santa Fe 292,165
Santiago del Estero (★ 200,000) 148,758
San Vincente (★ Buenos Aires) 55,803
Tandil 79,429
Tigre (★ Buenos Aires) 206,349
Trelew 52,372
Vicente López (★ Buenos Aires) 291,072
Villa Krause (★ San Juan) 66,693
Villa María 67,560
Villa Nueva (★ Mendoza) 164,670
Zárate 67,143

ARUBA

1987 E 64,763

• ORANJESTAD 19,800

AUSTRALIA

1989 E 16,833,100

Adelaide (★ 1,036,747) 12,340
Albury (★ 66,530) 40,730
Auburn (★ Sydney) 49,950
Ballarat (★ 80,090) 36,680
Bankstown (★ Sydney) 158,750
Bayswater (★ Perth) 46,426
Bendigo (★ 67,920) 32,050
Berwick (★ Melbourne) 64,100
Blacktown (★ Sydney) 210,900
Blue Mountains (★ Sydney) 70,800
Box Hill (★ Melbourne) 47,700
Brisbane (★ 1,273,511) 744,828
Broadmeadows (★ Melbourne) 105,500
Brunswick (★ Melbourne) 41,100
Camberwell (★ Melbourne) 87,700
Campbelltown (★ Sydney) 139,500
CANBERRA (★ 271,362) (1986 C) 247,194
Canning (★ Perth) 69,104
Canterbury (★ Sydney) 135,200
Caulfield (★ Melbourne) 70,100
Coburg (★ Melbourne) 54,500
Cockburn (★ Perth) 49,802
Coffs Harbour 47,890
Dandenong (★ Melbourne) 59,400
Darwin (★ 73,300) 63,900
Doncaster (★ Melbourne) 107,300
Enfield (★ Adelaide) 64,058
Essendon (★ Melbourne) 55,300
Fairfield (★ Sydney) 176,350
Footscray (★ Melbourne) 48,700
Frankston (★ Melbourne) 90,500
Geelong (★ 148,980) 13,190
Gosford 126,600
Gosnells (★ Perth) 71,862
Heidelberg (★ Melbourne) 63,500
Hobart (★ 181,210) 47,280
Holroyd (★ Sydney) 82,500
Hurstville (★ Sydney) 66,350
Ipswich (★ Brisbane) 75,283
Keilor (★ Melbourne) 103,700
Knox (★ Melbourne) 121,300
Kogarah (★ Sydney) 47,850
Lake Macquarie (★ Newcastle) 161,700
Launceston (★ 92,350) 32,150
Leichhardt (★ Sydney) 58,950
Liverpool (★ Sydney) 99,750
Logan (★ Brisbane) 142,222
Mackay (★ 50,885) 22,583
Malvern (★ Melbourne) 43,400
Marion (★ Adelaide) 74,631
Marrickville (★ Sydney) 84,650
Melbourne (★ 3,039,100) 55,300
Melville (★ Perth) 85,590
Mitcham (★ Adelaide) 63,301
Moorabbin (★ Melbourne) 98,900
Newcastle (★ 425,610) 130,940
Noarlunga (★ Adelaide) 77,352
Northcote (★ Melbourne) 49,100
North Sydney (★ Sydney) 53,400
Nunawading (★ Melbourne) 96,400
Oakleigh (★ Melbourne) 57,600
Parramatta (★ Sydney) 134,600
Penrith (★ Sydney) 152,650
Perth (★ 1,158,387) 82,413
Prahran (★ Melbourne) 43,900
Preston (★ Melbourne) 82,000
Randwick (★ Sydney) 119,200
Redcliffe (★ Brisbane) 48,123
Rockdale (★ Sydney) 88,200
Rockhampton (★ 61,694) 58,890
Ryde (★ Sydney) 94,400
Saint Kilda (★ Melbourne) 46,400
Salisbury (★ Adelaide) 106,129
Shoalhaven 64,070
Southport (★ 254,861) 135,408
South Sydney (★ Sydney) 74,100
Springvale (★ Melbourne) 88,700
Stirling (★ Perth) 181,556
Sunshine (★ Melbourne) 97,700
• Sydney (★ 3,623,550) 9,800
Tea Tree Gully (★ Adelaide) 82,324
Toowoomba 81,071
Townsville (★ 111,972) 83,339
Wagga Wagga 52,180
Wanneroo (★ Perth) 163,324
Waverley (★ Melbourne) 126,300
Waverley (★ Sydney) 61,850
West Torrens (★ Adelaide) 44,711
Willoughby (★ Sydney) 53,950
Wollongong (★ 236,690) 174,770
Woodville (★ Adelaide) 82,590
Woollahra (★ Sydney) 53,850

AUSTRIA / Österreich

1981 C 7,555,338

Bruck an der Mur (★ 52,000) 15,068
Graz (★ 325,000) 243,166
Innsbruck (★ 185,000) 117,287
Klagenfurt (★ 115,000) 87,321
Leoben (★ 52,000) 31,989
Linz (★ 335,000) 199,910
Neunkirchen (★ 45,000) 10,764
Salzburg (★ 220,000) 139,426
Sankt Pölten (★ 67,000) 50,419
Steyr (★ 65,000) 38,942
Villach (★ 65,000) 52,692
Wels (★ 76,000) 51,060
• WIEN (VIENNA) (★ 1,875,000) (1988 E) 1,482,800

BAHAMAS

1982 E 218,000

Freeport 25,000
• NASSAU 135,000

BAHRAIN / Al-Baḥrayn

1981 C 350,798

• AL-MANĀMAH (★ 224,643) 115,054
Al-Muharraq (★ Al-Manāmah) 57,688

BANGLADESH

1981 C 87,119,965

Barisāl 172,905
Begamganj 69,623
Bhairab Bāzār 63,563
Bogra 68,749
Brāhmanbāria 87,570
Chāndpur 85,656
Chittagong (★ 1,391,877) 980,000
Chuādanga 76,000
Comilla 184,132
• DHAKA (DACCA) (★ 3,430,312) 2,365,695
Dinājpur 96,718
Farīdpur 66,579
Gopālpur 31,725
Gulshan (★ Dhaka) 215,444
Jamālpur 91,815
Jessore 148,927
Jhenida 47,953
Khulna 648,359
Kishorganj 52,302
Kurīgrām 47,641
Kushtia 74,892
Mādārīpur 63,917
Mīrpur (★ Dhaka) 349,031
Mymensingh 190,991
Naogaon 52,975
Nārāyanganj (★ Dhaka) 405,562
Narsinghdi 76,841
Nawābganj 87,724
Noākhāli 59,065
Pābna 109,065
Patuākhāli 48,121
Rājshāhi 253,740
Rangpur 153,174
Saidpur 126,608
Sātkhira 52,156
Sherpur 48,214
Sirājganj 106,774
Sītākunda (★ Chittagong) 237,520
Sylhet 168,371
Tangail 77,518
Tongi (★ Dhaka) 94,580

BARBADOS

1980 C 244,228

• BRIDGETOWN (★ 115,000) 7,466

BELGIUM / België / Belgique

1987 E 9,864,751

Aalst (Alost) (★ Bruxelles) 77,113
Anderlecht (★ Bruxelles) 88,849
Antwerpen (★ 1,100,000) 479,748
Bastogne (▲ 11,699) 6,900
Brugge (Bruges) (★ 223,000) 117,755
• BRUXELLES (★ 2,385,000) 136,920
Charleroi (★ 480,000) 209,395
Etterbeek (★ Bruxelles) 44,240
Forest (★ Bruxelles) 48,266
Genk (★ Hasselt) 61,391
Gent (Gand) (★ 465,000) 233,856
Hasselt (★ 290,000) 65,563
Ixelles (★ Bruxelles) 76,241
Kortrijk (Courtrai) (★ 202,000) 76,216
La Louvière (★ 147,000) 76,340
Leuven (Louvain) (★ 173,000) 84,583
Liège (Luik) (★ 750,000) 200,891
Mechelen (Malines) (★ 121,000) 75,808
Molenbeek-St.-Jean (★ Bruxelles) 69,764
Mons (Bergen) (★ 242,000) 89,697
Mouscron (★ Lille, France) 53,713
Namur (★ 147,000) 102,670
Oostende (Ostende) (★ 122,000) 68,318
Roeselare (Roulers) 51,963
Saint-Gilles (★ Bruxelles) 42,482
Schaerbeek (★ Bruxelles) 104,919
Seraing (★ Liège) 61,731
Sint-Niklaas (Saint-Nicolas) 68,082
Spa 9,645
Tournai (Doornik) (▲ 66,998) 44,900
Uccle (★ Bruxelles) 75,876
Verviers (★ 101,000) 53,498
Waterloo (★ Bruxelles) 25,232
Woluwe-Saint-Lambert (Sint-Lambrechts-Woluwe) (★ Bruxelles) 47,887

BELIZE

1985 E 166,400

• Belize City 47,000
BELMOPAN 4,500

BENIN / Bénin

1984 E 3,825,000

Abomey 53,000
• COTONOU 478,000
Natitingou (1975 E) 51,000
Ouidah (1979 E) 53,000
Parakou 92,000
PORTO-NOVO 164,000

BERMUDA

1985 E 56,000

• HAMILTON (★ 15,000) 1,676

BHUTAN / Druk-Yul

1982 E 1,333,000

• THIMPHU 12,000

BOLIVIA

1988 E 6,992,400

Cochabamba 361,900
• LA PAZ 1,057,200
Oruro 174,300
Potosí 106,600
Santa Cruz 651,600
SUCRE 106,300
Tarija 69,900
Trinidad 49,600

BOPHUTHATSWANA

1987 E 1,819,242

• Ga-Rankuwa (1980 C) 48,300

C Census. E Official estimate. U Unofficial estimate.
• Largest city in country.

★ Population or designation of metropolitan area, including suburbs (see headnote).
▲ Population of an entire municipality, commune, or district, including rural area.

Mafikeng (★ 16,000) (1980 C) ... 6,500
MMABATHO (★ Mafikeng) (1977 E) ... 9,062

BOTSWANA

1987 E ... 1,169,000

Francistown (1986 E) ... 43,837
• GABORONE ... 107,677
Selebi Phikwe (1986 E) ... 41,382

BRAZIL / Brasil

1985 E ... 135,564,395

Alagoinhas (▲ 116,959) ... 87,500
Alegrete (▲ 71,898) ... 56,700
Alvorada ... 105,730
Americana ... 156,030
Anápolis ... 225,840
Apucarana (▲ 92,812) ... 73,700
Aracaju ... 360,013
Araçatuba ... 129,304
Araguari (▲ 96,035) ... 84,300
Arapiraca (▲ 147,879) ... 91,400
Araraquara (▲ 145,042) ... 87,500
Araras (▲ 71,652) ... 59,900
Araxá ... 61,418
Assis (▲ 74,238) ... 63,100
Bagé (▲ 106,155) ... 70,800
Barbacena (▲ 99,337) ... 80,200
Barra do Piraí (▲ 78,189) ... 55,700
Barra Mansa (★ Volta Redonda) ... 149,200
Barretos ... 80,202
Bauru ... 220,105
Bayeux (★ João Pessoa) ... 67,182
Belém (★ 1,200,000) ... 1,116,578
Belford Roxo (★ Rio de Janeiro) ... 340,700
Belo Horizonte (★ 2,950,000) ... 2,114,429
Betim (★ Belo Horizonte) ... 96,810
Blumenau ... 192,074
Boa Vista ... 66,028
Botucatu (▲ 71,139) ... 62,600
Bragança Paulista (▲ 105,099) ... 76,300
BRASÍLIA ... 1,567,709
Caçapava (▲ 64,213) ... 56,600
Cachoeira do Sul (▲ 91,492) ... 58,900
Cachoeirinha (★ Porto Alegre) ... 73,117
Cachoeiro de Itapemirim (▲ 138,156) ... 95,000
Campina Grande ... 279,929
Campinas (★ 1,125,000) ... 841,016
Campo Grande ... 384,398
Campos (▲ 366,716) ... 187,900
Campos Elyseos (★ Rio de Janeiro) ... 188,200
Canoas (★ Porto Alegre) ... 261,222
Carapicuíba (★ São Paulo) ... 265,856
Carazinho (▲ 62,108) ... 48,500
Cariacica (★ Vitória) ... 74,300
Caruaru (▲ 190,794) ... 152,100
Cascavel (▲ 200,485) ... 123,100
Castanhal (▲ 89,703) ... 71,200
Catanduva (▲ 80,309) ... 71,400
Caucaia (★ Fortaleza) ... 78,500
Cavaleiro (★ Recife) ... 106,600
Caxias (▲ 148,230) ... 66,300
Caxias do Sul ... 266,809
Chapecó (▲ 100,997) ... 64,200
Coelho da Rocha (★ Rio de Janeiro) ... 164,400
Colatina (▲ 106,260) ... 58,600
Colombo (★ Curitiba) ... 65,900
Conselheiro Lafaiete ... 77,958
Contagem (★ Belo Horizonte) ... 152,700
Corumbá (▲ 80,666) ... 65,800
Crato (▲ 86,371) ... 52,700
Criciúma (▲ 128,410) ... 85,900
Cruz Alta (▲ 71,817) ... 58,300
Cruzeiro ... 63,918
Cubatão (★ Santos) ... 98,322
Cuiabá (▲ 279,651) ... 220,400
Curitiba (★ 1,700,000) ... 1,279,205
Diadema (★ São Paulo) ... 320,187
Divinópolis ... 139,940
Dourados (▲ 123,757) ... 89,200
Duque de Caxias (★ Rio de Janeiro) ... 353,200
Embu (★ São Paulo) ... 119,791
Erechim (▲ 70,709) ... 54,300
Esteio (★ Porto Alegre) ... 58,964
Feira de Santana (▲ 355,201) ... 278,600
Ferraz de Vasconcelos (★ São Paulo) ... 68,831
Florianópolis (★ 365,000) ... 178,400
Fortaleza (★ 1,825,000) ... 1,582,414
Foz do Iguaçu (▲ 182,101) ... 124,900
Franca ... 182,820
Garanhuns ... 73,100
Goiânia (★ 990,000) ... 923,333
Governador Valadares (▲ 216,957) ... 192,300
Guaratinguetá (▲ 93,534) ... 80,400
Guarujá (★ Santos) ... 83,500
Guarulhos (★ São Paulo) ... 571,700
Ijuí (▲ 82,064) ... 64,400
Ilhéus (▲ 145,810) ... 79,400
Imperatriz (▲ 235,453) ... 119,500
Ipatinga (★ 270,000) ... 149,100
Ipiíba (★ Rio de Janeiro) ... 116,200
Itabira (▲ 81,771) ... 66,300
Itabuna (▲ 167,543) ... 142,200
Itajaí ... 104,232
Itajubá (▲ 69,675) ... 61,500
Itapecerica da Serra (★ São Paulo) ... 65,500
Itapetininga (▲ 105,512) ... 76,700
Itapevi (★ São Paulo) ... 66,825
Itaquaquecetuba (★ São Paulo) ... 91,366
Itaquari (★ Vitória) ... 163,900
Itaúna ... 61,446
Itu (▲ 92,786) ... 77,900
Ituiutaba (▲ 85,365) ... 74,900
Itumbiara (▲ 78,844) ... 57,200
Jaboatão (★ Recife) ... 82,900
Jacareí ... 149,061
Jaú (▲ 92,547) ... 74,500
Jequié (▲ 127,070) ... 92,100
João Pessoa (★ 550,000) ... 348,500
Joinvile ... 302,877
Juàzeiro (★ Petrolina) ... 78,600
Juàzeiro do Norte ... 159,806
Juiz de Fora ... 349,720
Jundiaí (▲ 313,652) ... 268,900
Lajes (▲ 143,246) ... 103,600
Lavras ... 52,100
Limeira ... 186,986
Linhares (▲ 122,453) ... 53,400
Londrina (▲ 346,676) ... 296,400
Lorena ... 63,230
Luziânia (▲ 98,408) ... 71,400
Macapá (▲ 168,839) ... 109,400
Maceió ... 482,195
Manaus ... 809,914
Marabá (▲ 133,559) ... 92,700
Marília (▲ 136,187) ... 116,100
Maringá ... 196,871
Mauá (★ São Paulo) ... 269,321
Mesquita (★ Rio de Janeiro) ... 161,300
Mogi das Cruzes (★ São Paulo) ... 144,800
Mogi-Guaçu (▲ 91,994) ... 81,800
Mogi-Mirim (▲ 63,313) ... 52,300
Monjolo (★ Rio de Janeiro) ... 113,900
Montes Claros (▲ 214,472) ... 183,500
Mossoró (▲ 158,723) ... 128,300
Muriaé (▲ 80,466) ... 57,600
Muribeca dos Guararapes (★ Recife) ... 171,200
Natal ... 510,106
Neves (★ Rio de Janeiro) ... 163,600
Nilópolis (★ Rio de Janeiro) ... 112,800
Niterói (★ Rio de Janeiro) ... 441,684
Nova Friburgo (▲ 143,529) ... 103,500
Nova Iguaçu (★ Rio de Janeiro) ... 592,800
Novo Hamburgo (★ Porto Alegre) ... 167,744
Olinda (★ Recife) ... 316,600
Osasco (★ São Paulo) ... 591,568
Ourinhos (▲ 65,841) ... 58,100
Paranaguá (▲ 94,809) ... 82,300
Paranavaí (▲ 75,511) ... 60,900
Parnaíba (▲ 116,206) ... 90,200
Parque Industrial (★ Belo Horizonte) ... 228,400
Passo Fundo (▲ 137,843) ... 117,500
Passos (▲ 79,393) ... 65,500
Patos ... 74,298
Patos de Minas (▲ 99,027) ... 69,000
Paulo Afonso (▲ 86,182) ... 75,300
Pelotas (▲ 277,730) ... 210,300
Petrolina (★ 225,000) ... 92,100
Petrópolis (★ Rio de Janeiro) ... 170,300
Pindamonhangaba (▲ 86,990) ... 64,100
Pinheirinho (★ Curitiba) ... 51,600
Piracicaba (▲ 252,079) ... 211,000
Poá (★ São Paulo) ... 66,006
Poços de Caldas ... 100,004
Ponta Grossa ... 223,154
Porto Alegre (★ 2,600,000) ... 1,272,121
Porto Velho (▲ 202,011) ... 152,700
Pouso Alegre (▲ 65,958) ... 58,300
Praia Grande (★ Santos) ... 67,800
Presidente Prudente ... 155,883
Queimados (★ Rio de Janeiro) ... 113,700
Recife (★ 2,625,000) ... 1,287,623
Ribeirão Prêto ... 383,125
Rio Branco (▲ 145,486) ... 109,800
Rio Claro ... 129,859
Rio de Janeiro (★ 10,150,000) ... 5,603,388
Rio Grande ... 164,221
Rio Verde (▲ 92,954) ... 59,400
Rondonópolis (▲ 101,642) ... 65,500
Salvador (★ 2,050,000) ... 1,804,438
Santa Bárbara d'Oeste ... 95,818
Santa Cruz do Sul (▲ 115,288) ... 60,300
Santa Maria (▲ 196,827) ... 163,900
Santana do Livramento (▲ 70,489) ... 60,100
Santarém (▲ 226,618) ... 120,800
Santa Rita (★ João Pessoa) ... 60,100
Santo André (★ São Paulo) ... 635,129
Santo Ângelo (▲ 107,559) ... 57,700
Santos (★ 1,065,000) ... 460,100
São Bernardo do Campo (★ São Paulo) ... 562,485
São Caetano do Sul (★ São Paulo) ... 171,005
São Carlos ... 140,383
São Gonçalo (★ Rio de Janeiro) ... 262,400
São João da Boa Vista (▲ 61,653) ... 50,400
São João del Rei (▲ 74,385) ... 61,400
São João de Meriti (★ Rio de Janeiro) ... 241,700
São José do Rio Prêto ... 229,221
São José dos Campos ... 372,578
São José dos Pinhais (★ Curitiba) ... 64,100
São Leopoldo (★ Porto Alegre) ... 114,065
São Lourenco da Mata (★ Recife) ... 65,936
São Luís (★ 600,000) ... 227,900
• São Paulo (★ 15,175,000) ... 10,063,110
São Vicente (★ Santos) ... 239,778
Sapucaia do Sul (★ Porto Alegre) ... 91,820
Sete Lagoas ... 121,418
Sete Pontes (★ Rio de Janeiro) ... 72,300
Sobral (▲ 112,275) ... 69,400
Sorocaba ... 327,468
Suzano (★ São Paulo) ... 128,924
Taboão da Serra (★ São Paulo) ... 122,112
Tatuí (▲ 69,358) ... 56,000
Taubaté ... 205,120
Teófilo Otoni (▲ 126,265) ... 82,700
Teresina (★ 525,000) ... 425,300
Teresópolis (▲ 115,859) ... 92,600
Timon (★ Teresina) ... 68,300
Tubarão (▲ 82,082) ... 70,400
Uberaba ... 244,875
Uberlândia ... 312,024
Uruguaiana (▲ 105,862) ... 91,500
Varginha ... 74,630
Vicente de Carvalho (★ Santos) ... 102,700
Vila Velha (★ Vitória) ... 91,900
Vitória (★ 735,000) ... 201,500
Vitória da Conquista (▲ 198,150) ... 145,800
Vitória de Santo Antão (▲ 100,450) ... 67,800
Volta Redonda (★ 375,000) ... 219,267

BRITISH VIRGIN ISLANDS

1980 C ... 12,034

• ROAD TOWN ... 2,479

BRUNEI

1981 C ... 192,832

• BANDAR SERI BEGAWAN (★ 64,000) ... 22,777
Seria ... 23,415

BULGARIA / Bălgarija

1989 E ... 8,986,636

Blagoevgrad ... 74,236
Burgas ... 200,464
Dimitrovgrad ... 57,102
Gabrovo ... 80,930
Haskovo ... 93,609
Jambol ... 97,414
Kărdžali ... 58,995
Kazanlăk ... 63,776
Kjustendil ... 55,620
Loveč ... 50,872
Mihajlovgrad ... 55,203
Pazardžik ... 83,451
Pernik ... 97,930
Pleven ... 136,287
Plovdiv ... 364,162
Razgrad ... 56,494
Ruse ... 190,720
Silistra ... 56,907
Sliven ... 109,432
• SOFIJA (★ 1,205,000) ... 1,136,875
Stara Zagora ... 158,151
Šumen ... 107,973
Tolbuhin ... 112,582
Varna ... 306,300
Veliko Tărnovo ... 71,709
Vidin ... 65,892
Vraca ... 81,992

BURKINA FASO

1985 C ... 7,964,705

Bobo Dioulasso ... 228,668
Koudougou ... 51,926
• OUAGADOUGOU ... 441,514
Ouahigouya ... 38,902

BURMA / Myanmar

1983 C ... 34,124,908

Bago (Pegu) ... 150,528
Chauk ... 51,437
Dawei (Tavoy) ... 69,882
Henzada ... 82,005
Kale ... 52,628
Lashio ... 88,590
Mandalay ... 532,949
Mawlamyine (Moulmein) ... 219,961
Maymyo ... 63,782
Meiktila ... 96,496
Mergui (Myeik) ... 88,600
Mogok ... 49,392
Monywa ... 106,843
Myingyan ... 77,060
Myitkyinā ... 56,427
Pakokku ... 71,860
Pathein (Bassein) ... 144,096
Prome (Pyè) ... 83,332
Pyinmana ... 52,962
Sagaing ... 46,212
Shwebo ... 52,185
Sittwe (Akyab) ... 107,621
Taunggyi ... 108,231
Thaton ... 61,790
Toungoo ... 65,861
• YANGON (RANGOON) (★ 2,800,000) ... 2,705,039
Yenangyaung ... 62,582
Magway ... 54,881

BURUNDI

1986 E ... 4,782,000

• BUJUMBURA ... 273,000
Gitega ... 95,000

CAMBODIA / Kâmpŭchéa

1986 E ... 7,492,000

Kâmpóng Saôm (1981 E) ... 53,000
• PHNUM PÉNH ... 700,000

CAMEROON / Cameroun

1986 E ... 10,446,409

Bafoussam (1985 E) ... 89,000
Bamenda (1985 E) ... 72,000
• Douala ... 1,029,731
Foumban (1985 E) ... 50,000
Garoua (1985 E) ... 96,000
Kumba (1985 E) ... 67,000
Maroua ... 103,653
Ngaoundéré (1985 E) ... 61,000
Nkongsamba ... 123,149
YAOUNDÉ ... 653,670

CANADA

1986 C ... 25,354,064

CANADA: ALBERTA

1986 C ... 2,375,278

Calgary (★ 671,326) ... 636,104
Edmonton (★ 785,465) ... 573,982
Lethbridge ... 58,841
Medicine Hat (★ 50,734) ... 41,804
Red Deer ... 54,425

CANADA: BRITISH COLUMBIA

1986 C ... 2,889,207

Burnaby (★ Vancouver) ... 145,161
Kamloops ... 61,773
Kelowna (★ 89,730) ... 61,213
Matsqui (★ 88,420) ... 51,449
Nanaimo (★ 60,420) ... 49,029
Prince George ... 67,621
Richmond (★ Vancouver) ... 108,492
Vancouver (★ 1,380,729) ... 431,147
Victoria (★ 255,547) ... 66,303

CANADA: MANITOBA

1986 C ... 1,071,232

Winnipeg (★ 625,304) ... 594,551

CANADA: NEW BRUNSWICK

1986 C ... 710,422

Fredericton (★ 65,768) ... 44,352
Moncton (★ 102,084) ... 55,468
Saint John (★ 121,265) ... 76,381

CANADA: NEWFOUNDLAND

1986 C ... 568,349

Saint John's (★ 161,901) ... 96,216

CANADA: NORTHWEST TERRITORIES

1986 C ... 52,238

Yellowknife ... 11,753

CANADA: NOVA SCOTIA

1986 C ... 873,199

Dartmouth (★ Halifax) ... 65,243
Halifax (★ 295,990) ... 113,577
Sydney (★ 119,470) ... 27,754

CANADA: ONTARIO

1986 C ... 9,113,515

Barrie (★ 67,703) ... 48,287
Brampton (★ Toronto) ... 188,498
Brantford (★ 90,521) ... 76,146
Burlington (★ Hamilton) ... 116,675
Cambridge (Galt) (★ Kitchener) ... 79,920
Cornwall (★ 51,719) ... 46,425
East York (★ Toronto) ... 101,085
Etobicoke (★ Toronto) ... 302,973
Gloucester (★ Ottawa) ... 89,810
Guelph (★ 85,962) ... 78,235
Hamilton (★ 557,029) ... 306,728
Kingston (★ 122,350) ... 55,050
Kitchener (★ 311,195) ... 150,604
London (★ 342,302) ... 269,140
Markham (★ Toronto) ... 114,597
Mississauga (★ Toronto) ... 374,005
Nepean (★ Ottawa) ... 95,490
Niagara Falls (★ Saint Catharines) ... 72,107
North Bay (★ 57,422) ... 50,623
North York (★ Toronto) ... 556,297
Oakville (★ Toronto) ... 87,107
Oshawa (★ 203,543) ... 123,651
OTTAWA (★ 819,263) ... 300,763
Peterborough (★ 87,083) ... 61,049
Saint Catharines (★ 343,258) ... 123,455
Sarnia (★ 85,700) ... 49,033
Sault Sainte Marie (★ 84,617) ... 80,905
Scarborough (★ Toronto) ... 484,676
Sudbury (★ 148,877) ... 88,717
Thunder Bay (★ 122,217) ... 112,272
• Toronto (★ 3,427,168) ... 612,289
Vaughan (★ Toronto) ... 65,058
Waterloo (★ Kitchener) ... 58,718
Windsor (★ 253,988) ... 193,111
York (★ Toronto) ... 135,401

CANADA: PRINCE EDWARD ISLAND

1986 C ... 126,646

Charlottetown (★ 53,868) ... 15,776

CANADA: QUÉBEC

1986 C ... 6,540,276

Beauport (★ Québec) ... 62,869
Brossard (★ Montréal) ... 57,441
Charlesbourg (★ Québec) ... 68,996
Chicoutimi (★ 158,468) ... 61,083
Drummondville (★ 56,283) ... 36,020
Gatineau (★ Ottawa) ... 81,244
Hull (★ Ottawa) ... 58,722
Jonquière (★ Chicoutimi) ... 58,467
La Salle (★ Montréal) ... 75,621
Laval (★ Montréal) ... 284,164
Longueuil (★ Montréal) ... 125,441
Montréal (★ 2,921,357) ... 1,015,420
Montréal-Nord (★ Montréal) ... 90,303
Québec (★ 603,267) ... 164,580
Sainte-Foy (★ Québec) ... 69,615
Saint-Hubert (★ Montréal) ... 66,218
Saint-Jean-sur-Richelieu (★ 59,958) ... 34,745
Saint-Laurent (★ Montréal) ... 67,002
Saint-Léonard (★ Montréal) ... 75,947
Shawinigan (★ 61,965) ... 21,470
Sherbrooke (★ 129,960) ... 74,438
Trois-Rivières (★ 128,888) ... 50,122
Verdun (★ Montréal) ... 60,246

CANADA: SASKATCHEWAN

1986 C ... 1,010,198

Regina (★ 186,521) ... 175,064
Saskatoon (★ 200,665) ... 177,641

C Census. E Official estimate. U Unofficial estimate.
• Largest city in country.
★ Population or designation of metropolitan area, including suburbs (see headnote).
▲ Population of an entire municipality, commune, or district, including rural area.

World Populations

CANADA: YUKON

1986 C	23,504
Whitehorse	15,199

CAPE VERDE / Cabo Verde

1990 C	336,798,000
Mindelo	47,050
• PRAIA	61,797

CAYMAN ISLANDS

1988 E	25,900
• GEORGE TOWN	13,700

CENTRAL AFRICAN REPUBLIC / République centrafricaine

1984 E	2,517,000
• BANGUI	473,817
Bouar (1982 E)	48,000

CHAD / Tchad

1988 E	5,428,000
Abéché	40,000
Moundou	100,000
• N'DJAMENA	500,000
Sarh	76,835

CHILE

1982 C	11,329,736
Antofagasta	185,486
Apoquindo (★ Santiago)	175,735
Arica	139,320
Calama	81,684
Cerrillos (★ Santiago)	67,013
Cerro Navia (★ Santiago)	137,777
Chillán	118,163
Concepción (★ 675,000)	267,891
Conchalí (★ Santiago)	157,884
Copiapó	69,045
Coquimbo	62,186
Coronel (★ Concepción)	65,918
Curicó	60,550
El Bosque (★ Santiago)	143,717
Huechuraba (★ Santiago)	56,313
Independencia (★ Santiago)	86,724
Iquique	110,153
La Cisterna (★ Santiago)	95,863
La Florida (★ Santiago)	191,883
La Granja (★ Santiago)	109,168
La Pintana (★ Santiago)	73,932
La Reina (★ Santiago)	80,452
La Serena	83,283
Las Rejas (★ Santiago)	147,918
Linares	46,433
Lo Barnechea (★ Santiago)	24,258
Lo Espejo (★ Santiago)	124,462
Lo Prado (★ Santiago)	103,575
Los Ángeles	70,529
Lota (★ Concepción)	47,133
Macul (★ Santiago)	113,100
Maipú (★ Santiago)	114,117
Ñuñoa (★ Santiago)	168,919
Osorno	95,286
Ovalle	43,023
Pedro Aguirre Cerda (★ Santiago)	145,207
Peñalolén (★ Santiago)	137,298
Providencia (★ Santiago)	115,449
Pudahuel (★ Santiago)	97,578
Puente Alto (★ Santiago)	109,239
Puerto Montt	84,410
Punta Arenas	95,332
Quilpué (★ Valparaíso)	84,136
Quinta Normal (★ Santiago)	128,989
Rancagua	139,925
Recoleta (★ Santiago)	164,292
Renca (★ Santiago)	93,928
San Antonio	61,486
San Bernardo (★ Santiago)	117,132
San Joaquín (★ Santiago)	123,904
San Miguel (★ Santiago)	88,764
San Ramón (★ Santiago)	99,410
• SANTIAGO (★ 4,100,000)	232,667
Talca	128,544
Talcahuano (★ Concepción)	202,368
Temuco	157,297
Valdivia	100,046
Vallenar	38,375
Valparaíso (★ 675,000)	265,355
Villa Alemana (★ Valparaíso)	55,766
Viña del Mar (★ Valparaíso)	244,899
Vitacura (★ Santiago)	72,038

CHINA / Zhongguo

1988 E	1,103,983,000
Abagnar Qi (▲ 100,700) (1986 E)	71,700
Acheng (1985 E)	100,304
Aihui (▲ 135,000) (1986 E)	76,700
Aksu (▲ 345,900) (1986 E)	1,431,000
Altay (▲ 141,700) (1986 E)	62,800
Anci (Langfang) (▲ 522,800) (1986 E)	122,100
Anda (▲ 425,500) (1986 E)	130,200
Ankang (1985 E)	89,188
Anqing (▲ 433,900) (1986 E)	213,200
Anshan	1,330,000
Anshun (▲ 214,700) (1986 E)	128,800
Anyang (▲ 541,900) (1986 E)	361,200
Baicheng (▲ 282,000) (1986 E)	198,600
Baiquan (1985 E)	50,996
Baiyin (▲ 301,900) (1986 E)	157,100
Baoding (▲ 535,100) (1986 E)	423,200
Baoji (▲ 359,500) (1986 E)	286,200
Baoshan (▲ 688,400) (1986 E)	52,300
Baotou (Paotow)	1,130,000
Baoying (1985 E)	50,479
Bei'an (▲ 440,500) (1986 E)	199,500
Beihai (▲ 175,900) (1986 E)	119,000
BEIJING (PEKING) (★ 7,320,000)	6,710,000
Beipiao (▲ 603,700) (1986 E)	180,900
Bengbu (▲ 612,600) (1986 E)	403,900
Benxi (Penhsi)	860,000
Bijie (1985 E)	54,871
Binxian (▲ 177,900) (1986 E)	86,700
Binxian (1982 C)	127,326
Boli (1985 E)	61,990
Bose (▲ 271,400) (1986 E)	82,000
Boshan (1975 U)	100,000
Boxian (1985 E)	63,222
Boxing (1982 C)	57,554
Boyang (1985 E)	60,688
Butha Qi (Zalantun) (▲ 389,500) (1986 E)	111,300
Cangshan (Bianzhuang) (1982 C)	79,334
Cangzhou (▲ 293,600) (1986 E)	196,700
Changchun (▲ 2,000,000)	1,822,000
Changde (▲ 220,800) (1986 E)	178,200
Changge (1982 C)	67,002
Changji (▲ 233,400) (1986 E)	110,500
Changqing (1982 C)	65,094
Changsha	1,230,000
Changshou (1985 E)	51,923
Changshu (▲ 998,000) (1986 E)	281,300
Changtu (1985 E)	49,937
Changyi (1982 C)	64,513
Changzhi (▲ 463,400) (1986 E)	273,000
Changzhou (Changchow) (▲ 500,740) (1986 E)	522,700
Chao'an (▲ 1,214,500) (1986 E)	265,400
Chaoxian (▲ 739,500) (1986 E)	116,800
Chaoyang, Guangdong prov. (1985 E)	85,968
Chaoyang, Liaoning prov. (▲ 318,900) (1986 E)	180,300
Chengde (▲ 330,400) (1986 E)	226,600
Chengdu (Chengtu) (▲ 2,960,000)	1,884,000
Chenghai (1985 E)	50,631
Chenxian (▲ 191,900) (1986 E)	143,500
Chifeng (Ulanhad) (▲ 882,900) (1986 E)	299,000
Chongqing (Chungking) (▲ 2,890,000)	2,502,000
Chuxian (▲ 365,000) (1986 E)	113,300
Chuxiong (▲ 379,400) (1986 E)	67,700
Da'an (1985 E)	70,552
Dachangzhen (1975 U)	50,000
Dalian (Dairen)	2,280,000
Dandong (1986 E)	579,800
Daqing (▲ 880,000)	640,000
Dashiqiao (1985 E)	68,898
Datong (1985 E)	55,529
Datong (▲ 1,040,000)	810,000
Dawa (1985 E)	142,581
Daxian (▲ 209,400) (1986 E)	142,000
Dehui (1985 E)	60,247
Dengfeng (1982 C)	49,746
Deqing (1982 C)	48,726
Deyang (▲ 753,400) (1986 E)	184,800
Dezhou (▲ 276,200) (1986 E)	161,300
Didao (1975 U)	50,000
Dinghai (1985 E)	50,161
Dongchuan (Xincun) (▲ 275,100) (1986 E)	67,400
Dongguan (▲ 1,208,500) (1986 E)	254,900
Dongsheng (▲ 121,300) (1986 E)	57,500
Dongtai (1985 E)	65,788
Dongying (▲ 514,400) (1986 E)	178,100
Dukou (▲ 551,200) (1986 E)	380,200
Dunhua (▲ 448,000) (1986 E)	217,100
Duyun (▲ 386,600) (1986 E)	123,800
Echeng (▲ 938,000) (1986 E)	217,400
Enshi (▲ 679,000) (1986 E)	84,300
Erenhot (1986 E)	7,200
Ergun Zuoqi (1985 E)	55,970
Feixian (1982 C)	73,246
Fengcheng (1985 E)	66,745
Foshan (▲ 312,700) (1986 E)	243,500
Fujin (1985 E)	60,948
Fuling (▲ 973,500) (1986 E)	166,300
Fushun (Funan)	1,290,000
Fuxian (Wafangdian) (▲ 960,700) (1986 E)	246,200
Fuxin	700,000
Fuyang (▲ 195,200) (1986 E)	143,400
Fuyu, Heilongjiang prov. (1985 E)	48,670
Fuyu, Jilin prov. (1985 E)	98,373
Fuzhou, Fujian prov. (▲ 1,240,000)	910,000
Fuzhou, Jiangxi prov. (▲ 171,800) (1986 E)	106,700
Gaixian (1985 E)	67,587
Ganhe (1985 E)	48,128
Ganzhou (▲ 346,000) (1986 E)	191,600
Gaoqing (Tianzhen) (1982 C)	70,411
Gaoyou (1985 E)	57,844
Gejiu (Kokiu) (▲ 341,700) (1986 E)	193,600
Golmud (1986 E)	60,300
Gongchangling (1982 C)	49,281
Guanghua (▲ 420,000) (1986 E)	104,400
Guangyuan (▲ 805,500) (1986 E)	162,200
Guangzhou (Canton) (▲ 3,420,000)	3,100,000
Guanxian, Shandong prov. (1982 C)	49,782
Guanxian, Sichuan prov. (1985 E)	65,039
Guilin (Kweilin) (▲ 457,500) (1986 E)	324,200
Guixian (1985 E)	61,970
Guiyang (Kweiyang) (▲ 1,430,000)	1,030,000
Haicheng (▲ 984,800) (1986 E)	210,700
Haifeng (1985 E)	50,401
Haikou (▲ 289,600) (1986 E)	209,200
Hailar (▲ 163,549) (1986 E)	180,000
Hailin (1985 E)	58,909
Hailong (Meihekou) (▲ 534,200) (1986 E)	117,500
Hailun (1985 E)	83,448
Haiyang (Dongcun) (1982 C)	77,098
Hami (Kumul) (▲ 270,300) (1986 E)	146,400
Hancheng (▲ 304,200) (1986 E)	66,600
Handan (▲ 1,030,000)	870,000
Hangu (1975 U)	100,000
Hangzhou (Hangchow)	1,290,000
Hanzhong (▲ 415,000) (1986 E)	151,700
Harbin	2,710,000
Hebi (▲ 321,600) (1986 E)	158,500
Hechi (▲ 266,800) (1986 E)	74,400
Hechuan (1985 E)	65,237
Hefei (▲ 930,000)	740,000
Hegang (1986 E)	588,300
Helong (1985 E)	62,665
Hengshui (▲ 286,500) (1986 E)	83,100
Hengyang (▲ 601,300) (1986 E)	419,200
Heshan (▲ 109,600) (1986 E)	42,000
Heze (Caozhou) (▲ 1,001,500) (1986 E)	115,400
Hohhot (▲ 830,000)	670,000
Hongjiang (▲ 67,000) (1986 E)	54,300
Horqin Youyi Qianqi (Ulan Hot) (▲ 192,100) (1986 E)	129,100
Hotan (▲ 122,800) (1986 E)	71,700
Houma (▲ 158,500) (1986 E)	67,000
Huadian (1985 E)	75,183
Huai'an (1985 E)	65,673
Huaibei (▲ 447,200) (1986 E)	252,100
Huaide (▲ 899,400) (1986 E)	187,600
Huaihua (▲ 427,100) (1986 E)	102,000
Huainan (▲ 1,110,000)	700,000
Huaiyin (Wangying) (▲ 382,500) (1986 E)	201,700
Huanan (1985 E)	66,596
Huanggang (1982 C)	65,961
Huangshi (▲ 431,713) (1986 E)	451,900
Huayun (Huarong) (▲ 313,500) (1986 E)	81,000
Huinan (Chaoyang) (1985 E)	52,429
Huizhou (▲ 182,100) (1986 E)	117,000
Hulan (1985 E)	74,989
Hunjiang (Badaojiang) (▲ 687,700) (1986 E)	442,600
Huzhou (▲ 964,400) (1986 E)	208,500
Jiading (1985 E)	60,718
Jiamusi (Kiamusze) (▲ 557,700) (1986 E)	429,800
Ji'an (▲ 184,300) (1986 E)	132,200
Jiangling (1985 E)	77,887
Jiangmen (▲ 231,700) (1986 E)	168,800
Jiangyin (1985 E)	66,476
Jiangyou (1985 E)	72,663
Jian'ou (1985 E)	55,180
Jiaohe (1985 E)	51,504
Jiaojiang (▲ 385,200) (1986 E)	82,300
Jiaoxian (1985 E)	51,869
Jiaozuo (▲ 509,900) (1986 E)	335,400
Jiawang (1975 U)	50,000
Jiaxing (▲ 686,500) (1986 E)	210,200
Jiayuguan (▲ 102,100) (1986 E)	73,800
Jiexiu (1985 E)	51,300
Jieyang (1985 E)	98,531
Jilin (Kirin)	1,200,000
Jinan (Tsinan) (▲ 2,140,000)	1,546,000
Jinchang (Baijiazui) (▲ 136,000) (1986 E)	90,500
Jincheng (▲ 612,700) (1986 E)	99,900
Jingdezhen (Kingtechen) (▲ 569,700) (1986 E)	304,000
Jingmen (▲ 946,500) (1986 E)	227,000
Jinhua (▲ 799,900) (1986 E)	147,800
Jining, Nei Monggol prov. (1986 E)	163,300
Jining, Shandong prov. (▲ 765,700) (1986 E)	222,600
Jinshi (▲ 219,700) (1986 E)	73,700
Jinxi (▲ 634,300) (1986 E)	223,100
Jinxian (1985 E)	95,761
Jinzhou (Chinchou) (▲ 810,000)	710,000
Jishou (▲ 194,500) (1986 E)	59,500
Jishu (1985 E)	75,587
Jiujiang (▲ 382,300) (1986 E)	248,500
Jiuquan (Suzhou) (▲ 269,900) (1986 E)	56,300
Jiutai (1985 E)	63,021
Jixi (▲ 820,000)	700,000
Jixian (1985 E)	59,725
Juancheng (1982 C)	54,110
Junan (Shizilu) (1982 C)	90,222
Junxian (▲ 423,400) (1986 E)	97,000
Juxian (1982 C)	51,666
Kaifeng (▲ 629,100) (1986 E)	458,800
Kaili (▲ 342,100) (1986 E)	96,600
Kaiping (1985 E)	54,145
Kaiyuan (▲ 342,100) (1986 E)	96,600
Kaiyuan (1985 E)	85,762
Karamay (▲ 168,868) (1986 E)	185,300
Kashi (▲ 194,500) (1986 E)	146,300
Keshan (1985 E)	65,088
Korla (▲ 219,000) (1986 E)	129,400
Kunming (▲ 1,550,000)	1,310,000
Kunshan (1985 E)	44,645
Kuqa (1985 E)	63,847
Kuytun (1986 E)	60,200
Laiwu (▲ 1,041,800) (1986 E)	143,500
Langxiang (1985 E)	64,658
Lanxi (1985 E)	53,236
Lanxi (▲ 606,800) (1986 E)	70,500
Lanzhou (Lanchow) (▲ 1,420,000)	1,297,000
Lechang (1986 E)	56,913
Lengshuijiang (▲ 277,600) (1986 E)	101,700
Lengshuitan (▲ 362,000) (1986 E)	60,900
Leshan (▲ 972,300) (1986 E)	307,300
Lhasa (▲ 107,700) (1986 E)	84,400
Lianyungang (Xinpu) (▲ 459,400) (1986 E)	288,000
Liaocheng (▲ 724,300) (1986 E)	119,000
Liaoyang (▲ 576,900) (1986 E)	442,600
Liaoyuan (▲ 771,577) (1986 E)	370,400
Liling (▲ 856,300) (1986 E)	107,100
Linfen (▲ 530,100) (1986 E)	157,600
Lingling (▲ 515,300) (1986 E)	72,700
Lingyuan (1985 E)	66,825
Linhai (1985 E)	52,653
Linhe (▲ 365,900) (1986 E)	99,800
Linkou (1985 E)	52,936
Linqing (▲ 603,000) (1986 E)	87,000
Linqu (1982 C)	84,196
Linxia (▲ 150,200) (1986 E)	72,900
Linyi (▲ 1,365,000) (1986 E)	190,000
Liuzhou	680,000
Longjiang (1985 E)	51,156
Longyan (▲ 378,500) (1986 E)	114,500
Loudi (▲ 254,300) (1986 E)	84,200
Lu'an (▲ 163,400) (1986 E)	122,600
Lufeng (1985 E)	53,015
Luohe (▲ 159,100) (1986 E)	102,300
Luoyang (Loyang) (▲ 1,090,000)	760,000
Luzhou (▲ 360,300) (1986 E)	237,800
Ma'anshan (▲ 367,000) (1986 E)	258,900
Manzhouli (1986 E)	116,600
Maoming (▲ 434,900) (1986 E)	118,600
Meixian (▲ 740,600) (1986 E)	169,100
Mengyin (1982 C)	70,602
Mianyang, Sichuan prov. (▲ 848,500) (1986 E)	233,900
Minhang (1975 U)	60,000
Mishan (1985 E)	54,919
Mixian (1982 C)	64,776
Mudanjiang (▲ 580,982)	650,000
Nahe (1985 E)	49,725
N'aizishen (1985 E)	51,982
Nancha (1975 U)	50,000
Nanchang (▲ 1,260,000)	1,090,000
Nanchong (▲ 238,100) (1986 E)	158,000
Nanjing (Nanking)	2,390,000
Nanning (▲ 1,000,000)	720,000
Nanpiao (1982 C)	67,274
Nanping (▲ 420,800) (1986 E)	157,100
Nantong (▲ 411,000) (1986 E)	308,800
Nanyang (▲ 294,800) (1986 E)	199,400
Neihuang (1982 C)	56,039
Neijiang (▲ 298,500) (1986 E)	191,100
Ning'an (1985 E)	49,334
Ningbo (▲ 1,050,000)	570,000
Ningyang (1982 C)	55,424
Nong'an (1985 E)	55,966
Nunjiang (1985 E)	59,276
Orogen Zizhiqi (1985 E)	48,042
Panshan (▲ 343,100) (1986 E)	248,100
Panshi (1985 E)	59,270
Pingdingshan (▲ 819,900) (1986 E)	363,200
Pingliang (▲ 362,500) (1986 E)	85,400
Pingxiang, Jiangxi prov. (▲ 1,286,700) (1986 E)	368,700
Pingyi (1982 C)	89,373
Pingyin (1982 C)	62,827
Potou (▲ 456,100) (1986 E)	59,000
Puqi (1985 E)	65,239
Putian (▲ 265,400) (1986 E)	64,600
Putuo (1985 E)	50,962
Puyang (▲ 1,086,100) (1986 E)	131,000
Qian Gorlos (1985 E)	79,494
Qingdao (Tsingtao)	1,300,000
Qinggang (1985 E)	43,075
Qingjiang, Jiangsu prov. (▲ 246,617) (1982 C)	150,000
Qingjiang, Jiangxi prov. (1985 E)	42,698
Qingyuan (1985 E)	51,756
Qinhuangdao (Chinwangtao) (▲ 436,000) (1986 E)	307,500
Qinzhou (▲ 923,400) (1986 E)	97,100
Qiqihar (Tsitsihar) (▲ 1,330,000)	1,180,000
Qitaihe (▲ 309,900) (1986 E)	166,400
Qixia (1982 C)	54,158
Qixian (1982 C)	53,041
Quanzhou (Chuanchou) (▲ 436,000) (1986 E)	157,000
Qujing (▲ 758,000) (1986 E)	135,000
Quxian (▲ 704,800) (1986 E)	124,000
Raoping (1985 E)	54,831
Rizhao (▲ 970,300) (1986 E)	93,300
Rongcheng (1982 C)	52,878
Rugao (1985 E)	50,643
Rui'an (1985 E)	57,993

C Census. E Official estimate. U Unofficial estimate.
• Largest city in country.

★ Population or designation of metropolitan area, including suburbs (see headnote).
▲ Population of an entire municipality, commune, or district, including rural area.

ISRAELI OCCUPIED TERRITORIES

1989 E	1,574,700
Al-Quds (Jerusalem) (★ Yerushalayim) (1976 E)	90,000
Arīḥā (Jericho) (1967 C)	6,829
Bayt Laḥm (Bethlehem) (1971 E)	25,000
• Ghazzah (1967 C)	118,272
Khān Yūnis (1967 C)	52,997
Nābulus (1971 E)	64,000
Rafaḥ (1967 C)	49,812

ITALY / Italia

1987 E	57,290,519
Afragola (★ Napoli)	59,397
Alessandria (▲ 96,014)	76,100
Altamura	54,784
Ancona	104,409
Andria	88,348
Arezzo (▲ 91,681)	74,200
Asti (▲ 75,459)	63,600
Avellino	56,407
Aversa (★ Napoli)	57,827
Bari (★ 475,000)	362,524
Barletta	86,954
Benevento (▲ 65,661)	54,400
Bergamo (★ 345,000)	118,959
Biella	51,788
Bitonto	51,962
Bologna (★ 525,000)	432,406
Bolzano	101,515
Brescia	199,286
Brindisi	92,280
Busto Arsizio (★ Milano)	78,056
Cagliari (★ 305,000)	220,574
Caltanissetta	62,352
Campobasso (▲ 50,801)	44,000
Carpi (▲ 60,614)	49,500
Carrara (★ Massa)	69,229
Caserta	65,974
Casoria (★ Napoli)	54,100
Castellammare di Stabia (★ Napoli)	68,491
Catania (★ 550,000)	372,486
Catanzaro	102,558
Cava de'Tirreni (★ Salerno)	52,028
Cerignola	53,463
Cesena (▲ 90,012)	72,600
Chieti	55,827
Cinisello Balsamo (★ Milano)	78,917
Civitavecchia	50,806
Collegno (★ Torino)	49,334
Cologno Monzese (★ Milano)	52,554
Como (★ 165,000)	91,738
Cosenza (★ 150,000)	106,026
Cremona	76,979
Crotone (▲ 61,005)	53,600
Cuneo (▲ 55,878)	47,900
Empoli (▲ 43,940)	33,200
Ercolano (★ Napoli)	62,783
Ferrara (▲ 143,950)	113,300
Firenze (★ 640,000)	425,835
Foggia	155,051
Foligno (▲ 53,568)	42,500
Forlì (▲ 110,482)	91,200
Gela	79,378
Genova (Genoa) (★ 805,000)	727,427
Giugliano in Campania (★ Napoli)	51,187
Grosseto (▲ 70,592)	56,400
Imola (▲ 61,587)	48,200
Imperia	41,481
L'Aquila (▲ 66,438)	42,200
La Spezia (★ 185,000)	108,937
Latina (▲ 98,479)	67,800
Lecce	100,981
Lecco	48,844
Legnano (★ Milano)	48,711
Livorno	174,065
Lucca	88,024
Manfredonia	57,707
Mantova (▲ 56,817)	49,000
Marsala	80,468
Massa (★ 145,000)	66,872
Matera	52,819
Messina	268,896
Mestre (★ Venezia)	189,700
• Milano (Milan) (★ 3,750,000)	1,495,260
Modena	176,880
Molfetta	64,519
Moncalieri (★ Torino)	62,306
Monza (★ Milano)	122,064
Napoli (Naples) (★ 2,875,000)	1,204,211
Nicastro (▲ 67,562)	52,100
Nocera Inferiore	48,151
Novara	102,742
Padova (★ 270,000)	225,769
Palermo	723,732
Parma	175,842
Paternò	45,513
Pavia	82,065
Perugia (▲ 146,713)	106,700
Pesaro (▲ 90,336)	78,700
Pescara	131,027
Piacenza	105,626
Pisa	104,384
Pistoia (▲ 90,689)	76,800
Pordenone	50,825
Portici (★ Napoli)	76,302
Potenza (▲ 67,114)	57,600
Pozzuoli (★ Napoli)	65,000
Prato (★ 215,000)	164,595
Quartu Sant'Elena	52,838
Ragusa	67,748
Ravenna (▲ 136,016)	86,500
Reggio di Calabria	178,821
Reggio nell'Emilia (▲ 130,086)	107,300
Rho (★ Milano)	50,876
Rimini (▲ 130,698)	114,600
Rivoli (★ Torino)	50,786
ROMA (★ 3,175,000)	2,815,457
Salerno (★ 250,000)	154,848
San Benedetto del Tronto	45,397
San Giorgio a Cremano (★ Napoli)	63,656
San Remo	60,797
San Severo	55,239
Sassari	120,152
Savona (★ 112,000)	62,300
Scandicci (★ Firenze)	54,367
Sesto Fiorentino (★ Firenze)	46,355
Sesto San Giovanni (★ Milano)	91,624
Siena	59,712
Siracusa	122,857
Taranto	244,997
Teramo (▲ 52,378)	36,000
Terni (▲ 111,157)	94,500
Torino (★ 1,550,000)	1,035,565
Torre Annunziata (★ Napoli)	57,508
Torre del Greco (★ Napoli)	105,066
Trapani (▲ 73,083)	63,000
Trento (▲ 100,202)	81,500
Treviso	85,083
Trieste (Triest)	239,031
Udine (★ 126,000)	100,211
Varese	88,353
Venezia (Venice) (★ 420,000)	88,700
Vercelli	51,008
Verona	259,151
Viareggio (▲ 59,146)	50,300
Vicenza	110,449
Vigevano	62,671
Viterbo (▲ 59,267)	47,900
Vittoria	54,795

IVORY COAST / Côte d'Ivoire

1983 E	9,300,000
• ABIDJAN	1,950,000
Bouaké	275,000
Daloa	70,000
Korhogo	125,000
Man	55,000
YAMOUSSOUKRO	80,000

JAMAICA

1982 C	2,190,357
• KINGSTON (★ 770,000) (1987 E)	646,400
Montego Bay	70,265
Portmore (★ Kingston)	73,426
Spanish Town (★ Kingston)	89,097

JAPAN / Nihon

1990 C	123,611,541
Abiko (★ Tōkyō)	120,629
Ageo (★ Tōkyō)	194,952
Aizu-wakamatsu	119,084
Akashi (★ Ōsaka)	270,728
Akishima (★ Tōkyō)	105,375
Akita	302,359
Akō	51,131
Amagasaki (★ Ōsaka)	498,998
Anan (▲ 59,045)	47,000
Anjō	142,217
Aomori	287,813
Arao (★ Ōmuta)	59,508
Asahikawa	359,069
Asaka (★ Tōkyō)	103,621
Ashikaga	167,687
Ashiya (★ Ōsaka)	87,528
Atami	47,290
Atsugi (★ Tōkyō)	197,292
Ayase (★ Tōkyō)	77,926
Beppu	130,323
Bisai (★ Nagoya)	55,881
Chiba (★ Tōkyō)	829,467
Chichibu	60,916
Chigasaki (★ Tōkyō)	201,672
Chikushino (★ Fukuoka)	70,303
Chiryū (★ Nagoya)	54,061
Chita (★ Nagoya)	75,434
Chitose	78,947
Chōfu (★ Tōkyō)	197,680
Chōshi	85,138
Daitō (★ Ōsaka)	126,460
Dazaifu (★ Fukuoka)	62,408
Ebetsu (★ Sapporo)	97,201
Ebina (★ Tōkyō)	105,816
Eniwa	55,613
Fuchū	45,738
Fuchū (★ Tōkyō)	209,419
Fuchū	50,061
Fuji (★ 370,000)	222,500
Fujieda (★ Shizuoka)	119,815
Fujiidera (★ Ōsaka)	65,924
Fujimi (★ Tōkyō)	94,858
Fujinomiya (★ Fuji)	117,093
Fujisawa (★ Tōkyō)	350,335
Fuji-yoshida	54,802
Fukaya (▲ 94,023)	75,600
Fukuchiyama (▲ 66,506)	56,700
Fukui	252,750
Fukuoka (★ 1,750,000)	1,237,107
Fukushima	277,526
Fukuyama	365,615
Funabashi (★ Tōkyō)	533,273
Fussa (★ Tōkyō)	58,053
Gamagōri	84,819
Gifu	410,318
Ginowan	75,899
Gotemba	79,560
Gushikawa	54,026
Gyōda	83,181
Habikino (★ Ōsaka)	115,035
Hachinohe	241,065
Hachiōji (★ Tōkyō)	466,373
Hadano (★ Tōkyō)	155,619
Hagi	50,619
Hakodate	307,251
Hamada	49,139
Hamakita	81,159
Hamamatsu	534,624
Hanamaki (▲ 70,514)	55,000
Handa (★ Nagoya)	99,550
Hannō (★ Tōkyō)	73,216
Hashima	61,460
Hasuda (★ Tōkyō)	59,703
Hatogaya (★ Tōkyō)	56,441
Hatsukaichi (★ Hiroshima)	63,441
Hekinan	65,901
Higashīhiroshima (★ Hiroshima)	94,206
Higashikurume (★ Tōkyō)	113,800
Higashimatsuyama	84,395
Higashimurayama (★ Tōkyō)	134,002
Higashiōsaka (★ Ōsaka)	518,251
Higashiyamato (★ Tōkyō)	75,124
Hikari (★ Tokuyama)	47,613
Hikone	99,518
Himeji (★ 660,000)	454,360
Himi (▲ 60,768)	51,400
Hino (★ Tōkyō)	165,935
Hirakata (★ Ōsaka)	390,790
Hiratsuka (★ Tōkyō)	245,944
Hirosaki (▲ 174,710)	133,800
Hiroshima (★ 1,575,000)	1,085,677
Hita (▲ 64,694)	57,100
Hitachi	202,145
Hōfu	117,639
Honjō	59,094
Hōya (★ Tōkyō)	95,148
Hyūga	58,448
Ibaraki (★ Ōsaka)	254,080
Ichihara (★ Tōkyō)	257,717
Ichikawa (★ Tōkyō)	436,597
Ichinomiya (★ Nagoya)	262,434
Ichinoseki (▲ 61,971)	50,100
Iida (▲ 91,859)	64,700
Iizuka (★ 110,000)	83,133
Ikeda (★ Ōsaka)	104,219
Ikoma (★ Ōsaka)	99,598
Imabari	123,114
Imari (▲ 60,887)	50,000
Ina (▲ 60,063)	49,500
Inagi (★ Tōkyō)	58,593
Inazawa (★ Nagoya)	96,277
Inuyama (★ Nagoya)	69,803
Iruma (★ Tōkyō)	137,585
Isahaya	90,678
Ise (Uji-yamada)	104,162
Isehara (★ Tōkyō)	89,568
Isesaki	115,939
Ishinomaki	121,980
Itami (★ Ōsaka)	186,132
Itō	71,223
Iwaki (Taira)	355,817
Iwakuni	109,534
Iwamizawa	80,423
Iwata	83,521
Iwatsuki (★ Tōkyō)	106,462
Izumi (★ Sendai)	124,216
Izumi (★ Ōsaka)	146,105
Izumi-ōtsu (★ Ōsaka)	67,037
Izumi-sano (★ Ōsaka)	88,862
Izumo (▲ 82,680)	69,600
Joetsu	130,114
Jōyō (★ Ōsaka)	84,770
Kadoma (★ Ōsaka)	142,288
Kaga	69,199
Kagoshima	536,685
Kainan (★ Wakayama)	48,598
Kaizuka (★ Ōsaka)	79,236
Kakamigahara	129,682
Kakegawa (▲ 72,795)	59,000
Kakogawa (★ Ōsaka)	239,803
Kamagaya (★ Tōkyō)	95,052
Kamaishi	52,483
Kamakura (★ Tōkyō)	174,299
Kameoka	85,283
Kamifukuoka (★ Tōkyō)	58,753
Kanazawa	442,872
Kani (★ Nagoya)	80,012
Kanoya (▲ 77,652)	61,500
Kanuma (▲ 90,044)	74,900
Karatsu (▲ 79,206)	70,500
Kariya (★ Nagoya)	120,121
Kasai	51,789
Kasaoka (▲ 59,618)	52,700
Kashihara (★ Ōsaka)	115,556
Kashiwa (★ Tōkyō)	305,060
Kashiwara (★ Ōsaka)	76,819
Kashiwazaki (▲ 88,309)	75,300
Kasuga (★ Fukuoka)	88,703
Kasugai (★ Nagoya)	266,599
Kasukabe (★ Tōkyō)	188,809
Katano (★ Ōsaka)	65,311
Katsuta	109,826
Kawachi-nagano (★ Ōsaka)	108,770
Kawagoe (★ Tōkyō)	304,860
Kawaguchi (★ Tōkyō)	438,667
Kawanishi (★ Ōsaka)	141,254
Kawasaki (★ Tōkyō)	1,173,606
Kesennuma	65,578
Kimitsu (▲ 89,243)	76,100
Kiryū	126,443
Kisarazu	123,434
Kishiwada (★ Ōsaka)	188,553
Kitaibaraki	51,092
Kitakyūshū (★ 1,525,000)	1,026,467
Kitami	107,247
Kitamoto (★ Tōkyō)	63,933
Kiyose (★ Tōkyō)	67,540
Kōbe (★ Ōsaka)	1,477,423
Kōchi	317,090
Kodaira (★ Tōkyō)	164,021
Kōfu	200,630
Koga (★ Tōkyō)	58,227
Koganei (★ Tōkyō)	105,888
Kokubunji (★ Tōkyō)	100,958
Komae (★ Tōkyō)	74,197
Komaki (★ Nagoya)	124,441
Komatsu	106,072
Kōnan (★ Nagoya)	93,836
Kōnosu (★ Tōkyō)	72,436
Kōriyama	314,651
Koshigaya (★ Tōkyō)	285,280
Kudamatsu (★ Tokuyama)	53,029
Kuki (★ Tōkyō)	66,852
Kumagaya	152,122
Kumamoto	579,305
Kunitachi (★ Tōkyō)	65,830
Kurashiki	414,692
Kurayoshi (▲ 51,835)	42,700
Kure (★ Hiroshima)	216,717
Kuroiso (▲ 52,346)	41,900
Kurume	228,350
Kusatsu (★ Ōsaka)	94,766
Kushiro	205,640
Kuwana (★ Nagoya)	97,911
Kyōto (★ Ōsaka)	1,461,140
Machida (★ Tōkyō)	349,030
Maebashi	286,261
Maizuru	96,329
Marugame	75,607
Matsubara (★ Ōsaka)	135,921
Matsudo (★ Tōkyō)	456,211
Matsue	142,931
Matsumoto	200,723
Matsusaka	118,727
Matsuyama	443,317
Mihara	85,518
Miki (★ Ōsaka)	76,509
Minō (★ Ōsaka)	122,133
Misato (★ Tōkyō)	128,377
Mishima (★ Numazu)	105,419
Mitaka (★ Tōkyō)	165,555
Mito	234,970
Miura (★ Tōkyō)	52,441
Miyako	58,505
Miyakonojō (▲ 130,155)	106,200
Miyazaki	287,367
Mobara	83,437
Moriguchi (★ Ōsaka)	157,365
Morioka	235,440
Moriyama	58,561
Mukō (★ Ōsaka)	52,932
Munakata	68,267
Muroran (★ 195,000)	117,852
Musashimurayama (★ Tōkyō)	65,555
Musashino (★ Tōkyō)	139,069
Mutsu	48,470
Nabari	68,933
Nagahama	55,482
Nagano	347,036
Nagaoka	185,938
Nagaokakyō (★ Ōsaka)	77,193
Nagareyama (★ Tōkyō)	140,059
Nagasaki	444,616
Nagoya (★ 4,800,000)	2,154,664
Naha	304,896
Nakama (★ Kitakyūshū)	49,216
Nakatsu	66,383
Nakatsugawa	53,722
Nanao	50,101
Nara (★ Ōsaka)	349,356
Narashino (★ Tōkyō)	151,472
Narita	86,708
Naruto	64,577
Naze	46,309
Neyagawa (★ Ōsaka)	256,521
Niigata	486,087
Niihama	129,151
Niitsu (▲ 64,005)	55,700
Niiza (★ Tōkyō)	138,919
Nishinomiya (★ Ōsaka)	426,919
Nishio	95,198
Nobeoka	130,615
Noboribetsu (★ Muroran)	55,575
Noda (★ Tōkyō)	114,476
Nōgata	62,532
Noshiro (▲ 55,915)	47,800
Numazu (★ 495,000)	211,731
Obihiro	167,389
Ōbu (★ Nagoya)	69,721
Ōdate (▲ 68,196)	58,500
Odawara	193,415
Ōgaki	148,281
Ōita	408,502
Ōkawa	45,705
Okaya	59,854
Okayama	593,742
Okazaki	306,821
Okegawa (★ Tōkyō)	69,030
Okinawa	105,852
Ōme (★ Tōkyō)	125,945
Ōmi-hachiman (★ Ōsaka)	66,068
Ōmiya (★ Tōkyō)	403,779
Ōmura	73,437
Ōmuta (★ 225,000)	150,461
Ōnojō (★ Fukuoka)	75,217
Onomichi	97,104
Ōsaka (★ 16,450,000)	2,623,831
Ōta	139,801
Otaru (★ Sapporo)	163,215
Ōtsu (★ Ōsaka)	260,004
Owariashi (★ Nagoya)	65,676
Oyama (▲ 142,263)	120,000
Sabae	62,284
Saga	169,964
Sagamihara (★ Tōkyō)	531,562
Saijō	56,823
Saiki	52,325
Sakado (★ Tōkyō)	95,736
Sakai (★ Ōsaka)	807,859
Sakaide	63,878
Sakata	100,808
Saku (▲ 62,005)	50,000
Sakura (★ Tōkyō)	144,688
Sakurai	60,261
Sanjō	85,824
Sano	83,484
Sapporo (★ 1,900,000)	1,671,765
Sasebo	244,693
Satte	54,339
Sayama (★ Tōkyō)	157,307
Sayama (★ Ōsaka)	54,323
Seki	68,386
Sendai, Kagoshima pref. (▲ 71,736)	58,000
Sendai, Miyagi pref. (★ 1,175,000)	918,378
Sennan (★ Ōsaka)	60,054
Seto	126,343
Settsu (★ Ōsaka)	87,465
Shibata (▲ 78,168)	63,600
Shibukawa	49,064
Shijōnawate (★ Ōsaka)	50,036
Shiki (★ Tōkyō)	63,492
Shimada (▲ 73,809)	64,500
Shimizu (★ Shizuoka)	241,524
Shimodate (▲ 66,030)	54,100
Shimonoseki (★ Kitakyūshū)	262,643
Shiogama (★ Sendai)	62,025
Shizuoka (★ 975,000)	472,199
Sōka (★ Tōkyō)	206,129
Suita (★ Ōsaka)	345,187
Suwa	52,465
Suzuka	174,103
Tachikawa (★ Tōkyō)	152,817
Tagajō (★ Sendai)	58,456
Tagawa	57,701
Tajimi (★ Nagoya)	94,036
Takaishi (★ Ōsaka)	65,084
Takamatsu	329,695
Takaoka (★ 220,000)	175,469
Takarazuka (★ Ōsaka)	201,863
Takasago (★ Ōsaka)	93,267
Takasaki	236,463
Takatsuki (★ Ōsaka)	359,867
Takayama	65,245
Takefu	70,188
Takikawa	49,591
Tama (★ Tōkyō)	144,490
Tamano	73,240
Tanabe (▲ 69,861)	59,100
Tanashi (★ Tōkyō)	75,141
Tatebayashi	76,223
Tenri	68,818
Tochigi	86,216
Toda (★ Tōkyō)	87,600
Tōkai (★ Nagoya)	97,359
Toki	64,946
Tokoname (★ Nagoya)	51,784
Tokorozawa (★ Tōkyō)	303,047
Tokushima	263,336
Tokuyama (★ 250,000)	110,900
• TŌKYŌ (★ 27,700,000)	8,163,127
Tomakomai	160,116
Tondabayashi (★ Ōsaka)	110,444
Toride (★ Tōkyō)	81,667
Tosu	55,878
Tottori	142,477
Toyama	321,459
Toyoake (★ Nagoya)	62,156
Toyohashi	337,988
Toyokawa	111,731
Toyonaka (★ Ōsaka)	409,843
Toyota	332,336
Tsu	157,178
Tsuchiura	127,470
Tsuruga	68,039
Tsuruoka	99,891
Tsushima (★ Nagoya)	59,345
Tsuyama	89,405
Ube (★ 230,000)	175,052
Ueda	119,435
Ueno (▲ 60,239)	51,400
Uji (★ Ōsaka) (1985 C)	165,411
Uozu	49,516
Urasoe	89,993
Urawa (★ Tōkyō)	418,267
Urayasu (★ Tōkyō)	115,675
Usa (▲ 50,830)	38,600
Ushiku	60,698
Utsunomiya	426,809
Uwajima	68,035
Wakayama (★ 495,000)	396,554
Wakkanai	48,232
Wakō (★ Tōkyō)	56,891
Warabi (★ Tōkyō)	73,620
Yachiyo (★ Tōkyō)	148,615
Yaizu (★ Shizuoka)	112,188
Yamagata	249,493
Yamaguchi	129,467
Yamato (★ Tōkyō)	194,870
Yamato-kōriyama (★ Ōsaka)	92,948
Yamato-takada (★ Ōsaka)	68,236
Yame (▲ 39,817)	32,800
Yao (★ Ōsaka)	277,724
Yashio (★ Tōkyō)	72,474
Yatsushiro (▲ 108,135)	88,300
Yawata (★ Ōsaka)	75,761
Yokkaichi	274,184

C Census. E Official estimate. U Unofficial estimate.
• Largest city in country.

★ Population or designation of metropolitan area, including suburbs (see headnote).
▲ Population of an entire municipality, commune, or district, including rural area.

Yokohama (★ Tōkyō) 3,220,350
Yokosuka (★ Tōkyō) 433,361
Yonago 131,453
Yonezawa 94,763
Yono (★ Tōkyō) 79,058
Yotsukaidō (★ Tōkyō) 72,157
Yukuhashi 65,713
Zama (★ Tōkyō) 112,100
Zushi (★ Tōkyō) 56,705

JERSEY
1986 C 80,212

• SAINT HELIER (★ 46,500) 27,083

JORDAN / Al-Urdun
1989 E 3,111,000

Al-Baqʻah (★ ʻAmmān) 63,985
• ʻAMMĀN (★ 1,450,000) 936,300
Ar-Ruṣayfah (★ ʻAmmān) 72,580
As-Salṭ 47,585
Az-Zarqāʼ (★ ʻAmmān) 318,055
Irbid 167,785

KENYA
1990 E 24,870,000

Eldoret (1979 C) 50,503
Kisumu (1984 E) 167,100
Machakos (1983 E) 92,300
Meru (1979 C) 72,049
Mombasa 537,000
• NAIROBI 1,505,000
Nakuru (1984 E) 101,700

KIRIBATI
1988 E 68,207

BAIRIKI 2,230
• Bikenibeu 4,580

KOREA, NORTH / Chosŏn-minjujuŭi-inmīn-konghwaguk
1981 E 18,317,000

Ch'ŏngjin 490,000
Haeju (1983 E) 213,000
Hamhŭng (1970 E) 150,000
Hŭngnam (1976 E) 260,000
Kaesŏng 259,000
Kanggye (1967 E) 130,000
Kimch'aek (Sŏngjin) (1967 E) 265,000
Namp'o 241,000
• P'YŎNGYANG (★ 1,600,000) 1,283,000
Sinŭiju 305,000
Songnim (1944 C) 53,035
Wŏnsan 398,000

KOREA, SOUTH / Taehan-min'guk
1985 C 40,448,486

Andong 114,216
Anyang (★ Sŏul) 361,577
Bucheon (★ Sŏul) 456,292
Changwŏn (★ Masan) 173,508
Chech'on 102,274
Cheju 202,911
Chinhae 121,341
Chinju 227,309
Ch'ŏnan 170,196
Ch'ŏngju 350,256
Chŏnju 79,323
Chŏnju, Chŏlla Pukdo prov. 426,473
Ch'unch'ŏn 162,988
Ch'ungju 113,331
Ch'ungmu 87,459
Inch'ŏn (★ Sŏul) (1989 E) 1,628,000
Iri 192,269
Kangnŭng 132,897
Kimch'ŏn 77,254
Kimhae 77,903
Kumi 142,094
Kŭmsŏng 58,897
Kunsan 185,649
Kwangju (1989 E) 1,165,000
Kwangmyŏng (★ Sŏul) 219,611
Kyŏngju 127,544
Masan (★ 625,000) 448,746
Mokp'o 236,085
Namwŏn 61,447
P'ohang 260,691
Pusan (★ 3,800,000) (1989 E) 3,773,000
P'yŏngt'aek (▲ 180,513) 63,400
Samch'ŏnp'o 62,466
Sangju (▲ 180,575) 28,300
Sŏgwipo 82,311
Sŏkch'o 69,501
Songjŏng (▲ 136,612) 35,300
Sŏngnam (★ Sŏul) 447,692
Songtan 66,357
• SŎUL (★ 15,850,000) (1989 E) 10,522,000
Sunch'ŏn (▲ 116,323) 121,958
Suwŏn (★ Sŏul) 430,752
T'aebaek 113,997
Taegu (1989 E) 2,207,000
Taejŏn (1989 E) 1,041,000
Tongduchŏn 68,633
Tonghae 91,691
Ŭijŏngbu (★ Sŏul) 162,700
Ulsan 551,014
Wŏnju 151,165
Yŏngch'ŏn 52,811
Yŏngju 84,742
Yŏsu 171,933

KUWAIT / Al-Kuwayt
1985 C 1,697,301

Abraq Khīṭān (★ Al-Kuwayt) 45,120
Al-Aḥmadī (★ 285,000) 26,899
Al-Farwānīyah (★ Al-Kuwayt) 68,701
Al-Fuḥayḥīl (★ Al-Aḥmadī) 50,081
Al-Jahrah (★ Al-Kuwayt) 111,222
• AL-KUWAYT (★ 1,375,000) 44,335
As-Sālimīyah (★ Al-Kuwayt) 153,359
Aṣ-Ṣulaybīyah (★ Al-Kuwayt) 51,314
Hawallī (★ Al-Kuwayt) 145,126
Qalīb ash-Shuyūkh (★ Al-Kuwayt) 114,771
South Khīṭān (★ Al-Kuwayt) 69,256
Subahiya (★ Al-Aḥmadī) 60,787

LAOS / Lao
1985 C 3,584,803

Savannakhét (1975 E) 53,000
• VIANGCHAN (VIENTIANE) 377,409

LATVIA
1989 C 2,681,000

Daugavoils 127,000
Jelgava (1987 E) 72,000
Jūrmala (★ Rīga) (1987 E) 65,000
Liepāja 114,000
Rēzekne (1979 C) 35,620
• RĪGA (★ 1,005,000) 915,000
Ventspils (1987 E) 52,000

LEBANON / Lubnān
1982 E 2,637,000

• BAYRŪT (★ 1,675,000) 509,000
Ṣaydā 105,000
Ṣūr (Tyre) (1970 E) 12,500
Ṭarābulus (Tripoli) 198,000

LESOTHO
1986 C 1,577,536

• MASERU 109,382

LIBERIA
1986 E 2,221,000

• MONROVIA 465,000

LIBYA / Lībiyā
1988 E 3,772,500

Al-Bayḍā (Beida) (1984 C) 67,120
Banghāzī 446,250
Darnah (1984 C) 62,179
Misrātah 121,669
• ṬARĀBULUS (TRIPOLI) 591,062
Ṭubruq (Tobruk) (1984 C) 75,282

LIECHTENSTEIN
1990 E 28,452

• VADUZ 4,874

LITHUANIA
1989 C 3,690,000

Alytus (1987 E) 71,000
Kapsukas (1979 C) 38,824
Kaunas 423,000
Klaipėda (Memel) 204,000
Panevėžys 126,000
Šiauliai 145,000
• VILNIUS 582,000

LUXEMBOURG
1985 E 366,000

Esch-sur-Alzette (★ 83,000) (1981 C) 25,142
• LUXEMBOURG (★ 136,000) 76,130

MACAU
1987 E 429,000

• MACAU 429,000

MADAGASCAR / Madagasikara
1984 E 9,731,000

• ANTANANARIVO (1985 E) 663,000
Antsirabe (▲ 95,000) 50,100
Antsiranana 100,000
Fianarantsoa 130,000
Mahajanga 85,000
Toamasina 100,000
Toliara 55,000

MALAWI / Malaŵi
1987 C 7,982,607

• Blantyre 331,588
LILONGWE 233,973

MALAYSIA
1980 C 13,136,109

Alor Setar 69,435
Batu Pahat 64,727
Butterworth (★ George Town) 77,982
George Town (Pinang) (★ 495,000) 248,241
Ipoh 293,849
Johor Baharu (★ Singapore) 246,395
Kelang 192,080
Keluang 50,315
Kota Baharu 167,872
Kota Kinabalu (Jesselton) 55,997
• KUALA LUMPUR (★ 1,475,000) 919,610
Kuala Terengganu 180,296
Kuantan 131,547
Kuching 72,555
Melaka 87,494
Miri 52,125
Muar (Bandar Maharani) 65,151
Petaling Jaya (★ Kuala Lumpur) 207,805
Sandakan 70,420
Seremban 132,911
Sibu 85,231
Taiping 146,000
Telok Anson 49,148

MALDIVES
1985 C 181,453

• MALE 46,334

MALI
1987 C 7,620,225

• BAMAKO 646,163
Gao 54,874
Kayes 48,216
Koutiala 48,010
Mopti 73,979
Ségou 88,877
Sikasso 73,050
Tombouctou (Timbuktu) 31,925

MALTA
1989 E 349,014

• VALLETTA (★ 215,000) 9,210

MARSHALL ISLANDS
1980 C 30,873

• Jarej-Uliga-Delap 8,583

MARTINIQUE
1982 C 328,566

• FORT-DE-FRANCE (★ 116,017) 99,844

MAURITANIA / Mauritanie / Mūrītāniyā
1987 E 2,007,000

• NOUAKCHOTT 285,000

MAURITIUS
1987 E 1,008,864

Beau Bassin-Rose Hill (★ Port Louis) 93,125
Curepipe (★ Port Louis) 64,243
• PORT LOUIS (★ 420,000) 139,730
Quatre Bornes (★ Port Louis) 65,480
Vacoas-Phoenix (★ Port Louis) 55,667

MAYOTTE
1985 E 67,205

• DZAOUDZI (★ 6,979) 5,865

MEXICO / México
1980 C 67,395,826

Acapulco [de Juárez] 301,902
Aguascalientes 293,152
Atlixco 53,207
Campeche 128,434
Cancún 33,273
Celaya 141,675
Chetumal 56,709
Chihuahua 385,603
Chilpancingo de los Bravo 67,498
Ciudad del Carmen 72,489
• CIUDAD DE MÉXICO (★ 14,100,000) 8,831,079
Ciudad Guzmán 60,938
Ciudad Juárez (★ El Paso, Tex., U.S.A.) 544,496
Ciudad Madero (★ Tampico) 132,444
Ciudad Mante 70,647
Ciudad Obregón 165,572
Ciudad Valles 65,609
Ciudad Victoria 140,161
Coatzacoalcos 127,170
Colima 86,044
Córdoba 99,972
Cuernavaca 192,770
Culiacán 304,826
Delicias 65,504
Durango 257,915
Ecatepec (★ Ciudad de México) 741,821
Ensenada 120,483
Fresnillo 56,066
Garza García (★ Monterrey) 81,974
Gómez Palacio (★ Torreón) 116,967
Guadalajara (★ 2,325,000) 1,626,152
Guadalupe (★ Monterrey) 370,524
Guanajuato 48,981
Guaymas 54,826
Hermosillo 297,175
Heroica Zitácuaro 47,520
Hidalgo del Parral 75,590
Iguala 66,005
Irapuato 170,138
La Paz 91,453
La Piedad de Cabadas 47,441
Las Choapas 35,807
León 593,002
Los Mochis 122,531
Matamoros (★ Brownsville, Tex., U.S.A.) 188,745
Mazatlán 199,830
Mérida 400,142
Mexicali (★ 365,000) 341,559
Minatitlán 106,765
Monclova 115,786
Monterrey (★ 2,015,000) 1,090,009
Morelia 297,544
Naucalpan de Juárez (★ Ciudad de México) 723,723
Navojoa 62,901
Nezahualcóyotl (★ Ciudad de México) 1,341,230
Nogales 65,603
Nuevo Laredo (★ Laredo, Tex., U.S.A.) 201,731
Oaxaca [de Juárez] 154,223
Ocotlán 48,931
Orizaba (★ 215,000) 114,848
Pachuca 110,351
Piedras Negras 67,455
Poza Rica 166,799
Puebla (★ 1,055,000) 835,759
Puerto Vallarta 38,645
Querétaro 215,976
Reynosa 194,693
Río Bravo 55,236
Salamanca 96,703
Saltillo 284,937
San Luis Potosí (★ 470,000) 362,371
San Luis Río Colorado 76,684
San Nicolás de los Garza (★ Monterrey) 280,696
Santa Catarina (★ Monterrey) 87,673
Soledad Díez Gutiérrez (★ San Luis Potosí) 49,173
Tampico (★ 435,000) 267,957
Tapachula 85,766
Tecomán 46,371
Tehuacán 79,547
Tepic 145,741
Tijuana (★ San Diego, Calif., U.S.A.) 429,500
Tlalnepantla (★ Ciudad de México) 778,173
Tlaquepaque (★ Guadalajara) 133,500
Toluca [de Lerdo] 199,778
Torreón (★ 575,000) 328,086
Tulancingo 53,400
Tuxpan 56,037
Tuxtla Gutiérrez 131,096
Uruapan del Progreso 122,828
Veracruz [Llave] (★ 385,000) 284,822
Villahermosa 158,216
Xalapa 204,594
Zacatecas 80,088
Zamora de Hidalgo 86,998
Zapopan (★ Guadalajara) 345,390

MICRONESIA, FEDERATED STATES OF
1985 E 94,534

• KOLONIA 6,306

MONACO
1982 C 27,063

• MONACO (★ 87,000) 27,063

MONGOLIA / Mongol Ard Uls
1989 E 2,040,000

Darchan (1985 E) 69,800
• ULAANBAATAR 548,400

MONTSERRAT
1980 C 11,606

• PLYMOUTH 1,568

MOROCCO / Al-Magreb
1982 C 20,419,555

Agadir 110,479
Beni-Mellal 95,003
Berkane 60,490
• Casablanca (Dar-el-Beida) (★ 2,475,000) 2,139,204
El-Jadida (Mazagan) 81,455
Fès (★ 535,000) 448,823
Kenitra 188,194
Khemisset 58,925
Khouribga 127,181
Ksar-el-Kebir 73,541
Larache 63,893
Marrakech (★ 535,000) 439,728
Meknès (★ 375,000) 319,783
Mohammedia (Fedala) (★ Casablanca) 105,120
Nador 62,040
Oued-Zem 58,744
Oujda 260,082
RABAT (★ 980,000) 518,616
Safi 197,309
Salé (★ Rabat) 289,391
Settat 65,203
Sidi Kacem 55,833
Sidi Slimane 50,457
Tanger (Tangier) (★ 370,000) 266,346
Tan-Tan 41,451
Taza 77,216
Temera (★ Rabat) 48,644
Tétouan 199,615

MOZAMBIQUE / Moçambique
1989 E 15,326,476

Beira 291,604
Chimoio (1986 E) 86,928
Inhambane (1986 E) 64,274
• MAPUTO 1,069,727
Nacala 101,615
Nampula 197,379
Pemba (1986 E) 50,215
Quelimane 78,520
Tete (1986 E) 56,178
Xai-Xai (1986 E) 51,620

C Census. E Official estimate. U Unofficial estimate.
• Largest city in country.
★ Population or designation of metropolitan area, including suburbs (see headnote).
▲ Population of an entire municipality, commune, or district, including rural area.

NAMIBIA

1988 E 1,760,000
• WINDHOEK 114,500

NAURU / Naoero

1987 E 8,000

NEPAL / Nepāl

1981 C 15,022,839
Bhaktapur 48,472
• KĀTHMĀNDAU (★ 320,000) 235,160
Wirātnagar 93,544

NETHERLANDS / Nederland

1989 E 14,880,000
Alkmaar (★ 121,000) (1987 E) 87,034
Almelo (1986 E) 62,421
Alphen aan den Rijn (1986 E) 55,812
Amersfoort (★ 130,158) (1986 E) 89,596
Amstelveen (★ Amsterdam) (1986 E) 68,090
• AMSTERDAM (★ 1,860,000) 696,500
Apeldoorn 147,300
Arnhem (★ 296,362) 129,000
Assen (1986 E) 47,462
Bergen op Zoom (1986 E) 46,103
Breda (★ 155,613) 121,400
Delft (★ 's-Gravenhage) (1986 E) 87,440
Den Helder (1986 E) 63,231
Deventer (1986 E) 64,806
Dordrecht (★ 202,126) 108,300
Ede (▲ 88,866) (1986 E) 46,700
Eindhoven (★ 379,377) 190,700
Emmen (▲ 91,775) (1986 E) 36,400
Enschede (★ 288,000) 145,200
Geleen (★ 177,243) (1986 E) 34,292
Gouda (1986 E) 60,927
Groningen (★ 206,781) 167,800
Haarlem (★ Amsterdam) 149,200
Haarlemmermeer (★ Amsterdam) (1987 E) 12,100
Heerlen (★ 266,617) (1986 E) 93,871
Helmond (1987 E) 63,909
Hengelo (★ Enschede) (1986 E) 76,694
Hilversum (★ Amsterdam) (1986 E) 86,125
Hoorn (1987 E) 53,788
IJmuiden (★ Amsterdam) (1986 E) 57,157
Kerkrade (★ Heerlen) (1986 E) 52,885
Leeuwarden (1986 E) 84,966
Leiden (★ 182,244) 109,200
Maastricht (★ 160,026) 116,400
Nieuwegein (★ Utrecht) (1987 E) 56,719
Nijmegen (★ 240,085) 145,400
Oss (1986 E) 50,343
Purmerend (★ Amsterdam) (1987 E) 52,257
Ridderkerk (★ Rotterdam) (1986 E) 46,419
Rijswijk (★ 's-Gravenhage) (1986 E) 48,886
Roosendaal (1986 E) 57,385
Rotterdam (★ 1,110,000) 576,300
Schiedam (★ Rotterdam) (1986 E) 69,078
'S-GRAVENHAGE (THE HAGUE) (★ 770,000) 443,900
's-Hertogenbosch (★ 189,067) (1986 E) 89,039
Soest (★ Amersfoort) (1986 E) 40,562
Spijkenisse (★ Rotterdam) (1987 E) 62,394
Tilburg (★ 224,934) 155,100
Utrecht (★ 518,779) 230,700
Venlo (★ 87,000) (1986 E) 63,475
Vlaardingen (★ Rotterdam) (1986 E) 75,536
Vlissingen (Flushing) (▲ 45,339) (1986 E) 26,000
Zaanstad (★ Amsterdam) 129,600
Zeist (★ Utrecht) (1986 E) 59,743
Zoetermeer (★ 's-Gravenhage) (1987 E) 85,349
Zwolle (1986 E) 88,438

NETHERLANDS ANTILLES / Nederlandse Antillen

1990 E 189,687
• WILLEMSTAD (★ 130,000) (1981 C) 31,883

NEW CALEDONIA / Nouvelle-Calédonie

1989 C 164,173
• NOUMÉA (★ 88,000) 65,110

NEW ZEALAND

1986 C 3,307,084
• Auckland (★ 850,000) 149,046
Christchurch (★ 320,000) 168,200
Dunedin (★ 109,000) 76,964
Hamilton (★ 101,814) 94,511
Invercargill (★ 52,807) 48,197
Lower Hutt (★ Wellington) 63,862
Manukau (★ Auckland) 177,248
Napier (★ 107,060) 49,428
Palmerston North (★ 67,405) 60,503
Rotorua (★ 52,001) 40,597
Takapuna (★ Auckland) 69,419
Tauranga (★ 59,435) 41,611
Waitemata (★ Auckland) 96,365
WELLINGTON (★ 350,000) 137,495

NICARAGUA

1985 E 3,272,100
Chinandega 75,000
Granada (1981 E) 64,642
León 101,000
• MANAGUA 682,000
Masaya 75,000
Matagalpa 68,000

NIGER

1988 C 7,250,383
Agadez 50,164
Maradi 112,965
• NIAMEY 398,265
Tahoua 51,607
Zinder 120,892

NIGERIA

1987 E 101,907,000
Aba 239,800
Abakaliki 56,800
Abeokuta 341,300
Ado-Ekiti 287,000
Afikpo 65,790
Agege 83,810
Akure 129,600
Amaigbo 53,690
Apomu 49,570
Aramoko 48,280
Asaba 47,410
Awka 88,800
Azare 50,020
Bauchi 68,840
Benin City 183,200
Bida 100,200
Calabar 139,800
Deba 110,600
Duku 52,880
Ede 245,200
Effon-Alaiye 122,300
Ejigbo 84,570
Emure-Ekiti 58,750
Enugu 252,500
Epe 80,560
Erin-Oshogbo 59,940
Eruwa 49,140
Fiditi 49,440
Gboko 49,390
Gbongan 53,990
Gombe 86,120
Gusau 126,200
Ibadan 1,144,000
Idah 50,550
Idanre 56,080
Ife 237,000
Ifon-Oshogbo 65,980
Igbasa-Odo 48,040
Igboho 85,230
Igbo-Ora 68,060
Igede-Ekiti 56,570
Ihiala 73,240
Ijebu-Igbo 78,680
Ijebu-Ode 124,900
Ijero-Ekiti 76,420
Ikare 112,500
Ikerre 195,400
Ikire 94,450
Ikirun 144,900
Ikole 71,860
Ikorodu 147,700
Ikot Ekpene 69,440
Ila 210,800
Ilawe-Ekiti 147,300
Ilesha 302,100
Ilobu 159,000
Ilorin 380,000
Inisa 95,630
Ipoti-Ekiti 53,220
Ise-Ekiti 82,580
Iseyin 173,500
Iwo 289,100
Jega (1985 E) 47,000
Jimeta 66,130
Jos 164,700
Kaduna 273,200
Kano 538,300
Katsina 165,000
Kaura Namoda 52,910
Keffi 57,790
Kishi 77,210
Kumo 118,200
Lafia 97,810
Lafiagi 57,580
• LAGOS (★ 3,800,000) 1,213,000
Lalupon 56,130
Lere 49,670
Maiduguri 255,100
Makurdi 98,350
Minna 109,300
Mubi 51,190
Mushin (★ Lagos) 266,100
Nguru 78,770
Nsukka 47,760
Ode-Ekiti 48,910
Offa 157,500
Ogbomosho 582,900
Oka 114,400
Oke-Mesi 55,040
Okwe 52,550
Olupona 65,720
Ondo 135,300
Onitsha 298,200
Opobo 64,620
Oron 62,260
Oshogbo 380,800
Owerri (1985 E) 37,000
Owo 146,600
Oyan 50,930
Oyo 204,700
Pindiga 64,130
Port Harcourt 327,300
Potiskum 56,490
Sapele 111,200
Shagamu 93,610
Shaki 139,000
Shomolu (★ Lagos) 120,700
Sokoto 163,700
Ugep 81,910
Umuahia 52,550
Uyo 60,500
Warri 100,700
Zaria 302,800

NIUE

1986 C 2,531
• ALOFI 811

NORTHERN MARIANA ISLANDS

1980 C 16,780
• Chalan Kanoa 2,678
Garapan 2,063

NORWAY / Norge

1987 E 4,190,000
Bærum (★ Oslo) (1985 E) 83,000
Bergen (★ 239,000) 209,320
Drammen (★ 73,000) (1985 E) 50,700
Fredrikstad (★ 52,000) (1983 E) 27,618
Hammerfest (1983 E) 7,208
Kristiansand (1985 E) 62,200
Narvik (1983 E) 19,080
• OSLO (★ 720,000) 452,415
Skien (★ 77,981) (1985 E) 46,700
Stavanger (★ 132,000) (1985 E) 94,200
Tromsø (1985 E) 47,800
Trondheim 135,010

OMAN / 'Umān

1981 E 919,000
• MASQAṬ (MUSCAT) 50,000
Maṭraḥ (1971 E) 14,000
Ṣūr (1980 E) 30,000

PAKISTAN / Pākistān

1981 C 84,253,644
Abbottābād (★ 65,996) 32,188
Ahmadpur East 56,979
Attock (★ 39,986) 26,233
Bahāwalnagar 74,533
Bahāwalpur (★ 180,263) 152,009
Bannu (★ 43,210) 35,170
Bhakkar 41,934
Chārsadda 62,530
Chīchāwatni 50,241
Chiniot 105,559
Chishtiān Mandi 61,959
Daska 55,555
Dera Ghāzi Khān 102,007
Dera Ismāīl Khān (★ 68,145) 64,358
Drigh Road Cantonment (★ Karāchi) 56,742
Faisalabad (Lyallpur) 1,104,209
Gojra 68,000
Gujrānwāla (★ 658,753) 600,993
Gujrānwāla Cantonment (★ Gujrānwāla) 57,760
Gujrāt 155,058
Hāfizābād 83,464
Hyderābād (★ 800,000) 702,539
Hyderābād Cantonment (★ Hyderābād) 48,990
ISLĀMĀBĀD (★ Rāwalpindi) 204,364
Jacobābād 79,365
Jarānwāla 69,459
Jhang Sadar 195,558
Jhelum (★ 106,462) 92,646
Kamālia 61,107
Kāmoke 71,097
• Karāchi (★ 5,300,000) 4,901,627
Karāchi Cantonment (★ Karāchi) 181,981
Kasūr 155,523
Khairpur 61,447
Khānewāl 89,090
Khānpur 70,589
Khāriān Cantonment (★ 51,506) 16,042
Khushāb 56,274
Kohāt (★ 77,604) 55,832
Lahore (★ 3,025,000) 2,707,215
Lahore Cantonment (★ Lahore) 245,474
Lārkāna 123,890
Leiah 51,482
Malir Cantonment (★ Karāchi) 47,588
Mandi Būrewāla 86,311
Mardān (★ 147,977) 141,842
Miānwāli 59,159
Mingāora 88,078
Mīrpur Khās 124,371
Multān (★ 732,070) 696,316
Muzaffargarh 53,000
Nawābshāh 102,139
Nowshera (★ 74,913) 38,875
Okāra (★ 153,483) 127,455
Pākpattan 69,820
Peshāwar (★ 566,248) 506,896
Peshāwar Cantonment (★ Peshāwar) 59,352
Quetta (★ 285,719) 244,842
Rahīmyār Khān (★ 132,635) 119,036
Rāwalpindi (★ 1,040,000) 457,091
Rāwalpindi Cantonment (★ Rāwalpindi) 337,752
Sādiqābād 63,935
Sāhīwal 150,954
Sargodha (★ 291,362) 231,895
Sargodha Cantonment (★ Sargodha) 59,467
Shekhūpura 141,168
Shikārpur 88,138
Shorkot (★ 50,568) 18,533
Siālkot (★ 302,009) 258,147
Sukkur 190,551
Tando Ādam 62,744
Turbat 52,337
Vihāri 53,799
Wāh Cantonment 122,335
Wazīrābād 62,725

PALAU / Belau

1986 C 13,873
• KOROR 8,629

PANAMA / Panamá

1990 C 2,315,047
Balboa (★ Panamá) 1,214
Colón (★ 96,000) 54,469
David 65,635
• PANAMÁ (★ 770,000) 411,549
San Miguelito (★ Panamá) 242,529

PAPUA NEW GUINEA

1987 E 3,479,400
Lae 79,600
• PORT MORESBY 152,100
Rabaul (1980 C) 14,954

PARAGUAY

1985 E 3,279,000
• ASUNCIÓN (★ 700,000) 477,100
Fernando de la Mora (★ Asunción) 80,000
Lambaré (★ Asunción) 84,000
Puerto Presidente Stroessner 64,000
San Lorenzo (★ Asunción) (1982 C) 74,632

PERU / Perú

1981 C 17,031,221
Arequipa (★ 446,942) 108,023
Ayacucho (★ 69,533) 57,432
Barranco (★ Lima) 46,478
Breña (★ Lima) 112,398
Cajamarca 62,259
Callao (★ Lima) 264,133
Cerro de Pasco (★ 66,373) 55,597
Chiclayo (★ 279,527) 213,095
Chimbote 223,341
Chorrillos (★ Lima) 141,881
Chosica 65,139
Cuzco (★ 184,550) 89,563
Huacho 43,398
Huancayo (★ 164,954) 84,845
Huánuco 61,812
Ica 114,786
Iquitos 178,738
Jesús María (★ Lima) 83,179
Juliaca 87,651
La Victoria (★ Lima) 270,778
• LIMA (★ 4,608,010) 371,122
Lince (★ Lima) 80,456
Magdalena (★ Lima) 55,535
Miraflores (★ Lima) 103,453
Pisco 55,604
Piura (★ 207,934) 144,609
Pucallpa 112,263
Pueblo Libre (★ Lima) 83,985
Puno 67,397
Rímac (★ Lima) 184,484
San Isidro (★ Lima) 71,203
San Martin de Porras (★ Lima) 404,856
Santiago de Surco (★ Lima) 146,636
Sullana 89,037
Surquillo (★ Lima) 134,158
Tacna 97,173
Talara 57,351
Trujillo (★ 354,301) 202,469
Tumbes 47,936
Vitarte (★ Lima) 145,504

PHILIPPINES / Pilipinas

1990 C 60,477,000
Angeles 236,000
Antipolo (▲ 68,912) (1980 C) 54,117
Bacolod 364,000
Bacoor (★ Manila) (1980 C) 90,364
Baguio 183,000
Baliuag (1980 C) 70,555
Biñan (★ Manila) (1980 C) 83,684
Binangonan (1980 C) 80,980
Bislig (▲ 81,615) (1980 C) 49,498
Bocaue (1980 C) 49,693
Butuan (▲ 228,000) 99,000
Cabanatuan (▲ 173,000) 75,700
Cagayan de Oro (▲ 340,000) 255,000
Cainta (★ Manila) (1980 C) 59,025
Calamba (▲ 121,175) (1980 C) 72,359
Caloocan (★ Manila) 746,000
Carmona (★ Manila) (1980 C) 65,014
Cavite (★ 175,000) 92,000
Cebu (★ 720,000) 610,000
Cotabato 127,000
Dagupan 122,000
Davao (▲ 850,000) 569,300
Dumaguete 80,000
General Santos (Dadiangas) (▲ 250,000) 157,600
Guagua (1980 C) 72,609
Iloilo 311,000
Isabela (Basilan) (▲ 49,891) (1980 C) 11,491
Jolo (1980 C) 52,429
Lapu-Lapu (Opon) 146,000
Las Piñas (★ Manila) (1984 E) 190,364
Legaspi (▲ 121,000) 63,000
Lucena 151,000
Mabalacat (▲ 80,966) (1980 C) 54,988
Makati (★ Manila) (1984 E) 408,991
Malabon (★ Manila) (1984 E) 212,930
Malolos (1980 C) 95,699
Mandaluyong (★ Manila) (1984 E) 226,670
Mandaue (★ Cebu) 180,000
Mangaldan (1980 C) 50,434
• MANILA (★ 6,800,000) 1,587,000
Marawi 92,000
Marikina (★ Manila) (1984 E) 248,183
Meycauayan (★ Manila) (1980 C) 83,579
Muntinglupa (★ Manila) (1984 E) 172,421
Naga 115,000
Navotas (★ Manila) (1984 E) 146,899
Olongapo 192,000
Pagadian (▲ 107,000) 52,400
Parañaque (★ Manila) (1984 E) 252,791
Pasay (★ Manila) 354,000
Pasig (★ Manila) (1984 E) 318,853

C Census. E Official estimate. U Unofficial estimate.
• Largest city in country.

★ Population or designation of metropolitan area, including suburbs (see headnote).
▲ Population of an entire municipality, commune, or district, including rural area.

Puerto Princesa (▲ 92,000) 52,000
Quezon City (★ Manila) 1,632,000
San Fernando (1980 C) 110,891
San Juan del Monte (★ Manila) (1984 E) 139,126
San Pablo (▲ 161,000) 83,900
San Pedro (1980 C) 74,556
Santa Cruz (1980 C) 60,620
Santa Rosa (★ Manila) (1980 C) 64,325
Tacloban 138,000
Tagbilaran 56,000
Tagig (★ Manila) (1984 E) 130,719
Taytay (★ Manila) (1980 C) 75,328
Valenzuela (★ Manila) (1984 E) 275,725
Zamboanga (▲ 444,000) 107,000

PITCAIRN

1988 C 59
• ADAMSTOWN 59

POLAND / Polska

1989 E 37,775,100
Będzin (★ Katowice) 77,300
Bełchatów 53,600
Biała Podlaska 50,900
Białystok 263,900
Bielsko-Biała 179,600
Bydgoszcz 377,900
Bytom (Beuthen) (★ Katowice) 228,000
Chełm 63,300
Chorzów (★ Katowice) 133,300
Częstochowa 254,600
Dąbrowa Górnicza (★ Katowice) 133,200
Dzierżoniów (Reichenbach) (★ 89,000) 37,700
Elbląg (Elbing) 124,600
Ełk 49,600
Gdańsk (Danzig) (★ 909,000) 461,500
Gdynia (★ Gdańsk) 250,200
Gliwice (Gleiwitz) (★ Katowice) 222,500
Głogów 70,100
Gniezno 68,900
Gorzów Wielkopolski (Landsberg an der Warthe) 121,500
Grudziądz 99,900
Inowrocław 75,100
Jastrzębie-Zdrój 102,200
Jaworzno (★ Katowice) 97,400
Jelenia Góra (Hirschberg) 92,700
Kalisz 105,600
• Katowice (★ 2,778,000) 365,800
Kędzierzyn Kozle 71,600
Kielce 211,100
Konin 78,500
Koszalin (Köslin) 105,600
Kraków (★ 828,000) 743,700
Krosno 48,300
Legionowo (★ Warszawa) 50,000
Legnica (Liegnitz) 102,800
Leszno 56,700
Łódź (★ 1,061,000) 851,500
Łomża 56,300
Lubin 78,800
Lublin (★ 389,000) 339,500
Mielec 58,600
Mysłowice (★ Katowice) 91,200
Nowy Sącz 75,100
Olsztyn (Allenstein) 158,800
Opole (Oppeln) 125,800
Ostrowiec Świętokrzyski 76,300
Ostrów Wielkopolski 71,200
Pabianice (★ Łódź) 74,400
Piekary Śląskie (★ Katowice) 68,200
Piła (Schneidemühl) (1988 E) 70,000
Piotrków Trybunalski 80,100
Płock 119,300
Poznań (★ 672,000) 586,500
Pruszków (★ Warszawa) 52,700
Przemyśl 67,300
Puławy 52,200
Racibórz (Ratibor) 61,700
Radom 223,600
Radomsko 49,700
Ruda Śląska (★ Katowice) 167,700
Rybnik 140,000
Rzeszów 148,600
Siedlce 69,200
Siemianowice Śląskie (★ Katowice) 79,200
Skarżysko-Kamienna 50,200
Słupsk (Stolp) 98,500
Sopot (★ Gdańsk) 47,800
Sosnowiec (★ Katowice) 258,700
Stalowa Wola 67,600
Starachowice 55,400
Stargard Szczeciński (Stargard in Pommern) 68,400
Suwałki 57,900
Świdnica (Schweidnitz) 61,800
Świętochłowice (★ Katowice) 58,700
Świnoujście (Swinemünde) 42,600
Szczecin (Stettin) (★ 449,000) 409,500
Tarnów 119,100
Tarnowskie Góry (★ Katowice) 72,700
Tczew 58,400
Tomaszów Mazowiecki 69,200
Toruń 199,600
Tychy (★ Katowice) 187,600
Wałbrzych (Waldenburg) (★ 207,000) 141,400
WARSZAWA (★ 2,323,000) 1,651,200
Włocławek 119,500
Wodzisław Śląski 109,800
Wrocław (Breslau) 637,400
Zabrze (Hindenburg) (★ Katowice) 201,400
Zamość 59,000
Zawiercie 55,700
Zgierz (★ Łódź) 58,500
Zielona Góra (Grünberg) 111,800
Żory 65,300

PORTUGAL

1981 C 9,833,014
Amadora (★ Lisboa) 95,518
Barreiro (★ Lisboa) 50,863
Braga 63,033
Coimbra 74,616
• LISBOA (★ 2,250,000) 807,167
Ponta Delgada 21,187
Porto (★ 1,225,000) 327,368
Setúbal 77,885
Vila Nova de Gaia (★ Porto) 62,469

PUERTO RICO

1980 C 3,196,520
Arecibo (★ 160,336) 48,779
Bayamón (★ San Juan) 185,087
Caguas (★ San Juan) 87,214
Carolina (★ San Juan) 147,835
Guaynabo (★ San Juan) 65,075
Mayagüez (★ 200,464) 82,968
Ponce (★ 232,551) 161,739
• SAN JUAN (★ 1,775,260) 424,600

QATAR / Qaṭar

1986 C 369,079
• AD-DAWḤAH (DOHA) (★ 310,000) 217,294
Ar-Rayyān (★ Ad-Dawḥah) 91,996

REUNION / Réunion

1982 C 515,814
• SAINT-DENIS (▲ 109,072) 84,400

ROMANIA / România

1986 E 22,823,479
Alba Iulia 66,100
Alexandria 52,802
Arad 187,744
Bacău 179,877
Baia Mare 139,704
Bîrlad 70,365
Bistrița 77,267
Botoșani 108,775
Brăila 235,620
Brașov 351,493
• BUCUREȘTI (BUCHAREST) (★ 2,275,000) 1,989,823
Buzău 136,080
Călărași 69,350
Cluj-Napoca 310,017
Constanța 327,676
Craiova 281,044
Deva 77,976
Drobeta-Turnu Severin 99,366
Focșani 86,411
Galați 295,372
Gheorghe Gheorghiu-Dej 52,329
Giurgiu 68,002
Hunedoara 88,514
Iași 313,060
Lugoj 53,665
Mediaș 72,816
Oradea 213,846
Petroșani (★ 76,000) 49,131
Piatra Neamț 109,393
Pitești 157,190
Ploiești (★ 310,000) 234,886
Reșița 105,914
Rîmnicu Vîlcea 96,051
Roman 72,415
Satu Mare 130,082
Sfîntu-Gheorghe 67,587
Sibiu 177,511
Slatina 76,714
Suceava 96,317
Timișoara 325,272
Tîrgoviște 91,990
Tîrgu Jiu 87,693
Tîrgu-Mureș 158,998
Tulcea 86,336
Turda 61,594
Vaslui 65,070
Zalău 57,283

RWANDA

1983 E 5,762,000
• KIGALI 181,600

SAINT HELENA

1987 C 5,644
• JAMESTOWN 1,413

SAINT KITTS AND NEVIS

1980 C 44,404
• BASSETERRE 14,725
Charlestown 1,771

SAINT LUCIA

1987 E 142,342
• CASTRIES 53,933

SAINT PIERRE AND MIQUELON / Saint-Pierre-et-Miquelon

1982 C 6,041
• SAINT-PIERRE 5,371

SAINT VINCENT AND THE GRENADINES

1987 E 112,589
• KINGSTOWN (★ 28,936) 19,028

SAN MARINO

1988 E 22,304
• SAN MARINO 2,777

SAO TOME AND PRINCIPE / São Tomé e Príncipe

1970 C 73,631
• SÃO TOMÉ 17,380

SAUDI ARABIA / Al-ʿArabīyah as-Suʿūdīyah

1980 E 9,229,000
Abhā (1974 C) 30,150
Ad-Dammām 200,000
Al-Hufūf (1974 C) 101,271
Al-Khubar (1974 C) 48,817
Al-Madīnah (Medina) 290,000
Al-Mubarraz (1974 C) 54,325
AR-RIYĀḌ (RIYADH) 1,250,000
Aṭ-Ṭāʾif 300,000
Buraydah (1974 C) 69,940
Ḥāʾil (1974 C) 40,502
• Jiddah 1,300,000
Khamīs Mushayṭ (1974 C) 49,581
Makkah (Mecca) 550,000
Najran (1974 C) 47,501
Tabūk (1974 C) 74,825

SENEGAL / Sénégal

1988 C 6,881,919
• DAKAR 1,447,642
Diourbel 77,548
Kaolack 152,007
Louga 52,763
Saint-Louis 160,689
Thiès 184,902
Ziguinchor 124,283

SEYCHELLES

1984 E 64,718
• VICTORIA 23,000

SIERRA LEONE

1985 C 3,515,812
Bo 59,768
• FREETOWN (★ 525,000) 469,776
Kenema 52,473
Koidu 82,474
Makeni 49,038

SINGAPORE

1989 E 2,685,400
• SINGAPORE (★ 3,025,000) 2,685,400

SOLOMON ISLANDS

1986 C 285,176
• HONIARA 30,413

SOMALIA / Somaliya

1984 E 5,423,000
Berbera 65,000
Hargeysa 70,000
Kismaayo 70,000
Marka 60,000
• MUQDISHO 600,000

SOUTH AFRICA / Suid-Afrika

1985 C 23,385,645
Alberton (★ Johannesburg) 66,155
Alexandra (★ Johannesburg) 67,276
Atteridgeville (★ Pretoria) 73,439
Bellville (★ Cape Town) 68,915
Benoni (★ Johannesburg) 94,926
Bloemfontein (★ 235,000) 104,381
Boksburg (★ Johannesburg) 110,832
Botshabelo (★ Bloemfontein) 95,625
Brakpan (★ Johannesburg) 46,416
CAPE TOWN (KAAPSTAD) (★ 1,790,000) 776,617
Carletonville (★ 120,499) 97,874
Daveyton (★ Johannesburg) 99,056
Diepmeadow (★ Johannesburg) 192,682
Durban (★ 1,550,000) 634,301
East London (Oos-Londen) (★ 320,000) 85,699
Edendale (★ Pietermaritzburg) 47,001
Elsies River (★ Cape Town) 70,067
Empumalanga (★ Durban) 47,938
Evaton (★ Vereeniging) 52,559
Galeshewe (★ Kimberley) 63,238
Germiston (★ Johannesburg) 116,718
Grassy Park (★ Cape Town) 50,193
Guguleto (★ Cape Town) 63,893
• Johannesburg (★ 3,650,000) 632,369
Kagiso (★ Johannesburg) 50,647
Katlehong (★ Johannesburg) 137,745
Kayamnandi (★ Port Elizabeth) 220,548
Kempton Park (★ Johannesburg) 87,721
Kimberley (★ 145,000) 74,061
Klerksdorp (★ 205,000) 48,947
Krugersdorp (★ Johannesburg) 73,767
Kwa Makuta (★ Durban) 71,378
Kwa Mashu (★ Durban) 111,593
Kwanobuhle (★ Port Elizabeth) 52,376
Kwa-Thema (★ Johannesburg) 78,640
Ladysmith (★ 31,670) 25,102
Lekoa (Shapeville) (★ Vereeniging) 218,392
Madadeni (★ Newcastle) 65,832
Mamelodi (★ Pretoria) 127,033
Mangaung (★ Bloemfontein) 79,851
Ntuzuma (★ Durban) 61,834
Nyanga (★ Cape Town) 148,882
Osizweni (★ Newcastle) 51,934
Paarl (★ Cape Town) 63,671
Parow (★ Cape Town) 60,294
Pietermaritzburg (★ 230,000) 133,809
Pinetown (★ Durban) 55,770
Port Elizabeth (★ 690,000) 272,844
PRETORIA (★ 960,000) 443,059
Randburg (★ Johannesburg) 74,347
Randfontein (★ Johannesburg) 43,763
Roodepoort-Maraisburg (★ Johannesburg) 141,764
Sandton (★ Johannesburg) 86,089
Soshanguve (★ Pretoria) 68,598
Soweto (★ Johannesburg) 521,948
Springs (★ Johannesburg) 68,235
Tembisa (★ Johannesburg) 149,282
Thabong (★ Welkom) 43,470
Uitenhage (★ Port Elizabeth) 54,987
Umlazi (★ Durban) 194,933
Vanderbijlpark (★ Vereeniging) 59,865
Vereeniging (★ 525,000) 60,584
Verwoerdburg (★ Pretoria) 49,891
Vosloosrus (★ Johannesburg) 52,061
Walvisbaai (Walvis Bay) (★ 16,607) 9,687
Welkom (★ 215,000) 54,488
Westonaria (★ Johannesburg) 46,523

SPAIN / España

1988 E 39,217,804
Alacant (Alicante) 261,051
Albacete 125,997
Alcalá de Guadaira 50,935
Alcalá de Henares (★ Madrid) 150,021
Alcobendas (★ Madrid) 73,455
Alcoi (Alcoy) 66,074
Alcorcón (★ Madrid) 139,796
Algeciras 99,528
Almería 157,644
Avilés (★ 131,000) 87,811
Badajoz (▲ 122,407) 106,400
Badalona (★ Barcelona) 225,229
Baracaldo (★ Bilbao) 113,502
Barcelona (★ 4,040,000) 1,714,355
Bilbao (★ 985,000) 384,733
Burgos 160,561
Cáceres 71,598
Cádiz (★ 240,000) 156,591
Cartagena (▲ 172,710) 70,000
Castelló de la Plana 131,809
Ciudad Real 56,300
Córdoba 302,301
Cornellà de Llobregat (★ Barcelona) 86,866
Coslada (★ Madrid) 68,765
Donostia (San Sebastián) (★ 285,000) 177,622
Dos Hermanas (▲ 68,456) 60,600
Elda 56,756
El Ferrol del Caudillo (★ 129,000) 86,503
El Prat de Llobregat (★ Barcelona) 64,193
El Puerto de Santa María (▲ 62,285) 49,900
Elx (Elche) (▲ 180,256) 158,300
Fuenlabrada (★ Madrid) 128,872
Gernika-Lumo (Guernica y Luno) (▲ 17,836) (1981 C) 12,214
Getafe (★ Madrid) 135,367
Gijón 262,156
Granada 263,334
Granollers (★ Barcelona) 49,045
Guadalajara 61,309
Huelva 137,826
Irún 54,886
Jaén 106,435
Jerez de la Frontera (▲ 183,007) 156,200
La Coruña 248,862
La Línea 60,956
Las Palmas de Gran Canaria (▲ 366,347) 319,000
Leganés (★ Madrid) 168,403
León (★ 159,000) 136,558
L'Hospitalet de Llobregat (★ Barcelona) 278,449
Linares 58,622
Lleida (Lérida) (▲ 109,795) 91,500
Logroño 119,038
Lugo (▲ 78,795) 68,700
• MADRID (★ 4,650,000) 3,102,846
Málaga 574,456
Manresa 65,607
Mataró 100,817
Mérida 52,368
Móstoles (★ Madrid) 181,648
Murcia (▲ 314,124) 149,800
Orense 106,042
Oviedo (▲ 190,073) 168,900
Palencia 76,692
Palma (▲ 314,608) 249,000
Pamplona 180,598
Parla (★ Madrid) 66,253
Portugalete (★ Bilbao) 57,813
Puertollano 52,284
Reus 83,800
Rubí (★ Barcelona) 48,807
Sabadell (★ Barcelona) 189,489
Salamanca 159,342
San Baudilio de Llobregat (★ Barcelona) 77,502
San Cristóbal de la Laguna (▲ 111,533) 25,900
San Fernando (★ Cádiz) 81,975
San Sebastián de los Reyes (★ Madrid) 51,653

C Census. E Official estimate. U Unofficial estimate.
• Largest city in country.

★ Population or designation of metropolitan area, including suburbs (see headnote).
▲ Population of an entire municipality, commune, or district, including rural area.

Santa Coloma de Gramanet (★ Barcelona) ... 136,042
Santa Cruz de Tenerife ... 215,228
Santander (▲ 190,795) ... 166,800
Santiago de Compostela (▲ 88,110) ... 68,800
Santurce-Antiguo (★ Bilbao) ... 52,334
Segovia ... 54,402
Sevilla (★ 945,000) ... 663,132
Talavera de la Reina ... 68,158
Tarragona (▲ 109,586) ... 63,500
Tarrasa (★ Barcelona) ... 161,410
Toledo ... 59,551
Torrejón de Ardoz (★ Madrid) ... 83,267
Torrent (★ València) ... 55,751
València (★ 1,270,000) ... 743,933
Valladolid ... 331,461
Vigo (▲ 271,128) ... 179,500
Vitoria (Gasteiz) ... 204,264
Zamora ... 62,047
Zaragoza ... 582,239

SPANISH NORTH AFRICA / Plazas de Soberanía en el Norte de África

1988 E ... 122,905

• Ceuta ... 67,188
Melilla ... 55,717

SRI LANKA

1986 E ... 16,117,000

Battaramulla (★ Colombo) (1981 C) ... 56,535
• COLOMBO (★ 2,050,000) ... 683,000
Dehiwala-Mount Lavinia (★ Colombo) ... 191,000
Galle ... 109,000
Jaffna ... 143,000
Kandy ... 130,000
Matale (1985 E) ... 57,000
Matara (1985 E) ... 57,000
Moratuwa (★ Colombo) ... 138,000
Negombo (1985 E) ... 76,000
Ratnapura (1985 E) ... 51,000
SRI JAYAWARDENEPURA (KOTTE) (★ Colombo) ... 104,000
Trincomalee (1985 E) ... 51,000

SUDAN / As-Sūdān

1983 C ... 20,564,364

Al-Fāshir (1973 C) ... 51,932
• AL-KHARṬŪM (★ 1,450,000) ... 476,218
Al-Kharṭūm Bahrī (★ Al-Kharṭūm) ... 341,146
Al-Qaḍārif (1973 C) ... 66,465
Al-Ubayyiḍ ... 140,000
'Atbarah ... 73,000
Būr Sūdān (Port Sudan) ... 206,727
Jūbā (1980 E) ... 116,000
Kassalā ... 143,000
Kūstī (1973 C) ... 65,257
Nyala (1973 C) ... 59,852
Umm Durmān (Omdurman) (★ Al-Kharṭūm) ... 526,287
Wad Madanī ... 141,000
Wāw (1980 E) ... 116,000

SURINAME

1988 E ... 392,000

• PARAMARIBO (★ 296,000) ... 241,000

SWAZILAND

1986 C ... 712,131

LOBAMBA ...
Manzini (★ 30,000) ... 18,084
• MBABANE ... 38,290

SWEDEN / Sverige

1990 E ... 8,527,036

Borås ... 101,231
Eskilstuna ... 89,460
Gävle (▲ 88,081) ... 67,500
Göteborg (★ 710,894) ... 431,840
Halmstad (▲ 79,362) ... 50,900
Helsingborg ... 108,359
Huddinge (★ Stockholm) ... 73,107
Järfälla (★ Stockholm) ... 56,386
Jönköping ... 110,860
Karlstad ... 76,120
Linköping ... 120,562
Luleå ... 67,903
Lund (★ Malmö) ... 86,412
Malmö (★ 445,000) ... 232,908
Mölndal (★ Göteborg) ... 51,767
Nacka (★ Stockholm) ... 63,114
Norrköping ... 119,921
Örebro ... 120,353
Södertälje (★ Stockholm) ... 81,460
Sollentuna (★ Stockholm) ... 50,606
Solna (★ Stockholm) ... 51,427
• STOCKHOLM (★ 1,449,972) ... 672,187
Sundsvall (▲ 93,404) ... 50,600
Täby (★ Stockholm) ... 56,553
Trollhättan ... 50,602
Tumba (★ Stockholm) ... 68,255
Umeå (▲ 90,004) ... 58,700
Uppsala ... 164,754
Västerås ... 118,386
Växjö (▲ 68,849) ... 45,500

SWITZERLAND / Schweiz / Suisse / Svizzera

1990 E ... 6,673,850

Aarau (★ 58,903) ... 15,881
Arbon (★ 41,639) ... 12,284
Baden (★ 71,769) ... 14,545
Basel (Bâle) (★ 575,000) ... 169,587
BERN (BERNE) (★ 298,363) ... 134,393
Biel (Bienne) (★ 83,133) ... 52,023
Fribourg (Freiburg) (★ 59,141) ... 33,962
Genève (Geneva) (★ 470,000) ... 165,404
Lausanne (★ 263,442) ... 122,600
Locarno (★ 42,350) ... 14,149
Lugano (★ 94,800) ... 26,055
Luzern (★ 163,026) ... 59,115
Neuchâtel (★ 66,457) ... 32,509
Sankt Gallen (★ 126,845) ... 73,191
Schaffhausen (★ 53,501) ... 33,956
Thun (★ 78,978) ... 37,707
Vevey (★ 65,074) ... 15,207
Winterthur (★ 108,918) ... 85,174
Zug (★ 68,698) ... 21,467
• Zürich (★ 870,000) ... 342,861

SYRIA / Sūrīyah

1988 E ... 11,338,000

Al-Ḥasakah (1981 C) ... 73,426
Al-Lādhiqīyah (Latakia) ... 249,000
Al-Qāmishlī ... 126,236
Ar-Raqqah ... 113,000
Dar'ā (1981 C) ... 49,534
Dārayyā (★ Dimashq) ... 53,204
Dayr az-Zawr ... 112,000
• DIMASHQ (DAMASCUS) (★ 1,950,000) ... 1,326,000
Dūmā (★ Dimashq) ... 66,130
Ḥalab (Aleppo) (★ 1,275,000) ... 1,261,000
Ḥamāh ... 222,000
Ḥimṣ ... 447,000
Idlib (1981 C) ... 51,682
Jaramānah (★ Dimashq) ... 96,681
Kābir aṣ Ṣaghīr ... 47,728
Madīnat ath Thawrah ... 58,151
Ṭarṭūs (1981 C) ... 52,589

TAIWAN / T'aiwan

1988 E ... 19,672,612

Changhua (▲ 206,603) ... 158,400
Chiai ... 254,875
Chilung ... 348,541
Chungho (★ T'aipei) ... 343,389
Chungli ... 247,639
Chutung ... 104,797
Fangshan (★ Kaohsiung) ... 276,259
Fengyüan (▲ 144,434) ... 115,300
Hsichih (★ T'aipei) (1980 C) ... 70,031
Hsinchu ... 309,899
Hsinchuang (★ T'aipei) ... 259,001
Hsintien (★ T'aipei) ... 205,094
Hualien ... 106,658
Ilan (▲ 81,751) (1980 C) ... 70,900
Kangshan (1980 C) ... 78,049
Kaohsiung (★ 1,845,000) ... 1,342,797
Lotung (1980 C) ... 57,925
Lukang (1980 C) ... 72,019
Miaoli (1980 C) ... 81,500
Nant'ou (1980 C) ... 84,038
P'ingchen (★ T'aipei) ... 134,925
P'ingtung (▲ 204,990) ... 167,600
Sanchung (★ T'aipei) ... 362,171
Shulin (★ T'aipei) (1980 C) ... 75,700
Tach'i (1980 C) ... 67,209
T'aichung ... 715,107
T'ainan ... 656,927
• T'AIPEI (★ 6,130,000) ... 2,637,100
T'aipeihsien (★ T'aipei) ... 506,220
T'aitung (▲ 109,358) ... 79,800
Taoyüan ... 220,255
T'oufen (1980 C) ... 66,536
T'uch'eng (★ T'aipei) ... 70,500
Yangmei (1980 C) ... 84,353
Yüanlin (▲ 116,936) ... 51,300
Yungho (★ T'aipei) ... 242,252
Yungkang (▲ 114,904) ... 59,600

TANZANIA

1984 E ... 21,062,000

Arusha ... 69,000
• DAR ES SALAAM ... 1,300,000
Dodoma ... 54,000
Iringa ... 67,000
Kigoma (1978 C) ... 50,044
Mbeya ... 93,000
Morogoro ... 72,000
Moshi ... 62,000
Mtwara (1978 C) ... 48,510
Mwanza (1978 C) ... 110,611
Tabora ... 87,000
Tanga ... 121,000
Ujiji (1967 C) ... 21,369
Zanzibar (1985 E) ... 133,000

THAILAND / Prathet Thai

1988 E ... 54,960,917

Chiang Mai ... 164,030
Chon Buri ... 47,286
Hat Yai ... 138,046
Khon Kaen ... 131,340
• KRUNG THEP (BANGKOK) (★ 7,025,000) (1989 E) ... 5,845,152
Nakhon Ratchasima ... 204,982
Nakhon Sawan ... 105,220
Nakhon Si Thammarat ... 72,407
Nonthaburi (★ Krung Thep) ... 218,354
Pattaya ... 56,402
Phitsanulok ... 77,675
Phra Nakhon Si Ayutthaya ... 60,847
Sakon Nakhon ... 25,110
Samut Prakan (★ Krung Thep) ... 73,327
Samut Sakhon ... 53,984
Saraburi ... 61,206
Songkhla ... 84,433
Trang ... 48,042
Ubon Ratchathani ... 100,374
Udon Thani ... 81,202
Yala ... 67,383

TOGO

1981 C ... 2,702,945

• LOMÉ (1984 E) ... 400,000

TOKELAU

1986 C ... 1,690

TONGA

1986 C ... 94,535

• NUKU'ALOFA ... 21,265

TRANSKEI

1987 E ... 3,081,770

• UMTATA (1978 E) ... 30,000

TRINIDAD AND TOBAGO

1990 C ... 1,234,388

• PORT OF SPAIN (★ 370,000) ... 50,878
San Fernando (★ 75,000) ... 30,092

TUNISIA / Tunis / Tunisie

1984 C ... 6,975,450

Ariana (★ Tunis) ... 98,655
Bardo (★ Tunis) ... 65,669
Ben Arous (★ Tunis) ... 52,105
Bizerte ... 94,509
Gabès ... 92,258
Gafsa ... 60,970
Hammam Lif (★ Tunis) ... 47,009
Houmt Essouk ... 92,269
Kairouan ... 72,254
Kasserine ... 47,606
La Goulette (★ Tunis) ... 61,609
Menzel Bourguiba ... 51,399
Sfax (★ 310,000) ... 231,911
Sousse (★ 160,000) ... 83,509
• TUNIS (★ 1,225,000) ... 596,654
Zarzis ... 49,063

TURKEY / Türkiye

1990 C ... 56,969,109

Adana ... 931,555
Adapazarı ... 174,353
Adıyaman ... 101,306
Afyon ... 98,618
Ağrı ... 57,837
Akhisar ... 74,002
Aksaray ... 92,038
Akşehir ... 51,669
Amasya ... 55,602
ANKARA (★ 2,650,000) ... 2,553,209
Antakya (Antioch) ... 124,443
Antalya ... 378,726
Aydın ... 106,603
Bafra ... 66,209
Balıkesir ... 171,967
Bandırma ... 77,211
Batman ... 148,121
Bilecik ... 23,050
Bolu ... 60,600
Burdur ... 56,095
Bursa ... 838,323
Çanakkale ... 53,887
Ceyhan ... 85,000
Çorlu ... 77,025
Çorum ... 116,260
Denizli ... 203,130
Diyarbakır ... 375,767
Edirne ... 102,325
Elazığ ... 211,720
Elbistan ... 55,114
Ereğli, Konya prov. ... 74,332
Ereğli, Zonguldak prov. ... 63,776
Erzincan ... 90,799
Erzurum ... 241,344
Eskişehir ... 413,305
Gaziantep ... 627,584
Gebze (★ İstanbul) ... 156,594
Gelibolu ... 18,052
Gemlik ... 50,212
Giresun ... 67,536
Gölcük ... 65,000
Gümüşhane ... 25,877
Hakkâri ... 30,261
İçel (Mersin) ... 420,750
İnegöl ... 71,095
İskenderun ... 156,198
Isparta ... 111,706
• İstanbul (★ 7,550,000) ... 6,748,435
İzmir (★ 1,900,000) ... 1,762,849
İzmit ... 254,768
Kadirli ... 55,193
Karabük ... 104,869
Karaman ... 76,682
Kars ... 79,496
Kastamonu ... 52,363
Kayseri ... 416,276
Kilis ... 81,469
Kırıkhan ... 69,323
Kırıkkale ... 203,666
Kırşehir ... 74,546
Kızıltepe ... 60,445
Konya ... 509,208
Kozan ... 54,934
Kütahya ... 131,286
Lüleburgaz ... 51,978
Malatya ... 276,666
Manisa ... 158,283
Maraş ... 229,066
Mardin ... 52,994
Muş ... 42,334
Nazilli ... 80,209
Nevşehir ... 52,514
Niğde ... 54,822
Nizip ... 58,259
Nusaybin ... 50,605
Ödemiş ... 511,110
Ordu ... 101,306
Osmaniye ... 122,315
Polatlı ... 61,026
Rize ... 51,586
Salihli ... 71,035
Samsun ... 301,412
Siirt ... 66,607
Silvan (Miyafarkin) ... 59,959
Sincan (★ Ankara) ... 92,262
Sinop ... 25,631
Sivas ... 219,122
Siverek ... 63,366
Söke ... 50,598
Soma ... 50,165
Tarsus ... 191,333
Tatvan ... 52,404
Tekirdağ ... 80,207
Tokat ... 83,174
Trabzon ... 144,805
Tunceli ... 24,584
Turgutlu ... 73,734
Turhal ... 71,406
Urfa ... 278,516
Uşak ... 104,980
Van ... 153,525
Viranşehir ... 58,394
Yalova (★ İstanbul) ... 72,874
Yarımca ... 64,526
Yozgat ... 51,360
Zonguldak (★ 220,000) ... 120,300

TURKS AND CAICOS ISLANDS

1990 C ... 12,350

• GRAND TURK ... 3,761

TUVALU

1979 C ... 7,349

• FUNAFUTI ... 2,191

UGANDA

1990 E ... 17,213,407

Jinja (1982 E) ... 55,000
• KAMPALA ... 1,008,707

UNION OF SOVIET SOCIALIST REPUBLICS / Sojuz Sovetskich Socialističeskich Respublik

1989 C ... 286,717,000

Abakan ... 154,000
Abovjan (1987 E) ... 53,000
Achtubinsk (1987 E) ... 53,000
Ačinsk ... 122,000
Akt'ubinsk ... 253,000
Alapajevsk (1987 E) ... 51,000
Alatyr' (1979 C) ... 45,313
Aleksandrija ... 103,000
Aleksandrov (1987 E) ... 66,000
Aleksin (1987 E) ... 72,000
Ali-Bajramly (1987 E) ... 51,000
Alma-Ata (★ 1,190,000) ... 1,128,000
Almalyk ... 114,000
Al'metjevsk ... 129,000
Amursk (1987 E) ... 54,000
Andižan ... 293,000
Angarsk ... 266,000
Angren ... 131,000
Antracit (★ Krasnyj Luč) (1987 E) ... 70,000
Anžero-Sudžensk ... 108,000
Apatity (1987 E) ... 80,000
Archangel'sk ... 416,000
Arkalyk (1987 E) ... 71,000
Armavir ... 161,000
Arsenjev (1987 E) ... 67,000
Art'om (1987 E) ... 73,000
Art'omovsk (1987 E) ... 91,000
Arzamas ... 109,000
Asbest (1987 E) ... 83,000
Aščabad ... 398,000
Astrachan' ... 509,000
Azov (1987 E) ... 81,000
Baku (★ 2,020,000) ... 1,150,000
Balakovo ... 198,000
Balašicha (★ Moskva) ... 136,000
Balašov (1987 E) ... 99,000
Balchaš (1987 E) ... 84,000
Baranoviči ... 159,000
Barnaul (★ 665,000) ... 602,000
Batajsk (★ Rostov-na-Donu) (1987 E) ... 98,000
Batumi ... 136,000
Bekabad (1987 E) ... 80,000
Belaja Cerkov' ... 197,000
Bel'cy ... 159,000
Belebej (1987 E) ... 51,000
Belgorod ... 300,000
Belgorod-Dnestrovskij (1987 E) ... 54,000
Belogorsk (1987 E) ... 71,000
Beloreck (1987 E) ... 75,000
Belovo (1987 E) ... 118,000
Bendery ... 130,000
Berd'ansk ... 132,000
Berdičev (1987 E) ... 89,000
Berdsk (★ Novosibirsk) (1987 E) ... 77,000
Berezniki ... 201,000
Ber'ozovskij (1987 E) ... 51,000
Bijsk ... 233,000
Birobidžan (1987 E) ... 82,000
Blagoveščensk ... 206,000
Bobrujsk ... 223,000
Bor (★ Nižnij Novgorod) (1987 E) ... 65,000
Borisoglebsk (1987 E) ... 69,000
Borisov ... 144,000
Boroviči (1987 E) ... 64,000
Br'anka (★ Stachanov) (1987 E) ... 65,000
Br'ansk ... 452,000
Bratsk ... 255,000
Brest ... 258,000
Brovary (★ Kijev) (1987 E) ... 73,000
Buchara ... 224,000
Bud'onnovsk (1987 E) ... 54,000
Bugul'ma (1987 E) ... 88,000
Buguruslan (1987 E) ... 53,000
Bujnaksk (1987 E) ... 53,000
Buzuluk (1987 E) ... 82,000
Čajkovskij (1987 E) ... 83,000
Čapajevsk (1987 E) ... 87,000
Čardžou ... 161,000
Čeboksary ... 420,000
Čechov (1987 E) ... 57,000
Čel'abinsk (★ 1,325,000) ... 1,143,000
Čelinograd ... 277,000
Čeremchovo (1987 E) ... 73,000
Čerepovec ... 310,000
Čerkassy ... 290,000
Čerkessk ... 113,000
Černigov ... 296,000
Černogorsk (1987 E) ... 80,000
Černovcy ... 257,000
Červonograd (1987 E) ... 71,000
Chabarovsk ... 601,000
Charcyzsk (★ Doneck) (1987 E) ... 69,000
Char'kov (★ 1,940,000) ... 1,611,000
Chasavjurt (1987 E) ... 74,000
Cherson ... 355,000
Chimki (★ Moskva) ... 133,000
Chmel'nickij ... 237,000
Chodžejli (1987 E) ... 55,000
Chodžent ... 160,000
Cholmsk (1987 E) ... 50,000
Čimkent ... 393,000
Čirčik (★ Taškent) ... 156,000
Čistopol' (1987 E) ... 65,000
Čita ... 366,000
Čusovoj (1987 E) ... 59,000
Denau (1987 E) ... 53,000
Derbent (1987 E) ... 83,000
Dimitrov (★ Krasnoarmejsk) (1987 E) ... 62,000
Dimitrovgrad ... 124,000

C Census. E Official estimate. U Unofficial estimate.
• Largest city in country.
★ Population or designation of metropolitan area, including suburbs (see headnote).
▲ Population of an entire municipality, commune, or district, including rural area.

Dmitrov (1987 E) 64,000
Dneprodzeržinsk (★ Dnepropetrovsk) 282,000
Dnepropetrovsk (★ 1,600,000) 1,179,000
Dolgoprudnyj (★ Moskva) (1987 E) 71,000
Domodedovo (★ Moskva) (1987 E) 51,000
Doneck (★ 2,200,000) 1,110,000
Drogobyč (1987 E) 76,000
Družkovka (★ Kramatorsk) (1987 E) 70,000
Dubna (1987 E) 64,000
Dušanbe 595,000
Džalal-Abad (1987 E) 74,000
Džambul 307,000
Džankoj (1987 E) 51,000
Dzeržinsk (★ Nižnij Novgorod) 285,000
Džezkazgan 109,000
Džizak 102,000
Ečmiadzin (★ Jerevan) (1987 E) 53,000
Ekibastuz 135,000
Elektrostal' 153,000
Elista (1987 E) 85,000
Engel's (★ Saratov) 182,000
Fastov (1987 E) 55,000
Feodosija (1987 E) 83,000
Fergana 200,000
Fr'azino (★ Moskva) (1987 E) 52,000
Frunze 616,000
Gatčina (★ Leningrad) (1987 E) 81,000
Georgijevsk (1987 E) 62,000
Georgiu-Dež (1987 E) 54,000
Gjandža 278,000
Gjandža 278,000
Glazov 104,000
Gomel' 500,000
Gori (1987 E) 62,000
Gorlovka (★ 710,000) 337,000
Gorno-Altajsk (1979 C) 39,917
Gr'azi (1979 C) 41,082
Grodno 270,000
Groznyj 401,000
Gubkin (1987 E) 75,000
Gukovo (1987 E) 72,000
Gulistan (1987 E) 51,000
Gurjev 149,000
Gus'-Chrustal'nyj (1987 E) 75,000
Iljičovsk (★ Odessa) (1987 E) 52,000
Inta (1987 E) 58,000
Irbit (1987 E) 53,000
Irkutsk 626,000
Išim (1987 E) 65,000
Išimbaj (1987 E) 67,000
Iskitim (1987 E) 69,000
Ivano-Frankovsk 214,000
Ivanovo 481,000
Ivantejevka (★ Moskva) (1987 E) 53,000
Iževsk 635,000
Izmail (1987 E) 90,000
Iz'um (1987 E) 63,000
Jakutsk 187,000
Jalta (1987 E) 89,000
Jangijul' (1987 E) 71,000
Jaroslavl' 633,000
Jefremov (1987 E) 58,000
Jegorjevsk (1987 E) 73,000
Jejsk (1987 E) 77,000
Jelec 120,000
Jenakijevo (★ Gorlovka) 121,000
Jerevan (★ 1,315,000) 1,199,000
Jessentuki (1987 E) 84,000
Jevpatorija 108,000
Joškar-Ola 242,000
Jurga (1987 E) 92,000
Južno-Sachalinsk 157,000
Kaliningrad (Königsberg) 401,000
Kaliningrad (★ Moskva) 160,000
Kaluga 312,000
Kaluš (1987 E) 67,000
Kamenec-Podol'skij 102,000
Kamensk-Šachtinskij (1987 E) 75,000
Kamensk-Ural'skij 209,000
Kamyšin 122,000
Kanaš (1987 E) 53,000
Kansk 110,000
Kara-Balta (1987 E) 55,000
Karaganda 614,000
Karši 156,000
Kaspijsk (1987 E) 61,000
Kattakurgan (1987 E) 63,000
Kazan' (★ 1,140,000) 1,094,000
Kemerovo 520,000
Kentau (1987 E) 60,000
Kerč' 174,000
Kijev (★ 2,900,000) 2,587,000
Kimry (1987 E) 61,000
Kinel' (1979 C) 40,873
Kinešma 105,000
Kiriši (1987 E) 51,000
Kirov 441,000
Kirovakan (1987 E) 169,000
Kirovo-Čepeck (1987 E) 89,000
Kirovograd 269,000
Kisel'ovsk (★ Prokopjevsk) 128,000
Kišin'ov 665,000
Kislovodsk 114,000
Kizel (1979 C) 40,157
Klimovsk (★ Moskva) (1987 E) 57,000
Klin (1987 E) 95,000
Klincy (1987 E) 72,000
Kokand 182,000
Kokčetav 137,000
Kol'čugino (1979 C) 43,686
Kolomna 162,000
Kolomyja (1987 E) 63,000
Kolpino (★ Leningrad) 142,000
Kommunarsk (★ Stachanov) 126,000
Komsomol'sk-na-Amure 315,000
Konotop (1987 E) 93,000
Konstantinovka 108,000
Kopejsk (★ Čel'abinsk) (1987 E) 99,000
Korkino (1981 E) 63,000
Korosten' (1987 E) 72,000
Korsakov (1979 C) 43,348
Kostroma 278,000
Kotlas (1987 E) 69,000
Kovel' (1987 E) 66,000
Kovrov 160,000
Kramatorsk (★ 465,000) 198,000
Krasnoarmejsk (★ 175,000) (1987 E) 70,000
Krasnodar 620,000
Krasnodon (1987 E) 52,000
Krasnogorsk (★ Moskva) (1987 E) 89,000
Krasnojarsk 912,000
Krasnokamensk (1987 E) 70,000
Krasnokamsk (1987 E) 58,000
Krasnoturjinsk (1987 E) 66,000
Krasnoufimsk (1979 C) 40,027
Krasnoural'sk (1979 C) 38,212
Krasnovodsk (1987 E) 59,000
Krasnyj Luč (★ 250,000) 113,000
Krasnyj Sulin (1979 C) 42,281
Kremenčug 236,000
Krivoj Rog 713,000
Kropotkin (1987 E) 73,000
Krymsk (1983 E) 50,000
Kstovo (★ (1987 E) 64,000
Kujbyšev (1987 E) 51,000
Kul'ab (1987 E) 71,000
Kumertau (1987 E) 62,000
Kungur (1987 E) 83,000
Kurgan 356,000
Kurgan-T'ube (1987 E) 55,000
Kursk 424,000
Kustanaj 224,000
Kušva (1979 C) 43,089
Kutaisi 235,000
Kuzneck (1987 E) 98,000
Kyzyl (1987 E) 80,000
Kzyl-Orda 153,000
Labinsk (1987 E) 58,000
Leninakan 120,000
Leningrad (★ 5,825,000) 4,456,000
Leninogorsk, Tatarskaja A. S. S. R. (1987 E) 61,000
Leninogorsk, Vostočno-Kazachstanskaja oblast' (1987 E) 69,000
Leninsk-Kuzneckij 165,000
Lida (1987 E) 81,000
Lipeck 450,000
Lisičansk (★ 410,000) 127,000
Livny (1987 E) 51,000
Lobn'a (★ Moskva) (1987 E) 59,000
Lozovaja (1987 E) 68,000
L'ubercy (★ Moskva) 165,000
Lubny (1987 E) 58,000
Luck 198,000
Lugansk 497,000
L'vov 790,000
Lys'va (1987 E) 77,000
Lytkarino (★ Moskva) (1987 E) 51,000
Machačkala 315,000
Magadan 152,000
Magnitogorsk 440,000
Majkop 149,000
Makejevka (★ Doneck) 430,000
Marganec (1987 E) 55,000
Margilan 125,000
Mariupol' (Ždanov) 517,000
Mary (1987 E) 89,000
Melitopol' 174,000
Meždurečensk 107,000
Miass 168,000
Michajlovka (1987 E) 58,000
Mičurinsk 109,000
Mineral'nyje Vody (1987 E) 75,000
Mingečaur (1987 E) 78,000
Minsk (★ 1,650,000) 1,589,000
Minusinsk (1987 E) 72,000
Mogil'ov 356,000
Molodečno (1987 E) 87,000
Mončegorsk (1987 E) 65,000
Moršansk (1987 E) 51,000
• MOSKVA (MOSCOW) (★ 13,100,000) 8,769,000
Mozyr' 101,000
Mukačevo (1987 E) 88,000
Murmansk 468,000
Murom 124,000
Mytišči (★ Moskva) 154,000
Naberežnyje Čelny 501,000
Nachičevan' (1987 E) 51,000
Nachodka 165,000
Nal'čik 235,000
Namangan 308,000
Naro-Fominsk (1987 E) 60,000
Navoi 107,000
Nazarovo (1987 E) 63,000
Nebit-Dag (1987 E) 85,000
Neftejugansk (1987 E) 86,000
Neftekamsk 107,000
Ner'ungri (1987 E) 68,000
Nevinnomyssk 121,000
Nežin (1987 E) 81,000
Nikolajev 503,000
Nikol'skij (1987 E) 64,000
Nikopol' 158,000
Nižnekamsk 191,000
Nižnevartovsk 242,000
Nižnij Novgorod (★ 2,025,000) 1,438,000
Nižnij Tagil 440,000
Noginsk 123,000
Nojabr'sk (1987 E) 77,000
Noril'sk 174,000
Novaja Kachovka (1987 E) 53,000
Novgorod 229,000
Novoaltajsk (★ Barnaul) (1987 E) 51,000
Novočeboksarsk 115,000
Novočerkassk 187,000
Novodvinsk (1987 E) 50,000
Novograd-Volynskij (1987 E) 52,000
Novokujbyševsk (★ Samara) 113,000
Novokuzneck 600,000
Novomoskovsk, Dnepropetrovsk oblast' (1987 E) 76,000
Novomoskovsk, Tula oblast' (★ 365,000) 146,000
Novopolock (1987 E) 90,000
Novorossijsk 186,000
Novošachtinsk 106,000
Novosibirsk (★ 1,600,000) 1,436,000
Novotroick 106,000
Novovolynsk (1987 E) 54,000
Novyj Urengoj (1987 E) 79,000
Nukus 169,000
Obninsk 100,000
Odessa (★ 1,185,000) 1,115,000
Odincovo (★ Moskva) 125,000
Okt'abr'skij 105,000
Omsk (★ 1,175,000) 1,148,000
Orechovo-Zujevo (★ 205,000) 137,000
Orenburg 547,000
Or'ol 337,000
Orša 123,000
Orsk 271,000
Oš 213,000
Osinniki (1987 E) 63,000
Partizansk (1979 C) 45,628
P'atigorsk 129,000
Pavlodar 331,000
Pavlograd 131,000
Pavlovo (1987 E) 72,000
Pavlovskij Posad (1987 E) 71,000
Pečora (1987 E) 64,000
Penza 543,000
Perm' (★ 1,160,000) 1,091,000
Pervomajsk (1987 E) 79,000
Pervoural'sk 142,000
Petrodvorec (★ Leningrad) (1987 E) 77,000
Petropavlovsk 241,000
Petropavlovsk-Kamčatskij 269,000
Petrozavodsk 270,000
Pinsk 119,000
Podol'sk (★ Moskva) 210,000
Polevskoj (1987 E) 71,000
Polock (1987 E) 80,000
Poltava 315,000
Poti (1977 E) 54,000
Priluki (1987 E) 73,000
Prochladnyj (1987 E) 53,000
Prokopjevsk (★ 410,000) 274,000
Prževal'sk (1987 E) 64,000
Pskov 204,000
Puškin (★ Leningrad) (1987 E) 97,000
Puškino (1987 E) 74,000
Ramenskoje (1987 E) 86,000
R'azan' 515,000
Razdan (1987 E) 56,000
Rečica (1987 E) 71,000
Reutov (★ Moskva) (1987 E) 68,000
Revda (1987 E) 66,000
Romny (1987 E) 53,000
Roslavl' (1987 E) 61,000
Rossoš' (1987 E) 55,000
Rostov-na-Donu (★ 1,165,000) 1,020,000
Roven'ki (1987 E) 68,000
Rovno 228,000
Rubcovsk 172,000
Rubežnoje (★ Lisičansk) (1987 E) 72,000
Rudnyj 124,000
Rustavi (★ Tbilisi) 159,000
Ruzajevka (1987 E) 53,000
Rybinsk 252,000
Rybnica (1987 E) 58,000
Ržev (1987 E) 70,000
Šachtinsk (1987 E) 62,000
Šacht'orsk (★ Torez) (1987 E) 73,000
Šachty 224,000
Šadrinsk (1987 E) 87,000
Safonovo (1987 E) 56,000
Salavat 150,000
Sal'sk (1987 E) 62,000
Samara (★ 1,505,000) 1,257,000
Samarkand 366,000
Saran' (1987 E) 64,000
Saransk 312,000
Sarapul 111,000
Saratov (★ 1,155,000) 905,000
Ščelkovo (★ Moskva) 109,000
Ščokino (1987 E) 70,000
Ščučinsk (1987 E) 53,000
Šeki (Nucha) (1987 E) 54,000
Semipalatinsk 334,000
Serov 104,000
Serpuchov 144,000
Sevastopol' 356,000
Ševčenko 159,000
Severodoneck (★ Lisičansk) 131,000
Severodvinsk 249,000
Severomorsk (1987 E) 55,000
Simferopol' 344,000
Slav'ansk (★ Kramatorsk) 135,000
Slav'ansk-Na-Kubani (1987 E) 57,000
Sluck (1987 E) 55,000
Smela (1987 E) 76,000
Smolensk 341,000
Snežnoje (★ Torez) (1987 E) 68,000
Soči 337,000
Sokol (1979 C) 45,424
Soligorsk (1987 E) 92,000
Solikamsk 110,000
Solncevo (★ Moskva) (1984 E) 62,000
Solnečnogorsk (★ Moskva) (1987 E) 53,000
Sosnovyj Bor (1987 E) 56,000
Šostka (1987 E) 87,000
Spassk-Dal'nij (1987 E) 60,000
Stachanov (★ 610,000) 112,000
Staryj Oskol 174,000
Stavropol' 318,000
Sterlitamak 248,000
Stryj (1987 E) 63,000
Stupino (1987 E) 73,000
Suchumi 121,000
Šuja (1987 E) 72,000
Sumgait (★ Baku) 231,000
Sumy 291,000
Surgut 248,000
Sverdlovsk, Sverdlovsk oblast' (★ 1,620,000) 1,367,000
Sverdlovsk, Vorosilovgrad oblast' (1987 E) 84,000
Svetlogorsk (1987 E) 68,000
Svetlovodsk (1987 E) 55,000
Svobodnyj (1987 E) 78,000
Syktyvkar 233,000
Syzran' 174,000
Taganrog 291,000
Taldy-Kurgan 119,000
Talnach (1987 E) 54,000
Tambov 305,000
Tašauz 112,000
Taškent (★ 2,325,000) 2,073,000
Tbilisi (★ 1,460,000) 1,260,000
Temirtau 212,000
Termez (1987 E) 72,000
Ternopol' 205,000
Tichoreck (1987 E) 67,000
Tichvin (1987 E) 70,000
Tiraspol' 182,000
Tobol'sk (1987 E) 82,000
Tokmak (1987 E) 71,000
Toljatti 630,000
Tomsk 502,000
Torez (★ 290,000) (1987 E) 88,000
Toržok (1987 E) 51,000
Troick (1987 E) 91,000
Tuapse (1987 E) 64,000
Tujmazy (1987 E) 54,000
Tula (★ 640,000) 540,000
Tulun (1987 E) 56,000
T'umen' 477,000
Turkestan (1987 E) 77,000
Tver' 451,000
Tyndinskij (1987 E) 61,000
Uchta 111,000
Ufa (★ 1,100,000) 1,083,000
Uglič (1979 C) 39,872
Ulan-Ude 353,000
Uljanovsk 625,000
Uman' (1987 E) 89,000
Ural'sk 200,000
Urgenč 128,000
Usolje-Sibirskoje 107,000
Ussurijsk 162,000
Ust'-Ilimsk 109,000
Ust'-Kamenogorsk 324,000
Ust'-Kut (1987 E) 58,000
Užgorod 117,000
Uzlovaja (★ Novomoskovsk) (1987 E) 63,000
V'az'ma (1987 E) 57,000
Velikije Luki 114,000
Verchn'aja Salda (1987 E) 56,000
Vičuga (1987 E) 51,000
Vinnica 374,000
Vitebsk 350,000
Vladikavkaz 300,000
Vladimir 350,000
Vladivostok 648,000
Volchov (1987 E) 51,000
Volgodonsk 176,000
Volgograd (Stalingrad) (★ 1,360,000) 999,000
Vologda 283,000
Vol'sk (1987 E) 66,000
Volžsk (1987 E) 60,000
Volžskij (★ Volgograd) 269,000
Vorkuta 116,000
Voronež 887,000
Voskresensk (1987 E) 80,000
Votkinsk 103,000
Vyborg (1987 E) 81,000
Vyksa (1987 E) 60,000
Vyšnij Voločok (1987 E) 70,000
Zagorsk 115,000
Žanatas (1987 E) 53,000
Zaporožje 884,000
Zelenograd (★ Moskva) 158,000
Železnodorožnyj (★ Moskva) (1987 E) 90,000
Železnogorsk (1987 E) 81,000
Zel'onodol'sk (1987 E) 93,000
Žigulevsk (1977 E) 50,000
Zima (1987 E) 51,000
Žitomir 292,000
Zlatoust 208,000
Žlobin (1987 E) 52,000
Žodino (1987 E) 51,000
Žoltyje Vody (1987 E) 61,000
Žukovskij 101,000
Zyr'anovsk (1987 E) 55,000

UNITED ARAB EMIRATES / Al-Imārāt al-ʿArabīyah Al-Muttaḥidah

1980 C 980,000

ABŪ ẒABY (ABU DHABI) 242,975
Al-ʿAyn 101,663
Ash-Shāriqah 125,149
• Dubayy 265,702
Ra's al-Khaymah 42,000

UNITED KINGDOM

1981 C 55,678,079

UNITED KINGDOM: ENGLAND

1981 C 46,220,955

Aldershot (★ London) 53,665
Ashton-under-Lyne (★ Manchester) 43,605
Aylesbury 51,999
Barnsley 76,783
Barrow-in-Furness 50,174
Basildon (★ London) 94,800
Basingstoke 73,027
Bath 84,283
Bebington (★ Liverpool) 62,618
Bedford 75,632
Beeston and Stapleford (★ Nottingham) 64,785
Benfleet (★ London) 50,783
Birkenhead (★ Liverpool) 99,075
Birmingham (★ 2,675,000) 1,013,995
Blackburn (★ 221,900) 109,564
Blackpool (★ 280,000) 146,297
Bognor Regis 50,323
Bolton (★ Manchester) 143,960
Bootle 70,860
Bournemouth (★ 315,000) 142,829
Bracknell (★ London) 52,257
Bradford (★ Leeds) 293,336
Brentwood (★ London) 51,212
Brighton (★ 420,000) 134,581
Bristol (★ 630,000) 413,861
Burnley (★ 160,000) 76,365
Burton upon Trent 59,040
Bury (★ Manchester) 61,785
Bury Saint Edmunds 30,563
Camberley see Frimley and Camberley
Cambridge 87,111
Cannock (★ Birmingham) 54,503
Canterbury 34,546
Carlisle 72,206
Carlton (★ Nottingham) 46,053
Chatham (★ London) 65,835
Cheadle and Gatley (★ Manchester) 59,478
Chelmsford (★ London) 91,109
Cheltenham 87,188
Cheshunt (★ London) 49,616
Chester 80,154
Chesterfield (★ 127,000) 73,352
Clacton-on-Sea 39,618
Colchester 87,476
Corby 48,704
Coventry (★ 645,000) 318,718
Crawley (★ London) 80,113
Crewe 59,097
Crosby (★ Liverpool) 54,103
Darlington 85,519
Dartford (★ London) 62,032
Derby (★ 275,000) 218,026
Dewsbury (★ Leeds) 49,612
Doncaster 74,727
Dover 33,461
Dudley (★ Birmingham) 186,513
Dunstable (★ Luton) 48,436
Durham 38,105
Eastbourne 86,715
Eastleigh (★ Southampton) 58,585
Ellesmere Port (★ Liverpool) 65,829
Epsom and Ewell (★ London) 65,830
Esher / Molesey (★ London) 46,688
Exeter 88,235
Fareham / Portchester (★ Portsmouth) 55,563
Farnborough (★ London) 48,063
Folkestone 42,949
Frimley and Camberley (★ London) 45,108
Gateshead (★ Newcastle) 91,429
Gillingham (★ London) 92,531
Gloucester (★ 115,000) 106,526
Gosport (★ Portsmouth) 69,664
Gravesend (★ London) 53,450
Grays (★ London) 45,881
Greasby / Moreton (★ Liverpool) 56,410
Great Yarmouth 54,777

C Census. E Official estimate. U Unofficial estimate.
• Largest city in country.

★ Population or designation of metropolitan area, including suburbs (see headnote).
▲ Population of an entire municipality, commune, or district, including rural area.

Grimsby (★ 145,000) 91,532
Guildford (★ London) 61,509
Halesowen (★ Birmingham) 57,533
Halifax 76,675
Harlow (★ London) 79,150
Harrogate 63,637
Hartlepool (★ Middlesbrough) 91,749
Hastings 74,979
Havant (★ Portsmouth) 50,098
Hemel Hempstead (★ London) 80,110
Hereford 48,277
Hertford (★ London) 21,350
High Wycombe (▲ 156,800) 69,575
Hove (★ Brighton) 65,587
Huddersfield (▲ 377,400) 147,825
Huyton-with-Roby (★ Liverpool) 62,011
Ipswich 129,661
Keighley (★ Leeds) 49,188
Kidderminster 50,385
Kingston upon Hull (★ 350,000) 322,144
Kingswood (★ Bristol) 54,736
Kirkby (★ Liverpool) 52,825
Lancaster 43,902
Leeds (★ 1,540,000) 445,242
Leicester (★ 495,000) 324,394
Lincoln 79,980
Littlehampton 46,028
Liverpool (★ 1,525,000) 538,809
• LONDON (★ 11,100,000) 6,574,009
Loughborough 44,895
Lowestoft 59,430
Luton (★ 220,000) 163,209
Macclesfield 47,525
Maidenhead (★ London) 59,809
Maidstone 86,067
Manchester (★ 2,775,000) 437,612
Mansfield (★ 198,000) 71,325
Margate 53,137
Middlesbrough (★ 580,000) 158,516
Middleton (★ Manchester) 51,373
Milton Keynes 36,886
Newcastle-under-Lyme (★ Stoke-on-Trent) 73,208
Newcastle upon Tyne (★ 1,300,000) 199,064
Northampton 154,172
Norwich (★ 230,000) 169,814
Nottingham (★ 655,000) 273,300
Nuneaton (★ Coventry) 60,337
Oldbury / Smethwick (★ Birmingham) 153,268
Oldham (★ Manchester) 107,095
Oxford (★ 230,000) 113,847
Penzance 18,501
Peterborough 113,404
Plymouth (★ 290,000) 238,583
Poole (★ Bournemouth) 122,815
Portsmouth (★ 485,000) 174,218
Preston (★ 250,000) 166,675
Ramsgate 36,678
Reading (★ 200,000) 194,727
Redditch (★ Birmingham) 61,639
Reigate / Redhill (★ London) 48,241
Rochdale (★ Manchester) 97,292
Rotherham (★ Sheffield) 122,374
Royal Leamington Spa (★ Coventry) 56,552
Royal Tunbridge Wells 57,699
Rugby 59,039
Runcorn (★ Liverpool) 63,995
Saint Albans (★ London) 76,709
Saint Helens 114,397
Sale (★ Manchester) 57,872
Salford (★ Manchester) 96,525
Salisbury 36,890
Scarborough 36,665
Scunthorpe 79,043
Sheffield (★ 710,000) 470,685
Shrewsbury 57,731
Slough (★ London) 106,341
Solihull (★ Birmingham) 93,940
Southampton (★ 415,000) 211,321
Southend-on-Sea (★ London) 155,720
Southport (★ Liverpool) 88,596
South Shields (★ Newcastle) 86,488
Stafford 60,915
Staines (★ London) 51,949
Stapleford see Beeston and Stapleford
Stevenage 74,757
Stockport (★ Manchester) 135,489
Stockton-on-Tees (★ Middlesbrough) 86,699
Stoke-on-Trent (★ 440,000) 272,446
Stourbridge (★ Birmingham) 55,136
Stratford-upon-Avon 20,941
Stretford (★ Manchester) 47,522
Sunderland (★ Newcastle) 195,064
Sutton Coldfield (★ Birmingham) 102,572
Swindon 127,348
Tamworth 63,260
Taunton 47,793
Torquay (★ 112,400) 54,430
Wakefield (★ Leeds) 74,764
Wallasey (★ Liverpool) 62,465
Walsall (★ Birmingham) 177,923
Walton and Weybridge (★ London) 50,031
Warrington 81,366
Washington (★ Newcastle) 48,856
Waterlooville (★ Portsmouth) 57,296
Watford (★ London) 109,503
West Bromwich (★ Birmingham) 153,725
Weston-super-Mare 60,821
Weybridge see Walton and Weybridge
Widnes 55,973
Wigan (★ Manchester) 88,725
Woking (★ London) 92,667
Wolverhampton (★ Birmingham) 263,501
Worcester 75,466
Worthing (★ Brighton) 90,687
York (★ 145,000) 123,126

UNITED KINGDOM: NORTHERN IRELAND

1987 E 1,575,200

Bangor (★ Belfast) 70,700
Belfast (★ 685,000) 303,800
Castlereagh (★ Belfast) 57,900
Londonderry (★ 97,200) 97,500
Lurgan (★ 63,000) (1981 C) 20,991
Newtownabbey (★ Belfast) 72,300

UNITED KINGDOM: SCOTLAND

1989 E 5,090,700

Aberdeen 210,700
Ayr (★ 100,000) (1981 C) 48,493
Clydebank (★ Glasgow) (1981 C) 51,832
Coatbridge (1981 C) 50,831
Cumbernauld (★ Glasgow) 50,300
Dundee 172,540
Dunfermline (★ 125,817) (1981 C) 52,105
East Kilbride (★ Glasgow) 69,500
Edinburgh (★ 630,000) 433,200
Falkirk (★ 148,171) (1981 C) 36,372
Glasgow (★ 1,800,000) 695,630
Greenock (★ 101,000) (1981 C) 58,436
Hamilton (★ Glasgow) (1981 C) 51,666
Irvine (★ 94,000) 55,900
Kilmarnock (★ 84,000) (1981 C) 51,799
Kirkcaldy (★ 148,171) (1981 C) 46,356
Motherwell (★ Glasgow) (1981 C) 30,616
Paisley (★ Glasgow) (1981 C) 84,330
Perth (1981 C) 41,916
Stirling (★ 61,000) (1981 C) 36,640

UNITED KINGDOM: WALES

1981 C 2,790,462

Cardiff (★ 625,000) 262,313
Cwmbran (★ Newport) 44,592
Llanelli 45,336
Merthyr Tydfil 38,893
Neath (★ Swansea) 48,687
Newport (★ 310,000) 115,896
Pontypool (★ Newport) 36,064
Port Talbot (★ 130,000) 40,078
Rhondda (★ Cardiff) 70,980
Swansea (★ 275,000) 172,433
Wrexham 39,929

UNITED STATES

1990 C 248,709,873

UNITED STATES: ALABAMA

1990 C 4,040,587

Anniston (★ 116,034) 26,623
Auburn 33,830
Birmingham (★ 907,810) 265,968
Decatur (★ 131,556) 48,761
Dothan (★ 130,964) 53,589
Florence (★ 131,327) 36,426
Gadsden (★ 99,840) 42,523
Huntsville (★ 238,912) 159,789
Mobile (★ 476,923) 196,278
Montgomery (★ 292,517) 187,106
Tuscaloosa (★ 150,522) 77,759

UNITED STATES: ALASKA

1990 C 550,043

Anchorage (★ 226,338) 226,338
Fairbanks 30,843
Juneau 26,751

UNITED STATES: ARIZONA

1990 C 3,665,228

Chandler (★ Phoenix) 90,533
Glendale (★ Phoenix) 148,134
Mesa (★ Phoenix) 288,091
Nogales 19,489
Phoenix (★ 2,122,101) 900,013
Scottsdale (★ Phoenix) 130,069
Sun City (★ Phoenix) 57,000
Tempe (★ Phoenix) 141,865
Tucson (★ 666,880) 405,390
Yuma (★ 106,895) 54,923

UNITED STATES: ARKANSAS

1990 C 2,350,725

Fayetteville (★ 113,409) 42,099
Fort Smith (★ 175,911) 72,798
Hot Springs National Park 32,462
Jonesboro 46,535
Little Rock (★ 513,117) 175,795
North Little Rock (★ Little Rock) 61,741
Pine Bluff (★ 85,487) 57,140

UNITED STATES: CALIFORNIA

1990 C 29,760,021

Alameda (★ San Francisco) 76,459
Alhambra (★ Los Angeles) 82,106
Anaheim (★ Los Angeles) 266,406
Arden (★ Sacramento) 62,900
Bakersfield (★ 543,477) 174,820
Baldwin Park (★ Los Angeles) 69,330
Bellflower (★ Los Angeles) 61,815
Berkeley (★ San Francisco) 102,724
Buena Park (★ Los Angeles) 68,784
Burbank (★ Los Angeles) 93,643
Calexico 18,633
Carmichael (★ Sacramento) 56,600
Carson (★ Los Angeles) 83,995
Cerritos (★ Los Angeles) 53,240
Chico (★ 182,120) 40,079
Chino (★ Los Angeles) 59,682
Chula Vista (★ San Diego) 135,163
Citrus Heights (★ Sacramento) 112,800
Compton (★ Los Angeles) 90,454
Concord (★ San Francisco) 111,348
Costa Mesa (★ Los Angeles) 96,357
Cucamonga (★ Los Angeles) 101,409
Daly City (★ San Francisco) 92,311
Downey (★ Los Angeles) 91,444
East Los Angeles (★ Los Angeles) 126,379
El Cajon (★ San Diego) 88,693
El Monte (★ Los Angeles) 106,209
Escondido (★ San Diego) 108,635
Eureka 27,025
Fairfield (★ San Francisco) 77,211
Fontana (★ Los Angeles) 87,535
Fountain Valley (★ Los Angeles) 53,691
Fremont (★ San Francisco) 173,339
Fresno (★ 667,490) 354,202
Fullerton (★ Los Angeles) 114,144
Gardena (★ Los Angeles) 49,847
Garden Grove (★ Los Angeles) 143,050
Glendale (★ Los Angeles) 180,038
Hacienda Heights (★ Los Angeles) 58,200
Hawthorne (★ Los Angeles) 71,349
Hayward (★ San Francisco) 111,498
Hemet (★ Los Angeles) 36,094
Huntington Beach (★ Los Angeles) 181,519
Huntington Park (★ Los Angeles) 56,065
Inglewood (★ Los Angeles) 109,602
Irvine (★ Los Angeles) 110,330
Lakewood (★ Los Angeles) 73,557
La Mesa (★ San Diego) 52,931
Lancaster (★ Los Angeles) 97,291
Livermore (★ San Francisco) 56,741
Lompoc (★ Santa Barbara) 37,649
Long Beach (★ Los Angeles) 429,433
Los Angeles (★ 14,531,529) 3,485,398
Lynwood (★ Los Angeles) 61,945
Merced (★ 178,403) 56,216
Mission Viejo (★ Los Angeles) 72,820
Modesto (★ 370,522) 164,730
Montebello (★ Los Angeles) 59,564
Monterey (★ Salinas) 31,954
Monterey Park (★ Los Angeles) 60,738
Mountain View (★ San Francisco) 67,460
Napa (★ San Francisco) 61,842
National City (★ San Diego) 54,249
Newport Beach (★ Los Angeles) 66,643
Norwalk (★ Los Angeles) 94,279
Oakland (★ San Francisco) 372,242
Oceanside (★ San Diego) 128,398
Ontario (★ Los Angeles) 133,179
Orange (★ Los Angeles) 110,658
Oxnard (★ Los Angeles) 142,216
Palm Springs (★ Los Angeles) 40,181
Palo Alto (★ San Francisco) 55,900
Pasadena (★ Los Angeles) 131,591
Pico Rivera (★ Los Angeles) 59,177
Pomona (★ Los Angeles) 131,723
Porterville (★ Visalia) 29,563
Rancho Cordova (★ Sacramento) 56,200
Redding (★ 147,036) 66,462
Redlands (★ Los Angeles) 60,394
Redondo Beach (★ Los Angeles) 60,167
Redwood City (★ San Francisco) 66,072
Richmond (★ San Francisco) 87,425
Riverside (★ Los Angeles) 226,505
Sacramento (★ 1,481,102) 369,365
Salinas (★ 355,660) 108,777
San Bernardino (★ Los Angeles) 164,164
San Diego (★ 2,949,000) 1,110,549
San Francisco (★ 6,253,311) 723,959
San Jose (★ San Francisco) 782,248
San Leandro (★ San Francisco) 68,223
San Mateo (★ San Francisco) 85,486
Santa Ana (★ Los Angeles) 293,742
Santa Barbara (★ 369,608) 85,571
Santa Clara (★ San Francisco) 93,613
Santa Cruz (★ San Francisco) 49,040
Santa Maria (★ Santa Barbara) 61,284
Santa Monica (★ Los Angeles) 86,905
Santa Rosa (★ San Francisco) 113,313
Santee (★ San Diego) 52,902
Simi Valley (★ Los Angeles) 100,217
South Gate (★ Los Angeles) 86,284
South San Francisco (★ San Francisco) 54,312
Stockton (★ 480,628) 210,943
Sunnyvale (★ San Francisco) 117,229
Thousand Oaks (★ Los Angeles) 104,352
Torrance (★ Los Angeles) 133,107
Upland (★ Los Angeles) 63,374
Vacaville (★ San Francisco) 71,479
Vallejo (★ San Francisco) 109,199
Ventura (San Buenaventura) (★ Los Angeles) 92,575
Visalia (★ 311,921) 75,636
Walnut Creek (★ San Francisco) 60,569
Watsonville (★ San Francisco) 31,099
West Covina (★ Los Angeles) 96,086
Westminster (★ Los Angeles) 78,118
Whittier (★ Los Angeles) 77,671
Yuba City (★ 122,643) 27,437

UNITED STATES: COLORADO

1990 C 3,294,394

Arvada (★ Denver) 89,235
Aurora (★ Denver) 222,103
Boulder (★ Denver) 83,312
Colorado Springs (★ 397,014) 281,140
Denver (★ 1,848,319) 467,610
Fort Collins (★ 186,136) 87,758
Grand Junction 29,034
Greeley (★ 131,821) 60,536
Lakewood (★ Denver) 126,481
Longmont (★ Denver) 51,555
Loveland (★ Fort Collins) 37,352
Pueblo (★ 123,051) 98,640
Westminster (★ Denver) 74,625

UNITED STATES: CONNECTICUT

1990 C 3,287,116

Bridgeport (★ New York, N.Y.) 141,686
Bristol (★ Hartford) 60,640
Danbury (★ New York, N.Y.) 65,585
East Hartford (★ Hartford) 50,452
Fairfield (★ New York, N.Y.) 52,400
Greenwich (★ New York, N.Y.) 58,000
Hamden (★ New Haven) 53,100
Hartford (★ 1,085,837) 139,739
Manchester (★ Hartford) 51,000
Meriden (★ New Haven) 59,479
Milford (★ New York, N.Y.) 48,168
New Britain (★ Hartford) 75,491
New Haven (★ 530,180) 130,474
New London (★ 266,819) 28,540
Norwalk (★ New York, N.Y.) 78,331
Stamford (★ New York, N.Y.) 108,056
Stratford (★ New York, N.Y.) 50,400
Torrington 33,687
Waterbury (★ 221,629) 108,961
West Hartford (★ Hartford) 59,100
West Haven (★ New Haven) 54,021

UNITED STATES: DELAWARE

1990 C 666,168

Dover 27,630
Wilmington (★ Philadelphia, Pa.) 71,529

UNITED STATES: DISTRICT OF COLUMBIA

1990 C 606,900

WASHINGTON (★ 3,923,574) 606,900

UNITED STATES: FLORIDA

1990 C 12,937,926

Boca Raton (★ West Palm Beach) 61,492
Carol City (★ Miami) 52,800
City of Sunrise (★ Miami) 64,407
Clearwater (★ Tampa) 98,784
Daytona Beach (★ 370,712) 61,921
De Land (★ Daytona Beach) 16,491
Fort Lauderdale (★ Miami) 149,377
Fort Myers (★ 335,113) 45,206
Fort Pierce (★ 251,071) 36,830
Fort Walton Beach (★ 143,776) 21,471
Gainesville (★ 204,111) 84,770
Hialeah (★ Miami) 188,004
Hollywood (★ Miami) 121,697
Jacksonville (★ 906,727) 635,230
Kendall (★ Miami) 53,100
Lakeland (★ 405,382) 70,576
Largo (★ Tampa) 65,674
Melbourne (★ 398,978) 59,646
Miami (★ 3,192,582) 358,548
Miami Beach (★ Miami) 92,639
Naples (★ 152,099) 19,505
Ocala (★ 194,833) 42,045
Orlando (★ 1,072,748) 164,693
Panama City (★ 126,994) 34,378
Pensacola (★ 344,406) 58,165
Plantation (★ Miami) 66,692
Pompano Beach (★ Miami) 72,411
Saint Petersburg (★ Tampa) 238,629
Sarasota (★ 277,776) 50,961
Tallahassee (★ 233,598) 124,773
Tampa (★ 2,067,959) 280,015
Venice (★ Sarasota) 16,922
West Palm Beach (★ 863,518) 67,643
Winter Haven (★ Lakeland) 24,725

UNITED STATES: GEORGIA

1990 C 6,478,216

Albany (★ 112,561) 78,122
Athens (★ 156,267) 45,734
Atlanta (★ 2,833,511) 394,017
Augusta (★ 396,809) 44,639
Columbus (★ 243,072) 178,681
Macon (★ 281,103) 106,612
Rome 30,326
Savannah (★ 242,622) 137,560
Valdosta 39,806
Warner Robins (★ Macon) 43,726

C Census. E Official estimate. U Unofficial estimate.
• Largest city in country.

★ Population or designation of metropolitan area, including suburbs (see headnote).
▲ Population of an entire municipality, commune, or district, including rural area.

World Populations

UNITED STATES: HAWAII

1990 C 1,108,229

Hilo 37,808
Honolulu (★ 836,231) 365,272

UNITED STATES: IDAHO

1990 C 1,006,749

Boise (★ 205,775) 125,738
Idaho Falls 43,929
Lewiston 28,082
Nampa 28,365
Pocatello 46,080

UNITED STATES: ILLINOIS

1990 C 11,430,602

Arlington Heights (★ Chicago) 75,460
Aurora (★ Chicago) 99,581
Bloomington (★ 129,180) 51,972
Champaign (★ 173,025) 63,502
Chicago (★ 8,065,633) 2,783,726
Cicero (★ Chicago) 67,436
Danville 33,828
Decatur (★ 117,206) 83,885
De Kalb 34,925
Des Plaines (★ Chicago) 53,223
East Saint Louis (★ Saint Louis, Mo.) 40,944
Elgin (★ Chicago) 77,010
Evanston (★ Chicago) 73,233
Galesburg 33,530
Joliet (★ Chicago) 76,836
Kankakee (★ 96,255) 27,575
Mount Prospect (★ Chicago) 53,170
Naperville (★ Chicago) 85,351
Oak Lawn (★ Chicago) 56,182
Oak Park (★ Chicago) 53,648
Peoria (★ 339,172) 113,504
Quincy 39,681
Rockford (★ 283,719) 139,426
Schaumburg (★ Chicago) 68,586
Skokie (★ Chicago) 59,432
Springfield (★ 189,550) 105,227
Waukegan (★ Chicago) 69,392
Wheaton (★ Chicago) 51,464

UNITED STATES: INDIANA

1990 C 5,544,159

Anderson (★ 130,669) 59,459
Bloomington (★ 108,978) 60,633
Columbus 31,802
Elkhart (★ 156,198) 43,627
Evansville (★ 278,990) 126,272
Fort Wayne (★ 363,811) 173,072
Gary (★ Chicago, Il.) 116,646
Hammond (★ Chicago, Il.) 84,236
Indianapolis (★ 1,249,822) 731,327
Kokomo (★ 96,946) 44,962
Lafayette (★ 130,598) 43,764
Marion 32,618
Michigan City 33,822
Muncie (★ 119,659) 71,035
Richmond 38,705
South Bend (★ 247,052) 105,511
Terre Haute (★ 130,812) 57,483

UNITED STATES: IOWA

1990 C 2,776,755

Ames 47,198
Cedar Rapids (★ 168,767) 108,751
Clinton 29,201
Council Bluffs (★ Omaha) 54,315
Davenport (★ 350,861) 95,333
Des Moines (★ 392,928) 193,187
Dubuque (★ 86,403) 57,546
Iowa City (★ 96,119) 59,738
Mason City 29,040
Sioux City (★ 115,018) 80,505
Waterloo (★ 146,611) 66,467

UNITED STATES: KANSAS

1990 C 2,477,574

Hutchinson 39,308
Kansas City (★ Kansas City, Mo.) 149,767
Lawrence (★ 81,798) 65,608
Manhattan 37,712
Olathe (★ Kansas City, Mo.) 63,352
Overland Park (★ Kansas City, Mo.) 111,790
Salina 42,303
Topeka (★ 160,976) 119,883
Wichita (★ 485,270) 304,011

UNITED STATES: KENTUCKY

1990 C 3,685,296

Bowling Green 40,641
Covington (★ Cincinnati, Oh.) 43,264
Frankfort 25,968
Lexington (★ 348,428) 225,366
Louisville (★ 952,662) 269,063
Owensboro (★ 87,189) 53,549
Paducah 27,256

UNITED STATES: LOUISIANA

1990 C 4,219,973

Alexandria (★ 131,556) 49,188
Baton Rouge (★ 528,264) 219,531
Bossier City (★ Shreveport) 52,721
Houma (★ 182,842) 96,982
Kenner (★ New Orleans) 72,033
Lafayette (★ 208,740) 94,440
Lake Charles (★ 168,134) 70,580
Metairie (★ New Orleans) 149,428
Monroe (★ 142,191) 54,909
New Iberia 31,828
New Orleans (★ 1,238,816) 496,938
Shreveport (★ 334,341) 198,525

UNITED STATES: MAINE

1990 C 1,227,928

Augusta 21,325
Bangor (★ 88,745) 33,181
Lewiston (★ 88,141) 39,757
Portland (★ 215,281) 64,358

UNITED STATES: MARYLAND

1990 C 4,781,468

Annapolis (★ Baltimore) 33,187
Baltimore (★ 2,382,172) 736,014
Bethesda (★ Washington, D.C.) 62,936
Columbia 75,883
Cumberland (★ 101,643) 23,706
Dundalk (★ Baltimore) 65,800
Hagerstown (★ 121,393) 35,445
Salisbury 20,592
Silver Spring (★ Washington, D.C.) 76,200
Towson (★ Baltimore) 49,445
Wheaton (★ Washington, D.C.) 58,300

UNITED STATES: MASSACHUSETTS

1990 C 6,016,425

Amherst 17,773
Boston (★ 4,171,643) 574,283
Brockton (★ Boston) 92,788
Brookline (★ Boston) 54,718
Cambridge (★ Boston) 95,802
Chicopee (★ Springfield) 56,632
Fall River (★ Providence) 92,703
Fitchburg (★ 102,797) 41,194
Framingham (★ Boston) 64,989
Lawrence (★ Boston) 70,207
Lowell (★ Boston) 103,439
Lynn (★ Boston) 81,245
Malden (★ Boston) 53,884
Medford (★ Boston) 57,407
New Bedford (★ 175,641) 99,922
Newton (★ Boston) 82,585
Northampton (★ Springfield) 29,289
Pittsfield (★ 79,250) 48,622
Quincy (★ Boston) 84,985
Somerville (★ Boston) 76,210
Springfield (★ 529,519) 156,983
Taunton 49,832
Waltham (★ Boston) 57,878
Weymouth (★ Boston) 54,063
Worcester (★ 436,905) 169,759

UNITED STATES: MICHIGAN

1990 C 9,295,297

Ann Arbor (★ Detroit) 109,592
Battle Creek (★ 135,982) 53,540
Benton Harbor (★ 161,378) 12,818
Clinton Township (★ Detroit) 77,900
Dearborn (★ Detroit) 89,286
Dearborn Heights (★ Detroit) 60,838
Detroit (★ 4,665,236) 1,027,974
East Lansing (★ Lansing) 50,677
Farmington Hills (★ Detroit) 74,652
Flint (★ 430,459) 140,761
Grand Rapids (★ 688,399) 189,126
Holland (★ Grand Rapids) 30,745
Jackson (★ 149,756) 37,446
Kalamazoo (★ 223,411) 80,277
Lansing (★ 432,674) 127,321
Livonia (★ Detroit) 100,850
Monroe (★ Detroit) 22,902
Muskegon (★ 158,983) 40,283
Pontiac (★ Detroit) 71,166
Port Huron (★ Detroit) 33,694
Redford Township (★ Detroit) 54,387
Roseville (★ Detroit) 51,412
Royal Oak (★ Detroit) 65,410
Saginaw (★ 399,320) 69,512
Saint Clair Shores (★ Detroit) 68,107
Sault Sainte Marie 14,689
Southfield (★ Detroit) 75,728
Sterling Heights (★ Detroit) 117,810
Taylor (★ Detroit) 70,811
Troy (★ Detroit) 72,884
Warren (★ Detroit) 144,864
Westland (★ Detroit) 84,724
Wyoming (★ Grand Rapids) 63,891

UNITED STATES: MINNESOTA

1990 C 4,375,099

Bloomington (★ Minneapolis) 86,335
Brooklyn Park (★ Minneapolis) 56,381
Duluth (★ 239,971) 85,493
Mankato 31,477
Minneapolis (★ 2,464,124) 368,383
Rochester (★ 106,470) 70,745
Saint Cloud (★ 190,921) 48,812
Saint Paul (★ Minneapolis) 272,235

UNITED STATES: MISSISSIPPI

1990 C 2,573,216

Biloxi (★ 197,125) 46,319
Columbus 23,799
Greenville 45,226
Gulfport (★ Biloxi) 40,775
Hattiesburg 41,882
Jackson (★ 395,396) 196,637
Laurel 18,827
Meridian 41,036
Natchez 19,460
Pascagoula (★ 115,243) 25,899
Vicksburg 20,908

UNITED STATES: MISSOURI

1990 C 5,117,073

Cape Girardeau 34,438
Columbia (★ 112,379) 69,101
Florissant (★ Saint Louis) 51,206
Independence (★ Kansas City) 112,301
Jefferson City 35,481
Joplin (★ 134,910) 40,961
Kansas City (★ 1,566,280) 435,146
Saint Charles (★ Saint Louis) 54,555
Saint Joseph (★ 83,083) 71,852
Saint Louis (★ 2,444,099) 396,685
Springfield (★ 240,593) 140,494

UNITED STATES: MONTANA

1990 C 799,065

Billings (★ 113,419) 81,151
Butte 33,336
Great Falls (★ 77,691) 55,097
Helena 24,569
Missoula 42,918

UNITED STATES: NEBRASKA

1990 C 1,578,385

Grand Island 39,386
Lincoln (★ 213,641) 191,972
Omaha (★ 618,262) 335,795

UNITED STATES: NEVADA

1990 C 1,201,833

Carson City 40,443
Las Vegas (★ 741,459) 258,295
Paradise (★ Las Vegas) 124,682
Reno (★ 254,667) 133,850
Sparks (★ Reno) 53,367
Sunrise Manor (★ Las Vegas) 95,362

UNITED STATES: NEW HAMPSHIRE

1990 C 1,109,252

Concord 36,006
Manchester (★ 147,809) 99,567
Nashua (★ Boston) 79,662
Portsmouth (★ 223,578) 25,925

UNITED STATES: NEW JERSEY

1990 C 7,730,188

Atlantic City (★ 319,416) 37,986
Bayonne (★ New York, N.Y.) 61,444
Bloomfield (★ New York, N.Y.) 45,061
Brick Township (★ New York, N.Y.) 66,473
Camden (★ Philadelphia, Pa.) 87,492
Cherry Hill (★ Philadelphia, Pa.) 69,319
Clifton (★ New York, N.Y.) 71,742
East Orange (★ New York, N.Y.) 73,552
Edison (★ New York, N.Y.) 88,680
Elizabeth (★ New York, N.Y.) 110,002
Irvington (★ New York, N.Y.) 59,774
Jersey City (★ New York, N.Y.) 228,537
Middletown (★ New York, N.Y.) 68,183
Newark (★ New York, N.Y.) 275,221
Passaic (★ New York, N.Y.) 58,041
Paterson (★ New York, N.Y.) 140,891
Trenton (★ Philadelphia, Pa.) 88,675
Union (★ New York, N.Y.) 51,000
Union City (★ New York, N.Y.) 58,012
Vineland (★ Philadelphia, Pa.) 54,780
Woodbridge (★ New York, N.Y.) 93,086

UNITED STATES: NEW MEXICO

1990 C 1,515,069

Albuquerque (★ 480,577) 384,736
Farmington 33,997
Las Cruces (★ 135,510) 62,126
Roswell 44,654
Santa Fe (★ 117,043) 55,859

UNITED STATES: NEW YORK

1990 C 17,990,455

Albany (★ 874,304) 101,082
Amherst (★ Buffalo) 45,600
Auburn 31,258
Binghamton (★ 264,497) 53,008
Buffalo (★ 1,189,288) 328,123
Cheektowaga (★ Buffalo) 84,387
Elmira (★ 95,195) 33,724
Glens Falls (★ 118,539) 15,023
Greece (★ Rochester) 64,600
Hicksville (★ New York) 40,174
Irondequoit (★ Rochester) 52,322
Ithaca 29,541
Jamestown (★ 141,895) 34,681
Kingston 23,095
Levittown (★ New York) 53,286
Lockport (★ Buffalo) 24,426
Middletown (★ New York) 24,160
Mount Vernon (★ New York) 67,153
Newburgh (★ New York) 26,454
New Rochelle (★ New York) 67,265
• New York (★ 18,087,251) 7,322,564
Niagara Falls (★ Buffalo) 61,840
Poughkeepsie (★ 259,462) 28,844
Rochester (★ 1,002,410) 231,636
Schenectady (★ Albany) 65,566
Syracuse (★ 659,864) 163,860
Town of Tonawanda (★ Buffalo) 65,284
Troy (★ Albany) 54,269
Utica (★ 316,633) 68,637
West Seneca (★ Buffalo) 47,866
Yonkers (★ New York) 188,082

UNITED STATES: NORTH CAROLINA

1990 C 6,628,637

Asheville (★ 174,821) 61,607
Burlington (★ 108,213) 39,498
Charlotte (★ 1,162,093) 395,934
Durham (★ Raleigh) 136,611
Fayetteville (★ 274,566) 75,695
Gastonia (★ Charlotte) 54,732
Goldsboro 40,709
Greensboro (★ 942,091) 183,521
Hickory (★ 221,700) 28,301
High Point (★ Greensboro) 69,496
Jacksonville (★ 149,838) 30,013
Kannapolis (★ Charlotte) 29,696
Raleigh (★ 735,480) 207,951
Rocky Mount 48,997
Salisbury (★ Charlotte) 23,087
Wilmington (★ 120,284) 55,530
Winston-Salem (★ Greensboro) 143,485

UNITED STATES: NORTH DAKOTA

1990 C 638,800

Bismarck (★ 83,831) 49,256
Fargo (★ 153,296) 74,111
Grand Forks (★ 70,683) 49,425
Minot 34,544

UNITED STATES: OHIO

1990 C 10,847,115

Akron (★ Cleveland) 223,019
Alliance (★ Canton) 23,376
Ashtabula 21,633
Brunswick (★ Cleveland) 28,230
Canton (★ 394,106) 84,161
Cincinnati (★ 1,744,124) 364,040
Cleveland (★ 2,759,823) 505,616
Cleveland Heights (★ Cleveland) 54,052
Columbus (★ 1,377,419) 632,910
Dayton (★ 951,270) 182,044
East Liverpool 13,654
Elyria (★ Cleveland) 56,746
Euclid (★ Cleveland) 54,875
Hamilton (★ Cincinnati) 61,368
Kettering (★ Dayton) 60,569
Lakewood (★ Cleveland) 59,718
Lancaster (★ Columbus) 34,507
Lima (★ 154,340) 45,549
Lorain (★ Cleveland) 71,245
Mansfield (★ 126,137) 50,627
Marion 34,075
Middletown (★ Cincinnati) 46,022
Newark (★ Columbus) 44,389
Parma (★ Cleveland) 87,876
Portsmouth 22,676
Sandusky 29,764
Springfield (★ Dayton) 70,487
Steubenville (★ 142,523) 22,125
Toledo (★ 614,128) 332,943
Warren (★ Youngstown) 50,793
Youngstown (★ 492,619) 95,732
Zanesville 26,778

UNITED STATES: OKLAHOMA

1990 C 3,145,585

Enid (★ 56,735) 45,309
Lawton (★ 111,486) 80,561
Midwest City (★ Oklahoma City) 52,267
Muskogee 37,708
Norman (★ Oklahoma City) 80,071
Oklahoma City (★ 958,839) 444,719
Tulsa (★ 708,954) 367,302

UNITED STATES: OREGON

1990 C 2,842,321

Corvallis 44,757
Eugene (★ 282,912) 112,669
Medford (★ 146,389) 46,951
Portland (★ 1,477,895) 437,319
Salem (★ 278,024) 107,786

UNITED STATES: PENNSYLVANIA

1990 C 11,881,643

Abington (★ Philadelphia) 59,300
Allentown (★ 686,688) 105,090
Altoona (★ 130,542) 51,881
Bensalem (★ Philadelphia) 59,900
Bethlehem (★ Allentown) 71,428
Bristol (★ Philadelphia) 10,405
Butler 15,714
Coatesville (★ Philadelphia) 11,038
Erie (★ 275,572) 108,718
Hanover (★ York) 14,399
Harrisburg (★ 587,986) 52,376
Haverford (★ Philadelphia) 51,800
Hazleton (★ Scranton) 24,730
Johnstown (★ 241,247) 28,134
Lancaster (★ 422,822) 55,551
Lebanon (★ Harrisburg) 24,800
Lower Merion Township (★ Philadelphia) 60,800
New Castle 28,334
Oil City 11,949
Penn Hills (★ Pittsburgh) 51,430
Philadelphia (★ 5,899,345) 1,585,577
Pittsburgh (★ 2,242,798) 369,879
Pottstown 21,831
Pottsville (★ Philadelphia) 16,603
Reading (★ 336,523) 78,380
Scranton (★ 734,175) 81,805
Sharon (★ 121,003) 17,493
State College (★ 123,786) 38,923
Uniontown (★ Pittsburgh) 12,034
Upper Darby (★ Philadelphia) 86,100
Washington (★ Pittsburgh) 15,864
Wilkes-Barre (★ Scranton) 47,523
Williamsport (★ 118,710) 31,933
York (★ 417,848) 42,192

C Census. E Official estimate. U Unofficial estimate.
• Largest city in country.

★ Population or designation of metropolitan area, including suburbs (see headnote).
▲ Population of an entire municipality, commune, or district, including rural area.

Blende, CO 81006 • *1,330*
Blennerhassett, WV 26101 • *2,924*
Blissfield, MI 49228 • *3,172*
Block Island, RI 02807 • *620*
Bloomer, WI 54724 • *3,085*
Bloomfield, CT 06002 • *7,120*
Bloomfield, IN 47424 • *2,592*
Bloomfield, IA 52537 • *2,580*
Bloomfield, MO 63825 • *1,800*
Bloomfield, NE 68718 • *1,181*
Bloomfield, NJ 07003 • *45,061*
Bloomfield, NM 87413 • *5,214*
Bloomfield Hills, MI 48302–04 • *4,288*
Bloomfield Township, MI 48302 • *42,137*
Bloomingdale, GA 31302 • *2,271*
Bloomingdale, IL 60108 • *16,614*
Bloomingdale, NJ 07403 • *7,530*
Bloomingdale, TN 37660 • *10,953*
Blooming Prairie, MN 55917 • *2,043*
Bloomington, CA 92316 • *15,116*
Bloomington, IL 61701–04 • *51,972*
Bloomington, IN 47401–08 • *60,633*
Bloomington, MN 55420 • *86,335*
Bloomington, TX 77951 • *1,888*
Bloomsburg, PA 17815 • *12,439*
Blossburg, PA 16912 • *1,571*
Blossom, TX 75416 • *1,440*
Blount □, AL • *39,248*
Blount □, TN • *85,969*
Blountstown, FL 32424 • *2,404*
Blountsville, AL 35031 • *1,527*
Blountville, TN 37617 • *2,605*
Blowing Rock, NC 28605 • *1,257*
Blue Ash, OH 45242 • *11,860*
Blue Diamond, NV 89004 • *420*
Blue Earth, MN 56013 • *3,745*
Blue Earth □, MN • *54,044*
Bluefield, VA 24605 • *5,363*
Bluefield, WV 24701 • *12,756*
Blue Grass, IA 52726 • *1,214*
Blue Hills, CT 06002 • *3,206*
Blue Island, IL 60406 • *21,203*
Blue Lake, CA 95525 • *1,235*
Blue Mound, IL 62513 • *1,161*
Blue Rapids, KS 66411 • *1,131*
Blue Ridge, GA 30513 • *1,336*
Blue Ridge, VA 24064 • *2,840*
Blue Ridge Summit, PA 17214 • *1,800*
Blue Springs, MO 64014–15 • *40,153*
Bluewell, WV 24701 • *2,752*
Bluff City, TN 37618 • *1,390*
Bluffdale, UT 84065 • *2,152*
Bluff Park, AL 35226 • *8,000*
Bluffton, IN 46714 • *9,020*
Bluffton, OH 45817 • *3,367*
Blythe, CA 92225–26 • *8,428*
Blytheville, AR 72315–19 • *22,906*
Boalsburg, PA 16827 • *2,206*
Boardman, OH 44512 • *38,596*
Boardman, OR 97818 • *1,387*
Boaz, AL 35957 • *6,928*
Boca Grande, FL 33921 • *1,200*
Boca Raton, FL 33431–34 • *61,492*
Boerne, TX 78006 • *4,274*
Bogalusa, LA 70427–29 • *14,280*
Bogart, GA 30622 • *1,018*
Bogata, TX 75417 • *1,421*
Boger City, NC 28092 • *1,373*
Bogota, NJ 07603 • *7,824*
Bohemia, NY 11716 • *9,556*
Boiling Springs, NC 28017 • *2,445*
Boiling Springs, PA 17007 • *1,978*
Boise, ID 83701–15 • *125,738*
Boise □, ID • *3,509*
Boise City, OK 73933 • *1,509*
Bolingbrook, IL 60440 • *40,843*
Bolivar, MO 65613 • *6,845*
Bolivar, NY 14715 • *1,261*
Bolivar, TN 38008 • *5,969*
Bolivar □, MS • *41,875*
Bollinger □, MO • *10,619*
Bolton Landing, NY 12814 • *1,600*
Bon Air, VA 23235 • *16,413*
Bonaventure, FL 33317 • *6,000*
Bond □, IL • *14,991*
Bondsville, MA 01009 • *1,992*
Bonduel, WI 54107 • *1,210*
Bondurant, IA 50035 • *1,584*
Bonham, TX 75418 • *6,686*
Bon Homme □, SD • *7,089*
Bonifay, FL 32425 • *2,612*
Bonita, CA 91903 • *12,542*
Bonita Springs, FL 33923 • *13,600*
Bonneauville, PA 17325 • *1,282*
Bonner □, ID • *26,622*
Bonners Ferry, ID 83805 • *2,193*
Bonner Springs, KS 66012 • *6,413*
Bonne Terre, MO 63628 • *3,871*
Bonneville □, ID • *72,207*
Bonney Lake, WA 98390 • *7,494*
Bonnie Doone, NC 28303 • *3,893*
Bono, AR 72416 • *1,220*
Booker, TX 79005 • *1,236*
Boomer, WV 25031 • *1,051*
Boone, IA 50036 • *12,392*
Boone, NC 28607 • *12,915*
Boone □, AR • *28,297*
Boone □, IL • *30,806*
Boone □, IN • *38,147*
Boone □, IA • *25,186*
Boone □, KY • *57,589*
Boone □, MO • *112,379*
Boone □, NE • *6,667*
Boone □, WV • *25,870*
Booneville, AR 72927 • *3,804*
Booneville, MS 38829 • *7,955*
Boonsboro, MD 21713 • *2,445*
Boonton, NJ 07005 • *8,343*
Boonville, CA 95415 • *1,000*
Boonville, IN 47601 • *6,724*
Boonville, MO 65233 • *7,095*
Boonville, NY 13309 • *2,220*
Boonville, NC 27011 • *1,009*
Boothbay Harbor, ME 04538 • *1,267*
Borden □, TX • *799*
Bordentown, NJ 08505 • *4,341*
Borger, TX 79007–08 • *15,675*
Boron, CA 93516 • *2,101*
Borrego Springs, CA 92004 • *2,244*
Boscobel, WI 53805 • *2,706*
Bosque □, TX • *15,125*
Bossert Estates, NJ 08505 • *1,830*
Bossier □, LA • *86,088*
Bossier City, LA 71111–13 • *52,721*
Boston, GA 31626 • *1,395*
Boston, MA 02101–99 • *574,283*
Boswell, PA 15531 • *1,485*
Botetourt □, VA • *24,992*
Bothell, WA 98011–12 • *12,345*
Botkins, OH 45306 • *1,340*
Bottineau, ND 58318 • *2,598*
Bottineau □, ND • *8,011*
Boulder, CO 80301–08 • *83,312*
Boulder, MT 59632 • *1,316*
Boulder □, CO • *225,339*
Boulder City, NV 89005–06 • *12,567*
Boulder Creek, CA 95006 • *6,725*
Boulder Hill, IL 60538 • *8,894*
Boulevard Heights, MD 20743 • *1,820*
Boundary □, ID • *8,332*
Bound Brook, NJ 08805 • *9,487*
Bountiful, UT 84010–11 • *36,659*
Bourbon, IN 46504 • *1,672*
Bourbon, MO 65441 • *1,188*
Bourbon □, KS • *14,966*
Bourbon □, KY • *19,236*
Bourbonnais, IL 60914 • *13,934*
Bourg, LA 70343 • *2,073*
Bourne, MA 02532 • *1,284*
Boutte, LA 70039 • *1,200*
Bovina, TX 79009 • *1,549*
Bowdon, GA 30108 • *1,981*
Bowie, MD 20715–21 • *37,589*
Bowie, TX 76230 • *4,990*
Bowie □, TX • *81,665*
Bowling Green, FL 33834 • *1,836*
Bowling Green, KY 42101–04 • *40,641*
Bowling Green, MO 63334 • *2,976*
Bowling Green, OH 43402 • *28,176*
Bowman, ND 58623 • *1,741*
Bowman, SC 29018 • *1,063*
Bowman □, ND • *3,596*
Box Butte □, NE • *13,130*
Box Elder, SD 57719 • *2,680*
Box Elder □, UT • *36,485*
Boxford, MA 01921 • *2,072*
Boyce, LA 71409 • *1,361*
Boyd □, KY • *51,150*
Boyd □, NE • *2,835*
Boyertown, PA 19512 • *3,759*
Boyes Hot Springs, CA 95416 • *5,973*
Boyle □, KY • *25,641*
Boyne City, MI 49712 • *3,478*
Boynton Beach, FL 33435–37 • *46,194*
Bozeman, MT 59715 • *22,660*
Bracken □, KY • *7,766*
Brackenridge, PA 15014 • *3,784*
Brackettville, TX 78832 • *1,740*
Braddock, PA 15104 • *4,682*
Braddock Heights, MD 21714 • *4,778*
Bradenton, FL 34201–10 • *43,779*
Bradenville, PA 15620 • *1,100*
Bradford, OH 45308 • *2,005*
Bradford, PA 16701 • *9,625*
Bradford, RI 02808 • *1,604*
Bradford, TN 38316 • *1,154*
Bradford, VT 05033 • *672*
Bradford □, FL • *22,515*
Bradford □, PA • *60,967*
Bradfordwoods, PA 15015 • *1,329*
Bradley, FL 33835 • *1,108*
Bradley, IL 60915 • *10,792*
Bradley, WV 25818 • *2,144*
Bradley □, AR • *11,793*
Bradley □, TN • *73,712*
Bradley Beach, NJ 07720 • *4,475*
Bradner, OH 43406 • *1,093*
Brady, TX 76825 • *5,946*
Braham, MN 55006 • *1,139*
Braidwood, IL 60408 • *3,584*
Brainerd, MN 56401 • *12,353*
Braintree, MA 02184 • *33,836*
Branch □, MI • *41,502*
Branch Village, RI 02895 • *400*
Branchville, SC 29432 • *1,107*
Brandenburg, KY 40108 • *1,857*
Brandon, FL 33510 • *57,985*
Brandon, MS 39042–43 • *11,077*
Brandon, SC 29611 • *2,170*
Brandon, SD 57005 • *3,543*
Brandon, VT 05733 • *1,902*
Brandywine, MD 20613 • *1,406*
Branford, CT 06405 • *27,603*
Branford Hills, CT 06405 • *3,460*
Branson, MO 65616 • *3,706*
Brantley, AL 36009 • *1,015*
Brantley □, GA • *11,077*
Brant Rock, MA 02020 • *1,850*
Bratenahl, OH 44108 • *1,356*
Brattleboro, VT 05301–04 • *8,612*
Brawley, CA 92227 • *18,923*
Braxton □, WV • *12,998*
Brazil, IN 47834 • *7,640*
Brazoria, TX 77422 • *2,717*
Brazoria □, TX • *191,707*
Brazos □, TX • *121,862*
Brea, CA 92621–22 • *32,873*
Breathitt □, KY • *15,703*
Breaux Bridge, LA 70517 • *6,515*
Breckenridge, CO 80424 • *1,285*
Breckenridge, MI 48615 • *1,301*
Breckenridge, MN 56520 • *3,708*
Breckenridge, TX 76024 • *5,665*
Breckenridge Hills, MO 63114 • *5,404*
Breckinridge □, KY • *16,312*
Brecksville, OH 44141 • *11,818*
Breese, IL 62230 • *3,567*
Bremen, GA 30110 • *4,356*
Bremen, IN 46506 • *4,725*
Bremen, OH 43107 • *1,386*
Bremer □, IA • *22,813*
Bremerton, WA 98310–15 • *38,142*
Bremond, TX 76629 • *1,110*
Brenham, TX 77833–34 • *11,952*
Brent, AL 35034 • *2,776*
Brent, FL 32503 • *21,624*
Brentwood, CA 94513 • *7,563*
Brentwood, MD 20722 • *3,005*
Brentwood, MO 63144 • *8,150*
Brentwood, NY 11717 • *45,218*
Brentwood, NY • *45,218*
Brentwood, OH 45231 • *3,568*
Brentwood, PA 15227 • *10,823*
Brentwood, SC 29405 • *2,000*
Brentwood, TN 37027 • *16,392*
Brevard, NC 28712 • *5,388*
Brevard □, FL • *398,978*
Brewer, ME 04412 • *9,021*
Brewster, MA 02631 • *1,818*
Brewster, NY 10509 • *1,566*
Brewster, OH 44613 • *2,307*
Brewster, WA 98812 • *1,633*
Brewster □, TX • *8,681*
Brewton, AL 36426–27 • *5,885*
Briarcliff Manor, NY 10510 • *7,070*
Brick [Township], NJ 08723 • *55,473*
Bridge City, LA 70094 • *8,327*
Bridge City, TX 77611 • *8,034*
Bridgehampton, NY 11932 • *1,997*
Bridgeport, AL 35740 • *2,936*
Bridgeport, CT 06601–50 • *141,686*
Bridgeport, IL 62417 • *2,118*
Bridgeport, MI 48722 • *8,569*
Bridgeport, NE 69336 • *1,581*
Bridgeport, OH 43912 • *2,318*
Bridgeport, PA 19405 • *4,292*
Bridgeport, TX 76026 • *3,581*
Bridgeport, WA 98813 • *1,498*
Bridgeport, WV 26330 • *6,739*
Bridger, MT 59014 • *692*
Bridgeton, MO 63044 • *17,779*
Bridgeton, NJ 08302 • *18,942*
Bridgetown, OH 45211 • *11,460*
Bridgeview, IL 60455 • *14,402*
Bridgeville, DE 19933 • *1,210*
Bridgeville, PA 15017 • *5,445*
Bridgewater, MA 02324 • *7,242*
Bridgewater, NJ 08807 • *5,630*
Bridgewater, VA 22812 • *3,918*
Bridgman, MI 49106 • *2,140*
Bridgton, ME 04009 • *2,195*
Brielle, NJ 08730 • *4,406*
Brigantine, NJ 08203 • *11,354*
Brigham City, UT 84302 • *15,644*
Brighton, AL 35020 • *4,518*
Brighton, CO 80601 • *14,203*
Brighton, IL 62012 • *2,270*
Brighton, MI 48116 • *5,686*
Brighton, NY 14610 • *34,455*
Brilliant, OH 43913 • *1,672*
Brillion, WI 54110 • *2,840*
Brinkley, AR 72021 • *4,234*
Briscoe □, TX • *1,971*
Bristol, CT 06010–11 • *60,640*
Bristol, IN 46507 • *1,133*
Bristol, NH 03222 • *1,483*
Bristol, RI 02809 • *21,625*
Bristol, TN 37620–25 • *23,421*
Bristol, VT 05443 • *1,801*
Bristol, VA 24201–03 • *18,426*
Bristol □, MA • *506,325*
Bristol □, RI • *48,859*
Bristol [Township], PA 19007 • *58,773*
Bristow, OK 74010 • *4,062*
Britt, IA 50423 • *2,133*
Britton, SD 57430 • *1,394*
Broadalbin, NY 12025 • *1,397*
Broad Brook, CT 06016 • *1,280*
Broadkill Beach, DE 19968 • *390*
Broadus, MT 59317 • *572*
Broadview, IL 60153 • *8,713*
Broadview Heights, OH 44141 • *12,219*
Broadview Park, FL 33314 • *6,109*
Broadwater □, MT • *3,318*
Broadway, VA 22815 • *1,209*
Brockport, NY 14420 • *8,749*
Brockton, MA 02401–05 • *92,788*
Brockway, PA 15824 • *2,207*
Brocton, NY 14716 • *1,387*
Brodhead, KY 40409 • *1,140*
Brodhead, WI 53520 • *3,165*
Brodheadsville, PA 18322 • *1,500*
Broken Arrow, OK 74011–14 • *58,043*
Broken Bow, NE 68822 • *3,778*
Broken Bow, OK 74728 • *3,961*
Bronson, MI 49028 • *2,342*
Bronx □, NY • *1,203,789*
Bronxville, NY 10708 • *6,028*
Brooke □, WV • *26,992*
Brookfield, CT 06804 • *1,500*
Brookfield, IL 60513 • *18,876*
Brookfield, MA 01506 • *2,968*
Brookfield, MO 64628 • *4,888*
Brookfield, VA 22021 • *2,100*
Brookfield, WI 53005 • *35,184*
Brookfield Center, CT 06804 • *1,400*
Brookhaven, MS 39601 • *10,243*
Brookhaven, PA 19015 • *8,567*
Brookhaven, WV 26505 • *3,836*
Brookings, OR 97415 • *4,400*
Brookings, SD 57006 • *16,270*
Brookings □, SD • *25,207*
Brooklawn, NJ 08030 • *1,805*
Brookline, MA 02146 • *54,718*
Brooklyn, CT 06234 • *1,400*
Brooklyn, IN 46111 • *1,162*
Brooklyn, IA 52211 • *1,439*
Brooklyn, OH 44144 • *11,706*
Brooklyn, SC 29720 • *1,850*
Brooklyn Center, MN 55429 • *28,887*
Brooklyn Park, MD 21225 • *10,987*
Brooklyn Park, MN 55443 • *56,381*
Brookneal, VA 24528 • *1,344*
Brook Park, OH 44142 • *22,865*
Brookport, IL 62910 • *1,070*
Brooks, KY 40109 • *2,464*
Brooks □, GA • *15,398*
Brooks □, TX • *8,204*
Brookshire, TX 77423 • *2,922*
Brookside, AL 35036 • *1,365*
Brookside, DE 19713 • *15,307*
Brookston, IN 47923 • *1,804*
Brooksville, FL 34601–14 • *7,440*
Brooksville, MS 39739 • *1,098*
Brookville, IN 47012 • *2,529*
Brookville, NY 11545 • *3,716*
Brookville, OH 45309 • *4,621*
Brookville, PA 15825 • *4,184*
Brookwood, NJ 08527 • *5,500*
Broomall, PA 19008 • *10,930*
Broome □, NY • *212,160*
Broomfield, CO 80020–21 • *24,638*
Broussard, LA 70518 • *3,213*
Broward □, FL • *1,255,488*
Browardale, FL 33311 • *6,257*
Brown □, IL • *5,836*
Brown □, IN • *14,080*
Brown □, KS • *11,128*
Brown □, MN • *26,984*
Brown □, NE • *3,657*
Brown □, OH • *34,966*
Brown □, SD • *35,580*
Brown □, TX • *34,371*
Brown □, WI • *194,594*
Brown City, MI 48416 • *1,244*
Brown Deer, WI 53209 • *12,236*
Brownfield, TX 79316 • *9,560*
Brownfields, LA 70811 • *5,229*
Browning, MT 59417 • *1,170*
Brownsburg, IN 46112 • *7,628*
Browns Mills, NJ 08015 • *11,429*
Brownstown, IN 47220 • *2,872*
Brownsville, FL 33142 • *15,607*
Brownsville, OR 97327 • *1,281*
Brownsville, PA 15417 • *3,164*
Brownsville, TN 38012 • *10,019*
Brownsville, TX 78520–26 • *98,962*
Brownville, LA 71291 • *1,700*
Brownville, NY 13615 • *1,138*
Brownwood, TX 76803–04 • *18,387*
Broxton, GA 31519 • *1,211*
Broyhill Park, VA 22042 • *3,600*
Bruce, MS 38915 • *2,127*
Bruceton, TN 38317 • *1,586*
Brule □, SD • *5,485*
Brundidge, AL 36010 • *2,472*
Brunswick, GA 31520–22 • *16,433*
Brunswick, ME 04011 • *14,683*
Brunswick, MD 21716 • *5,117*
Brunswick, MO 65236 • *1,074*
Brunswick, OH 44212 • *28,230*
Brunswick □, NC • *50,985*
Brunswick □, VA • *15,987*
Brush, CO 80723 • *4,165*
Brusly, LA 70719 • *1,824*
Bryan, OH 43506 • *8,348*
Bryan, TX 77801–06 • *55,002*
Bryan □, GA • *15,438*
Bryan □, OK • *32,089*
Bryans Road, MD 20616 • *3,809*
Bryant, AR 72022 • *5,269*
Bryantville, MA 02327 • *1,800*
Bryn Mawr, WA 98178 • *1,500*
Bryson City, NC 28713 • *1,145*
Buchanan, GA 30113 • *1,009*
Buchanan, MI 49107 • *4,992*
Buchanan, VA 24066 • *1,222*
Buchanan □, IA • *20,844*
Buchanan □, MO • *83,083*
Buchanan □, VA • *31,333*
Buckeye, AZ 85326 • *5,038*
Buckeye Lake, OH 43008 • *2,986*
Buckhannon, WV 26201 • *5,909*
Buckingham □, VA • *12,873*
Buckley, WA 98321 • *3,516*
Bucknell Manor, VA 22307 • *2,300*
Buckner, MO 64016 • *2,873*
Bucks □, PA • *541,174*
Bucksport, ME 04416 • *2,989*
Bucksport, SC 29527 • *1,022*
Bucyrus, OH 44820 • *13,496*
Buda, TX 78610 • *1,795*
Budd Lake 0L, NJ • *7,272*
Buechel, KY 40218 • *7,081*
Buena, NJ 08310 • *4,441*
Buena Park, CA 90620–24 • *68,784*
Buena Vista, CO 81211 • *1,752*
Buena Vista, FL 34691 • *3,000*
Buena Vista, GA 31803 • *1,472*
Buena Vista, VA 24416 • *6,406*
Buena Vista □, IA • *19,965*
Buffalo, IA 52728 • *1,260*
Buffalo, MN 55313 • *6,856*
Buffalo, MO 65622 • *2,414*
Buffalo, NY 14201–40 • *328,123*
Buffalo, OK 73834 • *1,312*
Buffalo, SC 29321 • *1,569*
Buffalo, TX 75831 • *1,555*
Buffalo, WY 82834 • *3,302*
Buffalo □, NE • *37,447*
Buffalo □, SD • *1,759*
Buffalo □, WI • *13,584*
Buffalo Center, IA 50424 • *1,081*
Buffalo Grove, IL 60089 • *36,427*
Buford, GA 30518 • *8,771*
Buhl, ID 83316 • *3,516*
Buhler, KS 67522 • *1,277*
Buies Creek, NC 27506 • *2,085*
Bullhead City, AZ 86430 • *21,951*
Bullitt □, KY • *47,567*
Bulloch □, GA • *43,125*
Bullock □, AL • *11,042*
Bull Shoals, AR 72619 • *1,534*
Buna, TX 77612 • *1,900*
Bunche Park, FL 33054 • *4,000*
Buncombe □, NC • *174,821*
Bunker Hill, IL 62014 • *1,722*
Bunker Hill, OR 97420 • *1,242*
Bunkerville, NV 89007 • *300*
Bunkie, LA 71322 • *5,044*
Bunnell, FL 32110 • *1,873*
Buras, LA 70041 • *1,600*
Burbank, CA 91501–10 • *93,643*
Burbank, IL 60459 • *27,600*
Burdickville, RI 02808 • *500*
Bureau □, IL • *35,688*
Burgaw, NC 28425 • *1,807*
Burgettstown, PA 15021 • *1,634*
Burgin, KY 40310 • *1,009*
Burien, WA 98062 • *25,089*
Burkburnett, TX 76354 • *10,145*
Burke, SD 57523 • *756*
Burke, VA 22015 • *57,734*
Burke □, GA • *20,579*
Burke □, NC • *75,744*
Burke □, ND • *3,002*
Burkesville, KY 42717 • *1,815*
Burleigh □, ND • *60,131*
Burleson, TX 76028 • *16,113*
Burleson □, TX • *13,625*
Burley, ID 83318 • *8,702*
Burlingame, CA 94010–11 • *26,801*
Burlingame, KS 66413 • *1,074*
Burlington, CO 80807 • *2,941*
Burlington, IA 52601 • *27,208*
Burlington, KS 66839 • *2,735*
Burlington, KY 41005 • *6,070*
Burlington, MA 01803 • *23,302*
Burlington, NJ 08016 • *9,835*
Burlington, NC 27215–17 • *39,498*
Burlington, ND 58722 • *995*
Burlington, VT 05401–04 • *39,127*
Burlington, WA 98233 • *4,349*
Burlington, WI 53105 • *8,855*
Burlington □, NJ • *395,066*
Burnet, TX 78611 • *3,423*
Burnet □, TX • *22,677*
Burnett □, WI • *13,084*
Burney, CA 96013 • *3,423*
Burnham, PA 17009 • *2,197*
Burns, OR 97720 • *2,913*
Burns, TN 37029 • *1,127*
Burns, WY 82053 • *254*
Burns Flat, OK 73624 • *1,027*
Burnsville, MN 55337 • *51,288*
Burnsville, NC 28714 • *1,482*
Burnt Hills, NY 12027 • *1,550*
Burr Ridge, IL 60521 • *7,669*
Burt □, NE • *7,868*
Burton, MI 48509 • *27,617*
Burton, OH 44021 • *1,349*
Burton, SC 29902 • *6,917*
Burtonsville, MD 20866 • *5,853*
Burwell, NE 68823 • *1,278*
Bushnell, FL 33513 • *1,998*
Bushnell, IL 61422 • *3,288*
Butler, AL 36904 • *1,872*
Butler, GA 31006 • *1,673*
Butler, IN 46721 • *2,601*
Butler, MO 64730 • *4,099*
Butler, NJ 07405 • *7,392*
Butler, PA 16001–03 • *15,714*
Butler, WI 53007 • *2,079*
Butler □, AL • *21,892*
Butler □, IA • *15,731*
Butler □, KS • *50,580*
Butler □, KY • *11,245*
Butler □, MO • *38,765*
Butler □, NE • *8,601*
Butler □, OH • *291,479*
Butler □, PA • *152,013*
Butner, NC 27509 • *4,679*
Butte, MT 59701–03 • *33,336*
Butte □, CA • *182,120*
Butte □, ID • *2,918*
Butte □, SD • *7,914*
Buttonwillow, CA 93206 • *1,301*
Butts □, GA • *15,326*
Buxton, NC 27920 • *1,300*
Buzzards Bay, MA 02532 • *3,250*
Byers, CO 80103 • *1,065*
Byesville, OH 43723 • *2,435*
Byfield, MA 01922 • *1,200*
Bylas, AZ 85530 • *1,219*
Byron, GA 31008 • *2,276*
Byron, IL 61010 • *2,284*
Byron, MN 55920 • *2,441*
Byron, WY 82412 • *470*

C

Cabarrus □, NC • *98,935*
Cabell □, WV • *96,827*
Cabin Creek, WV 25035 • *1,300*
Cabin John, MD 20818 • *1,690*
Cabool, MO 65689 • *2,006*
Cabot, AR 72023 • *8,319*
Cache, OK 73527 • *2,251*
Cache □, UT • *70,183*
Caddo □, LA • *248,253*
Caddo □, OK • *29,550*
Cadillac, MI 49601 • *10,104*
Cadiz, KY 42211 • *2,148*
Cadiz, OH 43907 • *3,439*
Cadott, WI 54727 • *1,328*
Cahaba Heights, AL 35243 • *4,778*
Cahokia, IL 62206 • *17,550*
Cairnbrook, PA 15924 • *1,081*
Cairo, GA 31728 • *9,035*
Cairo, IL 62914 • *4,846*
Cairo, NY 12413 • *1,273*
Calais, ME 04619 • *3,963*
Calaveras □, CA • *31,998*
Calavo Gardens, CA 91941 • *6,100*
Calcasieu □, LA • *168,134*
Calcutta, OH 43920 • *1,212*
Caldwell, ID 83605–06 • *18,400*
Caldwell, KS 67022 • *1,351*
Caldwell, NJ 07006 • *7,549*
Caldwell, OH 43724 • *1,786*
Caldwell, TX 77836 • *3,181*
Caldwell □, KY • *13,232*
Caldwell □, LA • *9,810*
Caldwell □, MO • *8,380*
Caldwell □, NC • *70,709*
Caldwell □, TX • *26,392*
Caledonia, MN 55921 • *2,846*
Caledonia, NY 14423 • *2,262*
Caledonia □, VT • *27,846*
Calera, AL 35040 • *2,136*
Calera, OK 74730 • *1,536*
Calexico, CA 92231–32 • *18,633*
Calhoun, GA 30701 • *7,135*
Calhoun □, AL • *116,034*
Calhoun □, AR • *5,826*
Calhoun □, FL • *11,011*
Calhoun □, GA • *5,013*
Calhoun □, IL • *5,322*
Calhoun □, IA • *11,508*
Calhoun □, MI • *135,982*
Calhoun □, MS • *14,908*
Calhoun □, SC • *12,753*
Calhoun □, TX • *19,053*
Calhoun □, WV • *7,885*
Calhoun City, MS 38916 • *1,838*
Calhoun Falls, SC 29628 • *2,328*
Caliente, NV 89008 • *1,111*
Califon, NJ 07830 • *1,073*
California, MD 20619 • *7,626*
California, MO 65018 • *3,465*
California, PA 15419 • *5,748*
Calipatria, CA 92233 • *2,690*
Calistoga, CA 94515 • *4,468*
Callahan □, TX • *11,859*
Callaway, FL 32401 • *12,253*
Callaway □, MO • *32,809*
Calloway □, KY • *30,735*
Calmar, IA 52132 • *1,026*
Calumet □, WI • *34,291*
Calumet City, IL 60409 • *37,840*
Calumet Park, IL 60643 • *8,418*
Calvert, TX 77837 • *1,536*
Calvert □, MD • *51,372*
Calvert City, KY 42029 • *2,531*
Calverton, MD 20705 • *12,046*

United States Populations and ZIP Codes

Calverton Park, MO 63136 • 1,404
Camanche, IA 52730 • 4,436
Camarillo, CA 93010–11 • 52,303
Camas, WA 98607 • 6,442
Camas □, ID • 727
Cambria, CA 93428 • 5,382
Cambria □, PA • 163,029
Cambrian Park, CA 95124 • 2,998
Cambridge, IL 61238 • 2,124
Cambridge, MD 21613 • 11,514
Cambridge, MA 02138 • 95,802
Cambridge, MN 55008 • 5,094
Cambridge, NE 69022 • 1,107
Cambridge, NY 12816 • 1,906
Cambridge, OH 43725 • 11,748
Cambridge City, IN 47327 • 2,091
Cambridge Springs, PA 16403 • 1,837
Camden, AL 36726 • 2,414
Camden, AR 71701 • 14,380
Camden, DE 19934 • 1,899
Camden, ME 04843 • 4,022
Camden, NJ 08101–10 • 87,492
Camden, NY 13316 • 2,552
Camden, OH 45311 • 2,210
Camden, SC 29020 • 6,696
Camden, TN 38320 • 3,643
Camden □, GA • 30,167
Camden □, MO • 27,495
Camden □, NJ • 502,824
Camden □, NC • 5,904
Camdenton, MO 65020 • 2,561
Camelot, WA 98002 • 4,900
Cameron, LA 70631 • 2,041
Cameron, MO 64429 • 4,831
Cameron, TX 76520 • 5,580
Cameron, WV 26033 • 1,177
Cameron, WI 54822 • 1,273
Cameron □, LA • 9,260
Cameron □, PA • 5,913
Cameron □, TX • 260,120
Cameron Park, CA 95682 • 11,897
Camilla, GA 31730 • 5,008
Camino, CA 95709 • 1,500
Camp □, TX • 9,904
Campbell, CA 95008–09 • 36,048
Campbell, FL 34746 • 3,884
Campbell, MO 63933 • 2,165
Campbell, OH 44405 • 10,038
Campbell □, KY • 83,866
Campbell □, SD • 1,965
Campbell □, TN • 35,079
Campbell □, VA • 47,572
Campbell □, WY • 29,370
Campbellsport, WI 53010 • 1,732
Campbellsville, KY 42718–19 • 9,577
Camp Hill, AL 36850 • 1,415
Camp Hill, PA 17011 • 7,831
Camp Point, IL 62320 • 1,230
Camp Springs, MD 20748 • 16,392
Camp Verde, AZ 86322 • 6,243
Canaan, CT 06018 • 1,194
Canadensis, PA 18325 • 1,200
Canadian, TX 79014 • 2,417
Canadian □, OK • 74,409
Canajoharie, NY 13317 • 2,278
Canal Fulton, OH 44614 • 4,157
Canal Winchester, OH 43110 • 2,617
Canandaigua, NY 14424–25 • 10,725
Canastota, NY 13032 • 4,673
Canby, MN 56220 • 1,826
Canby, OR 97013 • 8,983
Candler □, GA • 7,744
Candlewood Isle, CT 06812 • 1,100
Candlewood Shores, CT 06804 • 1,620
Cando, ND 58324 • 1,564
Caney, KS 67333 • 2,062
Canfield, OH 44406 • 5,409
Canisteo, NY 14823 • 2,421
Cannelton, IN 47520 • 1,786
Cannon □, TN • 10,467
Cannon Beach, OR 97110 • 1,221
Cannondale, CT 06897 • 1,500
Cannon Falls, MN 55009 • 3,232
Canon City, CO 81212 • 12,687
Canonsburg, PA 15317 • 9,200
Canterbury, DE 19943 • 500
Canton, CT 06019 • 1,563
Canton, GA 30114 • 4,817
Canton, IL 61520 • 13,922
Canton, MA 02021 • 18,182
Canton, MI 48187 • 57,047
Canton, MS 39046 • 10,062
Canton, MO 63435 • 2,623
Canton, NY 13617 • 6,379
Canton, NC 28716 • 3,790
Canton, OH 44701–99 • 84,161
Canton, PA 17724 • 1,966
Canton, SD 57013 • 2,787
Canton, TX 75103 • 2,949
Cantonment, FL 32533 • 3,200
Canutillo, TX 79835 • 4,500
Canyon, TX 79015 • 11,365
Canyon □, ID • 90,076
Canyon Lake, CA 92380 • 7,938
Canyon Lake, TX 78130 • 9,975
Canyonville, OR 97417 • 1,219
Capac, MI 48014 • 1,583
Cape Canaveral, FL 32920 • 8,014
Cape Charles, VA 23310 • 1,398
Cape Coral, FL 33904 • 74,991
Cape Elizabeth, ME 04107 • 8,854
Cape Girardeau, MO 63701–02 • 34,438
Cape Girardeau □, MO • 61,633
Cape May, NJ 08204 • 4,668
Cape May □, NJ • 95,089
Cape May Court House, NJ 08210 • 4,426
Cape Saint Claire, MD 21401 • 7,878
Capitola, CA 95010 • 10,171
Capitol Heights, MD 20743 • 3,633
Capitol View, SC 29209 • 10,456
Captain Cook, HI 96704 • 2,595
Captiva, FL 33924 • 1,200
Caraway, AR 72419 • 1,178
Carbon □, MT • 8,080
Carbon □, PA • 56,846
Carbon □, UT • 20,228
Carbon □, WY • 16,659
Carbondale, CO 81623 • 3,004
Carbondale, IL 62901–03 • 27,033
Carbondale, KS 66414 • 1,526
Carbondale, PA 18407 • 10,664
Carbon Hill, AL 35549 • 2,115
Cardington, OH 43315 • 1,770
Carencro, LA 70520 • 5,429
Carey, OH 43316 • 3,684
Caribou, ME 04736 • 9,415
Caribou □, ID • 6,963
Carle Place, NY 11514 • 5,107
Carleton, MI 48117 • 2,770
Carlin, NV 89822 • 2,220
Carlinville, IL 62626 • 5,416
Carlisle, AR 72024 • 2,253
Carlisle, IA 50047 • 3,241
Carlisle, KY 40311 • 1,639
Carlisle, OH 45005 • 4,872
Carlisle, PA 17013 • 18,419
Carlisle □, KY • 5,238
Carl Junction, MO 64834 • 4,123
Carlsbad, CA 92008–09 • 63,126
Carlsbad, NM 88220–21 • 24,952
Carlstadt, NJ 07072 • 5,510
Carlton, OR 97111 • 1,289
Carlton □, MN • 29,259
Carlyle, IL 62231 • 3,474
Carmel, CA 93921–23 • 4,239
Carmel, IN 46032 • 25,380
Carmel, NY 10512 • 3,395
Carmi, IL 62821 • 5,564
Carmichael, CA 95608–09 • 48,702
Carnation, WA 98014 • 1,243
Carnegie, OK 73015 • 1,593
Carnegie, PA 15106 • 9,278
Carney, MD 21234 • 25,578
Carneys Point, NJ 08069 • 7,686
Carnot, PA 15108 • 4,750
Caro, MI 48723 • 4,054
Carol City, FL 33055 • 53,331
Caroleen, NC 28019 • 1,100
Carolina Beach, NC 28428 • 3,630
Caroline □, MD • 27,035
Caroline □, VA • 19,217
Carol Stream, IL 60188 • 31,716
Carpentersville, IL 60110 • 23,049
Carpinteria, CA 93013–14 • 13,747
Carrabelle, FL 32322 • 1,200
Carrboro, NC 27510 • 11,553
Carrier Mills, IL 62917 • 1,991
Carrington, ND 58421 • 2,267
Carrizo Springs, TX 78834 • 5,745
Carrizozo, NM 88301 • 1,075
Carroll, IA 51401 • 9,579
Carroll □, AR • 18,654
Carroll □, GA • 71,422
Carroll □, IL • 16,805
Carroll □, IN • 18,809
Carroll □, IA • 21,423
Carroll □, KY • 9,292
Carroll □, MD • 123,372
Carroll □, MS • 9,237
Carroll □, MO • 10,748
Carroll □, NH • 35,410
Carroll □, OH • 26,521
Carroll □, TN • 27,514
Carroll □, VA • 26,594
Carrollton, AL 35447 • 1,170
Carrollton, GA 30117 • 16,029
Carrollton, IL 62016 • 2,507
Carrollton, KY 41008 • 3,715
Carrollton, MI 48724 • 6,521
Carrollton, MO 64633 • 4,406
Carrollton, OH 44615 • 3,042
Carrollton, TX 75006–08 • 82,169
Carrolltown, PA 15722 • 1,286
Carrollwood, FL 33618 • 11,400
Carson, CA 90749 • 83,995
Carson □, TX • 6,576
Carson City, MI 48811 • 1,158
Carson City, NV 89701–21 • 40,443
Carter □, KY • 24,340
Carter □, MO • 5,515
Carter □, MT • 1,503
Carter □, OK • 42,919
Carter □, TN • 51,505
Carteret, NJ 07008 • 19,025
Carteret □, NC • 52,556
Carter Lake, IA 51510 • 3,200
Cartersville, GA 30120 • 12,035
Carterville, IL 62918 • 3,630
Carterville, MO 64835 • 2,013
Carthage, IL 62321 • 2,657
Carthage, MS 39051 • 3,819
Carthage, MO 64836 • 10,747
Carthage, NY 13619 • 4,344
Carthage, TN 37030 • 2,386
Carthage, TX 75633 • 6,496
Caruthersville, MO 63830 • 7,389
Carver, MA 02330 • 1,500
Carver □, MN • 47,915
Carver Ranch Estates, FL 33023 • 5,600
Carville, LA 70721 • 1,108
Cary, IL 60013 • 10,043
Cary, NC 27511 • 43,858
Caryville, TN 37714 • 1,751
Casa de Oro, CA 92077 • 9,500
Casa Grande, AZ 85222 • 19,082
Casas Adobes, AZ 85704 • 12,155
Cascade, CO 80809 • 1,000
Cascade, ID 83611 • 877
Cascade, IA 52033 • 1,812
Cascade, MT 59421 • 729
Cascade □, MT • 77,691
Cascade Vista, WA 98058 • 7,800
Casey, IL 62420 • 2,914
Casey □, KY • 14,211
Cashion, AZ 85329 • 3,014
Cashmere, WA 98815 • 2,544
Casper, WY 82601–15 • 46,742
Caspian, MI 49915 • 1,031
Cass □, IL • 13,437
Cass □, IN • 38,413
Cass □, IA • 15,128
Cass □, MI • 49,477
Cass □, MN • 21,791
Cass □, MO • 63,808
Cass □, NE • 21,318
Cass □, ND • 102,874
Cass □, TX • 29,982
Cass City, MI 48726 • 2,276
Casselberry, FL 32707–08 • 18,911
Casselton, ND 58012 • 1,601
Cassia □, ID • 19,532
Cassopolis, MI 49031 • 1,822
Cassville, MO 65625 • 2,371
Cassville, WI 53806 • 1,144
Castanea, PA 17726 • 1,123
Castile, NY 14427 • 1,078
Castle Dale, UT 84513 • 1,704
Castle Hayne, NC 28429 • 1,182
Castle Hills, DE 19720 • 1,475
Castle Park, CA 92011 • 6,300
Castle Point, MO 63136 • 7,800
Castle Rock, CO 80104 • 8,708
Castle Rock, WA 98611 • 2,067
Castle Shannon, PA 15234 • 9,135
Castleton, VT 05735 • 600
Castleton on Hudson, NY 12033 • 1,491
Castlewood, VA 24224 • 2,110
Castro □, TX • 9,070
Castro Valley, CA 94546 • 48,619
Castroville, TX 78009 • 2,159
Caswell □, NC • 20,693
Catahoula □, LA • 11,065
Catalina Foothills, AZ 85718 • 1,470
Catasauqua, PA 18032 • 6,662
Cataumet, MA 02534 • 1,500
Catawba □, NC • 118,412
Catawissa, PA 17820 • 1,683
Cathedral City, CA 92234–35 • 30,085
Catlettsburg, KY 41129 • 2,231
Catlin, IL 61817 • 2,173
Catonsville, MD 21228 • 35,233
Catoosa, OK 74015 • 2,954
Catoosa □, GA • 42,464
Catron □, NM • 2,563
Catskill, NY 12414 • 4,690
Cattaraugus, NY 14719 • 1,100
Cattaraugus □, NY • 84,234
Cavalier, ND 58220 • 1,508
Cavalier □, ND • 6,064
Cave City, AR 72521 • 1,503
Cave City, KY 42127 • 1,953
Cave Creek, AZ 85331 • 2,925
Cave Junction, OR 97523 • 1,126
Cave Spring, VA 24018 • 24,053
Cavetown, MD 21720 • 1,533
Cayce, SC 29033 • 11,163
Cayuga, IN 47928 • 1,083
Cayuga □, NY • 82,313
Cayuga Heights, NY 14850 • 3,457
Cazenovia, NY 13035 • 3,007
Cecil □, MD • 71,347
Cedar □, IA • 17,381
Cedar □, MO • 12,093
Cedar □, NE • 10,131
Cedar Bluff, AL 35959 • 1,174
Cedar Bluff Two, TN 37722 • 2,000
Cedarburg, WI 53012 • 9,895
Cedar City, UT 84720–22 • 13,443
Cedar Crest, NM 87008 • 1,200
Cedaredge, CO 81413 • 1,380
Cedar Falls, IA 50613 • 34,298
Cedar Grove, NJ 07009 • 12,053
Cedar Grove, WV 25039 • 1,213
Cedar Grove, WI 53013 • 1,521
Cedar Hill, MO 63016 • 1,966
Cedar Hill, TX 75104 • 19,976
Cedar Hills, OR 97005 • 9,294
Cedarhurst, NY 11516 • 5,716
Cedar Lake, IN 46303 • 8,885
Cedar Rapids, IA 52401–10 • 108,751
Cedar Springs, MI 49319 • 2,600
Cedartown, GA 30125 • 7,978
Cedarville, NJ 08311 • 1,100
Cedarville, OH 45314 • 3,210
Celina, OH 45822 • 9,650
Celina, TN 38551 • 1,493
Celina, TX 75009 • 1,737
Celoron, NY 14720 • 1,232
Cementon, PA 18052 • 1,050
Center, CO 81125 • 1,963
Center, ND 58530 • 826
Center, TX 75935 • 4,950
Centerburg, OH 43011 • 1,323
Centereach, NY 11720 • 26,720
Center Line, MI 48015 • 9,026
Center Moriches, NY 11934 • 5,987
Center Point, AL 35215 • 22,657
Center Point, IA 52213 • 1,693
Centerville, IN 47330 • 2,398
Centerville, IA 52544 • 5,936
Centerville, MA 02632 • 9,190
Centerville, OH 45459 • 21,082
Centerville, PA 15417 • 3,842
Centerville, SD 57014 • 887
Centerville, TN 37033 • 3,616
Centerville, UT 84014 • 11,500
Central, NM 88026 • 1,835
Central, SC 29630 • 2,438
Central City, CO 80427 • 335
Central City, IL 62801 • 1,390
Central City, IA 52214 • 1,063
Central City, KY 42330 • 4,979
Central City, NE 68826 • 2,868
Central City, PA 15926 • 1,246
Central Falls, RI 02863 • 17,637
Central Heights, AZ 85501 • 1,500
Centralia, IL 62801 • 14,274
Centralia, MO 65240 • 3,414
Centralia, WA 98531 • 12,101
Central Islip, NY 11722 • 26,028
Central Park, WA 98520 • 2,669
Central Point, OR 97502 • 7,509
Central Square, NY 13036 • 1,671
Central Valley, CA 96019 • 4,340
Central Valley, NY 10917 • 1,929
Central Village, CT 06332 • 1,600
Centre, AL 35960 • 2,893
Centre □, PA • 123,786
Centre City, NJ 08051 • 2,070
Centre Hall, PA 16828 • 1,203
Centreville, AL 35042 • 2,508
Centreville, IL 62207 • 7,489
Centreville, MD 21617 • 2,097
Centreville, MI 49032 • 1,516
Centreville, MS 39631 • 1,771
Centreville, VA 22020 • 26,585
Century, FL 32535 • 1,989
Century Village, FL 33409 • 8,363
Ceredo, WV 25507 • 1,916
Ceres, CA 95307 • 26,314
Cerritos, CA 90703 • 53,240
Cerro Gordo, IL 61818 • 1,436
Cerro Gordo □, IA • 46,733
Chadbourn, NC 28431 • 2,005
Chadds Ford, PA 19317 • 1,200
Chadron, NE 69337 • 5,588
Chadwicks, NY 13319 • 2,000
Chaffee, MO 63740 • 3,059
Chaffee □, CO • 12,684
Chaffin, MA 01520 • 3,980
Chagrin Falls, OH 44022 • 4,146
Chalfonte, DE 19810 • 1,740
Challis, ID 83226 • 1,073
Chalmette, LA 70043–44 • 31,860
Chama, NM 87520 • 1,048
Chamberlain, SD 57325 • 2,347
Chambers □, AL • 36,876
Chambers □, TX • 20,088
Chambersburg, PA 17201 • 16,647
Chamblee, GA 30341 • 7,668
Champaign, IL 61820–21 • 63,502
Champaign □, IL • 173,025
Champaign □, OH • 36,019
Champion, OH 44481 • 5,270
Champlain, NY 12919 • 1,273
Champlin, MN 55316 • 16,849
Chandler, AZ 85224–27 • 90,533
Chandler, IN 47610 • 3,099
Chandler, OK 74834 • 2,596
Chandler, TX 75758 • 1,630
Chandler Heights, AZ 85227 • 1,000
Chanhassen, MN 55317 • 11,732
Channahon, IL 60410 • 4,266
Channel Lake, IL 60002 • 1,660
Channelview, TX 77530 • 25,564
Chantilly, VA 22021–22 • 29,337
Chanute, KS 66720 • 9,488
Chapel Hill, NC 27514–16 • 38,719
Chapel Square, VA 22003 • 2,400
Chapman, KS 67431 • 1,264
Chapmanville, WV 25508 • 1,110
Chappaqua, NY 10514 • 6,380
Chardon, OH 44024 • 4,446
Chariton, IA 50049 • 4,616
Chariton □, MO • 9,202
Charleroi, PA 15022 • 5,014
Charles □, MD • 101,154
Charles City, IA 50616 • 7,878
Charles City □, VA • 6,282
Charles Mix □, SD • 9,131
Charleston, AR 72933 • 2,128
Charleston, IL 61920 • 20,398
Charleston, MS 38921 • 2,328
Charleston, MO 63834 • 5,085
Charleston, SC 29401–22 • 80,414
Charleston, WV 25301–75 • 57,287
Charleston □, SC • 295,039
Charlestown, IN 47111 • 5,889
Charlestown, NH 03603 • 1,173
Charlestown, RI 02813 • 1,500
Charles Town, WV 25414 • 3,122
Charlevoix, MI 49720 • 3,116
Charlevoix □, MI • 21,468
Charlotte, MI 48813 • 8,083
Charlotte, NC 28201–41 • 395,934
Charlotte, TX 78011 • 1,475
Charlotte □, FL • 110,975
Charlotte □, VA • 11,688
Charlotte Hall, MD 20622 • 1,992
Charlotte Harbor, FL 33980 • 3,327
Charlottesville, VA 22901–08 • 40,341
Charlton □, GA • 8,496
Charlton City, MA 01508 • 1,400
Charter Oak, CA 91724 • 8,858
Chase □, KS • 3,021
Chase □, NE • 4,381
Chase City, VA 23924 • 2,442
Chaska, MN 55318 • 11,339
Chatfield, MN 55923 • 2,226
Chatham, IL 62629 • 6,074
Chatham, MA 02633 • 1,916
Chatham, NJ 07928 • 8,007
Chatham, NY 12037 • 1,920
Chatham, VA 24531 • 1,354
Chatham □, GA • 216,935
Chatham □, NC • 38,759
Chatom, AL 36518 • 1,094
Chatsworth, GA 30705 • 2,865
Chatsworth, IL 60921 • 1,186
Chattahoochee, FL 32324 • 4,382
Chattahoochee □, GA • 16,934
Chattanooga, TN 37401–22 • 152,466
Chattaroy, WV 25667 • 1,182
Chattooga □, GA • 22,242
Chautauqua □, KS • 4,407
Chautauqua □, NY • 141,895
Chauvin, LA 70344 • 3,375
Chaves □, NM • 57,849
Chazy, NY 12921 • 1,000
Cheatham □, TN • 27,140
Cheboygan, MI 49721 • 4,999
Cheboygan □, MI • 21,398
Checotah, OK 74426 • 3,290
Cheektowaga, NY 14225 • 84,387
Chehalis, WA 98532 • 6,527
Chelan, WA 98816 • 2,969
Chelan □, WA • 52,250
Chelmsford, MA 01824 • 32,388
Chelsea, MA 02150 • 28,710
Chelsea, MI 48118 • 3,772
Chelsea, OK 74016 • 1,620
Chelsea Estates, DE 19720 • 1,320
Cheltenham Township, PA 19012 • 35,509
Chemung □, NY • 95,195
Chenango □, NY • 51,768
Chenango Bridge, NY 13745 • 2,890
Cheney, KS 67025 • 1,560
Cheney, WA 99004 • 7,723
Cheneyville, LA 71325 • 1,005
Chenoa, IL 61726 • 1,732
Chenoweth, OR 97058 • 3,246
Chepachet, RI 02814 • 900
Cheraw, SC 29520 • 5,505
Cherokee, AL 35616 • 1,479
Cherokee, IA 51012 • 6,026
Cherokee, OK 73728 • 1,787
Cherokee □, AL • 19,543
Cherokee □, GA • 90,204
Cherokee □, IA • 14,098
Cherokee □, KS • 21,374
Cherokee □, NC • 20,170
Cherokee □, OK • 34,049
Cherokee □, SC • 44,506
Cherokee □, TX • 41,049
Cherokee Village, AR 72525 • 3,200
Cherry □, NE • 6,307
Cherry Hill, NJ 08002–03 • 69,319
Cherry Hills Village, CO 80110 • 5,245
Cherryland, CA 94541 • 11,088
Cherryvale, KS 67335 • 2,464
Cherry Valley, CA 92223 • 5,945
Cherry Valley, IL 61016 • 1,615
Cherry Valley, MA 01611 • 1,120
Cherryville, NC 28021 • 4,756
Chesaning, MI 48616 • 2,567
Chesapeake, OH 45619 • 1,073
Chesapeake, VA 23320–28 • 151,976
Chesapeake, WV 25315 • 1,896
Chesapeake Beach, MD 20732 • 2,403
Cheshire, CT 06410 • 25,684
Cheshire, MA 01225 • 1,100
Cheshire □, NH • 70,121
Chesilhurst, NJ 08089 • 1,526
Chesnee, SC 29323 • 1,280
Chester, CA 96020 • 2,082
Chester, CT 06412 • 1,563
Chester, IL 62233 • 8,194
Chester, MT 59522 • 942
Chester, NJ 07930 • 1,214
Chester, NY 10918 • 3,270
Chester, PA 19013–16 • 41,856
Chester, SC 29706 • 7,158
Chester, VT 05143 • 550
Chester, VA 23831 • 14,896
Chester, WV 26034 • 2,905
Chester □, PA • 376,396
Chester □, SC • 32,170
Chester □, TN • 12,819
Chester Depot, VT 05144 • 500
Chesterfield, IN 46017 • 2,730
Chesterfield, SC 29709 • 1,373
Chesterfield □, SC • 38,577
Chesterfield □, VA • 209,274
Chesterton, IN 46304 • 9,124
Chestertown, MD 21620 • 4,005
Chester Township, PA 19013 • 5,399
Chestnut Hill Estates, DE 19713 • 1,730
Chestnut Ridge, NY 10952 • 7,517
Cheswick, PA 15024 • 1,971
Cheswold, DE 19936 • 321
Chetek, WI 54728 • 1,953
Chetopa, KS 67336 • 1,357
Chevak, AK 99563 • 598
Cheverly, MD 20785 • 6,023
Cheviot, OH 45211 • 9,616
Chevy Chase, MD 20815 • 8,559
Chewelah, WA 99109 • 1,945
Cheyenne, WY 82001–09 • 50,008
Cheyenne □, CO • 2,397
Cheyenne □, KS • 3,243
Cheyenne □, NE • 9,494
Cheyenne Wells, CO 80810 • 1,128
Chicago, IL 60601–66 • 2,783,726
Chicago Heights, IL 60411 • 33,072
Chicago Ridge, IL 60415 • 13,643
Chickamauga, GA 30707 • 2,149
Chickasaw, AL 36611 • 6,649
Chickasaw □, IA • 13,295
Chickasaw □, MS • 18,085
Chickasha, OK 73018 • 14,988
Chico, CA 95926–28 • 40,079
Chicopee, MA 01013–22 • 56,632
Chicora, PA 16025 • 1,058
Chiefland, FL 32626 • 1,917
Childersburg, AL 35044 • 4,579
Childress, TX 79201 • 5,055
Childress □, TX • 5,953
Chilhowie, VA 24319 • 1,971
Chili Center, NY 14624 • 4,360
Chillicothe, IL 61523 • 5,959
Chillicothe, MO 64601 • 8,804
Chillicothe, OH 45601 • 21,923
Chillum, MD 20783 • 31,309
Chilton, WI 53014 • 3,240
Chilton □, AL • 32,458
Chimayo, NM 87522 • 2,789
China Grove, NC 28023 • 2,732
Chincoteague, VA 23336 • 3,572
Chinle, AZ 86503 • 5,059
Chino, CA 91708–10 • 59,682
Chinook, MT 59523 • 1,512
Chino Valley, AZ 86323 • 4,837
Chipley, FL 32428 • 3,866
Chippewa □, MI • 34,604
Chippewa □, MN • 13,228
Chippewa □, WI • 52,360
Chippewa Falls, WI 54729 • 12,727
Chisago □, MN • 30,521
Chisago City, MN 55013 • 2,009
Chisholm, ME 04239 • 1,653
Chisholm, MN 55719 • 5,290
Chittenango, NY 13037 • 4,734
Chittenden □, VT • 131,761
Choctaw, OK 73020 • 8,545
Choctaw □, AL • 16,018
Choctaw □, MS • 9,071
Choctaw □, OK • 15,302
Choteau, MT 59422 • 1,741
Chouteau, OK 74337 • 1,771
Chouteau □, MT • 5,452
Chowan □, NC • 13,506
Chowchilla, CA 93610 • 5,930
Chrisman, IL 61924 • 1,136
Christian □, IL • 34,418
Christian □, KY • 68,941
Christian □, MO • 32,644
Christiana, DE 19702 • 500
Christiana, PA 17509 • 1,045
Christiansburg, VA 24073 • 15,004
Christmas, FL 32709 • 1,200
Christopher, IL 62822 • 2,774
Chubbuck, ID 83202 • 7,791
Chugwater, WY 82210 • 192
Chula Vista, CA 91909–15 • 135,163
Church Hill, TN 37642 • 4,834
Churchill, OH 44505 • 7,700
Churchill □, NV • 17,938
Church Point, LA 70525 • 4,677
Churchville, NY 14428 • 1,731
Churubusco, IN 46723 • 1,781
Cibola □, NM • 23,794
Cicero, IL 60650 • 67,436
Cicero, IN 46034 • 3,268
Cimarron, KS 67835 • 1,626
Cimarron □, OK • 3,301
Cimarron Hills, CO 80906 • 11,160
Cincinnati, OH 45201–75 • 364,040
Cinnaminson, NJ 08077 • 14,583
Circle, MT 59215 • 805
Circle Pines, MN 55014 • 4,704
Circleville, OH 43113 • 11,666
Cisco, TX 76437 • 3,813
Citra, FL 32113 • 1,500
Citronelle, AL 36522 • 3,671
Citrus, CA 91702 • 9,481

Citrus □, FL • 93,515
Citrus Heights, CA 95610–11 • 107,439
City Of Sunrise, FL 33313 • 64,407
City View, SC 29611 • 1,490
Clackamas, OR 97015 • 2,578
Clackamas □, OR • 278,850
Claiborne, LA 71291 • 8,300
Claiborne □, LA • 17,405
Claiborne □, MS • 11,370
Claiborne □, TN • 26,137
Clair-Mel City, FL 33619 • 7,000
Clairton, PA 15025 • 9,656
Clallam □, WA • 56,464
Clanton, AL 35045 • 7,669
Clara City, MN 56222 • 1,307
Clare, MI 48617 • 3,021
Clare □, MI • 24,952
Claremont, CA 91711 • 32,503
Claremont, NH 03743 • 13,902
Claremore, OK 74017–18 • 13,280
Clarence, MO 63437 • 1,026
Clarendon, AR 72029 • 2,072
Clarendon, TX 79226 • 2,067
Clarendon □, SC • 28,450
Clarendon Hills, IL 60514 • 6,994
Claridge, PA 15623 • 1,200
Clarinda, IA 51632 • 5,104
Clarion, IA 50525 • 2,703
Clarion, PA 16214 • 6,457
Clarion □, PA • 41,699
Clark, NJ 07066 • 14,629
Clark, SD 57225 • 1,292
Clark □, AR • 21,437
Clark □, ID • 762
Clark □, IL • 15,921
Clark □, IN • 87,777
Clark □, KS • 2,418
Clark □, KY • 29,496
Clark □, MO • 7,547
Clark □, NV • 741,459
Clark □, OH • 147,548
Clark □, SD • 4,403
Clark □, WA • 238,053
Clark □, WI • 31,647
Clarkdale, AZ 86324 • 2,144
Clarke □, AL • 27,240
Clarke □, GA • 87,594
Clarke □, IA • 8,287
Clarke □, MS • 17,313
Clarke □, VA • 12,101
Clarkesville, GA 30523 • 1,151
Clarksburg, WV 26301–02 • 18,059
Clarksdale, MS 38614 • 19,717
Clarks Summit, PA 18411 • 5,433
Clarkston, GA 30021 • 5,385
Clarkston, MI 48346–48 • 1,005
Clarkston, WA 99403 • 6,753
Clarksville, AR 72830 • 5,833
Clarksville, DE 19970 • 500
Clarksville, IN 47129 • 19,833
Clarksville, IA 50619 • 1,382
Clarksville, TN 37040–43 • 75,494
Clarksville, TX 75426 • 4,311
Clarksville, VA 23927 • 1,243
Clarkton, MO 63837 • 1,113
Clatskanie, OR 97016 • 1,629
Clatsop □, OR • 33,301
Claude, TX 79019 • 1,199
Clawson, MI 48017 • 13,874
Claxton, GA 30417 • 2,464
Clay, KY 42404 • 1,173
Clay □, AL • 13,252
Clay □, AR • 18,107
Clay □, FL • 105,986
Clay □, GA • 3,364
Clay □, IL • 14,460
Clay □, IN • 24,705
Clay □, IA • 17,585
Clay □, KS • 9,158
Clay □, KY • 21,746
Clay □, MN • 50,422
Clay □, MS • 21,120
Clay □, MO • 153,411
Clay □, NE • 7,123
Clay □, NC • 7,155
Clay □, SD • 13,186
Clay □, TN • 7,238
Clay □, TX • 10,024
Clay □, WV • 9,983
Clay Center, KS 67432 • 4,613
Clay City, KY 40312 • 1,258
Claymont, DE 19702 • 9,800
Claypool, AZ 85532 • 1,942
Claysburg, PA 16625 • 1,399
Clayton, AL 36016 • 1,564
Clayton, DE 19938 • 1,163
Clayton, GA 30525 • 1,613
Clayton, MO 63105 • 13,874
Clayton, NJ 08312 • 6,155
Clayton, NM 88415 • 2,484
Clayton, NY 13624 • 2,160
Clayton, NC 27520 • 4,756
Clayton □, GA • 182,052
Clayton □, IA • 19,054
Clear Creek □, CO • 7,619
Clearfield, KY 40313 • 1,250
Clearfield, PA 16830 • 6,633
Clearfield, UT 84015 • 21,435
Clearfield □, PA • 78,097
Clearlake, CA 95422 • 11,804
Clear Lake, IA 50428 • 8,183
Clear Lake, SD 57226 • 1,247
Clearlake, WA 98235 • 1,100
Clear Lake Shores, TX 77565 • 1,096
Clearwater, FL 34615–30 • 98,784
Clearwater, KS 67026 • 1,875
Clearwater, SC 29822 • 4,731
Clearwater □, ID • 8,505
Clearwater □, MN • 8,309
Cleburne, TX 76031–33 • 22,205
Cleburne □, AL • 12,730
Cleburne □, AR • 19,411
Cle Elum, WA 98922 • 1,778
Cleland Heights, DE 19805 • 1,120
Clementon, NJ 08021 • 5,601
Clemmons, NC 27012 • 6,020
Clemson, SC 29631–33 • 11,096
Clendenin, WV 25045 • 1,203
Cleona, PA 17042 • 2,322
Clermont, FL 34711–12 • 6,910
Clermont □, OH • 150,187
Cleveland, GA 30528 • 1,653
Cleveland, MS 38732–33 • 15,384
Cleveland, OH 44101–99 • 505,616
Cleveland, OK 74020 • 3,156
Cleveland, TN 37311–12 • 30,354
Cleveland, TX 77327–28 • 7,124
Cleveland, WI 53015 • 1,398
Cleveland □, AR • 7,781
Cleveland □, NC • 84,714
Cleveland □, OK • 174,253
Cleveland Heights, OH 44118 • 54,052
Cleves, OH 45002 • 2,208
Clewiston, FL 33440 • 6,085
Cliffside Park, NJ 07010 • 20,393
Clifton, AZ 85533 • 2,840
Clifton, CO 81520 • 12,671
Clifton, IL 60927 • 1,347
Clifton, NJ 07011–15 • 71,742
Clifton, TX 76634 • 3,195
Clifton Forge, VA 24422 • 4,679
Clifton Heights, PA 19018 • 7,111
Clifton Knolls, NY 12065 • 5,636
Clifton Springs, NY 14432 • 2,175
Clinch □, GA • 6,160
Clint, TX 79836 • 1,035
Clinton, AR 72031 • 2,213
Clinton, CT 06413 • 3,439
Clinton, IL 61727 • 7,437
Clinton, IN 47842 • 5,040
Clinton, IA 52732–33 • 29,201
Clinton, KY 42031 • 1,547
Clinton, LA 70722 • 1,904
Clinton, ME 04927 • 1,485
Clinton, MD 20735 • 19,987
Clinton, MA 01510 • 7,943
Clinton, MI 49236 • 2,475
Clinton, MS 39056 • 21,847
Clinton, MO 64735 • 8,703
Clinton, NJ 08809 • 2,054
Clinton, NY 13323 • 2,238
Clinton, NC 28328 • 8,204
Clinton, OK 73601 • 9,298
Clinton, SC 29325 • 7,987
Clinton, TN 37716 • 8,972
Clinton, UT 84015 • 7,945
Clinton, WA 98236 • 2,000
Clinton, WI 53525 • 1,849
Clinton □, IL • 33,944
Clinton □, IN • 30,974
Clinton □, IA • 51,040
Clinton □, KY • 9,135
Clinton □, MI • 57,883
Clinton □, MO • 16,595
Clinton □, NY • 85,969
Clinton □, OH • 35,415
Clinton □, PA • 37,182
Clinton Township, MI 48043 • 85,866
Clintonville, WI 54929 • 4,351
Clintwood, VA 24228 • 1,542
Clio, AL 36017 • 1,365
Clio, MI 48420 • 2,629
Clive, IA 50322 • 7,462
Cloquet, MN 55720 • 10,885
Closter, NJ 07624 • 8,094
Cloud □, KS • 11,023
Clover, SC 29710 • 3,422
Cloverdale, CA 95425 • 4,924
Cloverdale, IN 46120 • 1,681
Cloverleaf, TX 77015 • 18,230
Cloverport, KY 40111 • 1,207
Clovis, CA 93612–13 • 50,323
Clovis, NM 88101–03 • 30,954
Clute, TX 77531 • 8,910
Clyde, NY 14433 • 2,409
Clyde, NC 28721 • 1,041
Clyde, OH 43410 • 5,776
Clyde, TX 79510 • 3,002
Clymer, PA 15728 • 1,499
Coachella, CA 92236 • 16,896
Coahoma, TX 79511 • 1,133
Coahoma □, MS • 31,665
Coal □, OK • 5,780
Coal City, IL 60416 • 3,907
Coal Fork, WV 25306 • 2,100
Coalgate, OK 74538 • 1,895
Coal Grove, OH 45638 • 2,251
Coalinga, CA 93210 • 8,212
Coalville, UT 84017 • 1,065
Coatesville, PA 19320 • 11,038
Coats, NC 27521 • 1,493
Cobb □, GA • 447,745
Cobden, IL 62920 • 1,090
Cobleskill, NY 12043 • 5,268
Cochise □, AZ • 97,624
Cochituate, MA 01778 • 6,046
Cochran, GA 31014 • 4,390
Cochran □, TX • 4,377
Cochranton, PA 16314 • 1,174
Cocke □, TN • 29,141
Cockeysville, MD 21030 • 18,668
Cockrell Hill, TX 75211 • 3,746
Cocoa, FL 32922–27 • 17,722
Cocoa Beach, FL 32931–32 • 12,123
Coconino □, AZ • 96,591
Coconut Creek, FL 33060 • 27,485
Codington □, SD • 22,698
Cody, WY 82414 • 7,897
Coeburn, VA 24230 • 2,165
Coeur d'Alene, ID 83814 • 24,563
Coffee □, AL • 40,240
Coffee □, GA • 29,592
Coffee □, TN • 40,339
Coffey □, KS • 8,404
Coffeyville, KS 67337 • 12,917
Cohasset, MA 02025 • 6,800
Cohoes, NY 12047 • 16,825
Cokato, MN 55321 • 2,180
Coke □, TX • 3,424
Cokeville, WY 83114 • 493
Colbert, OK 74733 • 1,043
Colbert □, AL • 51,666
Colby, KS 67701 • 5,396
Colby, WI 54421 • 1,532
Colchester, CT 06415 • 3,212
Colchester, IL 62326 • 1,645
Cold Bay, AK 99571 • 148
Cold Spring, KY 41076 • 2,880
Cold Spring, MN 56320 • 2,459
Cold Spring Harbor, NY 11724 • 4,789
Coldwater, MI 49036 • 9,607
Coldwater, MS 38618 • 1,502
Coldwater, OH 45828 • 4,335
Cole □, MO • 63,579
Colebrook, NH 03576 • 2,444
Cole Camp, MO 65325 • 1,054
Coleman, MI 48618 • 1,237
Coleman, TX 76834 • 5,410
Coleman □, TX • 9,710
Coleraine, MN 55722 • 1,041
Coles □, IL • 51,644
Colfax, CA 95713 • 1,306
Colfax, IA 50054 • 2,462
Colfax, LA 71417 • 1,696
Colfax, WA 99111 • 2,713
Colfax, WI 54730 • 1,110
Colfax □, NE • 9,139
Colfax □, NM • 12,925
College, AK 99701 • 11,249
Collegedale, TN 37315 • 5,048
College Park, GA 30337 • 20,457
College Park, MD 20740–41 • 21,927
College Place, WA 99324 • 6,308
College Station, AR 72053 • 3,800
College Station, TX 77840–45 • 52,456
Collegeville, PA 19426 • 4,227
Colleton □, SC • 34,377
Colleyville, TX 76034 • 12,724
Collier □, FL • 152,099
Collierville, TN 38017 • 14,427
Collin □, TX • 264,036
Collingdale, PA 19023 • 9,175
Collingswood, NJ 08108 • 15,289
Collingsworth □, TX • 3,573
Collins, MS 39428 • 2,541
Collins Park, DE 19720 • 2,100
Collinsville, AL 35961 • 1,429
Collinsville, CT 06022 • 2,591
Collinsville, IL 62234 • 22,446
Collinsville, OK 74021 • 3,612
Collinsville, VA 24078 • 7,280
Collinwood, TN 38450 • 1,014
Colmar Manor, MD 20722 • 1,249
Coloma, MI 49038 • 1,679
Colon, MI 49040 • 1,224
Colonia, NJ 07067 • 18,238
Colonial Beach, VA 22443 • 3,132
Colonial Heights, TN 37663 • 6,716
Colonial Heights, VA 23834 • 16,064
Colonial Park, PA 17109 • 13,777
Colonie, NY 12212 • 8,019
Colorado □, TX • 18,383
Colorado City, AZ 86021 • 2,426
Colorado City, CO 81019 • 1,149
Colorado City, TX 79512 • 4,749
Colorado Springs, CO 80901–99 • 281,140
Colquitt, GA 31737 • 1,991
Colquitt □, GA • 36,645
Colstrip, MT 59323 • 3,035
Colton, CA 92324 • 40,213
Columbia, CA 95310 • 1,799
Columbia, IL 62236 • 5,524
Columbia, KY 42728 • 3,845
Columbia, MD 21044–46 • 75,883
Columbia, MS 39429 • 6,815
Columbia, MO 65201–05 • 69,101
Columbia, PA 17512 • 10,701
Columbia, SC 29201–92 • 98,052
Columbia, TN 38401–02 • 28,583
Columbia □, AR • 25,691
Columbia □, FL • 42,613
Columbia □, GA • 66,031
Columbia □, NY • 62,982
Columbia □, OR • 37,557
Columbia □, PA • 63,202
Columbia □, WA • 4,024
Columbia □, WI • 45,088
Columbia City, IN 46725 • 5,706
Columbia City, OR 97018 • 1,003
Columbia Falls, MT 59912 • 2,942
Columbia Heights, MN 55421 • 18,910
Columbiana, AL 35051 • 2,968
Columbiana, OH 44408 • 4,961
Columbiana □, OH • 108,276
Columbine, CO 80123 • 23,969
Columbus, GA 31901–09 • 178,681
Columbus, IN 47201–03 • 31,802
Columbus, KS 66725 • 3,268
Columbus, MS 39701–05 • 23,799
Columbus, MT 59019 • 1,573
Columbus, NE 68601 • 19,480
Columbus, OH 43201–91 • 632,910
Columbus, TX 78934 • 3,367
Columbus, WI 53925 • 4,093
Columbus □, NC • 49,587
Columbus Grove, OH 45830 • 2,231
Columbus Junction, IA 52738 • 1,616
Colusa, CA 95932 • 4,934
Colusa □, CA • 16,275
Colver, PA 15927 • 1,024
Colville, WA 99114 • 4,360
Colwich, KS 67030 • 1,091
Comal □, TX • 51,832
Comanche, OK 73529 • 1,695
Comanche, TX 76442 • 4,087
Comanche □, KS • 2,313
Comanche □, OK • 111,486
Comanche □, TX • 13,381
Combee Settlement, FL 33801 • 5,463
Combined Locks, WI 54113 • 2,190
Comfort, TX 78013 • 1,477
Commack, NY 11725 • 36,124
Commerce, CA 90040 • 12,135
Commerce, GA 30529 • 4,108
Commerce, OK 74339 • 2,426
Commerce, TX 75428 • 6,825
Commerce City, CO 80022 • 16,466
Common Fence Point, RI 02871 • 860
Como, MS 38619 • 1,387
Compton, CA 90220–24 • 90,454
Comstock, MI 49041 • 5,600
Comstock Park, MI 49321 • 6,530
Concho □, TX • 3,044
Concord, CA 94518–24 • 111,348
Concord, MA 01742 • 4,680
Concord, MO 63128 • 19,859
Concord, NH 03301–03 • 36,006
Concord, NC 28025–27 • 27,347
Concord, TN 37901 • 3,420
Concordia, KS 66901 • 6,167
Concordia, MO 64020 • 2,160
Concordia □, LA • 20,828
Conecuh □, AL • 14,054
Conejos □, CO • 7,453
Conemaugh, PA 15909 • 1,470
Congers, NY 10920 • 8,003
Conklin, NY 13748 • 1,800
Conley, GA 30027 • 5,528
Conneaut, OH 44030 • 13,241
Connell, WA 99326 • 2,005
Connellsville, PA 15425 • 9,229
Connersville, IN 47331 • 15,550
Conover, NC 28613 • 5,465
Conrad, MT 59425 • 2,891
Conroe, TX 77301–05 • 27,610
Conshohocken, PA 19428 • 8,064
Constantia, NY 13044 • 1,140
Constantine, MI 49042 • 2,032
Continental, OH 45831 • 1,214
Contoocook, NH 03229 • 1,334
Contra Costa □, CA • 803,732
Converse, IN 46919 • 1,144
Converse, SC 29329 • 1,173
Converse, TX 78109 • 8,887
Converse □, WY • 11,128
Convoy, OH 45832 • 1,200
Conway, AR 72032 • 26,481
Conway, FL 32809 • 13,159
Conway, NH 03818 • 1,604
Conway, PA 15027 • 2,424
Conway, SC 29526–27 • 9,819
Conway □, AR • 19,151
Conway Springs, KS 67031 • 1,384
Conyers, GA 30207–08 • 7,380
Cook □, GA • 13,456
Cook □, IL • 5,105,067
Cook □, MN • 3,868
Cooke □, TX • 30,777
Cookeville, TN 38501–02 • 21,744
Coolidge, AZ 85228 • 6,927
Coon Rapids, IA 50058 • 1,266
Coon Rapids, MN 55433 • 52,978
Cooper, TX 75432 • 2,153
Cooper □, MO • 14,835
Cooper City, FL 33328 • 20,791
Cooper Road, LA 71107 • 11,050
Coopersburg, PA 18036 • 2,599
Cooperstown, NY 13326 • 2,180
Cooperstown, ND 58425 • 1,247
Coopersville, MI 49404 • 3,421
Coos □, NH • 34,828
Coos □, OR • 60,273
Coosa □, AL • 11,063
Coos Bay, OR 97420 • 15,076
Copake, NY 12516 • 1,200
Copiague, NY 11726 • 20,769
Copiah □, MS • 27,592
Coplay, PA 18037 • 3,267
Copperas Cove, TX 76522 • 24,079
Coquille, OR 97423 • 4,121
Coral Gables, FL 33134 • 40,091
Coral Hills, MD 20743 • 11,032
Coral Springs, FL 33065 • 79,443
Coral Terrace, FL 33157 • 23,255
Coralville, IA 52241 • 10,347
Coral Way Village, FL 33155 • 9,000
Coram, NY 11727 • 30,111
Coraopolis, PA 15108 • 6,747
Corbin, KY 40701–02 • 7,419
Corcoran, CA 93212 • 13,364
Corcoran, MN 55340 • 5,199
Cordaville, MA 01772 • 1,530
Cordele, GA 31015 • 10,321
Cordell, OK 73632 • 2,903
Cordova, AL 35550 • 2,623
Cordova, AK 99574 • 2,110
Cordova, NC 28330 • 1,200
Corinth, MS 38834 • 11,820
Corinth, NY 12822 • 2,760
Cornelia, GA 30531 • 3,219
Cornelius, NC 28031 • 2,581
Cornelius, OR 97113 • 6,148
Cornell, WI 54732 • 1,541
Corning, AR 72422 • 3,323
Corning, CA 96021 • 5,870
Corning, IA 50841 • 1,806
Corning, NY 14830 • 11,938
Cornville, AZ 86325 • 1,200
Cornwall, PA 17016 • 3,231
Cornwall on Hudson, NY 12520 • 3,093
Corona, CA 91718–20 • 76,095
Coronado, CA 92118 • 26,540
Coronado, CO 80229 • 6,890
Corpus Christi, TX 78401–82 • 257,453
Corrigan, TX 75939 • 1,764
Corriganville, MD 21524 • 1,020
Corry, PA 16407 • 7,216
Corsicana, TX 75110 • 22,911
Corson □, SD • 4,195
Corte Madera, CA 94925 • 8,272
Cortez, CO 81321 • 7,284
Cortez, FL 34215 • 4,509
Cortland, NY 13045 • 19,801
Cortland, OH 44410 • 5,666
Cortland □, NY • 48,963
Corunna, MI 48817 • 3,091
Corvallis, OR 97330–33 • 44,757
Corydon, IN 47112 • 2,661
Corydon, IA 50060 • 1,675
Coryell □, TX • 64,213
Coshocton, OH 43812 • 12,193
Coshocton □, OH • 35,427
Cosmopolis, WA 98537 • 1,372
Costa Mesa, CA 92626–28 • 96,357
Costilla □, CO • 3,190
Cottage Grove, MN 55016 • 22,935
Cottage Grove, OR 97424 • 7,402
Cottle □, TX • 2,247
Cottleville, MO 63338 • 2,936
Cotton □, OK • 6,651
Cottondale, AL 35453 • 1,960
Cotton Plant, AR 72036 • 1,150
Cottonport, LA 71327 • 2,600
Cotton Valley, LA 71018 • 1,130
Cottonwood, AL 36320 • 1,385
Cottonwood, AZ 86326 • 5,918
Cottonwood, CA 96022 • 1,747
Cottonwood, ID 83522 • 822
Cottonwood, UT 84121 • 11,554
Cottonwood □, MN • 12,694
Cottonwood Heights, UT 84121 • 28,766
Cotuit, MA 02635 • 1,750
Cotulla, TX 78014 • 3,694
Coudersport, PA 16915 • 2,854
Coulee Dam, WA 99116 • 1,087
Council, ID 83612 • 831
Council Bluffs, IA 51501–03 • 54,315
Council Grove, KS 66846 • 2,228
Country Club Hills, IL 60478 • 15,431
Country Homes, WA 99218 • 5,126
Countryside, IL 60525 • 5,716
Coupeville, WA 98239 • 1,377
Coushatta, LA 71019 • 1,845
Covedale, OH 45238 • 6,669
Covelo, CA 95428 • 1,057
Coventry, CT 06238 • 10,063
Coventry, DE 19720 • 1,165
Coventry, RI 02816 • 6,980
Covina, CA 91722–24 • 43,207
Covington, GA 30209 • 10,026
Covington, IN 47932 • 2,747
Covington, KY 41011–18 • 43,264
Covington, LA 70433–34 • 7,691
Covington, OH 45318 • 2,603
Covington, TN 38019 • 7,487
Covington, VA 24426 • 6,991
Covington □, AL • 36,478
Covington □, MS • 16,527
Cowan, TN 37318 • 1,738
Cowarts, AL 36321 • 1,400
Coweta, OK 74429 • 6,159
Coweta □, GA • 53,853
Cowley, WY 82420 • 477
Cowley □, KS • 36,915
Cowlitz □, WA • 82,119
Cowpens, SC 29330 • 2,176
Coxsackie, NY 12051 • 2,789
Cozad, NE 69130 • 3,823
Crab Orchard, WV 25827 • 2,919
Crabtree, PA 15624 • 1,000
Crafton, PA 15205 • 7,188
Craig, AK 99921 • 1,260
Craig, CO 81625–26 • 8,091
Craig □, OK • 14,104
Craig □, VA • 4,372
Craighead □, AR • 68,956
Craigsville, WV 26205 • 1,955
Cramerton, NC 28032 • 2,371
Cranbury, NJ 08512 • 1,255
Crandall, TX 75114 • 1,652
Crandon, WI 54520 • 1,958
Crane, AZ 85365 • 2,650
Crane, MO 65633 • 1,218
Crane, TX 79731 • 3,533
Crane □, TX • 4,652
Cranford, NJ 07016 • 22,624
Cranston, RI 02910 • 76,060
Craven □, NC • 81,613
Crawford, NE 69339 • 1,115
Crawford □, AR • 42,493
Crawford □, GA • 8,991
Crawford □, IL • 19,464
Crawford □, IN • 9,914
Crawford □, IA • 16,775
Crawford □, KS • 35,568
Crawford □, MI • 12,260
Crawford □, MO • 19,173
Crawford □, OH • 47,870
Crawford □, PA • 86,169
Crawford □, WI • 15,940
Crawfordsville, IN 47933 • 13,584
Crawfordville, FL 32327 • 1,110
Creedmoor, NC 27522 • 1,504
Creek □, OK • 60,915
Creighton, NE 68729 • 1,223
Creighton, PA 15030 • 1,658
Crenshaw □, AL • 13,635
Creola, AL 36525 • 1,896
Cresaptown, MD 21502 • 4,645
Crescent, OK 73028 • 1,236
Crescent City, CA 95531 • 4,380
Crescent City, FL 32112 • 1,859
Crescent Springs, KY 41016 • 2,179
Cresco, IA 52136 • 3,669
Cresskill, NJ 07626 • 7,558
Cresson, PA 16630 • 1,784
Cressona, PA 17929 • 1,694
Cresthaven, FL 33064 • 2,400
Crest Hill, IL 60435 • 10,643
Crestline, CA 92325 • 8,594
Crestline, OH 44827 • 4,934
Creston, IA 50801 • 7,911
Creston, OH 44217 • 1,848
Crestview, FL 32536 • 9,886
Crestview, HI 96797 • 1,000
Crestwood, IL 60445 • 10,823
Crestwood, KY 40014 • 1,435
Crestwood, MO 63126 • 11,234
Crestwood Village, NJ 08759 • 8,030
Creswell, OR 97426 • 2,431
Crete, IL 60417 • 6,773
Crete, NE 68333 • 4,841
Creve Coeur, IL 61611 • 5,938
Creve Coeur, MO 63141 • 12,304
Crewe, VA 23930 • 2,276
Cricket, NC 28659 • 2,015
Cridersville, OH 45806 • 1,885
Crisfield, MD 21817 • 2,880
Crisp □, GA • 20,011
Crittenden □, AR • 49,939
Crittenden □, KY • 9,196
Crocker, MO 65452 • 1,077
Crockett, CA 94525 • 3,228
Crockett, TX 75835 • 7,024
Crockett □, TN • 13,378
Crockett □, TX • 4,078
Crofton, MD 21114 • 12,781
Cromwell, CT 06416 • 1,100
Crook □, OR • 14,111
Crook □, WY • 5,294
Crookston, MN 56716 • 8,119
Crooksville, OH 43731 • 2,601
Crosby, MN 56441 • 2,073
Crosby, ND 58730 • 1,312
Crosby, TX 77532 • 1,811
Crosby □, TX • 7,304
Crosbyton, TX 79322 • 2,026
Cross □, AR • 19,225
Cross City, FL 32628 • 2,041
Crossett, AR 71635 • 6,282
Crosslake, MN 56442 • 1,132
Cross Lanes, WV 25313 • 10,878
Cross Plains, TN 37049 • 1,025
Cross Plains, TX 76443 • 1,063
Cross Plains, WI 53528 • 2,098
Crossville, AL 35962 • 1,350
Crossville, TN 38555 • 6,930
Croswell, MI 48422 • 2,174
Crothersville, IN 47229 • 1,687
Croton-on-Hudson, NY 10520 • 7,018
Crow Agency, MT 59022 • 1,446
Crowell, TX 79227 • 1,230
Crowley, LA 70526–27 • 13,983
Crowley, TX 76036 • 6,974

Crowley □, CO • 3,946
Crown Point, IN 46307 • 17,728
Crownpoint, NM 87313 • 2,108
Crow Wing □, MN • 44,249
Crozet, VA 22932 • 2,256
Crystal, MN 55428 • 23,788
Crystal Bay, NV 89402 • 1,200
Crystal Beach, FL 34681 • 1,450
Crystal City, MO 63019 • 4,088
Crystal City, TX 78839 • 8,263
Crystal Falls, MI 49920 • 1,922
Crystal Lake, CT 06029 • 1,200
Crystal Lake, FL 33803 • 5,300
Crystal Lake, IL 60014 • 24,512
Crystal Lawns, IL 60435 • 1,660
Crystal River, FL 32629 • 4,044
Crystal Springs, MS 39059 • 5,643
Cuba, IL 61427 • 1,440
Cuba, MO 65453 • 2,537
Cuba, NY 14727 • 1,690
Cuba City, WI 53807 • 2,024
Cucamonga, CA 91730 • 101,409
Cudahy, CA 90201 • 22,817
Cudahy, WI 53110 • 18,659
Cuero, TX 77954 • 6,700
Culberson □, TX • 3,407
Culbertson, MT 59218 • 796
Cullen, LA 71021 • 1,642
Cullman, AL 35055–56 • 13,367
Cullman □, AL • 67,613
Culloden, WV 25510 • 2,907
Cullowhee, NC 28723 • 1,200
Culpeper, VA 22701 • 8,581
Culpeper □, VA • 27,791
Culver, IN 46511 • 1,404
Culver City, CA 90230–33 • 38,793
Cumberland, KY 40823 • 3,112
Cumberland, MD 21501–05 • 23,706
Cumberland, WI 54829 • 2,163
Cumberland □, IL • 10,670
Cumberland □, KY • 6,784
Cumberland □, ME • 243,135
Cumberland □, NJ • 138,053
Cumberland □, NC • 274,566
Cumberland □, PA • 195,257
Cumberland □, TN • 34,736
Cumberland □, VA • 7,825
Cumberland Center, ME 04021 • 1,890
Cumberland Foreside, ME 04110 • 1,000
Cumberland Hill, RI 02864 • 6,379
Cuming □, NE • 10,117
Cumming, GA 30130 • 2,828
Cupertino, CA 95014–16 • 40,263
Currituck □, NC • 13,736
Curry □, NM • 42,207
Curry □, OR • 19,327
Curtisville, PA 15032 • 1,285
Curwensville, PA 16833 • 2,924
Cushing, OK 74023 • 7,218
Cusseta, GA 31805 • 1,107
Custer, SD 57730 • 1,741
Custer □, CO • 1,926
Custer □, ID • 4,133
Custer □, MT • 11,697
Custer □, NE • 12,270
Custer □, OK • 26,897
Custer □, SD • 6,179
Cut Bank, MT 59427 • 3,329
Cutchogue, NY 11935 • 1,730
Cuthbert, GA 31740 • 3,730
Cutler, FL 33157 • 16,201
Cutler Ridge, FL 33157 • 21,268
Cutlerville, MI 49508 • 11,228
Cut Off, LA 70345 • 5,325
Cuyahoga □, OH • 1,412,140
Cuyahoga Falls, OH 44221–24 • 48,950
Cynthiana, KY 41031 • 6,497
Cypress, CA 90630 • 42,655
Cypress Lake, FL 33919 • 10,491
Cypress Quarters, FL 34972 • 1,343
Cyril, OK 73029 • 1,072

D

Dacono, CO 80514 • 2,228
Dacula, GA 30211 • 2,217
Dade □, FL • 1,937,094
Dade □, GA • 13,147
Dade □, MO • 7,449
Dade City, FL 33525–26 • 5,633
Dadeville, AL 36853 • 3,276
Daggett □, UT • 690
Dagsboro, DE 19939 • 398
Dahlonega, GA 30533 • 3,086
Daingerfield, TX 75638 • 2,572
Dakota □, MN • 275,227
Dakota □, NE • 16,742
Dakota City, IA 50529 • 1,024
Dakota City, NE 68731 • 1,470
Dale, IN 47523 • 1,553
Dale □, AL • 49,633
Dale City, VA 22193 • 47,170
Daleville, AL 36322 • 5,117
Daleville, IN 47334 • 1,681
Dalhart, TX 79022 • 6,246
Dallam □, TX • 5,461
Dallas, GA 30132 • 2,810
Dallas, NC 28034 • 3,012
Dallas, OR 97338 • 9,422
Dallas, PA 18612 • 2,567
Dallas, TX 75201–99 • 1,006,877
Dallas □, AL • 48,130
Dallas □, AR • 9,614
Dallas □, IA • 29,755
Dallas □, MO • 12,646
Dallas □, TX • 1,852,810
Dallas Center, IA 50063 • 1,454
Dallas City, IL 62330 • 1,037
Dallastown, PA 17313 • 3,974
Dalton, GA 30720–22 • 21,761
Dalton, MA 01226–27 • 6,797
Dalton, OH 44618 • 1,377
Dalton, PA 18414 • 1,369
Dalton Gardens, ID 83814 • 1,951
Daly City, CA 94014–17 • 92,311
Damascus, MD 20872 • 9,817
Dana Point, CA 92629 • 31,896
Danbury, CT 06810–13 • 65,585
Danbury, TX 77534 • 1,447
Dandridge, TN 37725 • 1,540
Dane □, WI • 367,085
Dania, FL 33004 • 13,024
Daniels □, MT • 2,266
Danielson, CT 06239 • 4,441
Dannemora, NY 12929 • 4,005
Dansville, NY 14437 • 5,002
Dante, VA 24237 • 1,083
Danvers, MA 01923 • 24,174
Danville, AR 72833 • 1,585
Danville, CA 94526 • 31,306
Danville, IL 61832–34 • 33,828
Danville, IN 46122 • 4,345
Danville, KY 40422–23 • 12,420
Danville, OH 43014 • 1,001
Danville, PA 17821 • 5,165
Danville, VA 24540–43 • 53,056
Daphne, AL 36526 • 11,290
Darby, PA 19023 • 11,140
Darby Township, PA 19036 • 10,955
Dardanelle, AR 72834 • 3,722
Dare □, NC • 22,746
Darien, CT 06820 • 18,130
Darien, GA 31305 • 1,783
Darien, IL 60559 • 18,341
Darien, WI 53114 • 1,158
Darke □, OH • 53,619
Darley Woods, DE 19810 • 1,220
Darlington, SC 29532 • 7,311
Darlington, WI 53530 • 2,235
Darlington □, SC • 61,851
Darrington, WA 98241 • 1,042
Dartmouth Woods, DE 19810 • 1,970
Dassel, MN 55325 • 1,082
Dauphin □, PA • 237,813
Davenport, FL 33837 • 1,529
Davenport, IA 52801–09 • 95,333
Davenport, WA 99122 • 1,502
David City, NE 68632 • 2,522
Davidson, NC 28036 • 4,046
Davidson □, NC • 126,677
Davidson □, TN • 510,784
Davidsville, PA 15928 • 1,167
Davie, FL 33328 • 47,217
Davie □, NC • 27,859
Daviess □, IN • 27,533
Daviess □, KY • 87,189
Daviess □, MO • 7,865
Davis, CA 95616–17 • 46,209
Davis, OK 73030 • 2,543
Davis □, IA • 8,312
Davis □, UT • 187,941
Davison, MI 48423 • 5,693
Davison □, SD • 17,503
Davisville, RI 02852 • 500
Dawes □, NE • 9,021
Dawson, GA 31742 • 5,295
Dawson, MN 56232 • 1,626
Dawson □, GA • 9,429
Dawson □, MT • 9,505
Dawson □, NE • 19,940
Dawson □, TX • 14,349
Dawson Springs, KY 42408 • 3,129
Day □, SD • 6,978
Dayton, KY 41074 • 6,576
Dayton, MN 55327 • 4,443
Dayton, NV 89403 • 2,217
Dayton, NJ 08810 • 1,200
Dayton, OH 45401–90 • 182,044
Dayton, OR 97114 • 1,526
Dayton, TN 37321 • 5,671
Dayton, TX 77535 • 5,151
Dayton, WA 99328 • 2,468
Dayton, WY 82836 • 565
Daytona Beach, FL 32114–25 • 61,921
Dayville, CT 06241 • 1,500
Deadwood, SD 57732 • 1,830
Deaf Smith □, TX • 19,153
Deal, NJ 07723 • 1,179
Deale, MD 20751 • 4,151
Dearborn, MI 48120–26 • 89,286
Dearborn □, IN • 38,835
Dearborn Heights, MI 48127 • 60,838
De Baca □, NM • 2,252
De Bary, FL 32713 • 7,176
Decatur, AL 35601–03 • 48,761
Decatur, GA 30030–37 • 17,336
Decatur, IL 62521–26 • 83,885
Decatur, IN 46733 • 8,644
Decatur, MI 49045 • 1,760
Decatur, MS 39327 • 1,248
Decatur, TN 37322 • 1,361
Decatur, TX 76234 • 4,252
Decatur □, GA • 25,511
Decatur □, IN • 23,645
Decatur □, IA • 8,338
Decatur □, KS • 4,021
Decatur □, TN • 10,472
Decherd, TN 37324 • 2,196
Deckerville, MI 48427 • 1,015
Decorah, IA 52101 • 8,063
Dedham, MA 02026 • 23,782
Deep River, CT 06417 • 2,520
Deerfield, IL 60015 • 17,327
Deerfield, WI 53531 • 1,617
Deerfield Beach, FL 33441–43 • 46,325
Deer Lodge, MT 59722 • 3,378
Deer Lodge □, MT • 10,278
Deer Park, NY 11729 • 28,840
Deer Park, OH 45236 • 6,181
Deer Park, TX 77536 • 27,652
Deer Park, WA 99006 • 2,278
Defiance, OH 43512 • 16,768
Defiance □, OH • 39,350
De Forest, WI 53532 • 4,882
De Funiak Springs, FL 32433 • 5,120
De Graff, OH 43318 • 1,331
De Kalb, IL 60115 • 34,925
De Kalb, MS 39328 • 1,073
De Kalb, TX 75559 • 1,976
De Kalb □, AL • 54,651
De Kalb □, GA • 545,837
De Kalb □, IL • 77,932
De Kalb □, IN • 35,324
De Kalb □, MO • 9,967
De Kalb □, TN • 14,360
Delafield, WI 53018 • 5,347
Del Aire, CA 90250 • 8,040
Delanco, NJ 08075 • 3,316
De Land, FL 32720–24 • 16,491
Delano, CA 93215–16 • 22,762
Delano, MN 55328 • 2,709
Delavan, IL 61734 • 1,642
Delavan, WI 53115 • 6,073
Delavan Lake, WI 53115 • 2,177
Delaware, OH 43015 • 20,030
Delaware □, IN • 119,659
Delaware □, IA • 18,035
Delaware □, NY • 47,225
Delaware □, OH • 66,929
Delaware □, OK • 28,070
Delaware □, PA • 547,651
Delaware City, DE 19706 • 1,682
Delcambre, LA 70528 • 1,978
Del City, OK 73115 • 23,928
De Leon, TX 76444 • 2,190
De Leon Springs, FL 32130 • 1,481
Delevan, NY 14042 • 1,214
Delhi, LA 71232 • 3,169
Delhi, NY 13753 • 3,064
Delhi Hills, OH 45238 • 27,647
Dell Rapids, SD 57022 • 2,484
Dellwood, MO 63136 • 5,245
Del Mar, CA 92014 • 4,860
Delmar, DE 19940 • 962
Delmar, MD 21875 • 1,430
Delmar, NY 12054 • 8,360
Del Norte, CO 81132 • 1,674
Del Norte □, CA • 23,460
Del Park Manor, DE 19808 • 1,550
Delphi, IN 46923 • 2,531
Delphos, OH 45833 • 7,093
Delran, NJ 08075 • 14,811
Delray Beach, FL 33444–47 • 47,181
Del Rio, FL 33617 • 8,248
Del Rio, TX 78840–42 • 30,705
Delta, CO 81416 • 3,789
Delta, OH 43515 • 2,849
Delta, UT 84624 • 2,998
Delta □, CO • 20,980
Delta □, MI • 37,780
Delta □, TX • 4,857
Delta Junction, AK 99737 • 652
Deltaville, VA 23043 • 1,082
Deltona, FL 32725 • 50,828
Demarest, NJ 07627 • 4,800
Deming, NM 88030–31 • 10,970
Demopolis, AL 36732 • 7,512
Demorest, GA 30535 • 1,088
Demotte, IN 46310 • 2,482
Denham Springs, LA 70726–27 • 8,381
Denison, IA 51442 • 6,604
Denison, TX 75020–21 • 21,505
Denmark, SC 29042 • 3,762
Denmark, WI 54208 • 1,612
Dennis, MA 02638 • 2,500
Dennison, OH 44621 • 3,282
Dennis Port, MA 02639 • 2,775
Denny Terrace, SC 29203 • 1,885
Dent □, MO • 13,702
Denton, MD 21629 • 2,977
Denton, NC 27239 • 1,292
Denton, TX 76201–06 • 66,270
Denton □, TX • 273,525
Dentsville, SC 29204 • 11,839
Denver, CO 80201–95 • 467,610
Denver, IA 50622 • 1,600
Denver, PA 17517 • 2,861
Denver □, CO • 467,610
Denver City, TX 79323 • 5,145
Denville, NJ 07834 • 14,380
De Pere, WI 54115 • 16,569
Depew, NY 14043 • 17,673
Deposit, NY 13754 • 1,936
Depue, IL 61322 • 1,729
De Queen, AR 71832 • 4,633
De Quincy, LA 70633 • 3,474
Derby, CT 06418 • 12,199
Derby, KS 67037 • 14,699
Derby, NY 14047 • 1,200
Derby Line, VT 05830 • 855
De Ridder, LA 70634 • 9,868
Dermott, AR 71638 • 4,715
Derry, NH 03038 • 20,446
Derry, PA 15627 • 2,950
Derwood, MD 20855 • 1,500
Des Allemands, LA 70030 • 2,504
Des Arc, AR 72040 • 2,001
Deschutes □, OR • 74,958
Desert Hot Springs, CA 92240 • 11,668
Desha □, AR • 16,798
Deshler, OH 43516 • 1,876
Desloge, MO 63601 • 4,150
De Smet, SD 57231 • 1,172
Des Moines, IA 50301–95 • 193,187
Des Moines, WA 98188 • 17,283
Des Moines □, IA • 42,614
De Soto, IL 62924 • 1,500
De Soto, IA 50069 • 1,033
De Soto, KS 66018 • 2,291
De Soto, MO 63020 • 5,993
De Soto, TX 75115 • 30,544
De Soto □, FL • 23,865
De Soto □, LA • 25,346
De Soto □, MS • 67,910
Despard, WV 26301 • 1,018
Des Peres, MO 63131 • 8,395
Des Plaines, IL 60016–19 • 53,223
Destin, FL 32540–41 • 8,080
Destrehan, LA 70047 • 8,031
Detroit, MI 48201–44 • 1,027,974
Detroit Lakes, MN 56501–02 • 6,635
Deuel □, NE • 2,237
Deuel □, SD • 4,522
Devils Lake, ND 58301 • 7,782
Devine, TX 78016 • 3,928
Devola, OH 45750 • 2,736
Devon, PA 19333 • 6,620
Devonshire, DE 19810 • 2,120
Dewey, OK 74029 • 3,326
Dewey □, OK • 5,551
Dewey □, SD • 5,523
Dewey Beach, DE 19971 • 204
Deweyville, TX 77614 • 1,218
De Witt, AR 72042 • 3,553
De Witt, IA 52742 • 4,514
De Witt, MI 48820 • 3,964
De Witt, NY 13214 • 8,244
De Witt □, IL • 16,516
De Witt □, TX • 18,840
Dexter, ME 04930 • 2,650
Dexter, MI 48130 • 1,497
Dexter, MO 63841 • 7,559
Dexter, NY 13634 • 1,030
Diamond Bar, CA 91765 • 53,672
Diamond Hill, RI 02864 • 810
Diamond Lake, IL 60060 • 1,500
Diamond Springs, CA 95619 • 2,872
Diamondville, WY 83116 • 864
Diaz, AR 72043 • 1,363
D'Iberville, MS 39532 • 6,566
Diboll, TX 75941 • 4,341
Dickens □, TX • 2,571
Dickenson □, VA • 17,620
Dickey □, ND • 6,107
Dickinson, ND 58601–02 • 16,097
Dickinson, TX 77539 • 9,497
Dickinson □, IA • 14,909
Dickinson □, KS • 18,958
Dickinson □, MI • 26,831
Dickson, TN 37055 • 8,791
Dickson □, TN • 35,061
Dickson City, PA 18519 • 6,276
Dierks, AR 71833 • 1,263
Dighton, KS 67839 • 1,361
Dighton, MA 02715 • 1,100
Dillard, OR 97432 • 1,000
Dilley, TX 78017 • 2,632
Dillingham, AK 99576 • 2,017
Dillon, MT 59725 • 3,991
Dillon, SC 29536 • 6,829
Dillon □, SC • 29,114
Dillsboro, IN 47018 • 1,200
Dillsburg, PA 17019 • 1,925
Dilworth, MN 56529 • 2,562
Dimmit □, TX • 10,433
Dimmitt, TX 79027 • 4,408
Dimondale, MI 48821 • 1,247
Dingmans Ferry, PA 18328 • 1,200
Dinuba, CA 93618 • 12,743
Dinwiddie □, VA • 20,960
Dishman, WA 99213 • 9,671
District Heights-Forestville, MD 20747 • 6,704
Divernon, IL 62530 • 1,178
Divide □, ND • 2,899
Dixfield, ME 04224 • 1,300
Dix Hills, NY 11746 • 25,849
Dixie □, FL • 10,585
Dixon, CA 95620 • 10,401
Dixon, IL 61021 • 15,144
Dixon, MO 65459 • 1,585
Dixon □, NE • 6,143
Dixonville, PA 15734 • 1,000
Dobbs Ferry, NY 10522 • 9,940
Dobson, NC 27017 • 1,195
Docena, AL 35060 • 1,000
Dock Junction, GA 31520 • 7,094
Doddridge □, WV • 6,994
Dodge □, GA • 17,607
Dodge □, MN • 15,731
Dodge □, NE • 34,500
Dodge □, WI • 76,559
Dodge Center, MN 55927 • 1,954
Dodge City, KS 67801 • 21,129
Dodge Park, MD 20785 • 4,842
Dodgeville, WI 53533 • 3,882
Dolgeville, NY 13329 • 2,452
Dolomite, AL 35061 • 2,590
Dolores □, CO • 1,504
Dolton, IL 60419 • 23,930
Dona Ana, NM 88032 • 950
Dona Ana □, NM • 135,510
Donaldsonville, LA 70346 • 7,949
Donalsonville, GA 31745 • 2,761
Doneraile, SC 29532 • 1,276
Doniphan, MO 63935 • 1,713
Doniphan □, KS • 8,134
Donley □, TX • 3,696
Donna, TX 78537 • 12,652
Donora, PA 15033 • 5,928
Dooly □, GA • 9,901
Door □, WI • 25,690
Dora, AL 35062 • 2,214
Doraville, GA 30340 • 7,626
Dorchester □, MD • 30,236
Dorchester □, SC • 83,060
Dormont, PA 15216 • 9,772
Dorothy Pond, MA 01527 • 1,670
Dorr, MI 49323 • 1,450
Dorset, VT 05251 • 550
Dorsey, MD 21227 • 1,186
Dothan, AL 36301–04 • 53,589
Double Springs, AL 35553 • 1,138
Dougherty □, GA • 96,311
Douglas, AZ 85607–08 • 12,822
Douglas, GA 31533 • 10,464
Douglas, MI 49406 • 1,040
Douglas, WY 82633 • 5,076
Douglas □, CO • 60,391
Douglas □, GA • 71,120
Douglas □, IL • 19,464
Douglas □, KS • 81,798
Douglas □, MN • 28,674
Douglas □, MO • 11,876
Douglas □, NE • 416,444
Douglas □, NV • 27,637
Douglas □, OR • 94,649
Douglas □, SD • 3,746
Douglas □, WA • 26,205
Douglas □, WI • 41,758
Douglass, KS 67039 • 1,722
Douglasville, GA 30133–35 • 11,635
Dousman, WI 53118 • 1,277
Dover, AR 72837 • 1,055
Dover, DE 19901–03 • 27,630
Dover, FL 33527 • 2,606
Dover, MA 02030 • 2,163
Dover, NH 03820 • 25,042
Dover, NJ 07801 • 15,115
Dover, OH 44622 • 11,329
Dover, PA 17315 • 1,884
Dover, TN 37058 • 1,341
Dover-Foxcroft, ME 04426 • 3,077
Dover Plains, NY 12522 • 1,847
Dowagiac, MI 49047 • 6,409
Downers Grove, IL 60515–17 • 46,858
Downey, CA 90239–42 • 91,444
Downingtown, PA 19335 • 7,749
Downs, KS 67437 • 1,119
Downsville, NY 13755 • 1,100
Doylestown, OH 44230 • 2,668
Doylestown, PA 18901 • 8,575
Dracut, MA 01826 • 25,594
Drain, OR 97435 • 1,011
Draper, UT 84020 • 7,257
Drayton, ND 58225 • 961
Drayton, SC 29333 • 1,443
Drayton Plains, MI 48330 • 18,000
Dreamland Villa, AZ 85205 • 3,400
Dresden, OH 43821 • 1,581
Dresden, TN 38225 • 2,488
Dresslerville, NV 89410 • 180
Drew, MS 38737 • 2,349
Drew □, AR • 17,369
Drexel, NC 28619 • 1,746
Drexel, OH 45427 • 5,143
Drexel Hill, PA 19026 • 29,744
Dripping Springs, TX 78620 • 1,033
Druid Hills, GA 30333 • 12,174
Drumright, OK 74030 • 2,799
Dryden, NY 13053 • 1,908
Dry Ridge, KY 41035 • 1,601
Duarte, CA 91010 • 20,688
Dublin, CA 94568 • 23,229
Dublin, GA 31021 • 16,312
Dublin, OH 43017 • 16,366
Dublin, PA 18917 • 1,985
Dublin, TX 76446 • 3,190
Dublin, VA 24084 • 2,012
Du Bois, PA 15801 • 8,286
Dubois, WY 82513 • 895
Dubois □, IN • 36,616
Duboistown, PA 17701 • 1,201
Dubuque, IA 52001–04 • 57,546
Dubuque □, IA • 86,403
Duchesne, UT 84021 • 1,308
Duchesne □, UT • 12,645
Dudley, MA 01570–71 • 3,700
Due West, SC 29639 • 1,220
Dukes □, MA • 11,639
Dulce, NM 87528 • 2,438
Duluth, GA 30136 • 9,029
Duluth, MN 55801–16 • 85,493
Dumas, AR 71639 • 5,520
Dumas, TX 79029 • 12,871
Dumfries, VA 22026 • 4,282
Dumont, NJ 07628 • 17,187
Dunaire, GA 30032 • 7,170
Dunbar, PA 15431 • 1,213
Dunbar, WV 25064 • 8,697
Duncan, OK 73533–34 • 21,732
Duncan, SC 29334 • 2,152
Duncan Falls, OH 43734 • 1,200
Duncannon, PA 17020 • 1,450
Duncansville, PA 16635 • 1,309
Duncanville, TX 75116 • 35,748
Dundalk, MD 21222 • 65,800
Dundee, FL 33838 • 2,335
Dundee, IL 60118 • 3,728
Dundee, MI 48131 • 2,664
Dundee, NY 14837 • 1,588
Dundee, OR 97115 • 1,663
Dundy □, NE • 2,582
Dunedin, FL 34697–98 • 34,012
Dunellen, NJ 08812 • 6,528
Dunkirk, IN 47336 • 2,739
Dunkirk, NY 14048 • 13,989
Dunklin □, MO • 33,112
Dunlap, IN 46514 • 5,705
Dunlap, IA 51529 • 1,251
Dunlap, TN 37327 • 3,731
Dunleith, DE 19801 • 2,600
Dunmore, PA 18512 • 15,403
Dunn, NC 28334–35 • 8,336
Dunn □, ND • 4,005
Dunn □, WI • 35,909
Dunnellon, FL 32630 • 1,624
Dunn Loring Woods, VA 22180 • 2,800
Dunseith, ND 58329 • 723
Dunsmuir, CA 96025 • 2,129
Dunwoody, GA 30338 • 26,302
Du Page □, IL • 781,666
Duplin □, NC • 39,995
Dupont, CO 80024 • 5,200
Dupont, PA 18641 • 2,984
Dupont Manor, DE 19901 • 1,059
Duquesne, PA 15110 • 8,525
Du Quoin, IL 62832 • 6,697
Durand, IL 61024 • 1,100
Durand, MI 48429 • 4,283
Durand, WI 54736 • 2,003
Durango, CO 81301–02 • 12,430
Durant, IA 52747 • 1,549
Durant, MS 39063 • 2,838
Durant, OK 74701–02 • 12,823
Durham, CA 95938 • 1,500
Durham, CT 06422 • 2,650
Durham, NH 03824 • 9,236
Durham, NC 27701–22 • 136,611
Durham □, NC • 181,835
Duryea, PA 18642 • 4,869
Duson, LA 70529 • 1,465
Dutchess □, NY • 259,462
Duval □, FL • 672,971
Duval □, TX • 12,918
Duxbury, MA 02331–32 • 1,637
Dwight, IL 60420 • 4,230
Dyer, IN 46311 • 10,923
Dyer, TN 38330 • 2,204
Dyer □, TN • 34,854
Dyersburg, TN 38024–25 • 16,317
Dyersville, IA 52040 • 3,703
Dysart, IA 52224 • 1,230

E

Eagan, MN 55121 • 47,409
Eagar, AZ 85925 • 4,025
Eagle, CO 81631 • 1,580
Eagle, ID 83616 • 3,327
Eagle, NE 68347 • 1,047
Eagle, WI 53119 • 1,182
Eagle □, CO • 21,928
Eagle Grove, IA 50533 • 3,671
Eagle Lake, MN 56024 • 1,703
Eagle Lake, TX 77434 • 3,551
Eagle Lake, WI 53139 • 1,000
Eagle Pass, TX 78852–53 • 20,651
Eagle Point, OR 97524 • 3,008
Eagle River, WI 54521 • 1,374
Eagleton Village, TN 37801 • 5,331
Earle, AR 72331 • 3,393
Earlham, IA 50072 • 1,157
Earlimart, CA 93219 • 5,881
Earlington, KY 42410 • 1,833
Earlville, IL 60518 • 1,435
Early □, GA • 11,854
Earth, TX 79031 • 1,228
Easley, SC 29640–42 • 15,195
East Alton, IL 62024 • 7,063
East Arlington, VT 05252 • 600
East Aurora, NY 14052 • 6,647
East Bangor, PA 18013 • 1,006
East Barre, VT 05649 • 700
East Baton Rouge □, LA • 380,105

East Berlin, PA 17316 • *1,175*
East Bernard, TX 77435 • *1,544*
East Bethel, MN 55005 • *8,050*
East Billerica, MA 01821 • *3,830*
East Brady, PA 16028 • *1,047*
East Brewton, AL 36426 • *2,579*
East Bridgewater, MA 02333 • *3,270*
East Brookfield, MA 01515 • *1,396*
East Brooklyn, CT 06239 • *1,481*
East Brunswick, NJ 08816 • *43,548*
East Carbon, UT 84520 • *1,270*
East Carroll □, LA • *9,709*
Eastchester, NY 10709 • *18,537*
East Chicago, IN 46312 • *33,892*
East Cleveland, OH 44112 • *33,096*
East Compton, CA 90221 • *7,967*
East Dennis, MA 02641 • *1,500*
East Detroit, MI 48021 • *35,283*
East Douglas, MA 01516 • *1,945*
East Dubuque, IL 61025 • *1,914*
East Falmouth, MA 02536 • *5,577*
East Farmingdale, NY 11735 • *4,510*
East Feliciana □, LA • *19,211*
East Flat Rock, NC 28726 • *3,218*
East Gaffney, SC 29340 • *3,278*
Eastgate, WA 98007 • *4,434*
East Glenville, NY 12302 • *6,518*
East Granby, CT 06026 • *1,200*
East Grand Forks, MN 56721 • *8,658*
East Grand Rapids, MI 49506 • *10,807*
East Greenville, PA 18041 • *3,117*
East Greenwich, RI 02818 • *11,865*
East Half Hollow Hills, NY 11746 • *7,010*
Eastham, MA 02642 • *1,150*
East Hampton, CT 06424 • *2,167*
Easthampton, MA 01027 • *15,580*
East Hampton, NY 11937 • *1,402*
East Hanover, NJ • *9,926*
East Hartford, CT 06128 • *50,452*
East Haven, CT 06512 • *26,144*
East Helena, MT 59635 • *1,538*
East Hemet, CA 92343 • *17,611*
East Hills, NY 11576 • *6,746*
East Islip, NY 11730 • *14,325*
East Jordan, MI 49727 • *2,240*
Eastlake, OH 44094 • *21,161*
East La Mirada, CA 90638 • *9,367*
Eastland, TX 76448 • *3,690*
Eastland □, TX • *18,488*
East Lansing, MI 48823–26 • *50,677*
East Las Vegas, NV 89112 • *11,087*
East Liverpool, OH 43920 • *13,654*
East Longmeadow, MA 01028 • *12,905*
East Los Angeles, CA 90022 • *126,379*
East Lyme, CT 06333 • *1,200*
Eastman, GA 31023 • *5,153*
East Marietta, GA 30062 • *11,900*
East Marion, NY 11939 • *1,500*
East Matunuck, RI 02879 • *500*
East Meadow, NY 11554 • *36,609*
East Middlebury, VT 05740 • *500*
East Midvale, UT 84047 • *3,800*
East Millinocket, ME 04430 • *2,075*
East Moline, IL 61244 • *20,147*
East Montpelier, VT 05651 • *600*
East Naples, FL 33962 • *22,951*
East Newark, NJ 07029 • *2,157*
East Newnan, GA 30263 • *1,173*
East Norriton, PA 19401 • *13,324*
East Northport, NY 11731 • *20,411*
Easton, MD 21601 • *9,372*
Easton, PA 18042–44 • *26,276*
East Orange, NJ 07017–19 • *73,552*
East Orleans, MA 02643 • *1,850*
Eastover, SC 29044 • *1,044*
East Palatka, FL 32131 • *1,989*
East Palestine, OH 44413 • *5,168*
East Palo Alto, CA 94303 • *23,451*
East Patchogue, NY 11772 • *20,195*
East Pea Ridge, WV 25705 • *4,980*
East Peoria, IL 61611 • *21,378*
East Pepperell, MA 01463 • *2,296*
East Petersburg, PA 17520 • *4,197*
East Pittsburgh, PA 15112 • *2,160*
Eastpoint, FL 32328 • *1,577*
East Point, GA 30344 • *34,402*
Eastport, ME 04631 • *1,965*
Eastport, NY 11941 • *1,500*
East Porterville, CA 93257 • *5,790*
East Port Orchard, WA 98366 • *5,409*
East Prairie, MO 63845 • *3,416*
East Providence, RI 02914 • *50,380*
East Quogue, NY 11942 • *4,372*
East Richmond, CA 94805 • *5,100*
East Ridge, TN 37412 • *21,101*
East River, CT 06443 • *3,440*
East Rochester, NY 14445 • *6,932*
East Rockaway, NY 11518 • *10,152*
East Rockingham, NC 28379 • *4,158*
East Rutherford, NJ 07073 • *7,902*
East Saint Louis, IL 62201–08 • *40,944*
Eastsound, WA 98245 • *1,200*
East Spencer, NC 28039 • *2,055*
East Stroudsburg, PA 18301 • *8,781*
East Tawas, MI 48730 • *2,887*
East Templeton, MA 01438 • *1,300*
East Troy, WI 53120 • *2,664*
East Tustin, CA 92705 • *10,000*
East Vestal, NY 13902 • *6,310*
East View, WV 26301 • *1,222*
East Walpole, MA 02032 • *3,760*
East Wareham, MA 02538 • *1,500*
East Washington, PA 15301 • *2,126*
East Wenatchee, WA 98802 • *2,701*
East Windsor, NJ 08520 • *15,000*
Eastwood, MI 49001 • *6,340*
Eastwood Hills, UT 84106 • *1,200*
Eaton, CO 80615 • *1,959*
Eaton, IN 47338 • *1,614*
Eaton, OH 45320 • *7,396*
Eaton □, MI • *92,879*
Eaton Rapids, MI 48827 • *4,695*
Eatonton, GA 31024 • *4,737*
Eatontown, NJ 07724 • *13,800*
Eatonville, WA 98328 • *1,374*
Eau Claire, WI 54701–03 • *56,856*
Eau Claire □, WI • *85,183*
Ebensburg, PA 15931 • *3,872*
Eccles, WV 25836 • *1,162*
Echo Bay, NV 89040 • *120*
Echols □, GA • *2,334*
Eckhart Mines, MD 21528 • *1,333*
Eclectic, AL 36024 • *1,087*
Economy, PA 15005 • *9,519*
Ecorse, MI 48229 • *12,180*
Ector □, TX • *118,934*
Edcouch, TX 78538 • *2,878*
Eddy □, NM • *48,605*
Eddy □, ND • *2,951*
Eddystone, PA 19013 • *2,446*
Eddyville, IA 52553 • *1,010*
Eddyville, KY 42038 • *1,889*
Eden, NY 14057 • *3,088*
Eden, NC 27288 • *15,238*
Eden, TX 76837 • *1,567*
Eden Prairie, MN 55344 • *39,311*
Edenton, NC 27932 • *5,268*
Edgar, WI 54426 • *1,318*
Edgar □, IL • *19,595*
Edgartown, MA 02539 • *3,062*
Edgecombe □, NC • *56,558*
Edgefield, SC 29824 • *2,563*
Edgefield □, SC • *18,375*
Edgeley, ND 58433 • *680*
Edgemere, MD 21221 • *9,226*
Edgemont, SD 57735 • *906*
Edgemoor, DE 19802 • *5,853*
Edgerton, KS 66021 • *1,244*
Edgerton, MN 56128 • *1,106*
Edgerton, OH 43517 • *1,896*
Edgerton, WI 53534 • *4,254*
Edgerton, WY 82635 • *247*
Edgewater, AL 35224 • *1,120*
Edgewater, CO 80214 • *4,613*
Edgewater, FL 32132 • *15,337*
Edgewater, MD 21037 • *1,600*
Edgewater, NJ 07020 • *5,001*
Edgewater Park, NJ 08010 • *8,388*
Edgewood, IN 46011 • *2,057*
Edgewood, KY 41017 • *8,143*
Edgewood, MD • *3,470*
Edgewood, MD 21040 • *23,903*
Edgewood, OH 44004 • *5,189*
Edgewood, PA 15218 • *3,581*
Edgewood, WA 98372 • *2,650*
Edgeworth, PA 15143 • *1,670*
Edina, MN 55410 • *46,070*
Edina, MO 63537 • *1,283*
Edinboro, PA 16412 • *7,736*
Edinburg, TX 78539–40 • *29,885*
Edinburgh, IN 46124 • *4,536*
Edison, GA 31746 • *1,182*
Edison, NJ 08817–20 • *88,680*
Edmond, OK 73034 • *52,315*
Edmonds, WA 98020 • *30,744*
Edmondson Heights, MD 21207 • *4,750*
Edmonson □, KY • *10,357*
Edmonton, KY 42129 • *1,477*
Edmore, MI 48829 • *1,126*
Edmunds □, SD • *4,356*
Edna, TX 77957 • *5,343*
Edwards, MS 39066 • *1,279*
Edwards □, IL • *7,440*
Edwards □, KS • *3,787*
Edwards □, TX • *2,266*
Edwardsburg, MI 49112 • *1,142*
Edwardsville, IL 62025 • *14,579*
Edwardsville, KS 66113 • *3,979*
Edwardsville, PA 18704 • *5,399*
Effingham, IL 62401 • *11,851*
Effingham □, GA • *25,687*
Effingham □, IL • *31,704*
Egg Harbor City, NJ 08215 • *4,583*
Egypt, MA 02066 • *1,100*
Egypt Lake, FL 33614 • *14,580*
Ehrenberg, AZ 85334 • *1,500*
Elba, AL 36323 • *4,011*
Elbert □, CO • *9,646*
Elbert □, GA • *18,949*
Elberta, GA 31093 • *1,559*
Elberton, GA 30635 • *5,682*
Elbow Lake, MN 56531 • *1,186*
Elburn, IL 60119 • *1,275*
El Cajon, CA 92019–22 • *88,693*
El Campo, TX 77437 • *10,511*
El Centro, CA 92243–44 • *31,384*
El Cerrito, CA 94530 • *22,869*
Eldersburg, MD 21784 • *9,720*
Eldon, IA 52554 • *1,070*
Eldon, MO 65026 • *4,419*
Eldora, IA 50627 • *3,038*
El Dorado, AR 71730–31 • *23,146*
Eldorado, IL 62930 • *4,536*
El Dorado, KS 67042 • *11,504*
Eldorado, TX 76936 • *2,019*
El Dorado □, CA • *125,995*
El Dorado Hills, CA 95630 • *6,395*
El Dorado Springs, MO 64744 • *3,830*
Eldridge, IA 52748 • *3,378*
Eleanor, WV 25070 • *1,256*
Electra, TX 76360 • *3,113*
Eleele, HI 96705 • *1,489*
El Encanto Heights, CA 93117 • *7,700*
Elfers, FL 34680 • *12,356*
Elgin, IL 60120–23 • *77,010*
Elgin, ND 58533 • *765*
Elgin, OR 97827 • *1,586*
Elgin, TX 78621 • *4,846*
Elida, OH 45807 • *1,486*
Elizabeth, NJ 07201–08 • *110,002*
Elizabeth City, NC 27906–09 • *14,292*
Elizabethton, TN 37643–44 • *11,931*
Elizabethtown, KY 42701–02 • *18,167*
Elizabethtown, NC 28337 • *3,704*
Elizabethtown, PA 17022 • *9,952*
Elizabethville, PA 17023 • *1,467*
Elk □, KS • *3,327*
Elk □, PA • *34,878*
Elkader, IA 52043 • *1,510*
Elk City, OK 73644 • *10,428*
Elk Grove, CA 95624 • *17,483*
Elk Grove Village, IL 60009 • *33,429*
Elkhart, IN 46514–17 • *43,627*
Elkhart, KS 67950 • *2,318*
Elkhart, TX 75839 • *1,076*
Elkhart □, IN • *156,198*
Elkhart Lake, WI 53020 • *1,019*
Elkhorn, NE 68022 • *1,398*
Elkhorn, WI 53121 • *5,337*
Elkin, NC 28621 • *3,790*
Elkins, WV 26241 • *7,420*
Elkland, PA 16920 • *1,849*
Elk Mountain, WY 82324 • *174*
Elko, NV 89801–02 • *14,736*
Elko □, NV • *33,530*
Elk Point, SD 57025 • *1,423*
Elk Rapids, MI 49629 • *1,626*
Elkridge, MD 21227 • *12,953*
Elk River, MN 55330 • *11,143*
Elkton, KY 42220 • *1,789*
Elkton, MD 21921–22 • *9,073*
Elkton, VA 22827 • *1,935*
Elkview, WV 25071 • *1,047*
Ellaville, GA 31806 • *1,724*
Ellendale, DE 19941 • *313*
Ellendale, ND 58436 • *1,798*
Ellensburg, WA 98926 • *12,361*
Ellenton, FL 34222 • *2,573*
Ellenville, NY 12428 • *4,243*
Ellerbe, NC 28338 • *1,132*
Ellerslie, MD 21529 • *1,500*
Ellettsville, IN 47429 • *3,275*
Ellicott City, MD 21043 • *41,396*
Ellijay, GA 30540 • *1,178*
Ellington, CT 06029 • *1,500*
Ellinwood, KS 67526 • *2,329*
Elliott □, KY • *6,455*
Ellis, KS 67637 • *1,814*
Ellis □, KS • *26,004*
Ellis □, OK • *4,497*
Ellis □, TX • *85,167*
Ellisville, MS 39437 • *3,634*
Ellisville, MO 63011 • *7,545*
Ellport, PA 16117 • *1,243*
Ellsworth, KS 67439 • *2,294*
Ellsworth, ME 04605 • *5,975*
Ellsworth, PA 15331 • *1,048*
Ellsworth, WI 54011 • *2,706*
Ellsworth □, KS • *6,586*
Ellwood City, PA 16117 • *8,894*
Elma, WA 98541 • *3,011*
Elm City, NC 27822 • *1,624*
Elmer, NJ 08318 • *1,571*
Elm Grove, WI 53122 • *6,261*
Elmhurst, IL 60126 • *42,029*
Elmira, NY 14901–05 • *33,724*
El Mirage, AZ 85335 • *5,001*
Elmira Heights, NY 14903 • *4,359*
Elmont, NY 11003 • *28,612*
El Monte, CA 91731–34 • *106,209*
Elmora, PA 15737 • *1,500*
Elmore, OH 43416 • *1,334*
Elmore □, AL • *49,210*
Elmore □, ID • *21,205*
Elmwood, IL 61529 • *1,841*
Elmwood Park, IL 60635 • *23,206*
Elmwood Park, NJ 07407 • *17,623*
Elmwood Place, OH 45216 • *2,937*
Eloise, FL 33880 • *1,408*
Elon College, NC 27244 • *4,394*
Eloy, AZ 85231 • *7,211*
El Paso, IL 61738 • *2,499*
El Paso, TX 79901–99 • *515,342*
El Paso □, CO • *397,014*
El Paso □, TX • *591,610*
El Portal, FL 33138 • *2,457*
El Reno, OK 73036 • *15,414*
Elroy, WI 53929 • *1,533*
Elsa, TX 78543 • *5,242*
Elsberry, MO 63343 • *1,898*
El Segundo, CA 90245 • *15,223*
Elsmere, DE 19805 • *5,935*
Elsmere, KY 41018 • *6,847*
Elsmere, NY 12054 • *4,180*
El Sobrante, CA 94803 • *9,852*
Elton, LA 70532 • *1,277*
El Toro, CA 92630 • *62,685*
Elvins, MO 63601 • *1,391*
Elwood, IN 46036 • *9,494*
Elwood, KS 66024 • *1,079*
Elwood, NJ 08217 • *1,400*
Elwood, NY 11731 • *10,916*
Ely, MN 55731 • *3,968*
Ely, NV 89301 • *4,756*
Elyria, OH 44035–39 • *56,746*
Elysburg, PA 17824 • *1,890*
Emanuel □, GA • *20,546*
Emerson, GA 30137 • *1,201*
Emerson, NJ 07630 • *6,930*
Emery □, UT • *10,332*
Eminence, KY 40019 • *2,055*
Emmaus, PA 18049 • *11,157*
Emmet □, IA • *11,569*
Emmet □, MI • *25,040*
Emmetsburg, IA 50536 • *3,940*
Emmett, ID 83617 • *4,601*
Emmitsburg, MD 21727 • *1,688*
Emmonak, AK 99581 • *642*
Emmons □, ND • *4,830*
Empire, NV 89405 • *300*
Emporia, KS 66801 • *25,512*
Emporia, VA 23847 • *5,306*
Emporium, PA 15834 • *2,513*
Emsworth, PA 15202 • *2,892*
Encampment, WY 82325 • *490*
Encinitas, CA 92023–24 • *55,386*
Enderlin, ND 58027 • *997*
Endicott, NY 13760 • *13,531*
Endwell, NY 13760 • *12,602*
Enfield (Thompsonville), CT 06082–83 • *8,458*
Enfield, NH 03748 • *1,560*
Enfield, NC 27823 • *3,082*
England, AR 72046 • *3,351*
Engleside, VA 22309 • *24,058*
Englewood, CO 80110–12 • *29,387*
Englewood, FL 34223–24 • *15,025*
Englewood, NJ 07631–32 • *24,850*
Englewood, OH 45322 • *11,432*
Englewood, TN 37329 • *1,611*
Englewood Cliffs, NJ 07632 • *5,634*
Englishtown, NJ 07726 • *1,268*
Enid, OK 73701–06 • *45,309*
Enka, NC 28728 • *5,567*
Ennis, MT 59729 • *773*
Ennis, TX 75119–20 • *13,883*
Enoch, UT 84720 • *1,947*
Enola, PA 17025 • *5,961*
Enon, OH 45323 • *2,605*
Enoree, SC 29335 • *1,107*
Enosburg Falls, VT 05450 • *1,350*
Ensley, FL 32504 • *16,362*
Enterprise, AL 36330–31 • *20,123*
Enterprise, OR 97828 • *1,905*
Enterprise, WV 26568 • *1,058*
Enumclaw, WA 98022 • *7,227*
Ephraim, UT 84627 • *3,363*
Ephrata, PA 17522 • *12,133*
Ephrata, WA 98823 • *5,349*
Epping, NH 03042 • *1,384*
Epworth, IA 52045 • *1,297*
Erath, LA 70533 • *2,428*
Erath □, TX • *27,991*
Erial, NJ 08081 • *2,500*
Erick, OK 73645 • *1,083*
Erie, CO 80516 • *1,258*
Erie, IL 61250 • *1,572*
Erie, KS 66733 • *1,276*
Erie, PA 16501–65 • *108,718*
Erie □, NY • *968,532*
Erie □, OH • *76,779*
Erie □, PA • *275,572*
Erin, TN 37061 • *1,586*
Erlanger, KY 41018 • *15,979*
Erma, NJ 08204 • *2,045*
Errol Heights, OR 97266 • *10,487*
Erwin, NC 28339 • *4,061*
Erwin, TN 37650 • *5,015*
Escalon, CA 95320 • *4,437*
Escambia □, AL • *35,518*
Escambia □, FL • *262,798*
Escanaba, MI 49829 • *13,659*
Escatawpa, MS 39552 • *3,902*
Escondido, CA 92025–27 • *108,635*
Esmeralda □, NV • *1,344*
Esmond, RI 02917 • *4,320*
Espanola, NM 87532 • *8,389*
Esparto, CA 95627 • *1,487*
Esperance, WA 98043 • *11,236*
Espy, PA 17815 • *1,430*
Essex, CT 06426 • *2,500*
Essex, MD 21221 • *40,872*
Essex, MA 01929 • *1,507*
Essex, VT 05451 • *800*
Essex □, MA • *670,080*
Essex □, NJ • *778,206*
Essex □, NY • *37,152*
Essex □, VT • *6,405*
Essex □, VA • *8,689*
Essex Fells, NJ 07021 • *2,363*
Essex Junction, VT 05452–53 • *8,396*
Essexville, MI 48732 • *4,088*
Estacada, OR 97023 • *2,016*
Estelle, LA 70072 • *14,091*
Estell Manor, NJ 08319 • *1,404*
Estes Park, CO 80517 • *3,184*
Estherville, IA 51334 • *6,720*
Estill, SC 29918 • *2,387*
Estill □, KY • *14,614*
Estill Springs, TN 37330 • *1,408*
Etna, PA 15223 • *4,200*
Etowah, TN 37331 • *3,815*
Etowah □, AL • *99,840*
Ettrick, VA 23803 • *5,290*
Euclid, OH 44117 • *54,875*
Eudora, AR 71640 • *3,155*
Eudora, KS 66025 • *3,006*
Eufaula, AL 36027 • *13,220*
Eufaula, OK 74432 • *2,652*
Eugene, OR 97401–05 • *112,669*
Euless, TX 76039–40 • *38,149*
Eunice, LA 70535 • *11,162*
Eunice, NM 88231 • *2,676*
Eupora, MS 39744 • *2,145*
Eureka, CA 95501–02 • *27,025*
Eureka, IL 61530 • *4,435*
Eureka, KS 67045 • *2,974*
Eureka, MO 63025 • *4,683*
Eureka, MT 59917 • *1,043*
Eureka, NV 89316 • *650*
Eureka, SC 29706 • *1,738*
Eureka, SD 57437 • *1,197*
Eureka □, NV • *1,547*
Eureka Springs, AR 72632 • *1,900*
Eustis, FL 32726–27 • *12,967*
Eutaw, AL 35462 • *2,281*
Evangeline □, LA • *33,274*
Evans, CO 80620 • *5,877*
Evans, GA 30809 • *2,000*
Evans □, GA • *8,724*
Evans City, PA 16033 • *2,054*
Evansdale, IA 50707 • *4,638*
Evanston, IL 60201–04 • *73,233*
Evanston, WY 82930–31 • *10,903*
Evansville, IN 47701–37 • *126,272*
Evansville, WI 53536 • *3,174*
Evansville, WY 82636 • *1,403*
Evart, MI 49631 • *1,744*
Evarts, KY 40828 • *1,063*
Eveleth, MN 55734 • *4,064*
Everett, MA 02149 • *35,701*
Everett, PA 15537 • *1,777*
Everett, WA 98201–08 • *69,961*
Evergreen, AL 36401 • *3,911*
Evergreen, CO 80439 • *7,582*
Evergreen Park, IL 60642 • *20,874*
Everman, TX 76140 • *5,672*
Everson, WA 98247 • *1,490*
Ewa, HI 96706 • *3,780*
Ewa Beach, HI 96706–07 • *14,315*
Ewing Township, NJ 08618 • *34,185*
Excelsior Springs, MO 64024 • *10,354*
Exeter, CA 93221 • *7,276*
Exeter, NH 03833 • *9,556*
Exeter, PA 18643 • *5,691*
Exmore, VA 23350 • *1,115*
Experiment, GA 30223 • *3,762*
Eyota, MN 55934 • *1,448*

F

Fabens, TX 79838 • *5,599*
Factoryville, PA 18419 • *1,310*
Fairbank, IA 50629 • *1,018*
Fairbanks, AK 99701 • *30,843*
Fair Bluff, NC 28439 • *1,068*
Fairborn, OH 45324 • *31,300*
Fairburn, GA 30213 • *4,013*
Fairbury, IL 61739 • *3,643*
Fairbury, NE 68352 • *4,335*
Fairchance, PA 15436 • *1,918*
Fairdale, KY 40118 • *6,563*
Fairfax, CA 94930 • *6,931*
Fairfax, DE 19803 • *2,075*
Fairfax, MN 55332 • *1,276*
Fairfax, OK 74637 • *1,749*
Fairfax, SC 29827 • *2,317*
Fairfax, VA 22030–39 • *19,622*
Fairfax □, VA • *818,584*
Fairfield, AL 35064 • *12,200*
Fairfield, CA 94533 • *77,211*
Fairfield, CT 06430–32 • *53,418*
Fairfield, IL 62837 • *5,439*
Fairfield, IA 52556 • *9,768*
Fairfield, ME 04937 • *2,794*
Fairfield, NJ 07004 • *7,615*
Fairfield, OH 45014 • *39,729*
Fairfield, TX 75840 • *3,234*
Fairfield □, CT • *827,645*
Fairfield □, OH • *103,461*
Fairfield □, SC • *22,295*
Fairfield Bay, AR 72088 • *2,332*
Fair Grove, NC 27360 • *1,500*
Fairhaven, MA 02719 • *15,759*
Fair Haven, NJ 07704 • *5,270*
Fair Haven, VT 05743 • *2,432*
Fairhope, AL 36532–33 • *8,485*
Fair Lawn, NJ 07410 • *30,548*
Fairlawn, OH 44313 • *5,779*
Fairlawn, VA 24141 • *2,399*
Fairlea, WV 24902 • *1,743*
Fairless Hills, PA 19030 • *9,026*
Fairmont, IL 60441 • *2,260*
Fairmont, MN 56031 • *11,265*
Fairmont, NC 28340 • *2,489*
Fairmont, WV 26554–55 • *20,210*
Fairmount, IN 46928 • *3,130*
Fairmount, NY 13031 • *12,266*
Fairmount Heights, MD 20743 • *1,238*
Fair Oaks, CA 95628 • *26,867*
Fair Oaks, GA 30060 • *6,996*
Fairoaks, PA 15003 • *1,854*
Fair Plain, MI 49022 • *8,051*
Fairport, NY 14450 • *5,943*
Fairport Harbor, OH 44077 • *2,978*
Fairton, NJ 08320 • *1,359*
Fairview, MT 59221 • *869*
Fairview, NJ 07022 • *10,733*
Fairview, OK 73737 • *2,936*
Fairview, OR 97024 • *2,391*
Fairview, PA 16415 • *1,988*
Fairview, TN 37062 • *4,210*
Fairview Heights, IL 62208 • *14,351*
Fairview Park, IN 47842 • *1,446*
Fairview Park, OH 44126 • *18,028*
Fairview Shores, FL 32804 • *13,192*
Fairway, KS 66205 • *4,173*
Fairwood, WA 98058 • *2,000*
Fairwood, WA 99218 • *5,807*
Falconer, NY 14733 • *2,653*
Falcon Heights, MN 55113 • *5,380*
Falfurrias, TX 78355 • *5,788*
Falkville, AL 35622 • *1,337*
Fall Branch, TN 37656 • *1,203*
Fallbrook, CA 92028 • *22,095*
Fall City, WA 98024 • *1,582*
Fall Creek, WI 54742 • *1,034*
Fallon, NV 89406 • *6,438*
Fallon □, MT • *3,103*
Fall River, MA 02720–26 • *92,703*
Fall River □, SD • *7,353*
Falls □, TX • *17,712*
Falls Church, VA 22040–46 • *9,578*
Falls City, NE 68355 • *4,769*
Falls Creek, PA 15840 • *1,087*
Fallston, MD 21047 • *5,730*
Falls Township, PA 19054 • *36,083*
Falmouth, KY 41040 • *2,378*
Falmouth, ME 04105 • *7,610*
Falmouth, MA 02540 • *4,047*
Falmouth, VA 22405 • *3,541*
Fannin □, GA • *15,992*
Fannin □, TX • *24,804*
Fanwood, NJ 07023 • *7,115*
Fargo, ND 58102–09 • *74,111*
Faribault, MN 55021 • *17,085*
Faribault □, MN • *16,937*
Farley, IA 52046 • *1,354*
Farmer City, IL 61842 • *2,114*
Farmers Branch, TX 75234 • *24,250*
Farmersburg, IN 47850 • *1,159*
Farmersville, CA 93223 • *6,235*
Farmerville, LA 71241 • *3,334*
Farmingdale, ME 04345 • *2,070*
Farmingdale, NJ 07727 • *1,462*
Farmingdale, NY 11735 • *8,022*
Farmington, AR 72730 • *1,322*
Farmington, CT 06032 • *2,500*
Farmington, IL 61531 • *2,535*
Farmington, ME 04938 • *4,197*
Farmington, MI 48335–36 • *10,132*
Farmington, MN 55024 • *5,940*
Farmington, MO 63640 • *11,598*
Farmington, NH 03835 • *3,567*
Farmington, NM 87401–02 • *33,997*
Farmington, UT 84025 • *9,028*
Farmington Hills, MI 48331–34 • *74,652*
Farmingville, NY 11738 • *14,842*
Farmland, IN 47340 • *1,412*
Farmville, NC 27828 • *4,392*
Farmville, VA 23901 • *6,046*
Farragut, TN 37922 • *12,793*
Farrell, PA 16121 • *6,841*
Farwell, TX 79325 • *1,373*
Faulk □, SD • *2,744*
Faulkland Heights, DE 19808 • *1,300*
Faulkner □, AR • *60,006*
Faulkton, SD 57438 • *809*
Fauquier □, VA • *48,741*
Fayette, AL 35555 • *4,909*
Fayette, IA 52142 • *1,317*
Fayette, MS 39069 • *1,853*
Fayette, MO 65248 • *2,888*
Fayette, OH 43521 • *1,248*
Fayette □, AL • *17,962*
Fayette □, GA • *62,415*
Fayette □, IL • *20,893*
Fayette □, IN • *26,015*
Fayette □, IA • *21,843*
Fayette □, KY • *225,366*
Fayette □, OH • *27,466*
Fayette □, PA • *145,351*
Fayette □, TN • *25,559*
Fayette □, TX • *20,095*
Fayette □, WV • *47,952*
Fayetteville, AR 72701–03 • *42,099*
Fayetteville, GA 30214 • *5,827*
Fayetteville, NC 28301–14 • *75,695*
Fayetteville, PA 17222 • *3,033*
Fayetteville, TN 37334 • *6,921*
Fayetteville, WV 25840 • *2,182*
Fayville, MA 01745 • *1,000*
Federal Heights, CO 80221 • *9,342*
Federalsburg, MD 21632 • *2,365*
Federal Way, WA 98003 • *67,554*

United States Populations and ZIP Codes

Feeding Hills, MA 01030 • 5,470
Fellowship, NJ 08057 • 4,250
Fellsmere, FL 32948 • 2,179
Felton, CA 95041 • 5,350
Felton, DE 19943 • 683
Fennimore, WI 53809 • 2,378
Fennville, MI 49408 • 1,023
Fenton, MI 48430 • 8,444
Fentress □, TN • 14,669
Ferdinand, IN 47532 • 2,318
Fergus □, MT • 12,083
Fergus Falls, MN 56537-38 • 12,362
Ferguson, MO 63135 • 22,286
Fernandina Beach, FL 32034 • 8,765
Fern Creek, KY 40291 • 16,406
Ferndale, CA 95536 • 1,331
Ferndale, MD 21061 • 16,355
Ferndale, MI 48220 • 25,084
Ferndale, PA 15905 • 2,020
Ferndale, WA 98248 • 5,398
Fernley, NV 89408 • 5,164
Fern Park, FL 32730 • 8,294
Fernway, PA 16063 • 9,072
Ferriday, LA 71334 • 4,111
Ferris, TX 75125 • 2,212
Ferron, UT 84523 • 1,606
Ferry □, WA • 6,295
Ferry Farms, VA 22405 • 1,600
Fessenden, ND 58438 • 655
Festus, MO 63028 • 8,105
Fieldale, VA 24089 • 1,018
Fig Garden, CA 93704 • 9,000
Filer, ID 83328 • 1,511
Fillmore, CA 93015-16 • 11,992
Fillmore, UT 84631 • 1,956
Fillmore □, MN • 20,777
Fillmore □, NE • 7,103
Findlay, OH 45839-40 • 35,703
Finley, TN 38030 • 1,014
Finney □, KS • 33,070
Fircrest, WA 98466 • 5,258
Firebaugh, CA 93622 • 4,429
Firestone, CO 80520 • 1,358
Fisher, IL 61843 • 1,526
Fisher □, TX • 4,842
Fishers, IN 46038 • 7,508
Fishkill, NY 12524 • 1,957
Fiskdale, MA 01518 • 2,189
Fitchburg, MA 01420 • 41,194
Fitzgerald, GA 31750 • 8,612
Five Points, NM 87105 • 4,200
Flagler □, FL • 28,701
Flagler Beach, FL 32136 • 3,820
Flagstaff, AZ 86001-16 • 45,857
Flanders, NJ 07836 • 3,040
Flandreau, SD 57028 • 2,311
Flathead □, MT • 59,218
Flatonia, TX 78941 • 1,295
Flat River, MO 63601 • 4,823
Flat Rock, MI 48134 • 7,290
Flat Rock, NC 28731 • 1,200
Flatwoods, KY 41139 • 7,799
Fleetwood, PA 19522 • 3,478
Fleming □, KY • 12,292
Flemingsburg, KY 41041 • 3,071
Flemington, NJ 08822 • 4,047
Flemington, PA 17745 • 1,321
Fletcher, NC 28732 • 2,787
Fletcher, OK 73541 • 1,002
Flint, MI 48501-32 • 140,761
Flint City, AL 35601 • 1,033
Flippin, AR 72634 • 1,006
Flomaton, AL 36441 • 1,811
Flora, IL 62839 • 5,054
Flora, IN 46929 • 2,179
Flora, MS 39071 • 1,482
Florala, AL 36442 • 2,075
Floral City, FL 32636 • 2,609
Floral Park, NY 11001-05 • 15,947
Florence, AL 35630-33 • 36,426
Florence, AZ 85232 • 7,510
Florence, CA 90001 • 43,900
Florence, CO 81226 • 2,990
Florence, KY 41042 • 18,624
Florence, MS 39073 • 1,831
Florence, NJ 08518 • 4,203
Florence, OR 97439 • 5,162
Florence, SC 29501-06 • 29,813
Florence □, SC • 114,344
Florence □, WI • 4,590
Floresville, TX 78114 • 5,247
Florham Park, NJ 07932 • 8,521
Florida, NY 10921 • 2,497
Florida City, FL 33034 • 5,806
Florida Ridge, FL 32960 • 12,218
Florin, CA 95828 • 24,330
Florissant, MO 63031-34 • 51,206
Flossmoor, IL 60422 • 8,651
Flower Hill, NY 11050 • 4,490
Flowery Branch, GA 30542 • 1,251
Flowood, MS 39208 • 2,860
Floyd □, GA • 81,251
Floyd □, IN • 64,404
Floyd □, IA • 17,058
Floyd □, KY • 43,586
Floyd □, TX • 8,497
Floyd □, VA • 12,005
Floydada, TX 79235 • 3,896
Flushing, MI 48433 • 8,542
Flushing, OH 43977 • 1,042
Fluvanna □, VA • 12,429
Foard □, TX • 1,794
Folcroft, PA 19032 • 7,506
Foley, AL 36535-36 • 4,937
Foley, MN 56329 • 1,854
Folkston, GA 31537 • 2,285
Follansbee, WV 26037 • 3,339
Folly Beach, SC 29439 • 1,398
Folsom, CA 95630 • 29,802
Folsom, NJ 08037 • 2,181
Fonda, NY 12068 • 1,007
Fond du Lac, WI 54935-36 • 37,757
Fond du Lac □, WI • 90,083
Fontana, CA 92334-36 • 87,535
Fontana, WI 53125 • 1,635
Foothill Farms, CA 95841 • 17,135
Ford □, IL • 14,275
Ford □, KS • 27,463
Ford City, CA 93268 • 3,781
Ford City, PA 16226 • 3,413
Ford Heights, IL 60411 • 4,259
Fords, NJ 08863 • 14,392
Fords Prairie, WA 98531 • 2,480
Fordyce, AR 71742 • 4,729
Foreman, AR 71836 • 1,267
Forest, MS 39074 • 5,060
Forest, OH 45843 • 1,594
Forest □, PA • 4,802
Forest □, WI • 8,776
Forest Acres, SC 29206 • 7,197
Forest City, IA 50436 • 4,430
Forest City, NC 28043 • 7,475
Forest City, PA 18421 • 1,846
Forestdale, AL 35214 • 10,395
Forestdale, RI 02824 • 530
Forest Dale, VT 05745 • 350
Forest Grove, OR 97116 • 13,559
Forest Hill, TX 76119 • 11,482
Forest Hills, PA 15221 • 7,335
Forest Knolls, CA 94933 • 2,000
Forest Lake, MN 55025 • 5,833
Forest Park, GA 30050-51 • 16,925
Forest Park, IL 60130 • 14,918
Forest Park, LA 71291 • 1,400
Forest Park, OH 45240 • 18,609
Forked River, NJ 08731 • 1,950
Forks, WA 98331 • 2,862
Forney, TX 75126 • 4,070
Forrest, IL 61741 • 1,124
Forrest □, MS • 68,314
Forrest City, AR 72335 • 13,364
Forreston, IL 61030 • 1,361
Forsyth, GA 31029 • 4,268
Forsyth, IL 62535 • 1,275
Forsyth, MO 65653 • 1,175
Forsyth, MT 59327 • 2,178
Forsyth □, GA • 44,083
Forsyth □, NC • 265,878
Fort Ashby, WV 26719 • 1,288
Fort Atkinson, WI 53538 • 10,227
Fort Bend □, TX • 225,421
Fort Benton, MT 59442 • 1,660
Fort Bragg, CA 95437 • 6,078
Fort Branch, IN 47648 • 2,447
Fort Collins, CO 80521-26 • 87,758
Fort Covington, NY 12937 • 1,200
Fort Davis, TX 79734 • 1,100
Fort Defiance, AZ 86504 • 4,489
Fort Deposit, AL 36032 • 1,240
Fort Dodge, IA 50501 • 25,894
Fort Edward, NY 12828 • 3,561
Fort Fairfield, ME 04742 • 1,729
Fort Gaines, GA 31751 • 1,248
Fort Gibson, OK 74434 • 3,359
Fort Hall, ID 83203 • 2,681
Fort Kent, ME 04743 • 2,123
Fort Laramie, WY 82212 • 243
Fort Lauderdale, FL 33301-51 • 149,377
Fort Lee, NJ 07024 • 31,997
Fort Loramie, OH 45845 • 1,042
Fort Loudon, PA 17224 • 1,200
Fort Lupton, CO 80621 • 5,159
Fort Madison, IA 52627 • 11,618
Fort McKinley, OH 45426 • 9,740
Fort Meade, FL 33841 • 4,976
Fort Mill, SC 29715 • 4,930
Fort Mitchell, KY 41017 • 7,438
Fort Morgan, CO 80701 • 9,068
Fort Myers, FL 33901-19 • 45,206
Fort Myers Beach, FL 33931-32 • 9,284
Fort Myers Shores, FL 33905 • 5,460
Fort Oglethorpe, GA 30742 • 5,880
Fort Payne, AL 35967 • 11,838
Fort Pierce, FL 34945-54 • 36,830
Fort Pierre, SD 57532 • 1,854
Fort Plain, NY 13339 • 2,416
Fort Recovery, OH 45846 • 1,313
Fort Scott, KS 66701 • 8,362
Fort Shawnee, OH 45806 • 4,128
Fort Smith, AR 72901-17 • 72,798
Fort Stockton, TX 79735 • 8,524
Fort Sumner, NM 88119 • 1,269
Fort Thomas, KY 41075 • 16,032
Fortuna, CA 95540 • 8,788
Fort Valley, GA 31030 • 8,198
Fortville, IN 46040 • 2,690
Fort Walton Beach, FL 32547-48 • 21,471
Fort Washington Forest, MD 20744 • 1,010
Fort Wayne, IN 46801-99 • 173,072
Fort Wingate, NM 87316 • 950
Fort Worth, TX 76101-85 • 447,619
Fort Wright, KY 41011 • 6,570
Forty Fort, PA 18704 • 5,049
Fort Yukon, AK 99740 • 580
Fosston, MN 56542 • 1,529
Foster □, ND • 3,983
Foster City, CA 94404 • 28,176
Foster Village, HI 96818 • 3,700
Fostoria, OH 44830 • 14,983
Fountain, CO 80817 • 9,984
Fountain □, IN • 17,808
Fountain Hill, PA 18015 • 4,637
Fountain Inn, SC 29644 • 4,388
Fountain Place, LA • 9,200
Fountain Valley, CA 92708 • 53,691
Four Corners, OR 97301 • 12,156
Four Oaks, NC 27524 • 1,308
Fowler, CA 93625 • 3,208
Fowler, CO 81039 • 1,154
Fowler, IN 47944 • 2,333
Fowlerville, MI 48836 • 2,648
Foxboro, MA 02035 • 5,706
Fox Chapel, PA 15238 • 5,319
Fox Lake, IL 60020 • 7,478
Fox Lake, WI 53933 • 1,269
Fox Point, WI 53217 • 7,238
Fox River Grove, IL 60021 • 3,551
Frackville, PA 17931 • 4,700
Framingham, MA 01701 • 64,994
Franconia, VA 22310 • 19,882
Frankenmuth, MI 48734 • 4,408
Frankford, DE 19945 • 591
Frankfort, IL 60423 • 7,180
Frankfort, IN 46041 • 14,754
Frankfort, KY 40601-22 • 25,968
Frankfort, MI 49635 • 1,546
Frankfort, NY 13340 • 2,693
Frankfort, OH 45628 • 1,065
Franklin, IN 46131 • 12,907
Franklin, KY 42134-35 • 7,607
Franklin, LA 70538 • 9,004
Franklin, MA 02038 • 9,965
Franklin, NE 68939 • 1,112
Franklin, NH 03235 • 8,304
Franklin, NJ 07416 • 4,977
Franklin, NC 28734 • 2,873
Franklin, OH 45005 • 11,026
Franklin, PA 16323 • 7,329
Franklin, TN 37064-65 • 20,098
Franklin, TX 77856 • 1,336
Franklin, VA 23851 • 7,864
Franklin, WI 53132 • 21,855
Franklin □, AL • 27,814
Franklin □, AR • 14,897
Franklin □, FL • 8,967
Franklin □, GA • 16,650
Franklin □, ID • 9,232
Franklin □, IL • 40,319
Franklin □, IN • 19,580
Franklin □, IA • 11,364
Franklin □, KS • 21,994
Franklin □, KY • 43,781
Franklin □, LA • 22,387
Franklin □, ME • 29,008
Franklin □, MA • 70,092
Franklin □, MS • 8,377
Franklin □, MO • 80,603
Franklin □, NE • 3,938
Franklin □, NY • 46,540
Franklin □, NC • 36,414
Franklin □, OH • 961,437
Franklin □, PA • 121,082
Franklin □, TN • 34,725
Franklin □, TX • 7,802
Franklin □, VT • 39,980
Franklin □, VA • 39,549
Franklin □, WA • 37,473
Franklin Lakes, NJ 07417 • 9,873
Franklin Park, IL 60131 • 18,485
Franklin Park, PA 15143 • 10,109
Franklin Square, NY 11010 • 28,205
Franklinton, LA 70438 • 4,007
Franklinton, NC 27525 • 1,615
Franklinville, NJ 08322 • 1,020
Franklinville, NY 14737 • 1,739
Frankston, TX 75763 • 1,127
Frankton, IN 46044 • 1,736
Fraser, MI 48026 • 13,899
Frazee, MN 56544 • 1,176
Frazeysburg, OH 43822 • 1,165
Frazier Park, CA 93225 • 2,201
Frederic, WI 54837 • 1,124
Frederica, DE 19946 • 761
Frederick, MD 21701-02 • 40,148
Frederick, OK 73542 • 5,221
Frederick □, MD • 150,208
Frederick □, VA • 45,723
Fredericksburg, IA 50630 • 1,011
Fredericksburg, TX 78624 • 6,934
Fredericksburg, VA 22401-08 • 19,027
Fredericktown, MO 63645 • 3,950
Fredericktown, OH 43019 • 2,443
Fredericktown, PA 15333 • 1,052
Fredonia, AZ 86022 • 1,207
Fredonia, KS 66736 • 2,599
Fredonia, NY 14063 • 10,436
Fredonia, WI 53021 • 1,558
Freeborn □, MN • 33,060
Freeburg, IL 62243 • 3,115
Freedom, CA 95019 • 8,361
Freedom, PA 15042 • 1,897
Freedom, WY 83120 • 450
Freehold, NJ 07728 • 10,742
Freeland, MI 48623 • 1,421
Freeland, PA 18224 • 3,909
Freeman, SD 57029 • 1,293
Freemansburg, PA 18017 • 1,946
Freeport, IL 61032 • 25,840
Freeport, ME 04032 • 1,829
Freeport, NY 11520 • 39,894
Freeport, PA 16229 • 1,983
Freeport, TX 77541 • 11,389
Freer, TX 78357 • 3,271
Freestone □, TX • 15,818
Fremont, CA 94536-39 • 173,339
Fremont, IN 46737 • 1,407
Fremont, MI 49412 • 3,875
Fremont, NE 68025 • 23,680
Fremont, NC 27830 • 1,710
Fremont, OH 43420 • 17,648
Fremont □, CO • 32,273
Fremont □, ID • 10,937
Fremont □, IA • 8,226
Fremont □, WY • 33,662
French Island, WI 54601 • 4,478
French Lick, IN 47432 • 2,087
Frenchtown, NJ 08825 • 1,528
Fresno, CA 93701-94 • 354,202
Fresno □, CA • 667,490
Frewsburg, NY 14738 • 1,817
Friars Point, MS 38631 • 1,334
Friday Harbor, WA 98250 • 1,492
Fridley, MN 55432 • 28,335
Friend, NE 68359 • 1,111
Friendship, NY 14739 • 1,423
Friendswood, TX 77546 • 22,814
Frio □, TX • 13,472
Friona, TX 79035 • 3,688
Frisco, CO 80443 • 1,601
Frisco City, AL 36445 • 1,581
Fritch, TX 79036 • 2,335
Frontenac, KS 66762 • 2,588
Frontier □, NE • 3,101
Front Royal, VA 22630 • 11,880
Frostburg, MD 21532 • 8,075
Frostproof, FL 33843 • 2,808
Fruita, CO 81521 • 4,045
Fruit Heights, UT 84037 • 3,900
Fruitland, ID 83619 • 2,400
Fruitland, MD 21826 • 3,511
Fruitland Park, FL 34731 • 2,754
Fruitport, MI 49415 • 1,090
Fruitvale, CO 81504 • 1,070
Fruitvale, WA 98902 • 4,125
Fruitville, FL 34232 • 9,808
Fryeburg, ME 04037 • 1,580
Fulda, MN 56131 • 1,212
Fullerton, CA 92631-35 • 114,144
Fullerton, NE 68638 • 1,452
Fulton, IL 61252 • 3,698
Fulton, KY 42041 • 3,078
Fulton, MS 38843 • 3,387
Fulton, MO 65251 • 10,033
Fulton, NY 13069 • 12,929
Fulton □, AR • 10,037
Fulton □, GA • 648,951
Fulton □, IL • 38,080
Fulton □, IN • 18,840
Fulton □, KY • 8,271
Fulton □, NY • 54,191
Fulton □, OH • 38,498
Fulton □, PA • 13,837
Fultondale, AL 35068 • 6,400
Funkstown, MD 21734 • 1,136
Fuquay-Varina, NC 27526 • 4,562
Furnas □, NE • 5,553
Fyffe, AL 35971 • 1,094

G

Gabbs, NV 89409 • 667
Gadsden, AL 35901-05 • 42,523
Gadsden □, FL • 41,105
Gaffney, SC 29340-42 • 13,145
Gage □, NE • 22,794
Gages Lake, IL 60030 • 8,349
Gahanna, OH 43230 • 27,791
Gaines □, TX • 14,123
Gainesboro, TN 38562 • 1,002
Gainesville, FL 32601-14 • 84,770
Gainesville, GA 30501-07 • 17,885
Gainesville, TX 76240 • 14,256
Gaithersburg, MD 20877-79 • 39,542
Galax, VA 24333 • 6,670
Galena, AK 99741 • 833
Galena, IL 61036 • 3,647
Galena, KS 66739 • 3,308
Galesburg, IL 61401-02 • 33,530
Galesburg, MI 49053 • 1,863
Gales Ferry, CT 06335 • 1,191
Galesville, WI 54630 • 1,278
Galeton, PA 16922 • 1,370
Galeville, NY 13088 • 4,695
Galion, OH 44833 • 11,859
Gallatin, MO 64640 • 1,864
Gallatin, TN 37066 • 18,794
Gallatin □, IL • 6,909
Gallatin □, KY • 5,393
Gallatin □, MT • 50,463
Gallia □, OH • 30,954
Galliano, LA 70354 • 4,294
Gallipolis, OH 45631 • 4,831
Gallitzin, PA 16641 • 2,003
Gallup, NM 87301-05 • 19,154
Galt, CA 95632 • 8,889
Galva, IL 61434 • 2,742
Galveston, IN 46932 • 1,609
Galveston, TX 77550-54 • 59,070
Galveston □, TX • 217,399
Gambell, AK 99742 • 525
Gambier, OH 43022 • 2,073
Gambrills, MD 21054 • 1,200
Ganado, AZ 86505 • 3,400
Ganado, TX 77962 • 1,701
Gang Mills, NY 14870 • 2,738
Gantt, SC 29605 • 13,891
Gap, PA 17527 • 1,200
Garberville, CA 95440 • 1,200
Garden □, NE • 2,460
Gardena, CA 90247-49 • 49,847
Garden City, GA 31408 • 7,410
Garden City, ID 83704 • 6,369
Garden City, KS 67846 • 24,097
Garden City, MI 48135-36 • 31,846
Garden City, MO 64747 • 1,225
Garden City, NY 11530 • 21,686
Garden City Park, NY 11040 • 7,437
Gardendale, AL 35071 • 9,251
Garden Grove, CA 92640-45 • 143,050
Garden Home, OR 97223 • 5,500
Gardiner, ME 04345 • 6,746
Gardner, IL 60424 • 1,237
Gardner, KS 66030 • 3,191
Gardner, MA 01440 • 20,125
Gardnerville, NV 89410 • 2,177
Gardnerville Ranchos, NV 89410 • 7,455
Garfield, NJ 07026 • 26,727
Garfield □, CO • 29,974
Garfield □, MT • 1,589
Garfield □, NE • 2,141
Garfield □, OK • 56,735
Garfield □, UT • 3,980
Garfield □, WA • 2,248
Garfield Heights, OH 44125 • 31,739
Garfield Park, DE 19720 • 1,415
Garland, TX 75040-48 • 180,650
Garland, UT 84312 • 1,637
Garland □, AR • 73,397
Garner, IA 50438 • 2,916
Garner, NC 27529 • 14,967
Garnett, KS 66032 • 3,210
Garrard □, KY • 11,579
Garretson, SD 57030 • 924
Garrett, IN 46738 • 5,349
Garrett □, MD • 28,138
Garrettsville, OH 44231 • 2,014
Garrison, MD 21055 • 5,045
Garrison, ND 58540 • 1,530
Garvin □, OK • 26,605
Garwood, NJ 07027 • 4,227
Gary, IN 46401-11 • 116,646
Gary, WV 24836 • 1,355
Garysburg, NC 27831 • 1,057
Garyville, LA 70051 • 3,181
Garza □, TX • 5,143
Gas City, IN 46933 • 6,296
Gasconade □, MO • 14,006
Gasport, NY 14067 • 1,336
Gassville, AR 72635 • 1,167
Gaston, NC 27832 • 1,003
Gaston □, NC • 175,093
Gastonia, NC 28051-56 • 54,732
Gate City, VA 24251 • 2,214
Gates, NY 14624 • 30,000
Gates □, NC • 9,305
Gatesville, TX 76528 • 11,492
Gatlinburg, TN 37738 • 3,417
Gautier, MS 39553 • 10,088
Gaylord, MI 49735 • 3,256
Gaylord, MN 55334 • 1,935
Gearhart, OR 97138 • 1,027
Geary, OK 73040 • 1,347
Geary □, KS • 30,453
Geauga □, OH • 81,129
Geistown, PA 15904 • 2,749
Gem □, ID • 11,844
Genesee, ID 83832 • 725
Genesee, MI 48437 • 1,400
Genesee □, MI • 430,459
Genesee □, NY • 60,060
Geneseo, IL 61254 • 5,990
Geneseo, NY 14454 • 7,187
Geneva, AL 36340 • 4,681
Geneva, IL 60134 • 12,617
Geneva, IN 46740 • 1,280
Geneva, NE 68361 • 2,310
Geneva, NY 14456 • 14,143
Geneva, OH 44041 • 6,597
Geneva □, AL • 23,647
Geneva-on-the-Lake, OH 44041 • 1,626
Genoa, IL 60135 • 3,083
Genoa, NE 68640 • 1,082
Genoa, NV 89411 • 190
Genoa, OH 43430 • 2,262
Genoa City, WI 53128 • 1,277
Gentry, AR 72734 • 1,726
Gentry □, MO • 6,848
George, IA 51237 • 1,066
George □, MS • 16,673
Georgetown, CA 95634 • 2,000
Georgetown, CT 06829 • 1,694
Georgetown, DE 19947 • 3,732
Georgetown, IL 61846 • 3,678
Georgetown, IN 47122 • 2,092
Georgetown, KY 40324 • 11,414
Georgetown, MA 01833 • 2,100
Georgetown, OH 45121 • 3,627
Georgetown, SC 29440-42 • 9,517
Georgetown, TX 78626-28 • 14,842
Georgetown □, SC • 46,302
George West, TX 78022 • 2,586
Georgiana, AL 36033 • 1,933
Gering, NE 69341 • 7,946
Gerlach, NV 89412 • 200
Germantown, IL 62245 • 1,167
Germantown, MD 20874 • 41,145
Germantown, OH 45327 • 4,916
Germantown, TN 38138 • 32,893
Germantown, WI 53022 • 13,658
Gettysburg, PA 17325 • 7,025
Gettysburg, SD 57442 • 1,510
Giants Neck, CT 06357 • 1,200
Gibbon, NE 68840 • 1,525
Gibbstown, NJ 08027 • 5,404
Gibsland, LA 71028 • 1,224
Gibson □, IN • 31,913
Gibson □, TN • 46,315
Gibsonburg, OH 43431 • 2,579
Gibson City, IL 60936 • 3,396
Gibsonia, FL 33805 • 5,168
Gibsonia, PA 15044 • 3,500
Gibsonton, FL 33534 • 7,706
Gibsonville, NC 27249 • 3,441
Giddings, TX 78942 • 4,093
Gideon, MO 63848 • 1,104
Gifford, FL 32960 • 6,278
Gig Harbor, WA 98335 • 3,236
Gila □, AZ • 40,216
Gila Bend, AZ 85337 • 1,747
Gilbert, AZ 85234 • 29,188
Gilbert, MN 55741 • 1,934
Gilbert, OR 97266 • 4,000
Gilbertsville, PA 19525 • 3,994
Gilbertville, MA 01031 • 1,029
Gilchrist □, FL • 9,667
Gilcrest, CO 80623 • 1,084
Giles □, TN • 25,741
Giles □, VA • 16,366
Gilford Park, NJ 08753 • 8,668
Gillespie, IL 62033 • 3,645
Gillespie □, TX • 17,204
Gillett, WI 54124 • 1,303
Gillette, WY 82716-17 • 17,635
Gilliam □, OR • 1,717
Gilman, IL 60938 • 1,816
Gilman, VT 05904 • 500
Gilmer, TX 75644 • 4,822
Gilmer □, GA • 13,368
Gilmer □, WV • 7,669
Gilpin □, CO • 3,070
Gilroy, CA 95020-21 • 31,487
Girard, IL 62640 • 2,164
Girard, KS 66743 • 2,794
Girard, OH 44420 • 11,304
Girard, PA 16417 • 2,879
Girardville, PA 17935 • 1,889
Glacier □, MT • 12,121
Glades □, FL • 7,591
Glade Spring, VA 24340 • 1,435
Gladeview, FL 33138 • 15,637
Gladewater, TX 75647 • 6,027
Gladstone, MI 49837 • 4,565
Gladstone, MO 64118 • 26,243
Gladstone, NJ 07934 • 2,111
Gladstone, OR 97027 • 10,152
Gladwin, MI 48624 • 2,682
Gladwin □, MI • 21,896
Glasco, NY 12432 • 1,538
Glascock □, GA • 2,357
Glasford, IL 61533 • 1,115
Glasgow, KY 42141-42 • 12,351
Glasgow, MO 65254 • 1,295
Glasgow, MT 59230 • 3,572
Glasgow, VA 24555 • 1,140
Glasgow Village, MO 63137 • 5,199
Glassboro, NJ 08028 • 15,614
Glasscock □, TX • 1,447
Glassport, PA 15045 • 5,582
Glastonbury, CT 06033 • 7,082
Gleason, TN 38229 • 1,402
Glen Allen, VA 23060 • 9,010
Glen Avon, CA • 12,663
Glenbrook, NV 89413 • 400
Glen Burnie, MD 21061 • 37,305
Glen Burnie Park, MD 21061 • 3,260
Glen Carbon, IL 62034 • 7,731
Glencoe, AL 35905 • 4,670
Glencoe, IL 60022 • 8,499
Glencoe, MN 55336 • 4,648
Glen Cove, NY 11542 • 24,149
Glendale, AZ 85301-12 • 148,134
Glendale, CA 91201-14 • 180,038
Glendale, CO 80222 • 2,453
Glendale, MS 39401 • 1,329
Glendale, MO 63122 • 5,945
Glendale, OH 45246 • 2,445
Glendale, RI 02826 • 700
Glendale, SC 29346 • 1,049
Glen Dale, WV 26038 • 1,612
Glendale, WI 53209 • 14,088
Glendale Heights, IL 60139 • 27,973
Glendive, MT 59330 • 4,802
Glendo, WY 82213 • 195

Glendola, NJ 07719 • 2,340
Glendora, CA 91740 • 47,828
Glendora, NJ 08029 • 5,201
Glen Ellyn, IL 60137–38 • 24,944
Glen Gardner, NJ 08826 • 1,665
Glenham, NY 12527 • 2,832
Glen Head, NY 11545 • 6,870
Glen Lyon, PA 18617 • 2,082
Glenmora, LA 71433 • 1,686
Glenn □, CA • 24,798
Glennallen, AK 99588 • 451
Glenn Dale, MD 20769 • 9,689
Glenns Ferry, ID 83623 • 1,304
Glennville, GA 30427 • 3,676
Glenolden, PA 19036 • 7,260
Glenpool, OK 74033 • 6,688
Glen Raven, NC 27215 • 2,616
Glen Ridge, NJ 07028 • 7,076
Glen Rock, NJ 07452 • 10,883
Glen Rock, PA 17327 • 1,688
Glenrock, WY 82637 • 2,153
Glen Rose, TX 76043 • 1,949
Glens Falls, NY 12801 • 15,023
Glenside, PA 19038 • 8,704
Glen Ullin, ND 58631 • 927
Glenview, IL 60025 • 37,093
Glenville, WV 26351 • 1,923
Glenwood, AR 71943 • 1,354
Glenwood, IL 60425 • 9,289
Glenwood, IA 51534 • 4,571
Glenwood, MN 56334 • 2,573
Glenwood, VA 24541 • 2,276
Glenwood City, WI 54013 • 1,026
Glenwood Farms, VA 23223 • 3,200
Glenwood Hills, GA 30032 • 5,240
Glenwood Springs, CO 81601–02 • 6,561
Glidden, IA 51443 • 1,099
Globe, AZ 85501–02 • 6,062
Gloster, MS 39638 • 1,323
Gloucester, MA 01930–31 • 28,716
Gloucester, VA 23061 • 1,200
Gloucester □, NJ • 230,082
Gloucester □, VA • 30,131
Gloucester City, NJ 08030 • 12,649
Gloucester Point, VA 23062 • 8,509
Glouster, OH 45732 • 2,001
Gloversville, NY 12078 • 16,656
Gloverville, SC 29828 • 2,753
Glynn □, GA • 62,496
Gnadenhutten, OH 44629 • 1,226
Goddard, KS 67052 • 1,804
Godfrey, IL 62035 • 5,436
Goffstown, NH 03045 • 2,700
Gogebic □, MI • 18,052
Golconda, NV 89414 • 200
Gold Bar, WA 98251 • 1,078
Gold Beach, OR 97444 • 1,546
Golden, CO 80401–03 • 13,116
Goldendale, WA 98620 • 3,319
Golden Gate, FL 33999 • 14,148
Golden Glades, FL 33055 • 25,474
Golden Meadow, LA 70357 • 2,049
Golden Valley, MN 55427 • 20,971
Golden Valley □, MT • 912
Golden Valley □, ND • 2,108
Goldfield, NV 89013 • 600
Goldsboro, NC 27530–34 • 40,709
Goldthwaite, TX 76844 • 1,658
Goleta, CA 93117 • 28,600
Golf Manor, OH 45237 • 4,154
Goliad, TX 77963 • 1,946
Goliad □, TX • 5,980
Gonzales, CA 93926 • 4,660
Gonzales, LA 70737 • 7,003
Gonzales, TX 78629 • 6,527
Gonzales □, TX • 17,205
Gonzalez, FL 32560 • 7,669
Goochland □, VA • 14,163
Goodhue □, MN • 40,690
Gooding, ID 83330 • 2,820
Gooding □, ID • 11,633
Goodland, FL 33933 • 1,000
Goodland, IN 47948 • 1,033
Goodland, KS 67735 • 4,983
Goodlettsville, TN 37072 • 11,219
Goodman, MS 39079 • 1,256
Goodman, MO 64843 • 1,094
Goodsprings, NV 89019 • 150
Goodview, MN 55987 • 2,878
Goodwater, AL 35072 • 1,840
Goodwell, OK 73939 • 1,065
Goodyear, AZ 85338 • 6,258
Goose Creek, SC 29445 • 24,692
Gordo, AL 35466 • 1,918
Gordon, GA 31031 • 2,468
Gordon, NE 69343 • 1,803
Gordon □, GA • 35,072
Gordonsville, VA 22942 • 1,351
Gorham, ME 04038 • 3,618
Gorham, NH 03581 • 1,910
Gorman, TX 76454 • 1,290
Goshen, IN 46526 • 23,797
Goshen, NY 10924 • 5,255
Goshen, OH 45122 • 1,400
Goshen □, WY • 12,373
Gosnell, AR 72319 • 3,783
Gosper □, NE • 1,928
Gothenburg, NE 69138 • 3,232
Gould, AR 71643 • 1,470
Goulding, FL 32503 • 4,159
Goulds, FL 33170 • 7,284
Gouverneur, NY 13642 • 4,604
Gove □, KS • 3,231
Gowanda, NY 14070 • 2,901
Gower, MO 64454 • 1,249
Gowrie, IA 50543 • 1,028
Grace, ID 83241 • 973
Graceville, FL 32440 • 2,675
Gracewood, GA 30812 • 1,000
Grady □, GA • 20,279
Grady □, OK • 41,747
Grafton, MA 01519 • 1,520
Grafton, ND 58237 • 4,840
Grafton, OH 44044 • 3,344
Grafton, WV 26354 • 5,524
Grafton, WI 53024 • 9,340
Grafton □, NH • 74,929
Graham, CA 90002 • 10,600
Graham, NC 27253 • 10,426
Graham, TX 76046 • 8,986
Graham □, AZ • 26,554
Graham □, KS • 3,543
Graham □, NC • 7,196
Grainger □, TN • 17,095
Grain Valley, MO 64029 • 1,898
Grambling, LA 71245 • 5,484
Gramercy, LA 70052 • 2,412
Granbury, TX 76048–49 • 4,045
Granby, CT 06035 • 9,369
Granby, MA 01033 • 1,327
Granby, MO 64844 • 1,945
Grand □, CO • 7,966
Grand □, UT • 6,620
Grand Bay, AL 36541 • 3,383
Grand Blanc, MI 48439 • 7,760
Grand Caillou, LA 70360 • 1,400
Grand Canyon, AZ 86023 • 1,499
Grand Coteau, LA 70541 • 1,118
Grandfield, OK 73546 • 1,224
Grand Forks, ND 58201–06 • 49,425
Grand Forks □, ND • 70,683
Grand Haven, MI 49417 • 11,951
Grand Island, NE 68801–03 • 39,386
Grand Isle, LA 70358 • 1,455
Grand Isle □, VT • 5,318
Grand Junction, CO 81501–06 • 29,034
Grand Ledge, MI 48837 • 7,579
Grand Marais, MN 55604 • 1,171
Grand Prairie, TX 75050–54 • 99,616
Grand Rapids, MI 49501–99 • 189,126
Grand Rapids, MN 55744 • 7,976
Grand Saline, TX 75140 • 2,630
Grand Terrace, CA 92324 • 10,946
Grand Traverse □, MI • 64,273
Grandview, MO 64030 • 24,967
Grandview, WA 98930 • 7,169
Grandview Heights, OH 43212 • 7,010
Grandville, MI 49418 • 15,624
Granger, IN 46530 • 20,241
Granger, TX 76530 • 1,190
Granger, WA 98932 • 2,053
Grangeville, ID 83530 • 3,226
Granite, OK 73547 • 1,844
Granite □, MT • 2,548
Granite City, IL 62040 • 32,862
Granite Falls, MN 56241 • 3,083
Granite Falls, NC 28630 • 3,253
Granite Falls, WA 98252 • 1,060
Granite Quarry, NC 28072 • 1,646
Graniteville, MA 01886 • 1,010
Graniteville, SC 29829 • 1,158
Graniteville, VT 05654 • 500
Grant, NE 69140 • 1,239
Grant □, AR • 13,948
Grant □, IN • 74,169
Grant □, KS • 7,159
Grant □, KY • 15,737
Grant □, LA • 17,526
Grant □, MN • 6,246
Grant □, NE • 769
Grant □, NM • 27,676
Grant □, ND • 3,549
Grant □, OK • 5,689
Grant □, OR • 7,853
Grant □, SD • 8,372
Grant □, WA • 54,758
Grant □, WV • 10,428
Grant □, WI • 49,264
Grant Park, IL 60940 • 1,024
Grants, NM 87020 • 8,626
Grantsburg, WI 54840 • 1,144
Grants Pass, OR 97526–27 • 17,488
Grantsville, UT 84029 • 4,500
Grantville, GA 30220 • 1,180
Granville, IL 61326 • 1,407
Granville, NY 12832 • 2,646
Granville, OH 43023 • 4,353
Granville □, NC • 38,345
Grapeland, TX 75844 • 1,450
Grapevine, TX 76051 • 29,202
Grasonville, MD 21638 • 2,439
Grass Lake, IL 60002 • 2,191
Grass Valley, CA 95945 • 9,048
Gratiot □, MI • 38,982
Graves □, KY • 33,550
Gravette, AR 72736 • 1,412
Gray, GA 31032 • 2,189
Gray, LA 70359 • 1,500
Gray □, KS • 5,396
Gray □, TX • 23,967
Grayling, MI 49738 • 1,944
Graylyn Crest, DE 19810 • 4,380
Grays Harbor □, WA • 64,175
Grayslake, IL 60030 • 7,388
Grayson, KY 41143 • 3,510
Grayson □, KY • 21,050
Grayson □, TX • 95,021
Grayson □, VA • 16,278
Graysville, AL 35073 • 2,241
Graysville, TN 37338 • 1,301
Grayville, IL 62844 • 2,043
Great Barrington, MA 01230 • 2,810
Great Bend, KS 67530 • 15,427
Great Falls, MT 59401–06 • 55,097
Great Falls, SC 29055 • 2,307
Great Falls, VA 22066 • 6,945
Great Neck, NY 11020–27 • 8,745
Great Neck Estates, NY 11021 • 2,790
Greece, NY 14626 • 15,632
Greece, NY • 15,632
Greeley, CO 80631–34 • 60,536
Greeley □, KS • 1,774
Greeley □, NE • 3,006
Green, OR 97470 • 5,076
Green □, KY • 10,371
Green □, WI • 30,339
Greenacres, CA 93308 • 7,379
Green Acres, DE 19803 • 1,140
Greenacres, WA 99016 • 4,250
Greenacres City, FL 33463 • 18,683
Green Bay, WI 54301–24 • 96,466
Greenbelt, MD 20770 • 21,096
Greenbriar, VA 22033 • 6,200
Greenbrier, AR 72058 • 2,130
Green Brier, TN 37073 • 2,873
Greenbrier □, WV • 34,693
Green Brook, NJ 08812 • 2,380
Greencastle, IN 46135 • 8,984
Greencastle, PA 17225 • 3,600
Green Cove Springs, FL 32043 • 4,497
Greendale, IN 47025 • 3,881
Greendale, WI 53129 • 15,128
Greene, IA 50636 • 1,142
Greene, NY 13778 • 1,812
Greene □, AL • 10,153
Greene □, AR • 31,804
Greene □, GA • 11,793
Greene □, IL • 15,317
Greene □, IN • 30,410
Greene □, IA • 10,045
Greene □, MS • 10,220
Greene □, MO • 207,949
Greene □, NY • 44,739
Greene □, NC • 15,384
Greene □, OH • 136,731
Greene □, PA • 39,550
Greene □, TN • 55,853
Greene □, VA • 10,297
Greeneville, TN 37743–44 • 13,532
Greenfield, CA 93927 • 7,464
Greenfield, IL 62044 • 1,162
Greenfield, IN 46140 • 11,657
Greenfield, IA 50849 • 2,074
Greenfield, MA 01301–02 • 14,016
Greenfield, MO 65661 • 1,416
Greenfield, OH 45123 • 5,172
Greenfield, TN 38230 • 2,105
Greenfield, WI 53220 • 33,403
Greenfield Plaza, IA 50315 • 2,200
Green Forest, AR 72638 • 2,050
Green Harbor, MA 02041 • 1,900
Greenhills, OH 45218 • 4,393
Green Island, NY 12183 • 2,490
Green Lake, WI 54941 • 1,064
Green Lake □, WI • 18,651
Greenlawn, NY 11740 • 13,208
Greenlee □, AZ • 8,008
Greenock, PA 15047 • 2,500
Greenport, NY 11944 • 2,070
Green River, WY 82935 • 12,711
Green Rock, IL 61241 • 2,615
Greensboro, AL 36744 • 3,047
Greensboro, GA 30642 • 2,860
Greensboro, MD 21639 • 1,441
Greensboro, NC 27401–95 • 183,521
Greensburg, IN 47240 • 9,286
Greensburg, KS 67054 • 1,792
Greensburg, KY 42743 • 1,990
Greensburg, PA 15601 • 16,318
Green Springs, OH 44836 • 1,446
Greensville □, VA • 8,853
Greentown, IN 46936 • 2,172
Green Tree, PA 15220 • 4,905
Greenup, IL 62428 • 1,616
Greenup, KY 41144 • 1,158
Greenup □, KY • 36,742
Green Valley, AZ 85614 • 13,231
Green Valley, MD 21771 • 9,424
Greenview, SC 29203 • 5,515
Greenville, AL 36037 • 7,492
Greenville, CA 95947 • 1,396
Greenville, DE 19807 • 800
Greenville, GA 30222 • 1,167
Greenville, IL 62246 • 4,806
Greenville, KY 42345 • 4,689
Greenville, ME 04441 • 1,601
Greenville, MI 48838 • 8,101
Greenville, MS 38701–04 • 45,226
Greenville, NH 03048 • 1,135
Greenville, NY 10583 • 9,528
Greenville, NC 27834–36 • 44,972
Greenville, OH 45331 • 12,863
Greenville, PA 16125 • 6,734
Greenville, RI 02828 • 8,303
Greenville, SC 29601–16 • 58,282
Greenville, TX 75401–03 • 23,071
Greenville □, SC • 320,167
Greenwich, CT 06830–36 • 58,441
Greenwich, NY 12834 • 1,961
Greenwich, OH 44837 • 1,442
Greenwood, AR 72936 • 3,984
Greenwood, DE 19950 • 578
Greenwood, IN 46142 • 26,265
Greenwood, LA 71033 • 2,092
Greenwood, MS 38930 • 18,906
Greenwood, MO 64034 • 1,505
Greenwood, PA 16601 • 1,650
Greenwood, SC 29646–49 • 20,807
Greenwood □, KS • 7,847
Greenwood □, SC • 59,567
Greenwood Lake, NY 10925 • 3,208
Greenwood Village, CO 80111 • 7,589
Greer, SC 29650–52 • 10,322
Greer □, OK • 6,559
Gregg □, TX • 104,948
Gregory, SD 57533 • 1,384
Gregory □, SD • 5,359
Greilickville, MI 49684 • 1,060
Grenada, MS 38901 • 10,864
Grenada □, MS • 21,555
Gresham, OR 97030 • 68,235
Gresham Park, GA 30316 • 9,000
Gretna, FL 32332 • 1,981
Gretna, LA 70053–54 • 17,208
Gretna, NE 68028 • 2,249
Gretna, VA 24557 • 1,339
Greybull, WY 82426 • 1,789
Gridley, CA 95948 • 4,631
Gridley, IL 61744 • 1,304
Griffin, GA 30223–24 • 21,347
Griffith, IN 46319 • 17,916
Grifton, NC 28530 • 2,393
Griggs □, ND • 3,303
Griggsville, IL 62340 • 1,218
Grimes, IA 50111 • 2,653
Grimes □, TX • 18,828
Grindall Creek, VA 23234 • 1,710
Grinnell, IA 50112 • 8,902
Griswold, IA 51535 • 1,049
Groesbeck, OH 45239 • 6,684
Groesbeck, TX 76642 • 3,185
Grosse Ile, MI 48138 • 9,781
Grosse Pointe, MI 48236 • 5,681
Grosse Pointe Farms, MI 48236 • 10,092
Grosse Pointe Park, MI 48230 • 12,857
Grosse Pointe Woods, MI 48225 • 17,715
Grossmont, CA 91941 • 2,600
Groton, CT 06340 • 9,837
Groton, MA 01450 • 1,044
Groton, NY 13073 • 2,398
Groton, SD 57445 • 1,196
Grottoes, VA 24441 • 1,455
Grove, OK 74344 • 4,020
Grove City, FL 34224 • 2,374
Grove City, OH 43123 • 19,661
Grove City, PA 16127 • 8,240
Grove Hill, AL 36451 • 1,551
Groveland, FL 34736 • 2,300
Groveland, MA 01834 • 3,780
Groveport, OH 43125 • 2,948
Grover City, CA 93433 • 11,656
Groves, TX 77619 • 16,513
Groveton, NH 03582 • 1,255
Groveton, TX 75845 • 1,071
Groveton, VA 22303 • 19,997
Groveton Gardens, VA 22303 • 2,600
Grovetown, GA 30813 • 3,596
Groveville, NJ 08620 • 2,900
Gruetli-Laager, TN 37339 • 1,810
Grulla, TX 78548 • 1,335
Grundy, VA 24614 • 1,305
Grundy □, IL • 32,337
Grundy □, IA • 12,029
Grundy □, MO • 10,536
Grundy □, TN • 13,362
Grundy Center, IA 50638 • 2,491
Gruver, TX 79040 • 1,172
Guadalupe, AZ 85283 • 5,458
Guadalupe, CA 93434 • 5,479
Guadalupe □, NM • 4,156
Guadalupe □, TX • 64,873
Guernsey, WY 82214 • 1,155
Guernsey □, OH • 39,024
Gueydan, LA 70542 • 1,611
Guilford, CT 06437 • 2,588
Guilford, ME 04443 • 1,082
Guilford □, NC • 347,420
Guin, AL 35563 • 2,464
Gulf □, FL • 11,504
Gulf Breeze, FL 32561 • 5,530
Gulf Gate Estates, FL 34231 • 11,622
Gulfport, FL 33707 • 11,727
Gulfport, MS 39501–07 • 40,775
Gulf Shores, AL 36542 • 3,261
Gumboro, DE 19945 • 200
Gunnison, CO 81230 • 4,636
Gunnison, UT 84634 • 1,298
Gunnison □, CO • 10,273
Guntersville, AL 35976 • 7,038
Gurdon, AR 71743 • 2,199
Gurley, AL 35748 • 1,007
Gurnee, IL 60031 • 13,701
Gustine, CA 95322 • 3,931
Guthrie, KY 42234 • 1,504
Guthrie, OK 73044 • 10,518
Guthrie □, IA • 10,935
Guthrie Center, IA 50115 • 1,614
Guttenberg, IA 52052 • 2,257
Guttenberg, NJ 07093 • 8,268
Guymon, OK 73942 • 7,803
Gwinhurst, DE 19809 • 1,340
Gwinn, MI 49841 • 2,370
Gwinner, ND 58040 • 585
Gwinnett □, GA • 352,910
Gypsum, CO 81637 • 1,750

H

Haakon □, SD • 2,624
Habersham □, GA • 27,621
Hacienda Heights, CA 91745 • 52,354
Hackensack, NJ 07601–08 • 37,049
Hackettstown, NJ 07840 • 8,120
Hackleburg, AL 35564 • 1,161
Haddam, CT 06438 • 1,200
Haddonfield, NJ 08033 • 11,628
Haddon Heights, NJ 08035 • 7,860
Hadlock, WA 98339 • 1,752
Hagerman, NM 88232 • 961
Hagerstown, IN 47346 • 1,835
Hagerstown, MD 21740 • 35,445
Hahira, GA 31632 • 1,353
Hahnville, LA 70057 • 2,599
Hailey, ID 83333 • 3,687
Haines, AK 99827 • 1,238
Haines City, FL 33844 • 11,683
Hainesport, NJ 08036 • 1,250
Halawa Heights, HI 96701 • 7,000
Hale □, AL • 15,498
Hale □, TX • 34,671
Hale Center, TX 79041 • 2,067
Haledon, NJ 07508 • 6,951
Haleiwa, HI 96712 • 2,442
Hales Corners, WI 53130 • 7,623
Halethorpe, MD 21227 • 19,750
Haleyville, AL 35565 • 4,452
Half Hollow Hills, NY 11746 • 5,110
Half Moon, NC 28540 • 6,306
Half Moon Bay, CA 94019 • 8,886
Halfway, MD 21740 • 8,873
Halifax □, NC • 55,516
Halifax □, VA • 29,033
Haliimaile, HI 96768 • 841
Hall □, GA • 95,428
Hall □, NE • 48,925
Hall □, TX • 3,905
Hallandale, FL 33009 • 30,996
Hallettsville, TX 77964 • 2,718
Hallie, WI 54729 • 1,300
Hallock, MN 56728 • 1,304
Hallowell, ME 04347 • 2,534
Halls, TN 37918 • 6,450
Halls, TN 38040 • 2,431
Halls Crossroads, TN 37918 • 1,900
Hallstead, PA 18822 • 1,274
Hallsville, TX 75650 • 2,288
Halstead, KS 67056 • 2,015
Haltom City, TX 76117 • 32,856
Hamblen □, TN • 50,480
Hamburg, AR 71646 • 3,098
Hamburg, IA 51640 • 1,248
Hamburg, NJ 07419 • 2,566
Hamburg, NY 14075 • 10,442
Hamburg, PA 19526 • 3,987
Hamden, CT 06514 • 52,434
Hamel, MN 55340 • 3,096
Hamilton, AL 35570 • 5,787
Hamilton, IL 62341 • 3,281
Hamilton, MA 01936 • 1,000
Hamilton, MI 49419 • 1,000
Hamilton, MO 64644 • 1,737
Hamilton, MT 59840 • 2,737
Hamilton, NY 13346 • 3,790
Hamilton, OH 45011–18 • 61,368
Hamilton, TX 76531 • 2,937
Hamilton □, FL • 10,930
Hamilton □, IL • 8,499
Hamilton □, IN • 108,936
Hamilton □, IA • 16,071
Hamilton □, KS • 2,388
Hamilton □, NE • 8,862
Hamilton □, NY • 5,279
Hamilton □, OH • 866,228
Hamilton □, TN • 285,536
Hamilton □, TX • 7,733
Hamilton City, CA 95951 • 1,811
Hamilton Square, NJ 08690 • 10,970
Ham Lake, MN 55304 • 8,924
Hamlet, NC 28345 • 6,196
Hamlin, TX 79520 • 2,791
Hamlin, WV 25523 • 1,030
Hamlin □, SD • 4,974
Hammond, IN 46320–27 • 84,236
Hammond, LA 70401–04 • 15,871
Hammond, WI 54015 • 1,097
Hammonton, NJ 08037 • 12,208
Hampden, ME 04444 • 3,895
Hampden □, MA • 456,310
Hampden Highlands, ME 04444 • 1,540
Hampshire, IL 60140 • 1,843
Hampshire □, MA • 146,568
Hampshire □, WV • 16,498
Hampstead, MD 21074 • 2,608
Hampton, AR 71744 • 1,562
Hampton, GA 30228 • 2,694
Hampton, IA 50441 • 4,133
Hampton, NH 03842 • 7,989
Hampton, NJ 08827 • 1,515
Hampton, SC 29924 • 2,997
Hampton, TN 37658 • 2,236
Hampton, VA 23651–70 • 133,793
Hampton □, SC • 18,191
Hampton Bays, NY 11946 • 7,893
Hamtramck, MI 48212 • 18,372
Hana, HI 96713 • 683
Hanahan, SC 29406 • 13,176
Hanamaulu, HI 96715 • 3,611
Hanapepe, HI 96716 • 1,395
Hanceville, AL 35077 • 2,246
Hancock, MD 21750 • 1,926
Hancock, MI 49930 • 4,547
Hancock, NY 13783 • 1,330
Hancock □, GA • 8,908
Hancock □, IL • 21,373
Hancock □, IN • 45,527
Hancock □, IA • 12,638
Hancock □, KY • 7,864
Hancock □, ME • 46,948
Hancock □, MS • 31,760
Hancock □, OH • 65,536
Hancock □, TN • 6,739
Hancock □, WV • 35,233
Hand □, SD • 4,272
Hanford, CA 93230–32 • 30,897
Hankinson, ND 58041 • 1,038
Hanna, WY 82327 • 1,076
Hanna City, IL 61536 • 1,205
Hannibal, MO 63401 • 18,004
Hanover, IN 47243 • 3,610
Hanover, MA 02339 • 2,500
Hanover, NH 03755 • 6,538
Hanover, PA 17331 • 14,399
Hanover □, VA • 63,306
Hanover Center, MA 02339 • 1,000
Hanover Park, IL 60103 • 32,895
Hanover Township, NJ 07981 • 11,538
Hansen, ID 83334 • 848
Hansford □, TX • 5,848
Hanson, MA 02341 • 2,188
Hanson □, SD • 2,994
Hapeville, GA 30354 • 5,483
Happy Valley, OR 97236 • 1,519
Harahan, LA 70123 • 9,927
Haralson □, GA • 21,966
Harbeson, DE 19951 • 500
Harbor, OR 97415 • 2,143
Harbor Beach, MI 48441 • 2,089
Harborcreek, PA 16421 • 1,500
Harbor Springs, MI 49740 • 1,540
Hardee □, FL • 19,499
Hardeeville, SC 29927 • 1,583
Hardeman □, TN • 23,377
Hardeman □, TX • 5,283
Hardin, IL 62047 • 1,071
Hardin, MT 59034 • 2,940
Hardin □, IL • 5,189
Hardin □, IA • 19,094
Hardin □, KY • 89,240
Hardin □, OH • 31,111
Hardin □, TN • 22,633
Hardin □, TX • 41,320
Harding □, NM • 987
Harding □, SD • 1,669
Hardinsburg, KY 40143 • 1,906
Hardwick, GA 31034 • 8,800
Hardwick, VT 05843 • 1,400
Hardy □, WV • 10,977
Harford □, MD • 182,132
Hargill, TX 78549 • 1,030
Harker Heights, TX 76543 • 12,841
Harkers Island, NC 28531 • 1,759
Harlan, IN 46743 • 1,200
Harlan, IA 51537 • 5,148
Harlan, KY 40831 • 2,686
Harlan □, KY • 36,574
Harlan □, NE • 3,810
Harlem, FL 33440 • 2,826
Harlem, GA 30814 • 2,199
Harlem, MT 59526 • 882
Harleysville, PA 19438 • 7,405
Harlingen, TX 78550–52 • 48,735
Harlowton, MT 59036 • 1,049
Harmon □, OK • 3,793
Harmony, MN 55939 • 1,081
Harmony, PA 16037 • 1,054
Harmony, RI 02829 • 820
Harnett □, NC • 67,822
Harney □, OR • 7,060
Harper, KS 67058 • 1,735
Harper □, KS • 7,124
Harper □, OK • 4,063
Harpers Ferry, WV 25425 • 308
Harper Woods, MI 48225 • 14,903
Harrah, OK 73045 • 4,206
Harriman, TN 37748 • 7,119
Harrington, DE 19952 • 2,311
Harrington Park, NJ 07640 • 4,623
Harris, RI 02816 • 1,050
Harris □, GA • 17,788
Harris □, TX • 2,818,199
Harrisburg, AR 72432 • 1,943
Harrisburg, IL 62946 • 9,289
Harrisburg, OR 97446 • 1,939
Harrisburg, PA 17101–13 • 52,376
Harris Hill, NY 14221 • 4,577

Harrison, AR 72601–02 • 9,922
Harrison, MI 48625 • 1,835
Harrison, NJ 07029 • 13,425
Harrison, NY 10528 • 23,308
Harrison, OH 45030 • 7,518
Harrison, TN 37341 • 7,191
Harrison □, IN • 29,890
Harrison □, IA • 14,730
Harrison □, KY • 16,248
Harrison □, MS • 165,365
Harrison □, MO • 8,469
Harrison □, OH • 16,085
Harrison □, TX • 57,483
Harrison □, WV • 69,371
Harrisonburg, VA 22801 • 30,707
Harrison Township, MI 48045 • 24,685
Harrisonville, MO 64701 • 7,683
Harristown, IL 62537 • 1,319
Harrisville, RI 02830 • 1,654
Harrisville, UT 84404 • 3,004
Harrisville, WV 26362 • 1,839
Harrodsburg, KY 40330 • 7,335
Hart, MI 49420 • 1,942
Hart, TX 79043 • 1,221
Hart □, GA • 19,712
Hart □, KY • 14,890
Hartford, AL 36344 • 2,448
Hartford, CT 06101–99 • 139,739
Hartford, IL 62048 • 1,676
Hartford, KY 42347 • 2,532
Hartford, MI 49057 • 2,341
Hartford, SD 57033 • 1,262
Hartford, VT 05047 • 500
Hartford, WI 53027 • 8,188
Hartford □, CT • 851,783
Hartford City, IN 47348 • 6,960
Hartington, NE 68739 • 1,583
Hartland, ME 04943 • 1,038
Hartland, WI 53029 • 6,906
Hartley, IA 51346 • 1,632
Hartley □, TX • 3,634
Hartsdale, NY 10530 • 9,587
Hartselle, AL 35640 • 10,795
Hartshorne, OK 74547 • 2,120
Hartsville, SC 29550 • 8,372
Hartsville, TN 37074 • 2,188
Hartville, OH 44632 • 2,031
Hartwell, GA 30643 • 4,555
Harvard, IL 60033 • 5,975
Harvard, MA 01451 • 1,200
Harvey, IL 60426 • 29,771
Harvey, LA 70058 • 21,222
Harvey, MI 49855 • 1,377
Harvey, ND 58341 • 2,263
Harvey □, KS • 31,028
Harwich, MA 02645 • 4,399
Harwich Port, MA 02646 • 2,300
Harwinton, CT 06791 • 5,228
Harwood Heights, IL 60656 • 7,680
Hasbrouck Heights, NJ 07604 • 11,488
Haskell, AR 72015 • 1,342
Haskell, OK 74436 • 2,143
Haskell, TX 79521 • 3,362
Haskell □, KS • 3,886
Haskell □, OK • 10,940
Haskell □, TX • 6,820
Haslett, MI 48840 • 10,230
Hastings, MI 49058 • 6,549
Hastings, MN 55033 • 15,445
Hastings, NE 68901–02 • 22,837
Hastings, PA 16646 • 1,431
Hastings-on-Hudson, NY 10706 • 8,000
Hatboro, PA 19040 • 7,382
Hatch, NM 87937 • 1,136
Hatfield, MA 01038 • 1,234
Hatfield, PA 19440 • 2,650
Hatteras, NC 27943 • 1,000
Hattiesburg, MS 39401–07 • 41,882
Hatton, ND 58240 • 800
Haubstadt, IN 47639 • 1,455
Haughton, LA 71037 • 1,664
Hauppauge, NY 11788 • 19,750
Hauula, HI 96717 • 3,479
Havana, FL 32333 • 1,654
Havana, IL 62644 • 3,610
Havelock, NC 28532 • 20,268
Haven, KS 67543 • 1,198
Haverford [Township], PA 19083 • 52,371
Haverhill, MA 01830–35 • 51,418
Haverstraw, NY 10927 • 9,438
Havre, MT 59501 • 10,201
Havre de Grace, MD 21078 • 8,952
Havre North, MT 59501 • 1,110
Hawaii □, HI • 120,317
Hawaiian Gardens, CA 90716 • 13,639
Hawarden, IA 51023 • 2,439
Hawi, HI 96719 • 924
Hawkins □, TN • 44,565
Hawkinsville, GA 31036 • 3,527
Hawley, MN 56549 • 1,655
Hawley, PA 18428 • 1,244
Haworth, NJ 07641 • 3,384
Haw River, NC 27258 • 1,855
Hawthorne, CA 90250–51 • 71,349
Hawthorne, FL 32640 • 1,305
Hawthorne, NV 89415–16 • 4,162
Hawthorne, NJ 07506 • 17,084
Hawthorne, NY 10532 • 4,764
Hayden, CO 81639 • 1,444
Hayden, ID 83835 • 3,744
Hayes □, NE • 1,222
Hayesville, OR 97303 • 14,318
Hayfield, MN 55940 • 1,283
Hayfield, VA 22310 • 2,300
Hayfork, CA 96041 • 2,605
Haynesville, LA 71038 • 2,854
Hays, KS 67601 • 17,767
Hays □, TX • 65,614
Haysville, KS 67060 • 8,364
Hayti, MO 63851 • 3,280
Hayward, CA 94540–46 • 111,498
Hayward, WI 54843 • 1,897
Hayward Addition, SD 57106 • 1,000
Haywood □, NC • 46,942
Haywood □, TN • 19,437
Hazard, KY 41701 • 5,416
Hazardville, CT 06082 • 5,179
Hazel Crest, IL 60429 • 13,334
Hazel Dell, WA 98660 • 15,386
Hazel Green, AL 35750 • 2,208
Hazel Green, WI 53811 • 1,171
Hazel Park, MI 48030 • 20,051
Hazelwood, MO 63042–45 • 15,324
Hazelwood, NC 28738 • 1,678
Hazen, AR 72064 • 1,668
Hazen, ND 58545 • 2,818
Hazlehurst, GA 31539 • 4,202
Hazlehurst, MS 39083 • 4,221
Hazlet, NJ 07730 • 23,013
Hazleton, PA 18201 • 24,730
Headland, AL 36345 • 3,266
Healdsburg, CA 95448 • 9,469
Healdton, OK 73438 • 2,872
Healy, AK 99743 • 487
Heard □, GA • 8,628
Hearne, TX 77859 • 5,132
Heath, OH 43056 • 7,231
Heavener, OK 74937 • 2,601
Hebbronville, TX 78361 • 4,465
Heber City, UT 84032 • 4,782
Heber Springs, AR 72543 • 5,628
Hebron, IN 46341 • 3,183
Hebron, KY 41048 • 1,200
Hebron, NE 68370 • 1,765
Hebron, ND 58638 • 888
Hebron, OH 43025 • 2,076
Hector, MN 55342 • 1,145
Heeia, HI 96744 • 5,010
Heflin, AL 36264 • 2,906
Hegins, PA 17938 • 1,200
Helena, AL 35080 • 3,918
Helena, AR 72342 • 7,491
Helena, GA 31037 • 1,256
Helena, MT 59601–26 • 24,569
Helena, OK 73741 • 1,043
Hellam, PA 17406 • 1,375
Hellertown, PA 18055 • 5,662
Helmetta, NJ 08828 • 1,211
Helotes, TX 78023 • 1,535
Helper, UT 84526 • 2,148
Hemet, CA 92343–44 • 36,094
Hemlock, MI 48626 • 1,601
Hemphill, TX 75948 • 1,182
Hemphill □, TX • 3,720
Hempstead, NY 11550–54 • 49,453
Hempstead, TX 77445 • 3,551
Hempstead □, AR • 21,621
Henagar, AL 35978 • 1,934
Henderson, KY 42420 • 25,945
Henderson, LA 70517 • 1,543
Henderson, NV 89015–16 • 64,942
Henderson, NC 27536 • 15,655
Henderson, TN 38340 • 4,760
Henderson, TX 75652–53 • 11,139
Henderson □, IL • 8,096
Henderson □, KY • 43,044
Henderson □, NC • 69,285
Henderson □, TN • 21,844
Henderson □, TX • 58,543
Henderson's Point, MS 39571 • 1,114
Hendersonville, NC 28739 • 7,284
Hendersonville, TN 37075 • 32,188
Hendricks □, IN • 75,717
Hendry □, FL • 25,773
Hennepin □, MN • 1,032,431
Hennessey, OK 73742 • 1,902
Henniker, NH 03242 • 1,693
Henrico □, VA • 217,881
Henrietta, NY 14467 • 1,200
Henrietta, NC 28076 • 1,412
Henrietta, TX 76365 • 2,896
Henry, IL 61537 • 2,591
Henry □, AL • 15,374
Henry □, GA • 58,741
Henry □, IL • 51,159
Henry □, IN • 48,139
Henry □, IA • 19,226
Henry □, KY • 12,823
Henry □, MO • 20,044
Henry □, OH • 29,108
Henry □, TN • 27,888
Henry □, VA • 56,942
Henryetta, OK 74437 • 5,872
Henryville, IN 47126 • 1,132
Hephzibah, GA 30815 • 2,466
Heppner, OR 97836 • 1,412
Herculaneum, MO 63048 • 2,263
Hercules, CA 94547 • 16,829
Hereford, TX 79045 • 14,745
Herington, KS 67449 • 2,685
Heritage Village, CT 06488 • 9,700
Herkimer, NY 13350 • 7,945
Herkimer □, NY • 65,797
Hermann, MO 65041 • 2,754
Hermantown, MN 55811 • 6,761
Herminie, PA 15637 • 2,000
Hermiston, OR 97838 • 10,040
Hermitage, PA 16148 • 15,300
Hermosa Beach, CA 90254 • 18,219
Hernando, FL 32642 • 2,103
Hernando, MS 38632 • 3,125
Hernando □, FL • 101,115
Herndon, VA 22070–71 • 16,139
Herrin, IL 62948 • 10,857
Herscher, IL 60941 • 1,278
Hershey, PA 17033 • 11,860
Hertford, NC 27944 • 2,105
Hertford □, NC • 22,523
Hesperia, CA 92345 • 50,418
Hesston, KS 67062 • 3,012
Hettinger, ND 58639 • 1,574
Hettinger □, ND • 3,445
Hewitt, TX 76643 • 8,983
Hewlett, NY 11557 • 6,620
Heyburn, ID 83336 • 2,714
Heyworth, IL 61745 • 1,627
Hialeah, FL 33010–16 • 188,004
Hiawatha, IA 52233 • 4,986
Hiawatha, KS 66434 • 3,603
Hibbing, MN 55746–47 • 18,046
Hickman, KY 42050 • 2,689
Hickman, NE 68372 • 1,081
Hickman □, KY • 5,566
Hickman □, TN • 16,754
Hickory, NC 28601–03 • 28,301
Hickory □, MO • 7,335
Hickory Hills, IL 60457 • 13,021
Hicksville, NY 11801–05 • 40,174
Hicksville, OH 43526 • 3,664
Hico, TX 76457 • 1,342
Hidalgo, TX 78557 • 3,292
Hidalgo □, NM • 5,958
Hidalgo □, TX • 383,545
Higganum, CT 06441 • 1,692
Higginsville, MO 64037 • 4,693
High Bridge, NJ 08829 • 3,886
Highland, CA 92346 • 34,439
Highland, IL 62249 • 7,525
Highland, IN 46322 • 23,696
Highland, MI 48356–57 • 750
Highland, NY 12528 • 4,492
Highland □, OH • 35,728
Highland □, VA • 2,635
Highland Falls, NY 10928 • 3,937
Highland Heights, OH 44124 • 6,249
Highland Lakes, NJ 07422 • 4,550
Highland Park, IL 60035 • 30,575
Highland Park, MI 48203 • 20,121
Highland Park, NJ 08904 • 13,279
Highland Park, TX 75205 • 8,739
Highlands, NJ 07732 • 4,849
Highlands, TX 77562 • 6,632
Highlands □, FL • 68,432
Highland Springs, VA 23075 • 13,823
Highmore, SD 57345 • 835
High Point, NC 27260–65 • 69,496
High Ridge, MO 63049 • 2,380
High Spire, PA 17034 • 2,668
High Springs, FL 32643 • 3,144
Hightstown, NJ 08520 • 5,126
Highview, KY 40228 • 14,814
Highwood, IL 60040 • 5,331
Hilbert, WI 54129 • 1,211
Hildale, UT 84784 • 1,325
Hill □, MT • 17,654
Hill □, TX • 27,146
Hill City, KS 67642 • 1,835
Hillcrest, NY 10977 • 6,447
Hillcrest Center, CA 93306 • 26,900
Hillcrest Heights, MD 20748 • 17,136
Hilliard, FL 32046 • 1,751
Hilliard, OH 43026 • 11,796
Hillsboro, IL 62049 • 4,400
Hillsboro, KS 67063 • 2,704
Hillsboro, MO 63050 • 1,625
Hillsboro, NH 03244 • 1,826
Hillsboro, ND 58045 • 1,488
Hillsboro, OH 45133 • 6,235
Hillsboro, OR 97123–24 • 37,520
Hillsboro, TX 76645 • 7,072
Hillsboro, WI 54634 • 1,288
Hillsborough, CA 94010 • 10,667
Hillsborough, NC 27278 • 4,263
Hillsborough □, FL • 834,054
Hillsborough □, NH • 336,073
Hillsdale, MI 49242 • 8,170
Hillsdale, NJ 07642 • 9,750
Hillsdale □, MI • 43,431
Hillside, IL 60162 • 7,672
Hillside, NJ 07205 • 21,044
Hillside Heights, DE 19711 • 1,500
Hillsville, VA 24343 • 2,008
Hillview, KY 40229 • 6,119
Hilo, HI 96720–21 • 37,808
Hilton, NY 14468 • 5,216
Hilton Head Island, SC 29928 • 23,694
Hinckley, IL 60520 • 1,682
Hinds □, MS • 254,441
Hines, OR 97738 • 1,452
Hinesville, GA 31313 • 21,603
Hingham, MA 02043 • 5,454
Hinsdale, IL 60521–22 • 16,029
Hinsdale, NH 03451 • 1,718
Hinsdale □, CO • 467
Hinton, OK 73047 • 1,233
Hinton, WV 25951 • 3,433
Hiram, GA 30141 • 1,389
Hiram, OH 44234 • 1,330
Hitchcock, TX 77563 • 5,868
Hitchcock □, NE • 3,750
Hitchcock Lake, CT 06716 • 1,640
Hobart, IN 46342 • 21,822
Hobart, OK 73651 • 4,305
Hobbs, NM 88240–41 • 29,115
Hobe Sound, FL 33455 • 11,507
Hoboken, NJ 07030 • 33,397
Hockessin, DE 19707 • 2,430
Hocking □, OH • 25,533
Hockley □, TX • 24,199
Hodgeman □, KS • 2,177
Hodgenville, KY 42748 • 2,721
Hoffman Estates, IL 60194–95 • 46,561
Hogansville, GA 30230 • 2,976
Hohenwald, TN 38462 • 3,760
Ho-Ho-Kus, NJ 07423 • 3,935
Hoisington, KS 67544 • 3,182
Hoke □, NC • 22,856
Hokes Bluff, AL 35903 • 3,739
Holbrook, AZ 86025–29 • 4,686
Holbrook, MA 02343 • 11,041
Holbrook, NY 11741 • 25,273
Holcomb, KS 67851 • 1,400
Holden, MA 01520 • 4,040
Holden, MO 64040 • 2,389
Holden, WV 25625 • 1,246
Holden Heights, FL 32805 • 4,387
Holdenville, OK 74848 • 4,792
Holdrege, NE 68949 • 5,671
Holgate, OH 43527 • 1,290
Holiday, FL 34690 • 19,360
Holiday City at Berkeley, NJ 08757 • 5,750
Holladay, UT 84117 • 22,189
Holland, MI 49422–24 • 30,745
Holland, NY 14080 • 1,288
Holland, OH 43528 • 1,210
Holland, PA 18966 • 5,250
Holland, TX 76534 • 1,118
Hollandale, MS 38748 • 3,576
Holley, NY 14470 • 1,890
Holliday, TX 76366 • 1,475
Hollidaysburg, PA 16648 • 5,624
Hollins, VA 24019 • 13,305
Hollis, OK 73550 • 2,584
Hollister, CA 95023–24 • 19,212
Hollister, MO 65672 • 2,628
Holliston, MA 01746 • 12,622
Holly, MI 48442 • 5,595
Holly Hill, FL 32117 • 11,141
Holly Hill, SC 29059 • 1,478
Holly Springs, GA 30142 • 2,406
Holly Springs, MS 38634–35 • 7,261
Hollywood, FL 33019–29 • 121,697
Hollywood, SC 29449 • 2,094
Holmen, WI 54636 • 3,220
Holmes □, FL • 15,778
Holmes □, MS • 21,604
Holmes □, OH • 32,849
Holstein, IA 51025 • 1,449
Holt, AL 35404 • 4,125
Holt, MI 48842 • 11,744
Holt □, MO • 6,034
Holt □, NE • 12,599
Holton, KS 66436 • 3,196
Holtsville, NY 11742 • 14,972
Holtville, CA 92250 • 4,820
Holualoa, HI 96725 • 3,834
Holyoke, CO 80734 • 1,931
Holyoke, MA 01040–41 • 43,704
Homedale, ID 83628 • 1,963
Home Gardens, CA 91720 • 7,780
Homeland Park, SC 29621 • 6,569
Home Place, IN 46240 • 1,300
Homer, AK 99603 • 3,660
Homer, IL 61849 • 1,264
Homer, LA 71040 • 4,152
Homer, MI 49245 • 1,758
Homer, NY 13077 • 3,476
Homer City, PA 15748 • 1,809
Homerville, GA 31634 • 2,560
Homestead, FL 33030–35 • 26,866
Homestead, PA 15120 • 4,179
Hometown, IL 60456 • 4,769
Homewood, AL 35209 • 22,922
Homewood, IL 60430 • 19,278
Homewood, OH 45015 • 2,550
Hominy, OK 74035 • 2,342
Homosassa, FL 32646 • 2,113
Hondo, TX 78861 • 6,018
Honea Path, SC 29654 • 3,841
Honeoye Falls, NY 14472 • 2,340
Honesdale, PA 18431 • 4,972
Honey Brook, PA 19344 • 1,184
Honey Grove, TX 75446 • 1,681
Honeypot Glen, CT 06410 • 1,200
Honeyville, UT 84314 • 1,112
Honokaa, HI 96727 • 2,186
Honolulu, HI 96801–50 • 365,272
Honolulu □, HI • 836,231
Honomu, HI 96728 • 532
Hood □, TX • 28,981
Hood River, OR 97031 • 4,632
Hood River □, OR • 16,903
Hoodsport, WA 98548 • 1,100
Hooker, OK 73945 • 1,551
Hooker □, NE • 793
Hooksett, NH 03106 • 2,573
Hoonah, AK 99829 • 795
Hooper Bay, AK 99604 • 845
Hoopeston, IL 60942 • 5,871
Hoosick Falls, NY 12090 • 3,490
Hoover, AL 35216 • 39,788
Hooverson Heights, WV 26037 • 3,056
Hopatcong, NJ 07843 • 15,586
Hope, AR 71801 • 9,643
Hope, IN 47246 • 2,171
Hope, RI 02831 • 270
Hopedale, MA 01747 • 3,961
Hope Mills, NC 28348 • 8,184
Hope Valley, RI 02832 • 1,446
Hopewell, NJ 08525 • 1,968
Hopewell, VA 23860 • 23,101
Hopewell Junction, NY 12533 • 1,786
Hopkins, MN 55343–47 • 16,534
Hopkins, SC 29061 • 1,600
Hopkins □, KY • 46,126
Hopkins □, TX • 28,833
Hopkinsville, KY 42240–41 • 29,809
Hopkinton, MA 01748 • 2,305
Hopkinton, RI 02833 • 550
Hopwood, PA 15445 • 2,021
Hoquiam, WA 98550 • 8,972
Horicon, WI 53032 • 3,873
Hornell, NY 14843 • 9,877
Horn Lake, MS 38637 • 9,069
Horry □, SC • 144,053
Horse Cave, KY 42749 • 2,284
Horseheads, NY 14844–45 • 6,802
Horsham, PA 19044 • 15,051
Horton, KS 66439 • 1,885
Hortonville, WI 54944 • 2,029
Hot Spring □, AR • 26,115
Hot Springs, SD 57747 • 4,325
Hot Springs □, WY • 4,809
Hot Springs National Park, AR 71901–14 • 32,462
Hot Springs Village, AR 71901 • 6,361
Houghton, MI 49931 • 7,498
Houghton, NY 14744 • 1,740
Houghton □, MI • 35,446
Houghton Lake, MI 48629 • 3,353
Houghton Lake Heights, MI 48630 • 2,449
Houlton, ME 04730 • 5,627
Houma, LA 70360–64 • 96,982
Housatonic, MA 01236 • 1,184
Houston, DE 19954 • 487
Houston, MN 55943 • 1,013
Houston, MS 38851 • 3,903
Houston, MO 65483 • 2,118
Houston, PA 15342 • 1,445
Houston, TX 77001–99 • 1,630,553
Houston □, AL • 81,331
Houston □, GA • 89,208
Houston □, MN • 18,497
Houston □, TN • 7,018
Houston □, TX • 21,375
Houtzdale, PA 16651 • 1,204
Howard, SD 57349 • 1,156
Howard, WI 54303 • 9,874
Howard □, AR • 13,569
Howard □, IN • 80,827
Howard □, IA • 9,809
Howard □, MD • 187,328
Howard □, MO • 9,631
Howard □, NE • 6,055
Howard □, TX • 32,343
Howard City, MI 49329 • 1,351
Howard Lake, MN 55349 • 1,343
Howards Grove-Millersville, WI 53083 • 2,329
Howell, MI 48843–44 • 8,184
Howell □, MO • 31,447
Howland, ME 04448 • 1,304
Howland, OH 44484 • 6,732
Hoxie, AR 72433 • 2,676
Hoxie, KS 67740 • 1,342
Hoyt Lakes, MN 55750 • 2,348
Huachuca City, AZ 85616 • 1,782
Hubbard, OH 44425 • 8,248
Hubbard, OR 97032 • 1,881
Hubbard, TX 76648 • 1,589
Hubbard □, MN • 14,939
Hubbell, MI 49934 • 1,174
Huber Heights, OH 45424 • 38,696
Huber Ridge, OH 43081 • 5,255
Huber South, OH 45439 • 4,800
Hudson, FL 34667 • 7,344
Hudson, IL 61748 • 1,006
Hudson, IA 50643 • 2,037
Hudson, MA 01749 • 14,267
Hudson, MI 49247 • 2,580
Hudson, NH 03051 • 7,626
Hudson, NY 12534 • 8,034
Hudson, NC 28638 • 2,819
Hudson, OH 44236 • 5,159
Hudson, WI 54016 • 6,378
Hudson, WY 82515 • 392
Hudson □, NJ • 553,099
Hudson Falls, NY 12839 • 7,651
Hudson Lake, IN 46552 • 1,347
Hudsonville, MI 49426 • 6,170
Hudspeth □, TX • 2,915
Huerfano □, CO • 6,009
Hueytown, AL 35023 • 15,280
Huffakers, NV 89501 • 150
Hughes, AR 72348 • 1,810
Hughes □, OK • 13,023
Hughes □, SD • 14,817
Hughesville, MD 20637 • 1,319
Hughesville, PA 17737 • 2,049
Hugo, MN 55038 • 4,417
Hugo, OK 74743 • 5,978
Hugoton, KS 67951 • 3,179
Hulett, WY 82720 • 429
Hull, IA 51239 • 1,724
Hull, MA 02045 • 10,466
Humansville, MO 65674 • 1,084
Humble, TX 77338–39 • 12,060
Humboldt, IA 50548 • 4,438
Humboldt, KS 66748 • 2,178
Humboldt, NE 68376 • 1,003
Humboldt, TN 38343 • 9,651
Humboldt □, CA • 119,118
Humboldt □, IA • 10,756
Humboldt □, NV • 12,844
Hummels Wharf, PA 17831 • 1,069
Humphreys □, MS • 12,134
Humphreys □, TN • 15,795
Hunt □, TX • 64,343
Hunterdon □, NJ • 107,776
Huntertown, IN 46748 • 1,330
Huntingburg, IN 47542 • 5,242
Huntingdon, PA 16652 • 6,843
Huntingdon, TN 38344 • 4,180
Huntingdon □, PA • 44,164
Huntington, IN 46750 • 16,389
Huntington, MA 01050 • 1,200
Huntington, NY 11743 • 18,243
Huntington, TX 75949 • 1,794
Huntington, UT 84528 • 1,875
Huntington, VA 22303 • 7,489
Huntington, WV 25701–79 • 54,844
Huntington □, IN • 35,427
Huntington Bay, NY 11743 • 1,521
Huntington Beach, CA 92646–49 • 181,519
Huntington Park, CA 90255 • 56,065
Huntington Station, NY 11746 • 28,247
Huntington Woods, MI 48070 • 6,419
Huntley, IL 60142 • 2,453
Huntsville, AL 35801–24 • 159,789
Huntsville, AR 72740 • 1,605
Huntsville, MO 65259 • 1,567
Huntsville, TX 77340–44 • 27,925
Hurley, NM 88043 • 1,534
Hurley, NY 12443 • 4,644
Hurley, WI 54534 • 1,782
Hurlock, MD 21643 • 1,706
Huron, OH 44839 • 7,030
Huron, SD 57350 • 12,448
Huron □, MI • 34,951
Huron □, OH • 56,240
Hurricane, UT 84737 • 3,915
Hurricane, WV 25526 • 4,461
Hurst, TX 76053–54 • 33,574
Hurt, VA 24563 • 1,294
Hutchins, TX 75141 • 2,719
Hutchinson, KS 67501–05 • 39,308
Hutchinson, MN 55350 • 11,523
Hutchinson □, SD • 8,262
Hutchinson □, TX • 25,689
Huxley, IA 50124 • 2,047
Hyannis, MA 02601 • 14,120
Hyannis Port, MA 02647 • 1,100
Hyattsville, MD 20780–89 • 13,864
Hybla Valley, VA 22306 • 15,491
Hydaburg, AK 99922 • 384
Hyde, PA 16843 • 1,643
Hyde □, NC • 5,411
Hyde □, SD • 1,696
Hyde Park, NY 12538 • 2,550
Hyde Park, UT 84318 • 2,190
Hydeville, VT 05750 • 450
Hyndman, PA 15545 • 1,019
Hyrum, UT 84319 • 4,829

I

Iberia □, LA • 68,297
Iberville □, LA • 31,049
Ida, MI 48140 • 1,000
Ida □, IA • 8,365
Idabel, OK 74745 • 6,957
Ida Grove, IA 51445 • 2,357
Idaho □, ID • 13,783
Idaho Falls, ID 83401–15 • 43,929
Idaho Springs, CO 80452 • 1,834
Idalou, TX 79329 • 2,074
Ilion, NY 13357 • 8,888
Illmo, MO 63780 • 1,368
Imlay, NV 89418 • 250
Imlay City, MI 48444 • 2,921
Immokalee, FL 33934 • 14,120
Imperial, CA 92251 • 4,113
Imperial, NE 69033 • 2,007
Imperial, PA 15126 • 3,200
Imperial □, CA • 109,303
Imperial Beach, CA 91932–33 • 26,512
Incline Village, NV 89450 • 4,500
Independence, CA 93526 • 1,000
Independence, IA 50644 • 5,972
Independence, KS 67301 • 9,942
Independence, KY 41051 • 10,444
Independence, LA 70443 • 1,632
Independence, MO 64050–58 • 112,301
Independence, OH 44131 • 6,500

Independence, OR 97351 • 4,425
Independence, WI 54747 • 1,041
Independence □, AR • 31,192
Indiana, PA 15701 • 15,174
Indiana □, PA • 89,994
Indianapolis, IN 46201-90 • 731,327
Indian Harbour Beach, FL 32937 • 6,933
Indian Head, MD 20640 • 3,531
Indian Heights, IN 46902 • 3,669
Indian Hills, CO 80454 • 2,000
Indian Neck, CT 06405 • 2,430
Indianola, IA 50125 • 11,340
Indianola, MS 38751 • 11,809
Indian Ridge Estates, AZ 85715 • 1,260
Indian River □, FL • 90,208
Indian Rocks Beach, FL 34635 • 3,963
Indian Springs, NV 89018 • 1,164
Indiantown, FL 34956 • 4,794
Indian Trail, NC 28079 • 1,942
Indio, CA 92201-02 • 36,793
Ingalls Park, IL 60431 • 2,730
Ingham □, MI • 281,912
Ingleside, TX 78362 • 5,696
Inglewood, CA 90301-12 • 109,602
Inglewood, TX 98011 • 6,500
Ingram, PA 15205 • 3,901
Inkom, ID 83245 • 769
Inkster, MI 48141 • 30,772
Inman, KS 67546 • 1,035
Inman, SC 29349 • 1,742
Inniswold, LA 70809 • 1,100
Inola, OK 74036 • 1,444
Institute, WV 25112 • 1,400
Interlachen, FL 32148 • 1,160
International Falls, MN 56649 • 8,325
Inver Grove Heights, MN 55076-77 • 22,477
Inverness, CA 94937 • 1,422
Inverness, FL 32650-52 • 5,797
Inverness, IL 60067 • 6,503
Inverness, MS 38753 • 1,174
Inwood, FL 33880 • 6,824
Inwood, NY 11696 • 7,767
Inwood, WV 25428 • 1,360
Inyo □, CA • 18,281
Iola, KS 66749 • 6,351
Iola, WI 54945 • 1,125
Iona, ID 83427 • 1,049
Ione, CA 95640 • 6,516
Ionia, MI 48846 • 5,935
Ionia □, MI • 57,024
Iosco □, MI • 30,209
Iota, LA 70543 • 1,256
Iowa, LA 70647 • 2,588
Iowa □, IA • 14,630
Iowa □, WI • 20,150
Iowa City, IA 52240-46 • 59,738
Iowa Falls, IA 50126 • 5,424
Iowa Park, TX 76367 • 6,072
Ipswich, MA 01938 • 4,132
Ipswich, SD 57451 • 965
Iraan, TX 79744 • 1,322
Iredell □, NC • 92,931
Irion □, TX • 1,629
Irmo, SC 29063 • 11,280
Iron □, MI • 13,175
Iron □, MO • 10,726
Iron □, UT • 20,789
Iron □, WI • 6,153
Irondale, AL 35210 • 9,454
Irondequoit, NY 14617 • 52,322
Ironia, NJ 07845 • 1,110
Iron Mountain, MI 49801 • 8,525
Iron River, MI 49935 • 2,095
Ironton, MO 63650 • 1,539
Ironton, OH 45638 • 12,751
Ironwood, MI 49938 • 6,849
Iroquois □, IL • 30,787
Irvine, CA 92713-20 • 110,330
Irvine, KY 40336 • 2,836
Irving, TX 75060-63 • 155,037
Irvington, KY 40146 • 1,180
Irvington, NJ 07111 • 59,774
Irvington, NY 10533 • 6,348
Irwin, PA 15642 • 4,604
Irwin □, GA • 8,649
Isabella □, MI • 54,624
Isanti, MN 55040 • 1,228
Isanti □, MN • 25,921
Iselin, NJ 08830 • 16,141
Ishpeming, MI 49849 • 7,200
Islamorada, FL 33036 • 1,220
Island □, WA • 60,195
Island Heights, NJ 08732 • 1,470
Island Park, NY 11558 • 4,860
Island Park, RI 02871 • 1,240
Island Pond, VT 05846 • 1,222
Isla Vista, CA 93117 • 20,395
Isle of Palms, SC 29451 • 3,680
Isle of Wight □, VA • 25,053
Isleta, NM 87022 • 1,703
Islington, MA 02090 • 4,920
Islip, NY 11751 • 18,924
Islip Terrace, NY 11752 • 5,530
Issaquah, WA 98027 • 7,786
Issaquena □, MS • 1,909
Italy, TX 76651 • 1,699
Itasca, IL 60143 • 6,947
Itasca, TX 76055 • 1,523
Itasca □, MN • 40,863
Itawamba □, MS • 20,017
Ithaca, MI 48847 • 3,009
Ithaca, NY 14850-52 • 29,541
Itta Bena, MS 38941 • 2,377
Iuka, MS 38852 • 3,122
Iva, SC 29655 • 1,174
Ives Estates, FL 33162 • 13,531
Ivins, UT 84738 • 1,630
Ivoryton, CT 06442 • 2,200
Izard □, AR • 11,364

J

Jacinto City, TX 77029 • 9,343
Jack □, TX • 6,981
Jackpot, NV 89825 • 570
Jacksboro, TN 37757 • 1,568
Jacksboro, TX 76056 • 3,350
Jackson, AL 36545 • 5,819
Jackson, CA 95642 • 3,545
Jackson, GA 30233 • 4,076
Jackson, KY 41339 • 2,466
Jackson, LA 70748 • 3,891
Jackson, MI 49201-04 • 37,446
Jackson, MN 56143 • 3,559
Jackson, MS 39201-98 • 196,637
Jackson, MO 63755 • 9,256
Jackson, OH 45640 • 6,144
Jackson, SC 29831 • 1,681
Jackson, TN 38301-08 • 48,949
Jackson, WI 53037 • 2,486
Jackson, WY 83001-02 • 4,472
Jackson □, AL • 47,796
Jackson □, AR • 18,944
Jackson □, CO • 1,605
Jackson □, FL • 41,375
Jackson □, GA • 30,005
Jackson □, IL • 61,067
Jackson □, IN • 37,730
Jackson □, IA • 19,950
Jackson □, KS • 11,525
Jackson □, KY • 11,955
Jackson □, LA • 15,705
Jackson □, MI • 149,756
Jackson □, MN • 11,677
Jackson □, MS • 115,243
Jackson □, MO • 633,232
Jackson □, NC • 26,846
Jackson □, OH • 30,230
Jackson □, OK • 28,764
Jackson □, OR • 146,389
Jackson □, SD • 2,811
Jackson □, TN • 9,297
Jackson □, TX • 13,039
Jackson □, WV • 25,938
Jackson □, WI • 16,588
Jackson Center, OH 45334 • 1,398
Jacksonville, AL 36265 • 10,283
Jacksonville, AR 72076 • 29,101
Jacksonville, FL 32201-98 • 635,230
Jacksonville, IL 62650-51 • 19,324
Jacksonville, NC 28540-46 • 30,013
Jacksonville, OR 97530 • 1,896
Jacksonville, TX 75766 • 12,765
Jacksonville Beach, FL 32250 • 17,839
Jaffrey, NH 03452 • 2,558
Jal, NM 88252 • 2,156
Jamesburg, NJ 08831 • 5,294
James City, NC 28560 • 4,279
James City □, VA • 34,859
James Island, SC 29412 • 24,124
Jamestown, CA 95327 • 2,178
Jamestown, KY 42629 • 1,641
Jamestown, NY 14701-02 • 34,681
Jamestown, NC 27282 • 2,600
Jamestown, ND 58401-02 • 15,571
Jamestown, OH 45335 • 1,794
Jamestown, RI 02835 • 2,156
Jamestown, TN 38556 • 1,862
James Town, WY 82935 • 280
Janesville, CA 96114 • 1,200
Janesville, MN 56048 • 1,969
Janesville, WI 53545-47 • 52,133
Jarrettsville, MD 21084 • 2,148
Jasmine Estates, FL 34668 • 17,136
Jasonville, IN 47438 • 2,200
Jasper, AL 35501-02 • 13,553
Jasper, FL 32052 • 2,099
Jasper, GA 30143 • 1,772
Jasper, IN 47546-47 • 10,030
Jasper, TN 37347 • 2,780
Jasper, TX 75951 • 6,959
Jasper □, GA • 8,453
Jasper □, IL • 10,609
Jasper □, IN • 24,960
Jasper □, IA • 34,795
Jasper □, MS • 17,114
Jasper □, MO • 90,465
Jasper □, SC • 15,487
Jasper □, TX • 31,102
Jay, OK 74346 • 2,220
Jay □, IN • 21,512
Jean, NV 89019 • 150
Jeanerette, LA 70544 • 6,205
Jeannette, PA 15644 • 11,221
Jeff Davis □, GA • 12,032
Jeff Davis □, TX • 1,946
Jefferson, GA 30549 • 2,763
Jefferson, IA 50129 • 4,292
Jefferson, LA 70121 • 14,521
Jefferson, NC 28640 • 1,300
Jefferson, OH 44047 • 3,331
Jefferson, OR 97352 • 1,805
Jefferson, PA 15025 • 9,533
Jefferson, TX 75657 • 2,199
Jefferson, WI 53549 • 6,078
Jefferson □, AL • 651,525
Jefferson □, AR • 85,487
Jefferson □, CO • 438,430
Jefferson □, FL • 11,296
Jefferson □, GA • 17,408
Jefferson □, ID • 16,543
Jefferson □, IL • 37,020
Jefferson □, IN • 29,797
Jefferson □, IA • 16,310
Jefferson □, KS • 15,905
Jefferson □, KY • 664,937
Jefferson □, LA • 448,306
Jefferson □, MS • 8,653
Jefferson □, MO • 171,380
Jefferson □, MT • 7,939
Jefferson □, NE • 8,759
Jefferson □, NY • 110,943
Jefferson □, OH • 80,298
Jefferson □, OK • 7,010
Jefferson □, OR • 13,676
Jefferson □, PA • 46,083
Jefferson □, TN • 33,016
Jefferson □, TX • 239,397
Jefferson □, WA • 20,146
Jefferson □, WV • 35,926
Jefferson □, WI • 67,783
Jefferson City, MO 65101-10 • 35,481
Jefferson City, TN 37760 • 5,494
Jefferson Davis □, LA • 30,722
Jefferson Davis □, MS • 14,051
Jefferson Farms, DE 19720 • 3,130
Jefferson Manor, VA 22303 • 2,300
Jeffersontown, KY 40299 • 23,221
Jefferson Valley, NY 10535 • 6,420
Jefferson Village, VA 22042 • 2,500
Jeffersonville, GA 31044 • 1,545
Jeffersonville, IN 47129-31 • 21,841
Jeffersonville, KY 40337 • 1,854
Jeffersonville, OH 43128 • 1,281
Jeffrey City, WY 82310 • 1,882
Jellico, TN 37762 • 2,447
Jemez Pueblo, NM 87024 • 1,301
Jemison, AL 35085 • 1,898
Jena, LA 71342 • 2,626
Jenison, MI 49428-29 • 17,882
Jenkins, KY 41537 • 2,751
Jenkins □, GA • 8,247
Jenkintown, PA 19046 • 4,574
Jenks, OK 74037 • 7,493
Jennings, LA 70546 • 11,305
Jennings, MO 63136 • 15,905
Jennings □, IN • 23,661
Jennings Lodge, OR 97222 • 11,480
Jensen Beach, FL 34957-58 • 9,884
Jerauld □, SD • 2,425
Jericho, NY 11753 • 13,141
Jericho, VT 05465 • 1,300
Jermyn, PA 18433 • 2,263
Jerome, ID 83338 • 6,529
Jerome, PA 15937 • 1,074
Jerome □, ID • 15,138
Jersey □, IL • 20,539
Jersey City, NJ 07301-11 • 228,537
Jersey Shore, PA 17740 • 4,353
Jerseyville, IL 62052 • 7,382
Jessamine □, KY • 30,508
Jessup, MD 20794 • 6,537
Jessup, PA 18434 • 4,605
Jesup, GA 31545 • 8,958
Jesup, IA 50648 • 2,121
Jewell, IA 50130 • 1,106
Jewell □, KS • 4,251
Jewett City, CT 06351 • 3,349
Jim Hogg □, TX • 5,109
Jim Thorpe, PA 18229 • 5,048
Jim Wells □, TX • 37,679
Joanna, SC 29351 • 1,735
Jo Daviess □, IL • 21,821
John Day, OR 97845 • 1,836
Johnson, KS 67855 • 1,348
Johnson, VT 05656 • 1,470
Johnson □, AR • 18,221
Johnson □, GA • 8,329
Johnson □, IL • 11,347
Johnson □, IN • 88,109
Johnson □, IA • 96,119
Johnson □, KS • 355,054
Johnson □, KY • 23,248
Johnson □, MO • 42,514
Johnson □, NE • 4,673
Johnson □, TN • 13,766
Johnson □, TX • 97,165
Johnson □, WY • 6,145
Johnsonburg, PA 15845 • 3,350
Johnson City, NY 13790 • 16,890
Johnson City, TN 37601-15 • 49,381
Johnson Creek, WI 53038 • 1,259
Johnsonville, SC 29555 • 1,415
Johnston, IA 50131 • 4,702
Johnston, RI 02919 • 26,542
Johnston, SC 29832 • 2,688
Johnston □, NC • 81,306
Johnston □, OK • 10,032
Johnston City, IL 62951 • 3,706
Johnstown, CO 80534 • 1,579
Johnstown, NY 12095 • 9,058
Johnstown, OH 43031 • 3,237
Johnstown, PA 15901-09 • 28,134
Joliet, IL 60431-36 • 76,836
Jones, OK 73049 • 2,424
Jones □, GA • 20,739
Jones □, IA • 19,444
Jones □, MS • 62,031
Jones □, NC • 9,414
Jones □, SD • 1,324
Jones □, TX • 16,490
Jonesboro, AR 72401-03 • 46,535
Jonesboro, GA 30236-37 • 3,635
Jonesboro, IL 62952 • 1,728
Jonesboro, IN 46938 • 2,073
Jonesboro, LA 71251 • 4,305
Jonesborough, TN 37659 • 3,091
Jones Creek, TX 77541 • 2,160
Jonesport, ME 04649 • 1,525
Jonestown, MS 38639 • 1,467
Jonesville, LA 71343 • 2,720
Jonesville, MI 49250 • 2,283
Jonesville, NC 28642 • 1,549
Jonesville, SC 29353 • 1,205
Joplin, MO 64801-04 • 40,961
Joppatowne, MD 21085 • 11,084
Jordan, MN 55352 • 2,909
Jordan, NY 13080 • 1,325
Joseph, OR 97846 • 1,073
Josephine □, OR • 62,649
Joshua, TX 76058 • 3,828
Joshua Tree, CA 92252 • 3,898
Jourdanton, TX 78026 • 3,220
Juab □, UT • 5,817
Juanita, WA 98033 • 10,500
Judith Basin □, MT • 2,282
Judsonia, AR 72081 • 1,915
Julesburg, CO 80737 • 1,295
Julian, CA 92036 • 1,284
Junction, TX 76849 • 2,654
Junction City, KS 66441 • 20,604
Junction City, KY 40440 • 1,983
Junction City, OR 97448 • 3,670
Juneau, AK 99801-03 • 26,751
Juneau, WI 53039 • 2,157
Juneau □, WI • 21,650
Juniata □, PA • 20,625
Jupiter, FL 33458 • 24,986
Justice, IL 60458 • 11,137
Justin, TX 76247 • 1,234

K

Kaaawa, HI 96730 • 1,138
Kadoka, SD 57543 • 736
Kahaluu, HI 96725 • 380
Kahaluu, HI 96744 • 3,068
Kahoka, MO 63445 • 2,195
Kahuku, HI 96731 • 2,063
Kahului, HI 96732-33 • 16,889
Kailua, HI 96734 • 36,818
Kailua Kona, HI 96739-40 • 9,126
Kake, AK 99830 • 700
Kalaheo, HI 96741 • 3,592
Kalama, WA 98625 • 1,210
Kalamazoo, MI 49001-09 • 80,277
Kalamazoo □, MI • 223,411
Kalawao □, HI • 130
Kalispell, MT 59901 • 11,917
Kalkaska, MI 49646 • 1,952
Kalkaska □, MI • 13,497
Kalona, IA 52247 • 1,942
Kamas, UT 84036 • 1,061
Kamiah, ID 83536 • 1,157
Kamuela (Waimea), HI 96743 • 5,972
Kanab, UT 84741 • 3,289
Kanabec □, MN • 12,802
Kanawha □, WV • 207,619
Kandiyohi □, MN • 38,761
Kane, PA 16735 • 4,590
Kane □, IL • 317,471
Kane □, UT • 5,169
Kaneohe, HI 96744 • 35,448
Kankakee, IL 60901 • 27,575
Kankakee □, IL • 96,255
Kannapolis, NC 28081-83 • 29,696
Kansas City, KS 66101-19 • 149,767
Kansas City, MO 64101-99 • 435,146
Kapaa, HI 96746 • 8,149
Kapaau, HI 96755 • 1,083
Kaplan, LA 70548 • 4,535
Karnes □, TX • 12,455
Karnes City, TX 78118 • 2,916
Karns, TN 37921 • 1,458
Kasson, MN 55944 • 3,514
Kathleen, FL 33849 • 2,743
Katy, TX 77449-50 • 8,005
Kauai □, HI • 51,177
Kaufman, TX 75142 • 5,238
Kaufman □, TX • 52,220
Kaukauna, WI 54130 • 11,982
Kaumakani, HI 96747 • 803
Kaunakakai, HI 96748 • 2,658
Kay □, OK • 48,056
Kaycee, WY 82639 • 256
Kayenta, AZ 86033 • 4,372
Kaysville, UT 84037 • 13,961
Keaau, HI 96749 • 1,584
Kealakekua, HI 96750 • 1,453
Kealia, HI 96751 • 700
Keansburg, NJ 07734 • 11,069
Kearney, MO 64060 • 1,790
Kearney, NE 68847-48 • 24,396
Kearney □, NE • 6,629
Kearns, UT 84118 • 28,374
Kearny, AZ 85237 • 2,262
Kearny, NJ 07031-32 • 34,874
Kearny □, KS • 4,027
Keego Harbor, MI 48320 • 2,932
Keene, NH 03431 • 22,430
Keene, TX 76059 • 3,944
Keeseville, NY 12944 • 1,854
Keewatin, MN 55753 • 1,118
Keith □, NE • 8,584
Keizer, OR 97303 • 21,884
Kekaha, HI 96752 • 3,506
Keller, TX 76248 • 13,683
Kellogg, ID 83837 • 2,591
Kelseyville, CA 95451 • 2,861
Kelso, WA 98626 • 11,820
Kemmerer, WY 83101 • 3,020
Kemp, TX 75143 • 1,184
Kemper □, MS • 10,356
Kenai, AK 99611 • 6,327
Kenbridge, VA 23944 • 1,264
Ken Caryl, CO 80123 • 24,391
Kendall, FL 33156 • 87,271
Kendall □, IL • 39,413
Kendall □, TX • 14,589
Kendall Park, NJ 08824 • 7,127
Kendallville, IN 46755 • 7,773
Kenedy, TX 78119 • 3,763
Kenedy □, TX • 460
Kenilworth, IL 60043 • 2,402
Kenilworth, NJ 07033 • 7,574
Kenly, NC 27542 • 1,549
Kenmare, ND 58746 • 1,214
Kenmore, NY 14217 • 17,180
Kenmore, WA 98028 • 8,917
Kennebec □, ME • 115,904
Kennebunk, ME 04043 • 4,206
Kennebunkport, ME 04046 • 1,100
Kennedy Heights, LA 70094 • 2,000
Kennedy Township, PA 15108 • 7,152
Kenner, LA 70062-65 • 72,033
Kennesaw, GA 30144 • 8,936
Kennett, MO 63857 • 10,941
Kennett Square, PA 19348 • 5,218
Kennewick, WA 99336-37 • 42,155
Kennydale, WA 98056 • 2,000
Kenosha, WI 53140-44 • 80,352
Kenosha □, WI • 128,181
Kenova, WV 25530 • 3,748
Ken Rock, IL 61109 • 3,300
Kensett, AR 72082 • 1,741
Kensington, CA 94707 • 4,974
Kensington, CT 06037 • 8,306
Kensington, MD 20895 • 1,713
Kent, OH 44240 • 28,835
Kent, WA 98031-32 • 37,960
Kent □, DE • 110,993
Kent □, MD • 17,842
Kent □, MI • 500,631
Kent □, RI • 161,135
Kent □, TX • 1,010
Kentfield, CA 94904 • 6,030
Kentland, IN 47951 • 1,798
Kenton, DE 19955 • 232
Kenton, OH 43326 • 8,356
Kenton, TN 38233 • 1,366
Kenton □, KY • 142,031
Kentwood, LA 70444 • 2,468
Kentwood, MI 49508 • 37,826
Kenvil, NJ 07847 • 3,050
Kenwood, OH 45236 • 7,469
Kenyon, MN 55946 • 1,552
Kenyon, RI 02836 • 400
Keokea, HI 96790 • 900
Keokuk, IA 52632 • 12,451
Keokuk □, IA • 11,624
Keosauqua, IA 52565 • 1,020
Keota, IA 52248 • 1,000
Kerens, TX 75144 • 1,702
Kerhonkson, NY 12446 • 1,629
Kermit, TX 79745 • 6,875
Kern □, CA • 543,477
Kernersville, NC 27284-85 • 10,836
Kernville, CA 93238 • 1,656
Kerr □, TX • 36,304
Kerrville, TX 78028-29 • 17,384
Kershaw, SC 29067 • 1,814
Kershaw □, SC • 43,599
Ketchikan, AK 99901 • 8,263
Ketchum, ID 83340 • 2,523
Kettering, MD 20772 • 9,901
Kettering, OH 45429 • 60,569
Kettle Falls, WA 99141 • 1,272
Kewanee, IL 61443 • 12,969
Kewaskum, WI 53040 • 2,515
Kewaunee, WI 54216 • 2,750
Kewaunee □, WI • 18,878
Keweenaw □, MI • 1,701
Keya Paha □, NE • 1,029
Key Biscayne, FL 33149 • 8,854
Key Largo, FL 33037 • 11,336
Keyport, NJ 07735 • 7,586
Keyser, WV 26726 • 5,870
Keystone Heights, FL 32656 • 1,315
Key West, FL 33040-41 • 24,832
Kiana, AK 99749 • 385
Kidder □, ND • 3,332
Kiel, WI 53042 • 2,910
Kihei, HI 96753 • 11,107
Kilauea, HI 96754 • 1,685
Kilgore, TX 75662-63 • 11,066
Killdeer, ND 58640 • 722
Killeen, TX 76540-47 • 63,535
Killen, AL 35645 • 1,047
Kilmarnock, VA 22482 • 1,109
Kimball, NE 69145 • 2,574
Kimball □, NE • 4,108
Kimberly, AL 35091 • 1,096
Kimberly, ID 83341 • 2,367
Kimberly, WI 54136 • 5,406
Kimble □, TX • 4,122
Kincaid, IL 62540 • 1,353
Kinder, LA 70648 • 2,246
Kinderhook, NY 12106 • 1,293
King, NC 27021 • 4,059
King □, TX • 354
King □, WA • 1,507,319
King and Queen □, VA • 6,289
King City, CA 93930 • 7,634
King Cove, AK 99612 • 451
Kingfisher, OK 73750 • 4,095
Kingfisher □, OK • 13,212
King George □, VA • 13,527
Kingman, AZ 86401-02 • 12,722
Kingman, KS 67068 • 3,196
Kingman □, KS • 8,292
King of Prussia, PA 19406 • 18,406
Kings, MS 39180 • 1,165
Kings □, CA • 101,469
Kings □, NY • 2,300,664
King Salmon, AK 99613 • 696
Kingsburg, CA 93631 • 7,205
Kingsbury □, SD • 5,925
Kingsford, MI 49801 • 5,480
Kingsgate, WA 98011 • 14,259
Kingsland, GA 31548 • 4,699
Kingsland, TX 78639 • 2,725
Kingsley, IA 51028 • 1,129
Kings Mountain, NC 28086 • 8,763
Kings Park, NY 11754 • 17,773
Kings Park, VA 22151 • 6,000
Kings Park West, VA 22032 • 6,000
Kings Point, FL 33484 • 12,422
Kings Point, NY 11024 • 4,843
Kingsport, TN 37660-65 • 36,365
Kingston, ID 83839 • 1,000
Kingston, MA 02364 • 4,774
Kingston, NJ 08528 • 1,200
Kingston, NY 12401 • 23,095
Kingston, OH 45644 • 1,153
Kingston, OK 73439 • 1,237
Kingston, PA 18704 • 14,507
Kingston, RI 02881 • 6,504
Kingston, TN 37763 • 4,552
Kingston Springs, TN 37082 • 1,529
Kingstown, MD 21620 • 1,660
Kingstree, SC 29556 • 3,858
Kingsville, MD 21087 • 3,550
Kingsville (North Kingsville), OH 44048 • 1,243
Kingsville, TX 78363-64 • 25,276
King William □, VA • 10,913
Kingwood, TX 77339 • 37,397
Kingwood, WV 26537 • 3,243
Kinloch, MO 63140 • 2,702
Kinnelon, NJ 07405 • 8,470
Kinney □, TX • 3,119
Kinsey, AL 36301 • 1,679
Kinsley, KS 67547 • 1,875
Kinston, NC 28501-03 • 25,295
Kiowa, KS 67070 • 1,160
Kiowa □, CO • 1,688
Kiowa □, KS • 3,660
Kiowa □, OK • 11,347
Kipnuk, AK 99614 • 470
Kirby, TX 78219 • 8,326
Kirbyville, TX 75956 • 1,871
Kirkland, IL 60146 • 1,011
Kirkland, WA 98033-34 • 40,052
Kirksville, MO 63501 • 17,152
Kirkwood, DE 19708 • 350
Kirkwood, MO 63122 • 27,291
Kirtland, NM 87417 • 3,552
Kirtland, OH 44094 • 5,881
Kissimmee, FL 34741-46 • 30,050
Kit Carson □, CO • 7,140
Kitsap □, WA • 189,731
Kittanning, PA 16201 • 5,120
Kittery, ME 03904 • 5,151
Kittery Point, ME 03905 • 1,093
Kittitas □, WA • 26,725
Kittson □, MN • 5,767
Kitty Hawk, NC 27949 • 1,937
Klamath □, OR • 57,702
Klamath Falls, OR 97601-03 • 17,737
Klawock, AK 99925 • 722
Kleberg □, TX • 30,274
Klein, TX 77379 • 12,000
Klickitat □, WA • 16,616
Knightdale, NC 27545 • 1,884
Knights Landing, CA 95645 • 1,000
Knightstown, IN 46148 • 2,048
Knob Noster, MO 65336 • 2,261
Knott □, KY • 17,906
Knox, IN 46534 • 3,705
Knox, PA 16232 • 1,182
Knox □, IL • 56,393
Knox □, IN • 39,884
Knox □, KY • 29,676
Knox □, ME • 36,310

Knox □, MO • 4,482
Knox □, NE • 9,534
Knox □, OH • 47,473
Knox □, TN • 335,749
Knox □, TX • 4,837
Knox City, TX 79529 • 1,440
Knoxville, IL 61448 • 3,243
Knoxville, IA 50138 • 8,232
Knoxville, TN 37901–50 • 165,121
Kodiak, AK 99615 • 6,365
Kohler, WI 53044 • 1,817
Kokomo, IN 46901–04 • 44,962
Koloa, HI 96756 • 1,791
Konawa, OK 74849 • 1,508
Koochiching □, MN • 16,299
Koontz Lake, IN 46574 • 1,615
Kootenai □, ID • 69,795
Koppel, PA 16136 • 1,024
Kosciusko, MS 39090 • 6,986
Kosciusko □, IN • 65,294
Kossuth □, IA • 18,591
Kotlik, AK 99620 • 461
Kotzebue, AK 99752 • 2,751
Kountze, TX 77625 • 2,056
Kouts, IN 46347 • 1,603
Krebs, OK 74554 • 1,955
Kremmling, CO 80459 • 1,166
Krotz Springs, LA 70750 • 1,285
Kula, HI 96790 • 1,300
Kulpmont, PA 17834 • 3,233
Kuna, ID 83634 • 1,955
Kurtistown, HI 96760 • 910
Kutztown, PA 19530 • 4,704
Kwethluk, AK 99621 • 558
Kwigillingok, AK 99622 • 278
Kyle, TX 78640 • 2,225

L

Labadieville, LA 70372 • 1,821
La Barge, WY 83123 • 493
La Belle, FL 33935 • 2,703
Labette □, KS • 23,693
La Canada Flintridge, CA 91011 • 19,378
Lac du Flambeau, WI 54538 • 1,180
La Center, KY 42056 • 1,040
Lacey, WA 98503 • 19,279
Lackawanna, NY 14218 • 20,585
Lackawanna □, PA • 219,039
Laclede □, MO • 27,158
Lacombe, LA 70445 • 6,523
Lacon, IL 61540 • 1,986
Laconia, NH 03246–47 • 15,743
Lacoochee, FL 33537 • 2,072
Lac qui Parle □, MN • 8,924
La Crescent, MN 55947 • 4,311
La Crescenta, CA 91214 • 12,500
La Crosse, KS 67548 • 1,427
La Crosse, WI 54601–03 • 51,003
La Crosse □, WI • 97,904
La Cygne, KS 66040 • 1,066
Ladd, IL 61329 • 1,283
Ladera Heights, CA 90045 • 6,316
Ladoga, IN 47954 • 1,124
Ladson, SC 29456 • 13,540
Ladue, MO 63124 • 8,847
Lady Lake, FL 32159 • 8,071
Ladysmith, WI 54848 • 3,938
Lafayette, AL 36862 • 3,151
Lafayette, CA 94549 • 23,501
Lafayette, CO 80026 • 14,548
Lafayette, GA 30728 • 6,313
Lafayette, IN 47901–06 • 43,764
Lafayette, LA 70501–09 • 94,440
Lafayette, NC 28304 • 3,200
Lafayette, OR 97127 • 1,292
La Fayette, RI 02852 • 640
Lafayette, TN 37083 • 3,641
Lafayette □, AR • 9,643
Lafayette □, FL • 5,578
Lafayette □, LA • 164,762
Lafayette □, MS • 31,826
Lafayette □, MO • 31,107
Lafayette □, WI • 16,076
Lafayette Southwest, LA • 5,500
La Feria, TX 78559 • 4,360
Lafitte, LA 70067 • 1,507
La Follette, TN 37766 • 7,192
Lafourche □, LA • 85,860
La Grande, OR 97850 • 11,766
La Grange, GA 30240–41 • 25,597
La Grange, IL 60525 • 15,362
Lagrange, IN 46761 • 2,382
La Grange, KY 40031 • 3,853
La Grange, MO 63448 • 1,102
La Grange, NC 28551 • 2,805
Lagrange, OH 44050 • 1,199
La Grange, TX 78945 • 3,951
Lagrange □, IN • 29,477
La Grange Highlands, IL 60525 • 3,660
La Grange Park, IL 60525 • 12,861
Laguna Beach, CA 92651–54 • 23,170
Laguna Hills, CA 92653 • 46,731
Laguna Niguel, CA 92677 • 44,400
La Habra, CA 90631–33 • 51,266
Lahaina, HI 96761 • 9,073
La Harpe, IL 61450 • 1,407
Laie, HI 96762 • 5,577
Laingsburg, MI 48848 • 1,148
La Junta, CO 81050 • 7,637
Lake □, CA • 50,631
Lake □, CO • 6,007
Lake □, FL • 152,104
Lake □, IL • 516,418
Lake □, IN • 475,594
Lake □, MI • 8,583
Lake □, MN • 10,415
Lake □, MT • 21,041
Lake □, OH • 215,499
Lake □, OR • 7,186
Lake □, SD • 10,550
Lake □, TN • 7,129
Lake Alfred, FL 33850 • 3,622
Lake Andes, SD 57356 • 846
Lake Arrowhead, CA 92317 • 6,539
Lake Arthur, LA 70549 • 3,194
Lake Barcroft, VA 22041 • 8,686
Lake Bluff, IL 60044 • 5,513
Lake Butler, FL 32054 • 2,116
Lake Carmel, NY 10512 • 8,489
Lake Charles, LA 70601–29 • 70,580
Lake City, AR 72437 • 1,833
Lake City, FL 32055–56 • 10,005
Lake City, IA 51449 • 1,841
Lake City, MN 55041 • 4,391
Lake City, PA 16423 • 2,519
Lake City, SC 29560 • 7,153
Lake City, TN 37769 • 2,166
Lake Crystal, MN 56055 • 2,084
Lake Delta, NY 13440 • 1,980
Lake Delton, WI 53940 • 1,470
Lake Elmo, MN 55042 • 5,903
Lake Elsinore, CA 92330–31 • 18,285
Lake Erie Beach, NY 14006 • 4,509
Lakefield, MN 56150 • 1,679
Lake Forest, FL 33023 • 5,400
Lake Forest, IL 60045 • 17,836
Lake Geneva, WI 53147 • 5,979
Lake Grove, NY 11755 • 9,612
Lake Hamilton, AR 71913 • 1,331
Lake Havasu City, AZ 86403–05 • 24,363
Lake Helen, FL 32744 • 2,344
Lakehurst, NJ 08733 • 3,078
Lake in the Hills, IL 60102 • 5,866
Lake Jackson, TX 77566 • 22,776
Lake Katrine, NY 12449 • 1,998
Lakeland, FL 33801–13 • 70,576
Lakeland, GA 31635 • 2,467
Lakeland Highlands, FL 33801 • 9,972
Lakeland Village, CA 92330 • 5,159
Lake Linden, MI 49945 • 1,203
Lake Lorraine, FL 32569 • 6,779
Lake Luzerne, NY 12846 • 1,160
Lake Magdalene, FL 33612 • 15,973
Lake Mary, FL 32746 • 5,929
Lake Mills, IA 50450 • 2,143
Lake Mills, WI 53551 • 4,143
Lakemore, OH 44250 • 2,684
Lake Odessa, MI 48849 • 2,256
Lake Of The Woods □, MN • 4,076
Lake Orion, MI 48360–62 • 3,057
Lake Oswego, OR 97034–35 • 30,576
Lake Park, FL 33403 • 6,704
Lake Placid, FL 33852 • 1,158
Lake Placid, NY 12946 • 2,485
Lakeport, CA 95453 • 4,390
Lake Preston, SD 57249 • 663
Lake Providence, LA 71254 • 5,380
Lake Ridge, VA 22192 • 23,862
Lake Ronkonkoma, NY 11779 • 18,997
Lake Shore, MD 21122 • 13,269
Lakeside, CA 92040 • 39,412
Lakeside, CT 06488 • 1,200
Lakeside, FL 32073 • 29,137
Lakeside, OR 97449 • 1,437
Lakeside, VA 23228 • 12,081
Lakeside Park, KY 41017 • 3,131
Lakeside-Pinetop, AZ 85935 • 2,422
Lake Station, IN 46405 • 13,899
Lake Stevens, WA 98258 • 3,380
Lake Telemark, NJ 07866 • 1,121
Lakeview, GA 30741 • 5,237
Lake View, IA 51450 • 1,303
Lakeview, MI 48850 • 1,108
Lake View, NY 14085 • 1,460
Lakeview, NY 11552 • 5,476
Lakeview, OH 43331 • 1,056
Lakeview, OR 97630 • 2,526
Lake Villa, IL 60046 • 2,857
Lake Village, AR 71653 • 2,791
Lakeville, CT 06039 • 1,800
Lakeville, MA 02346 • 1,948
Lakeville, MN 55044 • 24,854
Lakeville, NY 14480 • 1,000
Lake Wales, FL 33853 • 9,670
Lake Wissota, WI 54729 • 2,175
Lakewood, CA 90711–16 • 73,557
Lakewood, CO 80215 • 126,481
Lakewood, IL 60014 • 1,609
Lakewood, IA 50211 • 1,950
Lakewood, NJ 08701 • 26,095
Lakewood, NY 14750 • 3,564
Lakewood, OH 44107 • 59,718
Lakewood, WA 98259 • 58,412
Lakewood Center, WA 98499 • 58,412
Lakewood Park, FL 34951 • 7,211
Lake Worth, FL 33460–67 • 28,564
Lake Zurich, IL 60047 • 14,947
Lakin, KS 67860 • 2,060
Lakota, ND 58344 • 898
La Luz, NM 88337 • 1,625
Lamar, CO 81052 • 8,343
Lamar, MO 64759 • 4,168
Lamar, PA 16848 • 1,200
Lamar, SC 29069 • 1,125
Lamar □, AL • 15,715
Lamar □, GA • 13,038
Lamar □, MS • 30,424
Lamar □, TX • 43,949
La Marque, TX 77568 • 14,120
Lamb □, TX • 15,072
Lambert, MS 38643 • 1,131
Lambertville, MI 48144 • 7,860
Lambertville, NJ 08530 • 3,927
La Mesa, CA 91941–44 • 52,931
La Mesa, NM 88044 • 900
Lamesa, TX 79331 • 10,809
La Mirada, CA 90637–38 • 40,452
Lamoille, NV 89828 • 110
Lamoille □, VT • 19,735
Lamoni, IA 50140 • 2,319
Lamont, CA 93241 • 11,517
La Moure, ND 58458 • 970
La Moure □, ND • 5,383
Lampasas, TX 76550 • 6,382
Lampasas □, TX • 13,521
Lanai City, HI 96763 • 2,400
Lanark, IL 61046 • 1,382
Lancashire, DE 19810 • 1,175
Lancaster, CA 93534–39 • 97,291
Lancaster, KY 40444 • 3,421
Lancaster, NH 03584 • 1,859
Lancaster, NY 14086 • 11,940
Lancaster, OH 43130 • 34,507
Lancaster, PA 17601–05 • 55,551
Lancaster, SC 29720–21 • 8,914
Lancaster, TX 75146 • 22,117
Lancaster, WI 53813 • 4,192
Lancaster □, NE • 213,641
Lancaster □, PA • 422,822
Lancaster □, SC • 54,516
Lancaster □, VA • 10,896
Lancaster Village, DE 19805 • 1,100
Landen, OH 45040 • 9,263
Lander, WY 82520 • 7,023
Lander □, NV • 6,266
Landess, IN 46944 • 1,500
Landis, NC 28088 • 2,333
Land O' Lakes, FL 34639 • 7,892
Landover, MD 20784 • 5,052
Landrum, SC 29356 • 2,347
Lane □, KS • 2,375
Lane □, OR • 282,912
Lanesboro, MA 01237 • 1,000
Lanett, AL 36863 • 8,985
Langdon, ND 58249 • 2,241
Langeloth, PA 15054 • 1,112
Langhorne, PA 19047 • 1,361
Langlade □, WI • 19,505
Langley, SC 29834 • 1,714
Langley Park, MD 20783 • 17,474
Langston, OK 73050 • 1,471
Lanham, MD 20706 • 5,000
Lanier □, GA • 5,531
Lansdale, PA 19446 • 16,362
Lansdowne, MD 21227 • 9,430
Lansdowne, PA 19050 • 11,712
L'Anse, MI 49946 • 2,151
Lansford, PA 18232 • 4,583
Lansing, IL 60438 • 28,086
Lansing, IA 52151 • 1,007
Lansing, KS 66043 • 7,120
Lansing, MI 48901–33 • 127,321
Lantana, FL 33462 • 8,392
La Palma, CA 90623 • 15,392
La Paz □, AZ • 13,844
Lapeer, MI 48446 • 7,759
Lapeer □, MI • 74,768
Lapel, IN 46051 • 1,742
La Place, LA 70068–69 • 24,194
La Plata, MD 20646 • 5,841
La Plata, MO 63549 • 1,401
La Plata □, CO • 32,284
Laporte, CO 80535 • 1,300
La Porte, IN 46350 • 21,507
La Porte, TX 77571–72 • 27,910
La Porte □, IN • 107,066
La Porte City, IA 50651 • 2,128
La Pryor, TX 78872 • 1,343
La Puente, CA 91744–49 • 36,955
Lapwai, ID 83540 • 932
Laramie, WY 82063–71 • 26,687
Laramie □, WY • 73,142
Larchmont, NY 10538 • 6,181
Larchmont North, NY 10538 • 11,240
Laredo, TX 78040–44 • 122,899
Largo, FL 34640–49 • 65,674
Larimer □, CO • 186,136
Larimore, ND 58251 • 1,464
La Riviera, CA 95826 • 10,986
Larkspur, CA 94939 • 11,070
Larksville, PA 18704 • 4,700
Larned, KS 67550 • 4,490
Larose, LA 70373 • 5,772
Larue □, KY • 11,679
La Salle, CO 80645 • 1,783
La Salle, IL 61301 • 9,717
La Salle □, IL • 106,913
La Salle □, LA • 13,662
La Salle □, TX • 5,254
Las Animas, CO 81054 • 2,481
Las Animas □, CO • 13,765
Las Cruces, NM 88001–08 • 62,126
Lassen □, CA • 27,598
Las Vegas, NV 89101–99 • 258,295
Las Vegas, NM 87701 • 14,753
Latah □, ID • 30,617
Lathrop, MO 64465 • 1,794
Lathrop Wells, NV 89020 • 350
Latimer □, OK • 10,333
Laton, CA 93242 • 1,415
Latrobe, PA 15650 • 9,265
Latta, SC 29565 • 1,565
Lauderdale □, AL • 79,661
Lauderdale □, MS • 75,555
Lauderdale □, TN • 23,491
Lauderdale Lakes, FL 33313 • 27,341
Lauderhill, FL 33313 • 49,708
Laughlin, NV 89028–29 • 140
Laughlintown, PA 15655 • 1,000
Laurel, DE 19956 • 3,226
Laurel, FL 34272 • 8,245
Laurel, MD 20707–09 • 19,438
Laurel, MS 39440–42 • 18,827
Laurel, MT 59044 • 5,686
Laurel, VA 23060 • 13,011
Laurel □, KY • 43,438
Laurel Bay, SC 29902 • 4,972
Laureldale, PA 19605 • 3,726
Laurel Hill, NC 28351 • 2,314
Laurence Harbor, NJ 08879 • 6,361
Laurens, IA 50554 • 1,550
Laurens, SC 29360 • 9,694
Laurens □, GA • 39,988
Laurens □, SC • 58,092
Laurinburg, NC 28352–53 • 11,643
Laurium, MI 49913 • 2,268
Lavaca, AR 72941 • 1,253
Lavaca □, TX • 18,690
La Vale, MD 21502 • 5,000
Lavallette, NJ 08735 • 2,299
La Vergne, TN 37086 • 7,499
La Verkin, UT 84745 • 1,771
La Verne, CA 91750 • 30,897
Laverne, OK 73848 • 1,269
La Vista, GA 30329 • 4,900
La Vista, NE 68128 • 9,840
Lavonia, GA 30553 • 1,840
Lawai, HI 96765 • 1,787
Lawndale, CA 90260–61 • 27,331
Lawnside, NJ 08045 • 2,841
Lawrence, IN 46226 • 26,763
Lawrence, KS 66044–46 • 65,608
Lawrence, MA 01840–45 • 70,207
Lawrence, NY 11559 • 6,513
Lawrence □, AL • 31,513
Lawrence □, AR • 17,457
Lawrence □, IL • 15,972
Lawrence □, IN • 42,836
Lawrence □, KY • 13,998
Lawrence □, MS • 12,458
Lawrence □, MO • 30,236
Lawrence □, OH • 61,834
Lawrence □, PA • 96,246
Lawrence □, TN • 35,303
Lawrenceburg, IN 47025 • 4,375
Lawrenceburg, KY 40342 • 5,911
Lawrenceburg, TN 38464 • 10,412
Lawrence Park, PA 16511 • 4,310
Lawrenceville, GA 30243–46 • 16,848
Lawrenceville, IL 62439 • 4,897
Lawrenceville, NJ 08648 • 6,446
Lawrenceville, VA 23868 • 1,486
Lawson, MO 64062 • 1,876
Lawsonia, MD 21817 • 1,326
Lawtell, LA 70550 • 1,014
Lawton, MI 49065 • 1,685
Lawton, OK 73501–07 • 80,561
Layton, UT 84040–41 • 41,784
Laytonville, CA 95454 • 1,133
Lea □, NM • 55,765
Leachville, AR 72438 • 1,743
Lead, SD 57754 • 3,632
Leadville, CO 80461 • 2,629
Leadwood, MO 63653 • 1,247
League City, TX 77573–74 • 30,159
Leake □, MS • 18,436
Leakesville, MS 39451 • 1,129
Lealman, FL 33714 • 21,748
Leavenworth, KS 66048 • 38,495
Leavenworth, WA 98826 • 1,692
Leavenworth □, KS • 64,371
Leavittsburg, OH 44430 • 2,220
Leawood, KS 66206 • 19,693
Lebanon, DE 19901 • 130
Lebanon, IL 62254 • 3,688
Lebanon, IN 46052 • 12,059
Lebanon, KY 40033 • 5,695
Lebanon, MO 65536 • 9,983
Lebanon, NH 03766 • 12,183
Lebanon, NJ 08833 • 1,036
Lebanon, OH 45036 • 10,453
Lebanon, OR 97355 • 10,950
Lebanon, PA 17042 • 24,800
Lebanon, TN 37087–88 • 15,208
Lebanon, VA 24266 • 3,386
Lebanon □, PA • 113,744
Lebanon Junction, KY 40150 • 1,741
Le Center, MN 56057 • 2,006
Le Claire, IA 52753 • 2,734
Lecompte, LA 71346 • 1,592
Lee, MA 01238 • 2,020
Lee □, AL • 87,146
Lee □, AR • 13,053
Lee □, FL • 335,113
Lee □, GA • 16,250
Lee □, IL • 34,392
Lee □, IA • 38,687
Lee □, KY • 7,422
Lee □, MS • 65,581
Lee □, NC • 41,374
Lee □, SC • 18,437
Lee □, TX • 12,854
Lee □, VA • 24,496
Leechburg, PA 15656 • 2,504
Leedom Estates, DE 19720 • 1,100
Leeds, AL 35094 • 9,946
Leelanau □, MI • 16,527
Lee Park, PA 18702 • 3,800
Leesburg, FL 34748–49 • 14,903
Leesburg, GA 31763 • 1,452
Leesburg, OH 45135 • 1,063
Leesburg, VA 22075 • 16,202
Lees Summit, MO 64063–64 • 46,418
Leesville, LA 71446 • 7,638
Leesville, SC 29070 • 2,025
Leetonia, OH 44431 • 2,070
Leetsdale, PA 15056 • 1,387
Leflore □, MS • 37,341
Le Flore □, OK • 43,270
Le Grand, CA 95333 • 1,205
Lehi, UT 84043 • 8,475
Lehigh □, PA • 291,130
Lehigh Acres, FL 33936 • 13,611
Lehighton, PA 18235 • 5,914
Leicester, MA 01524 • 3,200
Leipsic, DE 19901 • 236
Leipsic, OH 45856 • 2,203
Leisure City, FL 33033 • 19,379
Leitchfield, KY 42754–55 • 4,965
Leland, MS 38756 • 6,366
Le Mars, IA 51031 • 8,454
Lemay, MO 63125 • 18,005
Lemhi □, ID • 6,899
Lemmon, SD 57638 • 1,614
Lemmon Valley, NV 89501 • 4,100
Lemon Grove, CA 91945–46 • 23,984
Lemont, IL 60439 • 7,348
Lemont, PA 16851 • 2,613
Lemoore, CA 93245 • 13,622
Lena, IL 61048 • 2,605
Lenawee □, MI • 91,476
Lenexa, KS 66215 • 34,034
Lennox, CA 90304 • 22,757
Lennox, SD 57039 • 1,767
Lenoir, NC 28645 • 14,192
Lenoir □, NC • 57,274
Lenoir City, TN 37771 • 6,147
Lenox, IA 50851 • 1,303
Lenox, MA 01240 • 1,687
Leo, IN 46765 • 1,200
Leominster, MA 01453 • 38,145
Leon, IA 50144 • 2,047
Leon □, FL • 192,493
Leon □, TX • 12,665
Leonard, TX 75452 • 1,744
Leonardo, NJ 07737 • 3,720
Leonardtown, MD 20650 • 1,475
Leonia, NJ 07605 • 8,365
Leon Valley, TX 78238 • 9,581
Leoti, KS 67861 • 1,738
Lepanto, AR 72354 • 2,033
Le Roy, IL 61752 • 2,777
Le Roy, NY 14482 • 4,974
Leslie, MI 49251 • 1,872
Leslie, SC 29730 • 1,102
Leslie □, KY • 13,642
Lester Prairie, MN 55354 • 1,180
Le Sueur, MN 56058 • 3,714
Le Sueur □, MN • 23,239
Letcher □, KY • 27,000
Levelland, TX 79336–38 • 13,986
Levittown, NY 11756 • 53,286
Levittown, PA 19058 • 55,362
Levy □, FL • 25,923
Lewes, DE 19958 • 2,295
Lewis □, ID • 3,516
Lewis □, KY • 13,029
Lewis □, MO • 10,233
Lewis □, NY • 26,796
Lewis □, TN • 9,247
Lewis □, WA • 59,358
Lewis □, WV • 17,223
Lewis and Clark □, MT • 47,495
Lewisburg, OH 45338 • 1,584
Lewisburg, PA 17837 • 5,785
Lewisburg, TN 37091 • 9,879
Lewisburg, WV 24901 • 3,598
Lewisport, KY 42351 • 1,778
Lewiston, ID 83501 • 28,082
Lewiston, ME 04240–43 • 39,757
Lewiston, MN 55952 • 1,298
Lewiston, NY 14092 • 3,048
Lewiston, UT 84320 • 1,532
Lewistown, IL 61542 • 2,572
Lewistown, MT 59457 • 6,051
Lewistown, PA 17044 • 9,341
Lewisville, AR 71845 • 1,424
Lewisville, TX 75067 • 46,521
Lexington, IL 61753 • 1,809
Lexington, KY 40501–96 • 225,366
Lexington, MA 02173 • 28,974
Lexington, MS 39095 • 2,227
Lexington, MO 64067 • 4,860
Lexington, NE 68850 • 6,601
Lexington, NC 27292–93 • 16,581
Lexington, OH 44904 • 4,124
Lexington, OK 73051 • 1,776
Lexington, SC 29071–73 • 3,289
Lexington, TN 38351 • 5,810
Lexington, VA 24450 • 6,959
Lexington □, SC • 167,611
Lexington Park, MD 20653 • 9,943
Libby, MT 59923 • 2,532
Liberal, KS 67901–05 • 16,573
Liberty, IN 47353 • 2,051
Liberty, KY 42539 • 1,937
Liberty, MO 64068 • 20,459
Liberty, NY 12754 • 4,128
Liberty, NC 27298 • 2,047
Liberty, SC 29657 • 3,228
Liberty, TX 77575 • 7,733
Liberty □, FL • 5,569
Liberty □, GA • 52,745
Liberty □, MT • 2,295
Liberty □, TX • 52,726
Liberty Acres, CA 90250 • 4,700
Liberty Center, OH 43532 • 1,084
Liberty Lake, WA 99019 • 2,015
Libertyville, IL 60048 • 19,174
Licking, MO 65542 • 1,328
Licking □, OH • 128,300
Lidgerwood, ND 58053 • 799
Lighthouse Point, FL 33064 • 10,378
Ligonier, IN 46767 • 3,443
Ligonier, PA 15658 • 1,638
Lihue, HI 96766 • 5,536
Lilbourn, MO 63862 • 1,378
Lilburn, GA 30247 • 9,301
Lillington, NC 27546 • 2,048
Lilly, PA 15938 • 1,162
Lima, NY 14485 • 2,165
Lima, OH 45801–09 • 45,549
Limestone, ME 04750–51 • 1,245
Limestone □, AL • 54,135
Limestone □, TX • 20,946
Limon, CO 80828 • 1,831
Lincoln, AL 35096 • 2,941
Lincoln, AR 72744 • 1,460
Lincoln, CA 95648 • 7,248
Lincoln, DE 19960 • 500
Lincoln, IL 62656 • 15,418
Lincoln, KS 67455 • 1,381
Lincoln, ME 04457 • 3,399
Lincoln, MA 01773 • 2,860
Lincoln, NE 68501–72 • 191,972
Lincoln □, AR • 13,690
Lincoln □, CO • 4,529
Lincoln □, GA • 7,442
Lincoln □, ID • 3,308
Lincoln □, KS • 3,653
Lincoln □, KY • 20,045
Lincoln □, LA • 41,745
Lincoln □, ME • 30,357
Lincoln □, MN • 6,890
Lincoln □, MS • 30,278
Lincoln □, MO • 28,892
Lincoln □, MT • 17,481
Lincoln □, NE • 32,508
Lincoln □, NV • 3,775
Lincoln □, NM • 12,219
Lincoln □, NC • 50,319
Lincoln □, OK • 29,216
Lincoln □, OR • 38,889
Lincoln □, SD • 15,427
Lincoln □, TN • 28,157
Lincoln □, WA • 8,864
Lincoln □, WV • 21,382
Lincoln □, WI • 26,993
Lincoln □, WY • 12,625
Lincoln Acres, CA 91947 • 1,800
Lincoln City, OR 97367 • 5,892
Lincoln Heights, OH 45215 • 4,805
Lincoln Park, CO 81212 • 3,728
Lincoln Park, GA 30286 • 1,755
Lincoln Park, MI 48146 • 41,832
Lincoln Park, NJ 07035 • 10,978
Lincolnshire, IL 60069 • 4,931
Lincolnton, GA 30817 • 1,476
Lincolnton, NC 28092 • 6,847
Lincoln Village, CA 95207 • 4,236
Lincoln Village, OH 43228 • 9,958
Lincolnwood, IL 60645 • 11,365
Lincroft, NJ 07738 • 4,740
Linda, CA 95901 • 13,033
Lindale, GA 30147 • 4,187
Lindale, TX 75771 • 2,428
Linden, AL 36748 • 2,548
Linden, MI 48451 • 2,415
Linden, NJ 07036 • 36,701
Linden, TN 37096 • 1,099
Linden, TX 75563 • 2,375
Lindenhurst, IL 60046 • 8,038
Lindenhurst, NY 11757 • 26,879
Lindenwold, NJ 08021 • 18,734
Lindgren Acres, FL 33177 • 22,290
Lindon, UT 84042 • 3,818
Lindsay, CA 93247 • 8,338
Lindsay, OK 73052 • 2,947
Lindsborg, KS 67456 • 3,076
Lindstrom, MN 55045 • 2,461
Linesville, PA 16424 • 1,166
Lineville, AL 36266 • 2,394
Lingle, WY 82223 • 473
Linglestown, PA 17112 • 3,700

Linn, MO 65051 • 1,148
Linn □, IA • 168,767
Linn □, KS • 8,254
Linn □, MO • 13,885
Linn □, OR • 91,227
Lino Lakes, MN 55014 • 8,807
Linthicum Heights, MD • 2,950
Linthicum Heights, MD 21090 • 7,547
Linton, IN 47441 • 5,814
Linton, ND 58552 • 1,410
Linwood, NJ 08221 • 6,866
Lipscomb, AL 35020 • 2,892
Lipscomb □, TX • 3,143
Lisbon, IA 52253 • 1,452
Lisbon, ME 04250 • 1,240
Lisbon, NH 03585 • 1,246
Lisbon, ND 58054 • 2,177
Lisbon, OH 44432 • 3,037
Lisbon Falls, ME 04252 • 4,674
Lisle, IL 60532 • 19,512
Litchfield, CT 06759 • 1,378
Litchfield, IL 62056 • 6,883
Litchfield, MI 49252 • 1,317
Litchfield, MN 55355 • 6,041
Litchfield □, CT • 174,092
Litchfield Park, AZ 85340 • 3,303
Lithia Springs, GA 30057 • 11,403
Lithonia, GA 30058 • 2,448
Lititz, PA 17543 • 8,280
Little Canada, MN 55110 • 8,971
Little Chute, WI 54140 • 9,207
Little Compton, RI 02837 • 500
Little Creek, DE 19961 • 167
Little Falls, MN 56345 • 7,232
Little Falls, NJ 07424 • 11,294
Little Falls, NY 13365 • 5,829
Little Ferry, NJ 07643 • 9,989
Littlefield, TX 79339 • 6,489
Little River □, AR • 13,966
Little Rock, AR 72201–31 • 175,795
Little Silver, NJ 07739 • 5,721
Littlestown, PA 17340 • 2,974
Littleton, CO 80120–27 • 33,685
Littleton, MA 01460 • 2,867
Littleton, NH 03561 • 4,633
Little Valley, NY 14755 • 1,188
Live Oak, CA 95062 • 15,212
Live Oak, CA 95953 • 4,320
Live Oak, FL 32060 • 6,332
Live Oak, TX 78233 • 10,023
Live Oak □, TX • 9,556
Live Oak Manor, LA 70094 • 2,150
Livermore, CA 94550 • 56,741
Livermore, KY 42352 • 1,534
Livermore Falls, ME 04254 • 1,935
Livingston, AL 35470 • 3,530
Livingston, CA 95334 • 7,317
Livingston, MT 59047 • 6,701
Livingston, NJ 07039 • 26,609
Livingston, TN 38570 • 3,809
Livingston, TX 77351 • 5,019
Livingston □, IL • 39,301
Livingston □, KY • 9,062
Livingston □, LA • 70,526
Livingston □, MI • 115,645
Livingston □, MO • 14,592
Livingston □, NY • 62,372
Livingston Manor, NY 12758 • 1,482
Livonia, MI 48150–54 • 100,850
Livonia, NY 14487 • 1,434
Llangollen Estates, DE 19720 • 1,070
Llano, TX 78643 • 2,962
Llano □, TX • 11,631
Lloyd Harbor, NY 11743 • 3,343
Lochearn, MD 21207 • 25,240
Loch Lomond, VA 22110 • 3,292
Lockhart, FL 32810 • 11,636
Lockhart, TX 78644 • 9,205
Lock Haven, PA 17745 • 9,230
Lockland, OH 45215 • 4,357
Lockney, TX 79241 • 2,207
Lockport, IL 60441 • 9,401
Lockport, LA 70374 • 2,503
Lockport, NY 14094 • 24,426
Lockwood, MO 65682 • 1,041
Lockwood, MT 59101 • 3,967
Locust, NC 28097 • 1,940
Locust Grove, GA 30248 • 1,681
Locust Grove, OK 74352 • 1,326
Lodi, CA 95240–42 • 51,874
Lodi, NJ 07644 • 22,355
Lodi, OH 44254 • 3,042
Lodi, WI 53555 • 2,093
Logan, IA 51546 • 1,401
Logan, OH 43138 • 6,725
Logan, UT 84321 • 32,762
Logan, WV 25601 • 2,206
Logan □, AR • 20,557
Logan □, CO • 17,567
Logan □, IL • 30,798
Logan □, KS • 3,081
Logan □, KY • 24,416
Logan □, NE • 878
Logan □, ND • 2,847
Logan □, OH • 42,310
Logan □, OK • 29,011
Logan □, WV • 43,032
Logandale, NV 89021 • 500
Logansport, IN 46947 • 16,812
Logansport, LA 71049 • 1,390
Loganville, GA 30249 • 3,180
Lolo, MT 59847 • 2,746
Loma Linda, CA 92354 • 17,400
Lombard, IL 60148 • 39,408
Lomira, WI 53048 • 1,542
Lomita, CA 90717 • 19,382
Lompoc, CA 93436 • 37,649
Lonaconing, MD 21539 • 1,122
London, KY 40741 • 5,757
London, OH 43140 • 7,807
Londonderry, NH 03053 • 10,114
Londontown, MD 21037 • 6,992
Lone Grove, OK 73443 • 4,114
Lone Pine, CA 93545 • 1,818
Long □, GA • 6,202
Long Beach, CA 90801–88 • 429,433
Long Beach, IN 46360 • 2,044
Long Beach, MS 39560 • 15,804
Long Beach, NY 11561 • 33,510
Long Beach, WA 98631 • 1,236
Longboat Key, FL 34228 • 5,937
Long Branch, NJ 07740 • 28,658
Long Lake, IL 60041 • 2,888
Longmeadow, MA 01106 • 15,467
Longmont, CO 80501–02 • 51,555
Longport, NJ 08403 • 1,224
Long Prairie, MN 56347 • 2,786
Long Valley, NJ 07853 • 1,744
Long View, NC 28601 • 3,229
Longview, TX 75601–15 • 70,311
Longview, WA 98632 • 31,499
Longwood, FL 32750 • 13,316
Lonoke, AR 72086 • 4,022
Lonoke □, AR • 39,268
Lonsdale, MN 55046 • 1,252
Lonsdale, RI 02865 • 3,850
Loogootee, IN 47553 • 2,884
Lookout Mountain, TN 37350 • 1,901
Lorain, OH 44052–55 • 71,245
Lorain □, OH • 271,126
Lordsburg, NM 88045 • 2,951
Lorenzo, TX 79343 • 1,208
Loretto, PA 15940 • 1,072
Loretto, TN 38469 • 1,515
Loris, SC 29569 • 2,067
Lorton, VA 22079 • 15,385
Los Alamitos, CA 90720–21 • 11,676
Los Alamos, NM 87544 • 11,455
Los Alamos □, NM • 18,115
Los Altos, CA 94022–24 • 26,303
Los Altos Hills, CA 94022 • 7,514
Los Angeles, CA 90001–99 • 3,485,398
Los Angeles □, CA • 8,863,164
Los Banos, CA 93635 • 14,519
Los Fresnos, TX 78566 • 2,473
Los Gatos, CA 95030–32 • 27,357
Los Lunas, NM 87031 • 6,013
Los Molinos, CA 96055 • 1,709
Los Nietos, CA 90606 • 7,100
Los Osos, CA 93402 • 8,000
Los Padillas, NM 87105 • 2,400
Los Ranchos de Albuquerque, NM 87107 • 3,955
Los Serranos, CA 91709 • 7,099
Lost Hills, CA 93249 • 1,212
Loudon, TN 37774 • 4,026
Loudon □, TN • 31,255
Loudonville, NY 12211 • 10,822
Loudonville, OH 44842 • 2,915
Loudoun □, VA • 86,129
Louisa, KY 41230 • 1,990
Louisa, VA 23093 • 1,088
Louisa □, IA • 11,592
Louisa □, VA • 20,325
Louisburg, KS 66053 • 1,964
Louisburg, NC 27549 • 3,037
Louisiana, MO 63353 • 3,967
Louisville, CO 80027 • 12,361
Louisville, GA 30434 • 2,429
Louisville, IL 62858 • 1,098
Louisville, KY 40201–99 • 269,063
Louisville, MS 39339 • 7,169
Louisville, OH 44641 • 8,087
Loup □, NE • 683
Loup City, NE 68853 • 1,104
Love □, OK • 8,157
Loveland, CO 80537–39 • 37,352
Loveland, OH 45140 • 9,990
Loveland Park, OH 45140 • 1,357
Lovell, WY 82431 • 2,131
Lovelock, NV 89419 • 2,069
Loves Park, IL 61111 • 15,462
Loving, NM 88256 • 1,243
Loving □, TX • 107
Lovington, IL 61937 • 1,143
Lovington, NM 88260 • 9,322
Lowell, AR 72745 • 1,224
Lowell, IN 46356 • 6,430
Lowell, MA 01850–54 • 103,439
Lowell, MI 49331 • 3,983
Lowell, NC 28098 • 2,704
Lowellville, OH 44436 • 1,349
Lower Burrell, PA 15068 • 12,251
Lower Merion Township, PA 19003 • 59,629
Lower Paia, HI 96779 • 1,500
Lowndes □, AL • 12,658
Lowndes □, GA • 75,981
Lowndes □, MS • 59,308
Lowville, NY 13367 • 3,632
Loxley, AL 36551 • 1,161
Loyal, WI 54446 • 1,244
Loyall, KY 40854 • 1,100
Lubbock, TX 79401–99 • 186,206
Lubbock □, TX • 222,636
Lucas □, IA • 9,070
Lucas □, OH • 462,361
Lucasville, OH 45648 • 1,575
Luce □, MI • 5,763
Lucedale, MS 39452 • 2,592
Lucerne, CA 95458 • 2,011
Lucernemines, PA 15754 • 1,074
Lucerne Valley, CA 92356 • 1,300
Luck, WI 54853 • 1,022
Ludington, MI 49431 • 8,507
Ludlow, KY 41016 • 4,736
Ludlow, MA 01056 • 18,150
Ludlow, VT 05149 • 1,123
Ludowici, GA 31316 • 1,291
Lufkin, TX 75901–03 • 30,206
Lugoff, SC 29078 • 3,211
Lula, GA 30554 • 1,018
Luling, LA 70070 • 2,803
Luling, TX 78648 • 4,661
Lumber City, GA 31549 • 1,429
Lumberport, WV 26386 • 1,014
Lumberton, MS 39455 • 2,217
Lumberton, NC 28358–59 • 18,601
Lumpkin, GA 31815 • 1,250
Lumpkin □, GA • 14,573
Luna □, NM • 18,110
Luna Pier, MI 48157 • 1,507
Lund, NV 89317 • 330
Lunenburg, MA 01462 • 1,694
Lunenburg □, VA • 11,419
Luray, VA 22835 • 4,587
Lusk, WY 82225 • 1,504
Lutcher, LA 70071 • 3,907
Luther, OK 73054 • 1,560
Lutherville-Timonium, MD 21093 • 16,442
Lutz, FL 33549 • 10,552
Luverne, AL 36049 • 2,555
Luverne, MN 56156 • 4,382
Luxemburg, WI 54217 • 1,151
Luxora, AR 72358 • 1,338
Luzerne, PA 18709 • 3,206
Luzerne □, PA • 328,149
Lycoming □, PA • 118,710
Lyford, TX 78569 • 1,674
Lykens, PA 17048 • 1,986
Lyman, SC 29365 • 2,271
Lyman, WY 82937 • 1,896
Lyman □, SD • 3,638
Lynbrook, NY 11563 • 19,208
Lynch, KY 40855 • 1,166
Lynchburg, OH 45142 • 1,212
Lynchburg, TN 37352 • 4,721
Lynchburg, VA 24501–06 • 66,049
Lyncourt, NY 13208 • 4,516
Lynden, WA 98264 • 5,709
Lyndhurst, NJ 07071 • 18,262
Lyndhurst, OH 44124 • 15,982
Lyndon, KY 40222 • 8,037
Lyndonville, VT 05851 • 1,255
Lyndora, PA 16045 • 3,000
Lynn, IN 47355 • 1,183
Lynn, MA 01901–08 • 81,245
Lynn □, TX • 6,758
Lynne Acres, MD 21207 • 5,910
Lynnfield, MA 01940 • 11,274
Lynn Garden, TN 37665 • 7,213
Lynn Garden, TN 37665 • 3,950
Lynn Haven, FL 32444 • 9,298
Lynnwood, WA 98036–37 • 28,695
Lynwood, CA 90262 • 61,945
Lyon □, IA • 11,952
Lyon □, KS • 34,732
Lyon □, KY • 6,624
Lyon □, MN • 24,789
Lyon □, NV • 20,001
Lyon Mountain, NY 12952 • 1,000
Lyons, CO 80540 • 1,227
Lyons, GA 30436 • 4,502
Lyons, IL 60534 • 9,828
Lyons, KS 67554 • 3,688
Lyons, NE 68038 • 1,144
Lyons, NY 14489 • 4,280
Lytle, TX 78052 • 2,255

M

Mabank, TX 75147 • 1,739
Mableton, GA 30059 • 25,725
Mabscott, WV 25871 • 1,543
Mabton, WA 98935 • 1,482
MacClenny, FL 32063 • 3,966
Macedon, NY 14502 • 1,400
Macedonia, OH 44056 • 7,509
Machesney Park, IL 61111 • 19,033
Machias, ME 04654 • 1,773
Mackinac □, MI • 10,674
Mackinaw, IL 61755 • 1,331
Mackinaw City, MI 49701 • 875
Macomb, IL 61455 • 19,952
Macomb □, MI • 717,400
Macon, GA 31201–95 • 106,612
Macon, IL 62544 • 1,282
Macon, MS 39341 • 2,256
Macon, MO 63552 • 5,571
Macon □, AL • 24,928
Macon □, GA • 13,114
Macon □, IL • 117,206
Macon □, MO • 15,345
Macon □, NC • 23,499
Macon □, TN • 15,906
Macoupin □, IL • 47,679
Macungie, PA 18062 • 2,597
Madawaska, ME 04756 • 3,653
Madeira, OH 45243 • 9,141
Madelia, MN 56062 • 2,237
Madera, CA 93637–39 • 29,281
Madera □, CA • 88,090
Madill, OK 73446 • 3,069
Madison, AL 35758 • 14,904
Madison, AR 72359 • 1,263
Madison, CT 06443 • 2,139
Madison, FL 32340 • 3,345
Madison, GA 30650 • 3,483
Madison, IL 62060 • 4,629
Madison, IN 47250 • 12,006
Madison, ME 04950 • 2,956
Madison, MN 56256 • 1,951
Madison, MS 39110 • 7,471
Madison, NE 68748 • 2,135
Madison, NJ 07940 • 15,850
Madison, NC 27025 • 2,371
Madison, OH 44057 • 2,477
Madison, SD 57042 • 6,257
Madison, WV 25130 • 3,051
Madison, WI 53701–19 • 191,262
Madison □, AL • 238,912
Madison □, AR • 11,618
Madison □, FL • 16,569
Madison □, GA • 21,050
Madison □, ID • 23,674
Madison □, IL • 249,238
Madison □, IN • 130,669
Madison □, IA • 12,483
Madison □, KY • 57,508
Madison □, LA • 12,463
Madison □, MS • 53,794
Madison □, MO • 11,127
Madison □, MT • 5,989
Madison □, NE • 32,655
Madison □, NY • 69,120
Madison □, NC • 16,953
Madison □, OH • 37,068
Madison □, TN • 77,982
Madison □, TX • 10,931
Madison □, VA • 11,949
Madison Heights, MI 48071 • 32,196
Madison Heights, VA 24572 • 11,700
Madisonville, KY 42431 • 16,200
Madisonville, TN 37354 • 3,033
Madisonville, TX 77864 • 3,569
Madras, OR 97741 • 3,443
Madrid, IA 50156 • 2,395
Maeser, UT 84078 • 2,598
Magalia, CA 95954 • 8,987
Magdalena, NM 87825 • 861
Magee, MS 39111 • 3,607
Magna, UT 84044 • 17,829
Magnolia, AR 71753 • 11,151
Magnolia, MS 39652 • 2,245
Magnolia, NJ 08049 • 4,861
Magoffin □, KY • 13,077
Mahanoy City, PA 17948 • 5,209
Mahaska □, IA • 21,522
Mahnomen, MN 56557 • 1,154
Mahnomen □, MN • 5,044
Mahomet, IL 61853 • 3,103
Mahoning □, OH • 264,806
Mahopac, NY 10541 • 7,755
Mahwah, NJ 07430 • 7,500
Maiden, NC 28650 • 2,574
Maili, HI 96792 • 6,059
Maine, NY 13802 • 1,110
Maitland, FL 32751 • 9,110
Maize, KS 67101 • 1,520
Major □, OK • 8,055
Makaha, HI 96792 • 7,990
Makakilo City, HI 96706 • 9,828
Makawao, HI 96768 • 5,405
Makaweli, HI 96769 • 700
Malabar, FL 32950 • 1,977
Malad City, ID 83252 • 1,946
Malaga, NJ 08328 • 2,140
Malakoff, TX 75148 • 2,038
Malden, MA 02148 • 53,884
Malden, MO 63863 • 5,123
Malheur □, OR • 26,038
Malibu, CA 90264–65 • 10,000
Malone, NY 12953 • 6,777
Malta, MT 59538 • 2,340
Malvern, AR 72104 • 9,256
Malvern, IA 51551 • 1,210
Malvern, OH 44644 • 1,112
Malvern, PA 19355 • 2,944
Malverne, NY 11565 • 9,054
Mamaroneck, NY 10543 • 17,325
Mammoth, AZ 85618 • 1,845
Mammoth Lakes, CA 93546 • 4,785
Mammoth Spring, AR 72554 • 1,097
Mamou, LA 70554 • 3,483
Manahawkin, NJ 08050 • 1,594
Manasquan, NJ 08736 • 5,369
Manassas, VA 22110–11 • 27,957
Manassas Park, VA 22111 • 6,734
Manatee □, FL • 211,707
Manawa, WI 54949 • 1,169
Mancelona, MI 49659 • 1,370
Manchaug, MA 01526 • 1,000
Manchester, CT 06040 • 51,618
Manchester, GA 31816 • 4,104
Manchester, IA 52057 • 5,137
Manchester, KY 40962 • 1,634
Manchester, MD 21102 • 2,810
Manchester, MA 01944 • 5,424
Manchester, MI 48158 • 1,753
Manchester, MO 63011 • 6,542
Manchester, NH 03101–10 • 99,567
Manchester, NY 14504 • 1,598
Manchester, OH 45144 • 2,223
Manchester, PA 17345 • 1,830
Manchester, TN 37355 • 7,709
Manchester, VT 05254 • 561
Manchester Center, VT 05255 • 1,574
Mandan, ND 58554 • 15,177
Mandeville, LA 70448 • 7,083
Mangum, OK 73554 • 3,344
Manhasset, NY 11030 • 7,718
Manhattan, KS 66502 • 37,712
Manhattan, MT 59741 • 1,034
Manhattan Beach, CA 90266 • 32,063
Manheim, PA 17545 • 5,011
Manila, AR 72442 • 2,635
Manistee, MI 49660 • 6,734
Manistee □, MI • 21,265
Manistique, MI 49854 • 3,456
Manito, IL 61546 • 1,711
Manitou Springs, CO 80829 • 4,535
Manitowoc, WI 54220–21 • 32,520
Manitowoc □, WI • 80,421
Mankato, KS 66956 • 1,037
Mankato, MN 56001–03 • 31,477
Manlius, NY 13104 • 4,764
Manly, IA 50456 • 1,349
Mannford, OK 74044 • 1,826
Manning, IA 51455 • 1,484
Manning, SC 29102 • 4,428
Mannington, WV 26582 • 2,184
Manokotak, AK 99628 • 385
Manomet, MA 02345 • 1,500
Manor, TX 78653 • 1,041
Manorhaven, NY 11050 • 5,672
Mansfield, AR 72944 • 1,018
Mansfield, LA 71052 • 5,389
Mansfield, MA 02048 • 7,170
Mansfield, MO 65704 • 1,429
Mansfield, OH 44901–07 • 50,627
Mansfield, PA 16933 • 3,538
Mansfield, TX 76063 • 15,607
Mansfield Center, CT 06250 • 1,043
Manson, IA 50563 • 1,844
Mansura, LA 71350 • 1,601
Manteca, CA 95336 • 40,773
Manteno, IL 60950 • 3,488
Manti, UT 84642 • 2,268
Manton, MI 49663 • 1,161
Mantua, NJ 08051 • 1,350
Mantua, OH 44255 • 1,178
Mantua Hills, VA 22031 • 1,600
Manvel, TX 77578 • 3,733
Manville, NJ 08835 • 10,567
Manville, RI 02838 • 3,030
Many, LA 71449 • 3,112
Many Farms, AZ 86538 • 1,294
Maple Bluff, WI 53704 • 1,352
Maple Grove, MN 55369 • 38,736
Maple Heights, OH 44137 • 27,089
Maple Lake, MN 55358 • 1,394
Maple Plain, MN 55359 • 2,005
Maple Shade, NJ 08052 • 19,211
Mapleton, IA 51034 • 1,294
Mapleton, MN 56065 • 1,526
Mapleton, UT 84663 • 3,572
Maple Valley, WA 98038 • 1,211
Mapleville, RI 02839 • 1,300
Maplewood, MN 55109 • 30,954
Maplewood, MO 63143 • 9,962
Maplewood, NJ 07040 • 21,756
Maquoketa, IA 52060 • 6,111
Marana, AZ 85653 • 2,187
Marathon, FL 33050 • 8,857
Marathon, NY 13803 • 1,107
Marathon, WI 54448 • 1,606
Marathon □, WI • 115,400
Marble Falls, TX 78654 • 4,007
Marblehead, MA 01945 • 19,971
Marble Hill, MO 63764 • 1,447
Marbleton, WY 83113 • 634
Marbury, MD 20658 • 1,244
Marceline, MO 64658 • 2,645
Marcellus, MI 49067 • 1,193
Marco, FL 33937 • 9,493
Marcus, IA 51035 • 1,171
Marcus Hook, PA 19061 • 2,546
Marengo, IL 60152 • 4,768
Marengo, IA 52301 • 2,270
Marengo □, AL • 23,084
Marfa, TX 79843 • 2,424
Margate, FL 33063 • 42,985
Margate, MD 21060 • 1,900
Margate City, NJ 08402 • 8,431
Marianna, AR 72360 • 5,910
Marianna, FL 32446 • 6,292
Maricopa, AZ 85239 • 1,600
Maricopa, CA 93252 • 1,193
Maricopa □, AZ • 2,122,101
Mariemont, OH 45227 • 3,118
Marienville, PA 16239 • 1,400
Maries □, MO • 7,976
Marietta, GA 30060–68 • 44,129
Marietta, OH 45750 • 15,026
Marietta, OK 73448 • 2,306
Marin □, CA • 230,096
Marina, CA 93933 • 26,436
Marina del Rey, CA 90292 • 7,431
Marine City, MI 48039 • 4,556
Marinette, WI 54143 • 11,843
Marinette □, WI • 40,548
Maringouin, LA 70757 • 1,149
Marion, AL 36756 • 4,211
Marion, AR 72364 • 4,391
Marion, IL 62959 • 14,545
Marion, IN 46952–53 • 32,618
Marion, IA 52302 • 20,403
Marion, KS 66861 • 1,906
Marion, KY 42064 • 3,320
Marion, MA 02738 • 1,426
Marion, MS 39342 • 1,359
Marion, NY 14505 • 1,080
Marion, NC 28752 • 4,765
Marion, OH 43301–02 • 34,075
Marion, PA 17235 • 1,000
Marion, SC 29571 • 7,658
Marion, SD 57043 • 831
Marion, VA 24354 • 6,630
Marion, WI 54950 • 1,242
Marion □, AL • 29,830
Marion □, AR • 12,001
Marion □, FL • 194,833
Marion □, GA • 5,590
Marion □, IL • 41,561
Marion □, IN • 797,159
Marion □, IA • 30,001
Marion □, KS • 12,888
Marion □, KY • 16,499
Marion □, MS • 25,544
Marion □, MO • 27,682
Marion □, OH • 64,274
Marion □, OR • 228,483
Marion □, SC • 33,899
Marion □, TN • 24,860
Marion □, TX • 9,984
Marion □, WV • 57,249
Marionville, MO 65705 • 1,920
Mariposa, CA 95338 • 1,152
Mariposa □, CA • 14,302
Marissa, IL 62257 • 2,375
Marked Tree, AR 72365 • 3,100
Markesan, WI 53946 • 1,496
Markham, IL 60426 • 13,136
Markham, TX 77456 • 1,206
Markle, IN 46770 • 1,208
Marks, MS 38646 • 1,758
Marksville, LA 71351 • 5,526
Marlboro, NY 12542 • 2,200
Marlboro □, SC • 29,361
Marlborough, CT 06447 • 5,535
Marlborough, MA 01752 • 31,813
Marlborough, NH 03455 • 1,211
Marlene Village, OR 97005 • 1,500
Marlette, MI 48453 • 1,924
Marley, MD 21060 • 7,100
Marlin, TX 76661 • 6,386
Marlinton, WV 24954 • 1,148
Marlow, OK 73055 • 4,416
Marlow Heights, MD 20748 • 5,885
Marlton, NJ 08053 • 10,228
Marmaduke, AR 72443 • 1,164
Marmet, WV 25315 • 1,879
Maroa, IL 61756 • 1,602
Marquette, MI 49855 • 21,977
Marquette □, MI • 70,887
Marquette □, WI • 12,321
Marquette Heights, IL 61554 • 3,077
Marrero, LA 70072–73 • 36,671
Mars, PA 16046 • 1,713
Marseilles, IL 61341 • 4,811
Marshall, AR 72650 • 1,318
Marshall, IL 62441 • 3,555
Marshall, MI 49068 • 6,891
Marshall, MN 56258 • 12,023
Marshall, MO 65340 • 12,711
Marshall, TX 75670–71 • 23,682
Marshall, WI 53559 • 2,329
Marshall □, AL • 70,832
Marshall □, IL • 12,846
Marshall □, IN • 42,182
Marshall □, IA • 38,276
Marshall □, KS • 11,705
Marshall □, KY • 27,205
Marshall □, MN • 10,993
Marshall □, MS • 30,361
Marshall □, OK • 10,829
Marshall □, SD • 4,844
Marshall □, TN • 21,539
Marshall □, WV • 37,356
Marshallton, DE 19808 • 1,765
Marshalltown, IA 50158 • 25,178
Marshallville, GA 31057 • 1,457
Marshfield, MA 02050 • 4,002
Marshfield, MO 65706 • 4,374
Marshfield, WI 54449 • 19,291
Marshfield Hills, MA 02051 • 2,201
Mars Hill, ME 04758 • 1,500
Mars Hill, NC 28754 • 1,611
Marshville, NC 28103 • 2,020
Marsing, ID 83639 • 798
Marstons Mills, MA 02648 • 8,017
Mart, TX 76664 • 2,004
Martha Lake, WA 98012 • 10,155
Martin, SD 57551 • 1,151
Martin, TN 38237 • 8,600

Martin □, FL • 100,900
Martin □, IN • 10,369
Martin □, KY • 12,526
Martin □, MN • 22,914
Martin □, NC • 25,078
Martin □, TX • 4,956
Martinez, CA 94553 • 31,808
Martinez, GA 30907 • 33,731
Martinsburg, PA 16662 • 2,119
Martinsburg, WV 25401 • 14,073
Martins Ferry, OH 43935 • 7,990
Martinsville, IL 62442 • 1,161
Martinsville, IN 46151 • 11,677
Martinsville, VA 24112–15 • 16,162
Marvell, AR 72366 • 1,545
Maryland City, MD 20724 • 6,813
Maryland Heights, MO 63043 • 25,407
Marysville, CA 95901 • 12,324
Marysville, KS 66508 • 3,359
Marysville, MI 48040 • 8,515
Marysville, OH 43040 • 9,656
Marysville, PA 17053 • 2,425
Marysville, WA 98270 • 10,328
Maryville, MO 64468 • 10,663
Maryville, TN 37801–04 • 19,208
Mascot, TN 37806 • 2,138
Mascoutah, IL 62258 • 5,511
Mason, MI 48854 • 6,768
Mason, NV 89447 • 400
Mason, OH 45040 • 11,452
Mason, TX 76856 • 2,041
Mason, WV 25260 • 1,053
Mason □, IL • 16,269
Mason □, KY • 16,666
Mason □, MI • 25,537
Mason □, TX • 3,423
Mason □, WA • 38,341
Mason □, WV • 25,178
Masonboro, NC 28403 • 7,010
Mason City, IL 62664 • 2,323
Mason City, IA 50401 • 29,040
Masontown, PA 15461 • 3,759
Massac □, IL • 14,752
Massapequa, NY 11758 • 22,018
Massapequa Park, NY 11762 • 18,044
Massena, NY 13662 • 11,719
Massillon, OH 44646–48 • 31,007
Mastic, NY 11950 • 13,778
Mastic Beach, NY 11951 • 10,293
Masury, OH 44438 • 1,836
Matagorda □, TX • 36,928
Matamoras, PA 18336 • 1,934
Matawan, NJ 07747 • 9,270
Mather, PA 15346 • 1,300
Mathews □, VA • 8,348
Mathis, TX 78368 • 5,423
Matoaca, VA 23803 • 1,967
Mattapoisett, MA 02739 • 2,949
Matteson, IL 60443 • 11,378
Matthews, NC 28105–06 • 13,651
Mattituck, NY 11952 • 3,902
Mattoon, IL 61938 • 18,441
Mattydale, NY 13211 • 6,418
Matunuck, RI 02879 • 550
Maud, OK 74854 • 1,204
Maugansville, MD 21767 • 1,707
Maui □, HI • 100,374
Mauldin, SC 29662 • 11,587
Maumee, OH 43537 • 15,561
Maunaloa, HI 96770 • 405
Maunawili, HI 96734 • 4,847
Maury □, TN • 54,812
Mauston, WI 53948 • 3,439
Maverick □, TX • 36,378
Maxton, NC 28364 • 2,373
Maxwell Acres, WV 26041 • 1,000
Mayer, AZ 86333 • 1,800
Mayes □, OK • 33,366
Mayfield, KY 42066 • 9,935
Mayfield, PA 18433 • 1,890
Mayfield Heights, OH 44124 • 19,847
Mayflower, AR 72106 • 1,415
Mayflower Village, CA 91016 • 4,978
Maynard, MA 01754 • 10,325
Maynardville, TN 37807 • 1,298
Mayo, MD 21106 • 2,537
Mayodan, NC 27027 • 2,471
Mays Landing, NJ 08330 • 2,090
Maysville, KY 41056 • 7,169
Maysville, MO 64469 • 1,176
Maysville, OK 73057 • 1,203
Mayville, MI 48744 • 1,010
Mayville, NY 14757 • 1,636
Mayville, ND 58257 • 2,092
Mayville, WI 53050 • 4,374
Maywood, CA 90270 • 27,850
Maywood, IL 60153–54 • 27,139
Maywood, NJ 07607 • 9,473
Mazomanie, WI 53560 • 1,377
McAdoo, PA 18237 • 2,459
McAlester, OK 74501–02 • 16,370
McAllen, TX 78501–04 • 84,021
McAlmont, AR 72117 • 1,800
McAlpine, MD 21043 • 2,230
McArthur, OH 45651 • 1,541
McCall, ID 83638 • 2,005
McCamey, TX 79752 • 2,493
McCandless, PA 15237 • 28,781
McCaysville, GA 30555 • 1,065
McClain □, OK • 22,795
McCleary, WA 98557 • 1,235
McCloud, CA 96057 • 1,555
McClure, PA 17841 • 1,070
McColl, SC 29570 • 2,685
McComb, MS 39648 • 11,591
McComb, OH 45858 • 1,544
McCone □, MT • 2,276
McConnellsburg, PA 17233 • 1,106
McConnelsville, OH 43756 • 1,804
McCook, NE 69001 • 8,112
McCook □, SD • 5,688
McCormick, SC 29835 • 1,659
McCormick □, SC • 8,868
McCracken □, KY • 62,879
McCreary □, KY • 15,603
McCrory, AR 72101 • 1,971
McCulloch □, TX • 8,778
McCurtain □, OK • 33,433
McDermitt, NV 89421 • 373
McDonald □, MO • 16,938
McDonough, GA 30253 • 2,929
McDonough □, IL • 35,244
McDowell □, NC • 35,681
McDowell □, WV • 35,233
McDuffie □, GA • 20,119
McEwen, TN 37101 • 1,442
McFarland, CA 93250 • 7,005
McFarland, WI 53558 • 5,232
McGehee, AR 71654 • 4,997
McGill, NV 89318 • 1,258
McGrath, AK 99627 • 528
McGraw, NY 13101 • 1,074
McGregor, TX 76657 • 4,683
McHenry, IL 60050–51 • 16,177
McHenry □, IL • 183,241
McHenry □, ND • 6,528
McIntosh □, GA • 8,634
McIntosh □, ND • 4,021
McIntosh □, OK • 16,779
McKean □, PA • 47,131
McKee City, NJ 08232 • 1,200
McKeesport, PA 15130–35 • 26,016
McKees Rocks, PA 15136 • 7,691
McKenzie, TN 38201 • 5,168
McKenzie □, ND • 6,383
McKinley □, NM • 60,686
McKinleyville, CA 95521 • 10,749
McKinney, TX 75069–70 • 21,283
McLaughlin, SD 57642 • 780
McLean, VA 22101 • 38,168
McLean □, IL • 129,180
McLean □, KY • 9,628
McLean □, ND • 10,457
McLeansboro, IL 62859 • 2,677
McLennan □, TX • 189,123
McLeod □, MN • 32,030
McLoud, OK 74851 • 2,493
McMechen, WV 26040 • 2,130
McMinn □, TN • 42,383
McMinnville, OR 97128 • 17,894
McMinnville, TN 37110 • 11,194
McMullen □, TX • 817
McNairy □, TN • 22,422
McPherson, KS 67460 • 12,422
McPherson □, KS • 27,268
McPherson □, NE • 546
McPherson □, SD • 3,228
McQueeney, TX 78123 • 2,063
McRae, GA 31055 • 3,007
McRoberts, KY 41835 • 1,101
McSherrystown, PA 17344 • 2,769
Mead, WA 99021 • 2,150
Meade, KS 67864 • 1,526
Meade □, KS • 4,247
Meade □, KY • 24,170
Meade □, SD • 21,878
Meadowbrook, FL 32808 • 5,200
Meadowood, DE 19711 • 2,100
Meadville, PA 16335 • 14,318
Meagher □, MT • 1,819
Mebane, NC 27302 • 4,754
Mecca, CA 92254 • 1,966
Mechanic Falls, ME 04256 • 2,388
Mechanicsburg, OH 43044 • 1,803
Mechanicsburg, PA 17055 • 9,452
Mechanicsville, IA 52306 • 1,012
Mechanicsville, VA 23111 • 22,027
Mechanicville, NY 12118 • 5,249
Mecklenburg □, NC • 511,433
Mecklenburg □, VA • 29,241
Mecosta □, MI • 37,308
Medfield, MA 02052 • 5,985
Medford, MA 02155 • 57,407
Medford, NJ 08055 • 1,800
Medford, NY 11763 • 21,274
Medford, OK 73759 • 1,172
Medford, OR 97501–04 • 46,951
Medford, WI 54451 • 4,283
Medford Lakes, NJ 08055 • 4,462
Media, PA 19063–65 • 5,957
Mediapolis, IA 52637 • 1,637
Medical Lake, WA 99022 • 3,664
Medicine Bow, WY 82329 • 389
Medicine Lodge, KS 67104 • 2,453
Medina, NY 14103 • 6,686
Medina, OH 44256 • 19,231
Medina, WA 98039 • 2,981
Medina □, OH • 122,354
Medina □, TX • 27,312
Medway, MA 02053 • 3,890
Meeker, CO 81641 • 2,098
Meeker, OK 74855 • 1,003
Meeker □, MN • 20,846
Meeteetse, WY 82433 • 368
Mehlville, MO 63129 • 27,557
Meigs, GA 31765 • 1,120
Meigs □, OH • 22,987
Meigs □, TN • 8,033
Meiners Oaks, CA 93023 • 3,329
Melbourne, AR 72556 • 1,562
Melbourne, FL 32901–10 • 59,646
Melbourne Beach, FL 32951 • 3,021
Melcher, IA 50163 • 1,302
Mellette □, SD • 2,137
Melrose, FL 32666 • 1,700
Melrose, MA 02176 • 28,150
Melrose, MN 56352 • 2,561
Melrose Park, FL 33312 • 6,477
Melrose Park, IL 60160–63 • 20,859
Melville, LA 71353 • 1,562
Melville, NY 11747 • 12,586
Melvindale, MI 48122 • 11,216
Memphis, FL 34221 • 6,760
Memphis, MI 48041 • 1,221
Memphis, MO 63555 • 2,094
Memphis, TN 38101–87 • 610,337
Memphis, TX 79245 • 2,465
Mena, AR 71953 • 5,475
Menahga, MN 56464 • 1,076
Menands, NY 12204 • 4,333
Menard, TX 76859 • 1,606
Menard □, IL • 11,164
Menard □, TX • 2,252
Menasha, WI 54952 • 14,711
Mendenhall, MS 39114 • 2,463
Mendham, NJ 07945 • 4,890
Mendocino, CA 95460 • 1,008
Mendocino □, CA • 80,345
Mendota, CA 93640 • 6,821
Mendota, IL 61342 • 7,018
Mendota Heights, MN 55118 • 9,431
Menifee □, KY • 5,092
Menlo Park, CA 94025–28 • 28,040
Menno, SD 57045 • 768
Menominee, MI 49858 • 9,398
Menominee □, MI • 24,920
Menominee □, WI • 3,890
Menomonee Falls, WI 53051–52 • 26,840
Menomonie, WI 54751 • 13,547
Mentor, OH 44060–61 • 47,358
Mentor-on-the-Lake, OH 44060 • 8,271
Mequon, WI 53092 • 18,885
Meraux, LA 70075 • 8,000
Merced, CA 95339–44 • 56,216
Merced □, CA • 178,403
Mercedes, TX 78570 • 12,694
Mercer, PA 16137 • 2,444
Mercer, WI 54547 • 1,300
Mercer □, IL • 17,290
Mercer □, KY • 19,148
Mercer □, MO • 3,723
Mercer □, NJ • 325,824
Mercer □, ND • 9,808
Mercer □, OH • 39,443
Mercer □, PA • 121,003
Mercer □, WV • 64,980
Mercer Island, WA 98040 • 20,816
Mercersburg, PA 17236 • 1,640
Mercerville, NJ 08619 • 15,600
Merchantville, NJ 08109 • 4,095
Meredith, NH 03253 • 1,654
Meredosia, IL 62665 • 1,134
Meriden, CT 06450 • 59,479
Meridian, ID 83642 • 9,596
Meridian, MS 39301–09 • 41,036
Meridian, PA 16001 • 3,473
Meridian, TX 76665 • 1,390
Meridian Hills, IN 46260 • 1,728
Meridianville, AL 35759 • 2,852
Meriwether □, GA • 22,411
Merkel, TX 79536 • 2,469
Merriam, KS 66203 • 11,821
Merrick, NY 11566 • 23,042
Merrick □, NE • 8,042
Merrifield, VA 22031 • 8,399
Merrill, WI 54452 • 9,860
Merrillville, IN 46410 • 27,257
Merrimac, MA 01860 • 2,050
Merrimack, NH 03054 • 1,300
Merrimack □, NH • 120,005
Merritt Island, FL 32952–54 • 32,886
Merryville, LA 70653 • 1,235
Merton, WI 53056 • 1,199
Mesa, AZ 85201–16 • 288,091
Mesa □, CO • 93,145
Mescalero, NM 88340 • 1,159
Mesilla, NM 88046 • 1,975
Mesquite, NV 89024 • 1,871
Mesquite, TX 75149–50 • 101,484
Metairie, LA 70001–11 • 149,428
Metamora, IL 61548 • 2,520
Metcalfe, MS 38760 • 1,092
Metcalfe □, KY • 8,963
Methuen, MA 01844 • 39,990
Metlakatla, AK 99926 • 1,407
Metropolis, IL 62960 • 6,734
Metter, GA 30439 • 3,707
Metuchen, NJ 08840 • 12,804
Metzger, OR 97223 • 3,149
Mexia, TX 76667 • 6,933
Mexico, ME 04257 • 2,302
Mexico, MO 65265 • 11,290
Mexico, NY 13114 • 1,555
Meyersdale, PA 15552 • 2,518
Miami, AZ 85539 • 2,018
Miami, FL 33101–99 • 358,548
Miami, OK 74354–55 • 13,142
Miami □, IN • 36,897
Miami □, KS • 23,466
Miami □, OH • 93,182
Miami Beach, FL 33139 • 92,639
Miami Lakes, FL 33014 • 12,750
Miamisburg, OH 45342–43 • 17,834
Miami Shores, FL 33138 • 10,084
Miami Springs, FL 33166 • 13,268
Micco, FL 32958 • 8,757
Michigan Center, MI 49254 • 4,863
Michigan City, IN 46360 • 33,822
Middleboro (Middleborough Center), MA 02346 • 6,837
Middleburg, FL 32068 • 6,223
Middleburg, PA 17842 • 1,422
Middleburgh, NY 12122 • 1,436
Middleburg Heights, OH 44130 • 14,702
Middlebury, CT 06762 • 4,140
Middlebury, IN 46540 • 2,004
Middlebury, VT 05753 • 6,007
Middlefield, CT 06455 • 1,200
Middlefield, OH 44062 • 1,898
Middle Island, NY 11953 • 7,848
Middleport, NY 14105 • 1,876
Middleport, OH 45760 • 2,725
Middle River, MD 21220 • 24,616
Middlesboro, KY 40965 • 11,328
Middlesex, NJ 08846 • 13,055
Middlesex □, CT • 143,196
Middlesex □, MA • 1,398,468
Middlesex □, NJ • 671,780
Middlesex □, VA • 8,653
Middleton, ID 83644 • 1,851
Middleton, MA 01949 • 4,135
Middleton, WI 53562 • 13,289
Middletown, CA 95461 • 2,000
Middletown, CT 06457 • 42,762
Middletown, DE 19709 • 3,834
Middletown, IN 47356 • 2,333
Middletown, KY 40243 • 5,016
Middletown, MD 21769 • 1,834
Middletown, NJ 07718 • 62,298
Middletown, NY 10940 • 24,160
Middletown, OH 45042–44 • 46,022
Middletown, PA 17057 • 9,254
Middletown, RI 02840 • 3,350
Middletown, VA 22645 • 1,061
Middletown Township, PA 19037 • 6,866
Middleville, MI 49333 • 1,966
Midfield, AL 35228 • 5,559
Midland, MI 48640–42 • 38,053
Midland, PA 15059 • 3,321
Midland, TX 79701–12 • 89,443
Midland □, MI • 75,651
Midland □, TX • 106,611
Midland City, AL 36350 • 1,819
Midland Park, KS 67216 • 1,200
Midland Park, NJ 07432 • 7,047
Midland Park, SC 29405 • 1,300
Midlothian, IL 60445 • 14,372
Midlothian, TX 76065 • 5,141
Midvale, UT 84047 • 11,886
Midway, DE 19971 • 500
Midway, KY 40347 • 1,290
Midway, OR 97233 • 19,000
Midway, PA 15060 • 1,043
Midway, UT 84049 • 1,554
Midwest, WY 82643 • 495
Midwest City, OK 73110 • 52,267
Mifflin □, PA • 46,197
Mifflinburg, PA 17844 • 3,480
Mifflinville, PA 18631 • 1,329
Milaca, MN 56353 • 2,182
Milam □, TX • 22,946
Milan, GA 31060 • 1,056
Milan, IL 61264 • 5,831
Milan, IN 47031 • 1,529
Milan, MI 48160 • 4,040
Milan, MO 63556 • 1,767
Milan, NM 87021 • 1,911
Milan, OH 44846 • 1,464
Milan, TN 38358 • 7,512
Milbank, SD 57252 • 3,879
Milesburg, PA 16853 • 1,144
Miles City, MT 59301 • 8,461
Milford, CT 06460 • 48,168
Milford, DE 19963 • 6,040
Milford, IL 60953 • 1,512
Milford, IN 46542 • 1,388
Milford, IA 51351 • 2,170
Milford, ME 04461 • 2,228
Milford, MA 01757 • 23,339
Milford, MI 48380–82 • 5,511
Milford, NE 68405 • 1,886
Milford, NH 03055 • 8,015
Milford, NJ 08848 • 1,273
Milford, OH 45150 • 5,660
Milford, PA 18337 • 1,064
Milford, UT 84751 • 1,107
Mililani Town, HI 96789 • 29,359
Millard □, UT • 11,333
Millbrae, CA 94030 • 20,412
Millbrook, AL 36054 • 6,050
Millbrook, NY 12545 • 1,339
Millburn, NJ 07041 • 18,630
Millbury, MA 01527 • 4,940
Millbury, OH 43447 • 1,081
Mill City, OR 97360 • 1,555
Millcreek, UT 84109 • 32,230
Millcreek Township, PA 16505 • 46,100
Milledgeville, GA 31061 • 17,727
Milledgeville, IL 61051 • 1,076
Mille Lacs □, MN • 18,670
Millen, GA 30442 • 3,808
Miller, SD 57362 • 1,678
Miller □, AR • 38,467
Miller □, GA • 6,280
Miller □, MO • 20,700
Miller Place, NY 11764 • 9,315
Millersburg, OH 44654 • 3,051
Millersburg, PA 17061 • 2,729
Millers Falls, MA 01349 • 1,084
Millersport, OH 43046 • 1,010
Millersville, PA 17551 • 8,099
Mill Hall, PA 17751 • 1,702
Milliken, CO 80543 • 1,605
Millington, MI 48746 • 1,114
Millington, TN 38053 • 17,866
Millinocket, ME 04462 • 6,922
Millis, MA 02054 • 3,777
Millport, AL 35576 • 1,203
Mills, WY 82644 • 1,574
Mills □, IA • 13,202
Mills □, TX • 4,531
Millsboro, DE 19966 • 1,643
Millstadt, IL 62260 • 2,566
Milltown, NJ 08850 • 6,968
Millvale, PA 15209 • 4,341
Mill Valley, CA 94941–42 • 13,038
Millville, MA 01529 • 1,693
Millville, NJ 08332 • 25,992
Millville, UT 84326 • 1,202
Millwood, WA 99212 • 1,559
Milnor, ND 58060 • 651
Milo, ME 04463 • 2,129
Milpitas, CA 95035–36 • 50,686
Milroy, PA 17063 • 1,456
Milstead, GA 30207 • 1,500
Milton, DE 19968 • 1,417
Milton, FL 32570–71 • 7,216
Milton, MA 02186 • 25,725
Milton, NH 03851 • 1,000
Milton, NY 12547 • 1,140
Milton, PA 17847 • 6,746
Milton, VT 05468 • 1,578
Milton, WA 98354 • 4,995
Milton, WV 25541 • 2,242
Milton, WI 53563 • 4,434
Milton-Freewater, OR 97862 • 5,533
Milwaukee, WI 53201–95 • 628,088
Milwaukee □, WI • 959,275
Milwaukie, OR 97222 • 18,692
Mimosa Park, LA 70070 • 4,516
Mims, FL 32754 • 9,412
Mina, NV 89422 • 400
Minco, OK 73059 • 1,411
Minden, LA 71055 • 13,661
Minden, NE 68959 • 2,749
Minden, NV 89423 • 1,441
Mine Hill, NJ 07801 • 3,250
Mineola, NY 11501 • 18,994
Mineola, TX 75773 • 4,321
Miner, MO 63801 • 1,218
Miner □, SD • 3,272
Mineral □, CO • 558
Mineral □, MT • 3,315
Mineral □, NV • 6,475
Mineral □, WV • 26,697
Mineral Point, WI 53565 • 2,428
Mineral Springs, AR 71851 • 1,004
Mineral Wells, TX 76067 • 14,870
Minersville, PA 17954 • 4,877
Minerva, OH 44657 • 4,318
Minetto, NY 13115 • 1,252
Mineville, NY 12956 • 1,000
Mingo □, WV • 33,739
Mingo Junction, OH 43938 • 4,297
Minidoka □, ID • 19,361
Minier, IL 61759 • 1,155
Minneapolis, KS 67467 • 1,983
Minneapolis, MN 55401–80 • 368,383
Minnehaha □, SD • 123,809
Minneota, MN 56264 • 1,417
Minnetonka, MN 55345 • 48,370
Minocqua, WI 54548 • 1,280
Minonk, IL 61760 • 1,982
Minooka, IL 60447 • 2,561
Minot, ND 58701–02 • 34,544
Minquadale, DE 19720 • 790
Minster, OH 45865 • 2,650
Mint Hill, NC 28212 • 11,567
Minturn, CO 81645 • 1,066
Mio, MI 48647 • 1,500
Mira Loma, CA 91752 • 15,786
Miramar, FL 33023 • 40,663
Misenheimer, NC 28109 • 1,000
Mishawaka, IN 46544–46 • 42,608
Mishicot, WI 54228 • 1,296
Missaukee □, MI • 12,147
Mission, KS 66205 • 9,504
Mission, TX 78572 • 28,653
Mission Hills, KS 66205 • 3,446
Mission Viejo, CA 92691 • 72,820
Mississippi □, AR • 57,525
Mississippi □, MO • 14,442
Mississippi State, MS 39762 • 12,400
Missoula, MT 59801–07 • 42,918
Missoula □, MT • 78,687
Missouri City, TX 77459 • 36,176
Missouri Valley, IA 51555 • 2,888
Mitchell, IL 62040 • 1,320
Mitchell, IN 47446 • 4,669
Mitchell, NE 69357 • 1,743
Mitchell, SD 57301 • 13,798
Mitchell □, GA • 20,275
Mitchell □, IA • 10,928
Mitchell □, KS • 7,203
Mitchell □, NC • 14,433
Mitchell □, TX • 8,016
Mitchellville, IA 50169 • 1,670
Mizpah, NJ 08342 • 1,000
Moab, UT 84532 • 3,971
Moberly, MO 65270 • 12,839
Mobile, AL 36601–95 • 196,278
Mobile □, AL • 378,643
Mobridge, SD 57601 • 3,768
Mocanaqua, PA 18655 • 1,100
Mocksville, NC 27028 • 3,399
Modesto, CA 95350–56 • 164,730
Modoc □, CA • 9,678
Moenkopi, AZ 86045 • 1,200
Moffat □, CO • 11,357
Mogadore, OH 44260 • 4,008
Mohall, ND 58761 • 931
Mohave □, AZ • 93,497
Mohawk, NY 13407 • 2,986
Mohnton, PA 19540 • 2,484
Mojave, CA 93501–02 • 3,763
Mokena, IL 60448 • 6,128
Molalla, OR 97038 • 3,651
Moline, IL 61265 • 43,202
Molino, FL 32577 • 1,207
Momence, IL 60954 • 2,968
Monaca, PA 15061 • 6,739
Monahans, TX 79756 • 8,101
Monarch Mills, SC 29379 • 2,214
Moncks Corner, SC 29461 • 5,607
Mondovi, WI 54755 • 2,491
Monee, IL 60449 • 1,044
Monessen, PA 15062 • 9,901
Monett, MO 65708 • 6,529
Monette, AR 72447 • 1,115
Monfort Heights, OH 45239 • 9,745
Moniteau □, MO • 12,298
Monmouth, IL 61462 • 9,489
Monmouth, OR 97361 • 6,288
Monmouth □, NJ • 553,124
Monmouth Beach, NJ 07750 • 3,303
Monmouth Junction, NJ 08852 • 1,570
Mono □, CA • 9,956
Monon, IN 47959 • 1,585
Monona, IA 52159 • 1,520
Monona, WI 53716 • 8,637
Monona □, IA • 10,034
Monongah, WV 26554 • 1,018
Monongahela, PA 15063 • 4,928
Monongalia □, WV • 75,509
Monroe, GA 30655 • 9,759
Monroe, IA 50170 • 1,739
Monroe, LA 71201–13 • 54,909
Monroe, MI 48161 • 22,902
Monroe, NY 10950 • 6,672
Monroe, NC 28110–12 • 16,127
Monroe, OH 45050 • 4,490
Monroe, UT 84754 • 1,472
Monroe, WA 98272 • 4,278
Monroe, WI 53566 • 10,241
Monroe □, AL • 23,968
Monroe □, AR • 11,333
Monroe □, FL • 78,024
Monroe □, GA • 17,113
Monroe □, IL • 22,422
Monroe □, IN • 108,978
Monroe □, IA • 8,114
Monroe □, KY • 11,401
Monroe □, MI • 133,600
Monroe □, MS • 36,582
Monroe □, MO • 9,104
Monroe □, NY • 713,968
Monroe □, OH • 15,497
Monroe □, PA • 95,709
Monroe □, TN • 30,541
Monroe □, WV • 12,406
Monroe □, WI • 36,633
Monroe Center, CT 06468 • 7,900
Monroe City, MO 63456 • 2,701
Monroe Park, DE 19807 • 1,000
Monroeville, AL 36460–61 • 6,993
Monroeville, IN 46773 • 1,232
Monroeville, OH 44847 • 1,381
Monroeville, PA 15146 • 29,169
Monrovia, CA 91016 • 35,761
Monsey, NY 10952 • 13,986
Monson, MA 01057 • 2,101
Montague, CA 96064 • 1,415
Montague, MI 49437 • 2,276
Montague □, TX • 17,274
Mont Alto, PA 17237 • 1,395
Montauk, NY 11954 • 3,001
Mont Belvieu, TX 77580 • 1,323
Montcalm □, MI • 53,059
Montchanin, DE 19710 • 500
Montclair, CA 91763 • 28,434
Montclair, NJ 07042–44 • 37,729
Mont Clare, PA 19453 • 1,800
Monteagle, TN 37356 • 1,138
Montebello, CA 90640 • 59,564
Montecito, CA 93108 • 9,300

Montello, NV 89830 • 200
Montello, WI 53949 • 1,329
Monterey, CA 93940 • 31,954
Monterey, TN 38574 • 2,559
Monterey □, CA • 355,660
Monterey Park, CA 91754 • 60,738
Montesano, WA 98563 • 3,064
Montevallo, AL 35115 • 4,239
Montevideo, MN 56265 • 5,499
Monte Vista, CO 81144 • 4,324
Montezuma, GA 31063 • 4,506
Montezuma, IN 47862 • 1,134
Montezuma, IA 50171 • 1,651
Montezuma □, CO • 18,672
Montgomery, AL 36101–99 • 187,106
Montgomery, IL 60538 • 4,267
Montgomery, MN 56069 • 2,399
Montgomery, NY 12549 • 2,696
Montgomery, OH 45242 • 9,753
Montgomery, PA 17752 • 1,631
Montgomery, WV 25136 • 2,449
Montgomery □, AL • 209,085
Montgomery □, AR • 7,841
Montgomery □, GA • 7,163
Montgomery □, IL • 30,728
Montgomery □, IN • 34,436
Montgomery □, IA • 12,076
Montgomery □, KS • 38,816
Montgomery □, KY • 19,561
Montgomery □, MD • 757,027
Montgomery □, MS • 12,388
Montgomery □, MO • 11,355
Montgomery □, NY • 51,981
Montgomery □, NC • 23,346
Montgomery □, OH • 573,809
Montgomery □, PA • 678,111
Montgomery □, TN • 100,498
Montgomery □, TX • 182,201
Montgomery □, VA • 73,913
Montgomery City, MO 63361 • 2,281
Montgomery Village, MD 20879 • 32,315
Monticello, AR 71655 • 8,116
Monticello, FL 32344 • 2,573
Monticello, GA 31064 • 2,289
Monticello, IL 61856 • 4,549
Monticello, IN 47960 • 5,237
Monticello, IA 52310 • 3,522
Monticello, KY 42633 • 5,357
Monticello, MN 55362 • 4,941
Monticello, MS 39654 • 1,755
Monticello, NY 12701 • 6,597
Monticello, UT 84535 • 1,806
Monticello, WI 53570 • 1,140
Montmorency □, MI • 8,936
Montour □, PA • 17,735
Montour Falls, NY 14865 • 1,845
Montoursville, PA 17754 • 4,983
Montpelier, ID 83254 • 2,656
Montpelier, IN 47359 • 1,880
Montpelier, OH 43543 • 4,299
Montpelier, VT 05601–02 • 8,247
Montrose, AL 36559 • 1,400
Montrose, CO 81401–02 • 8,854
Montrose, MI 48457 • 1,811
Montrose, PA 18801 • 1,982
Montrose, VA 23231 • 6,405
Montrose □, CO • 24,423
Montvale, NJ 07645 • 6,946
Montville, CT 06353 • 16,673
Montville, NJ 07045 • 2,600
Monument, CO 80132 • 1,020
Monument Beach, MA 02553 • 1,800
Monument Heights, VA 23226 • 2,500
Moodus, CT 06469 • 1,170
Moody, TX 76557 • 1,329
Moody □, SD • 6,507
Moonachie, NJ 07074 • 2,817
Moorcroft, WY 82721 • 768
Moore, OK 73160 • 40,318
Moore □, NC • 59,013
Moore □, TN • 4,721
Moore □, TX • 17,865
Moorefield, WV 26836 • 2,148
Moore Haven, FL 33471 • 1,432
Mooreland, OK 73852 • 1,157
Moorestown, NJ 08057 • 16,500
Mooresville, IN 46158 • 5,541
Mooresville, NC 28115 • 9,317
Moorhead, MN 56560–61 • 32,295
Moorhead, MS 38761 • 2,417
Moorpark, CA 93020–21 • 25,494
Moose Lake, MN 55767 • 1,206
Moosic, PA 18507 • 5,339
Moosup, CT 06354 • 3,289
Mora, MN 55051 • 2,905
Mora, NM 87732 • 1,200
Mora □, NM • 4,264
Moraga, CA 94556 • 15,852
Moraine, OH 45439 • 5,989
Moravia, NY 13118 • 1,559
Morehead, KY 40351 • 8,357
Morehead City, NC 28557 • 6,046
Morehouse, MO 63868 • 1,068
Morehouse □, LA • 31,938
Morenci, AZ 85540 • 1,799
Morenci, MI 49256 • 2,342
Moreno Valley, CA 92387–88 • 118,779
Morgan, UT 84050 • 2,023
Morgan □, AL • 100,043
Morgan □, CO • 21,939
Morgan □, GA • 12,883
Morgan □, IL • 36,397
Morgan □, IN • 55,920
Morgan □, KY • 11,648
Morgan □, MO • 15,574
Morgan □, OH • 14,194
Morgan □, TN • 17,300
Morgan □, UT • 5,528
Morgan □, WV • 12,128
Morgan City, LA 70380–81 • 14,531
Morganfield, KY 42437 • 3,776
Morgan Hill, CA 95037–38 • 23,928
Morganton, NC 28655 • 15,085
Morgantown, KY 42261 • 2,284
Morgantown, MS 39120 • 3,288
Morgantown, WV 26502–07 • 25,879
Moriarty, NM 87035 • 1,399
Morningdale, MA 01505 • 1,130
Morocco, IN 47963 • 1,044
Moroni, UT 84646 • 1,115
Morrill □, NE • 5,423
Morrilton, AR 72110 • 6,551
Morris, AL 35116 • 1,136
Morris, IL 60450 • 10,270
Morris, MN 56267 • 5,613
Morris, OK 74445 • 1,216
Morris □, KS • 6,198
Morris □, NJ • 421,353
Morris □, TX • 13,200
Morrison, IL 61270 • 4,363
Morrison □, MN • 29,604
Morrison City, TN 37660 • 2,032
Morrisonville, IL 62546 • 1,113
Morrisonville, NY 12962 • 1,742
Morris Plains, NJ 07950 • 5,219
Morristown, NJ 07960–63 • 16,189
Morristown, TN 37813–16 • 21,385
Morrisville, NY 13408 • 2,732
Morrisville, PA 19067 • 9,765
Morrisville, VT 05661 • 1,984
Morro Bay, CA 93442–43 • 9,664
Morrow, GA 30260 • 5,168
Morrow, OH 45152 • 1,206
Morrow □, OH • 27,749
Morrow □, OR • 7,625
Morton, IL 61550 • 13,799
Morton, MS 39117 • 3,212
Morton, TX 79346 • 2,597
Morton, WA 98356 • 1,130
Morton □, KS • 3,480
Morton □, ND • 23,700
Morton Grove, IL 60053 • 22,408
Moscow, ID 83843 • 18,519
Moscow, PA 18444 • 1,527
Moses Lake, WA 98837 • 11,235
Mosheim, TN 37818 • 1,451
Mosinee, WI 54455 • 3,820
Moss Bluff, LA 70611 • 8,039
Moss Point, MS 39563 • 17,837
Motley □, TX • 1,532
Mott, ND 58646 • 1,019
Moulton, AL 35650 • 3,248
Moultrie, GA 31768 • 14,865
Moultrie □, IL • 13,930
Mound, MN 55364 • 9,634
Mound Bayou, MS 38762 • 2,222
Mound City, MO 64470 • 1,273
Moundridge, KS 67107 • 1,531
Mounds, IL 62964 • 1,407
Mounds View, MN 55432 • 12,541
Moundsville, WV 26041 • 10,753
Moundville, AL 35474 • 1,348
Mountainair, NM 87036 • 926
Mountain Brook, AL 35223 • 19,810
Mountain City, NV 89831 • 110
Mountain City, TN 37683 • 2,169
Mountain Grove, MO 65711 • 4,182
Mountain Home, AR 72653 • 9,027
Mountain Home, ID 83647 • 7,913
Mountain Iron, MN 55768 • 3,362
Mountain Lake, MN 56159 • 1,906
Mountain Lake Park, MD 21550 • 1,938
Mountain Lakes, NJ 07046 • 3,847
Mountain Park, GA 30087 • 11,025
Mountainside, NJ 07092 • 6,657
Mountain View, AR 72560 • 2,439
Mountain View, CA 94039–43 • 67,460
Mountain View, CO 80521 • 2,100
Mountain View, MO 65548 • 2,036
Mountain View, NM 87105 • 2,300
Mountain View, OK 73062 • 1,086
Mountain View, WY 82604 • 1,200
Mountain View, WY 82939 • 1,189
Mountain Village, AK 99632 • 674
Mount Airy, MD 21771 • 3,730
Mount Airy, NC 27030 • 7,156
Mount Angel, OR 97362 • 2,778
Mount Arlington, NJ 07856 • 3,630
Mount Ayr, IA 50854 • 1,796
Mount Carmel, IL 62863 • 8,287
Mount Carmel, PA 17851 • 7,196
Mount Carroll, IL 61053 • 1,726
Mount Clemens, MI 48043–46 • 18,405
Mount Dora, FL 32757 • 7,196
Mount Ephraim, NJ 08059 • 4,517
Mount Freedom, NJ 07970 • 1,920
Mount Gay, WV 25637 • 1,200
Mount Gilead, NC 27306 • 1,336
Mount Gilead, OH 43338 • 2,846
Mount Healthy, OH 45231 • 7,580
Mount Holly, NJ 08060 • 10,639
Mount Holly, NC 28120 • 7,710
Mount Holly Springs, PA 17065 • 1,925
Mount Hope, WV 25880 • 1,573
Mount Horeb, WI 53572 • 4,182
Mount Jackson, VA 22842 • 1,583
Mount Jewett, PA 16740 • 1,029
Mount Joy, PA 17552 • 6,398
Mount Juliet, TN 37122 • 5,389
Mount Kisco, NY 10549 • 9,108
Mountlake Terrace, WA 98043 • 19,320
Mount Lebanon, PA 15228 • 33,362
Mount Morris, IL 61054 • 2,919
Mount Morris, MI 48458 • 3,292
Mount Morris, NY 14510 • 3,102
Mount Olive, AL 35117 • 2,270
Mount Olive, IL 62069 • 2,126
Mount Olive, NC 28365 • 4,582
Mount Olympus, UT 84117 • 7,413
Mount Orab, OH 45154 • 1,929
Mount Penn, PA 19606 • 2,883
Mount Pleasant, IA 52641 • 8,027
Mount Pleasant, MI 48858–59 • 23,285
Mount Pleasant, NC 28124 • 1,027
Mount Pleasant, PA 15666 • 4,787
Mount Pleasant, SC 29464–65 • 30,108
Mount Pleasant, TN 38474 • 4,278
Mount Pleasant, TX 75455 • 12,291
Mount Pleasant, UT 84647 • 2,092
Mount Pocono, PA 18344 • 1,795
Mount Prospect, IL 60056 • 53,170
Mount Pulaski, IL 62548 • 1,610
Mountrail □, ND • 7,021
Mount Rainier, MD 20712 • 7,954
Mount Savage, MD 21545 • 1,640
Mount Shasta, CA 96067 • 3,460
Mount Sinai, NY 11766 • 8,023
Mount Sterling, IL 62353 • 1,922
Mount Sterling, KY 40353 • 5,362
Mount Sterling, OH 43143 • 1,647
Mount Union, PA 17066 • 2,878
Mount Vernon, GA 30445 • 1,914
Mount Vernon, IL 62864 • 16,988
Mount Vernon, IN 47620 • 7,217
Mount Vernon, IA 52314 • 3,657
Mount Vernon, KY 40456 • 2,654
Mount Vernon, MO 65712 • 3,726
Mount Vernon, NY 10550–53 • 67,153
Mount Vernon, OH 43050 • 14,550
Mount Vernon, TX 75457 • 2,219
Mount Vernon, WA 98273 • 17,647
Mount View, RI 02852 • 610
Mount Washington, KY 40047 • 5,226
Mount Wolf, PA 17347 • 1,365
Mount Zion, IL 62549 • 4,522
Moville, IA 51039 • 1,306
Moweaqua, IL 62550 • 1,785
Mower □, MN • 37,385
Moyock, NC 27958 • 1,400
Muenster, TX 76252 • 1,387
Muhlenberg □, KY • 31,318
Mukilteo, WA 98275 • 7,007
Mukwonago, WI 53149 • 4,457
Mulberry, AR 72947 • 1,448
Mulberry, FL 33860 • 2,988
Mulberry, IN 46058 • 1,262
Mulberry, NC 28659 • 2,339
Muldraugh, KY 40155 • 1,376
Muldrow, OK 74948 • 2,889
Muleshoe, TX 79347 • 4,571
Mullan, ID 83846 • 821
Mullens, WV 25882 • 2,006
Mullica Hill, NJ 08062 • 1,117
Mullins, SC 29574 • 5,910
Multnomah □, OR • 583,887
Mulvane, KS 67110 • 4,674
Muncie, IN 47302–08 • 71,035
Muncy, PA 17756 • 2,702
Munday, TX 76371 • 1,600
Mundelein, IL 60060 • 21,215
Munford, TN 38058 • 2,326
Munfordville, KY 42765 • 1,556
Munhall, PA 15120 • 13,158
Munising, MI 49862 • 2,783
Munster, IN 46321 • 19,949
Murfreesboro, AR 71958 • 1,542
Murfreesboro, NC 27855 • 2,580
Murfreesboro, TN 37129–33 • 44,922
Murphy, MO 63026 • 9,342
Murphy, NC 28906 • 1,575
Murphys, CA 95247 • 1,517
Murphysboro, IL 62966 • 9,176
Murray, KY 42071 • 14,439
Murray, UT 84107 • 31,282
Murray □, GA • 26,147
Murray □, MN • 9,660
Murray □, OK • 12,042
Murrells Inlet, SC 29576 • 3,334
Murrysville, PA 15668 • 17,240
Muscatine, IA 52761 • 22,881
Muscatine □, IA • 39,907
Muscle Shoals, AL 35661 • 9,611
Muscoda, WI 53573 • 1,287
Muscogee □, GA • 179,278
Muscoy, CA 92405 • 7,541
Muse, PA 15350 • 1,250
Muskego, WI 53150 • 16,813
Muskegon, MI 49440–45 • 40,283
Muskegon □, MI • 158,983
Muskegon Heights, MI 49444 • 13,176
Muskingum □, OH • 82,068
Muskogee, OK 74401–03 • 37,708
Muskogee □, OK • 68,078
Musselshell □, MT • 4,106
Mustang, OK 73064 • 10,434
Myerstown, PA 17067 • 3,236
Myrtle Beach, SC 29577–78 • 24,848
Myrtle Grove, FL 32506 • 17,402
Myrtle Point, OR 97458 • 2,712
Mystic, CT 06355 • 2,618
Mystic Island, NJ 08087 • 7,400

N

Naalehu, HI 96772 • 1,027
Naamans Gardens, DE 19810 • 1,500
Nabnasset, MA 01886 • 3,600
Nacogdoches, TX 75961–63 • 30,872
Nacogdoches □, TX • 54,753
Nags Head, NC 27959 • 1,838
Nahant, MA 01908 • 3,828
Nahunta, GA 31553 • 1,049
Nampa, ID 83651–53 • 28,365
Nanakuli, HI 96792 • 9,575
Nance □, NE • 4,275
Nanticoke, PA 18634 • 12,267
Nantucket, MA 02554 • 3,069
Nantucket □, MA • 6,012
Nanty Glo, PA 15943 • 3,190
Nanuet, NY 10954 • 14,065
Napa, CA 94558–59 • 61,842
Napa □, CA • 110,765
Napanoch, NY 12458 • 1,068
Naperville, IL 60540 • 85,351
Naples, FL 33939–42 • 19,505
Naples, NY 14512 • 1,237
Naples, TX 75568 • 1,508
Naples, UT 84078 • 1,334
Naples Park, FL 33963 • 8,002
Napoleon, ND 58561 • 930
Napoleon, OH 43545 • 8,884
Nappanee, IN 46550 • 5,510
Naranja, FL 33032 • 5,790
Narberth, PA 19072 • 4,278
Narragansett, RI 02882 • 3,721
Narrows, VA 24124 • 2,082
Naselle, WA 98638 • 1,000
Nash, TX 75569 • 2,162
Nash □, NC • 76,677
Nashua, IA 50658 • 1,476
Nashua, NH 03060–63 • 79,662
Nashville, AR 71852 • 4,639
Nashville, GA 31639 • 4,782
Nashville, IL 62263 • 3,202
Nashville, MI 49073 • 1,654
Nashville, NC 27856 • 3,617
Nashville, TN 37201–35 • 487,969
Nashwauk, MN 55769 • 1,026
Nassau, NY 12123 • 1,254
Nassau □, FL • 43,941
Nassau □, NY • 1,287,348
Nassau Shores, NY 11758 • 5,110
Natalia, TX 78059 • 1,216
Natchez, MS 39120–22 • 19,460
Natchitoches, LA 71457–58 • 16,609
Natchitoches □, LA • 36,689
Natick, MA 01760 • 30,100
National City, CA 91950–51 • 54,249
National Park, NJ 08063 • 3,413
Natrona □, WY • 61,226
Natrona Heights, PA 15065 • 12,200
Naugatuck, CT 06770 • 30,625
Nautilus Park, CT 06340 • 6,500
Nauvoo, IL 62354 • 1,108
Navajo □, AZ • 77,658
Navarre, OH 44662 • 1,635
Navarro □, TX • 39,926
Navasota, TX 77868–69 • 6,296
Navesink, NJ 07752 • 1,420
Nazareth, PA 18064 • 5,713
Neah Bay, WA 98357 • 1,300
Nebraska City, NE 68410 • 6,547
Nederland, CO 80466 • 1,099
Nederland, TX 77627 • 16,192
Nedrow, NY 13120 • 2,980
Needham, MA 02192 • 27,557
Needles, CA 92363 • 5,191
Needville, TX 77461 • 2,199
Neenah, WI 54956–57 • 23,219
Neffs, OH 43940 • 1,213
Negaunee, MI 49866 • 4,741
Neillsville, WI 54456 • 2,680
Nekoosa, WI 54457 • 2,557
Neligh, NE 68756 • 1,742
Nelson □, KY • 29,710
Nelson □, ND • 4,410
Nelson □, VA • 12,778
Nelsonville, OH 45764 • 4,563
Nemacolin, PA 15351 • 1,097
Nemaha □, KS • 10,446
Nemaha □, NE • 7,980
Nenana, AK 99760 • 393
Neodesha, KS 66757 • 2,837
Neoga, IL 62447 • 1,678
Neosho, MO 64850 • 9,254
Neosho □, KS • 17,035
Nephi, UT 84648 • 3,515
Neptune, NJ 07753 • 28,366
Neptune Beach, FL 32233 • 6,816
Neptune City, NJ 07753 • 4,997
Nesconset, NY 11767 • 10,712
Nescopeck, PA 18635 • 1,651
Neshoba □, MS • 24,800
Nesquehoning, PA 18240 • 3,364
Ness □, KS • 4,033
Ness City, KS 67560 • 1,724
Netcong, NJ 07857 • 3,311
Nether Providence Township, PA 19013 • 13,229
Nettleton, MS 38858 • 2,462
Nevada, IA 50201 • 6,009
Nevada, MO 64772 • 8,597
Nevada □, AR • 10,101
Nevada □, CA • 78,510
Nevada City, CA 95959 • 2,855
New Albany, IN 47150–51 • 36,322
New Albany, MS 38652 • 6,775
New Albany, OH 43054 • 1,621
Newark, AR 72562 • 1,159
Newark, CA 94560 • 37,861
Newark, DE 19711–15 • 25,098
Newark, NJ 07101–75 • 275,221
Newark, NY 14513 • 9,849
Newark, OH 43055–58 • 44,389
Newark Valley, NY 13811 • 1,082
New Athens, IL 62264 • 2,010
Newaygo, MI 49337 • 1,336
Newaygo □, MI • 38,202
New Baden, IL 62265 • 2,602
New Baltimore, MI 48047 • 5,798
New Bedford, MA 02740–48 • 99,922
Newberg, OR 97132 • 13,086
New Berlin, NY 13411 • 1,220
New Berlin, WI 53151 • 33,592
New Bern, NC 28560–64 • 17,363
Newbern, TN 38059 • 2,515
Newberry, FL 32669 • 1,644
Newberry, MI 49868 • 1,873
Newberry, SC 29108 • 10,542
Newberry □, SC • 33,172
New Bethlehem, PA 16242 • 1,151
New Bloomfield, PA 17068 • 1,092
New Boston, MI 48164 • 1,200
New Boston, OH 45662 • 2,717
New Boston, TX 75570 • 5,057
New Braunfels, TX 78130–33 • 27,334
New Bremen, OH 45869 • 2,558
New Brighton, MN 55112 • 22,207
New Brighton, PA 15066 • 6,854
New Britain, CT 06050–53 • 75,491
New Brockton, AL 36351 • 1,184
New Brunswick, NJ 08901–06 • 41,711
New Buffalo, MI 49117 • 2,317
Newburg, KY 40218 • 21,647
Newburgh, IN 47629–30 • 2,880
Newburgh, NY 12550–53 • 26,454
Newburgh Heights, OH 44105 • 2,310
Newburyport, MA 01950–52 • 16,317
New Canaan, CT 06840 • 17,864
New Carlisle, IN 46552 • 1,446
New Carlisle, OH 45344 • 6,049
New Carrollton, MD 20784 • 12,002
New Cassel, NY 11590 • 10,257
New Castle, AL 35119 • 1,100
New Castle, DE 19720 • 4,837
New Castle, IN 47362 • 17,753
Newcastle, OK 73065 • 4,214
New Castle, PA 16101–08 • 28,334
Newcastle, WY 82701 • 3,003
New Castle □, DE • 441,946
New City, NY 10956 • 33,673
Newcomerstown, OH 43832 • 4,012
New Concord, OH 43762 • 2,086
New Cumberland, PA 17070 • 7,665
New Cumberland, WV 26047 • 1,363
New Egypt, NJ 08533 • 2,327
Newell, IA 50568 • 1,089
Newell, WV 26050 • 1,724
New Ellenton, SC 29809 • 2,515
Newellton, LA 71357 • 1,576
New England, ND 58647 • 663
New Fairfield, CT 06812 • 4,600
Newfane, NY 14108 • 3,001
Newfield, NJ 08344 • 1,592
New Franklin, MO 65274 • 1,107
New Freedom, PA 17349 • 2,920
New Glarus, WI 53574 • 1,899
New Hampton, IA 50659 • 3,660
New Hanover □, NC • 120,284
New Hartford, CT 06057 • 1,269
New Haven, CT 06501–36 • 130,474
New Haven, IN 46774 • 9,320
New Haven, MI 48048 • 2,331
New Haven, MO 63068 • 1,757
New Haven, WV 25265 • 1,632
New Haven □, CT • 804,219
New Holland, GA 30501 • 1,200
New Holland, PA 17557 • 4,484
New Holstein, WI 53061 • 3,342
New Hope, AL 35760 • 2,248
New Hope, MN 55428 • 21,853
New Hope, NC 27604 • 5,694
New Hope, PA 18938 • 1,400
New Hyde Park, NY 11040 • 9,728
New Iberia, LA 70560–62 • 31,828
Newington, CT 06131 • 29,208
Newington, VA 22122 • 17,965
New Johnsonville, TN 37134 • 1,643
New Kensington, PA 15068 • 15,894
New Kent □, VA • 10,445
Newkirk, OK 74647 • 2,168
New Lenox, IL 60451 • 9,627
New Lexington, OH 43764 • 5,117
New Lisbon, WI 53950 • 1,491
Newllano, LA 71461 • 2,660
New London, CT 06320 • 28,540
New London, IA 52645 • 1,922
New London, NH 03257 • 3,180
New London, OH 44851 • 2,642
New London, WI 54961 • 6,658
New London □, CT • 254,957
New Madrid, MO 63869 • 3,350
New Madrid □, MO • 20,928
Newman, CA 95360 • 4,151
Newmanstown, PA 17073 • 1,410
Newmarket, NH 03857 • 4,917
New Market, TN 37820 • 1,086
New Market, VA 22844 • 1,435
New Martinsville, WV 26155 • 6,705
New Matamoras, OH 45767 • 1,002
New Miami, OH 45011 • 2,555
New Milford, CT 06776 • 5,775
New Milford, NJ 07646 • 15,990
Newnan, GA 30263–65 • 12,497
New Orleans, LA 70101–95 • 496,938
New Oxford, PA 17350 • 1,617
New Paltz, NY 12561 • 5,463
New Paris, IN 46553 • 1,007
New Paris, OH 45347 • 1,801
New Philadelphia, OH 44663 • 15,698
New Philadelphia, PA 17959 • 1,283
New Plymouth, ID 83655 • 1,313
Newport, AR 72112 • 7,459
Newport, DE 19804 • 1,240
Newport, KY 41071–76 • 18,871
Newport, ME 04953 • 1,843
Newport, MI 48166 • 1,100
Newport, MN 55055 • 3,720
Newport, NH 03773 • 3,772
Newport, NC 28570 • 2,516
Newport, OR 97365 • 8,437
Newport, PA 17074 • 1,568
Newport, RI 02840 • 28,227
Newport, TN 37821 • 7,123
Newport, VT 05855 • 4,434
Newport, WA 99156 • 1,691
Newport □, RI • 87,194
Newport Beach, CA 92657–63 • 66,643
Newport East, RI 02840 • 11,080
Newport Hills, WA 98002 • 14,736
Newport News, VA 23601–09 • 170,045
New Port Richey, FL 34652–56 • 14,044
New Prague, MN 56071 • 3,569
New Preston, CT 06777 • 1,217
New Providence, NJ 07974 • 11,439
New Richland, MN 56072 • 1,237
New Richmond, OH 45157 • 2,408
New Richmond, WI 54017 • 5,106
New River Station, NC 28542 • 9,732
New Roads, LA 70760 • 5,303
New Rochelle, NY 10801–05 • 67,265
New Rockford, ND 58356 • 1,604
New Salem, ND 58563 • 909
New Sarpy, LA 70078 • 2,946
New Sharon, IA 50207 • 1,136
New Smyrna Beach, FL 32168–70 • 16,543
New Tazewell, TN 37825 • 1,864
Newton, AL 36352 • 1,580
Newton, IL 62448 • 3,154
Newton, IA 50208 • 14,789
Newton, KS 67114 • 16,700
Newton, MA 02158 • 82,585
Newton, MS 39345 • 3,701
Newton, NJ 07860 • 7,521
Newton, NC 28658 • 9,304
Newton, TX 75966 • 1,885
Newton □, AR • 7,666
Newton □, GA • 41,808
Newton □, IN • 13,551
Newton □, MS • 20,291
Newton □, MO • 44,445
Newton □, TX • 13,569
Newton Falls, OH 44444 • 4,866
Newtown, CT 06470 • 1,800
New Town, ND 58763 • 1,388
Newtown, OH 45244 • 1,589
Newtown Square, PA 19073 • 11,366
New Ulm, MN 56073 • 13,132
Newville, PA 17241 • 1,349
New Washington, OH 44854 • 1,057
New Washoe City, NV 89701 • 2,875
New Waterford, OH 44445 • 1,278
New Whiteland, IN 46184 • 4,097
New Wilmington, PA 16142 • 2,706
New Windsor, NY 12553 • 8,898
New York, NY 10001–99 • 7,322,564
New York □, NY • 1,487,536
Nez Perce □, ID • 33,754
Niagara, WI 54151 • 1,999
Niagara □, NY • 220,756
Niagara Falls, NY 14301–05 • 61,840
Niantic, CT 06357 • 3,048
Nibley, UT 84321 • 1,167
Niceville, FL 32578 • 10,507
Nicholas □, KY • 6,725
Nicholas □, WV • 26,775
Nicholasville, KY 40356 • 13,603
Nicholls, GA 31554 • 1,003
Nichols Hills, OK 73116 • 4,020
Nickerson, KS 67561 • 1,137
Nicollet □, MN • 28,076
Nicoma Park, OK 73066 • 2,353
Nikishka, AK 99635 • 1,109
Niland, CA 92257 • 1,183

Niles, IL 60648 • 28,284
Niles, MI 49120 • 12,458
Niles, OH 44446 • 21,128
Ninety Six, SC 29666 • 2,099
Ninilchik, AK 99639 • 456
Niobrara □, WY • 2,499
Nipomo, CA 93444 • 7,109
Niskayuna, NY 12309 • 4,942
Nisswa, MN 56468 • 1,391
Nitro, WV 25143 • 6,851
Niwot, CO 80544 • 2,666
Nixa, MO 65714 • 4,707
Nixon, NV 89424 • 150
Nixon, TX 78140 • 1,995
Noank, CT 06340 • 1,406
Noble, OK 73068 • 4,710
Noble □, IN • 37,877
Noble □, OH • 11,336
Noble □, OK • 11,045
Nobles □, MN • 20,098
Noblesville, IN 46060 • 17,655
Nocatee, FL 33864 • 1,300
Nocona, TX 76255 • 2,870
Nodaway □, MO • 21,709
Noel, MO 64854 • 1,169
Nogales, AZ 85621 • 19,489
Nokomis, FL 34274–75 • 3,448
Nokomis, IL 62075 • 2,534
Nolan □, TX • 16,594
Nome, AK 99762 • 3,500
Noorvik, AK 99763 • 531
Nora Springs, IA 50458 • 1,505
Norco, CA 91760 • 23,302
Norco, LA 70079 • 3,385
Norcross, GA 30071 • 5,947
Norfolk, CT 06058 • 1,500
Norfolk, NE 68701 • 21,476
Norfolk, NY 13667 • 1,412
Norfolk, VA 23501–93 • 261,229
Norfolk □, MA • 616,087
Norland, FL 33169 • 22,109
Normal, IL 61761 • 40,023
Norman, OK 73069–72 • 80,071
Norman □, MN • 7,975
Normandy, MO 63121 • 4,480
Norridge, IL 60656 • 14,459
Norridgewock, ME 04957 • 1,496
Norris, TN 37828 • 1,303
Norris City, IL 62869 • 1,341
Norristown, PA 19401–09 • 30,749
North Adams, MA 01247 • 16,797
North Albany, OR 97321 • 4,325
North Amherst, MA 01059 • 6,239
North Amityville, NY 11701 • 13,849
Northampton, MA 01060–61 • 29,289
Northampton, PA 18067 • 8,717
Northampton □, NC • 20,798
Northampton □, PA • 247,105
Northampton □, VA • 13,061
North Andover, MA 01845 • 20,129
North Andrews Gardens, FL 33308 • 9,002
North Apollo, PA 15673 • 1,391
North Arlington, NJ 07032 • 13,790
North Atlanta, GA 30319 • 27,812
North Attleboro, MA 02760–63 • 16,178
North Auburn, CA 95603 • 10,301
North Augusta, SC 29841 • 15,351
North Aurora, IL 60542 • 5,940
North Babylon, NY 11703 • 18,081
North Baltimore, OH 45872 • 3,139
North Bay Shore, NY 11706 • 12,799
North Beach, MD 20714 • 1,173
North Bellmore, NY 11710 • 19,707
North Bellport, NY 11713 • 8,182
North Belmont, NC 28012 • 10,762
North Bend, NE 68649 • 1,249
North Bend, OR 97459 • 9,614
North Bend, WA 98045 • 2,578
North Bennington, VT 05257 • 1,520
North Bergen, NJ 07047 • 48,414
North Berwick, ME 03906 • 1,568
North Billerica, MA 01862 • 5,400
Northborough, MA 01532 • 5,761
North Braddock, PA 15104 • 7,036
North Branch, MI 48461 • 1,023
North Branch, MN 55056 • 1,867
North Branch, NJ 08876 • 2,620
North Branford, CT 06471 • 6,600
Northbridge, MA 01534 • 3,570
Northbrook, IL 60062 • 32,308
Northbrook, OH 45231 • 11,471
North Brookfield, MA 01535 • 2,635
North Brunswick, NJ 08902 • 31,287
North Brunswick Township, NJ 08902 • 31,287
North Caldwell, NJ 07006 • 5,832
North Canton, OH 44720 • 14,748
North Cape May, NJ 08204 • 3,574
North Charleston, SC 29406 • 70,218
North Chicago, IL 60064 • 34,978
North City, WA 98155 • 8,200
North Cohasset, MA 02025 • 1,045
North College Hill, OH 45239 • 11,002
North Collins, NY 14111 • 1,335
North Conway, NH 03860 • 2,032
North Corbin, KY 40701 • 1,601
North Crossett, AR 71635 • 3,358
North Dartmouth, MA 02747 • 8,080
North Decatur, GA 30033 • 13,936
North Dighton, MA 02764 • 1,174
North Druid Hills, GA 30033 • 14,170
North Eagle Butte, SD 57625 • 1,423
North East, MD 21901 • 1,913
North East, PA 16428 • 4,617
North Eastham, MA 02651 • 1,570
Northeast Henrietta, NY 14534 • 10,650
North Easton, MA 02356 • 4,420
North Fair Oaks, CA 94025 • 13,912
North Falmouth, MA 02556 • 3,150
Northfield, IL 60093 • 4,635
Northfield, MA 01360 • 1,322
Northfield, MN 55057 • 14,684
Northfield, NH 03276 • 1,375
Northfield, NJ 08225 • 7,305
Northfield, OH 44067 • 3,624
Northfield, VT 05663 • 1,889
Northfield Falls, VT 05664 • 600
North Fond du Lac, WI 54935 • 4,292
Northford, CT 06472 • 3,180
North Fort Myers, FL 33903 • 30,027
Northglenn, CO 80233 • 27,195
North Grafton, MA 01536 • 3,050
North Great River, NY 11722 • 3,964
North Grosvenordale, CT 06255 • 1,705
North Gulfport, MS 39501 • 4,966
North Haledon, NJ 07508 • 7,987
North Hampton, NH 03862 • 1,000
North Haven, CT 06473 • 22,249
North Highlands, CA 95660 • 42,105
North Hill, WA 98166 • 5,706
North Houston, TX 77086 • 12,800
North Hudson, WI 54016 • 3,101
North Industry, OH 44707 • 3,250
North Judson, IN 46366 • 1,582
North Kansas City, MO 64116 • 4,130
North Kingstown, RI 02852–54 • 2,750
North Kingsville, OH 44068 • 2,672
North La Junta, CO 81050 • 1,076
Northlake, IL 60164 • 12,505
North Las Vegas, NV 89030–31 • 47,707
North Lauderdale, FL 33068 • 26,506
North Lewisburg, OH 43060 • 1,160
North Liberty, IN 46554 • 1,366
North Liberty, IA 52317 • 2,926
North Lindenhurst, NY 11757 • 10,563
North Little Rock, AR 72114–20 • 61,741
North Logan, UT 84321 • 3,768
North Madison, OH 44057 • 8,699
North Manchester, IN 46962 • 6,383
North Mankato, MN 56001 • 10,164
North Massapequa, NY 11758 • 19,365
North Merrick, NY 11566 • 12,113
North Merrydale, LA 70812 • 4,000
North Miami, FL 33161 • 49,998
North Miami Beach, FL 33162 • 35,359
North Muskegon, MI 49445 • 3,919
North Myrtle Beach, SC 29582 • 8,636
North Naples, FL 33963 • 13,422
North New Hyde Park, NY 11040 • 14,359
North Ogden, UT 84404 • 11,668
North Olmsted, OH 44070 • 34,204
North Oxford, MA 01537 • 1,250
North Palm Beach, FL 33408 • 11,343
North Park, IL 61111 • 15,806
North Patchogue, NY 11772 • 7,374
North Pembroke, MA 02358 • 2,485
North Plainfield, NJ 07060 • 18,820
North Platte, NE 69101–03 • 22,605
Northport, AL 35476 • 17,366
North Port, FL 34287 • 11,973
Northport, NY 11768 • 7,572
North Prairie, WI 53153 • 1,322
North Providence, RI 02911 • 32,090
North Reading, MA 01864 • 11,455
North Richland Hills, TX 76118 • 45,895
Northridge, OH 45502 • 5,939
Northridge, OH 45414 • 9,448
North Ridgeville, OH 44039 • 21,564
North Riverside, IL 60546 • 6,005
North Royalton, OH 44133 • 23,197
North Salt Lake, UT 84054 • 6,474
North Sarasota, FL 34234 • 6,702
North Scituate, MA 02060 • 4,891
North Sioux City, SD 57049 • 2,019
North Springfield, OR 97477 • 5,451
North Springfield, VT 05150 • 750
North Springfield, VA 22151 • 8,996
North Star, DE 19711 • 1,030
North St. Paul, MN 55109 • 12,376
North Sudbury, MA 01776 • 2,630
North Syracuse, NY 13212 • 7,363
North Tarrytown, NY 10591 • 8,152
North Terre Haute, IN 47805 • 2,000
North Tewksbury, MA 01876 • 1,030
North Tonawanda, NY 14120 • 34,989
North Troy, VT 05859 • 723
North Tunica, MS 38676 • 1,314
Northumberland, PA 17857 • 3,860
Northumberland □, PA • 96,771
Northumberland □, VA • 10,524
North Uxbridge, MA 01538 • 1,500
Northvale, NJ 07647 • 4,563
North Valley Stream, NY 11580 • 14,574
North Vernon, IN 47265 • 5,311
North Versailles, PA 15137 • 12,302
Northview, MI 49505 • 13,712
Northview, OH 45322 • 10,337
Northville, MI 48167 • 6,226
Northville, NY 12134 • 1,180
North Wales, PA 19454 • 3,802
North Wantagh, NY 11793 • 12,276
North Warren, PA 16365 • 1,232
North Wildwood, NJ 08260 • 5,017
North Wilkesboro, NC 28659 • 3,384
North Windham, ME 04062 • 4,077
Northwood, IA 50459 • 1,940
Northwood, ND 58267 • 1,166
Northwood, OH 43619 • 5,506
Northwoods, MO 63121 • 5,106
North York, PA 17404 • 1,689
Norton, KS 67654 • 3,017
Norton, MA 02766 • 1,899
Norton, OH 44203 • 11,477
Norton, VA 24273 • 4,247
Norton □, KS • 5,947
Norton Shores, MI 49441 • 21,755
Nortonville, KY 42442 • 1,209
Norwalk, CA 90650–52 • 94,279
Norwalk, CT 06850–56 • 78,331
Norwalk, IA 50211 • 5,726
Norwalk, OH 44857 • 14,731
Norway, ME 04268 • 3,023
Norway, MI 49870 • 2,910
Norwell, MA 02061 • 1,200
Norwich, CT 06360 • 37,391
Norwich, NY 13815 • 7,613
Norwich, VT 05055 • 1,000
Norwood, MA 02062 • 28,700
Norwood, MN 55368 • 1,351
Norwood, NJ 07648 • 4,858
Norwood, NY 13668 • 1,841
Norwood, NC 28128 • 1,617
Norwood, OH 45212 • 23,674
Norwood, PA 19074 • 6,162
Norwoodville, IA 50317 • 1,200
Nottoway □, VA • 14,993
Novato, CA 94947–49 • 47,585
Novi, MI 48374–77 • 32,998
Nowata, OK 74048 • 3,896
Nowata □, OK • 9,992
Noxubee □, MS • 12,604
Nuckolls □, NE • 5,786
Nueces □, TX • 291,145
Nulato, AK 99765 • 359
Nunda, NY 14517 • 1,347
Nutley, NJ 07110 • 27,099
Nutter Fort, WV 26301 • 1,819
Nutting Lake, MA 01865 • 3,180
Nyack, NY 10960 • 6,558
Nye □, NV • 17,781
Nyssa, OR 97913 • 2,629

O

Oak Bluffs, MA 02557 • 1,124
Oak Brook, IL 60521 • 9,178
Oak Creek, WI 53154 • 19,513
Oakdale, CA 95361 • 11,961
Oakdale, GA 30080 • 1,080
Oakdale, LA 71463 • 6,832
Oakdale, MN 55128 • 18,374
Oakdale, NY 11769 • 7,875
Oakdale, PA 15071 • 1,752
Oakes, ND 58474 • 1,775
Oakfield, NY 14125 • 1,818
Oakfield, WI 53065 • 1,003
Oak Forest, IL 60452 • 26,203
Oak Grove, KY 42262 • 2,863
Oak Grove, LA 71263 • 2,126
Oak Grove, OR 97267 • 12,576
Oak Grove, SC 29073 • 7,173
Oak Harbor, OH 43449 • 2,637
Oak Harbor, WA 98277 • 17,176
Oak Hill, MI 49660 • 1,000
Oak Hill, OH 45656 • 1,831
Oak Hill, WV 25901 • 6,812
Oakhurst, OK 74050 • 2,200
Oakland, CA 94601–62 • 372,242
Oakland, IA 51560 • 1,496
Oakland, ME 04963 • 3,510
Oakland, MD 21550 • 2,078
Oakland, NE 68045 • 1,279
Oakland, NJ 07436 • 11,997
Oakland, RI 02830 • 600
Oakland □, MI • 1,083,592
Oakland City, IN 47660 • 2,810
Oakland Park, FL 33334 • 26,326
Oak Lawn, IL 60453–59 • 56,182
Oaklawn, KS 67216 • 4,200
Oakley, CA 94561 • 18,374
Oakley, KS 67748 • 2,045
Oaklyn, NJ 08107 • 4,430
Oakmont, PA 15139 • 6,961
Oak Orchard, DE 19966 • 350
Oak Park, CA 91301 • 5,000
Oak Park, IL 60301–05 • 53,648
Oak Park, MI 48237 • 30,462
Oak Ridge, FL 32809 • 15,388
Oakridge, OR 97463 • 3,063
Oak Ridge, TN 37830 • 27,310
Oakton, VA 22124 • 24,610
Oak Valley, NJ 08090 • 5,400
Oakville, CT 06779 • 8,741
Oakville, MO 63129 • 31,750
Oakwood, GA 30566 • 1,464
Oakwood, IL 61858 • 1,533
Oakwood, OH 45419 • 3,392
Oberlin, KS 67749 • 2,197
Oberlin, LA 70655 • 1,808
Oberlin, OH 44074 • 8,191
Obetz, OH 43207 • 3,167
Obion, TN 38240 • 1,241
Obion □, TN • 31,717
Oblong, IL 62449 • 1,616
O'Brien □, IA • 15,444
Ocala, FL 32670–78 • 42,045
Ocean □, NJ • 433,203
Oceana, WV 24870 • 1,791
Oceana □, MI • 22,454
Ocean Bluff, MA 02065 • 2,500
Ocean City, FL 32548 • 5,422
Ocean City, MD 21842 • 5,146
Ocean City, NJ 08226 • 15,512
Ocean Gate, NJ 08740 • 2,078
Ocean Grove, MA 02777 • 4,560
Oceano, CA 93445 • 6,169
Ocean Park, WA 98640 • 1,650
Ocean Port, NJ 07757 • 6,146
Oceanside, CA 92054–56 • 128,398
Oceanside, NY 11572 • 32,423
Ocean Springs, MS 39564–65 • 14,658
Ocean [Township], NJ 07712 • 23,570
Ocean View, DE 19970 • 606
Oceanville, NJ 08231 • 1,000
Ochiltree □, TX • 9,128
Ocilla, GA 31774 • 3,182
Ocoee, FL 34761 • 12,778
Oconee □, GA • 17,618
Oconee □, SC • 57,494
Oconomowoc, WI 53066 • 10,993
Oconto, WI 54153 • 4,474
Oconto □, WI • 30,226
Oconto Falls, WI 54154 • 2,584
Odebolt, IA 51458 • 1,158
Odell, IL 60460 • 1,030
Odem, TX 78370 • 2,366
Odenton, MD 21113 • 12,833
Odessa, DE 19730 • 303
Odessa, MO 64076 • 3,695
Odessa, TX 79760–68 • 89,699
Odin, IL 62870 • 1,150
Odon, IN 47562 • 1,475
O'Donnell, TX 79351 • 1,102
Oelwein, IA 50662 • 6,493
O'Fallon, IL 62269 • 16,073
O'Fallon, MO 63366 • 18,698
Ogallala, NE 69153 • 5,095
Ogden, IA 50212 • 1,909
Ogden, KS 66517 • 1,494
Ogden, UT 84401–14 • 63,909
Ogdensburg, NJ 07439 • 2,722
Ogdensburg, NY 13669 • 13,521
Ogemaw □, MI • 18,681
Ogle □, IL • 45,957
Oglesby, IL 61348 • 3,619
Oglethorpe, GA 31068 • 1,302
Oglethorpe □, GA • 9,763
Ogunquit, ME 03907 • 1,492
Ohatchee, AL 36271 • 1,042
Ohio □, IN • 5,315
Ohio □, KY • 21,105
Ohio □, WV • 50,871
Ohioville, PA 15059 • 3,865
Oil City, LA 71061 • 1,282
Oil City, PA 16301 • 11,949
Oildale, CA 93308 • 26,553
Oilton, OK 74052 • 1,060
Ojai, CA 93023–24 • 7,613
Okaloosa □, FL • 143,776
Okanogan, WA 98840 • 2,370
Okanogan □, WA • 33,350
Okarche, OK 73762 • 1,160
Okauchee, WI 53069 • 2,300
Okauchee Lake, WI 53058 • 3,819
Okawville, IL 62271 • 1,274
Okeechobee, FL 34972–74 • 4,943
Okeechobee □, FL • 29,627
Okeene, OK 73763 • 1,343
Okemah, OK 74859 • 3,085
Okemos, MI 48864 • 20,216
Okfuskee □, OK • 11,551
Oklahoma □, OK • 599,611
Oklahoma City, OK 73101–80 • 444,719
Oklawaha, FL 32179 • 1,200
Okmulgee, OK 74447 • 13,441
Okmulgee □, OK • 36,490
Okolona, KY 40219 • 18,902
Okolona, MS 38860 • 3,267
Oktibbeha □, MS • 38,375
Ola, AR 72853 • 1,090
Olathe, CO 81425 • 1,263
Olathe, KS 66061–62 • 63,352
Olcott, NY 14126 • 1,432
Old Bethpage, NY 11804 • 5,610
Old Bridge, NJ 08857 • 22,151
Old Forge, NY 13420 • 1,061
Old Forge, PA 18518 • 8,834
Oldham □, KY • 33,263
Oldham □, TX • 2,278
Old Harbor, AK 99643 • 284
Old Orchard Beach, ME 04064 • 7,789
Old Saybrook, CT 06475 • 1,820
Oldsmar, FL 34677 • 8,361
Old Tappan, NJ 07675 • 4,254
Old Town, ME 04468 • 8,317
Olean, NY 14760 • 16,946
Olive Branch, MS 38654 • 3,567
Olive Hill, KY 41164 • 1,809
Olivehurst, CA 95961 • 9,738
Oliver, PA 15472 • 3,271
Oliver □, ND • 2,381
Oliver Springs, TN 37840 • 3,433
Olivet, MI 49076 • 1,604
Olivette, MO 63132 • 7,573
Olivia, MN 56277 • 2,623
Olla, LA 71465 • 1,410
Olmito, TX 78575 • 1,400
Olmos Park, TX 78212 • 2,161
Olmsted □, MN • 106,470
Olmsted Falls, OH 44138 • 6,741
Olney, IL 62450 • 8,664
Olney, MD 20832 • 23,019
Olney, TX 76374 • 3,519
Olton, TX 79064 • 2,116
Olympia, WA 98501–07 • 33,840
Olympia Heights, FL 33175 • 36,900
Olyphant, PA 18447 • 5,222
Omaha, NE 68101–72 • 335,795
Omak, WA 98841 • 4,117
Omro, WI 54963 • 2,836
Onalaska, WI 54650 • 11,284
Onancock, VA 23417 • 1,434
Onarga, IL 60955 • 1,281
Onawa, IA 51040 • 2,936
Onaway, MI 49765 • 1,039
Oneco, FL 34264 • 6,417
Oneida, NY 13421 • 10,850
Oneida, OH 45042 • 1,650
Oneida, TN 37841 • 3,502
Oneida □, ID • 3,492
Oneida □, NY • 250,836
Oneida □, WI • 31,679
O'Neill, NE 68763 • 3,852
Oneonta, AL 35121 • 4,844
Oneonta, NY 13820 • 13,954
Onida, SD 57564 • 761
Onondaga □, NY • 468,973
Onset, MA 02558 • 1,461
Onslow □, NC • 149,838
Ontario, CA 91761–62 • 133,179
Ontario, OH 44862 • 4,026
Ontario, OR 97914 • 9,392
Ontario □, NY • 95,101
Ontonagon, MI 49953 • 2,040
Ontonagon □, MI • 8,854
Oolitic, IN 47451 • 1,424
Ooltewah, TN 37363 • 1,200
Oostburg, WI 53070 • 1,931
Opal Cliffs, CA 95062 • 5,940
Opa-Locka, FL 33054–56 • 15,283
Opelika, AL 36801–03 • 22,122
Opelousas, LA 70570–71 • 18,151
Opp, AL 36467 • 6,985
Opportunity, WA 99206 • 22,326
Oquawka, IL 61469 • 1,442
Oracle, AZ 85623 • 3,043
Oradell, NJ 07649 • 8,024
Oran, MO 63771 • 1,164
Orange, CA 92664–69 • 110,658
Orange, CT 06477 • 12,830
Orange, MA 01364 • 3,791
Orange, NJ 07050–52 • 29,925
Orange, TX 77630–31 • 19,381
Orange, VA 22960 • 2,582
Orange □, CA • 2,410,556
Orange □, FL • 677,491
Orange □, IN • 18,409
Orange □, NY • 307,647
Orange □, NC • 93,851
Orange □, TX • 80,509
Orange □, VT • 26,149
Orange □, VA • 21,421
Orange Beach, AL 36561 • 2,253
Orangeburg, SC 29115–16 • 13,739
Orangeburg □, SC • 84,803
Orange City, FL 32763 • 5,347
Orange City, IA 51041 • 4,940
Orange Grove, MS 39503 • 15,676
Orange Grove, TX 78372 • 1,175
Orange Lake, FL 32681 • 1,000
Orange Park, FL 32073 • 9,488
Orangevale, CA 95662 • 26,266
Orangeville, UT 84537 • 1,459
Orchard City, CO 81410 • 2,218
Orchard Homes, MT 59801 • 10,317
Orchard Mesa, CO 81501 • 5,977
Orchard Park, NY 14127 • 3,280
Orchards, WA 98662 • 8,828
Orchard Valley, WY 82007 • 3,321
Orcutt, CA 93455 • 1,500
Ord, NE 68862 • 2,481
Ordway, CO 81063 • 1,025
Oregon, IL 61061 • 3,891
Oregon, OH 43616 • 18,334
Oregon, WI 53575 • 4,519
Oregon □, MO • 9,470
Oregon City, OR 97045 • 14,698
Orem, UT 84057–59 • 67,561
Orfordville, WI 53576 • 1,219
Orient, NY 11957 • 1,000
Orinda, CA 94563 • 16,642
Orion, IL 61273 • 1,821
Oriskany, NY 13424 • 1,450
Orland, CA 95963 • 5,052
Orlando, FL 32801–72 • 164,693
Orland Park, IL 60462 • 35,720
Orleans, IN 47452 • 2,083
Orleans, IN 47452 • 2,161
Orleans, MA 02653 • 1,699
Orleans, VT 05860 • 806
Orleans □, LA • 496,938
Orleans □, NY • 41,846
Orleans □, VT • 24,053
Orlovista, FL 32811 • 5,990
Ormond Beach, FL 32174–76 • 29,721
Ormond By The Sea, FL 32174 • 8,157
Orofino, ID 83544 • 2,868
Orono, ME 04473 • 9,789
Orono, MN 55323 • 7,285
Orosi, CA 93647 • 5,486
Oroville, CA 95965–66 • 11,960
Oroville, WA 98844 • 1,505
Orrville, OH 44667 • 7,712
Orting, WA 98360 • 2,106
Ortonville, MI 48462 • 1,252
Ortonville, MN 56278 • 2,205
Orwell, OH 44076 • 1,258
Orwigsburg, PA 17961 • 2,780
Osage, IA 50461 • 3,439
Osage, WY 82723 • 350
Osage □, KS • 15,248
Osage □, MO • 12,018
Osage □, OK • 41,645
Osage Beach, MO 65065 • 2,599
Osage City, KS 66523 • 2,689
Osakis, MN 56360 • 1,256
Osawatomie, KS 66064 • 4,590
Osborne, KS 67473 • 1,778
Osborne □, KS • 4,867
Osburn, ID 83849 • 1,579
Osceola, AR 72370 • 8,930
Osceola, IN 46561 • 1,999
Osceola, IA 50213 • 4,164
Osceola, WI 54020 • 2,075
Osceola □, FL • 107,728
Osceola □, IA • 7,267
Osceola □, MI • 20,146
Osceola Mills, PA 16666 • 1,310
Oscoda, MI 48750 • 1,061
Oscoda □, MI • 7,842
Osgood, IN 47037 • 1,688
Oshkosh, WI 54901–04 • 55,006
Oskaloosa, IA 52577 • 10,632
Oskaloosa, KS 66066 • 1,074
Osprey, FL 34229 • 2,597
Osseo, MN 55369 • 2,704
Osseo, WI 54758 • 1,551
Ossian, IN 46777 • 2,428
Ossining, NY 10562 • 22,582
Osterville, MA 02655 • 2,911
Oswego, IL 60543 • 3,876
Oswego, KS 67356 • 1,870
Oswego, NY 13126 • 19,195
Oswego □, NY • 121,771
Otay, CA 92010 • 6,400
Oteen, NC 28805 • 1,400
Otego, NY 13825 • 1,068
Otero □, CO • 20,185
Otero □, NM • 51,928
Othello, WA 99327 • 4,638
Otis Orchards, WA 99027 • 3,200
Otoe □, NE • 14,252
Otsego, MI 49078 • 3,937
Otsego □, MI • 17,957
Otsego □, NY • 60,517
Ottawa, IL 61350 • 17,451
Ottawa, KS 66067 • 10,667
Ottawa, OH 45875 • 3,999
Ottawa □, KS • 5,634
Ottawa □, MI • 187,768
Ottawa □, OH • 40,029
Ottawa □, OK • 30,561
Ottawa Hills, OH 43606 • 4,543
Otterbein, IN 47970 • 1,291
Otter Tail □, MN • 50,714
Ottumwa, IA 52501 • 24,488
Ouachita □, AR • 30,574
Ouachita □, LA • 142,191
Ouray, CO 81427 • 644
Ouray □, CO • 2,295
Outagamie □, WI • 140,510
Overland, MO 63114 • 17,987
Overland Park, KS 66204 • 111,790
Overlea, MD 21206 • 12,137
Overlook, OH 45431 • 6,000
Overton, NV 89040 • 1,111
Overton, TX 75684 • 2,105
Overton □, TN • 17,636
Ovid, MI 48866 • 1,442
Owasso, OK 74055 • 11,151
Owatonna, MN 55060 • 19,386
Owego, NY 13827 • 4,442
Owen □, IN • 17,281
Owen □, KY • 9,035
Owensboro, KY 42301–03 • 53,549
Owensville, IN 47665 • 1,053
Owensville, MO 65066 • 2,325
Owensville, OH 45160 • 1,019
Owenton, KY 40359 • 1,306
Owings Mills, MD 21117 • 9,474
Owingsville, KY 40360 • 1,491
Owosso, MI 48867 • 16,322
Owsley □, KY • 5,036
Owyhee, NV 89832 • 908
Owyhee □, ID • 8,392
Oxford, AL 36203 • 9,362
Oxford, CT 06483 • 1,600
Oxford, GA 30267 • 1,945
Oxford, IN 47971 • 1,273
Oxford, KS 67119 • 1,143
Oxford, MA 01540 • 5,969
Oxford, MI 48370–71 • 2,929
Oxford, MS 38655 • 9,984
Oxford, NJ 07863 • 1,767
Oxford, NY 13830 • 1,738

Oxford, NC 27565 • *7,913*
Oxford, OH 45056 • *18,937*
Oxford, PA 19363 • *3,769*
Oxford □, ME • *52,602*
Oxnard, CA 93030–35 • *142,216*
Oxon Hill, MD 20745 • *36,267*
Oyster Bay, NY 11771 • *6,687*
Ozark, AL 36360–61 • *12,922*
Ozark, AR 72949 • *3,330*
Ozark, MO 65721 • *4,243*
Ozark □, MO • *8,598*
Ozaukee □, WI • *72,831*
Ozona, FL 34660 • *1,500*
Ozona, TX 76943 • *3,181*

P

Paauilo, HI 96776 • *620*
Pace, FL 32571 • *6,277*
Pacific, MO 63069 • *4,350*
Pacific, WA 98047 • *4,622*
Pacific □, WA • *18,882*
Pacifica, CA 94044 • *37,670*
Pacific Beach, WA 98571 • *1,200*
Pacific City, OR 97135 • *1,500*
Pacific Grove, CA 93950 • *16,117*
Pacific Palisades, HI 96782 • *10,000*
Packwood, WA 98361 • *1,010*
Pacolet, SC 29372 • *1,736*
Paddock Lake, WI 53168 • *2,662*
Paden City, WV 26159 • *2,862*
Paducah, KY 42001–03 • *27,256*
Paducah, TX 79248 • *1,788*
Page, AZ 86040 • *6,598*
Page □, IA • *16,870*
Page □, VA • *21,690*
Pageland, SC 29728 • *2,666*
Page Manor, OH 45431 • *9,300*
Pagosa Springs, CO 81147 • *1,207*
Pahala, HI 96777 • *1,520*
Pahoa, HI 96778 • *1,027*
Pahokee, FL 33476 • *6,822*
Pahrump, NV 89041 • *7,424*
Paia, HI 96779 • *2,091*
Paincourtville, LA 70391 • *1,550*
Painesville, OH 44077 • *15,699*
Painted Post, NY 14870 • *1,950*
Paintsville, KY 41240 • *4,354*
Pajarito, NM 87105 • *1,400*
Palacios, TX 77465 • *4,418*
Palatine, IL 60067 • *39,253*
Palatka, FL 32177 • *10,201*
Palestine, IL 62451 • *1,619*
Palestine, TX 75801–02 • *18,042*
Palisade, CO 81526 • *1,871*
Palisades Park, NJ 07650 • *14,536*
Palm Bay, FL 32905 • *62,632*
Palm Beach, FL 33480 • *9,814*
Palm Beach □, FL • *863,518*
Palm Beach Gardens, FL 33410 • *22,965*
Palm Coast, FL 32135 • *14,287*
Palmdale, CA 93550–51 • *68,842*
Palm Desert, CA 92260–61 • *23,252*
Palmer, AK 99645 • *2,866*
Palmer, MA 01069 • *4,069*
Palmer, MS 39401 • *2,765*
Palmer, TX 75152 • *1,659*
Palmer Lake, CO 80133 • *1,480*
Palmer Park, MD 20785 • *7,019*
Palmerton, PA 18071 • *5,394*
Palmetto, FL 34220–21 • *9,268*
Palmetto, GA 30268 • *2,612*
Palmetto Estates, FL 33157 • *12,293*
Palm Harbor, FL 34682–85 • *50,256*
Palm Springs, CA 92262–64 • *40,181*
Palm Springs, FL 33460 • *9,763*
Palm Springs North, FL 33015 • *5,300*
Palm Valley, FL 32082 • *9,960*
Palmyra, MO 63461 • *3,371*
Palmyra, NJ 08065 • *7,056*
Palmyra, NY 14522 • *3,566*
Palmyra, PA 17078 • *6,910*
Palmyra, WI 53156 • *1,539*
Palo Alto, CA 94301–09 • *55,900*
Palo Alto □, IA • *10,669*
Palo Pinto □, TX • *25,055*
Palos Heights, IL 60463 • *11,478*
Palos Hills, IL 60465 • *17,803*
Palos Park, IL 60464 • *4,199*
Palos Verdes Estates, CA 90274 • *13,512*
Pamlico □, NC • *11,372*
Pampa, TX 79065–66 • *19,959*
Pamplico, SC 29583 • *1,314*
Pana, IL 62557 • *5,796*
Panaca, NV 89042 • *700*
Panama, OK 74951 • *1,528*
Panama City, FL 32401–13 • *34,378*
Panama City Beach, FL 32407–08 • *4,051*
Pandora, OH 45877 • *1,009*
Panguitch, UT 84759 • *1,444*
Panhandle, TX 79068 • *2,353*
Panola □, MS • *29,996*
Panola □, TX • *22,035*
Panora, IA 50216 • *1,100*
Panthersville, GA 30032 • *9,874*
Paola, KS 66071 • *4,698*
Paoli, IN 47454 • *3,542*
Paoli, PA 19301 • *5,603*
Paonia, CO 81428 • *1,403*
Papaikou, HI 96781 • *1,634*
Papillion, NE 68046 • *10,372*
Paradise, CA 95969 • *25,408*
Paradise, NV 89109 • *124,682*
Paradise Hills, NM 87114 • *5,513*
Paradise Valley, AZ 85253 • *11,671*
Paradise Valley, NV 89426 • *150*
Paragould, AR 72450–51 • *18,540*
Paramount, CA 90723 • *47,669*
Paramount, MD 21740 • *1,878*
Paramus, NJ 07652–53 • *25,067*
Parchment, MI 49004 • *1,958*
Pardeeville, WI 53954 • *1,630*
Paris, AR 72855 • *3,674*
Paris, IL 61944 • *8,987*
Paris, KY 40361–62 • *8,730*
Paris, MO 65275 • *1,486*
Paris, TN 38242 • *9,332*
Paris, TX 75460–61 • *24,699*
Park □, CO • *7,174*
Park □, MT • *14,562*
Park □, WY • *23,178*
Park City, KS 67219 • *5,050*
Park City, UT 84060 • *4,468*
Parke □, IN • *15,410*
Parker, AZ 85344 • *2,897*
Parker, CO 80134 • *5,450*
Parker, FL 32401 • *4,598*
Parker, SD 57053 • *984*
Parker □, TX • *64,785*
Parker City, IN 47368 • *1,323*
Parkersburg, IA 50665 • *1,804*
Parkersburg, WV 26101–06 • *33,862*
Parkesburg, PA 19365 • *2,981*
Park Falls, WI 54552 • *3,104*
Park Forest, IL 60466 • *24,656*
Park Hills, KY 41015 • *3,321*
Parkin, AR 72373 • *1,847*
Parkland, WA 98444 • *20,882*
Park Layne, OH 45344 • *4,895*
Park Rapids, MN 56470 • *2,863*
Park Ridge, IL 60068 • *36,175*
Park Ridge, NJ 07656 • *8,102*
Park River, ND 58270 • *1,725*
Parkrose, OR 97230 • *21,108*
Parkston, SD 57366 • *1,572*
Parkville, MD 21234 • *31,617*
Parkville, MO 64152 • *2,402*
Parkwater, WA 99211 • *4,300*
Parkway, CA 95823 • *12,000*
Parkwood, NC 27713 • *4,123*
Parkwood, WA 98366 • *6,853*
Parlier, CA 93648 • *7,938*
Parma, ID 83660 • *1,597*
Parma, OH 44129 • *87,876*
Parma Heights, OH 44130 • *21,448*
Parmer □, TX • *9,863*
Parole, MD 21401 • *10,054*
Parowan, UT 84761 • *1,873*
Parrish, AL 35580 • *1,433*
Parshall, ND 58770 • *943*
Parsons, KS 67357 • *11,924*
Parsons, TN 38363 • *2,033*
Parsons, WV 26287 • *1,453*
Pasadena, CA 91101–09 • *131,591*
Pasadena, MD 21122 • *10,012*
Pasadena, TX 77501–08 • *119,363*
Pascagoula, MS 39567–68 • *25,899*
Pasco, WA 99301–02 • *20,337*
Pasco □, FL • *281,131*
Pascoag, RI 02859 • *5,011*
Paso Robles, CA 93446–47 • *18,583*
Pasquotank □, NC • *31,298*
Passaic, NJ 07055 • *58,041*
Passaic □, NJ • *453,060*
Pass Christian, MS 39571 • *5,557*
Pataskala, OH 43062 • *3,046*
Patchogue, NY 11772 • *11,060*
Paterson, NJ 07501–44 • *140,891*
Patrick □, VA • *17,473*
Patten, ME 04765 • *1,256*
Patterson, LA 70392 • *4,736*
Patterson, NY 12563 • *1,200*
Patton, PA 16668 • *2,206*
Paul, ID 83347 • *901*
Paulding, OH 45879 • *2,605*
Paulding □, GA • *41,611*
Paulding □, OH • *20,488*
Paullina, IA 51046 • *1,134*
Paulsboro, NJ 08066 • *6,577*
Pauls Valley, OK 73075 • *6,150*
Pawcatuck, CT 06379 • *5,289*
Paw Creek, NC 28130 • *1,700*
Pawhuska, OK 74056 • *3,825*
Pawling, NY 12564 • *1,974*
Pawnee, IL 62558 • *2,384*
Pawnee, OK 74058 • *2,197*
Pawnee □, KS • *7,555*
Pawnee □, NE • *3,317*
Pawnee □, OK • *15,575*
Pawnee City, NE 68420 • *1,008*
Paw Paw, MI 49079 • *3,169*
Pawtucket, RI 02860–65 • *72,644*
Paxton, IL 60957 • *4,289*
Paxton, MA 01612 • *1,550*
Payette, ID 83661 • *5,592*
Payette □, ID • *16,434*
Payne, OH 45880 • *1,244*
Payne □, OK • *61,507*
Paynesville, MN 56362 • *2,275*
Payson, AZ 85541 • *8,377*
Payson, IL 62360 • *1,114*
Payson, UT 84651 • *9,510*
Peabody, KS 66866 • *1,349*
Peabody, MA 01960–61 • *47,039*
Peace Dale, RI 02883 • *3,100*
Peach □, GA • *21,189*
Peach Orchard, GA 30906 • *13,800*
Peachtree City, GA 30269 • *19,027*
Pea Ridge, AR 72751 • *1,620*
Pearisburg, VA 24134 • *2,064*
Pearl, MS 39208 • *19,588*
Pearland, TX 77581 • *18,697*
Pearl City, HI 96782 • *30,993*
Pearl River, LA 70452 • *1,507*
Pearl River, NY 10965 • *15,314*
Pearl River □, MS • *38,714*
Pearsall, TX 78061 • *6,924*
Pearson, GA 31642 • *1,714*
Pecatonica, IL 61063 • *1,760*
Pecos, NM 87552 • *1,012*
Pecos, TX 79772 • *12,069*
Pecos □, TX • *14,675*
Peculiar, MO 64078 • *1,777*
Pedricktown, NJ 08067 • *1,500*
Peebles, OH 45660 • *1,782*
Peekskill, NY 10566 • *19,536*
Pegram, TN 37143 • *1,371*
Pekin, IL 61554–55 • *32,254*
Pekin, IN 47165 • *1,095*
Pelahatchie, MS 39145 • *1,553*
Pelham, AL 35124 • *9,765*
Pelham, GA 31779 • *3,869*
Pelham, NY 10803 • *6,413*
Pelham Manor, NY 10803 • *5,443*
Pelican Rapids, MN 56572 • *1,886*
Pella, IA 50219 • *9,270*
Pell City, AL 35125 • *8,118*
Pell Lake, WI 53157 • *2,018*
Pemberton, NJ 08068 • *1,367*
Pemberville, OH 43450 • *1,279*
Pembina □, ND • *9,238*
Pembroke, GA 31321 • *1,503*
Pembroke, MA 02359 • *2,000*
Pembroke, NC 28372 • *2,241*
Pembroke, VA 24136 • *1,064*
Pembroke Park, FL 33009 • *4,933*
Pembroke Pines, FL 33024 • *65,452*
Pemiscot □, MO • *21,921*
Pen Argyl, PA 18072 • *3,492*
Penbrook, PA 17103 • *2,791*
Pender, NE 68047 • *1,208*
Pender □, NC • *28,855*
Pendleton, IN 46064 • *2,309*
Pendleton, OR 97801 • *15,126*
Pendleton, SC 29670 • *3,314*
Pendleton □, KY • *12,036*
Pendleton □, WV • *8,054*
Pendley Hills, GA 30032 • *5,400*
Pend Oreille □, WA • *8,915*
Penfield, NY 14526 • *6,260*
Penn Acres, DE 19720 • *2,430*
Penn Hills, PA 15235 • *51,430*
Pennington, NJ 08534 • *2,537*
Pennington □, MN • *13,306*
Pennington □, SD • *81,343*
Pennington Gap, VA 24277 • *1,922*
Pennsauken, NJ 08110 • *34,733*
Pennsboro, WV 26415 • *1,282*
Pennsburg, PA 18073 • *2,460*
Penns Grove, NJ 08069 • *5,228*
Pennsville, NJ 08070 • *12,218*
Penn Yan, NY 14527 • *5,248*
Penobscot □, ME • *146,601*
Pensacola, FL 32501–26 • *58,165*
Pentwater, MI 49449 • *1,050*
Peoria, AZ 85345 • *50,618*
Peoria, IL 61601–56 • *113,504*
Peoria □, IL • *182,827*
Peoria Heights, IL 61614 • *6,930*
Peotone, IL 60468 • *2,947*
Pepeekeo, HI 96783 • *1,813*
Pepin □, WI • *7,107*
Pepperell, MA 01463 • *2,350*
Pepper Pike, OH 44124 • *6,185*
Pequannock, NJ 07440 • *12,844*
Perdido, AL 36562 • *1,200*
Perham, MN 56573 • *2,075*
Perkasie, PA 18944 • *7,878*
Perkins, OK 74059 • *1,925*
Perkins □, NE • *3,367*
Perkins □, SD • *3,932*
Perquimans □, NC • *10,447*
Perrine, FL 33157 • *15,576*
Perris, CA 92370 • *21,460*
Perry, FL 32347 • *7,151*
Perry, GA 31069 • *9,452*
Perry, IA 50220 • *6,652*
Perry, MI 48872 • *2,163*
Perry, NY 14530 • *4,219*
Perry, OH 44081 • *1,012*
Perry, OK 73077 • *4,978*
Perry, UT 84302 • *1,211*
Perry □, AL • *12,759*
Perry □, AR • *7,969*
Perry □, IL • *21,412*
Perry □, IN • *19,107*
Perry □, KY • *30,283*
Perry □, MS • *10,865*
Perry □, MO • *16,648*
Perry □, OH • *31,557*
Perry □, PA • *41,172*
Perry □, TN • *6,612*
Perry Hall, MD 21128 • *22,723*
Perry Heights, OH 44646 • *9,055*
Perryman, MD 21130 • *2,160*
Perrysburg, OH 43551–52 • *12,551*
Perryton, TX 79070 • *7,607*
Perryville, AR 72126 • *1,141*
Perryville, MD 21903 • *2,456*
Perryville, MO 63775 • *6,933*
Pershing □, NV • *4,336*
Person □, NC • *30,180*
Perth Amboy, NJ 08861–63 • *41,967*
Peru, IL 61354 • *9,302*
Peru, IN 46970 • *12,843*
Peru, NE 68421 • *1,110*
Peru, NY 12972 • *1,565*
Peshtigo, WI 54157 • *3,154*
Petal, MS 39465 • *7,883*
Petaluma, CA 94952–55 • *43,184*
Peterborough, NH 03458 • *2,685*
Petersburg, AK 99833 • *3,207*
Petersburg, IL 62675 • *2,261*
Petersburg, IN 47567 • *2,449*
Petersburg, MI 49270 • *1,201*
Petersburg, TX 79250 • *1,292*
Petersburg, VA 23801–05 • *38,386*
Petersburg, WV 26847 • *2,360*
Petersville, AL 35633 • *1,730*
Petoskey, MI 49770 • *6,056*
Petroleum □, MT • *519*
Petros, TN 37845 • *1,286*
Pettis □, MO • *35,437*
Pevely, MO 63070 • *2,831*
Pewaukee, WI 53072 • *4,941*
Pewee Valley, KY 40056 • *1,283*
Pharr, TX 78577 • *32,921*
Phelps, KY 41553 • *1,120*
Phelps, NY 14532 • *1,978*
Phelps □, MO • *35,248*
Phelps □, NE • *9,715*
Phenix City, AL 36867–69 • *25,312*
Philadelphia, MS 39350 • *6,758*
Philadelphia, NY 13673 • *1,478*
Philadelphia, PA 19101–96 • *1,585,577*
Philadelphia □, PA • *1,585,577*
Phil Campbell, AL 35581 • *1,317*
Philip, SD 57567 • *1,077*
Philippi, WV 26416 • *3,132*
Philipsburg, MT 59858 • *925*
Philipsburg, PA 16866 • *3,048*
Phillips, TX 79007 • *1,729*
Phillips, WI 54555 • *1,592*
Phillips □, AR • *28,838*
Phillips □, CO • *4,189*
Phillips □, KS • *6,590*
Phillips □, MT • *5,163*
Phillipsburg, KS 67661 • *2,828*
Phillipsburg, NJ 08865 • *15,757*
Philmont, NY 12565 • *1,623*
Philo, IL 61864 • *1,028*
Philomath, OR 97370 • *2,983*
Phoenix, AZ 85001–82 • *983,403*
Phoenix, IL 60426 • *2,217*
Phoenix, NY 13135 • *2,435*
Phoenix, OR 97535 • *3,239*
Phoenixville, PA 19460 • *15,066*
Piatt □, IL • *15,548*
Picayune, MS 39466 • *10,633*
Picher, OK 74360 • *1,714*
Pickaway □, OH • *48,255*
Pickens, MS 39146 • *1,285*
Pickens, SC 29671 • *3,042*
Pickens □, AL • *20,699*
Pickens □, GA • *14,432*
Pickens □, SC • *93,894*
Pickerington, OH 43147 • *5,668*
Pickett □, TN • *4,548*
Pico Rivera, CA 90660–61 • *59,177*
Piedmont, AL 36272 • *5,288*
Piedmont, CA 94611 • *10,602*
Piedmont, MO 63957 • *2,166*
Piedmont, OK 73078 • *2,522*
Piedmont, SC 29673 • *4,143*
Piedmont, WV 26750 • *1,094*
Pierce, ID 83546 • *746*
Pierce, NE 68767 • *1,615*
Pierce □, GA • *13,328*
Pierce □, NE • *7,827*
Pierce □, ND • *5,052*
Pierce □, WA • *586,203*
Pierce □, WI • *32,765*
Pierce City, MO 65723 • *1,382*
Pierceton, IN 46562 • *1,030*
Pierre, SD 57501 • *12,906*
Pierre Part, LA 70339 • *3,053*
Pierson, FL 32180 • *2,988*
Pierz, MN 56364 • *1,014*
Pigeon, MI 48755 • *1,207*
Pigeon Cove, MA 01966 • *1,660*
Pigeon Forge, TN 37863 • *3,027*
Piggott, AR 72454 • *3,777*
Pike □, AL • *27,595*
Pike □, AR • *10,086*
Pike □, GA • *10,224*
Pike □, IL • *17,577*
Pike □, IN • *12,509*
Pike □, KY • *72,583*
Pike □, MS • *36,882*
Pike □, MO • *15,969*
Pike □, OH • *24,249*
Pike □, PA • *27,966*
Pike Lake, MN 55811 • *1,004*
Pikesville, MD 21208 • *24,815*
Piketon, OH 45661 • *1,717*
Pikeville, KY 41501–02 • *6,324*
Pikeville, TN 37367 • *1,771*
Pilot Mountain, NC 27041 • *1,181*
Pilot Point, TX 76258 • *2,538*
Pilot Rock, OR 97868 • *1,478*
Pilot Station, AK 99650 • *463*
Pima, AZ 85543 • *1,725*
Pima □, AZ • *666,880*
Pimmit Hills, VA 22043 • *6,019*
Pinal □, AZ • *116,379*
Pinardville, NH 03045 • *4,654*
Pinckney, MI 48169 • *1,603*
Pinckneyville, IL 62274 • *3,372*
Pinconning, MI 48650 • *1,291*
Pine □, MN • *21,264*
Pine Bluff, AR 71601–13 • *57,140*
Pine Bluffs, WY 82082 • *1,054*
Pine Bridge, CT 06403 • *1,160*
Pine Bush, NY 12566 • *1,445*
Pine Castle, FL 32809 • *8,276*
Pine City, MN 55063 • *2,613*
Pinedale, WY 82941 • *1,181*
Pine Grove, PA 17963 • *2,118*
Pine Grove Mills, PA 16868 • *1,129*
Pine Hill, NJ 08021 • *9,854*
Pine Hills, FL 32808 • *35,322*
Pinehurst, MA 01866 • *6,614*
Pinehurst, NJ 08201 • *1,850*
Pinehurst, NC 28374 • *5,103*
Pine Island, MN 55963 • *2,125*
Pine Island, NY 10969 • *1,200*
Pine Knot, KY 42635 • *1,549*
Pine Lawn, MO 63120 • *5,092*
Pine Level, NC 27568 • *1,217*
Pinellas □, FL • *851,659*
Pinellas Park, FL 34664–66 • *43,426*
Pine Plains, NY 12567 • *1,312*
Pine Ridge, SD 57770 • *2,596*
Pinetops, NC 27864 • *1,514*
Pine Valley, CA 91962 • *1,297*
Pineville, KY 40977 • *2,198*
Pineville, LA 71360–61 • *12,251*
Pineville, NC 28134 • *2,970*
Pinewald, NJ 08721 • *1,700*
Pinewood, FL 33168 • *15,518*
Pinewood Park, FL 33168 • *8,300*
Piney Point, MD 20674 • *1,200*
Piney View, WV 25906 • *1,085*
Pinole, CA 94564 • *17,460*
Pinson, AL 35126 • *1,430*
Pioche, NV 89043 • *830*
Pioneer, OH 43554 • *1,287*
Pipestone, MN 56164 • *4,554*
Pipestone □, MN • *10,491*
Piqua, OH 45356 • *20,612*
Pirtleville, AZ 85626 • *1,364*
Piscataquis □, ME • *18,653*
Piscataway, NJ 08854–55 • *42,223*
Pisgah, OH 45069 • *15,660*
Pisgah Forest, NC 28768 • *1,899*
Pismo Beach, CA 93448–49 • *7,669*
Pitcairn, PA 15140 • *4,087*
Pitkin □, CO • *12,661*
Pitman, NJ 08071 • *9,365*
Pitt □, NC • *107,924*
Pittsboro, NC 27312 • *1,436*
Pittsburg, CA 94565 • *47,564*
Pittsburg, KS 66762 • *17,775*
Pittsburg, TX 75686 • *4,007*
Pittsburg □, OK • *40,581*
Pittsburgh, PA 15201–90 • *369,879*
Pittsfield, IL 62363 • *4,231*
Pittsfield, ME 04967 • *3,222*
Pittsfield, MA 01201–03 • *48,622*
Pittsfield, NH 03263 • *1,717*
Pittsford, VT 05763 • *650*
Pittston, PA 18640–44 • *9,389*
Pittsylvania □, VA • *55,655*
Piute □, UT • *1,277*
Pixley, CA 93256 • *2,457*
Placentia, CA 92670 • *41,259*
Placer □, CA • *172,796*
Placerville, CA 95667 • *8,355*
Plain City, OH 43064 • *2,278*
Plain City, UT 84404 • *2,722*
Plain Dealing, LA 71064 • *1,074*
Plainedge, NY 11714 • *8,739*
Plainfield, CT 06374 • *2,856*
Plainfield, IL 60544 • *4,557*
Plainfield, IN 46168 • *10,433*
Plainfield, NJ 07059–63 • *46,567*
Plainfield, VT 05667 • *600*
Plainfield Heights, MI 49505 • *5,000*
Plains, MT 59859 • *992*
Plains, PA 18705 • *4,694*
Plains, TX 79355 • *1,422*
Plainsboro, NJ 08536 • *1,560*
Plainview, MN 55964 • *2,768*
Plainview, NE 68769 • *1,333*
Plainview, NY 11803 • *26,207*
Plainview, TX 79072–73 • *21,700*
Plainville, CT 06062 • *17,392*
Plainville, KS 67663 • *2,173*
Plainville, MA 02762 • *5,857*
Plainwell, MI 49080 • *4,057*
Plaistow, NH 03865 • *1,850*
Plano, IL 60545 • *5,104*
Plano, TX 75074–75 • *128,713*
Plantation, FL 33317 • *66,692*
Plant City, FL 33564–67 • *22,754*
Plantersville, MS 38862 • *1,046*
Plantsite, AZ 85540 • *1,500*
Plantsville, CT 06479 • *7,050*
Plaquemine, LA 70764–65 • *7,186*
Plaquemines □, LA • *25,575*
Platte, SD 57369 • *1,311*
Platte □, MO • *57,867*
Platte □, NE • *29,820*
Platte □, WY • *8,145*
Platte City, MO 64079 • *2,947*
Platteville, CO 80651 • *1,515*
Platteville, WI 53818 • *9,708*
Plattsburg, MO 64477 • *2,248*
Plattsburgh, NY 12901 • *21,255*
Plattsmouth, NE 68048 • *6,412*
Pleasant Gap, PA 16823 • *1,699*
Pleasant Garden, NC 27313 • *2,228*
Pleasant Grove, AL 35127 • *8,458*
Pleasant Grove, UT 84062 • *13,476*
Pleasant Hill, CA 94523 • *31,585*
Pleasant Hill, IL 62366 • *1,030*
Pleasant Hill, IA 50301 • *3,671*
Pleasant Hill, MO 64080 • *3,827*
Pleasant Hill, OH 45359 • *1,066*
Pleasant Hills, PA 15236 • *8,884*
Pleasanton, CA 94566 • *50,553*
Pleasanton, KS 66075 • *1,231*
Pleasanton, TX 78064 • *7,678*
Pleasant Prairie, WI 53158 • *11,961*
Pleasants □, WV • *7,546*
Pleasant Valley, MO 64068 • *2,731*
Pleasant Valley, NY 12569 • *1,688*
Pleasant View, CO 80401 • *3,460*
Pleasant View, UT 84404 • *3,603*
Pleasantville, IA 50225 • *1,536*
Pleasantville, NJ 08232 • *16,027*
Pleasantville, NY 10570–72 • *6,592*
Pleasure Beach, CT 06385 • *1,356*
Pleasure Ridge Park, KY 40258 • *25,131*
Plentywood, MT 59254 • *2,136*
Plover, WI 54467 • *8,176*
Plum, PA 15239 • *25,609*
Plumas □, CA • *19,739*
Plumsteadville, PA 18949 • *1,200*
Plymouth, CT 06782 • *1,070*
Plymouth, FL 32768 • *2,700*
Plymouth, IN 46563 • *8,303*
Plymouth, MA 02360–61 • *7,258*
Plymouth, MI 48170 • *9,560*
Plymouth, MN 55441 • *50,889*
Plymouth, NH 03264 • *3,967*
Plymouth, NC 27962 • *4,328*
Plymouth, OH 44865 • *1,942*
Plymouth, PA 18651 • *7,134*
Plymouth, WI 53073 • *6,769*
Plymouth □, IA • *23,388*
Plymouth □, MA • *435,276*
Plymouth Township, PA 19401 • *17,168*
Poca, WV 25159 • *1,124*
Pocahontas, AR 72455 • *6,151*
Pocahontas, IA 50574 • *2,085*
Pocahontas □, IA • *9,525*
Pocahontas □, WV • *9,008*
Pocasset, MA 02559 • *2,200*
Pocatalico, WV 25320 • *2,450*
Pocatello, ID 83201–06 • *46,080*
Pocola, OK 74902 • *3,664*
Pocomoke City, MD 21851 • *3,922*
Poinsett □, AR • *24,664*
Point Clear, AL 36564 • *2,125*
Pointe Coupee □, LA • *22,540*
Point Hope, AK 99766 • *639*
Point Marion, PA 15474 • *1,344*
Point Pleasant, NJ 08742 • *18,177*
Point Pleasant, WV 25550 • *4,996*
Point Pleasant Beach, NJ 08742 • *5,112*
Poipu, HI 96756 • *975*
Polk, PA 16342 • *1,267*
Polk □, AR • *17,347*
Polk □, FL • *405,382*
Polk □, GA • *33,815*
Polk □, IA • *327,140*
Polk □, MN • *32,498*
Polk □, MO • *21,826*
Polk □, NE • *5,675*
Polk □, NC • *14,416*
Polk □, OR • *49,541*
Polk □, TN • *13,643*
Polk □, TX • *30,687*
Polk □, WI • *34,773*
Polk City, FL 33868 • *1,439*
Polk City, IA 50226 • *1,908*
Polo, IL 61064 • *2,514*
Polson, MT 59860 • *3,283*
Pomeroy, OH 45769 • *2,259*
Pomeroy, WA 99347 • *1,393*
Pomona, CA 91765–69 • *131,723*
Pomona, NJ 08240 • *2,624*
Pompano Beach, FL 33060–69 • *72,411*
Pompano Beach Highlands, FL 33060 • *17,915*
Pompton Lakes, NJ 07442 • *10,539*
Ponca City, OK 74601–04 • *26,359*
Ponchatoula, LA 70454 • *5,425*
Pondera □, MT • *6,433*
Ponte Vedra Beach, FL 32082 • *1,700*
Pontiac, IL 61764 • *11,428*
Pontiac, MI 48340–43 • *71,166*
Pontotoc, MS 38863 • *4,570*
Pontotoc □, MS • *22,237*

Pontotoc □, OK • 34,119
Pooler, GA 31322 • 4,453
Poolesville, MD 20837 • 3,796
Pope □, AR • 45,883
Pope □, IL • 4,373
Pope □, MN • 10,745
Poplar, MT 59255 • 881
Poplar Bluff, MO 63901 • 16,996
Poplarville, MS 39470 • 2,561
Poquonock Bridge, CT 06340 • 2,770
Poquoson, VA 23662 • 11,005
Portage, IN 46368 • 29,060
Portage, MI 49081 • 41,042
Portage, PA 15946 • 3,105
Portage, WI 53901 • 8,640
Portage □, OH • 142,585
Portage □, WI • 61,405
Portage Lakes, OH 44319 • 13,373
Portageville, MO 63873 • 3,401
Portales, NM 88130 • 10,690
Port Allegany, PA 16743 • 2,391
Port Allen, LA 70767 • 6,277
Port Angeles, WA 98362 • 17,710
Port Aransas, TX 78373 • 2,233
Port Arthur, TX 77640–43 • 58,724
Port Barre, LA 70577 • 2,144
Port Bolivar, TX 77650 • 1,600
Port Byron, IL 61275 • 1,002
Port Byron, NY 13140 • 1,359
Port Carbon, PA 17965 • 2,134
Port Charlotte, FL 33952 • 41,535
Port Chester, NY 10573 • 24,728
Port Clinton, OH 43452 • 7,106
Port Dickinson, NY 13901 • 1,785
Port Edwards, WI 54469 • 1,848
Porter, IN 46304 • 3,118
Porter, TX 77365 • 7,000
Porter □, IN • 128,932
Porterdale, GA 30270 • 1,278
Porterville, CA 93257–58 • 29,563
Port Ewen, NY 12466 • 3,444
Port Gibson, MS 39150 • 1,810
Port Henry, NY 12974 • 1,263
Port Hueneme, CA 93041–44 • 20,319
Port Huron, MI 48060–61 • 33,694
Port Isabel, TX 78578 • 4,467
Port Jefferson, NY 11777 • 7,455
Port Jefferson Station, NY 11776 • 7,232
Port Jervis, NY 12771 • 9,060
Portland, CT 06480 • 5,645
Portland, IN 47371 • 6,483
Portland, ME 04101–12 • 64,358
Portland, MI 48875 • 3,889
Portland, OR 97201–99 • 437,319
Portland, TN 37148 • 5,165
Portland, TX 78374 • 12,224
Port Lavaca, TX 77979 • 10,886
Port Monmouth, NJ 07758 • 3,800
Port Neches, TX 77651 • 12,974
Port Norris, NJ 08349 • 1,701
Port O'Connor, TX 77982 • 1,031
Portola, CA 96122 • 2,193
Port Orange, FL 32127 • 35,317
Port Orchard, WA 98366 • 4,984
Port Orford, OR 97465 • 1,025
Port Penn, DE 19731 • 300
Port Richey, FL 34667–74 • 2,523
Port Royal, SC 29935 • 2,985
Port Saint Joe, FL 32456 • 4,044
Port Saint Lucie, FL 34952 • 55,866
Port Salerno, FL 34992 • 7,786
Portsmouth, NH 03801–02 • 25,925
Portsmouth, OH 45662 • 22,676
Portsmouth, RI 02871 • 3,540
Portsmouth, VA 23701–09 • 103,907
Port St. John, FL 32922 • 8,933
Port Sulphur, LA 70083 • 3,523
Port Townsend, WA 98368 • 7,001
Portville, NY 14770 • 1,040
Port Vue, PA 15133 • 4,641
Port Washington, NY 11050 • 15,387
Port Washington, WI 53074 • 9,338
Port Wentworth, GA 31407 • 4,012
Posen, IL 60469 • 4,226
Posey □, IN • 25,968
Poseyville, IN 47633 • 1,089
Post, TX 79356 • 3,768
Post Falls, ID 83854 • 7,349
Postville, IA 52162 • 1,472
Poteau, OK 74953 • 7,210
Poteet, TX 78065 • 3,206
Poth, TX 78147 • 1,642
Potlatch, ID 83855 • 790
Potomac, MD 20851 • 45,634
Potomac Heights, MD 20640 • 1,524
Potomac Park, MD 21502 • 1,800
Potosi, MO 63664 • 2,683
Potsdam, NY 13676 • 10,251
Pottawatomie □, KS • 16,128
Pottawatomie □, OK • 58,760
Pottawattamie □, IA • 82,628
Potter □, PA • 16,717
Potter □, SD • 3,190
Potter □, TX • 97,874
Potter Valley, CA 95469 • 1,500
Pottstown, PA 19464 • 21,831
Pottsville, PA 17901 • 16,603
Poughkeepsie, NY 12601–03 • 28,844
Poulsbo, WA 98370 • 4,848
Poultney, VT 05764 • 1,731
Poway, CA 92064 • 43,516
Powder River □, MT • 2,090
Powder Springs, GA 30073 • 6,893
Powell, OH 43065 • 2,154
Powell, TN 37849 • 7,534
Powell, WY 82435 • 5,292
Powell □, KY • 11,686
Powell □, MT • 6,620
Powellhurst, OR 97236 • 28,756
Powellton, WV 25161 • 1,905
Power □, ID • 7,086
Poweshiek □, IA • 19,033
Powhatan □, VA • 15,328
Powhatan Point, OH 43942 • 1,807
Poydras, LA 70085 • 4,029
Poynette, WI 53955 • 1,662
Prague, OK 74864 • 2,308
Prairie □, AR • 9,518
Prairie □, MT • 1,383
Prairie City, IA 50228 • 1,360
Prairie City, OR 97869 • 1,117
Prairie du Chien, WI 53821 • 5,659
Prairie du Sac, WI 53578 • 2,380
Prairie Grove, AR 72753 • 1,761
Prairie View, TX 77446 • 4,004
Prairie Village, KS 66208 • 23,186
Pratt, KS 67124 • 6,687
Pratt □, KS • 9,702
Prattville, AL 36066–67 • 19,587
Preble □, OH • 40,113
Premont, TX 78375 • 2,914
Prentiss, MS 39474 • 1,487
Prentiss □, MS • 23,278
Prescott, AZ 86301–14 • 26,455
Prescott, AR 71857 • 3,673
Prescott, WI 54021 • 3,243
Presho, SD 57568 • 654
Presidio, TX 79845 • 3,072
Presidio □, TX • 6,637
Presque Isle, ME 04769 • 10,550
Presque Isle □, MI • 13,743
Preston, ID 83263 • 3,710
Preston, IA 52069 • 1,025
Preston, MN 55965 • 1,530
Preston □, WV • 29,037
Prestonsburg, KY 41653 • 3,558
Price, UT 84501 • 8,712
Price □, WI • 15,600
Prichard, AL 36610 • 34,311
Priest River, ID 83856 • 1,560
Primrose, RI 02895 • 500
Prince Edward □, VA • 17,320
Prince Frederick, MD 20678 • 1,885
Prince George □, VA • 27,394
Prince Georges □, MD • 729,268
Princes Lakes, IN 46164 • 1,055
Princess Anne, MD 21853 • 1,666
Princeton, FL 33032 • 7,073
Princeton, IL 61356 • 7,197
Princeton, IN 47670 • 8,127
Princeton, KY 42445 • 6,940
Princeton, MN 55371 • 3,719
Princeton, MO 64673 • 1,021
Princeton, NJ 08540–43 • 12,016
Princeton, NC 27569 • 1,181
Princeton, WV 24740 • 7,043
Princeton, WI 54968 • 1,458
Princeton Junction, NJ 08550 • 2,362
Princeville, IL 61559 • 1,421
Princeville, NC 27886 • 1,652
Prince William □, VA • 215,686
Prineville, OR 97754 • 5,355
Prior Lake, MN 55372 • 11,482
Proctor, MN 55810 • 2,974
Proctor, VT 05765 • 1,979
Proctorsville, VT 05153 • 480
Prophetstown, IL 61277 • 1,749
Prospect, CT 06712 • 6,807
Prospect, KY 40059 • 2,788
Prospect, OH 43342 • 1,148
Prospect, OR 97536 • 1,200
Prospect, PA 16052 • 1,122
Prospect Heights, IL 60070 • 15,239
Prospect Park, NJ 07508 • 5,053
Prospect Park, PA 19076 • 6,764
Prosperity, SC 29127 • 1,116
Prosperity, WV 25909 • 1,322
Prosser, WA 99350 • 4,476
Providence, KY 42450 • 4,123
Providence, RI 02901–40 • 160,728
Providence, UT 84332 • 3,344
Providence □, RI • 596,270
Provincetown, MA 02657 • 3,374
Provo, UT 84601–06 • 86,835
Prowers □, CO • 13,347
Prudenville, MI 48651 • 1,100
Prudhoe Bay, AK 99734 • 47
Pryor, OK 74361–62 • 8,327
Pueblo, CO 81001–19 • 98,640
Pueblo □, CO • 123,051
Puhi, HI 96766 • 1,210
Pukalani, HI 96788 • 5,879
Pulaski, NY 13142 • 2,525
Pulaski, TN 38478 • 7,895
Pulaski, VA 24301 • 9,985
Pulaski, WI 54162 • 2,200
Pulaski □, AR • 349,660
Pulaski □, GA • 8,108
Pulaski □, IL • 7,523
Pulaski □, IN • 12,643
Pulaski □, KY • 49,489
Pulaski □, MO • 41,307
Pulaski □, VA • 34,496
Pullman, WA 99163–65 • 23,478
Pumphrey, MD 21227 • 5,483
Punta Gorda, FL 33948–55 • 10,747
Punxsutawney, PA 15767 • 6,782
Purcell, OK 73080 • 4,784
Purcellville, VA 22132 • 1,744
Purvis, MS 39475 • 2,140
Pushmataha □, OK • 10,997
Putnam, CT 06260 • 6,835
Putnam □, FL • 65,070
Putnam □, GA • 14,137
Putnam □, IL • 5,730
Putnam □, IN • 30,315
Putnam □, MO • 5,079
Putnam □, NY • 83,941
Putnam □, OH • 33,819
Putnam □, TN • 51,373
Putnam □, WV • 42,835
Putney, VT 05346 • 1,100
Puyallup, WA 98371–74 • 23,875

Q

Quail Oaks, VA 23234 • 1,500
Quaker Hill, CT 06375 • 2,052
Quakertown, PA 18951 • 8,982
Quanah, TX 79252 • 3,413
Quarryville, PA 17566 • 1,642
Quartz Hill, CA 93536 • 9,626
Quartzsite, AZ 85346 • 1,876
Quay □, NM • 10,823
Quechee, VT 05059 • 550
Queen Annes □, MD • 33,953
Queen City, TX 75572 • 1,748
Queen Creek, AZ 85242 • 2,667
Queens □, NY • 1,951,598
Queensborough, WA 98021 • 4,850
Questa, NM 87556 • 1,707
Quidnessett, RI 02852 • 3,300
Quidnick, RI 02816 • 2,300
Quilcene, WA 98376 • 1,200
Quincy, CA 95971 • 2,700
Quincy, FL 32351 • 7,444
Quincy, IL 62301–06 • 39,681
Quincy, MA 02169 • 84,985
Quincy, MI 49082 • 1,680
Quincy, WA 98848 • 3,738
Quinebaug, CT 06262 • 1,031
Quinhagak, AK 99655 • 501
Quinlan, TX 75474 • 1,360
Quinton, OK 74561 • 1,133
Quitman, GA 31643 • 5,292
Quitman, MS 39355 • 2,736
Quitman, TX 75783 • 1,684
Quitman □, GA • 2,209
Quitman □, MS • 10,490
Quonochontaug, RI 02813 • 1,500

R

Rabun □, GA • 11,648
Raceland, KY 41169 • 2,256
Raceland, LA 70394 • 5,564
Racine, WI 53401–08 • 84,298
Racine □, WI • 175,034
Radcliff, KY 40159–60 • 19,772
Radford, VA 24141–43 • 15,940
Radnor Township, PA 19087 • 28,705
Raeford, NC 28376 • 3,469
Ragland, AL 35131 • 1,807
Rahway, NJ 07065–67 • 25,325
Rainbow City, AL 35901 • 7,673
Rainelle, WV 25962 • 1,681
Rainier, OR 97048 • 1,674
Rains □, TX • 6,715
Rainsville, AL 35986 • 3,875
Raleigh, MS 39153 • 1,291
Raleigh, NC 27601–61 • 207,951
Raleigh □, WV • 76,819
Raleigh Hills, OR 97225 • 6,066
Ralls, TX 79357 • 2,172
Ralls □, MO • 8,476
Ralston, NE 68127 • 6,236
Rambleton Acres, DE 19720 • 1,700
Ramblewood, NJ 08054 • 6,181
Ramona, CA 92065 • 13,040
Ramsay, MI 49959 • 1,075
Ramseur, NC 27316 • 1,186
Ramsey, MN 55303 • 12,408
Ramsey, NJ 07446 • 13,228
Ramsey □, MN • 485,765
Ramsey □, ND • 12,681
Ranchester, WY 82839 • 676
Rancho Cordova, CA 95670 • 48,731
Rancho Mirage, CA 92270 • 9,778
Rancho Palos Verdes, CA 90274 • 41,659
Rancho Rinconado, CA 95014 • 4,206
Ranchos de Taos, NM 87557 • 1,779
Rancocas Woods, NJ 08060 • 1,250
Rand, WV 25306 • 2,400
Randall □, TX • 89,673
Randallstown, MD 21133 • 26,277
Randleman, NC 27317 • 2,612
Randolph, ME 04345 • 1,949
Randolph, MA 02368 • 30,093
Randolph, NY 14772 • 1,298
Randolph, VT 05060 • 2,200
Randolph, WI 53956 • 1,729
Randolph □, AL • 19,881
Randolph □, AR • 16,558
Randolph □, GA • 8,023
Randolph □, IL • 34,583
Randolph □, IN • 27,148
Randolph □, MO • 24,370
Randolph □, NC • 106,546
Randolph □, WV • 27,803
Randolph Hills, MD 20852 • 4,180
Random Lake, WI 53075 • 1,439
Rangely, CO 81648 • 2,278
Ranger, TX 76470 • 2,803
Rankin, PA 15104 • 2,503
Rankin, TX 79778 • 1,011
Rankin □, MS • 87,161
Ransom □, ND • 5,921
Ransomville, NY 14131 • 1,542
Ranson, WV 25438 • 2,890
Rantoul, IL 61866 • 17,212
Raoul, GA 30510 • 1,400
Rapid City, SD 57701–09 • 54,523
Rapides □, LA • 131,556
Rapid Valley, SD 57701 • 5,968
Rappahannock □, VA • 6,622
Raritan, NJ 08869 • 5,798
Rathdrum, ID 83858 • 2,000
Raton, NM 87740 • 7,372
Ravalli □, MT • 25,010
Raven, VA 24639 • 2,640
Ravena, NY 12143 • 3,547
Ravenel, SC 29470 • 2,165
Ravenna, NE 68869 • 1,317
Ravenna, OH 44266 • 12,069
Ravenswood, WV 26164 • 4,189
Rawlins, WY 82301 • 9,380
Rawlins □, KS • 3,404
Ray, ND 58849 • 603
Ray □, MO • 21,971
Raymond, MS 39154 • 2,275
Raymond, NH 03077 • 2,516
Raymond, WA 98577 • 2,901
Raymondville, TX 78580 • 8,880
Raymore, MO 64083 • 5,592
Rayne, LA 70578 • 8,502
Raynham, MA 02767 • 3,709
Raynham Center, MA 02768 • 3,709
Raytown, MO 64133 • 30,601
Rayville, LA 71269 • 4,411
Reading, MA 01867 • 22,539
Reading, MI 49274 • 1,127
Reading, OH 45215 • 12,038
Reading, PA 19601–12 • 78,380
Reagan □, TX • 4,514
Real □, TX • 2,412
Reamstown, PA 17567 • 2,649
Rector, AR 72461 • 2,268
Red Bank, NJ 07701–04 • 10,636
Red Bank, SC 29073 • 6,112
Red Bank, TN 37415 • 12,322
Red Bay, AL 35582 • 3,451
Redbird, OH 44057 • 1,600
Red Bluff, CA 96080 • 12,363
Red Bud, IL 62278 • 2,918
Red Cloud, NE 68970 • 1,204
Redding, CA 96001–03 • 66,462
Redding, CT 06875 • 1,000
Redfield, AR 72132 • 1,082
Redfield, SD 57469 • 2,770
Redford, MI 48239 • 54,387
Redgranite, WI 54970 • 1,009
Red Hook, NY 12571 • 1,794
Redkey, IN 47373 • 1,383
Red Lake □, MN • 4,525
Red Lake Falls, MN 56750 • 1,481
Redlands, CA 92373–75 • 60,394
Red Lion, PA 17356 • 6,130
Red Lodge, MT 59068 • 1,958
Redmond, OR 97756 • 7,163
Redmond, WA 98052–53 • 35,800
Red Oak, GA 30272 • 2,800
Red Oak, IA 51566 • 6,264
Red Oak, TX 75154 • 3,124
Red Oaks, LA 70815 • 1,600
Red Oaks Mill, NY 12603 • 4,906
Redondo Beach, CA 90277–78 • 60,167
Red River □, LA • 9,387
Red River □, TX • 14,317
Red Springs, NC 28377 • 3,799
Red Willow □, NE • 11,705
Red Wing, MN 55066 • 15,134
Redwood, UT 84119 • 1,850
Redwood □, MN • 17,254
Redwood City, CA 94061–65 • 66,072
Redwood Falls, MN 56283 • 4,859
Redwood Valley, CA 95470 • 1,300
Reed City, MI 49677 • 2,379
Reedley, CA 93654 • 15,791
Reedsburg, WI 53959 • 5,834
Reedsport, OR 97467 • 4,796
Reedsville, PA 17084 • 1,030
Reedsville, WI 54230 • 1,182
Reedurban, OH 44710 • 6,650
Reese, MI 48757 • 1,414
Reeves □, TX • 15,852
Reform, AL 35481 • 2,105
Refugio, TX 78377 • 3,158
Refugio □, TX • 7,976
Rehoboth Beach, DE 19971 • 1,234
Reidland, KY 42001 • 4,054
Reidsville, GA 30453 • 2,469
Reidsville, NC 27320–23 • 12,183
Reinbeck, IA 50669 • 1,605
Reisterstown, MD 21136 • 19,314
Reliance, WY 82943 • 500
Remington, IN 47977 • 1,247
Remsen, IA 51050 • 1,513
Reno, NV 89501–70 • 133,850
Reno □, KS • 62,389
Renovo, PA 17764 • 1,526
Rensselaer, IN 47978 • 5,045
Rensselaer, NY 12144 • 8,255
Rensselaer □, NY • 154,429
Renton, WA 98055–59 • 41,688
Renville, MN 56284 • 1,315
Renville □, MN • 17,673
Renville □, ND • 3,160
Republic, MI 49879 • 1,100
Republic, MO 65738 • 6,292
Republic, PA 15475 • 1,400
Republic □, KS • 6,482
Reserve, LA 70084 • 8,847
Reston, VA 22090 • 48,556
Revere, MA 02151 • 42,786
Rexburg, ID 83440 • 14,302
Reynolds, GA 31076 • 1,166
Reynolds □, MO • 6,661
Reynoldsburg, OH 43068 • 25,748
Reynoldsville, PA 15851 • 2,818
Rhea □, TN • 24,344
Rhinebeck, NY 12572 • 2,725
Rhinelander, WI 54501 • 7,427
Rialto, CA 92376–77 • 72,388
Rice □, KS • 10,610
Rice □, MN • 49,183
Rice Lake, WI 54868 • 7,998
Rich □, UT • 1,725
Richardson, TX 75080–83 • 74,840
Richardson □, NE • 9,937
Richardson Park, DE 19804 • 1,100
Richardton, ND 58652 • 625
Richboro, PA 18954 • 5,332
Richfield, MN 55423 • 35,710
Richfield, UT 84701 • 5,593
Richfield Springs, NY 13439 • 1,565
Richford, VT 05476 • 1,425
Rich Hill, MO 64779 • 1,317
Richland, GA 31825 • 1,668
Richland, MO 65556 • 2,029
Richland, WA 99352 • 32,315
Richland □, IL • 16,545
Richland □, LA • 20,629
Richland □, MT • 10,716
Richland □, ND • 18,148
Richland □, OH • 126,137
Richland □, SC • 285,720
Richland □, WI • 17,521
Richland Center, WI 53581 • 5,018
Richland Hills, TX 76118 • 7,978
Richlands, VA 24641 • 4,456
Richlandtown, PA 18955 • 1,195
Richmond, CA 94801–08 • 87,425
Richmond, IL 60071 • 1,016
Richmond, IN 47374–75 • 38,705
Richmond, KY 40475–76 • 21,155
Richmond, ME 04357 • 1,775
Richmond, MI 48062 • 4,141
Richmond, MO 64085 • 5,738
Richmond, TX 77469 • 9,801
Richmond, UT 84333 • 1,955
Richmond, VT 05477 • 650
Richmond, VA 23201–94 • 203,056
Richmond □, GA • 189,719
Richmond □, NY • 378,977
Richmond □, NC • 44,518
Richmond □, VA • 7,273
Richmond Beach, WA 98160 • 5,000
Richmond Heights, FL 33156 • 8,583
Richmond Heights, MO 63117 • 10,448
Richmond Heights, OH 44143 • 9,611
Richmond Highlands, WA 98133 • 26,037
Richmond Hill, GA 31324 • 2,934
Rich Square, NC 27869 • 1,058
Richton, MS 39476 • 1,034
Richton Park, IL 60471 • 10,523
Richwood, OH 43344 • 2,186
Richwood, WV 26261 • 2,808
Riddle, OR 97469 • 1,143
Ridge, NY 11961 • 11,734
Ridgecrest, CA 93555 • 27,725
Ridgecrest, WA 98155 • 5,500
Ridgefield, CT 06877 • 6,363
Ridgefield, NJ 07657 • 9,996
Ridgefield, WA 98642 • 1,297
Ridgefield Park, NJ 07660 • 12,454
Ridgeland, MS 39157–58 • 11,714
Ridgeland, SC 29936 • 1,071
Ridgely, MD 21660 • 1,034
Ridgely, TN 38080 • 1,775
Ridgetop, TN 37152 • 1,132
Ridgeville, SC 29472 • 1,625
Ridgewood, NJ 07450–52 • 24,152
Ridgway, IL 62979 • 1,103
Ridgway, PA 15853 • 4,793
Ridley Park, PA 19078 • 7,592
Ridley Township, PA 19018 • 33,771
Rifle, CO 81650 • 4,636
Rigby, ID 83442 • 2,681
Riley □, KS • 67,139
Rimersburg, PA 16248 • 1,053
Rincon, GA 31326 • 2,697
Ringgold, GA 30736 • 1,675
Ringgold, LA 71068 • 1,856
Ringgold □, IA • 5,420
Ringling, OK 73456 • 1,250
Ringwood, NJ 07456 • 12,623
Rio, FL 34957 • 1,054
Rio Arriba □, NM • 34,365
Rio Blanco □, CO • 5,972
Rio Dell, CA 95562 • 3,012
Rio Del Mar, CA 95003 • 8,919
Rio Grande, NJ 08242 • 2,505
Rio Grande □, CO • 10,770
Rio Grande City, TX 78582 • 9,891
Rio Hondo, TX 78583 • 1,793
Rio Linda, CA 95673 • 9,481
Rio Rancho, NM 87124 • 32,505
Rio Vista, CA 94571 • 3,316
Ripley, MS 38663 • 5,371
Ripley, NY 14775 • 1,189
Ripley, OH 45167 • 1,816
Ripley, TN 38063 • 6,188
Ripley, WV 25271 • 3,023
Ripley □, IN • 24,616
Ripley □, MO • 12,303
Ripon, WI 54971 • 7,241
Rising Sun, DE 19934 • 540
Rising Sun, IN 47040 • 2,311
Rising Sun, MD 21911 • 1,263
Rison, AR 71665 • 1,258
Ritchie □, WV • 10,233
Rittman, OH 44270 • 6,147
Ritzville, WA 99169 • 1,725
Riverbank, CA 95367 • 8,547
Riverdale, CA 93656 • 1,980
Riverdale, GA 30274 • 9,359
Riverdale, IL 60627 • 13,671
Riverdale, MD 20737–38 • 5,185
Riverdale, NJ 07457 • 2,370
Riverdale, UT 84405 • 6,419
River Edge, NJ 07661 • 10,603
River Falls, WI 54022 • 10,610
River Forest, IL 60305 • 11,669
River Grove, IL 60171 • 9,961
Riverhead, NY 11901 • 8,814
River Heights, UT 84321 • 1,274
River Hills, WI 53217 • 1,612
River Oaks, TX 76114 • 6,580
River Pines, MA 01821 • 3,620
River Ridge, LA 70123 • 14,800
River Road, OR 97404 • 9,443
River Rouge, MI 48218 • 11,314
Riverside, AL 35135 • 1,004
Riverside, CA 92501–19 • 226,505
Riverside, IL 60546 • 8,774
Riverside, NJ 08075 • 7,974
Riverside, PA 17868 • 1,991
Riverside □, CA • 1,170,413
Riverton, IL 62561 • 2,638
Riverton, NJ 08077 • 2,775
Riverton, UT 84065 • 11,261
Riverton, VT 05663 • 150
Riverton, WY 82501 • 9,202
Riverton Heights, WA 98188 • 14,182
River Vale, NJ 07675 • 9,410
Riverview, FL 33569 • 6,478
Riverview, MI 48192 • 13,894
Rivesville, WV 26588 • 1,064
Riviera Beach, FL 33404 • 27,639
Riviera Beach, MD 21122 • 11,376
Roane □, TN • 47,227
Roane □, WV • 15,120
Roan Mountain, TN 37687 • 1,220
Roanoke, AL 36274 • 6,362
Roanoke, IL 61561 • 1,910
Roanoke, IN 46783 • 1,018
Roanoke, TX 76262 • 1,616
Roanoke, VA 24001–38 • 96,397
Roanoke □, VA • 79,332
Roanoke Rapids, NC 27870 • 15,722
Roaring Spring, PA 16673 • 2,615
Robbins, IL 60472 • 7,498
Robbinsdale, MN 55422 • 14,396
Robersonville, NC 27871 • 1,940
Robert Lee, TX 76945 • 1,276
Roberts, WI 54023 • 1,043
Roberts □, SD • 9,914
Roberts □, TX • 1,025
Robertsdale, AL 36567 • 2,401
Robertson □, KY • 2,124
Robertson □, TN • 41,494
Robertson □, TX • 15,511
Robertsville, NJ 07746 • 9,841
Robeson □, NC • 105,179
Robinson, IL 62454 • 6,740
Robinson, TX 76706 • 7,111
Robstown, TX 78380 • 12,849
Rochdale, MA 01542 • 1,105
Rochelle, GA 31079 • 1,510
Rochelle, IL 61068 • 8,769
Rochelle Park, NJ 07662 • 5,587
Rochester, IL 62563 • 2,676
Rochester, IN 46975 • 5,969
Rochester, MI 48306–09 • 7,130
Rochester, MN 55901–06 • 70,745
Rochester, NH 03867–68 • 26,630
Rochester, NY 14601–92 • 231,636
Rochester, PA 15074 • 4,156
Rochester, VT 05767 • 500
Rochester, WA 98579 • 1,150
Rochester Hills, MI 48309 • 61,766
Rock □, MN • 9,806
Rock □, NE • 2,019
Rock □, WI • 139,510
Rockaway, NJ 07866 • 6,243

Rockbridge □, VA • *18,350*
Rockcastle □, KY • *14,803*
Rock Creek, MN 55067 • *1,040*
Rock Creek 0M, OR • *8,282*
Rockdale, IL 60436 • *1,709*
Rockdale, MD 21207 • *5,885*
Rockdale, TX 76567 • *5,235*
Rockdale □, GA • *54,091*
Rock Falls, IL 61071 • *9,654*
Rockford, IL 61101–32 • *139,426*
Rockford, MI 49341 • *3,750*
Rockford, MN 55373 • *2,665*
Rockford, OH 45882 • *1,119*
Rock Hall, MD 21661 • *1,584*
Rock Hill, MO 63124 • *5,217*
Rock Hill, SC 29730–32 • *41,643*
Rockingham, NC 28379 • *9,399*
Rockingham □, NH • *245,845*
Rockingham □, NC • *86,064*
Rockingham □, VA • *57,482*
Rock Island, IL 61201–04 • *40,552*
Rock Island □, IL • *148,723*
Rockland, ME 04841 • *7,972*
Rockland, MA 02370 • *15,695*
Rockland □, NY • *265,475*
Rockledge, FL 32955–56 • *16,023*
Rockledge, PA 19111 • *2,679*
Rocklin, CA 95677 • *19,033*
Rockmart, GA 30153 • *3,356*
Rockport, IN 47635 • *2,315*
Rockport, ME 04856 • *1,100*
Rockport, MA 01966 • *4,690*
Rock Port, MO 64482 • *1,438*
Rockport, TX 78382 • *4,753*
Rock Rapids, IA 51246 • *2,601*
Rock River, WY 82083 • *190*
Rocksprings, TX 78880 • *1,339*
Rock Springs, WY 82901–02 • *19,050*
Rockton, IL 61072 • *2,928*
Rock Valley, IA 51247 • *2,540*
Rockville, IN 47872 • *2,706*
Rockville, MD 20847–59 • *44,835*
Rockville Centre, NY 11570–71 • *24,727*
Rockwall, TX 75087 • *10,486*
Rockwall □, TX • *25,604*
Rockwell, IA 50469 • *1,008*
Rockwell, NC 28138 • *1,598*
Rockwell City, IA 50579 • *1,981*
Rockwell Park, NC 28213 • *2,600*
Rockwood, MI 48173 • *3,141*
Rockwood, OR 97233 • *11,000*
Rockwood, PA 15557 • *1,014*
Rockwood, TN 37854 • *5,348*
Rocky Creek, FL 33615 • *7,800*
Rocky Ford, CO 81067 • *4,162*
Rocky Hill, CT 06067 • *14,559*
Rocky Mount, NC 27801–04 • *48,997*
Rocky Mount, VA 24151 • *4,098*
Rocky Point, NY 11778 • *8,596*
Rocky River, OH 44116 • *20,410*
Rodeo, CA 94572 • *7,589*
Roderfield, WV 24881 • *1,200*
Rodney Village, DE 19901 • *1,745*
Roebling, NJ 08554 • *2,415*
Roebuck, SC 29376 • *1,966*
Roeland Park, KS 66203 • *7,706*
Roessleville, NY 12205 • *10,753*
Roger Mills □, OK • *4,147*
Rogers, AR 72756–57 • *24,692*
Rogers, TX 76569 • *1,131*
Rogers □, OK • *55,170*
Rogers City, MI 49779 • *3,642*
Rogersville, AL 35652 • *1,125*
Rogersville, TN 37857 • *4,149*
Rogue River, OR 97537 • *1,759*
Rohnert Park, CA 94927–28 • *36,326*
Roland, IA 50236 • *1,035*
Roland, OK 74954 • *2,481*
Rolette □, ND • *12,772*
Rolla, MO 65401 • *14,090*
Rolla, ND 58367 • *1,286*
Rolling Fork, MS 39159 • *2,444*
Rolling Hills Estates, CA 90274 • *7,789*
Rolling Meadows, IL 60008 • *22,591*
Rollinsford, NH 03869 • *2,645*
Roma, TX 78584 • *8,059*
Rome, GA 30161–65 • *30,326*
Rome, IL 61562 • *1,902*
Rome, NY 13440 • *44,350*
Rome City, IN 46784 • *1,138*
Romeo, MI 48065 • *3,520*
Romeoville, IL 60441 • *14,074*
Romney, WV 26757 • *1,966*
Romulus, MI 48174 • *22,897*
Ronan, MT 59864 • *1,547*
Ronceverte, WV 24970 • *1,754*
Ronkonkoma, NY 11779 • *20,391*
Roodhouse, IL 62082 • *2,139*
Rooks □, KS • *6,039*
Roosevelt, NY 11575 • *15,030*
Roosevelt, UT 84066 • *3,915*
Roosevelt □, MT • *10,999*
Roosevelt □, NM • *16,702*
Roosevelt Park, MI 49441 • *3,885*
Rosamond, CA 93560 • *7,430*
Roscoe, IL 61073 • *2,079*
Roscoe, TX 79545 • *1,446*
Roscommon □, MI • *19,776*
Roseau, MN 56751 • *2,396*
Roseau □, MN • *15,026*
Roseboro, NC 28382 • *1,441*
Rosebud, TX 76570 • *1,638*
Rosebud □, MT • *10,505*
Roseburg, OR 97470 • *17,032*
Rosedale, MD 21237 • *18,703*
Rosedale, MS 38769 • *2,595*
Rose Hill, KS 67133 • *2,399*
Rose Hill, NC 28458 • *1,287*
Rose Hill, VA 22310 • *12,675*
Roseland, CA 95407 • *8,779*
Roseland, FL 32957 • *1,379*
Roseland, LA 70456 • *1,093*
Roseland, NJ 07068 • *4,847*
Roseland, OH 44906 • *3,000*
Roselle, IL 60172 • *20,819*
Roselle, NJ 07203 • *20,314*
Roselle Park, NJ 07204 • *12,805*
Rosemead, CA 91770 • *51,638*
Rosemont, CA 95826 • *22,851*
Rosemount, MN 55068 • *8,622*
Rosenberg, TX 77471 • *20,183*
Rosepine, LA 70659 • *1,135*
Roseto, PA 18013 • *1,555*
Roseville, CA 95678 • *44,685*
Roseville, IL 61473 • *1,151*
Roseville, MI 48066 • *51,412*
Roseville, MN 55113 • *33,485*
Roseville, OH 43777 • *1,847*
Rosewood Heights, IL 62024 • *4,821*
Rosiclare, IL 62982 • *1,378*
Roslyn Heights, NY 11577 • *6,405*
Ross, OH 45061 • *2,124*
Ross □, OH • *69,330*
Rossford, OH 43460 • *5,861*
Rossmoor, CA 90720 • *9,893*
Ross Township, PA 15237 • *33,482*
Rossville, GA 30741–42 • *3,601*
Rossville, IL 60963 • *1,334*
Rossville, IN 46065 • *1,175*
Rossville, KS 66533 • *1,052*
Roswell, GA 30075–77 • *47,923*
Roswell, NM 88201–02 • *44,654*
Rotan, TX 79546 • *1,913*
Rothschild, WI 54474 • *3,310*
Rothsville, PA 17543 • *2,097*
Rotterdam, NY 12303 • *21,228*
Roulette, PA 16746 • *1,500*
Round Lake, IL 60073 • *3,550*
Round Lake Beach, IL 60073 • *16,434*
Round Mountain, NV 89045 • *210*
Round Rock, TX 78664 • *30,923*
Roundup, MT 59072 • *1,808*
Rouses Point, NY 12979 • *2,377*
Routt □, CO • *14,088*
Rouzerville, PA 17250 • *1,188*
Rowan □, KY • *20,353*
Rowan □, NC • *110,605*
Rowland, NC 28383 • *1,139*
Rowland Heights, CA 91748 • *32,700*
Rowlett, TX 75088 • *23,260*
Rowley, MA 01969 • *1,144*
Roxboro, NC 27573 • *7,332*
Roy, UT 84067 • *24,603*
Royal Oak, MI 48067–73 • *65,410*
Royal Pines, NC 28704 • *1,600*
Royalton, IL 62983 • *1,191*
Royersford, PA 19468 • *4,458*
Royse City, TX 75089 • *2,206*
Royston, GA 30662 • *2,758*
Rubidoux, CA 92509 • *24,367*
Rugby, ND 58368 • *2,909*
Ruidoso, NM 88345 • *4,600*
Ruidoso Downs, NM 88346 • *920*
Ruleville, MS 38771 • *3,245*
Rumford, ME 04276 • *5,419*
Rumson, NJ 07760 • *6,701*
Runge, TX 78151 • *1,139*
Runnels □, TX • *11,294*
Runnemede, NJ 08078 • *9,042*
Rupert, ID 83350 • *5,455*
Rupert, WV 25984 • *1,104*
Rural Hall, NC 27045 • *1,652*
Rush □, IN • *18,129*
Rush □, KS • *3,842*
Rush City, MN 55069 • *1,497*
Rushford, MN 55971 • *1,485*
Rushmere, VA 23430 • *1,064*
Rush Springs, OK 73082 • *1,229*
Rushville, IL 62681 • *3,229*
Rushville, IN 46173 • *5,533*
Rushville, NE 69360 • *1,127*
Rusk, TX 75785 • *4,366*
Rusk □, TX • *43,735*
Rusk □, WI • *15,079*
Ruskin, FL 33570–73 • *6,046*
Russell, KS 67665 • *4,781*
Russell, KY 41169 • *4,014*
Russell, PA 16345 • *1,000*
Russell □, AL • *46,860*
Russell □, KS • *7,835*
Russell □, KY • *14,716*
Russell □, VA • *28,667*
Russell Springs, KY 42642 • *2,363*
Russellville, AL 35653 • *7,812*
Russellville, AR 72801 • *21,260*
Russellville, KY 42276 • *7,454*
Russellville, OR 97216 • *6,500*
Russellville, TN 37860 • *1,069*
Ruston, LA 71270–73 • *20,027*
Ruth, NV 89319 • *550*
Rutherford, NJ 07070–75 • *17,790*
Rutherford, TN 38369 • *1,303*
Rutherford □, NC • *56,918*
Rutherford □, TN • *118,570*
Rutherfordton, NC 28139 • *3,617*
Rutland, MA 01543 • *2,145*
Rutland, VT 05701–02 • *18,230*
Rutland □, VT • *62,142*
Rye, NH 03870 • *835*
Rye, NY 10580 • *14,936*
Rye Brook, NY 10573 • *7,765*

S

Sabattus, ME 04280 • *3,696*
Sabetha, KS 66534 • *2,341*
Sabina, OH 45169 • *2,662*
Sabinal, TX 78881 • *1,584*
Sabine □, LA • *22,646*
Sabine □, TX • *9,586*
Sac □, IA • *12,324*
Sacaton, AZ 85221 • *1,452*
Sac City, IA 50583 • *2,492*
Sachse, TX 75040 • *5,346*
Sackets Harbor, NY 13685 • *1,313*
Saco, ME 04072 • *15,181*
Sacramento, CA 95801–66 • *369,365*
Sacramento □, CA • *1,041,219*
Saddle Brook, NJ 07662 • *13,296*
Saddle River, NJ 07458 • *2,950*
Saegertown, PA 16433 • *1,066*
Safety Harbor, FL 34695 • *15,124*
Safford, AZ 85546 • *7,359*
Sagadahoc □, ME • *33,535*
Sagamore, MA 02561 • *2,589*
Sagamore Hills, OH 44067 • *4,700*
Sag Harbor, NY 11963 • *2,134*
Saginaw, MI 48601–08 • *69,512*
Saginaw, TX 76179 • *8,551*
Saginaw □, MI • *211,946*
Saguache □, CO • *4,619*
Saint Albans, VT 05478 • *7,339*
Saint Albans, WV 25177 • *11,194*
Saint Andrews, SC 29407 • *9,908*
Saint Andrews, SC 29210 • *25,692*
Saint Ann, MO 63074 • *14,489*
Saint Anne, IL 60964 • *1,153*
Saint Ansgar, IA 50472 • *1,063*
Saint Anthony, ID 83445 • *3,010*
Saint Anthony, MN 55418 • *7,727*
Saint Augustine, FL 32084–86 • *11,692*
Saint Bernard, OH 45217 • *5,344*
Saint Bernard □, LA • *66,631*
Saint Charles, IL 60174–75 • *22,501*
Saint Charles, MD 20601 • *28,717*
Saint Charles, MI 48655 • *2,144*
Saint Charles, MN 55972 • *2,642*
Saint Charles, MO 63301–03 • *54,555*
Saint Charles □, LA • *42,437*
Saint Charles □, MO • *212,907*
Saint Charles Mesa, CO 81006 • *7,050*
Saint Clair, MI 48079 • *5,116*
Saint Clair, MO 63077 • *3,917*
Saint Clair, PA 17970 • *3,524*
Saint Clair □, AL • *50,009*
Saint Clair □, IL • *262,852*
Saint Clair □, MI • *145,607*
Saint Clair □, MO • *8,457*
Saint Clair Shores, MI 48080–82 • *68,107*
Saint Clairsville, OH 43950 • *5,162*
Saint Cloud, FL 34769–73 • *12,453*
Saint Cloud, MN 56301–04 • *48,812*
Saint Croix □, WI • *50,251*
Saint Croix Falls, WI 54024 • *1,640*
Saint David, AZ 85630 • *1,500*
Saint Elmo, IL 62458 • *1,473*
Saint Francis, KS 67756 • *1,495*
Saint Francis, MN 55070 • *2,538*
Saint Francis, SD 57572 • *815*
Saint Francis, WI 53207 • *9,245*
Saint Francis □, AR • *28,497*
Saint Francisville, LA 70775 • *1,700*
Saint Francois □, MO • *48,904*
Sainte Genevieve, MO 63670 • *4,411*
Sainte Genevieve □, MO • *16,037*
Saint George, SC 29477 • *2,077*
Saint George, UT 84770–71 • *28,502*
Saint Georges, DE 19733 • *500*
Saint Helena, CA 94574 • *4,990*
Saint Helena □, LA • *9,874*
Saint Helens, OR 97051 • *7,535*
Saint Henry, OH 45883 • *1,907*
Saint Ignace, MI 49781 • *2,568*
Saint Ignatius, MT 59865 • *778*
Saint James, MN 56081 • *4,364*
Saint James, MO 65559 • *3,256*
Saint James, NY 11780 • *12,703*
Saint James □, LA • *20,879*
Saint James City, FL 33956 • *1,094*
Saint Jo, TX 76265 • *1,048*
Saint John, IN 46373 • *4,921*
Saint John, KS 67576 • *1,357*
Saint Johns, AZ 85936 • *3,294*
Saint Johns, MI 48879 • *7,284*
Saint Johns, MO 63114 • *7,466*
Saint Johns □, FL • *83,829*
Saint Johnsbury, VT 05819 • *6,424*
Saint Johnsville, NY 13452 • *1,825*
Saint John the Baptist □, LA • *39,996*
Saint Joseph, IL 61873 • *2,052*
Saint Joseph, LA 71366 • *1,517*
Saint Joseph, MI 49085 • *9,214*
Saint Joseph, MN 56374 • *3,294*
Saint Joseph, MO 64501–08 • *71,852*
Saint Joseph □, IN • *247,052*
Saint Joseph □, MI • *58,913*
Saint Landry □, LA • *80,331*
Saint Lawrence □, NY • *111,974*
Saint Leo, FL 33574 • *1,009*
Saint Louis, MI 48880 • *3,828*
Saint Louis, MO 63101–88 • *396,685*
Saint Louis □, MN • *198,213*
Saint Louis □, MO • *993,529*
Saint Louis Park, MN 55426 • *43,787*
Saint Lucie □, FL • *150,171*
Saint Maries, ID 83861 • *2,442*
Saint Martin □, LA • *43,978*
Saint Martinville, LA 70582 • *7,137*
Saint Mary □, LA • *58,086*
Saint Marys, AK 99658 • *441*
Saint Marys, GA 31558 • *8,187*
Saint Marys, IN 46556 • *1,800*
Saint Marys, KS 66536 • *1,791*
Saint Marys, OH 45885 • *8,441*
Saint Marys, PA 15857 • *5,511*
Saint Marys, WV 26170 • *2,148*
Saint Marys □, MD • *75,974*
Saint Marys City, MD 20686 • *3,200*
Saint Matthews, KY 40207 • *15,800*
Saint Matthews, SC 29135 • *2,345*
Saint Michael, MN 55376 • *2,506*
Saint Michaels, MD 21663 • *1,301*
Saint Paris, OH 43072 • *1,842*
Saint Paul, AK 99660 • *763*
Saint Paul, IN 47272 • *1,032*
Saint Paul, MN 55101–89 • *272,235*
Saint Paul, MO 63366 • *1,192*
Saint Paul, NE 68873 • *2,009*
Saint Paul, VA 24283 • *1,007*
Saint Paul Park, MN 55071 • *4,965*
Saint Pauls, NC 28384 • *1,992*
Saint Peter, MN 56082 • *9,421*
Saint Peters, MO 63376 • *45,779*
Saint Petersburg, FL 33701–84 • *238,629*
Saint Petersburg Beach, FL 33706 • *9,200*
Saint Rose, LA 70087 • *2,800*
Saint Simons Island, GA 31522 • *12,026*
Saint Stephen, SC 29479 • *1,697*
Saint Stephens, NC 28601 • *8,734*
Saint Tammany □, LA • *144,508*
Salamanca, NY 14779 • *6,566*
Sale Creek, TN 37373 • *1,050*
Salem, AR 72576 • *1,474*
Salem, IL 62881 • *7,470*
Salem, IN 47167 • *5,619*
Salem, MA 01970–71 • *38,091*
Salem, MO 65560 • *4,486*
Salem, NH 03079 • *12,000*
Salem, NJ 08079 • *6,883*
Salem, OH 44460 • *12,233*
Salem, OR 97301–14 • *107,786*
Salem, SD 57058 • *1,289*
Salem, UT 84653 • *2,284*
Salem, VA 24153 • *23,756*
Salem, WV 26426 • *2,063*
Salem, WI 53168 • *1,020*
Salem □, NJ • *65,294*
Salida, CO 81201 • *4,737*
Salina, KS 67401–02 • *42,303*
Salina, OK 74365 • *1,153*
Salina, UT 84654 • *1,943*
Salinas, CA 93901–15 • *108,777*
Saline, MI 48176 • *6,660*
Saline □, AR • *64,183*
Saline □, IL • *26,551*
Saline □, KS • *49,301*
Saline □, MO • *23,523*
Saline □, NE • *12,715*
Salineville, OH 43945 • *1,474*
Salisbury, CT 06068 • *1,600*
Salisbury, MD 21801–03 • *20,592*
Salisbury, MA 01952 • *3,729*
Salisbury, MO 65281 • *1,881*
Salisbury, NC 28144–46 • *23,087*
Sallisaw, OK 74955 • *7,122*
Salmon, ID 83467 • *2,941*
Salmon Creek, WA 98665 • *11,989*
Saltillo, MS 38866 • *1,782*
Salt Lake □, UT • *725,956*
Salt Lake City, UT 84101–90 • *159,936*
Salt Springs, FL 32113 • *1,500*
Saltville, VA 24370 • *2,300*
Saltwater, WA 98188 • *2,200*
Saluda, SC 29138 • *2,798*
Saluda □, SC • *16,357*
Salyersville, KY 41465 • *1,917*
Samoset, FL 34208 • *3,119*
Sampson □, NC • *47,297*
Samson, AL 36477 • *2,190*
Samtown, LA 71301 • *3,500*
San Andreas, CA 95249 • *2,115*
San Angelo, TX 76901–06 • *84,474*
San Anselmo, CA 94960 • *11,743*
San Antonio, TX 78201–99 • *935,933*
Sanatoga, PA 19464 • *5,534*
San Augustine, TX 75972 • *2,337*
San Augustine □, TX • *7,999*
San Benito, TX 78586 • *20,125*
San Benito □, CA • *36,697*
San Bernardino, CA 92401–27 • *164,164*
San Bernardino □, CA • *1,418,380*
Sanborn, IA 51248 • *1,345*
Sanborn □, SD • *2,833*
San Bruno, CA 94066 • *38,961*
San Carlos, AZ 85550 • *2,918*
San Carlos, CA 94070 • *26,167*
San Carlos Park, FL 33912 • *11,785*
San Clemente, CA 92672–74 • *41,100*
Sandalfoot Cove, FL 33433 • *14,214*
Sanders □, MT • *8,669*
Sanderson, TX 79848 • *1,128*
Sandersville, GA 31082 • *6,290*
Sand Hill, MA 02066 • *1,800*
Sandia, NM 87047 • *6,742*
San Diego, CA 92101–99 • *1,110,549*
San Diego, TX 78384 • *4,983*
San Diego □, CA • *2,498,016*
San Dimas, CA 91773 • *32,397*
Sandoval, IL 62882 • *1,535*
Sandoval □, NM • *63,319*
Sand Point, AK 99661 • *878*
Sandpoint, ID 83862–65 • *5,203*
Sand Springs, OK 74063 • *15,346*
Sandston, VA 23150 • *3,630*
Sandstone, MN 55072 • *2,057*
Sandusky, MI 48471 • *2,403*
Sandusky, OH 44870–71 • *29,764*
Sandusky □, OH • *61,963*
Sandwich, IL 60548 • *5,567*
Sandwich, MA 02563 • *2,998*
Sandy, OR 97055 • *4,152*
Sandy, UT 84070 • *75,058*
Sandy Hook, CT 06482 • *1,100*
Sandy Springs, GA 30328 • *67,842*
Sandy Springs, SC 29677 • *1,200*
San Felipe Pueblo, NM 87001 • *1,557*
San Fernando, CA 91340–46 • *22,580*
Sanford, FL 32771–73 • *32,387*
Sanford, ME 04073 • *10,296*
Sanford, NC 27330–31 • *14,475*
San Francisco, CA 94101–88 • *723,959*
San Francisco □, CA • *723,959*
Sangamon □, IL • *178,386*
Sanger, CA 93657 • *16,839*
Sanger, TX 76266 • *3,508*
Sanibel, FL 33957 • *5,468*
Sanilac □, MI • *39,928*
San Jacinto, CA 92383 • *16,210*
San Jacinto □, TX • *16,372*
San Joaquin □, CA • *480,628*
San Jose, CA 95101–96 • *782,248*
San Juan, TX 78589 • *10,815*
San Juan □, CO • *745*
San Juan □, NM • *91,605*
San Juan □, UT • *12,621*
San Juan □, WA • *10,035*
San Juan Capistrano, CA 92690–93 • *26,183*
San Leandro, CA 94577–79 • *68,223*
San Lorenzo, CA 94580 • *19,987*
San Luis, AZ 85634 • *4,212*
San Luis Obispo, CA 93401–12 • *41,958*
San Luis Obispo □, CA • *217,162*
San Manuel, AZ 85631 • *4,009*
San Marcos, CA 92069 • *38,974*
San Marcos, TX 78666–67 • *28,743*
San Marino, CA 91108 • *12,959*
San Mateo, CA 94401–04 • *85,486*
San Mateo □, CA • *649,623*
San Miguel □, CO • *3,653*
San Miguel □, NM • *25,743*
San Pablo, CA 94806 • *25,158*
San Patricio □, TX • *58,749*
Sanpete □, UT • *16,259*
San Rafael, CA 94901–15 • *48,404*
San Ramon, CA 94583 • *35,303*
San Remo, NY 11754 • *7,770*
San Saba, TX 76877 • *2,626*
San Saba □, TX • *5,401*
Sans Souci, SC 29609 • *7,612*
Santa Ana, CA 92701–08 • *293,742*
Santa Anna, TX 76878 • *1,249*
Santa Barbara, CA 93101–90 • *85,571*
Santa Barbara □, CA • *369,608*
Santa Clara, CA 95050–56 • *93,613*
Santa Clara, OR 97404 • *12,834*
Santa Clara, UT 84765 • *2,322*
Santa Clara □, CA • *1,497,577*
Santa Cruz, CA 95060–67 • *49,040*
Santa Cruz, NM 87567 • *975*
Santa Cruz □, AZ • *29,676*
Santa Cruz □, CA • *229,734*
Santa Fe, NM 87501–06 • *55,859*
Santa Fe, TX 77510 • *8,429*
Santa Fe □, NM • *98,928*
Santa Fe Springs, CA 90670–71 • *15,520*
Santa Margarita, CA 93453 • *1,200*
Santa Maria, CA 93454–56 • *61,284*
Santa Monica, CA 90401–11 • *86,905*
Santa Paula, CA 93060–61 • *25,062*
Santaquin, UT 84655 • *2,386*
Santa Rosa, CA 95401–09 • *113,313*
Santa Rosa, NM 88435 • *2,263*
Santa Rosa □, FL • *81,608*
Santa Venetia, CA 94901 • *6,000*
Santa Ynez, CA 93460 • *4,200*
Santee, CA 92071 • *52,902*
Santo Domingo Pueblo, NM 87052 • *2,866*
San Ygnacio, TX 78067 • *1,000*
Sappington, MO 63126 • *10,917*
Sapulpa, OK 74066–67 • *18,074*
Saraland, AL 36571 • *11,751*
Saranac, MI 48881 • *1,461*
Saranac Lake, NY 12983 • *5,377*
Sarasota, FL 34230–43 • *50,961*
Sarasota □, FL • *277,776*
Sarasota Springs, FL 34232 • *16,088*
Saratoga, CA 95070–71 • *28,061*
Saratoga, TX 77585 • *1,200*
Saratoga, WY 82331 • *1,969*
Saratoga □, NY • *181,276*
Saratoga Springs, NY 12866 • *25,001*
Sarcoxie, MO 64862 • *1,330*
Sardis, GA 30456 • *1,116*
Sardis, MS 38666 • *2,128*
Sargent □, ND • *4,549*
Sarpy □, NE • *102,583*
Sartell, MN 56377 • *5,393*
Satanta, KS 67870 • *1,073*
Satellite Beach, FL 32937 • *9,889*
Satsuma, AL 36572 • *5,194*
Saugerties, NY 12477 • *3,915*
Saugus, MA 01906 • *25,549*
Sauk □, WI • *46,975*
Sauk Centre, MN 56378 • *3,581*
Sauk City, WI 53583 • *3,019*
Sauk Rapids, MN 56379 • *7,825*
Sauk Village, IL 60411 • *9,926*
Saukville, WI 53080 • *3,695*
Sault Sainte Marie, MI 49783 • *14,689*
Saunders □, NE • *18,285*
Saunderstown, RI 02874 • *400*
Sausalito, CA 94965–66 • *7,152*
Savage, MD 20763 • *2,850*
Savage, MN 55378 • *9,906*
Savanna, IL 61074 • *3,819*
Savannah, GA 31401–20 • *137,560*
Savannah, MO 64485 • *4,352*
Savannah, TN 38372 • *6,547*
Savoonga, AK 99769 • *519*
Savoy, IL 61874 • *2,674*
Sawyer □, WI • *14,181*
Saxonburg, PA 16056 • *1,345*
Saxtons River, VT 05154 • *541*
Saybrook Manor, CT 06475 • *1,073*
Saydel, IA 50313 • *3,500*
Saylesville, RI 02865 • *3,510*
Saylorsburg, PA 18353 • *1,500*
Sayre, OK 73662 • *2,881*
Sayre, PA 18840 • *5,791*
Sayreville, NJ 08872 • *34,986*
Sayville, NY 11782 • *16,550*
Scalp Level, PA 15963 • *1,158*
Scappoose, OR 97056 • *3,529*
Scarborough, ME 04074 • *2,586*
Scarsdale, NY 10583 • *16,987*
Schaumburg, IL 60192–94 • *68,586*
Schenectady, NY 12301–09 • *65,566*
Schenectady □, NY • *149,285*
Schererville, IN 46375 • *19,926*
Schertz, TX 78154 • *10,555*
Schiller Park, IL 60176 • *11,189*
Schleicher □, TX • *2,990*
Schley □, GA • *3,588*
Schofield, WI 54476 • *2,415*
Schoharie, NY 12157 • *1,045*
Schoharie □, NY • *31,859*
Schoolcraft, MI 49087 • *1,517*
Schoolcraft □, MI • *8,302*
Schroon Lake, NY 12870 • *1,100*
Schulenburg, TX 78956 • *2,455*
Schurz, NV 89427 • *617*
Schuyler, NE 68661 • *4,052*
Schuyler □, IL • *7,498*
Schuyler □, MO • *4,236*
Schuyler □, NY • *18,662*
Schuylerville, NY 12871 • *1,364*
Schuylkill □, PA • *152,585*
Schuylkill Haven, PA 17972 • *5,610*
Scioto □, OH • *80,327*
Scituate, MA 02066 • *5,180*
Scobey, MT 59263 • *1,154*
Scotch Plains, NJ 07076 • *21,160*
Scotchtown, NY 10940 • *8,765*
Scotia, CA 95565 • *1,200*
Scotia, NY 12302 • *7,359*
Scotland, SD 57059 • *968*
Scotland □, MO • *4,822*
Scotland □, NC • *33,754*
Scotland Neck, NC 27874 • *2,575*
Scotlandville, LA 70807 • *15,113*
Scott, LA 70583 • *4,912*
Scott □, AR • *10,205*
Scott □, IL • *5,644*
Scott □, IN • *20,991*
Scott □, IA • *150,979*
Scott □, KS • *5,289*
Scott □, KY • *23,867*
Scott □, MN • *57,846*
Scott □, MS • *24,137*
Scott □, MO • *39,376*
Scott □, TN • *18,358*
Scott □, VA • *23,204*
Scott City, KS 67871 • *3,785*
Scott City, MO 63780 • *4,292*
Scottdale, GA 30079 • *8,636*
Scottdale, PA 15683 • *5,184*
Scott Lake, FL 33055 • *14,588*
Scottsbluff, NE 69361–63 • *13,711*
Scotts Bluff □, NE • *36,025*
Scottsboro, AL 35768 • *13,786*
Scottsburg, IN 47170 • *5,334*
Scottsdale, AZ 85250–71 • *130,069*
Scotts Valley, CA 95066–67 • *8,615*
Scottsville, KY 42164 • *4,278*

United States Populations and ZIP Codes

Scottsville, NY 14546 • 1,912
Scott Township, PA 15106 • 17,118
Scottville, MI 49454 • 1,287
Scranton, PA 18501–19 • 81,805
Screven □, GA • 13,842
Scurry □, TX • 18,634
Seabreeze, DE 19971 • 350
Sea Bright, NJ 07760 • 1,693
Seabrook, MD 20706 • 7,660
Seabrook, NJ 08302 • 1,457
Seabrook, TX 77586 • 6,685
Sea Cliff, NY 11579 • 5,054
Seadrift, TX 77983 • 1,277
Seaford, DE 19973 • 5,689
Seaford, NY 11783 • 15,597
Seaford, VA 23696 • 2,340
Seagate, NC 28403 • 5,444
Sea Girt, NJ 08750 • 2,099
Seagoville, TX 75159 • 8,969
Seagraves, TX 79359 • 2,398
Sea Isle City, NJ 08243 • 2,692
Seal Beach, CA 90740 • 25,098
Sealy, TX 77474 • 4,541
Seaman, OH 45679 • 1,013
Searchlight, NV 89029 • 430
Searcy, AR 72143 • 15,180
Searcy □, AR • 7,841
Searsport, ME 04974 • 1,151
Seaside, CA 93955 • 38,901
Seaside, OR 97138 • 5,359
Seaside Heights, NJ 08751 • 2,366
Seaside Park, NJ 08752 • 1,871
Seat Pleasant, MD 20743 • 5,359
Seattle, WA 98101–99 • 516,259
Sebastian, FL 32958 • 10,205
Sebastian □, AR • 99,590
Sebewaing, MI 48759 • 1,923
Sebree, KY 42455 • 1,510
Sebring, FL 33870–72 • 8,900
Sebring, OH 44672 • 4,848
Secaucus, NJ 07094 • 14,061
Security, CO 80911 • 6,660
Sedalia, MO 65301–02 • 19,800
Sedan, KS 67361 • 1,306
Sedgwick, KS 67135 • 1,438
Sedgwick □, CO • 2,690
Sedgwick □, KS • 403,662
Sedona, AZ 86336 • 7,720
Sedro Woolley, WA 98284 • 6,031
Seekonk, MA 02771 • 12,269
Seeley, CA 92273 • 1,228
Seelyville, IN 47878 • 1,090
Seguin, TX 78155–56 • 18,853
Seiling, OK 73663 • 1,031
Selah, WA 98942 • 5,113
Selawik, AK 99770 • 596
Selby, SD 57472 • 707
Selbyville, DE 19975 • 1,335
Selden, NY 11784 • 20,608
Seldovia, AK 99663 • 316
Selinsgrove, PA 17870 • 5,384
Sellersburg, IN 47172 • 5,745
Sellersville, PA 18960 • 4,479
Sells, AZ 85634 • 2,750
Selma, AL 36701–02 • 23,755
Selma, CA 93662 • 14,757
Selma, NC 27576 • 4,600
Selmer, TN 38375 • 3,838
Seminole, OK 74868 • 7,071
Seminole, TX 79360 • 6,342
Seminole □, FL • 287,529
Seminole □, GA • 9,010
Seminole □, OK • 25,412
Seminole Park, FL 34647 • 8,000
Semmes, AL 36575 • 2,250
Senath, MO 63876 • 1,622
Senatobia, MS 38668 • 4,772
Seneca, IL 61360 • 1,878
Seneca, KS 66538 • 2,027
Seneca, MO 64865 • 1,885
Seneca, PA 16346 • 1,300
Seneca, SC 29678–79 • 7,726
Seneca □, NY • 33,683
Seneca □, OH • 59,733
Seneca Falls, NY 13148 • 7,370
Sequatchie □, TN • 8,863
Sequim, WA 98382 • 3,616
Sequoyah □, OK • 33,828
Sergeant Bluff, IA 51054 • 2,772
Sesser, IL 62884 • 2,087
Seven Hills, OH 44131 • 12,339
Seven Oaks, SC 29210 • 15,722
Severn, MD 21144 • 24,499
Severna Park, MD 21146 • 25,879
Sevier □, AR • 13,637
Sevier □, TN • 51,043
Sevier □, UT • 15,431
Sevierville, TN 37862 • 7,178
Seville, OH 44273 • 1,810
Sewanee, TN 37375 • 2,128
Seward, AK 99664 • 2,699
Seward, NE 68434 • 5,634
Seward □, KS • 18,743
Seward □, NE • 15,450
Sewell, NJ 08080 • 1,870
Sewickley, PA 15143 • 4,134
Seymour, CT 06483 • 14,288
Seymour, IN 47274 • 15,576
Seymour, MO 65746 • 1,636
Seymour, TN 37865 • 7,026
Seymour, TX 76380 • 3,185
Seymour, WI 54165 • 2,782
Seymourville, LA 70764 • 2,891
Shackelford □, TX • 3,316
Shady Cove, OR 97539 • 1,351
Shady Side, MD 20764 • 4,107
Shadyside, OH 43947 • 3,934
Shady Spring, WV 25918 • 1,929
Shafter, CA 93263 • 8,409
Shaftsbury, VT 05262 • 700
Shaker Heights, OH 44120 • 30,831
Shakopee, MN 55379 • 11,739
Shaler Township, PA 15116 • 30,533
Shallowater, TX 79363 • 1,708
Shamokin, PA 17872 • 9,184
Shamokin Dam, PA 17876 • 1,690
Shamrock, TX 79079 • 2,286
Shannock, RI 02875 • 950
Shannon, GA 30172 • 1,703
Shannon, MS 38868 • 1,419
Shannon □, MO • 7,613
Shannon □, SD • 9,902
Shannontown, SC 29150 • 7,900
Sharkey □, MS • 7,066
Sharon, MA 02067 • 5,893
Sharon, PA 16146 • 17,493
Sharon, TN 38255 • 1,047
Sharon, WI 53585 • 1,250
Sharon Hill, PA 19079 • 5,771
Sharonville, OH 45241 • 13,153
Sharp □, AR • 14,109
Sharpes, FL 32922 • 3,348
Sharpley, DE 19803 • 1,250
Sharpsburg, MD 21782 • 659
Sharpsburg, NC 27878 • 1,536
Sharpsburg, PA 15215 • 3,781
Sharpsville, PA 16150 • 4,729
Shasta □, CA • 147,036
Shattuck, OK 73858 • 1,454
Shaw, MS 38773 • 2,349
Shawano, WI 54166 • 7,598
Shawano □, WI • 37,157
Shawnee, KS 66203 • 37,993
Shawnee, OK 74801–02 • 26,017
Shawnee □, KS • 160,976
Shawneetown, IL 62984 • 1,575
Sheboygan, WI 53081–83 • 49,676
Sheboygan □, WI • 103,877
Sheboygan Falls, WI 53085 • 5,823
Sheffield, AL 35660–62 • 10,380
Sheffield, IA 50475 • 1,174
Sheffield, MA 01257 • 1,100
Sheffield, PA 16347 • 1,294
Sheffield Lake, OH 44054 • 9,825
Shelbina, MO 63468 • 2,172
Shelburn, IN 47879 • 1,147
Shelburne Falls, MA 01370 • 1,996
Shelby, MI 49455 • 48,655
Shelby, MS 38774 • 2,806
Shelby, MT 59474 • 2,763
Shelby, NC 28150–51 • 14,669
Shelby, OH 44875 • 9,564
Shelby □, AL • 99,358
Shelby □, IL • 22,261
Shelby □, IN • 40,307
Shelby □, IA • 13,230
Shelby □, KY • 24,824
Shelby □, MO • 6,942
Shelby □, OH • 44,915
Shelby □, TN • 826,330
Shelby □, TX • 22,034
Shelbyville, IL 62565 • 4,943
Shelbyville, IN 46176 • 15,336
Shelbyville, KY 40065 • 6,238
Shelbyville, TN 37160 • 14,049
Sheldon, IL 60966 • 1,109
Sheldon, IA 51201 • 4,937
Sheldon, TX 77028 • 1,653
Shelley, ID 83274 • 3,536
Shell Lake, WI 54871 • 1,161
Shellman, GA 31786 • 1,162
Shell Rock, IA 50670 • 1,385
Shelter Island, NY 11964 • 1,193
Shelton, CT 06484 • 35,418
Shelton, WA 98584 • 7,241
Shenandoah, IA 51601 • 5,572
Shenandoah, PA 17976 • 6,221
Shenandoah, VA 22849 • 2,213
Shenandoah □, VA • 31,636
Shepherd, MI 48883 • 1,413
Shepherd, TX 77371 • 1,812
Shepherdstown, WV 25443 • 1,287
Shepherdsville, KY 40165 • 4,805
Sherborn, MA 01770 • 1,490
Sherburn, MN 56171 • 1,105
Sherburne, NY 13460 • 1,531
Sherburne □, MN • 41,945
Sheridan, AR 72150 • 3,098
Sheridan, CO 80110 • 4,976
Sheridan, IL 60551 • 1,288
Sheridan, IN 46069 • 2,046
Sheridan, OR 97378 • 3,979
Sheridan, WY 82801 • 13,900
Sheridan □, KS • 3,043
Sheridan □, MT • 4,732
Sheridan □, NE • 6,750
Sheridan □, ND • 2,148
Sheridan □, WY • 23,562
Sheridan Beach, WA 98155 • 6,518
Sherman, TX 75090–91 • 31,601
Sherman □, KS • 6,926
Sherman □, NE • 3,718
Sherman □, OR • 1,918
Sherman □, TX • 2,858
Sherrelwood, CO 80221 • 16,636
Sherrill, NY 13461 • 2,864
Sherwood, AR 72116 • 18,893
Sherwood, OR 97140 • 3,093
Sherwood Manor, CT 06082 • 6,357
Sherwood Park, DE 19808 • 2,000
Shiawassee □, MI • 69,770
Shickshinny, PA 18655 • 1,108
Shillington, PA 19607 • 5,062
Shiloh, OH 44878 • 11,607
Shiloh, PA 17404 • 8,245
Shiner, TX 77984 • 2,074
Shinglehouse, PA 16748 • 1,243
Shinnston, WV 26431 • 2,543
Ship Bottom, NJ 08008 • 1,352
Shippensburg, PA 17257 • 5,331
Shiprock, NM 87420 • 7,687
Shirley, MA 01464 • 1,559
Shirley, NY 11967 • 22,936
Shishmaref, AK 99772 • 456
Shively, KY 40216 • 15,535
Shoemakersville, PA 19555 • 1,443
Shore Acres, MA 02066 • 1,200
Shores Acres, RI 02852 • 410
Shoreview, MN 55112 • 24,587
Shorewood, IL 60435 • 6,264
Shorewood, MN 55331 • 5,917
Shorewood, WI 53211 • 14,116
Shorewood Hills, WI 53705 • 1,680
Short Beach, CT 06405 • 2,500
Shortsville, NY 14548 • 1,485
Shoshone, ID 83352 • 1,249
Shoshone □, ID • 13,931
Shoshoni, WY 82649 • 497
Show Low, AZ 85901 • 5,019
Shreve, OH 44676 • 1,584
Shreveport, LA 71101–10 • 198,525
Shrewsbury, MA 01545 • 23,400
Shrewsbury, MO 63119 • 6,416
Shrewsbury, NJ 07702 • 3,096
Shrewsbury, PA 17361 • 2,672
Shullsburg, WI 53586 • 1,236
Shungnak, AK 99773 • 223
Sibley, IA 51249 • 2,815
Sibley □, MN • 14,366
Sicklerville, NJ 08081 • 1,750
Sidney, IL 61877 • 1,027
Sidney, IA 51652 • 1,253
Sidney, MT 59270 • 5,217
Sidney, NE 69162 • 5,959
Sidney, NY 13838 • 4,720
Sidney, OH 45365 • 18,710
Siegle, LA 71291 • 1,600
Sierra □, CA • 3,318
Sierra □, NM • 9,912
Sierra Madre, CA 91024 • 10,762
Sierra Vista, AZ 85635–36 • 32,983
Siesta Key, FL 34242 • 7,772
Signal Hill, CA 90806 • 8,371
Signal Mountain, TN 37377 • 7,034
Sigourney, IA 52591 • 2,111
Sikeston, MO 63801 • 17,641
Siler City, NC 27344 • 4,808
Siloam Springs, AR 72761 • 8,151
Silsbee, TX 77656 • 6,368
Silt, CO 81652 • 1,095
Silver Bay, MN 55614 • 1,894
Silver Bow □, MT • 33,941
Silver City, NV 89428 • 100
Silver City, NM 88061–62 • 10,683
Silver Creek, NY 14136 • 2,927
Silverdale, WA 98383 • 7,660
Silver Grove, KY 41085 • 1,102
Silver Hill, MD 20746 • 1,580
Silver Lake, KS 66539 • 1,390
Silver Lake, MA 01887 • 2,900
Silver Lake, WI 53170 • 1,801
Silverpeak, NV 89047 • 190
Silver Spring, MD 20901–12 • 76,046
Silver Springs, FL 32688 • 1,082
Silver Springs, NV 89429 • 2,253
Silver Springs Shores, FL 32672 • 6,421
Silverton, NJ 08753 • 9,175
Silverton, OH 45236 • 5,859
Silverton, OR 97381 • 5,635
Silview, DE 19804 • 1,500
Silvis, IL 61282 • 6,926
Simi Valley, CA 93062–65 • 100,217
Simmesport, LA 71369 • 2,092
Simpson, PA 18407 • 1,670
Simpson □, KY • 15,145
Simpson □, MS • 23,953
Simpsonville, SC 29681 • 11,708
Simsbury, CT 06070 • 5,577
Sinclair, WY 82334 • 500
Sinton, TX 78387 • 5,549
Sioux □, IA • 29,903
Sioux □, NE • 1,549
Sioux □, ND • 3,761
Sioux Center, IA 51250 • 5,074
Sioux City, IA 51101–11 • 80,505
Sioux Falls, SD 57101–18 • 100,814
Siskiyou □, CA • 43,531
Sisseton, SD 57262 • 2,181
Sistersville, WV 26175 • 1,797
Sitka, AK 99835 • 8,588
Skagit □, WA • 79,555
Skagway, AK 99840 • 692
Skamania □, WA • 8,289
Skaneateles, NY 13152 • 2,724
Skiatook, OK 74070 • 4,910
Skokie, IL 60076–77 • 59,432
Skowhegan, ME 04976 • 6,990
Sky Lake, FL 32809 • 6,202
Skyland, NV 89448 • 660
Skyland, NC 28776 • 1,100
Skyway, WA 98178 • 8,500
Slackwoods, NJ 08638 • 8,100
Slater, IA 50244 • 1,268
Slater, MO 65349 • 2,186
Slater, SC 29683 • 1,000
Slatersville, RI 02876 • 2,330
Slatington, PA 18080 • 4,678
Slaton, TX 79364 • 6,078
Slayton, MN 56172 • 2,147
Sleepy Eye, MN 56085 • 3,694
Slickville, PA 15684 • 1,178
Slidell, LA 70458–61 • 24,124
Slinger, WI 53086 • 2,340
Slippery Rock, PA 16057 • 3,008
Sloan, NY 14225 • 3,830
Sloatsburg, NY 10974 • 3,035
Slocomb, AL 36375 • 1,906
Slope □, ND • 907
Smackover, AR 71762 • 2,232
Smethport, PA 16749 • 1,734
Smith □, KS • 5,078
Smith □, MS • 14,798
Smith □, TN • 14,143
Smith □, TX • 151,309
Smith Center, KS 66967 • 2,016
Smithers, WV 25186 • 1,162
Smithfield, NC 27577 • 7,540
Smithfield, PA 15478 • 1,000
Smithfield, UT 84335 • 5,566
Smithfield, VA 23430 • 4,686
Smith River, CA 95567 • 1,000
Smiths, AL 36877 • 1,700
Smithsburg, MD 21783 • 1,221
Smithton, IL 62285 • 1,587
Smithtown, NY 11787 • 25,638
Smithville, MO 64089 • 2,525
Smithville, OH 44677 • 1,354
Smithville, TN 37166 • 3,791
Smithville, TX 78957 • 3,196
Smyrna, DE 19977 • 5,231
Smyrna, GA 30080–82 • 30,981
Smyrna, TN 37167 • 13,647
Smyth □, VA • 32,370
Sneads, FL 32460 • 1,746
Sneedville, TN 37869 • 1,446
Snellville, GA 30278 • 12,084
Snohomish, WA 98290 • 6,499
Snohomish □, WA • 465,642
Snoqualmie, WA 98065 • 1,546
Snowflake, AZ 85937 • 3,679
Snow Hill, MD 21863 • 2,217
Snow Hill, NC 28580 • 1,378
Snyder, OK 73566 • 1,619
Snyder, TX 79549 • 12,195
Snyder □, PA • 36,680
Soap Lake, WA 98851 • 1,149
Socastee, SC 29577 • 10,426
Social Circle, GA 30279 • 2,755
Socorro, NM 87801 • 8,159
Socorro □, NM • 14,764
Soda Springs, ID 83276 • 3,111
Soddy-Daisy, TN 37379 • 8,240
Sodus, NY 14551 • 1,904
Sodus Point, NY 14555 • 1,190
Solana, FL 33950 • 1,128
Solana Beach, CA 92075 • 12,962
Solano □, CA • 340,421
Soldotna, AK 99669 • 3,482
Soledad, CA 93960 • 7,146
Solomons, MD 20688 • 1,500
Solon, IA 52333 • 1,050
Solon, OH 44139 • 18,548
Solvay, NY 13209 • 6,717
Somerdale, NJ 08083 • 5,440
Somers, CT 06071 • 9,108
Somerset, KY 42501–02 • 10,733
Somerset, MA 02725 • 17,655
Somerset, NJ 08873–75 • 22,070
Somerset, OH 43783 • 1,390
Somerset, PA 15501 • 6,454
Somerset, TX 78069 • 1,144
Somerset, WI 54025 • 1,065
Somerset □, ME • 49,767
Somerset □, MD • 23,440
Somerset □, NJ • 240,279
Somerset □, PA • 78,218
Somers Point, NJ 08244 • 11,216
Somersville, CT 06072 • 1,200
Somersworth, NH 03878 • 11,249
Somerton, AZ 85350 • 5,282
Somervell □, TX • 5,360
Somerville, MA 02143 • 76,210
Somerville, NJ 08876–77 • 11,632
Somerville, TN 38068 • 2,047
Somerville, TX 77879 • 1,542
Somonauk, IL 60552 • 1,263
Sonoma, CA 95476 • 8,121
Sonoma □, CA • 388,222
Sonora, CA 95370 • 4,153
Sonora, TX 76950 • 2,751
Soperton, GA 30457 • 2,797
Sophia, WV 25921 • 1,182
Soquel, CA 95073 • 9,188
Sorrento, LA 70778 • 1,119
Souderton, PA 18964 • 5,957
Sound Beach, NY 11789 • 9,102
South Acton, MA 01720 • 3,220
South Amboy, NJ 08879 • 7,863
South Amherst, MA 01002 • 5,053
South Amherst, OH 44001 • 1,765
Southampton, NY 11968–69 • 3,980
Southampton □, VA • 17,550
South Ashburnham, MA 01466 • 1,110
Southaven, MS 38671 • 17,949
South Barre, VT 05670 • 1,314
South Bay, FL 33493 • 3,558
South Belmar, NJ 07719 • 1,482
South Beloit, IL 61080 • 4,072
South Bend, IN 46601–80 • 105,511
South Bend, WA 98586 • 1,551
South Berwick, ME 03908 • 5,877
Southborough, MA 01772 • 1,450
South Boston, VA 24592 • 6,997
South Bound Brook, NJ 08880 • 4,185
South Bradenton, FL 34205 • 20,398
Southbridge, MA 01550 • 13,631
South Broadway, WA 98902 • 2,735
South Burlington, VT 05403 • 12,809
Southbury, CT 06488 • 3,000
South Charleston, OH 45368 • 1,626
South Charleston, WV 25303 • 13,645
South Chicago Heights, IL 60411 • 3,597
South Congaree, SC 29169 • 2,406
South Connellsville, PA 15425 • 2,204
South Dartmouth, MA 02748 • 9,850
South Daytona, FL 32121 • 12,482
South Decatur, GA 30034 • 19,350
South Deerfield, MA 01373 • 1,906
South Dennis, MA 02660 • 2,500
South Duxbury, MA 02332 • 3,017
South Easton, MA 02375 • 1,530
South Elgin, IL 60177 • 7,474
South El Monte, CA 91733 • 20,850
Southern Pines, NC 28387–88 • 9,129
South Euclid, OH 44121 • 23,866
South Fallsburg, NY 12779 • 2,115
South Farmingdale, NY 11735 • 15,377
Southfield, MI 48034 • 75,728
South Fork, PA 15956 • 1,197
South Fulton, TN 38257 • 2,688
South Gastonia, NC 28052 • 5,487
South Gate, CA 90280 • 86,284
Southgate, FL 34239 • 7,324
Southgate, KY 41071 • 3,266
South Gate, MD 21061 • 27,564
Southgate, MI 48195 • 30,771
South Glastonbury, CT 06073 • 1,570
Southglenn, CO 80122 • 43,087
South Glens Falls, NY 12801 • 3,506
South Grafton, MA 01560 • 2,610
South Hackensack, NJ 07606 • 2,229
South Hadley, MA 01075 • 5,340
South Hadley Falls, MA 01075 • 5,100
South Hamilton, MA 01982 • 2,720
South Haven, IN 46383 • 6,112
South Haven, MI 49090 • 5,563
South Hill, NY 14850 • 5,423
South Hill, VA 23970 • 4,217
South Hingham, MA 02043 • 4,080
South Holland, IL 60473 • 22,105
South Hooksett, NH 03106 • 3,638
South Hopkinton, RI 02813 • 900
South Houston, TX 77587 • 14,207
South Huntington, NY 11746 • 9,624
South Hutchinson, KS 67505 • 2,444
Southington, CT 06489 • 38,518
South International Falls, MN 56679 • 2,806
South Jacksonville, IL 62650 • 3,187
South Jordan, UT 84065 • 12,220
South Lake Tahoe, CA 95702 • 21,586
South Lancaster, MA 01561 • 1,772
South Laramie, WY 82070 • 1,500
South Laurel, MD 20708 • 18,591
South Lebanon, OH 45065 • 2,696
South Lockport, NY 14094 • 7,112
South Lyon, MI 48178 • 5,857
South Miami, FL 33143 • 10,404
South Miami Heights, FL 33157 • 30,030
South Milwaukee, WI 53172 • 20,958
South Nyack, NY 10960 • 3,352
South Ogden, UT 84403 • 12,105
Southold, NY 11971 • 5,192
South Orange, NJ 07079 • 16,390
South Paris, ME 04281 • 2,320
South Pasadena, CA 91030 • 23,936
South Patrick Shores, FL 32937 • 10,249
South Pekin, IL 61564 • 1,184
South Pittsburg, TN 37380 • 3,295
South Plainfield, NJ 07080 • 20,489
Southport, FL 32409 • 1,992
Southport, IN 46227 • 1,969
Southport, NY 14904 • 7,753
Southport, NC 28461 • 2,369
South Portland, ME 04106 • 23,163
South River, NJ 08882 • 13,692
South Royalton, VT 05068 • 700
South Saint Paul, MN 55075–77 • 20,197
South Salt Lake, UT 84115 • 10,129
South San Francisco, CA 94080–83 • 54,312
South San Gabriel, CA 91770 • 7,700
South San Jose Hills, CA 91744 • 17,814
South Sarasota, FL 34239 • 5,298
South Setauket, NY 11733 • 5,990
Southside, AL 35901 • 5,580
Southside Place, TX 77005 • 1,392
South Sioux City, NE 68776 • 9,677
South Stony Brook, NY 11790 • 6,120
South Streator, IL 61364 • 2,334
South Sumter, SC 29150 • 4,371
South Toms River, NJ 08757 • 3,869
South Torrington, WY 82240 • 300
South Tucson, AZ 85713 • 5,093
South Valley Stream, NY 11581 • 5,328
South Venice, FL 34293 • 11,951
South Walpole, MA 02071 • 1,300
South Waverly, PA 14892 • 1,049
South Wellfleet, MA 02663 • 2,300
South Westbury, NY 11590 • 9,732
Southwest Harbor, ME 04679 • 1,952
South Whitley, IN 46787 • 1,482
South Whittier, CA 90605 • 51,100
Southwick, MA 01077 • 1,170
South Williamsport, PA 17701 • 6,496
South Windham, CT 06266 • 1,644
South Windham, ME 04082 • 1,350
South Windsor, CT 06074 • 10,800
Southwood, CO 80120 • 2,050
Southwood Acres, CT 06082 • 8,963
South Woodstock, CT 06267 • 1,112
South Yarmouth, MA 02664 • 10,358
South Yuba City, CA 95991 • 8,816
South Zanesville, OH 43701 • 1,969
Spalding □, GA • 54,457
Spanaway, WA 98387 • 15,001
Spangler, PA 15775 • 2,068
Spanish Fork, UT 84660 • 11,272
Spanish Fort, AL 36527 • 3,732
Spanish Lake, MO 63138 • 20,322
Sparks, GA 31647 • 1,205
Sparks, NV 89431–36 • 53,367
Sparr, FL 32192 • 1,100
Sparta, GA 31087 • 1,710
Sparta, IL 62286 • 4,853
Sparta, MI 49345 • 3,968
Sparta (Lake Mohawk), NJ 07871 • 8,930
Sparta, NC 28675 • 1,957
Sparta, TN 38583 • 4,681
Sparta, WI 54656 • 7,788
Spartanburg, SC 29301–18 • 43,467
Spartanburg □, SC • 226,800
Spearfish, SD 57783 • 6,966
Spearman, TX 79081 • 3,197
Speedway, IN 46224 • 13,092
Spencer, IN 47460 • 2,609
Spencer, IA 51301 • 11,066
Spencer, MA 01562 • 6,306
Spencer, NC 28159 • 3,219
Spencer, TN 38585 • 1,125
Spencer, WV 25276 • 2,279
Spencer, WI 54479 • 1,757
Spencer □, IN • 19,490
Spencer □, KY • 6,801
Spencerport, NY 14559 • 3,606
Spencerville, MD 20868 • 1,780
Spencerville, OH 45887 • 2,288
Spicer, MN 56288 • 1,020
Spindale, NC 28160 • 4,040
Spink □, SD • 7,981
Spirit Lake, ID 83869 • 790
Spirit Lake, IA 51360 • 3,871
Spiro, OK 74959 • 2,146
Spokane, WA 99201–28 • 177,196
Spokane □, WA • 361,364
Spooner, WI 54801 • 2,464
Spotswood, NJ 08884 • 7,983
Spotsylvania □, VA • 57,403
Sprague, WV 25926 • 2,090
Spring, TX 77373 • 33,111
Spring Arbor, MI 49283 • 2,010
Springboro, OH 45066 • 6,590
Spring City, PA 19475 • 3,433
Spring City, TN 37381 • 2,199
Spring Creek 0M, NV • 5,866
Springdale, AR 72764–66 • 29,941
Springdale, OH 45246 • 10,621
Springdale, PA 15144 • 3,992
Springdale, SC 29169 • 3,226
Springer, NM 87747 • 1,262
Springerville, AZ 85938 • 1,802
Springfield, CO 81073 • 1,475
Springfield, FL 32401 • 8,715
Springfield, GA 31329 • 1,415
Springfield, IL 62701–94 • 105,227
Springfield, KY 40069 • 2,875
Springfield, MA 01101–05 • 156,983
Springfield, MI 49015 • 5,582
Springfield, MN 56087 • 2,173
Springfield, MO 65801–99 • 140,494
Springfield, NE 68059 • 1,426
Springfield, NJ 07081 • 13,240
Springfield, OH 45501–06 • 70,487
Springfield, OR 97477–78 • 44,683
Springfield, PA 19064 • 24,160
Springfield, SD 57062 • 834
Springfield, TN 37172 • 11,227
Springfield, VT 05156 • 4,207
Springfield, VA 22150 • 23,706
Spring Garden, PA 17403 • 11,127
Spring Green, WI 53588 • 1,283
Spring Grove, IL 60081 • 1,066
Spring Grove, MN 55974 • 1,153
Spring Grove, PA 17362 • 1,863
Spring Hill, FL 34606 • 31,117

Spring Hill, KS 66083 • 2,191
Springhill, LA 71075 • 5,668
Spring Hill, TN 37174 • 1,464
Spring Hope, NC 27882 • 1,221
Spring Lake, MI 49456 • 2,537
Spring Lake, NJ 07762 • 3,499
Spring Lake, NC 28390 • 7,524
Spring Lake Heights, NJ 07762 • 5,341
Spring Lake Park, MN 55432 • 6,532
Springvale, ME 04083 • 3,542
Spring Valley, IL 61362 • 5,246
Spring Valley, MN 55975 • 2,461
Spring Valley, NY 10977 • 21,802
Spring Valley, WI 54767 • 1,051
Springville, AL 35146 • 1,910
Springville, IA 52336 • 1,068
Springville, NY 14141 • 4,310
Springville, UT 84663–64 • 13,950
Spruce Pine, NC 28777 • 2,010
Spur, TX 79370 • 1,300
Staatsburg, NY 12580 • 1,100
Stafford, KS 67578 • 1,344
Stafford □, KS • 5,365
Stafford □, VA • 61,236
Stafford Springs, CT 06076 • 4,100
Stambaugh, MI 49964 • 1,281
Stamford, CT 06901–12 • 108,056
Stamford, NY 12167 • 1,211
Stamford, TX 79553 • 3,817
Stamford, VT 05352 • 400
Stamps, AR 71860 • 2,478
Stanaford, WV 25927 • 1,706
Stanberry, MO 64489 • 1,310
Standish, MI 48658 • 1,377
Stanfield, AZ 85272 • 1,700
Stanfield, OR 97875 • 1,568
Stanford, CA 94305 • 18,097
Stanford, KY 40484 • 2,686
Stanhope, NJ 07874 • 3,393
Stanislaus □, CA • 370,522
Stanley, NC 28164 • 2,823
Stanley, ND 58784 • 1,371
Stanley, VA 22851 • 1,186
Stanley, WI 54768 • 2,011
Stanley □, SD • 2,453
Stanleytown, VA 24168 • 1,563
Stanleyville, NC 27045 • 4,779
Stanly □, NC • 51,765
Stanton, CA 90680 • 30,491
Stanton, KY 40380 • 2,795
Stanton, MI 48888 • 1,504
Stanton, NE 68779 • 1,549
Stanton, TX 79782 • 2,576
Stanton □, KS • 2,333
Stanton □, NE • 6,244
Stanwood, WA 98292 • 1,961
Staples, MN 56479 • 2,754
Stapleton, AL 36578 • 1,300
Starbuck, MN 56381 • 1,143
Star City, AR 71667 • 2,138
Star City, WV 26505 • 1,251
Stargo, AZ 85540 • 1,038
Stark □, IL • 6,534
Stark □, ND • 22,832
Stark □, OH • 367,585
Starke, FL 32091 • 5,226
Starke □, IN • 22,747
Starkville, MS 39759 • 18,458
Starr □, TX • 40,518
Startex, SC 29377 • 1,162
State Center, IA 50247 • 1,248
State College, PA 16801–05 • 38,923
Stateline, NV 89449 • 1,379
State Line, PA 17263 • 1,253
Statesboro, GA 30458 • 15,854
Statesville, NC 28677 • 17,567
Statham, GA 30666 • 1,360
Staunton, IL 62088 • 4,806
Staunton, VA 24401 • 24,461
Stayton, OR 97383 • 5,011
Steamboat, NV 89511 • 450
Steamboat Springs, CO 80487 • 6,695
Stearns, KY 42647 • 1,550
Stearns □, MN • 118,791
Stebbins, AK 99671 • 400
Steele, AL 35987 • 1,046
Steele, MO 63877 • 2,395
Steele, ND 58482 • 762
Steele □, MN • 30,729
Steele □, ND • 2,420
Steeleville, IL 62288 • 2,059
Steelton, PA 17113 • 5,152
Steelville, MO 65565 • 1,465
Steger, IL 60475 • 8,584
Steilacoom, WA 98388 • 5,728
Stephens, AR 71764 • 1,137
Stephens □, GA • 23,257
Stephens □, OK • 42,299
Stephens □, TX • 9,010
Stephens City, VA 22655 • 1,186
Stephenson □, IL • 48,052
Stephenville, TX 76401 • 13,502
Sterling, AK 99672 • 3,802
Sterling, CO 80751 • 10,362
Sterling, IL 61081 • 15,132
Sterling, KS 67579 • 2,115
Sterling, MA 01564 • 1,250
Sterling, VA 22170 • 20,512
Sterling □, TX • 1,438
Sterling City, TX 76951 • 1,096
Sterling Heights, MI 48310–14 • 117,810
Sterlington, LA 71280 • 1,140
Steuben □, IN • 27,446
Steuben □, NY • 99,088
Steubenville, OH 43952 • 22,125
Stevens □, KS • 5,048
Stevens □, MN • 10,634
Stevens □, WA • 30,948
Stevenson, AL 35772 • 2,046
Stevenson, WA 98648 • 1,147
Stevens Point, WI 54481 • 23,006
Stevensville, MI 49127 • 1,230
Stevensville, MT 59870 • 1,221
Stewart □, GA • 5,654
Stewart □, TN • 9,479
Stewartstown, PA 17363 • 1,308
Stewartville, MN 55976 • 4,520
Stickney, IL 60402 • 5,678
Stigler, OK 74462 • 2,574
Stillwater, MN 55082–83 • 13,882
Stillwater, NY 12170 • 1,531
Stillwater, OK 74074–76 • 36,676
Stillwater □, MT • 6,536
Stilwell, OK 74960 • 2,663
Stinnett, TX 79083 • 2,166
Stirling, NJ 07980 • 1,800
Stockbridge, GA 30281 • 3,359
Stockbridge, MA 01262 • 2,408
Stockbridge, MI 49285 • 1,202
Stockdale, TX 78160 • 1,268
Stockholm, NJ 07460 • 1,200
Stockton, CA 95201–19 • 210,943
Stockton, IL 61085 • 1,871
Stockton, KS 67669 • 1,507
Stockton, MO 65785 • 1,579
Stoddard □, MO • 28,895
Stokes □, NC • 37,223
Stokesdale, NC 27357 • 2,134
Stollings, WV 25646 • 1,200
Stone □, AR • 9,775
Stone □, MS • 10,750
Stone □, MO • 19,078
Stoneboro, PA 16153 • 1,091
Stoneham, MA 02180 • 22,203
Stone Harbor, NJ 08247 • 1,025
Stone Mountain, GA 30083 • 6,494
Stoneville, NC 27048 • 1,109
Stonewall, LA 71078 • 1,266
Stonewall, MS 39363 • 1,148
Stonewall □, TX • 2,013
Stonewood, WV 26301 • 1,996
Stonington, CT 06378 • 1,100
Stonington, IL 62567 • 1,006
Stony Brook, NY 11790 • 13,726
Stony Point, NY 10980 • 10,587
Stony Point, NC 28678 • 1,286
Storey □, NV • 2,526
Storm Lake, IA 50588 • 8,769
Storrs, CT 06268 • 12,198
Story, WY 82842 • 700
Story □, IA • 74,252
Story City, IA 50248 • 2,959
Stottville, NY 12172 • 1,369
Stoughton, MA 02072 • 26,777
Stoughton, WI 53589 • 8,786
Stow, MA 01775 • 1,200
Stow, OH 44224 • 27,702
Stowe, PA 19464 • 3,598
Stowe, VT 05672 • 450
Stowe Township, PA 15136 • 7,681
Strabane, PA 15363 • 1,200
Strafford, MO 65757 • 1,166
Strafford □, NH • 104,233
Strasburg, CO 80136 • 1,005
Strasburg, OH 44680 • 1,995
Strasburg, PA 17579 • 2,568
Strasburg, VA 22657 • 3,762
Stratford, CT 06497 • 49,389
Stratford, DE 19720 • 1,950
Stratford, NJ 08084 • 7,614
Stratford, OK 74872 • 1,404
Stratford, TX 79084 • 1,781
Stratford, WI 54484 • 1,515
Stratford Landing, VA 22308 • 2,800
Strathmore, CA 93267 • 2,353
Strathmore, NJ 07747 • 7,060
Strawberry Point, IA 52076 • 1,357
Streamwood, IL 60103 • 30,987
Streator, IL 61364 • 14,121
Streetsboro, OH 44241 • 9,932
Stromsburg, NE 68666 • 1,241
Strongsville, OH 44136 • 35,308
Stroud, OK 74079 • 2,666
Stroudsburg, PA 18360 • 5,312
Struthers, OH 44471 • 12,284
Stryker, OH 43557 • 1,468
Stuart, FL 34994–97 • 11,936
Stuart, IA 50250 • 1,522
Stuarts Draft, VA 24477 • 5,087
Sturbridge, MA 01566 • 2,093
Sturgeon Bay, WI 54235 • 9,176
Sturgis, KY 42459 • 2,184
Sturgis, MI 49091 • 10,130
Sturgis, SD 57785 • 5,330
Sturtevant, WI 53177 • 3,803
Stutsman □, ND • 22,241
Stuttgart, AR 72160 • 10,420
Sublette, KS 67877 • 1,378
Sublette □, WY • 4,843
Sublimity, OR 97385 • 1,491
Succasunna, NJ 07876 • 7,750
Sudbury, MA 01776 • 1,860
Sudbury Center, MA 01776 • 2,590
Sudley, VA 22110 • 7,321
Suffern, NY 10901 • 11,055
Suffield, CT 06078 • 1,353
Suffolk, VA 23432–38 • 52,141
Suffolk □, MA • 663,906
Suffolk □, NY • 1,321,864
Sugar City, ID 83448 • 1,275
Sugar Creek, MO 64054 • 3,982
Sugarcreek, PA 16323 • 5,532
Sugar Grove, VA 24375 • 1,027
Sugar Hill, GA 30518 • 4,557
Sugar Land, TX 77478–79 • 24,529
Sugarland Run, VA 22170 • 9,357
Sugar Loaf, VA 24018 • 2,000
Sugar Notch, PA 18706 • 1,044
Suisun City, CA 94585 • 22,686
Suitland, MD 20746 • 35,400
Sulligent, AL 35586 • 1,886
Sullivan, IL 61951 • 4,354
Sullivan, IN 47882 • 4,663
Sullivan, MO 63080 • 5,661
Sullivan □, IN • 18,993
Sullivan □, MO • 6,326
Sullivan □, NH • 38,592
Sullivan □, NY • 69,277
Sullivan □, PA • 6,104
Sullivan □, TN • 143,596
Sullivans Island, SC 29482 • 1,623
Sully □, SD • 1,589
Sulphur, LA 70663–64 • 20,125
Sulphur, OK 73086 • 4,824
Sulphur Springs, TX 75482 • 14,062
Sultan, WA 98294 • 2,236
Sumiton, AL 35148 • 2,604
Summerfield, NC 27358 • 2,051
Summers □, WV • 14,204
Summersville, WV 26651 • 2,906
Summerville, GA 30747 • 5,025
Summerville, SC 29483–85 • 22,519
Summit, IL 60501 • 9,971
Summit, MS 39666 • 1,566
Summit, NJ 07901 • 19,757
Summit, TN 37363 • 8,307
Summit □, CO • 12,881
Summit □, OH • 514,990
Summit □, UT • 15,518
Summit Hill, PA 18250 • 3,332
Sumner, IL 62466 • 1,083
Sumner, IA 50674 • 2,078
Sumner, WA 98390 • 6,281
Sumner □, KS • 25,841
Sumner □, TN • 103,281
Sumter, SC 29150–54 • 41,943
Sumter □, AL • 16,174
Sumter □, FL • 31,577
Sumter □, GA • 30,228
Sumter □, SC • 102,637
Sunbury, OH 43074 • 2,046
Sunbury, PA 17801 • 11,591
Sun City, AZ 85351 • 38,126
Sun City, CA 92381 • 14,930
Sun City Center, FL 33573 • 8,326
Suncook, NH 03275 • 5,214
Sundance, WY 82729 • 1,139
Sundown, TX 79372 • 1,759
Sunflower □, MS • 32,867
Sunland Park, NM 88063 • 8,179
Sunny Isles, FL 33160 • 11,772
Sunnyside, CA 93727 • 5,000
Sunnyside, WA 98944 • 11,238
Sunnyvale, CA 94086–89 • 117,229
Sun Prairie, WI 53590 • 15,333
Sunray, TX 79086 • 1,729
Sunrise Manor, NV 89110 • 95,362
Sunset, FL 33143 • 15,810
Sunset, LA 70584 • 2,201
Sunset, UT 84015 • 5,128
Sunset Beach, HI 96712 • 800
Sun Valley, ID 83353–54 • 938
Sun Valley, NV 89433 • 11,391
Superior, AZ 85273 • 3,468
Superior, MT 59872 • 881
Superior, NE 68978 • 2,397
Superior, WI 54880 • 27,134
Superior, WY 82945 • 273
Suquamish, WA 98392 • 3,105
Surf City, NJ 08008 • 1,375
Surfside, FL 33154 • 4,108
Surfside Beach, SC 29575 • 3,845
Surgoinsville, TN 37873 • 1,499
Surprise, AZ 85374 • 7,122
Surrey, ND 58785 • 856
Surry □, NC • 61,704
Surry □, VA • 6,145
Susanville, CA 96130 • 7,279
Susquehanna, PA 18847 • 1,760
Susquehanna □, PA • 40,380
Sussex, NJ 07461 • 2,201
Sussex, WI 53089 • 5,039
Sussex □, DE • 113,229
Sussex □, NJ • 130,943
Sussex □, VA • 10,248
Sutherland, NE 69165 • 1,032
Sutherlin, OR 97479 • 5,020
Sutter □, CA • 64,415
Sutter Creek, CA 95685 • 1,835
Sutton, NE 68979 • 1,353
Sutton □, TX • 4,135
Suwanee, GA 30174 • 2,412
Suwannee □, FL • 26,780
Swain □, NC • 11,268
Swainsboro, GA 30401 • 7,361
Swampscott, MA 01907 • 13,650
Swannanoa, NC 28778 • 3,538
Swansboro, NC 28584 • 1,165
Swansea, IL 62221 • 8,201
Swanton, OH 43558 • 3,557
Swanton, VT 05488 • 2,360
Swanwyck Estates, DE 19720 • 1,320
Swarthmore, PA 19081 • 6,157
Swartz Creek, MI 48473 • 4,851
Swatara Township, PA 17111 • 19,700
Swayzee, IN 46986 • 1,059
Swedesboro, NJ 08085 • 2,024
Sweeny, TX 77480 • 3,297
Sweet Grass □, MT • 3,154
Sweet Home, OR 97386 • 6,850
Sweet Springs, MO 65351 • 1,595
Sweetwater, FL 33152 • 13,909
Sweetwater, TN 37874 • 5,066
Sweetwater, TX 79556 • 11,967
Sweetwater □, WY • 38,823
Sweetwater Creek, FL 33614 • 18,000
Swift □, MN • 10,724
Swisher □, TX • 8,133
Swissvale, PA 15218 • 10,637
Switzer, WV 25647 • 1,004
Switzerland, FL 32043 • 2,400
Switzerland □, IN • 7,738
Swoyerville, PA • 5,630
Sycamore, AL 35149 • 1,250
Sycamore, IL 60178 • 9,708
Sykesville, MD 21784 • 2,303
Sykesville, PA 15865 • 1,387
Sylacauga, AL 35150 • 12,520
Sylva, NC 28779 • 1,809
Sylvan Beach, NY 13157 • 1,119
Sylvania, GA 30467 • 2,871
Sylvania, OH 43560 • 17,301
Sylvan Lake, MI 48320 • 1,884
Sylvester, GA 31791 • 5,702
Syosset, NY 11791 • 18,967
Syracuse, IN 46567 • 2,729
Syracuse, KS 67878 • 1,606
Syracuse, NE 68446 • 1,646
Syracuse, NY 13201–90 • 163,860
Syracuse, UT 84075 • 4,658

T

Tabor City, NC 28463 • 2,330
Tacoma, WA 98401–99 • 176,664
Taft, CA 93268 • 5,902
Taft, TX 78390 • 3,222
Tahlequah, OK 74464–65 • 10,398
Tahoe City, CA 95730 • 1,300
Tahoka, TX 79373 • 2,868
Takoma Park, MD 20912 • 16,700
Talbot □, GA • 6,524
Talbot □, MD • 30,549
Talbotton, GA 31827 • 1,046
Talent, OR 97540 • 3,274
Taliaferro □, GA • 1,915
Talihina, OK 74571 • 1,297
Talladega, AL 35160 • 18,175
Talladega □, AL • 74,107
Tallahassee, FL 32301–17 • 124,773
Tallahatchie □, MS • 15,210
Tallapoosa, GA 30176 • 2,805
Tallapoosa □, AL • 38,826
Tallassee, AL 36078 • 5,112
Talleyville, DE 19803 • 6,346
Tallmadge, OH 44278 • 14,870
Tallulah, LA 71282–84 • 8,526
Tama, IA 52339 • 2,697
Tama □, IA • 17,419
Tamalpais Valley, CA 94941 • 5,000
Tamaqua, PA 18252 • 7,943
Tamarac, FL 33321 • 44,822
Tamiami, FL 33165 • 33,845
Tampa, FL 33601–97 • 280,015
Tanana, AK 99777 • 345
Taney □, MO • 25,561
Taneytown, MD 21787 • 3,695
Tangipahoa □, LA • 85,709
Taos, NM 87571 • 4,065
Taos □, NM • 23,118
Taos Pueblo, NM 87571 • 1,030
Tappahannock, VA 22560 • 1,550
Tappan, NY 10983 • 6,867
Tara Hills, CA 94564 • 6,000
Tarboro, NC 27886 • 11,037
Tarentum, PA 15084 • 5,674
Tariffville, CT 06081 • 1,477
Tarkio, MO 64491 • 2,243
Tarpey, CA 93727 • 4,000
Tarpon Springs, FL 34688–91 • 17,906
Tarrant, AL 35217 • 8,046
Tarrant □, TX • 1,170,103
Tarrytown, NY 10591 • 10,739
Tate, GA 30177 • 1,000
Tate □, MS • 21,432
Tattnall □, GA • 17,722
Taunton, MA 02780 • 49,832
Tavares, FL 32778 • 7,383
Tavernier, FL 33070 • 2,433
Tawas City, MI 48763–64 • 2,009
Taylor, AZ 85939 • 2,418
Taylor, MI 48180 • 70,811
Taylor, PA 18517 • 6,941
Taylor, TX 76574 • 11,472
Taylor □, FL • 17,111
Taylor □, GA • 7,642
Taylor □, IA • 7,114
Taylor □, KY • 21,146
Taylor □, TX • 119,655
Taylor □, WV • 15,144
Taylor □, WI • 18,901
Taylor Mill, KY 41015 • 5,530
Taylors, SC 29687 • 19,619
Taylorsville, IN 47280 • 1,044
Taylorsville, MS 39168 • 1,412
Taylorsville, NC 28681 • 1,566
Taylorville, IL 62568 • 11,133
Tazewell, TN 37879 • 2,150
Tazewell, VA 24651 • 4,176
Tazewell □, IL • 123,692
Tazewell □, VA • 45,960
Tchula, MS 39169 • 2,186
Teague, TX 75860 • 3,268
Teaneck, NJ 07666 • 37,825
Teaticket, MA 02536 • 2,600
Tecumseh, MI 49286 • 7,462
Tecumseh, NE 68450 • 1,702
Tecumseh, OK 74873 • 5,750
Tehachapi, CA 93561 • 5,791
Tehama □, CA • 49,625
Tekamah, NE 68061 • 1,852
Telfair □, GA • 11,000
Telford, PA 18969 • 4,238
Tell City, IN 47586 • 8,088
Teller □, CO • 12,468
Telluride, CO 81435 • 1,309
Temecula, CA 92390 • 27,099
Tempe, AZ 85280–85 • 141,865
Temperance, MI 48182 • 6,542
Temple, GA 30179 • 1,870
Temple, OK 73568 • 1,223
Temple, PA 19560 • 1,491
Temple, TX 76501–05 • 46,109
Temple City, CA 91780 • 31,100
Temple Terrace, FL 33617 • 16,444
Templeton, MA 01468 • 1,000
Tenafly, NJ 07670 • 13,326
Tenaha, TX 75974 • 1,072
Tenino, WA 98589 • 1,292
Tennessee Ridge, TN 37178 • 1,271
Tennille, GA 31089 • 1,552
Tensas □, LA • 7,103
Ten Sleep, WY 82442 • 311
Terra Alta, WV 26764 • 1,713
Terrebonne □, LA • 96,982
Terre Haute, IN 47801–08 • 57,483
Terre Hill, PA 17581 • 1,282
Terrell, TX 75160 • 12,490
Terrell □, GA • 10,653
Terrell □, TX • 1,410
Terrell Hills, TX 78209 • 4,592
Terry, MT 59349 • 659
Terry □, TX • 13,218
Terrytown, LA 70053 • 23,787
Terryville, CT 06786 • 5,426
Terryville, NY 11776 • 7,380
Tesuque, NM 87574 • 1,490
Teton □, ID • 3,439
Teton □, MT • 6,271
Teton □, WY • 11,172
Teton Village, WY 83025 • 250
Teutopolis, IL 62467 • 1,417
Tewksbury, MA 01876 • 10,540
Texarkana, AR 75502 • 22,631
Texarkana, TX 75501–05 • 31,656
Texas □, MO • 21,476
Texas □, OK • 16,419
Texas City, TX 77590–92 • 40,822
Texico, NM 88135 • 966
Thatcher, AZ 85552 • 3,763
Thayer, MO 65791 • 1,996
Thayer □, NE • 6,635
Thayne, WY 83127 • 267
The Colony, TX 75056 • 22,113
The Dalles, OR 97058 • 11,060
Theodore, AL 36582 • 6,509
The Plains, OH 45780 • 2,644
Thermalito, CA 95965 • 5,646
Thermopolis, WY 82443 • 3,247
The Village, OK 73120 • 10,353
The Village of Indian Hill, OH 45243 • 5,383
The Woodlands, TX 77380 • 29,205
Thibodaux, LA 70301–02 • 14,035
Thief River Falls, MN 56701 • 8,010
Thiensville, WI 53092 • 3,301
Thomas, OK 73669 • 1,246
Thomas □, GA • 38,986
Thomas □, KS • 8,258
Thomas □, NE • 851
Thomasboro, IL 61878 • 1,250
Thomaston, CT 06787 • 3,590
Thomaston, GA 30286 • 9,127
Thomaston, ME 04861 • 2,445
Thomasville, AL 36784 • 4,301
Thomasville, GA 31792 • 17,457
Thomasville, NC 27360–61 • 15,915
Thompson, ND 58278 • 930
Thompson Falls, MT 59873 • 1,319
Thomson, GA 30824 • 6,862
Thonotosassa, FL 33592 • 1,500
Thoreau, NM 87323 • 1,099
Thorndale, TX 76577 • 1,092
Thorndike, MA 01079 • 1,100
Thornton, CO 80229 • 55,031
Thorntown, IN 46071 • 1,506
Thornwood, NY 10594 • 7,025
Thorofare, NJ 08086 • 1,800
Thorp, WI 54771 • 1,657
Thorsby, AL 35171 • 1,465
Thousand Oaks, CA 91359–62 • 104,352
Three Forks, MT 59752 • 1,203
Three Oaks, MI 49128 • 1,786
Three Rivers, MA 01080 • 3,006
Three Rivers, MI 49093 • 7,413
Three Rivers, TX 78071 • 1,889
Throckmorton, TX 76083 • 1,036
Throckmorton □, TX • 1,880
Throop, PA 18512 • 4,070
Thunderbolt, GA 31404 • 2,786
Thurmont, MD 21788 • 3,398
Thurston □, NE • 6,936
Thurston □, WA • 161,238
Tiburon, CA 94920 • 7,532
Tice, FL 33905 • 3,971
Ticonderoga, NY 12883 • 2,770
Tierra Amarilla, NM 87575 • 900
Tiffin, OH 44883 • 18,604
Tift □, GA • 34,998
Tifton, GA 31793–94 • 14,215
Tigard, OR 97223 • 29,344
Tillamook, OR 97141 • 4,001
Tillamook □, OR • 21,570
Tillman □, OK • 10,384
Tillmans Corner, AL 36619 • 17,988
Tillson, NY 12486 • 1,688
Tilton, IL 61833 • 2,729
Tilton, NH 03276 • 1,380
Tiltonsville, OH 43963 • 1,517
Timberlake, VA 24502 • 10,314
Timberville, VA 22853 • 1,596
Timmonsville, SC 29161 • 2,182
Timpson, TX 75975 • 1,029
Tinley Park, IL 60477 • 37,121
Tinton Falls, NJ 07724 • 12,361
Tioga, LA 71477 • 1,200
Tioga, ND 58852 • 1,278
Tioga □, NY • 52,337
Tioga □, PA • 41,126
Tippah □, MS • 19,523
Tipp City, OH 45371 • 6,027
Tippecanoe □, IN • 130,598
Tipton, CA 93272 • 1,383
Tipton, IN 46072 • 4,751
Tipton, IA 52772 • 2,998
Tipton, MO 65081 • 2,026
Tipton, OK 73570 • 1,043
Tipton □, IN • 16,119
Tipton □, TN • 37,568
Tiptonville, TN 38079 • 2,149
Tishomingo, OK 73460 • 3,116
Tishomingo □, MS • 17,683
Titus □, TX • 24,009
Titusville, FL 32780–83 • 39,394
Titusville, PA 16354 • 6,434
Tiverton, RI 02878 • 7,259
Tivoli, NY 12583 • 1,035
Toast, NC 27049 • 2,125
Tobyhanna, PA 18466 • 1,200
Toccoa, GA 30577 • 8,266
Todd □, KY • 10,940
Todd □, MN • 23,363
Todd □, SD • 8,352
Todd Estates, DE 19713 • 2,000
Togiak, AK 99678 • 613
Tohatchi, NM 87325 • 661
Tok, AK 99780 • 935
Toledo, IL 62468 • 1,199
Toledo, IA 52342 • 2,380
Toledo, OH 43601–99 • 332,943
Toledo, OR 97391 • 3,174
Tolland, CT 06084 • 1,200
Tolland □, CT • 128,699
Tolleson, AZ 85353 • 4,434
Tolono, IL 61880 • 2,605
Toluca, IL 61369 • 1,315
Tomah, WI 54660 • 7,570
Tomahawk, WI 54487 • 3,328
Tomball, TX 77375 • 6,370
Tombstone, AZ 85638 • 1,220
Tom Green □, TX • 98,458
Tompkins □, NY • 94,097
Tompkinsville, KY 42167 • 2,861
Toms River, NJ 08753–57 • 7,524
Tonawanda, NY 14150–51 • 17,284
Tonawanda, NY 14223 • 65,284
Tonganoxie, KS 66086 • 2,347
Tonkawa, OK 74653 • 3,127
Tonopah, NV 89049 • 3,616
Tooele, UT 84074 • 13,887
Tooele □, UT • 26,601
Toole □, MT • 5,046
Toombs □, GA • 24,072
Topeka, KS 66601–99 • 119,883
Toppenish, WA 98948 • 7,419
Topsfield, MA 01983 • 2,711
Topsham, ME 04086 • 6,147
Topton, PA 19562 • 1,987
Toronto, OH 43964 • 6,127
Torrance, CA 90501–10 • 133,107
Torrance □, NM • 10,285
Torrington, CT 06790 • 33,687
Torrington, WY 82240 • 5,651
Totowa, NJ 07512 • 10,177
Touisset, MA 02777 • 1,520

Toulon, IL 61483 • 1,328
Towaco, NJ 07082 • 1,020
Towanda, KS 67144 • 1,289
Towanda, PA 18848 • 3,242
Tower City, PA 17980 • 1,518
Town and Country, WA 99210 • 4,921
Town Creek, AL 35672 • 1,379
Towner, ND 58788 • 669
Towner □, ND • 3,627
Town 'n Country, FL 33615 • 60,946
Towns □, GA • 6,754
Townsend, DE 19734 • 322
Townsend, MA 01469 • 1,164
Townsend, MT 59644 • 1,635
Towson, MD 21204 • 49,445
Tracy, CA 95376–78 • 33,558
Tracy, MN 56175 • 2,059
Tracy City, TN 37387 • 1,556
Tracyton, WA 98393 • 2,621
Traer, IA 50675 • 1,552
Trafford, PA 15085 • 3,345
Trail Creek, IN 46360 • 2,463
Traill □, ND • 8,752
Transylvania □, NC • 25,520
Travelers Rest, SC 29690 • 3,069
Traverse □, MN • 4,463
Traverse City, MI 49684 • 15,155
Travis □, TX • 576,407
Treasure □, MT • 874
Treasure Island, FL 33706 • 7,266
Trego □, KS • 3,694
Tremont, IL 61568 • 2,088
Tremont, PA 17981 • 1,814
Tremonton, UT 84337 • 4,264
Trempealeau, WI 54661 • 1,039
Trempealeau □, WI • 25,263
Trenton, FL 32693 • 1,287
Trenton, GA 30752 • 1,994
Trenton, IL 62293 • 2,481
Trenton, MI 48183 • 20,586
Trenton, MO 64683 • 6,129
Trenton, NJ 08601–91 • 88,675
Trenton, OH 45067 • 6,189
Trenton, TN 38382 • 4,836
Tresckow, PA 18254 • 1,033
Treutlen □, GA • 5,994
Trevorton, PA 17881 • 2,058
Triangle, VA 22172 • 4,740
Tri City, OR 97457 • 3,585
Trigg □, KY • 10,361
Tri Lakes, IN 46725 • 3,299
Trimble □, KY • 6,090
Trinidad, CO 81082 • 8,580
Trinidad, TX 75163 • 1,056
Trinity, AL 35673 • 1,380
Trinity, NC 27370 • 5,469
Trinity, TX 75862 • 2,648
Trinity □, CA • 13,063
Trinity □, TX • 11,445
Trion, GA 30753 • 1,661
Tripoli, IA 50676 • 1,188
Tripp □, SD • 6,924
Triumph, LA 70041 • 1,200
Trona, CA 93562 • 1,400
Trooper, PA 19401 • 5,137
Trotwood, OH 45426 • 8,816
Troup □, GA • 55,536
Trousdale □, TN • 5,920
Troutdale, OR 97060 • 7,852
Troutman, NC 28166 • 1,493
Troy, AL 36081 • 13,051
Troy, ID 83871 • 699
Troy, IL 62294 • 6,046
Troy, KS 66087 • 1,073
Troy, MI 48083–84 • 72,884
Troy, MO 63379 • 3,811
Troy, MT 59935 • 953
Troy, NH 03465 • 2,097
Troy, NY 12180–83 • 54,269
Troy, NC 27371 • 3,404
Troy, OH 45373 • 19,478
Troy, PA 16947 • 1,262
Troy, TN 38260 • 1,047
Truckee, CA 95734 • 3,484
Truman, MN 56088 • 1,292
Trumann, AR 72472 • 6,304
Trumansburg, NY 14886 • 1,611
Trumbull, CT 06611 • 32,000
Trumbull □, OH • 227,813
Trussville, AL 35173 • 8,266
Truth or Consequences (Hot Springs), NM 87901 • 6,221
Tryon, NC 28782 • 1,680
Tualatin, OR 97062 • 15,013
Tuba City, AZ 86045 • 7,323
Tuckahoe, NY 10707 • 6,302
Tucker, GA 30084 • 25,781
Tucker □, WV • 7,728
Tuckerman, AR 72473 • 2,020
Tuckerton, NJ 08087 • 3,048
Tucson, AZ 85701–51 • 405,390
Tucumcari, NM 88401 • 6,831
Tukwila, WA 98188 • 11,874
Tulare, CA 93274–75 • 33,249
Tulare □, CA • 311,921
Tularosa, NM 88352 • 2,615
Tulelake, CA 96134 • 1,010
Tulia, TX 79088 • 4,699
Tullahoma, TN 37388 • 16,761
Tulsa, OK 74101–94 • 367,302
Tulsa □, OK • 503,341
Tumwater, WA 98502 • 9,976
Tunica, MS 38676 • 1,175
Tunica □, MS • 8,164
Tunkhannock, PA 18657 • 2,251
Tununak, AK 99681 • 316
Tuolumne, CA 95379 • 1,686
Tuolumne □, CA • 48,456
Tupelo, MS 38801–03 • 30,685
Tupper Lake, NY 12986 • 4,087
Turley, OK 74156 • 2,930
Turlock, CA 95380–81 • 42,198
Turner, OR 97392 • 1,281
Turner □, GA • 8,703
Turner □, SD • 8,576
Turners Falls, MA 01376 • 4,731
Turtle Creek, PA 15145 • 6,556
Turtle Lake, ND 58575 • 681
Tuscaloosa, AL 35401–06 • 77,759
Tuscaloosa □, AL • 150,522
Tuscarawas □, OH • 84,090
Tuscola, IL 61953 • 4,155
Tuscola □, MI • 55,498
Tuscumbia, AL 35674 • 8,413
Tuskegee, AL 36083 • 12,257
Tustin, CA 92680–81 • 50,689
Tuttle, OK 73089 • 2,807
Tutwiler, MS 38963 • 1,391
Tuxedo Park, DE 19804 • 1,300
Twentynine Palms, CA 92277–78 • 11,821
Twiggs □, GA • 9,806
Twin City, GA 30471 • 1,466
Twin Falls, ID 83301–03 • 27,591
Twin Falls □, ID • 53,580
Twin Knolls, AZ 85207 • 5,210
Twin Lakes, CA 95060 • 5,379
Twin Lakes, WI 53181 • 3,989
Twin Rivers, NJ 08520 • 7,715
Twinsburg, OH 44087 • 9,606
Two Harbors, MN 55616 • 3,651
Two Rivers, WI 54241 • 13,030
Tybee Island, GA 31328 • 2,842
Tyler, MN 56178 • 1,257
Tyler, TX 75701–13 • 75,450
Tyler □, TX • 16,646
Tyler □, WV • 9,796
Tyler Heights, WV 25312 • 4,070
Tylertown, MS 39667 • 1,938
Tyndall, SD 57066 • 1,201
Tyrone, NM 88065 • 950
Tyrone, PA 16686 • 5,743
Tyrrell □, NC • 3,856
Tysons Corner, VA 22102 • 13,124

U

Ucon, ID 83454 • 895
Uhrichsville, OH 44683 • 5,604
Uinta □, WY • 18,705
Uintah □, UT • 22,211
Ukiah, CA 95482 • 14,599
Uleta, FL 33162 • 10,000
Ulster □, NY • 165,304
Ulysses, KS 67880 • 5,474
Umatilla, FL 32784 • 2,350
Umatilla, OR 97882 • 3,046
Umatilla □, OR • 59,249
Unadilla, GA 31091 • 1,620
Unadilla, NY 13849 • 1,265
Unalakleet, AK 99684 • 714
Unalaska, AK 99685 • 3,089
Uncasville, CT 06382 • 1,597
Underwood, AL 35630 • 1,950
Underwood, ND 58576 • 976
Unicoi □, TN • 16,549
Union, KY 41091 • 1,001
Union, MS 39365 • 1,875
Union, MO 63084 • 5,909
Union, NJ 07083 • 50,024
Union, OH 45322 • 5,501
Union, OR 97883 • 1,847
Union, SC 29379 • 9,836
Union, UT 84047 • 13,684
Union □, AR • 46,719
Union □, FL • 10,252
Union □, GA • 11,993
Union □, IL • 17,619
Union □, IN • 6,976
Union □, IA • 12,750
Union □, KY • 16,557
Union □, LA • 20,690
Union □, MS • 22,085
Union □, NJ • 493,819
Union □, NM • 4,124
Union □, NC • 84,211
Union □, OH • 31,969
Union □, OR • 23,598
Union □, PA • 36,176
Union □, SC • 30,337
Union □, SD • 10,189
Union □, TN • 13,694
Union Beach, NJ 07735 • 6,156
Union City, CA 94587 • 53,762
Union City, GA 30291 • 8,375
Union City, IN 47390 • 3,612
Union City, MI 49094 • 1,767
Union City, NJ 07087 • 58,012
Union City, OH 45390 • 1,984
Union City, OK 73090 • 1,000
Union City, PA 16438 • 3,537
Union City, TN 38261 • 10,513
Uniondale, NY 11553 • 20,328
Union Gap, WA 98903 • 3,120
Union Grove, WI 53182 • 3,669
Union Lake, MI 48386–87 • 8,500
Union Park, FL 32817 • 6,890
Union Pier, MI 49129 • 1,039
Union Point, GA 30669 • 1,753
Union Springs, AL 36089 • 3,975
Union Springs, NY 13160 • 1,142
Uniontown, AL 36786 • 1,730
Uniontown, KY 42461 • 1,008
Uniontown, OH 44685 • 1,500
Uniontown, PA 15401 • 12,034
Union Village, RI 02895 • 2,150
Unionville, CT 06085 • 3,500
Unionville, MO 63565 • 1,989
Universal City, TX 78148 • 13,057
University City, MO 63130 • 40,087
University Gardens, NY 11020 • 4,600
University Heights, IA 52240 • 1,042
University Heights, OH 44118 • 14,790
University Park, IL 60466 • 6,204
University Park, NM 88003 • 4,520
University Park, TX 75205 • 22,259
University Place, WA 98465 • 27,701
Upland, CA 91785–86 • 63,374
Upland, IN 46989 • 3,295
Upper Arlington, OH 43221 • 34,128
Upper Darby, PA 19082–83 • 84,054
Upper Dublin Township, PA 19034 • 22,348
Upper Greenwood Lake, NJ 07421 • 2,734
Upper Merion Township, PA 19406 • 26,138
Upper Moreland Township, PA 19090 • 25,874
Upper Providence Township, PA 19063 • 9,727
Upper Saddle River, NJ 07458 • 7,198
Upper Saint Clair, PA 15241 • 19,692
Upper Sandusky, OH 43351 • 5,906
Upshur □, TX • 31,370
Upshur □, WV • 22,867
Upson □, GA • 26,300
Upton, MA 01568 • 1,500
Upton, WY 82730 • 980
Upton □, TX • 4,447
Urbana, IL 61801 • 36,344
Urbana, OH 43078 • 11,353
Urbandale, IA 50322 • 23,500
Usquepaug, RI 02892 • 400
Utah □, UT • 263,590
Utica, MI 48315–18 • 5,081
Utica, MS 39175 • 1,033
Utica, NY 13501–05 • 68,637
Utica, OH 43080 • 1,997
Uvalde, TX 78801–02 • 14,729
Uvalde □, TX • 23,340
Uxbridge, MA 01569 • 3,340

V

Vacaville, CA 95687–88 • 71,479
Vacherie, LA 70090 • 2,169
Vadnais Heights, MN 55110 • 11,041
Vail, CO 81657–58 • 3,659
Valatie, NY 12184 • 1,487
Valdese, NC 28690 • 3,914
Valdez, AK 99686 • 4,068
Valdosta, GA 31601–04 • 39,806
Vale, OR 97918 • 1,491
Valencia, AZ 85326 • 1,200
Valencia □, NM • 45,235
Valencia Heights, SC 29205 • 4,122
Valentine, NE 69201 • 2,826
Valhalla, NY 10595 • 6,200
Valinda, CA 91744 • 18,735
Vallejo, CA 94589–92 • 109,199
Valle Vista, CA 92343 • 8,751
Valley, AL 36854 • 8,173
Valley, NE 68064 • 1,775
Valley □, ID • 6,109
Valley □, MT • 8,239
Valley □, NE • 5,169
Valley Center, KS 67147 • 3,624
Valley City, ND 58072 • 7,163
Valley Cottage, NY 10989 • 9,007
Valley Falls, KS 66088 • 1,253
Valley Falls, RI 02864 • 11,175
Valley Forge, PA 19481–82 • 1,500
Valley Mills, TX 76689 • 1,085
Valley Park, MO 63088 • 4,165
Valley Ridge, WA 98188 • 6,500
Valley Springs, SD 57068 • 739
Valley Station, KY 40272 • 22,840
Valley Stream, NY 11580–82 • 33,946
Valley View, PA 17983 • 1,749
Valparaiso, FL 32580 • 4,672
Valparaiso, IN 46383–84 • 24,414
Val Verda, UT 84010 • 3,712
Val Verde □, TX • 38,721
Van, TX 75790 • 1,854
Van Alstyne, TX 75095 • 2,090
Van Buren, AR 72956 • 14,979
Van Buren, ME 04785 • 2,759
Van Buren □, AR • 14,008
Van Buren □, IA • 7,676
Van Buren □, MI • 70,060
Van Buren □, TN • 4,846
Vance □, NC • 38,892
Vanceburg, KY 41179 • 1,713
Vancleave, MS 39564 • 3,214
Vancouver, WA 98660–68 • 46,380
Vandalia, IL 62471 • 6,114
Vandalia, MO 63382 • 2,683
Vandalia, OH 45377 • 13,882
Vandenberg Village, CA 93436 • 5,871
Vander, NC 28301 • 1,179
Vanderburgh □, IN • 165,058
Vandergrift, PA 15690 • 5,904
Van Horn, TX 79855 • 2,930
Van Lear, KY 41265 • 1,050
Vansant, VA 24656 • 1,187
Van Vleck, TX 77482 • 1,534
Van Wert, OH 45891 • 10,891
Van Wert □, OH • 30,464
Van Zandt □, TX • 37,944
Varina, VA 23231 • 2,500
Varnville, SC 29944 • 1,970
Vassar, MI 48768 • 2,559
Vaughn, MT 59487 • 2,270
Veazie, ME 04401 • 1,610
Veedersburg, IN 47987 • 2,192
Velda Rose Estates, AZ 85205 • 2,330
Velva, ND 58790 • 968
Venango □, PA • 59,381
Veneta, OR 97487 • 2,519
Venice, FL 34292–93 • 16,922
Venice, IL 62090 • 3,571
Venice Gardens, FL 34293 • 7,701
Ventnor City, NJ 08406 • 11,005
Ventura (San Buenaventura), CA 93001–07 • 92,575
Ventura □, CA • 669,016
Veradale, WA 99037 • 7,836
Verda, KY 40828 • 1,133
Verdi, NV 89439 • 1,140
Vergennes, VT 05491 • 2,578
Vermilion, OH 44089 • 11,127
Vermilion □, IL • 88,257
Vermilion □, LA • 50,055
Vermillion, SD 57069 • 10,034
Vermillion □, IN • 16,773
Vernal, UT 84078–79 • 6,644
Vernon, AL 35592 • 2,247
Vernon, CT 06066 • 30,200
Vernon, TX 76384 • 12,001
Vernon □, LA • 61,961
Vernon □, MO • 19,041
Vernon □, WI • 25,617
Vernon Hills, IL 60061 • 15,319
Vernonia, OR 97064 • 1,808
Vero Beach, FL 32960–68 • 17,350
Verona, MS 38879 • 2,893
Verona, NJ 07044 • 13,597
Verona, PA 15147 • 3,260
Verona, WI 53593 • 5,374
Versailles, IN 47042 • 1,791
Versailles, KY 40383 • 7,269
Versailles, MO 65084 • 2,365
Versailles, OH 45380 • 2,351
Vestal, NY 13850–51 • 5,530
Vestavia Hills, AL 35216 • 19,749
Vevay, IN 47043 • 1,393
Vian, OK 74962 • 1,414
Vicksburg, MI 49097 • 2,216
Vicksburg, MS 39180–82 • 20,908
Victor, NY 14564 • 2,308
Victoria, KS 67671 • 1,157
Victoria, TX 77901–05 • 55,076
Victoria, VA 23974 • 1,830
Victoria □, TX • 74,361
Victorville, CA 92392–93 • 40,674
Vidalia, GA 30474 • 11,078
Vidalia, LA 71373 • 4,953
Vidor, TX 77662 • 10,935
Vienna, GA 31092 • 2,708
Vienna, IL 62995 • 1,446
Vienna, VA 22180–83 • 14,852
Vienna, WV 26105 • 10,862
View Park, CA 90043 • 5,900
Vigo □, IN • 106,107
Vilas □, WI • 17,707
Villa Grove, IL 61956 • 2,734
Villa Hills, KY 41016 • 7,739
Villa Park, CA 92667 • 6,299
Villa Park, IL 60181 • 22,253
Villa Rica, GA 30180 • 6,542
Villas, NJ 08251 • 8,136
Ville Platte, LA 70586 • 9,037
Villisca, IA 50864 • 1,332
Vilonia, AR 72173 • 1,133
Vincennes, IN 47591 • 19,859
Vincent, AL 35178 • 1,767
Vine Grove, KY 40175 • 3,586
Vineland, NJ 08360 • 54,780
Vineyard Haven, MA 02568 • 1,762
Vinita, OK 74301 • 5,804
Vinton, IA 52349 • 5,103
Vinton, LA 70668 • 3,154
Vinton, VA 24179 • 7,665
Vinton □, OH • 11,098
Viola, NY 10952 • 4,504
Violet, LA 70092 • 8,574
Virden, IL 62690 • 3,635
Virginia, IL 62691 • 1,767
Virginia, MN 55792 • 9,410
Virginia Beach, VA 23450–67 • 393,069
Virginia City, NV 89440 • 920
Viroqua, WI 54665 • 3,922
Visalia, CA 93277–79 • 75,636
Vista, CA 92083–84 • 71,872
Vivian, LA 71082 • 4,156
Volcano, HI 96785 • 1,516
Volga, SD 57071 • 1,263
Volusia □, FL • 370,712

W

Wabash, IN 46992 • 12,127
Wabash □, IL • 13,111
Wabash □, IN • 35,069
Wabasha, MN 55981 • 2,384
Wabasha □, MN • 19,744
Wabasso, FL 32970 • 1,145
Wabaunsee □, KS • 6,603
Waco, TX 76701–16 • 103,590
Waconia, MN 55387 • 3,498
Wade Hampton, SC 29607 • 20,014
Wadena, MN 56482 • 4,131
Wadena □, MN • 13,154
Wadesboro, NC 28170 • 3,645
Wading River, NY 11792 • 5,317
Wadley, GA 30477 • 2,473
Wadsworth, IL 60083 • 1,826
Wadsworth, NV 89442 • 640
Wadsworth, OH 44281 • 15,718
Wagner, SD 57380 • 1,462
Wagoner, OK 74467 • 6,894
Wagoner □, OK • 47,883
Wahiawa, HI 96786 • 17,386
Wahkiakum □, WA • 3,327
Wahoo, NE 68066 • 3,681
Wahpeton, ND 58074–75 • 8,751
Waialua, HI 96791 • 3,943
Waianae, HI 96792 • 8,758
Waikapu, HI 96793 • 729
Wailua, HI 96746 • 2,018
Wailuku, HI 96793 • 10,688
Waimanalo, HI 96795 • 3,508
Waimea, HI 96712 • 600
Waimea, HI 96796 • 5,972
Wainwright, AK 99782 • 492
Waipahu, HI 96797 • 31,435
Waipio Acres, HI 96786 • 5,304
Waite Park, MN 56387 • 5,020
Wakarusa, IN 46573 • 1,667
Wake □, NC • 423,380
Wa Keeney, KS 67672 • 2,161
Wakefield, MA 01880 • 24,825
Wakefield, MI 49968 • 2,318
Wakefield, NE 68784 • 1,082
Wakefield, RI 02879–83 • 3,450
Wakefield, VA 23888 • 1,070
Wake Forest, NC 27587–88 • 5,769
Wakulla □, FL • 14,202
Walbridge, OH 43465 • 2,736
Walcott, IA 52773 • 1,356
Walden, NY 12586 • 5,836
Waldo, AR 71770 • 1,495
Waldo, FL 32694 • 1,017
Waldo □, ME • 33,018
Waldoboro, ME 04572 • 1,420
Waldport, OR 97394 • 1,595
Waldron, AR 72958 • 3,024
Waldwick, NJ 07463 • 9,757
Walhalla, ND 58282 • 1,131
Walhalla, SC 29691 • 3,755
Walker, LA 70785 • 3,727
Walker, MI 49504 • 17,279
Walker □, AL • 67,670
Walker □, GA • 58,340
Walker □, TX • 50,917
Walkersville, MD 21793 • 4,145
Walkerton, IN 46574 • 2,061
Walkertown, NC 27051 • 1,200
Walkerville, MT 59701 • 605
Wall, SD 57790 • 834
Wallace, ID 83873 • 1,010
Wallace, NC 28466 • 2,939
Wallace □, KS • 1,821
Walla Walla, WA 99362 • 26,478
Walla Walla □, WA • 48,439
Walled Lake, MI 48390 • 6,278
Wallen, IN 46806 • 1,000
Waller, TX 77484 • 1,493
Waller □, TX • 23,390
Wallingford, CT 06492 • 17,827
Wallingford, VT 05773 • 1,148
Wallington, NJ 07057 • 10,828
Wallis, TX 77485 • 1,001
Wallkill, NY 12589 • 2,125
Wallowa □, OR • 6,911
Walnut, CA 91789 • 29,105
Walnut, IL 61376 • 1,463
Walnut Cove, NC 27052 • 1,088
Walnut Creek, CA 94593–98 • 60,569
Walnut Park, CA 90255 • 14,722
Walnutport, PA 18088 • 2,055
Walnut Ridge, AR 72476 • 4,388
Walpole, MA 02081 • 5,495
Walsenburg, CO 81089 • 3,300
Walsh □, ND • 13,840
Walterboro, SC 29488 • 5,492
Walters, OK 73572 • 2,519
Walthall □, MS • 14,352
Waltham, MA 02154 • 57,878
Walthourville, GA 31333 • 2,024
Walton, IN 46994 • 1,053
Walton, KY 41094 • 2,034
Walton, NY 13856 • 3,326
Walton □, FL • 27,760
Walton □, GA • 38,586
Walworth, WI 53184 • 1,614
Walworth □, SD • 6,087
Walworth □, WI • 75,000
Wamac, IL 62801 • 1,501
Wamego, KS 66547 • 3,706
Wamesit, MA 01876 • 2,700
Wamsutter, WY 82336 • 240
Wanaque, NJ 07465 • 9,711
Wanchese, NC 27981 • 1,380
Wando Woods, SC 29405 • 5,253
Wantagh, NY 11793 • 18,567
Wapakoneta, OH 45895 • 9,214
Wapato, WA 98951 • 3,795
Wapello, IA 52653 • 2,013
Wapello □, IA • 35,687
Wappingers Falls, NY 12590 • 4,605
War, WV 24892 • 1,081
Ward, AR 72176 • 1,269
Ward □, ND • 57,921
Ward □, TX • 13,115
Warden, WA 98857 • 1,639
Ware, MA 01082 • 6,533
Ware □, GA • 35,471
Wareham, MA 02571 • 2,607
Warehouse Point, CT 06088 • 1,880
Ware Shoals, SC 29692 • 2,497
Waretown, NJ 08758 • 1,283
Warminster, PA 18974 • 35,463
Warner, OK 74469 • 1,479
Warner Robins, GA 31088 • 43,726
Warr Acres, OK 73132 • 9,288
Warren, AR 71671 • 6,455
Warren, IL 61087 • 1,550
Warren, IN 46792 • 1,185
Warren, MA 01083 • 1,516
Warren, MI 48089–93 • 144,864
Warren, MN 56762 • 1,813
Warren, OH 44481–85 • 50,793
Warren, PA 16365 • 11,122
Warren, RI 02885 • 11,385
Warren, VT 05674 • 350
Warren □, GA • 6,078
Warren □, IL • 19,181
Warren □, IN • 8,176
Warren □, IA • 36,033
Warren □, KY • 76,673
Warren □, MS • 47,880
Warren □, MO • 19,534
Warren □, NJ • 91,607
Warren □, NY • 59,209
Warren □, NC • 17,265
Warren □, OH • 113,909
Warren □, PA • 45,050
Warren □, TN • 32,992
Warren □, VA • 26,142
Warren Park, IN 46219 • 1,763
Warrensburg, IL 62573 • 1,274
Warrensburg, MO 64093 • 15,244
Warrensburg, NY 12885 • 3,204
Warrensville Heights, OH 44122 • 15,745
Warrenton, GA 30828 • 2,056
Warrenton, MO 63383 • 3,564
Warrenton, OR 97146 • 2,681
Warrenton, VA 22186 • 4,830
Warrenville, IL 60555 • 11,333
Warrenville, SC 29851 • 1,029
Warrick □, IN • 44,920
Warrington, FL 32507 • 16,040
Warrington, PA 18976 • 6,980
Warrior, AL 35180 • 3,280
Warroad, MN 56763 • 1,679
Warsaw, IL 62379 • 1,882
Warsaw, IN 46580–81 • 10,968
Warsaw, KY 41095 • 1,202
Warsaw, MO 65355 • 1,696
Warsaw, NY 14569 • 3,830
Warsaw, NC 28398 • 2,859
Warwick, NY 10990 • 5,984
Warwick, RI 02886–89 • 85,427
Wasatch □, UT • 10,089
Wasco, CA 93280 • 12,412
Wasco □, OR • 21,683
Waseca, MN 56093 • 8,385
Waseca □, MN • 18,079
Washakie □, WY • 8,388
Washburn, IL 61570 • 1,075
Washburn, IA 50706 • 1,400
Washburn, ME 04786 • 1,880
Washburn, ND 58577 • 1,506
Washburn, WI 54891 • 2,285
Washburn □, WI • 13,772
Washington, DC 20001–99 • 606,900
Washington, GA 30673 • 4,279
Washington, IL 61571 • 10,099
Washington, IN 47501 • 10,838
Washington, IA 52353 • 7,074
Washington, KS 66968 • 1,304
Washington, LA 70589 • 1,253
Washington, MO 63090 • 10,704
Washington, NJ 07882 • 6,474
Washington, NC 27889 • 9,075
Washington, PA 15301 • 15,864
Washington, UT 84780 • 4,198
Washington □, AL • 16,694
Washington □, AR • 113,409
Washington □, CO • 4,812
Washington □, FL • 16,919
Washington □, GA • 19,112
Washington □, ID • 8,550
Washington □, IL • 14,965
Washington □, IN • 23,717

Washington □, IA • 19,612
Washington □, KS • 7,073
Washington □, KY • 10,441
Washington □, LA • 43,185
Washington □, ME • 35,308
Washington □, MD • 121,393
Washington □, MN • 145,896
Washington □, MS • 67,935
Washington □, MO • 20,380
Washington □, NE • 16,607
Washington □, NY • 59,330
Washington □, NC • 13,997
Washington □, OH • 62,254
Washington □, OK • 48,066
Washington □, OR • 311,554
Washington □, PA • 204,584
Washington □, RI • 110,006
Washington □, TN • 92,315
Washington □, TX • 26,154
Washington □, UT • 48,560
Washington □, VT • 54,928
Washington □, VA • 45,887
Washington □, WI • 95,328
Washington Court House, OH 43160 • 12,983
Washington Park, FL 33314 • 6,930
Washington Park, IL 62204 • 7,431
Washington Terrace, UT 84403 • 8,189
Washington Township, NJ 07675 • 9,245
Washita □, OK • 11,441
Washoe □, NV • 254,667
Washoe City, NV 89701 • 400
Washougal, WA 98671 • 4,764
Washtenaw □, MI • 282,937
Wasilla, AK 99687 • 4,028
Waskom, TX 75692 • 1,812
Watauga, TX 76148 • 20,009
Watauga □, NC • 36,952
Watchung, NJ 07060 • 5,110
Waterbury, CT 06701–26 • 108,961
Waterbury, VT 05676 • 1,702
Waterbury Center, VT 05677 • 500
Waterford, CT 06385 • 17,930
Waterford, MI 48327–29 • 66,692
Waterford, NY 12188 • 2,370
Waterford, PA 16441 • 1,492
Waterford, WI 53185 • 2,431
Waterford Works, NJ 08089 • 1,200
Waterloo, IL 62298 • 5,072
Waterloo, IN 46793 • 2,040
Waterloo, IA 50701–07 • 66,467
Waterloo, NY 13165 • 5,116
Waterloo, WI 53594 • 2,712
Waterman, IL 60556 • 1,074
Waterproof, LA 71375 • 1,080
Watertown, CT 06795 • 20,456
Watertown, FL 32055 • 3,340
Watertown, MA 02172 • 33,284
Watertown, NY 13601–03 • 29,429
Watertown, SD 57201 • 17,592
Watertown, TN 37184 • 1,250
Watertown, WI 53094 • 19,142
Water Valley, MS 38965 • 3,610
Waterville, ME 04901–03 • 17,173
Waterville, MN 56096 • 1,771
Waterville, NY 13480 • 1,664
Waterville, OH 43566 • 4,517
Watervliet, MI 49098 • 1,867
Watervliet, NY 12189 • 11,061
Watford City, ND 58854 • 1,784
Wathena, KS 66090 • 1,160
Watkins Glen, NY 14891 • 2,207
Watkinsville, GA 30677 • 1,600
Watonga, OK 73772 • 3,408
Watonwan □, MN • 11,682
Watseka, IL 60970 • 5,424
Watsontown, PA 17777 • 2,310
Watsonville, CA 95076–77 • 31,099
Wattsville, SC 29360 • 1,324
Wauchula, FL 33873 • 3,253
Wauconda, IL 60084 • 6,294
Waukee, IA 50263 • 2,512
Waukegan, IL 60085–87 • 69,392
Waukesha, WI 53186–88 • 56,958
Waukesha □, WI • 304,715
Waukomis, OK 73773 • 1,322
Waukon, IA 52172 • 4,019
Waunakee, WI 53597 • 5,897
Waupaca, WI 54981 • 4,957
Waupaca □, WI • 46,104
Waupun, WI 53963 • 8,207
Wauregan, CT 06387 • 1,200
Waurika, OK 73573 • 2,088
Wausau, WI 54401–02 • 37,060
Wauseon, OH 43567 • 6,322
Waushara □, WI • 19,385
Wautoma, WI 54982 • 1,784
Wauwatosa, WI 53213 • 49,366
Waveland, MS 39576 • 5,369
Waverly, IL 62692 • 1,402
Waverly, IA 50677 • 8,539
Waverly, MI 48917 • 15,614
Waverly, NE 68462 • 1,869
Waverly, NY 14892 • 4,787
Waverly, OH 45690 • 4,477
Waverly, TN 37185 • 3,925
Waverly, VA 23890 • 2,223
Waxahachie, TX 75165 • 18,168
Waxhaw, NC 28173 • 1,294
Waycross, GA 31501 • 16,410
Wayland, MA 01778 • 2,550
Wayland, MI 49348 • 2,751
Wayland, NY 14572 • 1,976
Waylyn, SC 29405 • 2,400
Waymart, PA 18472 • 1,337
Wayne, MI 48184–88 • 19,899
Wayne, NE 68787 • 5,142
Wayne, NJ 07470–74 • 47,025
Wayne, WV 25570 • 1,128
Wayne □, GA • 22,356
Wayne □, IL • 17,241
Wayne □, IN • 71,951
Wayne □, IA • 7,067
Wayne □, KY • 17,468
Wayne □, MI • 2,111,687
Wayne □, MS • 19,517
Wayne □, MO • 11,543
Wayne □, NE • 9,364
Wayne □, NY • 89,123
Wayne □, NC • 104,666
Wayne □, OH • 101,461
Wayne □, PA • 39,944
Wayne □, TN • 13,935
Wayne □, UT • 2,177
Wayne □, WV • 41,636
Wayne City, IL 62895 • 1,099
Waynesboro, GA 30830 • 5,701
Waynesboro, MS 39367 • 5,143
Waynesboro, PA 17268 • 9,578
Waynesboro, TN 38485 • 1,824
Waynesboro, VA 22980 • 18,549
Waynesburg, OH 44688 • 1,068
Waynesburg, PA 15370 • 4,270
Waynesville, MO 65583 • 3,207
Waynesville, NC 28786 • 6,758
Waynesville, OH 45068 • 1,949
Waynewood, VA 22308 • 5,000
Wayzata, MN 55391 • 3,806
Weakley □, TN • 31,972
Weatherford, OK 73096 • 10,124
Weatherford, TX 76086–87 • 14,804
Weatherly, PA 18255 • 2,640
Weatogue, CT 06089 • 2,521
Weaver, AL 36277 • 2,715
Weaverville, CA 96093 • 3,370
Weaverville, NC 28787 • 2,107
Webb, AL 36376 • 1,039
Webb □, TX • 133,239
Webb City, MO 64870 • 7,449
Webberville, MI 48892 • 1,698
Weber □, UT • 158,330
Weber City, VA 24251 • 1,377
Webster, MA 01570 • 11,849
Webster, NY 14580 • 5,464
Webster, PA 15087 • 1,000
Webster, SD 57274 • 2,017
Webster □, GA • 2,263
Webster □, IA • 40,342
Webster □, KY • 13,955
Webster □, LA • 41,989
Webster □, MS • 10,222
Webster □, MO • 23,753
Webster □, NE • 4,279
Webster □, WV • 10,729
Webster City, IA 50595 • 7,894
Webster Groves, MO 63119 • 22,987
Websterville, VT 05678 • 600
Wedgewood, MO 63031 • 6,700
Weed, CA 96094 • 3,062
Weed Heights, NV 89447 • 230
Weedsport, NY 13166 • 1,996
Weehawken, NJ 07087 • 12,385
Weeping Water, NE 68463 • 1,008
Weigelstown, PA 17315 • 8,665
Weimar, TX 78962 • 2,052
Weippe, ID 83553 • 532
Weirsdale, FL 32195 • 1,500
Weirton, WV 26062 • 22,124
Weiser, ID 83672 • 4,571
Wekiva Springs, FL 32750 • 23,026
Welch, WV 24801 • 3,028
Welcome, SC 29611 • 6,560
Weld □, CO • 131,821
Weldon, NC 27890 • 1,392
Weleetka, OK 74880 • 1,112
Wellesley, MA 02181 • 26,615
Wellfleet, MA 02667 • 1,200
Wellford, SC 29385 • 2,511
Wellington, CO 80549 • 1,340
Wellington, FL 33414 • 20,670
Wellington, KS 67152 • 8,411
Wellington, NV 89444 • 280
Wellington, OH 44090 • 4,140
Wellington, TX 79095 • 2,456
Wellington, UT 84542 • 1,632
Wellman, IA 52356 • 1,085
Wells, ME 04090 • 1,200
Wells, MI 49894 • 1,150
Wells, MN 56097 • 2,465
Wells, NV 89835 • 1,256
Wells □, IN • 25,948
Wells □, ND • 5,864
Wellsboro, PA 16901 • 3,430
Wellsburg, WV 26070 • 3,385
Wellston, OH 45692 • 6,049
Wellsville, KS 66092 • 1,563
Wellsville, MO 63384 • 1,430
Wellsville, NY 14895 • 5,241
Wellsville, OH 43968 • 4,532
Wellsville, UT 84339 • 2,206
Wellton, AZ 85356 • 1,066
Welsh, LA 70591 • 3,299
Wenatchee, WA 98801–07 • 21,756
Wendell, ID 83355 • 1,963
Wendell, NC 27591 • 2,822
Wendover, UT 84083 • 1,127
Wenham, MA 01984 • 3,897
Wenonah, NJ 08090 • 2,331
Wentzville, MO 63385 • 5,088
Weslaco, TX 78596 • 21,877
Wesleyville, PA 16510 • 3,655
Wessington Springs, SD 57382 • 1,083
Wesson, MS 39191 • 1,510
West, TX 76691 • 2,515
West Acton, MA 01720 • 5,230
West Alexandria, OH 45381 • 1,460
West Allis, WI 53214 • 63,221
West Andover, MA 01810 • 1,970
West Athens, CA 90247 • 8,859
West Babylon, NY 11704 • 42,410
West Barnstable, MA 02668 • 1,000
West Baton Rouge □, LA • 19,419
West Bay Shore, NY 11706 • 4,907
West Bend, WI 53095 • 23,916
West Berlin, NJ 08091 • 2,970
West Billerica, MA 01862 • 1,920
West Blocton, AL 35184 • 1,468
Westborough, MA 01581 • 3,917
West Bountiful, UT 84087 • 4,477
West Boylston, MA 01583 • 3,130
West Bradenton, FL 34205 • 4,528
West Branch, IA 52358 • 1,908
West Branch, MI 48661 • 1,914
West Bridgewater, MA 02379 • 2,140
Westbrook, CT 06498 • 2,060
Westbrook, ME 04092 • 16,121
West Brookfield, MA 01585 • 1,419
West Burlington, IA 52655 • 3,083
Westbury, NY 11590 • 13,060
Westby, WI 54667 • 1,866
West Caldwell, NJ 07004 • 10,422
West Cape May, NJ 08204 • 1,026
West Carroll □, LA • 12,093
West Carrollton, OH 45449 • 14,403
West Carson, CA 90502 • 20,143
West Carthage, NY 13619 • 2,166
West Chatham, MA 02669 • 1,504
Westchester, FL 33136 • 29,883
Westchester, IL 60153 • 17,301
West Chester, PA 19380–82 • 18,041
Westchester □, NY • 874,866
West Chicago, IL 60185–86 • 14,796
West Columbia, SC 29169–72 • 10,588
West Columbia, TX 77486 • 4,372
West Compton, CA 90220 • 5,451
West Concord, MA 01742 • 5,761
West Concord, NC 28027 • 5,859
West Covina, CA 91790–93 • 96,086
West Crossett, AR 71635 • 2,019
West Dennis, MA 02670 • 2,307
West Des Moines, IA 50265 • 31,702
West Elmira, NY 14905 • 5,218
Westerly, RI 02891 • 16,477
Westernport, MD 21562 • 2,454
Western Springs, IL 60558 • 11,984
Westerville, OH 43081–82 • 30,269
West Fairview, PA 17025 • 1,403
West Falmouth, MA 02574 • 1,600
West Fargo, ND 58078 • 12,287
West Feliciana □, LA • 12,915
Westfield, IN 46074 • 3,304
Westfield, MA 01085–86 • 38,372
Westfield, NJ 07090–92 • 28,870
Westfield, NY 14787 • 3,451
Westfield, PA 16950 • 1,119
Westfield, WI 53964 • 1,125
Westford, MA 01886 • 1,200
West Fork, AR 72774 • 1,607
West Frankfort, IL 62896 • 8,526
West Freehold, NJ 07728 • 11,166
Westgate, FL 33401 • 2,100
West Gate, VA 22110 • 6,565
West Gate of Lomond, VA 22110 • 5,400
West Glens Falls, NY 12801 • 5,964
West Goshen, PA 19380 • 8,948
West Grove, PA 19390 • 2,128
Westham, VA 23229 • 3,200
West Hanover, MA 02339 • 1,700
West Hartford, CT 06127 • 60,110
West Haven, CT 06516 • 54,021
West Haven, OR 97225 • 3,400
West Haverstraw, NY 10993 • 9,183
West Hazleton, PA 18201 • 4,136
West Helena, AR 72390 • 9,695
West Hempstead, NY 11552 • 17,689
West Hollywood, CA 90069 • 36,118
Westhope, ND 58793 • 578
West Hyannisport, MA 02672 • 1,200
West Islip, NY 11795 • 28,419
West Jefferson, NC 28694 • 1,002
West Jefferson, OH 43162 • 4,504
West Jordan, UT 84084 • 42,892
West Kingston, RI 02892 • 1,150
West Lafayette, IN 47906–07 • 25,907
West Lafayette, OH 43845 • 2,129
Westlake, LA 70669 • 5,007
Westlake, OH 44145 • 27,018
Westlake Village, CA 91361 • 7,455
Westland, MI 48185 • 84,724
West Lawn, PA 19609 • 1,606
West Liberty, IA 52776 • 2,935
West Liberty, KY 41472 • 1,887
West Liberty, OH 43357 • 1,613
West Liberty, WV 26074 • 1,434
West Linn, OR 97068 • 16,367
West Long Branch, NJ 07764 • 7,690
West Marion, NC 28752 • 1,291
West Medway, MA 02053 • 1,940
West Melbourne, FL 32901 • 8,399
West Memphis, AR 72301 • 28,259
Westmere, NY 12203 • 6,750
West Miami, FL 33174 • 5,727
West Mifflin, PA 15122–23 • 23,644
West Milford, NJ 07480 • 25,430
West Milton, OH 45383 • 4,348
West Milwaukee, WI 53214 • 3,973
Westminster, CA 92683–84 • 78,118
Westminster, CO 80030–31 • 74,625
Westminster, MD 21157 • 13,068
Westminster, SC 29693 • 3,120
West Modesto, CA 95351 • 6,135
West Monroe, LA 71291–94 • 14,096
Westmont, CA 90044 • 31,100
Westmont, IL 60559 • 21,228
Westmont, NJ 08108 • 5,630
Westmont, PA 15905 • 5,789
Westmoreland, TN 37186 • 1,726
Westmoreland □, PA • 370,321
Westmoreland □, VA • 15,480
Westmorland, CA 92281 • 1,380
West Mystic, CT 06388 • 3,595
West Newton, PA 15089 • 3,152
West New York, NJ 07093 • 38,125
West Norriton, PA 19401 • 15,209
West Nyack, NY 10960 • 3,437
Weston, CT 06883 • 1,370
Weston, MA 02193 • 11,169
Weston, MO 64098 • 1,528
Weston, OH 43569 • 1,716
Weston, WV 26452 • 4,994
Weston, WI 54476 • 9,714
Weston □, WY • 6,518
West Orange, NJ 07052 • 39,103
Westover, WV 26505 • 4,201
West Palm Beach, FL 33401–20 • 67,643
West Pasco, WA 99301 • 7,312
West Paterson, NJ 07424 • 10,982
West Pawlet, VT 05775 • 350
West Pensacola, FL 32505 • 22,107
West Peoria, IL 61604 • 5,314
West Pittsburg, CA 94565 • 17,453
West Pittsburg, PA 16160 • 1,133
West Pittston, PA 18643 • 5,590
West Plains, MO 65775 • 8,913
West Point, CA 95255 • 1,500
West Point, GA 31833 • 3,571
West Point, IA 52656 • 1,079
West Point, KY 40177 • 1,216
West Point, MS 39773 • 8,489
West Point, NE 68788 • 3,250
West Point, NY 10996–97 • 8,024
West Point, UT 84015 • 4,258
West Point, VA 23181 • 2,938
Westport, CT 06880–83 • 24,407
Westport, IN 47283 • 1,478
Westport, WA 98595 • 1,892
West Portsmouth, OH 45662 • 3,551
West Puente Valley, CA 91744 • 20,254
West Reading, PA 19611 • 4,142
West Rutland, VT 05777 • 2,246
West Sacramento, CA 95691 • 28,898
West Saint Paul, MN 55118 • 19,248
West Salem, IL 62476 • 1,042
West Salem, OH 44287 • 1,534
West Salem, WI 54669 • 3,611
West Sayville, NY 11796 • 4,680
West Seneca, NY 14224 • 47,866
West Simsbury, CT 06092 • 2,149
West Slope, OR 97225 • 7,959
West Springfield, MA 01089–90 • 27,537
West Springfield, VA 22152 • 28,126
West Swanzey, NH 03469 • 1,055
West Terre Haute, IN 47885 • 2,495
West Union, IA 52175 • 2,490
West Union, OH 45693 • 3,096
West Unity, OH 43570 • 1,677
West University Place, TX 77005 • 12,920
West Upton, MA 01588 • 1,300
Westvale, NY 13219 • 5,952
West Valley City, UT 84120 • 86,976
Westview, FL 33168 • 9,668
West View, PA 15229 • 7,734
Westville, IL 61883 • 3,387
Westville, IN 46391 • 5,255
Westville, NJ 08093 • 4,573
Westville, OK 74965 • 1,374
West Wareham, MA 02576 • 2,059
West Warren, MA 01092 • 1,200
West Warwick, RI 02893 • 29,268
West Webster, NY 14580 • 8,690
Westwego, LA 70094–96 • 11,218
West Whittier, CA 90606 • 13,800
West Willow, MI 48198 • 4,300
Westwood, CA 96137 • 2,017
Westwood, KS 66205 • 1,772
Westwood, KY 41101 • 5,300
Westwood, MA 02090 • 6,500
Westwood, MI 49007 • 8,957
Westwood, NJ 07675 • 10,446
Westwood Lakes, FL 33165 • 11,522
West Wyoming, PA 18644 • 3,117
West Yarmouth, MA 02673 • 5,409
West Yellowstone, MT 59758 • 913
West York, PA 17404 • 4,283
Wethersfield, CT 06129 • 25,651
Wetumka, OK 74883 • 1,427
Wetumpka, AL 36092 • 4,670
Wetzel □, WV • 19,258
Wewahitchka, FL 32465 • 1,779
Wewoka, OK 74884 • 4,050
Wexford □, MI • 26,360
Weyauwega, WI 54983 • 1,665
Weymouth, MA 02188 • 54,063
Whalom, MA 01420 • 1,340
Wharton, NJ 07885 • 5,405
Wharton, TX 77488 • 9,011
Wharton □, TX • 39,955
Whatcom □, WA • 127,780
Wheatland, CA 95692 • 1,631
Wheatland, WY 82201 • 3,271
Wheatland □, MT • 2,246
Wheaton, IL 60187–89 • 51,464
Wheaton, MD 20902 • 58,300
Wheaton, MN 56296 • 1,615
Wheat Ridge, CO 80033–34 • 29,419
Wheeler, TX 79096 • 1,393
Wheeler □, GA • 4,903
Wheeler □, NE • 948
Wheeler □, OR • 1,396
Wheeler □, TX • 5,879
Wheelersburg, OH 45694 • 5,113
Wheeling, IL 60090 • 29,911
Wheeling, WV 26003 • 34,882
Whitacres, CT 06082 • 2,410
White □, AR • 54,676
White □, GA • 13,006
White □, IL • 16,522
White □, IN • 23,265
White □, TN • 20,090
White Bear Lake, MN 55110 • 24,704
White Bluff, TN 37187 • 1,988
White Castle, LA 70788 • 2,102
White Center, WA 98126 • 15,700
White City, OR 97503 • 5,891
White City, UT 84070 • 6,506
White Cloud, MI 49349 • 1,147
White Deer, TX 79097 • 1,125
Whitefield, NH 03598 • 1,041
Whitefish, MT 59937 • 4,368
Whitefish Bay, WI 53217 • 14,272
White Hall, AR 71602 • 3,849
White Hall, IL 62092 • 2,814
Whitehall, MI 49461 • 3,027
Whitehall, MT 59759 • 1,067
Whitehall, NY 12887 • 3,071
Whitehall, OH 43213 • 20,572
Whitehall, PA 15227 • 14,451
Whitehall, WI 54773 • 1,494
White Haven, PA 18661 • 1,132
White Horse, NJ 08610 • 9,397
White Horse Beach, MA 02381 • 1,200
Whitehouse, OH 43571 • 2,528
White House, TN 37188 • 2,987
White House Station, NJ 08889 • 1,400
White Island Shores, MA 02538 • 2,000
White Meadow Lake, NJ 07866 • 8,002
White Oak, MD 20901 • 18,671
White Oak, OH 45239 • 12,430
White Oak, PA 15131 • 8,761
White Pigeon, MI 49099 • 1,458
White Pine, MI 49971 • 1,142
White Pine, TN 37890 • 1,771
White Pine □, NV • 9,264
White Plains, MD 20695 • 3,560
White Plains, NY 10601–07 • 48,718
Whiteriver, AZ 85941 • 3,775
White River Junction, VT 05001 • 2,521
White Rock, NM 87544 • 6,192
White Salmon, WA 98672 • 1,861
Whitesboro, NY 13492 • 4,195
Whitesboro, TX 76273 • 3,209
Whitesburg, KY 41858 • 1,636
White Settlement, TX 76108 • 15,472
Whiteside □, IL • 60,186
White Sulphur Springs, MT 59645 • 963
White Sulphur Springs, WV 24986 • 2,779
Whiteville, NC 28472 • 5,078
Whiteville, TN 38075 • 1,050
Whitewater, WI 53190 • 12,636
Whitewood, SD 57793 • 891
Whitewright, TX 75491 • 1,713
Whitfield □, GA • 72,462
Whitfield Estates, FL 34243 • 3,152
Whiting, IN 46394 • 5,155
Whiting, WI 54481 • 1,838
Whitinsville, MA 01588 • 5,639
Whitley □, IN • 27,651
Whitley □, KY • 33,326
Whitley City, KY 42653 • 1,133
Whitman, MA 02382 • 13,534
Whitman, WV 25652 • 1,651
Whitman □, WA • 38,775
Whitman Square, NJ 08012 • 3,490
Whitmire, SC 29178 • 1,702
Whitmore Lake, MI 48189 • 3,251
Whitmore Village, HI 96786 • 3,373
Whitney, SC 29303 • 4,052
Whitney, TX 76692 • 1,626
Whitney Point, NY 13862 • 1,054
Whittier, AK 99693 • 243
Whittier, CA 90601–12 • 77,671
Whitwell, TN 37397 • 1,622
Wibaux, MT 59353 • 628
Wibaux □, MT • 1,191
Wichita, KS 67201–78 • 304,011
Wichita □, KS • 2,758
Wichita □, TX • 122,378
Wichita Falls, TX 76301–11 • 96,259
Wickenburg, AZ 85358 • 4,515
Wickliffe, OH 44092 • 14,558
Wickliffe, OH 44515 • 7,240
Wicomico □, MD • 74,339
Wiconisco, PA 17097 • 1,321
Widefield, CO 80911 • 12,112
Wiggins, MS 39577 • 3,185
Wilbarger □, TX • 15,121
Wilber, NE 68465 • 1,527
Wilberforce, OH 45384 • 2,639
Wilbraham, MA 01095 • 3,352
Wilburton, OK 74578 • 3,092
Wilcox, PA 15870 • 1,000
Wilcox □, AL • 13,568
Wilcox □, GA • 7,008
Wilder, ID 83676 • 1,232
Wilder, VT 05088 • 1,576
Wildorado, TX 79098 • 2,000
Wildwood, FL 34785 • 3,421
Wildwood, IL 60030 • 2,034
Wildwood, NJ 08260 • 4,484
Wildwood Crest, NJ 08260 • 3,631
Wilkes □, GA • 10,597
Wilkes □, NC • 59,393
Wilkes-Barre, PA 18701–73 • 47,523
Wilkesboro, NC 28697 • 2,573
Wilkin □, MN • 7,516
Wilkinsburg, PA 15221 • 21,080
Wilkinson □, GA • 10,228
Wilkinson □, MS • 9,678
Wilkins Township, PA 15145 • 7,487
Will □, IL • 357,313
Willacoochee, GA 31650 • 1,205
Willacy □, TX • 17,705
Willamina, OR 97396 • 1,717
Willard, MO 65781 • 2,177
Willard, NY 14588 • 1,339
Willard, OH 44890 • 6,210
Willard, UT 84340 • 1,298
Willcox, AZ 85643 • 3,122
Williams, AZ 86046 • 2,532
Williams, CA 95987 • 2,297
Williams □, ND • 21,129
Williams □, OH • 36,956
Williams Bay, WI 53191 • 2,108
Williamsburg, IA 52361 • 2,174
Williamsburg, KY 40769 • 5,493
Williamsburg, MA 01096 • 1,200
Williamsburg, OH 45176 • 2,322
Williamsburg, PA 16693 • 1,456
Williamsburg, VA 23185–88 • 11,530
Williamsburg □, SC • 36,815
Williamson, NY 14589 • 1,768
Williamson, WV 25661 • 4,154
Williamson □, IL • 57,733
Williamson □, TN • 81,021
Williamson □, TX • 139,551
Williamsport, IN 47993 • 1,798
Williamsport, MD 21795 • 2,103
Williamsport, PA 17701–03 • 31,933
Williamston, MI 48895 • 2,922
Williamston, NC 27892 • 5,503
Williamston, SC 29697 • 3,876
Williamstown, KY 41097 • 3,023
Williamstown, MA 01267 • 4,791
Williamstown, NJ 08094 • 10,891
Williamstown, PA 17098 • 1,509
Williamstown, VT 05679 • 650
Williamstown, WV 26187 • 2,774
Williamsville, IL 62693 • 1,140
Williamsville, NY 14221 • 5,583
Willimantic, CT 06226 • 14,746
Willingboro, NJ 08046 • 36,291
Willis, TX 77378 • 2,764
Williston, FL 32696 • 2,179
Williston, ND 58801–02 • 13,131
Williston, SC 29853 • 3,099
Williston Park, NY 11596 • 7,516
Willits, CA 95490 • 5,027
Willmar, MN 56201 • 17,531
Willoughby, OH 44094–95 • 20,510
Willoughby Hills, OH 44092 • 8,427
Willow Brook, CA 90222 • 32,772
Willowbrook, IL 60521 • 8,598
Willow Grove, PA 19090 • 16,325
Willowick, OH 44094 • 15,269
Willow Run, DE 19805 • 1,600
Willow Run, MI 48198 • 7,200
Willows, CA 95988 • 5,988
Willow Springs, IL 60480 • 4,509
Willow Springs, MO 65793 • 2,038
Willston, VA 22044 • 2,000
Wilmerding, PA 15148 • 2,222
Wilmette, IL 60091 • 26,690
Wilmington, DE 19801–99 • 71,529
Wilmington, IL 60481 • 4,743
Wilmington, MA 01887 • 17,654
Wilmington, NC 28401–12 • 55,530
Wilmington, OH 45177 • 11,199
Wilmington, VT 05363 • 550
Wilmington Island, GA 31410 • 11,230
Wilmington Manor, DE 19720 • 8,568
Wilmington Manor Gardens, DE 19720 • 1,500
Wilmore, KY 40390 • 4,215
Wilmot, AR 71676 • 1,047
Wilson, AR 72395 • 1,068

Wilson, NY 14172 • 1,307
Wilson, NC 27893–95 • 36,930
Wilson, OK 73463 • 1,639
Wilson, PA 18042 • 7,830
Wilson, WY 83014 • 500
Wilson □, KS • 10,289
Wilson □, NC • 66,061
Wilson □, TN • 67,675
Wilson □, TX • 22,650
Wilsonville, AL 35186 • 1,185
Wilsonville, OR 97070 • 7,106
Wilton, CT 06897 • 7,200
Wilton, IA 52778 • 2,577
Wilton, ME 04294 • 2,453
Wilton, NH 03086 • 1,165
Wilton, ND 58579 • 728
Wilton Manors, FL 33334 • 11,804
Wimauma, FL 33598 • 2,932
Winamac, IN 46996 • 2,262
Winchendon, MA 01475 • 4,316
Winchester, IL 62694 • 1,769
Winchester, IN 47394 • 5,095
Winchester, KY 40391–92 • 15,799
Winchester, MA 01890 • 20,267
Winchester, NV 89101 • 23,365
Winchester, NH 03470 • 1,735
Winchester, TN 37398 • 6,305
Winchester, VA 22601 • 21,947
Windber, PA 15963 • 4,756
Windcrest, TX 78239 • 5,331
Winder, GA 30680 • 7,373
Windgap, PA 18091 • 2,741
Windham, CT 06280 • 1,100
Windham, OH 44288 • 2,943
Windham □, CT • 102,525
Windham □, VT • 41,588
Wind Lake, WI 53185 • 3,000
Windom, MN 56101 • 4,283
Window Rock, AZ 86515 • 3,306
Wind Point, WI 53402 • 1,941
Windsor, CO 80550 • 5,062
Windsor, CT 06095 • 27,817
Windsor, IL 61957 • 1,143
Windsor, MO 65360 • 3,044
Windsor, NC 27983 • 2,056
Windsor, PA 17366 • 1,355
Windsor, VT 05089 • 3,478
Windsor, VA 23487 • 1,025
Windsor □, VT • 54,055
Windsor Heights, IA 50311 • 5,190
Windsor Hills, CA 90052 • 6,200
Windsor Locks, CT 06096 • 12,358
Windy Hill, SC 29506 • 1,622
Windy Hills, DE 19711 • 1,130
Winfield, AL 35594 • 3,689
Winfield, IA 52659 • 1,051
Winfield, KS 67156 • 11,931
Winfield, NJ 07036 • 1,785
Winfield, WV 25213 • 1,164
Wingate, NC 28174 • 2,821
Wink, TX 79789 • 1,189
Winkler □, TX • 8,626
Winlock, WA 98596 • 1,027
Winn □, LA • 16,269
Winnebago, IL 61088 • 1,840
Winnebago, MN 56098 • 1,565
Winnebago, WI 54985 • 1,433
Winnebago □, IL • 252,913
Winnebago □, IA • 12,122
Winnebago □, WI • 140,320
Winneconne, WI 54986 • 2,059
Winnemucca, NV 89445 • 6,134
Winner, SD 57580 • 3,354
Winneshiek □, IA • 20,847
Winnetka, IL 60093 • 12,174
Winnfield, LA 71483 • 6,138
Winnsboro, LA 71295 • 5,755
Winnsboro, SC 29180 • 3,475
Winnsboro, TX 75494 • 2,904
Winnsboro Mills, SC 29180 • 2,275
Winona, MN 55987 • 25,399
Winona, MS 38967 • 5,705
Winona, MO 65588 • 1,081
Winona □, MN • 47,828
Winona Lake, IN 46590 • 4,053
Winooski, VT 05404 • 6,649
Winslow, AZ 86047 • 8,190
Winslow, ME 04901 • 5,436
Winsted, CT 06098 • 8,254
Winsted, MN 55395 • 1,581
Winston, FL 33801 • 9,118
Winston, OR 97496 • 3,773
Winston □, AL • 22,053
Winston □, MS • 19,433
Winston-Salem, NC 27101–27 • 143,485
Winter Garden, FL 34787 • 9,745
Winter Haven, FL 33880–84 • 24,725
Winter Park, FL 32789–90 • 22,242
Winter Park, NC 28403 • 4,504
Winterport, ME 04496 • 1,274
Winters, CA 95694 • 4,639
Winters, TX 79567 • 2,905
Winterset, IA 50273 • 4,196
Winter Springs, FL 32708 • 22,151
Wintersville, OH 43952 • 4,102
Winterville, NC 28590 • 2,816
Winthrop, ME 04364 • 2,819
Winthrop, MA 02152 • 18,127
Winthrop, MN 55396 • 1,279
Winthrop Harbor, IL 60096 • 6,240
Winton, CA 95388 • 7,559
Wirt □, WV • 5,192
Wiscasset, ME 04578 • 1,350
Wisconsin Dells, WI 53965 • 2,393
Wisconsin Rapids, WI 54494–95 • 18,245
Wise, VA 24293 • 3,193
Wise □, TX • 34,679
Wise □, VA • 39,573
Wishek, ND 58495 • 1,171
Wisner, LA 71378 • 1,153
Wisner, NE 68791 • 1,253
Withamsville, OH 45245 • 5,000
Witherbee, NY 12998 • 1,000
Wittenberg, WI 54499 • 1,145
Wixom, MI 48393 • 8,550
Woburn, MA 01801 • 35,943
Wolcott, CT 06716 • 6,070
Wolcott, NY 14590 • 1,544
Wolfe □, KY • 6,503
Wolfeboro, NH 03894 • 2,783
Wolfe City, TX 75496 • 1,505
Wolf Lake, MI 49442 • 4,110
Wolf Point, MT 59201 • 2,880
Wolf Trap, VA 22182 • 13,133
Womelsdorf, PA 19567 • 2,270
Wonder Lake, IL 60097 • 6,664
Wood □, OH • 113,269
Wood □, TX • 29,380
Wood □, WV • 86,915
Wood □, WI • 73,605
Woodbine, GA 31569 • 1,212
Woodbine, IA 51579 • 1,500
Woodbine, NJ 08270 • 2,678
Woodbourne, NY 12788 • 1,155
Woodbourne, OH 45459 • 6,000
Woodbridge, CT 06525 • 7,924
Woodbridge, NJ 07095 • 17,434
Woodbridge, VA 22191–94 • 26,401
Woodbridge [Township], NJ 07095 • 17,434
Woodburn, IN 46797 • 1,321
Woodburn, OR 97071 • 13,404
Woodbury, CT 06798 • 1,212
Woodbury, GA 30293 • 1,429
Woodbury, MN 55125 • 20,075
Woodbury, NJ 08096 • 10,904
Woodbury, NY 11797 • 8,008
Woodbury, TN 37190 • 2,287
Woodbury □, IA • 98,276
Woodcliff Lake, NJ 07675 • 5,303
Wood Dale, IL 60191 • 12,425
Woodfield, SC 29206 • 8,862
Woodford □, IL • 32,653
Woodford □, KY • 19,955
Woodhaven, MI 48183 • 11,631
Woodlake, CA 93286 • 5,678
Woodland, CA 95695 • 39,802
Woodland, ME 04694 • 1,287
Woodland, WA 98674 • 2,500
Woodland Park, CO 80863 • 4,610
Woodlawn, KY 42001 • 1,600
Woodlawn, MD 21207 • 5,329
Woodlawn, MD 20784 • 5,329
Woodlawn, OH 45215 • 2,674
Woodlawn, VA 24381 • 1,689
Woodlynne, NJ 08107 • 2,547
Woodmere, NY 11598 • 15,578
Woodmont, CT 06460 • 1,770
Woodmoor, MD 21207 • 8,630
Woodridge, IL 60517 • 26,256
Wood-Ridge, NJ 07075 • 7,506
Wood River, IL 62095 • 11,490
Wood River, NE 68883 • 1,156
Woodruff, SC 29388 • 4,365
Woodruff, WI 54568 • 1,500
Woodruff □, AR • 9,520
Woods □, OK • 9,103
Woodsboro, TX 78393 • 1,731
Woods Cross, UT 84087 • 5,384
Woodsfield, OH 43793 • 2,832
Woods Hole, MA 02543 • 1,080
Woodside, CA 94062 • 5,035
Woodson □, KS • 4,116
Woodstock, GA 30188 • 4,361
Woodstock, IL 60098 • 14,353
Woodstock, NY 12498 • 1,870
Woodstock, VT 05091 • 1,037
Woodstock, VA 22664 • 3,182
Woodstown, NJ 08098 • 3,154
Woodsville, NH 03785 • 1,122
Woodville, FL 32362 • 2,760
Woodville, MS 39669 • 1,393
Woodville, OH 43469 • 1,953
Woodville, TX 75979 • 2,636
Woodward, IA 50276 • 1,197
Woodward, OK 73801–02 • 12,340
Woodward □, OK • 18,976
Woodway, TX 76710 • 8,695
Woonsocket, RI 02895 • 43,877
Woonsocket, SD 57385 • 766
Wooster, OH 44691 • 22,191
Worcester, MA 01601–15 • 169,759
Worcester □, MD • 35,028
Worcester □, MA • 709,705
Worland, WY 82401 • 5,742
Worth, IL 60482 • 11,208
Worth □, GA • 19,745
Worth □, IA • 7,991
Worth □, MO • 2,440
Wortham, TX 76693 • 1,020
Worthington, IN 47471 • 1,473
Worthington, KY 41183 • 1,751
Worthington, MN 56187 • 9,977
Worthington, OH 43085 • 14,869
Wrangell, AK 99929 • 2,479
Wray, CO 80758 • 1,998
Wrens, GA 30833 • 2,414
Wrentham, MA 02093 • 2,110
Wright, FL 32548 • 18,945
Wright □, IA • 14,269
Wright □, MN • 68,710
Wright □, MO • 16,758
Wright City, MO 63390 • 1,250
Wrightstown, NJ 08562 • 3,843
Wrightstown, WI 54180 • 1,262
Wrightsville, AR 72183 • 1,062
Wrightsville, GA 31096 • 2,331
Wrightsville, PA 17368 • 2,396
Wrightsville Beach, NC 28480 • 2,937
Wrightwood, CA 92397 • 3,308
Wurtsboro, NY 12790 • 1,048
Wyandanch, NY 11798 • 8,950
Wyandot □, OH • 22,254
Wyandotte, MI 48192 • 30,938
Wyandotte □, KS • 161,993
Wyanet, IL 61379 • 1,017
Wyckoff, NJ 07481 • 15,372
Wymore, NE 68466 • 1,611
Wynne, AR 72396–97 • 8,187
Wynnewood, OK 73098 • 2,451
Wyoming, DE 19934 • 977
Wyoming, IL 61491 • 1,462
Wyoming, MI 49509 • 63,891
Wyoming, MN 55092 • 2,142
Wyoming, OH 45215 • 8,128
Wyoming, PA 18644 • 3,255
Wyoming □, NY • 42,507
Wyoming □, PA • 28,076
Wyoming □, WV • 28,990
Wyomissing, PA 19610 • 7,332
Wythe □, VA • 25,466
Wytheville, VA 24382 • 8,038

X

Xenia, OH 45385 • 24,664

Y

Yadkin □, NC • 30,488
Yadkinville, NC 27055 • 2,525
Yakima, WA 98901–09 • 54,827
Yakima □, WA • 188,823
Yakutat, AK 99689 • 534
Yale, MI 48097 • 1,977
Yale, OK 74085 • 1,392
Yalobusha □, MS • 12,033
Yamhill □, OR • 65,551
Yancey □, NC • 15,419
Yanceyville, NC 27379 • 1,973
Yankton, SD 57078 • 12,703
Yankton □, SD • 19,252
Yaphank, NY 11980 • 5,000
Yardley, PA 19067 • 2,288
Yardville, NJ 08620 • 6,190
Yarmouth, ME 04096 • 3,338
Yarmouth, MA 02675 • 1,200
Yarnell, AZ 85362 • 1,500
Yates □, NY • 22,810
Yates Center, KS 66783 • 1,815
Yavapai □, AZ • 107,714
Yazoo □, MS • 25,506
Yazoo City, MS 39194 • 12,427
Yeadon, PA 19050 • 11,980
Yeagertown, PA 17099 • 1,150
Yell □, AR • 17,759
Yellow Medicine □, MN • 11,684
Yellow Springs, OH 45387 • 3,973
Yellowstone □, MT • 113,419
Yellowstone National Park, WY 82190 • 400
Yellowstone National Park □, MT • 52
Yellville, AR 72687 • 1,181
Yelm, WA 98597 • 1,337
Yerington, NV 89447 • 2,367
Yermo, CA 92398 • 1,092
Yoakum, TX 77995 • 5,611
Yoakum □, TX • 8,786
Yolo □, CA • 141,092
Yonkers, NY 10701–10 • 188,082
Yorba Linda, CA 92686 • 52,422
York, AL 36925 • 3,160
York, ME 03909 • 3,130
York, NE 68467 • 7,884
York, PA 17401–07 • 42,192
York, SC 29745 • 6,709
York □, ME • 164,587
York □, NE • 14,428
York □, PA • 339,574
York □, SC • 131,497
York □, VA • 42,422
Yorketown, NJ 07726 • 6,313
York Harbor, ME 03911 • 2,555
Yorklyn, DE 19736 • 600
Yorkshire, NY 14173 • 1,340
Yorktown, IN 47396 • 4,106
Yorktown, NY 10598 • 5,270
Yorktown, TX 78164 • 2,207
Yorktown, VA 23690–93 • 270
Yorktown Heights, NY 10598 • 7,690
Yorktown Manor, RI 02852 • 2,520
Yorkville, IL 60560 • 3,925
Yorkville, NY 13495 • 2,972
Yorkville, OH 43971 • 1,246
Yosemite National Park, CA 95389 • 1,073
Young □, TX • 18,126
Youngstown, NY 14174 • 2,075
Youngstown, OH 44501–15 • 95,732
Youngsville, LA 70592 • 1,195
Youngsville, PA 16371 • 1,775
Youngtown, AZ 85363 • 2,542
Youngwood, PA 15697 • 3,372
Ypsilanti, MI 48197–98 • 24,846
Yreka, CA 96097 • 6,948
Yuba □, CA • 58,228
Yuba City, CA 95991–92 • 27,437
Yucaipa, CA 92399 • 20,000
Yucca Valley, CA 92284–86 • 13,701
Yukon, OK 73099 • 20,935
Yulee, FL 32097 • 6,915
Yuma, AZ 85364–69 • 54,923
Yuma, CO 80759 • 2,719
Yuma □, AZ • 106,895
Yuma □, CO • 8,954

Z

Zachary, LA 70791 • 9,036
Zanesville, OH 43701–02 • 26,778
Zapata, TX 78076 • 7,119
Zapata □, TX • 9,279
Zavala □, TX • 12,162
Zebulon, GA 30295 • 1,035
Zebulon, NC 27597 • 3,173
Zeeland, MI 49464 • 5,417
Zeigler, IL 62999 • 1,746
Zelienople, PA 16063 • 4,158
Zenith, WA 98188 • 1,100
Zephyr Cove, NV 89448 • 1,700
Zephyrhills, FL 33539–44 • 8,220
Ziebach □, SD • 2,220
Zillah, WA 98953 • 1,911
Zilwaukee, MI 48604 • 1,850
Zimmerman, MN 55398 • 1,350
Zion, IL 60099 • 19,775
Zionsville, IN 46077 • 5,281
Zolfo Springs, FL 33890 • 1,219
Zumbrota, MN 55992 • 2,312
Zuni (Zuni Pueblo), NM 87327 • 5,857
Zwolle, LA 71486 • 1,779